France

Nicola Williams,

Alexis Averbuck, Oliver Berry, Jean-Bernard Carillet, Kerry Christiani,
Gregor Clark, Damian Harper, Anita Isalska, Catherine Le Nevez, Hugh
McNaughtan, Christopher Pitts, Daniel Robinson, Regis St Louis, Greg Ward

Contents

PHARE DES BALEINES,
ÎLE DE RÉ P647

CHÂTEAUNEUF-DU-PAPE
P834

Contents

ON THE ROAD

GALERIE DES GLACES, VERSAILLES P189

Contents

SPECIAL FEATURES

Welcome to France

France seduces travellers with its unfalteringly familiar culture, woven around cafe terraces, village-square markets and lace-curtained bistros with their plat du jour *(dish of the day) chalked on the board.*

Cultural Savoir Faire

France's world-class art and architecture seduce with iconic landmarks known the world over, and rising stars yet to be discovered. This country's cultural repertoire is staggering – in volume and diversity. And this is where the beauty of *la belle France* lies: when superstars such as Mademoiselle Eiffel, royal Versailles and the celebrity-ridden French Riviera have been ticked off, there's ample more to thrill. France is, after all, the world's top tourism destination with some 89 million visitors flocking each year to the land of the Gauls to feast on its extraordinary wealth of museums, galleries, *ateliers* (artist workshops) and hands-on cultural experiences.

Gastronomy

Food is of enormous importance to the French and the daily culinary agenda takes no prisoners: breakfasting on warm croissants from the *boulangerie* (bakery), stopping off at Parisian bistros, and market shopping are second nature to the French – and it would be rude to refuse. But French gastronomy goes far deeper than just eating exceedingly well. Its experiential nature means there is always something tasty to observe, learn and try. Be it flipping crêpes in Brittany or clinking champagne flutes in ancient Reims cellars, the culinary opportunities are endless.

Art de Vivre

The rhythm of daily life – dictated by the seasons in the depths of *la France profonde* (rural France) – exudes an intimacy that gets under your skin. Don't resist. Rather, live the French lifestyle. Embrace the luxury of simple, everyday rituals being transformed into unforgettable moments, be it a coffee and croissant in the Parisian cafe where Jean-Paul Sartre and Simone de Beauvoir met to philosophise, a stroll through the lily-clad gardens Monet painted, or a walk on a beach in Brittany scented with the subtle infusion of language, music and mythology brought by 5th-century Celtic invaders.

Outdoor Action

The *terroir* (land) of France weaves a varied journey from northern France's cliffs and sand dunes to the piercing blue sea of the French Riviera and Corsica's green oak forests. Outdoor action is what France's lyrical landscape demands – and there's something for everybody. Whether you end up walking barefoot across wave-rippled sand to Mont St-Michel, riding a cable car to glacial panoramas above Chamonix or cartwheeling down Europe's highest sand dune, France does not disappoint. Its great outdoors is thrilling, with endless opportunities and the next adventure begging to be had. *Allez!*

Why I Love France

By Nicola Williams, Writer

France has been home for two decades yet I still feel on holiday – which is a testament to how good the French *art de vivre* (art of living) is. From my Haute-Savoie house on Lake Geneva's southern shore, the Jura's dark-green hills and *un café* in the wisteria-draped village bar are my wake-up call. Weekends of endless possibilities punctuate the gentle rhythm of village life: art museums in Lyon and Paris, Alpine hiking and skiing, paddle boarding on the glittering lake, road trips to Beaujolais and Burgundy and other regions so different they could be another country. France's sheer variety is amazing.

For more about our writers, see p1024

Above: Château de Versailles Gardens & Park (p189)

France

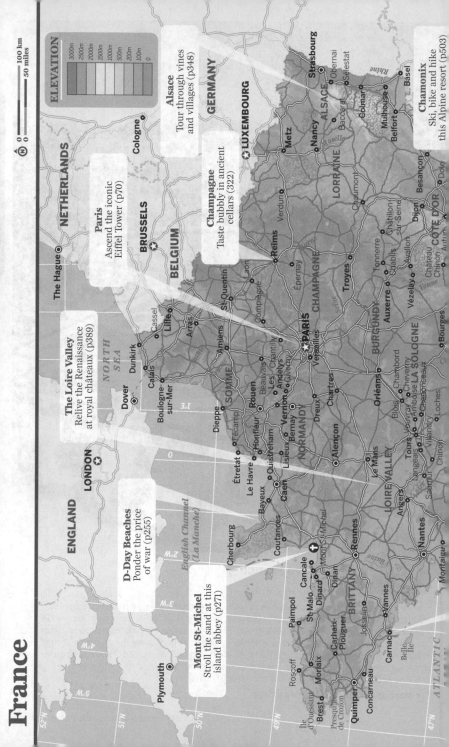

ELEVATION
3000m
2500m
2000m
1500m
1000m
500m
200m
100m
0

Paris
Ascend the iconic
Eiffel Tower (p70)

Alsace
Tour through vines
and villages (p348)

Champagne
Taste bubbly in ancient
cellars (322)

Chamonix
Ski, bike and hike
this Alpine resort (p503)

The Loire Valley
Relive the Renaissance
at royal châteaux (p389)

D-Day Beaches
Ponder the price
of war (p255)

Mont St-Michel
Stroll the sand at this
island abbey (p271)

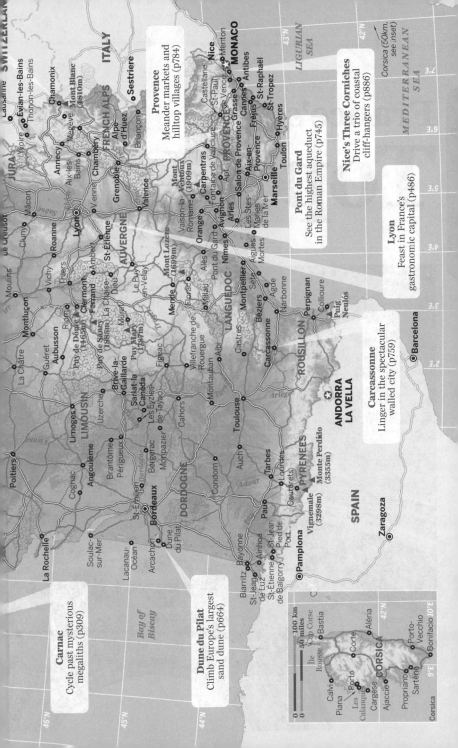

Carnac
Cycle past mysterious megaliths (p309)

Dune du Pilat
Climb Europe's largest sand dune (p664)

Provence
Meander markets and hilltop villages (p784)

Nice's Three Corniches
Drive a trio of coastal cliff-hangers (p886)

Pont du Gard
See the highest aqueduct in the Roman Empire (p745)

Lyon
Feast in France's gastronomic capital (p486)

Carcassonne
Linger in the spectacular walled city (p759)

France's
Top 15

1

Eiffel Tower

1 More than six million people visit the Eiffel Tower (p70) annually – and from an evening ascent amid twinkling lights over a flute of Champagne to a lazy lunch in one of its restaurants, every visit is magical. Gustave Eiffel only designed the graceful tower as a temporary exhibit for the 1889 Exposition Universelle, yet its distinctive art nouveau–laced silhouette is an icon of Paris' skyline. Best are the special occasions when all 324m of the iconic tower glows a different colour.

Mont St-Michel

2 The dramatic play of tides on this abbey-island in Normandy is magical and mysterious. Said by Celtic mythology to be a sea tomb to which souls of the dead were sent, Mont St-Michel (p274) is rich in legend and history, keenly felt as you make your way across the bridge – or barefoot across rippled sand – to this stunning architectural ensemble. Walk around it alone or, better still, hook up with a guide in nearby Genêts for a dramatic day hike across the bay.

JAN OTTO/GETTY IMAGES ©

NEIRFY/SHUTTERSTOCK ©

Champagne

3 Known-brand Champagne houses in the main towns of Reims and Épernay are famed the world over. But – our tip – much of Champagne's finest liquid gold is created by passionate, small-scale vignerons (winegrowers) in drop-dead-gorgeous villages, rendering the region's scenic driving routes the loveliest way of tasting fine bubbly amid rolling vineyards. Our favourite: exploring the region's best Champagne museum, the Musée de la Vigne et du Vin (p335), in Le Mesnil-sur-Oger, followed by a tasting and lunch in the village at Le Mesnil.

Loire Valley Châteaux

4 If it's aristocratic pomp and architectural splendour you're after, this regal valley is the place to linger. Flowing for more than 1000km into the Atlantic Ocean, the Loire is one of France's last *fleuves sauvages* (untamed rivers) and its banks provide a 1000-year snapshot of French high society. The valley is riddled with beautiful châteaux sporting glittering turrets and ballrooms, lavish cupolas and chapels. If you're seeking the perfect fairy-tale castle, head for moat-ringed Azay-le-Rideau (p415; pictured), Villandry and its gardens, and less-visited Château de Beauregard.

Chamonix Action

5 The birthplace of mountaineering and winter playground to the rich, famous and not-so-famous, this iconic ski resort in the French Alps has something for everyone. Snow-sports fiends fly down slopes on skis or boards in order to savour the breathtaking views of Mont Blanc and surrounding mountains. But there's absolutely no obligation to do so: nonskiers can hop aboard the Aiguille du Midi (p503; pictured above) cable car – and onwards to Italy aboard the Télécabine Panoramique Mont Blanc – for the ride of a lifetime above 3800m.

Dune du Pilat

6 The Dune du Pilat (p664) is a 'mountain' that has to be climbed – and gleefully romped down at speed. Not only is the coastal panorama from the top of Europe's largest sand dune a stunner – ogle at the Banc d'Arguin bird reserve and Cap Ferret across the bay – but nearby beaches have some of the Atlantic Coast's best surf. Cycle here from Arcachon and feast afterwards on locally farmed oysters and *crepinettes* (local sausages) at a 1930s hunting lodge redesigned by Philippe Starck, aka the-place-to-be-seen La Co(o)rniche.

Nice's Three Corniches

7 It's impossible to drive this dramatic trio of coastal roads (p886), each one higher and with more hairpin bends than the next, without conjuring up cinematic images of Grace Kelly, Alfred Hitchcock, the glitz of Riviera high life, and the glamour of the Monaco royal family – all while absorbing views of the sweeping blue sea fringing Europe's most mythical coastline. To make a perfect day out of it, shop for a picnic at the cours Saleya morning market before leaving Nice. Villefranche-sur-Mer (p886)

Carcassonne at Dusk

8 That first glimpse of La Cité's sturdy, stone, witch's-hat turrets above Carcassonne (p759) in the Languedoc is enough to make your hair stand on end. To properly savour this fairy-tale walled city, linger at dusk after the crowds have left, when the old town belongs to its 100 or so inhabitants and the few visitors staying at the handful of lovely hotels within its ramparts. Don't forget to look back when you leave to view the old city, beautifully illuminated, glowing in the warm night.

D-Day Beaches

9 A trip to these peaceful, broad stretches of fine sand and breeze-blown bluffs is one of France's most emotional journeys. On 6 June 1944 (the 75th anniversary is in 2019), beaches here became a cacophony of gunfire and explosions, the bodies of Allied soldiers lying in the sand as their comrades-in-arms charged inland. Just up the hill from Omaha Beach, the long rows of symmetrical gravestones at the Normandy American Cemetery & Memorial (p257) bear solemn, silent testimony to the profound price paid for France's liberation from Nazi tyranny.
Utah Beach (p259)

Pont du Gard

10 This Unesco World Heritage Site (p745) near Nîmes in southern France is gargantuan: 35 arches straddle the Roman aqueduct's 275m-long upper tier, containing a watercourse that was designed to carry 20,000 cu metres of water per day. View it from afloat a canoe on the River Gard or jig across the top. Oh, and don't forget your swimming gear for some post-Pont daredevil diving and high jumping from the rocks nearby. Flop afterwards on a floating deck a little way downstream.

Provençal Markets

11 No region is such a market-must. Be it fresh fish by the port in seafaring Marseille, early summer's strings of pink garlic, Cavaillon melons and cherries all summer long or wintertime's earthy 'black diamond' truffles, Provence thrives on a bounty of local produce – piled high each morning at the market. Every town and village has one, but those in Aix-en-Provence (p808) and Antibes are particularly atmospheric. Take your own bag to stock up on dried herbs, green and black olives marinated a dozen different ways, courgette flowers and tangy olive oils.

VOLPUTIN/SHUTTERSTOCK ©

Hilltop Villages

12 Impossibly perched on a rocky peak above the Mediterranean, gloriously lost in back country, fortified or château-topped... Southern France's portfolio of *villages perchés* is vast and impressive, and calls for go-slow touring – on foot, by bicycle or car. Most villages are medieval, built from golden stone and riddled with cobbled lanes, flower-filled alleys and hidden squares silent but for the glug of a fountain. Combine a village visit with lunch alfresco – La Table de Ventabren (p806) near Aix-en-Provence is one such dreamy address that you'll never want to leave.
Pérouges (p482)

Lyonnais Bouchons

13 The red-and-white checked tablecloths, closely packed tables and decades-old bistro decor could be anywhere in France. It's the local cuisine that makes Lyon's *bouchons* (small bistros) unique, plus the quaint culinary customs, such as totting up the bill on the paper tablecloth, or serving wine in a glass bottle wrapped with an elastic band to stop drips, or the 'shut weekends' opening hours. Various piggy parts drive Lyonnais cuisine (p487), but have faith – this French city is said to be the gastronomic capital of France. Quenelles (p487)

Carnac Megaliths

14 Pedalling past open fields dotted with the world's greatest concentration of mysterious megaliths (p310) gives a poignant reminder of Brittany's ancient human inhabitants. No one knows for sure what inspired these gigantic menhirs, dolmens, cromlechs, tumuli and cairns to be built. A sun god? Some phallic fertility cult? Post-ride, try to unravel the mystery from the soft-sand comfort of La Grande Plage, Carnac's longest and most popular beach, with a 2km-long stretch of pearly white sand.

Alsatian Wine Route

15 This is one of France's most popular drives – and for good reason. Motoring in this far northeast corner of France takes you through a kaleidoscope of lush green vines, perched castles and gentle mist-covered mountains. The only pit stops en route are half-timbered villages and roadside wine cellars, where fruity Alsace vintages can be swirled, tasted and bought. To be truly wooed, drive the Route des Vins d'Alsace (p356) in autumn, when vines are heavy with grapes waiting to be harvested and colours are at their vibrant best.

LEOKS/SHUTTERSTOCK ©

Need to Know

For more information, see Survival Guide (p973)

Currency
Euro (€)

Language
French

Visas
Generally not required for stays of up to 90 days (or at all for EU nationals); some nationalities need a Schengen visa.

Money
ATMs at every airport, most train stations and on every second street corner in towns and cities. Visa, MasterCard and Amex widely accepted.

Mobile Phones
European and Australian phones work, but only American cells with 900 and 1800 MHz networks are compatible; check with your provider before leaving home. Use a French SIM card to call with a cheaper French number.

Time
Central European Time (GMT/UTC plus one hour)

When to Go

Brittany & Normandy •
GO Apr–Sep

Paris
• GO May & Jun

• **French Alps**
GO late Dec–early Apr (skiing)
or Jun & Jul (hiking)

French Riviera •
GO Apr–Jun, Sep & Oct

Corsica •
GO Apr–Jun, Sep & Oct

Warm to hot summers, mild winters
Warm to hot summers, cold winters
Mild year-round
Mild summers, cold winters
Alpine climate

High Season
(Jul & Aug)

➡ Queues at big sights and on the road, especially August.

➡ Christmas, New Year and Easter equally busy.

➡ Late December to March is high season in Alpine ski resorts.

➡ Book tables and accommodation well in advance.

Shoulder
(Apr–Jun & Sep)

➡ Accommodation rates drop in southern France and other hot spots.

➡ Spring brings warm weather, flowers and local produce.

➡ The *vendange* (grape harvest) is reason to visit in autumn.

Low Season
(Oct–Mar)

➡ Prices up to 50% lower than high season.

➡ Sights, attractions and restaurants open fewer days and shorter hours.

➡ Hotels and restaurants in quieter rural regions (such as the Dordogne) are closed.

Useful Websites

France.fr (www.france.fr) Official country website.

France 24 (www.france24. com/en/france) French news in English.

Paris by Mouth (www.parisby mouth.com) Dining and drinking; one-stop site for where and how to eat in the capital with plenty of the latest openings.

David Lebovitz (www. davidlebovitz.com) American pastry chef in Paris and author of several French cookbooks; insightful postings and great France-related articles shared on his Facebook page.

French Word-a-Day (http:// french-word-a-day.typepad. com) Fun language learning.

Lonely Planet (www.lonely planet.com/france) Destination information, hotel bookings, traveller forum and more.

Important Numbers

France country code	☎33
International access code	☎00
Europe-wide emergency	☎112
Ambulance (SAMU)	☎15
Police	☎17

Exchange Rates

Australia	A$1	€0.64
Canada	C$1	€0.66
Japan	¥100	€0.76
New Zealand	NZ$1	€0.59
UK	UK£1	€1.14
USA	US$1	€0.85

For current exchange rates see www.xe.com.

Daily Costs
Budget: Less than €130

➡ Dorm bed: €18–30

➡ Double room in a budget hotel: €90

➡ Admission to many attractions first Sunday of month: free

➡ Lunch *menus* (set meals): less than €20

➡ Public transport: €1.60–7.50

Midrange: €130–220

➡ Double room in a midrange hotel: €90–190

➡ Lunch *menus* in gourmet restaurants: €20–40

➡ Car hire: €35–80

Top end: More than €220

➡ Double room in a top-end hotel: €190–350

➡ Top restaurant dinner: *menu* €65, à la carte €100–150

➡ Opera tickets: €15–150

Opening Hours

Opening hours vary throughout the year. We list high-season opening hours, but remember these longer summer hours often decrease in shoulder and low seasons.

Banks 9am–noon and 2pm–5pm Monday to Friday or Tuesday to Saturday

Bars 7pm–1am

Cafes 7am–11pm

Clubs 10pm–3am, 4am or 5am Thursday to Saturday

Restaurants Noon–2.30pm and 7pm–11pm six days a week

Shops 10am–noon and 2pm–7pm Monday to Saturday; longer, and including Sunday, for shops in defined ZTIs (international tourist zones)

Arriving in France

Aéroport de Charles de Gaulle (Paris) RER trains, buses and night buses to the city centre €6 to €17; taxi €50 to €55, 15% higher evenings and Sundays.

Aéroport d'Orly (Paris) Orlyval then RER trains, buses and night buses to the city centre €8.70 to €13.25; T7 tram to Villejuif–Louis Aragon then metro to centre (€3.80); taxi €30 to €35, 15% higher evenings and Sundays.

Getting Around

Transport in France is comfortable, quick, usually reliable and reasonably priced.

Train Run by the state-owned **SNCF** (p988), France's rail network is truly first-class, with extensive coverage of the country and frequent departures.

Car Meander away from cities (where parking is challenging) and a car comes into its own. Mooching along peaceful country lanes, past vineyards and fruit orchards, is one of France's greatest joys. Hire wheels at airports and train stations.

Bus Cheaper and slower than trains. Useful for more remote villages that aren't serviced by trains.

Bicycle Certain regions – the Loire Valley, the Luberon in Provence and Burgundy – beg to be explored by two wheels and have dedicated cycling paths, some along canal towpaths or between orchards and vineyards.

For much more on **getting around**, see p987

First Time France

For more information, see Survival Guide (p973)

Checklist

➡ Check passport validity and visa requirements.

➡ Arrange travel insurance.

➡ Check airline baggage restrictions.

➡ Book accommodation; reserve big-name restaurants.

➡ Buy tickets online for the Louvre, Eiffel Tower and other top sights.

➡ Download France-related travel apps and music.

What to Pack

➡ Two-pin travel plug (electrical adapter)

➡ Sunscreen, sunhat and sunglasses (southern France)

➡ Rainproof jacket and umbrella (northern France)

➡ Pocket knife with corkscrew (pack this in your checked-in luggage)

➡ Walking shoes – for hiking paths and cobbled streets

➡ Light scarf (to cover bare shoulders in churches)

➡ An adventurous appetite

Top Tips for Your Trip

➡ Almost every village and town has a weekly morning market brimming with fruit, veg and other regional produce – and there's no finer opportunity for mingling with locals! Take your own shopping bag or basket.

➡ To get the best out of a French road trip, avoid *autoroutes* (highways) and main roads. Opt instead for back roads and country lanes that twist past farms, châteaux, vineyards and orchards – scenic routes are highlighted in green on road maps (print and digital) published by French cartographer Michelin (www.viamichelin.com).

➡ For authentic local dining experiences, avoid restaurants that tout a *'menu touristique'* or display a sample meal of plastic food on the pavement outside. While it might be tempting to favour restaurants with a menu in English, the very best (and best-loved by locals) rarely offer a translation.

What to Wear

➡ Paris sports a mixed bag of styles. Dress smart-casual to avoid standing out. The further south, the more relaxed fashion becomes. No bikini tops or bare male chests unless you're on the beach.

➡ Countrywide, dress up rather than down in midrange restaurants, clubs and bars.

➡ If hitting the coast, know some municipalities in Corsica and the Côte d'Azur have had (contested) burkini bans in place – check the local rules.

Sleeping

Advance reservations are essential in high season.

B&Bs Enchanting properties with maximum five rooms.

Camping Wild and remote, to brash resorts with pools, slides etc.

Hostels New-wave hostels equal lifestyle spaces with private rooms.

Hotels Embrace every budget and taste; breakfast rarely included in rates.

Money Savers

Eat cheap Lunchtime *formules* (two courses) and *menus* (three courses) in restaurants are a snip of the price of evening dining.

Discount admission City museum passes provide cheaper admission to sights; free admission first Sunday of month in many cities.

Savvy sleeping It's cheaper for families staying in hotels to ask for a double room with extra bed rather than a triple. Families of four or more will find self-catering accommodation cheaper.

Picnic perfection With its bucolic scenery and outstanding produce, France is picnic paradise. Buy a baguette from the *boulangerie* (bakery) and fill it with Camembert, pâté or charcuterie (cold meats). Finish sweet with macarons (Paris), buttery *kouign amann* (Breton butter cake), cherries (southern France) or – for blue-blooded gourmets – Champagne and Reims' *biscuits roses*.

Bargaining

With the exception of the odd haggle at the market, little bargaining goes on in France.

Tipping

Hotels €1 to €2 per bag is standard; gratuity for cleaning staff is at your discretion.

Bars No tips for drinks served at bar; round to nearest euro for drinks served at table.

Restaurants For decent service tip 10%.

Pubic toilets For super-clean, sparkling toilets with music, €0.50 at most.

Tours For excellent guides, €1 to €2 per person.

Phrases to Learn Before You Go

English is increasingly widespread in Paris, Nice and other big tourist-busy cities, but step into *la France profonde* (rural France) and you'll need those French phrases you mastered before setting off. See Language (p998) for more information.

 What are the opening hours?
Quelles sont les heures d'ouverture?
kel son lay zer doo·vair·tewr

French business hours are governed by a maze of regulations, so it's a good idea to check before you make plans.

 I'd like the set menu, please.
Je voudrais le menu, s'il vous plait.
zher voo·dray ler mer·new seel voo play

The best-value dining in France is the two- or three-course meal at a fixed price. Most restaurants have one on the chalkboard.

 Which wine would you recommend?
Quel vin vous conseillez?
kel vun voo kon·say·yay

Who better to ask for advice on wine than the French?

 Can I address you with 'tu'?
Est-ce que je peux vous tutoyer?
es ker zher per voo tew·twa·yay

Before you start addressing someone with the informal 'you' form, it's polite to ask permission first.

 Do you have plans for tonight/tomorrow?
Vous avez prévu quelque chose ce soir/demain?
voo za·vay pray·vew kel·ker shoz ser swar/der·mun

To arrange to meet up without sounding pushy, ask friends if they're available rather than inviting them directly.

Etiquette

Conversation Use *vous* when speaking to anyone unknown or older than you; the informal *tu* is for friends, family and children.

Churches Dress modestly (cover shoulders).

Drinks Asking for *une carafe d'eau* (free jug of tap water) in restaurants is acceptable. Never end a meal with a cappuccino or cup of tea. Play French and order *un café* (espresso).

French kissing Exchange *bisous* (cheek-skimming kisses) – at least two, but in some parts of France it can be up to four.

Shopping Fondle fruit, veg, flowers or clothing in shops and you'll be greeted with a killer glare from the shop assistant.

Dining out Splitting the bill is deemed the height of unsophistication. The person who invites pays, although close friends often go Dutch. Never, ever, discuss money over dinner.

Gifts Take flowers (not chrysanthemums, which are only for cemeteries) or Champagne when invited to someone's home.

What's New

Contemporary Art & Gastronomy

Spring 2019 sees the opening of the Collection Pinault inside Paris' former grain market and stock exchange, Bourse de Commerce, with a restaurant by former triple-Michelin-starred chef Michel Bras. (p85)

Celebrations at Chambord

The Loire Valley's blockbuster castle celebrates its 500th birthday in 2019. Celebrity French designer Jacques Garcia heads the festivities, which will see part of the empty castle furnished as it was when the king and his itinerant court rocked up. Spend the night at the refurbished Relais de Chambord (p406), overlooking the château.

Fine Art Renaissance

Les beaux arts are enjoying a renaissance with the reopening of a trio of fine-art museums – in Nantes (p635), Besançon (p552) and Dijon (p431) – after years of renovation work. Collections of artistic and archaeological treasures amassed over the centuries, moreover, are now 100% accessible.

Dancing with Death

Eight years and €23 million later, the grand makeover of the Auvergne's magnificent Gothic abbey church in La Chaise-Dieu is complete. Its 14th-century fresco of skeletons dancing with death has never been such a brilliant blood-red. (p581)

Maritime Bordeaux

Bordeaux is landing itself another landmark museum (p651) in early 2019: a seven-storey ocean liner of a marine-and-maritime history museum, in the edgy Bassins à Flot 'hood.

Turtle Watch

Watch as turtles waltz underwater and marine biologists tend to injuries (for later release into the Med) at this new outdoor turtle pool (p889) neighbouring Monaco's Musée Océanographique.

A New Tramway for Nice

Nice's new east–west tramline (p861), from September 2019, translates as a state-of-the-art, direct transport link between both airport terminals and downtown.

Civilians in Wartime Memorial

Normandy marks the 75th anniversary of D-Day in 2019 with an evocative museum recalling civilian life during WWII. War artefacts, survivor stories, interactive tablets and films get under the skin of the horrific conflict and aftermath. (p264)

Alpine Hotel Makeovers

The centuries-old charm of Alpine overnights never tires: in Chamonix, discover the faux-vintage chic of Pointe Isabelle (p510), named after a female explorer, or ubercool designer bunkroom Terminal Neige (p509) by a glacial sea of ice. Hôtel Avancher (p533) is Val d'Isère's sassy kid on the block.

Digital Art

A former foundry in Paris forms the blank canvas for the dazzling digital art projections at the capital's first museum dedicated to the genre, L'Atelier des Lumières (p102).

Slow Down!

As of 1 July 2018, the speed limit (p19) on undivided national and departmental roads will be 80km/h (instead of 90km/h).

For more recommendations and reviews, see lonelyplanet.com/France

If You Like...

Gorgeous Villages

There is no humbler pleasure than exploring villages of gold stone, pink granite or whitewash. Cobbled lanes ensnare ornate fountains, flowery squares and houses strung with wisteria, vines or drying peppers.

Pérouges Day trip it from Lyon for cider and *galettes de Pérouges* (thin, sugar-crusted tarts) between yellow-gold medieval stone. (p482)

St-Émilion A Unesco-listed medieval village perched dramatically amid Bordeaux vines. (p661)

St-Jean Pied de Port Ancient pilgrim outpost en route to Santiago de Compostela in Spain. (p689)

Yvoire On Lake Geneva's southern shore, this flowery, fortified Savoyard village is a privileged address. (p517)

The Luberon A part of Provence lavishly strewn with hilltop villages; Bonnieux, Gordes and red-rock Roussillon are pure brilliance. (p836)

Èze Fuses a stunning hilltop village with sweeping Riviera panoramas. (p886)

The Dordogne Extraordinary *bastides* (fortified hilltop towns) at every turn. (p588)

Cordes-sur-Ciel The beautiful village to be in the Toulouse area. (p733)

Locronan Breton stunner, best savoured off-season when you can have it all to yourself. (p302)

Wine Tasting

Be it tasting in cellars, watching grape harvests or sleeping *au château,* French wine culture demands immediate road-testing.

Bordeaux The Médoc, St-Émilion and Cognac set connoisseurs' hearts aflutter. (p650)

Burgundy Sample renowned vintages in Beaune, the Côte d'Or and Chablis. (p429)

Châteauneuf-du-Pape Vines planted by 14th-century popes yield southern France's most illustrious red. (p834)

Gigondas Taste raved-about reds in this gold-stone village in Provence. (p833)

Route des Vins d'Alsace Pair wine tasting with castle-topped villages in this storybook region, rich in rieslings, pinots and sylvaners. (p356)

Beaujolais Gentle cycling and wine tasting through bucolic vine-ribboned hills near Lyon. (p494)

Arbois Discover the potent, liquid gold of the Jura's memorable *vin jaune;* if red is more your cup of tea, search out the region's less-known Poulsard reds. (p554)

Castles

The Loire Valley is the prime stop for French châteaux, dripping in period gold leaf. But venture elsewhere and you'll be surprised by what hides behind lumbering stone walls.

Versailles France's largest and grandest château, a stone's throw from Paris. (p189)

Chambord Renaissance castle of preposterous proportion where no one ever lived. (p402)

Azay-le-Rideau Classic French château with moat, turrets and sweeping staircase. (p415)

Villandry The formal French gardens framing this Renaissance Loire Valley château are glorious. (p414)

Cathar fortresses Now ruined, these dramatic, heat-sizzled hilltop castles in Languedoc evoke 13th-century persecution. (p774)

Château de Foix A château in Vallée de l'Ariège with amazing views of the Pyrenees. (p713)

Château Gaillard Magnificent, ruined bastion built in Normandy by Richard the Lionheart; to-die-for River Seine views. (p242)

Coastal Paths

From white cliff to red rock, pebble cove to golden sand strip, France's coastline is dramatically different. Explore on a windswept *sentier du littoral* (coastal trail), scented with sea salt and herbal scrub.

St-Tropez This *sentier du littoral* leads from fishing coves to celebrity-laced sands. (p878)

Sentier Nietzsche Spectacular, steep rocky footpath in Èze near Nice where the German philosopher once hung out. (p887)

Corsica Hike from Bonifacio to a lighthouse, or past Genoese watchtowers along Cap Corse's Customs Officers' Trail. (p898)

Côte d'Opale Savour opal blues from windswept clifftops near Cap Blanc-Nez and Cap Gris-Nez. (p217)

Atlantic island capers Fall in love with Brittany's Belle Île or Île d'Ouessant; hobnob with Parisians on chic Île de Ré. (p313)

Île de Porquerolles Mediterranean island beauty strung with sea-facing cycling and hiking trails. (p887)

Sentier du Littoral One of the Basque Country's best-kept secrets, linking Bidart and Hendaye. (p683)

Markets

Art nouveau hangar or tree-shaded village square... French markets spill across an enticing mix of spaces. Every town and village has one – they operate in the mornings, at least once a week. Bring your own bag.

Les Halles This market and Croix Rousse are Lyon's two celebrated market divas, endowed with stalls heaving with

Top: Wine tasting, Chablis (p457)

Bottom: St-Jean Pied de Port (p689)

fruit, veg, meat and runny St-Marcellin cheese. (p493)

Place des Lices No town square is as celebrity-studded as St-Tropez. (p879)

Marché des Capucins Enjoy oysters and white wine at Bordeaux's historic covered market. (p659)

Marché Couvert Once a bishop's palace, now a temple to local produce in Metz. (p381)

Uzès Languedoc's most splendid farmers market. (p746)

Carpentras This Friday-morning *marché* steals the Provençal market show; nearby Apt is the Saturday-morning star. (p833)

Marché Victor Hugo Lunch with locals on the 1st floor of Toulouse's covered food market. (p725)

St-Girons Riverside extravaganza of food, crafts, antiques and delectable Pyrenean produce. (p716)

Amboise Lovely Loire Valley outdoor market. (p413)

Islands & Beaches

The country's 3427km-long coastline morphs from white chalk cliffs (Normandy) to treacherous promontories (Brittany) to broad expanses of fine sand (Atlantic coast) and pebbly or sandy beaches (Mediterranean coast).

Îles d'Hyères France's only marine national park and a pedestrian paradise fringed with near-tropical beaches. (p887)

Plage de Pampelonne Stars love this hip beach in St-Tropez, darling, and for good reason – it's glam and golden. (p879)

Île de Ré Follow the flock from Paris to this chic, beach-laced island off France's west coast. (p647)

Belle Île Its name means 'Beautiful Island' and that is just what this island off the coast of Brittany is. (p313)

Plage de Palombaggia Near Porto-Vecchio, this is a Corsican beauty to die for, along with nearby Plage de Santa Giulia. (p923)

Les Landes Surfers' secret backed by dunes on the Atlantic Coast. (p674)

Côte d'Opale Rousing, wind-buffeted beaches across from the white cliffs of Dover. (p217)

Gorges de l'Ardèche River beaches are all the rage and those around Pont d'Arc are great fun; arrive by kayak. (p499)

Incredible Train Journeys

There is nothing quite like watching mountains, valleys, gorges and rivers jog past kaleidoscope-style from the window of an old-fashioned steam train or mountain railway.

Train du Montenvers Ride this historic rack-and-pinion train from Chamonix to Montenvers, then catch a cable car to the Mer de Glace, France's biggest glacier. (p506)

Tramway du Mont Blanc Travel in the shade of Europe's biggest mountain aboard France's highest train from St-Gervais-Le-Fayet. (p513)

Le Train Jaune Mind-blowing Pyrenean scenery aboard a mountain train in Roussillon. (p779)

Train des Pignes Narrow-gauge railway from Nice. (p856)

Chemin de Fer Touristique du Haut-Quercy Savour the sun-baked vineyards, oak

forests and rivers of the Lot in southwest France aboard a vintage steam train. (p629)

La Vapeur du Trieux Journey riverside on this steam train from a Breton harbour to an artists' village. (p289)

Le Petit Train de la Rhune Chug past miniature Pottok ponies to the summit of the most famous Basque mountain. (p688)

Chemin de Fer de la Corse Cross from coast to coast, via Corsica's mountainous interior, on this awesome single-track railway. (p900)

Rural Escapes

Solitude is sweet and there's ample opportunity to stray off the beaten track *sans* the crowds.

Marais Poitevin Paddle by boat through this tranquil, bird-filled wetland dubbed 'Green Venice'. (p642)

Vallée d'Aspe The 21st century has yet to reach this quiet valley, sprinkled with tiny hamlets and rural farms, in the Pyrenees. (p704)

Essoyes Watch vine-streaked landscapes of Champagne fade into watercolour distance in this riverside village, Renoir's summer home. (p343)

Le Crotoy The mood is laid-back and the panorama superb in this picturesque fishing town on the northern bank of the Baie de Somme. (p225)

Forêt de Paimpont Recharge your batteries in this Breton forest, far from the coastal crowds. (p317)

À la Crécia Experience life on a farm at a rural retreat in Parc Naturel Régional du Vercors in the French Alps. (p543)

Train du Montenvers (p513)

Domaine de la Palissade Trek on horseback through this remote, coastal nature park in the Camargue, kissed pink by salt pans and flamingos. (p816)

Massif des Maures Chestnut forest, right next door to – but a million miles away from – the French Riviera glitz. (p884)

Mountain Vistas

On sunny days, views from atop France's highest mountains are breathtaking. Cable cars and mountain railways often take out the legwork.

Aiguille du Midi, Chamonix If you can handle the height (3842m), unforgettable summit views of the French, Swiss and Italian Alps await. (p503)

Pic Blanc, Alpe d'Huez Scale the 3330m peak year-round by cable car – magical views ripple across the French Alps into Italy and Switzerland. (p546)

Massif de l'Estérel, French Riviera Stupendous views of red rock, green forest and big blue – only on foot! (p877)

Ballon d'Alsace See where Alsace, Franche-Comté and Lorraine converge from this rounded, 1247m-high mountain. (p371)

Puy de Dôme, Auvergne Gulp at extinct volcanoes, pea-green and grassy, from this windswept summit reached by foot or cog railway. (p571)

Cirque de Gavarnie Near Lourdes, a mind-blowing mountain amphitheatre ringed by icy Pyrenean peaks. (p709)

Pic du Midi Eye-popping panorama of the entire Pyrenees; catch a cable car from La Mongie. (p711)

Month by Month

January

With New Year festivities done and dusted, head to the Alps. Crowds on the slopes thin out once school's back, but January remains busy. On the Mediterranean, mild winters are wonderfully serene in a part of France that's mad busy the rest of the year.

🏃 Vive le Ski!

Grab your skis, hit the slopes. Most resorts in the Alps, Pyrenees, Jura and Auvergne open mid- to late December, but January is the start of the ski season in earnest. Whether a purpose-built station or Alpine village, there's a resort to match every mood and moment. (p50)

🍴 Truffle Season

No culinary product is more aromatic or decadent than black truffles. Hunt them in the Dordogne and Provence – the season runs late December to March, but January is the prime month.

February

Crisp, cold weather in the mountains – lots of china-blue skies now – translates as ski season in top gear. Alpine resorts get mobbed by families during the February school holidays and accommodation is at its priciest.

🎊 Nice Carnival

Nice makes the most of its mild climate with this crazy Lenten carnival. As well as parade and costume shenanigans, merrymakers pelt each other with blooms during the legendary flower battles. Dunkirk in northern France celebrates Mardi Gras with equal gusto. (p855)

🎊 Citrus Celebrations

Menton on the French Riviera was once Europe's biggest lemon producer, hence its exotic Fête du Citron. These days it has to ship in a zillion lemons from Spain to sculpt into gargantuan carnival characters. (p896)

March

The ski season stays busy thanks to ongoing school holidays (until mid-March) and warmer temperatures. Down south, spring ushers in the bullfighting season and *Pâques* (Easter).

🎊 Féria d'Arles

In France's hot south, four days of open-air dancing, music and concerts alfresco enliven the Féria d'Arles, a flamboyant street festival held at Easter in Arles to open the town's highly controversial bullfighting season. (p811)

April

Dedicated ski fiends can carve glaciers in the highest French ski resorts until mid-April or later at highest altitudes. Then it's off with the ski boots and on with the hiking gear as peach and almond trees flower pink against a backdrop of snowcapped peaks.

🏃 Fête de la Transhumance

During the ancient Fête de la Transhumance in April or May, shepherds walk their flocks of sheep up to green summer pastures; St-Rémy de Provence's fest is the best known. Or head to villages in the Pyrenees and Auvergne to witness this transit. (p28)

May

There is no lovelier month to travel in France, as the first melons ripen in Provence and outdoor markets burst with new-found colour. Spring is always in.

🎎 May Day

No one works on 1 May, a national holiday that incites summer buzz, with *muguets* (lilies of the valley) sold at roadside stalls and given to friends for good luck. In Arles, Camargue cowboys prove their bull-herding and equestrian skills at the Fête des Gardians. (p811)

🎎 Fêtes de Jeanne d'Arc

Orléans residents have celebrated the liberation of their city by Joan of Arc since 1430. Festivities include a four-day medieval market, costume parades, concerts and, on 8 May, a cathedral service and military parade (including tanks). (p395)

☆ Festival de Cannes

In mid-May, film stars and celebrities walk the red carpet at Cannes, Europe's biggest cinema extravaganza. (p863)

☆ Monaco Grand Prix

How fitting that Formula One's most glamorous rip around the streets is in one of the world's most glam countries at Monaco's Formula One Grand Prix. (p889)

🎎 Pèlerinage des Gitans

Roma flock to the Camargue on 24 and 25 May and again in October for a flamboyant fiesta of street music, dancing and dipping their toes in the sea. (p818)

June

As midsummer approaches, the festival pace quickens alongside a rising temperature gauge, which tempts the first bathers into the sea. Looking north, nesting white storks shower good luck on farmsteads in Alsace.

☆ Fête de la Musique

Orchestras, crooners, buskers and bands fill streets with free music during France's vibrant nationwide celebration of music on 21 June (www.fetedelamusique.culture.fr).

☆ Paris Jazz Festival

No festival better evokes the brilliance of Paris' interwar jazz age than this annual fest in the Parc Floral de Paris. (p118)

July

If lavender's your French love, now is the time to catch it flowering in Provence. But you won't be the only one. School's out for the summer, showering the country with teems of tourists, traffic and too many *complet* (full) signs strung in hotel windows.

🎎 Bastille Day

Join the French in celebrating the storming of the Bastille on 14 July 1789 – countrywide there are fireworks displays, balls, processions, parades and lots of hoo-ha all round.

🏃 Tour de France

The world's most prestigious cycling race ends on av des Champs-Élysées in Paris on the third or fourth Sunday of July, but you can catch it for two weeks before all over France – the route changes each year but the French Alps are a hot spot. (p118)

☆ Festival d'Avignon

Rouse your inner thespian with Avignon's legendary performing-arts festival. Street acts in its fringe fest are as inspired as those on official stages. (p823)

☆ Jazz à Juan

Jive to jazz cats in Juan-les-Pins at this mythical Riviera music fest, which has been around for 50-odd years. Jazz à Juan requires tickets, but the fringe 'Off' part of the music festival does not. (p871)

August

It's that crazy summer month when the French join everyone else on holiday. Paris, Lyon and other big cities empty; traffic jams at motorway toll booths test the patience of a saint; and temperatures soar. Avoid. Or don your party hat and join the crowd!

🎇 Festival Interceltique de Lorient

Celtic culture is the focus of the Festival Interceltique de Lorient, when hundreds of thousands of Celts from Brittany and abroad flock to Lorient to celebrate just that. (p309)

🍷 Route du Champagne en Fête

There's no better excuse for a flute or three of bubbly than during the first weekend in August when Champagne toasts its vines and vintages with the Route du Champagne en Fête. Free tastings, cellar visits, music and dancing. (p343)

☆ Hestiv'Òc

Ramp up the summer with four days of revelry in the Pyrenean town of Pau, featuring performances and music on stages in the centre of town (www.hestivoc.com). The best feature: it's entirely *gratuit* so won't cost you a single centime. (p695)

September

As sun-plump grapes hang heavy on darkened vines and that August madness drops off as abruptly as it began, a welcome tranquillity falls across autumnal France. This is the start of France's *vendange* (grape harvest).

🏰 Braderie de Lille

The mountains of empty mussel shells engulfing

the streets after three days of mussel-munching have to be seen to be believed. Then there's the real reason for visiting Lille in the first weekend in September – its huge flea market is Europe's largest. (p211)

🏃 Rutting Season

Nothing beats getting up at dawn to watch mating stags, boar and red deer at play. Observatory towers are hidden in thick forest around Château de Chambord. (p402)

October

The days become shorter, the last grapes are harvested and the first sweet chestnuts fall from trees. With the changing of the clocks on the last Sunday of the month, there's no denying it's winter.

🎇 Nuit Blanche

In one last-ditch attempt to stretch out what's left of summer, museums, monuments, cultural spaces, bars and clubs rock around the clock during Paris' so-called White Night, aka one fabulous long all-nighter! (p118)

November

It's nippy now. Toussaint (All Saints' Day) on 1 November ushers in the switch to shorter winter opening hours for many sights. Many restaurants close two nights a week, making dining out on Monday a challenge in some towns.

🍷 Beaujolais Nouveau

At the stroke of midnight on the third Thursday in November the first bottles of cherry-red Beaujolais *nouveau* are cracked open – and what a party it can be in Beaujolais, Lyon and other places nearby! (p495)

🍷 Vente aux Enchères des Vins des Hospices de Beaune

The grandest of the many wine fests in Burgundy's prestigious Côte d'Or, this three-day extravaganza see the Hospices de Beaune hold a private auction of wine, the proceeds of which go to charity. (p447)

December

Days are short and it's cold everywhere bar the south of France. But there are Christmas school holidays and festive celebrations to bolster sun-deprived souls, not to mention some season-opening winter skiing in the highest-altitude Alpine resorts from mid-December.

☆ Fête des Lumières

France's biggest and best light show, on and around 8 December, transforms the streets and squares of Lyon into an open stage. (p483)

🏰 Alsatian Christmas Markets

Visitors meander between fairy-light-covered craft stalls, mug of *vin chaud* (warm mulled wine) in gloved hand, at Alsace's traditional pre-Christmas markets.

Itineraries

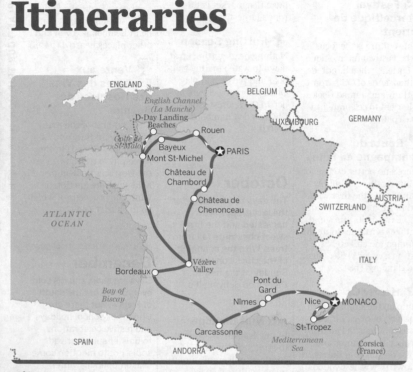

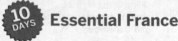

10 DAYS Essential France

For a taste of quintessential France, follow this 10-day 'best of' itinerary.

No place screams 'France!' more than **Paris**. Spend two days in the capital, allowing time for cafe lounging, bistro lunches and waterside strolls along the Seine and Canal St-Martin. On day three, enjoy Renaissance royalty at **Château de Chambord** and **Château de Chenonceau** in the Loire Valley. Or spend two days in Normandy, marvelling at **Rouen's** Notre Dame cathedral, the **Bayeux** tapestry, sea-splashed **Mont St-Michel** and – should modern history be your passion – the **D-Day landing beaches**.

Day five, zoom south for world-class cave art in the **Vézère Valley**. Key sites are around the towns of Les Eyzies-de-Tayac-Sireuil and Montignac. Or base yourself in Sarlat-la-Canéda, showcasing some of France's best medieval architecture and a fabulous food market. Day seven, experience 12 hours in **Bordeaux**, not missing wine tasting in its stunning La Cité du Vin and its sparkling new seafaring Musée de la Mer et de la Marine. Next day, drive three hours to walled **Carcassonne**, Roman **Nîmes** and the **Pont du Gard**. Finish on the French Riviera with a casino flutter in Grace Kelly's **Monaco**, a portside aperitif in Brigitte Bardot's **St-Tropez** and a stroll through Henri Matisse's **Nice**.

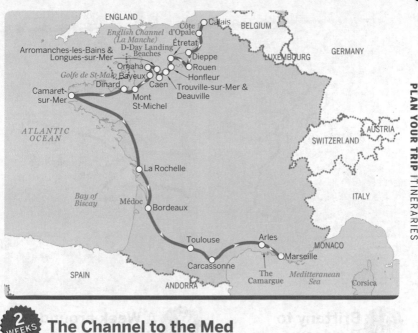

2 WEEKS The Channel to the Med

France has 3427km of coastline, handsomely spread along the Atlantic and the Mediterranean, and a trip from coast to coast uncovers a wealth of dramatically contrasting seascapes, port cities and quaint coastal villages.

Step off the boat in **Calais** and be seduced by cliffs, sand dunes and windy beaches on the spectacular **Côte d'Opale**. Speed southwest, taking in a fish lunch in **Dieppe**, a sensational cathedral visit in **Rouen** or a picturesque cliffside picnic in **Étretat** en route to your overnight stop: your choice of the pretty Normandy seaside resorts of **Honfleur**, **Trouville-sur-Mer** or **Deauville**. Spend two days here: a boat trip beneath the Pont de Normandie, shopping for fresh fish and seafood at Trouville-sur-Mer's waterfront fishmonger, and hobnobbing with Parisians on Deauville's star-studded boardwalk are essentials.

Devote day three to Normandy's D-Day landing beaches. Start with Le Mémorial – Un Musée pour la Paix in **Caen**, the best museum devoted to the Battle of Normandy, then follow a westward arc along the beach-laced coast, taking in caisson-strewn sands at **Arromanches-les-Bains**, gun installations at **Longues-sur-Mer** and the 7km-long stretch of 'bloody **Omaha**'. Come dusk, rejuvenate spent emotions over fresh scallops and *calvados* (apple-flavoured brandy). Or, skip the beaches and go for the stunning representation of 11th-century warfare embroidered across 70m of tapestry in **Bayeux**.

Day four and iconic **Mont St-Michel** beckons – hiking barefoot across the sands here is exhilarating. End the week in Brittany with a flop in an old-fashioned beach tent in **Dinard** and a bracing stroll on spectacular headlands around **Camaret-sur-Mer**.

Week two begins with a long drive south to chic **La Rochelle** for a lavish seafood feast. Spend a night here, continuing the gourmet theme as you wend your way south through Médoc wine country to **Bordeaux**. Next morning, stop in La Ville Rose, **Toulouse**, through which runs the undisputed queen of canals, Canal du Midi, and/or **Carcassonne** before hitting the Med. The Camargue – a wetland of flamingos, horses and incredible birdlife – is a unique patch of coast to explore and Van Gogh thought so too. Follow in his footsteps around **Arles**, before continuing onto the ancient, enigmatic and totally fascinating port city of **Marseille**.

1 WEEK Brittany to Bordeaux

For an exhilarating dose of Breton culture, Atlantic sea air and outstanding wine full of southern sun, there is no finer trip.

It starts fresh off the boat in **St-Malo**, a walled city with sturdy Vauban ramparts that beg exploration at sunset. Walk across at low tide to Île du Grand Bé and lap up great views atop a 14th-century tower in pretty St-Servan. Motor along the Côte d'Émeraude the next day, stopping in picturesque seaside town **Dinard** en route to captivating Breton port **Roscoff**, 200km west. Devote day four to discovering Brittany's famous cider and megaliths around **Carnac**, the enchanting medieval town of **Vannes** overlooking the glittering island-studded Golfe du Morbihan, and the turreted medieval castle in **Josselin**. Push south along the Atlantic coast, stopping in **Nantes** if you like big cities (and riding mechanical elephants), or continuing to the peaceful waterways of 'Green Venice', aka the **Marais Poitevin**. **Bordeaux** is your final destination for day six, from where a bevy of Bordeaux wine-tasting trips tempt. End the journey atop Europe's highest sand dune, **Dune du Pilat**, near oyster-famed **Arcachon**.

1 WEEK A Week around Paris

What makes capital city **Paris** even more wonderful is the extraordinarily green and nonurban journey of Renaissance châteaux and sparkling wine that unfurls within an hour of the city.

Day one has to be France's grandest castle, **Château de Versailles**, and its vast gardens. Second day, feast on France's best-preserved medieval basilica and the dazzling blue stained glass in **Chartres**, an easy train ride away. Small-town **Chantilly** is a good spot to combine a laid-back lunch with a Renaissance château, formal French gardens and – if you snagged tickets in advance – an enchanting equestrian performance. On the fourth day, catch the train to elegant **Reims** in the heart of the Champagne region. Scale its cathedral for dazzling views before tucking into the serious business of Champagne tasting. Dedicated bubbly aficionados can hop the next day to **Épernay**, France's other great Champagne city. On day six, enjoy a lazy start then catch an afternoon fountain show at **Château de Vaux-le-Vicomte**, followed by a candlelit tour of the chateau. End the week with a look at futuristic **La Défense** or, for those with kids, **Disneyland Resort Paris**.

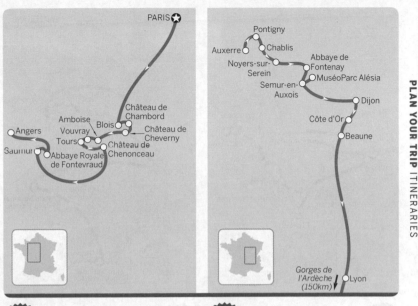

5 DAYS — Along the Loire Valley

For five days of aristocratic pomp and architectural splendour within spitting distance of transport hub **Paris**, there is no finer destination than the château-studded Loire Valley – a Unesco World Heritage destination.

Make your first base the regal city of **Blois**, from where you can take an organised château tour: queen of all castles **Château de Chambord** and the charmingly classical **Château de Cheverny** make a great combo. Day three, follow France's longest river southwest to **Amboise**, final home of Leonardo da Vinci. If wine is a love, build some *dégustation* (tasting) of local **Vouvray** wines in vineyards into your itinerary on the way to solidly bourgeois **Tours**, an easy hop from Amboise. From here **Château de Chenonceau** is beautifully strung across the River Cher 34km east. End your trip with France's elite riding school in **Saumur** and the movingly simple abbey church **Abbaye Royale de Fontevraud** – or push on northwest to **Angers** with its massive black-stone fortress and Apocalypse tapestry. Château de Verrières in Saumur is a befitting overnight address in this château-rich neck of the woods.

6 DAYS — Burgundy & Beyond

Red-wine lovers can enjoy the fruits of Burgundy with this delightful motoring tour.

Begin in the Roman river port of **Auxerre**, 170km southeast of Paris. Explore its ancient abbey and Gothic cathedral, and cycle along towpaths. On day two consider an easy bike ride to pretty **Pontigny**, 25km north. Stay overnight or push on to **Chablis**, where bags more bike rides and gentle hikes between Burgundy vineyards await – allow ample time here to taste the seven *grands crus* of this well-known winemaking town. Day four, meander south to the picture-postcard village of **Noyers-sur-Serein**, then head east to the breathtaking, Unesco-listed **Abbaye de Fontenay**, before winding up for the night in **Semur-en-Auxois**. **MuséoParc Alésia**, where Julius Caesar defeated Gaulish chief Vercingétorix in 52 BC, is not far from here and makes for a fascinating day out. On the last day, discover **Dijon** and its beautiful medieval and Renaissance buildings. From here, should you have more time, take a road trip through the winemaking area of **Côte d'Or** to **Beaune**, or south to **Lyon** in the Rhône Valley and beyond to the rugged **Gorges de l'Ardèche**.

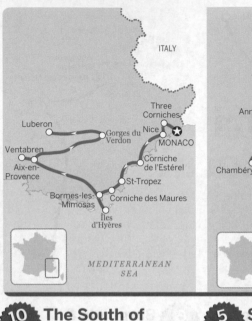

10 DAYS The South of France

For sun, sea and celebrity action, hit France's hot south.

Start in **Nice**, star of the coastline that unfurls in a pageant of belle époque palaces and iconic sands. Drive along the Riviera's trio of legendary **corniches** – coastal views are mind-blowing – and on day three train it to glitzy **Monaco**. Motor southwest next, breaking for a stroll and a few snaps on the red-rock **Corniche de l'Estérel** en route to fishing port **St-Tropez**, where million-dollar yachts jostle for space with street artists. Rise early next morning for the place des Lices market and spend the afternoon on sandy Plage de Pampelonne. Day six is a toss-up between a dramatic drive along the **Corniche des Maures** to **Bormes-les-Mimosas** or a boat trip to the *très belle* **Îles d'Hyères**. Head inland next to **Aix-en-Provence**, a canvas of graceful 19th-century architecture, stylish cafes and squares. From Aix, it's a hop and a skip to **Ventabren**, where lunch or dinner alfresco at La Table de Ventabren is what eating in Provence is all about. Devote your last two days to the wild **Gorges du Verdon**, Europe's largest canyon, two hours' drive northeast, or gentle **Luberon** with its hilltop villages.

5 DAYS Summer in the Alps

A trip to the French Alps often translates as one week of skiing in one place. Yet take time to explore the region after the snow has melted – summer is best – and you'll be pleasantly surprised.

Warm up with old-town ambling, lakeside strolling and warm-weather swimming in fairy-tale **Annecy**, a beautiful medieval town just 45km from Geneva, Switzerland. Day two, shift to **Chamonix** at the foot of Mont Blanc, Europe's highest peak: ride a cable car up to the **Aiguille du Midi** or, if the sky is not crystal-clear, ride a cog railway up to the **Mer de Glace** glacier. Yet more unforgettable views of Mont Blanc seduce along hiking trails in the chic, picturesque Alpine villages of **St-Gervais and Megève**. Let the adrenalin rip, or push on via the ancient Savoyard stronghold of **Chambéry** to the **Parc National de la Vanoise**, where spectacular mountain biking in **Les Trois Vallées** will please the most jaded outdoor junkie. A fitting finale to your Alpine foray is the stunning drive through the **Parc National des Écrins** to **Briançon**, perhaps the loveliest of all the medieval villages in the French Alps, famous for its Vauban fortifications.

Plan Your Trip
Eat & Drink Like a Local

Indulging in France's extraordinary wealth of gastronomic pleasures is reason alone to travel here – cruising around inspires hunger, gastronomic adventure and experimental know-how. Take time to delve into local culinary traditions, with both taste buds and hands, and you'll be rewarded with a far richer and tastier travel experience.

Food Experiences
Meals of a Lifetime

Restaurant Guy Savoy (p154) Triple-Michelin-starred Paris flagship of Guy Savoy, at home in the gorgeously refurbished neoclassical Monnaie de Paris.

La Table de Plaisance (p662) Twin-Michelin-star gastronomy in the wine-rich town of St-Émilion.

Le Vieux Logis (p599) Local Dordogne products, including seasonal truffles, crafted into creative cuisine; in season, join a truffle hunt or the chef at the truffle market.

Le Coquillage (p287) Triple-starred Michelin temple set to French perfection in a château in Brittany; cooking school too.

La Fleur de Sel (p269) A celebration of the underrated culinary riches of Normandy, prepared by a talented Honfleur native in his hometown.

Yoann Conte (p522) Polished, double-Michelin-starred restaurant in a baby-blue house on the shore of Lake Annecy.

L'Oustau de Baumanière (p822) Legendary hotel-restaurant, with two Michelin stars, in Les Baux-de-Provence.

Flaveur (p859) Food becomes art at this double-Michelin-starred restaurant in Nice.

The Year in Food

Feasting happens year-round, and what's cooking changes with the seasons.

Spring (March–May)
Markets burst with asparagus, artichokes and fresh goat's cheese, Easter cooks up traditional lamb for lunch and the first strawberries redden.

Summer (June–August)
Melons, cherries, peaches, apricots, fresh figs, garlic and tomatoes brighten market stalls. Breton shallots are hand-harvested, and on the Atlantic and Mediterranean coasts, diners gorge on seafood and shellfish.

Autumn (September–November)
The Camargue's nutty red rice is harvested. Normandy apples fall from trees to make France's finest cider and the chestnut harvest begins in the Ardèche, Cévennes and Corsica. In damp woods, mushrooming and the game season begin.

Winter (December–February)
Nets are strung beneath silvery groves in Provence and Corsica to catch olives. Pungent markets in the Dordogne and Provence sell black truffles, and in the Alps, skiers dip into cheese fondue. Christmas means Champagne and oysters, foie gras, chestnut-stuffed turkey and yule logs.

Regional Cuisine

Café Lavinal (p661) Outstanding Bordeaux and French classics in a gourmet, winegrowing village in the Médoc.

La Bastide de Moustiers (p846) Legendary table of Provence.

Le Suquet (p758) Gastronomic, Aveyronnais cuisine from southwestern France.

Chez Auguste (p373) Alsatian and bistro fare with locals.

Le Musée (p488) Lyonnais classics *bouchon* (small bistro) style.

Ma Table en Ville (p473) Sensational, traditional Burgundian cooking.

Cheap Treats

Croque monsieur Toasted ham-and-cheese sandwich; cheesy *croques madames* are egg-topped.

Chestnuts Served piping hot in paper bags on street corners in winter.

Socca Chickpea-flour pancake typical to Nice in the French Riviera.

Pan bagnat Crusty Niçois tuna sandwich dripping in fruity green olive oil.

Flammekueche (*tarte flambée* in French) Alsatian thin-crust pizza dough topped with sour cream, onions and bacon.

Ice cream By the best *glaciers* (ice-cream makers) in France: Berthillon (p147) in Paris, La Maison du Glacier (p653) in Bordeaux; Glaces Geronimi (p916) and Raugi (p901) in Corsica; La Martinière (p648) in St-Martin de Ré in Ile de Ré. Myrtle, chestnut, lavender, artichoke or Camembert ice anyone?

Crêpes Large, round, thin sweet pancakes cooked at street-corner stands while you wait.

Galettes Savoury, usually gluten-free crêpes, made with buckwheat flour and typically served with *fromage* (cheese) and *jambon* (ham).

Pissaladière Traditional Niçois 'pizza' topped with salty anchovies and sweet caramelised onions.

Beignets au brocciu Corsican deep-fried doughnuts, sweet or savoury, filled with the island's local cream cheese.

Gougères Utterly irresistible, cheesy pastry puffs typical in Burgundy, usually served with an aperitif but delicious as a cheap snack too.

Dare to Try

Andouillette Big fat sausage made from minced pig intestine; try it in Troyes or Lyon, France's gastronomic heart and known for its piggy cuisine.

Oursins (sea urchins) Caught and eaten west of Marseille in February.

Epoisses de Bourgogne Create a stink with France's undisputed smelliest cheese from Burgundy.

Escargots (snails) Eat them in Burgundy, shells stuffed with garlic and parsley butter, and oven-baked.

Cuisses de grenouilles (frogs' legs) Catching wild frogs and frog farming have been outlawed in France since 1980, but frogs' legs are imported from Southeast Asia, ensuring this French culinary tradition is alive and kicking.

Foie (liver) Die-hard aficionados in the Dordogne eat fresh fattened duck or goose liver, raw and chilled, with a glass of sweet Monbazillac wine.

Pieds de cochon (pig trotters) Just that, or go for the oven-baked trotters of a *mouton* (sheep) or *veau* (calf).

Presskopf Alsatian head cheese or brawn, made with a calf or pig's head.

Beuchelle à la tourangelle Old-world dish from Tours in the Loire Valley, combining calf sweetbreads and kidneys with cream and mushrooms.

Local Specialities

Gourmet appetites know no bounds in France, paradise for food lovers with its varied cuisine, markets and local gusto for dining well. Go to Burgundy for hearty wine-based cooking, Brittany and the Atlantic Coast for seafood, and Basque Country for a slice of Spanish spice.

Normandy

Cream, apples and cider are the essentials of Norman cuisine, which sees mussels simmered in cream and a splash of cider to make *moules à la crème normande* and tripe thrown in the slow pot with cider and vegetables to make *tripes à la mode de Caen*. Creamy Camembert is the local cow's-milk cheese, and on the coast *coquilles St-Jacques* (scallops) and *huîtres* (oysters) rule the seafood roost. Apples are the essence of the region's main tipples: tangy cider and the potent *calvados*

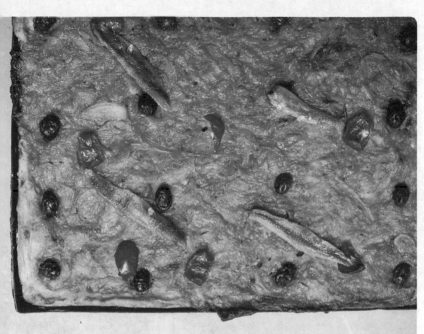

Pissaladière (p858)

(apple-flavoured brandy), exquisite straight or splashed on apple sorbet.

Burgundy

Vine-wealthy Burgundy honours a culinary trinity of beef, red wine and Dijon mustard. Begin with *oeufs en meurette* (wine-poached eggs) or snails, traditionally served by the dozen and oven-baked in their shells with butter, garlic and parsley. Savour bœuf bourguignon (beef marinated and cooked in young red wine with mushrooms, onions, carrots and bacon), followed by the pick of Burgundy AOC cheeses.

Wine tasting in the Côte d'Or vineyards, source of world-famous Côte de Nuits and Côte de Beaune wines, is obligatory when in Burgundy; laid-back Irancy, less known around the globe but much-loved by locals, is an insider favourite.

The Dordogne

This southwest region is fabulously famous for its indulgent black truffles and poultry, especially ducks and geese, who are typically force-fed to ensure suitably fattened livers to go into foie gras (literally 'fattened liver'). *Pâté de foie gras* (duck- or goose-liver pâté)

is served straight or flavoured with Cognac and truffles. *Confit de canard* and *confit d'oie* are duck or goose joints cooked very slowly in their own fat. Snails are another tasty treat – savour one stuffed with foie gras. Walnuts from the region's abundant walnut groves go into *eau de noix* (caramel-coloured walnut liqueur).

Lyon

Lyon is dubbed France's gastronomic capital. And while it doesn't compete with France's capital when it comes to variety of international cuisine, it certainly holds its own when it comes to titillating taste buds with the unusual and inventive. Take the age-old repertoire of feisty, often pork-driven dishes served in the city's legendary *bouchons* (small bistros): breaded fried tripe, big fat *andouillettes* (pig-intestine sausage), silk-weaver's brains (a herbed cheese spread, not brains at all) – there is no way you can ever say Lyonnais cuisine is run of the mill. A lighter, less meaty speciality is *quenelle de brochet*, a poached dumpling made of freshwater fish (usually pike) and served with sauce Nantua (a cream and freshwater-crayfish sauce).

SHAIITH/SHUTTERSTOCK ©

Top: Galettes
Bretonnes (p716)

Bottom: Escargots
(snails; p36)

SENSATIONAL SEAFOOD ON THE COAST

Perard (p224) One of France's most famous seafood restaurants in the fabled beach resort of Le Touquet.

La Co(o)rniche (p665) Atlantic Coast oysters and seafood platters overlooking Europe's largest sand dune.

Le Matahari (p909) Corsican tropical paradise cooking up Mediterranean fusion.

Le Kaiku (p687) Gastronomic seafood with a Basque twist in St-Jean de Luz.

Le Coquillage (p287) Château dining with a Michelin-starred chef near Cancale, Brittany.

Equally fine is the Lyonnais wine list where very fine Côtes de Rhône reds vie for attention with local Brouilly and highly esteemed Mâcon reds from nearby Burgundy. In *bouchons,* local Beaujolais is mixed with a dash of blackcurrant liqueur to make a blood-red *communard* aperitif.

Alsace

No Alsatian dish is more classic than *choucroute alsacienne* or *choucroute garnie* – sauerkraut flavoured with juniper berries and served hot with sausages, bacon, pork and/or ham knuckle. It's meaty, Teutonic and served in *winstubs* (traditional Alsatian taverns). *Wädele braisé au pinot noir* (ham knuckles braised in wine) also come with sauerkraut. Crack open a bottle of light citrusy sylvaner, crisp dry Alsatian riesling or full-bodied pinot noir to accompany either, and round off the filling feast with a *tarte alsacienne,* a scrumptious custard tart made with local fruit such as mirabelles (sweet yellow plums) or *quetsches* (a variety of purple plum). Beer might be big in Alsace but it's a big no-no when it comes to sauerkraut. Sweet tooths will adore Alsatian gingerbread and *kougelhopf* (sugared, ring-shaped raisin cake).

Provence & the Côte d'Azur

Cuisine in this sun-baked land is laden with tomatoes, melons, cherries, peaches, olives, Mediterranean fish and Alpine cheese. Farmers gather at the weekly market to sell their fruit and vegetables, woven garlic plaits, dried herbs displayed in stubby coarse sacks, and olives stuffed with a multitude of edible sins. *À la Provençal* still means anything with a generous dose of garlic-seasoned tomatoes, while a simple *filet mignon* sprinkled with olive oil and rosemary fresh from the garden makes the same magnificent Sunday lunch it did generations ago.

Yet there are exciting culinary contrasts in this region, which see fisherfolk return with the catch of the day in seafaring Marseille; grazing bulls and paddy fields in the Camargue; lambs in the Alpilles; black truffles in the Vaucluse; cheese made from cow's milk in Alpine pastures; and an Italianate accent to cooking in seaside Nice.

Bouillabaisse, Marseille's mighty meal of fish stew, is Provence's most famous contribution to French cuisine. The chowder must contain at least three kinds of fresh saltwater fish, cooked for about 10 minutes in a broth containing onions, tomatoes, saffron and various herbs, and eaten as a main course with toasted bread and *rouille* (a spicy red mayonnaise of olive oil, garlic and chilli peppers).

The fish stew *bourride* is similar to bouillabaisse but has fewer ingredients, a less prescriptive recipe, and often a slightly creamier sauce. It's usually served with aïoli.

When in Provence, do as the Provençaux do: drink pastis. An aniseed-flavoured, 45%-alcohol drink, it was invented in Marseille by industrialist Paul Ricard in 1932. Amber-coloured in the bottle, it turns milky white when mixed with water. An essential lunch or dinner companion is a chilled glass of the region's irresistibly pink, AOC Côtes de Provence rosé wine.

Brittany

Brittany is a paradise for seafood lovers (think lobster, scallops, sea bass, turbot, mussels and oysters from Cancale) as well as kids, thanks to the humble crêpe and *galette,* an ancient culinary tradition that has long ruled Breton cuisine. Pair a sweet wheat-flour pancake or savoury buckwheat *galette* with *une bolée* (a stubby terracotta goblet) of apple-rich Breton cider, and taste buds enter gourmet heaven. Royal Guillevic and ciders produced by the Domaine de Kervéguen are excellent quality, artisanal ciders to try. If cider is not your cup of tea, order a local beer like Coreff or nonalcoholic *lait ribot* (fermented milk). *Chouchen* (hydromel), a fermented honey liqueur, is a typical Breton aperitif.

Cheese is not big, but *la beurre de Bretagne* (Breton butter) is. Traditionally sea-salted and creamy, a knob of it naturally goes into crêpes, *galettes* and the most outrageously buttery cake you're likely to ever taste in your life – *kouign amann* (Breton butter cake). Bretons, unlike the rest of the French, even butter their bread. Butter handmade by Jean-Yves Bordier – buy it at his shop in St-Malo (p284) – ends up on tables of top restaurants around the world.

Seaweed is another Breton culinary curiosity, and 80% of French shallots are grown here.

Languedoc-Roussillon

No dish better evokes Languedoc than *cassoulet,* an earthy cockle-warming stew of white beans and meat that fires passionate debate. Everyone knows best which type of bean and meat hunk should be thrown in the *cassole,* the traditional earthenware dish it is cooked and brought to the table in. Otherwise this region's trademark cuisine *campag-*

narde (country cooking) sees fisherfolk tending lagoon oyster beds on the coast, olives being pressed in gentle hills inland, blue-veined 'king of cheeses' ripening in caves in Roquefort, geese and gaggles of ducks fattening around Toulouse, sheep munching in salty marsh meadows around Montpellier, and mushrooms growing in forests.

In Uzès, *croquignoles* (shortbread biscuits adorned with a sweet almond or hazelnut and covered in orange syrup after baking) are a sweet treat. A Spanish accent gives cuisine in neighbouring Roussillon a fiery twist of exuberance.

Basque Country

Among the essential ingredients of Basque cooking are the deep-red Espelette chillies that add bite to many dishes, including the dusting on the signature *jambon de Bayonne,* the locally prepared Bayonne ham. Eating out in this part of France near Spain is a delight thanks to its many casual *pintxo* (tapas) bars serving garlic prawns, spicy chorizo and other local dishes tapas-style. Wash the whole lot down with a glass of local cider (*sidrea* in Basque), lighter and more sparkling than ciders in northern France, best poured in a glass at arm's length. *Izarra* is a much-loved herbal liqueur.

Basques love cakes, especially *gâteau basque* (cake filled with cream or cherry jam). Then there's Bayonne chocolate...

THE PERFECT CHEESEBOARD

Treat your taste buds to the perfect balance of cheese by taking at least one of each type from the cheeseboard:

Goat's cheese *(fromage de chèvre)* Made from goat's milk.

Soft cheese *(fromage à pâté molle)* Moulded or rind-washed, the classic soft cheese that everyone knows is Camembert from Normandy made from unpasteurised cow's milk. Munster from Alsace is a fine-textured, rind-washed cheese.

Semihard cheese *(fromage à pâté demi-dure)* Among the finest uncooked, pressed cheese is Tomme de Savoie, made from pasteurised or unpasteurised cow's milk near the Alps; and St-Nectaire, a strong-smelling pressed cheese with a complex taste.

Hard cheese *(fromage à pâté dure)* Must-taste cooked and pressed cheeses are Beaufort, a fruity cow's-milk cheese from Rhône-Alpes; Comté, made with raw cow's milk in Franche-Comté; emmental, a cow's-milk cheese made all over France; and Mimolette, an Edam-like bright-orange cheese from Lille aged for as long as 36 months.

Blue cheese *(fromage à pâté persillée)* 'Marbled' or with veins that resemble *persil* (parsley).

Bouillabaisse (p795)

Corsica

The hills and mountains of the island of Corsica have always been ideal for raising stock, and the dense Corsican underbrush called the *maquis* is made up of shrubs mixed with wild herbs. These raw materials come together to create aromatic trademark Corsican dishes like *stufatu* (fragrant mutton stew), *premonata* (beef braised with juniper berries) and *lonzo* (Corsican sausage cooked with white beans, white wine and herbs).

How to Eat & Drink

It pays to know what and how much to eat, and when – adopting the local culinary pace is key to savouring every last exquisite moment of the French day.

When to Eat

Petit déjeuner (breakfast) The French kick-start the day with a tartine (slice of baguette smeared with unsalted butter and jam) and *un café* (es-

presso), long milky *café au lait* or – especially for kids – hot chocolate. In hotels you get a real cup but in French homes, coffee and hot chocolate are drunk from a cereal bowl – perfect bread-dunking terrain. Croissants (eaten straight, never with butter or jam) are a weekend treat along with brioches (sweet breads), *pains au chocolat* (chocolate-filled croissants) and other *viennoiserie* (sweet baked goods).

Déjeuner (lunch) A meal few French would go without. The traditional main meal of the day, lunch translates as a starter and main course with wine, followed by an espresso. Sunday lunch is a long, languid affair taking several hours. Indeed, a fully fledged, traditional French meal – *déjeuner* or *dîner* – can comprise six courses, each accompanied by a different wine. Standard restaurant lunch hours are noon to 2.30pm.

Aperitif The *apéro* (predinner drink) is sacred. Urban cafes and bars get packed out from around 5pm onwards as workers relax over a chit-chat-fuelled *kir* (white wine sweetened with blackcurrant syrup), glass of red or beer. Come weekends, a leisurely noon-time *apéro* before lunch is equally acceptable – and oh so pleasurable.

Goûter An afternoon snack, devoured with particular relish by French children. A slab of milk chocolate inside a wedge of baguette is a traditional favourite.

Dîner (dinner) Traditionally lighter than lunch, but a meal that is increasingly treated as the main meal of the day. Standard restaurant times are 7pm to 10.30pm.

Where to Eat

Auberge Country inn serving traditional fare, often attached to a small hotel.

Ferme auberge Working farm that cooks up meals from local farm products; usually only dinner and frequently only by reservation.

Bistro (also spelled *bistrot*) Anything from a pub or bar with snacks and light meals to a small, fully fledged restaurant.

Neobistro Trendy in Paris and large cities where this contemporary take on the traditional bistro embraces everything from checked-tablecloth tradition to contemporary minimalism.

Brasserie Much like a cafe except it serves full meals, drinks and coffee from morning until 11pm or later. Typical fare includes *choucroute* (sauerkraut) and *moules frites* (mussels and fries).

Restaurant Born in Paris in the 18th century, restaurants today serve lunch and dinner five or six days a week.

Buffet (or *buvette*) Kiosk, usually at train stations and airports, selling drinks, filled baguettes and snacks.

Cafe Basic light snacks as well as drinks.

Crêperie (also *galetterie*) Casual address specialising in sweet crêpes and savoury *galettes* (buckwheat crêpes).

Salon de thé Trendy tearoom often serving light lunches (quiche, salads, cakes, tarts, pies and pastries) as well as green, black and herbal teas.

Table d'hôte (literally 'host's table') Some of the most charming B&Bs serve *table d'hôte* too, a delicious homemade meal of set courses with little or no choice.

Winstub Cosy wine tavern in Alsace serving traditional Alsatian cooking and local wines.

Estaminet Flemish-style eatery of Flanders and *le nord*, cooking up regional fare.

Etiquette

Table reservations To snag a table in the best addresses, particularly at weekends, booking a table well in advance by telephone or email is vital.

MENU DECODER

Carte	Menu, as in the written list of what's cooking, listed in the order you'd eat it: starter, main course, cheese then dessert.
Menu	Not at all what it means in English, *le menu* in French is a two- or three-course meal at a fixed price. It's by far the best-value dining and most bistros and restaurants chalk one on the board. Lunch *menus* – usually incredibly good value – occasionally include a glass of wine and/or coffee; dinner *menus* in gastronomic restaurants sometimes pair a perfectly matched glass of wine with each course.
À la carte	Order whatever you fancy from the menu (as opposed to choosing a fixed *menu*).
Formule	Not to be confused with a *menu*, une *formule* is a cheaper lunchtime option comprising a main plus starter or dessert.
Plat du jour	Dish of the day, invariably good value.
Menu enfant	Two- or three-course kids' meal at a fixed price (generally for children up to the age of 12); usually includes a soft drink.
Menu dégustation	Fixed-price tasting *menu* served in many top-end restaurants, consisting of five to seven modestly sized courses.
Amuse-bouche	A complimentary savoury morsel intended to excite and ignite taste buds, served in top-end and gastronomic restaurants at the very beginning of a meal.
Entrée	Starter, appetiser.
Plat	Main course.
Fromage	Cheese, accompanied with fresh bread (never crackers and no butter); always served after the main course and *before* dessert.
Dessert	Just that, served *after* cheese.

Bread Order a meal and within seconds a basket of fresh bread will be brought to the table. Butter is rarely an accompaniment, and when it is (occasionally in top-end addresses), it will be *doux* (unsalted). Except in upmarket places, don't expect a side plate – simply put it on the table. And yes, in bistros and other casual diners, it is perfectly acceptable to mop up what's left of that delicious sauce on your plate with a bread chunk.

Water Asking for *une carafe d'eau* (jug of tap water) is acceptable. Should bubbles be your cup of tea, ask for *de l'eau gazeuze* (some fizzy mineral water). Perrier is the most popular French brand.

Coffee Never end a meal with a cappuccino, *café au lait* or cup of tea, which, incidentally, never comes with milk in France. Play French and order *un café* (espresso).

Dress Smart casual is best, particularly in Paris and on the French Riviera where local hipsters dress up for dinner. In provincial towns and rural France, anything goes providing you're well-covered. No bikini tops or bare male chests *s'il vous plaît*.

Picnic Perfect

France might have Michelin-starred restaurants aplenty to thrill your taste buds, but some of the most memorable foodie experiences can be had by just finding a fine picnic spot to soak up the views, sunshine and stunning local produce. Picnic-hamper suggestions:

Baguette French simplicity at its best: buy a baguette from the *boulangerie (bakery)*, stuff it with a chunk of Camembert, pâté and *cornichons* (miniature gherkins), or a few slices of *rosette de Lyon* or other salami and, *voilà,* picnic perfection!

DOGGY BAGS

Don't be shy in asking for a doggy bag! Since 1 January 2016 restaurants are officially obliged to provide a doggy bag to customers wanting to take the remains of their meal home. The law applies to any restaurant serving more than 180 meals a day.

In a similar food-waste tackling vein, restaurants producing more than 10 tonnes of waste a year now have to recycle it.

If you're sweet-toothed, do it the French-kid way – wedge a slab of milk chocolate inside.

Macarons No sweeter way to end a gourmet picnic, most famously from Ladurée (p136) in Paris who, in 2017, opened its first specialised picnic boutique (p155).

Kouign amann The world's most buttery, syrupy cake, aka Breton butter cake.

Fruit Big juicy black cherries from Apt, peaches, apricots and tomatoes from the Rhône Valley, Provence and the Riviera.

Provençal olives or peppers Marinated and stuffed morsels sold at market stalls.

Kougelhopf and gingerbread Try the Alsatian sugared, ring-shaped raisin cake, or treat yourself to gingerbread.

Champagne From Reims and *biscuits roses* (pink ladyfinger sponge biscuits).

Country produce Pâté, walnuts and foie gras from the Dordogne.

Plan Your Trip
Travel with Children

Be it the kid-friendly extraordinaire capital or rural hinterland, France spoils families with its rich mix of cultural sights, activities and entertainment – some paid for, some free. To get the most out of travelling en famille, plan ahead.

Best Regions for Kids

Paris
Interactive museums, choice dining for every taste and budget, and beautiful green parks seemingly at every turn make the French capital a top choice for families.

Normandy
Beaches, boats and some great stuff for history-mad kids and teens give this northern region plenty of family allure.

Brittany
More beaches, boats, pirate-perfect islands and bags of good old-fashioned outdoor fun. Enough said.

French Alps & the Jura Mountains
Winter in this mountainous region in eastern France translates as one giant outdoor (snowy) playground – for all ages.

French Riviera & Monaco
A vibrant arts scene, a vivacious cafe culture and a beach-laced shore riddled with seafaring activities keeps kids of all ages on their toes.

Corsica
Sailing, kayaking, walking, biking, or simply dipping your toes or snorkel mask in clear turquoise waters: life on this island is fairy-tale *belle* (beautiful).

France for Kids

Savvy parents can find kid-appeal in almost every sight in France, must-sees included. Skip the formal guided tour of Mont St-Michel, for example, and hire a walking guide to lead you and the children barefoot across the sand to the abbey; trade the day-time queues at the Eiffel Tower for a tour after dark with teens; don't dismiss wine tasting in Provence or Burgundy outright – rent bicycles and turn it into a family bike ride instead. The opportunities are endless.

Musuems & Monuments

Many Paris museums organise creative *ateliers* (workshops) for children, parent-accompanied or solo. Workshops are themed, require booking, last 1½ to two hours, and cost €5 to €20 per child. French children have no school Wednesday afternoon, so most workshops happen at that time, week-ends and during school holidays. Most cater for kids aged seven to 14 years, but in Paris art activities at the Louvre start at four years and at the Musée d'Orsay, five years.

Countrywide, when buying tickets at museums and monuments, ask about children's activity sheets – most have something to hook kids. Another winner is to arm your gadget-mad child (from six years) with an audioguide. Older children can check out what apps a museum or monument might have for smartphones and tablets.

Outdoor Activities

Once the kids are out of nappies, skiing in the French Alps is the obvious family choice. Ski school École du Ski Français (www.esf.net) initiates kids in the art of snow plough (group or private lessons, half or full day) from four years old, and many resorts open fun-driven *jardins de neige* (snow gardens) to children from three years old. Families with kids aged under 10 will find smaller resorts including Les Gets, Avoriaz (car-free), La Clusaz, Chamrousse and Le Grand Bornand easier to navigate and better value than larger ski stations. Then, of course, there is all the fun of the fair off-piste: ice skating, sledging, snowshoeing, mushing, indoor swimming pools...

The French Alps and Pyrenees are prime walking areas. Tourist offices have information on easy, well-signposted family walks, or get in touch with a local guide. In Chamonix, the cable-car ride and two-hour hike to Lac Blanc followed by a dip in the Alpine lake is a DIY family favourite; as are the mountain-discovery half-days for ages three to seven, and outdoor-adventure days for ages eight to 12 run by Cham' Aventure (p507). As with skiing, smaller places such as the Parc Naturel Régional du Massif des Bauges cater much better to young families than the big names everyone knows.

White-water sports and canoeing are doable for children aged seven and older; the French Alps, Provence and Massif Central are key areas. Mountain biking is an outdoor thrill that teens can share – try Morzine. Or dip into some gentle sea kayaking around *calanques* (deep rocky inlets), below cliffs and into caves in the Mediterranean, a family activity suitable for kids aged four and upwards. Marseille in Provence and Bonifacio on Corsica are hot spots to rent the gear and get afloat.

Entertainment

Tourist offices can tell you what's on – and the repertoire is impressive: puppet shows alfresco, children's theatres, children's films at cinemas Wednesday afternoon and weekends, street buskers, illuminated monuments after dark, an abundance of music festivals and so on. Sure winners are the *son et lumière* (sound-and-light) shows projected on some Renaissance châteaux in the Loire Valley; the papal palace in Avignon; and cathedral façades in Rouen, Chartres

IMAGE: MARTIN-DM / GETTY IMAGES ©

Musée du Louvre (p81)

and Amiens. Outstanding after-dark illuminations that never fail to enchant include Paris' Eiffel Tower and Marseille's MuCEM.

Dining Out

French children, accustomed to three-course lunches at school, expect a starter *(entrée)*, main course *(plat)* and dessert as their main meal of the day. They know the difference between Brie and Camembert, and eat lettuce, grated carrot and other salads no problem. Main meals tend to be meat and veg or pasta, followed by dessert and/or a slice of cheese. Classic French mains loved by children include *gratin dauphinois* (sliced potatoes oven-baked in cream), *escalope de veau* (breaded pan-fried veal) and bœuf bourguignon. Fondue and *raclette* (melted cheese served with potatoes and cold meats) become favourites from about five years, and *moules frites* (mussels and fries) a couple of years later.

Children's *menus* (fixed meals at a set price) are common, although anyone in France for more than a few days will soon tire of the ubiquitous spaghetti bolognaise or *saucisse* (sausage), or *steak haché* (beef burger) and *frites* (fries) followed by ice

Crêpes with raspberries

selling hot chestnuts. *Galettes* (savoury buckwheat crêpes) make for an easy light lunch, as does France's signature croque monsieur (toasted cheese-and-ham sandwich) served by most cafes and brasseries. *Goûter* (afternoon snack), devoured after school around 4.30pm, is golden for every French child and *salons de thé* (tearooms) serve a mouth-watering array of cakes, pastries and biscuits. Or go local: buy a baguette, rip off a chunk and pop a chunk of chocolate inside.

Baby requirements are easily met. The choice of infant formula, soy and cow's milk, nappies (diapers) and jars of baby food in supermarkets and pharmacies is similar to any developed country, although opening hours are more limited (few shops open Sunday). Organic *(bio)* baby food is harder to find.

Drinks

Buy a fizzy drink for every child sitting at the table and the bill soars. Opt instead for a free *carafe d'eau* (jug of tap water) with meals and *un sirop* (flavoured fruit syrup) in between – jazzed up with *des glaçons* (some ice cubes) and *une paille* (a straw). Every self-respecting cafe and bar in France has dozens of syrup flavours to choose from: pomegranate-fuelled grenadine and pea-green *menthe* (mint) are French-kid favourites, but there are peach, raspberry, cherry, lemon and a rainbow of others too. Syrup is served diluted with water and, best up, costs a good €2 less than a coke. Expect to pay around €1.50 a glass.

cream that most feature. Don't be shy in asking for a half-portion of an adult main – restaurants generally oblige. In budget and midrange places you can ask for a plate of *pâtes au beurre* (pasta with butter) for fussy or very young eaters.

Bread, specifically slices of baguette, accompanies every meal and in restaurants is brought to the table before or immediately after you've ordered – to the glee of children who wolf it down while they wait. Wait for the fight to begin over who gets the *quignon* (the knobbly end bit, a hit with teething babies!).

It is perfectly acceptable to dine *en famille* after dark provided the kids don't run wild. Few restaurants open their doors, however, before 7.30pm or 8pm, making brasseries and cafes – many serve food continuously from 7am or 8am until midnight – more appealing for families with younger children. Some restaurants have high chairs and supply paper and pens for children to draw with while waiting for their meal.

France is fabulous snack-attack terrain. Parisian pavements are rife with crêpe stands and wintertime stalls

Children's Highlights
Gastronomic Experiences

Ladurée, Paris (p136) Cakes too beautiful to eat over afternoon tea at this historic tearoom.

Berthillon, Paris (p147) Ice cream in dozens of different crazy flavours; regional master ice-cream makers include Geronimi (p916) and Raugi (p901) in Corsica; La Maison du Glacier (p653) in Bordeaux; La Martinière (p648) in St-Martin de Ré.

Meert, Lille (p211) Waffles with sweet vanilla cream, served since the 18th century.

La Cité du Vin, Bordeaux (p650) Grape-juice tasting; parents taste the alcoholic equivalent.

La Bicyclette Bleue, La Dombes (p497) Frogs' legs and a lakeside bike ride.

Moutarderie Fallot, Beaune (p444) Hand-mill mustard seeds with stone at this mustard factory.

Musée du Champignon, Saumur (p420) Get acquainted with fabulous fungi at the mushroom farm in a cave.

L'Atelier du Chocolat, Bayonne (p673) Watch chocolate being made in this Basque chocolate factory and museum.

Roquefort Société, Roquefort (p773) Taste 'mouldy' cheese after a visit to the cheese-maturing cellars dug into the Languedoc hillside.

Energy Burners

French Alps (p502) and the Pyrenees (p693) Skiing, snowboarding, sledging and dog-mushing (from four years).

Aiguille du Midi, Chamonix (p503) Glide up this mountain peak by gondola and cross glaciers into Italy (from four years).

Île de Ré (p647) and Île de Porquerolles (p887) Explore an island by bike (over five years) or parent-pulled bike trailer (over one year).

Gorges du Verdon (p844), Gorges du Tarn (p768) and Gorges de l'Ardèche (p499) White-water sports (over seven years).

Pont du Gard, Nîmes (p745) Canoe (over seven years) beneath a Roman aqueduct, or along the Dordogne River around La Roque Gageac.

Parc National des Cévennes, Languedoc (p766) Donkey trek (over 10 years) like Robert Louis Stevenson.

Camargue, Provence (p808) Ride horses with cowboys.

Acrobastille, Grenoble (p539) Zip between trees on wires (from five years).

Val Thorens, French Alps (p526) Fly along the world's highest zip wire (from eight years).

Domaine du Rayol, Corniche des Maures (p885) Embark on a snorkelling safari on the French Riviera or snorkel off island shores on Porquerolles, Port-Cros and Corsica (from six years).

Best Free Stuff

Fort St-Jean, Marseille (p785) Crazy about castles? No fortress is finer to explore.

> ### ADMISSION PRICES
> •
>
> There is no rule on how much and from what age children pay – many museums and monuments are free to under 18 years. In general, under fives don't pay (a noteworthy exception is Paris' must-do Cité des Sciences et de l'Industrie which costs from two years). Some museums offer money-saving family tickets, worth buying once you count two adults and two children or more.

Route des Vins d'Alsace, Alsace (p356) Watch fairy tales come to life before your eyes in half-timbered, castle-topped villages.

Miroir d'Eau, Bordeaux (p650) Frolicking barefoot in the world's largest reflecting pool. Fountain dipping is also big in Lyon (place des Terreaux), Dijon (place de la Libération) and Paris (place de la République).

Dune du Pilat, Atlantic Coast (p664) Run wild on the largest 'sandcastle' any child is ever likely to see.

Festival Off, Avignon (p823) World-class freebie festival that kids love; Lyon's Fête des Lumières (p483) and the Carnaval de Nice (p855) are other memorable favourites.

Maison Natale de Pierre Fermat, Toulouse Area (p726) Learn about the life and works of 17th-century mathematician Pierre de Fermat through puzzles and games at this fun house museum.

Wildlife Watch

Pointe du Hourdel, Baie de Somme (p225) Admire colonies of sandbank-lounging seals in northern France.

Parc National de la Vanoise, French Alps (p535) Come face-to-face with ibex, chamois and cuddly, kid-pleasing marmots.

Parc Polaire, Jura (p559) Close encounters with scampering chamois, Greenland huskies, horned stags, yaks and wild horses.

Parc National du Mercantour (p843), **Parc Animalier des Monts de Guéret** (Loups de Chabrières; ☎05 55 81 23 23; www.loups-chabrieres.com; Guéret; adult/child €10/7.50; ⏱10am-7pm Jul & Aug, shorter hours rest of year, closed Dec & Jan) and Les Loups du Gévaudan (p768) Wolves.

Musée Océanographique de Monaco (p889)

Réserve Ornithologique du Teich, near Arcachon (Bird Reserve; ☑05 56 22 80 93; www. reserve-ornithologique-du-teich.com; La Teich; adult/child €8.90/6.70; ☉10am-8pm Jul & Aug, to 7pm mid-Apr–Jun & 1-15 Sep, to 6pm mid-Sep–mid-Apr) Observe storks and kingfishers.

NaturOparC, Hunawihr (p364) Discover the springtime joy of hatchling storks in Alsace.

Réserve de Bisons d'Europe, Mende (p768) Watch European bison at close quarters.

Parc des Oiseaux, La Dombes (p497) Marvel at hundreds of local and exotic birds at this well-organised bird park near Lyon.

Maison des Vautours, Haut-Languedoc (p772) Watch vultures soar through mountain skies in the wild Grands Causses; the Parc National des Pyrénées (p703) and the Gorges du Verdon (p844) in Provence are other spots vultures love.

Rainy Days

Musée des Égouts, Paris (Map p76; ☑01 53 68 27 81; http://equipement.paris.fr/musee-des-egouts-5059; place de la Résistance, 7e; adult/child €4.40/3.60; ☉11am-5pm Mon-Wed, Sat & Sun; Ⓜ Alma Marceau or RER Pont de l'Alma) Romp through sewage tunnels with rats.

Musée Océanographique de Monaco (p889) Stunning museum with aquarium dating to 1910.

Le Petit Musée Fantastique de Guignol, Lyon (p476) Immerse yourself in the enchanting world of puppetry.

Aquarium La Rochelle (p643) This Atlantic Coast aquarium is among France's finest; find others in Paris, Boulogne-sur-Mer, St-Malo, Montpellier, Brest, Lyon and Biarritz.

Les Catacombes, Paris (p107) Ogle at thousands upon thousands of skulls (from 14 years).

Aven Armand, Languedoc (p771) Discover the world's largest collection of stalactites.

Vézère Valley, Dordogne (p605) Play cavepeople in caves riddled with prehistoric art.

Cité de l'Océan, Biarritz (p674) Delve into the depths of the ocean in southwest France.

Micropolis, near Millau (p772) Inspect insects, lots of insects, in Languedoc.

Musée du Bonbon Haribo, Uzès (p746) Sweeter than sweet, sweet museum.

Le Train Jaune, Pyrenees (p779) Watch spectacular Pyrenean scenery unfold aboard this mythical mountain train.

Citadelle de Besançon, Besançon (p550) Far more than a fabulous set of rambling ancient walls: insect house and zoo too.

Tech Experiences

Les Machines de l'Île de Nantes (p635) Fly on a heron or ride a house-sized mechanical elephant at this fantastical workshop like no other.

Cité des Sciences, Paris (p114) Sign up for a hands-on science workshop at the capital's leading science museum (from three years).

Palais de la Découverte, Paris (p80) The other key address for budding young scientists (from 10 years) in the capital.

Le Vaisseau, Strasbourg (p351) Science is never boring at this interactive science and technology museum in northern France.

Jean Luc Lagardère Airbus factory, Toulouse (p723) Learn how planes are built (from six years).

Cité de l'Automobile and Cité du Train, Mulhouse (p372) Enter wannabe-mechanic heaven at these two museums.

Funiculaire du Capucin, Massif Central (p575) This 100 year-old funicular is one mighty cool way to climb the mountain of Le Mont-Dore.

L'Aventure Michelin, Clermont-Ferrand (p563) Map-making, shiny cars, flashy TV screens and lots of interactive displays geared towards kids.

Theme Parks

Cité de l'Espace, Toulouse (p723) Explore the depths of outer space and discover what life is like as an astronaut.

Disneyland, Paris (p188) Throw yourself into the magical world of Disney, with its five themed lands and bonanza of a-thrill-a-minute rides and shows.

Vulcania, Massif Central (p573) Thrills, spills and highly educative stuff too about Auvergne's long-extinct volcanoes.

Futuroscope, Poitiers (p641) Space-age cinematic experiences for all ages at this huge, film-themed fun park.

Musée Parc des Dinosaures et de la Préhistoire, Languedoc-Roussillon (p755) Take a stroll in the woods but be warned, life-size dinosaur models lurk where you least expect them.

TOP WEBSITES

Familiscope (www.familiscope.fr) Definitive family-holiday planner: endless activity, outing and entertainment listings.

Tots to Travel (http://totstotravel.co.uk) Self-catering properties vetted by a team of trained mums.

Baby-friendly Boltholes (www.babyfriendlyboltholes.co.uk) This London-based enterprise specialises in sourcing charming and unique family accommodation.

Baby Goes 2 (www.babygoes2.com) Why, where, how-to travel guide aimed squarely at families.

Planning

Accommodation

In Paris and larger towns and cities, serviced apartments equipped with washing machine and kitchen are suited to families with younger children. Countrywide, hotels with family or four-person rooms can be hard to find and need booking in advance. Functional, if soulless, chain hotels such as Formule 1, found on the outskirts of most large towns, always have a generous quota of family rooms and make convenient overnight stops for motorists driving from continental Europe or the UK (Troyes is a popular stopover for Brits en route to the Alps). Parents with just one child and/or a baby in tow will have no problem finding hotel accommodation – most midrange hotels have baby cots and are happy to put a child's bed in a double room for a minimal extra cost.

In rural France, family-friendly B&Bs and *fermes auberges* (farm stays) are convenient. For older children, tree houses decked out with bunk beds and Mongolian yurts create a real family adventure.

Camping is huge with French families: check into a self-catering mobile home, wooden chalet or tent; sit back on the verandah with glass of wine in hand and watch as your kids – wonderfully oblivious to any barriers language might pose – run around with new-found French friends.

Plan Your Trip
Activities

From Alpine glaciers, rivers and canyons to the volcanic peaks of the Massif Central – not to mention 3427km of coastline stretching from Italy to Spain and from the Basque country to the Straits of Dover – France's spirit-lifting landscapes beg outdoor escapes. Or move inside and try your hand at perfumery, knife-making or another traditional French craft.

Best Outdoor Experiences

Best Off-Piste Descent
Whoop as you make a 2800m vertical descent on La Vallée Blanche in Chamonix – it's the ride of a lifetime.

Best Long-Distance Hike
Scale the wildest heights of the Pyrenees on the GR10, taking you from the Mediterranean to the Atlantic.

Best Cycling
Cruise past turreted châteaux and trace the curves of France's longest river in the Loire Valley.

Best Surf
Grab your board and hit the fizzing surf on the Atlantic Coast. Hossegor and Capbreton, north of Bayonne in French Basque Country, are big-wave heaven.

Best Kayaking & Canyoning
Make a splash in the astonishingly turquoise water of the Gorges du Verdon, Europe's largest canyon.

Skiing & Snowboarding

Just whisper the words 'French Alps' to a skier and watch their eyes light up. These mountains are the crème de la crème of European skiing, with the height edge, Mont Blanc views and more phenomenal pistes than you could ever hope to ski in a lifetime. Return time and again and you'll still never ski them all!

When to Go

The ski season goes with the snow, generally running from some time in December to around mid-April: the higher you go, the more snow-sure the resort and the longer the season. Crowds and room rates skyrocket during school holidays (Christmas, February half-term, Easter), so avoid these times if you can. There is summer glacier skiing in two resorts: Les Deux-Alpes and Val d'Isère (Espace Killy) from roughly mid-June to August.

Where to Go

Two of the world's largest ski areas are in France – Les Portes du Soleil, with 650km of runs, and Les Trois Vallées, with 600km of runs – as well as Europe's highest resort, Val Thorens (p531), at 2300m. Crowned by Mont Blanc, Chamonix skiing is the stuff of legend, especially the do-before-you-die La Vallée Blanche (p506), a high-level 2.8km off-piste descent. Speed is of the essence in the glacier-licked free-rider favourites of Les Deux Alpes (p544) and Val d'Isère (p532), as well as Alpe d'Huez (p545), where the brave can tackle Europe's longest black run, the 16km La Sarenne.

Beginners and intermediates will find tamer skiing and boarding in the Pyrenees and Le Mont-Dore in Massif Central. Cross-country *(ski de fond)* is big in the thickly forested Jura, the host of the famous **Transjurassienne race** (www.transjurassienne.com; ⊙2nd weekend in Feb), and at the Espace Nordique Sancy (p575) in the Massif Central, with 250km of trails to glide and skate on.

Ski Passes, Tuition & Equipment Hire

Prices for ski passes *(forfaits)* covering one or more ski areas vary according to the popularity of the resort, but can be anything from €32 to €54 per day and €120 to €282 per week (six days). Passes are hands-free with a built-in chip that barriers detect, and can be prebooked online – a wise idea if you want to beat the slope-side queues. Children usually pay half-price and under-fives ski for free (proof of age required).

All-inclusive rental will set you back around around €34/180 per one/six days for skiing or snowboarding equipment, and €15/65 for cross-country. Most resorts have one or more ski schools with certified instructors. Group lessons cost roughly €45/170 for one/six half-days. Kids can start learning from the age of four.

Information

Where to Ski and Snowboard (Chris Gill and Dave Watts; www.wheretoskiandsnowboard.com) Up-to-the minute guide to the slopes.

If You Ski (www.ifyouski.com) Resort guides, ski deals and the lowdown on ski hire and schools.

Météo France (www.meteofrance.com) Weather and daily avalanche forecast during the ski season.

France Montagnes (www.france-montagnes. com) Official website of French ski resorts, with guides, maps, snow reports and more.

École du Ski Français (ESF; www.esf.net) The largest ski school in the world, with first-class tuition. Search by region.

Club Alpin Français (French Alpine Club; www. ffcam.fr) Umbrella organisation for local mountain sports clubs, with experienced guides in all manner of winter sports.

SKI RUN CLASSIFICATIONS

Green Easy-peasy runs for absolute beginners.

Blue Gentle, well-groomed runs for novices.

Red Intermediate – groomed but steeper and narrower than blue runs.

Black Difficult runs for experts, often with moguls and steep, near-vertical drops.

Walking & Hiking

The French have been die-hard hikers for centuries, due no doubt to the sheer variety of their country's landscape – alpine mountains, flamingo-pink wetlands, cliff-laced coastal paths, cavernous gorges, mythical forests – that begs deeper exploration on foot. Some of Europe's most inspirational trails are here and communing with the wild is not hard to do.

When to Go

There is some form of walking available year-round in France. Spring and autumn are great seasons to hike in Corsica and on the French Riviera, which swelter in summer. The season is short and sweet in the Alps, running from mid-June to September.

Where to Go

Hikers have a high time of it in the Alps, with mile after never-ending mile of well-marked trails. Lifts and cable cars take the sweat out of hiking here in summer. Chamonix (p503) is the trailhead for the epic 10-day, three-country Tour de Mont Blanc, but gentler paths, such as the Grand Balcon Sud (p508), also command Mont Blanc close-ups. Some of the finest treks head into the more remote, glacier-capped wilds of the Parc National des Écrins (p543), with 700km of trails – many following old shepherd routes – and the equally gorgeous Parc National de la Vanoise (p535).

But the Alps are tip-of-the-iceberg stuff. Just as lovely are walks threading through the softly rounded heights of the Vosges and through the forest-cloaked hills of Jura spreading down to Lake Geneva.

Skiing in La Vallée Blanche (p506)

The extinct volcanoes in the Auvergne, interwoven with 13 Grandes Randonnées (long-distance footpaths), and the mist-shrouded peaks and swooping forested valleys of the Parc National des Pyrénées (p703) offer fine walking and blissful solitude. In the Cévennes, you can follow in Robert Louis Stevenson's footsteps on the GR70 Chemin de Stevenson (p766) from Le Puy to Alès – with or without a donkey.

Corsica is a hiker's paradise – the GR20, the 15-day trek that crosses the island north to south, is one of France's most famous, but there are dozens of shorter, easier walks. Or combine walking with swimming on the *sentiers littoraux* in the Alpes-Maritimes. More bracing hikes await on the GR21 skirting the chalky cliffs of Côte d'Albâtre in Normandy, the Côte d'Opale's GR120 taking in the colour-changing seascapes of the English Channel, and Brittany's Presqu'île de Crozon peninsula with 145km of signed trails woven around rocky outcrops and clear ocean views.

Paths & Trails

In all, the French countryside is criss-crossed by a staggering 120,000km of *sentiers balisés* (marked walking paths), which pass through every imaginable terrain in every region of the country. These range from blockbuster legendary hikes of magnificent, snow axe- and crampon-proportion (like the 10-day Tour de Mont Blanc in the French Alps), to timeless pilgrim trails along mellow fields and country lanes (such as the Chemins de Saint-Jacques de Compostelle or Way of St James to Santiago de Compostela in Spain) and short family walks around frosted lakes or in forests filled with giant sequoias and pine trees. Gentler trails in the French Alps follow old shepherd routes, while those along the Breton coast track ancient smuggler paths.

No permit is needed to hike. Trails cater to all ages and abilities, and are generally well-maintained and signposted. Bear in mind, though, that there is no substitute for a decent map and/or compass.

In southern France and on the island of Corsica, paths in heavily forested areas – including some *sentiers du littoral* (coastal paths) – are closed between 1 July and 15 September due to the high risk of forest fire. Always check with the local tourist office before setting out.

In the French Alps and Pyrenees, summertime lifts and cable cars open July and August to transport hikers up to higher altitudes.

GR Footpaths

The best-known walking trails are the *sentiers de grande randonnée* (GR trails), long-distance paths marked by red-and-white-striped track indicators. GR trails include:

GR70 Follow the trail from Le Puy to Alès in the sun-baked Cévennes.

GR20 France's most famous GR trail: a 15-day trek crossing Corsica's untamed interior from north to south.

GR21 Exhilarating, windswept hikes along the chalky cliffs of Normandy's Côte d'Albâtre.

GR120 Coastal hikes along the spectacular, 140km-long Côte d'Opale, northern France.

GR30 Nine-day loop covering 189km through the uncanny, grass-green moonscape of giant molehills in the volcanic Auvergne.

GR34 Celebrated 'Customs' Officer' trail stretching for 2000km along the Atlantic Coast, taking in Mont St-Michel and seafaring Brittany.

Trail Information

Local tourist offices have mountains of information on walking in their area. They can put you in touch with local hiking guides, and set you up with short walking itineraries in their neck of the woods. Tourist offices often sell walking guides and books. Some helpful online resources:

Grande Randonnée (www.grande-randonnee.fr) A good source of information (in French) on France's long-distance footpaths.

GR-Infos (www.gr-infos.com) Information in English on France's long-distance footpaths.

Parcs Nationaux de France (French National Parks; www.parcsnationaux.fr) First port of call if you are planning a visit to one of France's six hiking-rich national parks.

Parcs Naturels Régionaux de France (French Regional Nature Parks; www.parcs-naturels-regionaux.tm.fr) Has the low-down on walking and hiking in France's 48 regional nature parks.

Maps & Guides

Fédération Française de Randonnée Pédestre (www.ffrandonnee.fr) Publishes detailed French-language topo guides – trail booklets of major routes with topographic maps.

IGN (www.ign.fr) Publishes reliable, well-written topographic trail guides; buy them at tourist offices and in bookshops.

Guides RandOxygène (https://randoxygene.departement06.fr) An excellent resource for hiking in southern France's Alpes-Maritime *département* (adminstrative region); its maps and guides are both indispensable.

Bretagne Rando (www.bretagne-rando.com) Essential resource for maps, guides and itineraries along Brittany's beautiful coastal paths.

Pyrandonnées (www.pyrandonnees.fr) Walking in the Pyrenees.

Cycling

Be it family-friendly peddalling along disused railway lines, canals and vineyards or powering it with the hardcore set up an Alpine mountain pass, cycling in France is brilliantly big and varied. Spring to autumn is the best season for cycling; summer in the Alps and the sun-baked south is hot.

When to Go

Slip into a bicycle saddle to maximise breezes when the heat turns up. Summer is prime time for road cycling on the coast and mountain biking – *vélo tout terrain* (VTT) – in the French Alps and Pyrenees, with the season running from mid-June to September. Elsewhere, there's some form of cycling available year-round, be it in vine-ribboned valleys or along France's great waterways.

Where to Go

France is fabulous freewheeling country, with routes leading along its lushly wooded valleys and mighty rivers begging to be explored in slow motion. The options are boundless, but among the best are the soothingly lovely, château-studded Loire Valley where **Loire à Vélo** (www.loireavelo.fr) maintains 800km of signposted routes from Cuffy to the Atlantic; the peaceful towpaths shadowing the 240km, Unesco-listed Canal du Midi (p727), many of which form part of the stunning **Canal des 2 Mers en Vélo** (http://en.canaldes2mersavelo.com) cycling route linking the Atlantic with the Med via canals; and Provence's 236km **Autour du Luberon** *véloroute* (bike path) linking one gold-stone village to another. Pair wine tasting with a pedal through the vines in Burgundy (www.burgundy-by-bike.com), Bordeaux, the Beaujolais region, the southern Rhône Valley or the Route des Vins d'Alsace. Bicycle trails also criss-cross the sun-baked Île de Ré, dangling off the Atlantic coast.

Naturally, if you're up for a challenge, the gruelling inclines and exhilarating descents of the Alps and Pyrenees will appeal.

Resorts such as Alpe d'Huez (p545), Morzine (p514) and Les Deux Alpes (p544) are downhill heaven, as is the Parc National des Pyrénées (p703), where ski stations open up to mountain bikers in summer with *sentiers balisés* (marked trails) and obstacle-riddled bike parks for honing technique. Most cable cars let you take your bike for free or a nominal fee with a valid lift pass.

In Megève, seasoned downhill competitor Alexandre at Bike Addict (p514) organises bespoke mountain-bike itineraries for families, hardened cyclists and everyone in between. Expect to pay around €80/245 for a two-hour lesson/day excursion.

Provence is the other popular mountain-biking region. North of Nice in the Vallée de la Roya, **VTT Sospel** (www.mountnpass.com/destination/sospel-peille) maintains a network of 150km around Sospel for experienced riders. Beginners (minimum 10 years) and less experienced riders should head to the Ventoux Bike Park (p832), with ramps and jumps in a forest. Southwest in

---

ALTERNATIVE ACTIVITIES

Sick of eating cheese, strolling between vines or peddalling breathlessly up one Alpine *col* (mountain pass) too many? Try your hand at one of these lesser-known activities:

Perfumery The Provençal town of Grasse is the spot to test your *nez* (nose) during a perfume-making workshop at **Fragonard** (La Fabrique des Fleurs; ☑04 93 77 94 30; www.fragonard.com; Les 4 Chemins, rte de Cannes; ⊘9am-6pm Feb-Oct, 9am-1pm & 2-6pm Nov-Jan) or **Galimard** (☑04 93 09 20 00; www.galimard.com; 73 rte de Cannes; workshops from €49; ⊘9am-12.30pm & 2-6pm); in Nice, contact **The French Way** (☑06 27 35 13 75; www.thefrenchway.fr).

Knife Making Learn how to craft your very own traditional knife with a skilled craftspeople at Atelier Le Thiers (p580) or Robert David Coutellerie (p580) in tiny town Thiers in rural Auvergne.

Factory Tours Meet the makers firsthand. See how artisans hand-craft accordions at Maugein (p620) in Tulle, 28km northeast of Brive-la-Gaillarde in Limousin; how sardines are tinned at Conservarie La Belle-Iloise (p311) in Brittany; or how traditional *dragées* (sugared almonds) are made in Verdun (p387) or *fruits confits* (candied fruits) in Apt (p836).

Arts & Crafts In the capital, budding fashion designers of all ages can make their very own Paris-chic bag at a **Kasia Dietz** (www.kasiadietzworkshops.com; workshops €115-150) bag-making workshop.

Be a Cowboy for a Day at the **Manade Salierène** (☑04 66 86 45 57; www.manade salierene.com; D37, Mas de Capellane; weeklong course €700, gîte per night €80; ⊘Apr-Aug; ⚘) in the Camargue, the wild west of Provence.

Beer Brewing Forget wine. Brewing your very own French beer is the new *grand cru*. La Beer Fabrique (p115) in Paris is a good place to start.

French Table Decoration, Embroidery, Backstage Cabaret Tours... you name it, you can pretty much do it with Meeting the French (p116), an inspired grassroots organisation that puts curious visitors in touch with on-the-ground creatives.

Languedoc, Duverbike (p773) is a similar park with thrilling hollows, double bumps etc. Both parks rent VTT bikes and organise guided mountain-bike rides.

Bike hire is widely available and costs €10 to €15 per day for a classic bike up to €35 for a top-of-the-range mountain bike or ebike, and from €50 to €90 for the sort of high-end road bike you would need for tackling a mountainous section of Le Tour. Tourist office websites are a good first port of call for route maps and itineraries.

Véloroutes & Voies Vertes

With a vast network of cycling paths designed especially for cyclists, France is pure two-wheeling joy. *Véloroutes* are designated cycling paths while *voies vertes* ('greenways') stretch for thousands of kilometres along old canal towpaths, disused logging roads, decommissioned railway lines and so on. *Voies vertes* are open to walkers and horse riders as well as cyclists, and many sections are paved to ensure a silky-smooth ride.

A growing number of *pistes cycables* (cycling lanes) link neighbouring towns and villages, and rural France enjoys an extensive network of secondary and tertiary roads with relatively light traffic.

In the French Alps and Pyrenees, road cyclists labour up gruelling, hairpin-laced *cols* (mountains passes) and down exhilarating bone-chilling descents. Tackling these hills with a mountain bike – *vélo tout terrain* (VTT) – or even an electric bike (increasingly widespread) might be seen as the soft option, but it sure is easier on the leg muscles.

Maps & Itineraries

Local tourist offices are the obvious first port of call for route maps and itineraries.

Freewheeling France (www.freewheelingfrance. com) Comprehensive site covering routes and nearby accommodation, bike hire and tours, and loads of practical tips.

Union Touristique Les Amis de la Nature (www. amis-nature.org) Details on local, regional and long-distance *véloroutes* (cycling routes) around France.

Fédération Française de Cyclisme (French Cycling Federation; www.ffc.fr) Going strong since 1881, this is the authority on competitive cycling and mountain biking in France, including freeriding, cross-country and downhill.

Cycling at Château de Chambord (p402)

VeloMap (www.velomap.org) For free Garmin GPS cycling maps.

Véloroutes et Voies Vertes (www.af3v.org) The inside scoop on 250 signposted *véloroutes* and *voies vertes* for cycling, plus an interactive map to pinpoint them.

Information

Alsace à Vélo (www.alsaceavelo.fr) Comprehensive resource on peddalling along Alsace's numerous wine trails.

Burgundy by Bike (www.burgundy-by-bike.com) Pair wine tasting with a pedal between vineyards in wine-rich Burgundy.

Cycling Bretagne (https://cycling.brittanytourism.com) Cycling routes and tours and reams of practical advice on cycling in Brittany.

La Provence à Vélo (www.provence-a-velo.fr) Tip-top route resource for cyclists in Provence; lots of suggested routes covering the Mont Ventoux area.

Véloloisir Provence (www.veloloisirprovence. com) Superb cycling resource, detailing a range of colour-coded road and mountain-bike routes around the Luberon, Verdon and other areas.

Adventure & Water Sports

Kayaking & Canoeing

Kayaking and canoeing are available up and down the country, with some of the best options (including the looking-glass Lake Annecy) in the French Alps, the Vézère Valley, the Dronne, the River Gard and the Gorges de l'Ardèche. Startlingly turquoise water and sheer, forest-cloaked cliffs make the Gorges du Tarn and Gorges du Verdon highly scenic spots for a paddle. Sea kayakers prefer the ragged, cove-indented Parc National des Calanques and Corsica's islet-speckled waters. Expect to pay around €10 to €15 for kayak or canoe rental per day, and €25/50 for a half-/full-day excursion.

Surfing, Kitesurfing & Sailing

The wave-thrashed, wind-lashed Atlantic coast – Arcachon and Cap Ferret, for instance – and Capbreton in the French Basque Country, make surfers swoon. You'll find some of Europe's best surf in ocean-battered Biarritz and nearby Hossegor, which hosts the 10-day Quiksilver Pro France on the ASP World Surfing Tour in late September and early October. Group lessons are available everywhere for between €30 and €45. For surf spots and schools, visit www.surfingfrance.com.

Kitesurfers, meanwhile, catch breezes on the French Riviera and Corsica (around Porto-Vecchio), where outfits offer courses as well as equipment rental.

St-Malo is the hot spot to land-yacht (€35 for 90 minutes); contact its all-rounder **Surf School** (www.surfschool.org; 2 av de la Hoguette; lessons per hr from €35).

Stand-Up PaddleBoarding

Grab a board, bring along your balance and a Zen mind, and away you go – cruising on a stand-up paddleboard across glittering Alpine lakes (Lake Annecy is a scenic favourite), around island fortresses in the Atlantic and from one *calanque* (rocky outlet) to another in the Med. Rent boards for fun along the Promenade des Anglais in Nice on the French Riviera, or sign up for a more serious ocean encounter on the Atlantic Coast with Antioche Kayak (p646) near La Rochelle; in Corsica with **Bonif' Kayak** (☑06 27 11 30 73; www.bonifacio-kayak.com; Plage de Piantarella; kayak rental per hr from €8, excursions from €35) or Club Nautique d'Île Rousse (p907); or in Sète with Kayak Med (p753). Life jackets and waterproof containers are generally provided. Expect to pay around €15 per hour for board rental and from €25 per hour for tuition.

Canyoning & White-Water Rafting

For a thrill, little beats throwing yourself down a foaming river in a raft or a waterfall while rappelling – cue white-water rafting and canyoning. Canyoning operators are found in mountainous, ravine-riddled areas – from the French Alps to Aiguilles de Bavella (p925) in Corsica.

White-water rafting is another sure-fire way to get the heart pumping. France's most scenic options on this front include the cliff-flanked limestone wilderness of the Gorges de l'Ardèche and the mind-blowingly spectacular Gorges du Verdon, Europe's largest canyon, where you can also hydrospeed and gorge float. A half-day outing for either activity will set you back around €50.

Regions at a Glance

Few appreciate quite how varied France is. The largest country in Europe after Russia and Ukraine, hexagon-shaped France is hugged by water or mountains along every side except its north-eastern boundary – an instant win for lovers of natural beauty, the coast and great outdoors. Winter snow sports and summer hiking and biking rule the Alps in eastern France and the Pyrenees lacing the 450km-long border with Spain in the southwest. For *très belle* beach holidays, the coastal regions of Normandy and Brittany (northern France), the Atlantic Coast (with oyster-rich islands and waves for surfers), Corsica, and the French Riviera (Côte d'Azur), Provence and Languedoc-Roussillon on the hot Mediterranean deliver every time. Then there's food and wine, most exceptional in Burgundy, Provence, the Dordogne and Rhône Valley.

Paris

Food
Art
Shopping

Bistro Dining

Tables are jammed tight, chairs spill onto busy pavements outside, dishes of the day are chalked on the blackboard, and cuisine is simple and delicious. Such is the timeless joy of bistro dining in the capital.

Museums & Galleries

All the great masters star in Paris' priceless portfolio of museums. But not all the booty is stashed inside: buildings, metro stations, parks and other public art give *Mona Lisa* a good run for her money.

Fashion & Flea Markets

Luxury fashion houses, edgy boutiques, Left Bank designer-vintage and Europe's largest flea market: Paris really is the last word in fabulous shopping.

p64

Around Paris

Châteaux
Cathedrals
Green Spaces

A Taste of Royalty

Château de Versailles – vast, opulent and *very* shimmery – has to be seen to be believed. Fontainebleau, Chantilly and Vaux-le-Vicomte are other fabled addresses in French royalty's little black book.

Sacred Architecture

An architectural heavyweight near Paris is Chartres' cathedral, one of Western architecture's greatest achievements, with stained glass in awesome blue – at its most dazzling on sunlit days.

Urban Green

Parisians take air in thick forests outside the city: Forêt de Fontainebleau, an old royal hunting ground, is a hot spot for rock climbing and family walks. Chantilly means manicured French gardens and upper-class horse racing.

p186

Lille, Flanders & the Somme

Architecture
History
Coastline

Flemish Style

Breaking for a glass of strong local beer between old-town meanders around extravagant Flemish Renaissance buildings is a highlight of northern France. Lille and Arras are the cities to target if you have limited time.

Gothic to WWI

Amiens evokes serene contemplation inside one of France's most awe-inspiring Gothic cathedrals, and emotional encounters in WWI cemeteries.

Coastal Capers

Hiking along the Côte d'Opale – a wind-buffeted area of white cliffs, gold sand and ever-changing sea and sky – is dramatic and beautiful, as is a Baie de Somme bicycle ride past lounging seals.

p205

Normandy

Food
Coastline
Battlefields

Calvados & Camembert

This coastal chunk of northern France is a pastoral land of butter and soft cheeses. Its exotic fruits: Camembert, cider, fiery *calvados* (apple-flavoured brandy) and super-fresh seafood.

Cliffs & Coves

Chalk-white cliff to dune-lined beach, rock spire to pebble cove, coastal path to tide-splashed island-abbey Mont St-Michel: few coastlines are as inspiring.

D-Day Beaches

Normandy has long played a pivotal role in European history. But it was during WWII's D-Day landings that Normandy leaped to global importance. Museums, memorials, cemeteries and endless stretches of soft golden sand evoke that dramatic day in 1944.

p238

Brittany

Food
Walking
Islands

Crêpes & Cider

These two Breton culinary staples are no secret, but who cares? Devouring caramel-doused buckwheat pancakes in the company of homemade cider is a big reason to visit Brittany.

Wild Hikes

With its wild dramatic coastline, islands, medieval towns and thick forests laced in Celtic lore and legend, this proud and fiercely independent region promises exhilarating walks.

Breton Beauties

Brittany's much-loved islands, dotted with black sheep and crossed with craggy coastal paths and windswept cycling tracks, are big draws. Don't miss dramatic Île d'Ouessant or the very aptly named Belle Île.

p277

Champagne

Champagne
Walking
Drives

Bubbly Tasting

Gawp at a Champagne panorama from atop Reims' cathedral then zoom in close with serious tasting at the world's most prestigious Champagne houses in Reims and Épernay.

Vineyard Trails

Nothing quite fulfils the French dream like easy day hikes through neat rows of vineyards, exquisite picture-postcard villages bedecked in flowers and a gold-stone riverside hamlet right out of a Renoir painting.

Majestic Motoring

No routes are more geared to motorists and cyclists than the Champagne Routes, fabulously picturesque and well-signposted driving itineraries taking in the region's wealthy winemaking villages, hillside vines and traditional cellars.

p322

Alsace & Lorraine

Battlefields
City Life
Villages

Emotional Journeys

Surveying the dazzling symmetry of crosses on the Verdun battlefields is painful. Memorials, museums, cemeteries, forts and an ossuary mark out the journey.

Urban Icons

From the sublime (Strasbourg's cathedral) to the futuristic (Centre Pompidou in Metz), this northeast chunk of France steals urbanite hearts with its city squares, architecture, museums and Alsatian dining.

Chocolate-Box Villages

There is no lovelier way of getting acquainted with this part of France than travelling from hilltop castles to half-timbered villages framed by vines – with your foot light on the pedal.

p345

Loire Valley

Châteaux
History
Cycling

Royal Architecture

Endowed with dazzling structural and decorative gems from medieval to Renaissance and beyond, the Loire's lavish châteaux sweep most visitors off their feet.

Tempestuous Tales

This region is a dramatic storyteller: through spectacular castles, fortresses, apocalyptic tapestries and court paintings, the gore and glory, political intrigue and sex scandals of medieval and Renaissance France unfold.

Riverside Trails

The River Loire is France's longest, best-decorated river. Pedalling riverside along the flat from château to château is one of the valley's great joys – not to mention tasting the fruits of the vineyards that fan out from its banks.

p389

Burgundy

Wine
History
Outdoors

Reds & Whites

Meander between vines and old-stone villages along Burgundy's *grand cru* (wine of exceptional quality) vineyard route. But this region is not just about Côte d'Or reds. Taste whites in Chablis and Mâcon also.

Medieval History

Nowhere is Burgundy's past as one of medieval Europe's mightiest states evoked more keenly than in the dashingly handsome capital Dijon. Complete the medieval history tour with abbeys Cluny and Cîteaux, Fontenay, Tournus, Vézelay and Autun.

Great Outdoors

Hiking and biking past vineyards or cruising in a canal boat is the good life. Pedal the towpath to gloriously medieval Abbaye de Fontenay, open a bottle of Chablis and savour the best of Burgundy.

p429

Lyon & the Rhône Valley

Food
Roman Sites
Cycling

Famous Flavours

No city in France excites taste buds more than Lyon. Savour local specialities in a checked-tableclothed *bouchon* (small bistro), washed down by local Côtes de Rhône wine poured from a Lyonnais *pot* (bottle).

Roman Remains

Not content with lavishing two majestic amphitheatres on Lyon (catch a concert alfresco after dark during Les Nuits de Fourvière – magical!), the Romans gifted the Rhône Valley with a third in jazz-famed Vienne.

Two-Wheel Touring

Pedalling between vineyards in Beaujolais country or around frog-filled lakes swamped with birdlife in La Dombes is a simple pleasure of valley life.

p474

French Alps & the Jura Mountains

Food
Outdoors
Farmstays

Culture & Cuisine

Fondue is the tip of the culinary iceberg in this Alpine region, where cow's milk flavours dozens of cheeses. Around chic Lake Annecy, chefs woo with wild herbs and lake perch.

Adrenaline Rush

Crowned by Mont Blanc (4810m), the French Alps show no mercy in their insanely challenging ski trails and mountain-bike descents. Did we mention Europe's longest black downhill piste and the world's highest zip line?

Back to Nature

Feel the rhythm of the land with an overnight stay on a farm. Bottle-feed calves, collect the eggs, eat breakfast in a fragrant garden or before a wood-burning stove, and feel right at home.

p502

Auvergne

Volcanoes
Architecture
Outdoors

Volcanic Landscape

The last volcano erupted in 5000 BC but their presence is still evident: mineral waters bubble up from volcanic springs in Vichy and Volvic; volcanic stone paints Clermont-Ferrand black; and ancient craters pocket rich green hills in the Parc Naturel Régional des Volcans d'Auvergne.

Belle Époque

A string of early-20th-century spa towns including Vichy and La Bourboule add understated elegance to this region's otherwise deeply provincial bow.

Hiking & Skiing

Walking is the best way to explore this unique landscape – an uncanny, grass-green moonscape of giant molehills crossed with trails. Then there are the little-known ski slopes of Le Mont-Dore.

p560

The Dordogne, Limousin & the Lot

Food
Hilltop Towns
Cruises

Mouth-Watering Markets

Black truffles, foie gras and walnuts... eat your heart out in this fertile part of central and southwest France, where the fruits of the land are piled high at a bevy of atmospheric weekly markets.

Mighty Bastides

Dordogne's collection of 13th-century fortified towns and villages is a joy to explore, and valley views from the top of these clifftop *bastides* are uplifting. Start with Monpazier and Domme.

Meandering Waterways

Be it aboard a canoe, raft or *gabarre* (traditional flat-bottomed boat), cruising quietly along the region's rivers is an invitation to see *la belle France* at her most serene.

p586

Atlantic Coast

Port Towns
Wine
Outdoors

Town Life

Make a hip dining rendezvous in an old banana-ripening warehouse in Nantes, or take in bright-white limestone arcades and islands in the fortified port of La Rochelle, and brilliant art museums in wine-rich Bordeaux.

Wonderful Wines

France's largest winegrowing region, Bordeaux, encompasses the Médoc with its magnificent châteaux and medieval hamlet of St-Émilion. The wine is wonderful.

Rural Retreats

Paddling emerald-green waterways in the Marais Poitevin, pedalling sun-baked Île de Ré and wandering between weathered, wooden oyster shacks in Arcachon Bay are what this tranquil region is all about – slowing the pace right down.

p633

French Basque Country

Food
Activities
Culture

Culture & Cuisine

With its fiestas, traditional *pelota* (ball games), tapas and famous Bayonne ham, this exuberant Basque region beneath the mist-soaked Pyrenees feels very close to neighbouring Spain.

Surf's Up

Riding waves in the glitzy beach resort of Biarritz or on surfer beaches in Les Landes are good reasons to visit this sun-slicked coastal region, snug in France's most southwestern corner.

A Timeless Pilgrimage

For centuries pilgrims have made their way across France to the quaint walled town of St-Jean Pied de Port, and beyond to Santiago de Compostela in Spain. Do the same, on foot or by bicycle.

p667

The Pyrenees

Outdoors
Scenery
History

Mountain Adventures

Make Parc National des Pyrénées your playground. Vigorous hikes to lofty heights, good-value downhill skiing and racy white-water sports will leave you wanting more.

Jaw-Dropping Views

France's last wilderness has rare flora and fauna, snow-kissed peaks, vulture-specked skies, waterfalls and lakes. Top views include those from Pic du Jer, Pic du Midi, Lescun, Cirque de Gavarnie, Lac de Gaube and pretty much every valley going.

Rare & Holy Cities

That same elegance that saw well-to-do 19th-century English and Americans winter in Pau still attracts guests today. Then there is sacred Lourdes, a provincial pilgrim city.

p693

Toulouse Area

Food
History
Cruises

Cassoulet & Armagnac

In Toulouse be sure to try *cassoulet* (rich bean, pork and duck stew), a classic dish found simmering on the stove in most local kitchens. Begin the experience with an aperitif and end with an Armagnac brandy.

Towns with Tales

Red-brick Toulouse's historic mansions, quintessential fortified town Montauban, Gothic Albi, Moissac's Romanesque abbey: this compact region is packed with historical tales and historic architecture.

Canal du Midi

Pop a cork out of a bottle of Vin de Pays d'Oc and savour the go-slow, lush-green loveliness of the Canal du Midi. Stroll or pedal its towpaths, soak in a spa or simply rent a canal boat and drift.

p717

Languedoc-Roussillon

Culture
Roman Sites
Outdoors

Neighbouring Spain

Roussillon is a hot, dusty, lively region, long part of Catalonia at the eastern end of the Pyrenees. Celebrate a traditional fiesta in Perpignan, and modern art and *sardane* (Catalan folk dance) in Céret.

Aqueducts & Amphitheatres

Nîmes' amphitheatre and Pont du Gard are two of the Roman Empire's best-preserved sites. Catch a show in Nîmes, canoe on the Gard.

Footpaths & Waterways

Try canoeing beneath the Pont du Gard, cycling towpaths to Carcassonne, boating the Canal du Midi, climbing up to Cathar fortresses, donkey trekking in the Cévennes, or hiking gorges in Haut-Languedoc.

p738

Provence

Food
Villages
Modern Art

Eating & Drinking

Sip pastis over *pétanque* (boules, a variant of bowls), spend all evening savouring bouillabaisse (fish stew), mingle over buckets of herbs and marinated olives at the market, hunt truffles, and taste Bandol reds and Côtes de Provence rosé.

Sensual Sauntering

Travelling *à la provençal* is a sensual journey past scented lavender fields and chestnut forests, through apple-green vineyards and silvery olive groves, and around markets, chapels and medieval villages perched on rocky crags.

Avant-Garde

Provence itself is an art museum and has the roll-call to prove it: Matisse, Renoir, Picasso, Cézanne, Van Gogh and Signac all painted and lived here.

p784

The French Riviera & Monaco

Seaside Resorts
Glamour
Coastline

Coastal Queen

Urban grit, old-world opulence, art that moves and a seaside promenade everyone loves – Nice, queen of the French Riviera, will always be belle of the seaside ball.

Party Time

Enjoy the Riviera high life: trail film stars in Cannes, watch Formula One, meet high society in Monaco, guzzle champers in St-Tropez, frolic on sandy beaches, dine between priceless art, dance until dawn...

Magnificent Scenery

With its glistening sea, idyllic beaches and coastal paths, this part of the Med coast begs wonderful walks. Cicadas sing on Cap Ferrat, while the sun turns the Massif de l'Estérel a brilliant red.

p847

Corsica

Drives
Hiking
Boat Trips

Postcard Home

Corsican coastal towns are impossibly picturesque – alley-woven Bastia, Italianate Bonifacio, celeb-loved Île Rousse, chichi Calvi – but it is the hair-raising coastal roads that wend their way past medieval Genoese watchtowers and big blue views that really scream, 'Send a postcard home!'.

Great Outdoors

Hiking high-altitude mountain trails once the preserve of bandits and *bergers* (shepherds) is a trail-junkie favourite, as are the cliff-hanging Gorges de Spelunca and beautiful pink, ochre and ginger Calanques de Piana.

The Big Blue

Nowhere does the Med seem bluer. Hop on deck in Porto, Bonifacio, Calvi or Porto-Vecchio for a boat excursion, or view sapphire waters through a mask while diving and snorkelling.

p898

On the Road

Paris

POP 2.2 MILLION

Best Places to Eat

➜ Tomy & Co (p153)

➜ Restaurant AT (p149)

➜ Restaurant Guy Savoy (p154)

➜ Bouillon Racine (p153)

➜ Berthillon (p147)

Best Places to Stay

➜ L'Hôtel (p131)

➜ Hôtel Henriette (p132)

➜ Hôtel Ritz Paris (p123)

➜ Generator Hostel (p123)

➜ Hôtel Particulier Montmartre (p125)

Why Go?

Paris has a timeless familiarity for first-time and frequent visitors, with instantly recognisable architecture – the Eiffel Tower, the Arc de Triomphe guarding glamorous Champs-Élysées, gargoyled Notre Dame cathedral, lamplit bridges spanning the Seine, cafes spilling onto wicker-chair-lined terraces. Dining is a quintessential part of any Parisian experience, whether at neighbourhood bistros, Michelin-starred temples of gastronomy, *boulangeries* (bakeries) or street markets. Shopping is also essential in this stylish city, from vintage fashion through to emerging designers and *haute-couture* houses. And Paris is one of the world's great art repositories, with priceless treasures showcased in palatial museums. But against this back-drop, Paris' real magic lies in the unexpected: hidden parks, unsung museums and hidden boutiques, bistros and cafes where local life unfolds.

When to Go
Paris

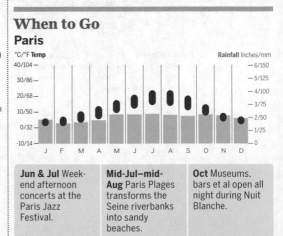

Jun & Jul Week-end afternoon concerts at the Paris Jazz Festival.

Mid-Jul–mid-Aug Paris Plages transforms the Seine riverbanks into sandy beaches.

Oct Museums, bars et al open all night during Nuit Blanche.

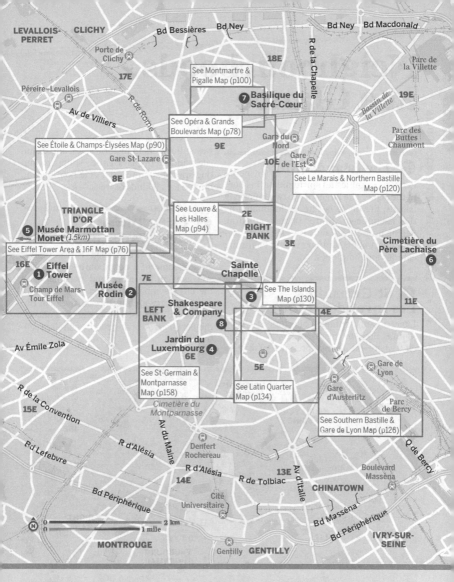

Paris Highlights

❶ Eiffel Tower (p70) Ascending at dusk for the best views of the City of Light.

❷ Musée Rodin (p106) Indulging in a Parisian moment in the sculpture-filled gardens of this romantic art museum.

❸ Sainte-Chapelle (p102) Taking in the magical sparkle of stained glass in the sun.

❹ Jardin du Luxembourg (p110) Lounging with locals in the city's most popular park.

❺ Musée Marmottan Monet (p74) Marvelling in peace at Monet masterpieces in one of Paris' least sung museums.

❻ Cimetière du Père Lachaise (p97) Paying respects at the world's most visited cemetery.

❼ Basilique du Sacré-Cœur (p88) Admiring the city of Paris laid out at your feet.

❽ Shakespeare & Company (p179) Attending a reading at this mythical bookshop and hobnobbing over coffee afterwards.

Neighbourhoods at a Glance

❶ The Islands (p102)

Paris' geographic and spiritual heart is here in the Seine. The larger of the two inner-city islands, the Île de la Cité, is dominated by the magnificent Notre Dame cathedral. Serene little Île St-Louis is graced with elegant apartments and hotels, and charming eateries and boutiques.

❷ St-Germain & Les Invalides (p106)

Literary buffs, antique collectors and fashionistas flock to this legendary part of the city, where the former presence of writers such as Sartre, de Beauvoir and Hemingway still lingers in historic cafes, and exquisite window displays entice shoppers into tiny specialist stores and chic boutiques to browse for all kinds of treasures.

❸ Eiffel Tower & Western Paris (p68)

Home to very well-heeled Parisians, this grande dame of a neighbourhood is where you can get up close and personal with the city's symbolic tower as well as more contemporary architecture in the high-rise business district of La Défense just outside the *périphérique* (ring road) encircling central Paris.

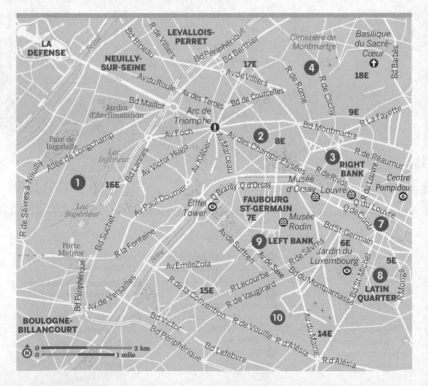

④ Champs-Élysées & Grands Boulevards (p75)

Baron Haussmann famously reshaped the Parisian cityscape around the Arc de Triomphe, from which 12 avenues radiate like the spokes of a wheel, including the glamorous Champs-Élysées.

⑤ Bastille & Eastern Paris (p101)

Fabulous markets, intimate bistros and cutting-edge drinking and dancing venues make this neighbourhood one of the best places to discover the Parisians' Paris.

⑥ Montmartre & Northern Paris (p85)

Montmartre's lofty views, wine-producing vines and hidden village squares have lured painters from the 19th century onwards. Crowned by the Sacré-Cœur basilica, Montmartre is the city's steepest *quartier*. The grittier neighbourhoods of Pigalle and Canal St-Martin are a trove of hip drinking, dining and shopping.

⑦ Louvre & Les Halles (p81)

Paris' splendid line of monuments, the *axe historique* (historic axis; also called the grand axis), passes through the Tuileries gardens before reaching IM Pei's glass pyramid at the entrance to the world's most visited museum, the Louvre. Nearby, the Forum des Halles shopping mall and park has recently emerged from a much-needed makeover.

⑧ Latin Quarter (p103)

So named because international students communicated in Latin here until the French Revolution, the Latin Quarter remains the hub of academic life in Paris. Centred on the Sorbonne's main university campus, this lively area is also home to outstanding museums and churches, along with Paris' beautiful art deco mosque and botanic gardens.

⑨ Le Marais, Ménilmontant & Belleville (p96)

Fashionable bars and restaurants, emerging designers' boutiques, the city's thriving gay and Jewish communities, and excellent museums all squeeze into Le Marais' warren of narrow medieval lanes. Neighbouring Ménilmontant has some of the city's most happening nightlife, while hilly Belleville is a vibrant multicultural neighbourhood with one of Paris' most colourful street markets.

⑩ Montparnasse & Southern Paris (p107)

Fabled Montparnasse has brasseries from its mid-20th-century heyday and re-energised backstreets buzz with local life. The residential 15e harbours some beautiful parks, while the 13e is enjoying a brilliant renaissance. Long-time home to Paris' largest Chinatown, it is now also the premium *arrondissement* for edgy street art.

History

Paris was born in the Seine in the 3rd century BC, when the Parisii tribe of Celtic Gauls settled on what is now the Île de la Cité. Centuries of conflict between the Gauls and Romans ended in 52 BC, and in AD 508 Frankish king Clovis I made Paris the seat of his united Gaul kingdom. In the 9th century France was beset by Scandinavian Vikings. In the centuries that followed, these 'Norsemen' started pushing towards Paris, which had risen rapidly in importance. Construction had begun on the cathedral of Notre Dame in the 12th century, the Louvre was built as a riverside fortress around 1200, Sainte-Chapelle was consecrated in 1248 and the Sorbonne opened its doors in 1253.

Many of the city's most famous buildings and monuments were erected during the Renaissance at the end of the 15th century. But in less than a century, Paris was again in turmoil, as clashes between Huguenot (Protestant) and Catholic groups increased, culminating in the St Bartholomew's Day massacre in 1572. Louis XIV (the Sun King) ascended the throne in 1643 at the age of five and ruled until 1715, virtually emptying the national coffers with his ambitious building and battling. His greatest legacy is the palace at Versailles. The excesses of Louis XVI and his queen, Marie Antoinette, in part led to an uprising of Parisians on 14 July 1789 and the storming of the Bastille prison – triggering the French Revolution.

◉ Sights

◉ Eiffel Tower & Western Paris

The Eiffel Tower may get top billing here, but it's the incredible assortment of museums that ensures you'll be a repeat visitor. Most destinations are found on the Right Bank of the Seine, with stars such as the Musée Guimet, Cité de l'Architecture and Palais de Tokyo mixed in with smaller attractions, such as the Musée Yves Saint Laurent Paris. Further west is the Musée Marmottan Monet and the leafy expanse of the Bois de Boulogne. Paris' business district is also located in the western suburbs. Begun in the 1950s, La Défense is the only place in Paris where you'll see skyscrapers.

Eiffel Tower   LANDMARK
See p70.

Parc du Champ de Mars   PARK
(Map p76; Champ de Mars, 7e; Ⓜ École Militaire or RER Champ de Mars–Tour Eiffel) Running southeast from the Eiffel Tower, the grassy Champ de Mars – an ideal summer picnic spot – was originally used as a parade ground for the cadets of the 18th-century **École Militaire**, the vast French-classical building at the southeastern end of the park, which counts Napoléon Bonaparte among its graduates. The steel-and-etched-

---

PARIS IN ...
....

Two Days

Kick off with a morning cruise or tour, then concentrate on the most Parisian of sights and attractions: **Notre Dame**, the **Louvre**, the **Eiffel Tower** and the **Arc de Triomphe**. In the late afternoon have a coffee or glass of wine on the av des Champs-Élysées before making your way to Montmartre for dinner. The following day take in such sights as the **Musée d'Orsay**, **Sainte-Chapelle**, **Conciergerie**, **Musée National du Moyen Âge** or **Musée Rodin**. Dine in soulful St-Germain before hitting the Latin Quarter's jazz clubs.

Four Days

Be sure to visit at least one Parisian street market and consider a cruise along **Canal St-Martin**, bookended by visits to the **Cimetière du Père Lachaise** and **Parc de la Villette**. By night, take in a concert, opera or ballet at the **Palais Garnier** or **Opéra Bastille**, and a bar and club crawl in Le Marais and its vibrant surrounds.

One Week

With one week in the French capital, you can see a good many of the major sights covered in this chapter and take excursions from Paris proper further afield to areas around Paris such as **Versailles**.

glass **Wall for Peace Memorial** (Map p76; http://wallforpeace.org; Ⓜ École Militaire or RER Champ de Mars–Tour Eiffel), erected in 2000, is by Clara Halter.

★ **Musée du Quai Branly**   MUSEUM
(Map p76; ☑ 01 56 61 70 00; www.quaibranly.fr; 37 quai Branly, 7e; adult/child €10/free; ☺ 11am-7pm Tue, Wed & Sun, 11am-9pm Thu-Sat; Ⓜ Alma Marceau or RER Pont de l'Alma) A tribute to the diversity of human culture, Musée du Quai Branly's highly inspiring overview of indigenous and folk art spans four main sections – Oceania, Asia, Africa and the Americas. An impressive array of masks, carvings, weapons, jewellery and more make up the body of the rich collection, displayed in a refreshingly unorthodox interior without rooms or high walls. Look out for excellent temporary exhibitions and performances.

Palais de Chaillot   HISTORIC BUILDING
(Map p76; place du Trocadéro et du 11 Novembre, 16e; Ⓜ Trocadéro) The two curved, colonnaded wings of this building (built for the 1937 International Expo) and central terrace afford an exceptional panorama of the **Jardins du Trocadéro**, Seine and Eiffel Tower. The eastern wing houses the standout **Cité de l'Architecture et du Patrimoine** (Map p76; www.citechaillot.fr; 1 place du Trocadéro et du 11 Novembre, 16e; adult/child €8/free; ☺ 11am-7pm Wed & Fri-Sun, to 9pm Thu; Ⓜ Trocadéro), devoted to French architecture and heritage, as well as the **Théâtre National de Chaillot** (Map p76; ☑ 01 53 65 30 00; http://theatre-chaillot.fr; 1 place du Trocadéro, 16e; Ⓜ Trocadéro), staging dance and theatre. The **Musée de la Marine** (Maritime Museum; Map p76; ☑ 01 53 65 69 69; www.musee-marine.fr; 17 place du Trocadéro et du 11 Novembre, 16e; Ⓜ Trocadéro), closed for renovations until 2021, and the **Musée de l'Homme** (Museum of Humankind; Map p76; ☑ 01 44 05 72 72; www.museedelhomme.fr; 17 place Trocadéro et du 11 Novembre, 16e; adult/child €10/free; ☺ 10am-6pm Wed-Mon; Ⓜ Passy, léna) are housed in the western wing.

Flame of Liberty Memorial   MONUMENT
(Map p90; place de l'Alma, 8e; Ⓜ Alma Marceau) This bronze sculpture, a replica of the one topping the Statue of Liberty, was placed here in 1987 as a symbol of friendship between France and the USA. More famous is its location, above the place d'Alma tunnel where, on 31 August 1997, Diana, Princess of Wales, was killed in a car accident.

★ **Musée Guimet des Arts Asiatiques**   GALLERY
(Map p90; ☑ 01 56 52 53 00; www.guimet.fr; 6 place d'Iéna, 16e; adult/child €8.50/free; ☺ 10am-6pm Wed-Mon; Ⓜ Iéna) Connoisseurs of Japanese ink paintings and Tibetan thangkas won't want to miss the Musée Guimet, the largest Asian art museum in France. Observe the gradual transmission of both Buddhism and artistic styles along the Silk Road in pieces ranging from 1st-century Gandhara Buddhas from Afghanistan and Pakistan to later Central Asian, Chinese and Japanese Buddhist sculptures and art.

Palais de Tokyo   GALLERY
(Map p90; ☑ 01 81 97 35 88; www.palaisdetokyo.com; 13 av du Président Wilson, 16e; adult/child €12/free; ☺ noon-midnight Wed-Mon; Ⓜ Iéna) The Tokyo Palace, created for the 1937 Exposition Internationale des Arts et Techniques dans la Vie Moderne (International Exposition of Art and Technology in Modern Life), has no permanent collection. Instead, its shell-like interior of concrete and steel is a stark backdrop to interactive contemporary-art exhibitions and installations. Its bookshop is fabulous for art and design magazines, and its eating and drinking options are magic.

Musée d'Art Moderne de la Ville de Paris   GALLERY
(Map p90; ☑ 01 53 67 40 00; www.mam.paris.fr; 11 av du Président Wilson, 16e; ☺ 10am-6pm Tue, Wed & Fri-Sun, 10am-10pm Thu; Ⓜ Iéna) FREE The permanent collection at Paris' modern-art museum displays works representative of just about every major artistic movement of the 20th and (nascent) 21st centuries, with works by Modigliani, Matisse, Braque and Soutine. The real jewel, though, is the room hung with canvases by Dufy and Bonnard. Look out for cutting-edge temporary exhibitions (not free).

Musée Yves Saint Laurent Paris   MUSEUM
(Map p90; ☑ 01 44 31 64 00; www.museeyslparis.com; 5 av Marceau, 16e; adult/child €10/7; ☺ 11am-6pm Tue-Thu, Sat & Sun, to 9pm Fri; Ⓜ Alma - Marceau) Housed in the legendary designer's studios (1974–2002), this museum holds retrospectives of YSL's avant-garde designs, from early sketches to finished pieces. Temporary exhibitions give an insight into the creative process of designing a *haute couture* collection and the history of fashion throughout the 20th century. The building can only accommodate a small number of visitors at a time, so buy tickets online or expect to queue.

TOP SIGHT
EIFFEL TOWER

There are different ways to experience the Eiffel Tower, from an evening ascent amid twinkling lights to a meal in one of its two restaurants. And even though some 6.2 million people come annually, few would dispute that each visit is unique – and something that simply has to be done when in Paris.

Metal Asparagus

Named after its designer, Gustave Eiffel, the Tour Eiffel was built for the 1889 Exposition Universelle (World's Fair). It took 300 workers, 2.5 million rivets and two years of nonstop labour to assemble. Upon completion the tower became the tallest human-made structure in the world (324m or 1063ft) – a record held until the completion of the Chrysler Building in New York (1930). A symbol of the modern age, it faced massive opposition from Paris' artistic and literary elite, and the 'metal asparagus', as some Parisians snidely called it, was originally slated to be torn down in 1909. It was spared only because it proved an ideal platform for the transmitting antennas needed for the newfangled science of radiotelegraphy.

1st Floor

Of the tower's three floors, the 1st (57m) has the most space but the least impressive views. The glass-enclosed **Pavillon Ferrié** – open since summer 2014 – houses an immersion film along with a small cafe and souvenir shop, while the outer walkway features a discovery circuit to help visitors learn more about the tower's ingenious design. Check out the sections of glass flooring that

DON'T MISS
→ 2nd-floor panorama

→ Top-floor Champagne bar

PRACTICALITIES
→ Map p76

→ ☎ 08 92 70 12 39

→ www.toureiffel.paris

→ Champ de Mars, 5 av Anatole France, 7e

→ adult/child lift to top €25/6.30, lift to 2nd fl €16/4, stairs to 2nd fl €10/2.50

→ ⊙ lifts & stairs 9am-12.45am mid-Jun–Aug, lifts 9.30am-11.45pm, stairs 9.30am-6.30pm Sep–mid-Jun

→ Ⓜ Bir Hakeim or RER Champ de Mars–Tour Eiffel

proffer a dizzying view of the ant-like people walking on the ground far below.

This level also hosts the restaurant **58 Tour Eiffel** (Map p76; ☑ 01 76 70 04 86; www.restaurants-toureiffel.com; 1st fl, Eiffel Tower, menus lunch €37.20, dinner €93.70-113.70; ⏲ 11.30am-4.30pm & 6.30-11pm; ⚲ ⚑).

Not all lifts stop at the 1st floor (check before ascending), but it's an easy walk down from the 2nd floor should you accidentally end up one floor too high.

2nd Floor

Views from the 2nd floor (115m) are the best – impressively high but still close enough to see the details of the city below. Telescopes and panoramic maps placed around the tower pinpoint locations in Paris and beyond. Story windows give an overview of the lifts' mechanics, and the vision well allows you to gaze through glass panels to the ground. Also up here are toilets, a souvenir shop and the Michelin-starred restaurant Jules Verne (p133).

Top Floor

Views from the wind-buffeted top floor (276m) stretch up to 60km on a clear day, though at this height the panoramas are more sweeping than detailed. Celebrate your ascent with a glass of bubbly (€13 to €22) from the Champagne bar (open noon to 5.15pm and 6.15pm to 10.45pm). Afterwards peep into Gustave Eiffel's restored top-level office where lifelike wax models of Eiffel and his daughter Claire greet Thomas Edison.

To access the top floor, take a separate lift on the 2nd floor (closed during heavy winds).

Ticket Purchases & Queuing Strategies

Ascend as far as the 2nd floor (either on foot or by lift), from where it is lift-only to the top floor. Pushchairs must be folded in lifts and you are not allowed to take bags or backpacks larger than aeroplane-cabin size.

Buying tickets in advance online usually means you avoid the monumental queues at the ticket offices. Print your ticket or show it on a smartphone screen. If you can't reserve your tickets ahead of time, expect waits of well over an hour in high season.

Stair tickets can't be reserved online. They are sold at the south pillar, where the staircase can also be accessed: the climb consists of 360 steps to the 1st floor and another 360 steps to the 2nd floor.

If you have reservations for either restaurant, you are granted direct access to the lifts.

NIGHTLY SPARKLES

Every hour on the hour, the entire tower sparkles for five minutes with 20,000 6-watt lights. They were first installed for Paris' millennium celebration in 2000 – it took 25 mountain climbers five months to install the current bulbs and 40km of electrical cords. For the best view of the light show, head across the Seine to the Jardins du Trocadéro.

Slapping a fresh coat of paint on the tower is no easy feat. It takes a 25-person team 18 months to complete the 60-tonnes-of-paint task, redone every seven years. Painted red and bronze since 1968, it's had six different colours throughout its lifetime, including yellow.

MAN ON A WIRE

In 1989 tightrope artist Philippe Petit walked up an inclined 700m cable across the Seine, from Palais Chaillot to the Eiffel Tower's 2nd floor. The act, performed before an audience of 250,000 people, was held to commemorate the French Republic's bicentennial.

Greater Paris

COURBEVOIE

Île de la Grande Jatte

Seine

Cimetière de Levallois

LEVALLOIS-PERRET

CLICHY

Cimetière Sud

ST-OUEN

6 Bd Bessières

Bd Périphérique

Porte de Clichy

NEUILLY-SUR-SEINE

La Défense (200m)

Av Charles de Gaulle

Bd Bineau

Péreire–Lavallois

Av de Villiers

Bd Gouvion St-Cyr

17E

R de Rome

27

Jardin d'Acclimatation

10 12

Marc St-James

Lac Pour le Patinage

Allée de Longchamp

Bois de Boulogne

18

Lac Inférieur

Neuilly-Porte Maillot

71

Pl du Maillot de Lattre de Tassigny

Av de la Grande Armée

See Étoile & Champs-Élysées Map (p90)

Gare St-Lazare

Charles de Gaulle–Étoile

8E

Auber

61

Avenue Foch

Av Foch

36

Av Victor Hugo

Av Kléber

Av Marceau

Av des Champs-Élysées

TRIANGLE D'OR

Av Gabriel

Q des Tuileries

Musée Marmottan Monet

16E

4

Jardin du Ranelagh

Avenue Henri Martin

Boulain-Villiers

See Eiffel Tower Area & 16e Map (p76)

Jardins du Trocadéro

15

Musée d'Orsay

31

Musée d'Orsay

7E

Lac Supérieur

Av Mozart

Avenue du Président Kennedy

Champ de Mars–Tour Eiffel

Av de la Motte-Picquet

Av du Maréchal Galliéni

See St-Germain & Montparnasse Map (p158)

Porte d'Auteuil

28 17

19 44

Javel

Av Émile Zola

67

55

39

Av de Saxe

Av de Suffren

LEFT BANK

6E

Ste-Périne

Parc André Citroën

7

22

R de la Croix Nivert

R Lecourbe

R de Vaugirard

25

Gare Montparnasse

Boulevard Victor

Bd Victor

45 43

15E

R de la Convention

R de Vouillé

Bd Pasteur

49

Les Catacombes

2

70

Issy–Val de Seine

Bd Périphérique

Bd Lefebvre

46

Parc Georges Brassens

23

R d'Alésia

47

26

Av du Maine

Denfert Rochereau

Île St-Germain

Parc Départemental de l'Île St-Germain

Sq de la Porte de la Plaine

Mobile en Ville

R d'Alésia

14E

Jacques Henri Lartigue

Sq Jean Moulin

Issy Ville

VANVES

MALAKOFF

MONTROUGE

Parc Rodin

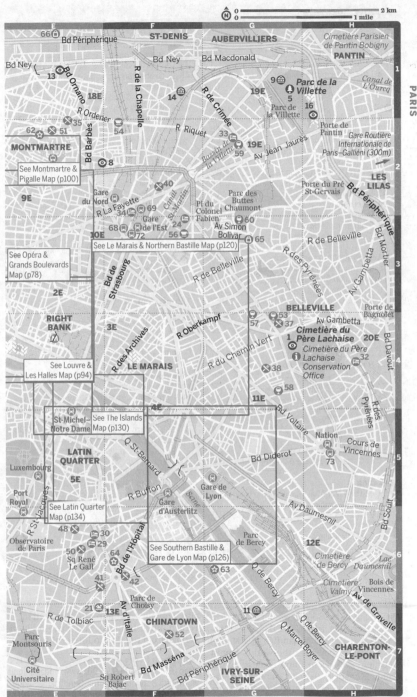

0 _____ 2 km
0 _____ 1 mile

ST-DENIS
AUBERVILLIERS
Cimetière Parisien de Pantin Bobigny
PANTIN

Bd Périphérique
Bd Ney
Bd Macdonald
Canal de L'Ourcq

Bd Ney
Bd Ornano
18E
R Ordener
R de la Chapelle
R de Crimée
19E
Parc de la Villette
Parc de la Villette
Porte de Pantin
Gare Routière Internationale de Paris–Galliéni (300m)

MONTMARTRE
Bd Barbès
R Riquet
Bassin de la Villette
19E
Av Jean Jaurès

See Montmartre & Pigalle Map (p100)

LES LILAS
Bd Périphérique

9E
Gare du Nord
R La Fayette
Canal St-Martin
Pl du Colonel Fabien
Parc des Buttes Chaumont
Porte du Pré St-Gervais

See Opéra & Grands Boulevards Map (p78)

10E
Gare de l'Est
Av Simon Bolivar
R de Belleville
Bd Mortier
Av Gambetta

See Le Marais & Northern Bastille Map (p120)

2E
Bd de Strasbourg
R de Belleville

RIGHT BANK
3E
R des Archives
R Oberkampf
BELLEVILLE
Porte de Bagnolet
20E
Bd Davout

LE MARAIS
R du Chemin Vert
Cimetière du Père Lachaise
Cimetière du Père Lachaise Conservation Office

See Louvre & Les Halles Map (p94)

11E
Bd Voltaire
R des Pyrénées

4E
St-Michel–Notre Dame
See The Islands Map (p130)
Bd Diderot
Nation
Cours de Vincennes

LATIN QUARTER
5E
Q St-Bernard
Luxembourg
See Latin Quarter Map (p134)
R Buffon
Gare de Lyon
Av Daumesnil
Bd Soult

Port Royal
R St-Jacques
Gare d'Austerlitz
Seine
Parc de Bercy
12E

Observatoire de Paris
Bd de l'Hôpital
Sq René Le Gall
See Southern Bastille & Gare de Lyon Map (p126)
Q de Bercy
Cimetière de Bercy
Lac Daumesnil

Parc Montsouris
R de Tolbiac
13E
Av d'Italie
CHINATOWN
Cimetière Valmy
Bois de Vincennes
Av de Gravelle

Cité Universitaire
Sq Robert Bajac
Bd Masséna
Bd Périphérique
IVRY-SUR-SEINE
Q Marcel Boyer
CHARENTON-LE-PONT

Parc de Choisy

Parc de Bercy

Greater Paris

★ **Musée Marmottan Monet**　　GALLERY
(Map p72; ☑ 01 44 96 50 33; www.marmottan.fr; 2 rue Louis Boilly, 16e; adult/child €11/7.50; ☺10am-6pm Tue, Wed & Fri-Sun, to 9pm Thu; Ⓜ La Muette) This museum showcases the world's largest collection of works by impressionist painter Claude Monet (1840-1926) – about 100 – as well as paintings by Gauguin, Sisley, Pissarro, Renoir, Degas, Manet and Berthe Morisot. It also contains an important collection of French, English, Italian and Flemish illuminations from the 13th to 16th centuries.

Fondation Louis Vuitton　　GALLERY
(Map p72; ☑ 01 40 69 96 00; www.fondationlouis vuitton.fr; 8 av du Mahatma Gandhi, 16e; adult/child €16/5; ☺hours vary with exhibit; Ⓜ Les

BOIS DE BOULOGNE

The 845-hectare **Bois de Boulogne** (bd Maillot, 16e; M Porte Maillot) owes its informal layout to Baron Haussmann, who, inspired by London's Hyde Park, planted 400,000 trees here in the 19th century. Along with various gardens and other sights, the park has 15km of cycle paths and 28km of bridle paths through 125 hectares of forested land.

Be warned that the area becomes a distinctly adult playground after dark, especially along the Allée de Longchamp running northeast from the Étang des Réservoirs (Reservoirs Pond), where prostitutes cruise for clients.

The Bois de Boulogne is served by metro lines 1 (Porte Maillot, Les Sablons), 2 (Porte Dauphine), 9 (Michel-Ange-Auteuil) and 10 (Michel-Ange-Auteuil, Porte d'Auteuil), and the RER C (Avenue Foch, Avenue Henri Martin). Vélib' stations are found near most of the park entrances, but not within the park itself.

Jardin d'Acclimatation (Map p72; ☑ 01 40 67 90 85; http://jardindacclimatation.fr; av du Mahatma Gandhi; admission €3.50, per attraction €2.90; ⊙ 11am-6pm Mon-Fri, 10am-6pm Sat & Sun; M Les Sablons) Families adore this green, flowery amusement park on the Bois de Boulogne's northern fringe. There are swings, roundabouts, playgrounds, a paddling pool, a petting zoo and puppet shows several times per week (included in the admission fee), along with dozens of attractions, such as boat, pony and funfair rides, and a miniature train to/from Porte Maillot, which cost extra. A full-scale renovation in 2017 and 2018 added 17 new attractions.

Lac Inférieur (Map p72; ☑ 06 95 14 00 01; Carrefour du Bout des Lacs; 1hr €10, plus deposit €50; ⊙ noon-5pm Mon-Fri, 10am-6pm Sat & Sun mid-Feb–Oct; M Avenue Henri Martin) Rent an old-fashioned rowing boat to explore Lac Inférieur, the largest of Bois de Boulogne's lakes – romance guaranteed.

Parc de Bagatelle (rte de Sèvres à Neuilly, 16e; adult/child Jun-Oct €6/3, Nov-May free; ⊙ 9.30am-8pm Apr-Sep, shorter hours rest of year; M Porte Maillot) Few Parisian parks are as romantic as this, created as the result of a wager between Marie Antoinette and the Count of Artois. Irises bloom in May, roses between June and October, and – perhaps most magnificently of all – water lilies in August. The *pièce de résistance* is the château itself, built for the younger brother of Louis XVI in the 18th century.

Pré Catelan (Catelan Meadow; rte de Suresnes, 16e; ⊙ 9.30am-8pm Apr-Oct, Jardin Shakespeare 2-4pm, shorter hours Nov-Mar; M Ranelagh) FREE These gardens squirrel away a wonderful Jardin Shakespeare where plants, flowers and trees mentioned in Shakespeare's plays are cultivated. Watch out for summer performances in the attached open-air theatre.

Jardin des Serres d'Auteuil (☑ 01 40 72 16 16; av de la Porte d'Auteuil, 16é; ⊙ 8am-8.30pm summer, shorter hours rest of year; M Porte d'Auteuil) FREE Garden with impressive conservatories, which opened in 1898 and are home to a large collection of tropical plants, at the southeastern end of the park

Fondation Louis Vuitton (p74)

Sablons) Designed by Frank Gehry, this striking contemporary art centre in the Bois de Bologne opened its doors in late 2014. Emerging behind the Jardin d'Acclimatation (p75), the glass-panelled building hosts temporary shows like the MOMA in Paris, the Sergei Shchukin collection and Art/Africa. Check online for the latest exhibit.

A **shuttle** (Map p90; 44 ave Friedland, 8e; round trip €2) runs between the Arc de Triomphe and the museum during opening hours.

⊙ Champs-Élysées & Grands Boulevards

Strolling down the Champs-Élysées from the Arc de Triomphe will leave you in the museum-rich neighbourhood surrounding the unparalleled vistas of place de la Concorde. Just west of the square are three architectural beauties from fin-de-siècle Paris: the Grand Palais, Petit Palais and Palais de la Découverte. North of Concorde is place de la Madeleine, with its neoclassical Église de la Madeleine. Further east towards the Grands Boulevards

Eiffel Tower Area & 16e

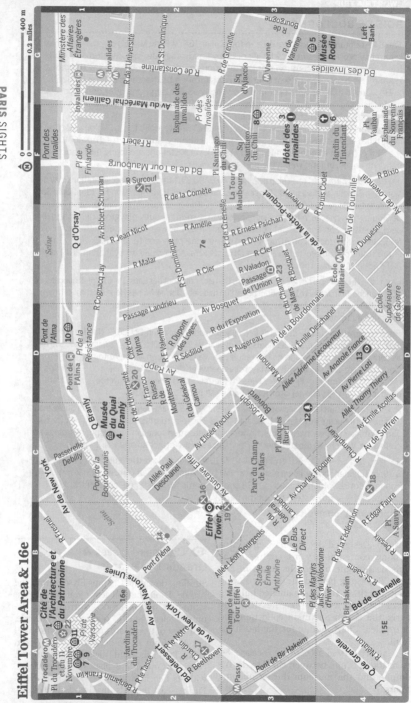

0 — 0.2 miles
0 — 400 m

Trocadéro
Pl du Trocadéro
et du 11
Novembre

Cité de
l'Architecture et
du Patrimoine 1

R de Tasse
R de Belfort
R des Nations Unies
Av des Nations Unies
Benjamin Franklin
R Franklin
Pl de
Varsovie
16e
Jardins
du Trocadéro
R Beethoven
R Chardin
R Vineuse
Pl du
Chaillot
7 9
11
22

Av de New York
Passerelle
Debilly
Pont de la
Bourdonnais
Seine
Av de New York
Pont d'Iéna
Pont de Bir Hakeim

Cité de
l'Alma
Pont de
l'Alma
Q d'Orsay
Seine
Pont des
Invalides
Ministère des
Affaires
Étrangères
Invalides
Invalides

10

Pl de la
Résistance
Pl de
Finlande
R Cognacq-Jay
R de l'Université
R Jean Nicot
R Robert Schuman
Av du Maréchal Galliéni
Esplanade des
Invalides

Musée
du Quai
Branly 4
Q Branly
R de l'Université
Av Franco
Russe
R de
Montessuy
Av Rapp
R du Général
Camou
Cité de
l'Alma
R E Valentin
R Dupont
des Loges
R Sédillot
R St-Dominique
R Malar
Passage Landrieu
R Amélie
R de la Comète
R Surcouf
21
R de Grenelle
Bd de la Tour Maubourg
R Fabert
R de Constantine
R St-Dominique

Pl des
Invalides
Esplanade des
Invalides
La Tour
Maubourg
Pl Santiago
du Chili
Sq Santiago
du Chili
Sq
d'Ajaccio
R de Grenelle
R de Varenne
R de Varenne
R de Bourgogne
Musée
Rodin 5
Left
Bank
Bd des Invalides

Hôtel des
Invalides 3 1
8
6
Jardin de
l'Intendant
Pl
Vauban
Esplanade
du Souvenir
Français
R Bixio
R Lowendal
Av de Lowendal
R Louis Codet
Av de Tourville
Av de Ségur

R St-Dominique
R Cler
R Valadon
Passage
de l'Union 23
R Ernest Psichari
R Duvivier
R Cler
R Bosquet
R du Champ
de Mars
Av de la Motte Picquet
Av Duquesne
École
Militaire 15
École
Supérieure
de Guerre
École
R Augereau
Av de la Bourdonnais
Av Émile Deschanel
Av Anatole France 13

R du Champ
de Mars
R de l'Exposition
R Marinoni
Passage
de l'Union
Av Bosquet

Parc du Champ
de Mars
Av Joseph
Bouvard
Pl Jacques
Rueff
Allée Adrienne Lecouvreur
Av Pierre Loti
Allée Thomy Thierry
Av Émile Acollas
Av de Suffren
R de Champfleury
12
18

Allée Paul
Deschanel
Av Élisée Reclus
Av Gustave Eiffel
16

Eiffel
Tower 2
19
14

Allée Léon Bourgeois
R du
Général
Lambert
Le Bus
Direct
Stade
Émile
Anthoine
Champ de Mars-
Tour Eiffel
R Jean Rey
Pl des Martyrs
Juifs du Vélodrome
d'Hiver
Av Charles Floquet
R de la Fédération
R Edgar Faure
Pl
A Sauvy
R Desaix
R St-Saëns
Bd de Grenelle
15E
Q de Grenelle
M Bir-Hakeim
M Passy
M Nélaton

Eiffel Tower Area & 16e

is the legendary Palais Garnier, the city's 19th-century opera house.

★ Arc de Triomphe   LANDMARK
(Map p90; www.paris-arc-de-triomphe.fr; place Charles de Gaulle, 8e; viewing platform adult/child €12/free; ⊘10am-11pm Apr-Sep, to 10.30pm Oct-Mar; Ⓜ Charles de Gaulle–Étoile) If anything rivals the Eiffel Tower (p70) as the symbol of Paris, it's this magnificent 1836 monument to Napoléon's victory at Austerlitz (1805), which he commissioned the following year. The intricately sculpted triumphal arch stands sentinel in the centre of the Étoile (Star) roundabout. From the viewing platform on top of the arch (50m up via 284 steps and well worth the climb) you can see the dozen avenues.

Avenue des Champs-Élysées   STREET
(Map p90; 8e; Ⓜ Charles de Gaulle–Étoile, George V, Franklin D Roosevelt, Champs-Élysées–Clemenceau)

No trip to Paris is complete without strolling this broad, tree-shaded avenue lined with luxury shops. Named for the Elysian Fields ('heaven' in Greek mythology), the Champs-Élysées was laid out in the 17th century and is part of the *axe historique,* linking place de la Concorde with the Arc de Triomphe. It's where presidents and soldiers parade on Bastille Day, where the Tour de France holds its final sprint, and where Paris turns out for organised and impromptu celebrations.

Place de la Concorde   SQUARE
(Map p90; 8e; Ⓜ Concorde) Paris spreads around you, with views of the Eiffel Tower (p70), the Seine and along the Champs-Élysées, when you stand in the city's largest square. Its 3300-year-old pink granite obelisk was a gift from Egypt in 1831. The square was first laid out in 1755 and originally named after King Louis XV, but its royal associations meant that it took centre stage during the Revolution – Louis XVI was the first to be guillotined here in 1793.

Grand Palais   GALLERY
(Map p90; ☎01 44 13 17 17; www.grandpalais.fr; 3 av du Général Eisenhower, 8e; adult/child €14/free; ⊘10am-8pm Thu-Mon, to 10pm Wed; Ⓜ Champs-Élysées–Clemenceau) Erected for the 1900 Exposition Universelle (World's Fair), the Grand Palais today houses several exhibition spaces beneath its huge 8.5-tonne art nouveau glass roof. Some of Paris' biggest shows (Renoir, Chagall, Turner) are held in the Galeries Nationales, lasting three to four months. Hours, prices and exhibition dates vary significantly for all galleries. Reserving a ticket online for any show is strongly advised. Note that the Grand Palais will close for renovations from late 2020 to mid-2024.

Petit Palais   GALLERY
(Musée des Beaux-Arts de la Ville de Paris; Map p90; ☎01 53 43 40 00; www.petitpalais.paris.fr; av Winston Churchill, 8e; suggested donation €2; ⊘10am-6pm Tue-Sun, to 9pm Fri; Ⓜ Champs-Élysées–Clemenceau) FREE This architectural stunner was built for the 1900 Exposition Universelle, and is home to the Musée des Beaux-Arts de la Ville de Paris (City of Paris Museum of Fine Arts). It specialises in medieval and Renaissance *objets d'art*, such as porcelain and clocks, tapestries, drawings, and 19th-century French paintings and sculpture; there are also paintings by such artists as Rembrandt, Colbert, Cézanne, Monet, Gauguin and Delacroix.

Opéra & Grands Boulevards

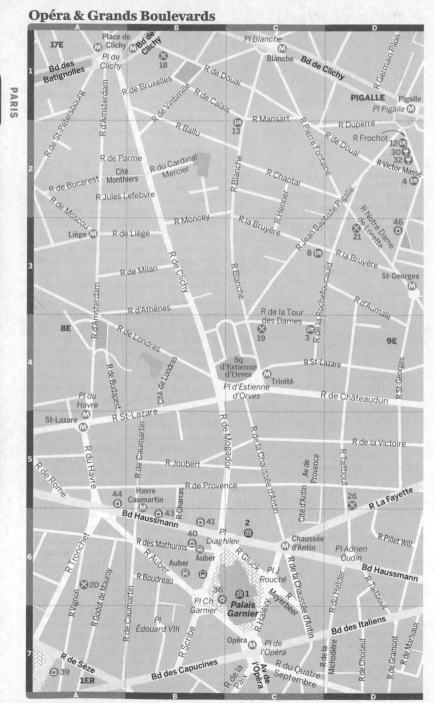

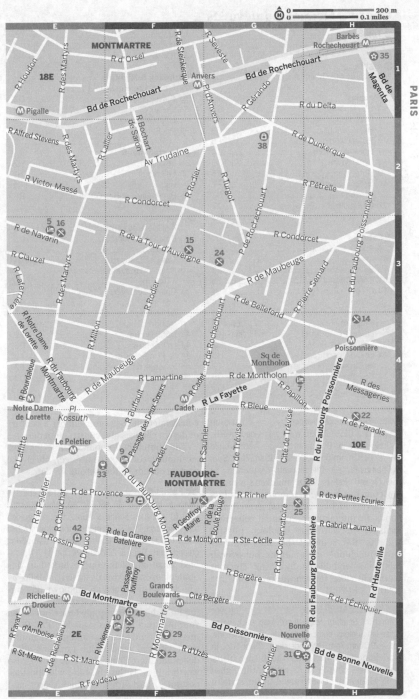

MONTMARTRE

18E

Barbès Rochechouart ⭐ 35

Bd de Magenta

R d'Orsel

R de Steinkerque

R Séveste

Bd de Rochechouart

Anvers
Pl d'Anvers

R Gérando

R du Delta

Ⓜ Pigalle

Bd de Rochechouart

R Houdon

R des Martyrs

R Alfred Stevens

R des Martyrs

R Lallier

R Bochart
de Saron

Av Trudaine

R de Dunkerque
38

R Victor Massé

R Condorcet

R Rodier

R Turgot

R Pétrelle

5 16
R de Navarin

R de la Tour d'Auvergne

15

24

P de Rochechouart

R Condorcet

R du Faubourg Poissonnière

R Clauzel

R des Martyrs

R Rodier

R de Maubeuge

14

R Milton

R de Bellefond

R Pierre Semard

Poissonnière Ⓜ

R Notre Dame
de Lorette

R du Faubourg
Montmartre

R de Maubeuge

R Lamartine

R Cadet

Sq de
Montholon

R de Montholon

7

R des
Messageries

R Bourdaloue

Ⓜ

**Notre Dame
de Lorette**

Pl
Kossuth

R Buffault

Passage des Deux Sœurs

Cadet Ⓜ

R La Fayette

R Bleue

R Papillon

22
R de Paradis

R Laffitte

Le Peletier
Ⓜ

9

R Cadet

R Saulnier

R de Trévise

Cité de Trévise

10E

R le Peletier

33

R du Faubourg Montmartre

**FAUBOURG-
MONTMARTRE**

28

R du Faubourg Poissonnière

R Chauchat

R de Provence

37

17

R Richer

R des Petites Écuries

25

42

R Rossini

R Drouot

R de la Grange
Batelière

R Geoffroy
Marie

R de la
Boule Rouge

R de Montyon

R Ste-Cécile

R du Conservatoire

R Gabriel Laumain

R d'Hauteville

6

**Richelieu-
Drouot** Ⓜ

Bd Montmartre

Passage
Jouffroy

**Grands
Boulevards**

Cité Bergère

R Bergère

R de l'Échiquier

Bd Poissonnière

**Bonne
Nouvelle** Ⓜ

R Favart

R
d'Amboise

2E

R de Richelieu

10 45

27

R Vivienne

R Montmartre

29

23

R d'Uzès

R du Sentier

31
34

Bd de Bonne Nouvelle

R St-Marc

R St-Marc

R Feydeau

11

Opéra & Grands Boulevards

Palais de la Découverte　　MUSEUM
(Mapp90; ☎0156432020; www.palais-decouverte.fr; av Franklin D Roosevelt, 8e; adult/child €9/7; ☺9.30am-6pm Tue-Sat, 10am-7pm Sun; Ⓜ Champs-Élysées–Clemenceau) Attached to the Grand Palais, this children's science museum has excellent temporary exhibits (eg moving lifelike dinosaurs) as well as a hands-on, interactive permanent collection focusing on astronomy, biology, physics and the like. Some of the older exhibits have French-only explanations, but overall this is a dependable family outing. The museum will close for renovations from late 2020 to mid-2024.

Église de la Madeleine　　CHURCH
(Church of St Mary Magdalene; Map p90; www.eglise-lamadeleine.com; place de la Madeleine, 8e; ☺9.30am-7pm; Ⓜ Madeleine) Place de la Madeleine is named after the 19th-century neoclassical church at its centre, the Église de la Madeleine. Constructed in the style of a massive Greek temple, 'La Madeleine' was consecrated in 1842 after almost a century of design changes and construction delays.

The church is a popular venue for classical-music concerts (some free); check the posters outside or the website for dates.

★ **Palais Garnier**　　HISTORIC BUILDING
(Map p78; ☎08 92 89 90 90; www.operadeparis.fr; cnr rues Scribe & Auber, 9e; self-guided tours adult/child €12/8, guided tours adult/child €15.50/8.50; ☺self-guided tours 10am-5pm, guided tours 11am & 2.30pm; Ⓜ Opéra) The fabled 'phantom of the opera' lurked in this opulent opera house designed in 1860 by Charles Garnier (then an unknown 35-year-old architect). Reserve a spot on a 90-minute English-language guided tour, or visit on your own (audioguides available; €5). Don't miss the Grand Staircase and gilded auditorium with red velvet seats, a massive chandelier and Marc Chagall's ceiling mural. Also worth a peek is the museum, with posters, costumes, backdrops, original scores and other memorabilia.

⊙ Louvre & Les Halles

History and culture meet head on along the banks of the Seine in the 1er *arrondissement* (city district), home to some of the most important sights for visitors to Paris, including the world-renowned Louvre and Centre Pompidou.

It was in this same neighbourhood that Louis VI created *halles* (markets) in 1137 for the merchants who converged on the city centre to sell their wares, and for more than 800 years they were, in the words of Émile Zola, the 'belly of Paris'. The wholesalers were moved lox, stock and cabbage out to the suburbs in 1971.

★ Musée du Louvre
MUSEUM

(Map p94; ☑ 01 40 20 53 17; www.louvre.fr; rue de Rivoli & quai des Tuileries, 1er; adult/child €15/free; ◷ 9am-6pm Mon, Thu, Sat & Sun, to 9.45pm Wed & Fri; Ⓜ Palais Royal–Musée du Louvre) It isn't until you're standing in the vast courtyard of the Louvre, with sunlight shimmering through the glass pyramid and crowds milling about beneath the museum's ornate façade, that you can truly say you've been to Paris. Holding tens of thousands of works of art – from Mesopotamian, Egyptian and Greek antiquities to masterpieces by artists such as da Vinci (including his incomparable *Mona Lisa*), Michelangelo and Rembrandt – it's no surprise that this is one of the world's most visited museums.

The **Sully Wing** is at the eastern end of the complex; the **Denon Wing** stretches 800m along the Seine to the south; and the northern **Richelieu Wing** parallels rue de Rivoli. Long before its modern incarnation, the vast Palais du Louvre originally served as a fortress constructed by Philippe-Auguste in the 12th century (medieval remnants are still visible on the lower ground floor, Sully); it was rebuilt in the mid-16th century as a royal residence in the Renaissance style. The Revolutionary Convention turned it into a national museum in 1793.

The paintings, sculptures and artefacts on display in the Louvre have been amassed by subsequent French governments. Among them are works of art and artisanship from all over Europe and priceless collections of antiquities. The Louvre's *raison d'être* is essentially to present Western art (primarily French and Italian, but also Dutch and Spanish) from the Middle Ages to about 1848 – at which point the Musée d'Orsay (p108) takes over – as well as works from

SENSATIONAL CITY VIEW

La Défense's landmark edifice is the marble **Grande Arche de la Défense** (☑ 01 40 90 52 20; www.lagrandearche.fr; 1 Parvis de la Défense; adult/child €15/7; ◷ 10am-7pm; Ⓜ La Défense) , a cube-like arch built in the 1980s to house government and business offices. The arch marks the western end of the *axe historique* (historic axis), though Danish architect Johan-Otto von Sprekelsen deliberately placed the Grande Arche fractionally out of alignment. After several years of renovations, it reopened in 2017, with spectacular views from the rooftop.

Temporary photojournalism exhibits are held in the museum (adult/child €19/11).

ancient civilisations that formed the West's cultural foundations.

When the museum opened in the late 18th century it contained 2500 paintings and *objets d'art*; the 'Grand Louvre' project inaugurated by the late president François Mitterrand in 1989 doubled the museum's exhibition space, and both new and renovated galleries have opened in recent years devoted to objets d'art such as the crown jewels of Louis XV (Room 66, 1st floor, Apollo Gallery, Denon). The Islamic art galleries (lower ground floor, Denon) are in the restored Cour Visconti.

The richness and sheer size of the place can be overwhelming. However, there's an array of innovative, entertaining self-guided thematic trails (1½ hours; download trail brochures in advance from the website) ranging from a Louvre masterpieces trail to the art of eating, plus several for kids (hunt lions, galloping horses). Even better are the Louvre's self-paced multimedia guides (€5). More formal, English-language **guided tours** (☑ 01 40 20 52 63; adult/child €12/9; ◷ 11am & 2pm except 1st Sun of month;) depart from the Hall Napoléon, which has free English-language maps.

For many, the star attraction is Leonardo da Vinci's *La Joconde*, better known as *Mona Lisa* (Room 6, 1st floor, Denon). This entire section of the 1st floor of the Denon Wing, in fact, is hung with masterpieces – Rooms 75 and 77 have enormous French paintings from Ingres, Delacroix (*Liberty Leading the People*) and Géricault (*The Raft of the Medusa*), while Rooms 1, 3, 5 and 8 contain

The Louvre

A HALF-DAY TOUR

Successfully visiting the Louvre is a fine art. Its complex labyrinth of galleries and staircases spiralling across three wings and four floors renders discovery a snakes-and-ladders experience. Initiate yourself with this three-hour itinerary – a playful mix of *Mona Lisa*–obvious and up-to-the-minute unexpected.

Arriving in the newly renovated ❶ **Cour Napoléon** beneath IM Pei's glass pyramid, pick up colour-coded floor plans at an information stand, then ride the escalator up to the Sully Wing and swap passport or credit card for a multimedia guide (there are limited descriptions in the galleries) at the wing entrance.

The Louvre is as much about spectacular architecture as masterful art. To appreciate this, zip up and down Sully's Escalier Henri II to admire ❷ **Venus de Milo**, then up parallel Escalier Henri IV to the palatial displays in ❸ **Cour Khorsabad**. Cross Room 1 to find the escalator up to the 1st floor and the opulent ❹ **Napoléon III apartments**. Next traverse 25 consecutive galleries (thank you, floor plan!) to flip conventional contemplation on its head with Cy Twombly's ❺ **The Ceiling**, and the hypnotic ❻ **Winged Victory of Samothrace**, which brazenly insists on being admired from all angles. End with the impossibly famous ❼ **Raft of the Medusa**, ❽ **Mona Lisa** and ❾ **Virgin & Child**.

TOP TIPS

➡ Don't even consider entering the Louvre's maze of galleries without a floor plan, free from the information desk in the Hall Napoléon.

➡ The Denon Wing is always packed; visit on late nights (Wednesday or Friday) or trade Denon in for the notably quieter Richelieu Wing.

➡ Tickets to the Louvre are valid for the whole day, meaning that you can nip out for lunch.

BRIAN KINNEY /SHUTTERSTOCK ©

Napoléon III Apartments
1st Floor, Richelieu
Napoléon III's gorgeous gilt apartments were built from 1854 to 1861, featuring an over-the-top decor of gold leaf, stucco and crystal chandeliers that reaches a dizzying climax in the Grand Salon and State Dining Room.

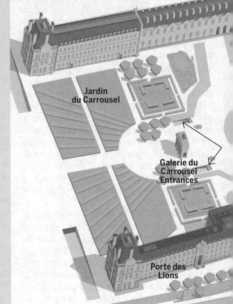

Jardin du Carrousel

Galerie du Carrousel Entrances

Porte des Lions

LOUVRE AUDITORIUM

Classical-music concerts are staged several times a week at the Louvre Auditorium (off the main entrance hall). Don't miss the Thursday lunchtime concerts featuring emerging composers and musicians. The season runs from September to April or May, depending on the concert series.

Mona Lisa
Room 6, 1st Floor, Denon
No smile is as enigmatic or bewitching as hers. Da Vinci's diminutive *La Joconde* hangs opposite the largest painting in the Louvre – sumptuous, fellow Italian Renaissance artwork *The Wedding at Cana*.

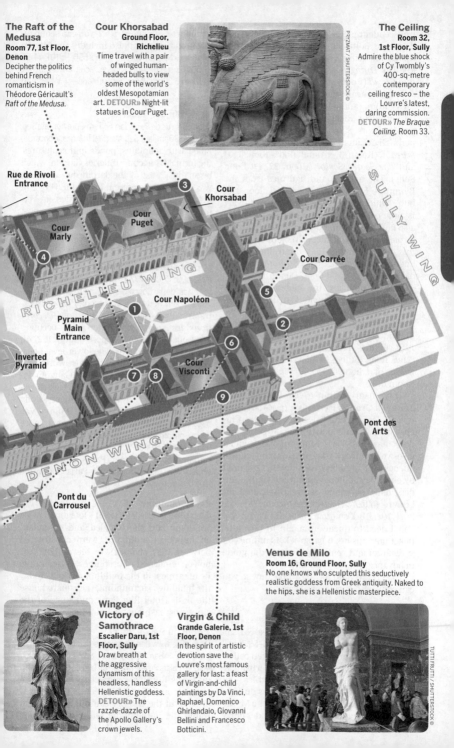

The Raft of the Medusa
Room 77, 1st Floor, Denon
Decipher the politics behind French romanticism in Théodore Géricault's *Raft of the Medusa*.

Cour Khorsabad
Ground Floor, Richelieu
Time travel with a pair of winged human-headed bulls to view some of the world's oldest Mesopotamian art. **DETOUR»** Night-lit statues in Cour Puget.

P7Z7MAT / SHUTTERSTOCK ©

The Ceiling
Room 32, 1st Floor, Sully
Admire the blue shock of Cy Twombly's 400-sq-metre contemporary ceiling fresco – the Louvre's latest, daring commission. **DETOUR»** *The Braque Ceiling*, Room 33.

Rue de Rivoli Entrance

SULLY WING

③ Cour Khorsabad

Cour Puget

Cour Marly

④

Cour Carrée

RICHELIEU WING

① Cour Napoléon

⑤

Pyramid Main Entrance

②

Inverted Pyramid

⑥

Cour Visconti

⑦ ⑧

⑨

Pont des Arts

DENON WING

Pont du Carrousel

Venus de Milo
Room 16, Ground Floor, Sully
No one knows who sculpted this seductively realistic goddess from Greek antiquity. Naked to the hips, she is a Hellenistic masterpiece.

Winged Victory of Samothrace
Escalier Daru, 1st Floor, Sully
Draw breath at the aggressive dynamism of this headless, handless Hellenistic goddess. **DETOUR»** The razzle-dazzle of the Apollo Gallery's crown jewels.

Virgin & Child
Grande Galerie, 1st Floor, Denon
In the spirit of artistic devotion save the Louvre's most famous gallery for last: a feast of Virgin-and-child paintings by Da Vinci, Raphael, Domenico Ghirlandaio, Giovanni Bellini and Francesco Botticini.

TUTTI FRUTTI / SHUTTERSTOCK ©

transcendent pieces by Raphael, Titian, Botticini and Botticelli. On the ground floor of the Denon Wing, take time for Michelangelo's *The Dying Slave* and Canova's *Psyche and Cupid* (Room 4).

Others, meanwhile, will prefer the treasures from antiquity: the Mesopotamia (ground floor, Richelieu) and Egypt (ground and 1st floors, Sully) collections are both superb. Highlights include the *Code of Hammurabi* (Room 3, ground floor, Richelieu) and *The Seated Scribe* (Room 22, 1st floor, Sully). The mosaics and figurines from the Byzantine Empire (lower ground floor, Denon), which merge into the state-of-the-art Islamic collection in the Cour Visconti, are also notable. Topping the list of ancient masterpieces are the armless Greek duo, the *Venus de Milo* (Room 16, ground floor, Sully) and the *Winged Victory of Samothrace* (top of Daru staircase, 1st floor, Denon).

Also of note are the gilded-to-the-max Napoléon III Apartments (1st floor, Richelieu), Dutch masters Vermeer (Room 38, 2nd floor, Richelieu) and Rembrandt (Room 31, 2nd floor, Richelieu), and the 18th- and 19th-century French painting collection (2nd floor, Sully), which features iconic works like Ingres' *The Turkish Bath* (off Room 60).

The main entrance is through the 21m-high **Grande Pyramide** (place du Louvre, 1er), a glass pyramid designed by the Chinese-born American architect IM Pei. If you don't have the Paris Museum Pass (which gives you priority), you can avoid the longest queues (for security) outside the pyramid by entering the Louvre complex via the underground shopping centre **Carrousel du Louvre** (http://carrouseldulouvre.com; 99 rue de Rivoli, 1er; ☉8.30am-11pm, shops 10am-8pm; 🛜). You'll need to queue up again to buy your ticket once inside; buying tickets online (€2 surcharge) and renting a multimedia guide in advance will save you time.

Tickets are valid for the whole day, so you can come and go as you please.

Musée des Arts Décoratifs GALLERY
(Map p94; ✍01 44 55 57 50; www.lesartsdecoratifs. fr; 107 rue de Rivoli, 1er; adult/child €11/free; ☉11am-6pm Tue-Sun, to 9pm Thu; Ⓜ Palais Royal–Musée du Louvre) A trio of privately administered collections – Applied Arts & Design, Advertising & Graphic Design, and Fashion & Textiles – sit in the Rohan Wing of the vast Palais du Louvre. They are collectively known as the Musée des Arts Décoratifs; admission includes entry

to all three. For an extra €2, you can scoop up a combo ticket that also includes the **Musée Nissim de Camondo** (Map p90; ✍01 44 55 57 50; 63 rue de Monceau, 8e; adult/child €9/free; ☉10am-5.30pm Wed-Sun; Ⓜ Monceau, Villiers) in the 8e.

★**Jardin des Tuileries** PARK
(Map p94; rue de Rivoli, 1er; ☉7am-9pm Apr-late Sep, 7.30am-7.30pm late Sep-Mar; Ⓜ Tuileries, Concorde) Filled with fountains, ponds and sculptures, the formal 28-hectare Tuileries Garden, which begins just west of the Jardin du Carrousel, was laid out in its present form in 1664 by André Le Nôtre, architect of the gardens at Versailles. The Tuileries soon became the most fashionable spot in Paris for parading about in one's finery. It now forms part of the Banks of the Seine Unesco World Heritage Site.

Musée de l'Orangerie MUSEUM
(Map p90; ✍01 44 77 80 07; www.musee-orangerie. fr; place de la Concorde, 1er; adult/child €9/free; ☉9am-6pm Wed-Mon; Ⓜ Concorde) Monet's extraordinary cycle of eight enormous *Decorations des Nymphéas* (Water Lilies) occupies two huge oval rooms purpose-built in 1927 on the artist's instructions. The lower level houses more of Monet's impressionist works and many by Sisley, Renoir, Cézanne, Gauguin, Picasso, Matisse and Modigliani, as well as Derain's *Arlequin et Pierrot*. The orangery, along with photography gallery **Jeu de Paume** (Map p90; ✍01 47 03 12 50; www.jeudepaume.org; 1 place de la Concorde, 1er; adult/child €10/free; ☉11am-9pm Tue, to 7pm Wed-Sun; Ⓜ Concorde), is all that remains of the former Palais des Tuileries, which was razed during the Paris Commune in 1871. Audioguides cost €5.

Place Vendôme SQUARE
(Map p94; Ⓜ Tuileries, Opéra) Octagonal place Vendôme and the arcaded and colonnaded buildings around it were constructed between 1687 and 1721. In March 1796 Napoléon married Josephine, Viscountess Beauharnais, in the building at No 3. Today the buildings surrounding the square house the posh Hôtel Ritz Paris and some of the city's most fashionable boutiques.

Jardin du Palais Royal GARDENS
(Map p94; www.domaine-palais-royal.fr; 2 place Colette, 1er; ☉8am-10.30pm Apr-Sep, to 8.30pm Oct-Mar; Ⓜ Palais Royal–Musée du Louvre) The Jardin du Palais Royal is a perfect spot to sit, contemplate and picnic between boxed hedges, or shop in the trio of beautiful arcades that frame the garden: the **Galerie de Valois**

(east), **Galerie de Montpensier** (west) and **Galerie Beaujolais** (north). However, it's the southern end of the complex, polka-dotted with sculptor Daniel Buren's 260 black-and-white striped columns, that has become the garden's signature feature.

★**Église St-Eustache** CHURCH
(Map p94; www.st-eustache.org; 2 impasse St-Eustache, 1er; ⊙9.30am-7pm Mon-Fri, 9am-7.15pm Sat & Sun; M Les Halles or RER Châtelet–Les Halles) Just north of the gardens adjoining the city's old marketplace, now the Forum des Halles, is one of Paris' most beautiful churches. Majestic, architecturally magnificent and musically outstanding, St-Eustache was constructed between 1532 and 1632 and is primarily Gothic. Artistic highlights include a work by Rubens, Raymond Mason's colourful bas-relief of market vendors (1969) and Keith Haring's bronze triptych (1990) in the side chapels.

Bourse de Commerce MUSEUM
(Map p94; www.collectionpinaultparis.com; 2 rue de Viarmes, 1er; M Les Halles or RER Châtelet–Les Halles) Paris' newest art museum is housed in the eye-catching Bourse de Commerce, an 18th-century rotunda that once held the city's grain market and stock exchange. Japanese architect Tadao Ando designed the ambitious new interior, where three floors of galleries will display contemporary art from the $1.4 billion collection of François Pinault, who previously teamed up with Ando to open the Palazzo Grassi and Punta della Dogana in Venice. It's slated to open in early 2019.

Forum des Halles NOTABLE BUILDING
(Map p94; www.forumdeshalles.com; 1 rue Pierre Lescot, 1er; ⊙shops 10am-8pm Mon-Sat, 11am-7pm Sun; M Les Halles or RER Châtelet–Les Halles) Paris' main wholesale food market stood here for nearly 800 years before being replaced by this underground shopping mall in 1971. Long considered an eyesore by many Parisians, the mall's exterior was finally demolished in 2011 to make way for its golden-hued translucent canopy, unveiled in 2016. Below, four floors of stores (more than 100), some 20 eateries and entertainment venues including cinemas and a swimming pool extend down to the city's busiest metro hub.

Spilling out from the canopied centre, the new Nelson Mandela Garden (opened May 2018) has *pétanque* (a variant on the game of bowls) courts and chess tables, a central patio and pedestrian walkways. The project

GREEN PARIS

On the corner of rue des Petits Carreaux (the northern extension of foodie street rue Montorgueil), the extraordinary *mur végétal* ('vertical garden') **L'Oasis d'Aboukir** (Map p94; 83 rue d'Aboukir, 2e; M Sentier) was installed on a 25m-high blank building façade by the modern innovator of the genre, French botanist Patrick Blanc, in 2013. It's since flourished to cover a total surface area of 250 sq metres in greenery. Subtitled *Hymne à la Biodiversité* (Ode to Biodiversity), the 'living wall' incorporates some 7600 plants from 237 different species.

has also opened up the shopping centre, allowing for more natural light.

Centre Pompidou MUSEUM
See p86.

⊙ **Montmartre & Northern Paris**
The hilltop neighbourhood of Montmartre safeguards some of Paris' most iconic sights, including the white-domed Sacré-Cœur basilica and a Parisian vineyard. The *quartier's* museums evoke its fabled artistic heritage and it's easy to stroll between them. West, past place de Clichy and beyond to Parc Monceau, there are a couple of excellent lesser-known art museums at home in historic mansions. Canal St-Martin, a sight in itself with its vintage bridges and canal boats, flows to the east.

Basilique du Sacré-Cœur BASILICA
See p88.

★**Le Mur des je t'aime** PUBLIC ART
(Map p100; www.lesjetaime.com; Sq Jehan Rictus, place des Abbesses ,18e; ⊙8am-9.30pm Mon-Fri, from 9am Sat & Sun mid-May–Aug, shorter hours Sep–mid-May; M Abbesses) Few visitors can resist a selfie in front of Montmartre's 'I Love You' wall, a public artwork created in a small park by artists Frédéric Baron and Claire Kito in the year 2000. Made from 511 dark-blue enamel tiles, the striking mural features the immortal phrase 'I love you' 311 times in nearly 250 different languages (the red fragments, if joined together, would form a heart). Find a bench beneath a maple tree and brush up your language skills romantic-Paris-style.

TOP SIGHT
CENTRE POMPIDOU

The Centre Pompidou has amazed and delighted visitors ever since it opened in 1977, not just for its outstanding collection of modern art but also for its radical architectural statement. The dynamic and vibrant arts centre delights and enthrals with its irresistible cocktail of galleries and exhibitions, hands-on workshops, dance performances, bookshop, design boutique, cinemas, a research library and other entertainment venues.

Musée National d'Art Moderne

Europe's largest collection of modern art fills the bright and airy, well-lit galleries of the National Museum of Modern Art, covering two complete floors of the Pompidou. For art lovers, this is one of the jewels of Paris. On a par with the permanent collection are the two temporary exhibition halls (on the ground floor/basement and the top floor), which showcase some memorable blockbuster exhibits. Also of note is the fabulous children's gallery on the 1st floor.

The permanent collection changes every two years, but the basic layout generally stays the same. The 5th floor showcases artists active between 1905 and 1970 (give or take a decade); the 4th floor focuses on more contemporary creations, roughly from the 1990s onward.

The dynamic presentation of the 5th floor mixes up works by Picasso, Matisse, Chagall and Kandinsky with lesser-known contemporaries from as far afield as Argentina and Japan, as well as more famous cross-Atlantic names such as Arbus, Warhol, Pollock and Rothko.

DON'T MISS

➡ The Musée National d'Art Moderne

➡ Cutting-edge temporary exhibitions

➡ The 6th floor and its sweeping panorama of Paris

PRACTICALITIES

➡ Map p120

➡ ☎ 01 44 78 12 33

➡ www.centrepompidou.fr

➡ place Georges Pompidou, 4e

➡ museum, exhibitions & panorama adult/child €14/free, panorama only ticket €5/free

➡ ⏰ 11am-9pm Wed-Mon, temporary exhibits to 11pm Thu

➡ Ⓜ Rambuteau

One floor down on the 4th, you'll find monumental paintings, installation pieces, sculpture and video taking centre stage. The focus here is on contemporary art, architecture and design.

Architecture & Views

Former French President Georges Pompidou wanted an ultracontemporary artistic hub and he got it: competition-winning architects Renzo Piano and Richard Rogers designed the building inside out, with utilitarian features like plumbing, pipes, air vents and electrical cables forming part of the external façade.

Viewed from a distance (such as from Sacré-Cœur), the Centre Pompidou's primary-coloured, box-like form amid a sea of muted grey Parisian rooftops makes it look like a child's Meccano set abandoned on someone's elegant living-room rug. Although the Centre Pompidou is just six storeys high, the city's low-rise cityscape means stupendous views extend from its roof (reached by external escalators enclosed in tubes). Rooftop admission is included in museum and exhibition admission – or buy a panorama ticket (€5) just for the roof.

Atelier Brancusi

West of the Centre Pompidou main building, this reconstruction of the studio (55 rue de Rambuteau, 4e; incl in admission to Centre Pompidou €14/free; ◷ 2-6pm Wed-Mon) of Romanian-born sculptor Constantin Brancusi (1876–1957) – known for works such as *The Kiss* and *Bird in Space* – contains over 100 sculptures in stone and wood. You'll also find drawings, pedestals and photographic plates from his original Paris studio.

Tours & Guides

Guided tours in English take place at 2pm on Saturday and sometimes Sunday (€4.50; reserve online). The museum no longer provides audioguides; instead, visitors are encouraged to download the Centre Pompidou app (which unfortunately receives only so-so reviews) and bring headphones.

Above left: Centre Pompidou, by Studio Piano & Rogers, architects

DRINKS WITH A VIEW

Georges' outdoor terrace on the 6th floor is a fabulous spot for a drink with a view, though it's not so great for dining.

The full-monty Pompidou experience is as much about hanging out in the busy streets and squares around it, packed with souvenir shops and people, as absorbing the centre's contents. West of the Centre Pompidou, fun-packed place Georges Pompidou and its nearby pedestrian streets attract bags of buskers, musicians, jugglers and mime artists. Don't miss place Igor Stravinsky with its fanciful mechanical fountains of skeletons, hearts, treble clefs, and a big pair of ruby-red lips by Jean Tinguely and Niki de Saint Phalle.

TOP TIP

Rooftop entry is included in museum and exhibition admission; alternatively, buy a panorama ticket (€5) just for the roof.

TOP SIGHT
BASILIQUE DU SACRÉ-CŒUR

More than just a place of worship, the distinctive dove-white domed Basilique du Sacré-Cœur (Sacred Heart Basilica) is a veritable experience. Reached by 270 steps, the parvis (forecourt) in front of the basilica provides a postcard-perfect city panorama. Buskers and street artists perform on the steps, while picnickers spread out on the hillside park.

History

It may appear to be a place of peacefulness and quiet contemplation today, but Sacré-Cœur's foundations were laid amid bloodshed and controversy. Its construction began in 1875, in the wake of France's humiliating defeat by Prussia and the subsequent chaos of the Paris Commune. Following Napoléon III's surrender to von Bismarck in September 1870, angry Parisians, with the help of the National Guard, continued to hold out against Prussian forces – a harrowing siege that lasted four long winter months. By the time a ceasefire was negotiated in early 1871, the split between the radical working-class Parisians (supported by the National Guard) and the conservative national government (supported by the French army) had become insurmountable.

Over the next several months, the rebels, known as Communards, managed to overthrow the reactionary government and take over the city. It was a particularly chaotic and bloody moment in Parisian history, with mass executions on both sides and a wave of rampant destruction that spread throughout Paris. Montmartre was a key Communard stronghold. It was on the future site of Sacré-Cœur that the rebels won their first victory and it was consequently the first neighbourhood to be targeted when the French army returned in full force in May 1871. Ultimately, many Communards were buried alive in the gypsum mines beneath the Butte.

The Basilica

Within the historical context, the construction of an enormous basilica to expiate the city's sins seemed like a gesture of peace and forgiveness – indeed, the seven million French francs needed to construct the church's foundations came solely from the contributions of local Catholics. However, the Montmartre location was certainly no coincidence: the conservative old guard desperately wanted to assert its power in what was then a hotbed of revolution. The battle between the two camps – Catholic versus secular, royalist versus republican – raged on and in 1882 the construction of the basilica was even voted down by the city council on the grounds that it would continue to fan the flames of civil war. It was overturned in the end by a technicality.

The Romano-Byzantine–style basilica's travertine stone exudes calcite, ensuring it remains white despite weathering and pollution. Six successive architects oversaw construction of the basilica, and it wasn't until 1919 that Sacré-Cœur was finally consecrated, contrasting the surrounding area's bohemian lifestyle.

While criticism of its design and white travertine stone has continued throughout the decades (one poet called it a giant baby's bottle for angels), the interior is enlivened by the glittering apse mosaic *Christ in Majesty*, designed by Luc-Olivier Merson in 1922 and one of the largest in the world.

On Sundays, you can hear the organ being played during Mass and Vespers.

The Dome & Crypt

Outside, to the west of the main entrance, 300 spiralling steps lead you to the basilica's dome, which affords one of Paris' most spectacular panoramas; it's said you can see for 30km on a clear day. Weighing in at 19 tonnes, the bell in the tower above, called La Savoyarde, is the largest in France.

The huge chapel-lined crypt is closed indefinitely to the public.

A PLACE OF PILGRIMAGE

In a sense, atonement here has never stopped: a prayer 'cycle' that began in 1885 before the basilica's completion still continues around the clock, with perpetual adoration of the Blessed Sacrament continually on display above the high altar.

Try to visit early morning or at sunset when crowds are a little thinner. For the best views, pick a blue-sky day to visit; don't even consider climbing to the top of the dome in bad weather.

DIVINE INTERVENTION?

In 1944, 13 Allied bombs were dropped on Montmartre, falling just next to Sacré-Cœur. Although the stained-glass windows all shattered from the force of the explosions, miraculously no one died and the basilica sustained no other damage.

Étoile & Champs-Élysées

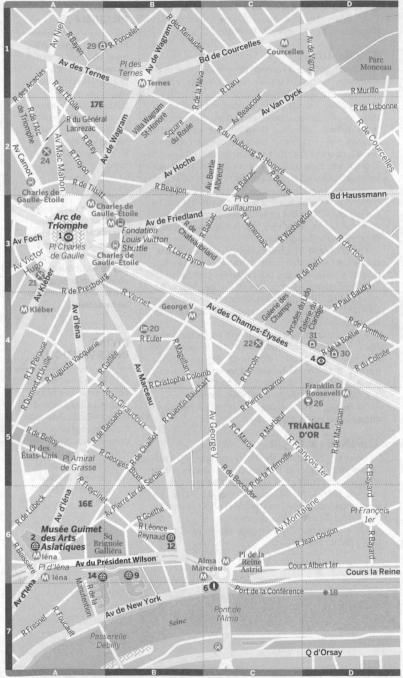

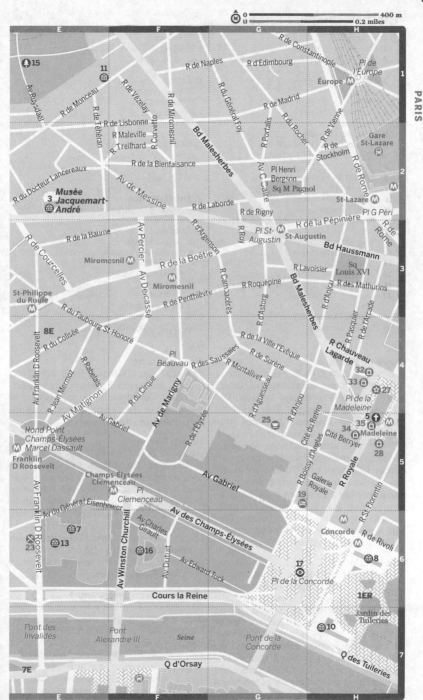

0   400 m
0   0.2 miles

E **F** **G** **H**

15
11

R de Naples
R d'Edimbourg
R de Constantinople
Pl de l'Europe
Europe

Av Ruysdaël
R de Monceau
R de Vézelay
R de Miromesnil
R du Général Foy
R de Madrid
R de Stockholm
R de Vienne
Gare St-Lazare

R de Téhéran
R de Lisbonne
R Corvetto
R Portalis
R du Rocher
R de Rome

R Maleville
R Treilhard
Bd Malesherbes
R de la Bienfaisance
Av C Saire
Pl Henri Bergson
Sq M Pagnol
St-Lazare

R du Docteur Lancereaux
Av de Messine
R de Laborde
R de Rigny
Pl G Péri

Musée Jacquemart-André
3

R de la Baume
R d'Argenson
Pl St-Augustin
R de la Pépinière
R de Rome

St-Augustin
R Roy
Bd Haussmann

R de Courcelles
Av Percier
R de la Boétie
R Lavoisier
Sq Louis XVI
R des Mathurins

Miromesnil
Av Decassé
R Cambacérès
R Roquépine
Bd Malesherbes
R d'Anjou

St-Philippe du Roule
Miromesnil
R de Penthièvre
R d'Astorg
R Pasquier
R de l'Arcade

R du Faubourg St-Honoré
8E
R du Colisée
R de la Ville l'Evêque
R Chauveau Lagarde
32
33
27

Av Franklin D Roosevelt
R Rabelais
Pl Beauvau
R des Saussaies
R de Surène
R Montalivet
Pl de la Madeleine
5
35

R Jean Mermoz
Av de Marigny
R d'Aguesseau
R d'Anjou
Cité du Retiro
34
Madeleine
28

Av Matignon
R du Cirque
R de l'Elysée
25
Cité Berryer

Rond Point Champs-Élysées Marcel Dassault
Av Gabriel
R Boissy d'Anglas
R Royale

Franklin D Roosevelt
Champs-Élysées Clemenceau
Pl Clemenceau
Galerie Royale
19

Av du Général Eisenhower
Av Charles Girault
Av des Champs-Élysées
Av Gabriel
Concorde
R de Rivoli
R St-Florentin

7
23
13
16
Av Dutuit
Av Edward Tuck
17
Pl de la Concorde
8

Cours la Reine
1ER
Jardin des Tuileries

Pont des Invalides
Pont Alexandre III
Seine
Pont de la Concorde
10

7E
Q d'Orsay
Q des Tuileries

E **F** **G** **H**

Étoile & Champs-Élysées

Musée de Montmartre MUSEUM
(Map p100; ☑ 01 49 25 89 39; www.museedemont
martre.fr; 12 rue Cortot, 18e; adult/child €9.50/5.50,
garden only €4; ☉ 10am-7pm Apr-Sep, to 6pm Oct-
Mar; Ⓜ Lamarck–Caulaincourt) This delightful
'village' museum showcases paintings, lithographs and documents illustrating Montmartre's bohemian, artistic and hedonistic past –
one room is dedicated entirely to the French
cancan. It's housed in a 17th-century manor
where several artists, including Renoir and
Raoul Dufy, had their studios in the 19th century. You can also visit the studio of painter
Suzanne Valadon, who lived and worked here
with her son Maurice Utrillo and partner André Utter between 1912 and 1926.

Clos Montmartre VINEYARD
(Map p100; 18 rue des Saules, 18e; Ⓜ Lamarck–
Caulaincourt) Epitomising Montmartre's
enchanting village-like atmosphere, the
quartier has its own small vineyard. Planted
in 1933, its 2000 vines produce an average
of 800 bottles of wine a year. Each October
the grapes are pressed, fermented and bottled in Montmartre's town hall, then sold by
auction to raise funds for local community
projects. It's closed to the public except for a
handful of special events.

Place du Tertre SQUARE
(Map p100; 18e; Ⓜ Abbesses) Today filled with
visitors, buskers and portrait artists, place
du Tertre was originally the main square of
the village of Montmartre before it was incorporated into the city proper.

Espace Dalí GALLERY
(Map p100; ☑ 01 42 64 40 21; www.daliparis.com;
11 rue Poulbot, 18e; adult/child €12/9; ☉ 10am-
6pm Sep-Jun, to 8pm Jul & Aug; Ⓜ Abbesses) More
than 300 works by Salvador Dalí (1904–89),
the flamboyant Catalan surrealist printmak-
er, painter, sculptor and self-promoter, are
on display at this basement museum located
just west of place du Tertre. The collection includes Dalí's strange sculptures, lithographs,
and many of his illustrations and furniture,
including the famous *Mae West Lips Sofa*.

★ **Musée Jacquemart-André** MUSEUM
(Map p90; ☑ 01 45 62 11 59; www.musee-jacquemart-
andre.com; 158 bd Haussmann, 8e; adult/child
€13.50/10.50; ☉ 10am-6pm, to 8.30pm Mon during
temporary exhibitions; Ⓜ Miromesnil) The home of
art collectors Nélie Jacquemart and Édouard
André, this opulent late-19th-century residence combined elements from different
eras – seen here in the presence of Greek and

Roman antiquities, Egyptian artefacts, period furnishings and portraits by Dutch masters. Its 16 rooms offer an absorbing glimpse of the lifestyle of Parisian high society: from the library, hung with canvases by Rembrandt and Van Dyck, to the marvellous Jardin d'Hiver – a glass-paned garden room backed by a magnificent double-helix staircase.

Parc Monceau PARK
(Map p90; 35 bd de Courcelles, 8e; ⊙7am-10pm May-Aug, to 9pm Sep, to 8pm Oct-Apr; Ⓜ Monceau) Marked by a neoclassical rotunda at its main bd Courcelles entrance, beautiful Parc Monceau sprawls over 8.2 lush hectares. It was laid out by Louis Carrogis Carmontelle in 1778–79 in English style with winding paths, ponds and flower beds. An Egyptian-style pyramid is the only original folly remaining today, but other distinctive features include a bridge modelled after Venice's Rialto, a Renaissance arch and a Corinthian colonnade. There are play areas, a carousel and scheduled puppet shows for kids.

★**Parc de la Villette** PARK
(Map p72; www.lavillette.com; 211 av Jean Jaurès, 19e; ⊙6am-1am; Ⓜ Porte de la Villette, Porte de Pantin) Spanning 55 hectares, this vast city park is a cultural centre, kids playground and landscaped urban space at the intersection of two canals, the Ourcq and the St-Denis. Its futuristic layout includes the colossal mirror-like sphere of the Géode cinema and the bright-red cubical pavilions known as *folies*. Among its themed gardens are the Jardin du Dragon (Dragon Garden), with a giant dragon's tongue slide for kids, Jardin des Dunes (Dunes Garden) and Jardin des Miroirs (Mirror Garden).

La REcyclerie CULTURAL CENTRE
(Map p72; www.larecyclerie.com; 83 bd Ornano, 18e; ⊙8am-midnight Mon-Thu, to 2am Fri & Sat, to 10pm Sun early Jan–mid-Dec; Ⓜ Porte de Clignancourt) 🖉 An abandoned Petite Ceinture train station has been repurposed as an eco-hub with an urban farm along the old railway line, featuring community vegetable and herb gardens and chickens. They provide ingredients for the mostly vegetarian cafe-canteen (tables stretch trackside in summer and the station houses a cavernous dining space). In turn, food scraps replenish the chickens and gardens. Beehives on the roof produce honey. Look out for regular upcycling and repair workshops, flea markets and various other events.

DON'T MISS

PARISIAN STREET ART
....

For a guided tour of the city's vibrant street art and the low-down on both its history and current scene, hook up with **Street Art Paris** (📞 09 50 75 19 92; http://streetartparis.fr; 2½hr tour €20). Tours take place in Belleville and Montmartre and on the Left Bank. Inspired to have a bash yourself? Book into a 2½-hour mural workshop (€35).

Art 42 (Map p72; www.art42.fr; 96 bd Bessières, 17e; ⊙tours in English 7pm Tue, 4pm 1st Sun of month; Ⓜ Porte de Clichy) Street art and post-graffiti now have their own dedicated space at this 'anti-museum', with works by Banksy, Bom.K, Miss Van, Swoon and Invader (who's behind the Space Invader motifs on buildings all over Paris), among other boundary-pushing urban artists. Compulsory guided tours, generally lasting 1½ to two hours, lead you through 4000 sq metres of subterranean rooms sheltering some 150 works. Entry's free but you need to reserve tours online (ideally several weeks in advance, although last-minute cancellations can arise).

Galerie Itinerrance (Map p72; http://itinerrance.fr; 24 bd du Général d'Armée Jean Simon, 13e; ⊙noon-7pm Tue-Sat; Ⓜ Bibliothèque) Testament to the 13e's ongoing creative renaissance, this gallery showcases graffiti and street art, and can advise on self-guided and guided street-art tours of the neighbourhood that take in many landmark works by artists represented by the gallery. Exhibitions and events change regularly.

L'Aerosol (Map p72; www.laerosol.fr; 54 rue de l'Évangile, 18e; adult/child €5/3; ⊙11am-9pm Wed-Sun; Ⓜ Marx Dormoy) Street art is showcased at this cavernous museum inside a former SNCF freight railway station. French and international artists here include Mr Chat, Speedy Graphito, Invader and Banksy. You can test out your own tagging skills on the walls outside (BYO aerosols) or ask about taking a street-art course. Festivals, food trucks and a summer roller nightclub also set up here.

Louvre & Les Halles

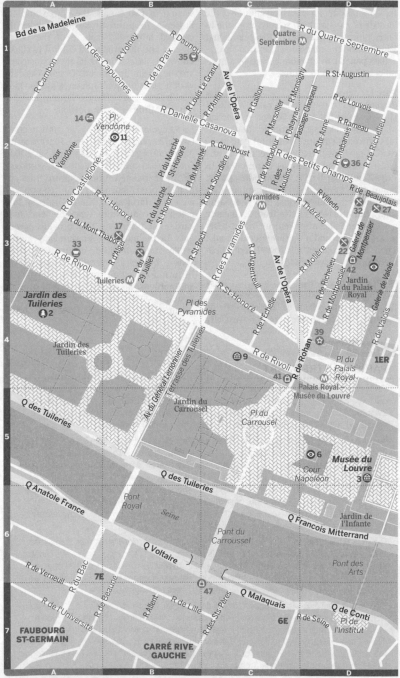

Map content:

A | **B** | **C** | **D**

Bd de la Madeleine

R Cambon

R des Capucines

R Volney

R de la Paix

R Daunou

35

R Louis Le Grand

R d'Antin

Av de l'Opéra

Quatre Septembre M

R du Quatre Septembre

R St-Augustin

R de Louvois

R Gaillon

R Marsollier

R Monsigny

Passage Choiseul

R Dalayrac

R Rameau

R Ste-Anne

R Chabanais

R de Richelieu

14

Pl Vendôme

11

Cour Vendôme

R Danielle Casanova

R du Marché St-Honoré

R Gomboust

R des Petits Champs

R de Ventadour

R des Moulins

36

Pl du Marché St-Honoré

R de la Sourdière

Pyramides M

R Villedo

R de Beaujolais

32

27

R de Castiglione

R St-Honoré

R du Mont Thabor

17

R St-Roch

R des Pyramides

R Thérèse

R Molière

R de Richelieu

22

42

7

Galerie de Montpensier

33

R d'Alger

R du 29 Juillet

31

Tuileries M

R d'Argenteuil

R St-Honoré

Av de l'Opéra

Jardin du Palais Royal

Galerie de Valois

Jardin des Tuileries

2

Pl des Pyramides

R de l'Echelle

R de Montpensier

39

1ER

Jardin des Tuileries

Av du Général Lemonnier

Terrasse des Tuileries

9

R de Rivoli

R de Rohan

41

Pl du Palais Royal

M

Palais Royal – Musée du Louvre

Q des Tuileries

Jardin du Carrousel

Pl du Carrousel

6

Cour Napoléon

Musée du Louvre

3

Q Anatole France

Pont Royal

Seine

Q des Tuileries

Q Francois Mitterrand

Jardin de l'Infante

Q Voltaire

Pont du Carroussel

Pont des Arts

R de Verneuil

R du Bac

7E

R de Beaune

R Allent

R de Lille

47

Q Malaquais

Q de Conti

R de l'Université

R des Sts-Pères

6E

R de Seine

Pl de l'Institut

FAUBOURG ST-GERMAIN

CARRÉ RIVE GAUCHE

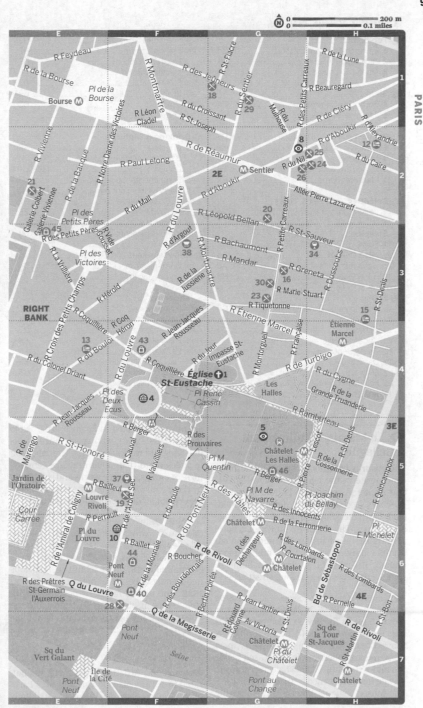

Louvre & Les Halles

◉ Le Marais, Ménilmontant & Belleville

The majority of sights in this neighbourhood concentrate in the narrow, medieval streets and sheltered squares of Le Marais, which are easily accessed on foot. Museums here include an increasing number of cutting-edge art galleries. The Cimetière du Père Lachaise sprawls northeast in the 20e, and although traditional sights beyond Le Marais are more limited, Belleville in particular is home to some of the city's most striking street art.

★ **Musée National Picasso**   MUSEUM
(Map p120; ☑ 01 85 56 00 36; www.museepicasso paris.fr; 5 rue de Thorigny, 3e; adult/child €12.50/ free; ☉10.30am-6pm Tue-Fri, from 9.30am Sat & Sun; Ⓜ Chemin Vert, St-Paul) One of Paris' most treasured art collections is showcased inside the mid-17th-century Hôtel Salé, an exquisite private mansion owned by the city since 1964. The Musée National Picasso is a staggering art museum devoted to Spanish artist Pablo Picasso (1881-1973), who spent much of his life living and working in Paris. The collection includes more than 5000 drawings, engravings, paintings, ceramic works and sculptures by the *grand maître* (great master), although they're not all displayed at the same time.

Hôtel de Ville   ARCHITECTURE
(Map p120; www.paris.fr; place de l'Hôtel de Ville, 4e; Ⓜ Hôtel de Ville) FREE Paris' beautiful town hall was gutted during the Paris Commune of 1871 and rebuilt in luxurious neo-Renaissance style between 1874 and 1882. The ornate façade is decorated with 108 statues of illustrious Parisians, and the outstanding temporary exhibitions (admission free; enter at 29 rue de Rivoli) have a Parisian theme.

Place des Vosges   SQUARE
(Map p120; 4e; Ⓜ Bastille, Chemin Vert) Inaugurated in 1612 as place Royale and thus Paris' oldest square, place des Vosges is a strikingly

elegant ensemble of 36 symmetrical houses with ground-floor arcades, steep slate roofs and large dormer windows arranged around a leafy square with four symmetrical fountains and an 1829 copy of a mounted statue of Louis XIII. The square received its present name in 1800 to honour the Vosges *département* (administrative division) for being the first in France to pay its taxes.

★**Maison de Victor Hugo** MUSEUM
(Map p120; ☎ 01 42 72 10 16; www.maisonsvictor
hugo.paris.fr; 6 place des Vosges, 4e; ☉10am-6pm Tue-Sun; Ⓜ Bastille) FREE Between 1832 and 1848 the celebrated novelist and poet Victor Hugo lived in an apartment in Hôtel de Rohan-Guéménée, a townhouse overlooking one of Paris' most elegant squares. Hugo moved here a year after the publication of *Notre Dame de Paris* (The Hunchback of Notre Dame), completing *Ruy Blas* during his stay. It's now a museum devoted to his life and works, with an impressive collection of his personal drawings and portraits. Temporary exhibitions command an admission fee.

Musée Carnavalet MUSEUM
(Map p120; www.carnavalet.paris.fr; 23 rue de Sévigné, 3e; Ⓜ St-Paul, Chemin Vert) FREE Paris' history museum, spanning Gallo-Roman times onwards, rambles over a pair of remarkable *hôtels particuliers* (private mansions), the 1560-built **Hôtel Carnavalet** and 1688-built **Hôtel Le Peletier de St-Fargeau**.

The museum is closed entirely until 2020 for major renovations that will make it more accessible, including for travellers with disabilities, but the courtyards remain open to the public while work's under way.

Musée des Arts et Métiers MUSEUM
(Map p120; www.arts-et-metiers.net; 60 rue de Réaumur, 3e; adult/child €8/free, 6-9.30pm Thu & 1st Sun of month free; ☉10am-6pm Tue, Wed & Fri-Sun, to 9.30pm Thu; Ⓜ Arts et Métiers) The Arts and Crafts Museum, dating to 1794 and Europe's oldest science and technology museum, is a must for families – or anyone with an interest in how things tick or work. Housed inside the sublime 18th-century priory of St-Martin des Champs, some 2400 instruments, machines and working models from the 18th to 20th centuries are displayed across three floors. In the priory's attached church is Foucault's original pendulum, introduced to the world at the Universal Exhibition in Paris in 1855.

DON'T MISS

WATERSIDE STROLL

The tranquil, 4.5km-long **Canal St-Martin** (Map p120; Ⓜ République, Jaurès, Jacques Bonsergent) was inaugurated in 1825 to provide a shipping link between the Seine and Paris' northeastern suburbs. Emerging from below ground near place de la République, its towpaths take you past locks, bridges and local neighbourhoods. Come for a romantic stroll, cycle, picnic lunch or dusk-time drink. From the iron footbridge by the intersection of rue de la Grange aux Belles and quai de Jemmapes, watch the vintage road bridge swing open to let canal boats pass.

★**Mémorial de la Shoah** MUSEUM
(Map p120; www.memorialdelashoah.org; 17 rue Geoffroy l'Asnier, 4e; ☉10am-6pm Sun-Wed & Fri, to 10pm Thu; Ⓜ Pont Marie, St-Paul) FREE Established in 1956, the Memorial to the Unknown Jewish Martyr has metamorphosed into the Memorial of the Shoah – 'Shoah' is a Hebrew word meaning 'catastrophe' and it's synonymous in France with the Holocaust. Museum exhibitions relate to the Holocaust and German occupation of parts of France and Paris during WWII. The actual memorial to the victims stands at the entrance. The wall is inscribed with the names of 76,000 men, women and children deported from France to Nazi extermination camps.

★**Cimetière du Père Lachaise** CEMETERY
(Map p72; ☎ 01 55 25 82 10; www.pere-lachaise.com; 16 rue du Repos & 8 bd de Ménilmontant, 20e; ☉8am-6pm Mon-Fri, from 8.30am Sat, from 9am Sun mid-Mar–Oct, shorter hours Nov–mid-Mar; Ⓜ Père Lachaise, Gambetta) Opened in 1804, Père Lachaise is today the world's most visited cemetery. Its 70,000 ornate tombs of the rich and famous form a verdant, 44-hectare sculpture garden. The most visited are those of 1960s rock star Jim Morrison (division 6) and Oscar Wilde (division 89). Pick up cemetery maps at the **conservation office** (Bureaux de la Conservation; ☉8.30am-12.30pm & 2-5pm Mon-Fri; Ⓜ Philippe Auguste, Père Lachaise) near the main bd de Ménilmontant entrance. Other notables buried here include composer Chopin, playwright Molière, poet Apollinaire, and writers Balzac, Proust, Gertrude Stein and Colette.

Cimetière du Père Lachaise

A HALF-DAY TOUR

There is a certain romance to getting lost in Cimetière du Père Lachaise, a jungle of graves spun from centuries of tales. But to search for one grave among one million in this 44-hectare land of the dead is no joke – narrow the search with this itinerary.

From the main bd de Ménilmontant entrance (metro Père Lachaise or Philippe Auguste), head up av Principale, turn right onto av du Puits and collect a map from **❶ the Bureaux de la Conservation**.

Backtrack along av du Puits, turn right onto av Latérale du Sud, scale the stairs and bear right along chemin Denon to New Realist artist **❷ Arman**, film director **❸ Claude Chabrol** and **❹ Chopin**.

Follow chemin Méhul downhill, cross av Casimir Périer and bear right onto chemin Serré. Take the second left (chemin Lebrun – unsigned), head uphill and near the top leave the footpath to weave through graves on your right to rock star **❺ Jim Morrison**. Back on chemin Lauriston, continue uphill to roundabout **❻ Rond-Point Casimir Périer**.

Admire the funerary art of contemporary photographer **❼ André Chabot**, av de la Chapelle. Continue uphill for energising city views from the **❽ chapel** steps, then zig-zag to **❾ Molière & La Fontaine**, on chemin Molière.

Cut between graves onto av Tranversale No 1 – spot potatoes atop **❿ Parmentier's** headstone. Continue straight onto av Greffulhe and left onto av Tranversale No 2 to rub **⓫ Monsieur Noir's** shiny crotch.

Navigation to **⓬ Édith Piaf** and the **⓭ Mur des Fédérés** is straightforward. End with angel-topped **⓮ Oscar Wilde** near the Porte Gambetta entrance.

TOP TIPS

➡ Père Lachaise is a photographer's paradise any time of the day or year, but best are sunny autumn mornings after the rain.

➡ Cemetery-lovers will appreciate themed guided tours (two hours) led by entertaining cemetery historian Thierry Le Roi (www.necro-romantiques.com).

BRUNO DE HOGUES / GETTY IMAGES ©

Chopin, Division 11

Add a devotional note to the handwritten letters and flowers brightening the marble tomb of Polish composer/pianist Frédéric Chopin (1810–49), who spent his short adult life in Paris. His heart is buried in Warsaw.

Monuments aux Morts

Main Entrance

av du Puits

av Latérale du Sud

chemin Denon

chemin Méhul

av Principale

Bureaux de la Conservation

Porte du Repos

av Casimir Périer

chemi Maiso

chemin

73

Jim Morrison, Division 6

The original bust adorning the disgracefully dishevelled grave of Jim Morrison (1943–71), lead singer of The Doors, was stolen. Pay your respects to rock's greatest legend – no chewing gum or padlocks please.

HUANG ZHENG / SHUTTERSTOCK ©

André Chabot, Division 20

Contemporary photographer André Chabot (b 1941) shoots funerary art, hence the bijou 19th-century chapel he's equipped with monumental granite camera – and a QR code – in preparation for the day he departs.

Molière & La Fontaine, Division 25

Parisians refused to leave their local *quartier* for Père Lachaise so in 1817 the authorities moved in popular playwright Molière (1622–73) and poet Jean de la Fontaine (1621–95). The marketing strategy worked.

Oscar Wilde, Division 89

Irish writer Oscar Wilde (1854–1900) was forever scandalous: check the enormous packet of the sphinx on his tomb, sculpted by British-American sculptor Jacob Epstein 11 years after Wilde died.

BRUNO DE HOGUES / GETTY IMAGES ©

BRUNO DE HOGUES / GETTY IMAGES ©

ALIZADA STUDIOS / SHUTTERSTOCK ©

Monsieur Noir, Division 92

Cemetery sex stud Mr Black, alias 21-year-old journalist Victor Noir (1848–70), was shot by Napoléon III's nephew in a botched duel. Urban myth means women rub his crotch to boost fertility.

Mur des Fédérés, Division 76

This plain brick wall was where 147 Communard insurgents were lined up and shot in 1871. Equally emotive is the sculpted walkway of commemorative war memorials surrounding the mass grave.

Édith Piaf, Division 97

The archbishop of Paris might have refused Parisian diva Édith Piaf (1915–63) the Catholic rite of burial, but that didn't stop more than 100,000 mourners attending her internment at Père Lachaise.

IRINA KLYUCHNIKOVA / SHUTTERSTOCK ©

Map labels

av des Combattants Étrangers morts pour la France

Porte Gambetta Entrance

av Circulaire

84

88

89

14

Crematorium

Chapel

av Tranversale No 3

av Tranversale No 2

av Tranversale No 1

av de Saint Morys

50

51

chemin Berthole

21

7

chemin Molière

20

24

25

9

26

10

42

41

39

93

92

11

av Greffülhe

94

95

av Pacthod

Rond-Point Casimir Périer

6

chemin Lauriston

14

5

6

chemin Lebrun

la Chapelle

Commemorative war memorials

12

97

13

76

96

av Circulaire

Porte de la Réunion

Montmartre & Pigalle

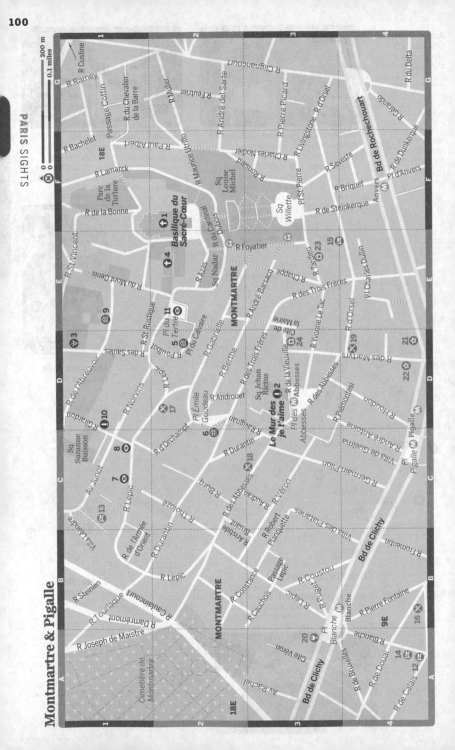

0 200 m
0 0.1 miles

18E

R Custine
R Ramey
Passage Cottin
R Bachelet
R du Chevalier de la Barre
R Mullet
R Feutrier
R André del Sarte
R Clignancourt
R Pierre Picard
R d'Orsel
R du Delta
R de Gérando
Bd de Rochechouart
R de Dunkerque
Pl d'Anvers

R Lamarck
Parc de la Turlure
R de la Bonne
R Paul Albert
R Maurice Utrillo
R Ronsard
R Charles Nodier
R Livingstone – R d'Orsel
R Seveste
R Briquet
R de Steinkerque
Anvers
Sq Louise Michel

R St-Vincent
Basilique du Sacré-Cœur [1]
R du Cardinal Dubois
[4]
Sq Nadar
R Azaïs
R Foyatier
R Chappe
R André-Barsacq
R Tardieu
Pl St-Pierre
Sq Willette
[23]
[15]
Pl Charles Dullin

R de l'Abreuvoir
[3]
R du Mont Cenis
R des Saules
Pl du Tertre
[5] [11]
Pl du Calvaire
R St-Rustique
R Poulbot
R Gabrielle
R des Trois Frères
MONTMARTRE
R des Trois Frères
Cité de la Mairie
R Yvonne Le Tac
R d'Orsel
[9]

[10]
R Girardon
R Norvins
R Lepic
R Berthe
R Jehan Rictus
[24]
R de la Vieuville
R des Abbesses
Abbesses
R des Martyrs
[19]
[21]
[22]

Sq Suzanne Buisson
Av Junot
[7] [8]
R d'Orchampt
Pl Émile Goudeau
R Androuet
[6]
R Ravignan
Le Mur des Je t'aime [2]
Pl des Abbesses
R de la Vieuville
R Houdon
R Piémontési
R André Antoine
Pigalle
Pl Pigalle

[13]
Villa Léandre
R de l'Armée d'Orient
R Durantin
R Tholozé
R Burq
[18]
R des Abbesses
R Aristide Bruant
R Audran
R Véron
R Durantin
R Germain Pilon
R Germain Pilon
Villa de Guelma

R Steinlen
R Tourlaque
R Caulaincourt
R Damrémont
R Joseph de Maistre
R Lepic
R Constance
Passage Lepic
R Cauchois
R Robert Planquette
R Coustou
R Puget
R Pierre Fontaine
9E
[16]

Cimetière de Montmartre
Av Rachel
MONTMARTRE
18E
Cité Véron
[20]
Pl Blanche
Blanche
R Blanche
Bd de Clichy
R de Bruxelles
R de Douai
[14]
[12]
R de Calais

Bd de Clichy
R Fromentin

Montmartre & Pigalle

◉ Bastille & Eastern Paris

Historic place de la Bastille – at the intersection of the 4e, 11e and 12e *arrondissements,* and being transformed from a busy roundabout into a much more pedestrian-friendly zone by mid-2019 – is the obvious place to start exploring. Take a waterside stroll south along the city's only pleasure port, Port de l'Arsenal. Southeast of here is the busy Gare de Lyon station area, with the unusual Promenade Plantée, which can be followed on foot for 4.5km to Bois de Vincennes on the far eastern fringe of this neighbourhood. Several key sights are clustered in and around the green urban woodland.

Place de la Bastille　　　　　　　SQUARE
(Map p120; 12e; Ⓜ Bastille) A 14th-century fortress built to protect the city gates, the Bas-

tille ecame a prison under Cardinal Richelieu, which was mobbed on 14 July 1789, igniting the French Revolution. At the centre of the square is the 52m-high **Colonne de Juillet** (Map p120; www.colonne-de-juillet. fr; place de la Bastille, 12e; Ⓜ Bastille) a green-bronze column topped by a gilded, winged Liberty. Revolutionaries from the uprising of 1830 are buried beneath; the crypt will open to the public as part of a major redevelopment that will link the square to Bassin de l'Arsenal.

As part of the works, which are due for completion in 2019, the location of the old fortress prison of the Bastille will be marked on the ground (currently you can see a triple row of paving stones that traces the building's outline on the ground between bd Henri IV and rue St-Antoine). The foundations are also marked below ground in the Bastille metro station, on the platform of line 5. When complete, the square's overhaul will reduce traffic by 40%, making it pedestrian- and cyclist-friendly.

Promenade Plantée　　　　　　　PARK
(La Coulée Verte René-Dumont; Map p126; cnr rue de Lyon & av Daumesnil, 12e; ⊙ 8am-9.30pm Mon-Fri, from 9am Sat & Sun Mar-Oct, 8am-5.30pm Mon-Fri, from 9am Sat & Sun Nov-Feb; Ⓜ Bastille, Gare de Lyon, Daumesnil) The disused 19th-century Vincennes railway viaduct was reborn as the world's first elevated park, planted with a fragrant profusion of cherry trees, maples, rose trellises, bamboo corridors and lavender. Three storeys above ground, it provides a unique aerial vantage point on the city. Along the first, northwestern section, above av Daumesnil, art-gallery workshops beneath the arches form the Viaduc des Arts (p179). Staircases provide access (lifts/elevators here invariably don't work).

Ground Control　　　　　　ARTS CENTRE
(Map p126; www.groundcontrolparis.com; 81 rue du Charolais, 12e; ⊙ noon-midnight Wed-Fri, 11am-midnight Sat, 11am-10pm Sun; Ⓜ Gare de Lyon) An industrial area that once housed a postal sorting centre was transformed into a pop-up cultural space and will now operate year-round until at least 2020. Spread across a 4500-sq-metre hall and 1500-sq-metre terrace are an urban kitchen garden with gardening workshops, a plant shop and veggie stand, yoga, reiki and meditation classes, 19 bars, cafes and restaurants (some inside old buses and

trains), 13 shops and galleries, DJ sets, live-music gigs and kids' play areas.

Bois de Vincennes
PARK

(bd Poniatowski, 12e; M Porte de Charenton, Porte Dorée) In the southeastern corner of Paris, Bois de Vincennes encompasses some 995 hectares. Originally royal hunting grounds, the woodland was annexed by the army following the Revolution and then donated to the city in 1860 by Napoléon III. A fabulous place to escape the Parisian concrete, Bois de Vincennes also contains a handful of notable sights including a bona fide royal château, **Château de Vincennes** (☑ 01 48 08 31 20; www.chateau-de-vincennes.fr; 1 av de Paris, Vincennes; adult/child €9/free; ⊘ 10am-6pm mid-May–mid-Sep, to 5pm mid-Sep–mid-May; M Château de Vincennes), with massive fortifications and a moat.

Paris' largest, state-of-the-art zoo, the **Parc Zoologique de Paris** (Zoo de Vincennes; ☑ 08 11 22 41 22; www.parczoologiquedeparis. fr; cnr av Daumesnil & rte de Ceinture du Lac Daumesnil, 12e; adult/child €22/16.50; ⊘ 9.30am-8.30pm May-Aug, shorter hours Sep-Apr; M Porte Dorée), is also here, as is the magnificent **Parc Floral de Paris** (☑ 01 49 57 24 81; www. parcfloraldeparisjeux.com; Esplanade du Chateau de Vincennes or rte de la Pyramide; adult/child €2.50/1.50; ⊘ 9.30am-8pm Apr-Sep, to 6.30pm Oct, to 5pm Nov-Feb, to 6.30pm Mar; M Château de Vincennes), a botanical park with exciting playgrounds for older children. The wood also has a lovely lake, with boats to rent and ample green lawns to picnic on.

DON'T MISS

DIGITAL ART

A former foundry dating from 1835 that supplied iron for the French navy and railroads now houses Paris' first digital art museum, **L'Atelier des Lumières** (Map p120; www.atelier-lumieres. com; 38-40 rue St-Maur, 11e; adult/child €14.50/9.50; ⊘ 10am-6pm Sun-Thu, to 10pm Fri & Sat; M Voltaire), opened in 2018. The 1500-sq-metre La Halle mounts dazzling light projections that take over the bare walls. Long programs lasting around 30 minutes are based on historic artists' works; there's also a shorter contemporary program. Screenings are continuous. In the separate Le Studio space, you can discover emerging and established digital artists.

⊙ The Islands

Île de la Cité was the site of the first settlement in Paris (c 3rd century BC) and later the centre of Roman Lutetia. The island remained the hub of royal and ecclesiastical power, even after the city spread to both banks of the Seine in the Middle Ages. Smaller Île St-Louis was actually two uninhabited islets called Île Notre Dame (Our Lady Isle) and Île aux Vaches (Cows Island) in the early 17th century – until a building contractor and two financiers worked out a deal with Louis XIII to create one island and build two stone bridges to the mainland.

★Cathédrale
Notre Dame de Paris
CATHEDRAL

(Map p130; ☑ 01 42 34 56 10, towers 01 53 10 07 00; www.notredamedeparis.fr; 6 Parvis Notre Dame – place Jean-Paul-II, 4e; cathedral free, adult/ child towers €10/free, treasury €5/3; ⊘ cathedral 7.45am-6.45pm Mon-Fri, to 7.15pm Sat & Sun, towers 10am-6.30pm Sun-Thu, 10am-11pm Fri & Sat Jul & Aug, 10am-6.30pm Apr-Jun & Sep, 10am-5.30pm Oct-Mar, treasury 9.45am-5.30pm; M Cité) Paris' most visited unticketed site, with upwards of 14 million visitors per year, is a masterpiece of French Gothic architecture. The focus of Catholic Paris for seven centuries, its vast interior accommodates 6000 worshippers.

Highlights include its three spectacular rose windows, treasury and bell towers, which can be climbed. From the North Tower, 400-odd steps spiral to the top of the western façade, where you'll find yourself face-to-face with frightening gargoyles and a spectacular view of Paris.

★Sainte-Chapelle
CHAPEL

(Map p130; ☑ 01 53 40 60 80, concerts 01 42 77 65 65; www.sainte-chapelle.fr; 8 bd du Palais, 1er; adult/child €10/free, joint ticket with Conciergerie €15; ⊘ 9am-7pm Apr-Sep, to 5pm Oct-Mar; M Cité) Try to save Sainte-Chapelle for a sunny day, when Paris' oldest, finest stained glass is at its dazzling best. Enshrined within the Palais de Justice (Law Courts), this gem-like Holy Chapel is Paris' most exquisite Gothic monument. It was completed in 1248, just six years after the first stone was laid, and was conceived by Louis IX to house his personal collection of holy relics, including the famous Holy Crown (now in Notre Dame).

Conciergerie
MONUMENT

(Map p130; ☑ 01 53 40 60 80; www.paris-conciergerie. fr; 2 bd du Palais, 1er; adult/child €9/free, joint ticket with Sainte-Chapelle €15; ⊙ 9.30am-6pm; Ⓜ Cité) A royal palace in the 14th century, the Conciergerie later became a prison. During the Reign of Terror (1793–94) alleged enemies of the Revolution were incarcerated here before being brought before the Revolutionary Tribunal next door in the **Palais de Justice**. Top-billing exhibitions take place in the Rayonnant Gothic **Salle des Gens d'Armes**, Europe's largest surviving medieval hall.

Pont Neuf
BRIDGE

(Map p130; Ⓜ Pont Neuf) Paris' oldest bridge, misguidingly named 'New Bridge', has linked the western end of Île de la Cité with both riverbanks since 1607, when the king, Henri IV, inaugurated it by crossing the bridge on a white stallion. View the bridge's arches (seven on the northern stretch and five on the southern span), decorated with 381 *mascarons* (grotesque figures) depicting barbers, dentists, pickpockets, loiterers etc, from a spot along the river or afloat.

Square du Vert-Galant
PARK

(Map p130; place du Pont Neuf, 1er; ⊙ 24hr; Ⓜ Pont Neuf) Chestnut, yew, black walnut and weeping willow trees grace this picturesque park at the westernmost tip of the Île de la Cité, along with migratory birds including mute swans, pochard and tufted ducks, black-headed gulls and wagtails. Sitting at the islands' original level, 7m below their current height, the waterside park is reached by stairs leading down from the Pont Neuf. It's romantic at any time of day, but especially so in the evening as the sun sets over the river.

⊙ Latin Quarter

The Latin Quarter's Roman and medieval roots can be seen throughout the neighbourhood. Natural history buffs won't want to miss the museums making up the Muséum National d'Histoire Naturelle in the beautifully green Jardin des Plantes. Watch for the partial reopening after extensive renovation of the neighbourhood's premier museum and France's finest medieval-history museum, the Musée National du Moyen Âge.

★ Panthéon
MAUSOLEUM

(Map p134; ☑ 01 44 32 18 00; www.paris-pantheon.fr; place du Panthéon, 5e; adult/child €9/free; ⊙ 10am-6.30pm Apr-Sep, to 6pm Oct-Mar; Ⓜ Maubert-Mutualité or RER Luxembourg) The Panthéon's stately neoclassical dome is an icon of the Parisian skyline. Its vast interior is an architectural masterpiece: originally an abbey church

dedicated to Ste Geneviève and now a mausoleum, it has served since 1791 as the resting place of some of France's greatest thinkers, including Voltaire, Rousseau, Braille and Hugo. A copy of Foucault's pendulum, first hung from the dome in 1851 to demonstrate the rotation of the earth, takes pride of place.

The first woman to be interred in the Panthéon based on achievement was two-time Nobel Prize–winner Marie Curie (1867–1934), reburied here, along with her husband, Pierre, in 1995. Also interred here are resistance fighters Pierre Brossolette and Jean Zay, as well as the symbolic interments of resistance fighters Germaine Tillion and Geneviève de Gaulle-Anthonioz, with soil from their graves. In July 2018, Auschwitz survivor, feminist icon and human rights activist Simone Veil became the fifth woman to be interred in the Panthéon.

Musée National du Moyen Âge
MUSEUM

(Map p134; ☑ 01 53 73 78 16; www.musee-moyen age.fr; 6 place Paul Painlevé, 5e; adult/child €8/free; ⊙ 9.15am-5.45pm Wed-Mon; Ⓜ Cluny–La Sorbonne) Undergoing renovation until late 2020, the National Museum of the Middle Ages is considered one of Paris' top small museums. It showcases a series of sublime treasures, from medieval statuary, stained glass and *objets d'art* to its celebrated series of tapestries, *The Lady with the Unicorn* (1500). Other highlights include ornate 15th-century mansion Hôtel de Cluny and the *frigidarium* (cold room) of an enormous Roman-era bathhouse.

Jardin des Plantes
PARK

(Map p126; www.jardindesplantes.net; place Valhubert & 36 rue Geoffroy-St-Hilaire, 5e; ⊙ 7.30am-8pm early Apr–mid-Sep, shorter hours rest of year; Ⓜ Gare d'Austerlitz, Censier Daubenton, Jussieu) Founded in 1626 as a medicinal herb garden for Louis XIII, Paris' 24-hectare botanic gardens – visually defined by the double alley of plane trees that runs the length of the park – are an idyllic spot to stroll around, break for a picnic (watch out for the automatic sprinklers!) and escape the city concrete for a spell. Three museums from the **Muséum National d'Histoire Naturelle** (Map p134; www.mnhn.fr; place Valhubert & 36 rue Geoffroy-St-Hilaire, 5e; Ⓜ Gare d'Austerlitz, Censier Daubenton, Jussieu) and a small zoo, **La Ménagerie** (Le Zoo du Jardin des Plantes; Map p134; www.zoodujardindesplantes.fr; 57 rue Cuvier, 5e; adult/child €13/10; ⊙ 9am-6pm Mon-Sat, to 6.30pm Sun Mar-Oct, to 5pm or 5.30pm Nov-Feb; Ⓜ Gare d'Austerlitz), add to its appeal.

Notre Dame

TIMELINE

1160 Maurice de Sully becomes bishop of Paris. Mission: to grace growing Paris with a lofty new cathedral.

1182–90 The ❶ **choir with double ambulatory** is finished and work starts on the nave and side chapels.

1200–50 The ❷ **west façade**, with rose window, three portals and two soaring towers, goes up. Everyone is stunned.

1345 Some 180 years after the foundation stone was laid, the Cathédrale de Notre Dame is complete. It is dedicated to notre dame (our lady), the Virgin Mary.

1789 Revolutionaries smash the original ❸ **Gallery of Kings**, pillage the cathedral and melt all its bells except the great bell Emmanuel. The cathedral becomes a Temple of Reason then a warehouse.

1831 Victor Hugo's novel *The Hunchback of Notre Dame* inspires new interest in the half-ruined Gothic cathedral.

1845–64 Architect Viollet-le-Duc undertakes its restoration. Twenty-eight new kings are sculpted for the west façade. The heavily decorated ❹ **portals** and ❺ **spire** are reconstructed. The neo-Gothic ❻ **treasury** is built.

1860 The area in front of Notre Dame is cleared to create the parvis, an al fresco classroom where Parisians can learn a catechism illustrated on sculpted stone portals.

1935 A rooster bearing part of the relics of the Crown of Thorns, St Denis and Ste Geneviève is put on top of the cathedral spire to protect those who pray inside.

1991 The architectural masterpiece of Notre Dame and its Seine-side riverbanks become a Unesco World Heritage Site.

2013 Notre Dame celebrates 850 years since construction began with a bevy of new bells and restoration works.

Virgin & Child
Spot all 37 artworks representing the Virgin Mary. Pilgrims have revered the pearly cream sculpture of her in the sanctuary since the 14th century. Light a devotional candle and write some words to the *Livre de Vie* (Book of Life).

PAL TERAVAGIMOV PHOTOGRAPHY / GETTY IMAGES ©

North Rose Window
See prophets, judges, kings and priests venerate Mary in vivid blue and violet glass, one of three beautiful rose blooms (1225–70), each almost 10m in diameter.

Flying Buttresses

Choir Screen
No part of the cathedral weaves biblical tales more evocatively than these ornate wooden panels, carved in the 14th century after the Black Death killed half the country's population. The faintly gaudy colours were restored in the 1960s.

DIGITAL IMAGINATION / GETTY IMAGES ©

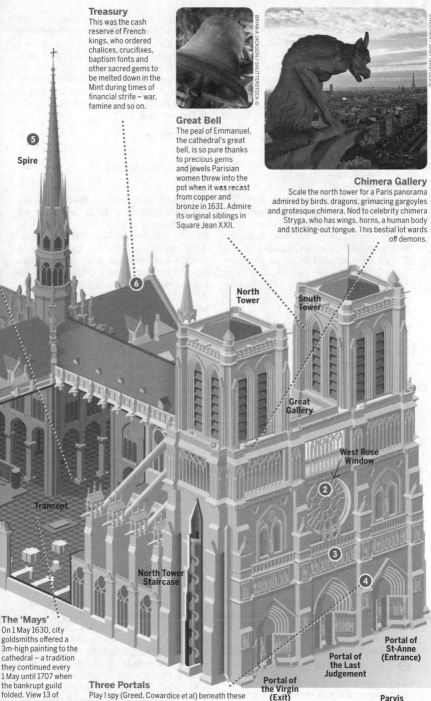

Treasury
This was the cash reserve of French kings, who ordered chalices, crucifixes, baptism fonts and other sacred gems to be melted down in the Mint during times of financial strife – war, famine and so on.

5 Spire

BRIAN A JACKSON ©

SYADCHKA / SHUTTERSTOCK ©

Great Bell
The peal of Emmanuel, the cathedral's great bell, is so pure thanks to precious gems and jewels Parisian women threw into the pot when it was recast from copper and bronze in 1631. Admire its original siblings in Square Jean XXII.

Chimera Gallery
Scale the north tower for a Paris panorama admired by birds, dragons, grimacing gargoyles and grotesque chimera. Nod to celebrity chimera Stryga, who has wings, horns, a human body and sticking-out tongue. This bestial lot wards off demons.

6

North Tower

South Tower

Great Gallery

West Rose Window

2

North Tower Staircase

3

4

Transept

The 'Mays'
On 1 May 1630, city goldsmiths offered a 3m-high painting to the cathedral – a tradition they continued every 1 May until 1707 when the bankrupt guild folded. View 13 of these huge artworks in the side chapels.

Three Portals
Play I spy (Greed, Cowardice et al) beneath these sculpted doorways, which illustrate the seasons, life and the 12 vices and virtues alongside the Bible.

Portal of the Virgin (Exit)

Portal of the Last Judgement

Portal of St-Anne (Entrance)

Parvis Notre Dame

Mosquée de Paris   MOSQUE

(Map p134; ☎ 01 45 35 97 33; www.mosqueede paris.net; 2bis place du Puits de l'Ermite, 5e; adult/ child €3/2; ⊙ 9am-noon & 2-7pm Sat-Thu Apr-Sep, 9am-noon & 2-6pm Sat-Thu Oct-Mar; Ⓜ Place Monge) Paris' central mosque, with a striking 26m-high minaret, was completed in 1926 in an ornate art deco Moorish style. You can visit the interior to admire the intricate tile work and calligraphy. A separate entrance leads to the wonderful North African–style **hammam** (Turkish bathhouse; Map p134; ☎ 01 43 31 14 32; www.la-mosquee. com; 39 rue Geoffroy-St-Hilaire, 5e; admission €18, spa package from €43; ⊙ 10am-9pm Wed-Mon; Ⓜ Place Monge), **restaurant** (Map p134; ☎ 01 43 31 14 32; www.restaurantauxportesdelorient. com; 39 rue Geoffroy-St-Hilaire, 5e; mains €10-28; ⊙ kitchen noon-midnight; Ⓜ Censier Daubenton, Place Monge) and **tearoom** (Map p134; ☎ 01 43 31 38 20; www.restaurantauxportesdelorient.com; 39 rue Geoffroy-St-Hilaire, 5e; ⊙ noon-midnight; Ⓜ Censier Daubenton), and a small souk (actually more of a gift shop). Visitors must be modestly dressed.

★ Institut du Monde Arabe   MUSEUM

(Arab World Institute; Map p134; ☎ 01 40 51 38 38; www.imarabe.org; 1 place Mohammed V, 5e; adult/ child €8/4; ⊙ 10am-6pm Tue-Fri, to 7pm Sat & Sun; Ⓜ Jussieu) The Arab World Institute was jointly founded by France and 18 Middle Eastern and North African nations in 1980, with the aim of promoting cross-cultural dialogue. It hosts temporary exhibitions and a fascinating museum of Arabic culture and history (4th to 7th floors). The stunning building, designed by French architect Jean Nouvel, was inspired by latticed-wood windows *(mashrabiya)* traditional to Arabic architecture: thousands of modern-day photoelectrically sensitive apertures cover its sparkling glass façade.

Musée de la Sculpture en Plein Air   MUSEUM

(quai St-Bernard, 5e; Ⓜ Gare d'Austerlitz) FREE Along quai St-Bernard, this open-air sculpture museum (also known as the Jardin Tino Rossi) has more than 50 late-20th-century unfenced sculptures, and makes a great picnic spot. A salad beneath a César or a baguette beside a Brancusi is a pretty classy way to see the Seine up close.

◉ St-Germain & Les Invalides

Chart-topping sights in this stately neighbourhood include the impressionist-art-filled Musée d'Orsay, massive military complex Hôtel des Invalides (home to Napoléon's tomb) and romantic, sculpture-strewn Musée Rodin. Look out for smaller, lesser-known gems too, such as the Musée National Eugène Delacroix, and some exquisite churches. Allow ample time for ambling in the city's most beautiful park, timeless Jardin du Luxembourg.

Musée d'Orsay   MUSEUM

See p108.

Jardin du Luxembourg   PARK

See p110.

★ Église St-Germain des Prés   CHURCH

(Map p158; ☎ 01 55 42 81 18; www.eglise-saint germaindespres.fr; 3 place St-Germain des Prés, 6e; ⊙ 9am-7.45pm; Ⓜ St-Germain des Prés) Paris' oldest standing church, the Romanesque St Germanus of the Fields, was built in the 11th century on the site of a 6th-century abbey and was the main place of worship in Paris until the arrival of Notre Dame. It's since been altered many times. The oldest part, **Chapelle de St-Symphorien,** is to the right as you enter; St Germanus (496–576), the first bishop of Paris, is believed to be buried there.

★ Musée Rodin   MUSEUM, GARDEN

(Map p76; ☎ 01 44 18 61 10; www.musee-rodin.fr; 79 rue de Varenne, 7e; adult/child €10/free, garden only €4/free; ⊙ 10am-5.45pm Tue-Sun; Ⓜ Varenne or Invalides) Sculptor, painter, sketcher, engraver and collector Auguste Rodin donated his entire collection to the French state in 1908 on the proviso that it dedicate his former workshop and showroom, the beautiful 1730 Hôtel Biron, to displaying his works. They're now installed not only in the magnificently restored mansion itself, but also in its rose-filled garden – one of the most peaceful places in central Paris and a wonderful spot to contemplate his famous work *The Thinker*.

Prepurchase tickets online to avoid queuing.

★ Hôtel des Invalides   MONUMENT, MUSEUM

(Map p76; www.musee-armee.fr; 129 rue de Grenelle, 7e; adult/child €12/free; ⊙ 10am-6pm; Ⓜ Varenne, La Tour Maubourg) Flanked by the 500m-long Esplanade des Invalides lawns, Hôtel des Invalides was built in the 1670s by Louis XIV to house 4000 *invalides* (disabled war veterans). On 14 July 1789, a mob broke into the building and seized 32,000 rifles before heading on to the prison at Bastille and the start of the French Revolution.

Admission includes entry to all Hôtel des Invalides sights (temporary exhibitions cost extra). Hours for individual sites can vary – check the website for updates.

In the **Cour d'Honneur**, the nation's largest collection on the history of the French military is displayed at the **Musée de l'Armée** (Army Museum; Map p76; www.musee-armee.fr; 129 rue de Grenelle, 7e; included in Hôtel des Invalides entry; ⊙10am-6pm Apr-Oct, to 5pm Nov-Mar; M Varenne, La Tour Maubourg). South is **Église St-Louis des Invalides**, once used by soldiers, and **Église du Dôme** (Map p76; www.musee-armee.fr; 129 rue de Grenelle, 7e; included in Hôtel des Invalides entry; ⊙10am-7pm Jul & Aug, to 6pm Apr-Jun, Sep & Oct, to 5pm Nov-Mar; M Varenne), with a dazzling golden dome (1677–1735). Scale models of towns and châteaux across France fill the **Musée des Plans-Reliefs**.

Atmospheric classical concerts (ranging from €5 to €30) take place regularly here year-round.

Monnaie de Paris   MUSEUM
(Map p158; ☑01 40 46 56 66; www.monnaiedeparis.fr; 11 quai de Conti, 6e; adult/child €10/free; ⊙11am-7pm Tue & Thu-Sun, to 9pm Wed; M Pont Neuf) The 18th-century royal mint, Monnaie de Paris, houses the **Musée du 11 Conti**, an interactive museum exploring the history of French coinage from antiquity onwards, plus edgy contemporary-art exhibitions. The impeccably restored, neoclassical building, with one of the longest façades on the Seine stretching 116m long, squirrels away five sumptuous courtyards, the Hôtel de Conti designed by Jules Hardouin-Mansart in 1690, engraving workshops, the original foundry (now the museum boutique), Guy Savoy's flagship restaurant (p154) and the fashionable cafe **Frappé by Bloom** (Map p158; ☑07 89 83 79 58; http://frappe.bloom-restaurant.fr; 2 rue Guénégaud, 6e, Monnaie de Paris; ⊙8.30am-7pm Tue & Wed, 8.30am-midnight Thu & Fri, 10.30am-midnight Sat, 10.30am-7pm Sun; M Pont Neuf).

Église St-Sulpice   CHURCH
(Map p158; ☑01 42 34 59 98; www.pss75.fr/saint-sulpice-paris; place St-Sulpice, 6e; ⊙7.30am-7.30pm; M St-Sulpice) FREE In 1646 work started on the twin-towered Church of St Sulpicius, lined inside with 21 side chapels, and it took six architects 150 years to finish. It's famed for its striking Italianate façade with two rows of superimposed columns, its Counter-Reformation-influenced neoclassical decor, its frescoes by Eugène Delacroix –

and its setting for a murderous scene in Dan Brown's *The Da Vinci Code*. You can hear the monumental, 1781-built organ during 10.30am Mass on Sunday or the occasional Sunday-afternoon concert.

Musée National Eugène Delacroix   MUSEUM
(Map p158; ☑01 44 41 86 50; www.musee-delacroix.fr; 6 rue de Furstenberg, 6e; adult/child €7/free; ⊙9.30am-5pm Wed-Mon, to 9pm 1st Thu of month; M Mabillon) In a courtyard off a pretty tree-shaded square, this museum is housed in the romantic artist's home and studio at the time of his death in 1863. It contains a collection of his oil paintings, watercolours, pastels and drawings, including many of his more intimate works, such as *An Unmade Bed* (1828) and his paintings of Morocco. A ticket from the Musée du Louvre (p81) allows same-day entry here (you can also buy tickets here and skip the Louvre's ticket queues).

As well as the Musée du Louvre, you can see Delacroix's works at the Musée d'Orsay (p108) and frescoes at Église St-Sulpice.

⊙ Montparnasse & Southern Paris

This vast swath of southern Paris is a perfect place to explore if you're looking for a local experience away from the tourist crowds. There are also some big-hitting sights here, too, from the creepy skull-and-bone-packed underground tunnels of Les Catacombes to France's national library, Bibliothèque Nationale de France, and the world's largest campus for start-ups.

★**Les Catacombes**   CEMETERY
(Map p72; ☑01 43 22 47 63; www.catacombes.paris.fr; 1 av Colonel Henri Roi-Tanguy, 14e; adult/child €13/free, online booking incl audioguide €29/5; ⊙10am-8.30pm Tue-Sun; M Denfert Rochereau) Paris' most macabre sight is its underground tunnels lined with skulls and bones. In 1785 it was decided to rectify the hygiene problems of Paris' overflowing cemeteries by exhuming the bones and storing them in disused quarry tunnels and the Catacombes were created in 1810. After descending 20m (via 130 narrow, dizzying spiral steps), follow dark, subterranean passages to the ossuary (1.5km in all). Exit via a minimalist all-white 'transition space' with gift shop onto 21bis av René Coty, 14e. Buy tickets in advance online to avoid queuing.

TOP SIGHT
MUSÉE D'ORSAY

After the Louvre, this eye-catching art gallery, at home in a former railway station overlooking the River Seine, is a one-stop shop for some of the world's most celebrated paintings by impressionist, postimpressionist and art nouveau artists. The museum's cavernous interiors, vintage monumental clocks and contemporary styled galleries are as dazzling as the art itself.

Paintings

Most visitors make a beeline for the world's largest collection of impressionist and postimpressionist art, the highlights of which include Manet's *On the Beach* and *Woman with Fans;* Monet's gardens at Giverny and *Rue Montorgueil, Paris, Celebration of June 30, 1878;* Cézanne's card players, *Green Apples* and *Blue Vase;* Renoir's *Ball at the Moulin de la Galette* and *Young Girls at the Piano;* Degas' ballerinas; Toulouse-Lautrec's cabaret dancers; Pissarro's *The Seine and the Louvre;* Sisley's *View of the Canal St-Martin;* and Van Gogh's self-portraits, *Bedroom in Arles* and *Starry Night over the Rhône.* Less high-profile but classified a National Treasure is James Tissot's 1868 painting *The Circle of the Rue Royale.*

Decorative & Graphic Arts

Household items such as hat and coat stands, candlesticks, desks, chairs, bookcases, vases, pot-plant holders, free-standing screens, wall mirrors, water pitchers, plates,

DON'T MISS

➡ The building

➡ Painting collections

➡ Decorative-arts collections

➡ Sculptures

➡ Graphic-arts collections

PRACTICALITIES

➡ Map p72

➡ ☎ 01 40 49 48 14

➡ www.musee-orsay.fr

➡ 1 rue de la Légion d'Honneur, 7e

➡ adult/child €12/free

➡ ⊙ 9.30am-6pm Tue, Wed & Fri-Sun, to 9.45pm Thu

➡ Ⓜ Assemblée Nationale, RER Musée d'Orsay

goblets and bowls become works of art in the hands of their creators, who incorporated exquisite design elements from the era.

Drawings, pastels and sketches from major artists are another of the d'Orsay's lesser-known highlights. Look for Georges Seurat's *The Black Bow* (c 1882), which uses crayon on paper to define forms by contrasting between black and white, and Paul Gaugin's poignant self-portrait (c 1902–03), drawn near the end of his life.

Sculptures

The cavernous former station is a magnificent setting for sculptures, including works by Degas, Gaugin, Camille Claudel, Renoir and Rodin.

History

The Gare d'Orsay railway station was designed by competition-winning architect Victor Laloux. Even on its completion, just in time for the 1900 Exposition Universelle, painter Edouard Detaille declared that the new station looked like a Palais des Beaux Arts. But although it had its own hotel and all the mod cons of the day – including luggage lifts and passenger elevators – by 1939 the increasing electrification of the rail network meant the platforms were too short for mainline trains, and within a few years all rail services ceased.

The station was used as a mailing centre during WWII, and in 1962 Orson Welles filmed Franz Kafka's *The Trial* in the then-abandoned building. Fortunately, it was saved from being demolished and replaced with a hotel complex by a Historical Monument listing in 1973, before the government set about establishing the palatial museum.

Transforming the languishing building into the country's premier showcase for art from 1848 to 1914 was the grand project of President Valéry Giscard d'Estaing, who signed off on it in 1977. The museum opened its doors in 1986.

Far from resting on its laurels, major renovations at the Musée d'Orsay between 2008 and 2011 incorporated a re-energised layout and increased exhibition space. World-renowned paintings now gleam from richly coloured walls that create an intimate, stately home-like atmosphere, with high-tech illumination literally casting the masterpieces in a new light.

PARIS MUSÉE D'ORSAY

GUIDED TOURS

For a thorough introduction to the museum, 90-minute 'Masterpieces of the Musée d'Orsay' guided tours (€6) in English run at 11.30am and 2.30pm on Tuesday and 11.30am from Wednesday to Saturday.

Kids under 13 years aren't permitted on adult tours; look out for family tours (six to 12 years; €4.50) and themed children's workshops (six to eight years; €7) instead. An audioguide costs €5.

BIG VIEWS

Look down on Paris (spot Montmartre's Sacré-Cœur) through the former railway station's two giant glass clock faces – one in the museum cafe and another immediately after the impressionist galleries.

The museum is busiest on Tuesday and Sunday, followed by Thursday and Saturday. Save time by buying tickets online and head directly to entrance C.

TOP SIGHT
JARDIN DU LUXEMBOURG

Playing the quintessential French *flâneur* (indulgent stroller or meanderer) in this romantic city park is a classic 'I'm in Paris!' moment. Elegant and timeless in equal measure, the 23-hectare large garden squirrels away a lush medley of pea-green lawns and crunchy gravel paths, formal terraces and chestnut groves, ornamental ponds and orchards – with their own charm in every season.

DON'T MISS

➡ Grand Bassin

➡ Puppet shows

➡ Orchards

➡ Palais du Luxembourg

➡ Musée du Luxembourg

History

The Jardin du Luxembourg's history stretches further back than Napoléon's dedication. The gardens are a backdrop to the Palais du Luxembourg, built in the 1620s for Marie de Médici, Henri IV's consort, to assuage her longing for the Pitti Palace in Florence. The Palais is now home to the French Senate, which, in addition to parliamentary-assembly activities like voting on legislation, is charged with promoting the palace and its gardens.

Numerous overhauls over the centuries have given the Jardin du Luxembourg a blend of traditional French- and English-style gardens that is unique in Paris.

All of the gardens' nostalgic childhood activities are still here today, as well as modern play equipment, tennis and other sporting and games venues.

PRACTICALITIES

➡ Map p158

➡ www.senat.fr/visite/jardin

➡ ⊙ hours vary

➡ Ⓜ Mabillon, St-Sulpice, Rennes, Notre Dame des Champs, RER Luxembourg

Grand Bassin

It is for good reason that the Luxembourg Gardens hold a place in the heart of every Parisian: for centuries, this is where children (and grown-up 'children') have come to while away a weekend afternoon chasing **toy sailboats** (sailboat rental per 30min €4; ⊙ 11am-6pm Apr-Oct) on the octagonal **Grand Bassin**, a serene ornamental pond. Nearby, younger children and tots can take **pony rides** (☎ 06 07 32 53 95; www.animaponey.com; 600m/900m pony ride €6/8.50; ☺ 3-6pm Wed, Sat, Sun & school holidays) or romp around the **playgrounds** (adult/child €1.50/2.50; ☺ hours vary) – the green half is for kids aged seven to 12 years, the blue half for under-sevens.

Puppet Shows

Puppetry is an ancient tradition in France and alfresco puppet shows at the Jardin du Luxembourg's bijou Théâtre du Luxembourg (p172) are as entertaining as marionette shows come – regardless of whether you speak French or are a child. Show times vary; check the program online and arrive 30 minutes before.

Orchards

Dozens of apple varieties grow in the **orchards** in the gardens' south. Bees have produced honey in the nearby apiary, the **Rucher du Luxembourg**, since the 19th century. The annual Fête du Miel (Honey Festival) offers two days of tasting and buying its sweet harvest around late September in the ornate **Pavillon Davioud** (55bis rue d'Assas, 6e).

Palais du Luxembourg

The **Palais du Luxembourg** (www.senat.fr; rue de Vaugirard, 6e) was built in the 1620s and has been home to the Sénat (French Senate) since 1958. It's occasionally visitable by guided tour.

East of the palace is the ornate, Italianate **Fontaine des Médici**, built in 1630. During Baron Haussmann's 19th-century reshaping of the roads, the fountain was moved 30m and the pond and dramatic statues of the giant bronze Polyphemus discovering the white-marble lovers Acis and Galatea were added.

Musée du Luxembourg

Top-billing temporary art exhibitions, such as 'Cézanne et Paris', are invariably held in the beautiful **Musée du Luxembourg** (☎ 01 40 13 62 00; http://museeduluxembourg.fr; 19 rue de Vaugirard, 6e; most exhibitions €13; ☺ 10.30am-7pm Sat-Thu, to 10pm Fri).

Around the back of the museum, lemon and orange trees, palms, grenadiers and oleanders shelter from the cold in the palace's **orangery**. Nearby, the heavily guarded **Hôtel du Petit Luxembourg** was where Marie de Médicis lived while the Palais du Luxembourg was being built. The president of the Senate has called it home since 1825.

PICNICS IN THE PARK

If you're planning on having a picnic, forget bringing a blanket – the elegantly manicured lawns are off limits apart from a small wedge on the southern boundary. Instead, do as Parisians do, and corral one of the iconic 1923-designed green metal chairs and find your own favourite part of the park.

The Jardin du Luxembourg plays a pivotal role in Victor Hugo's *Les Misérables:* the novel's lovers Marius and Cosette meet here for the first time.

SCULPTURES

The gardens are studded with over 100 sculptures. Look out for statues of Stendhal, Chopin, Baudelaire and Delacroix.

DON'T MISS

BIRD'S-EYE CITY VIEWS

Ballon de Paris (Map p72; ☑ 01 44 26 20 00; www.ballondeparis.com; 2 rue de la Montagne de la Fage, 15e, Parc André Citroën; adult/child €12/6; ⊙ 9am-9pm May-Aug, shorter hours Sep-Apr; M Balard, Lourmel) Drift up and up but not away – this helium-filled balloon in Parc André Citroën remains tethered to the ground as it lifts you 150m into the air for spectacular panoramas over Paris. The balloon plays an active environmental role, changing colour depending on the air quality and pollution levels. From September to April, the last 'flight' is 30 minutes before the park closes. Confirm ahead any time of year as the balloon doesn't ascend in windy conditions.

Tour Montparnasse (Map p158; www.tourmontparnasse56.com; 33 av du Maine, 15e; adult/child €17/9.50; ⊙ 9.30am-11.30pm Apr-Sep, to 10.30pm Oct-Mar; M Montparnasse Bienvenüe) Spectacular views unfold from this 210m-high smoked-glass-and-steel office block, built in 1973. (Bonus: it's about the only spot in the city you can't see this startlingly ugly skyscraper, which dwarfs low-rise Paris.) A speedy elevator whisks visitors up in 38 seconds to the indoor observatory on the 56th floor, with multimedia displays. Finish with a hike up the stairs to the 59th-floor open-air terrace (with a sheltered walkway) and bubbly at the terrace's Champagne bar.

★ **Cimetière du Montparnasse** CEMETERY
(Map p158; www.paris.fr; 3 bd Edgar Quinet, 14e; ⊙ 8am-6pm Mon-Fri, 8.30am-6pm Sat, 9am-6pm Sun; M Edgar Quinet) FREE This 19-hectare cemetery opened in 1824 and is Paris' second largest after Père Lachaise (p97). Famous residents include writer Guy de Maupassant, playwright Samuel Beckett, sculptor Constantin Brancusi, photographer Man Ray, industrialist André Citroën, Captain Alfred Dreyfus of the infamous Dreyfus Affair, legendary singer Serge Gainsbourg and philosopher-writers Jean-Paul Sartre and Simone de Beauvoir.

★ **Station F** RESEARCH CENTRE
(Map p126; https://stationf.co/fr/campus; 55 bd Vincent Auriol, 13e; ⊙ tours noon Mon, Wed & Fri; M Chevaleret, Bibliothèque) FREE The world's largest start-up campus was unveiled with much pomp and ceremony by French president, Emmanuel Macron, in mid-2017. At any one time, some 3000 resident entrepreneurs from all over the world beaver away on ground-breaking new ideas and businesses, supported by 30 high tech incubators and accelerators in this unique start-up ecosystem. Guided tours take visitors on a 45-minute waltz through the gargantuan steel, glass and concrete hangar – a railway depot constructed in 1927–29 to house new trains servicing nearby Gare d'Austerlitz.

Bibliothèque Nationale de France LIBRARY
(Map p126; ☑ 01 53 79 59 59; www.bnf.fr; 11 quai François Mauriac, 13e; €3-9; ⊙ 10am-7pm Tue-Sat, 1-7pm Sun, closed 2 weeks in Sep; M Bibliothèque) With four glass towers shaped like half-open books, the National Library of France, opened in 1995, was one of President Mitterand's most ambitious and costliest projects. Some 12 million tomes are stored on 420km of shelves and the library can accommodate 2000 readers and 2000 researchers. Excellent temporary exhibitions (entrance E) revolve around 'the word' – from storytelling to bookbinding and French heroes. Exhibition admission includes free same-day access to the reference library.

No expense was spared to carry out the library's grand design, which many claimed defied logic. Books and historical documents are shelved in the sunny, 23-storey and 79m-high towers, while patrons sit in artificially lit basement halls built around a 'forest courtyard' of 140 50-year-old pines, trucked in from the countryside.

🏃 Activities

As Paris gears up to host the 2024 Summer Olympics and Summer Paralympics, you'll find increasing opportunities to watch spectator sports or take part yourself. To unwind with the Parisians, check out the city's green spaces, where you can thwack a tennis ball, stroll in style, admire art, or break out some wine and cheese.

Cycling

Everyone knows that the Tour de France races up the Champs-Élysées at the end of July every year, but you don't need Chris Froome's leg muscles to enjoy Paris on two wheels. Between the Paris bike-share scheme Vélib' (p183), and the hundreds of kilometres of urban bike paths, cycling around the city

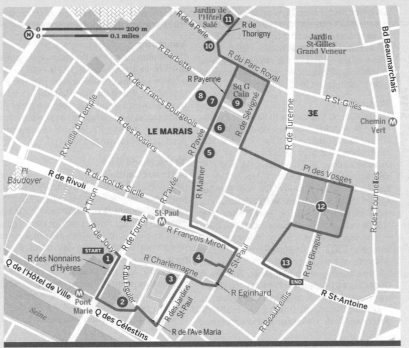

City Walk
Medieval Marais Meanderings

START HÔTEL D'AUMONT
END HÔTEL DE SULLY
LENGTH 2.6KM; TWO HOURS

While Henri IV was busy building place Royale (today's place des Vosges), aristocrats were commissioning gold-brick *hôtels particuliers* (private mansions) – the city's most beautiful Renaissance structures that lend the Marais a particular architectural harmony.

At 7 rue de Jouy stands majestic ❶ **Hôtel d'Aumont**, built in 1648 for a councillor of the king. Continue south along rue des Nonnains d'Hyères and turn left onto rue de l'Hôtel de Ville; at 1 rue du Figuier is ❷ **Hôtel de Sens**, the oldest Marais mansion, with geometric gardens and a neogothic turret. It was begun around 1475 for the archbishops of Sens and restored in 1930 (look for the cannonball lodged above the main gate during the 1830 Trois Glorieuses).

Head northeast along rue des Jardins de St-Paul. To the left, two truncated towers are all that remain of Philippe-Auguste's ❸ **enceinte**, a fortified wall built between 1190 and 1209 and

once guarded by 77 towers. Cross rue Charlemagne, duck into rue Eginhard and follow it to rue St-Paul and ❹ **Église St-Paul St-Louis** (1641). At the end of rue St-Paul, turn left, then walk north up rue Malher and rue Pavée, the first cobbled road in Paris. At No 24 is the late Renaissance ❺ **Hôtel Lamoignon**, built for Diane de France (1538–1619), the legitimised daughter of Henri II.

North along rue Payenne is the back of the ❻ **Musée Carnavalet** (p97; closed for renovations until 2020); the Revolutionary-era 'Temple of Reason' ❼ **Chapelle de l'Humanité** at No 5; and the rear of the ❽ **Musée Cognacq-Jay**. From grassy ❾ **Square George Cain** opposite 11 rue Payenne, walk northwest to more spectacular 17th-century *hôtels particuliers:* ❿ **Hôtel de Libéral Bruant** at 1 rue de la Perle, and Hôtel Salé, housing the ⓫ **Musée National Picasso** (p96).

Retrace your steps to rue du Parc Royal, walk south down rue de Sévigné and follow rue des Francs Bourgeois eastwards to end with sublime ⓬ **place des Vosges** (p96) and the 17th-century aristocratic mansion ⓭ **Hôtel de Sully**.

has never been easier. Sign up for one of the great city **bike tours** (Map p120; ☑ 06 18 80 84 92; www.bikeabouttours.com; Le Peloton Café, 17 rue du Pont Louis-Philippe, 4e; M Hôtel de Ville) or hire a bike yourself (p184). Some streets are closed to vehicle traffic on Sundays – great news for cyclists! Bring your own helmet.

Skating

The next-most popular activity after cycling has to be skating, whether on the street or on ice. Rent a pair of in-line skates at **Nomadeshop** (Map p126; ☑ 01 44 54 07 44; www.nomadeshop.com; 37 bd Bourdon, 4e; half-/full-day skate rental from €5/8; ⊙ 11am-1.30pm & 2.30-7.30pm Tue-Fri, 10am-7pm Sat, noon-6pm Sun Apr-Oct, closed Sun Nov-Mar; M Bastille) and join the Friday-evening skate, **Pari Roller** (Map p158; www.pari-roller.com; place Raoul Dautry, 14e; ⊙ 10pm-1am Fri, arrive 9.30pm; M Montparnasse Bienvenüe) **FREE**, that zooms through the Paris streets or for a more laid-back experience, join the Sunday-afternoon skate, **Rollers & Coquillages** (Map p126; www.rollers-coquillages. org; place de la Bastille; ⊙ 2.30pm Sun; M Bastille).

During the winter holidays several temporary outdoor rinks are installed around Paris. Venues change from year to year; check www.paris.fr for locations.

Swimming

If you plan to go swimming at either your hotel or in a public pool, you'll need to don a *bonnet de bain* (bathing cap) – even if you don't have any hair. You shouldn't need to buy one ahead of time as they are generally sold at most pools. Men are required to wear skin-tight trunks (Speedos); loose-fitting Bermuda shorts are not allowed.

★**Piscine de la Butte aux Cailles**   SWIMMING
(Map p72; ☑ 01 45 89 60 05; http://equipement. paris.fr/piscine-de-la-butte-aux-cailles-2927; 5 place Paul Verlaine, 13e; adult/child €3.50/2, 10 entrances €28/16; ⊙ hours vary; M Place d'Italie) Built in 1924, this art deco gem of a swimming pool complex – a historical monument to boot – takes advantage of the lovely warm artesian well water nearby. It has a spectacular vaulted indoor pool and, since its 2017 renovation, is the only complex in Paris to have a Nordic pool. In the depths of winter this is where Parisians come to

---

MUSEUMS FOR CHILDREN

Cité des Sciences (Map p72; ☑ 01 40 05 80 00; www.cite-sciences.fr; 30 av Corentin Cariou, Parc de la Villette, 19e; per attraction adult/child €12/9; ⊙ 10am-6pm Tue-Sat, to 7pm Sun, La Géode 10.30am-8.30pm Tue-Sun; M Porte de la Villette) Paris' top museum for kids has a host of hands-on exhibits for children aged two and up, a special-effects cinema La Géode, a planetarium and a retired submarine. Various combination tickets can be booked online. Advance reservations are essential for weekend and school-holiday visits, and for the fabulous Cité des Enfants educative play sessions (1½ hours, ages two to seven years or five to 12 years) year-round. Packing a picnic is also a good idea.

Musée en Herbe (Map p94; ☑ 01 40 67 97 66; www.musee-en-herbe.com; 23 rue de l'Arbre-Sec, 1er; €6; ⊙ 10am-7pm; ♿; M Louvre Rivoli, Pont Neuf) One of the city's great backstreet secrets, this children's museum is a surprise gem for art lovers of every age. Its permanent exhibition changes throughout the year and focuses on the work of one artist or theme through a series of interactive displays.

Captions are in English as well as French, children get a *jeu de piste* (activity sheet) to guide and entertain, and additional workshops and guided visits for kids and adults – think hands-on art workshops, afternoon tea, early-evening aperitifs and so on (€6 to €10; reserve in advance) – add to the playful experience.

Galerie des Enfants (Map p134; www.galeriedesenfants.fr; 36 rue Geoffroy-St-Hilaire, 5e; adult/child €11/9; ⊙ 10am-6pm Wed-Mon; M Censier Daubenton) This hands-on science museum tailored to children from ages six to 12 is located in the **Grande Galerie de l'Évolution** (Map p134; ☑ 01 40 79 54 79; www.grandegaleriedelevolution.fr; 36 rue Geoffroy-St-Hilaire, 5e; adult/child €9/free, with Galeries des Enfants €11/9; ⊙ 10am-6pm Wed-Mon; M Censier Daubenton), part of the Muséum National d'Histoire Naturelle (p103), within the Jardin des Plantes (p103). All exhibitions are in French and English.

PARISIAN PLAYGROUND
....

A breath of fresh air, the **Parc Rives de Seine** (Map p72; btwn Musée d'Orsay & Pont de l'Alma, 7e; ☺ information point noon-7pm Tue-Sun May-Sep, shorter hours Oct-Apr; Ⓜ Solférino, Assemblée Nationale, Invalides) is a 2.3km-long expressway-turned-riverside promenade on the Left Bank is a favourite spot in which to run, cycle, skate, play board games or take part in a packed program of events. Equally it's simply a great place to hang out – in a Zzz shipping-container hut (reserve at the information point just west of the Musée d'Orsay), on the archipelago of floating gardens, or at the burgeoning restaurants and bars (some floating aboard boats and barges).

Together with an equivalent 3.3km pedestrian stretch on the Right Bank, between the Tuileries and Henry IV tunnels, these fun car-free promenades on both sides of the River Seine form part of the **Parc Rives de Seine** (Map p120; btwn Bassin de l'Arsenal, 4e & quai des Tuileries, 1er; Ⓜ Quai de la Rapéé, Pont Marie or Pont Neuf), created in April 2017.

swim 25m laps in a five-lane outdoor pool, heated to a toasty 28°C.

Piscine Joséphine Baker   SWIMMING
(Map p126; ☑ 01 56 61 96 50; www.piscine-baker.fr; quai François Mauriac, 13e; adult/child €6.20/3.10; ☺ 7-9am & 10am-11pm Mon-Fri, 10am-8pm Sat & Sun Jun-Sep, shorter hours rest of year; Ⓜ Quai de la Gare) Floating on the Seine, this striking swimming pool is named after the 1920s American singer. The 25m-by-10m, four-lane pool and large sun deck are especially popular in summer when the roof slides back. Also here is a children's paddling pool. In July and August, plus weekends from late May to September, admission is limited to two hours.

Boules

You'll often see groups of earnest Parisians playing boules (France's most popular traditional game, similar to lawn bowls) in the Jardin du Luxembourg and other parks and squares with suitably flat, shady patches of gravel. The **Arènes de Lutèce** (Map p134; 49 rue Monge, 5e; ☺ 8am-9.30pm May-Aug, to 8.30pm Apr & Sep, shorter hours rest year; Ⓜ Place Monge) FREE *boulodrome* in a 2nd-century Roman amphitheatre in the Latin Quarter is a fabulous spot to absorb the scene. There are usually places to play at Paris Plages (p118).

🡒 Courses

La Cuisine Paris   COOKING
(Map p120; ☑ 01 40 51 78 18; www.lacuisineparis. com; 80 quai de l'Hôtel de Ville, 4e; 2hr cooking class/walking tours from €69/80; Ⓜ Pont Marie, Hôtel de Ville) Classes in English range from how to make bread and croissants to macarons as well as market classes and gourmet 'foodie walks'.

Le Cordon Bleu   COOKING
(Map p72; ☑ 01 85 65 15 00; www.cordonbleu.edu/ paris; 13-15 quai André Citroën, 15e; Ⓜ Javel–André Citroën or RER Javel) One of the world's foremost culinary arts schools, the Le Cordon Bleu campus overlooks the Seine and **Statue of Liberty** (Map p72; Île aux Cygnes; Ⓜ Javel–André Citroën), with views of the nearby Eiffel Tower from its terrace. Prices start at €140 for themed three-hour classes (food and wine pairing, vegetarian cuisine, éclairs, choux pastry etc) and €470 for two-day courses.

Wine Tasting in Paris   WINE
(Map p134; ☑ 06 76 93 32 88; www.wine-tasting-in-paris.com; 14 rue des Boulangers, 5e; tastings from €46; ☺ tastings 5-7.30pm Tue, Thu & Sat; Ⓜ Jussieu) Find this wine-tasting school on a winding cobblestone backstreet. With the knowledgeable Thierry from wine-rich Burgundy at the helm, themed tastings and tours do not disappoint. The comprehensive French Wine Tour (€62, 2½ hours, six wines) covers tasting methodology, wine vocabulary and French winegrowing regions. Foodies will adore the tasty, lunchtime cheese–wine pairing (€46, 1½ hours, four wines).

La Beer Fabrique   BREWING
(Map p120; ☑ 01 71 27 71 02; www.labeerfabrique. com; 6 rue Guillaume Bertrand, 11e; 2/4hr brewing course €60/160; ☺ by reservation; Ⓜ Rue St-Maur) During a two-hour course at this brewing school, you'll brew your own beer (and take it away with you, along with three of La Beer Fabrique's own beers), and enjoy six tastings accompanied by charcuterie. Four-hour courses will see you brew 15L of beer that you also get to take with you. Instruction is in English and French.

☞ Tours

★ Parisien d'un Jour – Paris Greeters
WALKING

(https://greeters.paris; by donation) See Paris through local eyes with these two- to three-hour city tours. Volunteers – mainly knowledgable Parisians passionate about their city – lead groups to their favourite spots. Minimum two weeks' notice is needed.

Meeting the French
CULTURAL, TOURS

(☏ 01 42 51 19 80; www.meetingthefrench.com; tours & courses from €15) Cosmetics workshops, backstage cabaret tours, fashion-designer showroom visits, French table decoration, art embroidery classes, market tours, baking with a Parisian baker – the repertoire of cultural and gourmet tours and behind-the-scenes experiences offered by Meeting the French is truly outstanding. All courses and tours are in English.

THATMuse
TOURS

(www.thatmuse.com; per person excl museum admission Louvre/Musée d'Orsay €25/35) Organises treasure hunts in English and French in the Louvre (p81) and Musée d'Orsay (p108). Participants (up to five people, playing alone or against another team) have to photograph themselves in front of 20 to 30 works of art ('treasure'). Hunts typically last 1½ to two hours.

Set in Paris
WALKING

(Map p134; ☏ 09 84 42 35 79; http://setinparis.com; 3 rue Maître Albert, 5e; 2hr tours €25; ☺ tours 10am & 3pm; Ⓜ Maubert-Mutualité) From its cinema-style 'box office' HQ in the Latin Quarter, Set in Paris offers themed walking tours (Hemingway, Coco Chanel, French markets...). Its two-hour 'Paris Movie Tour' covers locations throughout Paris where films including *The Devil Wears Prada, The Bourne Identity, The Three Musketeers, The Hunchback of Notre Dame, Ratatouille, Before Sunset,* several James Bond instalments and many others were shot.

Bateaux-Mouches
BOATING

(Map p90; ☏ 01 42 25 96 10; www.bateaux-mouches. fr; Port de la Conférence, 8e; adult/child €13.50/6; Ⓜ Alma Marceau) Bateaux-Mouches, the largest river cruise company in Paris, is a favourite with tour groups. Departing just east of the Pont de l'Alma on the Right Bank, cruises (70 minutes) run regularly from 10am to 10.30pm April to September and every 40 minutes from 11am to 9.20pm the rest of the year. Commentary is in French and English.

Vedettes du Pont Neuf
BOATING

(Map p130; ☏ 01 46 33 98 38; www.vedettesdu pontneuf.com; square du Vert Galant, 1er; adult/ child €14/7; ☺ 10.30am-9pm; Ⓜ Pont Neuf) One-hour cruises depart year-round from Vedettes' centrally located dock at the western tip of Île de la Cité; commentary is in French and English. Tickets are cheaper if you buy in advance online (adult/child €10/5). Check the website for details of its one-hour lunch cruises (adult/child €41/35), two-hour dinner (€71/35) and Champagne cruises (adult/ child €104/35).

Paris Canal Croisières
CRUISE

(Map p72; ☏ 01 42 40 96 97; www.pariscanal. com; quai Anatole France, 7e; adult/child €22/14; ☺ Mar–mid-Nov; Ⓜ Solférino, RER Musée d'Orsay) Seasonal 2½-hour Seine-and-canal cruises depart from quai Anatole France near the Musée d'Orsay (morning cruises) and from Parc de la Villette (afternoon cruises).

Fat Tire Bike Tours
CYCLING

(☏ 01 82 88 80 96; www.fattiretours.com; tours from €34) Offers day and night bicycle tours of the city, both in central Paris and further afield to Versailles (p189) and Monet's Garden (p194) in Giverny.

Left Bank Scooters
TOURS

(☏ 06 78 12 04 24; www.leftbankscooters.com; 3hr tours per 1st/2nd passenger from €200/50) Runs a variety of scooter tours around Paris, both day and evening, as well as trips out to Versailles and sidecar tours. Car or motorcycle licence required. Also **rents scooters** (☏ 06 78 12 04 24; www.leftbankscooters.com; 50/125cc scooters per 24hr €70/80).

✸ Festivals & Events

January

Paris Cocktail Week
FOOD & DRINK

(https://pariscocktailweek.fr; ☺ Jan) Each of the 75-plus cocktail bars all over the city that take part in late January's Paris Cocktail Week creates signature cocktails especially for the event. There are also workshops, guest bartenders, masterclasses and food pairings. Sign up for a free pass for cut-price cocktails.

May

French Open
SPORTS

(www.rolandgarros.com; ☺ late May-early Jun; Ⓜ Porte d'Auteuil) The glitzy Grand Slam tournament Les Internationaux de France de Tennis hits up from late May to early June at Stade Roland Garros.

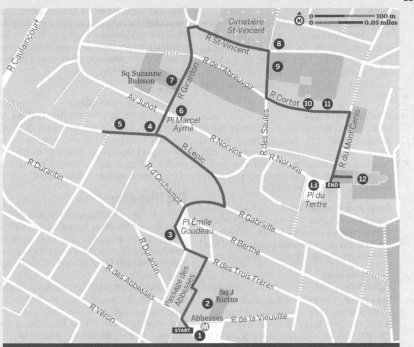

City Walk
Mythic Montmartre

START ABBESSES METRO STATION
END PLACE DU TERTRE
LENGTH 1KM; ONE HOUR

Begin on **❶ place des Abbesses**, where Hector Guimard's iconic art nouveau metro entrance (1900) still stands. Deep underground, beneath a maze of gypsum mines, it's one of Paris' deepest metro stations. Learn how to say 'I love you!' in another language or 10 with **❷ Le Mur des je t'aime** (p85), hidden in a park, Sq Jehan Rictus, on place des Abbesses.

Head up passage des Abbesses to place Émile Goudeau. At No 11bis you'll find **❸ Le Bateau Lavoir**, where Max Jacob, Amedeo Modigliani and Pablo Picasso – who painted his seminal *Les Demoiselles d'Avignon* (1907) here – once had art studios.

Continue the climb up rue Lepic to Montmartre's two surviving windmills: **❹ Moulin Radet** (now a restaurant) and, 50m west, **❺ Moulin Blute Fin**. In the 19th century, the latter became the open-air dance hall Le Moulin de la Galette, immortalised by Renoir in *Bal du Moulin de la Galette* (in the Musée d'Orsay).

Just north, on place Marcel Aymé, you'll see a man pop out of a stone wall. This **❻ Passe-Muraille sculpture** portrays Dutilleul, the hero of Marcel Aymé's short story *Le Passe-Muraille*. Aymé lived in the adjacent building from 1902 until 1967. Continue along rue Girardon to Sq Suzanne Buisson, home to a **❼ statue of St Denis**, the 3rd-century martyr and patron saint of France beheaded by Roman priests.

After passing by Cimetière St-Vincent you'll come upon celebrated cabaret **❽ Au Lapin Agile**, with a mural of a rabbit jumping out of a cooking pot by caricaturist André Gill. Opposite is **❾ Clos Montmartre** (p92), a vineyard dating from 1933, which produces an average of 800 bottles of wine each October.

Uphill is Montmartre's oldest building, onetime home to painters Renoir, Utrillo and Raoul Dufy, it's now the **❿ Musée de Montmartre** (p85). Continue past composer **⓫ Eric Satie's former residence** (No 6) and turn right onto rue du Mont Cenis; you'll soon come to historic **⓬ Église St-Pierre de Montmartre**. End on busy **⓭ place du Tertre** (p92), the former main square of the village.

June

Paris Beer Week
BEER

(http://parisbeerweek.fr; ⊘early Jun) Craft beer's popularity in Paris peaks during Paris Beer Week, held over 10 days. Events take place across the city's bars, pubs, breweries, specialist beer shops and other venues.

Fête de la Musique
MUSIC

(https://fetedelamusique.culturecommunication. gouv.fr; ⊘21 Jun) This national music festival welcomes in summer on the solstice with fabulous staged and impromptu live performances of jazz, reggae, classical and more. Held at venues all over the city.

Paris Jazz Festival
MUSIC

(www.parisjazzfestival.fr; ⊘ Jun-Jul; M Château de Vincennes) Jazz concerts swing every Saturday and Sunday afternoon in the Parc Floral de Paris during the Paris Jazz Festival.

July & August

Paris Plages
BEACH

(www.paris.fr; ⊘mid-Jul–mid-Aug) 'Paris Beaches' sets up along Paris' riverbanks in two main zones, the Parc Rives de Seine and the Bassin de la Villette (with swimming pools in the canal).

Bastille Day
CULTURAL

(⊘14 Jul) The capital celebrates France's national day with a morning military parade along av des Champs-Élysées, accompanied by a fly-past of fighter aircraft and helicopters. *Feux d'artifice* (fireworks) light up the sky above the Champ de Mars by night.

Tour de France
SPORTS

(www.letour.com; ⊘late Jul) The last of 21 stages of this prestigious, 3500km-long cycling event finishes with a race up the av des Champs-Élysées on the third or fourth Sunday of July – as it has done since 1975.

Rock en Seine
MUSIC

(www.rockenseine.com; ⊘late Aug; M Pont de St-Cloud, 🚲 Parc de St-Cloud) Headlining acts rock the Domaine National de St-Cloud, on the city's southwestern edge, at this popular three-day music festival.

October

Nuit Blanche
CULTURAL

(⊘early Oct) From sundown until sunrise on the first Saturday and Sunday of October, museums stay open all night, along with bars and clubs, for one 'White Night'.

Fête des Vendanges de Montmartre
WINE

(www.fetedesvendangesdemontmartre.com; ⊘Oct) This five-day festival taking in the second weekend in October celebrates Montmartre's grape harvest with costumes, concerts, food events and a parade.

December

Le Festival du Merveilleux
CULTURAL

(www.arts-forains.com; ⊘Dec-Jan; M Cour St-Émilion) The magical private museum Musée des Arts Forains, filled with fairground attractions of yesteryear, opens from late December to early January, with enchanting rides, attractions and festive shows.

🛏 Sleeping

Paris' wealth of accommodation spans all budgets, but it's often *complet* (full) well in advance. Reservations are recommended year-round and essential during the warmer months (April to October) and all public and school holidays.

Although marginally cheaper, accommodation outside central Paris is invariably a false economy given travel time and costs. Choose somewhere within Paris' 20 *arrondissements* to experience Parisian life the moment you step out the door.

🛏 Eiffel Tower & Western Paris

Not surprisingly, this very chic neighbourhood has little in the way of midrange accommodation. If you're in the mood for boutique luxury, however, you're in the right place.

Hôtel Molitor
HISTORIC HOTEL €€€

(☑01 56 07 08 50; www.mltr.fr; 13 rue Nungesser et Coli, 16e; d/ste from €300/600; ✱@🛜🏊; M Michel Ange Molitor) Famed as Paris' swishest swimming pool in the 1930s (where the bikini made its first appearance, no less) and a hot spot for graffiti art in the 1990s, the Molitor is one seriously legendary address. The art deco complex, built in 1929 and abandoned from 1989, has been restored to stunning effect.

Hôtel Félicien
BOUTIQUE HOTEL €€€

(Map p72; ☑01 55 74 00 00; www.hotelfelicienparis. com; 21 rue Félicien David, 16e; d €300-369, ste from €500; ✱@🛜; M Mirabeau) The price–quality ratio at this chic boutique hotel, squirrelled away in a 1930s building, is excellent – expect online rates to start around €200. Exquisitely designed rooms feel more five star than four, with 'White' and 'Silver' suites on the hotel's top 'Sky floor' (rooftop jacuzzi included). Romantics, eat your heart out.

🛏 Champs-Élysées & Grands Boulevards

The Champs-Élysées is home to deluxe palace hotels and global chains, though there are options here with more personality. Heading east the choices increase; the area between the Grands Boulevards and Pigalle is a beautiful neighbourhood and, being less touristy than the Champs-Élysées, a great place to immerse yourself in the city's charms and day-to-day life.

BVJ Opéra
HOSTEL €

(Map p78; ☎01 42 36 88 18; www.bvjhostelparis.com; 1 rue de la Tour des Dames, 9e; dm/d €39/49 incl breakfast; 🛜; Ⓜ Trinité) Clean rooms at this Bureau des Voyages de la Jeunesse (BVJ) hostel might be monastic, but that's negated by its decent location near the Palais Garnier and Grands Boulevards department stores, and its 19th-century building opening to a cobbled courtyard. Lockers and wi-fi both cost extra (per day €2). There's no sign.

Hôtel Monte Carlo
HOTEL €

(Map p78; ☎01 47 70 36 75; www.hotelmontecarlo.fr; 44 rue du Faubourg Montmartre, 9e; s €107, d €145-155, tr €195; 🛜; Ⓜ Le Peletier) A unique budget hotel, the Monte Carlo is a fabulous deal, with 20 colourful, personalised rooms and a great neighbourhood location. The cheaper rooms don't have private bathroom, but overall it outclasses many of the other choices in its price range. Prices for a double drop below €100 in low season. Wi-fi can be iffy.

Hôtel Chopin
HISTORIC HOTEL €

(Map p78; ☎01 47 70 58 10; www.hotelchopin.fr; 46 passage Jouffroy, 9e; d €90-160; @🛜; Ⓜ Grands Boulevards) Dating from 1846, the 36-room Chopin is inside one of Paris' most delightful 19th-century *passages couverts* (covered shopping arcades). The rooms don't have much in the way of personality (and the cheaper rooms are small and dark), but the belle époque location is beautiful.

Hôtel du Temps
BOUTIQUE HOTEL €€

(Map p78; ☎01 47 70 37 16; http://hotel-du-temps.fr; 11 rue de Montholon, 9e; d €195-215; ✳🛜; Ⓜ Poissonnière) This artsy boutique hotel is loaded with personality, from the flea-market furniture and white-parquet flooring to the patterned green tiling in the lobby. It's a 10-minute walk from the Gare du Nord; check out the secret basement bar where guests can play the piano over cocktails.

Hôtel Joyce
DESIGN HOTEL €€

(Map p78; ☎01 55 07 00 01; www.astotel.com; 29 rue la Bruyère, 9e; d €200-235; ✳@🛜; Ⓜ St-Georges) 🏵 Located in a lovely residential area between Montmartre and Opéra, this place has all the modern design touches (iPod docks, individually styled rooms, a sky-lit breakfast room fitted out with old Range Rover seats) and makes some ecofriendly claims – it relies on 50% renewable energy and uses organic products.

★ Hôtel Ekta
DESIGN HOTEL €€€

(Map p90; ☎01 53 76 09 05; www.hotelekta.com; 52 rue Galilée, 8e; d €325-525; ✳@🛜; Ⓜ George V) Psychedelic zebra stripes give this 1970s-style fashionista an unusually playful personality, especially in a neighbourhood where sleeping choices tend more towards the classical. Rooms are smallish but modern – smart TVs, Nespresso coffee makers and phone chargers are some of the amenities available. Online rates can drop to €100 in low season, a steal for a room off the Champs-Élysées.

★ Hôtel de Crillon
HISTORIC HOTEL €€€

(Map p90; ☎01 44 71 15 00; www.rosewoodhotels.com; 10 place de la Concorde, 8e; d/ste from €970/1750; ✳@🛜🏊; Ⓜ Concorde) Built in 1758 by Louis XV–commissioned architect Jacques-Ange Gabriel and transformed into a hotel in 1909, this palatial address at the foot of the Champs-Élysées opposite the Jardin des Tuileries reopened in 2017 after four years of renovations. Its original splendour has been retained throughout its sumptuous rooms and suites, three restaurants and opulent bar.

🛏 Louvre & Les Halles

The area encompassing the Musée du Louvre and the Forum des Halles is a central though busy area to base yourself. While it is more disposed to welcoming top-end travellers, there are some decent midrange places and even a budget pick or two to choose from.

Hôtel Vivienne
HOTEL €

(Map p78; ☎01 42 33 13 26; www.hotel-vivienne.com; 40 rue Vivienne, 2e; d €100-150, tr & q €200; @🛜; Ⓜ Grands Boulevards) This refurbished two-star hotel is amazingly good value for Paris. While the 45 rooms are not huge, they have all the mod cons; some even boast little balconies. Family rooms accommodate up to two children on a sofa bed. Not all rooms have air-con.

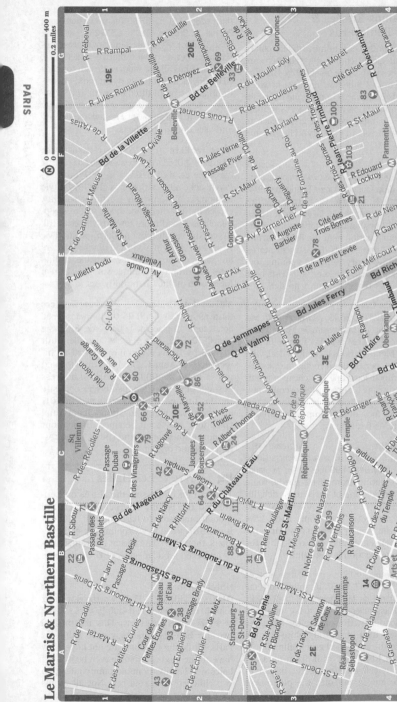

Le Marais & Northern Bastille

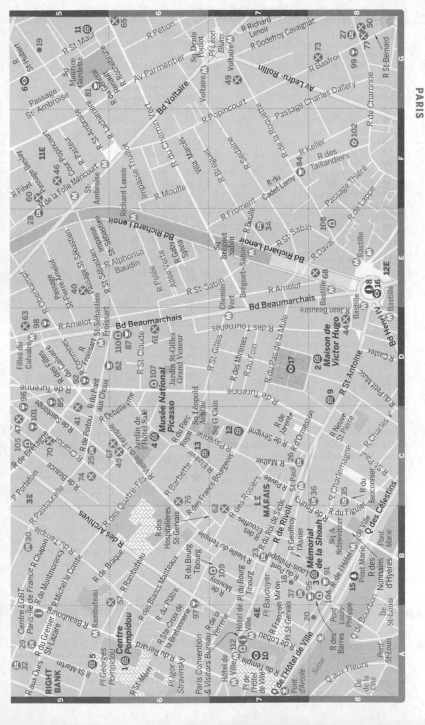

Le Marais & Northern Bastille

Hôtel Tiquetonne   HOTEL €

(Map p94; ☑ 01 42 36 94 58; www.hoteltiquetonne. fr; 6 rue Tiquetonne, 2e; d €80, without shower €65; @ 🛜; Ⓜ Étienne Marcel) What heart-warmingly good value this 45-room cheapie is. This serious, well-tended address has been in the hotel biz since the 1900s and is much loved by a loyal clientele of all ages. Rooms range across seven floors, are spick and span, and sport an inoffensive mix of vintage decor – roughly 1930s to 1980s, with brand-new bathrooms and parquet flooring in recently renovated rooms.

★ Hoxton   DESIGN HOTEL €€

(Map p78; ☑ 01 85 65 75 00; www.thehoxton. com; 30-32 rue du Sentier, 2e; d €239-549; 🏵 🛜; Ⓜ Bonne Nouvelle) One of the hottest hotel openings of 2017, the Parisian outpost of designer hotel The Hoxton occupies a grand 18th-century former residence. Its 172 striking rooms come in four sizes: Shoebox (from 13 sq metres), Cosy (from 17 sq metres),

Roomy (from 21 sq metres) and Biggy (from 32 sq metres). All have intricate cornicing and reclaimed oak floors.

★ Edgar   BOUTIQUE HOTEL €€

(Map p94; ☑ 01 40 41 05 19; www.edgarparis.com; 31 rue d'Alexandrie, 2e; d €235-275; 🏵 🛜; Ⓜ Strasbourg St-Denis) Thirteen playful rooms, each decorated by a different team of artists or designers, await the lucky few who secure a reservation at this former convent/seamstress workshop. 'Milagros' conjures up all the magic of the Far West, while 'Dream' echoes the rich imagination of childhood with surrealist installations. Breakfast is served in the popular downstairs restaurant, and the hidden tree-shaded square is a fabulous location.

★ Hôtel Crayon   BOUTIQUE HOTEL €€€

(Map p94; ☑ 01 42 36 54 19; www.hotelcrayon.com; 25 rue du Bouloi, 1er; s/d €311/347; 🏵 🛜; Ⓜ Les Halles, Louvre-Rivoli) Line drawings by French artist Julie Gauthron bedeck walls and doors at this creative boutique hotel. *Le crayon* (the pencil) is the theme, with 26 rooms sporting a different shade of each floor's chosen colour – we love the coloured-glass shower doors, and the books on the bedside table guests can swap and take home. Online deals often slash rates by up to 50%.

★**Hôtel Ritz Paris**　HISTORIC HOTEL €€€
(Map p94; ☑ 01 43 16 30 30; www.ritzparis.com; 15 place Vendôme, 1er; d from €1000, ste from €1900; P❋@🛜🛏; Ⓜ Opéra) The Ritz reopened in all its glory in mid-2016 after a four-year, €400 million head-to-toe renovation that painstakingly restored its original features while incorporating 21st-century technology. It's once again Paris' most rarefied address, with a manicured French formal garden and a world-first Chanel spa (Coco Chanel lived here). Also reinvigorated are its prestigious Ritz Escoffier cookery school and legendary Bar Hemingway (p161).

🛏 **Montmartre & Northern Paris**

Montmartre, in the 18e, is one of the most charming neighbourhoods in Paris and makes an ideal base. Every taste and budget is well catered for and the hilly streets mean many hotels have a view – of Montmartre and Sacré-Cœur or the Paris skyline stretching away to the south; check top-floor availability when deciding where to stay. Accommodation in Pigalle, which straddles the 18e and the northern part of the 9e, continues to up its game, with a brilliant choice of stylish and boutique 'life-style' addresses on offer.

★**Generator Hostel**　HOSTEL €
(Map p72; ☑ 01 70 98 84 00; www.generatorhostels. com; 9-11 place du Colonel Fabien, 10e; dm/d from €33/92; ❋@🛜; Ⓜ Colonel Fabien) From the 9th-floor rooftop bar overlooking Sacré-Cœur and the stylish ground-floor cafe-restaurant to the vaulted basement bar-club styled like a Paris metro station, and supercool bathrooms with 'I love you' tiling, this ultra-contemporary hostel near Canal St-Martin is sharp. Dorms have USB sockets and free lockers, and the best doubles have fabulous terraces with views. Women-only dorms are available.

St Christopher's Canal　HOSTEL €
(Map p72; ☑ 01 40 34 34 40; www.st-christophers. co.uk/paris-hostels; 159 rue de Crimée, 19e; dm from

€26, d from €117, with shared bathroom €87; @ 🛜; M Riquet, Laumière) This is one of Paris' most up-to-date hostels, with modern design and four- to 12-bed dorms, including female-only dorms. Doubles come with or without en-suite bathroom. Other perks include canal-side cafe, bar, bike rental and organised day trips. Daily prices vary wildly; reserve in advance to secure reasonable prices. No kitchen but rates include breakfast.

St Christopher's Gare du Nord   HOSTEL €
(Map p72; ☑ 01 70 08 52 22; www.st-christophers. co.uk/paris-hostels; 5 rue de Dunkerque, 10e; dm/s/d from €29/87/107; @ 🛜; M Gare du Nord) Steps from Gare du Nord, St Christopher's is a modern backpacker hostel with six light-filled floors and 580 beds. Dorms (including women-only dorms) sleep four to 10 but beds are pricey unless you reserve months in advance. Facilities include a laundry and Belushi's bar and restaurant with live music. No kitchen; breakfast included.

Hôtel du Nord – Le Pari Vélo   HOTEL €
(Mapp120; ☑ 0142016600; www.hoteldunord-lepari velo.com; 47 rue Albert Thomas, 10e; s/d €73/86; 🛜; M Jacques Bonsergent) Offering fantastic value given its prized location near place de la République, this perennial favourite has 23 rooms decorated with flea-market antiques and free bikes for guests to borrow to ride around town. Served in a vaulted stone cellar, breakfast (€8) includes locally baked bread and pastries along with homemade jams.

Hôtel Eldorado   HOTEL €
(Map p72; ☑ 01 45 22 35 21; www.eldoradohotel. fr; 18 rue des Dames, 17e; d from €100, with shared bathroom from €65; 🛜; M Place de Clichy) Bohemian Eldorado is a welcoming, reasonably well-run hotel with 33 colourfully decorated rooms above the **Bistro des Dames** (Map p72; ☑ 01 45 22 13 42; 18 rue des Dames, 17e; mains €16-24; ⊙ noon-2.30pm & 7-11pm; M Place

---

ℹ️ BOOKING SERVICES

Lonely Planet (www.lonelyplanet. com/france/paris/hotels) Reviews of Lonely Planet's top choices.

Paris Attitude (www.parisattitude. com) Thousands of apartment rentals, professional service, reasonable fees.

Haven In (https://havenin.com) Charming Parisian apartments for rent.

---

de Clichy), with a private garden. Rooms facing the back can be quite noisy as they look out onto the restaurant terrace, which stays open until 2am – earplugs may be a good idea. Cheaper-category rooms have washbasins only. Breakfast costs €12.

★ Le Pigalle   DESIGN HOTEL €€
(Map p78; ☑ 01 48 78 37 14; www.lepigalle.paris; 9 rue Frochot, 9e; d €120-280; ✳ @ 🛜; M Pigalle) This offbeat lifestyle hotel's edgy design reflects the neighbourhood's legendary nightlife, while carefully thought-out details like a postcard taped on the bathroom wall and a key ring jangling with Paris souvenirs add personalised touches to the 40 stylish rooms. Each has an iPad loaded with music, and larger rooms have vintage turntables with an eclectic vinyl collection.

★ Hôtel Providence   BOUTIQUE HOTEL €€
(Map p120; ☑ 01 46 34 34 04; www.hotelprovidence paris.com; 90 rue René Boulanger, 10e; d from €163; ✳ @ 🛜; M Strasbourg–St-Denis) This luxurious hideaway, in a 19th-century townhouse in the increasingly trendy 10e, is exquisite. Its 18 rooms (seven with balconies) have rich House of Hackney velvet wallpaper and vintage flea-market finds; the smallest aren't nearly as 'Mini' (by Paris standards) as the name implies. Bespoke cocktail bars in each room come complete with suggested recipes and ingredients.

Joke Hôtel   DESIGN HOTEL €€
(Map p100; ☑ 01 40 40 71 71; www.astotel.com/ hotel; 69 rue Blanche, 9e; s/d from €136/151; ✳ @ 🛜; M Blanche) No joke. This fabulous childhood-themed hotel is a serious contender for Paris' best-value, most fun address, where you can play 'scrabble' or spin the wheel of fortune above your bed each night, hunt for coins stuck in the lobby floor, or check out the toys and board games. Rates include breakfast and all-day complimentary (nonalcoholic) drinks, cakes and fruit.

Hôtel Amour   DESIGN HOTEL €€
(Map p78; ☑ 01 48 78 31 80; www.hotelamourpar is.fr; 8 rue de Navarin, 9e; s/d from €145/195; 🛜; M St-Georges, Pigalle) Craving romance in Paris? The inimitable black-clad Amour ('Love') in south Pigalle plays on its long-ago incarnation as a brothel, featuring darkened hallways, original design and nude artwork (some more explicit than others) in each of its 24 rooms (none have TVs, but that's

not the point here). The hip ground-floor **bistro** (Map p78; mains €14-26, weekend brunch €21; ☺8am-midnight; ☺) has a leafy summer patio garden.

Grand Amour Hôtel   DESIGN HOTEL €€
(Map p120; ☑01 44 16 03 10; www.hotelamour paris.fr; 18 rue de la Fidélité, 10e; s/d from €145/195; ☺; ⓜGare de l'Est) Younger sister to Pigalle's Hôtel Amour, this lifestyle hotel mixes vintage furniture from the flea market with phallic-symbol carpets and the striking B&W nude photography of graffiti artist André Saraiva. The result is an edgy hideaway for lovers in one of Paris' most up-and-coming neighbourhoods. Breakfast is served in the hotel **bistro** (Map p120; ☑01 44 16 03 30; mains €16-30, weekend brunch €21; ☺8am-12.30am; ☺☺), a trendy drinking and dining address in itself.

Môm'Art   BOUTIQUE HOTEL €€
(Map p100; ☑01 82 52 26 26; www.hotelmomart. com; 42 rue d'Orsel, 18e; d €180-230, ste €350; ✱☺; ⓜAnvers) Run by the same family since 1971 but stunningly made over (and renamed) in 2018, this four-star Montmartre hotel has just 25 rooms (including one suite), giving it a high level of intimacy. Generously sized rooms come in four different styles, including 'Artistes' rooms with modern-art motifs. There's an interior courtyard, a fitness area, a spa, a destination restaurant and a craft cocktail bar.

R Kipling Hotel   BOUTIQUE HOTEL €€
(Map p78; ☑01 55 31 91 99; www.kipling-hotel. com; 65 rue Blanche, 9e; s/d from €182/199; ✱☺; ⓜBlanche) Themed around Nobel Prize–winning writer Rudyard Kipling, this spellbinding hotel evokes his famous works like *The Jungle Book* in its beautifully wall-papered guest lounge and library, and its 40 rooms done out in pastel blues and greens and whimsical prints such as fluttering butterflies. Several higher-category rooms have balconies overlooking south Pigalle's rooftops.

Hôtel Joséphine   BOUTIQUE HOTEL €€
(Map p100; ☑01 55 31 90 75; www.hotel-josephine. com; 67 rue Blanche, 9e; s/d from €108/142; ✱☺; ⓜBlanche) Life's a cabaret at this novel, four-star boutique address in Pigalle. Named after 1920s cabaret star Josephine Baker, the hotel has 41 rooms with richly patterned wallpapers broken up by solid colours and 1930s period furniture and light fittings. Black-and-white cabaret photos decorate

walls, and downstairs in the sociable library-lounge there's an honesty bar, free coffee and board games.

Grand Hôtel Pigalle   DESIGN HOTEL €€
(Map p78; ☑01 85 73 12 00; www.grandpigal le.com; 29 rue Victor Massé, 9e; d from €186; ✱@☺; ⓜPigalle) Created by the pioneering Experimental group, which has shaken up Paris' contemporary cocktail scene, this outrageously hip address in south Pigalle (aka 'SoPi') is a sophisticated lifestyle hotel with cocktail 'minibars' in its 37 beautifully crafted rooms, and a fabulous restaurant–wine bar with a menu from lauded Italian chef Giovanni Passerini.

★Hôtel Particulier Montmartre   BOUTIQUE HOTEL €€€
(Map p100; ☑01 53 41 81 40; www.hotel-particulier-montmartre.com; Pavillon D, 23 av Junot, 18e; ste €390-590; ✱☺; ⓜLamarck–Caulaincourt) Hidden down a stone-paved alley behind a high wall, this mansion is one of the city's most magical addresses. Its five sweeping designer suites are decorated with retro flea-market finds, but it's the garden, designed by landscape architect Louis Benech, and fashionable cocktail bar (p163) that really stun. Ring the buzzer outside the unmarked black-gated entrance at No 23.

🛏 Le Marais, Ménilmontant & Belleville

In an area as fashionable as Le Marais, there's no shortage of exquisite boutique and designer properties, but you'll also find options for all budgets here, from dorms and budget hotels to good-value midrange addresses. Moving east into the ethnically diverse 'hoods of Ménilmontant and Belleville, pickings are slimmer but prices inevitably drop.

★Les Piaules   HOSTEL €
(Map p120; ☑01 43 55 09 97; www.lespiaules.com; 59 bd de Belleville, 11e; dm/d from €35/105; @☺; ⓜCouronnes, Belleville) Run by hip, witty staff, this brilliant hostel is the Belleville hot spot to mingle with locals over Parisian craft beer at the stunning ground-floor bar, cosy up in front of the wood-burner, or soak up the sun and panoramic views from the roof terrace. Dorms are fitted with custom bunks and ample bedside plugs; rooftop doubles have sleek all-white decor.

Southern Bastille & Gare de Lyon

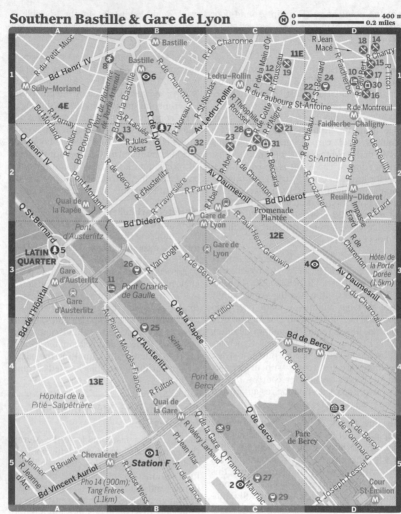

MIJE Fourcy

HOSTEL €

(Map p120; ☑ 01 42 74 23 45; www.mije.com; 6 rue de Fourcy, 4e; dm/s/d €35.50/65/85; ☏; Ⓜ St-Paul, Pont Marie) Behind the elegant front door of this *hôtel particulier*, Fourcy welcomes guests with clean rooms and a summer garden to breakfast/hang out in. It's one of three Marais hostels run by the Maison Internationale de la Jeunesse et des Étudiants – the others are **MIJE Le Fauconnier** (Map p120; ☑ 01 42 74 23 45; 11 rue du Fauconnier, 4e; dm/s/d €35.50/65/85; @☏; Ⓜ St-Paul, Pont Marie) and **MIJE Maubuisson** (Map p120; ☑ 01 42 74 23 45; 12 rue des Barres, 4e; dm/s/d €35.50/65/85; @☏; Ⓜ Hôtel de Ville, Pont Marie). Rates include breakfast; evening meals are available in the vaulted cellar.

Cosmos Hôtel

HOTEL €

(Map p120; ☑ 01 43 57 25 88; www.cosmos-hotel-paris.com; 35 rue Jean-Pierre Timbaud, 11e; s/d from €67/72; ☏; Ⓜ Parmentier, Goncourt) Cheap, brilliant value and just footsteps from the nightlife of rue JPT, Cosmos is a shining star with retro style on the budget-hotel scene that, unlike most other hotels in the same price bracket, has been treated to a thoroughly modern makeover

Southern Bastille & Gare de Lyon

this century. Breakfast is basic but is also budget priced, costing just €8.

★ Hôtel Georgette
DESIGN HOTEL €€
(Map p120; ☎01 44 61 10 10; www.hotelgeorgette.com; 36 rue du Grenier St-Lazare, 3e; d from €240; ❄️🛜; Ⓜ️Rambuteau) Taking inspiration from the Centre Pompidou around the corner, this vivacious hotel's 19 rooms reflect major 20th-century artistic movements, including pop art, op art, Dada, new realism and street art, with lots of bold colours and funky touches like Andy Warhol–inspired Campbell's-soup-can lampshades. Art exhibitions regularly take place in the bright lobby. It's gay-friendly and all-welcoming.

Hôtel Jules & Jim
DESIGN HOTEL €€
(Map p120; ☎01 44 54 13 13; www.hoteljulesetjim.com; 11 rue des Gravilliers, 3e; d from €240; ❄️@🛜; Ⓜ️Arts et Métiers) The subtle oyster-grey entrance to this hotel named after the cult 1962 Truffaut film hints at the sophisticated interior design inside. Its 23 contemporary rooms mix raw concrete with marble, wood, glass and other beautiful materials. Jim rooms open onto a fabulous interior courtyard with an outdoor fireplace; 8th-floor Sous les Toits rooms have balconies, some looking out to Montmartre.

Hôtel Emile
DESIGN HOTEL €€
(Map p120; ☎01 42 72 76 17; www.hotelemile.com; 2 rue Malher, 4e; s/d/ste from €139/157/211; ❄️🛜; Ⓜ️St-Paul) Prepare to be dazzled – literally. Retro B&W, geometrically patterned carpets, curtains, wallpapers and drapes dress this chic hotel, wedged between boutiques and restaurants in Le Marais. Pricier 'top floor' doubles look out over Parisian roofs and chimney pots. Breakfast (included in the price) is on bar stools in the lobby; open the cupboard to find the 'kitchen'.

Hôtel Fabric
DESIGN HOTEL €€
(Map p120; ☎01 43 57 27 00; www.hotelfabric.com; 31 rue de la Folie Méricourt, 11e; d/tr from €247/445; ❄️@🛜; Ⓜ️St-Ambroise) Honouring its industrial heritage as a 19th-century textile factory, four-star Hôtel Fabric has steely pillars propping up the red-brick lounge area with dining tables where breakfast (€18) is served, and vintage touches include a Singer sewing machine. Darkly carpeted corridors open to 33 bright rooms with beautiful textiles and cupboards made from upcycled packing crates.

Hôtel Caron de Beaumarchais
BOUTIQUE HOTEL €€
(Map p120; ☎01 42 72 34 12; www.carondebeaumarchais.com; 12 rue Vieille du Temple, 4e; d from

€196; ❄ ☎; M Hôtel de Ville, St-Paul) The attention to detail at this antique-filled, 19-room hotel is impressive. From the period card table set as if time stopped halfway through a game, to the harp and well-worn sheet music propped on the music stand, along with chandeliers and silk wallpapers, the decor evokes the life and times of the 18th-century playwright after whom the hotel is named.

★ Les Bains   DESIGN HOTEL €€€
(Map p120; ☑ 01 42 77 07 07; www.lesbains-paris.com; 7 rue du Bourg l'Abbé, 3e; d/ste from €392/715; ❄ @ ☎; M Étienne Marcel, Rambuteau) Opened in 1885 as thermal baths (frequented by Marcel Proust among others), in 1978 this iconic address morphed into the Bains-Douches nightclub, made famous by David Bowie, Mick Jagger and a galaxy of celebs. Today it's probably Paris' most fabulous lifestyle hotel, with 39 bespoke rooms – some opening to balconies or terraces – showcasing vintage treasures, luxury fabrics and eclectic design.

Its history is recalled at its club (midnight to dawn Thursday to Saturday), with concerts, DJs and a swimming pool. Sunday brunch (€35) is the hot ticket at the modern French restaurant. Breakfast costs €20.

★ Hôtel du Petit Moulin   BOUTIQUE HOTEL €€€
(Map p120; ☑ 01 42 74 10 10; www.hoteldupetit moulin.com; 29-31 rue de Poitou, 3e; d €250-395; ❄ ☎; M St-Sébastien–Froissart) A bakery at the time of Henri IV, this scrumptious 17-room hotel was designed from head to toe by Christian Lacroix. Choose from medieval and rococo Marais rooms sporting exposed beams and dressed in toile de Jouy wallpaper, or more modern surrounds with contemporary murals and heart-shaped mirrors just this side of kitsch.

🛏 Bastille & Eastern Paris

The relatively untouristy neighbourhood east of place de la Bastille has a handful of budget choices and French chains (Ibis et al), along with an increasing number of boutique and/or designer properties.

Mama Shelter   DESIGN HOTEL €
(Map p72; ☑ 01 43 48 48 48; www.mamashelter.com; 109 rue de Bagnolet, 20e; s/d/tr/q from €119/129/209/289; ❄ @ ☎; 🚌 76, M Gambetta, Alexandre Dumas) This former car park was coaxed into its current zany incarnation by designer Philippe Starck. Its 170 cutting-edge rooms feature iMacs, catchy colour schemes,

polished-concrete walls and free movies on demand. A rooftop terrace, pizzeria and huge restaurant with live music and all-you-can-eat Sunday brunch add to its street cred. Book as early as possible to get the best deal.

★ Hôtel Paris Bastille Boutet   HOTEL €€
(Map p126; ☑ 01 40 24 65 65; www.sofitel.com; 22-24 rue Faidherbe, 11e; d/ste from €199/279; P ❄ @ ☎ ☰; M Faidherbe-Chaligny) A joinery workshop and later a chocolate factory, the Boutet retains its original 1926 mosaic-tiled façade and art deco canopy, and acknowledges its industrial heritage in its timber-panelled hallways. Ten of its 80 rooms and suites have spectacular terraces. There's a *hammam*, gym and two beauty treatment rooms, but the biggest bonus is the sky-lit swimming pool with a counter current.

Hôtel Exquis   DESIGN HOTEL €€
(Map p120; ☑ 01 56 06 95 13; https://hotelexquis paris.com; 71 rue de Charonne, 11e; d from €161; ❄ ☎; M Charonne) Surrealism is the theme of this excellent-value hotel amid a cluster of top-choice dining addresses. A unique work of surrealist art decorates each of its 42 rooms, where beautiful colour palettes, designer lighting and bathrooms with twinkling tile lights woo guests. Breakfast (€14) is handily served from 7am to 11am.

★ Maison Bréguet   BOUTIQUE HOTEL €€€
(Map p120; ☑ 01 58 30 32 31; www.maisonbreguet.com; 8 rue Bréguet, 11e; d/ste from €357/464; ❄ ☎ ☰; M Bréguet–Sabin) Local creatives were involved in the evolution of this former factory turned five-star property, which opened in 2018: artists' works hang on the walls, writers selected the library's books and films, and musicians put together playlists (performances also often take place here). Some of its 53 art deco-influenced rooms and suites have terraces; the two-storey deluxe suite has a private garden.

🛏 The Islands

The islands are a delightful place to stay, but choice is limited and budget accommodation nonexistent.

Hôtel des 2 Îles   HISTORIC HOTEL €€
(Map p130; ☑ 01 43 26 13 35; www.deuxiles-paris-hotel.com; 59 rue St-Louis en l'Île, 4e; s/d €230/263; ❄ ☎; M Pont Marie) A venerable 17th-century building shelters this intimate three-star hotel with 17 classical rooms sporting patterned wallpaper, screen-printed fabrics,

original Portuguese *azulejos* (blue-and-white ceramic tiles) in some bathrooms, and ancient wooden beams. Breakfast (€14) is served in the vaulted stone cellar with fireplace (not functioning) and terracotta-tiled floor. Top-floor rooms peep out over Parisian rooftops and chimney pots.

Hôtel de Lutèce   HOTEL €€
(Map p130; ☑ 01 43 26 23 52; www.paris-hotel-lutece.com; 65 rue St-Louis en l'Île, 4e; s/d/tr €230/245/310; ❄ ☎; M Pont Marie) An elegant lobby-salon, with ancient fireplace, wood panelling, antique furnishings and traditional board games to borrow, welcomes guests at the lovely Lutèce, a country-style three-star hotel with 23 tastefully decorated rooms stacked up on six floors. Those overlooking the village-like street – with *fromagerie* (cheese shop), greengrocer's and chocolate shop – are more atmospheric than those facing the interior courtyard. Breakfast €14.

★ Hôtel du
Jeu de Paume   BOUTIQUE HOTEL €€€
(Map p130; ☑ 01 43 26 14 18; http://jeudepaumehotel.com; 54 rue St-Louis en l'Île, 4e; s/d €205/305; ❄ ☎; M Pont Marie) Romantically set in a courtyard off Île St-Louis' main street, this chic, contemporary four-star hotel occupies a 17th-century royal tennis court. Its 30 rooms are each inspired by a different modern artist. Panton chairs add a design edge to the historic beamed, exposed-stone-walled house, and its leafy patio garden is divine. Facilities include a wellness centre. Breakfast €18.

🛏 Latin Quarter

This lively neighbourhood has plenty of options in all price categories. Some areas, especially just across the bridge from Notre Dame and around place St-Michel, are exceptionally central. Note that the months of March to June and October are very busy with students and professors attending conferences and seminars, so book well ahead if you're visiting then.

★ Hôtel Diana   HOTEL €
(Map p134; ☑ 01 43 54 92 55; http://hotel-diana-paris.com; 73 rue St-Jacques, 5e; s €78-98, d €105-145, tr €160-195; ☎; M Maubert-Mutualité) Footsteps from the Sorbonne, two-star Diana is budget-traveller gold. Owner extraordinaire, Thérèse Cheval, has been at the helm here since the 1970s and the pride and joy she invests in the hotel is boundless. Spacious rooms sport a stylish contemporary decor with geometric-patterned fabrics, the odd

retro furniture piece, and courtesy tray with kettle and white-mug twinset. Breakfast €10.

★ Hôtel Port Royal   HOTEL €
(Map p72; ☑ 01 43 31 70 06; www.port-royal-hotel.fr; 8 bd de Port-Royal, 5e; d €95-100, s/d without bathroom €56/58; ☎; M RER Port Royal) This elegant, fourth-generation family hotel, run by great-granddaughter Isabelle and her Uncle Thierry today, wins the prize for the most polished, squeaky-clean budget hotel in Paris (even the cleaners are second generation). Its 46 rooms, stacked across six floors, enjoy impeccably maintained vintage furnishings. The *bijou* courtyard garden – the spot to breakfast (€8) alfresco on warm days – is a summertime bonus.

★ Familia Hôtel   HOTEL €€
(Map p134; ☑ 01 43 54 55 27; www.familiahotel.com; 11 rue des Écoles, 5e; s/d/tr €110/134/152; ❄ ☎; M Cardinal Lemoine) Staff at this friendly, third-generation family-run hotel proudly tell you that nothing ever changes at the Familia. Indeed, the sepia murals of Parisian landmarks, flower-bedecked windows, and exposed rafters and stone walls are clearly from a past era. Some of the 32 rooms have weeny balconies; those on the 6th floor peep at Notre Dame. Breakfast €7.

Hôtel La Lanterne   BOUTIQUE HOTEL €€
(Map p134; ☑ 01 53 19 88 39; www.hotel-la-lanterne.com; 12 rue de la Montagne Ste-Geneviève, 5e; d from €175; ❄ @ ☎ ≋; M Maubert-Mutualité) A stunning swimming pool and *hammam* in a vaulted stone cellar, a topiary-filled courtyard garden, contemporary guest rooms (some with small balconies) with black-and-white photos of Parisian architecture, amenities including Nespresso machines, and an honesty bar make this a jewel of a boutique hotel. Breakfast (€25) is a choice of hot and cold buffets and includes Mariage Frères teas.

Hôtel Atmosphères   DESIGN HOTEL €€
(Map p134; ☑ 01 43 26 56 02; www.hotelatmospheres.com; 31 rue des Écoles, 5e; d from €132; ❄ @ ☎; M Maubert-Mutualité) Striking images by award-winning French photographer Thierry des Ouches are permanently exhibited at this design hotel where 56 glam rooms evoke different Parisian 'atmospheres' – nature, monuments, Paris by night, the metro-inspired 'urban' and colourful *salon de thé* (tearoom)–style 'macaron'. A small gym, sauna and water massage bed are tucked away in the basement. Express/buffet breakfast €9/16.

The Islands

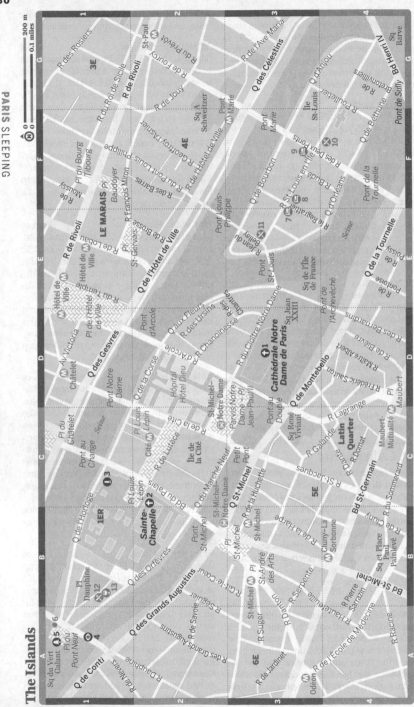

The Islands

🛏 St-Germain & Les Invalides

St-Germain is one of the most quintessentially Parisian neighbourhoods, with a bevy of enchanting history-steeped jewels and swish designer digs to prove it. On the downside, bar a couple of notable exceptions, accommodation doesn't come cheap here. Les Invalides is less epicentral and more residential but, alas, no cheaper.

★ **Hôtel du Dragon** HOTEL €
(Map p158; ☎ 01 45 48 51 05; www.hoteldudragon.com; 36 rue du Dragon, 6e; d €95-150, tr €130-180; ☎; Ⓜ St-Sulpice) It's hard to believe that such a gem of a budget hotel still exists in this ultra-chic part of St-Germain. A family affair for the last five generations, today the ever-charming Roy runs the 28-room Dragon with his children, Sébastien and Marie-Hélène. Spotlessly clean rooms are decidedly large by Paris standards, often with exposed wooden beams and lovely vintage furnishings.

Hôtel Le Clément HOTEL €
(Map p158; ☎ 01 43 26 53 60; http://hotelclementparis.com; 6 rue Clément, 6e; s/d from €88/99; ❄ ☎; Ⓜ St-Germain des Prés) Excellent value for the style and tranquillity it offers, the Clément has 28 stylish rooms (with beautiful printed wallpapers and fabrics), some overlooking the Marché St-Germain. Rooms on the top floor have sloping ceilings. The proprietors know

what they're doing – this place has been in the same family for over a century. Breakfast €14.

★ **Hôtel Le Comtesse** BOUTIQUE HOTEL €€
(Map p76; ☎ 01 45 51 29 29; www.comtesse-hotel.com; 29 av de Tourville, 7e; d from €229; ❄ @ ☎; Ⓜ École Militaire) A five-star view of Mademoiselle Eiffel seduces guests in every single room at The Countess, an utterly charming boutique hotel at home in a 19th-century building with alluring wrought-iron balconies. Colour palettes are playful, and the feathered quill pen adorning the desk in each room is one of many cute touches. Breakfast (€19) is served in the glamorous, boudoir-styled cafe with pavement terrace.

Le Bellechasse DESIGN HOTEL €€
(Map p72; ☎ 01 45 50 22 31; www.lebellechasse.com; 8 rue de Bellechasse, 7e; d €149-440; ❄ ☎; Ⓜ Solférino) Handily placed near the Seine and Musée d'Orsay, 33-room Le Bellechasse is an enticing, sensorial feast. Entrancing room themes by fashion designer Christian Lacroix – including St-Germain, with brocades, zebra striping and faux-gold leafing; Tuileries, with trompe l'œil and palms; and Jeu de Paume, with giant playing-card motifs – create the impression you've stepped into a larger-than-life oil painting.

★ **L'Hôtel** BOUTIQUE HOTEL €€€
(Map p158; ☎ 01 44 41 99 00; www.l-hotel.com; 13 rue des Beaux Arts, 6e; d from €323; ❄ @ ☎ ☀; Ⓜ St-Germain des Prés) In a quiet quayside street, this 20-room establishment is the stuff of romance, Parisian myths and urban legends. Rock- and film-star patrons fight to sleep in the Oscar Wilde Suite, decorated with a peacock motif, where the Irish playwright died in 1900. A stunning, modern swimming pool occupies the ancient cellar.

🛏 Montparnasse & Southern Paris

This sprawling neighbourhood has everything from hostels and cheapie old-school hotels through to stunning designer properties. Bear in mind that some areas are out of the way and/or are not well served by metro, although there are usually buses instead.

3 Ducks Hostel HOSTEL €
(Map p72; ☎ 01 48 42 04 05; http://3ducks.fr; 6 place Étienne Pernet, 15e; dm/d/q from €29.95/99/144; ❄ ☎; Ⓜ Félix Faure) A lively bar (open day and night to guests and nonguests), courtyard BBQ and no curfew

or lockout give this reinvigorated hostel, a 10-minute walk from the Eiffel Tower, a good-time vibe. Facilities are excellent (self-catering kitchen, small lockers, plus a luggage room and multiple USB outlets and a lamp per bed), there's a women-only dorm and freebies include breakfast.

Arty Paris HOSTEL €

(Map p72; ☑ 01 40 34 40 34; www.artyparis. fr; 62 rue des Morillons, 15e; dm/s/d/q from €26/55/75/115; @ 🛜; Ⓜ Porte de Vanves) Flags add a dashing splash of colour to the delicious, caramel-brick façade of this design hostel-hotel, tucked away in the staunchly local 15e but moments from the T3 tram, and zippy buses to St-Germain, the Louvre and Montmartre. Inside, it is all geometric wallpapers, parquet flooring and funky colour schemes. Guests have use of a superb kitchen, making it a family favourite too.

Hôtel Carladez Cambronne HOTEL €

(Map p72; ☑ 01 47 34 07 12; www.hotelcarladez. com; 3 place du Général Beuret, 15e; d €106-158; 🛜; Ⓜ Vaugirard) On a quintessentially Parisian cafe-clad square, this very good-value hotel has comfortable rooms with attractive wallpapers and fabrics. Higher-priced superior rooms come with bathtubs, more space and tend to be quieter. Communal coffee- and tea-making facilities let you make yourself at home. Breakfast €10. Check its website for last-minute deals.

Hôtel de la Loire HOTEL €

(Map p72; ☑ 01 45 40 66 88; www.hoteldela loire-paris.com; 39bis rue du Moulin Vert, 14e; d €110-125, with shared bath €80; Ⓟ 🛜; Ⓜ Alésia) Obviously, at these prices don't expect luxury, but do expect a warm welcome and clean, colourful en-suite rooms (18 all-up) at this budget hotel of old. The lovely vil-lage-like location on a quiet, quaint lane near Denfert-Rochereau makes it easy to reach both major airports and Gare du Nord, and there's a pretty table-set garden. Breakfast €8.50.

★ Hôtel Henriette DESIGN HOTEL €€

(Map p72; ☑ 01 47 07 26 90; www.hotelhenri-ette.com; 9 rue des Gobelins, 13e; s €69-209, d €79-309, tr €89-339, q €129-499; ❋ 🛜; Ⓜ Les Gobelins) Interior designer Vanessa Scoffier scoured Paris' flea markets to source Platner chairs, 1950s lighting and other unique vintage pieces for the 32 rooms at bohemian Henriette – one of the Left Bank's most stunning boutique addresses. Guests can mingle in the light-flooded glass atrium and adjoining plant-filled patio with wrought-iron furniture.

Afternoon tea and cake and an early-evening aperitif with savoury tasting board is an intrinsic part of any stay. Breakfast €14.

Off Paris Seine HOTEL €€

(Map p126; ☑ 01 44 06 62 66; www.offparisseine. com; 85 quai d'Austerlitz, 13e; d from €169; 🛜 ❋; Ⓜ Gare d'Austerlitz) Should the idea of being gently rocked to sleep take your fancy, check into Paris' first floating hotel by the highly recommended Parisian Elegancia hotel group. The sleek, 80m-long catamaran-design structure moored by Pont Charles de Gaulle sports sun terraces overlooking the Seine, a chic bar with silver beanbags by a 15m-long dipping pool, lounge and 58 stunningly appointed rooms and suites.

✕ Eating

The inhabitants of some cities rally around local sports teams, but in Paris they rally around *la table* – and everything on it. Pistachio macarons, shots of tomato consommé,

---

ℹ️ FOOD BLOGGERS & WEBSITES

David Lebovitz (www.davidlebovitz.com) Expat US pastry chef and cookbook author. Good insights and recommendations.

Le Fooding (https://lefooding.com) The French movement that's giving Michelin a run for its money. Le Fooding's mission is to shake up the ossified establishment, so expect a good balance of quirky, under-the-radar reviews and truly fine dining.

La Fourchette (www.thefork.com) Website offering user reviews and great deals of up to 50% off in Paris restaurants.

Paris by Mouth (https://parisbymouth.com) Capital dining and drinking with articles and recommendations searchable by *arrondissement*.

Paris Food Affair (www.parisfoodaffair.com) Keep tabs on Paris' evolving foodie scene.

STREET TALK: FOOD TRUCKS

Street food continues to take the city by storm as food trucks roll out across Paris. Find the day's location online.

Le Camion Qui Fume (p138) This 'smoking truck' serving gourmet burgers started the local food-truck craze.

Cantine California (www.cantinecalifornia.com; burger & fries €16, tacos 3 for €13.50) This roving food truck serves up organic burgers, tacos and homemade desserts.

KimPop (www.facebook.com/kimpopfoodtruck; dishes €5.50-12.50) Korean food truck KimPop serves soup, pork, beef or tofu *bibimbap* ('mixed rice') salad bowls and *kimbap* (sushi-style rolls) and more.

Le Beau Caillou (http://lebeaucaillou.com; dishes €7-9) *Accras* (fried fish), meat- or fish-curry-filled *roti* (flatbread) and *gallo pinto* (rice and beans) are among the Caribbean dishes on offer here.

La Cabane de Cape Cod (www.facebook.com/cabanecapecod; dishes €11-16) Choose from classic fish and chips, salmon gravlax, tuna tataki and other seafood dishes.

Currywurst Paris-Berlin (http://curry-wurst.fr; dishes €5-7) Try German currywurst (chopped sausage slathered in curry sauce), fluffy pretzels and caffeine-packed Fritz-kola.

---

decadent bœuf bourguignon, a goocy wedge of Camembert running onto the cheese plate...food isn't fuel here; it's the reason you get up in the morning.

✖ Eiffel Tower & Western Paris

In addition to the pickings of the 16e *arrondissement,* the many restaurants of Les Invalides and the buzzing market street of rue Cler (7e) are a short walk from the Eiffel Tower. For a truly memorable experience, dine in the icon itself.

Les Deux Abeilles　　　　　　CAFE €
(Map p76; ✆ 01 45 55 64 04; 189 rue de l'Université, 7e; lunch menu €24, salads €15-20; ☺ 9am-7pm Mon-Sat; Ⓜ Alma Marceau or RER Pont d'Alma) There is no lovelier sanctuary from the Eiffel Tower crowds than this old-fashioned tearoom, the elegant love child of a mother-and-daughter team who greet regulars with a *bisou* (kiss). Delicious homemade cakes and *citronnade* (ginger lemonade) aside, the Two Bees cook up quiches, tarts and salads ensuring every table is full by 1pm. Breakfast and brunch available too.

Atelier Vivanda　　　　　　FRENCH €€
(Map p72; ✆ 01 40 67 10 00; www.ateliervivanda.com; 18 rue Lauriston, 16e; 2-/3-course meal €32/38, mains €28; ☺ noon-2.30pm & 7.30-10.30pm Mon-Fri; Ⓜ Charles de Gaulle–Étoile) A micro outpost of carnivore heaven, tucked away down an inconspicuous side street 10

minutes from the Arc de Triomphe. The Atelier focuses uniquely on high-quality meat and poultry; the three-course meal is a deal in this neighbourhood. You can also get frogs' legs, snails and fondue in season. Reserve.

★ L'Astrance　　　　　　GASTRONOMY €€€
(Map p76; ✆ 01 40 50 84 40; www.astrancerestaurant.com; 4 rue Beethoven, 16e; 3-/5-course lunch menus €75/170, 7-course dinner menu €250; ☺ 12.15-1.15pm & 8.15-9.15pm Tue-Fri, closed Aug; Ⓜ Passy) It's almost two decades since Pascal Barbot's dazzling cuisine at the triple-Michelin-starred L'Astrance made its debut, but it's shown no signs of losing its cutting edge. Look beyond the complicated descriptions on the menu and expect exquisite elements making up intricate plates that are as spectacular as the artworks adorning Paris' grand galleries. Reserve one to two months in advance.

Le Jules Verne　　　　　　GASTRONOMY €€€
(Map p76; ✆ 01 45 55 61 44; www.lejulesverne-paris.com; 2nd fl, Eiffel Tower, Champ de Mars, 7e; 5-/6-course menus €190/230, 3-course lunch menu €105; ☺ noon-1.30pm & 7-9.30pm; Ⓜ Bir Hakeim or RER Champ de Mars–Tour Eiffel) Book way ahead (online only) to feast on Michelin-starred cuisine and the most beautiful view of Paris at this magical spot on the Eiffel Tower's 2nd floor, accessed by a private lift (elevator) in the south pillar. Cuisine is contemporary, with a five- or six-course 'experience' menu allowing you to taste the best of chef Pascal Féraud's stunning gastronomic repertoire.

Latin Quarter

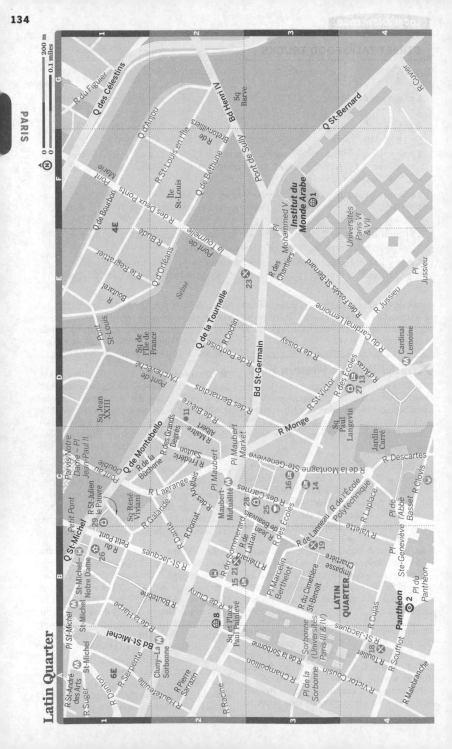

N

0   200 m
0   0.1 miles

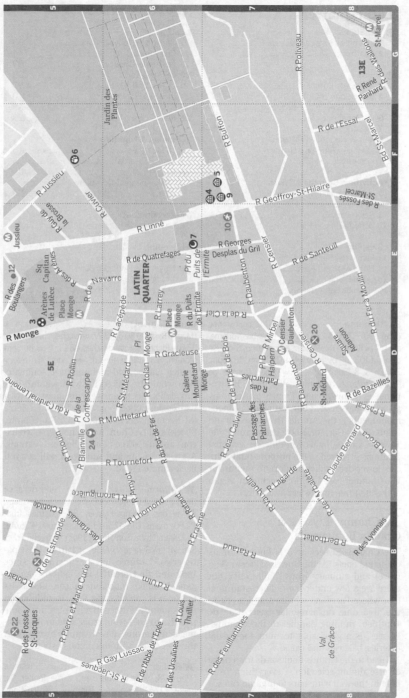

Latin Quarter

Bustronome   GASTRONOMY **€€€**
(Map p90; ☏09 54 44 45 55; www.bustronome.
com; 2 av Kléber, 16e; 4-course lunch €65, 6-course
dinner €100; ⊘by reservation 12.15pm, 12.45pm,
7.45pm & 8.45pm; 🖉🖝; Ⓜ Kléber, Charles de
Gaulle–Étoile) A true moveable feast, Bustronome is a voyage into French gastronomy
aboard a glass-roofed bus, with Paris' famous
monuments – the Arc de Triomphe, Grand
Palais, Palais Garnier, Notre Dame and Eiffel
Tower – gliding by as you dine on seasonal
creations prepared in the purpose-built vehicle's lower-deck galley. Children's menus for
lunch/dinner cost €40/50; vegetarian, vegan
and gluten-free menus are available.

✗ Champs-Élysées & Grands Boulevards

The Champs-Élysées area is known for its
big-name chefs (Alain Ducasse, Pierre Gagnaire) and culinary icons (Taillevent), but
there are a few under-the-radar restaurants
too, where Parisians who live and work in
the area dine on a regular basis. Rue de
Ponthieu, running parallel to the Champs-
Élysées, is a good spot to hunt for casual
eateries, bakeries and cafes.

Head to the Grands Boulevards for a more
diverse dining selection – everything from
hole-in-the-wall wine bars to organic cafes.

Chéri Charlot   SANDWICHES **€**
(Map p78; ☏09 80 41 78 27; www.chericharlot.com;
33 rue Richer, 9e; sandwiches €8-13; ⊘noon-3pm
Mon-Fri, 6.30-10pm Tue-Fri; Ⓜ Cadet) If every
French cheese had a charcuterie soulmate,
who would be paired up with whom? This
tiny deli seeks to answer this question with
its excellent choice of sandwiches: Le Serra
(St-Nectaire, Serrano ham), Le Rai (Comté,
Speck) and Le Chon (Reblochon, smoked bacon) are just some of its delicious creations.
A glass of wine and sandwich will set you
back a mere €9.50.

★ Ladurée   PASTRIES **€€**
(Map p90; ☏01 40 75 08 75; www.laduree.com;
75 av des Champs-Élysées, 8e; pastries from
€2.60, mains €18-47, 2-/3-course menu €35/42;
⊘7.30am-11pm Sun-Thu, 7.30am-midnight Fri &
Sat; 🖝; Ⓜ George V) One of Paris' oldest patisseries, Ladurée has been around since
1862 and first created the lighter-than-air,
ganache-filled macaron in the 1930s. Its
tearoom is the classiest spot to indulge on
the Champs. Alternatively, pick up some
pastries to go – from croissants to its trademark macarons, it's all quite heavenly. A
three-course children's menu costs €19.

★ Richer   BISTRO **€**
(Map p78; www.lericher.com; 2 rue Richer, 9e;
mains €17-21; ⊘noon-2.30pm & 7.30-10.30pm;

Ⓜ Poissonnière, Bonne Nouvelle) Run by the same team as across-the-street neighbour **L'Office** (Map p78; ☑ 01 47 70 67 31; www. office-resto.com; 3 rue Richer, 9e; 2-/3-course lunch menus €22/27, mains €23-29; ☺ noon-2pm & 7.30-10.30pm Mon-Fri), Richer's pared-back, exposed-brick decor is a smart setting for genius creations including smoked-duck-breast ravioli in miso broth, and quince-and-lime cheesecake for dessert. It doesn't take reservations, but it serves snacks and Chinese tea, and has a full bar (open until midnight). Fantastic value.

Mamou
BISTRO €€

(Map p78; ☑ 01 44 63 09 25; 42 rue Taitbout, 9e; 2-/3-course lunch menu €19/22, mains €21-26; ☺ noon-2.30pm Mon-Fri, 7.30-10.30pm Wed-Fri; Ⓜ Chaussée d'Antin) Fans of *haute cuisine* sans *haute* attitude should seek out this casual bistro by the Palais Garnier (p80). Chef Romain Lalu, who previously worked at Michelin-starred icons, runs the kitchen, and diners can expect all the playful flavour combos of a chef free to follow his whims, such as salmon gravlax with beetroot. There's an excellent natural wine selection. Reserve ahead.

Le Hide
FRENCH €€

(Map p90; ☑ 01 45 74 15 81; www.lehide.fr; 10 rue du Général Lanrezac, 17e; 2-/3-course menus €36/48; ☺ 6-10.30pm Mon-Sat; Ⓜ Charles de Gaulle–Étoile) A perpetual favourite, Le Hide is a tiny neighbourhood bistro serving scrumptious traditional French fare: snails, seared duck breast with celery purée and truffle oil, baked shoulder of lamb, and monkfish with *beurre blanc* (white sauce). Unsurprisingly, this place fills up faster than you can scamper down the steps of the nearby Arc de Triomphe (p77) – reserve well in advance.

Détour
FRENCH €€

(Map p78; ☑ 01 45 26 21 48; www.facebook. com/DetourRestaurant; 15 rue de la Tour des Dames, 9e; lunch menu €28, dinner menu €35-50; ☺ noon-1.30pm Wed-Sat, 7.30-10.30pm Tue-Sat; Ⓜ Trinité) As the name suggests, Adrien Cachot's 16-seat neobistro is off the beaten path, both literally and figuratively. Diners choose between just two options (meat or fish), leaving the rest in the hands of the highly original chef. Expect dishes like sweet carrots puréed with miso and topped with shaved Mimolette, or veal tartare with coffee vinaigrette and truffled egg cream.

Lasserre
GASTRONOMY €€€

(Map p90; ☑ 01 43 59 02 13; www.restaurant-lasserre.com; 17 av Franklin D Roosevelt, 8e; 3-course lunch menu €60, tasting menu €190, mains €85-130; ☺ noon-2pm Thu & Fri, 7-10pm Tue-Sat; Ⓜ Franklin D Roosevelt) Since 1942, this exceedingly elegant restaurant in the Triangle d'Or has hosted style icons, including Audrey Hepburn, and is still a superlative choice for a Michelin-starred meal to remember. A bellhop-attended lift (elevator), white-and-gold chandeliered decor, extraordinary retractable roof and flawless service set the stage for inspired creations such as roast blue lobster *à la Parisienne* with tarragon sauce. Observe the dress code.

🍴 Louvre & Les Halles

The dining scene in central Paris is excellent, and there is no shortage of choices, from eat-on-the-go bakeries to casual foodie favourites to Michelin-starred cuisine. By all means reserve a table at a big-name restaurant, but also try wandering market streets like rue Montorgueil or, for something different, sample ramen or udon at one of the innumerable Japanese noodle shops along rue St-Anne.

Fou de Pâtisserie
PATISSERIE €

(Map p94; 45 rue Montorgueil, 2e; ☺ 11am-8pm Mon-Fri, 10am-8pm Sat, 10am-6pm Sun; Ⓜ Les Halles, Sentier or RER Châtelet–Les Halles) Single-name patisseries scatter across the city, but for a greatest-hits range from its finest pastry chefs – Cyril Lignac, Christophe Adam (L'Éclair de Génie), Jacques Genin, Pierre Hermé and Philippe Conticini included – head to this one-stop concept shop. A Paris first, it's the brainchild of the publishers of pastry magazine *Fou de Pâtisserie* (also sold here).

Stohrer
PATISSERIE €

(Map p94; www.stohrer.fr; 51 rue Montorgueil, 2e; ☺ 7.30am-8.30pm; Ⓜ Étienne Marcel, Sentier) Opened in 1730 by Nicolas Stohrer, the Polish pastry chef of queen consort Marie Leszczyńska (wife of Louis XV), Stohrer's house-made specialities include its own inventions, the *baba au rhum* (rum-soaked sponge cake) and *puits d'amour* (caramel-topped, vanilla cream–filled puff pasty). The beautiful pastel murals were added in 1864 by Paul-Jacques-Aimé Baudry, who also decorated the Palais Garnier's Grand Foyer.

Salatim
ISRAELI €

(Map p94; ☑ 01 42 36 30 03; www.facebook.com/ SalatimParis; 15 rue des Jeûneurs, 2e; mains €8-16;

8.30am-4pm Sun, Mon & Fri, 8.30am-11pm Tue-Thu; M Sentier) Chipped plates and organised chaos reign at Yariv Berreby's overflowing sardine-tin-sized eatery. It takes its name from the Hebrew word for salad, and you'd be remiss not to try the eponymous mixed plate (eggplant caviar, pickled red cabbage, hummus etc). But don't overlook the sandwiches, *limonana* (iced mint lemonade) or Wednesday's chicken schnitzel. If you can't get a seat, the takeaway window beckons.

Hero
KOREAN €

(Map p120; ☑ 01 42 33 38 01; www.quixotic-projects. com; 289 rue St-Denis, 2e; cocktails €8-12, chicken €12.50-18; ☺ noon-2.30pm & 7-11pm Tue-Sun; M Strasbourg-St-Denis) The creative team behind Le Mary Céleste (p165) and Glass (Map p78; www.quixotic-projects.com/venue/glass; 7 rue Frochot, 9e; ☺ 7pm-4am Sun-Thu, to 5am Fri & Sat; M Pigalle) have also designed this unique drinking and dining space. Hero cooks up *yangnyeom* (crispy fried Korean chicken) in sweet and sour, garlicky or fiery *gochujang* sauces. Tasty salads and snacks pad out the menu, all to be washed down with a truly fabulous cocktail or shot of traditional Korean *soju* (distilled rice liquor).

Le Camion Qui Fume
BURGERS €

(Map p78; http://lecamionquifume.com; 168 rue Montmartre, 2e; burgers €9-11; ☺ noon-11pm Sun-Thu, to midnight Fri & Sat; M Grands Boulevards) The sedentary outpost of the famous food truck (https://lecamionquifume.com; burger & fries €13-15), Le Camion Qui Fume has staked a claim on lively rue Montmartre, and judging by the late-night crowds,

business is good. The Camion's claim to fame is gourmet burgers made with high-grade French beef and freshly baked buns, but you'll also appreciate the draught beer, friendly service and smothered chilli cheese fries.

★ Maison Maison
MEDITERRANEAN €€

(Map p94; ☑ 09 67 82 07 32; www.facebook.com/ maisonmaisonparis; opposite 16 quai du Louvre, 1er; 2-/3-course lunch menu €20/25, small plates €7-16; ☺ 10am-2am Wed-Sun, 6pm-2am Tue; M Pont Neuf) Halfway down the stairs by Pont Neuf is this wonderfully secret space beneath the *bouquinistes* (used-book sellers), where you can watch the *bateaux-mouches* (excursion boats) float by as you dine on artful creations such as beetroot and pink-grapefruit-cured bonito or gnocchi with white asparagus and broccoli pesto. In nice weather, cocktails at the glorious riverside terrace are not to be missed.

★ Uma
FUSION €€

(Map p94; ☑ 01 40 15 08 15; www.uma-restaurant. fr; 7 rue du 29 Juillet, 1er; 2-/3-course lunch €25/29, 7-/9-course dinner €67/82; ☺ 12.30-2.30pm & 7.30-10.30pm Mon-Sat; M Tuileries) Embark on a culinary voyage at Uma, where chef Lucas Felzine infuses contemporary French sensibilities with Nikkei: Peruvian-Japanese fusion food. The lunch menu comes with two exquisitely prepared starters (think ceviche with daikon radish or smoked duck with lychees); grab a table upstairs to spy on the open kitchen. Mezcal, pisco and vodka cocktails served until 1.30am. Reserve.

DON'T MISS

BEST BOULANGERIES
....

Poilâne (Map p158; ☑ 01 45 48 42 59; www.poilane.com; 8 rue du Cherche Midi, 6e; ☺ 7am-8.30pm Mon-Sat; M Sèvres-Babylone) Turning out distinctive wood-fired, rounded sourdough loaves since 1932.

Du Pain et des Idées (p140) Traditional bakery near Canal St-Martin with an exquisite 1889 interior.

Le Grenier à Pain (Map p100; www.legrenierapain.com; 38 rue des Abbesses, 18e; ☺ 7.30am-8pm Thu-Mon; M Abbesses) Perfect Montmartre picnic stop.

Pain Pain (Map p100; www.pain-pain.fr; 88 rue des Martyrs, 18e; sandwiches & pastries €2.20-5.25; ☺ 7am-8pm Tue-Sat, 7.30am-7.30pm Sun; M Abbesses) Fantastic breads and pastries from a 'Best Baguette in Paris' winner.

Huré (Map p120; ☑ 01 42 72 32 18; www.hure-createur.fr; 18 rue Rambuteau, 3e; pastries €1.50-5, sandwiches €5.50-9.50; ☺ 6.30am-8.30pm Tue-Sat; M Rambuteau) Contemporary bakery with a graffitied red-brick wall.

★ **Balagan** ISRAELI €€

(Map p94; ☑ 01 40 20 72 14; www.balagan-paris. com; 9 rue d'Alger, 1er; lunch menus from €24, mains €23-28; ⊘ noon-2pm Mon-Sat, 7-10pm daily; Ⓜ Tuileries) Cool navy blues and creamy diamond tiling contrast with the chic vibe at this Israeli hot spot. Come here to sample delectable small plates: deconstructed kebabs, crispy halloumi cheese with dates, onion confit Ashkenazi chicken liver or, our favourite, a spicy, succulent tuna tartare with fennel, cilantro, capers and pistachios. Mains, such as the sea bream black pasta, are just as praiseworthy.

Chez La Vieille FRENCH €€

(Map p94; ☑ 01 42 60 15 78; www.chezlavieille.fr; 1 rue Bailleul, 1er; mains €24-26; ⊘ noon-2.30pm Fri & Sat, 6-10.30pm Tue-Sat; Ⓜ Louvre–Rivoli) In salvaging this history-steeped eatery within a 16th-century building, star chef Daniel Rose pays homage to the former wholesale markets, the erstwhile legendary owner Adrienne Biasin (many of her timeless dishes have been updated, from terrines and rillettes to veal blanquette), and the soul of Parisian bistro cooking itself. Dine at the street-level bar or upstairs in the peacock-blue dining room.

Bambou SOUTHEAST ASIAN €€

(Map p94; ☑ 01 40 28 98 30; www.bambouparis. com; 23 rue des Jeûneurs, 2e; mains €18-29; ⊘ noon-2.30pm & 7-11pm, bar to 1am; ☑; Ⓜ Sentier) This spectacular Southeast Asian restaurant occupies a 500-sq metre former fabric warehouse, with vintage birdcages and a giant metal dragon adorning the main dining room, a downstairs billiards room/bar, a vast terrace and a Zen-like garden. Chef Antonin Bonnet's specialities include squid with black pepper and basil, and aromatic shrimp pad thai.

★ **Frenchie** BISTRO €€€

(Map p94; ☑ 01 40 39 96 19; www.frenchie-restaurant.com; 5 rue du Nil, 2e; 4-course lunch menu €45, 5-course dinner menu €74, with wine €175; ⊘ 6.30-11pm Mon-Fri, noon-2.30pm Thu & Fri in summer; Ⓜ Sentier) Tucked down an inconspicuous alley, this tiny bistro with wooden tables and old stone walls is always packed and for good reason: excellent-value dishes are modern, market-driven and prepared with unpretentious flair by French chef Gregory Marchand. Reserve well in advance or arrive early and pray for a cancellation (it does happen). Alternatively, head to Frenchie Bar à Vins (Map p94; 6 rue du Nil, 2e; dishes €9-23; ⊘ 6.30-11pm), located just next door.

No reservations at Frenchie Bar à Vins – write your name on the sheet of paper strung outside and wait for your name to be called.

During the day, swing by its adjacent deli-style takeaway outlet **Frenchie to Go** (Map p94; ☑ 01 40 26 23 43; www.frenchietogo. com; 9 rue du Nil, 2e; dishes €8-18; ⊘ 8.30am-4.30pm Mon-Fri, 9.30am-5.30pm Sat & Sun; ☎).

★ **Verjus** MODERN AMERICAN €€€

(Map p94; ☑ 01 42 97 54 40; http://verjusparis. com; 52 rue de Richelieu, 1er; menu €78, with wine €133; ⊘ 7-11pm Mon-Fri; Ⓜ Bourse, Pyramides) Opened by American duo Braden Perkins and Laura Adrian, Verjus was born out of their former clandestine supper club, the Hidden Kitchen. The restaurant builds on that tradition, offering a chance to sample some excellent, creative cuisine in a casual space. The tasting menu is a series of small plates, using ingredients sourced straight from producers. Reserve well in advance.

If you're just after an aperitif or a prelude to dinner, the downstairs **Verjus Bar à Vins** (Map p94; 47 rue de Montpensier, 1er; ⊘ 6-11pm Mon-Fri; Ⓜ Bourse, Pyramides) serves a handful of charcuterie and cheese plates. For lunch or a more casual dinner, don't miss nearby **Ellsworth** (Map p94; ☑ 01 42 60 59 66; www.ellsworthparis.com; 34 rue de Richelieu, 1er; 2-/3-course lunch menu €22/28, mains €12-30; ⊘ 12.15-2.15pm & 7-10.30pm Mon-Sat, 11.30am-3pm Sun; Ⓜ Pyramides), Verjus' sister restaurant.

Le Grand Véfour GASTRONOMY €€€

(Map p94; ☑ 01 42 96 56 27; www.grand-vefour. com; 17 rue de Beaujolais, 1er; lunch/dinner menu €115/315, mains €99-126; ⊘ noon-2.30pm & 7.30-10.30pm Mon Fri; Ⓜ Pyramides) Holding two Michelin stars, this 18th-century jewel on the northern edge of the Jardin du Palais Royal has been a dining favourite since 1784; the names ascribed to each table span Napoléon and Victor Hugo to Colette (who lived next door). Expect a voyage of discovery from chef Guy Martin in one of the most beautiful restaurants in the world.

✖ Montmartre & Northern Paris

Western Paris' culinary scene evolves slowly, but once you cross over that invisible border somewhere in the middle of the 9th *arrondissement,* it's a different world, with a constant flurry of new openings in south Pigalle, along Canal St-Martin and in the cosmopolitan 10e west of place de la République: young chefs here head up some of the most exciting dining venues in Paris today. *Rues commerçantes* (shopping streets) where food stalls set up on the pavement outside shops include rue des Martyrs and, in the 17e, rue Poncelet.

★ Du Pain et des Idées
BAKERY €

(Map p120; www.dupainetdesidees.com; 34 rue Yves Toudic, 10e; breads €1.20-7, pastries €2.50-6.50; ⊙6.45am-8pm Mon-Fri; M Jacques Bonsergent) This traditional bakery with an exquisite interior from 1889 is famed for its naturally leavened bread, orange-blossom brioche and *escargots* (scroll-like 'snails') in four sweet flavours. Its mini savoury *pavés* (breads) flavoured with Reblochon cheese and fig, or goat's cheese, sesame and honey, are perfect for lunch on the run. A wooden picnic table sits on the pavement outside.

Fric-Frac
SANDWICHES €

(Map p120; ☏01 42 85 87 34; www.fricfrac. fr; 79 quai de Valmy, 10e; sandwiches €11.50-15; ⊙noon-3pm & 7.30-11pm Tue-Fri, noon-11pm Sat & Sun; M Jacques Bonsergent) Traditional snack croque monsieur (toasted cheese-and-ham sandwich) gets a contemporary makeover at this quayside space. Gourmet Winnie (Crottin de Chavignol cheese, dried fruit, chestnut honey, chives and rosemary) and exotic Shaolin (king prawns, lemongrass paste, shiitake mushrooms and Thai basil) are among the creative combos served with salad and fries. Eat in or head to the canal.

Sunken Chip
FAST FOOD €

(Map p120; ☏01 53 26 74 46; www.thesunkenchip. com; 39 rue des Vinaigriers, 10e; fish & chips €12-14; ⊙noon-2.30pm & 7-10pm Mon-Fri, noon-3.30pm & 7-10pm Sat & Sun; M Jacques Bonsergent) It's hard to argue with the battered, fried goodness at this ideally located fish-and-chip shop near Canal St-Martin. Nothing is frozen here: it's all line-caught fish fresh from Brittany (three varieties per day), accompanied by thick-cut chips (peeled and chopped *sur place*), brown malt vinegar and minty mushy peas. Pickled eggs and onions are optional. Takeaway is available.

Ten Belles
CAFE €

(Map p120; www.tenbelles.com; 10 rue de la Grange aux Belles, 10e; dishes €3-7; ⊙8am-5pm Mon-Fri, 9am-6pm Sat & Sun; ☏; M Jacques Bonsergent) A stone's skim from the canal, this lively cafe with mezzanine seating and pavement tables overflows with regulars drinking Parisian-roasted Belleville Brûlerie coffee and dining on homemade soups, salads, filled focaccia, toasted sandwiches and tartines (open-faced sandwiches) as well as home-baked scones, cookies and cakes.

Holybelly 5
CAFE €

(Map p120; www.holybellycafe.com; 5 rue Lucien Sampaix, 10e; dishes €6.50-16.50; ⊙9am-5pm; ☏♪; M Jacques Bonsergent) Light-filled Holybelly's regulars never tire of its outstanding coffee, cuisine and service. Sarah Mouchot's breakfast pancakes (with eggs, bacon, bourbon butter and maple syrup) and chia-seed porridge are legendary, while her lunch menu features everything from beetroot gnocchi to slow-cooked pork belly with sweet potato purée. Wash them down with a Bloody Mary or Deck & Donohue beer. No reservations.

52 Faubourg St-Denis
CAFE, BISTRO €

(Map p120; www.faubourgstdenis.com; 52 rue du Faubourg St-Denis, 10e; mains €17-20; ⊙kitchen noon-2.30pm & 7-11pm, bar 8am-midnight, closed Aug; ☏; M Château d'Eau) With its polished concrete floors, stone walls and exposed ducting, this contemporary neighbourhood cafe-restaurant is a brilliant space to hang out in, from breakfast through to lunch, dinner and drinks. Creative cuisine might include tuna sashimi salad with beetroot jelly, egg-yolk ravioli with ham and mushrooms or lamb-shoulder pie with cinnamon fig jus. No reservations.

★ Le Verre Volé
BISTRO €

(Map p120; ☏01 48 03 17 34; www.leverrevole.fr; 67 rue de Lancry, 10e; mains €11-22, sandwiches €7.90; ⊙bistro 12.30-2.30pm & 7.30-11.30pm, wine bar 10am-2am; ☏; M Jacques Bonsergent) The tiny 'Stolen Glass' – a wine shop with a few tables – is one of Paris' most popular wine bar–restaurants, with outstanding natural and unfiltered wines and expert advice. Unpretentious, hearty *plats du jour* are excellent. Reserve in advance for meals, or stop by to pick up a gourmet sandwich (such as mustard-smoked burrata with garlic-pork sausage) and a bottle.

Le Petit Château d'Eau
FRENCH €

(Map p120; ☏01 42 08 72 81; 34 rue du Château d'Eau, 10e; mains €13.50-17.50; ⊙kitchen noon-3pm Mon, noon-3pm & 7-11.30pm Tue-Sat, bar 8am-3.30pm Mon, to 2am Tue-Fri, 9am-2am Sat; M Jacques Bonsergent) Scarcely changed in a century, with lemon- and lime-tiled walls, horseshoe-shaped zinc bar and burgundy banquettes, this neighbourhood treasure endures in defiance of the post-industrial co-working cafes that have sprung up around it. Classical cooking ranges from duck with honey sauce to beef entrecôte with roast garlic potatoes. You can also just stop by for a morning coffee or afternoon kir.

★ **Abattoir Végétal** VEGAN €
(Map p72; 61 rue Ramey, 18e; 3-course lunch menu €18, mains €13-16, Sun brunch adult/child €25/5; ⊙9am-6pm Tue & Wed, 9am-11.45pm Thu & Fri, 10am-11.45pm Sat, 10.30am 4.30pm Sun; ⑤⬆; Ⓜ Jules Joffrin) Mint-green wrought-iron chairs and tables line the pavement outside the 'plant slaughterhouse' (it occupies a former butcher shop), while the light, bright interior has bare-bulb downlights, distempered walls and greenery-filled hanging baskets. Each day there's a choice of three raw and cooked organic dishes per course, cold-pressed juices and craft beers from Parisian brewery BapBap.

L'affineur Affiné CHEESE €
(Map p78; ⬆09 66 94 22 15; www.laffineuraffine. com; 51 rue Notre Dame de Lorette, 9e; cheese platters €6.50-39, weekend brunch €20; ⊙kitchen noon-2.30pm Mon, noon-2.30pm & 5.30-9pm Wed-Sat, 11.30am-2pm & 5.30-7pm Sun, shop 10.30am-2.30pm Mon, to 9pm Wed-Sat, to 7pm Sun; Ⓜ St-Georges) With 120 French cheeses, this *fromagerie* (cheese shop) is a fabulous place to stock up and taste them at its on-site *bar à fromages* (cheese bar). Let the staff know your preferences and they'll prepare platters of two to 15 varieties, with charcuterie available as well as paired wines. Weekend brunch is a multicourse feast.

★ **Marrow** BISTRO €€
(Map p120; ⬆09 81 34 57 00; 128 rue du Faubourg St-Martin, 10e; mains €11-19; ⊙6-10pm Tue-Sat, bar to 2am, closed Aug; Ⓜ Gare de l'Est) Hay-smoked quail with peat vinaigrette, grilled octopus and fennel confit, and breaded roast bone marrow are among the adventurous flavour combinations from Hugo Blanchet, who partnered with mixologist Arthur Combe to open this neobistro that's taking Paris' foodie scene by storm. Rough stone walls, blonde wood tables and a small pavement terrace create a relaxed backdrop.

Abri BISTRO €€
(Map p78; ⬆01 83 97 00 00; 92 rue du Faubourg Poissonnière, 9e; lunch/dinner menus €26/49; ⊙12.30-2pm Mon, 12.30-2pm & 7.30-10pm Tue-Fri, 12.30-3pm & 7.30-10pm Sat; Ⓜ Poissonnière) It's no bigger than a shoebox and the decor is borderline nonexistent, but that's all part of the charm. Katsuaki Okiyama is a seriously talented chef with an artistic flair, and his surprise tasting menus (three courses at lunch, six at dinner) are exceptional. On Saturdays, a giant gourmet sandwich is all that's served for lunch. Reserve months in advance.

Le Bistrot de la Galette BISTRO €€
(Map p100; ⬆01 46 06 19 65; www.bistrotdela galette.fr; 102ter rue Lepic, 18e; mains €14-17; ⊙11am-10pm Tue-Sun; Ⓜ Abbesses, Lamarck–Caulaincourt) 🍴 In the shadow of Montmartre windmill Moulin de la Galette, this vintage fitted bistro is the creation of pastry chef Gilles Marchal, who uses locally hand-milled flour in *feuilletés* (delicately laminated pastry puffs) that accompany most dishes, such as *galette parisienne* (roast ham, sautéed mushrooms and Comté) and *galette provençale* (shredded roast lamb, aubergine, garlic and sun-dried tomatoes).

LOCAL KNOWLEDGE

RUE MONTORGUEIL

A splinter of the historic Les Halles, rue Montorgueil was once the oyster market and the final stop for seafood merchants hailing from the coast. Immortalised by Balzac in *La Comédie humaine,* this compelling strip still draws Parisians to eat and shop – it's lined with *fromageries* (cheese shops), cafes, and street stalls selling fruit, veg and other foodstuffs.

At No 78, **Au Rocher de Cancale** (Map p94; ⬆01 42 33 50 29; 78 rue Montorgueil, 2e; dozen oysters €20, seafood platter €30; ⊙8am-2am; Ⓜ Sentier, Les Halles, or RER Châtelet–Les Halles) is the last remaining legacy of the old oyster market. This 19th-century timber-lined restaurant first opened in 1804 at No 59. Feast on oysters and seafood from Cancale in Brittany as well as other *plats du jour* (daily dishes).

Bonhomie
TAPAS €€

(Map p120; ☎ 09 83 88 82 51; www.bonhomie.paris; 22 rue d'Enghien, 10e; tapas €9-23; ◷ kitchen 8.30am-10pm Mon-Fri, from 10.30am Sat & Sun, bar to 2am daily; ☒ Bonne Nouvelle) Good-time Bonhomie serves home-brewed beer and creative cocktails (Pina Sage, with sage-infused mezcal, almond liqueur and sherry; Bon Americano, with dry vermouth, bitters and rhubarb soda), but the biggest draw is the food. Small plates whipped up in its open kitchen might include mussels with gin sauce, beetroot tartare or scallops with trout roe and artichoke *crème*.

Le Bel Ordinaire
MEDITERRANEAN €€

(Map p78; ☎ 01 46 27 46 67; www.lebelordinaire. com; 54 rue de Paradis, 10e; 2-/3-course midweek lunch menus €18/22, dishes €5-15; ◷ kitchen noon-2.30pm & 7-10.30pm, bar 11am-11.30pm; ☏; ☒ Poissonnière) Floor-to-ceiling, wall-to-wall open shelves lined with bottles and gourmet products (hams, cheeses, shellfish, preserves, straw baskets of farm eggs and fresh fruit and vegetables) fire up your appetite for tapas-style small plates, such as tuna gravlax with grated apple, smoked burrata with sesame pesto, cuttlefish-ink risotto with blue cheese, at this contemporary wine bar. Over 300 winemakers are represented.

Belle Maison
SEAFOOD €€

(Map p78; ☎ 01 42 81 11 00; 4 rue de Navarin, 9e; mains lunch €11-14, dinner €22-26; ◷ 12.30-2pm & 7.30-10pm Tue-Sat; ☒ St-Georges) With a hip blue-and-white-tiled decor and happening SoPi (south Pigalle) location, Belle Maison is named after a small beach on Île d'Yeu, off France's Atlantic coast, where its owners holiday. Breton scallops with parsnip purée, line-caught whiting with Cévennes onion brûlée, Earl Grey–marinated mullet, and grilled mackerel with crispy wasabi root and miso caramel are among its seafood specialities.

Flesh
BARBECUE €€

(Map p100; ☎ 01 42 81 21 93; www.flesh-restaurant. com; 25 rue de Douai, 9e; mains €12-36; ◷ noon-10.30pm Mon-Fri, from 12.30pm Sat & Sun; ☒ Blanche) This trendy address with spartan interior and hip Pigalle crowd specialises in meats and seafood, charcoal-barbecued to smoky perfection. Angus beef, free-range chicken, suckling lamb and other quality meats and cuts come in two sizes – big or XL – in the company of garlic-spiked fries and some fantastic veggie dishes.

La Bulle
MODERN FRENCH €€

(Map p72; ☎ 01 85 15 21 58; www.restolabulle.fr; 48 rue Louis Blanc, 10e; 2-/3-course lunch menus €18.50/24, 3-/6-course dinner menus €36/55, mains €21-28; ◷ noon-3pm & 7.30-11.30pm Mon-Thu, noon-3.30pm & 7.30-11.45pm Fri & Sat; ☒ Louis Blanc) It's worth detouring a couple of blocks west of Canal St-Martin to this contemporary corner bistro with lime-green seating on a sunny pavement terrace. Creative *fait maison* (homemade) cuisine includes duck with chanterelles and pickled figs, wild boar with quince jus and spiced chocolate mousse with orange cake and cranberry sauce, accompanied by outstanding all-natural French wines.

Matière à.
MODERN FRENCH €€

(Map p120; ☎ 09 70 38 61 48; www.matiere-a.com; 15 rue Marie et Louise, 10e; 2-/3-course lunch menus €21/25, 4-course dinner menus €46; ◷ noon-2pm & 7.30-11pm Mon-Fri, 7.30-11pm Sat; ☒ Goncourt, Jacques Bonsergent) The short but stunning seasonal menu changes daily at this unique space. *Table d'hôte*–style dining (consisting of a set menu with a fixed price) for up to 14 is around a shared oak table lit by dozens of naked light bulbs. In the kitchen is young chef Anthony Courteille, who prides himself on doing everything *fait maison* (homemade), including bread and butter to die for. Reservations essential.

Aspic
BISTRO €€€

(Map p78; ☎ 09 82 49 30 98; 24 rue de la Tour d'Auvergne, 9e; 7-course tasting menu €65, with wine €100; ◷ 7.30-9.30pm Tue-Sat; ☒ Anvers) Chef Quentin Giroud ditched the high-flying world of finance for the stoves, and this small vintage-style space with a semi-open kitchen is testament to his conviction. Weekly changing, no-choice tasting menus feature inspired creations such as peppercorn pancetta with kaffir lime butter, warm octopus with cashew purée, skin-on plaice with popcorn capers, and celeriac with mustard shoots and grated raw cauliflower.

✗ Le Marais, Ménilmontant & Belleville

Packed with eateries of every imaginable type, Le Marais is one of Paris' premier dining neighbourhoods with many restaurants and bistros requiring a reservation. Despite the huge concentration of eating addresses, new openings pop up seemingly every week. Multi-ethnic Belleville is tops for Asian

farc. Some of the Bastille and Eastern Paris neighbourhood's best neobistros are within easy walking distance of Cimetière du Père Lachaise.

★ Jacques Genin
PASTRIES €

(Map p120; ☑ 01 45 77 29 01; www.jacquesgenin. fr; 133 rue de Turenne, 3e; pastries €9; ⊗ 11am-7pm Tue-Fri & Sun, to 7.30pm Sat; Ⓜ Oberkampf, Filles du Calvaire) Wildly creative *chocolatier* Jacques Genin is famed for his flavoured caramels, *pâtes de fruits* (fruit jellies) and exquisitely embossed *bonbons de chocolat* (chocolate sweets). But what completely steals the show at his elegant chocolate showroom is the *salon de dégustation* (aka tearoom), where you can order a pot of outrageously thick hot chocolate and legendary Genin *millefeuille*, assembled to order.

★ La Maison Plisson
CAFE, DELI €

(Map p120; www.lamaisonplisson.com; 93 bd Beaumarchais, 3e; mains €8-15; ⊗ 9.30am-9pm Mon, from 8.30am Tue-Sat, 9.30am 8pm Sun; Ⓜ St-Sébastien–Froissart) Framed by glass-canopied wrought-iron girders, this gourmand's dream includes a covered-market-style, terrazzo-floored food hall filled with exquisite, mostly French produce: meat, vegetables, cheese, wine, chocolate, jams, freshly baked breads and much more. If your appetite's whet, its cafe, opening to twin terraces, serves charcuterie, foie gras and cheese planks, bountiful salads and delicacies such as olive-oil-marinated, Noilly Prat–flambéed sardines.

★ Breizh Café
CRÊPES €

(Map p120; ☑ 01 42 72 13 77; www.breizhcafe.com; 109 rue Vieille du Temple, 3e; crêpes & galettes €6.80-18.80; ⊗ 11.30am-11pm Mon-Sat, to 10pm Sun; Ⓜ St-Sébastien–Froissart) Everything at the Breizh ('Breton' in Breton) is 100% authentic, including its organic-flour crêpes and *galettes* (savoury buckwheat crêpes) that top many Parisians' lists for the best in the city. Other specialities include Cancale oysters and 20 types of cider. Tables are limited and there's often a wait; book ahead or try its deli, L'Épicerie (Map p120; ☑ 01 42 71 39 44; 111 rue Vieille du Temple, 3e; crêpes & galettes €6.80-18.80; ⊗ 11.30am-10pm), next door.

L'As du Fallafel
FELAFEL €

(Map p120; 34 rue des Rosiers, 4e; takeaway €5.50-8.50, mains €12-18; ⊗ noon-midnight Sun-Thu, to 4pm Fri; ⚐; Ⓜ St-Paul) The lunchtime queue stretching halfway down the street from this place says it all. This Parisian favourite, 100% worth the inevitable wait, is the address for kosher, perfectly deep-fried falafel (chickpea balls) and turkey or lamb shawarma sandwiches. Do as every Parisian does and get them to take away.

La Cantine de Merci
FRENCH €

(Map p120; ☑ 01 42 77 00 33; www.merci-merci. com; 111 bd Beaumarchais, 3e; mains €16-21; ⊗ 10am-7.30pm; Ⓜ St-Sébastien–Froissart) Adjacent to the designer kitchen gadgets in the homewares section of hip concept store Merci (p178), this chic canteen serves zesty salads, seasonal soups, rustic risottos and savoury tarts along with a creative array of cakes. Industrial downlights are suspended over the tables, while big picture windows frame a leafy green courtyard garden.

Okomusu
JAPANESE €

(Map p120; ☑ 01 57 40 97 27; www.okomusu.com; 11 rue Charlot, 3e; mains €11-18; ⊗ 7.30 10pm Tue-Thu, noon-2.30pm & 7.30-10pm Fri & Sat, noon-2.30pm Sun; Ⓜ St-Sébastien–Froissart) Once full – which happens within seconds of chef Hiroko Tabuchi opening her *table d'hôte* – all eyes are on the chef as she deftly whips up her speciality *okonomiyaki* (a wheat-flour pancake with cabbage, chives, ginger, dried fish shavings and pork, prawn or squid), while hungry diners sit at the bar. Vegetarians can order a nonmeat version.

★ Au Passage
BISTRO €€

(Map p120; ☑ 01 43 55 07 52; www.restaurant-aupassage.fr; 1bis passage St-Sébastien, 11e; small plates €9-18, meats to share €25-70; ⊗ 7-10.30pm Tue-Sat; Ⓜ St-Sébastien-Froissart) Rising-star chefs continue to make their name at this *petit bar de quartier* (little neighbourhood bar). Choose from a good-value, uncomplicated selection of *petites assiettes* (small tapas-style plates) of cold meats, raw or cooked fish, vegetables and so on, and larger meat dishes such as slow-roasted lamb shoulder or *côte de bœuf* (rib steak) to share. Reservations are essential.

Bøti
BISTRO €€

(Map p72; ☑ 06 65 49 12 29; 74 bd de Ménilmontant, 20e; 2-/3-course menus lunch €13/16, dinner €22/25; ⊗ noon-3pm & 7-11pm Tue-Sat; Ⓜ Père Lachaise) There's always at least one vegetarian option (such as roast beetroot and purple-carrot crumble) on the small but superb weekly menu at this welcoming little stone-walled bistro footsteps from Père Lachaise, along with meat and poultry dishes like confit spiced lamb shoulder or duck terrine with pickled lotus root. Wines are excellent; artisanal beers include a quinoa-based gluten-free brew. Cash only.

La Cave de l'Insolite
BISTRO €€

(Map p120; ☑ 01 53 36 08 33; www.lacavedel insolite.fr; 30 rue de la Folie Méricourt, 11e; 2-/3-course midweek lunch menus €18/20, mains €18-21; ⊙ noon-2.30pm & 7.30-10.30pm Tue-Sat, to 10pm Sun; ☎; M St-Ambroise, Parmentier) Brothers Axel and Arnaud, who have worked at some of Paris' top addresses, run this rustic-chic wine bar with barrels, timber tables and a wood-burning stove. Duck pâté with cider jelly, haddock rillettes with lime and endive confit, and beef with mushroom and sweetbread sauce are among the seasonal dishes; its 100-plus hand-harvested wines come from small-scale French vineyards.

Robert et Louise
FRENCH €€

(Map p120; ☑ 01 42 78 55 89; www.robertetlouise. com; 64 rue Vieille du Temple, 4e; 2-course lunch menus €14, mains €13-26; ⊙ 7-11pm Tue & Wed, noon-3pm & 7-11pm Thu & Fri, noon-11pm Sat & Sun; M Rambuteau) Going strong since 1958, this wonderfully convivial 'country inn' with red gingham curtains and rustic timber beams offers simple and inexpensive French food, including *côte de bœuf* (side of beef for two or three people) cooked on an open fire. Arrive early to snag the farmhouse table next to the fireplace – the makings of a real jolly Rabelaisian evening.

Le Clown Bar
FRENCH €€

(Map p120; ☑ 01 43 55 87 35; www.clown-bar-paris. com; 114 rue Amelot, 11e; mains €28-34; ⊙ kitchen noon-2.30pm & 7-10.30pm Wed-Sun, bar 8am-2am; M Filles du Calvaire) The former staff dining room of the city's winter circus, the 1852-built Cirque d'Hiver, is a historic monument with colourful clown-themed ceramics and mosaics, painted glass ceilings and its original zinc bar. Modern French cuisine spans line-caught whiting with whelks to Mesquer pigeon stuffed with anchovies. The pavement terrace gets packed out on sunny days.

Pierre Sang
FRENCH €€

(Map p120; ☑ 09 67 31 96 80; www.pierresang.com; 55 rue Oberkampf, 11e; 2-/3-/5-course lunch menus €20/25/35, 5-course dinner menus €39; ⊙ noon, 7pm & 9.30pm; ☞; M Parmentier, Oberkampf) At *Top Chef* finalist Pierre Sang's flagship, modern French cuisine has a strong fusion lilt thanks to his French and Korean background, and the vibe is casual and fun. He

also has a neighbouring French–Korean *atelier* annex at 6 rue Gambey, and experimental 'signature' restaurant at 8 rue Gambey. Kids under eight years eat free here and at the *atelier*.

Derrière
FRENCH €€

(Map p120; ☑ 01 44 61 91 95; www.derriere-resto.com; 69 rue des Gravilliers, 3e; 2-/3-course lunch menus €25/30, mains €22-38, Sun brunch €38, with Champagne €56; ⊙ noon-2.30pm & 7.30-11.30pm Mon-Sat, noon-4pm & 7.30-11.30pm Sun; M Arts et Métiers) Play table tennis, sit on the side of the bed, glass of Champers in hand, or lounge between bookcases at this apartment-style restaurant in a beautiful courtyard (idyllic for lunch in the sunshine). Chilled vibe aside, Derrière ('behind') is deadly serious in the kitchen. Classic French bistro dishes and more inventive creations are excellent, as is Sunday's buffet brunch.

Istr
SEAFOOD, BRETON €€

(Map p120; ☑ 01 43 56 81 25; 41 rue Notre Dame de Nazareth, 3e; half-dozen oysters €12-20, mains €13-25, 2-/3-course lunch menus €19/24; ⊙ kitchen noon-2.30pm & 6-10pm Tue-Fri, 6-11pm Sat, bar to 2am Tue-Sat; M Temple) Fabulously patterned wallpaper and a gleaming zinc bar set the stage for innovative Breton-inspired cuisine. The region's famed *istr* ('oyster' in Breton) is the star of the show here, served plain, as a Bloody Mary–style shot, or with sauces such as soy and ginger. Other creations include buckwheat chips with smoked haddock fishcakes. It doubles as a rocking bar.

Anahi
SOUTH AMERICAN €€

(Map p120; ☑ 01 83 81 38 00; www.anahi-paris. com; 49 rue Volta, 3e; mains €16-39, 2-/3-course midweek lunch menus €29/35; ⊙ 7-11pm Sun-Thu, to 11.30pm Fri & Sat; M Temple) History infuses Anahi, a 1920s butcher that became an '80s fashion-magnet steakhouse and is now overseen by rare meat importer and restaurateur Riccardo Giraudi. Original features include its glorious art deco painted-glass ceiling, reflected in soaring mirrored columns. Premium charcoal-grilled steaks are the house speciality; other South American dishes include black Angus empanadas, wagyu quesadillas, Kagoshima tostadas and sea bass ceviche.

Brasserie Bofinger
BRASSERIE €€

(Map p120; ☑ 01 42 72 87 82; www.bofinger paris.com; 5-7 rue de la Bastille, 4e; 2-/3-course menus €26/32, mains €19.50-29.50; ⊙ noon-3pm & 6.30pm-midnight Mon-Fri, noon-3.30pm &

LOCAL KNOWLEDGE

BEST VEGETARIAN & VEGAN

••

Abattoir Végétal (p141) Plant-filled vegan cafe in Montmartre.

Le Potager de Charlotte (Map p78; ☑ 01 44 65 09 63; www.lepotagerdecharlotte.fr; 12 rue de la Tour d'Auvergne, 9e; mains €14.50-16, Sunday brunch €29; ⊙ 7-10.30pm Wed & Thu, noon-2.30pm & 7-10.30pm Fri & Sat, 11am-3pm Sun; ☑; Ⓜ Cadet) Gourmet vegan restaurant.

Soul Kitchen (Map p72; ☑ 01 71 37 99 95; 33 rue Lamarck, 18e; 3-course lunch menus €14, snacks €3-4.50; ⊙ 8.30am-6pm Tue-Fri, 10am-6.30pm Sat & Sun; 🛜☑♿; Ⓜ Lamarck–Caulaincourt) Market-driven vegetarian dishes.

Raw Cakes (Map p72; ☑ 09 86 12 73 48; 83 rue Daguerre, 14e; mains €10-15; ⊙ 10am-8pm Mon, 11am-10pm Tue-Thu, 10am-4pm Fri, noon-7pm Sun; Ⓜ Gaîté) Not only cakes but yes, it's all raw.

Bob's Juice Bar (Map p120; ☑ 09 50 06 36 18; www.bobsjuicebar.com; 15 rue Lucien Sampaix, 10e; dishes €3.50-6, pastries €1.75-3; ⊙ 8am-3pm Mon-Fri, 8.30am-4pm Sat; ☑; Ⓜ Jacques Bonsergent) Pioneering Parisian veggie address.

Gentle Gourmet Café (Map p126; ☑ 01 43 43 48 49; https://gentlegourmet.fr; 24 bd de la Bastille, 12e; 2-/3-course lunch menu €23/30, mains €21-25; ⊙ noon-2.30pm & 6.30-10pm Tue-Sun; 🛜☑♿; Ⓜ Quai de la Rapée, Bastille) 🍃 All of the dishes are vegan and most are organic at this light-filled cafe.

6.30pm-midnight Sat, noon-11pm Sun; 🛜♿; Ⓜ Bastille) Founded in 1864, Bofinger is reputedly Paris' oldest brasserie, though its polished art nouveau brass, glass and mirrors indicate redecoration a few decades later. Alsatian-inspired specialities include six kinds of *choucroute* (sauerkraut), along with oysters (€11 to €35 per half-dozen) and magnificent seafood platters (€30 to €140). Ask for a seat downstairs beneath the *coupole* (stained-glass dome).

🍴 Bastille & Eastern Paris

Bastille dining tends to swing between a highly lauded group of up-and-coming chefs, who run the hip new neobistros that have reinspired Parisian cooking, and the die-hard traditionalists, who rarely venture beyond the much-loved standards of French cuisine. The neighbourhood caters to all budgets, tastes and time constraints – along with the area's sensational markets, speciality food shops and *boulangeries*, you'll find gourmet burger, sandwich and pizza addresses in the mix too.

CheZaline   SANDWICHES €
(Map p120; 85 rue de la Roquette, 11e; sandwiches €5.50-8.50; ⊙ 11am-5.30pm Mon-Fri; Ⓜ Voltaire) A former horse-meat butcher's shop (*chevaline*, hence the spin on the name; look for the gold horse head above the door) is now a fabulous deli for baguettes filled with ingredients such

as Prince de Paris ham and housemade garlic pesto, salads and homemade terrines. There's a handful of seats (and plenty of parks nearby). Prepare to queue at lunchtime.

Mokonuts   CAFE €
(Map p126; ☑ 09 80 81 82 85; 5 rue St-Bernard, 11e; dishes €2-3.50, mains €7-18; ⊙ 8.45am-6pm Mon-Fri, closed Aug; 🛜☑; Ⓜ Faidherbe-Chaligny) Much-loved hole-in-the-wall Mokonuts, with a beautiful mosaic-tiled floor, makes a cosy refuge for snacks like flourless chocolate layer cake, clementine almond cake and pecan pie. Other treats include white-chocolate and roasted-almond cookies, while sea bream with chickpeas and capers, and lamb shoulder with hummus are among the all-organic lunchtime mains. Natural wines and craft beers feature on the drinks list.

Café Mirabelle   CAFE €
(Map p72; https://cafemirabelleparis.wixsite.com; 16 rue la Vacquerie, 11e; dishes €2-7.50; ⊙ 8am-6pm Wed-Fri, from 9am Sat & Sun; 🛜; Ⓜ Philippe Auguste, Voltaire) A black-and-white stencilled outline of Paris' skyline stretches across one wall of this charming cafe, whose home-baked treats include custard- and banana-filled croissants, Grand Marnier gateau and lemon meringue pie. Its *gianduja* (choc-hazelnut) hot chocolate is a winter warmer; in summer, cool down with a freshly squeezed juice. Granola with seasonal berries makes a great start to the day.

Nanina
CHEESE €

(Map p120; ☑ 06 12 67 04 76; 24bis rue Basfroi, 11e; 3-course lunch menu €11.50, dishes €2.50-9; ⊙ 10am-8.30pm Mon-Thu, to 10pm Fri & Sat; Ⓜ Voltaire) Nanina's creamy mozzarella and ricotta, made from Auvergne-sourced buffalo milk and handmade here on the premises, supply some of Paris' most prestigious restaurants. You can taste the cheeses here on their own, on focaccia bread or as part of a lunch *menu* that might include lasagne or pasta. Staff are happy to show you around and explain the cheese-making process.

★ Le Servan
BISTRO €€

(Map p120; ☑ 01 55 28 51 82; http://leservan. com; 32 rue St-Maur, 11e; 3-course lunch menu €27, mains €25-38; ⊙ 7.30-10.30pm Mon, noon-2.30pm & 7.30-10.30pm Tue-Fri; Ⓜ Voltaire, Rue St-Maur, Père Lachaise) Ornate cream-coloured ceilings with moulded cornices and pastel murals, huge windows and wooden floors give this neighbourhood neobistro near Père Lachaise a light, airy feel on even the greyest Parisian day. Sweetbread wontons, cockles with chilli and sweet basil, and roast pigeon with tamarind jus are among the inventive creations on the daily changing menu. Reserve to avoid missing out.

Buffet
BISTRO €€

(Map p126; ☑ 01 83 89 63 82; www.restaurantbuffet. fr; 8 rue de la Main d'Or, 11e; 2-/3-course lunch menu €16.50/19, small plates €5-15; ⊙ 7.30-11pm Tue, noon-2.30pm & 7.30-11pm Wed-Sat; Ⓜ Ledru-Rollin) Tucked away on a charming Bastille backstreet behind a mulberry-coloured façade, Buffet has burgundy leather seating, wooden tables, mirrors and terrazzo floors. Despite its name, there's no smorgasbord but a short daily changing blackboard menu of bistro dishes like lemon sole with hand-cut chips, lamb shoulder with prunes, and chestnut and chocolate mousse that belies the complexity of the cooking.

Les Déserteurs
FRENCH €€

(Map p126; ☑ 01 48 06 95 85; 46 rue Trousseau, 11e; menus €30-49; ⊙ 7.30-9.45pm Tue, 12.30-2pm & 7.30-9.45pm Wed-Sat; Ⓜ Ledru-Rollin) Deserting their previous workplace, Les Déserteurs' chef Daniel Baratier and sommelier Alexandre Céret have combined their talents here at their own premises. In a contemporary space with high blonde oak tables, grey-painted walls and open kitchen, they serve exquisitely presented multicourse *menus* (no à la carte) with an emphasis on market-sourced vegetables, complemented by small-scale, pan-European wines.

Le Bistrot Paul Bert
BISTRO €€

(Map p126; ☑ 01 43 72 24 01; 18 rue Paul Bert, 11e; 2-/3-course lunch/dinner menu €19/41; ⊙ noon-2pm & 7.30-11pm Tue-Sat, closed Aug; Ⓜ Faidherbe-Chaligny) When food writers list Paris' best bistros, Paul Bert's name consistently pops up. The timeless vintage decor and classic dishes such as *steak-frites* (steak and chips) and hazelnut-cream Paris-Brest pastry reward those booking ahead. Look for its siblings in the same street: **L'Écailler du Bistrot** (Map p126; ☑ 01 43 72 76 77; 22 rue Paul Bert, 11e; oysters per half-dozen €9-20, mains €32-46, seafood platters per person from €40; ⊙ noon-2.30pm & 7.30-11pm Tue-Sat) for seafood; **La Cave Paul Bert** (Map p126; ☑ 01 58 53 50 92; 16 rue Paul Bert, 11e; ⊙ noon-midnight, kitchen noon-2pm & 7.30-11.30pm), a wine bar with small plates; and **Le 6 Paul Bert** (Map p126; ☑ 01 43 79 14 32; www.le6paulbert.com; 6 rue Paul Bert, 12e; 6-course menu €60, mains €24-35; ⊙ noon-2pm & 7.30-11pm Tue-Sat) for modern cuisine.

★ Septime
GASTRONOMY €€€

(Map p120; ☑ 01 43 67 38 29; www.septime-charonne.fr; 80 rue de Charonne, 11e; 4-course lunch menu with/without wine €70/42, 7-course dinner menu with/without wine €135/80; ⊙ 7.30-10pm Mon, 12.15-2pm & 7.30-10pm Tue-Fri; Ⓜ Charonne) The alchemists in Bertrand Grébaut's Michelin-starred kitchen produce truly beautiful creations, served by blue-aproned waitstaff. The menu reads like an obscure shopping list: each dish is a mere listing of three ingredients, while the mystery *carte blanche* dinner *menu* puts you in the hands of the innovative chef. Reservations require planning and perseverance – book at least three weeks in advance.

Its nearby wine bar **Septime La Cave** (Map p120; www.septime-charonne.fr; 3 rue Basfroi, 11e; ⊙ 4-11pm; Ⓜ Charonne) is ideal for a pre- or post-meal drink. For stunning seafood tapas, its sister restaurant **Clamato** (Map p120; http://clamato-charonne.fr; 80 rue de Charonne, 11e; tapas €8-16, dozen oysters €18-48; ⊙ 7-11pm Wed-Fri, from noon Sat & Sun; Ⓜ Charonne) is right next door.

Le Chardenoux
BISTRO €€€

(Map p126; ☑ 01 43 71 49 52; www.restaurantle chardenoux.com; 1 rue Jules Vallès, 11e; 2-/3-course lunch menus €25/30, 3-course dinner menu €41; ⊙ noon-2.30pm & 7-11pm; Ⓜ Charonne) Dating from 1908, this picture-perfect Parisian bistro with a polished-timber façade, patterned tiled floors, marble-topped tables, mirrored walls, bevelled frosted-glass screens and a centrepiece zinc bar is a listed historic monument. Star chef Cyril Lignac recreates classical French dishes: Aubrac beef tartare and *frites* (fries), chicken in white wine, and brioche toast with poached pears and hazelnut caramel.

It's across the road from Lignac's combined chocolate boutique and tearoom **La Chocolaterie Cyril Lignac** (Map p126; www.cyrillignac.com; 25 rue Chanzy, 11e; pastries €1.40-4; ☺8am-7pm; ⓂCharonne), to the east, and from his bakery/pastry shop **La Pâtisserie** (Map p126; www.gourmand-croquant.com; 24 rue Paul Bert, 11e; pastries €3-6.50; ☺7am-7pm Mon, to 8pm Tue-Sun; ⓂCharonne, Faidherbe-Chaligny), to the south.

Table FRENCH €€€
(Map p126; ☑01 43 43 12 26; www.tablerestaurant.fr; 3 rue de Prague, 12e; 2-/3-course lunch menu €25/29, mains €39-69; ☺noon-3pm & 7.45-10.30pm Mon-Fri, 7.30-10pm Sat; ⓂLedru-Rollin) Unusual and rare artisan products sourced from all over France decide the day's menu at Michelin-starred Table, styled like a contemporary *table d'hôte*, with diners seated at the curvaceous zinc bar while talented food writer and chef Bruno Verjus performs in his open kitchen. Delicious meats are spit-roasted on the rotisserie and Verjus delights in talking food with diners.

✖ The Islands

Île St-Louis is a pleasant if pricey and often touristy place to dine. Otherwise barren of decent eating places, Île de la Cité has a handful of lovely addresses on its western tip.

Self-caterers will find a couple of *fromageries*, chocolate shops and a small grocery store on rue St-Louis en l'Île, 4e.

★Berthillon ICE CREAM €
(Map p130; www.berthillon.fr; 29-31 rue St-Louis en l'Île, 4e; 1/2/3/4 scoops takeaway €3/4.50/6/7.50; ☺10am-8pm Wed-Sun, closed mid-Feb–early Mar & Aug; ⓂPont Marie) Founded here in 1954, this esteemed *glacier* (ice-cream maker) is still run by the same family today. Its 70-plus all-natural, chemical-free flavours include fruit sorbets (pink grapefruit, raspberry and rose) and richer ice creams made from fresh milk and eggs (salted caramel, candied Ardèche chestnuts, Armagnac and prunes, gingerbread, liquorice, praline and pine

kernels). Watch for tempting new seasonal flavours.

★Café Saint Régis CAFE €
(Map p130; ☑01 43 54 59 41; www.cafesaintregisparis.com; 6 rue Jean du Bellay, 4e; breakfast & snacks €3.50-15.50, mains €18-32; ☺6.30am-2am, kitchen 8am-midnight; ☞; ⓂPont Marie) Waiters in long white aprons, a ceramic-tiled interior and retro vintage decor make hip Le Saint Régis a deliciously Parisian hang-out any time of day – for eating or drinking. From breakfast pastries, organic eggs and bowls of fruit-peppered granola to mid-morning pancakes or waffles, lunchtime salads, burgers, dusk-time oysters and late-night cocktails, it is the hobnobbing hot spot on the islands.

Le Caveau du Palais MODERN FRENCH €€
(Map p130; ☑01 43 26 04 28; www.caveaudupalais.fr; 19 place Dauphine, 1er; mains €20-27; ☺noon-2.30pm & 7-10pm; ⓂPont Neuf) Even when the western Île de la Cité shows few other signs of life, the Caveau's half-timbered dining areas and (weather permitting) alfresco terrace are packed with diners tucking into bountiful fresh fare: pan-seared scallops with artichokes, grilled codfish with smoked haddock cream and coriander-spiced cauliflower, or vegetable risotto.

More informal dishes are served at its adjacent wine bar, **Le Bar du Caveau** (Map p130; www.barducaveau.fr; 17 place Dauphine, 1er; ☺bar 8am-6.30pm Mon-Fri, kitchen noon-4pm Mon-Fri).

✖ Latin Quarter

From chandelier-lit palaces loaded with history to cheap-eat student haunts, the 5e *arrondissement* caters to every budget and culinary taste. Rue Mouffetard is famed for its food market and food shops, though you'll have to trek down side streets for the neighbourhood's best meals. Other busy eat streets lined with cafes, restaurants and takeaway joints include rue St-Séverin, rue de la Harpe and delightfully car-free rue du Pot de Fer.

★Café de la Nouvelle Mairie CAFE €
(Map p134; ☑01 44 07 04 41; 19 rue des Fossés St-Jacques, 5e; mains €10-20; ☺8am-midnight Mon-Fri, kitchen noon-2.30pm & 8-10.30pm Mon-Thu, 8-10pm Fri; ⓂCardinal Lemoine) Shhhh... just around the corner from the Panthéon (p103) but hidden away on a small, fountained square, this hybrid cafe-restaurant

BRUNCH IN LE MARAIS

Café Pinson (Map p120; ☎ 09 83 82 53 53; www.cafepinson.fr; 6 rue du Forez, 3e; 2-course lunch menus €17.50, mains €13.50-14.50, Sun brunch €27; ⊘ 9am-10pm Mon-Fri, from 10am Sat, noon-6pm Sun; ☎ ⁊; Ⓜ Filles du Calvaire) Tucked down a narrow Haut Marais side street, this stylish cafe with an interior by celebrity designer Dorothée Meilichzon sees a fashionable lunchtime crowd flock for its organic vegetarian and vegan dishes such as beetroot-stuffed squash with vegetable crumble and chia pudding with cranberry sauce. Freshly squeezed juices are excellent, as is Sunday brunch (noon and 2.30pm).

Café Méricourt (Map p120; www.cafemericourt.com; 22 rue de la Folie Méricourt, 11e; 2-course midweek lunch menus €15, mains €8.50-14; ⊘ 9am-6pm; ☎ ⁊; Ⓜ St-Ambroise) With a pretty peppermint-green façade and airy, plant-filled interior, Méricourt is a delightful backstreet find. Breakfast (honey-ricotta pancakes with roasted pineapple, spinach-wrapped eggs with feta, congee rice porridge) is served until 3pm, with lunch options from 11am. Parisian-roasted coffee, homemade ginger beer and lemonade, natural wines and Bloody Marys and Mimosas make it easy to while away a few hours.

Biglove Caffè (Map p120; www.bigmammagroup.com; 30 rue Debelleyme, 3e; pizza & pasta €13-18, weekend brunch €7-14; ⊘ noon-2.30pm & 7-10.30pm Mon-Fri, 9am-4.30pm & 7-10.30pm Sat & Sun; Ⓜ Filles du Calvaire) Weekend brunch is the big event at this Italian-run cafe: expect blackberry pancakes with ricotta and maple syrup; avocado toast with prosciutto and lemon; eggs Benedict with homemade brioche and feta. Throughout the week, drop by for wood-fired, gluten-free pizzas (black truffle and mushroom or burrata, pesto and potato) and regularly changing pastas. No reservations.

Goku (Map p120; ☎ 01 85 15 28 11; www.gokuasiancanteen.fr; 27 bd du Temple, 3e; tapas €4-9, mains €16-17, Sun brunch €25; ⊘ noon-3pm & 7-11pm Tue-Sat, noon-7pm Sun; Ⓜ Oberkampf, République) Fronted by a bamboo-fringed terrace, Goku is a sizzling address for pan-Asian flavours. It serves everything from tapas-style *kimchi* (Korean fermented vegetables), sake- and ginger-marinated yakitori skewers and coconut-coated chicken satay through to mains such as Bulgogi grilled pork with sesame and coriander dressing. Sunday's Asian brunch is hugely popular.

Soya (Map p120; ☎ 01 85 15 27 84; www.soya-cantine-bio.fr; 20 rue de la Pierre Levée, 11e; 2-/3-course weekday lunch menus €19/23, mains €16-20, weekend brunch €29; ⊘ 7-11pm Tue, noon-4pm & 7-11pm Wed-Sat, 11.30am-4pm Sun; ⁊; Ⓜ Goncourt) In an industrial *atelier* (workshop) with bare cement, metal columns and big windows, Soya is a 100% *cantine bio* (organic eatery) in what was once a staunchly working-class district. All dishes here are vegetarian and many are vegan, such as shiitake and ginger garam masala curry or couscous, quinoa and candied grapes. On weekends, the brunch buffet brims with fresh salads.

and wine bar is a tip-top neighbourhood secret, serving natural wines by the glass and delicious seasonal bistro fare from oysters and ribs (*à la française*) to grilled lamb sausage over lentils. It takes reservations for dinner but not lunch – arrive early.

★**OnoPoké**   HAWAIIAN €
(Map p134; ☎ 09 82 29 81 87; www.onopoke.fr; 167 rue St-Jacques, 5e; mains €9.50-15; ⊘ noon-5pm Mon & Tue, noon-5pm & 7.30-9.30pm Wed, noon-9.30pm Thu & Fri, 12.30-9.30pm Sat; Ⓜ Cardinal Lemoine) Head here for creative beans, grains, pulses and veg topped with raw or smoked fish (tuna, salmon, white fish) and your cho-

sen sprinkling of fried onions, chilli, sunflower seeds or wasabi-laced sesame seeds. Always rammed with cent-smart students from the neighbouring Sorbonne, OnoPoké cooks turbo-sized salad bowls inspired by traditional Hawaiian *poke* (raw diced fish with sushi rice) in a hip, laid-back space.

★**La Bête Noire**   MEDITERRANEAN €
(Map p158; ☎ 06 15 22 73 61; www.facebook.com/labetenoireparis; 58 rue Henri Barbusse, 5e; mains lunch €12-15, dinner €20, brunch €25; ⊘ 8am-5pm Tue, 8am-11pm Wed-Fri, 9.30am-5.30pm Sat & Sun; ☎ ⁊; Ⓜ RER Port Royal) Funky music and a small, fashionably minimalist interior with open kitchen ensure bags of soul at

this off-the-radar *'cantine gastronomique'*, a showcase for the sensational home cooking of passionate chef-owner Maria. Inspired by her Russian-Maltese heritage, she cooks just one meat and one vegetarian dish daily using seasonal products sourced from local farmers and small producers, washed down with Italian wine.

Croq' Fac
SANDWICHES €

(Map p134; 160 rue St-Jacques, 5e; sandwich menu €5.50; ⊙8am-7pm Mon-Sat; Ⓜ Cardinal Lemoine) Latin Quarter students pack out this *sandwicherie* (sandwich bar) at lunchtime and for good reason. Delicious, made-to-measure sandwiches embrace dozens of bread types (wraps, ciabatta, panini, bagels, *pan bagnat* etc) and fillings (the world's your oyster). Arrive before noon to ensure a table – inside or on the people-watching pavement terrace – or takeaway.

Les Papilles
BISTRO €€

(Map p158; ☑ 01 43 25 20 79; www.lespapillesparis. fr; 30 rue Gay Lussac, 5e; 2-/4-course menus €28/35; ⊙noon-2pm & 7-10.30pm Tue-Sat; Ⓜ Raspail or RER Luxembourg) This hybrid bistro, wine cellar and *épicerie* (specialist grocer) with a sunflower-yellow façade is one of those fabulous Parisian dining experiences. Meals are served at simply dressed tables wedged beneath bottle-lined walls, and fare is market driven: each weekday cooks up a different *marmite du marché* (market casserole). But what really sets it apart is its exceptional wine list.

Le Pré Verre
BISTRO €€

(Map p134; ☑ 01 43 54 59 47; www.lepreverre.com; 8 rue Thénard, 5e; lunch menu €16.50, mains €18-21; ⊙noon-2pm & 7.30-10.30pm Tue-Sat; 🛜📶; Ⓜ Maubert-Mutualité) Noisy, busy and buzzing, this jovial bistro plunges diners into the heart of a Parisian's Paris. Long the stronghold of the legendary Delacourcelle brothers, current owner Jean-François Paris continues to woo foodies with a predominantly organic kitchen and buzzing pavement terrace. At lunchtime join the flock for the fabulous-value *formule dejéuner* (lunch menu), which spices up French classics with the odd 'exotic' ingredient.

Prosper et Fortunée
MODERN FRENCH €€

(Map p72; ☑ 01 43 37 70 39; 50 rue Broca, 5e; menus €55; ⊙from 8.30pm Tue-Thu, from 6:30pm Fri & Sat, closed Aug; Ⓜ Les Gobelins) 🍴 Eric Lévy's 15-seat premises is effectively a clandestine supper club where you can watch the chef prepare daily changing dishes (raw mackerel with yuzu and lemon confit; prime fillet with black radish) using mostly organic premium produce in his open kitchen. Dinner kicks off at a fixed time (8.30pm Tuesday to Thursday, 6.30pm and 9pm Friday and Saturday); reservations essential weekends.

Le Coupe-Chou
FRENCH €€

(Map p134; ☑ 01 46 33 68 69; www.lecoupechou. com; 9 & 11 rue de Lanneau, 5e; menu lunch €15, 2-/3-course dinner €27/33, mains €17.50-29.50; ⊙noon-1.30pm & 7-10.30pm Mon-Sat, 7-10.30pm Sun Sep-Jun, 7-10.30pm Jul & Aug; Ⓜ Maubert-Mutualité) This maze of candlelit rooms inside a vine-clad 17th-century townhouse is overwhelmingly romantic. Ceilings are beamed, furnishings are antique, open fireplaces crackle and background classical music mingles with the intimate chatter of diners. As in the days when Marlene Dietrich dined here, reservations are essential. Timeless French dishes include Burgundy snails, steak tartare and bœuf bourguignon.

★Restaurant AT
GASTRONOMY €€€

(Map p134; ☑ 01 56 81 94 08; www.atsushitanaka. com; 4 rue du Cardinal Lemoine, 5e; 6-course lunch menu €55, 12-course dinner tasting menu €105; ⊙12.15-2pm & 8-9.30pm Mon-Sat; Ⓜ Cardinal Lemoine) Trained by some of the biggest names in gastronomy (Pierre Gagnaire included), chef Atsushi Tanaka showcases abstract artlike masterpieces incorporating rare ingredients (charred bamboo, kohlrabi turnip cabbage, juniper berry powder, wild purple fennel, Nepalese Timut pepper) in a blank-canvas-style dining space on stunning outsized plates. Ingeniously, dinner menus can be paired with wine (€70) or juice (€45). Reservations essential.

✖ St-Germain & Les Invalides

This neighbourhood's streets are lined with everything from quintessential Parisian bistros to chic designer restaurants and flagship establishments with Michelin-starred chefs. Some charming places hide inside Cour du Commerce St-André, a glass-covered passageway built in 1735 to link two *jeu de paume* (old-style tennis) courts. For snacks and fast food to munch on the move, head to rue St-André des Arts, a lively street peppered with taco, kebab, Lebanese, crêpe and falafel takeaways.

The Seine

The lifeline of Paris, the Seine sluices through the city, spanned by 37 bridges. Its Unesco World Heritage–listed riverbanks offer picturesque promenades, parks, activities and events, including sandy summertime beaches. After dark, watch the river dance with the watery reflections of city lights and tourist-boat floodlamps.

Paris' riverbanks are reborn and rocking. On the Left Bank cars have been banned from a 2.3km stretch of riverside quays between Pont de l'Alma and the Musée d'Orsay (originally known as Les Berges de Seine), since 2013. And in mid-2017 another 3.3km stretch of expressway across the water on the Right Bank (between the Tuileries and Henry IV tunnels) was pedestrianised to form the ground-breaking Parc Rives de Seine.

Dotted with restaurants and bars (some aboard boats), this is the alfresco hot spot to watch the world go by. There are giant chessboards, hopscotches, ball-game courts, boules pitches, a skate ramp, a kids' climbing wall and a 100m running track. Floating gardens on artificial islands have hammocks where you can soak up the mythical river's reclaimed serenity. Parisian lovers whispering on hidden staircases, musicians strumming mellow tunes in the summer sun, joggers, cyclists, in-line skaters – they are all here, on the Seine's revitalised riverbanks.

1. Statue of Henry IV in Square du Vert-Galant (p103)
2. Cathédrale Notre Dame de Paris (p102)
3. Pont Neuf (p103)

SEINE-SIDE HIGHLIGHTS

Picnics Idyllic spots include the Musée de la Sculpture en Plein Air (p106) and Square du Vert-Galant (p102).

Bridges Stroll the historic Pont Neuf (p103), or busker-filled Pont St-Louis or Pont au Double (p171).

Beaches Lounge along summer's Paris Plages (p118).

Islands Île de la Cité and Île St-Louis (p102) are enchanting; Île aux Cygnes is a little-known gem.

Cruises Board Bateaux-Mouches (p116) or hop on and off the Batobus (p184).

Cosi

SANDWICHES €

(Map p158; ☑01 46 33 35 36; www.cosiparis.com; 54 rue de Seine, 6e; sandwiches €5.50-8.50; ⊙noon-11pm; ☎♪; Ⓜ Mabillon) Cosi is the local institution for a sandwich with attention-grabbing names like Stonker, Naked Willi or Rocket Scientist and equally creative fillings (tandoori turkey with cheddar and oven-roast tomatoes, curried turkey and apple, roast veggies). Eat upstairs with classical music and a glass of well-chosen wine from La Dernière Goutte (p180), or take away. Homemade foccacia comes warm from the oven.

L'Avant Comptoir du Marché

TAPAS €

(Map p158; 15 rue Lobineau, 6e; tapas €3.50-20; ⊙noon-11pm; Ⓜ Mabillon) Top chef Yves Camdeborde stars again with this porcine-specialist tapas bar wedged in one corner of the Marché St-Germain covered market-shopping complex. A flying, fire-engine-red pig is the ceiling's centrepiece, surrounded by suspended menus listing dishes such as Bayonne ham croquettes, Bigorre pâté and shots of Béarnaise pig's blood; wines are chalked on the blackboard. No reservations.

Camdeborde's neighbouring addresses include bistro **Le Comptoir** (Map p158; ☑01 44 27 07 97; www.hotel-paris-relais-saint-germain.com; 9 Carrefour de l'Odéon, 6e; lunch mains €14-30, dinner menu €60; ⊙noon-6pm & 8.30-11.30pm Mon-Fri, noon-11pm Sat & Sun; Ⓜ Odéon), tapas bar **L'Avant Comptoir de la Terre** (Map p158; www.hotel-paris-relais-saint-germain.com; 3 Carrefour de l'Odéon, 6e; tapas €5-10; ⊙noon-11pm; Ⓜ Odéon) and seafood tapas bar **L'Avant Comptoir de la Mer** (Map p158; ☑01 42 38 47 55; www.hotel-paris-relais-saint-germain.com; 3 Carrefour de l'Odéon, 6e; tapas €5-25, oysters per 6 €17; ⊙noon-11pm; Ⓜ Odéon).

Simple

FRENCH €

(Map p158; ☑01 45 44 79 88; 86 rue du Cherche-Midi, 6e; bowls & mains €15-20; ⊙noon-6.30pm Tue-Fri, to 7pm Sat; ☎; Ⓜ St-Placide) Amid the many eateries on fashionable rue du Cherche-Midi, Simple stands out for its simple salads, soups and detox veggie bowls. Everything, in fact, is super healthy at this fully organic lunch spot. Dozens of fresh flowers in vases decorate wooden tables inside and the pavement terrace is a perfect spot to people-watch over an Omega 3 *assiette* (plate) or gluten-free fish bowl.

Freddy's

FRENCH €

(Map p158; 54 rue de Seine, 6e; small plates €6-10; ⊙noon-midnight; Ⓜ Mabillon) Run by the same team as neighbouring neobistro **Semilla** (Map p158; ☑01 43 54 34 50; www.semillaparis.com; 54 rue de Seine, 6e; 2-/3-course weekday lunch menu €34/40, mains €24-40; ⊙12.30-2.30pm & 7-11pm Mon-Sat, to 10pm Sun, closed early–mid-Aug; Ⓜ Mabillon), this buzzing no-reservation wine bar serves creative small plates (smoked artichoke with hazelnut butter, fire-roasted duck hearts, mushroom cappuccino, chicken teriyaki, grilled sardines) that pair with some fantastic small-scale producer-sourced wines. Herringbone timber floors, exposed stone walls and bar-stool seating give it a warm, welcoming vibe.

LOCAL KNOWLEDGE

BEST CRÊPES

Breizh Café (p143) Among the most authentic Breton crêpes in town.

Crêpe Dentelle (Map p94; ☑01 40 41 04 23; 10 rue Léopold Bellan, 2e; crêpes €8.20-15, lunch menu €12; ⊙noon-3pm & 7.30-11pm Mon-Fri; Ⓜ Sentier) Superb crêpes by Les Halles.

Crêperie Pen-Ty (Map p78; ☑01 48 74 18 49; 65 rue de Douai, 9e; galettes €4-15, crêpes €4.90-10.40; ⊙noon-2.30pm & 7.30-11.15pm Mon-Fri, 12.30-4pm & 6.30-11.30pm Sat, to 10.30pm Sun; Ⓜ Place de Clichy) Northern Paris' best crêperie, with traditional Breton aperitifs.

Little Breizh (Map p158; ☑01 43 54 60 74; www.facebook.com/LittleBreizhCreperie; 11 rue Grégoire de Tours, 6e; crêpes €5-15; ⊙noon-2.30pm & 7-10.30pm Tue-Sat; ♪; Ⓜ Odéon) Innovative twists such as Breton sardines.

Crêperie Josselin (Map p158; ☑01 43 20 93 50; 67 rue du Montparnasse, 14e; crêpes €5-10.50; ⊙11am-11.30pm Wed-Sun; ♨; Ⓜ Edgar Quinet) In the 'Little Brittany' neighbourhood near Gare Montparnasse.

Le Pot O'Lait (Map p134; 41 rue Censier, 5e; lunch menus €11.50-14-90, crêpes €5-12; ⊙11am-2.30pm & 7-10.30pm Tue-Sat; ♨; Ⓜ Censier Daubenton) Great *galettes* and sweet crêpes in the Latin Quarter.

FAVOURITE FOOD MARKETS

Marché d'Aligre (Map p126; rue d'Aligre, 12e; ⊘8am-1pm Tue-Sun; Ⓜ Ledru-Rollin) A favourite with chefs and locals, this chaotic street market's stalls are piled with fruit, vegetables and seasonal delicacies such as truffles. Behind them, specialist shops stock cheeses, coffee, chocolates, meat, seafood and wine. More are located in the adjoining covered market hall, **Marché Beauvau** (Map p126; place d'Aligre, 12e; ⊘9am-2pm & 4-7.30pm Tue-Sat, 9am-2pm Sun; Ⓜ Ledru-Rollin). The small but bargain-filled flea market Marché aux Puces d'Aligre (p179) takes place on the square.

Marché Bastille (Map p120; bd Richard Lenoir, 11e; ⊘7am-2.30pm Thu, to 3pm Sun; Ⓜ Bastille, Bréguet–Sabin) If you only get to one open-air street market in Paris, this one – stretching between the Bastille and Richard Lenoir metro stations – is among the very best. Its 150-plus stalls are piled high with fruit and vegetables, meats, fish, shellfish, cheeses and seasonal specialities such as truffles. You'll also find clothing, leather handbags and wallets, and a smattering of antiques.

Marché des Enfants Rouges (Map p120; 39 rue de Bretagne & 33bis rue Charlot, 3e; ⊘8.30am-1pm & 4-7.30pm Tue-Sat, 8.30am-2pm Sun, individual stall hours vary; Ⓜ Filles du Calvaire) Built in 1615, Paris' oldest covered market is secreted behind an inconspicuous green-metal gate. A glorious maze of 20-odd food stalls selling ready-to-eat dishes from around the globe (Moroccan couscous, Japanese bento boxes and more), as well as produce, cheese and flower stalls, it's a great place to meander and to dine with locals at communal tables.

Marché de Belleville (Map p120; bd de Belleville, 11e & 20e; ⊘7am-2.30pm Tue & Fri; Ⓜ Belleville) Belleville Market has filled busy thoroughfare bd de Belleville with open-air fruit, veg and other fresh-produce stalls since 1860. Food shopping aside, it provides a fascinating insight into the large, vibrant community of this eastern neighbourhood, home to artists, students and immigrants from Africa, Asia and the Middle East.

La Crèmerie　　　　　　FRENCH €
(Map p158; ☑01 43 54 99 30; 9 rue des Quatre-Vents, 6e; small plates €7-20; ⊘11am-2pm & 6-10pm Tue-Sat, 6-10pm Sun & Mon; Ⓜ Odéon) Beneath an original glass-covered ceiling, this marble-walled *caviste* (wine cellar) is a delicious flashback to 1880s Paris. With a stock of 400-odd wines and an exquisite array of France's finest gourmet goods, it is a delightful spot for an early-evening *apéro* (predinner drink) accompanied by tapas-style dishes (smoked-trout terrine, goat's cheese and olives, black-pudding-topped toast) or a fully-fledged meal.

Anima　　　　　　ITALIAN €
(Map p158; ☑01 40 47 90 41; https://anima.paris; 87 rue du Cherche-Midi, 6e; pizza €9-25, mains €13-18; ⊘noon-2.30pm & 7.30-11pm; Ⓜ Sèvres-Babylone) Dress on trend to ensure you don't look out of place at this sleek, fashionable Italian restaurant opened by David Lahner (of **Racines** (Map p78; ☑01 40 13 06 41; www.racinesparis.com; 8 passage des Panoramas, 2e; mains €20-28; ⊘noon-2.30pm & 7.30-10pm Mon-Fri; Ⓜ Grands Boulevards, Richelieu–Drouot) fame) and Marco Marzilli in a former tapestry workshop. Large cathedral windows lend the industrial-inspired space bags of natural light, Pierre Frey fabrics paper the walls and Sunday is fresh-pasta day. Roberto from Naples ensures fantastic thin-crust pizza.

★**Bouillon Racine**　　　　BRASSERIE €€
(Map p158; ☑01 44 32 15 60; www.bouillonracine.com; 3 rue Racine, 6e; 2-course weekday lunch menu €16.90, 3-course menu €35, mains €16-27.50; ⊘noon-11pm; ⛨; Ⓜ Cluny-La Sorbonne) Inconspicuously situated in a quiet street, this heritage-listed art nouveau 'soup kitchen', with mirrored walls, floral motifs and ceramic tiling, was built in 1906 to feed market workers. Despite the magnificent interior, the food – inspired by age-old recipes – is no afterthought but superbly executed (stuffed, spit-roasted suckling pig, pork shank in Rodenbach red beer, scallops and shrimps with lobster coulis).

★**Tomy & Co**　　　　GASTRONOMY €€
(Map p76; ☑01 45 51 46 93; 22 rue Surcouf, 7e; 2-course lunch menu €27, 3-course/tasting dinner menu €47/68, mains wine pairings €45; ⊘noon-2pm & 7.30-9.30pm Mon-Fri; Ⓜ Invalides) Tomy Gousset's restaurant near Mademoiselle Eiffel has been a sensation since day one. The

French-Cambodian chef works his magic on inspired seasonal dishes using produce from his organic garden. Winter ushers in aromatic black truffles (themed tasting menu €95). The spectacular desserts – chocolate tart with fresh figs, Cambodian palm sugar and fig ice cream anyone? – are equally seasonal. Reservations essential.

★**L'Étable Hugo Desnoyer** FRENCH €€
(Map p158; ☑ 01 42 39 89 27; www.hugodesnoyer. com; 15 rue Clément, 6e; lunch menu €24.50, mains €30-40; ⊗ noon-2.30pm & 7.30-10.30pm Tue-Sat; Ⓜ Mabillon) Duck beneath the elegant stone arches of Marché St-Germain (p180) to uncover the stylish steakhouse of Paris' superstar butcher Hugo Desnoyer. Vegetarians be warned, there are some delicious veggie dishes too, but some of the walls in the sharp design interior are clad in ginger-and-cream cow-hide and the menu is essentially for meat lovers.

★**Epoca** ITALIAN €€
(Map p72; ☑ 01 43 06 88 88; http://epoca.paris; 17 rue Oudinot, 7e; 2-course lunch menu €20, pasta/mains €16/20; ⊗ noon-2.30pm & 7.30-10.30pm Mon-Thu, to 11pm Fri & Sat; Ⓜ Sèvres-Babylone) Star of the French TV show *Top Chef,* Italian chef Denny Imbroisi, is the creative talent behind this A-lister-chic Italian bistro with a sharp, black-and-white interior evocative of 1930s art deco. The short, stylish menu features the best of Italian regional cooking: begin with a Roman deep-fried artichoke or Sicilian squid, perhaps, followed by spaghetti with goat's cheese and black pepper or saffron-laced Milanese risotto.

★**Huîtrerie Regis** SEAFOOD €€
(Map p158; http://huitrerieregis.com; 3 rue de Montfaucon, 6e; dozen oysters from €26; ⊗ noon-2.30pm & 6.30-10.30pm Mon-Fri, noon-10.45pm Sat, noon-10pm Sun; Ⓜ Mabillon) Hip, trendy, tiny and white, this is the spot for slurping oysters on crisp winter days – inside or on the tiny pavement terrace sporting sage-green Fermob chairs. Oysters arrive live from the Bassin de Marennes-Oléron and come only by the dozen. Wash them down with a glass of chilled Muscadet. No reservations, so arrive early.

★**Clover** BISTRO €€
(Map p158; ☑ 01 75 50 00 05; www.clover-paris. com; 5 rue Perronet, 7e; 2-/3-course lunch menu €37/47, 3-/5-course dinner menu €60/73; ⊗12.30-2pm & 7-10pm Tue-Fri, 12.30-2.30pm & 7-10pm Sat; Ⓜ St-Germain des Prés) Dining at hot-shot chef Jean-François Piège's casual

bistro is like attending a private party: the galley-style open kitchen adjoining the 20 seats (online reservations open just 15 days in advance) is part of the dining-room decor, putting customers at the front and centre of the culinary action. Light, luscious dishes range from tomato gazpacho with pea sorbet to cabbage leaves with smoked herring *crème* and chestnuts.

★**Anicia** FRENCH €€
(Map p158; ☑ 01 43 35 41 50; http://anicia-bistrot. com; 97 rue du Cherche Midi, 6e; 2-/3-course weekday lunch menu €24/29, 3-/5-course dinner menu €49/58, mains €27-34; ⊗ noon-10.30pm Tue-Sat; Ⓜ Duroc, Vaneau) It is essential to make an advance online booking at this glorious 'bistro nature', showcase for the earthy but refined cuisine of chef François Gagnaire who ran a Michelin-starred restaurant in the foodie town of Puy-en-Velay in the Auvergne before uprooting to the French capital. He still sources dozens of regional products – Puy lentils, Velay snails, St-Nectaire cheese – from small-time producers in central France, to stunning effect.

★**Niébé** FUSION €€
(Map p158; ☑ 01 43 29 43 31; www.restaurant niebe.com; 16 rue del a Grande Chaumière, 6e; 2-/3-course weekday lunch menu €17/22, mains €19-22; ⊗ noon-3pm & 7.30pm-midnight Tue-Sat; Ⓜ Vavin) Inviting sunflower-yellow walls set the tone at this new Left Bank hot spot for soul food. Ex-chef at the Brazilian Embassy, Rosilène Vitorino, oversees a menu that fuses Brazilian, Creole and African cuisine. Best up, there are two menus: classic (starring Creole blood sausage with sweet potato and kumquat purée) and vegan (with dishes like sautéed tofu with black rice in a coconut coulis).

Restaurant Guy Savoy GASTRONOMY €€€
(Map p158; ☑ 01 43 80 40 61; www.guysavoy. com; 11 quai de Conti, 6e, Monnaie de Paris; lunch menu via online booking €130, tasting menu €415; ⊗ noon-2pm & 7-10.30pm Tue-Fri, 7-10.30pm Sat; Ⓜ Pont Neuf) If you're considering visiting a three-Michelin-star temple to gastronomy, this should certainly be on your list. The world-famous chef needs no introduction (he trained Gordon Ramsay, among others) but his flagship, entered via a red-carpeted staircase, is ensconced in the gorgeously refurbished neoclassical Monnaie de Paris (p107). Monumental cuisine to match includes Savoy icons such as artichoke and black-truffle soup with layered brioche.

LOCAL KNOWLEDGE

GLUTEN-FREE ESSENTIALS

In a city known for its bakeries, it's only right that there's **Chambelland** (Map p120; ☑ 01 43 55 07 30; www.chambelland.com; 14 rue Ternaux, 11e; lunch menus €10-12, pastries €2.50-5.50; ☉ 9am-8pm Tue-Sat, to 6pm Sun; Ⓜ Parmentier) – a 100% gluten-free bakery with serious breads to die for. Using rice and buckwheat flour milled at the bakery's very own mill in southern France, this pioneering bakery creates exquisite cakes and pastries as well as sourdough loaves and brioches (sweet breads) peppered with nuts, seeds, chocolate and fruit. Make a meal of it and stop here for lunch at one of the handful of formica tables in this youthful space, strewn with sacks of rice flour and books. There is always a salad (summer) or homemade soup (winter) on the boil, served of course with a designer chunk of crunchy focaccia, perhaps of brown linseed-laced loaf. Or grab a sandwich – to eat in or take away.

Combining the French genius for pastries with a 100% gluten-free kitchen, **Helmut Newcake** (Map p78; ☑ 09 81 31 28 31; www.helmutnewcake.com; 28 rue Vignon, 9e; plats du jour €6.80-11.50; ☉ 11am-7pm Tue-Sat; Ⓜ Madeleine) is one of those Parisian addresses that some will simply have to hang on to. Eclairs, fondants, cheesecake and tarts are some of the dessert options, while you can count on lunch (salads, quiches, soups, pizzas) to be scrumptious and market driven. Takeaway only.

✖ Montparnasse & Southern Paris

Since the 1920s bd du Montparnasse has been one of the city's premier avenues for enjoying Parisian pavement life, with legendary brasseries and cafes.

The down-to-earth 15e cooks up fabulous bistro fare – along rues de la Convention, de Vaugirard, St-Charles and du Commerce, and south of bd de Grenelle.

In Chinatown, try av de Choisy, av d'Ivry and rue Baudricourt.

Villagey Butte aux Cailles, 13e, is chock-a-block with interesting addresses: rue de la Butte aux Cailles and rue des Cinq Diamants are the main foodie streets. Vibrant food markets fill the nearby bd Auguste Blanqui every Tuesday and Friday morning.

★ Ladurée Picnic   PASTRIES, DELI €

(Map p72; ☑ 01 70 22 45 20; www.laduree.fr; 16 rue Linois, 15e; Centre Commercial Beaugrenelle; breakfast/lunch menu €14.50/9.50, sandwiches/salads from €2.40/5.50; ☉ 9.30am-8.30pm Mon-Sat, 10am-7pm Sun; Ⓜ Charles Michels) The first of its kind, Ladurée Picnic specialises in just that – picnics, albeit exceedingly fine, gourmet picnics to take away in the famous patisserie's signature peppermint-green packaging. Luxury salads include lobster or aromatic salmon; there are flavoured waters like ginger and coriander and mint and cucumber; and the rainbow of cakes and macarons are simply out of this world.

La Tropicale   ICE CREAM €

(Map p72; ☑ 01 42 16 87 27; www.latropicaleglacier.com; 180 bd Vincent Auriol, 13e; ice cream per 1/2/3 scoops €3/5/7, lunch menus €8-12; ☉ noon-8pm Mon-Fri, 3-8pm Sat & Sun summer, noon-3.30pm Mon, Tue & Thu, noon-7pm Wed & Sat winter; ♿; Ⓜ Place d'Italie) 🍦 Pistachio and orange-flower, lemon and absinthe, and mandarin spiced with timut pepper are among the exciting favours at this exceptional ice-creamery near place d'Italie. Ice cream is made on-site in the tiny space, and seasonal flavours incorporate gorgeous tropical spices sourced by the creative Cambodian owner and ice-cream maker, Thai-Thanh, on her many travels.

Lunchtime ushers in a couple of equally tasty, vegetarian savoury tarts and inventive *plats du jour* (dishes of the day) such as sage-spiced risotto with roast pumpkin, feta and ginger-saffron ice cream. Arrive early to ensure a pew at one of the handful of tables inside.

Thieng Heng   VIETNAMESE, SANDWICHES €

(Map p72; ☑ 01 45 82 92 95; 50 av d'Ivry, 13e; sandwiches €2.70-3.50; ☉ 8.30am-7pm; Ⓜ Porte d'Ivry, Maison Blanche) You'll know you're in the vicinity of this takeaway joint when you see crowds of locals munching on giant *banh mi* (Vietnamese stuffed baguettes), which have earned Thieng Heng a cult following. Fillings include grilled marinated meats, such as pork or chicken, pickled veggies, fresh herbs and sweet, salty or spicy sauces. If you're famished, there's a super-size option.

ℹ RUE CLER

Pick up fresh bread, sandwich fillings, pastries and wine for a picnic along the typically Parisian commercial street rue Cler, 7e, which buzzes with local shoppers, especially on weekends.

Interspersed between the *boulangeries* (bakeries), *fromageries* (cheese shops), grocers, butchers, delis and other food shops (many with pavement stalls), lively cafe terraces overflow with locals.

★ Le Saut du Crapaud   BISTRO €

(Map p72; ✆ 01 85 15 28 35; www.lesautducrapaud. fr; 16 rue des Plantes, 14e; 2-/3-course lunch menu €16/20, dinner menu €35; ☺ 7-10.30pm Mon-Fri, noon-2.30pm & 7-10.30pm Sat, 11.30am-3pm Sun; Ⓜ Mouton-Duvernet) Locals pack out this quirky neighbourhood bistro, showcase for the casual Franco-Mexican cuisine of Mexican banker-turned-chef Marco Paz. Cooking pots and guitars adorn the stylish vintage interior and the menu features creative dishes like steak coriander and lime-laced steak tartare, tuna with orange, and baby cuttlefish pan-fried with tequila and black pudding. Sunday brunch (€22.50) is a fabulously vibrant affair, spilling outside in summer.

La Butte aux Piafs   BISTRO €

(Map p72; ✆ 09 70 38 55 11; www.labutteauxpiafs-paris.fr; 31 bd Auge Blanqui, 13e; mains €14.10-16.90; ☺ noon-midnight Mon-Fri, noon-3.30pm & 6pm-midnight Sat; Ⓜ Place d'Italie) A cinematic cluster of cherry-red chairs flag the pavement terrace of this neighbourhood bistro, *the* spot to lap up the quietly fashionable vibe of La Butte aux Cailles. Inside, flip-down cinema seats mix with an eclectic jumble of vintage seating, while menus featuring burgers, meal-sized salads and creative starters come bound in the sleeve of a vinyl single.

Le Petit Pan   MODERN FRENCH €

(Map p72; ✆ 01 42 50 04 04; www.lepetitpan.fr; 18 rue Rosenwald, 15e; 2-/3-course lunch menu €16.50/20.50, small plates €2.50-13; ☺ noon-2.30pm & 7-11.30pm Tue-Sat; Ⓜ Porte de Vanves) Parisians working in the 'hood fill this casual bistro to bursting at lunchtime thanks to a fantastic-value lunchtime menu, but it's after dusk that the gourmet action kicks in with small plates of tapas *à la française* designed for sharing. Think cured ham, duck pâté with pork trotters or duck hearts fried in ginger, washed down with superb wines by the glass.

The lunchtime menu includes gourmet sandwiches, quiches and salads. To sink your teeth into a serious hunk of meat, nip across the street to big sister restaurant **Le Grand Pan** (Map p72; ✆ 01 42 50 02 50; www. legrandpan.fr; 20 rue Rosenwald, 15e; mains €14-30; ☺ noon-2pm & 7.30-11pm Mon-Fri).

★ Le Beurre Noisette   BISTRO €€

(Map p72; ✆ 01 48 56 82 49; www.restaurant beurrenoisette.com; 68 rue Vasco de Gama, 15e; 2-/3-course lunch menu €23/32, 3-/5-/7-course dinner menu €36/46/56, mains lunch/dinner €18/21; ☺ noon-2pm & 7-10.30pm Tue-Sat; Ⓜ Lourmel) *Beurre noisette* (brown butter sauce, named for its hazelnut colour) features in dishes such as tender veal loin with homemade fries and caramelised pork belly tender with braised red cabbage and apple, at pedigreed chef Thierry Blanqui's neighbourhood neobistro. Filled with locals, the chocolate-toned dining room is wonderfully convivial – be sure to book. Fantastic value.

★ Le Cassenoix   MODERN FRENCH €€

(Map p76; ✆ 01 45 66 09 01; www.le-cassenoix. fr; 56 rue de la Fédération, 15e; 3-course menu €34; ☺ noon-2.30pm & 7-10.30pm Mon-Fri; Ⓜ Bir Hakeim) The Nutcracker is everything a self-respecting neighbourhood bistro should be. *'Tradition et terroir'* (tradition and provenance) dictate the menu that inspires owner-chef Pierre Olivier Lenormand to deliver feisty dishes such as braised veal chuck with mashed potato and caramelised onions or grilled hake with parsnips and hazelnut-parmesan crumble. Vintage ceiling fans add to the wonderful retro vibe. Book ahead.

L'Accolade   BISTRO €€

(Map p72; ✆ 01 45 57 73 20; www.laccoladeparis.fr; 208 rue de la Croix Nivert, 15e; 2-/3-course lunch menu €19.50/24.50, 4-course dinner menu €35; ☺ noon-2.30pm Mon, noon-2pm & 7-10.30pm Tue-Fri, 7-10.30pm Sat; Ⓜ Convention) Seasonal market products reign supreme at this neighbourhood bistro where rising star Nicolas Tardivel woos a local crowd with his creative, modern French 'bistronomie' – bistro-style gastronomy. The lunchtime *plat du jour,* at €15 including coffee, is an excellent deal. Should you be open to temptation, the vanilla millefeuille, glazed with salted butter caramel, is sublime.

Simone Le Resto BISTRO €€
(Map p72; ✆01 43 37 82 70; www.simoneparis.com; 33 bd Arago, 13e; 2-/3-course lunch menu €18/22, tasting menu €49; ⊗noon-2.30pm & 7.30-10.30pm Tue-Fri, 7.30-10.30pm Sat; Ⓜ Les Gobelins) A generous smattering of pavement-terrace tables flags this vibrant neobistro with tattooed chef Mathia Di Gino in the kitchen and knowledgeable duo Julian and Charles out front. Daily *menus* created in the open kitchen ooze seasonal products. An exceptional selection of all-natural and biodynamic wines that pair perfectly with each course are also available at Simone's nearby wine shop and bar, **Simone La Cave** (Map p72; 48 rue Pascal, 13e; ⊗5-11pm Tue-Sat; Ⓜ Les Gobelins), which hosts weekly fantastic tastings.

Le Clos Y MODERN FRENCH €€
(Map p158; ✆01 45 49 07 35; www.leclosy.com; 27 av du Maine, 15e; 2-/3-course lunch menu €31/36, dinner menu €65; ⊗noon-2pm & 7.30-10pm Tue-Sat; Ⓜ Montparnasse Bienvenüe) One of Paris' rapidly rising star chefs Yoshitaka Ikeda creates utterly original *menus* that change daily but might start with foie gras ice cream and move on to perch sashimi with beetroot, apple and powdered olive oil; green peas in pea jelly with mascarpone; smoked salmon and egg with raspberry foam; and Madeira-marinated beef with butternut squash and carrot purée.

Le Dôme BRASSERIE €€€
(Map p158; ✆01 43 35 25 81; www.restaurant-ledome.com; 108 bd du Montparnasse, 14e; mains €42-67, seafood platters €85-148; ⊗noon-3pm & 7-11pm; Ⓜ Vavin) A 1930s art deco extravaganza of the formal white-tablecloth and bow-tied waiter variety, monumental Le Dôme is one of the swishest places around for shellfish platters laden with fresh oysters, king prawns, crab claws and much more, followed by traditional creamy homemade *millefeuille* for dessert, wheeled in on a trolley and cut in front of you.

🍷 Drinking & Nightlife

For the French, drinking and eating go together like wine and cheese, and the line between a cafe, *salon de thé* (tearoom), bistro, brasserie, bar and even *bar à vins* (wine bar) is blurred. The line between drinking and clubbing is often nonexistent – a cafe that's quiet mid-afternoon might have DJ sets in the evening and dancing later on.

🍷 Eiffel Tower & Western Paris

Ogling the illuminated Eiffel Tower aside, being in the wealthy and predominantly residential 16e after dark doesn't translate to much when it comes to buzzing bars and clubs. The pace picks up around Palais de Tokyo, and the lively bars and cafes of St-Germain are a short metro ride away.

★**St James Paris** BAR
(Map p72; www.saint-james-paris.com; 43 av Bugeaud, 16e; ⊗7pm-1am; 🛜; Ⓜ Porte Dauphine) Hidden behind a stone wall, this historic mansion-turned-hotel opens its bar nightly to nonguests – and the setting redefines extraordinary. Winter drinks are in the wood-panelled library; summer drinks are on the impossibly romantic 300-sq-metre garden terrace with giant balloon-shaped gazebos (the first hot-air balloons took flight here). It has over 70 cocktails and an adjoining Michelin-starred restaurant.

PARIS' OLDEST RESTAURANT & CAFE

St-Germain claims both the city's oldest restaurant and its oldest cafe.

À la Petite Chaise (Map p158; ✆01 42 22 13 35; www.alapetitechaise.fr; 36 rue de Grenelle, 6e; 2-/3-course lunch menu €25/33, 3-course dinner menu €26, mains €21; ⊗noon-2pm & 7-11pm; Ⓜ Sèvres-Babylone) In 1860 wine merchant Georges Rameau took the innovative move of serving food (to accompany his wares) to customers coming to his shop – and so the oldest restaurant still standing in the capital was born. The kitchen remains firmly grounded in timeless French classics like onion soup and pan-fried calf kidneys.

Le Procope (Map p158; ✆01 40 46 79 00; www.procope.com; 13 rue de l'Ancienne Comédie, 6e; 2-/3-course menu €21.90/28.90; ⊗11.30am-midnight Sun-Wed, to 1am Thu-Sat; Ⓜ Odéon) If you ever wondered what Voltaire, Molière and Balzac dined on in the heady days of 17th-century Paris, reserve a table at this chandelier-posh restaurant where very little has changed since the day it first opened its doors in 1686. Coq au vin or calf's-head casserole in veal stock are tasty blasts from the past.

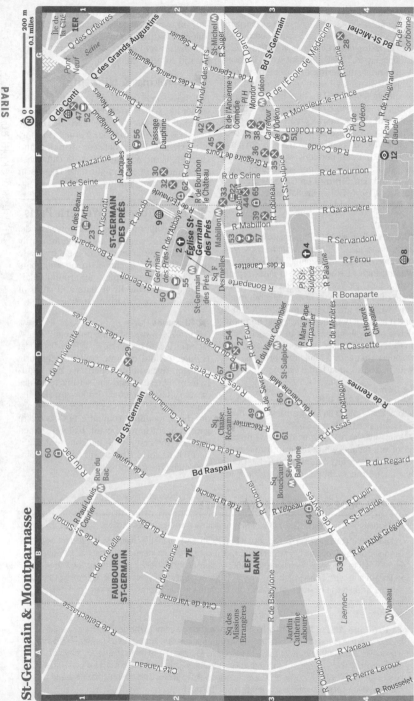

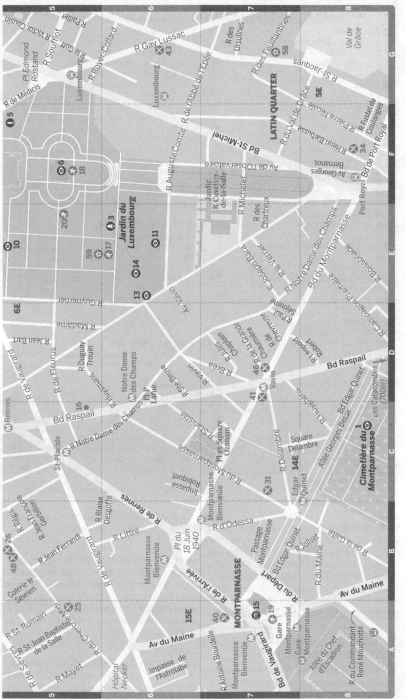

St-Germain & Montparnasse

Top Sights
1 Cimetière du Montparnasse C8
2 Église St-Germain des Prés E2
3 Jardin du Luxembourg E6

Sights
4 Église St-Sulpice E3
5 Fontaine des Médici F5
6 Grand Bassin F5
7 Monnaie de Paris F1
8 Musée du Luxembourg E4
9 Musée National Eugène Delacroix E2
10 Orangery E5
11 Orchards E6
12 Palais du Luxembourg F4
13 Pavillon Davioud E6
14 Rucher du Luxembourg E6
15 Tour Montparnasse A7

Activities, Courses & Tours
16 Alliance Française C5
17 Children's Playgrounds E6
18 Grand Bassin Toy Sailboats F5
19 Pari Roller A7
20 Pony Rides E5

Sleeping
21 Hôtel du Dragon D3
22 Hôtel Le Clément F3
23 L'Hôtel E1

Eating
24 À la Petite Chaise C2
25 Anicia A5
26 Anima B5
27 Aux Prés D3
28 Bouillon Racine G4
29 Clover D1
30 Cosi F2
31 Crêperie Josselin C7
32 Freddy's F2
33 Huîtrerie Regis F2
34 La Bête Noire F8
35 La Crèmerie F3
36 L'Amaryllis de Gérard Mulot F3
37 L'Avant Comptoir de la Mer F3
38 L'Avant Comptoir de la Terre F3
39 L'Avant Comptoir du Marché E3
40 Le Clos Y A7
Le Comptoir .... (see 38)
41 Le Dôme D7
42 Le Procope F2
43 Les Papilles G6
44 L'Étable Hugo Desnoyer F3
45 Little Breizh F2
46 Niébé D7
47 Restaurant Guy Savoy F1
Semilla .... (see 32)
48 Simple B5

Drinking & Nightlife
49 Au Sauvignon C3
50 Café de Flore E2
51 Cod House F3
52 Frappé by Bloom F1
53 Frog & Princess E3
54 Le Bar des Prés D3
55 Les Deux Magots E2
56 Prescription Cocktail Club F2
57 Tiger E3

Entertainment
58 Café Universel G7
59 Théâtre du Luxembourg E5

Shopping
60 Deyrolle C1
61 Hermès C3
62 La Dernière Goutte F2
63 La Grande Épicerie de Paris B4
64 Le Bon Marché B3
65 Marché Saint-Germain F3
66 Poilâne D3
67 Sabbia Rosa D3

Yoyo CLUB

(Map p90; http://yoyo-paris.com; 13 av du Président Wilson, 16e; hours vary; M léna) Deep in the basement of the Palais de Tokyo, Yoyo has an edgy, raw-concrete Berlin-style vibe and a capacity of 800. Techno and house dominate, with diversions into hip hop, electro, funk, disco, R&B and soul. Hours can vary; check the website to see what's happening when.

Champs-Élysées & Grands Boulevards

The Champs-Élysées is home to a mix of exclusive nightspots, tourist haunts and a handful of large dance clubs that party all night. As a rule, you'll want to look as chic as possible to get in the door.

PanPan BAR

(Map p78; 01 42 46 36 06; 32 rue Drouot, 9e; 10am-2am Mon-Fri, 6pm-2am Sat; M Le Peletier) This unassuming locals' hang-out doesn't even bother with a sign, but it keeps things interesting with activities, like blind taste tests, throughout the week. Happy hour from 6pm to 8pm.

Zig Zag Club CLUB

(Map p90; http://zigzagclub.fr; 32 rue Marbeuf, 8e; 11.30pm-7am Fri & Sat; M Franklin D Roosevelt) With star DJs, a great sound and light system, and a spacious dance floor, Zig Zag has some of the hippest electro beats in western Paris. It can be pricey, but it still fills up quickly, so don't start the party too late.

🍸 Louvre & Les Halles

The area north of Les Halles is a prime destination for night owls. Cocktails predominate, but you'll also find wine and Champagne bars, studenty hang-outs, open-till-dawn local dives and a smattering of fun nightclubs. Rue St-Sauveur, rue Tiquetonne and rue Montmartre are the best streets to explore.

★ Bar Hemingway   COCKTAIL BAR

(Map p94; www.ritzparis.com; Hôtel Ritz Paris, 15 place Vendôme, 1er; ⊙ 6pm-2am; 🛜; Ⓜ Opéra) Black-and-white photos and memorabilia (hunting trophies, old typewriters and framed handwritten letters by the great writer) fill this snug bar inside the Ritz (p123). Head bartender Colin Field mixes monumental cocktails, including three different Bloody Marys made with juice from freshly squeezed seasonal tomatoes. Legend has it that Hemingway himself, wielding a machine gun, helped liberate the bar during WWII.

★ Danico   COCKTAIL BAR

(Map p94; www.facebook.com/danicoparis; 6 rue Vivienne, 2e; ⊙ 6pm-2am; Ⓜ Bourse) While not exactly a secret, Danico still feels like one – first you'll need to find the hidden, candlelit backroom in **Daroco** (Map p94; ☑ 01 42 21 93 71; www.daroco.fr; 6 rue Vivienne, 2e; mains €14-40; ⊙ noon-2.30pm & 7-11.30pm; 🖉; Ⓜ Bourse) before you get to treat yourself to one of Nico de Soto's extravagant cocktails. Chia seeds, kombucha tea, ghost peppers and pomegranate Champagne are some of the more unusual ingredients you'll find on the drink list.

★ Experimental Cocktail Club   COCKTAIL BAR

(ECC; Map p94; www.experimentalevents.com; 37 rue St-Sauveur, 2e; ⊙ 7pm-2am; Ⓜ Réaumur

Sébastopol) With a black curtain façade, this retro-chic speakeasy – with sister bars in London, Ibiza, New York and, *bien sûr,* Paris – is a sophisticated flashback to those *années folles* (crazy years) of Prohibition New York. Cocktails (€13 to €15) are individual and fabulous, and DJs keep the party going until dawn at weekends. It's not a large space, however, and fills to capacity quickly.

★ Le Garde Robe   WINE BAR

(Map p94; ☑ 01 49 26 90 60; 41 rue de l'Arbre Sec, 1er; ⊙ 12.30-2.30pm & 6.30pm-midnight Tue-Fri, 4.30pm-midnight Mon-Sat; Ⓜ Louvre Rivoli) Le Garde Robe is possibly the world's only bar to serve alcohol alongside a detox menu. While you probably shouldn't come here for the full-on cleansing experience, you can definitely expect excellent, affordable natural wines, a casual atmosphere and a good selection of food, ranging from cheese and charcuterie plates to adventurous options (tuna gravlax with black quinoa and guacamole).

Matamata   COFFEE

(Map p94; ☑ 01 71 39 44 58; www.matamata coffee.com; 58 rue d'Argout, 2e; ⊙ 8am-5pm Mon-Fri, 9am-5.30pm Sat & Sun; 🛜; Ⓜ Sentier) Beans from Parisian roastery Café Lomi are expertly brewed at this small, two-level space with tables and light fittings made from recycled timber and repurposed metal, and subtropical fern wallpaper. Homemade cakes, such as carrot or banana, go with its exceptional coffee, sandwiches, salads and house-toasted granola. In summer, cool down with a cold-drip coffee over ice.

Frog & Underground   PUB

(Map p78; www.frogpubs.com; 173 rue Montmartre, 2e; ⊙ 8am-1am Sun-Wed, to 3am Thu, to 5am Fri & Sat; 🛜; Ⓜ Grands Boulevards) FrogPubs has been brewing in Paris since 1993, and this central new rue Montmartre venue is its best yet. Spread over a cavernous ground

---

LOCAL KNOWLEDGE

BEST PAVEMENT TERRACES

Chez Prune (p162) The boho cafe that put Canal St-Martin on the map.

L'Ebouillanté (Map p120; www.ebouillante.fr; 6 rue des Barres, 4e; ⊙ noon-10pm Tue-Sun Jun-Aug, to 7pm Tue-Sun Sep-May; 🛜; Ⓜ Pont Marie, Hôtel de Ville) A contender for Paris' prettiest cafe terrace (and its best homemade ginger lemonade).

Café des Anges (Map p120; ☑ 01 47 00 00 63; www.cafedesangesparis.com; 66 rue de la Roquette, 11e; ⊙ 7.30am-2am; 🛜; Ⓜ Bastille) The terrace of this 11e cafe buzzes night and day.

Shakespeare & Company Café (p166) Live the Parisian Left Bank literary dream.

LOCAL KNOWLEDGE

BEST SPECIALIST COFFEE

Belleville Brûlerie (Map p72; ☏ 09 83 75 60 80; http://cafesbelleville.com; 10 rue Pradier, 19e; ⊙ 11.30am-6.30pm Sat; Ⓜ Pyrénées) Ground-breaking roastery with Saturday-morning tastings and cuppings.

Beans on Fire (Map p120; www.thebeansonfire.com; 7 rue du Général Blaise, 11e; ⊙ 8.30am-5pm Mon-Fri, 9.30am-6pm Sat & Sun; ☏; Ⓜ St-Ambroise) Collaborative roastery and cafe.

La Caféothèque (p164) Coffee house and roastery with an in-house coffee school.

Coutume Café (p167) Artisan roastery with a flagship Left Bank cafe.

Honor (Map p90; www.honor-cafe.com; 54 rue du Faubourg St-Honoré, 8e; ⊙ 9am-6pm Mon-Sat; Ⓜ Madeleine) Outdoor coffee bar in an elegant rue du Faubourg St-Honoré courtyard.

Café Lomi (Map p72; ☏ 09 80 39 56 24; www.lomi.paris; 3ter rue Marcadet, 18e; ⊙ 8am-6pm Mon-Fri, 10am-7pm Sat & Sun; Ⓜ Marcadet–Poissonnière) Coffee roastery and cafe in the multi-ethnic La Goutte d'Or neighbourhood.

floor and opening to a terrace, a vaulted cellar with a dance floor and upstairs lounge (spanning 370 sq metres in all), its exciting beers include a wonderfully crisp dry-hopped Hopster pale ale.

Harry's New York Bar　　　COCKTAIL BAR
(Map p94; ☏ 01 42 61 71 14; http://harrysbar.fr; 5 rue Daunou, 2e; ⊙ noon-2am Mon-Sat, 4pm-1am Sun; Ⓜ Opéra) One of the most popular American-style bars in the prewar years, Harry's once welcomed writers including F Scott Fitzgerald and Ernest Hemingway, who no doubt sampled the bar's unique cocktail and creation: the Bloody Mary. The Cuban mahogany interior dates from the mid-19th century and was brought over from a Manhattan bar in 1911.

There's a basement piano bar called Ivories where George Gershwin supposedly composed *An American in Paris* and, for the peckish, old-school hot dogs and generous club sandwiches to snack on. Its enduring tagline is 'Tell the Taxi Driver Sank Roo Doe Noo'.

Le Rex Club　　　CLUB
(Map p78; ☏ 01 42 36 10 96; www.rexclub.com; 5 bd Poissonnière, 2e; ⊙ midnight-7am Wed-Sat; Ⓜ Bonne Nouvelle) Attached to the art deco Grand Rex cinema, this is Paris' premier house and techno venue where some of the world's hottest DJs strut their stuff on a 70-speaker, multidiffusion sound system.

📍 Montmartre & Northern Paris

Crowded around place Pigalle at the foot of Montmartre you'll find an eclectic selection of nightlife options, from local cafes and hipster dives to dance clubs and hostess bars. In contrast, the trend around the Canal St-Martin is more barista-run cafes, though wonderful summer nights (and days) see everyone decamp to the canalside quays with blankets, baguettes and bottles of wine. In the 10e, parallel rue du Faubourg St-Martin and rue du Faubourg St-Denis and surrounding streets are speckled with hip cafes, cocktail bars and hybrid bistro-bars.

La Fontaine de Belleville　　　COFFEE
(Map p72; www.lafontaine.cafesbelleville.com; 31-33 rue Juliette Dodu, 10e; ⊙ 8am-10pm; Ⓜ Colonel Fabien) Beans roasted by Belleville Brûlerie are the toast of Paris and the roastery has since opened its own cafe near Canal St-Martin, updating a long-standing local corner spot with gold lettering, woven sky-blue-and-cream bistro chairs and matching tables, and retaining its vintage fittings. Spectacular coffee is complemented by sandwiches, salads and small sharing plates.

Chez Prune　　　BAR
(Map p120; 36 rue Beaurepaire, 10e, cnr quai de Valmy; ⊙ 8am-2am Mon-Sat, 10am-2am Sun; Ⓜ Jacques Bonsergent, République) This boho cafe put Canal St-Martin on the map and its good vibes, original mosaic-tiled interior and rough-around-the-edges look show no sign of disappearing in the near future. Chez Prune remains one of those timeless classic Paris addresses, fabulous for hanging out and people-watching any time of day. Weekend brunch buzzes.

★ Pavillon Puebla　　　BEER GARDEN
(Map p72; www.leperchoir.tv; Parc des Buttes Chaumont, 39 av Simon Bolivar, 19e; ⊙ 6pm-2am Wed-Fri, from noon Sat, noon-10pm Sun; ☏; Ⓜ Buttes Chaumont) Strung with fairy lights, this rus-

tic ivy-draped cottage's two rambling terraces in the Parc des Buttes Chaumont evoke a *guinguette* (old-fashioned outdoor tavern/dance venue), with a 21st-century vibe provided by its Moroccan decor, contemporary furniture, and DJ beats from Thursdays to Saturdays. Alongside mostly French wines and craft beers, cocktails include its signature Spritz du Pavillon (Aperol, Prosecco and soda).

★ Le Syndicat
COCKTAIL BAR

(Map p120; www.syndicatcocktailclub.com; 51 rue du Faubourg St-Denis, 10e; ◔6pm-2am Mon-Sat, from 7pm Sun; Ⓜ Château d'Eau) Plastered top to bottom in peeling posters, an otherwise unmarked façade conceals one of Paris' hottest cocktail bars, but it's no fly-by-night. Le Syndicat's subtitle, Organisation de Défense des Spiritueux Français, reflects its impassioned commitment to French spirits. Ingeniously crafted (and named) cocktails include Saix en Provence (Armagnac, chilli syrup, lime and lavender).

★ Le Très Particulier
COCKTAIL BAR

(Map p100; ☏01 53 41 81 40; www.hotel-particulier-montmartre.com; Pavillon D, 23 av Junot, 18e; ◔6pm-2am; Ⓜ Lamarck–Caulaincourt) The clandestine cocktail bar of boutique Hôtel Particulier Montmartre (p125) is an entrancing spot for a summertime alfresco cocktail. Ring the buzzer at the unmarked black gated entrance and make a beeline for the 1871 mansion's flowery walled garden (or, if it's raining, the adjacent conservatory-style interior). DJs spin tunes from 9.30pm Wednesday to Saturday and from 7pm on Sunday.

★ Gravity Bar
COCKTAIL BAR

(Map p120; 44 rue des Vinaigriers, 10e; ◔6pm-2am Tue-Sat; Ⓜ Jacques Bonsergent) Gravity's stunning wave-like interior, crafted from slats of plywood descending to the curved concrete bar, threatens to distract from the business at hand – serious cocktails, such as Back to My Roots (Provence herb-infused vodka, vermouth, raspberry purée and lemon juice), best partaken in the company of excellent and inventive tapas-style small plates such as clam gnocchi.

CopperBay
COCKTAIL BAR

(Map p120; www.copperbay.fr; 5 rue Bouchardon, 10e; ◔6pm-2am Tue-Sat; Ⓜ Strasbourg–St-Denis) This sleek cocktail bar's polished pale-wood decor, floor-to-ceiling windows and glistening copper fixtures and fittings inject a generous dose of design flair into proceedings.

The cocktail menu mixes classics with house specials such as L'Orangeraie (Japanese pepper-infused gin, ginger, lemon juice and orange blossom water) and Le Bouillon (coriander-infused vodka, red lentil purée, verjus, mezcal and zaatar syrup).

Lipstick
COCKTAIL BAR

(Map p78; www.lipstickparis.com; 5 rue Frochot, 9e; ◔6pm-5am Tue-Sat; Ⓜ Pigalle) If the name isn't a clue, the decor certainly is: its bordello-like leopard-print lounges, red velour drapes and a pole in the centre of the bar reflect its former incarnation as a brothel in this gentrifying red-light district. Stupendous cocktails include Queen P (rose syrup, gin, Aperol, ginger ale and grapefruit juice).

Happy hour, from 6pm to 10pm, gets the party started; DJs play on Fridays and Saturdays from 11pm.

La Machine du Moulin Rouge
CLUB

(Map p100; www.lamachinedumoulinrouge.com; 90 bd de Clichy, 18e; admission €9-16; ◔midnight-6am Fri & Sat, variable Sun-Thu; Ⓜ Blanche) Part of the original Moulin Rouge (well, the boiler room, anyway), this club packs 'em in on weekends with a dance floor, a concert hall, a Champagne bar and an outdoor terrace. Check the agenda online for weekday soirées and happenings.

📍 Le Marais, Ménilmontant & Belleville

Le Marais is a spot *par excellence* when it comes to a good night out – the lively scene embraces everything from gay-friendly and gay-only venues to arty cafes, eclectic bars and raucous pubs. Rue Oberkampf and parallel rue

---

DON'T MISS

THE MOST FAMOUS HOT CHOCOLATE IN TOWN

Clink china with lunching ladies, their posturing poodles and half the students from Tokyo University at **Angelina** (Map p94; ☏01 42 60 82 00; www.angelina-paris.fr; 226 rue de Rivoli, 1er; ◔7.30am-7pm Mon-Fri, 8.30am-7.30pm Sat & Sun; Ⓜ Tuileries) , a grande-dame tearoom dating from 1903. Decadent pastries are served here, but it's the super-thick 'African' hot chocolate (€8.20), which comes with a pot of whipped cream and a carafe of water, that prompts the constant queue for a table.

Jean-Pierre Timbaud are hubs of the Ménilmontant bar crawl, a scene that is edging out steadily through cosmopolitan Belleville.

The Hood
CAFE

(Map p120; www.thehoodparis.com; 80 rue Jean-Pierre Timbaud, 11e; ⊘9.30am-5.30pm Mon & Wed-Fri, 10am-6pm Sat & Sun; 🛜; MParmentier) First and foremost this light-filled local hang-out is about the coffee (Parisian-roasted Belleville Brûlerie beans are brewed to absolute perfection here), but it takes its music just as seriously with a great vinyl collection, spontaneous jam sessions and acoustic Sunday-afternoon 'folkoff' gigs. Fantastic lunches might include cinnamon-roasted chicken with red cabbage and soba noodles. Ask about English-language coffee-brewing workshops.

La Caféothèque
COFFEE

(Map p120; ☑01 53 01 83 84; www.lacafeotheque.com; 52 rue de l'Hôtel de Ville, 4e; ⊘8.30am-7.30pm Mon-Fri, from noon Sat & Sun; 🛜; MPont Marie, St-Paul) From the industrial grinder to elaborate tasting notes, this coffee house

LGBTIQ PARIS

The city known as 'gay Paree' lives up to its name. Paris is so open that there's less of a defined 'scene' here than in other cities where it's more underground. While Le Marais is the mainstay of gay and lesbian nightlife, you'll find LGBTIQ venues throughout the city attracting a mixed crowd.

Le Marais, especially the areas around the intersection of rue Ste-Croix de la Bretonnerie and rue des Archives, and eastwards to rue Vieille du Temple, has long been Paris' main centre of gay nightlife and is still the epicentre of gay and lesbian life in Paris. There's also a handful of bars and clubs within walking distance of bd de Sébastopol. The lesbian scene is less prominent than its gay counterpart, and centres on a few cafes and bars, particularly along rue des Écouffes. Bars and clubs are generally all gay- and lesbian-friendly.

Best Drinking & Nightlife

Open Café (Map p120; www.opencafe.fr; 17 rue des Archives, 4e; ⊘11am-2am Sun-Thu, to 3am Fri & Sat; MHôtel de Ville) The wide terrace is prime for talent-watching.

Gibus Club (Map p120; ☑01 77 15 73 09; www.gibusclub.fr; 18 rue du Faubourg du Temple, 11e; admission €12-25; ⊘11pm-7am Thu-Sat; MRépublique) One of Paris' biggest gay parties.

La Champmeslé (Map p94; 4 rue Chabanais, 2e; ⊘4pm-dawn Mon-Sat; MPyramides) Cabaret nights, fortune-telling and art exhibitions attract an older lesbian crowd.

Guided Tours

For an insider's perspective of gay life in Paris and recommendations on where to eat, drink, sightsee and party, take a tour with the Gay Locals (www.thegaylocals.com; 3hr tour from €180, 2½hr gay or lesbian bar crawl €50). English-speaking residents lead tours of Le Marais as well as private tours of other popular neighbourhoods and customised tours based on your interests.

Events

By far the biggest event on the gay and lesbian calendar is Gay Pride Day, in late June, when the annual Marche des Fiertés (Gay Pride March; www.gaypride.fr; ⊘Jun or Jul) through Paris via Le Marais provides a colourful spectacle, and plenty of parties take place.

Year-round, check gay and lesbian websites or ask at gay bars and other venues to find out about events.

Information

Centre LGBT Paris-Île de France (Map p120; ☑01 43 57 21 47; www.centrelgbtparis.org; 63 rue Beaubourg, 3e; ⊘centre & bar 3.30-8pm Mon-Fri, 1-7pm Sat, library 6-8pm Mon-Wed, 5-7pm Fri & Sat; MRambuteau) is the single best source of information for gay and lesbian travellers in Paris, with a large library of books and periodicals and a sociable bar. It also has details of hotlines, helplines, gay and gay-friendly medical services and politically oriented activist associations.

and roastery is serious. Grab a seat, and pick your bean, filtration method (Aeropress, V60 filter, piston or drip) and preparation style. The in-house coffee school has tastings of different *crus* and various courses including two-hour Saturday-morning tasting initiations (five *terroirs*, five extraction methods) for €60 (English available).

Boot Café
COFFEE
(Map p120; 19 rue du Pont aux Choux, 3e; ☉10am-6pm; 🛜; Ⓜ St-Sébastien–Froissart) The charm of this three-table cafe is its façade. An old cobbler's shop, its original washed-blue exterior, 'Cordonnerie' lettering and fantastic red-boot sign above it are beautifully preserved. The excellent coffee is roasted in Paris, to boot.

★ Le Perchoir
ROOFTOP BAR
(Map p72; 🖉01 48 06 18 48; www.leperchoir.tv; 14 rue Crespin du Gast, 11e; ☉6pm-2am Tue-Fri, from 4pm Sat; 🛜; Ⓜ Ménilmontant) Sunset is the best time to head up to this 7th-floor bar for a drink overlooking Paris' rooftops, where DJs spin on Saturday nights. Greenery provides shade in summer; in winter, it's covered by a sail-like canopy and warmed by fires burning in metal drums. It's accessed off an inner courtyard via a lift (or a spiralling staircase).

★ Candelaria
COCKTAIL BAR
(Map p120; www.quixotic-projects.com; 52 rue de Saintonge, 3e; ☉bar 6pm-2am, taqueria noon-10.30pm Sun-Wed, to 11.30pm Thu-Sat; Ⓜ Filles du Calvaire) A lime-green *taqueria* serving homemade tacos, quesadillas and tostadas conceals one of Paris' coolest cocktail bars through an unmarked internal door. Phenomenal cocktails made from agave spirits, including mezcal, are inspired by Central and South America, such as a Guatemalan El Sombrerón (tequila, vermouth, bitters, hibiscus syrup, pink-pepper-infused tonic and lime). Weekend evenings kick off with DJ sets.

Le Mary Céleste
COCKTAIL BAR
(Map p120; www.quixotic-projects.com/venue/mary-celeste; 1 rue Commines, 3e; ☉6pm-2am, kitchen 7-11.30pm; Ⓜ Filles du Calvaire) Snag a stool at the central circular bar at this uber-popular brick-and-timber-floored cocktail bar or reserve one of a handful of tables online. Innovative cocktails such as Ahha Kapehna (grappa, absinthe, beetroot, fennel and Champagne) are the perfect partners to tapas-style 'small plates' (grilled duck hearts, devilled eggs) to share.

PasDeLoup
COCKTAIL BAR
(Map p120; 🖉09 54 74 16 36; www.pasdeloupparis.com; 108 rue Amelot, 11e; ☉6pm-1am Mon-Wed, to 2am Thu-Sat, to midnight Sun; Ⓜ Filles du Calvaire) Next to the Cirque d'Hiver Bouglione (Winter Circus), a small front bar with timber shelving gives way to a larger space out back where epicureans head for stunning cocktails such as Gardenia (absinthe, St-Germain elderflower liqueur, freshly squeezed OJ and lime) accompanied by superbly gourmet small plates and a loungey retro soundtrack. Happy hour runs from 6pm to 8pm.

Little Red Door
COCKTAIL BAR
(Map p120; 🖉01 42 71 19 32; www.lrdparis.com; 60 rue Charlot, 3e; ☉6pm-2am Sun-Thu, to 3am Fri & Sat; Ⓜ Filles du Calvaires) Behind an inconspicuous timber façade, a tiny crimson doorway is the illusionary portal to this low-lit, bare-brick drinking den filled with flickering candles. Ranked among the World's 50 Best Bars, it's a must for serious mixology fans. Its annual collection of 11 cocktails, in themes from 'art' to 'architecture', are intricately crafted from ingredients such as glacier ice and paper syrup.

Café Charbon
BAR
(Map p120; www.lecafecharbon.fr; 109 rue Oberkampf, 11e; ☉8am-2am Mon-Wed, to 5am Thu, to 6am Fri & Sat; 🛜; Ⓜ Parmentier) Canopied by a gold-stencilled navy-blue awning, Charbon was the first of the hip bars to catch on in Ménilmontant and it remains one of the best. It's always crowded and worth heading to for the belle époque decor (high ceilings, chandeliers and leather booths) and sociable atmosphere. Happy hour is 5pm to 8pm; DJs and musicians play Friday and Saturday.

Cinéma Café Merci
CAFE
(Map p120; www.merci-merci.com; 111 bd Beaumarchais, 3e; ☉11am-2pm Mon-Sat; Ⓜ St-Sébastien–Froissart) Dedicated to the seventh art, this street-level cafe inside concept store Merci (p178) is graced with retro film posters and projects vintage films on one wall. Its *citronnade maison* – extra tart and tongue-tickling, homemade lemonade – and freshly squeezed fruit juices are worth every cent; alternatively, you can get a glass of Champagne to accompany its excellent lunchtime salads and cheese/charcuterie platters.

Wild & the Moon
JUICE BAR
(Map p120; www.wildandthemoon; 55 rue Charlot, 3e; ☉8am-8pm Mon-Fri, from 9am Sat & Sun; Ⓜ Filles du Calvaire) 🌿 Nut milks, vitality

shots, smoothies, cold-pressed juices and raw food are the specialities of this sleek juice bar. All-vegan, ethically sourced ingredients are fresh, seasonal and organic; dishes such as avocado slices on almond and rosemary crackers are served all day.

Bastille & Eastern Paris

Bastille invariably draws a crowd, particularly along rue de Lappe, 11e, which is awash with raucous bars. Continue further east and the options become much more stylish and appealing, with wine bars, intimate clubs and backstreet cocktail dens.

★ Le Baron Rouge   WINE BAR

(Map p126; ☎ 01 43 43 14 32; www.lebaronrouge. net; 1 rue Théophile Roussel, 12e; ⊗ 5-10pm Mon, 10am-2pm & 5-10pm Tue-Fri, 10am-10pm Sat, 10am-4pm Sun; M Ledru-Rollin) Just about the ultimate Parisian wine-bar experience, this wonderfully unpretentious local meeting place, where everyone is welcome, has barrels stacked against the bottle-lined walls and serves cheese, charcuterie and oysters in season. It's especially busy on Sunday after the Marché d'Aligre wraps up. For a small deposit, you can fill up 1L bottles straight from the barrel for less than €5.

★ Concrete   CLUB

(Map p126; www.concreteparis.fr; 69 Port de la Rapée, 12e; ⊗ Thu-Sun; M Gare de Lyon) Moored by Gare de Lyon on a barge on the Seine, this wild-child club with two dance floors is famed for introducing an 'after-hours' element to Paris' somewhat staid clubbing scene, with the country's first 24-hour licence. Watch for world-class electro DJ appearances and all-weekend events on social media.

Outland   CRAFT BEER

(Map p72; https://outland-beer.com; 6 rue Émile Lepeu, 11e; ⊗ 6pm-2am Mon-Sat, to midnight Sun; M Charonne) Of the 12 beers on tap at this artisanal beer bar, eight are Outland's own, brewed just east of central Paris in Fontenay-sous-Bois near the Bois de Vincennes. Among them are a double IPA, a session pale ale, a porter and a fabulously fermented plum göse. Soak them up with tapas like duck liver pâté, organic burrata and stuffed calamari.

Bluebird   COCKTAIL BAR

(Map p126; 12 rue St-Bernard, 11e; ⊗ 6pm-2am; M Faidherbe-Chaligny) The ultimate neighbourhood hang-out, Bluebird is styled like a 1950s apartment with retro decor, a giant fish tank

along one wall, and a soundtrack of smooth lounge music. Cocktail recipes date from the 1800s and early 1900s and change seasonally, but the menu always features six gin-based creations, six with other spirits, and three low-alcohol wine- and Champagne-based drinks.

Latin Quarter

Rive Gauche romantics, well-heeled cafe-society types and students by the gallon drink in the 5e *arrondissement,* where nostalgic haunts, swish bars and new-generation coffee shops ensure a deluge of early-evening happy hours and a quintessential Parisian soirée.

★ Nuage   CAFE

(Map p134; ☎ 09 82 39 80 69; www.nuagecafe.fr; 14 rue des Carmes, 5e; per hr/day €5/25; ⊗ 8.30am-7pm Mon-Fri, 11am-8pm Sat & Sun; 🛜; M Maubert-Mutualité) One of a crop of co-working cafes to mushroom in Paris, Nuage (Cloud) lures a loyal following of nomadic digital creatives with its cosy, home-like spaces in an old church (and subsequent school where Cyrano de Bergerac apparently studied). Payment is by the hour or day, craft coffee is by Parisian roaster Coutume (p167) and gourmet snacks stave off hunger pangs.

★ Shakespeare & Company Café   CAFE

(Map p134; ☎ 01 43 25 95 95; www.shakespeareandcompany.com; 2 rue St-Julien le Pauvre, 5e; ⊗ 9.30am-7pm Mon-Fri, to 8pm Sat & Sun; 🛜; M St-Michel) 🖉 Instant history was made when this literary-inspired cafe opened in 2015 adjacent to magical bookshop Shakespeare & Company (p179), designed from long-lost sketches to fulfil a dream of late bookshop founder George Whitman from the 1960s. Organic chai tea, turbo-power juices and specialist coffee by Café Lomi (p162) marry with soups, salads, bagels and pastries by Bob's Bake Shop (of Bob's Juice Bar; p145).

★ Little Bastards   COCKTAIL BAR

(Map p134; ☎ 01 43 54 28 33; www.facebook. com/lilbastards; 5 rue Blainville, 5e; ⊗ 6pm-2am Mon-Thu, 6pm-4am Fri & Sat; M Place Monge) Only house-creation cocktails (€12) are listed on the menu at uberhip Little Bastards – among them Balance Ton Cochon (bacon-infused rum, egg white, lime juice, oak wood–smoked syrup and bitters) and Deep Throat (Absolut vodka, watermelon syrup and Pernod). The bartenders will mix up classics too if you ask.

🍷 St-Germain & Les Invalides

St-Germain's Carrefour de l'Odéon has a cluster of lively bars and cafes. Rues de Buci, St-André des Arts and de l'Odéon enjoy a fair slice of night action with arty cafes and busy pubs, while place St-Germain des Prés buzzes with the pavement terraces of fabled literary cafes. Rue Princesse attracts a student crowd with its bevy of pubs, microbreweries and cocktail bars.

Les Invalides is a day- rather than nighttime venue, with government ministries and embassies outweighing drinking venues. Particularly in summer, however, look out for bars along the Seine's river banks in the Parc Rives de Seine (p115).

★ Coutume Café
COFFEE
(Map p72; ☑ 01 45 51 50 47; www.coutumecafe. com; 47 rue de Babylone, 7e; ⏰ 8.30am-5.30pm Mon-Fri, 9am-6pm Sat & Sun; 🛜; Ⓜ St-François Xavier) 🍴 The Parisian coffee revolution is thanks in no small part to Coutume, artisanal roaster of premium beans for scores of establishments around town. Its flagship cafe – a bright, light-filled, post-industrial space – is ground zero for innovative preparation methods including cold extraction and siphon brews. Couple some of Paris' finest coffee with a tasty, seasonal cuisine and the place is always packed out.

Be it porridge and fruit or pancakes for *petit dej* (breakfast), a bowl of homemade soup and tartine laden with fresh veggies or weekend brunch (€12), Coutume is an excellent spot to eat all day too. No reservations at weekends.

★ Les Deux Magots
CAFE
(Map p158; ☑ 01 45 48 55 25; www.lesdeux magots.fr; 170 bd St-Germain, 6e; ⏰ 7.30am-1am, Ⓜ St-Germain des Prés) If ever there was a cafe that summed up St-Germain des Prés' early-20th-century literary scene, it's this former hang-out of anyone who was anyone. You'll spend substantially more here than elsewhere to sip *un café* (€4.70) in a wicker-woven bistro chair on the pavement terrace shaded by dark-green awnings and geraniums spilling from window boxes, but it's an undeniable piece of Parisian history.

Café de Flore
CAFE
(Map p158; ☑ 01 45 48 55 26; http://cafedeflore. fr; 172 bd St-Germain, 6e; ⏰ 7.30am-1.30am; Ⓜ St-Germain des Prés) The red upholstered benches, mirrors and marble walls at this art deco

---

ℹ CLUBBING WEBSITES

Track tomorrow's hot 'n' happening soirée with these finger-on-the-pulse Parisian-nightlife links:

Paris DJs (www.parisdjs.com) Free downloads to get you in the groove.

Paris Bouge (www.parisbouge.com) Comprehensive listings site.

Sortir à Paris (www.sortiraparis.com) Click on 'Soirées & Bars', then 'Nuits Parisiennes'.

Tribu de Nuit (www.tribudenuit.com) Parties, club events and concerts galore.

landmark haven't changed much since the days when Jean-Paul Sartre and Simone de Beauvoir essentially set up office here, writing in its warmth during the Nazi occupation. Watch for monthly English-language *philocafé* (philosophy discussion) sessions.

★ Au Sauvignon
WINE BAR
(Map p158; ☑ 01 45 48 49 02; http://ausavignon. com; 80 rue des Sts-Pères, 7e; ⏰ 8am-11pm Mon-Sat, 9am-10pm Sun; Ⓜ Sèvres-Babylone) Grab a table in the evening light at this wonderfully authentic wine bar or head to the quintessential bistro interior, with original zinc bar, tightly packed tables and hand-painted ceiling celebrating French viticultural tradition. A plate of *casse-croûtes au pain Poilâne* (toast with ham, pâté, terrine, smoked salmon and foie gras) is the perfect accompaniment.

★ Le Bar des Prés
COCKTAIL BAR
(Map p158; ☑ 01 43 25 87 67; www.lebardespres. com; 25 rue du Dragon, 6e; ⏰ noon-2.30pm & 7-11pm; Ⓜ St-Sulpice) Sake-based craft cocktails and tantalising shared plates (€18 to €24) by a Japanese chef create buzz at the stylish cocktail-bar arm of Cyril Lignac's foodie empire on rue du Dragon – his glam, 1950s-styled **bistro** (Map p158; ☑ 01 45 48 29 68; www.restaurantauxpres.com; 27 rue du Dragon, 6e; 2-/3-course menu €38/49; ⏰ noon-2.30pm & 7-11pm) is right next door. The scallops with caramelised miso, avocado and fresh coriander are heavenly, as is the yellow tail sashimi, jellied eel and other sushi.

★ Cod House
COCKTAIL BAR
(Map p158; ☑ 01 42 49 35 59; www.thecodhouse. fr; 1 rue de Condé, 6e; ⏰ noon-3pm & 7.30pm-2am Mon-Sat; Ⓜ Odéon) 'Oh my cod!' screams the turquoise-neon 'tag' on the wall, and indeed,

this achingly cool cocktail bar with a gold-and-blue, Scandinavian-style interior does excite. Sake-based cocktails play around with matcha-infused cachaça, cinammon-infused pisco, homemade lemongrass syrup and fresh yuzu. Creative small plates (€5 to €16) titillate taste buds with shrimp tempura, yellowtail carpaccio with fresh chilli and a yuzu sauce, and deep-fried chicken ravioli.

Tiger
COCKTAIL BAR

(Map p158; www.tiger-paris.com; 13 rue Princesse, 6e; ⊙6.30pm-2am Mon-Sat; M Mabillon) Suspended bare-bulb lights and fretted timber make this split-level space a stylish spot for specialist gins (130 varieties). Signature cocktails include a Breakfast Martini (gin, triple sec, orange marmalade and lemon juice) and Oh My Dog (white-pepper-infused gin, lime juice, raspberry and rose cordial and ginger ale). Dedicated G&T aficionados can work their way through a staggering 1040 combinations.

Prescription Cocktail Club
COCKTAIL BAR

(Map p158; ☑09 50 35 72 87; www.prescription cocktailclub.com; 23 rue Mazarine, 6e; ⊙7pm-2am Mon-Thu, 7pm-4am Fri & Sat, 8pm-2am Sun;

M Odéon) With bowler and flat-top hats as lampshades and a 1930s speakeasy New York air to the place, this cocktail club – run by the same mega-successful team as Experimental Cocktail Club (p161) – is very Parisian-cool. Getting past the doorman can be tough, but once in, it's friendliness and old-fashioned cocktails all round.

🍷 Montparnasse & Southern Paris

The comings and goings of the Gare Montparnasse and its historic brasseries keep things lively. Southwest of place d'Italie, rue de la Butte aux Cailles and the surrounding Butte aux Cailles molehill have a plethora of fabulous options popular with students and locals; places here have a loyal clientele and lack the pretension of more trendsetting neighbourhoods.

Especially in summer, you can't beat the floating bars and clubs on the Seine.

★ Café Oz Rooftop
BAR, CLUB

(Map p126; ☑01 44 24 39 34; www.facebook.com/cafeozrooftop; 34 quai d'Austerlitz, 13e, Les Docks; ⊙3pm-2am Tue & Wed, to 4am Thu-Sat; M Gare

---

BEER TALK

Beer hasn't traditionally had a high profile in France and mass-produced varieties such as Kronenbourg 1664 (5.5%), brewed in Strasbourg, dominate. Paris' growing *bière artisanale* (craft beer) scene, however, is going from strength to strength, with an increasing number of city breweries, such as **Brasserie BapBap** (Map p120; ☑01 77 17 52 97; www. bapbap.paris; 79 rue St-Maur, 11e; guided tours €15; ⊙guided tours 11am Sat, shop 6-8pm Tue-Fri, from 3pm Sat; M Rue St-Maur) and **Brasserie la Goutte d'Or** (Map p72; ☑09 80 64 23 51; www.brasserielagouttedor.com; 28 rue de la Goutte d'Or, 18e; ⊙5-7pm Thu & Fri, from 2pm Sat; M Château Rouge, Barbès-Rochechouart) FREE, microbreweries and cafes offering limited-production brews on tap and by the bottle. The city's artisan-beer festival, Paris Beer Week (p118), takes place in brasseries, bars and specialist beer shops, usually in early June. An excellent resource for hopheads is www.hoppyparis.com.

Our favourite addresses for a jar include:

Paname Brewing Company (Map p72; www.panamebrewingcompany.com; 41bis quai de la Loire, 19e; ⊙11am-2am; 🛜; M Crimée, Laumiere) Craft-brewery taproom in a 19th-century waterside granary with a floating pontoon.

Balthazar (Map p72; 20 bd Ménilmontant, 20e; ⊙5pm-1.30am Thu-Sat; M Père Lachaise) Crowdfunded microbrewery with guest Parisian beers.

Outland (p166) Artisan beer bar serving Outland's own beers.

Le Triangle (Map p120; www.triangleparis.com; 13 rue Jacques Louvel-Tessier, 10e; ⊙6-10.30pm Tue-Sat; M Goncourt) Microbrewery with shiny kettles and sharing plates.

Frog & Princess (Map p158; ☑01 40 51 77 38; www.frogpubs.com; 9 rue Princesse, 6e; ⊙5pm-1am Mon-Wed, to 2am Thu & Fri, noon-2am Sat, noon-1am Sun; 🛜; M Mabillon) Long-established microbrewery on a hopping nightlife street.

d'Austerlitz) Chilling with the hip crowd, with beer or cocktail in hand, between potted palms and colourful orange parasols in this alfresco rooftop bar is very much what summer in the city is all about. River views are glorious, multicoloured surfboards inject a touch of Australian beach culture and the dance floor throbs after dark. Pizzas, burgers, wraps and snacks too.

★ **Le Batofar** CLUB
(Map p126; ☑ 01 53 60 37 85; www.batofar.fr; opposite 11 quai François Mauriac, 13e; ⊙ 6pm-7am Wed-Sat, to midnight Sun-Tue; Ⓜ Quai de la Gare, Bibliothèque) Closed for renovation at the time of writing, this much-loved, red-metal tugboat promises to be even more fabulous when it reopens. Its rooftop bar is a place to be seen in summer; it has a respected restaurant; and its club provides memorable underwater acoustics for edgy, experimental music and live performances (mostly electro-oriented but hip hop, new wave, rock, punk and jazz, too).

La Dame de Canton CLUB
(Map p126; www.damedecanton.com; opposite 11 quai François Mauriac, 13e; ⊙ 7pm-midnight Tue-Thu, to 2am Fri, 2pm-5am Sat; Ⓜ Bibliothèque) This floating *boîte* (club) aboard a three-masted Chinese junk with a couple of world voyages under its belt bobs beneath the Bibliothèque Nationale de France. Concerts cover pop and indie to electro, hip hop, reggae and rock; afterwards DJs keep the crowd hyped. There's also a popular bar and restaurant with wood-fired pizzas served on the terrace from May to September.

☆ Entertainment

Catching a performance in Paris is a treat. French and international opera, ballet and theatre companies and cabaret dancers take to the stage in fabled venues, while elsewhere a flurry of young, passionate, highly creative musicians, thespians and other artists make the city's fascinating fringe art scene what it is.

Cabarets
Whirling lines of high-kicking, feather-boa-clad dancers at grand-scale cabarets like cancan creator Moulin Rouge are a quintessential fixture on Paris' entertainment scene – for everyone but Parisians. Still, the dazzling sets, costumes and dancing guarantee an entertaining evening (or matinee).

Tickets to these spectacles start at around €90 (from around €165/190 with lunch/

dinner), with the option of Champagne. Reserve ahead.

Moulin Rouge CABARET
(Map p100; ☑ 01 53 09 82 82; www.moulinrouge.fr; 82 bd de Clichy, 18e; show only from €87, lunch & show from €165, dinner & show from €190; ⊙ show only 2.45pm, 9pm & 11pm, lunch & show 1.45pm, dinner & show 7pm; Ⓜ Blanche) Immortalised in Toulouse-Lautrec's posters and later in Baz Luhrmann's film, Paris' legendary cabaret twinkles beneath a 1925 replica of its original red windmill. Yes, it's packed with bus-tour crowds, but from the opening bars of music to the last high cancan kick, it's a whirl of fantastical costumes, sets, choreography and Champagne. Book in advance and dress smartly (no trainers or sneakers).

No entry for children under six years.

Live Music
Festivals for just about every musical genre ensure that everyone gets to listen in. Street music is a constant in this busker-filled city, with summer adding stirring open-air concerts along the Seine and in city parks to the year-round serenade of accordions.

★ **Philharmonie de Paris** CONCERT VENUE
(Map p72; ☑ 01 44 84 44 84; www.philharmoniedeparis.fr; 221 av Jean Jaurès, 19e; ⊙ box office noon-6pm Tue-Fri, 10am-6pm Sat & Sun, plus concerts; Ⓜ Porte de Pantin) Major complex the Cité de la Musique – Philharmonie de Paris hosts an eclectic range of concerts, from classical to North African and Japanese, in the **Philharmonie** (Map p72; ⊙ noon-6pm Tue-Fri, from 10am Sat & Sun, plus concerts; Ⓜ Porte de Pantin) building's Grande Salle Pierre Boulez, with an audience capacity of 2400 to 3600. The adjacent Cité de la Musique's Salle des Concerts has a capacity of 900 to 1600.

★ **EP7** ARTS CENTER
(Map p72; ☑ 01 43 45 68 07; https://ep7.paris; 133 av de France, 13e; ⊙ 7.30am-2am; 🔊; Ⓜ Bibliothèque) It is impossible to miss the façade of this brand-new cultural cafe and concert venue – the capital's first piece of 'interactive architecture', unveiled in early 2018. Contemporary works of pixel art prance across 12 giant screens covering the façade, creating a dazzling digital gallery. Inside the cultural cafe, named after the vintage vinyl format 'extended play', find art exhibitions and happenings, DJ sets, a trendy bistro serving local, fresh, seasonal cuisine (menu €26) and a late-night bar with Seine view.

★**La Seine Musicale** CONCERT VENUE
(☑01 74 34 54 00; www.laseinemusicale.com; Île Seguin, Boulogne-Billancourt; Ⓜ Pont de Sèvres) A landmark addition to Paris' cultural offerings, La Seine Musicale opened on the Seine island of Île Seguin in 2017. Constructed of steel and glass, the egg-shaped auditorium has a capacity of 1150, while the larger, modular concrete hall accommodates 6000. Ballets, musicals and concerts from classical to rock are all staged here, alongside exhibitions.

★**Café Universel** JAZZ, BLUES
(Map p158; ☑01 43 25 74 20; www.facebook.com/cafeuniverseljazzbar; 267 rue St-Jacques, 5e; ☺8.30pm-1.30am Tue-Sat; 🎤; Ⓜ Censier Daubenton or RER Port Royal) Café Universel hosts a brilliant array of live concerts with everything from bebop and Latin sounds to vocal jazz sessions. Plenty of freedom is given to young producers and artists, and its convivial, relaxed atmosphere attracts a mix of students and jazz lovers. Concerts are free, but you should tip the artists when they pass the hat around.

Caveau de la Huchette JAZZ, BLUES
(Map p134; ☑01 43 26 65 05; www.caveaudelahuchette.fr; 5 rue de la Huchette, 5e; admission €13-15; ☺9pm-2.30am Sun-Thu, to 4am Fri & Sat; Ⓜ St-Michel) Housed in a medieval *caveau* (cellar) used as a courtroom and torture chamber during the Revolution, this club is where virtually all the jazz greats (Georges Brassens, Thibault...) have played since the end of WWII. It attracts its fair share of tourists, but the atmosphere can be more electric than at the more serious jazz clubs. Sessions start at 10pm.

ⓘ **TEATIME IN PARIS**
....

Mariage Frères (Map p120; www.mariagefreres.com; 30, 32 & 35 rue du Bourg Tibourg, 4e; ☺10am-8pm; Ⓜ Hôtel de Ville) Paris' oldest and finest tearoom, founded in 1854.

L'Amaryllis de Gérard Mulot (Map p158; ☑01 43 26 91 03; www.gerard-mulot.com; 12 rue des Quartre Vents, 6e; lunch menu €25, afternoon tea €15; ☺11am-6.30pm Tue-Sat; Ⓜ Odéon) Wonderful tearoom by patisserie maestro Gérard Mulot.

La Mosquée (p106) Sip sweet mint tea and nibble delicious pastries at Paris' mosque.

Le Divan du Monde LIVE MUSIC
(Map p100; ☑01 40 05 08 10; www.divandumonde.com; 75 rue des Martyrs, 18e; Ⓜ Pigalle) Take some cinematographic events and *nouvelles chansons françaises* (new French songs). Add in soul/funk fiestas, air-guitar face-offs and rock parties of the Arctic Monkeys/Killers/Libertines persuasion... You may now be getting some idea of the inventive, open-minded approach at this excellent cross-cultural venue in Pigalle.

La Cigale LIVE MUSIC
(Map p100; ☑01 49 25 89 99; www.lacigale.fr; 120 bd de Rochechouart, 18e; Ⓜ Pigalle) Now classed as a historical monument, this music hall dates from 1887 but was redecorated a century later by Philippe Starck. Artists who have performed here include Ryan Adams, Ibrahim Maalouf and the Dandy Warhols.

Badaboum LIVE MUSIC
(Map p120; ☑01 48 06 50 70; http://badaboum.paris; 2bis rue des Taillandiers, 11e; ☺bar 7pm-2am Wed & Thu, to 6am Sat, club & concerts vary; Ⓜ Ledru-Rollin) The onomatopoeically named Badaboum hosts a mixed bag of concerts on its up-close-and-personal stage, but focuses on electro, funk and hip hop. Great atmosphere, super cocktails and a chill-out room upstairs.

L'Alimentation Générale LIVE MUSIC
(Map p120; ☑01 43 55 42 50; www.alimentation-generale.net; 64 rue Jean-Pierre Timbaud, 11e; admission Wed, Thu & Sun free, Fri & Sat €10; ☺7pm-2am Wed, Thu & Sun, to 5am Fri & Sat; Ⓜ Parmentier) This true hybrid, known as the Grocery Store to Anglophones, is a massive space, fronted at street level by its in-house Italianate canteen-bar with big glass windows and retro 1960s Belgian furniture. But music is the big deal here, with an impressive line-up of live gigs and DJs spinning pop, rock, electro, soul and funk to a packed dance floor.

Cinema

The film lover's ultimate city, Paris has some wonderful movie houses to catch new flicks, avant-garde cinema and priceless classics.

Foreign films (including English-language films) screened in their original language with French subtitles are labelled 'VO' (*version originale*). Films labelled 'VF' (*version française*) are dubbed in French.

L'Officiel des Spectacles lists the full crop of Paris' cinematic pickings and screening times; online, check out http://cinema.le parisien.fr.

DON'T MISS

BUSKERS IN PARIS

Paris' gaggle of clowns, mime artists, living statues, acrobats, in-line skaters, buskers and other street entertainers can be loads of fun and cost substantially less than a theatre ticket (a few coins in the hat is appreciated). Some excellent musicians perform in the long, echo-filled corridors of the metro (artists audition for the privilege). Outside, you can be sure of a good show at the following:

Place Georges Pompidou, 4e The huge square in front of the Centre Pompidou.

Pont St-Louis, 4e The bridge linking Paris' two islands.

Pont au Double, 4e The pedestrian bridge linking Notre Dame with the Left Bank.

Place Joachim du Bellay, 1er Musicians and fire-eaters near the Fontaine des Innocents.

Parc de la Villette, 19e African drummers at the weekend.

Place du Tertre, 18e Montmartre's original main square is Paris' busiest busker stage.

The city's film archive, the **Forum des Images** (Map p94; ☑ 01 44 76 63 00; www.forumdes images.fr; Forum des Halles, 2 rue du Cinéma, Porte St-Eustache, 1er; cinema tickets adult/child €6/4; ⊙ 12.30-9pm Tue-Fri, 2-9pm Sat & Sun; Ⓜ Les Halles or RER Châtelet Les Halles), screens films set in Paris.

First-run tickets cost around €11.50 for adults (€13.50 for 3D). Students and over 60s get discounted tickets (usually around €8.50) from 7pm Sunday to 7pm Friday. Discounted tickets for children and teens have no restrictions. Most cinemas have across-the-board discounts before noon.

Fondation Jérôme Seydoux-Pathé CINEMA

(Map p72; ☑ 01 83 79 18 96; www.fondation-jerome seydoux-pathe.com; 77 av des Gobelins, 13e; tickets adult/child €6.50/4.50; ⊙ 1-8pm Tue, 1-7pm Wed-Fri, 11.30am-7pm Sat; Ⓜ Place d'Italie) This striking cinema with a small exhibition (€3) devoted to the history of cinema is a brilliant addition to the Paris flick scene. Where else can you watch silent B&W movies to the sound of a live pianist? The Pathé Foundation is hidden in a former theatre and cinema dating to 1869, but only the façade – sculpted by Rodin – remains. The rest of the building is an unbelievable, five-storey, contemporary 'slug' of a creation by world-class architect Renzo Piano.

Le Louxor CINEMA

(Map p78; ☑ 01 44 63 96 98; www.cinemalouxor.fr; 170 bd de Magenta, 10e; tickets adult/child €9.70/5; Ⓜ Barbès-Rochechouart) Built in neo-Egyptian art deco style in 1921 and saved from demolition by a neighbourhood association seven decades later, this historical monument is a palatial place to catch a new release, classic, piano-accompanied 'ciné-concert', short-film festival, special workshop (such as sing-alongs) or live-music performance. Don't miss a drink at its bar, which opens onto an elevated terrace overlooking Sacré-Cœur.

La Cinémathèque Française CINEMA

(Map p126; ☑ 01 71 19 33 33; www.cinematheque. fr; 51 rue de Bercy, 12e; tickets adult/child €6.50/4; ⊙ 2.30-9pm or later Wed-Sun; Ⓜ Bercy) This **national institution** (Map p126; adult/child €5/2.50, with film €8; ⊙ noon-7pm Wed-Mon) is a temple to the 'seventh art' and always screens its foreign offerings in their original versions. Up to 10 films a day are shown, usually retrospectives (eg Spielberg, Altman, Eastwood) mixed in with related but more obscure films.

Le Grand Rex CINEMA

(Map p78; ☑ 01 45 08 93 89; www.legrandrex.com; 1 bd Poissonnière, 2e; tours adult/child €11/9, cinema tickets adult/child €11/4.50; ⊙ tours 10am-6pm Wed, Sat & Sun, extended hours during school holidays; Ⓜ Bonne Nouvelle) Blockbuster screenings and concerts aside, this 1932 art deco cinematic icon runs 50-minute behind-the-scenes tours (English soundtracks available) during which visitors – tracked by a sensor slung around their neck – are whisked up (via a lift) behind the giant screen, tour a soundstage and experiment in a recording studio. Whizz-bang special effects along the way will stun adults and kids alike.

Opera & Ballet

France's Opéra National de Paris and Ballet de l'Opéra National de Paris perform at Paris' two opera houses, the Palais Garnier and Opéra Bastille. The season runs between September and July.

Palais Garnier
OPERA, BALLET

(Map p78; place de l'Opéra, 9e; M Opéra) The city's original opera house (p80) is smaller than its Bastille counterpart, but has perfect acoustics. Due to its odd shape, some seats have limited or no visibility – book carefully. Ticket prices and conditions (including last-minute discounts) are available from the box office (Map p78; ☑ international calls 01 71 25 24 23, within France 08 92 89 90 90; www. operadeparis.fr; cnr rues Scribe & Auber; ☉10am-6.30pm Mon-Sat). Online flash sales are held from noon on Wednesdays.

Opéra Bastille
OPERA

(Map p126; ☑ international calls 01 71 25 24 23, within France 08 92 89 90 90; www.operadeparis.fr; 2-6 place de la Bastille, 12e; ☉ box office 11.30am-6.30pm Mon-Sat, 1hr prior to performances Sun; M Bastille) Paris' premier opera hall, Opéra Bastille's 2745-seat main auditorium also stages ballet and classical concerts. Online tickets go on sale up to three weeks before telephone or box-office sales (from noon on Wednesdays; online flash sales offer significant discounts). Standing-only tickets (*places débouts*; €5) are available 90 minutes before performances. French-language 90-minute guided tours (Map p126; ☑ within France 08 92 89 90 90; www.operadeparis.fr; 2-6 place de la Bastille, 12e; M Bastille) take you backstage.

Significant discounts are available for those aged under 28.

Theatre

Theatre productions, including those originally written in other languages, are invariably performed in French. Only occasionally do English-speaking troupes play at smaller venues in and around town. Consult *L'Officiel des Spectacles* (www.offi.fr) for details.

Non-French speakers should check out Theatre in Paris (TIP; ☑ 01 85 08 66 89; www. theatreinparis.com; tickets €20-100; ☉ phone enquiries 10am-7pm Mon-Fri), whose bilingual hosts provide an English-language program and direct you to your seats. Typically there are upwards of 10 shows on offer, from French classics to contemporary comedies and Broadway-style productions with English surtitles. Book via its English online ticketing platform.

Théâtre du Luxembourg
THEATRE

(Map p158; ☑ 01 43 29 50 97; www.marionnettesduluxembourg.fr; Jardin du Luxembourg; tickets €6.40; ☉ Wed, Sat & Sun, daily during school holidays; M Notre Dame des Champs) You don't have to be a kid or be able to speak French to be delighted by marionette shows, which have entertained audiences in France since the Middle Ages. The lively puppets perform in the Jardin du Luxembourg's Théâtre du Luxembourg. Show times vary; check the program online and arrive half an hour ahead.

Comédie Française
THEATRE

(Map p94; ☑ 01 44 58 15 15; www.comedie-francaise. fr; place Colette, 1er; M Palais Royal–Musée du Louvre) Founded in 1680 under Louis XIV, this state-run theatre bases its repertoire on the works of classic French playwrights. The theatre has its roots in an earlier company directed by Molière at the Palais Royal.

🔒 Shopping

Paris has it all: broad boulevards lined with international chains, luxury avenues studded with designer fashion houses, famous *grands magasins* (department stores) and fabulous markets. But the real charm lies in strolling the city's backstreets, where tiny speciality shops and quirky boutiques

---

ⓘ WHAT'S ON & TICKETS

Paris' top listings guide, *L'Officiel des Spectacles* (www.offi.fr; €1), is published in French but is easy to navigate. It's available from newsstands on Wednesday, and is crammed with everything that's on in the capital.

The most convenient place to purchase concert, theatre and other cultural and sporting-event tickets is from electronics and entertainment megashop Fnac (☑ 08 92 68 36 22; www.fnactickets.com), whether in person at the *billeteries* (ticket offices) or by phone or online. There are branches throughout Paris, including in the Forum des Halles. Tickets generally can't be refunded.

On the day of performance, theatre, opera and ballet tickets are sold for half price (plus €3.50 commission) at the central Kiosque Théâtre Madeleine (Map p90; www. kiosqueculture.com; opposite 15 place de la Madeleine, 8e; ☉12.30-7.30pm Tue-Sat, to 3.45pm Sun; M Madeleine).

selling everything from strawberry-scented wellington boots to heavenly fragranced candles are wedged between cafes, galleries and churches.

🔒 Champs-Élysées & Grands Boulevards

Global chains line the Champs-Élysées, but it's the luxury fashion houses in the Triangle d'Or and on rue du Faubourg St-Honoré that have made Paris famous. The area around Opéra and the Grands Boulevards is where you'll find flagship *grands magasins*.

⭐ **Galeries Lafayette**   DEPARTMENT STORE
(Map p78; 📞 01 42 82 34 56; http://haussmann. galerieslafayette.com; 40 bd Haussmann, 9e; ⏲ 9.30am-8.30pm Mon-Sat, 11am-7pm Sun; 📶; Ⓜ Chaussée d'Antin or RER Auber) Grande-dame department store Galeries Lafayette is spread across the main store (its magnificent stained-glass dome is over a century old), **men's store** (Map p78; bd Haussmann, 9e), and **homewares store** (Map p78; bd Haussmann, 9e) with a **gourmet emporium** (Map p78; bd Haussmann, 9e).

Catch modern art in the 1st-floor **gallery** (Map p78; 📞 01 42 82 81 98; www.galeriedesgaleries. com; ⏲ 11am-7pm Tue-Sun; Ⓜ Chaussée d'Antin or RER Auber) ⒻⓇⒺⒺ, take in a **fashion show** (Map p78; 📞 bookings 01 42 82 81 98; ⏲ 3pm Fri Mar-Jun & Sep-Dec by reservation), ascend to a free, wind-swept rooftop panorama or take a break at one of its 24 restaurants and cafes.

The main store will stay open during renovations by architect Amanda Levete's studio AL_A. On the av des Champs-Élysées, a new Galeries Lafayette **store** (Map p90; www.galerieslafayette.com; 52 av Champs-Élysées; Ⓜ Franklin D Roosevelt) is under construction and is expected to open in 2019.

Le Printemps   DEPARTMENT STORE
(Map p78; 📞 01 42 82 50 00; www.printemps.com; 64 bd Haussmann, 9e; ⏲ 9.35am-8pm Mon-Sat, to 8.45pm Thu, 11am-7pm Sun; 📶; Ⓜ Havre Caumartin) Famous department store Le Printemps encompasses Le Printemps de la Mode, for women's fashion, and **Le Printemps de l'Homme** (Map p78; rue de Provence, 9e; Ⓜ Havre Caumartin), for men's fashion, both with established and up-and-coming designer wear. Le Printemps de la Beauté et Maison, for beauty and homewares, offers a staggering display of perfume, cosmetics and accessories.

There's a free panoramic rooftop terrace and luxury eateries, including Ladurée.

ℹ️ LES SOLDES

Paris' twice-yearly *soldes* (sales) generally last five to six weeks, starting around mid-January and again around mid-June.

Guerlain   PERFUME
(Map p90; 📞 spa 01 45 62 11 21; www.guerlain.com; 68 av des Champs-Élysées, 8e; ⏲ 10.30am-8pm Mon-Sat, noon-8pm Sun; Ⓜ Franklin D Roosevelt) Guerlain is Paris' most famous parfumerie, and its shop (dating from 1912) is one of the most beautiful in the city. With its shimmering mirror-and-marble art deco interior, it's a reminder of the former glory of the Champs-Élysées. For total indulgence, make an appointment at its heavenly spa.

À la Mère de Famille   FOOD & DRINKS
(Map p78; 📞 01 47 70 83 69; www.lameredefamille.com; 35 rue du Faubourg Montmartre, 9e; ⏲ 9.30am-8pm Mon-Sat, 10am-7.30pm Sun; Ⓜ Le Peletier) Founded in 1761, this is the original location of Paris' oldest chocolatier. Its beautiful belle époque façade is as enchanting as the rainbow of sweets, caramels and chocolates inside.

Place de la Madeleine   FOOD & DRINKS
(Map p90; place de la Madeleine, 8e; Ⓜ Madeleine) Ultragourmet food shops garland place de la Madeleine; many have in-house dining options. Notable names include truffle dealers **La Maison de la Truffe** (Map p90; 📞 01 42 65 53 22; www.maison-de-la-truffe.com; 19 place de la Madeleine, 8e; ⏲ 10am-10pm Mon-Sat); luxury food shop **Hédiard** (Map p90; 📞 01 43 12 88 88; www.hediard.fr; 21 place de la Madeleine, 8e), which is reopening in 2019 after head-to-toe renovations; mustard specialist **Boutique Maille** (Map p90; www.maille.com; 6 place de la Madeleine, 8e; ⏲ 10am-7pm Mon-Sat); Paris' most famous caterer, **Fauchon** (Map p78; 📞 01 70 39 38 00; www.fauchon.fr; 26 & 30 place de la Madeleine, 8e; ⏲ 10am-8.30pm Mon-Sat), with mouth-watering delicacies from foie gras to jams, chocolates and pastries; and extravagant chocolate sculptures at **Patrick Roger** (Map p90; 📞 09 67 08 24 47; www.patrickroger.com; 3 place de la Madeleine, 8e; ⏲ 10.30am-7.30pm).

Hôtel Drouot   ART, ANTIQUES
(Map p78; 📞 01 48 00 20 20; www.drouot.com; 7-9 rue Drouot, 9e; ⏲ 11am-6pm Mon-Fri, to 11pm Thu; Ⓜ Richelieu Drouot) Selling everything from antiques and jewellery to rare books and

BRUNO DE HOGUES/GETTY IMAGES ©

Marché d'Aligre (p153) **2.** Ladurée (p136), Champs-Élysées **3.** Galeries Lafayette (p173)

Paris Shopping

Paris has it all: broad boulevards lined with flagship fashion houses and international labels, famous *grands magasins* (department stores) and fabulous markets. But the real charm of Parisian shopping lies in strolling the backstreets, where tiny speciality shops and quirky boutiques sell everything from strawberry-scented wellington boots to heaven-scented candles.

Fashion is Paris' forte. Browse *haute couture* creations in the Étoile and Champs-Élysées neighbourhood (p173), particularly within the Triangle d'Or (Golden Triangle). For original streetwear and vintage gear, head for Le Marais, particularly the Haut Marais (p178). Small boutiques fill St-Germain's chic streets (p179). You'll also find adorable children's wear and accessories. Parisian fashion doesn't have to break the bank: there are fantastic bargains at secondhand and vintage boutiques, along with outlet shops selling previous seasons' collections, surpluses and seconds by top-line designers.

But fashion is just the beginning. Paris is an exquisite treasure chest of gourmet food (including cheeses, macarons and foie gras), wine, tea, books, beautiful stationery, art, art supplies, antiques and collectables. Ask for *un paquet cadeau* – free (and very beautiful) gift wrapping offered by most shops.

UNIQUE SHOPPING EXPERIENCES

Passages couverts Paris' 19th-century glass-roofed covered passages were the precursors to shopping malls.

Flea markets Lose yourself in the maze of *marchés* (markets) at the enormous Marché aux Puces de St-Ouen (p177).

Street markets Scores of colourful street markets take place every week.

Grands magasins One-stop department-store shopping in resplendent art nouveau surrounds.

PARIS' RIVERSIDE BOOKSELLERS

With some 3km of forest-green boxes lining the Seine – containing over 300,000 secondhand (and often out-of-print) books, rare magazines, postcards and old advertising posters – Paris' *bouquinistes* (used-book sellers) are as integral to the cityscape as Notre Dame. Many open only from spring to autumn (and many shut in August), but year-round you'll still find some to browse.

Bouquinistes (Map p94; quai Voltaire, 7e, to quai de la Tournelle, 5e, & Pont Marie, 4e, to quai du Louvre, 1er; ⊘ 11.30am–dusk) have been in business since the 16th century, when they were itinerant peddlers selling their wares on Parisian bridges; back then their sometimes subversive (eg Protestant) materials could get them into trouble with the authorities. By 1859 the city had finally wised up: official licences were issued, space (10m of railing) was rented and eventually the permanent green boxes were installed.

Today, *bouquinistes* (the official count ranges from 200 to 240) are allowed to have four boxes, only one of which can be used to sell souvenirs. Look hard enough and you just might find some real treasures: old comic books, forgotten first editions, maps, stamps, erotica and prewar newspapers – as in centuries past, it's all there, waiting to be rediscovered.

art, Paris' most established auction house has been in business for more than a century. Viewings are from 11am to 6pm the day before and from 11am to noon the morning of the auction. Pick up the catalogue *Gazette de l'Hôtel Drouot,* published Fridays, in-house or at newsstands.

🏠 Louvre & Les Halles

The 1er and 2e *arrondissements* are mostly about fashion. Indeed the Sentier district is something of a garment heaven, while rue Étienne Marcel, place des Victoires and rue du Jour flaunt prominent labels and shoe shops. Nearby rue Montmartre and rue Tiquetonne are the streets to shop for streetwear and avant-garde designs; the easternmost part of the 1er around Palais Royal, for fancy period and conservative label fashion.

La Samaritaine   DEPARTMENT STORE
(Map p94; ☑ 01 56 81 28 40; www.lasamaritaine. com; 19 rue de la Monnaie, 1er; Ⓜ Pont Neuf) One of Paris' four big department stores, the 10-storey La Samaritaine is finally emerging from its much contested and drawn-out 14-year overhaul. Pritzker Prize–winning Japanese firm Sanaa has preserved much of the gorgeous art nouveau and art deco exterior, in addition to the glass ceiling topping the central Hall Jourdain. It's slated to open in 2019.

Passage des Panoramas   MALL
(Map p78; btwn 10 rue St-Marc & 11 bd Montmartre, 2e; ⊘ 6am–midnight, shop hours vary; Ⓜ Grands Boulevards, Richelieu Drouot) Built in 1800, this

is the oldest covered arcade in Paris and the first to be lit by gas (1817). It's a bit faded now, but retains a real 19th-century charm with several outstanding eateries, a theatre from where spectators would come out to shop during the interval, and autograph dealer Arnaud Magistry (at No 60).

Didier Ludot   FASHION & ACCESSORIES
(Map p94; ☑ 01 42 96 06 56; www.didierludot.fr; 24 Galerie de Montpensier, 1er; ⊘ 10.30am–7pm Mon-Sat; Ⓜ Palais Royal–Musée du Louvre) In the rag trade since 1975, collector Didier Ludot sells the city's finest couture creations of yesteryear, hosts exhibitions and has published a book portraying the evolution of the little black dress.

L'Exception   DESIGN
(Map p94; ☑ 01 40 39 92 34; www.lexception. com; 24 rue Berger, 1er; ⊘ 10am–8pm Mon-Sat, 11am–7pm Sun; Ⓜ Les Halles or RER Châtelet–Les Halles) Over 400 different French designers come together under one roof at this light-filled concept store, which showcases rotating collections of men's and women's fashion along with accessories including lingerie and swimwear, shoes, eyewear, gloves, hats, scarves, belts, bags, watches and jewellery. It also sells design books, cosmetics, candles, vases and other gorgeous homewares, and has a small in-house coffee bar.

Legrand Filles & Fils   FOOD & DRINKS
(Map p94; ☑ 01 42 60 07 12; www.caves-legrand. com; 1 rue de la Banque, 2e; ⊘ 11am–7pm Mon, 10am–7.30pm Tue-Sat; Ⓜ Bourse) Tucked inside

Galerie Vivienne since 1880, Legrand sells fine wine and all the accoutrements: corkscrews, tasting glasses, decanters etc. It also has a fancy wine bar, *école du vin* (wine school; courses from €60 for two hours) and *éspace dégustation* with several tastings a month, including ones accompanied by live concerts; check its website for details.

E Dehillerin   HOMEWARES
(Map p94; ☑ 01 42 36 53 13; www.edehillerin.fr; 18-20 rue Coquillière, 1er; ⊙ 9am-12.30pm & 2-6pm Mon, 9am-6pm Tue-Sat; Ⓜ Les Halles) Founded in 1820, this extraordinary two-level store – more like an old-fashioned warehouse than a shiny, chic boutique – carries an incredible selection of professional-quality *matériel de cuisine* (kitchenware). Poultry scissors, turbot poacher, professional copper cookware or an Eiffel Tower–shaped cake tin – it's all here.

🏠 Montmartre & Northern Paris

There's a growing number of boutiques in Pigalle but the finest strips for fashion shoppers are rue Beaurepaire and rue de Marseille by Canal St-Martin. While Montmartre has its fair share of keyring-filled souvenir shops, there are some exquisite specialist boutiques selling everything from handcrafted jewellery to antique perfume bottles, vinyl and vintage fashion. The enormous Marché aux Puces de St-Ouen flea market sprawls to the neighbourhood's north, while gourmet shops line rue des Martyrs.

**★ Marché aux
Puces de St-Ouen**   MARKET
(Map p72; www.marcheauxpuces-saintouen.com; rue des Rosiers, St-Ouen; ⊙ Sat-Mon; Ⓜ Porte de Clignancourt) Spanning 9 hectares, this vast flea market was founded in 1870 and is said to be Europe's largest. Over 2000 stalls are grouped into 15 *marchés* selling everything from 17th-century furniture to 21st-century clothing. Each market has different opening hours – check the website for details. There are kilometre upon kilometre of 'freelance' stalls; come prepared to spend some time.

★ Belle de Jour   FASHION & ACCESSORIES
(Map p100; www.belle-de-jour.fr; 7 rue Tardieu, 18e; ⊙ 11am-1pm & 2-7pm Tue-Fri, 11am-1pm & 2-6pm Sat; Ⓜ Anvers, Abbesses) Be whisked back in time to the elegance of belle époque Paris is at this Montmartre shop specialising in

perfume bottles. Gorgeous 19th-century atomisers, smelling salts and powder boxes in engraved or enamelled Bohemian, Baccarat and Saint-Louis crystal share shelf space with more contemporary designs. Whether you're after art deco or art nouveau, pink-frosted or painted glass, it's here.

★ Fromagerie Alléosse   CHEESE
(Map p90; www.fromage-alleosse.com; 13 rue Poncelet, 17e; ⊙ 9am-1pm & 3.30-7pm Tue-Sat, 9am-1pm Sun; Ⓜ Ternes) On stall-filled foodie street rue Poncelet, heady *fromagerie* Alléosse has its own cheese-ripening *caves* (cellars) spanning 300 sq metres with four separate environments. Its 250-plus cheeses are grouped into five main categories: *fromage de chèvre* (goat's milk), *fromage à pâte persillée* (veined or blue), *fromage à pâte molle* (soft), *fromage à pâte demi-dure* (semihard) and *fromage à pâte dure* (hard).

Balades Sonores   MUSIC
(Map p78; www.baladessonores.com; 1-3 av Trudaine, 9e; ⊙ noon-8pm Mon-Sat; Ⓜ Anvers) One of Paris' best vinyl shops, Balades Sonores sprawls over two adjacent buildings. The ground floor of 1 av Trudaine stocks contemporary pop, rock, metal, garage and all genres of French music. Its basement holds secondhand blues, country, new wave and punk from the '60s to '90s. Next door, No 3 has soul, jazz, funk, hip hop, electronica and world music.

O/HP/E   DESIGN
(Map p120; 27 rue du Château d'Eau, 10e; ⊙ 2-7.30pm Tue, 8.30am-7.30pm Wed-Fri, 9.30am-7.30pm Sat, to 6.30pm Sun; Ⓜ Jacques Bonsergent) White-on-white concept store O/HP/E stocks chic homewares – ceramics, textiles, light fittings, candles and kitchenware (rolling pins, mats, chopping boards, chopsticks et al) – along with cosmetics, stationery and gifts. Also here is an *épicerie* with gourmet delicacies (preserves, nougats, sugar-coated olives and chocolates) and a cafe with baked treats such as hazelnut praline tarts.

Spree   FASHION & ACCESSORIES
(Map p100; ☑ 01 42 23 41 40; www.spree.fr; 16 rue de la Vieuville, 18e; ⊙ 11am-7.30pm Tue-Sat, 3-7pm Sun & Mon; Ⓜ Abbesses) Allow plenty of time to browse this super-stylish boutique-gallery, with a carefully selected collection of designer fashion put together by stylist Roberta Oprandi and artist Bruni Hadjadj. What makes shopping here fun is that all the furniture –

vintage 1950s to 1980s pieces by Eames and other midcentury designers – is also for sale, as is the contemporary artwork on the walls.

Pigalle   FASHION & ACCESSORIES
(Map p78; www.pigalle-paris.com; 7 rue Henry Monnier, 9e; ⏱noon-8pm Mon-Sat, from 2pm Sun; Ⓜ St-Georges) Pick up a hoodie emblazoned with the black-and-white Pigalle logo from this leading Parisian menswear brand, created by designer and basketball player Stéphane Ashpool, who grew up in the 'hood.

🔒 Le Marais, Ménilmontant & Belleville

Le Marais has an ever-expanding fashion presence, with tiny *ateliers* and boutiques with rising and just-established designers at work. In the Haut Marais, young designers have colonised the upper reaches of the 3e on and around rue Charlot and rue de Turenne. To the south, in the 4e, rue des Francs Bourgeois and rue François Miron have well-established boutique shopping for clothing, hats, home furnishings and stationery. Place des Vosges is lined with high-end art and antique galleries. Both areas form one of Paris' ZTIs (international tourist zones) with late-night and Sunday trading.

★**Merci**   GIFTS & SOUVENIRS
(Map p120; ☎01 42 77 00 33; www.merci-merci.com; 111 bd Beaumarchais, 3e; ⏱10am-7.30pm; Ⓜ St-Sébastien–Froissart) 🌿 A Fiat Cinquecento marks the entrance to this unique concept store, which donates all its profits to a children's charity in Madagascar. Shop for fashion, accessories, linens, lamps and nifty designs for the home. Complete the experience with a coffee in its hybrid used-bookshop-cafe,

a juice at its Cinéma Café (p165) or lunch in its stylish La Cantine de Merci (p143).

★**Empreintes**   DESIGN
(Map p120; www.empreintes-paris.com; 5 rue de Picardie, 3e; ⏱11am-7pm Mon-Sat; Ⓜ Temple) Spanning more than 600 sq metres over four floors, this design emporium has over 1000 items for sale at any one time from more than 6000 emerging and established French artists and designers. Handcrafted jewellery, fashion and art are displayed alongside striking homewares (ceramics, cushions, furniture, lighting and more). Upstairs there's a cafe and a reference library. The basement houses a projection room.

★**Kerzon**   HOMEWARES, COSMETICS
(Map p120; www.kerzon.paris; 68 rue de Turenne, 3e; ⏱11.30am-8pm Tue-Sat; Ⓜ St-Sébastien–Froissart) Candles made from natural, biodegradable wax in Parisian scents such as Jardin du Luxembourg (with lilac and honey), Place des Vosges (rose and jasmine) and Parc des Buttes-Chaumont (cedar and sandalwood) make aromatic souvenirs of the city. The pretty white and sage-green boutique also stocks room fragrances, scented laundry liquids, and perfumes, soaps, bath oils and other toiletries.

★**Fromagerie Goncourt**   CHEESE
(Map p120; ☎01 43 57 91 28; 1 rue Abel Rabaud, 11e; ⏱9am-1pm & 4-8.30pm Tue-Fri, 9am-8pm Sat; Ⓜ Goncourt) Styled like a boutique, this contemporary *fromagerie* is a must-discover. Clément Brossault ditched a career in banking to become a *fromager* and his cheese selection – 70-plus types – is superb. Cheeses flagged with a bicycle symbol are varieties he discovered in situ during a two-month French cheese tour he embarked on as part of his training.

Candora   PERFUME
(Map p120; ☎01 43 48 76 05; www.candora.fr; 1 rue du Pont Louis-Philippe, 4e; ⏱2-7pm Tue-Sat; Ⓜ Pont Marie) At this brother-and-sister-run parfumerie near the Seine you can have bespoke scents made up in just 10 minutes. Or learn how to create fragrances yourself during a perfume-making workshop for adults and children. Workshops in English take place at 2.30pm on Tuesday and Friday, last 90 minutes (€79/54 per adult/child) and include a 15mL bottle.

🔒 Bastille & Eastern Paris

Superb markets aside, Bastille and eastern Paris are not really known for shopping, but there's a select choice of unique boutiques and specialist shops. Key fashion brands have stores on the western end of trendy rue de Charonne, between av Ledru-Rollin and rue du Faubourg St-Antoine, and arts and crafts studio-showrooms are tucked under the viaduct arches beneath the Promenade Plantée.

Marché aux Puces d'Aligre   MARKET
(Map p126; place d'Aligre, 12e; ⊗8am-1pm Tue-Sun; Ⓜ Ledru-Rollin) Smaller but more central than Paris' other flea markets, the Marché aux Puces d'Aligre, adjoining the Marché d'Aligre (p153) street market, has a jumble of furniture, antiques, retro homewares, books, vintage and new clothes, and bric-a-brac.

La Cocotte   HOMEWARES
(Map p126; www.lacocotteparis.com; 5 rue Paul Bert, 11e; ⊗noon-7pm Tue-Sat; Ⓜ Faidherbe-Chaligny) If the gourmet restaurants along rue Paul Bert have inspired you to get into the kitchen, stop by the boutique of designers Andrea Wainer and Laetitia Bertrand for stylish, often Paris-and/or French-themed accoutrements such as tea towels, oven mitts, aprons, mugs, shopping bags and more, many incorporating La Cocotte's signature hen motif.

La Manufacture de Chocolat   FOOD
(Map p120; www.lechocolat-alainducasse.com; 40 rue de la Roquette, 11e; ⊗9.30am-6pm Mon-Fri; Ⓜ Bastille) If you dine at superstar chef Alain Ducasse's restaurants, the chocolate will have been made here at Ducasse's own chocolate factory (the first in Paris to produce 'bean-to-bar' chocolate), which he set up with his former executive pastry chef Nicolas Berger. Deliberate over ganaches, pralines and truffles and no fewer than 44 flavours of chocolate bar.

Viaduc des Arts   ARTS & CRAFTS
(Map p126; www.leviaducdesarts.com; 1-129 av Daumesnil, 12e; ⊗hours vary; Ⓜ Bastille, Gare de Lyon) Located beneath the red-brick arches of the Promenade Plantée (p101) elevated park, the Viaduc des Arts' line-up of traditional artisans and contemporary designers – including furniture and tapestry restorers, interior designers, cabinetmakers, violin- and flute-makers, embroiderers and jewellers – carry out antique renovations and create new items using time-honoured methods.

🔒 Latin Quarter
Bookworms will love this part of the Left Bank, home to some wonderful bookshops.

Other student-frequented shops include camping stores, comic shops, old-school vinyl shops where collectors browse for hours and cheap, colourful homewares stores, interspersed with the occasional *droguerie-quincaillerie* (hardware store) – easily spotted by the jumble of laundry baskets, buckets etc piled on the pavement out the front.

★ Shakespeare & Company   BOOKS
(Map p134; ☑01 43 25 40 93; www.shakespeareandcompany.com; 37 rue de la Bûcherie, 5e; ⊗10am-10pm; Ⓜ St-Michel) Enchanting nooks and crannies overflow with new and secondhand English-language books. The original shop (12 rue l'Odéon, 6e; closed by the Nazis in 1941) was run by Sylvia Beach and became the meeting point for Hemingway's 'Lost Generation'. Readings by emerging and illustrious authors take place at 7pm most Mondays and there's a wonderful cafe (p166) next door.

★ Le Bonbon au Palais   FOOD
(Map p134; ☑01 78 56 15 72; www.bonbonsaupalais.fr; 19 rue Monge, 5e; ⊗10.30am-7.30pm Tue-Sat; Ⓜ Cardinal Lemoine) Kids and kids-at-heart will adore this sugar-fuelled *tour de France*. The school-geography-themed boutique stocks rainbows of artisan sweets from around the country. Old-fashioned glass jars brim with treats such as *calissons* (diamond-shaped, icing-sugar-topped ground fruit and almonds from Aix-en Provence), *rigolettes* (fruit-filled pillows from Nantes), *berlingots* (striped, triangular boiled sweets from Carpentras and elsewhere) and *papalines* (herbal liqueur-filled pink-chocolate balls from Avignon).

Mayette la Boutique de la Magie   GAMES, HOBBIES
(Map p134; ☑01 43 54 13 63; www.mayette.com; 8 rue des Carmes, 5e; ⊗2-7.30pm Tue-Sat; Ⓜ Maubert-Mutualité) One of a kind, this magic shop established in 1808 is said to be the world's oldest. Since 1991 it's been in the hands of world-famous magic pro Dominique Duvivier. Professional and hobbyist magicians flock here to discuss king sandwiches, reverse assemblies, false cuts and other card tricks with Duvivier and his daughter, Alexandra.

🔒 St-Germain & Les Invalides
The northern wedge of the 6e between Église St-Germain des Prés and the Seine is a dream

to mooch around with its bijou art galleries, antique shops, stylish vintage clothes shops and designer boutiques (Vanessa Bruno, Isabel Marant et al). St-Germain's style continues along the western half of bd St-Germain and rue du Bac with a striking collection of contemporary furniture, kitchen and design shops. Gourmet food and wine shops galore make it a foodie's paradise.

Marché Saint-Germain
MARKET

(Map p158; http://marchesaintgermain.com; 4-6 rue Lobineau, 6e; ⏱8am-8pm Tue-Sat, to 1.30pm Sun; Ⓜ Mabillon) New life has been breathed into St-Germain's stunning covered market following a 2017 refit. A food market has been here since 1486 and it became covered in the 1880s. Today's arcaded building, with dazzling Apple and Nespresso stores tucked beneath its arches, dates to the late 20th century. Duck inside to uncover down-to-earth vendors selling fresh fruit, veg, meat, poultry and exceptional cheeses.

★ Le Bon Marché
DEPARTMENT STORE

(Map p158; ☑01 44 39 80 00; http://lebonmarche. com; 24 rue de Sèvres, 7e; ⏱10am-8pm Mon-Wed, Fri & Sat, 10am-8.45pm Thu, 11am-8pm Sun; Ⓜ Sèvres-Babylone) Built by Gustave Eiffel as Paris' first department store in 1852, this is the epitome of style, with a superb concentration of men's and women's fashions, homewares, stationery, books and toys. Break for a coffee, afternoon tea with cake or a light lunch at the Rose Bakery tearoom on the 2nd floor.

The icing on the cake is its glorious **food hall** (Map p158; www.lagrandeepicerie.com; 36 rue de Sèvres, 7e; ⏱8.30am-9pm Mon-Sat, 10am-8pm Sun; Ⓜ Sèvres-Babylone).

★ Magasin Sennelier
ARTS & CRAFTS

(Map p94; ☑01 42 60 72 15; www.magasinsen nelier.com; 3 quai Voltaire, 7e; ⏱2-6.30pm Mon, 10am-12.45pm & 2-6.30pm Tue-Sat; Ⓜ St-Germain des Prés) Cézanne and Picasso were among the artists who helped develop products for this venerable 1887-founded art supplier on the banks of the Seine, and it remains an exceptional place to pick up canvases, brushes, watercolours, oils, pastels, charcoals and more. The shop's forest-green façade with gold lettering, exquisite original timber cabinetry and glass display cases also fuel artistic inspiration.

★ Cantin
CHEESE

(Map p76; ☑01 45 5043 94; www.cantin.fr; 12 rue du Champs de Mars, 7e; ⏱2-7.30pm Mon, 8.30am-7.30pm Tue-Sat, 8.30am-1pm Sun; Ⓜ École Militaire)

🍃 Opened in 1950 and still run by the same family today, this exceptional shop stocks cheeses only made in limited quantities on small rural farms. They're then painstakingly ripened in Cantin's own cellars (from two weeks up to two years) before being displayed for sale. Should you want to know how to concoct the perfect cheeseboard, Cantin runs informative tasting workshops.

Sabbia Rosa
FASHION & ACCESSORIES

(Map p158; ☑01 45 48 88 37; 73 rue des Sts-Pères, 6e; ⏱10am-7pm Mon-Sat; Ⓜ St-Germain des Prés) Only French-sourced fabrics (silk from Lyon, lace from Calais) are used by lingerie designer Sabbia Rosa for her ultra-luxe range at this upmarket boutique, open since 1976. Every piece is unique; items can be custom-made in 48 hours. The list of celebrity clients reads like a who's who: Serge Gainsbourg, Madonna, Naomi Campbell, Claudia Schiffer and George Clooney have all shopped here.

Hermès
FASHION & ACCESSORIES

(Map p158; ☑01 42 22 80 83; www.hermes.com; 17 rue de Sèvres, 6e; ⏱10.30am-7pm Mon-Sat; Ⓜ Sèvres-Babylone) A stunning art deco swimming pool (originally belonging to neighbouring Hôtel Lutetia, no less) now houses luxury label Hermès' inaugural concept store. Retaining its original mosaic tiles and iron balustrades, the vast, tiered space showcases new directions in home furnishings, including fabrics and wallpaper, along with classic lines such as its signature scarves. Its cafe, Le Plongeoir (the Diving Board), is equally chic.

La Dernière Goutte
WINE

(Map p158; ☑01 43 29 11 62; www.laderniEregoutte. net; 6 rue du Bourbon le Château, 6e; ⏱3.30-8pm Mon, 10.30am-1.30pm & 3-8pm Tue-Fri, 10.30am-8pm Sat, 11am-7pm Sun; Ⓜ Mabillon) 'The Last Drop' is the brainchild of Cuban-American sommelier Juan Sánchez, whose tiny wine shop is packed with exciting, mostly organic French *vins de propriétaires* (estate-bottled wines) made by small independent producers. Wine classes lasting two hours (two white tastings, five red) regularly take place in English (per person €55); phone for schedules and reservations. Free tastings with winemakers take place most Saturdays.

Deyrolle
ANTIQUES, HOMEWARES

(Map p158; ☑01 42 22 30 07; www.deyrolle.com; 46 rue du Bac, 7e; ⏱10am-1pm & 2-7pm Mon, 10am-7pm Tue-Sat; Ⓜ Rue du Bac) Overrun with creatures such as lions, tigers, zebras and storks, taxidermist Deyrolle opened in 1831. In addition to stuffed animals (for rent and sale), it stocks minerals, shells, corals and crustaceans, stand-mounted ostrich eggs and pedagogical storyboards. There are also rare and unusual seeds (including many old types of tomato), gardening tools and accessories.

ℹ Information

DANGERS & ANNOYANCES

Overall, Paris is well lit and safe, and random street assaults are rare.

➡ Stay alert for pickpockets and take precautions: don't carry more cash than you need, and keep credit cards and passports in a concealed pouch.

➡ Beware of scams such as fake petitions.

➡ Metro stations best avoided late at night include Châtelet Les Halles, Château Rouge, Gare du Nord, Strasbourg St-Denis, Réaumur Sébastopol, Stalingrad and Montparnasse Bienvenüe. Marx Dormoy, Porte de la Chapelle and Marcadet–Poissonniers can be sketchy day and night.

➡ *Bornes d'alarme* (alarm boxes) are located in the centre of metro/RER platforms and some station corridors.

MEDICAL SERVICES

Paris has some 50 hospitals, including the following:

Hôpital Hôtel Dieu (☑ 01 42 34 88 19; www. aphp.fr; 1 Parvis Notre Dame – place Jean-Paul-II, 4e; Ⓜ Cité) One of the city's main government-run public hospitals; after 8pm use the emergency entrance on rue de la Cité.

L'Institut Hospitalier Franco-Britannique (IHFB; ☑ 01 47 59 59 59; www.ihfb.org; 4 rue Kléber, Levallois-Perret; Ⓜ Anatole France) Private, English-speaking option.

Pharmacies (chemists) are marked by a large illuminated green cross outside. At least one in each neighbourhood is open for extended hours; find a complete night-owl listing on the Paris Convention & Visitors Bureau website (www. parisinfo.com).

Pharmacie Bader (☑ 01 43 26 92 66; www. pharmaciebader.com; 10-12 bd St-Michel, 6e; ◷ 8.30am-9pm; Ⓜ St-Michel)

Pharmacie de la Mairie (☑ 01 42 78 53 58; www.pharmacie-mairie-paris.com; 9 rue des Archives, 4e; ◷ 9am-8pm; Ⓜ Hôtel de Ville)

Pharmacie Les Champs (☑ 01 45 62 02 41; Galerie des Champs-Élysées, 84 av des Champs-Élysées, 8e; ◷ 24hr; Ⓜ George V)

TOURIST INFORMATION

Paris Convention & Visitors Bureau (Paris Office de Tourisme; Map p120; ☑ 01 49 52 42 63; www.parisinfo.com; 29 rue de Rivoli, 4e; ◷ 9am-7pm; 🛜; Ⓜ Hôtel de Ville) Paris' main tourist office is at the Hôtel de Ville. It sells tickets for tours and several attractions, plus museum and transport passes.

ℹ Getting There & Away

AIR

Aéroport de Charles de Gaulle (CDG; ☑ 01 70 36 39 50; www.parisaeroport.fr) Most international airlines fly to Aéroport de Charles de Gaulle, 28km northeast of central Paris. (The airport is commonly called 'Roissy' after the suburb in which it's located.)

Aéroport d'Orly (ORY; ☑ 01 70 36 39 50; www. parisaeroport.fr) Aéroport d'Orly is located 19km south of central Paris, but despite being closer to the centre than Aéroport de Charles de Gaulle, it's used less frequently by international airlines and public-transport options aren't quite as straightforward. If you're travelling with heavy luggage or young kids, consider a taxi.

That will change by 2024, when metro line 14 will be extended to the airport. A TGV station is due to arrive here in 2025.

Aéroport de Beauvais (BVA; ☑ 08 92 68 20 66; www.aeroportbeauvais.com) Aéroport de Beauvais is 75km north of Paris and is served by a few low-cost airlines – but before you snap up that bargain, consider whether the post-arrival journey is worth it.

BUS

Eurolines (Map p134; ☑ 08 92 89 90 91; www. eurolines.fr; 55 rue St-Jacques, 5e; ◷ 9.30am-6.30pm Mon-Fri, 10am-1pm & 2-5pm Sat; Ⓜ Cluny-La Sorbonne) connects all major European capitals to Paris' international bus terminal, **Gare Routière Internationale de Paris-Galliéni** (28 av du Général de Gaulle, Bagnolet; Ⓜ Galliéni). The terminal is in the eastern suburb of Bagnolet; it's about a 15-minute metro ride to the more central République station.

Major European bus company Flixbus (www.flix bus.com) uses western **Parking Pershing** (Map p72; 16-24 bd Pershing, 17e; Ⓜ Porte Maillot).

TRAIN

Paris is the central point in the French rail network, Société Nationale des Chemins de Fer Français (SNCF), with six train stations that handle passenger traffic to different parts of France and Europe. Each is well connected to the Paris public-transport system, the Régie Autonome des Transports Parisiens (RATP). To buy onward tickets from Paris, visit a station or go to Oui.SNCF (www.oui.sncf). Most trains – and all high-speed Trains à Grande Vitesse (TGV) – require advance reservations. The earlier you book, the better your chances of securing a discounted fare. Main-line stations in Paris have left-luggage offices and/or *consignes* (lockers) for a maximum of 72 hours.

Gare du Nord (www.gares-sncf.com; rue de Dunkerque, 10e; Ⓜ Gare du Nord) The terminus

ⓘ MUSEUM DISCOUNTS & PASSES

Almost all museums and monuments in Paris have discounted tickets (tarif réduit) for students and seniors (generally over 60 years), provided they have valid ID. Children often get in for free; the cut-off age for 'child' is anywhere between six and 18 years. EU citizens under 26 years get in for free at national monuments and museums.

Paris Museum Pass (http://en.parismuseumpass.com; two/four/six days €48/62/74) Gets you into 50-plus venues in and around Paris; a huge advantage is that pass holders usually enter larger sights at a different entrance, meaning you bypass (or substantially reduce) ridiculously long ticket queues.

Paris Passlib' (www.parisinfo.com; two/three/five days €109/129/155) Sold at the Paris Convention & Visitors Bureau (p181) and on its website, this handy city pass covers unlimited public transport in zones 1 to 3, admission to some 50 museums in the Paris region (aka a Paris Museum Pass), temporary exhibitions at most municipal museums, a one-hour **Bateaux Parisiens** (Map p76; ☑ 08 25 01 01 01; www.bateauxparisiens.com; Port de la Bourdonnais, 7e; adult/child €15/7; Ⓜ Bir Hakeim or RER Pont de l'Alma) boat cruise along the Seine, and a one-day hop-on, hop-off open-top bus sightseeing service around central Paris' key sights with L'Open Tour (p184). There's an optional €20 supplement for a skip-the-line ticket to levels one and two of the Eiffel Tower.

for northbound domestic trains as well as several international services. Located in northern Paris.

Eurostar (www.eurostar.com) The London–Paris line runs from St Pancras International to Gare du Nord. Voyages take 2¼ hours.

Thalys (www.thalys.com) Trains pull into Paris' Gare du Nord from Brussels, Amsterdam and Cologne.

Gare de Lyon (bd Diderot, 12e; Ⓜ Gare de Lyon) The terminus for trains from Lyon, Provence, the Côte d'Azur, the French Alps, Italy, Spain and Switzerland. Located in eastern Paris.

Gare de l'Est (www.gares-sncf.com; place du 11 Novembre 1918, 10e; Ⓜ Gare de l'Est) The terminus for trains from Luxembourg, southern Germany (Frankfurt, Munich, Stuttgart) and points further east (including a weekly Moscow service); there are regular and TGV Est trains to areas of France east of Paris (Champagne, Alsace and Lorraine). Located in northern Paris.

Gare d'Austerlitz (bd de l'Hôpital, 13e; Ⓜ Gare d'Austerlitz) The terminus for a handful of trains from the south, including services from Orléans, Limoges and Toulouse. High-speed trains to/from Barcelona and Madrid also use Austerlitz. Current renovations will continue until 2021. Located in southeastern Paris.

Gare Montparnasse (av du Maine & bd de Vaugirard, 15e; Ⓜ Montparnasse Bienvenüe) The terminus for trains from the southwest and west, including services from Brittany, the Loire Valley, Bordeaux, Toulouse, and Spain and Portugal. Some of these services will move to Gare d'Austerlitz (by 2021, once refurbishment is complete). Located in southern Paris.

Gare St-Lazare (www.gares-sncf.com; rue Intérieure, 8e; Ⓜ St-Lazare) The terminus for trains from Normandy. Located in Clichy, northwestern Paris.

ⓘ Getting Around

TO/FROM THE AIRPORTS
Aéroport Charles de Gaulle

Bus

There are six main bus lines.

Le Bus Direct line 2 (www.lebusdirect.com, €17, one hour, every 30 minutes from 5.45am to 11pm) Links the airport with the Arc de Triomphe via the **Eiffel Tower** (Map p76; www.lebusdirect.com; 16-20 av de Suffren, 15e; Ⓜ Bir-Hakeim or RER Champ de Mars–Tour Eiffel) and Trocadéro.

Le Bus Direct line 4 (€17, 50 to 80 minutes, every 30 minutes from 6am to 10.30pm from the airport, 5.30am to 10.30pm from Montparnasse) Links the airport with **Gare Montparnasse** (Map p158; www.lebusdirect.com; rue du Commandant René Mouchotte, 14e; Ⓜ Montparnasse Bienvenüe; 80 minutes) in southern Paris via **Gare de Lyon** (Map p126; www.lebusdirect.com; 20bis bd Diderot, 12e; Ⓜ Gare de Lyon; 50 minutes) in eastern Paris.

Noctilien buses 140 and 143 (€8 or four metro tickets) Part of the RATP night service, Noctilien has two buses that link CDG with **Gare de l'Est** (Map p72; rue du 8 Mai 1945, 10e; Ⓜ Gare de l'Est) in northern Paris via nearby **Gare du Nord** (Map p72; 170 rue La Fayette, 10e; Ⓜ Gare du Nord): bus 140 (1am to 4am; from Gare de l'Est 1am to 3.40am) takes 80 minutes, and bus 143 (12.32am to 4.32am; from Gare de l'Est 12.55am to 5.08am) takes 55 minutes.

RATP bus 350 (€6 or three metro tickets, 70 minutes, every 30 minutes from 5.30am to 11pm) Links the airport with **Gare de l'Est** (Map p72; www.ratp.fr; bd de Strasbourg, 10e, Gare de l'Est; €5.70, direct from driver €6; Ⓜ Gare de l'Est).

RATP bus 351 (€6 or three metro tickets, 70 minutes, every 30 minutes from 5.30am to 11pm) Links the airport with **place de la Nation** (Map p72; 2 av du Trône, 12e; M Nation) in eastern Paris.

Roissybus (€12.50, one hour, from CDG every 15 to 20 minutes from 6am to 12.30am; from Paris every 15 minutes from 5.15am to 12.30am) Links the airport with **Opéra** (Map p78; 11 rue Scribe, 9e; M Opéra).

Taxi

→ A taxi to the city centre takes 40 minutes. Since 2016, fares have been standardised to a flat rate: €50 to the Right Bank and €55 to the Left Bank. The fare increases by 15% between 7pm and 7am and on Sundays.

→ Only take taxis at a clearly marked rank. Never follow anyone who approaches you at the airport and claims to be a driver.

Train

CDG is served by the RER B line (€11.40, child four to nine €7.90, approximately 50 minutes, every 10 to 20 minutes), which connects with central Paris stations including Gare du Nord, Châtelet–Les Halles and St-Michel–Notre Dame. Trains run from 4.50am to 11.50pm (from Gare du Nord 4.53am to 12.15am) every six to 15 minutes.

Aéroport d'Orly

Bus

Two bus lines serve Orly:

Le Bus Direct line 1 (€12, one hour, every 20 minutes from 5.50am to 11.30pm from Orly, 4.50am to 10.30pm from the Arc de Triomphe) Runs to/from the Arc de Triomphe (one hour) via **Gare Montparnasse** (p182; 40 minutes), **La Motte-Picquet** (Map p72; www.lebusdirect.com; 88 av de Suffren, 15e; M La Motte-Picquet–Grenelle) and Trocadéro.

Orlybus (€8.70, 30 minutes, every 15 to 20 minutes from 6am to 12.30am from Orly, 5.35am to midnight from Paris) Runs to/from place **Denfert-Rochereau** (Map p72; 3 place Denfert-Rochereau, 14e; M Denfert-Rochereau) in southern Paris.

Taxi

A taxi to the city centre takes roughly 30 minutes. Standardised flat-rate fares since 2016 mean a taxi costs €30 to the Left Bank and €35 to the Right Bank. The fare increases by 15% between 7pm and 7am and on Sunday.

Train

There is currently no direct train to/from Orly; you'll need to change halfway. Note that while it is possible to take a shuttle to the RER C line, this service is quite long and not recommended.

RER B (€13.25, children four to nine €6.60, 35 minutes, every four to 12 minutes) This line connects Orly with the St-Michel–Notre Dame, Châtelet–Les Halles and Gare du Nord stations in the city centre. In order to get from Orly to the RER station (Antony), you must first take the Orlyval automatic train. The service runs from 6am to 11.35pm. You only need one ticket to take the two trains.

Tram

Tramway T7 (€1.90, 40 minutes, every six minutes from 5.30am to 12.30am) This tramway links Orly with Villejuif–Louis Aragon metro station in southern Paris; buy tickets from the machine at the tram stop as no tickets are sold on board.

Aéroport Paris-Beauvais

Shuttle

The Beauvais *navette* (shuttle bus; €17, 1¼ hours) links the airport with **Parking Pershing** (p181) on central Paris' western edge; services are coordinated with flight times. See the airport website for details and tickets.

Taxi

A taxi to central Paris during the day/night costs around €170/210 (probably more than the cost of your flight!).

BICYCLE

The **Vélib'** (☎ 01 76 49 12 34; www.velib-metropole.fr; day/week subscription for up to 5 people €5/15, standard bike hire up to 30/60min free/€1, electric bike €1/2) bike-share scheme changed operators in 2018; check the website for the latest information. When the handover is complete, it will put tens of thousands of bikes (30% of which will be electric) at the disposal of Parisians and visitors at some 1400 stations throughout Paris, accessible around the clock.

→ To get a bike, you first need to purchase a one- or seven-day subscription either at the docking stations or online.

→ The terminals require a credit card with an embedded smart chip (which precludes many North American cards), and, even then, not all foreign chip-embedded cards will work. Alternatively, you can purchase a subscription online before you leave your hotel.

→ After you authorise a deposit (€300) to pay for the bike should it go missing, you'll receive an ID number and PIN code and you're ready to go.

→ Bikes are rented in 30-minute intervals. If you return a bike before a half-hour is up and then take a new one, you will not be charged for a standard bicycle (electric bikes incur charges).

→ Standard bikes are suitable for cyclists aged 14 and over, and are fitted with gears, an anti-theft lock with key, reflective strips and front/

ℹ TOURIST PASSES

The Mobilis and Paris Visite passes are valid on the metro, the RER, SNCF's suburban lines, buses, night buses, trams and the Montmartre funicular railway. No photo is needed, but write your full name and date of use on the ticket. Passes are sold at larger metro and RER stations, SNCF offices in Paris and the airports. Passes operate by date (rather than 24-hour periods), so activate them early in the day for the best value.

Mobilis Allows unlimited travel for one day and costs €7.50 (for two zones) to €17.80 (five zones). Buy it at any metro, RER or SNCF station in the Paris region. Depending on how many times you plan to take the metro in a day, a *carnet* (book of 10 tickets) might work out cheaper.

Paris Visite Allows unlimited travel as well as discounted entry to certain museums, and other discounts and bonuses. The 'Paris+Suburbs+Airports' pass includes transport to/from the airports and costs €25.25/38.35/53.75/65.80 for one/two/three/five days. The cheaper 'Paris Centre' pass, valid for zones 1 to 3, costs €12/19.50/26.65/38.35 for one/two/three/five days. Children aged four to 11 years pay half price.

rear lights. Bring your own helmet (they are not required by law).

➡ Electric bikes are also for those aged over 14. They have a top speed of 25km/h and a range of 50km.

Rentals

Most rental places will require a deposit (usually €150 for a standard bike, €300 for electric bikes). Take ID and your bank or credit card.

Freescoot (🖉 01 44 07 06 72; www.freescoot. com; 63 quai de la Tournelle, 5e; 50/125cc scooters per 24hr from €65/75, bicycle/tandem/electric-bike rental per 24hr from €25/40/50; 🕙 9am-1pm & 2-7pm mid-Apr–mid-Sep, closed Sun & Wed mid-Sep–mid-Apr; Ⓜ Maubert-Mutualité)

Gepetto et Vélos (🖉 01 43 54 19 95; www. gepetto-velos.com; 28 rue des Fossés St-Bernard, 5e; bike rental per hr/day/weekend €4/16/20, tandem €8/30/45; 🕙 9am-7pm Tue-Sat; Ⓜ Cardinal Lemoine)

Paris à Vélo, C'est Sympa (🖉 01 48 87 60 01; www.parisvelosympa.fr; 22 rue Alphonse Baudin, 11e; half-day/full day/24hr bike from €12/15/20, electric bike €20/30/40; 🕙 9.30am-1pm & 2-6pm Mon-Fri, 9am-7pm Sat & Sun Apr-Oct, shorter hours Nov-Mar; Ⓜ Richard Lenoir)

BOAT

Batobus (www.batobus.com; adult/child 1-day pass €17/8, 2-day pass €19/10; 🕙 10am-9.30pm late Apr-Aug, shorter hours Sep-late Apr) runs glassed-in trimarans that dock every 20 to 25 minutes at nine small piers along the Seine: Beaugrenelle, Eiffel Tower, Musée d'Orsay, St-Germain des Prés, Notre Dame, Jardin des Plantes/Cité de la Mode et du Design, Hôtel de Ville, Musée du Louvre and Champs-Élysées.

Buy tickets online, at ferry stops or at tourist offices. Two-day passes must be used on consecutive days. You can also buy a Pass+ that includes **L'Open Tour** (🖉 01 42 66 56 56; www.

paris.opentour.com; 1-day pass adult/child €33/17, night tour €27/17) buses, to be used on consecutive days. A two-day pass per adult/child costs €46/21; a three-day pass is €50/21.

CAR & MOTORCYCLE

Driving in Paris is defined by the triple hassle of navigation, heavy traffic and limited parking. Petrol stations are also difficult to locate and access. A car is unnecessary to get around, but if you're heading out of the city on an excursion, then one can certainly be useful. A Crit'Air Vignette (compulsory anti-pollution sticker) is also required in most instances. If you plan on hiring a car, it's best to do so online and in advance.

Scooters

Cityscoot (www.cityscoot.eu; per 1/100min €0.28/25; 🕙 7am-11pm) Electric mopeds with a top speed of 45km/h are available to rent as part of Paris' scooter-sharing scheme, with all bookings via smartphones. No subscriptions are necessary. Any driver's licence (including a foreign-issued licence) is valid for those born before 1 January 1988; anyone born after that date requires a current EU driver's licence.

Freescoot (p184) Rents 50/125cc scooters in various intervals. Prices include third-party insurance as well as helmets, locks, rain gear and gloves. A motorcycle licence is required for 125cc scooters but not for 50cc scooters, though you must be at least 23 years old and leave a credit-card deposit of €1000.

Left Bank Scooters (p116) Rents Vespa XLV scooters including insurance, helmet and wet-weather gear; scooters can be delivered to and collected from anywhere in Paris. You must be at least 20 years old and have a car or motorcycle licence. Credit-card deposit is €1000.

PUBLIC TRANSPORT
Bus

Buses can be a scenic way to get around – and there are no stairs to climb, meaning they are more widely accessible – but they're slower and less intuitive to figure out than the metro.

Paris' bus system, operated by the RATP, runs from approximately 5am to 1am Monday to Saturday; services are drastically reduced on Sunday and public holidays. Hours vary substantially depending on the line.

➡ Normal bus rides embracing one or two bus zones cost one metro ticket; longer rides require two or even three tickets.

➡ Transfers to other buses – but not the metro – are allowed on the same ticket as long as the change takes place 1½ hours between the first and last validation. This does not apply to Noctilien services.

➡ Whatever kind of single-journey ticket you have, you must validate it in the ticket machine near the driver. If you don't have a ticket, the driver can sell you one for €2 (correct change required).

➡ If you have a Mobilis or Paris Visite pass, flash it at the driver when you board.

Metro & RER

Paris' underground network is run by RATP and consists of two separate but linked systems: the metro and the Réseau Express Régional (RER) suburban train line. The metro has 14 numbered lines; the RER has five main lines (but you'll probably only need to use A, B and C). When buying tickets consider how many zones your journey will cover; there are five concentric transport zones rippling out from Paris (zone 5 being the furthest); if you travel from Charles de Gaulle airport to Paris, for instance, you will have to buy a ticket for zones 1 to 5.

For information on the metro, RER and bus systems, visit www.ratp.fr. Metro maps of various sizes and degrees of detail are available for free at metro ticket windows; several can also be downloaded for free from the RATP website.

➡ The same RATP tickets are valid on the metro, the RER (for travel within the city limits), buses, trams and the Montmartre funicular.

➡ A ticket – white in colour and called Le Ticket t+ – costs €1.90 (half price for children aged four to nine years) if bought individually; a carnet (book) of 10 costs €14.90 for adults.

➡ Tickets are sold at all metro stations. Some automated machines take notes and coins, though not all. Ticket windows accept most credit cards; however, machines do not accept credit cards without embedded chips (and even then, not all foreign chip-embedded cards are accepted).

➡ One ticket lets you travel between any two metro stations (no return journeys) for a period of 1½ hours, no matter how many transfers are required. You can also use it on the RER for travel within zone 1, which encompasses all of central Paris.

➡ Transfers from the metro to buses or vice versa are not possible.

➡ Always keep your ticket until you exit from your station; if you are stopped by a ticket inspector, you will have to pay a fine if you don't have a valid ticket.

TAXI

➡ The *prise en charge* (flagfall) is €4. Within the city limits, it costs €1.07 per kilometre for travel between 10am and 5pm Monday to Saturday (*Tarif A;* white light on taxi roof and meter).

➡ At night (5pm to 10am), on Sunday from 7am to midnight and in the inner suburbs, the rate is €1.29 per kilometre (*Tarif B;* orange light).

➡ Travel in the city limits and inner suburbs on Sunday night (midnight to 7am Monday) and in the outer suburbs is at *Tarif C,* €1.56 per kilometre (blue light).

➡ The minimum taxi fare for a short trip is €7.10.

➡ There are flat-fee fares to/from the major airports (Charles de Gualle from €50, Orly from €30).

➡ A fifth passenger incurs a €4 surcharge.

➡ There's no additional charge for luggage.

➡ Flagging down a taxi in Paris can be difficult; it's best to find an official taxi stand.

➡ To order a taxi, call or reserve online with **Taxis G7** (☎ 3607, 01 41 27 66 99; www.g7.fr) or **Alpha Taxis** (☎ 01 45 85 85 85; www.alpha-taxis-paris.fr).

➡ An alternative is private driver system Uber taxi (www.uber.com/fr/cities/paris); you order and pay via your phone. However, official taxis continue to protest about the service and there have been instances of Uber drivers and passengers being harassed.

Motorbike Taxis

For speed seekers, the hot choice is a *taxi moto* (motorbike taxi), whereby you leap on the back of a bike, driver and helmet provided, and zip past the traffic at lightning speed. Companies include **Paris Motos** (☎ 06 75 67 56 75; www.parismotos.fr) and **Taxi Moto Paris** (☎ 06 64 65 61 86; http://taxi-motos-paris.com).

Around Paris

Best Places to Eat

➡ Le Jardin des Plumes (p195)

➡ L'Axel (p203)

➡ Le Tripot (p203)

➡ La Cour (p192)

➡ Le Vertugadin (p200)

➡ La Table du 11 (p193)

Best Places to Sleep

➡ La Demeure du Parc (p197)

➡ Le Grand Monarque (p203)

➡ La Ferme de la Canardière (p199)

Why Go?

Whether you're taking day trips from Paris or continuing further afield, a trove of treasures awaits in the areas around the French capital.

The Île de France *région* – the 12,000-sq-km 'Island of France' shaped by five rivers – and surrounding areas contain some of the most extravagant châteaux in the land. At the top of everyone's list is the palace at Versailles, the opulence and extravagance of which partly spurred the French Revolution, but the châteaux in Fontainebleau and Chantilly are also breathtaking. Many beautiful and ambitious cathedrals are also here, including the glorious cathedral crowning the medieval old city of Chartres. In Giverny, Monet's home and gardens provide a picturesque insight into the inspiration for his seminal paintings.

Yet Paris' surrounds don't only hark back to the past. Also here is every kid's favourite, Disneyland Resort Paris, which now has more attractions than ever.

When to Go
Chartres

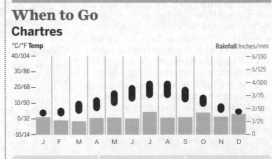

Mid-Apr–mid-Oct
Chartres' landmarks light up during Chartres en Lumières.

Mid-May–early Oct Candlelight visits are magical at the Château de Vaux-le-Vicomte.

Mid-Jun–mid-Sep
Fountains dance to classical music in Versailles' gardens some summer evenings.

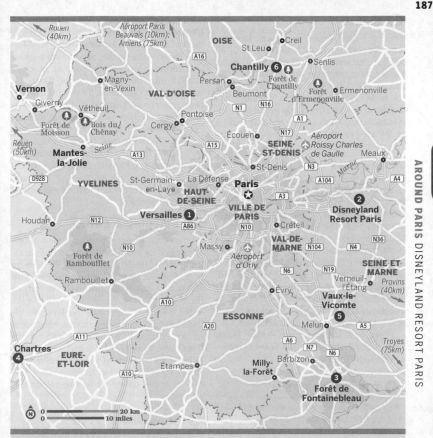

Around Paris Highlights

1 Château de Versailles
(p189) Reliving the glory of
the 17th- and 18th-century
kingdom of France at the
opulent palace.

**2 Disneyland Resort
Paris** (p188) Following an
adorable aspiring chef, rat
Rémy, in his quest to prepare
a Parisian meal aboard Walt
Disney Studios Park's larger-
than-life *Ratatouille* ride.

**3 Forêt de
Fontainebleau** (p196)
Hiking, cycling, horse riding
or rock climbing in one of
France's loveliest forests.

**4 Cathédrale Notre
Dame** (p200) Gazing at
the hypnotic blue stained-
glass windows at the
awe-inspiring cathedral in
Chartres.

**5 Château de Vaux-le-
Vicomte** (p197) Visiting the
interior of this 17th-century
château and its collection of
carriages.

6 Château de Chantilly
(p198) Viewing the
extraordinary artworks
inside the lake-set château
where the namesake
whipped cream was created.

Disneyland Resort Paris

It took almost €4.6 billion to turn the beet
fields 32km east of Paris into Europe's first
Disney theme park. What started out as
Euro-Disney in 1992 today comprises the
traditional Disneyland Park theme park,
the film-oriented Walt Disney Studios
Park, and the hotel-, shop- and restau-
rant-filled Disney Village. And kids – and
kids-at-heart – can't seem to get enough.

◉ Sights

Basic one-day admission fees at **Disneyland Resort Paris** (🏨hotel bookings 01 60 30 60 30, restaurant reservations 01 60 30 40 50; www.disneylandparis.com; adult/child 1 day single park €63/56, 1 day both parks €83/76, 2 days both parks €150/133; ⊘ hours vary) include unlimited access to attractions in either Disneyland Park or Walt Disney Studios Park. A multitude of multiday passes, special offers and packages are always available.

Disneyland Park   AMUSEMENT PARK
(Disneyland Resort Paris; ⊘ 10am-11pm May-Sep, to 8pm Oct-Apr, hours can vary) Disneyland Park has five themed *pays* (lands): the 1900s-styled **Main Street USA**; **Frontierland**, home of the legendary Big Thunder Mountain ride; **Adventureland**, which evokes exotic lands in rides including the Pirates of the Caribbean and Indiana Jones and the Temple of Peril; **Fantasyland**, crowned by Sleeping Beauty's castle; and the high-tech **Discoveryland**, with massive-queue rides such as Space Mountain: Mission 2 and Buzz Lightyear Laser Blast.

Three new themed areas – *Star Wars*, Marvel and *Frozen*-inspired Snow Queen – will be built from 2021.

ℹ️ TOP DISNEY TIPS

➡ Crowds peak during European school holidays; visit www.schoolholidays europe.eu to avoid them if possible.

➡ Pre-plan your day on Disney's website or the excellent www.dlpguide.com, working out which rides and shows you really want to see.

➡ Buy tickets in advance to avoid the ticket queue.

➡ The free Disneyland Paris app provides real-time waiting time for attractions but note that free wi-fi is only available in limited areas within the park.

➡ Once in, reserve your time slot on the busiest rides using FastPass, the park's ride reservation system (limited to one reservation at a time).

➡ Disney hotel guests are often entitled to two 'Magic Hours' in Disneyland Park (usually from 8am, May to October) before opening to the public, although not all rides run during these hours.

Walt Disney Studios Park   AMUSEMENT PARK
(Disneyland Resort Paris; ⊘ 10am-9pm Jun-Sep, to 8pm Oct-May, hours can vary) Disneyland Resort Paris' sound stage, production backlot and animation studios provide an up-close insight into the production of films, TV programs and cartoons. There are behind-the-scenes tours, larger-than-life characters and spine-tingling rides like the Twilight Zone Tower of Terror, as well as the out-sized *Ratatouille* ride, based on the winsome 2007 film about a rat who dreams of becoming a top Parisian chef, which offers a multisensory rat's perspective of Paris' rooftops and restaurant kitchens aboard a trackless 'ratmobile'.

🛏 Sleeping & Eating

The resort's seven American-styled hotels are linked by free shuttle bus to the parks. Rates vary hugely, according to the season, packages and promotional deals. Plenty of chain-style hotels are also in the vicinity of the resort.

No picnic hampers or coolers are allowed but you can bring snacks, sandwiches, water bottles (refillable at water fountains) and the like. The resort also has 29 themed restaurants of varying quality and value; reservations are recommended and can be made online up to two months in advance.

ℹ️ Information

Tourist Office (📞 01 60 43 33 33; www.visit parisregion.com; place François Truffaut; ⊘ 9am-8.45pm) Near the RER and TGV train stations.

ℹ️ Getting There & Away

Disneyland is easily reached by RER A (€7.60, 40 minutes to one hour, frequent), which runs from central Paris to Marne-la-Vallée/Chessy, Disneyland's RER station.

TGV trains run directly from Charles de Gaulle airport terminal 2 to Disneyland's Marne-la-Vallée/Chessy TGV station (from €24, nine minutes, up to two per hour).

Shuttle buses link Charles de Gaulle and Orly airports (€23, 45 minutes to one hour, six daily) with the resort. From central Paris (Gare du Nord, Opéra and Châtelet–Les Halles) one shuttle a day runs, departing from Gare du Nord at 8.20am and returning from Disneyland Park at 8pm.

By car, follow route A4 from Porte de Bercy (direction Metz-Nancy) and take exit 14.

Versailles

POP 87,550

Louis XIV transformed his father's hunting lodge into the monumental Château de Versailles in the mid-17th century, and it remains France's most famous and grand palace. Situated in the leafy, bourgeois suburb of Versailles, 22km southwest of central Paris, the Baroque château was the kingdom's political capital and the seat of the royal court from 1682 up until the fateful events of 1789 when revolutionaries massacred the palace guard. Louis XVI and Marie Antoinette were ultimately dragged back to Paris, where they were ingloriously guillotined.

◉ Sights

★**Château de Versailles** PALACE
(☎01 30 83 78 00; www.chateauversailles.fr; place d'Armes; adult/child passport ticket incl estate-wide access €20/free, with musical events €27/free, palace €18/free except during musical events; ☉9am-6.30pm Tue-Sun Apr-Oct, to 5.30pm Tue-Sun Nov-Mar; ⓂRER Versailles-Château–Rive Gauche) Amid magnificently landscaped formal gardens (p189), this splendid and enormous palace was built in the mid-17th century during the reign of Louis XIV – the Roi Soleil (Sun King) – to project the absolute power of the French monarchy, which was then at the height of its glory. The château has undergone relatively few alterations since its construction, though almost all the interior furnishings disappeared during the Revolution and many of the rooms were rebuilt by Louis-Philippe (r 1830–48).

Some 30,000 workers and soldiers toiled on the structure, the bills for which all but emptied the kingdom's coffers.

Work began in 1661 under the guidance of architect Louis Le Vau (Jules Hardouin-Mansart took over from Le Vau in the mid-1670s); painter and interior designer Charles Le Brun; and landscape artist André Le Nôtre, whose workers flattened hills, drained marshes and relocated forests as they laid out the seemingly endless gardens, ponds and fountains.

Le Brun and his hundreds of artisans decorated every moulding, cornice, ceiling and door of the interior with the most luxurious and ostentatious of appointments: frescoes, marble, gilt and woodcarvings, many with themes and symbols drawn from Greek and Roman mythology. The King's Suite of the Grands Appartements du Roi et de la Reine (King's and Queen's State Apartments), for example, includes rooms dedicated to Hercules, Venus, Diana, Mars and Mercury. The opulence reaches its peak in the **Galerie des Glaces** (Hall of Mirrors), a 75m-long ballroom with 17 huge mirrors on one side and, on the other, an equal number of windows looking out over the gardens and the setting sun.

The current €400 million restoration program is the most ambitious yet, and until it's completed in 2020, at least a part of the palace is likely to be clad in scaffolding when you visit.

Château de Versailles Gardens & Park GARDENS
(www.chateauversailles.fr; place d'Armes; free except during musical events; ☉gardens 8am-8.30pm Apr-Oct, to 6pm Nov-Mar, park 7am-8.30pm Apr-Oct, 8am-6pm Nov-Mar) The section of the vast gardens nearest the palace, laid out between 1661 and 1700 in the formal French style, is famed for its geometrically aligned terraces, flower beds, tree-lined paths, ponds and fountains. The 400-odd statues of marble, bronze and lead were made by the most talented sculptors of the era. The English-style Jardins du Petit Trianon are more pastoral and have meandering, sheltered paths.

Oriented to reflect the sunset, the **Grand Canal**, 1.6km long and 62m wide, is traversed by the 1km-long Petit Canal, creating a cross-shaped body of water with a perimeter of more than 5.5km.

On the southwestern side of the palace, the **Orangerie**, built under the Parterre du Midi (Southern Flowerbed), shelters tropical plants in winter.

The gardens' largest fountains include the 17th-century **Bassin de Neptune**, a dazzling mirage of 99 spouting gushers 300m north of the palace, whose straight side abuts a small pond graced by a winged dragon (Grille du Dragon). On the same days as the Grandes Eaux Musicales fountain displays, the Bassin de Neptune flows for 10 minutes.

At the eastern end of the Grand Canal, the **Bassin d'Apollon** was built in 1688. Emerging from the water in the centre is Apollo's chariot, pulled by rearing horses.

Versailles

A DAY IN COURT

Visiting Versailles – even just the State Apartments – may seem overwhelming at first, but think of it as a house where people ate, drank, worked, slept and conspired and you'll be on the right path.

Some two decades into his long reign, Louis XIV began turning his father's hunting lodge into a palace large enough to house his entire court (to keep closer tabs on the 6000-strong army of courtiers). Sparing no expense, the Sun King employed the greatest artists and craftspeople of the day and by 1682 he'd created the most extravagant dormitory in history.

The royal schedule was as accurate and predictable as a Swiss watch. By following this itinerary of rooms you can recreate the king's day, starting with the ❶ **King's Bedchamber** and the ❷ **Queen's Bedchamber**, where the royal couple was roused at about the same time. The royal procession then leads through the ❸ **Hall of Mirrors** to the ❹ **Royal Chapel** for morning Mass and returns to the ❺ **Council Chamber** for late-morning meetings with ministers. After lunch the king might ride or hunt or visit the ❻ **King's Library**. Later he could join courtesans for an 'apartment evening' starting from the ❼ **Hercules Drawing Room** or play billiards in the ❽ **Diana Drawing Room** before supping at 10pm.

VERSAILLES BY NUMBERS

Rooms 700 (11 hectares of roof)

Windows 2153

Staircases 67

Gardens and parks 800 hectares

Trees 200,000

Fountains 50 (with 620 nozzles)

Paintings 6300 (measuring 11km laid end to end)

Statues and sculptures 2100

Objets d'art and furnishings 5000

Visitors 5.3 million per year

VICHIE81 / SHUTTERSTOCK ©

Queen's Bedchamber
Chambre de la Reine
The queen's life was on constant public display and even the births of her children were watched by crowds of spectators in her own bedchamber. DETOUR » The Guardroom, with a dozen armed men at the ready.

Guardroom

South Wing

LUNCH BREAK

Contemporary French cuisine at Alain Ducasse's restaurant Ore, or a picnic in the park.

Hercules Drawing Room
Salon d'Hercule
This salon, with its stunning ceiling fresco of the strong man, gave way to the State Apartments, which were open to courtiers three nights a week. DETOUR» Apollo Drawing Room, used for formal audiences and as a throne room.

TAKVAN URK / SHUTTERSTOCK ©

Hall of Mirrors
Galerie des Glaces
The solid-silver candelabra and furnishings in this extravagant hall, devoted to Louis XIV's successes in war, were melted down in 1689 to pay for yet another conflict. DETOUR» The antithetical Peace Drawing Room, adjacent.

WALTER G./SHUTTERSTOCK ©

King's Bedchamber
Chambre du Roi
The king's daily life was anything but private and even his *lever* (rising) at 8am and *coucher* (retiring) at 11.30pm would be witnessed by up to 150 sycophantic courtiers.

Council Chamber
Cabinet du Conseil
This chamber, with carved medallions evoking the king's work, is where the monarch met his various ministers (state, finance, religion etc) depending on the days of the week.

King's Library
Bibliothèque du Roi
The last resident, bibliophile Louis XVI, loved geography and his copy of *The Travels of James Cook* (in English, which he read fluently) is still on the shelf here.

Diana Drawing Room
Salon de Diane
With walls and ceiling covered in frescoes devoted to the mythical huntress, this room contained a large billiard table reserved for Louis XIV, a keen player.

Peace Drawing Room

Hall of Mirrors

Marble Courtyard

Apollo Drawing Room

trance

Entrance

North Wing

To Royal Opera

Royal Chapel
Chapelle Royale
This two-storey chapel (with gallery for the royals and important courtiers, and the ground floor for the B-list) was dedicated to St Louis, patron of French monarchs. DETOUR» The sumptuous Royal Opera.

COATO / BUDGET TRAVEL ©

SAVVY SIGHTSEEING
Avoid Versailles on Monday (closed), Tuesday (Paris' museums close, so visitors flock here) and Sunday, the busiest day. Also, book tickets online so you don't have to queue.

Domaine de Marie-Antoinette   PALACE
(Marie Antoinette's Estate; www.chateauversailles.
fr; Château de Versailles; adult/child €12/free, free
with passport ticket; ⊙noon-6.30pm Tue-Sun
Apr-Oct, to 5.30pm Tue-Sat Nov-Mar) Northwest
of Versailles' main palace is the Domaine
de Marie-Antoinette. Admission includes
the pink-colonnaded **Grand Trianon**, built
in 1687 for Louis XIV and his family to escape the rigid etiquette of the court; the
ochre-coloured 1760s **Petit Trianon**, redecorated in 1867 by consort of Napoléon III,
Empress Eugénie, who added Louis XVI–
style furnishings; and the 1784-completed
Hameau de la Reine (Queen's Hamlet), a
mock village of thatched cottages where
Marie Antoinette played milkmaid.

Versailles Stables   STABLES
(av Rockefeller) The **Grandes Écuries** (Big Stables; www.bartabas.fr; av Rockefeller) are the stage
for the prestigious **Académie du Spectacle
Équestre** (Academy of Equestrian Arts; ☑01 39
02 62 70; http://bartabas.fr; 1 av Rockefeller; training session adult/child €15/10; ⊙by reservation).
It presents spectacular **Reprises Musicales
equestrian shows** (Musical Equestrian Shows;
☑08 92 68 18 91; http://bartabas.fr; av Rockefeller;
adult/child from €25/16; ⊙6pm Sat, 3pm Sun), for
which tickets sell out weeks in advance; book
ahead online. In the stables' main courtyard
is a new *manège* where horses and their riders train. Show tickets and training sessions
include a stable visit.

The **Petites Écuries** (Little Stables; av Rockefeller) `FREE` are today used by Versailles'
School of Architecture.

Salle du Jeu de Paume   HISTORIC BUILDING
(www.versailles-tourisme.com; 1 rue du Jeu de
Paume; admission free, guided tours €10; ⊙2-
5.45pm Tue-Sun, guided tours in French 3pm &
4.30pm 1st Sat of month) In May 1789 Louis
XVI convened the États-Généraux, made
up of more than 1118 deputies representing
the nobility, clergy and the Third Estate
('common people'), to moderate dissent.
Denied entry, the Third Estate's reps met
separately on this 1686-built royal tennis
court, formed a National Assembly and
took the Serment du Jeu de Paume (Tennis
Court Oath), swearing not to dissolve it until Louis XVI accepted a new constitution.

Less than a month later, a mob in Paris
stormed the prison at Bastille.

🐾 Tours

Château de Versailles Guided Tours   TOURS
(☑01 30 83 77 88; www.chateauversailles.fr; Château de Versailles; tours €10, plus palace entry;
⊙English-language tours 9.30am Tue-Sun) To access areas that are otherwise off limits and to
learn more about Versailles' history, prebook
a 1½-hour guided tour of the Private Apartments of Louis XV and Louis XVI and the
Opera House or Royal Chapel. Tours also
cover the most famous parts of the palace.

Paris City Vision   BUS
(www.pariscityvision.com; adult/child half-day tour
including palace entry from €58/33, full day from
€81/50) Guided half-day and full-day minibus trips from Paris to Versailles.

City Discovery   BUS
(www.city-discovery.com; day trips from Paris adult/
child from €58/33) Offers various Versailles
trips from Paris.

Other options from Paris include Disneyland Resort Paris (including entry to both
parks from €102/97).

🍴 Eating

Rue de Satory is lined with restaurants and
cafes. More local options can be found on
and around rue de la Paroisse, where you'll
also find Versailles' **markets** (rue de la Paroisse; ⊙food market 7am-2pm Tue, Fri & Sun, covered market 7am-7.30pm Tue-Sat, to 2pm Sun, flea
market 11am-7pm Wed, Thu & Sat).

La Cour   CAFE €
(☑01 39 02 33 09; www.versailles-lacour.fr; 7 rue
des Deux Portes; 2-course lunch menus €15, Sun
brunch €24; ⊙noon-6pm Wed-Sat, 11am-3pm Sun)
Framed by a royal-blue façade and painted
with giant flower murals inside, this charmer is hidden in a little courtyard that fills
with tables in warm weather. Everything is
made fresh daily, including quiches, tarts,
salads, sandwiches, pastries and OJ. Book
ahead for Sunday brunch, which features
smoked salmon, scrambled eggs with feta
and pancakes with maple syrup.

Angelina   CAFE €
(www.angelina-paris.fr; Domaine de Marie-
Antoinette, Château de Versailles; dishes €5-10.30;
⊙10am-6pm Tue-Sun Apr-Oct, to 5pm Tue-Sun
Nov-Mar) Eateries within the Versailles estate
include tearoom Angelina, famed for its decadent hot chocolate. It also serves quiches,

ⓘ TOP VERSAILLES TIPS

Versailles is one of the country's most popular destinations, with over five million visitors annually; advance planning will make visiting more enjoyable.

➡ Monday is out for obvious reasons (it's closed).

➡ By noon, queues for tickets and entering the château spiral out of control: arrive early morning and avoid Tuesday, Saturday and Sunday, its busiest days.

➡ Prepurchase tickets on the château's website or at Fnac (p172) branches and head straight to Entrance A.

➡ Versailles is free on the first Sunday of every month from November to March.

➡ Prams/buggies, metal-frame baby carriers and luggage aren't allowed inside the palace.

➡ Prebook a guided tour (p192) to access areas that are otherwise off limits as well as the most famous parts of the palace.

➡ The estate is so vast that the only way to see it all is to hire a four-person **electric car** (☑ 01 39 66 97 66; www.versailles-tourisme.com; car hire per hr €34; ⊘ 10am-6.45pm Apr-Oct, to 5.30pm Feb & Mar, to 5pm Nov & Dec) or hop aboard the **shuttle train** (www.train-versailles.com; adult/child €8/6.10, audioguide €4; ⊘ every 20min 11.10am-6.50pm Apr-Oct, to 5.10pm Nov-Mar); you can also rent a **bike** (☑ 01 39 66 97 66; www.chateauversailles.fr; bike hire per hr/day €8.50/20; ⊘ 10am-6.45pm Apr-Oct, to 5.30pm mid-Feb–Mar, to 5pm early–mid-Nov) or a **rowboat** (☑ 01 39 66 97 66; www.versailles-tourisme.com; boat hire per 30 min/hr €13/17; ⊘ 10am-6.45pm Jul & Aug, shorter hrs Mar-Jun & Sep–mid-Nov).

➡ Try to time your visit for the **Grandes Eaux Musicales** (www.chateauversailles-spectacles.fr; Château de Versailles; adult/child €9.50/8; ⊘ 9am-7pm Tue, Sat & Sun mid-May–late Jun, 9am-7pm Sat & Sun Apr–mid-May & late Jun-Oct) or the after-dark **Grandes Eaux Nocturnes** (www.chateauversailles-spectacles.fr; Château de Versailles; adult/child €24/20; ⊘ 8.30-11.30pm Sat mid-Jun–mid-Sep), truly magical 'dancing water' displays – set to music composed by Baroque- and classical-era composers – throughout the grounds in summer.

➡ Organ concerts in the palace chapel (free) take place at 3pm, 3.30pm and 5.30pm on Thursdays; check the website for other performances.

➡ Other events and performances are listed online.

➡ Audioguides are included in admission.

➡ Free apps can be downloaded from the website.

gourmet sandwiches, salads, a soup of the day and spectacular pastries. In addition to this branch by the Petit Trianon, there's another inside the palace.

La Table du 11   GASTRONOMY €€€

(☑ 09 83 34 76 00; www.latabledu11.com; 10 rue de Satory; 3-course lunch menu €44, 5-/7-course dinner menus €75/95; ⊘ 12.30-1.30pm & 7.30-9.30pm Tue-Sat) For an appropriately sumptuous meal in this stately town, Michelin-starred La Table du 11 fits the bill. Dark-blue flooring matches its façade; dishes on the daily changing menu might include roast onion with a garlic, parmesan and onion tuile and onion foam, lobster with white truffle, radish leaves and mushrooms, and caramelised apple with Chantilly cream and liquorice powder.

ⓘ Information

Tourist Office (☑ 01 39 24 88 88; www.versailles-tourisme.com; 2bis av de Paris; ⊘ 9.30am-6pm Mon, 8.30am-7pm Tue-Sun Apr-Oct, 11am-5pm Mon, 8.30am-6pm Tue-Sun Nov-Mar) Sells the passport to Château de Versailles and detailed visitor's guides.

ⓘ Getting There & Away

BUS

Bus 171 (€2 or one t+ metro/bus ticket, 35 minutes) links Paris' Pont de Sèvres metro station (15e) with place d'Armes at least every 15 minutes from 5am to 12.30am.

From the Eiffel Tower, Versailles Express (www.versaillesexpress.com; return €24, 45 minutes, 7.45am, 9.45am and 1.30pm) runs to the Château de Versailles; reserve ahead online.

CAR & MOTORCYCLE
Follow the A13 from Porte d'Auteuil and take the exit marked 'Versailles Château'.

TRAIN
Versailles has several train stations; the most convenient way to reach the château is to take RER C5 (return €7.10, 40 minutes, frequent) from Paris' Left Bank RER stations to Versailles-Château–Rive Gauche station.

Giverny

POP 518

The tiny country village of Giverny, 74km northwest of Paris, is a place of pilgrimage for devotees of impressionism, though the summer months herald the tour-bus crowds, who shatter the bucolic peace. Monet lived here from 1883 until his death in 1926, in a rambling house – surrounded by flower-filled gardens – that's now the immensely popular Maison et Jardins de Claude Monet.

Note that the principal sights are closed from November to Easter, along with most accommodation and restaurants, so there's little point visiting out of season, although you will have the streets and a few sights all to yourself.

⊙ Sights

★Maison et Jardins de Claude Monet
MUSEUM, GARDEN

(✏ 02 32 51 28 21; www.fondation-monet.com; 84 rue Claude Monet; adult/child €9.50/5.50, incl Musée des Impressionnismes Giverny €17/9; ⊙ 9.30am-6pm Easter-Oct) Monet's home for the last 43 years of his life is now a delightful house-museum. His pastel-pink house and Water Lily studio stand on the periphery of the **Clos Normand**, with its symmetrically laid-out gardens bursting with flowers. Monet bought the **Jardin d'Eau** (Water Garden) in 1895 and set about creating his trademark lily pond, as well as the famous **Japanese bridge** (since rebuilt).

The charmingly preserved house and beautiful bloom-filled gardens (rather than Monet's works) are the draws here.

Draped with purple wisteria, the Japanese bridge blends into the asymmetrical foreground and background, creating the intimate atmosphere for which the 'painter of light' was renowned.

Seasons have an enormous effect on Giverny. From early to late spring, daffodils, tulips, rhododendrons, wisteria and irises appear, followed by poppies and lilies.

By June, nasturtiums, roses and sweet peas are in flower. Around September, there are dahlias, sunflowers and hollyhocks.

Combined tickets with Paris' Musée Marmottan Monet (p74) cost €20.50/12 per adult/child, and combined adult tickets with Paris' Musée de l'Orangerie (p84) cost €18.50.

Musée des Impressionnismes Giverny
GALLERY

(✏ 02 32 51 94 65; www.mdig.fr; 99 rue Claude Monet; adult/child €7.50/5, incl Maison et Jardins de Claude Monet €17/9; ⊙ 10am-6pm Easter-Oct) About 100m northwest of the Maison et Jardins de Claude Monet is the Giverny Museum of Impressionisms. It was set up in partnership with the Musée d'Orsay, among other institutions, and the pluralised name reinforces its coverage of all aspects of impressionism and related movements in its permanent collection and temporary exhibitions. Lectures, readings, concerts and documentaries also take place regularly. The audioguide is €4. Admission on the first Sunday of the month is free.

🛏 Sleeping & Eating

Le Clos Fleuri
B&B €€

(✏ 02 32 21 36 51; www.giverny-leclosfleuri.fr; 5 rue de la Dîme; s/d €105/110; ⊙ Apr-Oct; 🅿🖥) Big rooms with king-size beds and exposed wood beams overlook the hedged gardens of this delightful B&B within strolling distance of the Maison et Jardins de Claude Monet. Each of its three rooms is named after a different flower; green-thumbed host Danielle speaks fluent English. Cash only.

La Pluie de Roses
B&B €€

(✏ 02 32 51 10 67; www.givernylapluiederoses.fr; 14 rue Claude Monet; s/d from €120/130; 🅿🖥) You'll be won over by this adorable private home cocooned in a dreamy, peaceful garden. Inside, the three rooms (two of which can accommodate families) are so comfy it can be hard to wake up, but the superb breakfast on a verandah awash with sunlight is always further motivation to cast off the duvet. Payment is by cash only.

La Musardière
HOTEL €€

(✏ 02 32 21 03 18; www.lamusardiere.fr; 123 rue Claude Monet; d €85-99, f €149, 3-course menus €26-36; ⊙ hotel Feb–mid-Dec, restaurant noon-10pm Apr-Oct; 🅿🖥) This two-star 10-room hotel dating back to 1880 and evocatively called the 'Idler' is set amid a lovely garden less than 100m northeast of the Maison et Jardins de Claude Monet. Breakfast costs €11 (or €13 in-room) and savouring a crêpe in the hotel restaurant is a genuine treat. Family rooms sleep three or four people.

★ Le Jardin des Plumes   MODERN FRENCH €€€
(☏ 02 32 54 26 35; www.jardindesplumes.fr; 1 rue du Milieu; 3-/5-course menus €48/78, tasting menus €98, mains €36-40; ☺ 12.15-1.30pm & 7.30-9pm Wed-Sun, hotel closed Mon & Tue Nov-Mar; P 🖐 🖐) This gorgeous sky-blue-trimmed property's airy white dining room is a handsome stage for chef Eric Guerin's exquisite and inventive Michelin-starred cuisine, which justifies the trip from Paris alone.

There are also four rooms (€195 to €215) and four suites (€295 to €370), combining vintage and contemporary furnishings. It's less than 10 minutes' walk to the Maison et Jardins de Claude Monet.

❶ Information

Tourist Office (☏ 02 32 64 45 01; www.normandie-giverny.fr; 80 rue Claude Monet; ☺ 10am-5.45pm Easter-Oct) By the Maison et Jardins de Claude Monet.

❶ Getting There & Around

The closest train station is at Vernon, from where shuttle buses, taxis and cycle/walking tracks run to Giverny.

BICYCLE

Rent bikes (cash only) at the **Café L'Arrivée de Giverny** (☏ 02 32 21 16 01; 1-3 place de la Gare, Vernon; per day €14; ☺ 8am-11pm), opposite the train station in Vernon, from where Giverny is a signposted 5km along a direct (and flat) cycle/walking track.

BUS

Shuttle buses (single/return €5/10, 20 minutes, four daily Monday to Friday Easter to October, five daily Saturday and Sunday Easter to October) meet most trains from Paris at Vernon. There are limited seats, so arrive early for the return trip from Giverny. Tickets are sold on board; cash or credit card accepted. Check the live shuttle schedule on www.sngo-giverny.fr; there is free wi-fi on board.

TAXI

Taxis (☏ 02 32 51 10 24) usually wait outside the train station in Vernon and charge around €15 for the one-way trip to Giverny. There's no taxi rank in Giverny, however, so you'll need to phone for one for the return trip to Vernon. It is preferable to take the shuttle bus back to Vernon.

TRAIN

From Paris' Gare St-Lazare there are up to 15 daily trains to Vernon (from €9, 45 minutes to one hour), 7km to the west of Giverny. Trains also run to/from Rouen in Normandy (from €7, one to 1½ hours, at least every two hours).

Fontainebleau
POP 14,132

Fresh air fills your lungs on arriving in the classy town of Fontainebleau. It's enveloped by the 280-sq-km Forêt de Fontainebleau, which is as big a playground today as it was in the 16th century, with superb walking and rock-climbing opportunities. Situated 68km southeast of Paris, the town grew up around its magnificent château, one of the most beautifully decorated and furnished in France. Although it's less crowded and pressured than Versailles, exploring it can still take the best part of a day. You'll also find a cosmopolitan drinking and dining scene, thanks to the town's lifeblood, the international graduate business school INSEAD.

◉ Sights

★ Château de Fontainebleau   PALACE
(☏ 01 60 71 50 70; www.musee-chateau-fontaine bleau.fr; place du Général de Gaulle; adult/child €12/free, 1st Sun of month Sep-Jun free; ☺ 9.30am-6pm Wed-Mon Apr-Sep, to 5pm Wed-Mon Oct-Mar) The resplendent, 1900-room Château de Fontainebleau's list of former tenants and guests reads like a who's who of French royalty and aristocracy. Every square centimetre of wall and ceiling space is richly adorned with wood panelling, gilded carvings, frescoes, tapestries and paintings.

Visits take in the **Grands Appartements** (State Apartments), which contain several outstanding rooms. An informative 1½-hour multimedia guide (€3) leads you around the main areas.

The first château on this site was built in the early 12th century and enlarged by Louis IX a century later. Only a single medieval tower survived the energetic Renaissance-style reconstruction undertaken by François I (r 1515–47), whose superb artisans, many of them brought from Italy, blended Italian and French styles to create what is known as the First School of Fontainebleau. The *Mona Lisa* once hung here amid other fine works of art in the royal collection.

During the latter half of the 16th century, the château was further enlarged by Henri

FORÊT DE FONTAINEBLEAU

Unfolding 500m south of the Château de Fontainebleau (p195) and surrounding the town (covering 280 sq km in all), the Forêt de Fontainebleau (Fontainebleau Forest) is one of the Île-de-France's loveliest woods. The many trails here include parts of the GR1 and GR11.

Rock-climbing enthusiasts have long come to the forest's sandstone ridges, rich in cliffs and overhangs, to hone their skills before setting off for the Alps. There are different grades marked by colours, starting with white ones, which are suitable for children, and going up to death-defying black boulders. The website Bleau.info (www.bleau.info) has stacks of information in English on climbing in Fontainebleau. Two gorges worth visiting are the Gorges d'Apremont, 7km northwest near Barbizon, and the Gorges de Franchard, a few kilometres south of Gorges d'Apremont. Contact **Top Loisirs** (☑01 60 74 08 50; www.toploisirs.fr; guided rock climbing per half-/full day from €40/55, canoe/kayak hire per half-/full day from €25/35; ☺9am-6pm, hours can vary) about equipment hire and instruction; pick-ups in Fontainebleau are possible by arrangement. The company also offers canoeing and kayaking on the edge of the forest.

Fontainebleau's tourist office (p197) sells maps, walking guides and climbing guides.

II (r 1547–59), Catherine de Médicis and Henri IV (r 1589–1610), whose Flemish and French artists created the Second School of Fontainebleau. Even Louis XIV got in on the act: it was he who hired landscape artist André Le Nôtre, celebrated for his work at Versailles, to redesign the gardens.

Fontainebleau was beloved by Napoléon Bonaparte, who had a fair bit of restoration work carried out. Napoléon III was another frequent visitor. During WWII the château was turned into a German headquarters. After it was liberated by Allied forces under US General George Patton in 1944, part of the complex served as the Allied and then NATO headquarters from 1945 to 1965.

The spectacular **Chapelle de la Trinité** (Trinity Chapel), the ornamentation of which dates from the first half of the 17th century, is where Louis XV married Marie Leszczyńska in 1725 and where the future Napoléon III was christened in 1810. **Galerie François 1er**, a jewel of Renaissance architecture, was decorated from 1533 to 1540 by Il Rosso, a Florentine follower of Michelangelo. In the wood panelling, François I's monogram appears repeatedly along with his emblem, a dragon-like salamander. The **Musée Chinois de l'Impératice Eugénie** (Chinese Museum of Empress Eugénie) consists of four drawing rooms created in 1863 for the Asian art and curios collected by Napoléon III's wife.

The **Salle de Bal**, a 30m-long ballroom dating from the mid-16th century that was also used for receptions and banquets, is renowned for its mythological frescoes, mar-

quetry floor and Italian-inspired coffered ceiling. Its large windows afford views of the Cour Ovale (Oval Courtyard) and the gardens. The gilded bed in the 17th- and 18th-century **Chambre de l'Impératrice** (Empress' Bedroom) was never used by Marie Antoinette, for whom it was built in 1787. The gilding in the **Salle du Trône** (Throne Room), which was the royal bedroom before the Napoléonic period, is decorated in golds, greens and yellows.

As successive monarchs added their own wings to the château, five irregularly shaped courtyards were created. The oldest and most interesting is the **Cour Ovale** (Oval Courtyard), no longer oval but U-shaped due to Henri IV's construction work. It incorporates the keep, the sole remnant of the medieval château. The largest courtyard is the **Cour du Cheval Blanc** (Courtyard of the White Horse), from where you enter the château. Napoléon, about to be exiled to Elba in 1814, bade farewell to his guards from the magnificent 17th-century double-horseshoe staircase here. For that reason the courtyard is also called the Cour des Adieux (Farewell Courtyard).

Château de Fontainebleau Gardens & Park
GARDENS

(☺9am-7pm May-Sep, to 6pm Mar, Apr & Oct, to 5pm Nov-Feb) **FREE** On the northern side of the Château de Fontainebleau is the formal **Jardin de Diane**, created by Catherine de Médicis. Le Nôtre's formal, 17th-century **Jardin Français** (French Garden), also known as the Grand Parterre, is east of the **Cour de la Fontaine** (Fountain Courtyard) and the **Étang des Carpes** (Carp Pond). The informal **Jardin Anglais** (English Garden), created in 1812, is west of the pond. Excavated in 1609, the **Grand Canal** predates the Versailles canals by more than 50 years.

🛏 Sleeping & Eating

Restaurants are prevalent in the town centre; rue Montebello has a large concentration. For fabulous food shops such as *fromageries* (cheese shops) and *boulangeries* (bakeries), head to rue des Sablons and rue Grande. Fontainebleau's **market** (place de la République; ⏰7am-2pm Tue, Fri & Sun) takes place three times a week.

★**La Demeure du Parc**   BOUTIQUE HOTEL €€
(📞01 60 70 20 00; www.lademeureduparc.fr; 36 rue Paul Séramy; s/d/ste from €132/174/321; ❄🛜) A wisteria-draped courtyard garden with chestnut and apple trees is the centrepiece of this charming 27-room hotel. Deluxe-category rooms have their own terraces; ground-floor suites open onto small private gardens. The pick are the suites such as the literary-themed Bibliothèque and travel-themed Voyage (with its own telescope). Its contemporary French restaurant, **La Table du Parc** (📞01 60 70 20 00; www.lademeureduparc.fr; 36 rue Paul Séramy; 5-course vegetarian dinner menu €57, 6-course dinner menu €72, mains €25-44; ⏰12.15-2pm & 7-9.30pm Wed-Sat, 12.15-2pm Sun; 🛜), is one of Fontainebleau's finest.

Baby cots, high chairs and babysitting services are available.

Dardonville   PASTRIES, BAKERY €
(www.dardonville-fontainebleau.com; 24 rue des Sablons; pastries €1.60-4; ⏰7am-1.30pm & 3.15-7.30pm Tue-Sat, 7am-1.30pm Sun) Melt-in-your-mouth macarons, in flavours including poppy seed and gingerbread, are refreshingly inexpensive at this beloved patisserie-*boulangerie*. Queues also form out the door for its amazing breads and great picnic treats like mini quiches and tarts.

Crêperie Ty Koz   CRÊPES €
(📞01 64 22 00 55; www.creperiety-koz.com; 18 rue de la Cloche; crêpes & galettes €3-13; ⏰noon-2pm & 7-10pm Tue-Thu, noon-2pm & 7-10.30pm Fri & Sat) Tucked away in a cobbled courtyard, this Breton hidey-hole cooks up authentic sweet crêpes and *simple* (single thickness) and *pourleth* (double thickness) *galettes* (savoury buckwheat crêpes). Wash them down with traditional Val de Rance cider.

Le Ferrare   BRASSERIE €
(📞01 60 72 37 04; 23 rue de France; 2-/3-course menus €12.50/14.50; ⏰8am-4pm Mon, to 10.30pm Tue-Thu, to midnight Fri & Sat; 🛜) Locals pile into this bar-brasserie, which has a blackboard full of Auvergne specialities such as *tripoux* (sheep's tripe) with *aligot* (potato and melted cheese) and bargain-priced *plats du jour* (daily specials).

★**L'Axel**   GASTRONOMY €€€
(📞01 64 22 01 57; www.laxel-restaurant.com; 43 rue de France; 2-/3-course lunch menus €35/42, dinner menus €60-110, mains €45-58; ⏰7.15-9.30pm Wed, 12.15-2pm & 7.15-9.30pm Thu-Sun) Chef Kunihisa Goto has gained a Michelin star for his inspired flavour combinations: turbot with candied artichoke and yuzu-butter sauce, veal sweetbreads with cinnamon-roasted carrot purée, and mango mousse in a white-chocolate coconut sphere with banana and passionfruit sorbet. Book several weeks ahead.

ℹ Information

Tourist Office (📞01 60 74 99 99; www.fontainebleau-tourisme.com; 4 rue Royale; ⏰10am-6pm Mon-Sat, 10am-1pm & 2-5pm Sun May-Oct, 10am-6pm Mon-Sat, 10am-1pm Sun Nov-Apr; 🛜) In a converted petrol station west of the château, with information on the town and forest.

ℹ Getting There & Away

Importantly, train tickets to Fontainebleau/Avon are sold at Paris' Gare de Lyon's SNCF Transilien counter/Billet Île-de-France machines, *not* SNCF mainline counters/machines. On returning to Paris, tickets include travel to any metro station.

Up to 40 daily SNCF Transilien (www.transilien.com) commuter trains link Paris' Gare de Lyon with **Fontainebleau/Avon station** (place de la Gare) (€8.85, 40 minutes).

By car, take the A6 from Paris to the Fontainebleau exit.

Vaux-le-Vicomte

The privately owned **Château de Vaux-le-Vicomte** (📞01 64 14 41 90; www.vaux-le-vicomte.com; D215, Maincy; adult/child château & gardens €16.50/10.50, garden only €10/7, candlelight visits incl entry €19.50/13.50; ⏰10am-7pm mid-Mar-early Nov, candlelight visits 5-11pm Sat mid-May-early Oct) and its fabulous formal gardens, 20km north of Fontainebleau and 61km southeast of Paris, were designed and built by Le Brun, Le Vau and Le Nôtre between

1656 and 1661 as a precursor to their more ambitious work at Versailles.

The château's beautifully furnished interior is topped by a striking dome. Don't miss the stables' collection of 18th- and 19th-century carriages at the Musée des Équipages, or if at all possible, a candlelight visit.

During the same period as the candlelight visits, there are elaborate *jeux d'eau* (fountain displays) in the gardens from 3pm to 6pm on the second and last Saturday of the month. In the vaulted cellars an exhibition looks at Le Nôtre's landscaping of the gardens.

The beauty of Vaux-le-Vicomte turned out to be the undoing of its original owner, Nicolas Fouquet, Louis XIV's minister of finance. It seems that Louis, seething that he'd been upstaged at the château's official opening, had Fouquet thrown into prison, where the unfortunate minister died in 1680.

ⓘ Getting There & Away

Vaux-le-Vicomte is not an easy place to reach by public transport. The château is 6km northeast of Melun and 15km southwest of Verneuil-l'Étang.

Melun is served by RER line D2 from Paris' Gare de Lyon (€8.70, 40 minutes, frequent). Trains link Paris' Gare de l'Est (direction Provins; €8.70, 35 minutes, hourly) to Verneuil-l'Étang, from where the **Châteaubus shuttle** (☑ 01 64 14 41 90; adult/child return day €10/5, evening €25/20; ⊙ noon-6pm mid-Mar–early Nov, to 11.30pm Sat May-early Oct) links Verneuil-l'Étang station with Château de Vaux-le-Vicomte (35 minutes, hourly). On Saturdays from mid-May to early October, the last bus returns directly to Gare de Lyon in Paris. Reserve ahead via the château's website and bring cash for the bus.

At other times, you'll have to take a taxi. One-way day/evening prices are €18/32 from Melun, and €28/46 from Verneuil-l'Étang.

By car, follow the A6 from Paris and then the A5 (direction Melun), and take the 'St-Germain Laxis' exit. From Fontainebleau take the N6 and N36.

Chantilly

POP 10,861

The elegant old town of Chantilly, 50km north of Paris, is small and select. Its imposing, heavily restored château is surrounded by parkland, gardens and the Forêt de Chantilly, offering a wealth of walking opportunities. Chantilly's racetrack is one of the most prestigious hat-and-frock addresses in Europe, and deliciously sweetened thick *crème Chantilly* was created here.

◉ Sights

Château de Chantilly   CHATEAU

(☑ 03 44 27 31 80; www.domainedechantilly.com; off rue du Connétable; domain pass adult/child €17/10, domain & show pass €30/24; ⊙ 10am-6pm late Mar-Oct, 10.30am-5pm Wed-Mon Nov-Dec & Feb-Mar) A storybook vision amid an artificial lake and magnificent gardens, the Château de Chantilly contains a superb collection of paintings within the Musée Condé.

Left shambolic after the Revolution, the restored château consists of the attached Petit and Grand Châteaux, entered through the same vestibule. The estate's Grandes Écuries (Grand Stables) (p199) are just to the west.

From Easter to October, visit the estate aboard a little 'train' (adult/child €5/3.50, 11am to 6pm) or hire four-person golf carts (€32 per hour).

The **Petit Château**, containing the Appartements des Princes (Princes' Suites), was built around 1560 for Anne de Montmorency (1492–1567), who served six French kings as *connétable* (high constable), diplomat and warrior, and died doing battle with Protestants in the Counter-Reformation. The highlight here is the **Cabinet des Livres**, a repository of 700 manuscripts and more than 30,000 volumes, including a Gutenberg Bible and a facsimile of the *Très Riches Heures du Duc de Berry*, an illuminated manuscript dating from the 15th century that illustrates the calendar year for both the peasantry and the nobility. The **chapel**, to the left as you walk into the vestibule, has woodwork and stained-glass windows dating from the mid-16th century.

The adjoining Renaissance-style **Grand Château**, completely demolished during the Revolution, was rebuilt by the Duke of Aumale, son of King Louis-Philippe, from 1875 to 1885. It contains the **Musée Condé**, a series of 19th-century rooms adorned with paintings and sculptures haphazardly arranged according to the whims of the duke – he donated the château to the Institut de France on the condition the exhibits were not reorganised and would remain open to the public. The most remarkable works, hidden in the Sanctuaire (Sanctuary), include paintings by Filippino Lippi, Jean Fouquet and (it's thought) Raphael.

Guided tours (45 minutes; €3) of the lavish **Appartements Privés du Duc et de la Duchesse d'Aumale** (the Duke and Duchess' private suites) are available in English by prior reservation.

Château de Chantilly Gardens GARDENS
(Château de Chantilly; admission incl in domain pass, gardens & park only adult/child €8/5; ⊙10am-8pm late Mar-Oct, 10.30am-6pm Wed-Mon Nov-Dec & Feb-Mar) Sprawling over 115 hectares, the wondrous gardens of the Château de Chantilly encompass the formal Jardin Français (French Garden), with flower beds, lakes and a Grand Canal all laid out by Le Nôtre in the mid-17th century, northeast of the main building; and the 'wilder' Jardin Anglais (English Garden), begun in 1817, to the west. East of the Jardin Français is the rustic Jardin Anglo-Chinois (Anglo-Chinese Garden), created in the 1770s.

The foliage and silted-up waterways of the Jardin Anglo-Chinois surround the **hameau**, a mock village dating from 1774, whose mill and half-timbered buildings inspired the Hameau de la Reine (Queen's Hamlet) at Versailles. *Crème Chantilly* (sugar-whipped cream) was invented here.

Grandes Écuries STABLES
(Grand Stables; www.domainedechantilly.com; 7 rue du Connétable) The Grandes Écuries, built between 1719 and 1740 to house 240 horses and 400-plus hounds, stand west of the château near Chantilly's famous hippodrome (racecourse), inaugurated in 1834. The stables contain the **Musée Vivant du Cheval** (Living Horse Museum; ☑03 44 27 31 80; www.domainedechantilly.com; 7 rue du Connétable; entry incl in domain-only & domain & show pass; ⊙10am-6pm late Mar-Oct, 10.30am-5pm Wed-Mon Nov-Dec & Feb-Mar), included in domain-only and domain and show passes; displays span riding equipment to rocking horses.

Visitors big and small will be mesmerised by the half-hour equestrian show included in the combined domain and show pass. **One-hour shows** (☑03 44 27 31 80; www.domainedechantilly.com; Grandes Écuries; adult/child €21/17) take place from late March to October.

The stables' pampered equines live in luxurious wooden stalls built by Louis-Henri de Bourbon, the seventh Prince de Condé, who was convinced he would be reincarnated as a horse (hence the extraordinary grandeur).

Forêt de Chantilly FOREST
Once a royal hunting estate, the 63-sq-km Forêt de Chantilly is criss-crossed by walking and riding trails. Long-distance trails here include the **GR11**, which links the Château de Chantilly with the town of **Senlis**; the **GR1**, from **Luzarches** (famed for its cathedral, parts of which date from the 12th

---

CHÂTEAU DE WHIPPED CREAM

Like every self-respecting French château three centuries ago, the palace at Chantilly had its own *hameau* (hamlet) complete with *laitier* (dairy), where the lady of the household and her guests could play at being milkmaids. But the cows at the Chantilly dairy took their job rather more seriously than their fellow bovines at other faux *crémeries* (dairy shops), and the *crème Chantilly* served at the hamlet's teas became the talk (and envy) of aristocratic 18th-century Europe. The future Habsburg emperor Joseph II paid a clandestine visit to this 'temple de marbre' (marble temple), as he called it, to taste it himself in 1777.

Chantilly (or more properly *crème Chantilly*) is whipped unpasteurised cream with a twist. It's beaten with icing and vanilla sugars to the consistency of a mousse and dolloped on berries.

---

century) to Ermenonville; and the **GR12**, which heads northeast from four lakes known as the Étangs de Commelles to the Forêt d'Halatte.

Chantilly's tourist office (p200) stocks maps and guides.

🛏 Sleeping

La Ferme de la Canardière B&B €€
(☑03 44 62 00 96; https://fermecanardiere.fr; 20 rue du Viaduc; s €110-130, d €145-165, f €235; 🅿🛜❄) Delicately embroidered cushions and cherrywood furniture add to the romantic ambience of this three-room family-run property on a 27-hectare estate, which is everything a French B&B should be. Allow plenty of time for breakfast (included in the price) on the terrace in summer before plunging into the pool. An open fireplace warms the lounge in chilly weather.

Hôtel de Londres HOTEL €€
(☑01 64 22 20 21; www.hoteldelondres.com; 1 place du Général de Gaulle; d €138-228; ❄@🛜) Classy, cosy and beautifully kept, the 'Hotel London' faces the château. Its 16 rooms are furnished in warm reds and royal blues. Most have air-conditioning and the priciest rooms (such as room 5) have balconies overlooking the palace. Breakfast is €16.

✕ Eating

Try sugar-whipped *crème Chantilly* in cafes and restaurants throughout town. Chantilly's **market** (place Omer Vallon; ⊙8.30am-12.30pm Wed & Sat) takes place on Wednesday and Saturday.

ID Cook L'Atelier Gourmand DELI €
(www.idcook-chantilly.fr; 78 rue du Connétable; ⊙10.30am-2pm & 4-8pm Tue-Fri, 10.30am-8pm Sat, 10.30am-1.30pm Sun) If it's not market day (and even if it is), this deli is a fabulous spot to pick up ingredients for a forest picnic. Charcuterie, smoked and marinated fish, foie gras, premade salads, preserves, cheeses, breads, chocolates, beer, wine and much more cram the shelves.

Le Boudoir FRENCH €
(☑03 44 55 44 49; www.leboudoir-chantilly.fr; 100 rue du Connétable; lunch menus €8.50-11.50, dishes €4.50-10; ⊙11am-6pm Mon, 10am-7pm Tue-Sat, 11am-7pm Sun) As a certified partner of Parisian gourmet emporium Fauchon (p173), you can be sure of the quality at this charming tearoom. With comfy sofas, a sunny pavement terrace and a shaded courtyard garden, it's a perfect place to try *crème Chantilly* (including on hot chocolate) or to enjoy a light lunch (salads, savoury tarts and so on).

Le Vertugadin FRENCH €€
(☑03 44 57 03 19; http://vertugadin.com; 44 rue du Connétable; 3-course menu €32, mains €22-36; ⊙7.15-10pm Tue, noon-2pm & 7.15-10pm Wed-Sat, noon-2pm Sun; ☒) This elegant white-shuttered townhouse serves classical cuisine such as meat, game and terrines accompanied by sweet onion chutney. A warming fire roars in the hearth in winter, and summer welcomes diners to the walled garden.

ⓘ Information

Tourist Office (☑03 44 67 37 37; www.chantilly-tourisme.com; 73 rue du Connétable; ⊙9.30am-12.30pm & 1.30-5.30pm Mon & Wed-Sat, 9.30am-12.30pm Tue, 10.30am-1pm & 2.30-5pm Sun May-Sep, 9.30am-12.30pm & 1.30-5.30pm Mon & Wed-Sat, 9.30am-12.30pm Tue Oct-Apr) Can help with accommodation and has details of walks through town, along Chantilly's two canals and around the racecourse, as well as walking and mountain-bike trails in the forest.

ⓘ Getting There & Away

RER D (direction Creil) links Gare de Lyon, Châtelet–Les Halles and Gare du Nord with Chantilly-Gouvieux train station (€8.70, 25 to 45 minutes, up to four hourly). High-speed TGV trains are planned to arrive in 2020.

Driving from Paris, the fastest route is via the Autoroute du Nord (A1/E19); use exit 7 (signposted Chantilly). The N1 then N16 from Porte de la Chapelle/St-Denis is cheaper.

Chartres

POP 41,588

Step off the train in Chartres, 91km southwest of Paris, and the two very different steeples – one Gothic, the other Romanesque – of its glorious 13th-century cathedral loom above. Follow them to check out the cathedral's dazzling blue stained-glass windows and its collection of relics, including the Sainte Voile (Holy Veil) said to have been worn by the Virgin Mary when she gave birth to Jesus, which have lured pilgrims since the Middle Ages.

After visiting the town's museums, don't miss a stroll around Chartres' carefully preserved old city. Adjacent to the cathedral, staircases and steep streets lined with half-timbered medieval houses lead downhill to the narrow western channel of the Eure River, romantically spanned by footbridges.

⊙ Sights

Allow 1½ to two hours to walk the signposted *circuit touristique* (tourist circuit), taking in Chartres' key sights. Free town maps from the tourist office also mark the route.

★**Cathédrale Notre Dame** CATHEDRAL
(www.cathedrale-chartres.org; place de la Cathédrale; ⊙8.30am-7.30pm daily year-round, also to 10pm Tue, Fri & Sun Jun-Aug) One of Western civilisation's crowning architectural achievements, the 130m-long Cathédrale Notre Dame de Chartres is renowned for its brilliant-blue stained-glass windows and sacred holy veil. Built in the Gothic style during the first quarter of the 13th century to replace a Romanesque cathedral that had been devastated by fire – along with much of the town – in 1194, effective fundraising and donated labour meant construction took only 30 years, resulting in a high degree of architectural unity.

Today, it is France's best-preserved medieval cathedral, having been spared post-medieval modifications, the ravages of war and the Reign of Terror.

The cathedral's west, north and south entrances have superbly ornamented triple

Chartres

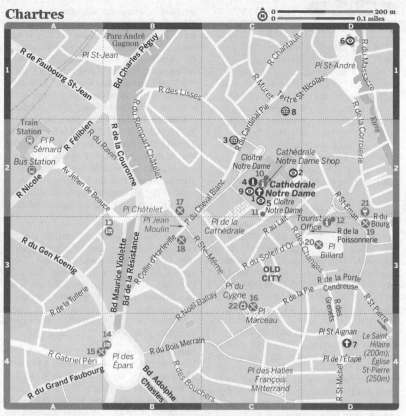

Chartres

portals, but the west entrance, known as the **Portail Royal** (Cathédrale Notre Dame), is the only one that predates the fire. Carved from 1145 to 1155, its superb statues, whose features are elongated in the Romanesque style, represent the glory of Christ in the centre, and the Nativity and the Ascension to the right and left, respectively. The structure's other

THE HOLY VEIL

The most venerated object in Chartres' cathedral is the Sainte Voile, the 'Holy Veil' said to have been worn by the Virgin Mary when she gave birth to Jesus. It originally formed part of the imperial treasury of Constantinople but was offered to Charlemagne by the Empress Irene when the Holy Roman Emperor proposed marriage to her in 802. Charles the Bald presented it to the town in 876; the cathedral was built because the veil survived the 1194 fire.

main Romanesque feature is the 105m-high **Clocher Vieux** (Old Bell Tower; Cathédrale Notre Dame), also called the Tour Sud (South Tower). Construction began in the 1140s; it remains the tallest Romanesque steeple still standing.

A visit to the 112m-high **Clocher Neuf** (New Bell Tower; Cathédrale Notre Dame; adult/child €7.50/free; ⊙9.30am-12.30pm & 2-4.30pm Mon-Sat, 2-4.30pm Sun), also known as the Tour Nord (North Tower), is worth the ticket price and the climb up the long spiral stairway (350 steps). A 70m-high platform on the lacy flamboyant **Gothic spire**, built from 1507 to 1513 by Jehan de Beauce after an earlier wooden spire burned down, affords superb views of the three-tiered flying buttresses and the 19th-century copper roof, turned green by verdigris.

The cathedral's 176 extraordinary **stained-glass windows**, almost all of which date back to the 13th century, form one of the most important ensembles of medieval stained glass in the world. The three most exquisite windows, dating from the mid-12th century, are in the wall above the west entrance and below the rose window. Survivors of the fire of 1194 (they were made some four decades before), the windows are revered for the depth and intensity of their tones, famously known as 'Chartres blue'.

In Chartres since 876, the venerated **Sainte Voile** (Holy Veil) – a yellowish bolt of silk draped over a support, which is believed to have been worn by the Virgin Mary when she gave birth to Jesus – is displayed at the end of the cathedral's north aisle behind the choir.

The cathedral's 110m **crypt** (Cathédrale Notre Dame; adult/child €3/2.40; ⊙up to 5 tours daily), a

tombless Romanesque structure built in 1024 around a 9th-century predecessor, is the largest in France. Thirty-minute tours in French (with a written English translation) start at the cathedral-run **shop** (⊘02 37 21 59 08; www.cathedrale-chartres.org; Cathédrale Notre Dame; ⊙8.30am-7.30pm) selling souvenirs, from April to October. At other times they begin at the shop below the Clocher Neuf in the cathedral.

Guided tours (⊘Anne Marie Woods 02 37 21 75 02, Malcolm Miller 02 37 28 15 58; tours €10; ⊙noon & 2.45pm Mon-Sat Apr-Oct, by request Nov-Mar) of the cathedral, in English, with Chartres experts Malcolm Miller or Anne Marie Woods, depart from the shop.

Multilingual audioguides cost €3.20 for Clocher Neuf and €4.20 for the cathedral, or €6.20 for both.

Centre International du Vitrail MUSEUM (www.centre-vitrail.org; 5 rue du Cardinal Pie; adult/child €7/5.50; ⊙9.30am-12.30pm & 1.30-6pm Mon-Fri, 10am-12.30pm & 2.30-6pm Sat, 2.30-6pm Sun) After viewing the stained glass in Chartres' cathedral, nip into the town's International Stained-Glass Centre, in a half-timbered former granary, to see superb examples close up.

Musée des Beaux-Arts MUSEUM (www.chartres.fr/culture/musee-des-beaux-arts; 29 Cloître Notre Dame; adult/child €3.40/1.70; ⊙10am-12.30pm & 2-8pm Thu, 10am-12.30pm & 2-6pm Fri & Sat, 2-6pm Sun May-Oct, shorter hrs Nov-Apr) Chartres' fine-arts museum, accessed via the gate next to Cathédrale Notre Dame's north portal, is in the former Palais Épiscopal (Bishop's Palace), built in the 17th and 18th centuries. Its collections include 16th-century enamels of the Apostles made for François I, paintings from the 16th to 19th centuries and polychromatic wooden sculptures from the Middle Ages.

◉ Old City

Chartres' beautiful medieval old city is northeast and east of the cathedral. Highlights include the 12th-century **Collégiale St-André** (place St-André), a Romanesque church that's now an exhibition centre; **rue de la Tannerie** and its extension **rue de la Foulerie**, lined with flower gardens, mill-races and the restored remnants of riverside trades: wash houses, tanneries and the like; and **rue des Écuyers**, with many structures dating from around the 16th century.

Église St-Pierre CHURCH
(www.cathedrale-chartres.org; place St-Pierre; ⊙8.30am-6pm) Flying buttresses hold up the 12th- and 13th-century Église St-Pierre. Once part of a Benedictine monastery founded in the 7th century, it was outside the city walls and thus vulnerable to attack; the fortress-like, pre-Romanesque bell tower attached to it was used as a refuge by monks, and dates from around 1000. The fine, brightly coloured clerestory windows in Église St-Pierre's nave, choir and apse date from the early 14th century.

Église St-Aignan CHURCH
(www.cathedrale-chartres.org; place St-Aignan; ⊙8.30am-6pm) Église St-Aignan is interesting for its wooden barrel-vault roof (1625), arcaded nave and painted interior of faded blue and gold floral motifs (c 1870). The stained glass and the Renaissance Chapelle de St-Michel date from the 16th and 17th centuries.

⚑ Festivals & Events

Chartres en Lumières LIGHT SHOW
(www.chartresenlumieres.com; ⊙dusk-1am mid-Apr–mid-Oct) During the warmer months, some two dozen Chartres landmarks are spectacularly lit every night. You can also see them from aboard **Le Petit Chart' Train late circuits** (www.lepetittraindechartres. fr; adult/child €6.50/3.50, late circuits €7.50/4.50; ⊙10.45am-2pm late Mar-Oct, late circuits 10.30pm early Jun–mid-Aug, hrs vary mid-Apr–early Jun & mid-Aug–early Oct) or on **night walking tours** (☑02 37 18 26 26; www.chartres-tourisme.com; adult/child €13/6.50; ⊙by reservation 9.30pm Sat mid-Apr–early Oct) in English, bookable through Chartres' tourist office.

🛏 Sleeping

Chartres is a convenient stop between Paris and the Loire Valley.

Hôtel du Bœuf Couronné HOTEL €€
(☑02 37 18 06 06; www.leboeufcouronne.com; 15 place Châtelet; d from €92; 🛜) The red-curtained entrance lends a theatrical air to this two-star Logis guesthouse in the centre of everything. Its summertime terrace restaurant has cathedral-view dining and the XV bar mixes great cocktails. Cathedral views also extend from some of its 17 modern rooms.

Le Grand Monarque HOTEL €€
(☑02 37 18 15 15; www.bw-grand-monarque. com; 22 place des Épars; d/f from €127/157.50; ✴@🛜) With teal-blue shutters gracing its 1779 façade, a lovely stained-glass ceiling and a treasure trove of period furnishings, old B&W photos and knick-knacks, the epicentral Grand Monarque is a historical gem. Some rooms have air-conditioning; staff are charming. A host of hydrotherapy treatments are available at its spa. Its elegant restaurant, Georges (p204), has a Michelin star.

Family rooms have sofa beds; cots and babysitting services are available. Ask about cooking courses in English (1½ hours from €30; kids' courses available).

🍴 Eating & Drinking

Food shops and restaurants surround the **covered market** (Covered Market; place Billard; ⊙7am-1pm Wed & Sat, organic market 5-8pm Wed), just off rue des Changes, south of the cathedral.

La Passacaille ITALIAN €
(☑02 37 21 52 10; www.lapassacaille.fr; 30 rue Ste-Même; 2-/3-course menus €17.80/20.90, pizzas €12-16, pastas €10.50-15.50; ⊙11.45am-2pm & 6.45-10pm Thu & Sun-Tue, 11.45am-2pm & 6.45-10.30pm Fri & Sat; 🔾) This welcoming spot has particularly good pizzas (try the Montagnarde with tomato, mozzarella, Reblochon cheese, potatoes, red onions, cured ham and crème fraîche) and homemade pasta with toppings including *pistou* (pesto) also made on the premises. Tables spill onto the square out front in summer.

La Chocolaterie PASTRIES €
(www.lachocolaterie-chartres.fr; 2 place du Cygne; dishes €3.80-6.50; ⊙8am-7.30pm Tue-Sat, from 10am Sun & Mon) Soak up local life overlooking the open-air **flower market** (place du Cygne; ⊙8am-7pm Tue, Thu & Sat). This tearoom/patisserie's hot chocolate and macarons (flavoured with orange, apricot, peanut, pineapple and so on) are sublime, as are its sweet homemade crêpes and miniature madeleine cakes.

Le Tripot BISTRO €€
(☑02 37 36 60 11; http://letripot.wixsite.com/ chartres; 11 place Jean Moulin; 2-/3-course lunch menus €15/18, 3-course dinner menus €32-44, mains €13-22; ⊙noon-1.45pm & 7.30-9.15pm Wed-Sat, noon-1.45pm Sun) Tucked off the tourist trail and easy to miss even if you do chance down its narrow street, this atmospheric space with low, beamed ceilings is a treat for authentic and adventurous French fare like saddle of rabbit stuffed with snails or grilled turbot in truffled hollandaise sauce. Locals are on to it, so booking ahead is advised.

Les Feuillantines
MODERN FRENCH €€

(🖉02 37 30 22 21; https://restaurantles feuillantines.eatbu.com; 4 rue du Bourg; menus €25-36, mains €20-22; ⏱noon-1.30pm & 7-9.30pm Tue-Sat) Take a seat in the sleek interior or beneath a market umbrella in the rear courtyard to dine on superb dishes such as sea bream with potatoes and tomato emulsion, bacon-wrapped veal with lentils, roast duck with butternut squash and cider jus, before finishing with its house-speciality chocolate sphere served with orange sorbet and sweet Chantilly cream.

L'Escalier
BAR

(🖉07 86 09 50 38; 1 rue du Bourg; ⏱4pm-1am Thu, to 2am Fri & Sat; 🛜) On a steep corner near its namesake staircase in Chartres' hilly old city, this deceptively large, very local spot has a wonderful terrace. Look out for live jazz performances.

Le Saint-Hilaire
MODERN FRENCH €€

(🖉02 37 30 97 57; www.restaurant-saint-hilaire. fr; 11 rue du Pont St-Hilaire; 2-course midweek lunch menu €21, €2-/3-course menus €36/46; ⏱noon-2pm & 7-9.30pm Tue-Sat) At this pistachio-painted, wood-beamed charmer, local products are ingeniously used in dishes such as snails with leeks and Nottonville Abbey goat's cheese crème, and cinnamon candied pear with gingerbread. Don't miss its lobster menu in season, or the aromatic cheese platters any time of year.

Georges
GASTRONOMY €€€

(🖉02 37 18 15 15; www.bw-grand-monarque. com; 22 place des Épars; 4-/5-/7-course menus €56/78/98; ⏱noon-2pm & 7.30-10pm Tue-Sat) Even if you're not staying at lavish hotel Le Grand Monarque (p203), its refined Georges restaurant is worth seeking out for its Michelin-starred multicourse *menus* and mains such as ginger-marinated salmon with pickled veggies and crustacean bouillon, or blackberry-marinated roast lamb with chestnut purée and green beans. Desserts (confit of grapefruit with Campari gelato, for instance) are inspired.

ℹ️ Information

Tourist Office (🖉02 37 18 26 26; www. chartres-tourisme.com; 8-10 rue de la Poissonnerie; ⏱10am-6pm Mon-Sat, to 5.30pm Sun) Housed in the half-timbered Maison du Saumon, a former fish merchant's premises dating from the 16th century, with an exhibition on Chartres' history. Rents 1½-hour English-language audioguide tours (€5.50/8.50 per one/ two) of the medieval city as well as binoculars (€2), fabulous for seeing details of the cathedral close up.

The **Cathédrale Notre Dame Shop** (p202) is also helpful.

ℹ️ Getting There & Away

Frequent SNCF trains link Paris' Gare Montparnasse (€16, 55 to 70 minutes) with Chartres' **train station** (place Pierre Semard), some of which stop at Versailles-Chantiers (€13.50, 45 to 60 minutes). The **bus station** (place Pierre Semard) is next to the train station.

If you're driving from Paris, follow the A6 from Porte d'Orléans (direction Bordeaux–Nantes), then the A10 and A11 (direction Nantes) and take the 'Chartres' exit.

Lille, Flanders & the Somme

POP 5.97 MILLION

Best Places to Eat

➡ Perard (p224)
➡ Meert (p211)
➡ La Marie Galante (p219)
➡ La Sirène (p219)
➡ La Matelote (p222)

Best Places to Stay

➡ Hôtel L'Arbre Voyageur (p211)
➡ Château du Romerel (p227)
➡ Hôtel Barrière Le Westminster (p224)
➡ Hôtel Marotte (p235)
➡ La Corne d'Or (p216)

Why Go?

Hauts-de-France (Upper France) is one of the country's least heralded regions, but with dramatic land and sea views, deeply rooted culture, culinary traditions that include freshly caught seafood, age-old Flemish recipes and locally brewed beers, it competes with the best France has to offer.

This fascinating area comprises the former *régions* of Nord-Pas-de-Calais and Picardie, taking in the home territories of the Ch'tis (residents of France's northern tip) and the Picards. Its capital, Lille, is awash with magnificent architecture, outstanding museums, creative enterprises and an energetic student vibe. Arras, Amiens and Laon captivate with Gothic treasures, and Compiègne preserves the dazzle of Napoléon III's Second Empire.

Beyond the cities, WWI memorials and cemeteries marking the 1914 to 1918 front lines have a heartbreaking beauty. Outdoors enthusiasts will love the wildlife-filled estuaries of the Baie de Somme, and the Côte d'Opale's activity-packed resorts, including fabled Le Touquet, and wide, often-empty beaches.

When to Go
Lille

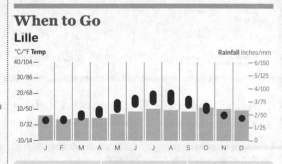

Feb & Mar Pre-Lenten carnivals bring out marching bands and costumed revellers.

Jun–Aug Splendid weather makes summer a perfect time to explore the Côte d'Opale.

Sep The world's largest flea market, the Braderie, takes over Lille on the first weekend in September.

Lille, Flanders & the Somme Highlights

1 Lille (p207) Discovering one of France's finest collections of art in French Flanders' engaging capital.

2 Amiens (p233) Marvelling at Amiens' breathtaking Gothic cathedral.

3 Côte d'Opale (p217) Rambling along the spectacular, windswept coast facing the White Cliffs of Dover.

4 Historial de la Grande Guerre (p228) Pondering the horror and sacrifice of WWI in Péronne.

5 La Cité Souterraine de Naours (p232) Exploring a Roman-quarried cave system used by wartime troops.

6 Cassel (p215) Enjoying Flemish landscapes, architecture and cuisine.

7 Baie de Somme (p225) Spotting seals lounging on the sandbanks of this magical area.

8 Arras (p216) Joining the Saturday market at place des Héros.

9 Ring of Remembrance memorial (p230) Reflecting on the human price of WWI.

10 Compiègne (p236) Visiting the palace where Napoléon III hosted hunting parties.

History

In the Middle Ages, the Nord *département* (the sliver of France along the Belgian border), together with much of Belgium and part of the Netherlands, belonged to a feudal principality known as Flanders (Flandre or Flandres in French, Vlaanderen in Dutch). French Flanders takes in the areas of French Westhoek (around Dunkirk) and Walloon Flanders (around Lille).

Today, many people in the French Westhoek area still speak French Flemish (French Flemish: *Fransch vlaemsch;* French: *flamand français;* Dutch: *Frans-Vlaams*), a regional language that closely resembles West Flemish, though it differs to standard Dutch, which was based on northern Netherlands dialects. In Walloon Flanders, the traditional language is *picard,* also known as *ch'ti, chtimi* or *rouchi.*

The area south of the Somme estuary and Albert, Picardy (Picardie), historically centred on the Somme *département,* which saw some of the bloodiest fighting of WWI. The popular British WWI love song 'Roses of Picardy' was penned here in 1916 by Frederick E Weatherley.

In 2016, the former *régions* of Nord-Pas-de-Calais and Picardie merged, becoming the *région* of Hauts-de-France.

ⓘ Getting There & Away

By Eurostar train (www.eurostar.com) Lille is just 90 minutes from London's St Pancras International train station. Eurotunnel Le Shuttle (www.eurotunnel.com) can get you and your car from Folkestone to Calais, via the Channel Tunnel, in a mere 35 minutes. Frequent car ferries link Dover with Calais (90 minutes) and Dunkirk (two hours).

On the Continent, superfast Eurostar and TGV trains connect Lille with Brussels (35 minutes), and TGVs make travel from Lille to Paris' Gare du Nord (one hour) and Charles de Gaulle Airport (50 minutes) a breeze.

LILLE

POP 233,900

Capital of the Hauts-de-France *région,* Lille may be France's most underrated metropolis. Recent decades have seen the country's fourth-largest city (by greater urban area) transform from an industrial centre into a glittering cultural and commercial hub. Highlights include its enchanting old town with magnificent French and Flemish architecture, renowned art museums, stylish shopping, outstanding cuisine, a nightlife scene bolstered by 67,000 university students, and some 1600 designers in its environs.

In 2020, Lille will become the World Design Capital (the first French city to do so), with design agencies and other creative enterprises opening their doors to the public, and exhibitions and festivities throughout the year.

Thanks to the Eurostar and the TGV, Lille makes an easy, environmentally sustainable weekend destination from London, Paris, Brussels and beyond.

◉ Sights & Activities

★ Palais des Beaux Arts   MUSEUM
(Fine Arts Museum; ☑ 03 20 06 78 00; www.pba-lille.fr; place de la République; adult/child €7/4; ☻ 2-6pm Mon, 10am-6pm Wed-Sun; Ⓜ République-Beaux-Arts) Inaugurated in 1892, Lille's illustrious Fine Arts Museum claims France's second-largest collection after Paris' Musée du Louvre. Its cache of sublime 15th- to 20th-century paintings include works by Rubens, Van Dyck and Manet. Exquisite porcelain and faience (pottery), much of it of local provenance, is on the ground floor, while in the basement you'll find classical archaeology, medieval statuary and 18th-century scale models of the fortified cities of northern France and Belgium.

Musée d'Art Moderne, d'Art Contemporain et d'Art Brut – LaM   MUSEUM
(☑ 03 20 19 68 68; www.musee-lam.fr; 1 allée du Musée, Villeneuve-d'Ascq; adult/child €7/5, 1st Sun of month free; ☻ museum 10am-6pm Tue-Sun, sculpture park 9am-6pm Tue-Sun) Colourful, playful and just plain weird works of modern and contemporary art by masters such as Braque, Calder, Léger, Miró, Modigliani and Picasso are the big draw at this renowned museum and sculpture park in the Lille suburb of Villeneuve-d'Ascq, 9km east of Gare Lille-Europe. Take metro line 1 to Pont de Bois, then bus L4 six stops to 'LaM'.

★ La Piscine Musée d'Art et d'Industrie   GALLERY
(☑ 03 20 69 23 60; www.roubaix-lapiscine.com; 23 rue de l'Espérance, Roubaix; ☻ 11am-6pm Tue-Thu, 11am-8pm Fri, 1-6pm Sat & Sun; Ⓜ Gare Jean Lebas) An art deco municipal swimming pool built between 1927 and 1932 is now an innovative museum showcasing fine arts (paintings, sculptures, drawings) and applied arts (furniture, textiles, fashion) in a delightfully watery environment: the pool is still filled and sculptures are reflected in the water. Reopening in

Lille

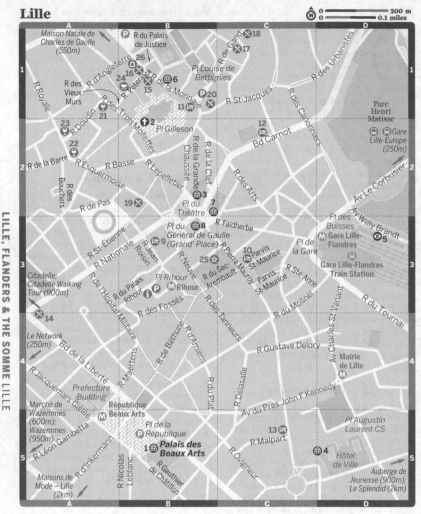

October 2018 with a new wing and 2000 sq metres of additional exhibition space; check the website for updated entry prices. It's 12km northeast of Gare Lille-Europe in Roubaix.

Hôtel de Ville
HISTORIC BUILDING

(📞03 20 49 50 00; www.lille.fr; place Augustin Laurent CS; belfry adult/child €7/5.50; ⏰belfry 10am-1pm & 2-5.30pm; Ⓜ Mairie de Lille) Built between 1924 and 1932, Lille's city hall is topped by a slender, 104m-high belfry that was designated a Unesco-listed monument in 2004. Climbing 100 steps leads to a lift that whisks you to the top for a stunning panorama over the town.

An audioguide costs €2; binoculars are available for €1. Ring the doorbell to gain entry.

Wazemmes
AREA

(Ⓜ Gambetta) For an authentic taste of grassroots Lille, head to the ethnically diverse, family-friendly *quartier populaire* (working-class quarter) of Wazemmes, 1.3km southwest of place du Général de Gaulle, where old-school proletarians and immigrants live harmoniously alongside students and trendy *bobos* (bourgeois bohemians).

The neighbourhood's focal point is the cavernous **Marché de Wazemmes**

Lille

LILLE, FLANDERS & THE SOMME LILLE

(www.halles-wazemmes.com; place de la Nouvelle Aventure; ⊙ covered market 8am-8pm Tue-Sat, to 3pm Sun; street market 7am-2pm Tue, Thu & Sun; Ⓜ Gambetta), Lille's favourite food market. The adjacent outdoor market is the place to be on Sunday morning – it's a real carnival scene. Rue des Sarrazins and rue Jules Guesde are lined with shops, restaurants and Tunisian bakeries, many owned by, and catering to, the area's North African residents.

Wazemmes is famed for its outdoor concerts and street festivals, including La Louche d'Or (The Golden Ladle; 1 May), a soup festival that has spread to cities across Europe.

Maison Natale de Charles de Gaulle · MUSEUM
(☎ 03 59 73 00 30; www.charles-de-gaulle.org; 9 rue Princesse; adult/child incl audioguide €6/free; ⊙ 10am-noon & 2-5pm Wed-Sat, 1.30-5pm Sun; Ⓜ Rihour) The upper-middle-class house in which Charles de Gaulle was born in 1890 is now a museum presenting the French general and president in the context of his times, with an emphasis on his connection to French Flanders. Displays include de Gaulle's baptismal robe and some evocative newsreels.

Musée de l'Hospice Comtesse GALLERY
(☎ 03 28 36 84 00; www.lille.fr; 32 rue de la Monnaie; adult/child €3.60/free, audioguide €2; ⊙ 2-6pm Mon, 10am-6pm Wed-Sun; Ⓜ Rihour) Within a red-brick 15th- and 17th-century poorhouse, this absorbing museum features ceramics, earthenware wall tiles, religious art, 17th- and 18th-century paintings and furniture, and a detailed exhibit on the history of Lille. A rood screen separates the Salle des Malades (Hospital Hall), hosting contemporary art exhibitions, from a mid-17th-century chapel (look up to see a mid-19th-century painted ceiling).

Le Tripostal ARTS CENTRE
(☎ 03 20 14 47 60; www.facebook.com/letripo; av Willy Brandt; prices vary; ⊙ 10am-7pm Wed-Sat, hours can vary; Ⓜ Gare Lille-Flandres) Splashed with street art murals, this cavernous red-brick postal sorting centre was transformed into an arts centre in 2004, when Lille was the European Capital of Culture. Changing art and photography exhibitions (most free) usually feature local artists; there's also a bar, canteen-style restaurant, a kids' play area and a design shop. Look out too for events such as DJ sets, live music gigs and workshops.

Citadelle FORTRESS
(https://citadellelille.fr; av du 43e Régiment d'Infanterie; 🚌 10) At the northwestern end of bd de la Liberté, this massive, star-shaped fortress was designed by renowned 17th-century French military architect Vauban after France captured Lille in 1667, and completed in 1670. Made of some 60 million bricks, it now serves as the headquarters of the 12-nation, NATO-certified Rapid Reaction Corps – France. The only way to visit is by **guided tour** (☎ 03 59 57 94 00; www.lilletourism.com; av du 43e Régiment d'Infanterie; €7.50; ⊙ 3pm & 4.30pm Sun Jun-Aug, 3rd Sun of month Sep-May; 🚌 10).

Outside the 2.2km-long ramparts is central Lille's largest public park, the Parc de la Citadelle, spanning 60 hectares.

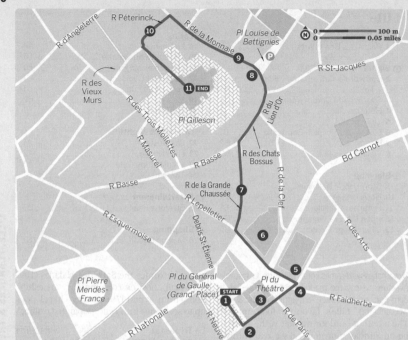

🏃 City Walk
Lille Discovery Stroll

START PLACE DU GÉNÉRAL DE GAULLE
END CATHÉDRALE NOTRE-DAME-DE-LA-
TREILLE
LENGTH 1KM; ONE HOUR

The best place to begin a discovery stroll through Lille's Flemish heart is the city's focal point, **❶ place du Général de Gaulle** (the Grand Place), where you can admire the art deco home of **❷ La Voix du Nord** (the leading regional newspaper), crowned by a gilded sculpture of the Three Graces. The goddess-topped victory column (1845) in the fountain commemorates the city's successful resistance to the Austrian siege of 1792. On warm evenings, Lillois come here by the thousands to take in the urban vibe and sip a local beer.

The adjacent **❸ Vieille Bourse** (the old stock exchange), is ornately decorated with caryatids and cornucopia, a Flemish Renaissance extravaganza. Built in 1653, it consists of 24 separate houses set around a richly ornamented interior courtyard that hosts a used-book market. In the afternoon, especially on weekends, locals gather here to play (chess).

Just east of the Vieille Bourse, impressive **❹ place du Théâtre** is dominated by the Louis XVI–style **❺ Opéra** (p214) and the neo-Flemish **❻ Chambre de Commerce**, topped by a 76m-high spire sporting a gilded clock. Both were built in the early 20th century. Look east along rue Faidherbe and you'll see Gare Lille-Flandres at the far end.

Vieux Lille (Old Lille) begins just north of here. It's hard to believe today, but in the late 1970s much of this quarter was a half-abandoned slum dominated by empty, dilapidated buildings. Head north past the outdoor cafes to **❼ rue de la Grande Chaussée**, lined with Lille's chicest shops. Continue north along **❽ rue de la Monnaie** (named after a mint constructed here in 1685), whose old brick residences now house boutiques and the **❾ Musée de l'Hospice Comtesse** (p209).

Turning left (west) on tiny **❿ rue Péterinck** and then left again will take you to the 19th-century neogothic **⓫ Cathédrale Notre-Dame-de-la-Treille**, which has a strikingly modern (some would say jarring) west façade (1999) that looks better from inside or when illuminated at night.

✨ Festivals & Events

Braderie de Lille   MARKET
(www.braderie-de-lille.fr; ⊘ early Sep) On the first
weekend in September, Lille's entire city centre – 200km of footpaths – is transformed
into what's billed as the world's largest
flea market. It runs nonstop – yes, all night
long – from 2pm on Saturday to 11pm on
Sunday, when street sweepers emerge to
tackle the mounds of mussel shells and old
frites (fries) left behind by the merrymakers.

Marché de Noël   CHRISTMAS MARKET
(www.noel-a-lille.com; place Rihour; ⊘ mid-Nov–
late Dec) The neoclassical and Flemish build
ings of place Rihour provide a magical backdrop for one of France's most enchanting
Christmas markets. In the lead-up to Christmas, some 90 wooden stalls sell decorations,
spiced biscuits, mulled wine and other seasonal treats; a funfair also sets up here.

🛏️ Sleeping

Auberge de Jeunesse   HOSTEL €
(🖉 03 20 57 08 94; www.hifrance.org; 235 bd
Paul Painlevé; dm incl breakfast & sheets €25;
@ 🛜; Ⓜ Porte de Valenciennes) With a façade
sporting the colours of Europe, Lille's
youth hostel opened in 2015. The 55 spartan rooms have metal bunks, lockers and
showers (with timer buttons), but only 12
have attached toilets. There's bike storage,
a laundry and a self-catering kitchen. Wi-
fi is available only in the lobby. It's 1.7km
southeast of Gare Lille-Flandres.

★ Hôtel L'Arbre Voyageur   DESIGN HOTEL €€
(🖉 03 20 20 62 62; http://hotelarbrevoyageur.com;
45 bd Carnot; d/f/ste from €119/214/219; ✳ 🛜;
Ⓜ Gare Lille-Flandres) 🌿 Behind a fretted glass-
and-steel façade in the former Polish Consulate's post-Soviet building, the 2016-opened
Hôtel L'Arbre Voyageur has 48 stylised rooms
(including four suites) with custom-made
furniture and minibars stocked with free soft
drinks, and a bamboo- and palm-filled courtyard. Green initiatives span solar panels to
a free drink for guests who don't want their
linen changed every day.

Grand Hôtel Bellevue   HISTORIC HOTEL €€
(🖉 03 20 57 45 64; www.grandhotelbellevue.com;
5 rue Jean Roisin; d from €138, with city views from
€219; ✳ @ 🛜; Ⓜ Rihour) Opened in 1913, this
venerable establishment has 60 spacious
rooms with high ceilings, all-marble bathrooms, gilded picture frames and a mix of
inlaid-wood antiques and ultramodern furnishings. Higher-priced rooms have sweeping

views of place du Général de Gaulle. A lavish
buffet is laid on at breakfast (€16).

Hôtel de la Treille   HOTEL €€
(🖉 03 20 55 45 46; www.hoteldelatreille.com; 7-9
place Louise de Bettignies; s/d from €93/109; 🛜;
Ⓜ Gare Lille-Flandres) In a superb spot smack
in the middle of Vieux Lille, a few steps from
dining and shopping options galore, Hôtel
de la Treille's 42 stylish rooms offer views of
the lively square out front, the cathedral or a
quiet interior courtyard.

Hôtel Brueghel   HOTEL €€
(🖉 03 20 06 06 69; www.hotel-brueghel-lille.com;
5 parvis St-Maurice; s/d/apt from €79/90/250;
🛜; Ⓜ Gare Lille-Flandres) Hôtel Brueghel's
1930s-styled wood-panelled lobby has charm
in spades, as does the tiny, old-fashioned lift
that trundles guests up to 61 quiet rooms
with modern furnishings and art posters
on the walls. Some south-facing rooms have
sunny views of the adjacent church. It also
rents two city-centre apartments.

★ L'Hermitage Gantois   HOTEL €€€
(🖉 03 20 85 30 30; www.hotelhermitagegantois.
com; 224 rue Pierre Mauroy; d/ste from €169/442;
🅿 @ 🛜 ⊠; Ⓜ Mairie de Lille) This five-star hotel creates enchanting, harmonious spaces
by complementing its rich architectural
heritage, such as the Flemish-Gothic façade,
with refined ultramodernism. The 89 rooms
are sumptuous, with Philippe Starck accessories alongside Louis XV–style chairs
and bathrooms that sparkle with Carrara
marble. The still-consecrated chapel dates
from 1637; there's a 12m pool and *hammam*
(Turkish steambath).

🍴 Eating

The city has a flourishing culinary scene.
Keep an eye out for *estaminets* (traditional
Flemish eateries, with antique knick-knacks
on the walls and plain wooden tables) serving Flemish specialities.

Dining hot spots in Vieux Lille include
rue de Gand, home to small, moderately
priced French and Flemish restaurants, and
rue de la Monnaie and its side streets, alleys
and courtyards.

★ Meert   PASTRIES €
(🖉 03 20 57 07 44; www.meert.fr; 27 rue Esquermoise; waffles & pastries €3-7.60, tearoom dishes €4.50-
11.50, restaurant mains €26-32; ⊘ shop 2-7.30pm
Mon, 9.30am-7.30pm Tue-Fri, 9am-7.30pm Sat,
9am-7pm Sun, tearoom 2-7pm Mon, 9.30am-10pm
Tue-Fri, 9am-10pm Sat, 9am-6.30pm Sun, restaurant

noon-2.30pm & 7.30-10pm Tue-Sat, 11am-2pm Sun; ☎; Ⓜ Rihour) Famed for its *gaufres* (waffles) made with Madagascar vanilla, Meert has served kings, viceroys and generals since 1761. The sumptuous chocolate shop's coffered ceiling, painted wooden panels, wrought-iron balcony and mosaic floor date from 1839. Its *salon de thé* (tearoom) is a delightful spot for a morning Arabica or a mid-afternoon tea. Also here is a French gourmet restaurant.

Papà Raffaele   PIZZA €

(www.facebook.com/paparaffaelepizzeria; 5 rue St-Jacques; pizza €7.50-14; ⊙ noon-2pm & 7-10pm Mon-Thu, noon-2pm & 6.30-11pm Fri, noon-3pm & 6.30-11pm Sat & Sun; 🍴🖥; Ⓜ Gare Lille-Flandres) The queues at Papà Raffaele are as legendary as its pizzas (it doesn't take reservations), so come early or late to this post-industrial space with recycled timber tables, vintage chairs and cured meats hanging from the ceiling. Wood-fired pizzas (like Cheesus Christ, with six cheeses) are made with Naples-sourced ingredients; coffee, craft beers and wine are all Italian. Takeaway's available.

La Clairière   VEGAN €

(☏ 03 20 11 23 16; www.facebook.com/LaClairiere-Lille; 75 bd de la Liberté; 2-/3-course midweek lunch menus €14/18, 2-/3-course dinner menus €16/20, mains €11-12, Sun brunch €22; ⊙ noon-2.30pm Tue-Thu, noon-2.30pm & 7.30-10pm Fri & Sat, noon-2pm Sun; ☎🍴🖥; Ⓜ Rihour, République–Beaux Arts) In a bare-timber space with mezzanine seating, La Clairière creates colourful, 100% organic

---

ⓘ **SHOP TALK**

The snazziest fashion and homewares boutiques are in Vieux Lille, in the area bounded by rue de la Monnaie, rue Esquermoise, rue de la Grande Chausée and rue d'Angleterre. Design shops concentrate on rue du Faubourg des Poste, 3km southwest of the centre.

Keep an eye out for gourmet shops with locally made specialities such as chocolate. At **Maison Benoit** (☏ 03 20 31 69 03; https://maison-benoit.com; 77 rue de la Monnaie; ⊙ 10am-7pm Mon-Sat, 9.30am-1pm Sun; Ⓜ Rihour), second-generation artisan chocolatier Dominique Benoit creates pralines and other chocolates using traditional techniques and inspired flavour pairings, such as Cointreau and caramel, Bavarian vanilla and cherries, Périgord walnuts and chicory...

---

vegan cuisine made from sustainable produce (no palm oil). Most is locally sourced, including herbs and flowers grown in its planter boxes on the pavement out front. Menu highlights include roast butternut pumpkin stuffed with chestnuts, soy beans and carrots, and a squash, quinoa and mushroom crumble.

Le Bistrot Lillois   FRENCH, FLEMISH €

(☏ 03 20 14 04 15; 40 rue de Gand; mains €13-24; ⊙ noon-2pm & 7.30-10pm Tue-Sat; Ⓜ Rihour) Dishes both Flemish and French are served here under hanging hops. The highlight of the menu is *os à moëlle* (bone marrow); Flemish dishes worth trying include *carbonade flamande* (braised beef slow-cooked with beer, onions, brown sugar and gingerbread) and *potjevleesch* (jellied chicken, pork, veal and rabbit; served cold). Book ahead for dinner, or try arriving promptly at 7.30pm.

★ L'Assiette du Marché   FRENCH €€

(☏ 03 20 06 83 61; www.assiettedumarche.com; 61 rue de la Monnaie; 2-/3-course menus €19.50/25, mains €16-25; ⊙ noon-2.30pm & 7-10.30pm Mon-Fri, to 11pm Sat & Sun; Ⓜ Rihour) Entered via a grand archway, a 12th-century aristocratic mansion – a mint under Louis XIV, hence the street's name, and a listed historical monument – is the romantic setting for contemporary cuisine (tuna carpaccio with Champagne vinaigrette, roast duckling with glazed turnips and smoked garlic). Dine under its glass roof, in its intimate dining rooms, or on its cobbled courtyard in summer.

Le Barbier qui Fume   BARBECUE €€

(☏ 03 20 06 99 35; www.lebarbierquifume.fr; 69 rue de la Monnaie; 3-course lunch/dinner menu €17.40/28, mains €15-29.50; ⊙ 10.30am-3pm & 6-11pm Mon-Fri, 10.30am-11pm Sat, 11am-4pm Sun; Ⓜ Rihour) Charred aromas waft from this former barber shop (hence the name, the Smoking Barber), which now houses a ground-floor butcher and upstairs restaurant specialising in premium meats (pork knuckle, lamb shoulder, beef ribs) and poultry (pigeon, duck) smoked onsite over beechwood. There's a handful of tables next to the butcher's counter, and more out on the terrace.

Le Clair de Lune   FRENCH €€

(☏ 03 20 51 46 55; www.restaurant-leclairdelune.fr; 50 rue de Gand; 2-/3-course midweek lunch menus €16/20, dinner menus €28/36, mains €20; ⊙ noon-2pm & 7-10pm Mon, Tue & Thu, noon-2pm & 7-10.30pm Fri, noon-2.30pm & 7-10.30pm Sat, 12.30-2.30pm & 7-10pm Sun; Ⓜ Rihour) Creations such as duck carpaccio with gingerbread vinaigrette, beef

THE GIANTS

In far northern France and nearby Belgium, *géants* (giants) – wickerwork body masks up to 8.5m tall animated by someone (or several someones) inside – emerge for local carnivals and on feast days to dance and add to the general merriment. Each has a name and a personality, usually based on the Bible, legends or local history. Giants are born, baptised, grow up, marry and have children, creating, over the years, complicated family relationships. They serve as important symbols of town, neighbourhood and village identity.

Medieval in origin – and also found in places such as the UK, Catalonia, the Austrian Tyrol, Mexico, Brazil and India – giants have been a tradition in northern France since the 16th century. More than 300 of the creatures now 'live' in French towns, including Arras, Boulogne, Calais, Cassel, Dunkirk and Lille. France and Belgium's giants were recognised by Unesco as 'masterpieces of the oral and intangible heritage of humanity' in 2005.

Your best chance to see them is at pre-Lenten carnivals, during Easter and at festivals held from May to September, often on weekends. Dates and places appear in the free, annual poster-brochure *C'est quand les géants?*, available at tourist offices and online at www.calendrier-des-geants.eu.

---

fillet with red wine and chocolate jus, and guinea fowl with smoked bacon *crème* have seen Sébastien Defrance's elegant restaurant awarded the prestigious title Maître Restaurateur, a French government recognition of quality local produce and homemade cooking, in 2017. Around half of the 50-strong wine list is available by the glass.

🍷 Drinking & Nightlife

Lille is a bastion of the area's long-standing tradition of beer brewing; look out for beers from the region around town. Small, stylish bars line rue Royale and rue de la Barre, while university students descend on the bars along rue Masséna and rue Solférino, as far southeast as Marché Sébastopol. In warm weather, cafes on place du Général de Gaulle and place du Théâtre spill onto table-filled terraces.

Tamper   COFFEE
(☑03 20 39 28 21; 10 rue des Vieux Murs; ⊙9am 6pm Wed-Sat, to 5pm Sun; 🛜; MRihour) Beans roasted by Berlin's The Barn are brewed using filter, Aeropress, siphon or piston methods at this hip cafe with bare-brick walls and vintage American jazz on the turntable. It also serves iced teas and coffee, fresh OJ, homemade lemonade and smoothies, along with pastries and cakes. Granola, eggs and French toast are among the options at breakfast; at lunch there are quiches, tartines (open sandwiches), salads and soups.

★La Capsule   CRAFT BEER
(☑03 20 42 14 75; www.bar-la-capsule.fr; 25 rue des Trois Mollettes; ⊙5.30pm-1am Mon-Wed, 5.30pm-3am Thu & Fri, 4pm-3am Sat, 5.30pm-midnight Sun; 🛜; MRihour) Spread across three levels – a vaulted stone cellar, beamed-ceilinged ground floor and an upper level reached by a spiral staircase – Lille's best craft beer bar has 28 varieties on tap and over 100 by the bottle. Most are French (such as Lille's Lydéric and Paris' BapBap) and Belgian (eg Cantillon), but small-scale brewers from around the world are also represented.

L'Illustration Café   BAR
(☑03 20 12 00 90; 18 rue Royale; ⊙noon-1am Mon & Tue, 12.30pm-1am Wed, noon-3am Thu & Fri, 2.30pm-3am Sat, 3pm-1am Sun; MRihour) Adorned with art nouveau woodwork and changing exhibits by local painters, this laid back bar attracts artists, musicians, budding intellectuals and teachers in the mood to read, exchange weighty ideas or just shoot the breeze. The mellow soundtrack mixes jazz, blues, indie rock, French *chansons* and African and Cuban beats. Check the Facebook page for details of concerts.

Le Privilège   GAY
(www.facebook.com/privilege.lille; 2 rue Royale; ⊙5pm-1am Sun-Wed, 5pm-3am Thu & Fri, 3pm-3am Sat; 🛜; MRihour) In a former bookshop, Lille's premier gay bar has a vaulted cellar, ground-floor bar/dance floor strung with mirrored disco balls, and an upper-level bar. Most nights see DJs spinning disco, pop and electronica. Tuesdays is retro ('80s and '90s tunes); on Wednesdays it hosts drag karaoke.

Le Network   CLUB
(☑03 20 40 04 91; www.lenetwork.fr; 15 rue du Faisan; ⊙10.30pm-7am Tue, Wed, Fri & Sat, 9.30pm-7am Thu, 7pm-7am Sun; MRépublique–Beaux Arts) Central Lille's hottest club has two dance floors, three bars, plenty of flashing lights and

space for 700 revellers. On most nights the music is three-quarters house and electronic and a quarter R&B. Dress up as the door policy is pretty strict. Admission ranges from free to €15 (including a drink), depending on what's happening.

☆ Entertainment

Lille's free French-language entertainment guide *Sortir* (http://hautsdefrance.sortir.eu), issued every Wednesday, is available at the tourist office, cinemas, event venues and bookshops. For arts exhibitions and events, check www.lille3000.com.

Lille's **Opéra** (⌕ tickets 08 20 48 90 00; www.opera-lille.fr; place du Théâtre; Ⓜ Rihour) hosts opera, dance and classical concerts.

Buy entertainment tickets at **Fnac** (www.fnacspectacles.com; 20 rue St-Nicolas; ⊙ 10am-7.30pm Mon-Sat; Ⓜ Rihour).

Le Splendid   LIVE MUSIC
(⌕ 03 20 33 20 17; www.le-splendid.com; 1 place du Mont de Terre; Ⓜ Porte de Valenciennes) A former cinema with balcony seating is now one of Lille's best live music venues, with a capacity of 900. Local and international rock, indie and pop acts all play here; there are around 70 to 100 concerts per year.

ℹ Information

Tourist Office (⌕ 03 59 57 94 00; www.lilletourism.com; 3 rue du Palais Rihour; ⊙ 9.30am-1pm & 2-6pm Mon-Sat, 10am-12.30pm & 1.15-4.30pm Sun; Ⓜ Rihour)

ℹ Getting There & Away

AIR

Aéroport de Lille (LIL; www.lille.aeroport.fr; rte de L'Aéroport, Lesquin) is situated 11km southeast of the centre. It's linked to destinations around France and southern Europe by a variety of low-cost carriers. To get to/from the city centre (Gare Lille-Europe), you can take a shuttle bus (return €8, 20 minutes, hourly).

> ### ℹ LILLE CITY PASS
> ....
> The Lille City Pass (24/48/72 hours €25/35/45) gets you into almost all the museums in greater Lille and affords unlimited use of public transport. The 72-hour option throws in sites in the surrounding area, including Arras, Dunkirk and Cassel, and free use of regional TER trains for 24 hours. Buy it at Lille's tourist office or through its website.

BUS

Lille's **bus station** (bd de Turin; Ⓜ Gare Lille-Flandres) is just outside Gare Lille-Europe. **Isilines** (www.isilines.fr) and **Ouibus** (https://fr.ouibus.com) operate domestic services to destinations throughout France. **Eurolines** (www.eurolines.com) and **Flixbus** (www.flixbus.com) run international services to destinations including London.

TRAIN

Lille's two main train stations, Gare Lille-Flandres and the newer Gare Lille-Europe, are 400m apart on the eastern edge of the city centre. They are one stop apart on metro line 2.

Gare Lille-Europe (☎; Ⓜ Gare Lille-Europe) Topped by what looks like a 20-storey ski boot, this ultramodern station handles Eurostar trains to London, TGV/Thalys/Eurostar trains to Brussels-Midi, half of the TGVs to Paris Gare du Nord and most province-to-province TGVs.

Gare Lille-Flandres (☎; Ⓜ Gare Lille-Flandres) This renovated, older-style station is used by half of the TGVs to Paris Gare du Nord and all intraregional TER services.

Services include the following:

Brussels-Midi By TGV €30, 35 minutes, at least 12 daily

Charles de Gaulle Airport €41 to €59, one hour, at least hourly

London (St Pancras International) By Eurostar €110 to €180, 90 minutes, 10 daily

Nice-Ville €155, 7½ hours, one direct daily

Paris Gare du Nord €47 to €63, one hour, at least hourly

ℹ Getting Around

BICYCLE

Operated by Transpole, Lille's bike-sharing scheme **V-Lille** (www.transpole.fr; day/week subscription €1.60/7, 1st 30min free, every subsequent 30min €1; ⊙ 24hr) has 2200 bikes at stations across town.

PUBLIC TRANSPORT

Lille's two speedy metro lines (1 and 2), two tramways (R and T), two Citadine shuttles (C1, which circles the city centre clockwise, and C2, which goes counterclockwise) and many urban and suburban bus lines – several of which cross into Belgium – are run by Transpole (www.transpole.fr).

Public transport tickets (€1.60, plus €0.20 for a reusable ticket) are sold on buses but must be purchased before boarding a metro or tram; there are ticket machines at each stop. A Pass' Journée (24-hour pass) costs €4.80 and needs to be time-stamped each time you board; two- to seven-day passes are also available. A Pass Soirée, good for unlimited travel after 7pm, costs €2.20.

Transpole has a **ticket office** (⌕ 03 20 40 40 40; www.transpole.fr; Gare Lille-Flandres;

⊙ 6.30am-8pm Mon-Fri, 9am-8pm Sat;
Ⓜ Gare Lille-Flandres) adjacent to the Gare
Lille-Flandres metro station.

FLANDERS & ARTOIS

Cassel

POP 2320

Perched at the summit of French Flanders'
highest hill – though at 176m it's hardly
Mont Blanc – the fortified, quintessentially Flemish village of Cassel offers panoramic views of the verdant Flanders plain.

Because of its elevated position, Cassel
served as Maréchal Ferdinand Foch's headquarters at the beginning of WWI. In 1940
it was the site of intensive rearguard resistance by British troops defending Dunkirk
during the evacuation.

Cassel's citizens are enormously proud of
Reuze Papa and Reuze Maman, the resident
géants (giants; p213) which are wickerwork
body masks animated by people inside; who
are feted each Easter Monday.

⊙ Sights

The **Grand' Place**, Cassel's focal point, is
ringed by austere red-brick buildings with
steep slate roofs.

Musée de Flandre   GALLERY
(⤢03 59 73 45 60; www.museedeflandre.
fr; 26 Grand' Place; adult/child €5/free; ⊙10am-
12.30pm & 2-6pm Tue-Fri, 10am-6pm Sat & Sun)
The Museum of Flanders has a worthwhile,
well-presented collection of Flemish art,
both old and modern, including canvases in
the 15th-century Flemish primitive style and
two dramatic paintings of the Battle of Cassel (1677). Multimedia guides are free.

🛏 Sleeping & Eating

Hôtel Le Foch   HOTEL €
(⤢03 28 42 47 73; www.hotel-foch.net; 41 Grand'
Place; s/d/cottage €63/73/150; 🛜) Some
of Hôtel Le Foch's six spacious rooms
have views of the square and all have antique-style beds. The restaurant serves
excellent traditional French cuisine (two-/
three-course *menus* €19/25) but it's closed
on Friday and Sunday evenings. The hotel's
owners also rent a three-bedroom cottage
sleeping six in the grounds of their own
residence 500m northeast.

NORTHERN BREWS

French Flanders brews some truly excellent *bière blonde* (lager) and *bière
ambrée* (amber beer) with an alcohol
content of up to 8.5%.

While in the area, beer lovers should
be sure to try some of these local varieties, which give Belgian brewers a run
for their money: 3 Monts, Amadeus,
Ambre des Flandres, Brasserie des 2
Caps, Ch'ti, Enfants de Gayant, Grain
d'Orge, Hellemus, Jenlain, L'Angélus, La
Wambrechies, Moulins d'Ascq, Raoul,
Septante 5, St-Landelin, Triple Secret
des Moines and Vieux Lille.

★ **'T Kasteelhof**   FLEMISH €
(⤢03 28 40 59 29; 8 rue St-Nicolas; mains €7-13;
⊙11am-10pm Thu-Sun, closed Jan & early Oct) At
the 'highest *estaminet* (traditional Flemish
restaurant) in Flanders', facing Cassel's hilltop windmill, you can quaff Flemish beer
(including Kassels Bier, only available here),
sip *vin de chicorée* (made with red wine and
chicory) and dine on dishes such as *carbonade* (braised beef stewed with beer). For
dessert, try the chicory *crème brûlée*. The
tiny shop sells Flemish edibles.

ℹ Information

Tourist Office (⤢03 28 40 52 55; www.
coeurdeflandre.fr; 20 Grand' Place; ⊙9.30am-
12.30pm & 2-6pm Mon-Sat, 11am-12.30pm &
2-6pm Sun Jul & Aug, 9.30am-noon & 2-6pm
Tue-Sat, 2-6pm Sun Apr-Jun, Sep & Oct,
9.30am-noon & 2-6pm Tue-Sat Nov-Feb)

ℹ Getting There & Away

Cassel is midway between Calais (59km) and
Lille (49km). The village is served by trains from
Dunkirk (€6.80, 25 minutes, up to five daily) and
Lille (€11.10, 40 minutes, up to two per hour);
the station is 2.5km downhill from the centre.

Arras

POP 40,720

An unexpected gem of a city, Artois' former
capital Arras (the final 's' is pronounced) has
an exceptional ensemble of Flemish-style arcaded buildings – the main squares are especially lovely at night – and two subterranean
WWI sites. The city makes a good base for
visits to the Battle of the Somme memorials.

◉ Sights & Activities

★ Grand' Place & Place des Héros   SQUARE

Arras' two ancient market squares, the Grand' Place and the almost-adjacent, smaller place des Héros (also known as the Petite Place), are surrounded by 17th- and 18th-century Flemish Baroque houses topped by curvaceous gables. Although the structures vary in decorative detail, their 345 sandstone columns form a common arcade unique in France. Like 80% of Arras, both squares – especially handsome at night – were heavily damaged during WWI, so many of the gorgeous façades were reconstructed after the war.

Hôtel de Ville   HISTORIC BUILDING

(☑ 03 21 51 26 95; place des Héros; city hall tours adult/child €4.20/3, belfry adult/child €3.10/2.10, boves tour €5.40/3.20; ⊘ 9am-6.30pm Mon-Sat, 10am-1pm & 2.30-6.30pm Sun early Apr–mid-Sep, shorter hours mid-Sep–early Apr, boves closed Jan) Arras' Flemish Gothic city hall dates from the 16th century but was completely rebuilt after WWI. Four *géants* (giants) live in the lobby. For a panoramic view, take the lift (plus 43 stairs) up the 75m-high, Unesco-listed belfry. Or, for a subterranean perspective, head down into the *souterrains* (caves) under the square, also known as *boves*, which were turned into British command posts, hospitals and barracks during WWI.

Tours of the *boves* (40 minutes; in English upon request) generally begin at 11am, with at least two more departures in the afternoon. City hall tours run at 3pm Sunday year-round, with an additional tour at 3pm Monday to Friday July and August. Tickets are sold at the tourist office (on the ground floor).

Carrière Wellington   HISTORIC SITE

(Wellington Quarry; ☑ 03 21 51 26 95; www.carrierewellington.com; rue Arthur Delétoille; tours adult/child €7/3.30; ⊘ 10am-12.30pm & 1.30-6pm, closed Jan) Staging ground for the spring 1917 offensive, Wellington Quarry is a 20m-deep network of old chalk quarries expanded during WWI by tunnellers from New Zealand. Hourlong guided tours in French and English combine imaginative audiovisuals, evocative photos and period artefacts. Signs painted in black are British and from WWI; those in red are French from WWII, when the site was used as a bomb shelter. It's signposted 1km south of the train station. Access is by lift (no stairs).

The temperature in the tunnels is a constant 11°C; bring a jacket.

🛏 Sleeping

Place du Maréchal Foch, in front of the train station, has a number of midrange hotels.

★ La Corne d'Or   B&B €€

(☑ 03 21 58 85 94; www.lamaisondhotes.com; 1 place Guy Mollet; s/d/ste/loft incl breakfast from €110/125/140/145; 🐕) Occupying a magnificent *hôtel particulier* (private mansion) built in 1748, this romantic B&B is filled with antiques, art and books on WWI. Some of the five imaginatively designed rooms and suites still have their original woodwork, gilded mirrors, marble fireplaces and stained glass. Australian host Rodney, formerly of Australia's Department of Veterans' Affairs, is a great resource.

Hôtel Les 3 Luppars   HOTEL €€

(☑ 03 21 60 02 03; www.hotel-les3luppars.com; 49 Grand' Place; s/d/tr/q from €88/105/115/125; @🐕) Occupying the Grand' Place's only non-Flemish-style building (it's Gothic and dates from the 1400s), Les 3 Luppars (derived from 'Leopards') has a private courtyard and 42 rooms, 10 with fine views of the square. The decor is uninspired, but the location is great and the atmosphere is welcoming. Amenities include a sauna (€6 per person).

Grand Place Hôtel   DESIGN HOTEL €€

(☑ 03 91 19 19 79; http://grandplacehotel.fr; 23 Grand' Place; d/ste/apt/loft from €102/120/150/170; ❄🐕) Behind one of the Grand' Place's few Flemish Baroque façades to escape wartime damage, this 2015-opened hotel has a dozen rooms done out in stylish black and white. Some suites and the apartments sleep four, while the loft sleeps six; apartments and the loft also come with kitchenettes.

🍴 Eating

Lots of restaurants are tucked away under the arches of the Grand' Place, place des Héros and – connecting the two – rue de la Taillerie.

Marché à Arras   MARKET €

(place des Héros, Grand' Place & place de la Vacquerie; ⊘ 8am-1pm Wed & Sat) Arras' twice-weekly food market stretches across the city's three central squares; Saturday's market is especially huge.

Le Petit Rat Porteur   BRASSERIE €

(☑ 03 21 51 29 70; 11 rue de la Taillerie; mains €10-18.50; ⊘ noon-2pm & 7-9.30pm Tue-Sat, noon-2pm Sun) Beloved for its marvellous vaulted cellar and friendly staff, this buzzing brasserie has a great range of salads alongside regional standards including *potjevleesch* (aspic potted meat) and *waterzooi* (chicken stew).

Assiette au Bœuf
GRILL €

(☑ 03 21 15 11 51; http://assietteauboeuf.fr; 56 Grand' Place; menus lunch €12-15.50, dinner €17-19.50; ☺ noon-2.30pm & 7-11pm; ⚐) Hugely popular with locals for its great-value steaks, this Grand' Place restaurant also serves burgers and mixed grills.

La Faisanderie
FRENCH €€

(☑ 03 74 11 64 69; www.restaurant-la-faisanderie.com; 45 Grand' Place; 3-course midweek lunch menu €25, 2-/3-course dinner menu €31/36, mains €16-19; ☺ 7-9.30pm Tue, noon-1.30pm & 7-9.30pm Wed-Sat, noon-1.30pm Sun) In a superb vaulted brick cellar, this formal restaurant serves a range of classical dishes prepared with carefully selected ingredients: oysters *naturelles*, Pernod-flambéed prawns, beef fillet with morel sauce or turbot with seared endives and beer sauce. The wine list is outstanding.

ℹ Information

Tourist Office (☑ 03 21 51 26 95; www.explorearras.com; place des Héros; ☺ 9am-6.30pm Mon-Sat, 10am-1pm & 2.30-6.30pm Sun early Apr-mid-Sep, shorter hours mid-Sep–early Apr; ☎)

ℹ Getting There & Around

BICYCLE
Arras is setting up a shared bicycle scheme; contact the tourist office for details.

TRAIN
Arras' station is 750m southeast of the two main squares.

Amiens €13.10, 45 minutes, five to 10 daily
Lens €4.60, 15 minutes, up to two per hour
Lille-Flandres €11.50, 40 minutes, up to two per hour
Paris Gare du Nord (TGV) €33, one hour, seven to 13 daily

Lens

POP 26,840

A brash 2012-opened branch of Paris' renowned Louvre, the Louvre-Lens, is the main reason to visit this former coal-mining town.

◉ Sights

Louvre-Lens
MUSEUM

(☑ 03 21 18 62 62; www.louvrelens.fr; 99 rue Paul Bert; temporary exhibitions adult/child €10/5; ☺ 10am-6pm Wed-Mon) FREE The innovative Louvre-

Lens, opened in 2012, showcases hundreds of treasures from Paris' venerable Musée du Louvre in state-of-the-art exhibition spaces. The centrepiece, the 120m-long Galerie du Temps, displays a semi-permanent collection of 200-plus objects from the dawn of civilisation to the mid-1800s. Unlike the original Louvre, the collection here can easily be taken in and savoured in a single afternoon.

The glass-walled Pavillon de Verre is used for themed temporary exhibits that change three times a year. For kids 11 and under there are 1½-hour art workshops (in French). A third Louvre site opened in Abu Dhabi in 2017.

Free half-hourly shuttle buses link the Louvre-Lens with Lens' train station. Unless you're dining at the museum's gourmet restaurant (or you have a disability) it's not possible to park onsite; the nearest car parks are 400m west on rue Paul Bert or Bollaert-Delelis Stadium, 1km east.

ℹ Getting There & Away

Lens is served by TGV trains from Paris' Gare du Nord (€33, 1¼ hours, three to five daily) and regional TER trains from Lille-Flandres (€8.30, 45 minutes, up to five daily) and Arras (€4.60, 15 minutes, at least hourly).

CÔTE D'OPALE

Stretching 120km from the Belgian border to the Baie de Somme (Somme estuary), the sublimely beautiful Opal Coast – named for the interplay of greys and blues in the sea and sky – features lofty chalk cliffs, rolling green hills, windswept beaches, scrub-dotted sand dunes and charming seaside towns that have been a favourite of British beach lovers since the Victorian era.

The coast is dotted with the remains of Nazi Germany's Atlantic Wall, a line of fortifications, artillery emplacements and massive, reinforced concrete bunkers built to prevent the Allied invasion that in the end took place in Normandy.

Calais to Boulogne

The most spectacular section of the Côte d'Opale is between Calais and Boulogne-sur-Mer. This 40km stretch, a mirror image of the White Cliffs of Dover, can be visited by car (take the D940), on foot (the GR120 trail, marked with red and white blazes, hugs the coast) or by local bus.

To the south, the relatively flat coastline is broken by the estuaries, wetlands and tidal marshes created by the Canche, Authie and Somme rivers. Much of this area is privately owned – and used for hunting ducks and teals – but there are several attractive beach resorts and plenty of excellent spots for bird-watching and seal spotting.

◉ Sights

Cap Blanc-Nez   LANDMARK

Southwest of Calais, just past Sangatte, the coastal dunes give way to cliffs that culminate in windswept, 134m-high Cap Blanc-Nez, which affords breathtaking views of the Bay of Wissant, the port of Calais, the Flemish countryside (pockmarked by Allied bomb craters, such as those on the slopes of Mont d'Hubert) and the distant chalk cliffs of Kent. A grey stone obelisk honours the WWI Dover Patrol. Paths lead to a number of massive WWII German bunkers.

Cap Gris-Nez   LANDMARK

Topped by a lighthouse and a radar station that keeps track of the hundreds of ships that pass by here each day, the 49m-high cliffs of Cap Gris-Nez are only 28km from the white cliffs of the English coast. The name, which means 'grey nose' in French, is a corruption of the archaic English 'craig ness', meaning 'rocky promontory'. The area is a stopping-off point for millions of migrating birds. The car park is a good starting point for hikes.

Musée du Mur de l'Atlantique   MUSEUM

(Atlantic Wall Museum; ☑03 21 32 97 33; www.batterietodt.com; rte du Musée, Hameau de Haringzelle, Audinghen; adult/child €8.80/5.50; ⊙10am-6.30pm Jul & Aug, 2-6pm Mon, 10am-6pm Tue-Sun Apr-Jun, Sep & Oct, 2-5.30pm Feb, Mar & early–mid-Nov) WWII hardware including a massive, rail-borne German artillery piece with a range of 86km is displayed at this well-organised museum, housed in a colossal German pillbox. It's located 400m off the D940 from the Maison du Site des Deux Caps tourist office. Last admission is one hour before closing.

Musée 39-45   MUSEUM

(☑03 21 87 33 01; www.musee3945.com; 2 rue des Garennes, Ambleteuse; adult/child €8.90/5.90; ⊙10am-7pm Jul & Aug, to 6pm Apr-Jun, Sep & Oct, 10am-6pm Sat & Sun Mar & Nov) Popular period songs play as you stroll past dozens of life-size tableaux of WWII military and civilian life at this museum. The dashing but wildly impractical French officers' dress uniforms of 1931 hint at possible reasons that France fared so badly on the battlefield in 1940. The museum also screens archival films.

🛏 Sleeping & Eating

Hôtel-Restaurant L'Escale   HOTEL €

(☑03 21 85 25 00; www.hotel-lescale.com; 4 rue de la Mer, Escalles; d/tr from €77/107; ⊙closed early Jan-early Feb; 🅿🛜) Welcoming and cosy-modern, this family-run hotel in the tiny village of Escalles has 44 rooms spread across three buildings with bright feature walls in shades of red and purple, matching bedspreads and fabrics. Three rooms are wheelchair accessible. The restaurant serves French classics (especially fish) that you can wash down with a local 2 Caps craft beer.

DUNKIRK

In 1940, Dunkirk (French: Dunkerque; French Flemish: Duunkerke, meaning 'church of the dunes') became world famous thanks to the heroic evacuation of Allied troops. Destroyed by German attacks, it was rebuilt after the war – though, alas, during one of the most uninspired periods in the history of Western architecture. While the modern city has precious little charm, it does offer visitors worthwhile museums, a family-friendly beach and colourful pre-Lent carnivals.

On clear days, from the top of Dunkirk's landmark 58m-high belfry, **Le Beffroi** (☑03 28 66 79 21; www.dunkerque-tourisme.fr; rue de l'Amiral Ronarch; adult/child €3.50/2.50; ⊙10-11.45am & 2-5.45pm Mon-Fri, 10am-5.45pm Sat, 10-11.30am & 2-3.30pm Sun), you can see as far as Dover on a clear day. A Unesco World Heritage–listed monument since 2004, the 15th-century tower is serviced by a lift that whisks visitors up to its 50 bells, which chime every 15 minutes.

★ **La Marie Galante** SEAFOOD €€

(✉️ 03 21 83 02 32; http://la-marie-galante. business.site; 173 rue Edouard Quenu, Audresselles; mains €16.50-33, seafood platters €16-62; ⏱️ noon-1.30pm & 6.30-8pm Tue & Thu-Sat, noon-1.30pm & 6.30-7.30pm Sun Feb-Dec) All the seafood here is from the surrounding waters, including Audresselles crab and lobster. Piled-high seafood platters are the house speciality but there are also superb mains such as lobster medallions with Champagne sauce, freshly shucked oysters, or sole with garlic and herb butter. The red-roofed building is framed by blue shutters and fronted by an umbrella-shaded terrace.

★ **La Sirène** SEAFOOD €€€

(✉️ 03 21 32 95 97; www.lasirene-capgrisnez.com; 376 rue de la Plage, Audinghen; 3-course menu €30, mains €16-26, seafood platters €23.50-74; ⏱️ noon-2pm & 7.30-9pm Tue-Sat, noon-2pm Sun Apr-Aug, noon-2pm & 7.30-9pm Tue-Fri, 7.30-9pm Sat Sep-Mar; 🖥️) At the foot of Cap Gris-Nez, this whitewashed beachfront cottage has picture windows with glorious sea views. All of the fresh seafood is sourced from Audresselles and Boulogne-sur-Mer, oysters, prawns, langoustines, lobster, whelks, mussels and succulent crab included. Reserve ahead in summer and for Sunday lunch year-round.

ℹ️ Information

Maison du Site des Deux Caps (✉️ 03 21 21 62 22; www.lesdeuxcaps.fr; Ferme d'Haringzelle, Audinghen; ⏱️ 9.30am-6pm Jul & Aug, 10am-12.30pm & 2-6pm Apr-Jun, Sep & Oct, 10am-12.30pm & 2-5.30pm Tue-Sat Feb, Mar, Nov & Dec) Serves as an information centre for the 'two capes', the area around and between Cap Blanc-Nez and Cap Gris-Nez, and sells hiking maps. From April to October it rents out bicycles, both standard (per half-/whole day €7/10) and electric (€10/15).

Wissant Tourist Office (✉️ 03 21 82 48 00; http://terredes2capstourisme.fr; 1 place de la Mairie, Wissant; ⏱️ 9.30am-12.30pm & 1.30-6pm Jul & Aug, 9.30am-12.30pm & 2-6pm Mon-Sat, 10am-noon & 3-6pm Sun Apr-Jun & Sep, 10am-noon & 2-4.30pm Mon-Fri, 10am-noon Sat Oct-Mar)

ℹ️ Getting There & Away

The northern section of the Côte d'Opale, between Calais and Boulogne-sur-Mer, is served by buses run by Pass Pass (www.passpass.fr; €1 to all destinations, up to five daily).

Calais

POP 72,590

A mere 34km from the English port of Dover (Douvres in French), Calais makes a convenient launching pad for exploring the majestic Côte d'Opale. Beaches extend around the town centre, whose handful of museums are well worth a look.

◉ Sights

Cité Internationale de la Dentelle et de la Mode MUSEUM

(International Centre of Lace & Fashion; ✉️ 03 21 00 42 30; www.cite-dentelle.fr; 135 quai du Commerce; adult/child €7/5; ⏱️ 10am-6pm Wed-Mon Apr-Oct, to 5pm Wed-Mon Nov-Mar) Innovative exhibits trace the history of lacemaking – the industry that once made Calais a textile powerhouse – from hand knotting (some stunning samples are on display) through the Industrial Revolution. The highlight is watching a century-old mechanical loom with 3500 vertical threads and 11,000 horizontal threads bang, clatter and clunk according to instructions provided by perforated Jacquard cards. Signs are in English and French.

Hôtel de Ville TOWER, ARCHITECTURE

(✉️ 03 21 46 20 53; www.calais.fr; place du Soldat Inconnu; Hôtel de Ville adult/child €3/1.50, belfry €5/3, combination ticket €7/4; ⏱️ 10am-noon & 2-5.30pm, closed Mon Oct–mid-Apr) Inaugurated in 1925, Calais' Hôtel de Ville (city hall) melds Flemish and Renaissance styles, as does its 78m-high, Unesco-listed *beffroi* (belfry) topped by gilded statues that glint in the sun. A lift zips you to the top of the belfry for 360-degree views. Timber panelling, stained glass and a magnificent garden are highlights of the Hôtel de Ville, as is the Rodin sculpture out front.

Burghers of Calais STATUE

(place du Soldat Inconnu) In front of Calais' ornate Hôtel de Ville stands the first cast of Rodin's famous sculpture *Les Bourgeois de Calais* (The Burghers of Calais; 1889), which portrays six local leaders (burghers) in 1347 as they surrender to besieging English forces, knowing they will soon be executed – but hoping their sacrifice will mean their fellow Calaisiens will be spared.

Musée Mémoire 1939–1945 MUSEUM

(✉️ 03 21 34 21 57; www.musee-memoire-calais. com; Parc St-Pierre; adult/child incl audioguide €8/6; ⏱️ 10am-6pm May-Sep, 11am-5pm Mon & Wed-Sat Feb-Apr, Oct & Nov) Housed in a massive concrete bunker built as a German naval headquarters, this WWII museum displays thousands of period artefacts, including weapons, uniforms and proclamations across 22 themed rooms. It's situated in the middle of flowery Parc St-Pierre.

Beaches

Blériot Plage
BEACH

This broad, gently sloping sandy beach stretching for 8km is safe for swimming and gets packed in summer.

Plage de Calais
BEACH

Children can splash in the shallow, clear waters of Calais' cabin-lined city beach (patrolled by lifeguards in summer), while its fine sand is ideal for sunbathing. From the beach, you can watch huge car ferries as they sail majestically to and from Dover.

🛌 Sleeping

Centre Européen de Séjour
HOSTEL €

(☑ 03 21 34 70 20; www.auberge-jeunesse-calais. com; rue du Maréchal de Lattre de Tassigny; s/tw incl breakfast €33/50; 🛜) Great for meeting fellow travellers, this efficiently run, 162-bed youth hostel is just 150m southeast of the beach and 1km northwest of the city centre. There's a bar, a lounge area with table football and a pool table, and 84 modern (if spartan) one- to three-bed rooms; bathrooms are attached but shared by two rooms.

Hôtel Meurice
HOTEL €

(☑ 03 21 34 57 03; www.hotel-meurice.fr; 5-7 rue Edmond Roche; d/f from €79/139; 🛜) 🐾 Dating from the 1950s after the earlier 1771-built hotel was destroyed in WWII, Hôtel Meurice received a facelift in 2018, including the installation of solar panels. A carpeted staircase with wrought-iron balustrades leads to its 39 rooms (there's also a lift); family rooms have a double and two single beds. Studded leather armchairs are strewn throughout its timber-panelled bar.

Le Cercle de Malines
B&B €

(☑ 03 21 96 80 65; www.lecercledemalines.fr; 12 rue de Malines; s/d/f incl breakfast from €71/85/150; 🛜) Built in 1884, this stately townhouse has been elegantly furnished in a modern spirit, with generous public areas and a wisteria-draped walled garden. Among its five spacious rooms, top choices are La Leavers, with its claw-footed Victorian bathtub, and Guipure, with a private sauna; family room Chantilly sleeps four. Rooms are on the 1st and 2nd floors (no lift).

🍴 Eating

Restaurants ring place d'Armes, Calais' main public square, and also line adjacent rue Royale.

⭐ Le Grand Bleu
FRENCH €€

(☑ 03 21 97 97 98; www.legrandbleu-calais.com; 8 rue Jean-Pierre Avron; 2-/3-course midweek lunch menus €19/22, 3-course dinner menus €22-42, mains €19-27; ⊗ noon-2pm & 7-9pm Mon & Thu-Sat, noon-2pm Tue, Wed & Sun) Run by talented *avantgardiste* chef Matthieu Colin (formerly of Paris institution Ledoyen), royal-blue-painted Le Grand Bleu is known for its *cuisine élaborée* (creatively transformed versions of traditional dishes) such as veal samosas with sweetbreads and red carrots or snails with chorizo butter. The weekday *menus* offer fabulous value. Book a table on the luminous terrace to enjoy harbour views.

Histoire Ancienne
BISTRO €€

(☑ 03 21 34 11 20; www.histoire-ancienne.com; 20 rue Royale; 2- & 3-course menus €16-27; ⊗ noon-2pm Mon, noon-2pm & 6.45-9.30pm Tue-Sat; 🛜) Bistro-style French dishes, such as grilled pig's trotters with *Béarnaise* sauce, sea bass with *beurre blanc* (emulsified butter sauce), and port-poached prunes with liquorice ice cream, are served in a classic dining room with a zinc bar.

Restaurant Aquar'Aile
SEAFOOD €€

(☑ 03 21 34 00 00; http://aquaraile.fr; 255 rue Jean Moulin; 3-/4-course menus €33/48, seafood platters per person €44-58; ⊗ noon-2pm & 6.30-9.30pm Mon-Sat, noon-2pm Sun) A 20th-century apartment block framed by lurid green-glass balconies is the unlikely setting for sublime seafood. Occupying the top floor, the dining room has white-clothed tables, and panoramic windows overlooking the port, beach and Dover beyond. Try prized Marennes-Oléron oysters, monkfish with crushed celery and watercress emulsion, salt crust–baked whiting, brown-butter sole *meunière*, or lobster bouillabaisse.

ℹ️ Information

Tourist Office (☑ 03 21 96 62 40; www.calais-cotedopale.com; 12 bd Georges Clemenceau; ⊗ 10am-6pm Mon-Sat, to 5pm Sun May-Aug, 10am-6pm Mon-Fri, to 5pm Sat Sep-Apr; 🛜) Has brochures on Calais and the Côte d'Opale and sells the discount Visit'Pass (€11), which provides entry into most major sights. It's just north across the bridge from the train station.

ℹ Getting There & Away

BOAT

Each day, up to 50 car ferries from Dover dock at Calais' car-ferry terminal, situated about 1.5km northeast of place d'Armes. It's patrolled by police and surrounded by high, concertina-topped fences to prevent stowaways on ferries to the UK.

Two companies, **P&O Ferries** (www.poferries.com; av du Commandant Cousteau) and **DFDS Seaways** (www.dfdsseaways.co.uk; av du Commandant Cousteau), operate regular trans-Channel services. P&O accepts foot passengers; DFDS only takes passengers with vehicles.

BUS

Buses run by Pass Pass (www.passpass.fr) link Calais with Boulogne-sur-Mer via the beautiful Côte d'Opale (€1 to all destinations, up to five daily). The bus stop, marked by a blue-and-yellow sign, is right outside Calais' city-centre train station, Gare Calais-Ville.

Eurolines (www.eurolines.com) and Flixbus (www.flixbus.com) link Calais with London.

CAR & MOTORCYCLE

To reach the Channel Tunnel's high-security vehicle-loading area at Coquelles, 6km southwest of Calais' town centre, follow the road signs on the A16 to 'Tunnel Sous La Manche' (Tunnel Under the Channel) and get off at exit 42.

TRAIN

Calais has two train stations, linked by free shuttle buses.

Gare Calais-Fréthun A TGV station 10km southwest of town near the Channel Tunnel entrance; has direct TGVs to Paris' Gare du Nord (€33 to €66, two hours, hourly or better) as well as the Eurostar to London St Pancras (€117 to €201, one hour, two daily).

Gare Calais-Ville In the city centre; has direct services to Boulogne-sur-Mer (€8.50, 40 minutes, at least hourly) and Lille-Flandres (€19, 1½ hours, at least hourly).

Boulogne-sur-Mer

POP 42,540

Boulogne-sur-Mer's Haute-Ville (Upper City) is perched high above the rest of town, and girded by a 13th-century wall. Centred on the Grande Rue and rue Adolphe Thiers, the Basse-Ville (Lower City) is a bustling if uninspiring assemblage of postwar structures, but its waterfront is home to Nausicaá, one of the world's largest aquariums, with beaches stretching along the coast nearby. As France's most important fishing port, just-landed seafood is a highlight of visiting.

◉ Sights & Activities

Boulogne's wide beach begins just north of Nausicaá aquarium, across the mouth of the Liane from a whirring wind farm on the former site of a steelworks. Other fine beaches include Le Portel, 2.5km southwest of Boulogne (take bus C), and Equihen Plage, about 5km to the south (take bus A). All are easily accessible by bike.

★**Nausicaá** AQUARIUM
(☑ 03 21 30 99 99; www.nausicaa.fr; bd Ste-Beuve; adult/child €19/12.50; ⊙ 9.30am-6.30pm, closed 3 weeks Jan) At this vast manta ray–shaped aquarium – one of the world's largest – huge tanks with floor-to-ceiling windows make you feel as though you're swimming with the sharks. All-up there are more than 60,000 creatures, including sea turtles, California sea lions, South American caimans and African penguins, some of them hatched right here. Kids of all ages can engage with ecologically conscious exhibits and activities, including fish petting, feeding sessions and sea lion shows throughout the day. Signage is in English.

A new wing opened in 2018 with a 21m-long underwater viewing window, an underwater tunnel and a balcony providing bird's eye views.

Haute-Ville HISTORIC SITE
(Ville Fortifiée) Boulogne's hilltop Upper City is an island of centuries-old buildings and cobblestone streets. You can walk all the way around this 'Fortified City' atop the ancient stone walls – look for signs for the Promenade des Remparts.

Highlights here include the **Basilique Notre Dame** (rue de Lille; basilica free, crypt adult/child €5/3; ⊙ basilica 10am-noon & 2-6pm Apr-Aug, shorter hours Sep-Mar, crypt 10am-6pm May-Sep, 10am-12.30pm & 2-5.30pm Oct-Apr), the **Château-Musée** (Castle Museum; ☑ 03 21 10 02 20; 1 rue de Bernet; adult/child €5/3; ⊙ museum 10am-6pm Wed-Mon May-Sep, 10am-12.30pm & 2.30-5.30pm Wed-Mon Oct-Apr, courtyard 7am-7pm daily), the neoclassical **Hôtel Desandrouin** (Palais Impérial; 3 place Godefroy de Bouillon) and the 18th-century **Hôtel de Ville** (place de la Résistance; ⊙ 8am-noon & 2-6pm Mon-Thu) FREE with a medieval belfry.

🛏 Sleeping & Eating

Hôtel La Matelote HOTEL €€
(☑ 03 21 30 33 33; www.la-matelote.com; 70 bd Ste-Beuve; s/d/ste from €120/130/265; P ❋ @ ☎ ☲)

Boulogne-sur-Mer

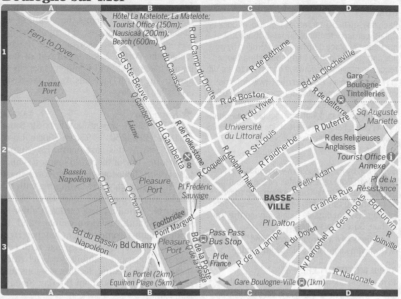

Boulogne's plushest hotel offers old-world character, professional service and amenities such as a *hammam,* a dry sauna and a tiny jacuzzi pool. The 35 rooms are decorated in rich tones of gold, milk chocolate, maroon, cream and brass and have modern wooden furnishings. Prestige doubles have sea views; the six suites open onto balconies. Breakfast costs €16.

Its **restaurant** (☑ 03 21 30 33 33; 80 bd Ste-Beuve; 3-/4-/6-/7-course menus €50/68/70/82; ⏰ noon-2pm & 7.30-9.30pm Fri-Wed, 7.30-9.30pm Thu; 🛜) has a Michelin star.

Les Terrasses de l'Enclos
B&B €€

(☑ 03 91 90 05 90; www.enclosdeleveche.com; L'enclos de l'Évêché, 6 rue de Pressy; d/f incl breakfast from €90/140; 🛜) An imposing 19th-century mansion next to the basilica has been turned into an elegant B&B with a cobbled courtyard. The five spacious rooms have hardwood floors and contemporary furnishings, along with some vintage pieces; the family room sleeps four (one double bed and two singles). Check-in is strictly from 5pm.

Quai 42
SEAFOOD €

(☑ 03 21 92 05 06; 42 bd Gambetta; tapas €2.50-10; ⏰ 11am-3pm & 6-11pm Tue-Sun) Seafood tapas (oysters, cod croquettes, flash-fried calamari) makes the perfect accompaniment to the by-the-glass wines (seven whites, seven reds and seven rosés) at this contemporary wine bar set back from bd Gambetta on a pedestrianised square, with upturned barrels inside and out. Live acoustic music plays on Friday and Saturday evenings from June to September.

L'Îlot Vert
BISTRO €€

(☑ 03 21 92 01 62; www.lilotvert.fr; 36 rue de Lille; 2-course lunch menu €25, 3-/4-/6-course dinner menus €33/52/66; ⏰ noon-2pm & 7-9.30pm Mon, Tue & Thu-Sat) 'Bistronomique' cuisine and contempoary design make this chic spot stand out. Dishes on the daily changing menu (no à la carte) might include smoked turbot with samphire foam, *dorade* (gilt-head bream) with wild garlic emulsion, confit pork with micro herbs and mini *galettes* (savoury buckwheat crêpes), and pineapple-and-mint tart with caramel meringue. Its cobbled, ivy-draped rear courtyard has umbrella-shaded tables.

🛈 Information

Tourist Office (☑ 03 21 10 88 10; www.visit boulogne.com; bd Ste-Beuve; ⏰ 10am-12.30pm & 2-5.30pm Mon-Sat year-round, plus 10.30am-1pm & 2.30-5pm Sun Apr–mid-Nov; 🛜) Situated outside the Nausicaá aquarium. Helpful staff and plenty of English brochures.

Tourist Office Annexe (📞 03 91 90 54 95; www.visitboulogne.com; Square Auguste Mariette-Pacha; ⊙10.30am-12.30pm & 2-5pm Mon-Sat Apr–mid-Nov) Just outside the Haute-Ville.

ℹ Getting There & Around

BICYCLE
Cycléco (📞 03 91 18 34 48; quai de la Poste, forum Jean Noël; per hr/day standard bike from €2/9, electric bike from €4/15; ⊙10am-6.30pm Apr-Oct, by reservation 9.30am-6pm Wed, Sat & Sun Nov-Mar) Hires out regular and electric bicycles in the warm season, ideal for getting to the beaches at Equihen Plage and Le Portel.

BUS
Buses run by Pass Pass (www.passpass.fr) link Boulogne's **place de France** with Calais via the Côte d'Opale (€1 to all destinations, up to five daily).

TRAIN
The main train station, Gare Boulogne-Ville, is 1.2km southeast of the Basse-Ville (take bus F). Destinations with direct services include:
Amiens €21.90, 1½ hours, seven to nine daily
Calais-Ville €8.50, 40 minutes, at least hourly
Lille-Flandres or Lille-Europe €22.90, one hour, five to eight daily
Paris Gare du Nord €47 to €66, three to four hours, five to eight daily

Le Touquet
POP 4290

Utterly unlike any other French beach resort, fashionable Le Touquet Paris-Plage is surrounded by thatched-roofed villas and other striking architecturally designed mansions nestled unfenced among sprawling woodlands planted with pine, elm, poplar and alder trees.

Le Touquet, as it's most commonly known, has a long and illustrious history as a playground for wealthy Parisians and well-to-do Brits. Reminders of its early 20th century heyday include the 1913-built Casino de la Forêt (now the Palais de Congrès) and the fabled 1928-built Hôtel Westminster (now the Hôtel Barrière Le Westminster). Today, it remains a popular high-end holiday destination for its wide promenade stretching along the magnificent sandy beach, lush forest, extensive sports facilities, upmarket boutiques and gastronomy.

◎ Sights & Activities

A beachside water park with slides, an equestrian centre offering horse riding along the beach, polo, kitesurfing, SUP (stand-up paddle boarding), blokarting (sand yachting), sailing, cycling, tennis and three golf courses are among the variety of sports and activities on offer in Le Touquet. The tourist office (p224) has comprehensive information, along with details of luxurious spas.

Tour Paris-Plage   SCULPTURE
(bd de la Plage) Designed by French artist Alain Godon (b 1964), this 9.5m-high sculpture made from polystyrene on a metal frame, coated with beach sand, depicts an abstract version of Paris' Eiffel Tower in the style of a giant sandcastle. It was unveiled in 2017 to

A SACRED DETOUR: VALLÉE DE L'AUTHIE

Nestled in the bucolic Authie valley 27km northeast of Le Crotoy, the strikingly beautiful 12th-century **Abbaye de Valloires** (📞03 22 29 62 33; www.abbaye-valloires.com; Argoules; abbey & gardens tour adult/child €14.50/9, abbey tour €8/5, gardens admission €9.50/5.50; ⏰ tours by reservation mid-Mar–mid-Nov, gardens 10am-7pm May-Sep, 10.30am-6pm Apr & Oct–mid-Nov, accommodation year-round), rebuilt between 1687 and 1756, merits a detour for its harmonious Cistercian architecture and Baroque interiors. One of northern France's most intact old monasteries, it retains its cloister, sacristy, chapter house and refectory. The church has a magnificent organ loft and a wrought-iron choir screen. Covering 8 hectares, the landscaped gardens have over 5000 plants including rare apple trees and roses.

The complex has been owned since the 1920s by a not-for-profit association that still runs foster and nursing homes on the premises, which is why visitors must join a guided tour; call ahead for details on English tours. Year-round, the abbey welcomes overnight guests in 16 large, simply furnished rooms and suites; singles/doubles/suites start at €65/70/110. The on-site restaurant serves dishes using organic produce from the kitchen gardens and can arrange picnic baskets.

commemorate Le Touquet's 105-year anniversary and honour its Parisian connections.

Palais de Congrès HISTORIC BUILDING
(place de l'Hermitage) Nowadays this 1913-built beauty is Le Touquet's Palais de Congrès (convention centre), but in the town's early-20th-century golden era it was the high-rolling Casino de la Forêt, which served as the inspiration for the fictional Royale-les-Eaux casino in Ian Fleming's inaugural James Bond novel, *Casino Royale*. The original casino is long gone, but the convention centre has a gambling area with slot machines and table games.

🛏 Sleeping & Eating

Restaurants and gourmet food shops cluster along rue St-Jean and nearby streets. Dating from the early 1930s, the town's semicircular **covered market** (31 rue Jean Monnet; ⏰ produce market 8.15am-1.30pm Mon, Thu & Sat Jul & Aug, 9am-1.30pm Thu & Sat Sep-Jun, fish market 8.15am-1pm Fri & Sat year round) is a listed historical monument.

⭐**Hôtel Barrière**
Le Westminster HISTORIC HOTEL €€€
(📞03 21 05 48 48; www.hotelsbarriere.com; av du Verger; s/d/ste from €136/233/644; 🅿❄@ 🛜🏊) Built between 1924 and 1928, Le Touquet's best-known hotel is a town landmark with a magnificent red-brick art deco façade. Named for the Duchess of Westminster, its former guests include Sean Connery (who signed on to his first James Bond film here). Its 115 rooms and suites are classically furnished; amenities include a spa, indoor pool and Michelin-starred restaurant.

Les Canailles BISTRO €€
(📞03 21 05 03 03; http://lescanailles-letouquet.com; 73 rue de Paris; 2-/3-course menus €28/32, mains €18; ⏰ 7-11pm Tue-Fri, noon-3pm & 7-11pm Sat & Sun) At this chic wine bar/bistro, with corks strewn in the window, over 90 all-natural wines are available by the glass or bottle and pair perfectly with seasonally changing gourmet dishes: raw mackerel, pomegranate and peanuts or beef tartare with buckwheat and Jerusalem artichoke, mains such as confit pig breast with mustard pickles, and delectable desserts.

⭐**Perard** SEAFOOD €€€
(📞03 21 05 13 33; www.perard-letouquet.fr; 67 rue de Metz; 3-/4-course menus €28/38, mains €23-36, oysters per half-dozen €10-25, seafood platters per person €37.50-55.50; ⏰ noon-2.30pm & 7-10pm; 🍴) One of France's most famous seafood restaurants, frequented by a host of celebrities, 1960s-opened Perard combines a casual oyster bar with seating at high stools, a fishmonger and a restaurant with a retractable glass roof. It's renowned for its sublime lobster bouillabaisse (€76 for two people); other menu highlights might include skate-wing with capers and samphire or monkfish with morels.

ℹ Information

Tourist Office (📞03 21 06 72 00; www.letouquet.com; Pavillon Cousteau, 370 av Louis Aboudaram; ⏰ 9am-1pm & 2-6pm Mon-Sat, 10am-1pm & 2-6pm Sun)

ℹ Getting There & Away

Le Touquet–Côte d'Opale Airport (LTQ; 📞03 21 05 03 99; www.aeroport-letouquet.com; allée de la Royale Air Force) is located 2.9km south-east of Le Touquet. From June to September, Lyddair (www.lyddair.com) serves Lydd Airport in Kent, England; the flight time is 15 minutes. The airport has a Hertz car-rental desk.

The nearest train station, Étaples-Le Touquet, is 6km east of Le Touquet. The two towns are linked by *navettes* (shuttle buses; €1).

BAIE DE SOMME

Famed for its galloping tides and the seals that lounge on the Pointe du Hourdel sand-banks, this sparkling estuary – the largest in northern France, at 72 sq km – affords delightful, watery views as the cycle of the tides exposes and conceals vast expanses of marshland and sand. The area's wetlands provide hugely important habitats for hun-dreds of bird species. You can explore the bay by boat, kayak, outrigger canoe and – at low tide with a guide – on foot.

Both Le Crotoy, on the northern bank, and St-Valery-sur-Somme, on the south side, make excellent bases for exploring the area.

Le Crotoy

POP 2080

Occupying a wonderfully picturesque spot on the northern bank of the Baie de Somme, laid-back Le Crotoy is a lovely place to relax. Its broad, sandy beach is the only one in north-ern France to have a southerly exposure, giv-ing it more sunshine than others in the area. Jules Verne wrote *Twenty Thousand Leagues Under the Sea* (1870) while living here.

Experienced operator **Promenade en Baie** (☑ 03 22 27 47 36; www.promenade-en-baie.com; 5 allée des Soupirs; adult/child 2hr walk €12/6, 3hr walk €15/7, 5hr walk €18/7; ☺ by reservation) runs excel-lent two- to eight-hour guided walks through and around the estuary, including seal-watching rambles at Pointe du Hourdel. De-parture times depend on the tides.

🛏 Sleeping & Eating

Several restaurants can be found along rue de la Porte du Pont and the waterfront's promenade Jules Noiret.

Les Tourelles   HOTEL €€
(☑ 03 22 27 16 33; www.lestourelles.com; 2-4 rue Pierre Guerlain; d/tr/q from €93/161/181; ☺ closed 3 weeks Jan; @ 🤶) Overlooking Le Crotoy's beach, this atmospheric old-time hotel has 35 rooms, 13 with fabulous bay views; try room

33, which occupies one of the cone-roofed *tourelles* (turrets). Five rooms are accessible by lift. Kids aged four to 14 can stay in a dor-mitory with 10 bunks (€32 per child including breakfast).

The restaurant serves excellent seafood, most of it locally sourced.

Le Carré Gourmand   FRENCH €€
(☑ 03 22 27 46 72; www.facebook.com/lecarre gourmandbaiedesomme; 53 rue de la Porte du Pont; 3-course menu €29.50; ☺ 12.15-2pm & 7.15-9.30pm Mon & Thu-Sat, 12.15-2pm Sun year-round, plus 7.15-9.30pm Sun Jul & Aug; 🖉) Each day offers a different three-course blackboard menu at this intimate restaurant with exposed bricks, crisp tablecloths and a shady street-side terrace. Artistically presented dishes incorporate ingredients from the area such as *agneau de pré-salé* (salt marsh lamb), Le Crotoy duck, and Baie de Somme kelp and samphire. The small, local wine list compris-es just four whites and four reds.

ⓘ Information

Tourist Office (☑ 03 22 27 05 25; www.crotoy-baiedesomme.com; 1 rue Carnot; ☺ 9.30am-12.30pm & 2-6pm Mon-Sat, 10am-12.30pm & 2-5.30pm Sun Jun-Aug, shorter hours Sep-May) Can book boating and walking tours of the Baie de Somme.

ⓘ Getting There & Away

The SNCF train station in Noyelles-sur-Mer, 9km southeast of Le Crotoy, has direct services to Am-iens (€11.40, 40 minutes, six to eight daily) and Boulogne-sur-Mer (€12.90, 50 minutes, five to six daily). From late March to October (and some winter weekends), steam trains run by the not-for-profit **Chemin de Fer de la Baie de Somme** (p226), link Noyelles-sur-Mer with Le Crotoy.

Year-round, Trans 80 (www.trans80.fr) buses connect Le Crotoy with Noyelles-sur-Mer (€1.50, 15 minutes, up to eight daily).

St-Valery-sur-Somme

POP 2820

A cargo and fishing port as late as the 1980s, St-Valery-sur-Somme has a charming mari-time quarter, a pocket-size walled city with cobbled streets, a white-sand beach and a scenic promenade that stretches along the seafront. Like an impressionist seascape, the deep brick reds of St-Valery's houses are complemented by sea hues that range from sparkling blue to overcast grey, and are accented by dashes of red, white and blue

WORTH A TRIP

STOP WITH THE BIRDS

An astonishing 300 bird species have been sighted at the 2-sq-km **Parc du Marquenterre Bird Sanctuary** (☎ 03 22 25 68 99; www.parcdumarquenterre.fr; 25bis chemin des Garennes, St-Quentin-en-Tourmont; adult/child €10.50/7.90, binoculars €4/2; ⊗ 10am-7pm Apr-Sep, to 6pm early Feb-Mar & Oct, to 5pm Nov-early Feb), an important migratory stopover between the UK, Iceland, Scandinavia and Siberia and the warmer climes of West Africa. Three marked walking circuits (2km to 6km) take you to marshes, dunes, meadows, freshwater ponds, a brackish lagoon and 13 observation posts. Year-round, the park's guides – carrying telescopes on tripods – are happy to help visitors, especially kids, spot and identify birds. It's situated 9.5km northwest of Le Crotoy.

The park consists of land reclaimed from the sea in the 1960s by the construction of Dutch-style polders. Birds can be seen here year-round. Some species spend the winter, others migrate through in spring and autumn, and yet others – including white storks, grey herons, night herons, cattle egrets, little egrets, pied avocets and Eurasian spoonbills – nest from March or April to June or July. Allow at least two hours for a visit.

One-hour guided introductory walks (free) begin daily at 10.30am and 2pm; call ahead if you'd like a tour in English. The immediate vicinity has a number of lovely day-hike paths, including Sentier des Crocs (15km). The park rents out bicycles (€15/11 for a whole/half day) for rides in the area, like the Circuit de l'Avocette. Other tours include early-morning or evening birdsong tours outside of park opening hours, horse-drawn carriage rides along the seashore and bird photography lessons; prices for adults/children start from €18/10.

from flapping French flags. Grey and harbour seals can often be spotted off Pointe du Hourdel, 8km northwest of town.

◉ Sights & Activities

In the quaint, seaside **Quartier des Marins**, the narrow lanes (like rue de Moulins) are lined with miniature houses made of brick, many whimsically decorated with marine motifs. Up the hill is the walled **Cité Médiévale** (or Ville Médiévale; medieval town), whose narrow alleyways are paved with cobblestones and smooth pebbles.

Tides (www.maree.info) have long set the pace of maritime life here and still do, at least as far as outdoor activities on the bay are concerned. High tide is a whopping 8m to 11m above low tide; high tides with a coefficient of 100 or more submerge the entire bay, including the salt marshes.

Église St-Martin de St-Valery-sur-Somme CHURCH
(www.amiens.catholique.fr; 16 rue de la Porte de Nevers; ⊗ 8am-6pm Jul & Aug, to 5pm Sep-Jun) FREE St-Valery-sur-Somme's Église St-Martin was built from shingle and flint, giving it a chequerboard appearance, guarded by fantastical gargoyles. Construction started in 1488 and the church was consecrated in 1500, but wasn't completed until 1559. Inside are four models of 17th-century war ships. The stained-glass windows date from the 19th century.

Chemin de Fer de la Baie de Somme RAIL
(CFBS; ☎ 03 22 26 96 96; www.cfbs.eu; quai Lejoille; return to Le Crotoy adult/child €14.50/10.50; ⊗ daily late Mar-Oct, weekends only Nov, Feb & early–mid-Mar) Kids and adults alike will relish an old-time train ride. Staffed by passionate volunteers, the not-for-profit CFBS runs one to three round trips a day around the bay to Le Crotoy and west to Cayeux-sur-Mer. Passengers travel on trains assembled from the group's collection of historic steam and diesel engines, carriages, wagons and autorails, all dating from 1889 to 1954.

⚐ Tours

Rando-Nature en Somme WALKING
(☎ 03 22 26 92 30; www.randonature-baiedesomme.com; quai Perret; adult/child €13/7; ⊗ daily Mar-Oct, reduced hours Nov-Feb) This well-regarded outfit offers guided nature walks on the estuary, including Traversons la Baie ('we cross the bay'; 7km to 8km one-way depending on tides) and Les Phoques et la Baie (seal-watching at Pointe du Hourdel; 5km return). Circuits begin at seven *points de rendez-vous* (meeting places) around the bay – the website has details. Reserve ahead.

Bateaux de la Baie de Somme BOATING
(☎ 03 22 60 74 68; www.bateau-baie-somme.com; quai Perret; adult €13-22, child €9-15; ⊗ late

Mar–mid-Nov & school holidays Feb) Offers boat excursions around the bay lasting 40 minutes to two hours. For some real excitement, go seal-watching on a 12-person open-air Zodiac (€35 per person for one hour). Departure times are determined by the tides.

Sleeping & Eating

Rue de la Ferté has the highest concentration of restaurants. Local specialities include *agneau de pré-salé* (salt marsh lamb), available from June to mid-February, and seaweed and other delicacies foraged from the coast.

Relais Guillaume de Normandy HISTORIC HOTEL €
(☎03 22 60 82 36; www.relais-guillaume-de-normandy.com; 46 quai du Romerel; s/d/tr from €71/82/92; ⊙closed mid-Dec–mid-Jan; P) Right on the waterfront in a mock Tudor mansion from the early 1900s, this vintage hotel has a five-storey tower and period touches such as a mosaic entryway and creaky wooden stairs. Half of the 14 rooms have bay views. The in-house restaurant (closed Tuesdays) serves traditional French cuisine. Breakfast costs €12.50. Reserve well ahead in summer and on weekends.

Au Vélocipède B&B €€
(☎03 22 60 57 42; http://auvelocipede.fr; 1 rue du Puits Salé; s/d/tr incl breakfast from €95/105/150;) Two townhouses facing the church have been transformed into this swish B&B. The eight supremely comfortable rooms are huge, with stripped-back wooden floors, hip furnishings and modern slate-and-cream bathrooms. Those up in the attic (Vélo 3 and Vélo 4) are especially romantic, with sloped ceilings and exposed timber beams.

There's a rustic-chic **restaurant** (☎03 22 60 57 42; http://auvelocipede.fr; 1 rue du Puits Salé; mains €16-19, 3-course dinner menu €34; ⊙noon-6pm Wed-Fri, Sun & Mon, noon-6pm & 7.30-9pm Sat Apr-Sep, shorter hours Nov-Mar;) on-site.

Hôtel Les Pilotes BOUTIQUE HOTEL €€
(☎03 22 60 80 39; www.lespilotes.fr; 62 rue de la Ferté; d/tr/f from €119/178/204;) Pass beneath a lobby chandelier made entirely of white feathers to reach this hotel's 25 uniquely decorated rooms, which sport 1960s-inspired furnishings and fabrics. Higher-priced rooms come with large windows overlooking the bay; street-facing rooms can be noisy due to the cobblestones. Breakfast (€11) includes fresh fruit and pastries. Family rooms sleep up to four; baby cots are available.

BEACH TALK

A 3.5km promenade runs along the waterfront. The **Sentier du Littoral**, marked with yellow blazes, takes walkers west to Le Hourdel (8.5km) and around the bay to Le Crotoy (14km).

St-Valery-sur-Somme's sandy beach is at the western end of town but currents can be strong; there's a safer swimming beach 12km further west at Cayeux-sur-Mer.

Its waterfront **restaurant** (mains €15-28; ⊙noon-2.30pm & 7-9.30pm Jul & Aug, noon-2.30pm & 7-9.30pm Wed-Sat, noon-2.30pm Sun Feb-Jun & Sep-Dec) specialises in local produce.

★ **Château du Romerel** B&B €€€
(☎03 22 26 54 10; https://chateauduromerel.com; 15 quai du Romerel; d incl breakfast from €180, apt from €223; P) Four forested hectares envelop this 1870-built château with five spacious, beautifully furnished rooms, and two self-catering apartments sleeping up to four. Breakfast on the terrace in summer or by the open fire in winter. The honesty bar stocks regional wines and liqueurs; three-course evening meals (€35) are served by candlelight. The shaded outdoor pool opens from June to September.

Le Nicol's SEAFOOD €€
(☎03 22 26 82 96; nicols@wanadoo.fr; 15 rue de la Ferté; 2-/3-course dinner menus €18/22, mains €11-24, seafood platters per person €19-26; ⊙9.30am-3pm & 5.30-10pm Apr-Sep, 9.30am-3pm & 5.30-10pm Tue, Wed & Fri-Sun, 9.30am-3pm Thu Oct-Mar;) In a charming mustard-coloured building opening to a pavement terrace, Le Nicol's serves delicious fish, seafood and paella dishes, but the real crowd-pleasers are the whopping bowls of mussels (800g before cooking), available nine different ways including *moules à la salicorne* (mussels cooked with samphire), accompanied by crispy *frites* (fries).

Information

Tourist Office (☎03 22 60 93 50; www.tourisme-baiedesomme.fr; 2 place Guillaume Le Conquérant; ⊙9.30am-12.30pm & 2.30-6pm Apr-Sep, 10am-12.30pm & 2.30-5pm Tue-Sun Oct-Mar;) Has details on outdoor activities and excellent English brochures, including cycling maps. Sells tickets for guided walks of the estuary.

ℹ️ Getting There & Away

By car, St-Valery-sur-Somme is 64km northwest of Amiens and 14km around the bay from Le Crotoy.

The closest SNCF train station is 6km to the east in Noyelles-sur-Mer, which has direct services to Amiens (€11.40, 40 minutes, six to eight daily) and Boulogne-sur-Mer (€12.90, 50 minutes, five to six daily). From late March to October (and some winter weekends), steam trains run by the not-for-profit **Chemin de Fer de la Baie de Somme** (p226) link Noyelles-sur-Mer with St-Valery-sur-Somme.

Year-round, buses run by Trans 80 (www. trans80.fr) connect St-Valery-sur-Somme with Noyelles-sur-Mer (€1.50, 15 minutes, up to six daily) and Cayeux-sur-Mer (€1.50, 15 minutes, up to six daily).

SOMME BATTLEFIELDS MEMORIALS

The First Battle of the Somme, a WWI Allied offensive waged in the villages and woodlands northeast of Amiens, was designed to relieve pressure on the beleaguered French troops at Verdun. On 1 July 1916, British, Commonwealth and French troops 'went over the top' in a massive assault along a 34km front. But German positions proved virtually unbreachable, and on the first day of the battle an astounding 19,240 British troops were killed and another 38,230 were wounded. Most casualties were infantrymen mown down by German machine guns. By the time the offensive was called off in mid-November, over one million men on both sides had been killed or wounded. The British had advanced 12km, the French 8km.

The Battle of the Somme has become a symbol of the meaningless slaughter of WWI, and its killing fields – along with those of the Battle of Arras and Western Front sectors further north – are now sites of pilgrimage. Each year, thousands of visitors from Australia, Canada, Great Britain, New Zealand, South Africa and other Commonwealth nations follow the **Circuit du Souvenir** (Remembrance Trail; www.somme-battlefields.com).

Convenient bases for exploring the area include Amiens, Arras and the small towns of Péronne, Albert and Pozières.

👁️ Sights

⭐ **Historial de la Grande Guerre**   MUSEUM
(Museum of the Great War; 📞 03 22 83 14 18; www. historial.org; Château de Péronne, place André Audinot, Péronne; adult/child incl audioguide €9/4.50;

🕐 9.30am-6pm Apr-Oct, to 5pm Thu-Tue Nov–mid-Dec & late Jan-Mar) For historical and cultural context, the best place to begin a visit to the Somme battlefields is the outstanding Historial de la Grande Guerre in Péronne, 60km east of Amiens. Located inside the town's fortified medieval château, this award-winning museum tells the story of the war chronologically, with equal space given to the German, French and British perspectives on what happened, how and why.

Its unique collection of visually engaging material includes period films and the bone-chilling engravings by Otto Dix, which capture the aesthetic sensibilities, enthusiasm, naive patriotism and unimaginable violence of the time. The proud uniforms of various units and armies are shown laid out on the ground, as if on freshly (though bloodlessly) dead soldiers.

A second museum is located in Thiepval (p230), 8km northeast of Albert.

Beaumont-Hamel
Newfoundland Memorial   MEMORIAL
(📞 03 22 76 70 86; www.veterans.gc.ca; rue de l'Église, Beaumont-Hamel; 🕐 visitor centre noon-6pm Mon, 10am-6pm Tue-Sun Apr-Sep, 11am-5pm Mon, 9am-5pm Tue-Sun Oct-Mar) **FREE** This evocative memorial preserves part of the Western Front in the state it was in at fighting's end. The zigzag trench system, which still fills with mud in winter, is clearly visible, as are countless shell craters and the remains of barbed-wire barriers. Canadian students based at the Welcome Centre, which resembles a Newfoundland fisher's house, give free guided tours on the hour (except from mid-December to mid-January). It's 9km north of Albert; follow the signs for 'Memorial Terreneuvien'.

The memorial to the 29th Division, to which the volunteer Royal Newfoundland Regiment belonged, stands at the entrance to the site. On 1 July 1916, this regiment stormed entrenched German positions and was nearly wiped out; until a few years ago, a plaque noted bluntly that 'strategic and tactical miscalculations led to a great slaughter'. A path leads to an orientation table at the top of the Caribou mound, where a bronze caribou statue is surrounded by plants native to Newfoundland.

Vimy Ridge Canadian
National Historic Site   MEMORIAL
(📞 03 21 50 68 68; www.cheminsdememoire.gouv. fr; chemins des Canadiens, Vimy; 🕐 memorial site 24hr, visitor centre 10am-6pm May-Oct, 9am-5pm

Somme Battlefields & Memorials

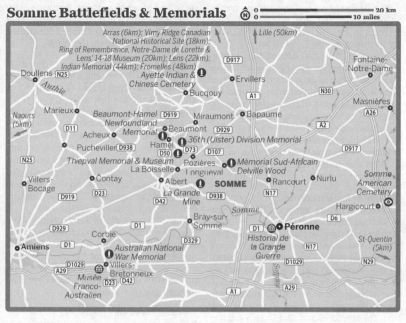

Nov-Apr) **FREE** After the war, the French attempted to erase signs of battle and return northern France to agriculture and normalcy. Conversely, the Canadians remembered their fallen by preserving part of the crater-pocked battlefield as it was when the guns fell silent. The resulting chilling, eerie moonscape of Vimy, 11km north of Arras, is a poignant place to comprehend the hell of the Western Front. During visitor centre opening hours, bilingual Canadian students lead free guided tours of reconstructed tunnels and trenches.

Of the more than 66,000 Canadians who died in WWI, 3598 lost their lives in April 1917 taking Vimy Ridge. Its highest point – site of a heavily fortified German position – was later chosen as the site of Canada's national WWI memorial, built from 1925 to 1936. It features 20 allegorical figures, carved from huge blocks of white Croatian limestone, that include a cloaked, downcast female figure representing a young Canada grieving for her dead. The names of 11,285 Canadians who 'died in France but have no known graves', listed alphabetically and within each letter by rank, are inscribed around the base.

In the surrounding forest, the zigzag trench system is clearly visible, as are countless shell craters. Because human remains still lie buried among the trees, the entire site has been declared a graveyard.

Fromelles (Pheasant Wood) Cemetery & Museum
CEMETERY, MUSEUM

(☏ 03 59 61 15 14; www.musee-bataille-fromelles.fr; 2 rue de la Basse Ville, Fromelles; cemetery free, museum adult/child €6.50/4; ⊙ cemetery 24hr, museum 9.30am-5.30pm Wed-Mon early Mar–mid-Jan) The death toll was horrific – 1917 Australians and 519 Britons killed in just one day of fighting – yet the Battle of Fromelles was largely forgotten until 2008, when the remains of 250 of the fallen were discovered. They are now buried in the Fromelles (Pheasant Wood) Cemetery. Next door, the Musée de la Bataille de Fromelles evokes life in the trenches with reconstructed bunkers, photographs and biographies.

On 19 July 1916, a poorly planned offensive using inexperienced Australian and British troops was launched to divert German forces from the Battle of the Somme. After the surviving Australians retreated to their pre-battle front lines, hundreds of their comrades-in-arms lay wounded in no man's land. For three days the survivors made heroic efforts to rescue them, acts of bravery commemorated by the *Cobbers* sculpture in the Australian Memorial Park, 2km northwest of the museum. Ross McMullin, writing for the Australian War Memorial (www.awm.gov.au), described the battle as the worst 24 hours in Australia's entire history.

It is likely that one of the soldiers on the victorious German side was a 27-year-old corporal in the 16th Bavarian Reserve Infantry Regiment named Adolf Hitler.

After the failed and catastrophic assault, the Germans buried many of the Australian and British dead in mass graves behind their lines. Most were reburied after the war, but five pits were not found for more than 90 years. DNA testing has established the identity of 144 Australians.

The 'Battle of Fromelles Walking Guide' has details on a 10km walking or driving tour of 10 WWI sites near Fromelles, which is 18km west of Lille.

★ Ring of Remembrance   MEMORIAL
(L'Anneau de la Mémoire; www.lens14-18.com; chemin du Mont de Lorette, Ablain-St-Nazaire; ⊙8.30am-11pm Apr-Nov, to 8pm Dec-Mar) FREE It's hard not to be overwhelmed by the waste and folly of the Western Front as you walk past panel after panel engraved with 579,606 tiny names: WWI dead from both sides who are listed in strict alphabetical order, without reference to nationality, rank or religion. Across the road from the memorial is a vast French military cemetery, Notre-Dame de Lorette; 6000 unidentified French soldiers are interred in the base of the Lantern Tower (1921). It's 13km west of Lens.

Lens' 14-18 Museum   MUSEUM
(⊉03 21 74 83 15; www.lens14-18.com; 102 rue Pasteur, Souchez; audioguide €3; ⊙10am-1pm & 2-5pm Tue-Sun) FREE Housed in four black concrete cubes, this 2015-opened WWI museum provides an in-depth introduction to WWI on the Western Front. Over 300 extraordinary photos, carefully selected by historians from French, British and German archives, detail daily life and death in the trenches; also on display are some 60 hours of archival film. It's situated 2km west (down the hill) from the Ring of Remembrance (Notre-Dame de Lorette), on a hill overlooking Lens.

Musée Franco-Australien   MUSEUM
(Franco-Australian Museum; ⊉03 22 96 80 79; www.museeaustralien.com; 9 rue Victoria, Villers-Bretonneux; adult/child €6/3; ⊙9.30am-5.30pm Apr-Oct, to 4.30pm Nov-late Dec & mid-Jan–Mar) Some 2400 Australian soldiers were killed or wounded in the April 1918 assault that wrested Villers-Bretonneux from German control. In the 1920s, Australian children donated funds to rebuild the town's primary school, creating bonds of friendship that remain strong to this day. Part of Victoria School is now a museum featuring highly personal artefacts donated by Australian ex-servicemen and their families. It's located 20km east of Amiens via the D1029.

Somme American Cemetery   CEMETERY
(⊉03 23 66 87 20; www.abmc.gov; rue de la Libération, Bony; ⊙9am-5pm) FREE In late September 1918, just six weeks before the end of WWI, American units – flanked by their British, Canadian and Australian allies – launched an assault on the Germans' heavily fortified Hindenburg Line. Some of the fiercest fighting took place near the village of Bony, 24km east of Péronne, on the sloping site now occupied by the 1844 Latin crosses and Stars of David of this serene cemetery. The small Visitors Building has information on the battle.

One regiment of the 27th Infantry Division, a National Guard unit from New York, suffered 337 dead and 658 wounded on a single day. The names of 333 men whose remains were never recovered are inscribed on the walls of the Memorial Chapel, reached through massive bronze doors.

Thiepval Memorial
& Museum   MEMORIAL, MUSEUM
(⊉03 22 74 60 47; www.historial.org; rue de l'Ancre, Thiepval; memorial free, museum adult/child €6/3; ⊙memorial 10am-5pm Tue-Sun Mar-Nov, museum 9.30am-6pm Mar-Oct, to 5pm Nov-early Dec & mid-Jan–Feb) Its silhouette instantly recognisable from afar, this 45m-high memorial to the missing of the Somme, 7.5km northeast of Albert, is inscribed with the names of more than 72,000 British and South African soldiers whose remains were never recovered or identified. Designed by Edwin Lutyens, it was built from 1928 to 1932 on the site of a German stronghold that was stormed on 1 July 1916, the first day of the Battle of the Somme.

The museum, run by Péronne's outstanding Historial de la Grande Guerre (p228), opened in 2016; displays include uniforms and large installations such as a replica of French fighter ace Georges Guynemer's aeroplane. The visitor centre's bookshop has an excellent selection of English books on WWI.

Its adjacent joint French and Commonwealth cemetery expresses Franco-British fraternity in death as in life.

Ulster Memorial Tower   MEMORIAL
(⊉03 22 74 81 11; www.somme14-18.com; rte de St-Pierre-Divion, Thiepval; ⊙10am-5pm Tue-Sun Mar-Nov) FREE The 5000 Ulstermen who perished in the Battle of the Somme are commemorated by this 21m-high Gothic-style tower, an exact

replica of Helen's Tower at Clanboye, County Down, where the Ulster Division trained. Dedicated in 1921, it has long been a Unionist pilgrimage site; a black obelisk known as the Orange Memorial to Fallen Brethren (1994) stands in an enclosure behind the tower. It's 1.2km northwest of Thiepval.

Virtually untouched since the war, nearby Thiepval Wood can be visited on a guided tour (donation requested); check the website for times and dates.

Neuve-Chapelle Indian Memorial   MEMORIAL
(www.cwgc.org; 413 rue du Bois, Richebourg; ⊘24hr) FREE The Mémorial Indien, 27km southwest of Lille, records the names of 4700 soldiers and labourers of the Indian Army who 'have no known grave'. The 15m-high column, flanked by two tigers, is topped by a lotus capital, the British Crown and the Star of India. The units (31st Punjabis, 11th Rajputs, 2nd King Edward's Own Gurkha Rifles) and the ranks of the fallen – Sepoy (infantry private), Havildar (sergeant) – are engraved on the walls.

La Grande Mine   LANDMARK
(Lochnagar Crater Memorial; www.lochnagarcrater. org; rte de la Grande Mine, La Boisselle; ⊘24hr) FREE Just outside the hamlet of La Boisselle, 4.5km northeast of Albert, this enormous crater looks like the site of a meteor impact. Some 100m across and 30m deep, it was created on the morning of the first day of the First Battle of the Somme (1 July 1916) by 27 tonnes of ammonal (an explosive made from ammonium nitrate and aluminium powder) laid by British sappers in order to create a breach in the German front lines.

Mémorial Sud-Africain Delville Wood   MEMORIAL, MUSEUM
(South African National Memorial & Museum; ☏03 22 85 02 17; www.delvillewood.com; rte de Ginchy, Longueval; ⊘memorial 24hr, museum 10am-5.30pm Apr–mid-Oct, to 4pm Feb, Mar & mid-Oct–Nov, closed Dec, Jan & South African public holidays) FREE The memorial (1926) and star-shaped museum (1986), a replica of Cape Town's Castle of Good Hope, stand in the middle of Delville Wood, where in July 1916 the 1st South African Infantry Brigade was nearly wiped out in hand-to-hand fighting that obliterated all the trees. In 2016, the names of all the South Africans who died in WWI were inscribed on a memorial wall.

During the 1916 offensive, pre-existing paths through Delville Wood were named for well-known streets in London and Edinburgh. Today, the area is still considered a cemetery because so many bodies were never recovered. Inside the museum, apartheid-era bronze murals portray black members of the South African Native Labour Corps (black South Africans were banned from combat roles) without shirts – despite the often chilly European weather. The memorial and museum are 15km east of Albert.

Ayette Indian & Chinese Cemetery   CEMETERY
(www.cwgc.org; Vieux Chemin de Bucquoy, Ayette; ⊘24hr) FREE Towards the end of WWI, tens of thousands of Chinese labourers were recruited by the British government to perform noncombat jobs in Europe, including the gruesome task of recovering and burying Allied war dead. Some 80 of these *travailleurs chinois* (Chinese labourers) and Indians who served with British forces are buried in this Commonwealth cemetery, which is 15km south of Arras, just off the D919 at the southern edge of the village of Ayette.

Many Chinese labourers died in the Spanish flu epidemic of 1918–19. Their gravestones are etched in Chinese and English with inscriptions such as 'A good reputation endures forever', 'A noble duty bravely done' and 'Faithful unto death'. The nearby graves of Indians are marked in Hindi or Arabic.

Australian National War Memorial   MEMORIAL, MUSEUM
(https://sjmc.gov.au; rte de Villers-Bretonneux, Fouilloy; ⊘memorial 24hr, museum 9.30am-6pm mid-Apr–Oct, to 5pm Nov–mid-Apr) FREE During WWI, 416,809 Australians – 8% of the country's population – volunteered for overseas military service; 46,000 met their deaths on the Western Front (14,000 others perished elsewhere). The names of 10,722 Australian soldiers whose remains were never found are engraved at the base of the Australian National War Memorial's 32m-high tower, which stands atop a hill where Australian and British troops repulsed a German assault in April 1918. Behind the tower, the Sir John Monash Centre museum has interactive displays.

The viewing area atop the tower, damaged by German gunfire in 1940, affords panoramic views of a large Commonwealth cemetery with 779 Australian graves and the one-time battlefield. An Anzac Day Dawn Service is held here every 25 April at 5.30am. The memorial is 3km north of Villers-Bretonneux along the D23.

LILLE, FLANDERS & THE SOMME SOMME BATTLEFIELDS MEMORIALS

SUBTERRANEAN DISCOVERY

Believed to date from the 3rd century AD, this extraordinary underground 'city' of quarried tunnels **La Cité Souterraine de Naours** (Caves of Naours; ☑ 03 22 93 71 78; http://citesouterrainedenaours.fr; 5 rue des Carrières, Naours; adult/child incl audioguide €11/7, incl 90min guided tour €12/9; ☺ 10am-6.30pm Jul & Aug, 10am-5.30pm Tue-Fri, 10am-6.30pm Sat & Sun Apr-Jun, Sep & Oct, 11am-4.30pm Tue-Sun Feb, Mar & Nov) was started by the Romans and expanded over the centuries, incorporating 28 galleries and 300 rooms, including three chapels, multiple town squares, a bakery (with working ovens) and livestock barns. Only rediscovered in 1887, it was used by Allied forces in WWI, and as a Nazi HQ in WWII. The temperature below ground is a constant 9.5°C; bring a jacket (and a torch/flashlight).

Soldiers' graffiti from both wars can be seen throughout the cave system. Guided tours are in English and French. The site is 18km north of Amiens.

Fricourt German Cemetery CEMETERY (www.volksbund.de; 21 rue de Pozières, Fricourt; ☺ 24hr) **FREE** A stark reminder of the extensive loss of life on all sides of WWI, this cemetery is the burial place of 17,027 fallen German soldiers. Only 5000 of the graves are individual; the remainder of the dead lie in four mass graves. Many remains were interred from other cemeteries around the Somme in 1920.

🏃 Activities

Aero Dom SCENIC FLIGHTS (☑ 07 83 54 39 01; www.aero-dom.fr; rte de Paris, Roupy; 20/30/60min flight €80/100/175; ☺ by reservation) If you have a head for heights, get a swooping aerial view over the Somme battlefields and memorials aboard a gyrocopter flight, where you sit behind the pilot in an open cockpit. Itineraries can be customised depending on your interest. Heated jackets and helmets are provided. Flights depart 24km southeast of Péronne.

Amiens Balloon BALLOONING (☑ 06 07 68 74 44; www.amiensballoon.com; 7 rue du Laboureur, Sains-en-Amiénois; per person €220; ☺ by reservation) Float over the Somme aboard a hot-air balloon, with commentary in English and French. Flight time is one hour but the whole experience lasts four hours; bring a jacket and wear flat shoes. Children under 1.2m tall (and expectant mothers) aren't permitted. The departure point is 11km south of Amiens; routes depend on wind direction.

👉 Tours

Tourist offices (including those in Amiens, Arras, Albert and Péronne) can help book tours of battlefield sites and memorials. Recommended tour companies:

Battlefields Experience (☑ 03 22 76 29 60; www.thebattleofthesomme.co.uk; half-/full day per person incl museum entry fees €65/130)

Chemins d'Histoire (☑ 06 23 67 77 64; www.cheminsdhistoire.com; full day per person from €120)

Sacred Ground Tours (☑ 06 75 66 59 02; www.sacredgroundtours.com.au; full day per person from €200)

Terres de Mémoire (☑ 03 22 84 23 05; www.terresdememoire.com; full day per person from €130)

True Blue Digger Tours (☑ 06 01 33 46 76; http://trueblue-diggertours.com; half-day per person from €55)

Walkabout Digger Tours (☑ 06 64 54 16 63; http://walkaboutdiggertours.free.fr; full day per person from €120)

🛏 Sleeping & Eating

Amiens and Arras have a good range of accommodation options, but many visitors choose to stay in small hotels or B&Bs situated in towns closer to the battlefields, such as Péronne, Albert or Pozières. The latter towns all have ample restaurants and shops selling picnic supplies.

Au Vintage B&B € (☑ 03 22 75 63 28; www.chambres-dhotes-albert.com; 19 rue de Corbie, Albert; d incl breakfast €80-85; 🅿 🛜) This delightful B&B, in a brick mansion from 1920, has two atmospheric rooms with old wooden floors, antique furnishings and marble fireplaces. Evelyne and Jacky are delightful, cultured hosts who enjoy sharing their knowledge about the battlefields with their guests; ask to see their three vintage cars. Reserve well ahead.

Butterworth Farm B&B € (☑ 03 22 75 26 46; www.butterworth-cottage.com; rte de Bazentin (D73), Pozières; s/d/q incl breakfast €65/80/110; 🅿 🛜) Run by Bernard, the mayor of Pozières, and his wife, Marie, this B&B on their family farm has six individually decorated rooms with themes such as Out of Africa.

Guests can unwind in the garden filled with flowers and herbs; copious breakfasts include quiche and freshly squeezed orange juice.

La Basilique
HOTEL €€

(☑ 03 22 75 04 71; www.hotelbasiliquesomme.fr; 3-5 rue Gambetta, Albert; d/tr from €92/102; ☎) In the heart of Albert, right across the square from the basilica, this well-kept hotel has 10 neat rooms with French windows, bright bathrooms and richly patterned feature walls. The in-house restaurant specialises in *cuisine du terroir* (regional specialities made with quality local ingredients) such as duck breast with sour-cherry sauce (two-/three-course *menus* €18/22). Breakfast costs €10.

Hôtel Le Saint-Claude
HOTEL €€

(☑ 03 22 79 49 49; www.hotelsaintclaude.com; 42 place du Commandant Louis Daudré, Péronne; s/d/tr from €76/93/125; ☎) Originally a *relais de poste* (coaching inn), the Saint-Claude is in the centre of Péronne just 200m from the medieval château housing the Historial de la Grande Guerre. The 40 contemporary rooms are decorated in chic greys and creams and have ultramodern bathrooms; some have château views. The walled courtyard is a suntrap.

ⓘ Information

Albert Tourist Office (☑ 03 22 75 16 42; www.tourisme-paysducoquelicot.com; 9 rue Gambetta, Albert; ☺ 9am-12.30pm & 1.30-6.30pm Mon-Fri, 9am-12.30pm & 2-6.30pm Sat, 9am-1pm Sun May-Aug, 9am-12.30pm & 1.30-5pm Mon-Fri, 9am-noon & 2-5pm Sat Sep-Apr)

Péronne Tourist Office (☑ 03 22 84 42 38; www.hautesomme-tourisme.com; 16 place André Audinot, Péronne; ☺ 9.30am-12.30pm & 1.30-6.30pm Mon-Sat, 10am-noon & 2-5pm Sun Jul & Aug, 9am-12.30pm & 2-6pm Mon-Fri, 9am-noon & 2-6pm Sat Apr-Jun, Sep & Oct, shorter hour Nov-Mar)

ⓘ Getting There & Around

You'll need your own transport (a car or bike) to visit most of the Somme battlefields and memorials. Bicycles can be rented at the **tourist office** in Albert (standard bike half-/full day €8/12, electric bike €15/25).

Villers-Bretonneux has rail services to/from Amiens (€4, 15 minutes, up to 10 daily). The train station is 600m southeast of the Musée Franco-Australien (take rue de Melbourne) and a walkable 3km south of the Australian National War Memorial (a round-trip taxi from Villers-Bretonneux costs around €25).

Albert is linked by train to Amiens (€7, 25 minutes, up to two per hour) and Arras (€8, 25 minutes, every two hours).

AMIENS

POP 133,450

One of France's mightiest Gothic cathedrals is reason enough to visit Amiens, the former capital of Picardy. The mostly pedestrianised city centre, tastefully rebuilt after WWII, is complemented by lovely green spaces along the Somme River. Jules Verne lived the last 34 years of his life here; his former home is now a museum. Some 30,000 students from the Université de Picardie Jules Verne give the town a youthful energy. Amiens is an ideal base for visits to many of the Battle of the Somme memorials.

⊙ Sights & Activities

Place Gambetta, the city's commercial hub, is three blocks southwest of the cathedral. Amiens' Quartier Anglais (English Quarter), 1.5km southeast of the train station, is a little piece of England built in the 1890s for the British managers of a textile factory (part of Sebastian Faulks' novel *Birdsong* is set here).

★ Cathédrale Notre Dame
CATHEDRAL

(www.cathedrale-amiens.fr; 30 place Notre Dame; cathedral free, north tower adult/child €6/free, treasury €3.50/free, tower & treasury €8/free, audioguide €4; ☺ cathedral 8.30am-5.15pm daily, north tower to mid-afternoon Wed-Mon) A Unesco World Heritage Site, the largest Gothic cathedral in France (at 145m long) and the largest in the world by volume was begun in 1220 to house the skull of St John the Baptist. It's renowned for its soaring Gothic arches (42.3m high over the transept), unity of style and immense interior; look for the 17th-century statue known as the *Ange Pleureur* (Crying Angel), behind the Baroque high altar.

The octagonal, 234m-long labyrinth on the black-and-white floor of the nave is easy to miss as the soaring vaults draw the eye upward. Part of the skull of St John the Baptist, framed in gold and jewels, can be seen in the *trésor* (treasury). Plaques in the south transept honour American, Australian, British, Canadian and New Zealand soldiers who perished in WWI.

To get a sense of what you're seeing, hire a multilingual audioguide at Amiens' tourist office (p235). Weather permitting, visitors willing to brave 307 steps can climb the north tower for spectacular views; tickets are sold in the boutique to the left as you walk through the west façade. The cathedral is closed to visitors during religious ceremonies.

A free 45-minute light show bathes the cathedral's façade in vivid medieval colours

Amiens

Amiens

◎ Top Sights
1 Cathédrale Notre Dame B2

◎ Sights
2 Beffroi d'Amiens A2
3 Maison de Jules Verne B4

🛏 Sleeping
4 Grand Hôtel de l'Univers C3

5 Hôtel Marotte................................... B3
6 Hôtel Victor Hugo C2

✖ Eating
7 Halle au Frais A1
8 Le Tire Bouchon C1
9 Marché sur l'Eau C1

nightly from mid-June to the third weekend in September, and from early December to 1 January. The photons start flying at 10.45pm in June, 10.30pm in July, 10pm in August, 9.45pm in September and 7pm in December.

Maison de Jules Verne MUSEUM
(Maisons des Illustres; ☎ 03 22 45 45 75; www.amiens.fr; 2 rue Charles Dubois; adult/child €7.50/4, audioguide €2; ◷ 10am-12.30pm & 2-6.30pm Mon & Wed-Fri, 2-6.30pm Tue, 11am-6.30pm Sat & Sun mid-Apr–mid-Oct, to 6pm, closed Tue mid-Oct–mid-Apr) Jules Verne (1828–1905) wrote some of his

best-known works of brain-tingling – and eerily prescient – science fiction under the eaves of this turreted home, where he lived from 1882 to 1900. The 700 models, prints, posters and other items inspired by Verne's boundless imagination afford a fascinating opportunity to check out the future as he envisioned it over a century ago, when going around the world in 80 days sounded utterly fantastic.

Beffroi d'Amiens TOWER
(place au Fil; belfry & cathedral tour adult/child €6/3, belfry only €4/2) Constructed between

1406 and 1410, Amiens' massive square belfry – a Unesco-listed monument – has a mid-18th-century top reaching 52m, which was rebuilt after it was damaged in 1940 by German bombing. The tourist office runs two guided tours per month, one including a cathedral tour, plus night-time visits in July and August – check the website and reserve well ahead.

Hortillonnages Cruises
BOATING

(📋 03 22 92 12 18; http://leshortillonnages-amiens.fr; 54 bd Beauvillé; adult/child €6/5; ⏰ 9am-noon & 1.30-6pm Apr-Oct) Covering some 3 sq km, Amiens' market gardens have supplied the city with vegetables and flowers since the Middle Ages. Today, their peaceful *rieux* (waterways), home to seven working farms, more than 1000 private gardens and countless water birds, can be visited on tours aboard gondola-like 12-person boats.

From mid-June to mid-October, the Hortillonnages host contemporary art installations accessible on foot, by bicycle or by rental *barque* (boat).

🛏 Sleeping & Eating

Le Quatorze
B&B €

(📋 06 16 89 19 87; www.lequatorze.fr; 14 av de Dublin; s/d incl breakfast €65/75; 🛜) Laure offers the perfect B&B experience 1.5km southeast of the train station in the Quartier Anglais (English Quarter). The five rooms are full of old-time touches (original tiles, wooden flooring, marble fireplaces) spanning two floors. All have private bathrooms; two are across the hall from the rooms. Amenities include a guest kitchen, laundry facilities and a rambling English-style garden.

Hôtel Victor Hugo
HOTEL €

(📋 03 22 91 57 91; www.hotel-a-amiens.fr; 2 rue de l'Oratoire; d from €52; 🛜) This bargain-priced, family-run hotel has 10 simple but comfortable rooms. The best-value rooms – if you don't mind a long stair climb – are under the eaves on the top floor, offering rooftop views and streaming natural light.

⭐ Hôtel Marotte
BOUTIQUE HOTEL €€

(📋 03 60 12 50 00; www.hotel-marotte.com; 3 rue Marotte; d/q from €166/325; 🅿️❄️🛜) Modern French luxury is at its most romantic at this boutique hotel. All 12 light-drenched rooms are huge (at least 35 sq metres), but the two sauna suites (100 sq metres), sporting free-standing stone bathtubs weighing 1.5 tonnes, are really luxury apartments; one opens to a rooftop terrace.

Grand Hôtel de l'Univers
HOTEL €€

(📋 03 22 91 52 51; www.hotel-univers-amiens.com; 2 rue de Noyon; d €95-125; @🛜) Built in 1875, this venerable, Best Western–affiliated hostelry has a superb parkside location. The 40 soundproofed rooms, set around a three-storey atrium, are immaculate and very comfortable; those on the 2nd floor come with balconies. Spacious corner rooms such as room 26 are flooded with natural light.

Le Tire Bouchon
FRENCH €

(📋 06 83 52 58 42; www.facebook.com/letirebouchon80; 1 bd du Cange; 2-/3-course menus €16/19, mains €12.50-16, sharing plates €3-11; ⏰ kitchen 11.30am-3pm & 6.30-10.30pm, bar 11.30am-midnight Sun-Thu, to 1am Fri, to 3am Sat) With a table-filled riverside terrace, this contemporary wine bar is ideal for a glass and small sharing plate such as bone marrow with lemon zest, duck and fig terrine or sardine rillettes with capers, but it also has more substantial dishes such as steak tartare or the house special burger with Somme-produced Rollot cheese. Live music, especially blues and jazz, plays on weekends.

ℹ Information

Tourist Office (📋 03 22 71 60 50; www.visit-amiens.com; 23 place Notre Dame; ⏰ 9.30am-6.30pm Mon-Sat, 10am-noon & 2-5pm Sun Apr-Sep, 9.30am-6pm Mon-Sat, 10am-noon & 2-5pm Sun Oct-Mar; 🛜)

ℹ Getting There & Around

BICYCLE

Amiens' **Vélam** (📋 08 20 20 02 99; www.velam.amiens.fr; subscription per day €1, 1st 30min free, per subsequent 30 min €1) bike-sharing scheme has 26 bike stations around town.

BUS

Regional bus services operate from Amiens' **bus station**, just north of the train station.

TRAIN

Amiens is an important rail hub, with the following direct services:

Arras €13.10, 45 minutes, hourly
Boulogne-sur-Mer €21.70, 1¾ hours, seven to nine daily
Compiègne €14.20, 1¼ hours, eight to 13 daily
Laon €19, 1½ hours, five to 11 daily
Lille-Flandres €22.20, 1½ hours, six to 12 daily
Paris Gare du Nord €22.80, one to 1½ hours, 14 to 21 daily
Rouen €21.40, 1¼ hours, four to seven daily

SNCF buses link Amiens' train station with the Haute-Picardie TGV station (€10, 45 minutes, six to eight daily), 40km east of the city.

ℹ️ PICNIC PERFECT

Stock up on a picnic of local produce at the market before heading out for the day to the Somme battlefields and memorials.

Marché sur l'Eau (place Parmentier; ⊙ 8am-1pm Sat) Fruit and veggies grown in the city's market gardens, the Hortillonnages, are sold at this one-time floating market, now held on dry land.

Halle au Frais (www.leshalles-amiens.fr; 22b rue du Général Leclerc; ⊙ 9am-7pm Tue-Sat, to 12.30pm Sun) Two dozen stalls sell picnic supplies, including cheeses, breads and wine, at this covered market within Amiens' Les Halles shopping complex.

COMPIÈGNE

POP 40,730

Just 60km north of Paris' Charles de Gaulle Airport, the prosperous 'imperial city' of Compiègne reached its glittering zenith under Emperor Napoléon III (r 1852–70), whose legacy is alive and well in his opulent *palais* (palace) and the adjacent gardens and forests. Both the 1918 armistice that ended WWI and the French surrender of 1940 were signed in a wooded area just outside town.

On 23 May 1430, Joan of Arc (Jeanne d'Arc) – honoured by two statues in the partly medieval city centre – was captured at Compiègne by the Burgundians, who later sold her to their English allies.

⊙ Sights

★ Palais de Compiègne   PALACE
(Palais Impérial; ☑ 03 44 38 47 00; http://palaisde compiegne.fr; place du Général de Gaulle; adult/child €7.50/free; ⊙ palace 10am-6pm Wed-Mon, Grands Appartements 10am-6pm Wed-Mon mid-Mar–Oct, to 4pm Nov–mid-Mar, park 8am-7pm daily mid-Apr–mid-Sep, to 6pm daily Mar–mid-Apr & mid-Sep–Oct, to 5pm daily Nov-Feb) This 1337-room palace, originally built for Louis XV, hosted Napoléon III's dazzling hunting parties, which drew aristocrats from all around Europe. A single ticket grants access to the sumptuous Grands Appartements, where highlights include the empress's bedroom and a ballroom lit by 15 chandeliers (English audioguide available); the Musée du Second Empire, illustrating the lives of Napoléon III and his family; and the Musée de la Voiture, featuring vehicles that predate the internal combustion engine.

The Musée de l'Impératrice, which stars Eugénie (Napoléon III's wife), is closed for renovations until at least late 2018. From about April to mid-November, you can have lunch or a drink in the Jardin des Roses (rose garden). Almost all parts of the palace are now wheelchair accessible.

Stretching southeast from the château, the 20-hectare, English-style Petit Parc links up with the Grand Parc and the Forêt de Compiègne, a forest that surrounds Compiègne on the east and south and is criss-crossed by rectilinear paths. The area is a favourite venue for hiking and cycling (maps and bike-rental details available at the tourist office) as well as horse riding.

Mémorial de l'Internement et de la Déportation – Camp de Royallieu   MUSEUM
(Internment & Deportation Memorial; ☑ 03 44 96 37 00; www.memorial-compiegne.fr; 2bis av des Martyrs de la Liberté; adult/child incl audioguide €5/ free; ⊙ 10am-6pm Wed-Mon) Situated about 3km southwest of the city centre, the French military base of Royallieu was used as a Nazi transit and internment camp known as Frontstalag 122 from 1941 to 1944; three of the 24 original barracks now house a memorial museum.

Clairière de l'Armistice   HISTORIC SITE
(Armistice Clearing; ☑ 03 44 85 14 18; www.musee-armistice-14-18.fr; rte de Soissons; adult/child €5/3; ⊙ 10am-6pm Jan-Nov, to 5.30pm Dec) The armistice that put an end to WWI was signed in a thick forest 6.5km east of Compiègne, inside the railway carriage of the Allied supreme commander. On 22 June 1940, in the same railway car, the French were forced to sign the armistice that recognised Nazi Germany's domination of France. These momentous events are commemorated with monuments, memorabilia, newspaper clippings and 800 stereoscopic (3D) photos.

Taken to Berlin for exhibition, the railway carriage used in 1918 and 1940 was destroyed in April 1945 on Hitler's personal orders, lest it be used for a third surrender – his own. The wooden rail wagon now on display is of the same type as the original, though some of the interior furnishings, hidden during WWII, were the ones actually used in 1918.

🛏️ Sleeping & Eating

Accommodation is limited but the town can easily be visited on a day trip from Paris. Most of Compiègne's rather lacklustre hotels can be found near the train station and along the Oise River. Room prices drop on Friday, Saturday and Sunday nights.

Hôtel du Nord
HOTEL €€

(☎03 44 83 22 30; www.hoteldunordcompiegne.com; 1 place de la Gare; d/tr from €94/111; 🛜) Around the corner from the train station, this well-run establishment has 20 quiet but compact rooms, some with little balconies and river views. Downstairs, its excellent restaurant, **La Table d'Elisa** (☎03 44 83 22 30; 1 place de la Gare; 3-/4-course menus €38/45, mains €19-35; ☺noon-2pm & 7-9.30pm Mon-Fri, 7-9.30pm Sat, noon-2pm Sun; 🛜🅿♿), serves seafood and other local specialities with a creative twist.

★ Les Accordailles
BISTRO €

(☎03 44 40 03 45; 24 rue d'Ulm; 2-/3-course lunch menus €13/16, 3-course dinner menu €20, mains €12-16.50; ☺10.30am-3.30pm & 6.30-11pm Tue-Sat year-round, plus 10.30am-3.30pm Sun & Mon Jul & Aug; 🅿♿) 🍴 Everything at this bistro facing the Palais de Compiègne is organic, including the wines and liqueurs. Morel-stuffed chicken breast with truffled potato gratin, and *entrecôte* (rib steak) with garlic butter and roasted figs are standouts; every day there are vegetarian options such as Camembert and calvados (apple-flavoured brandy) *tartines* and vegan choices like beetroot mousse with quinoa and root vegetables.

Bistrot du Terroir
FRENCH €€

(☎03 44 40 06 36; http://bistrotduterroircompiegne.fr; 13 rue Eugène Floquet; 2-/3-course lunch menus €18.90/31.90, 3-course dinner menus €23.90-31.90, mains €14-24; ☺noon-2pm & 7-10pm Mon-Sat) Tucked away on a side street near the tourist office, this cosy little place serves excellent French cuisine such as scrumptious *carré d'agneau rôti* (roasted rack of lamb) or duck-liver Quercy sausage *cassoulet* (slow-cooked casserole). For dessert try the crème brûlée in variations such as blueberry.

ℹ️ Information

Tourist Office (☎03 44 40 01 00; www.compiegne-tourisme.fr; place de l'Hôtel de Ville; ☺9.15am-12.15pm & 1.45-6.15pm Mon-Sat, 10am-12.15om & 2.15-5pm Sun Apr-Sep, 1.45-5.15pm Mon, 9.15am-12.15pm & 1.45-5.15pm Tue-Sat Oct-May)

ℹ️ Getting There & Away

Compiègne's train station, 1km northwest of the château, has direct services to Paris' Gare du Nord (€15.40, 50 minutes, at least hourly) and Amiens (€14.20, one hour, at least hourly).

LAON

POP 25,280

Enclosed within a 7km-long wall pierced by three fortified gates, Laon's medieval Ville Haute (Upper City) has a magnificent Gothic **cathedral** (rue du Cloître; ☺9am-9pm Jul & Aug, to 6pm Sep-Jun) and 84 listed historic monuments, the densest concentration anywhere in France. The narrow streets, alleyways and courtyards reward keen-eyed wandering. About 100 vertical metres below sits the Ville Basse (Lower City), completely rebuilt after being flattened in WWII.

The **tourist office** (☎03 23 20 28 62; www.tourisme-paysdelaon.com; Hôtel-Dieu de Laon, place du Parvis, Ville Haute; ☺10am-6pm Jun-Aug, 10am-12.30pm & 1.30-5.30pm Mon-Sat, 1.30-5.30pm Sun Sep-May; 🛜) has an excellent walking-tour map of Laon (free) and audioguides (€5) for walks around the cathedral (one hour) and the Cité Médiévale (medieval city; one to four hours). It's next to the cathedral in a 12th-century hospital decorated with 13th-century frescoes. About 20km south of Laon along the D18 highway, the 30km-long ridge known as the Chemin des Dames was the site of fierce fighting during WWI at the Second Battle of the Aisne, a bloody French offensive, in 1917.

ℹ️ Getting There & Away

The train station, in the Ville Basse, has direct services to Paris' Gare du Nord (€24.10, 1½ hours, eight to 14 direct daily), Amiens (€19, 1½ hours, four to 12 daily) and Reims (€10.40, 45 minutes, three to 12 daily).

WORTH A TRIP

A FRENCH-AMERICAN MUSEUM

Inside the 1612-built Château de Blérancourt, 33km northeast of Compiègne, the **Musée Franco-Américain** (☎03 23 39 60 16; http://museefrancoamericain.fr; Château de Blérancourt, Blérancourt; museum adult/child €6/4.50, gardens free; ☺museum 10am-12.30pm & 2-5.30pm Wed-Mon, gardens 8am-7pm) reopened in 2017 after a decade of archaeological excavations and renovations. The two countries' relationship over the centuries is chronicled through art, historical exhibits and the Jardins du Nouveau Monde, which is planted with flowers, shrubs and trees native to the Americas, including Virginia magnolia, maple, oak and sweetgum trees, chosen for their autumn foliage.

Normandy

POP 3.3 MILLION

Best Places to Eat

➜ La Fleur de Sel (p269)

➜ L'Espiguette (p243)

➜ Marché aux Poissons (p266)

➜ L'Alchimie (p254)

➜ Les Voiles d'Or (p246)

Best Places to Stay

➜ Hôtel de Bourgtheroulde (p243)

➜ Château de la Ferrière (p253)

➜ La Maison de Famille (p264)

➜ La Petite Folie (p268)

➜ Les Cabanes du Clos Masure (p243)

Why Go?

From the Norman invasion of England in 1066 to the D-Day landings of 1944, Normandy has long played an outsized role in European history. This rich and often brutal past is brought vividly to life by the spectacular and iconic island monastery of Mont St-Michel; the incomparable Bayeux Tapestry, world-famous for its cartoon scenes of 11th-century life; and the transfixing cemeteries and memorials along the D-Day beaches, places of solemn pilgrimage.

Lower-profile charms include a variety of dramatic coastal landscapes, plenty of pebbly beaches, some of France's finest museums, quiet pastoral villages and architectural gems ranging from Rouen's medieval old city – home of Monet's favourite cathedral – to the maritime charms of Honfleur to the striking postwar modernism of Le Havre.

Camembert, apples, cider, cream-rich cuisine and the very freshest fish and seafood provide further reasons to visit this accessible and beautiful region of France.

When to Go

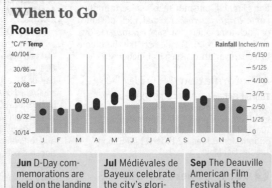

Rouen

Jun D-Day commemorations are held on the landing beaches. 2019 sees the landing's 75th anniversary

Jul Médiévales de Bayeux celebrate the city's glorious history with medieval re-enactments.

Sep The Deauville American Film Festival is the accessible cousin of Cannes.

Normandy Highlights

1 Rouen's old town (p240)
Strolling among half-timbered houses and Gothic churches.

2 Bayeux Tapestry (p251)
Travelling back to 1066 with the world's oldest comic strip.

3 D-Day Beaches (p255)
Pondering the price of freedom at the landing sites and nearby war cemeteries.

4 Mont St-Michel (p271)
Watching the tide rush in from the ramparts and the extraordinary monastery.

5 La Fleur de Sel (p269) Feasting at one of Normandy's best eateries, in charming Honfleur.

6 Caen (p262) Exploring the mighty castle ramparts and historic sights of this handsome and sights-packed town.

7 Étretat (p248)
Marvelling at the famous twin cliffs and free-standing limestone arches.

SEINE-MARITIME

The Seine-Maritime *département* (administrative division) stretches along the chalk-white cliffs of the Côte d'Albâtre (Alabaster Coast) from Le Tréport via Dieppe to Le Havre, France's second-busiest port (after Marseille). With its history firmly bound up with the sea, the region offers visitors an engaging mix of small seaside villages and dramatic clifftop walks.

When you fancy a break from the bracing sea air, head inland to the lively, ancient and good-looking metropolis of Rouen, a favourite haunt of Claude Monet and Simone de Beauvoir and one of the most intriguing and history-infused cities in France's northeast.

Rouen

POP 111,000

With its soaring Gothic cathedral, beautifully restored medieval quarter, imposing ancient churches, excellent museums and vibrant cultural life, Rouen is one of Normandy's most engaging and historically rich destinations.

The city has endured a turbulent history. It was devastated by fire and plague several times during the Middle Ages, and was occupied by the English during the Hundred Years War. The young French heroine Joan of Arc (Jeanne d'Arc) was tried for heresy and burned at the stake in the central square in 1431. And during WWII, Allied bombing raids laid waste to large parts of the city, especially south of the cathedral.

◉ Sights & Activities

Cathédrale Notre Dame CATHEDRAL
(www.cathedrale-rouen.net; place de la Cathédrale; ⊘2-7pm Mon, 9am-7pm Tue-Sat, 8am-6pm Sun Apr-Oct, shorter hours Nov-Mar) Rouen's stunning Gothic cathedral, built between the late 12th and 16th centuries, was famously the subject of a series of canvases painted by Monet at various times of the day and year. The 75m-tall **Tour de Beurre** (Butter Tower) was financed by locals in return for being allowed to eat butter during Lent – or so the story goes. A free sound-and-light spectacular is projected on the façade every night from June (at 11pm) to late September (at 9.30pm).

★ Historial Jeanne d'Arc MUSEUM
(☑02 35 52 48 00; www.historial-jeannedarc.fr; 7 rue St-Romain; adult/child €10.50/7.50; ⊘10am-6pm Tue-Sun) For an introduction to the great 15th-century heroine and the events that earned her fame – and shortly thereafter condemnation – don't miss this excellent site. It's less of a museum, and more of an immersive, theatre-like experience, where you walk through medieval corridors and watch (and hear via headphones, in seven languages) the dramatic retelling of Joan's visions, her victories, the trial that sealed her fate, and the mythologising that followed in the years after her death.

Église St-Maclou CHURCH
(place Barthélémy; ⊘10am-noon & 2-5.30pm Sat & Sun) This supreme example of the Flamboyant Gothic–style church was built between 1437 and 1521, but much of the decoration dates from the Renaissance. The church was heavily damaged in WWII and later restored. Note the detailed wood panelling in the porch of the church; also observe how many of the statues on the exterior stonework of the church are missing their heads (victims of the French Wars of Religion). Half-timbered houses that incline at curious angles can be found on nearby side streets.

Musée des Beaux-Arts GALLERY
(☑02 35 71 28 40; www.mbarouen.fr; esplanade Marcel Duchamp; ⊘10am-6pm Wed-Mon) FREE Housed in a very grand structure flung up in 1870, Rouen's simply outstanding fine-arts museum features canvases by Rubens, Modigliani, Pissarro, Renoir, Sisley (lots) and, of course, several works by Monet, as well as a fine collection of Flemish oils. There's also one jaw-dropping painting by Caravaggio as well as a very serene cafe. Drop your bag in the lockers provided and follow the route through the galleries, arranged chronologically.

Musée Le Secq des Tournelles MUSEUM
(☑02 35 71 28 40; www.museelesecqdestournelles. fr; 2 rue Jacques Villon; ⊘2-6pm Wed-Mon) FREE Home to one of the world's premier collections of wrought iron, this riveting (excuse the pun) museum is an astonishing sight, showcasing the extraordinary skills of pre-industrial iron- and locksmiths, in a magnificent setting across two floors within a desanctified 16th-century church. There's everything from elaborate penknives to candle snuffs, beds, fortified chests, candelabra, miniature pistols and intricate keys.

Musée de la Céramique MUSEUM
(☑02 35 07 31 74; www.museedelaceramique.fr; 1 rue du Faucon; ⊘2-6pm Wed-Mon) FREE The Ceramics Museum, housed in a 17th-century building with a fine courtyard, is known for

Rouen

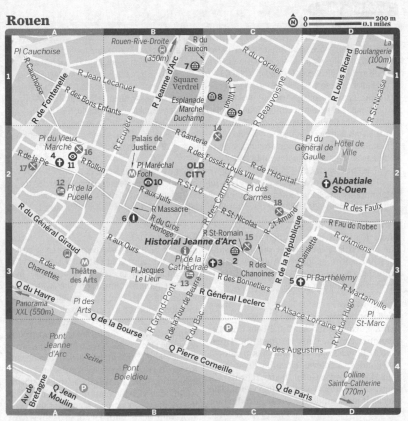

Rouen

⊚ Top Sights

⊚ Sights

🛏 Sleeping

🍴 Eating

its 16th- to 19th-century faience (tin-glazed earthenware) and porcelain. Don't miss sculptural pieces such as the exquisite celestial sphere (1725) on the upper floor.

Place du Vieux Marché   SQUARE
The old city's main thoroughfare, rue du Gros Horloge, runs from the cathedral west to place du Vieux Marché, where 19-year-old Joan of Arc was burned at the stake for heresy in 1431.

Église Jeanne d'Arc   CHURCH
(place du Vieux Marché; ⊘10am-noon & 2-6pm, closed Fri & Sun mornings) Dedicated in 1979, the thrillingly bizarre Église Jeanne d'Arc, with its fish-scale exterior, marks the spot

LES ANDELYS

From Rouen, a lovely day trip can be made to the landlocked Eure *département* (www.eure-tourisme.fr) where Richard the Lionheart's brooding 12th-century castle **Château Gaillard** (☑ 02 32 54 41 93; adult/child €3.20/2.70; ⊘ 10am-1pm & 2-6pm Wed-Mon late Mar-Oct) affords breathtaking panoramas of the majestic River Seine. Beneath it slumbers the pretty village of Les Andelys, 40km south of Rouen. **La Chaîne d'Or** (☑ 02 32 54 00 31; www.hotel-lachainedor.com; 25 rue Grande, Petit Andely; weekday lunch menus €23.50-31, other menus €51-68, mains €26-36; ⊘ noon-1.30pm & 7.30-8.30pm Thu-Tue year-round, closed Tue, Wed & Sun mid-Oct–mid-Apr) is one of the most classy, traditional and romantic French restaurants for kilometres around and the adjoining 12-room hotel is a gem of a rustic hideaway, should you not want to leave.

The **tourist office** (☑ 02 32 54 41 93; www.lesandelys-tourisme.fr; rue Raymond Phélip; ⊘ 10am-noon & 2-6pm Mon-Sat, 10am-1pm Sun, shorter hours Oct-Mar) in Petit Andely has information on walking routes around town. From Rouen take a train to Gaillon-Aubevoye, then hop on bus 290 (€2) for the 30-minute onward journey.

where Joan of Arc was burned at the stake. The church is a lot prettier on the inside, with one entire staggered wall devoted to stained glass, faced by a well-designed semicircle of knee-height pews.

Gros Horloge   TOWER

(rue du Gros Horloge; adult/child €7/3.50; ⊘ 10am-1pm & 2-7pm Tue-Sun Apr-Oct, 2-6pm Nov-Mar) Spanning rue du Gros Horloge, the Great Clock's Renaissance archway has a gilded, one-handed medieval clock face on each side. High above, a Gothic belfry, reached via spiral stairs, affords spectacular views. The excellent audioguide is a great introduction to Rouen's colourful history and is available in eight languages.

Palais de Justice   ARCHITECTURE

(place Maréchal Foch & rue aux Juifs) The ornately Gothic Law Courts, little more than a shell at the end of WWII, have been restored to their early-16th-century glory. On rue Jeanne d'Arc, however, you can still see the very pock-marked façade, which shows the damage sustained during bombing raids in 1944. Around the corner on pedestrianised rue aux Juifs, you can peer in the spire- and gargoyle-adorned courtyard.

★ Abbatiale St-Ouen   CHURCH

(place du Général de Gaulle; ⊘ 10am-noon & 2-6pm Tue-Thu, Sat & Sun) This largely empty 14th-century abbey is a gloriously sublime and quite stunning example of the Rayonnant Gothic style, with a colossal interior dappled with the light from the gorgeous stained glass; it's quite a mind-blowing spectacle. The entrance is through the lovely garden on the south side, facing rue des Faulx.

Panorama XXL   GALLERY

(☑ 02 35 52 95 25; www.panoramxxl.com; quai de Boisguilbert; adult/child €9.50/6.50; ⊘ 10am-7pm Tue-Sun May-Aug, to 6pm Tue-Sun Sep-Apr) In a large, circular column on the waterfront, Panorama XXL is a massive 360-degree exhibition offering in-depth exploring of one astonishing landscape, created with photographs, drawings, digital images and recorded audio. Past years have featured the Great Barrier Reef, Amazonia, Ancient Rome and Rouen in 1431 – often with sunrise and sunset generating different moods, as well as storms. A 15m-high viewing platform in the middle of the room gives a vantage point over the scene.

A joint ticket with Historial Jeanne d'Arc is €15 for adults and €12 for children.

Colline Sainte-Catherine   HILL

(rue Henri Rivière) To size up Rouen, climb this hill rising up next to the Seine. It's a 15-minute walk to the summit, from where Monet once painted a view of the city. Sunrise or sunset casts the city in a fine photographic light, but wear good shoes as the climb can be slippery. As you walk along rue Henri Rivière, look out for the concrete steps to your right straight after the long brown building, which lead to wooden steps up the hill.

🛏 Sleeping

Auberge de Jeunesse Robec   HOSTEL €

(☑ 02 35 08 18 50; www.fuaj.org; 3 rue du Tour; dm €25-35; ⊘ reception 8-11.45am & 5.30-10pm; 🛜) The two- to eight-bed rooms at this modern, 88-bed hostel are comfortable and functional. It's set 2km east of the cathedral off rte de Darnétal; from the city centre, take bus T2 or T3 to the 'Auberge de Jeunesse' stop.

★ La Boulangerie
D&D €

(📱 06 12 94 53 15; www.laboulangerie.fr; 59 rue St-Nicaise; s from €67, d €77-92; 🛜) Tucked away in a quiet side street 1.2km northeast of the cathedral, this adorable B&B sits above a historic bakery with three bright, pleasingly decorated rooms to its name, decorated with artwork and exposed beam ceilings. Charming host Aminata is a gold mine of local information. Parking available nearby for €5; breakfast is included.

Les Cabanes du Clos Masure
COTTAGE €€

(📱 07 70 36 84 21; www.cabanesclosmasure.fr; 873 rue du Bornier; r incl breakfast €140) Sleep in the rustling treetops in wood cabins located some 30 minutes northeast of Rouen at this fun place. It's also a working farm with cows and chickens running about, and a good choice for families with small children (cabins are small but cosy and sleep up to six). Breakfast is put in a basket, which you hoist up.

Hôtel Le Cardinal
HOTEL €€

(📱 02 35 70 24 42; www.cardinal-hotel.fr; 1 place de la Cathédrale; s/d from €78/88; 🛜) Facing the cathedral's famous west façade and with large portraits of namesake cardinals overlooking the small lobby, this 15-room hotel is one of the best midrange deals in central Rouen. All but two of the bright rooms have romantic cathedral views, and eight doubles come with balconies or terraces, including the suites. Buffet breakfast is €10.

Hôtel de Bourgtheroulde
LUXURY HOTEL €€€

(📱 02 35 14 50 50; www.hotelsparouen.com; 15 place de la Pucelle; r €165-370; 🅿🛜🐾🏊) Rouen's finest hostelry (owned for the last five years by the Marriott) serves up a sumptuous mix of early-16th-century architecture – Flamboyant Gothic, to be precise – and sleek, modern luxury. The 78 rooms are spacious and gorgeously appointed. Amenities include a pool (18m), sauna and spa in the basement; the Atrium Bar has live piano music on Saturday evening.

✖ Eating

Hallettes du Vieux Marché
MARKET €

(place du Vieux Marché; ⊙ 7am-7pm Tue-Sat, 7.30am-1pm Sun) This covered market by the Église Jeanne d'Arc has an excellent *fromagerie* (cheese shop) as well as fishmongers and other purveyors of foods.

Dame Cakes
PASTRIES €

(📱 02 35 07 49 31; www.damecakes.fr; 70 rue St-Romain; lunch menus €16-20, tea & cake €9; ⊙ 10.30am-7pm Mon-Sat; 🍴) Walk through the grand and historic, early-20th-century façade and you'll discover a delightfully civilised selection of pastries, cakes and chocolates. From noon to 3pm you can tuck into delicious quiches, gratins and salads in the attached *salon de thé* (tearoom). Lovely.

Citizen
CAFE €

(4 rue de l'Écureuil; mains €7-13, Sat brunch €22; ⊙ 9am-7pm Mon-Fri, from 11am Sat) Citizen is undeniably hip with its black lines, industrial fixtures and groovy tunes playing overhead. More important is the excellent coffee, and the tasty bites on hand (granola, fresh fruit and *fromage blanc* (white cheese) for breakfast; smoked salmon salad for lunch), plus beers from Brooklyn Brewery. The outdoor seating on the plaza is popular when the sun is out.

★ L'Espiguette
BISTRO €

(📱 02 35 71 66 27; 25 place St-Amand; weekday lunch menus €13, mains €17-24; ⊙ noon-10pm Tue-Sat) This charmingly decorated eatery serves excellent bistro classics – think *osso bucco* (veal casserole), fillet of sole, beef tartare – with the day's offerings up on a chalkboard. It's quite popular with locals, so reserve ahead, even at lunchtime (the lunch *menu* is a great deal). Grab a seat at one of the outdoor tables on a warm day.

Bar à Huîtres
SEAFOOD €

(place du Vieux Marché; mains €10-16, oysters per half-dozen/dozen from €10/17; ⊙ 10am-2pm Tue-Sat) Grab a seat at the horseshoe-shaped bar at this casual but polished eatery located inside Rouen's covered market for uberfresh seafood. Specials change daily based on what's fresh, from giant shrimp to dorado and fillet of sole, but each is cooked up to perfection. Don't neglect the restaurant's namesake – the satisfying *huîtres* (oysters) with several different varieties on offer.

Les Nymphéas
GASTRONOMY €€€

(📱 09 74 56 46 19; www.lesnympheas-rouen.fr; 7 rue de la Pie; weekday lunch menus €27, other menus €40-77, mains €33-58; ⊙ 12.15-2pm Tue-Sun, 7-9pm Tue-Sat) With its formal tables arrayed under 16th-century beams, Les Nymphéas has long been a top address for fine dining in Rouen. Young chef Alexandre Dessaux serves up French cuisine that manages to be both traditional and creative. Reservations are a must on weekends. A vegan menu is available for either €30 or €39.

ℹ️ Information

Tourist Office (☎ 02 32 08 32 40; www.
rouentourisme.com; 25 place de la Cathédrale;
🕐 9am-7pm Mon-Sat, 9.30am-12.30pm &
2-6pm Sun May-Sep, 9.30am-12.30pm & 1.30-
6pm Mon-Sat Oct-Apr)

ℹ️ Getting There & Around

BICYCLE

Cy'clic (☎ 08 00 08 78 00; http://cyclic.rouen.
fr; 🕐 5am-1am), Rouen's version of Paris' Vélib',
lets you rent a city bike from 24 locations. Credit-card registration for one/seven days costs
€1/7, plus a deposit of €150. Use is free for the
first 30 minutes; the second/third/fourth and
subsequent half-hours cost €1/2/4 each.

BUS

Rouen is not very well served by buses, although
there's a useful, but very slow, service to Le Havre
(€2, three hours, four to five daily) from the **bus
station** (☎ 02 32 08 19 75; 11 rue des Charrettes).

TRAIN

The train station, **Rouen-Rive-Droite**, is 1.2km
north of the cathedral. In the city centre, train
tickets are available at the **Boutique SNCF** (cnr
rue aux Juifs & rue Eugène Boudin; 🕐 12.30-
7pm Mon, from 10am Tue-Sat). Direct services
include the following:

Caen €28, 1¾ hours, five or six daily

Dieppe €12, 45 minutes, 10 to 16 daily Monday
to Saturday, seven Sunday

> **WORTH A TRIP**
>
> ### MEDIEVAL MEANDER
> ●
>
> With its ghostly white-stone ruins
> glowing against bright green grass
> and dark green trees, the **Abbaye de
> Jumièges** (☎ 02 35 37 24 02; www.
> abbayedejumieges.fr; Jumièges; adult/
> child €6.50/free; 🕐 9.30am-6.30pm mid-
> Apr–mid-Sep, 9.30am-1pm & 2.30-5.30pm
> mid-Sep–mid-Apr) is one of Normandy's
> most evocative medieval relics. The
> church was begun in 1020, and William
> the Conqueror attended its consecration
> in 1067. The abbey declined during the
> Hundred Years War but enjoyed a renais-
> sance under Charles VII, flourishing until
> revolutionaries booted out the monks
> in 1790 and allowed the buildings to be
> mined for construction material.
>
> Jumièges is 28km from Rouen. To get
> there, take the westbound D982 and
> then, from Duclair, the D65.

Le Havre €16, one hour, 16 to 20 daily Monday
to Saturday, 10 Sunday

Paris Gare St-Lazare €10 to €24.10, 1¼ to
1½ hours, 25 daily Monday to Friday, 13 to 18
Saturday and Sunday

Dieppe

POP 30,600

A seaside resort since 1824, Dieppe hasn't
been chic for over a century, but the town's
lack of cuteness and pretension can be refreshing. During WWII, the city was the focal point of the only large-scale Allied raid
on Nazi-occupied France before D-Day, a
catastrophic event commemorated in one of
the town's top museums.

Dieppe was one of France's most important ports in the 16th and 17th centuries,
when ships regularly sailed from here to West
Africa and Brazil. Many of the earliest French
settlers in Canada set sail from Dieppe.

👁️ Sights & Activities

Château-Musée   MUSEUM
(☎ 02 35 06 61 99; www.dieppe.fr; rue de Chastes;
adult/child €4.50/free; 🕐 10am-noon & 2-5pm
Wed-Sun Oct-May, 10am-6pm Wed-Sun Jun-Sep)
Built between the 14th and 18th centuries,
this imposing clifftop castle affords spectacular views of the coast. Inside, the museum explores the city's maritime history as
well as displaying a remarkable collection
of carved ivory. There are also local scenes
painted by artists such as Pissarro and Renoir between 1870 and 1915, when Dieppe
was at the height of its popularity with the
fashionable, holidaying classes.

Cité de la Mer   MUSEUM
(Estran; ☎ 02 35 06 93 20; www.estrancitedelamer.
fr; 37 rue de l'Asile Thomas; adult/child €7.50/4;
🕐 9.30am-6pm Mon-Fri, 9.30am-12.30pm & 1.30-
6pm Sat & Sun) The 'City of the Sea' brings
Dieppe's long maritime and fishing history
to life, with kid-friendly exhibits that include
model ships and a fish-petting *bassin tactile*.
Sea creatures native to the English Channel
swim in a dozen aquariums. Ask for an English-language brochure at the ticket desk.

Dieppe Canadian War Cemetery   CEMETERY
(Cimetière Canadien; www.cwgc.org) Many of the
Canadians who died in the Dieppe Raid of
1942 are buried at this peaceful site framed
by rolling fields. The cemetery is situated
4km towards Rouen; from the centre, take
av des Canadiens (the continuation of av
Gambetta) south and follow the signs.

THE DIEPPE RAID

On 19 August 1942 a mainly Canadian force of over 6000, backed up by 300 ships and 800 aircraft, landed on 20km of beaches between Berneval-sur-Mer and Varengeville-sur-Mer. The objectives: to help the Soviets by drawing Nazi military power away from the Eastern Front and – so the film *Dieppe Uncovered* revealed in 2012 – to 'pinch' one of the Germans' new, four-rotor Enigma encoding machines (the effort failed). The results of the Dieppe Raid were nothing short of catastrophic: 73% of the men who took part ended up killed, wounded or missing-in-action. But lessons learnt at great cost here proved invaluable in planning the Normandy landings two years later.

For insights into the operation, visit Dieppe's **Memorial du 19 Août 1942** (www.dieppe-operationjubilee-19aout1942.fr; place Camille St-Saëns; adult/child €3.50/free; ⊙ 2-6.30pm Wed-Mon late May-Sep, to 6pm Thu, Fri, Sat, Sun & holidays late Mar–mid-May, Fri, Sat & Sun Oct–mid-Nov, closed mid-Nov–Mar).

Beach
BEACH

(🏖) Dieppe's often-windy, beach is a 1.8km-long stretch of smooth pebbles, rather like the beach at Brighton across the channel. The vast lawns were laid out in the 1860s by that seashore-loving imperial duo, Napoléon III and his wife, Eugénie. The area has several play areas for kids.

👉 Tours

Ville de Dieppe
BOATING

(📞 06 09 52 37 38; www.bateau-ville-de-dieppe.com; quai Henri IV; adult €9-18, child €5.50-14; ⊙ weekends & school holidays Apr-Nov & mid-Jul–mid-Aug) Hop aboard one of these boat excursions (35 to 90 minutes) along the dramatic cliffs of the Côte d'Albâtre to get the coastline in perspective. The company also offers sea fishing.

🛏 Sleeping

Villa Les Capucins
B&B €

(📞 02 35 82 16 52; www.villadescapucins.jimdo. com; 11 rue des Capucins; d/tr €80/100) Run by a retired lady, this B&B is a good surprise, not least for the marvellous sense of peacefulness that envelops the property (it's a former convent) – all just a two-minute walk east of the harbour. The four rooms are nicely appointed with antique furniture, framed artwork and homey touches, and the ravishing landscaped garden is perfect for unwinding.

Les Arcades
HOTEL €

(📞 02 35 84 14 12; www.lesarcades.fr; 1-3 arcades de la Bourse; d €75-92; 📶) Perched above a colonnaded arcade from the 1600s, this well-managed and long-established place enjoys a great location by the port. The decor, in tans and browns, is unexciting, but 12 of the 21 rooms have fine port views (the cheaper ones face the road). Breakfast is €10.

Hôtel de la Plage
HOTEL €€

(📞 02 35 84 18 28; www.plagehotel-dieppe.com; 20 bd de Verdun; d €77-119, f €95-130; P 📶) One of several somewhat faded seafront places, this hotel has 40 modern, mod-con rooms of varying shapes and sizes, including family rooms; those at the front have balconies and afford knockout views of the sea. Cheaper rooms face into the courtyard. Parking €8.

🍴 Eating

Dieppe has a decent range of quality seafood restaurants. Quai Henri IV, along the north side of the harbour, is lined with touristy choices.

Le Turbot
FRENCH €

(📞 02 35 82 63 44; 12 quai Calc; mains €18-27, menus €16; ⊙ 12.15-2.30pm & 7.15-9.30pm Tue-Sat) A prime place for lunch or dinner, this family-run Norman bistro decked out in sea paraphernalia serves outstanding seafood. Fresh-off-the-boat dishes, such as monkfish, Dover sole, scallops, and ray in cream sauce and capers, vie with deftly prepared meat dishes. At €17, the prix-fixe *menu* (which also includes a buffet selection of seafood entrées) is good value.

À La Marmite Dieppoise
SEAFOOD €€

(📞 02 35 84 24 26; 8 rue St-Jean; menus €21-44, mains €16-36; ⊙ noon-2pm Tue-Sun, plus 7-9pm Tue-Sat) This Dieppe institution is applauded for its hearty and rich *marmite dieppoise* (cream-sauce stew made with mussels, prawns and four kinds of fish – though you can also order it with lobster), served in a rustic dining room: it's a dish to remember. Other specialities include Normandy-style fish and, from October to May, scallops.

NORMANDY DIEPPE

OFF THE BEATEN TRACK

COASTAL CAPERS

On the plateau above the cliffs, walkers can follow the dramatic long-distance **GR21 Hiking Trail** (www.gr-infos.com), which parallels the coast from Le Tréport all the way to Le Havre. *Le Pays des Hautes Falaises* ('Land of the High Cliffs') is a free map available at tourist offices, detailing 46 coastal and inland walking circuits ranging from 6km to 22km.

Les Voiles d'Or   GASTRONOMY €€€

(📞 02 35 84 16 84; www.lesvoilesdor.fr; 2 chemin des Falaise; mains €35-38, lunch menus €39, dinner menus €56; ⏰ noon-1pm Wed-Sun, plus 8-9pm Wed-Sat) For cutting-edge cuisine concocted from top-quality ingredients, this Michelin-starred place is worth seeking out. Chef Christian Arhan has a soft spot for local seafood but the menu also includes savoury meat dishes. Just next door is Villa Bali-Dieppe (same owners), an excellent B&B featuring three rooms decorated in a Balinese style (doubles €130). It's near Église Notre-Dame de Bon Secours.

ℹ Information

Tourist Office (📞 02 32 14 40 60; www.dieppe tourisme.com; Pont Jehan Ango; ⏰ 9am-1pm & 2-5pm Mon-Sat year-round, plus 9.30am-1pm & 2-5.30pm Sun May-Sep)

ℹ Getting There & Away

BOAT

DFDS Seaways (www.dfdsseaways.co.uk) runs trans-Channel car ferries linking Dieppe's **ferry terminal** (Terminal Transmanche; quai de la Marine), on the eastern side of the port's entrance channel, with the English port of Newhaven.

TRAIN

The train station is just south of the harbour. Services include the following:

Le Havre €28, two to three hours, eight to 11 daily

Paris Gare St-Lazare €32, two to three hours, nine daily Monday to Friday, two to four Saturday and Sunday

Rouen €12, 45 minutes, 10 to 16 daily Monday to Saturday, seven Sunday

To get to Paris and Le Havre, you have to change trains in Rouen.

Côte d'Albâtre

Stretching along the Norman coast for 130km, the vertical, bone-white cliffs of the Côte d'Albâtre (Alabaster Coast) are strikingly reminiscent of the limestone cliffs of Dover, right across the Channel. The dramatic coastline, sculpted over aeons by wind and waves, is dotted with attractive villages, fishing harbours, resort towns, pebbly beaches, eroded rock forms and gorgeous gardens.

St-Valery-en-Caux

POP 4200

This delightful coastal village, 32km west of Dieppe, has a large fishing and pleasure port, a lovely beach and half a dozen hotels. It is also the site of a Franco-British WWII cemetery. In January 1945, a runaway troop train crashed here, killing 89 American soldiers.

🛏 Sleeping & Eating

La Maison des Galets   HOTEL €

(📞 02 35 97 11 22; www.lamaisondesgalets.fr; 6 rue des Remparts, St-Valery-en-Caux; s €50, d €70-80; 📶) The spacious lobby is classic 1950s, with leather couches and lovely sea panoramas. Upstairs, the 14 rooms are pretty and simply furnished, with nautical touches and shiny, all-tile bathrooms, with pricier rooms getting views of the waters. La Maison des Galets is situated 100m west of the casino.

Restaurant du Port   SEAFOOD €€

(📞 02 35 97 08 93; 18 quai d'Amont, St-Valery-en-Caux; menus €27-49, mains €13-38; ⏰ 12.15-2pm Tue-Sun, plus 7.30-9pm Tue, Wed, Fri & Sat) A treat for lovers of fish and seafood (*fruits de mer*), this restaurant down by the port has been doing good business since 1989. À la carte offerings include oysters, fresh crab and turbot marinated in hollandaise sauce. The seafood platters (€43) are a sight to behold.

ℹ Getting There & Away

For freedom of movement, most travellers arrive in St-Valery-en-Caux by car. If you're relying on public transport, bus 61 (€2, four to seven daily, one hour) provides regular service to/from Dieppe.

Fécamp

POP 19,300

Fécamp is a lively fishing port with an attractive harbour, dramatic cliffs and a long monastic history. It is best known for producing Bénédictine, a fiery 'medicinal elixir' concocted here by a Venetian monk in 1510. Lost during the Revolution, the recipe was rediscovered in the 19th century.

The Abbatiale de la Ste-Trinité was a sacred place of pilgrimage during the Middle Ages for drops of Jesus' blood enshrined there.

⊙ Sights & Activities

Abbatiale de la Ste-Trinité ABBEY
(place des Ducs Richard; ⊙ 9am-7pm Apr-Sep, 9am-noon & 2-5pm Oct-Mar) Built from 1175 to 1220 by Richard the Lionheart, towering Abbatiale de la Ste-Trinité was the most important pilgrimage site in Normandy until the construction of Mont St-Michel, thanks to the drops of Jesus' blood that, legend has it, miraculously floated to Fécamp in the trunk of a fig tree, landing on a beach nearby. Across from the abbey are the remains of a fortified **château** built in the 10th and 11th centuries by the earliest dukes of Normandy.

Palais de la Bénédictine LIQUEUR FACTORY
(🖉 02 35 10 26 10; www.benedictinedom.com; 110 rue Alexandre Le Grand; adult/child €12/7, guided tour adult/child €18/10; ⊙ ticket sales 10.30-11.30am & 2.30-4.30pm mid-Dec–mid-Apr, longer hours mid-Apr–mid-Dec, closed early Jan–mid-Feb) This ornate, neo-Renaissance factory, opened in 1900, is where all the Bénédictine liqueur in the world is made. Self-guided tours take you to a mini-museum of 13th- to 19th-century religious artworks and then to the production facilities (visible through glass), where you can admire copper alembics and touch and smell some of the 27 herbs, many from East Asia and Africa, used to make the famous *digestif*. There's a tasting at the end. Guided tours are also available.

Les Pêcheries MUSEUM
(Musée de Fécamp; 🖉 02 35 28 31 99; 3 quai Capitaine Jean Recher; adult/child €7/free; ⊙ 11am-7pm May-Sep, 11am-5.30pm Wed-Mon Oct-Apr) Fécamp's new flagship museum is a terrific addition to town, situated in the middle of the harbour, 300m northwest of the tourist office and showcasing local history, the town's fishing industry, local artists and traditional Norman life. The dramatic, glassed-in observation platform on top offers great views across Fécamp. The audioguide is €2.

Plage de Fécamp BEACH
Fécamp's 800m-long, smooth-pebble breezy beach stretches southward from the narrow channel connecting the port with the open sea. In July and August it's loads of fun, and you can rent catamarans, kayaks, paddle boats and windsurfers.

Cap Fagnet VIEWPOINT
The highest point on the Côte d'Albâtre, Cap Fagnet (110m) towers over Fécamp from the north, offering fantastic views up and down the coast. The site of an important German *blockhaus* and radar station during WWII, today it's topped by a chapel and there are five wind turbines a short walk to the east (there's a plan to erect 83 more turbines offshore, due to generate power from 2021). Cap Fagnet is a 1.5km walk from the centre.

🛌 Sleeping

Camping de Renéville CAMPGROUND €
(🖉 02 35 28 20 97; www.campingderenéville.com; chemin de Nesmond; tent & 2 adults from €14; ⊙ Apr-Oct) Dramatically situated on the western cliffs overlooking the beach, this campground also rents out two- and six-person chalets (from €280 per week). In July and August the tent rate goes up to €17.

Hôtel Vent d'Ouest HOTEL €
(🖉 02 35 28 04 04; www.hotelventdouest.tm.fr; 3 rue Gambetta; d €57-65, q €95) Small and welcoming, with a smart breakfast room and 15 pleasant rooms decorated in yellow and blue. Call ahead if you'll be checking in after 8pm. The hotel is situated 200m east (up the hill) from the port, next to Église St-Étienne. Buffet breakfast is €8.

Le Grand Pavois HOTEL €€
(🖉 02 35 10 01 01; www.hotel-grand-pavois.com; 15 quai de la Vicomté; r/ste from €103/149; P 🖥) This reliable three-star hotel has a fine location overlooking the marina, and it's an easy stroll to the beach. The welcome is warm, and the spacious rooms have attractive furnishings and comfortable mattresses, though the big windows – and the view! – are undoubtedly the best features.

🍴 Eating

Tourist-oriented crêperies and restaurants, many specialising in fish and mussels, line the south side of the port, along quai de la Vicomté and nearby parts of quai Bérigny.

Le Daniel's FRENCH €€
(🖉 02 76 39 95 68; 5 place Nicolas Selle; lunch menus €15-17, dinner menus €24-40; ⊙ noon-2pm & 7-9pm Tue-Sat) Tucked down a narrow lane just a short stroll from the marina, this delightful spot serves up market-fresh fare that highlights delicacies from the region including Valmont trout, creamy rich oysters and braised veal. The service is warm, and the plates are beautifully presented – great value. Just be sure to call ahead for a table as it's not big.

DON'T MISS

VEULES-LES-ROSES

With its wonderfully relaxing atmosphere and lovely setting, Veules-les-Roses is one of the Côte d'Albâtre's gems. The pebbly beach is never too crowded and the flowery village is supremely picturesque, with elegant mansions and an imposing church. The small river running through the village adds to the bucolic appeal – it also makes it into the record books as France's shortest river flowing into the sea. Look out for the *cressonnières* (ponds where watercress is grown). You can find Veules-les-Roses 8km east of St-Valery-en-Caux.

Most travellers arrive in Veules-les-Roses by car. If using public transport, take a train to Dieppe and transfer to bus 61 operated by VTNI (www.vtni76.fr).

La Marée   SEAFOOD €€

(☑02 35 29 39 15; www.restaurant-maree-fecamp. fr; 77 quai Bérigny; mains €17-27, menus €19-29.50; ☺noon-2pm Tue-Sun, plus 7.30-8.30pm or later Tue, Wed, Fri & Sat; ☼) Locals claim that you won't find better seafood anywhere in town here: fish and seafood – that's all that matters at quayside La Marée, Fécamp's premier address for maritime dining, with outside terrace.

❶ Information

Tourist Office (☑02 35 28 51 01; www.fe-camptourisme.com; quai Sadi Carnot; ☺9am-6pm Mon-Fri, from 10am Sat & Sun; ☼) Has useful English-language brochures and maps and free luggage lockers. Situated at the eastern end of the pleasure port, across the parking lot from the train station.

❶ Getting There & Around

BICYCLE

The tourist office rents bicycles for €9/14/40 per day/weekend/week.

BUS

Scenic bus 24, operated by **Keolis** (☑02 35 28 19 88; www.keolis-seine-maritime.com), goes to Le Havre's train station (€2, 1½ hours, seven or more daily) via Étretat and various small villages. The tourist office has schedules.

TRAIN

Fécamp's train station is a block east of the eastern end of the pleasure port. Destinations include the following:

Le Havre €8, one to 1½ hours, eight to 15 daily
Paris Gare St-Lazare from €20, 2¾ hours, six to nine daily
Rouen from €11, 1½ hours, 10 to 13 daily

You usually have to change trains at Bréauté-Beuzeville, connected to Fécamp by an 18km rail spur.

Étretat

POP 1500

The small and delightful village of Étretat's dramatic coastal scenery – it's framed by twin cliffs – made it a favourite of painters such as Camille Corot, Eugène Boudin, Gustave Courbet and Claude Monet. With the vogue for sea air at the end of the 19th century, fashionable Parisians came and built extravagant villas.

Étretat has never gone out of style and still swells with visitors every weekend, who sit on the shingle beach, wander up and down the shoreline or clamber up to the fantastic vantage points above the chalk cliffs.

◉ Sights & Activities

The pebbly **beach** is separated from the town centre by a dyke. To the left as you face the sea, you can see the **Falaise d'Aval**, renowned for its beautiful arch – and the adjacent **Aiguille**, a needle of rock poking high up from the waves.

To the right as you face the sea towers the **Falaise d'Amont**, atop which a memorial marks the spot where two aviators were last seen before attempting to cross the Atlantic in 1927.

The tourist office has a map of trails around town and can also provide details on sail-powered cruises aboard a **two-masted schooner** (March to October).

⌂ Sleeping

★**Detective Hôtel**   HOTEL €

(☑02 35 27 01 34; www.detectivehotel.com; 6 av Georges V; d €59-129; ☼) Run by a former detective with an impressive moustache, this establishment was inspired by Sherlock Holmes and Hercule Poirot. Each of the 14 charming rooms bears the name of a fictional gumshoe whose time and place have inspired the decor. In some, the first mystery you'll face is how to find the secret door to the hidden bathroom. Utterly original.

❶ Information

Tourist Office (☑02 35 27 05 21; www.etretat. net; place Maurice Guillard; ☺9.30am-6.30pm mid-Jun–mid Sep, 10am-noon & 2-6pm Mon-Sat mid-Sep–mid-Jun, Sun during school holidays)

ⓘ Getting There & Away

Keolis (p248) Scenic bus 24 (seven or more daily) goes to Le Havre's train station (€2, one hour) and to Fécamp (€2, 30 minutes).

Le Havre

POP 176,000

A Unesco World Heritage Site since 2005 and a regular port of call for cruise ships, Le Havre is a love letter to modernism, evoking, more than any other French city, France's postwar energy and optimism. All but obliterated in September 1944 by Allied bombing raids that killed 3000 civilians, the centre was completely rebuilt by the Belgian architect Auguste Perret – mentor to Le Corbusier – whose bright, airy modernist vision remains, miraculously, largely intact.

Attractions include a museum full of captivating impressionist paintings, a soaring modernist church with a mesmerising stained-glass tower, hilltop gardens with views over the city and a medieval church that rose again from the ashes of war.

◉ Sights

★ **Musée Malraux**   GALLERY
(MuMa; ☑ 02 35 19 62 62; www.muma-lehavre.fr/en; 2 bd Clemenceau; adult/under 26yr €7/free; ☉11am-6pm Tue-Fri, to 7pm Sat & Sun) Near the waterfront, this luminous and tranquil space houses a fabulous collection of vivid impressionist works – the finest in France outside Paris – by masters such as Monet (who grew up in Le Havre), Pissarro, Renoir and Sisley. You'll also find works by the Fauvist painter Raoul Dufy, born in Le Havre, and paintings by Eugène Boudin, a mentor of Monet and another Le Havre native.

Église St-Joseph   CHURCH
(bd François 1er; ☉10am-6pm) Perret's masterful, 107m-high Église St-Joseph, visible from all over town, was built using bare concrete from 1951 to 1959. Some 13,000 panels of coloured glass make the soaring, sombre interior particularly striking when it's sunny. Stained-glass artist Marguerite Huré created a cohesive masterpiece in her collaboration with Perret, and her use of shading and colour was thoughtfully conceived, evoking different moods depending on where the sun is in the sky – and the ensuing colours created by the illumination.

Jardins Suspendus   GARDENS
(rue du Fort; gardens free, greenhouses €2; ☉10.30am-8pm Apr-Sep, to 5pm Oct-Mar) The Jardins Suspendus (Hanging Gardens) is an old hilltop fortress transformed into a beautiful set of gardens, whose greenhouses and outdoor spaces feature exquisite flowers, trees and grasses from five different continents, as fine views range over the harbour. It's a 30-minute uphill walk from the centre, or you can catch bus 1 along bd François 1er near the beach.

Le Volcan   CULTURAL CENTRE
(Espace Oscar Niemeyer; ☑ 02 35 19 10 10; www.levolcan.com; place du Général de Gaulle; ☉ library 10am-7pm) Le Havre's most conspicuous landmark, designed by Brazilian architect Oscar Niemeyer and opened in 1982, is also the city's premier cultural venue. One look and you'll understand how it got its name, which means 'the volcano' – it's quite a sight, especially framed against a blue sky. Extensive renovations saw the complex reopen with a new concert hall and an ultramodern *mediathèque* (multimedia library). It's situated at the western end of the Bassin du Commerce, the city centre's former port.

Appartement Témoin   ARCHITECTURE
(☑ 02 35 22 31 22; 181 rue de Paris; adult/child €5/free; ☉ tours 3.30pm & 4.30pm Wed & Fri, 2.30pm, 3.30pm & 4.30pm Sat, 10.30am, 11.30am, 2.30pm, 3.30pm & 4.30pm Sun) Furnished in impeccable early-1950s style, this lovingly furnished bourgeois apartment can be visited on a one-hour guided tour that starts at 181 rue de Paris (Maison du Patrimoine). The apartment is a remarkable time capsule of the postwar boom days that Le Havre experienced, complete with clothes, newspapers, furniture and appliances exactly as one would have seen entering a downtown apartment in the decade of the city's reconstruction. Reservations are recommended as there are 19 places per visit.

Cathédrale Notre-Dame   CHURCH
When Le Havre's concrete expanses and straight lines overpower you, stop by this lovely Baroque church, which somehow eluded the intense bombing efforts of the Royal Air Force. The cathedral originally dates to the early 16th century and is the oldest building in the centre of town; the interior is a repository of calm.

🛏 Sleeping

Hôtel le Petit Vatel HOTEL €
(☎ 02 35 41 72 07; www.lepetitvatel.com; 86 rue
Louis Brindeau; s/d €60/70; @🛜) This central spot earns high marks for comfortable
rooms, a good location and very kind staff.
Rooms receive decent natural light, the
mattresses are fresh, and the tiled bathrooms are spick and span. There's a small,
sunny lounge on the ground floor. Breakfast is €9.

Hôtel Oscar HOTEL €
(☎ 02 35 42 39 77; www.hotel-oscar.fr; 106 rue
Voltaire; s €49-79, d €50-109; 🛜) A treat for
architecture aficionados, this bright and
very central hotel brings Auguste Perret's
mid-20th-century legacy alive. The rooms
are authentic retro, with hardwood floors
and large windows, as is the tiny 1950s
lounge. Reception closes at 8.30pm. It's
situated across the street from Le Volcan,
with some rooms looking straight onto it.
Breakfast is €9.

★**Hôtel Vent d'Ouest** BOUTIQUE HOTEL €€
(☎ 02 35 42 50 69; www.ventdouest.fr; 4 rue
de Caligny; d €100-150, ste €170, apt €185; 🛜)
This terrific and very stylish four-star establishment is all nautical downstairs and
has cheerfully painted rooms upstairs arranged with sisal flooring and attractive
furnishings; ask for one with a balcony.
There are lovely common areas where you
can while away the hours with a book when
the weather inevitably sours, including an
enticing cafe-bar with leather armchairs.

OFF THE BEATEN TRACK

NATURE WATCH

Inland from Utah Beach, to the south
and southwest, is the 1480-sq-km
**Parc Naturel Régional des Marais
du Cotentin et du Bessin** (www.
parc-cotentin-bessin.fr) , a vast expanse of
waterways, marshes, moors and hedgerows. The Maison du Parc (visitor centre)
is in St-Côme-du-Mont, 50km west of
Bayeux just off the N13.

For details on hiking and cycling in
the park and elsewhere in the Manche
département, visit www.manche-
tourism.com and click on 'Walks, Rambles & Rides' under the 'Explore' tab.

✖ Eating

Halles Centrales MARKET €
(rue Voltaire; ⊗8.30am-7.30pm Mon-Sat, 9am-1pm
Sun) The food stalls at Le Havre's main market include a patisserie, a *fromagerie* and
many tempting fruit stands; there's also a
small supermarket here. You can find it a
block west of Le Volcan.

★**La Taverne Paillette** BRASSERIE €€
(☎02 35 41 31 50; www.taverne-paillette.com; 22 rue
Georges Braque; lunch menus €15.50-31.20, mains
€16-26; ⊗noon-midnight daily) Solid brasserie
food is served up at this Le Havre institution
whose origins, in a former incarnation, go
back to the late 16th century. Think bowls
overflowing with mussels, generous salads,
gargantuan seafood platters and, in the Alsatian tradition, eight types of *choucroute* (sauerkraut). Diners leave contentedly well-fed
and many are here for its famous beer too.

Les Pieds Dans L'Eau SEAFOOD €€
(☎02 35 47 97 45; promenade de la Plage; mains
€13-20; ⊗noon-10pm) Amid the many simple
restaurants set on the beach promenade, this
place always draws a crowd for its reasonably priced seafood plates and ample prix-fixe
menus. The mussels (served seven different
ways) are a highlight, as are the oysters and
grilled *dorade* (gilt-head bream).

La Petite Auberge FRENCH €€€
(☎02 35 46 27 32; www.lapetiteauberge-lehavre.fr;
32 rue de Ste-Adresse; mains €27-45, menus €25-
43; ⊗noon-9.30pm Tue & Thu-Sat, 7.30-9.30pm
Wed, noon-4pm Sun) This absolute gem of a
place has a low-beamed dining room that
whispers of romance, while the dishes rarely
fail to satisfy. The à la carte menu is limited (typically just two seafood and two meat
dishes), but serves as a showcase for seasonal ingredients. There's a kids menu for €11.

ℹ Information

Maison du Patrimoine (☎02 35 22 31 22; 181
rue de Paris; ⊗2-6pm Mon-Sat, 10am-1pm
& 2-6pm Sun) The tourist office's city centre
annexe has an exhibition on Perret's postwar
reconstruction of the city.

Tourist Office (☎02 32 74 04 04; www.
lehavretourisme.com; 186 bd Clemenceau;
⊗2-6pm Mon, 10am-12.30pm & 2-6pm Tue-Sat
Nov-Mar, 9.30am-1pm & 2-7pm Apr-Nov) Has a
map in English for a two-hour walking tour of Le
Havre's architectural highlights and details on
cultural events. Situated at the western edge of
the city centre, one block south of the La Plage
tram terminus.

ℹ Getting There & Away

BOAT
Le Havre's car ferry terminal, situated 1km southeast of Le Volcan, is linked with the English port of Portsmouth via **Brittany Ferries** (www.brittany-ferries.co.uk). Ferries depart daily from late March to early November.

BUS
The bus station is next to the train station.
Bus Verts (☑09 70 83 00 14; www.busverts.fr) Heading south, bus 20 (four to six daily) goes to Honfleur (€4.90, 30 minutes) and Deauville and Trouville (€4.90, one hour).
Keolis (p248) For the Côte d'Albâtre, take scenic bus 24 (seven or more daily) to Étretat (€2, one hour) and Fécamp (€2, 1½ hours).

TRAIN
The train station, Gare du Havre, is 1.5km east of Le Volcan, at the eastern end of bd de Strasbourg. The tram stop out front is called 'Gares'. Destinations include the following:
Fécamp €8, 45 to 75 minutes, seven to 11 daily
Paris Gare St-Lazare €30, 2¼ hours, 15 daily Monday to Friday, seven to nine Saturday and Sunday
Rouen €16, one hour, 16 to 20 daily Monday to Saturday, 10 Sunday

CALVADOS

The Calvados *département* (www.calvados-tourisme.com) stretches from Honfleur in the east to Isigny-sur-Mer in the west and includes Caen, Bayeux and the D-Day beaches. The area is famed for its rich pastures and farm products, including butter, cheese, cider and an eponymous apple brandy.

The origins of the name 'Calvados' are opaque. One (tenuous) theory points to a (possibly mythical) ship of the Spanish Armada sent by King Philip II of Spain to attack England called *San El Salvador,* which was shipwrecked off the Normandy coast. Another more convincing argument attests the name derives from a pair of rocks off the Normandy coast known as *calva dorsa.*

Bayeux
POP 13,900
Two cross-Channel invasions, almost 900 years apart, gave Bayeux a front-row seat at defining moments in Western history. The dramatic story of the Norman invasion of England in 1066 is told in 58 vivid scenes by the world-famous and quite astonishing Bayeux Tapestry, embroidered just a few years after William the Bastard, Duke of Normandy, became William the Conqueror, King of England.

On 6 June 1944, 160,000 Allied troops, supported by almost 7000 naval vessels, stormed ashore along the coast just north of town. Bayeux was the first French town to be liberated (on the morning of 7 June 1944) and is one of the few places in Calvados to have survived WWII practically unscathed.

A very attractive and historic town, Bayeux makes an ideal base for exploring the D-Day beaches and is crammed with 13th- to 18th-century buildings plus a fine Gothic cathedral.

◉ Sights

A 'triple ticket' good for all three of Bayeux' outstanding municipal museums costs €15/13.50 for an adult/child (€12/10 for two museums).

★ Bayeux Tapestry   MUSEUM
(☑02 31 51 25 50; www.bayeuxmuseum.com; 15bis rue de Nesmond; adult/child incl audioguide €9.50/5; ⊙9.30am-12.30pm & 2-5.30pm Mon-Sat, 10am-1pm & 2-5.30pm Sun Feb, Mar, Nov & Dec, to 6pm Apr-Jun, Sep & Oct, 9am-7pm Mon-Sat, 9am-1pm & 2-6pm Sun Jul & Aug, closed Jan) The world's most celebrated embroidery depicts the conquest of England by William the Conqueror in 1066 from an unashamedly Norman perspective. Commissioned by Bishop Odo of Bayeux, William's half-brother, for the opening of Bayeux' cathedral in 1077, the well-preserved cartoon strip tells the dramatic, bloody tale with verve and vividness as well as some astonishing artistry. Particularly incredible are its length – nearly 70m long – and fine attention to detail.

★ Musée d'Art et
d'Histoire Baron Gérard   MUSEUM
(MAHB; ☑02 31 92 14 21; www.bayeuxmuseum.com; 37 rue du Bienvenu; adult/child €7.50/5; ⊙9.30am-6.30pm May-Sep, 10am-12.30pm & 2-6pm Oct-Apr, closed 3 weeks in Jan) Make sure you drop by this museum – one of France's most gorgeously presented provincial museums – where exhibitions cover everything from Gallo-Roman archaeology through medieval art to paintings from the Renaissance and on to the 20th century, including a fine work by Gustave Caillebotte. Other highlights include impossibly

Bayeux

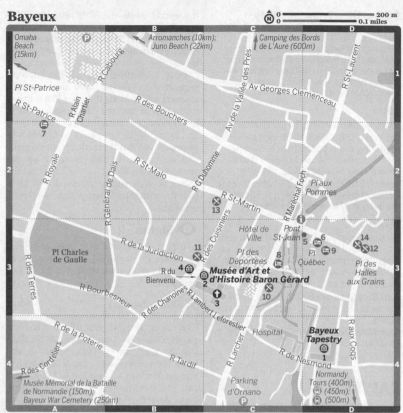

Bayeux

fine local lace and Bayeux-made porcelain. The museum is housed in the former bishop's palace.

A joint ticket for admission to the Musée d'Art et d'Histoire Baron Gérard and either the Bayeux Tapestry or the Musée Mémorial de la Bataille de Normandie is €12 (or €15 for all three).

Cathédrale Notre Dame   CATHEDRAL
(rue du Bienvenu; ⊙ 8.30am-7pm) Most of Bayeux' spectacular Norman Gothic cathedral dates from the 13th century, though the crypt (take the stairs on the north side of the choir), the arches of the nave and the lower parts of the entrance towers are 11th-century Romanesque. The central tower was added in the 15th century; the copper dome dates from the 1860s. The crypt, with its colourful frescoes, is a highlight. Several plaques and stained-glass windows commemorate American and British sacrifices during the world wars.

Musée Mémorial de la Bataille de Normandie
MUSEUM

(Battle of Normandy Memorial Museum; ☑ 02 31 51 46 90; www.bayeuxmuseum.com; bd Fabien Ware; adult/child €7.50/5; ⊙ 9.30am-6.30pm May-Sep, 10am-12.30pm & 2-6pm Oct-Apr, closed 3 weeks in Jan) Using well-chosen photos, personal accounts, dioramas and wartime objects, this first-rate museum offers an excellent introduction to the Battle of Normandy. The 25-minute film is screened in both French and English. A selection of hardware – tanks and artillery pieces – is displayed outside.

Bayeux War Cemetery
CEMETERY

(bd Fabien Ware) The largest of the 18 Commonwealth military cemeteries in Normandy, this peaceful cemetery contains 4848 graves of soldiers from the UK and 10 other countries, including a few from Germany. Across the road is a memorial to 1807 Commonwealth soldiers whose remains were never found; the Latin inscription across the top reads: 'We, once conquered by William, have now liberated the Conqueror's native land'.

Conservatoire de la Dentelle
MUSEUM

(Lace Conservatory; ☑ 02 31 92 73 80; http://dentelle debayeux.free.fr; 6 rue du Bienvenu; ⊙ 9.30am-12.30pm & 2.30-6pm Mon-Sat, to 5pm Mon & Thu) FREE Lacemaking (dentellerie), brought to Bayeux by nuns in 1678, once employed 5000 people. The industry is sadly long gone, but at the Conservatoire you can watch some of France's most celebrated lacemakers create intricate designs using dozens of bobbins and hundreds of pins; a small shop also sells some of their delicate creations. The half-timbered building housing the workshop, decorated with carved wooden figures, dates from the 1400s.

🛏 Sleeping

Camping des Bords de L'Aure
CAMPGROUND €

(☑ 02 31 92 08 43; www.camping-bayeux.fr; bd d'Eindhoven; campsite from €13) This three-star municipal campground in the north of Bayeux has 140 pitches pleasantly located near the River Aure. There's free access for campers to the municipal swimming pool, a short walk to the south. You can also rent out mobile homes (from €75 per night). Click on the website for a map of the campground.

Hôtel Reine Mathilde
HOTEL €

(☑ 02 31 92 08 13; www.hotel-bayeux-reinemathil de.fr; 23 rue Larcher; d/ste from €50/90, studio from €95; 🛜) Occupying a superbly central location, this friendly hotel has comfortable accommodation, with an assortment of sleek and spacious rooms in the annexe, a converted barn by the Aure River. Rooms, named after historic figures, are attractively designed with beamed ceilings, and elegant lines, excellent lighting and modern bathrooms; studios come with a small kitchenette. A decent restaurant is also on-site.

Hotel Churchill
HOTEL €€

(☑ 02 31 21 31 80; www.hotel-churchill.fr; 14-16 rue St-Jean; d €125-157, ste €179; 🛜) Run by the affable ex–French first division footballer Eric Pean, this terrific 46-room old town place by the cathedral has very decent accommodation with new carpets and 14 spotless modern rooms in the new extension. The hotel arranges daily morning shuttle bus trips to Mont St-Michel (€65, including admission).

Hôtel d'Argouges
HOTEL €€

(☑ 02 31 92 88 86; www.hotel-dargouges.com; 21 rue St-Patrice; s/d €120/141, ste €210-295; ⊙ closed Dec & Jan; P 🛜) Occupying a very stately 18th-century residence with a lush little garden, this graceful and serene hotel has 28 comfortable rooms with exposed beams, thick walls and Louis XVI–style furniture, plus very welcoming and professional service, with excellent English spoken. The breakfast room, hardly changed since 1734, still has its original wood panels and parquet floors.

Villa Lara
BOUTIQUE HOTEL €€€

(☑ 02 31 92 00 55; www.hotel-villalara.com; 6 place du Québec; d €200-420, ste €380-570; P ❄ 🛜) This modern and very elegant 28-room hotel concocts an appealing blend of minimalist colour schemes, top-quality fabrics and decor juxtaposing 18th- and 21st-century tastes. Amenities include a bar, a gym and a comfortable library-lounge with a fireplace. Most rooms have cathedral views and are well-equipped and decorated most tastefully, with attractive bathrooms.

Château de la Ferrière
HISTORIC HOTEL €€€

(☑ 02 31 21 13 39; www.chateaudelaferriere.com; Vaux-sur-Aure; d incl breakfast from €220; P 🛜) Located between Bayeux and Longues-sur-Mer, this splendid 18th-century château – set in 13.4 hectares of lawn and woodland – is a handsome and elegant base for exploring the D-Day beaches and nearby sights. The huge rooms are littered with antique furniture and long curtains that reach either wooden or parquet floors, with lovely views extending over the gardens.

✕ Eating

★ La Reine Mathilde
PASTRIES €

(☑ 02 31 92 00 59; 47 rue St-Martin; cakes from €2.50; ⊙ 9am-7.30pm Tue-Sun) With a vast expanse of glass in its windows and set with white-painted cast-iron chairs, this sumptuously decorated patisserie and *salon de thé* (tearoom), ideal for a sweet breakfast or a relaxing cup of afternoon tea, hasn't changed much since it was built in 1898. Size up the sweet offerings on display and tuck in.

Chez Paulette
INTERNATIONAL €

(☑ 09 80 32 03 94; 44 rue des Cuisiniers; menus €10.50-15.50; ⊙ noon-6pm Tue & Wed, to 9.30pm Thu-Sat) This colourful cafe-restaurant throwback to the '60's is an enticing – and lovingly curated – jumble of Beatles-era wallpaper, old phones, crockery, polka-dot tablecloths, furniture, broken TVs and wall clocks. It's a fun addition to Bayeux and the food (a bit of a jumble as well, from fish and chips to soup, quiche and bagel sandwiches) is tops too. A small boutique conjoins it.

Au Ptit Bistrot
MODERN FRENCH €€

(☑ 02 31 92 30 08; 31 rue Larcher; lunch menus €17-20, dinner menus €29-35, mains €18-22; ⊙ noon-2pm & 7-9pm Tue-Sat) Near the cathedral, this friendly, welcoming eatery whips up creative, beautifully prepared dishes that highlight the Norman bounty without pretension. Recent hits include braised beef cheek with red wine, polenta, grapefruit tapenade and vegetables or roasted pigeon with mushrooms and mashed parsnip. The kids menu is €11. Reservations essential.

L'Alchimie
MODERN FRENCH €€

(☑ 02 14 08 03 97; 49 rue St-Jean; lunch menus €13-18; ⊙ noon-1.30pm & 7-10pm Mon- Wed, Fri & Sat, 7-10pm Thu) On a street lined with restaurants, L'Alchimie has a simple but elegant design that takes nothing from the beautifully presented dishes. Choose from the day's specials listed on a chalkboard menu, which might include hits such as *brandade de morue* (baked codfish pie) or *pastilla de poulet au gingembre et cumin* (chicken pastilla with ginger and cumin). Book ahead.

La Rapière
FRENCH €€

(☑ 02 31 21 05 45; www.larapiere.net; 53 rue St-Jean; lunch menus €16-21, dinner menus €36-49, mains €20-28; ⊙ noon-1.30pm Tue & Thu-Sat, plus 7-8.15pm Tue-Sat, closed mid-Dec–early Feb) Housed in a late-1400s mansion composed of stone walls and big wooden beams, this atmospheric restaurant specialises in Normandy staples such as terrines, duck and veal with Camembert. The various fixed-price *menus* assure a splendid meal on any budget.

ℹ Information

Tourist Office (☑ 02 31 51 28 28; www.bayeux-bessin-tourisme.com; Pont St-Jean; ⊙ 9am-7pm Mon-Sat, 10am-1pm & 2-6pm Sun Jul & Aug, shorter hours rest of year)

ℹ Getting There & Around

BICYCLE

Vélos (☑ 02 31 92 89 16; www.velosbayeux.com; 5 rue Larcher; adult bike per half-/full day from €7.50/10, child bike per half-/full day from €7.50/5; ⊙ 8am-8.30pm) Year-round bike rental from a fruit and veggie store a few paces from the tourist office.

BUS

Bus Verts (p251) Buses 70 and 74 (bus 75 in July and August) link Bayeux' train station and place St-Patrice with many of the villages, memorials and museums along Omaha, Gold and Juno D-Day beaches.

TRAIN

Bayeux' train station is 1km southeast of the cathedral. Direct services include the following:

Caen €6, 15 to 20 minutes, at least hourly

Cherbourg €20, one hour, 15 daily Monday to Friday, eight to 10 daily Saturday and Sunday

Pontorson (Mont St-Michel) €24, 1¾ hours, three daily

To get to Deauville, change at Lisieux. For Paris Gare St-Lazare and Rouen, you may have to change at Caen.

DON'T MISS

GET UP CLOSE

The cable-stayed **Pont de Normandie** (car one-way €5.40) bridge opened in 1995, stretching in a soaring 2km arch over the Seine between Le Havre and Honfleur. It's a typically French affair, as much sophisticated architecture as engineering, with two huge inverted-V-shaped columns holding aloft a delicate net of cables. Crossing it is quite a thrill – and the views of the Seine are magnificent. In each direction there's a narrow footpath and a bike lane.

D-Day Beaches

Code-named 'Operation Overlord', the D-Day landings were the largest seaborne invasion in history. Early on the morning of 6 June 1944, swarms of landing craft – part of an armada of more than 6000 ships and boats – hit the beaches of northern Normandy and tens of thousands of Allied soldiers began pouring onto French soil.

The majority of the 135,000 Allied troops who arrived in France that day stormed ashore along 80km of beaches north of Bayeux, code-named (from west to east) Utah, Omaha, Gold, Juno and Sword. The landings on D-Day – known as 'Jour J' in French – were followed by the 76-day Battle of Normandy, during which the Allies suffered 210,000 casualties, including 37,000 troops killed. German casualties are believed to

have been around 200,000; another 200,000 German soldiers were taken prisoner. About 14,000 French civilians also died.

Caen's Le Mémorial (p262) and Bayeux' Musée Mémorial (p253) provide comprehensive overviews of the events of D-Day. Dozens of villages near the landing beaches have museums focusing on local events; all but a few are privately owned.

You can join a tour, but if you've got wheels, just follow the D514 along the D-Day coast or several signposted circuits around the battle sites – look for signs reading 'D-Day–Le Choc' in the American sectors and 'Overlord-L'Assaut' in the British and Canadian sectors. The area is also sometimes called the Côte de Nacre (Mother-of-Pearl Coast). A free booklet called *The D-Day Landings and the Battle of Normandy,* available from tourist offices, has details on the eight major visitors' routes.

THE BATTLE OF NORMANDY

In early 1944, an Allied invasion of continental Europe seemed inevitable. Hitler's disastrous campaign on the Russian front and the Luftwaffe's inability to control the skies over Europe had left Germany vulnerable. Both sides knew a landing was coming – the only questions were where and, of course, when.

Several sites were considered by Allied command. After long deliberation, it was decided that the beaches along Normandy's northern coast – rather than the even more heavily fortified coastline further north around Calais, where Hitler was expecting an attack – would serve as a surprise spearhead into occupied Europe.

Code-named 'Operation Overlord', the invasion began on the night of 5 June 1944 when three paratroop divisions were dropped behind enemy lines. At about 6.30am on the morning of 6 June, six amphibious divisions stormed ashore at five beaches, backed up by an unimaginable 6000 sea craft and 13,000 aeroplanes. The initial landing force involved some 45,000 troops; 15 more divisions were to follow once successful beachheads had been established.

The narrow Straits of Dover had seemed the most likely invasion spot to the Germans, who'd set about heavily reinforcing the area around Calais and the other Channel ports. Allied intelligence went to extraordinary lengths to encourage the German belief that the invasion would be launched north of Normandy: double agents, leaked documents and fake radio traffic, buttressed by phony airfields and an entirely fictitious American army group, supposedly stationed in southeast England, all suggested the invasion would centre on the Pas de Calais.

Because of the tides and unpredictable weather patterns, Allied planners had only a few dates available each month in which to launch the invasion. On 5 June, the date chosen, the worst storm in 20 years set in, delaying the operation. The weather had improved only marginally the next day, but General Dwight D Eisenhower, Allied commander-in-chief, gave the go-ahead: 6 June would be D-Day.

In the hours leading up to D-Day, French Resistance units set about disrupting German communications. Just after midnight on 6 June, the first Allied troops were on French soil. British commandos and glider units captured key bridges and destroyed German gun emplacements, and the American 82nd and 101st Airborne Divisions landed west of the invasion site. Although the paratroops' tactical victories were few, they caused confusion in German ranks and, because of their relatively small numbers, the German high command was convinced that the real invasion had not yet begun.

The Battle of Normandy

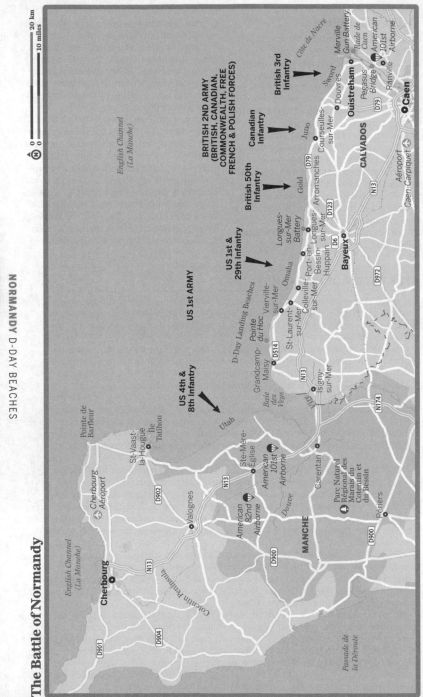

NORMANDY D-DAY BEACHES

The Battle of Normandy

English Channel (La Manche)

Cherbourg
Pointe de Barfleur
Cherbourg Aéroport
St-Vaast-la-Hougue
Île Tatihou

Coutin Peninsula

D901
D904
N13
D902

Valognes
Ste-Mère-Église
American 101st Airborne
American 82nd Airborne

MANCHE

Carentan
Douve
D900

Parc Naturel Régional des Marais du Cotentin et du Bessin

Périers

D900

Passade de la Déroute

US 4th & 8th Infantry

Utah

Baie des Veys

Grandcamp-Maisy

D-Day Landing Beaches

Pointe du Hoc

D514

N13

Isigny-sur-Mer

Vierville-sur-Mer
St-Laurent-sur-Mer
Omaha
Colleville-sur-Mer
Port-en-Bessin
Longues-sur-Mer
Longues-sur-Mer Battery
Huppain

N174

US 1st ARMY

US 1st & 29th Infantry

Bayeux

D6
D123
D972

Arromanches
Gold

British 50th Infantry

BRITISH 2ND ARMY
(BRITISH, CANADIAN, COMMONWEALTH, FREE FRENCH & POLISH FORCES)

Courseulles-sur-Mer
Juno

Canadian Infantry

D79

CALVADOS

Aéroport Caen-Carpiquet

N13

Côte de Nacre

Sword
Douvres

British 3rd Infantry

Ouistreham
Merville Gun Battery
Rade de Caen
American 101st Airborne
Pegasus Bridge
Ranville

D79
D79

Caen

English Channel (La Manche)

20 km
10 miles

Maps of the D-Day beaches are available at *tabacs* (tobacconists), newsagents and bookshops in Bayeux and elsewhere. When visiting the D-Day sites, do not leave valuables in your car.

☞ Tours

Accessible and handy introductions to the beaches, guided minibus tours – lots of local companies offer them – can be an excellent way to get a sense of the D-Day beaches and their place in history. The Bayeux tourist office (p254) can handle reservations or book online for Caen.

Tours by Le Mémorial – Un Musée pour la Paix BUS
(☑ 02 31 06 06 45; www.memorial-caen.fr; tours with/without lunch €131/95; ☺ tours 1pm, closed 3 weeks in Jan) Excellent year-round minibus tours (four to five hours) depart at 1pm, to take in Pointe du Hoc, Omaha Beach, the American cemetery and the artificial British harbour at Arromanches. There are cheaper tours in full-size buses from June to August. Rates include entry to Le Mémorial – Un Musée pour la Paix. There's a choice of two tours, one including lunch.

Normandy Sightseeing Tours TOURS
(☑ 02 31 51 70 52; www.normandy-sightseeing-tours.com; 6 rue St-Jean, Bayeux; adult/child morning €60/40, full-day €100/60) This experienced Bayeux-based outfit offers informative morning tours of the various D-Day beaches and cemeteries, as well as all-day excursions. Check the website for further details.

Normandy Tours TOURS
(☑ 02 31 92 10 70; www.normandy-landing-tours.com; 26 place de la Gare, Bayeux; adult/student €72/62) Offers well-regarded four- to five-hour tours of the main sites starting at 8.15am and 1.15pm on most days, as well as personally tailored trips. Based at Bayeux' Hôtel de la Gare, facing the train station.

❶ Getting There & Away

Bus Verts (p251) links Bayeux' train station and place St-Patrice with many of the villages along the D-Day beaches.

Bus 70 (two to four daily Monday to Saturday, more frequently and on Sunday and holidays in summer) goes to Colleville-sur-Mer (Omaha Beach and the American Cemetery; €2.10 to €2.50, 35 minutes); some services continue to Pointe du Hoc near Cricqueville-en-Bessin (€4.20 to €4.90) and Grandcamp-Maisy (€4.20 to €4.90).

Bus 74 (bus 75 in July and August; three or four daily Monday to Saturday, more frequently and on Sunday and holidays in summer) heads to Arromanches (€2.10 to €2.50, 10 minutes), Gold Beach (Ver-sur-Mer; €3.10 to €3.70, 30 minutes) and Juno Beach (Courseulles-sur-Mer; €3.10 to €3.70, one hour).

Omaha Beach

The most brutal fighting on D-Day took place on the 7km stretch of coastline around Vierville-sur-Mer, St-Laurent-sur-Mer and Colleville-sur-Mer, 15km northwest of Bayeux, known as 'Bloody Omaha' to US veterans. More than seven decades on, little evidence of the carnage unleashed here on 6 June 1944 remains, except for the harrowing American cemetery and concrete German bunkers, though at very low tide you can see a few remnants of the Mulberry Harbour.

These days Omaha is a peaceful place, a beautiful stretch of fine golden sand partly lined with dunes and summer homes. Circuit de la Plage d'Omaha, trail-marked with a yellow stripe, is a self-guided tour along the beach.

◉ Sights

Normandy American Cemetery & Memorial MEMORIAL
(☑ 02 31 51 62 00; www.abmc.gov; Colleville-sur-Mer; ☺ 9am-6pm mid-Apr–mid-Sep, to 5pm mid-Sep–mid-Apr) FREE White marble crosses and Stars of David stretch off in seemingly endless rows at the Normandy American Cemetery, situated on a now-serene bluff overlooking the bitterly contested sands of Omaha Beach. The **visitor centre** has an excellent multimedia presentation on the D-Day landings, told in part through the stories of individuals' courage and sacrifice. Free 45-minute English-language tours of the cemetery, also focusing on personal stories, depart daily at 2pm and, from mid-April to mid-September, at 11am.

Featured in the opening scenes of Steven Spielberg's *Saving Private Ryan*, this place of pilgrimage is one of the largest American war cemeteries in Europe and is an incredibly emotional sight, containing the graves of 9387 American soldiers, including 33 pairs of brothers who are buried side-by-side (another 12 pairs of brothers are buried separately or memorialised here). Only about 40% of American war dead from the fighting in Normandy are interred in this cemetery – the rest were repatriated at the request of their families.

Overlooking the gravestones is a large colonnaded memorial centred on a statue called *The Spirit of American Youth,* maps explaining the order of battle, and a wall honouring 1557 Americans whose bodies were not found (men whose remains were recovered after the memorial was inaugurated are marked with a bronze rosette). A small, white-marble **chapel** stands at the intersection of the cross-shaped main paths through the cemetery.

The Normandy American Cemetery & Memorial is 17km northwest of Bayeux; by car, follow the signs to the 'Cimetière Militaire Americain'. There is a large car park on site.

Overlord Museum　　　　MUSEUM
(☑ 02 31 22 00 55; www.overlordmuseum.com; D514, Colleville-sur-Mer; adult/child €7.80/5.70; ⊙ 10am-5.30pm mid-Feb–Mar, Oct & Nov, to 6.30pm Apr, May & Sep, 9.30am-7pm Jun-Aug, closed Jan–mid-Feb) This excellent museum has an astonishing collection of restored WWII military equipment from both sides; the human dimension of the war is brought movingly to life with photos, audio clips, letters and personal stories and recollections. The museum is situated just up the hill from the Normandy American Cemetery & Memorial. You could easily spend a few hours here, so plan your visit accordingly as you will need time for both the museum and the cemetery.

Arromanches-les-Bains

In order to unload the vast quantities of cargo needed by the invasion forces without having to capture – intact! – one of the heavily defended Channel ports (a lesson of the 1942 Dieppe Raid), the Allies set up prefabricated marinas, code-named Mulberry Harbours, off two of the landing beaches. A total of 146 massive cement caissons were towed over from England and sunk to form two semi-circular breakwaters in which floating bridge spans were moored. In the three months after D-Day, the Mulberries facilitated the unloading of a mind-boggling 2.5 million men, four million tonnes of equipment and 500,000 vehicles.

Today, Arromanches-les-Bains is an important D-Day stop for the remains of the Mulberry Harbours caissons visible in the waters and the exhibits at the Musée du Débarquement, dedicated to the history of the artificial harbours and their significance in the war effort.

⊙ Sights

Mulberry Harbours Caissons　　RUINS
The harbour established at Omaha was completely destroyed by a ferocious gale (the worst storm to lash the Normandy coast in four decades) just two weeks after D-Day, but the impressive remains of three dozen caissons belonging to the second, Port Winston (named after Churchill), can still be seen off Arromanches-les-Bains, 10km northeast of Bayeux. At low tide you can even walk out to one of the caissons from the beach, but they are being gradually eroded by the sea.

**Arromanches 360°
Circular Cinema**　　　　THEATRE
(☑ 02 31 06 06 44; www.arromanches360. com; chemin du Calvaire; adult/child €6/5.50; ⊙ 10am-between 5pm & 6pm, from 9.30am May-Aug, closed 3 weeks in Jan & Mon mid-Nov–mid-Feb) The best view of Port Winston and nearby Gold Beach is from the hill east of town, site of the popular Arromanches 360° Circular Cinema, which screens archival footage of the Battle of Normandy every half-hour (on the hour and at half past the hour); it is run by Caen's Le Mémorial – Un Musée pour la Paix (p262). Entrance is free for WWII veterans. Check the website for details of guided tours (adult/child €2.50/2), held at noon and 4pm.

Musée du Débarquement　　MUSEUM
(Landing Museum; ☑ 02 31 22 34 31; www.musee-arromanches.fr; place du 6 Juin; adult/child €8/5.90; ⊙ 9am-12.30pm & 1.30-6pm Apr-Sep, 10am-12.30pm & 1.30-5pm Oct-Dec, Feb & Mar, closed Jan) Down in Arromanches itself and right on the beach, the Musée du Débarquement makes for a very informative stop before visiting the beaches. Dioramas, models and two films explain the logistics and importance of the artificial harbour of Port Winston. Guided tours are available in English, French and German. At the time of writing, the museum was preparing for a June 2019 relaunch, to mark the 75th anniversary of D-Day; new features will include a model of Port Winston.

Juno Beach

Dune-lined Juno Beach, 12km east of Arromanches around Courseulles-sur-Mer, was stormed by Canadian troops on D-Day. A Cross of Lorraine marks the spot where General Charles de Gaulle came ashore shortly after the landings. He was followed by Winston Churchill on 12 June and King

George VI on 16 June. A bunker is by the beach, which can be accessed on tours, led by the Juno Beach Centre.

◉ Sights

Juno Beach Centre   MUSEUM
([☎]02 31 37 32 17; www.junobeach.org; voie des Français Libres, Courseulles-sur-Mer; adult/child €7/5.50, incl guided tour of Juno Beach €11/9, temporary exhibit only €3; ⊘9.30am-7pm Apr-Sep, 10am-6pm Oct & Mar, 10am-5pm Nov-Dec & Feb, closed Jan) Juno Beach's only specifically Canadian museum, the nonprofit Juno Beach Centre, has multimedia exhibits on Canada's role in the war effort and the landings; at the time of writing, the temporary collection displayed 52,022 bright red poppies, one for each Canadian who died in France. There is also a short film screened before visitors enter the permanent collection. Guided tours of Juno Beach (€5.50) are available from April to October.

Bény-sur-Mer Canadian War Cemetery   CEMETERY
(www.cwgc.org; D35) The Bény-sur-Mer Canadian War Cemetery is 4km south of Courseulles-sur-Mer near Reviers.

Longues-sur-Mer

Part of the Nazis' Atlantic Wall, the massive concrete casemates and 150mm German guns at Longues-sur-Mer, 6km west of Arromanches, were designed to hit targets some 20km away, including both Gold Beach (to the east) and Omaha Beach (to the west). Seven and a half decades after their installation, the guns and their stolid concrete casemates survive and constitute one of the highlights along the coast. In their now silent and disused form, they serve as a fitting testament to the collapse of the German occupation.

Parts of the classic D-Day film *The Longest Day* (1962) were filmed both here and at Pointe du Hoc. On clear days, Bayeux' cathedral, is visible 8km to the south.

ℹ Information

Longues Tourist Office ([☎]02 31 21 46 87; www.bayeux-bessin-tourisme.com; Site de la Batterie; ⊘10am-1pm & 2-6pm, closed Nov Mar) Has details on guided tours (adult/child €5/3) to the German artillery batteries at Longues-sur-Mer, available on weekends from April to October (and daily in July and August). View the excellent website for a full list of events in the region.

Utah Beach

Situated midway between Bayeux and Cherbourg, this beach – the Allies' right (western) flank on D-Day – stretches for 5km near the village of La Madeleine. It was taken, with only light resistance, by the US 4th Infantry Division. D-Day events are commemorated by a number of monuments and the impressive **Musée du Débarquement de Utah Beach** (Utah Beach Landing Museum; [☎]02 33 71 53 35; www.utah-beach.com; Ste-Marie du Mont; adult/child €8/4; ⊘9.30am-7pm Jun-Sep, 10am-6pm Oct-May, closed Jan), a few kilometres inland in Ste-Marie du Mont.

POINTE DU HOC RANGER MEMORIAL

At 7.10am on 6 June 1944, 225 US Army Rangers under the command of Lieutenant Colonel James Earl Rudder scaled the impossibly steep, 30m-high cliffs of Pointe du Hoc. Their objective was to disable five 155mm German artillery guns perfectly placed to rain shells onto the beaches of Utah and Omaha. Unbeknown to Rudder and his team, the guns had been transferred inland shortly before, but they nevertheless managed to locate the massive artillery pieces and put them out of action.

By the time the Rangers were finally relieved on 8 June – after repelling fierce German counterattacks for two days – 81 of the rangers had been killed and 58 more had been wounded.

Today the memorial **site** ([☎]02 31 51 90 70; www.abmc.gov; ⊘9am-6pm mid-Apr–mid-Sep, to 5pm rest of year), which France turned over to the US government in 1979, looks much as it did right after the battle, with the earth still pitted with huge bomb craters. The German command post (topped by a dagger-shaped memorial) and several concrete bunkers and casemates, scarred by bullet holes and blackened by flame-throwers, can be explored.

As you face the sea, Utah Beach is 14km to the left. A visitor centre with multimedia exhibits can be explored.

KARTOUCHKEN/SHUTTERSTOCK ©

1. Gun Battery at Longues-sur-Mer (p259) **2.** D-Day Monument, Omaha Beach (p257) **3.** Sherman tank, Utah Beach (p259) **4.** Normandy American Cemetery & Memorial (p257)

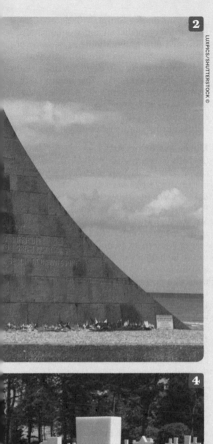

LUXPICS/SHUTTERSTOCK ©

Normandy D-Day Sites

The bravery and sacrifice of Operation Overlord – the 6 June 1944 Allied landings known in history as D-Day – is still a palpable presence in Normandy, and nowhere more so than on the broad, quiet beaches: Utah, Omaha, Gold, Juno and Sword. Still dotted with German pillboxes, these beaches were where American, British, Canadian, Commonwealth, Polish, Free French and other soldiers stormed ashore in the early morning, beginning the long-awaited liberation of France.

As you gaze out over the brilliant golden sand from the Normandy American Cemetery, a place of solemn pilgrimage, or the Channel coast's quiet seaside villages, it's hard to picture the death and heroism that occurred here – but the relics of war and a number of excellent museums help put the world-changing events into historical and human context.

UNMISSABLE D-DAY BATTLE SITES

Omaha Beach (p257) Site of the landings' most ferocious fighting, 'bloody Omaha' should not be missed.

Normandy American Cemetery & Memorial (p257) This vast war cemetery is deeply moving.

Le Mémorial – Un Musée pour la Paix (p262) The best single museum devoted to the Battle of Normandy.

Bayeux War Cemetery (p253) The largest of Normandy's Commonwealth war cemeteries is next to a memorial for the many men whose remains were never found.

Caen

POP 109,300

Founded by William the Conqueror in the 11th century, Caen – capital of the Basse Normandie region – was massively damaged during the 1944 Battle of Normandy, but considerable history and heritage survives to make it a very good-looking city, especially in its central areas. Visitors will discover the imposing bastions of a superb medieval château, two ancient abbeys and a clutch of excellent museums, including an outstanding and enthralling museum of war and peace, largely dedicated to D-Day, WWII and its aftermath.

With its decent hotels, superb collection of restaurants, atmospheric streets and manageable size, Caen is a terrific place to explore; the easygoing city is also a launchpad to the nearby D-Day sights spread out along the coast.

◉ Sights

★ Le Mémorial – Un Musée pour la Paix

MEMORIAL

(Memorial – A Museum for Peace; ☑02 31 06 06 44; www.memorial-caen.fr; esplanade Général Eisenhower; adult/child €19.80/17.50, family pass €51; ⊙9am-7pm Apr-Sep, 9.30am-6pm Oct-Dec, 9am-6pm Feb-Mar, closed 3 weeks in Jan, shut most Mon in Nov & Dec) For a very insightful and vivid account of the entire war, with special focus on the Battle of Normandy, Le Mémorial is unparalleled – it's one of Europe's premier WWII museums. A hugely impressive affair, the museum uses film, animation and audio testimony, as well as many original artefacts, to graphically evoke the realities of war, the trials of occupation and the joy of liberation. It is situated 3km northwest of the city centre, reachable by bus 2 from place Courtonne.

Château de Caen

CHATEAU

(www.musee-de-normandie.caen.fr; ⊙8am-10pm; Ⓟ) FREE Looming above the centre of the city, Caen's magnificent castle walls – massive battlements overlooking a now dry moat – were established by William the Conqueror, Duke of Normandy, in 1060. Visitors can walk around the ramparts and visit the 12th-century Église St-Georges (Château de Caen), which holds an information centre with a diorama of the castle, and the Échiquier (Exchequer; ☑02 31 30 47 60; Château de Caen), which dates from about 1100 and is one of the oldest civic buildings in Normandy. The castle affords splendid visuals over the town at sunset.

The Jardin des Simples (Château de Caen) is a garden of medicinal and aromatic herbs cultivated during the Middle Ages, some of them poisonous. There are also two worthwhile museums in the castle grounds, and a good restaurant-cafe. The mighty 12th-century donjon (keep) only survives today as vestiges and foundations. Tours of the castle are provided by the tourist office (p264) during summer, but only in French.

Musée des Beaux-Arts

GALLERY

(Fine Arts Museum; ☑02 31 30 47 70; www.mba.caen.fr; Château de Caen; adult/child €3.50/free, incl temporary exhibition €5.50; ⊙9.30am-12.30pm & 2-6pm Mon-Fri, 11am-6pm Sat & Sun Jun-Oct, 9.30am-12.30pm & 2-6pm Wed-Fri, 11am-6pm Sat & Sun Nov-May) This excellent and well-curated museum takes you on a tour through the history of Western art from the 15th to 21st centuries, including works depicting landscapes and interiors found around Normandy. The collection includes works by Rubens, Tintoretto, Géricault, Monet, Bonnard, Boudin, Dufy and Courbet, among many others. Situated inside the Château de Caen.

Abbaye-aux-Hommes

ABBEY

(Abbaye-St-Étienne; ☑02 31 30 42 81; rue Guillaume le Conquérant; church free, cloisters €2; ⊙church 9.30am-1pm & 2-7pm Mon-Sat, 2-6.30pm Sun, cloister 8.30am-5pm Mon-Fri, 9.30am-1pm & 2-5.30pm Sat & most Sun) Caen's most important medieval site is the Men's Abbey – now city hall – and, right next door, the magnificent, multi-turreted Église St-Étienne (St Stephen's Church), with its Romanesque nave, Gothic choir and William the Conqueror's tomb (rebuilt; the original was destroyed by a 16th-century Calvinist mob and, in 1793, by fevered revolutionaries).

The complex is 1km southwest of the Château de Caen; to get there by car, follow the signs to the 'Hôtel de Ville'.

Abbaye-aux-Dames

ABBEY

(Abbaye-de-la-Trinité; ☑02 31 06 98 98; place Reine Mathilde) Highlights at the Women's Abbey complex in the east of the town centre, once run by the Benedictines, include Église de la Trinité – look for Matilda's tomb behind the main altar and the striking pink stained-glass windows just beyond. Free tours (at 2.30pm and 4pm daily) take you through the interior, but you can snoop around the courtyard and the church on your own at other times, except during Mass.

Caen

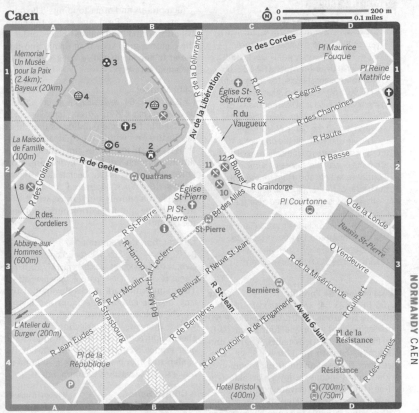

Caen

◎ Sights

⊗ Eating

1944 Radar Museum   MUSEUM

(📞 02 31 06 06 45; www.musee.radar.fr; rte de Basly, Douvres-la-Délivrande; adult/child €5.50/free; ⊙10am-6pm Tue-Sun May–mid-Sep) Located 5km north of Caen within two restored German bunkers (bunker H 622 and bunker L 479), this museum is interesting for anyone of a technical bent or those who wish to understand more about the role of radar in WWII. You can see a large German *Würzburg* radar antenna as well as three other radars in what was one of the most important German radar stations in Normandy. The site was captured by British forces on 17 June 1944.

🛏 Sleeping

Hotel Bristol   HOTEL €

(📞 02 31 84 59 76; www.hotelbristolcaen.com; 31 rue du 11 Novembre; s/d from €75/85; 🛜) The centrally located Hotel Bristol has well-maintained contemporary, rather neutrally toned rooms with comfortable beds and huge windows. It's the friendly and welcoming service, however, that really sets this place apart from other similarly priced options. Breakfast is €9.50; parking is €10 per night.

WORTH A TRIP

CAEN DAY TRIPPER

The new, highly informative and timely (for the 75th anniversary of D-Day) **Civilians in Wartime Memorial** (☑ 02 31 06 06 45; www.memorial-falaise.fr; Falaise; adult/child €7.50/6.50; ⊙ 10am-5.30pm Feb-Oct) in the town of Falaise, 41km southeast of Caen, gets you under the skin of being a civilian during the battle of Normandy. The life of civilians in the conflict is brought into stark relief through relics and artefacts of war, the stories of survivors, interactive tablets and a film that reveals the horror of the conflict and its aftermath. The museum is located near the Château de Falaise.

A €28 ticket includes the Civilians in Wartime Memorial, Le Mémorial – Un Musée pour la Paix in Caen and the Arromanches 360° Circular Cinema.

★ **La Maison de Famille**   B&B €€
(☑ 06 61 64 88 54; www.maisondefamille.sitew.com; 4 rue Elie de Beaumont; d/ste €75/105; [P] [⟨wifi⟩]) This grand and adorable four-room B&B, overflowing with personality, charm and history (it dates to the 17th century), occupies three floors of an imposing townhouse. Added perks include a lovely breakfast in a fine dining room, private parking and a marvellous staircase. The attic apartment is atmospheric, while the suite has access to the peaceful garden.

✗ Eating

Dolly's   CAFE €
(☑ 02 31 94 03 29; 16-18 av de la Libération; mains from €9; ⊙ 11am-11pm Tue, from 10am Wed & Sun, 10am-1am Thu-Sat; [⟨wifi⟩]) This colourful British-style cafe is popular and often full, so it can be a bit of a struggle to get a seat, but it's the place for greasy fry-up brekkies, burgers, fish and chips (€13.50), plus salads and healthier fare for the body-conscious and vegetarians. Service is brusque. If it's too full of elbows, a smaller **takeout branch** (☑ 02 50 54 23 23; 18 rue Montoir-Poissonnerie; ⊙ 11am-7.30pm Tue-Thu, to 11pm Fri & Sat; [✗]) is nearby.

L'Atelier du Burger   BURGERS €
(☑ 02 31 50 13 44; www.latelier-duburger.fr; 27 rue Écuyère; mains €7.50-9; ⊙ noon-2.30pm & 7-11.30pm; [⟨wifi⟩]) Near the end of bar-lined rue Écuyère, this place does a busy trade in juicy, thick burgers piled high with guacamole, grilled onions and other toppings. The burgers are truly top-form, and so are the chips. It's an informal and relaxed place: order at the counter, grab your own drink, and take a seat in the stone-walled back room or on the small terrace.

Café Mancel   FRENCH €€
(☑ 02 31 86 63 64; www.cafemancel.com; Château de Caen; menus €18-25; ⊙ noon-10pm Tue-Sat, to 2pm Sun) In the same building as the Musée des Beaux-Arts within the Château de Caen, this stylish place serves up delicious, traditional French cuisine – everything from pan-fried Norman-style beefsteak to hearty Caen-style *tripes*, delivered by attentive staff. There's a lovely sun terrace, which also makes a fine spot for a drink outside of busy meal times.

Le Bouchon du Vaugueux   FRENCH €€
(☑ 02 31 44 26 26; www.bouchonduvaugueux.com; 12 rue Graindorge; lunch menus €17-25, dinner menus €23-35; ⊙ noon-2pm & 7-10pm Tue-Sat; [✗]) The giant wine cork marks the spot at this tiny *bistrot gourmande* (gourmet bistro), which matches creative modern cooking with a first-rate wine selection (from €4 a glass), sourced from small producers all over France. Staff are happy to translate the chalkboard menu and there's a kids menu too (€9). Reservations recommended.

À Contre Sens   MODERN FRENCH €€
(☑ 02 31 97 44 48; www.acontresenscaen.fr/a-contre-sens; 8 rue des Croisiers; mains €30-38, menus €26-56; ⊙ noon-1.15pm Wed-Sat, plus 7.30-9.15pm Tue-Sat) À Contre Sens' stylish interior and serene atmosphere belie the hotbed of seething creativity happening in the kitchen. Under the helm of chef Anthony Caillot, meals are thoughtfully crafted and superbly presented. Expect dishes such as seaweed risotto with apple and coriander or veal rubbed with herbs, endive and ham.

ⓘ Information

Tourist Office (☑ 02 31 27 14 14; www.caen-tourisme.fr; 12 place St-Pierre; ⊙ 9.30am-6.30pm Mon-Sat, 9.30am-1.30pm Sun Apr-Sep, 9.30am-1pm & 2-6pm Mon-Sat Oct-Feb, to 6.30pm Mar)

ⓘ Getting There & Around

BOAT

Brittany Ferries (www.brittany-ferries.co.uk) links the English port of Portsmouth with Ouistreham, 14km northeast of Caen.

BUS

Bus 20, run by Caen-based **Bus Verts** (☑09 70 83 00 14; www.busverts.fr; place Courtonne; ⊙7.30am-7pm Mon-Fri, 9am-7pm Sat), links the bus station (next to the train station) with Deauville and Trouville-sur-Mer (€4.90, two hours, four to seven daily); bus 20 also runs, along with the faster Prestobus 39 to Honfleur (bus 20, €4.20 to €4.90, 2½ hours, seven to 13 daily; express Prestobus 39 (€12.10, one hour, one or two daily) and Le Havre (bus 20 €4.20 to €4.90, 2½ hours; express Prestobus bus 39 €17, 1½ hours, six to 10 daily). When arriving or departing, your Bus Verts ticket is valid for an hour on Caen's local buses and trams.

Twisto (www.twisto.fr) Local bus 61 links Caen with the ferry port of Ouistreham.

TRAIN

The train station is 1.5km southeast of the Château de Caen. Services include the following:

Bayeux €6, 15 to 20 minutes, at least hourly

Cherbourg €24, 1¼ hours, eight to 15 daily

Deauville & Trouville (via Lisieux) €16, 1¼ to two hours, six to 11 daily

Paris Gare St-Lazare €37, two hours, 13 daily

Pontorson (Mont St-Michel) €28, 1¾ hours, three daily

Rouen from €28, 1¾ hours, five or six daily

Deauville

POP 3800

Good-looking and chic Deauville has been a playground of well-heeled Parisians ever since it was founded by Napoléon III's half-brother, the Duke of Morny, in 1861. Expensive, flashy and brash, it's packed with designer boutiques, deluxe hotels and meticulously tended public gardens, and hosts two racetracks (Deauville-La Touques Racecourse and Deauville-Clairefontaine Racecourse) and the high-profile Deauville American Film Festival.

The port town is 15km southwest of Honfleur, separated from equally popular Trouville-sur-Mer by the River Touques, which flows into the sea here. Deauville is hugely popular with denizens of Paris, who flock here year-round on weekends – and all week long from June to September and during Paris' school holidays.

🏃 Activities

The rich and beautiful strut their stuff along the beachside **Promenade des Planches**, a 643m-long boardwalk that's lined with a row of 1920s cabins named after famous Americans (mainly film stars). After swimming in the nearby 50m **Piscine Olympique** (Olympic swimming pool; ☑02 31 14 02 17; bd de la Mer, Deauville; weekday/weekend from €4/6; ⊙10am-2pm & 3.30-7pm Mon-Sat, 9am-4pm Sun, closed 2 weeks in Jan & 3 weeks in Jun), filled with seawater heated to 28°C, they – like you – can head to the beach, hundreds of metres wide at low tide; walk across the street to their eye-popping, neo-something mansion; or head down the block to the spectacularly Italianate casino.

✲ Festivals & Events

Deauville American Film Festival FILM (www.festival-deauville.com; ⊙Sep) Deauville has a fair bit of Beverly Hills glitz and glamour so it's an appropriate venue for an annual festival celebrating American cinema, running since 1975. Held for 10 days from early September; tickets cost €35 for one day or €160 for the whole festival. Students to the age of 26 can get tickets for one day/whole festival for €16/110.

🛏 Sleeping & Eating

There's not a great selection of hotels in Deauville – there's a superior selection in Trouville-sur-Mer next door. Prices are highest and reservations are recommended in July and August, and year-round on weekends and holidays; and lowest (we're talking half off) from October to Easter, except during Paris' school holidays, and most of the year on weekdays.

L'Essentiel FUSION €€ (☑02 31 87 22 11; 29 rue Mirabeau; lunch menus €27-32, dinner menus €69, mains €31-39; ⊙noon-2pm & 7.30-11pm Thu-Mon) One of Deauville's top dining rooms, L'Essentiel serves up an imaginative blend of French ingredients with Asian and Latin American accents. Start off with codfish croquettes with sweet potato aioli before moving on to scallops with broccoli yuzu, or wagyu flank steak with roasted turnips and smoked cashew juice.

Le Comptoir et la Table MODERN FRENCH €€€ (☑02 31 88 92 51; www.lecomptoiretlatable.fr; 1 quai de la Marine, Deauville; mains €28-42; ⊙noon-2.30pm & 7-10.30pm Thu-Tue) Seasonal ingredients fresh from the market are transformed into delicious dishes, some of Italian inspiration, served in appealingly maritime surroundings. Specialities include risotto with cream of truffles and scallops, and grilled lobster. A further plus is the attentive service. You can find Le Comptoir et la Table along the waterfront, about four blocks northwest of the Deauville-Trouville bridge.

ℹ Information

Deauville Tourist Office (☏ 02 31 14 40 00; www.indeauville.fr; quai de la Gare; ⊙10am-6pm Mon-Sat, 10am-1pm & 2-5pm Sun)

ℹ Getting There & Away

BUS

Deauville and Trouville's joint bus station is next to the Trouville-Deauville train station.

Bus Verts (p251) Bus 20 goes to Caen (€4.90, two hours, seven to 12 daily), Honfleur (€2.50, 30 minutes, four to seven daily) and Le Havre (€4.90, 1¼ hours, four to seven daily).

TRAIN

The Trouville-Deauville train station is in Deauville, right next to Pont des Belges (the bridge to Trouville). Getting here usually requires a change at Lisieux (€8, 20 minutes, nine to 12 daily), though there are two or three direct trains a day to Paris Gare St-Lazare (€35, two hours). Destinations that require a change of trains include Caen (€16, 1¼ to two hours, six to 11 daily) and Rouen (from €24, 1¼ to two hours, five to eight daily).

Trouville-sur-Mer

POP 4800

Unpretentious Trouville-sur-Mer – usually known simply as Trouville – is both a veteran beach resort, graced with impressive mansions from the late 1800s, and a working fishing port. Popular with middle-class French families, the town was frequented by painters and writers during the 19th century (eg Mozin and Flaubert), lured by the 2km-long sandy beach and the laid-back seaside ambience.

The port town is right next to Deauville and is similarly very popular with Parisians, who descend on Trouville-sur-Mer at weekends and during the summer, vastly swelling the population.

◎ Sights & Activities

Trouville has a waterfront casino, a wide beach and **Promenade des Planches** (boardwalk). At the latter, 583m long and outfitted with Bauhaus-style pavilions from the 1930s, you can swim in a freshwater swimming pool and windsurf; there's also a playground for kids. Trouville's most impressive 19th-century villas are right nearby.

Musée Villa Montabello   MUSEUM
(☏ 02 31 88 16 26; 64 rue du Général Leclerc; adult/child €3/free, Sun free; ⊙ 2-5.30pm Wed-Mon Apr–mid-Nov, from 11am Sat, Sun & holidays) In a grand mansion dating to 1865, this municipal museum recounts Trouville's history and features works by Charles Mozin, Eugène Isabey and Charles Pecrus. The Musée Villa Montabello is situated 1km northeast of the tourist office, near the beach (and signed off the beach). The two towns and beach scenes of Trouville and Deauville play a starring role in the impressionist works in the small permanent collection.

🛏 Sleeping

La Maison Normande   HOTEL €
(☏ 02 31 88 12 25; www.la-maison-normande.com; 4 place de Lattre de Tassigny; d €55-85; ☏) The 17 rooms in this late-17th-century half-timbered Norman house vary considerably in size and style and are eminently serviceable, offering very good value indeed. Prices rise slightly a bit on Friday and Saturday. Breakfast is €8.50.

Le Flaubert   HOTEL €€
(☏ 02 31 88 37 23; www.flaubert.fr; rue Gustave Flaubert; d incl breakfast €129-179, ste €199-299; ☏) With a fresh and breezy seafront perspective and lovely, bright accommodation, Le Flaubert is a peach. Each room has its own personality, with ample wood, wicker chairs and the occasional pastel shade, but it's the position right by the beach that seals it. Sea-view rooms go like hot cakes, so book early in summer. Parking is €12 per day.

Le Fer à Cheval   HOTEL €€
(☏ 02 31 98 30 20; www.hotel-trouville.com; 11 rue Victor Hugo; s €64-80, d €92-105, ste from €170; ☏) Ensconced in three beautiful turn-of-the-20th-century buildings, this very welcoming 34-room hotel has comfortable, modern rooms with big double-glazed windows, stylish decor and bright bathrooms. It's situated two short blocks inland from the riverfront. Breakfast is either a buffet in the breakfast room or a continental version served in your room. Prices rise on Fridays and Saturdays.

🍴 Eating

There are lots of restaurants and buzzing brasseries along riverfront bd Fernand Moureaux; many specialise in fresh fish, mussels and seafood. The area has a fantastic atmosphere on summer evenings. Inland, check out the small restaurants and cafes along and near rue d'Orléans and on pedestrianised rue des Bains.

Marché aux Poissons   SEAFOOD €
(Fish Market; bd Fernand Moureaux; ⊙8am-7.30pm) The sizeable Marché aux Poissons is *the* place

in Trouville to head for fresh oysters with lemon (from €9 to €16 a dozen) and other maritime delicacies. Even if you don't have access to a kitchen, there's cooked peel-and-eat shrimp, mussels, sea urchins and scallops, to enjoy at a table out front. Located on the waterfront 250m south of the casino.

Les Vapeurs
BRASSERIE €€

(☑ 02 31 88 15 24; 160 bd Fernand Moureaux; mains €18-38; ⊙ noon-11.30pm) Across from the fish market, Les Vapeurs has been going strong in Trouville since 1927. The huge menu is a showcase for seafood platters, oysters (from €15 for six), mussels in cream sauce, grilled haddock, lobster and classic brasserie fare (like steak tartare). It's served amid an old-time ambience, with black-and-white photos, a touch of neon and wicker chairs at the outdoor tables in front. There are dishes for the young ones too.

Tivoli Bistro
BISTRO €€

(☑ 02 31 98 43 44; 27 rue Charles Mozin; menus €30; ⊙ 12.15-2pm & 7.15-9.30pm Fri-Tue) You won't find a cosier place in Trouville than this much-loved hideaway, tucked away on a narrow side street a block inland from the riverfront. It's famous for its delicious *sole meunière* (Dover sole; €32.50) and exquisite homemade terrine, or you can just stop by for a quick serving of delicious *moules marinière* (€12).

ℹ Information

Trouville Tourist Office (☑ 02 31 14 60 70; www.trouvillesurmer.org; 32 bd Fernand Moureaux; ⊙ 10am-6pm Mon-Sat, to 1.30pm Sun Sep-Jun, 9.30pm-7pm Mon-Sat, 10am-6pm Sun Jul & Aug) Has a free map of Trouville and sells map-brochures for two self-guided architectural tours (€4) of town and also two rural walks (€1).

Honfleur

POP 8200

Long a favourite with painters such as Monet, Normandy's most charming port town is a popular day-trip destination for Parisian families. Though the centre can be overrun with visitors on warm weekends and in summer, it's hard not to love the rugged maritime charm of the Vieux Bassin (Old Harbour), which evokes maritime Normandy of centuries past.

In the 16th and 17th centuries, Honfleur was one of France's most important ports for commerce and exploration. Some of the earliest French expeditions to Brazil and New-foundland began here, and in 1608, Samuel de Champlain set sail from Honfleur to found Québec City.

◉ Sights

Honfleur is spread around the roughly rectangular Vieux Bassin and, along its southeast side, the Enclos, the once-walled old town. Église Ste-Catherine is northwest of the Vieux Bassin (up the hill).

Honfleur is superb for aimless ambling, especially if you have a walking map from the tourist office. One option is to head north from the Lieutenance along quai des Passagers to **Jetée de l'Ouest** (Western Jetty), which forms the west side of the Avant Port, out to the broad mouth of the Seine. Possible stops include the **Jardin des Personnalités**, a park featuring figures from Honfleur history; the beach; and **Naturospace** (☑ 02 31 81 77 00; www.naturospace.com; bd Charles V; adult/child €9/7; ⊙ 10am-5pm Feb-Mar & Oct–mid-Nov, to 6.30pm Apr-Sep), a lush greenhouse filled with free-flying tropical butterflies and birds that's situated 500m northwest of the Lieutenance.

The tourist office also has audioguides (€5; in English, French and German) for a 1½-hour walking tour of the town.

Le Pass Musées (adult €13) gets you into all four municipal museums for less than the price of two.

Vieux Bassin
HISTORIC SITE

The old harbour, with its bobbing pleasure boats, is Honfleur's focal point. On the west side, quai Ste-Catherine is lined with tall, taper-thin houses – many protected from the elements by slate tiles – dating from the 16th to 18th centuries. The **Lieutenance** (12 place Ste-Catherine), at the mouth of the old harbour, was once the residence of the town's royal governor. Just northeast of the Lieutenance is the **Avant Port**, home to Honfleur's dozen fishing vessels, which sell their catch at the **Marché au Poisson** (Fish Market; Jetée de Transit; ⊙ 8am-noon or later Thu-Sun).

Small children will get a kick out of a ride on the carousel, situated opposite the Lieutenance.

Église Ste-Catherine
CHURCH

(place Ste-Catherine; ⊙ 9am-5.15pm or later) Initially intended as a temporary structure, this extraordinary wooden church was built by local shipwrights during the late 15th and early 16th centuries after its stone predecessor was destroyed during the Hundred Years War. Wood was used so money would be left over to strengthen the city's fortifications, though there are elements of stone (such as some of the pillar bases). From the inside, the remarkable twin naves and double-vaulted roof resemble two overturned ships' hulls.

★Les Maisons Satie MUSEUM
(☎02 31 89 11 11; www.musees-honfleur.fr/maison-satie.html; 67 bd Charles V & 90 rue Haute; adult/child €6.20/free; ⏲10am-7pm Wed-Mon May-Sep, 11am-6pm Wed-Mon Oct-Apr) This unusual and intriguing complex captures the whimsical spirit of the eccentric avant-garde composer Erik Satie (1866–1925), who lived and worked in Honfleur and was born in one of the two half-timbered *maisons Satie* (Satie houses). Visitors wander through the beguiling rooms, each concealing a surreal surprise, as a headset plays Satie's strangely familiar music. Les Maisons Satie is situated 350m northwest of the northern end of the Vieux Bassin.

Musée Eugène Boudin GALLERY
(☎02 31 89 54 00; www.musees-honfleur.fr; 50 rue de l'Homme de Bois; adult/child Jun-Oct €8/free, Nov-May €6/free; ⏲10am-1pm & 2-6pm Wed-Mon Jun-Oct, 2.30-5.30pm Wed-Mon, 10am-noon Sat & Sun Nov-May) This museum features superb 19th- and 20th-century paintings of Normandy's towns and coast, including works by Dubourg, Dufy and Monet. One room is devoted to Eugène Boudin, an early impressionist and marine painter (he was the son of a sailor), who was born in Honfleur in 1824 and whom Baudelaire called the 'king of skies' for his luscious skyscapes.

Musée d'Ethnographie et d'Art Populaire Normand MUSEUM
(☎02 31 89 14 12; www.musees-honfleur.fr; rue de la Prison; adult/child €4.20/free, incl Musée de la Marine €5.30/free; ⏲10am-noon & 2-6.30pm Tue-Sun Apr-Sep, 2.30-5.30pm Tue-Fri, 10am-noon & 2.30-5.30pm Sat & Sun mid-Feb–Mar & Oct-late Nov, closed late Nov–mid-Feb) Through multiple rooms, this museum gathers together exhibits on domestic and economic life in 16th- to 19th-century Normandy portraying traditional costumes, furniture and housewares. It's located in two adjacent 16th-century buildings: a one-time prison and a house, hence the name of the street. A pass for access to Musée d'Ethnographie et d'Art Populaire Normand, Musée Eugène Boudin and the **Musée de la Marine** (quai St-Étienne; adult/child €4.20/free, incl Musée d'Ethnographie €5.30/free; ⏲10am-noon & 2-6.30pm Tue-Sun Apr-Sep, 2.30-5.30pm Tue-Fri, 10am-noon Sat & Sun mid-Feb–Mar, Oct & Nov, closed Dec–mid-Feb) is €13.

Sleeping

Hôtel Monet HOTEL €
(☎02 31 89 00 90; www.hotel-monet-honfleur.com; rue Charriere du Puits; incl breakfast d/f from €65/100; P 📶) Up the hill, out of the action and run by welcoming Sylvie and Christophe, this delightful and small hotel has modern, neat rooms with a sweet, small cafe in the lobby. All rooms come with terrace, with breakfast served either in your room or on your terrace.

★La Petite Folie B&B €€
(☎06 74 39 46 46; www.lapetitefolie-honfleur.com; 44 rue Haute; d incl breakfast €145-195, apt €195-275; 📶) Penny Vincent, an American who moved to France from San Francisco, and her French husband Thierry are the gracious hosts at this elegant home, built in 1830 and still adorned by the original stained glass and tile floors. Each room has a different design, with original artwork, and the best are filled with vintage furnishings and overlook the pretty garden.

La Cour Ste-Catherine BOUTIQUE HOTEL €€
(☎02 31 89 42 40; www.coursaintecatherine.com; 74 rue du Puits; r €120, ste €120-150, apt €150-200; 📶) With a lovely courtyard garden that flowers with tulips and *Magnolia grandiflora*, this charming and tranquil place has adorable rooms, some charmingly tucked away under the eaves of the garret. There are six rooms and two apartments in all, with breakfast included.

Le Fond de la Cour B&B €€
(☎06 72 20 72 98; www.lefonddelacour.com; 29 rue Eugène Boudin; d €99-150, cottage from €145; 📶) Watched over by a dog, a cat and some chickens, rooms here (including a studio and a cottage, which sleeps up to four) are light, airy and immaculate. The energetic Amanda, a native of Scotland, goes to great lengths to make you feel at home. Breakfast, with eggs, croissants, crêpes, bread and Normandy cheese, is included in all room rates.

À l'École Buissonnière B&B €€
(☎06 16 18 43 62; www.a-lecole-buissonniere.com; 4 rue de la Foulerie; d/ste from €100/120; 📶) Occupying a former girls' school built in the 1600s, this handsomely restored B&B has five luxurious rooms with antique wood furnishings, some with terrace for sun-catching. For lunch, stop by the *bar à fromages*

(cheese bar), or ask your hosts to prepare a picnic lunch (€25). Guests can also borrow a bike (no charge). Parking is €10 per night.

La Maison de Lucie   BOUTIQUE HOTEL €€€

(📞 02 31 14 40 40; www.lamaisondelucie.com; 44 rue des Capucins; s/d €170/200, ste €250-330; 🅿🛜) This marvellous and intimate nine-room, three-suite hideaway is a gem. Some bedrooms, panelled in oak, have Moroccan-tile bathrooms and fantastic views across the harbour to the Pont de Normandie. The shady terrace is a glorious place for a summer breakfast. A chic jacuzzi-spa (€40 for two people, 45 minutes) in the old brick-vaulted cellar rounds it off. No lift.

✖ Eating

Marché   MARKET €

(place Ste-Catherine; ⊙ 9am-noon Wed & Sat) A traditional food market on Saturday, a *biologique* (organic) market on Wednesday. There's usually a vendor selling made-to-order crêpes. The market is next to Église Ste-Catherine.

La Cidrerie   CRÊPES €

(📞 02 31 89 59 85; 26 place Hamelin; mains €8-12; ⊙ noon-2.30pm & 7-9.30pm Thu-Mon) For an inexpensive and casual meal, La Cidrerie is a superb choice, serving up a winning combination of piping-hot *galettes* (savoury buckwheat crêpes) and fizzy Norman ciders served in bowls. You can choose from over a dozen savoury options, then finish with a dessert crêpe (try one with homemade caramel sauce). There's also warm cider – perfect if (when) the weather sours.

Bistro des Artistes   FRENCH €€

(📞 02 31 89 95 90; 14 place Berthelot; mains €20-28; ⊙ noon-2.30pm & 7-9.30pm Thu-Tue) This small and dainty eatery near Église Ste-Catherine is managed by Anne-Marie Carneiro, who greets guests, waits tables and cooks. Service can therefore be a bit slow, but dishes are magnificent, and everything is made in-house, including the hearty bread brought to your table. The menu – on a chalkboard – changes frequently, but features beautifully turned-out dishes.

L'Endroit   FRENCH €€

(📞 02 31 88 08 43; www.restaurantlendroithonfleur. com; 3 rue Charles et Paul Bréard; weekday lunch menus €25.50, other menus €32.50, mains €24-26; ⊙ noon-1.30pm & 7.30-9pm Wed-Fri, noon-2pm & 7.30-10pm Sat, noon-2pm & 7.30-9.30pm Sun; 🛜) In an eclectic and artfully designed space with an open kitchen, L'Endroit serves beautifully prepared dishes that showcase the bounty of Normandy fields and coastline. The menu is brief, with just a few roasted meats and seafood dishes on offer, but the high-quality cooking, friendly service and appealing surrounds (including a secret roof terrace for smokers) wins plaudits.

★ La Fleur de Sel   GASTRONOMY €€€

(📞 02 31 89 01 92; www.lafleurdesel-honfleur.com; 17 rue Haute; menus €32-62; ⊙ noon-1.30pm & 7.15-9pm Wed-Sun) Honfleur-raised Vincent Guyon cooked in some of Paris' top kitchens before returning to his hometown to make good and open his own (now celebrated) restaurant. Guyon uses the highest-quality locally

---

CAMEMBERT COUNTRY

Some of the most enduring names in the pungent world of French *fromage* come from Normandy, including Pont L'Évêque, Livarot and, most famous of all, Camembert, all of which are named after towns south of Honfleur, on or near the D579.

It's thought that monks first began experimenting with cheesemaking in the Pays d'Auge area of Normandy sometime in the 11th century, but the present-day varieties didn't emerge until around the 17th century. The invention of Camembert is generally credited to Marie Harel, who was supposedly given the secret of soft cheesemaking by an abbot from Brie on the run from revolutionary mobs in 1790. Whatever the truth of the legend, the cheese was a huge success at the local market in Vimoutiers, and the *fabrication* of Camembert quickly grew from cottage production into a veritable industry. The distinctive round wooden boxes, in which Camembert is wrapped, have been around since 1890; they were designed by a local engineer to protect the soft disc of cheese during its bruising long-distance travel.

If you're interested in seeing how the cheese is made, you can take a tour of **Maison du Camembert** (📞 02 33 12 10 37; www.maisonducamembert.com; adult/child €4/2; ⊙ 10am-noon & 2-5pm daily May-Sep, Wed-Sun Apr & Oct, closed Nov-late Mar), an early-19th-century farm restored by Président, one of the largest Camembert producers. It's in the centre of the town of Camembert, about 60km south of Honfleur.

sourced ingredients and plenty of invention (with roast meats and wild-caught seafood featuring ginger and kaffir-lime vinaigrettes, Camembert foams and hazelnut tempura) in his beautifully crafted dishes. Reserve ahead.

SaQuaNa GASTRONOMY €€€

(☑ 02 31 89 40 80; 22 place Hamelin; menus from €100; ☺ 12.30-2.30pm & 7.30-9.30pm Thu-Sat) This celebrated two-Michelin-starred restaurant dazzles with its exquisite, brilliantly inventive dishes. Chef Alexandre Bourdas trained in Japan (*sakana* means fish in Japanese, but also plays on French artistry in the realm of '*SAveur* (flavour), *QUalité* (quality) and *NAture*'), and he brings elements of the Far East to fresh, locally sourced ingredients.

ⓘ Information

Tourist Office (☑ 02 31 89 23 30; www.ot-honfleur.fr; quai Lepaulmier; ☺ 9.30am-12.30pm & 2-6pm Mon-Sat Sep-Jun, 9.30am-7pm Jul & Aug, also 10am-5pm Sun Easter-Sep; ☏)

ⓘ Getting There & Away

The **bus station** (quai Lepaulmier), two blocks east of the tourist office, has schedules posted in the window.

Bus Verts (p251) Services include Deauville and Trouville-sur-Mer (€2.50, 30 minutes, four to seven daily), Caen (bus 20 €4.20 to €4.90, 2½ hours, seven to 13 daily; express Prestobus 39 €12.10, one hour, one or two daily) and Le Havre (€4.90, 30 minutes, four to six daily).

MANCHE

The Manche *département* (www.manchetourisme.com) encompasses the entire Cotentin Peninsula, stretching from Utah Beach northwest to Cherbourg and southwest to magnificent Mont St-Michel. The peninsula's northwest corner has unspoiled stretches of rocky coastline sheltering tranquil bays and villages. The fertile inland areas, crisscrossed by hedgerows, produce an abundance of beef, dairy products and apples.

The British crown dependencies of Jersey and Guernsey lie 22km and 48km offshore, respectively.

Cherbourg

POP 41,000

At the tip of the Cotentin Peninsula, the port city of Cherbourg plays host to French warships, transoceanic cargo ships, cruise liners, yachts and passenger ferries from Britain and Ireland. It's a far cry from the romantic locale portrayed in Jacques Demy's 1964 musical film *Les Parapluies de Cherbourg* (The Umbrellas of Cherbourg), but it's home to an outstanding aquarium-cum-sea-museum.

During WWII, Cherbourg's port was destroyed by the Germans shortly after D-Day to prevent it from falling into Allied hands.

⊙ Sights

★ **Cité de la Mer** AQUARIUM

(☑ 02 33 20 26 69; www.citedelamer.com; allée du Président Menut, Gare Maritime Transatlantique; adult/child €18/13; ☺ 9.30am-6pm or 7pm Feb-Sep, 10am-6pm Oct-Dec, closed many Mon in Nov & Dec, closed in Jan; ⊞) Cherbourg's art-deco Gare Maritime Transatlantique (Transatlantic Ferry Terminal), built from 1928 to 1933, was designed so travellers could walk from their train directly to their ocean liner. These days it is still used by cruise ships such as the *Queen Mary 2*, but most of the complex houses a fine aquarium featuring Europe's deepest fish tank. The complex is situated 1km northeast of the tourist office.

🛏 Sleeping

Auberge de Jeunesse HOSTEL €

(☑ 02 33 78 15 15; www.fuaj.org; 55 rue de l'Abbaye; dm incl breakfast €23; ☺ reception 9am-1pm & 6-11pm; ☏) Located 1km northwest of the tourist office, this excellent, 99-bed hostel is housed in the French navy's old archives complex. Rooms have two to five beds; there's a small kitchen for self-caterers. To get there, take bus 3 or 5 to the Chantier stop. It's closed for three weeks during the Christmas period.

Hôtel de la Renaissance HOTEL €

(☑ 02 33 43 23 90; www.hotel-renaissance-cherbourg.com; 4 rue de l'Église; d €55-75, f €70-115; ℗ ☏) Staff here are welcoming, and most of the 12 large, well-kept rooms have great views of the port. The Renaissance is situated 400m northwest of the tourist office and by the Basilique de la Trinité. Reception closes at 9pm. Breakfast is €8, the garage is €6.50.

★ **L'Erguillère** HOTEL €€

(☑ 02 33 52 75 31; www.hotel-lerguillere.com; 4 port Racine, St-Germain-des-Vaux; r €110-158; ☏) The building itself is nothing special at this nine-room place in Port Racine (reputed to be the smallest port in the country), but the astonishing sea views and adorable (smallish) bedrooms are, at this breezy spot above the small St Martin cove, 25km west of Cherbourg.

Owner Nicolas pushes the boat out to make guests feel at home. Breakfast is €16.50.

Eating

Restaurants can be found along quai de Caligny, a block or two north of the tourist office, and along the streets leading inland from there, including rue Tour Carrée.

Le Commerce   BRASSERIE €
(☑ 02 33 53 18 20; www.brasserie-du-commerce. fr; 42 rue François la Vieille; mains €9-16, menus €14-18; ⊗ 11am-midnight Mon-Sat) When you (or your wallet) need a break from gourmet dining, head to this brash and boisterous brasserie, where pan-fried salmon, steak, chicken fajitas and other filling dishes are served in ample portions. It's a local favourite of all ages and open long hours, plus it's good value for money.

Au Tire-Bouchon   FRENCH €€
(☑ 02 33 53 54 69; www.restaurant-autirebouchon. com; 17 rue Notre-Dame; lunch menus €11.90-14.20, dinner menus €20-26, mains €15-21; ⊗ noon-2pm & 7-10pm Tue-Sat) At this convivial bistro and wine bar, specialities include oysters, tartines (open sandwiches; €11 to €12) and the *salade tire-bouchon* (a salad with ham, foie gras and salmon). There's a menu for youngsters at €7.20. Au Tire-Bouchon is a bit hard to find – from quai de Caligny, follow the signs to 'Parking Notre-Dame'.

Le Plouc 2   FRENCH €€
(☑ 02 33 01 06 46; 59 rue du Blé; menus €21-36; ⊗ noon-2pm & 7-9.30pm Tue-Fri, 7-9.30pm Sat & Mon, noon-2pm Sun) Locals keep coming back for Le Plouc 2's creative versions of traditional French favourites, prepared with seasonal ingredients and served in a cosy, wood-beamed dining room.

★ Le Pily   GASTRONOMY €€€
(☑ 02 33 10 19 29; www.restaurant-le-pily.com; 39 rue Grande Rue; menus €45.50-80; ⊗ noon-1.45pm & 7-9pm Mon-Sat, 7-9pm Sun Sep–mid-Jun, noon-1.45pm & 7-9pm Tue-Sat, 7-9pm Mon mid-Jun–Aug) Young chef Pierre Marion is at the helm of the town's best restaurant, which has been serving Cherbourg gastronomes for over a decade. Expect a lively menu of seafood and meat dishes, with great care taken in the balancing of flavours and skilled presentation on the plate.

Information

Tourist Office (☑ 02 33 93 52 02; www. cherbourgtourisme.com; 14 quai Alexandre III;

⊗ 9.30am-7pm Mon-Sat, 10am-5pm Sun mid-Jun–mid-Sep, 10am-12.30pm & 2-6pm Mon-Sat mid-Sep–mid-Jun)

Getting There & Away

BOAT
Cherbourg's **ferry terminal** is 2km northeast of the tourist office.

Brittany Ferries (www.brittany-ferries.co.uk) Has services to the English ports of Poole and Portsmouth.

Irish Ferries (www.irishferries.com) Goes to the Irish ports of Rosslare and Dublin.

Stena Line (www.stenaline.ie) Sails to Rosslare.

TRAIN
The train station is at the southern end of Bassin du Commerce (inner harbour), just west of the Les Éléis shopping mall. Direct services include the following:

Bayeux €20, one hour, 15 daily Monday to Friday, eight to 10 daily Saturday and Sunday

Caen €24, 1¼ hours, eight to 15 daily

Paris Gare St-Lazare €52, three hours, eight daily Monday to Friday, four or five daily Saturday and Sunday

Pontorson (Mont St-Michel) €32, 2½ to 3½ hours, three to five daily (via Lison)

Mont St-Michel
POP 44

It's one of France's most iconic images: the slender spires, stout ramparts and rocky outcrops of Mont St-Michel rising dramatically from the sea – or towering over slick, shimmering sands laid bare by the receding tide. Despite vast numbers of tourists, both the rock-top abbey and the narrow alleys below still manage to transport visitors back to the Middle Ages.

The bay around Mont St-Michel is famed for having Europe's highest tidal variations; the difference between low and high tides – only about six hours apart – can reach an astonishing 15m. The Mont is only completely surrounded by the sea every month or two, when the tidal coefficient is above 100 and high tide is above 14m (check online before you go, if this is what you want to see). Regardless of the time of year, the waters sweep in at an astonishing clip, said to be as fast as a galloping horse.

History

Bishop Aubert of Avranches is said to have built a devotional chapel on the summit of the island in 708, following his vision of

Mont St-Michel

TIMELINE

708 Inspired by a vision of ❶ **St Michael**, Bishop Aubert is inspired to 'build here and build high'.

966 Richard I, Duke of Normandy, gives the Mont to the Benedictines. The three levels of the ❷ **abbey** reflect their monastic hierarchy.

1017 Development of the abbey begins. Pilgrims arrive to honour the cult of St Michael. They walk barefoot across the mudflats and up the ❸ **Grande Rue** to be received in the almonry (now the bookshop).

1203 The monastery is burnt by the troops of Philip Augustus, who later donates money for its restoration and the Gothic 'miracle', ❹ **La Merveille**, is constructed.

1434 The Mont's ❺ **ramparts** and fortifications ensure it withstands the English assault during the Hundred Years War. It is the only place in northern France not to fall.

1789 After the Revolution, monasticism is abolished and the Mont is turned into a prison. During this period the ❻ **treadmill** is built to lift up supplies.

1878 The Mont is linked to the mainland by a causeway.

1979 The Mont is declared a Unesco World Heritage Site.

2014 The causeway is replaced by a ❼ **bridge**.

TOP TIPS

➡ Pick up a picnic lunch at the supermarket in La Caserne to avoid the Mont's overpriced fast food.

➡ Allow 30 to 45 minutes to an hour to get from the parking lot in La Caserne to the Mont.

➡ If you step off the island pay close attention to the tides – they can be dangerous and whisk you away.

➡ Don't forget to pick up the Abbey's excellent audioguide – it tells some great stories.

MOR65, MAURO PICCARDI/SHUTTERSTOCK ©

Abbey
The abbey's three levels reflect the monastic order: monks lived isolated in church and cloister, the abbot entertained noble guests at the middle level, and lowly pilgrims were received in the basement. Tip: night visits run from mid-July to August, while admission is free the first Sunday of the month November to March.

Treadmill
The giant treadmill was powered hamster-like by half a dozen prisoners, who, marching two abreast, raised stone and supplies up the Mont.

West Terrace

Chapelle St-Aubert

Tour Gabriel

Les Fanils

JULIA KUZNETSOVA/SHUTTERSTOCK ©

Ramparts
The Mont was also a military garrison surrounded by machi-colated and turreted walls, dating from the 13th to 15th centuries. The single entrance, Porte de l'Avancée, ensured its security in the Hundred Years War. Tip: Tour du Nord (North Tower) has the best views.

BEST VIEWS

The view from the Jardin des Plantes in nearby Avranches is unique, as are the panoramas from Pointe du Grouin du Sud near the village of St-Léonard.

St Michael Statue & Bell Tower

A golden statue of the winged St Michael looks ready to leap heavenward from the bell tower. He is the patron of the Mont, having inspired St Aubert's original devotional chapel.

La Merveille

The highlights of La Merveille are the vast refectory hall lit through embrasured windows, the Knights Hall with its elegant ribbed vaulting, and the cloister (above), which is one of the purest examples of 13th-century architecture to survive here.

ELENA ELISSEEVA/SHUTTERSTOCK ©

ÎLOT DE TOMBELAINE

Occupied by the English during the Hundred Years War, this islet is now a bird reserve. From April to July it teems with exceptional birdlife.

Gardens

Tour du Nord

① ④ ②

⑥

Église St-Pierre

Cemetery

Chemin des Remparts

③

Tour de l'Arcade

Toilets

Tour du Roi

Porte des Fanils

Tourist Office

Porte de l'Avancée (Entrance)

⑦

Grande Rue

The main thoroughfare of the small village below the abbey, Grande Rue has charm despite its rampant commercialism. Don't miss the famous Mère Poulard shop here, for souvenir cookies.

SARANYA33/SHUTTERSTOCK ©

Bridge

In 2014 the Mont's 136-year-old causeway was replaced by a bridge designed to allow seawater to circulate and thus save the island from turning into a peninsula.

the Archangel Michael, whose gilded figure, perched on the tip of the abbey's spire. In 966, Richard I, Duke of Normandy, gave Mont St-Michel to the Benedictines, who turned it into a centre of learning and, in the 11th century, into something of an ecclesiastical fortress, with a military garrison at the disposal of both abbot and king.

In the 15th century, during the Hundred Years War, the English blockaded and besieged Mont St-Michel three times. The fortified abbey withstood these assaults and was the only place in western and northern France not to fall into English hands. After the Revolution, Mont St-Michel was turned into a prison. In 1966, the abbey was symbolically returned to the Benedictines as part of the celebrations marking its millennium. Mont St-Michel and the bay became a Unesco World Heritage Site in 1979.

In recent decades, sand and silt built up hugely around the causeway – created in 1879 – linking the Mont to the mainland, threatening to turn the island into a permanent peninsula. To restore the site's 'maritime character', in 2014 the causeway was replaced by a 2km pedestrian and vehicle (primarily the shuttle buses) bridge designed to allow the tides and the River Couësnon (kweh-*no*) – whose new *barrage* (dam) stores up high-tide water and then releases it at low tide – to flush away accumulated sediments. For the latest, see www.projetmontsaintmichel.fr.

⊙ Sights & Activities

The Mont's one main street, the **Grande Rue**, leads up the slope – past souvenir shops, eateries and a forest of elbows – to the abbey. The staircases and tiny passageways that meander up the hill from the Grande Rue – one, opposite Restaurant La Croix Blanche, is just 50cm wide – will take you to the diminutive parish church, a tiny cemetery and other Mont-sized surprises. Finding your way around is easier if you pick up a detailed map of the Mont at the tourist office or the abbey's ticket counter.

Be prepared for lots of steps, some of them spiral – alas, it's one of the least wheelchair-accessible sites in France.

★**Abbaye du Mont St-Michel**   ABBEY
(☑ 02 33 89 80 00; www.abbaye-mont-saint-michel. fr/en; adult/child incl guided tour €10/free; ☺ 9am-7pm May-Aug, 9.30am-6pm Sep-Apr, last entry 1hr before closing) The Mont's star attraction is the stunning ensemble crowning its top: the

abbey. Most areas can be visited without a guide, but it's worth taking the 1¼-hour tour included in the ticket; English tours (usually) begin at 11am and 3pm from October to March, with three or four daily tours in spring and summer. You can also take a one-hour audioguide tour (€3), available in 10 languages. Admission is free the first Sunday of the month from November to March.

Benedictine monks hold services in the abbey at 6.50am from Tuesday to Friday; at 7.50am on Saturday, Sunday and holidays; at 11.15am on Sunday; at noon from Tuesday to Saturday; and at 6.20pm from Tuesday to Friday.

From Monday to Saturday from mid-July to August there are illuminated *nocturnes* (night-time visits) with live chamber music from 7pm to midnight.

Église Abbatiale   CHURCH
(Abbey Church) Built on the rocky tip of the mountain cone, the transept rests on solid rock, while the nave, choir and transept arms are supported by the rooms below. This church is famous for its mix of architectural styles: the nave and south transept (11th and 12th centuries) are solid Norman Romanesque, while the choir (late 15th century) is Flamboyant Gothic.

La Merveille   HISTORIC SITE
(The Marvel) The buildings on the northern side of the Mont are known as 'The Marvel'. The famous **cloître** (cloister) is surrounded by a double row of delicately carved arches resting on granite pillars. The early-13th-century, barrel-roofed **réfectoire** (dining hall) is illuminated by a wall of recessed windows – remarkable given that the sheer drop precluded the use of flying buttresses. The Gothic **Salle des Hôtes** (Guest Hall), dating from 1213, has two enormous fireplaces.

Other features to look out for include the **promenoir** (ambulatory), with one of the oldest ribbed vaulted ceilings in Europe, and the **Chapelle de Notre Dame sous Terre** (Underground Chapel of Our Lady), one of the abbey's oldest rooms, rediscovered in 1903.

The masonry used to build the abbey was brought to the Mont by boat and pulled up the hillside using ropes.

★**Chemin des Remparts**   WALKING
For spectacular views of the bay and people trudging through the mud at low tide, you can walk along the top of the entire eastern section of the Mont's ramparts, from Tour du Nord (North Tower) to the Porte du Roy.

☞ Tours

When the tide is out (the tourist office has tide tables), you can walk all the way around Mont St-Michel, a distance of about 1km, with a guide (doing so on your own is very risky). Straying too far from the Mont can be dangerous: you could get stuck in wet sand – from which Norman soldiers are depicted being rescued in one scene of the Bayeux Tapestry – or be overtaken either by the incoming tide or by water gushing from the new dam's eight sluice gates.

Experienced outfits offering guided walks into – or even across – the bay are based across the bay from Mont St-Michel in Genêts. Local tourist offices have details on other guiding companies. Reserve ahead. A good choice is **Découverte de la Baie du Mont-Saint-Michel** (☑ 02 33 70 83 49; www. decouvertebaie.com; 1 rue Montoise, Genêts; adult/ child from €8/5).

🛏 Sleeping

The most convenient hotels – most run by formulaic chains – are in La Caserne, 2km south of the Mont itself. The only way to drive into La Caserne is to get a gate code when you make your reservation. If you stay here or in a nearby B&B, you'll save the €12 parking fee. If you stay up on the Mont itself, you'll have to leave your car in La Caserne.

Camping du Mont St-Michel CAMPGROUND €
(☑ 02 33 60 22 10; www.camping-montsaintmichel. com/fr/camping-mont-saint-michel; campsite from €15; ☉Mar-Oct) Located in La Caserne and putting you well within walking distance of Mont St-Michel, placing a tent here costs €15 for one person and €18 for two; in the high season, it's €4 more per tent.

Auberge de Jeunesse HOSTEL €
(Centre Duguesclin; ☑ 02 33 60 18 65; www.fuaj. org; 21 bd du Général Patton, Pontorson; dm €15; ☉reception 8am-noon & 5-8.30pm, hostel closed Oct-Mar) This 62-bed hostel has four- to six-bed rooms and kitchen facilities: it's not located on Mont St-Michel, but in Pontorson, linked to the rest of France by train and to the Mont by shuttle bus.

Vent des Grèves B&B €
(☑ Estelle 02 33 48 28 89; www.ventdesgreves. com; 7-9 chemin des Dits, Ardevon; s/d €48/58) Offering outstanding value, this friendly, family-run B&B has five modern rooms, furnished simply, with magical views of the Mont. It's located an easily walkable 1km east of the shuttle stop in La Caserne.

SANTÉ!

Equal parts gallery, wine bar and taxidermy shop, **Le Ballon Rouge** (☑ 02 33 94 34 06; 9 rue du Port; ☉10.30am-1pm & 3-8.30pm Tue, Thu & Sat, 4-8.30pm Wed, 10.30am-1pm & 3pm-1am Fri) near the waterfront embodies Cherbourg's most creative side. Stop in for a look at the changing artwork for sale, chat with the quirky owner, and enjoy an evening tipple amid half-deflated balloons, stuffed foxes and wildly eclectic tunes played on vinyl (from alt rock to old French marching songs).

La Bourdatière B&B €
(☑ 02 33 68 11 17; www.la-bourdatiere.com; 8 rue Maurice Desfeux, Beauvoir; d from €45; ☉Apr-Oct) This charming stone farmhouse in Beauvoir village, around an hour on foot from Mont St-Michel, is excellent value. The decor of the four rooms is nothing special, but comfy enough and the rural setting and blissful gardens are tough to top, especially when compared to the more identikit hotels.

★**La Jacotière** B&B €€
(☑ 02 33 60 22 94; www.lajacotiere.fr; 46 rue de la Côte, Ardevon; d €78-95, studio €100-122; P ♠) Built as a farmhouse in 1906, this superbly situated and very popular family-run B&B has five comfortable rooms and one studio apartment. With views of Mont St-Michel, it's situated just 300m east of the shuttle stop in La Caserne.

Hotel Gabriel HOTEL €€
(☑ 02 33 60 14 13; https://hotels.le-mont-saint-michel.com/en/hotel-gabriel/; rte du Mont St-Michel; d from €99, r for 5 incl breakfast from €162; P ♠) Hotel Gabriel serves up lodging with a dash of style, courtesy of its boldly painted (if somewhat small) rooms with touches of pop art sprinkled about. The location is unbeatable: it's in La Caserne, just steps from the causeway (and shuttle stop) leading to Mont St-Michel.

Hôtel Du Guesclin HOTEL €€
(☑ 02 33 60 14 10; www.hotelduguesclin.com; Grande Rue, Mont St-Michel; d €100-130; ☉closed Wed night & Thu Apr-Jun & Oct–mid-Nov, hotel closed mid-Nov–Mar; ♠) One of the most affordable hotels on the Mont itself, the Hôtel Du Guesclin (geck-*la*) has 10 old-style rooms, five with priceless views of the bay. Not all rooms have wi-fi access, so check.

COUTANCES

The lovely old town of Coutances makes for a nice detour on the way to Mont St-Michel from the D-Day beaches or Cherbourg. Its splendid, twin-towered Gothic **cathedral** (http://cathedralecoutances.free.fr; parvis Notre-Dame; ☉ 8.30am-noon & 2-5.30pm) includes several 13th-century windows and a 14th-century fresco of St Michael skewering the dragon, and the nearby **Jardin des Plantes de Coutances** (rue Quesnel Morinière; ☉ 9am-8pm Apr-Jun, to 11pm Jul & Aug, to 10pm Sep, to 6pm Oct, Feb & Mar, to 5pm Nov-Jan) is a delight to meander with its impeccably landscaped, flower-filled beds first planted in the mid-19th century.

TER trains connect Coutances with Caen, Cherbourg and Pontorson (the nearest station to Mont St-Michel).

✖ Eating

The Grande Rue is jammed with crêperies and sandwich shops. Many of the eating options on the Mont are overpriced, overbooked and overbusy.

Crêperie La Sirène CRÊPES €
(☎ 02 33 60 08 60; Grande Rue; crêpes €4-11; ☉ 11.45am-5pm Sep-Dec & mid-Feb–Jun, to 9.30pm Jul & Aug, closed Jan–mid-Feb) This decent crêperie is located near the bottom of Grande Rue, up a 15th-century staircase from the souvenir shop.

Les Terrasses Poulard FRENCH €€
(☎ 02 33 89 02 02; www.terrasses-poulard.fr; Grand Rue; menus €19-29; ☉ noon-2pm & 7-9pm) Amid cast-iron chandeliers and copper pots hung from the walls and part of the hotel of the same name, this bright and buzzing, always packed eatery serves up the usual assortment of bistro classics, as well as *galettes* (including a more affordable *galette* menu for €16); there's a kids menu for €9. The waterfront views are a nice bonus.

ℹ Information

La Caserne Tourist Office (☎ 02 14 13 20 15; www.bienvenueaumontsaintmichel.com; La Caserne parking lot; ☉ 10am-6pm) Just before you approach the bridge, this is a handy port of call for brochures and info, with left-luggage lockers and an ATM.

Mont St-Michel Tourist Office (☎ 02 33 60 14 30; www.ot-montsaintmichel.com; bd Avancée, Corps de Garde des Bourgeois; ☉ 9.30am-7pm Jul & Aug, to 6.30pm Mon-Sat, 9.30am-12.30pm & 1.30-6pm Sun Apr, May, Jun & Sep, shorter hours rest of year; 🛜) You can check the tide tables here, change money and buy a map of the Mont (€3). Next door are toilets and an ATM.

ℹ Getting There & Away

For all manner of details on getting to the Mont, see www.bienvenueaumontsaintmichel.com.

BUS

Intercity buses stop next to the Mont's parking lot in La Caserne, very near the shuttles to the Mont. Bus 1 (every hour or two, more frequently in July and August), operated by **Transdev** (☎ 02 14 13 20 15), links La Caserne with the village of Beauvoir (€3.20, five minutes) and the train station in Pontorson (€3.20, 18 minutes); times are coordinated with the arrival in Pontorson of some trains from Caen and Rennes.

Keolis Emeraude (☎ 02 99 26 16 00; www.destination-montsaintmichel.com) has buses to the train stations in Rennes (€15, 1¼ hours, four daily) and Dol de Bretagne (€8, 30 minutes, one or two daily); times are coordinated with TGVs to/from Paris.

CAR & MOTORCYCLE

Cars must be left in one of the parking lots (two/24 hours €6.30/11.70) situated east of La Caserne's hotel strip. If you find space, you could park your car for free further away in the village of Beauvoir, but it's a longer walk.

TRAIN

The town of Pontorson, 7km south of the La Caserne parking area, is the area's main rail hub, connected to Mont St-Michel by shuttle bus (€3.20). Services from Pontorson include:

Bayeux €24, 1¾ hours, three daily

Caen €28, 1¾ hours, three daily

Cherbourg €32, 2½ to 3½ hours, three to five daily (via Lison)

Rennes €15, 50 minutes, three or four daily

ℹ Getting Around

The parking area next to La Caserne is 2.5km south of Mont St-Michel. To get from there to the Mont, you can either walk or take the shuttle bus (free with your car park ticket) that lets you off 300m from the Mont's main gate. Shuttles run 24 hours a day – regularly from 7am to 1am, when summoned by phone after that. Count on spending 45 minutes to an hour to get from the parking lot to the abbey. A shuttle (€2.80) also runs from the train station in Pontorson to Mont St-Michel. A horse-drawn carriage from the La Caserne Tourist Office area to Mont St-Michel is €5.30.

Brittany

POP 3.27 MILLION

Best Places to Eat

➡ Le Vivier (p311)

➡ Breizh Café (p283)

➡ La Table Breizh Café (p287)

➡ Le Coquillage (p287)

Best Places to Stay

➡ Le 14 Saint-Michel (p317)

➡ La Maison Pavie (p288)

➡ Le Keo – La Maison des Capitaines (p296)

➡ Kastell Dinn (p298)

Why Go?

Brittany is for explorers. Its wild, dramatic coastline, medieval towns and thick forests make an excursion here well worth the detour off the beaten track. This is a land of prehistoric mysticism, proud tradition and culinary wealth, where fiercely independent locals celebrate Breton culture, and Paris feels a long way away indeed.

The entire region (Breizh in Breton) has a wonderfully undiscovered feel once you go beyond world-famous sights such as stunning St-Malo, regal Dinard and charming Dinan. Unexpected gems – including the little-known towns of Roscoff, Quimper and Vannes, the megaliths of Carnac, the rugged coastlines of Finistère, the Presqu'Île de Crozon and the Morbihan Coast – reveal there's far more to Brittany than delicious crêpes and homemade cider. Its much-loved islands are also big draws – don't miss the stars: dramatic Île d'Ouessant and the aptly named Belle Île. And wherever you go, keep an eye out for *korrigans* (fairies or spirits).

When to Go
Brest

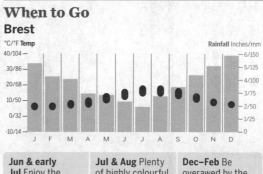

Jun & early Jul Enjoy the beaches, outdoor adventures and sunshine before the crowds.

Jul & Aug Plenty of highly colourful festivals and events await you throughout the region.

Dec–Feb Be overawed by the elements during a wild winter storm along the Finistère coastline.

Brittany Highlights

1 **St-Malo** (p279) Strolling along historic ramparts with panoramic views.

2 **Megaliths** (p310) Cycling past fields prehistoric megaliths around Carnac.

3 **Coastlines** (p297) Exploring the scenic Presqu'île de Crozon and Pointe du Raz.

4 **Belle Île** (p313) Getting away from it all and frolicking in sun and sea.

5 **Vannes** (p314) Joining a vibrant Breton city in its *joie de vivre*, history and coastal sights.

6 **Île de Batz** (p291) Hiking and biking to your heart's content on this car-free islet.

7 **Quiberon** (p311) Looking for beaches along the raw, wild and sublime Côte Sauvage.

8 **Josselin** (p316) Touring the turreted medieval castle over the fairy-tale forest village.

9 **Cancale** (p287) Tucking into freshly shucked oysters on a casual harbourfront.

10 **Dinan** (p287) Getting lost in the higgledy-piggledy old town.

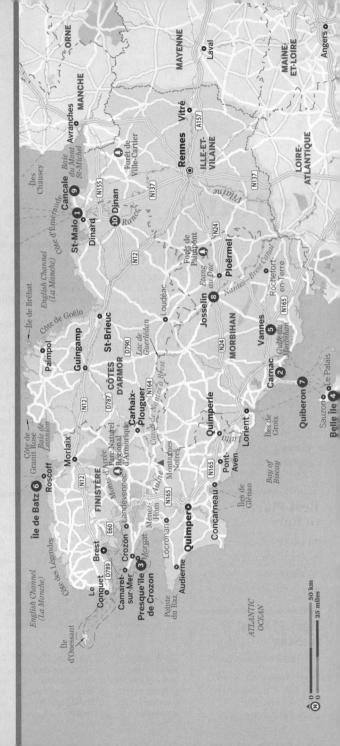

History

Brittany's earliest known neolithic tribes left a legacy of menhirs and dolmens clustered across the region that continue to baffle historians. Celts arrived in the 6th century BC, naming their new homeland Armor ('the land beside the sea') and ultimately the region was conquered by Julius Caesar in 56 BC. Following the withdrawal of the Romans in the 5th century AD, another influx of Celts – driven from what is now Britain and Ireland by the Anglo-Saxon invasions – settled in Brittany, bringing Christianity with them.

In the 9th century, Brittany's national hero Nominoë (also spelled Nomenoë) revolted against French rule. Wedged between two more-powerful kingdoms, the duchy of Brittany was continually contested by France and England until a series of strategic royal weddings finally saw the region become part of France in 1532.

However, Brittany has retained a separate regional identity. A drive for cultural and linguistic renewal is afoot, and a consciousness exists of Brittany's place within a wider Celtic culture embracing Ireland, Wales, Scotland, Cornwall and Galicia in Spain.

❶ Getting There & Away

Ferries link St-Malo with the Channel Islands and the English ports of Portsmouth, Plymouth and Poole. From Roscoff there are ferries to Plymouth (UK), Cork and Rosslare (Ireland), and Bilbao (Spain). Alternatively, airports in Brest, Quimper, Rennes, Dinard and, further to the south, Nantes, serve the UK and Ireland, as well as other European and domestic destinations.

Brittany's major towns and cities have rail connections, but routes leave the interior poorly served. The opening of the TGV line between Le Mans and Rennes in 2017 has cut approximately 40 minutes off train travel times to Paris. A handy website for calculating transit in the region whether by train, bus or boat is www.breizhgo.com.

The bus network is extensive, if generally infrequent, meaning that your own wheels are the best way to see the area, particularly out-of-the-way destinations.

With gently undulating, well-maintained roads, an absence of road tolls and relatively little traffic outside the major towns, driving in Brittany is a real pleasure. Cycling is also extremely popular, and bike-rental places are never hard to find.

NORTH COAST

Enveloped by belle époque beach resorts, fishing villages and wave-splashed headlands, Brittany's central-north coast splendidly spans the *départements* of Ille-et-Vilaine and Côtes d'Armor. Verdant shallows give rise to the name Côte d'Émeraude (Emerald Coast) to the east; westwards, boulders blush in profusion along the Côte de Granit Rose, while a scattering of charming offshore islands begs for exploration.

St-Malo

POP 46,589

The enthralling mast-filled port town of St-Malo is a dramatic sight. With one of the world's greatest tidal ranges, brewing storms under blackened skies see waves lash the top of the ramparts ringing its beautiful walled city. Hours later, the blue sky merges with the deep cobalt sea as the tide recedes, exposing broad beaches and creating land bridges to granite outcrop islands.

Construction of the walled city's fortifications began in the 12th century. The town became a key port during the 17th and 18th centuries as a base for both merchant ships and government-sanctioned privateers (pirates, basically) against the constant threat of the English. These days, English arrivals are tourists, for whom St-Malo, a short ferry hop from the Channel Islands, is a summer haven.

The pretty fishing port of St-Servan sits 2km south of the walled city and many sights are located there.

◉ Sights

A combined ticket (per adult/child €13/6) gives you access to St-Malo's four major monuments: Musée d'Histoire de St-Malo (p280), Musée International du Long Cours Cap-Hornier (p281), **Musée Jacques Cartier** (☑ 02 99 40 97 73; www.musee-jacques-cartier.fr; rue David MacDonald Stewart; adult/child €6/3; ☉ tours 10am, noon, 2.30pm & 6pm Jun-Sep, shorter hours rest of year) and Mémorial 39–45 (p281). It can be purchased at any of the participating museums and is valid for the duration of your stay in St-Malo.

◉ Intra-Muros

The tangle of streets in the walled city of St-Malo, known as Intra-Muros ('within the walls'), are a highlight of a visit to Brittany. Grand merchants' mansions and sea

St-Malo & St-Servan

N 0 ——— 200 m
0 ——— 0.1 miles

★ **Château de St-Malo** CASTLE
(Map p282; place Chateaubriand; ⊙10am-
12.30pm & 2-6pm Apr-Sep, 10am-noon & 2-6pm
Tue-Sun Oct-Mar) Château de St-Malo was
built by the dukes of Brittany in the 15th
and 16th centuries, and is now the home
of the **Musée d'Histoire de St-Malo** (Map
p282; ☎02 99 40 71 57; www.ville-saint-malo.
fr/culture/les-musees; place Chateaubriand,
Château de St-Malo; adult/child €6/3; ⊙10am-
12.30pm & 2-6pm Apr-Sep, 10am-noon & 2-6pm
Tue-Sun Oct-Mar), which examines the life
and history of the city, while the lookout
tower offers eye-popping views of the old
city.

Cathédrale St-Vincent CATHEDRAL
(Map p282; place Jean de Châtillon; ⊙9.30am-
6pm) The city's centrepiece was constructed between the 12th and 18th centuries.
During the ferocious fighting of August
1944, the cathedral was badly mauled, with
much of its original structure (including
its spire) reduced to rubble. The cathedral
was subsequently rebuilt and reconsecrat-
ed in 1971. A mosaic plaque on the floor
of the nave marks the spot where Jacques
Cartier received the blessing of the bishop
of St-Malo before his 'voyage of discovery'
to Canada in 1535.

◎ Beyond the Walls

Fort National RUINS
(Map p280; www.fortnational.com; adult/child
€5/3; ⊙Easter, Jun-Sep & school holidays, hours
vary) The St-Malo ramparts' northern
stretch looks across to the remains of this
former prison, built by Vauban in 1689.
Standing atop a rocky outcrop, the fort
can is only accessible at low tide, so check
online or with the tourist office (p284) for
tour times.

captains' houses line the narrow lanes, and
open squares are tucked in its heart. For the
best panoramas, stroll along the **jetty** that
pokes out to sea off the southwestern tip of
Intra-Muros from the end of which you'll
get the wide-angle view – or, to zoom in,
clamber along the top of the **ramparts** (Map
p282), which surround the town.

Though you'd never guess it from the
cobblestone streets and reconstructed monuments in 17th- and 18th-century style, during August 1944, the battle to drive German
forces out of St-Malo destroyed around 80%
of the old city, which has been painstakingly
restored since then.

BRITTANY ST-MALO

Fort de la Cité d'Alet   FORT

(Map p280; allée Gaston Buy, St-Servan; ⊙ 24hr) FREE Constructed in the mid-18th century, Fort de la Cité d'Alet was used as a German base during WWII; one of the bunkers now houses this memorial, which depicts St-Malo's violent WWII history and liberation. A visit is an evocative and moving experience.

Mémorial 39–45   MONUMENT

(Map p280; ☑ 02 99 82 41 74; www.ville-saint-malo. fr; Fort de la Cité d'Alet, St-Servan; adult/child €6/3; ⊙ guided visits 10.15am, 11am, 2pm, 3pm & 4.30pm Jul & Aug, 2.30pm, 3.15pm & 4.30pm Tue-Sun Apr-Jun & Sep, shorter hours Oct) One of the bunkers of the Fort de la Cité d'Alet now houses this memorial, which depicts St-Malo's violent WWII history and liberation, and includes a 45-minute film in French on the Battle of St-Malo (not shown on every tour). Some guided visits are conducted in English; call ahead to confirm times.

Musée International du
Long Cours Cap-Hornier   MUSEUM

(Museum of the Cape Horn Route; Map p280; ☑ 02 99 40 71 58; www.ville-saint-malo.fr; Tour Solidor, quai Sébastopol, St-Servan; adult/child €6/3; ⊙ 10am-12.30pm & 2-6pm daily Apr-Sep, 10am-noon & 2-6pm Tue-Sun Oct-Mar) Housed in the 14th-century Tour Solidor, this museum presents the life of the hardy sailors who followed the dangerous Cape Horn route around the southern tip of South America. Don't miss the superb views from atop the tower.

Grand Aquarium   AQUARIUM

(☑ 02 99 21 19 00; www.aquarium-st-malo.com; av Général Patton; adult/child €16.50/12; ⊙ 9.30am-9pm mid Jul–mid-Aug, 9.30am-8pm early Jul & late Aug, 10am-6pm mid-Jan–Jun & Sep-Dec; ⊕; ☐ C1, C2) Containing over 600 species of marine creature, this very popular aquarium about 4km south of the city centre features a 'Nautibus' ride – a simulated descent aboard an underwater submarine – and a *bassin tactile* (touch pool), where kids can touch rays and turbots. The exhibits on local marine life, tropical reefs and mangrove forests are also very strong. Allow around two hours for a visit.

⊙ Beaches

You can splash in the protected tidal **swimming pool** west of the city walls at **Plage de Bon Secours** (Map p282) or climb its ladder to jump off into the sea. It's also a great place to catch sunset.

The **Plage des Bas Sablons** (Map p280) is south of the Intra-Muros in the fishing port of St-Servan.

The much larger **Grande Plage** stretches northeast along the isthmus of Le Sillon. Less-crowded **Plage de Rochebonne** is another 1km to the northeast, along Grande Plage.

⟳ Tours

Compagnie Corsaire   BOATING

(Map p282; ☑ 08 25 13 81 00; www.compagnie corsaire.com; Cale de Dinan; ⊙ Apr-Sep) Compagnie Corsaire runs four-hour *pêche en mer* (deep-sea fishing) trips (€43.50). Boat tours and ferries leave from just outside Porte de Dinan and include: Bay of St-Malo (adult/child €21.20/12.70, 1½ hours), Cap Fréhel (adult/child €31.50/18.90), Dinan (adult/child €33.50/20.10), Île Cézembre (adult/child €15.90/9.50) and Îles Chausey (adult/child €34.80/20.90). Check online for schedules and itineraries.

The company also runs a Bus de Mer shuttle service (adult/child return €8.50/5.60, 10 minutes) between St-Malo and Dinard.

🛏 Sleeping

🛏 Intra-Muros

Hôtel San Pedro   HOTEL €

(Map p282; ☑ 02 99 40 88 57; www.sanpedro-hotel.com; 1 rue Ste-Anne; s €53-60, tw €73, d €66-81; 🛜) Tucked at the back of the old city, the San Pedro has a cool, crisp, neutral-toned decor

---

DON'T MISS

LOW-TIDE COASTAL ENCOUNTER

At low tide, cross the beach to walk out via Porte des Bés to **Île du Grand Bé** (Map p280; ☑ 06 08 27 51 20; fort guided tours adult/child €6/4; ⊙ fort by reservation, depending on tides & weather), the rocky islet where the great St-Malo-born, 18th-century writer Chateaubriand is buried. About 100m beyond Grand Bé is the privately owned, Vauban-built, 17th-century **Fort du Petit Bé**. Once the tide rushes in, the causeway remains impassable for about six hours; check tide times with the tourist office (p284) so you don't get trapped on the island.

BRITTANY ST-MALO

Intra-Muros

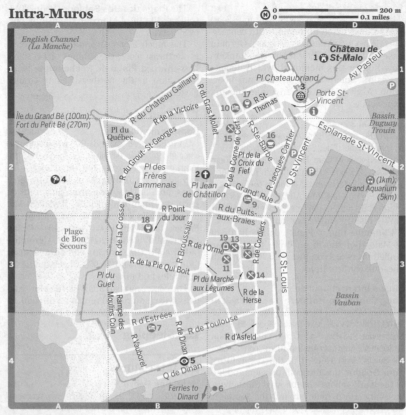

Intra-Muros

◎ Top Sights

◎ Sights

✈ Activities, Courses & Tours

🛏 Sleeping

✗ Eating

🍸 Drinking & Nightlife

🛍 Shopping

with subtle splashes of yellow paint, friendly service, great breakfast (€8.50), private parking (€10) and a few bikes available for free.

It features 12 rooms on four floors served by possibly the smallest lift in existence; two rooms come with partial sea views.

Le Nautilus HOTEL €
(Map p282; ☑02 99 40 42 27; www.hotel-lenautilus-saint-malo.com; 9 rue de la Corne de Cerf; s €52-76, d €59-98, tw €68-104, tr €82-110, f €92-116; ⊘ Feb-Nov; 🖥) With efficient, friendly service and comfortable albeit smallish rooms (appropriately enough for the name), this super-central two-star abode offers excellent value. Decor is spruce with smartly finished bathrooms and light yellow walls, while the lift is an unexpected bonus for a hotel in this price range.

Hôtel Quic en Groigne HOTEL €€
(Map p282; ☑02 99 20 22 20; www.quic-en-groigne.com; 8 rue d'Estrées; d/f €67/30; ⊘ mid-Feb–Dec; 🖥) This lovely hotel has 15 clean and simple-style rooms and affords not only good value, but also excellent service and an ideal location on a quiet, old-town street just a short walk from a beach. The icing on the cake: the convenience of secure parking (€14; five spaces only) in a city where parking can be downright hellish.

★ La Maison des Armateurs HOTEL €€
(Map p282; ☑02 99 40 87 70; www.maisondesarmateurs.com; 6 Grand' Rue; d €99-290, f/ste €170/430; ⊘ closed Dec; ❀🖥) La Maison des Armateurs is enthusiastically run by a very helpful French-American couple. Despite the austere granite-fronted setting, the inside of this sassy four-star hotel is all sexy, modern minimalism: stylish furniture throughout, gleaming bathrooms with power showers and cool chocolate, pale orange and neutral grey tones. Families can plump for the super-sized suites. Check the website for deals.

🛏 Beyond the Walls

Camping de la Cité d'Alet CAMPGROUND €
(Map p280; ☑02 99 81 60 91; www.ville-saint-malo.fr/camping-la-cite-dalet/; allée Gaston Buy, St-Servan; 2-person tent €17; ⊘ Apr–mid-May & Jul–mid-Sep; 🖥) Perched on a peninsula, this campground has panoramic 360-degree views and is close to beaches and some lively bars, but facilities are very basic – toilets only.

**Auberge de Jeunesse –
Éthic Étapes Patrick Varangot** HOSTEL €
(☑02 99 40 29 80; www.centrevarangot.com; 37 av du Révérend Père Umbricht, Paramé; dm incl breakfast €25.20; @🖥; 🚌3) This efficient hostel scores high on amenities, with a well-equipped communal kitchen, a restaurant, a bar, laundry service, private parking and free sports facilities. It has 285 beds, with each room accommodating two to five beds and an en-suite bathroom. It's in a calm neighbourhood, a five-minute walk from Plage de Rochebonne. Breakfast is served between 6am and 9.15pm.

Maison Angélus B&B €€
(☑02 99 40 66 79; www.maisonangelus.com; 82 av Pasteur; d €115-130; 🖥) This delightful three-room B&B, housed inside a tastefully restored 19th-century building, is a tranquil respite from the crowds, ideally situated just a two-minute stroll from the Grande Plage. You'll love the cosy lounge areas and the backyard garden oasis. Your Italian hosts, Giulio and Cristina, complete the charming picture, and serve a delicious breakfast and a superb Italian dinner (€40).

★ Le Valmarin HISTORIC HOTEL €€
(Map p280; ☑02 99 81 94 76; www.levalmarin.com; 7 rue Jean XXIII, St-Servan; s €80-125, d €85-165, f €149-230; 🖥) If you're yearning for an aristocratic overlay to your St-Malo experience then this peaceful 18th-century mansion should do the job nicely. It has 12 high-ceilinged rooms dressed in late-19th-century style, and glorious gardens full of flowers and shade trees. Minus: some bathrooms feel a bit dated. It's a soothing escape from the St-Malo hubbub, on the edge of the village-like St-Servan quarter.

✕ Eating

St-Malo boasts superb places to eat, but also beware of the many mediocre tourist-style eateries (mainly those around the Porte St-Vincent and Grande Porte). For a seat at the best restaurants in town, it's essential to book ahead in high season and on weekends.

Market mornings are Tuesday and Friday in the Intra-Muros at the **Halle au Blé** (Map p282; ⊘ 8am 1pm Tue & Fri) market hall.

Breizh Café CRÊPES €
(Map p282; ☑02 99 56 96 08; www.breizhcafe.com; 6 rue de l'Orme; crêpes €10-15, menu €15.80; ⊘ noon-2pm & 7-10pm Wed-Sun) This will be one of your most memorable meals in Brittany, from the delicious menu at this international name to the excellent service. The creative chef combines traditional Breton ingredients and *galette* and crêpe styles with Japanese flavours, textures and presentation, where seaweed and delightful seasonal pickles meet local ham, organic eggs and roast duck.

L'Absinthe MODERN FRENCH €€
(Map p282; ☑02 99 40 26 15; www.restaurant-absinthe-cafe.fr; 1 rue de l'Orme; lunch menu €19,

DON'T MISS

FRANCE'S WORLD-FAMOUS BUTTER

Casual **Bistro Autour du Beurre** (Map p282; ☑ 02 23 18 25 81; www.lebeurrebordier. com; 7 rue de l'Orme; 3-course weekday lunch menu €22, mains €19-26; ☺ noon-2pm & 7-10pm Tue-Sat Jul & Aug, noon-2pm Tue & Wed, plus 7-10pm Thu-Sat Sep-Oct, Apr & Jun, noon-2pm Tue-Thu, plus 7-10pm Fri & Sat Nov-Mar) in showcases the cheeses and butters handmade by the world-famous Jean-Yves Bordier; you'll find his **shop** (Map p282; ☑ 02 99 40 88 79; www.lebeur-rebordier.com; 9 rue de l'Orme; ☺ 9am-1pm & 3.30-7.30pm Mon-Sat, 9am-1pm Sun Jul & Aug, closed Mon Sep-Jun) next door. At the bistro, the butter sampler and bottomless bread basket are just the start to creative, local meals that change with the seasons.

The establishment is in one of the few completely intact buildings from before WWII.

dinner menu €29-47, mains €18-29; ☺ noon-1.30pm & 7-9pm Sun-Thu, noon-1.30pm & 7-9.30pm Fri & Sat) Secreted away along a quiet St-Malo street, this superb eatery is housed in a 17th-century building. Ingredients fresh from the market are whipped into shape by talented chef Stéphane Brebel, and served in cosy, alluring surrounds. The wine list is another hit, with an all-French cast from white to red and rosé. The menu for little gastronomes is €13.

Le Cambusier　　　MODERN FRENCH €€
(Map p282; ☑ 02 99 20 18 42; www.cambusier.fr; 6 rue des Cordiers; mains €22-26, dinner menu €29-38; ☺ noon-2pm Thu-Tue, 7-9pm Mon, Tue & Thu-Sat) With its ambient lighting, honey-coloured parquet flooring and large B&W shots of fishermen enlivening the dining room, Le Cambusier can do no wrong. Run by a talented husband-and-wife team, it's known across the city for its upmarket take on classic French cuisine. Since *madame* is also a sommelier, let things rip with the list of well-chosen French tipples. Under-12 foodies' menu is €14.

Le Chalut　　　SEAFOOD €€
(Map p282; ☑ 02 99 56 71 58; 8 rue de la Corne de Cerf; mains €27-29, menus €29-79; ☺ 12.15-1.15pm & 7.15-9.15pm Wed-Sun) This unremark-able-looking blue-painted establishment is, in fact, St-Malo's most celebrated restaurant,

with one Michelin star and a large following of gastronomic devotees. Its kitchen overflows with the best the Breton coastline has to offer – buttered turbot, line-caught sea bass, crab and scallops. Feel like shelling out? Plump for the 'all lobster' menu.

🍷 Drinking & Nightlife

La Cafe du Coin d'en Bas de la Rue du Bout de la Ville d'en Face du Port... La Java　　　CAFE
(Map p282; ☑ 02 99 56 41 90; www.lajavacafe.com; 3 rue Ste-Barbe; ☺ 8.20am-8.45pm Mon-Fri, to 9.45pm Sat, 8.45am-8.45pm Sun mid-Jul–mid-Aug, shorter hours rest of year) This extraordinary and rather deranged cafe is a splendid experience. Think part museum, part toyshop and part work of art from an ever-so-slightly-twisted mind. Traditional French accordion music plays as the eyes of hundreds of dolls and puppets keep watch from shelves. And the drinks? Ah, well they're actually quite sane – 100 different kinds of coffee and beer.

L'Aviso　　　BAR
(Map p282; 12 rue Point du Jour; ☺ 6pm-3am Thu-Tue) This cosy place with jazzy tunes in the air serves more than 300 beers, mostly from Brittany and Belgium, with more than 10 – including two Breton beers – on tap as well. If you can't decide, ask the friendly owner/connoisseur.

L'Alchimiste　　　BAR
(Map p282; 7 rue St-Thomas; ☺ 5pm-1am Tue-Sun) Mellow tunes fill this magical and alluring place lined with old books. Take a seat at the bar draped on the wall behind with a red-tasselled theatre curtain, on the carved-timber mezzanine (including a pulpit), where a pile of books helps support the ceiling, or in the wood-heated basement (though the downstairs has little if any character).

ℹ️ Information

Tourist Office (Map p282; ☑ 08 25 13 52 00; www.saint-malo-tourisme.com; esplanade St-Vincent; ☺ 9am-7.30pm Mon-Sat, 10am-7pm Sun Jul & Aug, shorter hours rest of year; 🐾)

ℹ️ Getting There & Around

BICYCLE

Hire bicycles and different sized scooters at **Cycles Nicole** (☑ 02 99 56 11 06; www.cycles nicole.com; 11 rue du Président Robert Schuman, Paramé; bicycle/scooter per day €12/30; ☺ 9am-noon & 2-6.45pm Tue-Sat).

BOAT

Brittany Ferries (www.brittany-ferries.com) sails between St-Malo and Portsmouth, and Condor Ferries (www.condorferries.co.uk) runs to/from Poole via Jersey or Guernsey, with connections to Portsmouth. Ferries leave from the **Gare Maritime du Naye** (Map p280; Terre-Plein du Naye), 1km south of the Intra-Muros, which is served by the town-centre *navette* (shuttle).

Compagnie Corsaire (p281) runs a Bus de Mer shuttle service (adult/child return €8.50/5.60, 10 minutes, at least half-hourly) between St-Malo and Dinard, April to September. Outside the July–August peak season, both frequency and cost fall.

BUS

All intercity buses stop at the bus station alongside the train station. **Keolis St-Malo** (☑ 02 99 40 19 22; www.ksma.fr) has local buses, and services to Cancale (€1.30, 30 minutes, every 30 to 40 minutes Monday to Saturday and every 2½ hours Sunday). **Illenoo** (p320) services run to Dinard (€2.70, 30 minutes, hourly) and Rennes (€6.20, one to 1½ hours, three to six daily). **Tibus** (☑ 08 10 22 22 22; www.tibus.fr) buses serve Dinan (€2, 50 minutes, three to eight daily).

TRAIN

St-Malo trains include services to Dinan (€10, one hour, nine daily; change in Dol de Bretagne), Paris Montparnasse (€74, 2¾ hours, three direct TGVs daily) and Rennes (€15, 45 minutes to one hour, roughly hourly).

Dinard

POP 10,438

Visiting Dinard 'in season' is a little like stepping into one of the canvases Picasso painted here in the 1920s. Belle époque mansions built into the cliffs form a timeless backdrop to the beach dotted with blue-and-white-striped bathing tents and the beachside carnival. Views across to St-Malo are brilliant.

Out of season, when holidaymakers have packed up their buckets and spades, the town is decidedly dormant, but wintry walks along the coastal paths are spectacular.

◉ Sights & Activities

Plage de l'Écluse (Grande Plage) is the most popular beach, but when it gets too crowded, savvy Dinardais take refuge at the town's smaller beaches, including **Plage du Prieuré**, 1km to the south, and **Plage de St-Énogat**, 1km to the west.

Barrage de la Rance   BRIDGE
Built in 1966, this 750m bridge over the Rance estuary carries the D168 between St-Malo and Dinard, lopping a good 30km off the journey. A feat of hydroelectrics, the Usine Marémotrice de la Rance (below the bridge) generates electricity by harnessing the lower estuary's extraordinarily high tidal range – a difference of 13.5m between high and low tide. There is a drawbridge, while the tidal power station was the world's first when constructed and, until 2011, the largest on the planet.

BRITTANY DINARD

BRETON LANGUAGE REDUX

Throughout Brittany you'll see bilingual Breton street and transport signs, and many other occurrences of the language popping up. Even though all Breton speakers also speak French, this is seen as an important gesture to normalising the use of a language that was stigmatised (and even banned) throughout much of the early and mid-20th century.

Historically speaking, Breton is a Celtic language related to Cornish and Welsh, and more distantly to Irish and Scottish Gaelic. Following on from the French Revolution, the government banned the teaching of Breton in schools, punishing children who spoke their mother tongue. Between 1950 and 1990 there was an 80% reduction in Breton usage.

The seeds of the language's revival were planted in the 1960s, particularly after France's May 1968 protests, driven by the younger generation rebelling against the oppression of their cultural heritage. Bringing about the rebirth of the language, no longer passed on generationally, wasn't straightforward. As Breton is more often spoken than written (with regional differences in both within Brittany), settling on a standardised language for teaching in schools remains a complex issue.

Breton now extends beyond its former boundaries. Originally, residents of Basse Bretagne (Lower Brittany, in the west) spoke Breton variants, while Haute Bretagne (Upper Brittany, in the east, including areas such as St-Malo) spoke Gallo, a Latinate language similar to French. But today you'll find Breton signage in Rennes' metro stations and many other parts of the east as well.

🛏 Sleeping & Eating

Dinard's prices match its historical cachet: budget travellers may want to consider staying in St-Malo and catching the ferry across.

Dinard's enticing open-air markets – hotspot for picnic shopping – spill across esplanade de la Halle on Tuesday, Thursday and Saturday.

Camping Le Port Blanc   CAMPGROUND €
(☑ 02 99 46 10 74; www.camping-port-blanc.com; rue du Sergent Boulanger; site per 2 adults from €20.60; ☉ Apr-Sep; 🛜) This campground is close to the beach, about 2km west of Plage de l'Écluse, with direct access to another beach.

Hôtel de la Plage   HOTEL €€
(☑ 02 99 46 14 87; www.hoteldelaplage-dinard. com; 3 bd Féart; d €62-139; 🛜) Attractive, fresh rooms with modern bathrooms and an enviable location a stone's throw away from the beach make this one of the best deals in town. Pricier rooms boast terrific sea views. Breakfast is €11.50.

Castelbrac   BOUTIQUE HOTEL €€€
(☑ 02 99 80 30 00; www.castelbrac.com; 17 av Georges V; d €274-645, ste €729-1104; ❄ @ 🛜) Sink into the lap of luxury at this grand hotel enjoying sweeping views of the water and St-Malo beyond. Rooms are luxemodern with a spa, private summertime boat, and fine restaurant (*menus* €28-€85) to match.

Le Balafon   MODERN FRENCH €€
(☑ 02 99 46 14 81; www.lebalafon-restaurant-dinard.fr; 31 rue de la Vallée; mains €18-25, lunch/dinner menu €18/29-39; ☉ noon-2pm & 7-9.30pm Tue-Sat, noon-2pm Sun) Away from the seafront tourist bustle, this quality, modern, neighbourhood bistro serves freshly made meals using produce from the nearby market. The lunch *menu* consists of a couple of well-chosen and presented dishes. It's totally unpretentious, well priced and many locals rate it the best place in town. In fair weather, sit in the inviting courtyard.

La Passerelle du Clair de Lune   MODERN FRENCH €€
(☑ 02 99 16 96 37; www.la-passerelle-restaurant. com; 3 av Georges V; menu €28-39; ☉ noon-2pm & 8-9.30pm Thu-Mon) This intimate little restaurant serves up inventive and delectable French dishes with mouth-watering views over the water, coupled with welcoming service and a lovely ambience.

ℹ Information

Tourist Office (☑ 02 99 46 94 12; www. dinardemeraudetourisme.com; 2 bd Féart; ☉ 9.30am-12.30pm & 2-6pm Mon-Sat; 🛜) Books accommodation for free, runs walking tours and offers maps of self-guided tours of Dinard's architecture.

ℹ Getting There & Around

AIR

Dinard–Pleurtuit–St-Malo Airport (www. dinard.aeroport.fr; Pleurtuit), 6.5km south of Dinard, is served by Ryanair (www.ryanair.com) with flights to/from London Stansted, East Midlands. Aurigny Air (www.aurignynew.com) flies from Guernsey. There's no public transport; a daytime/evening taxi from Dinard to the airport costs around €17/25.

BOAT

Compagnie Corsaire (p281) runs a Bus de Mer shuttle service (adult/child return €8.50/5.60, 10 minutes, at least half-hourly) between St-Malo and Dinard, April to September, operating at least half-hourly. Outside July/August, both frequency and cost fall.

BUS

Illenoo (p320) buses connect Dinard and the train station in St-Malo (€2.70, 30 minutes, hourly). Le Gallic bus stop, outside the tourist office, is the most convenient. Buses also travel to Rennes (€6.20, two hours, hourly).

Cancale

POP 5332

Tucked into the curve of a shimmering shell-shaped bay, the idyllic and tranquil little fishing port of Cancale, 14km east of St-Malo, is famed for its offshore *parcs à huîtres* (oyster beds) that stretch for kilometres around the surrounding coastline. The excellent oysters themselves are shipped across northern France. There's not much of a beach, but the waterfront is a very relaxing place to stroll and soak up the atmosphere. You can – or should, rather – carry on to sublime Pointe du Grouin, 7km north of town, full of trekking trails.

⊙ Sights

Ferme Marine   FARM
(☑ 02 99 89 69 99; www.ferme-marine.com; corniche de l'Aurore; adult/child €7.70/4.40; ☉ guided tours in English 2pm, in French 11am, 3pm & 5pm Jul–mid-Sep, 3pm only mid-Feb–Jun & mid-Sep–Oct) If you ever wanted to crack open the science and art of *ostréiculture* (oyster farming), this well-organised and informative museum, a

couple of kilometres southwest of the port, is the place. Tours include an oyster tasting.

🛏 Sleeping & Eating

Les Chambres Breizh Café   B&B €€
(📞02 99 89 61 76; www.breizhcafe.com; 7 quai Thomas; d €118-138; 🕸) You'll need to book early to bag your spot at this delightful *maison d'hôte* right on the harbourfront. It offers five fancy rooms all christened after apple varieties, ranging from coquettish Guillevic (balcony, views of the oyster parks) to sexy Kermerien (full-frame bay views, gleaming bathrooms) and amply sized Rouget de Dol (a two-room suite, ideal for families).

★Breizh Café   CRÊPES €
(📞02 99 89 61 76; www.breizhcafe.com; 7 quai Thomas; mains €5-14; 🕑noon-10pm) Not your average crêperie, the Breizh Café is renowned for its gourmet crêpes and *galettes* made from organic flours. The cappuccino-and-cream decor gives it a fresh, modern feel, and the crêpes are really first-class. Where else could you savour a *galette* stuffed with langoustines and cheese? Wash it all down with a tipple from their wide range of top-notch local ciders.

Le Troquet   SEAFOOD €€
(📞02 99 89 99 42; www.restaurantletroquet-cancale.fr; 19 quai Gambetta; mains €18-39, lunch/other menu €28/41; 🕑noon-2pm & 7-9pm Sat-Wed, daily Jul & Aug) Of the dozens of waterside restaurants at the port, this sleek and well-established contemporary *troquet* (bistro) run by *artisan cuisinier* Laurent Helleu is the pick of the shoal. His *raison d'être* is straightforward: locally bought, market-fresh ingredients, cooked with a minimum of fuss to bring forth natural flavours. Unsurprisingly, seafood features heavily. Don't miss the killer *far breton* (Breton cake).

★La Table Breizh Café   JAPANESE €€€
(📞02 99 89 56 46; www.breizhcafe.com; 7 quai Thomas; lunch €38-48, dinner €75-135; 🕑noon-1.30pm & 7.30-9pm Thu-Mon) This Michelin-starred restaurant is a triumph. Raphaël-Fumio Kudaka has created a menu of wonder with Breton ingredients at this fantastic outpost of Japanese cuisine, with such delights as *fruits de mer* in *kabosu-koshō* (citrus fruit and pepper) vinaigrette with dried plums and rice salad, blue lobster with *yuzu* sauce and yellow chicken supreme seasoned with *miso* and sesame vinaigrette.

FRESH OYSTERS

One of the most authentic seafood experiences you'll ever have awaits you in Cancale. Local fishers sell their catch directly from stalls clustered by the Pointe des Crolles lighthouse at **Marché aux Huîtres** (www.marcheauxhuitres-cancale.com; 1 rue des Parcs; 12 oysters from €5; 🕑9am-6pm). Point to the ones you want, and they'll be shucked, dashed with lemon and served before your eyes, and *voilà*, one perfect lunch. Oysters are numbered according to size and quality.

★Le Coquillage   GASTRONOMY €€€
(📞02 99 89 64 76; www.maisons-de-bricourt.com; rte du Buot au Point du Jour, Le Buot; lunch menu €35, other menus €75-140; 🕑noon-2pm & 7-9pm) Superchef Olivier Roellinger's sumptuous restaurant is housed in the impressive Château Richeux, 4km south of Cancale. Roellinger's creations have earned him three Michelin stars (though he renounced them in 2008), and the food takes in culinary highlights of Brittany and Normandy, all beautifully cooked and imaginatively served. Book well ahead.

ℹ Information

Tourist Office (📞02 99 89 63 72; www.cancale-tourisme.fr; 44 rue du Port; 🕑9.30am-1pm & 2.30-6pm or 7pm; 🕸) In July and August, there's also an annexe on quai Gambetta.

ℹ Getting There & Away

Buses stop behind the church on place Lucidas and at Port de la Houle, next to the fish market. **Keolis St-Malo** (p285) has year-round services to and from St-Malo (€1.30, 30 minutes, every 30 to 40 minutes Monday to Saturday and every 2½ hours Sunday). Most visitors arrive by car, to make the trip up to Pointe du Grouin.

Dinan

POP 11,440

Set high above the fast-flowing Rance River, the gorgeous narrow – and sometimes plunging – cobblestone streets lined with crooked, creaking half-timbered houses of Dinan's old town are straight out of the Middle Ages. This guarantees a tourist bonanza in the warmer months, of course, but choose anything slightly off-season and you may find the place deserted. Even when it's busy, by around 6pm, someone seemingly waves a magic wand and

DON'T MISS

POINTE DU GROUIN

A short 4km drive north or exhilarating 7km coastal hike along the GR34 coastal hiking trail from Cancale brings you to this sublime and stormy headland. Rock cleaves the water and fantastic views range over islands and rocks to the sea beyond, while Mont St-Michel is visible to your east. Wander around the well-worn trails and hike around here to your heart's content. An old German pillbox here has been converted into an **ornithological observatory** and displays information on local bird life in its entrance.

most of the crowds vanish and a sense of calm settles once more over the charming town.

⊙ Sights

Vieux Pont   HISTORIC SITE
Be sure to head downhill along **rue du Jerzual and rue du Petit Fort** to the Vieux Pont (Old Bridge). From here, the bridge, a pretty little **port**, hemmed by restaurants and cafes, extends northwards, and the 19th-century **Viaduc de Dinan** soars high above to the south.

Basilique St-Sauveur   CHURCH
(place St-Sauveur; ⊙9am-6pm, closed during services) The soaring chancel of the Basilique St-Sauveur is Flamboyant Gothic, but the south side of the church is Romanesque, while other periods and styles get their say too. The church contains a 14th-century gravestone in its north transept reputed to contain the heart of Bertrand du Guesclin, a 14th-century knight noted for his hatred of the English and his fierce battles to expel them. Ironically, today Dinan is home to one of the largest English expat communities in Brittany!

Tour Ste-Catherine   TOWER
(rue Michel) FREE The 14th-century Tour Ste-Catherine is just east of Basilique St-Sauveur and beyond the tiny **Jardin Anglais** (English Garden), a former cemetery and nowadays a pleasant little park. The 16m-high tower has great views over the viaduct and port.

Tour de l'Horloge   TOWER
(☑02 96 87 02 26; rue de l'Horloge; adult/child €4/2.50; ⊙10am-6.30pm Jun-Sep, 2-6pm Apr-May) Climb up to the little balcony of this 15th-century clock tower whose chimes ring every quarter-hour.

Château-Musée de Dinan   MUSEUM
(☑02 96 39 45 20; rue du Château; adult/child €5/free; ⊙10am-6.30pm Jun-Sep, shorter hours rest of year, closed Jan & Feb) The town's museum is atmospherically housed in the keep of Dinan's ruined 14th-century château, showcasing the town's history, with information sheets in various languages.

⏦ Sleeping

**Camping Municipal
Châteaubriand**   CAMPGROUND €
(☑02 96 39 11 96; 103 rue Chateaubriand; per adult/tent/car €3.10/3.70/3.10; ⊙Jun-Sep) With 48 pitches, this campground at the foot of the ramparts is the closest to the old town, but is only open during the summer months.

★La Maison Pavie   B&B €€
(☑02 96 84 45 37; www.lamaisonpavie.com; 10 place St-Sauveur; d €105-155; ☎) If you ever dreamt of staying in a 15th-century half-timbered house, look no further than this sumptuous B&B in the heart of Dinan. The building's medieval character and historic ambience have been lovingly preserved while modern comforts and designer fittings have been added – you have to see the architectural elements and furnishings of the rooms to believe them.

Hôtel Arvor   HOTEL €€
(☑02 96 39 21 22; www.hotelarvordinan.com; 5 rue Pavie; d €82-135, tr & f from €125; ⊙Feb-Dec; ☎) It's hard to believe that this smart establishment was once a Jacobin convent, but they manage to get in modern bathrooms, a few fancy decorative touches and calming colour tones. The charming tearoom is a great place to relax after a long day's sightseeing. Service is excellent and it's an all-round good deal, considering the location and ambience.

✗ Eating

Crêperie Ahna   CRÊPES €
(☑02 96 39 09 13; 7 rue de la Poissonnerie; mains from €5; ⊙noon-2pm & 7-9.30pm Mon-Sat) This elegant scarlet eatery has been run by the same family for four generations and deserves its reputation as one of the best crêperies in town. Unusual delights include a *galette* with duck and snail butter (better than it sounds!). They also serve grilled meats and excellent ice creams.

La Courtine   BISTRO €€
(☑02 96 39 74 41; 6 rue de la Croix; mains €15-18, 2-3-course set lunch with glass of wine €14/16.50,

2-3-course set dinner €21/28.50; ⊙ noon-1.30pm Thu-Tue, 7.45-11.30pm Mon & Thu-Sat) This snug bistro with wood beams and stone walls serves classic French dishes. Its *souris d'agneau confite au cidre* (lamb shank stewed in cider) is not to be scoffed at, but the entire menu is a winner and the set meals are good value. There's also a good list of well-chosen French tipples, available by the glass.

Le Cantorbery
FRENCH €€

(☑ 02 96 39 02 52; 6 rue Ste-Claire; mains €18-28, menus €34-44; ⊙ noon-1.45pm Thu-Tue, 7-9.30pm Mon, Tue & Thu-Sat) This intimate restaurant in a 17th-century house is perfect for wining and dining your beloved over a romantic meal. Its traditional menu – based on beef, grilled fish and seafood, including *coquilles St-Jacques* (scallops) from St-Brieuc – changes with the seasons.

ⓘ Information

Tourist Office (☑ 02 96 87 69 76; www. dinan-tourisme.com; 9 rue du Château; ⊙ 9.30am-7pm Mon-Sat, 10am-12.30pm & 2-6pm Sun; 🛜) In the 16th-century Hôtel Kératry. Free map in several languages plots two walking itineraries around town.

ⓘ Getting There & Away

BUS

Buses leave from place Duclos and the bus stop at the train station at Place du 11 Novembre 1918. **Illenoo** (☑ 08 10 35 10 35; www.illenoo-services. fr) runs several daily services to Dinard (€3.90, 30 minutes) and Rennes (€6.20, 1¼ hours).

TRAIN

Change in Dol de Bretagne for trains to Rennes (from €15.70, 1¼ hours, nine daily) and St-Malo (€10, one hour, nine daily).

Paimpol
POP 7900

Set around a former fishing harbour, now a boating harbour, Paimpol is rich in history. It was the one-time home port of the Icelandic fishery, when the town's fishermen would set sail to the seas around Iceland for seven months or more at a stretch. Pierre Loti's 1886 novel *Pêcheur d'Islande* (*An Iceland Fisherman*) describes the experience. Paimpol is also rich in legends – the fishermen lost at sea are recalled in folk tales and *chants de marins* (sea shanties).

⊙ Sights & Activities

La Vapeur du Trieux
TOURIST TRAIN

(☑ 02 96 20 52 06; www.vapeurdutrieux.com; Gare de Paimpol, av du Général de Gaulle; adult/child return €26/13; ⊙ May-Sep) Steam-engine buffs and lovers of fine scenery will be in seventh heaven aboard the chuffing carriages of this 1922 steam train that plies the old railway line between Paimpol and the artists' town of Pontrieux, where there's time for a pleasant meal and a stroll before the return journey. Reserve at least one day ahead; tickets are cheaper bought online. Check the website for the times of trains, which usually leave at 9.45am or 11am.

Abbaye de Beauport
ABBEY

(☑ 02 96 55 18 58; www.abbaye-beauport.com; rte de Kérity; adult/child €6/3.50; ⊙ 10.30am-2.30pm & 2-6pm Apr-Jun, 10.30am-7pm Jul-Sep, 2-6pm Oct-Mar) If you have wheels (or you're up for a glorious 1½-hour walk along the seashore from the town harbour), head 3.5km east of Paimpol to this romantic 18th-century abbey, which also hosts art and sculpture exhibitions. En route, stop at the **Pointe de Guilben** for beautiful bay views. A delightful walk goes around the abbey grounds, down

---

ÎLE DE BRÉHAT

Île de Bréhat, a tiny island 8km to the north of Paimpol, stretches just 5km from north to south. It's known for its beautiful coastline (but beaches are sparse) and an unusually balmy climate. The most idyllic time to visit is in spring, when gorgeous Mediterranean wildflowers bloom in its gentle microclimate – it is known as the island of flowers.

Bréhat is completely car-free, so the only way to get around is by bike or on foot. For more on the island and the services available, see www.brehat-infos.fr.

Vedettes de Bréhat (☑ 02 96 55 79 50; www.vedettesdebrehat.com; Pointe L'Arcouest) operates ferries to Île de Bréhat from Pointe L'Arcouest, 6km north of Paimpol; adult/child return fares are €10.30/8.80. The trip takes 10 minutes. Bikes cost €16 return to transport, which is only possible on certain journeys. It's cheaper to rent a bike on the island; shops line the right-hand side of the road when you get off the boat.

BRITTANY PAIMPOL

by the sea, looping past the fields and cows and back to the car park. The tourist office (p290) has a free map.

Musée de la Mer
MUSEUM

(Sea Museum; ☑ 02 96 22 02 19; https://museemer-paimpol.fr; 11 rue de Labenne; adult/child €4.10/free; ⏰ 2-6.30pm) This excellent little museum in a former cod-drying factory charts the Paimpol region's maritime history. Peruse nautical artefacts, from seine nets and canvas sails to vintage posters and fishing outfits.

🛏 Sleeping & Eating

Paimpol's Tuesday-morning **market** spreads over place Gambetta and place du Martray. On weekends, vendors sell freshly shucked oysters at quai Duguay Trouin.

Hôtel de la Marne
HOTEL €

(☑ 02 96 16 33 41; www.hoteldelamarne-paimpol.fr; 30 rue de la Marne; d €55-100; 🛜) This granite inn ranks as highly in the dining stakes as it does in the sleeping. All rooms are beautifully and very neatly modernised and the restaurant cooks up top-notch regional cuisine (*menus* €29 to €85) with tip-top presentation and ace desserts. It's 650m southwest of the harbour.

ℹ Information

Tourist Office (☑ 02 96 20 83 16; www.paimpol-goelo.com; place de la République; ⏰ 9.30am-7.30pm Mon-Sat, 9.30am-12.30pm & 4.30-6.30pm Sun Jul & Aug, closed Sun Sep-Jun; 🛜) Sells local rambling guides.

ℹ Getting There & Away

BUS

Tibus (p285) runs eight buses daily to and from St-Brieuc (€2, 1½ hours), setting off from the train station. In summer, most continue to Pointe L'Arcouest.

TRAIN

There are five daily trains between Paimpol and Guingamp (€7.90, one hour), where you can pick up connections to Brest, St-Brieuc and Rennes.

FINISTÈRE

France's westernmost *département,* Finistère (www.finisterebrittany.com) has a wind-whipped rocky beach and cove-strewn coastline dotted with lighthouses and beacons lashed by the waves. Wild and mysterious, Finistère is, for many travellers, the most enticing edge of an already enticing region.

The etymology of the name Finistère literally emerges from 'end of the earth' (the Latin *Finis Terræ*) – an extremely apt name for this domain, especially as one approaches the raw shore which is redolent of the west coast of Ireland. Swaths of this beautiful land are preserved in the **Parc Naturel Régional d'Armorique** (www.pnr-armorique.fr).

Finistère's southern extent, called Cornouaille, takes its name from early Celts who sailed from Cornwall and other parts of Britain to settle here, and today it is a centre of Breton language, customs and culture.

Roscoff
POP 3523

If you sail in by ferry, Roscoff (Rosko in Breton) provides a captivating first glimpse of Brittany, with granite houses dating from the 16th century lining the pretty docks, a superb Gothic church and a surrounding landscape of emerald-green fields full of cauliflowers, onions and artichokes. This onion-producing region gave rise to the 'Johnnies' who made a lucrative itinerant trade exporting their agricultural produce to the UK, where they travelled the roads by bicycle.

◉ Sights

★ Église Notre Dame de Kroaz-Batz
CHURCH

(2 rue Albert de Mun; ⏰ 9am-noon & 2-7pm) With its spectacular Renaissance belfry rising above the flat landscape, the most arresting sight in Roscoff is this unique church at the heart of the old town, a 16th-century Flamboyant Gothic structure and one of Brittany's most impressive churches.

Le Jardin Exotique de Roscoff
GARDENS

(☑ 02 98 61 29 19; www.jardinexotiqueroscoff.com; Le Ruveic; adult/child €6/3; ⏰ 10am-7pm Jul & Aug, shorter hours Sep-Nov & Mar-Jun, closed Dec-Feb) Wander through 3500 species of exotic plants (many from the southern hemisphere) at this impressive garden on the coast; for an exhaustive list of plants in the garden, consult the website. It's a well-sign-posted 1.5km walk southeast from the town centre.

Maison des Johnnies et de l'Oignon de Roscoff
MUSEUM

(⌲ 02 98 61 25 48; 48 rue Brizeux; adult/child €4/free; ⊙ tours 11am, 3pm & 5pm Tue-Fri mid-Sep–mid-Jun, 3pm & 5pm mid-Jun–mid-Sep) Photographs at this popular museum trace Roscoff's roaming pink-onion farmers, known as 'Johnnies', from the early 19th century. The onion farmers gave rise to the classic British stereotype of Frenchmen in berets carrying strings of onions on bicycles, as much of their business was in the UK. Today, the itinerant trade has largely vanished, though a few survive. Visit is by guided tour only; call ahead, tour times change.

Centre de Découverte des Algues
MUSEUM

(⌲ 02 98 69 77 05; quai d'Auxerre; ⊙ 10am-12.30pm & 2.30-7pm Mon-Sat) FREE Learn all about local seaweed harvesting at this enthusiastically run museum, which also organises guided walks and gives regular free lectures (often in English and German). There's also a shop.

🛏 Sleeping

Camping Aux Quatre Saisons
CAMPGROUND €

(⌲ 02 98 69 70 86; www.camping-aux4saisons. fr; allée des Chênes Verts, Perharidy; sites €15.70; ⊙ Easter-Sep; 🐾🏊) Close to a long sandy beach in the grounds of a lovely 19th-century mansion, this popular seafront campground has a heated swimming pool and is approximately 3km southwest of Roscoff.

Hôtel aux Tamaris
HOTEL €€

(⌲ 02 98 61 22 99; www.hotel-aux-tamaris.com; 49 rue Édouard Corbière; d €59-119; 🕸) This smart, family-run place in an old granite building overlooking the water at the western end of town is an excellent choice, with well-equipped, light, seabreeze-filled rooms, all with a pleasant maritime aura and yacht sails for ceilings. Rooms with sea views cost more than the land-side ones. Expect locally sourced goodies at breakfast (€7 to €11). Bikes for hire.

Le Temps de Vivre
BOUTIQUE HOTEL €€

(⌲ 02 98 19 33 19; www.letempsdevivre.net; 19 place Lacaze Duthiers; s €120, d €153-200; 🕸) This lovely, glamorous place is hidden away in a lovely stone mansion complete with its own tower just opposite the Église Notre Dame de Kroaz-Batz. With a great blend of modern and traditional decor, plus friendly staff, this is one of Roscoff's best options.

Some rooms have fantastic sea views, family rooms are available and excellent offers are on the website. The hotel has bike rental.

🍴 Eating

⭐ Le Surcouf
BRASSERIE €€

(⌲ 02 98 69 71 89; www.surcoufroscoff.fr; 14 rue Amiral Réveillère; lunch menu €14, dinner menu €19-30; ⊙ noon-2pm & 6.30-9.30pm Thu-Mon) Bang in the heart of Roscoff, this brasserie serves excellent seafood. You can choose your own crab and lobster from the window tank, tuck into the classic fish soup or opt for a heaped platter of fresh shellfish. Plate-glass windows keep things light and bright, and the dining room has a steady chatter.

⭐ Le Brittany
GASTRONOMY €€€

(⌲ 02 98 69 70 78, www.hotel-hrittany.com; bd Ste-Barbe; menus €59-105, mains €38-46) Splash out on the best of Breton seafood at this Michelin-starred restaurant on the seafront at the east end of town. Chef Loïc Le Bail sources top local ingredients and crafts creative, artfully presented dishes in a formal dining room with views of the sea. The kids' menu is €16 to €22.

WORTH A TRIP

ÎLE DE BATZ

The Roscoff area may be light on beaches, but don't despair: you can bounce over the waves to the fabulous offshore island of Île de Batz (www.iledebatz. com) and discover brilliant sand beaches (without the crowds). The biggest and best, **Grève Blanche**, lace the island's northern shore.

A half-day is all you need to walk around this tiny speck of paradise (no cars allowed), but we suggest that you spend a night on the island to soak up its divine atmosphere. Lap up the joys of its mild island climate in the **Jardins Georges Delaselle** (⌲ 02 98 61 75 65; www.jardin-georgesdelaselle.fr; adult/child €5/2.50; ⊙ 11am-6pm Apr-Oct), luxuriant gardens dating from 1897 with over 1500 plants from all five continents.

Ferries (adult/child return €9/4.50, child under four €2, bike €9, 15 minutes each way), run by three different companies, sail between Roscoff and Île de Batz every 30 minutes between 8am and 8pm in July and August, with less frequent sailings the rest of the year.

NATURAL WONDER

Running along the coast from Penvern to Trégastel and Ploumanach lies one of Brittany's natural wonders: a delightful and breezy coastline of pink-, salmon- and russet-coloured granite known as the **Côte de Granit Rose**. Plan time to walk among the marvellously shaped and hued natural boulders and the sepia and coral-coloured beaches.

ⓘ Information

Tourist Office (✆ 02 98 61 12 13; www.ro-scoff-tourisme.com; quai d'Auxerre; ⊙ 9.15am-12.30pm & 1.30-7pm Mon-Sat, 10am-12.30pm & 2.30-7pm Sun Jul & Aug, 9.15am-noon & 2-6pm Mon-Sat Sep-Jun; ⓦ) Next to the handsome lighthouse.

ⓘ Getting There & Away

BOAT

Brittany Ferries (✆ Roscoff 02 98 29 28 13, reservations in UK 0044 330 159 7000; www.brittany-ferries.com) links Roscoff to Plymouth, England (five to nine hours, one to three daily), Cork, Ireland (14 hours, one weekly April to October) and Bilbao, Spain (21 hours, one weekly, no sailings mid-July to early August).

Irish Ferries (✆ Roscoff 02 98 61 17 17, Rosslare, Ireland +353 53 913 3158; www.irishferries.com) sails to Rosslare, Ireland (17½ hours, five weekly).

Boats leave from Port de Bloscon, about 2km east of the town centre.

BUS

The bus and train stations are together on rue Ropartz Morvan. **Buses** (p297) also depart from the ferry terminal (Port de Bloscon) and pass by the town centre. Services include Brest (€2, 1½ to two hours, up to four daily) and Morlaix (€2, 40 minutes, several daily).

TRAIN

Nine daily trains and SNCF buses go to Morlaix (€5, 35 minutes), where you can make connections to Brest, Quimper and St-Brieuc.

Morlaix

POP 16,263

At the bottom of a deep valley sluicing through northeastern Finistère, Morlaix is a good-looking town that makes a fine gateway to the coast. The narrow, finger-like town centre is filled with ancient half-timbered houses that spill down to a small port at the end of a large coastal inlet. Towering above all else is an imposing, arched 58m-high **viaduct** (Viaduc; ⊙ 7.30am-7.30pm Mon-Fri, 10am-7.30pm Sat-Sun), dating from 1861 – it's a truly astonishing sight.

◉ Sights & Activities

Maison de la Duchesse Anne   MUSEUM
(✆ 02 98 88 23 26; www.mda-morlaix.com; 33 rue du Mur; adult €2; ⊙ 11am-6pm Mon-Sat, 2-6pm Sun Jul & Aug, 11am-6pm Mon-Sat May, Jun & Sep) This magnificent 15th-century home (which, despite the name, has nothing to do with Duchess Anne) overlooking place Allende, is one of the finest examples of the local building style. The highlight is a staircase engraved with the faces of the building's patron saints.

Musée de Morlaix   MUSEUM
(✆ 02 98 88 68 88; www.musee.ville.morlaix.fr; place des Jacobins; adult/child €3/free; ⊙ 10am-6pm Jul-Sep, 10am-noon & 2-5pm Tue-Sat Oct-Jun) Closed for restoration till 2019, this museum showcases the area's history, archaeology and art, which also incorporates the beautifully preserved half-timbered house **La Maison à Pondalez** (✆ 02 98 88 68 88; 9 Grand' Rue; incl in ticket for Musée de Morlaix; ⊙ 10am-12.30pm & 2-6pm Jul-Sep, 10am-noon & 2-5pm Tue-Sat Oct-Jun).

Château du Taureau   FORTRESS
(✆ 02 98 62 29 73; www.chateaudutaureau.com; cruise & admission adult/child €15/9; ⊙ Apr-Sep) Sail out to this amazing petite prison-fortress constructed in the 16th century by Vauban, on a small islet in the Bay of Morlaix. Most departures are from Kelenn beach in Carantec (15km northwest of Morlaix), while a few leave from the port of Diben in Plougasnou (17km north of Morlaix). Check online for schedules.

A joint ticket with the Cairn of Barnenez (p293) gets you a reduced fee for both sights.

Le Léon à Fer et à Flots   BOATING
(✆ 02 98 62 07 52; www.aferaflots.org; adult/child €32/17; ⊙ Apr-Sep) A great way to see the area by land and sea, this tour combines a boat trip through the islands of the Baie de Morlaix and a picturesque train trip between Roscoff and Morlaix.

🛏 Sleeping

Ty Pierre   B&B €
(✆ 02 98 63 25 75, 07 81 26 03 17; http://lenaj.free.fr/typierre/index.htm; 1bis place de Viarmes; s/d/tr with shared bathroom €34/50/65; ⊙ Mar-Dec; ⓦ) Knick-knacks and artefacts picked up by

Pierre-Yves Jacquet on his Asian travels now decorate this quirky *chambre d'hôte*'s five spacious rooms. At this price there's no lift (count on climbing up three or four floors), and most rooms don't have their own bathroom (they're just along the wide corridors). All in all, it's very simple but practical. Lunch and dinner are available (€20). Bike rental is €15 per day.

★**Manoir de Ker-Huella** B&B €€
(☑ 06 18 23 07 63, 02 98 88 05 52; http://manoird-ekerhuella.monsite-orange.fr; 78 voie d'accès au port; d from €92; ☎) Built in 1898 by the then-director of the railways (the train station is very close by), this wonderful grey-stone manor house is set in park-like gardens high above the town and is today a well-run *chambre d'hôte*. Despite the size of the building, there are actually only four guest rooms, all named after heroines from classic novels.

🍴 Eating & Drinking

Rue Ange de Guernisac has several enticing restaurants. Morlaix's excellent **Saturday market** fills the centre of the old town all day.

Atipik Bilig CRÊPES €
(☑ 02 98 63 38 63; 1 rue Ange de Guernisac; mains €5-13; ☺ noon-2pm & 7-9.30pm Tue-Sat) Tucked inside a two-storey, 16th-century timbered house in the old town, this enticing and recommended crêperie whips up sweet crêpes, savoury *galettes,* substantial salads, *tartines* and cooling glasses of Breton cider. The outdoor tables occupy a prime location alongside picturesque rue Ange de Guernisac.

Grand Café de la Terrasse BRASSERIE €
(☑ 02 98 88 20 25; 31 place des Otages; mains €12-20; ☺ 8am-midnight Mon-Sat) In the heart of town, Morlaix's showpiece is this magnificent 1872-established brasserie with an original central spiral staircase, around which a galaxy of locals sip tea, coffee or down something stronger, or sup on classic brasserie fare. A hubbub within, it's quite a sight to behold and staff are snappy but polite. The outdoor area abuts a busy road.

Le Viaduc FRENCH €€
(☑ 02 98 63 24 21; www.le-viaduc.com; 3 rampe St-Melaine; mains €19.50, lunch menu €16.50, other menus €24-32; ☺ noon-1.30pm & 7-9.30pm Tue-Sat, noon-1.30pm Sun Sep-Jun, noon-2pm & 7-10pm daily Jul & Aug) A sterling reputation props up this ode to contemporary Breton cuisine, named after the nearby viaduct and framed by a stylish interior featuring grey-stone

DON'T MISS

MORLAIX MEANDER

Cairn of Barnenez (☑ 02 98 67 24 73; www.barnenez.fr; rte de Barnenez, Plouezoc'h; adult/child €6/free; ☺ 10am-12.30pm & 2-6.30pm May-Jun, 10am-6.30pm Jul-Aug, 10am-12.30pm & 2-5.30pm Sep-Apr) is an enormous ancient series of hilltop tombs is set spectacularly overlooking the Bay of Morlaix, on the edge of the modern-day village of Plouezoc'h, 10km north of Morlaix. Built between 4500 and 3900 BC, the cairn measures 75m and comprises two sets of tombs, built in successive eras but attached to each other. You can walk through the centre of the cairn, where it was once, amazingly, used as a source of stones in the 1950s.

walls, wood-panelled ceilings and groovy lighting. On the menu are fish and meat dishes, all skilfully cooked and presented.

Le Tempo BAR
(☑ 02 98 63 29 11; quai de Tréguier, Port de Plaisance; ☺ 10am-1am Mon-Fri, 5pm-1am Sat) A spacious, bright and welcoming bar-brasserie overlooking the boats and the harbour, Le Tempo has a blackboard full of brasserie staples and plenty of brews on offer. Otherwise, just drop by for a restorative coffee. Well worth the detour.

ℹ Information

Tourist Office (☑ 02 98 62 14 94; www.tourisme-morlaix.fr; 10 place Charles de Gaulle; ☺ 9am-7pm Mon-Sat, 10am-6pm Sun Jul & Aug, 9am-12.30pm & 2-6.30pm Mon-Sat Sep-Jun; ☎) Has a handy map of walking itineraries around town.

ℹ Getting There & Away

Morlaix's renovated bus-train transfer station opened in early 2017, and it's on the main Paris train line. Services include Brest (€10.50, 45 minutes, 16 daily), Paris Montparnasse (€77 to €92, three hours, seven daily) and SNCF bus or train to Roscoff (€5, 30 minutes, seven daily).

Brest

POP 143,458
A major port and military base, and a large town, Brest is big, bold and dynamic. Destroyed by Allied air attacks during WWII, Brest was swiftly rebuilt after the war in utilitarian fashion. Though it won't win any

beauty contests, it's a lively port and a university town, home to an elaborate aquarium and makes itself the gateway to the sea-swept Île d'Ouessant.

◉ Sights

Océanopolis   AQUARIUM
(☑02 98 34 40 40; www.oceanopolis.com; port de Plaisance du Moulin Blanc; adult/child €21/13.35; ☺9.30am-7pm mid-Jul–mid-Aug, 9.30am-5pm Tue-Sun mid-Aug–Mar, 9.30am-6pm Apr–mid-Jul, closed most of Jan; ⓗ; ◻3) If you've kids in tow, bring them here. Much more than just an aquarium, this enormous 'aquatic world' is divided into three pavilions containing polar, tropical and temperate ecosystems. Highlights are the shark tanks, mangrove and rainforest sections, colourful tropical reefs, seals and the penguin display. The numerous films and interactive displays are educational for children and adults alike. It's about 3km east of the city centre.

Musée de la Marine   MUSEUM
(Naval Museum; ☑02 98 22 12 39; www.musee-marine.fr; rue du Château, Château de Brest; adult/child €7/free; ☺10am-6.30pm Apr-Sep, 1.30-6.30pm Wed-Mon Oct-Mar, closed Jan) Get to grips with Brest's maritime military history and briny past at this museum housed within the fortified 13th-century Château de Brest, built to defend the harbour on the Penfeld River. Following the 1532 union of Brittany and France, the castle and its harbour became a royal fortress. The castle was heavily refortified by Vauban in the mid-17th century with his trademark combination of defensive towers and ramparts, from which extend striking views of the harbour and the naval base.

Tour Tanguy   MUSEUM
(☑02 98 00 87 93; place Pierre Péron; ☺10am-noon & 2-7pm Jun-Sep, 2-5pm Wed, Thu, Sat & Sun Oct-May) FREE Inside this 14th-century tower, displays on Brest's history include a sobering reminder of what Brest looked like on the eve of WWII. One display documents the visit of three Siamese ambassadors in 1686, who presented gifts to the court of Louis XIV; rue de Siam was named in their honour.

✿ Festivals & Events

Astropolis   MUSIC
(www.astropolis.org; ☺early Jul) Brest's electronic music fest.

🛏 Sleeping

Hôtel de la Rade   HOTEL €
(☑02 98 44 47 76; www.hoteldelarade.com; 6 rue de Siam; d €58-69; ☎) This good-value, welcoming and very central place has smart and stylishly simple rooms with small yet functional bathrooms. Rooms at the back have superb views onto the harbour. Secure parking is available for bicycles. Weekend (Friday to Sunday) prices are lowest (€58) and overall prices drop even further to €49 in July and August – check the website.

Hôtel Continental   HOTEL €€
(☑02 98 80 50 40; www.oceaniahotels.com; 41 rue Émile Zola; d €120-155; ❄☎) Every business-person's favourite base in Brest, this retro downtown hotel offers plenty of atmosphere, thanks to its monumental art deco lobby, stained-glass windows and 73 large, luminous, stylish and tidy rooms, some with balcony. Considerable reductions on room rates apply at weekends, while booking through their website can make up to 50% savings. Breakfast is €15.

✗ Eating

Le Potager de Mémé   HEALTH FOOD €
(☑09 51 44 14 78; www.lepotagerdememe.com; 44 rue de Lyon; mains €7-12, menus €15.50-18.50; ☺11.30am-2.30pm Mon-Sat, 7-9pm Fri & Sat) 🖉 A fabulous lunch address wedged between shops, Le Potager de Mémé (Grandma's vegetable garden) is uber-cool, ultra-healthy and great value. Pick from zesty salads, soups, tarts and savoury *tartines* (slices of bread with toppings), all made with locally sourced, organic products. Mmmm, vegetarian quiche with sheep's-milk cheese.

Crêperie du Roi Gradlon   CRÊPES €
(☑02 98 80 17 28; 19 rue Fautras; menu €10; ☺10am-3pm & 6-10pm) The crêpes at this very popular, homey and affordable crêperie really are worth writing home about. Service is very friendly, but it can get packed.

Ô Zinc   MODERN FRENCH €
(☑02 98 43 08 52; 48 rue de Lyon; mains €13-18, lunch menus €16-18; ☺noon-2pm Tue-Sat, 7.45-10pm Thu-Sat) This contemporary bistro with a pinch of post-industrial flavour (suspended lamps, zinc tabletops and walls done up in greys) cooks up just a few starters, three or four mains and a handful of desserts – and none disappoint.

La Chaumière
MODERN FRENCH €€

(☑ 02 98 44 18 60; www.lachaumiere-brest.com; 25 rue Émile Zola; mains €12-20, menus €18-33; ⊗ noon-2pm Mon-Fri, 7.30-9pm Tue-Sat) Creative cuisine is what gives this modern-meets-traditional restaurant, with a big fireplace and contemporary furnishings, a high profile. Breton chef René Botquelen turns out succulent concoctions prepared with top-quality ingredients. A vegetarian *menu* is available for €15.

Le Crabe Marteau
SEAFOOD €€

(☑ 02 98 33 38 57; www.crabemarteau.fr; 8 quai de la Douane; mains €17-23; ⊗ noon-2.30pm & 7-10.30pm Mon-Sat) This eatery down by the port is famous for one thing and one thing only: crab (served with potatoes); savour them from the terrace facing the island ferries or in a rustically nautical interior. The seasonally adjusted menu also includes oysters and freshly caught fish.

❶ Information

Tourist Office (☑ 02 98 44 24 96; www.brest-metropole-tourisme.fr; place de la Liberté; ⊗ 9.30am-7pm Mon-Sat, to 1.30pm Sun Jul & Aug, 9.30am-6pm Mon-Sat Sep-Jun; 🛜)

❶ Getting There & Away

AIR
Brest's **airport** (BES; ☑ 02 98 32 86 00; www.brest.aeroport.fr; off D67, Guipavas) has regular domestic and international flights. These include Finist Air flights to Île d'Ouessant; Air France to Paris, London, Nice and Lyon; Ryanair serving Marseille; Flybe to Birmingham and Southampton; easyJet to Lyon; Aegean Air to Heraklion, Crete; Chalair Aviation to Caen and Bordeaux; and Vueling to Barcelona.

A **Bibus shuttle** (☑ 02 98 80 30 30; www.bibus.fr; ticket €1.50, day pass €3.95) connects the airport to the Tram line A at Porte de Guipavas (€1.50, seven to 10 per day). Buy tickets on board. A taxi to the centre costs around €22 by day, €32 at night.

BOAT
Ferries to Île d'Ouessant leave from Port de Commerce.

Le Brestoâ (☑ 07 78 37 03 23; www.lebrestoa.com; quai de la Douane) connects Brest's Port de Commerce with Le Fret on the Crozon Peninsula (one way adult/child €9.50/7.50, 30 minutes, twice daily Tuesday to Sunday, April to September).

BUS
Brest's **bus station** (☑ 02 98 44 46 73; www.viaoo29.fr; place du 19e Régiment d'Infanterie)

is beside the train station, and buses serve the whole region, including Le Conquet (€2, 45 minutes, six daily) and Roscoff (€2, 1½ hours, four daily).

TRAIN
For Roscoff, change trains at Morlaix; Brest is the terminus of the Paris train line.

Morlaix €10.50, 30-45 mins, 16 daily
Paris Montparnasse €75-90, 3½ hours, around 10 daily
Quimper €9, 1½ hours, (SNCF bus or train) 11 daily
Rennes €28-40, 2 hours, 10 daily

Île d'Ouessant

POP 891

An old Breton saying captures raw wildness of Île d'Ouessant: *'Qui voit Molène, voit sa peine, qui voit Ouessant, voit son sang'* ('Those who see Molène, see their sorrow, those who see Ouessant, see their blood'). On a stormy winter day there's a palpable end-of-the-world feeling to the island (known as Enez Eusa in Breton, meaning 'Island of Terror', and Ushant in English). However, if you come on a sunny day, the place can seem like a little paradise, with turquoise waters, abundant wildflowers and not much to do but walk and picnic. The peace and calm of the island is best experienced by hiking its 45km craggy coastal path or hiring a bike and cycling. While Ouessant can be visited as a day trip (as masses of people do), spend the night to fully allow its other-worldly nature to truly sink in.

◉ Sights & Activities

Plage de Corz, 600m south of Lampaul, is the island's best beach. Another good spot to stretch out is **Plage du Prat**. Both are easily accessible by bike from Lampaul or Port du Stiff.

Musée des Phares et des Balises
LIGHTHOUSE, MUSEUM

(Lighthouse & Beacon Museum; ☑ 02 98 48 80 70; www.pnr-armorique.fr; Phare du Créac'h; adult/child €4.30/3; ⊗ 10.30am-6pm Jul & Aug, 11.30am-5pm Apr-Jun & Sep, 1.30-5.30pm Tue-Sun Oct-Mar) The black-and-white-striped Phare de Créac'h is one of the world's most powerful lighthouses. Beaming two white flashes every 10 seconds and visible for more than 60km, it serves as a beacon for more than 50,000 ships entering the Channel each year. At its base is the island's highly educational main museum, which tells the story of these vital navigational aids. There are also displays devoted to the numerous ships that have been wrecked off the island. A joint ticket with Écomusée d'Ouessant is €7.

Écomusée d'Ouessant
MUSEUM

(Maison du Niou Huella; ☑ 02 98 48 86 37; www.pnr-armorique.fr; lieu-dit Niou Huella, north of D81; adult/child €3.80/2.80; ⊙ 10.30am-6pm Jul & Aug, 11am-5pm Apr-Jun & Sep, 1.30-5.30pm Tue-Sun Oct-Mar) Two traditional local houses make up this small but rewarding ecomuseum. One re-creates a traditional homestead, furnished like a ship's cabin, with furniture fashioned from driftwood and painted in bright colours to mask imperfections; the other explores the island's history and customs.

🛏 Sleeping

Camping Municipal
Penn Ar Bed
CAMPGROUND €

(☑ 02 98 48 84 65; www.ot-ouessant.fr/location-ouessant/camping/182-camping-municipal-penn-ar-bed.html; rte du Stiff (D81), Stang Ar Glann; per person/tent €3.50/3.30; ⊙ Apr-Sep) About 500m east of Lampaul, this sprawling 100-pitch place looks more like a football field than a campground; facilities are basic.

Auberge de Jeunesse
HOSTEL €

(☑ 02 98 48 84 53; www.auberge-ouessant.com; La Croix Rouge; dm incl breakfast €22, s €38; ⊙ reception 7.30am-1pm & 6-8pm Feb-Nov; 🛜) This friendly and welcoming hostel on the hill above Lampaul has two- to six-person rooms and a small communal kitchen. Sheets cost an extra €5.40 per stay. It's popular with school and walking groups; reservations are essential.

La Duchesse Anne
HOTEL €

(☑ 02 98 48 80 25; www.hotelduchesseanne.fr; Le Keo; r €55-65; ⊙ Mar-Oct; 🛜) A really good choice, idyllically set on a cliff next to Baie de Lampaul on the edge of town, with unpretentious yet neat doubles, of which four (pricier) have staggering sunset-facing sea views. It also boasts one of the island's best restaurants (*menus* €13.50 to €28) with a terrace overlooking the ocean, so you have all you need.

⭐ Le Keo – La Maison des Capitaines
B&B €€

(☑ 06 01 39 67 08; www.lekeoouessant.com; Le Keo; d €79-96; ⊙ Apr-Oct; 🛜) This welcoming and individual townhouse B&B in the heart of Lampaul has an interior brimming with creative trappings and its four rooms all boast unique decor. Two have swoon-inducing sea views, and one features a *lit clos* (traditional Breton bed). The fantastic breakfast room has original wood panelling, and there's a lovely small garden.

🍴 Eating

Ty Korn
SEAFOOD €

(☑ 02 98 48 87 33; Lampaul; mains €11-30; ⊙ noon-1.30pm & 7.30-9.30pm Tue-Sat) The ground floor of this hyperfriendly and very popular place is a bar serving Breton buckwheat beers (made from the same *blé noire* as Breton *galettes*). Upstairs is an excellent restaurant with seafood a speciality. Save room for their divine *tiramisu breton* (biscuit with apples, mascarpone and salty caramel sauce). Opening hours can vary, though the bar stays open until 1am.

Ar Piliguet
MODERN FRENCH €€

(☑ 02 98 03 14 64; http://arpiliguet.bzh; Lampaul; mains €17-25, six-course menu €72; ⊙ noon-2.30pm & 7-9.30pm Wed-Sun Mar-Oct, daily Jul & Aug) For picturesque, flavour-rich dining, head to Ar Piliguet, beautifully set in a traditional house behind the tourist office. Dishes are packed with fresh, local ingredients – enjoy them on

MEETING THE MOLÉNAIS

Scarcely 1km across, Île Molène (www.molene.fr) feels even more remote than its neighbour Île d'Ouessant. It's carless, virtually treeless, home to a declining population of just 169 people (inhabitants are known as Molénais) and its electricity supply depends on a single diesel generator. The island's only village is Le Bourg, a hamlet of whitewashed fishing cottages clustered around a granite quay, with a church. Needless to say, the island can only be explored on foot.

A half-day is all you really need to walk the island's circumference. Another option, which also allows you to investigate the nearby islets, is to hire a kayak or canoe, which can be arranged from the port on arrival. The island has several *chambres d'hôte,* a campground, a hotel and a list of other properties to rent – check the website for more information.

All ferries to Ouessant stop here en route.

the terrace or in a snug interior full of stone and artistic flourishes. Vegetarians are well catered for and there's a good wine selection.

ℹ Information

Tourist Office (☏ 02 98 48 85 83; www.ot-ouessant.fr; place de l'Église; ☉ 9am-6.30pm Mon-Sat, 10am-12.30pm Sun mid-Jul–mid-Aug, 10am-noon & 2-6pm Mon-Sat rest of year; ☏) Sells walking brochures and has information on operators offering horse riding, sailing and other activities. The office can also provide a list of accommodation choices.

ℹ Getting There & Around

AIR

Finist Air (☏ 02 98 84 64 87; www.finistair.fr; Kerlaouen) flies from Brest's airport to **Ouessant** (☏ 02 98 48 82 09; Kerlaouen) in a mere 15 minutes. There are two daily flights on weekdays and one on Saturdays (one way adult/child €70/41), with no flights between 14 July and 12 August.

BICYCLE

Bike-hire operators have kiosks at the Port du Stiff ferry terminal and compounds just up the hill, as well as outlets in Lampaul. The going rate for town bikes is €10 to €15 per day. Cycling on the coastal footpath is forbidden – the fragile turf is strictly reserved for walkers.

BOAT

Ferries for Île d'Ouessant depart from Brest and the tiny town of Le Conquet (Brittany's most westerly point). In high summer, reserve ferry tickets at least two days in advance and check in 45 minutes before departure to avoid enormous lines.

Penn Ar Bed (☏ 02 98 80 80 80; www.pennarbed.fr; return adult/child €34.90/24.90) sails from the Port de Commerce in Brest (2½ hours), from Le Conquet (1½ hours) and from Camaret-sur-Mer (one hour). Boats run between the first two and the island two to five times daily from May to September and once daily between October and April. Boats run from Camaret two to six times per week in July and August, and once weekly in May, June and early September. A bike costs €15.50.

Finist'mer (☏ 08 25 13 52 35; www.finist-mer.fr; adult/child return €34/26.50) runs high-speed boats from Le Conquet (40 minutes), Lanildut (35 minutes) and Camaret (1½ hours) one to three times per day, with more sailings during the peak season of July and August.

BUS

Penn Ar Bed (☏ 08 10 81 00 29; www.viaoo29.fr) buses link Brest with Le Conquet (€2, 45 minutes, hourly).

Presqu'île de Crozon

Stretching westwards into the Atlantic, the anchor-shaped Presqu'île de Crozon (or Crozon Peninsula) is one of the most scenic spots in Brittany. In previous centuries, this multifingered spit of land was a key strategic outpost; crumbling forts and ruined gun batteries can still be seen on many headlands, but these days it's the tucked-away coves, secluded and inviting beaches, thrilling panoramas, charming B&Bs and clifftop trails that attract thousands of visitors in summer.

Landévennec

POP 359

The Aulne River flows into the Rade de Brest beside the pretty village of Landévennec, home to the ruined Benedictine **Abbaye St-Guenol**. The abbey **museum** (☏ 02 98 27 35 90; www.musee-abbaye-landevennec.fr; Landévennec; adult/child €6/3; ☉ 10.30am-7pm daily Jul-Sep, shorter hours Mar-May & Oct, closed Nov-Feb) here records the history of the settlement, founded by St Guenolé in 485 and the oldest Christian site in Brittany.

Crozon & Morgat

POP 7909

The peninsula's largest town, Crozon is the area's practical hub, but though the town centre is pleasant enough there's little reason to hang around.

On the water 2km south of Crozon, Morgat was built as a summer resort in the 1930s by the Peugeot brothers (of motor-vehicle fame), and it retains something of a period feel. It's one of the prettier resorts in this part of Brittany, with colourful houses piled up at one end of a long sandy beach – La Plage de Morgat – that has very safe bathing.

◉ Sights & Actvities

Morgat has a picturesque beach, **Plage de Morgat**, that's popular with families, protected by a breakwater and marina. To the west, there's sunbathing aplenty on the 2km-long **Plage de la Palue** and nearby **Plage de Lostmarc'h**, but swimming is forbidden due to strong currents. Further north, **Plage de Goulien** is another wonderful stretch of golden sand.

Cap de la Chèvre   NATURAL FEATURE
The peninsula's most southerly point, Cap de la Chèvre is 8km south of Morgat, and offers stupendous panoramas of the Baie de

MEET A BEEKEEPER

The intriguing **Ferme Apicole de Térénez** (☑ 02 98 81 06 90; www.fermeapicole.com; Térénez, Rosnoën; ⏱ 9am-8pm), 8km west of Le Faou on the D791, is abuzz with live bees that you can view in its honey museum. Depending on the season, you might also see busy-bee *apiculteurs* (beekeepers) Irène and Stéphane Brindeau using environmentally friendly cold-extraction methods to draw out the all-natural honey from giant combs. There's honey tasting and you can buy honey, nougat and other homemade honey products like *hydromel* (*chouchen* in Breton; a fermented alcoholic drink made from honey and water).

They also have B&B – no pun intended – accommodation, with single/double rooms from €35/42 and triple rooms from €45-60. Bikes are free for guests.

Douarnenez and the Pointe du Raz. You'll be amazed by the contrast between the Mediterrean-like eastern side of the peninsula and the much wilder western shore, which is clearly Atlantic.

Pointe de Dinan   NATURAL FEATURE
The cliffs of Pointe de Dinan, 6.5km west of Crozon, provide a dramatic outlook over the sands of Anse de Dinan and the rock formations locally known as the Château de Dinan, which are linked to the mainland by a natural archway.

Coastal Hike   WALKING
The coastline between Morgat and Cap de la Chèvre is gorgeous. Beyond the marina at the southern end of Morgat's beach, the coastal path offers an excellent 13km hike (part of the GR34) along the sea cliffs to Cap de la Chèvre, lassoing in some of the most scenic spots in the area. It takes roughly five hours to complete (one way), but you can also walk smaller sections.

The route takes you past an old fort and through sweet-scented pine forests overlooking numerous little coves (most inaccessible) with water that, on a sunny day, glows electric blue. Be sure to pause at the picture-perfect **Île Vierge** – you'll be smitten with this idyllic cove lapped by turquoise waters and framed by lofty cliffs. The lazy summer-day feel is dramatically shattered on

reaching Cap de la Chèvre and the wind-exposed, western side of the peninsula.

🛏 Sleeping

Les Pieds dans l'Eau   CAMPGROUND €
(☑ 02 98 27 62 43; www.campinglespiedsdansleau-crozon.fr; St-Fiacre; per person/tent/car €4.75/5/2.50; ⏱ mid-Mar–mid-Oct; 🛜) 'Camping feet in the water' (almost literally, at high tide) is one of 16 campgrounds along the peninsula; it also has mobile homes, chalets and bungalows for rent (two nights minimum).

⭐ **Kastell Dinn**   CABIN €
(☑ 02 98 27 26 40, 06 62 52 96 61; www.sejour-insolitebretagne.com; Kerlouantec; d €70-95) Looking for something extra special and different? This marvellous and incredibly atmospheric little hideaway in the tiny hamlet of Kerlouantec, 2km southwest of Crozon, offers two free-standing 'shipshape' units set in decommissioned fishing boats (yes!) and one *roulotte* (caravan), as well as two rooms in a traditional Breton *longère* (long house). There's also a fully equipped shared kitchen.

Hôtel de la Baie   HOTEL €
(☑ 02 98 27 07 51; www.hoteldelabaie-crozon-morgat.com; 46 bd de la Plage; d €55-98, studio €89.50-149.50; 🛜) One of the *very* few places to remain open year-round and one of the best deals about, this friendly, family-run spot on Morgat's promenade has clean and pleasant rooms; pricier rooms have views over the sea, while studio apartments with kitchenette are also available.

🍴 Eating

⭐ **Le Mutin Gourmand**   FRENCH €€
(☑ 02 98 27 06 51; www.lemutingourmand.fr; place de l'Église; menus €29-84, mains €25-32; ⏱ noon-1.30pm Wed-Sun, 7-8.45pm Tue-Sun Jul & Aug, closed Sun dinner rest of year) There's no sea view (it's in Crozon's town centre), but this is the gourmet choice. With its intimate dining room, charming welcome and delicious cuisine, Le Mutin Gourmand has honed the art of dining to perfection. The chef works with local, carefully chosen ingredients, so whatever season it is, you'll be in for a treat. The kids' menu is €10.

The associated **Le Bistrot du Mutin**, in a nearby annex, has very affordable *menus* (lunch *menu* €19).

Saveurs et Marées   SEAFOOD €€
(☑ 02 98 26 23 18; www.saveurs-maree-crozon.fr; 52 bd de la Plage; lunch menu €14-19.50, dinner menu €19.50-46; ⏱ noon-2pm & 7-10pm Tue-Sun)

Our pick of Morgat's clutch of restaurants has sweeping windows with full-on views of the sea from its breezy contemporary dining room and lovely sunny terrace. Tuck into consistently good, locally caught seafood (including succulent lobster).

ℹ️ Information

Crozon Tourist Office (📞 02 98 27 07 92; www.tourisme-presquiledecrozon.fr; bd de Pralognan; ⊙ 9.30am-1pm & 2-7pm Mon-Sat, 10am-1pm Sun Jul & Aug, 9.30am-noon & 2-6pm Mon-Sat Sep-Jun)

Morgat Tourist Office (📞 02 98 27 29 49; www.morgat.fr; place d'Ys; ⊙ 9.30am-12.30pm & 3-7pm Mon-Wed, 2.30-7.30pm Thu-Sun Jul-Aug, 9.30am-noon Mon Jun & Sep)

ℹ️ Getting There & Around

BICYCLE

Rent a bike in summer at the open-air stall in front of Morgat's tourist office for €12 per day, or year-round with **Point Bleu** (📞 02 98 27 22 11; www.point-bleu.fr; 10 bvd Pierre Mendes France, Crozon; per day €12; ⊙ 9.30am-noon & 2-7pm Mon-Sat, 10am-noon Sun).

BUS

Penn Ar Bed (p297) bus 34 connects Crozon with Camaret-sur-Mer (€2; 25 minutes; two daily) and Le Faou (€4; 40 minutes; two daily), and bus 37 goes to Quimper (€4; one hour; two daily). The bus stops in Crozon near the **tourist office** (p299).

Camaret-sur-Mer

POP 2647

At the western edge of the Presqu'île de Crozon, Camaret is a classic fishing village – or at least it was early in the 20th century, when it was France's largest crayfish port. Nowadays, abandoned fishing boats dot the attractive harbour, which is populated by clanking yacht masts and lined by cafes.

Overlooked by a 17th-century red-brick watchtower, Camaret remains an enchanting spot that attracts artists who run an ever-increasing number of galleries throughout town.

◎ Sights

★ Pointe de Pen-Hir   NATURAL FEATURE

Three kilometres southwest of Camaret, this spectacular and sublime headland is bounded by steep, sheer sea cliffs. On a peninsula known for its breathtaking scenery, this might be the most impressive lookout of them all. The series of offshore rock stacks are known as **Tas de Pois**. There are also two WWII memorials, and just inland 80 neolithic menhirs comprise the **Alignements de Lagatjar**. There are plenty of short walks in the area, as well as a handful of small cove beaches.

Chapelle Notre-Dame-de-Rocamadour   CHURCH

(⊙ 10am-5pm daily, Sat & Sun only during school holidays) Its timber roof like an inverted ship's hull, the 17th-century Chapelle Notre-Dame-de-Rocamadour at the **Pointe de Rocamadour** is dedicated to the sailors of Camaret, who have adorned it with votive offerings of oars, lifebuoys and model ships.

ℹ️ Information

Tourist Office (📞 02 98 27 93 60; www.camaretsurmer-tourisme.fr; 15 quai Kléber; ⊙ 9am-noon & 2-6pm Mon-Sat, plus 10am-noon Sun Jul & Aug) Located on the waterfront.

ℹ️ Getting There & Away

BOAT

Le Brestoâ (p295) connects Brest's Port de Commerce with Le Fret on the Crozon Peninsula (one way adult/child €9.50/7.50, 30 minutes, twice daily Tuesday to Sunday April to September) – handy to avoid the huge overland journey round the coast. Check the timetable as there's often only one boat on Sundays.

Penn Ar Bed (p297) sails between Camaret and Île d'Ouessant (return adult/child €34.90/24.90, one hour) two to six times per week in July and August, and once weekly in May, June and early September. It also has high-season boats to Île de Sein.

BUS

Five buses daily run from Quimper to Crozon (€2, 1¼ hours), continuing to Camaret (€2) and stopping at the port; up to four daily go from Camaret and Crozon to Brest (€2, 1¼ hours).

ℹ️ CATCHING THE WAVE

Feel like hitting the waves slamming onto the wild shores of Brittany, but not sure how? Head to **École de Surf de Bretagne** (www.ecole-surf-bretagne.fr) surf school at one of 12 outfits around Brittany (see the website for details). Courses range from a 1½-hour session (€40) to a full-time weeklong program (€280).

BORIS STROUJKO/SHUTTERSTOCK ©

City walls and beach, St-Malo (p279) **2.** Fresh oysters (p287) om the Breton coast **3.** Île d'Ouessant (p295)

3

Breton Coast

Brittany's rugged coastline is one of the region's best-kept secrets. With brilliant sandy beaches framing traditional fishing villages, rocky cliffs towering above the churning swell of the North Atlantic, and loads of outdoor activities to keep you occupied, there's plenty to discover.

Superb Stretches of Sand

Don't associate Brittany with beaches? Think again... Yes, the water may be freezing, but the sand is spectacular and the backing sublime at St-Malo (p279) and Quiberon (p311). Alternatively, find your own patch of sand on the beaches of Belle Île (p313).

Hiking the Coasts

Get out into nature on the coastal hiking trail from Morgat to Cap de la Chèvre (p297). For a challenge, walk the 45km coastal path on Île d'Ouessant (p295) or the 95km path around Belle Île (p313).

Coastal Villages

Find your own quiet bliss in the village life of charming Camaret-sur-Mer (p299), the fishing port of Roscoff (p290) and, our personal favourite, oyster-rich hideaway Cancale (p286).

Island Life

Take the ferry to Île d'Ouessant (p295), with its rugged coastal path and great activities, or head out of season to Belle Île (p313), the southern coast's star. To get off the beaten track, head to Île de Batz (p291).

Get Active!

You can dive, windsurf and hire catamarans in Dinard (p285); canoe or kayak in Paimpol (p289), St-Malo (p279), Îles de Glénan (p306) and Quiberon (p311); and hire bikes pretty much anywhere, though we recommend Presqu'île de Crozon (p297) and any of Brittany's islands. You can also learn to surf at schools (p299) around Brittany.

Locronan

POP 838

Locronan may be no secret, and tourists flock here by the busload in summer, but that shouldn't deter you from visiting this quintessentially Breton village that has barely changed in appearance since the mid-18th century. With its splendid cobbled streets and traditional architecture, it's perhaps the prettiest village in this region of France, so it's little wonder that its old-world ambience and photogenic granite houses have made it hugely popular with film crews.

Locronan is also famous for hosting one of Brittany's oldest *pardons* (religious processions), the Petite Troménie, and for its more ambitious sibling, the Grande Troménie, which takes place every six years.

◉ Sights

★ Église St-Ronan   CHURCH
(place de l'Église; ⊘ 9am-7pm) At the core of Locronan, this beautiful and very sacred church dates from the 15th century. It contains the tomb of St Ronan, as well as a green wooden pulpit that is a marvel to behold, carved and painted with scenes from the saint's life in Brittany. Ronan was an ascetic pilgrim from Ireland who established a hermitage in the woods here, around which the village eventually formed.

Musée Municipal d'Art et d'Histoire   MUSEUM
(☑ 02 98 51 80 80; www.locronan-tourisme.bzh/musee-art-et-histoire-locronan; place de la Mairie; adult/child €5/free; ⊘ 10am-12.30pm & 1.30-6pm Mon-Sat, 2-6pm Sun Apr-Sept) Situated next to the small town hall (off the main square near the church), this museum is largely dedicated to the history of the linen industry. It brought prosperity to the village, but then died out because of mechanisation. There are also examples of Breton paintings upstairs.

⚜ Festivals & Events

Petite Troménie   RELIGIOUS
(⊘ 2nd Sun in Jul) Barefooted pilgrims bearing saintly banners and singing traditional songs follow a 4km route from the church to a sacred grove, following the path taken by St Ronan. This highly colourful event attracts huge crowds of onlookers, so try to catch it.

Every six years sees the Grande Troménie (the next one is in 2019), which follows a 12km route, past 12 stations.

⛏ Sleeping & Eating

Camping Locronan   CAMPGROUND €
(☑ 02 98 91 87 76; www.camping-locronan.fr; rue de la Troménie; site from €12; ⊘ Apr-Sep; 🛜🏊) With an indoor swimming pool, this campground is situated in a lovely wooded setting, with 100 pitches as well as mobile homes and activities for children.

Le Prieuré   HOTEL €€
(☑ 02 98 91 70 89; www.hotel-le-prieure.com; 11 rue du Prieuré; s/d/tr/q from €58/72/85/95; 🛜) The only hotel in Locronan, the two-star, 15-room Le Prieuré is a pleasant choice with comfy and cosy rooms – it can be oversubscribed in summer, so book ahead. The hotel has a decent restaurant too, serving seafood and local cuisine. Breakfast is €10, or €11 if served in your room.

BRITTANY'S MOST UNFORGETTABLE SUNSET

Few places in France can match **Pointe du Raz** for its coastal splendour: on every side gorse-cloaked cliffs plummet to the waves 70m below, gulls trace lazy arcs overhead, and a statue gazes out to sea towards the île de Sein and the winking light of the Ar Men lighthouse. On a stormy day, with giant waves hurling themselves at the cliff faces, it feels like the end of the world. On a clear day, the sunsets are quite unbelievable.

The area is a nationally protected reserve and trails criss-cross the land, but be careful on trails that have severe, unprotected drop-offs. A car park, cafes and a high-season **visitor centre** (Maison de la Pointe du Raz et du Cap-Sizun; ☑ 02 98 70 67 18; www.pointeduraz.com; 10.30am-6pm Apr-Jun & Sep, to 7pm Jul-Aug, to 5.30pm Oct) are behind the point proper; shuttle buses ferry visitors the last 800m, or you can just walk the scenic coast path.

In high season only, **Penn Ar Bed** (☑ 02 98 90 88 89; www.viaoo29.fr) bus 53B from Quimper continues past Audierne on to the car park at Pointe du Raz (€2, three daily Monday to Saturday, 1¼ hours), but it's easier and more sensible to visit with your own wheels. There is a car-park fee of €6.50.

ℹ Getting There & Away

Penn Ar Bed (p297) bus 37 connects Locronan to Quimper (€2; 25 minutes, two daily) and Camaret-sur-Mer (€6; one hour, two daily). **QUB** (p305) lines 21 and 23 serve Quimper (25 minutes). The bus stops in Locronan on rue du Prieuré.

Quimper

POP 66,926

Small enough to feel like a village, with its slanted half-timbered houses and narrow cobbled streets, and large enough to buzz as the troubadour of Breton culture and arts, Quimper (kam-pair) is Finistère's thriving capital. With some excellent museums, standout crêperies, a history of faience (pottery) production, one of Brittany's loveliest old quarters and a delightful setting along the Odet River, Quimper deserves serious exploration.

◎ Sights & Activities

Cathédrale St-Corentin CHURCH
(place St-Corentin; ⊙8.30am-noon & 1.30-6.30pm Mon-Sat, 8.30am-noon & 2-6.30pm Sun) At the centre of the city rises Quimper's dramatic Gothic cathedral, with its distinctive dip in the middle where it was built to conform to the land. It is said to symbolise Christ's inclined head as he was dying on the cross. Construction began in 1239, but the cathedral's imposing twin spires weren't added until the 19th century. High on the west facade, look out for an equestrian statue of King Gradlon, the city's mythical 5th-century founder.

★ Musée Départemental Breton MUSEUM
(✍ 02 98 95 21 60; http://musee-breton.finistere.fr; 1 rue du Roi Gradlon; adult/child €5/free, free weekends Oct-Jun; ⊙10am-7pm mid-Jun–mid-Sep, 9.30am-5.30pm Tue-Fri, 2-5.30pm Sat & Sun mid-Sep–mid-Jun) Beside the Cathédrale St-Corentin, recessed behind a magnificent stone courtyard, this superb museum over several floors showcases Breton history, furniture, crafts and archaeology, in a former bishop's palace. Don't miss the fascinating displays of traditional costumes – some beautifully elaborate – and the splendid ceramics and painting, and don't overlook the **Tour de Rohan**, up a spiral staircase. There are also temporary exhibitions: when we visited, there was a fascinating display of art

work by talented Quimper illustrator Marguerite Chabay.

Musée des Beaux-Arts GALLERY
(✍ 02 98 95 45 20; www.mbaq.fr; 40 place St-Corentin; adult/child €5/3; ⊙10am-6pm Jul & Aug, 9.30am-noon & 2-6pm Wed-Mon Apr-Jun, Sep & Oct, shorter hours Nov-Mar) The ground-floor rooms of the town's main art museum are home to 16th- to 20th-century European paintings, and upper levels include a room dedicated to Quimper-born poet Max Jacob with sketches by Picasso. There's also a section devoted to the Pont-Aven school.

Vedettes de l'Odet BOATING
(✍ 02 98 57 00 58; www.vedettes-odet.com; av du Corniguel; adult/child from €16/13; ⊙Apr-Sep) Vedettes de l'Odet runs boat trips, including one around the îles Glénan and a promenade cruise from Quimper's Port de Corniguel along the serene Odet estuary to Bénodet. You can stop for a look about Bénodet and then hop on a boat back. The company also offers a shorter one-hour cruise along the Odet River, its cheapest and handy if you've not much time.

🛏 Sleeping

Hôtel Gradlon HOTEL €€
(✍ 02 98 95 04 39; www.hotel-gradlon.com; 30 rue de Brest; d €60-150, ste €114-190, f €132-220; ⊙mid-Jan–mid-Dec; 🛜) The bland, sterile facade belies a charming country-manor interior, where excellent service prevails. Rooms are not large, but are well furnished and quite varied, with plenty of character and individual touches. Bathrooms tend towards the large and modern. Cheapest prices can be angled for in winter when all's slow; breakfast costs €12. No lift.

Best Western Hôtel Kregenn HOTEL €€
(✍ 02 98 95 08 70; www.hotel-kregenn.fr; 13 rue des Réguaires; d €109-180, ste €199-214; ✳ 🛜) A timber-decked courtyard and a guest lounge with oversized mirrors and white leather sofas shows Quimper's coolest hotel. Some of the contemporary plush rooms – decked out in warm colours – come with ancient stone walls. Buffet breakfast is €13; parking is €7.

Hôtel Manoir des Indes HOTEL €€
(✍ 02 98 55 48 40; www.manoir-hoteldesindes.com; 1 allée de Prad ar C'hras; s €89-171, d €155-190; 🛜 ✷) Fabulously located in an old manor house 5km west of the centre of Quimper, this excellent place has been lovingly

Quimper

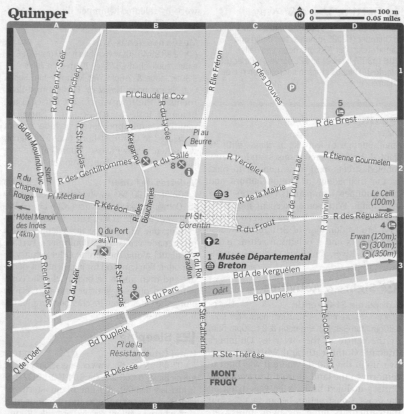

Quimper

◎ Top Sights
1 Musée Départemental Breton	C3

◎ Sights
2 Cathédrale St-Corentin	C3
3 Musée des Beaux-Arts	C2

◎ Sleeping
4 Best Western Hôtel Kregenn	D3
5 Hôtel Gradlon	D1

◎ Eating
6 Crêperie du Quartier	B2
7 Halles St-François	A3
8 La Krampouzerie	B2
9 L'Épée	B3

restored with the globe-trotting original owner in mind. Decor is minimalist and modern, with Asian *objets d'art* and lots of exposed wood and oodles of character, plus a subterranean swimming pool.

✖ Eating

As a bastion of Breton culture, Quimper has a bewildering choice of exceptional crêperies, all centred on, fittingly, place au Beurre and also rue du Sallé. You'll be spoiled for choice. The covered market **Halles St-François** (www.halles-cornouaille.com; 16 quai du Stéïr; ⏱ 7am-7.30pm Mon-Sat, to 1pm Sun) in the old town has a slew of salad and sandwich options. **Open-air markets** are on Wednesday and Saturday and surround the covered market.

Crêperie du Quartier   CRÊPES **€**
(☏ 02 98 64 29 30; 16 rue du Sallé; mains €6-9; ⏱ noon-2pm & 7-9pm Mon-Sat) In a town where the humble crêpe is king, and in a street stuffed with crêperies, this cosy stone-lined place is one of the best. Its wide-ranging and lip-smackingly good menu includes a *galette* of the week and, to follow up, you can go for a crêpe stuffed with apple, caramel, ice cream, almonds and Chantilly.

La Krampouzerie
CRÊPES €

(🖉 02 98 95 13 08; 9 rue du Sallé; mains €4.50-9; ⏱ 11.45am-3pm & 6.45-10pm Tue-Sat) 🍴 Crêpes and *galettes* made from organic flours and eggs and regional ingredients such as *algues d'Ouessant* (seaweed), Roscoff onions and homemade ginger caramel are king here, all served and washed down with Breton cider or apple juice. In summer, tables on the square out the front launch a street-party atmosphere.

★ L'Épée
CAFE €€

(🖉 02 98 95 28 97; http://cafedelepee.fr; 14 rue du Parc; mains €12-32, menus €15.50-39; ⏱ brasserie noon-2.30pm & 7-10.30pm Mon-Sat, cafe 10.30am-midnight Mon-Sat, noon-2.30pm Sun) This good-looking Quimper institution is one of Brittany's oldest brasseries and hits the mark with its buzzy, contemporary dining areas, efficient service and good vibe. Despite the hip interior, the food is never an afterthought. Superbly executed dishes include duck breast, lamb shank, shellfish and salads, and you can always just stop by for a drink. There's a €10 kids' menu.

ℹ Information

Tourist Office (🖉 02 98 53 04 05; www. quimper-tourisme.bzh; 8 rue Élie Fréron; ⏱ 9am-7pm Mon-Sat, 10am-12.45pm & 3-5.45pm Sun Jul & Aug, shorter hours rest of year; 🛜) Sells the Pass Quimper (€12), which gives admission to four museums, sights or tours from a list of participating organisations. Arranges walking tours.

ℹ Getting There & Around

AIR

Quimper's **airport** (UIP; 🖉 02 98 94 30 30; www.quimper.aeroport.fr; rue de l'Aéroport, Pluguffan), 10km southwest of town, has direct flights to Paris, Figari (Corsica), London and Nice-Côte d'Azur. It is served by **QUB** (🖉 02 98 95 26 27; www.qub.fr; single/day ticket €1.30/3.90) bus 25 from Quimper.

BUS

Penn Ar Bed (p297) has regular buses to Brest (€6, 1¼ hours), Concarneau (€2, 45 minutes) and Camaret-sur-Mer (€2, 1¼ hours). The bus station is next to the train station.

TRAIN

Quimper is on major lines to Vannes, Rennes and Paris, and a minor line north to Landerneau and Brest:

Brest €9, 1½ hours, (SNCF bus or train) 11 daily

Nantes €38.60, 2½ hours, 3 direct daily

Paris Montparnasse €67-108, 4¾ hours, 9 direct daily

Rennes €32-40, 2 hours, 11 direct daily

Vannes €18-27.50, 1½ hours, 15 daily

Concarneau
POP 19,568

The sheltered harbour of Concarneau (Konk-Kerne in Breton), 24km southeast of Quimper, radiates out from its trawler port, which brings in close to 200,000 tonnes of *thon* (tuna) from the Indian Ocean and off the African coast (the adjacent Atlantic is too cold). Jutting out into the port, and circled by medieval walls, the supremely picturesque old town – Ville Close – is quite amazing, and one of Brittany's most popular spots in summer, and the town itself is good-looking enough.

The coast to the west of Concarneau is fun to explore if you have your own wheels, as it's cut by inlets and dotted with picturesque harbours such as Ste-Marine (a good place to stop for a coffee or meal in one of the port cafes). Concarneau is also a jumping-off point for the Îles de Glénan.

◉ Sights

★ Ville Close (Walled City)
HISTORIC SITE

This special walled town, fortified in the 14th century and modified by the architect Vauban two centuries later, sits on a small island linked to place Jean Jaurès by a stone footbridge. Just past the citadel's clock tower and main gate, look out for the 18th-century **Tour du Gouverneur**, which is one of the access points for strolling the ramparts . As you continue, rue Vauban leads to place St-Guénolé and the former church – and later hospice – of the same name.

On the way you will pass stone houses converted into shops, crêperies, ice-cream stalls and galleries. Indeed, the best way to explore the island is to wander at will. The eastern side of the island has a small hilly park, and there's a passenger ferry (€1) that runs across the inlet to the opposite quay at place Duquesne. The Ville Close is thronged in summer and on weekends.

Musée de la Pêche
MUSEUM

(Fisheries Museum; 🖉 02 98 97 10 20; www.musee-peche.fr; 3 rue Vauban; adult/child €5/free; ⏱ 10am-7pm Jul & Aug, 10am-6pm Tue-Sun Apr-Jun & Sep, 2-5.30pm Tue-Sun Feb, Mar, Nov & Dec, closed Jan) This excellent museum, just inside the main western gate of the Ville Close, delves into Concarneau's seafaring traditions using everything from archive film to scale models and vintage boats. You can even clamber aboard the museum's very own fishing vessel, the retired *L'Hémérica,* permanently docked just outside the city walls.

🏖 Beaches

Concarneau's best beach is **Plage des Sables Blancs** (🔲3), northwest of the town centre. **Plage du Cabellou** (🔲2), about 7km south of town, is a decent spot for sunbathing and swimming, with views back to Concarneau; take bus 2, southbound, which continues all the way to scenic **Pointe du Cabellou** (🔲2) and its old fort.

🛏 Sleeping

Auberge de Jeunesse Éthic Étapes   HOSTEL €
(📲 02 98 97 03 47; www.aj-concarneau.org; quai de la Croix; dm incl breakfast €18; 🛜) Fall asleep listening to the waves at this functional and central waterfront hostel at the southern tip of Concarneau. Digs are in four- to six-bed dorms. Extras include a wrap-around barbecue terrace, a self-catering kitchen and pastries for breakfast. Lunch and dinner is €11.

Hôtel des Halles   HOTEL €
(📲 02 98 97 11 41; www.hoteldeshalles.com; place de l'Hôtel de Ville; s/tr/f €64/100/110, d €74-98,; 🛜) The location is superb – just a few steps from Ville Close – and though this 22-room hotel tends towards the mainstream and ordinary, its rooms are cheered by their use of colour and suitably nautical decor, while service is positive. The organic breakfast (€11) includes homemade jams; garage parking is €9.

DON'T MISS

ÎLES DE GLÉNAN
···

Sapphire waters, idyllic white-sand beaches and no crowds – Bora Bora? No: Îles de Glénan. This archipelago of around a dozen mini-islands lies just 20km south of Concarneau and never fails to impress in fine weather. Visitors are only allowed on Île de St-Nicolas. **Vedettes de l'Odet** (📲 02 98 57 00 58; www.vedettes-odet.com/en; Port de Plaisance, Concarneau) runs scenic cruises around the islands from Concarneau and other coastal towns. Optional activities include sea kayaking and glass-bottom-boat tours as well as diving.

Hôtel de France et d'Europe   HOTEL €€
(📲 02 98 97 00 64; www.hotel-france-europe.com; 9 av de la Gare; s/d/tr/q from €80/87/108/130; 🛜) This faintly stylish, comfortable and serviceable place is just two blocks north of the harbour. There's no 'wow' factor – just plain, good-value lodging in a handy location. Precious perks include private parking (car/bicycle per day €8/2), a shady terrace and a fitness room.

Les Sables Blancs   BOUTIQUE HOTEL €€
(📲 02 98 50 10 12; www.hotel-les-sables-blancs.com; plage des Sables Blancs; d €135-235; 🛜) If you want to get out of town, this contemporary west-facing hotel, right on the 'white sands' of the beach of the same name, has tastefully decorated rooms with fabulous sea views and a good restaurant. The catch? The 'standard' rooms are a bit boxy and prices can inflate rather unappealingly in summer.

🍴 Eating

Tourist-focused cafes, pizzerias and crêperies line the waterfront, and there are more inside the walls of Ville Close, but other restaurants are secreted away down the back streets.

There's a **covered market** on place Jean Jaurès and a busy **open-air market** in the same square on Monday (smaller) and Friday (larger) mornings.

Le Petit Chaperon Rouge   CRÊPES €
(📲 02 98 60 53 32; 7 place Duguesclin; mains €4-12; ⊙ noon-1.30pm Tue-Sun, 7.15-9.15pm Tue-Sat) This cute and inviting crêperie enjoys a cosy setting and a bumper and enticing selection of savoury *galettes* and sweet crêpes.

Le Flaveur   MODERN FRENCH €€
(📲 02 98 60 43 47; 4 rue Duquesne; lunch menu €17-19.90, dinner menu €28.50, mains €18-23; ⊙ noon-1.30pm & 7.15-9pm Tue-Wed & Fri-Sat, noon-1.30pm Sun) Le Flaveur is tucked temptingly away from the hustle and bustle down a quiet street near the harbour. Meals range from strictly local dishes through to broader French cuisine. The menu changes regularly so specific pointers are tricky. If it's available, enquire about the *pigeonneau royal* (royal pigeon), endorsed by locals as 'almost gastronomic' – meaning delectable, but affordable.

🛍 Shopping

Atelier-Boutique Valérie Le Roux   CERAMICS
(📲 02 98 50 82 13; www.valerieleroux.com; 4 rue Duguay Trouin; ⊙ 9.30am-noon & 1-7pm Tue-Sat) This terrific shop is a delight, filled with

hand-painted and glazed pottery bottles, bowls, tiles and all manner of other bright and colourful things in fresh, child-like patterns. What's on display is truly eye-catching and makes the perfect gift.

ⓘ Information

Tourist Office (☎ 02 98 97 01 44; www.tourismeconcarneau.fr; quai d'Aiguillon; ☺ 9am-12.30pm & 2-6pm Mon-Sat; ☎) Has information on the myriad walking and cycling circuits in the area.

ⓘ Getting There & Away

Concarneau is on the route run by **L'Été Évasion** (☎ 02 98 56 82 82; www.autocars-ete.com; €2) between Quimper (40 minutes) and Quimperlé (55 minutes). Services run up to 10 buses daily, and stop at the port.

Pont-Aven

POP 2901

Breton villages don't come much prettier than Pont-Aven, a former port and mill town cradled at the end of a wooded creek about 20km east of Concarneau. In the 19th century, its charms were discovered by artists. American painters were among the first to uncover it, but things really took off when France's Paul Gauguin and Émile Bernard set up a colony here in the 1850s and captured the beauty of the little village and the surrounding countryside.

At the village's **Musée de Pont-Aven** (☎ 02 98 06 14 43; www.museepontaven.fr; place Julia; adult/child €8/free; ☺ 10am-7pm Jul & Aug, 10am-6pm Tue-Sun Apr-Jun, Sep & Oct, 2-5.30pm Tue-Sun Mar, Nov & Dec, closed Jan) interactive exhibits delve in to the life and art of Gauguin and others. Some excellent temporary exhibitions bring masterpieces to town and the museum has a lovely garden and a shop.

Since the 1960s, Pont-Aven has again become a magnet for artists seeking fresh air and country inspiration. Today there are over 60 galleries around town.

🛏 Sleeping & Eating

Les Ajoncs d'Or HOTEL €
(☎ 02 98 06 02 06; www.ajoncsdor-pontaven.com; 1 place Julia; d €70-80, tr/q €87/97; ☎) A good deal for Pont-Aven, this venerable two-star hotel is a decent and well-priced choice, with cosy beds, tiled bathrooms and nice furnishings, all kept clean and presentable. There's an attached restaurant and breakfast is an extra €9.50.

Sur Le Pont MODERN FRENCH €€
(☎ 02 98 06 16 16; www.surlepont-pontaven.fr; 11 place Paul Gauguin; mains €16-23, lunch/dinner menu from €26/33; ☺ 12.30-2pm Thu-Tue, 7.30-9pm Thu-Mon) You couldn't wish for a more perfect setting, lodged in a stylishly renovated building by the Pont-Aven bridge. A just-so palette of cool greys, beiges, blacks and whites creates the feel of an elegant bistro, and the mood is relaxed and joyous. Dishes are refined takes on Breton cooking with an emphasis on seafood.

ⓘ Information

Tourist Office (☎ 02 98 06 87 90; www.pontaven.com; 3 rue des Meunières; ☺ 9.30am-noon & 2.30-6pm Mon-Sat; ☎) Pick up a free walking-trail map to see the spots where the masters set up their easels. Can also help with accommodation.

ⓘ Getting There & Away

Pont-Aven is 16km east of Concarneau. **Buses** (p297) (€2, five daily Monday to Saturday, two on Sunday) connect Pont-Aven with Quimperlé in the east (30 minutes), Concarneau (30 minutes) and Quimper (one hour). Buses depart Port-Aven from Place de l'Hôtel de Ville in the centre of town.

GOLFE DU MORBIHAN

In the crook of Brittany's southern coastline, the Golfe du Morbihan (Morbihan Coast; www.morbihan.com) is a haven of around 40 islands, plus beaches, oyster beds and bird life. Its shallow waters form a breathtakingly beautiful inland sea that's easily accessible from Vannes. Some islands are barely sandy specks of land, while others harbour communities of fishermen, farmers and artistic types seduced by the island lifestyle.

The area is perhaps best known for its profusion of magnificent and mystifying Celtic megaliths – a must for a visit to Brittany. They rise majestically throughout most of the *département,* charging the area with a sense of ancient mystery.

Further inland lies the handsome town of Josselin, well-known for its huge castle, medieval contours and scenic riverine perch on the River Oust. For further doses of ancient charm, the picture-postcard town of Rochefort-en-Terre is well worth a day's exploration to fully soak up its historic flavours.

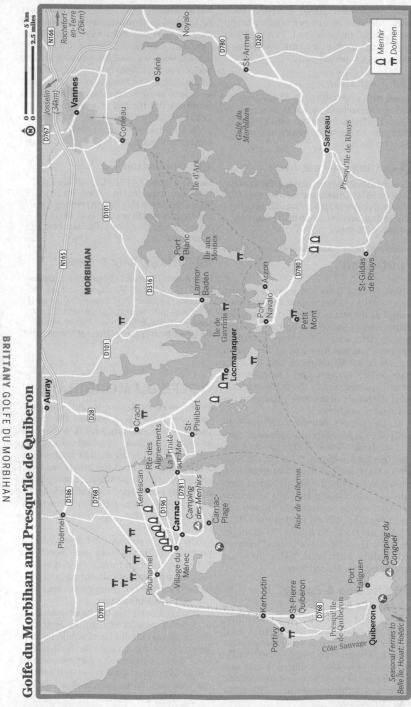

BRITTANY GOLFE DU MORBIHAN

Golfe du Morbihan and Presqu'île de Quiberon

Carnac
POP 4334

Carnac is firmly on the map for its astonishing and almost other-worldly collection of megalithic sites. Predating Stonehenge by around 100 years, Carnac (Garnag in Breton) tops it with the sheer number of ancient sites found in the vicinity, making this the world's greatest concentration of megalithic sites. There are no fewer than 3000 of these upright stones erected between 5000 and 3500 BC.

Off the trail, you can hike through the woods and soak up some of the area's primordial energy. Go in search of a giant menhir, duck down through a passage to a tumulus vault or climb up an abandoned mill for panoramic views of the ancient stones. This is one of the most important sights in the whole country.

Carnac, some 32km west of Vannes, comprises the old stone village Carnac-Ville and, 1.5km south, the seaside resort of Carnac-Plage, bordered by the 2km-long sandy beach.

🏄 Beaches

Not only is Carnac a fantastic open-air museum that appeals to culture vultures, but it's also a superb playground for beachy types. **Grande Plage** is Carnac's longest and most popular beach and is excellent for sunbathing – it's a 2km-long stretch of white sand 2km south of Carnac-Ville. To the west, **Plage de Légenèse** and **Plage de St-Colomban** are smaller and quieter. St-Colomban appeals to windsurfers.

🛏 Sleeping

Camping des Menhirs CAMPGROUND €
(📞 02 97 52 94 67; www.lesmenhirs.com; 7 allée St-Michel, Carnac-Plage; adult/site from €9/33; ⊙ mid-May–late Sep; 🖥🖳) Carnac and its surrounds have more than 15 camp grounds, including this luxury complex of 100-sq-metre sites, with 332 pitches as well as some fantastic mobile homes. Just 300m north of the beach, this is very much the glamorous end of camping and more of a resort, with amenities such as a sauna, cocktail bar, sports facilities and entertainment.

Le Ratelier INN €
(📞 02 97 52 05 04; www.le-ratelier.com; 4 chemin du Douet; s/d from €61, f from €85; 🖥) This vine-clad former farmhouse has eight rooms – with low ceilings, fabric-covered walls and traditional timber furnishings – is in a quiet

street south of the church. The cheapest rooms have showers only and shared toilets. Those with private bathrooms feel a tad compact due to the cubicle shower and toilets plonked in the corner. Breakfast is €8.

⭐Dihan B&B €€
(📞 02 97 56 88 27; www.dihan-evasion.org; Kerganiet, Ploëmel; tent/tree house from €65/90) 🌿 For the ultimate eco-escape, don't miss fantastic Dihan, secluded in a leafy dell outside Ploëmel (follow the signs from the village), 8km north of Carnac. Run by fun-loving Myriam and Arno Le Masle, a farmhouse and barn house the guest rooms, while the grounds shelter yurts, bubble tents and tree houses and even a whimsical wonkily shaped 'house'.

⭐Plume au Vent B&B €€
(📞 06 16 98 34 79; www.plume-au-vent.com; 4 venelle Notre-Dame, Carnac-Ville; d €85-100, q €145-160; 🛜) Forget about tacky seaside hotels, this two-room B&B on a *venelle* (little street) in the town centre is more like something from an interior-design magazine. It's all mellow shades of blues and greys, with hundreds of neatly bound books, knick-knacks discovered washed up on the high-tide line and polished concrete showers and sinks. A great find.

🍴 Eating

Chez Marie CRÊPES €
(📞 02 97 52 07 93; 3 place de l'Église, Carnac-Ville; mains €6-13, menus €10-15; ⊙ noon-2pm & 7-10pm Wed-Sun) Established in 1959, this Carnac institution churns out savoury *galettes* and sweet crêpes in a charmingly traditional stone house opposite the church. Connoisseurs recommend its flambéed specialities, especially the Arzal *galette*, with scallops, apples and cider. There's a kids' menu (for

---

FESTIVAL FUN

Celtic communities from Ireland, Scotland, Wales, Cornwall, the Isle of Man and Galicia in northwest Spain congregate with Bretons at the **Festival Interceltique de Lorient** (📞 02 97 21 24 29; www.festival-interceltique.bzh; rue Pierre Guergadic, Lorient; ⊙ early Aug) over 10 days in early August. Upwards of 600,000 people descend on the city of Lorient, about 30km northwest of Carnac, so book well ahead if you're planning to stay in town for the festival.

DON'T MISS

CARNAC'S MYSTERIOUS MEGALITHS

Two perplexing questions arise from the Brittany's neolithic menhirs, dolmens, crom-lechs, tumuli and cairns. Just *how* did the original constructors hew, then haul, these blocks (the heaviest weighs 300 tonnes), millennia before the wheel and the mechanical engine reached Brittany? And *why*? Theories and hypotheses abound, but common consensus is that they served some kind of sacred purpose – a spiritual impulse that has motivated so much monument-building by humankind.

Just north of Carnac is a vast array of monoliths arranged in several distinct align-ments, all visible from the road, though fenced for controlled admission. There are also several spectacular sites around the Golfe du Morbihan, including Cairn de Gavrinis (p312), Locmariaquer Megaliths (p312) and Cairn de Petit Mont (p312).

The main information point for the Carnac alignments is the **Maison des Méga-lithes** (☑ 02 97 52 29 81; www.menhirs-carnac.fr; rte des Alignements, D196; tour adult/child €9/5; ☺ 9.30am-7pm Jul & Aug, 9.30am-6pm Sep, Apr & Jun, 10am-1pm & 2-5pm Oct-Mar), which explores the history of the site and has a rooftop viewpoint overlooking the *aligne-ments*. Due to severe erosion, the sites are fenced off to allow the vegetation to regener-ate, and certain areas are accessible only by guided tour. The Maison can organise one hour guided visit, several times daily in French and weekly in English during the summer.

The best way to appreciate the stones' sheer numbers is to walk or cycle between the Ménec and Kerlescan groups, with menhirs almost continuously in view. Between June and September, seven buses a day run between the two sites, as well as Carnac-Ville and Carnac-Plage.

On the other side of the road from the Maison des Mégalithes, the largest menhir field – with 1099 stones – is the **Alignements du Ménec** (rte des Alignements), 1km north of Carnac-Ville. From here, the D196 heads northeast for about 1.5km to the equally impressive **Alignements de Kermario** (rte de Kerlescan), parts of which are open year-round. Climb the stone **Moulin de Kermaux** (rte de Kerlescan) midway along the site to view the alignment from above.

The massive burial mound of a neolithic chieftain dating from 3800 BC, the astonish-ing **Tumulus de Kercado** (rte de Kerlescan) lies just east of Kermario and 500m to the south of the D196; look for the signs. Deposit your fee (€1) in an honour box at the entry hut that you walk through to reach the site. About 300m east of the Kercado turnoff along the D196 lies the parking area for the **Géant du Manio**.

The easternmost of the major groups is the **Alignements de Kerlescan** (rte de Kerlescan), a smaller grouping also accessible in winter.

Tumulus St-Michel (chemin du Tumulus, Carnac-Ville), 400m northeast of the Carnac-Ville tourist office, and accessed off the D781 at the end of rue du Tumulus, is a gigantic burial mound with a church on top. It dates back to at least 5000 BC and offers sweep-ing views (exterior access only).

Be sure to visit the **Musée de Préhistoire** (☑ 02 97 52 22 04; www.museedecarnac. fr; 10 place de la Chapelle, Carnac-Ville; adult/child €6/3; ☺ 10am-6.30pm Jul & Aug, 10am-12.30pm & 2-6pm Wed-Mon Apr-Jun & Sep, shorter hours Oct-Mar) to see the incredible neo-lithic artefacts found throughout the region.

under 10s) for €7.50, as well as a list of beers, ciders, wines and cocktails.

★**La Côte** GASTRONOMY €€€
(☑ 02 97 52 02 80; www.restaurant-la-cote.com; impasse Parc Er Forn, Kermario; lunch menu €26, dinner menu €39-58; ☺ 12.15-2.15pm Wed-Sun, 7.15-9.15pm Wed-Sat) Top recommendation on the Morbihan Coast goes to this Carnac res-taurant run by Carnacois *maître-cuisinier* Pierre Michaud, who has won plaudits for his inventive cuisine that combines the very

best Breton ingredients. The setting is an-other draw, with an elegant dining room and a soothing terrace overlooking a small fish pond. Find it in a quiet property close to the Alignements de Kermario.

ⓘ Information

Tourist Office (☑ 02 97 52 13 52; www.ot-carnac.fr; 74 av des Druides, Carnac-Plage; ☺ 9.30am-7pm Mon-Sat, 3-7pm Sun Jul-Aug, 9.30-12.30pm & 2-6pm Mon-Sat, 3-6pm Sun Apr-Jun & Sep, shorter hours rest of year; ☎) This office in Carnac-Plage, next to the church, has an excellent map of nearby neolithic sites and a smartphone app.

ⓘ Getting There & Around

BICYCLE

Hire bikes and cycle buggies from **A Bicyclette** (☑ 02 97 52 75 08; www.velocarnac.com; 93bis av des Druides, Carnac-Plage; bicycle per day from €10, buggy per hour from €8) down near the beach.

BUS

The main bus stops are in Carnac-Ville, outside the police station on rue St-Cornély, and in Carnac-Plage, beside the tourist office. **TIM** (☑ 08 00 88 10 87; www.tim-morlaix.com; ticket €2) runs a daily bus (line 1) to Auray (30 minutes), Vannes (80 minutes) and Quiberon (30 minutes).

TRAIN

The nearest useful train station is in Auray, 12km to the northeast. SNCF has an office in the **tourist office** where you can buy advance tickets.

Quiberon

POP 5112

Quiberon (Kiberen in Breton) sits right at the southern tip of a thin, 14km-long peninsula, called the **Presqu'île de Quiberon**, flanked on the western side by the rocky, sublime and wave-lashed **Côte Sauvage** (Wild Coast). A thin ribbon of isthmus – **l'isthme de Penthièvre** – links the peninsula to the mainland. The setting is superb, with a heady mix of lovely rock-strewn beaches and dramatic, rugged inlets; the town of Quiberon is also pleasant, but finding a parking spot in the high season can be trying. Even so, it's wildly popular in summer and is also the departure point for ferries to Belle Île (p313). For outdoorsy types, there are plenty of water sports available, from diving and snorkelling to sea kayaking, surfing and *char à voile* (sand yachting). The highlight is, however, driving down the Route Côtière (D186A) along the Côte Sauvage, stopping off at the various beaches.

🏃 Activities & Tours

Grande Plage   BEACH

Grande Plage is a long, family-friendly and attractive, sheltered sweep of sand; bathing spots towards the peninsula's tip are less crowded.

Sillages   KAYAKING

(☑ 06 81 26 75 08; www.kayak-sillages.com; 9 av de Groix, St-Pierre-Quiberon; adult/child from €20/16; ⊙ daily by reservation) What about a morning paddle far from the crowds along the Côte Sauvage? This reputable outfit based in St-Pierre-Quiberon (look for the 'Base Nautique') runs guided kayaking tours for all levels – beginners are welcome.

Conserverie La Belle-Iloise   CANNERY TOUR

(☑ 02 97 50 59 08; www.labelleiloise.fr; zone d'Activités Plein Ouest, bd Plein Ouest; ⊙ high-season tours 10.30am, 11.30am, 2.30pm, 3.30pm, 4.30pm & 5pm Mon-Fri, 10.30am, 11.30am, 2.30pm, 3.30pm & 4.30pm Sat, fewer tours low season) **FREE** Take a 45-minute guided tour of this former sardine cannery before replenishing your supplies of tinned tuna, mackerel, sardines and fish spread in the adjacent shop. It's north of the train station.

🛏 Sleeping & Eating

Camping du Conguel   CAMPGROUND €

(☑ 02 97 50 19 11; www.campingduconguel.com; bd de la Teignouse, Plage Conguel; sites from €29; ⊙ Apr-Oct; 🛜 ⊛) This splashy option with an aqua park that has water slides is one of the peninsula's 15 campgrounds. Just 2km east of the town centre, it's beside Plage du Conguel. There are also caravans to rent (from €45).

★ Le Petit Hôtel du Grand Large   BOUTIQUE HOTEL €€

(☑ 02 97 30 91 61; www.lepetithoteldugrandlarge.fr; 11 quai St-Ivy, Portivy; d €115-135; 🛜) This intimate hotel is a soothing escape, offering six spiffy, well-lit rooms facing the sea. Top choices are room 4, with its bathroom set in a turret, and room 5, for its wide balcony. It's in Portivy, an adorable, quiet seaside town a few kilometres north of Quiberon. Breakfast is €13.

★ Le Vivier   SEAFOOD €

(☑ 02 97 50 12 60; rte du Prado, Côte Sauvage; mains €9-30; ⊙ noon-3pm & 7-8pm Tue-Sun Feb-Nov, plus Mon Jul & Aug) The seafood is superb, but almost secondary at this convivial but busy eatery dramatically perched on a small cliff on the blustery Côte Sauvage; bookings are essential for the top tables, squeezed onto a sunny terrace hovering above the rocky coastline. The menu is plain and unpretentious – think fish soup, salads, mussels, smoked fish and oysters (€8.50 for a half dozen).

DON'T MISS

NEOLITHIC DISCOVERIES IN THE GULF

The land and islands around the Golfe du Morbihan are dotted with an astonishing array of neolithic sites, which are of interest not only to archaeologists but also to anyone with an eye for the sublime and mysterious.

Within the bay itself, the largest island is the 6km-long Île aux Moines. Nearby Île d'Arz is smaller – just 3km long and 1km wide – but it's the most scenic of the lot and features secluded sands and coastal walks. Tempted to stay? Both islands have a slew of B&Bs and eateries.

The most unusual of neolithic sites, the **Locmariaquer megaliths** (☑ 02 97 57 37 59; www.site-megalithique-locmariaquer.fr; rte de Kerlognan, Locmariaquer; adult/child €6/free; ☻ 10am-7pm Jul & Aug, 10am-6pm May & Jun, 10am-12.30pm & 2-5.15pm Sep-Apr) on the eastern edge of the village of Locmariaquer, 13km south of Auray, sit in an area rich in dolmens. This one features three distinct forms. A giant broken menhir (20m long and the tallest in Western Europe) was made from a type of granite that indicates it was transported (it is not understood how) several kilometres. The Table des Marchand dolmen boasts an incredible geometric carving in its interior, while an enormous tumulus covers multiple graves.

One of the most special neolithic ruins along the Morbihan coast is the **Cairn de Gavrinis** (☑ 02 97 57 19 38; Île de Gavrinis; boat trip & tour adult/child €18/8; ☻ 9.30am-12.30pm & 1.30-6.30pm Apr-Sep), a giant cairn is out on the island of the same name. Dating from 4000 BC and measuring more than 50m in diameter, the beautifully situated tomb is well known for its profusion of intricate engravings. You access the site on a 15-minute boat trip from the harbour at Larmor-Baden (14km southeast of Auray), and it's important to reserve tickets in advance.

On the southern shore of the Rhuys Peninsula, on the southern edge of the Golfe du Morbihan, the **Cairn de Petit Mont** (☑ 06 03 95 90 78; www.morbihan.fr/petit-mont; rue du Petit Mont, Arzon; adult/child €7/3; ☻ 11am-6.30pm Jul & Aug, 2.30-6.30pm Thu-Tue Apr-Jun & Sep) is a broad neolithic tomb built between 4500 and 2500 BC. Scale the mound for sweeping views of the entire Golfe du Morbihan and its hypnotic offshore islands.

Lots of companies offer scenic cruises and ferry services to Île aux Moines and Île d'Arz and beyond. In high season, check with **Navix** (☑ 02 97 46 60 00; www.navix.fr; ☻ Apr-Sep) and **Compagnie du Golfe** (☑ 02 97 01 22 80; www.compagnie-du-golfe.fr; 7 allée Loïc Caradec, Vannes; cruise adult/child from €16.80/11.80; ☻ Apr-Sep). Year-round **Bateaux-Bus du Golfe** (☑ 02 97 44 44 40; www.ile-arz.fr; 7 allée Loic Caradec; adult/child return €10.40/5.70; ☻ 6.30am-8pm) runs 10 to 14 boats per day between Vannes port or Conleau and Île d'Arz. **Izenah Croisières** (☑ 02 97 26 31 45; www.izenah-croisieres.com; adult/child return €5.20/2.90) runs boats from the port at Baden to Île aux Moines year-round.

ℹ Information

Tourist Office (☑ 02 97 50 07 84; www.quiberon.com; 14 rue de Verdun; ☻ 9am-7pm Mon-Sat, 10am-1pm & 2-5pm Sun Aug, shorter hours rest of year; ☎)

ℹ Getting There & Around

BICYCLE

Cycles Loisirs (☑ 02 97 50 31 73; www.cycles loisirs.free.fr; 32 rue Victor Golvan; touring/mountain bikes per day from €9.50/13, kids' bikes per day from €7), 200m north of the tourist office, rents out touring and mountain bikes. **Cyclomar** (☑ 02 97 50 26 00; www.cyclomar. fr; 47 place Hoche; touring/mountain bikes per day from €11/13.5, scooters incl helmet per day from €39.50), around 200m south of the tourist

office, rents out bikes at similar prices, as well as scooters. It also runs an operation from the train station during July and August.

BOAT

Compagnie Océane (p314) runs ferries between Quiberon and Belle Île, and Houat and Hoëdic islands. Park at **Sémaphore car park** (☑ 02 97 30 59 45; 66 av du Général de Gaulle; parking 4hr/24hr/36hr €4.80/13.70/16; ☻ Apr-Sep) 1.5km north of the harbourfront, and take the free shuttle to the port.

BUS

Quiberon is connected by **TIM** (p311) bus line 1 with Carnac (45 minutes), Auray (1¼ hours) and Vannes (1¾ hours). Buses stop at the train station and at place Hoche, near the tourist office and the beach.

In July and August only, a train runs several times a day between Auray and Quiberon (€6.40, 45 minutes). In June, an SNCF bus service links Quiberon and Auray train stations (€3.65, 50 minutes) at least seven times a day.

Belle Île

POP 5270

Belle Île (in full, Belle-Île-en-Mer, 'beautiful island in the sea') does indeed live up to its name: rugged cliffs and rock stacks line the island's west coast while picturesque pastel ports nestle along the eastern side. For sunbathers and outdoorsy types, there is no shortage of lovely beaches and activities.

Accessed by ferries from Quiberon, the island sees its modest population swell tenfold in summer. But as it's Brittany's largest offshore island (at 20km by 9km), there's room to escape the crowds.

Belle Île has two main settlements: the main port of Le Palais is on the east side of the island, while smaller (and even more charming) Sauzon is in the northeast.

◉ Sights & Activities

Citadelle Vauban & Musée
d'Art et d'Histoire   FORT
(☑ 02 97 31 85 54; www.citadellevauban.com; Porte du Donjon, Le Palais; adult/child €8/5; ⊙ 9am-7pm Jul & Aug, shorter hours Sep-Dec & Feb-Jun) The dramatic citadel, strengthened by the architect Vauban in 1682, dominates little Le Palais port. Inside, the informative museum's displays concentrate on the history of the island's defensive system, though there are also sections on the local fishing trade and island life. There's also a very smart hotel here and a restaurant.

★ Aiguilles de Port Coton   NATURAL FEATURE
Just off the western side of the island, these magnificent rock stacks – depicted in a series of celebrated canvases by Claude Monet in 1886 – resemble *aiguilles* (needles) and are a must-see for panorama-lovers and photographers. The name Port Coton comes from the way the sea foams around the rocks, creating foam like cotton wool.

Pointe des Poulains   NATURAL FEATURE
The island's northernmost point juts out dramatically at Pointe des Poulains. Flanked by craggy cliffs and affording sublime views, this windswept headland is Belle Île's loftiest lookout, and was once the home of French actress

(and sculptor) Sarah Bernhardt. Her former fortress home is open to the public as a museum from April to October; there is a lighthouse here too, closer to the Pointe itself.

🏖 Beaches & Caves

Belle Île is blessed with some lovely beaches, including the lengthy **Plage des Grands Sables**, **Plage de Donnant**, and sheltered **Plage d'Herlin**, on the south side, which is better for children.

Belle Île's fretted western coast has spectacular rock formations and caves, including **Grotte de l'Apothicairerie** (off D30).

🛏 Sleeping & Eating

Camping Bordénéo   CAMPGROUND €
(☑ 02 97 31 88 96; www.bordeneo.com; Bordénéo, Le Palais; per adult/car/site €7.35/2.70/11.35; ⊙ Apr-Sep; 🤶🏊) This modern, well-equipped campground is delightfully located in Bordénéo, about 2km northwest of Le Palais off the road to Sauzon. The heated pool is a big plus, and there are mobile homes for hire.

Auberge de Jeunesse   HOSTEL €
(☑ 02 97 31 81 33; www.fuaj.org/belle-ile-en-mer; Haute Boulogne, Le Palais; dm from €17; ⊙ Apr-Sep; 🤶) This modern, well-equipped and functional 96-bed, HI-affiliated hostel, with a self-catering kitchen, is a few hundred metres north of the citadel. Its rooms are all twins with bunk beds and shared toilets. Meals are available; you'll need to reserve ahead, as it's popular.

Hôtel Vauban   HOTEL €
(☑ 02 97 31 45 42; www.hotel-vauban-belleile.com; 1 rue des Remparts, Le Palais; d €70-94; 🤶) This comfy two-star place has 16 multicoloured rooms splashed with driftwood, perched high on Le Palais' ramparts. It has jaw-dropping views of the harbour below, though cheaper rooms face the garden. The owners do hiking packages, which include several nights' stay and all meals, including a picnic lunch. Room prices are way lower in low season. Breakfast is an additional €12.

★ La Villa de Jade   B&B €€
(☑ 02 97 31 53 00; www.villadejade.com; Taillefer, Le Palais; d €160-200, house per week €1300; 🤶) Manuel and Valérie are the widely travelled, bilingual couple behind La Villa de Jade. They have created a one-of-a-kind, gorgeous B&B in a stunningly renovated villa, perfectly placed slap-bang on a clifftop with plunging

views of the sea, 2km north of Le Palais. The four rooms ooze charm with mix-and-match furniture, family photos, colourful touches and wood floors.

Les Embruns CRÊPES €
(☑ 0297316478; www.creperielesembruns-sauzon. fr; quai Jospeh Naudin, Sauzon; mains €5-11; ☺ noon-9.30pm Apr-Oct) ∅ In business for over 30 years, this tempting crêperie is one of the best on the harbourfront. It prepares perfectly buttered Breton crêpes and *galettes,* as well as scrumptious fillings such as *oranges confites de maison* (homemade candied orange), and finger-licking ice creams. Most ingredients are organic and locally sourced. In summer, tables spill onto a pavement terrace.

ⓘ Information

Tourist Office (☑ 02 97 31 81 93; www.belle-ile.com; quai Bonnelle, Le Palais; ☺ 9am-1pm & 2-7pm Mon-Sat, to 1pm Sun Jul & Aug, shorter hours rest of year; ☎) On the left as you leave the ferry in Le Palais.

ⓘ Getting There & Away

Travelling to Belle Île can involve a bit of planning, as taking a car on the ferry is prohibitively expensive for a short trip (a small car starts at €170 return *plus* passenger fares) and needs to be booked well ahead, even outside peak season.

The shortest crossing to Belle Île is from Quiberon. **Compagnie Océane** (☑ 08 20 05 61 56, 02 97 35 02 00; www.compagnie-oceane.fr; adult/child single from €15/6.50) operates car/ passenger ferries (45 minutes) year-round, and fast passenger ferries to Le Palais and Sauzon in July and August. There are up to 10 crossings a day in July and August. Fares and frequencies are reduced off-season.

It is also possible to make the trip from Vannes (and Locmariaquer and Port-Navalo) on **Navix** (p312), which operates ferries to Le Palais three to five times per week between April and September (adult/child return €30/25 from Vannes, 2½ hours).

Vannes

POP 53,558

Overlooking the Golfe du Morbihan, Vannes is one of the unmissable towns of Brittany. Spectacular fortifications encircle Vannes' meandering alleys and cobbled squares, and lead down to a sparkling marina lined with cafes and townhouses. The city still preserves much of its medieval atmosphere, though it's

not a museum piece but a vibrant place with a lively bar and restaurant scene year-round. Vannes is also an excellent base for exploring the glittering island-studded Golfe du Morbihan and the mesmerising neolithic sites in the vicinity.

⊙ Sights

★ **Ramparts** HISTORIC SITE
Vannes' old town is surrounded by imposing ramparts and gates, which are in turn lined by a moat and, on the eastern edge, simply spectacular flower-filled gardens (p314). Tucked away behind rue des Vierges, stairs lead to the accessible section of the ramparts from which you can see the black-roofed **Vieux Lavoirs** (Old Laundry Houses) along the water. Or walk rue Francis Decker, on the wall's eastern exterior, to take it all in.

Cathédrale St-Pierre CATHEDRAL
(place St-Pierre) On the eastern side of place St-Pierre looms the 13th-century Gothic Cathédrale St-Pierre, being ambitiously restored in parts at the time of writing. Inside, look for paintings of St Vincent Ferrier, a preacher and saint who died in Vannes is 1419.

La Cohue – Musée des Beaux-Arts GALLERY
(☑ 02 97 01 63 00; place St-Pierre; adult/child €6.30/4.30, free Sun; ☺ 1.30-6pm daily Jun-Sep, Tue-Sun Oct-May) Opposite the cathedral, the building called La Cohue has variously been a produce market, a law court and the seat of the Breton parliament. Today it's a well-curated museum of fine arts, displaying 19th-century paintings, sculptures and engravings, and rotating exhibitions of cutting-edge contemporary art.

Musée d'Histoire et d'Archéologie MUSEUM
(☑ 02 97 01 63 00; 2 rue Noë; adult/child €6.30/4.30, free Sun; ☺ 1.30-6pm Jun-Sep) Housed inside the 16th-century Château Gaillard, this small but intriguing museum contains precious neolithic artefacts unearthed throughout the region, opening a window to an understanding of the early history of this area of France.

The ticket price includes La Cohue – Musée des Beaux-Arts.

Jardins des Remparts GARDENS
(rue Francis Decker; ☺ 24hr) These beautifully manicured gardens lie just outside the walls of the town and are a gorgeous place to relax and take in some astonishing views.

VANNES DAYTRIPPER: ROCHEFORT-EN-TERRE

For an architectural trip into the Middle Ages, make a beeline for delightful Rochefort-en-Terre. It's a photogenic town of narrow, cobbled streets and lovely squares lined with grand, granite mansions, slate-roofed houses and flower-filled window boxes – not to mention a smattering of art galleries and the mandatory crêperies that fill these parts.

Its picture-book perch on a rocky outcrop above the River Gueuzon is equally enchanting, though it can be packed in summer. As befits any medieval Breton town, it also boasts a lovely **castle**, which is sadly not open to the public, but is home to the eccentric sci-fi/fantasy **Naia Museum** (☑ 02 97 40 12 35; www.naiamuseum.com; rue des Scourtets; adult/child €6/4; ☺ 10.30am-6.30pm Tue-Sun Apr-Jun & Sept, to 7pm July-Aug, 2-6pm Oct, 10.30am-6.30pm Nov, 2-6pm Feb-early Mar, shut Jan & 3 weeks Mar) in one of its out-buildings. The town's superb **church** (rue Notre-Dame de la Tronchaye) was originally built in the 10th century.

Rochefort-en-Terre is around 40km east of Vannes along the N166, the D775, then the D777. TIM (p311) bus 9 serves Vannes (€2, 1¼ hours, four daily). The bus stops on rue St-Roch in Rochefort-en-Terre.

🛏 Sleeping

Le Bretagne HOTEL €
(☑ 02 97 47 20 21; www.hotel-lebretagne-vannes.com; 36 rue du Mené; s/d from €55/59; 🛜) This small and thin hotel is easy to miss, but the 12 rooms inside are a steal. They may be small, but they're neat and bright, with good colours, excellent bedding and clean bathrooms. Top picks are rooms at the back, with stupendous views of the ramparts. Service is friendly and breakfast costs between €7 and €9.

La Villa Garenne B&B €€
(☑ 06 76 01 80 83; www.chambresdhotes-vannes.fr; 3 rue Monseigneur Tréhiou; d €80-125, apt €140-160; 🛜) A stone's throw from the imposing ramparts, this very attractive option has five charmingly and uniquely decorated rooms in a handsome stone building. They're light, airy and furnished with great taste, and breakfasts come in for warm praise.

⭐**Hôtel Villa Kerasy** BOUTIQUE HOTEL €€€
(☑ 02 97 68 36 83; www.villakerasy.com; 20 av Favrel-et-Lincy; s & d €99-220, ste from €298; ☺ closed mid-Nov–mid-Dec; 🛜) From the outside this may seem little more than a large Breton house, but beyond the entrance is an exotic world of spices and far-away tropical sea ports. Rooms are individually decorated in Indian and Far Eastern styles, and the garden, crowded with Buddha statues and ponds filled with lazy koi carp, is a little slice of Sri Lanka or Japan.

🍴 Eating

There's no shortage of appealing restaurants in Vannes. Rue des Halles and its offshoots are lined with tempting eateries; classic and contemporary brasseries are around the port. Book ahead in high season and on weekends.

Market days are Wednesday and Saturday mornings.

Dan Ewen CRÊPES €
(☑ 02 97 42 44 34; 3 place Général de Gaulle; mains €3-10, menus €10-18; ☺ 11.30am-2pm & 6.30-9pm Mon-Sat) A near-life-size statue of a smiling Breton lady bearing a tray greets you at the entrance of this popular stone and dark-wood crêperie. Generous fillings include frangipani, or flambéed options topped with *crème Chantilly*. You can wash it all down with a *boule* (goblet) of local cider. To tempt in the young ones, a €6.90 kids' menu is at hand.

Brasserie des Halles BRASSERIE €
(☑ 02 97 54 08 34; www.brasseriedeshallesvannes.com; 9 rue des Halles; mains €11-21.50, menus €16-21; ☺ noon-2.30pm & 7-11pm) Atmospherically set in a 16th-century building in the heart of the old town, this buzzing brasserie has a varied menu of fish and meat dishes, as well as pastas, salads, oysters and other shellfish. It's an equally good spot for a drink (there's a good choice of beers) while browsing the art, and the €9 kids' menu makes it popular with families.

⭐**Restaurant de Roscanvec** GASTRONOMY €€€
(☑ 02 97 47 15 96; www.roscanvec.com; 17 rue des Halles; lunch menu €25-30, dinner menu €55-70; ☺ 12.15-2pm Tue-Sun, 7.45-9.15pm Tue-Sat Jul & Aug, closed Tue Sep-Jun) Hidden among the timber-frame houses of the old city, this stellar restaurant is overseen by one of Brittany's most talented names, Thierry Seychelles, whose cooking has been championed by most of the major culinary critics.

Rightly so: his trademark six-course 'Hedonist Menu' (€70) combines seasonal French classics with global flavours, and the lunch *menu* is a gourmet steal. Book ahead.

ⓘ Information

Tourist Office (☑ 08 25 13 56 10, 02 97 47 24 34; www.tourisme-vannes.com; quai Eric Tabarly; ⊙ 9.30am-7pm Mon-Sat, 10am-6pm Sun Jul & Aug, 9.30am-12.30pm & 1.30-6pm Mon-Sat Sep-Jun; ☎) In a modern building on the marina.

ⓘ Getting There & Away

BUS

The small bus station is opposite the train station. **TIM** (p311) has services throughout the region, including line 1 to Carnac (€2, 80 minutes) and on to Quiberon (€2, 1¾ hours, eight daily), and line 9 to Rochefort-en-Terre (€2, 1¼ hours).

TRAIN

Vannes is on the train line running east to Quimper and west to Rennes, Nantes or Paris. The TGV line between Le Mans and Rennes opened in July 2017, cutting approximately 40 minutes off train travel times to Paris.

Nantes €23.40, 1½ hours, 5 direct daily

Quimper from €18, 1½ hours, 15 daily

Paris Montparnasse €48-85.60, 2½ hours, 10 direct daily

Rennes €16-19.50, 1-1½, 15 daily

EASTERN & CENTRAL BRITTANY

The one-time frontier between Brittany and France, fertile and bucolic eastern Brittany fans out around the region's lively and engaging capital, Rennes. The *département* of Ille-et-Vilaine indeed gets its name from the two rivers (L'Ille and La Vilaine) that flow together in the city of Rennes itself. Central Brittany conceals within its bosom the enchanting and mysterious Forêt de Paimpont, sprinkled with villages and wreathed in ancient Breton myth and legend.

Josselin

POP 2626

The storybook village of Josselin lies on the banks of the River Oust, 43km northeast of Vannes, in the shadow of an enormous, cone-turreted 14th-century castle that was the long-time seat of the counts of Rohan.

Today, visitors in their thousands continue to fall under its spell. The little town's heart is place Notre-Dame, a beautiful square of 16th-century half-timbered houses.

◉ Sights

★**Château de Josselin**   CASTLE
(☑ 02 97 22 36 45; www.chateaujosselin.com/en; place de la Congrégation; adult/child €9/5.50; ⊙ 11am-6pm daily mid-Jul–Aug, 2-6pm Apr–mid-Jul & Sep, 2-5.30pm Sat & Sun only Oct) Guarded by its three round towers and overlooking the canal, the extraordinary town château is an formidable sight that remains the home of the Rohan family today. Beyond the entrance gate, the castle fans out into tree-filled grounds and a central courtyard, which affords a great view of the castle's Flamboyant Gothic facade. The château is filled with treasures, including a medieval-style dining room, a 3000-tome library and a grand *salon* filled with Sèvres porcelain, Gobelins carpets and an astronomical clock.

Basilique Notre-Dame du Roncier   CHURCH
(place Notre-Dame; ⊙ 9am-6pm) Ringed by some highly impressive gargoyles, parts of the Basilique Notre-Dame du Roncier date from the 12th century, including its Romanesque pillars. The 60m tower, however, was built in 1949; you can climb it for free when the door is open off the place de la Mairie. Superb 15th- and 16th-century stained glass illuminates the south aisle. If you're lucky you'll be there while the organist is playing the 17th-century organ.

⏢ Sleeping & Eating

Domaine de Kerelly Camping   CAMPGROUND €
(☑ 02 97 22 22 20; www.camping-josselin.com; Le Bas de la Lande, Josselin-Guégon; site for 1/2 people €11/14; ⊙ Apr-Sep; ☎⊠) This peaceful spot is 2km west of Josselin, on the south bank of the River Oust, and offers plenty of shady spots to pitch your tent. You can also rent mobile homes from as little as €30. There's a pool, mini-golf and a bar.

Le Clos des Devins   B&B €
(☑ 02 97 75 67 48, 06 88 84 77 05; www.leclosdes devins.fr; 11 rue des Devins; d €60-70; ☎) A beautiful 18th-century private mansion complete with fabulous walled garden underpins this gem of a *chambre d'hôte*, 250m north of the church. Conscientious owner, Madame Astruc, has artfully decorated the three charming rooms with both modern touches and lovely antiques. Each room has its own

personality; our favourite is the Abricotine, which has a drop-dead-gorgeous roof terrace overlooking the garden.

★ Le 14 Saint-Michel B&B €€
(☎06 89 37 26 07, 02 97 22 24 24; www.le14stmichel.com; 14 rue St-Michel; s €72-95, d €85-115, f €125-170; 📶) This outstanding *chambre d'hôte* fills a grand townhouse in the historic centre. Spacious, stylish rooms (including a two-room family suite) ooze romance, and there's a superb garden at the back. Breakfast is sumptuous, and the welcoming hostess, Viviane, also does *tables d'hôte* (€32) with local, seasonal products. It's a haven of charm and serenity, and some rooms have views of the countryside.

La Table d'O MODERN FRENCH €€
(☎02 97 70 61 39; https://latabledo.eatbu.com; 9 rue Glatinier; lunch menu from €15.50, dinner menu €24-34, mains €15.50-22; ⏲noon-1.15pm & 7.30-8.45pm Tue & Thu-Fri, noon-1.15pm & 7.30-9pm Sat, noon-1.15pm Wed) This pleasant family-run place offers an interesting and varied menu of local cooking with a sprinkle of fusion on top, making it a local favourite. The sweeping views of the town and valley from the terrace are fantastic for a summer lunch. It's 250m west of the château.

Information

Tourist Office (☎02 97 22 36 43; www.josselin-tourisme.com; 21 rue Olivier de Clisson; ⏲10am-6pm Jul & Aug, 10am-noon Tue-Sat, 1.30-5.30pm Mon-Sat Apr-Jun & Sep, shorter hours Oct-Mar; 📶) Offers a useful map of local sights and list of *chambres d'hôte*.

Getting There & Away

Keolis Armor (☎02 99 26 16 00; www.keolis-armor.fr) runs several daily buses to Rennes (€15.30; 1½ hours), and SNCF has buses to Rennes (€15.30; 90 minutes) as well. The nearest train station is in Pontivy, also served by Keolis buses (€7.70, 30 minutes). Buses stop on Rue St-Jacques in Josselin.

Forêt de Paimpont

Legendary for being the site of Brocéliande – the place where King Arthur received his magic sword, Excalibur, from the Lady of the Lake – the bewitching Paimpont Forest is about 40km southwest of Rennes. This is also the magical forest where the Lady entombed the mythical wizard Merlin (his tomb can be found here to this day). Although some dispute the link between Paimpont and the mythical Brocéliande, Paimpont is an enchanting setting all the same and, with its local stories and themes focusing on those medieval tales, the place hums with mystery.

The best base for exploring the forest is the lakeside village of Paimpont and having a car is the best way to go.

Sights & Activities

Some 95% of the forest is private land, but the tourist office (p318), beside the 13th-century **Abbaye de Paimpont** (3 esplanade de Brocéliande; ⏲9am-6pm, not accessible to visitors during church services), has a free map outlining a 62km-long driving circuit with numerous short walks along the way that are accessible to the public. It also sells more-detailed walking and cycling guides, and has guided tours (adult/child from €7.50/4) in summer. Some areas are closed for hunting in winter, and the tourist office has a map showing what's open.

Tombeau de Merlin TOMB
(Tomb of Merlin; La Marette, Paimpont; ⏲24hr) FREE The Tomb of Merlin is worth hunting out, secluded and lying quietly amid a grove of trees. According to legend, the Lady of the Lake circled Merlin nine times, casting a spell that captivated and entrapped the mythical wizard at this spot. Today, all that remains of the tomb are three large, ancient and mossy rocks, but the setting is most peaceful. Offerings to the sorcerer are often left here, displayed on the ground or arrayed on the stones themselves.

Sleeping & Eating

Camping Municipal de Paimpont CAMPGROUND €
(☎02 99 07 89 16; www.camping-paimpont-broceliande.com; rue du Chevalier Lancelot du Lac, Paimpont; site €3.20-3.80, adult €3.60-4.30, car €1.90-2.30; ⏲Apr-Sep) Campers can set up their tents at this rural campground, 800m north of Paimpont and the lake, where 90 pitches are available. There are also chalets available from €150 for two nights at the weekend, from €170 for three nights midweek or from €280 for seven nights. Prices vary according to the season.

La Corne de Cerf B&B €
(☎02 99 07 84 19; http://corneducerf.bcld.net; Le Cannée; s/d/tr €55/65/85; ⏲Apr-Nov; 📶) For garden lovers – flowers all around – and history vultures, friendly Annick and Robert's

three-room house is tranquil, elegantly homey and secluded. Each room has its own clear personality, comfortable beds, soft colours and privacy; the room at the top has a big window with long views over the garden. It's in Le Cannée, about 3km south of Paimpont.

★ Le Relais de Brocéliande   HOTEL €€

(☑ 02 99 07 84 94; www.le-relais-de-broceliande.fr; 5 rue des Forges, Paimpont; d €84-128; 🛜) In an historic but thoroughly modernised building right at the heart of Paimpont, this hotel has comfy guest rooms – clean and bright with good bedding and clean bathrooms, a top-notch spa and efficient staff. Perks also include a renowned restaurant (lunch *menus* €15 to €18, dinner *menus* €28 to €34) serving fresh, seasonal cuisine, so you won't have to stray far.

Crêperie du Porche   CRÊPES €

(☑ 02 99 07 81 88; www.creperie-du-porche.fr; 26 rue du Général de Gaulle; mains from €6.90) This handy crêperie is a good choice, right in the heart of Paimpont. To get you in the Arthurian mood, the tasty *galettes* are named topically: La Lancelot, La Kamelott, La Roi Arthur; crêpes follow a similar script (eg La Guenièvre). In summer, you can sit out the front or take a table on the grass in the pleasant garden around the back.

Les Forges de Paimpont   FRENCH €€

(☑ 02 99 06 81 07; www.restaurant.forges-de-paimpont.com; Les Forges, Plélan-le-Grand; lunch menu €16-35, dinner €23-35, mains €13-18.50; ⊙ noon-2pm Wed-Sun, 7-9pm Wed-Sat) This rustic country inn has a cosy interior and a menu rooted in the traditions of the *terroir*. The excellent-value €23 set menu may include quail, deer, duck, pigeon or grilled ribsteak. Find the restaurant in the hamlet of Les Forges, near Plélan-le-Grand, 4km southeast of Paimpont.

ℹ Information

Tourist Office (☑ 02 99 07 84 23; www.tourisme-broceliande.com; place du Roi Judicaël, Paimpont; ⊙ 9.30am-7pm Jul-Aug, 9.30am-noon & 2-6pm Apr, May, Jun & Sep-Oct, 9.30am-12.30pm & 2-5pm Wed-Sun Nov-Mar; 🛜) Beside the Abbaye de Paimpont.

ℹ Getting There & Away

Illenoo (p320) bus line 1a connects the centre of Paimpont and the bus station by the train station in Rennes (€5, one hour, nine daily Monday to Saturday).

It's by far the best approach to explore the forest with your own wheels, giving total freedom of movement in what is quite a large area.

Rennes

POP 217,309

A crossroads since Roman times, Brittany's vibrant capital sits at the junction of highways linking northwestern France's major cities. It's a beautifully set-out city, with an elaborate and stately centre and a superb medieval quarter that's a joy to get lost in. At night, this student city has no end of lively places to pop in for a pint, while the restaurant selection is superb.

⊙ Sights

Cathédrale St-Pierre   CATHEDRAL

(rue de la Monnaie; ⊙ 9.30am-noon & 3-6pm; Ⓜ République, Ste-Anne) Crowning Rennes' old town is the 17th-century cathedral, which has an impressive, if dark, neoclassical interior adorned with a fabulous ceiling.

Palais du Parlement de Bretagne   HISTORIC BUILDING

(☑ reservations 02 99 67 11 66; place du Parlement de Bretagne; adult/child €7.20/free; Ⓜ République) This 17th-century former seat of the rebellious Breton parliament has, in more recent times, been home to the Palais de Justice. In 1994 this building was destroyed by a fire started by demonstrating fishermen. It was reopened in 2004 after a major restoration and now houses the Court of Appeal. Daily guided tours (request in advance for a tour in English) take you through the ostentatiously gilded rooms. Tour bookings must be made through the tourist office (p320).

★ Musée des Beaux-Arts   MUSEUM

(☑ 02 23 62 17 45; www.mbar.org; 20 quai Émile Zola; adult/child €6/free; ⊙ 10am-5pm Tue-Fri, to 6pm Sat & Sun; Ⓜ République) Extensive collections span the 15th century to the present at the Museum of Fine Arts, plus there is a section devoted to antiquities. The Pont-Aven school is featured, as is a 'curiosity gallery' of antiques and illustrations amassed in the 18th century. It also hosts ever-changing temporary exhibitions.

Champs Libres   CULTURAL CENTRE

(☑ 02 23 40 66 00; www.leschampslibres.fr; 10 cours des Alliés; all-sight pass adult/child €11/7; ⊙ noon-7pm Tue-Fri, 2-7pm Sat & Sun; Ⓜ Charles

Rennes

N 0 ———— 200 m
0 ———— 0.1 miles

Rennes

◎ Top Sights
1 Musée des Beaux-Arts D3

◎ Sights
2 Cathédrale St-Pierre A2
3 Palais du Parlement de
Bretagne C2

⌂ Sleeping
4 Hôtel de Nemours B4

✖ Eating
5 Cafe Albertine B4
6 Le Café du Port A3

◯ Drinking & Nightlife
7 Le Bar'Hic A2
8 Oan's Pub A3

de Gaulle) Rennes' futuristic cultural centre is home to the **Musée de Bretagne** (☏ 02 23 40 66 00; www.musee-bretagne.fr; adult/child €6/4; ◷ noon-7pm Tue-Fri, 2-7pm Sat & Sun; M Charles de Gaulle), with displays on Breton history and culture. Under the same roof is **Espace des Sciences** (☏ 02 23 40 66 40; www.espace-sciences.org; 10 cours des Alliés; adult €5.50-9.50, child €3.50-5; ◷ noon-7pm Tue-Fri, 2-7pm Sat & Sun; ☍; M Charles de Gaulle), an interactive science museum, along with a planetarium, a temporary exhibition space and a library.

🛏 Sleeping

Auberge de Jeunesse   HOSTEL €
(☏ 02 99 33 22 33; www.hifrance.org; 10-12 canal St-Martin; dm incl breakfast €22.90; ◷ 7am-1am, closed late-Dec-mid-Jan; ☍; ☐ 12, M Ste-Anne) Rennes' well-equipped youth hostel has a self-catering kitchen and a pleasant canalside setting 2km north of the centre. Digs are in one- to five-bed rooms; breakfast is continental. Take the bus from place de la Mairie.

BRITTANY RENNES

★ Hôtel de Nemours
HOTEL €€

(☎ 02 99 78 26 26; www.hotelnemours.com; 5 rue de Nemours; s/d/tw from €63/73/93; ❄ 🛜; Ⓜ République) This excellent three-star abode, ideally located near place de la République, ranks among the best options in town. Stylish and tidy rooms, a cosy-chic lobby and friendly staff round out a great bet.

✕ Eating

Rennes has a wide choice of excellent restaurants, but it's worth booking ahead at the smarter choices. Rues St-Malo and St-Georges are the city's two main 'eat streets'; the latter in particular specialises in crêperies.

Rennes' daily market **Halles Centrales** (www.les-halles-liberte.fr) is at place Honoré Commeurec, and the large **Saturday morning market** fills the place des Lices. The tourist office has a list of other weekly markets.

Cafe Albertine
CAFE €

(☎ 02 99 51 03 04; 10 rue Jean Denis Lanjuinais; snacks from €4; ⏱ 9.30am-6.30pm Mon-Sat; 🛜 🚼) A lovely spot for breakfast, Cafe Albertine is bright as a new pin and a relaxing environment for a pick-me-up coffee or a snack. There are friendly smiles from the waiting staff, while kids' books lie scattered on shelves in the corner and there are high chairs if you've a tot in tow.

Le Café du Port
BISTRO €

(☎ 02 99 30 01 43; 3 rue le Bouteiller; mains €9-14, menu €20; ⏱ noon-2pm & 7.30-10pm Mon-Sat; Ⓜ République) Market-fresh produce and great value are the name of the game at this laid-back, modern bistro that also doubles as a popular spot for an early-evening drink. Garrulous locals fill the outdoor seating area, which is tented in winter.

★ L'Atelier des Gourmets
FRENCH €€

(☎ 02 99 67 53 84; www.latelierdesgourmets-rennes.fr; 12 rue Nantaise; mains €16-17, lunch/dinner menu €13/31; ⏱ 12.30-1.30pm & 7.30-9.30pm Tue-Thu, to 10pm Fri & Sat; Ⓜ République) This very smart bistro garners serious accolades in a city where talent is in no short supply and competition is fierce. The chef has created a choice institution in the heart of Rennes, adeptly blending the best of high-end bistro fare with solid regional cuisine in a succinct menu.

🍷 Drinking & Nightlife

Rue St-Michel – nicknamed 'rue de la Soif' (Thirsty St) for its bars, pubs and cafes – is the best-known drinking strip, but it can get rowdy late at night.

Le Bar'Hic
BAR

(24 place des Lices; ⏱ 5pm-3am Tue-Sat, 9pm-3am Sun & Mon; Ⓜ Ste-Anne) This inviting bar is a good place for getting a bit of local vibe. It fills up at night, when students and young hipsters stream in for the music events – usually live bands. Earlier in the evening it's much quieter. In warm weather, bag a seat on the terrace and watch the world go by.

Oan's Pub
PUB

(☎ 02 99 31 07 51; 1 rue Georges Dottin; ⏱ 5pm-1am Mon-Fri, noon-1am Sat; Ⓜ République) Locals habitually turn up with instruments for impromptu Celtic jam sessions at this cosy cave-like, stone-walled pub with Brittany-brewed Coreff beer on tap. It can get pretty full, but there's a terrace out the front to help mop up the crowds in summer and add breathing space.

ℹ Information

Tourist Office (☎ 02 99 67 11 11; www.tourisme-rennes.com; 11 rue St-Yves; ⏱ 9am-6pm Mon-Sat, 11am-1pm & 2-6pm Sun; 🛜; Ⓜ République) Located in a superb old church, with huge amounts of information on the city and its architecture. It offers an audioguide to the city, smartphone apps and a walking map (€0.20). There's also a video presentation of the fire at the Parliament building in 1994 and its aftermath and restoration.

ℹ Getting There & Around

AIR

Rennes' **airport** (RNS; ☎ 02 99 29 60 00; www.rennes.aeroport.fr; av Joseph le Brix) is 8km southwest of the city centre. It offers direct flights to many domestic and European destinations. Bus 57 connects place de la République and the airport, every 20 minutes daily. A taxi costs about €20.

BUS

The **bus station** (place de la République) is adjacent to the train station. **Illenoo** (☎ 0810 35 10 35; www.illenoo-services.fr) offers many daily services in eastern Brittany, including both Dinan and Dinard (€6.20, 1½ hours, 14 daily Monday to Friday, six Saturday, five Sunday) and Paimpont (€5, one hour, nine daily Monday to Friday, five Saturday).

METRO

Rennes has a single-line metro system, run by **STAR** (☑ 09 70 82 18 00; www.star.fr; 12 rue du Pré Botté; single journey €1.50, 24hr pass €4). The metro A line runs northwest to southeast, with a second line (B line) under construction to begin service in 2019, running southwest to northeast. Tickets are interchangeable with the bus.

Main stations include République (place de la République) in the centre, Ste-Anne (old town) and Gares (the train and regional bus stations).

TRAIN

Rennes is a major transport hub for northeast France. The new TGV track to Le Mans has cut travel times to the east by about 40 minutes.

As part of this project, the train station in Rennes is being completely rebuilt. Until it is complete (possibly in 2019), the area around the station is chaotic and ever-changing, so plan for extra time. It's easiest to reach by metro, since the streets are often blocked by construction.

Brest €28-40, 2 hours, 10 daily

Dinan €15.70, 1¼ hours, 9 daily

Nantes €18, 1¼ hours, 9 daily

Paris Montparnasse €70-80, 1½ hours, 24 daily

Quimper €32-40, 2 hours, 11 direct daily

St-Malo €15, ¾-1 hours, roughly hourly

Vannes €18-25, 1-1½ hours, 14 daily

Vitré

POP 18,080

With its narrow cobbled streets, half-timbered houses and colossal castle topped by witch's-hat turrets, Vitré rivals Dinan as one of Brittany's best-preserved medieval towns. It has far fewer tourists and a more laissez-faire village air than most spots, especially during the slow season when it is virtually empty. The modern outskirts are sprawling, but the historic centre is precious and wandering at will is the way to go.

⊙ Sights

Château de Vitré   CASTLE
(☑ 02 99 75 04 54; place du Château; adult/child €6/free; ⊙ 10am-6pm Jul & Aug, 10am-12.30pm & 2-6pm Apr-Jun & Sep, shorter hours Oct-Mar) Dominating the town, Vitré's medieval castle rises on a rocky outcrop overlooking the River Vilaine, and is one of the most impressive in Brittany – a real fairy tale of spires and drawbridges. Beyond the twin-turreted gateway, you'll discover a triangular inner courtyard and a warren of semi-furnished rooms.

Don't miss the top of the tower of San Lorenzo where paintings by Raoul David and others reimagine Vitré and you can wander around a circular walkway.

🛏 Sleeping & Eating

Le Minotel   HOTEL €
(☑ 02 99 75 11 11; www.leminotel.fr; 47 rue de la Poterie; s/t/f €56/81/91, d €66-76,; 🕿) Not far from the traditional style train station and the castle, this 15-room hotel is superb value given its coveted location. Freshly maintained rooms are decked out in beige and chocolate hues and have modern bathrooms. Opt for the more-spacious, dearer rooms; the cheaper ones are pocket-sized. A cheerful breakfast room rounds things off. Breakfast is €9; parking is €5.

Hôtel du Château   HOTEL €
(☑ 02 99 74 58 59; 5 rue Rallon; s €51-64, d €57-70, tr/q €68/71; 🕿) Wake up to the aroma of freshly baked bread and, on upper floors (choose room 12, 14 or 15), fantastic vistas of the castle at this family-run hotel at the base of the ramparts. The rooms are simple and the bathrooms minuscule, but the friendly owners are a great source of local information; there's a nice courtyard for breakfast (€9).

Auberge du Château   CRÊPES €
(☑ 02 99 75 01 83; 34 rue d'En Bas; mains €6-13; ⊙ noon-2pm Tue-Sun, 7-9pm Tue-Sat) For crêpes, *galettes*, salads and *tartines* washed down with beer or cider, look no further than this restaurant, which occupies an atmospheric and charming timber-framed house not far below the castle. Outdoor seating flung outside in summer adds to the welcoming refrain.

ⓘ Information

Tourist Office (☑ 02 99 75 04 46; www.bretagne-vitre.com; place Général de Gaulle; ⊙ 9.30am-12.30pm & 2-6.30pm Mon-Sat, 10am-12.30pm & 3-6pm Sun Jul & Aug, shorter hours rest of year; 🕿) Right next door to the handsome train station; helpful, central and supplied with useful info.

ⓘ Getting There & Away

Vitré is 37km due east of Rennes along the N157 and the D857. Frequent trains travel between Vitré and Rennes (from €8, 20 to 35 minutes, 23 per day). Three direct trains a day serve Paris Montparnasse (€40 to €85, two hours).

BRITTANY VITRÉ

Champagne

POP 1.3 MILLION

Best Places to Eat

➜ Anna-S – La Table Amoureuse (p329)

➜ L'Assiette Champenoise (p329)

➜ La Grillade Gourmande (p338)

➜ Claire et Hugo (p342)

➜ Le Valentino (p342)

Best Places to Stay

➜ Les Telliers (p328)

➜ Château Les Crayères (p328)

➜ Maison M (p341)

➜ La Villa Eugène (p337)

➜ Hostellerie La Montagne (p343)

Why Go?

Champagne arouses the senses: the eyes feast on vines parading up hillsides and vertical processions of tiny, sparkling bubbles; the nose breathes in damp soil and the heavenly bouquet of fermentation; the ears rejoice at the clink of glasses and the barely audible fizz; and the palate tingles with every sip. The imagination and the intellect are engaged as Champagne cellar visits reveal the magical processes – governed by the strictest of rules – that transform the world's most pampered pinot noir, pinot meunier and chardonnay grapes into this Unesco World Heritage–listed region's most fabled wines.

Despite the prestige of their vines, the people of Champagne offer a warm, surprisingly easygoing welcome, both in the stylish cities and along the Champagne Routes, which wend their way through villages to family-run cellars and vineyards.

When to Go
Reims

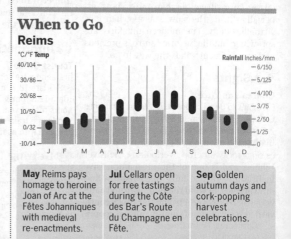

May Reims pays homage to heroine Joan of Arc at the Fêtes Johanniques with medieval re-enactments.

Jul Cellars open for free tastings during the Côte des Bar's Route du Champagne en Fête.

Sep Golden autumn days and cork-popping harvest celebrations.

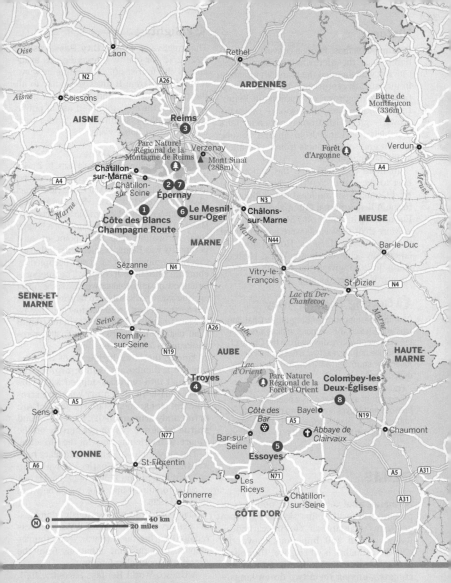

Champagne Highlights

1 **Côte des Blancs Champagne Route** (p335) Rambling through hillside vineyards, comely villages and family-run wineries.

2 **Épernay** (p336) Toasting the end of a cellar tour with a glass of fizz.

3 **Cathédrale Notre Dame** (p324) Climbing the tower of Reims' Gothic wonder for 360-degree views across France's flattest region.

4 **16th-Century Troyes** (p340) Slipping back to the Middle Ages wandering half-timbered backstreets.

5 **Atelier Renoir** (p344) Treading in Renoir's impressionistic footsteps in Essoyes.

6 **Musée de la Vigne et du Vin** (p335) Marvelling at Champagne-making techniques in Le Mesnil-sur-Oger.

7 **Avenue de Champagne** (p336) Revelling in the mansions and Champagne houses of Épernay.

8 **Mémorial Charles de Gaulle** (p343) Discovering mid-20th-century France in Colombey-les-Deux-Églises.

History

Champagne's most famous convert to Christianity was the Merovingian warrior-king Clovis I, who founded the Frankish kingdom in the late 5th century and began the tradition of holding royal coronations in Reims. In the Middle Ages, the region – especially Troyes – grew rich from commercial fairs at which merchants from around Europe bought and sold products from as far afield as the Mediterranean.

In more recent history, the region was host to the end of WWII in Europe, when Nazi Germany surrendered unconditionally to the Allied Supreme Commander, General Eisenhower, in Reims on 7 May 1945.

More than a few corks were popped when the Champagne Hillsides, Houses and Cellars finally achieved Unesco World Heritage status in 2015, giving the region's precious vineyards protected status.

❶ Getting There & Away

Champagne, just north of Burgundy's Châtillonnais and Chablis wine regions, makes a refreshing stopover if you're driving from the Channel ports, Lille or Paris eastward to Lorraine or Alsace, or southeastward towards Dijon, Lyon or Provence.

France's rail lines radiate out from Paris like the spokes of a wheel and, as it happens, Reims, Épernay and Troyes are each on a different spoke (more or less). Thanks to the TGV Est Européen line, Reims can be visited on a day trip from Paris.

REIMS

POP 186,971

No matter what you have read, nothing can prepare you for that first skyward glimpse of Reims' gargantuan Gothic cathedral. Rising golden and imperious above the city, the cathedral is where, over the course of a millennium (816 to 1825), some 34 sovereigns – among them two dozen kings – began their reigns.

Meticulously restored after WWI and again following WWII, Reims is endowed with handsome pedestrian boulevards, Roman remains, art-deco cafes and a flourishing fine-dining scene that counts among it four Michelin-starred restaurants. Along with Épernay, it is the most important centre of Champagne production, and a fine base for exploring the Montagne de Reims Champagne Route (p331).

◉ Sights

The great-value **Reims City Pass**, costing €22/32/42 for one/two/three days, is available at the tourist office or online at www.reimscitypass.com. It gives you entry to all the major museums and attractions, guided tours of the city, unlimited use of public transport, plus discounts on activities such as Champagne house visits.

★ **Cathédrale Notre Dame**   CATHEDRAL
(☑ 03 26 47 81 79; www.cathedrale-reims.fr; 2 place du Cardinal Luçon; tower adult/child €8/free, incl Palais du Tau €11/free; ⊙ 7.30am-7.30pm, tower tours 10am, 11am & 2-5pm Tue-Sat, 2-5pm Sun May-Aug, 10am, 11am & 2-4pm Sat, 2-4pm Sun Sep, Oct & mid-Mar–Apr) Imagine the extravagance of a French royal coronation. The focal point of such pomposity was Reims' resplendent Gothic cathedral, begun in 1211 on a site occupied by churches since the 5th century. The interior is a rainbow of stained-glass windows; the finest are the western façade's great rose window, the north transept's rose window and the vivid Marc Chagall creations (1974) in the central axial chapel. The tourist office (p330) rents audioguides for self-paced tours.

Among the other highlights of the interior are a flamboyant **Gothic organ case** (15th and 18th centuries) topped with a figure of Christ, a 15th-century wooden **astronomical clock**, and a statue of **Joan of Arc in full body armour** (1901); there's a second **statue** (place du Parvis) of her outside on the square, to the right as you exit the cathedral.

The most famous event to take place here was the coronation of Charles VII, with Joan of Arc at his side, on 17 July 1429. This is one of 25 coronations that took place between 1223 and 1825.

The cathedral was seriously damaged by artillery and fire during WWI, and was repaired during the interwar years, thanks, in part, to significant donations from the American Rockefeller family.

A Unesco World Heritage Site since 1991, the cathedral celebrated its 800th anniversary in 2011. To get the most impressive first view, approach the cathedral from the west, along rue Libergier. Here your gaze will be drawn to the heavily restored architectural features of the façade, lavishly encrusted with sculptures. Among them is the 13th-century *L'Ange au Sourire* (Smiling Angel), presiding beneficently above the central portal.

Feeling as strong as Goliath? (Look for his worn figure up on the west façade, held in place with metal straps.) Then consider climbing

250 steps up the cathedral tower on a one-hour tour. Book at the Palais du Tau.

★ **Palais du Tau** MUSEUM
(www.palais-du-tau.fr; 2 place du Cardinal Luçon; adult/child €8/free, incl cathedral tower €11/free; ⊙9.30am-6.30pm Tue-Sun May–mid-Sep, 9.30am-12.30pm & 2-5.30pm Tue-Sun mid-Sep–Apr) A Unesco World Heritage Site, this lavish former archbishop's residence, redesigned in neoclassical style between 1671 and 1710, was where French princes stayed before their coronations – and where they threw sumptuous banquets afterwards. Now a museum, it displays truly exceptional statuary, liturgical objects and tapestries from the cathedral, some in the impressive, Gothic-style **Salle de Tau** (Great Hall). Treasures worth seeking out include the 9th-century talisman of Charlemagne and St Rémi's golden, gem-encrusted chalice, which dates from the 12th century.

Basilique St-Rémi BASILICA
(place du Chanoine Ladame; ⊙9am-7pm) This 121m-long former Benedictine abbey church, a Unesco World Heritage Site, mixes Romanesque elements from the mid-11th century (the worn but stunning nave and transept) with early Gothic features from the latter half of the 12th century (the choir, with a large triforium gallery and, way up top, tiny clerestory windows). Next door is the Musée St-Rémi.

The abbey church is named in honour of Bishop Remigius, who baptised Clovis and 3000 Frankish warriors in 498. The 12th-century-style chandelier has 96 candles, one for each year of the life of St Rémi, whose tomb (in the choir) is marked by a mausoleum from the mid-1600s.

Musée St-Rémi MUSEUM
(http://musees-reims.fr; 53 rue Simon; adult/child €5/free; ⊙10am-noon & 2-6pm Tue-Sun) Housed in a 17th- and 18th-century abbey, this museum homes in on local Gallo-Roman archaeology, 16th-century Flemish tapestries, medieval sculpture and 16th- to 19th-century military history. The centrepiece is the early-18th-century cloister built to replace the original Romanesque one, which dated to the 12th century.

Musée des Beaux-Arts GALLERY
(http://musees-reims.fr; 8 rue Chanzy; adult/child €5/free; ⊙10am-noon & 2-6pm Wed-Mon) Lodged in an 18th-century abbey, this museum's rich collection stars one of four versions of Jacques-Louis David's world-famous

ART DECO REIMS

The vaulted **Halles du Boulingrin** (rue de Mars) were a symbol of Reims' emergence from the destruction of WWI when they began service as the city's main food market in 1929. Following a major restoration project, the Halles were reopened in all their art-deco glory in September 2012. Besides sheltering a **food market** (⊙food market 7am-1pm Wed, 7am-1pm & 4-8pm Fri, 6am-2pm Sat), they provide a unique backdrop for exhibitions and cultural events.

Thanks to a donation from the US-based Carnegie Foundation, the lobby of the **Bibliothèque** (2 place Carnegie; ⊙10am-1pm & 2-7pm Tue, Wed & Fri, 2-7pm Thu, 10am-1pm & 2-6pm Sat) boasts gorgeous 1920s mosaics, stained glass, frescoes and an extraordinary chandelier – duck inside for a look.

The tourist office (p330) also has a brochure on art-deco sites around Reims.

The Death of Marat (yes, the bloody corpse in the bath-tub), 27 works by Camille Corot (only the Louvre has more), 13 portraits by German Renaissance painters Cranach the Elder and the Younger, lots of Barbizon School landscapes, some art-nouveau creations by Émile Gallé, and two works each by Monet, Gauguin and Pissarro

Musée Hôtel Le Vergeur MUSEUM
(www.museelevergeur.com; 36 place du Forum; adult/child €5/free; ⊙2-6pm Tue-Sun) Highlights in this 15th-century townhouse include a series of furnished period rooms (kitchen, smoking room, Napoléon III's bedroom), some 50 wood engravings by Albrecht Dürer and a stunning Renaissance façade facing the interior garden.

Musée de la Reddition MUSEUM
(http://musees-reims.fr; 12 rue Franklin Roosevelt; adult/child €5/free; ⊙10am-6pm Wed-Mon) The original Allied battle maps are still affixed to the walls of US General Dwight D Eisenhower's headquarters, where Nazi Germany, represented by General Alfred Jodl, surrendered unconditionally at 2.41am on 7 May 1945, thus ending WWII. Displays include military uniforms and photographs. A 12-minute film is screened in French, English and German.

Reims

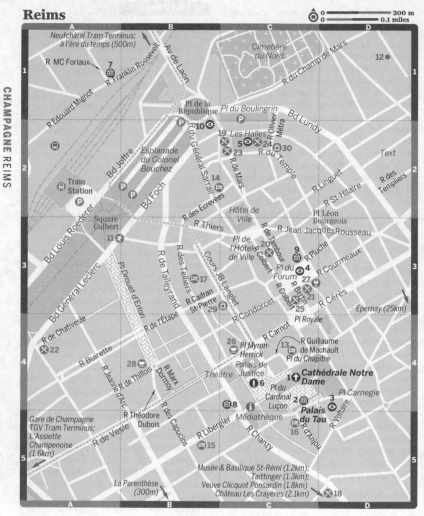

Porte de Mars
HISTORIC SITE

(Mars Gate; place de la République) For a quick trip back to Roman Gaul, check out the massive Porte de Mars, a three-arched triumphal gate built in the 2nd century AD. The gate was undergoing total renovation at the time of writing and was expected to reopen in all its glory in 2019.

Cryptoportique
HISTORIC SITE

(place du Forum; ⊙ 2-6pm May-Sep) FREE One of Reims' Roman standouts, the below-street-level Cryptoportique is thought to have been used for grain storage in the 3rd century AD.

👉 Tours

Mumm
WINE

(☑ 03 26 49 59 70; www.mumm.com; 34 rue du Champ de Mars; tours incl tasting €20-39; ⊙ tours 9.30am-1pm & 2-6pm daily, shorter hours & closed Sun Oct-Mar) Mumm (pronounced 'moom'), the only *maison* (house) in central Reims, was founded in 1827 and is now the world's third-largest Champagne producer (almost eight million bottles a year). Engaging and edifying guided tours take you through cellars filled with 25 million bottles of fine bubbly and conclude with a tasting. Wheelchair accessible. Phone ahead if possible.

Reims

★ **Taittinger**   WINE
(☏ 03 26 85 45 35; https://cellars-booking.taittinger.
fr; 9 place St-Niçaise; tours €19-55; ⊘ tours 10am-
4.30pm) The headquarters of Taittinger are a
highly atmospheric place to come for a clear,
straightforward presentation on how Champagne is actually made – there's no claptrap
about 'the Champagne mystique' here. A
spiral staircase twists down to the cellars occupying 4th-century *crayères* (Gallo-Roman
chalk quarries); other bits were excavated by
13th-century Benedictine monks and became
the cellars of St-Niçaise Abbey.

Buy tickets in advance online. The standard *'L'instant premier'* includes a tasting of
Brut Réserve; more expensive tours include
tastings of the Comtes de Champagne white
and rosé. It's situated 1.5km southeast of
Reims centre; take the Citadine 1 or 2 bus to
the St-Niçaise or Salines stops.

★ **Veuve Clicquot Ponsardin**   WINE
(☏ 03 26 89 53 90; www.veuveclicquot.com; 1
place des Droits de l'Homme; public tours & tastings €26-53, private tour & tasting €250; ⊘ tours
9.30am, 10.30am, 12.30pm, 1.30pm, 2pm, 3.30pm
& 4.30pm Tue-Sat Mar-Dec) One of the most
impressive cellar tours in the region is offered by Veuve Clicquot, a venerable *maison* founded in 1772. Veuve Cliquot has the
largest network of *crayères* in Reims, a
24km maze of tunnels and vaults deep below the ground. Guides lead you deep into

the cavernous, pyramid-shaped *crayères*,
used for chalk excavation in Gallo-Roman
times and now harbouring millions of
bottles of Champagne, one of which (the
yellow-label brut) you get to taste on the
1½-hour public tours.

The *maison* rose to fame under Madame Clicquot (1777–1866), nicknamed the
'Grande Dame of Champagne'. One of the
first businesspeople to tap into the wine industry, the widowed 27 year old evolved the
Champagne-making process using the first
riddling table, frequently turning the bottles
so the yeast would gather near the cork and
removing this frozen plug (disgorgement).
This resulted in a clearer Champagne with
finer bubbles.

Tickets can be purchased in advance
online.

✦ Festivals & Events

Fêtes Johanniques   CULTURAL
(⊘ May) Reims pays homage to heroine Joan
of Arc with medieval re-enactments on a
weekend in mid-May. The line-up is packed
with activities from jousting and street markets to falconry and craft displays.

🛏 Sleeping

Chambre d'Hôte Cathédrale   B&B €
(☏ 03 26 91 06 22; 21 place du Chapitre; s/d/tr
without bathroom €55/65/80) The cathedral
bells are your wake-up call at this sweet and

MAKING CHAMPAGNE

Champagne is made from the red pinot noir (38%), the black pinot meunier (35%) or the white chardonnay (27%) grape. Each vine is vigorously pruned and trained to produce a small quantity of high-quality grapes. Indeed, to maintain exclusivity (and price), the designated areas where grapes used for Champagne can be grown and the amount of wine produced each year are limited.

Making Champagne according to the traditional method (*méthode champenoise*) is a complex procedure. There are two fermentation processes, the first in casks and the second after the wine has been bottled and had sugar and yeast added. Bottles are then aged in cellars for two to five years, depending on the *cuvée* (vintage).

During the two months in early spring that the bottles are aged in cellars kept at 12°C, the wine turns effervescent. The sediment that forms in the bottle is removed by *remuage*, a painstakingly slow process in which each bottle, stored horizontally, is rotated slightly every day for weeks until the sludge works its way to the cork. Next comes *dégorgement:* the neck of the bottle is frozen, creating a blob of solidified Champagne and sediment, which is then removed.

simple B&B. Rooms are immaculate and old-fashioned, with stripy wallpaper, heavy wood furnishings and shared bathrooms.

Hôtel Azur
B&B €

(☏03 26 47 43 39; www.hotel-azur-reims.com; 9 rue des Ecrevées; s €55-85, d €79-109, tr €109, q €119; P⊛) Slip down a side street in the heart of Reims to reach this petite B&B, which extends a heartfelt welcome. Rooms are cheerfully painted and immaculately kept, and breakfast is served on the garden patio when the sun's out. There's no lift, so be prepared to lug your bags.

★ Les Telliers
B&B €€

(☏09 53 79 80 74; https://telliers.fr; 18 rue des Telliers; s €68-85, d €80-121, tr €117-142, q €133-163; P⊛) Enticingly positioned down a quiet alley near the cathedral, this bijou B&B extends one of Reims' warmest *bienvenues* (welcomes). The high-ceilinged rooms are big on art-deco character, and handsomely decorated with ornamental fireplaces, polished oak floors and the odd antique. Breakfast costs an extra €9 and is a generous spread of pastries, fruit, fresh-pressed juice and coffee.

Le Clos des Roys
B&B €€

(☏06 75 28 34 85; www.leclosdesroys.fr; 3 rue d'Anjou; d €100-120; ⊛) But a stone's throw from the cathedral, this historic home turned B&B is made all the homelier by hosts Marie Anne and Gérard. The quiet, countrified rooms are done out in soft greys and taupes. Top billing goes to the Charles VII room with its free-standing tub. Fresh pastries, fruit and waffles are served at breakfast.

La Demeure des Sacres
B&B €€

(☏06 79 06 80 68; 29 rue Libergier; d €170, ste €245-270; ⊛) Nuzzled in an art-deco townhouse close to the cathedral, this B&B harbours four wood-floored rooms and suites, with pleasing original features like marble fireplaces and free-standing bath-tubs. The Royal Suite has cracking cathedral views. Homemade treats (preserves, crêpes and the like) appear at breakfast, which is included in the room rate. There's a secluded garden for post-sightseeing moments.

★ Château Les Crayères
LUXURY HOTEL €€€

(☏03 26 24 90 00; www.lescrayeres.com; 64 bd Henry-Vasnier; d €395-755; P⊛@⊛) Such class! If you've ever wanted to stay in a palace, this romantic château on the fringes of Reims is the real McCoy. Manicured lawns sweep the graceful turn-of-the-century estate, where you can play golf or tennis, dine in two-Michelin-starred finery, and stay in the lap of luxury in exuberantly furnished, chandelier-lit interiors – all at a price, naturally.

L'Assiette Champenoise
BOUTIQUE HOTEL €€€

(☏03 26 84 64 64; www.assiettechampenoise. com; 40 av Paul-Vaillant-Couturier, Tinqueux; r €265-370, ste €470-780; P⊛⊛⊛⊛) Occupying a stout mansion, this five-star pad is often fully booked with gastronomes, here for the three-Michelin-starred restaurant (p329). Modern-minimalist rooms and suites sport a smattering of designer flourishes. Swishest of all is the Terrace Suite with private whirlpool. There's a chic bar for predinner drinks and an indoor pool. It's 2km west of central Reims in the suburb of Tinqueux.

✕ Eating

A tempting array of delis, patisseries and chocolatiers line rue de Mars, near Halles du Boulingrin (p325). Place du Forum is a great place to watch the world drift languidly by at bistros, cafes and bars with pavement seating.

Chez Jérôme BISTRO €

(📋 03 26 24 36 73; 23 rue de Tambour; menus €15-20; ⊙11am-6pm Tue-Fri, to 10.30pm Sat) So cosy it's like stepping into a friend's eccentric dining room, this bistro is run with passion by the inimitable one-man-band that is Jérôme – cook, waiter and chief bottle-washer. Made according to the chef's whim and what's available, the tasty, unfussy *menus* are prepared with seasonal, market-fresh ingredients. Everything, from the vintage lights to ceramics and furnishings, is for sale.

à l'ère du temps CRÊPES €

(📋 03 26 06 16 88; www.aleredutemps.com; 123 av de Laon; lunch menus €9.90, mains €7-14; ⊙noon-2pm & 7-9.30pm Tue-Sat) A short stroll north of place de la République brings you to this sweet and simple crêperie. It does a roaring trade in homemade crêpes, *galettes* (savoury buckwheat crêpes) and gourmet salads.

La Cave aux Fromages CHEESE €

(12 place du Forum; ⊙8.30am-1pm & 3.30-7.30pm Tue-Sat) Run by the knowledgable Charlet family, this fabulous shop is *fromage* heaven, with cheeses carefully sourced from all four corners of France. Among them is the regional speciality Cendré de Champagne, a creamy, smoky cheese matured in beech ash.

Le Bocal SEAFOOD €

(📋 03 26 47 02 51; 27 rue de Mars; mains €13-18; ⊙12.30-2pm & 7.30-9.30pm Tue-Sat) Winningly fresh seafood is the big deal at this tiny eatery set above a fishmongers: try sardines tossed in chilli butter, home-smoked salmon or hot oysters with parmesan.

Anna-S – La Table Amoureuse FRENCH €€

(📋 03 26 89 12 12; www.annas-latableamoureuse.com; 6 rue Gambetta; 3-course lunch €18.50, dinner menus €36-50; ⊙noon-1.30pm & 7-9pm Tue & Thu-Sat, noon-1.30pm Wed & Sun) So what if the decor is chintzy – there is a reason why this bistro is as busy as a beehive. Friendly service and a menu packed with well-done classics – Arctic char with Champagne jus, fillet of veal in rich, earthy morel sauce – hit the mark every time. The three-course lunch is a steal at €18.50.

l'Alambic FRENCH €€

(📋 03 26 35 64 93; www.restaurant-lalambic.fr; 63 bis rue de Chativesle; mains €14-25; ⊙noon-2pm & 7-9.30pm Tue-Fri, 7-9.30pm Sat & Mon; 📵) ⊘ Ideal for an intimate dinner, this vaulted cellar dishes up well-prepared French classics – along the lines of home-smoked trout with horseradish, cod fillet with Champagne-laced *choucroute* (sauerkraut) and pigeon served two ways with Reims mustard sauce. Save room for terrific desserts such as crème brûlée with chicory ice cream. The *plat du jour* (dish of the day) is a snip at €11.

Brasserie Le Boulingrin BRASSERIE €€

(📋 03 26 40 96 22; www.boulingrin.fr; 29 31 rue de Mars; menus €22-45; ⊙noon-2.30pm & 7-11pm Mon-Sat) A genuine, old-time brasserie – the decor and zinc bar date back to 1925 – whose ambience and cuisine make it an enduring favourite. From September to June, the culinary focus is on *fruits de mer* (seafood) such as Breton oysters.

★L'Assiette Champenoise GASTRONOMY €€€

(📋 03 26 84 64 64; www.assiettechampenoise.com; 40 av Paul-Vaillant-Couturier, Tinqueux; menus €95-315; ⊙noon-2pm & 7.30-10pm Thu-Mon) Heralded far and wide as one of Champagne's finest tables and crowned with the holy grail of three Michelin stars, L'Assiette Champenoise is headed up by chef Arnaud Lallemen. Listed by ingredients, his intricate, creative dishes rely on outstanding produce and play up integral flavours – be they Breton scallops, or milk-fed lamb with preserved vegetables. One for special occasions.

★Racine JAPANESE €€€

(📋 03 26 35 16 95; www.racine.re; 8 rue Colbert; tasting menus €75-100; ⊙12.15-2pm & 7.15-9pm Fri-Mon, 7.15-9pm Thu) With strong Japanese roots and a generous pinch of love for his adopted home, chef Kazuyuki Tanaka creates menus that sing with bright flavours and are delivered with finesse at slick, monochrome, Michelin-starred Racine. They're listed in the modern, ingredient-driven way, so turbot with squash and pistachio, pineapple with lemon and Champagne ice cream, and the like.

🍷 Drinking & Nightlife

Le Wine Bar by Le Vintage WINE BAR

(http://winebar-reims.com; 16 place du Forum; ⊙6pm-12.30am Tue-Thu, to 1.30am Fri & Sat) This bijou wine bar is a convivial spot to chill over a glass of wine or Champagne (some 500 are offered) with a tasting plate of charcuterie and cheese. The friendly brothers who own the place are happy to give recommendations.

Café du Palais CAFE
(www.cafedupalais.fr; 14 place Myron-Herrick; ⏰8.30am-8.30pm Tue-Fri, 9am-9.30pm Sat) Run by the same family since 1930, this art-deco cafe is *the* place to sip a glass of Champagne. Lit by a skylight is an extraordinary collection of bric-a-brac – from the inspired to the kitsch.

Waïda TEAHOUSE
(5 place Drouet d'Erlon; ⏰7.30am-7.30pm Tue-Fri, 7.30am-8pm Sat, 8am-2pm & 3.30-7.30pm Sun) A tearoom and confectioner with old-fashioned mirrors, mosaics and marble. This is a good place to pick up a box of Reims' famous *biscuits roses* (pink ladyfinger sponge biscuits), traditionally nibbled with Champagne, rainbow-bright macarons and divine *religieuses* (cream-filled puff pastries).

🛍 Shopping

Trésors de Champagne WINE
(www.boutique-tresors-champagne.com; 2 rue Olivier Métra; ⏰2-7pm Tue & Wed, 10.30am-12.30pm & 2-7pm Thu, 10.30am-12.30pm & 2-9.30pm Fri & Sat) Strikingly illuminated by Champagne bottles, this swish wine boutique-cum-bar plays host to 27 vintners and more than 200 Champagnes. There is a different selection available to taste each week. Keep an eye out, too, for tasting workshops posted on the website.

Maison Fossier FOOD
(www.fossier.fr; 25 cours Jean-Baptiste Langlet) You either love or hate *biscuits roses de Reims,* (pink ladyfinger sponge biscuits), which have been doing the rounds since Maison Fossier perfected them in 1756 and swiftly became supplier to the king. Buy them here (a 100g box costs €2.50).

In the 19th century, it was the done thing to dunk them in Champagne, which was sweeter back then, and some still do today, though sommeliers might tut.

ⓘ Information

The **tourist office** (☎03 26 77 45 00; www.reims-tourisme.com; 6 rue Rockefeller; ⏰10am-5pm Mon-Sat, 10am-12.30pm & 1.30-5pm Sun; 📶) has stacks of information on the Champagne region and Reims (plus free city maps), as well as some incredibly cool giant cork stools where you can perch while using the free wi-fi.

ⓘ Getting There & Around

BICYCLE

As of 2018, Reims has a new self-service bike-rental scheme courtesy of Gobee.bike. To locate a bike, visit http://gobeebike.fr and download the app, then scan your code to unlock. Rental costs €0.50 for 30 minutes.

BUS

Regional buses to nearby towns and villages are operated by **Marne Mobilité** (www.marne mobilite.fr). The website has details of timetables and fares. The **bus station** is outside the train station's northern (back) entrance. The best way to get to Troyes is by taking **Courriers de l'Aube** (www.courriersdelaube.fr; €15, 2¼ hours, up to 13 daily) bus line 140.

Two circular bus lines, the clockwise 1 and the anticlockwise 2 (single ticket €1.60, all-day ticket *journée* €4), serve most of the major sights of Reims. Most **Citura** (www.citura.fr) lines begin their last runs at about 9.50pm; five night lines operate until 12.15am.

TRAIN

Reims train station, 1km northwest of the cathedral, was renovated in 2010; the bullet marks on the façade date from both world wars. Frequent services run to Paris Gare de l'Est (€28 to €61, 46 minutes to one hour, 12 to 17 daily). Direct services also go to Épernay (€7.20, 30 minutes, 16 daily) and Laon (€10.40, 35 to 47 minutes, three to nine daily). The journey to Troyes (€36 to €64, 2½ to 3½ hours, 10 daily) involves at least one change.

FIZZ OF THE FUTURE

Thanks to Champagne's protected (Appellation d'Origine Contrôlée) status, only the stuff that's made in the region, which is subjected to rigorous laws and controls, can actually call itself Champagne – anything else is just sparkling wine by a different name.

But that hasn't stopped some of the major Champagne houses from latching on to the global thirst for fizz and casting their gazes further afield. In 2011, Moët & Chandon began establishing a winery in the Ningxia Hui autonomous region in northwestern China, thereby kick-starting something of a new trend.

More recently Taittinger planted its first vines on English soil in Kent in spring 2017. Quick to recognise the rise of British sparkling wine, the Champagne house aims to have its first ready by 2023 under the name Domaine Evremond.

ℹ WHICH CHAMPAGNE?

Blanc de Blancs Champagne made using only chardonnay grapes. Fresh and elegant, with very small bubbles and a bouquet reminiscent of 'yellow fruits' such as pear and plum.

Blanc de Noirs A full-bodied, deep golden Champagne made solely with black grapes (despite the colour). Often rich and refined, with great complexity and a long finish.

Rosé Pink Champagne (mostly served as an aperitif), with a fresh character and summer fruit flavours. Made by adding a small percentage of red pinot noir to white Champagne.

Prestige Cuvée The *crème de la crème* of Champagne. Usually made with grapes from *grand cru* vineyards and priced and bottled accordingly.

Millésimé Vintage Champagne produced from a single crop during an exceptional year. Most Champagne is nonvintage.

MARNE

The bucolic Marne *département* is famed for its Champagne routes, which wend their way among neat rows of hillside vines, through hilltop forests and across lowland crop fields. Along the way, they call on winemaking villages and hamlets, some with notable churches or museums, others quite ordinary, most without a centre or even a cafe. At almost every turn, beautiful panoramas unfold and small-scale, family-run Champagne wineries welcome travellers in search of bubbly.

Many producers prefer that visitors phone ahead but, if you haven't, don't be shy about knocking on the door. More and more young vignerons (winegrowers) speak English. Almost all producers are closed around the *vendange* (grape harvest, from late August to October), when bringing in the crop eclipses all other activities.

ℹ Getting There & Around

Car is by far the best means to explore and Champagne lends itself perfectly to a road trip. Getting around the villages can range from slow and laborious to nigh impossible without your own wheels.

The Champagne Routes, which follow secondary and tertiary rural roads, are signposted but there are so many twists and turn-offs that setting off without a map would be unwise. Bookshops and tourist offices sell Michelin's yellow-jacketed, 1:150,000-scale *Aisne, Ardennes, Marne* map (No 306).

Montagne de Reims Champagne Route

Linking Reims with Épernay by skirting the Parc Naturel Régional de la Montagne de Reims, a regional park covering the forested Reims Mountain plateau, this meandering, 70km route passes through vineyards planted mainly with pinot noir vines. Villages en route include Verzenay, the apt, humorously named **Bouzy** and Ay.

Verzenay

POP 1076

With vines spreading like a ribbed blanket over the hillsides and top-of-the-beanstalk views from its lighthouse, Verzenay makes an attractive stop on the **Montagne de Reims Champagne Route** (www.tourisme-en-champagne.co.uk). Its vines are planted mostly with pinot noir grapes – 100% *grand cru* (wine of exceptional quality).

◉ Sights & Activities

Phare & Musée de Verzenay   VIEWPOINT
(Verzenay Lighthouse; www.lepharedeverzenay.com; D26; lighthouse adult/child €3/2, museum €8/4, combined ticket €9/5; ◷10am-5pm Tue-Fri, to 5.30pm Sat & Sun, closed Jan) For the region's best introduction to the art of growing grapes and the cycles of the seasons, head to the Phare de Verzenay, on a hilltop at the eastern edge of the village. Exactly 101 spiral stairs lead to the top of the lighthouse, constructed as a publicity stunt in 1909, which rewards visitors with unsurpassed 360-degree views of vine, field and forest – and, if you're lucky, a tiny TGV zipping by in the distance.

Moulin de Verzenay   HISTORIC SITE
(Verzenay Windmill; D26) The Moulin de Verzenay, on the western edge of town, was used as an observation post during WWI and by the US Army during WWII. The interior is closed but the nearby hill offers valley views.

Étienne & Anne-Laure Lefevre   WINE
(📞03 26 97 96 99; www.champagne-etienne-lefevre.com; 30 rue de Villers; ◷10am-noon & 2-6pm Mon-Fri,

Routes of the Marne

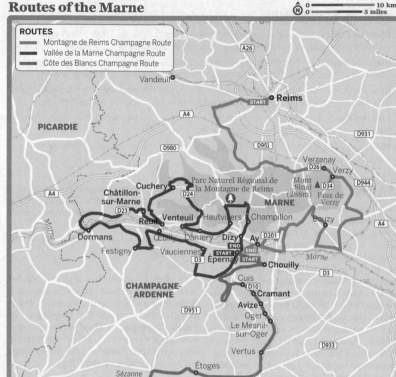

ROUTES
- Montagne de Reims Champagne Route
- Vallée de la Marne Champagne Route
- Côte des Blancs Champagne Route

to 5pm Sat) Étienne and Anne-Laure Lefevre run group tours of their family-owned vineyards and cellars – if you're on your own, ring ahead to see if you can join a prearranged tour. There are no flashy videos or multimedia shows – the emphasis is firmly on the nitty-gritty of Champagne production.

Parc Naturel Régional de la Montagne de Reims

Spreading across bijou winegrowing villages, lushly wooded hills and Champagne vines, the 500-sq-km Montagne de Reims Regional Park is best known for a botanical curiosity: 800 spectacularly contorted dwarf beech trees known as **faux de Verzy**. The best way to appreciate the park is by striking out on foot or by bicycle.

To get a good look at the park's trees, which have tortuously twisted trunks and branches that hang down like an umbrella,

take the Balade des Faux forest walk from 'Les Faux' parking lot, 2km up D34 from Verzy (situated on D26).

Across D34, a 500m gravel path leads through the forest to a *point de vue* (panoramic viewpoint) – next to a concrete WWI bunker – atop 288m-high Mont Sinaï.

Reims and Épernay – both with train stations and car rentals – are the major gateways to the park. You'll need your own car to get around and explore its off-the-beaten-track corners.

Vallée de la Marne Champagne Route

A stronghold of pinot meunier vines, this 90km itinerary winds from Épernay to Dormans, heading more or less west along the hillsides north of the River Marne via Œuilly, then circles back to the east along the river's south bank via Châtillon-sur-Marne and

BUBBLES IN A TREEHOUSE

Squirrelled away deep in the forest of the Parc Naturel Régional de la Montagne de Reims, this slick, Nordic-cool **Perching Bar** (www.facebook.com/perchingbar; Forêt de Brise-Charrette, Verzy; ⊙noon-2pm & 4-8pm Wed-Sun mid-Apr–mid-Dec) commands broad views from a treehouse over valley and vine – and we just love those swings! It's accessed via wooden walkways raised above the trees. Your €17 gets you a glass of Champagne. The bar champions both the *grandes maisons* and small producers.

Hautvillers. The GR14 long-distance walking trail and its variants (eg GR141) pass through the area.

Hautvillers

POP 806

Perched above a sea of emerald vines and ablaze with forsythia and tulips in spring, Hautvillers is where Dom Pierre Pérignon (1638–1715) is popularly believed to have created Champagne. The village is one of Champagne's prettiest, with ubiquitous medieval-style wrought-iron signs providing pictorial clues to the activities taking place on the other side of the wall.

Astonishing vineyard views await a few hundred metres north of the centre along rte de Fismes (D386); south along rte de Cumières (a road leading to D1); and along the GR14 long-distance walking trail (red-and-white markings) and local vineyard footpaths (yellow markings).

◉ Sights & Activities

Guided tours including a Champagne tasting (€9) and half-day electric bike tours of the surrounding vineyards (€45) can be arranged by the tourist office.

Volière des Cigognes Altavilloises   BIRD SANCTUARY
(rue des Côtes de l'Héry; ⊙24hr; 🚗) FREE Hautvillers is twinned with the Alsatian town of Eguisheim, which explains why several storks (including one rare black one) live here, an easy 500m walk towards Épernay from place de la République. It's a great opportunity to get a close-up view of these majestic birds. In most years, storklings hatch here in late April and May.

Église Abbatiale   CHURCH
(rue de l'Abbaye; ⊙9am-6.30pm Mon-Fri, 10am-6.30pm Sat & Sun) Part of a former Benedictine abbey, the Abbaye St-Pierre d'Hautvillers, founded in AD 650 by St Nivard, bishop of Reims, this church is liberally decorated with 17th-century woodwork. This is where the good monk Dom Pérignon is buried. Note the tomb in front of the altar.

🛏 Sleeping & Eating

Le Clos des Armoiries   B&B €€
(📞06 81 46 01 22; 74 rue des Côtes de l'Héry; s/d €170/190; 🅿🛜) This fetching, vine-swaddled country mansion positions you right in the heart of Champagne country. Behind white-painted shutters are rooms that have been tastefully done out with original beams, muted colour schemes and plush fabrics. The views are fab and the setting is pin-drop peaceful. Free bike rental is a nice touch.

★ Au 36   WINE BAR
(www.au36.net; 36 rue Dom Pérignon; ⊙10.30am-6pm Apr-Oct, 10.30am-4pm Fri-Tue Nov-Dec & Mar) This slinky wine boutique has a 'wall' of Champagne, innovatively arranged by aroma, and a laid-back upstairs tasting room. A two-/three-glass tasting costs €13/17, while a six-glass tasting for two people costs €38. A tasting platter of Champagne specialities costs €19.

ⓘ Information

The attractive main square is place de la République. Here you'll find the helpful **tourist office** (📞03 26 57 06 35; www.tourisme-hautvillers. com; place de la République; ⊙9.30am-1pm & 1.30-5.30pm Mon-Sat, 10am-4pm Sun, shorter hours winter), where you can pick up excellent free maps for several vineyard walks. One-hour guided tours cost €3 (with a Champagne tasting €5).

Châtillon-sur-Marne

POP 845

Sloping picturesquely down a hillside and braided with vines, Châtillon-sur-Marne reclines sleepily in the Vallée de la Marne. Woven with narrow streets, it's a pretty base for striking out on vineyard walks and its cellars also produce Champagnes worth lingering for.

◉ Sights

Albert Levasseur   WINERY
(📞03 26 58 11 38; www.champagne-levasseur. fr; 6 rue Sorbier, Cuchery; ⊙by appointment only) FREE You're assured a warm – and

English-speaking – welcome and a fascinating cellar tour at Albert Levasseur, run by a friendly Franco-Irish couple, which turns grapes grown on 4.2 hectares into 35,000 to 40,000 bottles of Champagne each year. Try to phone or email ahead if possible. Situated in the hamlet of Cuchery (population 438), 7.5km northeast of Châtillon-sur-Marne on D24.

Pope Urban II
STATUE

The highest point in Châtillon-sur-Marne is crowned by a 25m-high statue of Pope Urban II, dedicated in 1887, a particularly successful local boy (1042–99) best known to history for having launched the bloody First Crusade. The orientation table near the base offers excellent views of the Marne Valley and is a super spot for a picnic.

🛏 Sleeping & Eating

Grab a quick bite to eat on central place Urbain II. For more restaurant choice, you might want to venture into Épernay or Reims.

Domaine du Moulin de l'Étang
B&B €€

(📞 03 26 58 72 95; Moulin de l'Étang; d €120-130; 🅿🛜) Ah, such peace! This squat 18th-century farmhouse B&B reclines in the prettiest setting of vineyards and pond-speckled gardens. Rooms are furnished in nouveau-rustic style, with stone walls, earthy hues and natural fabrics. The lovely owner prepares great breakfasts and can advise on local Champagne *dégustations* (tastings).

ⓘ Information

Tourist Office (📞 03 26 58 32 86; www.tourisme-chatillon-marne.fr; 4 rue de l'Église; ⊙10am-1pm & 2.30-6.30pm Tue-Sun, 2.30-6.30pm Mon, shorter hours Oct-Mar)

Œuilly
POP 621

Blink and you'll miss dinky Œuilly, 15km west of Épernay, just off D3, on the **Vallée de la Marne Champagne Route**, but that would be a shame. This cute grey-stone village, flower-draped in summer, is topped by a 13th-century church.

To get a sense of winegrowing life a century ago, drop by the **Écomusée d'Œuilly** (www.ecomusee-oeuilly.fr; cour des Maillets; adult/child €7/4; ⊙ tours 10.30am & 2pm Wed-Mon) whose three sections showcasing traditional viticulture methods and country life include a schoolroom, c 1900.

Lunch afterwards on a cracking value €13 *menu du jour* at **Le G'Houlot Champenois** (📞 03 26 51 46 22; 4 rue de la Libération; menus €13; ⊙ 9.30am-8.30pm Mon-Thu, to 11.30pm Fri & Sat), with sweet-and-simple tiled floors, marble-topped tables and summertime terrace.

Côte des Blancs Champagne Route

This 100km route, planted almost exclusively with white chardonnay grapes (the name means 'hillside of the whites'), begins along Épernay's majestic av de Champagne and then heads south to Sézanne and beyond. Stops en route include Cramant (of giant Champagne bottle fame), Avize and Le Mesnil-sur-Oger. The gently rolling landscape is at its most attractive in late summer and autumn.

Avize
POP 1814

Right in the heart of Blancs des Blancs country and surrounded by rows of immaculately tended vines, which yield the chardonnay grapes that go into producing some of the world's finest fizz, Avize is lauded far and wide for its outstanding Champagnes. It's home to a highly regarded school of wine and some excellent cellars.

⊙ Sights

Sanger Cellars
WINE

(📞 03 26 57 79 79; www.sanger.fr; 33 rue du Rempart du Midi; tour incl 2-/4-/9-flute tasting €10/17.50/30, full-day masterclass €60; ⊙8am-noon & 2-5pm Mon-Fri) At the Sanger Cellars, tours of the Avize Viti Campus' (p335) impressive production facilities take in traditional equipment and the latest high-tech machinery, such as a gadget that removes sediment from the necks of bottles after *remuage* (riddling) by an automated *gyropalette*. Tours include a tasting.

ⓘ INSTA SELFIE

The mammoth Champagne bottle dominating the northern entrance to **Cramant**, a pretty village 9km southeast of Épernay on D10, is one hell of a magnum. When taking that perfect Instagram selfie, stand right next to it to get a true sense of scale.

Champagnes are sold at discounted *prix départ cave* (cellar-door prices) and profits are reinvested in the school. The entrance is on the D19; if the door is locked, push the intercom button.

Avize Viti Campus
WINERY

(Champagne High School of Winemaking; www. avizeviticampus.fr; rue d'Oger) Many past, present and future Champagne makers learn, or are learning, their art and science at the Avize Viti Campus run by the Ministry of Agriculture. As part of their studies, students produce quite excellent bubbly, made with grapes from some of Champagne's most prestigious parcels and sold under the label Champagne Sanger (www.sanger.fr). Sanger was established shortly after WWI, and the name is from '*sans guerre*' ('without war'), pronounced sahn-*gher*.

Église St-Nicolas
CHURCH

(rue de l'Église, D10) Once the abbey church of a Benedictine convent, Église St-Nicolas mixes Romanesque, Flamboyant Gothic and Renaissance styles. There are no specific opening times – turn up and hopefully you'll be able to go inside.

From here, aptly named rue de la Montagne leads up the hill (towards Grauves), past an oversized Champagne bottle, to Parc Vix (D19), which affords panoramic vineyard views; a map sign details a 6.5km, two-hour walk through forest and field.

🛏 Sleeping & Eating

Les Avisés
HISTORIC HOTEL €€€

(☑ 03 26 57 70 06; www.selosse-lesavises.com; 59 rue de Cramant; d €250-390, menus €39-62) Housed in a splendid neoclassical manor, Les Avisés is a touch of class in the heart of Champagne. Overlooking the park or vineyards, rooms manage the delicate act of combining historic and contemporary, with muted colours and clean lines. Regional cuisine is prepared with flair and served with top-quality wines (some produced on the estate) in the intimate restaurant.

Oger

POP 558

The tiny hamlet of Oger is known for its *grand cru* fields, prize-winning flower gardens and the **Musée du Mariage** (www.champagne-henry-devaugency.fr; 1 rue d'Avize, D10; adult/child €8/free; ⊙ 9.30am-noon & 2-6pm Tue-Sun) featuring colourful and often gaudy objects

associated with 19th-century marriage traditions. The collection was assembled by the parents of the owner of Champagne Henry de Vaugency (founded 1732), an eighth-generation Champagne grower. An explanatory sheet in English is available. The price of entry includes a Champagne tasting.

Le Mesnil-sur-Oger

POP 1077

This comely winegrowing village on the **Côte des Blancs Champagne Route** is among the most famous, with 100% of its chardonnay vines producing the superlative *grand cru* Champagnes. It's worth the pilgrimage alone for an insight into Champagne making and its history at the Musée de la Vigne et du Vin.

◎ Sights

★ Musée de la Vigne et du Vin
MUSEUM

(☑ 03 26 57 50 15; www.champagne-launois.fr; 2 av Eugène Guillaume, cnr D10; adult incl 3 flutes €12; ⊙ tours 10am & 3pm Mon-Fri, 10.30am Sat & Sun) This museum is so outstanding that it's worth planning your day around a two-hour tour. Assembled by a family that has been making Champagne since 1872, this extraordinary collection of century-old Champagne-making equipment includes objects so aesthetically ravishing that you'll want to reach out and touch them. Among the highlights is a massive 16-tonne oak-beam grape press from 1630. The museum can only be visited by tour; these are available in French and English. Call ahead or book online.

🛏 Sleeping & Eating

Champagne Baradon Michaudet
B&B €

(☑ 03 26 57 19 70; www.champagne baradon-michaudet.com; 58 Grand'Rue; s €66-78, d €75-90, tr €95, q €116; ℗) Stay with the Champagne makers at this attractive little B&B, with four rooms and one *gîte* (self-catering apartment) big enough to accommodate a family. The decor is delightfully old school, with florals, flounces and wood beams, and it's not every day you find *grand cru* Champagne in your minibar! The friendly hosts put on a generous spread at breakfast.

La Gare
FRENCH €€

(☑ 03 26 51 59 55; www.lagarelemesnil.com; 3 place de la Gare; menus €18-26; ⊙ noon-1.30pm Mon-Wed, noon-1.30pm & 7-9pm Thu-Sat; 🅿) Decked out like a station, La Gare prides itself on serving bistro-style grub prepared with seasonal produce, simple as pork tenderloin with cider and potatoes, grilled salmon with hollandaise and beef cooked in red wine. There's a €9 menu for *les petits*.

ÉPERNAY

POP 24,456

Prosperous Épernay, the self-proclaimed *capitale du Champagne* and home to many of the world's most celebrated Champagne houses, is the best place for touring cellars and sampling bubbly. The town also makes an excellent base for exploring the Champagne Routes.

Beneath the streets in 110km of subterranean cellars, more than 200 million bottles of Champagne, just waiting to be popped open on some sparkling occasion, are being aged. In 1950 one such cellar – owned by the irrepressible Mercier family – hosted a car rally without the loss of a single bottle!

◉ Sights

★ Avenue de Champagne   STREET

Épernay's handsome av de Champagne fizzes with *maisons de champagne* (Champagne houses). The boulevard is lined with mansions and neoclassical villas, rebuilt after WWI. Peek through wrought-iron gates at Moët's private **Hôtel Chandon**, an early-19th-century pavilion-style residence set in landscaped gardens, which counts Wagner among its famous past guests. The haunted-looking **Château Perrier**, a redbrick mansion built in 1854 in neo–Louis XIII style, is aptly placed at number 13! It's set to open as a new Champagne museum in 2019.

A REASON TO CELEBRATE

The Champagne region really had a reason to crack open the fizz and pop corks when it finally achieved Unesco World Heritage status in 2015. The accolade refers to three specific areas: the historic vineyards of Hautvillers, Aÿ and Mareuil-sur-Aÿ; St-Nicaise Hill in Reims; and the av de Champagne and Fort Chabrol in Épernay.

⚲ Tours

★ Atelier 1834: Champagne Boizel   WINE

(☑ 03 26 55 91 49; www.boizel.com; 46 av de Champagne; tours incl 2 Champagne tastings €22-40; ⊙ 10am-1pm & 2.30-5.30pm Mon-Fri, 10am-1pm & 2.30-6pm Sat) This wonderfully intimate Champagne house is still run with passion and prowess by the Boizel family, with a winemaking tradition dating to 1834. Unlike many of the *maisons* that open their doors to the public, these are still very much working cellars. Hidden away here are the real treasures – several bottles (still drinkable, apparently) hailing from 1834.

★ Moët & Chandon   WINE

(☑ 03 26 51 20 20; www.moet.com; 20 av de Champagne; 1½hr tour with tasting €25-40, 10-17yr €10; ⊙ tours 9.30-11.30am & 2-4.30pm) Flying the Moët, French, European and Russian flags, this prestigious *maison* is the world's biggest producer of Champagne. It has frequent 90-minute tours that are among the region's most impressive, offering a peek at part of its 28km labyrinth of *caves* (cellars).

Mercier   WINE

(☑ 03 26 51 22 22; www.champagnemercier.fr; 68-70 av de Champagne; adult incl 1/2/3 glasses €18/22/25, 12-17yr €8; ⊙ tours 9.30-11.30am & 2-4.30pm, closed mid-Dec–mid-Feb) France's most popular brand was founded in 1847 by Eugène Mercier, a trailblazer in the field of publicity stunts and the virtual creator of cellar tours. Everything at this Champagne house is flashy, including the 160,000L barrel that took two decades to build (for the 1889 Universal Exposition), the lift that transports you 30m underground and the laser-guided touring train.

The Mercier cellars were closed for renovation at the time of research and are set to reopen in 2019.

Champagne Georges Cartier   WINE

(☑ 03 26 32 06 22; www.georgescartier.com; 9 rue Jean Chandon-Moët; adult incl 6-glass tasting €15, cellar tour & 1-glass tasting €12.50, cellar tour & 6-glass tasting €23.50; ⊙ 10am-7pm Tue-Thu & Sun, 10am-8pm Fri & Sat) Hewn out of the chalk in the 18th century, the warren of cellars and passageways at Champagne Georges Cartier is incredibly atmospheric. Look out for the fascinating graffiti (both in French and German) dating to when the cellars were used as bunkers during WWII. Tours are followed by a Champagne tasting of one to six glasses.

Champagne Domi Moreau BUS

(📱 06 30 35 51 07, after 7pm 03 26 59 45 85; www. champagne-domimoreau.com; 11 rue du Bas, Mancy; tours €35; ⊘ tours 2.30pm except Wed, Sun & Aug) Nathalie and Max run scenic and insightful three-hour minibus tours, in French and English, of nearby vineyards. Pick-up is across the street from the tourist office (p338). Call ahead for reservations.

🛌 Sleeping

La Villa St-Pierre HOTEL €

(📱 03 26 54 40 80; www.villasaintpierre.fr; 1 rue Jeanne d'Arc; d €65-120, tr €102-113, q €119-132; 🛜) Expect a warm, family-style *bienvenue* at this early-20th-century townhouse turned B&B. A recent makeover has spruced up the 11 rooms, the pick of which have separate sitting areas and fine views over Épernay to the vine-cloaked hills beyond. The downside to top-floor rooms is having to lug your bags. Breakfast costs an additional €14.

Magna Quies B&B €€

(📱 06 73 25 66 60; www.magnaquies-epernay. jimdo.com; 49 av de Champagne; d/tr/q €160/200/240; 🅿) Nestled in a shuttered manor house on the Avenue de Champagne (p336), this family-run B&B extends the warmest of welcomes. The trio of sunny, wood-floored rooms, in shades of grey, pink and brown, command fine views of the vineyards. Rates include a generous breakfast spread of pastries, fresh fruit and cold cuts.

Hôtel Jean Moët HISTORIC HOTEL €€

(📱 03 26 32 19 22; www.hoteljeanmoet.com; 7 rue Jean Moët; d €168-212, ste €235-265; 🎛❄🛜🏊) Housed in a beautifully converted 18th-century mansion, this old-town hotel is big on atmosphere, with its skylit tearoom and revamped antique-meets-boutique-chic rooms. Exposed beams add a dash of romance and there are modern comforts like Nespresso makers. Champagne cellar C. Comme (p338) awaits downstairs.

Le Clos Raymi HISTORIC HOTEL €€

(📱 03 26 51 00 58; www.closraymi-hotel.com; 3 rue Joseph de Venoge; d €120-195; 🛜) Staying at this atmospheric place is like being a personal guest of Monsieur Chandon of Champagne fame, who occupied this luxurious townhouse over a century ago. The seven romantic, parquet-floored rooms – styles include Provençal, Tuscan and Champagne – have giant beds, high ceilings and French windows. In winter, there's often a fire in the art-deco living room.

DOM PÉRIGNON

Everyone who visits Moët & Chandon invariably stops to strike a pose next to the statue of **Dom Pérignon** (av de Champagne) after whom the prestige *cuvée* is named. The Benedictine monk (c 1638–1715) played a pivotal role, in making Champagne what it is – perfecting the process of using a second, in-the-bottle fermentation to make ho-hum wine sparkle.

★**La Villa Eugène** BOUTIQUE HOTEL €€€

(📱 03 26 32 44 76; www.villa-eugene.com; 84 av de Champagne; d €173-275, ste €305-398; 🅿❄🛜🏊) Sitting handsomely astride the Avenue de Champagne (p336) in its own grounds with an outdoor pool, La Villa Eugène is a class act. It's in a beautiful 19th-century town mansion that once belonged to the Mercier family. The roomy doubles exude understated elegance, with soft, muted hues and the odd antique. Splash out more for a private terrace or four-poster bed.

🍴 Eating

Épernay's main eat street is rue Gambetta and adjacent place de la République. For picnic fixings, head to rue St-Thibault.

Covered Market MARKET €

(Halle St-Thibault; rue Gallice; ⊘ 7am-12.30pm Wed & Sat) Picnic treats galore.

Lunch Time SANDWICHES €

(📱 03 26 54 33 32; www.lunchtime-epernay.com; 43 rue Général Leclerc; sandwiches €4-7; ⊘ 8am-6pm Mon-Fri, to 4pm Sat) For breakfast, baguettes, club sandwiches or the quiche of the day with a salad, this sweet and simple cafe is the go-to place in Épernay. It also does smoothies, fresh juices, good coffee – even Champagne!

Pâtisserie Vincent Dallet PASTRIES €

(www.chocolat-vincentdallet.fr; 26 rue Général Leclerc; pastries €2-5, light meals €8-18; ⊘ 7.30am-7.45pm Tue-Sun) A sweet dream of a chocolaterie, patisserie and tearoom, with delectable pralines, macarons and pastries. A *champenoise* speciality is the 'Baba', vanilla cream topped by a cork-shaped pastry flavoured with Champagne. Or go straight for a *café gourmand*, coffee with a selection of mini desserts.

TASTE LIKE A PRO

You can taste Champagne anywhere but you might get more out of one of the two-hour workshops at **Villa Bissinger** (☑ 03 26 55 78 78; www.villabissinger.com; 15 rue Jeanson, Ay), home to the International Institute for the Wines of Champagne. Besides covering the basics like names, producers, grape varieties and characteristics, the workshop includes a tasting of four different Champagnes. The institute is in Ay, 3.5km northeast of Épernay. Call ahead to secure your place.

★ **La Grillade Gourmande**   FRENCH €€
(☑ 03 26 55 44 22; www.lagrilladegourmande. com; 16 rue de Reims; lunch menus €21, dinner menus €33-59, mains €20-26; ⊗ noon-1.45pm & 7.30-9.30pm Tue-Sat) This chic, red-walled, art-slung bistro is an inviting spot to try char-grilled meats and dishes rich in texture and flavour, such as crayfish pan-fried in Champagne and lamb cooked in rosemary and honey until meltingly tender. Diners spill out onto the covered terrace in the warm months. Both the presentation and service are flawless.

La Cave à Champagne   FRENCH €€
(☑ 03 26 55 50 70; www.la-cave-a-champagne. com; 16 rue Gambetta; menus €22-40; ⊗ noon-2pm & 7-10pm Thu-Mon; ☑) 'The Champagne Cellar' is well regarded by locals for its humble *champenoise* cuisine (snail-and-pig's-trotter casserole, fillet of beef in pinot noir), served in a warm, traditional, bourgeois atmosphere. Pair these dishes with inexpensive regional Champagnes and wines.

Le Théâtre   FRENCH €€
(☑ 03 26 58 88 19; www.epernay-rest-letheatre. com; 8 place Mendès-France; menus €26-51; ⊗ noon-2pm & 7.30-9pm Mon & Thu-Sat, noon-2pm Tue & Sun) Sidling up to Épernay's **theatre** (☑ box office 03 26 51 15 99; http://theatrelesalmanazar.fr; place Mendès-France; tickets €9-35), Le Théâtre raises a curtain on a delightfully old-school brasserie with splashes of high-ceilinged art-nouveau charm. The Belgian chef, Lieven Vercouteren, prides himself on using superb seasonal produce in *menus* that might begin, say, with pheasant terrine with juniper berries and move on to mains such as tender leg of lamb with seasonal vegetables.

⚲ Drinking & Nightlife

★ **C. Comme**   WINE BAR
(☑ 03 26 32 09 55; www.c-comme.fr; 8 rue Gambetta; 2-/4-/6-glass Champagne tasting €13/26.60/37.50; ⊗ 10am-8pm Mon, Tue & Thu, 3-8pm Wed, 10am-midnight Fri & Sat) The downstairs cellar has a stash of 400 different varieties of Champagne; sample them in the softly lit bar-bistro upstairs. Accompany with a tasting plate of regional cheese, charcuterie and rillettes (pork pâté). We love the funky bottle-top tables and relaxed ambience.

ⓘ Information

Tourist Office (☑ 03 26 53 33 00; www. ot-epernay.fr; 7 av de Champagne; ⊗ 9am-12.30pm & 1.30-7pm Mon-Sat, 10.30am-1pm & 2-4.30pm Sun mid-Apr–mid-Oct, 9.30am-12.30pm & 1.30-5.30pm Mon-Sat mid-Oct–mid-Apr; ☏) The team here hands out English brochures and maps with walking, cycling and driving tour options. Staff can also make cellar visit reservations. Free wi-fi.

ⓘ Getting There & Around

BICYCLE

The **tourist office** rents out bikes (city/children's/electric bicycles €20/11/30 per day). Pick up cycling maps and map-cards (€0.50) here.

TRAIN

The **train station** (place Mendès-France) has direct services to Reims (€7.20, 27 minutes, 14 daily) and Paris Gare de l'Est (€24 to €69, 1¼ to 2¾ hours, seven daily).

TROYES

POP 60,009

In polls of France's most romantic towns, Troyes invariably makes the grade – and with good reason. Its astonishingly intact, ludicrously pretty historic centre wings you back to the Middle Ages, with its warren of cobbled streets, fine ensemble of half-timbered houses in pastel hues once home to wealthy textile merchants, and uplifting Gothic churches. Often overlooked, it's one of the best places to get a sense of what Europe looked like back when Molière was penning his plays and the Three Musketeers were swashbuckling.

Troyes punches well above its weight culturally, too, with a raft of fascinating galleries and museums, homing in on everything from apothecaries to tools, hosiery and 16th-century art.

◉ Sights

★ 16th-Century Troyes   AREA

Half-timbered houses – some with lurching walls and floors that aren't quite level – line many streets in the old city, rebuilt after a devastating fire in 1524. The best place for aimless ambling is the area bounded by (clockwise from the north) rue du Général de Gaulle, the Hôtel de Ville, rue Général Saussier and rue de la Pierre. Of special interest are (from southwest to northeast) **rue de Vauluisant**, **rue de la Trinité**, **rue Champeaux** and **rue Paillot de Montabert**.

★ Cathédrale St-Pierre
et St-Paul   CATHEDRAL

(place St-Pierre; ◷ 9.30am-12.30pm & 2-6pm Mon-Sat, 2-6pm Sun Apr-Oct, to 5pm Nov-Mar) All at once imposing and delicate with its filigree stonework, Troyes' cathedral is a stellar example of *champenoise* Gothic architecture. The flamboyant **west façade** dates from the mid-1500s, while the 114m long interior is illuminated by a spectacular series of 180 **stained-glass windows** (13th to 17th centuries) that shine when it's sunny. Also notable is the fantastical **Baroque organ** (1730s) sporting musical *putti* (cherubs), and a tiny **treasury** with enamels from the Meuse Valley.

★ Maison de l'Outil et de
la Pensée Ouvrière   MUSEUM

(MOPO; http://mopo3.com; 7 rue de la Trinité; adult/child €7/3.50; ◷ 10am-6pm daily, closed Tue Oct-Mar) Worn to a sensuous lustre by generations of skilled hands, the 11,000 hand tools on display here – each designed to perform a single, specialised task with exquisite efficiency – bring to life a world of manual skills made obsolete by the Industrial Revolution. The collection is housed in the magnificent Renaissance-style Hôtel de Mauroy, built in 1556. Videos show how the tools were used and what they were used for. A catalogue in English is available at the reception.

Hôtel de Vauluisant   MUSEUM

(4 rue de Vauluisant; adult/child €3/free; ◷ 10am-1pm & 2-6pm Wed-Sun Apr-Oct, to 5pm Nov-Mar) This haunted-looking, Renaissance-style mansion shelters a twinset of unique museums. The **Musée de l'Art Champenois** is a repository for the evocative paintings, stained glass and statuary (stone and wood) of the Troyes School, which flourished here during the economic prosperity and artistic ferment of the early 16th century. The **Musée de la Bon**neterie (Hosiery Museum) showcases the sock-strewn story of Troyes' 19th-century knitting industry, with exhibits from knitting machines and looms to bonnets and embroidered silk stockings.

Ruelle des Chats   STREET

Off rue Champeaux (between Nos 30 and 32), a stroll along tiny ruelle des Chats (Alley of the Cats), as dark and narrow as it was four centuries ago – the upper floors almost touch – is like stepping back into the Middle Ages. The stones along the base of the walls were designed to give pedestrians a place to stand when horses clattered by. See if you can spot the namesake cat in the stonework.

Église Ste-Madeleine   CHURCH

(rue Général de Gaulle; ◷ 9.30am-12.30pm & 2-6pm Mon-Sat, 2-6pm Sun Apr-Oct, to 5pm Nov-Mar) Troyes' oldest and most interesting neighbourhood church has an early Gothic nave and transept and a Renaissance-style choir and tower. The highlights here are the splendid Flamboyant Gothic **rood screen** (early 1500s), dividing the transept from the choir, and the 16th-century **stained glass** in the presbytery portraying scenes from Genesis. In the nave, the statue of a deadly serious **Ste Marthe** (St Martha), around the pillar from the wooden pulpit, is considered a masterpiece of the 15th-century Troyes School.

Basilique St-Urbain   CHURCH

(place Vernier; ◷ 9.30am-12.30pm & 2-6pm Mon-Sat, 2-6pm Sun Apr-Oct, to 5pm Nov-Mar) Begun in 1262 by the Troyes-born Pope Urban IV, whose father's shoemaker shop once stood on this spot, this church is exuberantly Gothic both inside and out, and has some fine 13th-century stained glass. In the chapel off the south transept arm is **La Vierge au Raisin** (Virgin with Grapes), a graceful, early-14th-century stone statue of Mary and the Christ child.

Église St-Pantaléon   CHURCH

(rue de Vauluisant; ◷ 9.30am-12.30pm & 2-6pm Mon-Sat, 2-6pm Sun Apr-Oct, to 5pm Nov-Mar) Faded with age and all the more enigmatic for it, this Renaissance-style, cruciform church, with its barrel-vaulted wood ceiling, is a great place to see the work of the 16th-century Troyes School – check out the sculptures attached to the columns of the nave. The west façade was added in the 18th century. History sheets are available.

Troyes

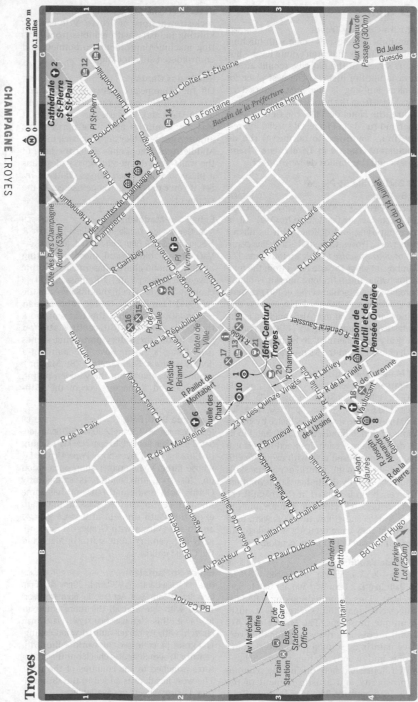

Cathédrale
St-Pierre
et St-Paul

R du Cloître St-Étienne

Q La Fontaine

Q du Comte Henri

Bassin de la Préfecture

Bd Jules
Guesde

Aux Oiseaux de
Passage (300m)

R du 14 Juillet

R Richard Gontilbue

Pl St-Pierre

R Boucherat

R de la Cité

R-Salengro

Q des Comtes de Champagne

Q Dampierre

R Hennequin

Côte des Bars Champagne
Route (53km)

Bd Gambetta

R Garnbey

R Raymond Poincaré

R Louis Ulbach

Pl
Vernier

R Urbain IV

R George-Clemenceau

R Pithou

R de la Halle

Pl de
la Halle

R de la République

Hôtel de
Ville

R Champeaux

16th-Century
Troyes

R Général Saussier

Maison de
l'Outil et de la
Pensée Ouvrière

R Champeaux

R Émile Zola

R de la Trinité

R Larivey

R de Turenne

R de Vauluisant

R Molé

R Aristide
Briand

R Paillot de
Montabert

R Clé Huez

Ruelle des
Chats

23 R des Quinze Vingts

R Brunneval

R Juvénal
des Ursins

R Joseph

R Alexandre

R Guivet

R de la
Pierre

Pl Jean
Jaurès

R de la Monnaie

R du Palais de Justice

R Jaillant Deschainets

R de la Paix

R Jules Lebocey

R de la Madeleine

R Général de Gaulle

R Agence

Bd Gambetta

Av Pasteur

R Paul Dubois

Bd Carnot

Pl Général
Patton

Bd Victor Hugo

Free Parking
Lot (250m)

Bd Carnot

Av Maréchal
Joffre

Pl de
la Gare

Bus
Station
Office

Train
Station

R Voltaire

200 m
0.1 miles

N

G F E D C B A

1 2 3 4

Troyes

Apothicairerie de l'Hôtel-Dieu-le-Comte   MUSEUM

(www.musees-troyes.com; quai des Comtes de Champagne; adult/child €3/free; ⊙10am-1pm & 2-6pm Tue-Sun Apr-Oct, to 5pm Nov-Mar) If you come down with an old-fashioned malady – scurvy, perhaps, or unbalanced humours – the place to go is this fully outfitted, wood-panelled pharmacy from 1721. Rare majolica and earthenware pharmaceutical jars share shelf space with decorative pill boxes and bronze mortars.

La Cité du Vitrail   MUSEUM

(www.cite-vitrail.fr; 1 rue Roger Salengro; ⊙9.30am-12.30pm & 1.30-5pm Tue-Sun; ⊕) **FREE** Housed in the barn of the 18th-century Hôtel-Dieu-le-Comte, this free museum dazzles with 25 works of stained glass reaching from the 12th to the 21st century – all visible at eye level. A highlight (quite literally) is the 16th-century *Tree* by Jessé of Laines-aux-Bois. There are regular workshops for children; see the website for details.

🛏 Sleeping

★ Maison M   B&B €€

(☑06 80 27 21 03, 03 25 46 30 97; http://maisonmtroyes.com; 3 quai la Fontaine; d €115-160; ❋🛜) Michelle and Bruno are your hosts at this boutique-flavoured guesthouse, a tasteful melange of 19th-century features and furnishings and chic modern design. Most of the spacious, sunny, wood-floored rooms face gardens, and breakfast is a small feast of local produce. Whether you want to rent a bike or arrange a Champagne tasting, just say the word.

Le Jardin de la Cathédrale   B&B €€

(☑06 63 10 32 32; www.jardindelacathedrale.com; 12 place St-Pierre; d €180-210; ℗🛜) Tucked behind the cathedral, this delightful little B&B lodges in a stone-walled 18th-century house, with oodles of history, style and soul-stirring views. Laetitia is your charming host, tending to the beautiful courtyard garden, revealing her flair for design in four suites furnished with bold colours, beams and antiques, and serving delicious breakfasts with fresh pastries, organic jams and homemade yoghurt.

Le Relais St-Jean   HISTORIC HOTEL €€

(☑03 25 73 89 90; www.relais-st-jean.com; 51 rue Paillot de Montabert; d €98-159, ste €169-215; ℗❋🛜) On a narrow medieval street in the heart of the old city, this hotel combines half-timbered charm with 24 contemporary rooms, a mini tropical hothouse, a jacuzzi in the 16th-century cellar, a small fitness centre and facilities for people with disabilities. There's direct access from the underground car park (€10).

La Maison de Rhodes   HISTORIC HOTEL €€€

(☑03 25 43 11 11; www.maisonderhodes.com; 18 rue Linard Gonthier; r €209-429; 🛜❋) Once home to the Knights Templar, this half-timbered pile sits proudly on its 12th-century foundations. Creaking staircases lead to 11 spacious rooms, with beams and stone floors, which positively ooze medieval character; iPod docks and wi-fi suddenly wing you back into the 21st century. The gardens, courtyard and gourmet restaurant invite lingering. Breakfast will set you back an extra €23.

✗ Eating

Locals are enormously proud of the city's specialities: *andouillettes de Troyes* (sausages made with strips of pigs' intestines) and *tête de veau* (calf's head served without the brain). As far as most nonlocals are concerned, they're an acquired taste.

Covered Market   MARKET €
(www.marchedeshalles.fr; place de la Halle; ⊙8am-12.45pm & 3.30-7pm Mon-Thu, 7am-7pm Fri & Sat, 9am-1pm Sun) Fruit, veggies, bread, charcuterie, fish and cheese, glorious cheese.

★ Claire et Hugo   BURGERS €
(☑06 52 94 70 77; www.facebook.com/Claire-et-Hugo; place de la Halle; mains €10-14; ⊙noon-2pm & 7-9pm Mon-Fri) Meet Claire and Hugo, the dynamic duo behind this double-decker-bus street-food venture, which does the rounds in Troyes and around. Everything on the menu is homemade: from the burgers and *frites* to the bread, sauces, macarons and brownies. They're on place de la Halle on Mondays; see their Facebook page for other locations.

Tout Simplement   BISTRO €
(☑03 25 40 83 72; www.resto-toutsimplement.fr; 29 place Alexandre Israël; mains €12-19; ⊙noon-2pm & 7-10pm Tue-Sat) Chipper staff keep the good vibes and food coming at this contemporary wine bar-bistro in the half-timbered heart of Troyes, which spills out onto a terrace in summer. Their famous *rillettes* (pâtés) – chicken, aubergine and grilled almonds, for instance – are a tasty prelude to mains such as creamy scallop risotto.

Aux Oiseaux de Passage   FRENCH €
(☑06 87 11 57 75; www.auxoiseauxdepassage.com; 24bis mail des Charmilles; menus €14.50-21; ⊙noon-1.30pm & 7-9.30pm Tue-Sat, 11.30am-1.30pm Sun; ☑♦) A 10-minute amble east of central Troyes, on the banks of the Seine, this artsy, family-friendly cafe brims with books, board games, art and mismatched furniture. Come for the relaxed boho vibe, great coffee and homemade cake, Sunday brunch (€20), great-value, season-driven *menus* (plenty of choice for vegetarians), and chilled music. Look out for the odd gig at weekends.

ⓘ CITY PASS

Le Pass' Troyes (€15), sold at the tourist offices, gets you free entry to five of the big museums, chocolate tasting, an old-city tour (with a guide or audioguide) and discounts at various factory outlet shops.

★ Le Valentino   FRENCH €€
(☑03 25 73 14 14; http://levalentino.com; 35 rue Paillot de Montabert; menus €28-58; ⊙noon-1.30pm & 7.30-9.30pm Tue-Sat) What could be more romantic than a *table à deux* in the cobbled courtyard of this rose-hued, 17th-century modern French restaurant? The chef juggles flavours skilfully in market-driven specialities such as roasted monkfish with pak choi, ginger and pink pepper, and quail with red grape jelly and pear chutney.

Ô des Lys   FRENCH €€
(☑03 25 41 11 09; www.restaurant-odeslys.com; 14 rue de Turenne; 2-/3-course lunches €14/17, dinner menus €29.50-39.50; ⊙noon-1.30pm Tue & Sun, noon-1.30pm & 7-9pm Thu-Sat) A talented husband–wife team shakes the pans at this sweet, bistro in the heart of historic Troyes. Classic French home cooking with a pinch of love is brought to tightly packed tables – with starters like escargots with parsnip cream preluding mains like pollack fillet in a herb crust with Champagne sauce and desserts like *tarte tatin* (upside-down caramelised apple pie).

🍷 Drinking & Nightlife

The hum of chatter fills the open-air bars and cafes around rue Champeaux and half-timbered place Alexandre Israël on warm evenings.

Chez Gus   CAFE
(29 rue Molé; ⊙10am-7pm Mon-Sat) Riding the new wave of retro-style coffee shops, vintage-cool Chez Gus is one of the hippest hang-outs in town for an espresso, smoothie, speciality tea or snacks from sandwiches to pancakes, waffles and croque monsieur. It's a nicely chilled spot to while away an hour or so, with a book exchange and board games.

Chez Philippe   WINE BAR
(www.bullesetdouceurs.com; 11 rue Champeaux; ⊙5pm-1.30am Tue-Sat, 6-10pm Sun) This is one of the chicest Champagne bars in town, with its lilac walls, cosy living-room feel and quirky scattering of vintage furniture. Black-and-white photos of the 10 vignerons (winegrowers) who supply Champagne from the Côte des Bar region adorn the walls, and the terrace is humming on warm evenings.

Dixi Café   BAR
(12 rue Pithou; ⊙5pm-midnight Sun-Tue, to 1.30am Wed-Sat) A convivial neighbourhood bar that draws an arty crowd, including students. The house speciality is *rhum arrangé*. Has live music – rock, reggae, jazz, French *chansons* – on weekends from about 10pm.

ℹ️ Information

Tourist Office (☑ 03 25 82 62 70; www.
tourisme-troyes.com; 16 rue Aristide Briand;
⊙ 9.30am-6.30pm Mon-Sat, 10am-1pm & 2-6pm
Sun May-Oct, 9.30am-12.30pm & 2-6pm Mon-
Sat Nov-Apr; 🛜) Free wi-fi.

ℹ️ Getting There & Away

BUS

The best way to get to Reims (€15, 2¼ hours, up
to 13 daily), without a change in Paris, is taking
bus line 140 with Courriers de l'Aube (www.cour-
riersdelaube.fr). Departures are from the very
last bus berth to the right as you approach the
train station; a schedule is posted. The **bus station office** (☑ 03 25 71 28 42; ⊙ 8.30am-noon &
2-6.30pm Mon-Fri) is in the train station.

TRAIN

Troyes is on the rather isolated train line that links
Mulhouse (€56 to €115, four to six hours, 13 daily)
in Alsace with Paris Gare de l'Est (€11 to €28, 1½
hours, 10 to 14 daily). To get to Dijon (€25 to €35,
two to four hours), change in Culmont or St-Flor-
entin-Vergigny.

CÔTE DES BAR CHAMPAGNE ROUTE

The 220km Côte des Bar Champagne Route
does curlicues and loop-the-loops through
austere fields, neat vineyards and forestland
in an area 30km to 50km east and southeast
of Troyes. Great for a deliciously leisurely
drive, it passes through stone-built villages
that are bedecked with flowers in the spring.

If you're in the Côte des Bar on the last
weekend in July, you're in luck, as this is
when the region hosts the **Route du Champagne en Fête** (www.routeduchampagne.com;
⊙ late Jul). A celebratory flute, costing €25 and
sold at local tourist offices, is your ticket to
free tastings at the *caves ouvertes* (open cellars) of more than 20 top Champagne houses.

Colombey-les-Deux-Églises

POP 729

Charles de Gaulle lived in this village from
1934 – except, obviously, during WWII – until his death in 1970. It is named after two
historic *églises* (churches), one a parish
church, the other a Cluniac priory.

The hill just north of town (on D619) is
crowned by a 43.5m-high **Croix de Lorraine**
(Lorraine Cross), erected in 1972, the symbol
of France's WWII Resistance.

🔘 Sights

Mémorial Charles de Gaulle   MEMORIAL
(http://memorial-charlesdegaulle.fr; adult/child
€13.50/8; ⊙ 9.30am-7pm May-Sep, 10am-5.30pm
Wed-Mon Oct-Apr) The impressive Mémorial
Charles de Gaulle presents graphic, easily di-
gestible exhibits, rich in photos, which form
an admiring biography of France's greatest
modern statesman. Displays help visitors
untangle such complicated mid-20th-
century events as the Algerian war and the
creation of the Fifth Republic, and consider
the ways in which De Gaulle's years in power
(1958–69) affected French culture, style and
economic growth. Audioguides are available. The site affords breathtaking, sublime
views of the Haute-Marne countryside.

La Boisserie   MUSEUM
(www.charles-de-gaulle.org; adult/child €5.50/4;
⊙ 10am-1pm & 2-6.30pm Apr-Sep, 10am-12.30pm
& 2-5.30pm Wed-Mon Oct-Mar) People flock by
the coach-load to visit Charles de Gaulle's
vine-swathed home, La Boisserie, its elegant
antique furnishings unchanged since he was
laid to rest in the village-centre *cimetière*
(graveyard). Tours (English brochure available; price included in admission) begin at
the ticket office, situated across D23 from
the house, on the Colombey's southern edge.

🛏️ Sleeping

Hostellerie La Montagne   BOUTIQUE HOTEL €€
(☑ 03 25 01 51 69; www.hostellerielamontagne.com;
10 rue de Pisseloup; d €105-170) This boutique
guesthouse exudes vintage-chic charm and
offers quirky designer twists in its individually decorated rooms, some of which sport
free-standing bath-tubs for a lingering soak.
The big deal here, however, is its double act
of excellent restaurants (*menus* €28 to €100),
playing up winningly fresh seasonal produce
– among them a Michelin-starred number
with Jean-Baptiste Natali at the helm.

ℹ️ Information

Tourist Information Point (☑ 03 25 03 12 42;
http://colombey-les-deux-eglises.com; 10 place
de l'Église; ⊙ 9.30am-12.30pm & 2.30-6pm
Thu-Mon)

Essoyes

POP 741

It's easy to see why Renoir loved Essoyes, so
much that he spent his last 25 summers here:
it's one of the area's comeliest villages, with

WORTH A TRIP

AN ABBEY DETOUR

Bernard de Clairvaux (1090–1153), nemesis of Abelard and preacher of the Second Crusade, founded this hugely influential Cistercian monastery **Abbaye de Clairvaux Monastery** (www.abbayedeclairvaux.com; Clairvaux; adult/child €8.50/free; ☉ tours 10.30am, 2pm & 4.30pm Mon & Tue, 10.30am, 11.45am, 1.30pm, 2pm, 3pm, 4pm & 5pm Wed-Sun Jul-early Sep, shorter hours rest of year) in 1115. Since Napoléon's time, the complex has served as one of France's highest-security prisons. Several historic abbey buildings are open to the public. Tours take in 12th-century structures, built in the austere Cistercian tradition, but more interesting is the 18th-century **Grand Cloître**, where you can see collective 'chicken coop' cells (from the 1800s) and individual cells (used until 1971).

Past 'guests' have included Carlos the Jackal; two prisoners who staged a revolt here in 1971 were guillotined. For security reasons, visitors need to bring ID, mobile phones must be switched off and photography is prohibited. The abbey is on D396, 8km south of Bayel and 6km north of A5 exit 23.

neat stone houses, a riverfront that glows golden in the late afternoon sun and landscapes of vineyards and flower-flecked meadows that unfold in an almost artistic way.

◎ Sights & Activities

Espace des Renoir   MUSEUM
(Renoir Centre; www.renoir-essoyes.fr; 9 place de la Mairie; adult/child incl Atelier Renoir €14/7; ☉ 10am-12.30pm & 1.30-6pm Wed-Sun Jun-Aug, shorter hours rest of year) The Renoir trail in Essoyes begins at the Espace des Renoir, which also houses the tourist office. The centre screens a 15-minute film about the artist and displays temporary exhibitions of mostly contemporary art.

Atelier Renoir   HISTORIC BUILDING
(Renoir's Studio; www.renoir-essoyes.fr; 9 place de la Mairie; adult/child incl Espace des Renoir €14/7; ☉ 10am-12.30pm & 1.30-6pm Wed-Sun Jun-Aug, shorter hours rest of year) The Atelier Renoir has displays zooming in on the hallmarks of Renoir's work (the female form, the vibrant use of colour and light), alongside original pieces such as his antiquated wheelchair and the box he used to carry his paintings to Paris. Perhaps loveliest of all is the studio garden, particularly in spring to early summer when it bursts forth with tulips, anemones and roses.

Circuit Découverte   WALKING
You can slip into the shoes of great impressionist Renoir on Essoyes' standout *circuit découverte,* a marked trail that loops around the village, taking in viewpoints that inspired the artist, the family home and the cemetery where he lies buried, his grave marked by a contemplative bronze bust. The trail begins at the Espace des Renoir.

🛏 Sleeping & Eating

Les Demoiselles   HOTEL €
(☎ 03 25 29 08 59; https://les-demoiselles-essoyes. com; 1 rue Pierre-Renoir; d €78-95, tr €98, q €108; ☎🖳) The pick of the places to stay in Essoyes is this hotel, whose sleekly modern rooms in muted colours have tea- and coffee-making facilities. In summer there's a pleasant terrace and an outdoor pool. Its **restaurant** (menus €18-45, mains €18; ☉ 12.15-1.30pm & 7-9pm; 🍴) also happens to be the best in town.

❶ Information

Tourist office (☎ 03 25 29 21 27; www.ot-essoyes.fr; Espace des Renoir, 9 place de la Mairie; ☉ 9am-12.30pm & 1.30-5.30pm, closed Sat & Sun Oct-May)

Les Riceys

POP 1376

Running along both banks of the picturesque River Laigne, the commune of Les Riceys consists of three adjacent villages (Ricey-Bas, Ricey-Haute-Rive and Ricey-Haut). The commune is famous for its three churches, and for growing grapes belonging to three different Appellation d'Origine Contrôlée (AOC) wines. Its best-known product is rosé des Riceys, an exclusive pinot noir rosé that can be made only in particularly sunny years and was a special favourite of Louis XIV. Annual production of this – when there is any – hovers around 65,000 bottles. Lots of Champagne wineries are nestled along and near D70.

For more information, including details on walking circuits through vine and vale, contact the **tourist office** (☎ 03 25 29 15 38; www. tourisme-cotedesbar.com; 14 place des Héros de la Résistance, Ricey-Haut; ☉ 9am-5pm Mon, Tue, Thu & Fri).

Alsace & Lorraine

POP 4.2 MILLION

Best Places to Eat

➡ L'Imaginarium (p383)

➡ Chez Auguste (p373)

➡ Winstub S'Kaechele (p353)

➡ La Fourchette des Ducs (p357)

➡ Auberge du Parc Carola (p363)

Best Places to Stay

➡ Villa Élyane (p367)

➡ Hôtel d'Haussonville (p377)

➡ Cour du Corbeau (p352)

➡ La Villa Haute Corniche (p356)

➡ Hôtel de la Cathédrale (p381)

Why Go?

Alsace is a cultural one-off. With its Germanic dialect and French sense of fashion, love of foie gras and *choucroute* (sauerkraut), fine wine *and* beer, this region often leaves you wondering quite where you are. Where are you? Why, in the land of living fairy tales, of course, where vineyards fade into watercolour distance, hilltop castles send spirits soaring higher than the region's emblematic storks and half-timbered villages garlanded with geraniums look fresh-minted for a Disney film set.

Lorraine has high culture and effortless grace thanks to its historic roll call of dukes and art-nouveau pioneers, who had an eye for grand designs and good living. The art and architecture in blessedly underrated cities like Nancy and Metz leave visitors spellbound, while the region's WWI battlefields render visitors speechless time and again with their painful beauty.

When to Go
Strasbourg

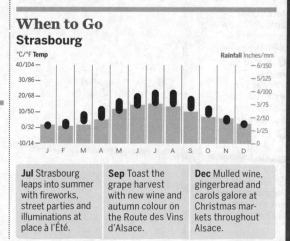

Jul Strasbourg leaps into summer with fireworks, street parties and illuminations at place à l'Été.

Sep Toast the grape harvest with new wine and autumn colour on the Route des Vins d'Alsace.

Dec Mulled wine, gingerbread and carols galore at Christmas markets throughout Alsace.

Alsace & Lorraine Highlights

1 **Petite Venise** (p366) Wandering this canal-laced neighbourhood of Colmar.

2 **Cathédrale Notre-Dame** (p348) Getting a gargoyle's-eye view of Strasbourg from its colossal Gothic cathedral.

3 **Verdun Battlefields** (p384) Surveying the cross-studded landscape in the early morning.

4 **Musée de l'École de Nancy** (p374) Appreciating art-nouveau grace at this prominent French exponent.

5 **Château du Haut Kœnigsbourg** (p362) Peering across the vines from the hilltop perch of this medieval castle.

6 **Hunawihr** (p364) Wishing for luck (or bountiful babies) spotting storks at this sanctuary.

7 **Centre Pompidou-Metz** (p380) Contemplating avant-garde art at this innovative gallery.

8 **Massif des Vosges** (p371) Diverging from the beaten track to forgotten villages and misty, forested hills.

9 **Vallée de Munster** (p371) Dairy-hopping this cheese-mad valley.

10 **Riquewihr** (p364) Going for a lantern-lit dusk stroll in lanes ripe for a bedtime story.

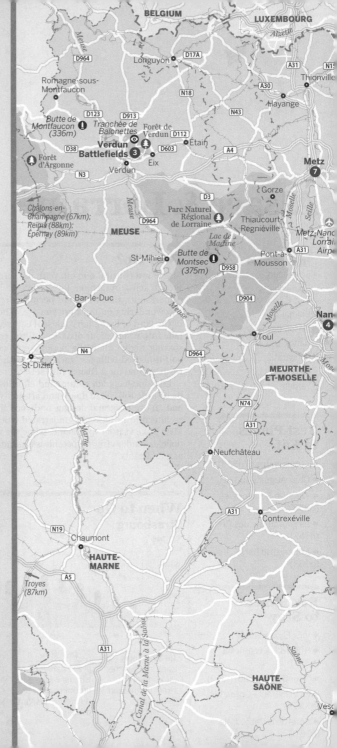

ALSACE

Ask the French what they think of Alsace and watch them grow misty-eyed with nostalgia and affection for this most idiosyncratic of regions, which borders Switzerland to the south and Germany to the east. So hard to nail in terms of its character, it proudly guards its own distinct identity, language, cuisine, history and architecture – part French, part German, 100% Alsatian. Here the candy-coloured towns and villages look as though they've popped up from a children's bedtime story, the gently rolling countryside, striped with vines, is nothing short of idyllic, and everywhere locals swear by centuries-old traditions.

Strasbourg

POP 276,170

Strasbourg is the perfect overture to all that is idiosyncratic about Alsace – walking a fine tightrope between France and Germany and between a medieval past and a progressive future, it pulls off its act in inimitable Alsatian style.

Tear your gaze away from that mesmerising Gothic cathedral for just a minute and you'll be roaming the old town's twisting alleys lined with crooked half-timbered houses à la Grimm; feasting in the cosiest of *winstubs* (Alsatian taverns) by the canals in Petite France; and marvelling at how a city that does Christmas markets and gingerbread so well can also be home to the glittering EU Quarter and France's second-largest student population. But that's Strasbourg for you: all the sweeter for its contradictions and cross-cultural quirks.

◉ Sights

Take a DIY spin of Strasbourg's cathedral and the old city with one of the tourist office's (p355) 1½-hour audioguides (adult/child €5.50/2.75), available in five languages.

★ **Cathédrale Notre-Dame**   CATHEDRAL
(www.cathedrale-strasbourg.fr; place de la Cathédrale; adult/child astronomical clock €3/2, platform €5/3; ⏰ 9.30-11.15am & 2-5.45pm, astronomical clock noon-12.45pm, platform 9am-7.15pm; 🚊 Grand'Rue) Nothing prepares you for your first glimpse of Strasbourg's Cathédrale Notre-Dame, completed in all its Gothic grandeur in 1439. The lace-fine façade lifts the gaze little by little to flying buttresses, leering gargoyles and a 142m spire. The interior is exquisitely lit by 12th- to 14th-century **stained-glass windows**, including the western portal's jewel-like rose window. The Gothic-meets-Renaissance **astronomical clock** strikes solar noon at 12.30pm with a parade of figures portraying the different stages of life and Jesus with his apostles.

★ **Grande Île**   HISTORIC SITE
(🚊 Grand'Rue) History seeps through the twisting lanes and cafe-rimmed plazas of Grande Île, Strasbourg's Unesco World Heritage–listed island bordered by the River Ill. These streets – with their photogenic line-up of wonky, timber-framed houses in sherbet colours – are made for aimless ambling. They cower beneath the soaring magnificence of the cathedral and its sidekick, the gingerbready 15th-century **Maison Kammerzell** (rue des Hallebardes; 🚊 Grand'Rue), with its ornate carvings and leaded windows. The alleys are at their most atmospheric when lantern-lit at night.

★ **Palais Rohan**   HISTORIC BUILDING
(2 place du Château; adult/child per museum €6.50/free, all 3 museums €12/free; ⏰ 10am-6pm Wed-Mon; 🚊 Grand'Rue) Hailed as a 'Versailles in miniature', this opulent 18th-century residence is loaded with treasures. The basement **Musée Archéologique** takes you from the Palaeolithic period to AD 800. On the ground floor is the **Musée des Arts Décoratifs**, where rooms adorned with Hannong ceramics and gleaming silverware evoke the lavish lifestyle of the nobility in the 18th century. On the 1st floor, the **Musée des Beaux-Arts'** collection of 14th- to 19th-century art includes El Greco, Botticelli and Flemish Primitive works.

Petite France   AREA
(🚊 Grand'Rue) Criss-crossed by narrow lanes, canals and locks, Petite France is where artisans plied their trades in the Middle Ages. The half-timbered houses, sprouting veritable thickets of scarlet geraniums in summer, and the riverside parks attract the masses, but the area still manages to retain its Alsatian charm, especially in the early morning and late evening. Drink in views of the River Ill and the **Barrage Vauban** (Vauban Dam; ⏰ viewing terrace 7.15am-9pm, shorter hours winter; 🚊 Faubourg National) FREE from the much-photographed **Ponts Couverts** (Covered Bridges; 🚊 Musée d'Art Moderne) and their trio of 13th-century towers.

DON'T MISS

EU ENCOUNTERS

Should the inner workings of the EU intrigue you, you can sit in on debates ranging from lively to yawn-a-minute at the **Parlement Européen** (European Parliament; www.europarl.europa.eu; rue Lucien Fèbvre; 🚊 Parlement Européen); dates are available from the tourist office or on the website. For individuals it's first come, first served (bring ID).

A futuristic glass crescent, the Council of Europe's **Palais de l'Europe** (Palace of Europe; 📞 03 88 41 20 29; www.coe.int; av de l'Europe; 🚊 Droits de l'Homme) across the River Ill can be visited on free one-hour weekday tours; phone ahead for times and reservations.

It's just a hop across the Canal de la Marne to the swirly silver **Palais des Droits de l'Homme** (European Court of Human Rights; www.echr.coe.int; Allée des Droits de l'Homme; 🚊 Droits de l'Homme), the most eye-catching of all the EU institutions.

The EU buildings sit 2km northeast of Grande Île (central Strasbourg), close to Parc de l'Orangerie (p351), a flowery park designed in the 17th century by Le Nôtre of Versailles fame. A family magnet with its playgrounds and swan-dotted lake, it's also the spot to rent row boats on Lac de l'Orangerie in summer. Take tram line E to the Droits de l'Homme stop.

Musée d'Art Moderne et Contemporain
GALLERY

(MAMCS; www.musees.strasbourg.eu; 1 place Hans Jean Arp; adult/child €10/free; ⏱ 10am-6pm Tue-Sun; 🚊 Musée d'Art Moderne) This striking glass-and-steel cube showcases an outstanding fine-art, graphic-art and photography collection. Besides modern and contemporary works of the Kandinsky, Picasso, Magritte, Monet and Rodin ilk, you'll encounter pieces by Strasbourg-born artists, including the curvaceous creations of Hans Jean Arp and the evocative 19th-century works of Gustave Doré. The 1st-floor **Art Café** is graced by bold frescoes by Japanese artist Aki Kuroda and has a terrace overlooking the River Ill and Petite France.

Musée de l'Œuvre Notre-Dame
MUSEUM

(www.musees.strasbourg.eu; 3 place du Château; adult/child €6.50/free; ⏱ 10am-6pm Tue-Sun; 🚊 Grand'Rue) Occupying a cluster of sublime 14th- and 16th-century buildings, this museum harbours one of Europe's premier collections of Romanesque, Gothic and Renaissance sculpture (including many originals from the cathedral), plus 15th-century paintings and stained glass. *Christ de Wissembourg* (c 1060) is the oldest work of stained glass in France.

Grande Mosquée de Strasbourg
MOSQUE

(Strasbourg Grand Mosque; 6 rue Averroès; 🚊 Laiterie) Designed by Italian architect Paolo Portoghesi and opened in September 2012, France's biggest mosque (accommodating 1500 worshippers) sits on a bend in the River Ill and is topped by a copper dome and flanked by wings resembling a flower in bud. More than just another landmark, it took 20 years of political to-ing and fro-ing for this project to come to fruition and its completion is considered the beginning of a new era for Muslims and religious tolerance in France.

Musée Alsacien
MUSEUM

(www.musees.strasbourg.eu; 23 quai St-Nicolas; adult/child €6.50/free; ⏱ 10am-6pm Wed-Mon; 🚊 Porte de l'Hôpital) Spread across three typical houses from the 1500s and 1600s, with creaky floors and beautifully restored wood-panelled interiors, this museum dips into rural Alsatian life over the centuries. Costumes, toys, ceramics, folk art, furniture and even a tiny 18th-century synagogue are on display in the museum's two dozen rooms.

Musée Historique
MUSEUM

(www.musees.strasbourg.eu; 2 rue du Vieux Marché aux Poissons; adult/child €6.50/free; ⏱ 10am-6pm Tue-Sun; 🚊 Grand'Rue) Trace Strasbourg's history from its beginnings as a Roman military camp called Argentoratum at this engaging museum, housed in a 16th-century slaughterhouse. Highlights include a painting of the first-ever performance of 'La Marseillaise', France's national anthem (which, despite its name, was written in Strasbourg in 1792); a 1:600-scale model, created in the 1720s to help Louis XV visualise the city's fortifications; and a Gutenberg Bible from 1485.

River Ill
WATERFRONT

(🚊 Grand'Rue) The leafy paths that shadow the River Ill and its canalised branch, the Fossé du Faux-Rempart, are great for an impromptu picnic or a romantic stroll.

Strasbourg

ALSACE & LORRAINE STRASBOURG

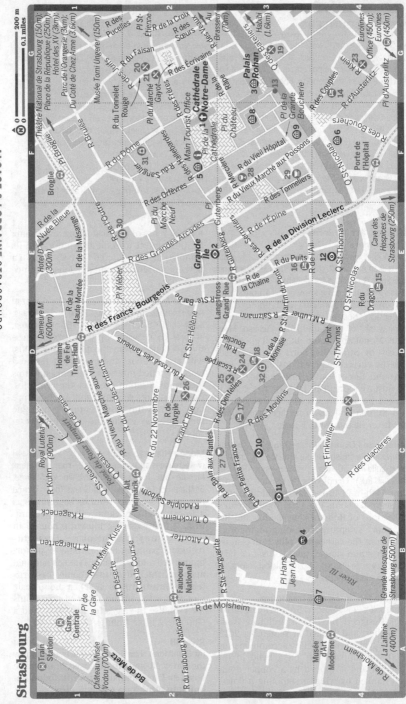

Scale: 0–200 m / 0–0.1 miles

Map labels include:

Train Station, Gare Centrale, Pl de la Gare, Château Musée Vodou (700m), Bd de Metz, R Kuhn, Royal Lutetia (900m), R Thiergarten, R du Maire Kuss, R Déserte, R de la Course, Faubourg National, R du Faubourg National, R de Molsheim, R Ste-Marguerite, Pl Hans Jean Arp, Musée d'Art Moderne, La Laiterie (400m), R de Moisheim, Grande Mosquée de Strasbourg (500m), River III, R des Glacières, R Finkwiller, Pont St-Thomas, Q St-Nicolas, Cave des Hospices de Strasbourg (250m), Porte de l'Hôpital, R des Bouchers, Pl d'Austerlitz, Eurolines (450m); Office (450m); Eurolines (450m), Pl d'Austerlitz, R Klein, R d'Austerlitz, R des Couples, R de la Grande Boucherie, Pl de la Grande Boucherie, Palais Rohan, Habibi (1.6km), Q des Bateliers, Q des Pêcheurs, Au Vieux Strasbourg, R Brasseur (70m), R des Soeurs, R de la Croix, Pl St-Étienne, R des Pucelles, Théâtre National de Strasbourg (150m); Place de la République (250m); Hôtel des XV (3km); Parc de l'Orangerie (3km); Du Côté de Chez Anne (3.6km), R du Faisan, Pl du Marché Gayot, R du Marché Rouge, R des Écrivains, Cathédrale Notre-Dame, Musée Tomi Ungerer (150m), R du Tonnelet Rouge, Pl du Faisan, R des Frères, R des Juifs, R Brûlée, R du Dôme, Broglie, Pl Broglie, R de la Nuée Bleue, Hotel D (300m), R de l'Outre, R de la Mésange, Pl du Marché Neuf, R des Grandes Arcades, R des Orfèvres, R des Hallebardes, R du Sanglier, Main Tourist Office, Pl de la Cathédrale, R Mercière, R du Vieil Hôpital, R du Château, Pl du Château, Pl de la Grande Boucherie, R de la Râpe, R du Vieux Marché aux Poissons, R des Tonneliers, Grande Île, R Gutenberg, R des Serruriers, R de l'Épine, R de la Division Leclerc, R du Puits, R du Puits, Q St-Thomas, R du Vieux Marché aux Vins, R du 22 Novembre, R des Francs-Bourgeois, R Kléber, Pl Kléber, R de la Haute Montée, Demeure M (600m), Homme de Fer Tram Hub, Grand Rue, Langstross Grand Rue, R Ste-Barbe, R Ste-Hélène, R de la Chaîne, R Salzmann, R St-Martin du Pont, R de la Monnaie, R M Luther, Pont St-Thomas, R des Dentelles, R de l'Escarpée, R du Bouclier, R de l'Argile, R des Moulins, R du Bain aux Plantes, R du Bain aux Plantes, Q de la Petite France, R du Fossé des Tanneurs, Q Desaix, Q St-Jean, Q Kellermann, Q Turckheim, Q Altorffer, Q Adolphe Seyboth, Alt Winmärik, R Kageneck, R du Dragon, R St-Nicolas

Château Musée Vodou (700m)

Strasbourg

Cave des Hospices de Strasbourg WINERY
(www.vins-des-hospices-de-strasbourg.fr; 1 place
de l'Hôpital; ◎8.30am-noon & 1.30-5.30pm Mon-
Fri, 9am-12.30pm Sat; ◎Porte de l'Hôpital) FREE
Founded in 1395, this brick-vaulted wine
cellar nestles deep in the bowels of Strasbourg's hospital. A hospice back in the days
when wine was considered a cure for all
ills, today the cellar bottles first-rate Alsatian wines from rieslings to sweet muscats.
One of its historic barrels is filled with a

1472 vintage. Take tram A or D to Porte de
l'Hôpital. From here it is a three-minute
walk south on rue d'Or.

Le Vaisseau MUSEUM
(www.levaisseau.com; 1bis rue Philippe Dollinger;
adult/child €8/7; ◎10am-6pm Tue-Sun; ◎Win-
ston Churchill) Science is *never* boring at this
interactive science and technology museum, 2.5km southeast of central Strasbourg.
There are plenty of hands-on activities to
amuse little minds, from crawling through
an ant colony to creating cartoons and
broadcasting the news. Take tram line B, C
or F to the Winston Churchill stop.

Jardin des Deux Rives GARDENS
(Two-Shores Garden; ◎9am-7pm; ◎Aristide
Briand) An expression of flourishing Franco-German friendship, Strasbourg and its
German neighbour Kehl have turned former
customs posts and military installations
into this 60-hectare garden, whose play areas, promenades and parkland straddle the
Rhine. The centrepiece is Marc Mimram's
sleek (and hugely expensive) **suspension
bridge**, which has proved a big hit with pedestrians and cyclists. From the tram stop,
walk east or take bus 21 for three stops.
It is 3km southeast of central Strasbourg
(Grande Île).

◉ Neustadt

Place de la République SQUARE
(◎République) Many of Strasbourg's grandest public buildings, constructed when the
city was ruled by the German Reich, huddle
northeast of the Grande Île area in the so-
called imperial quarter of Neustadt, part
of the city's Unesco World Heritage status
since 2017. The neighbourhood centres on
this stately square, bounded by the **Théâtre National de Strasbourg** (TNS; ◎03 88
24 88 24; www.tns.fr; 1 av de la Marseillaise; ◎box
office 1-7pm Mon-Sat; ◎République). It stretches
eastwards to **Parc de l'Orangerie** (◎Droits
de l'Homme) and is dominated by sturdy
neo-Renaissance buildings inspired by
late-19th-century Prussian tastes.

Musée Tomi Ungerer MUSEUM
(www.musees.strasbourg.eu; 2 av de la Marseillaise;
adult/child €6.50/free; ◎10am-6pm Wed-Mon;
◎République) A tribute to one of Strasbourg's
most famous sons – award-winning illustrator and cartoonist Tomi Ungerer – this museum, just northeast of Grande Île, is housed
in the fetching Villa Greiner. The collection

discloses the artist's love of dabbling in many genres, from children's-book illustrations to satirical drawings and erotica.

👉 Tours

Batorama
BOATING

(www.batorama.fr; rue de Rohan; adult/child €13/7.50; ⏱ tours half-hourly 9.45am-9.15pm, shorter hours winter; 🚊 Grand'Rue) This outfit runs scenic 70-minute boat trips, which glide along the storybook canals of Petite France, taking in the Barrage Vauban (p348) and the glinting EU institutions. Tours depart from rue de Rohan, the quay behind Palais Rohan (p348).

🎊 Festivals & Events

Marché de Noël
CHRISTMAS

(Christmas Market; www.noel.strasbourg.eu; ⏱ last Sat Nov-31 Dec) Mulled wine, spicy *bredele* (biscuits) and a Santa-loaded children's village are all part and parcel of Strasbourg's sparkly Marché de Noël.

🛏 Sleeping

It can be tricky to find last-minute accommodation from Monday to Thursday when the European Parliament is in plenary session (see www.europarl.europa.eu for dates). Book ahead for December, when beds are at a premium because of the Christmas market. The tourist office (p355) can advise about same-night room availability; if you drop by, staff are happy to help reserve a room.

Hôtel Patricia
HOTEL €

(☏ 03 88 32 14 60; www.hotelpatricia.fr; 1 rue du Puits; s €41, d €55-67, tr €62-75; 🛜; 🚊 Grand'Rue) The high-ceilinged, wood-floored rooms here are nothing fancy and the cheaper rooms have shared bathrooms, but you can't beat Hôtel Patricia for value. And given how central it is, this big, rambling townhouse bang in the heart of Grande Île (p348) is surprisingly quiet.

⭐ Cour du Corbeau
BOUTIQUE HOTEL €€

(☏ 03 90 00 26 26; www.cour-corbeau.com; 6-8 rue des Couples; r €157-275, ste €220-260; ❄🛜; 🚊 Porte de l'Hôpital) A 16th-century inn lovingly converted into a boutique hotel, Cour du Corbeau wins you over with its half-timbered charm and its location, just steps from the river. Gathered around a courtyard, rooms blend original touches such as oak parquet and Louis XV furnishings with mod cons including flat-screen TVs.

Hotel des XV
BOUTIQUE HOTEL €€

(☏ 03 88 79 76 10; www.hoteldesxv.com; 46 rue du Conseil des Quinze; d €160-220, breakfast €19; 🅿🛜; 🚊 Conseil des Quinze) Housed in a beautifully revamped villa near Parc de l'Orangerie (p351), boutiquey Hotel des XV is a chic number. Monochrome interiors, geometric prints and art-deco-style furnishings are enlivened with bursts of teal or mustard, and swish yet understated rooms come with little luxuries like Nespresso makers and robes. Breakfast is great, with fresh pastries and fruit, and eggs to order.

Hôtel du Dragon
HOTEL €€

(☏ 03 88 35 79 80; www.dragon.fr; 12 rue du Dragon; r €80-154; @🛜❄; 🚊 Porte de l'Hôpital) Step through a tree-shaded courtyard and into the, ahhh…blissful calm of this bijou hotel. The Dragon receives glowing reviews for its crisp interiors, attentive service and prime location near Petite France (p348).

Du Coté de Chez Anne
BOUTIQUE HOTEL €€

(☏ 03 88 41 80 77; www.du-cote-de-chez-anne. com; 4 rue de la Carpe Haute; d €165-185; 🅿🛜; 🚊 Robertsau Boecklin) A dash of boutique style on Strasbourg's leafy northeastern fringes, this half-timbered farmhouse sits in flower-strewn gardens and conceals gorgeous rooms designed with the utmost grace and beautiful fabrics – from summery florals to gilded glamour. Some rooms have romantic touches like freestanding bathtubs. Take tram E from place de la République to Robertsau Boecklin, a seven-minute walk away.

Hotel D
BOUTIQUE HOTEL €€

(☏ 03 88 15 13 67; www.hoteld.fr; 15 rue du Fossé des Treize; d €129-224, ste €219-359; 🅿❄🛜; 🚊 République) Splashes of bold colour and daring design have transformed this townhouse into a nouveau-chic boutique hotel. The slick, spacious rooms are dressed in soothing tones and no comfort stone has been left unturned – you'll find robes, Nespresso machines and iPod docks even in the standard ones. A fitness room and sauna invite relaxation.

Le Bouclier d'Or
BOUTIQUE HOTEL €€€

(☏ 03 88 13 73 55; www.leboucllierdor.com; 1 rue du Bouclier; d €200-350; ❄🛜; 🚊 Grand'Rue) This bijou family-run hotel nestles in a gorgeously restored 16th-century building in Petite France (p348). It has been decorated with lots of loving care – whether you opt for an ever-so-snug 'Alsatian' room with beams and warm colours, or a grand, chandelier-lit 'bourgeoise' room furnished with antiques. After a day pounding the cobbles, your feet will be grateful for the spa.

Hôtel Régent Petite France DESIGN HOTEL €€€
(☑ 03 88 76 43 43; www.regent-hotels.com; 5 rue des Moulins; r €170-300; ✳ @ 🛜; 🚋 Alt Winmärik) Once an ice factory and now Strasbourg's hottest design hotel, this waterfront pile is quaint on the outside and ubercool on the inside. The sleek rooms, dressed in muted colours and plush fabrics, sport shiny marble bathrooms. Work your relaxed look in the sauna, chic restaurant and Champagne bar with dreamy river views.

🍴 Eating

Restaurants abound on Grande Île: try canalside Petite France for Alsatian fare and half-timbered romance; Grand'Rue for curbside kebabs and *tarte flambée* (thin Alsatian-style pizza topped with crème fraîche, onions and lardons); and rue des Veaux or rue des Pucelles for hole-in-the-wall eateries serving the world on a plate. Stepping across the river, pedestrianised rue d'Austerlitz is lined with patisseries and bistros.

Chez Victor FAST FOOD €
(☑ 09 82 48 56 88; 19 rue des Frères; ⊘ 11am-3pm Mon, 11am-3pm & 6-9pm Tue-Fri, 11.30am-4.30pm Sat; ☑; 🚋 Broglie) Victor is almost single-handedly reinventing fast food in this corner of Strasbourg, with his wholesome tartines (open sandwiches), salads and soups, which he prepares fresh with your fillings of choice

right before your eyes in his open-plan kitchen. And all for pocket-money prices.

Winstub S'Kaechele FRENCH €
(☑ 03 88 22 62 36; www.skaechele.fr; 8 rue de l'Argile; mains €12.50-18.50; ⊘ 7-9.30pm Mon, 11.45am-1.30pm & 7-9.30pm Tue-Fri; 🚋 Grand'Rue) Traditional French and Alsatian grub doesn't come more authentic than at this snug, amiable *winstub* (wine tavern), run with love by couple Karine and Daniel. Cue wonderfully cosy evenings spent in stone-walled, lamp-lit, wood-beamed surrounds, huddled over dishes such as escargots oozing Roquefort, fat pork knuckles braised in pinot noir, and *choucroute garnie* (sauerkraut garnished with meats).

Binchstub ALSATIAN €
(☑ 03 88 13 47 73; www.binchstub.fr; 6 rue du Tonnelet Rouge; tarte flambée €10-15; ⊘ 6.30pm-1am; 🚋 Broglie) Cooked to thin, crisp perfection, the *Flammekueche (tarte flambée)* at Binchstub is in a league of its own. Locally sourced farm ingredients go into toppings such as goat's cheese, thyme and honey, and Bleu d'Auvergne cheese with pear and rocket.

Perles de Saveurs FRENCH €€
(☑ 03 88 22 19 81; www.perlesdesaveurs.fr; 9 rue des Dentelles; mains €18.50-23, menus €28-37; ⊘ noon-2pm & 7-10pm Tue-Sat; 🚋 Grand'Rue) Tucked away in a Petite France (p348) courtyard, this cheerful restaurant is vibrantly graced with the comical paintings of local artists Elisa and Marie-Hélène. Clean, snappy flavours dominate the modern French menu, along

---

PASS THE CHOCOLATE

Strasbourg is now sweeter than ever, as it's one of the main stops on **La Route du Chocolat et des Douceurs d'Alsac** (Alsace Chocolate and Sweets Road), stretching 80km north to Bad Bergzabern and 125km south to Heimsbrunn near Mulhouse. Pick up a map at the tourist office (p355) to pinpoint Alsace's finest patisseries, chocolateries, macaron shops and confectioners. The following are three sweet Strasbourg favourites to get you started:

Mireille Oster (www.mireille-oster.com; 14 rue des Dentelles; ⊘ 10am-7pm Mon & Sun, 9am-7pm Tue-Sat; 🚋 Grand'Rue) Cherubs adorn this heavenly shop where Strasbourg's *pain d'épices* (gingerbread) fairy Mireille Oster tempts with handmade varieties featuring figs, amaretto, cinnamon and chocolate. Have a nibble before you buy.

Christian (www.christian.fr; 12 rue de l'Outre; ⊘ 7am-6.30pm Mon-Sat; 🚋 Broglie) Sumptuous truffles and pralines, weightless macarons and edible Strasbourg landmarks – renowned chocolatier Christian's creations are mini works of art.

Maison Alsacienne de Biscuiterie (www.maison-alsacienne-biscuiterie.com; 16 rue du Dôme; ⊘ 10am-7pm Mon, 9am-7pm Tue-Sat, 10am-6pm Sun; 🚋 Broglie) Bakes scrumptious Alsatian gingerbread, macarons, raisin-stuffed *kougelhopf* and *sablés* (butter cookies) flavoured with nuts and spices.

WORTH A TRIP

ODE TO ART NOUVEAU

A stunning, romantic tribute to French art-nouveau designer René Lalique, the **Musée Lalique** (www.musee-lalique.com; rue du Hochberg, Wingen-sur-Moder; adult/child €6/3; ☉10am-7pm, closed Mon Oct-Mar) harbours a collection assembling exquisite gem-encrusted and enamelled jewellery, perfume bottles, stoppers and sculpture. Complementing it are flower and wooded gardens, making the connection, as Lalique did, between art and the natural world. Located in the northern Vosges, 60km north of Strasbourg, the museum can easily be visited on a half-day trip by taking the train to Wingen-sur-Moder (€10.80, 44 minutes). Alternatively, it's an hour's drive.

the lines of marinated salmon with avocado and lime caviar, sea bass with sweet potatoes, ginger and coriander, and 'deconstructed' *tarte au citron* – all top quality.

La Cuiller à Pot
FRENCH €€
(☑ 03 88 35 56 30; www.lacuillerapot.com; 18b rue Finkwiller; mains €22.50-26.50; ☉noon-1.30pm & 7-9.30pm Tue-Fri, 7-9.30pm Sat; ☐Musée d'Art Moderne) Run by a talented husband-and-wife team, this little Alsatian dream of a restaurant rustles up fresh regional food. Its well-edited menu goes with the seasons but might include such dishes as fillet of wild turbot with saffron sauce, and homemade gnocchi and escargots in parsley jus. Quality is second to none.

L'Eveil des Sens
BISTRO €€
(☑ 03 88 32 81 01; http://eveil-des-sens.com; 2 rue Escarpée; menus €29-39; ☉noon-2pm & 7.15-10pm Mon & Wed-Sun; ☐Grand'Rue) With a name pledging to awaken your senses, this Petite France (p348) bistro promises great things – and it delivers. Tables draped in white linen and flowers create an intimate, romantic mood for dishes big on integral flavours: marinated salmon with Granny Smith apple and wasabi, wine-braised pork cheeks with Emmental crumble, Munster tiramisu with a pinch of cumin, and the like.

★1741
GASTRONOMY €€€
(☑ 03 88 35 50 50; www.1741.fr; 22 quai des Bateliers; 3-course lunch menus €42, 3-/5-course dinner menus €95/129; ☉noon-2pm & 7-10pm Thu-Mon; ☐Porte de l'Hôpital) A team of profoundly passionate chefs run the show at this Michelin-starred number facing the River Ill. Murals, playful fabrics and splashes of colour add warmth to the dining room, where waiters bring well-executed, unfussy dishes, such as sea bass with Jerusalem artichoke and Alsatian venison with root vegetables, to the table. Service is excellent, as is the wine list.

Le Gavroche
MEDITERRANEAN €€€
(☑ 03 88 36 82 89; www.restaurant-gavroche. com; 4 rue Klein; menus €37-95; ☉noon-2pm & 7.30-9.30pm Mon-Fri; ☒; ☐Porte de l'Hôpital) Nathalie and Benoît Fuchs give food a pinch of creativity and southern sunshine at intimate, softly lit Le Gavroche, awarded a Michelin star. Mains like veal in a mint crust with crispy polenta, and turbot with spelt and shellfish risotto are followed by zingy desserts such as lime tart with lemon-thyme sorbet. There's a children's menu.

🍷 Drinking & Nightlife

Strasbourg's beer-thirsty students keep the scene lively and the bars and clubs pumping at weekends. Among the city's legion of pubs and bars is a glut of student-oriented places on the small streets east of the cathedral such as rue des Juifs, rue des Frères and rue des Sœurs.

★Sthélline
TEAHOUSE
(http://sthelline.fr; 10 rue des Tonneliers; ☉9am-6.30pm Tue-Sat; ☐Porte de l'Hôpital) A little cocoon of warmth and bonhomie bang in the heart of Strasbourg, this literary cafe and tea room is lined with novels (feel free to browse) and does a fine line in fragrant speciality teas, from green and Darjeeling to rooibos and rare yellow tea – all served ceremonially in pretty pots and with mini-timers.

Café Bretelles
CAFE
(http://suspenders.fr; 36 rue du Bain aux Plantes; ☉9am-6pm Mon-Sat, to 5pm Sun; ☐Alt Winmärik) Huddled away in Petite France, this chilled-out haunt has Italian coffee worth raving about – served with an artistic flourish – relaxed vibes and good music. The baristas know their stuff when it comes to speciality coffees, which are best enjoyed with a slice of cake or breakfast (€5.50 to €7.50).

La Popartiserie
BAR
(www.lapopartiserie.com; 3 rue de l'Ail; ☉2-10pm Tue-Sat; ☐Grand'Rue) Emerging urban artists from various countries showcase their edgy work at this gallery, wine bar and concert venue. There are regular free gigs, including

pop and jazz Fridays, and exhibitions, and the inner courtyard is a nicely chilled spot for drinks. Keep your eyes peeled for street art in this area, too.

Code Bar
COCKTAIL BAR

(39 rue du Vieil Hôpital; ⊘6pm-4am; 🚊Langstross/Grand Rue) At the top of the cocktail bar pile, the intimate, backlit Code Bar knows its mixology, with creative, attractively presented concoctions that reach from 'Voodoo', a spicy rum and coconut number, to the refreshing 'Gin Snatch' – gin, fresh basil, pink grapefruit and elderflower soda.

Au Brasseur
MICROBREWERY

(www.aubrasseur.fr; 22 rue des Veaux; ⊘11am-1am; 🚊Gallia) Copper vats shine at this easygoing microbrewery, which is perfect for a pint. It has been a boozer in some shape or form since 1746. Today, there's a good buzz and a fine selection of brews – from malty dark beers to hoppy IPAs. These pair well with snacks like *Flammekueche*.

☆ Entertainment

Cultural event listings appear in the free monthly Spectacles (www.spectacles-publications.com, in French), available at the tourist office.

La Laiterie
LIVE MUSIC

(www.artefact.org; 13 rue du Hohwald; 🚊Laiterie) Reggae, metal, punk, *chanson,* blues – Strasbourg's premier concert venue covers the entire musical spectrum and stages some 200 gigs a year. Tickets are available at the door and online. La Laiterie is just a five-minute walk (500m) south of Petite France along rue de Molsheim.

ℹ Information

Tourist Office (🕾03 88 52 28 28; www.otstrasbourg.fr; 17 place de la Cathédrale; ⊘9am-7pm; 🚊Grand'Rue)

ℹ Getting There & Around

AIR

Strasbourg's international **airport** (SXB; www.strasbourg.aeroport.fr) is 17km southwest of the city centre (towards Molsheim), near the village of Entzheim. The airport is served by major carriers such as Air France, KLM, Iberia and budget airline Ryanair (London Stansted). Flights link Strasbourg to cities elsewhere in Europe, including London, Amsterdam, Madrid and Vienna, and domestic destinations including Paris, Nice, Lille and Lyon.

A speedy shuttle train links the airport to the train station (€4.30, nine minutes, four hourly); the ticket also covers your onward tram journey into the city centre.

BICYCLE

A world leader in bicycle-friendly planning, Strasbourg has an extensive and ever-expanding *réseau cyclable* (cycling network). The **tourist office** stocks free maps.

The city's 24-hour, self-rental **Vélhop** (www.velhop.strasbourg.eu; per hour/day €1/5) system can supply you with a bike. Pay by card and receive a code to unlock your bike. There's a refundable deposit of €150 per bike. Helmets are not available. There are 20 automatic rental points, plus outlets including the following:

City Centre (3 rue d'Or; ⊘8am-7pm Mon-Fri, 9.30am-12.30pm & 2-5.30pm Sat; 🚊Porte de l'Hôpital)

Rotonde (rue de la Rotonde; ⊘24hr; 🚊Rotonde)

Train Station (⊘9am-12.30pm & 1-6.30pm Mon-Fri, 9.30am-12.30pm & 2-5.30pm Sat; 🚊Gare Centrale) Situated on Level -1. Adjacent is an 820-place bicycle parking lot (€1 for 24 hours).

BUS

The **Eurolines office** (🕾08 92 89 90 91; www.eurolines.com; place de l'Étoile; ⊘9.30am-6.30pm Mon-Fri, to 4.30pm Sat; 🚊Étoile Bourse) is situated south of Grande Île on place de l'Étoile. Take tram line A or D to the Étoile Bourse stop. **Eurolines buses** (place de l'Étoile; 🚊Étoile Bourse) arrive and depart from the same square.

ℹ CENT SAVERS

The Strasbourg Pass (adult/child €21.50/15), a coupon book valid for three consecutive days, includes a visit to one museum, access to the cathedral platform and astronomical clock, half a day's bicycle rental and a boat tour, plus hefty discounts on other tours and attractions.

The money-saving Strasbourg Pass Musées (day pass adult/child €12/6, three-day pass €18/12; www.musees.strasbourg.eu) offers entry to all the Musées de la Ville de Strasbourg. You can purchase both passes from the tourist office and the latter directly from the city's museums. Admission to all of Strasbourg's museums (www.musees-strasbourg.eu) and the cathedral's platform is free on the first Sunday of the month.

Strasbourg city bus 21 links the Jean Jaurès tram terminus with Kehl (€1.70, 13 minutes), the German town just across the Rhine.

TRAIN

Built in 1883, the Gare Centrale was given a 120m-long, 23m-high glass façade and underground galleries in order to welcome the TGV Est Européen in grand style. On the Grande Île, tickets are available at the **SNCF Boutique** (www.voyages-sncf.com; 5 rue des Francs-Bourgeois; 🚊 Grand'Rue).

If you take the Eurostar via Paris or Lille, London is just 5¼ hours away. Direct services include the following:

Basel SNCF €24.70, 1¼ hours, 25 daily

Brussels-Nord €135 to €206, 5¼ hours, 10 daily

Karlsruhe €26 to €36.80, 39 to 70 minutes, 16 daily

Stuttgart €50 to €81, 1¼ to 2¼ hours, 11 daily

Destinations within France:

Lille €128 to €151, four hours, 17 daily

Lyon €54 to €194, 4½ hours, 14 daily

Marseille €85 to €208, 6¾ hours, 16 daily

Metz €27.80, 1½ hours, 16 daily

Nancy €26.80, 1½ hours, 12 daily

Paris €90 to €113, 1¾ hours, 19 daily

From Strasbourg, there are trains to Route des Vins destinations including the following:

Colmar €12.60, 30 minutes, 30 daily

Dambach-la-Ville €9.40 to €10.30, one hour, 12 daily

Obernai €6.50, 29 to 31 minutes, 20 daily

Sélestat €9.20, 17 to 33 minutes, 46 daily

Route des Vins d'Alsace

Green and soothingly beautiful, this is one of France's most evocative **drives** (Alsace Wine Route; www.route-des-vins-alsace.com). Vines march up hillsides to castle-topped crags and the mist-enshrouded Vosges, and every mile or so there's a roadside *cave* (wine cellar) or half-timbered village to enjoy. Corkscrewing through glorious countryside, the route stretches 170km from Marlenheim, 21km west of Strasbourg, southwards to Thann, 46km southwest of Colmar.

Local tourist offices can supply you with the excellent English-language map/brochure The Alsace Wine Route, and Alsace Grand Cru Wines, detailing Alsace's 50 most prestigious Appellation d'Origine Contrôlée (AOC) winegrowing microregions. The signposted Route des Vins comprises several minor, lightly trafficked roads (D422, D35, D18 and so on).

Obernai

POP 10,822

A vision of half-timbered, vine-draped, ring-walled loveliness, the wine-producing town of Obernai sits 31km south of Strasbourg. Give the summertime crowds the slip by ducking down cool, flower-bedecked alleyways, such as ruelle des Juifs, next to the tourist office.

⊙ Sights & Activities

A number of winegrowers have cellars a short walk from town (the tourist office has a map).

Place du Marché   SQUARE
Life spirals around this market square, put to use each Thursday morning, where you'll find the 16th-century **hôtel de ville** (town-hall building) embellished with Baroque trompe l'œil; the Renaissance **Puits à Six Seaux** (Six Bucket Well), just across rue du Général Gouraud; and the bell-topped, 16th-century **Halle aux Blés** (Corn Exchange).

Ramparts   HISTORIC SITE
Stretch your legs by strolling around Obernai's 13th-century ramparts, accessible from the square in front of the twin-spired, neo-Gothic **Église St-Pierre et St-Paul**.

Sentier Viticole du Schenkenberg   WALKING
This 1.5km wine route meanders through vineyards and begins at the hilltop cross north of town; to get there, follow the yellow signs from the cemetery behind Église St-Pierre et St-Paul.

🛏 Sleeping & Eating

Le Gouverneur   HISTORIC HOTEL €
(☏ 03 88 95 63 72; www.hotellegouverneur.com; 13 rue de Sélestat; s €55-80, d €65-150, tr €78-135, q €88-130; 🅿 🛜) Overlooking a courtyard, this old-town hotel strikes a perfect balance between half-timbered rusticity and contemporary comfort. Its petite rooms have a boutiquey feel, with bursts of vivid colour and art-slung walls. The family-friendly team can provide cots and high chairs free of charge.

La Villa Haute Corniche   B&B €€
(☏ 07 87 75 44 37, 03 88 83 10 46; https://villa-hautecorniche.com; 25 rue de la Haute Corniche; d €107-137; 🅿 🛜 ❄) On a tremendously scenic perch above Obernai, with views of the Vosges and Alsace plains, this B&B has a

boutiquey feel thanks to owner Anthony's attention to detail. The four rooms are impeccably tasteful – dark-wood parquet, textured fabrics, fur throws and eye-catching art – and open onto terraces. Breakfast is a fine spread of farm-fresh eggs and cheeses, pastries and fruits.

It's a 1.5km (20-minute) walk northwest of central Obernai, or a quick taxi ride.

Winstub Le Freiberg   ALSATIAN €
(✆03 88 95 53 77; www.le-freiberg.com; 46 rue du Général Gouraud; mains €14-20; ⊙noon-2pm & 7-10pm Thu-Tue) Brimming with warmth and bonhomie, this *winstub* is a rustic ensemble of timber beams, red-checked tablecloths, heart-carved wooden chairs and stone walls. It's popular, too, thanks to its solid menu of dishes prepared with regional ingredients, from pork cheeks braised in pinot noir to plump local duck breast in blackberry sauce.

La Fourchette des Ducs   GASTRONOMY €€€
(✆03 88 48 33 38; www.lafourchettedesducs.com; 6 rue de la Gare; menus €120-155; ⊙7-9.30pm Tue-Sat, noon-1.30pm Sun) A great believer in fastidious sourcing, chef Nicolas Stamm serves regional cuisine with gourmet panache and a signature use of herbs to a food-literate crowd at this two-Michelin-starred restaurant. The tasting *menus* go with the seasons, featuring specialities such as Alsatian pigeon with *baerewecke* (spiced fruit cake) and veal with truffles and Menton lemon jus – simple but sublime.

ⓘ Information

The central **tourist office** (✆03 88 95 64 13; www.tourisme-obernai.fr; place du Beffroi; ⊙9am-12.30pm & 2-6pm Mon-Fri, 9.30am-12.30pm & 2-6pm Sat & Sun, shorter hours in low season) provides info on the town and its surrounds. You can also rent an electric bike here for €13/20 per half/full day.

ⓘ Getting There & Away

The train station is about 300m east of the old town. There are at least hourly TER train connections from Obernai to Colmar (€9.50 to €17.20, one hour to 70 minutes) and Strasbourg (€6.50, 31 to 39 minutes).

Mittelbergheim

POP 657

Serene, untouristy and set on a hillside, Mittelbergheim sits amid a sea of sylvan-

> ### TALK LOCAL
>
> The roots of Alsatian (Elsässisch) go back to the 4th century, when Germanic Alemanni tribes assimilated the local Celts (Gauls) and Romans. Similar to the dialects spoken in nearby Germany and Switzerland, it has no official written form (spelling is something of a free-for-all) and pronunciation varies considerably. Yet despite heavy-handed attempts by the French and Germans to impose their language on the region by restricting (or even banning) Alsatian, you'll still hear it used in everyday life by people of all ages, especially in rural areas.

er grapevines and seasonal wild tulips, its tiny streets lined with sand-hued, red-roofed houses.

👁 Sights & Activities

Each of Mittelbergheim's *caves* (cellars) has an old-fashioned wrought-iron sign hanging out the front.

Domaine Gilg   WINE
(www.domaine-gilg.com; 2 rue Rotland; ⊙8am-noon & 1.30-6pm Mon-Fri, to 5pm Sat, 9.30-11.30am Sun) Nip into this friendly, family-run winery to taste award-winning wines, including *grand cru* sylvaners, pinots and rieslings.

Sentier Viticole   WALKING
From the car park on the D362 at the upper edge of the village next to the cemetery, a vineyard trail wriggles across the slopes towards the perky twin-towered **Château du Haut Andlau** and the lushly forested Vosges.

🛏 Sleeping & Eating

Hôtel Gilg   HISTORIC HOTEL €
(✆03 88 08 91 37; www.hotel-gilg.com; 1 rte du Vin; r €68-98; 🕸) For a dose of old-fashioned romance, check into this 17th-century half-timbered pile. A spiral staircase leads up to spacious, homey rooms in warm tones, some with wooden beams. The elegantly rustic restaurant (*menus* €35 to €56) serves classic French and Alsatian cuisine. Breakfast costs an extra €9.

Place du Marché (p356), Ober

N 0 ▬▬▬ 5 km
   0 ▬▬▬ 2.5 miles

Marlenheim

BAS-RHIN

Molsheim

Rosheim

Obernai

Mittelbergheim

D35

Dambach-
la-Ville

Château du Haut
Kœnigsbourg

D18

Ribeauvillé   Bergheim
Hunawihr
Riquewihr
Kaysersberg
D415

Katzenthal

Colmar

HAUT-
RHIN

2 DAYS Route des Vins d'Alsace

Weaving through lyrical landscapes, this road trip takes in the best of the vine-strewn Route des Vins d'Alsace.

From the gateway town of **Marlenheim**, a well-marked lane leads through bucolic countryside to medieval **Molsheim**, centred on a square dominated by the step-gabled Renaissance *metzig* (butcher's shop). Continue south to **Rosheim**, where the striking Romanesque Église St-Pierre-St-Paul raises eyebrows with its, ahem, copulating gargoyles! Step inside for a moment of quiet contemplation before swinging south to pretty, half-timbered **Obernai** to explore the market square and château-topped vineyard trail. Views of the forest-cloaked Vosges unfold as you meander south to the sleepy hamlet of **Mittelbergheim**, pausing to taste the local *grand cru* wines at award-winning Domaine Gilg (p357). Even higher peaks slide into view as you cruise south to cellar-studded **Dambach-la-Ville**, embraced by 14th-century town walls, and catch your first tantalising glimpse of the turrets of 900-year-old **Château du Haut Kœnigsbourg** (p362). After detouring for astounding views from the castle ramparts – which reach to the Black Forest and Alps on cloudless days – rewind time roaming the cobbled streets in half-timbered **Bergheim**. Curving alleys hide cosy *winstubs* (wine taverns) in tower-speckled **Ribeauvillé** nearby. You'll definitely see storks in **Hunawihr** at the NaturOparC wildlife reserve (p364); visit in spring to coo over hatchlings. Allow time for serendipitous strolls in fairest-of-them-all **Riquewihr** – pure fairy-tale stuff with its procession of half-timbered houses painted pastel colours as bright as the macarons sold by its patisseries. Contemplate the Renaissance town hall and the house of Nobel Peace Prize–winner Albert Schweitzer in riverside **Kaysersberg**, then wend your way south to little-known **Katzenthal** for organic wine tasting and vineyard walks at family-run Vignoble Klur (p366). Wrap up your tour with culture and Michelin-starred dining in canal-woven **Colmar**, the enchanting Alsatian wine capital and birthplace of Statue of Liberty creator Frédéric Auguste Bartholdi (p366).

5 Terres Hotel & Spa
SPA HOTEL €€

(☑03 88 08 28 44; www.sofitel.com; 1 place de l'Hôtel de Ville, Barr; d €142-183, ste €206-308; P 🛜 ⊠) A 16th-century half-timbered house has undergone a dramatic transformation to become this slick boutique spa hotel. The rooms are a clever fusion of old (beams, stone walls) and new (contemporary lighting, minimalist decor). Suites have arresting views over the vines. Besides a bar serving local biodynamic wines, there's a romantically lit spa in the hotel's vaults and a well-regarded restaurant.

The hotel is 1.7km north of Mittelbergheim in Barr; it's a five-minute drive on the D362.

Am Lindeplatzel
FRENCH €€

(☑03 88 08 10 69; http://am-lindeplatzel.fr; 71 rue Principale; mains €17.50-24, menus €30-52; ⊘noon-2pm & 7-9pm Fri-Tue) Creative riffs on Alsatian cuisine go down a treat at this nouveau-chic restaurant, run by a talented couple who take pride in local sourcing. Dishes like fricassee of Alsatian snails with roasted almonds, and rack of lamb with foraged wild garlic are expertly paired with regional wines. The two-course lunch is a steal at €10.

❶ Getting There & Away

The closest train station is in Barr, 1.5km north of town (approximately a 20-minute walk). From here, frequent trains run to Obernai (€2.60, eight minutes), Sélestat (€4.10, 23 minutes) and Strasbourg (€7.70, 40 minutes).

STORKS OF ALSACE
∙∙∙∙∙∙∙∙∙∙∙∙∙∙∙∙∙∙∙∙∙∙∙∙∙∙∙∙∙∙∙∙∙∙∙∙∙∙

White storks (cigognes), prominent in local folklore, are Alsace's most beloved symbols. Believed to bring luck (as well as babies), they winter in Africa and then spend summer in Europe, feeding in the marshes and building twig nests on church steeples and rooftops.

In the mid-20th century, environmental changes reduced stork numbers catastrophically. By the early 1980s, only two pairs were left in the wild, so research and breeding centres were set up to establish a year-round Alsatian stork population. The program has been a huge success and today Alsace is home to more than 400 pairs – some of which you are bound to spot (or hear bill-clattering) on the Route des Vins d'Alsace.

Dambach-la-Ville
POP 2061

Ringed by vines and sturdy ramparts, this flowery village has some 60 *caves* but manages to avoid touristic overload. The renowned Frankstein *grand cru* vineyards cover the southern slopes of four granitic hills west and southwest of Dambach.

◉ Sights & Activities

Some of the eye-catching half-timbered houses, painted in ice-cream colours like pistachio, caramel and raspberry, date from before 1500.

Ramparts
HISTORIC SITE

A gentle stroll takes in the 14th-century, pink-granite ramparts, originally pierced by four gates, three still holding aloft watchtowers and bearing quintessentially Alsatian names: Ebersheim, Blienschwiller and Dieffenthal.

Sentier Viticole du Frankstein
WALKING

It's a pleasant 1½-hour walk through the vineyards on this trail, which begins 70m up the hill from the tourist office (p360), on rue du Général de Gaulle. The path meanders among the hallowed vines, passing by hillside **Chapelle St-Sébastien** (Steinhausen; ⊘9am-7pm), known for its Romanesque tower and Gothic choir.

🛏 Sleeping & Eating

Le Vignoble
HISTORIC HOTEL €

(☑03 88 92 43 75; www.hotel-vignoble-alsace. fr; 1 rue de l'Église; s/d €69/79; 🛜) Housed in a beautifully converted 18th-century barn, this hotel has comfortable wood-beamed rooms in fresh lemon and lime hues. It's well situated in the village centre. Breakfast will set you back an extra €10.

Le Pressoir de Bacchus
FRENCH €€

(☑03 88 92 43 01; 50 rte des Vins, Blienschwiller; menus €15-48; ⊘noon-1.45pm Mon, 7-8.45pm Wed, noon-1.45pm & 7-8.45pm Thu-Sun) Good, honest Alsatian grub, cooked with passion and served with a smile, is the deal at this snug, wood-beamed bistro. Local wines marry well with classics like garlicky escargots and *choucroute garnie* (sauerkraut with smoked meats). It's 2.5km north of Dambach-la-Ville on the D35.

❶ Information

Tourist Office (☑03 88 92 61 00; www.pays-de-barr.com; place du Maré; ⊘9.30am-noon

& 2-5.30pm Mon-Fri, 10am-noon Sat) In the Renaissance-style *hôtel de ville*. Hands out walking-tour maps and has details on cycling to nearby villages.

ℹ️ Getting There & Away

The train station is about 1km east of the old town. Dambach-la-Ville has hourly services to Sélestat (€2.60, 10 minutes), Colmar (€6.70, 40 minutes) and Strasbourg (€10.30, 36 minutes to one hour).

Sélestat

POP 19,546

Wedged between Strasbourg, 50km to the north, and Colmar, 23km to the south, Sélestat is an enticing jumble of colourful half-timbered houses and church spires, including that of Gothic **Église St-Georges** (place St-Georges; ☉ 8am-7pm).

The town's claim to cultural fame is its incomparable **Bibliothèque Humaniste** (Humanist Library; ☑ 03 88 58 07 20; 1 rue de la Bibliothèque; ☉ 10am-12.30pm & 1.30-6pm Tue-Sun May-Sep & Dec, from 1.30-5.30pm Tue-Sun Feb-Apr & Oct & Nov), a library founded in 1452, whose stellar collection features a 7th-century book of Merovingian liturgy, a copy of *Cosmographiae Introductio* (printed in 1507), in which the New World is referred to as 'America' for the first time, and the first written mention of the Christmas tree (1521).

🛏️ Sleeping & Eating

Le Domaine des Remparts   B&B €
(☑ 03 88 92 94 43; www.gite-alsace-selestat.fr; 9 bd Vauban; d €67-92, ste €88-105, q €145-160; P 🛜) You'll receive a heartfelt *bienvenue* at this pink-hued B&B on the southern fringes of town, which centres on an inner courtyard. Homely touches, warm colours and wooden beams afford the rooms an air of cosiness, and the owners will lend you a bike for free. A generous breakfast is included in room rates.

L'Illwald   BOUTIQUE HOTEL €€
(☑ 03 90 56 11 40; www.illwald.fr; Le Schnellenbuhl; s €100, d €120-160; P 🛜 ✖️) Serenely set against the wooded backdrop of the Illwald (p362) nature reserve, this charmingly rustic, half-timbered farmhouse harbours warm-hued rooms furnished with antiques and lots of attention to detail. The wood-panelled restaurant (mains €17 to €23) plays up organic ingredients in classic dishes, and there's an outdoor pool for summer swims. Organic jams, local cheeses and fresh pastries appear at breakfast. The hotel is a 6km drive south of Sélestat on the D424.

WORTH A TRIP

NATZWEILER-STRUTHOF

About 25km west of Obernai, off the D130, stands **Natzweiler-Struthof** (www.struthof.fr; Natzwiller; adult/child €6/3; ☉ 9am-6.30pm, closed Christmas-Feb), the only Nazi concentration camp on French territory. Today the sombre remains of the camp are still surrounded by guard towers and concentric, once-electrified, barbed-wire fences. The four *crématoire* (crematorium ovens), the *salle d'autopsie* (autopsy room) and the *chambre à gaz* (gas chamber), 1.7km from the camp gate, bear grim witness to the atrocities committed here.

In all, some 22,000 of the prisoners (40% of the total) interned here and at nearby annexe camps died; many were shot or hanged. In early September 1944, as US Army forces approached, the 5517 surviving inmates were sent to Dachau.

Le Schatzy   INTERNATIONAL €€
(☑ 03 88 82 48 76; www.le-schatzy.com; 8 rue des Chevaliers; mains €23-25; ☉ noon-2pm & 7-9pm Mon & Thu-Sat, noon-2pm Sun & Tue) Contemporary backlighting and furnishings put a modern spin on this beamed bistro. The vibe is laid-back and the menu offers fresh seasonal produce in well-prepared dishes such as red mullet in a Cajun crust and duck breast in sweet spices with orange-infused turnip confit. Save space for the delectable desserts.

ℹ️ Information

Tourist Office (☑ 03 88 58 87 20; www.selestat-haut-koenigsbourg.com; 10 bd du Général Leclerc; ☉ 9.30am-noon & 2-5.30pm Mon-Sat)

ℹ️ Getting There & Around

The tourist office rents out bicycles (two hours/half-day/day €7/9/14; deposit €150) from June to October.

The train station is 1km west of the **Bibliothèque Humaniste** (p361). Train is the fastest way to reach destinations including Strasbourg (€9.20, 20 to 41 minutes, twice hourly), Colmar (€5.20, 11 minutes, hourly) and Obernai (€5.40, 35 minutes, hourly).

Bergheim

POP 2038

Enclosed by a sturdy 14th-century ring wall, overflowing with geraniums and enlivened by half-timbered houses in vivid pastels,

DON'T MISS

AROUND SÉLESTAT: NATURE WATCH

Illwald (rte de Marckolsheim; 🅿) On the southeastern fringes of Sélestat, this nature reserve is a mix of deciduous forest and wetlands. It attracts plenty of wildlife, including kingfishers, beavers and France's largest population of wild deer (some 400 pairs at last count). Interwoven with footpaths, it's a quiet place for a stroll. It's a five-minute drive from town via the D159 and D424.

Cigoland (www.cigoland.fr; rte de Sélestat, Kintzheim; adult/child €17/15; ⊘10am-6pm Apr-early Nov; 🅿) One place you're guaranteed to glimpse Alsace's emblematic bringers of good fortune (and their babies) is at this theme park, home to 120 bill-clattering storks along with farm animals and free-roaming deer. Besides floating in ducks and riding toy trains and carousels, you can rise high in a giant stork's nest. It's a 10-minute drive/30-minute walk west of central Sélestat.

Montagne des Singes (www.montagnedessinges.com; Kintzheim; adult/child €9/5.50; ⊘10am-6pm, shorter hours autumn/spring, closed mid-Nov–late Mar; 🅿) Kids love to feed popcorn (special monkey popcorn, of course) to the free-roaming Barbary macaques and their cheeky infants at this 2.4-hectare woodland park. Take the D35 to Kintzheim, 7km west of Sélestat.

Bergheim is a joy to behold. But things have not always been so cheerful: overlords, stampeding invaders, women burnt at the stake for witchcraft – this tiny village has seen the lot.

Stroll the cobbled streets of the well-preserved medieval centre or follow the 2km path that circumnavigates the town's ramparts. Bergheim's *grand cru* wine labels are Kanzlerberg and Altenberg de Bergheim.

◉ Sights

Château du Haut Kœnigsbourg   CHATEAU
(www.haut-koenigsbourg.fr; Orschwiller; adult/child €9/5; ⊘9.15am-6pm, shorter hours winter) On its fairy-tale perch above vineyards and hills, the turreted red-sandstone Château du Haut Kœnigsbourg is worth a detour for the wraparound panorama from its ramparts, taking in the Vosges, the Black Forest and, on cloud-free days, the Alps. Audioguides delve into the turbulent 900-year history of the castle, which makes a very medieval impression despite having been reconstructed, with German imperial pomposity, by Kaiser Wilhelm II in 1908.

Medieval Centre   AREA
A stroll through the cobbled streets of the well-preserved medieval centre takes in the early Gothic **church**; the wall-mounted **sundial** (44 Grand'Rue), dating from 1711; and the imposing, turreted **Porte Haute**, Bergheim's last remaining town gate.

🛏 Sleeping & Eating

La Cour du Bailli   HISTORIC HOTEL €€
(☎03 89 73 73 46; www.cour-bailli.com; 57 Grand'Rue; r €89-205; 🅿) Draped around a 16th-century courtyard, La Cour du Bailli has countrified studios and apartments, all with kitchenettes. Factor in downtime in the pool and stone-built spa, which pampers with luscious vinotherapy treatments. The atmospheric cellar restaurant (*menus* €14 to €35) serves regional grub like *choucroute garnie* and Munster cheese gratin. There's no lift, so be prepared to lug your bags.

Wistub du Sommelier   FRENCH €€
(☎03 89 73 69 99; www.wistub-du-sommelier. com; 51 Grand'Rue; menus €18-45; ⊘noon-2pm & 7-9.30pm Mon, Tue, Fri & Sat, noon-2pm Sun) Behind an ornate 18th-century façade lies this traditionally elegant bistro, where parquet floors, wooden beams and a *Kachelofen* (tiled oven) create a delightfully cosy ambience. The menu pairs fine regional wines with dishes such as *choucroute garnie* (sauerkraut with smoked meats) or lighter flavours like salmon with mussels in saffron sauce. The two-course €18 lunch including coffee is good value.

❶ Information

Tourist Office (☎03 89 73 31 98; 1 place du Dr Walter; ⊘9.30am-noon & 2-6pm Mon, 4-6pm Wed-Fri, 9am-noon & 2-7pm Sat, 10am-1pm & 5-7pm Sun, shorter hours low season)

ⓘ Getting There & Away

Bus 109 runs between Colmar's main train station and Bergheim (€4.05, 40 minutes) several times daily. Visit www.vialsace.eu for timetables and itineraries.

Ribeauvillé

POP 4940

Nestled snugly in a valley, presided over by a castle and with winding alleys brimming with half-timbered houses, medieval Ribeauvillé is a Route des Vins must. The local *grand cru* wines are Kirchberg de Ribeauvillé, Osterberg and Geisberg.

⊙ Sights & Activities

Vieille Ville   AREA
(Grand'Rue) Along the main street that threads through the old town, keep an eye out for the 17th-century **Pfifferhüs** (Fifers' House; 14 Grand'Rue), which once housed the town's fife-playing minstrels; the **hôtel de ville** and its Renaissance fountain; and the nearby, clock-equipped **Tour des Bouchers** (Butchers' Bell Tower).

★ **Cave de Ribeauvillé**   WINERY
(☑ 03 89 73 20 35; www.vins-ribeauville.com; 2 rte de Colmar; ⊙ 8am-noon & 2-6pm Mon-Fri, 9.30am-12.30pm & 2.30-6.30pm Sat & Sun) **FREE** France's oldest winegrowers' cooperative, which brings together 40 vintners, was founded in 1895. The huge, contemporary building contains a viniculture museum, informative brochures and free tastings of its excellent wines, made with all seven of the grape varieties grown in Alsace. You can also stock up on wine (from €6 per bottle) here. On weekends it's staffed by local winegrowers. It's just across two roundabouts north of the tourist office.

Castle Ruins   WALKING
West and northwest of Ribeauvillé, the ruins of three 12th- and 13th-century hilltop castles – **St-Ulrich** (530m), **Giersberg** (530m) and **Haut Ribeaupierre** (642m) – can be reached on a hike (three hours return) beginning at place de la République (at the northern tip of Grand'Rue).

🛏 Sleeping

Au Lion   HOTEL €
(☑ 03 89 73 67 69; https://au-lion.com; 6 place de la Sinne; d €50-90, tr €80-115) Looking as pretty as can be, this pink-fronted, half-timbered hotel is a cut above most of the other budget places in town. The surprisingly modern rooms (including quads, family rooms and apartments) are spacious and warm hued, some with sloping ceilings and beams lending character. The restaurant speciality is *tarte flambée* (€8 to €13).

Hôtel de la Tour   HISTORIC HOTEL €€
(☑ 03 89 73 72 73; www.hotel-la-tour.com; 1 rue de la Mairie; s €80, d €86-115; ⓢ) Ensconced in a stylishly converted winery, this half-timbered hotel has quaint, comfy rooms, some with views of the Tour des Bouchers. Breakfast will set you back an extra €10.50 per person.

Le Clos Saint Vincent   BOUTIQUE HOTEL €€€
(☑ 03 89 73 67 65; www.leclossaintvincent.com; Osterbergweg; s €170-285, d €190-285, tr €310-335; ℗ ⓢ ⊠) Gasp you might as you crest the hill and gaze out across the vines and the wooded peaks of the Vosges near this elegant guesthouse. The sound is silence and the smart, light-drenched rooms capitalise on those incredible views, as does the restaurant, serving French cuisine inspired by the seasons. An indoor pool and a little spa area invite relaxation.

🍴 Eating

Auberge du Parc Carola   INTERNATIONAL €€
(☑ 03 89 86 05 75; www.auberge-parc-carola.com; 48 rte de Bergheim; menus €32-64, kids' menu €13; ⊙ noon-1.30pm & 7-9.30pm Thu-Mon; 🐾) Quaint on the outside, slick on the inside, this *auberge* (country inn) is all about surprises. Much-lauded chef Michaela Peters is behind the stove, and flavours ring true in seasonal showstoppers like roe deer with spiced red cabbage and Black Forest ham, and Alsatian wild boar tartine with Granny Smith apples. Tables are set up under the trees in summer.

Wistub Zum Pfifferhüs   FRENCH €€
(☑ 03 89 73 62 28; 14 Grand'Rue; menus €26-54; ⊙ noon-1.30pm & 6.30-8.30pm Fri-Tue) If it's good old-fashioned Alsatian grub you're after, look no further than this snug wine tavern, which positively radiates rustic warmth with its beams, dark wood and checked tablecloths. Snag a table for copious dishes including *choucroute garnie* (sauerkraut with smoked meats), pork knuckles and *coq au riesling* (chicken braised in riesling and herbs).

ⓘ Information

Tourist Office (☑ 03 89 73 23 23; www.ribeauville-riquewihr.com; 1 Grand'Rue; ⊙ 9.30am-noon & 2-6pm Mon-Sat, 9.30am-12.30pm Sun, shorter hours winter; ⓢ) Free wi-fi.

ℹ Getting There & Away

A fairly frequent service runs from Ribeauvillé's central bus station to Route des Vins destinations including Colmar (€4.10, 37 minutes) and Riquewihr (€2.70, 13 minutes). Timetables are available online at www.vialsace.eu.

Hunawihr

POP 611

You're guaranteed to see storks in the quiet walled hamlet of Hunawihr, 1km south of Ribeauvillé. On a hillside just outside the centre, the 16th-century fortified church has been a simultaneum – serving both the Catholic and Protestant communities – since 1687.

◉ Sights & Activities

NaturOparC WILDLIFE RESERVE
(www.centredereintroduction.fr; rte de Ribeauvillé; adult/child €10.50/9.50; ⊙10am-6.30pm, closed early Nov-late Mar; 🐾) 🐾 Set amid the vines, this delightful centre is home base for 200 free-flying storks; visit in spring and you're guaranteed to see hatchlings. Cormorants, otters and sea lions show off their fishing prowess several times each afternoon. The park's other resident critters include beaver-like coypus and increasingly rare great hamsters of Alsace. Visit the website for up-to-date feeding times.

Jardins des Papillons GARDENS
(www.jardinsdespapillons.fr; adult/child €8/5.50; ⊙10am-6pm, closed Nov-Easter; 🐾) Stroll among exotic free-flying butterflies at these pretty gardens, situated around 500m east of Hunawihr. A walk among the wildflowers here reveals not only rare species of butterfly but also birds, bees, tropical frogs, chameleons and stick insects aplenty.

ℹ Getting There & Away

Bus 106 provides a fairly frequent service between Hunawihr and Colmar (€4.35, 33 minutes).

Riquewihr

POP 1136

The competition is stiff, but Riquewihr is, just maybe, the most enchanting town on the Route des Vins. Medieval ramparts enclose its walkable centre, a photogenic maze of twisting lanes, hidden courtyards and half-timbered houses – each brighter and lovelier than the last. Of course, its chocolate-box looks also make it popular, so arrive in the early morning or the evening to appreciate the town at its peaceful best.

◉ Sights & Activities

Dolder HISTORIC SITE
(www.musee-riquewihr.fr; €3, incl Tour des Voleurs €7; ⊙2-6pm Sat & Sun Apr-Nov, daily Jul–mid-Aug) This late-13th-century stone and half-timbered gate, topped by a 25m bell tower, is worth a look for its panoramic views and small local-history museum.

Tour des Voleurs HISTORIC SITE
(Thieves' Tower; €5, incl Dolder €7; ⊙10.30am-1pm & 2-6pm Easter-Oct) Rue des Juifs (site of the former Jewish quarter) leads down the hill to this medieval stone tower. Inside is a gruesome torture chamber with English commentary and an old-style winegrower's kitchen.

Sentier Viticole des Grands Crus WALKING
A yellow-marked 2km trail takes you out to acclaimed local vineyards Schœnenbourg (north of town) and Sporen (southeast of town), while a 15km trail with red markers takes you to five nearby villages. Both trails can be picked up next to Auberge du Schœnenbourg, 100m to the right of the *hôtel de ville*.

🛏 Sleeping & Eating

Le Sarment d'Or HISTORIC HOTEL €€
(📞03 89 86 02 86; http://riquewihr-sarment-dor.fr; 4 rue du Cerf; d €90-110) Yes, you'll have to schlep your bags up a spiral staircase, but frankly it's a small price to pay for staying at this 17th-century, rose-tinted abode. Rooms are simple with a dash of rusticity, and the restaurant (*menus* €28 to €38) serves regional food cooked with precision and finesse.

Hôtel de la Couronne HISTORIC HOTEL €€
(📞03 89 49 03 03; www.hoteldelacouronne.com; 5 rue de la Couronne; s €58-72, d €65-137; 📶) With its 16th-century tower and flowing wisteria, this central choice is big on old-world character. Rooms are country style with crisp floral fabrics, low oak beams and period furnishings; many have views over the rooftops to the hills beyond. There's no lift.

Bastion de Riquewihr B&B €€
(📞06 42 02 81 21; www.bastion-riquewihr.com; 21 rue des Remparts; apt €105-112; 🅿📶) Harking back to 1807, this B&B is housed in an enticingly cosy half-timbered building, which once belonged to a vintner and cooper. The place creaks with history and is full of low-beamed, lovingly furnished nooks and crannies. Martine, your kindly host, keeps the spacious, characterful apartments spick and span.

Au Trotthus
FRENCH €€

(📞 03 89 47 96 47; www.trotthus.com; 9 rue des Juifs; dinner menus €32-64; ⏱7-10pm Mon, noon-2pm & 7-10pm Tue & Thu-Sat, noon-2pm Sun) Lodged in a 16th-century winemaker's house, this snug wood-beamed restaurant is overseen by a chef with exacting standards. The market-driven modern French menu might include such delicacies as veal and braised endive with teriyaki sauce, and roast salmon with porcini mushrooms, chorizo chips and crustacean jus.

⭐ Table du Gourmet
GASTRONOMY €€€

(📞 03 89 49 09 09; www.jlbrendel.com; 5 rue de la Première Armée; menus €38-115; ⏱noon-1.30pm & 7-9.30pm Thu-Mon) Jean-Luc Brendel is the culinary force behind this Michelin-starred venture. A 16th-century house given a slinky, scarlet-walled makeover is the backdrop for specialities made with herbs and little-heard-of vegetables from the restaurant's medieval garden. The menu swings with the seasons from asparagus to truffles, and dishes sing with intense, natural flavours – prepared with care, served creatively.

ℹ Information

Tourist Office (📞 03 89 73 23 23; www.ribeauville-riquewihr.com; 2 rue de la 1ère Armée; ⏱9.30am-noon & 2-6pm Mon-Sat, 10.30am-1.30pm Sun, shorter hours winter; 🛜) Free wi-fi.

ℹ Getting There & Away

Bus 106 runs several times daily from Riquewihr to Ribeauvillé (€2.80, 18 minutes) and Colmar (€3.90, 25 minutes).

Kaysersberg
POP 2701

Kaysersberg, 10km northwest of Colmar, is an instant heart-stealer with its backdrop of gently sloping vines, hilltop castle and 16th-century fortified bridge spanning the gushing River Weiss.

Footpaths lead in all directions through glens and vineyards. A 10-minute walk above town, the remains of the massive, crenulated **Château de Kaysersberg** stand surrounded by vines; other destinations include Riquewihr and Ribeauvillé (four hours). These paths begin through the arch to the right as you face the entrance to the old town's Hôtel de Ville.

🛏 Sleeping & Eating

Hôtel Constantin
HOTEL €

(📞 03 89 47 19 90; www.hotel-constantin.com; 10 rue du Père Kohlmann; s €59, d €70-88, tr €102-116; 🅿🛜) Originally a winegrower's house in the heart of the old town, this old-school hotel has 20 no-frills rooms with wood furnishings.

Le Chambard
BOUTIQUE HOTEL €€€

(📞 03 89 47 10 17; www.lechambard.fr; 9-13 rue du Général de Gaulle; d €224-299, ste €360; 🅿✳🛜🏊) A splash of five-star luxury in the heart of this little wine-growing village, Le Chambard offers elegantly contemporary quarters with balcony or terrace, a terrific spa and indoor pool for relaxing after exploring the Route des Vins, a cosy *winstub* (wine tavern) and two-Michelin-starred restaurant, **64°** (5-course lunch menus €58, 5- to 8-course dinner menus €132-188; ⏱7-9pm Tue & Wed, noon-1.30pm & 7-9pm Thu-Sun). Breakfast will set you back an extra €30.

L'Alchémille
GASTRONOMY €€€

(📞 03 89 27 66 41; www.lalchemille.fr; 53 rte de Lapoutroie; 2-/3-course lunch €24/32, tasting menus €49-79; ⏱noon-2pm & 7.15-9pm Wed-Sat, noon-2pm Sun) As the name suggests, you can expect culinary alchemy at this strikingly minimalist Michelin-starred restaurant, with its bare wood tables, slate floor and monochrome colour scheme. Each of chef Jérôme Jaegle's dishes is an edible work of art (and is presented as such). Season-inspired menus reveal a profound love of nature and a playful use of herbs and flowers.

ℹ Information

Tourist Office (📞 03 89 78 22 78; www.kaysersberg.com; 39 rue du Général de Gaulle; ⏱9.30am-noon & 2-5.30pm Mon-Sat; 🛜)

ℹ Getting There & Away

Bus 145 runs several times daily between Kaysersberg and Colmar (€3.75, 38 minutes).

Katzenthal
POP 535

Close-to-nature Katzenthal, 5km south of Kaysersberg, is great for tiptoeing off the tourist trail for a while. *Grand cru* vines ensnare the hillside, topped by the medieval ruins of **Château du Wineck**, where walks through forest and vineyard begin.

🛏 Sleeping & Eating

Vignoble Klur   APARTMENT €
(☑ 03 89 80 94 29; www.klur.net; 105 rue des Trois Épis; apt €110-160) 🍴 Specialising in organic, biodynamic wines, family-run Vignoble Klur is a relaxed choice for tastings, Alsatian cookery classes and vineyard walks. The light-drenched, well-equipped apartments are great for back-to-nature holidays, and you can unwind in the sauna after a long day's walking and wine tasting. Le KatZ bistro pairs wines with dishes that make the most of local farm produce.

À l'Agneau   FRENCH €€
(☑ 03 89 80 90 25; www.agneau-katzenthal.com; 16 Grand'Rue; menus €21-52, mains €17-24; ⊙ noon-2pm & 7-10pm Fri-Tue, 7-10pm Thu; 🔟) Market-driven *menus* and a cocoon-like setting of dark-wood panelling and lamp lighting draw locals to À l'Agneau. This family-run affair serves beautifully cooked food, whether you opt for Alsatian classics such as escargots and braised pork knuckles, or seasonal dishes like pigeon cooked two ways with truffle jus or langoustines in cream of asparagus. Wine pairing is reasonably priced.

ℹ Getting There & Away

Bus 145 operates several times a day between Colmar and Katzenthal. See www.vialsace.eu for timetables and itineraries. The village is 8km west of Colmar on the D415.

Colmar

POP 67,956

The capital of the Alsace wine region, Colmar looks for all the world as though it has been plucked from the pages of a medieval folk tale. At times the Route des Vins d'Alsace fools you into thinking it's 1454, and here, in the alley-woven heart of the old town, the illusion is complete. Half-timbered houses in chalk-box colours crowd dark cobblestone lanes and bridge-laced canals, which have most day-trippers wandering around in a daze of neck-craning, photo-snapping, gasp-eliciting wonder.

Quaintness aside, Colmar's illustrious past is clearly etched in its magnificent churches and museums, which celebrate local legends from Bartholdi (of Statue of Liberty fame) to the revered Issenheim Altarpiece.

👁 Sights

Petite Venise   AREA
(Little Venice; rowboats per 30min €6) If you see just one thing in Colmar, make it the Little Venice quarter. Canal connection aside, it doesn't resemble Venice in the slightest, but it's truly lovely in its own right, whether explored on foot or by rowboat. The backstreets are punctuated by impeccably restored half-timbered houses in sugared-almond shades, many ablaze with geraniums in summer. Take a mosey around rue des Tanneurs, with its rooftop verandahs for drying hides, and quai de la Poissonnerie, the former fishers' quarter.

⭐ Musée d'Unterlinden   GALLERY
(www.musee-unterlinden.com; 1 rue d'Unterlinden; adult/child €13/8; ⊙ 10am-6pm Mon, Wed & Fri-Sun, to 8pm Thu) Gathered around a Gothic-style Dominican cloister, this revamped museum hides a prized medieval stone statue collection, late-15th-century prints by Martin Schongauer plus an ensemble of Upper Rhine Primitives. Its stellar modern-art collection contains works by Monet, Picasso and Renoir. The star attraction, however, is the late-Gothic **Rétable d'Issenheim** (Issenheim Altarpiece), by painter Mathias Grünewald and sculptor Nicolas de Haguenau. Hailed as one of the most profound works of faith ever created, the altarpiece realistically depicts New Testament scenes.

Église des Dominicains   CHURCH
(place des Dominicains; adult/child €1.50/0.50; ⊙ 10am-1pm & 3-6pm Sun-Thu, 10am-6pm Fri & Sat mid-Mar–Dec) Lit by late-medieval stained glass, this desanctified Gothic church shelters the celebrated triptych *La Vierge au Buisson de Roses* (The Virgin in the Rose Bush), painted by Martin Schongauer in 1473.

Musée Bartholdi   MUSEUM
(www.musee-bartholdi.fr; 30 rue des Marands; adult/child €6/free, audioguide €2; ⊙ 10am-noon & 2-6pm Wed-Mon Mar-Dec) In the house where Frédéric Auguste Bartholdi was born

---

DON'T MISS

BOATING PETITE VENISE

Rowboats depart next to **Pont Rue de Turenne** (rue de Turenne) and are a relaxed way to see Petite Venise from the water. The bridge is also the best spot to see the canals light up after dark.

in 1834, this museum pays homage to the sculptor who captured the spirit of a nation with his Statue of Liberty. Look out for the full-size plaster model of Lady Liberty's left ear (the lobe is watermelon-sized!) and the Bartholdi family's sparklingly bourgeois apartment. A ground-floor room shows 18th- and 19th-century Jewish ritual objects.

Maison des Têtes   HISTORIC BUILDING
(House of the Heads; 19 rue des Têtes) True to its name, this step-gabled house, built in 1609 for a wealthy wine merchant, is festooned with 106 grimacing faces and heads of animals, devils and cherubs.

Ancienne Douane   HISTORIC SITE
(place de l'Ancienne Douane) At the southern tip of rue des Marchands is this late-medieval customs house, with loggia and variegated tile roof, which now hosts temporary exhibitions and concerts.

Collégiale St-Martin   CHURCH
(place de la Cathédrale; ⊘ 8.30am-6.30pm) Delicate stonework guides the eye to the polychrome mosaic roof and Mongol-style copper spire of this Gothic church. Its jewel-like stained-glass windows cast kaleidoscopic patterns.

Musée du Jouet   MUSEUM
(www.museejouet.com; 40 rue Vauban; adult/child €5/4; ⊘ 10am-5pm) Kids of every age delight at the sight of toys from generations past – from demure 1950s Barbies to Gaultier-clad dolls and Hornby train sets – at this museum.

Statue of Liberty Replica   LANDMARK
(rte de Strasbourg) Prepare for *déjà vu* as you approach Colmar on the rte de Strasbourg (N83), 3km north of the old town, and spy the spitting image of the Statue of Liberty, albeit on a smaller scale. Bearing her torch aloft, this 12m-high, copper-green replica was erected to mark the centenary of the death of local lad Frédéric Auguste Bartholdi (1834–1904), creator of the NYC statue.

We wonder how this little lady (four times smaller than her big sister across the Pond) feels about her humble home on a roundabout. New York Harbour it isn't, but she's an icon nonetheless.

✨ Festivals & Events

Marché de Noël   CHRISTMAS
(Christmas Market; www.noel-colmar.com; ⊘ late Nov-Dec) Colmar's snow globe of a Marché de Noël glitters from late November to 31 December. The entire city goes to town with festive sparkle, and five markets brim with gifts,

---

CYCLING THE VINES

Colmar is a great base for slipping onto a bicycle saddle to pedal along the Route des Vins and the well-marked Franco-German trails of the nearby Rhine (www.2rives3ponts.eu, in French). Get your two-wheel adventure started by clicking onto www.haute-alsacetourisme.com, with detailed information on everything from bicycle hire to luggage-free cycling holidays, itinerary ideas and downloadable route maps.

If you'd rather join a group, **Bicyclette Go** (☎ 06 87 47 44 31; www.bicyclettego com; 2 impasse du Tokay, Voegtlinshoffen), 12km south of Colmar, arranges all-inclusive half-day to two-week cycling tours in the region, many of which are customised. Half-day tours complete with wine tasting start at €40 per person.

---

hand-crafted decorations and gingerbread hearts. An open-air ice rink takes over place Rapp.

Festival International de Colmar   CULTURAL
(www.festival-colmar.com; ⊘ Jul) Orchestras strike up at 22 concerts in historic venues across Colmar, including Musée d'Unterlinden (p366), during the 10-day Festival International de Colmar.

🛏 Sleeping

Maison Martin Jund   GUESTHOUSE €
(☎ 03 89 41 58 72; www.martinjund.com; 12 rue de l'Ange; r €39-87, apt €80-100; 🛜) Surrounding a courtyard in the backstreets of the old town, this rosy half-timbered house shelters an organic winery and bright, well-kept studios, many with living rooms and kitchenettes. Breakfast is well worth the extra €8, with croissants, organic apple juice, homemade jams and Vosges cheese.

★ **Villa Élyane**   B&B €€
(☎ 06 99 04 55 23; www.villa-elyane.com; 26a rue Camille Schlumberger; d €145-235, ste €230-285; 🅿✳🛜) This graceful late-19th-century villa manages the careful balancing act of combining original art-nouveau features with modern comforts such as in-room iPod docks and espresso makers. Regional organic produce and fresh-squeezed juice make breakfast a delight. A garden, a sauna, a ping-pong table and bike rental boost the guesthouse's family appeal.

Colmar

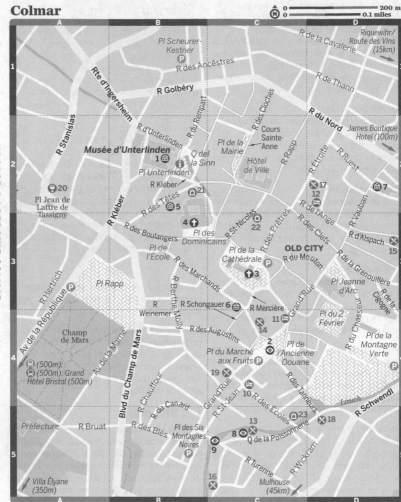

★ **Gîte L'Âme d'Antan** APARTMENT €€
(☑ 03 89 27 58 62; 1 rue des Écoles; apt €111-137, cleaning fee €45) Perched nest-like above the old-town bustle, this gorgeous attic apartment (sleeping three) is spacious, silent and equipped with dining area, kitchen and living room. The friendly owner, Annik, has furnished it with love, using family heirlooms and personal details – note the shutter headboard and her grandmother's hand-embroidered pillows. Towels and bed linen cost €20 extra per person. Minimum three-night stay.

James Boutique Hotel BOUTIQUE HOTEL €€
(☑ 03 89 21 93 70; www.james-hotel.com; 15 rue St-Éloi; d €136-181; ᴾ⊚) A sassy newcomer to Colmar's sleeping scene, this boutique hotel is a two-minute stroll north of the historic centre. The decor is nouveau-chic, with little details from geometric patterned rugs and tiles to richly coloured fabrics. The spacious rooms and suites come with Nespresso makers and kettles. Breakfast (€17) is a highly decent spread, with scrambled eggs and homemade cakes.

Colmar

ALSACE & LORRAINE COLMAR

Hôtel St-Martin HISTORIC HOTEL €€
(☑ 03 89 24 11 51; www.hotel-saint-martin.com; 38 Grand'Rue; d €75-140, f €120-160, ste €140-180; ❄❞) What a location! Right on the place de l'Ancienne Douane, this 14th-century patrician house captures the elegance of yesteryear in rooms dressed with handcrafted furniture. Choose a top-floor room for rooftop views. Family rooms are available.

Hôtel les Têtes HISTORIC HOTEL €€€
(☑ 03 89 24 43 43; www.la-maison-des-tetes.com; 19 rue des Têtes; r €190-340; ❄❞) Luxurious but never precious, this hotel occupies the magnificent Maison des Têtes. Each of its 21 rooms has rich wooden panelling, an elegant sitting area, a marble bathroom and romantic views. With its wrought ironwork and stained glass, the restaurant provides a sumptuously historic backdrop for French-Alsatian specialities (mains €39 to €65).

✗ Eating

The old town is liberally sprinkled with bistros and *winstubs,* especially place de l'Ancienne Douane, rue des Marchands and Petite Venise. And for a town of its moderate size, it packs a mighty gastronomic punch, with no fewer than three Michelin-starred restaurants.

La Soi ALSATIAN €
(www.lasoicolmar.fr; 17 rue des Marands; tarte flambée €7.50-12; ⊙ noon-2pm & 7-10pm Thu-Tue) A *winstub* (wine tavern) in the best of Alsatian traditions, La Soi whips up mighty fine *Flammekueche (tarte flambée)* with just the right amount of crunch in cosy, wood-lined surrounds. You might, say, opt for a 'For-

estière', with cream, onions, Tomme cheese, diced bacon, mushrooms and wild garlic.

L'Arpège FRENCH €
(☑ 03 89 24 29 64; www.larpegebio.com; 24 rue des Marands; lunch menus €15-17, mains €17-25; ⊙ noon-2pm Tue-Sat, 7-10pm Thu-Sat; ☑) ⌇ Discreetly tucked away at the back of a courtyard in a 15th-century house and with pretty garden seating when the weather is fine, L'Arpège places the accent on well-balanced, organic food. It's a convivial spot for dishes ranging from salads through to roast lamb with thyme jus and rabbit cooked in red wine. There's also a separate vegetarian menu.

★La Table du Brocanteur FRENCH €€
(☑ 03 89 23 45 57; 23 rue d'Alspach; mains €20-23; ⊙ 7-9.30pm Wed, noon-2pm & 7-9.30pm Thu-Sat, noon-2pm Sun) Tucked down a backstreet, this half-timbered house is decorated with milk pails, clogs and an attic's worth of other rustic knick-knacks. Bright flavours like scallop carpaccio and tender beef steak with confit shallots marry well with local wines.

Le Quai 21 MEDITERRANEAN €€
(☑ 03 89 58 58 58; www.restaurant-quai21.fr; 21 Quai de la Poissonnerie; mains €27-29; ⊙ noon-2pm & 7-9pm Tue-Sat) This canalside restaurant on the edge of Petite Venise (p366) is a winner, with its trad-meets-contemporary decor of exposed stone, clean-lined bistro furnishings and pops of electric blue. The succinct menu has a Mediterranean slant – a nod to the chef's native Italy – and is underscored by simplicity in dishes like line-caught pollock with spinach, nuts and Jerusalem artichoke.

Le Petit Bidon FRENCH €€

(☑ 03 89 24 97 93; http://petitbidon.com; 14 rue Étroite; mains €22-25; ⊙ 7-9pm Mon, noon-1.30pm & 7-9pm Tue-Fri) What a delight this nouveau-rustic bistro is, with its friendly welcome and bright interior sporting bare wood tables and milk-pail-lined shelves. The menu puts a refined spin on seasonal flavours in dishes such as smoked trout with lentils, white cheese and truffle, cod loin with leek carbonara and lamb rump with Mauritian spices.

Le Caveau Saint Pierre FRENCH €€

(☑ 03 89 41 99 33; http://lecaveausaintpierre-colmar.com; 24 rue de la Herse; mains €16-20, menus €26-32; ⊙ noon-2pm & 6.30-9.30pm Thu-Mon; ⊕) Squirrelled away in the canal-laced heart of Petite Venise (p366), this half-timbered restaurant is enticingly rustic, with low beams, stone walls and checked tablecloths. *Choucroutes* (such as with fresh fish or cider apples and blood sausage) and *tartes flambées* (thin Alsatian-style pizzas) are bang on the money, as are specialities like pork cheeks in beer sauce. There's a €10.50 children's menu.

★ **JY'S** GASTRONOMY €€€

(☑ 03 89 21 53 60; www.jean-yves-schillinger.com; 17 quai de la Poissonnerie; lunch menus €45, dinner menus €78-124; ⊙ noon-1.45pm & 7-9.45pm Tue-Sat) Jean-Yves Schillinger runs the stove at this two-Michelin-starred restaurant in Petite Venise (p366). Behind a trompe-l'œil façade lies an urban-cool, lounge-style restaurant,

with flattering lighting and chesterfield sofas. Every flavour shines in seasonal dishes cooked with imagination and delivered with panache, be it barbecued oysters with algae butter and chorizo or Alsatian pigeon breast with bitter chocolate and Moroccan spice.

🍷 Drinking & Nightlife

★ **Japadeunon** WINE BAR

(24 rue Stanislas; ⊙ 5.30pm-1.30am) This new, bottle-lined wine bar is a drop of sophistication. Here you can sample and quaff wines from Alsace and elsewhere (from €3 per glass), and there are special evenings devoted to little-heard-of winemakers. The wines are accompanied by sharing plates of local cheese, pâte and charcuterie.

ℹ️ Information

Tourist Office (☑ 03 89 20 68 92; www.tourisme-colmar.com; place Unterlinden; ⊙ 9am-6pm Mon-Sat, 10am-1pm Sun; 🛜) Free wi-fi for 45 minutes.

ℹ️ Getting There & Around

AIR

Trinational **EuroAirport** (MLH or BSL; ☑ +33 3 89 90 31 11; www.euroairport.com) is 60km south of Colmar.

An airport shuttle bus service operates between St-Louis and the airport (€2.60, eight minutes, every 20 or 30 minutes) and frequent

---

DON'T MISS

THE EPICURE TOUR

Colmar is an exceptional city for all-out indulgence. So go, assemble your gourmet picnic:

Marché Couvert (rue des Écoles; ⊙ 8am-6pm Tue-Thu, 8am-7pm Fri, 8am-5pm Sat, 10am-2pm Sun) Bag Munster cheese, pretzels, pastries, wild-boar *saucisson* (dry-cured sausage or salami) and more at this 19th-century market hall.

Fromagerie St-Nicolas (www.fromagerie-st-nicolas.com; 18 rue St-Nicolas; ⊙ 2-7pm Mon, 10am-12.30pm & 2-7pm Tue-Thu, 9am-7pm Fri, 9am-6.30pm Sat) Follow your nose to pungent Munster, Tomme and ripe Camembert. BYOB (bring your own baguette) and the staff here will make you a sandwich.

Choco en Têtes (www.chocolat-en-tetes.com; 7 rue des Têtes; ⊙ 2-6.30pm Mon, 9.30am-12.30pm & 2-6.30pm Tue-Sat) Edible art describes this chocolatier's seasonally inspired truffles and pralines. Kids love the chocolate stork eggs.

Pâtisserie Gilg (www.patisserie-gilg.com; 60 Grand'Rue; patisserie & desserts €3-5; ⊙ 9am-6.45pm Tue-Fri, to 6pm Sat, to 12.30pm Sun) Bitter-chocolate cake, desserts with fresh fruit, nuts or caramel, rainbow-hued macarons, magnificent *millefeuilles*: Gilg is Colmar's patisserie par excellence.

Maison Martin Jund (www.martinjund.com; 12 rue de l'Ange; ⊙ tastings 9am-noon & 1.30-6.30pm Mon-Fri, 9am-noon & 2-6pm Sat) Need something to wash it all down? Head to this organic winery to taste home-grown pinots, rieslings and sylvaners.

WORTH A TRIP

THE STAR OF CITADELS

Shaped like an eight-pointed star, the fortified town of Neuf-Brisach was commissioned by Louis XIV in 1697 to strengthen French defences and prevent the area from falling to the Habsburgs. It was conceived by Sébastien Le Prestre de Vauban (1633–1707).

A Unesco World Heritage Site since 2008, the citadel of Neuf-Brisach has remarkably well-preserved fortifications. The **Musée Vauban** (7 place de Belfort; adult/child €2.50/1.65; ⊙ 10am-noon & 2-5pm Wed-Mon May-Oct), below the porte de Belfort gate, tells the history of the citadel through models, documents and building plans.

Neuf-Brisach is just 4km from its German twin Breisach am Rhein on the banks of the Rhine. To reach Neuf-Brisach, 16km southeast of Colmar, follow the signs on the D415. Buses 1076 and 301 also run between the town and Colmar's main station (€4.15, 40 minutes).

trains run between Colmar and St-Louis (€13.40, 39 minutes).

BUS

Public buses are not the quickest way to explore Alsace's Route des Vins, but they *are* a viable option; destinations served include Riquewihr, Hunawihr, Ribeauvillé, Kaysersberg and Eguisheim.

The open-air bus terminal is to the right as you exit the train station. Timetables are posted and are also available at the tourist office or online (www.l-k.fr, in French).

Line 1076 goes to Neuf-Brisach (€3.75, 30 minutes), continuing on to the German city of Freiburg (€8.70, 1¼ hours, seven daily Monday to Friday, four daily weekends).

TRAIN

Colmar train connections:

Basel €14.40, 46 minutes, 25 daily

Mulhouse €8.90, 21 to 38 minutes, 38 daily

Paris Gare de l'Est; €90 to €115, 2¼ to three hours, 17 daily

Strasbourg €12.90, 32 to 36 minutes, 30 daily

Route des Vins destinations departing from Colmar include Dambach-la-Ville (€6.70, 27 minutes to one hour) and Obernai (€9.50, one to 1½ hours), both of which require a change of trains at Sélestat (€5.20, 10 minutes, 30 daily).

About 20 daily TER trains (10 daily on weekends) link Colmar with the Vallée de Munster towns of Munster (€4.30, 22 to 37 minutes) and Metzeral (€5.40, 35 to 50 minutes).

Massif des Vosges

La vie en Vosges is in many ways the good life and the region is a fine place to tiptoe away from the well-trodden trail. This little-known swath of softly rounded, lushly forest-cloaked heights, pastures, lakes and dairy farms has its own special allure.

The remote 3000-sq-km **Parc Naturel Régional des Ballons des Vosges** (www.

parc-ballons-vosges.fr) is surmounted by 1424m **Grand Ballon**, the highest peak in the range. Situated 20km southwest of Grand Ballon as the crow flies (by road, take the D465 from St-Maurice), the 1247m-high **Ballon d'Alsace** (www.ballondalsace.fr) marks the meeting point of the Alsace, Franche-Comté and Lorraine *régions*.

Partly built during WWI to supply French frontline troops, the **Route des Crêtes** (Route of the Crests; www.massif-des-vosges.com) takes you to the Vosges' highest *ballons* (bald, rounded mountain peaks) and to several WWI sites. Mountaintop lookouts afford spectacular views of the Alsace plain, the Black Forest across the Rhine in Germany and – on clear days – the Alps and Mont Blanc.

The **Vallée de Munster**, northeast of the park, is one of the region's loveliest valleys.

Munster

POP 4645

Spread around gently rolling hills and famous for its notoriously smelly and eponymous cheese, streamside Munster, meaning 'monastery', is a relaxed base for exploring the Vallée de Munster (the long-distance hiking trail GR531 passes by here).

⊙ Sights & Activities

Enclos aux Cigognes   WILDLIFE RESERVE
(Stork Enclosure; chemin du Dubach; ⊙ 24hr) FREE
About 20 storks live year-round in the Enclos aux Cigognes, and more hang out on top of it. It's 250m behind the Renaissance *hôtel de ville;* on foot, cross the creek and turn left.

🛏 Sleeping & Eating

Hôtel Deybach   HOTEL €
(☑ 03 89 77 32 71; www.hotel-deybach.com; 4 chemin du Badischhof; s €56-70, d €65-80, tr €84-95; P 🛜) You are made to feel instantly welcome

at family-run Hôtel Deybach, which has fresh, simple rooms with town or country views and a flowery garden for relaxing moments. Breakfast costs an additional €11.

Patisserie Gilg
CAFE €

(11 Grand'Rue; cakes & pastries €2-5; ⊙7.30am-6.30pm Tue-Fri, 7am-6pm Sat, 7.30am-12.30pm Sun) Skip dinner and go straight for dessert at this tearoom famous for its delectable *kougelhopf* (a ring-shaped marble cake), petits fours and pastries.

A l'Agneau d'Or
FRENCH €€

(☑ 03 89 77 34 08; http://m.fache.free.fr; 2 rue St-Grégoire; mains €23-27; ⊙noon-2pm & 7-9pm Wed-Sun) Brimming with bonhomie, A l'Agneau d'Or is a fine choice for robustly seasoned, attractively presented Alsatian dishes, such as *choucroute au gratin* with Munster cheese and pork cheeks slow-braised in pinot noir – all served in intimate, candlelit surrounds.

ℹ Information

Maison du Parc Naturel Régional des Ballons des Vosges (☑ 03 89 77 90 34; www.parc-ballons-vosges.fr; 1 cour de l'Abbaye; ⊙10am-noon & 1.30-5.30pm Tue-Sun mid-Jun–mid-Sep, shorter hours rest of year) The regional park's visitors centre has ample information in English. To get here, walk through the arch from place du Marché.

Tourist Office (☑ 03 89 77 31 80; www.vallee-munster.eu; 1 rue du Couvent; ⊙9.30am-noon & 2-6pm Mon-Fri, 10am-noon & 2-4pm Sat) Information on the Munster valley, including visits to cheesemakers. Sells hiking maps and topo-guides in French. To get here, walk through the arch from place du Marché.

ℹ Getting There & Around

Cycle Hop Evasion (☑ 06 07 16 56 35; 5 rue de la République; city bike per half-/full day €10/14, mountain bike €14/18, e-bike €22/28; ⊙9.30am-6.30pm Mon-Sat) rents out bikes, arranges guides and provides details on cycling routes.

Trains run approximately twice hourly from Munster to Colmar (€4.30, 22 to 30 minutes) and Strasbourg (€15.70, one to 1½ hours).

Mulhouse

POP 111,167

The dynamic industrial city of Mulhouse (moo-looze), 57km south of Colmar, was allied with nearby Switzerland before voting to join Revolutionary France in 1798. Largely rebuilt after the ravages of WWII, it has little of the quaint Alsatian charm that you find further north, but the city's world-class industrial museums are well worth a stop.

◎ Sights

Ecomusée d'Alsace
MUSEUM

(www.ecomusee-alsace.fr; Ungersheim; adult/child €15/10; ⊙10am-6pm, closed Jan–mid-Mar) Ecomusée d'Alsace is a fascinating excursion into Alsatian country life and time-honoured crafts. Smiths, cartwrights, potters and coopers do their thing in and among 70 historic Alsatian farmhouses – a veritable village – brought here and painstakingly reconstructed for preservation (and so storks can build nests on them). Ungersheim is 17km northwest of Mulhouse. Take tram 1 to Rattachement, then bus 54 to the Ecomusée stop. The closest train station is in Bollwiller, 3km north.

Musée de l'Impression sur Étoffes
MUSEUM

(Museum of Textile Printing; www.musee-impression.com; 14 rue Jean-Jacques Henner; adult/child €10/5; ⊙10am-noon & 2-6pm Tue-Sun) Once known as the 'French Manchester', Mulhouse is fittingly home to this peerless collection of six million textile samples – from brilliant cashmeres to intricate silk screens – which makes it very popular with fabric designers. It's one long block northeast of the train station.

Musée du Papier Peint
MUSEUM

(www.museepapierpeint.org; 28 rue Zuber, Rixheim; adult/child €8.50/free; ⊙10am-noon & 2-6pm, closed Mon Nov-Apr) More stimulating than it sounds, this is a treasure trove of wallpaper (some of the scenic stuff is as detailed as an oil painting) and the machines used to produce it since the 18th century. To reach it, take bus 18 from the train station to Temple stop, or the Rixheim exit on the A36.

Cité de l'Automobile
MUSEUM

(http://citedelautomobile.com; 192 av de Colmar; adult/child €13/10.50; ⊙10am-6pm) An ode to the automobile, this striking glass-and-steel museum showcases 400 rare and classic motors, from old-timers such as the Bugatti Royale to Formula 1 dream machines. There's a kids' corner for would-be mechanics. By car, hop off the A36 at the Mulhouse Centre exit. By public transport, take bus 10 or tram 1 from Mulhouse to the Musée de l'Automobile stop.

Cité du Train
MUSEUM

(www.citedutrain.com; 2 rue Alfred de Glehn; adult/child €12/9.50; ⊙10am-6pm) Trainspotters are in their element at Europe's largest railway museum, displaying SNCF's prized collection of locomotives and carriages. Take bus 20 from the train station or, if driving, the Mulhouse-Dornach exit on the A35.

🛏 Sleeping

Hotel du Musée Gare HOTEL €
(☑ 03 89 45 47 41; www.hotelmuseegare.com; 3 rue de l'Est; d €49-98, tr €105-198, q €115-218; P 🛜) Sitting opposite the Musée de l'Impression sur Étoffes (p372) and very close to the train station, this lovingly restored townhouse outclasses most of Mulhouse's hotels with its 19th-century flair, attentive service and spacious, high-ceilinged rooms. Free parking is a bonus. Buffet breakfast costs an extra €9.80.

Hotel Bristol HOTEL €€
(☑ 03 89 42 12 31; www.hotelbristol.com; 18 av de Colmar; d €55-150, ste €150-200, tr €85-130, q €95-145; P 🛜) This central hotel is a decent midrange base for exploring Mulhouse. The modern, revamped 'comfort' rooms are worth the upgrade from the old-style 'standard' rooms, which could do with a little TLC. A buffet breakfast with cold cuts, cheeses and pastries costs €9.50.

Villa Eden VILLA €€€
(☑ 06 74 37 19 38, 03 89 44 50 72; www.villa-eden. fr; 99 av de la 1ère Division Blindée; s €170-190, d €195-230; P 🛜🏊) A far cry from the anonymity of many of Mulhouse's hotels, this shuttered villa sits above the city's zoo and botanical gardens. It's a secluded spot to escape the bustle of the centre, with gardens, an outdoor pool and individually designed rooms (from 'Zen' to 'sweet chocolate') with plenty of light, space and comfort.

🍴 Eating & Drinking

Enquête de Goûts CAFE
(35 rue des Trois Rois; ⊙ 9am-7pm Tue-Thu, to 11pm Fri, to 7pm Sat) Crammed with crime novels and mismatched furniture, this quirky hole-in-the-wall bookshop also does a fine line in breakfasts, coffee, tea and two-course lunches (€11.50).

Zum Sauwadala FRENCH €
(☑ 03 89 45 18 19; 13 rue de l'Arsenal; mains €12-21; ⊙ noon-2pm & 7-11pm Tue-Sat, 7-11pm Mon) Two little pigs guide the way to this snug bistro – the very essence of Alsace quaintness with its dark timber, checked tablecloths and roll-me-out-the-door hearty grub. The menu is packed with classics – Spätzle (egg pasta), pork trotters and choucroute (garnished sauerkraut) – all of which marry nicely with a glass of local pinot noir. The plat du jour goes for €8.50.

⭐Chez Auguste BISTRO €€
(☑ 03 89 46 62 71; www.chezauguste.com; 11 rue Poincaré; menus €20-25, mains €15-22; ⊙ noon-2pm & 7-10pm Tue-Sat) Overflowing with regulars, this casually sophisticated bistro always has a good buzz. The concise menu excels in classics including scallops with orange-infused carrot purée and pistachio, confit pork cheeks slow-cooked for six hours, and chocolate fondant. Service is faultless.

ℹ Information

Mulhouse's helpful tourist office (☑ 03 89 35 48 48; www.tourism-mulhouse.com; 1 av Robert Schuman; ⊙ 10am-1pm & 2-6pm Mon-Sat, 10am-3pm Sun; 🛜) is just north of the old town. Free wi-fi.

ℹ Getting There & Around

BICYCLE
Mulhouse has an automatic bike-rental system, Velocité (www.velocite.mulhouse.fr), with 40 stands across the city – the online map shows where. The first half-hour is free and it costs €1/3 per day/week thereafter (deposit €150).

TRAIN
France's second train line, linking Mulhouse with Thann, opened in 1839. The train station (10 av du Général Leclerc) is just south of the centre. Trains run at least hourly to Basel (€7.70, 23 to 31 minutes), Colmar (€8.90, 19 to 37 minutes), St-Louis (€6.30, 14 to 20 minutes) and Strasbourg (€19.20, 53 minutes).

LORRAINE

Wedged between the plains and vines of Champagne and the hilly, thickly wooded Massif des Vosges, Lorraine is fed by the Meurthe, Moselle and Meuse Rivers – hence the names of three of its four départements (the fourth is Vosges).

Cities like Metz, with its outstanding galleries and jewel-like Gothic cathedral, and Nancy with its art-nouveau sophistication and uplifting Unesco World Heritage square, are a terrific starting point. From here, you can strike out into more uncharted territory. A hard-hitting journey heads west to the cross-stippled battlefields of Verdun, where the longest battle of WWI unravelled.

ALSACE & LORRAINE LORRAINE

Nancy

POP 104,321

Delightful Nancy has an air of refinement found nowhere else in Lorraine. With a resplendent central square, fine museums, formal gardens and shop windows sparkling with Daum and Baccarat crystal, the former capital of the dukes of Lorraine catapults you back to the riches of the 18th century, when much of the city centre was built.

Nancy has long thrived on a combination of innovation and sophistication. The art-nouveau movement flourished here (as the Nancy School) thanks to the rebellious spirit of local artists, who set out to prove that everyday objects could be drop-dead gorgeous.

◉ Sights

The tourist office offers multilingual audioguide tours (€7.50) of the historic centre (two hours) and the art-nouveau quarters (up to three or four hours). A €30 deposit is required. Alternatively download a free MP3 tour online (www.nancy-tourisme.fr).

★ Place Stanislas   SQUARE
Nancy's crowning glory is this grand neoclassical square and Unesco World Heritage Site. Designed by Emmanuel Héré in the 1750s, it was named after the enlightened, Polish-born duke of Lorraine, whose statue stands in the middle. The square is home to an opulent ensemble of pale-stone buildings, including the hôtel de ville and Opéra National de Lorraine (p379), as well as gilded wrought-iron gateways by Jean Lamour and rococo fountains by Guibal – look out for the one of a trident-bearing Neptune.

Place de la Carrière   SQUARE
Adjoining place Stanislas – on the other side of Nancy's own Arc de Triomphe, built in the mid-1750s to honour Louis XV – is this quiet square. Once a riding and jousting arena, it is now graced by four rows of linden trees and stately rococo gates in gilded wrought iron.

★ Musée des Beaux-Arts   GALLERY
(http://mban.nancy.fr; 3 place Stanislas; adult/child €7/4.50, audioguide €3; ◉10am-6pm Wed-Mon) Lodged in a regal 18th-century edifice, Nancy's standout gallery occupies art lovers for hours. A wrought-iron staircase curls gracefully up to the 2nd floor, where a chronological spin begins with 14th- to 17th-century paintings by the likes of Perugino, Tintoretto and Jan van Hemessen. The 1st floor spot-

lights 17th- to 19th-century masterpieces of the Rubens, Monet, Picasso and Caravaggio ilk. A collection of Jean Prouvé furnishings, impressionist and modern art and a dazzling Daum crystal collection hide in the basement.

Highlights in the 1st- and 2nd-floor picture galleries include Mello da Gubbio's 14th-century altarpiece, Perugino's Renaissance *Madonna and Child with two Angels* (1505), Rubens' lucid, large-scale *Transfiguration* (1603), showing Jesus radiant on a mountain, and Caravaggio's dramatic chiaroscuro *Annunciation* (1607).

The basement Jean Prouvé Collection homes in on the pared-down aesthetic of Nancy-born architect and designer Jean Prouvé (1901–84), and displays a selection of Prouvé's furniture, architectural elements, ironwork and graphic works. Here you will also find the peerless Daum Collection, which is displayed in a dark, spotlit gallery that shows off the glassware to great effect and is cleverly set against the backdrop of Nancy's late-medieval city walls. Trace Daum through the ages – from the sinuous, naturalistic forms of art nouveau to the clean colours and restrained lines of contemporary crystal.

The downstairs picture gallery wings you into the 19th and 20th centuries with an excellent portfolio of works, among them Eugène Delacroix' *Battle of Nancy* (1831), Monet's dreamy *Étretat, Sunset* (1883) and Picasso's *Homme et femme* (1971), one of his final portraits.

Musée de l'École de Nancy   MUSEUM
(School of Nancy Museum; www.ecole-de-nancy. com; 36-38 rue du Sergent Blandan; adult/child €6/4; ◉10am-6pm Wed-Sun) A highlight of a visit to Nancy, the Musée de l'École de Nancy brings together an exquisite collection of art-nouveau interiors, curvaceous glass and landscaped gardens. It's housed in a 19th-century villa about 2km southwest of the centre; to get there take bus 6 (Painlevé stop) or bus 6, 7 or 8 (Nancy Thermal stop).

Musée Lorrain   MUSEUM
(www.musee-lorrain.nancy.fr; 64 & 66 Grande Rue; adult/child €6/4; ◉10am-12.30pm & 2-6pm Tue-Sun) Once home to the dukes of Lorraine, the regal Renaissance Palais Ducal now shelters the Musée Lorrain. The rich fine arts and history collection spotlights medieval statuary, engravings and lustrous faience (glazed pottery). The regional art and folklore collection occupies a 15th-century former Franciscan monastery. Inside, the

ART NOUVEAU TRAIL

In 1900, glassmaker and ceramist Émile Gallé founded the École de Nancy, one of France's leading art-nouveau movements, joining creative forces with masters of decorative arts and architecture such as Jacques Gruber, Louis Majorelle and the Daum brothers. Banks, villas, pharmacies, brasseries – wherever you wander in Nancy, you're bound to stumble across their handiwork, from sinuous grillwork to curvaceous stained-glass windows and doorways that are a profusion of naturalistic ornament.

Slip back to this genteel era by picking up the free *Art Nouveau Itineraries* brochure and map at the tourist office (p379), covering four city strolls. Lucien Weissenburger's 1911 **Brasserie Excelsior** (☑ 03 83 35 24 57; www.brasserie-excelsior.com; 50 rue Henri Poincaré; menus €29-59; ⊗ 8am-12.30am Tue-Sat, to 11pm Sun & Mon; ⊞) and the 1908 **Chambre de Commerce** (rue Henri Poincaré) with wrought iron by Louis Majorelle are central standouts. Close to the Musée de l'École de Nancy lies the whimsical Villa Majorelle (p375), built by Henri Sauvage in 1901 and bearing the hallmarks of Majorelle (furniture) and Gruber (stained glass). The centrepiece is the Les Blés dining room with its vine-like stone fireplace. Advance telephone bookings are essential.

Gothic **Église des Cordeliers** and the 17th-century **Chapelle Ducale**, modelled on the Medici Chapel in Florence, served as the burial place of the dukes of Lorraine.

Villa Majorelle   MUSEUM
(☑ 03 83 17 86 77; www.ecole-de-nancy.com; 1 rue Louis-Majorelle; adult/child €6/4; ⊗ guided tours 2.30pm & 3.45pm Sat & Sun May-Oct) The whimsical Villa Majorelle, built by Henri Sauvage in 1901, bears the hallmarks of Majorelle (furniture) and Gruber (stained glass). The centrepiece is **Les Blés dining room**, with its vine-like stone fireplace. Advance telephone bookings are essential.

Vieille Ville   AREA
A saunter through the charming old town takes in the silver-turreted, 14th-century **Porte de la Craffe**, Nancy's oldest city gate, and **place St-Epvre**, dominated by ornate neo Gothic **Basilique St-Epvre**.

Parc de la Pépinière   PARK
(⊗ 6.30am-10.30pm, shorter hours winter) On a hot summer's day, escape the crowds in this formal garden, with ornamental fountains, a rose garden and a Rodin sculpture of Baroque landscape painter Claude Lorrain.

Muséum-Aquarium de Nancy   MUSEUM
(www.museumaquariumdenancy.eu; 34 rue Ste-Catherine; adult/child €5/3; ⊗ 9am-noon & 2-6pm Tue-Sun) Bang in the centre of town, this museum brings together a natural history museum and aquarium under one rather stylish art-deco roof. Its tanks swirl with tropical and temperate fish and the zoology collection contains 600 specimens. Come on the first Sunday of the month and entry is free.

✳ Festivals & Events

Jazz Pulsations   MUSIC
(www.nancyjazzpulsations.com; 10 rue Baron Louis; ⊗ mid-Oct) Get your groove on to live jazz, blues and Latin at the 10-day Jazz Pulsations. Events are held at numerous venues across town including Théâtre de la Manufacture.

Fêtes de St-Nicolas   CHRISTMAS MARKET
(place Charles III; ⊗ late Nov-late Dec) The Fêtes de St-Nicolas bring festive twinkle, carols, shows, carousels and handicrafts to the city centre, revolving mostly around place Charles III.

🛏 Sleeping

**Chambres des Quatre
Coins du Monde**   B&B €
(☑ 03 83 96 46 83; www.chambresdesquatrecoins dumonde.fr; 247 av de la Libération; s/d €80/90) You'll receive a warm *bienvenue* at this lovely homestyle B&B on Nancy's fringes. As the name alludes, there are four rooms themed on different places around the world – in this case New York, Marrakesh, Bali and... Baccarat. In summer, the substantial breakfast is served on the garden terrace. Bus 5 to St-Mansuy stops out front.

La Résidence   HOTEL €
(☑ 03 83 40 33 56; www.hotel-laresidence-nancy. com; 30 bd Jean-Jaurès; d €73-84, q €115; 🅿 🛜) This convivial hotel is one of Nancy's best deals, with an inviting salon and a leafy courtyard for alfresco breakfasts. The snappy rooms have ultramodern bathrooms and flat-screen TVs. The hotel is situated 1km south of the train station (p379). Tram 1 stops at Mon Désert and Garenne, both a two-minute walk from the hotel.

Nancy

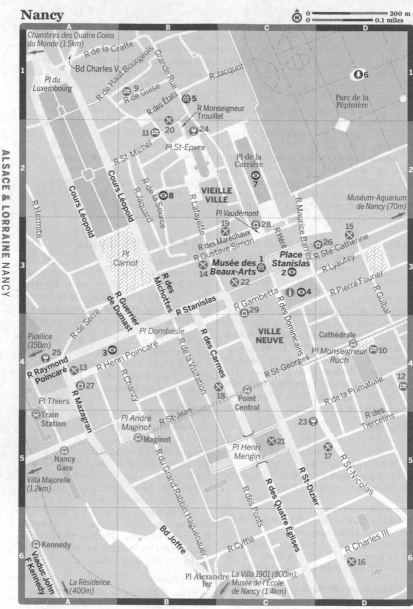

Hôtel des Prélats HISTORIC HOTEL €€
(03 83 30 20 20; www.hoteldesprelats.com; 56 place Monseigneur Ruch; s €79-99, d €119-145, ste €249;) It's not every day you get to sleep in a 17th-century former bishop's palace right next to the cathedral. This elegant hotel plays up the romance in rooms with stained-glass windows, four-poster beds and shimmery drapes. Service is as polished as the surrounds.

Nancy

Hôtel de Guise　　　HISTORIC HOTEL €€
(☑ 03 83 32 24 68; www.hoteldeguise.com; 18 rue de Guise; s €69-100, d €80-140; 🐾) Boutique chic meets 17th-century elegance at this hotel, tucked down an old-town backstreet. A wrought-iron staircase sweeps up to grand-meets-modern rooms, with antique furnishings and heavy drapes. There's a walled garden for quiet moments.

La Villa 1901　　　B&B €€
(☑ 06 30 03 21 62; www.lavilla1901.fr; 63 av du Général Leclerc; s €145-165, d €165-185, tr €195-215; 🐾) Taking a leaf out of the chic interiors book, this B&B combines art nouveau with contemporary design flourishes and boho flair to beautiful effect. The richly hued rooms and suites feature homestyle touches like fireplaces and iPod docks, and there's a garden for time out. Breakfast (included in the rate) is a treat, with fresh pastries, juice and preserves.

Maison de Myon　　　B&B €€
(☑ 03 83 46 56 56; www.maisondemyon.com; 7 rue Mably; s €115, d €140-150, apt €165-195; 🐾) Slip behind the cathedral to reach this stately 17th-century house turned boutique B&B. A wrought-iron staircase leads to light-filled, wooden-floored rooms flaunting antique furnishings, one-of-a-kind art and ornamental fireplaces. Each room takes its name from its polished-concrete bathroom (sand, turquoise, mandarin and so on). The wisteria-draped courtyard is a calm breakfast spot.

★ **Hôtel d'Haussonville**　　　HISTORIC HOTEL €€€
(☑ 03 83 35 85 84; www.hotel-haussonville.fr; 9 rue Monseigneur Trouillet; d €149-239; 🐾) Centred on an ornately carved courtyard, this sublime Renaissance mansion snuggles down a backstreet in the heart of Nancy's Vieille Ville (p375). The seven individually designed rooms are decorated with impeccable taste, done out with parquet floors, elegant drapes and ornamental fireplaces. It's worth shelling out the extra €17 for breakfast.

✖ Eating

Restaurant-speckled rue des Maréchaux dishes up French, Italian, tapas, seafood, Indian and Japanese, while rue St-Nicolas is a great street for on-the-hoof snacking, with everything from pizza to Thai and kebabs. Grande Rue is peppered with intimate bistros.

Marché Couvert　　　MARKET €
(place Henri Mengin; ⊙7am-7pm Tue-Sat) A fresh-produce feast for the picnic basket, with several snack stands offering inexpensive lunches.

Pidélice　　　SANDWICHES €
(25 rue Raymond-Poincaré; pidélices €6-7, menus €9.50-12; ⊙11.30am-2.30pm & 7-10.30pm Mon-Fri, 7-10.30pm Sun) Is it a pizza? Is it a sandwich? Well, a *pidélice* is kind of both, served hot, crunchy and stuffed with gourmet fillings – from feta and olives to steak with melted cheese – prepared with organic ingredients. The walls are covered with quirky photos of moustaches; see if you can snap a better one.

L'Appétit Bio
FAST FOOD €

(☑ 09 86 26 22 53; www.lappetit-bio.fr; 153 rue St-Dizier; mains €8-9.50, menus €12; ⊙11.30am-2pm & 6.30-9pm Tue-Sat; 🖊🖼) 🍃 Healthy and 100% organic fast food is the raison d'être of L'Appétit Bio, which makes the most of fresh local produce in its tasty burgers, soups and quiches. There's plenty of choice for vegetarians, vegans and kids.

Voyou
BURGERS €

(☑ 03 72 14 87 25; www.voyou-burger.com; 20 rue Stanislas; burgers €14.90; ⊙noon-1.45pm & 7-10.15pm Tue-Sat; 🖼) Hip, split-level, doodle-daubed Voyou is hands-down the best place in town for a gourmet burger you can properly sink your teeth into. On the menu are burgers made from quality meat, served in organic buns, with toppings like *raclette*, rösti and caramelised onions, plus a veggie option. All come with proper *frites* and salad.

Le Bouche à Oreille
BISTRO €

(☑ 03 83 35 17 17; http://restaurant-bouche-a-oreille.fr; 42 rue des Carmes; menus €11-24, mains €13-21; ⊙7-10pm Mon, noon-1.30pm & 7-10pm Tue-Thu, noon-1.30pm & 7-10.30pm Fri, 7-10.30pm Sat; 🖼) Resembling an overgrown doll's house, this knick-knack-filled bistro specialises in cheese-based dishes such as *raclette, tartiflette* (creamy, cheesy potato bake with onions and lardons) and fondue. There's a €10 kids' menu.

L'Artisan Épicier
INTERNATIONAL €

(www.artisan-epicier.com; 26 rue St-Nicolas; mains €8, menus €12.90; ⊙10am-7pm Tue-Sat) Trading in spices, herbs and top-quality condiments, this friendly, modern, jar-lined bistro naturally uses these to flavour appetising day specials like chicken tagines, which go for a wallet-friendly €8. The *menu*, including dessert and tea or coffee, will set you back €12.90.

Inévitable
MODERN FRENCH €€

(☑ 03 83 36 36 36; www.bistorant-inevitable.fr; 17 rue Gustave Simon; lunch menus €20, dinner mains €22; ⊙noon-2pm & 8-10pm Thu, Fri & Mon, 8-10pm Sat) You can expect a warm welcome at this slick, monochrome bistro, which keeps its menu seasonal, simple and regional, along the lines of market-fresh fish with braised fennel and bergamot confit.

Le V-Four
BISTRO €€

(☑ 03 83 32 49 48; www.levfour.fr; 10 rue St-Michel; menus €21-78; ⊙noon-1.30pm & 7.30-11.30pm Tue-Sat, noon-1.30pm Sun) With just a handful of tables, this petite bistro is all about intimacy and understated sophistication. Mulberry chairs and crisp white tablecloths set the scene for original creations such as grilled scallops with Jerusalem artichoke and truffle. The three-course lunch is a steal at €21. Book ahead.

Le Gentilhommiere
FRENCH €€

(☑ 03 83 32 26 44; www.lagentilhommierenancy.fr; 29 rue des Maréchaux; menus €26-40; ⊙noon-2pm & 7-10pm Mon-Fri, 7-10pm Sat) Warm-hued, subtly lit Le Gentilhommiere stands head and shoulders above most of the restaurants on rue des Maréchaux. Specialities like scallop tartlet with beetroot and liquorice vinaigrette and pike-perch fillets with Lorraine truffle risotto reveal true depth of flavour.

La Maison dans le Parc
FRENCH €€€

(☑ 03 83 19 03 57; www.lamaisondansleparc.com; 3 rue Ste-Catherine; menus €39-98; ⊙noon-1.30pm & 7-10pm Wed-Sat, noon-1.30pm Sun) Shining with one Michelin star, this restaurant is Nancy's bastion of fine dining. Service is faultless and the ambience one of urban sophistication, with clean lines, monochrome hues and floor-to-ceiling windows. A smartly dressed crowd pours in for chef Françoise Mutel's artistically presented, intensely flavoured creations, simple as sea-bass tartare with oysters and caviar, and Iberian pork with sweet garlic.

🍷 Drinking & Nightlife

Nancy's buoyant nightlife concentrates on bar-dotted Grande Rue; the spectacularly illuminated place Stanislas and laid-back place St-Epvre in the Vieille Ville (p375) are the best spots for sundowners.

Le Ch'timi
BAR

(17 place St-Epvre; ⊙10am-2am Mon-Sat, to 9pm Sun) On three brick-and-stone levels, Le Ch'timi is *the* place to go for beer. It's a beloved haunt of students, who come for the 200 brews, 16 of them on tap.

La Quincaillerie
BAR

(2 rue St-Nicolas; ⊙4pm-2am Mon-Sat) 'The hardware store' is more kid-in-a-candy-shop stuff for anyone into their flavoured rums, which reach from bergamot to mint and basil here. The windows brim with flagons filled with brightly coloured spirits that are expertly mixed into signature cocktails. It's cosily stylish, with slouchy sofas for lingering over a killer mojito plus a pavement terrace for summer imbibing.

Rhumerie la Plantation
BAR

(www.rhumerielaplantation.fr; 8 rue Raymond Poincaré; ⊙6pm-midnight Tue, to 2am Wed-Sat) The mixologists sure know their stuff at this upbeat, backlit bar, especially when they are shaking speciality rums into creative cocktails. The vibe is mellow and there are regular events – from jam sessions and folk gigs to exhibitions and tastings.

☆ Entertainment

Details on cultural events appear in French in Spectacles (www.spectacles-publications. com).

Opéra National de Lorraine OPERA
(☑03 83 85 33 11; www.opera-national-lorraine. fr; 1 rue Ste-Catherine) A harmonious blend of neoclassical and art-nouveau styles, this is Nancy's lavish stage for opera and classical music. The resident orchestra performs at *concerts apéritifs* (€9), held at 11am roughly one Sunday a month.

🛍 Shopping

Nancy's grand thoroughfares are rue St-Dizier, rue St-Jean and rue St-Georges. Grande Rue is studded with idiosyncratic galleries and antique shops.

Lefèvre-Lemoine FOOD
(47 rue Henri Poincaré; ⊙9.30am-7pm Mon-Sat, to 12.30pm Sun) They don't make sweet shops like this 1840s treasure any more, where a bird chirps a welcome as you enter. One of the old-fashioned sweet tins made a cameo appearance in the film *Amélie*. *Bergamotes de Nancy* (bergamot boiled sweets), caramels, nougat, gingerbread, glazed *mirabelles* (plums) – how ever will you choose?

Maison des Sœurs Macarons FOOD
(www.macaron-de-nancy.com; 21 rue Gambetta; ⊙2-7pm Mon, 9.30am-12.30pm & 2-7pm Tue Fri, 9am-7pm Sat) When Nancy's Benedictine nuns hit hard times during the French Revolution, they saw the light in heavenly macarons. They're still made to the original recipe (egg whites, sugar, Provençal almonds) at this old-world confectioner. A dozen box (€8.50) makes a great gift.

L'Épicerie du Goût FOOD & DRINKS
(www.epicerie-du-gout.fr; 4 place Vaudémont; ⊙10am-1pm & 3.30-8pm Mon-Fri, 10am-1pm & 2.30-8pm Sat) This family-run grocery store on the edge of the old town is crammed with Lorraine delicacies. Cheeses, smoked *saucisson*, macarons, *mirabelles* (plums) in every guise, beer, preserves – you'll find it all here.

ⓘ CITY PASS

The good-value Nancy City Pass (€12), valid for 10 days, gets you an audioguide tour of the city, a 24-hour transport ticket and a 50% discount on bike rental. Various other discount passes include Le Museo Pass, valid for 10 days and costing €15, which gets you entry to six of the city's major museums.

ⓘ Information

Tourist Office (☑03 83 35 22 41; www.nancy-tourisme.fr; place Stanislas; ⊙9am-6.30pm Mon-Sat, 10am-5pm Sun Apr-Oct, shorter hours rest of year; 🛜) Inside the **Hôtel de Ville** (p374). Has free brochures detailing walking tours of the city centre and art-nouveau architecture. Free wi-fi.

ⓘ Getting There & Around

BICYCLE
Nancy is easy to navigate by bicycle. **Vélostan** (www.velostanlib.fr; per day/week €1.50/5; ⊙24hr) has rental sites inside the **train station** and near the Musée de l'École de Nancy in **Espace Thermal** (rue du Sergent Blandan), as well as 29 rental points where you can hire bikes 24/7. An €80 deposit is required.

TRAIN
The **train station** (place Thiers) is on the line linking Paris with Strasbourg. Destinations include:
Baccarat €11.70, 38 to 48 minutes, 15 daily
Metz €11.50, 38 to 53 minutes, 48 daily
Paris €77 to €90, 1½ hours, 13 daily
Strasbourg €26.80, 1½ hours, 12 daily

Baccarat
POP 4460
Bisected by the Moselle River, Baccarat, 60km southeast of Nancy, seems like any other quaint French town on the surface of things, with its historic centre of shuttered houses. But its glitzy Baccarat *cristallerie* (crystal glassworks), founded in 1764, whose craftsmanship dazzles in the Musée Baccarat and Église St-Rémy (p380), really puts it on the map.

◉ Sights

Musée Baccarat MUSEUM
(www.baccarat.fr; cours des Cristalleries; adult/child €5/free; ⊙10am-noon & 2-6pm Tue-Sun) The Musée Baccarat displays 1100 exquisite pieces

of handmade lead crystal. The boutique out front is almost as dazzling as the museum.

Église St-Rémy CHURCH
(1 av de Lachapelle; ⊙ 8am-5pm) On the bank of the park-lined River Meurthe, the dark concrete sanctuary of Église St-Rémy, built in the mid-1950s, is austere on the outside and kaleidoscopic on the inside – dramatically lit by 20,000 Baccarat crystal panels.

ℹ Information
The **tourist office** (📞 03 83 75 13 37; www. tourisme-lunevillois.com; 13 rue du Port; ⊙ 9am-12.30pm & 1.30-6pm) has info on the surrounds and hiking maps.

ℹ Getting There & Away
Trains run from Baccarat to Nancy (€11.70, 38 to 50 minutes, 15 daily). By car, Baccarat makes an easy stop on the way from Nancy to Colmar via the Vosges' Col du Bonhomme.

Metz
POP 119,775

Sitting astride the confluence of the Moselle and Seille rivers, Lorraine's graceful capital, Metz (pronounced 'mess'), is ready to be feted. Though the city's Gothic marvel of a cathedral (p380), superlative art collections and Michelin star–studded dining scene long managed to sidestep the world spotlight, all that changed with the show-stopping arrival of Centre Pompidou-Metz (p380). Yet the Pompidou is but the prelude to Metz's other charms: buzzy pavement cafes and shady riverside parks, a beautiful old town built from golden Jeumont stone and a regal Quartier Impérial (p380) up for Unesco World Heritage status.

◉ Sights

★ Centre Pompidou-Metz GALLERY
(www.centrepompidou-metz.fr; 1 parvis des Droits de l'Homme; adult/child €7/free; ⊙ 10am-6pm Mon & Wed-Thu, to 7pm Fri-Sun) Designed by Japanese architect Shigeru Ban, with a curved roof resembling a space-age Chinese hat, the architecturally innovative Centre Pompidou-Metz is the star of Metz' art scene. The satellite branch of Paris' Centre Pompidou draws on Europe's largest modern-art collection to stage ambitious temporary exhibitions, such as the figurative cubist creations of French artist and sculptor Fernand Léger and the bold avant-garde works of German Bauhaus artist Oskar Schlemmer. The dynamic space

also hosts cultural events, talks and youth projects.

★ Cathédrale St-Étienne CATHEDRAL
(www.cathedrale-metz.fr; place St-Étienne; audioguide €7, combined ticket treasury & crypt adult/child €4/2; ⊙ 8am-6pm, treasury & crypt 9.30am-12.30pm & 1.30-5.30pm Mon-Sat, 2-6pm Sun) The lacy golden spires of this Gothic cathedral crown Metz' skyline. Exquisitely lit by kaleidoscopic curtains of 13th- to 20th-century stained glass, the cathedral is nicknamed 'God's lantern' and its sense of height is spiritually uplifting. Notice the flamboyant **Chagall windows** in startling jewel-coloured shades of ruby, gold, sapphire, topaz and amethyst in the ambulatory, which also harbours the **treasury**. A sculpture of the **Graoully** ('grau-lee'), a dragon said to have terrified pre-Christian Metz, lurks in the 15th-century **crypt**.

Musée La Cour d'Or MUSEUM
(http://musee.metzmetropole.fr; 2 rue du Haut Poirier; adult/child €5/free; ⊙ 9am-12.30pm & 1.45-5pm Wed-Mon) Delve into the past at this trove of Gallo-Roman antiquities, hiding remnants of the city's Roman baths and a statue of the Egyptian goddess Isis unearthed right here in Metz. Your visit continues with art from the Middle Ages, paintings from the 15th century onwards, and artefacts revealing the history of Metz' ancient Jewish community. A room-by-room brochure in English is available.

Quartier Impérial AREA
The stately boulevards and bourgeois villas of the German Imperial Quarter, including rue Gambetta and av Foch, are the brainchild of Kaiser Wilhelm II. Philippe Starck lamp posts contrast with Teutonic sculptures, whose common theme is German imperial might, at the monumental Rhenish neo-Romanesque train station (p384), completed in 1908. The massive main **post office** (9 rue Gambetta; ⊙ 8.30am-noon & 1.30-6pm Mon-Fri, 8.30am-12.30pm Sat), built in 1911 of red Vosges sandstone, is as solid and heavy as the cathedral is light and lacy.

Built to trumpet the triumph of Metz' post-1871 status as part of the Second Reich, the architecture is a whimsical mix of art-deco, neo-Romanesque and neo-Renaissance influences. The area's unique ensemble of Wilhelmian architecture has made it a candidate for Unesco World Heritage status.

Place de la Comédie
SQUARE

Bounded by one of the channels of the Moselle, this neoclassical square is home to the city's 18th-century **Théâtre**, France's oldest theatre still in use. During the Revolution, place de l'Égalité (as it was then known) was the site of a guillotine that lopped the heads off 63 'enemies of the people'. Only open during services, the neo-Romanesque **Temple Neuf** church was constructed under the Germans in 1904.

Église St-Pierre-aux-Nonnains
CHURCH

(Esplanade) Originally built around AD380 as part of a Gallo-Roman spa complex, Église St-Pierre-aux-Nonnains is a fine example of a pre-medieval basilica, tracing almost 2000 years of history. Now a cultural centre, it can only be admired from the outside.

Place St-Louis
SQUARE

On the eastern edge of the city centre, triangular place St-Louis is surrounded by medieval arcades and merchants' houses dating from the 14th to 16th centuries.

Metz Plage
BEACH

(1 allée de Metz Plage; ⊙ 11am-8pm late Jul–mid-Aug; ▣) **FREE** You might not have packed your bucket and spade for a trip to Metz, but you can head to this makeshift 'beach' on the banks of the Moselle in summer. Besides a pool with splashy fun for the kids, there's a program of sports and activities.

Riverside Park
PARK

(quai des Régates) In summer, pedal boats and rowboats can be rented on quai des Régates. The promenade leads through a leafy riverside park, with statues, ponds, swans and a fountain. It's the ideal picnic spot.

🛏 Sleeping

Péniche Alclair
HOUSEBOAT €

(☑ 06 37 67 16 18; www.chambrespenichemetz.com; allée St-Symphorien; s/d incl breakfast €75/80; 🕲) What a clever idea: this old barge has been revamped into a stylish blue houseboat, with two cheerful wood-floored rooms and watery views. Breakfast is served in your room or on the sundeck. It's a 15-minute stroll south of the centre along the river.

Les Chambres de l'Ile
B&B €

(☑ 06 13 23 28 33; 15 rue de l'Horticulture, Longeville-lès-Metz; s/d/tr/q €70/80/100/120; ℗🕲) You'll feel immediately *chez vous* (at home) at this sweet, friendly B&B on an island in the Moselle River. The parquet-floored,

MARKET MUST

If only every market were like Metz' grand **Marché Couvert** (Covered Market; place de la Cathédrale; ⊙ 7am-7pm Tue-Sat). Once a bishop's palace, now a temple to fresh local produce, this is the kind of place where you pop in for a baguette and struggle out an hour later with bags overflowing with charcuterie, ripe fruit, pastries and five different sorts of *fromage*.

Make a morning of it, stopping for an early, inexpensive lunch and a chat with the market's larger-than-life characters. Chez Mauricette (p383) tempts with such Lorraine goodies as herby *saucisson*, local charcuterie and *mirabelle* (plum) pâté. Its neighbour, **Soupes á Soups** (Maré Couvert; soups €3-5; ⊙ 7am-6.30pm Tue-Sat), ladles out homemade soups, from mussel to creamy mushroom varieties.

warm-coloured rooms overlook gardens, and homemade preserves, fresh-pressed juice and pastries feature at breakfast. Note that the minimum stay is two nights.

Cécil Hôtel
HOTEL €

(☑ 03 87 66 66 13; www.cecilhotel-metz.com; 14 rue Pasteur; s €64-75, d €74-95, tr €98-100; ℗🕲) Built in 1920, this family run hotel's smallish rooms are neat, petite and decorated in warm colours, though light sleepers should specify that they want a quiet room. Breakfast costs an extra €9 and parking €10 per day.

★ Hôtel de la Cathédrale
HISTORIC HOTEL €€

(☑ 03 87 75 00 02; www.hotelcathedrale-metz.fr; 25 place de Chambre; d €72-120; 🕲) You can expect a friendly welcome at this classy little hotel, occupying a 17th-century townhouse in a prime spot right opposite the cathedral. Climb the wrought-iron staircase to your classically elegant room, with high ceilings, hardwood floors and antique trappings. Book well ahead for a cathedral view. Breakfast will set you back €11.

La Citadelle
LUXURY HOTEL €€

(☑ 03 87 17 17 17; www.citadelle-metz.com; 5 av Ney; d €134-233, ste €290; ℗🕲) A slick conversion of a 16th-century military arsenal and barracks, La Citadelle sits in a tranquil park in the heart of the city. The contemporary rooms flaunt arched windows, red walls and eye-catching fabrics. Best of all, for anyone seriously

Metz

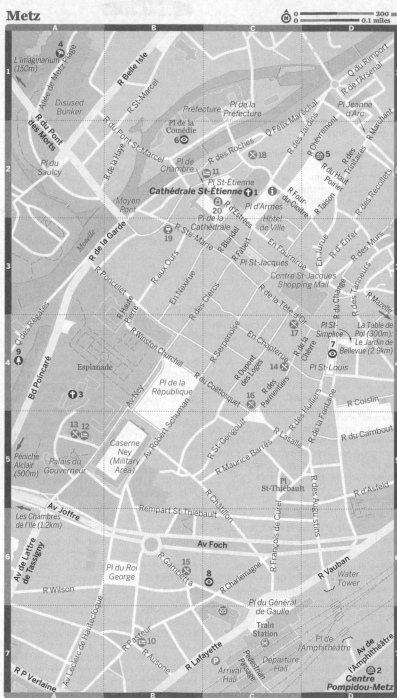

N

0 — 200 m
0 — 0.1 miles

L'Imaginarium
(150m)

4

Allée de Metz Plage

Disused
Bunker

R du Pont
des Morts

R Belle Isle

R St-Marcel

Pl du
Saulcy

Préfecture

Pl de la
Préfecture

R du Pont St-Marcel

Pl de la
Comédie

6

R de la Haye

Q Félix Maréchal

Q des Jardins

Pl Jeanne
d'Arc

R de l'Arsenal

Q du Rimport

R Marchant

R Chèvremont

5

R du Haut
Poirier

R des
Trinitaires

R des Recollets

R des Roches

18

Pl de
Chambre

11

Pl St-Étienne

Cathédrale St-Étienne **1**

Moyen
Pont

Moselle

R de la Garde

R Poncelet

R Haute
Pierre

R Ste-Marie

19

Pl de la
Cathédrale

R d'Estrées

R Blondel

R Fabert

R aux Ours

En Nexirue

R des Clercs

En Nexirue

R Winston Churchill

Av Ney

Pl d'Armes

Hôtel
de Ville

R Four-
du-Cloître

R Raison

En Fournirue

Pl St-Jacques

Centre St-Jacques
Shopping Mall

En Jurue

R d'Enfer

R des Murs

R des Tanneurs

R du Change

R Mazelle

Pl St-
Simplice

17

En Chaplerue

R de la Chèvre

7

Pl St-
Louis

La Table de
Pol (300m);
Le Jardin de
Bellevue (2.9km)

R de la Tête d'Or

R Serpenoise

Q des Régates

9

Bd Poincaré

Esplanade

3

R du Coëtlosquet

Av Robert Schuman

Pl de la
République

R Dupont
des Loges

14

Pl St-Louis

16

R des
Parmentiers

R des Huiliers

R de la Fontaine

R Coislin

R du Cambout

13 **12**

Caserne
Ney
(Military
Area)

Palais du
Gouverneur

Péniche
Alcair
(500m)

R St-Gengoulf

R des Augustins

Pl
St-Thiébault

R d'Asfeld

Av Joffre

Les Chambres
de l'Ile (1.2km)

Av de Lattre
de Tassigny

R Wilson

R Châtillon

Rempart St-Thiébault

R Maurice Barrès

R Lasalle

R François de Curel

Av Foch

Pl du Roi
George

R Gambetta

15

8

R Charlemagne

R Vauban

Water
Tower

R Lafayette

Av Leclerc de Hautecloque

R Pasteur

10

R Ausone

Pl du Général
de Gaulle

Train
Station

Arrival
Hall

Pedestrian
Passage

Departure
Hall

Pl de
l'Amphithéâtre

Av de
l'Amphithéâtre

2
**Centre
Pompidou-Metz**

R P Verlaine

Metz

into their food, is the easy access to Michelin-starred Le Magasin aux Vivres (p384).

✖ Eating

Metz has scores of appetising restaurants, many along and near the river. Place St-Jacques becomes one giant open-air cafe when the sun's out. Cobbled rue Taison and the arcades of place St-Louis shelter moderately priced bistros, pizzerias and cafes.

Pâtisserie Claude Bourguignon   PASTRIES €
(www.bourguignonmetz.fr; 31 rue de la Tête d'Or; snacks €3-8; ☺ 9.15am-7pm Tue-Sat, 9am-12.30pm Sun) Oh, the temptation! The window display says it all at this smart tearoom/chocolatier/patisserie, with an irresistible array of tarts (try *mirabelle* – plum), éclairs, quiches, ganaches and pralines.

Chez Mauricette   DELI €
(Maré Couvert; sandwiches €3.50-4.50, light meals €7-11; ☺ 7am-6.30pm Tue-Sat) At Chez Mauricette, Mauricette tempts with such Lorraine goodies as herby *saucisson*, local charcuterie and *mirabelle* (plum) pâté.

★ L'Imaginarium   FRENCH €€
(☑ 03 87 30 14 40; http://imaginarium-restaurant.com; 2 rue de Paris; mains €21-23; ☺ noon-2pm & 7-10pm Wed-Sat, noon-2pm Sun & Tue; ⓘ) Decorated with one-of-a-kind artworks, this sleek, monochrome bistro by the river is one of Metz' top foodie addresses. The season-driven menu emphasises clean, bright flavours in dishes such as salmon with pumpkin velouté and crispy hazelnuts, and duck breast in a peanut crust with artichoke. There's a €17 children's menu.

Les Caves Saint-Clement   FRENCH €€
(☑ 03 87 63 92 92; www.caves-saint-clement-metz.fr; 6 rue Gambetta; menus €17-40; ☺ 10am-7pm Tue-Thu, to 11pm Fri & Sat) This *caviste* (wine merchant) is a delight, with bistro seating in a bright, open-plan, lavender-accented dining area. Market-fresh ingredients go into unfussy yet well-prepared dishes – homemade *jambon persille* (ham terrine with parsley), say, or fresh tagliatelle tossed in butter, Parmesan and herbs. Even better is the lack of marked-up wine prices – simply choose your bottle from the shelf.

Les Copains d'Abord   FRENCH €€
(☑ 03 87 76 21 46; http://restaurantlescopains dabordmetz.fr; 32 rue du Coëtlosquet; mains €17-26, 2-course lunch €17.90; ☺ noon-1.30pm & 7-9.30pm Tue-Sat) Winningly fresh ingredients shine in regional cuisine, matched with an impressive array of wines, at Les Copains d'Abord. Dishes such as pike-perch with ravioli and morel sauce, and lamb cooked with spring vegetables and herbs speak profoundly of the seasons. Alternatively, opt for sharing boards of top-quality *fromage* and charcuterie.

Le Petit Frontalier   FRENCH €€
(☑ 03 87 37 31 49; http://le-petit-frontalier.fr; 3 rue des Parmentiers; menus €35-48; ☺ noon-2pm & 7-10pm Wed-Sat, noon-2pm Sun) Huddled away in an old-town backstreet, this bright, modern bistro draws on the best of seasonal, regional produce. Dishes like crispy suckling pig and lamb in a tangy Comté cheese crust are nicely cooked and presented. Save room for enticing desserts such as tarte tatin with *mirabelle* plums and almond cream.

La Table de Pol   FRENCH €€
(☑ 03 87 62 13 72; www.latabledepol.fr; 1/3 rue du Grand-Wad; menus €18.50-43, mains €20-25; ☺ noon-2pm & 7-9pm Tue-Sat) Intimate lighting and cheek-by-jowl tables keep the mood

METZ DAY TRIPPER

The largest single Maginot Line bastion in the Metz area was the 1000-man **Fort du Hackenberg** (www.maginot-hackenberg.com; adult/child €10/5; ☺ tours 2.30pm Mon-Fri, 9.30am & 2-3.30pm Sat, 2-3.30pm Sun late Mar–mid-Nov, shorter hours rest of year), whose 10km of galleries were designed to be self-sufficient for three months and, in battle, to fire 4 tonnes of shells a minute. An electric trolley takes visitors along 4km of tunnels – always at 12°C – past subterranean installations. Tours last two hours. The fort is around 35km northeast of Metz via the D2 or A35.

The fort is probably best seen as a day trip from Metz – there's a smattering of places to eat in nearby Thionville.

mellow in this friendly bistro, which serves winningly fresh modern French dishes prepared with market produce, along the lines of lamb filet mignon in a herb crust and cod fillet with asparagus – all cooked to a T.

Restaurant Thierry INTERNATIONAL €€
(☎ 03 87 74 01 23; www.restaurant-thierry.fr; 5 rue des Piques; menus €25.50-42.50; ☺ noon-2.30pm & 7-10.30pm, closed Wed & Sun) Combining the historic backdrop of a 16th-century townhouse with the lighting, bohemian flair and subtly spiced cuisine of Morocco, this is one of Metz' most coveted tables. An aperitif in the candlelit salon works up an appetite for global flavours such as swordfish with risotto and red curry, and tagine of lamb with olives and dried fruit.

Le Magasin aux Vivres GASTRONOMY €€€
(☎ 03 87 17 17 17; 5 av Ney; menus €38-125; ☺ noon-2pm & 7.30-10pm Tue-Fri, 7.30-10pm Sat) Conjurer of textures and seasonal flavours, chef Christophe Dufossé makes creative use of local produce at this sophisticated Michelin-starred restaurant. Moselle wines work well with specialities such as plump scallops with fresh truffle, Jerusalem artichoke millefeuille and roasted hazelnuts, and salt-crusted sea bass with seaweed and thyme and bay-leaf sauce. The three-course lunch is a snip at €38.

Le Jardin de Bellevue FRENCH €€€
(☎ 03 87 37 10 27; www.lejardindebellevue.com; 58 rue Claude Bernard; mains €35-38, menus €31-87; ☺ noon-1.30pm & 7.30-9.30pm Wed-Fri, 7.30-9.30pm Sat, noon-1.30pm Tue & Sun; ☼) Worth the 3km trek out of town, Le Jardin de Bellevue is a class act. The backdrop is sophisticated, with white-linen-draped tables, shades of taupe and orange and fresh flowers. The food itself has a seasonal slant, be it scallop carpaccio with crab cannelloni or perfectly cooked Vosges pigeon – presented and served with finesse.

🍷 Drinking & Nightlife

Some 22,000 resident students keep Metz' vibe young and upbeat after dark. For an alfresco sundowner or two, try the bars and open-air cafes lining place de Chambre and place St-Jacques.

Bazaar Sainte Marie BAR
(www.bsm-metz.com; 2bis rue Ste-Marie; ☺ 6pm-2am Tue-Sat) Retro-chic bar with red walls, vintage sofas, a relaxed vibe and old-school music. Check the website for details of gigs, exhibitions and DJ nights.

🛈 Information

Tourist Office (☎ 03 87 39 00 00; www.tourisme-metz.com; 2 place d'Armes; ☺ 9am-7pm Mon-Sat, 10am-4pm Sun, shorter hours winter; ☂) In a one-time guardroom built in the mid-1700s. Free walking-tour and cycling maps, and free wi-fi. Can make room bookings for a €1.50 fee.

🛈 Getting There & Around

BICYCLE

Rent city and mountain bikes cheaply from nonprofit **Mob d'Emploi** (www.mobemploi.com; 7 place du Général de Gaulle; per half day/full day/week €3/4/10, deposit per bike €250; ☺ 8.30am-6.30pm Mon-Fri, 10am-6.30pm Sat, 2-8pm Sun). Helmets and locks are free; rental options include kids' bikes, electro bikes, child carriers and even a tandem.

TRAIN

Metz' ornate early-20th-century **train station** (place du Général de Gaulle) has a super-sleek TGV linking Paris with Luxembourg. Direct services:

Luxembourg €16.90, 55 minutes, 40 daily
Nancy €11.50, 38 to 53 minutes, 48 daily
Paris €77 to €82, 1½ hours, 15 daily
Strasbourg €27.80, 1½ hours, 16 daily
Verdun €15.40, 1½ hours, three direct daily

Verdun

POP 18,393

The unspeakable atrocities that took place in and around Verdun between 21 February and 18 December 1916, the longest battle of WWI, have turned the town's name into a byword for wartime slaughter and futile sacrifice.

Such a dark past means that Verdun always has an air of melancholy, even when the sun bounces brightly off the River Meuse and the town's shuttered houses. Go to the moonscape hills of the Verdun battlefields, scarred with trenches and shells; walk through the stony silence of the cemeteries as the morning mist rises, and you will understand why. Time has healed and trees have grown, but the memory of *l'enfer de Verdun* (the hell of Verdun) has survived. And, some say, may it never be forgotten.

History

After the annexation of Lorraine's Moselle *département* and Alsace by Germany in 1871, Verdun became a front-line outpost. Over the next four decades it was turned into the most important and heavily fortified element in France's eastern defence line.

During WWI, Verdun itself was never taken by the Germans, but the evacuated town was almost totally destroyed by artillery bombardments. In the hills to the north and east of Verdun, the brutal combat – carried out with artillery, flame-throwers and poison gas – completely wiped out nine villages. During the last two years of WWI, more than 800,000 soldiers (some 400,000 French and almost as many Germans, along with thousands of the Americans who arrived in 1918) lost their lives in this area.

⊙ Sights

The money-saving Pass Champ de Bataille (adult/child €25/15), available at the tourist office, gives discounted entry to the Ossuaire de Douaumont, Fort de Douaumont (p386), Fort de Vaux (p386), Mémorial de Verdun and the Citadelle Souterraine.

The **tourist office** (☑ 03 29 86 14 18; www.tourisme-verdun.fr; place de la Nation; ⊙9am-7pm Mon-Sat, 10am-5pm Sun, shorter hours winter; 🖥) provides a huge range of guided tours in and around Verdun, including four-hour tours of the battlefields (adult/child €27/20). See https://en.tourisme-verdun.com/guided-tours for the lowdown on prices, times and bookings.

Citadelle Souterraine   HISTORIC SITE
(☑ 03 29 84 84 42; www.citadelle-souterraine-verdun.fr; av du Soldat Inconnu; adult/child €9/5; ⊙9am-6pm, closed Jan) Comprising 7km of underground galleries, this cavernous sub-

terranean citadel was designed by military engineer Sébastien Le Prestre de Vauban in the 17th century and completed in 1838. In 1916 it was turned into an impregnable command centre in which 10,000 *poilus* (French WWI soldiers) lived, waiting to be dispatched to the front. About 10% of the galleries have been converted into an audiovisual re-enactment of Verdun's WWI history. Half-hour, battery-powered-car tours, available in six languages, should be booked ahead.

Centre Mondial de la Paix   MUSEUM
(World Centre for Peace; www.cmpaix.eu; place Monseigneur Ginisty; adult/child €5/2.50; ⊙10am-12.30pm & 2-6pm) Set in Verdun's handsomely classical former bishop's palace, built in 1724, this museum's permanent exhibition touches upon wars, their causes and solutions; human rights; and the fragility of peace.

⊙ Out of Town

Much of the Battle of Verdun was fought 5km to 8km (as the crow flies) northeast of Verdun. Today, the forested area – still a jumble of trenches and artillery crates – can be explored via signposted paths leading to dozens of war remnants.

Mémorial de Verdun   MEMORIAL
(http://memorial-verdun.fr; 1 av du Corps Européen, Fleury; adult/child €11/7; ⊙9.30am-7pm, shorter hours winter) The village of Fleury, wiped off the face of the earth in the course of being captured and recaptured 16 times, is now the site of this memorial. It tells the story of '300 days, 300,000 dead, 400,000 wounded', with insightful displays of war artefacts and personal items. Downstairs you'll find a recreation of the battlefield as it looked on the day the guns finally fell silent.

In the grassy crater-pocked centre of what was once Fleury, a few hundred metres down the road from the memorial, signs among the low ruins indicate the village's former layout.

Ossuaire de Douaumont   MEMORIAL
(www.verdun-douaumont.com; ⊙9am-6pm Mon-Fri, 10am-6pm Sat & Sun, shorter hours winter) FREE Rising like a gigantic artillery shell above 15,000 crosses that bleed into the distance, this sombre, 137m-long ossuary, inaugurated in 1932, is one of France's most important WWI memorials. A ticket to the 20-minute **audiovisual presentation** (adult/child €6/3) on the battle also lets you climb the 46m-high **bell tower**. Out front,

the French military **cemetery** is flanked by memorials to Muslim and Jewish soldiers (to the east and west, respectively) who died fighting for France in WWI.

The ossuary contains the bones of about 130,000 unidentified French and German soldiers collected from the Verdun battlefields and buried together in 52 mass graves according to where they fell. Each engraved stone denotes a missing soldier, while a touching display of photographs shows Verdun survivors – as they were in WWI and as they were later in life.

Fort de Douaumont
FORT

(adult/child €4/2; ⊙10am-6.30pm, shorter hours winter) Sitting high on a hill, this is the strongest of the 38 fortresses and bastions built along a 45km front to protect Verdun. When the Battle of Verdun began, 400m-long Douaumont – whose 3km network of cold, dripping galleries was built between 1885 and 1913 – had only a skeleton crew. By the fourth day it had been captured easily, a serious blow to French morale; four months later, it was retaken by colonial troops from Morocco.

Charles de Gaulle, then a young captain, was wounded and taken prisoner near here in 1916. It's free to take in the sweeping country views from the fort's crater-pocked roof.

Fort de Vaux
FORT

(Vaux-devant-Damloup; adult/child €4/2; ⊙10am-6.30pm, shorter hours winter) Located in crater-scarred countryside 10km northeast of Verdun, this fort was constructed between 1881 and 1884. It was the second fort – Douaumont (p386) was the first – to fall in the Battle of Verdun, and became the site of the bloodiest battle for two months. Weak with thirst, Major Raynal and his troops surrendered to the enemy on 7 June 1916. You can gain an insight into past horrors by taking a tour of its dank interior and observation points.

Tranchée des Baïonnettes
MEMORIAL

FREE On 12 June 1916, two companies of the 137th Infantry Regiment of the French army were sheltered in their *tranchées* (trenches), *baïonnettes* (bayonets) fixed, waiting for a ferocious artillery bombardment to end. It never did – the incoming shells covered their positions with mud and debris, burying them alive. They were found three years later, when someone spotted several hundred bayonet tips sticking out of the ground. Today the site is marked by a simple memorial that is always open. The tree-filled valley across the D913

is known as the **Ravin de la Mort** (Ravine of Death).

🛏 Sleeping

Hôtel Montaulbain
HOTEL €

(☑03 29 86 00 47; www.hoteldemontaulbain.fr; 4 rue de la Vieille Prison; d €87-100, f €144; 🐾) It requires very little detective work to pin down this central hotel, which is run with charm and an eye for detail. Overlooking an inner courtyard, the 11 revamped rooms are compact, spotless and understated yet chic in look and feel.

Le Château de Puxe
GUESTHOUSE €

(☑03 82 22 76 21; www.chateau-puxe.com; 18 rue du Château, Puxe; s €57-62, d €77-80, tr €95; 🅿🐾) Fancy spending the night in a bona-fide château but without the steep price tag? *Et voilà*: 17th-century Le Château de Puxe fits the bill nicely. Midway between Verdun and Metz, it has peaceful and expansive grounds to explore and elegant wood-floored, antique-furnished rooms. Freshly baked bread and homemade jams appear at breakfast. All things considered, it's a bargain.

Château des Monthairons
HISTORIC HOTEL €€

(☑03 29 87 78 55; www.chateaudesmonthairons. fr; 26 rte de Verdun; d €110-250, apt €300-390; 🅿🐾) Reclining in its own beautifully tended grounds, this turreted vision of a 19th-century château has grand rooms dressed in flouncy florals and antique furnishings. Some have sweeping views of the Meuse Valley, others crank up the romance with four-poster beds. There's a highly regarded restaurant and spa on site. It's a 15-minute drive south of Verdun via the D34.

Les Jardins du Mess
HOTEL €€

(☑03 29 80 14 18; www.lesjardinsdumess.fr; 22 quai de la République; d €139-175, tr €209, q €289; 🅿🐾) What a clever idea: take the old military mess and give it an ultramodern makeover and new lease of life as Verdun's swankiest four-star hotel, sitting astride the banks of the Meuse. In a graceful 19th-century building topped off with a mansard roof, Les Jardins du Mess has spacious, tastefully minimalist rooms in earthy tones with pops of bright colour.

🍴 Eating

Brasseries and fast-food joints line up along riverside quai de Londres (a plaque on the wall near rue Beaurepaire explains the origin of the name, which refers to the City of London choosing Verdun as the most poignant location to reunite the two countries in the aftermath of WWI).

Marché Couvert
MARKET

(place du Maré Couvert; ⊙ 7.30am-1pm Fri, 8am-noon Sun) Bountiful produce from the surrounding Meuse region is for sale at this twice-weekly market, held in a 19th-century hall.

L'Esprit Bistro
FRENCH €

(✐ 07 71 75 73 06; http://esprit-bistrot-verdun. com; 5 rue de la Grange; mains €14-20; ⊙ 7-10pm Mon, noon-2pm & 7-10pm Tue, Wed, Fri & Sat) Such good old-fashioned, family-run bistros are a dying breed. No-nonsense L'Esprit goes for the classic look, with red-and-white checked tablecloths, tightly packed seating and day specials chalked on a board. Dishes like beef cheek confit, lamb shanks slow-cooked in thyme, and red mullet with creamy risotto are bang on the money. The *plat du jour* goes for €9.80.

Le Clapier
BISTRO €€

(✐ 03 29 86 20 14; 34 rue des Gros Degrés; mains €15-33; ⊙ noon-1.30pm & 7-10.30pm Tue-Sat; 🖈) The chef's penchant for Provence's balmy climes shines through on the menu at this cosy lime-walled bistro, whose name translates as 'the rabbit hutch'. Specialities like crumbly Brie tart and herb-infused leg of lamb are expertly paired with Meuse wines.

Chez Mamie
FRENCH €€

(✐ 03 29 86 45 50; 52 av de la 42ème Division; menus €12-30; ⊙ noon-2pm Mon, noon-2pm & 7-10pm Wed-Sun; ✐🖈) The clue's in the name: family-run Chez Mamie does indeed dish up the kind of wholesome, hearty grub your French gran might make. Pull up a chair at one of the checked-cloth tables for satisfying dishes such as scallops with bacon and fat, stubby pork trotters. Vegetarian and children's options are available.

Château des Monthairons
FRENCH €€€

(✐ 03 29 87 78 55; www.chateaudesmonthairons.fr; 26 rte de Verdun; lunch menus €28, dinner menus €48-102; ⊙ noon-2pm & 7-9pm Wed-Sun, 7-9pm Tue; 🖈) It's not every day you get to dine at a bona-fide castle, so it's worth the 15-minute drive south of Verdun to this whimsically turreted château overlooking parkland. Chef Benoit Thouvenin puts his own creative spin on French cuisine in dishes such as confit pork cheeks with leeks and saffron-mustard sauce and iced parfait with Verdun *dragées* (sugared almonds).

LOCAL KNOWLEDGE

MORE SWEET THAN BITTER

Verdun's sweet claim to fame is as the *dragée* (sugared almond) capital of the world. In 1220 a local pharmacist dabbling with almonds, sugar and honey created the tooth-rotting delights that later graced the tables of royalty and nobility – Napoléon and Charles de Gaulle included. **Braquier** (www.dragees-braquier. com; 50 rue du Fort de Vaux; ⊙ 9am-noon & 1.30-7pm Mon-Sat, 9am-noon & 2-7pm Sun) **FREE** has been making Verdun's celebrated *dragées* since 1783 and offers free guided tours of its factory. Or buy a box at the more central **shop** (3 rue Pasteur; ⊙ 2-7pm Mon, 10am-noon & 2-7pm Tue-Sat).

ⓘ Information

Tourist Office (p385) Friendly tourist office with guided tours, info on Verdun and the surrounding region, and free maps of the battlefields. Free wi-fi.

ⓘ Getting There & Around

BICYCLE

Bikes are an excellent way to tour the Verdun battlefields. At the train station, **TiV' vélo** (www. bus-tiv.com; place Maurice Genevoix; half day/ day/week €1/2/5; ⊙ 9am-noon & 2-6pm Mon-Fri) rents out bicycles. You'll need to pay a €100 deposit.

TRAIN

Verdun's poorly served train station, designed by Gustave Eiffel and built in 1868, has direct services to Metz (€15.80, 1½ hours, three direct daily). Five buses a day go to the Gare Meuse TGV station (€4.50, 30 minutes), from where direct TGVs whisk you to Paris' Gare de l'Est (€44, one hour).

Romagne-sous-Montfaucon

POP 194

This remote village in the countryside northwest of Verdun would be easy to overlook were it not for its huge and deeply saddening WWI cemetery, where a sea of crosses stretches to infinity. The surrounding landscape is pockmarked with the craters of artillery shells – some of which are still churned up on a daily basis. The heart-tugging museum here, Romagne '14-'18 (p388), is one of the most fascinating of its kind.

⊙ Sights

More than one million American troops participated in the Meuse-Argonne Offensive of late 1918, the last Western Front battle of WWI. The fighting northwest of Verdun, in which more than 26,000 Americans died, convinced the Kaiser's government to cable US President Woodrow Wilson with a request for an armistice. The film *Sergeant York* (1941) is based on events that took place here. The website of the Meuse *département's* tourism board – www.tourisme-meuse.com – offers background on the region and its WWI sites.

Apart from Romagne '14-'18 (p388), all of the sites are managed by the American Battle Monuments Commission (www.abmc. gov) and are open from 9am to 5pm daily.

★ **Meuse-Argonne**
American Cemetery   CEMETERY
(www.abmc.gov; ⊙9am-5pm) The largest US military cemetery in Europe is this WWI ground, where 14,246 soldiers lie buried – a sobering sea of white crosses reaching as far as the eye can see. The cemetery is located 41km northwest of Verdun along the D38 and D123.

Romagne '14-'18   MUSEUM
(☑03 29 85 10 14; www.romagne14-18.com; 2 rue de l'Andon; museum adult/child €5/free; ⊙noon-6pm Thu-Tue) This heart-rending museum, which, in the words of owner Jean-Paul de Vries, is all about 'life stories' and 'the human being behind the helmet'. Artefacts are shown in the state in which they were found – rust, dirt and all. The museum is a 40-minute drive northwest of Verdun via the D964 and D123.

⊙ Out of Town

The American Memorial trail continues in the countryside surrounding Romagne-sous-Montfaucon.

Lorraine American Cemetery   CEMETERY
(www.abmc.gov; St-Avold; ⊙9am-5pm) Verdun had a significant military presence from the end of WWII until Charles de Gaulle pulled France out of NATO's integrated military command in 1966. Surrounded by woodland and set in landscaped grounds, this is the largest US WWII military cemetery in Europe. The cemetery is a 30-minute drive east of Metz via the A4 motorway.

Butte de Montfaucon   MEMORIAL
(www.abmc.gov; Montfaucon-en-Argonne; ⊙9am-5pm) Commemorating the 1918 Meuse-Argonne Offensive, this 336m-high mound is topped by a 58m-high Doric column crowned by a statue symbolising liberty. Ascend 234 steps to reach the observation platform. The memorial is a 40-minute drive northwest of Verdun via the D38 and D19.

St-Mihiel American Cemetery   CEMETERY
(www.abmc.gov; Thiaucourt-Regniéville; ⊙9am-5pm) In this WWI cemetery, the graves of 4153 American soldiers who died in the 1918 Battle of St-Mihiel radiate towards a central sundial topped by a white American eagle. The cemetery is 40km southeast of Verdun on the outskirts of Thiaucourt-Regniéville.

Butte de Montsec   MEMORIAL
(www.abmc.gov; Montsec; ⊙9am-5pm) This 375m-high mound, site of a US monument with a bronze relief map, is surrounded by a round neoclassical colonnade. The monument commemorates the achievements of the American soldiers who fought here in 1917 and 1918. It's a 50-minute drive south of Verdun via the D964.

❶ Getting There & Away

You'll need your own wheels to reach Romagne-sous-Montfaucon, which is 38km northwest of Verdun via the D964.

---

❶ BATTLEFIELD OVERNIGHT

Housed in a bijou villa framed by gardens, B&B **Villa Nantrisé** (☑03 29 84 73 85; 46 rue de l'Argonne, D998; d/apt/f €75/95/125; [P] �📶)is brilliantly placed for exploring the WWI American memorials around Romagne-sous-Montfaucon. Rooms are old-fashioned but spotlessly kept, and the welcome is heartfelt, with little touches including free bike rental and homemade jams at breakfast.

The Loire Valley

POP 2.7 MILLION

Best Places to Eat

➡ Le Gambetta (p421)

➡ Les Années 30 (p418)

➡ Amboise's Sunday Food Market (p413)

➡ Le Lièvre Gourmand (p396)

➡ Le Boeuf Noisette (p421)

Best Places to Stay

➡ Château de Brissac (p428)

➡ Château de Verrières (p421)

➡ Château de Beaulieu (p421)

➡ Demeure de la Vignole (p422)

➡ Le Vieux Manoir (p413)

Why Go?

If it's French splendour, style and gastronomy you seek, the Loire Valley will exceed your expectations, no matter how great. Poised on the crucial frontier between northern and southern France, and just a short train or autoroute ride from Paris, the region was once of immense strategic importance. Kings, queens, dukes and nobles came here to establish feudal castles and, later on, sumptuous pleasure palaces – that's why this fertile river valley is sprinkled with hundreds of France's most opulent aristocratic estates. With crenellated towers, soaring cupolas and glittering banquet halls, the region's châteaux, and the villages and vineyards that surround them, attest to over a thousand years of rich architectural and artistic creativity. The Loire Valley is also known for its outstanding wines (red, white, rosé and sparkling) and lively, sophisticated cities, including Orléans, Blois, Tours and Angers – yet more reasons why the entire area is an enormous Unesco World Heritage Site.

When to Go
Tours

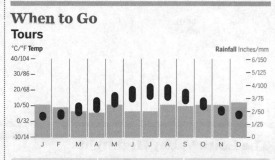

Late Apr–early May The Fêtes de Jeanne d'Arc in Orléans culminate with parades on 8 May.

May & Jun Cycle verdant back roads and bike paths from château to château.

Sep & Oct Go wine tasting during harvest season; the châteaux are less crowded now.

The Loire Valley Highlights

1 **Château de Chambord** (p402) Climbing the staircase to the turreted rooftop of the Loire's most exuberant château.

2 **Château de Chenonceau** (p411) Admiring elegant arches and fabulous art.

3 **Saumur** (p419) Enjoying fantastic food, great local wines and equestrian virtuosity.

4 **Château d'Azay-le-Rideau** (p415) Appreciating the gardens and fine furnishings of this serene island château.

5 **Château de Chaumont-sur-Loire** (p406) Immersing yourself in striking modern art and avant-garde gardens.

6 **Tours** (p407) Exploring super museums by day and partying by night.

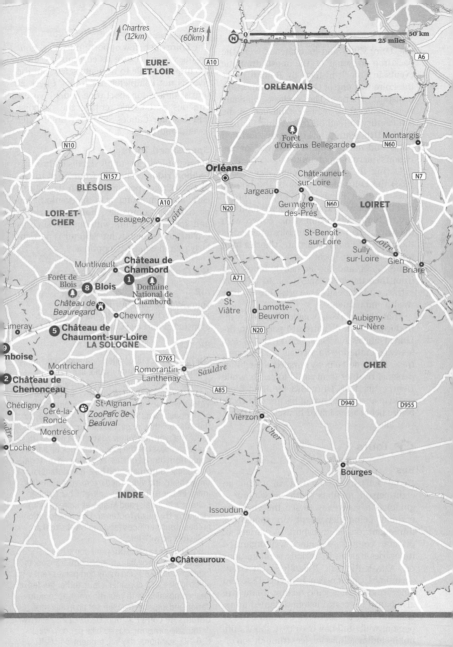

⑦ Château de Villandry (p414) Wandering the meticulously tended flower and vegetable gardens.

⑧ Château Royal de Blois (p399) Following the transition, over just two decades, from Flamboyant Gothic to early Renaissance.

⑨ Château Gaillard (p413) Strolling through harmonious, Renaissance-style gardens in Amboise.

⑩ Château d'Angers (p425) Searching for dragons, angels and allegories in Angers' sensational medieval Apocalypse Tapestry.

History

The Loire Valley and its châteaux were the backdrop to some of the most dramatic events in French history. By Roman times the Loire was one of Gaul's most important transport arteries. The earliest châteaux were medieval fortresses established in the 9th century to fend off marauding Vikings. By the 11th century massive walls, fortified keeps and moats were must-haves for the region's querulous potentates.

During the Hundred Years War (1337–1453) the Loire marked one of the boundaries between French and English forces, and the area was ravaged by fierce fighting. After Charles VII regained his crown with the help of Joan of Arc, the Loire emerged as the centre of French court life. Charles took up residence in Loches with his mistress, Agnès Sorel, and the French nobility, and from then the aristocracy took to building extravagant châteaux as expressions of their wealth and influence.

François I (r 1515–47) made his mark by introducing ornate Renaissance palaces to the Loire. François' successor, Henri II (r 1547–59), his wife, Catherine de Médicis, and his mistress, Diane de Poitiers, pursued their bitter personal rivalries from castle to castle, while Henri's son Henri III (r 1573–89) used Blois' castle to assassinate two of his greatest rivals before being assassinated himself less than a year later.

☞ Tours

Bus

If you don't have your own car, taking an eight-person minibus (with or without a guide) is a good way to see the châteaux without being dependent on sometimes infrequent public transport. A variety of private companies offer well-organised itineraries, taking in various combinations of Azay-le-Rideau, Villandry, Cheverny, Chambord, Chenonceau, Langeais, Ussé and vineyards offering wine tasting. Many are also happy to create custom-designed tours. Half-day trips cost between €25 and €40 per person, while full-day trips cost about €60, not including admission fees (though you often get slight discounts). Reserve at the tourist offices in Tours (p410) or Amboise (p414), from where most tours depart, or via their websites (under 'Excursions'); last-minute spots are often available.

Boat

The Loire offers few opportunities to get out on the water because its currents are often too unpredictable to navigate safely, but the river is not completely off limits. Check at tourist offices for short (one-hour) boat excursions and kayak rentals; the Amboise and Saumur/Candes-St-Martin areas offer several options.

Specialised Tours

Tourist offices can supply details on **hot-air-balloon rides** (generally from April to October, weather permitting, with departures early in the morning or in the evening), run by a dozen companies, **helicopter rides**, and specialised tours with themes such as cycling and wine tasting. Saumur is particularly rich in equestrian options.

ⓘ Getting There & Around

AIR

Tours–Val de Loire Airport (www.tours. aeroport.fr) has Ryanair flights to London's Stansted airport and Dublin.

BICYCLE

The mostly flat Loire Valley is fabulous cycling country – there's nothing quite like pedalling through villages, vineyards and forests on your way from one château to the next. **La Loire à Vélo** (www.cycling-loire.com) maintains 800km of signposted routes from Nevers all the way to the Atlantic; they're part of the Eurovelo 6 bike route that you can follow east all the way to the Bulgarian coast of the Black Sea. Pick up a free guide from tourist offices, or download material (including route maps and bike-hire details) from the website. Individual *départements,* including Indre-et-Loire (Touraine), Loir-et-Cher (Blois), Loiret (Orléannais) and Maine-et-Loire (Anjou), also have their own routes and accommodation guides. Tourist offices (and their websites) are well stocked with info.

If you'd like to cycle but want some help, **Bagafrance** (www.bagafrance.com) transports luggage and bikes, and many companies rent electric bikes. Or consider a tour, either guided or unaccompanied, with your itinerary, accommodation and luggage transfer set up in advance. **Détours de Loire** (☏ Tours 02 47 61 22 23; www. detoursdeloire.com; classic bike per day/week €16/60, additional day €5, tandem €46/140, electric €35/155) Has rental and return locations up and down the Loire, including in Amboise, Angers, Blois (year-round), Nantes, Orléans, Saumur and Tours (year-round). Bikes can be picked up and dropped off at your hotel for a small surcharge; emergency repairs en route are free. Kids' bikes are available. Can also arrange luggage transport and self-guided bike tours.

Les Châteaux à Vélo (www.chateauxavelo. co.uk) Funded by 65 Loire municipalities, this organisation maintains 400km of marked bike routes around Blois, Chambord, Cheverny and Chaumont-sur-Loire. Get route maps, a useful mobile app and the latest weather reports from the website, or pick up brochures at local tourist offices.

Wheel Free (p396) Delivers and picks up classic and electric bikes to/from various points along the Loire. Prices drop if you rent for several days. The office is about 2.5km southeast of central Orléans, on the southern side of the Loire.

TRAIN

Tours is the Loire Valley's main rail hub. TGV trains connect St-Pierre-des-Corps (4km east of Tours) with Paris' Gare Montparnasse (one hour), Charles de Gaulle Airport (1¾ hours), Nantes (1½ hours) and Bordeaux (2¾ hours). Orléans, Blois, Amboise and other Loire towns also have quick, direct rail links to Paris. TGVs from Angers to Paris' Gare Montparnasse (1½ hours) go via Le Mans.

ORLÉANAIS

Taking its name from the historic city of Orléans, famed for its close association with Joan of Arc, the Orléanais is the northeastern gateway to the Loire Valley. Upriver (southwest) from Orléans are the ecclesiastical treasures of St-Benoît-sur-Loire and Germigny-des-Prés, while to the south lies the marshy Sologne, once a favourite hunting ground for France's kings and princes.

Orléans

POP 114,375

There's a big-city buzz on the broad boulevards and in the sparkling boutiques and elegant buildings of Orléans, 100km south of Paris. An important settlement by the time of the Roman conquest, the city sealed its place in history in 1429 when a young peasant girl by the name of Jeanne d'Arc (Joan of Arc) rallied the armies of Charles VII and brought about a spectacular rout against the besieging English forces, a key turning point in the Hundred Years War. Six centuries later, the Maid of Orléans still exerts a powerful hold on the French imagination – all around town, you'll find statues (at least seven), stained-glass windows and museum exhibits dedicated to her exploits. Other attractions in the old city include an outstanding art museum and a breathtaking cathedral.

◉ Sights

A single €6 ticket, valid all day, gets you into five city-run museums, including the Musée des Beaux-Arts, the Maison de Jeanne d'Arc, the Musée d'Histoire et d'Archéologie and, from 2019, the renovated Muséum d'Orléans pour la Biodiversité et l'Environnement (MOBE).

★**Cathédrale Ste-Croix**　　　CATHEDRAL
(www.orleans.catholique.fr; place Ste-Croix; ◉9.15am–5pm or later, to 8pm Sun-Wed & to 11pm Thu-Sat Jul & Aug) In a country of jaw-dropping churches, Gothic-style Cathédrale Ste-Croix still raises a gasp. Originally built in the 13th century, it underwent tinkering by successive monarchs after being partly destroyed by Protestants in 1568. Joan of Arc prayed here on 8 May 1429 and was greeted with a procession of thanks for saving the town; 10 extraordinarily vivid stained-glass windows (1893) illustrate her life. The most picturesque way to approach the 130m-long cathedral is along rue Jeanne d'Arc.

★**Musée des Beaux-Arts**　　　GALLERY
(⌨02 38 79 21 83; www.orleans-metropole.fr; 1 rue Fernand Rabier; adult/child €6/free; ◉10am-6pm Tue-Sat, 1-6pm Sun) Orléans' five-level fine-arts museum is a treat, with an excellent collection of Italian, Flemish and Dutch paintings (including works by Correggio, Velázquez and Bruegel) as well as a huge collection of work by French artists such as Léon Cogniet (1794–1880), Orléans-born Alexandre Antigna (1817–78) and Paul Gauguin (1848–1903), who spent some of his youth here. Other rare treasures include a set of 18th-century pastels by Maurice Quentin de la Tour and a self-portrait by Jean-Baptiste Chardin.

ⓘ ORLÉANS WITNESSES

As you wander around the old city, keep an eye out for Témoins d'Orléans (Orléans Witnesses) – rusty columns, installed in 2017, delicately incised with scenes from the history of the city. Embedded in each one is a QR code – use your smartphone's QR reader to access historical information in French and English.

Orléans

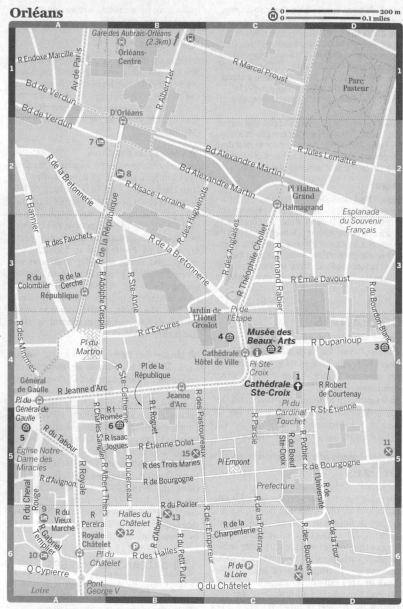

Hôtel Groslot   HISTORIC BUILDING
(📞 02 38 79 22 30; www.orleans-metropole.fr; place de l'Étape; ⏰ 10am-noon & 2-6pm Oct-Jun, 9am-7pm Jul-Sep) FREE The Renaissance-style Hôtel Groslot was built between 1530 and 1550 as a private mansion for lawyer and bailiff Jacques Groslot; it became Orléans' city hall during the Revolution. The neo-Renaissance interior decor (1850s) is extravagant, especially the ornate bedroom – now used for weddings – in which 17-year-old François II died in 1560. Salle Jeanne d'Arc

Orléans

◉ Top Sights
1 Cathédrale Ste-Croix............................C4
2 Musée des Beaux-Arts.......................C4

◉ Sights
3 CERCIL – Musée-Mémorial des
   Enfants du Vel d'Hiv..........................D4
4 Hôtel Groslot...C4
5 Maison de Jeanne d'Arc.....................A5
6 Musée d'Histoire et
   d'Archéologie...................................B5

◉ Sleeping
7 Hôtel Archange.....................................A2
8 Hôtel de l'Abeille................................B2
9 Hôtel Marguerite A6
10 Les Trois Maillets...............................A6

⊗ Eating
11 Chez Jules D5
12 Halles Châtelet B6
13 La Parenthèse......................................B6
14 Le Lièvre Gourmand...........................C6
15 Ver di Vin...B5

is richly decorated with images of St Joan. The gardens behind the building are lovely.

Maison de Jeanne d'Arc   MUSEUM
(☑ 02 38 68 32 63; www.jeannedarc.com.fr; 3 place du Général de Gaulle; adult/child €6/frce; ⊙ 10am-1pm & 2-6pm Tue-Sun Apr-Sep, 2-6pm Tue-Sun Oct-Mar) An excellent 15-minute film (in French or English) tracing Joan of Arc's origins, accomplishments and historical impact is the main attraction at the Maison de Jeanne d'Arc, a 1960s reconstruction of the 15th-century house that hosted her between April and May 1429 (the original was destroyed by German bombing in 1940). The world's largest Joan of Arc research centre is upstairs.

Musée d'Histoire et d'Archéologie   MUSEUM
(☑ 02 38 79 25 60; www.orleans-metropole.fr; 21 rue Ste-Catherine; adult/child €6/free; ⊙ 10am-1pm & 2-6pm Tue-Sun Apr-Sep, 1-6pm Tue-Sun Oct-Mar) The centrepiece of this history museum, in the Renaissance-style Hôtel Cabu, is an extraordinary collection of Celtic and Gallo-Roman bronzes, recovered from the Loire's sandy bottom. Our favourites: an almost-life-size horse and wild boar. Another room is dedicated to rare Orléans-made porcelain from the 18th and 19th centuries. Plasticised sheets in each room provide information in English.

CERCIL – Musée-Mémorial des Enfants du Vel d'Hiv   MUSEUM
(☑ 02 38 42 03 91; www.cercil.fr; 45 rue du Bourdon-Blanc; adult/child €4/free; ⊙ 2-8pm Tue, 2-6pm Wed-Fri & Sun) Between 1941 and 1943, more than 16,000 Jews were interned in two camps about 50km northeast of Orléans, Beaune-la-Rolande and Pithiviers. The adults were deported first, and only after authorisation had arrived from Berlin were 4400 parent-less, terrified children loaded onto trains and sent to Auschwitz and Sobibor;

only 26, all adolescents, survived. Exhibits (in French) document the deportation and serve as a moving memorial for the children. A detailed booklet in English is available.

✦ Festivals & Events

Fêtes de Jeanne d'Arc   CULTURAL
(www.orleans-metropole.fr; ⊙ 29 Apr-8 May) The Orléanais have celebrated the liberation of their city by Joan of Arc since 1430. Festivities include a medieval market (5 to 8 May), costume parades, concerts and, on 8 May (also a national holiday commemorating the surrender of Nazi Germany), a morning prayer service in the cathedral (at 10am) and a military parade (starts at 2.50pm at the cathedral).

🛏 Sleeping

Les Trois Maillets   B&B €
(☑ 06 28 43 29 14; 4 rue des Trois Maillets; d €85, additional person €17.50; 🛜) Two charming rooms, each with space for up to four people, are available in a Renaissance-era building. Eugénie's welcome is warm, and breakfasts are delicious and copious.

Hôtel Archange   BOUTIQUE HOTEL €
(☑ 02 38 54 42 42; www.hotelarchange.com; 1 bd de Verdun; d €55-90, 5-person ste €139; 🛜) Cherub murals and armchairs shaped like hands greet you at this exuberant hotel. Splashy colour schemes spice up the 22 themed rooms, whose wooden floors are kept squeaky-clean by robots. The double-thick windows are remarkably effective against tram noise. Great value.

★ Hôtel de l'Abeille   HISTORIC HOTEL €€
(☑ 02 38 53 54 87; www.hoteldelabeille.com; 64 rue Alsace-Lorraine; d €98-135, q €180-210; 🛜) Floorboards creak and vintage posters adorn the lobby walls at this classic, 23-room hotel,

built in 1903 and run by the same family since 1919 (that's four generations). The atmosphere is deliciously old-fashioned, from the real oak parquet and wildly ornate wallpapers to the hefty antique furniture. No lift.

Hôtel Marguerite
HOTEL €€

(☑ 02 38 53 74 32; www.hotel-marguerite.fr; 14 place du Vieux Marché; d €70-110, q €125-155; @ ☎) This cheerful 25-room establishment wins points for its friendly reception and central location. 'Superior' rooms are both more spacious and more modern than the standard ones. The bright breakfast room is presided over by a plaster Sologne deer, made by a local artist. Parking up the block in an underground lot (€3) is a breeze. Offers free locked bike parking.

✗ Eating

Orléans' main dining street, rue de Bourgogne, has plenty of places to eat and drink, including a cluster of Indian restaurants around No 151. For more cafes, head to parallel rue du Poirier.

Halles Châtelet
MARKET €

(www.halleschatelet.fr; place du Châtelet; ⊙ 7.30am-7.30pm Tue-Sat, 8am-1pm Sun) A covered food market with about two dozen stalls, including three excellent fromageries and a boulangerie.

La Parenthèse
FRENCH €€

(☑ 02 38 62 07 50; www.restaurant-la-parenthese. com; 26 place du Châtelet; menus lunch €19, dinner €28-32; ⊙ noon-1.30pm & 7.30-9.30pm Tue-Sat) Youthful chef David Sterne turns fresh produce from nearby market stalls, including heritage vegetables, into old-fashioned, family-style French cuisine, creating seasonal menus that change every two months. Choose from relaxed sidewalk seating or three refined dining rooms. Book well ahead by phone.

Chez Jules
FRENCH €€

(☑ 02 38 54 30 80; www.chezjulesorleans.fr; 135 rue de Bourgogne; lunch menus €16-19.50, other menus €25-35; ⊙ noon-1.45pm & 7-9.30pm Tue-Sat) A great address for *cuisine française familiale* (French family-style cuisine). Reimagined four times a year, the menu features local products such as Orléans mustard, Sologne truffles and Surôtin, an aperitif made with sureau flowers macerated in red or white wine. Specialities include duckling perfumed with coffee and, for dessert, poached pear drizzled with chocolate sauce.

Ver di Vin
FRENCH

(☑ 02 38 54 47 42; www.verdivin.com; 2 rue des Trois Maries; menu €35; ⊙ dinner 7.30-10pm, wine & snacks 7pm-midnight or 1am Tue-Sat; ☎) Hidden away in a vaulted medieval cellar, this *restaurant à vin* is known for the excellence of both its *cuisine de maison traditionelle* (traditional French home cooking) and its wine list; 30 vintages are available by the glass. Specialities, some with subtle Japanese influences, include *feuilleté de caille* (quail wrapped in pastry) and dishes prepared with mushrooms.

★ Le Lièvre Gourmand
GASTRONOMY €€€

(☑ 02 38 53 66 14; www.lelievregourmand.com; 28 quai du Châtelet; lunch menu €39, other menus €49-74; ⊙ from 8pm Mon & Wed, from noon & from 8pm Thu-Sun) You'll get the perfect amuse-bouche with your aperitif upstairs in the *salon* while you decide on a set of French, Asian and fusion courses, each a creative duo of hot and cold. Delicate foams and infusions in unexpected combinations use seasonal ingredients, such as new asparagus in spring. It's a good idea to book ahead.

ℹ Information

Tourist Office (☑ 02 38 24 05 05; www. tourisme-orleans.com; 2 place de l'Étape; ⊙ 9.30am or 10am-12.30pm & 2-6pm or 7pm Mon-Sat, 10am-1pm Sun, no midday closure Apr-Sep; ☎)

ℹ Getting There & Around

BICYCLE

Vélo+ (☑ 08 00 00 83 56; www.agglo-veloplus. fr; registration per 24hr €1, first 30min free, subsequent hours €1-2) On-street, 24/7 bike-hire system, with 35 stations around town (eg at the train station and the cathedral). For rides out of town, try **Wheel Free** (☑ 02 38 44 26 85; www.wheel-free.fr; 44 rue du Géneral de Gaulle, St-Jean le Blanc; mountain/electric bike rental per day €17.85/29.85; ⊙ Apr-Sep), which rents, delivers and picks up classic and electric bikes.

BUS

Rémi (☑ 08 00 00 45 00; www.remi-centre valdeloire.fr/loiret) links Orléans' **bus station** (Gare Routière; 2 rue Marcel Proust; ⊙ information desk 8.30am-12.30pm & 3.30-7pm Mon-Fri) with destinations around the Loiret *département*, including Châteauneuf-sur-Loire, Germigny-des-Prés, St-Benoît-sur-Loire and Sully-sur-Loire (all line 3); and Beaugency (line 9). Buy tickets (€2.40 for all destinations) on board.

TRAIN

The city's two stations, **Orléans-Centre** and **Gare des Aubrais-Orléans** (the latter is 2.5km north), are linked to each other by tram and frequent shuttle trains; many trains stop at both stations.

Blois-Chambord €11.50, 25 to 40 minutes, 15 to 25 daily.

Paris Gare d'Austerlitz €21.40, one to 1¾ hours, hourly Monday to Friday, less frequently Saturday and Sunday.

Tours €20.70, 1¼ hours, every two hours.

Orléans to Sully-sur-Loire

Upriver from Orléans, a number of pretty towns – among them Châteauneuf-sur-Loire, Germigny-des-Prés, St-Benoît-sur-Loire and Sully-sur-Loire – make excellent day-trip destinations.

North of Orléans lies the 350-sq-km **Forêt d'Orléans**, one of the few places in France where you can still spot wild ospreys, as well as deer and wild boar.

◉ Sights

Musée de la Marine de Loire MUSEUM
(☎ 02 38 46 84 46; www.musee-marinedeloire. fr; 1 place Aristide Briand, Châteauneuf-sur-Loire; adult/child €5/3; ☺ 10am-6pm Wed-Mon Apr-Oct, 2-6pm Wed-Mon Nov-Mar) Well-presented exhibits tell the story of how a river that's basically non-navigable was used for commerce using ultra-shallow-draft (70cm) boats. Displays include a collection of model boats and ancient riverine artefacts. The ticket counter can supply you with an excellent museum guide in English. Occupies the former stables of the town's park-encircled château, now the town hall.

★**Oratoire de Germigny-des-Prés** CHURCH
(☎ tourist office 02 38 58 27 97; www.tourisme-loire-foret.com; Germigny-des-Prés; ☺ 9am-6.30pm Apr-Sep, 10am-5pm Oct-Mar) FREE One of France's few Carolingian-era churches, this exceptional oratory – sadly, over-restored in the mid-19th century – is

---

WINE IN THE LOIRE VALLEY

Splendid scenery and densely packed vineyards make the Loire Valley an outstanding wine-touring destination, with a range of excellent reds, rosés, whites, dessert wines and crémants (sparkling wines). Equipped with *Sur la Route des Vins de Loire* (On the Loire Wine Route), a free map from the winegrowers association (www.vinsvaldeloire.fr), or the *Loire Valley Vineyards* booklet, available at area tourist offices and *maisons des vins* (wine visitor centres), you can put together a web of wonderful wine-tasting itineraries, drawing from over 320 wine cellars.

Anjou and Saumur alone have 30 Appellation d'Origine Contrôlée (AOC) designations, and Touraine has 23, including some lively gamays (fruity, light-bodied wines). The Vins du Val de Loire website (www.vinsvaldeloire.fr) has a complete primer.

The predominant red is cabernet franc, though you'll also find cabernet sauvignon, pinot noir and others. Appellations (AOCs) include Anjou, Saumur-Champigny, Bourgueil and Chinon.

For whites, Vouvray's chenin blancs are excellent, and Sancerre and the appellation across the Loire River, Pouilly-Fumé, produce great sauvignon blancs. Cour-Cheverny is made from the lesser-known romorantin grape. Savennières, near Angers, has both a dry and a sweet chenin blanc.

The bubbly appellation Crémant de Loire spans many communities, but you can easily find it around Montrichard (eg Château Monmousseau); other bubblies include Saumur Brut and Vouvray.

One of the most densely packed stretches for wine tasting along the Loire River itself is around Saumur. Towns with multiple tasting rooms (from west to east) include St-Hilaire-St-Florent (where you'll find Ackerman, Langlois-Château and Veuve Amiot), Souzay Champigny (home to Château Villeneuve and Clos des Cordeliers) and Parnay (Château de Parnay and Château de Targé).

Just east of Tours, another hot spot includes Rochecorbon (home to Blanc Foussy), Vouvray (Domaine Huet l'Echansonne, Château Moncontour and several others) and Montlouis-sur-Loire. You'll find a cave des producteurs representing multiple producers in each of the latter two towns.

Designate a driver (or hop on your bike), grab your map, and explore!

renowned for its unusual Maltese-cross layout and gilt-and-silver mosaic of the biblical Ark of the Covenant (early 9th century; see Exodus 25:10-21). Audioguides (€3) and information sheets in several languages are available at the adjacent tourist office (p398), or you can download the audio tour from its website. Signs are in French and English.

Abbaye de St-Benoît-sur-Loire MONASTERY
(Abbaye de Fleury; ☑ 02 38 35 72 43; www. abbaye-fleury.com; 1 rue de l'Abbaye, St-Benoît-sur-Loire; ☺ 6.30am-10pm) Home to about 40 Benedictine monks, this abbey – shut down during the Revolution and reopened in 1944 – is known for its Romanesque basilica, whose 11th-century crypt houses the relics of St Benedict (480–547). Visitors are welcome to attend prayers (held six times a day), chanted by the monks in haunting Gregorian monophony – a spiritual experience even if you're not religious. From about December to Easter, all services (except for Sunday Mass) are held in the crypt.

Château de Sully-sur-Loire CHATEAU
(☑ 02 38 36 36 86; www.chateausully.fr; Sully-sur-Loire; adult/child €8/5, with guided tour €10/6; ☺ 10am-7pm daily Jul & Aug, 10am-6pm Tue-Sun May, Jun & Sep, 1.30-5.30pm Tue-Sun Feb-Apr & Oct-Dec, closed Jan) With its machicolated ramparts (featuring holes for pouring boiling liquid on attackers), soaring round turrets and steeply pitched roof, this fairy-tale castle was built, starting in 1395, to defend one of the Loire's crucial crossings. Today, 19 rooms are richly decorated with furnishings dating from the Middle Ages to the 19th century. One side of the glassy moat is lined with two-century-old bald cypresses, brought from the USA by General Lafayette, hero of the American Revolution, in the late 1700s.

ℹ Information

Val de Loire & Forêt d'Orléans Tourist Office
(☑ 02 38 58 44 79; www.tourisme45-loire-et-foret.fr; 3 place Aristide Briand, Châteauneuf-sur-Loire; ☺ 10am-12.30pm & 2-6pm Wed-Sat Oct-Apr, plus Tue May-Sep, plus 10am-12.30pm Sun Jul & Aug)

ℹ Getting There & Away

Châteauneuf-sur-Loire, Germigny-des-Prés, St-Benoît-sur-Loire and Sully-sur-Loire are linked to Orléans by Rémi bus 3.

La Sologne

For centuries the boggy wetland and murky woods of La Sologne have been one of France's great hunting grounds, with deer, boar, pheasants and stags roaming the forest, and eels, carp, pike and perch (and, more recently, caviar-producing sturgeon) filling the 300 *étangs* (ponds). François I established the region as a royal playground, but floods and the Wars of Religion turned it into a malaria-infested swamp; only in the mid-19th century, after it was drained under Napoléon III, did La Sologne again become *à la mode*.

In winter the region can be desolate, with drizzle and thick fog, but in summer it's a riot of wildflowers and makes great country to explore on foot or – on a network of quiet backroads known as the Rte des Étangs – by bike. Trails, including the GR31 and the GR3C, criss-cross the area, but stick to the signposted routes during hunting season (late September to February).

For info on hikes and walks in La Sologne, contact the **tourist office** (☑ 02 54 76 43 89; www.sologne-tourisme.fr; place de la Paix, Romorantin-Lanthenay; ☺ 9.30am-12.30pm or 1pm & 2-6pm or 6.30pm Mon-Sat, closed Mon morning Sep-Jun; ☎) in Romorantin-Lanthenay, 42km southeast of Blois, or St-Viâtre's **Maison des Étangs** (☑ 02 54 88 23 00; www.maison-des-etangs.fr; 2 rue de la Poste, St-Viâtre; adult/child incl tour €5/3; ☺ 10am-noon & 2-6pm Apr-Oct, 2-6pm Wed & Sat Nov-Mar). Exhibits at the latter explore La Sologne's 3000 étangs (ponds) – all of them human-made over the past millennium.

On the last weekend in October, the annual **Journées Gastronomiques de Sologne** (www.jgs.romorantin.net; Romorantin-Lanthenay; adult/child €5/3) fill the streets of Romorantin with local delicacies like stuffed trout, wild-boar pâté and freshly baked *tarte tatin,* the upside-down apple tart accidentally created in 1888 by two sisters in nearby Lamotte-Beuvron.

ℹ Getting There & Away

Non-direct trains and train-bus combos link Romorantin-Lanthenay with Tours (€16.50, 1½ hours, four to eight daily). **Rémi** (p402) bus 4 connects Romorantin-Lanthenay with Blois (€2, one hour, six daily Monday to Friday, two Saturday, one Sunday).

BLÉSOIS

The peaceful, verdant countryside around the former royal seat of Blois is home to some of France's finest châteaux, including graceful Cheverny, smaller Beauregard and the cupola-capped *château extraordinaire* to top them all, Chambord.

Blois

POP 46,350

Towering above the northern bank of the Loire, Blois' royal château, one-time feudal seat of the powerful counts of Blois, offers a gripping introduction to some key periods in French history and architecture. Parts of the city still have a medieval vibe, and Blois makes an excellent base for visits to the châteaux, villages and towns of the central Loire Valley.

◉ Sights

Billets combinés (combo tickets; €15.50 to €26.50), sold at the château, Maison de la Magie and Fondation du Doute, can save you some cash.

★**Château Royal de Blois** CHATEAU
(🎫 02 54 90 33 33; www.chateaudeblois.fr; place du Château; adult/child €12/6.50, audioguide €4; ⊗9am-6.30pm or 7pm Apr-Oct, 10am-5pm Nov-Mar) Seven French kings lived in Blois' royal château, whose four grand wings were built during four distinct periods in French architecture: Gothic (13th century), Flamboyant Gothic (1498–1501), early Renaissance (1515–20) and classical (1630s). You can easily spend a half-day immersing yourself in the château's dramatic and bloody history and its extraordinary architecture. In July and August there are free tours in English (at 10.30am, 1.15pm and 3pm).

The most famous part of the **Gothic wing** is the richly painted **Hall of the States-General**, from the 13th century. Along one wall, interactive screens illustrate the development of the château over the centuries.

In the **Renaissance wing** you'll find the extraordinary spiral **loggia staircase**, decorated with fierce salamanders and curly Fs, heraldic symbols of François I. Other highlights include the **Queen's Bedchamber**, in which Catherine de Médicis (Henri II's machiavellian wife) died in 1589, and the **King's Bedchamber**, setting for one of the bloodiest episodes in the château's history. In 1588 Henri III had his arch-rival, Duke Henri I de Guise, murdered by royal bodyguards (the king is said to have hidden behind a tapestry while the dastardly deed was done). He had the duke's brother, the Cardinal de Guise, killed the next day. The bloodletting of the Wars of Religion continued when Henri III himself was murdered just eight months later by a vengeful monk. Dramatic and very graphic oil paintings illustrate these gruesome events next door in the **Council Room**.

The **Musée des Beaux-Arts** (Fine Arts Museum), in the Flamboyant Gothic **Louis XII wing** (look for his heraldic emblem, the porcupine), displays 300 16th- to 19th-century paintings, sculptures and tapestries.

Admission includes use of an augmented-reality tablet computer called a HistoPad. Kids aged five to 12 can guide their parents through the château with the interactive **Parcours Enfants** (Path for Children) app; wi-fi is available to download it.

From late April to late September, a **sound-and-light show** (Sound & Light Show; 🎫 02 54 90 33 33; Château Royal de Blois; adult/child €10.50/6.50; ⊗10pm or 10.30pm late Apr-late Sep) brings the château's history and architecture to life with dramatic lighting and narration; an all-new 360-degree *spectacle* was inaugurated in 2018.

★**Maison de la Magie** MUSEUM
(🎫 02 54 90 33 33; www.maisondelamagie.fr; 1 place du Château; adult/child €10/6.50; ⊗10am-12.30pm & 2-6.30pm Apr-Aug & mid-Oct–early Nov, 2-6.30pm daily plus 10am-12.30pm Sat & Sun 1st 2 weeks Sep; 🖐) This museum of magic occupies the one-time home of watchmaker, inventor and conjurer Jean Eugène Robert-Houdin (1805–71), after whom the American magician Harry Houdini named himself. Dragons emerge roaring from the windows every half-hour, while inside the museum has exhibits on Robert-Houdin and the history of magic, displays of optical trickery, and several daily magic shows.

Old City HISTORIC SITE
Blois' medieval and Renaissance old town is well worth a stroll. The façade of **Maison des Acrobates** (3bis place St-Louis) – one of Blois' few surviving 15th-century houses – is decorated with wooden sculptures of figures from medieval farces. The **Hôtel de Villebrême** (13 rue Pierre de Blois), another 15th-century townhouse, is nearby.

The Gothic-style **Cathédrale St-Louis** (place St-Louis; ⊗9am or 10am-6pm or 7pm), rebuilt after a terrible storm in 1678, has a western façade mixing late-Gothic and

Blois

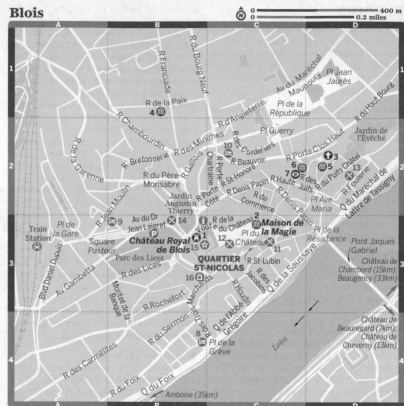

Blois

◎ Top Sights

◎ Sights

🛏 Sleeping

✗ Eating

✪ Entertainment

🛍 Shopping

neoclassical elements. The church's stained glass, bearing enigmatic Latin inscriptions, was created by Dutch artist Jan Dibbets in 2000.

Lovely panoramas unfold across town from the peaceful **Jardins de l'Évêché** (the gardens behind the cathedral) and from the top of the **Escalier Denis Papin**, a grand staircase linking rue du Palais with the commercial precinct around rue Denis Papin.

Fondation du Doute
GALLERY

(☑ 02 54 55 37 40; www.fondationdudoute.fr; 14 rue de la Paix; adult/child €7.50/3.50; ⊙ 2-6.30pm Wed-Sun mid-Apr–early Nov, plus Tue Jul & Aug, 2-6.30pm Fri-Sun winter, closed late Dec-early Feb) Avant-garde from the floorboards to the roof, this museum showcases the art and 'state of mind' of the 1960s Fluxus movement, inspired in part by the American composer John Cage, which mocked the elitism of 'high art' and sought to bring art to the people, in part through humour. Works by 50 artists 'invite visitors to call preconceptions into question'. Situated 750m north of the château.

🛏 Sleeping

Hôtel Anne de Bretagne
HOTEL €

(☑ 02 54 78 05 38; www.hotelannedebretagne.com; 31 av du Dr Jean Laigret; s/d/tr/q €60/69/76/95, winter s/d €45/55; ⊙ reception 7am-11pm; P 🛜) This ivy-covered hotel, in a great location midway between the train station and the château, has friendly staff, a cosy piano-equipped *salon* and 29 brightly coloured rooms with bold bedspreads. A packed three-course picnic lunch costs €11.50. Rents out bicycles (€16) and has free enclosed bike parking.

Côté Loire
HOTEL €

(☑ 02 54 78 07 86; www.coteloire.com; 2 place de la Grève; d €62-105; 🛜) This aptly named hotel, in a 15th- and 16th-century building facing the river, has eight spotless rooms decorated in subdued tones, some with 500-year-old beams and/or great Loire views. The restaurant (closed Sunday and Monday; lunch/dinner *menus* €23/33) serves French cuisine in a rustic dining room and, when it's warm, on a lovely terrace. No lift.

★ La Maison de Thomas
B&B €€

(☑ 09 81 84 44 59; www.lamaisondethomas.fr; 12 rue Beauvoir; s/d/tr €91/101/121; 🛜) A friendly welcome and five spacious rooms with large windows, high ceilings and exposed beams await you at this beautiful B&B, on a pedestrianised street midway between the château and the cathedral. There's bike storage in the interior courtyard and a wine cellar where you can sample local vintages, most of them organic.

🍴 Eating

Food Market
MARKET €

(place Louis XII; ⊙ 8am-1pm Sat) The perfect place to assemble a picnic.

Les Planches
ITALIAN €

(☑ 02 54 55 08 00; 5 rue Grenier à Sel; mains €11.50-14.50; ⊙ noon-1.30pm & 7-9pm Tue-Sat; 🛜🍴) Hidden away on a tiny stone-paved square, Les Planches is a Blois favourite for its toasted bruschettas (open-face Italian sandwiches) and meal-size salads. Romantic, with a purple light on each table. It stays open later in summer.

Le Triboulet
GRILL €€

(☑ 02 54 74 11 23; www.letriboulet.com; 18 place du Château; menus €18.50-22.50, child's menu €10.80; ⊙ noon-2pm & 7-9pm daily Jul & Aug, closed Sun dinner & Mon Sep-Jun, also closed Sun lunch mid-Sep–Easter) Succulent beef, mutton and *andouillette* sausages, grilled on an open wood fire right in the dining room, keep connoisseurs coming back to this traditional French restaurant and its spacious terrace. Dishes are made with local products, such as mushrooms from the Sologne. Has a good selection of Touraine wines.

L'Orangerie du Château
GASTRONOMY €€€

(☑ 02 54 78 05 36; www.orangerie-du-chateau.fr; 1 av du Dr Jean Laigret; menus €40-86; ⊙ noon-1.45pm & 7-9.15pm Tue-Sat; P) This Michelin-starred restaurant serves *cuisine gastronomique inventive* inspired by both French tradition and culinary ideas brought from faraway lands. The excellent wine list comes on a tablet computer. For dessert try the house speciality, *soufflé chaud* (hot soufflé).

ℹ Information

Tourist Office (☑ 02 54 90 41 41; www.blois chambord.co.uk; 6 rue de la Voûte du Château; ⊙ 9am-7pm Apr-Sep, 10am-12.30pm & 2-5pm Mon-Sat, plus Sun school holidays, Oct-Mar)

DON'T MISS

BOUTIQUE SHOPPING

One of just a handful of artisanal umbrella makers in France, Nathalie Fraudeau uses skills learned in Normandy and six specialised machines to craft each *parapluie* (umbrella) and *ambrelle* (parasol). Visitors are welcome to drop by and watch her work at **La Maison des Parapluies** (☑ 02 54 46 99 92; www.lamaisondes parapluies.com; 2 rue des Fossés du Château; full-size umbrella €75-100, collapsible €55-70; ⊙ 2.30-7pm Mon, 9.30am-1pm & 2.30-7pm Tue-Sat). Special orders (including umbrellas with a customised photo printed on the dome) take a couple of days.

ⓘ Getting There & Away

BUS

The tourist office has a brochure detailing public-transport options to nearby châteaux.

A *navette* (shuttle bus; €6) run by **Rémi** (☑ 02 54 58 55 44; www.remi-centrevaldeloire.fr) makes it possible to do a Blois–Chambord–Cheverny–Beauregard–Blois circuit on Wednesday, Saturday and Sunday from early April to 5 November. From early April to August, this line runs daily during school-holiday periods and on public holidays.

TRAIN

Blois-Chambord train station (av Dr Jean Laigret) is 600m west (up the hill) from Blois' château.

Amboise €7.20, 20 minutes, 15 to 20 daily.
Orléans €11.50, 25 to 56 minutes, 17 to 24 daily.
Paris Gare d'Austerlitz €18 to €32.40, 1½ hours, five direct daily.
Tours €11.20, 30 to 46 minutes, 16 to 22 daily.

Around Blois

★ **Château de Chambord**   CHATEAU
(☑ info 02 54 50 40 00, tour & show reservations 02 54 50 50 40; www.chambord.org; adult/child €13/free, parking distant/near €4/6; ⊙ 9am-6pm Apr-Oct, to 5pm Nov-Mar; 🚻) One of the crowning achievements of French Renaissance architecture, the Château de Chambord – with 426 rooms, 282 fireplaces and 77 staircases – is the largest, grandest and most visited château in the Loire Valley. Begun in 1519 by François I (r 1515–47) as a weekend hunting retreat, it quickly grew into one of the most ambitious – and expensive – building projects ever under-

---

ⓘ CHÂTEAUX PASS

You can save money on visits to many Blésois châteaux – and avoid waiting in line – by buying a **Pass' Châteaux** multi-site discount ticket. For information, contact the tourist offices in Blois and at Chambord, Chaumont and Cheverny. Popular combinations include the following:

➡ Blois–Chambord–Cheverny €31

➡ Blois–Chenonceau–Chambord–Cheverny €44

➡ Blois–Chaumont–Chambord–Cheverny €46.50

➡ Blois–Chambord–Amboise–Clos Lucé €45.50

---

taken by a French monarch. A French-style **formal garden** opened in 2017.

Construction was repeatedly halted by financial problems, design setbacks and military commitments (not to mention the kidnapping of the king's two sons in Spain). Ironically, when Chambord was finally finished after three decades of work, François found his elaborate palace too draughty, preferring instead the royal apartments in Amboise and Blois. In the end he stayed here for just 72 days during his entire 32-year reign. Still, Chambord's 500th anniversary will be celebrated with great pomp in 2019.

Inside the main building, a film (subtitled in five languages) provides an excellent introduction to the château's history and architecture. On the ground floor you can visit 18th-century **kitchens**, while the 1st floor is where you'll find the most interesting (though lightly furnished) rooms, including the **royal bedchambers**. Rising through the centre of the structure, the world-famous **double-helix staircase** – very possibly designed by the king's chum Leonardo da Vinci – ascends to the great lantern tower and the rooftop, where you can marvel at a veritable skyline of cupolas, domes, turrets, chimneys and lightning rods and gaze out across the vast grounds.

To get a sense of what you're looking at and add virtual-reality furnishings to some of the rooms, pick up a Histopad tablet computer (€6.50, 1½ hours), available in 12 languages and in versions for both kids (including a treasure hunt) and adults. From July to September there are hour-long guided tours (adult/child €5/3) in English – ask at the ticket counter for times. Outdoor spectacles held in the warm season include a 45-minute **equestrian show** (☑ 02 54 50 50 40; www.chambord.org; adult/child €14.50/11, adult incl château €24; ⊙ 10.45am &/or 4pm Tue-Sun late Apr-Sep, plus Mon early Jul-late Aug) featuring horses and riders in colourful, François I–themed dress and birds of prey.

From about April to December there are several places to eat just past the new entrance pavilion, plus a cafe inside. In winter dress warmly – the castle is no easier to heat now than it was five centuries ago.

Chambord is 16km east of Blois, 45km southwest of Orléans and 18km northeast of Cheverny.

Château de Cheverny   CHATEAU
(☑ 02 54 79 96 29; www.chateau-cheverny.fr; av du Château; château & gardens adult/

CHAMBORD: EXPLORING THE ESTATE

The 54-sq-km hunting reserve around Château de Chambord (p402) – the largest walled park in Europe – is reserved for the exclusive use of very high-ranking French government officials. About 10 sq km of the *domaine* (estate), north and northwest of the château, is open to the public, with marked trails for walkers, cyclists and horse riders.

Hire bikes, *rosalies* (pedal carts), *golfettes* (electric golf carts), rowboats and electric boats at a **rental kiosk** (☑ 02 54 50 40 00; www.chambord.org; hire bicycle 1/4hr €6/15, rowboat 1hr €12, golf cart 45min €25; ⊙ 10am-6.30pm Apr-early Nov) near the *embarcadère* (dock) midway between the chateau and its entrance pavilion. April to early November, carriage rides (adult/child €11/6) begin at the château's *écuries* (stables).

The reserve is a great place for wildlife spotting, especially during the deer mating season between mid-September and mid-October. Five observatories let you discreetly view the park's residents; set out at dawn or dusk to maximise your chances of spotting stags, boars, red deer and wild sheep. To visit parts of the reserve normally closed to the public, take a 1½-hour **Land Rover safari tour** (☑ 02 54 50 50 40; www.chambord. org; adult/child €18/12; ⊙ up to 6 times a day summer, 1-3 times a day winter) conducted by French-speaking guides; most speak at least a bit of English. Call ahead to book.

child €11.50/8.20; ⊙ 9.15am-6.30pm Apr-Sep, 10am-5pm Oct-Mar) Perhaps the Loire's most elegantly proportioned château, Cheverny represents the zenith of French classical architecture: a perfect blend of symmetry, geometry and aesthetic order. Inside are some of the most sumptuous and beautifully furnished rooms anywhere in the Loire Valley, virtually unchanged for generations because the de Vibraye family has lived here, almost continuously, ever since the château's construction in the early 1600s by Jacques Hurault, an attendant to Louis XII.

Highlights downstairs include the formal **dining room**, with 34 painted wooden panels depicting the story of Don Quixote. Upstairs are the **king's bedchamber**, with ceiling murals and tapestries illustrating stories from Greek mythology, and a **children's playroom** complete with toys from the time of Napoléon III. The **arms room** is full of pikestaffs, claymores, crossbows and suits of armour – including a tiny gilded one made to measure for a four-year-old duke – and a mid-17th-century Gobelins tapestry that's so well preserved you can still see the reds.

The de Vibrayes' fabulous **art collection** includes a portrait of Jeanne of Aragon by Raphael's studio, an 18th-century De la Tour pastel, and works by a who's who of court painters. In the downstairs Gallerie, keep your eyes open for a certificate signed by US president George Washington.

Behind the main château, the 18th-century **orangerie** – where many priceless artworks, including (apparently) the *Mona Lisa,* were stashed during WWII – is now

a **tearoom** (open April to mid-November), with thick, creamy hot chocolate (€4.90) prepared according to Madame de Vibraye's special recipe. During low-season school holidays there's a **cafe** near the kennels. The **Labyrinthe** (maze), near the orangerie, reopened in 2018.

In the gardens about 50m beyond the giant sequoia (planted around 1870), the **kennels** house around 100 hunting dogs, a cross between Poitevins and English foxhounds. Feeding time, known as the **Soupe des Chiens**, showcases the extraordinary relationship between the dogs and their *piqueux* (handler); it begins at 11.30am daily from April to mid-October, and on Monday, Wednesday, Thursday and Friday from mid-October to March (on other days the dogs are out hunting).

Fans of **Tintin** might find the Château de Cheverny's façade strangely familiar: Hergé used it as a model (minus the two end towers) for Moulinsart (Marlinspike) Hall, the ancestral home of Tintin's irascible sidekick, Captain Haddock. Devotees large and small may enjoy **Les Secrets de Moulinsart** (Château de Cheverny; combo ticket incl château adult/child €16/12.10; 🚻), whose interactive exhibits explore the world of Tintin with recreated scenes, thunder and other special effects.

The château's self-guided-tour brochure is available in 13 languages. Kids aged seven to 14 may enjoy *Secrets of Cheverny,* a free booklet of puzzles and games.

Cheverny is 14km southeast of Blois and 18km southwest of Chambord.

LEOKS/SHUTTERSTOCK ©

1. Jardin d'Ornement, Château de Villandry (p414) 2. Moat-encircled Château de Sully-sur-Loire (p398) 3. Diane de Poitiers' Bedroom, Château de Chenonceau (p411) 4. Château d'Ussé (p417)

VIACHESLAV LOPATIN/SHUTTERSTOCK ©

Châteaux of the Loire Valley

The Loire Valley is the place to see castles, but with so many glorious options, what's the best way to spend your time?

For sheer architectural splendour, you can't top the big three: François I's country extravaganza Chambord (p402); Renaissance-era, river-spanning Chenonceau (p411); and the supremely graceful Cheverny (p402).

If you're looking for solitude, chances are that off-the-beaten-track châteaux, such as Brissac (p428), Brézé (p425) and Beauregard, will be much quieter.

For historical significance, at the top of the list are the royal château of Blois (p399), spanning four distinct periods of French architecture; Amboise (p412), home to a succession of French monarchs; the Forteresse Royale de Chinon (p417), where Joan of Arc held her momentous first rendezvous with the future King Charles VII; the forbidding Château d'Angers (p425), with its fantastic tapestry of the Apocalypse; and pastoral Le Clos Lucé (p412), where Leonardo da Vinci spent his final years.

Looking for a picture-perfect setting? Our choices are the moat-ringed Château d'Azay-le-Rideau (p415) and the Château de Sully-sur-Loire (p398), and the stunning formal gardens at Villandry (p414) and Chaumont-sur-Loire (p406).

For literary connections, try Château d'Ussé (p417), the inspiration for Sleeping Beauty; or the Château de Montsoreau (p423), setting for a classic Alexandre Dumas novel.

TOP TIPS

➡ In the summer, go first thing or late in the day to avoid the coach-tour crowds.

➡ Buy multi-château combo tickets, or pre-purchase tickets at tourist offices, for slight savings and to avoid queues.

➡ Remember that château ticket offices close from 30 to 60 minutes before the châteaux themselves.

Château de Chaumont-sur-Loire

CHATEAU

(☑02 54 20 99 22; www.domaine-chaumont.fr; adult/child Apr-Oct €18/12, Jan-Mar, Nov & Dec €12/7; ⊙9.30am or 10am-5pm or 6pm Nov-Mar, to 8pm Apr-Oct) Set on a strategic bluff with sweeping views along the Loire, Chaumont-sur-Loire is known for three things: the **château** itself, which has a medieval exterior (cylindrical towers, a sturdy drawbridge) and an interior courtyard that is very much of the Renaissance; world-class exhibitions of striking **contemporary art**; and the **Festival International des Jardins** (⊙late Apr-early Nov), for which 30 magnificent gardens are created each year by jury-selected teams led by visual artists, architects, set designers and landscape gardeners.

A defensive château was first built on this spot in the late 900s, but most of the present castle was constructed between 1468 and 1566. Following the death of Henri II in 1559, Catherine de Médicis (his widow) forced Diane de Poitiers (his mistress and her 2nd cousin) to accept Chaumont in exchange for the grander surroundings of Chenonceau. Savvy Diane earned considerable sums from Chaumont's vast landholdings but stayed here only occasionally.

In the second half of the 18th century, the château's owner, Jacques-Donatien Le Ray, a supporter of the American Revolution and an intimate of Benjamin Franklin's, removed the decrepit north wing. In 1875 Princess de Broglie, heiress to the Say sugar fortune, bought the château and thoroughly renovated and furnished it.

The most impressive furnished room is the **Council Chamber**, with its series of eight 16th-century tapestries and a 17th-century majolica-tiled floor from a palace in Palermo.

Don't miss the brick **Écuries** (stables), an outbuilding constructed in 1877 to house the Broglies' horses in equine luxury. A fine collection of 19th-century equestrian gear and horse-drawn carriages of surprisingly varied design, and installations of contemporary art, are displayed inside.

It's a good idea to rent an informative **audiovideo guide** (a tablet computer; €4), available in 10 languages for adults and four languages for kids; the app can be downloaded from iTunes and Google Play.

The Château de Chaumont is 19km southwest of Blois. Trains link Onzain, a 2.5km walk across the Loire from the château, with Blois (€3.70, eight to 12 minutes, nine to 19 daily) and Tours (€8.80, 28 minutes, 10 to 18 daily).

🛏 Sleeping & Eating

★ Relais de Chambord

BOUTIQUE HOTEL €€

(☑02 54 81 01 01; www.relaisdechambord.com; place St-Louis, Chambord; d from €165; P ❋ @ ☎) At home in the Château de Chambord's former kennels in front of the castle, this four-star hotel offers larger-than-life views of the château from some rooms and a sensational bar and restaurant terrace. Contemporary rooms are country-chic, dining is modern French and the hotel has a spa. Guests can borrow electric bicycles to cruise around the vast private estate. Rates include breakfast.

La Levraudière

B&B €

(☑02 54 79 81 99; www.lalevraudiere.fr; 1 chemin de la Levraudière, Cheverny; d €85-95, 4/5-person ste €150/160; ☎ ❋) In a peaceful 1892 farmhouse, amid 3.5 hectares of grassland, La Levraudière's four spacious rooms are comfortable and homey and come with queen-size beds. Sonia Maurice, the friendly owner, speaks English and is happy to arrange bike rental and supply cycling maps. The B&B is 1.5km south of the Château de Cheverny (p402), just off the D102.

A 10m swimming pool was added in 2017. A homemade, Sologne-style dinner that includes four courses, an aperitif, wine and coffee costs €30.

La Madeleine de Proust

FRENCH €€

(☑02 54 20 94 80; http://lamadeleinedeproust.business.site; 31-33 rue du Maréchal Leclerc, Chaumont-sur-Loire; 2/3-course menus €23/30; ⊙noon-1.45pm & 7-8.45pm Mon & Thu-Sat, noon-1.45pm Tue & Sun) Excellent homemade French cuisine served impeccably and with a warm smile.

Max Vauché Chocolate Factory

FOOD & DRINK

(☑02 54 46 07 96; www.maxvauche-chocolatier.com; 22 Les Jardins du Moulin, Bracieux; tour adult/child €4.70/3.70; ⊙shop 10am-12.30pm & 2-7pm Tue-Sat, 3-6.30pm Sun Sep-Jun, plus 10am-12.30pm & 2-7pm Mon Jul & Aug) For scrumptious chocolate, head to sleepy Bracieux, 8km south of the Château de Chambord (p402), where Max Vauché has a production facility, shop and *salon du chocolat* (chocolate cafe; open Saturday & Sunday year-round plus Tuesday to Friday in July and August). Visitors can sample and compare dark chocolate made with cacao from places like Madagascar, Sao Tomé, New Guinea and Vietnam.

THE LOIRE VALLEY BLOIS

TOURAINE

Often dubbed the 'Garden of France', the Touraine region is known for its rich food, tasty cheeses and famously pure French accent, as well as a first-rate line-up of glorious châteaux: some medieval (Langeais and Loches), others Renaissance (Azay-le-Rideau, Villandry and Chenonceau). The vibrant capital, Tours, offers plenty of good restaurants, château tours and public-transport options.

Tours

POP 136,000

Bustling Tours is a smart and vivacious city, with an impressive medieval quarter, fine museums, well-tended parks and a university of some 30,000 students. Combining the sophisticated style of Paris with the conservative sturdiness of central France, Tours makes an ideal staging post for exploring the castles of the Touraine.

⊙ Sights

Tours' focal point is grand, semicircular **place Jean Jaurès**, adorned with fountains, formal gardens and imposing public buildings (the town hall and the courthouse). **Vieux Tours** (the old city) occupies the narrow streets around place Plumereau (locally known as place Plum'), which is about 400m west of **rue Nationale**, the city's majestic main commercial thoroughfare.

★ Musée du Compagnonnage   MUSEUM
(🕿 02 47 21 62 20; www.museecompagnonnage.fr; 8 rue Nationale & 1 square Prosper Merimée; adult/child €5.80/4; ⊙ 9am-12.30pm & 2-6pm, closed Tue mid-Sep–mid-Jun) This extraordinary museum – an absolute gem! – spotlights France's renowned *compagnonnages,* guild organisations of skilled craftspeople who have created everything from medieval cathedrals to the Statue of Liberty. Dozens of professions – from carpentry to saddle-making to locksmithing – are celebrated here with items handcrafted from wood, wrought iron, bronze, stone, brick, clay and leather; standouts include exquisite wooden architectural models of elaborate towers and a miniature wrought-iron gate that took 14 years to make.

★ Musée des Beaux-Arts   GALLERY
(🖉 02 47 05 68 73; www.mba.tours.fr; 18 place François Sicard; adult/child €6/3; ⊙ 9am-12.45pm & 2-6pm Wed-Mon) This superb fine-arts museum, in a gorgeous 18th-century archbishop's palace, features paintings, sculpture, furniture and *objets d'art* from the 14th to 20th centuries. Highlights include paintings by Delacroix, Degas and Monet, a rare Rembrandt miniature and a Rubens *Madonna and Child.* Outside there's a magnificent cedar of Lebanon planted in 1804 and a flowery garden.

Cathédrale St-Gatien   CHURCH
(www.paroisse-cathedrale-tours.fr; place de la Cathédrale; ⊙ 8.30am-8pm or 8.30pm) With its flying buttresses, gargoyles and twin Renaissance-style towers (70m) – and, inside, Gothic vaulting, dazzling stained glass and huge baroque organ – this cathedral cuts a striking figure. Near the entrance you can pick up an English brochure on its architecture and history; English signs in the choir explain the luminous stained glass, some from the 13th century, other parts from the 21st.

On the north side is the **Cloître de la Psalette** (place de la Cathédrale; adult/child €3.50/free; ⊙ 9.30am or 10am-12.30pm & 2-5pm or 6pm, closed Sun morning, also closed Mon & Tue Oct-Mar), built from 1442 to 1524 (that's why it's partly Flamboyant Gothic and partly Renaissance). It once served as a scriptorium (for the copying of manuscripts) and a school of Gregorian chanting. A **music-and-light show** is projected on the west façade twice nightly in July (10.45pm and 11.15pm) and August (10.15pm and 10.45pm) and on the first two weekends of September (10pm and 10.30pm).

Basilique St-Martin   CHURCH
(www.basiliquesaintmartin.fr; rue Descartes; ⊙ 7.30am-7pm, to 9pm Jul & Aug) In the Middle Ages, Tours was an important pilgrimage city thanks to the relics of soldier-turned-evangelist St Martin (c 317–97). In the 5th century a basilica was constructed above his tomb; in the 13th century it was replaced by an enormous Romanesque church, of which only two towers, **Tour Charlemagne** and **Tour de l'Horloge** (Clock Tower), remain. Modern-day Basilique St-Martin, a domed, neo-Byzantine structure, was built from 1886 to 1925.

Jardin Botanique   GARDENS
(🖉 02 47 21 62 67; www.tours.fr; 35 bd Tonnellé; ⊙ 7.45am-7.30pm Mar-May, Sep & Oct, to 9pm Jun-Aug, to 5.30pm Nov-Feb; 👫) FREE Founded in 1843, Tours' delightful 5-hectare botanical gardens have a tropical greenhouse, a medicinal herb garden, a small zoo and playgrounds. Situated 2km west of place Jean Jaurès, the gardens are served by Fil Bleu bus 15 from place Jean Jaurès or bus 4 from the riverfront; get off at the Bretonneau or Tonnellé stops.

Tours

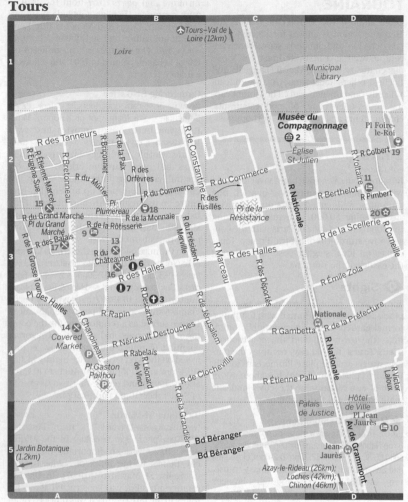

🛏 Sleeping

★ Hôtel l'Adresse   BOUTIQUE HOTEL €

(📞 02 47 20 85 76; www.hotel-ladresse.com; 12 rue de la Rôtisserie; s from €59, d €80-125; 🌊 @ 🛜) Looking for Parisian stylishness in provincial Tours? L'Adresse is the address! On a pedestrianised street in the old quarter, this place has 17 rooms (renovated in 2017) – finished in calm creams, tans and light browns – with designer sinks, sparkling bathrooms, ultra-soundproofed windows and, on the 3rd floor, 17th-century rafters. No lift.

★ Hôtel Ronsard   BOUTIQUE HOTEL €

(📞 02 47 05 25 36; www.hotel-ronsard.com; 2 rue Pimbert; s €63-77, d €73-85; 🌊 @ 🛜) A favourite of musicians performing at the nearby **Grand Théâtre** (📞 box office 02 47 60 20 20; www. operadetours.fr; 34 rue de la Scellerie; ⏰ box office 10.30am-1pm & 2-5.45pm Tue-Sat, theatre closed early Jul-early Sep), this quiet, 20-room hotel, built in 1920, offers easy comfort and good value. Staircases are lined with colourful photographs of theatre and opera performances, while the sleek rooms are decorated in muted tones of grey, brown and cream. No lift.

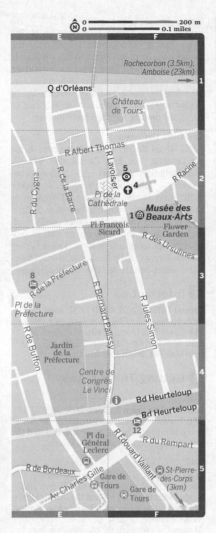

N 0 ⎯⎯⎯⎯ 200 m
0 ⎯⎯⎯⎯ 0.1 miles

Tours

◎ Top Sights
1 Musée des Beaux-Arts	F2
2 Musée du Compagnonnage	C2

◎ Sights
3 Basilique St-Martin	B3
4 Cathédrale St-Gatien	F2
5 Cloître de la Psalette	F2
6 Tour Charlemagne	B3
7 Tour de l'Horloge	B3

⊟ Sleeping
8 Alcôve des Beaux Arts	E3
9 Hôtel l'Adresse	A3
10 Hôtel Oceania L'Univers Tours	D5
11 Hôtel Ronsard	D2
12 Hôtel Val de Loire	F5

✕ Eating
13 Barju	B3
14 Halles de Tours	A4
15 L'Atelier Gourmand	A2
16 Le Timbre Poste	B3
17 Le Zinc	A3

♦ Drinking & Nightlife
18 Les Trois Orfèvres	B3
19 Pale	D2

✦ Entertainment
20 Grand Théâtre	D3

THE LOIRE VALLEY TOURS

marble fireplaces and one with direct garden access, blend antique furnishings, modern touches and large windows. Rooms on the 3rd floor have AC. No lift.

Hôtel Oceania L'Univers Tours HOTEL €€€
(☑ 02 47 05 37 12; www.oceaniahotels.com/hotel-lunivers-tours; 5 bd Heurteloup; d €200-245; P ✳ @ ⊛ ≋) Everyone from Ernest Hemingway to Winston Churchill to Thomas Edison has bunked at L'Univers since it opened in 1846. Check out the lobby's balcony frescos before heading up to the 91 tasteful rooms, renovated in 2017. Amenities include pool, spa, *hammam* and fitness centre. Discounts available by phone and on the website.

✕ Eating

Halles de Tours MARKET €
(www.halles-de-tours.com; place Gaston Pailhou; ⊙ 7am-1pm & 3-7.30pm Tue-Sat, no midday closure Fri & Sat, 8am-1pm Sun; ∅) This is Tours' 'gastronomic heart'. Market stalls – 38 of them – sell everything you could want for a picnic, including fine cheese, wine and prepared dishes.

Alcôve des Beaux Arts B&B €
(☑ 02 47 05 05 00; www.hoteldesartstours.com; 40 rue de la Préfecture; s/d €65/77; ☎) A delightful place with charming management, this B&B has four rooms, all of them spacious, bright and spotless; the colour scheme is tasteful and subdued. Excellent value in a great location. No lift.

Hôtel Val de Loire HOTEL €
(☑ 02 47 05 37 86; www.hotelvaldeloire.fr; 33 bd Heurteloup; d €68-88, q €108-128; ✳ ☎) Bright-red banisters, friendly staff and upbeat rooms welcome you to this very central hotel. The 14 well-kept rooms, four with (non-working)

Le Timbre Poste
CRÊPES €

(📋02 47 64 84 14; www.letimbreposte.fr; 10 rue du Châteauneuf; lunch menu €11.90, crêpes €3-11; ⊙noon-1.45pm & 7-9.30pm Tue-Sat, closed holidays) Acclaimed by locals as one of Tours' best purveyors of savoury buckwheat galettes, sweet crêpes, and *cidre* (apple cider; €3.50/8 per glass/pitcher) from Normandy and Brittany, this restaurant also serves creative salads, including one in which chèvre (goat cheese) meets honey. The intimate dining room is decorated with old French postage stamps and postcards.

⭐Le Zinc
FRENCH €€

(📋02 47 20 29 00; lezinc37@gmail.com; 27 place du Grand Marché; menus €20.90-25.90; ⊙7.30-10.30pm Mon, noon-2pm & 7.30-10.30pm or 11pm Tue-Sat; 🛜🍴) This intimate restaurant, with just a dozen tables, garners rave reviews for its outstanding traditional French cuisine, prepared *à l'ancienne* (old style, like your grandmother would have). Each dish – saltwater fish, duck breast, steak, rice pudding with caramel sauce – is prepared with exemplary finesse using market-fresh ingredients from the nearby Halles (p409). Excellent value.

L'Atelier Gourmand
FRENCH €€

(📋02 47 38 59 87; www.lateliergourmand.fr; 37 rue Étienne Marcel; lunch/dinner menus €20/27; ⊙noon-1.45pm & 7.30-10.30pm or 11pm Tue-Fri, 7.30-11pm Sat) Using Touraine-grown products and spices that chef David Bironneau brings back in his suitcase from faraway lands, this restaurant serves French cuisine that's as contemporary as its violet-and-aubergine colour scheme. Specialities include *côte de veau* (veal chops) and *escargots de la Touraine* (snails); some dishes feature intriguing blends of sweet and savoury.

Barju
FUSION €€€

(📋02 47 64 91 12; www.barju.fr; 15 rue du Change; lunch menu €21, dinner menus €25-80; ⊙noon-2pm & 7.30-10pm) The French cuisine here, served in bright, contemporary rooms, is infused with *inspiration asiatique* (inspiration from Asia). Chef Julien Perrodin's focus is on fish, and seafood brought in fresh from Cancale and St-Malo in Brittany, including blue lobster, *encornet* (squid), abalone, and *lisettes* (small mackerels) with rice vinegar.

🍷 Drinking & Nightlife

In Vieux Tours, place Plumereau and adjacent rue du Commerce and rue du Grande Marché are loaded with drinking dens that get stuffed to bursting on warm summer nights.

Pale
PUB

(opposite 81 rue Colbert & 18 place Foire-le-Roi; ⊙1pm-2am; 🛜) This genuinely Irish pub – the owner hails from the Emerald Isle – is hugely popular with both locals and students from English-speaking lands. Has 18 beers on tap, 40 whiskies, darts and, every Thursday or Friday at 9.30pm, live music (mostly jazz or rock); for details, see the Facebook page.

Les Trois Orfèvres
CLUB

(📋02 47 64 02 73; www.3orfevres.com; 6 rue des Orfèvres; Wed free, Thu-Sat after 1am €3; ⊙midnight-6am Wed-Sat) An underground (literally) nightspot where DJs (every night) and bands (about one Thursday or Friday a month, starting between 7.30pm and 8.30pm) quake the cellar walls with pop and rock, and students as well as older habitués hang out in force. Dress is very casual. Things really get going around 2am. For concert details, see the Facebook page.

ℹ️ Information

Tourist Office (📋02 47 70 37 37; www.tours-tourisme.fr; 78-82 rue Bernard Palissy; ⊙8.30am-7pm Mon-Sat, 10am-12.30pm & 2.30-5pm Sun Apr-Sep, 9am-12.30pm & 1.30-6pm Mon-Sat, 10am-1pm Sun Oct-Mar; 🛜)

ℹ️ Getting There & Away

AIR

Tours–Val de Loire Airport (TUF; 📋02 47 49 37 00; www.tours.aeroport.fr; 40 rue de l'Aéroport), 6km northeast of the centre, is linked to Dublin and London Stansted by Ryanair.

BUS

Rémi (📋02 47 31 14 00; www.remi-centre-valdeloire.fr; all destinations €2.40) operates buses to destinations around the Indre-et-Loire *département* from Tours' **intercity bus station** (Halte Routière; 📋02 47 05 30 49; 9 place du Général Leclerc; ⊙ticket counter 7am-7pm Mon-Fri, to 6.30pm Sat). Destinations include Amboise (one hour, seven daily Monday to Saturday), served by line C.

TRAIN

Tours is the Loire Valley's main rail hub. Regular trains and a few TGVs use the city-centre train station, **Tours-Centre** (place du Général Leclerc; 🛜); other TGV trains stop only at **St-Pierre-des-Corps**, 3km east and linked to Tours-Centre by frequent shuttle and TER trains. Some destinations, including Paris, Angers and Orléans, are served by trains from both stations.

Bicycles can be taken aboard almost all trains, so you can train it out and pedal back or vice versa.

Direct services from Tours-Centre include the following:

Amboise €5.70, 13 to 23 minutes, 13 to 22 daily.

Angers €19, one hour, four to nine daily.

Azay-le-Rideau €5.90, 26/41 minutes by train/bus, six to eight daily.

Blois €11.20, 30 to 46 minutes, 16 to 22 daily.

Chenonceaux €7, 25 minutes, nine to 11 daily.

Chinon €9.90, 45 minutes by train, 1¼ hours by SNCF bus, six to eight daily.

Langeais €5.70, 17 minutes, six to 10 daily.

Loches €9.60, one hour, one or two trains plus five to 13 SNCF buses daily.

Orléans €20.70, 1¼ hours, every two hours.

Paris Gare d'Austerlitz €25.50, 2¼ hours, four Intercités trains daily.

Paris Gare Montparnasse €52.50, 1¼ hours, four to seven TGVs daily.

Saumur €12.30, 45 minutes, eight to 13 daily.

ⓘ Getting Around

Options for bicycle hire include **Détours de Loire** (☏ 02 47 61 22 23; www.detoursdeloire.com; 35 rue Charles Gille; per half-day/day/week from €10/16/60; ⊙ 9am-1pm & 2-7pm Mon-Sat Apr-Oct, plus 9.30am-12.30pm & 6-7pm Sun May-Sep, 9.30am-1pm & 2-6.30pm Tue-Sat Nov-Mar) and **Roue Lib'** (☏ 07 70 64 23 84; http://rouelib.eu; 55 rue Bernard Palissy; per day bicycle/tandem/electric €15/30/35; ⊙ 8am-6pm Apr-Sep, 10am-1pm & 2-6.30pm Oct-Mar).

At **Accueil Vélo et Rando** (☏ 02 47 64 66 38; www.mobilite.tours-metropole.fr; 31 bd Heurteloup; ⊙ 9am-7pm daily May-Sep, to 5pm Tue-Sat Oct-Apr), an innovative, government-financed resource centre for cyclists and hikers, you can repair or tune up your bike (free), shower (€2), leave your stuff in a locker (€3 per day), and pick up free/for-sale cycling and walking brochures/guides, some of them in English.

Chenonceaux

Spanning the languid Cher River atop a graceful arched bridge, **Château de Chenonceau** (☏ 02 47 23 90 07; www.chenonceau.com; adult/child €14/11, with audioguide €18/14.50; ⊙ 9am-6.30pm or later Apr-Oct, to 5pm or 6pm Nov-Mar) is one of France's most elegant châteaux. It's hard not to be moved and exhilarated by the glorious setting, the formal gardens, the magic of the architecture and the château's fascinating history, shaped by a series of powerful women. The interior is decorated with rare furnishings and an **art collection** that includes works by Tintoretto, Correggio, Rubens, Murillo, Van Dyck and Ribera (look for an extraordinary portrait of Louis XIV).

WORTH A TRIP

VOUVRAY

Renowned chenin-blanc (aka pineau de la Loire) vineyards carpet the area above the cliffs behind **Vouvray**, a small town 11km east of – and across the river from – Tours.

Wine cellars sprinkle the region and Vouvray's **tourist office** (☏ 02 47 52 68 73; www.tourismevouvray-valdeloire.com; 12 rue Rabelais, Vouvray; ⊙ 9.30am-1pm & 2-5.30pm or 6.30pm Mon-Sat, 9.30am-12.30pm Sun mid-Apr–mid-Sep, 9.30am-1pm & 2-5.30pm Tue-Sat mid-Sep–mid-Apr; ☎), in the nondescript town centre, has a list of cellars that welcome visitors to taste and buy the Vouvray AOC's dry, semi-dry, sweet and sparkling white wines. To admire the vineyards afloat, hop aboard a **NaviLoire** (☏ 06 37 49 92 61, 02 47 52 68 88; www.naviloire.com; 56 quai de la Loire, Rochecorbon; adult/child €10.50/7; ⊙ mid-Mar–Oct) cruise along the Loire. Cruises last 50 minutes and depart from opposite the tourist office in **Rochecorbon**, 4km west of Vouvray, on the D952.

This spectacular complex is largely the work of several remarkable women (hence its nickname, Le Château des Dames). The initial phase of construction started in 1515 for Thomas Bohier, a court minister of Charles VIII's, although much of the work and design was actually overseen by his wife, Katherine Briçonnet.

The distinctive arches and the eastern **formal garden** were added by Diane de Poitiers, mistress of Henri II. Following Henri's death Catherine de Médicis, the king's scheming widow, forced Diane (her second cousin) to exchange Chenonceau for the rather less grand Château de Chaumont. Catherine completed the château's construction and added the yew-tree maze and the western **rose garden**. Louise of Lorraine's most singular contribution was her black-walled **mourning room** (restored in 2018) on the top floor, to which she retreated when her husband, Henri III, was assassinated in 1589.

Chenonceau had an 18th-century heyday under the aristocratic Madame Dupin, who made the château a centre of fashionable society; guests included Voltaire and Rousseau. During the Revolution, at the age of 83, she was able to save the château from destruction at the hands of angry mobs thanks to quick thinking and some strategic concessions.

The château's pièce de résistance is the 60m-long, chequerboard-floored **Grande Galerie** over the Cher, scene of many an elegant party hosted by Catherine de Médicis and Madame Dupin. Used as a military hospital during WWI, it served from 1940 to 1942 as an escape route for *résistants,* Jews and other refugees fleeing from the German-occupied zone (north of the Cher) to the Vichy-controlled zone (south of the river). The upper level of the gallery, the Galerie Médicis, has a well-presented exhibition (in French and English) on the château's colourful history and the women who moulded it.

The excellent 45-minute audioguide (not available on some holiday weekends), available in 11 languages, has a nicely done version for kids aged seven to 12 (in French and English). There's a great deal to see, so plan on spending at least half a day here. From mid-March to mid-November, dining choices include a gastronomic French restaurant called L'Orangerie (menus €32 and €39.50, mains €20 to €26) and a salon de thé (tearoom) serving breakfast until 11.30am and afternoon tea from 3pm to 5pm. There's wine tasting in an outbuilding, in the Cave des Dômes.

The château is 33km east of Tours, 13km southeast of Amboise and 40km southwest of Blois. From the town of Chenonceaux (spelt with an x), just outside the château grounds, trains go to Tours (€7, 25 minutes, nine to 11 daily).

POST-CHATEAU DRINK

Perched quietly beneath an imposing 12th-century *donjon* (keep), the town of Montrichard, 9km east of Chenonceau, is a perfect spot for a fizzy break. Just outside town, **Caves Monmousseau** (🖰02 54 32 35 15; www.monmousseau.com; 71 rue de Vierzon, Montrichard; ⊙10am-noon & 2-5.30pm Mon-Sat Nov-Mar, 10am-12.30pm & 1.30-6pm Apr-Oct, no midday closure Jul & Aug) has extensive wine cellars, carved into the tufa stone, creating the perfect 12°C environment for ageing *crémant* (sparkling wine). One-hour tours (adult/child €4.50/free), starting at 10am and 2pm from April to October, explain the *méthode traditionelle* (the traditional way to make bubbly, adopted from Champagne) and end with a tasting.

Amboise

POP 13.370

Elegant Amboise, childhood home of Charles VIII and final resting place of the incomparable Leonardo da Vinci, is gorgeously situated on the southern bank of the Loire, guarded by a soaring château. With some seriously posh hotels, outstanding dining and one of France's most vivacious weekly markets (on Sunday morning), Amboise is a convivial base for exploring the Loire countryside and nearby châteaux by car or bicycle.

◎ Sights

As you walk up to Le Clos Lucé, keep an eye out for the **habitats troglodytiques** (cave houses) carved into the rock face overlooking rue Victor Hugo. Pedestrian-only **rue Nationale** is packed with attractive boutiques.

★**Château Royal d'Amboise**   CHATEAU
(🖰02 47 57 00 98; www.chateau-amboise.com; place Michel Debré; adult/child €11.70/7.80, incl audioguide €15.70/10.80; ⊙9am-5.45pm Dec-Feb, to btwn 6.30pm & 8pm Mar-Nov, last entry 1hr before closing) Perched atop a rocky escarpment above town, Amboise's castle was a favoured retreat for all of France's Valois and Bourbon kings. Only a few of the château's original structures survive, but you can still visit the furnished Logis (Lodge) – Gothic except for the top half of one wing, which is Renaissance – and the Flamboyant Gothic Chapelle St-Hubert (1493), where Leonardo da Vinci's presumed remains have been buried since 1863. The ramparts afford thrilling views of the town and river.

★**Le Clos Lucé**   HISTORIC BUILDING
(🖰02 47 57 00 73; www.vinci-closluce.com; 2 rue du Clos Lucé; adult/child €15.50/11, mid-Nov–Feb €13.50/10.50; ⊙9am-7pm or 8pm Feb-Oct, 9am or 10am-6pm Nov-Jan, last entry 1hr before closing; 🖰) It was at the invitation of François I that Leonardo da Vinci (1452–1519), aged 64, took up residence in this grand manor house, built in 1471. An admirer of the Italian Renaissance, the French monarch named Da Vinci 'first painter, engineer and king's architect', and the Italian spent his time here sketching, tinkering and dreaming up ingenious contraptions.

★**Château Gaillard**   CHATEAU
(🖰02 47 30 33 29; www.chateau-gaillard-amboise.fr; 95-97 av Léonard de Vinci & 29 allée du Pont Moulin; adult/child €12/8; ⊙1-7pm Apr-early Nov) The

most exciting Loire château to open to visitors in years, Gaillard is the earliest expression of the Italian Renaissance in France. Begun in 1496, the château was inspired by the refined living that Charles VIII fell in love with during his Italian campaign. The harmonious, Renaissance-style **gardens** were laid out by master gardener Dom Pacello (1453–1534), an Italian Benedictine monk who brought the first orange trees to France.

Pagode de Chanteloup
HISTORIC SITE

(www.pagode-chanteloup.com; adult/child €9.90/7.90; ⊙10am-6pm late Mar-Sep, to 7pm Jun-Aug, 2-5pm Oct–mid-Nov; ⊞) Three kilometres south of Amboise, this seven-storey, vaguely Asian 'pagoda' (44m) was built between 1775 and 1778, when blending classical French architecture and Chinese motifs was all the rage. Clamber to the top for glorious views. From May to September, picnic baskets (adult/child €12.50/7) are available, and you can rent rowboats (€5 per hour) and – great for kids – play 18th-century outdoor games.

🛏 Sleeping

Camping Municipal de l'Île d'Or
CAMPGROUND €

(☑02 47 57 23 37; www.camping-amboise.com; Île d'Or; sites per adult/child/tent €3.40/2.30/4.10; ⊙Apr-Sep; ▦) Lovely 291-site campground on the Île d'Or, the island opposite the château. Facilities include pool, tennis courts, ping-pong, canoe hire and kids' playground.

Éthic Étapes Île d'Or
HOSTEL €

(Centre Charles Péguy; ☑02 47 30 60 90; www.iledor-amboise.fr; 1 rue Commire, Île d'Or; s/d/f incl breakfast €30/50/76; ⊙reception 10am-noon & 3-8.30pm Mon-Fri, 5-8.30pm Sat; @🗢) Spartan but efficient, this 114 bed hostel – totally renovated in 2017 and 2018 – is 600m northwest of the entrance to the château, at the downriver tip of Île d'Or. The 30 rooms have space for one to six people, industrial-strength furnishings and attached bath; most beds are bunks. Amenities include free washers and dryers and locked bicycle parking.

★ Le Vieux Manoir
B&B €€

(☑02 47 30 41 27; www.le-vieux-manoir.com; 13 rue Rabelais; d €150-220, f €330, cottages €260-310; ⊙mid-Mar–Oct; ▣✳🗢) Set in a lovely walled garden, this restored mansion has oodles of old-time charm; the six rooms and two cottages, decorated with antiques, get lots of natural light. Expat American owners Gloria and Bob (he a Bechtel engineer, she

a spirited ex-'60s radical who once ran an award-winning Boston B&B) are generous with their knowledge of the area.

Le Clos d'Amboise
HISTORIC HOTEL €€€

(☑02 47 30 10 20; www.leclosamboise.com; 27 rue Rabelais; d €169-309, 6-person ste €249-369; ▣✳🗢⛱) Overlooking a lovely garden with a 200-year-old cedar and a heated pool, this posh pad – most of it built in the 17th century – offers country living in the heart of town. Stylish features abound, from luxurious fabrics to antique furnishings. Half of the 20 rooms still have their original, now non-functioning, marble fireplaces.

Château de Pray
HOTEL €€€

(☑02 47 57 23 67; www.chateaudepray.fr; rue du Cèdre, Chargé; d €159-270, q €230-285; ⊙restaurant 7-9pm Wed, noon-1.30pm & 7-9pm Thu-Sun, plus Tue & Wed evenings Jun-Sep; ▣🗢) What better way to experience the Loire vibe than to stay in a 16th-century château? The 19 rooms here, each named after a famous visitor, are brimming with antique furnishings and old-fashioned charm. Has a Michelin-starred French *gastronomique* restaurant (four/five-course *menus* €59/72). Situated 3.5km northeast of Amboise's town centre, 300m off the D751.

🍴 Eating

★ Sunday Food Market
MARKET €

(quai du Général de Gaulle; ⊙8am-1pm Sun, small market 8am-1pm Fri) Voted France's *marché préféré* (favourite market) a few years back, this riverfront extravaganza, 400m southwest of the château, hosts 200 to 300 stalls selling both edibles and durables. Worth timing your visit around.

Bigot
PASTRIES €

(☑02 47 57 04 46; www.maisonbigot-amboise.com; cnr rue Nationale & place du Château; breakfast €12-18, lunch menu €15.50; ⊙8.30am or 9am-7pm or 7.30pm Tue-Sun, to 8pm & open Mon Easter-Oct; 🗢🍴) Founded by Madame Bigot's grandfather in 1913, this *salon de thé*, *pâtisserie* and *chocolaterie* is known for its *puits d'amour* (puff pastry filled with custard cream and rum), tarte tatin, chocolates, homemade ice cream and light meals (omelettes, quiches, meal-size salads). Perfect for a sweet or savoury break.

Le Patio
MODERN FRENCH €€

(☑02 47 79 00 00; 14 rue Nationale; menus lunch €19, dinner €32; ⊙noon-2pm & 7-9pm Thu-Mon, daily Jul & Aug; 🗢) The friendly staff here serve creative, beautifully presented French cuisine that garners rave reviews. Specialities include *cromesquis d'escargots* (crunchy fried balls of Burgundy snails) and slow-cooked lamb shank. Has a superb wine list, a glass-roofed courtyard and a Facebook page.

L'Écluse
FRENCH €€

(☑ 02 47 79 94 91; www.ecluse-amboise.fr; rue Racine; lunch menu €19, other menus €25-39; ☺ noon-1.30pm & 7-9pm Tue-Sat) On the banks of the bubbling L'Amasse (or La Masse) River next to an *écluse* (river lock), L'Écluse has been generating enthusiasm and glowing reviews since the moment it opened in 2017. The sharply focused menu is made up of just three entrées, three mains and three desserts, expertly prepared with fresh seasonal products from a dozen Loire-area producers.

Auberge de Launay
FRENCH €€

(☑ 02 47 30 16 82; www.aubergedelaunay.com; 9 rue de la Rivière, Limeray; lunch/dinner menus €19.50/36; ☺ 12.15-1.30pm & 7-9pm Tue-Fri, 7-9pm Sat, 12.15-1.30pm Sun, closed 20 Dec–Jan; ☜) Renowned for its traditional *gourmande* cuisine and cosy atmosphere, this country inn is 7.5km northeast of Amboise (just off the D952). Herbs from the garden are used in classic French dishes, accompanied by libations from a superb wine list, local cheeses and scrumptious desserts. Local specialities include *beuchelle à la tourangelle* (an old-world dish combining calf sweetbreads and kidneys, cream and mushrooms).

Also has 15 decent guest rooms (doubles €55 to €98).

ⓘ Information

Tourist Office (☑ 02 47 57 09 28; www.amboise-valdeloire.co.uk; quai du Général de Gaulle; ☺ 9am or 10am-6pm or 7pm Mon-Sat, 10am-1pm & 2-5pm Sun Apr-Oct, 10am-12.30pm & 2-5pm Mon-Sat Nov-Mar; ☜) Sells cycling maps and discount combo tickets for area châteaux (also available online). You can leave your bag(s) for €2.

ⓘ Getting There & Around

BICYCLE

Amboise is a great base for cycling along the Loire. To rent a bike, try **Détours de Loire** (☑ 02 47 30 00 55; www.detoursdeloire.com; quai du Général de Gaulle; half-day/day/week €10/16/60; ☺ Apr-Sep), in an oval pavilion by the river, or **Cycles Richard** (☑ 02 47 57 01 79; 2 rue de Nazelles; day/week €14/60, electric bike per day €38; ☺ 9am-noon & 2.30-6.30pm Tue-Sat year-round), directly across the river from the town centre.

BUS

Run by **Rémi** (p410), bus line C links Amboise's Théâtre with Tours' Halte Routière (bus station; one hour, eight daily Monday to Saturday) and Chenonceau (22 minutes, one or two daily Monday to Saturday), from where trains go to Tours.

TRAIN

Amboise's **train station** (bd Gambetta) is 1.5km north of the château, on the opposite side of the Loire.

Blois €7.20, 20 minutes, 15 to 20 daily.

Paris €18.50 to €60.50, two hours; a handful of direct trains go to Gare d'Austerlitz, other trains serve Gare Montparnasse.

Tours €5.70, 13 to 23 minutes, 13 to 22 daily.

Villandry

The six glorious landscaped gardens *à la française* of **Château de Villandry** (☑ 02 47 50 02 09; www.chateauvillandry.com; 3 rue Principale; chateau & gardens adult/child €11/7, gardens only €7/5, cheaper Dec-Feb, audioguide €4; ☺ 9am-5pm or 6.30pm year-round, château interior closed mid-Nov–late Dec & early Jan-early Feb) are some of France's finest, with more than 6 hectares of cascading flowers, ornamental vines, manicured lime trees, razor-sharp box hedges and tinkling fountains. Try to visit when the gardens – all of them organic – are blooming, between April and October. Tickets are valid all day (get your hand stamped). The website has details on special events.

The original gardens and château were built by Jean Le Breton, who served François I as finance minister and ambassador to Italy (and supervised the construction of Chambord). During his ambassadorial service, Le Breton became enamoured with the art of Italian Renaissance gardening, later creating his own ornamental masterpiece at newly constructed Villandry. The current gardens, tended by 10 full-time expert gardeners, were recreated starting in 1908.

Wandering the pebbled walkways, you'll see the classical **Jardin d'Eau** (Water Garden), the hornbeam **Labyrinthe** (Maze) and the **Jardin d'Ornement** (Ornamental Garden), which depicts various aspects of love (fickle, passionate, tender and tragic) using geometrically pruned hedges and coloured flowerbeds. The **Jardin du Soleil** (Sun Garden) is a looser array of gorgeous multicoloured and multiscented perennials. But for many the highlight is the 16th-century-style **Jardin des Simples** (Kitchen Garden), where cabbages, leeks and carrots are laid out to create nine geometrical, colour-coordinated squares.

After the gardens, the Renaissance château (built in the 1530s), surrounded by a watery moat, is a bit of a let-down. Nevertheless, highlights include the Oriental drawing room, with a gilded Moorish ceiling taken from a 15th-century palace near Toledo, and a gallery of Spanish and Flemish art. Best of all are the bird's-eye views across the gardens and the nearby Loire and Cher Rivers from the top of the 12th-century *donjon* (the only remnant of the original medieval château) and three *belvédères* (hillside panoramic viewpoints).

Near Villandry's parking area you'll find a branch of Tours' **tourist office** (in an all-wood pavilion), several restaurants, a *boulangerie* and two places to stay.

The château is 16km southwest of Tours and 11km northeast of Azay-le-Rideau. Trains link Savonnières, 4km northeast of Villandry, with Tours (€3.50, 13 minutes, two or three daily).

Langeais

POP 4340

No castle in the Loire is more authentically medieval in architecture and furnishings than the Château de Langeais, the focal point of a peaceful village with lovely walking streets and a bustling Sunday-morning market.

The most medieval of the Loire châteaux, **Château de Langeais** (☑ 02 47 96 72 60; www.chateau-de-langeais.com; adult/child €9.80/5; ☉ 9.30am-6.30pm Apr–mid-Nov, 10am-5pm mid-Nov–Mar) – built in the 1460s – looks much as it did at the tail end of the Middle Ages, with crenellated ramparts and massive towers dominating the surrounding village; original 15th-century furniture fills its flag-stoned chambers. In one room, a life-size wax-figure tableau portrays the marriage of Charles VIII and Anne of Brittany, held here on 6 December 1491, which brought about the historic union of France and Brittany.

Langeais, superbly preserved inside and out, presents two faces to the world. From the town you see a fortified castle, nearly windowless, with machicolated walls rising forbiddingly from the **drawbridge**, opened and closed by hand at the start and end of each workday. But the sections facing the courtyard have large windows, ornate dormers

and decorative stonework designed for more refined living.

Among the château's many fine, if faded, Flemish and Aubusson **tapestries**, look out for one from 1530 depicting astrological signs; three intricate panels with mille-fleurs ('thousand flowers') motifs; and seven panels from the famous Les Neuf Preux series, whose nine 'worthy knights' represent the epitome of medieval courtly honour. In each room, plasticised sheets in eight languages provide information.

The **Chemin de Ronde** (Parapet Walk) gives you a knight's-eye view from the ramparts; gaps underfoot (machicolations) enabled boiling oil, rocks and ordure to be dumped on attackers. Across the château's courtyard, climb to the top of the ruined stone keep, constructed by great 10th-century builder Foulques Nerra (Fulk III), count of Anjou.

❶ Getting There & Away

Langeais is 31km southwest of Tours and 10km west of Villandry. Its train station, 400m from the château, is on the line linking Tours (€5.70, 17 minutes, six to 10 daily) with Saumur (€8.30, 25 minutes, six to 10 daily).

Azay-le-Rideau

Romantic, moat-ringed **Château d'Azay-le-Rideau** (☑ 02 47 45 42 04; www.azay-le-rideau.fr; adult/child €10.50/free, audioguide €3; ☉ 9.30am-11pm Jul & Aug, to 6pm Apr–Jun & Sep, 10am-5.15pm Oct–Mar) is celebrated for its elegant turrets, perfectly proportioned windows, delicate stonework and steep slate roofs. Built in the early 1500s on a natural island in the middle of the Indre River, it is one of the Loire's loveliest castles: Honoré de Balzac called it a 'multifaceted diamond set in the River Indre'. The famous, Italian-style loggia staircase overlooking the central courtyard is decorated with the salamanders and ermines of François I and Queen Claude.

The interior decor is mostly 19th century, created by the Marquis Charles de Biencourt (who bought the château after the Revolution) and his heirs. The **Salon de Biencourt** was given historically coherent furnishings – plucked from the extensive collection of the French government – and comprehensively restored to its 19th-century glory in 2016. The lovely English-style **gardens** were restored and partly replanted from 2015 to 2017; the Jardin des Secrets (April to September) features heritage vegetables and flowers.

Audioguides are available in five languages; one-hour guided tours in French are free. In the Pressoir (the outbuilding to the right as you exit the ticket-sales hall), there's a very worthwhile exposition on construction methods and materials, decorative motifs and the restoration of antique furnishings; the videos of experts at work are fascinating.

A number of places to eat are located within a few hundred metres of the château, in the attractive, stone-built village centre.

Azay-le-Rideau is 26km southwest of Tours. The D84 and D17, on either side of the Indre, are great for countryside cycling. The train station, 2.5km west of the château, is linked to Tours (€5.90, 26/41 minutes by train/bus, six to eight daily) and Chinon (€5.30, 20 minutes, six to 11 daily).

Loches

POP 6300

Loches, on the Indre River, spirals picturesquely up from the modern town – through ancient stone gates – to the citadel, a forbidding medieval stronghold established by Foulques Nerra in the 10th century and later updated by Charles VII. In 1429 Joan of Arc met with Charles VII here and persuaded him to march north to claim the French crown. These days Loches is a sleepy place, great for a day of mellow exploration. The town is known for its bustling open-air food market.

◉ Sights

To reach Loches' fortress from the modern town centre, walk through **Porte Picois** and you'll be inside the **Ville-Basse** (lower city). Continue up rue du Château and through **Porte Royale** and you'll enter the Cité Royale (royal city), also known as the **Citadelle** (citadel) and the **Ville-Haute** (upper city).

Across the Indre River, **Beaulieu-lès-Loches** is home to the 11th- and 12th-century abbey whose church (interior closed) is the final resting place of citadel-builder Foulques Nerra. It can be reached on foot via a marked 7.5km circuit (the tourist office has a map).

★ **Cité Royale de Loches** CITADEL
(📞 02 47 59 01 32; www.citeroyaleloches.fr; ⊙ 24hr) Loches' vast hilltop citadel is the size of a small town – a few lucky people even live here! Inside you can visit the **Logis Royal** (Royal Lodge; Cité Royale; incl Donjon adult/child €9/7; ⊙ 9am-7pm Apr-Sep, 9.30am-5pm Oct-Mar) and the **Donjon et Cachots** (Forteresse; Cité Royale; incl Logis Royal adult/child €9/7; ⊙ 9am-7pm Apr-Sep, 9.30am-5pm Oct-Mar) – the same ticket is good for both – and a Romanesque **church** (Cité Royale; ⊙ 9am-7pm Apr-Sep, 9.30am-5pm Oct-Mar) FREE. The ensemble is great for kids who are into knights, castles and dungeons.

🛏 Sleeping & Eating

Food Market MARKET €
(rue de la République; ⊙ 8am or 9am-12.30pm Wed & Sat) Fills rue de la République and surrounding streets.

La Demeure Saint-Ours B&B €
(📞 06 33 74 54 82; www.saintours.eu; 11 rue du Château, Ville Basse; d €65-75; 🛜) Ensconced in a 16th-century town house, this B&B has three attractive, quiet rooms – accessed via a creaky, 16th-century wooden staircase – with wood-beam ceilings, 200-year-old *tommettes* (red hexagonal floor tiles) and

---

BALZAC IN SACHÉ

Meander down the Indre Valley along the tiny D84, passing mansions, villages and troglodyte caves, and 7km east of Azay-le-Rideau you'll come to sweet Saché. Once home to American sculptor Alexander Calder (one of his red-and-blue mobiles sits in the town square), it still celebrates the life of long-time resident Honoré de Balzac (1799–1850), author of *La Comédie Humaine*. The Renaissance manor house where he frequent stayed is now the **Musée Balzac** (📞 02 47 26 86 50; www.musee-balzac.fr; rue du Château; adult/child €6/5; ⊙ 10am-6pm or 7pm daily Apr-Sep, 10am-12.30pm & 2-5pm Wed-Mon Oct-Mar), a museum with rooms furnished in the style of Balzac's time, manuscripts, letters, 1st editions and lithographs.

Lunch afterwards on fish, hare, quail, veal sweetbreads, lobster and other timeless, Balzac-era dishes at the aptly named **Auberge du XII Siècle** (📞 02 47 26 88 77; auberge12emesiecle@orange.fr; 1 rue du Château; menus €28-95; ⊙ 7.30-9pm Tue, noon-1.30pm & 7.30-9pm Wed-Sat, noon-1.30pm Sun), in an ancient half-timbered homestead in Saché. Saché is 25km southwest of Tours and 18km southeast of Langeais.

DON'T MISS

SLEEPING BEAUTY

The creamy white towers and slate roofs of the **Château d'Ussé** (☑ 02 47 95 54 05; www.chateaudusse.fr; Rigny-Ussé; adult/child €14/4, audioguide €3; ☺10am-6pm or 7pm, closed mid-Nov–mid-Feb) offer sweeping views across the flat Loire countryside, the flood-prone Indre River and French-style formal gardens designed by André Le Nôtre, landscape architect of Versailles. The château's main claim to literary fame is that it served as the inspiration for Charles Perrault's classic fairy tale, *La Belle au Bois Dormant* (Sleeping Beauty).

Built on top of an 11th-century fortress (part of whose cellar you can visit), the modern-day château – a mix of medieval and Renaissance styles – dates mainly from the 15th to 17th centuries. In the gardens, the mostly Gothic chapel (1528) has a Renaissance-style doorway; inside, signs tell the story of the depredations visited upon Ussé during the French Revolution. Nearby, films on the château's upkeep and gardens can be seen inside three caves, while the stables display horse-drawn carriages and a tiny cart, designed to be pulled by a dog, that once amused privileged children.

The town of Rigny-Ussé is 12km northeast of Chinon.

an old-time vibe. Situated midway between Porte Picois and Porte Royale. Great value.

La Gerbe d'Or   FRENCH €
(☑ 02 47 91 67 63; www.restaurantlagerbedor.fr; 22 rue Balzac; lunch menu €13.90, dinner menus €23.50-37.50, child's menu €9.50; ☺noon-2pm Tue & Sun, noon-2pm & 7.30-9.30pm Wed-Sat; ☑) Serves delicious dishes that bring together traditional French savoir faire, fresh local ingredients and flavours from Italy and East Asia. The braised beef and the roasted duck breast are standouts. For dessert, try the roasted apple with dried fruit and almond panna cotta.

ℹ️ Information

Tourist Office (☑ 02 47 91 82 82; www.loches-valdeloire.com; place de la Marne; ☺9am or 10am-12.30pm & 2pm to btwn 5pm & 7pm Mon-Sat year-round, plus 10am-12.30pm & 2.30-5pm Sun Apr-Sep) Has information on Loches and southern Touraine, including charming villages such as Chédigny, famed for its roses. Situated a block from the train station, next to the river.

ℹ️ Getting There & Away

Loches is 68km southwest of Blois and 42km southeast of Tours. Trains and SNCF buses link the train station, across the Indre River from the tourist office, with Tours (€9.60, one hour, one or two trains plus five to 13 SNCF buses daily).

Chinon

POP 8070

Dominated by its towering medieval castle, Chinon is etched into France's collective memory both as the favourite fortress of

Henry II (1133–89), king of England, and as the venue for Joan of Arc's first meeting with Charles VII, in 1429. Below the château is an appealing medieval quarter, a warren of narrow lanes whose white tufa houses are topped with black slate roofs, giving the town its characteristic high-contrast aspect.

Surrounding the town is one of the Loire's main wine-producing areas, and Chinon AOC (www.chinon.com) cabernet-franc vineyards stretch along both banks of the Vienne River. Chinon makes a good base for wine-cellar visits.

◉ Sights

★**Forteresse Royale de Chinon**   FORTRESS
(☑ 02 47 93 13 45; www.forteressechinon.fr; adult/child €9/7; ☺9.30am-7pm May-Aug, to 5pm or 6pm Sep-Apr) Surrounded by massive walls, this hilltop castle – offering fabulous views across town, river and countryside – is split into three sections separated by dry moats. The ticket counter and shop are inside the 12th-century **Fort St-Georges**. Pass under the 14th-century **Tour de l'Horloge** (Clock Tower) and you'll come to the **Château du Milieu** (Middle Castle), vestige of a time when the Plantagenet court of Henry II and Eleanor of Aquitaine assembled here. Finally, **Fort du Coudray** sits on the tip of the promontory.

In the Château du Milieu, the restored south wing of the **Logis Royaux** (Royal Lodgings) has a multimedia exhibit, scale models of the castle, Joan of Arc memorabilia and archaeological finds; it's scheduled to be upgraded in 2019. In the garden you can see scale models of a *trébuchet* and a *bricole*, used in the Middle Ages to catapult projectiles at the enemy. At the far end, the

---

ⓘ CENT SAVER

Save your ticket stub! Buying a full-priced ticket at Azay-le-Rideau, Brézé, Chinon, Fontevraud, Langeais, Montsoreau or Villandry will get you reduced-price admission at the others.

---

round, 13th-century **Tour du Coudray** was used to imprison Knights Templar in the early 1300s (find their graffiti inside) and hosted Joan of Arc in 1429.

The castle gives visitors neat booklets whose embedded chips activate about two dozen audio and video commentaries (in four languages) around the site; out-of-doors, look for wooden benches. Also has iPad Mini audiovisual guides (€3), with versions in French and English for adults, kids and people with limited mobility. The ticket counter can supply you with a map of town.

Cité Médiévale   HISTORIC SITE

(Medieval Town) François Rabelais (c 1494–1553), whose works include the Gargantua and Pantagruel series, spent part of his childhood in Chinon; you'll see Rabelais-related names dotted all around the old town, whose narrow cobblestone streets and alleys present a fine cross-section of medieval architecture, best seen along rue Voltaire and its western continuation, rue Haute St-Maurice.

Musée Le Carroi   MUSEUM

(🖉 02 47 93 18 12; www.chinon-vienne-loire.fr; 44 rue Haute St-Maurice; adult/child €2/free; ⏰ 2pm or 2.30-6pm or 6.30pm Fri-Sun late Feb–mid-Nov, plus Wed, Thu & Mon May–mid-Sep) Refurbished in 2018, this museum features exhibits on the art and archaeology of Chinon and its environs as well as contemporary art, displayed in the turreted, 14th- to 16th-century États-Généraux (States-General) building.

Musée Rabelais   MUSEUM

(La Devinière; 🖉 02 47 95 91 18; www.musee-rabelais.fr; 4 rue de la Devinière, Seuilly; adult/child €6/5; ⏰ 10am-7pm Jul & Aug, 10am-12.30pm & 2-6pm Apr-Jun & Sep, to 5pm Wed-Mon Oct-Mar) La Devinière, the prosperous farm where François Rabelais (1483 or 1494–1553) – doctor, Franciscan friar, theoretician, author and all-around Renaissance man – lived for part of his childhood, inspired settings for some of his five satirical, erudite Gargantua and Pantagruel novels. Surrounded by vineyards and open farmland, the farmstead has a few exhibits on Rabelais' life and genius,

including early editions of his works and an original 1951 Matisse charcoal portrait (the other four portraits are facsimiles). The English brochure is excellent.

Situated 8.5km southwest of Chinon and 1.4km northeast of the centre of Seuilly.

🛏 Sleeping

Hôtel Diderot   HISTORIC HOTEL €

(🖉 02 47 93 18 87; www.hoteldiderot.com; 4 rue de Buffon; d €70-103, q €169; 🅿 🛜) This gorgeous town house is tucked amid luscious rose-filled gardens and crammed with polished antiques. The owners – Jean-Pierre, who's French, and Jamie, who hails from Florida – impart the sort of charm you'd expect for twice the price. The 26 cheerful rooms are all individually styled, some with flowery wallpaper. No lift. Situated 250m north of place Jeanne d'Arc.

Hôtel de France   HOTEL €€

(🖉 02 47 93 33 91; www.bestwestern.com; 47 place du Général de Gaulle; d €99-139, apt €175; ❄ 🛜) Impeccably run by the same couple since 1979, this Best Western–affiliated hotel, right in the centre of town, has 30 rooms, most arrayed around an inner courtyard. Tastefully decorated in a contemporary style, many have views of the château. Offers enclosed bicycle parking. No lift.

🍴 Eating

Food Market   MARKET €

(place Jeanne d'Arc; ⏰ 7am-1.30pm Thu) Fruit, vegetables, cheeses and other picnic supplies.

★ Les Années 30   FRENCH €€

(🖉 02 47 93 37 18; www.lesannees30.com; 78 rue Haute St-Maurice; lunch menu €19.50, dinner menus €27-47, veg menu €23; ⏰ 12.15-1.30pm & 7.30-9.30pm Thu-Mon; 🖉) Expect the kind of meal you came to France for, with exquisite attention to flavours and detail, served in relaxed intimacy. The offerings range from *ris de veau* (veal sweetbreads) to venison (during the winter hunting season) to Guayaquil chocolate mousse. There's a golden-lit downstairs dining room, with an elegantly grey-and-white counterpart upstairs; in summer you can dine outside.

La Part des Anges   FRENCH €€

(🖉 02 47 93 99 93; www.lapartdesanges-chinon.com; 5 rue Rabelais; menus €18-29; ⏰ noon-1.30pm & 7.30-8.15pm Wed-Sat, noon-1.30pm Sun) 'Between traditional and creative' – that's how chef Virginie describes the delicious dishes she prepares using vegetables that are both local and organic. The wines are, too: almost all come from the Chinon AOC. Excellent value.

ℹ Information

Tourist Office (✉ 02 47 93 17 85; www.chinon-valdeloire.com; 1 rue Rabelais; ⊗ 9.30am-1pm & 2-6pm or 7pm daily May-Sep, 10am-12.30pm & 2-6pm Mon-Sat Oct-Apr) Has a free walking-tour brochure and details on bike rental, kayaking, boat trips and hot-air balloons. Sells slightly reduced-price château tickets. Has a **summer kiosk** (av François Mitterrand; ⊗ 10am-1pm & 2-5pm or 6pm Jun–mid-Sep) up near the château.

ℹ Getting There & Away

The train station, 1km southeast of place du Général de Gaulle and the tourist office, is linked with Tours (€9.90, 45 minutes by train, 1¼ hours by SNCF bus, six to eight daily) and Azay-le-Rideau (€5.30, 20 minutes, six to 11 daily). SNCF buses also stop in the centre of town.

ANJOU

As you float down the Loire and enter Anjou, fortified châteaux give way to chalky-white tufa cliffs concealing an astonishing subterranean world of wine cellars, mushroom farms and (literally) underground art. Up on the surface, black slate roofs pepper the vine-rich land, which produces some of the Loire's best wines.

Angers, the historic capital of Anjou, is famous for its powerful dukes, the fortified hilltop château they left behind, and the stunning medieval Apocalypse Tapestry. Other architectural gems in Anjou include the medieval Abbaye Royale de Fontevraud, delightful riverside villages such as Candes-St-Martin, and some lovely châteaux. Europe's highest concentration of troglodyte dwellings dots the banks of the Loire around cosmopolitan Saumur.

To take in the Anjou wine country by car, head northwest from Saumur along route D751 towards Gennes, or southeast on route D947 through Souzay-Champigny and Parnay. From Angers, cut southwest to Savennières.

Saumur

POP 27,300

There's an air of sparkly Parisian sophistication in Saumur but also a sense of relaxed contentment. The local wines are world famous, the restaurants may be the Loire Valley's best, the spot is gorgeous – and the Saumurois know it. The town is renowned for the École Nationale d'Équitation, a national riding school that's home to the crack Cadre Noir equestrian corps. Soft white tufa cliffs stretch along the riverbanks east and west of town, pierced by *habitations troglodytes* (cave dwellings).

◉ Sights & Activities

Six wineries based in and around Saumur offer tours, among them **Langlois-Chateau** (✉ 02 41 40 21 42; www.langlois-chateau.fr; 3 rue Léopold Palustre, St-Hilaire-St-Florent; tours adult/child €5/free; ⊗ shop 10am-12.30pm & 2-6.30pm daily Apr–mid-Oct).

★ **École Nationale d'Équitation**   FARM
(✉ 02 41 53 50 60; www.cadrenoir.fr; av de l'École Nationale d'Équitation, St-Hilaire-St-Florent; tours adult/child €8/6; ⊗ tours 2.30pm & 4pm Mon, 10am, 11am, 2.30pm & 4pm Tue-Fri, 10am & 11am Sat early Feb-early Nov, more frequently mid-Apr–mid-Sep; ⊕) One of the world's premier equestrian academies, the prestigious French National Riding School is home to the **Cadre Noir**, an elite group of riding instructors that's also an equestrian display team. Superb tours take you behind the scenes; kids will love to pat the horses in their spacious stalls – several stomp their feet insistently if you don't caress them! Commentary is in French, but written information is available in eight languages; call ahead for details on tours in English.

Tours (one hour) take visitors around the spacious campus, built in 1980, and stop by the *manège* (riding arena), which has mirrors mounted on the walls, like a ballet studio. It's often possible to see horses and riders training (no photography); watch carefully and you'll get a sense of the incredibly intimate collaboration between horse and rider.

The riders and horses of the Cadre Noir, founded in 1825, are famous for their astonishing discipline and acrobatic prowess, all performed without stirrups. The school trains about 150 students – they're headed for careers as riding instructors – as well as their horses, 350 in number. France's Olympic eventing team trains here; the 2016 team, which won gold in Rio, included a member of the Cadre Noir.

You can recognise members of the Cadre Noir by their distinctive black *(noir)* jackets and hats (*képis* for men, *bicornes* for women), gold spurs and the three golden wings on their whips. Look closely at their collar insignia and at the gold buttons of their tunic: a flaming grenade means they're members of the French military, a sun that they are civilians. Saumur has been an equestrian centre since 1593.

The school is 4.5km due west of Saumur, just outside sleepy St-Hilaire-St-Florent. There is no public transport.

Château de Saumur   CHATEAU

(☑ 02 41 40 24 40; www.chateau-saumur.fr; adult/child €6/4, Jul & Aug €7/5; ⊙ 10am-1pm & 2-5.30pm Tue-Sun Apr–mid-Nov, to 6.30pm & no midday closure Jun–mid-Sep) Soaring above the town's rooftops, Saumur's fairy-tale castle was largely built in the 13th century by Louis XI, and has served variously as a fortress for protection from the Normans, a Renaissance palace, a Protestant stronghold and an army barracks. Today it houses Saumur's municipal museum, whose exhibits include outstanding collections of faience (earthenware) and equestrian gear, housed in the adjacent abbey church.

Musée des Blindés   MUSEUM

(☑ 02 41 83 69 95; www.museedesblindes.fr; 1043 rte de Fontevraud; adult/child €8.50/5.50; ⊙ 10am or 11am-5pm or 6pm year-round) Housed in a one-time cigarette factory, this non-profit museum displays more than 200 *blindés* (tanks) and other military vehicles – some in

working order – from 17 countries. For anyone interested in military history, the collection offers an exceptional opportunity to see tanks from all sides in WWI, WWII and the Cold War, including French models rarely seen overseas, the world's largest collection of WWII-era German vehicles and Soviet Bloc tanks. Near the exit, children can climb inside three troop-transport vehicles.

🛏 Sleeping

Camping l'Île d'Offard   CAMPGROUND €

(☑ 02 41 40 30 00; www.saumur-camping.com; rue de Verden; 2-person sites €19-43, 4-person cabins without bathroom €38-71; ⊙ mid-Mar–Oct; 🛜🐕🏊) Very pretty campground on an island opposite the château. Cyclists and hikers get discounts; riverside and castle-view sites cost extra. Amenities include spa, Jacuzzi, *hammam*, heated pool and activities for kids. Cabins have a seven-day minimum on some dates.

★ Hôtel de Londres   HOTEL €

(☑ 02 41 51 23 98; www.lelondres.com; 48 rue d'Orléans; d €79-109, q €99-115, apt €120; 🅿✳@🛜) Built as an *hôtel de grand standing* (luxury hotel) and named in honour of the British capital in 1837, this family-run hotel – entirely renovated in 2017 – has 29 spacious rooms decorated in jolly colours and

---

MUSHROOM MADNESS

Mushroom lovers – or those open to being seduced by the charms of *champignons* – can learn more about their favourite fungi, tour caves and taste samples in the Saumur area.

Musée du Champignon (☑ 02 41 50 31 55; www.musee-du-champignon.com; rte de Gennes, St-Hilaire-St-Florent; adult/child €9/7; ⊙ 10am-6pm or 7pm mid-Feb–mid-Nov) Get acquainted with some fabulous fungi at this mushroom museum, where you can see about a dozen varieties growing in glowing shades of orange, yellow, tan, brown and white. The shop sells shiitake-flavoured beer. Situated inside a cave at the western edge of St-Hilaire-St-Florent, 4.5km northwest of Saumur.

Le Saut aux Loups (☑ 02 41 51 70 30; www.troglo-sautauxloups.com; D947, Montsoreau; menus €21-23; ⊙ restaurant noon-2.30pm mid-Feb–mid-Nov, plus 7-9.30pm Jul & Aug, cave 10am-6pm mid-Feb–mid-Nov; 🌱) A great place to tour mushroom caves (adult/child €7/5.50), whose informative exhibits – a great intro to 'shroom farming – were redone in 2018, and tuck into fungi, including *galipettes* (stuffed extra-large button mushrooms; five for €14). Has plenty of veggie options. Situated 11km southeast of Saumur, at the western edge of Montsoreau.

La Cave aux Moines (☑ 02 41 67 95 64; www.cave-aux-moines.com; D751, Préban, Chêne-hutte-Trèves-Cunault; menus €21-26; ⊙ restaurant noon-1.30pm & 7-9pm daily mid-Jun–mid-Sep, 7-9pm Fri, noon-1.30pm & 7-9pm Sat & Sun rest of year, mushroom beds 10am-6pm mid-Jun–mid-Sep, noon-4pm Sat & Sun rest of year; 🛜🌱) Besides offering tours of their extensive, underground *champignonnière* (mushroom beds; adult/child €6/3), La Cave has a restaurant with all manner of *galipettes*, snails and *fouées* (local breads baked in a wood-fired oven). Situated 10km northwest of Saumur.

two family-friendly apartments, all with big windows and gleaming bathrooms. Sunday brunch is served from 11.30am to 3pm. Offers special massages for cyclists. Excellent value.

★ **Château de Beaulieu**   B&B €€
(📱 02 41 50 83 52; www.chateaudebeaulieu.fr; 98 rte de Montsoreau; d incl breakfast €120-160, q €190; ☺ mid-Mar–mid-Nov; 🅿 🤚 ☀) Gregarious Dublin natives Mary and Conor welcome you with Irish warmth to their 1727 château. The five rooms are comfortably done up (bathrooms were upgraded in 2018), and the mood among guests is one of extended family. Sun yourself by the pool (next to the little vineyard) or play three-ball billiards in the grand salon. Situated 2.5km southeast of Saumur.

★ **Château de Verrières**   HERITAGE HOTEL €€€
(📱 02 41 38 05 15; www.chateau-verrieres.com; 53 rue d'Alsace; d €169-335, ste €375; ☺ closed Dec & Jan; 🅿 @ 🤚 ☀) Built by the widow of one of Napoleon III's generals, this splendid belle époque mansion (1896) is surrounded by a 2-hectare English-style park. It's sumptuous throughout, with carved-wood balustrades, marble fireplaces and, in the 10 spacious rooms, antique writing desks and cast-iron bathtubs. The magnificent, wood-panelled Salle de Musique has a window directly over the fireplace.

✖ Eating

Le 30 Février   VEGETARIAN €
(📱 02 41 51 12 45; 9 place de la République; mains €7.60-13.80; ☺ noon-2pm & 7-10.30pm Tue-Sat, plus Sun evening & Mon Jun-Sep; 🤚 ✍) An utterly unpretentious vegan restaurant whose pizza, pasta and mains (€8) - a cooked cereal (quinoa, rice or buckwheat) accompanied by raw seasonal veggies (eg carrots, cabbage and beets) - get excellent reviews for taste, healthfulness and value. Gluten-free options are available.

★ **Le Boeuf Noisette**   FRENCH €€
(📱 09 81 73 73 10; 29 rue Molière; menus €23-28; ☺ noon-2.30pm & 7-10pm Tue & Thu-Sun, 7-10pm Wed; 🤚) Since opening in 2016, talented young chef Delphine Rémy has been earning enthusiastic reviews for cuisine she describes as *française, locale et fraîche* (French, local and fresh). Her flagship dish is tender Rouge des Prés *boeuf* (beef) served with *beurre noisette* (hazelnut-coloured butter sauce made with drippings and spices). For dessert, try the orange cake generously doused with triple sec.

L'Escargot   FRENCH €€
(📱 02 41 51 20 88; 30 rue du Maréchal Leclerc; lunch/dinner menus from €20/31; ☺ 12.30-1.30pm & 7.30-9.30pm Thu, Fri, Sun & Mon, 7.30-9.30pm Sat; 🤚) A Saumur fixture for more than half a century, this family-run place is all about traditional recipes done really well, such as escargots with 'three butters' (flavoured with herbs, walnuts and Roquefort) or *carré d'agneau rôti à l'ail et au thym* (loin of lamb roasted with garlic and thyme).

Le Pot de Lapin   MODERN FRENCH €€
(📱 02 41 67 12 86; 35 rue Rabelais; mains €14-25; ☺ noon-2pm & 7-9.30pm Tue-Sat; 🤚) Mellow music wafts from the cheery dining room, decorated with winemaking tools, through the wine bar and onto the street-side terrace as chef Olivier Thibault works the tables, proposing perfect wine pairings. Start with a local bubbly, then move on to foie gras with onion-and-fruit chutney, monkfish with cream or Rouge des Prés beef. Situated 1km southeast of the centre.

★ **Le Gambetta**   GASTRONOMY €€€
(📱 02 41 67 66 66; www.restaurantlegambetta.fr; 12 rue Gambetta; menus lunch €29, dinner €38-109; ☺ noon-1.30pm & 7.15-9pm Tue & Thu-Sat, noon-1.30pm Sun) This is one to write home about: a truly outstanding restaurant that combines refined elegance with knock-your-socks-off creative French cuisine. Some *menus* include wine pairings perfectly chosen to complement the parade of gorgeously presented *gastronomique* dishes, punctuated by surprise treats from the kitchen. Reserve ahead at weekends and in summer.

☆ Entertainment

★ **Cadre Noir**   EQUESTRIAN SHOW
(📱 02 41 53 50 80; www.cadrenoir.fr; l'École Nationale d'Équitation; Matinale adult/child €19/13, Gala €35/15; ☺ specific dates Mar-early Nov) The Cadre Noir equestrian display team puts on two types of astonishingly graceful show: **Matinales**, hour-long training demonstrations with commentary; and - this is what it's most famous for - ballet-like **Galas** that showcase horses' and riders' extraordinary skills. Headsets provide simultaneous translation into English. Reserve by phone or online, or via Saumur's tourist office.

ℹ Information

Tourist Office (📱 02 41 40 20 60; www.saumur-tourisme.com; 8bis quai Carnot; ☺ 9.15am-12.30pm & 2-6pm or 7pm Mon-Sat) year-round, 10.30am–noon or 12.30pm Sun early Feb–mid-Nov, plus Sun afternoon Easter-Sep; 🐎) Can supply you with a city map, information on horse-riding options, a list of sites open in winter and slightly reduced-price châteaux tickets. Has a free left-luggage service. Situated on the riverfront one block southwest of the bridge.

Maison des Vins (📞 02 41 38 45 83; 7 quai Carnot; ⏰10.30am-1pm & 2.30pm or 3-6.30pm or 7pm Tue-Sat, closed holidays) Run by a local winegrowers federation, this is an excellent place to sample and purchase Saumur-area wines and get details on vineyard visits. Situated next to the tourist office.

ⓘ Getting There & Around

BICYCLE

Détours de Loire (📞 02 41 53 01 01; www.detoursdeloire.com; 10 rue de Rouen; half-day/day/week €10/16/60; ⏰Apr-Sep) Bike-rental outfit with locations all along the Loire.

BUS

Agglobus (📞 02 41 51 11 87; www.agglobus.fr; single/day ticket €1.40/3.80) Saumur's local bus company runs *lignes estivales* (summer lines) that link the train station and the city centre (place Roosevelt) with Turquant and the Abbaye Royale de Fontevraud; line 1B operates two or three times a day on Saturday and Sunday from early June to mid-September, daily from 10 July to August. Also from 10 July to August, on-demand minibuses (reserve at least four hours ahead) go twice a day to the École Nationale d'Équitation and the Château de Brézé. The tourist office has details.

Anjou Bus (p428) Lines 4 and 17 serve Angers and intermediate points, including Chênehutte-Trèves-Cunault and Gennes. The tourist office has details.

TRAIN

Saumur's station is across the river from the town centre, 1.3km from the tourist office.

Angers €9.10, 21 to 36 minutes, nine to 19 daily.

Paris Gare Montparnasse €42.10 to €72.40, two to three hours, eight to 16 daily (requires one transfer).

Tours €12.30, 45 minutes, eight to 13 daily.

East of Saumur

Some of the Loire's most exquisite scenery, including riverside tufa bluffs punctuated by cave houses, stretches along the D947 southeast of Saumur. Many of the renowned wine producers here, both small and large, offer free tastings at their cellars from spring to early autumn; see www.saumur-champigny.com (click 'Winemakers & Estates') for details that include websites and whether you need to phone ahead. Note that winegrowers are especially busy during the *vendanges* (grape harvest) from late August to October.

TURQUANT
POP 580

Ten kilometres southeast of Saumur, the picturesque and easily strollable village of Turquant is one of the best places in the Loire Valley to see troglodyte dwellings. Many have now been spruced up and converted into shops, galleries or restaurants.

Les Pommes Tapées (📞 02 41 51 48 30; https://pommes-tapees.fr; 11 rue des Ducs d'Anjou; adult/child €6.50/4; ⏰10.30am-6.30pm late Feb-early Nov) is one of the last places in France producing traditionally made dried apples. See displays on how it's done, visit the tufa caves, sample the wares (€1) and buy some to take home. Tours begin between 10.30am and noon, and 2pm and 5.30pm.

🛏 Sleeping & Eating

⭐ **Demeure de la Vignole**   DESIGN HOTEL €€
(📞 02 41 53 67 00; www.demeure-vignole.com; 3 impasse Marguerite d'Anjou; d €120-165, 4-person ste €220; ⏰closed mid-Nov–mid-Feb; 🅿❄🏊) This swish hotel has 12 richly decorated rooms, five of them inside caves. The 15m heated swimming pool (open 24 hours) is carved into the rock face, too. Very homey, and a wonderful change from the ordinary.

Bistroglo   BISTRO €€
(📞 02 41 40 22 36; www.bistroglo.com; Atelier 3, rue du Château Gaillard; menus €19-25; ⏰10.30am-9pm Tue-Sat, to 6pm Sun Apr-Sep; 🐎) At this bistro-style restaurant, situated *en troglo* (troglodyte, ie built into the cliff face) – artisanal beers and local wines are an excellent prelude to traditional French cuisine, including Loire Valley favourites such as *galipettes* (stuffed extra-large button mushrooms).

L'Hélianthe   FRENCH €€
(📞 02 41 51 22 28; www.restaurant-helianthe.fr; ruelle Antoine Cristal; mains €16; ⏰noon-2pm & 7-9pm Thu-Tue mid-Mar–mid-Nov, 7-9pm Fri, noon-2pm & 7-9pm Sat & Sun mid-Nov–mid-Mar) Carved into a cliff behind Turquant's *mairie* (town hall), this atmospheric restaurant has a hearty menu firmly based on local products and classic French flavours. Specialities include Loire fish casserole and dishes made with heritage vegetables such as *panais* (parsnip), *topinambours* (Jerusalem artichoke) and *vitelottes* (purple potatoes).

THE GREEN FAIRY: ABSINTHE

Some of France's most distinctive liqueurs are distilled in the Loire Valley, including the aniseedy (and allegedly hallucinogenic) brew known as absinthe. Distilled using a heady concoction of natural herbs, true absinthe includes three crucial components: green anise, fennel and the foliage of *Artemisia absinthium* (wormwood, used as a remedy since the time of the ancient Egyptians). Legend has it that absinthe was created by a French doctor (the wonderfully named Dr Pierre Ordinaire) in the late 1790s, and the recipe was acquired by the father-and-son team who established the first major absinthe factory, Maison Pernod-Fils, in 1805.

The drink's popularity exploded in the 19th century, when it was discovered by bohemian poets and painters (as well as French troops, who were given it as an antimalarial drug). Seriously potent (it's 62% to 72% alcohol by volume), absinthe's traditional green colour and supposedly psychoactive effects led to its popular nickname, 'the green fairy'; everyone from Rimbaud to Vincent van Gogh sang its praises. Ernest Hemingway invented his own absinthe cocktail, ominously dubbed 'Death in the Afternoon'.

But the drink's reputation was ultimately its downfall: fearing widespread psychic degeneration, governments around the globe banned it in the early 20th century (France in 1915). In the 1990s a group of dedicated absintheurs reverse-engineered the liqueur, chemically analysing century-old bottles that had escaped the ban. In 2011 absinthe again became legal in France. It's traditionally mixed with cold water streamed through a sugar cube – you can try it at **Distillerie Combier** (☑02 41 40 23 02; www.combier.fr; 48 rue Beaurepaire; tours adult/child €5/free; ☉tours 10.30am, 2.30pm & 4pm or 4.30pm Tue-Sun Apr-Oct, plus Mon Jun-Sep, shop 10am-12.30pm & 2-7pm Tue-Sat, plus Sun Apr-Sep & Dec, plus Mon Jun-Sep & Dec) in Saumur.

ℹ Information

Regional Park Visitors Centre (☑02 41 38 38 88; www.parc-loire-anjou-touraine.fr; 15 av de la Loire, Montsoreau; ☉9.30am-1pm & 2-6pm or 7pm daily Apr-Oct, Sat & Sun Mar, no midday closure Jul & Aug) Provides maps and information on activities throughout the 2530-sq-km Parc Naturel Régional Loire-Anjou-Touraine, a regional park established to protect the landscape, extraordinary architectural patrimony and culture of this section of the Loire Valley. The same building houses the local tourist office. Situated 2.5km southeast of Turquant.

CANDES-ST-MARTIN
POP 227

The picturesque village of Candes-St-Martin, about 1.5km southeast of Montsoreau, occupies an idyllic spot at the confluence of the Vienne and Loire Rivers. St Martin died here in 397, turning little Candes into a major pilgrimage destination.

For great panoramas, climb the tiny streets above the church, past inhabited cave dwellings, or head down to the benches and path along the waterfront.

◉ Sights & Activities

Collégiale St-Martin   CHURCH
(place de l'Église; ☉8.45am-6pm, to 7pm summer) This soaring, crenellated village church, built in the Gothic style from 1175

to 1240, venerates the spot where St Martin died in 397 and was buried for a while (his body was later spirited off to Tours). Enter via the exceptional side porch, decorated with two rows of statues.

Château de Montsoreau-Musée d'Art Contemporain   CHATEAU
(☑02 41 67 12 60; www.chateau-montsoreau. com; passage du Marquis de Geoffre, Montsoreau; adult/child €9.50/5.50; ☉10am-7pm daily Jul-Sep, noon-6pm or 7pm Wed-Mon mid-Feb-Jun & Oct-early Nov, closed weekdays mid-Mar & early Oct) Converted into a museum of conceptual art in 2016 – the focus is on the Art & Language movement – the Renaissance-style Château de Montsoreau, beautifully situated overlooking the Loire, was built in 1455 by one of Charles VII's advisers; it later became famous thanks to an Alexandre Dumas novel, *La Dame de Montsoreau*. There are spectacular river views from the rooftop. Find it 2km northwest of Candes in Montsoreau.

ℹ Getting There & Away

Candes-St-Martin is midway between Saumur and Chinon (about 14km from each) and about 2km southeast of Montsoreau. From Saumur take the scenic D947, from Chinon the D751.

SAUMUR DAY TRIPPER

The gorgeous D751 from Saumur to **Gennes** (population 2300) follows the banks of the Loire, sweeping through glades and along 8km of tiny white-stone villages belonging to the commune of **Chênehutte-Trèves-Cunault** (population 1050).

From Gennes, take the tiny D132 to **Le Thoureil** (population 461), a picturesque riverside hamlet with a wonderful restaurant, **La Route du Sel** (🖉 02 41 45 75 31; www. authoureil.fr; 55 quai des Mariniers, Le Thoureil; lunch/dinner menus from €17.50/33.50; 🕑 noon-2.30pm Tue, Wed & Sun, noon-2.30pm & 7-9.30pm Thu-Sat Sep-Jun, daily except Mon evening Jul & Aug; 🛜). Chef Marie, from an old Saumur winegrowing family, and London-born Daniel (in the dining room) serve up traditional French home cooking made with fresh Anjou products (smoked Loire eel is a speciality), accompanied by Tina artisanal beer from Saumur and sparkling wine from the family vineyards. Save room for the transcendent *gâteau de Marie*, a sesame-encrusted chocolate extravaganza.

FONTEVRAUD-L'ABBAYE
POP 1570

The charming, stone-built village of Fontevraud-l'Abbaye has been known since the Middle Ages for its superb abbey.

👁 Sights

★ Abbaye Royale de Fontevraud
HISTORIC SITE

(🖉 02 41 51 45 11; www.fontevraud.fr; adult/child €11/7.50, audioguide €4.50; 🕑 9.30am-6.30pm Apr-Oct, to 5.30pm Nov, Dec, Feb & Mar) The highlight of this 12th-century abbey complex is the vast but movingly simple church, notable for its soaring pillars, Romanesque domes and polychrome *gisants* (funerary effigies) of four illustrious Plantagenets: Henry II, king of England (r 1154–89); his wife, Eleanor of Aquitaine (who retired to Fontevraud following Henry's death); their son Richard the Lionheart; and Richard's brother King John's wife Isabelle of Angoulême. Signs are in English.

In the church's crypt, opened in 2016, you can see the archaeological excavations of earlier churches; the entrance is in the left transept arm, behind the white cube.

The cloister is surrounded by one-time dormitories, workrooms and prayer halls; the Salle Capitulaire (chapter room), with murals of the Passion of Christ by Thomas Pot; and a wonderful Gothic-vaulted refectory, where the nuns would eat in silence while being read the Scriptures. Both the nuns and the monks of Fontevraud were, exceptionally, governed by an abbess, generally a lady of noble birth who had retired from public life. Outside, there are medieval-style gardens and a multi-chimneyed, missile-shaped kitchen (closed for restoration until 2020), built entirely from stone to make it fireproof.

In 1804, by Napoleonic decree, Fontevraud was turned into a notoriously harsh prison, a role it played until 1963. Author Jean Genet was imprisoned for stealing (but not here) and, based on that experience, wrote *Miracle de la Rose* (1946), which is set at Fontevraud.

An iPad 'game of discovery' (€4.50), for kids aged eight to 14, recreates a day in the life of a medieval nun or a Fontevraud prisoner.

A new modern-art museum, housing the superb collection of industrialist Léon Cligman and his wife, Martine Martine, is due to open in the abbey in 2019. Highlights will include works by Delacroix, Derain, Dufy, Corot, Degas, Toulouse-Lautrec and de Vlaminck.

🛏 Sleeping & Eating

Fontevraud l'Hôtel
DESIGN HOTEL €€

(🖉 02 46 46 10 10; www.hotel-fontevraud.com; d/q Fri & Sat €170/210, Sun-Thu €145/180; 🕑 restaurant 7.30-9.30pm Thu & Fri, noon-2pm & 7.30-9.30pm Sat, noon-2pm Sun, plus other days Apr-Oct; @🛜) Ultramodern meets medieval at this luxurious hotel, situated on the abbey (p424) grounds in a one-time priory (the vehicle entrance is around the side of the complex). The 54 sleek rooms are decorated in muted beiges and whites. The Michelin-starred gastronomic restaurant (menus €68 to €108, with wine €33 extra) serves seriously haute cuisine, conceived by award-winning chef Thibaut Ruggeri.

Guests enjoy exclusive access to the abbey grounds at night.

Chez Teresa
CAFE €

(🖉 02 41 51 21 24; www.lettersandlunches-fromtheloire.com; 6 av Rochechouart; lunch menus €12.50; 🕑 noon-8pm; 🛜) English expats Tere-

TROGLODYTES: C LIFE

For centuries the creamy-white tufa cliffs around Saumur have provided shelter and storage for local inhabitants, leading to the development of a unique *culture troglodyte* (cave-dwelling culture). The naturally cool caves were turned into houses (*habitations troglodytes*) and incorporated into castles: some are still used by vintners and mushroom farmers. Many of the Loire's grandest châteaux were built from white tufa, and the quarrying, naturally, created caves.

Lots of caves can be found along the Loire east and west of Saumur (eg around Turquant), in Amboise and around the town of Doué-la-Fontaine. Stop by the Saumur **tourist office** (p421) for a complete list. Bring something warm to wear, as caves remain cool (13°C) year-round.

Rochemenier (☑ 02 41 59 18 15; www.troglodyte.fr; 14 rue du Musée, Louresse-Rochemenier; adult/child €6.50/4; ⊙ 9.30am-7pm May-Sep, 10am-6pm Tue-Sun Oct-Nov & Feb-Apr, closed Dec & Jan)

Troglodytes et Sarcophages (☑ 06 77 77 06 94; www.troglo-sarcophages.fr; 1 rue de la Croix Mordret, Doué-la-Fontaine; adult/child €5.40/3.70; ⊙ 10am-12.30pm & 2.30-7pm early Jul-late Aug, tours 2.30pm, 3.30pm & 4.30pm Tue-Sun early Apr-early Jul & late Aug-Sep)

Le Mystère des Faluns (Les Perrières; ☑ 02 41 59 71 29; www.les-perrieres.com; 7 rue d'Anjou, Doué-la-Fontaine; adult/child €7/4.50; ⊙ 10am-12.30pm & 2-6pm Tue-Sun mid-Feb-early Nov, 10am-7pm daily mid-Jun–mid-Sep; 🎦)

Château de Brézé (☑ 02 41 51 60 15; www.chateaudebreze.com; rue de l'Amiral Maillé-Brézé, Brézé; adult/child €11.80/6.20, incl tour €17.90/10; ⊙ 10am-6pm or 7pm Feb-Dec)

sa and Tony offer a welcome as cosy-warm as tea at this frilly little tearoom, half a block from the abbey, which is stuffed with bric-a-brac from across the Channel. In the afternoon, pop by for a cuppa, little triangular sandwiches, scones with cream and jam, and cake, all for €9.80. The double room upstairs costs €65, breakfast included.

❶ Getting There & Away

Fontevraud-l'Abbaye is 16km southwest of Saumur along the D947, whose most attractive section runs along the south bank of the Loire between Saumur and Montsoreau.

Angers

POP 151,000

An intellectual centre in the 1400s and a lively university city today, Angers – the historical seat of the Plantagenet dynasty and the dukes of Anjou – makes an engaging western gateway to the Loire Valley. The mostly pedestrianised old town supports a thriving cafe culture, thanks in part to the dynamic presence of over 39,000 students, as well as some excellent places to eat. The city is famous for two sets of breathtaking tapestries, one from the 14th century, the other from the 20th.

◉ Sights

⭐**Château d'Angers** CHATEAU
(☑ 02 41 86 48 77; www.chateau-angers.fr; 2 promenade du Bout-du-Monde; adult/child €9/free, audioguide €3; ⊙ 9.30am-6.30pm May-Aug, 10am-5.30pm Sep-Apr) Looming above the river, this forbidding medieval castle – seat of power of the once-mighty counts of Anjou – is ringed by moats, 2.5m-thick walls and 17 scarily massive round towers. The centrepiece is the stunning **Tenture de l'Apocalypse** (Apocalypse Tapestry), a 104m-long series of tapestries commissioned in 1375 to illustrate the story of the final battle between good and evil, as prophesied in the Bible's Book of Revelation.

Quartier de la Cité HISTORIC SITE
One of the earliest examples of Angevin (Plantagenet) architecture in France, Gothic **Cathédrale St-Maurice** (place Monseigneur Chappoulie; ⊙ 8am-7pm) is distinguished by its striking Norman portal and nave (mid-1100s), 13th- to 15th-century stained glass, humongous organ and supremely baroque baldachin (1758) over the high altar. From the square in front, a monumental staircase, **Montée St-Maurice**, leads down to a new **riverside esplanade** (under construction at the time of research) and a **gourmet covered market** (set to open in 2020).

Angers

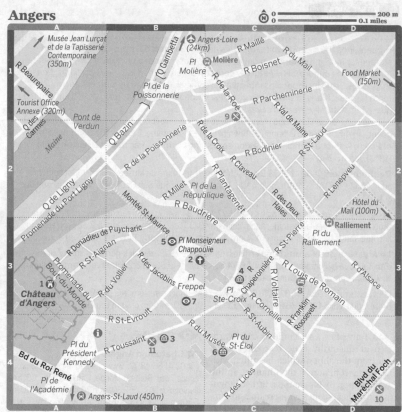

THE LOIRE VALLEY ANGERS

Angers

Right behind the cathedral stands the **Maison d'Adam** (place Ste-Croix), one of the city's best-preserved medieval houses (c 1500), which is decorated with a riot of carved, bawdy wooden sculptures.

Musée des Beaux-Arts GALLERY
(☑ 02 41 24 18 48; www.musees.angers.fr; 14 rue du Musée; adult/child €6/free; ☺10am-6pm Tue-Sun) Has a superior 14th- to 20th-century collection (mainly paintings) that ranges from French masters Ingres, Fragonard and Watteau to the Florentine Lorenzo Lippi to Flemish and Dutch Golden Age painters such as Jacob Jordaens. Also has a section on the history of Angers and hosts two special expositions a year. The exuberant sculpture in the courtyard, *L'Arbre aux Serpents* (Serpent Tree) by Niki de Saint Phalle, was restored in 2017.

Galerie David d'Angers MUSEUM
(☑ 02 41 05 38 90; www.musees.angers.fr; 33bis rue Toussaint; adult/child €4/free; ☺10am-6pm Tue-Sun) The Angers-born sculptor Pierre-Jean David (1788–1856), aka David d'Angers, is renowned for his lifelike sculptures, which

adorn public monuments such as the Panthéon in Paris and can be seen in the Louvre and Paris' Père Lachaise cemetery. Here in the 12th-century Toussaint Abbey, flooded with light thanks to a striking glass-and-girder ceiling, you can admire original plaster studio casts and drawings of most of his creations.

★ Musée Jean Lurçat et de la Tapisserie Contemporaine   MUSEUM

(✎ 02 41 24 18 45; www.musees.angers.fr; 4 bd Arago; adult/child €6/free; ⊙ 10am-6pm Tue-Sun) Inspired by the Apocalypse Tapestry in the château (p425), Jean Lurçat (1892–1966) began his epic tapestry masterpiece, *Le Chant du Monde* (Song of the World; 1957–61), just 12 years after the slaughter of WWII; scenes depict everything from the delights of Champagne to space exploration to nuclear holocaust. A quintessentially mid-20th-century meditation on the human condition, it is exuberant but contemplative, and only guardedly optimistic. The museum also exhibits a changing kaleidoscope of beautiful 20th-century and 21st-century tapestries.

☞ Tours

Cointreau Distillery   DISTILLERY

(✎ 02 41 31 50 50; www.cointreau.com; 2 bd des Bretonnières, St-Barthélemy-d'Anjou; 2hr tour adult/child €12/4.50; ⊙ boutique 11am-6pm Tue-Sat, tours Tue-Sat May-Oct, Sat Nov) To discover some (but not all) of the secret of how Cointreau is made, take a tour of the distillery, source of all 15 million bottles of the bitter-orange liqueur produced each year. Reserve ahead by phone. Situated in an industrial zone 3km east of Angers' city centre (served by Irigo bus 6).

⌷ Sleeping

★ Hôtel du Mail   HISTORIC HOTEL €

(✎ 02 41 25 05 25; www.hoteldumail.fr; 8 rue des Ursules; d €83-103, tr/q €113/123; ℗ ☎) Rose-adorned carpets and bright-red walls greet you at this attractive hotel, arrayed around a quiet courtyard in a converted 17th-century convent. The 25 rooms have antique-style furnishings, creative light fixtures and white-tile bathrooms; superior rooms are spacious, and most have large windows. No lift. Situated 250m east of place du Ralliement.

Hôtel Continental   HOTEL €

(✎ 02 41 86 94 94; www.hotellecontinental.com; 14 rue Louis de Romain; s €77, d €86-90; ✳ ☎) Wedged into a triangular corner building smack in the city centre, this ecologically certified, metro-style hotel has 25 rooms decked out with cosy pillows and sunny colours. Breakfast is organic and fair trade.

✗ Eating

Food Market   MARKET €

(place Mendès-France & place du Général Leclerc; ⊙ 8am-1.30pm Sat) This huge weekly market sells edibles and, at nearby place Louis Imbach, flea-market goods.

Au Goût du Jour   MODERN FRENCH €

(✎ 02 41 23 73 19; restaurant.augoutdujour@gmail.com; 14 rue de la Roë; 2-/3-course lunch menus €16/19, dinner €22/25; ⊙ noon-1pm & 7.30-9pm Tue-Fri, 7.30-9pm Sat) This intimate restaurant is notable for its red ceiling and old-time French cuisine, prepared with the freshest organic ingredients and served with organic wines. The good-value chalkboard *menu*, which changes every two weeks, consists of just three entrées, three main dishes and three desserts. It's a good idea to reserve.

Villa Toussaint   FUSION €€

(✎ 02 41 88 15 64; www.lavillatoussaint.fr; 43 rue Toussaint; lunch menu €16, mains €14.80-22.60; ⊙ noon-2pm & 7.15-10pm Tue-Sat; ☎ ✎) Combining pan-Asian flavours with classic French ingredients, this highly regarded restaurant serves fusion food in a chic, glass-roofed dining room and on a tree-shaded deck. Reserve unless you'll be arriving right when it opens. There's a Facebook page.

Le Favre d'Anne   GASTRONOMY €€€

(✎ 02 41 36 12 12; www.lefavredanne.fr; 21 bd du Maréchal Foch; lunch menus €49, dinner menus €70-105; ⊙ noon-1.30pm & 7.30-9.30pm Wed-Sat; ✎) Chef Pascal Favre d'Anne shut a Michelin-starred restaurant in order to travel around Asia for a year – he's a Lonely Planet fan, by the way – and then opened this place. Incredibly, he got his Michelin star back almost immediately. The *gastronomique* menu is inspired by his travels but uses the freshest local products, eg pigeons. Reserve ahead.

ⓘ ANGERS CITY PASS

Swing by the tourist office (p428) to pick up the **Angers City Pass** (€15/23/29 for 24/48/72 hours), good for entry to about 20 Angers-area châteaux and museums and the **Terra Botanica gardens** (www.terrabotanica.fr), as well as tram and bus use and four hours of parking for the price of two.

WORTH A TRIP

ANGERS DAY TRIPPER

South of Angers, the Maine (France's shortest major river) joins the Loire for the final leg of its journey to the Atlantic. The river banks immediately west of this confluence remain the source of some of the valley's most notable wines, including Savennières (grown near the pretty village of the same name) and Coteaux du Layon. The area due south of Angers, between Gennes, Brissac-Quincé and Savennières, makes for great back-roads exploration.

Owned by the Brissac family for 18 generations (since 1502), the seven-storey **Château de Brissac** (☑ 02 41 91 22 21; www.chateau-brissac.fr; Brissac-Quincé; adult/child incl tour €10/4.50, gardens only €5/free; ☺ tours begin 10-11.30am & 2-4.30pm Apr-Oct, no midday closure Jul & Aug, also 2pm & 4pm Wed-Mon Feb & Christmas school holidays), the tallest castle in France, has 204 rooms, many of them sumptuously furnished with antique furniture, Flemish tapestries and twinkling crystal chandeliers. The serene 70-hectare gardens, which can be explored on five themed paths, have 19th-century stables, and vineyards boasting four AOC vintages (three rosés and one red). Guided tours are in French; a written text is available in six languages. Non-guided visits may be possible in July and August. From May to September, three of the château's bedrooms turn into an opulent **B&B** (€390 to €450 per room) – ideal for a honeymoon or a very special family vacation! Situated 19km southeast of Angers.

Owned and lived in by the same Irish family and its descendants since 1749, the elegant, Renaissance-style **Château de Serrant** (☑ 02 41 39 13 01; www.chateau-serrant.net; St-Georges-sur-Loire; tour adult/child €11/6.50; ☺ 10am-5.15pm & tours 5 times a day Wed-Sun late Feb-early Nov, open daily & tours hourly Jul & Aug), built on medieval foundations, is notable for its 12,000-tome library, huge kitchens, domestics' dining room and Chambre Empire, an extravagant domed bedroom designed for Napoléon (he stuck around for just two hours). To see the most interesting sections you have to take a 1¼-hour tour (in French with reference text available in six languages), but you can visit the ground floor, two Louis XV–style rooms on the 1st floor, the chapel and the English-style gardens on your own (adult/child €8/free). Situated 20km west-southwest of Angers.

To experience rural France at its most pastoral, drop by the **Auberge de Montrivet** (Ferme de Montrivet; ☑ 02 41 45 32 02; www.auberge-montrivet.fr; Montrivet, commune of Denée; d/q €60/100; ☺ daily year-round), a working family farm, to sleep and/or dine – you're assured of a warm and very French welcome. Note that the four rooms are *very* simple. Delicious country-style French meals (€19 per person) are made with duck, chicken and veggies grown right here; phone a day ahead to reserve. Situated in the hamlet of Montrivet (the first T is silent; the second, oddly, is not), 22km south of Angers and 5km southeast of the centre of the village of Denée, home to a 10th-century brick-and-stone church.

ⓘ Information

Tourist Office (☑ 02 41 23 50 00; www.angers loiretourisme.com; 7 place du Président Kennedy; ☺ 9am or 10am-5.30pm, 6pm or 7pm, closed Tue morning & Sun afternoon Oct-Apr; 🛜) Very helpful, with luggage lockers big enough for backpacks, locked bicycle parking boxes (€2), public toilets, and loads of info on sights, activities (including cycling) and transport. Sells the Angers City Pass.

Tourist Office Annexe (38 bd Henri Arnauld; ☺ mid-Apr–mid-Sep)

ⓘ Getting There & Around

BICYCLE

The tourist office annexe, down by the river, rents bikes (€15 per day) and can supply you with cycling maps.

BUS

Angers' **gare routière** (bus station) is next to the train station. **Anjou Bus** (☑ 02 41 36 29 46; www.anjoubus.fr; tickets €2-6.20) serves destinations within the Maine-et-Loire *département*.

TRAIN

Angers-St-Laud Train Station is 600m south of the château and the tourist office.

Nantes €11.50 to €20, 35 to 54 minutes, two or three per hour.

Paris' Gare Montparnasse €47 to €80, 1½ hours, hourly.

Saumur €9.10, 21 to 36 minutes, nine to 19 daily.

Tours €19, one hour, four to nine daily.

Burgundy

POP 1.64 MILLION

Best Places to Eat

➜ Au Fil du Zinc (p458)

➜ Ma Table en Ville (p473)

➜ L'Age de Raisin (p436)

➜ Le Millésime (p439)

➜ Comptoir Cuisine (p467)

Best Places to Stay

➜ Les Jardins de Loïs (p447)

➜ Villa Louise Hôtel (p442)

➜ Château de Villette (p465)

➜ Moulin Renaudiots (p467)

➜ Le Clos de l'Abbaye (p471)

Why Go?

Burgundy (Bourgogne in French) offers some of France's most gorgeous countryside: rolling green hills dotted with mustard fields and medieval villages. The region's towns and its dashingly handsome capital, Dijon, are heirs to a glorious architectural heritage that goes back to the Renaissance, the Middle Ages and into the mists of Gallo-Roman and Celtic antiquity.

Two great French passions, wine and food, come together here in a particularly enticing way. Burgundy's vineyards have been granted Unesco World Heritage status in recognition of the region's centuries-old history of viticulture and the remarkable diversity of its winegrowing *terroir* (land).

Burgundy's four *départements* (Côte d'Or, Yonne, Saône-et-Loire and Nièvre) are a paradise for lovers of the great outdoors. You can cycle through venerable vineyards, hike the wild reaches of the Parc Naturel Régional du Morvan, glide along tranquil waterways in a canal boat, or float above it all in a hot-air balloon.

When to Go
Dijon

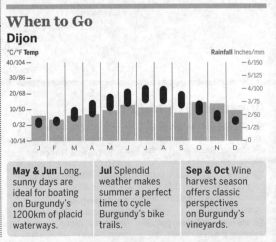

May & Jun Long, sunny days are ideal for boating on Burgundy's 1200km of placid waterways.

Jul Splendid weather makes summer a perfect time to cycle Burgundy's bike trails.

Sep & Oct Wine harvest season offers classic perspectives on Burgundy's vineyards.

Burgundy Highlights

1 **Beaune** (p444) Sampling Burgundy's most renowned vintages in Beaune, heart of the vine-carpeted Côte d'Or.

2 **Dijon** (p431) Basking in the glory of the Burgundy dukes on the medieval streets of the region's capital.

3 **Noyers-sur-Serein** (p459) Watching the mist rise off the river and the sun peek over the medieval battlements of this multiturreted village.

4 **Abbaye de Fontenay** (p451) Conjuring up medieval monastic life at this tranquil Cistercian abbey.

5 **Autun** (p466) Contemplating Gislebertus' *Temptation of Eve*, a masterpiece of 12th-century stone carving.

6 **Vézelay** (p461) Exploring countryside and cobblestoned lanes to reach the medieval basilica atop this hilltop village.

7 **Bibracte** (p464) Feeling the spirit of the ancient Gauls at Vercingétorix's stronghold.

8 **Chablis** (p456) Strolling or cycling through the vineyards that produce Burgundy's most famous white wine.

CÔTE D'OR

The Côte d'Or *département* is named after one of the world's foremost winegrowing regions, which stretches from Dijon, bursting with cultural riches, south to the wine town of Beaune and beyond. West of Dijon, other worthwhile destinations include the walled, hilltop town of Semur-en-Auxois, the idyllic Cistercian monastic site Abbaye de Fontenay and the historic Alésia battlefield where Julius Caesar finally vanquished the Gauls in 52 BC. In the far northwest of the *département*, on the border with Champagne, Châtillon-sur-Seine displays some stunning Celtic treasures.

Dijon

POP 159,168

With its compact and pedestrian-friendly centre, lively street scene and aesthetically pleasing ensemble of half-timbered houses and polychrome tile roofs, Dijon is one of France's most appealing cities. Filled with elegant medieval and Renaissance buildings that hark back to the city's 14th- and 15th-century heyday as the capital of the Duchy of Burgundy, the historic centre is wonderful for strolling, especially if you like to leaven your cultural enrichment with excellent food, fine wine and shopping.

History

Dijon served as the capital of the duchy of Burgundy from the 11th to 15th centuries, enjoying a golden age during the 14th and 15th centuries under Philippe-le-Hardi (Philip the Bold), Jean-sans-Peur (John the Fearless) and Philippe-le-Bon (Philip the Good). During their reigns, some of the finest painters, sculptors and architects from around the continent were brought to Dijon, turning the city into one of the great centres of European art.

◉ Sights

The Owl's Trail (€3.50), available in 11 languages at the tourist office, details a self-guided city-centre walking tour; the route is marked on the pavement with bronze triangles. All of Dijon's municipal museums are free except, occasionally, for special exhibitions. Major churches are open from 8am to 7pm.

Palais des Ducs et des États de Bourgogne   PALACE
(Palace of the Dukes & States of Burgundy; place de la Libération) Once home to Burgundy's powerful dukes, this monumental palace with a neoclassical façade overlooks place de la Libération, old Dijon's magnificent central square dating from 1686. The palace's eastern wing houses the outstanding Musée des Beaux-Arts, whose entrance is next to the **Tour de Bar**, a squat 14th-century tower that once served as a prison. The remainder of the palace houses municipal offices that are off-limits to the public.

★ Musée des Beaux-Arts   MUSEUM
(☑ 03 80 74 52 09; http://beaux-arts.dijon.fr; 1 rue Rameau; audioguide €4, guided tour €6; ⊘ 10am-6.30pm Jun-Sep, 9.30am-6pm Oct-May, closed Tue year-round) **FREE** Nearing the end of a nine-year renovation, these sprawling galleries in Dijon's monumental Palais des Ducs are works of art in themselves and constitute one of France's most outstanding museums. The star attraction is the wood-panelled **Salle des Gardes**, which houses the ornate, carved late-medieval sepulchres of dukes John the Fearless and Philip the Bold. Other sections focus on Egyptian art, the Middle Ages in Burgundy and Europe, and six centuries of European painting, from the Renaissance to modern times.

The museum's highlights include a fine collection of 13th- and 14th-century primitives that reveal how medieval artistic and aesthetic sensibilities varied between Italy, Switzerland and the Rhineland; a smattering of old masters such as Lorenzo Lotto; quite a few naturalistic sculptures by the Dijon-born artist François Rude (1784–1855); works by Manet, Monet, Matisse and Rodin; and the incomparable Pompon Room, tucked off a back staircase, packed with stylised modern sculptures of animals by François Pompon (1855–1933), who was born in Saulieu, Burgundy. In the courtyard, the ducal kitchens (1433) often host exhibitions of works by local artists.

Tour Philippe le Bon   TOWER
(place de la Libération; adult/child €3/1.50; ⊘ guided tours every 45min 10.30am-noon & 1.45-5.30pm Tue-Sun Apr–mid-Nov, hourly 2-4pm Tue, 11am-4pm Sat & Sun mid-Nov–Mar) Adjacent to the ducal palace, this 46m-high, mid-15th-century tower affords fantastic views over the city. On a clear day you can see all the way to Mont Blanc. Dijon's tourist office (p437) handles reservations.

Église Notre Dame   CHURCH
(place Notre-Dame; ⊘ 8am-7pm) A block north of the Palais des Ducs, this church was built between 1220 and 1240. Its extraordinary

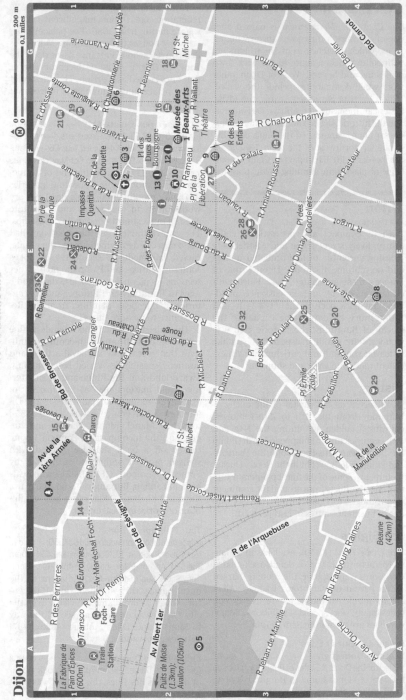

Dijon

Musée des Beaux-Arts

200 m
0.1 miles

Dijon

façade's three tiers are lined with leering gargoyles separated by two rows of pencil-thin columns. Atop the church, the 14th-century **Horloge à Jacquemart**, transported from Flanders in 1383 by Philip the Bold who claimed it as a trophy of war, chimes every quarter-hour.

Hôtel de Vogüé
HISTORIC BUILDING
(8 rue de la Chouette) Behind Église Notre Dame, the 17th-century Hôtel de Vogüé is renowned for the ornate carvings around the arches of its exquisitely proportioned Renaissance courtyard. It's worth walking through the pink stone archway for a peek.

Rue de la Chouette
STREET
Around the north side of Église Notre Dame, this street is named after the small stone owl (chouette) carved into the exterior corner of the chapel diagonally across from No 24. Said to grant happiness and wisdom to those who stroke it, it has been worn smooth by generations of fortune-seekers.

Maison des Cariatides
HISTORIC BUILDING
(28 rue Chaudronnerie) Its Renaissance-style façade bursting with stone caryatids, soldiers and vines, Maison des Cariatides is one of Dijon's finest buildings. Dating to the early 17th century, it was built by the Pouffiers, a wealthy family of local coppersmiths and merchants.

Musée Archéologique
MUSEUM
(☎ 03 80 48 83 70; http://archeologie.dijon.fr; 5 rue Docteur Maret; ◎ 9.30am-12.30pm & 2-6pm Wed-Mon Apr-Oct, Wed, Sat & Sun only Nov-Mar) FREE Truly surprising Celtic, Gallo-Roman and Merovingian artefacts are displayed here, including a particularly fine 1st-century AD bronze of the Celtic river goddess Sequana standing on a dual-prowed boat. Upstairs, the early-Gothic hall (12th and 13th centuries), with its ogival arches held aloft by two rows of columns, once served as the dormitory of a Benedictine abbey.

Musée de la Vie Bourguignonne
MUSEUM
(☎ 03 80 48 80 90; http://vie-bourguignonne.dijon.fr; 17 rue Ste-Anne; ◎ 9.30am-12.30pm & 2-6pm Wed-Mon) FREE Housed in a 17th-century Cistercian convent, this museum explores village and town life in Burgundy in centuries past with evocative tableaux illustrating dress, customs and traditional crafts. On the 1st floor, a whole street has been re-created, complete with 19th-century pharmacy and numerous antique-filled shops (grocer, furrier, hat-maker, clock-maker, toy store and more).

Musée Magnin
GALLERY
(☎ 03 80 67 11 10; www.musee-magnin.fr; 4 rue des Bons-Enfants; adult/child incl audioguide €3.50/free, during special exhibitions €5.50/free; ◎ 10am-12.30pm & 1.30-6pm Tue-Sun) In 1938, art collectors Jeanne and Maurice Magnin turned their

FAMILY FUN IN DIJON'S PRETTIEST SQUARE

There's no greater kid magnet than the fountains in Dijon's pretty place de la Libération. Shooting up out of the ground at irregular intervals, these jets of water arrayed in long symmetrical rows prove irresistible for youngsters, who can't help but run through them and test their water-dodging skills, especially at night when everything is illuminated with multicoloured lights. Parents can either join in the fun or retreat to one of the cafes ringing the square for a glass of wine and inspirational views of the ducal palace, all the while watching their kids bliss out in traffic-free safety.

historic townhouse over to the state to display, in perpetuity, the excellent collection they had amassed over a period of 55 years. Works include fine examples of the Italian Renaissance, and Flemish and medieval painting.

Jardin Darcy   PARK

Dijon has plenty of green spaces that are perfect for picnics, including this inviting park between the train station and the historic centre.

Jardin de l'Arquebuse   GARDENS

A delightful place for a Sunday stroll, this 5-hectare park south of the train station encompasses the colourful flower beds and rose trellises of Dijon's botanical gardens, along with an arboretum, a stream and a pond.

Puits de Moïse   SCULPTURE

(Well of Moses; Centre Hospitalier Spécialisé La Chartreuse, 1 bd Chanoine Kir; adult/child €3.50/2.50; ⊗ 9.30am-12.30pm & 2-6pm Apr-Sep, to 4.30pm Oct-Mar) This famous grouping of six Old Testament figures, carved from 1395 to 1405 by court sculptor Claus Sluter and his nephew Claus de Werve, is on the grounds of a psychiatric hospital 1km west of the train station; grab a bike from Diviavélodi (p437) or take bus 3 towards Fontaine d'Ouche.

👉 Tours

The tourist office has scads of information on tours of the city and the nearby wine regions, and can make bookings.

English-language minibus tours operated by **Authentica Tours** (📞 06 87 01 43 78; www.authentica-tours.com; group tours per person €65-130) and **Wine & Voyages** (📞 03 80 61 15 15; www.wineandvoyages.com; tours €63-120) introduce the Côte d'Or vineyards. Reserve by phone, internet or via the tourist office.

🛏 Sleeping

Hôtel Le Chambellan   HOTEL €

(📞 03 80 67 12 67; www.hotel-chambellan.com; 92 rue Vannerie; s €44-59, d €59-66, q from €79, s/d with shared bathroom €37/39; 🛜) Fresh off a 2018 renovation, this budget favourite in the heart of medieval Dijon has a whole new look, mixing modern flair (remodelled bathrooms, bold colours, phone-charging ports, spiffy new reading lamps) with the three Ps – *poutres, pierre, parquet* (exposed beams, stone and wood floors) – that epitomise owner Christophe Comte's long-standing fondness for the rustic.

Hôtel Le Jacquemart   HOTEL €

(📞 03 80 60 09 60; www.hotel-lejacquemart.fr; 32 rue Verrerie; s €58-62, d €67-75, q €89-95; 🛜) In the heart of old Dijon, this two-star hotel has tidy, comfortable rooms and friendly staff. Rooms 5 and 6, in a 17th-century annexe just across the street, are larger and better equipped than those within the hotel's original core, and combine vintage touches (stone walls, beamed ceiling) with modern conveniences.

Hôtel du Palais   HOTEL €

(📞 03 80 65 51 43; www.hoteldupalais-dijon.fr; 23 rue du Palais; s €39-65, d €65-105, q €79-109, breakfast €9.90; ✳🛜) This inviting three-star in a 17th-century *hôtel particulier* (private mansion) offers excellent value. The 13 rooms range from cosy, inexpensive 3rd-floor doubles tucked under the eaves to spacious, high-ceilinged family suites with abundant natural light. The location is unbeatable, on a quiet side street five minutes' walk from central place de la Libération.

Le Petit Tertre   APARTMENT €€

(📞 03 80 52 74 07; www.lepetit-tertre.fr; 41 rue Verrerie; s apt €65-93, d apt €83-111; ✳🛜) For homey digs in the heart of medieval Dijon, this ensemble of four impeccably maintained apartments in a lovingly renovated family home is hard to beat. Each unique unit reflects the creative vision of the Franco-Japanese owners, with welcoming features that range from kitchen facilities, parquet floors and spacious bathrooms to a four-poster canopy bed or a Burgundian stone fireplace.

Grand Hôtel La Cloche
HOTEL €€

(✆ 03 80 30 12 32; www.hotel-lacloche.fr; 14 place Darcy; s/d/ste from €129/165/379; ✴ @ 🕿 ☲) Well placed on a large park between the train station and Dijon's historic centre, this newly revamped historic five-star offers Dijon's most business-friendly accommodation. Sleek soundproofed rooms decorated with bold colour splashes offer every imaginable comfort, while the common spaces retain crystal chandeliers and other vintage touches. There's a restaurant, a spa, a pool and a garden out back.

Hôtel des Ducs
HOTEL €€

(✆ 03 80 67 31 31; www.hoteldesducs.com; 5 rue Lamonnoye; d €89-134, apt €120-160; 🅿 ✴ @ 🕿) The new owners at this three-star hotel smack-dab in Dijon's medieval centre have poured plenty of time and money into recent renovations. The result: eight spacious self-catering apartments done up in contemporary designs, to complement the comfortable modern hotel rooms next door. The ample breakfast includes organic free-trade coffee, eggs, bacon, sausage and homemade black-currant jam

★La Cour Berbisey
B&B €€€

(✆ 03 45 83 12 38; www.lacourberbisey.fr; 31 rue Berbisey; r €169, junior ste €229, ste €289; 🕿 ☲) An arched red doorway in an ivy-draped wall leads to this luxurious B&B, easily Dijon's classiest midcity accommodation. Three enormous suites with parquet floors, beamed ceilings and tall French-shuttered windows are complemented by a lone junior suite and one smaller but equally comfortable double. Other upscale touches include an indoor swimming pool, sauna and antique-filled salon. Breakfast is included.

✕ Eating

Find loads of restaurants on buzzy rue Berbisey, around place Émile Zola, on rue Amiral Roussin and around the perimeter of the covered market. In warm months, outdoor cafes and brasseries (restaurants) fill place de la Libération.

TFTF
ALSATIAN €

(Tout Feu Tout Flam; ✆ 0380339451; www.facebook.com/tftfdijon; 40 rue Amiral Roussin; flammekueche €8-15; ☉ noon-2pm Fri & Sat, 6pm-2am Tue-Sat) Tables spill out onto the sidewalk at this bustling new resto-bar in Dijon's pedestrianised centre. The menu revolves around delicious *flammekueche* (*tarte flambée*

in French), the classic Alsatian flatbread topped with everything from crème fraiche, onions and lardons (smoked pork) to ham and truffle oil. Free-flowing glasses of beer keep things buzzing late into the evening.

Café de l'Industrie
BRASSERIE €

(✆ 03 80 30 20 81; 15 rue des Godrans; lunch menu €14; ☉ 6.30am-1am Tue-Sat) For a no-nonsense, good-value lunch, head one block west of Dijon's market and grab a sidewalk table at this convivial corner brasserie, where hearty *plats du jour* go for just €10. In the evenings it switches over to a bar, serving platters of cheese and charcuterie along with Burgundian wines.

Le Piano Qui Fume
MODERN FRENCH €€

(✆ 09 70 35 84 63, 03 80 30 35 45; www.lepianoquifume.com; 36 rue Berbisey; lunch menus €13.50-20, dinner menus €31-35; ☉ noon-1.45pm Mon, Tue & Thu-Sat, plus 7-9.45pm Thu-Sat) Market cuisine, carefully chosen ingredients, reasonably priced wines and a lovely contemporary dining room with traditional touches (exposed brick walls and beams) are the hallmarks of this popular hideaway. The lunchtime *plat du jour* (daily special) is brilliant value at €9.90.

Chez Léon
BURGUNDIAN €€

(✆ 03 80 50 01 07; www.restochezleon.fr; 20 rue des Godrans; lunch menus €16-20, dinner menus €26-31; ☉ noon-2pm & 7-10.30pm Tue-Sat) From *bœuf bourguignon* (beef marinated in young red wine) to *andouillettes* (chitterling sausages), this family-run eatery offers the perfect primer course in hearty regional fare celebrated in a cosy and joyful atmosphere. There's outdoor seating in warmer months.

DZ'Envies
BURGUNDIAN €€

(✆ 03 80 50 09 26; www.dzenvies.com; 12 rue Odebert; mains €17-22, lunch menus €14-21, dinner menus €32-40; ☉ noon-2pm & 7-10pm Mon-Sat) This zinging restaurant with cheery decorative touches is a good choice if you're tired of heavy Burgundian classics. The menu always involves seasonal, fresh ingredients, and dishes are imaginatively prepared and beautifully presented. At €21, the lunchtime 'I love Dijon' *menu* is a steal.

★La Maison des Cariatides
GASTRONOMY €€€

(✆ 03 80 45 59 25; www.thomascollomb.fr/la-maison-des-cariatides; 28 rue Chaudronnerie; 2-/3-course lunch menu €25/29, dinner menu €58; ☉ noon-1.30pm & 7.30-9pm Tue-Sat; 🕿) This renovated 17th-century mansion with exposed beams, stone walls and refined mod-

LOCAL KNOWLEDGE

SWEET TALK: DIJON GINGERBREAD

Around the time of the French Revolution, Mulot & Petitjean founded one of several bakeries making Dijon's famous *pain d'épices* (gingerbread). Nine generations later, the founders' descendants have converted part of their factory into the interactive museum **La Fabrique de Pain d'Épices** (☑ 03 80 66 30 80; www.mulotpetitjean.fr; 6 bd de l'Ouest; adult/child €8/free; ☺ 10am-12.30pm & 2-6.30pm Tue-Sat), opened in 2017. English-language audio guides and animated talking heads tell you the history of *pain d'épices* and take you through the production process. Afterwards, taste the goods, including Mulot & Petitjean's companion product – *jacquelines* – meringue-covered treats filled with nougat or hazelnut pralines. They run several outlets, including one on place Bossuet (p436).

The *pain d'épices* tradition in France dates back to the Middle Ages, when Crusaders brought the recipe and the necessary spices back from the Middle East. In those days, spices served as currency, the basis for the modern French term *espèces*, meaning 'cash'!

ern decor makes a delightful spot to savour top-of-the-line French and regional cuisine, complemented by an extensive selection of Burgundian wines. There's also pleasant terrace seating out back. The two- to three-course lunch menu offers excellent value.

🍷 Drinking & Nightlife

Lively bar-hopping neighbourhoods include rue Berbisey and the streets surrounding Les Halles.

★ L'Age de Raisin
WINE BAR

(☑ 03 80 23 24 82; 67 rue Berbisey; ☺ 6pm-2am Tue-Sat) Stone walls, red-and-white-checked tablecloths and gracious service set the mood at this cosiest of Dijon wine bars. With late hours and a wealth of local vintages hand-selected by affable owners Jeff and Nadine, it doubles as a bistro, serving fabulous home-cooked *plats du jour* built from locally sourced organic produce. Reserve ahead at dinnertime; it fills up fast!

La Causerie des Mondes
CAFE

(☑ 03 80 49 96 59; www.facebook.com/lacauserie desmondes; 16 rue Vauban; ☺ 8.30am-7.30pm Tue-Sat) Tucked behind a half-timbered façade in Dijon's pedestrian zone, this eclectically decorated cafe is beloved for its multipage list of teas and its enticing line-up of hot chocolates. Kick back on pillows decorated with cats in Elizabethan ruffs and sip a *doudou royal* (double espresso with Nutella and whipped cream). Juices and veggie-friendly lunch *menus* (€16) also draw devoted crowds.

Café Gourmand
CAFE

(☑ 0380368751; www.facebook.com/cafegourmand dijon; 9 place de la Libération; ☺ 10am-midnight Mon-Sat, to 8pm Sun) You simply couldn't ask for a better backdrop for sipping aperitifs than this sidewalk cafe-restaurant on sprawling place de la Libération, facing the dramatic façade of Dijon's ducal palace. It's especially sweet when the sun catches the terrace full force in late afternoon, and you can watch the comings and goings of tourists, locals, and kids playing in the fountains.

🛍 Shopping

The main shopping area is along pedestrianised rue de la Liberté and perpendicular rue du Bourg.

★ Les Halles
MARKET

(rue Quentin; ☺ 8am-1pm Tue & Thu-Sat) Northwest of Palais des Ducs is Dijon's fabulous 19th-century covered market, Les Halles. Enshrined as a national monument in 1975 (when it narrowly escaped the wrecking ball), its dozens of stalls buzz with activity four mornings a week, with Saturdays drawing the biggest crowds. It's the perfect place to mingle with Dijonnais locals while stocking up for a picnic of fresh produce, cheeses and charcuterie.

Mulot & Petitjean
FOOD

(☑ 03 80 30 07 10; www.mulotpetitjean.fr; 13 place Bossuet; ☺ 2-7pm Mon, 9am-noon & 2-7pm Tue-Sat) The sweet-toothed will lose all self-control at this Dijon institution dating to 1796. Housed in a suitably gingerbready half-timbered building, it's famous for its scrumptious *pain d'épices* (gingerbread made with honey and spices). The goodies are made at a factory (p436) nearby.

Moutarde Maille
FOOD

(☑ 03 80 30 41 02; www.maille.com; 32 rue de la Liberté; ☺ 10am-7pm Mon-Sat) When you enter the factory boutique of this mustard company, tangy odours assault your nostrils. Three-dozen varieties of mustard fill the shelves (cassis, truffle, celery etc), along with a host of rotating flavours for you to sample.

ℹ️ Information

Tourist Office (📞 08 92 70 05 58; www.destinationdijon.com; 11 rue des Forges; ⏰ 9.30am-6.30pm Mon-Sat, 10am-6pm Sun Apr-Sep, 9.30am-1pm & 2-6pm Mon-Sat, 10am-4pm Sun Oct-Mar; 📶) Helpful office offering maps, themed walking tours (€8 to €12), and guided vineyard tours (from €65).

ℹ️ Getting There & Around

BICYCLE

DiviaVélodi (www.divia.fr; subscription fee per day/week €1.50/7, rental first 30min free, each additional 30min €2), Dijon's version of Paris' Vélib' automatic rental system, has 400 city bikes at 40 sites around town. Insert a credit card, get a passcode, choose a PIN and go.

BUS

Transco (📞 03 80 11 29 29; www.mobigo-bourgogne.com; single ticket/day pass €1.50/6.60) Buses stop in front of the train station. Tickets, sold on board, cost the same regardless of destination. Bus 44 goes to Nuits-St-Georges (45 minutes) and Beaune (1¼ hours).

Eurolines (📞 08 92 89 90 91; www.eurolines.fr; 53 rue Guillaume Tell) International bus travel. Office just outside the train station.

TRAIN

Connections from Dijon's train station include the following:

Lyon-Part Dieu Regional train/TGV from €32/37, two/1½ hours, hourly

Marseille TGV from €81, 3¾ hours, two direct daily

Paris Gare de Lyon Regional train/TGV from €35/61, three/1½ hours, hourly

Côte d'Or Vineyards

Burgundy's most renowned vintages come from the vine-covered region of the Côte d'Or (literally Golden Hillside, but it is actually an abbreviation of Côte d'Orient or Eastern Hillside), the narrow, eastern slopes of a range of hills made of limestone, flint and clay that runs south from Dijon for about 60km. The exquisite terrain with its patchwork of immaculate hand-groomed vines is dotted with peaceful stone villages where every house seems to hold a vintner.

An oenophile's nirvana, the Côte d'Or vineyards are divided into two areas, Côte de Nuits to the north and Côte de Beaune to the south. The Côte de Nuits is noted for its powerful red wines, while the Côte de Beaune produces top-quality dry whites and delicate reds.

Côte de Nuits

The Côte de Nuits winegrowing area extends from Marsannay-la-Côte, just south of Dijon, to Corgoloin, a few kilometres north of Beaune. All told, it's only a span of 30km, but with so many picturesque villages, vineyards and other attractions along the way, you could easily spend the better part of a day here, including stops for wine tasting, sightseeing and lunch.

Highlights include **Fixin**, with its distinctive polychrome bell tower; **Gevrey-Chambertin**, where every other doorway seems to harbour its own winery; **Chambolle-Musigny**, with its old stone houses and fine restaurants tucked photogenically up against a rocky hillside; **Vougeot**, home to a venerable 16th-century wine-producing château where you can tour the historic wine presses; and **Nuits-St-Georges**, the Côte de Nuits' biggest town, where you'll find another cluster of fine restaurants and a pair of museums focused on the region's winemaking tradition and its famous blackcurrant liqueur, *crème de cassis*.

Wine can be bought direct from the winegrowers, many of whom offer tastings, allowing you to sample two or three vintages, but at many places, especially the better-known

---

ℹ️ BRINGING IT BACK HOME

Dreaming of bringing a dozen or two bottles of Burgundian wine home with you, but running out of room in your suitcase? Help is at hand for overseas visitors who get a little carried away with their wine purchases. Companies such as **Côte d'Or Imports** (📞 03 80 61 15 15; www.cotedorpdx.com) work with vineyards throughout Burgundy and can facilitate fully insured, door-to-door shipments to the US or Canada for roughly €15 per bottle (depending on volume); shipments to Australia and New Zealand are also available for about €20 per bottle, plus duty – not a bad deal if you're buying the expensive stuff!

BURGUNDY WINE BASICS

Burgundy's epic vineyards extend approximately 258km from Chablis in the north to the Mâconnais region in the south and comprise 100 AOCs (Appellations d'Origine Contrôlée). Each region has its own appellations and traits, embodied by a concept called *terroir*, the earth imbuing its produce, such as grapes, with unique qualities. However, some appellations, such as Crémant de Bourgogne (a light, sparkling white or rosé) and Bourgogne Aligoté, are produced in several regions.

Wine Regions

Here's an ever-so-brief survey of some of Burgundy's major growing regions:

Côte d'Or vineyards The northern section, the Côte de Nuits, stretches from Marsannay-la-Côte south to Corgoloin and produces reds known for their robust, full-bodied character. The southern section, the Côte de Beaune, lies between Ladoix-Serrigny and Santenay and produces great reds and whites. Appellations from the area's hilltops are the Hautes-Côtes de Nuits and Hautes-Côtes de Beaune.

Chablis & Grand Auxerrois Four renowned chardonnay white wine appellations from 20 villages around Chablis. Part of the Auxerrois vineyards, Irancy produces excellent pinot noir reds. The Tonnerrois vineyards produce good, affordable reds, whites and rosés.

Châtillonnais Approximately 20 villages around Châtillon-sur-Seine producing red and white wines.

Côte Chalonnaise The southernmost continuation of the Côte de Beaune's slopes is noted for its excellent reds and whites.

Mâconnais Known for rich or fruity white wines, including the Pouilly-Fuissé chardonnay.

Want to Know More?

Tourist offices provide brochures including *The Burgundy Wine Road* and a useful map, *Roadmap to the Wines of Burgundy*. A handy website is www.bourgogne-wines.com.

Lots of books are available at Beaune's Athenaeum de la Vigne et du Vin (p449). Look for these:

➡ *Côte d'Or: A Celebration of the Great Wines of Burgundy* and *My Favorite Burgundies* by Clive Coates.

➡ *The Wines of Burgundy* by Sylvain Pitiot and Jean-Charles Servant. Excellent overview.

➡ *The Climats and Lieux-dits of the Great Vineyards of Burgundy* by Marie-Hélène Landrieu-Lussigny and Sylvain Pitiot. Classic atlas of Burgundian vinicultural place names, translated into English in 2014.

➡ *The Great Domaines of Burgundy* and *Grand Cru: the Great Wines of Burgundy Through the Perspective of Its Finest Vineyards* by Remington Norman.

➡ *Inside Burgundy* by Jasper Morris.

➡ *The Finest Wines of Burgundy* by Bill Nanson.

➡ *The Cook's Atelier* by Marjorie Taylor and Kendall Smith Franchini

Take a Class!

Wine-tasting classes can help you make the most of your time in Burgundy.

École des Vins de Bourgogne (☑ 03 80 26 35 10; www.ecoledesvins-bourgogne.com; 6 rue du 16e Chasseurs) Offers a variety of courses (from a three-hour, €75 fundamentals class to a three-day, €780 wine-taster's certificate program) to refine your viticultural vocabulary as well as your palate.

Sensation Vin (☑ 03 80 22 17 57; www.sensation-vin.com; 1 rue d'Enfer; tasting sessions/excursions from €35/275; ⊙ 10am-6pm Sun-Fri, to 7pm Sat) Offers a €35, 1½-hour essentials class, half- and full-day tasting sessions and personalised wine-tasting circuits through the area's most famous vineyards.

ones, you have to make advance reservations. Lists of estates and caves open to the public are available from local tourist offices.

◉ Sights

Château du Clos de Vougeot
MUSEUM, CASTLE

(☎03 80 62 86 09; www.closdevougeot.fr; rue de la Montagne, Vougeot; adult/child €7.50/2.50; ⊙9am-6.30pm Sun-Fri, to 5pm Sat Apr-Oct, 10am-5pm Nov-Mar) A mandatory stop on your tour of Burgundy's vineyards, this magnificent wine-producing château (estate) provides a wonderful introduction to Burgundy's wine-making techniques. Originally the property of the Abbaye de Cîteaux, the 16th-century country castle served as a getaway for the abbots. Tours offer a chance to discover the workings of enormous ancient wine presses and casks.

Cassissium
MUSEUM

(☎03 80 62 49 70; www.cassissium.fr; 8 passage Montgolfier, Nuits-St-Georges; adult/child €9.50/6.50; ⊙10am-1pm & 2-7pm Apr–mid-Nov, 10.30am-1pm & 2.30-5pm Tue-Sat mid-Nov–Mar) This museum and factory worships all things liqueur, with a particular focus on the blackcurrant, from which cassis is made. There's fun for the whole family: movies, displays, a 30-minute guided tour and a tasting with nonalcoholic fruit syrups for the kids. In the industrial area east of N74.

L'Imaginarium
MUSEUM

(☎03 80 62 61 40; www.imaginarium-bourgogne. com; av du Jura, Nuits-St-Georges; adult incl basic/ grand cru tasting €10/21, child €7; ⊙2-7pm Mon, 10am-7pm Tue-Sun; last admission 5pm) This gleaming modern museum is a good place to learn about Burgundy wines and winemaking techniques, with movies, exhibits and interactive displays, followed by your choice of tastings, from regional wines to *grands crus* (wine of exceptional quality).

🛏 Sleeping

Maison des Abeilles
B&B €

(☎03 80 62 95 42; www.chambres-beaune.fr; 4 rue Pernand, Magny-lès-Villers; d €70-90, q €115-130; 🎧) Food- and wine-lovers Céline and Tony maintain these six impeccably clean *chambres d'hôte* in Magny-lès-Villers, a small village off rte des Grands Crus between Côte de Nuits, Haute Côte de Nuits and Côte de Beaune. Rooms have colourful linen, and breakfasts (included) are a feast of breads and homemade jams. The vast, flowery garden out back is another plus.

Hôtel de Vougeot
HOTEL €€

(☎03 80 62 01 15; www.hotel-vougeot.com; 18 rue du Vieux Château, Vougeot; d €88-133; 🅿🎧) What's not to love in this gracious country manor? The 16 rooms are comfortable and impeccably maintained, many with rustically stylish features such as stone walls or exposed beams. Angle for one of the 10 rooms with a view of the Vougeot vineyards.

Les Deux Chèvres
HOTEL €€€

(☎03 80 51 48 25; www.lesdeuxchevres.com; 23 rue de L'Eglise, Gevrey-Chambertin; r €185-285; 🎧) After a day exploring the vineyards, this luxurious converted winery in viticulture mecca Gevrey-Chambertin invites guests to unwind in the stone-walled fireplace room, relax on the spacious back patio, and snuggle under Egyptian cotton sheets and goosedown duvets. The eight unique rooms range from a lower-priced upstairs unit with vineyard views, to a bright superior with clawfoot tub to a three-bedroom apartment.

🍴 Eating

⭐ Le Millésime
MODERN FRENCH €€

(☎03 80 62 80 37; www.restaurant-le-millesime. com; 1 rue Traversière, Chambolle-Musigny; lunch menu €20, dinner menus €33-65; ⊙noon-2pm & 7-9.30pm Tue-Sat) This renowned venture is located in an exquisitely renovated *maison de village* in the picturesque heart of tiny Chambolle-Musigny. The chef combines fresh local ingredients and exotic flavours in his excellent creations. Dark-wood floors, well-spaced tables and a warm welcome create an easy air.

Chez Guy & Family
MODERN FRENCH €€

(☎03 80 58 51 51; www.chez-guy.fr; 3 place de la Mairie, Gevrey-Chambertin; lunch/dinner menus from €18/32; ⊙noon-2pm & 7-9.30pm Tue-Sat) Its dining room is large and light, and there's a tempting choice of dishes on the fixed-price *menus,* complemented by one of the finest wine lists in the entire Côte de Nuits region. Signature seasonal specialities include tender duckling, rabbit leg and pollack.

Le Chambolle
BURGUNDIAN €€

(☎03 80 62 86 26; www.restaurant-lechambolle. com; 28 rue Caroline Aigle, Chambolle-Musigny; menus €27-39; ⊙12.15-1.30pm Thu-Tue, plus 7.15-8.30pm Fri-Tue) This unpretentious backroads gem creates traditional Burgundian cuisine with the freshest ingredients. Look for it on the D122, a bit west of Vougeot in gorgeous Chambolle-Musigny.

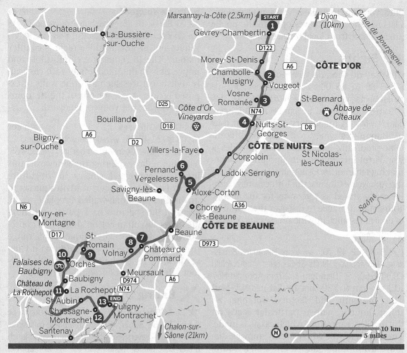

Driving Tour
Route des Grands Crus

START GEVREY-CHAMBERTIN
FINISH PULIGNY-MONTRACHET
LENGTH 55KM; ONE DAY

Burgundy's most famous wine route, the Route des Grands Crus (www.road-of-the-fine-burgundy-wines.com) follows the tertiary roads west of the N74, wending through seas of cascading vineyards dotted with stone-built villages, church steeples and château turrets. Signposted in brown, the route provides a grand tour of the world-renowned Côte de Nuits and Côte de Beaune.

Coming from Dijon, the Côte de Nuits begins in earnest just south of Marsannay-la-Côte. Most of the area's *grand cru* (wine of exceptional quality) vineyards lie between ❶**Gevrey-Chambertin** and Vosne-Romanée. In ❷**Vougeot**, stop at the historic château. ❸**Vosne-Romanée** is famed for its Romanée Conti wines, among Burgundy's most prestigious and priciest. Continuing south, visit the Côte de Nuits' largest town, ❹**Nuits-St-Georges**, home to the Imaginarium wine museum.

On the Côte de Beaune, the impossibly steep coloured-tile roof of Château Corton-André in ❺**Aloxe-Corton** is easy to spot, just off the one-lane main street. From here, a brief detour northwest brings you to photogenic ❻**Pernand-Vergelesses**, nestled in a little valley hidden from the N74. The views down over the town and vineyards are spectacular.

South of Beaune, ❼**Château de Pommard**, surrounded by a stone wall, is on the D973 on the northeast edge of town. Wander quaint ❽**Volnay** to its hillside church. Off the main track, ❾**St-Romain** is a bucolic village, where vineyard meets pastureland, forests and cliffs. Hiking trails from here include the spectacular Sentier des Roches, a circuit that follows part of the GR7, and the D17 along the top of the Falaises de Baubigny (Baubigny cliffs). Then, via the hillside hamlet of ❿**Orches**, which has breathtaking vineyard views, travel to the fantastic 15th-century ⓫**Château de la Rochepot**. For a pretty finale to your journey, drive down to the villages of ⓬**Chassagne-Montrachet** and ⓭**Puligny-Montrachet**, where you'll have the chance to sample the world's most opulent whites.

La Cabotte
MODERN FRENCH €€€

(📞03 80 61 20 77; www.restaurantlacabotte.fr; 24 Grande Rue, Nuits-St-Georges; lunch menu €19.50, dinner menus €30-75; ⏱12.15-1.30pm & 7.15-9pm Tue-Sat) This intimate restaurant serves up refined, inventive versions of French dishes. No artifice or posing here, just excellent, if sometimes surprising, food.

🏷 Shopping

Le Caveau des Musignys
WINE

(📞03 80 62 84 01; 1 rue Traversière, Chambolle-Musigny; ⏱9.30am-6pm Wed-Sun, by appointment Mon & Tue) Directly below the fabulous Les Millésimes restaurant, this place represents more than 100 Côte de Nuits and Côte de Beaune winegrowers.

ℹ Information

Nuits-St-Georges Tourist Office (📞03 80 62 11 17; www.ot-nuits-st-georges.fr; 3 rue Sonoys, Nuits-St-Georges; ⏱9.30am-12.30pm & 2-6pm Mon-Sat, 10.30am-1pm Sun Jun-Sep, shorter hrs & closed Sun Oct-May)

Gevrey-Chambertin Tourist Office (📞03 80 34 38 40; www.ot-gevreychambertin.fr; 1 rue Gaston Roupnel, Gevrey-Chambertin; ⏱9.30am-12.30pm & 1.30-6pm Mon-Fri, to 5.30pm Sat, 10am-12.30am & 1.30-4pm Sun May-Sep, shorter hrs & closed Sun Oct-Apr)

ℹ Getting There & Away

Transco (📞03 80 11 29 29; www.mobigo-bourgogne.com) provides regular bus connections between Dijon and Beaune on its line 44, stopping in Nuits-St-Georges, Vougeot, Gevrey-Chambertin and other Côte de Nuits villages along the way.

Côte de Beaune

Welcome to one of the most prestigious winegrowing areas in the world. The Côte de Beaune area extends from **Ladoix-Serrigny**, just a few kilometres north of Beaune, to **Santenay**, about 18km south of the city. It includes the delightful villages of **Pernand-Vergelesses**, **Aloxe-Corton**, **Savigny-lès-Beaune**, **Chorey-lès-Beaune**, **Pommard**, **Volnay**, **Meursault**, **Puligny-Montrachet** and **Chassagne-Montrachet**, which boast Burgundy's most fabled vineyards. If you're looking for an upscale wine château experience, you've come to the right place.

⊙ Sights

★ Château de la Rochepot
CASTLE

(📞07 60 50 25 62; www.chateau-de-la-rochepot.com; La Rochepot; adult/child self-guided €8.50/6.50; ⏱10am-5.30pm Wed-Mon Mar-Jun & Sep-Nov, 10am-6.30pm daily Jul & Aug) Conical towers and multicoloured tile roofs rise from thick woods above the ancient village of La Rochepot. This marvellous medieval fortress offers fab views of surrounding countryside, and the interiors are a fascinating combination of the utilitarian (weapons) and the luxe (fine paintings). Visitors receive a multilingual handout and are free to tour the château on their own.

Château de Meursault
WINERY

(📞03 80 26 22 75; www.chateau-meursault.com; 5 rue du Moulin Foulot, Meursault; tour incl 7-/9-wine tasting €21.50/27; ⏱10am-noon & 2-6pm Oct-Apr, 10am-6.30pm May-Sep) One of the prettiest of the Côte de Beaune châteaux, Château de Meursault has beautiful grounds and produces some of the most prestigious white wines in the world. Guided tours visit the estate's vast labyrinth of underground caves, the oldest dating to the 12th century; the 500-sq-metre 16th-century cellar is particularly impressive.

Château de Pommard
WINERY

(📞03 80 22 07 99; www.chateaudepommard.com; 15 rue Marey Monge, Pommard; guided tour incl 4-wine tasting €25; ⏱9.30am-6.30pm Mon-Fri) For many red-wine lovers, a visit to this superb château 3km south of Beaune is the ultimate Burgundian pilgrimage. The impressive cellars contain many vintage bottles. If the tour

DON'T MISS

CYCLING THROUGH VINES

The 23km **Voie des Vignes** (Vineyard Way), a bike route marked by rectangular green-on-white signs, goes from Beaune's Parc de la Bouzaize via Pommard, Volnay, Meursault, Puligny-Montrachet and Chassagne-Montrachet to Santenay, where you can turn north and continue another 13km to Nolay, or pick up the southbound Voie Verte (Green Way) to Cluny. Beaune's tourist office sells the detailed bilingual *Guide Rando Cyclo* map (€3); alternatively you can download a rough PDF route guide at www.la-bourgogne-a-velo.com.

BURGUNDY CÔTE D'OR VINEYARDS

has whetted your appetite, you can sample Burgundian specialities at the on-site restaurant. The château offers several other wine-related experiences, including a 2½-hour glimpse into the secrets of the sommelier, a chance to help with the wine harvest, and a kids' introduction to vineyard ecology followed by a fruit juice tasting.

Château de Savigny   MUSEUM, CASTLE
(☑ 03 80 21 55 03; www.chateau-savigny.com; Savigny-lès-Beaune; adult/child €11/5; ◷ 9am-6.30pm mid-Apr–mid-Oct, 9am-noon & 2-5.30pm rest of yr) Drop in for wine tasting and stay to see the unexpected collection of race cars, motorcycles, airplanes and fire trucks. Last admission is 90 minutes before closing time.

🏃 Activities

You'll find plenty of wine-tasting opportunities in the wine-producing villages. You can stop at the famous wine châteaux or you may prefer to drop in at more laid-back small wineries – look for signs.

Château Corton C   WINE
(☑ 03 80 26 28 79; www.corton-andre.com; rue Cortons, Aloxe-Corton; ◷ 10am-1pm & 2-6.30pm Apr-Oct, shorter hrs Nov-Mar) FREE With its splendid cellars and colourful tiled roofs, this high-flying château (formerly known as Château Corton-André) is a wonderful place for a free tasting session in atmospheric surrounds.

Caveau de Puligny-Montrachet   WINE
(☑ 03 80 21 96 78; www.caveau-puligny.com; 1 rue de Poiseul, Puligny-Montrachet; 6-wine tasting €20; ◷ 9.30am-noon & 2-7pm daily Mar-Oct, 10am-noon & 3-6pm Tue-Sun Nov-Feb) Sample the town's namesake bijou appellation along with other fine local wines in this comfortable, relaxed wine bar and cellar in the lovely town of Puligny-Montrachet. Knowledgeable hosts Julien Wallerand and Emilien Masuyer provide excellent advice (in good English).

🛌 Sleeping

★ Villa Louise Hôtel   HOTEL €€
(☑ 03 80 26 46 70; www.hotel-villa-louise.fr; 9 rue Franche, Aloxe-Corton; d €98-194, ste €205-244; P @ ⓢ ☀) In the pretty village of Aloxe-Corton, this tranquil mansion houses elegant, modern rooms, each of them dreamily different. The expansive garden stretches straight to the edge of the vineyard and a separate gazebo shelters the sauna and pool. Genteel Louise Perrin presides, and has a private *cave*, perfect for wine tastings. Breakfast costs €17.

Hotel Les Charmes   HOTEL €€
(☑ 03 80 21 63 53; www.hotellescharmes.com; 10 place du Murger, Meursault; s €107-130, d €120-140; ⓢ ⓦ ☀) In the heart of Meursault village, this family-run inn has simple, comfortable rooms in two categories: smaller Villages units and more spacious Grands Crus. Charming features not visible from the street include a huge backyard where owls and other birds gather at nesting boxes set up by owners Emmanuel and Pascale, and an inviting pool with chaises longues for relaxing.

La Maison d'Olivier Leflaive   BOUTIQUE HOTEL €€€
(☑ 03 80 21 37 65; www.olivier-leflaive.com; place du Monument, Puligny-Montrachet; d €185-265; ◷ closed Christmas-early Feb; P ✳ @ ⓢ) Occupying a tastefully renovated 17th-century village house in the heart of Puligny-Montrachet, this venerable boutique venture delivers top service and classy comfort. The 13 spacious rooms and suites come equipped with top-quality linens, flat-screen TVs and modern bathrooms. Best of all, the hotel offers personalised wine tours and tastings, and an acclaimed restaurant right downstairs.

La Cueillette   HERITAGE HOTEL €€€
(☑ 03 80 20 62 80; www.lacueillette.com; Château de Cîteaux, rue de Cîteaux, Meursault; r €209-365; ✳ ⓢ ☀) This grand old dame of a château, now converted into a hotel and spa, provides luxurious digs on the edge of Meursault village. The best rooms have private terraces overlooking the vineyards, while even guests in simpler units have access to amenities including the swimming pool and the elegant downstairs bar-salon with plush leather couches and rich burgundy-tone walls.

🍴 Eating

Excellent restaurants are tucked away in the villages of the Côte de Beaune. It's generally best to reserve ahead.

Le Chevreuil – La Maison de la Mère Daugier   MODERN FRENCH €€
(☑ 03 80 21 23 25; www.lechevreuil.fr; place de la République, Meursault; menus €25-48; ◷ noon-1.30pm & 7.15-9pm Mon, Tue & Thu-Sat) At this country-chic dining room in the heart of Meursault village, Chef Tiago is known for taking the cream of traditional Burgundian and giving it a 21st-century spin. For a taste of local tradition, don't miss the house's signature *terrine chaude de la mère Daugier*, a delectable blend of slow-cooked meats in a top-secret marinade, served here since 1872.

BURGUNDY OUTDOORS

Tasting fine wines often involves hanging out in dimly lit cellars, but Burgundy is also a paradise for lovers of the great outdoors.

The **Comité Régional de Tourisme de Bourgogne** (www.burgundy-tourism.com) publishes excellent brochures on outdoors options (including *Burgundy by Bike,* available at tourist offices) and has a list of boat-rental companies.

Hiking & Cycling

Burgundy has thousands of kilometres of walking and cycling trails, including sections of the GR2, GR7 and GR76. Varied local trails take you through some of the most ravishingly beautiful winegrowing areas in France, among them the vineyards of world-renowned Côte d'Or, Chablis and the Mâconnais (in Saône-et-Loire).

Rural footpaths criss-cross the Parc Naturel Régional du Morvan and some depart from the Morvan Visitors Centre, but you can also pick up trails from the Abbaye de Fontenay, Autun, Avallon, Cluny, Noyers-sur-Serein and Vézelay.

You can cycle on or very near the *chemin de halage* (towpath) of the Canal de Bourgogne all the way from Dijon to Migennes (225km). The section from Montbard to Tonnerre (65km) passes by Château d'Ancy-le-Franc; between Montbard and Pouilly-en-Auxois (58km), spurs go to the Abbaye de Fontenay and Semur-en-Auxois.

For details on Burgundy's planned 800km of *véloroutes* (bike paths) and *voies vertes* (green ways), including maps and guides, see www.burgundy-by-bike.com or stop at a tourist office.

Canal & River Boating

Few modes of transport are as relaxing as a houseboat on Burgundy's 1200km of placid waterways, which include the rivers Yonne, Saône and Seille and a network of canals, including the Canal de Bourgogne, the Canal du Centre, the Canal Latéral à la Loire and the Canal du Nivernais (www.canal-du-nivernais.com). Rental companies offer boats from late March to mid-November (canals close for repairs in winter).

France Afloat (Burgundy Cruisers; ☑ 03 86 81 54 55; www.franceafloat.com; 1 quai du Port, Vermenton) Based in Vermenton (25km southeast of Auxerre), with a second base in Tonnerre.

Locaboat Holidays (☑ 03 86 91 72 72; www.locaboat.com; Port au Bois, Joigny) Based in Joigny (27km northwest of Auxerre), with additional bases in Montbard, Mâcon and St-Léger-sur-Dheune (27km southwest of Beaune).

Hot-Air Ballooning

From about April to October you can take a stunning *montgolfière* (hot-air balloon) ride over Burgundy. Book through the Beaune and Dijon tourist offices. Some veteran outfits:

Air Adventures (☑ 06 08 27 95 39; www.airadventures.fr; rue de la Chaume, Civry-en-Montagne; ⊘ Apr-Oct) Based just outside Pouilly-en-Auxois, 50km west of Dijon.

Air Escargot (☑ 03 85 87 12 30; www.air-escargot.com; ⊘ Apr-Oct) In Remigny, 16km south of Beaune.

Le Cellier Volnaysien   BURGUNDIAN €€
(☑ 03 80 21 61 04; www.restaurant-lecelliervolnaysien.com; 2 place de l'Église, Volnay; menus €19.90-32.50; ⊘ noon-1.30pm Thu-Tue, 7.30-9pm Sat) Solid Burgundian cooking in a cosy stone-walled, vaulted dining room in the heart of Volnay.

Les Roches   BURGUNDIAN €€
(☑ 03 80 21 21 63; www.les-roches.fr; Bas Village, St-Romain; menus €29; ⊘ noon-1.30pm & 7-8.30pm Thu-Mon) Tucked between the hills along St-Romain's main street, this sweet little spot with a pleasant outdoor setting serves farm-fresh fare and well-executed Burgundian specialities, including snails and bœuf bourguignon.

★ **Auprès du Clocher**   GASTRONOMY €€€
(☑ 03 80 22 21 79; www.aupresduclocher.com; 1 rue Nackenheim, Pommard; lunch menu €26, dinner menus €32-72; ⊘ noon-1.30pm & 7-9pm Thu-Mon) Celebrated chef Jean-Christophe Moutet rustles up unforgettable gastronomic delights at Auprès du Clocher, in the heart of Pommard.

The ingredients are Burgundian, but imagination renders them into something new and elegant, accompanied by a superb wine list. The best tables enjoy direct views of the church bell tower for which the restaurant is named.

La Table d'Olivier Leflaive   BISTRO €€€
(☑ 03 80 21 37 65; www.olivier-leflaive.com; 10 place du Monument, Puligny-Montrachet; mains €21-30, dégustation menus €65-90; ⊙ 12.30-2pm & 7.30-9pm Mon-Sat Feb-Dec) This is *the* address in Puligny-Montrachet. The trademark four-course 'Repas Dégustation' (tasting menu) combines seasonal French classics with global flavours, and comes paired with six to nine wines served in 6cl glasses.

Le Charlemagne   GASTRONOMY €€€
(☑ 03 80 21 51 45; www.lecharlemagne.fr; 1 rte des Vergelesses, Pernand-Vergelesses; lunch menus €37-115, dinner menus €62-115; ⊙ noon-1.30pm & 7-9.30pm Thu-Mon) Vineyard views are perhaps even more mind-blowing than the imaginatively prepared dishes melding French cuisine with Asian techniques and ingredients. Look for it at the entrance of Pernand-Vergelesses. On Mondays, Thursdays and Fridays a cheaper lunch menu is offered (€37 to €42).

🛈 Getting There & Away

Bus 20, operated by **Côte & Bus** (☑ 03 80 21 85 09; www.coteetbus.fr; tickets €1.50), runs between Beaune and several Côte de Beaune wine villages, including Pommard, Meursault, St-Romain and La Rochepot.

Beaune

POP 22,418

Beaune (pronounced similarly to 'bone'), 44km south of Dijon, is the unofficial capital of the Côte d'Or. This thriving town's raison d'être and the source of its joie de vivre is wine: making it, tasting it, selling it, but most of all, drinking it. Consequently Beaune is one of the best places in all of France for wine tasting, and one of Burgundy's top tourist destinations.

The jewel of Beaune's old city is the magnificent Hôtel-Dieu, France's most splendiferous medieval charity hospital. Hidden beneath the city's streets is a labyrinth of wine cellars dating back several centuries, where some of the world's most prestigious wines repose.

⦿ Sights

The amoeba-shaped old city is enclosed by thick stone ramparts and a stream, which is in turn encircled by a one-way boulevard with seven names. The ramparts, which shelter wine cellars, are lined with overgrown gardens and ringed by a pathway that makes for a lovely stroll.

★**Hôtel-Dieu des Hospices de Beaune**   HISTORIC BUILDING
(☑ 03 80 24 45 00; www.hospices-de-beaune.com; 2 rue de l'Hôtel-Dieu; adult/child €7.50/3; ⊙ 9am-6.30pm mid-Mar–mid-Nov, 9-11.30am & 2-5.30pm rest of yr) Built in 1443, this magnificent Gothic hospital (until 1971) is famously topped by stunning turrets and pitched rooftops covered in multicoloured tiles. Interior highlights include the barrel-vaulted **Grande Salle** (look for the dragons and peasant heads up on the roof beams); the mural-covered **St-Hughes Room**; an 18th-century **pharmacy** lined with flasks once filled with elixirs and powders; and the multipanelled masterpiece **Polyptych of the Last Judgement** by 15th-century Flemish painter Rogier van der Weyden, depicting Judgment Day in glorious technicolour.

Maison des Climats   MUSEUM
(www.climats-bourgogne.com; Porte Marie de Bourgogne, 6 bd Perpreuil; ⊙ 9.30am-noon & 1.30-5.30pm Mon-Sat, 10am-noon & 1.30-4.30pm Sun) **FREE** Opened in 2017 to celebrate the two-year anniversary of Unesco's recognition of Burgundy's vineyards as a World Heritage Site, this free interpretive centre adjacent to the tourist office is a must-see for anyone interested in French wine. Exhibits include a 25-minute film, a wealth of bilingual educational displays focused on Burgundy's winegrowing traditions and wine-related terminology, and a nifty 9m-long map allowing visitors to explore the Côte de Beaune and Côte de Nuits *climats* (wine-growing parcels) in precise detail.

Moutarderie Fallot   FACTORY
(Mustard Mill; ☑ 03 80 22 10 10; www.fallot.com; 31 rue du Faubourg Bretonnière; adult/child €10/8; ⊙ tasting room 9.30am-6pm Mon-Sat, tours by arrangement) In business since 1840, Burgundy's last family-run stone-ground-mustard company offers guided tours through its mustard museum, focusing on mustard's history, folklore and traditional production techniques, with kid-friendly opportunities for hand-milling mustard seeds. Another tour focuses on Fallot's modern mustard-production facility. Reserve tours ahead at Beaune's tourist office. Drop-ins can sample and purchase more than a dozen varieties in the *dégustation* room.

Beaune

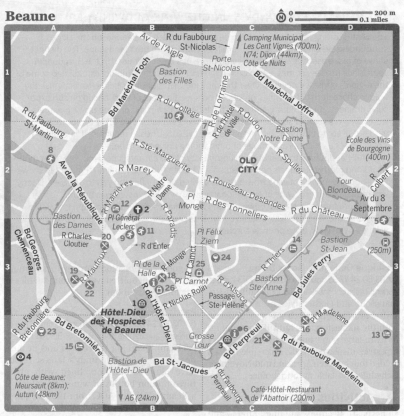

Beaune

◉ Top Sights
1 Hôtel-Dieu des Hospices de Beaune.... B3

◉ Sights
2 Basilique Collégiale Notre Dame...... B2
3 Maison des Climats.................................C4
4 Moutarderie Fallot.................................A4

◉ Activities, Courses & Tours
5 Bourgogne Randonnées D3
6 Chemins de Bourgogne.......................C4
7 Cook's Atelier.......................................C2
8 La Cave de l'Ange Gardien A2
9 Maison Joseph Drouhin........................B3
10 Patriarche Père et Fils..........................B1
   Safari Tours....................................(see 6)
11 Sensation Vin.......................................B3
   Vinéatours.....................................(see 6)

◉ Sleeping
12 Abbaye de Maizières B2

13 Chez Marie...D4
14 Hôtel des Remparts C3
15 Les Jardins de Loïs..............................A4

◉ Eating
16 Bistrot des Cocottes D4
17 Caves Madeleine C4
18 Food Market..B3
19 La Lune..A3
20 La Maison du Colombier.......................B3
21 Le Bacchus C4
22 Loiseau des Vignes...............................A3

◉ Drinking & Nightlife
23 La Dilettante A4
24 Le Bistrot du Coin................................C3

◉ Shopping
25 Alain Hess Fromager............................B3
26 Athenaeum de la Vigne et du Vin B3

THE CLIMATS: BURGUNDY'S UNIQUE WINE-GROWING HERITAGE

The wine-growing regions of the Côte de Nuits and Côte de Beaune, on the slopes surrounding Beaune, are deeply culturally entwined with their landscape. The distinct sense of place associated with local viticulture has been ingrained in the Burgundian spirit since medieval times, when Cistercian and Benedictine monks established some of the region's earliest vineyards. Over the centuries, Burgundians began to recognise the unique characteristics of wines produced on specific plots of land, based on sun exposure, drainage, microclimate and soil type. Individual *climats,* or winegrowing parcels, were given names and set apart with paths, *meurgers* (stone walls) and *cabottes* (vineyard huts), some of which survive to this day. In 2015, Unesco recognised Burgundy's 1247 *climats* as a 'cultural heritage of outstanding universal value'.

To fully appreciate the beauty and complexity of the *climats,* check out the giant multicoloured map at Beaune's new Maison des Climats (p444). The 9m-long display shows the elaborate mosaic of winegrowing plots in vivid detail, allowing you to discover exactly where that *grand cru* (wine of exceptional quality) you just tasted was grown.

For more fun with *climats,* download the free Balades en Bourgogne app from Côte d'Or Tourisme, which provides audio commentary on the viticultural history of each village as you walk, drive or cycle through.

Basilique Collégiale Notre Dame CHURCH
(☑03 80 24 77 95, tour info 03 80 26 21 34; place Général Leclerc; ☺9.30am-5.30pm) Built in Romanesque and Gothic styles from the 11th to 15th centuries, this church was once affiliated with the monastery of Cluny. It's notable for its extra-large porch and the five 15th-century tapestries displayed inside, accessible by a €3 guided tour between April and mid-November (schedules available at tourist office).

🏃 Activities

Underneath Beaune's buildings, streets and ramparts, millions of dusty bottles of wine are being aged to perfection in cool, dark cellars. Wine-tasting options abound.

Maison Joseph Drouhin WINE
(☑03 80 24 84 05; www.drouhin.com; place du Général Leclerc; guided tour & tasting €38; ☺tours 10am, 2pm & 4pm) This well-run tour explores the original 13th-century cellars of Beaune's Notre-Dame basilica, where the Drouhin family has operated its wine business for four generations. Fascinating historical tidbits along the way are almost as good as the wine tasting itself.

La Cave de l'Ange Gardien WINE
(☑03 80 24 21 29; www.lacavedelangegardien. com; 38 bd Maréchal Foch; tasting session €10) Beaune's most convivial wine-tasting experience is offered by the affable, bilingual Pierre and Nicole Jaboulet-Vercherre, whose family roots in the local winemaking business go back to 1834. Blind tastings of 10 wines last two hours or longer, with plenty

of good conversation thrown in as groups of a dozen people converge around tables in the long cellar room.

Patriarche Père et Fils WINE
(☑03 80 24 53 78; www.patriarche.com; 7 rue du Collège; audioguide tour €17; ☺9.30-11.15am & 2-5.15pm) Spanning 2 hectares and in business since 1780, Burgundy's largest cellars have 5km of corridors lined with about three million bottles of wine. (The oldest is a Beaune Villages AOC from 1904!) Visitors armed with multilingual audioguides can tour the premises in 60 to 90 minutes, tasting 10 wines along the way and taking the *tastevin* (tasting cup) home.

☞ Tours

The tourist office (p449) handles reservations for **hot-air-balloon rides,** and for **vineyard tours** run by companies including **Chemins de Bourgogne** (☑06 60 43 68 86; www.chemins-de-bourgogne.com; tours from €58), **Safari Tours** (☑06 33 40 19 14; www.burgundytourism-safaritours.com; tours from €45) and **Vinéatours** (☑06 73 38 37 19; www.burgundywine-tour.com; tours from €63).

🎊 Festivals & Events

Festival International Opéra Baroque & Romantique MUSIC
(www.festivalbeaune.com; ☺Jul) Held over four weekends in July, this is one of the most prestigious baroque opera festivals in Europe. Performances (Friday to Sunday) are held at the Basilique Collégiale Notre Dame and the Hôtel-Dieu des Hospices de Beaune.

Vente aux Enchères des Vins des Hospices de Beaune WINE

(Hospices de Beaune Wine Auction; www.hospices-de-beaune.com; ⊙ mid-Nov) On the third weekend in November, the Vente aux Enchères des Vins des Hospices de Beaune is the grandest of the Côte d'Or's many wine festivals. As part of this three-day extravaganza, the Hospices de Beaune holds a *vente aux enchères* (private auction) of wines from its endowment, 61 hectares of prime vineyards bequeathed by benefactors; proceeds go to medical facilities and research.

🛏 Sleeping

Beaune and the surrounding wine-growing villages offer a nice mix of midrange and top-end sleeping options. For budget accommodation, Dijon is a much better bet.

Camping Municipal Les Cent Vignes CAMPGROUND €

(☑ 03 80 22 03 91; campinglescentvignes@mairie-beaune.fr; 10 rue Auguste Dubois; per adult/child/site €4.80/2.50/6.90; ⊙ mid-Mar–Oct; 🛜) A flowery, well-equipped campground 700m north of the centre.

★ Les Jardins de Loïs B&B €€

(☑ 03 80 22 41 97; www.jardinsdelois.com; 8 bd Bretonnière; r €160, ste €185-195, 2-/4-person apt €280/350; P🛜) An unexpected oasis in the middle of the city, this luxurious B&B encompasses several ample rooms, including two suites and a 135-sq-metre top-floor apartment with gorgeous views of Beaune's rooftops. The vast garden, complete with rose bushes and fruit trees, makes a dreamy place to sit and enjoy wine grown on the hotel's private domaine. Drivers, rejoice – there's free parking!

Chez Marie B&B €€

(☑ 06 64 63 48 20; www.chezmarieabeaune.com; 14 rue Poissonnerie; d €85-120, tr/q €145/170; 🛜) At this peaceful haven on a residential street within a five-minute stroll of central Beaune, Marie and Yves make visitors feel right at home, sharing conversation and travel-planning advice (especially for cyclists) over breakfast in the sweet central garden. The four rooms, including two family-friendly apartments with kitchenettes, are impeccably simple and airy. Bikes are also available for rent.

In late 2018, Marie and Yves will embark on an open-ended round-the-world sailing journey with their young son; armchair travellers can follow their adventures on the website. Meanwhile, the B&B will remain open, watched over by a capable crew of family members who have been stepping in for years during similar bouts of wanderlust!

Hôtel des Remparts HISTORIC HOTEL €€

(☑ 03 80 24 94 94; www.hotel-remparts-beaune.com; 48 rue Thiers; d €70-150, ste €159-179; P🌸🛜) Set around two delightful courtyards, rooms in this 17th-century townhouse have red-tiled or parquet floors and simple antique furniture. Some rooms come with exposed beams and a fireplace, while others have air-con. Distinguished proprietress Madame Épailly presides over a regular regimen of renovations that keep everything up to snuff. Friendly staff can also hire out bikes. Breakfast costs €13.

Abbaye de Maizières HISTORIC HOTEL €€€

(☑ 03 80 24 74 64; www.hotelabbayedemaizieres.com; 19 rue Maizières; d €159-255, ste €350-468; 🌸@🛜) This character-laden, four-star establishment inside a 12th-century abbey oozes history, yet all 12 rooms have been

BURGUNDY CÔTE D'OR VINEYARDS

LEARN TO COOK LOCAL

Burgundy's rich, hearty cuisine combines smoky flavours and fresh ingredients. Why not take the opportunity to learn a few of the local techniques? Courses range from the informal to the chic.

➜ After a morning trip to the market, prepare and share a seven-course lunch with the dynamic mother-daughter duo who run **the Cook's Atelier** (☑ 06 84 83 16 18; www.thecooksatelier.com; 43 rue de Lorraine; all-day course incl lunch & wine pairings €395) in Beaune.

➜ The refurbished 17th-century kitchen at Château d'Ancy-le-Franc (p459) makes an evocative venue for four-hour classes from top chefs, followed by lunch accompanied by Burgundy wines.

➜ Join Michelin-starred chef Laurent Peugeot in the kitchen of his award-winning Le Charlemagne (p444), in the heart of Côte d'Or wine country.

➜ The proprietress of La Cimentelle (p461), Nathalie, will teach you how to make a *repas gastronomique* in a half-day course.

luxuriously modernised. Some rooms boast Cistercian stained-glass windows and exposed beams; those on the top floor offer views over Beaune's famed multicoloured tile roofs. There's no lift, but the friendly staff will help haul your luggage upstairs.

✖ Eating

Beaune harbours a host of excellent restaurants; you'll find many around place Carnot, place Félix Ziem and place Madeleine. Reserve ahead, especially in high season.

Food Market   MARKET €
(place de la Halle; ☉ 7am-1pm Wed & Sat) Beaune's Saturday food market is an elaborate affair, with vendors displaying their wares both indoors and on the cobblestones of place de la Halle. There's a much smaller *marché gourmand* (gourmet market) on Wednesday morning.

Bistrot des Cocottes   BISTRO €
(✐ 03 80 24 02 60; 3 place Madeleine; mains €13.50-20; ☉ 11.30am-11pm Tue-Sat) Tucked away on place Madeleine's quieter side, this classy-casual restaurant scores points for its all-day service (a rarity in Beaune, with snacks served between 4pm and 7pm), and its friendly and attentive waitstaff. But the clincher is the well-prepared, reasonably priced bistro fare, from grilled salmon with leek fondue to beef carpaccio with olive oil, basil and parmesan.

★ Caves Madeleine   FRENCH €€
(✐ 03 80 22 93 30; 8 rue du Faubourg Madeleine; mains €23-25; ☉ noon-1.30pm & 7.15-9.45pm Mon, Tue & Thu-Sat) Focusing on fresh-from-the-farm meat and vegetables produced within a 100km radius of Beaune, this cosy little restaurant changes its menu daily. Reserve ahead for a private table, or enjoy a more convivial experience at the long shared table backed by well-stocked wine racks.

Le Bacchus   BURGUNDIAN €€
(✐ 03 80 24 07 78; 6 rue du Faubourg Madeleine; menus lunch €14-16.50, dinner €23-31; ☉ noon-1.30pm & 7-9pm Tue-Sat) The welcome is warm and the food exceptional at this small restaurant just outside Beaune's centre. Multilingual co-owner Anna works the tables while her partner Olivier whips up market-fresh *menus* that blend classic flavours (steak with Fallot mustard) with tasty surprises (gazpacho with tomato-basil ice cream). Save room for desserts such as Bourbon vanilla crème brûlée, flambéed at your table.

La Maison du Colombier   TAPAS €€
(✐ 03 80 26 16 26; www.maisonducolombier.com; 1 rue Charles Cloutier; tapas & small plates €8-22; ☉ 6pm-midnight Mon-Fri) For a supremely cosy evening out, head for this 'gastro-bar' in candlelit 16th-century surrounds. Grab a seat beside the brick-walled open kitchen, on the sidewalk out front, or amid the labyrinth of stone-vaulted interior rooms to enjoy *tartines*, tapas-sized plates of cheese, charcuterie, salmon tataki and more, all accompanied by a good (if pricey) selection of wines.

La Lune   FUSION €€
(✐ 03 80 20 77 42; la.lune.restaurant@gmail.com; 32 rue Maufoux; items €6-27; ☉ 6pm-1am Tue-Sat) Grab a counter seat and enjoy chef Seiichi Hirobe's one-man show as he prepares French-Japanese fusion treats such as tuna tartare with poached egg and lotus root, or grilled scallops with *umeboshi* (Japanese pickled plum) sauce. The abundance of fresh veggies offers a nice break from Beaune's normally richer cuisine, and long hours keep the place hopping well past midnight.

Loiseau des Vignes   GASTRONOMY €€€
(✐ 03 80 24 12 06; www.bernard-loiseau.com; 31 rue Maufoux; lunch menus €25-35, dinner menus €59-119; ☉ noon-2pm & 7-10pm Tue-Sat) For an upscale meal with your significant other, this Michelin-starred culinary shrine is the place to go. Expect exquisite concoctions ranging from caramelised pigeon to *quenelles de sandre* (pike-fish dumplings). At lunchtime even the most budget-conscious can indulge thanks to bargain-priced midday *menus*. In summer, the verdant garden is a plus.

🍷 Drinking & Nightlife

Le Bistrot du Coin   WINE BAR
(✐ 06 99 42 65 43; 2 place Ziem; ☉ 5pm-midnight Tue-Fri, from 10am Sat) This delightfully unpretentious corner bar boasts only a single stool inside, but that doesn't keep locals from crowding in day and night for glasses of wine, hard cider and platters of cheese and charcuterie. In warmer weather, the scene moves out under the trees on the square in front.

La Dilettante   WINE BAR
(✐ 03 80 21 48 59; 11 rue du Faubourg Bretonnière; ☉ noon-midnight Mon, Tue & Thu, to 1am Fri & Sat) One of the few places in Beaune that does a booming business even in the dead of winter, this relaxed wine bar serves a fabulous selection of wines and low-key nibbles such as croque monsieurs, soups, salads and small plates of cheese, Iberian ham and local charcuterie.

🛍 Shopping

Athenaeum de la Vigne et du Vin   BOOKS
(☑ 03 80 25 08 30; www.athenaeumfr.com; 5 rue
de l'Hôtel-Dieu; ⊙10am-7pm) This fabulous
bookshop stocks thousands of titles, including many in English, covering everything
from wine tasting to oenology (the art and
science of winemaking) to gastronomy to
wine literature and essays. There's also a
nice selection of wine-related gifts.

Alain Hess Fromager   FOOD
(☑ 03 80 24 73 51; www.fromageriealainhess.com;
7 place Carnot; ⊙9am-12.15pm & 2.30-7.15pm Mon-
Fri, 8.30am-7.15pm Sat year-round, plus 10am-1pm
Sun Easter-Dec) This treasure trove of gourmet regional foodstuffs, including cheeses,
mustards and wines, will tempt the devil
in you. Don't miss the Délice de Pommard,
the house's signature cheese. Also look for
Burgundy's famous Appellation d'Origine
Protégée (AOP) cheeses: strong, creamy,
orange-skinned Époisses, invented by
16th-century Cistercian monks; and elegant
little wheels of soft white Chaource.

ℹ Information

Tourist Office (☑ 03 80 26 21 30; www.
beaune-tourisme.fr; 6 bd Perpreuil; ⊙9am-
6.30pm Mon-Sat, to 6pm Sun Apr-Oct,
shorter hrs Nov-Mar) Has lots of brochures
about the town and nearby vineyards. An
annexe (www.beaune-tourisme.fr; 1 rue de
l'Hôtel-Dieu; ⊙10am-1pm & 2-6pm daily Apr-
Oct, to 5.30pm Mon-Sat Nov-Mar) opposite
the Hôtel-Dieu keeps shorter hours.

ℹ Getting There & Around

BICYCLE

Bourgogne Randonnées (☑ 03 80 22 06
03; www.bourgogne-randonnees.fr; 7 av du 8
Septembre; bikes per day/week from €19/96;
⊙9am-noon & 1.30-6pm Mon-Sat, 10am-noon
& 2-6pm Sun Mar-Oct) Rents everything you
need to explore the area by bike (bikes, helmets, panniers, baby seats, tandems) and offers excellent advice on local cycling itineraries.

BUS

Bus 44, operated by **Transco** (p441), links
Beaune with Dijon (€1.50, 1¼ hours, seven
Monday to Saturday, two on Sunday), stopping
at Côte d'Or villages such as Gevrey-Chambertin, Vougeot, Nuits-St-Georges and Aloxe-
Corton. In Beaune, buses stop along the boulevards around the old city. Services are reduced
in July and August. Get timetables online or at
the tourist office.

TRAIN

Beaune's train station is located around 250m
east of the old town along av du 8 Septembre.
Trains connect the following places:
Dijon €10, 20 to 30 minutes, 40 daily
Lyon Part-Dieu from €27.20, 1¾ hours, 16 daily
Mâcon €15, 55 minutes, 19 daily
Nuits-St-Georges €5, 10 minutes, 20 daily
Paris €35, 3½ hours, five direct daily

WORTH A TRIP

ABBAYE DE CITEAUX

Rising from bucolic fields between Dijon and Beaune, the restored 11th-century **Abbaye
de Cîteaux** (☑ 03 80 61 32 58; www.citeaux-abbaye.com; D996, St-Nicolas-lès-Cîteaux; adult/
child guided tour €7.50/5, video €3/1.50, tour & video €8.50/6; ⊙tours 10.30am-4.30pm Wed-Sat,
12.15-4.30pm Sun late Apr–early Oct) – founded in 1098 as the original abbey of the Cistercian
monks – is well worth visiting for its historical significance. Seasonal 1¼-hour guided tours
(in French, with printed English commentary) depart hourly, and reservations are essential;
phone or email ahead. There's also an audiovisual presentation on monastic life, available
with or without the tour. The boutique sells edibles from monasteries around France, including the abbey's own cheese.

In contrast to the showy Benedictines of Cluny, the medieval Cistercian order was
known for its austerity, discipline and humility, and for the productive manual labour of
its monks, one result of which was ground-breaking wine-producing techniques. The abbey enjoyed phenomenal growth in the 12th century under St Bernard (1090–1153), and
some 600 Cistercian abbeys soon stretched from Scandinavia to the Near East. Cîteaux
was virtually destroyed during the Revolution and the monks didn't return until 1898, but
today it is home to about 35 monks. Visitors may attend daily prayers and Sunday Mass
(10.30am) year-round.

The abbey, 13km east of Nuits-St-Georges via the D116 or D8, is best reached by private vehicle or by taxi from the Nuits-St-Georges train station.

Pays d'Auxois

West of Dijon, along and around the Canal de Bourgogne, the Pays d'Auxois is a rolling land of mustard fields, wooded hills and escarpments dotted with fortified hilltop towns, including Semur-en-Auxois. Tucked into this verdant landscape are a pair of exceptional historical sites, the Cistercian abbey of Fontenay and the MuséoParc Alésia historical museum.

Semur-en-Auxois & Around

POP 4462

Don't miss Semur-en-Auxois, an incredibly picturesque, small fortress town. Perched on a granite spur and surrounded by a hairpin turn in the River Armançon, it is guarded by four massive pink-granite bastions, and the centre is laced with cobbled lanes flanked by attractive houses. At night the ramparts are illuminated, which adds to the appeal.

BURGUNDY PAYS D'AUXOIS

◉ Sights

Most of the old city was built when Semur was an important religious centre boasting six monasteries. Just beyond the tourist office, pass through two concentric medieval gates, **Porte Sauvigne** (1417) and fortified **Porte Guillier** (14th century) to reach pedestrianised **rue Buffon**, lined with 17th-century houses. Further on, the **Promenade du Rempart** affords panoramic views from atop Semur's medieval battlements. Don't worry about the menacing cracks in the 44m-high **Tour de la Orle d'Or** – they've been there since 1589!

Collégiale Notre Dame   CHURCH
(⊘ 9am-6.30pm Apr-Oct, to 5.45pm Nov-Mar) A stained-glass window (1927) and a plaque commemorating American soldiers who fell in France in WWI are inside this twin-towered, Gothic collegiate church.

MuséoParc Alésia   ARCHAEOLOGICAL SITE
(www.alesia.com; Alise-Ste-Reine; adult/child museum €10/6, Gallo-Roman site €4/2.50, both €12/7; ⊘ 10am-5pm mid-Feb–Mar & Nov, to 6pm Apr-Jun, Sep & Oct, to 7pm Jul & Aug; 🅿) This sensational interactive museum and historic theme park is well worth the drive from Dijon (67km) or Semur-en-Auxois (16km). This was the historic site of Alésia, the camp where Vercingétorix, the chief of the Gaulish coalitions, was defeated by Julius Caesar after a long siege. The defeat marked the end of the Gal-

lic/Celtic heritage in France. You can visit the well-organised interpretative centre as well as the vestiges of the Gallo-Roman city that developed after the battle.

Grand Forge du Buffon   HISTORIC SITE
(📞 03 80 92 10 35; www.grandeforgedebuffon.fr; adult/child €8/6.50; ⊘ 10am-12.30pm & 2.30-6pm Wed-Mon Apr-Jun & Sep–mid-Nov, 10am-6pm daily Jul & Aug) The beautiful Grand Forge de Buffon sits 23km north of Semur-en-Auxois on the pastoral banks of the Brenne Canal. One of the first fully integrated factories, it was built in 1778 by Georges-Louis Leclerc, the Count of Buffon and a mathematician and naturalist. The forge's existing buildings include a blast furnace that was used for casting molten metals and a supply channel with paddlewheel. Take the D980 north from Semur-en-Auxois, then the D905, following signs for the village of Buffon.

🛏 Sleeping & Eating

Hôtel des Cymaises   HOTEL €
(📞 03 80 97 21 44; www.hotelcymaises.com; 7 rue du Renaudot; s €69-75, d/tr/q €79/92/113; 🅿 🛜) In the heart of the old town, this grand 18th-century *maison bourgeoise* has comfortable, slightly worn rooms, some with exposed wooden beams, and a bright verandah for breakfast. There's free parking in the courtyard, and a relaxing garden out back.

⭐**La Porte Guillier**   B&B €€
(📞 03 80 97 31 19; www.laporteguillier.com; 5bis rue de l'Ancienne Comédie; d €100-120, tr/q €140/170; 🛜) To really soak up the town's atmosphere, stay at this delightful B&B housed in a fortified stone gateway dating from the 14th century. Three generously sized rooms sport plenty of charming old furniture, and two enjoy stellar views of medieval Semur's main street. Nothing too standard, nothing too studied; a very personal home with good breakfasts brimming with organic specialities.

Pâtisserie Alexandre   PASTRIES €
(📞 03 80 97 08 94; rue de la Liberté; ⊘ 7.30am-7pm Tue-Fri, 7am-1pm & 2-7pm Sat, 7am-1pm Sun) The speciality at this historic patisserie is *granit rose de l'auxois,* a pink confection laden with sugar, orange-infused chocolate, cherries, almonds and hazelnuts.

ℹ Information

The **tourist office** (📞 03 80 97 05 96; www.tourisme-semur.fr; 2 place Gaveau; ⊘ 9.30am-12.15pm & 2-6pm Mon-Sat year-round, plus

DON'T MISS

UNESCO WORLD TREASURE: FONTENAY

Founded in 1118 and enshrined as a Unesco World Heritage site, **Abbaye de Fontenay** (Fontenay Abbey; ☑ 03 80 92 15 00; www.abbayedefontenay.com; adult/child self-guided tour €10/7, guided tour €12.50/7.90; ⊙ 10am-6pm Apr-Oct, 10am-noon & 2-5pm Nov-Mar) offers a fascinating glimpse of the austere, serene surroundings in which Cistercian monks lived lives of contemplation and manual labour. Set at road's end in a bucolic wooded valley beside a tranquil stream, this restored masterpiece of medieval monastic architecture includes an unadorned Romanesque church, a barrel-vaulted monks' dormitory, and Europe's earliest metallurgical forge, complete with a working reconstruction of the hydraulic hammer used by 13th-century monks.

A self-guided tour, with printed information in six languages, is available year-round. From April to October, optional guided tours (in French with multilingual handout) are available at 10am, 11am, noon, 1.45pm, 2.45pm, 4pm and 5pm.

From the parking lot, the GR213 trail forms part of two verdant walking circuits: one to Montbard (13km return), the other (11.5km) through Touillon and Le Petit Jailly. Maps and extensive guides to plant life are available in the abbey shop.

Fontenay is 25km north of Semur-en-Auxois. The nearest train station is Montbard, where fast trains connect regularly with Dijon (€15, 35 minutes). A taxi from Montbard to the abbey costs about €15 (more on Sundays and holidays).

Sun Jun–mid-Sep; 🛜) has a free walking-tour brochure in English.

🛈 Getting There & Away

Transco (p441) operates bus 49 (two to six daily) to Dijon (€1.50, 1½ hours) and Avallon (€1.50, 40 minutes). Bus 70 goes to Montbard (€1.50, 20 minutes, three to nine daily) on the Paris–Dijon rail line.

Châtillon-sur-Seine

POP 5813

On the northern fringes of Burgundy, Châtillon-sur-Seine has a picturesque old quarter by the river, well-preserved buildings and a not-to-be-missed archaeology museum. It's also a good base if you want to explore the atmospheric Forêt de Châtillon and the Châtillonnais vineyards.

⊙ Sights

★**Musée du Pays Châtillonnais Trésor de Vix**   MUSEUM
(☑ 03 80 91 24 67; www.musee-vix.fr; 14 rue de la Libération; adult/child €7/3.50; ⊙ 10am-5.30pm Wed-Mon Sep-Jun, daily Jul & Aug) Châtillon's main claim to fame is the **Trésor de Vix** (Vix Treasure), a collection of Celtic, Etruscan and Greek objects from the 6th century BC on display at the Musée du Pays Châtillonnais. The outstanding collection includes an exquisitely ornamented, jaw-droppingly massive Greek krater; easily the largest known bronze vessel from the ancient world, it's 1.64m high, with a weight of 208.6kg and a capacity of 1100L!

The treasure was discovered in 1953 in the tomb of the Dame de Vix, a Celtic princess who controlled the trade in Cornish tin in the 6th century. Mined in Cornwall, the tin was brought by boat up the Seine as far as Vix and then carried overland to the Saône and the Rhône, whence river vessels conveyed it south to Marseille and its most eager consumers, the Greeks.

🐾 Activities

Wine Tasting

Among the wines produced in the Châtillonnais vineyards, north of town, is Burgundy's own bubbly, Crémant de Bourgogne. Follow the 120km-long **Route du Crémant** (www.routeducremant.fr), marked by white-on-brown signs to the vineyards, and allow plenty of time for a wine tasting. The tourist office (p452) can supply you with the useful map/brochure, *Route du Crémant* (free). The Champagne region's Côte des Bar vineyards are just a few kilometres further north.

Walking

The town's commercial centre, rebuilt after WWII, is bordered by two branches of the Seine, here hardly more than a stream. For an enjoyable walk with fine views, start at the lovely green park surrounding **Source de la Douix** and climb up to the crenellated 16th-century **Tour de Gissey**.

The immense **Forêt de Châtillon** begins a few kilometres southeast of Châtillon. This peaceful haven is covered mainly by broad-leaved trees, including beeches and hornbeams, and criss-crossed by walking trails.

🛏 Sleeping & Eating

Châtillon has some good informal eateries, including a pair of pizzerias and a crêperie.

Sylvia Hôtel   HOTEL €
(📞03 80 91 02 44; www.sylvia-hotel.com; 9 av de la Gare; r €47-84; 🅿 @ 🛜) At the western edge of town, this elegant mansion offers 16 simple yet welcoming rooms, a delightful garden and a bright upstairs sitting room with billiard table.

ℹ Information

Tourist Office (📞03 80 91 13 19; www.chatillonnais-tourisme.fr; 1 rue du Bourg; ⊙9am-noon & 2-6pm Mon-Sat Sep-Jun, 9am-7pm Mon-Sat & 10am-1pm Sun Jul & Aug)

ℹ Getting There & Away

Bus 50, operated by **Transco** (p441), goes to Dijon (€1.50, 1¾ hours, two to four daily). SNCF buses go to the TGV train station in Montbard (€10, 40 minutes, three to eight daily).

CHEESE PAIRINGS
• •

What else would you pair with your glass of wine but one of Burgundy's Appellation d'Origine Protégé (AOP) cheeses? There are three, all made with cow's milk.

➡ Époisses – Invented in the 16th century by the monks at Abbaye de Cîteaux, Époisses is a soft, round, orange-skinned white cheese. It takes a month to make, using washes of salt water, rainwater and Marc de Bourgogne (local pomace brandy), resulting in a strong, creamy flavour.

➡ Soumaintrain – Milder than Époisses, Soumaintrain has a spicy burst at the end of a tasting. Similar in appearance to Époisses.

➡ Chaource – These elegant little wheels of soft white cheese can be quite fluid when young. A bit like Camembert, they are ideal with sparkling wines.

YONNE

The Yonne *département*, roughly midway between Dijon and Paris, has long been Burgundy's northern gateway. The verdant countryside harbours the magical hilltop village of Vézelay (a Unesco World Heritage site), the white-wine powerhouse Chablis, and the picturesque medieval town of Noyers-sur-Serein, along with off-the-beaten-track treasures in places like Tonnerre and La Puisaye. Canal boats cruise from the ancient river port of Auxerre and other towns throughout the region.

Auxerre

POP 36,569

The alluring riverside town of Auxerre (oh-sair) has been a port since Roman times. The old city clambers up the hillside on the west bank of the River Yonne. Wandering through the maze of its cobbled streets you come upon Roman remains, Gothic churches and timber-framed medieval houses. Views span a jumble of belfries, spires and steep tiled rooftops.

The area south of the city, anchored by the pretty town of Irancy, is known for its ruby-red wines. Auxerre also makes a good base for exploring northern Burgundy, including Chablis, and is an excellent place to hire a canal boat. Quiet backroads and walking trails thread through the forests, fields, pastures and vineyards of the surrounding Auxerrois and Tonnerrois countryside, making for some appealing walking and cycling.

⊙ Sights

Get wonderful city views from **Pont Paul Bert** (1857) and the arched footbridge opposite the main tourist office. For a self-guided architectural walking tour, pick up a copy of the *In the Steps of Cadet Roussel* brochure (€1.50) from the tourist office (p455).

Abbaye St-Germain   ABBEY
(📞03 86 18 02 90; www.auxerre.culture.gouv.fr; place St-Germain; guided tours €4.50-7.50; ⊙9am-noon & 2-6pm Apr-Sep, to 5pm Oct-Mar, closed Tue year-round) This ancient abbey with its dramatic flying buttresses began as a basilica above the tomb of St Germain, the 5th-century bishop who made Auxerre an important Christian centre. By medieval times it was attracting pilgrims from all over Europe. The **crypt**, accessible by tour (in French, with English handout),

Auxerre

N 0 ———————— 200 m
0 ———————— 0.1 miles

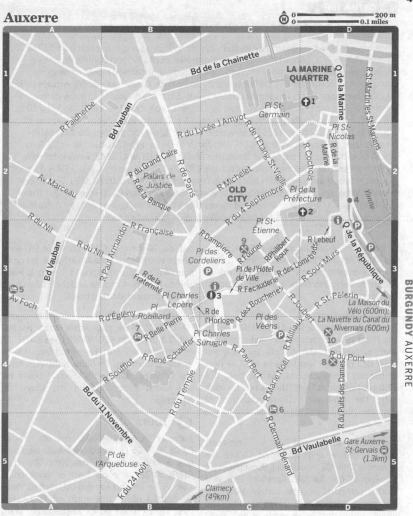

BURGUNDY AUXERRE

Auxerre

◎ Sights
1 Abbaye St-Germain	D1
2 Cathédrale St-Étienne	D2
3 Tour de l'Horloge	C3

◐ Activities, Courses & Tours
4 Bateaux Touristiques de l'Auxerrois	D2

◉ Sleeping
5 Hôtel Le Parc des Maréchaux	A3
6 La Maison des Randonneurs	C4
7 Le Relais des Saints Pères	B4

◈ Eating
8 Bistro L'Aspérule	D4
9 La Pause Gourmande	C3
10 La P'tite Beursaude	D4

contains some of Europe's finest examples of Carolingian architecture. Supported by 1200-year-old oak beams, the walls and vaulted ceiling are decorated with 9th-century frescoes; the innermost sanctum houses St Germain's tomb.

WORTH A TRIP

IRANCY & COULANGES-LA-VINEUSE WINE COUNTRY

Ask locals where they go to taste western Burgundy's wines and many say: **Irancy**. This relatively new AOC (Appellation d'Origine Contrôlée, as of 1999) predominantly uses a pinot noir grape, and the growing villages are extremely picturesque. Set in rolling hills and spring-blooming cherry orchards, Irancy and nearby **Coulanges-la-Vineuse**, which has its own appellation, lie 13km south of Auxerre. Explore and you'll find many domaines from which to sample. In Irancy you can visit organic producer **Thierry Richoux** (☑ 03 86 42 21 60; 73 rue Soufflot, Irancy; ⊙ 9.30am-noon & 1.30-6pm). In Coulanges-la-Vineuse stop by **Clos du Roi** (☑ 03 86 42 25 72; www.closduroi.com; 17 rue André Vildieu, Coulanges-la-Vineuse; tours incl wine-tasting from €7; ⊙ 8am-7pm Mon-Fri, 9am-7pm Sat, 10am-noon & 3-5pm Sun) or, in the heart of the village, **Domaine Maltoff** (☑ 03 86 42 32 48; www.maltoff.com; 20 rue d'Aguesseau, Coulanges-la-Vineuse; s/d/q €70/80/135; ☎), which is also a B&B. Just north of Irancy, another worthwhile stop is **Domaine Bersan** (☑ 03 86 53 33 73; www.bersan.fr; 20 rue du Docteur Tardieux, St-Bris-le-Vineux; ⊙ 8.30am-noon & 1.30-6pm Mon-Sat, 10am-12.15pm Sun) in **St-Bris-le-Vineux**, a winery that's been in the same family for more than five centuries; ask to tour the medieval cellars below the tasting room.

Housed around the abbey's cloister, the **Musée d'Art et d'Histoire** (admission free) displays rotating contemporary art exhibits, prehistoric artefacts and Gallo-Roman sculptures.

Tour de l'Horloge   TOWER
(btwn place de l'Hôtel de Ville & rue de l'Horloge) In the heart of Auxerre's partly medieval commercial precinct, the golden, spire-topped Tour de l'Horloge was built in 1483 as part of the city's fortifications. On the beautiful 17th-century clock faces (there's one on each side), the sun-hand indicates the time of day; the moon-hand shows the day of the lunar month.

Cathédrale St-Étienne   CATHEDRAL
(place St-Étienne; crypt adult/child €3/free, son et lumière show €5; ⊙ cathedral 9am-6pm, crypt 9am-1pm & 2-6pm Tue-Sat, 2-6pm Sun) This vast Gothic cathedral and its stately 68m-high bell tower dominate Auxerre's skyline. The choir, ambulatory and some of the vivid stained-glass windows date from the 1200s. The 11th-century Romanesque **crypt** is ornamented with remarkable frescoes, including a scene of *Christ à Cheval* (*Christ on Horseback*; late 11th century) unlike any other known in Western art. In July and August an hour-long **son et lumière (sound-and-light) show** is held Wednesday through Saturday at 10pm inside the cathedral.

⚡ Activities

Cycling options include the towpath along the Canal du Nivernais to Clamecy (about 60km) and Decize (175km); see www.burgundy-by-bike.com for a map. **La Navette du Ca-** nal du Nivernais (☑ 03 86 46 24 99; www.navette-nivernais.fr; 1 place Achille Ribain; per cyclist from €45), a trailer-equipped minivan, is available to transport cyclists and their bikes back to their original starting point.

La Maison du Vélo   CYCLING, BOATING
(☑ 03 86 46 24 99; place Achille Ribain; per 1hr/half/full day boats €20/60/85, bikes €4/11/20; ⊙ 9am-noon & 2-6pm Easter–mid-Sep) Down by the waterfront, La Maison du Vélo rents out bicycles along with electric boats for self-guided excursions on the Canal du Nivernais.

☞ Tours

Bateaux Touristiques de l'Auxerrois   BOATING
(☑ 06 30 37 66 17; www.bateaux-auxerrois.com; 1 quai de la République; 60min/90min/2hr cruise €12/16.50/23, three-hour lunch or dinner cruise €64; ⊙ Tue-Sun mid-Apr–mid-Oct) Across from the tourist office, this outfit offers a variety of river cruises on its 75-passenger boat, *L'Hirondelle*.

🛏 Sleeping

La Maison des Randonneurs   HOSTEL €
(☑ 03 86 41 43 22; www.maison-rando.fr; 5 rue Germain Bénard; dm/tw €19/38; ☎) Bordering a leafy park within easy walking distance of Auxerre's centre, this hostel is amazingly good value. It features three types of dorms (six-bed, four-bed and three-bed) along with singles and bunk-bed twins. Other perks include free wi-fi, bike hire (per day €18), laundry service (per machine €2) and a communal kitchen. Check-in is between 4pm and 7pm.

Le Relais des Saints Pères B&B€

(☏06 49 82 97 87; www.relaissaintsperes.fr; 12 rue Belle Pierre; d €70-90, q €130; �) This recently launched B&B in a 17th-century building with powder-blue shutters offers three comfortable doubles and a family room under the eaves, all within easy walking distance of the medieval city's attractions. Breakfast, including fresh-squeezed juice, seasonal jams and hot chocolate, is served on the outdoor terrace in good weather. Bikes (free) and childcare (per hour €10) are available.

Domaine Dessus Bon Boire B&B€

(☏03 86 53 89 99; www.dessusbonboire.com; 19 rue de Vallan, Vaux; s/d/tr/q €56/64/75/95; ☎) In sleepy riverside Vaux, 6km south of Auxerre, this family-run B&B offers impeccable rooms and plenty of peace and quiet. Friendly owners Catherine and André Donat, who have worked in organic viticulture since 2000, organise tours to local vineyards and share their extensive knowledge of the region's wines.

Hôtel Le Parc des Maréchaux HISTORIC HOTEL €€

(☏03 86 51 43 77; www.hotel-parcmarechaux.com; 6 av Foch; r €89-139; ⓟ☀☎⛱) Decorated in opulent 19th-century style and offering solid four-star amenities, this mansion of château-like proportions is a fine choice. The rooms, bar and common areas all brim with character. Opt for the quieter rooms that overlook the spacious private park out back. The pool is open from May to September.

✕ Eating

★**La Pause Gourmande** MEDITERRANEAN €€

(☏03 86 33 98 87; www.lapausegourmande-89.com; 1 rue Fourier; menu €25, incl 2 glasses of wine €32; ☺9am-5.30pm Tue & Thu-Sat, to 1.30pm Wed) This sweet, unpretentious lunchtime eatery near the cathedral features an ever-changing monthly *menu* built around fresh local produce and delectable desserts. Many of the gorgeously presented dishes come adorned with edible flowers from the greenhouse of friendly young owners David and Magali. Before noon and after 1.30pm, it doubles as a *salon de thé*, serving fine home-baked pastries.

La P'tite Beursaude BURGUNDIAN €€

(☏03 86 51 10 21; www.laptitebeursaude.fr; 55 rue Joubert; lunch menus €21-22, dinner menus €29-32; ☺noon-1.45pm Fri-Mon, 7.30-9pm Wed-Mon) Waitresses wearing traditional Morvan dress serve excellent fish and meat dishes at this cosy eatery in the medieval centre.

Ample dinner *menus* and bargain-priced lunches offer an introduction to Burgundian *cuisine du terroir* (traditional cuisine deeply connected to the land), which may include rib steak with Époisses cheese and *œufs en meurette* (poached eggs in red-wine sauce).

Bistro L'Aspérule FUSION €€

(☏03 86 33 24 32; www.restaurant-asperule.fr; 34 rue du Pont; lunch menus €22-30, dinner menus €29-34; ☺noon-1.30pm & 7.30-9pm Fri-Tue) Expect inventive cuisine with a Japanese twist at the classy bistro of Michelin-starred chef Keigo Kimura. From house-marinated salmon to breaded pork cutlets to Earl Grey crème brûlée, everything is beautifully presented, with lots of seasonal produce in the mix.

❶ Information

Tourist Office (☏03 86 52 06 19; www.ot-auxerre.fr; 1-2 quai de la République; ☺9.30am-12.30pm & 2-6pm; ☎) The main branch of Auxerre's well-run tourist office is on the riverfront just below the cathedral. Offers bike and boat rentals and free wi-fi. There is also a **branch** (☏03 86 51 03 26; www.ot-auxerre.fr; 7 place de l'Hôtel de Ville; ☺9.30am-12.30pm & 2-6pm) on place de l'Hôtel de Ville.

❶ Getting There & Away

BUS

TransYonne (☏08 00 30 33 09; www.yonne.fr/Territoire/Transports-dans-l-Yonne) runs infrequent buses (€2 regardless of destination) from Auxerre to Pontigny (line 2, 35 to 50 minutes), Chablis (line 4, 30 minutes), Tonnerre (line 4, one hour) and Avallon (line 6, one to 1¼ hours).

TRAIN

Trains run from **Gare Auxerre-St-Gervais** (rue Paul Doumer), 1km east of the centre:

Avallon €10, 50 minutes, two daily

Dijon €30, two hours, 10 to 13 daily

Paris Gare de Bercy €30, 1¾ hours, 10 to 14 daily

Sermizelles-Vézelay €10, 40 minutes, three daily

La Puisaye

The countryside west of Auxerre, known as La Puisaye, is a lightly populated landscape of woods, winding creeks and dark hills. The area is best known as the birthplace of Colette (1873–1954), author of *La Maison de Claudine* and *Gigi* (and 50 other novels) and is of particular interest because much of her work explores her rural Burgundian childhood.

◉ Sights

Chantier Médiéval de Guédelon   CASTLE

(☑ 03 86 45 66 66; www.guedelon.fr; D955, Treigny; adult/child €14/12; ☺ 10am-6pm Apr-Jun, to 7pm Jul & Aug, to 5.30pm Thu-Tue mid- to late-Mar, Sep & Oct) At this unique medieval building site, a team of skilled artisans, aided by archaeologists, has been diligently working since 1997 to build a fortified castle using only 13th-century techniques. No electricity or power tools here: stone is quarried on-site using iron hand tools forged by a team of blacksmiths, who also produce vital items such as door hinges. Clay for tiles is fired for three days using locally cut wood, and mortar is transported in freshly woven wicker baskets.

You can tour the site on your own or sign up for a guided visit (€3) in French or English. Wear closed shoes, as the site is often a sea of muck. Child-oriented activities include stone carving (using especially soft stone).

Guédelon is 45km southwest of Auxerre and 7km southwest of St-Sauveur-en-Puisaye, with plenty of signposts to guide you as you draw near. Admission is discounted if you purchase online.

Château de Ratilly   CASTLE

(☑ 03 86 74 79 54; www.chateauderatilly.fr; Treigny; adult/child €4/free; ☺ 10am-6pm late Jun–mid-Sep, reduced hrs rest of year) The elegant 13th-century Château de Ratilly sits in verdant countryside near Treigny. Interior rooms display a collection of pottery by the Pierlot family and host a changing series of excellent contemporary art exhibitions and concerts. Don't miss the magnificent 17th-century dovecote, with its original ladders and more than 1000 nesting holes for birds.

Musée Colette   MUSEUM

(☑ 03 86 45 61 95; www.musee-colette.com; Château de St-Sauveur, St-Sauveur-en-Puisaye; adult/child €7/5; ☺ 10am-6pm Wed-Mon Apr-Oct) Colette, author of *La Maison de Claudine* and *Gigi*, lived till the age of 18 in the tiny town of St-Sauveur-en-Puisaye, 40km southwest of Auxerre. The Musée Colette, in the village château, displays letters, manuscripts, two furnished rooms from her apartment in Paris' Palais Royal and photos featuring her iconic hairdo.

ⓘ Getting There & Away

To explore La Puisaye, you'll need your own vehicle. St-Sauveur is about 40km southwest of Auxerre via the D965 and D955. To reach Chantier Médiéval de Guédelon, continue 6km southwest of St-Sauveur on the D955; for Château de Ratilly, follow the series of signposted back roads 3.5km south from Guédelon.

Chablis

POP 2370

The well-to-do, picturesque town of Chablis, 20km east of Auxerre, has made its fortune growing, ageing and marketing the dry white wines that have carried its name to the four corners of the earth.

Chablis is made exclusively from chardonnay grapes and originated with the monks of Pontigny. Now it is divided into four AOCs: Petit Chablis, Chablis, Chablis Premier Cru and, most prestigious of all, Chablis Grand Cru. The seven *grands crus* are lovingly grown on just 1 sq km of land on the hillsides northeast of town.

◉ Sights

Southeast along rue Porte Noël are the twin bastions of Porte Noël (1778), formerly Chablis' southern town gate.

Nearby villages worth exploring include **Courgis**, which offers great views; **Chichée** and **Chemilly**, both on the River Serein; and **Chitry-le-Fort**, famous for its fortified church. The gorgeous hillside village of **Fleys** has a number of wineries.

Abbaye de Pontigny   ABBEY

(☑ 03 86 47 54 99; www.abbayedepontigny.com; Pontigny; guided tours €5; ☺ abbey 9am-7pm year-round, shop & grounds 10am-6pm Apr-Oct, 9.30am-4.30pm Nov-Mar) **FREE** Founded in 1114, Abbaye de Pontigny rises from the lush mustard fields 15km north of Chablis. The spectacular *abbatiale* (abbey church) is one of the last surviving examples of Cistercian architecture in Burgundy. The simplicity and purity of its white-stone construction reflect the austerity of the Cistercian order. On summer days sunshine filtering through the high windows creates an amazing sense of peace and tranquillity. *Discovering Pontigny* (€2.50), on sale in the gift shop, points out fascinating architectural details.

The Gothic sanctuary, 108m long and lined with 23 chapels, was built in the mid-12th century; the wooden choir screen, stalls and organ loft were added in the 17th and 18th centuries. Monks here were the first to perfect the production of Chablis wine.

🏃 Activities

Wine can be tasted and purchased at dozens of places around Chablis; the tourist office (p458) has a comprehensive list.

La Chablisienne
WINE

(☎ 03 86 42 89 98; www.chablisienne.com; 8 bd Pasteur; ⊙ 11am-6pm Apr, May, Sep & Oct, to 7pm Jun-Aug) To sample multiple vintages under one roof, try the cooperative cellar La Chablisienne, which carries six of Chablis' seven *grands crus*.

Walking

An amble through Chablis' vineyard-cloaked hills is the perfect way to connect with the *terroir* before tippling. Vineyard walks from Chablis include the **Circuit des Grands Crus** (8km), the **Circuit des Clos** (13km to 24km, depending on your route) and the **Circuit du Moulin des Roches** (15.5km to 33km). The tourist office (p458) sells topoguides and IGN maps.

Cycling

Cycling is a great way to tour the Chablis countryside. One flat, lush option is the 45km **Chemin de Serein**, which follows the old Tacot rail line southeast to Noyers-sur-Serein and L'Isle-sur-Serein. The tourist office (p458) hires **bikes** (per hour/half-day/full day €4/11/20) from Easter to early November.

👉 Tours

Au Coeur du Vin
WINE

(☎ 03 86 18 96 35, 06 80 68 23 76; www.aucoeur duvin.com; 1 rue Neuve du Prieuré, Chichée; tours €70-150) Tour the vineyards in a vintage Citroën 2CV.

Chablis Vititours
WINE

(☎ 06 11 47 82 98; www.chablis-vititours.fr, 1 chemin des Vignes, Aigremont; 90min/half-day/full-day tour €25/75/150) Tour the vineyards in an air-conditioned minibus.

🛏 Sleeping

La Menuiserie
B&B €

(☎ 0686743785, 0386188620; http://lamenuiserie. pagesperso-orange.fr; 11 rue du Panonceau; s/d/q from €40/60/100; P🖥) This is a peach of a B&B. Picture this: a former *menuiserie* (joiner's workshop) that has been renovated with a happy respect for the spirit of the place shelters one inviting room complete with exposed beams and stone walls. An upstairs mezzanine sleeps up to four additional people. Prices drop by 10% if you stay two nights or more.

Chambres d'Hôtes du Faubourg St-Pierre
B&B €

(☎ 03 86 42 83 90; www.faubourg-saint-pierre. com; 17 rue Jules Rathier; d from €80; P🖥) Occupying a stately townhouse, this B&B is of a standard that puts many hotels to shame. The mansion's character has been lovingly preserved during refurbishment and the three rooms are large, bright and romantic. Our choice is 'Pauline', with honey-coloured parquet flooring and a marble fireplace.

⭐ Maison du Moulin des Roches
B&B €€

(☎ 06 73 20 80 50; www.chablis-maisondu moulindesroches.fr; chemin du Moulin des Roches; d/q €125/195; 🖥) This lovingly renovated B&B, 1km outside Chablis beside an old mill on the River Serein, offers two spacious, elegantly appointed doubles and a pair of two-room family suites. Guests have access to a high-ceilinged fireplace room, a gym and (for a €60 surcharge) a relaxing *hammam*. Owners Thierry and Anne serve gourmet breakfasts featuring fresh-squeezed juice, local cheeses and home-grown fruit.

Hôtel du Vieux Moulin
BOUTIQUE HOTEL €€

(☎ 03 86 42 47 30; www.larochewines.com; 18 rue des Moulins; d €150-195, ste €245; P❄🖥) Housed in an 18th-century mill smack in the centre of Chablis, the understated and very contemporary five rooms and two suites afford luscious views of a branch of the Serein. The breakfast room has *grand cru* views. Breakfast is €12.

🍴 Eating

Le Syracuse
BURGUNDIAN, PIZZA €

(19 rue Mal de Lattre; pizzas €10-12, plat du jour €12.50; ⊙ noon-2pm Tue-Sun, 7-9pm Fri & Sat) Friendly and refreshingly down-to-earth, Le Syracuse serves everything from pizza to solid Burgundian *plats du jour* (€12.50, or €18.50 including coffee, dessert and a glass of Chablis). Take your pick of its two attractive settings: the stone-vaulted interior dining room or the sunny front terrace.

Les Trois Bourgeons
BISTRO €€

(☎ 03 86 46 63 23; http://les-trois-bourgeons. restaurant-chablis.fr; 10 rue Auxerroise; lunch menus €17-22, dinner menu €30; ⊙ noon-2pm & 7.30-9.30pm Tue-Sat) This recently launched spin-off of Au Fil du Zinc, Chablis' top table, offers the classic *bistronomique* experience – gastronomic dining with bistro atmosphere and prices. Run by a trio of Japanese chefs who honed their skills in Michelin-starred restaurants, it serves up everything from Burgundian meat-based classics to oysters to local trout.

★ **Au Fil du Zinc** MODERN FRENCH €€€
(☑ 03 86 33 96 39; http://au-fil-du-zinc.restaurant-chablis.fr; 18 rue des Moulins; 3-/5-/7-course menu €37/47/60; ⊙noon-1pm & 7.30-9pm Thu-Mon) At Chablis' top table, exquisite *menus* with nods to Japanese cuisine are served in a long open dining area perched over the River Serein, and on the adjoining terrace in summer. A nine-page list of Chablis wines complements a menu that changes every 10 days, making abundant use of seasonal vegetables, local fish, meat and cheeses. Desserts are phenomenal.

▼ Drinking & Nightlife

Wine bars and tasting rooms abound in the town centre.

S Chablis WINE BAR
(☑ 03 86 46 32 85; www.schablis.com; 8 rue Auxerroise; ⊙11am-6pm Mon, Tue, Thu & Fri, to 7pm Sat, 10am-4pm Sun) English-speaking owners Arnaud and Guillaume run this combination wine shop, tasting room and self-proclaimed *oenobistro*, where you can enjoy 3cl sampler glasses of Petit Chablis, Chablis, Premier Cru and Grand Cru wines accompanied by local cheeses, charcuterie or chocolates.

ℹ Information

Tourist Office (☑ 03 86 42 80 80; www.tourisme-chablis.fr; 1 rue du Maréchal de Lattre de Tassigny; ⊙10am-12.30pm & 1.30-6pm) Has free maps of town and the surrounding vineyards.

ℹ Getting There & Away

Chablis is 20km (20 minutes) east of Auxerre via the D965. **TransYonne** (p455) offers a very limited bus service between Auxerre and Chablis – exploring the region is much more convenient with your own vehicle.

Tonnerre

POP 4998

Tiny Tonnerre is full of surprises. The ancient Celtic spring at its heart is pure magic, and the recently opened Chevalier d'Éon museum, devoted to one of France's most colourful 18th-century figures, makes this a worthwhile detour for anyone passing near. Beyond the town's less inspiring outskirts, the surrounding Tonnerrois vineyards produce some excellent wines, and a pair of nearby châteaux offer a glimpse of the region's engaging Renaissance history.

◉ Sights

Fosse Dionne SPRING
(rue de la Fosse Dionne) Some 200L of water per second gushes from Fosse Dionne, a natural spring near the centre of Tonnerre that was sacred to the Celts and whose vivid blue-green tint hints at its great depth. Legend has it that a serpent lurks at the bottom. Forming a picturesque backdrop behind the great circular pool are a mid-18th-century washing house, a semicircle of ancient homes and a steep forested hillside.

Musée Chevalier d'Éon MUSEUM
(☑ 06 86 37 25 63; 22 rue du Pont; ⊙guided tours 10.30am, 3pm & 5pm Fri-Sun Apr–early Nov) Tonnerre's newest attraction is this house-museum, once home to the colourful Chevalier d'Éon, a gender-bending 18th-century diplomat and spy. The chevalier spent nearly half of his life assuming the role of a woman and dressing accordingly, spreading the fame of Tonnerre's wines across Europe during stints in St Petersburg and London. Access is by guided visit only (in French), led by the affable Philippe Luyt.

🛏 Sleeping

La Ferme de Fosse Dionne B&B €
(☑ 03 86 54 82 62; www.ferme-fosse-dionne.fr; 11 rue de la Fosse Dionne; s/d €69/82) In a late-18th-century farmhouse just above Fosse Dionne, this delightful hostelry has a *salon de thé* (tearoom) and antique shop. Owners Marina and Gérard speak French, English and Russian, and also offer dorm beds (per person €29) in their *gîte d'étape* (walkers' lodge) next door.

ℹ Information

The **tourist office** (☑ 03 86 55 14 48; www.tourisme-tonnerre.fr; 12 rue Général Campenon; ⊙9am-noon & 2-5pm Tue-Sat Sep-Jun, daily Jul & Aug) has maps of the city and the surrounding Tonnerrois vineyards, along with walking tour info.

ℹ Getting There & Away

By rail, Tonnerre is linked to Dijon (€20, one hour, 10 to 12 daily) and Auxerre (€10, 50 minutes, two direct trains daily; otherwise transfer in Laroche-Migennes).

TransYonne (p455) runs infrequent buses (€2 regardless of destination) to Chablis (line 4, 35 minutes), Auxerre (line 4, one hour), Noyers-sur-Serein (line 5, 30 minutes) and Avallon (line 5, 1¼ hours).

TOP THREE: CASTLE ENCOUNTERS

Château de Maulnes (📞 03 86 72 84 77; www.maulnes.fr; Cruzy-le-Châtel; adult/child €5/3; ⏱ 2-6pm Sat & Sun Easter-Jun & Sep, 10.30am-noon & 2-6pm daily Jul & Aug) The only château in France built on a pentagonal plan, and buttressed by five towers, the Renaissance-era Château de Maulnes, 24km east of Tonnerre, is a fascinating sight, though fans of interior decoration may find it disappointing: the rooms are entirely bare, and parts of the structure are obscured by scaffolding due to ongoing restoration work.

Château d'Ancy-le-Franc (📞 03 86 75 14 63; www.chateau-ancy.com; Ancy-le-Franc; adult/child €9/6, incl grounds $13/8, guided tour €1 extra; ⏱ 10.30am-12.30pm & 2-6pm Tue-Sun Apr-Sep, to 5pm Oct–mid-Nov, no midday closure Jul & Aug) The Italian Renaissance makes a cameo appearance at this imposing château, built in the 1540s by celebrated Italian architect Serlio. The richly painted interior, like the 32m-mural in the **Pharsale Gallery**, is mainly the work of Italian artists brought to Fontainebleau by François I. English-language handouts are available for self-guided tours. Don't miss Diane de Poitiers' private apartments on the ground floor, with their recently restored late-16th-century frescoes. Ancy-le-Franc is 19km southeast of Tonnerre (a 20-minute drive via the D905).

For a unique culinary experience, sign up for one of the cooking courses taught by top local chefs in the château's historic kitchens. The four-hour experience, including a multicourse lunch and pairings of Burgundy wines, costs €120 per person (minimum eight participants).

Château de Tanlay (📞 03 86 75 70 61; www.chateaudetanlay.fr; 2 Grande Rue Basse, Tanlay; adult/child €10/5; ⏱ tours 10am, 11.30am, 2.15pm, 3.15pm, 4.15pm & 5.15pm Wed-Mon late-Mar–mid-Nov) Dominating the northern edge of the tranquil riverside village of Tanlay, the elegant French Renaissance-style Château de Tanlay is surrounded by a wide moat and elaborately carved outbuildings. Guided tours of the interior are offered in French and English; highlights include the **Grande Galerie**, whose walls and ceiling are completely covered with *trompe l'œil*. Look for it 10km east of Tonnerre, via the D905 and D965.

Noyers-sur-Serein

POP 620

A must-see on any Burgundy itinerary, the picturesque medieval village of Noyers (nwa-yair), 30km southeast of Auxerre, is surrounded by rolling pastureland, wooded hills and a sharp bend in the River Serein.

Stone ramparts and fortified battlements enclose much of the village and, between the two imposing **stone gateways**, cobbled streets lead past 15th- and 16th-century gabled houses, wood and stone archways and several art galleries. Lines carved into the façade of the 18th-century **mairie** (town hall), next to the library, mark the level of historic floods.

Noyers makes a delightful base for walking. A pretty path runs along the village's eastern edge between the old town walls and the river, eventually climbing to a ruined hilltop château. The tourist office can provide information on several longer hikes in the region.

🏃 Activities

For a beautiful walk, take **chemin des Fossés** just outside Noyers' clock-topped southern gate, and follow it northeastwards between the River Serein and the village's 13th-century fortifications, 19 of whose original 23 towers are extant. A few hundred metres beyond the last tower, climb the marked trail to Noyers' ruined hilltop château (the site of ongoing excavations), then follow signs to the **Belvédère Sud** for spectacular perspectives on the town and the valley below.

🛏 Sleeping & Eating

Le Tabellion　　　　　　　B&B €
(📞 03 86 82 62 26, 06 86 08 39 92; www.noyers-tabellion.fr; 5 rue du Jeu de Paume; d €92; 🛜) Friendly, knowledgeable and multilingual owner Rita Florin runs this attractive B&B in a former notary's office right next to the church. The three tastefully furnished and charmingly rustic rooms are rife with personality, and there's a delightful garden at the back.

Côté Serein ACCOMMODATION SERVICES €€
(📞06 42 07 43 64; www.noyers-sur-serein.fr; 11 rue de Venoise; r €85-130; 📶🅿) Hosts Lionel and Marie-Noëlle rent out these 21 beautifully appointed rooms, suites and apartments in three historic Noyers buildings. Highlights include the Tour Madame, an atmospheric tower built into Noyers' medieval walls, complete with private panoramic terrace overlooking the River Serein, and the Loge, a two-level apartment in the town centre with its own full kitchen and plush living room.

Guests enjoy free use of rowboats and kayaks, and are welcomed (over a glass of Chablis) with oodles of tips for exploring the local area, including walking itineraries through the surrounding vineyards. Eleven of the rooms are housed within the charming Domaine de Venoise inside the old-town walls, while the Clos Malo, an additional ensemble of nine rooms outside the walls, comes with its own enclosed grassy courtyard and swimming pool.

Les Granges CAFE €
(📞03 86 55 45 91; www.lesgrangesnoyers.wix. com/les-granges; 7 promenade du Pré de l'Échelle; snacks from €5; ⊙7-10pm Fri, noon-6.30pm Sat-Mon) Harpist Haude Hodanger runs this inviting little tearoom between the river and the town's southern gate, serving sweet and savoury treats such as boeuf bourguignon, slow-roasted leg of lamb, trout with wild berries, zucchini tarts, fruit or chocolate charlottes and lemon pies, all accompanied by teas, coffees and local wines.

⭐ **Restaurant**
La Vieille Tour MODERN FRENCH €€
(📞03 86 82 87 36; rue Porte Peinte; menus €19-27; ⊙noon-2pm & 7.15-9pm Fri-Tue; 🖋) Adjacent to the clock tower at the entrance to the historic centre, young chefs Laurens and Hélène serve a delicious, unpretentious and ever-changing menu featuring creative takes on Burgundian staples. Vegetarian options are also available.

ℹ Information

Tourist Office (📞03 86 82 66 06; www. tourisme-serein.fr; 12 place de l'Hôtel de Ville; ⊙9.30am-1pm & 2-5.30pm Mon-Sat)

ℹ Getting There & Away

Travel in the area is most efficient with your own vehicle. Many of northern Burgundy's top attractions are within a 30- to 45-minute drive, including Auxerre, Vézelay, Abbaye de Fontenay and Semur-en-Auxois, making Noyers an excellent home base.

The LR05 bus, operated by **TransYonne** (p455), offers very limited 'on-demand' service from Noyers to Avallon and Tonnerre. The closest train stations are at Tonnerre (20 minutes by taxi) and Montbard (TGV station, 30 minutes by taxi)

Avallon

POP 7053

The once-strategic walled town of Avallon, on a picturesque hilltop overlooking the green terraced slopes of two River Cousin tributaries, was a stop on the coach road from Paris to Lyon in centuries past. At its most animated during the Saturday morning market, the city makes a good base for exploring Vézelay and the Parc Naturel Régional du Morvan.

◉ Sights & Activities

A pathway descends from the ancient gateway **Petite Porte**, affording fine views over the Vallée du Cousin. You can walk around the walls, with their 15th- to 18th-century towers, ramparts and bastions. For a bucolic walk or bike ride in the **Vallée du Cousin**, take the shaded, one-lane D427, which follows the gentle rapids of the River Cousin through forests and lush meadows. The tourist office sells hiking maps and has information on Parc Naturel Régional du Morvan.

Collégiale St-Lazare CHURCH
(rue Bocquillot; ⊙9am-noon & 2-6pm) Eight centuries ago, masses of pilgrims flocked here thanks to a piece of the skull of St Lazarus, believed to provide protection from leprosy. The early-12th-century church once had three portals, but one was crushed when the northern belfry came a-tumblin' down in 1633; the two remaining portals are grandly decorated in Romanesque style, though much of the carving has been damaged.

Musée de l'Avallonnais MUSEUM
(📞03 86 34 03 19; 5 rue du Collège; adult/child €3/ free, Wed free; ⊙2-6pm Wed-Mon Apr-Sep, Sat & Sun Oct, Feb & Mar, closed Nov-Jan) Founded in 1862, this wonderful small museum displays a series of expressionist watercolours by Georges Rouault (1871–1958) and an excellent art-deco silver collection by renowned designer and jeweller Jean Després (1889–1980). Upstairs, don't miss the permanent exhibition on the Yao people.

🛏 Sleeping

Camping Municipal
Sous Roche   CAMPGROUND €
(📞 03 86 34 10 39; www.campingsousroche.com;
sites per adult/child/tent/car €4.40/3/3.30/3.30;
☺ Apr–mid-Oct; 🛜🏊) Avallon's verdant,
well-maintained campground is 2km southeast of the old city, just across the road from
the River Cousin's forested banks. As of
2018, it boasts a brand-new heated swimming pool, along with a play structure, RV
hookups and wastewater disposal.

Hôtel Les Capucins   HOTEL €
(📞 03 86 34 06 52; www.avallonlescapucins.com; 6
av Président Doumer; d €54-68, q €92; ❄🛜) On
a quiet, plum-tree-lined side street near the
train station, Avallon's best-value hotel has
25 spotless, well-appointed rooms. Cheapest
are the 3rd-floor rooms under the eaves;
most comfortable are the newer units out
back. The attached **restaurant** (av Président
Doumer; 3-course menus €18-36; ☺ noon-2pm &
7-9.30pm) serves up well-prepared Burgundian dishes. There's free parking adjacent to
the small terrace and back garden. Breakfast
costs €8.50.

⭐ La Cimentelle   B&B €€
(📞 03 86 31 04 85; www.lacimentelle.com; 4 rue
de la Cimentelle, Étaule; s €80-110, d €96-125, q
€116-225; 🛜🏊) Situated on shady, extensive
grounds 6km north of Avallon, this château
houses two fantastic family apartments and
three luxuriously appointed rooms, each one
a bit different. One favourite, Hippolyte, has
a free-standing claw-foot tub in front of a
fireplace. Don't miss the spectacularly sited
swimming pool and the sumptuous *tables
d'hôte* (€46 including drinks). Nathalie, your
amenable hostess, speaks English.

🍴 Eating

Dame Jeanne   TEAHOUSE €
(📞 03 86 34 58 71; www.damejeanne.fr; 59 Grande
Rue Aristide Briand; snacks €9-13; ☺ 8am-7pm,
closed Thu & Sun; 🛜) Folks come from the
countryside for sweet and savoury breakfasts, delicious lunches or special pastry
treats accompanied by tea, hot chocolate,
coffee and wine. Sit in the back garden or
the cheerful 17th-century salon; it's just
north of the tourist office.

Le Vaudésir   BURGUNDIAN €€
(📞 03 86 34 14 60; www.levaudesir.com; 84 rue
de Lyon; menus €20-38; ☺ noon-1.30pm Tue-Sun,
7-9.30pm Tue & Thu-Sat) Freshness and value

for money are the hallmarks of this sophisticated bistro, 800m from the centre on the
road to Lyon. Dishes range from the quintessentially Burgundian (escargots in parsley-
cream sauce) to original inventions like
creamy risotto with Charolais beef chorizo.
There's outdoor seating in summer.

Auberge du Pot d'Etain   BURGUNDIAN €€€
(📞 03 86 33 88 10; www.potdetain.com; 24 rue
Bouchardat, L'Isle-sur-Serein; menus €29-50;
☺ noon-1.30pm Wed-Sun, 7-8.30pm Tue-Sat,
closed Feb & 2 weeks in Oct; 🛜) For a special
treat, stop in at this unexpected gastronomic
gem in the modest village of L'Isle-sur-Serein, 15km north of Avallon. The classically
Burgundian menu revolves around fresh
local meats, fish and vegetables, while the
epic 60-page wine list has been recognised
as one of France's top five. The *auberge* also
shelters nine immaculate, comfy, country-
style rooms (€65 to €98).

❶ Information

Tourist Office (📞 03 86 34 14 19; www.
avallon-morvan.com; 6 rue Bocquillot;
☺ 9.30am-12.30pm & 2-6pm Mon-Sat Sep-Jun,
10am-6.30pm Mon-Sat & 10am-noon & 2-4pm
Sun Jul & Aug; 🛜) Just south of the clock tower;
has free wifi.

❶ Getting There & Away

BUS

Transco (p441) operates bus 49 from the train
station to Dijon (€1.50, two hours, three to five
daily). Schedules are available online or at the
tourist office.

TRAIN

From the SNCF station about 1km northeast of the
centre, trains serve the following destinations:
Auxerre €10, 50 minutes, two daily
Paris Gare de Bercy €35, 2¾ hours, three daily
Sermizelles-Vézelay €5, 10 minutes, two daily

Vézelay

POP 440

The tiny hilltop village of Vézelay – a Unesco World Heritage Site – is one of France's
architectural gems. Perched on a rocky spur
crowned by a medieval basilica and surrounded by a sublime patchwork of vineyards, sunflower fields and cows, Vézelay
seems to have been lifted from another age.
One of the main pilgrimage routes to Santiago de Compostela in Spain starts here.

DON'T MISS

BEYOND THE BASILICA: VÉZELAY'S HIDDEN HILLSIDE CHAPEL

Vézelay's imposing hilltop basilica naturally commands the lion's share of tourists' attention, but a lesser-known treasure lies hidden just out back. Accessible by a lovely 15-minute stroll down a signposted trail behind the basilica, the Romanesque **Chapelle Ste-Croix** (La Cordelle; ⏱variable) – affectionately nicknamed 'La Cordelle' after the rope belts of the Franciscan monks who adopted this spot in the 13th century – slumbers on an idyllic hillside, with espaliered grapevines climbing its stone façade. This beautiful, simple chapel was built to commemorate Bernard de Clairvaux' preaching of the Second Crusade on this very spot in 1146. Nowadays there's no sign of the throngs that filled the fields nearly nine centuries ago. Rather, the chapel has become an off-the-beaten-track refuge for pilgrims and others seeking a place for peaceful meditation in the heart of the Burgundian countryside.

Bordering the northwestern tip of the Parc Naturel Régional du Morvan, the surrounding region harbours a handful of historic sites and quaint villages.

◉ Sights & Activities

The **park** behind the Basilique Ste-Madeleine affords wonderful views of the Vallée de Cure and nearby villages. A dirt road leads north to the old and new **cemeteries**.

Southeast of Vézelay at the base of the hill, the tiny village of **St-Père** has a Flamboyant Gothic church and an archaeological museum housing ancient Fontaines Salées finds. About 2km further south, the village of **Pierre-Perthuis** (literally 'pierced stone') is named after a natural stone arch; nearby, a graceful stone bridge (1770) spans the River Cure underneath a modern highway bridge.

★**Basilique Ste-Madeleine**   CHURCH
(www.basiliquedevezelay.org; ⏱7am-8pm)
Founded in the AD 880s on a former Roman and Carolingian site, Vézelay's stunning hilltop basilica was rebuilt between the 11th and 13th centuries. On the famous 12th-century tympanum, visible from the narthex (enclosed porch), Romanesque carvings show an enthroned Jesus radiating his holy spirit to the Apostles. The nave has typically Romanesque round arches and detailed capitals, while the transept and choir (1185) have Gothic ogival arches. The mid-12th-century crypt houses a reliquary reputedly containing one of Mary Magdalene's bones.

The church has had a turbulent history. Damaged by the great fire of 1120, trashed by the Huguenots in 1569, desecrated during the Revolution and repeatedly struck by lightning, by the mid-1800s it was on the point of collapse. In 1840 the architect Viollet-le-Duc undertook the daunting task of rescuing the structure. His work, which included reconstructing the western façade and its doorways, helped Vézelay, previously a ghost town, spring back to life.

Visitors are welcome to observe prayers or Mass. Concerts of sacred music are held in the nave from June to September; the tourist office (p464) and its website have details.

Musée Zervos   GALLERY
(☏03 86 32 39 26; www.musee-zervos.fr; 14 rue St-Étienne; adult/child €5/free; ⏱10am-6pm Wed-Mon mid-Mar–mid-Nov, daily Jul & Aug) This fantastic museum in the exquisite townhouse of Nobel Prize–winning pacifist writer Romain Rolland (1866–1944) holds the collection of Christian Zervos (1889–1970), an art critic, gallerist and friend of many modern art luminaries. He and his wife Yvonne collected paintings, sculptures and mobiles by Calder, Giacometti, Kandinsky, Léger, Miró and Picasso (for whom he created a pivotal 22-volume catalogue).

Maison Jules Roy   HISTORIC BUILDING
(☏03 86 33 35 01; Le Clos du Couvent; ⏱2-6pm Wed-Sun Apr-Oct) **FREE** Up near the top of town, the former home of Algerian-born writer Jules Roy (1907–2000) is an enchanting spot with fine views of the basilica. Walk around the beautiful gardens and see the writer's study.

Fontaines Salées   SPRING
(☏03 86 33 37 36; www.saint-pere.fr; adult/child €6/3; ⏱10am-12.30pm & 1.30-6.30pm Apr-Jun, Sep & Oct, 10am-6.30pm Jul & Aug) Located along the D958, 5km southeast of Vézelay, these ancient saltwater springs served as a salt production site in Neolithic times, then later a Celtic sanctuary (2nd century BC) and Roman baths (1st century AD). Tickets allow access to **Le Musée Archéologique** (☏03 86 33 37 31; St-Père; ⏱10.15am-12.15pm & 2.30-6.25pm, closed Nov-Mar) in St-Père, which holds finds from the site.

🏃 Activities

Vezélay is popular with walkers, in part due to its status as a major trailhead for the Chemin St-Jacques, the legendary medieval pilgrimage route to Santiago de Compostela, Spain (www.compostelle.asso.fr). The surrounding area is crisscrossed with well-maintained trails passing through lovely, pastoral landscapes. **Promenade des Fossés** circumnavigates Vézelay's medieval ramparts. A footpath with fine views of the basilica links Porte Neuve, on the northern side of the ramparts, with the village of **Asquins** (ah-kah) and the River Curc. The GR13 trail also passes by Vézelay.

AB Loisirs   OUTDOORS
(☑ 03 86 33 38 38; www.abloisirs.com; rue Gravier, St-Père; ☺ by arrangement) A few kilometres southeast of Vézelay in St-Père, this well-established outfit rents mountain bikes (€25 per day) and kayaks (€16 to €38), and leads outdoor activities such as rafting (€49), cave exploration (half-day €39) and hot-air-balloon rides (per person from €195). Bikes can be brought to your hotel. It's best to phone ahead.

🎆 Festivals & Events

Rencontres Musicales de Vézelay   MUSIC
(www.rencontresmusicalesdevezelay.com; ☺ Aug) This not-to-be-missed festival of classical music is held at various venues for four days in mid- to late August.

🛏 Sleeping

Auberge de Jeunesse et
Camping de l'Ermitage   CAMPGROUND, HOSTEL €
(☑ 06 38 77 15 33, 03 86 33 24 18; www.camping-auberge-vezelay.com; route de l'Étang; dm €16-18, sites per adult/child/tent/car €3/1.50/2/1; ☺ camping Apr-Oct, hostel year-round) For thrifty visitors who don't mind a short trek into town, this well-maintained venture 1km south of Vézelay is manna from heaven. After recent renovations, it now shelters well-equipped four- to 10-bed dorms with individual kitchenettes and gleaming en-suite bathrooms, flanked by a spacious, grassy camping area.

Cabalus   GUESTHOUSE €
(☑ 03 86 33 20 66; www.cabalus.com; rue St-Pierre; r €42-62) Atmospheric Cabalus offers four spacious rooms with sturdy beams, ancient tiles and stone walls in a 12th-century building right next to the cathedral. Decoration is sparse, reception can be rather dour, and cheaper rooms have shared toilets, but it's hard to beat for location, price and quirky rustic charm. Organic breakfasts (€10) are served at the cafe downstairs.

Au Moulin de Vézelay   B&B €
(☑ 03 86 32 37 80; www.gite-vezelay.fr; 48 Grand Rue, Soeuvres; d €67-88, q €118-140; ☎ ⚡) In tranquil countryside 9km south of Vézelay, this former mill has cosy rooms, a swimming pool, extensive grounds along a stream and nearby walking paths.

Hôtel SY Les Glycines   BOUTIQUE HOTEL €€
(☑ 03 86 47 29 81; www.vezelay-laterrasse.com; rue St-Pierre; r €67-181; ☎) Named for the wisteria that cascades over the front terrace, this lovingly renovated 18th-century house near the hilltop offers 13 rooms in various configurations. Most come with period features such as brick tile floors or exposed wood beams; some also have vintage mirrors, stone fireplaces, canopy beds or tapestries, and two boast basilica views.

Hôtel SY La Terrasse   BOUTIQUE HOTEL €€
(☑ 03 86 33 25 50; www.vezelay-laterrasse.com; 2 place de la Basilique; r €95-143; ☎) This recently renovated six-room hotel enjoys a plum position opposite the basilica, complemented by numerous modern amenities: top-quality bedding, sparkling new bathroom fixtures and large flat-screen

---

WORTH A TRIP

VAUBAN'S CHATEAU

Le Château de Bazoches (☑ 03 86 22 10 22; www.chateau-bazoches.com; Bazoches; adult/child €9.50/5; ☺ 2-6pm mid-Feb–mid-Mar, 9.30am-noon & 2-6pm mid-Mar–Jun & Sep, to 5pm Oct–mid-Nov, 9.30am-6pm Jul & Aug) sits magnificently on a hillside with views to Vézelay, 12km to the north. Built in the 13th century and visited by royalty including Richard the Lionheart, it was acquired by field marshal and military strategist Marquis de Vauban in 1675. The château displays a decent collection of 17th- and 18th-century paintings and furniture.

The real appeal for French history buffs will be the chance to see the very room where Vauban, the most acclaimed military architect of his time, drafted plans for 300 fortified towns all over France. The château is still owned by his descendants.

TVs. Unique touches include direct basilica views from the bath-tub in room 2 and a 12th-century stone window frame above the bed in room 4. The restaurant downstairs is among Vézelay's best.

✖ Eating

Restaurant SY La Terrasse
BISTRO €

(☏03 86 33 25 50; www.vezelay-laterrasse.com; place de la Basilique; mains €14-18, lunch menus €19-22.50; ⊙7-10pm Mon, noon-3pm & 7-10pm Tue-Sun) Stone walls, decorative tiled floors, smooth jazz and a roaring fire on chilly nights make this one of Vézelay's cosiest eateries. Menu options range from simple (the house special burger with pesto and parmesan) to fancier fare (wine-glazed scallops or rib steak with sautéed mushrooms). The bar, well-stocked with whiskeys, wines and rum, is a great spot for a nightcap.

À la Fortune du Pot
BURGUNDIAN €€

(☏03 86 33 32 56; www.fortunedupot.com; 6 place du Champ du Foire; menus €20-25; ⊙noon-3pm & 7-10pm Thu-Mon) Well placed in the square at the foot of Vézelay's main street, this French-Colombian-run restaurant with English iPad menus is at its best in sunny weather, when tables spill out onto the terrace. Build your own two- to three-course *menu* featuring Burgundian classics such as escargots, *tarte à l'Époisses* (Époisses cheese tart) and bœuf bourguignon.

Le Bougainville
FRENCH €€

(☏03 86 33 27 57; 26 rue St-Etienne; menus €30-34; ⊙noon-2pm & 7-9pm Thu-Mon; ☑) The smiling owner serves rich French and Burgundian specialities such as Charolais beef

BEER STOP

Microbrasserie **Brasserie de Vézelay** (☏03 86 34 98 38; www.brasseriedeveze-lay.com; rue du Gravier, St-Père; ⊙11am-9pm daily May-Oct, 1-5pm Mon-Fri, 2-6pm Sat Nov-Apr), is 3km southeast of Vézelay near the River Cure, and brews fine beers, all made according to Germany's strict purity law, using organic malt, hops, yeast and water from the adjoining Morvan park. Children can frolic on the grassy lawn while their parents sample the award-winning stout, *hefeweizen* and *rauchbier*. There's live music on the outdoor terrace in summer.

and tripe sausages. If you're growing weary of heavy regional dishes, fear not – Le Bougainville is also noted for its *Menu du Jardinier* (€28), which features vegetarian options – a rarity in Burgundy!

ⓘ Information

Tourist Office (☏03 86 33 23 69; www.vezelay tourisme.com; 12 rue St-Étienne; ⊙10am-1pm & 2-6pm Mon-Sat; ☏) Sells hiking maps and offers free wi-fi.

ⓘ Getting There & Away

Two daily SNCF buses go to tiny Sermizelles train station, 10km north of Vézelay (€5, 15 minutes). From Sermizelles, trains run south to Avallon (€5, 10 minutes) or north to Auxerre (€10, 40 minutes) and Paris Gare de Bercy (€35, 2½ hours).

PARC NATUREL RÉGIONAL DU MORVAN

The 2990-sq-km Morvan Regional Park, bounded more or less by Avallon, Vézelay, Corbigny, Luzy, Autun and Saulieu, and straddling Burgundy's four *départements* (with the majority in the Nièvre), encompasses 700 sq km of dense woodland, 13 sq km of lakes, and vast expanses of rolling farmland broken by hedgerows, stone walls and stands of beech, hornbeam and oak. The sharp-eyed can observe some of France's largest and most majestic birds of prey perched on trees as they scan for field rodents.

The park is also home to a museum and numerous other sites that pay tribute to the French *Résistance* fighters who defended the region during WWII.

◉ Sights

Several museums and historic sites around the park, collectively known as the **Écomusée du Morvan**, explore traditional Morvan life and customs. The most important of these are located in the village of St-Brisson.

For spectacular panoramic views of the Morvan, climb to **Le Signal d'Uchon**, a 681m granite outcrop at the park's southeastern corner, 22km south of Autun (a 30-minute drive).

★Bibracte
ARCHAEOLOGICAL SITE

(☏03 85 86 52 35; www.bibracte.fr; St-Léger-sous-Beuvray; ⊙year-round) FREE For anyone who's ever read an Astérix comic book and wondered how France's Celtic people really lived, Bibracte is a must-see. This hilltop stronghold of the ancient Gauls, together with the attached **Museum of Celtic Civilisation** (St-Léger-sous-Beuvray; adult/child incl audio guide €7.50/5.50; ⊙10am-6pm mid-Mar–mid-Nov, to 7pm Jul & Aug), offers a compelling portrayal of pre-Roman France in the years prior to Caesar's arrival. Crowning beautiful Mont Beuvray, 25km west of Autun, the site boasts expansive views and numerous walking trails, including the GR13, through high-altitude fields and 1000 hectares of forest.

Bibracte served as the capital of the Celtic Aedui people during the 1st and 2nd centuries BC. It was here, in 52 BC, that Vercingétorix was declared chief of the Gaulish coalition shortly before his defeat by Julius Caesar at Alésia. Caesar himself also resided here before the city decamped to Augustodunum (Autun). Stone remnants include ancient ramparts and several complexes of buildings, all in varying states of excavation. The adjacent museum explores the fascinating history of the site and its Celtic inhabitants.

You'll need your own wheels to reach Bibracte. The nearest train stations are at Autun, 25km to the east, and Étang-sur-Arroux, 17km to the southeast.

Musée de la Résistance en Morvan MUSEUM
(☑03 86 78 72 99; www.museeresistancemorvan. fr; St-Brisson; adult/child €6.50/4, combined ticket with Maison des Hommes et des Paysages €8.50/6.50; ⊙10am-1pm & 2-6pm daily Jul & Aug, closed Sat morning & Tue Apr-Jun & Sep–mid-Nov, closed mid-Nov–Mar) Commemorating the Morvan's role as a major stronghold for the Resistance during WWII, this museum chronicles key events and characters with photos, maps, letters, Vichy-era propaganda posters and other artefacts.

Maison des Hommes et des Paysages MUSEUM
(☑03 86 78 79 10; www.parcdumorvan.org; St-Brisson; adult/child €4.50/3.50, combined ticket with Musée de la Résistance €8.50/6.50; ⊙10am-1pm & 2-6pm daily Jul & Aug, closed Sat morning & Tue Apr-Jun & Sep–mid-Nov, closed mid-Nov–Mar) This thoughtfully organised museum invites visitors to contemplate the interplay between humans and the Morvan's landscapes over the centuries. Exhibits include a room-sized maquette of the park and the Salle des Panoramas, where touchscreens offer a chance to scan through photos of the region past and present. Displays are mainly in French.

🏃 Activities

The Morvan (a Celtic name meaning 'Black Mountain') offers an abundance of options to fans of outdoor activities. On dry land choose from **walking** (the park has more than 2500km of marked trails), **mountain biking**, **horse riding**, **rock climbing** and **orienteering**. On water, there's **rafting**, **canoeing** and **kayaking** on several lakes and the Chalaux, Cousin, Cure and Yonne rivers, along with excellent trout **fishing** in the River Méchet. Lac de Pannecière, Lac de St-Agnan and Lac des Settons have water-sports centres.

Guided walks of the park, some at night (eg to observe owls), are available from April to October, and there are children's activities in July and August. **Boat tours** are available at Lac des Settons.

In the mood for **swimming**? Head for Lac des Settons or Lac de St-Agnan, which offer 'beaches' (a loose term by anyone's standards).

The Morvan Visitors Centre has a comprehensive list of outdoor operators.

🛌 Sleeping & Eating

There's a good choice of campgrounds and B&Bs, as well as a few hotels, in the park. The Morvan Visitors Centre has a list of lodgings.

★Château de Villette B&B €€€
(☑03 86 30 09 13; www.chateaudevillette.eu; Poil; d €195-265, q €340-410, self-catering cottages per week €1250-1950; 🛜🐾) Set in a 5-sq-km private estate 11km south of Bibracte, this delightful 16th- and 18th-century château offers a glimpse of the luxurious life of Burgundy's landed aristocracy. After waking up in a ravishingly furnished period room, suite or cottage, you can cycle or look for escargots in the rolling countryside, play tennis or relax by the stress-melting pool. Reserve ahead.

Table d'hôte dinners (€55, on request) receive warm praise.

ⓘ Information

Morvan Visitors Centre (Maison du Parc; ☑03 86 78 79 57; http://tourisme.parcdumorvan.org; St-Brisson; ⊙10am-12.30pm & 2-5.30pm daily Apr–mid-Nov, Wed-Fri mid-Nov–Mar) Surrounded by hills, forests and lakes, Espace St-Brisson is a clearing house of park information, including hiking and cycling maps and guides. By car, follow the 'Maison du Parc' signs 14km west from Saulieu to St-Brisson. The website has details of local festivals, outdoor activities and lodging. Another useful site is www.patrimoinedumorvan.org (in French).

ℹ️ Getting There & Away

Park headquarters in St-Brisson is 33km south of Avallon via the D10 and 45km north of Autun via the D980 and D20. The easiest way to reach the park is by private vehicle. Limited public transport from Autun to the park is sometimes available in July and August; see the Mobigo website (www.mobigo-bourgogne.com) for details.

SAÔNE-ET-LOIRE

Midway between Dijon and Lyon, Burgundy's southernmost *département* Saône-et-Loire is an inviting land of rolling green fields criss-crossed by hedgerows and dotted with indigenous Charolais beef cattle. During the region's medieval heyday it was home to the largest church in all of Christendom, the magnificent abbey of Cluny. These days it's a sleepier place, but pretty châteaux and little-known Romanesque chapels still sit around every bend, hinting at Saône-et-Loire's long history and making this a delightful destination for a road trip.

Other regional highlights include the cathedral and Gallo-Roman ruins at Autun and the winegrowing villages around Mâcon, which produce some of France's finest whites. Several rivers, the Canal du Centre and some fabulous bike paths also meander through Saône-et-Loire's forests and pastureland.

Autun

POP 14,843

Autun is a low-key town, but almost two millennia ago (when it was known as Augustodunum) it was one of the most important cities in Roman Gaul, boasting 6km of ramparts, four monumental gates, two theatres, an amphitheatre and a system of aqueducts. Beginning in AD 269, the city was repeatedly sacked by barbarian tribes and its fortunes declined, but things improved considerably in the Middle Ages, making it possible to construct an impressive cathedral. The hilly area around Cathédrale St-Lazare, reached via narrow cobblestone streets, is known as the old city.

If you have a car, Autun is an excellent base for exploring the southern parts of the Parc Naturel Régional du Morvan.

◉ Sights & Activities

Autun's key sights surround the cathedral at the top of the old town. The city's Roman ruins are more widely dispersed around the urban periphery.

For a stroll along the city walls (part-Roman but mostly medieval), walk from av du Morvan south to the 12th-century **Tour des Ursulines** and follow the walls to the northeast. The **chemin des Manies** leads out to the Pierre de Couhard, where you can pick up the **Circuit des Gorges**, three marked forest trails ranging from 4.7km to 11.5km (IGN map 2925 SB Autun – Le Creusot).

The **water-sports centre** based at Plan d'Eau du Vallon (an artificial lake east of the centre) rents kayaks, paddle boats and bikes.

★ **Cathédrale St-Lazare**　　CATHEDRAL
(place du Terreau; chapter room adult/child €2/free; ⊙ cathedral 8am-6pm year-round; chapter room 10am-noon Tue-Sat & 2-6pm Tue-Sun Apr-Oct) Originally Romanesque, this cathedral was built in the 12th century to house the sacred relics of St Lazarus. Over the main doorway, the famous **Romanesque tympanum** shows the Last Judgment surrounded by zodiac signs, carved in the 1130s by Gislebertus, whose name is inscribed below Jesus' right foot. Ornamental capitals by Gislebertus and his school, described in a multilingual handout, adorn the columns of the nave; several especially exquisite capitals are displayed at eye level upstairs in the chapter room.

Musée Rolin　　MUSEUM
(🖉 03 85 54 21 60; 3 rue des Bancs; adult/child €6.50/free; ⊙ 10am-1pm & 2-6pm Wed-Mon Apr-Sep, 10am-noon & 2-5pm Wed-Mon Oct-Dec, Feb & Mar, closed Jan) Don't miss this superb collection of Gallo-Roman artefacts, 12th-century Romanesque art, 15th-century paintings and modern art including work by Maurice Denis, Jean Dubuffet and Joan Miró. The indisputable masterpiece here is the *Temptation of Eve,* an unusually sensual (for its time) stone bas-relief by Gislebertus, recently returned from a two-year stint at the Louvre.

Théâtre Romain　　ARCHAEOLOGICAL SITE
(Roman Theatre; ⊙ 24hr) **FREE** Let your imagination run wild at this ancient theatre, designed to hold 16,000 people; try picturing the place filled with cheering (or jeering), toga-clad spectators. From the top look southwest to see the **Pierre de Couhard** (Rock of Couhard), the 27m-high remains of a Gallo-Roman pyramid that was probably a tomb.

Temple de Janus　　ARCHAEOLOGICAL SITE
FREE Long associated (wrongly) with the Roman God Janus, this 24m-high temple in the

middle of farmland 800m north of the train station is thought to have originally been a site for Celtic worship. It exudes an imposing, mysterious energy, despite the fact that only two of its massive walls still stand.

🛏 Sleeping & Eating

★ Maison Sainte-Barbe
B&B €€

(📞 03 85 86 24 77; www.maisonsaintebarbe.com; 7 place Sainte-Barbe; s/d €85/90, ste €130-144; 🛜) Smack-dab in the old city in a 15th-century townhouse, this colourful, spotless B&B has five spacious, light-filled rooms, including one with fine views of the cathedral and a two-bedroom suite that's perfect for families. The icing on the cake? Delicious included breakfasts (served by the fireside in chilly weather), along with a verdant courtyard out back.

★ Moulin Renaudiots
B&B €€

(📞 03 85 86 97 10; www.moulinrenaudiots.com; chemin du Vieux Moulin; d €140-165; ⊘ late Mar–mid-Nov; 🅿🛜🏊) The exterior of this old water mill, run by friendly French-American couple Evelyne and Trevor, is 17th-century stately; inside, it's a minimalist's dream, with vast bedrooms, tasteful colour schemes and luxurious linens. The large, gracious garden comes with a swimming pool, perfect for an aperitif before a sumptuous *table d'hôte* meal (€54, Saturdays and Mondays). It's 3km southeast of Autun.

★ Comptoir Cuisine
BURGUNDIAN €€

(📞 03 85 54 30 60; 13 place du Terreau; lunch menu €21, dinner menus €25-29; ⊘ noon-1.15pm & 7.15-9pm Tue-Sat) After pursuing other gastronomic ventures far and wide, dynamic young chef Philippe Latrasse returned to his native Autun in 2017 to launch this intimate, modern bistro with only 24 place settings. The simple menu features three market-fresh mains each day: one meat, one fish and one veggie, all finished off with exquisite desserts.

Le Monde de Don Cabillaud
SEAFOOD €€

(📞 07 60 94 21 10; 4 rue des Bancs; menus €30-37; ⊘ noon-1.30pm & 7-9pm Tue-Sat) This convivial restaurant is renowned for its seafood dishes, prepared in a variety of styles and presented with a minimum of fuss by Italo-French chef-owner Vincent Bevacqua. Oh, and if you're wondering how such super-fresh seafood makes it way to inland Burgundy, It's all sourced from the same supplier used by the trio of Michelin-starred restaurants in nearby Tournus!

WORTH A TRIP

AUTUN DAY TRIPPER

Château de Sully (📞 03 85 82 09 86; www.chateaudesully.com; adult/child €8.90/4, gardens only €4.40/2; ⊘ 10am-5pm Apr–early Nov, hourly guided tours in French 10.30am-4.30pm Sun-Fri, to 3.30pm Sat) Hidden away in the countryside 15km northeast of Autun, this Renaissance-style château has a beautifully furnished interior and a lovely English-style garden. It was the birthplace of Marshal MacMahon, Duke of Magenta and president of France from 1873 to 1879, whose ancestors fled Ireland several centuries ago and whose descendants still occupy the property. With advance notice, guided visits in English can be arranged. You'll need your own vehicle to get here. From Autun, follow the D973 and D326.

ℹ Information

Tourist Office (📞 03 85 86 80 38; www.autun-tourisme.com; 13 rue Général Demetz; ⊘ 9.30am-7pm Jul & Aug, 9.30am-12.30pm & 2-6pm Mon-Sat Apr-Jun, Sep & Oct, 10am-12.30pm & 2-5.30pm Tue-Sat Nov-Mar) Sells a self-guided walking-tour brochure (€2) and hiking maps. Has information on the Parc Naturel Régional du Morvan. From June to September, it operates an annexe beside the cathedral.

ℹ Getting There & Away

Buscéphale (📞 03 80 11 29 29; www.mobigo-bourgogne.com) runs one to seven daily buses to the nearby Le Creusot TGV station (line 5; €2, 65 minutes), where TGVs depart regularly for Paris (from €67, 80 minutes) and Lyon (from €18, 45 minutes). They run from the train station and stop at place du Champ de Mars.

Autun's downtown **train station** (av de la République) is on a slow tertiary line that requires a change of train to get almost anywhere. Destinations in Burgundy include Beaune (€15, 1¼ hours) and Dijon (€20, 1¾ hours).

Tournus

POP 6030

Tournus, on the Saône, is known for its 10th-to 12th-century Romanesque abbey church, **Abbatiale St-Philibert** (www.tournus.fr/le-site-abbatial-de-saint-philibert; ⊘ 8.30am-7pm May-Sep, to 6pm Oct-Apr). The city is surrounded by scenic countryside, best viewed along small rural roads such as the D14, D15, D82 and D56, which pass through tiny villages,

Medieval Art & Architecture

Burgundy, once a powerful duchy and a major ecclesiastical centre, attracted the foremost European artists and builders of the Middle Ages. Now graced with a bounty of excellent museums and monumental architecture, Burgundy offers a trail of human accomplishment through its rolling emerald hills.

The Cistercians

Burgundy's clergy established a series of abbeys and churches that remain some of the world's best examples of Romanesque architecture. The austere Cistercian order was founded at the Abbaye de Cîteaux in 1098 by monks seeking to live St Benedict's teachings: pax, ora et labora (peace, pray and work). Their spectacular 1114 Abbaye de Pontigny is one of the finest surviving examples of Cistercian architecture in Burgundy – the purity of its white stone reflects the simplicity of the order. Further south, the Abbaye de Fontenay (founded in 1118), a Unesco World Heritage Site, sits in a peaceful forested valley perfect for contemplation.

The Benedictines

Cluny's 12th-century Benedictine abbey, now a sprawling ruin woven into the fabric of the town, once held sway over 1100 priories and monasteries stretching from Poland to Portugal. Aside from its imposing central towers, it's only a shell of its former self, but visitors can still conjure up its full original grandeur with the help of a virtual-reality video presentation.

1. Abbaye de Pontigny (p456) 2. Romanesque tympanum, Cathédrale St-Lazare (p466) 3. Cloister, Abbaye de Fontenay (p451)

Autun & Vézelay

The 12th-century Cathédrale St-Lazare (p466) in Autun is world-renowned for its deceptively austere Gislebertus carvings: a fantastic tympanum of the Last Judgement and extraordinary capitals depicting Bible stories and Greek mythology. The adjacent Musée Rolin holds another Gislebertus masterpiece, *The Temptation of Eve*, whose sensitive (and sensual) portrayal of its female subject is nothing short of revolutionary for its time.

Vézelay's Basilique Ste-Madeleine (p471), another Unesco World Heritage Site, was founded in the 880s. A traditional starting point for the Chemin de St-Jacques trail to Santiago de Compostela, Spain, it is adorned with Romanesque carvings and attracts both religious and artistic pilgrims. Nearby,

the medieval walls and turrets of Noyers-sur-Serein and Semur-en-Auxois are some of the finest remnants of Burgundy's more secular past.

The Dukes of Burgundy

Last but not least, let's not forget the royals. Dijon was home to the powerful Dukes of Burgundy (with fabulous names including John the Good, Philip the Bold and John the Fearless), and flourished into one of the art capitals of Europe. Explore the dukes' monumental palace (p431) in central Dijon, home to an excellent fine-arts museum. Or head south to Beaune, where Nicolas Rolin, chancellor to Philip the Good, established a hospital-cum-palace, Hôtel-Dieu des Hospices de Beaune (p444), that houses Rogier van der Weyden's fantastic (and fantastical) *Polyptych of the Last Judgement*.

many with charming churches of their own. The medieval hilltop village of **Brancion**, with its 12th-century church and **château** (☎03 85 32 19 70; www.chateau-de-brancion.fr; adult/child €6/3, audioguide €2; ⏰10am-12.30pm & 1-6.30pm Apr-Sep, to 5pm Oct–mid-Nov, closed mid-Nov–Mar) 12km west of Tournus, is a lovely place to wander, while Chardonnay is, as one would expect, surrounded by vineyards. There's a panoramic view from 579m **Mont St-Romain**, 22km southwest of town.

For a bite to eat there is one address: Michelin-starred **Aux Terrasses** (☎03 85 51 01 74; www.aux-terrasses.com; av du 23 Janvier; lunch menu €26, other menus €40-95; ⏰noon-1.30pm & 7-9pm Tue-Sat) where chef Jean-Michel Carrette carries forth his father's legacy, taking classic ingredients like Charolais beef, Bresse poultry and produce from small local producers and transforming them into works of art. The lunchtime *Menu du Marché* offers superb value. Or indulge in a multi-course dinner with wine pairings and trundle off to sleep at the hotel next door.

❶ Getting There & Away

The train station is just north and across the D906 from Tournus' abbey. Trains run north to Beaune (€10, 35 minutes) and Dijon (€15, one hour), and south to Mâcon (€5, 20 minutes) and Lyon (€18.60, 1¼ hours). **Buscéphale** (p473) also runs one bus daily in each direction between the train stations in Tournus and Mâcon (€2, 50 minutes).

Cluny

POP 5156

The remains of Cluny's great abbey – Christendom's largest church until the construction of St Peter's Basilica in the Vatican – are fragmentary and scattered, barely discernible among the houses and green spaces of the modern-day town. But with a bit of imagination, it's possible to picture how things looked in the 12th century, when Cluny's Benedictine abbey, renowned for its wealth and power and answerable only to the pope, held sway over 1100 priories and monasteries stretching from Poland to Portugal.

The village of Cluny and the green countryside surrounding it make a pleasant place to linger for a day or two. There are several other worthwhile places to visit nearby. Cormatin, 14km to the north, is home to a lavish Renaissance-style château, while Paray-le-Monial, about 50km to the west of

Cluny, makes an interesting side trip for its 11th-century Romanesque basilica.

⊙ Sights

★**Église Abbatiale** CHURCH
(Abbey Church; ☎03 85 59 15 93; www.cluny-abbaye.fr; place du 11 Août 1944; combined ticket with Musée d'Art et d'Archéologie adult/child €9.50/free; ⏰9.30am-7pm Jul & Aug, to 6pm Apr-Jun & Sep, to 5pm Oct-Mar) Cluny's vast abbey church, built between 1088 and 1130, once extended from the map table in front of the **Palais Jean de Bourbon** to the trees near the octagonal **Clocher de l'Eau Bénite** (Tower of the Holy Water) and the adjoining square **Tour de l'Horloge** (Clock Tower) – a staggering 187m! A short film (multilingual headsets available) helps visitors envision the grandeur of the medieval abbey while exploring its scant ruins. English-language audioguides (€3) and self-guided tour booklets are available.

Abbey visitors also have access to the grounds of the adjacent **École Nationale Supérieure d'Arts et Métiers**, an institute for training mechanical and industrial engineers that's centred on an 18th-century cloister. At the far edge of the grounds, don't miss the 13th-century **Farinier** (flour storehouse), under whose soaring wood-framed roof a series of eight finely carved capitals from the abbey's choir are now housed.

Tour des Fromages TOWER
(rue Mercière; adult/child €2.50/1.50; ⏰9.30am-6.30pm May-Sep, shorter hrs Oct-Apr) To better appreciate the abbey's vastness, climb the 120 steps to the top of this tower, once used to ripen cheeses. Access is through the tourist office.

Musée d'Art et d'Archéologie MUSEUM
(rue de l'Abbatiale; combined ticket with Église Abbatiale adult/child €9.50/free; ⏰9.30am-7pm Jul & Aug, to 6pm Apr-Jun & Sep, to 5pm Oct-Mar) For an enlightening historical perspective on Cluny and its abbey, start your visit at this archaeological museum inside the Palais Jean de Bourbon. Displays include a historically accurate scale model of the entire Cluny complex, a reproduction of the abbey's façade as it looked in the Middle Ages overlaid with scant remnants of its original stone carvings, and some superb Romanesque clerestories and other stonework salvaged from medieval houses around town. A combined ticket covers the museum and abbey.

CYCLING THE GREEN WAY

An old railway line and parts of a former canal towpath have been turned into the **Voie Verte** (www.bourgogne-du-sud.com/index.php/la-voie-verte.html), a series of paved 'greenways' around the Saône-et-Loire *département* that have been designed for walking, cycling and in-line skating. From Cluny, the Voie Verte heads north, via vineyards and valleys, to Givry (42km) and Santenay, where you can pick up the **Voie des Vignes** (Vineyard Way) to Beaune, or circle back around to Cluny on the 145km **Grande Boucle de Bourgogne** loop ride. Tourist offices have the free cycling map, *Voies Vertes et Cyclotourisme – Bourgogne du Sud*. Also log onto www.burgundy-by-bike.com.

Haras National FARM
(National Stud Farm; ☑ 03 85 32 09 73; www.equivallee-haras-cluny.fr/haras-national-de-cluny; 2 rue Porte des Prés; guided tour adult/child €7/free; ☺ Apr–early Nov) Founded by Napoléon in 1806, the Haras National houses some of France's finest thoroughbreds, ponies and draught horses. A regular schedule of afternoon guided tours runs from April to early November (days and hours vary by month; see website for details). From mid-July through August, reserve ahead for the special Wednesday afternoon equestrian demonstrations known as *mercredis au Haras* (adult/child €9.50/5.50) and the Spectacle de l'Été, an annually changing horse show that takes place on Tuesday and Friday evenings (adult/child €18/10).

🛏 Sleeping

Cluny Séjour HOSTEL €
(☑ 03 85 59 08 83; www.cluny-sejours.fr; 22 rue Porte de Paris; dm €22.50, d €60-80; ℗) Half hostel and half hotel, this former Benedictine monastery is a winning budget option with its clean, bright two- to five-bed rooms, helpful staff and prime location. Optional breakfast and towel rental cost €4.70 and €2, respectively.

★ **Le Clos de l'Abbaye** B&B €
(☑ 03 85 59 22 06; www.closdelabbaye.fr; 6 place du Marché; s €65-75, d €70-80, q €125-150; 🛜) At this handsome old house directly across the square from the abbey, the three spacious, comfortable and stylishly decorated bedrooms and two family-friendly suites are flanked by a lovely garden with facilities for kids. Gracious owners Claire and Pascal are excellent tour advisers who direct guests to little-known treasures. There's a wonderful Saturday morning market just outside the front door.

La Pierre Folle B&B €
(☑ 03 85 59 20 14; www.lapierrefolle.com; D980; s/d/tr/q €75/85/105/125, ste s/d/tr €92/105/125; 🛜) Surrounded by rolling fields near the main highway 3km south of town, this immaculate B&B offers four spacious, comfortable rooms and one suite. Friendly owners Véronique and Luigi are generous with information about the local area, and serve delicious breakfasts as well as Italian-influenced, four-course *table d'hôte* dinners (€28, Friday and Sunday, book ahead).

Hôtel de Bourgogne HISTORIC HOTEL €€
(☑ 03 85 59 00 58; www.hotel-cluny.com; place de l'Abbaye; s €89, d €99-136, ste €136-166; ☺ Feb-Nov; ℗🛜) This family-run hotel sits right next to the remains of the abbey. Built in 1817, it has a casual lounge area, 13 antique-furnished rooms and three family-friendly apartments. Breakfast (€11) is served in an enchanting courtyard. Parking costs €10.

🍴 Eating

Le Pain sur la Table BAKERY €
(☑ 03 85 59 24 50; www.lepainsurlatable.fr; 1 Pont de l'Étang; daily specials €12; ☺ bakery 8am-7pm Tue-Sat, lunch noon-2pm Tue-Sat; ✍) A local favourite, this organic bakery near the bridge at Cluny's southern edge doubles as an informal restaurant serving healthy soups, sandwiches and other light meals. The daily-changing lunch menu always includes at least one vegetarian appetiser and main dish. Outside of the midday hours, it's a great spot for coffee and fresh-baked pastries.

★ **La Halte de l'Abbaye** BURGUNDIAN €€
(☑ 03 85 59 28 49; 3 rue Porte des Prés; menus €17-29; ☺ noon-3pm Thu-Sun plus 7-9.15pm Fri & Sat mid-Feb–Nov) Artisanal *andouillette* sausage, Charolais steak tartare and even *tête de veau* (calf's head) are among the classic Burgundian dishes on the menu at this family-run spot just outside the abbey gates.

Hard-working owners Franck and Séverine offer nonstop service throughout the afternoon, making it a convenient break between sightseeing stints.

★ La Table d'Héloïse
BURGUNDIAN €€

(☑ 03 85 59 05 65; www.hostelleriedheloise.com/restaurant-cluny; 7 rue de Mâcon; lunch menu €21, dinner menus €33-52; ⊙ 12.15-1.45pm Fri-Tue, 7.30pm-8.45pm Mon, Tue & Thu-Sat) South of town, this family-run restaurant with a charmingly cosy, newly remodelled interior is a terrific place to sample firmly traditional Burgundian specialities, from the dexterously prepared *fricassée d'escargots* (snail stew) to the tender Charolais rumpsteak to the ripe Époisses cheese and the devastatingly delicious homemade desserts. Book ahead for a table on the light-filled verandah overlooking the Grosne river.

Restaurant de l'Abbaye
THAI, BURGUNDIAN €€

(☑ 03 85 59 11 14; www.abbaye-cluny.fr; 14ter av Charles de Gaulle; menus €23-34; ⊙ 11.30am-2pm Thu-Mon, 6.30-9pm Wed-Mon) Authentic Thai food in the middle of Burgundy? Yes, thanks to an enterprising French-Thai couple who recently opened this unconventional fusion restaurant at Cluny's Hôtel de l'Abbaye. You'll find plenty of straightforward Thai and Burgundian classics on the menu, complemented by more innovative 'Bourgi-thai' offerings that span the culinary gulf in between. Escargot *nems* (spring rolls), anyone?

ℹ Information

Tourist Office (☑ 03 85 59 05 34; www.cluny-tourisme.com; 6 rue Mercière; ⊙ 9.30am-6.30pm May-Sep, shorter hrs Oct-Apr; 🛜) Has free wifi.

ℹ Getting There & Away

The bus stop on rue Porte de Paris is served by **Buscéphale** (☑ 03 80 11 29 29; www.mobigobourgogne.com; tickets €2). All local buses cost €2. Line 7 (five to eight daily) goes to Mâcon (40 minutes), the Mâcon-Loché TGV station (25 minutes) and Cormatin (20 minutes). Line 9 also runs to Mâcon (30 minutes) and Paray-le-Monial (one hour) once or twice daily. Schedules are posted at the bus stop and tourist office.

Mâcon

POP 34,294

The town of Mâcon, 70km north of Lyon on the west bank of the Saône, sits at the heart of the Mâconnais, Burgundy's southernmost winegrowing area, which produces mainly dry whites. The city has a pair of museums, some excellent restaurants and a small but pleasant-enough historic centre consisting of a narrow strip of pedestrian-friendly streets near the riverfront.

Beyond these urban attractions, Mâcon's main appeal lies in the surrounding countryside. If you're after top-quality Mâconnais wines, head to the nearby villages of Fuissé, Vinzelles and Pouilly, which produce the area's best whites. For a bird's eye perspective on the entire region, don't miss the easy climb to the summit of Roche de Solutré, 10km west of town.

⊙ Sights & Activities

Maison de Bois
HISTORIC BUILDING

(rue Dombey) The all-wood Maison de Bois, facing 95 rue Dombey and built around 1500, is decorated with carved wooden figures, some of them very cheeky indeed.

Musée des Ursulines
MUSEUM

(☑ 03 85 39 90 38; 5 rue de la Préfecture; adult/child €4.50/free; ⊙ 10am-noon & 2-6pm Tue-Sat, 2-6pm Sun) Musée des Ursulines, housed in a 17th-century Ursuline convent, features Gallo-Roman archaeology, 16th- to 20th-century paintings, and displays about 19th-century Mâconnais life. There's also a section devoted to the life and times of the Mâcon-born Romantic poet and left-wing politician Alphonse de Lamartine (1790–1869).

Château de Fuissé
WINE

(☑ 03 85 35 61 44; www.chateau-fuisse.fr; Le Plan, Pouilly-Fuissé; ⊙ 8am-noon & 1.30-5.30pm Mon-Thu, to 4.30pm Fri, by reservation Sat & Sun) Pouilly-Fuissé is famous for its prestigious white wines. For the ultimate experience, reserve ahead for tastings at this magnificent estate, 9km southwest of Mâcon.

Musée Départemental de Préhistoire de Solutré
MUSEUM

(☑ 03 85 35 85 24; Solutré; adult/child €5/free; ⊙ 10am-6pm Apr-Sep, to 5pm Oct-Mar) The Musée de Préhistoire de Solutré displays finds from one of Europe's richest prehistoric sites, occupied from 35,000 to 10,000 BC. A lovely 20-minute walk from here will get you to the top of the rocky outcrop known as the Roche de Solutré, from where Mont Blanc can sometimes be seen, especially at sunset. The museum is about 10km west of Mâcon.

🛏 Sleeping

La Source des Fées   B&B €€
(☑ 03 85 35 67 02; www.lasourcedesfees.fr; route du May, Fuissé; r €128-168; 🛜) If you fancy staying overnight in the Mâconnais vineyards, make a beeline for these *chambres d'hôte* in pretty Fuissé village. Tucked into the courtyard of a winegrowing domaine, the three doubles and two spacious family suites share access to a jacuzzi and some nice walking loops. Dinners (€29.50) can be arranged, with preferential pricing on wine from the onsite cellars.

Hôtel d'Europe et d'Angleterre   HOTEL €€
(☑ 03 85 38 27 94; www.hotel-europe angleterre-macon.com; 92-109 quai Jean-Jaurès; r €82-175, ste €128-209; P 🌸 🛜) This grand old dame of a riverfront hotel is Mâcon's best city-centre option, with three-star amenities and suites overlooking the Saône.

🍴 Eating

Mâcon boasts a bevy of excellent restaurants one block inland from the river, plus a lively Saturday-morning market. For an especially memorable experience, seek out the fine-dining establishments tucked away in the Mâconnais vineyards.

L'Ethym' Sel   BURGUNDIAN €€
(☑ 03 85 39 48 84; 10 rue Gambetta; lunch menus €16.50-19, dinner menus €35-54; ⊙ noon-1.45pm Thu-Tue, 7-9.30pm Mon & Thu-Sat Sep-Jun; noon-1.45pm & 7-9.30pm Tue-Sat Jul & Aug) Two blocks south of the tourist office, this modern bistro showcases French and Burgundian specialities including locally sourced Charolais steak. The €19 three-course lunch *menu* (also available as a dinner *menu* till 9pm on weekdays) offers spectacular value; local Mâcon wines are attractively priced.

⭐ Ma Table en Ville   BURGUNDIAN €€€
(☑ 03 85 30 99 91; www.matableenville.fr; 50 rue de Strasbourg; lunch menus €19-25, dinner menus €39-58; ⊙ 11.45am-1.30pm & 7.30-9pm) Balancing top-of-the-line gastronomy with an unfailingly welcoming atmosphere, this husband-and-wife venture is a total gem. Chef Gilles Bérard brings decades of experience in some of France's finest Michelin-starred restaurants to his weekly changing, market-fresh menus, while Laurence attends to diners, sharing her exhaustive knowledge of artisanal Mâconnais wines. Colourful modern artwork fills the bright dining area, enhancing the relaxed feel.

L'O des Vignes   GASTRONOMY €€€
(☑ 03 85 38 33 40; www.lodesvignes.fr; rue du Bourg, Fuissé; lunch menu €27, dinner menus €46-70; ⊙ noon-2pm & 7.30-10pm Thu-Mon) For a gastronomic experience among the Mâconnais vineyards, look no further. Burgundy-born chef Sébastien Chambru builds his *menus* around seasonal produce, incorporates culinary influences from his wide-ranging international career, and complements it all with AOC white wines of the local Pouilly-Fuissé appellation. It's 9km southwest of Mâcon via the D172.

ℹ Information

Across the street from the 18th-century town hall, the **tourist office** (☑ 03 85 21 07 07; www.macon-tourism.com; 1 place St-Pierre; ⊙ 9.30am-noon & 2-6pm Mon-Sat Apr-Jun & Oct, Tue-Sat Nov-Mar; 9am-7pm Mon-Sat & 10am-6pm Sun Jul-Sep) has information on accommodation and visiting vineyards including the Route des Vins Mâconnais-Beaujolais.

ℹ Getting There & Away

BUS

Buscéphale (☑ 03 80 11 29 29; www.mobigo-bourgogne.com; tickets €2) bus lines 7 and 9 serve Cluny (30 to 40 minutes, €2) six to 10 times daily. Ouibus (www.ouibus.com) runs to Dijon (€8, two hours) and Lyon's St-Exupéry airport (€9, 1½ hours). All buses stop just outside Mâcon-Ville train station.

TRAIN

From Mâcon-Ville station, trains run at least hourly along the main line linking Dijon (€20, 1¼ to 1¾ hours), Beaune (€15, one hour) and Lyon Part-Dieu (from €13.10, 55 minutes). The fastest service to Paris (€70, 1¾ hours) is from Mâcon-Loché TGV station, 5km southwest of town.

Lyon & the Rhône Valley

POP 3.92 MILLION

Best Places to Eat

➡ La Cuisinerie (p486)

➡ Au 14 Février (p496)

➡ Les Halles de Lyon Paul Bocuse (p493)

➡ Restaurant Pic (p499)

➡ L'Espace PH3 (p498)

➡ Le Comptoir des Dombes (p497)

Best Places to Stay

➡ Mob Hotel (p484)

➡ Auberge de Clochemerle (p495)

➡ Prehistoric Lodge (p501)

➡ Cour des Loges (p484)

➡ La Maison de la Pra (p499)

Why Go?

At the crossroads of central Europe and the Atlantic, the Rhineland and the Mediterranean, grand old Lyon is France's third-largest metropolis and its gastronomic capital. Savouring timeless traditional dishes in checked-tableclothed *bouchons* (small bistros) creates unforgettable memories – as do the majestic Roman amphitheatres of Fourvière, the cobbled Unesco-listed streets of Vieux Lyon, and the audacious modern architecture of the new Confluence neighbourhood.

North of Lyon, Beaujolais produces illustrious wines, while the picturesque hilltop village of Pérouges is a perennial film location. Downstream, the Rhône forges past Vienne's Roman ruins and the centuries-old Côtes du Rhône vineyards, opening to sunny vistas of fruit orchards, lavender fields and the distant Alps as it continues south past Valence and Montélimar, eventually reaching the rugged Gorges de l'Ardèche, where the Ardèche River tumbles to the gates of Languedoc and Provence.

When to Go

Lyon

Jun–Jul Live performances in ancient Gallo-Roman theatres in Vienne's or Lyon.

Nov Celebrate the tapping of the first bottles of Beaujolais nouveau, the third Thursday in November.

Early Dec See Lyon spectacularly illuminated during the Fête des Lumières.

Lyon & the Rhône Valley Highlights

1 Lyon (p476) Delving into Lyon's hidden labyrinth of *traboules* (secret passageways) and sampling Lyonnais specialities in a *bouchon*.

2 Beaujolais (p494) Touring the vine-ribboned hills of this delightfully peaceful winegrowing region.

3 Vienne (p497) Seeing dramatic Gallo-Roman ruins, including a perfectly preserved Corinthian-columned temple.

4 Gorges de l'Ardèche (p499) Canoeing along these scenic gorges, including beneath the stunning natural stone bridge Pont d'Arc.

5 Caverne du Pont d'Arc (p500) Gazing with awe at this replica cave housing brilliantly reproduced prehistoric paintings.

6 La Dombes (p496) Driving or biking around a lake-dotted region, famous for its great restaurants.

7 Montélimar (p499) Visiting 14th-century battlements, strolling tree-shaded avenues and tasting delectable nougat in this sun-drenched town near the edge of Provence.

8 Pérouges (p482) Strolling the cobbled alleyways of this achingly picturesque medieval village.

LYON

POP 514,000

Commanding a strategic spot at the confluence of the Rhône and the Saône Rivers, Lyon has been luring people ever since the Romans named it Lugdunum in 43 BC. Commercial, industrial and banking powerhouse for the past 500 years, Lyon is France's third-largest city, and offers today's urban explorers a wealth of enticing experiences.

Outstanding museums, a dynamic cultural life, busy clubbing and drinking scenes, a thriving university and fantastic shopping lend the city a distinctly sophisticated air, while adventurous gourmets can indulge in their wildest gastronomic fantasies. Don't leave the city without sampling some Lyonnais specialities in a *bouchon* – the quintessential Lyon experience.

◉ Sights

A number of sights lie in the city centre, which occupies a long peninsula between the rivers known as Presqu'île. Rising to the north of the Presqu'île is the hillside Croix Rousse, which also harbours worthwhile museums and buildings. West across the Saône sits the medieval quarter of Vieux Lyon, which has plenty of attractions and sights, including museums and religious buildings.

◉ Vieux Lyon

Lyon's Unesco-listed old town, with its narrow streets and medieval and Renaissance houses, is divided into three quarters: St-Paul (north), St-Jean (middle) and St-Georges (south).

ⓘ LYON CITY CARD

The excellent-value **Lyon City Card** (www.lyoncitycard.com; 1/2/3 days adult €25/35/45, child €17/24/31) offers free admission to every Lyon museum, the roof of Basilique Notre Dame de Fourvière, guided city tours, Guignol puppet shows and river excursions (April to October), along with numerous other discounts.

The card also includes unlimited citywide transport on buses, trams, the funicular and the metro. Full-price cards are available at the tourist office and some hotels, or save 10% by booking online and presenting your confirmation number at the tourist office.

Lovely old buildings line rue du Bœuf, rue St-Jean and rue des Trois Maries. Crane your neck upwards to see gargoyles and other cheeky stone characters carved on window ledges along rue Juiverie, home to Lyon's Jewish community in the Middle Ages.

Cathédrale St-Jean-Baptiste   CATHEDRAL
(www.cathedrale-lyon.fr; place St-Jean, 5e; ⊙ cathedral 8.15am-7.45pm Mon-Fri, 8am-7pm Sat & Sun, treasury 9.30am-noon & 2-6pm Tue-Sat; Ⓜ Vieux Lyon) Lyon's partly Romanesque cathedral was built between the late 11th and early 16th centuries. The portals of its Flamboyant Gothic facade, completed in 1480 (and recently renovated), are decorated with 280 square stone medallions. Inside, the highlight is the astronomical clock in the north transept.

Musées Gadagne   MUSEUM
(☑ 04 78 42 03 61; www.gadagne.musees.lyon. fr; 1 place du Petit Collège, 5e; adult/child €8/free, both museums €9/free; ⊙ 11am-6.30pm Wed-Sun; Ⓜ Vieux Lyon) Housed in a 16th-century mansion built for two rich Florentine bankers, this twin-themed exhibition space incorporates an excellent local history museum, **Musée d'Histoire de Lyon**, that chronicles the city's layout as its silk-weaving, cinema and transportation evolved, and an international puppet museum, **Musée des Marionettes du Monde**, that pays homage to Lyon's iconic puppet, Guignol. On the 4th floor, a cafe adjoins tranquil, terraced gardens, here since the 14th century.

Le Petit Musée Fantastique de Guignol   MUSEUM
(☑ 04 78 37 01 67; www.le-petit-musee-fantastique-de-guignol.boutiquecardelli.fr; 6 rue St-Jean, 5e; adult/child €5/3; ⊙ 10.30am-12.30pm & 2-6.30pm Tue-Sun, 2-6pm Mon; Ⓜ Vieux Lyon) The star of this tiny, two-floor museum is Guignol, the Lyonnais puppet famous for its slapstick antics and political commentary. Various animated scenes as well as an audioguide give details about the beloved puppet.

◉ Fourvière

More than two millennia ago, the Romans built the city of Lugdunum on the slopes of Fourvière. Today this prominent hill on the Saône's western bank is topped by a showy 19th-century basilica and the **Tour Métallique** (montée Nicolas de Lange; 🚡 Fourvière, Minimes), an Eiffel Tower–like structure (minus its bottom two-thirds) built in 1893 and used as a TV transmitter.

LYON'S HIDDEN LABYRINTH

Deep within Vieux Lyon and Croix Rousse, dark, dingy *traboules* (secret passages) wind their way through apartment blocks, under streets and into courtyards. In all, 315 passages link 230 streets, with a combined length of 50km.

A couple of Vieux Lyon's *traboules* date from Roman times, but most were constructed by *canuts* (silk weavers) in the 19th century to transport silk in inclement weather. Resistance fighters found them equally handy during WWII.

Genuine *traboules* (derived from the Latin *trans ambulare,* meaning 'to pass through') cut from one street to another. Passages that fan out into a courtyard or cul-de-sac aren't *traboules* but *miraboules* (two of the finest examples are at 16 rue Bœuf and 8 rue Juiverie, both in Vieux Lyon).

Vieux Lyon's most celebrated *traboules* include those connecting 27 rue St-Jean with 6 rue des Trois Maries and 54 rue St Jean with 27 rue du Bœuf (push the intercom button to buzz open the door).

Step into Croix Rousse's underworld at 9 place Colbert, crossing cour des Voraces – renowned for its monumental seven-storey staircase – to 14bis montée St-Sébastien, and eventually emerging at 29 rue Imbert Colomès. From here a series of other *traboules* zigzags down the slope most of the way to place des Terreaux.

For more detailed descriptions and maps of Lyon's *traboules,* download the free iPhone app **Traboules de Lyon** or pick up a copy of the French-language guidebook *200 Cours et Traboules dans les Rues de Lyon* by Gérald Gambier (€9.90, available at Lyon's tourist office) available at the tourist office (p493). Many guided walking **tours** (☑04 72 77 69 69; www.visiterlyon.com; tours adult/child €13/8; ☺ by reservation) run by Lyon's tourism guides also visit *traboules*.

Footpaths wind uphill to Fourvière from Vieux Lyon, but the funicular is the least taxing way up; catch it just up the escalators from the Vieux Lyon metro station.

Basilique Notre Dame de Fourvière CHURCH
(☑04 78 25 13 01; www.fourviere.org; place de Fourvière, 5e; rooftop tour adult/child €10/5; ☺basilica 7am-7pm, tours 9am-12.30pm & 2-6pm Mon-Fri, 9am-12.30pm & 2-4.45pm Sat, 2-4.45pm Sun Apr-Nov; 🚠Fourvière) Crowning the hill, with stunning city panoramas from its terrace, this superb example of late-19th-century French ecclesiastical architecture is lined with magnificent mosaics. From April to November, free 30-minute discovery visits take in the main features of the basilica and crypt; otherwise, 90-minute rooftop tours ('Visite Insolite') climax on the stone-sculpted roof. Reserve tickets in advance online for the latter.

Musée Gallo-Romain de Fourvière MUSEUM
(☑04 73 38 49 30; www.museegalloromain.grandlyon.com; 17 rue Cléberg, 5e; adult/child €4/free; ☺11am-6pm Tue-Fri, from 10am Sat & Sun; 🚠Fourvière) For an enlightening historical perspective on the city's past, start your visit at this archaeological museum located on the hillside of Fourvière. It hosts a wide-ranging collection of ancient artefacts found in the Rhône Valley as well as superb mosaics.

Théâtre Romain ARCHAEOLOGICAL SITE
(rue Cléberg, 5e; 🚠Fourvière, Minimes) Lyon's Roman theatre, built around 15 BC and enlarged in AD 120, sat an audience of 10,000. Romans held poetry readings and musical recitals in the smaller, adjacent *odéon*.

⊙ Presqu'île

Lyon's city centre lies on this peninsula, 500m to 800m wide, bounded by the rivers Rhône and Saône.

Musée des Beaux-Arts MUSEUM
(☑04 72 10 17 40; www.mba-lyon.fr; 20 place des Terreaux, 1er; adult/child €8/free; ☺10am-6pm Wed, Thu & Sat-Mon, 10.30am-6pm Fri; Ⓜ Hôtel de Ville) This stunning and eminently manageable museum showcases France's finest collection of sculptures and paintings outside of Paris, from antiquity onwards. Highlights include works by Rodin, Monet and Picasso. Pick up a free audioguide and be sure to stop for a drink or meal on the delightful stone terrace off its cafe-restaurant or take time out in its tranquil cloister garden.

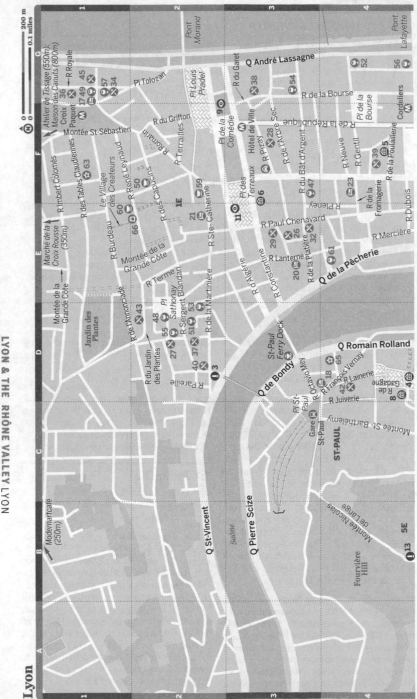

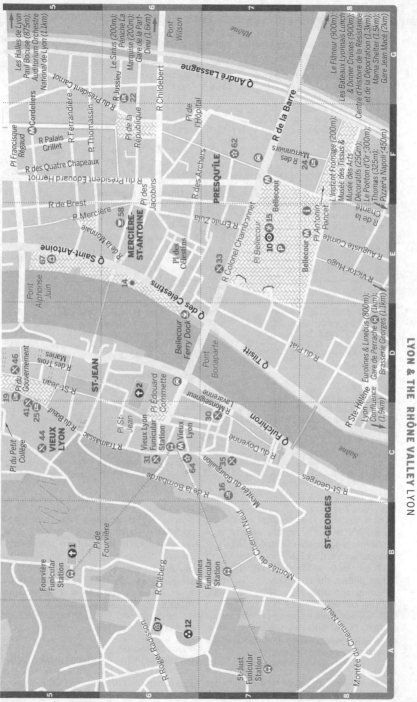

Lyon

Place des Terreaux   SQUARE

(Ⓜ Hôtel de Ville) The centrepiece of the Presqu'île's beautiful central square is a 19th-century **fountain** made of 21 tonnes of lead and sculpted by Frédéric-Auguste Bartholdi (of Statue of Liberty fame). The four horses pulling the chariot symbolise rivers galloping seawards. The **Hôtel de Ville** fronting the square's east side was built in 1655 but was given its present ornate façade in 1702. Daniel Buren's polka-dot 'forest' of 69 **granite fountains** are embedded in the ground across much of the square.

Opéra de Lyon   ARCHITECTURE

(www.opera-lyon.com; 1 place de la Comédie, 1er; Ⓜ Hôtel de Ville) Lyon's neoclassical 1831-built opera house was modernised in 1993 by renowned French architect Jean Nouvel, who added the striking semi-cylindrical glass-domed roof. On its northern side, boarders and bladers buzz around the fountains of **place Louis Pradel**, surveyed by the **Homme de la Liberté** (Man of Freedom) on roller skates, sculpted from scrap metal by Marseille-born César Baldaccini.

For drinks with a magnificent view, head up to the 7th-floor terrace bar Les Muses.

Place Bellecour   SQUARE

(Ⓜ Bellecour) One of Europe's largest public squares, gravel-strewn place Bellecour was laid out in the 17th century. In the centre is an equestrian statue of Louis XIV.

RIVERSIDE MAKEOVERS

Much to the joy of resident Lyonnais, the riverbanks north of the Confluence have been treated to a serious makeover. The Rhône's Rive Gauche (Left Bank), once the domain of high-speed traffic and car parks, has been extensively redeveloped in the past decade to provide Lyon with landscaped walking, cycling and inline skating paths, along with tiered seating where locals lounge on sunny days. Known as the **Berges du Rhône**, the project spans 10 hectares, along more than 5km of riverfront.

A separate riverside beautification project, **Les Rives de Saône** (www.lesrivesde saone.com), is spreading north along the Saône. A 15km stretch of pedestrian walkway between the Confluence and Île Ste-Barbe, north of Lyon, has already been completed; future phases of the project will eventually open up 50km of the Saône's banks for public recreational use.

From December to March, a 60m-high Ferris wheel provides a fine view over the city.

Musée des Tissus   MUSEUM
(☑ 04 78 38 42 00; www.mtmad.fr; 34 rue de la Charité, 2e; adult/child €10/7.50; ⓘ 10am-6pm Tue-Sun; Ⓜ Ampère) Extraordinary Lyonnais and international silks are showcased here. Ticket includes admission to the adjoining **Musée des Arts Décoratifs** (☑ 04 78 38 42 00; www.mtmad.fr; 34 rue de la Charité, 2e; adult/child €10/7.50; ⓘ 10am-6pm Tue-Sun; Ⓜ Ampère), which displays 18th-century furniture, tapestries, wallpaper, ceramics and silver.

Musée de l'Imprimerie   MUSEUM
(☑ 04 78 37 65 98; www.imprimerie.lyon.fr; 13 rue de la Poulaillerie, 2e; adult/child €6/free; ⓘ 10.30am-6pm Wed-Sun; Ⓜ Cordeliers) From early equipment through to computerised technology, this absorbing museum traces the history of the city's printing industry.

◉ Croix Rousse

Independent until it became part of Lyon in 1852, and retaining its own distinct character with its bohemian inhabitants and lush outdoor food market, the hilltop quarter of Croix Rousse slinks north up the steep *pentes* (slopes) from place des Terreaux.

Following the introduction of the mechanical Jacquard loom in 1805, Lyonnais *canuts* (silk weavers) built tens of thousands of workshops in the area, with large windows to let in light and hefty wood-beamed ceilings more than 4m high to accommodate the huge new machines. Weavers spent 14 to 20 hours a day hunched over their looms breathing in silk dust. Two-thirds were illiterate and everyone was paid a pittance;

strikes in 1830–31 and 1834 resulted in the deaths of several hundred weavers.

Nowadays, most workshops have long since been converted into chic loft apartments, but a few have been saved by the Soierie Vivante association (www.soierie-vivante.asso.fr).

Hidden Croix Rousse gems include **place Bertone**, a leafy square that doubles as an open-air stage for ad-hoc summer entertainment; the **Jardin Rosa Mir** (http://rosa.mir.free.fr; enter via 87 Grande Rue de la Croix Rousse, 4e; ⓘ 2-5.30pm Sat Apr-Oct; Ⓜ Hénon) **FREE**, a walled garden decorated with thousands of seashells; and the panoramic **Parc de La Cerisaie** (rue Chazière, 4e; Ⓜ Croix Rousse).

Maison des Canuts   WORKSHOP
(☑ 04 78 28 62 04; www.maisondescanuts.com; 10-12 rue d'Ivry, 4e; adult/child €7.50/4.50; ⓘ 10am-6.30pm Mon-Sat, guided tours 11am & 3.30pm Mon & Sat mid-Mar–mid-Oct; Ⓜ Croix Rousse) On a 50-minute guided tour, learn about weavers' labour-intensive life and the industry's evolution, see manual looms in use, and browse the silk boutique. Guided tours in English run at 11am on Saturday from May to September.

Atelier de Tissage   WORKSHOP
(☑ 04 78 27 17 13; www.soierie-vivante.asso.fr; 12bis rue Justin Godart, 4e; guided tour adult/child €7/free, combined ticket with Atelier de Passementerie €10/free; ⓘ guided tours 3pm & 5pm Tue-Sat; Ⓜ Croix Rousse) Accessible strictly by guided tour, this wonderful old workshop houses looms that produce large fabrics. It's best visited in conjunction with the nearby **Atelier de Passementerie** (☑ 04 78 27 17 13; www.soierie-vivante. asso.fr; 21 rue Richan, 4e; guided tour adult/child €7/free, combined ticket with Atelier de Tissage €10/free; ⓘ boutique 2-6.30pm Tue, 9am-noon & 2-6.30pm Wed-Sat, guided tours & demonstrations 2pm & 4pm Tue-Sat; Ⓜ Croix Rousse).

WORTH A TRIP

PÉROUGES

French film buffs will recognise photogenic Pérouges (pop 1200). Situated on a hill 30km northeast of Lyon, this enchanting yellow-stone medieval village has long been used as a set for films such as *Les Trois Mousquetaires* (*The Three Musketeers*). It's worth braving the summertime crowds to stroll its uneven cobbled alleys, admire its half-timbered stone houses and liberty tree on place de la Halle (planted in 1792), and wolf down *galettes de Pérouges* (warm, thin-pizza-crust-style, sugar-crusted tarts) with cider.

Should you be unable to tear yourself away, overnight at **Le Grenier à Sel** (☏ 04 74 46 71 90, 06 98 87 62 16; www.hebergement-perouges.fr; rue des Rondes; d €80-98, q €130; 🛜), a medieval town house with five romantic rooms mixing modern and vintage. 'Gargouille' has its own terrace and inspirational countryside views, while nest-cosy 'Remparts' is the couples' favourite.

Pérouges **tourist office** (☏ 09 67 12 70 84; www.perouges.org; 9 rte de la Cité; ⊙ 10am-5pm May-Aug, 10.30am-noon & 2-5pm Mon-Fri, 2-5pm Sat & Sun Apr, Sep & Oct, closed Sat & Sun Nov-Mar) is on the main road opposite the village entrance.

Cars Philibert (☏ 0810 744 744; www.philibert-transport.fr) runs bus 132 (€2, one hour) two to seven times daily from central Lyon to the Pérouges turnoff on route D4 (a 15-minute walk from the village).

◉ La Confluence

Lyon's newest neighbourhood lies at Presqu'île's southern tip where the Rhône and the Saône meet. The former industrial wasteland has been brought back to life by a multimillion-euro urban-renewal project, recognised for its cutting-edge, environmentally sustainable design.

Phase One has seen the whimsical remodelling of existing buildings, including the **Pavillon des Douanes** (customs house), whose balconies are now surmounted by pairs of giant orange frogs, and **La Sucrerie**, a converted 1930s sugar warehouse that houses a nightclub (p491) on its top floor and hosts art exhibits during Lyon's **Biennale d'Art Contemporain** (www.labiennalede lyon.com; ⊙ Sep-Dec).

New buildings to watch for include **Ycone**, an innovative residential tower by Jean Nouvel, and **French Tech Totem**, which will house tech start-ups inside the redesigned Halle Girard.

Musée des Confluences   MUSEUM
(☏ 04 28 38 12 12; www.museedesconfluences.fr; 86 quai Perrache, 6e; adult/child €9/free; ⊙ 11am-7pm Tue, Wed & Fri, to 10pm Thu, 10am-7pm Sat & Sun; 🚇 T1) This eye-catching building, designed by the Viennese firm Coop Himmelb(l)au, is the crowning glory of the Confluence. This ambitious science-and-humanities museum is housed in a futuristic steel-and-glass transparent crystal. Its distorted structure is one of the city's iconic landmarks.

Its artfully displayed permanent exhibitions are arranged thematically into four sections. The 'Origins' exhibition focuses on the origins of the Earth and the various theories of evolution; the 'Eternity' exhibition is devoted to death rites; the 'Societies' exhibition explores how human groups are organised and interact; and the 'Species' exhibition is devoted to natural history. Leave plenty of time to also explore the excellent temporary exhibitions.

Aquarium du Grand Lyon   AQUARIUM
(☏ 04 72 66 65 66; www.aquariumlyon.fr; 7 rue Stéphane Déchant, La Mulatière; adult/child €15/11; ⊙ 11am-7pm Wed-Sun Sep-Jun, daily Jul, Aug & school holidays; 🚢 Maison du Confluent) Just west of the Confluence, Lyon's well-thought-out aquarium is home to some 300 marine species, including more than 5000 fish. Bus 15 links it with place Bellecour. You get a 10% discount if you buy your ticket online.

◉ Rive Gauche

The Rhône's Rive Gauche (Left Bank) harbours parks, museums and day-to-day Lyonnais amenities, including the city's university and transport hubs.

Parc de la Tête d'Or   PARK
(www.loisirs-parcdelatetedor.com; bd des Belges, 6e; ⊙ 6.30am-10.30pm mid-Apr–mid-Oct, to 8.30pm rest of yr; 🚌 C1, C5, Ⓜ Masséna) If you're museumed out, head to this lovely space north of the centre, which provides a green haven for

nature lovers and families. Spanning 117 hectares, France's largest urban park was landscaped in the 1860s. It's graced by a lake (rent a row boat), botanic gardens with greenhouses, rose gardens, a zoo and a tourist train. Take bus C1 (from Part-Dieu train station) or bus C5 (from place Bellecour and Hôtel de Ville) to the Parc Tête d'Or-Churchill stop.

Musée d'Art Contemporain GALLERY
(☑0472691717; www.mac-lyon.com; 81 quai Charles de Gaulle, 6e; adult/child €8/free; ⊙11am-6pm Wed-Sun; 🚌C1, C4, C5) Lyon's contemporary-art museum mounts edgy temporary exhibitions and a rotating permanent collection of post-1960 art. It sometimes closes for several weeks between exhibitions, so check to make sure there's something on. Buses stop right out front.

Centre d'Histoire de la Résistance et de la Déportation MUSEUM
(☑04 78 72 23 11; www.chrd.lyon.fr; 14 av Berthelot, 7e; adult/child €8/free; ⊙10am-6pm Wed-Sun; Ⓜ Perrache, Jean Macé) The WWII headquarters of Gestapo commander Klaus Barbie evokes Lyon's role as the 'Capital of the Resistance' through moving multimedia exhibits. The museum includes sound recordings of deportees and Resistance fighters, plus a varied collection of everyday objects associated with the Resistance (including the parachute Jean Moulin used to re-enter France in 1942).

Musée Lumière MUSEUM
(☑04 78 78 18 95; www.institut-lumiere.org; 25 rue du Premier Film, 8e; adult/child €7/6; ⊙10am-6.30pm Tue-Sun; Ⓜ Monplaisir-Lumière) Cinema's glorious beginnings are showcased at the art nouveau home of Antoine Lumière, who moved to Lyon with sons Auguste and Louis in 1870. The brothers shot the first reels of the world's first motion picture, *La Sortie des Usines Lumières (Exit of the Lumières Factories)* here on 19 March 1895.

👉 Tours

The tourist office (p493) offers an outstanding choice of tours.

LyonExplorer WALKING
(☑07 69 61 34 29; www.lyonexplorer.com; place Bellecour; ⊙tour at 10am Mon, Wed & Fri; Ⓜ Bellecour) Energetic Lyon local Nico leads these fascinating 2½-hour walking and storytelling tours that take you to some of the lesser-known

spots around the city. The meeting spot is on place Bellecour near the statue of Louis XIV. The tour is free, though tips are highly encouraged.

Les Bateaux Lyonnais BOATING
(Croisière Promenade; ☑04 78 42 96 81; www.lesbateauxlyonnais.com; 2 quai des Célestins, 2e; river excursions adult/child from €14/8; ⊙daily Apr-Oct; Ⓜ Bellecour, Vieux Lyon) From April to October, river excursions depart from Lyon City Boat's dock along the Saône. Advance bookings are essential for lunch and dinner **cruises** (Croisière Restaurant; ☑04 78 42 96 81; www.lyoncityboat.com; 16 quai Claude Bernard, 7e; 2½hr lunch/dinner cruise €50/59, 5½hr lunch cruise €69; ⊙Tue-Sun by reservation; Ⓜ Ampère, Guillotière, 🚋T1), which leave from a separate dock on the Rhône.

⭐ Festivals & Events

⭐Fête des Lumières WINTER FESTIVAL
(Festival of Lights; www.fetedeslumieres.lyon.fr; ⊙Dec) Over four days around the Feast of the Immaculate Conception (8 December), magnificent sound-and-light shows are projected onto key buildings, while locals illuminate window sills with candles. This is Lyon's premier festival, and it's so colourful that it's worth timing your trip around it. Note that every hotel is fully booked.

Nuits de Fourvière PERFORMING ARTS
(Fourvière Nights; ☑04 72 57 15 40; www.nuits defourviere.com; ⊙Jun & Jul) A diverse program of open-air theatre, music and dance concerts atmospherically set in Fourvière's Roman amphitheatre from early June to late July.

🛏 Sleeping

Lyon's tourist office (p493) runs a free reservation service (http://book.lyon-france.com/en/accommodation) and occasionally offers deals like free breakfasts or discounts on multinight stays.

Chambres d'hôte (B&Bs) and rental apartments are increasingly popular; umbrella organisations include **Gîtes de France** (www.gites-bed-and-breakfast-rhone.com) and **Chambres Lyon** (www.chambreslyon.com). Other interesting websites include **Mon Hôtel Particulier Lyon** (www.mon-hotel-particulier-lyon.com) and **Loges Vieux Lyon** (www.loges-vieux-lyon.com).

THE PLACE TO BE

A stellar new addition to Lyon, the **Mob Hotel** (🖉 04 58 55 55 88; www.mobhotel. com; 55 quai Rambaud, 2e; d/ste from €120/170; P 🛜; 🚇 T1) is a magnet for designers and the creative set. Metal lacework encases the avant-garde building overlooking the Saône, while the inside is a playful mixture of polished concrete, pale blond woods, artful lighting and subtle pastels. Book a Master Mob room for a balcony and ample space.

The 1st-floor terrace is the place to be on warm days, and the restaurant serves excellent pizzas made from organic, locally sourced ingredients. Regular events include yoga and Pilates classes, as well as DJ-fuelled parties on weekends.

🛏 Vieux Lyon

Auberge de Jeunesse du Vieux Lyon   HOSTEL €

(🖉 04 78 15 05 50; www.hifrance.org; 41-45 montée du Chemin Neuf, 5e; dm incl breakfast €20-27; ⏱reception 7am-1pm, 2-8pm & 9pm-1am; @🛜; 🚇Vieux Lyon, 🚇Minimes) Stunning city views unfold from the terrace of Lyon's Hostelling International-affiliated hostel, and from many of the (mostly four- and six-bed) dorms. Bike parking and kitchen facilities are available, and there's an on-site bar. Try for a dorm with city views. To avoid the tiring 10-minute climb from Vieux Lyon metro station, take the funicular to Minimes station and walk downhill.

★ Lyon Renaissance   APARTMENT €€

(🖉 04 27 89 30 58; www.lyon-renaissance.com; 16 rue du Bœuf, 5e; apt €95-115; 🛜; 🚇Vieux Lyon) Friendly owners Françoise and Patrick rent these two superbly situated Vieux Lyon apartments with beamed ceilings and kitchen facilities. The smaller 3rd-floor walk-up (Côté Cour) sleeps two, with windows overlooking a pretty tree-shaded square. A second unit (Côté Jardin), opposite Vieux Lyon's most famous medieval tower, has a spacious living room with ornamental fireplace and fold-out couch, plus a mezzanine with double bed.

Artelit   APARTMENT €€

(🖉 04 78 42 84 83; www.dormiralyon.com; 16 rue du Bœuf, 5e; d €140-250, apt €150-250; 🛜; 🚇Vieux Lyon) Run by Lyonnais photographer Frédéric Jean, the three spacious tower rooms and self-catering apartment of this delightful *chambre d'hôte* have centuries of history behind every nook and cranny. They're right in the heart of Vieux Lyon but still feel very quiet. If you fall in love with the artworks, you can buy them to take home. Good English is spoken.

Collège Hotel   HOTEL €€

(🖉 04 72 10 05 05; www.college-hotel.com; 5 place St-Paul, 5e; d €130-190; P ✳ @ 🛜; 🚇Vieux Lyon, Hôtel de Ville) With an art deco facade, stylishly minimalist guestrooms and school-themed decor throughout, this four-star hotel is one of Vieux Lyon's unique lodging options. It shelters 40 luminous rooms, 10 of which come with balconies. Enjoy breakfast on the rooftop garden terrace, or in the *salle de classe petit dejeuner,* bedecked like a classroom of yesteryear. It also has private parking (€20, 15 spaces).

★ Cour des Loges   HOTEL €€€

(🖉 04 72 77 44 44; www.courdesloges.com; 2-8 rue du Bœuf, 5e; d €250-450, ste €430-580; ✳@🛜✉; 🚇Vieux Lyon) Four 14th- to 17th-century houses wrapped around a *traboule* (secret passage) with preserved features such as Italianate loggias make this an exquisite place to stay. Individually decorated rooms draw guests with designer bathroom fittings and bountiful antiques, while decadent facilities include a spa, a Michelin-starred restaurant (*menus* €105 to €145), a swish cafe and a cross-vaulted bar.

🛏 Presqu'île

Away Hostel   HOSTEL €

(🖉 04 78 98 53 20; www.awayhostel.com; 21 rue Alsace Lorraine, 1er; dm €25-30, d €95; @🛜; 🚇Croix-Paquet) One of Lyon's best new budget sleeps, Away Hostel has attractive, sunny rooms with tall ceilings, wood floors and oversized windows. The cafe is a good place to meet other travellers, and there are loads of events going on (walking tours, yoga brunches, communal dinners).

Ho36 Lyon Opéra   HOSTEL €

(🖉 04 78 28 11 01; www.ho36hostels.com; 9 rue Ste-Catherine, 1er; dm €25-27, d €80; 🛜; 🚇Hôtel de Ville) Representing a new wave of affordable lodging that doesn't sacrifice design smarts, Ho36 has transformed an old two-star hotel into an atmospheric spot with stylish doubles and a few good-value dorms. It has a bar, a guest kitchen and a handsome interior patio.

Hôtel Le Boulevardier
HOTEL €

(☑ 04 78 28 48 22; www.leboulevardier.fr; 5 rue de la Fromagerie, 1er; d €79-110; ✽ 🛜; Ⓜ Hôtel de Ville, Cordeliers) Le Boulevardier is a bargain 14-room hotel with snug, spotless rooms. It sports quirky touches such as old skis and tennis racquets adorning the hallways. No two rooms are alike; some have exposed brick walls and wooden ceilings. It's up a steep spiral staircase above a cool little cafe, which doubles as reception.

★ Jardin d'Hiver
B&B €€

(☑ 04 78 28 69 34; www.guesthouse-lyon.com; 10 rue des Marronniers, 2e; s/d €110/130, apt per week from €520; ✽ 🛜; Ⓜ Bellecour) Chic and centrally located, this 3rd-floor B&B (no lift) has two spacious rooms replete with modern conveniences – one in understated purple and pistachio, the other in vivid purple and orange. Friendly owner Annick Bournonville serves 100% organic breakfasts in the foliage-filled breakfast room. In the same building, her son rents out apartments with kitchen and laundry facilities. English and Spanish are spoken.

Grand Hôtel des Terreaux
HOTEL €€

(☑ 04 78 27 04 10; www.hotel-lyon-grandhotel desterreaux.fr; 16 rue Lanterne, 1er; s €108-120, d €150-270; ✽ 🛜 ❄; Ⓜ Hôtel de Ville) This four-star venture ideally positioned southwest of place des Terreaux is fair value, especially if you can score a promotional deal online. It offers neat, well-equipped rooms with retro-chic decor. Its distinctive characteristic is the lovely indoor pool next to the breakfast room. No private parking.

Hotel Carlton
HOTEL €€€

(☑ 04 78 42 56 51; www.sofitel.com; 4 rue Jussieu, 2e; r from €170; @ 🛜; Ⓜ Cordeliers, Bellecour) This vintage hotel tempts with soundproofed rooms done up in brilliant reds, lovingly restored with period furniture, mouldings and wallpaper. Options range from 15-sq-m 'Cocoon' units to circular 40-sq-m corner suites, many overlooking pedestrianised place de la République. A sauna, spa and sumptuous breakfast featuring traditional Lyonnais specialities add to the appeal.

🛏 Rive Gauche

Le Flâneur
HOSTEL €

(☑ 09 81 99 16 97; www.leflaneur-guesthouse. com/en; 56 rue Sébastien Gryphe, 7e; dm/s/d from €19/45/60; 🛜; Ⓜ Saxe-Gambetta) The dorm rooms are simple, but the welcome is warm

---

LOCAL KNOWLEDGE

TOP THREE: BREAKFAST, BRUNCH OR CAFE-LIGHT LUNCH

When a quick bite in between sights is needed, try one of these favourite cafes – hot spots for breakfast, brunch or a light lunch.

L'Instant (☑ 04 78 29 85 08; www.linstant-patisserie.fr; 3 place Marcel Bertone, 4e; pastries €2-3.50, weekend brunch €22; ☺ 8am-7pm; 🛜; Ⓜ Croix Rousse) A great place in Croix Rousse to start the day, this hybrid cafe-pastry shop overlooking lovely place Marcel Bertone packs a punch. Stop in for a tea or coffee coupled with one of the delightful in-house *tartes* (there's also brunch on weekends). The mellow setting and relaxed urban vibe add to the appeal. Ample outdoor seating on warm days.

Diploid (☑ 04 69 67 58 93; www.diploid.fr; 18 rue de la Platière, 2er; mains €8-13, brunch menu €23; ☺ 9am-7pm Mon-Fri, 10am-7pm Sat, 11am-7pm Sun; Ⓜ Hôtel de Ville) One of the best places in town for a filling breakfast, Diploid serves up fluffy pancakes and French toast as well as lovely pastries and great coffees amid exposed stone walls and basket-style light fixtures. The small friendly cafe also has changing lunch specials. Brunch on Sunday is a big draw (reserve ahead).

In Cuisine (☑ 04 72 41 18 00; www.incuisine.fr; 1 place Bellecour, 2e; mains €10.50, menu €16.50; ☺ 2.30-6.30pm Mon, 10am-7pm Tue-Sat; Ⓜ Bellecour) Equal parts bookstore, cafe and restaurant, this foodie haven has an astonishing selection of culinary, gastronomic and wine titles. It also offers demonstrations, tastings, cooking courses and lunch (from noon to 2pm) in its tearoom. The menu changes daily; it specialises in market-fresh cuisine with a twist.

ℹ COLD COMFORT

It's hard to resist the 150 flavours at ice-cream shop **Terre Adélice** (🖉 04 78 03 51 84; www.terre-adelice.eu; 1 place de la Baleine, 5e; 1/2/3 scoops €2.70/4.90/6.70; ⊙1-11pm May-Sep, 1-6.30pm Sun-Thu, to 11pm Fri & Sat Oct, Mar & Apr, 2-6pm Fri-Sun Nov-Feb; Ⓜ Vieux Lyon), both divine and daring, on Vieux Lyon's main pedestrian thoroughfare. Play it safe with Valrhona dark chocolate, organic pistachio or vanilla from Madagascar, experiment gently with cardamom, Grand Marnier or lavender, or take a walk on the wild side with a scoop of wasabi, yoghurt and pepper or tomato-basil.

at this convivial hostel on the Rive Gauche (left bank). The huge and bar lounge area is perhaps the best feature here, and setting for occasional concerts (jazz, Balkan folk), workshops, art openings, discussions and other community events.

★**Mama Shelter**   HOTEL €€

(🖉 04 78 02 58 00; www.mamashelter.com/en/lyon; 13 rue Domer, 7e; r €79-323; 🅿❋@🛜; Ⓜ Jean Macé) Lyon's branch of this trendy hotel chain has sleek decor, carpets splashed with calligraffiti, firm beds, plush pillows, modernist lighting and big-screen Macs offering free in-room movies. A youthful crowd fills the long bar at the low-lit restaurant. The residential location 2km outside the centre may feel remote, but it's only three metro stops from Gare de la Part-Dieu and place Bellecour.

✖ Eating

A flurry of big-name chefs presides over a sparkling restaurant line-up that embraces all genres: French, fusion, fast and international, as well as traditional Lyonnais *bouchons* (small bistros).

✖ Vieux Lyon

Vieux Lyon has a surfeit of restaurants, most aimed at tourists.

★**La Cuisinerie**   FUSION €

(🖉 04 78 60 91 86; www.lacuisinerie.com; 16 rue St-Georges; lunch menu €11-17, small plates €6-13; ⊙noon-2pm & 7pm-midnight Mon-Sat; ✖; Ⓜ Vieux Lyon) A charming new addition to Vieux Lyon's St-Georges neighbourhood, La Cuisinerie has a deliciously innovative menu of tapas-sized plates with global influences. You can sample a wide range of flavours (including vegetarian dishes) in small plates like chicken and goat cheese *churros,* crayfish ravioli, or smoked salmon blinis with wasabi cream, among dozens of other options.

★**Daniel et Denise**   BOUCHON €€

(🖉 04 78 42 24 62; www.danieletdenise.fr; 36 rue Tramassac, 5e; mains €17-29, 2-course lunch menu €21, dinner menus €33-51; ⊙noon-2pm & 7.30-9.30pm Tue-Sat; Ⓜ Vieux Lyon) One of Vieux Lyon's most dependable and traditional eateries, this classic spot is run by award-winning chef Joseph Viola. Come here for elaborate variations on traditional Lyonnais themes.

★**Cinq Mains**   NEOBISTRO €€

(🖉 04 37 57 30 52; www.facebook.com/cinqmains; 12 rue Monseigneur Lavarenne, 5e; menu lunch/dinner €19/33; ⊙noon-1.30pm & 7.30-9.30pm; Ⓜ Vieux Lyon) When young Lyonnais Grégory Cuilleron and his two friends opened this neobistro in early 2016, it was an instant hit. They're working wonders at this cool loft-like space with a mezzanine, serving up tantalising creations based on what they find at the market. A new generation of chefs, and a new spin for Lyonnais cuisine.

Les Terrasses de Lyon   FRENCH €€€

(🖉 04 72 56 56 02; www.villaflorentine.com/en/restaurant.html; 25 montée St-Barthélémy, 5e; lunch menu €49, dinner menus €76-115; ⊙noon-1.15pm & 7.30-9.15pm Tue-Sat; Ⓜ Vieux Lyon) Offering sweeping views over the city, this superbly located restaurant serves up imaginative and beautifully executed dishes, including foie gras with shrimp and crispy salad, or breast of veal with green cabbage and cancoillotte cheese. A thoughtful touch is the excellent *menu maraîcher,* a vegetarian tasting menu.

✖ Presqu'île

In the Presqu'île, cobbled rue Mercière and rue des Marronniers – both in the 2e (metro Bellecour) – are chock-a-block with sidewalk terraces in summer. In the 1er, the tangle of streets south of the opera house, including rue du Garet, rue Neuve and rue Verdi, is equally jam-packed with eateries.

Le Potager des Halles   NEOBISTRO, TAPAS €

(🖉 04 78 00 24 84; www.lepotagerdeshalles.com; 3 rue de la Martinière, 1er; mains €14-21; ⊙noon-2pm & 7.30-10pm Tue-Sat; Ⓜ Hôtel de Ville) Opposite the colourful Fresque des Lyonnais, this gourmet bistro is a dreamy spot for a tasty lunch or to

DON'T MISS

LYONNAIS BOUCHONS
••

A *bouchon* might be a 'bottle stopper' or 'traffic jam' elsewhere in France, but in Lyon it's a small, friendly bistro that cooks up traditional cuisine using regional produce. *Bouchons* originated in the first half of the 20th century when many large bourgeois families had to let go of their in-house cooks, who then set up their own restaurant businesses. The first of these *mères* (mothers) was Mère Guy, followed by Mère Filloux, Mère Brazier (under whom Paul Bocuse trained) and others. Choose carefully – not all *bouchons* are as authentic as they first appear. Many of the best are certified by the organisation Les Authentiques Bouchons Lyonnais – look for the metal plate on their façades depicting traditional puppet Gnafron (Guignol's mate) with his glass of Beaujolais.

Kick-start a memorable gastronomic experience with a *communard,* a blood-red aperitif of Beaujolais wine mixed with *crème de cassis* (blackcurrant liqueur), named after the supporters of the Paris Commune killed in 1871. When ordering wine with your meal, ask for a *pot* – a classically Lyonnais 46cL glass bottle adorned with an elastic band to prevent wine drips – of local Brouilly, Beaujolais, Côtes du Rhône or Mâcon, costing around €9 to €12; a smaller, 25cL version called a *fillette* costs between €5 and €7.

Next comes the entrée, perhaps *tablier de sapeur* ('fireman's apron'; actually meaning breaded, fried tripe), *salade de cervelas* (salad of boiled pork sausage sometimes studded with pistachio nuts or black truffle specks), or *caviar de la Croix Rousse* (lentils in creamy sauce). Hearty main dishes include *boudin blanc* (veal sausage), *boudin noir aux pommes* (blood sausage with apples), quenelles (feather-light flour, egg and cream dumplings), *quenelles de brochet* (pike dumplings served in a creamy crayfish sauce), *andouillette* (sausage made from pigs' intestines), *gras double* (a type of tripe), *pieds de mouton/veau/couchon* (sheep/calf/pig trotters) and *poulet au vinaigre* (chicken cooked in vinegar).

For the cheese course, choose between a bowl of *fromage blanc* (a cross between cream cheese and natural yoghurt); *cervelle de canut* ('brains of the silk weaver'; *fromage blanc* mixed with chives and garlic), which originated in Croix Rousse and accompanied every meal for 19th-century weavers; or local St Marcellin ripened to gooey perfection.

Desserts are grandma-style: think *tarte aux pommes* (apple tart), or the Lyonnais classic *tarte aux pralines,* a brilliant rose-coloured confection made with crème fraiche and crushed sugar-coated almonds.

Little etiquette is required in *bouchons*. Seldom do you get clean cutlery for each course, and mopping your plate with a chunk of bread is fine. In the most popular and traditional spots, you'll often find yourself sitting elbow-to-elbow with your fellow diners at a long row of tightly wedged tables. Advance reservations are recommended.

Several classics worth seeking out:

Le Garet (☑ 04 78 28 16 94; 7 rue du Garet, 1er; lunch/dinner menus €20/28; ☺ noon-1.30pm & 7.30-9pm Mon-Fri; Ⓜ Hôtel de Ville)

Chez Hugon (☑ 04 78 28 10 94; www.bouchonlyonnais.fr; 12 rue Pizay, 1er; menu €28; ☺ noon-2pm & 7.30-9.30pm Mon-Fri; Ⓜ Hôtel de Ville)

Le Poêlon d'Or (☑ 04 78 37 65 60; www.lepoelondor-restaurant.fr; 29 rue des Remparts d'Ainay, 2e; lunch menus €18-20, dinner menus €27-33; ☺ noon-2pm & 7.30-10pm Mon-Fri; Ⓜ Ampère-Victor Hugo)

Chez Paul (☑ 04 78 28 35 83; www.bouchonchezpaul.fr; 11 rue Major Martin, 1er; lunch menus €16-20, dinner menus €18-27; ☺ noon-2pm & 7.30-9.30pm Mon-Sat; Ⓜ Hôtel de Ville)

Le Tire Bouchon (☑ 09 83 22 88 47; www.letirebouchon-lyon.fr; 16 rue du Bœuf, 5e; lunch menus €15-18, dinner menus €27-39; ☺ noon-2pm Wed-Sun, 7-10.30pm Tue-Sat; Ⓜ Vieux Lyon)

Café des Fédérations (☑ 04 78 28 26 00; www.restaurant-cafedesfederations-lyon.com; 8-10 rue Major Martin, 1er; lunch/dinner menus €21/29; ☺ noon-1.30pm & 7.45-9pm Mon-Sat, noon-1.30pm Sun; Ⓜ Hôtel de Ville)

Les Fines Gueules (☑ 04 78 28 99 14; www.fines-gueules.fr; 16 rue Lainerie, 5e; menu €29-33, mains €18-28; ☺ noon-1.45pm & 7-10pm Tue-Sat; Ⓜ Vieux Lyon)

LYON & THE RHÔNE VALLEY LYON

WORTH A TRIP

THE POPE OF FRENCH CUISINE

Some 7km north of Lyon, this tri-ple-Michelin-starred **Restaurant Paul Bocuse** (📞04 72 42 90 90; www.bocuse. com; 40 quai de la Plage, Collonges au Mont d'Or; menus €175-275; ⊗noon-1.30pm & 8-9pm)was the flagship of the city's most decorated chef, Paul Bocuse. Although Bocuse is no longer around, his recipes continue to dazzle foodies, with the likes of escargots with parsley butter, thyme-roasted rack of lamb and Bocuse's signature *soupe aux truffes noires VGE* (truffle soup created for French president Valéry Giscard d'Estaing in 1975).

while away an evening. Happy diners throng the high-ceilinged main dining room, cosy up-stairs balcony and sidewalk tables, lingering over wine and creative seasonal dishes.

L'Instant Fromage CHEESE €
(📞04 78 92 93 54; www.linstant-fromage.fr; 31 rue Ste-Hélène, 2e; lunch menu €11, mains €9-16; ⊗noon-2pm & 6.30-10pm Tue-Sat; 🛜; ⓂAmpère-Victor Hugo, Bellecour) This sweet hideaway with checked tablecloths is a cheese-lover's dream. Sample individual portions of three-dozen French cheeses (cow, sheep and goat) from the chalkboard menu, or let them surprise you with an *ardoise découverte* (five cheeses for €13.50). It also has a nice selection of charcuterie, tartines (open-faced sandwiches) and salads.

★**Le Musée** BOUCHON €€
(📞04 78 37 71 54; 2 rue des Forces, 2e; lunch mains €14, lunch menus €19-26, dinner menus €23-32; ⊗noon-1.30pm & 7.30-9.30pm Tue-Sat; ⓂCordeliers) Housed in the stables of Lyon's former Hôtel de Ville, this delightful *bouchon* serves a splendid array of meat-heavy Lyonnais classics, including a divine *poulet au vinaigre* (chicken cooked in vinegar). The daily changing *menu* features 10 appetisers and 10 main dishes, plus five scrumptious desserts, all served on cute china plates at long family-style tables.

Chez Albert FRENCH €€
(📞04 78 27 95 56; 10 place Fernand Rey; menu lunch/dinner €18/28; ⊗noon-1.30pm & 8-10pm

Mon-Fri; 🖉; ⓂHôtel de Ville) The bright purple exterior is an apt introduction to the bold flavours of Chez Albert, a local favourite. Inside, the walls are strung with cooking implements, oil paintings and myriad roosters. None of this distracts from the changing hand-scrawled menu of roast meats and seafood, creative casseroles and Asian-accented salads (helpful English-speaking staff can guide you).

Pizzeria Napoli ITALIAN €€
(📞04 78 37 23 37; http://pizzeria-napoli-lyon.com; 45 rue Franklin, 2e; mains €13-24; ⊗noon-2pm & 7-11pm Tue-Sat; 🖉; ⓂAmpère) In business since 1966, family-owned Pizzeria Napoli serves some of Lyon's best pizzas, topped with quality ingredients and fired up in a wood-burning oven.

Le Bouchon des Filles FRENCH €€
(📞04 78 30 40 44; 20 rue Sergent Blandan, 1er; menu €27; ⊗7-10pm daily & noon-1.30pm Fri-Sun; ⓂHôtel de Ville) This contemporary ode to Lyon's legendary culinary *mères* (mothers) is run by an enterprising crew of young women with deep roots in the local *bouchon* scene and a flair for fine cooking. The light and fluffy quenelles are among the best you'll find in Lyon, and the rustic-chic decor, with wooden beams and deep red walls, is warm and welcoming.

Thomas MODERN FRENCH €€
(📞04 72 56 04 76; www.restaurant-thomas. com; 6 rue Laurencin, 2e; lunch menu €22, dinner menu €47; ⊗11am-2pm & 6pm-midnight Mon-Fri; ⓂAmpère) One of Lyon's savviest chefs, Thomas Ponson, infuses his cooking with a panoply of flavours. He gives taste buds the choice between formal dining at his eponymous restaurant; more casual fare in his Bouchon Thomas; and more casual still at his tapas-inspired Bistrot Thomas.

Brasserie Georges BRASSERIE €€
(📞04 72 56 54 54; www.brasseriegeorges.com; 30 cours de Verdun, 2e; mains €19-27, menus €23-28; ⊗11.30am-11pm Sun-Thu, to midnight Fri & Sat; ⓂPerrache) Opened as a brewery in 1836 (and still offering three homebrews on tap), Georges' cavernous 1924 art deco interior can feed 2000 a day! Famous customers include Rodin, Balzac, Hemingway, Zola, Verne and Piaf; food spans onion soup, sauerkraut with smoked pork belly, roasted sea bass, Lyonnais specialities and a smattering of vegetarian options.

✖ Croix Rousse

Croix Rousse is a great neighbourhood for foodies, with a range of affordable eateries with bags of character.

Les Mauvaises Herbes   VEGETARIAN €
(✔ 04 27 01 52 26; 3 rue du Jardin des Plantes; plat du jour €12, small plates around €9; ⊙ noon-11pm; 🛜; Ⓜ Croix-Paquet) A creative spot dreamed up by three eco-minded Lyonnais friends, this sunny, easy-going place serves up excellent organic fare, most of which is vegan. At lunchtime, you can stop in for changing specials, or come back in the evening for good wines (or teas), plus small plates of smoked lentil and walnut terrine, smooth hummus, or flavour-packed Brussels sprouts.

★ L'Ourson qui Boit   FUSION €€
(✔ 04 78 27 23 37; 23 rue Royale, 1er; lunch/dinner menu €20/32; ⊙ noon-1.30pm & 7.30-9.30pm Mon, Tue & Thu-Sat; Ⓜ Croix Paquet) On the fringes of Croix Rousse, Japanese chef Akira Nishigaki puts his own splendid spin on French cuisine, with plenty of locally sourced fresh vegetables and light, clean flavours. The ever-changing *menu* of two daily appetisers and two main dishes is complemented by good wines, attentive service and scrumptious desserts. Well worth reserving ahead.

Next door, you can sample Akira Nishigaki's imaginatively delicious pastries at **L'Ourson qui Boit – Pâtisserie** (✔ 04 78 72 90 54; 2 rue Roger Violi, 1er; pastries €3.50; ⊙ 10.30am-7pm Mon, Tue & Thu-Sat; Ⓜ Croix Paquet).

La Bonâme de Bruno   MODERN FRENCH €€
(✔ 04 78 30 83 93; www.restaurant-labonamede bruno.com; 5 Grande Rue des Feuillants; lunch menus €16-19, dinner menus €30-39; ⊙ noon-2pm Tue-Fri, 8-9.30pm Tue-Sat; Ⓜ Croix Paquet) Great food and atmosphere come together at this airy yet intimate eatery that's somewhere on the continuum between bistro and gastronomic. The high-ceilinged, parquet-floored dining room conjures the spirit of a 19th-century dance studio, while the *menus,* prepared with enthusiasm and creativity, change regularly based on Bruno's whims. Desserts are especially memorable.

Le Canut et Les Gones   BISTRO €€
(✔ 04 78 29 17 23; www.lecanutetlesgones.com; 29 rue de Belfort, 4e; lunch menus €19-27, dinner menu €32; ⊙ noon-1.30pm & 7.30-9.30pm Tue-Sat; Ⓜ Croix Rousse) With three cosy rooms and funky retro decor featuring dozens of antique clocks, this laid-back neighbourhood eatery draws a savvy local crowd with creative cuisine built around produce from Croix Rousse's market.

La Mère Brazier   GASTRONOMY €€€
(✔ 04 78 23 17 20; www.lamerebrazier.fr; 12 rue Royale; lunch menus €57-70, dinner menus €125-160; ⊙ noon-1pm & 8-9pm Mon-Fri Sep-Jul; Ⓜ Croix Paquet) Chef Mathieu Viannay has reinvented the mythical early-20th-century restaurant that earned Mère Eugénie Brazier Lyon's first trio of Michelin stars in 1933 (a copy of the original guidebook takes pride of place). Vianney is doing admirable justice to Brazier's legacy, claiming two Michelin stars himself for his assured cuisine accompanied by an impressive wine list.

🍷 Drinking & Nightlife

Lyon's beer-thirsty students keep the scene lively and the bars and clubs pumping at weekends. Vieux Lyon has an extraordinary concentration of British and Irish pubs. For

---

DON'T MISS

DRINKS AFLOAT

Along quai Victor Augagneur on the Rhône's left bank, a string of *péniches* (barges with onboard bars) serve drinks from mid-afternoon onwards, with many of them rocking until the wee hours with DJs and/or live bands. To study your options, stroll the quayside between Pont Lafayette and Pont de la Guillotière.

Le Sirius (✔ 04 78 71 78 71; www.lesirius.com; 4 quai Victor Augagneur, 3me; ⊙ 5pm-1am; Ⓜ Place Guichard, Cordeliers) Set in a *péniche* on the Rhône, Le Sirius draws a party crowd to its DJ-fuelled nights and concerts. Check online for its latest line-up, which leans towards jazz, hip hop, reggae, African rhythms and swing.

Péniche La Marquise (www.marquise.net; 20 quai Victor Augagneur, 3e; ⊙ 1pm-1am Sun-Wed, to 5am Fri & Sat; Ⓜ Place Guichard) This popular barge bar hosts all-night live shows and DJ sets featuring jazz, techno, hip hop and more. On sunny days, the terrace is a fine place to be.

SPECIALIST COFFEE & TEA

La Boîte à Café – Café Mokxa (www.cafemokxa.com; 3 rue de l'Abbé Rozier, 1er; ⊙7.30am-7pm Mon-Fri, 9am-7pm Sat, 10am-7pm Sun; 🛜; Ⓜ Croix Paquet, Hôtel de Ville) A favourite haunt of Lyonnais caffeine fiends and students, this laid-back place on the Croix Rousse slopes roasts its own beans and serves Sunday brunch. In summer, tables spill onto charming, circular place du Forez. It also serves superb pastries.

Slake (http://slake-coffee.com; 9 rue de l'Ancienne Préfecture; ⊙8am-7pm Mon-Fri, from 10am Sat, from 11am Sun; 🛜; Ⓜ Bellecour) A buzzing and decidedly hip coffee house around the corner from place des Jacobins, Slake makes beautiful lattes (the kind with artful designs atop) as well as other caffeinated goodness. All go nicely with the pastries and tarts. Come at lunchtime for soups, salads and sandwiches. There's also Sunday brunch (€22).

Sofffa (www.facebook.com/hellosofffa; 17 rue Ste-Catherine, 1er; ⊙9am-7pm Mon-Fri, from 2pm Sat; Ⓜ Hôtel de Ville) A novel concept in Lyon, Sofffa charges by time (€5 the first hour, €2 each subsequent half-hour) during which your coffees and snacks are free. A smattering of leather armchairs, mismatched tables and art-covered stone walls set the scene for chitchat and/or people-watching.

Torü (📞09 86 57 25 45; www.facebook.com/toruteashop; 23 rue René Leynaud, 1er; ⊙10am-7pm Tue-Fri, 11am-7pm Sat, to 4pm Sun; Ⓜ Croix-Paquet) Tapping into the latest craving in Lyon, this elegant spot has an impressive tea list, plus a photogenic wall of canisters packed with loose-leaf goodness for tea shoppers. The relaxing setting is just right for a perfectly brewed morning or afternoon pick-me-up.

offbeat bars, scout out alternative Croix Rousse.

Many establishments start as a relaxed place for a drink (and often serve food, too), morphing into jam-packed bars and/or live-music and dancing venues as the night wears on.

🍸 Presqu'île

L'Antiquaire
COCKTAIL BAR

(📞06 34 21 54 65; 20 rue Hippolyte Flandrin, 1er; ⊙5pm-1am Tue & Wed, to 3am Thu-Sat, 6.30pm-1am Sun & Mon; Ⓜ Hôtel de Ville) Old-time jazz, flickering candles and friendly suspenders-wearing barkeeps set the mood in this atmospheric speakeasy-style bar. The painstakingly prepared cocktails are first-rate (try a Penicillin made from scotch, ginger, honey, lemon and peat whiskey) and are best sipped slowly at one of the dark wood and leather booths.

Bar du Passage
COCKTAIL BAR

(📞04 78 28 11 16; www.le-passage.com/bar; 8 rue de Plâtre, 1er; ⊙7pm-1am Tue & Wed, to 3am Thu-Sat; Ⓜ Hôtel de Ville) Like a vestige from another time, the low-lit Bar du Passage impresses with its mural-covered ceiling, stuffed leather armchairs and vintage jazz soundtrack. The cocktails are pricey (€13 to €15), but nicely balanced. To get here, find the Restaurant du Passage sign, walk to the back of the alley and ring the buzzer.

Dam's Pub
BAR

(www.damspub.com; 4 place Sathonay, 1er; ⊙7am-1am; Ⓜ Hôtel de Ville) A staple of Lyon's easy-going pub scene, Dam's is a lively spot for a pint no matter the hour. It has good beers on tap (including the Belgian ale Saint Stefanus), televised sport, decent pub grub and a well-placed terrace overlooking place Sathonay.

Le Vin des Vivants
WINE BAR

(www.levindesvivants.fr; 6 place Fernand Rey, 1er; ⊙6.30-9pm Tue & Wed, to 11.30pm Thu-Sat; Ⓜ Hôtel de Ville) This relaxed stone-walled corner bar on a pretty backstreet square specialises in organic wines.

La Maison M
CLUB

(📞04 72 00 87 67; http://mmlyon.com; 21 place Gabriel Rambaud, 1er; ⊙7.30pm-4am Wed-Sat; Ⓜ Hôtel de Ville) A fantastic addition to Lyon's nightlife scene, La Maison M has three separate spaces: a tropical-style bar near the entrance, a dance floor to the left and a cosy lounge off to the right. DJ parties feature nights of samba (with Brazilian cocktails to match), cumbia, hip hop and new-wave disco.

⚑ Croix Rousse

Modernartcafé　　　　　　　　　BAR
(http://modernartcafe.free.fr; 65 bd de la Croix
Rousse, 4e; ⊙5pm-1am Mon-Sat; 🛜; Ⓜ Croix
Rousse) Changing art on the walls, weekend
brunch and various photography-, music- and
video-driven events make this art bar a linchpin of Croix Rousse's creative community.

Groom　　　　　　　　　　　　　BAR
(www.groomlyon.com; 6 rue Roger Violi, 1er;
⊙7.30pm-1am Tue, Wed & Sun, to 2am Thu, to
4am Fri & Sat; Ⓜ Croix-Paquet) This downstairs
cocktail den has a winning formula of great
cocktails and friendly staff, plus an excellent
line-up of bands and DJs throughout the
week. Recent draws include swing dancing,
indie rock, funk and jazz.

☆ Entertainment

The leading what's-on guide with both
print and online editions is Le Petit Bulletin
(www.petit-bulletin.fr/lyon). Other helpful
websites with entertainment listings include
www.lyon-france.com/L-Agenda and www.
lyonclubbing.com (both in French).

Tickets are sold at **Fnac Billetterie** (www.
fnacspectacles.com; 85 rue de la République, 2e;
⊙10am-7.30pm Mon-Sat; Ⓜ Bellecour).

Opéra de Lyon　　　　　　　　　OPERA
(www.opera-lyon.com; place de la Comédie, 1er;
Ⓜ Hôtel de Ville) Lyon's premier venue for opera, ballet and classical music.

**Auditorium Orchestre
National de Lyon**　　　　　CLASSICAL MUSIC
(📞04 78 95 95 95; www.auditorium-lyon.com;
149 rue Garibaldi, 3e; ⊙Sep-Jun; Ⓜ Part-Dieu,
Ⓜ Part-Dieu-Servient, Part-Dieu-Villette) Built in
1975, this spaceship-like auditorium houses
the National Orchestra of Lyon, along with
workshops, jazz and world-music concerts.

La Clef de Voûte　　　　　　　　JAZZ
(📞04 78 28 51 95; www.laclefdevoute.fr; 1 place
Chardonnet; ⊙7pm-midnight Wed-Mon; Ⓜ Croix-
Paquet) One of Lyon's most atmospheric
music venues, La Clef de Voûte is set in a
stone-walled, candelit cellar dating from the
18th century. Aside from an excellent line-up
of live jazz, there's cheese and antipasti platters, and good wines by the glass. Concerts
start at 8.30pm

★Le Sucre　　　　　　　　　LIVE MUSIC
(www.le-sucre.eu; 50 quai Rambaud, 2e;
⊙8.30pm-midnight Wed & Thu, 6.30pm-1am Fri, to
5am Sat, 4-11pm Sun; 🚊T1) Down in the Confluence neighbourhood, Lyon's most innovative club hosts DJs, live shows and eclectic
arts events on its super-cool roof terrace
atop a 1930s sugar factory, La Sucrière.

Le Transbordeur　　　　　　LIVE MUSIC
(www.transbordeur.fr; 3 bd de Stalingrad, Villeurbanne; ⊙Wed-Sat; 🚊Cité Internationale/Transbor-
deur) In an old industrial building near the
Parc de la Tête d'Or's northeastern corner, Lyon's prime concert venue draws international
acts on the European concert-tour circuit.

Hangar du Premier Film　　　　CINEMA
(www.institut-lumiere.org; 25 rue du Premier Film,
8e; Ⓜ Monplaisir-Lumière) This former factory
and birthplace of cinema now screens films
of all genres and eras in their original languages. From approximately June to September, the big screen moves outside.

ⓘ LGBT LYON

Declared France's most gay-friendly city in 2014 by the magazine Têtu, Lyon has scads of
venues.

Guys' favourite places to party include **United Café** (www.united-cafe.com; impasse de
la Pêcherie, 1er; ⊙midnight-5am; Ⓜ Hôtel de Ville), **Le XS Bar** (19 rue Claudia, 2e; ⊙5pm-3am;
Ⓜ Cordeliers), **L'Imperial** (📞06 44 87 35 75; 24 rue Royale; ⊙11pm-6am Thu-Sat; Ⓜ Croix
Paquet) and the city's oldest gay bar, **La Ruche** (22 rue Gentil, 2e; ⊙5pm-1am; Ⓜ Cordeliers).
Lesbian venues are limited to **Le L Bar** (19 rue du Garet, 1er; ⊙6pm-2am Mon-Sat; Ⓜ Hôtel de
Ville). For up-to-the-minute listings, visit the website Hétéroclite (www.heteroclite.org), or
check with the **Centre LGBTI de Lyon** (📞04 78 27 10 10; www.centrelgbtilyon.org; 19 rue des
Capucins, 1er; Ⓜ Croix Paquet), which organises social events.

Lyon's **Lesbian & Gay Pride** (www.fierte.net; ⊙Jun) march and festivities hit the
streets each year in June. In March, the city hosts a popular week-long LGBT film festival,
Écrans Mixtes (www.festival-em.org; ⊙Mar).

GUIGNOL: LYON'S HISTORIC PUPPETS

The history of Lyon's famous puppet, Guignol, is intertwined with that of the city. In 1797, out-of-work silk-weaver Laurent Mourguet took up dentistry (ie pulling teeth). To attract patients, he set up a puppet show in front of his chair, initially featuring the Italian Polichinelle (who became Punch in England). Success saw Mourguet move into full-time puppetry, creating Guignol in about 1808 and devising shows revolving around working-class issues, the news of the day, social gossip and satire.

Today this little hand-operated glove puppet pops up all over his home town, including on the **Fresque des Lyonnais** (cnr rue de la Martinière & quai St-Vincent, 1er; MHôtel de Ville) mural and at puppet museums.

Guignol's highly visual, slapstick-style antics appeal equally to children and adults (theatres also stage some adult-only evening performances). Shows are in French but also incorporate traditional Lyonnais dialect, such as the words *quinquets* (eyes), *picou* (nose), *bajafler* (talking nonstop) and *gones* (kids, and, by extension, all Lyonnais).

In addition to **Puppet Theatre** (Le Véritable Guignol du Parc; ☑06 12 42 48 71; http://theatre-guignol-lyon.fr; place de Guignol, 6e; adult/child €4/3.50; ⊙3pm, 4pm & 5pm Wed, Sat & Sun; ⊡C1, C5, MMasséna) performances at Parc de la Tête d'Or, Lyon has three dedicated Guignol theatres:

Théâtre La Maison de Guignol (☑04 72 40 26 61; www.lamaisondeguignol.fr; 2 montée du Gourguillon, 5e; tickets adult/child €11/9; ⊙Wed, Sat & Sun; MVieux Lyon) Quaint St-Georges theatre.

Guignol, un Gone de Lyon (☑04 72 32 11 55; www.guignol-un-gone-de-lyon.com; 65 bd des Canuts, 4e; adult/child €9.50/7.50; ⊙performances 3.30pm Wed, Sat & Sun Oct-Jun; MHénon) In Croix Rousse; puppeteers give audiences a behind-the-scenes peek at the props and puppets after certain performances.

Théâtre Le Guignol de Lyon (☑04 78 29 83 36; www.guignol-lyon.net; 2 rue Louis Carrand, 5e; adult/child €10/7.50; MVieux Lyon) In Vieux Lyon. Check individual websites for ticket prices (around €10 or €11) and schedules (typically Wednesdays and weekends, with extra dates added during school holidays).

🛍 Shopping

Vieux Lyon's narrow streets are dotted with galleries, and antiquarian and secondhand bookshops.

High-street chains line rue de la République and rue Victor Hugo, while upmarket boutiques and design houses stud rue du Président Édouard Herriot, rue de Brest and the streets between place des Jacobins and place Bellecour. More cluster between art galleries and antique shops around rue Auguste Comte, 2e.

Le Village des Créateurs FASHION & ACCESSORIES (☑04 78 27 37 21; www.villagedescreateurs.com; Passage Thiaffait, 19 rue René Leynaud, 1er; ⊙workshop 2-7pm by reservation Wed-Sat, boutique 1-7pm Wed-Sat; MCroix Paquet) Housed in an arcaded courtyard on the Croix Rousse slopes, this innovative cluster of workshop-boutiques showcases the artwork of a dozen up-and-coming local designers. The workshops can be visited by advanced reservation or you can pick up items from the adjacent shop,

VDC/B, which serves as a sales outlet, specialising in clothing and accessories.

Les Puces du Canal MARKET (www.pucesducanal.com; 3 rue Eugène Pottier, Villeurbanne; ⊙7am-3pm Thu & Sun, 8am-3pm Sat; 🛑; ⊡Le Roulet) With more than 400 exhibitors showcasing their wares in the northeastern suburb of Villeurbanne, France's second-biggest flea market is a fun place to browse, especially for antiques and furniture. Sunday draws the biggest crowds. You'll also find a few snack stands and sit-down restaurants.

From downtown Lyon, take metro line A east to the Laurent Bonnevay stop, then transfer to bus 7 northbound and get off at Le Roulet. Alternatively, on Monday through Saturday, catch metro A to Charpennes, then transfer onto bus 37 to Le Roulet.

Pôle de Commerces et de Loisirs Confluence SHOPPING CENTRE (www.confluence.fr; 112 cours Charlemagne, 2e; ⊙10am-8pm Mon-Sat; 🚋Montrochet) This vast complex of over 100 restaurants and shops (mostly outlets of major international companies) constitutes the commercial hub of Lyon's new Confluence neighbourhood.

ⓘ Information

Tourist Office (📞 04 72 77 69 69; www. lyon-france.com; place Bellecour, 2e; ⊙9am-6pm; 🛜; Ⓜ Bellecour) In the centre of Presqu'île, Lyon's exceptionally helpful, multilingual and well-staffed main tourist office offers a variety of city walking tours and sells the Lyon City Card (www.lyoncitycard.com).

ⓘ Getting There & Away

AIR

Lyon-St-Exupéry Airport (LYS; www.lyonaeroports.com) Located 25km east of the city, with 40 airlines (including many budget carriers) serving more than 120 direct destinations across Europe and beyond.

BUS

International bus companies **Eurolines** (📞 08 92 89 90 91; www.eurolines.fr; Gare de Perrache, 2e; ⊙6.30am-9.15pm Mon-Sat, noon-4pm & 8.15-10pm Sun; Ⓜ Perrache) and **Linebús** (📞 04 72 41 72 27; www.linebus.es; Gare de Perrache; ⊙7am-9pm Mon-Sat, noon-4pm Sun; Ⓜ Perrache) offer services to Spain, Portugal, Italy and Germany from the Centre d'Échange building at the north end of the Perrache train complex. Follow signs for 'Cars Grandes Lignes' and 'Galerie A: Gare Routière Internationale'.

TRAIN

Lyon has two main-line train stations: **Gare de la Part-Dieu** (place Charles Béraudier, 3e; Ⓜ Part-Dieu), 1.5km east of the Rhône, and **Gare de Perrache** (cours de Verdun Rambaud, 2e; Ⓜ Perrache). Some local trains stop at **Gare St-Paul** (www.ter.sncf.com/rhone-alpes; 11bis place St-Paul, 5e; Ⓜ Vieux Lyon) and **Gare Jean**

Macé (www.ter.sncf.com/rhone-alpes; place Jean Macé, 7e; Ⓜ Jean Macé). There's also a TGV station at Lyon-St-Exupéry Airport. Buy tickets at the stations or at the **SNCF Boutique** (2 place Bellecour; ⊙10am-6.45pm Tue-Fri, to 5.45pm Sat; Ⓜ Bellecour) downtown.

Destinations by direct TGV include the following:

Dijon €32, 1½ hours, at least six daily

Lille-Europe €90, three hours, at least eight daily

Marseille €52, 1¾ hours, every 30 to 60 minutes

Paris Charles de Gaulle Airport €88, two hours, at least 11 daily

Paris Gare de Lyon €75, two hours, every 30 to 60 minutes

ⓘ Getting Around

TO/FROM THE AIRPORT

Lyon-St-Exupéry Airport The **Rhônexpress** (www.rhonexpress.fr; adult/youth/child €16.10/13.40/free) tramway links the airport with the Part-Dieu train station in under 30 minutes. It's a five- to 10-minute walk from the arrivals hall; follow the red signs with the Rhônexpress train logo. Trams depart every 15 minutes between 6am and 9pm, and half-hourly from 5am to 6am and 9pm to midnight. Online purchases and round-trip travel qualify for discounts.

By taxi, the 30- to 45-minute trip between the airport and the city centre costs around €53 during the day and €68 between 7pm and 7am.

BICYCLE

Pick up a red-and-silver bike at one of the 300-odd bike stations throughout the city and drop it off at another with Lyon's **Vélo'v** (www.velov. grandlyon.com; 1st 30min free, next 30min €1, each subsequent 30min period €2) bike-rental scheme. Start by paying a one-time flat fee for a *carte courte durée* (short-duration card, €1.50 for 24 hours, €5 for seven days). Once equipped with the card, you're entitled to unlimited rentals.

DON'T MISS

LYONNAIS FOOD MARKETS

Food shopping in Lyon is an unmissable part of the city's experience. And with so many urban spaces and parks, there are plenty of picnic spots too.

Lyon's famed indoor food market **Les Halles de Lyon Paul Bocuse** (📞 04 78 62 39 33; www.hallespaulbocuse.lyon.fr; 102 cours Lafayette, 3e; ⊙7am-10.30pm Tue-Sat, to 4.30pm Sun; Ⓜ Part-Dieu) has more than 60 stalls selling their renowned wares. Pick up a round of impossibly runny St Marcellin from legendary cheesemonger Mère Richard, and a knobbly Jésus de Lyon from pork butcher Collette Sibilia. Or enjoy a sit-down lunch of local produce at the stalls, lip-smacking *coquillages* (shellfish) included.

Lyon has two main outdoor food markets: the **Marché de la Croix Rousse** (bd de la Croix Rousse, 1er; ⊙6am-1pm Tue-Sun; Ⓜ Croix Rousse) and the **Marché St-Antoine** (quai St-Antoine, 1er; ⊙6am-1pm Tue-Sun; Ⓜ Bellecour, Cordeliers). Each has more than 100 vendors.

Pay all fees with a chip-enabled credit card using machines installed at bike stations.

BOAT

Le Vaporetto (☎ 08 20 20 69 20; www.confluence.fr/notrenavettevaporetto; 1-way adult/child €4/2; ☺ mid-Mar–Dec) operates *navettes* (passenger ferry boats) to Lyon's new Confluence neighbourhood. Boats (€4) depart every 80 minutes between 10.20am and 9pm from riverbank docks on the Saône near place St-Paul and place Bellecour. Heading north, boats depart the Confluence dock between 9.30am and 8.10pm. Travel time is 30 minutes from the **St-Paul dock** (quai de Bondy, 5e; Ⓜ Hôtel de Ville, Vieux Lyon) and 20 minutes from the **Bellecour dock** (quai des Célestins, 2e; Ⓜ Bellecour, Vieux Lyon).

PUBLIC TRANSPORT

Buses, trams, a four-line metro and two funiculars linking Vieux Lyon to Fourvière and St-Just are operated by TCL (www.tcl.fr), which has information offices dispensing transport maps at major metro stations throughout Lyon. Public transport runs from around 5am to midnight.

Tickets valid for all forms of public transport cost €1.90 (€16.90 for a *carnet* of 10) and are available from bus and tram drivers as well as machines at metro entrances. Tickets allowing two consecutive hours of travel after 9am or unlimited travel after 7pm cost €3, and an all-day ticket costs €5.80. Bring coins, as machines don't accept notes (or some international credit cards). Time-stamp tickets on all forms of public transport or risk a fine.

Holders of the Lyon City Card (www.lyoncitycard.com; 1/2/3/4 days adult €25/35/45/55, child €17/24/31/38) receive free unlimited access to Lyon's transport network for the duration of the card's validity.

TAXI

Taxis hover in front of both train stations, on the place Bellecour end of **rue de la Barre (2e)**, at the northern end of rue du **Président Édouard Herriot (1er)** and along **quai Romain Rolland in Vieux Lyon (5e)**.

Allo Taxi (☎ 04 78 28 23 23; www.allotaxi.fr)
Taxis Lyonnais (☎ 04 78 26 81 81; www.tl.fr)

NORTH OF LYON

Lush green hills, lakes and vineyards unfold to the north of cosmopolitan Lyon.

Beaujolais

Ah, Beaujolais, where the unhurried life is complemented by rolling vineyards, beguiling villages, old churches, splendid estates

and country roads that twist into the hills. This rural paradise is within easy reach of Lyon, which is a mere 50km to the southeast.

An oenophile's nirvana, the region is synonymous with its fruity red wines, especially its 10 premium *crus,* and the Beaujolais Nouveau, drunk at the tender age of just six weeks. Vineyards stretch south from Mâcon along the right bank of the Saône for some 50km. Renowned wine-producing villages include Brouilly, Villié-Morgon, Fleurie, Juliénas, Moulin-à-Vent and St-Amour Bellevue. Be sure to factor in plenty of time for wine tasting.

⊙ Sights & Activities

Salles-Arbuissonnas-en-Beaujolais Priory   HISTORIC BUILDING
(Musée le Prieuré; ☎ 04 74 07 31 94; rue du Chapitre, Salles-Arbuissonnas-en-Beaujolais; museum adult/child €5/free; ☺ museum 10am-12.30pm & 2-6pm Wed-Sun Apr-Oct) For architecture buffs, this 10th-century priory founded by the monks of Cluny is a must. It's notable for its superb Roman cloister and elaborate porch. Adjacent to the building is a small museum that displays art exhibits and Gallo-Roman artefacts and also explores monastic life in past centuries in Salles-Arbuissonnas.

La Maison du Terroir Beaujolais   MUSEUM
(☎ 04 74 69 20 56; www.lamaisonduterroirbeaujolais.com; place de l'Hôtel de Ville, Beaujeu; admission incl wine tasting €7; ☺ 10am-12.30pm & 2-6pm Wed-Mon Mar-Dec) This exhibition space has a series of rooms with audiovisual displays that highlight the wine, food and culture of the Beaujolais. If you'd rather not visit the galleries, it's worth exploring the shop, which is packed with gourmet regional foodstuffs, including cheeses, jams, charcuterie and, of course, Beaujolais wine. Also rents bikes (half-/full day €14/19).

Beaujolais Greenway   PARK
(Voie Verte du Beaujolais) Set on a converted railway line, this new greenway runs for 15km between Beaujeu and Belleville. It's paved and mostly flat, making it ideal for cycling, inline skating or running. From Beaujeu, you can access the greenway about 1km southeast of the tourist office. Hire bikes are available at La Maison du Terroir Beaujolais.

Wine Tasting

Château de Juliénas   WINE
(☎ 06 85 76 95 41, 04 74 04 49 98; www.chateaudejulienas.com; Juliénas; tours from €6; ☺ by reservation) A beauty of a castle, the

16th-century Château de Juliénas occupies a delightful estate. You can arrange tours and tastings by phoning ahead. No doubt you'll be struck by the cellars, the longest in the region.

Caveau du Moulin à Vent WINE
(☑ 03 85 35 58 09; www.moulin-a-vent.net; 1673 rte du Moulin à Vent, Moulin à Vent, Romanèche Thorins; ☉ 10am-12.30pm & 2.30-7pm daily Jul & Aug, 10am-12.30pm & 2.30-6pm Thu-Mon Sep–mid-Dec & Mar-Jun) Dubbed the 'King of Beaujolais', the Moulin à Vent ('windmill') appellation is a particularly charming wine to sample in situ: its Caveau du Moulin à Vent, across the road from the windmill, provides a prime wine-tasting opportunity.

Caveau de Morgon WINE
(☑ 04 74 04 20 99; http://morgon-fr.cabanova.com; Château Fontcrenne, rue du Château de Fontcrenne, Villié-Morgon; ☉ 10am-noon & 2-6pm Feb-Dec) Morgon wine, anybody? Expand your knowledge of the local appellation with a tasting session at this vaulted cellar, which occupies a grandiose 17th-century château in the heart of town – it can't get more atmospheric than that.

**Domaine des Vignes du Paradis –
Pascal Durand** WINE
(☑ 03 85 36 52 97; www.saint-amour-en-paradis.com; En Paradis, St-Amour Bellevue; ☉ 10am-6pm) Not to be missed in St-Amour is this award-winning domaine run by fifth-generation vintners. It welcomes visitors to its intimate cellars and sells St-Amour wines at unbeatable prices.

🛏 Sleeping

The Beaujolais villages and their vineyard-stitched surrounds have some charming, if rather expensive, hotels and B&Bs. If you're on a budget, consider a day trip from Lyon, Mâcon or Villefranche-sur-Saône.

Les Folies de la Serve B&B €
(☑ 06 95 99 68 55; www.lesroulottes.com; La Serve, Ouroux; caravan/d €70/€100; ☉ Apr–mid-Nov; 🅿🤶) Run by traditional caravan-maker Pascal and his wife Pascaline, this unique place has a trio of romantically furnished 1920s to 1950s caravans amid the B&B's fields (€3 to €5 extra per night for heating). Bathrooms are provided in the main farmhouse, which has two whimsical en-suite guestrooms.

★ L'Auberge du Paradis BOUTIQUE HOTEL €€
(☑ 03 85 37 10 26; www.aubergeduparadis.fr; Le Plâtre Durand, Le Bourg, St-Amour-Bellevue; d €150-260, menu €74; ☉ restaurant 7.30-9pm Wed-Sun;

BEAUJOLAIS NOUVEAU

At the stroke of midnight on the third Thursday (ie Wednesday night) in November – as soon as French law permits – the *libération* (release) or *mise en perce* (tapping; opening) of the first bottles of cherry-bright Beaujolais Nouveau is celebrated around France and the world. In Beaujeu, 64km northwest of Lyon, there's free Beaujolais Nouveau for all as part of the **Sarmentelles de Beaujeu** (www.sarmentelles.com; ☉ Nov), a giant street party that kicks off the day before Beaujolais Nouveau for five days of wine tasting, live music and dancing.

🅿✳🤶🛁) Beaujolais' iconic, much-beloved inn occupies a village house restyled into an urban-chic, design-led boutique hotel. Oh, and there's the fantastic Michelin-starred restaurant: its creative, inspired cooking (expect top-quality ingredients served with a symphony of spices) draws diners from afar.

★ Les Buis du Chardonnet B&B €€
(☑ 04 74 03 64 76; www.lesbuisduchardonnet.com; Chardonnet, 399 rte des Andrés, Cogny; s/d €79/90; 🅿🤶) 🍃 If you're after hush and seclusion, this B&B with a green ethos – it was built as a positive-energy home – is the answer. The trio of sunny rooms have great picture windows and command superlative views of the vineyards. Madame Perroud is a former English teacher and willingly shares her great knowledge of all things Beaujolais – in perfect English, of course.

★ Auberge de Clochemerle HOTEL €€
(☑ 04 74 03 20 16; www.aubergedeclochemerle.fr; 12 rue Gabriel Chevallier, Vaux-en-Beaujolais; d €60-185, q €200, restaurant menus €42-88; 🅿🤶) A pleasant combination of modern and traditional, this atmospheric hotel smack dab in the centre of Vaux-en-Beaujolais has 12 stylishly refitted rooms, some with vineyard views. Dining at its Michelin-starred restaurant is a treat. Chef Romain creates elaborate Beaujolais meals using the best local ingredients, and his wife Delphine is a renowned sommelier – wine pairings are an adventure in themselves. Brilliant value.

🍴 Eating

With such fine wine flowing, dining well is a given. Most wine-growing villages have great bistros and inns where you can sample

WORTH A TRIP

LAZY LUNCH CALL

Occupying a lovingly restored inn, **Le Thou** (📞 04 74 98 15 25; www.lethou. com; Le Village, Bouligneux; menus €29-62; ⊙ noon-1.30pm & 7-8.30pm Wed-Sat, noon-1.30pm Sun) is headed up by chef Stéphane Konig, who is known for his creative (and sometimes surprising) take on regional staples. Where else in the world could you sample a *tarte à la grenouille* (frog pie)? Well-spaced tables, colourful paintings adorning the walls and a warm welcome create an easy air.

Bonus: there's a garden terrace in the warm months. Find Le Thou in Bouligneux, about 4km northwest of Villars-les-Dombes.

regional cuisine. Many B&Bs can also prepare tasty dinners on request. For foodies, a smattering of Michelin-starred restaurants await; some of the best fine-dining addresses are attached to hotels.

Joséphine à Table   FRENCH €

(📞 03 85 37 10 26; www.josephineatable.fr; Le Plâtre Durand, St-Amour-Bellevue; lunch menu €15, mains €15-20; ⊙ noon-2pm & 7.30-10pm Tue-Sat; 🍴) This easy-going, much-loved bistro always packs a crowd for its excellent-value cooking, which showcases the region's stellar produce. Corks on the ceiling and corkscrews at every table are a subtle reminder that you're in wine country (with a great wine menu, of course).

La Terrasse du Beaujolais   FRENCH €€

(📞 04 74 69 90 79; www.la-terrasse-du-beaujolais. fr; La Terrasse, Chiroubles; menus €26-69; ⊙ noon-2pm & 7-8.30pm Mar-Aug, closed Mon Sep-Nov, closed Mon-Thu Dec-Feb) That view! Perched high above Chiroubles at an altitude of 760m, this well-known venture offers a sensational panorama over the entire Beaujolais region, the Saône valley and the Alps. Food-wise, it's no less impressive, with hearty regional dishes, including *coq au beaujolais* (chicken cooked in Beaujolais wine) and *andouillette* (chitterlings). End on a sweet high with one of the excellent homemade desserts.

★ Au 14 Février   FUSION €€€

(📞 03 85 37 11 45; www.sa-au14fevrier.com; Le Plâtre Durant, St-Amour Bellevue; menus €65-120; ⊙ noon-2pm & 7.30-9pm Fri-Mon, 7.30-9pm Thu) For a gastronomic experience in the Beaujolais area, look no further than this gem of a restaurant. A true alchemist, Japanese chef Masafumi Hamano has got the magic formula right, fusing French with Japanese to create stunning, colourful cuisine, perfectly matched with French wines. It's housed in a traditional *maison de village* that has been entirely refurbished and modernised.

ℹ Information

Tourist Office (📞 04 74 69 22 88; www. beaujolaisvignoble.com; place de l'Hôtel de Ville, Beaujeu; ⊙ 9.30am-12.30pm & 2.30-6pm Tue-Sun Mar-Nov) Beaujeu's tourist office provides information on wine cellars where you can taste and buy local wine. It can also help with accommodation.

Around 35km north of Lyon, the Villefranche-sur-Saône **tourist office** (📞 04 74 07 27 40; www.villefranche-beaujolais.fr; 96 rue de la Sous-Préfecture, Villefranche-sur-Saône; ⊙ 9am-6pm Mon-Sat May-Sep, 10am-5pm Mon-Sat Oct-Apr) has info on southern Beaujolais.

ℹ Getting There & Around

To explore the delightful backroads and vineyards of Beaujolais, it's best to have your own set of wheels (and a non-drinking driver!).

For outdoorsy types, it's also possible to rent bikes at **La Maison du Terroir Beaujolais** (p494) in Beaujeu. It costs €14/19 for a half-/full day.

To get here by public transport, catch a train from Lyon to Belleville (€9.90, 35 minutes), where bus 235, operated by **Les Cars du Rhône** (📞 08 00 10 40 36; www.carsdurhone.fr), travels 10 times a day – weekdays only – to Beaujeu (€2, 25 minutes).

La Dombes

Known as the land of a thousand lakes, La Dombes is a bucolic region that's famed for its farm-fresh produce. People come from far and wide to sample frogs' legs, local chicken or carp at one of the area's many inns. Located just east of the Beaujolais region, this marshy area invites leisurely walks and bike rides through peaceful countryside that seems like little changed over the centuries.

In fact, these *étangs* (shallow lakes) were created from malarial swamps over the past 600 years by farmers. Today they are used as fish ponds and then drained to grow crops on the fertile lakebed. While it's not big on sights, this rural territory makes an idyllic counterpoint to the bustle of Lyon, 40km to the southwest.

Observe local and exotic birds, including dozens of pairs of storks, at the 35-hectare

Parc des Oiseaux (✆04 74 98 05 54; www.parcdesoiseaux.com; RD 1083, Villars-les-Dombes; adult/child €19/14; ⊙9.30am-6pm Apr-early Nov), a landscaped bird park comprising 24 protected habitats on the edge of Villars-les-Dombes.

Most visitors explore the area as a day trip from Pérouges or Lyon. Favourite lunch spots cooking up tried-and-true La Dombes frogs' legs include **Le Comptoir des Dombes** (✆04 72 88 50 69; www.lecomptoirdesdombes.com; Le Village, Lapeyrouse-Mornay; mains €14-22, lunch menu €16, menus €24-38; ⊙noon-1.30pm Wed-Mon & 7-9pm Thu-Sat) in the village of Lapeyrouse and **La Bicyclette Bleue** (✆04 74 98 21 48; www.labicyclettebleue.fr; Le Pont, Joyeux; mains €20, lunch menu €14, dinner menus €24-42; ⊙noon-1.30pm & 7.30-9pm Wed-Sun, closed Dec-Feb), known for its dining-biking combo. Rent wheels to explore 12 mapped lakeland trails.

Villars-les-Dombes' train station is linked to Lyon's Part-Dieu (€8.10, 40 minutes, at least hourly), but you really need your own wheels – two or four – to explore the area.

SOUTH OF LYON

South of Lyon, the Rhône flows past an incongruous mix of vineyards and nuclear power plants, but the landscapes grow more tantalising as you continue downriver towards Provence. Along the way there are several worthwhile stops for Lyon-based day trippers.

Vienne

POP 29,200

France's Gallo-Roman heritage is alive and well in this laid-back riverfront city, whose old quarter hides spectacular Roman ruins, including a temple and a theatre. The theatre relives its glory days as a performance venue

each summer during Vienne's two-week jazz festival – a must for music lovers.

◉ Sights

Musée Gallo-Romain   MUSEUM
(✆04 74 53 74 01; www.musees-gallo-romains.com; D502, St-Romain-en-Gal; adult/child €6/free; ⊙10am-6pm Tue-Sun) Across the Rhône from Vienne, the Musée Gallo-Romain highlights Vienne's historical importance, with several rooms full of dazzling mosaics and models of ancient Vienne, surrounded by the actual excavated remains of the Gallo-Roman city.

Temple d'Auguste et de Livie   HISTORIC SITE
(place Charles de Gaulle) FREE Best of all the Roman monuments in Vienne is this striking Roman temple right in the heart of the old town. Take a look at the superb Corinthian columns. It was built around 10 BC to honour Emperor Augustus and his wife, Livia.

Théâtre Romain   THEATRE
(✆04 74 85 39 23; www.musees-vienne.fr; rue du Cirque; adult/child €3/free; ⊙9.30am-1pm & 2-6pm Tue-Sun) This vast, well-preserved Roman amphitheatre was built around AD 40–50 at the base of Mt Pipet, on the eastern fringes of the old town. At that time, it was one of the largest theatres in the Roman empire – it was designed to seat 11,000 spectators. It's a key venue during Vienne's Jazz Festival in June and July.

✸ Festivals & Events

Jazz Festival   MUSIC
(www.jazzavienne.com; ⊙late Jun-early Jul) This two-week jazz festival held in late June/early July is said to be one of France's finest international jazz festivals, and it does attract some very big names, including Youssou N'Dour, Marcus Miller and Lisa Simone. Most concerts are held in the fabulous surrounds of the Roman theatre.

LYON & THE RHÔNE VALLEY VIENNE

WORTH A TRIP

CONDRIEU & CÔTE RÔTIE

Wine buffs, take note: the Rhône Valley boasts two appellations that rank among the most prestigious in France: Condrieu and Côte Rôtie. While Condrieu is beloved of white-wine (vioginer) aficionados, Côte Rôtie is a hallowed name among red-wine connoisseurs. Most of the Côte Rôtie vineyards, which extend over three villages, including Ampuis, are devoted to the syrah grape. Mixed with a bit of viognier, the Côte Rôtie produces rich reds, known for their robust, full-bodied character. A few kilometres further south, the Condrieu winegrowing area is a bit larger, and includes the small town of Condrieu. In all villages belonging to these appellations, you'll pass plenty of producers offering *dégustation* (tasting) en route. Both areas are within easy reach of Vienne.

FAMILY FAVE: DEATH BY CHOCOLATE

On the main road in Tain l'Hermitage, the **Cité du Chocolat Valrhona** (☑ 04 75 09 27 27; www.citeduchocolat.com; 12 av du Président Roosevelt, Tain l'Hermitage; adult €9-10.50, child €7.50-8.50; ☉ 9am-7pm Mon-Sat, 10am-6.30pm Sun) is a chocoholic's dream come true. This vast complex run by famous chocolatier Valrhona, one of the world's leading chocolate manufacturers, takes you through each stage of the production process thanks to extremely well-thought-out interactive displays, workshops and hands-on exhibits. Of course, the supersized adjoining boutique is a treasure trove of chocolate goodies. And yes, it includes tastings.

🛏️ Sleeping & Eating

Rue des Clercs and its offshoots, as well as place Charles de Gaulle, are lined with tempting eateries and lively bars.

Ibis Budget　　　　　　HOTEL **€**
(☑ 04 74 87 09 68; www.ibis.com; place Camille Jouffray; d €50-60; P✻🛜) Yes, we know it's a chain hotel, but this abode gets by on its super-handy location, a waddle away from restaurants, monuments and the train station, and its private parking (€5). It offers functional chain-hotel rooms with off-the-shelf furnishings and small bathrooms.

★ Hôtel de la Pyramide　　　HOTEL **€€€**
(☑ 04 74 53 01 96; www.lapyramide.com; 14 bd Fernand-Point; d €200-300, ste €350-460; P✻@🛜) Relax into the lap of luxury at this apricot-coloured villa overlooking La Pyramide (a 15.5m-tall obelisk dating from the Roman times). It contains beautifully appointed rooms and a few top-notch suites. Foodies, rejoice: facilities include a gastronomic restaurant (*menus* €67 to €180). This tasteful haven is in a quiet neighbourhood on the southern outskirts of town.

★ L'Espace PH3　　　MODERN FRENCH **€€**
(☑ 04 74 53 01 96; www.lapyramide.com; 14 bd Fernand Point; mains €23-24, lunch menu €24; ☉ noon-1.30pm & 7.30-9.30pm) Overseen by two-Michelin-starred chef Patrick Henriroux, L'Espace PH3 offers an affordable gastronomic menu, serving a small selection of French classics with a creative twist. The lunch *menu* is a steal. In summer, meals are served out on the superb garden terrace.

ℹ️ Information

Tourist Office (☑ 04 74 53 70 10; www.vienne-tourisme.com; 2 cours Brillier; ☉ 9am-noon & 1.30-6pm Tue-Sun, 10am-noon & 1.30-6pm Mon) Has details of museums and historical sites in the Viennois area. It also offers bike hire (€3/5 per half-/full day).

ℹ️ Getting There & Away

Trains link Vienne with Lyon's three main stations (€7.30, 20 to 30 minutes, at least hourly) as well as Valence Centre (€14, 50 minutes, at least hourly). All trains to Valence TGV station require changing at Valence Centre.

Valence

POP 62,500

Welcome to the Midi (as the French call the south)! With its warm weather, honey-coloured light, relaxed atmosphere and generous cuisine, it's easy to see why Valence advertises itself as the northern gateway to Provence. Its quaint old town is well endowed with eateries, convivial cafes and historic buildings, and the Musée de Valence will appeal to culture aficionados.

⊙ Sights & Activities

Musée de Valence　　　　MUSEUM
(☑ 04 75 79 20 80; www.museedevalence.fr; 4 place des Ormeaux; adult/child €6/free; ☉ 2-6pm Tue, 10am-6pm Wed-Sun) This great museum adjoining the cathedral offers a comprehensive and well-organised collection of art and archaeology from the Rhône Valley. Of particular interest are the superb mosaics and artefacts dating from the Roman era, as well as the series of red chalk sketches and paintings by Hubert Robert (1733–1808). There is also a lovely vaulted gallery. For knockout views of the city and the Rhône Valley, head to the top floor, which has a *belvédère* (viewpoint).

Cathédrale St-Apollinaire　　CATHEDRAL
(place des Ormeaux; ☉ 8am-6pm) A major landmark in the old town, this impressive cathedral dates from the late 11th century but was largely destroyed in the Wars of Religion before being reconstructed in the 17th century. The square bell tower is a more recent addition – it was built in the 19th century.

L'École Scook　　　　COOKING
(☑ 04 75 44 14 14; www.anne-sophie-pic.com/scook; 243 av Victor Hugo; ☉ by reservation) Serious foodies will want to sign up at three-Michelin-star chef Anne-Sophie Pic's cutting-edge cooking school, Scook. It offers 1½-hour (from

€65) and three-hour courses (from €112), plus courses for kids from six years old upwards (€42 per 90 minutes). It also provides wine-tasting classes. See the website for dates.

Sleeping & Eating

Les Négociants HOTEL €
(☑ 04 75 44 01 86; www.hotelvalence.com; 27 av Pierre Semard; d €45-78; P ☎) This well-run venture with modernised rooms is definitely good value. The cheaper doubles have minuscule bathrooms and don't have air-con but are perfectly serviceable. It's just steps from the railway station and a five-minute stroll from the historic centre. There's private parking (€7) about 300m away. Another draw is the on-site restaurant.

★ La Maison de la Pra B&B €€
(☑ 04 75 43 69 73; www.maisondelapra.com; 8 rue de l'Équerre; d €125-200; P ✼ ☎) Such charm! If you've ever wanted to stay in a 16th-century *hôtel particulier* (master's house), this bijou B&B enticingly positioned in a quiet alley near the town hall is the real McCoy. It offers five stadium-sized suites with beamed ceilings, period furniture and artworks. They're smack in the centre but still feel very quiet. Good English is spoken.

Maison Pic HOTEL €€€
(☑ 04 75 44 15 32; www.anne-sophie-pic.com; 285 av Victor Hugo; d €280-430, ste €380-600; ☺ Feb-Dec; P ✼ @ ☎) The Pic family's truffle-coloured, 1889-established inn has ultra-chic rooms mixing antique, contemporary and cutting-edge design. It is often fully booked with gastronomes, here for the three-Michelin-starred **Restaurant Pic** (☑ 04 75 44 15 32; www.anne-sophie-pic.com/content/anne-sophie-pic-le-restaurant; 285 av Victor Hugo; lunch menu €120, dinner menus €180-340; ☺ noon-1.30pm & 7.30-9.30pm Wed-Sat, noon-1.30pm Sun) or the less formal bistro **André** (☑ 04 75 44 15 32; www.anne-sophie-pic.com/content/andre; 285 av Victor Hugo; mains €22-32, menus €33-69; ☺ noon-2pm & 7.30-10pm). One downside: its location, on a busy road about 2km south of the old town, isn't exactly five-star.

Maison Nivon BAKERY €
(☑ 04 75 44 03 37; www.maison-nivon-valence.fr; 17 av Pierre Semard; suisses from €2; ☺ 6am-7pm Tue-Sun) In business since 1856, this venerable bakery near the train station is one of the best places to sample Valence's classic orange-rind-flavoured shortbread in the shape of a Vatican Swiss guard. Ask for a *suisse*!

ℹ Information

Tourist Office (☑ 04 75 44 90 40; www.valence-romans-tourisme.com; 11 bd Bancel; ☺ 9.30am-12.30pm & 1.30-6pm Mon-Sat; ☎) Located two blocks north of the train station.

ℹ Getting There & Away

From Valence Centre station (also known as Valence-Ville), there are trains at least hourly to the following destinations (many also stop at Valence TGV Rhône-Alpes Sud station, 10km east):

Avignon Centre €22, about 1¼ hours

Grenoble €16.10, about one hour

Lyon (Gare Part-Dieu or Gare Jean-Macé) from €19, 35 minutes (TGV) to 1¼ hours

Marseille from €37, 1¼ (TGV) to 2½ hours

Montélimar €11.10, 30 minutes

Gorges de l'Ardèche

Be prepared to fall on your knees in awe: the steep and spectacular limestone Gorges de l'Ardèche cut a curvaceous swath through the high scrubland along the serpentine Ardèche River, a tributary of the Rhône. The main gorges begin near **Vallon-Pont-d'Arc** and empty into the Rhône Valley near **St-Martin-d'Ardèche**. En route, they pass beneath the Pont d'Arc, a sublimely beautiful stone arch created by the river's torrents.

From Vallon-Pont-d'Arc, the area's main hub, the scenic riverside D290 zigzags for 29km along the canyon's rim, with 29 *belvédères* (panoramic viewpoints) revealing dazzling vistas of horseshoe bends, and kayakers in formation far below. However, it can turn into a chaotic traffic jam in midsummer.

Vallon-Pont-d'Arc is also the main base for visiting the Caverne du Pont d'Arc, which houses replicas of prehistoric paintings.

MONTÉLIMAR NOUGAT

An appealing place (once you're through its industrial outskirts), Montélimar boasts an atmospheric old town and a grassy, tree-shaded, cafe-lined promenade that carves a C-shape through its centre. The town is 46km south of Valence in the sunny section of the Drôme *département*, known as Drôme Provençale. An obligatory stop for sweet tooths, Montélimar is famous for its delectable nougat, which took off after WWII when motorists travelling to the French Riviera stopped here to buy the sweeter-than-sweet treat to munch en route.

ST-ÉTIENNE

Down-to-business St-Étienne (pop 170,000), 62km southwest of Lyon, is drawing on its Industrial Revolution origins and its history of arms, bicycle, textile and ribbon production to reinvent itself as a 'design city'. It still preserves fascinating vestiges from its past, including an old coal mine you can visit not far from the town centre at the **Musée de la Mine** (☑ 04 77 43 83 23; http://musee-mine.saint-etienne.fr; Parc Joseph Sanguedolce, bd Franchet d'Esperey; guided tour adult/child €7/free; ⊙ 9am-12.30pm & 2-6pm Tue-Sun).

St-Étienne hosts the forward-looking **Biennale Internationale Design** (www.biennale-design.com) fair for one month kicking off in March every odd-numbered year. Otherwise, delve into its design scene at the **Cité du Design** (☑ 04 77 49 74 70; www.citedudesign.com; 3 rue Javelin Pagnon; adult/child €5/4, guided tour adult/child €6.50/5.50; ⊙ 10am-6pm Tue-Sun, guided tours 3pm Sat & Sun) and contemporary art at the **Musée d'Art Moderne et Contemporain** (MAM; ☑ 04 77 79 52 52; www.mam-st-etienne.fr; rue Fernand Léger, St-Priest-en-Jarez; adult/child €6/4.50; ⊙ 10am-6pm Wed-Mon), 2.5km north in St-Priest-en-Jarez.

Should you consider an overnight, **La Villa Roassieux** (☑ 06 52 76 40 90, 04 77 41 20 87; www.villaroassieux.fr; 5 passage Jean Baptiste Corot; s €95-120, d €115-145, ste from €145; P ✿ ☎ ✈) – a country-chic B&B with heated saltwater pool in a vintage manor southeast of the centre – is the address.

Hourly (or more frequent) trains link St-Étienne with Lyon's Gare de la Part-Dieu (€11.70, 50 minutes) or Gare Perrache.

⊙ Sights

★ Caverne du Pont d'Arc   MUSEUM
(☑ 04 75 94 39 40; www.cavernedupontdarc.fr; Plateau du Razal; adult/child €15/7.50; ⊙ 8.30am-7pm mid-Apr-Aug, 9am-7pm Sep, 9.30am-6pm Oct-Dec & Feb-mid-Apr) This unique complex about 7km northeast of Vallon-Pont-d'Arc takes you on an incredible journey back in time. The biggest replica cave in the world, it was built a few kilometres north of the original Grotte Chauvet site and contains 1000 painstakingly reproduced paintings as well as around 450 bones and other debris. An hour-long tour takes visitors along a raised walkway, past panels displaying hundreds of breathtakingly sophisticated drawings of various animal species, including lions, panthers, rhinoceros and mammoths.

The original Grotte Chauvet, which was discovered in 1994 and is now a Unesco World Heritage Site, is not open to the public. It's the oldest known and best-preserved cave decorated by humans; the actual paintings date back 36,000 years. Specialists used 3D modelling techniques and a high-precision scanner to create a three-dimensional digital model of the original cave. Due to visitor limitations, it often sells out – buy your ticket online a few days in advance.

Pont d'Arc   NATURAL FEATURE
(Vallon-Pont-d'Arc) Spanning the Ardèche Gorge, this striking natural bridge is a must-see when visiting the area. Located 5km south of Vallon-Pont-d'Arc, this 54m-high arch makes a fine destination for a scenic walk (with routes beginning in Vallon-Pont-d'Arc). In the summer, it's also popular destination for kayaking.

Grotte de la Madeleine   CAVE
(☑ 04 75 04 22 20; www.grottemadeleine.com; D290, rte touristique des Gorges; adult/child €11/6.50; ⊙ 10am-7pm Jul & Aug, to 6pm Mar-Jun & Sep, to 5pm Oct & Nov) The Ardèche plateau is riddled with caves. One of the most atmospheric is Grotte de la Madeleine, which features impressive and colourful stalactite formations. A light and play show adds to the thrill. Near the ticket office you'll find one of the most spectacular *belvédères*, with awesome views of the gorges.

🏃 Activities

Vallon-Pont-d'Arc is the main water-sports base (April to September); its tourist office has lists of lots of local operators. Options range from 8km half-day trips to 32km full-day or overnight trips (the latter involve camping in the gorge). Tariffs and trip durations depend on how far you want to travel. Most outfits charge roughly similar rates: around €24/35 for a half-/full-day descent. Return transport is included in rental prices. Safety kit is provided, but you'll get wet, so dress appropriately. Minimum age is seven. Book in advance to secure online discounts. Some operators are also based in St-Martin d'Ardèche.

Base Nautique du Pont d'Arc   WATER SPORTS
(☑ 04 75 37 17 79; www.canoe-ardeche.com; D290, rte touristique des Gorges, Vallon-Pont-d'Arc; per adult/child half-day €23/15, full day €35/21, 2-day €50/32; ☺Apr-Oct) Hire canoes and kayaks through Base Nautique du Pont d'Arc. Options range from 8km half-day trips to 32km full-day or overnight camping trips. Minimum age is seven, and online discounts are available with advance booking.

🛏 Sleeping

Most accommodation is located in or around the main towns of Vallon-Pont-d'Arc and St-Martin d'Ardèche, at the western and eastern ends of the gorges respectively. In summer, make sure you book ahead.

Camping du Pont d'Arc   CAMPGROUND €
(☑ 04 75 88 00 64; www.campingdupontdarc. com; D290, rte touristique des Gorges; campsites €16-28) Adjacent to stunning Pont d'Arc, this tree-shaded campground has its own riverside beach and offers boat trips down the gorges.

★Le Belvédère   HOTEL €
(☑ 04 75 88 00 02; www.hotel-ardeche-belvedere. com; D290, rte touristique des Gorges; d €65-135, q €130-190; ☺Apr-Oct; P❋🛜🏊) Just 300m away from the Pont d'Arc, the aptly named Belvédère (Lookout) has 30 rooms that have been sleekly refitted. Half of the rooms have views of the gorges, and some come with a balcony. Facilities include a swimming pool, a canoe/kayak rental outlet and a well-regarded on-site restaurant (mains €17 to €22).

★Prehistoric Lodge   LODGE €€
(☑ 04 75 87 24 42; www.prehistoric-lodge.com; D290, rte touristique des Gorges; d €105-125, lodge d €115-175; ☺Apr-Oct; P❋) By far the most unusual sleeping option in the Gorges de l'Ardèche, this good find offers eight luxury safari tents (called 'lodges') and four modern, snazzily decorated rooms with private terraces. Best of all, it's in a verdant property right on the river's edge, with direct access to a swimming area and superlative gorge views.

Jardins de Prasserat   FARMSTAY €€
(☑ 06 86 68 03 02; Ferme de Prasserat, off D579, Vallon Pont d'Arc; d €75-110; P🛜) Some 2.5km northwest of Vallon Pont d'Arc, this delightfully rustic farmhouse offers three pleasant rooms with views over the gardens or rolling hills in the distance. Bruno, the kind-hearted owner, has a wealth of information on the area, and spreads a fine breakfast that includes homemade jams and sometimes eggs from his own hens.

---

❶ STRIDE OUT!

The **Sentier Aval des Gorges**, which descends 2km to the river, then follows the gorge for another 10km, is a great way to experience the beauty of the gorges. Shorter walks on the plateau above the gorges afford sensational views. The tourist office in Vallon-Pont-d'Arc has leaflets and maps.

🍴 Eating

Places to eat are limited in the gorges themselves, although there are a few tiny villages with seasonal restaurants and roadside snack bars dotted along the route – but you might find it more convenient to pack a picnic.Vallon-Pont-d'Arc and St-Martin d'Ardèche both have plenty of eating options.

Le Chelsea   MODERN FRENCH €
(☑ 04 75 88 01 40; www.lechelsea.com; 45 bd Peschaire-Alizon, Vallon-Pont-d'Arc; mains €17-19, menus €22-31; ☺noon-2pm Tue, noon-2pm & 7-9pm Thu-Mon) No, it's not a pub, but a traditional *maison de village* (old stone terraced house) with a snug, colourful dining room and an inviting, leafy terrace in warm weather. Enjoy wholesome meat or fish dishes served with fresh seasonal vegetables.

Le Jardin d'Eden   MODERN FRENCH €€
(☑ 04 75 88 36 91; www.facebook.com/jardinde denrestaurant; 185 rue Henri Barbusse, Vallon-Pont-d'Arc; mains €17-23; ☺noon-2pm & 7-9pm Wed-Sun) Formerly a cinema, it's amazing what a renovation and an ownership change can do for a place. The young team at the helm blends regional cuisine with contemporary style; the risotto and tartares are especially good. Save room for the splendid desserts – the *dôme gourmand* is amazing.

❶ Information

Tourist Office (☑ 04 28 91 24 10; www. vallon-pont-darc.com; Pôle de la Gare Routière, Vallon-Pont-d'Arc; ☺9am-noon & 2-5pm Mon-Fri, 9am-noon Sat; 🛜) Has some useful leaflets on walking itineraries and lists of canoeing and kayaking outlets. In the village centre.

❶ Getting There & Away

Four daily SNCF buses link Vallon-Pont-d'Arc's Gare Routière (located next to the tourist office) with Montélimar's train station (€11.40, 1¼ hours) and Valence's TGV station (€21.50, 2½ hours).

French Alps & the Jura Mountains

Best Places to Eat

➡ Yoann Conte (p522)

➡ Les Louvières (p558)

➡ Restaurant Grain de Sel (p556)

➡ Le Clin d'Oeil (p516)

➡ Le Cap Horn (p511)

Best Places to Stay

➡ Petit Hôtel Confidentiel (p524)

➡ Les Cinq Frères (p533)

➡ Hôtel Les Bruyères (p530)

➡ Le Grand Hôtel (p540)

➡ Camping Les Dômes de Miage (p513)

Why Go?

High up in the French Alps, it's enthralling to imagine the forces that shaped these colossal peaks. The African and Eurasian tectonic plates collided some 35 million years ago, forcing the land skyward into a 1000km chain of saw-edged mountains.

Rumbling across seven European countries, the Alps reach their maximum height in France, at Mont Blanc (4810m). Buckling northwest along the Swiss border are the less mighty Jura Mountains, where life unfolds along slower rhythms: winemaking, cross-country skiing and tinkling cow bells.

Routes into the Alps' otherworldly realms are many: aboard cable cars that fly to knee-trembling heights, or in the company of mountain guides who set out into wintry oblivion. Europe's biggest, and arguably most prestigious, ski resorts are here, melting into meadow-draped hiking country each summer. Winter or summer, this forbidding terrain commands respect: the French Alps' mirror lakes, ice-cold rivers and crevasse-scarred glaciers form one of Europe's true epics.

When to Go
Grenoble

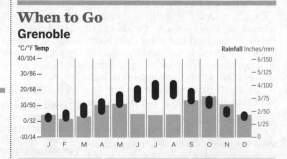

Dec–Feb Ski season begins, Venetian carnival livens up Annecy, and *vin jaune* is poured in Jura.

Mar & Apr Long sunny days meet enduring snow; brace yourself for end-of-season parties.

Jul & Aug The Tour de France whizzes by, and it's hiking prime time.

SAVOIE

The mountainous Savoie extends from Lake Geneva's southern shores to western Europe's highest peak, mighty Mont Blanc (4810m).

Savoie has been a magnet for health-conscious, well-heeled jet-setters since an 18th-century thermal spa boom in still-chic towns like Aix-les-Bains and Évian-les-Bains. Today, winter sports are Savoie's *raison d'être*. Snowheads travel far and wide for resorts that are among the largest and most snow-sure in Europe. The *crème de la crème* are Les Trois Vallées, Chamonix and Val d'Isère, which glitter with premium accommodation and restaurants. Slightly easier on the wallet and still accessing wondrous snow are Les Portes du Soleil and St-Gervais. Come summer, mountain bikers and hikers venture to the rugged, cave-speckled regional parks of Chartreuse, Vanoise and Bauges.

Almost as pleasing is Savoie's traditional cuisine, a farmhouse menu of melted cheese, *saucisson sec* (dried sausage) and herbal liqueurs – burned off rapidly by mountain adventures (we hope).

Chamonix

POP 8906 / ELEV 1035M

Mountains loom large almost everywhere you look in Chamonix. Skiers and sightseers are launched by cable car to heights of 3842m on the Mont Blanc massif, while the glacial void of La Vallée Blanche – one of Europe's most fêted off-piste adventures – beckons to the brave. Skiers and boarders have a choice of pistes along the valley, while in summer the same lifts access hiking and biking trails.

Chamonix has a long history as a winter-sports hub. Rediscovered as a tourist destination by Brits William Windham and Richard Pococke in 1741, Chamonix hosted the first ever Winter Olympics in 1924.

For all the desolate beauty of the mountains, downtown Chamonix hums with life. Streets are lined with Michelin-starred restaurants, sports gear stores and some of the French Alps' fanciest hotels. And if you do the nightlife justice, it'll exhaust you as much as the mountains.

⊙ Sights

★ Aiguille du Midi   VIEWPOINT
The great rocky fang of the Aiguille du Midi (3842m), rising from the Mont Blanc massif, is one of Chamonix' most distinctive features. The 360-degree views of the French, Swiss and Italian Alps from the summit are (quite literally) breathtaking. Year-round, you can float via cable car from Chamonix to the Aiguille du Midi on the vertiginous **Téléphérique de l'Aiguille du Midi** (www.compagnie dumontblanc.co.uk; place de l'Aiguille du Midi; adult/child return to Aiguille du Midi €61.50/52.30, to Plan de l'Aiguille €32.50/27.60; ☉1st ascent btwn 6.30am & 8.10am, last btwn 4pm & 5.30pm, mid-Dec–early Nov). Dress warmly: even in summer, temperatures at the top rarely rise above -10°C (in winter prepare for -25°C).

Up top, you can take in the view in literally every direction (including straight down), thanks to the glass-floored **Step into the Void**). Halfway up, **Plan de l'Aiguille** (2317m) is a terrific place to start hikes or to paraglide.

From the Aiguille du Midi, between late May and September, you can continue for a further 50 minutes of mind-blowing scenery – think glaciers and spurs, seracs and shimmering ice fields – in the smaller bubbles of the **Télécabine Panoramique Mont Blanc** (☑04 50 53 22 75; www.mont blancnaturalresort.com; Aiguille du Midi; adult/child return from Chamonix €89/75.70; ☉7.30am-4.30pm Jul & Aug, 8am-4pm Jun, 9am-3.30pm Sep) to Pointe Helbronner (3466m) on the France–Italy border. The **SkyWay Monte Bianco** (www.montebianco.com; Pointe Helbronner; single/return €37/49; ☉6.30am-4.30pm Jul & Aug, 8.30am-4pm Sep–mid-Nov & Dec–May, 7.30am-4.20pm Jun) cable car can then take you a further 4km to the Val d'Aosta ski resort of Courmayeur, on the Italian side of Monte Bianco.

Le Brévent   VIEWPOINT
The highest peak on the western side of the Chamonix Valley, Le Brévent (2525m) has tremendous views of the Mont Blanc massif, myriad hiking trails through a nature reserve, ledges to paraglide from and some vertiginous black runs.

Reach it by linking the **Télécabine de Planpraz** (☑04 50 53 22 75; www.compagnie dumontblanc.co.uk; 29 rte Henriette d'Angeville; adult/child return €32.50/27.60; ☉from 8.50am Dec-Apr, Jun-Sep & late Oct-Nov), 400m west of the tourist office, with the **Téléphérique du Brévent** (www.compagniedumontblanc.co.uk; from Planpraz return adult/child €14.50/12.30; ☉mid-Dec–mid-Apr & mid-Jun–mid-Sep). Plenty of family-friendly trails begin at **Planpraz** (2000m), and the Liaison cable car connects to the adjacent ski fields of La Flégère.

French Alps & the Jura Mountains Highlights

1 Chamonix
(p503) Feeling your heart hammer from high-altitude cable cars or the legendary Vallée Blanche.

2 Les Trois Vallées (p526)
Thundering across the world's biggest ski area before frolicking in après-ski bars.

3 Annecy (p518)
Navigating the medieval lanes of 'Alpine Venice' towards its stately château.

4 Portes du Soleil
(p514) Being spoilt for (snowy) choice between tree-lined runs, border-crossing trails and the infamously steep 'Swiss Wall'.

5 Route des Vins du Jura (p549)
Sipping golden *vin jaune* (a slow-matured regional wine) amid bucolic vines.

6 Parc National des Écrins (p543)
Tackling almost 700km of hiking trails among lakes and craggy peaks.

7 Val d'Isère (p532) Zipping through snow by day, spa-soaking or fine-dining by night.

8 Besançon (p549) Surveying distant peaks from 17th-century ramparts.

9 Chambéry (p523) Wandering between centuries-old mansions and a magnificent castle.

10 Briançon (p547) Tackling the best ski area you've never heard of, then retreating to a fairy-tale citadel.

★ **Mer de Glace**   GLACIER

France's largest glacier, the 200m-deep 'Sea of Ice', flows 7km down the northern side of Mont Blanc, scarred with crevasses formed by the immense pressure of its 90m-per-year movement. The Train du Montenvers (p513), a picturesque, 5km-long cog railway opened in 1909, links Gare du Montenvers with Montenvers (1913m), from where a cable car descends to the glacier and, 420 stairs later, the **Grotte de Glace** FREE. Also worth a visit is the **Glaciorium**, an exhibition on the formation (and future) of glaciers.

Musée Alpin   MUSEUM

(☑ 04 50 53 25 93; www.facebook.com/museealpin chamonixcc; 89 av Michel Croz; adult/child €5.90/ free; ☺ 2-6pm Wed-Mon Sep, late Dec–May, 10am-noon & 2-7pm Wed-Mon Jul, Aug & school holidays) This diverting two-level museum allows you to wander through Chamonix history, from butter moulds and farming tools of yore to the dawn of the 18th-century tourism boom. There's mountain history galore, including the early days of the high mountain guides and fascinating stories of the first female alpinists, as well as 19th-century oil paintings of the valley's timeless landscape.

Hang on to your entrance ticket, it shaves a euro off the price of the Musée des Cristaux.

Musée des Cristaux   MUSEUM

(☑ 04 50 55 53 93; www.mineralogie-chamonix. org; 615 allée Recteur Payot; adult/child €5.90/ free; ☺ 2-6pm Sep-Jan & May, 10am-1pm & 2-6pm Apr, Jun-Aug & school holidays) Beautifully lit collections of crystals, many from around Mont Blanc, are exposed within this small

museum. The adjoining **Espace Tairraz** focuses on the art and science of mountaineering with creative interactive displays and photos and videos of seemingly impossible ascents. Situated behind the church.

🏃 **Activities**

Winter

Thrilling descents, glorious off-piste terrain and unbeatable Mont Blanc views – skiing in Chamonix is so fantastic that skiers don't even mind that accessing the slopes involves lots of land transport to and from the lifts.

Best for beginners are **Le Tour & Vallorcine, Les Planards, Les Chosalets, Les Houches** and **La Vormaine**. For speed and challenge, it has to be **Brévent-Flégère** (1030m to 2525m), above Chamonix, and **Les Grands Montets** (1235m to 3300m), accessible from the attractive village of Argentière, 9km north of the town. Boarders seeking big air zip across to the kickers and rails at **Les Grands Montets snow park** and the natural halfpipe in **Le Tour**.

Chamonix' ski season runs from mid-December to mid-April.

La Vallée Blanche   SKIING

This jaw-dropping 2800m descent is the ride of a lifetime and probably Europe's most famous off-piste experience. Beginning at the Aiguille du Midi, the 20km route darts over the crevasse-riddled Mer de Glace glacier and returns to Chamonix through the forest. Skiers must be confident on red pistes and in good physical shape; the reward is access to a landscape of eerie, unearthly beauty. The

---

ℹ **TREK PLANNER**

It takes three years of rigorous training to become an *accompagnateur en moyenne montagne* (mountain leader) and a full five years to be certified as a *guide de haute montagne* (high-mountain guide), though many train for a decade. Only the latter are authorised to lead groups on to glaciers or on mountaineering climbs requiring specialised equipment. Recommended companies include the following:

Compagnie des Guides de Chamonix (☑ 04 50 53 00 88; www.chamonix-guides.com; 190 place de l'Église, Maison de la Montagne; ☺ 8.30am-noon & 2.30-7.30pm mid-Dec–late Apr & mid-June–mid-Sep, closed Sun & Mon rest of year)

Association Internationale des Guides du Mont Blanc (☑ 04 50 53 27 05; www. guides-du-montblanc.com; 9 passage de la Varlope)

Chamonix Experience (☑ 04 50 93 23 14; www.chamex.com; 610 rte Blanche; ☺ 9am-noon & 3-7pm Dec–early May, Jun-Sep)

Office de Haute Montagne (OHM; ☑ 04 50 53 22 08; www.chamoniarde.com; 190 place de l'Église, Maison de la Montagne; ☺ 9am-noon & 3-6pm Mon-Sat) Inside the Maison de Montagne, providing information on trails, hiking conditions, weather forecasts and refuges (mountain huts), plus topoguides and maps that are free to consult.

CHILD'S PLAY

There's plenty to amuse *les petits* (the little ones) around Chamonix. In the warm season, kids will love getting close to free-roaming chamois, ibex and whistling marmots at the **Parc de Merlet** (www.parcdemerlet.com; 2495 chemin de Merlet, Les Houches; adult/child €8/5; ⊙10am-6pm Tue-Sun May, Jun & Sep, 9.30am-7.30pm Jul & Aug, by reservation mid-Dec–mid-Mar), 13km by road (5km on foot) southwest of central Chamonix in Coupeau (across the Arve River from Les Houches). Or treat them to a fun-packed day on the beginner ski area or 1.3km luge at the **Parc de Loisirs de Chamonix** (☑04 50 53 08 97; www.chamonix parc.com; 351 chemin du Pied du Grépon; ski passes per day adult/child €22.50/20.50, 1/10 luge rides €5.50/45; ⊙ski area 9am-5pm winter, Alpine Coaster 10am-6.30pm Jul & Aug, reduced hours Apr-Jun & Sep-Oct; ⛄), near the chairlift in Les Planards, 500m east of Gare du Montenvers.

Cham' Aventure (☑04 50 53 55 70; www.cham-aventure.com; 190 place de l'Église, Maison de la Montagne; ⊙hours vary; ⛄) has a wide variety of day-long and half-day outdoor programs tailored for children aged three to seven, eight to 12, and 13 to 17 – biking, canyoning, treasure hunts and more (from €40).

Back in Chamonix, the indoor **ice skating rink** (☑04 50 53 12 36; 165 rte de la Patinoire; adult/child €6.50/4.80, skate hire €4.30; ⊙2-5pm daily term time, 3-7pm Fri-Wed & longer hours Thu in school holidays) provides amusement when the weather packs up, as do sports activities at the adjacent **Centre Sportif Richard Bozon** (☑04 50 53 23 70; www.chamonix. net/english/leisure/sport-centers/richard-bozon; 214 av de la Plage; ⊙noon-7.30pm Mon-Fri, 2-7.30pm Sat & Sun), with indoor and (in summer) outdoor swimming pools.

---

route can only be tackled with a *guide de haute montagne* (specially trained mountain guide).

École de Ski Français
SKIING

(ESF; ☑04 50 53 22 57; www.esfchamonix.com; place de l'Eglise, Maison de la Montagne; ⊙8.15am-7pm Dec-Apr) This 200-instructor branch of the French Ski School has been helping people hurl themselves down the slopes of Chamonix-Mont Blanc since 1945.

Lift Passes

Chamonix Le Pass (1/2/6 days €51.50/100/258.50) Gets you up to most Chamonix ski domains, around 118km of pistes.

Mont Blanc Multipass (1/2/6 days €63/77/126) In summer, this pass affords access to all operating lifts.

Mont Blanc Unlimited Pass (1/2/6 days €63.50/125/306) A worthwhile investment for serious skiers, this pass grants access to all lifts in the Chamonix Valley, Courmayeur in Italy and Verbier in Switzerland, plus the Aiguille du Midi cable car and the Montenvers–Mer de Glace train.

Details of all passes can be viewed and purchases made online at www.montblancnaturalresort.com.

Summer

When enough snow melts (usually some time in June), hikers can take their pick of 350km of spectacular marked trails, many easy to get to by cable car (running mid-June to September). In June and July there's enough light to walk until at least 9pm.

Balcon (literally 'balcony') trails, both *grand* and *petit*, run along both sides of the valley. The challenging Grand Balcon Nord (p509) is up around 2000m, while the three-hour **Petit Balcon Sud** (from Argentière to Servoz) is slightly above the valley's villages at 1250m.

Lac Blanc
HIKING

This jewel-like glacial lake (2352m), surrounded by the razor peaks of the Aiguilles Rouges, is usually accessible to hikers from June through October. Two gentle hours from **Télésiège de l'Index** (www.compagnie dumontblanc.co.uk; adult/child return from Les Praz €29/24.70; ⊙Dec-Apr & Jun-Sep) leads along the western valley to stunning **Lac Blanc**. There's also the steeper trail from the **Téléphérique de la Flégère** (☑04 50 53 22 75; www.compagniedumontblanc.co.uk; 35 rte des Tines; return adult/child from Les Praz €18/15.30; ⊙8.45am-4pm Dec-Apr, Jun–mid-Sep & late Oct).

Reserve a place at the **Refuge du Lac Blanc** (☑06 02 05 08 82; www.refugedulacblanc.fr; Les Houches; dm incl half-board adult/child €56/50; ⊙mid-Jun–Sep), a wooden chalet famed for its top-of-Europe Mont Blanc views.

For a calf-stiffening challenge, experienced trekkers can take the 1050 vertical-metre hike from Argentière (3½ hours one way).

Chamonix

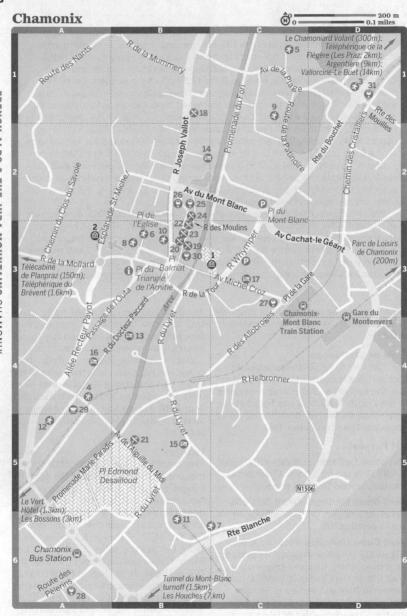

Le Chamoniard Volant (300m);
Téléphérique de la
Flégère (Les Praz; 2km);
Argentière (9km);
Vallorcine-Le Buet (14km)

Route des Nants

R de la Mummery

R Joseph Vallot

Promenade du Fori

Av de la Page

Route de la Patinoire

Rte du Bouchet

Chemin des Cristalliers

Rte des Mouilles

Av du Mont Blanc

Pl du Mont Blanc

Chemin du Clos du Savoie

Esplanade St-Michel

Pl de l'Eglise

R des Moulins

Av Cachat-le Géant

Parc de Loisirs de Chamonix (200m)

R Whymper

R de la Mollard

Pl Balmat

Av Michel Croz

Pl du Triangle de l'Amitié

R de la Tour

Pl de Gare

Chamonix-Mont Blanc Train Station

Gare du Montenvers

Allée Recteur Payot

Passage de l'Oufa

R du Docteur Paccard

R du Lyret

R Arrot

R des Allobroges

R Helbronner

Av de l'Aiguille du Midi

R du Lyret

Pl Edmond Desailloud

N1506

Promenade Marie-Paradis

R du Lyret

Le Vert
Hôtel (1.3km);
Les Bossons (3km)

Rte Blanche

Chamonix
Bus Station

Route des Pèlerins

Tunnel du Mont-Blanc
turnoff (1.5km);
Les Houches (7km)

Grand Balcon Sud Trail

HIKING

This easygoing trail skirts the western side of the valley at an altitude of around 2000m, commanding terrific views across the valley to Mont Blanc. To avoid hoofing it 900m up the slope, take the Téléphérique de la Flégère (p507) from Les Praz or the Télécabine de Planpraz (p503) from Chamonix; walking between the two takes about two hours.

Chamonix

Grand Balcon Nord Trail   HIKING

(☺Jun-Oct) Summer walking trails you can pick up at **Plan de l'Aiguille** – halfway up the Téléphérique de l'Aiguille du Midi (p503) – include the challenging Grand Balcon Nord, which takes you to the dazzling Mer de Glace, from where you can walk or take the Train du Montenvers (p513) down to Chamonix.

Cycling

Lower-altitude trails, such as the **Petit Balcon Sud** (1250m) from Argentière to Servoz, are perfect for biking. Most outdoor-activity specialists arrange guided mountain-biking expeditions. Talk to well-established bike 'n' board shop **Zero G** (☑04 50 53 01 01; www.zerogchamonix.com; 90 ave Ravanel-le-Rouge; ☺9am-12.30pm & 3.30-7pm) about gear hire and trail advice.

Paragliding

On clear days in summer and winter, the sky above Chamonix is speckled with colourful paragliders wheeling down from the heights. Tandem flights from Planpraz (2000m) start at around €110 per person; from the Aiguille du Midi (experienced flyers only), count on €295. **AirSports Chamonix** (☑06 76 90 03 70; www.airsportschamonix.fr; 24 av de la Plage; ☺10am-7pm) and **Summits** (☑04 50 53 50 14; www.summits.fr; 81 rue Joseph Vallot; tandem flights from €110; ☺9.15am-7.15pm Jun-Sep) are trusted local operators; book a couple of days ahead.

🛏 Sleeping

Le Chamoniard Volant   HOSTEL €

(☑04 50 53 14 09; www.chamoniard.com; 45 rte de la Frasse; dm/sheets €22/5.50; ☺10am-10pm; P) Long a favourite of low-budget climbing groups and luxury-averse skiers, this basic place has 67 places in dorm rooms of four to 15 bunk beds; bathrooms and showers are down the hall. Self-caterers can use the kitchen, and reasonable meals (including packed lunches from €7.20) are available.

Route de la Frasse is 1km north of town, along rte du Bouchet.

Le Vert Hôtel   HOTEL €

(☑04 50 53 13 58; www.verthotel.com; 964 rte des Gaillands; d €55-120, q €85-190; P 🐕) This lively hotel has 21 compact rooms – all with new bathrooms, some with fantastic Aiguille du Midi views. There's also a more-than-decent restaurant (dinner *menu* €22.50) and in-house ski rental. In winter, the bar regularly hosts international DJs (Gilles Peterson and Krafty Kuts, to name two).

Navettes (shuttle buses) to central Chamonix, 2km to the northeast, stop right outside.

Terminal Neige   HOTEL €€

(Refuge du Montenvers; ☑04 50 53 87 70; http://montenvers.terminal-neige.com; Le Montenvers; half-board dm €80-100, d €190-270, tr €275-395, q €360-500; ☺Nov-Sep; @ 🐕) There's just one way to access this iconic mountain address, overlooking the shimmering ice of Mer de Glace –

by the Train du Montenvers (p513) cog railway. Its 20 designer-chic, wood-panelled rooms have glacier views, and hikers and families are well-catered for with an insanely stylish 10-bed dorm, cosy duplex rooms for five or seven, and five-person bunk-bed rooms. Rates include dinner and breakfast.

The Grand Hôtel du Montenvers first opened its doors in 1880 to provide food and shelter for Chamonix's early mountaineers, and was remodelled in 2017 as a chic boutique hotel and glamorous hostel of sorts by the luxury Maisons et Hôtels Sibuet group.

Hôtel de l'Arve
HOTEL **€€**

(☎04 50 53 02 31; www.hotelarve-chamonix.com; 60 impasse des Anémones; d/f from €180/250; ☼Dec-Oct; P🅿🛜) 🍴 Overlooking the Arve River, this third-generation family hotel has quiet, compact rooms, tastefully decorated with chocolate brown drapes and liberal splashes of blond wood. A sauna, games room and gym (with a climbing wall) promote a convivial feel...as does the homemade afternoon tea. The ample breakfast buffet (Savoyard cheese, local jams and fresh pastries) costs €12.

Hôtel Aiguille du Midi
HOTEL **€€**

(☎04 50 53 00 65; www.hotel-aiguilledumidi. com; 479 chemin Napoléon, Les Bossons; d €80-212; ☼mid-Dec–early Apr & mid-May–Sep; 🛜📶) Run by the same family since 1908, this welcoming hotel has stunning views of the Aiguille du Midi and Mont Blanc. There are 40 pine-panelled rooms, an outdoor heated pool and a clay tennis court for summer fun, and a very good restaurant, accessible on half-board packages. Bus and train stops to Chamonix, 3km northeast, are right around the corner.

Hôtel Richemond
HOTEL **€€**

(☎04 50 53 08 85; www.richemond.fr; 228 rue du Docteur Paccard; s/d/q €68/105/136; ☼mid-Dec-mid-Apr & mid-Jun–mid-Sep; P🅿🛜) In a grand old building constructed in 1914 (and run by the same family ever since), this hotel – as friendly as it is central – has 52 spacious rooms with views of either Mont Blanc or Le Brévent; some are pleasantly old-fashioned (retaining original furniture and cast-iron bath-tubs), others are recently renovated in white, black and beige. Outstanding value.

Hotel L'Oustalet
HOTEL **€€**

(☎04 50 55 54 99; www.hotel-oustalet.com; 330 rue du Lyret; s €105-125, d €118-160, q €162-215; ☼mid-Dec–mid-May & mid-Jun–Sep; P🅿🛜📶) A

block from the Aiguille du Midi cable car, this lift-equipped hotel has 15 plain but well-maintained rooms, snugly built of thick pine, opening on to balconies with Mont Blanc views. To unwind, curl up by the fire with a *chocolat chaud* (hot chocolate) or loll about in the jacuzzi, *hammam* or sauna – or, in summer, dip into the garden pool.

Pointe Isabelle
HOTEL **€€**

(☎04 50 53 12 87; http://pointeisabelle.com; 165 av Michel Croz; s €70-140 d €84-248; P🅿🛜) Named for 19th-century British mountaineer Isabella Straton, whose grandchildren opened the hotel, this pleasing spot lies just west of Chamonix train station. Loosely vintage in theme (but with a whiff of business-hotel efficiency), Pointe Isabelle has rooms with a striking violet colour scheme, very comfy beds and glossy modern bathrooms.

★ Grand Hôtel des Alpes
HISTORIC HOTEL **€€€**

(☎04 50 55 37 80; www.grandhoteldesalpes.com; 75 rue du Docteur Paccard; d/ste from €175/294; ☼mid-Dec–mid-Apr & mid-June–late Sep; P🅿🛜📶) Exuding belle époque charm, this buttercup and powder-blue hotel is one of the prettiest buildings in Chamonix. Established in 1840, the hotel's 30 rooms have a classic style: flowing drapes, wood-panelled ceilings and glossy marble bathrooms. There's a glamorous-feeling wellness centre and in winter, a scrumptious teatime cake buffet (4pm to 6pm) greets skiers back from the slopes.

🍴 Eating

Pizzeria des Moulins
PIZZA **€**

(☎06 47 07 75 10, 06 68 70 99 82; www.facebook. com/pizzeriadesmoulins; 107 rue des Moulins; mains from €15; ☼noon-2.30pm & 6.30-11pm) Cham's best pizzas, piled with buffalo mozzarella, forest mushrooms and Savoyard ham, puff up in the oven of this little gourmet joint. Reservations are essential for dining in, but you can always get takeaway if (or rather, when) they're packed with ravenous diners.

Hibou Deli
DELI **€**

(☎04 50 96 65 13; www.hibou-chamonix.com; 416 rue Joseph Vallot; mains €8-14; ☼11am-8.30pm Mon-Sat mid-Dec–early May & mid-Jun–early Oct; 🖊📶) This minuscule shopfront kitchen nourishes fondue-weary diners with big portions of sticky miso aubergine, cauliflower korma and other earthy dishes inspired by North African and Asian cuisine. There are a few tiny stools to perch on but you might prefer to grab and go. Plentiful vegetarian and gluten-free options, too.

A TRADITIONAL FOREST LUNCH

A wooden forest chalet is the setting for Chef Claudy's **Crèmerie du Glacier** (☑ 04 50 54 07 52; www.lacremerieduglacier.fr; 766 chemin de la Glacière; lunch menus €17-22, fondues €15-20; ☺ noon-2pm & 7-9pm mid-Dec–mid-May & late Jun–mid-Sep, closed Wed in winter), where you can taste *croûte aux fromages* (bread drenched in a secret white-wine sauce, topped with cheese and baked) and other cheesy Savoyard delights including *gratin d'oeufs* (creamy baked eggs) and half a dozen kinds of fondue (the best with forest mushrooms). Reserve by phone and follow the signpost from the roundabout near the bridge at the southern entrance to Argentière.

To get here, you have several options. In winter, ski down on Piste de la Pierre à Ric (red) or cross-country ski over on Piste de la Moraine. In summer, hike over from the Petit Balcon Nord trail, 15 minutes away. In winter or summer, walk or drive east for about 1km from the base of Téléphérique Lognan-Les Grands Montets; if you're equipped with snow tyres, take one-lane chemin de la Glacière.

Les Vieilles Luges (☑ 06 84 42 37 00; http://lesvieillesluges.com; Les Houches; menus €20-35; ☺ noon-2pm Dec-Apr; ☑) is a 250-year-old farmhouse, strung with farming tools and vintage sledges, which can only be reached on skis or by 20-minute hike from the Maison Neuve chairlift. Hunker under low wood beams to savour *diots* (smoked sausages) and house special *farçon* (potato bake with prunes, wrapped in bacon), while supping *vin chaud* (mulled wine) warmed over a wood fire. Book ahead and bring cash. Vegetarian, and sometimes vegan, versions of *farçon* are offered, too. In summer, the restaurant is only open by reservation (minimum 25 people).

Le GouThé
DELI €

(☑ 04 50 78 36 20; www.legouthe.weebly.com; 95 rue des Moulins; light mains €4-8; ☺ 9am-6.30pm Jun-Apr; ☑) This relaxed, welcoming tearoom serves more than a dozen kinds of hot chocolate including cardamom-spiced, Grand Marnier-laced and 'chocomiel' (with a dash of honey). Salads, quiche and savoury crêpes are also offered, while fruit tarts like apple, *myrtille* (bilberry) and pear are priced by length (€0.49 per centimetre), enforcing hurried, hungry calculations by diners.

Munchie
FUSION €€

(☑ 04 50 53 45 41; www.streamcreek.com/munchie; 87 rue des Moulins; mains €23-29; ☺ 7pm-2am winter & summer) Franco-Japanese-Scandinavian fusion may not be the most obvious recipe for success, but this casual, Swedish-skippered restaurant has been making diners happy since 1997. There's a sharing plate concept with sushi plates like little works of art, and the excellent seafood and passion-fruit ceviche, teriyaki duck and alcoholic Oreo milkshakes have brought local acclaim. Reservations recommended.

★ Le Cap Horn
FRENCH, SEAFOOD €€€

(☑ 04 50 21 80 80; www.caphorn-chamonix.com; 74 rue des Moulins; lunch/dinner menus from €23/42; ☺ noon-3pm & 7-10.30pm; ☑) Housed in a candelit, two-storey chalet decorated with model sailing boats – joint homage to the Alps and Cape Horn – this highly praised restaurant, opened in 2012, serves French and Asian dishes such as pan-seared duck breast with honey and soy sauce, an ample sushi menu, and a marvellous range of seafood like red tuna *taquitos* and fish stew. Reserve for dinner Friday and Saturday in winter and summer.

Le Comptoir Nordique
SCANDINAVIAN €€€

(☑ 04 50 53 57 64; www.lecomptoirnordique.fr; 151 av de l'Aiguille du Midi; lunch menus €21-32, dinner menus €39-59; ☺ noon-1.30pm & 7-9pm; ☑ ☑) This design-conscious diner marries Scandinavian style with crisp Nordic flavours. Within, the Comptoir is defined by clean lines and slate tiles. Seafood rules the menu, with the likes of *fisksoppa* (fish stew) and rye-breaded perch, and desserts are original and highly memorable: zesty blood-orange fondant and waffles laden with Icelandic yoghurt.

Le Chaudron
FRENCH €€€

(☑ 04 50 53 40 34; 79 rue des Moulins; mains €28-33; ☺ 7-9.30pm or later mid-Dec–Apr & mid-Jun–Sep) Making stylish use of a 100-year-old mule stable (the faux cowhide recalling its rustic origins), the Cauldron offers Savoyard cuisine with a twist, in a cosy setting. There's fondue (of course), while dishes like scallops in Champagne sauce, lobster ravioli and barbecued *entrecôte* (premium beef steak) are refined without ever feeling fussy.

🍷 Drinking & Nightlife

Whether you're looking for a glammed-up cocktail bar, a spit-and-sawdust pub, or something in between, Chamonix nightlife rocks. For a bar crawl, head (along with the locals) to central rue des Moulins, where wall-to-wall watering holes keep buzzing until about 1am.

★ Chambre Neuf   BAR

(📞 04 50 53 00 31; www.facebook.com/chambre. neuf; 272 av Michel Croz; ⊙7am-1am; 🛜) A favourite among seasonal workers letting off steam, 'Room 9' boasts the most spirited (rather, loudest) après-ski party in Cham (from 3pm or 4pm). There's live rock music (from Sunday to Friday), dancing on the tables, and themed events (if DJ sets or circus-themed parties sound like your jam). Action spills out of the front door and the terrace opens in spring.

MBC   MICROBREWERY

(Micro Brasserie de Chamonix; 📞 04 50 53 61 59; www.mbchx.com; 350 rte du Bouchet; ⊙4pm-2am Mon-Fri, 10am-2am Sat & Sun) This Canadian-run microbrewery is one of Chamonix' most unpretentious and gregarious watering holes, pouring its own locally made blonde, stout, pale ale, German-style wheat beer and mystery beer of the month. Soaking it up is a menu of huge burgers, poutine (chips with cottage cheese and gravy) and vegetarian choices. Eclectic live music (usually from 9pm) could mean anything from soul to hard rock. Enormously satisfying.

Bistrot des Sports   PUB

(📞 04 50 53 00 46; 182 rue Joseph Vallot; ⊙8am-2am) In the 19th century, climbing parties used to assemble in the Bistrot des Sports before setting out to conquer Mont Blanc. A merry medley of mountaineers, skiers and tourists still gather in this welcoming bar and brasserie, whose worn wooden benches and retro sports posters whisper to the good old days. Closes earlier if it's not busy.

La Jonction   CAFE, BAR

(📞 06 34 02 96 88; www.facebook.com/jonction coffee; 75 av Ravanel le Rouge; ⊙8am-8pm; 🛜) A friendly, low-key place to mingle with fellow skiers and hikers, La Jonction pours excellent coffee by day, and – when après-ski hour arrives – mixes more than a dozen different gin and tonics (including a warming spiced gin with ginger ale). Whether it's to be coffee or cocktails, their dark, hoppy Guinness cake is an ideal accompaniment.

Bar'd Up   BAR

(123 rue des Moulins; ⊙3pm-late) This Anglophone dive bar borrows Irish, English and Aussie insignia in its bid to be the friendliest, grungiest place in Cham. Setting the scene are a pool table, sports screenings, stray surf boards and a low ceiling. Accommodating staff reel you in, and the reasonably priced drinks and music (live and recorded) finish you off.

Les Caves   BAR

(📞 04 50 21 80 80; www.caphorn-chamonix.com; 80 rue des Moulins; ⊙6pm-2am mid-Dec–Oct) Spread over four levels with cosy hidden corners, this futuristic/rustic disco chalet – stone archways, fancy disco balls, sleek leatherette seats – transforms itself from suave jazz and cocktail bar into a buzzing danceteria after 10.30pm.

Jekyll & Hyde   PUB

(📞 04 50 55 99 70; www.facebook.com/jekyll chamonix; 71 rte des Pélerins, Chamonix Sud; ⊙4pm-2am Mon-Fri, opens earlier Sat & Sun; 🛜) This British-owned après-ski mainstay has a split personality: upstairs the 'Jekyll' has really good pub food (from seafood tapas and sweet 'n' sour duck to plenty of veggie options), live music, DJs and comedy; check their Facebook page for events. Downstairs, the 'Hyde' is cosier and more relaxed. Both have good Irish beer and a friendly vibe.

ℹ️ Information

Tourist Office (📞 04 50 53 00 24; www. chamonix.com; 85 place du Triangle de l'Amitié; ⊙9am-7pm mid-Jun–mid-Sep & mid-Dec-Apr, 9am-12.30pm & 2-6pm rest of year, closed Sun Oct & Nov; 🛜)

ℹ️ Getting There & Away

BUS

It's worth dropping by the **bus station** for timetables and reservations (highly recommended) or you can book tickets online on Ouibus (www. ouibus.com). Direct services reach Annecy (from €10, 1½ hours, six daily) and Lyon Perrache (from €26, 3½ hours to 4½ hours, at least one daily).

International routes include the following:

Geneva, Switzerland (airport and bus station) One-way €19, 1½ to two hours, eight daily in winter, at least four at other times. Book tickets through Ouibus.

Courmayeur, Italy Adult/child €15/7.50, 45 minutes, four daily. Run by Savda (www.savda. it), with onward connections to Aosta and Milan.

CAR & MOTORCYCLE

Chamonix is linked to Courmayeur in Italy's Val d'Aosta by the 11.5km-long **Tunnel de Mont Blanc** (www.atmb.com; toll one way/return €44.40/55.40).

When the Col des Montets (between Argentière and Vallorcine) is closed by snow, signs will direct you to drive through the rail tunnel. Current conditions can be found at www.chamonix.com.

The valley's only car-hire company is **Europcar** (☑ 04 50 53 63 40; www.europcar.com; 36 place de la Gare; ⊙ 8.30am-noon & 2-6pm Mon-Sat).

TRAIN

The scenic, narrow-gauge **Mont Blanc Express** (www.mont-blanc-express.com) glides from the Swiss town of Martigny to Chamonix, taking in Argentière and Vallorcine en route.

For destinations around France, including Lyon, Annecy and Paris, you'll need to change trains at St-Gervais-Le-Fayet first (€11.40, 45 minutes, hourly).

To reach the cable car to the Mer de Glace, take the scenic cog train to Montenvers (1913m) from the **Gare du Montenvers** (☑ 04 50 53 22 75; www.montblancnaturalresort.com; 35 place de la Mer de Glace; adult/child return €32.50/27.60; ⊙ 10am-4.30pm late Dec–mid-Mar, to 5pm mid-Mar–Apr).

❶ Getting Around

BUS

Public buses run by Chamonix Bus (www.chamonix-bus.com) serve all the towns, villages, ski lifts and attractions in the Chamonix Valley, from Argentière (Col des Montets in summer) in the northeast, to Servoz and Les Houches in the southwest.

The buses all travel circuits that include the **bus station** (☑ 04 50 53 01 15; 234 av Courmayeur, Chamonix Sud; ⊙ ticket 8am-noon & 1.15-6.30pm in winter, shorter hours rest of year) in Chamonix Sud throughout the year, and have added destinations and are more frequent in winter (mid-December to mid-April) and summer (late June to early September).

All buses are free with a Carte d'Hôte (Guest Card), except the wintertime Chamo' Nuit night buses linking Chamonix with Argentière and Les Houches (last departures from Chamonix 11.30pm or midnight; €2).

Megève/St-Gervais

An upmarket Alpine paradise twinned with a sedate, all-season retreat, Megève/St-Gervais makes much of its mountainous location, 15km due west of Mont Blanc (4810m).

Megève was developed in the 1920s for Baroness de Rothschild of the famous banking family. Today it's an Alpine daydream made real: horse-drawn carriages and exquisitely arranged boutique windows spill into cobbled, medieval-style streets lined with chalets. In winter, Megève attracts a well-off crowd (including lots of families), but the scene is very laid-back in summer. Set beautifully in wooded hills, the well-equipped **Camping Les Dômes de Miage** (Nature & Lodge Camping; ☑ 04 50 93 45 96; www.natureandlodge.fr; 197 rte des Contamines, St-Gervais; unpowered sites €22.20-27.60, powered sites €26.80-32.20; ⊙ mid-May–mid-Sep; 🛜) is an ideal spot if you want to wake up to Mont Blanc.

Slightly lower down the valley, unpretentious St-Gervais-les-Bains is linked to Chamonix by the legendary Mont Blanc Express train. Most of the town is undistinguished 20th-century sprawl, but the lovely central square, with its baroque church, has a distinctly Alpine feel.

Both villages access the 445km **Domaine Évasion Mont Blanc** ski area.

🏃 Activities

Megève's Palais des Sports has plenty of active distractions year-round. The Bureau des Guides (p514) can organise a huge range of all-season outdoor activities, from ice or rock climbing to canyoning and trail running.

Tramway du Mont Blanc　　　CABLE CAR
(☑ 04 50 53 22 75; www.montblancnaturalresort.com; av de la Gare, St-Gervais; return to Bellevue/Nid d'Aigle €32.50/37.50; ⊙ 4-6 departures daily mid-Dec–early Apr, 8 daily early Jun–mid-Sep) France's highest rack-and-pinion railway, first chiselled into the mountain in 1907, ascends from St-Gervais-Le-Fayet (590m) to Bellevue (1900m; one hour). In summer, when you can hike back down, it climbs all the way to Nid d'Aigle (2372m), on the cusp of the Bionnassay glacier (80 minutes).

Le Palais des Sports　　　HEALTH & FITNESS
(☑ 04 50 21 59 09; www.megeve.fr/index.php/sport; 247 rte du Palais des Sports, Megève; ⊙ 10am-7.30pm Thu-Tue, to 9.30pm Wed) This impressive multipurpose sports centre stays open all year, offering an Olympic-sized ice-skating rink (€9), swimming (€15) and even a sheet (court) for the obscure Olympic sport of curling (€20 including gear hire). Too active? Stake out a spot in the saunas or *hammam,* or dunk into 34°C hot tubs (from €15).

DON'T MISS

THE VILLAGE POTTER

The **Atelier du Potier** (☑ 04 50 47 71 41; 18 chemin du Vieux Pont, St-Gervais; ⊙ hours vary), a rambling, poster-plastered workshop and gallery, is tucked away near the church in the centre of St-Gervais. Local legend Monsieur Baranger can often be seen at his wheel, where he throws pots, plates, ornaments and vases. Hours are irregular but the workshop usually opens in mornings and afternoons (he'll hang a sign if he goes for a siesta).

Bureau des Guides OUTDOORS
(☑ 04 50 21 55 11; www.guides-megeve.com; 76 rue Ambroise Martin, Maison de la Montagne, Megève; ⊙ 9.30am-12.30pm & 3-7pm, closed Sat & Sun low season) Open throughout the year, the Mountain Guides organise a huge range of outdoor activities, from ice or rock climbing to canyoning and trail running. Join a group for a half-day of snowshoeing (€25) or a day of dangling from via-ferrata ladders (€92), or get a private guide for paragliding (€200), glacier hiking (€340) or tackling the storied Vallée Blanche (€400).

Winter

Having the Mont Blanc massif as a backdrop makes for fabulously scenic **skiing**. Between 850m and 2353m high, pistes are accessible both from Megève (www.ski-megeve.com) and, via the St-Gervais-Bettex cable car, from near the centre of St-Gervais (www.ski-saintgervais.com). About 325km of the area's downhill runs are divided between three separate collections of slopes: **Mont d'Arbois-St-Gervais**, **Le Jaillet-Combloux-La Giettaz** and **Rochebrune-Cote 2000**. Skiing here is mostly for beginners and cruisy intermediates, though there are also some black runs.

Lift pass prices vary by area and duration: bank on €30 for a day in Megève/St-Gervais and €47 for the entire **Domaine Évasion Mont Blanc**, whose 445km of pistes include surrounding villages. Look out for family rates and online discounts (like spring skiing price cuts).

Summer

In summer, both towns make superb bases for **hiking**, with trails for walkers and hikers of all levels, including young children. Panoramic trails abound, including many in the Bettex, Mont d'Arbois and Mont Joly (2525m) areas. Tourist offices sell IGN hiking maps.

Some of the best **mountain-biking** terrain, with downhill runs accessible by lift, is between Val d'Arly, Mont Blanc and Beaufortain. In Megève, several winter-sports gear-rental shops hire out bikes in summer. Megève-based **Bike Addict** (☑ 06 83 27 89 73; www.bike-addict-megeve.com; 2-hr lesson/day excursion €80/245) can arrange bespoke MTB itineraries for families, hardened cyclists and everything in between.

ℹ Information

Megève Tourist Office (☑ 04 50 21 27 28; www.megeve.com; 70 rue de Monseigneur Conseil; ⊙ 9am-7pm late Dec–mid-Apr, Jul & Aug, 9am-12.30pm & 2-6.30pm Mon-Sat rest of year; 🛜)
St-Gervais Tourist Office (☑ 04 50 47 76 08; www.saintgervais.com; 43 rue du Mont-Blanc; ⊙ 9am-12.30pm & 2-6pm or later Mon-Sat, also Sun during school holidays; 🛜)

ℹ Getting There & Away

BUS

From late December to March and from June through September, Megevexpress (www.megevexpress.com) offers door-to-door transfers between Geneva Airport and Megève or St-Gervais (€35, 1½ hours). Cheaper services from Geneva Airport to St-Gervais-Le-Fayet train station (from €25, 1½ hours, from four daily) can be booked through Ouibus (www.ouibus.com). Reserve at least 24 hours ahead.

TRAIN

The train station nearest Megève is 12km north in Sallanches; take bus 83 to the railhead (€3.50, 25 minutes, six to 10 daily Monday to Saturday, also Sunday in ski season and July and August).

The St-Gervais-Le-Fayet train station is 2km northwest of the centre of St-Gervais. If you're heading to Chamonix, change here for the Mont Blanc Express. Geneva requires changing trains in Bellegarde, Vallorcine or La Roche-sur-Foron (it's better to get a bus).

Destinations include the following:
Annecy €16, 1½hr, 10 daily
Chamonix €11.40, 45min, almost hourly
Lyon (change in Annecy) €38.10, 3¾-4hr, 10 daily
Paris Gare de Lyon (change in Annecy) €94-115, 5½-7hr, 1-2 per hr

Les Portes du Soleil

For winter-sports fans across Europe, Les Portes du Soleil have a winning formula.

France's second-largest ski area (after Les Trois Vallées), the gigantic 'Gates of the Sun' have high-altitude terrain that gathers powder snow (1000m to 2466m), picturesque tree-fringed runs, exciting après-ski and easy access to Geneva airport. There's also the novel possibility of skiing in and out of Switzerland within a day (no passport needed).

A dozen villages access Les Portes du Soleil but **Morzine** (1000m), the big daddy for nightlife and gastronomy, is best-known. Further up the valley is car-free **Avoriaz** (1800m), a purpose-built ski resort chock full of 1960s apartment blocks. Horse-drawn sleighs romantically ferry new arrivals to and from the village centre. Arriving by road via Cluses, you hit the smaller ski station of **Les Gets** (1172m), whose easy access to sheltered, tree-lined ski runs has made it a favourite with families.

◉ Sights & Activities

Abbaye d'Aulps   ABBEY
(www.abbayedaulps.fr; rte de l'Abbaye, St-Jean-d'Aulps; adult/child €6.50/3.50; ⊙10am-7pm mid-Jun–mid-Sep, 2-6.30pm late Sep–Oct & mid-Dec–early Jun) The eerie skeleton of an 11th-century Cistercian abbey stands on this hilly site, accompanied by a visitors centre that illuminates the daily lives of monks. By road, it's 8km north of Morzine.

Bureau des Guides   OUTDOORS
(⌐04 50 75 96 65; www.guides-morzine.com; 23 Taille de Mas du Pleney, Morzine) This 15-strong team of mountain guides can lead you off-piste skiing, or organise warm-weather frolics such as hiking, biking, rock and via ferrata climbs, canyoning and paragliding, and the tough **Noire de Morzine**, Morzine's heart-stopping 3.2km, 500-vertical-metre bike descent from the top of the Pléney cable car (p517).

Winter
The stats speak for themselves at this gigantic snow-sports resort. Les **Portes du Soleil's** 196 ski lifts access 286 ski runs, between 450km and 650km of downhill slopes (depending on how they're measured). A single transfrontier ski pass covers it all (per day/week €52/293). Most snowheads go for the full package but if you aren't a confident skier, you can trim the price by confining your skiing to one area, such as **Morzine–Les Gets** (per day €40) or **Avoriaz** (per day €43). There are early-bird deals if you buy online, and there's 30% off passes late in the season.

Frequent powder, nursery slopes for little kids, toboggan runs, indoor pool and spa complexes, children's clubs and snow play areas make Les Portes du Soleil a great choice for families. **Morzine** offers ideal beginner and intermediate terrain, with scenic runs through the trees for windy days. The snow-sure slopes of higher-elevation **Avoriaz** are great for intermediate skiers but can also challenge the more advanced. Plus, it's freestyle heaven for **snowboarders**, with dozens of snow parks to play in and a fantastic superpipe near the top of the Prodains cable car.

The area's most famous piste is **Le Pas de Chavanette**, better known as the *Mur Suisse* (Swiss Wall), on the border with Switzerland (reached from Avoriaz). This ice-gathering slope is no ordinary black run: it's steep, mogulled and has a hair-raising incline around 35° to 40° at the top.

Summer
In summer, the slopes attract **mountain bikers** to 650km of trails, including invigorating routes such as the 80km circular Enduro Tour des Portes du Soleil. **Walkers** can pick and choose from 800km of marked trails. The extensive summer lift network (late June to early September, €27/122 per day/week) takes the slog out of reaching higher altitudes.

🛏 Sleeping & Eating

Fleur des Neiges   HOTEL €€
(⌐04 50 79 01 23; www.hotel-fleur-des-neiges.fr; 227 Taille de Mas de Nant Crue, Morzine; per person per week incl breakfast/half-board €745/927; ⊙mid-Dec–mid-Apr & late Jun–early Sep; P🛜🏊) A *grande dame* of Morzine's hotel scene since 1951, family-run Fleur des Neiges has a winning formula: a cheerful welcome, big breakfasts and 31 natural-timber rooms made jolly with red-checked bedspreads, each with a mountain-facing balcony. There's

> **DON'T MISS**
>
> ### PARTY ON THE SLOPES
> Festival atmosphere, spring skiing euphoria and epic mountain views combine at **Rock the Pistes** (http://rockthepistes.com; ⊙late Mar), a five-day live music event. There are five day-time concerts – pop, rock, soul, shoegaze, you name it – up on the slopes and dozens in Morzine, Avoriaz and Châtel.

❶ CENT SAVER

Les Portes du Soleil's hottest summer deal is the **Multi Pass**, which costs €2/12 per one/six days if you're staying here and €9 per day for day trippers. Available from early June to early September, the pass covers cable cars and chairlifts (some of which only run from late June) for hikers, as well as access to sporting facilities such as tennis courts, ice rinks and swimming pools.

a sauna, heated pool and a lounge where you can play board games in front of an open fire.

★ The Farmhouse   BOUTIQUE HOTEL €€€

(Le Mas de la Coutettaz; ☑ 04 50 79 08 26; www.the farmhouse.fr; 429 chemin de la Coutettaz, Morzine; d incl half-board €224-478; ☺ mid-Dec–mid-Apr & Jun–mid-Sep; ☎) This welcoming British-owned guesthouse has 11 individually decorated rooms spread across a gorgeous pre-Revolutionary manor house, the oldest building in Morzine. Dining is a lavish, candlelit affair around one huge banquet table; in summer it's a B&B, and in winter (when a one-week minimum may apply) it offers half-board.

★ Le Clin d'Oeil   FRENCH €€

(☑ 04 50 79 03 10; www.restaurant-leclin.com; 63 rte du Plan, Morzine; lunch/dinner menus from €17/33; ☺ noon-2pm & 7-9.30pm Mon-Fri, 7-9.30pm Sat & Sun; ☑ ☷) Armed with cornerstones of cuisine from France's southwest, like *cassoulet* (rich bean, pork and duck stew), Le Clin d'Oeil transplants southerly sunshine straight to the Alps. Venison, scallops and cheese-laden vegetarian dishes are impeccably presented, though it's hard to beat their *menu tout canard* (featuring two rich duck courses). Bubbly service from endlessly helpful staff lifts Le Clin d'Oeil above its competition.

La Ferme de la Fruitière   FRENCH €€

(☑ 04 50 79 12 39; www.alpage-morzine.com; 337 rte de la Plagne, Morzine; mains €18-22; ☺ noon-2pm & 6pm-midnight mid-Dec–mid-Apr & mid-Jun–mid-Sep) Savoyard cheese becomes a high-end experience at this pine-walled dining room, arranged around a central fireplace. Mannerly service and a comprehensive wine list accompany exceptionally presented fondue and other Alpine specialities. Swirl an aperitif, inhale the garlic-scented air, and contemplate golden wheels of Abondance, Reblochon and Tomme cheese, all made in the cellar downstairs.

⬤ Drinking & Nightlife

Morzine is the focal point of the Portes du Soleil's nightlife scene, which pops during winter, simmers gently in summer, and evaporates during the shoulder seasons. Avoriaz and Les Gets have more of a family focus, though both have a great choice of cafes and bars.

★ Bec Jaune   CRAFT BEER

(☑ 04 50 79 08 44; http://becjaunebrewery.com; 220 rte de la Combe à Zore, Morzine; ☺ 4.30-11.30pm mid-Dec–mid-Apr & mid-Jun–mid-Sep) Vats of home-brewed IPA, porter and German-style beer glint temptingly from Morzine's trendiest expat hangout and après-ski joint, while vegetarian and vegan bar snacks (€5 to €11) are a boon for anyone suffering Savoyard ham fatigue.

Le Tremplin   BAR

(☑ 04 50 79 12 31; www.hotel-tremplin.com; 166 Taille de Mas du Pleney, Morzine; ☺ 4-8pm) Skiers along Stade du Pleney and Piste B will see this colourful bar from the slopes as they glide back into Morzine village. This classic après-ski meet-up spot has speedy table service. There is an outdoor terrace with a stage for live rock, jazz and DJ sets, surrounded by wooden seats (with blankets).

❶ Information

Avoriaz Tourist Office (☑ 04 50 74 02 11; www.avoriaz.com; 44 promenade des Festivals, Avoriaz; ☺ 9am-7pm mid-Dec–mid-Apr, Jul & Aug, 9am-noon & 2-6pm Mon-Thu, to 5pm Fri May, Jun & Sep-Nov) Can book self-catering chalets and studios.

Morzine Tourist Office (☑ 04 50 74 72 72; www.morzine-avoriaz.com; 26 place du Baraty, Morzine; ☺ 8.30am-7.30pm mid-Dec–mid-Apr & mid-Jun–mid-Sep, 9am-noon & 2-6pm Mon-Sat rest of year; ☎) Has excellent brochures in English and can help find accommodation through **Morzine Réservation** (☑ 04 50 79 11 57; www.resa-morzine. com; Office du Tourisme, 26 place du Baraty, Morzine; ☺ 8.30am-7.30pm Mon-Sat mid-Dec–mid-Apr & mid-Jun–mid-Sep, 9am-noon & 2-6pm Mon-Fri rest of year).

❶ Getting There & Away

Les Portes du Soleil is straightforward to get to from **Geneva airport** (GVA; Aéroport International de Genève; www.gva.ch), 83km to the west. A plethora of buses and shared taxis run

---

from the airport to the resorts. Door-to-door transfers need to be booked in advance and start at around €25. Morzexpress (www.morzexpress.com) is a reliable operator.

Altibus (www.altibus.com) line 91 links Les Portes du Soleil's three resorts with the railheads of Thonon-les-Bains (€8 to €15, one hour, one to six daily) and Cluses (€8, one hour, one to 10 daily). It's worth calling (08 20 32 03 68), or asking a tourist office to do so, to ensure the bus service is running, particularly if you're planning to travel at weekends or the very beginning or end of ski season.

Within the Morzine area, free shuttle buses serve all the lifts between mid-December and mid-April, including a dainty miniature train that trundles between the Super Morzine lift and **Pléney** (Taille de Mas du Pleney, Morzine; 1/5/8 trips in summer €5.10/18.20/30.70).

Évian-les-Bains

POP 8968

Standing regally on the southern shore of Lake Geneva (Lac Léman), Évian-les-Bains was favourite country retreat for the Dukes of Savoy and remains a popular spa destination, particularly in summer.

Old-world glamour and modern-day commercialism clash in Évian. The world-famous mineral water, which takes at least 15 years to trickle down through the Chablais Mountains, is an arm of multinational food corporation Danone but it can be freely sipped at taps beneath a lacy colonnade. The town is jewelled with attractive belle époque buildings, but the casino, resorts and busy centre rather distract from lake-shore serenity.

◉ Sights & Activities

Évian is compact and easily explored on foot. Facing the **lakefront promenade** (along quai Baron de Blonay and quai Paul Léger) are impressive Victorian and belle époque buildings, including the **Palais Lumière** (☑04 50 83 15 90; www.ville-evian.fr/fr/culture/palais-lumiere; quai Charles-Albert-Besson; ⊙Tue-Sun 10am-7pm, 2-7pm Mon); the **Villa Lumière** (☑04 50 83 10 00; www.ville-evian.fr; rue de la Source de Clermont; ⊙9-11am & 1.30-5pm Mon-Fri) FREE; the **Théâtre** (☑04 50 26 85 00; http://ville-evian.fr/fr/culture/spectacles; quai Besson) and the **Casino** (☑04 50 26 87 87; www.casino-evian.com; quai Baron-de-Blonay; ⊙10am-2am Mon-Thu, to 3am Fri-Sun).

Source Cachat SPRING
(20 av des Sources; ⊙24hr) FREE Locals take pleasure in hauling huge canisters to these outdoor taps and filling them with Évian water, straight from the source. The taps are framed by pink-and-white neoclassical archways resembling an iced cake.

Thermes d'Évian SPA
(☑04 50 75 02 30; www.lesthermesevian.com; place de la Libération; gym session/massage from €15/41; ⊙9am-7.30pm Mon-Fri, to 6pm Sat) Making much of the healing properties of Évian water, this spa invites visitors to be sprinkled with, dunked in or hydromassage jetted by mineral-rich H_2O. Rather than feeling decadent, the spa evokes a fancy hospital but facilities are very good: a gym, pool, aqua-fitness classes and personal trainers on hand. Reserve ahead, bring a swimsuit, bathing cap and flip-flops, and find the complex 700m east of the tourist office.

WORTH A TRIP

YVOIRE

Petite fortified village Yvoire dozes on the southern shore of Lake Geneva, 26km west of Évian-les-Bains. Still accessed through 14th-century **Porte de Rovorée** (though sadly no longer beneath a portcullis), the historic core is jam-packed with medieval treasures. Amid beautifully weather-worn facades and spires is the privately owned 14th-century **Château d'Yvoire** – all earning Yvoire a place on the official list of 'the Most Beautiful Villages of France'.

Across the street, in the château's old *potager* (veggie garden), the walled **Jardin des Cinq Sens** (Garden of Five Senses; ☑04 50 72 88 80; www.jardin5sens.net; rue du Lac; adult/child €12/7; ⊙10am-6.30pm mid-Apr–early Oct; 🖝) is designed to be experienced through sight, touch, sound, scent and (within reason!) taste. There's a maze, kids' activities, and more than 1300 plant species.

Don't leave without sampling a sweet or savoury crêpe with hams, cheeses and smoked salmon expertly folded within at **Crêperie d'Yvoire** (☑04 50 72 80 78; 1 rue de l'Église; mains from €5; ⊙noon-9pm Feb-Nov).

FRENCH ALPS & THE JURA MOUNTAINS ÉVIAN-LES-BAINS

CGN Cruises BOATING
(www.cgn.ch; place du Port; one-way €19.95) Join local commuters for the scenic, 35-minute boat ride to the Swiss city of Lausanne. Boats depart every hour or two.

ℹ️ Information

Tourist Office (☎ 04 50 75 04 26; www.evian-tourisme.com; place de la Port d'Allinges; ☺9am-noon & 2-6pm Mon-Fri, to 5pm Sat Oct-Apr, 9am-noon & 2-6.30pm Mon-Sat, 10am-noon & 3-6pm Sun May-Sep; 🛜)

ℹ️ Getting There & Away

Évian is about an hour's drive northeast of Geneva. Direct trains reach Thonon-les-Bains (€2.60, eight minutes, at least 12 daily) and Annecy (€17.20, two hours, at least eight daily). For Annecy (€17.50, two hours, at least six daily) or Geneva (from €10.10, 1¾ hours, three daily), change trains in Annemasse.

Transdev Haute-Savoie (http://transdevhaute savoie.com) runs buses to Geneva from Monday to Saturday (€10.50, 1¾ hours, two to seven per day).

Annecy

POP 125,694 / ELEV 447M

Nestled by the northwestern shore of its namesake lake, Annecy is the jewel of the Haute-Savoie. From its crowning Château d'Annecy down to its gurgling canals, Annecy's Vieille Ville (Old Town) is infused with antique charm. Made great by the medieval Counts of Geneva and augmented by the Dukes of Savoy, Annecy still has numerous 16th- and 17th-century buildings, now painted in shades of peach and rose and housing restaurants, bakeries and boutiques. Canals trickle through town, earning Annecy its reputation as an 'Alpine Venice'.

Lac d'Annecy, speckled with swans and rowing boats, is said to have the cleanest waters in Europe, and Annecy's outdoorsy residents revel in all this nature. They row the lake, zip through town on rollerblades and bicycles, and, in winter, drive to nearby ski areas like La Clusaz (p520). After a few lungfuls of mountain air, you might feel compelled to join them.

◉ Sights

The free leaflet *Promenades en Ville* (Town Walks), available from the tourist office (p522), details four 1½-to-2-hour walks around Annecy. Each stroll is themed: canals, the lake, the old town, and Annecy's lesser-known side.

Vieille Ville AREA
It's a pleasure simply to wander aimlessly around Annecy's medieval Old Town, where emerald-green canals flow beneath stone bridges and pastel-painted 16th- and 17th-century buildings bask in sunlight. This jumble of narrow pedestrian-only streets and pretty canals gave Annecy its nickname 'Venice of the Alps'.

Château d'Annecy CASTLE
(☎ 04 50 33 87 34; www.musees.agglo-annecy.fr; place du Château; adult/child €5.50/3; ☺10am-noon & 2-5pm Wed-Mon Oct-May, 10.30am-6pm daily Jun-Sep) With commanding views across the ochre rooftops of the Vieille Ville (Old Town) to the Massif des Bauges, the Château d'Annecy is at once imposing and elegant, a marriage between medieval defensive and decorative architectural styles. Residence of the counts of Geneva during the 13th and 14th centuries, a military barracks in the 1940s, and classified as a historical monument in the 1950s, today it's filled with regional art, from medieval sculpture and Savoyard furniture to Alpine landscape painting and contemporary art.

Palais de l'Isle MUSEUM
(☎ 04 56 49 40 37; www.musees.agglo-anne cy.fr; 3 passage de l'Île; adult/child €3.80/2; ☺10.30am-6pm daily Jul-Sep, 10am-noon & 2-5pm Wed-Mon Oct-Jun) Sitting on a triangular islet surrounded by the Canal du Thiou, the Palais de l'Isle has been a lordly residence, a courthouse, a mint and a prison, according to records dating back to the 14th century. Chambers within this stocky stone building now house permanent exhibits on local history, from medieval coins to the industrial 19th century, plus occasional temporary art exhibits.

A combination ticket grants entry to the Palais and Château d'Annecy for €7.20 (or €4 for under-25s); buy it at either venue.

🏃 Activities

Sunbathing & Swimming

When the sun's out, the beaches fringing the lake beckon. Some are patrolled in July and August, including **Plage d'Albigny** (av du Petit Port) `FREE` and **Plage des Marquisats** (rue des Marquisats) `FREE`, when they can become very crowded.

Annecy

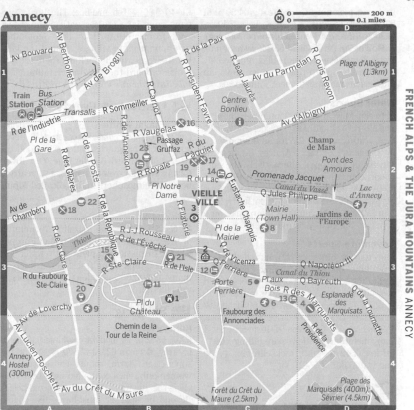

Annecy

◉ Sights
1 Château d'Annecy	B3
2 Palais de l'Isle	C3
3 Vieille Ville	B2

◉ Activities, Courses & Tours
4 Annecy Plongée	D3
5 Compagnie des Bateaux	C3
6 Cyclable	C3
7 Pedal Boat Rental	D2
8 Roll'n Cy	C3
9 Takamaka	A3

◉ Sleeping
10 Hôtel Central	B2
11 Hôtel du Château	B3
12 Hôtel du Palais de l'Isle	C3

13 Le Boutik	C3
14 Splendid Hôtel	C2

◉ Eating
15 Food Market	B3
16 La Ciboulette	B2
17 La Cuisine des Amis	C2
Le Potron-Minet	(see 12)
18 L'Esquisse	A2
19 L'Étage	B2

◉ Drinking & Nightlife
20 Beer O'Clock	A3
21 Captain Pub	B3
22 Folie Royale	A2
23 Le Barista	B2

Cycling & Blading

Biking and blading are big, with 46km of cycling track encircling the lake (aside from a gap on the eastern shore between Menthon and Perroix, awaiting construction). Another gentle path, once a railway grade, leads all the way to Albertville, 44km to the southeast. There are several bike rental operators in town, including **Cyclable** (☑04 50 51 51 50; www.velo-annecy.fr; 8 place aux Bois; ☺10am-12.30pm & 2.30-7pm Mar-Sep, 10am-7pm Jul & Aug).

Roll'n Cy (☑06 28 34 66 34; www.roll-n-cy. org; ☺8pm Fri Mar–mid-Dec) FREE runs weekly rollerblading group rides through town, an unconventional way to meet some locals.

Water Sports

Between May and mid-September, there is **pedalo rental** (quai Jules Philippe; ☺May–mid-Sep), costing around €15 for an hour, offered by the shore of Lac d'Annecy (at or near Jardins de l'Europe. Alternatively, the safety-conscious diving pros at **Annecy Plongée** (☑04 50 45 40 97; www.annecyplongee.com; 6 rue des Marquisats; ☺9am-noon & 2-7pm Tue-Fri, 9am-7pm Sat) can help you take the plunge on a dive into the lake's pristine waters.

Adventure Sports

The tourist office (p522) has listings of mountain biking, canyoning, ballooning and other adrenaline-sport operators in and around Annecy. An enormous range is offered by **Takamaka** (☑04 50 45 60 61; https:// annecy.takamaka.fr; 23 rue du Faubourg Ste-Claire; ☺9am-noon & 2-6pm Mon-Fri, 10am-5pm Sat & Sun), including tandem paragliding (€95), rafting (€42 to €62), rock climbing (€49) and water-skiing (€42).

☞ Tours

Compagnie des Bateaux   BOATING
(☑04 50 51 08 40; www.annecy-croisieres.com; 2 place aux Bois; 1hr lake cruises adult/child €14.40/9.80; ☺Feb–mid-Dec) The Boat Company runs lake cruises with commentary and, from mid-April to late September, two-hour trips to villages around the lake. For the romantically inclined there are also cruises aboard the 'floating restaurant' MS *Libellule* (*menus* €56.60 to €91.10).

✷ Festivals & Events

★ **Carnaval Vénitien**   CARNIVAL
(Venetian Carnival; ☺late Feb or early Mar) Revellers clad in ballgowns and masks flood the streets of Annecy's Vieille Ville (Old Town) for this two-day event, creating a surreal and beautiful atmosphere in the so-called 'Alpine Venice'.

Fête du Lac   FIREWORKS
(☺first Sat of Aug) This dazzling 70 minutes of fireworks over the lake is one of Europe's largest displays, complete with water jets and a booming soundtrack, and attracts as many as 200,000 goggle-eyed spectators to the lakeshore.

🛏 Sleeping

Annecy Hostel   HOSTEL €
(☑09 53 12 02 90; http://annecyhostel.fr; 32 av de Loverchy; dm from €23, d €55-70; @🛜) Bright, super-clean dorm rooms (mixed-sex and women-only) elicit contented sighs from travellers rocking up at this well-managed hostel. Beyond backpacker must-haves like shared kitchens, lockers and clean bathrooms, further perks include a TV lounge and a back

---

LOCAL KNOWLEDGE

ANNECY DAY TRIP: TO THE SNOW!

Hankering for a snowy day trip? Annecy is less than an hour from three ski resorts. Perched on the northwest side of the Chaîne des Aravis, **La Clusaz** (www.laclusaz.com; one-day lift pass adult/child €37.80/29.50; ☺Dec-Apr) gathers reliable snow to pad out its 125km of pistes, served by 49 lifts. Topping out at 2600m, the resort is best for intermediate and experienced skiers, with just a few green and black runs for beginners and pros.

Six kilometres north, **Le Grand Bornand** (☑04 50 02 78 00; www.legrandbornand.com; one-day pass adult/child €36.50/29; ☺Dec-Apr) has a 29-lift ski area, between 1000m and 2100m elevation, comprising more than a dozen each of green, blue and red pistes (with just a few black runs for advanced skiers) plus almost 70km of cross-country trails.

Best for beginners is Semnoz (p526; elevation 1700m), less than 30 minutes' drive from Annecy. The piste and lift network are limited, but there are lift tickets for just two hours (adult/child €9.20/7.40) if you only want a taste of the snow. In summer there's luge, biking and hiking.

In ski season Transdev (www.transdevsavoie.com) offers bus transfers from Annecy to La Clusaz (€8, 50 minutes, six to 10 daily) and Le Grand Bornand (€8, 1¼ hours, six to 10 daily). Local buses reach Semnoz from Annecy (€5.60, 45 minutes, three daily) but timetables vary depending on season; ask at Annecy's tourist office (p522).

garden that's perfect for socialising – with table tennis, a pool table and a bar serving local and imported beers between 3pm and 11pm.

★ Hôtel Central
BOUTIQUE HOTEL €

(☑ 04 50 45 05 37; 6bis rue Royale; d/tr from €70/85; ☜) Forget the prosaic name – this canalside hotel, occupying an 18th-century building in the pedestrianised heart of the city, has the most eccentric and visually entertaining digs in Annecy. Whether awash in sultry violet, following a zany safari theme or unabashedly kaleidoscopic in colour, each of the rooms has its own peculiar charm.

Hôtel du Château
HOTEL €€

(☑ 04 50 45 27 66; www.annecy-hotel.com; 16 rampe du Château; s/d/tr/q €69/99/119/129; ℗☜) Just across the square from the château's imposing gatehouse, this family-run hotel has a panoramic breakfast terrace and 16 neat rooms with rustic pine furniture and a sunny colour scheme. Four have lovely lake views.

Le Boutik
DESIGN HOTEL €€

(☑ 04 50 44 04 40; www.leboutikhotel.com; 2 rue des Marquisats; d €110-170; ☜) Each of Le Boutik's rooms has its own theme, ranging from loosely literary (the haughty 'Oscar Wilde' and book-lined 'Grey') to travel (like the brick-and-suitcase homage, 'New York'). Find the main entrance on rue de la Providence, above a boutique selling (of course) designer homewares.

Splendid Hôtel
BOUTIQUE HOTEL €€

(☑ 04 50 45 20 00; www.hotel-annecy-lac.fr; 4 quai Eustache Chappuis; d €123-137, ste from €250; ✲@☜) The aptly named Splendid's 58 rooms have a contemporary feel, with cream walls, crimson throws and polished wooden floors, but modern trimmings like coffee makers. Cushioned headboards and Rococo-style trimmings add decadence to the pricier 'executive' rooms. Whether you need an extra bed, stroller rental or a babysitter, the friendly staff can oblige.

Hôtel du Palais de l'Isle
HISTORIC HOTEL €€

(☑ 04 50 45 86 87; www.palaisannecy.com; 13 rue Perrière; s/d/ste from €114/139/306; ✲☜) In a warren-like 18th-century building in the centre of the old town, this hotel leans towards nostalgia with parchment-effect wallpaper and regal maroon hues, but keeps things up to date where it matters: tastefully modern bathrooms, minibars and a sleek lounge-bar. Rooms have views of the palais, the château or the old town's rooftops.

🍴 Eating

Food Market
MARKET €

(cnr rues Ste-Claire & de la République; ☉7am-1pm Sun, Tue & Fri) Snaking along rue Ste-Claire, this open-air food market reels you in with the scent of garlic-fried frogs' legs and Savoyard cheeses. Honey, homemade gingerbread and mind-boggling quantities of *saucisson sec* (dried regional sausage) will tempt self-caterers, plus there's grab-and-go food such as steaming sausages and turceens of *choucroute garnie* (dressed cabbage stew).

Le Potron-Minet
CRÊPES €

(☑ 04 50 32 60 59; www.facebook.com/LePotronMinetAnnecy; 9 rue Perrière; mains from €10; ☉noon-2pm & 7-9pm Tue-Sat) This outstanding bistro puts a gourmet spin on *galettes* (traditional buckwheat-flour crêpes). Try seafood *galette* La Breizh or the enormous Napolitaine, with fresh mozzarella, pesto and Savoyard ham. Also on offer are tartines (open sandwiches laden with bacon, artichokes, melted cheese and all manner of toppings), plus high-quality burgers and steak tartare.

L'Étage
FRENCH €€

(☑ 04 50 51 03 28; www.letageannecy.com; 13 rue du Pâquier; lunch menus €19, dinner menus €28-37; ☉noon-2.15pm & 7-10.30pm) The vintage-inspired decor and bar-side tables scream 'brasserie', but l'Étage, within a 17th-century building, has loftier aspirations, serving sophisticated interpretations of traditional recipes. Great-value *menus* offer French classics, while *à la carte* choices include truffled fondue and *farçon savoyard* (a ham-wrapped savoury potato cake). Inconsistent service is the only downside, but on the whole L'Étage deserves its excellent local reputation.

La Cuisine des Amis
MOROCCAN, FRENCH €

(☑ 04 50 10 10 80; www.lacuisinedesamisannecy.fr; 9 rue du Pâquier; mains €14-22, lunch menus €14.90; ☉noon-2pm & 7-10.30pm Jun-Sep, closed dinner Sun & Mon Oct-May; ☷) If your group is torn about where to dine, the Moroccan and French dishes served in this airy *salon* setting will please all palates. The menu is evenly split between cheesy Savoyard specialities and Moroccan classics like couscous royale and *tajine* of lamb and figs. The lunchtime dish of the day is a steal at €9.90.

COFFEE, TEA & CHOCOLATE

Le Barista (☏09 84 29 61 44; www.barista-cafe.fr; 2 passage Gruffaz; ☺9.30am-6.30pm Tue-Fri, 9am-7pm Sat; ☏) Hidden in a canalside arcade, this speciality coffee joint takes its time in pouring the perfect cappuccino. Though tiny, it attracts an animated mix of office workers, European backpackers and homesick Antipodeans in search of a coffee culture to remind them of home. Tempting selection of cookies and muffins, too.

Folie Royale (☏04 50 52 28 58; 13 rue Royale; ☺9am-7pm Mon-Sat) This handsome *salon de thé* has a master chocolatier staining his apron out back, as he hand-dips squares of ganache into chocolate, dices nougat and rolls marzipan into dainty logs. There are over 30 teas and tisanes with which to wash down his creations, or you can mainline: the hot chocolate is thick, rich and lip-smacking. Trust us, ask for a small hot chocolate (€2.80) – there really can be too much of a good thing.

La Ciboulette GASTRONOMY €€€
(☏04 50 45 74 57; www.laciboulette-annecy.com; Cour du Pré Carré, 10 rue Vaugelas; menus €39-130; ☺noon-1pm & 7.30-8.45pm Tue-Sat) With 30 years in business and a Michelin star, there's no mistaking La Ciboulette's *haute cuisine* credentials. Chef Georges Paccard prepares seasonally driven combinations like turbot with Provence asparagus, and nut-crumbed veal with mushroom and potato ravioli. A voluminous wine menu, best perused in the flowery courtyard, rounds out an elegant package.

L'Esquisse GASTRONOMY €€€
(☏04 50 44 80 59; www.esquisse-annecy.fr; 21 rue Royale; lunch menus €36, dinner menus €44-72; ☺12.15-1.15pm & 7.30-9pm Mon, Tue & Thu-Sat) A talented husband-and-wife team runs the show at this intimate Michelin-starred restaurant. Their passion shines through in the service, wine list and carefully composed *menus* in which each course – parsnip and orange consommé, Basque-style black pudding, flower-garnished desserts – resembles a miniature work of art. Reserve ahead.

★**Yoann Conte** GASTRONOMY €€€
(☏04 50 09 97 49; www.yoann-conte.com; 13 Vieille rte des Pensières, Veyrier-du-Lac; lunch menus €98-179, dinner menus €210-249; ☺noon-1.30pm & 7-8.30pm Wed-Sun, plus 7-8.30pm Tue in summer) Virtuoso chef Yoann Conte nods to regional cuisine with smoked *féra* (white fish from Lake Léman) and corn-flour farfalle (butterfly pasta) with morels, while Corsican citrus and Greek olive oils widen the balance of flavours. For sensory immersion in this polished, double Michelin-starred restaurant, the 'Conte Vents et Marées' – a 12-element 'winds and seas' menu – aims to tell a story through food.

🍷 Drinking & Nightlife

Beer O'Clock BAR
(☏04 50 65 83 78; www.facebook.com/beeroclock74; 18 rue du Faubourg Ste-Claire; ☺5pm-1am Tue-Sat, to 11pm Sun; ☏) This laid-back, high-tech establishment serves beer like petrol stations sell gasoline: you only pay for what you pump. After buying credit on a computerised magnetic card, you can drink as much or as little of the 12 brews on offer as you like – a fantastic way to compare and savour lots of microbrews side by side.

Captain Pub PUB
(☏04 11 88 99 80; www.captain-pub.fr; 11 rue du Pont Morens; ☺11am-2.30am Wed-Sun; ☏) It's best not to examine too closely this convivial boozer's Irish pub credentials. But after a genuine welcome and finding a seat in the warren of convivial nooks, it's impossible not to feel at home. Huddle up for a dozen beers on tap and scores of whiskies and cocktails like 'Blue Champagne'; you can enjoy premium views from canalside outdoor tables.

ℹ Information

Tourist Office (☏04 50 45 00 33; www.lac-annecy.com; 1 rue Jean Jaurès, courtyard of Centre Bonlieu; ☺9am-12.30pm & 1.45-6pm Mon-Sat year-round, plus Sun mid-May–mid-Sep, 9am-12.30pm Sun Apr & early Oct & Dec)

ℹ Getting There & Around

BICYCLE

Bikes can be hired from **Vélonecy** (☏04 50 51 38 90; www.velonecy.com; place de la Gare; ☺9am-1pm & 2-6.30pm Mon-Sat), situated at the train station. A day's hire including helmet is €21 (or just €4 if you're under 26 years old). Electric bikes are offered too, from €31. Staff can supply you with a bike-path map. Deposit of €250 required. In July and August reserve two or three days ahead.

BUS

The ticket office for the **bus station** (Gare Routière; rue de l'Industrie) is inside the train station.

Transalis (📞 04 50 51 08 51; www.transalis. fr) handles services from Annecy to Geneva (lines T72 and T73, €10.50, 1½ hours, up to 15 daily Monday to Friday, six to eight Saturday and Sunday).

Altibus (www.altibus.com) sends buses from Annecy to villages around Lac d'Annecy, including Veyrier-du-Lac (30 minutes, every hour or two between 7am and 7.40pm), Menthon-St-Bernard (25 minutes, five to eight services Monday to Saturday) and Talloires (30 minutes, five to eight services Monday to Saturday). Tickets cost €1.50 each way. Other destinations include the ski resorts of La Clusaz (€8, 1¼ hours, eight to 12 daily) and Le Grand Bornand (€8, 1½ hours, eight to 12 daily).

There are direct Altibus services to Geneva airport (€14, 1½ hours, six to 12 daily). Direct buses to Lyon-Saint-Exupéry airport (€12, 1½ hours, five or six daily) can be booked through www.ouibus.com.

TRAIN

Services from Annecy's **train station** (place de la Gare) include the following.

Aix-les-Bains €8.50, 40min, at least hourly (direct)

Chambéry €10.70, 50min, at least hourly (direct)

Lyon Part-Dieu €27.60, 2hr, 8 direct, more via Chambéry

Paris Gare de Lyon €76-110, 3¾hr, 2-5 direct, more via Lyon or Chambéry

Chamonix €24.90, 2½hr, 6 daily, all via St Gervais Les Bains Le Fayet

---

Chambéry

POP 59,697 / ELEV 270M

Huddled between Chartreuse and Massif des Bauges regional parks, the attractive town of Chambéry is often forgotten by visitors to the French Alps. Chambéry was Savoy's capital from the 13th century until 1563, when the Dukes relocated to Turin. Past centuries have enriched the town, 12km south of Lac du Bourget, with elaborate *hôtels particuliers* (grand townhouses), a medieval château and a one-of-a-kind *trompe l'œil*–decorated cathedral.

◉ Sights

★ **Ville Ancienne** AREA

Chambéry's medieval Old Town reveals its beauty gradually. Rush through its lanes and you risk missing hidden courtyards, murals and well-preserved 14th- to 18th-century *hôtels* (town houses), many of which are inhabited by modern Chambériens. Streets worth wandering include tiny **rue du Sénat de Savoie**, cobbled **rue Juiverie** and boutique-dotted **rue de la Métropole**. To peep inside private residences and uncover lesser-known corners, enquire about walking tours at **Hôtel de Cordon** (📞04 79 70 15 94; 71 rue St Réal; ⊙2-6pm Tue-Sat school holidays, 2-6pm Wed, Fri & Sat rest of year) **FREE**; usually at 2.30pm on weekends (€6, French only).

Fontaine des Éléphants FOUNTAIN

(place des Éléphants) With its four carved elephants, this 17.6m-high fountain looks like the model for an old Indian postage stamp. It was sculpted in 1838 in honour of Général de Boigne (1751–1830), who made his fortune in the East Indies and was honoured posthumously with this monument for bestowing some of his wealth on the town. Locally, the elephants – whose front halves sprout from the statue – are lovingly referred to as the *quatre sans cul* (the rear-less four).

Château des Ducs de Savoie CASTLE

(📞04 79 70 15 94; place du Château; ⊙gardens 9am-6pm Mon-Fri mid-Feb–Jun & Sep-Dec, plus Sat & Sun Jul & Aug, exhibition 9am-noon & 1.30-6pm Tue-Fri, 10.30am-6pm Sat & Sun, closed Jan–mid-Feb) Medieval walls, Gothic tracery, *trompe l'œil* detailing…Chambéry's château has acquired a wealth of styles since its founding in the 11th century. Once home to the counts and dukes of Savoy, the stately stronghold has housed the Préfecture and Conseil Général of the Savoie *département* since 1860. The **gardens** and **Cour d'Honneur** (courtyard) are open free of charge; to see 14th- and 15th-century **Tour Trésorerie** (Treasury Tower) and stained glass inside **Ste-Chapelle**, built in the 15th century to house the Turin Shroud, take a tour.

Cathédrale St-François de Sales CATHEDRAL

(📞04 79 33 25 00; www.catholiques-chambery. paroisse.net; 6 rue Métropole; ⊙8.45am-noon & 2-6pm Mon-Sat, 9am-12.15pm & 3-8pm Sun) All is not as it seems inside Chambéry's 15th-century Franciscan cathedral, decorated with 6000 sq metres of *trompe l'œil* painting. The largest such feature in any building in Europe, the decorations – created by 19th-century artists Sevesi and Vicario – deceive the eyes into seeing Gothic vaults, an ornate carved ceiling and a mystical labyrinth that leads believers to Jerusalem.

Musée des Beaux-Arts　　　GALLERY
(☑ 04 79 33 75 03; www.chambery.fr/musees; place du Palais de Justice; special exhibitions adult/child €5.50/2.50; ⊙10am-6pm Tue-Sun) **FREE** Occupying a former corn exchange, Chambéry's grand fine-arts museum exhibits mostly 14th- to 18th-century Italian works. There's a particular emphasis on Florentine and Sienese paintings from the Renaissance, including pieces by Caravaggio, Titian and Ghirlandaio; exhibitions are laid out in the light-flooded upper floor of this elegant 19th-century gallery. Also worth a look are the many dramatic landscapes of Chambéry and the Alps painted between 1799 and 1975.

Musée des Charmettes　　HISTORIC BUILDING
(Maison de Jean-Jacques Rousseau; ☑ 04 79 33 39 44; www.chambery.fr/musees; 890 chemin des Charmettes; audioguides €1; ⊙10am-6pm Tue-Sun) **FREE** Geneva-born philosopher, composer and writer Jean-Jacques Rousseau, a key figure of the Enlightenment and the French Revolution, lived the happiest years of his life in this serene country house between 1736 and 1742. It's laden with original features, like 18th-century wallpaper and fainting couches. Even those with little interest in the life of Rousseau might find their interest piqued by stories of his 'instruction' under Madame de Warens, who took the much-younger philosopher as her lover here. It's a steep 2km southeast of central Chambéry.

ⓘ WATCH THIS SPACE!
....
Due for a grand reopening in 2020, **Musée Savoisien** (☑ 04 56 42 43 43; www.musee-savoisien.fr; sq de Lannoy de Bissy) housed in a Franciscan monastery was closed to undergo a massive renovation when we passed through. When it reopens its doors, visitors can expect a showcase of the turbulent history, rich culture and diverse ethnography of Savoie.

🛏 Sleeping

Inter-Hôtel des Princes　　　HOTEL €€
(☑ 04 79 33 45 36; www.hoteldesprinces.com; 4 rue de Boigne; s/d/tr/q from €75/89/139/159; ⏃) This dapper family hotel is one of the oldest in town, squirrelled away in a 1471-built convent that once guarded the Shroud of Turin. Rooms feel simultaneously homely and swish, with Alpine prints, artfully arranged driftwood and heart-shaped ornaments. A spa and sauna, bookable for €16 per person (45 minutes), tips the balance from cosiness to utter chic.

★Petit Hôtel Confidentiel　BOUTIQUE HOTEL €€€
(☑ 04 79 26 24 17; www.petithotelconfidentiel. com; 10 rue de la Trésorerie; d €320-360, ste €400-890; Ⓟ❄⏃) Starting from the ground-floor *épicerie* (grocery) once frequented by 18th-century luminary JJ Rousseau, this five-star, family-run boutique hotel has steadily colonised a 15th-century building in the lee of the château. There's a choice of design-conscious doubles, individually decorated in midnight-black or along Scandinavian themes, and opulent suites with two-person bath-tubs and ultramodern ethanol fireplaces.

🍴 Eating

Pedestrian **rue du Sénat de Savoie** and **rue Bonivard**, flowing from the covered market, are where to find cheese shops, chocolate makers and delicatessens. Some of the many restaurants around **place Monge** serve Savoyard treats such as fondue and *tartiflette* (potatoes, cheese and bacon baked in a casserole). For cheap eats, head to **rue de la République**.

Marché des Halles　　　　　FOOD
(Covered Market; place de Genève; ⊙7am-1.30pm Tue-Sat) More than two-dozen local producers assemble in Chambéry's covered market, selling regional specialities like charcuterie and cheese, alongside butchers, fishmongers, florists, Vietnamese takeaway food and more.

La Cerise sur le Chapô　　　CRÊPES €
(☑ 04 79 60 86 70; 83 rue de la République; mains €8-14; ⊙noon-2pm Wed-Sun, 7-10pm Tue-Sat) This trim crêperie is evangelical about the health benefits of its protein-rich traditional *galettes* (savoury buckwheat crêpes), which arrive attractively laden with goat's cheese, salmon and leek, and – our favourite – salted caramel and baked apple.

★Les Halles FRENCH €€
(☎04 79 60 01 95; www.restaurant-les-halles-chambery.com; 15 rue Bonivard; lunch menus €14-18, dinner menus €27-36; ⊙noon-2pm & 7-10pm Tue-Sat) Swift service and charmingly retro decor set the tone at Les Halles, where regional and classic French dishes are executed simply and with finesse. Risotto of Parmesan and Savoyard ham, steak tartare, and a cinnamon-scented duck *à l'orange* are standouts, and they pair beautifully with the house Savoie and Rhône Valley wines.

L'Atelier FRENCH, TAPAS €€
(☎04 79 70 62 39; www.atelier-chambery.com; 59 rue de la République; lunch menus €21, dinner menus €32-40; ⊙noon-2pm & 7-10pm Tue-Sat) Chef Gilles Herard – who's worked in the kitchens of gastronomic princes like Alain Ducasse and Paul Bocuse – works the stoves in this brick-vaulted wine bar-bistro. Tapas-style options include charcuterie plates and a globe-spanning platter of gourmet spring rolls, burritos and samosas. Dinner *menus* balance rustic French and Italian flavours.

Information

Tourist Office (☎04 79 33 42 47; www.chambery-tourisme.com; 5bis place du Palais de Justice; ⊙9am-12.30pm & 2-6pm Mon-Sat)

Getting There & Around

BICYCLE

City-run **Vélostation** (☎04 79 96 34 13; www.velostation-chambery.fr; sq Paul Vidal, Parc du Verney; bike rental per hr/day €2/6; ⊙8am-7pm Mon-Fri, 1.30-7pm Sat, 9am-7pm Sun Apr-Oct, shorter hours Nov-Mar) rents out seven-speed city bikes with discounts for those aged under 26.

Staff can supply you with a cycling map featuring scenic routes like the 40km **Balcons de Chambéry** circuit.

AIR

Chambéry Savoie Mont Blanc Airport (☎04 79 54 49 54; www.chambery-airport.com; off D1201, Viviers-du-Lac; 📶), 10km north of Chambéry at the southern tip of Lac du Bourget, has seasonal flights (mainly December to April) to Amsterdam, Rotterdam, Stockholm and several British regional airports.

BUS

Adjacent to the train station, the **bus station** (place de la Gare) has services to Aix-les-Bains (50 minutes) via the beaches along Lac du Bourget from late June to early September (the 'Ligne des Plages'). Tickets cost €1.60.

WORTH A TRIP

BIRD'S EYE LAKE VIEW

Twenty-three generations of the De Menthon family have lived within 1000-year-old **Château de Menthon-St-Bernard** (☎07 81 74 39 72; www.chateau-de-menthon.com; allée du Château, Menthon-St-Bernard; guided tours adult/child €9.50/5; ⊙2-6pm Fri-Sun May, Jun & Sep, noon-6pm daily Jul & Aug; 👪). The birthplace of St Bernard in 1008 – and supposedly one of the inspirations for Walt Disney's *Sleeping Beauty* castle – the château clings to a forested hillside, 12km south of Annecy. Tours of the medieval interior take in tapestry-adorned *salons* and a magnificent library, stacked with more than 12,000 volumes dating to before the Revolution. But it's the sparkling Lac d'Annecy panorama that leaves many visitors speechless.

TRAIN

Direct services from Chambéry's **train station** (Gare de Chambéry-Challes-les-Eaux; www.gares-sncf.com; place de la Gare) include the following:

Annecy €10.70, 1 hour, hourly

Geneva from €18.40, 1½ hours, four to six per day

Grenoble €12.40, 1 hour, hourly

Lyon Part-Dieu €19.10, 1½ hours, almost hourly

Paris Gare de Lyon from €68, 3 hours, four to 10 daily

Around Chambéry

Chambéry is wedged between two protected nature parks brimming with mellow hiking, mountain biking, snowshoeing and cross-country skiing adventures.

Parc Naturel Régional de Chartreuse PARK
(☎04 76 88 75 20; www.parc-chartreuse.net) Limestone promontories, dense forests and a powerful liqueur are the signature features of this 767-sq-km regional park. The 1300km of marked walking trails are a major incentive to visit, but the namesake liqueur is an even bigger draw. The Caves de la Chartreuse (p526) introduce the history of monk-made Chartreuse liqueur (including tastings); 24km east is the **Musée de la Grande Chartreuse** (☎04 76 88 60 45; www.musee-grande-chartreuse.fr; La Correrie, St-Pierre-de-Chartreuse; adult/child €8.50/3.90;

LOCAL KNOWLEDGE

CHARTREUSE: THE MONASTIC LIQUEUR

Either acid green or radioactive yellow, Chartreuse may be the brightest, most shockingly hued herbal elixir of the cocktail and digestif world. Mixologists sing its praises and in ski resorts it adds a splash of Alpine fire to hot chocolate (known as 'Green Chaud'). Its surge in global popularity in recent years might have something to do with it being hailed as 'the only liqueur so good they named a colour after it' in Quentin Tarantino's 2007 thriller *Death Proof*. It certainly isn't because the Carthusian monks who make it have been brashly broadcasting its wonders, for this is a liqueur shrouded in secrecy and silence.

The production of Chartreuse began in 1737 and, at first, it was intended as a medicine. The green version is produced by macerating 130 hard-to-find mountain herbs, roots and plants in alcohol and leaving the mixture to age in oak casks.

Today, Chartreuse's exact ingredients remain a closely guarded secret, and word has it only two monks know the recipe. Perhaps closest to the original is the Elixir Végétal (69% alcohol), sold as a tonic, but potent, spicy, chlorophyll-rich Chartreuse Green (55% alcohol) and milder, sweeter Chartreuse Yellow (40% alcohol) are much better known. You can taste these otherworldly liqueurs, bone up on their history and tour barrel-lined cellars at the **Caves de la Chartreuse** (☑04 76 05 81 77; www.chartreuse.fr; 10 bd Edgar-Kofler, Voiron; ☉9am-11.30am & 2-6pm daily Apr-Oct, Mon-Fri Nov-Mar) **FREE** distillery, 25km northwest of Grenoble (or 45km southwest of Chambéry).

☉10am-6.30pm Mon-Wed, Fri & Sat, 2-6.30pm Sun Jun-Aug, 2-6pm Fri-Wed Apr, May, Sep-Nov), delving into the monks' secretive lives.

It's simplest to have private transport to reach and explore the park. Otherwise, Transisère (www.transisere.fr) runs irregular buses between Grenoble and St-Pierre-de-Chartreuse (line 7000, €5.60, 1¼ hours) and between Chambéry to Voiron (line 7010, €5.60, 1½ hours).

Parc Naturel Régional du Massif des Bauges   PARK

(☑04 79 54 86 40; www.parcdesbauges.com) Less touristed than other regional natural parks in the French Alps, the Massif des Bauges' jigsaw of peaks and meadows is invigorating terrain for walkers and mountain bikers. The park makes an easy day-trip from Annecy or Chambéry, but for immersion in its 900 sq km there are numerous farmstays; ask at the park's main **tourist office** (☑04 79 54 84 28; www.lesbauges.com; av Denis Therme, Le Châtelard; ☉9am-noon & 2-6pm Mon-Sat May-Sep, to 5pm Mon-Wed, Fri & Sat Oct-Apr; ⓢ) in Le Châtelard, 36km northeast of Chambéry.

It's most convenient to explore the park with a car, as bus services are very limited.

The villages of École, Doucy-en-Bauges and Ste-Reine are all starting points for walking trails, along which you might spot chamois, the park's emblem. Also within the park are **Semnoz** (☑04 50 01 20 30; www.semnoz.fr; Viuz-la-Chiésaz; five-hour pass adult/child €13.40/10/70; ☉9am-5pm Dec-Apr), a ski

retreat ideal for families (30 minutes' drive from Annecy), and Chambéry's favourite weekend retreat for snow-lovers, **Savoie Grand Révard** (www.savoiegrandrevard.com; per day cross-country ski pass adult/child €8.50/5, downhill ski pass €19/15; ☉late Dec–mid-Mar).

Irregular buses link Chambéry and park villages like Le Châtelard and École; browse bus schedules on www.lesbauges.com.

Les Trois Vallées

This is the big one you've heard all about: vast, fast and by most measures, the largest ski area in the world. It's impossible to tire of all this terrain: depending on how it's reckoned, there are more than 600km of pistes and more than 180 lifts linking eight resorts and three parallel valleys. Among these are **Val Thorens**, Europe's highest ski village at a heady 2300m; wealthy and ever-so-British **Méribel** (elevation 1450m), founded by Scotsman Colonel Peter Lindsay in 1938; and playground of the super-rich **Courchevel**, which stretches over three purpose-built resorts at 1550m, 1650m and 1850m and is a fave of the Moët-at-five brigade and ultra-wealthy Russians.

In between are a number of lesser-known Alpine villages – **Le Praz** (Courchevel-Le Praz; 1300m), **St-Martin de Belleville** (1450m) and *très anglais* **La Tania** (1400m); all are linked by speedy lifts to higher-elevation slopes.

Activities

Winter

Les Trois Vallées is blessed with some of the world's best ski-able terrain. The pistes here are vast and varied enough to satisfy even the most demanding skiers. The season here is also among the longest in France, running from early December to late April (or early May in Val Thorens). Save time queuing by buying your pass online at www.les3vallees. com. You'll pay in the region of €61/300 for a one-/six-day pass for Les Trois Vallées, less if you're skiing at the beginning or end of the season (or sticking to one valley).

Sunny, relaxed **Méribel** is intermediate heaven, with 150km of cruisy (mostly blue and red) runs, more than 40 ski lifts, two slalom stadiums, an Albertville Olympic run, two **snow parks** with jumps, pipes and rails, and plenty of activities for kids. Packed with Brits and *seasonaires* (seasonal workers), it's also famous for après-ski partying.

With a wide plateau of cruisy green and blue runs, tree-fringed **Courchevel** is paradise for beginners. Lifts begin in glitzy Courchevel 1850, the highest of the valley's hub villages (where you can practically ski down into a designer boutique). Courchevel's 150km of well-groomed pistes, served by 58 lifts, include a few knee-trembling black *couloirs* (steep gullies). The 2km-long floodlit **toboggan run** through the forest, illuminated from 5pm to 7.30pm, is a fun après-ski alternative.

Watched over by glacier-licked peaks, **Val Thorens**, purpose-built in the 1960s, is the highest valley of the three and enjoys the longest season. Largely tree-less and exposed, most skiing is above 2000m – on blue-sky days, the terrain feels vast and open, but clouds seem to descend in an instant. There's excellent off-piste terrain, a **snow park** and Europe's longest **toboggan run** (one run, with sledge and helmet, costs €15.50 and takes 45 minutes), a drop of 700m over its 6km.

Off-piste skiers seeking guidance should head for **La Croisette**, at the top of the Verdons ski lift: the **Maison de la Montagne** houses both the **ESF** (☑ 04 79 08 07 72; www. esfcourchevel.com; 110 rue de la Croisette, Courchevel 1850; 2hr private lesson €140; ☺ 9am-7pm Dec-Apr; ♿) and the **Bureau des Guides** (☑ 06 23 92 46 12; www.guides-courchevel.com; Maison de la Montagne, rue de La Croisette, Courchevel 1850; ☺ 9am-7pm Mon-Sat Dec-Apr, shorter hours Jul & Aug).

La Tyrolienne   ADVENTURE SPORTS
(Plan Bouchet; €52; ☺ Dec-Mar) Accessible only to skiers (and in clear weather), this is the world's highest zip line. From the top of the Bouchet chair lift, those who dare fly 1300m in one minute and 45 seconds at speeds of up to 100km/h, dangling more than 200m above the ice.

Aquamotion   WATER SPORTS
(☑ 09 71 00 73 00; www.aquamotion-courchevel. com; 1297 rte des Eaux Vives; adult/child €26/16; ☺ 10am-8.30pm Mon & Thu-Sun, to 10.30pm Tue & Wed Dec-Apr; ♿) No, the Starship Enterprise hasn't landed in Courchevel – it's a state-of-the-art aquatic complex, with mountain views visible from the waters of the 25m pool. Loll around by the wave-making machines, hop onto the 45m slide, or stump up for the wellness centre, complete with saunas, spas, mineral pools and massage. Other distractions include a gym and climbing wall.

Summer

Summer (mid-June to August) sprinkles wild flowers over the pastures of Les Trois Vallées and transforms the mountains into a playground for **hiking**, **paragliding** and **via ferrata** fixed-cable routes – for the last, there is one at Levassaix (near Les Menuires) and another at Le Cochet (St-Martin de Belleville). Scenic walks include a four-hour return hike to **Refuge du Saut** (2126m), a steep climb for magnificent valley views, and family-friendly two-hour **Circuit des Lacs** from Val Thorens.

The resorts are criss-crossed by hundreds of kilometres of circuits and downhill runs for **mountain bikers** – Val Thorens alone has 120km of trails. IGN biking maps and details on bike rental outlets (there's at least one in each station) are available at tourist offices. The Bureau des Guides can assist with summer activities.

🛏 Sleeping & Eating

Tourist offices run accommodation services in **Courchevel** (☑ 0479080029; http://booking. courchevel.com), **Méribel** (☑ 04 79 00 50 00; http://reservation.meribel.net; rte du Centre) and **Val Thorens** (☑ 04 79 00 01 06; http://book. valthorens.com; Grand Rue, Maison de Val Thorens).

Michelin star-spangled Courchevel (eight restaurants and counting) is heaven for gastronomes, but even by gourmet standards restaurants are stratospherically expensive (menus from €100). Fortunately the villages also have midrange Savoyard restaurants and bar-bistros (particularly Méribel).

SERGEY BERESTETSKY/SHUTTERSTOCK ©

1. Château de Menthon-St-Bernard (p525) **2.** Parc National des Écrins (p543) **3.** Skiing, La Vallée Blanche (p506)
4. Paragliding over Lake Annecy (p520)

Mountain Highs

You're tearing down the Alps on your mountain bike, a deep blue sky overhead; you're hiking through flowery pastures tinkling with cowbells; you're slaloming on a glacier while it slowly slithers down the flanks of Mont Blanc – everywhere the scenery makes you feel glad to be alive!

Downhill Skiing

Glide to off-piste heaven on the legendary Vallée Blanche (p506), zigzag like an Olympic pro down black pistes in Val d'Isère (p532), or take your pick of Les Portes du Soleil's (p514) 650km of runs.

Magical Views

Take in breathtaking panoramas of shimmering Mont Blanc from the Aiguille du Midi (p503) or contemplate the ethereal loveliness of the Grand Balcon Sud trail (p508). Lake Annecy spreads out like a mirror before the fairest castle of them all: Château de Menthon-St-Bernard (p525).

Sky High

The sky is blue, the mountain air brisk and pure – just the day to go paragliding or hang-gliding above glistening Lake Annecy (p518).

Alpine Hiking

There's nothing quite like donning a backpack and hitting the trails in the Alps' national parks. The rugged wilderness of Parc National des Écrins (p518) and the snowcapped majesty of Parc National de la Vanoise (p535) will leave you awestruck.

On the Edge

For an adrenaline buzz, few adventures beat racing down Morzine's heart-pumping mountain-bike route, La Noire de Morzine (p515). Not enough of a challenge? Head to Chamonix (p503) to summit one of the area's spectacular 'four-thousanders'.

Budget travellers can stick to crêpes and self-catering; each resort has at least one supermarket. Dining down in Les Allues or Brides-les-Bains is cheaper.

Book ahead, especially on Wednesday, Thursday and Friday nights.

🛏 Méribel

Le Roc
HOTEL €€

(🛏 La Taverne 04 79 00 36 18; www.hotelleroc.com; rte du Centre, Méribel; d/tr from €125/140; ☺ Dec-Apr, Jul & Aug) For some of the cheapest beds in central Méribel, this is the place to come. The 12 smallish rooms are situated directly over the late-opening and lively La Taverne (🛏 04 79 00 36 18; www.alpine-bars.com; rte du Centre, Méribel; ☺ 8am-1.30am Dec-Apr, hours vary rest of year; 📶) bar, so they're not recommended for families or light sleepers though renovation was on the cards when we passed through. Reception is in the bar.

La Fromagerie
FRENCH, SWISS €€

(🛏 04 79 08 55 48; Galerie des Cimes, Méribel; mains €14-30; ☺ 7-10pm ski season, Jul & Aug) The scent of cheese invading your nostrils will tell you instantly if this restaurant and cheese-mongers is for you. Herein is the ultimate primer on Alpine cheese: a choice of *raclettes* (sweet and creamy Savoyard style or a fruitier Swiss variety), various fondue recipes (perhaps the half-and-half blend of Gruyère and Vacherin), or goat's cheese piled on toast.

Evolution
INTERNATIONAL €€

(🛏 04 79 00 44 26; www.evolutionmeribel.com; rte Albert Gacon, Méribel; breakfast/lunch/dinner mains from €5.50/16/22; ☺ 8.30am-1.30am; 📶🛏🛏) With a busy entertainment program, hearty food, and boot-proof wooden floors, Evolution is a beacon that calls skiers in from the cold. Until 11.30am there's generous English breakfasts, smoked salmon and oaty granolas, lunch service brings burgers from vegetarian to Thai-style fish, while dinner has something for all tastes: five-spice duck, paneer salad and hulking steaks. Kids' menus available.

🛏 Courchevel

Hôtel Tournier
HOTEL €€

(🛏 04 79 04 16 35; www.hoteltournier.com; rue des Verdons, Courchevel 1850; d €139-195, extra bed €35; ☺ Dec-Apr; 📶) Decorated in kitschy 'chalet' accents (timber, taupe and faux deer heads) the Tournier has 34 of the cheapest rooms in Courchevel 1850. Rooms are small and thin-walled but the dead-centre location, just a block from Parking La Croisette, is a huge plus…as long as you bring ear-plugs.

Le Chabichou
HOTEL €€€

(🛏 04 79 08 00 55; www.chabichou-courchevel. com; rue des Chenus, Courchevel 1850; d incl breakfast six nights €640-900, s/d incl breakfast per night from €180/245; ☺ Dec-Apr, Jul & Aug; 🅿 @ 📶 🛏) Washed as white as the goat's cheese for which it is named, this handsome, slopeside hotel and spa manages to quietly blend modern amenities with wood-panelled charm throughout its public areas and 41 tasteful rooms. There's a six-night minimum stay during the ski season.

🛏 Les Menuires

★ Hôtel Les Bruyères
DESIGN HOTEL €€

(🛏 04 79 00 75 10; www.bruyeres-hotel-menuires. com; Quartier Les Bruyères, Les Menuires; d/f from €115/180; ☺ mid-Dec-Apr; 🅿 📶) Splashes of orange and acid lime add zest to the sumptuous contemporary rooms at Les Bruyères, at the foot of the pistes in Les Menuires (4km north of Val Thorens). Every room has

---

ℹ BUDGET BRIDES-LES-BAINS

Linked directly to Méribel by the 25-minute **Télécabine de l'Olympe** (☺ 8.30am-5pm mid-Dec–early Feb, to 5.30pm mid-Feb–mid-Apr), the little spa town of Brides-les-Bains is a great-value alternative to staying in the valleys. Simple and spotlessly clean rooms fill former convent **Hôtel Savoy** (🛏 04 79 55 20 55; www.savoy-hotel-brides.com; place de l'Église, Brides-les-Bains; d incl breakfast from €67; ☺ late Dec–Oct; 🅿 📶 🛏), one of several decent midrangers in town. Two-hundred metres west of the hotel is **Le Bis 'Trop' Savoyard** (🛏 06 82 52 20 27; www.lebistrop.com; rue Aristide Briand, Brides-les-Bains; mains €15-27; ☺ 4.30pm-midnight; 🛏), where Alpine specialities get reverent treatment, along with freshly made sushi, pumpkin and coconut risotto, and chicken gratinated (nay, drowned) in Reblochon cheese. There's a small après-ski scene, too: sedate but sophisticated **Amélie Bar** (🛏 04 79 55 30 15; www.hotel-amelie.com; rue Emile Machet, Brides-les-Bains; ☺ 3-11pm Dec-Apr, Jul & Aug) is between the Olympe lift and the centre of town.

a balcony that leans towards the mountains, and service is both efficient and warm.

La Marmite
FRENCH €€

(☑04 79 00 74 75; www.lamarmite-lesmenuires. fr; Immeuble Bellevue, Les Menuires; mains €19-28; ☺noon-2pm & 7-9pm Dec-Apr, Jul & Aug) Likeable La Marmite, trendily decked out in slate and timber, makes generous use of Alpine produce: truffled fondue and *ravioles du Dauphiné* (pasta bulging with Comté cheese) are highlights. But chef Christian also borrows recipes from elsewhere in France (duck in orange sauce, seared trout on butternut velouté) and throws in gourmet burgers, including a truly original vegetarian variety.

🛏 Les Allues

La Croix Jean-Claude
HOTEL €€

(☑04 79 08 61 05; www.croixjeanclaude.com; rte de la Resse, Les Allues; d/ste incl breakfast from €154.50/219; ☺Jun-Apr; 🛜) Far from the madding crowd in sleepy Les Allues, La Croix Jean-Claude is one of the oldest hotels in Meribel valley. Sixteen homely, floral-trimmed rooms show some signs of age but the excellent restaurant downstairs – a riot of Alpine decoration – more than makes up for it (half-board is available from €118 per person).

🛏 La Tania

Le Farçon
FRENCH €€€

(☑04 79 08 80 34; www.lefarcon.fr; Immeuble le Kalinka, La Tania; lunch/dinner menus from €42/68; ☺noon-1.30pm & 7.30-9.30pm mid-Nov–Apr, Tue-Sun noon-1.30pm & 7.30-9.30pm mid-Jun–mid-Sep) The carefully crafted *menus* of Michelin-starred chef Julien Machet contain delights such as asparagus with apple sorbet, suckling pig with a *Béarnaise* reduction and Reblochon pie, and the walk-in wine cellar is a cave of delights. Reservations are always a good idea (enquire 48 hours in advance).

🍷 Drinking & Nightlife

⭐ Jack's Bar
BAR

(☑04 79 00 30 94; www.jacksbarmeribel.com; rte de la Chaudanne, Méribel; ☺noon-2am Dec-Apr; 🛜) Jack's Bar plays it cool, but it's the slickest après-ski operator in town: stand-up comedy, themed nights, and live music from 5pm to 7pm from Monday to Friday. All-day food service has truffle-oil-drizzled pizzas, Reblochon macaroni and other sophisticated Alpine fillers, while the cocktails include quality winter warmers (amaretto and hot cranberry hits the spot). Happy hour is 4pm.

⭐ Le Rond Point
BAR

(☑04 79 00 37 51; www.alpine-bars.com; off rte du Plateau, Méribel; ☺9.30am-7pm Dec-Apr; 🛜) It would be an omission to leave Méribel without skiing straight up to the terrace of the 'Ronnie', shuffling to the bar in ski boots, and ordering the house speciality, toffee vodka, perhaps sloshed into *chocolat chaud* (hot chocolate). Snow-kissed fir trees provide the view until live music lights up the stage (most nights from 5pm to 6.30pm).

La Folie Douce
BAR

(☑04 79 00 04 27; www.lafoliedouce-valthorens. com; Piste Plein Sud, Val Thorens; ☺9am-5.15pm Dec-Apr; 🛜) There's no escaping La Folie Douce. These piste-side après-ski bars are notorious for building nightclub atmosphere in broad daylight. Around 2pm, follow the gleeful whoops below the top of Plein Sud lift, plant a bottle of rosé in the snow, sway with cyber-costumed dancers, stomp boots to the rhythms of the resident DJ, and emerge dazed, wondering how it's only 5pm.

There's also a good restaurant, La Fruitière, on-site.

ℹ Information

Courchevel 1850 Tourist Office (☑04 79 08 00 29; www.courchevel.com; rue du Rocher; ☺8.30am-6pm Mon-Fri, to 6.30pm Sat & Sun winter & school holidays, 9am-noon & 2.30-6.30 Sat, Sun, Wed & Thu summer; 🛜) Courchevel's main tourist office. Has other offices at Courchevel 1650m, 1550m and 1300m.

Méribel Tourist Office (☑04 79 08 60 01; www.meribel.net; rte du Centre; ☺9am-6.30pm Dec-Apr, 9am-noon & 2-6.30pm Jul & Aug, 9am-6.30pm Mon-Fri, 9am-noon & 2-6.30pm Sat & Sun rest of year; 🛜) Has the low-down on winter and summer activities.

Val Thorens Tourist Office (☑04 79 00 08 08; www.valthorens.com; Grand Rue, Maison de Val Thorens; ☺8.30am-7pm winter & summer, 8.30am-12.15pm & 2pm-7pm Mon-Fri spring & autumn) Has plenty of information in English.

ℹ Getting There & Away

BUS

In winter, Altibus (04 79 68 32 96; www.altibus. com) links all three Les Trois Vallées resorts with the following airports:

Chambéry ticket €39, 2½ to four hours

Geneva adult/child €90/45, 3½ hours, three daily Sunday to Friday, six Saturday

Lyon–St-Exupéry adult/child €73/37, 3¼ to four hours

For all airport buses, reserve 48 hours ahead.

From Moûtiers (the nearest rail station), Transdev Savoie (www.transdevsavoie.com) runs buses to Val Thorens, Méribel and Courchevel (lines T3, T4 and T5, respectively). All three cost €13, adult, one-way, and run at least three times per day in winter. Services drop to one daily on weekdays outside winter, and most services disappear altogether in high summer.

TRAIN

Six kilometres north of Brides-les-Bains is the nearest railhead, Moûtiers (Moûtiers-Salins-Brides-les-Bains).

Chambéry €14.80, 1¼ to 2 hours, hourly Monday to Friday, 13 per day Saturday and Sunday. Direct or via Montmelian.

Paris Gare de Lyon from €92.20, 4½ to six hours, hourly Monday to Friday, four Saturday and Sunday. Via Lyon or Aix-les-Bains.

On weekends from mid-December to early April, Eurostar (www.eurostar.com) operates direct overnight and day trains from London to Moûtiers (from €96.50, seven hours).

Val d'Isère

Wild off-piste skiing and beginner-friendly slopes, Michelin-starred gastronomy and farmhouse cooking, soothing spas and unbridled nightlife...all are gathered in twinkly Val d'Isère, 32km southeast of Bourg St-Maurice.

Val d'Isère's ability to be simultaneously chic and traditional, fast-paced and relaxed, has propelled it to stardom as the resort of choice for skiers and boarders with cash to splash. Val d'Isère has all the enchantment of an Alpine village but with world-class leisure facilities and swanky hotels.

The combined terrain of Val d'Isère and the lakeside *commune* of **Tignes** form the enormous **Espace Killy** (www.espacekilly.com; adult 1-/6-day pass €57/285, child 1-/6-day pass €46/228) ski area, named after Jean-Claude Killy, who grew up in Val d'Isère and won three slalom and downhill golds at the 1968 Winter Olympics in Grenoble. Popular with Brits, Danes and Swedes, the resort is accessible only by a sinuous access road clinging to the heights of the upper Tarentaise Valley.

 Activities

Winter

Val d'Isère and Tignes together form Espace Killy (p532), a giant for its scale – altitudes between 1550m and 3456m, 300km of pistes – and the length of its season (from late November until very early May). It's easy to leave behind queuing bottlenecks, even in peak season, and there's a great mix of beginner, intermediate and advanced skiing as well as miles of glorious, easily accessible off-piste. The piste gradings tend to assume good levels of skiing – look out for (moderate) blue runs that feel red, and (intermediate) red runs that seem to be expert-level.

The many ski schools include well-regarded **Top Ski** (📞04 79 06 14 80, 07 82 85 88 89; www.topski.fr; Immeuble Les Andes, av Olympique, Val Village; ⏰8.30am-7.30pm Dec-Apr) and the **ESF** (📞La Daille 04 79 06 99 99, Val Village 04 79 06 02 34; www.esfvaldisere.com; place des Dolomites, Val Village; ⏰9.30am-12.30pm & 2.30-5pm Dec-Apr). **Ski touring** in the area is fabulous, especially in Parc National de la Vanoise.

At 2500m, the **snow park** is on the back of Bellevarde mountain. Graded from green (easy) to black (experts only), it has rails, jumps and a boardercross course – everything a freestyle rider could ask for. Other winter options range from ice climbing to mushing, and ice skating to winter paragliding – or you can head to the Centre Aquasportif (p532) for swimming pools (great for kids), sports facilities and a spa. For more children's activities and creche facilities, head to the **Village des Enfants** (📞04 79 40 09 81; www.village-des-enfants.fr; Rond Point des Pistes, Val Village; child 3-13yr 1/5 half-days €32/135; ⏰9am-5.30pm Sun-Fri mid-Dec–Apr, Jul & Aug; 👶).

You can buy lift passes online or in person from **STVI** (rue de la Legettaz; ⏰8.30am-5pm Dec-Apr). Three free chairlifts on the lower slopes let novices find their feet without having to purchase a lift ticket: the village chairlift, Savonette and Les Lanches. Under 5s and over-75s ski for free.

Centre Aquasportif   SPA
(📞04 79 04 26 01; www.centre-aquasportif.com; rte de la Balme, Val Village; day/week pass €19/76; ⏰10am-9pm Fri-Wed, to 10pm Thu Dec-Apr, 11am-9pm Jul & Aug) Situated next to the Téléphérique Olympique, this glass-and-stone complex is great for a post-slope unwind. Besides pools with jets and bubble beds, it offers first-class sports facilities, a climbing wall and a spa area with saunas, steam rooms and whirlpools.

Summer

Espace Killy is one of only two places in France (the other is Les Deux Alpes) that still has **summer skiing** (between early

June and mid-July): here it's on the Grande Motte and Pissaillas glaciers, near Tignes and Val d'Isère, respectively. A day's lift pass costs a cut-down €28.

The valleys and trails that wend their way from Val d'Isère into the nearby Parc National de la Vanoise are a hiker's dream. If you fancy more of a challenge, you can play (safely) among the cliffs at La Daille's two **via ferrata** fixed-cable routes; both have a beginner-level section followed by a tougher section only for the experienced. For canyoning, mountaineering or rock climbing with a guide, contact the **Bureau des Guides** (🗹03 77 08 09 76; www.guides-montagne-valdisere.com; Galerie des Cimes, av Olympique, Val Village; ⊘hours vary).

Mountain biking (Vélo Tout Terrain, or VTT) is big in Val (but forbidden within the national park), with an assortment of downhill (green, blue, red and black), endurance and cross-country circuits. Bikes can be rented at local sport shops. Five lifts are open to downhill cyclists as well as hikers (€10 per day).

The summer season runs from late June to the first weekend in September. Stop by the tourist office for details on family-friendly activities, including pony rides.

🛏 Sleeping

★ Les Cinq Frères   BOUTIQUE HOTEL €€€
(🗹04 79 06 00 03; www.les5freres.com; rue Nicolas Bazile, Val Village; d incl breakfast €285-365, f incl breakfast €398-495; ⊘Dec-Apr & mid-Jun–Aug; 🛜) Situated 150m up the main street from the tourist office, this family hotel has been going strong since 1936. Named for the five sons of its founder, rooms offer unpolished luxury – distressed wood, old sleds, a mix of Baroque and ultramodern design flourishes – plus a lovely lounge area and a playroom for kids.

Hôtel Avancher   SPA HOTEL €€€
(🗹04 79 06 02 00; www.hotel-lavancher.com; rte du Prariond; d/ste from €184/300; ⊘Dec-Apr & Jun-Sep; 🅿🛜) The welcome is always warm and attentive at the Avancher. Remodelled in 2017, its rooms are bright and contemporary, with sleek bathrooms, good soundproofing and plenty of natural light. There's a lounge with board games, and a ski/mountain bike workshop, but it's the luxury touches that make this a top address: a top-class restaurant, steamy *hammam* and outdoor rooftop sauna.

🍴 Eating

Le Barillon   FRENCH €
(🗹04 79 41 13 92; cnr rue de la Daille & rue des Étroits, La Daille; mains from €16; ⊘7-10pm Dec–Apr & mid-Jun–Aug) Inside the quaintest stone cottage you've ever seen, ample Savoyard dishes are hauled onto tables by enormously friendly staff. At this family-run restaurant no corners are cut in preparing the *raclette*, a full half-moon of cheese, but there's duck confit and cured salmon to tempt you away from the classics.

Restaurant L'Avancher   FRENCH, INTERNATIONAL €€
(🗹04 79 06 02 00; www.avancher.com/restaurant-and-bar; rte du Prariond, Val d'Isère; mains €23-29; ⊘7-9.30pm Tue-Sun Dec-Apr, Jul & Aug) Even if you aren't staying at the chic Hôtel Avancher (p533), it's worth booking a table at its classy restaurant. Borrowing influences from across Europe (and beyond), the upmarket bistro meals – like seared Iberico pork with parsnip velouté, and outstanding ceviche – are both well-priced and beautifully presented.

L'Edelweiss   FRENCH, FUSION €€
(🗹06 10 28 70 64; www.restaurant-edelweiss-valdisere.com; Piste Mangard, Le Fornet; 2-/3-course menus €25/30; ⊘9.30am-4pm Dec-Apr) Perched halfway up Le Fornet's Mangard blue run, this wood-and-stone chalet has wondrous views around the valley. And at this *restaurant d'altitude* (le up on the slopes), the food matches the prospect: lamb saddle stuffed with olives, scallop and salmon linguini, wok-fried veggies and Sichuan-spiced duck. It's good value, and reservations are strongly recommended.

★ L'Atelier d'Edmond   GASTRONOMY, FRENCH €€€
(🗹04 79 00 00 82; www.atelier-edmond.com; rue du Fornet, Le Fornet; menus €115-175; ⊘7-9.30pm Tue, noon-2pm & 7-9.30pm Wed-Sun mid-Dec–Apr) Candlelight bathes stone walls, low beams and family heirlooms in this gorgeous double-Michelin-starred restaurant, where locally sourced ingredients are imaginatively transformed into dishes such as pork and snail rissoles, smoked pigeon with cacao nibs, and oysters every which way. The beautifully plated desserts belong in an art gallery. Call ahead to secure one of the Atelier's limited seats.

Find it 2km east of Val Village, across from the Téléphérique du Fornet ski lift.

FARM TALK

Part of Val d'Isère's charm is that it's a real village with year-round residents. Claudine is one of them and she runs **La Fermette de Claudine** (☑ 04 79 06 13 89; www.lafermette declaudine.com; Val Village; ☉ 7am-8pm mid-Dec–Apr, Jul & Aug) – walk in the door of this *fromagerie*-cum-delicatessen and you'll be enveloped by the heady odours of Alpine cheeses and artisanal sausages. Other delectables include yoghurt and small-batch Génépi (an Alpine herbal liqueur made with various species of Artemisia, aka wormwood). You'll find it 100m across the roundabout from the tourist office.

Sensational, hardcore dairy goodness – including seven varieties of raclette (smoked, blue and goat's cheese among the choices) – is served up at **L'Étable d'Alain** (☑ 04 79 06 13 02; www.lafermedeladroit.fr; rue des Barmettes; mains €18-38; ☉ 7-10pm Mon, noon-2pm & 7-10pm Tue-Sun Dec-Apr; 🖪); book two or three days ahead for dinner and, to find it, head 1km from central Val d'Isère, towards the Col de l'Iseran. The adjacent family dairy farm, **La Ferme de l'Adroit** (☑ 04 79 06 13 02; www.lafermedeladroit.com; rue des Barmettes; ☉ 8.30am & 5.30pm Mon, Wed, Fri school holidays), is open to visitors at morning cheese-making and afternoon milking; ask ahead to make sure it's visiting season.

🍷 Drinking & Nightlife

★ La Folie Douce   BAR

(☑ 04 79 06 21 08; www.lafoliedouce.com; La Daille; ☉ 9am-5pm mid-Dec–mid-Apr) Why wait until you're back down in the village to party? From 2.30pm every day, DJs, singers, choreographed dancers and live bands fuel a riotous après-ski bash on this outdoor terrace at the top of the La Daille cable car. Ibiza in the snow!

★ Cocorico   BAR

(☑ 04 79 24 60 04; www.cocoricovaldisere.com; chemin du Charvet, Val Village; ☉ 2-8pm Dec-Apr) The indie-rock alternative to après-ski stalwart La Folie Douce is Cocorico. The large outdoor deck, strung with fairy lights, stages excellent bands before morphing into a packed dance floor when DJs start up around 6pm. It's only a short stumble back to the main road in Val d'Isère.

La Cave...sur le Comptoir   WINE BAR

(☑ 04 79 22 27 81; www.facebook.com/lacavesur lecomptoir; av Olympique; ☉ 4.30pm-1am Dec-Apr) This intimate, wood-eaved den is the sophisticate's choice for après-ski. Hunker down between book-lined walls and be served top-notch wines by the glass with generous taster plates of cheese or charcuterie (or half and half, €16).

ℹ Information

Tourist Office (☑ 04 79 06 06 60; www. valdisere.com; place Jacques Mouflier, Val Village; ☉ 8.30am-7.30pm Sun-Fri, to 9pm Sat Dec-Apr & Jun-Aug; 🛜)

ℹ Getting There & Around

TO/FROM THE AIRPORT

Chambéry airport During ski season, Altibus (www.altibus.com) offers direct buses (one-way €39, 2½ hours, six daily Thursday, Saturday and Sunday).

Geneva airport Altibus has direct bus services (one-way/return €75/127, four hours, at least daily from early December to mid-April). Another option is booking a transfer (return €69, 3½ hours) through Ben's Bus (www.bensbus. co.uk), which also serves Grenoble airport (return €71, 3¾ hours).

Lyon–St-Exupéry airport There are seasonal Altibus services (one-way/return €73/115, 3½ hours, three or four daily Friday, Saturday and Sunday) from December through April, or take the train to Bourg St-Maurice (five hours, via Grenoble or Chambéry) then an onward bus to Val Village (line T14, €13, one hour, four to seven daily in season).

Advance reservations are essential during school holiday periods and can be made online or by phone.

BUS

From December through April, Belle Savoie Express (www.mobisavoie.fr) regularly links the railhead of Bourg St-Maurice, 32km northwest of Val d'Isère, with Val d'Isère (line T14, €13, one hour) and Tignes (line T15, €13, 1¼ hours).

During the ski season and in summer, free shuttles link the various parts of Val d'Isère, including La Daille, Val Village (the central village), Le Fornet and numerous ski lifts.

The *train rouge* (red train, actually a bus) goes from La Daille through Val Village to Le Fornet; it's every 10 minutes during the day and every 25 minutes between 8pm and 2.40am.

Belle Savoie Express (www.mobisavoie.fr) has ski-season buses linking Val d'Isère with Tignes (€6.50, 30 minutes, three to six daily) from December to April.

CAR & MOTORCYCLE

The roads up to Val d'Isère, outfitted with lots of *paravalanche* (avalanche protection) shelters, are narrow, winding and can get traffic-clogged.

Col de l'Iseran (2764m), on the D902 southeast to Bonneval-sur-Arc, and **Col du Petit-St-Bernard** (2188m), northeast of Bourg St-Maurice towards to the Aosta valley in Italy, are blocked by snow for all but the summer months.

TRAIN

Bourg St-Maurice, the nearest railhead, has train connections to destinations all over France (eg Chambéry and Lyon-Part Dieu) and seasonal bus links to Val d'Isère.

From mid-December to early April on weekends, **Eurostar** (www.eurostar.com) operates direct daytime and overnight services between Bourg St-Maurice and London (from €87, 7½ to nine hours).

Parc National de la Vanoise

Rippling between the Tarentaise and Maurienne Valleys is Parc National de la Vanoise. Designated France's first national park in 1963, the 529-sq-km park has more than 100 peaks surpassing 3000m. At its highest points, this is a desolate landscape of glaciers and lichen-spattered rock; at lower altitudes, Alpine meadows and spruce forests flourish. Marmots, chamois and France's largest colony of *bouquetins* (Alpine ibexes) – around 1800 – graze freely beneath the larch trees while 125 bird species wheel overhead. Amplifying the drama are historical fortifications like stocky **Fort Victor-Emmanuel** and **Fort Marie Thérèse**.

Along the southern edge of the park (west to east), **Termignon**, **Lanslebourg-Mont-Cenis** and **Bonneval-sur-Arc** are good bases. The former two have more shops and restaurants, while quaint Bonneval has a middle-of-nowhere charm.

In winter, the seasonal closure of the Col de l'Iseran blocks direct road access from Val d'Isère, thereby protecting the sizeable **Val Cenis ski area** from crowds.

🏃 Activities

Winter

Termignon, Lanslebourg-Mont-Cenis and other Vanoise villages are jumping-off points to the **Val Cenis ski station** (www.valcenis.ski), home to 125km of mostly easy and intermediate (blue and red) pistes between 1500m and 2800m. Mostly families, beginners and locals arrive to pound these pistes – after all, high-octane mountain thrills and nightlife are close by in Val d'Isère and Les Trois Vallées. Still, there are enough challenging runs here to entertain skiers and boarders who prioritise scenic pistes and country towns over thumping après-ski. Lift passes are good value at €35.50/175 for one/six days.

Summer

With 400km of marked trails, the park is hiker's heaven, although heavy snow can make walking trails inaccessible for all but a fraction of the year – usually June to late September. Speak to a tourist office, especially if you're planning a hike at the start or end of the season. The **Grand Tour de Haute Maurienne** (www.haute-maurienne-vanoise.com), a 10-day hike around the upper reaches of the valley, takes in national-park highlights. The GR5 and GR55 cross it, and other trails snake east into Italy's Grand Paradiso National Park.

🛏 Sleeping & Eating

Auberge d'Oul B&B €

(☏ 04 79 05 87 99; www.auberge-oul.com; Bonneval-sur-Arc; dm incl breakfast €26-29, d/tr/q incl breakfast €68/100/130; ⊙ mid-Jun–mid-Sep & mid-Dec–Apr) Smack on the village square, this flowery-balconied, slate-walled *gîte* (self-catering cottage) has a simple seven-person dorm and two plain but cosy *chambres d'hôte* (guest rooms) on the 2nd floor. The half-board option (per person €19.50) offers great-value mountain meals, from classic fondues to herbed lamb rack.

★ La Cabane FRENCH €€

(☏ 04 79 05 34 60; Bonneval-sur-Arc; mains €13.50-24.50; ⊙ noon-2pm & 7-9pm ski season, shorter hours Jul & Aug) Juicy *diots* (local sausages) in white wine are most popular at this welcoming wood-walled den, but the range of Savoyard cheese dishes is highly worthwhile. Try *moelleux de revard* (baked, spruce-wrapped cheese), or the sweet but strangely refreshing *chevrotine* (hot goat's cheese encrusted with honey and walnut, served with apple slices and rosemary-dusted potatoes). Reservations recommended.

ℹ Information

The tourist offices in **Lanslebourg** (📞 04 79 05 99 06; www.haute-maurienne-vanoise.com; 89 rue du Mont-Cenis, Lanslebourg; ⊙ 9am-noon & 2-6.30pm mid-Dec–Mar, Jul & Aug, shorter hours rest of year) and **Bonneval-sur-Arc** (📞 04 79 05 99 06; www.bonneval-sur-arc.com; Bonneval-sur-Arc; ⊙ 9am-noon & 2-6.30pm late Dec–Mar, to 6pm Apr, late Jun–Aug) stock practical information on walking, limited skiing (cross-country and downhill) and other activities in and around the park. **Termignon-la-Vanoise**, 6km west of Lanslebourg, houses the national park's small information centre, the **Maison de la Vanoise** (📞 04 79 20 51 67; www.parcnation-al-vanoise.fr; place de la Vanoise, Termignon; ⊙ 9am-noon & 2-6pm late Jun–early Sep, late Dec–Mar & school holidays, shorter hours rest of year; 🛜).

ℹ Getting There & Away

Trains serving the Arc River valley leave from Chambéry and run as far as Modane (€17.90, 1½ hours, almost hourly), 23km southwest of Lanslebourg. Travelling between Moûtiers (Les Trois Vallées) and Modane (€22.30, three hours, five daily) requires backtracking and changing trains in St-Pierre d'Albigny.

From Modane, Transdev Savoie (www.trans-devsavoie.com) runs three to four daily buses (one or none in the low season) to/from Termignon (€7.80, 35 minutes), Val Cénis-Lanslebourg (€13, 45 minutes) and Bonneval-sur-Arc (€13, 1¼ hours). Book through Altibus (www.altibus.com).

DAUPHINÉ

Named for the dolphin (*dauphin*) that graced the coat of arms of its prior rulers, the historic region of Dauphiné encompasses the territories south and southwest of Savoie, stretching from the Rhône River in the west to the Italian border in the east. It

---

ℹ WINTER ROAD WARNING

In winter the D1006 from Modane to Lanslebourg is cleared of snow, but east of here the D902 is unsalted. We don't recommend driving on to Bonne-val-sur-Arc unless you're equipped with winter tyres or snow chains.

---

roughly corresponds to the *départements* of Isère, Drôme and Hautes-Alpes.

Mountain-backed Grenoble is Dauphiné's cultural centre and largest city. Barely a few kilometres southwest extends Parc Naturel Régional du Vercors, scarred with gorges and caves. East of here is rugged, glacier-carved Parc National des Écrins, with whopping, world-class ski resorts Les Deux Alpes and Alpe d'Huez on its northern flank.

Standing sentinel over lesser-loved winter sports area Serre Chevalier is Briançon, an underrated fortress town connected to Italy by a hair-raising mountain road.

Grenoble

POP 160,649 / ELEV 215M

Haloed by mountains, France's self-styled 'Capital of the Alps' unites city pleasures and breathtaking nature. Every road leading out of Grenoble brushes a different regional park. The Isère River slices through the city, girding the clifftop Bastille and a ravishing set of riverside museums. On the opposite bank, Grenoble fizzes: a historic quarter lined with cafes and shops, world-class galleries and an efficient tram system zipping between neighbourhoods both glamorous and gritty.

Though it's surrounded by land preserved for nature, Grenoble is an engine of industry – thanks in part to an economic boost from the 1968 Winter Olympics held here. Since then, high-tech industries have carved out niches in Grenoble, fuelled by the university's reputation for maths and computer sciences. Students (more than 45,000) and culturally engaged locals stimulate an arts scene and nightlife that are the envy of the French Alps.

⊙ Sights

The pedestrian-friendly city centre is on the left (south) bank of the Isère River, between the Musée de Grenoble (to the east) and Pont de la Porte de France (a bridge). To the north, Fort de la Bastille, a vast hilltop fortress, towers over the area from across the river. The train and bus stations are 500m southwest of Pont de la Porte de France.

⭐ **Musée de Grenoble** MUSEUM
(📞 04 76 63 44 44; www.museedegrenoble.fr; 5 place de Lavalette; adult/child €8/free; ⊙ 10am-6.30pm Wed-Mon) For lovers of European art, this museum is an uplifting place to get lost for a day. There's an even spread of artistic

eras on display: an antiquities wing with statuettes from ancient Egypt and Greece, and mostly European art from medieval religious paintings to an impressive assembly of 20th-century luminaries like Bonnard, Ernst, Léger, Magritte, Miró, Modigliani and Soutine.

★ Musée Archéologique   MUSEUM
(☑ 04 76 44 78 68; www.musee-archeologique-grenoble.fr; place Saint-Laurent; ☺10am-6pm Wed-Sun) FREE This highly impressive museum unveils the secrets of a 12th-century church and cloister using light effects, a haunting choral soundtrack and an informative audioguide. Interactive, self-guided visits allow you to explore parts of the time-worn sanctuary at your own pace, from images projected on its lofty walls to 4th-century amphora burials in the basement.

Fort de la Bastille   FORTRESS
(www.bastille-grenoble.com) FREE After a fun ride in the téléphérique (p539), or a steep, hour-long climb, the reward is a magnificent mountain panorama from Grenoble's stocky fortress, built during the first half of the 19th century to strengthen the city against Alpine rival the Duchy of Savoy. On the viewing platform known as the Belvédère Vauban, panels (in French and English) indicate what you're looking at. On clear days you can see not only the peaks of the Vercors but also the snowy hump of Mont Blanc.

The fort complex has its own tourist office (p541), a couple of places to eat, and a number of walking trails, including the GR9, start or pass by.

Musée des Troupes de Montagne   MUSEUM
(French Alpine Troops Museum; ☑04 76 44 33 65; www.museedestroupesdemontagne.fr; Fort de la Bastille; adult/child €3/free; ☺11am-6pm Tue-Sun Feb-Dec) Though the subject is niche, this museum exploring France's elite Alpine regiments, which date to 1888, is riveting. An audioguide (in French, English, German or Italian) enlivens displays of military gear, tales of WWII resistance, and brings you right up to present-day mountain troops.

Musée Dauphinois   MUSEUM
(☑04 57 58 89 01; www.musee-dauphinois.fr; 30 rue Maurice Gignoux; ☺10am-6pm Wed-Mon Sep-May, to 7pm Jun-Aug) FREE This ever-evolving museum unleashes a century of regional history on visitors. Suits of armour are back-lit in brightly coloured rooms, 3-D family trees and highland traditions are reimagined

as cutting-edge modern art. The museum, occupying a 17th-century convent, has permanent exhibitions on skiing and rural lifestyles, but installations constantly change. You're sure to find something interesting in this impressive collection.

Cathédrale Notre Dame   CATHEDRAL
(www.cathedraledegrenoble.fr; place Notre Dame; ☺10am-7.30pm Mon-Fri, 9.30am-10.30pm Sat, 9.30am-6pm Sun) The rose-brick rib vaults of Grenoble's elegant cathedral rise from the site of a 4th-century church. Its present form dates to the 1200s, though its interior Gothic styling was added in later centuries.

Musée de l'Ancien Évêché   MUSEUM
(☑04 76 03 15 25; www.ancien-eveche-isere.fr; 2 rue Très Cloîtres; ☺9am-6pm Mon, Tue, Thu & Fri, 1-6pm Wed, 11am-6pm Sat & Sun) FREE A runthrough of regional history, from prehistory through medieval times to the 20th century, is presented within the atmospheric walls of the 13th-century Bishops' Palace. The building, its walls built atop 3rd-century Roman foundations, is sometimes more interesting than its displays; a highlight is the vaulted chapel. Bonus: there are enjoyable views over the cathedral as you wander around.

Musée de la Résistance et
de la Déportation de l'Isère   MUSEUM
(☑04 76 42 38 53; www.resistance-en-isere.fr; 14 rue Hébert; ☺9am-6pm Mon & Wed-Fri, 1.30-6pm Tue, 10am-6pm Sat & Sun) FREE This thoughtfully curated exhibition presents the history of Grenoble's vigorous resistance to Italian and then German forces during WWII, with plenty of translation into English and German. Mournfully lit, the permanent exhibition features emotive displays on the region's *résistants* (Resistance fighters) and the fates of the thousand local Jews – including 80 children – sent to Nazi camps.

Le Magasin   MUSEUM
(Centre National d'Art Contemporain; ☑04 76 21 95 84; www.magasin-cnac.org; 155 cours Berriat; adult/child €4/2.50; ☺2-7pm Wed-Sun late Apr–mid-Oct) A cavernous glass-and-steel warehouse built by Gustave Eiffel has been turned into one of France's leading centres of contemporary art. Many of the cutting-edge temporary exhibitions were designed specifically for this space. It's situated about 2km west of the centre; to get there, take tram A to the Berriat–Le Magasin stop.

Grenoble

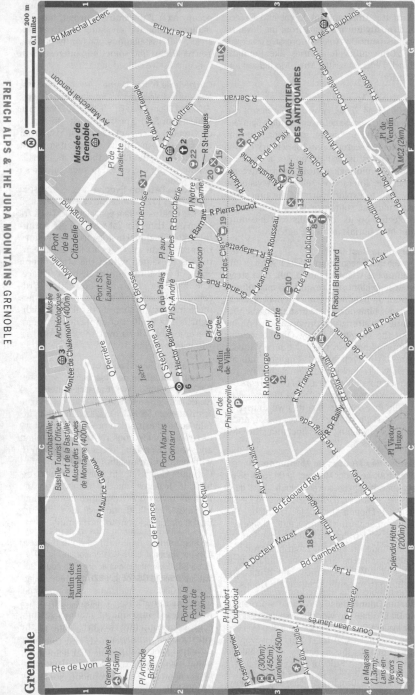

Grenoble

FRENCH ALPS & THE JURA MOUNTAINS GRENOBLE

Activities

Grenoble is well set up for exploring on two wheels: bikes can easily be hired from 32 **Métrovélo** (☑04 76 85 08 94; www.metrovelo.fr; place de la Gare) stations across the city.

Acrobastille   ADVENTURE SPORTS
(☑06 84 34 53 78; www.acrobastille.fr; Fort de la Bastille; adult/child €27/20; ☺Mar-Nov; 🚗) Adrenaline junkies can head to the Bastille (p537) for one of Acrobastille's two 300m-long zip lines (kids aged 11 and over). There's also Spélcobox (a caving simulator with 120m of dark tunnels), Mission Bastille (a puzzle-packed labyrinth worthy of Indiana Jones), and, for kids aged five and up, some rope-climbing activities. Weather conditions can alter opening hours.

Téléphérique Grenoble-Bastille   CABLE CAR
(☑04 76 44 33 65; www.bastille-grenoble.fr; quai Stéphane Jay; adult/child one-way €5.60/3.20, return €8.20/4.50; ☺11am-6.30pm Tue-Sun Feb-Apr & Oct-Dec, 9.30am or 11am-7.30pm daily May-Sep, closed Jan) Hop into a clear-panelled spherical pod for dreamy views of Grenoble's red roofs and magnificent mountains on this cable-car ride up to the Bastille. *Les bulles* ('the bubbles'), as they're known, have been floating along the 610m cable since 1934, making them the world's first urban cable car system for sightseers.

Maison de la Montagne   OUTDOORS
(☑04 57 04 27 00; www.grenoble-montagne.com; 14 rue de la République; ☺9.30am-12.30pm & 1-6pm Mon-Fri, 10am-1pm & 2-5pm Sat) This city-run centre provides advice on the perennial action of the Dauphiné Alps – including ski touring, ice climbing (on frozen waterfalls), hiking, rock climbing, biking, canyoning, paragliding and caving – plus weather and avalanche bulletins, and help planning overnight stays in the mountains. It also has maps on sale and a library of guidebooks to consult.

Also here is the **Bureau des Guides** (☑04 38 37 01 71; www.guide-grenoble.com; 14 rue de la République, Maison de la Montagne; ☺9.30am-12.30pm & 1-6pm Mon-Fri, 10am-1pm & 2-5pm Sat), which can help climbers, hikers, canyoneers, off-piste skiers and ice climbers of all levels explore Les Alpes.

Club Alpin Français   OUTDOORS
(☑04 76 87 03 73; www.cafgrenoble.com; 32 av Félix Viallet; ☺3-5pm Tue, 5-7pm Mon, Wed-Fri) The French Alpine Club runs outings and mountain day trips. details are posted in its front window and on its website, and casual purchasers of a €8 'Discovery Card' can join in. This branch runs most of the *refuges* (overnight mountain stays) in the Isère *département*.

Festivals & Events

Les Détours de Babel   MUSIC
(☑04 76 89 07 16; www.detoursdebabel.fr; ☺late Mar–mid-Apr) This impressive three-week festival of jazz and world music has a mix of big names (ticketed) and free concerts. Expect a programme that leaps from avant-garde orchestral music to Balkan brass bands, via Francophone soul and psychedelic rock.

Cabaret Frappé   MUSIC
(www.cabaret-frappe.com; ⊘ mid-/late Jul) This much-loved free festival brings a week of fresh-air concerts (from rock and pop to electronica) to the Jardin la Ville.

🛏 Sleeping

HI Hostel Grenoble   HOSTEL €
(Auberge de Jeunesse Grenoble Agglomération; ☑ 04 76 09 33 52; www.hifrance.org; 10 av du Grésivaudan, Échirolles; dm/d incl breakfast from €18/56.60; P @ 🛜) The parkside suburb setting might not have the charm of the town centre, but friendly English-speaking staff at HI Grenoble run it like clockwork. The topnotch facilities include a bar, kitchen, games room, sun deck and laundry. It's 5km south of the train station. Non-HI-members must buy a full membership to stay.

The hostel is served by the Express 3 and C2 buses; get off at 'La Quinzaine' stop.

★ Le Grand Hôtel   HOTEL €€
(☑ 04 76 51 22 59; www.grand-hotel-grenoble. fr; 5 rue de la République; d/ste from €134/170; ❄ @ 🛜) Like the service, rooms at Le Grand Hôtel are refined and sleek. Rooms are attired with high-quality bed sheets, spotless bathrooms and modern-art chairs, and triple-glazed windows ensure a peaceful night despite an enviable central location. A contemporary, businessy feel prevails but a few design throwbacks, like original mosaic tiles on the main stairs, hark back to decades past.

Hôtel de l'Europe   HISTORIC HOTEL €€
(☑ 04 76 46 16 94; www.hoteleurope.fr; 22 place Grenette; d/f from €97/130; ❄ 🛜) With more than two centuries of history behind it, dead-central Hôtel de l'Europe lays claim to being Grenoble's oldest hotel. Though venerable, its 39 crisp white rooms are modern, brightened by flashes of magenta and crimson, and most have wrought-iron balconies. It's worth saying *oui* to the breakfast buffet (€9.50 per person) of mostly local produce.

Splendid Hôtel   HOTEL €€
(☑ 04 76 46 33 12; www.splendid-hotel.com; 22 rue Thiers; s €49-72, d €72-149, tr €98-149, studio €149; P ❄ 🛜) 🍴 Family-run Splendid offers a more personal touch than most of Grenoble's business-focussed hotels. Its 45 rooms are individually designed (and a matter of preference, depending on your taste for fuchsia), some with hydromassage showers. More minimalist are the studios, self-contained with kitchenettes and desk space. Enclosed parking costs €6.90 per night.

🍴 Eating

As the one-time capital of Dauphiné, Grenoble is the place to sample *gratin dauphinois*. The original recipe calls for finely sliced potatoes oven-baked in milk, cream and butter, with a sprinkling of salt, pepper and garlic. A pinch of nutmeg or cayenne is widespread, depending on the chef's taste, though further alterations would be frowned on (and adding cheese is heresy).

Halles Ste-Claire   MARKET €
(place Ste-Claire; ⊘ 7am-1pm Tue-Sun, 3-7pm Fri & Sat) Built in 1874, this covered market is crammed with local cheeses, patisserie, wine and deli fare including quenelles (breadcrumbed torpedoes of fish) and *boudins blancs* (white sausages). There are butchers and fishmongers for self-caterers, and plenty of fruit and veg stalls outside.

La Festina Lente   VEGETARIAN, CAFE €
(☑ 04 76 54 53 84; rue Saint-Hugues; mains €12; ⊘ noon-2pm Mon-Fri, 10.30am-3pm Sat & Sun; 🍴) 🍴 In a setting somewhere between your great-aunt's living room and a garden centre, this grungy but loveable cafe offers mostly vegetarian and vegan set lunches, mostly platters of taster dishes like soup, savoury crumbles, salads and cheese. Produce is all organic and locally sourced, while hand-stitched place settings and one-of-a-kind curios create a nostalgic atmosphere

La Petite Idée   FRENCH €
(☑ 04 76 47 52 95; www.la-petite-idee.fr; 7 cours Jean Jaurès; lunch menus €16-20, dinner menus €20-32; ⊘ noon-2pm & 7-10pm Tue-Sun) Regional cuisine takes centre stage at this small and friendly restaurant, like trout in Vercors-style sauce (lemon and capers), gratin of Beaufort cheese ravioli, and Chartreuse ice cream dowsed with an extra glug of liqueur.

La Tête à l'Envers   FRENCH €
(☑ 04 76 51 13 42; 12 rue Chenoise; mains €8-16; ⊘ noon-2pm Thu & Fri, 7.30-10.30pm Tue-Sat) Tipping French cuisine upside down (sometimes literally), little La Tête à l'Envers has an ever-changing menu that presents seasonal ingredients in unexpected contexts (spicy desserts, fruity mains) – occasionally you'll be asked to guess what you're eating. Book ahead.

Au Clair de Lune
VEGETARIAN, FRENCH €€

(📞04 76 24 61 17; 54 rue Trés Cloitres; lunch mains/dinner menus from €13/22; ⏱noon-1.30pm Mon, noon-1.30pm & 7.30-9pm Tue-Sat; 🖊) 🍴 This tiny restaurant is freshening the palates of cheese-fatigued *grenoblois* with its vegetarian-leaning menu, from stuffed cabbage to creamy spinach risotto. It's not entirely meatless (as is clear from specials like Thai-style bream) but the emphasis is green in all senses: vegan pastries, organic ingredients and a menu that shifts with the seasons. Book ahead, even for lunch.

La Cuisine des Tontons
FRENCH €€

(📞04 76 25 25 00; 9 rue Bayard; menus €19.90-29.90; ⏱noon-2pm & 7.30-10pm Tue-Sat) Reserve ahead for the generous *menus* at this whimsically decorated bistro – decked out in homage to the 1963 French caper flick *Les Tontons Flingeurs*. Carnivores will be rapt over its seven different versions of *tartare*, from classic to Roquefort, and specials like five-spiced duck and rosemary lamb.

Le Petit Bouche
BISTRO €€

(📞04 76 43 10 39; www.facebook.com/pg/petitbouchegrenoble; 16 rue Docteur Mazet; lunch plats du jour €8.60, menus €20-30; ⏱11.45am-1.45pm & 6.30-9pm Mon-Fri) Festooned with vintage bric-a-brac, with time-scuffed floors and a narrow open bar-kitchen, Le Petit Bouche enjoys a loyal following. Its classic bistro fare, such as *andouillette* (plump, coarse sausage made from pigs' intestines) and *magret de canard* (seared fatty duck breast), is great value and there's always one veggie option.

Auberge Napoléon
FRENCH €€€

(📞04 76 87 53 64; www.auberge-napoleon.fr; 7 rue Montorge; menus €49-75; ⏱7-10pm Mon-Sat) If you dream of mannerly service in an 18th-century French *salon*, this is your place. Mirrors, baroque trimmings and white tablecloths establish the decadent tone, which is amplified by creations like foie gras–topped oysters, squid ink ravioli and juicy Iberico pork.

🍷 Drinking & Nightlife

Depending on where you go, you'll find nightlife both raucous and refined. Students power a bar scene that's big on happy hours and quick-acting cocktails, but sophisticated wine and beer joints are easy to find, too. Rue Auguste Gaché and around place Notre-Dame are good places to start. Also look around place aux Herbes, place Claveyson and place St-André (they're close to each other, a block south of the river).

★ Le 365
COCKTAIL BAR

(📞04 76 51 73 18; www.facebook.com/bar.le.365; 3 rue Bayard; ⏱6pm-1am or 2am Wed-Sat) Good-humoured mixologists preside over a fabulous cocktail list at this chic and ever-so-slightly risqué bar. Sip one of myriad mojito varieties – strawberry-basil and the Chartreuse variety were our favourites – and marvel at the nipple tassels on the wall. Go early if you want a seat.

Le Zinc
WINE BAR

(📞04 76 03 07 44; www.lezincbar.com; 5 rue Auge Gaché; ⏱6-10pm Mon, 6pm-midnight Tue & Wed, 6pm-1am Thu Sat) Evoking an old-timey train station, complete with looming clock and retro tiled floor, Le Zinc is a favourite among local wine lovers. The owners are especially passionate about local and organic varieties, and the fulsome wine list assembles dozens of winning drops (we love the robust, charcoal-noted red Languedoc). And the name? 'Zinc' stands for 'Ze Independent Natural Cellar' (really).

Les BerThom
BEER HALL

(📞04 76 01 81 17; www.lesberthom.com; 1 rue Saint Hugues; ⏱5pm-1am Mon-Wed, to 2am Thu-Sat, to midnight Sun) Ten or more beers on tap, an industrial feel, and a mixed crowd of students and seasoned hop-heads: lively Les BerThom is beer heaven. Glug a Grisette for something bright and blonde, a hoppy Vedette, or even gluten-free beers by the bottle. Attentive table service, despite perennial crowds, makes it all the harder to leave.

Kai-Iwi
CAFE

(www.facebook.com/kaiiwicafegrenoble; 5 rue des Clercs; ⏱8.30am-7pm Wed-Sat, 8.30am-3pm Sun, 11am-7pm Tue; 🖥) This welcoming coffee joint might just brew the best cup in Grenoble. The decor is pure New Zealand kitsch, and food follows the same theme (try avocado on toast or the whopping 'All Blacks breakfast'). NZ beer, cider and sauvignon blanc also feature, should you fancy a pre-dinner drink.

ℹ️ Information

Tourist Office (📞04 76 42 41 41; www.grenoble-tourisme.com; 14 rue de la République; ⏱1-6pm Mon, 9am-6pm Tue-Fri, 9am-1pm & 2-6pm Sat, 9am-noon Sun Oct-Apr, 9am-7pm Mon-Sat, to noon Sun May-Sep; 🖥)
Bastille Tourist Office (📞04 76 89 46 45; ⏱1.30-6.30pm Wed, Sat & Sun Apr-Sep, to 5.30pm Oct-Dec & Feb-Mar, daily in school holidays)

ⓘ GRENOBLE PASS

The **Grenoble Pass** (24/48/72 hours €19/33/48), sold at the tourist office, can save you money if you plan on visiting multiple ticketed sites in and around town. It includes free entry to major museums like the Musée de Grenoble and Musée Stendhal, free public transport, as well as discounts on other attractions. Learn more on www.grenoblepass.com.

ⓘ Getting There & Away

AIR

Some 45km northwest of the city by road, **Grenoble Isère Airport** (☑ 04 76 65 48 48; www.grenoble-airport.com; St-Étienne-de-St-Geoirs) handles flights to and from multiple UK destinations, plus Poland, Ireland, Sweden and the Netherlands.

BUS

Eurolines (www.eurolines.com; 11 place de la Gare; ⏰ 9am-noon & 2-6pm Mon-Fri), which runs international buses, has a desk at the Grenoble **bus station** (11 place de la Gare).

Transaltitude (www.transaltitude.fr) has frequent buses to various ski stations during the ski season, including Alpe d'Huez and Les Deux Alpes (from €15, 1½ to 1¾ hours, three to nine per day) and Chamrousse (from €12, one hour, usually one to three per day).

Transisère (www.transisere.fr) can get you to Bourg d'Oisans (bus 3000; €8.40, 1½ to two hours, at least three daily).

Transdev Dauphiné (www.transdevdauphine.com) has services to Briançon via Serre Chevalier (€20, 2½ hours, up to four daily). It's faster than the train.

TRAIN

The **train station** (1 place de la Gare) is about 1km west of the centre and is linked to the centre by tram lines A and B.

Grenoble has direct rail links to major towns around the Rhône-Alpes (and beyond). Destinations include:

Annecy €21, 1¾ hours, hourly

Chambéry €12.40, 1 hour, at least hourly

Geneva (Switzerland) €28.20, 2¼ hours, 5 daily

Lyon €22.80, 1½ hours, at least hourly

If travelling to/from Paris, change trains in Lyon Part Dieu or Chambéry. Marseille and the south require a change of trains in Valence.

Around Grenoble

Grenoble is within striking distance of two gorgeous, mountainous nature parks designed for cross-country skiing, walking, caving, wildlife watching and 'go slow' ambling in a refreshingly unhurried part of the world.

Parc Naturel Régional du Vercors

There's high drama almost immediately upon entering Parc Naturel Régional du Vercors. The roads dart around needlepoint bends, duck into tunnels burrowed through sheer cliffs, and emerge amid sleepy hamlets. Topping it all is the Réserve Naturelle des Hauts-Plateaux, at 170 sq km, France's largest terrestrial nature reserve.

In this 2062-sq-km mosaic of oak forests, highland plateaux and serrated peaks, rewards are rich for lovers of nature. Chamois perch on cliffs, 75 different types of orchid peep out from tree roots, and birds of prey soar above. There's also history pocketed in the limestone: numerous caves were hideouts for the French Resistance during WWII. Hikers can ply 3000km of trails or, come winter, strap on snowshoes and follow a guide through snow-blanketed meadows.

It's easy to dip into the park from Grenoble, just a few kilometres northeast. Approaching from the west, Pont-en-Royans makes a good base.

⊙ Sights & Activities

Grotte de la Luire   CAVE
(☑ 04 75 48 25 83; www.grottedelaluire.com; Le passage, off D622, Saint-Agnan-en-Vercors; adult/child €9/6.50; ⏰ mid-Dec–mid-Nov) Filled with karst springs and enormous, spectacularly lit chambers, the Grotte de la Luire was used as an emergency hospital during WWII. When it's open, up to five tours depart daily (a dozen daily in July and August), but days of operation vary greatly throughout the year: check the website to be certain.

Gorges du Furon   CANYON
Canyoning, abseiling and walking are all popular in the spectacular Gorges du Furon, carved through the Vercors limestone by the rushing Furon River. You'll see the gorges (in fact, pass through them) just before you reach Lans-en-Vercors, on the D531 from Grenoble.

Les Accompagnateurs Nature et Patrimoine WALKING
(06 35 95 23 08; www.accompagnateur-ver-
cors.com) Leaving from the tourist offices of
Villard de Lans (p543) or Lans-en-Vercors,
these walks in the Vercors park are conducted by knowledgeable guides. In spring, summer and autumn they offer half-day (adult/
child €17/11) and day walks (adult/child
€27/20) among Alpine wild flowers and
wildlife, while half-day snowshoeing tours
(adult/child €21/16) are available in winter.

Sleeping & Eating

Au Gai Soleil de Mont-Aiguille HOTEL €
(04 76 34 41 71; www.hotelgaisoleil.com; La Rich-
ardière, Chichilianne; d €69-76;) At the foot of
striking Mont Aiguille, this simple inn has
fabulous views, superb access to local hiking
routes, a rustic country restaurant, a spa and
two massage rooms for treating weary muscles at trail's end (spa access €15).

À la Crécia B&B €
(04 76 95 46 98; www.gite-en-vercors.com; 436
chemin des Cléments, Les Cléments, Lans-en-Vercors; s/d/tr/q incl breakfast €58/69/89/109)
Renovated by Véronique and Pascal, this
16th-century farm has been endowed with
five wood-panelled guest rooms and ecoconscious additions like solar panels. Kids
will adore the on-site menagerie of sheep
and pigs; and optional dinners, served in
a rustic dining room, assemble farm-fresh
produce like local cheeses and homemade
cakes (*menus* from €19). It's 2km south of
Lans-en-Vercors' tourist office.

Information

Tourist Office (04 76 95 10 38; www.villard
delans.com; 101 place Mûrc Ravaud, Villard de
Lans; 9am-12.30pm & 2-6.30pm Jul & Aug,
shorter hours Sep-Jun;)

Getting There & Away

Buses 5100 and 5110 (€5.60), run by Transisère
(www.transisere.fr), link Grenoble with Lans-
en-Vercors (45 minutes, nine daily) and Villard
de Lans (1¼ hours, four to seven daily). The trip,
which passes through the looming **Gorges du
Furon** (p542), is quite beautiful.

Parc National des Écrins

France's second-largest national park,
Parc National des Écrins (www.ecrins-parc
national.fr) stretches between the towns

of Bourg d'Oisans, Briançon and Gap. Glacial action and the thrashing Durance and
Drac rivers carved out this 918 sq km expanse of mountains and moraines. More
than 100 peaks, topping out at 4102m Barre
des Écrins, rise above more than 40 glaciers, beech forests, waterfalls and flower-
sprinkled alpine meadows. Stomping
ground for hikers between mid-June and
mid-September, the park has almost 700km
of trails, some following footpaths used by
shepherds and smugglers for centuries.

Approaching from the north of the park,
Bourg d'Oisans (50km southeast of Grenoble) is a good jumping-off point. Briançon
and Gap (respectively, east and south of the
park) are also suitable places to gather info
and picnic supplies before lacing up your
hiking boots.

Activities

Among the park's 676km of walking paths
are options long and short, to suit all levels of fitness. Popular (and unchallenging)
half-day hikes include the **Lac du Lauzon**
circuit (three hours) or the stream-side path
to **La Cabane de Jas Lacroix** (three hours).
Families might consider an hour-long ramble around the **Tombeau du Poète** (Poet's
Tomb) or the easy 90-minute walk to **Dor-
millouse** village. For a longer trail, the medium-difficulty **Grande Cabane** trail (five
hours) reaches outstanding views of a glacial valley and the tough **Col des Tourettes**
(6½ hours) rewards hikers with a craggy
mountain pass speckled with chamois.

The national park's free mobile app (iOs/
Android) is very handy for planning hikes
around the park, including maps, trail recommendations (you can filter by length or
difficulty) and info on flora and fauna. Trail
info can be downloaded for offline use.
Find more info on http://rando.ecrins-parc-
national.fr or search for 'Rando Écrins'
(French) or 'Écrins Trekking' (English).

Less of the park is accessible in winter
but visitors can ply a number of walking,
snowshoeing or cross-country skiing trails.
Experience is recommended, as is a guide;
get in touch with a Maison du Parc (p547).

Information

There are several tourist offices in towns around
the national park and seven Maisons du Parc
providing park-specific info, including **Maison
du Parc** (p547) in Bourg d'Oisans.

ℹ️ Getting There & Away

Rando Écrins (04 92 502 505; http://rando.ecrins-parcnational.fr/en/pages/transport) has details of bus services designed to take hikers from Gap, Briançon and Bourg d'Oisans into the park during summer. Reserve 36 hours in advance. Ask locally if driving in winter, as mountain passes may close due to snow.

Les Deux Alpes

POP 1894 / ELEV 1650M

Les Deux Alpes has come a long way since sleepy rural towns Venosc and Mont-de-Lans merged to create this gigantic mountain playground. France's second-oldest winter sports resort has grown from a single tow-rope lift into a 425-hectare ski area served by 47 lifts.

Testament to the tourism explosion of the 1970s and '80s, Les Deux Alpes is clogged with functional architecture and Lego-like blocks – meaning it's arguably less of a charmer than other Alpine ski hubs. But devotees are too busy gazing mountain-ward to notice. Good beginner ski areas, plenty of intermediate terrain, and convenient access to daredevil La Grave have all given Les Deux Alpes a loyal following. In summer, pistes metamorphose into adrenaline-pumping mountain bike trails...or you can continue skiing up high on the glacier.

👁️ Sights & Activities

Contact the Bureau des Guides (p545) for ice climbing, snowshoeing and off-piste skiing in winter, and via-ferrata expeditions, canyoning, glacier walks and mountain biking in summer.

Grotte de Glace   CAVE
(Ice Cave; adult/child €5.50/4.50; ⏰10am-3.30pm winter & summer) Rainbow-lit caverns, tunnelled 30m into the Glacier des Deux Alpes, delight pint-sized visitors with ice statues of prehistoric and mythic beasts; grown-up guests might be less excited. To get there, take the Jandri Express lift to 3200m (itself a 25-minute, €26 journey).

👁️ Winter

Les Deux Alpes' winter season runs from December to April. The main **skiing** domain lies below (ie west of) the summit of **La Meije** (3983m), one of the highest peaks in the Parc National des Écrins. Lots of lifts (per day/six days €50/250 for an adult, €40/200 for a child) come right into the village, and

five beginners' lifts – great for kids – are free. The higher you go, the easier the pistes are.

Free-riders come from far and wide to tackle the breathtaking, near-vertical **Vallons de la Meije** descent in **La Grave** (☑️04 76 79 91 09; www.la-grave.com; cable car adult/student €49/38; ⏰9am-4.30pm Dec-Apr), 23km (by road) east of Les Deux Alpes on the other side of the mountain. The stuff of myth, the off-piste run plummets from 3800m to 1400m and is strictly for experienced, avalanche-aware off-piste riders. A guide is strongly recommended; contact the local tourist office (p545) or Bureau des Guides (p545) in Les Deux Alpes.

Other winter options include ice skating, careening around on an ice bumper car (for kids) and going on a *motoneige* (snowmobile) expedition; the tourist office (p545) has details.

👁️ Summer

Thanks to the **Glacier des Deux-Alpes** (2900m to 3600m), Les Deux Alpes is one of only two places in France where you can **ski** on a glacier in summer (the other is Espace Killy, above Val d'Isère and Tignes). When it's clear, the 360-degree panorama takes in much of southeastern France, including Mont Blanc, the Massif Central and Mont Ventoux. The season runs from late June to early September. Note that a ski day skews earlier than in winter, with lifts between 7am and 1pm – exact timings depend on the weather. A day pass, valid for skiing and the **snow park** (and for other activities in the afternoon), costs €40.10/32.10 for an adult/child.

You can combine morning skiing with **mountain biking** on scores of nail-biting descents (in winter they're ski pistes) and cross-country trails up to an elevation of 3200m. A day pass to six bike-accessible lifts costs €25.50/20.40 per adult/child. Many ski shops rent out Alp-ready mountain bikes in the summer.

Les Deux Alpes also offers numerous **hiking trails** and plenty of opportunities for **paragliding** as well as ice skating, swimming, summer luge, tennis etc.

🛏️ Sleeping & Eating

Hotel Serre-Palas   HOTEL €
(☑️04 76 80 56 33; www.hotelserre-palas.fr; 13 place de l'Alpe de Venosc; d €55-105; 🅿️) With a snug bar for après-ski and marvellous views of the Écrins national park, this spick-and-span chalet is excellent value. Lodgings vary by size and character, including dinky but

comfortable standard rooms, a few with balconies (€75) and the spacious, wood-eaved 'Charme' room (from €100). There's wi-fi in parts of the hotel.

★ **Hotel Côte Brune** HOTEL €€
(☑ 04 76 80 54 89; www.hotel-cotebrune.fr; 6 rue des Côtes Brunes; s/d/tr/q from €95/130/195/220; ☎) You can ski in and out of this hotel, which has a luxurious ochre-toned spa and sprawling slopeside terrace bar. The 18 rooms have cheerful Alpine accents like faux-fur cushions, distressed wooden furniture and cherry-red throws, and the south-facing ones have balconies. Three rooms can sleep a family of four.

Le Raisin d'Ours FRENCH €€
(☑ 04 76 79 29 56; 98 av de la Muzelle; mains €16-24; ☺ noon-2pm & 7-10pm; 🖪) This rustic restaurant serves upmarket Alpine cuisine – pork knuckle in Munster cheese, roasted Camembert with calvados – along with well-executed Italian pasta dishes and seafood. It's accompanied by wines from around France and a satisfying roster of desserts like *fromage blanc aux myrtilles* (soft cheese with forest bilberries), and a magnificent apple tart. The mood is relaxed, the service attentive.

🍷 Drinking & Nightlife

★ **Polar Bear** PUB
(www.thepolarbearpub.com; 104 av de la Muzelle; ☺ 12.30pm-1.30am) Follow the totemic wooden polar bears into this snug chalet-style boozer. A hanging brazier keeps punters toasty, as do the Irish coffees and *vin chaud* (mulled wine). There's a range of European beers (including Guinness on tap), regular live music and 'shot skis' (if you must). Arrive early, this place gets packed.

Smithy's Tavern BAR
(☑ 04 76 11 36 79; www.smithystavern.com; 7 rue du Cairou; ☺ bar 6pm-late, restaurant 6-11pm; ☎) At the bottom of the Venosc lift is this rocking, English-owned pub, one of the premier (and longest-running) party spots in town. The low, timbered ceiling and battle-scarred bar oversee themed and fancy-dress nights, live music (usually Wednesdays) and the latest happy hours around (between midnight and 2am on Mondays, and 10pm to midnight on Tuesdays and Thursdays).

Smokey Joe's BAR
(6 place des Deux Alpes; ☺ 11am-2am late Nov–late Apr & mid-Jun–Aug; ☎) Live music, laid-back punters and plenty of elbow room make Smokey Joe's, at the bottom of the Jandri

Express lift, an easy après-ski option. There's also foosball, pool, and a staff of native English speakers. The star of the Tex-Mex menu is the fall-off-the-bone barbecue ribs (you might need to share).

ℹ **Information**

Maison des Deux Alpes is home to the **Tourist Office** (☑ 04 76 79 22 00; www.les2alpes.com; Maison des Deux Alpes, 4 place des Deux Alpes; ☺ 8am-7pm late Nov–late Apr & mid-Jun–Aug, 9am-noon & 2-6pm Mon-Fri in low season; ☎), **ESF** (☑ 04 76 79 21 21; www.esf2alpes.com; Maison des Deux Alpes, 4 place des Deux Alpes; ☺ 8.30am-6.30pm mid-Dec–mid-Apr, shorter hours early Dec & late Apr) and **Bureau des Guides** (☑ 04 76 11 36 29; www.guides2alpes. com; Maison des Deux Alpes, 4 place des Deux Alpes; ☺ 3.30-6.30pm).

If you're planning to ski the La Grave area or stay nearby, contact the **tourist office** (☑ 04 76 79 90 05; www.lagrave-lameije.com; D1091, La Grave; ☺ 9am-noon & 2-6pm daily mid-Dec–Apr & Jun-Sep, 9am-noon Mon-Fri May, Oct–mid-Dec; ☎) 23km east of Les Deux Alpes.

ℹ **Getting There & Away**

By road, Les Deux Alpes is 67km southeast of Grenoble and 19km southeast of Bourg d'Oisans.

By reservation, transfers are available between Les Deux Alpes and Grenoble airport (from €31.50, 1¾ to 2¼ hours) with **Ben's Bus** (www.bensbus.co.uk) and Lyon–Saint-Exupéry airport (from €32, 3½ hours) with **Ouibus** (www. ouibus.com).

In season (December to April), Transaltitude (www.transaltitude.fr) runs direct buses from Les Deux Alpes to Grenoble's bus station (€18, 1¾ hours, four to eight per day). Buy tickets online or from the **Agence Transisère VFD** (☑ 04 76 80 51 22; 112 av de la Muzelle; ☺ 3-6pm Tue-Sat).

Alpe d'Huez

ELEV 1860M
With high altitudes, reliable snow and almost 250km of pistes, Alpe d'Huez's enormous popularity is no mystery. Officially 'Alpe d'Huez Grand Domaine', this vast ski area encompasses neighbouring resorts Auris-en-Oisans, Huez-en-Oisans, Oz-en-Oisans, Vaujany and Villard Reculas. It's popular for families and first-timers, while pros can enjoy one of the world's longest black (advanced) runs as well as challenging skiing around Pic Blanc (3330m).

Ski season lasts from early December to late April, when the sun on its south-facing slopes can become a problem. Some of the ski lifts feel like they haven't been updated since the 1968 Winter Olympics, but it's hard to find fault with this crowd-pleasing resort.

Summer brings a mix of hikers and mountain bikers – and, often, the Tour de France. Alpe d'Huez is (in)famous for its incredibly steep, 14km access road, whose 21 hairpin curves are a regular highlight of the annual cycling race.

🏃 Activities

For adventure activities such as ice climbing, mountain climbing, via ferrata and glacier hiking, contact the **Bureau des Guides** (☑ 04 76 80 42 55; www.guidesalpedhuez.com; Rond-Point des Pistes, Chalet ESF; ☺ 9.30am-12.30pm & 2.30-5.30pm).

Winter

Alpe d'Huez's terrain, between 1250m and 3330m, has something for all abilities. The majority of pistes are at beginner and intermediate level. The main ski area, around the **Marmottes I** and **Bergers** lifts, is ideal for beginners. Sheltered, tree-lined **Vaujany 1250** is worth considering in bad weather. Intermediate boarders and skiers should head to **Dôme des Petites Rousses** for a plethora of red runs.

The **Pic Blanc** (3330m), Alpe d'Huez's highest point, commands magical panoramas that reach across one-fifth of France. Accessible winter and summer via the Tronçon and Pic Blanc cable cars, it's possible to ski more than two vertical kilometres from this awesome eyrie.

Then there's Europe's longest black run, the breathtakingly sheer, 16km **La Sarenne** (also accessed from the Pic Blanc car). Ski passes cost €52.50/267 for one/six days.

Summer

In summer, marked **hiking trails** lead up and across the slopes to views of jewel-like lakes such as **Lac Blanc**, **Lac de la Fare** and **Lac du Milieu**. The **Col du Lac Blanc** and **Face des Rousses** walks both take an hour to reach views of the lakes. For a longer, medium-difficulty hike, try the four-hour **Les Alpages** route for an eyeful of the Vallée de la Romanche.

For **mountain-biking** enthusiasts, the area is downhill heaven. Alpe d'Huez, and surrounding villages like Bourg d'Oisans, access more than 250km of trails to rattle and roll down, and three bike parks. In summer, lifts to the trails operate from late June

to late August, and a one-day lift pass costs €17.50 (€14.50 for kids) for both pedestrians and cyclists.

ℹ️ Information

Information hub **Maison de l'Alpe** (place Paganon; ☺ 8.45am-7pm Dec-Apr, Jul & Aug, 9am-noon & 2-5pm Mon-Fri Sep-Nov, May-Jun; 🐀) sells ski passes and houses the helpful **tourist office** (☑ 04 76 11 44 44; www.alpedhuez.com; place Paganon; ☺ 8.45am-7pm Dec-Apr, Jul & Aug, 9am-noon & 2-5pm Mon-Fri Sep-Nov, May-Jun; 🐀), **accommodation reservation centre** (☑ 04 76 11 59 90; www.reservation.alpedhuez.com; place Paganon, La Maison de l'Alpe) and **ESF** (☑ 04 76 80 31 69; www.esf-alpedhuez.com; place Paganon, La Maison de l'Alpe; ☺ 9am-7pm daily Dec-Apr, 9am-12.30pm & 1.30-5pm Mon, Tue, Thu & Fri May-Nov).

ℹ️ Getting There & Away

Alpe d'Huez is 64km southeast of Grenoble. From late December to March, Transaltitude (www.transaltitude.fr) buses link Alpe d'Huez with Grenoble's train and bus stations (€15, 1½ to 2 hours, three to eight daily) via Bourg d'Oisans.

Bourg d'Oisans

POP 3239 / ELEV 720M

There's a towering mountain or glacier-gouged valley in almost every direction out of Bourg d'Oisans. This agreeable village of slate-grey houses, set beneath the Grandes Rousses massif, is a good base for hikes into Parc National des Écrins or day-trips to a number of ski resorts, including Alpe d'Huez and Les Deux Alpes – that is, if you aren't deterred by the steep, serpentine roads to the resorts.

But Bourg's true passion is cycling. This valley village is a great starting point for numerous downhill trails in the national park as well as the legendary 21-bend access road to Alpe d'Huez, an iconic section of the Tour de France route.

◉ Sights & Activities

For information on the area, check out http://oisans.com and www.bikes-oisans.com, which have details on trails, maps and bike hire. For details on activities such as kayaking on the Drac's turquoise waters, rock climbing, via-ferrata routes and paragliding, contact the tourist office.

Musée des Minéraux et de la Faune des Alpes
MUSEUM

(☑04 76 80 27 54; www.musee-bourgdoisans. fr; place de l'Église; adult/child €5.50/2.40; ⊙2-6pm Sat & Sun Oct-Dec, 2-6pm Wed-Mon Apr-Sep & school holidays) Glittering cases of minerals and natural history displays are given a lift by great lighting and original presentation at this diverting museum. After being dazzled by crystals mined from these very mountains, bone up on regional flora and fauna like ibex and chamois.

Cycles et Sports
CYCLING

(☑04 76 79 16 79; www.cyclesetsports.com; rue du Général de Gaulle; ⊙8.30am-7pm daily May-Sep, 9am-noon & 2-6pm Mon-Sat Oct-Apr) For those mad enough to tackle the remorseless climb up Alpe d'Huez (21 bends, an ascent of nearly 1220m, and an average incline of 7.9%) this boutique operation hires out high-end road bikes for between €39 and €90 per day.

🛏 Sleeping & Eating

★ Hôtel des Alpes
HOTEL €

(☑04 76 80 00 16; www.hoteldesalpesoisans.com; 21 rue Général de Gaulle; d €60-80; 🛜) Well-heated, wooden-floored rooms are packed into this slender building in the centre of town. Standard rooms are plain but pleasingly large, while deluxe rooms have designer bathrooms, writing desks and a royal colour scheme of cream and maroon. Even cosier is the dinky spa (€8.50, by reservation), with jacuzzi and sauna to soothe cycling-sore muscles. The breakfast buffet costs €9.

Ferme Noémie
B&B €

(☑04 76 11 06 14; www.fermenoemie.com; chemin Pierre Polycarpe, Les Sables; campsites €10.50-25, apt per week €275-850; ⊙campground late Apr-Oct; 🅿) Five kilometres north of Bourg d'Oisans, run by British couple Melanie and Jeremy Smith, Ferme Noémie has barn-conversion apartments with four to six beds and old-fashioned campsites. There's wi-fi at reception, washing machines on site (€4) and an option for breakfast croissants delivered right to your tent. Prices depend on seasonal demand.

Five-metre luxury tents (prices vary), billed as 'camping for softies', sleep up to four people. To get there from the D1091, follow the signs for about 500m.

La Muzelle
FRENCH €€

(☑04 76 79 58 02; http://lamuzelle.com; 43 av de la République; lunch menus €15, dinner menus €24-29; ⊙noon-2pm & 6.30-10.30pm) A cut above the rest of Bourg d'Oisans' restaurants, La Muzelle fills its menu with perfectly seared tuna, beefy mains from burgers to steaks, and a good selection of pizzas. If you've been burning serious calories on the slopes or cycle trails, consider restoring the balance with a bacon-stuffed baked Camembert. The setting's simple but service is sunny.

🛈 Information

Maison du Parc (☑04 76 80 00 51; www. ecrins-parcnational.fr; 120 rue Gambetta; ⊙10am-noon & 3-6pm daily Jul & Aug, 9am-11am & 1.30-5pm Mon-Fri (except Wed afternoon) Sep-Jun)

Tourist Office (☑04 76 80 03 25, www.bourg doisans.com; 31 quai Girard; ⊙9am-noon & 2-6pm Mon-Sat Sep-Jun, 9am-7pm Jul & Aug; 🛜)

🛈 Getting There & Away

From December to April, Transisère (www. transisere.fr) bus line 3020 runs from Grenoble's bus station (€5.60, one hour) through Bourg d'Oisans to Alpe d'Huez (€3.20, 45 minutes) between two and four times daily. Line 3030 from Grenoble also reaches Bourg d'Oisans en route to Les Deux Alpes (€3.20, one hour) three to nine times per day.

During the same period, **LER bus** (p549) line 35 runs twice daily to/from Bourg, on the way between Grenoble (€6.50, one hour) and Briançon (€15.90, 1¾ hours).

Briançon

POP 12,370 / ELEV 1326M

It's a rare pleasure to retreat to a hilltop citadel after a day of epic hiking or skiing. Briançon, surrounded by mountains and capped with a fairy-tale fortress, manages equal doses of culture and outdoor pursuits. Technically France's highest city, it flies under the mass tourism radar because of its inconvenient road access compared to other Alpine resorts – despite being only 15 zigzagging kilometres from Italy.

Briançon is the northwestern gateway town to Parc National des Écrins' 676km of hiking trails. Even closer is the Serre Chevalier (p548) ski area, less than 2km from its crowning Cité Vauban (p547), a star-shaped old town girded by high walls.

⊙ Sights

Cité Vauban
HISTORIC SITE

(Vieille Ville) Surrounded by mighty starburst-shaped ramparts, Briançon's hilltop old town looks much as it did centuries ago, its winding cobbled lanes lined with Italianate, pastel-painted townhouses. The steep main street, the **Grande Rue** – also known as the **Grande Gargouille** (Great Gargoyle) because of its gushing rivulet – was laid out in 1345. You can walk all the way around the interior of Vauban's upper ramparts, enjoying spectacular views, by following the streets marked as the **chemin de Ronde**.

Vauban Fortifications   HISTORIC SITE
Situated at the confluence of five river valleys, Briançon was highly vulnerable to attack by France's Alpine arch-rival of the 17th century, the Duchy of Savoy. After an especially damaging raid in 1692, vast effort was expended on constructing hilltop fortresses to defend the remote town, under the instructions of master military planner Vauban. These marvels of engineering, along with a dozen other Vauban sites in France, were given Unesco World Heritage status in 2008.

Perched atop a rocky crag high above the Cité Vauban, the **Fort du Château** (1326m) can be visited on foot from late April to November. Across the 55m-high **Pont d'Asfeld** (erected 1731), a graceful stone bridge over the Durance River, **Fort des Trois Têtes** (1435m) can be seen on a walking tour in the warm season. The **Fort des Salettes** (1400m) is accessible on foot or on guided snowshoe tours; ask at the **Service du Patrimoine** (04 92 20 29 49; www.ville-briancon.fr; Porte de Pignerol, Cité Vauban; tours adult/child €6.20/4.60; 10am-noon & 2-5.30pm Tue-Fri & Sun Sep-Jun, Mon-Sat Jul & Aug), inside the Cité Vauban's main gate.

Activities

Serre Chevalier   SKIING
(www.serre-chevalier.com; one-day pass adult/child €49.90/40; Dec-Apr) The Serre Chevalier ski area links 13 villages and 250km of pistes along the Serre Chevalier Valley between Briançon and Le Monêtier-les-Bains, 15km northwest. To get to the slopes (and warm-season trails) directly from Briançon, take the **Télécabine du Prorel** lift, located by the river – on the western edge of Ste-Catherine – 1.8km from the Cité Vauban.

**Bureau des Guides et
Accompagnateurs de Briançon**   OUTDOORS
(04 92 20 15 73; www.guides-briancon.fr; 24 rue Centrale; 10am-noon & 3-7pm Mon-Fri, 3-7pm Sat, 10am-1pm Sun in summer, 5-7pm rest of year) Organises off-piste outings, snowshoeing and ice climbing in winter; and trekking, mountain climbing, mountaineering, via-ferrata climbs, glacier traverses, mountain biking and canyoning in summer.

Sleeping

Hotel Edelweiss   HOTEL €
(04 92 21 02 94; www.hotel-edelweiss-briancon.fr; 32 av de la République; s/d/tr/q €54/66/86/96;) An excellent bet if you're on a tight budget. The 20 spacious rooms, some in a building from 1890, are plain but perfectly clean. There's a lounge where you can curl up with a book, and the helpful owners can arrange everything from ski passes to babysitters. It's 400m downhill from the Cité Vauban.

Hôtel de la Chaussée   HISTORIC HOTEL €€
(04 92 21 10 37; www.hotel-de-la-chaussee.com; 4 rue Centrale, Ste-Catherine; s/d/tr/q €80/95/105/135;) The Bonnaffoux family has run this place with charm and efficiency for five generations – since 1892, in fact. Rooms fulfil every Alpine chalet fantasy: wooden shutters, soft lighting and a furnishings that wouldn't look out of place in a doll's house.

Eating

★ **Au Plaisir Ambré**   FRENCH €€
(04 92 52 63 46; www.auplaisirambre.com; 26 Grande Rue; menus €30-45; noon-1.15pm by reservation & 7-9.15pm Fri-Tue) At this refined old-town restaurant, the leisurely pace of service is essential, if only to let your taste buds catch up with chef Michaël Chassigneux's innovative creations. Pan-fried mullet surfs on celery foam, juicy scallops swim in coffee emulsion, and local lamb is stirred into Madras-style curry, served with quintessentially French potato mille feuille…and somehow it all works beautifully.

★ **Pâtisserie Turin**   DESSERTS, ITALIAN €
(04 92 21 14 00; www.patisserieturin.com; 25 Grande Rue, Cité Vauban; snacks from €2.50; 8am-6.30pm Tue-Sat, to 6pm Sun) It's hard to overstate how seriously this all-Italian baker and chocolate-maker takes its craft. Order a *caffè marocchino* (espresso with milk foam and cocoa powder) in the adjoining tea room and deliberate between raspberry gateaux, nougats, chocolate Florentines and macarons. Peruse the voluminous tea list of imperial Chinese blends and Japanese green teas while you recover from sugar-shock.

Le Gastrologue   FRENCH €€
(04 92 20 49 62; 20 av Vauban, Cité Vauban; mains €16, menus €23-38; noon-1pm & 7-8.30pm;) Whimsical Gastrologue rotates its cuisine depending on which herbs and edible flowers the kindly owners have picked that week. Featuring on the hand-drawn menu you

might find rabbit confit, gratinated *crozets* (the Dauphiné's square-shaped pasta), and always vegetarian options like *ravioles du Champsaur* (cheese and potato dumplings).

❶ Information

There's a **tourist office** (☑ 04 92 21 08 50; www.ville-briancon.fr; Maison des Templiers, 1 place du Temple, Cité Vauban; ⊙ 9am-noon & 2-6pm Mon-Sat, 10.30am-12.30pm & 2.30-5.30pm Sun; 🛜) inside the Cité Vauban, chock-full of free maps and pamphlets on regional attractions. Room availability information is posted on the door. There's also a **tourist office** (☑ 04 92 24 98 98; www.ville-briancon.fr; rue Centrale, Ste-Catherine; ⊙ 9am-noon & 2-6pm Mon-Sat, 10am-noon & 2-5pm Sun) in the lower town.

For info on Parc National des Écrins, stop by the **Maison du Parc** (☑ 04 92 21 42 15; www.ecrins-parcnational.fr; place du Médecin Général Blanchard; ⊙ 10.30am-6.30pm Jul & Aug, 2-6pm Mon-Fri Sep-Jun) at the bottom of the Cité Vauban's Grande Rue.

❶ Getting There & Away

BUS

The bus station is next to the train station. **LER bus** (Lignes Express Régionales; ☑ 08 21 20 22 03; www.info-ler.fr) 35, run by the Provence-Alpes-Côte d'Azur *région*, links Briançon with Grenoble (€20.70, three hours, one to three daily) via Bourg d'Oisans. LER bus 29 goes to Gap (€14.40, two hours, one to three daily Monday to Saturday), Aix-en-Provence (€39.10, 5½ hours, one or two daily Monday to Saturday) and Marseille (€43.50, six hours, one or two daily Monday to Saturday).

CAR & MOTORCYCLE

The **Col de Montgenèvre** (1854m), linking Briançon with neighbouring Italy, is kept open year-round, as is the **Col du Lautaret** (2058m) between Briançon and Grenoble. Both, though, occasionally get snow-bogged and forced to close in bad weather.

TRAIN

The **train station** (av du Général de Gaulle), terminus of a rail spur that heads northeast from Gap, is 1.5km southwest of the Cité Vauban and less than 1km south of the lower, modern town (Ste-Catherine). It is linked to the rest of town by infrequent local TUB bus 3.

Gap €15.70, 1¼ hours, 6 direct daily

Grenoble €34.30, 4½ hours, 4 daily, all via Gap or Veynes

Marseille €47.70, 4½, hours, 3 direct daily, more via Gap

Paris (Austerlitz) from €67, 11½ hours, 1 direct daily (night train)

Paris (Gare de Lyon) from € 82.30, 7½–9 hours, 5 daily, all via Valence or Gap

To Grenoble, the bus is much faster than the train. The fastest way to get to Paris is to take a bus to the Italian town of Oulx (€7.50, one hour, four daily from December to mid-April) – reserve 36 hours ahead on 04 92 50 25 05 or via www.05voyageurs.com – and then a TGV to Paris' Gare de Lyon (€69-116, 4¾ hours, three daily).

THE JURA MOUNTAINS

Brooding landscapes and inspiring hikes define the sparsely populated Jura Mountains. Extending along the Franco–Swiss border from Lake Geneva northeast to Belfort, these sub-alpine mountains lent their name to the Jurassic period in geology, when they formed. Rising highest is **Crêt de la Neige** (1720m), in the southwest of the Parc Naturel Régional du Haut-Jura.

In summer, *fruitières* (dairies) and vineyards sell prized regional produce like Comté cheese and unmistakable *vin jaune* (regional gold-coloured wine) to a mostly French influx of hikers and bikers. Winter attracts cross-country skiers to Les Rousses and Métabief, while the best limber up in the regional park for the **Transjurassienne**, France's toughest cross-country ski race.

Cultural sights, mostly overlooked by foreign tourists, provide opportunities to catch your breath: the citadels of Belfort and Besançon, modernist architecture in Arc-et-Senans and Ronchamp, and legacies of home-grown luminaries like Victor Hugo and biologist Louis Pasteur.

Besançon

POP 116,676 / ELEV 250M

Capped with a citadel and folded into a bend in the Doubs River, Besançon is a pleasant surprise. Unshowy and laid-back, the capital of the Doubs *département* nonetheless offers a broad spectrum of culture: 18th-century town houses, many now housing hotels and restaurants; active contemporary arts and local music scenes; and monuments to homegrown luminaries like Victor Hugo.

In Gallo-Roman times, Besançon (then Vesontio) was an important stop on the trade routes linking Italy, the Alps and the Rhine, and some remains of this period survive.

◉ Sights

For a lovely stroll, you can walk paths along either bank of the Doubs River, where it encircles the old city. For an alternative view, 1¼-hour river cruises (p552) ply the water.

★ **Citadelle de Besançon**   CITADEL
(☎ 03 81 87 83 17; www.citadelle.com; 99 rue des Fusillés de la Résistance; adult/child €10.80/8.70; ⊙ 10am-5pm Feb, Mar, Oct-Dec, 9am-6pm Apr-Jun & Sep, 9am-7pm Jul & Aug; 🅿 ♿) Dominating the city from Mt St-Etienne, more than 100 vertical metres above the old town, the 17th-century Citadelle de Besançon – designed by Vauban for Louis XIV – commands sweeping views of the city and the serpentine Doubs River. Along with 11 other similarly impressive military architectural sites, the 12-hectare Citadelle was recognised as a Unesco World Heritage Site in 2008.

English and German booklets are available at the entrance, including pamphlets aimed at kids. Entry includes audioguides (in French, English and German).

For an introduction to the citadel's architecture, head to **St-Etienne Chapel**, where a 15-minute multimedia presentation illuminates Besançon's history. The **chemin de Rond** lets you walk along 600m of the citadel's outer ramparts.

The **Musée de la Résistance et de la Déportation** is one of France's most in-depth and comprehensive WWII museums. Each room has an information sheet in English but the 20 rooms of evocative photos,

Besançon

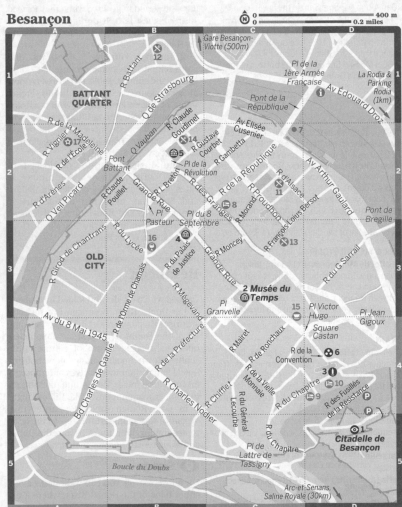

documents and artefacts are best visited with a free audioguide. Some of the photographs are unsuitable for young children. During WWII, the Germans imprisoned British civilians in the citadel, and German firing squads executed about 100 resistance fighters here. Nearby, the three-floor **Musée Comtois** presents local life in centuries past, including food, religion and a colourful puppet theatre.

Kids are sure to be fascinated by the **Insectarium**, with creepy-crawlies such as tarantulas, scorpions and stick insects; the small **Aquarium**, where you can admire goldfish and koi; the ho-hum **Noctarium**, where a few nocturnal rodents like dormice and voles snuffle around; a six-room **biodiversity exhibition**; and a **zoo**. There's a restaurant, snack bar and vending machines around the site.

If you don't fancy the uphill trudge, take Ginko bus 27 (€1.40) from the city centre or Parking Rodia, which runs from April to mid-October (find schedules on www.ginko. voyage).

★ **Musée du Temps**   MUSEUM
(☑ 03 81 87 81 50; www.mdt.besancon.fr; 96 Grande Rue; adult/child €5/free; ☉ 9.15am-noon & 2-6pm Tue-Sat, 10am-6pm Sun) Literal and figurative interpretations of time are woven together at the Musée du Temps, which places allegorical paintings about the passage of time next to 18th-century wall clocks and early astronomical equipment. The result is beautifully thought-provoking, and the philosophical questions it raises are best pondered while gazing out from the **tower**, which houses a Foucault's pendulum.

Porte Noire   RUINS
(Black Gate; square Castan) Erected in AD 175 in honour of Marcus Aurelius, this 16.5m-high Roman triumphal arch stands very near where the columns of a Roman theatre and the vestiges of an aqueduct (all still visible) were discovered in the late 19th-century.

Cathédrale St-Jean   CATHEDRAL
(☑ 03 81 83 34 62; www.cathedrale-besancon. fr; 10ter rue de la Convention; ☉ 9am-7pm, to 6.30pm winter) The earliest parts of Besançon's cathedral date to 1127. Though heavily modified in ensuing centuries, following a 13th-century fire and the collapse of its bell tower in 1724, Romanesque capitals still sit atop its interior columns. On the wall hangs *La Vierge aux Saints* (1512), painted by Italian Renaissance virtuoso Fra Bartolomeo; flick the switch to illuminate it. The cathedral's best-known treasure is its **astronomical clock** (☑ 03 81 81 12 76; www.horloge-astronomique-besancon.fr; rue du Chapitre; adult/child €3.50/ free; ☉ guided tours hourly 9.50-11.50am & 2.50-4.50pm Wed-Mon Apr-Sep, Thu-Mon Oct-Mar).

Musée des Beaux-Arts et d'Archéologie   MUSEUM
(☑ 03 81 87 80 67; www.mbaa.besancon.fr; 1 place de la Révolution; adult/child €5/free; ☉ 9.30am-noon & 2-6pm Mon & Wed-Fri, 9.30am-6pm Sat & Sun) France's oldest public museum, founded in 1694, is famous for its stellar collection of local Gallo-Roman archaeology; its Cabinet des Dessins, with some 6000 drawings from the 15th to 20th centuries, including masterpieces by Dürer, Delacroix and Rodin; and its 14th- to 20th-century paintings, with standouts by Titian, Rubens, Goya and Matisse.

Besançon

When we passed through, the museum was preparing to reopen in November 2018 after extensive renovations.

⟲ Tours

Vedettes de Besançon　　　　BOATING
(☑ 06 64 48 66 80; www.vedettesdebesancon.com; Pont de la République; adult/child €12/9; ☺ Apr-Oct; ♿) This 1¼-hour river cruise with commentary is a relaxed way to see Besançon from the Doubs' hairpin curve and the 375m-long boat tunnel that goes underneath the citadel. Local food is served on some launches (breakfast/*menu* from €16/38, or cheese plates from €31).

⊨ Sleeping

Résidence Charles Quint　APARTMENT, GUESTHOUSE €
(☑ 03 81 82 00 21; www.residence-charlesquint. com; 3 rue du Chapitre; d/apt €85/115; ᴘ ☎) Slumbering behind the cathedral, in the shade of the citadel, this discreetly grand 18th-century town house has double rooms with period furniture and sumptuous fabrics, and self-catering apartments with marbled bathrooms and an antique feel. The highlight is the peaceful private garden, erupting with flowers in summer and shaded by huge trees. Minimum three-night stay.

★**Hôtel de Paris**　　　DESIGN HOTEL €€
(☑ 03 81 81 36 56; www.besanconhoteldeparis.com; 33 rue des Granges; s/d/ste from €74/92/139; ᴘ ☎) Sleep in the same 18th-century coaching inn as renowned novelists George Sand and Colette. Rococo styling and ornate wallpaper add antique glamour to otherwise modern rooms, while the dining hall – a wonder of stained glass and flowing drapes – couldn't be a more chic place to start the day (breakfast €13).

L'Annexe　　　　　APARTMENT €€
(☑ 06 09 48 78 86; www.lannexe-apparthotel.com; 11 rue du Chapitre; per week €495-695; ☎) These classy apartments are within the handsome walls of a converted 18th-century town house – once used by canons from the nearby cathedral. Apartments sleep between two and six people, and they're equipped with full kitchen, excellent beds and modern fittings like coffee makers and washing machines.

✕ Eating

Marché Beaux-Arts　　　　MARKET €
(☑ 03 81 62 04 18; www.facebook.com/marche beauxarts; place de la Révolution; snacks from €4; ☺ 7am-7pm Tue-Sat, 8am-1pm Sun) This covered food market showcases cheese, charcuterie, fruit and veg from around the Jura. It's a bustling, workaday place where locals do their shopping, lined with butchers, fishmongers and deli produce like dried mushrooms. If you aren't self-catering, you can grab Vietnamese spring rolls, wedges of cheese and organic ciders to go.

★**Les Tables d'Antan**　　　　FRENCH €
(☑ 03 81 83 04 42; http://lestablesdantan.fr; 18 rue Bersot; mains €12-28; ☺ noon-2pm Wed-Sat, 7-9pm Mon-Sat; ☑) Thoughtful service adds finesse to Les Tables d'Antan's rustic cuisine, served beneath dangling farm tools and cartwheels. Potato or pasta *gratins* (creamy bakes) emerge steaming, salads assemble generous quantities of Morteau sausage, bleu de Gex cheese and other regional produce, but the *crumbles salés* (savoury crumbles) are the menu's high point, loaded with smoked trout, duck confit or ratatouille.

Le Poker d'As　　　　FRENCH €€
(☑ 03 81 81 42 49; www.restaurant-lepokerdas.fr; cnr rue d'Alsace & rue du Clos St-Amour; menus €24.50-45; ☺ noon-1.30pm & 7.30-9.30pm Tue-Sat) With its thoughtful blend of traditional and creative French fare – turbot on a bed of chorizo and tomato; chicken with morels and *vin jaune* (a regional slow-matured wine); and confit lemon tart – the family kitchen at the 'Poker Ace' has a winning hand.

★**Le Saint-Pierre**　　　　FRENCH €€€
(☑ 03 81 81 20 99; www.restaurant-saintpierre. com; 104 rue Battant; menus €44-78; ☺ noon-1.30pm Mon-Fri, 7.30-9pm Mon-Sat) Crisp white tablecloths, exposed stone and subtle lighting create an understated backdrop for Le Saint-Pierre's intense flavours: roast lamb in crushed tomato, sea bass with forest mushrooms, and ornate dessert plates, all expertly paired with regional wines.

🍷 Drinking & Nightlife

Students keep Besançon's live-music scene fizzing, while merry-makers from all walks of life fill the pubs around the northern end of the Grande Rue (eg along tiny rue Claude Pouillet) and, across the river, in the more diverse and gritty Battant quarter.

Green Man　　　　　WINE BAR
(☑ 03 81 50 99 59; www.facebook.com/Thegreen manbar; 21 rue Pasteur; ☺ 7am-midnight Mon-Fri, 10am-midnight Sat) Formerly trading heavily on an Irish pub theme, these days the Green Man is a genteel, convivial place for coffee or an

WORTH A TRIP

SALTY SIGHTS

The Jura has salt to thank for its early wealth. The focal point of sleepy **Arc-et-Senans**, 35km southwest of Besançon, is an 18th-century former saltworks. The **Saline Royale** (Royal Saltworks; 03 81 54 45 45; www.salineroyale.com; Grande Rue; adult/child €9.80/5; 10am-noon & 2-5pm Nov-Mar, 9am-6pm Apr, May, Sep & Oct, to 7pm Jul & Aug) was conceived as an 'ideal city' by creator Claude-Nicolas Ledoux. A masterpiece of early industrial-age design with columns, neoclassical archways and elegant outbuildings, the saltworks has been preserved as a monument to industrial France and now houses museums, a cafe and three-star **guest rooms** (03 81 54 45 17; www.salineroyale.com; Saline Royale, Grande Rue; s/d/tr €84/113/135; Mar-Oct; P).

Fifteen kilometres southeast of Arc-et-Senans lies **Salins-les-Bains**. The town owes its name and fortune to salt water, which fuelled a medieval salt trade and spa industry. The salt museum at the **Grande Saline** (03 84 73 10 92; www.salinesdesalins.com; place des Salines, Salins-les-Bains; museum adult/child €4/free, with tour €8/free; 9.30am-12.30pm & 2-6pm Apr-Jun, Sep & Oct, to 7pm Jul & Aug, shorter hours Nov-Mar) exhibits salt pans and pumps, and hour-long guided tours in French delve into salt-processing history (between two and 12 times daily, depending on season). English-language tours are at 12.15pm between July and mid-September.

aperitif, decorated with musical instruments and folksy touches like mounted antlers and sometimes vibrating with live folk or rock. A cheerful scrum forms at the bar, where classy local wines are served by the glass.

Café des Félins CAFE
(www.cafedesfelins.fr; 135 Grande Rue; noon-8pm Wed-Sat, from 3pm Sun) Cats prowl, loiter and generally reign supreme at this concept cafe, which serves a fittingly cosy range of hot chocolates, cookies and tartines (open-faced, melted sandwiches, €12). Importing the Japanese 'cat cafe' concept, this is the place to de-stress, surrounded by furry friends. No children.

⭐ Entertainment

Les Passagers du Zinc LIVE MUSIC
(03 81 81 54 70; www.lespassagersduzinc.com; 5 rue Vignier; from €5; 4pm-1am Tue & Wed, to 2am Thu-Sat) Behind an anonymous, black-shuttered shopfront lies one of Besançon's best venues for live music. Opening only when a gig's on (usually between 9pm and midnight on Thursday, Friday or Saturday – it could be punk, psychedelic rock, synth-pop or electro), it has battered leather sofas and a suitably grungy vibe.

ℹ Information

The **tourist office** (03 81 80 92 55; www.besancon-tourisme.com; 2 place de la 1ère Armée Française, Parc Micaud; 10am-12.30pm & 1.30-6pm Mon-Sat, 10am-1pm Sun Sep-Jun, 10am-6pm daily Jul & Aug;) is located at the northwestern end of the Parc Micaud. It may return to the **Hôtel de Ville** (03 81 61 50 50;

www.besancon.fr; place du 8 Septembre), after restoration is completed following an arson attack.

ℹ Getting There & Around

BICYCLE

VéloCité (www.velocite.besancon.fr; per hr/day €1/4) Besançon's credit-card-operated automatic bike-rental system has 30 pick-up and drop-off sites across the city. If your trip is under 30 minutes, it's free.

TRAIN

The train station, **Gare Besançon-Viotte** (Besançon Train Station; 2 av de la Paix), is 800m north (up the hill) from northern edge of the city centre. Buy tickets online (http://oui.sncf/billet-train) or at the **Boutique SNCF** (2 av de la Paix, Gare Besançon-Viotte; 8am-7pm Mon-Sat, 10.50am-7pm Sun).

Services include the following (direct unless stated otherwise):

Arc-et-Senans €5, 25 minutes, 18 daily

Arbois €10, 40 minutes, 13 daily

Belfort €15, 1 hour, one or two per hr

Dijon €15-22, 1 hour, two or three per hr

Paris-Gare de Lyon €56-90, 2½-3¼ hours, three direct daily (10 via Dijon)

Connections to major cities are often cheaper and/or quicker from **Gare TGV Besançon Franche-Comté**, on the TGV line linking Dijon with Mulhouse. Situated 10km northwest of the centre, it's a 15-minute hop by train from Gare Besançon-Viotte (€5, every one or two hours).

To reach Geneva (Switzerland) by train (from €61, three to 5½ hours), you'll need to change in Dole or Lyon Part Dieu.

South of Besançon

Southwest of Besançon is wine and cheese country, home of sweet nutty Comté cheese and the delightful **Route des Vins du Jura** (www.jura-vins.com) wine trail through 80km of chardonnay, savagnin and pinot noir vineyards, time-worn stone villages and darkly wooded slopes. It's also strongly identified with scientific pioneer Louis Pasteur, who was born in Dole, raised in Arbois and worked in Besançon. Southeast of the latter, chateau life kicks in.

Arbois

POP 3407

Vin jaune, a slowly fermented golden wine, is the prime source of pride for the town of Arbois, 40km southeast of Besançon. An astonishing number of the honey-coloured stone houses lining the banks of the Cuisance River house restaurants and wineries. Arbois is prettiest in summer but at all times of year you'll see locals passing through to haul crates of *vin jaune* into their car boots.

◉ Sights & Activities

The 2.5km-long **Chemin des Vignes** walking trail and the 8km-long **Circuit des Vignes** mountain-bike route meander through the vines. Both trails (marked with orange signs) begin at the top of the steps next to Arbois' Château Pécauld; a booklet with details is available at the tourist office.

High above Arbois, 3km southeast, is tiny **Pupillin**, a cute yellow-brick village famous for its wine production. Some 10 different *caves* (wine cellars) are open to visitors.

Musée de la Vigne et du Vin du Jura   MUSEUM

(☑ 03 84 66 40 45; www.arbois.fr; rue des Fossés; adult/child €3.50/free; ⊙10am-noon & 2-6pm Wed-Mon Mar-Oct, 2-6pm Wed-Mon Nov-Feb) The history behind the Jura's prized *vin jaune* (barrel-matured wine with a distinctive yellow hue) is told at this understated museum, between the turrets of the golden-hued Château Pécauld. Methods of viticulture are explained in detail between these 13th-century walls, including a short video presentation.

★ Festivals & Events

La Percée du Vin Jaune   WINE

(www.percee-du-vin-jaune.com; entry & 10 tasting tickets €20; ⊙early Feb) The festival of the 'Opening of the Yellow Wine' cracks open the vintage produced six years and three months earlier. Villages take turns holding the two-day celebration, during which the Jura's nectar of the gods is blessed and rated. *Vin jaune* (the region's barrel-matured, golden-hued wine) aficionados enjoy street tastings, cooking competitions, cellar visits and auctions.

⌂ Sleeping & Eating

★**Closerie les Capucines**   B&B €€

(☑ 03 84 66 17 38; www.closerielescapucines.com; 7 rue de Bourgogne; d/q incl breakfast from €125/250; ⊙Feb-Dec; @ 🕸 ☀) A 17th-century stone convent has been lovingly transformed into this boutique B&B, with five rooms remarkable for their pared-down elegance, a tree-shaded garden by the river, a plunge pool and sauna.

Edouard Hirsinger   DESSERTS €

(☑03 84 66 06 97; www.chocolat-hirsinger. com; place de la Liberté; ⊙8am-7.30pm Fri-Tue)

LIQUID GOLD

Legend has it that *vin jaune* (literally, 'yellow wine') was invented when a winemaker came across a forgotten barrel, six years and three months after he'd filled it, and discovered that its contents had been miraculously transformed into gold-coloured wine.

A long, undisrupted fermentation process gives Jura's signature wine its unique characteristics. Savagnin grapes are harvested late and their sugar-saturated juice left to ferment for a minimum of six years and three months in oak barrels. A thin layer of yeast forms over the wine, preventing too much oxidisation; there are no top-ups to compensate for wine that evaporates (known as *la part des anges*, 'the angels' share'). In the end, 100L of grape juice ferments down to just 62L of *vin jaune* (lucky angels!) which is then bottled in a special 0.62L bottle called a *clavelin*.

Vin jaune is renowned for ageing extremely well, with prime vintages keeping for more than a century. A 1774 vintage was bought for a cool 46,000 Swiss francs when auctioned off by Christie's in 2012...many locals insist that it should have fetched a higher price.

REPUBLIC OF SAUGEAIS

A perfect example of the *département* of Doubs' ironic sense of humour is its self-declared micronation, 12km northeast of Pontarlier.

The **République du Saugeais** began as a prank on an administrative official in 1947. Locals enjoyed the joke so much that there are still road signs marking the border of this so-called republic, though their novelty bank notes and postage stamps are a rarity these days.

While you're here, make time for the **Abbaye de Montbenoît** (🗷Montbenoît tourist office 03 81 38 10 32; www.montbenoit.fr; 4 rue du val Saugeais, Montbenoît; €5; ⊙tours 10am-5.30pm Jul & Aug, by arrangement with tourist office Sep-Jun), whose Renaissance-style tower – emblazoned with a horseback knight – instantly impresses. Tours, run by the adjoining tourist office, lead inside the 800-year-old abbey. Explore the double-columned **cloisters** and admire a 12th-century **church**, whose wooden stalls bear ornate carvings. Sculpted in the 16th century, several of the decorations 'warn' monks against the temptations of women (look out for a humiliated Aristotle, being ridden like a pony).

Browse displays of ornate éclairs, coffee-almond 'Opéra' cake, and ginger ganache enveloped in the darkest chocolate. The choice of expertly made chocolates, tarts and liqueur-drenched desserts is enormous. Frankly, they had us at 'absinthe marzipan'.

⭐**La Balance Mets et Vins**　FRENCH €€
(🗷03 84 37 45 00; www.labalance.fr; 47 rue de Courcelles; weekday lunch menus €17.50-19.80, dinner menus from €29; ⊙noon-2pm Wed-Sun, 7-9pm Tue-Sat, open Tue lunch & Sun evenings Jul & Aug; 🗷) Inside a charismatic 18th-century building, La Balance uses local, organic produce to produce signature dishes such as coq au vin with morel mushrooms, and crème brûlée with *vin jaune*, while the meat-free platter assembles 10 different preparations of seasonal vegetables. The well-priced wine list emphasises *vin jaune* and other Jura varieties.

ℹ Information

Arbois' **tourist office** (🗷03 84 66 55 50; http://tourisme.arbois.com; 17 rue de l'Hôtel de Ville; ⊙10am-12.30 & 2-5.30pm Mon-Sat, also 10am-noon Sun Apr-Sep; 🗟) is located on the southern side of the main bridge over La Cuisance, opposite the church.

ℹ Getting There & Away

Trains run to Arbois from Besançon (€10, 40 to 50 minutes, one per hour between 6.30am and 8pm) on their way to Poligny (€5, 10 minutes).

Poligny

POP 4104

Tucked behind limestone cliffs, picturesque Poligny, 60km southwest of Besançon, is the soul and centre of the Jura's Comté cheese industry. Dozens of *fruitières* (cheese co-

operatives) are open to the public, where visitors can sample batons of firm, golden Comté, which is produced in greater quantities than any other French *Appellation d'Origine Contrôlée* (AOC) cheese.

Learn how 450L of milk is transformed into a 40kg wheel of tangy Comté cheese and have a nibble at the **Maison du Comté** (🗷03 84 37 78 40; www.maison-du-comte.com; av de la Résistance; adult/child €5/3; ⊙2-5pm Tue-Sun Apr-Jun, Sep & Oct, 10am-noon & 2-5.30pm Jul & Aug). Between two and nine guided tours leave per day, depending on the season.

Should wine be your achilles heel, **Caveau des Jacobins** (🗷03 84 37 14 58; 1 rue Hyacinthe Friant; ⊙10am-noon & 2.30-6.30pm Tue-Sat & 10am-noon Sun Jul & Aug, closed Sun rest of year) in a 13th-century Gothic convent – abandoned by the Jacobins (Dominicans) after the Revolution and nabbed by local winemakers in 1907 – makes for an unforgettably atmospheric place to sample the wines of Jura.

The **tourist office** (🗷03 84 37 24 21; www.poligny-tourisme.com; 20 place des Déportés; ⊙10am-12.30pm & 1.30-6pm Mon-Sat) has details on cheesemakers and wineries in the region, plus accommodation, dining and events.

ℹ Getting There & Away

Poligny's train station is about 15 minutes' walk northwest of the centre. There are regular trains to Besançon (€10, one hour, eight to 12 daily), Arbois (€5, 10 minutes, eight to 12 daily) and Lons-le-Saunier (€5, 20 minutes, at least hourly).

Baume-les-Messieurs

POP 194

Along the descent into Baume-les-Messieurs, the road corkscrews down into a basin of black cliffs. Mossy boulders, clifftop woodlands and waterfalls provide a spectacular natural backdrop to this village of honey-coloured stone, most famous for its Benedictine abbey. It's 18km southwest of Poligny.

◉ Sights

Grottes de Baume
CAVE

(Baume Caves; ☑ 03 84 48 23 02; www.baume-lesmessieurs.fr; adult/child €8.50/5.50; ☉ tours 10.30am-12.30pm & 1.30-5pm, 6pm or 7pm Apr-Sep) The 30-million-year-old Grottes de Baume are secreted away in the cliffs 2km south of Baume-les-Messieurs. On guided tours, visitors can weave their way along 2.5km of passageways, with stalactites dangling above and limestone crags looming from the shadows. Allow an hour for the tour, bring a sweater, and listen out for the flutter of resident bats.

If you plan on visiting the Abbaye Impériale too, note that a combined ticket costs €13/6 per adult/child.

Abbaye Impériale
MONASTERY

(Imperial Abbey; ☑ 03 84 44 99 28; www.baume-lesmessieurs.fr; adult/child €8/5; ☉ tours 10am-noon & 2-6pm Apr-Sep) Baume-les-Messieurs' abandoned Benedictine Abbaye Impériale has an exquisite polychrome Flemish altarpiece dating from the 16th century (the time when the abbey, which grew from a simple 7th-century monastic cell, was at its apogee).

Cascades des Tufs
WATERFALL

Near the Grottes de Baume, the Tufs waterfalls slosh dramatically over limestone boulders into the Dard River. There are picturesque walking trails nearby.

🛏 Sleeping & Eating

Le Grand Jardin
B&B €

(☑ 03 84 44 68 37; www.legrandjardin.fr; 6 place Guillaume de Poupet; s/d/tr/q incl breakfast from €64/70/92/112; ☉ closed Tue & Wed Sep-Jun; ℗) Opposite the abbey are three sunny, wood-floored rooms in a 16th-century house, backed by carefully tended gardens.

French and Franc-Comtoise dishes, such as rabbit stuffed with Morteau sausage and char (a type of fish) with absinthe, are prepared with a personal touch in the restaurant (menus €28 to €47).

ℹ Getting There & Away

It's easiest to reach Baume-les-Messieurs, 18km southwest of Poligny, with your own wheels.

Trains from Besançon reach Domblans-Voiteur, 6.5km north of Baume (€15, 1¼ hours, four daily). Irregular local buses link Voiteur (1.5km southeast of the train station) with Baume (€2, 25 minutes, four to five daily Monday to Friday); download schedules from Jurago (http://jurago.fr).

ROUTE PASTEUR

The **Route Pasteur** (www.terredelouispasteur.fr) meanders through picturesque wine and dairy country while tracking landmarks in the life of pioneering biochemist Louis Pasteur (1822–95), who developed the first rabies vaccine and, of course, pasteurisation. Driving the route end to end takes 90 minutes, but allow a day for museums, strolls and lunch.

Begin in the handsome medieval city of Dole, Pasteur's birthplace and former capital of Franche-Comté (50km west of Besançon along the A36). A scenic stroll along the Canal des Tanneurs brings you to Pasteur's childhood home, which now houses the **Musée Pasteur** (La Maison Natale de Pasteur; ☑ 03 84 72 20 61; www.amisdepasteur.fr; 43 rue Pasteur, Dole; adult/child €5.30/free; ☉ 2-6pm Feb-Apr, Oct & Nov, 9.30am-12.30pm & 2-6pm May-Sep; ♿), an atmospheric museum where you can see Pasteur's cot and first drawings, and play games based around life and work. Only 100m west you can ponder Pasteur's legacy over lunch at **Restaurant Grain de Sel** (☑ 03 84 71 97 36; www.restaurant-graindesel.fr; 67 rue Pasteur, Dole; lunch menus from €17, dinner menus €27-50; ☉ noon-1.30pm Thur-Tues, also 7-9pm Thur-Sat & Mon; ♿), whose ever-evolving menus make daring use of seasonal produce.

From here, the route wends southeast through Franche-Comté to Molain, and there are a few short detours worth your while: at Mont Poupet (851m), a walking trail marks where Pasteur performed experiments to prove that bacteria were air-borne. Marnoz is the village of origin of Pasteur's mother's family, and Aiglepierre is where he went to school.

The highlight (and a possible finishing point) is the major wine-producing town of Arbois, 12km shy of Molain, where Louis Pasteur's family settled in 1827. His laboratory and workshops can be seen at the **Maison de Louis Pasteur** (☑ 03 84 66 11 72; www.terredelouispasteur.fr; 83 rue de Courcelles; adult/child €6.80/4.20; ☉ 2-6pm Feb-Apr, Oct & Nov, 9.30am-12.30pm & 2-6pm May-Sep), still decorated with original 19th-century fixtures and fittings.

Belfort

POP 49,519

Unsung but uncommonly attractive, Belfort's historic centre is a checker-board of brick towers and ochre and rose-pink houses. Looming above the skyline astride the Vauban-built citadel is a monumental lion, the symbol of the town. This sphinx-like statue honours Belfort's 103 days of tenacious resistance to the Prussian siege of 1870–71, thanks to which it managed to remain French and escape being annexed to Prussia.

Belfort makes a convenient stopover on the way from Alsace to Burgundy or the Alps.

◉ Sights

★ Lion du Belfort
MONUMENT

(allée du Souvenir Français; ⊘ viewing platform 10am-12.30pm & 2-6pm) Belfort's icon is a monumental lion statue that sits astride the citadel, scowling down on the town. Created by Frédéric Auguste Bartholdi, best known for designing the Statue of Liberty, the red sandstone lion – almost 11m high – represents the spirit of the French army's resistance during the Siege of Belfort during the Franco-Prussian War (1870–71).

Musée de l'Aventure Peugeot
MUSEUM

(⧉03 81 99 42 03; www.museepeugeot.com; Carrefour de l'Europe, Sochaux; adult/child €9/5; ⊙10am-6pm) Nineteenth-century industry is paid homage in aptly vintage style, within this museum 14km south of Belfort. Before Peugeot was a household name, the company was a family business. Not just motor cars but pepper mills, corsets, razor blades, washing machines and more, all bore the Peugeot name. The museum, crammed with classic cars, may be brand HQ, but it's an enjoyable ride through history.

Reserve ahead for a weekday tour of the ultramodern Peugeot factory, one of Europe's largest car plants (adult/child €18/12, no children younger than 12).

★✪ Festivals & Events

★ Les Eurockéennes
MUSIC

(www.eurockeennes.fr; ⊙ Jul) A huge, three-day open-air alternative rock festival held on the first weekend in July. Its varied, international line-up of electronic, metal, pop, jazz and indie artists, plus camping, will set you back only €122.

🛏 Sleeping & Eating

Hôtel Vauban
HOTEL €

(⧉03 84 21 59 37; www.hotel-vauban.com; 4 rue du Magasin; s/d/tr €75/80/93; 🛜) Hosts Guy and Marie have turned Hôtel Vauban into a home away from home for travellers passing through. More than 200 whimsical oil paintings by local artists cover its walls. The mid-sized rooms are made bright and welcoming with flashes of lime green, wall decals and fuzzy rugs, and there's a lovely flower garden out back. Add breakfast for €9.

Grand Hôtel du Tonneau d'Or
HISTORIC HOTEL €€

(⧉03 84 58 57 56; www.tonneaudor.fr; 1 rue du Général Reiset; d €97-105, tr €133; 🅿 ❄ 🛜) A belle époque hotel right in the city centre, the grand (if gently faded) 'Golden Barrel' combines its original Corinthian columns, huge stained-glass windows and a sweeping central staircase with 52 large, modern rooms, some with a view of the Lion du Belfort.

Aux Trois Maillets
BRASSERIE €

(⧉03 84 28 06 01; http://auxtroismaillets.fr; 3 place d'Armes; mains €11-25; ⊙10am-3pm & 6-11pm Mon-Fri, 10am-11pm Sat & Sun; 🖉) More distinguished than the average brasserie, the 'Three Mallets' serves up exemplary omelettes, platters of Haut-Doubs ham and sausage, and steaks cooked to perfection.

ⓘ Information

Tourist Office (⧉03 84 55 90 90; www.belfort-tourisme.com; 2bis rue Clémenceau; ⊙9am-12.30pm & 2-5.30pm Tue-Fri, 10am-12.30pm & 2-5pm Sat, 2-5.30pm Sun & Mon summer, reduced hours rest of year)

ⓘ Getting There & Away

Belfort's **train station** (6 av Wilson) has direct links to Besançon (€5, 1¼ hours, every one or two hours), and direct and indirect TGVs and TERs to Paris-Gare de Lyon (from €50, 2½ to four hours, one or two every hour).

Belfort-Montbéliard TGV station, 10km southeast of the city centre, is a stop on the LGV Rhin-Rhône service linking Marseille (from €80, 4½ hours) with Mulhouse (from €7, 30 minutes), from where there are direct trains to Basel (Switzerland).

Parc Naturel Régional du Haut-Jura

Sprawled along the France-Switzerland border, just west of Lac Léman (Lake Geneva), the 1780-sq-km Haut-Jura Regional Park entices hikers and skiers to its pine-furred wilds. Dozens of villages, in the *départements* of Ain, Doubs and Jura, are dotted around the park. **Les Rousses** is best for winter sports (especially cross-country skiers), while **Lajoux** and **Mijoux** are good starting points for walking and mountain-biking.

Activity in Parc Naturel Régional du Haut-Jura hinges on summer rambles and winter sports; expect whisper-quiet villages during the shoulder seasons.

◉ Sights & Activities

Col de la Faucille (1323m; open year-round), a serpentine 13km east of Lajoux and 25km north of Geneva Airport, has incredible views across Lake Geneva to the snowy Alps beyond.

Maison du Parc du Haut-Jura MUSEUM
(☑ 03 84 34 12 30; www.parc-haut-jura.fr; 29 Qua le Village, Lajoux; adult/child €5/3; ⊙ 9am-1pm & 2-6pm Tue-Fri & Sun, 9am-1pm Sat Jul, Aug & school holidays, 2-6pm Tue-Fri rest of year; ⊞) Part-museum, part-tourist office, the Maison du Parc is an excellent place to learn about the Jura's flora and fauna, as well as browse old-fangled skis and get maps and advice on exploring the park. Listening posts share locals' stories and there are tactile exhibits themed around geology and the climate (great for kids). It's in Lajoux, 19km east of the park's largest town, St-Claude.

🛏 Sleeping & Eating

★ La Mainaz CHALET €€€
(☑ 04 50 41 31 10; www.la-mainaz.com; Col de la Faucille, Gex; d/q from €185/359; ⓟ⊛⊛) Every imaginable luxury is available at La Mainaz: chic chalet-style rooms with coffee machines, ultramodern anthracite-walled bathrooms, and a high-gastronomy restaurant (*menus* €100 to €145). But it's the panoramic views of Lake Geneva and Mont Blanc that make the soul soar. Skis affixed to the bedroom walls wrench you out of your reverie, reminding you to head out on the mountain.It's 20km south of Les Rousses (direction Geneva).

★ Les Louvières INTERNATIONAL €€
(☑ 03 84 42 09 24; http://leslouvieres.com; Pratz; 2-/3-course menus €41/49; ⊙ noon-2pm Wed-Sun, 7.30-9pm Wed-Sat; ⊅) ⊘ The 'wolf's lair' is both elegant and creatively modern, with gorgeous Jura views and delicious, *gastronomique* cuisine. Chef Philippe Vaufrey is fond of adding Thai spice, ginger and mango to accent local produce like burbot (a freshwater fish), beef and rich pâtés. Reserve ahead by phone. Find the lair between Pratz and Moirans, 1.8km along a one-lane road from the D470 (follow the signs).

ⓘ Information

Tourist Office (☑ 03 84 60 02 55; www.lesrousses.com; 495 rue Pasteur, Les Rousses; ⊙ 9am-noon & 2-6pm Mon-Sat mid-Jun–Aug, hours vary rest of year) The go-to source for information on culture, activities and accommodation in the park. Check the website for the complex, season-dependent opening hours. There are also summer-only tourist offices in **Bois-d'Amont** and **Lamoura** villages, and

---

DON'T MISS

RONCHAMP

Bringing to mind a ship's sail or a lighthouse summoning the faithful, modernist **Chapelle de Notre-Dame du Haut** (☑ 03 84 20 65 13; www.collinenotredameduhaut.com; 13 rue de la Chapelle, Ronchamp; adult/child €8/4; ⊙ 9am-6pm Apr & May, to 7pm Jun-Oct, 10am-5pm Nov-Mar; ⓟ) (1955) roosts hilltop above the small town of Ronchamp, 20km west of Belfort. Visionary architect Le Corbusier was initially reluctant to design the sanctuary; views of the Jura Mountains from this age-old Marian pilgrimage site changed his mind.

Stepping inside the concrete chapel instantly cuts off the outside world, while rough interior walls and sombre lighting make the stained-glass windows seem all the more jewel-like. Also on site are various outbuildings, including an oratory, pilgrim accommodation and a small **Peace Pyramid** honouring locals lost in WWII.

Regular direct trains connect Ronchamp with Belfort (€5, 20 minutes). Change trains in Belfort for links to/from Besançon.

HOT BOX, JÉSUS & CHRISTMAS TREE LIQUEUR

It's hot, soft and packed in a box. Vacherin du Haut Doubs is a cheese made with *lait cru* (unpasteurised milk), which derives its unique grassy taste from the spruce bark in which it's wrapped. Connoisseurs poke a hole in the soft-rinded cheese and sprinkle in some chopped garlic and white wine, before baking it for half an hour to create a *boîte chaude* (hot box), best served with boiled potatoes. Just as rich is *le jésus de Morteau* – a small, fat Morteau sausage, smoked with pinewood sawdust in a traditional *tuyé* (mountain hut).

Another standout of the Doubs *département* is *liqueur de sapin* (fir-tree liqueur) produced in Mouthe, 15km southwest of Métabief (and known as 'France's Siberia' for sub-zero temperatures including a record low of -36.7°C). *Glace au sirop de sapin* (fir-tree ice cream) also comes from this area. Sampling either is rather like ingesting a Christmas tree.

an office in **Prémanon**, open in summer and school holidays.

Maison du Parc du Haut-Jura (p558) A museum brimming with resources on the regional park.

ℹ️ Getting There & Away

Public transport is scant in the High Jura. The local bus network, **Jurago** (www.jurago. fr), connects Lons-le-Saunier with St-Claude. Inter-village services run between Bois-d'Amont and Les Rousses (line 702) and Mijoux, Lajoux and Lamoura (line 701). It's a flat €2 per journey. Note that these infrequent services are timed for school kids and shoppers.

In winter, some villages are connected by a free *navette* (shuttle bus) service; get timetables at the **tourist office**.

Métabief & Around

POP 1179 / ELEV 1000M

Fresh air and farmland characterise Métabief for much of the year. But a blanketing of winter snow transforms the area into a ski zone, while summer brings mountain bikers.

Winter and summer lifts take you almost to the top of Mont d'Or (1463m), the area's highest peak, where a fantastic 180-degree panorama stretches over the Swiss plain to Lake Geneva (Lac Léman) and all the way from the Matterhorn to Mont Blanc.

🔘 Sights & Activities

Station de Métabief   SKIING
(www.station-metabief.com; day pass adult/child €28/24; ⏱ late Dec–early Mar) Though Métabief is primarily known for its cross-country skiing – 214km in the wider Métabief-Mont d'Or area – its small downhill ski station has an even mix of green, blue and red runs among its 37km of pistes (and just a couple of blacks). The terrain stretches between 950m and 1430m, so the season is short, and good snow conditions are needed.

Parc Polaire   WILDLIFE RESERVE
(📞 03 81 69 20 20; www.parcpolaire.com; Cernois Veuillet et les Fo, Chaux-Neuve; adult/child €9.50/6.50; ⏱ 10am-5pm Sep-Jun, to 6.30pm Jul & Aug; 🚗) Get close to scampering chamois, Greenland huskies and wild horses on two-hour guided walking tours around this nature park in Chaux-Neuve, 25km southwest of Métabief. Fantastically caring staff ensure a safe distance – that is, fenced off from yaks, several feet from horned stags, but within belly-rubbing distance of husky dogs.

Château de Joux   CASTLE
(📞 03 81 69 47 95; www.chateaudejoux.com; La Cluse-et-Mijoux; adult/child €7.50/4.50; ⏱ 10am-noon & 2-5.30pm Apr-Jun & Sep-Nov, 10am-5.30pm Jul & Aug) Clinging to a limestone outcrop, Château de Joux, 10km north of Métabief, used to guard the route between Switzerland and France. Its foundations date to 1034, though medieval towers and Vauban-era walls have fortified it over subsequent centuries.

Audioguides and printed information are available in multiple languages. Guided tours, full of gripping tales, are in French but groups of 10 or more can book a foreign-language tour (reserve well in advance).

There's also an impressive 700-item collection of 18th- and 19th-century weapons (undergoing renovation when we passed through).

Less than 1km south of the castle along the main road is the **Auberge du Château de Joux** (📞 03 81 69 40 41; http://aubergedu-chateaujoux.wixsite.com/aubergechateaujoux; 127 Au Frambourg, La Cluse-et-Mijoux; s/d/tr/f from €70/80/100/120; 🅿🛜), a worthy stop for its modern, monochrome guest rooms and **restaurant**, open daily, whose great-value *menus* (from €14) grant access to a magnificent dessert buffet.

Auvergne

Best Places to Eat

➡ Le Flamboyant (p566)
➡ Le Sisisi (p564)
➡ La Golmotte (p576)
➡ Entrez les Artistes (p584)
➡ Le Drac (p578)

Best Places to Stay

➡ La Demeure d'Hortense (p568)
➡ 5 Chambres en Ville (p563)
➡ Ermitage St-Vincent (p584)
➡ Aux 500 Diables (p579)
➡ Le Clos Saint François (p580)
➡ Alta Terra (p577)

Why Go?

Explosive history slumbers underground in the Auvergne. This land-locked region was scorched by ancient volcanoes, which left behind chains of cinder cones and mirror lakes, overlooked by the Massif Central mountain range.

Two great green lungs of protected land define the Auvergne: westerly, mountainous Parc Naturel Régional des Volcans d'Auvergne, and to its east Parc Naturel Régional Livradois-Forez, its picturesque villages lost amid woodlands and farms. Cultural splendour is strung in between: retro-glamorous Vichy, colourful Pays d'Issoire, and dreamy villages along the Allier River. East of here, petrified lava plumes tower over pilgrimage town Le Puy-en-Velay, surely one of the most dramatic skylines in France.

After hikes to Romanesque churches (or ice-fishing, or cross-country skiing...) the Auvergne's treasured cuisine tastes all the better. Mirroring the region's rough charisma, meals are hearty and utterly free of pretension.

When to Go
Clermont-Ferrand

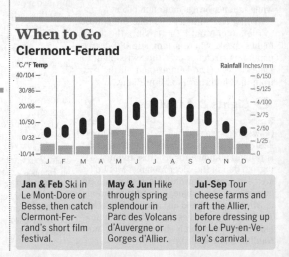

Jan & Feb Ski in Le Mont-Dore or Besse, then catch Clermont-Ferrand's short film festival.

May & Jun Hike through spring splendour in Parc des Volcans d'Auvergne or Gorges d'Allier.

Jul-Sep Tour cheese farms and raft the Allier, before dressing up for Le Puy-en-Velay's carnival.

Auvergne Highlights

1 Puy de Dôme (p571)
Surveying volcanic landscapes from the Panoramique train or on a guided crater hike.

2 Gorges de l'Allier (p584)
Road-tripping between crumbling stone villages.

3 Chapelle St-Michel d'Aiguilhe (p581) Climbing to a cave chapel for sublime Le Puy-en-Velay views.

4 Clermont-Ferrand (p562)
Getting lost in the old town's maze of lava-stone townhouses and Gothic spires.

5 Le Mont-Dore (p574)
Pounding pistes or hiking hills around this ski-and-spa town.

6 Musée de la Coutellerie (p580) Watching artisans work in France's knife-making capital.

7 Vichy (p566) Sliding into

thermal waters and exploring belle-époque buildings.

8 Cheese Trails (p569) Driving to dairy farms like St Nectaire and Ambert to buy cheese .

9 Pays d'Issoire (p570)
Marvelling at ornate churches and geological oddities.

10 La Chaise-Dieu (p580)
Craning your neck at Gothic splendour.

CLERMONT-FERRAND

POP 141,398 / ELEV 358M

In Clermont-Ferrand, the skyline is as moodily Gothic as the ambience is sunny and good-humoured. Dark volcanic stone gave the city its distinctive hue, layered into its 18th-century townhouses, dozens of fountains and the magnificent twin-turreted cathedral at its cobblestoned heart. As the Auvergne's largest city, Clermont-Ferrand is a hub not only for business but cuisine, with plenty of restaurants serving modernised *cuisine auvergnate*, and culture (in the form of fizzing art, film and live-music scenes). Beyond the winding lanes of its old town, the Auvergne's capital is an industrial powerhouse, home to the Michelin automotive empire.

This free-spirited city is a convenient base for trips to the slumbering volcanoes of the Parc Naturel Régional des Volcans d'Auvergne, as well as to neighbouring towns such as Thiers and Riom.

◉ Sights

★ **Cathédrale Notre Dame**   CATHEDRAL
(place de la Victoire; tower €2; ⊘ 7.30am-noon & 2-6pm Mon-Sat, 9.30am-noon & 3-7.30pm Sun) Clermont-Ferrand's skyline broods with

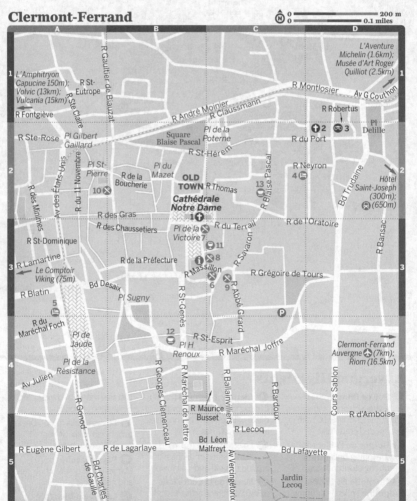

Clermont-Ferrand

volcanic stone, but its most impressive edifice is Cathédrale Notre-Dame, whose 108m twin spires pierce the sky like blackened spears. Its façade, with snarling gargoyles and Gothic tracery, was constructed between the 13th and 19th centuries. Within, lift your gaze to the 1527 **jacquemart clock**, with the faun-like god Mars and Time beating out the hours, and intricate **rose windows**, restored in the early 20th century.

In summer, climb **Tour de la Bayette** for 360-degree views.

★ **Musée d'Art Roger Quilliot**　　GALLERY
(📌04 43 76 25 25; place Louis-Deteix, Montferrand; adult/child €5/free; ⏰10am-6pm Tue-Fri, 10am-noon & 1-6pm Sat & Sun) Housed in an Ursuline convent 3km northeast of central Clermont, the city's premier gallery takes design cues from NYC's Guggenheim, its white spiral staircase linking various centuries of European art. Head upstairs for 17th-century European masterworks, or down for the medieval art annexe, packed with religious art relics dating back to the 7th century. Take tram A from place de Jaude.

Basilique Notre Dame du Port　　CHURCH
(rue du Port; ⏰8am-noon & 2-6pm Mon-Sat, 9am-noon & 3-8pm Sun) This architectural gem has all the key elements of a Romanesque church: semi-circular arches, a bulky silhouette and a broad headpiece. But its distinctive decorations set it apart, and

strengthened the case for granting it Unesco World Heritage status in 1998. Floral and geometric patterns of black volcanic stone are smoothly set in its peachy sandstone. Its exterior playfully combines neoclassical columns, terracotta tiles and medieval reliefs. The exterior is best admired from the **belvédère** (⏰2-5pm) FREE; follow signs across the street.

L'Aventure Michelin　　MUSEUM
(📌04 73 98 60 60; https://laventure.michelin.com; audioguide €2; ⏰10am-6pm Tue-Sun Sep-Dec & Feb-Jun, 10am-7pm daily Jul & Aug; ♿) Yes, it's a temple dedicated to the Auvergne's world-famous tyre brand, but the 'Michelin Adventure' is a crowd-pleasing attraction. Gallery spaces are decked out like 19th-century streets to evoke the early days of the Michelin brothers, whose designs would revolutionise transport worldwide. Some displays are somewhat niche (want to compare a 1919 cord tyre with the 1923 model?) but the museum answers interesting questions about map-making and car manufacture in colourful, interactive ways. Written explanations are in French and English.

🛏 Sleeping

Hôtel Saint-Joseph　　HOTEL €
(📌04 73 92 69 71; www.hotelsaintjoseph.fr; 10 rue de Maringues; s/d/tr/f €41/53/77/79; @ 🖥) The double-glazed rooms at this small hotel near the Friday morning St-Joseph market offer the best budget value in Clermont: they're smallish, and soundproofing could be better, but they're kept very clean.

★ **5 Chambres en Ville**　　B&B €€
(📌07 81 16 60 95; www.5-chambresenville.com; 8 rue Neyron; r €90-130; 🅿 ❄ 🖥) This classy B&B offers five pristine rooms, all uniquely styled and awash with pastel colours. Each unit has an ample bed dressed with high-quality linens and plenty of natural light; the more expensive pair on the top floor offer romantic features, like a recessed bath-tub. Our pick is 'Maud', with its dreamy view of Notre Dame du Port.

★ **Hôtel Le Lion**　　HOTEL €€
(📌04 73 17 60 80; www.hotel-le-lion-clermont.fr; 16 place de Jaude; s/d/ste from €83/93/113; ❄ 🖥) Punching well above its midrange price tag, Le Lion has a royal-blue colour scheme and offers royal treatment to match. Staff bend over backwards to make guests feel at home – easy

enough in the spacious, design-conscious rooms, whose excellent soundproofing is thoroughly tested by their location overlooking lively place de Jaude.

✖ Eating

Marché St-Pierre
MARKET

(Covered Market; www.marche-saint-pierre.com; place St-Pierre; ⊘7am-7pm Mon-Sat) The chunky building might bring to mind a jumble of Lego bricks, but this covered market is packed with fresh local produce and organic vegetables. Best buys include Auvergnat cheeses, the *pâte de fruits* (fruit jelly) pick 'n' mix, bottles of herbal liqueur, and jams from bilberry to quince (the latter is excellent with cheese).

★ Le Sisisi
BISTRO €

(✐04 73 14 04 28; www.lesisisi.com; 14 rue Massillon; lunch menus €15.50, mains €18-20; ⊘noon-1.30pm Tue-Fri, 8-10pm Tue-Sat) Just off cathedral square, this understated little restaurant has Clermont's most coveted tables. Le Sisisi's deft balance of sweet and savoury – spiced honey duck breast, ray fillet with vanilla potatoes – builds on local produce but gives ingredients new energy. Desserts also surprise the taste buds, like the mille-feuille with salted caramel and rum-sloshed mojito sundae.

Bistrot de la Butte
BISTRO, FRENCH €

(✐04 73 92 21 56; www.lebistrotdelabutte.fr; 2 rue Terrail; lunch menus from €13.50; ⊘10am-midnight Mon-Sat) Defying the myth that restaurants on a main square are often tourist traps, this exceptional bistro pulls seasonal produce into dishes that feel unrushed, despite fast, friendly service. Whether melt-in-the-mouth beef bourguignon or roast chicken with spiced risotto, you can't go wrong with their daily specials. Bag a window table

---

ⓘ CLERMONT PASS

Planning to visit L'Aventure Michelin (p563), take a ride on the Panoramique des Dômes (p573) and check out one of the town's art or natural history museums? Save money by grabbing the 72-hour **Clermont Pass** (€18.50), available at the tourist office, which grants access to all three, and throws in a guided city tour and local public transport (plus some other discounts).

---

upstairs and you'll have a VIP view of Clermont's cathedral.

La Table au Plafond
FRENCH, TAPAS €€

(✐09 83 01 57 15; www.latableauplafond.wixsite.com/contactez-nous; 7 place de la Victoire; tapas from €4.50, menus from €21; ⊘noon-2pm & 7-10pm Tue-Sat) Chefs here seem to have enormous fun designing tapas-style nibbles like 'cappuccino' (vegetable stew with a ham foam), mini burgers with *raclette* cheese, and Japanese *maki* with cabbage and pâté. Sharer plates of cheese and cured meats are beautifully assembled, too. And yes – look up to see a table on the ceiling, after which this free-spirited restaurant is named.

Avenue
FRENCH €€

(✐04 73 90 44 64; www.restaurant-avenue.fr; 10 rue Massillon; lunch menus €14-27, mains €19-25; ⊘noon-2pm & 7.30-9.30pm Tue-Sat) Avenue's ever-changing menu focuses on local market produce, lovingly plated with barely a pink peppercorn out of place. Original combinations range from cod on a bed of aubergine and dates to tuna and mango *ceviche*, with desserts as varied as honeyed Brie de Meaux cheese and passion fruit tart. There's always a well-priced *plat du jour* (€10) for weekday lunches.

L'Amphitryon Capucine
GASTRONOMY €€€

(✐04 73 31 38 39; www.amphitryoncapucine.com; 50 rue Fontgiève; lunch menus €21-25, dinner menus €33-85; ⊘noon-1.45pm & 7.30-9.30pm Tue-Sat) Wear your spiffiest suit for this restaurant *gastronomique*, 800m northwest of the cathedral. Its *menus* nod to Italian and Asian flavours (*conchiglie* pasta stuffed with slow-cooked lamb, coconut panna cotta) but its strength is classic French cuisine, such as *ris de veau* (lamb heart) and pork with Le Puy lentils.

🍷 Drinking & Nightlife

Le Bar d'O
WINE BAR

(✐04 73 91 43 14; 5 place de la Victoire; ⊘8am-10pm Mon & Tue, to midnight Wed-Sat) The wine connoisseur's choice. Bar d'O has an ambient soundtrack that, with each subsequent glass of Côtes du Ventoux, will lull you into a pleasant daze.

101 Club
CLUB

(www.oneoooneclub.com; 3 rue du Coche; ⊘midnight-5.30am Thu-Sat) This club near place de Jaude is hallowed ground for Clermont music fans: it was a new-wave and alt-rock

SPECIALIST COFFEE & TEA

Australian Coffee House (☑ 04 63 22 63 49; 35 rue St-Esprit; ☉ 9am-7pm Tue-Sat) We know, you're travelling *à la française*, but this Aussie-inspired coffee place pours the best brews in Clermont-Ferrand (from €2.80). The crowd's a mix of laptop-huggers, lunching office workers and artistic types, who arrive to idle over a flat white and homemade desserts, particularly the daily cheesecake. There are veg-based lunches, too (like goat's cheese salad and quinoa tabbouleh).

Les Goûters de Justine (11bis rue Blaise Pascal; ☉ noon-7pm Wed-Fri, 2.30-7pm Sat) The twinkly-eyed proprietress, presiding over her table of homemade cakes, is largely what makes this teahouse one of the most beloved spots in Clermont's old town. Arches of volcanic stone and a jumble of old-fashioned furniture establish a genteel, time-worn atmosphere in which to sip a *chocolat chaud à l'ancienne* (foamy old-style hot chocolate) while eavesdropping on local gossip.

haunt in the '80s, became a rock club in the '90s, and today hosts electro nights with funk, synth and techno played on the decks, often by resident DJ Syrob. Concerts charge entry (from €8) but club nights are often free.

ℹ Information

Tourist Office (☑ 04 73 98 65 00; www. clermont-fd.com; place de la Victoire; ☉ 9am-7pm Mon-Fri, from 10am Sat & Sun Jul & Aug, 9am-6pm Mon-Fri, 10am-1pm & 2-6pm Sat & Sun Sep-June; ☎) Opposite the cathedral, this efficient tourist office has city maps and ample free literature, plus suggestions on walking tours and local apps. Occasional art exhibitions liven the place up, too.

ℹ Getting There & Around

AIR

Clermont-Ferrand Auvergne Airport (www. clermont-aeroport.com; off D769, Aulnat) 7km east of the city centre by road. Domestic destinations include Paris, Nice and Ajaccio (Corsica); international flights go to Porto, Amsterdam and Marrakesh, among other destinations.

T2C (www.t2c.fr; single ticket/24hr pass/ carnet of 10 €1.50/4.90/13.50) bus 20 travels to/from the airport several times daily (€1.50, 30-40 minutes). A **taxi** (☑ 04 73 19 53 53; www.taxiradio-clermontferrand.fr) from the centre costs roughly €20.

BICYCLE

C.vélo (☑ 04 73 92 65 08; www.c-velo.fr; subscription per day/week €1/5 plus €1 per half-hour of use) Find more than 40 self-service bike-hire stations around town, including at the train station and place de Jaude.

TRAIN & BUS

Clermont-Ferrand is the region's main rail and long-distance bus hub, with ample direct trains several times daily to Lyon (€12-36, 2½-3¼ hours), Paris Bercy (€63-113, 3½-4½ hours), Volvic €4-90, 30 minutes), Vichy €11.10, 30 minutes) and elsewhere. Le Mont-Dore (€7.40-11.70, 1¾ hours) is served by SNCF bus.

AROUND CLERMONT-FERRAND

Riom

Between the brawny Chaîne des Puys and the wide-open Limagne plain lies Riom, a handsome medieval market town. Pilgrims have long processed into Riom to venerate the relics of locally-born Saint Amable, but the town owes its stately appearance to its time as an administrative capital. Riom steadily acquired *hôtels particuliers* during the Renaissance and into the 18th century, many of them fashioned from inky volcanic rock.

The modern town has sprawled to 50 times the size of the original medieval market town, but its historic core is the primary reason to pass through.

◉ Sights

★**Musée Mandet**   GALLERY
(☑ 04 73 38 18 53; www.musees-riom.com; 14 rue de l'Hôtel de Ville; adult/child €3/free, Wed free; ☉ 10am-noon & 2-5.30pm Tue-Sun, to 6pm Jul & Aug) Dating back to 1866, the Musée Mandet's splendid collection of art is arranged across two atmospheric *hôtels particuliers* (town houses). Exploring these beautifully restored

buildings is part of the charm, while the art on display is impressively broad in scope: antique Egyptian art, medieval religious works, Dutch masters and cutting-edge modern installations each have their own space.

Tour de l'Horloge
TOWER

(5 rue de l'Horloge; adult/child €1/free, Wed free; ◷10am-noon & 2-5pm Tue-Sun, to 6pm daily Jul & Aug) If you do one thing in Riom, it's likely to be climbing the 128 stairs of this Renaissance belfry to reach panoramic views of volcanic-stone houses and rolling farmland. Breaking up the ascent are a few simple displays on the town's history and development.

Basilique St-Amable
CHURCH

(rue St-Amable; ◷9am-6pm) This ornate Romanesque church dates back to the 13th century, though its Gothic flourishes (such as the bell tower) were added in the 19th century. The basilica honours Riom-born Saint Amable, said to have ousted demons from their unlucky human hosts and commanded powers over fire and snakes.

Musée Régional d'Auvergne
MUSEUM

(⌨04 73 38 17 31; www.musees-riom.com; 10bis rue Delille; adult/child €3/free; ◷guided tours 2.30pm & 4pm Tue-Sun, closed mid-Nov–mid-May) This 4000-object collection is a thorough primer on local traditions, with a focus on rural customs in the 19th century (expect plenty of antique farming implements and peasant garb). Guided tours only (in French).

🛏 Sleeping & Eating

Hôtel Pacifique
HOTEL €

(⌨04 73 38 15 65; www.hotel-lepacifique-riom.com; 52 av de Paris; s/d/tr/q €59/67/85/98; P🕏🗐) This welcoming three-star has bold, colourful rooms and cosy common areas decorated with velvet armchairs and relics of Auvergne's past.

L'Antre 2
FRENCH €

(⌨04 73 63 11 06; www.lantre2.fr; 15 rue du Marthuret; mains €14-18; ◷noon-2pm & 7-10pm Tue-Sun) This historic grocer's shop has been transformed into an understated eatery where salads, steaks and fish are beautifully turned out and always served with a regional twist. We especially like the plaice poached in St-Pourçain wine and seared steak covered in smooth and salty *bleu de Laqueuille* cheese.

★ Le Flamboyant
FRENCH €€

(⌨04 73 63 07 97; www.restaurant-le-flamboyant.com; 21bis rue de l'Horloge; mains €20-38, lunch/

dinner menus from €20/33; ◷noon-2pm Tue-Fri, 7-9.30pm Tue-Sat) Near Riom's clock tower, chef Hervé Klein accents local ingredients with flavours from India, Japan and beyond. Be surprised by seven courses selected by the chef (€100) or snap up a weekday lunch *menu*, featuring regional flavours like salmon in Cantal cheese or lamb in thyme jus. Save room for desserts like green tea and grapefruit tart or 'chocolate cube'.

ℹ Information

Tourist Office (⌨04 73 38 59 45; www.tourisme-riomlimagne.fr; 27 place de la Fédération; ◷9.30am-12.30pm & 2-5.30pm Mon-Sat, to 6.30pm Jul & Aug, 10am-12.30pm Sun, shorter hours Nov-Mar)

ℹ Getting There & Away

Riom is 14km north of Clermont-Ferrand and connected to the city by frequent trains (€3.60, 10 minutes). There are also direct trains from Vichy (€8.80, 20 minutes, at least hourly), 40km northeast. The train station, Riom-Châtel-Guyon, is 1km southeast of the tourist office.

Vichy

POP 25,068

Cradled in a bend in the Allier River, water has long defined the regal spa town of Vichy. During its belle-époque heyday, visitors flocked to sip its reputedly healing waters and plunge into thermal springs. Vichy has kept its reputation as a health retreat, helped along by the internationally known cosmetic brand named for the town, which prides itself on using local mineral water in its products.

Landscaped gardens that date to the 18th and 19th centuries, and art-deco buildings such as the opera (p567) and Église St-Blaise (p568) enhance the town's feeling of time-worn glamour. A seam of confectionery shops grew around the industry for the town's signature sweetie, the *pastille de Vichy*. So in the midst of a wellness capital, there is plenty of opportunity to snack between meals and double up on desserts – just what the doctor ordered.

⦿ Sights & Activities

Parc des Sources
GARDENS

Vichy's centrepiece is the huge Parc des Sources, the town's oldest park. Dating to the mid-18th century, the park is lined with chestnut and plane trees and encircled by

Vichy

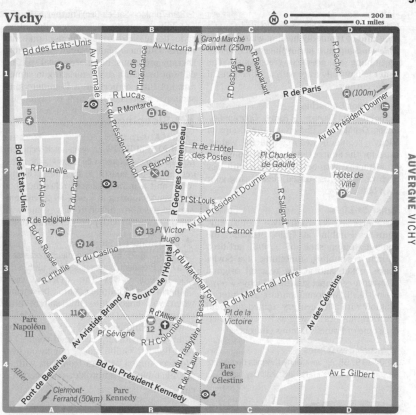

Vichy

⊙ Sights

⊛ Activities, Courses & Tours

⊜ Sleeping

⊗ Eating

⊜ Drinking & Nightlife

⊛ Entertainment

⊝ Shopping

700m of wrought-iron-canopied colonnade, added in the 19th century.

With **Les Célestins** (☎ 04 70 30 82 35; www.vichy-spa-hotel.com; 111 bd des États-Unis; half-day pass €40; ☺ 9am-8pm Mon-Sat, to 4pm Sun) and the Hall des Sources (p568) at its northern end, and the **opera** (☎ 04 70 30 50 30; www.opera-vichy.com; 1 rue du Casino) and casino (p569) at its southern end, the Parc des Sources is an ideal starting point to explore Vichy's spa history and belle-époque architecture.

Hall des Sources

SPRING

(Parc des Sources; ⊙ 6.15am-7pm) FREE Chug a mouthful of reputedly healing waters at the Hall des Sources, a late-19th-century atrium resembling an art-deco greenhouse. The water is naturally fizzy with a saline tang, if you're curious.

Source des Célestins

SPRING

(bd du Président Kennedy; ⊙ 8am-8.30pm Apr-Sep, to 6pm Oct-Mar) FREE For unlimited sips of Vichy's reputedly healing mineral waters, head for the Source des Célestins, housed in an attractive 19th-century atrium with lacy archways and rose-tinted glass. Bring your own bottle.

Église St-Blaise

CHURCH

(rue d'Allier; ⊙ 8am-7pm) Two contrasting churches combine at Église St-Blaise: the concrete outer shell of a 1931 art-deco church, resembling something of a Soviet space rocket, and at the rear an original 17th-century chapel guarding Vichy's *Vierge noire* (black Madonna statue). The interior is aglow with 20th-century stained glass and bronzed mosaics, as well as frescoes depicting some of France's famous churches.

Thermes des Dômes

SPA

(☑ 04 70 97 39 59; www.vichy-thermes-domes-hotel.com; 132 bd des États-Unis; half-day pass €22; ⊙ 8am-7pm Mon-Sat Feb-Dec) The thermal 'cures' unfolding beneath this grand Byzantine-style dome tend to be intense, multiday affairs with meal plans, exercise and hydrotherapy programs. But more casual spa fans can opt for half a day luxuriating in saunas and hot tubs, or perhaps a 15-minute massage treatment (€55).

🛏 Sleeping

Citotel Arverna

HOTEL €

(☑ 04 70 31 31 19; www.arverna-hotels-vichy.com; 12 rue Desbrest; d/f from €64/130; P ✴ ☎) This central hotel boasts a charming lounge room and a mini-library to relax in, when you aren't snoozing in one of its 23 contemporary, pastel-drenched rooms, some with balconies and all with plenty of natural light.

★ La Demeure d'Hortense

B&B €€

(☑ 04 70 96 73 66; www.demeure-hortense.fr; 62 av du Président Doumer; s/d/ste €105/€115-135/€145-150; ✴ ☎) The welcome from Catherine and Philippe couldn't be warmer when you check into this stately 19th-century mansion with plenty of original features. Wind your way up the marble stairs to individually decorated rooms like light-flooded 'Guilin' and – our favourite – Morocco-tinged 'Ménara' (complete with an Islamic table and embroidered slippers).

DON'T MISS

VICHY'S SWEET TREATS

Sweet-toothed travellers may well find Vichy a dream destination. What began with *pastilles de Vichy*, hard candies originally devised to settle the stomach, grew into a confectionery trade that has allowed *chocolateries*, patisseries and sweet boutiques to bloom across Vichy.

The town's signature sweeties, octagonal *pastilles de Vichy*, date to 1825. They were originally made with bicarbonate of soda to soothe digestive troubles. Hype grew when Eugénie, wife of Napoléon III, developed a passion for these moreish sweets. Salts extracted from Vichy mineral water were soon included in the recipe, mixed with sugar and flavoured with mint, lemon or aniseed, and *pastilles* remain firmly established as an after-dinner refresher across the Auvergne.

In their traditional blue-checked tins, *pastilles* are a favourite gift or souvenir, sold by numerous confectioners. But don't limit yourself: there are also *carreaux de Vichy*, layers of almond paste and fruit jelly pressed into colourful cubes. **Vichy-Prunelle** (☑ 04 70 98 20 02; www.vichy-prunelle.com; 36 rue Montaret; ⊙ 9am-noon & 2-7pm Mon-Sat, 10am-noon & 2.30-6.30pm Sun) sells a mouth-watering assortment, along with house speciality *délices de prunelle*, squares of pistachio marzipan and candied fruit, plus homemade *guimauves* (marshmallows) in flavours from blackcurrant to vanilla. Another sugary trove is **Aux Marocains** (☑ 04 70 98 30 33; www.auxmarocains.com; 33 rue Georges Clemenceau; ⊙ 3-7pm Mon, 9.45am-12.15pm & 2.30-7pm Tue-Sat, 10.30am-12.15pm & 3-7pm Sun), a 19th-century boutique whose shelves are heavy with *marrons glacés* (candied chestnuts), nougat and fruit-studded *pâte d'amande* (marzipan).

Aletti Palace Hôtel
HOTEL €€€

(☑ 04 70 30 20 20; www.hotel-aletti.fr; 3 place Joseph Aletti; s/d/ste from €130/150/230; ❋ ☎ ☜) Time travel to a more glamorous era at this luxurious hotel by the Parc des Sources (p566). Get comfy in the downstairs bar, where stained-glass windows cast a soft light over sleek leather sofas, or plunge into the heated outdoor pool (summer only). Either way, you'll retreat to romantic lodgings with marbled bathrooms, warm maroon decor and plenty of space.

✖ Eating

Grand Marché Couvert
MARKET €

(Covered Market; ☑ 04 70 30 55 75; www.legrandmarchecouvert-vichy.fr; place PV Léger; ⊙ 7am-1pm Tue-Sun, 4-7pm Fri & Sat) Bump elbows with hungry locals at this food market 500m northwest of Vichy's train station. There are no touristy souvenirs inside this 6800-sq-m market hall, only stalls piled high with fruit, veg, meat and wonderfully whiffy local cheeses.

L'Hippocampe
SEAFOOD €€

(☑ 04 70 97 68 37; www.restaurant-hippocampe.com; 3 bd de Russie; mains €25, lunch/dinner menus from €22/32; ⊙ noon-2pm Wed-Sun, 7.30-9.30pm Tue-Sat) Thoughtfully dressed and perfectly cooked, the seafood at L'Hippocampe is fit for Neptune's table. The weekday lunch *menu* is good value, though you won't regret splashing out on oysters with candied ginger, lobster roasted in olive butter or sole *meunière*. Desserts like Grand Marnier soufflé and pear-chocolate millefeuille are similarly refined.

★ La Table d'Antoine
GASTRONOMY €€€

(☑ 04 70 98 99 71; www.latabledantoine.com; 8 rue Burnol; mains €27-34, lunch menus €26.90, dinner menus €39.90-69.90; ⊙ 12.15-1pm Tue-Sun, 7.30-8.45pm Tue, Wed, Fri & Sat) Abstract portraits and high-backed chairs create a boutique feel at this temple to French fine dining. Choose from flavour pairings like char in calamondin sauce or beef with Cantal-drenched onions. Desserts are just as inventive, like lime-honey crêpe cake or spiced fruit tart with a sorbet of St-Pourçain wine. Tasting *menus* are worth every cent. Reserve well ahead.

☕ Drinking & Nightlife

★ Keck's Nature Shop
CAFE

(☑ 04 70 59 32 19; www.keckscafe.com; cnr rue d'Allier & rue Porte de France; ⊙ 9.30am-

---

AUVERGNE'S CHEESE TRAILS

Among countless dairy delights produced in the Auvergne's fragrant pastures are five Appellation d'Origine Protégée (AOP) cheeses. From mild to intense, these are: semi-hard, cheddar-like Cantal and nutty Salers; rich, semi-soft St-Nectaire; smooth blue cheese Fourme d'Ambert; and powerful Bleu d'Auvergne.

The **Routes des Fromages** (www.fromages-aop-auvergne.com) plot out almost 40 regional cheese producers. You can tramp across fields to buy wedges of cheese at farmhouse dairies, bring your kids to watch early-morning milkings, or join a tasting tour. The Auvergne's cheese trails are best explored during the summer, when many producers open their doors to tourists. The website has maps, complete with contact details for all dairies. The most classic, tourist-friendly cheese experiences are in Ambert and St-Nectaire.

8.30pm Tue & Wed, to 9pm Thu, Sat & Sun, to 10pm Fri) This Canadian-run cafe draws inspiration from far and wide in its hot chocolate menu. The 'Frambiosuisse', raspberry-tinged hot chocolate served with Gruyère cheese, is as filling as it sounds, though the orange-scented dark chocolate 'Russe', with a side of Russian biscuits, comes a close second. Coffees, teas and deli goods on sale, too.

☆ Entertainment

Casino du Grand Café
CASINO

(☑ cafe 04 70 97 16 45; www.casinovichygrandcafe.com; 7 rue du Casino; ⊙ 10am-3am, gambling from 8pm) Vichy's original casino, opened in 1865, was one of the first in France. Today punters can play blackjack, roulette or feed coin-slot machines in the annex of the now-closed original.

ℹ Information

Tourist office (☑ 0.15 per min 08 25 77 10 10; www.vichy-tourisme.com; 19 rue du Parc; ⊙ 9.30am-7pm Mon-Sat, 10am-noon & 2.30-7pm Sun Jul & Aug, 9.30am-noon & 1.30-6.30pm Mon-Sat, 3-6pm Sun Apr-Jun & Sep, 9.30am-noon & 1.30-6pm Mon-Sat Jan-Mar & Oct-Dec) Pick up a map at the tourist office next to the Parc des Sources for a self-guided tour of belle-époque architecture.

ⓘ Getting There & Away

Destinations reached by direct train include the following.

Clermont-Ferrand €11.10, 35 min, half-hourly

Lyon Part-Dieu €29.30, 2 hours, 5-8 per day

Paris Gare de Bercy €54, 3-4 hours, up to 7 per day

Riom €8.70, 25 min, every one or two hours

There are more Paris services if you change trains in Lyon Part Dieu.

Pays d'Issoire

The Pays d'Issoire is arguably the most colourful strip of the Auvergne, nestled between the green expanses of two regional natural parks. There's an almost Mediterranean feel to the region's coral-roofed villages and vine-cloaked meadows.

At its heart is main town Issoire, home to the Auvergne's most flamboyantly decorated Romanesque church. Equally dazzling is the Vallée des Saints, a geological marvel of ochre-and-red fairy chimneys. Fortified villages such as Montpeyroux and Usson are worthwhile detours as much for their medieval ramparts as their 360-degree views across rolling hills.

⊙ Sights & Activities

Abbatiale St-Austremoine   CHURCH

(place St-Paul, Issoire; ⊙8am-8pm) Issoire is the proud home of the Auvergne's most extravagantly decorated Romanesque church. The exterior of this 12th-century edifice is festooned with geometric patterns in white-and-black lava stone, dappled across great ornamental arches. Twelve signs of the zodiac in stone relief have been beautifully restored. Inside, blood-red columns are crowned with depictions from Christ's life, from the Last Supper to the Resurrection, all painted in vivid colour.

Usson   VILLAGE

Designed as an impregnable citadel, the village of Usson roosts atop a volcanic plume, 8km east of Issoire. The daughter of Henry II and Catherine de Médici, Marguerite de Valois (known as 'la reine Margot'), was imprisoned here by her brother, but after her release she remained in Usson to restore its castle and assemble a court of advisers. The fortified stone-and-slate village still feels frozen in time, and enjoys a peerless panorama of the Chaîne des Puys.

Vallée des Saints   WALKING

(Boudes) Natural stone chimneys frame this 6km walking circuit in the village of Boudes, a 17km drive southwest of Issoire. Rock formations ranging from red-clay cliffs to 30m-high turrets bring to mind a US national park. Allow at least 1½ hours for the walk. The tourist office (p571) in Issoire can supply information on the trail and other walks nearby.

Donjon de Montpeyroux   HISTORIC BUILDING

(☑04 73 96 62 68; www.montpeyroux63.com; rue de la Grande Charreyre, Montpeyroux; adult/child €2.50/free; ⊙10am-12.30pm & 2-7pm Tue-Sun May-Aug, shorter hours Sep, 2-5.30pm Tue-Sun Oct-early Nov & Apr) This castle keep is the stocky centrepiece of the medieval walled town of Montpeyroux, 12km north of Issoire. Montpeyroux's fortifications were built as a place to retreat during fires and attacks. Visitors can climb up the 33m-high tower, built in the 12th century, for a vantage point over the village's labyrinth of sandstone lanes, and across the Chaîne des Puys and Monts du Cantal.

🛏 Sleeping & Eating

Le Diapason   BOUTIQUE HOTEL €€

(☑04 73 71 71 71; www.lediapason.fr; rue du plateau de la Chaux, Le Broc; s/d from €115/130; ⊙Tue-Sat Jun-Sep; P✻🞋) Five kilometres south of Issoire, this luxurious seasonal retreat has an intriguing silhouette: the ultra-modern building has an industrial iron exterior that towers above the coral rooftops of Le Broc village. Its six light-filled rooms are decked out with wood panels, sleek white furnishings and marbled bathrooms.

Equally impressive is the modern French restaurant (lunch/dinner from €28/35) serving *mer* (sea) and *terre* (land) *menus* a world away from the Auvergne's usual farmhouse cuisine: try char with smoked salsify or goose encrusted with Medjool dates and quinoa.

L'Air 2 Rien   FRENCH €€

(☑04 73 71 16 21; www.facebook.com/LAir2Rien. fr; 3 rue Notre Dame du Ponteil, Issoire; mains €18-24; ⊙noon-2pm & 7-10pm Tue-Sat) Size isn't everything, and this pocked-sized restaurant ably balances Auvergne specialities (perfectly seasoned steaks, local cheese platters) with inspiration from around France (like Provence-style beef *tartare* and scallops dressed with hazelnut vinaigrette). Just as beautifully plated are L'Air 2 Rien's desserts: homemade *moelleux du chocolat* with cream of pistachio is definitely worth the wait.

ℹ Information

Tourist Office (☑ 04 73 89 15 90; www.
issoire-tourisme.com; 9 place St-Paul; ⊙9am-
12.30pm & 2-6pm, longer hours in Jul & Aug)

ℹ Getting There & Away

Direct trains serve Issoire from Clermont-
Ferrand (€8, 40 minutes, every one to two
hours) and Le Puy-en-Velay (€20.20, 1¾ hours,
three daily, with more trains via Arvant).

PARC NATUREL RÉGIONAL DES VOLCANS D'AUVERGNE

The Auvergne's most exhilarating views
are among the volcanic cones, snow-lashed
peaks and crater lakes of its Parc Naturel
Régional des Volcans (www.parcdesvolcans.
fr). One of France's largest regional natural parks at 3897 sq km, this photogenic
section of the Massif Central mountains is
a geological jigsaw of granite plateaus and
glacier-sculpted valleys, puckered by dozens
of sleeping volcanoes.

Outdoor exploration is the *parc*'s main
pursuit, with countless places to hike, bike
and (snowfall permitting) ski. Quick to
the rescue of stiff leg muscles are thermal
spas, some with Roman origins. Farm-style
cooking is another draw, especially when
St-Nectaire and Salers cheeses are involved.

Regional history is also worthy of note.
Fortifications such as Volvic's **Château de
Tournoël** (☑ 04 73 33 53 06; www.tournoel.com;
rue des Remparts; adult/child €8/3; ⊙10.30am-
12.30pm & 2-6pm Jul & Aug) and epic Château
de Murol (p578) bear witness to a battle-torn
medieval past, while palatial spas and townhouses in Le Mont-Dore and La Bourboule
were left behind by the 19th century's afflu-
ent leisure class.

Volvic

POP 4418

Volvic is caught between its world-famous
mineral water brand and an old-timey town
centre, packed with regal grey buildings
and fountains of volcanic stone. Beyond the
water-bottling plant and its glossy **visitors
centre** (☑ 04 73 64 51 24; www.espaceinfo.volvic.
tr; rue des Sources; ⊙10am-12.15pm & 2-6pm
Mon-Fri, 2.30-6pm Sat & Sun Apr-Sep, to 6.30pm
Jul & Aug, afternoons only Oct) **FREE**, Volvic is
overlooked by medieval fortress Château de
Tournoël, a stopping point along the scenic
GR441 walking trail. A number of excellent
walks spider out from this peaceful town,
but there's little to detain you beyond a day.

Volvic's **tourist office** (☑ 04 73 33 58 73;
www.volvic-tourisme.com; place de l'Église; ⊙9am-
noon & 1.30-5pm Tue-Sat) faces the village's
central square, place de l'Église. Trains reach
Volvic station (3km west of the centre) from
Clermont-Ferrand (€4.90, 30 minutes, four to
six daily).

Puy de Dôme

Puy de Dôme (1465m) is the best-known of
the Auvergne's dormant volcanoes. Part of the
Unesco-listed Chaîne des Puys, a 40km string
of lava domes now carpeted in green, Puy de
Dôme is the focal point for hikes, scenic train
rides and paragliding. Nearby, a volcano-
themed amusement park and excavated volcanic sight amp up the geological wonder.

DON'T MISS

UNESCO WORLD HERITAGE: CHAINE DES PUYS

Gazing at the *parc naturel*'s still lakes and wildflower meadows, it's hard to imagine that
this pastoral part of the Auvergne was forged by volcanic activity. In the northernmost
part of the region, the 80-odd lava domes and cinder cones of the **Chaîne des Puys** – a
Unesco World Heritage site since 2018 – were created by volcanic blasts that finally died
down 10,000 years ago. But the Chaîne des Puys' volcanic hills are young whippersnap-
pers compared to the craggy **Massif du Sancy**, formed nearly five million years ago,
and the **Monts du Cantal** further south, formed by a nine-million-year-old volcano that
collapsed inwards.

There hasn't been a rumble in seven millennia, but traces of the region's explosive
beginnings are everywhere, from the geothermal springs that bubble into the spas of La
Bourboule and Le Mont-Dore, to the black stone that gives a distinctively Auvergnat air
to architecture in Clermont-Ferrand, Salers and beyond.

A relative youngster (in geological terms, at least) at 10,000 years old, Puy de Dôme has long acted as a spiritual lightning rod. The remains of a Gallo-Roman temple, rediscovered in 1873, stand on the summit (now crowned with a TV antenna). Whether you visit in sunshine or midwinter, when the hills are kissed by snow, you are guaranteed one of France's prettiest panoramas.

◉ Sights & Activities

★ Panoramique des Dômes   RAIL
(📞 04 73 87 43 05; www.panoramiquedesdomes.fr; Orcines; adult/child one-way €11.60/6.80, return €14.30/8.30; ⊙9am-7pm Apr-Jun & Sep, to 9pm Jul & Aug, 10am-5pm Wed-Sun Oct-Mar) Rattling up a railway track astride Puy de Dôme, this pleasure train (inaugurated in 1907) hoists visitors to the 1465m summit after a leisurely 15-minute journey. Views are sublime, especially on clear days: the pouting cinder cones of the Chaîne des Puys melt into the verdant Limagne plain. Departures are two or three times per hour (or hourly in winter).

Temple de Mercure   RUIN, MUSEUM
(📞 04 73 62 21 46; ⊙mid-Mar–Dec) FREE An enigmatic imprint of the distant past stands atop the summit of Puy de Dôme: a 1st-century Gallo-Roman temple undergoing gradual restoration. Constructed here to allow it to be visible all the way from Augustonemetum (now Clermont-Ferrand), the temple lay in ruins until its rediscovery in the 19th century. There's a visitors centre that explains the region's Roman history.

★ Volcan de Lemptégy   VOLCANO
(📞 04 73 62 23 25; www.auvergne-volcan.com; off D941; adult/child on foot €11.50/9.50, by train €15.70/12.70; ⊙9.30am-6pm Apr-Sep, longer hours Jul & Aug, shorter hours Oct) Feel the Auvergne's smouldering terrain beneath your feet at this mined volcanic site, across the main road from amusement park Vulcania (p573). In summer, at weekends and during school holidays, a motorised 'train' chugs for 3km along the scorched scarlet soil, weaving past boulders flung out of the belly of this ancient volcano. Year-round, the site is visitable on guided walks. Lemptégy's geological forces are further explained through a short 'dynamic 3D' film (spoiler: expect bumps and jolts). Allow 2¾ hours.

Vulcania   AMUSEMENT PARK
(📞 04 73 19 70 00; www.vulcania.com; rte de Mazayes, off D941, St-Ours-les Roches; adult/child €28/19.50; ⊙10am-6pm Apr–early Nov, closed Mon & Tue Apr & Sep-Nov; 🚻) The Auvergne's long-extinct volcanoes are brought back to life in spectacular style at Vulcania theme park, 15km west of Clermont on the D941. Combining an educational museum with thrills and spills, highlights include 12-minute 'dynamic 3D' film *Awakening of the Auvergne Giants*, depicting volcanic eruptions complete with air blasts and water spray, a Tornado Alley audiovisual, and the Cité des Enfants (Kids' City), with activities specially geared for three- to seven-year-olds.

❶ Getting There & Away

It's a 13km drive west from Clermont-Ferrand to the Puy de Dôme (follow signs for Orcines).

In July and August (and by 48-hour advance reservation in April, May and late October), a **shuttle bus** (📞 06 85 92 04 45; www.puy-de-dome.fr; €3) runs twice daily between Clermont-Ferrand's SNCF station via place de Jaude to the Panoramique train station and Vulcania.

---

❶ HIKERS' NOTES

Some walkers skip the railway and hike to the top of Puy de Dôme along the **Chemin des Muletiers**. The steep 6km path, believed to have once been trodden by pilgrims heading to the Temple de Mercure (p573), takes roughly 1½ hours if you start from the lower Panoramique station, or half that if you begin at the **Col de Ceyssat Parking** (D68) FREE.

Orcines has bakeries and a convenience store, if you need picnic supplies. Otherwise, the classiest spot to eat is **1911 Restaurant** (📞 04 73 87 43 02; menus €35-45; ⊙noon-2pm late-Mar–Oct, noon-2pm Wed-Sun Nov & Dec, plus 7-9pm Jul & Aug), on the Puy de Dôme summit..

For bird's-eye views, consider booking a hang-gliding adventure with **Aero Parapente** (📞 06 61 24 11 45; www.aeroparapente.fr; one-/two-flight package €80/150; ⊙Feb-Oct).

Orcival

POP 234 / ELEV 870M

Snoozing soundly between Puy de Dôme and Le Mont-Dore, dinky Orcival is best known for its formidable 12th-century **Basilique Notre-Dame** (place de la Basilique; ⊙8.30am-6pm Oct-Mar, to 7.30pm Apr-Sep). Relics of the Virgin Mary drew pilgrims to Orcival centuries before the basilica was built but it was a 12th-century icon, the Virgin of Orcival, that cemented the village's status as a pilgrimage site. The statue continues to be the focus of veneration each Ascension Day.

For hikers, this romantic village of stone houses is an access point to verdant (and often precipitous) walking trails. For an intimate encounter with the landscape, hook up with Christophe and Isabelle at **Aluna Voyages** (☑06 74 28 70 98; www.aluna-voyages. com; ☷) to forage for berries, edible flowers and mushrooms, then whip up a meal with your findings (one/three days from €45/375, April to October).

Orcival **tourist office** (☑04 73 65 89 77; www.auvergnevolcansancy.com; place de la Basilique; ⊙9am-noon & 2-6pm Mon-Sat May-Sep, 10am-12.30pm & 2-5pm Sun Jul & Aug, shorter hours rest of year; ☷) is opposite the basilica. The town is not served by public transport so you'll need your own wheels.

Col de Guéry

Lost in the mists above spa-and-ski towns Le Mont-Dore and La Bourboule is the Col de Guéry. If you can manage the spine-chilling serpentine route to this mountain pass – winter tyres essential if there's snow – you'll have pristine hiking and snowshoeing territory at your feet. Above the pass gleams Lac de Guéry, the highest lake in the Auvergne at 1268m, filled with trout and perch. This is the only lake in France that allows *pêche blanche* (ice-fishing).

Even if you aren't sticking around, it's worth stopping to admire the **Roches Tuilière et Sanadoire** (off D983; ℙ) – slumbering volcanoes, sculpted by glacial movement millennia ago. It's an easy pull-over if you're driving between Le Mont-Dore and Orcival.

Should you be tempted to stay, **Auberge du Lac de Guéry** (☑04 73 65 02 76; www. auberge-lac-guery.fr; d/f/ste from €85/135/145; ⊙Feb–mid-Oct; ℙ☷) on the lake's southern edge is comfortable inn with cosy if una-dorned rooms and unbeatable access to hiking, fishing and cross-country skiing.

Le Mont-Dore

POP 1328 / ELEV 1050M

The Auvergne's most elegant winter-sports base has a glint of 19th-century glamour among its fondue restaurants and gear-hire shops. Nestled in a narrow valley 44km southwest of Clermont-Ferrand, and 4km north of Puy de Sancy (1886m), the town originally rose to prominence as a spa resort. Its bedomed Thermes (p574) (bathhouses) continue to draw *curistes*, who partake of the reputedly healing mountain waters.

Hiking trails, some reached by nerve-jangling funicular and cable-car rides, thread the surrounding mountains. Winter snow conditions can be hit or miss, but for a mix of fresh air and cultural enrichment, you could do worse than joining the loyal throng of skiers who come here.

◉ Sights & Activities

Thermes du Mont-Dore   HISTORIC BUILDING
(☑04 73 65 05 10; lemontdore@chainethermale. fr; 1 place du Panthéon; ⊙6.30am-12.30pm & 2-5.30pm Mon-Fri, 6.30am-12.30pm Sat mid-Apr-early Nov) Le Mont-Dore's graceful 19th-century buildings grew from its centuries-old spa heritage, which long pre-dates its reputation as a ski hub. See the source of its hot springs on a 45-minute guided tour of the grand bathhouses (French only; adult/child €3.50/2.50; 2pm, 3pm and 4pm Monday to Friday). You'll admire neo-Byzantine architecture, including gold-leaf-dappled tilework, be shown 'treatment rooms' (the vapours are thought to cure respiratory ailments), and take a sip of the water – brace yourself for a warmish, metallic-flavoured mouthful.

Funiculaire du Capucin   FUNICULAR
(☑04 73 65 01 25; rue René Cassin; one way/return adult €4.70/6.20, child €3.80/4.70; ⊙10am-12.10pm & 2-5.40pm Wed-Sun May-early Oct, to 6.40pm daily Jul & Aug) Built in 1898, France's oldest funicular railway (and listed historic monument) sets off every 20 minutes, crawling at 1m per second to the plateau of Les Capucins (1245m). Various trails lead off the plateau, including an easy 2km walk to volcanic dome Pic du Capucin (1468m), following part of the long-distance GR30, and a steep 1km downhill back to town.

Téléphérique du Sancy CABLE CAR
(one-way/return adult €7.50/9.90, child €5.60/7.40; ⊙9am-noon & 1.30-5pm late Dec-Jun & early–mid-Sep, 9am-6pm Jul & Aug) From this cable car's upper station (1780m), it's a short climb along a maintained trail and staircase to Puy de Sancy's snowcapped summit, where fabulous views unfold over the northern peaks and the Monts du Cantal.

🛏 Sleeping

**Camping Domaine de
la Grande Cascade** CAMPGROUND €
(⏰04 73 65 06 23; www.camping-grandecascade.com; rte de Besse; 2-person site €14.10, per additional person €4.30; ⊙late May-late Sep; 🐾) This is a stunning spot to pitch a tent, just 15 minutes' walk from a 30m waterfall, with marvellous views of the mountains. At 1250m elevation, this campground is prone to chilly conditions but you can always warm up in the jacuzzi (€2). Reach the campground by taking D36 south out of Le Mont-Dore for 3km. There's wi-fi at reception.

**Auberge de Jeunesse
HI Le Mont-Dore** HOSTEL €
(⏰04 73 65 03 53; www.hifrance.org; 100 rte du Sancy; per person incl breakfast/half-board/full board €20.40/33/45.60; ⊙mid-Dec–mid-Nov; 🐾) Usually jammed with skiers and hikers, this excellent hostel is right below the Puy de Sancy cable car, 3.5km south of town. Facilities include squeaky-clean two- to six-bed dorms with en-suite bathrooms, a guest kitchen and laundry, bike sheds, ski and snowshoe rentals, and an in-house bar. Book way ahead in winter, especially for one of the seven double rooms.

★ **Grand Hôtel** HOTEL €
(⏰04 73 65 02 64; www.hotel-mont-dore.com; 2 rue Meynadier; d €68-72, tr/ste €90, q €100; ⊙mid-Dec–mid-Nov; 🅿🐾) The romantic ambience of this turreted 1850 hotel is amply delivered within its rooms, which have a sharp modern design and comfortable wrought-iron beds. The best have balconies looking towards the mountains. Meanwhile, time spent in the spa (€6) is the perfect balm for calf muscles that ache from exertion up in the mountains.

SKING IN LE MONT-DORE

Le Mont-Dore isn't as high, nor as snow-sure, as similar-sized resorts in the Alps, but there are some excellent skiing opportunities such as Station du Mont-Dore (p575). You can also reach the ski fields of Super-Besse (p575) from here (weather and lifts permitting).

Other popular bases include spa town La Bourboule, 7km west of Le Mont-Dore, and tiny Besse-et-Saint-Anastaise, 30km southwest, with a lost-in-time old town of Renaissance and Gothic buildings and a pocket-sized ski museum brimming with vintage ski gear, ice skates, snowshoes and wintry miscellany across three centuries.

Station du Mont-Dore (www.sancy.com/commune/mont-dore; day pass adult/child €32.50/22.80; ⊙9am-5pm mid-Dec–mid-Apr) Four kilometres above Le Mont-Dore extend 84km of downhill ski runs, with terrain to suit beginners through to intermediate skiers (hardened snow-heads venture off-piste). You can also reach the ski fields of Super-Besse from here (weather and lifts permitting). Parking places close to the lifts fill quickly; consider the free shuttle bus from Le Mont-Dore instead.

Super Besse (https://superbesse.sancy.com; day pass adult/child €32.50/22.80; ⊙9am-5pm mid-Dec–mid-Apr) Glide down 43km of downhill pistes at Super Besse (1350-1800m), 7km west of Besse off D978. Better suited to intermediate skiers than the Mont-Dore side, Besse offers lift passes for weekenders as well as two-hour ski tickets (adult/child €23/16.10) if you only want a quick taster. This isn't among France's most snow-sure areas so check online webcams before venturing out.

Espace Nordique Sancy (⊙Jan-Mar) Glide along 250km of cross-country ski trails at this Nordic skiing space north of Super Besse. Prices depend on which of the nine sectors of trails you want to tackle (adult/child from €8.50/3.90); find maps on www.sancy.com. With altitudes up to 1560m and fickle weather, it's worth asking locally about snow conditions before setting your heart on schussing among frost-rimmed forests.

OFF THE BEATEN TRACK

LAC PAVIN

Six kilometres southwest of Besse-et-St-Anastaise, the landscape bewitches: the extraordinarily beautiful crater **Lac Pavin** (off D978), enclosed by a fuzz of pine trees, was blasted out of the earth by a volcanic explosion nearly seven millennia ago. Today it attracts trout fishers and walkers; the trail around the shore takes less than an hour. There's pedalo rental in summer (half-/full day €5.50/10). Winter, when the lake has a frosty halo, is even more beautiful.

Should you fall in love with this sultry scape, converted farmhouse **Auberge de la Petite Ferme** (☑04 73 79 51 39; www.auberge-petite-ferme.com; Le Faux; s/d/tr/ste from €83/90/110/159; P 🤚), on the lake-bound road from Besse, is the Zen spot to fling open your window shutters each morning to views of rolling pastures and taste fresh air in the breakfast buffet (€11.50) of cheeses, yoghurts and local honey.

🍴 Eating & Drinking

La Petite Boutique du Bougnat   DELI €
(1 & 4 rue Montlosier; ⊙9am-12.30pm & 2.30-7pm) The biggest lure of this impressive delicatessen is its mind-boggling array of *saucissons d'Auvergne*, local dried sausage in incarnations from duck to kangaroo and flavours as varied as forest berry and goat's cheese. Liqueurs, wines and jams are on sale too, and there are dairy delights in the cheese shop on the opposite side of the street.

La Tasse Carrée   TEAHOUSE €
(☑04 73 22 14 74; www.facebook.com/latasse carree; 47 rue Meynadier; ⊙noon-6pm Tue-Sat, from 2pm Sun) Fluffy toy heads are mounted on the walls of this welcoming *salon de thé* in a cutesy send-up of a hunting lodge. Choose a tea blend to suit your personality – *l'Intrépide*, perhaps, or *l'Enigmatique* – and agonise over the choice between frangipane tarts, spiced scones and rum-orange cake.

Chez Pépé Jean   FRENCH €
(☑04 73 22 16 44; 3 place Charles De Gaulle; mains €12-20; ⊙noon-2pm & 7-9pm Fri-Tue, noon-2pm Wed) Hearty and wholesome dishes receive elegant presentation in this self-styled 'bistrovergnat' – that is, a restaurant with the simplicity of a bistro but a cosiness (and cheese selection) that is unmistakeably Auvergne. Try the 'St Nectiflette', a variation on Alpine potato bake *tartiflette* but with a gooey layer of St Nectaire cheese.

⭐ La Golmotte   FRENCH €€
(☑04 73 65 05 77; www.aubergelagolmotte.com; rte D996, Le Barbier; menus €18.50-39; ⊙noon-2pm Wed-Sun, 7-9pm Wed-Sat) This farm-style inn is well worth the 3km trek up the main road towards Col de Guéry. Regional classics like cheesy *truffade* and *pounti* (a prune-studded savoury cake) are offered beneath its wooden rafters, but so are booze-drenched recipes like scallops in cider butter and pork cheeks stewed in red wine. Reservations recommended.

ℹ Information

Tourist Office (☑04 73 65 20 21; www.sancy. com; av de la Libération; ⊙9am-12.30pm & 2-6pm Mon-Sat, 9.30am-12.30pm & 2-5.30pm Sun, closed Sun Nov; 🤚)

ℹ Getting There & Away

Direct SNCF buses connect Le Mont-Dore with Clermont-Ferrand (€7.40, 1¾–2 hours, two daily) and there are train and bus connections via Laqueuille (€11.70, 1½ hours, three daily).

Monts du Cantal

Three million years ago Europe's broadest stratovolcano, almost 80km in diameter, blew its top and left behind the saw-tooth peaks of the Monts du Cantal. Rising highest in this southerly part of Parc Naturel Régional des Volcans d'Auvergne are **Puy Mary** (1787m), **Plomb du Cantal** (1858m) and **Puy de Peyre Arse** (1806m).

Meadows and farmland have long since carpeted over the Monts du Cantal's explosive beginnings, but the region hasn't been fully tamed. Wilder and more sparsely populated than other parts of the Auvergne, the Monts du Cantal are easily reached from **Murat**, 15km east, or with an overnight stop in Dienne or Lavigerie.

◉ Sights & Activities

Ambling through Murat's daydream of an old town to admire its 14th-century **Église Collégiale Notre-Dame** (place Gandilhon Gens d'Armes; ◷ 9.30am-7pm Apr-Oct, 10.30am-5pm Nov-Mar) is a Murat must.

Le Lioran   SKIING
(◷ tourist office 04 71 49 50 08; www.lelioran. com; day pass adult/child €32/21.90; ◷ late Dec–Mar) This 150-hectare ski station (1160m to 1850m), 12km west of Murat, is geared towards middle-of-the-road skiers. Just over half of its 44 pistes are blue (easy) or red (intermediate) and there's a snowpark, with an inflatable mattress for those trying jumps for the first time. Snow cannons top up most slopes but ask locally about conditions before heading out.

⌨ Sleeping & Eating

★ Alta Terra   B&B €
(◷ 04 71 20 83 03; www.altaterra-cantal.com; Pradel, Lavigerie; d/q from €72/110; ℗ 🛜) Antique skis and creaking wooden eaves give a chalet feel to this exemplary family-run B&B in Lavigerie, a 15km drive northwest of Murat. Slide into the outdoor Nordic hot tub (especially satisfying with snow outside), or soothe your muscles in the *hammam* and sauna (no extra charge).

Reserve ahead for dinner, a deftly assembled spread of regional flavours with options for vegetarian, vegan and gluten-free diners (€20-25).

**Instants d'Absolu
Ecolodge & Spa**   BOUTIQUE HOTEL €€
(◷ 04 71 20 83 09; www.ecolodge-france.com; Lac du Pêcher, Chavagnac; d/ste from €135/180; ◷ mid-Apr–mid-Nov & mid-Dec–mid-Mar; ℗ ✳ 🛜) ⌀ This 300-year-old lakeside farm, in the peaceful wilds 16km north of Murat, was remodelled with sustainability in mind – carpets from recycled fibres, ecologically

sound paintwork, and meticulous recycling. So with a clear conscience, slide into an outdoor hot tub, stretch out in the sauna, or flop onto a bed in one of 12 individually designed rooms (deliberately TV-free).

ⓘ Information

Tourist Office (◷ 04 71 20 09 47; www.haute sterrestourisme.fr; place de l'Hôtel de Ville; ◷ 9.30am-6.30pm Mon-Sat, 10am-12.30pm & 2-6pm Sun Jul & Aug, shorter hours rest of year)

ⓘ Getting There & Away

Direct trains connect Murat with Clermont-Ferrand (€21.50, 1¾ hours, four to six daily) and Issoire (€15.70, one hour, four daily).

Change trains in Arvant for services to other parts of the Auvergne, including Le Puy-en-Velay and Langeac (Gorges d'Allier).

Salers

POP 335 / ELEV 950M

Gastronomy and stately architecture lift Salers into the esteem of local diners and tourists alike. Huddled against the western edge of the Monts du Cantal, Salers' 16th-century town centre glimmers darkly with a warren of lava-stone townhouses and fairy-tale towers. The town is a good starting point for rambles to **Puy Violent** (1592m) and **Puy Mary** (1787m), but hikes are generally undertaken to work up sufficient appetite for Salers beef and the local Appellation d'Origine Protégée (AOP) cheese.

◉ Sights

Salers' picturesque central square, **place Tyssandier d'Escous**, is named for the 19th-century agronomist who developed the Salers breed of cattle. Encircling his statue are turreted, lava-rock buildings that date from Salers' 16th-century heyday as a

---

LOCAL KNOWLEDGE

WHAT'S THE BEEF IN SALERS?

Ask a local what to eat during your travels in the Auvergne and the answers will likely be cheese (first and foremost), followed by Salers beef. Renowned across France for its rich, gamey flavour, Salers beef is sizzled and seared with reverence in practically every restaurant in town. About 5km north of Salers, housed in a 17th-century barn, the **Maison de la Salers** (◷ 04 71 40 54 00; www.maisondelasalers.fr; Le Fau, St-Bonnet-de-Salers; adult/ child €7/4.50; ◷ 10am-noon & 2-6pm Feb-Oct) is a museum dedicated to the magnificence of these long-horned cattle. If that isn't enough beef, time a visit for the **Transhumance** (St-Paul-de-Salers; ◷ late May), in which farmers drive hundreds of bell-jingling, long-horned Salers dairy cattle through their village, 3km east of Salers.

regional administrative centre. From here, walk up to the leafy **Esplanade de Barrouze** for a panoramic view.

Pick up the free *Pays de Salers* map from the tourist office (p578) for a walking tour of historic buildings.

Musée de Salers · MUSEUM
(☑ 04 71 40 75 97; rue des Templiers; adult/child €5/free; ⊙ 10am-12.30pm & 2-5.30pm Mon-Thu & Sun, 2-5.30pm Sat mid-Apr–mid-Oct) Uncover Salers' history in one of the most enigmatic buildings in town. This former Knights Templar house exposes local history and traditions among its Gothic vaults and echoing stone walls.

🛏 Sleeping & Eating

Hôtel Saluces · HISTORIC HOTEL €€
(☑ 04 71 40 70 82; www.hotel-salers.fr; rue de la Martille; d €85-100, tr/q from €128/158; ⊙ mid-Dec–mid-Nov; 🐾) Formerly a 17th-century manor house, Hôtel Saluces has been restored with a simple yet refined touch. Each of its eight spacious rooms has unique features – a traditional fireplace in 'La Meneau', a big modern bath-tub in 'La Flanelle' – and there's an interior courtyard and adjoining crêperie plus a *salon de thé* to unwind in.

★ Le Drac · CRÊPES, FRENCH €
(☑ 04 71 40 72 12; www.ledrac.supersite.fr; place Tyssandier d'Escous; menus €13-22; ⊙ noon-2pm & 7-9pm) Named for a hairy, mischievous gnome, this cellar restaurant is a winning address thanks to well-executed regional cuisine and faultless service. Top billing goes to juicy Salers beef served with cheesy *truffade*, but *galettes* (buckwheat pancakes) bulging with Cantal cheese and draped with *jambon sec* (cured ham) come a close second.

La Diligence · FRENCH €€
(☑ 04 71 40 75 39; www.ladiligence-salers.com; rue de Beffroi; mains/menus from €15/23; ⊙ noon-3.30pm & 7-10.30pm Tue-Sat late-Mar–Oct) Loosen your belt for generous servings of regional delicacies such as pork with lentils, *pounti* (bacon- and prune-studded savoury cake) and *bourriols* (thick buckwheat pancakes) crammed with Cantal cheese at this restaurant in the village's historic centre. Our pick: Salers beef cooked on a *pierrade* (a stone grill placed on your table), followed by a fruit tart.

ℹ Information

Tourist Office (☑ 04 71 40 58 08; www.salers-tourisme.fr; place Tyssandier d'Escous; ⊙ 9.30am-noon & 2-6pm Jun-Sep, 9.30am-noon & 2-5.30pm Mon-Sat Oct-May)

ℹ Getting There & Away

Salers is on the D680, 43km west of Murat (21km west of the Pas de Peyrol) at the foot of Puy Mary. You'll need your own vehicle to get here.

Be aware that the Pas de Peyrol usually closes from November to May. It's still possible to drive to Salers from the eastern part of Parc Naturel Régional des Volcans d'Auvergne, but plan for a lengthy detour via Riom-ès-Montagnes.

Murol
POP 574 / ELEV 850M

Bisected by a gargling river and enclosed by forests, the stone village of Murol slows the pulse. Glowering over the town is magnificent 12th-century **Château de Murol** (☑ 04 73 88 82 50; www.murolchateau.com; adult/child €9/4.50; ⊙ 10am-7pm Apr-Sep, to 6pm Feb, Mar & Oct–mid-Nov, 2-5pm late Nov–Dec & early Feb; 🅿), a reminder of past battles. The only siege these days is the summer rush to 60-hectare **Lac Chambon** (🅿), a playground for families 1.5km west of Murol.

🛏 Sleeping & Eating

Camping les Bombes · CAMPGROUND €
(☑ 04 73 88 64 03; www.camping-les-bombes.com; Chemin de Pétary, Chambon-sur-Lac; tent site from €13, per extra adult/child €5.20/4.20; ⊙ late Apr–mid-Sep; 🅿🏊) Just 10 minutes' walk east of Lac Chambon's indigo waters is this efficiently run campground, with a choice of verdant tent sites and wooden chalets. Mini-golf, table tennis, a heated outdoor pool and acres of green space provide little incentive to leave the grounds, and there are regular activities for kids, from treasure hunts to singalongs.

Aux 500 Diables · BOUTIQUE HOTEL €€
(☑ 04 73 88 81 71; www.500diables.com; Moneaux, off D636, Chambon-des-Neiges; d €129; 🅿🏊❄) ✎ Designed for minimum impact on its fragile environment, the rooms adjoining **Aux 500 Diables Restaurant** (☑ 04 73 88 81 71; www.500diables.com; Moneaux, off D636, Chambon-des-Neiges; mains €17-25, menus from €35; ⊙ noon-2pm & 7-9pm Fri & Sat, other hours vary) are fresh and contemporary. Some feel economic in size, but they're tastefully decorated with earth tones, charcoal bathrooms and most have windows that survey deer grazing the highland meadows.

ST-NECTAIRE

The must-try product in foodie St-Nectaire, 6km east of Murol, is its eponymous cheese, sold at local dairies and featuring on restaurant menus baked whole, melting atop steaks, or served *nature* on cheese plates. Pick some up at the **Maison du Fromage** (☑04 73 88 57 96; www.maison-du-fromage.com; rte de Murol, St-Nectaire-le-Haut; tours adult/child €5.50/4.50; ⊘10am-noon & 2-7pm), where you can learn its history on a 35-minute guided tour. At out-of-town **La Ferme Bellonte** (☑04 73 88 52 25; www.st-nectaire.com/ferme-bellonte; rue du 10 août 1944, Farges; ⊘milking 7-8am & 4-5pm Apr-Oct, 6-7am & 3-4pm Nov-Mar; cheese-making 8.30-9.30am & 5.30-7pm Apr-Oct, 7.30-8.30am & 5-6pm Nov-Mar; ⊕) FREE, 3km northeast of St-Nectaire, you can see cows being milked or admire fresh batches of cheese being pressed into moulds, before taking a round of cheese away with you (€16.50).

Remnants of the belle-époque town's former life as a spa surge forth at **Fontaines Pétrifiantes** (☑04 73 88 50 80; www.fontaines-petrifiantes.fr; 1 av du Roux, St-Nectaire-le-Bas; adult/child €6/3; ⊘9.30am-noon & 2-7pm mid-May–mid-Sep, to 6pm mid-Dec–early May & late Sep–early Dec) where the Papon family use St-Nectaire's natural hot springs to make art. Calcium-heavy water lashing against an object gradually causes a mineral build-up; using a 14m-high waterfall, the Papon family let artistic moulds get drenched until mineral sculptures take shape. The well-designed museum and showroom are truly original and there's a gift shop full of mineral art.,

❶ Information

The **tourist office** (☑04 73 88 62 62; www.sancy.com; rue de Jassaguet, Murol; ⊘9am-noon & 2-6pm Mon-Sat May-Sep, also 9am-noon Sun Apr, Jul & Aug, closed Oct-Mar except school holidays; ☏) also runs a summer-only **tourist office** (☑04 73 78 65 10; www.sancy.com; Plage Chambon, Chambon-sur-Lac; ⊘10am-1pm & 2-6.30pm Jul & Aug; ☏) by Lac Chambon's main beach.

❶ Getting There & Away

Murol and its surrounds have scant public transport (the closest train station is in Le Mont-Dore, a 19km drive west), so you're better off with a rental car.

In winter, main roads are kept clear but it's worth paying attention to snow forecasts if you're taking the lonely, winding road to Chambon-des-Neiges.

PARC NATUREL RÉGIONAL LIVRADOIS-FOREZ

Extending between the plains of Limagne and the Monts du Forez, Parc Naturel Régional Livradois-Forez is a showcase for the placid beauty of rural France. Formerly a centre of logging and agriculture, the Livradois-Forez is now 3200 sq km of protected land. Its conifer forests, meadows and moors are interrupted by elegantly ramshackle villages, some of them (like La Chaise-Dieu) guarding remarkable cultural riches.

But it's the artisans of Livradois-Forez who have truly made a name for their towns. Thiers remains proud of its centuries of knife-making, paper production rolls on near Ambert, and countless dairies employ traditional methods to churn out cheeses such as Fourme d'Ambert, one of France's oldest, and creamy *fromage aux artisons*.

❶ Information

Maison du Tourisme (Park Information Office; ☑04 73 95 56 49; www.vacances-livradois-forez.com; 28 av Rhin et Danube, off D906, Olliergues; ⊘10am-12.30pm & 2-6pm Mon-Sat Jul & Aug, closed Mon & Tue Apr-May, limited hours rest of year) One of several regional park information centres with information on walking trails, mountain-bike routes and regional handicrafts.

Thiers

POP 11,805

France is as proud of its artisans as its artists, and nowhere is that more obvious than in the knife-making town of Thiers. Blades have been fashioned here for six centuries, in the early days by harnessing the power of the Durolle river. Thiers still sharpens around 70% of French knives, and more than 100 knife producers continue to operate in town.

In Thiers' historic centre, narrow stone lanes are still strung with weather-beaten workshop signs and every imaginable shape of blade glints from shop windows. The charming old town, with an excellent museum, knife-making courses and old-timey restaurants, is deserving of a detour.

◉ Sights & Activities

You might not have endured the punishing years of training of Thiers' master knife-makers, but you can make your own souvenir blade under their tutelage if you reserve a spot at a knife-making workshop. Established in 1919, Robert David Coutellerie (☑ 04 73 80 07 77; www.robert-david.com; 94 av des États Unis; adult/child €30/15; ☺ 10am, 2pm & 4pm Mon-Sat by reservation) offers knife classes, as does popular Atelier Le Thiers (☑ 09 80 31 30 21; www.atelierlethiers.com; 2 rue Alexandre Dumas; adult/child €30/11; ☺ by reservation 10am, 2pm & 4pm Mon-Sat mid-Apr–Sep). Kids can join in and make a blunt-edged butter knife.

★ Musée de la Coutellerie   MUSEUM
(☑ 04 73 80 58 86; 23 & 58 rue de la Coutellerie; adult/child €5.80/2.85, combined ticket with Vallée des Rouets €7/3.05; ☺ 10am-noon & 2-6pm Feb-Dec, closed Mon Oct-May; 🅿) Split across two buildings, this museum gives an entertaining account of cutlery-making history. In number 23, a kid-friendly sound-and-light show evokes the dazzling, deafening conditions of a medieval workshop. Continue down the street to number 58 to see sparks fly in a knife-making demonstration on centuries-old equipment. Demos are in French only, but written information is available in other languages on request. In summer, pair a trip to the museum with visiting open-air Vallée des Rouets (p580), 4km northeast of Thiers.

Vallée des Rouets   MUSEUM
(Valley of the Waterwheels; off D2089; adult/child €4.15/2.05; ☺ noon-6pm Jun & Sep, to 7pm Jul & Aug) About 4km northeast of Thiers is the Vallée des Rouets, an open-air museum dedicated to the knife-makers who once toiled here in front of water-driven grindstones, a method abandoned in the 1930s. In July and August a free shuttle-bus runs here from Thiers.

❶ Information

Tourist Office (☑ 04 73 80 65 65; www.thiers-tourisme.fr; 1 place du Pirou; ☺ 10am-noon & 2-5pm Mon-Sat Oct-Apr, 9.30am-12.30pm & 2-6pm Mon-Sat May, Jun & Sep, to 7pm Jul & Aug)

❶ Getting There & Away

Direct trains reach Thiers from Clermont-Ferrand (€9.60, 45 minutes, up to nine daily) and Vichy (€9, 45 minutes, up to six daily). Thiers train station is a 1km walk north of the tourist office.

La Chaise-Dieu

POP 619 / ELEV 1082M

The *raison d'être* of La Chaise-Dieu (literally 'the seat of God') is its monumental, 14th-century abbey-church – its beautifully restored Gothic arches and medieval artwork are likely to be the high point of any church-hopping itinerary through Parc Naturel Régional Livradois-Forez.

For Pope Clement VI, a humble tomb simply wouldn't do. The pope commissioned a palatial church to shelter his final resting place and the resulting Église Abbatiale de St-Robert (www.abbaye-chaise-dieu.com; La Chaise-Dieu; ☺ 10.15am-noon & 2-6pm Jun-Sep, from 9am Mar-May & Oct, 9am-noon & 2-5pm Nov-Apr), completed in 1352, is an imposing sight: two square towers crown its restrained Gothic façade, behind which a cavernous interior, framed

---

WORTH A TRIP

A CHEESE LOVER'S MUST: AMBERT

Creamy blue Fourme d'Ambert, recognisable by its tall, cylindrical shape, is one of the Auvergne's five Appellation d'Origine Protégée (AOP) cheeses. The best way to pay homage to this *fromage* is at the Maison de la Fourme d'Ambert (☑ 04 73 82 49 23; www.maison-fourme-ambert.fr; 29 rue des Chazeaux; adult/child €6/4.50; ☺ 10am-12.30pm & 2-6.30pm Tue-Sat Apr-Oct, daily Jul & Aug), within a 14th-century building in the cheese's town of origin. Join a 45-minute guided tour about the cheese's history and manufacture, then enjoy a three-cheese tasting, including a drink (€3.50). Book ahead for tours in English and, in July and August, for hands-on workshops (from €10) on butter-churning and cheese-making.

Ambert is an easy day-trip by car from Thiers (50km), Issoire (60km) or La Chaise-Dieu (30km).

ℹ SENSATIONAL SLEEPS

Bed down in a restful, wooden-floored room overlooking a 12th-century church at **Auberge du Ripailleur** (🖉 04 73 72 83 20; www.aubergeduripailleur.com; Le Bourg, Dorel'Église; s/d/tr €55/65/85; 🔊), a cheerful inn 8km north of La Chaise-Dieu in tiny Dorel'Église. It's worth getting breakfast (€7) or opting for half-board (from €15): half the fun is eating here (the name means to eat one's fill). Expect French comfort food like confit duck, coq au vin and plenty of outstanding local cheese.

Combining historic walls, French soul food and a lost-in-time village 14km west of La Chaise-Dieu, it's hard to imagine a more atmospheric place to stay than **Le Clos Saint François** (🖉 04 71 01 23 95; www.leclosstfrancois.com; Le Bourg, Beaune-sur-Arzon; s/d incl breakfast €50/€60-70) 🥐. Its four sizeable rooms, each decorated with a flair for antiques, are housed in a restored late-17th-century convent; ask to see the chapel. Breakfast is a fine spread of homemade jams and organic produce, and there's an ample evening meal (€22) cooked up by owner Karine, who couldn't be a more effusive host.

by 18m-high rib vaults, harbours treasures including the massive 17th-century **organ** (a focal point of the town's **Sacred Music Festival** (Festival de la Chaise-Dieu; www.chaise-dieu.com; events from €10; ☺ Aug)) and Clement VI's marble **tomb**.

Don't miss the celebrated *Danse Macabre* fresco, painstakingly restored in recent years as part of a €23m renovation over a period of eight years. It shows different members of 14th-century society tormented by Death, who is represented as a succession of dancing skeletons.

Behind the church is **Salle de l'Echo** – an architectural oddity that allows people on opposite sides of the chamber to hear each other talking, without being overheard by those in between. It's thought to have been built to enable monks to hear lepers' confessions without contracting the dreaded disease.

Aside from its main attraction, La Chaise-Dieu, 38km northwest of Le Puy-en-Velay, has little detain you other than some charming inns in surrounding villages.

SNCF buses run once or twice each weekday between La Chaise-Dieu and Le Puy-en-Velay (€9.80, one hour).

LE PUY-EN-VELAY

POP 18,909 / ELEV 630M

With two volcanic pillars thrusting above its rooftops, it would be impossible to mistake Le Puy-en-Velay for anywhere else in France. Topped with a 10th-century church and a vermillion statue of the Virgin Mary, these stone pinnacles tower hundreds of feet high, like two sacred rockets in the middle of blast-off.

Since the Middle Ages, Le Puy has been the starting point of the Via Podiensis, the oldest French route of the Way of St James. Le Puy's cathedral, a focal point for pilgrims, is also perched on a volcanic hill in the core of the alluring old town.

Le Puy is the proud home of two of the Auvergne's great gastronomic boasts: lentils grown in volcanic soil – gilded with Appellation d'Origine Protégée designation – and Verveine du Velay, an aromatic green liqueur. Le Puy was also a historic centre for lace-making; the craft remains greatly admired and fuels a modest souvenir trade.

⊙ Sights

Between April and mid-November, three of Le Puy's major sights (Chapelle St-Michel d'Aiguilhe, Notre Dame de France and the Forteresse de Polignac) can be visited on the joint Pass'Espace **museum pass** (adult/child €9.50/5.50). Buy it at any of the sights or from the tourist office.

★ **Chapelle St-Michel d'Aiguilhe** CHURCH
(www.rochersaintmichel.fr; off rue du Rocher; adult/child €3.50/2; ☺ 9am-6.30pm May-Sep, 9.30am-5.30pm Oct–mid-Nov & late Mar–Apr, 2-5pm Feb–mid-Mar & school holidays) Le Puy's oldest chapel, first established in the 10th century, and rebuilt several times since, teeters atop an 85m-high volcanic plug, reached by climbing 268 craggy stairs. Stepping through its polychrome doorway into the cave-like interior is a nearmystical experience – the chapel follows the natural contours of the rock, and the unusual carvings and 12th-century frescoes create an otherworldly atmosphere.

Cathédrale Notre Dame
CATHEDRAL

(📞 04 71 09 79 77; www.cathedraledupuy.org; rue de la Manécanterie; ⊙ 6.30am-7pm) A chequerboard of grey and white stone perched on a volcanic stone crag, Le Puy's cathedral is the monumental starting point for pilgrims embarking on the French Way of St James route. An exquisite blend of architectural styles, the cathedral's entryway is framed by Romanesque arches. Inside are Roman-era frescoes, (some 5.5m high), Baroque statues, an organ dating to 1689, and one of the Auvergne's most famous *Vierges noires* (black Madonnas).

Cathédrale Notre Dame Cloister
HISTORIC SITE

(📞 04 71 05 45 52; www.cathedrale-puy-en-velay. monuments-nationaux.fr; rue du Cloître; adult/child €6/free; ⊙ 9am-noon & 2-6.30pm mid-May–mid-Sep, to 5pm rest of year) A peaceful 12th-century cloister adjoins Le Puy's cathedral, its multicoloured bricks and columns alluding to strong Moorish influences. Upstairs is a fine collection of embroidered religious artwork and vestments, accompanied by absorbing audiovisual displays about their origins.

Notre Dame de France
MONUMENT

(adult/child €4/2; ⊙ 9am-7pm May-Sep, 10am-5pm Feb-Apr & Oct–mid-Nov, 2-5pm Sun late Nov–Jan) At 16m tall and weighing a svelte 110 tonnes, this crimson Notre Dame de France (Virgin Mary) statue makes an imposing guardian over Le Puy. Since 1860, she has been watching over the city from the Rocher Corneille, a 757m-high volcanic pillar. You can share her view by climbing a ladder right inside her haloed head. The statue was fashioned from 213 cannons captured during the Crimean War.

Le Camino
MUSEUM

(Musée de St-Jacques de Compostelle; 📞 04 71 09 06 00; www.lecamino.org; 2 rue de la Manécanterie; adult/child €3/1.50; ⊙ 2-6pm Apr-Jun & Sep–Oct, 11am-7.30pm Jul & Aug) Interesting for armchair travellers, as well as committed walkers about to undertake the multiweek journey to Santiago de Compostela, this museum in the restored 16th-century Hôtel St-Vidal traces the 1700km Chemin de St-Jacques (Way of Saint James) pilgrimage route. Rotating exhibitions of contemporary art are also hosted here; check the website to see what's on.

Musée Hôtel-Dieu
MUSEUM

(📞 04 71 07 00 00; www.hoteldieu.info; 2 rue Becdelièvre; adult/child €6/free; ⊙ 1.30-6.30pm Tue-Sat mid-Apr–early Nov) Within this museum and cultural centre, the highlight is a 19th-century pharmacy, elegantly panelled in walnut and wild cherry wood. Upstairs, French-language interactive exhibits focus on the architecture, history and natural history of the Haute-Loire.

AUVERGNE LE PUY-EN-VELAY

OFF THE BEATEN TRACK

LA MONTAGNE PROTESTANTE

East of Le Puy-en-Velay, roads meander towards the Haut-Lignon plateau. Skirted by Le Testavoyre (1436m) and Mont Mézenc (1753m), and enveloped with evergreen forest, the area is nicknamed 'La Montagne Protestante' on account of its historic Protestant majority. The population is low, but the communities and their histories are remarkable.

Le Chambon-sur-Lignon, 45km east of Le Puy-en-Velay, is renowned for highly organised resistance during World War II. Residents used the lonely, sparse character of the plateau to their advantage in a village-wide effort to hide Jews, saving thousands from Nazi death camps. Evocative displays and audiovisual presentations at **Lieu de Mémoire** (📞 04 71 56 56 65; www.memoireduchambon.com; 23 rte du Mazet; adult/child €5/3; ⊙ 10am-12.30pm & 2-6pm Tue-Sun May-Sep, 2-6pm Wed-Sat Mar-Apr & Oct-Nov) paint a vivid picture of an extraordinarily resilient wartime community.

Seven kilometres north is Tence, a stop along the Way of St James pilgrimage route. Fourteen kilometres further east lies St-Bonnet-le-Froid, marked firmly on the maps of French foodies, thanks to Michelin-starred celebrity chef Régis Marcon, who works with regional earthy flavours at **Restaurant Régis et Jacques Marcon** (menus €135-210) and more affordable bistro **La Coulemelle** (📞 04 71 65 63 62; www.regismarcon.fr; place de l'Église, St-Bonnet-le-Froid; menus €32-50; ⊙ noon-2pm & 7.30-10pm Wed-Mon mid-Feb–Dec; 🅿 🍴), named after a mushroom no less.

A road-trip is a pleasant way to sample each village's distinct character.

Le Puy-en-Velay

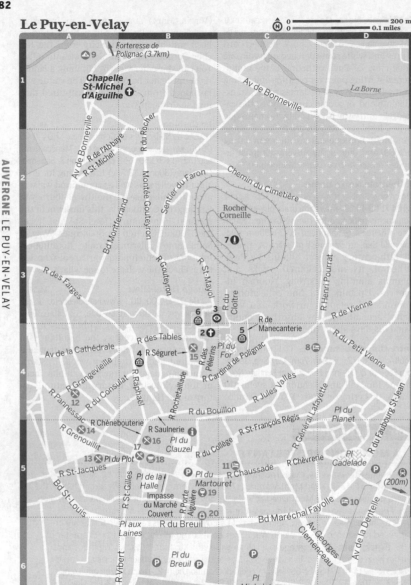

Keep an eye on the website for temporary exhibitions. In recent years the Hôtel-Dieu has displayed work by riveting contemporary artists, and hosted a major Picasso exhibition.

Centre d'Enseignement de la Dentelle au Fuseau

MUSEUM

(☎ 04 71 02 01 68; www.ladentelledupuy.com; 38-40 rue Raphaël; adult/child €4.50/free; ☉ 9am-noon & 1.30-5.30pm Mon-Fri, 9.30am-4.30pm Sat) Le Puy is famed for the intricacy and

Le Puy-en-Velay

beauty of its lace, and this workshop-museum – led by formidable lace expert Mick Fouriscot – showcases remarkable examples of the delicate craft, plus old photographs of the region's lace-makers across centuries. Nimble-fingered travellers can sign up for lace-making classes (from €18 per hour, book in advance). There's an adjoining shop filled with pretty souvenirs and books.

Forteresse de Polignac CASTLE
(☑04 71 04 06 04; www.forteressedepolignac.fr; adult/child €5/3.50; ☺10am-7pm Jul & Aug, 10am-noon & 1.30-6pm Apr-Jun, Sep & Oct, to 5pm early Nov, 1.30-5pm Feb & Mar) Sprouting from the sharp crags of a volcanic dome northwest of Le Puy, this late-11th-century castle was built by the powerful Polignac family, who once controlled access to the city from the north, and to whom the fortress has belonged for a millennium. It's ringed by a practically continuous wall dotted with lookout towers and a 32m-high rectangular keep. It's a 5km drive from Le Puy.

🎎 Festivals & Events

⭐ **Fête du Roi de l'Oiseau** STREET CARNIVAL
(www.roideloiseau.com; ☺3rd weekend in Sep) This Renaissance-themed street party dates back to a competition first recorded in 1524. Le Puy's most skilled archer, the first to shoot a straw bird from a high tower, was rewarded with year-long tax exemption, dining with nobles, and the title of 'roi de l'oiseau' (bird king). The present-day festival resurrects 16th-century costumes, food and music (and an archery contest).

🛏 Sleeping

Camping Bouthezard CAMPGROUND €
(☑04 71 09 55 09; www.aquadis-loisirs.com/camping-de-bouthezard; chemin de Bouthezard; pitch/adult/child from €16.90/3.50/1.60; ☺Apr-Oct; ℗🐕) Le Puy's campground enjoys an attractive berth beside the Borne river, overlooked by the towering Chapelle St-Michel d'Aiguilhe across the road. Facilities include washing machines, badminton and table tennis, and the option for croissant delivery in the mornings. There's wi-fi in the reception area.

Auberge de Jeunesse HOSTEL €
(☑04 71 05 52 40; www.hifrance.org/auberge-de-jeunesse/le-puy-en-velay.html; 9 rue Jules Vallès; dm €14.70; ℗🐕) Bright and clean, this hostel offers great value for its prime position below the cathedral. Dorms sleep three to nine people; there are facilities for disabled travellers, plus there are washing machines to blitz the trail dust from your clothes. Simple breakfasts of cereals, bread and orange juice cost €4.50 per head, and the on-site parking is free.

⭐ **L'Epicurium** B&B €
(☑06 24 41 56 10; www.l-epicurium.com; 5 rue du Bessat; d/f from €64/99; 🐕) This gastronomy-obsessed guesthouse has six spacious lodgings renovated with minimalist flair: ceilings are high, tones are neutral, and there are period features like wooden beams and chimney places. Creaky floors are also part of the old-world charm. Breakfast involves a toothsome range of homemade jams, and you can add a three-course meal (€18) or a gourmet picnic (€10).

DRIVING THE GORGES DE L'ALLIER

Roads that meander along the bends of the Allier River, weathered stone villages, imposing abbeys... the Gorges de l'Allier beg to be experienced on a lazy drive. Begin in Sauges, 43km west of Le Puy-en-Velay. Regionally, the town is best known for the *Bête du Gévaudan* (Beast of Gévaudan), an 18th-century lupine legend blamed for a series of bloodcurdling attacks; today he's remembered in a **museum** (☑04 71 77 64 22; www.musee-bete-gevaudan.com; rue de la Tour; adult/child €5.50/3.50; ☺10am-noon & 2.30-6.30pm Jul & Aug, 2.30-6.30pm late Jun & early Sep).

Follow D585 for 20km north until St-Arcons-d'Allier, before turning south along D48 to St-Julien-des-Chazes, whose weathered church is set against a picturesque backdrop of sheer basalt cliffs. Back in St-Arcons, luxuriate in the peaceful surrounds a little longer by booking a room at **Le Moulin Ferme-Auberge** (☑04 71 74 03 09; www.gite-aubergedumoulin.com; dm/d/tr/q €20/80/95/105; P) ✿, a converted 15th-century mill.

Leave St-Arcons on the northbound D585 and after 5km you'll reach Langeac, the best place in the gorges to seize some oars. Talk to **Tonic Aventure** (☑04 71 77 25 64; www.tonic-aventure.fr; Base l'Ile d'Amour (riverside); ☺Apr–mid-Oct) about canoe rental, or (if you time it right) consider hopping aboard the scenic **Train des Gorges de l'Allier** (☑04 71 77 70 17; www.train-gorges-allier.com; adult/child €15-29/11-17; ☺Jul & Aug). Failing that, stop for a no-frills *menu* at **Bistrot de Lucas** (☑04 71 76 41 31; 46 av Danton; menus €13; ☺8am-8pm Mon-Fri, to 3pm Sat).

Fourteen kilometres further northwest along D585 is Lavoûte-Chilhac, with a photogenic bridge and huddle of stone houses. A 4km detour east on D4 leads to the fortified hilltop town of Chilhac; follow signs around town for a ramble to its basalt cliffs.

Taking D41 out of Chilhac, follow the northbound turn along N102 until you see signs for Lavaudieu (15km in all), whose centrepiece is a majestic Benedictine abbey.

Drive northwest along D20 then meander west on D588 to architecturally rich Brioude. Its highlight is the **Basilique de St-Julien** (rue de Notre Dame; ☺9am-7pm Jul & Aug, to 5.30pm Sep-Jun), a wonder of peachy stone and volcanic rock decoration, and the Auvergne's largest Romanesque church. Four kilometres south of here you can sleep as peacefully as a monk in Vieille-Brioude, home to **Ermitage St-Vincent** (☑06 80 67 17 45; www.ermitage-saintvincent.fr; 9 place de l'Église; d/tr/q/f from €68/88/108/128; P 🛜), a converted presbytery next to the village church.

Hôtel Le Régina HOTEL €€

(☑04 71 09 14 71; www.hotelrestregina.com; 34 bd Maréchal Fayolle; s €69, d €76-110, ste €115-130; P❄🛜) Travel photography and zany murals, from Cola bottles and New York City's Chrysler building to Donald Duck, liven up this modern hotel. Situated five minutes' walk from Le Puy's train station, the hotel's double-glazed windows do a decent job of insulating against the noisy main road, but ask for a room on the *côté calme* (the quiet side).

✕ Eating

Weekly Market MARKET €

(place du Plot; ☺8am-1pm Sat) Shop for fresh fruit, regional wines and delectable dairy products at Le Puy's excellent Saturday market, which has taken place since the 15th century. Some of the local cheeses aren't sold anywhere else.

Crêperie La Maison de Flo CRÊPES €

(☑06 01 49 95 69; 4 impasse du Marché Couvert; menus €14.90; ☺noon-3pm Mon-Thu, to 10pm Fri & Sat; ☝) ✿ A rare healthy-eating gem in the heart of one of France's major cheese regions, Florence's crêperie delights with friendly, personalised service and a nourishing menu of thoughtfully sourced organic produce. Platters of braised tofu, kale and lentil-loaded patties are filling, but it's flourless chocolate cake that hits the spot. There are options for vegan and gluten-free diners.

★ Entrez les Artistes FRENCH €

(☑04 71 09 71 78; 29 rue Pannessac; menus €14-25; ☺noon-2pm Tue-Sat, 7-9pm Thu-Sat) Chef Pascale Suc pours heart, soul and lovingly selected local ingredients into the meals at this small, simple restaurant. The atmosphere is jolly, Le Puy lentils are seasoned to perfection, portions are ample from steaks to homemade *mousse au chocolat*, and there's a healthy wine cellar awash with fine French drops.

L'Âme des Poètes
FRENCH €

(☏ 04 71 05 66 57; www.restaurantlepuy.com; 16 rue Séguret; mains €14-16; ⊘ noon-2pm Thu-Tue & 7-9pm Thu-Sat; ✍) Chef Corinne Moreau is evangelical about nutrition, so vegetarian proteins and organic fruits are the bedrock of the menu. The house speciality, lentil lasagne with fennel, deserves top billing, though spring rolls and veggie burgers are also adroitly prepared. In warm weather, book ahead for dinner on the deck, fringed by roses and glowing under the setting sun.

★ Restaurant Tournayre
FRENCH €€

(☏ 04 71 09 58 94; www.restaurant-tournayre.com; 12 rue Chênebouterie; lunch menus €30, dinner menus €45-58, mains €22-35; ⊘ noon-1.30pm & 7.30-9.30pm Wed-Sat, noon-1.30pm Sun) One of Le Puy's best addresses for food and form. Its atmospheric setting, within a 12th- to 16th-century *hôtel particulier* (townhouse), sets the tone, but the food will dominate conversation. Citrus cod and chicken with horn-of-plenty mushrooms feature on the lunchtime *menu du marché*. Come evening, decadent options include lobster ravioli and sea bass on pumpkin foam.

Bambou et Basilic
FRENCH €€€

(☏ 04 71 09 25 59; www.bambou-basilic.com; 18 rue Grangevieille; lunch menu €24.50, dinner menus €30-65; ⊘ noon-1.30pm & 7.15-9pm Wed-Sun Mar-Nov, noon-1.30pm & 7.15-9pm Wed-Sat, noon-1.30pm Sun Dec-Feb) Smart service and a light gourmet touch bring locals flocking for tables at Bambou et Basilic. Monochrome decor seems designed not to distract from the eating: pork chops with chestnut cream, zander on artichoke purée, and everything prettily arranged. Dainty desserts like *financier de pistache* (crisp pistachio cake) with a tart sorbet beautifully complete the meal.

🍷 Drinking & Nightlife

Café Alami
COFFEE

(place du Plot; ⊘ 8am-noon & 2-5.30pm) This easy-going little cafe is an Aladdin's cave for coffee fans. Beans originating from Ethiopia, the Caribbean and beyond are displayed on its packed shelves and lovingly ground on-site by the gregarious owner (coffee of the day €2).

ℹ Information

Tourist Office (☏ 04 71 09 38 41; www.lepuyenvelay-tourisme.fr; 2 place du Clauzel; ⊘ 8.30am-7pm daily Jul & Aug, 8.30am-noon & 1.30-6.15pm Mon-Fri, to 5.30pm Sat, shorter hours Sun Apr-Jun & Sep, 8.30am-noon & 1.30-5.45pm Mon-Fri, to 5pm Sat, 10am-noon Sun Oct-Mar; 🛜)

ℹ Getting There & Away

SNCF bus and train links operate between Le Puy and Clermont-Ferrand (€25.40, 2¾ hours, up to six daily, change in Arvant or St Étienne and Thiers). There are direct trains to Lyon as well as services via St Étienne (€25.40, 2¼–3½ hours, five to 10 daily).

Connections to Paris transit via Lyon or St Étienne (€95-115, 4½ to five hours, six daily).

DON'T MISS

VERVAINE DU VELAY

Sip free samples of Le Puy's famous green liqueur and buy a bottle of your preferred drop at **Espace Pagès Maison Verveine du Velay** (☏ 04 71 02 46 80; www.verveine.com; 29 place du Breuil; ⊘ 10am-12.30pm & 2.30-6pm Tue-Sat Oct-Dec & Jan-Mar, 10am-1pm & 2-7pm Mon-Sat Jul & Aug) tasting room and boutique. First concocted in 1859 as a digestive tonic, it's a top-secret mix of 32 plants and herbs. These days verveine is glugged across the world as an aperitif or stirred into cocktails (it's delicious with pineapple juice).

Let your taste buds decide between the 55%-proof original, honeyed yellow verveine, a Cognac-strengthened 'Extra' variety, or refreshing citrus-scented 'Petite Verte'.

Espace Pagès is also packed with other regional produce, from verveine-flavoured macarons to tea infusions and condiments.

For a verveine cocktail, continue through the passageway to **Pub La Distillerie** (☏ 04 71 04 91 12; www.brasserie-la-distillerie.fr; 11 rue Porte Aiguière; ⊘ 9am-late Mon-Sat).

Alternatively, for an in-depth understanding of this green elixir, take a 45-minute guided tour of the **distillery** (☏ 04 71 03 04 11; www.verveine.com; St-Germain Laprade; guided tour adult/child €6.40/2.60; ⊘ 10.30am, 2.30pm, 3.30pm & 4.30pm Mon-Sat Jul & Aug, by reservation Jun & Sep), 7km east along the N88 in St-Germain Laprade (summer only).

The Dordogne, Limousin & the Lot

POP 1.34 MILLION

Best Places to Eat

➜ Le Vieux Logis (p599)

➜ Les Truffières (p598)

➜ Le Petit Paris (p602)

➜ La Tour des Vents (p595)

➜ Philippe Redon (p616)

Best Places to Stay

➜ Hôtel La Grézalide (p631)

➜ Manoir de Malagorse (p629)

➜ Château de Maraval (p601)

➜ Bel Estiu (p612)

➜ Moulin de Latreille (p628)

Why Go?

The Dordogne, Limousin and the Lot are the heart and soul of *la belle France,* a land of dense oak forests, winding rivers, emerald-green fields and famously rich country cooking. It's the stuff of which French dreams are made: turreted châteaux and medieval villages line the riverbanks, wooden-hulled *gabarres* (traditional flat-bottomed, wooden boats) ply the waterways, and market stalls overflow with pâté, truffles, walnuts, cheeses and fine wines.

The Dordogne *département* has a bevy of *bastides* (fortified towns) and fantastic medieval castles, as well as Europe's most spectacular cave paintings, and probably the best cuisine. To the northeast, Limousin – now part of the larger Nouvelle Aquitaine *région* – is the most rural, strewn with farms and hamlets, as well as the porcelain centre, Limoges. To the south, the Lot *département* is ribboned with rivers to cruise and caverns to explore, plus dramatic hilltop villages and medieval settlements.

When to Go
Limoges

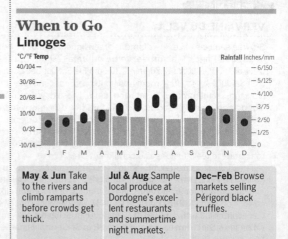

May & Jun Take to the rivers and climb ramparts before crowds get thick.

Jul & Aug Sample local produce at Dordogne's excellent restaurants and summertime night markets.

Dec–Feb Browse markets selling Périgord black truffles.

The Dordogne, Limousin & the Lot Highlights

1 **Vézère Valley** (p605)
Admiring the ancient artwork of prehistoric Europeans.

2 **Village Markets** (p595)
Sampling the region's rich local produce at abundant markets, such as Issigeac's and Martel's.

3 **Historic Castles** (p599)
Wandering the ramparts of medieval fortresses, such as Château de Castelnaud.

4 **Sarlat-la-Canéda** (p602)
Exploring historic russet-stone streets.

5 **Rocamadour** (p627)
Following in the footsteps of centuries of pilgrims at the cliff-face sanctuaries.

6 **River Cruising** (p600)
Plying local waterways aboard a *gabarre* near La Roque Gageac, Bergerac or Brantôme.

7 **Musée Gallo-Romain Vesunna** (p589) Strolling an excavated 1st-century Roman *domus* in Périgueux.

8 **Limoges** (p613) Shopping for French porcelain at renowned china factories.

9 **Medieval Cities** (p631)
Traipsing through still-vibrant towns from the Middle Ages, including Figeac and Cahors.

THE DORDOGNE

Few regions sum up the attractions of France better than the Dordogne. With its rich food, heady history, château-studded countryside and picturesque villages, the Dordogne has long been a favourite getaway for French families on *les grandes vacances*. It's also famous for having some of France's finest prehistoric cave art, which fill the caverns and rock shelters of the Vézère Valley.

Part of the historic area that was called Aquitaine, its strategic importance through the ages is illustrated by the many *bastides* (fortified towns) and fortresses throughout. Today it's known to the French as the Périgord, and is divided into four colour-coded areas: Périgord Pourpre (purple) for the winegrowing regions around Bergerac; Périgord Noir (black) for the dark oak forests around the Vézère Valley and Sarlat-la-Canéda; Périgord Blanc (white) after the limestone hills around the capital, Périgueux; and Périgord Vert (green) for the forested regions of the north.

Périgueux

POP 29,829

Founded by Gallic tribes, and later developed by the Romans into the important city of Vesunna, Périgueux remains the Dordogne's biggest (and busiest) town, with a lively cafe and restaurant scene, and plenty of shopping. Get past its suburban sprawl to its centre, and you discover a thoroughly charming old town dotted with medieval buildings and Renaissance mansions, radiating out from the Gothic Cathédrale St-Front.

Reminders of the city's Roman past fill the Cité quarter – the original 'old town'. You can visit a ruined garden-filled amphitheatre and triumphal tower, as well as a grand villa at the city's excellent Gallo-Roman museum.

◉ Sights

The tourist office (p591) has a great walking tour map (€0.50) and offers guided tours (adult/child €6/3).

◉ Puy St-Front

The area around the cathedral, known as Puy St-Front, encompasses the city's most impressive medieval streets and buildings.

★ **Cathédrale St-Front**   CATHEDRAL
(place de la Clautre; ⊙8.30am-7pm) Périgueux' most distinctive landmark is most notable for its five creamy Byzantine tower-topped domes (inspired by either St Mark's Basilica in Venice or the church of the Holy Apostles of Constantinople, depending on whom you ask). Built in the 12th century on the site of two earlier basilicas, it was sacked in the Wars of Religion, and redesigned and rebuilt by Abadie (the architect of Paris' Sacré Cœur) in the late 19th century.

A striking bell tower remains from the 12th-century church, and informed the design of Abadie's domes. The interior is laid out in a Greek cross, and the cloisters date from the 12th to 16th centuries.

The best views of the cathedral are from **Pont des Barris** just to the east.

St-Front Quarter   AREA
North of the cathedral is this fabulous tangle of cobblestone streets lined with medieval houses. The best examples are along rue du Plantier, rue de la Sagesse, rue de la Miséricorde and rue Aubergerie; many are marked with French/English placards.

Rue Limogeanne, a super shopping street, has graceful Renaissance buildings at nos 3, 5 and 12. Around the corner, the 15th-century **Maison du Pâtissier** (17 rue Éguillerie) is elaborately carved. Nearby **Galerie Daumesnil** is a series of linked courtyards within 15th- to 17th-century townhouses.

Puy St-Front used to be surrounded by medieval fortifications. Now, only the 15th-century Tour Mataguerre remains.

DON'T MISS

MARKET DAYS

Folks come from far and wide for Périgueux' bustling markets.

Wednesday & Saturday Market (place de la Clautre; ⊙8am-1pm Wed & Sat) Périgueux' wonderful street markets explode into action on Wednesday and Saturday, taking over place du Coderc, place de la Clautre and place de l'Ancienne Hôtel de Ville. All sorts of *gourmandise* are available.

Marchés au Gras (place St-Louis; ⊙9am-1pm Wed & Sat mid-Nov–early-Mar) Browse local winter delicacies, such as truffles (December to February), wild mushrooms and foie gras.

Musée d'Art et d'Archéologie du Périgord · MUSEUM

(☑05 53 06 40 70; www.perigueux-maap.fr; 22 cours Tourny; adult/child €5.50/3.50; ⊙10.30am-5.30pm Mon & Wed-Fri, 1-6pm Sat & Sun) The city's museum displays fine Roman mosaics, prehistoric scrimshaw, medieval stonework from the Cathédrale St-Front, and interesting art (mainly from the 19th and 20th centuries).

⊙ La Cité

The La Cité neighbourhood, west of the modern-day city centre, is the site of ancient Vesunna, among the most important cities in Roman Gaul.

★ Musée Gallo-Romain Vesunna · MUSEUM

(☑05 53 53 00 92; www.perigueux-vesunna.fr; 20 rue du 26e Régiment d'Infanterie, Parc de Vésone; adult/child €6/4, audioguide €1; ⊙10am-7pm Jul & Aug, shorter hr rest of year) Part of the park that contains the Tour de Vésone, this sleek museum designed by French architect Jean Nouvel encompasses a 1st-century Roman *domus* (townhouse) uncovered in 1959. Light floods in through the glass-and-steel structure, and walkways circumnavigate the enormous excavated complex; it's still possible to make out the central fountain, supporting pillars and the underfloor hypocaust system, as well as original mosaic murals, jewellery, pottery and even a water pump.

A joint ticket with the Musée d'Art et d'Archéologie du Périgord costs €9/6 per adult/child.

Roman Amphitheatre · RUINS

FREE The ruins of the city's amphitheatre, designed to hold more than 20,000 baying spectators, was one of the largest such structures in Gaul. Today the tops of the arches have been revealed and embrace a peaceful park and fountain, the **Jardin des Arènes** (⊙7.30am-9pm Apr-Sep, to 6.30pm Oct-Mar) **FREE**, popular with local families.

Tour de Vésone · RUINS

(⊙park 7.30am-9pm Apr-Sep, to 6.30pm Oct-Mar) **FREE** This 24.5m-high *cella* (inner shrine) is the last remaining section of a massive 2nd-century Gallo-Roman temple dedicated to the local goddess Vesunna.

Église St-Étienne de la Cité · CHURCH

(place de la Cité; ⊙8am-6pm) The Église St-Étienne de la Cité was built in the 11th century on the site of the Roman temple to Mars. Périgueux' cathedral until 1669, it only has two of its original four powerfully built domed bays (each different from the others).

ⓘ RIVERSIDE BIKING

Walkers and cyclists should check out the paved **Voie Verte**, which runs along the Isle River for some 30km (Périgueux is roughly in the middle). Hire bikes at the **Véloc Café** (☑06 33 48 22 89; 7 av Daumesnil; bicycles per 4/8hr €20/30; ⊙7.30am-8.30pm Mon-Sat, to 1pm Sun) and pick up a map detailing sights and activities along the way at the tourist office.

🛏 Sleeping

The choice of accommodation in Périgueux leaves a lot to be desired, with apartment rentals and chain hotels the primary options. The tourist office has lists of B&Bs and campgrounds.

Hôtel des Barris · HOTEL €

(☑05 53 53 04 05; www.hoteldesbarris.com; 2 rue Pierre Magne; s/d €60/67; 🖭) Beside the broad River Isle, this Logis hotel is the best value in Périgueux, as long as you can get a river-view room (the ones by the busy road are noisy). Higher-end rooms have air-conditioning, but only two have cathedral views. Reception closes in the middle of the day.

Bristol Hôtel · HOTEL €

(☑05 53 08 75 90; www.bristolfrance.com; 37-39 rue Antoine Gadaud; d €80-100, tr €110; ❀@🖭) The Bristol's boxy façade has little appeal, but look beyond the exterior and you'll find renovated, spacious rooms with all mod cons, super-friendly staff, and a central location. Find it half a block north of rue Gambetta, on the western edge of the Puy St-Front quarter. There's free parking.

🍴 Eating

Pierrot Gourmet · DELI €

(☑05 53 53 35 32; www.pierrotgourmet.com; 6 rue de l'Hôtel de Ville; mains €9.90, menus €15; ⊙11.30am-6pm Tue-Sat; 🖭) This lovely deli serves regional dishes canteen-style in the buzzy dining room, or boxed up to go for the perfect gourmet picnic. Specialities include cep (a type of mushroom) flans, duck parmentier, Périgueux pâté, and sinful gingerbread tiramisu.

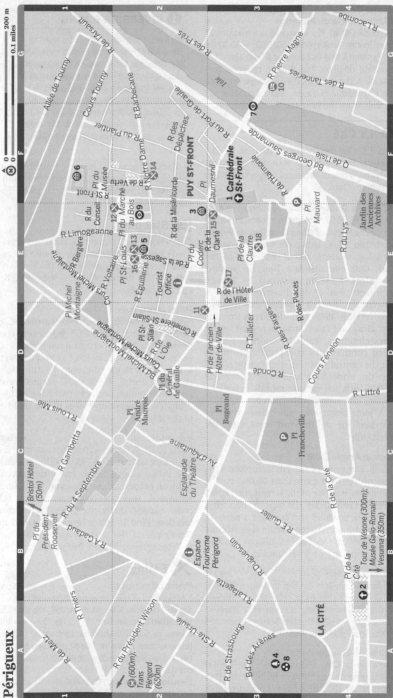

Périgueux

Périgueux

★ **Café de la Place**   BRASSERIE, CAFE €
(✑05 53 08 21 11; www.cafedelaplace24.com; 7 place du Marché au Bois; mains €9.50-20; ⊕restaurant noon-2.30pm & 7-10.30pm, bar 8am-2am) You simply couldn't hope to find a more lively Gallic spot. Cutlery clatters beneath classic brasserie trappings – spinning fans, shiny brass fittings, burnished wooden bar – and there's nowhere better in town for people-watching over a *petit café* or perfectly decadent *steak-frites*.

Au Phil des Saisons   CAFE €
(✑05 53 09 53 64; 3 pl de l'Ancien Hôtel de Ville; meals €7-14.90; ⊕8.30am-6pm) Create your own salads, grab a thick slice of quiche or juice up at this colourful pay-at-the-counter cafe. Continuous service.

La Ferme St-Louis   FRENCH €€
(✑05 53 53 82 77; 2 place St-Louis; lunch/dinner menus from €17/32; ⊕noon-2pm & 7-9.30pm daily Apr-Sep, closed Sun, Mon & Wed Oct-Mar) Specialises in local products such as duck foie gras. Dine in the intimate stone room with the tinkle of glasses, or under plane trees on the square.

Le Troquet   BISTRO €€
(✑05 53 35 81 41; www.letroquet-perigueux.fr; 4 rue Notre Dame; mains €15-23; ⊕noon-2pm &

7.30-10pm Tue-Sat) Locals in the know reserve ahead at this shoebox-small alleyway bistro great for authentic market cuisine.

★ **L'Essentiel**   GASTRONOMY €€€
(✑05 53 35 15 15; www.restaurant-perigueux. com; 8 rue de la Clarté; lunch menus €29-47, dinner menus €45-81; ⊕noon-1.30pm & 7.30-9.30pm Tue-Sat) At Michelin-starred L'Essentiel, it feels like you're dining inside an aristocratic friend's living room, with floral wallpaper and orange velour chairs providing a suitably posh setting for Périgueux' top gourmet cuisine. Chef Eric Vidal, a Tulle native, prepares meals steeped in local flavours: Quercy lamb, cockerel and local rare-breed pigs regularly feature on the *menus*, often with a truffly, nutty touch.

ℹ Information

Espace Tourisme Périgord (✑05 53 35 50 24; www.dordogne-perigord-tourisme. fr; 25 rue du Président Wilson; ⊕9am-noon & 2-5pm Mon-Fri) Dordogne *département* information.

Tourist Office (✑05 53 53 10 63; www. tourisme-perigueux.fr; 9bis place du Coderc; ⊕9am-7pm Mon-Sat, 10am-6pm Sun Jul & Aug, shorter hr rest of year; 🖱) Helpful, with loads of info and a smartphone app.

ℹ Getting There & Away

BUS

Péribus (✑05 53 53 30 37; www.peribus.fr; tickets €1.25) operates local buses, including a shuttle that runs from place Faidherbe to St-Front on Wednesday and Saturday market days.

Further afield, **Trans Périgord** (✑05 53 08 43 13; www.transperigord.fr; 19 rue Denis Papin; 1/10 tickets €2/14) runs weekday buses to destinations including Sarlat (line 7; 1½ hours, two daily), Montignac (line 7 and 8A; 1¾ hours, two daily), Bergerac (line 3; 1¼ hours, four daily), and Brantôme (line 1B; 50 minutes, one daily).

TRAIN

The **train station** (rue Denis Papin), 1km northwest of the old town, is served by Péribus lines GBE, 4 and 5. Getting to Bergerac (€25.70, nine daily) requires a change in Libourne, and Sarlat-la-Canéda (€16.30, three daily) requires a change in Le Buisson.

Bordeaux €22.50, 1½ hours, 13 daily
Brive-la-Gaillarde €14, one hour, seven daily
Les Eyzies-de-Tayac-Sireuil €8.50, 35 minutes, five daily
Limoges €18, 1½ hours, six daily

WORTH A TRIP

CHÂTEAU LIFE

For a dash of high-end château living, head 8km northeast of Périgueux to Château des Reynats. Its glass-encased **Bistro La Verrière** (Château des Reynats; ☑ 05 53 03 53 59; www.chateau-hotel-perigord.com; 15 ave des Reynats, Chancelade; lunch menus €19-26, dinner menus €26-44; ☉ noon-2pm & 7-9.30pm; ☏) cooks up refined seasonal cuisine in a relaxed atmosphere surrounded by verdant gardens. There's also a high-end gastronomic restaurant, **L'Oison**, open for dinner (Monday to Saturday, mains €26-38), and you can stay over in unique castle rooms (doubles from €135).

Brantôme

POP 2181

Beautiful Brantôme sits on a small island in a bend in the River Dronne, with five medieval bridges and romantic riverfront architecture, thus earning its tagline 'Venice of the Périgord'. Its impressive abbey is built into a mainland cliff face, and it's surrounded by parks and willow-filled woodland, making Brantôme an enchanting spot to while away an afternoon or embark on a boat ride.

◉ Sights

Abbaye de Brantôme LANDMARK
(bd Charlemagne) Brantôme's most illustrious landmark is the former Benedictine Abbey, built and rebuilt from the 11th to 18th centuries and now occupied by the town hall. Look for the detached 11th-century Romanesque bell tower, built into the rock, and the oldest in the Limousin style. Next door is the Gothic church.

Grottes de l'Abbaye CAVE
(☑ 05 47 45 30 12; bd Charlemagne; adult/child €6/4; ☉ 10am-7pm Jul & Aug, shorter hr rest of year) Behind the former abbey – Brantôme's most illustrious landmark and now the town hall – lie moody caves, originally a place of pagan worship and then part of Brantôme's first 8th-century abbey. Its most famous feature is a 15th-century rock frieze thought to depict the Last Judgment. The ticket also includes entrance to a small museum in the same building, which displays the work of the 'spiritualism' painter Fernand Desmoulin.

🏃 Activities

Plenty of outfitters hire out one-person kayaks, stand-up paddleboards and multi-person canoes for a self-guided paddle down the Dronne. They also offer half-day trips from Fontaine (4km upriver), Verneuil (8km upriver) and Bourdeilles (12km downriver), plus a full-day trip from Verneuil to Bourdeilles (20km).

Allo Canoës BOATING
(☑ 05 32 14 09 02; www.allocanoes.com; Le Chatenet; kayak/canoe rental per hr from €10/14, half-day €17-29, full day €25-38; ☉ Apr-Oct) Hire a kayak or canoe for a self-guided trip. Located 1.5km south of the abbey.

Brantôme Canoë BOATING
(☑ 05 53 05 77 24; www.brantomecanoe.com; 14 av André Maurois; kayak/SUP/canoe rental per hr from €10/12/14, half-day €16-29, full day €25-40; ☉ Apr-Oct) Beside the main car-park. Also rents stand-up paddleboards for self-guided sessions.

🛏 Sleeping & Eating

Bluebell Guesthouse B&B €
(☑ 05 53 03 96 51; 17 av Dr Devillard; d €80; ☏) This welcoming English-run mansion sits a five-minute walk south of Brantôme's central hubbub, and thus affords a gentle escape with gardens, silence and three modest guest rooms.

★ Hostellerie Les Griffons HOTEL €€
(☑ 05 53 45 45 35; www.griffons.fr; Bourdeilles; d from €105; ☉ Apr-Nov; ☏) In the riverside town of Bourdeilles, 9km southwest of Brantôme along the D78, this charming converted mill perched over the river drips with character. Medieval fireplaces, solid beams and higgledy-piggledy layouts characterise the rooms. Its riverside restaurant (three-course *menus* €32-45) opens onto a lovely waterfront terrace, and is renowned throughout the region.

Le Bistrot Saint Pierre BISTRO €
(☑ 05 53 13 33 90; 25 rue Victor Hugo; mains €12-20; ☉ 9am-3pm Thu-Tue, 6pm-midnight Thu-Mon) Floor-to-ceiling windows brighten up this airy, modern bistro, the local choice for a casual meal: think hearty salads, *magret de canard* (duck breast with honey) and duck burgers. Good cider selection.

Moulin de l'Abbaye GASTRONOMY €€€
(☑ 05 53 05 80 22; www.moulinabbaye.com; 1 rte de Bourdeilles; lunch/3-course/4-course menus

€39/70/90; ⊘noon-1.40pm Wed-Sun, 7.30-9.30pm Wed-Sun Apr-Oct) Choose between this extravagant gastronomic restaurant at a carefully converted water mill at the foot of the abbey, and its two sister bistros: **Au Fil de l'Eau** (☑05 53 05 73 65; www.fildeleau.com; quai Bertin 21; menus €22-29; ⊘noon-2pm Thu-Tue, 7.30-9.30pm Mon, Tue & Thu-Sat May-Sep), specialising in fish, and **Au Fil du Temps** (☑05 53 05 75 27; www.fildutemps.com; 1 chemin du Vert Galant; menus €19-39; ⊘noon-2pm Thu-Tue, 7.30-9.30pm Fri, Sat, Mon & Tue Apr-Oct) with traditional Périgordian roasted meats. At the main gourmet restaurant, terraces overlook the river, and 20 equally luxe rooms are on offer upstairs (rooms €205 to €425).

🛍 Shopping

Truffle Market   MARKET

(place du Marché; ⊘6am-noon Fri Dec-Feb) Brântome has a weekly winter market of the local delicacy, the black Périgord truffle.

ℹ Information

Tourist Office (☑05 53 05 80 63; www.perigord-dronne-belle.fr; 2 rue Puyjoli de Meyjounissas; ⊘10am-6pm Jun-Sep, shorter hr rest of year) Large office across the bridge from the abbey.

ℹ Getting There & Away

Brantôme is 27km north of Périgueux along the D939. From Monday to Friday, two **Trans Périgord** (www.transperigord.fr) buses per day run from the police station in Brantôme centre to Périgueux (€2, 50 minutes).

Bergerac

POP 27,419

Rich vineyards and rolling fields surround pretty cream-stone Bergerac, a good gateway to the Dordogne and one of the most prestigious winegrowing areas of the Aquitaine. The sweet town's main claim to fame is dramatist and satirist Savinien Cyrano de Bergerac (1619–55), whose romantic exploits – and oversized nose – have inspired everyone from Molière to Steve Martin. Despite the legend (largely invented by 19th-century playwright Edmond Rostand), Cyrano's connection with the town is tenuous – he's thought to have stayed here only a few nights, if at all.

Bergerac's riverfront old town and lively cafe scene make it fun to explore.

◉ Sights & Activities

The prettiest parts of Bergerac's fine old town are place de la Mirpe, with its tree-shaded square and timber houses, and place Pelissière, where a jaunty statue of Cyrano de Bergerac gazes up at the nearby Église St-Jacques, a former pilgrimage point. The *ancien* (old) port wraps beautifully along the river. Rue St-Clar arcs inland and is lined with half-timbered houses. The tourist office has a good, free walking-tour map.

Musée de la Ville   MUSEUM

(☑05 53 57 80 92; 5 rue des Conférences; adult/child €3/free; ⊘10am-noon & 1-6pm Jun-Sep, shorter hr rest of year) Wonderfully musty displays of vintage winemaking equipment and scale models of local river boats.

Musée du Tabac   MUSEUM

(☑05 53 63 04 13; 10 rue de l'Ancien Pont; adult/child €4/free; ⊘10am-1pm & 2-6pm Jun-Sep, shorter hr rest of year) Inside the 17th-century Maison Peyrarède, the displays span 3000 years of history and include a collection of ornate pipes.

Gabarres de Bergerac   BOATING

(☑05 53 24 58 80; www.gabarres.fr; quai Salvette; adult/child €9.50/6.50; ⊘Easter-Oct) Atmospheric 50-minute cruises from the quay.

🛏 Sleeping

Le Colombier de Cyrano et Roxane   B&B €

(☑05 53 57 96 70; www.lecolombierdecyrano.fr; 17 rue du Grand Moulin, place de la Mirpe; d €79-89; 🛜) One of several sweet *chambres d'hôte* in Bergerac's old town, this 16th-century blue-shuttered stone building has three colourful rooms and a flower-filled terrace where you can doze in the hammock.

REGIONAL PARKS

This corner of France is renowned for its natural beauty, with huge swathes protected in three *parcs naturels régionaux*: **Périgord-Limousin** (www.pnr-perigord-limousin.fr) in the northwest, **Millevaches en Limousin** (www.pnr-millevaches.fr) in the east and **Causses de Quercy** (www.parc-causses-du-quercy.org) in the south. All three offer a wealth of outdoor activities. Tourist offices stock walking leaflets, mountain biking guides, and horseback-riding information.

BERGERAC WINE COUNTRY

The broad, flat area south of Bergerac is covered in vineyards. Seven Appellations d'Origine Contrôlées (AOCs) hail from this region, which abuts Bordeaux wine country to the west, and represent some of the Dordogne's best wines. Pick up the *Wines of Bergerac* guide-map from local tourist offices or the **Maison des Vins** (☑ 05 53 63 57 55; www.vins-bergeracduras.fr; 1 rue des Récollets; ⊘ complimentary tastings 10am-12.30pm & 2-7pm Tue-Sat Feb-Jun & Sep-Dec, daily Jul & Aug, closed Jan) in Bergerac, and hit the wine-tasting trail.

Château Montdoyen (☑ 05 53 58 85 85; www.chateau-montdoyen.com; Le Puch, Monbazillac; ⊘ complimentary tastings 9.30am-6pm Mon-Fri) This fun family-run winery makes a full range of excellent wines, from Bergerac AOC reds, to whites with intriguing names like Divine Miséricorde (sauvignon blanc and sauvignon gris), to a delicious rosé, and outstanding Monbazillac sweet white. Find it 10km south of Bergerac, off the D933.

Château d'Elle (☑ 05 53 61 66 62; www.chateaudelle.com; 323 chemin de la Briasse, Bergerac; ⊘ complimentary tastings 10am-8pm) Jocelyne Pécou, one of the few Bergerac female vintners (hinted at in the winery's name), produces robust red Pécharmant AOC, 5km east of Bergerac centre.

Château de la Jaubertie (☑ 05 53 58 32 11; www.chateau-jaubertie.com; Colombier; ⊘ complimentary tastings 10am-5pm Mon-Sat May–mid-Sep) This historic monument and former royal hunting lodge in pretty fields off the N21 south of Monbazillac produces a range of organic AOC Bergerac wines.

Château de Monbazillac (☑ 05 53 63 65 00; www.chateau-monbazillac.com; Monbazillac; tour and tasting adult/child €7.50/3.75; ⊘ 10am-7pm Jun-Sep, shorter hr rest of year, closed Jan) Often crowded because of its grand 16th-century château (best seen from outside), this vineyard specialises in sweet white Monbazillac AOC.

★ **Château Les Farcies du Pech'** B&B €€
(☑ 06 75 28 01 90; www.farciesdupech.com; Farcies Nord, Pécharmant; d €110; ⊘ mid-Mar–mid-Nov) Part of a group of four renowned wineries (www.vignoblesdubard.com), this beautiful château-vineyard 2km north of Bergerac is definitely the choice for oenophiles. All five rooms scream rustic chic, with original stonework and vintage character. The proprietor serves a lovely home-cooked French brekkie in the dining room and can arrange tours of the vineyards.

Château les Merles BOUTIQUE HOTEL €€
(☑ 05 53 63 13 42; www.lesmerles.com; Tuilières, Mouleydier; d €150-210, ste €250, apt €350; @ 🖥 🗷) Behind its 19th-century neoclassical façade, this château 15km east of Bergerac is a study in modish minimalism. Monochrome colour schemes including black-and-white sofas and artfully chosen antiques run throughout the rooms, most of which would look more at home in Paris than deep in the Dordogne. From the nine-hole golf course to the ravishing restaurant (dinner *menus* from €30), it's a royal retreat.

✖ Eating

Bergerac and the surrounding wine country are loaded with great eateries to fit any budget. Market days are Wednesday and Saturday.

Fleur d'Oranger CAFE €
(☑ 05 53 63 40 36; 30 rue de la Résistance; meals €10-15; ⊘ 8.45am-7pm Tue-Sat) Sweet potato soup, leek curry and three varieties of tartines (open-faced sandwiches) – plus ice cream and milkshakes in summer months – make this address a good one to remember.

★ **Villa Laetitia** FRENCH €€
(☑ 05 53 61 00 12; www.villa-laetitia.fr; 21 rue de l'Ancien Pont; lunch menus €20-24, dinner menus €36; ⊘ noon-2pm Tue-Sun, 7-9pm Tue-Sat) Book ahead for a seat with in-the-know locals in the soft, cream-stone dining room where charming waitstaff serve delicious local cuisine, made in the open kitchen at the rear. Expect farm-fresh ingredients and delicious Périgord classics exquisitely presented.

La Ferme de Biorne FRENCH €€
(☑ 05 53 57 67 26; www.ferme-biorne.com; Lunas; lunch/dinner menu from €16/21; ⊘ Tue-Sun Apr-Oct by reservation only) This rural *ferme auberge*

(farm restaurant), 12km northwest of Bergerac, raises its own birds for the restaurant table, including goose, quail and duck for its foie gras. Cosy *gîtes* (€510 for four people per week in summer) are also available.

★ **La Tour des Vents**　　GASTRONOMY €€€
(☑ 05 53 58 30 10; www.tourdesvents.com; Le Moulin de Malfourat, Monbazillac; lunch menus €39, dinner menus €49-89; ⊙ noon-1.15pm Wed-Sun, 7.30-9.15pm Wed-Sun; ✈) Chef Damien Fagette creates elaborate *périgourdine* meals using the freshest seasonal ingredients, and friendly staff serve them to the dining room or terrace with panoramic views of Bergerac wine country. Dishes include foie gras with local strawberries, port *gelée* and balsamic vinegar.

L'Imparfait　　FRENCH €€€
(☑ 05 53 57 47 92; www.imparfait.com; 8-10 rue des Fontaines; lunch menus from €29, dinner menus €39-49; ⊙ noon-2pm & 7-10pm) Chef Hervé Battiston has made this sweet little restaurant a favourite, thanks to artful French food served up in a pretty 12th-century cloister. Reserve ahead.

🍷 Drinking & Nightlife

Le Plus Que Parfait　　BAR
(☑ 05 53 61 95 11; 12 rue des Fontaines; ⊙ 9am-1pm Tue-Sat, 11am-11pm Sun & Mon) Cleverly located across the street from the Imperfect, the lively Pluperfect serves up a winning selection of Belgian brews, cocktails and the occasional live concert.

ℹ Information

Tourist Office (☑ 05 53 57 03 11; www.bergerac-tourisme.com; 97 rue Neuve d'Argenson; ⊙ 9.30am-1pm & 2-6.30pm Mon-Sat Sep-Jun, plus Sun Jul & Aug; 🛜)

ℹ Getting There & Around

AIR
Bergerac's **airport** (EGC; ☑ 05 53 22 25 25; www.bergerac.aeroport.fr), 4km southeast of town, is served by Air France and budget carriers including Ryanair. Destinations include Paris Orly, Bristol, Brussels Charleroi, Edinburgh, London Stansted, London Gatwick, East Midlands, Liverpool, Birmingham, Exeter, Leeds Bradford, Southampton and Rotterdam.

Taxis (05 53 23 32 32), which cost about €15, and rental cars are the only option for getting into town.

BUS
Trans Périgord (www.transperigord.fr) line 3 connects Bergerac with Périgueux (€2, 1¼ hours, four Monday to Friday).

TRAIN
Bergerac is on the regional line between Bordeaux (€17.70, 1½ hours, seven daily) and Sarlat (€13.20, one to 1½ hours, six daily). For other destinations, change at Le Buisson or Libourne.

Issigeac
POP 760
Bastides (fortified towns) abound in the area southeast of Bergerac, and one of the best is wonderful Issigeac. The medieval village is a joy to explore, especially at its magnificent Sunday morning market. An agricultural area as well, it produces everything from foie gras to three AOC strawberry varieties. Look out for the delicious walnut-rind cheese, called *echourgnac*, made by nuns at Abbaye d'Echourgnac.

Issigeac's predominantly 13th- to 18th-century historic buildings were constructed

ℹ TOP MARKETS
Throughout the region local markets fill medieval cobbled streets and overflow with wintertime black truffles, walnuts, chestnuts, cheese, honey and seasonal produce, from asparagus to strawberries. Baskets and clothing also feature at some. **Summertime night markets** are fantastic: bring your own plates and cutlery and dine at tables set up under the stars.

Monday Ste-Alvère, Beaumont-du-Périgord (night), Beynac

Tuesday Beaumont-du-Périgord, Brive-la-Gaillarde, Le Bugue

Wednesday Périgueux, Sarlat-la-Canéda, Bergerac, Martel, Cahors, Cadouin

Thursday Monpazier, Issigeac (night)

Friday Brantôme, St-Pompon

Saturday Périgueux, Sarlat-la-Canéda, Brive-la-Gaillarde, Bergerac, Beaumont-du-Périgord, Villefranche-du-Périgord, Martel, Cahors, Figeac, St-Pompon (night)

Sunday Issigeac, St-Cyprien, Daglan

on top of a former 4th-century Roman villa, later a 7th-century Benedictine abbey. The tourist office has a free walking-tour leaflet. There's also an antique fair in August.

Sleeping & Eating

Issigeac has few places to eat; however, the tour de force is its magnificent Sunday morning market, which seems to fill every lane.

Passé et Présent B&B €
(05 53 63 35 31; www.passe-et-present.com; 14 Grand Rue, Issegeac; d €50-70; ⊛ 🕾) Impeccably designed antique-filled rooms fill a pretty ancient townhouse in Issegeac's centre. Take your tea in its rose-filled courtyard.

★**Shabby Chic Corner** CAFE €
(05 53 57 88 20; www.boheme-est-la-marquise. com; 3 rue Ernest Esclangon; ⊙ 9.30am-6pm Sun) Wonderful Nathalie has a lovely sewing atelier and shop around the corner, and a quaint, country-French-style *salon de thé* (tearoom) here. She bakes everything from scratch, and the place is open (and packed) for Sunday market days.

ℹ Information

Tourist Office (05 53 58 79 62; www. pays-des-bastides.com; place du Château; ⊙10am-noon & 2-5pm Tue-Sat, 10am-12.30pm Sun; 🕾) .

ℹ Getting There & Away

Issigeac is located 18km south of Bergerac on the D14, and is best reached with your own wheels.

Monpazier

POP 502

One of the Dordogne's best-preserved *bastides* is beautiful Monpazier. Founded in 1284 by a representative of Edward I (King of England and Duke of Aquitaine), it had a turbulent time during the Wars of Religion and the Peasant Revolts of the 16th century, but despite numerous assaults and campaigns, the town has survived wonderfully intact, with original walls, gates and a church.

TRUFFLES: BLACK PEARLS OF PÉRIGORD

While the Dordogne is famed for all of its gourmet goodies, for some culinary connoisseurs there's only one that matters: the black Périgord truffle (*Tuber melanosporum*), often dubbed *le diamant noir* (black diamond) or, hereabouts, *la perle noire du Périgord*.

A subterranean fungus that grows naturally in chalky soils (in the Dordogne around the roots of oak or hazelnut trees), it is notoriously capricious: a good truffle spot one year can be inexplicably bare the next, which makes large-scale farming practically impossible. The art of truffle hunting is a matter of luck, judgment and hard-earned experience, with specially trained dogs (and sometimes pigs) helping in the search.

The height of truffle season is between December and March, when you'll find them on local menus and when special **truffle markets** are held around the Dordogne, such as Périgueux' Marchés au Gras (p588), Brantôme (p593) and Sarlat (p602). Leading local chefs head 35km south of Périgueux to St-Alvère's **marché aux truffes** (rue Pasteur, Sainte Alvère; ⊙from 10am Mon Dec-Feb) where top harvests fetch as much as €1000 a kilogram, still a bargain by retail standards. Truffles are classified by quality and size, with the *brumale* species of truffles garnering lower prices.

Alternatively, book with local truffle expert Edouard Aynaud at **Truffière de Péchalifour** (05 53 29 20 44; www.truffe-perigord.com; Péchalifour; tours adult €8-10, child free-€5; ⊙tours 10.45am Wed-Sat Jul & Aug, by reservation rest of year) for a truffle-hunting tour, meal or stay at his *truffière* (truffle-growing area), just north of St-Cyprien.

Sorges, 23km northeast of Périgueux, has an **Écomusée de la Truffe** (05 53 05 90 11; N21, Sorges; adult/child €5/2.50; ⊙9.30am-6.30pm Mon-Fri, 9.30am-12.30pm & 2.30-6.30pm Sat & Sun mid-Jun–Sep, shorter hr rest of year) and a 3km trail through the local *truffières*, while **La Truffe Noire de Sorges** (06 08 45 09 48; www.truffe-sorges.com; Domaine de Saleix, Sorges; tours €10-25; ⊙by reservation Dec-Feb & Jun-Sep) runs truffle-themed tours followed by a tasting (tour in English on request). Sample the local speciality, or stay over, at **Auberge de la Truffe** (05 53 05 02 05; www.auberge-de-la-truffe.com; 21 rue Nationale, Sorges; lunch/dinner menus from €14.50/26.50; ⊙noon-2pm Wed-Sun, 7.30-9.30pm daily Easter-Oct; 🕾).

FORTIFIED VILLAGES IN THE DORDOGNE

If your curiosity is piqued by the *bastide* towns of Issigeac and Monpazier, be sure to roam the countryside in search of some less well-known but equally beautiful villages.

Beaumont-du-Périgord (15km east of Issigeac) features a large central square, fortified church, and Monday night market. One of its *bastide* gates leads straight into the countryside, and the tourist office has lists of walks and maps.

Belvès (16km northeast of Monpazier) has yellow-gold houses strung across a gorgeous hilltop, while **Villefranche-du-Périgord** (20km southeast of Monpazier), is another *bastide* with an enormous covered market in the central square. Teeny **Prats-du-Périgord** is for Romanesque architecture lovers, with its moody, fortified Église St-Maurice.

⊙ Sights

★ Place des Cornières SQUARE

From the town's three gateways, Monpazier's flat, grid-straight streets lead to the arcaded market square (also known as place Centrale), surrounded by an ochre-hued collection of stone houses that reflect centuries of building and rebuilding. In one corner is an old *lavoir* once used for washing clothes. Thursday is market day, as it has been since the Middle Ages.

Bastideum MUSEUM

(✆ 05 53 57 12 12; www.bastideum.fr; 8 rue Galmot; adult/child €4.80/2.80; ⊙ 10am-7pm Jul & Aug, shorter hr Apr-Jun & Sep-Oct) This small interpretative centre is a good stop for history buffs interested in reading up on *bastides*, or, for a bit more family fun, playing one of the two dozen plus 'medieval' games.

Château de Biron CHATEAU

(✆ 05 53 63 13 39; www.semitour.com; D53; adult/child €8.30/5.40, joint ticket with Cadouin €11.90/7.10; ⊙ 10am-7.30pm Jul & Aug, shorter hr rest of year, closed Jan) Eight kilometres south of Monpazier, this much-filmed château is a glorious mishmash of styles, having been fiddled with by eight centuries of successive heirs. The castle was finally sold in the early 1900s to pay for the extravagant lifestyle of a particularly irresponsible son. It's notable for its slate turrets and double loggia staircase, supposedly modelled on one at Versailles.

🛏 Sleeping & Eating

Chez Edèll B&B €

(✆ 05 53 63 26 71; www.chezedell.com; 2 rue Notre Dame; d €70, apt €80; 🛜) Cosy up in this diminutive but welcoming guesthouse in the middle of Monpazier. Rooms have balconies with sweeping country views, and a refrigerator – perfect for stocking up at the weekly market. A self-catering apartment is a superb deal.

Cabanes Perchées dans les Arbres TREEHOUSE €€

(✆ 06 87 05 48 75; www.cabanes-perchees-dans-les-arbres.com; Rousille, Capdrot; treehouse incl breakfast €155-195; ❄) Six treehouses await adventurers south of Monpazier, with marvellous countryside panoramas from the balconies and luxury add-ons like outdoor hot tubs, a spa and cocoon-like bunks for the kids. Dinners (€25) can be hauled up to your perch for the full experience. It's 2.5km southeast of town.

Hôtel Edward 1er HOTEL €€

(✆ 05 53 22 44 00; www.hoteledward1er.com; 5 rue St-Pierre; tw €143-202, d €155-225; ⊙ Apr-Oct; 🛜🏊) Rooms in this tower-topped mansion get more luxurious the more you pay: top-of-the-line suites have a choice of jacuzzi or Turkish bath, and views of surrounding hills. It feels slightly dated considering the price, but the owners are fun, and there's an excellent restaurant (*menus* €31.50 to €51), for which you should book ahead.

Bistrot 2 BISTRO €€

(✆ 05 53 22 60 64; www.bistrot2.fr; Foirail Nord; lunch/dinner menus from €16/22; ⊙ noon-10pm Jul & Aug, shorter hr rest of year, closed Nov-Mar) Modern dining in an old-town setting with a wisteria-covered terrace right opposite a medieval gateway. Food is French with an adventurous slant.

ⓘ Information

Tourist Office (✆ 05 53 22 68 59; www.pays-des-bastides.com; place des Cornières; ⊙ 10am-12.30pm & 2-6pm Jun-Sep, reduced hr rest of year) Distributes a good walking-tour map of town.

ⓘ Getting There & Away

Monpazier is 50km southwest of Sarlat and 50km southeast of Bergerac. There is no public transport.

ⓘ TRIP PLANNER: ONLINE RESOURCES

Regional tourism websites are packed with information, from accommodation and activities to local festivals.

Dordogne (www.dordogne-perigord-tourisme.fr)

Limousin (www.tourismelimousin.com)

Haute-Vienne (www.tourisme-haute-vienne.com)

Creuse (www.tourisme-creuse.com)

Corrèze (www.tourismecorreze.com)

The Lot (www.tourisme-lot.com)

The Dordogne Valley

Lush meadows and green woods roll out along the meandering banks of the Dordogne, one of France's most iconic and idyllic rivers. In centuries gone by, the valley marked an important frontier during the Hundred Years' War, and the hilltops are studded with defensive châteaux, as well as heavily fortified towns. These days it's a picture of French tranquillity, perfect country to explore by bike or, better still, by paddle.

Trémolat & Around

POP 637

Little Trémolat sits in a dramatic bend of the River Dordogne. Besides the beautiful, forested landscape, the area is home to several top restaurants and wine experiences, and there are a handful of interesting sights nearby.

◉ Sights

Cloître de Cadouin HISTORIC SITE

(☑ 05 53 63 36 28; www.semitour.com; Cadouin; adult/child €7/4.10, joint ticket with Château de Biron €11.90/7.10; ☉ 10am-7pm Jul & Aug, shorter hr rest of year) This Unesco-listed 12th-century Cistercian abbey and its Gothic cloister hide in the forest just south of the Dordogne, along the River Bélingou.

Château de Lanquais CHATEAU

(☑ 06 10 79 12 69; www.chateaudelanquais.fr; Lanquais; adult/child €8/6; ☉ 10am-7pm Jul & Aug, shorter hr rest of year) This château, with portions dating from as early as the 12th century, though much of it is in the later Italian Renaissance style, is fully kitted out with period furnishings.

Gouffre de Proumeyssac CAVE

(☑ 05 53 07 85 85; www.gouffre-proumeyssac.com; Audrix, Le Bugue; adult/child €10.50/6.90; ☉ 9am-7pm Jul & Aug, reduced hr rest of year, closed Jan) In high season, reserve ahead for a guided tour of this vast cave with sparkling stalactites. It has an aerial basket for viewing the cavern.

🛏 Sleeping

Auberge de Jeunesse Cadouin HOSTEL €

(☑ 05 53 73 28 78; www.hifrance.org; Cadouin; dm incl breakfast €17; ☉ reception 8am-noon & 4-9pm; 🛜) Set in part of Cadoin's 12th-century cloister, this youth hostel certainly has a special location. Rooms are monastic, however, and you will have trouble reaching the village, 13km south of Trémolat, without your own wheels. Wi-fi is iffy in rooms. Cash only if you haven't paid in advance.

★ Le Vieux Logis BOUTIQUE HOTEL €€€

(☑ 05 53 22 80 06; www.vieux-logis.com; Trémolat; r €210-395; ❄ @ 🛜 ☲) Make a reservation at this luxurious vine-covered manor for total immersion in the French countryside. A one-time tobacco farm, the hotel now has 25 personalised rooms (of which 11 are suites) and perfectly manicured grounds to explore, along with a lap pool and Michelin-starred restaurant (p599).

🍴 Eating

Don't miss a foodie stop at one of the Trémolat area restaurants. They offer some of the best, most diverse menus in the region.

★ Au Fil de l'Eau FRENCH €€

(☑ 05 53 61 79 76; www.au-fil-de-leau.net; 32 av de Cahors, Couze St-Front; lunch menus €15, dinner menus €27-48; ☉ noon-2pm Wed-Sun, 7.30-9pm Wed-Sat) It's well worth stopping in the nondescript village of Couze St-Front for the warm welcome and riverside dining at Au Fil de l'Eau. Jazzy tunes tinkle as a parade of fresh, seasonal dishes is served; super-popular with locals. Reserve ahead to get a seat at the giant windows overlooking the river.

★ Les Truffières FRENCH €€

(☑ 05 53 27 30 44; www.auberge-les-truffieres.fr; Bosredon; lunch/dinner menus from €22/32; ☉ noon-1.30pm Tue-Sun, 7.30-9.30pm Tue-Sat May–mid-Sep, dinner only mid-Sep–Apr) Reserve ahead for fantastic local cuisine prepared by lively Yanick and his son Aurélian on a farm in the hills above Trémolat. The dining room feels like the country home it is, and the dishes are tops: from classic garlic soup to homemade foie gras.

★ **Le Vieux Logis** GASTRONOMY €€€
(☑ 05 53 22 80 06; www.vieux-logis.com; Trémolat; lunch menus €53, 4-course menus from €80; ⊙ noon-1.30pm & 7.30-9pm, closed Wed & Thu mid-Oct–mid-Apr) Folks come from far and wide for chef Vincent Arnould's refined, beautifully presented creative cuisine of the Périgord. The ceiling soars over the elegant dining room, or dine alfresco under a canopy of sculpted trees. Every dish is a surprising treat, and the wine list matches. There's also the excellent **Bistrot de la Place** (*menus* lunch/dinner from €17/35).

🛍 Shopping

Julien de Savignac WINE
(☑ 05 53 07 10 31; www.julien-de-savignac.com; av de la Libération, D51, Le Bugue; ⊙ 9am-7pm Mon-Sat, to noon Sun) One of Dordogne's best wine shops is in Le Bugue, just south of the town centre. Check the website for other branches.

ℹ Getting There & Away

Trémolat is 35km east of Bergerac and 44km west of Sarlat, and best reached with your own wheels.

Beynac-et-Cazenac & Around

POP 552

Beynac, as it is known by locals, and its environs make up one of the Dordogne's most dramatic landscapes, with the two opposing fortresses of Beynac and Castelnaud facing off across the gloriously broad river, plied by pleasure craft in summer.

Scenes from the Lasse Hallström–directed movie *Chocolat* (2000), starring Johnny Depp and Juliette Binoche, were filmed along rue de l'Ancienne Poste in Beynac, and part of Luc Besson's *The Messenger: The Story of Joan of Arc* (1999) was filmed in the fortress.

◉ Sights

★ **Château de Castelnaud** CASTLE
(☑ 05 53 31 30 00; www.castelnaud.com; Castelnaud-la-Chapelle; adult/child €9.80/4.90; ⊙ 9am-8pm Jul & Aug, 10am-7pm Apr-Jun & Sep, shorter hr rest of year) The massive ramparts and metre-thick crenellated walls of this quintessential medieval fortress (occupied by the English during the Hundred Years War) contain an elaborate **museum of medieval warfare** with displays of daggers, spiked halberds, archaic cannons and enormous crossbows. Climb the dark 16th-century

artillery tower stairs to see the exhibits and reach the rugged 13th-century *donjon* (keep). From the upper terrace a fantastic view encompasses the Dordogne Valley all the way to Castelnaud's arch-rival, the Château de Beynac, 4km to the north.

★ **Château de Beynac** CHATEAU
(☑ 05 53 29 50 40; www.chateau-beynac.com; Beynac-et-Cazenac; adult/child €8/4; ⊙ 10am-7pm Apr-Sep, to 6.30pm Oct-Mar, closed Jan) Towering gloriously atop a limestone bluff, this 12th-century fortress' panoramic position above the Dordogne made it a key defensive position during the Hundred Years War. Apart from a brief interlude under Richard the Lionheart, Beynac remained fiercely loyal to the French monarchy, often placing it at odds with the English-controlled stronghold of nearby Castelnaud. Protected by 200m cliffs, a double wall and double moat, it presented a formidable challenge for would-be attackers, though it saw little direct action.

Highlights include the château's Romanesque **keep**, a grand **Salle des États** (State Room) and frescoed 15th-century **chapel**, and the 16th- and 17th-century **apartments** built to lodge castle barons. From the battlements, there's a fantastic view along the Dordogne.

The impressive fortress is rather bare-bones inside; buy the information booklet to add context.

Château des Milandes MUSEUM
(☑ 05 53 59 31 21; www.milandes.com; Castelnaud-la-Chapelle; adult/child €11/7; ⊙ 9.30am-8pm Jul & Aug, shorter hr rest of year, closed Jan-Mar) This 15th-century château, 3km southwest of Beynac, is famous for its fabulous former owner: glamorous dancer, singer and music-hall star Josephine Baker (1906–75), who took Paris by storm in the 1920s with her risqué performances. Baker purchased the castle in 1936 and lived here until 1958. It houses a super museum documenting her life with original photos and memorabilia including a fantastic costume collection, and her songs play throughout.

Baker was awarded the Croix de Guerre and the Legion of Honour for her work with the French Resistance during WWII, and was later active in the US civil-rights movement. She is also remembered for her 'Rainbow Tribe' – 12 children from around the world adopted as 'an experiment in brotherhood'.

From April to November free 30-minute daily **birds of prey displays** feature the château's owls, falcons and eagle.

⚡ Activities

Bike Bus
CYCLING

(☑ 05 53 31 10 61; www.bike-bus.com; Rte de Daglan, Castelnaud-La-Chapelle; adult/child bike rental per day from €10/20) An excellent way to explore the surrounding countryside, whether on a bike path or mountain-bike trail. Great advice for route selection, including the 30km tri-sport loop (bike-canoe-foot).

Gabarres de Beynac
BOATING

(☑ 05 53 28 51 15; www.gabarre-beynac.com; Beynac-et-Cazenac; adult/child €8.50/4.50; ⊘ every 30min 10am-6pm May-Sep, 11am-5pm Apr & Oct) Gabarres de Beynac does 50-minute flat-bottomed boat trips departing from Beynac-et-Cazenac; kids cruise for free in the mornings.

Montgolfière Châteaux
BALLOONING

(☑ 06 71 14 34 96; www.montgolfiere-chateaux. com; Beynac-et-Cazenac; 1hr aloft adult/child from €180/120) Lovely Monsieur Lionel Druet takes you soaring over Dordogne châteaux in hot-air balloons.

ℹ Information

Tourist Office (☑ 05 53 29 43 08; www.sarlat-tourisme.com; Beynac-et-Cazenac; ⊘10am-1pm & 2-6pm Jul & Aug, shorter hr rest of year)

ℹ Getting There & Away

Beynac is 12km southwest of Sarlat; there is no public transport.

La Roque Gageac

POP 467

La Roque Gageac's row of amber buildings and flourishing gardens built into the cliff face along the River Dordogne live up to all the ad-jectives: stunning, breathtaking! And it's an idyllic launch pad for a cruise or canoe trip.

⊙ Sights

Troglodyte Fort
FORT

A warren of meandering lanes leads up to La Roque's dramatic fort, where a series of defensive positions constructed by medieval engineers were carved out of overhanging cliffs. The fort has been shut down indefinitely following a partial collapse of one area.

★ Jardins de Marqueyssac
GARDENS

(☑ 05 53 31 36 36; www.marqueyssac.com; Vézac; adult/child €9.80/4.90; ⊘9am-8pm Jul & Aug, 10am-7pm Apr-Jun & Sep, shorter hr rest of year) Horticulture fans won't want to miss these famous manicured gardens, stretching along a rocky bluff overlooking the Dordogne Valley. Signposted paths lead through painstakingly clipped box hedges and decorative topiary to the gardens' breathtaking *belvédère* (viewpoint), with sightlines to area castles, the Dordogne and La Roque Gageac. Thursday nights in July and August, the entire place is alight with candles (adult/child €15/7.50). Find the entrance 3km west of La Roque Gageac.

There's also a 45-minute **via ferrata** (www.viaferrata-marqueyssac.com) along the cliff face – included in the garden admission.

⚡ Activities

Paddling along the river, especially along this particular stretch, offers a changing panorama of soaring cliffs, castles and picturesque villages. Canoe operators based near La Roque Gageac and Cenac, including **Canoë Vacances** (☑05 53 28 17 07; www.canoevacances.com; Lespinasse; canoe rental per person €15-23), **Canoë Loisirs**

GABARRE CRUISES

One of the best ways to explore the gorgeous scenery of the Dordogne River is aboard a *gabarre*, a flat-bottomed, wooden boat used to transport freight up and down the rivers of the Périgord and Lot Valley. *Gabarres* were a common sight in this part of France until the early 20th century, when they were eclipsed by the rise of the railway and the automobile.

From April to October, traditional *gabarres* cruise from several points along the river, including Bergerac, Brantôme, Beaulieu-sur-Dordogne and the quay at La Roque Gageac. La Roque Gageac's operators include **Gabarres Caminade** (☑ 05 53 29 40 95; www. gabarrecaminade.fr; D703; 1hr trip adult/child €10/8) and **Gabarres Norbert** (☑ 05 53 29 40 44; www.gabarres.com; D703; 1hr trip adult/child €10/8; ⊘Apr-Oct). Standard trips last about an hour and cost around €10/8 per adult/child; advance reservations are recommended. **Gabarres de Beynac** does slightly shorter, cheaper trips departing from Beynac-et-Cazenac, and kids cruise free in the mornings.

(☑ 05 53 28 23 43; www.destination-perigord-loisirs.com; Pont de Vitrac, Vitrac; canoe rental per person €15-27) and **Canoë Dordogne** (☑ 05 53 29 58 50; www.canoesdordogne.fr; D703; canoe rental per person €7-24), offer self-guided trips of between one and five hours, depending on your destination.

The quay is also a launch point for river cruises aboard a traditional *gabarre*.

🛏 Sleeping & Eating

La Belle Étoile   HOTEL €
(☑ 05 53 29 51 44; www.belleetoile.fr; D703; d €68-82, ste €150; ⊗ Apr-Oct; ☎) This riverside hotel has a prime position in La Roque, in an amber stone building with views across the water from higher-priced rooms (others overlook the village). Expect traditional wooden furniture and understated fabrics. The **restaurant** (menus €29-50; ⊗ 12.30-1.30pm Tue & Thu-Sun, 7.30-9pm Tue-Sun) is renowned for its sophisticated French food, and opens onto a vine-shaded terrace with a fabulous view.

Hôtel La Treille   FRENCH €€
(☑ 05 53 28 33 19; www.latreille-perigord.com; D703, Vitrac; menus €32-65; ⊗ 12.15-2pm & 7.15-8.45pm Jul & Aug, closed Mon & Tue lunch rest of year; ☎) Gourmet food is dished up riverside at this sweet, small hotel (double/family rooms from €59/76) in Vitrac, 6.5km east of La Roque Gageac. It's one of the few local restaurants open on Sunday nights.

ⓘ Getting There & Away

La Roque Gageac is 15km south of Sarlat, via the D46 and D703. There's no public transport.

Domme & Around

POP 923

Commanding an unparalleled view across the surrounding countryside from an outcrop above the Dordogne, Domme was a perfect defensive stronghold – a fact not lost on Philippe III of France, who founded the town in 1281 as a bastion against the English. Still one of the area's best preserved *bastides*, Domme retains most of its 13th-century ramparts and three original gateways. The imposing cliff-top position is best appreciated from esplanade du Belvédère and the adjacent promenade de la Barre, which offer panoramic views across the valley. Domme can be overrun in high season, so plan to see the town and view and get out quick.

👁 Sights & Activities

Grottes Naturelles   CAVE
(place de la Halle; adult/child incl museum €8.50/6; ⊗ 4-20 tours daily Feb-Oct) Honeycombing the stone underneath the village is a series of large caves decorated with ornate stalactites and stalagmites. Get tickets, which include admission to the small **L'Oustal du Périgord** (place de la Halle; ⊗ 9.30am-7pm Jul & Aug, shorter hr rest of year), a folk museum, at the tourist office near the entrance to the caves.

★ Fabrice le Chef   COOKING
(☑ 06 83 22 61 92; www.fabricelechef.fr; Daglan; 2-3hr class per person €50) Learn how to cook delicious Périgord cuisine from Fabrice, or have him come cook for you! He also has a great **restaurant** (lunch/dinner *menus* from €15/25) in Daglan, serving seasonal, creative cuisine.

🛏 Sleeping

La Guérinière   B&B €€
(☑ 05 53 29 91 97; www.la-gueriniere-dordogne.com; Baccas, Cénac-et-St-Julien; d €105, q €180; ☎☀) Surrounded by 6 hectares of grounds in the valley 4km south of Domme along the D46, this family-friendly B&B's rooms are all named after flowers: our faves are Mimosa, with its sloping roof and chinoiserie wardrobe, and the supersized Bleuet room. Book ahead for *tables d'hôte* (set *menus* €28 including wine) that use mostly organic produce.

La Tour de Cause   B&B €€
(☑ 05 53 30 30 51; www.latourdecause.com; Pont de Cause, Castelnaud-la-Chapelle; d €110; ☎☀) Nico and Igor have painstakingly renovated a historic manor house and barn into a comfortable B&B with modern bathrooms and luxe linens. Find it 8km east of Domme on the D50, or 2km south of Castelnaud on the D57. Cash only; three-night minimum in summer.

★ Château de Maraval   DESIGN HOTEL €€€
(☑ 06 06 94 37 61; www.chateaudemaraval.fr; Lieu-dit Maraval, Cénac-et-Saint-Julien; d €195; ⊗ Feb-Dec; ✦☎☀) Here's your chance to combine historic elegance (a grand château in lush grounds) with contemporary luxury (modern rooms kitted out with design tapestries, sleek furnishings and high-concept bathrooms). This friendly escape just south of Domme in Cénac pampers with high-thread-count linens, spa facilities and an idyllic pool.

✕ Eating

⭐ Le Petit Paris
FRENCH €€

(📞 05 53 28 41 10; www.le-petit-paris.fr; Daglan; menus €28-45; ⏱ noon-1.30pm Tue-Sun, 7-8.45pm Tue-Sat late Feb–mid-Nov) Friendly staff serve you on little Daglan's central square, promoting an elegant 'there's all the time in the world' feel, while wowing with impeccable seasonal local cuisine. Spring brings lovely asparagus; the rest of the year find tender Limousin beef, falling off the bone, or duck cassoulet. It's 11km south of Domme.

Cabanoix et Châtaigne
FRENCH €€

(📞 05 53 31 07 11; www.restaurantcabanoix.com; 3 rue Geoffroy de Vivans; lunch/dinner menus from €26/29; ⏱ 12.15-1.30pm & 7.15-9pm Thu-Mon Feb-Oct) This diminutive, welcoming restaurant is your best bet in the centre of Domme. All dishes are created seasonally, with an emphasis on local duck and produce. It's best to reserve ahead for a spot.

L'Envie des Mets
MODERN FRENCH €€

(📞 05 53 28 26 53; St-Pompon; 2/3-course menus €26/32; ⏱ noon-2pm Tue-Sat, 7-9pm Thu-Sat) Reserve ahead for the popular restaurant where Laétitia whips up cutting-edge seasonal *périgourdine* cuisine in St-Pompon, 16km southwest of Domme.

⭐ Le Saint Martial
GASTRONOMY €€€

(📞 05 53 29 18 34; www.lesaintmartial.com; St-Martial-de-Nabirat; menus €36-80; ⏱ noon-1.30pm & 7.30-9pm Wed-Sun; ❄) Details, details. Valérie and Jean-Marc Réal get them all right at this small restaurant in low-key St-Martial-de-Nabirat, 8km south of Domme. The church bells chime lightly and the terrace stretches out in the sun as you enjoy a steady procession of beautifully presented local dishes. Book well ahead.

ℹ Information

Tourist Office (📞 05 53 31 71 00; www. tourisme-domme.com; place de la Halle; ⏱ 9.30am-6.30pm May-Sep, shorter hr rest of year) Sells tickets to local sights.

ℹ Getting There & Away

Domme is 18km south of Sarlat along the D46. There are no public transport options. In high season, park at the edge of the village and walk in, or take the **mini-train** (www.domme-perigord. com; adult/child €5/3) from the Porte des Tours parking lot.

Sarlat-la-Canéda
POP 9030

A picturesque tangle of honey-coloured buildings, alleyways and secret squares make up the beautiful town of Sarlat-la-Canéda. Boasting some of the region's best-preserved medieval architecture, it's a popular base for exploring the Vézère Valley, and a favourite location for film directors. It's also firmly on the tourist radar, and you might find it difficult to appreciate the town's charms among the summer throngs, especially on market days.

Well-known markets sell a smorgasbord of goose-based products, and Sarlat hosts an annual goose festival, the Fest'Oie (early March).

◉ Sights

⭐ Weekly Markets
MARKET

(place de la Liberté; ⏱ 8.30am-1pm Wed & Sat) For an introductory French market experience, visit Sarlat's heavily touristed Saturday market, which takes over the streets around Cathédrale St-Sacerdos. Depending on the season, delicacies include local mushrooms and duck- and goose-based products such as foie gras. The Wednesday version is a smaller affair. An atmospheric, largely organic **night market** (place du 14 Juillet; ⏱ 6-10pm Thu) operates on Thursdays.

Marché aux Truffes
MARKET

(⏱ from 9am Sat Dec-Feb) Get *truffe noir* (black truffle) at the winter-morning Marché aux Truffes.

⭐ Place du Marché aux Oies
SQUARE

A life-size statue of three bronze geese stands in the centre of beautiful place du Marché aux Oies (Goose Market Sq), where live geese are still sold during the Fest'Oie. The square's architecture is exceptional.

Église Ste-Marie
MARKET

(place de la Liberté; elevator adult/child €4/1) Église Ste-Marie was ingeniously converted by acclaimed architect Jean Nouvel, whose parents still live in Sarlat, into the town's touristy **Marché Couvert** (Covered Market; place de la Liberté; ⏱ 8.30am-2pm daily mid-Apr–mid-Nov, closed Mon, Thu & Sun rest of year). Its **panoramic elevator** (buy tickets at tourist office) offers 360-degree views across Sarlat's countryside.

Cathédrale St-Sacerdos
CATHEDRAL

(place du Peyrou; ⏱ 9am-6pm) Once part of Sarlat's Cluniac abbey, the original abbey church was built in the 1100s, redeveloped

Sarlat-la-Canéda

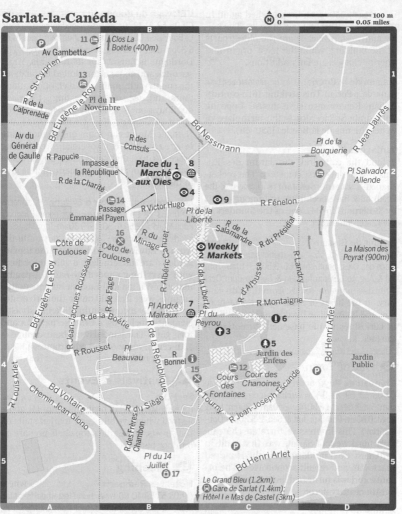

Sarlat-la-Canéda

⊚ Top Sights
1 Place du Marché aux Oies	B2
2 Weekly Markets	C3

⊚ Sights
3 Cathédrale St-Sacerdos	C4
4 Église Ste-Marie	B2
5 Jardin des Enfeus	C4
6 Lanterne des Morts	C4
7 Maison de la Boétie	B3
8 Manoir de Gisson	B2
9 Marché aux Truffes	C2

🛏 Sleeping
10 Hôtel La Couleuvrine	D2
11 Hôtel Les Remparts	A1
12 Le Porche de Sarlat	C4
13 Plaza Madeleine	A1
14 Villa des Consuls	B2

🍽 Eating
15 Chez les Gaulois	B4
16 Le Quatre Saisons	B3

🛍 Shopping
Marché Couvert	(see 4)
17 Organic Market	B5

in the early 1500s, and remodelled again in the 1700s, so it's a real mix of styles. The belfry and western façade are the oldest parts of the building, while the nave, organ and interior chapels are later additions.

Maison de la Boétie
HISTORIC BUILDING

(3 rue de la Boétie) This striking 16th-century Italian Renaissance–style house opposite Cathédrale St-Sacerdos is the birthplace of writer Étienne de la Boétie (1530–63).

Jardin des Enfeus
PARK

Behind the cathedral, the Jardin des Enfeus was Sarlat's first cemetery. The rocket-shaped **Lanterne des Morts** (Lantern of the Dead) may have been built to honour a visit by St Bernard in 1147, one of the founders of the Cistercian order.

Manoir de Gisson
HISTORIC BUILDING

(☏05 53 28 70 55; www.manoirdegisson.com; place des Oies; adult/child €6/3.50; ⊙10am-7pm Jul & Aug, to 6.30pm Apr-Jun & Sep, to 6pm Oct) Tour this mansion, dating from the 13th century, in the heart of Sarlat to get a taste of how the bourgeoisie lived. There's a cabinet of curiosities in the basement to entertain the kids.

◉ Out of Town

Château de Puymartin
CHATEAU

(☏05 53 59 29 97; www.chateau-de-puymartin. com; adult/child €8.50/4; ⊙10am-6.30pm Jul & Aug, 10.30am-6pm Apr-Jun & Sep, 2-5.30pm Oct–mid-Nov) This impressive turreted château, 8km northwest of Sarlat, was first built in 1270, destroyed in 1358 during the Hundred Years War, and rebuilt around 1450. The ornate interior is furnished lavishly with mostly 19th-century decor.

Moulin de la Tour
FARM

(☏05 53 59 22 08; www.moulindelatour.com; Ste-Nathalene; ⊙9.30am-noon & 2-6.30pm Mon, Wed & Fri Apr-Sep, to 6pm Wed & Fri Oct-Mar) The humble *noix* (walnut) has been a prized product of the Dordogne for centuries, and is still used in many local recipes – cakes, puddings, pancakes and breads, as well as liqueurs and *huile de noix* (walnut oil). At the Moulin de la Tour, the region's last working watermill, you can watch walnut oil being made and stock up with nutty souvenirs. Don't miss the *cerneaux de noix au chocolat* (chocolate-covered walnuts) and *gâteau de noix* (walnut cake).

L'Elevage du Bouyssou
FARM

(☏05 53 31 12 31; www.elevagedubouyssou.com; Le Bouyssou, Carsac-Aillac; ⊙shop 8am-6pm, tours 6.30pm daily Jul & Aug, Mon-Sat rest of year) The Dordogne is famous for its foie gras. You'll see duck and goose farms dotted throughout the countryside, many of which offer guided tours and *dégustation* (tasting). L'Elevage du Bouyssou is a family-run farm to the north of Carsac-Aillac. Owners Denis and Nathalie Mazet run tours and demonstrate *la gavage* – the controversial force-feeding process (p103) that helps fatten up the goose livers. You can also buy homemade foie gras in the shop.

Les Jardins du Manoir d'Eyrignac
GARDENS

(☏05 53 28 99 71; www.eyrignac.com; Eyrignac; adult/child €12.50/6.50; ⊙9.30am-7pm May-Sep, shorter hr rest of year) While it's not quite the work of Edward Scissorhands, these topiary gardens are nonetheless a labour of love, with everything clipped by hand. A combination of Italian and English influences, the grounds were first laid out in the 18th century, gradually incorporating different stylistic elements, including a Chinese pavilion and torii gate. The gardens are built around a 17th-century manor (no admittance) 13.5km northeast of Sarlat.

✷ Festivals & Events

Fest'Oie
FOOD & DRINK

(⊙early Mar) Sarlat hosts this annual goose festival when live birds and market stalls fill the streets, and Sarlat's top chefs prepare an outdoor banquet.

⛉ Sleeping

Hôtel Les Remparts
HOTEL €

(☏05 53 59 40 00; www.hotel-lesremparts-sarlat. com; 48 av Gambetta; d/tr/q from €70/86/106; ⊙Mar-Nov; 🛜) Just outside the old town centre on a busyish street, this simple stone hotel has to be one of the best deals in Sarlat. Rooms lack sparkle; simple furniture and the odd reclaimed roof beam are all you should expect.

Hôtel La Couleuvrine
HOTEL €

(☏05 53 59 27 80; www.la-couleuvrine.com; 1 place de la Bouquerie; d €80-100, q €135; 🛜) Originally part of Sarlat's city wall, this rambling hotel with a sunny terrace has rooms jammed along creaky corridors. Superior and family rooms are more spacious.

Hôtel Le Mas de Castel HOTEL €

(📞 05 53 59 02 59; www.hotel-lemasdecastel.com; rte du Sudalissant; d €85-100, q €105-135; ✿Mar-Nov; @🅿🛜🏊) This former farmhouse 3km south of town makes a delightful escape from the hectic hum of central Sarlat. Some of its 14 sunny rooms open to the flower-filled courtyard and pool; one has self-catering facilities.

⭐**Villa des Consuls** APARTMENT €€

(📞 05 53 31 90 05; www.villaconsuls.fr; 3 rue Jean-Jacques Rousseau; d €110-125, apt €145-320; @🛜) Despite its Renaissance exterior, the enormous rooms here are modern through and through, with shiny wood floors and sleek furnishings. Several delightful self-contained apartments dot the town, all offering the same mix of period plushness – some also have terraces overlooking the town's rooftops.

⭐**La Maison des Peyrat** HOTEL €€

(📞 05 53 59 00 32; www.maisondespeyrat.com; Le Lac de la Plane; r €69-125; ✿Apr–mid-Nov) This beautifully renovated 17th-century house, formerly a nuns' hospital and later an aristocratic hunting lodge, is set on a hill about 1.5km from Sarlat centre. Ten generously sized rooms are decorated in modern farmhouse style; the best have views over gardens and the countryside beyond. Good restaurant, too.

Le Porche de Sarlat APARTMENT €€

(📞 06 80 15 27 21; www.appart-hotel-sarlat.fr; 6 cour des Fontaines; apt €140-175; ❄🛜) Superb modern apartments fill this townhouse as central as could be in medieval Sarlat. Some have views of the cathedral or the cours des Fontaines, and small private gardens or terraces. All have full kitchens and high-quality fittings. There is a €52 cleaning charge.

Plaza Madeleine HOTEL €€

(📞 05 53 59 10 41; www.hoteldelamadeleine-sarlat.com; 1 place de la Petite Rigaudie; d €165-250; ❄🛜🏊) This elegant hotel offers an attractive mix of modern and traditional touches. Classy rooms subtly evoke a bygone era, with vintage-style phones and shuttered windows, while a solarium and Finnish sauna create a modern boutique feel.

✖ Eating

Chez les Gaulois FRENCH €

(📞 05 53 59 50 64; 9 rue Tourny; mains €12-14.50; ✿noon-2pm & 7-9pm Jul & Aug, Tue-Sat rest of year) The best of Sarlat's budget picks, come here for charcuterie, potatoes, salads and Savoy cheeses (fondue and Raclette) and nary a duck in sight.

Le Quatre Saisons FRENCH €€

(📞 05 53 29 48 59; 2 côte de Toulouse; menus €16-28; ✿noon-1.30pm & 7-8.30pm Jul & Aug, shorter hr rest of year, closed Dec-Mar; 🍴) A reliable local favourite, hidden in a beautiful stone house on a narrow alley leading uphill from rue de la République. The food is honest and unfussy, taking its cue from market ingredients and regional flavours. The most romantic tables have cross-town views.

⭐**Le Grand Bleu** GASTRONOMY €€€

(📞 05 53 31 08 48; www.legrandbleu.eu; 43 av de la Gare; lunch menus €25, dinner menus €54-125; ✿12.30-2pm Thu-Sun, 7.30-9.30pm Tue-Sat) This eminent Michelin-starred restaurant run by chef Maxime Lebrun is renowned for its creative cuisine, with elaborate *menus* making maximum use of luxury produce: truffles, lobster, turbot and scallops, with a wine list to match. Cooking courses are also available. Located 1.5km south of the centre.

ℹ Information

Tourist Office (📞 05 53 31 45 45; www.sarlat-tourisme.com; 3 rue Tourny; ✿9am-7.30pm Mon-Sat, 10am-1pm & 2-6pm Sun Jul & Aug, shorter hr rest of year; 🛜)

ℹ Getting There & Around

BICYCLE

Hire bikes for around €17 for half a day from **Liberty Cycle** (📞 07 81 24 78 79; www.liberty-cycle.com; D704; half-day bicycle/electric-cycle €17/25; ✿10am-6pm Apr-Oct).

TRAIN

The **train station** (av de la Gare) is 1.3km south of the old city. Many destinations require a change at Le Buisson or Libourne.

Bergerac €13.20, one hour, five daily

Bordeaux €28.20, 2½ hours, three daily

Les Eyzies €10.10, 1½ to two hours depending on connections, five daily

Périgueux €16.30, 1½ to three hours depending on connections, five daily

The Vézère Valley

North of the Dordogne, the placid River Vézère winds through lush green meadows and softly blowing willow trees, creating a gorgeous tiny valley flanked by limestone cliffs that conceal dozens of subterranean caverns and indented *abris* (shelters). This valley is famous for its wonderfully preserved prehistoric sites, and especially for

Vézère & Dordogne Valleys

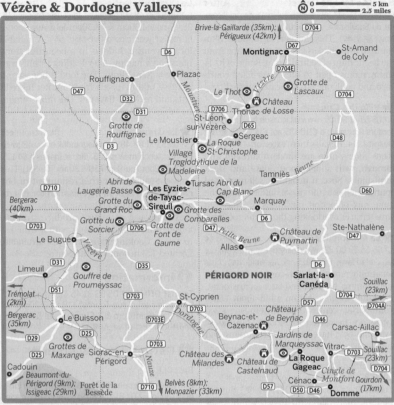

its incredible collection of cave paintings – the highest concentration of Stone Age art found in Europe. The paintings and etchings were mostly created by Cro-Magnon people between around 15,000 BC and 10,000 BC, and range in style and artistry from simple scratched lines to complex multicoloured frescoes.

Most of the key sites are around the towns of Les Eyzies-de-Tayac-Sireuil and Montignac, which are both set up for visitors, though Montignac is by far the more charming. Neither has particularly good restaurants. Visits can also be done as day-trips from elsewhere in the Dordogne.

Les Eyzies-de-Tayac-Sireuil & Around

POP 815

At the heart of the Vézère Valley, Les Eyzies (as it's known locally) makes an uninspiring

introduction to the wonders of the Vézère, with postcard sellers and souvenir shops lining the small main street. Still, the town has an excellent museum of prehistory, and many major sites are within a short drive.

⊙ Sights

LES EYZIES TOWN

Musée National de Préhistoire   MUSEUM
(🖵 05 53 06 45 65; www.musee-prehistoire-eyzies.fr; 1 rue du Musée; adult/child €6/4.50, 1st Sun of month free; ⊙ 9.30am-6.30pm daily Jul & Aug, 9.30am-6pm Wed-Mon Jun & Sep, shorter hr rest of year) Inside a marvellous modern building alongside the cliffs, this museum provides a fine prehistory primer, with the most comprehensive collection of prehistoric finds in France. Highlights include a huge gallery of Stone Age tools, weapons and jewellery, and skeletons of some of the animals that once roamed the Vézère (including bison, woolly rhinoceros,

giant deer and cave bears). A collection of carved reliefs on the 1st floor includes a famous frieze of horses and a bison licking its flank.

Abri Pataud
HISTORIC SITE

(☑ 05 53 06 92 46; www.mnhn.fr; 20 rue du Moyen Âge; adult/child €5/free; ⏰ 10am-noon & 1-6pm Jul & Aug, shorter hr rest of year, closed mid-Oct–Mar) About 250m north of the Musée National de Préhistoire, this Cro-Magnon *abri* (shelter) was inhabited over a period of 15,000 years starting some 37,000 years ago and now displays bones and other excavated artefacts. The ibex carved into the ceiling dates from about 19,000 BC. Admission includes a one-hour guided tour (some in English).

EAST OF LES EYZIES

★ Grotte de Font de Gaume
HISTORIC SITE

(☑ 05 53 06 86 00; www.sites-les-eyzies.fr; 4 av des Grottes; adult/child €10/free; ⏰ guided tours 9.30am-5.30pm Sun-Fri mid-May–mid-Sep, 9.30am-12.30pm & 2-5.30pm Sun-Fri mid-Sep–mid-May) This extraordinary cave contains the only original polychrome (as opposed to single-colour) paintings still open to the public. About 14,000 years ago, prehistoric artists created the gallery of more than 200 delicately engraved, painted figures, including bison, reindeer, horses, and mammoths, although only about 25 are included in the fantastically atmospheric tour. Look out for the famous Chapelle des Bisons, a scene of courting reindeer and stunningly realised horses, several caught in mid-movement.

Font de Gaume is such a rare and valuable site that there is always talk of the cave being closed for its own protection. Visitor numbers are limited to 78 per day, and as of our last visit, it was no longer possible to reserve in advance. Unless you come out of season, you must line up very early to get a ticket (only one per person). Guided tours are in English twice a day in summer. The ticket office and cave are 1km east of Les Eyzies on the D4.

★ Grotte des Combarelles
HISTORIC SITE

(☑ 05 53 06 97 72; www.sites-les-eyzies.fr; adult/child €10/free; ⏰ guided tours 9.30am-5.30pm Sun-Fri mid-May–mid-Sep, 9.30am-12.30pm & 2-5.30pm Sun-Fri mid-Sep–mid-May) This narrow, very long cave 1.5km east of Font de Gaume was the first rediscovered in the valley, in 1901, and is renowned for its animal engravings. Look out for mammoths, horses and reindeer, and human figures, as well as a fantastic mountain lion that seems to leap from the rock face.

Only 42 people are allowed in daily; go early to buy tickets at the Font de Gaume ticket office for 45-minute, seven-person tours.

Abri de Cap Blanc
HISTORIC SITE

(☑ 05 53 59 60 30; www.sites-les-eyzies.fr; adult/child €8/free; ⏰ guided tours 10am-6pm Sun-Fri mid-May–mid-Sep, 10am-12.30pm & 2-5.30pm Sun-Fri mid-Sep–mid-May) While most of the Vézère's caves contain engravings and paintings, this overhanging cliff-face contains a handful of unusual large carvings in relief, shaped using simple flint tools some 14,000 years ago. The frieze of horses and bison is a fascinating complement to the caves, albeit on a smaller scale. It's 7.5km east of Les Eyzies. Tickets available on-site or at Font de Gaume ticket office.

NORTH & WEST OF LES EYZIES

★ Grotte de Rouffignac
HISTORIC SITE

(☑ 05 53 05 41 71; www.grotted erouffignac.fr; Rouffignac-St-Cernin-de-Reilhac; adult/child €7.80/5.10; ⏰ 9-11.30am & 2-6pm Jul & Aug, 10-11.30am & 2-5pm Apr-Jun, Sep & Oct, closed Nov-Mar) Hidden in woodland 18km north of Les Eyzies, this tri-level cave is one of the most complex and rewarding to see in the Dordogne. Board an electric train to explore a 1km maze of tunnels in the massive cavern plunging 8km into the earth.

Highlights include the frieze of 10 mammoths in procession, one of the largest cave paintings ever discovered, and the Great Ceiling, with more than 65 figures from ibex to aurochs. You'll also see dens of long-extinct cave bears, and 17th-century graffiti.

Tickets are only sold at the cave and do sell out, so arrive by 9am in July and August to get tickets for any time that day. April to June and September to October, afternoon tickets are only available after 2pm.

Grotte du Grand Roc
CAVE

(☑ 05 53 06 92 70; www.semitour.com; adult/child €7.80/5.30; ⏰ 10am-7.30pm Jul & Aug, shorter hr rest of year) Around 3km northwest of Les Eyzies along the D47, this cave contains an array of glittering stalactites and stalagmites. A joint ticket (adult/child €11/6) includes adjacent **Abri de Laugerie Basse**, a rock shelter originally occupied by Cro-Magnon people and still used until recent times.

Grotte du Sorcier
HISTORIC SITE

(☑ 05 53 07 14 37; www.grotted usorcier.com; St-Cirq; adult/child €7/3.50; ⏰ 10am-7.30pm Jul & Aug, shorter hr rest of year, closed mid-Nov–Mar)

ⓘ TOP TIPS FOR CAVE VISITS

Summer crowds make it difficult to get tickets and to absorb the otherworldly atmosphere of the caves; some of the valley's sites are closed in winter, making spring and autumn the best times to visit. Getting tickets is always a bit of a competition, especially for the best sites. Most have timed entry due to guided tours, but each has its own rules for ticket acquisition (check websites), and often sell out in high season (especially those with visitor limitations, such as Font de Gaume).

Visiting the Caves

➡ Ticket sales stop 45 minutes to two hours before caves close.

➡ Follow all rules so as not to damage these sensitive sites.

➡ Bring warm clothing as the caves can be chilly.

Font de Gaume, Combarelles & Abri de Cap Blanc

➡ These caves do not offer advance reservations. Tickets are only sold on the day of the tour (42 to 78 tickets, depending on the cave).

➡ It's one ticket per adult/child present, so you cannot send one person to buy four tickets, for example.

➡ The Font de Gaume (p607) box office also sells Combarelles (p607) and Abri de Cap Blanc (p607) tickets (Cap Blanc also sold at the sight), as a well as the rarely open Abri de Laugerie-Haute, Abri du Poisson, Abri du Moustier, Gisement de la Ferrassie and Gisement de la Micoque.

➡ People line up *early*.

Lascaux IV

➡ As of our last visit, these were the only tickets that could be bought in advance, via the website. Tickets can only be reserved online up to two days before your visit.

➡ A certain number of tickets are only sold on site, so if you can't get a reservation online, show up early and you may be able to get a same- or next-day ticket.

About 8km west of Les Eyzies, near the hamlet of St-Cirq, this privately owned cave features several animal engravings dating from around 15,000 BC to 17,000 BC, but it's best known for a human figure known as the *Sorcier* (Sorceror), who's endowed with a phallus of truly enormous proportions, possibly indicating his shamanic status.

🏃 Activities

Prehistoric Art & Cave Tour   TOURS
(📞 05 53 07 26 04; www.caveconnection.fr; per day for 1 person €270, per additional person €20, maximum €370) Expert prehistoric anthropologist Christine Desdemaines-Hugon tailors cave tours for everyone from the Smithsonian to private individuals. She writes about Dordogne cave art in *Stepping-Stones: A Journey through the Ice Age Caves of the Dordogne*. Cave tickets not included, but she helps to acquire the often-hard-to-get tickets.

Canoës Vallée Vézère   BOATING
(📞 05 53 05 10 11; www.canoesvalleevezere.com; 1-3 promenade de la Vézère; canoe/kayak rentals from €17/19; ⊙ Apr-Sep) Organises 10km to 26km self-guided canoe and kayak trips including a shuttle. The company can also arrange overnight hikes.

Animation Vézère Canoë Kayak   BOATING
(📞 05 53 06 92 92; www.vezere-canoe.com; Pont des Eyzies; SUP/canoe/kayak rentals from €12/17/19; ⊙ Apr-Oct) Canoe, kayak and stand-up paddleboard (SUP) rentals, including a shuttle to your departure point. Also organises overnight hikes.

🛏 Sleeping & Eating

Camping La Rivière   CAMPGROUND €
(📞 05 53 06 97 14; www.lariviereleseyzies.com; 3 rte du Sorcier; 2-person campsite €25.25; ⊙ mid-Apr–Oct; 🅿 @ 🛜 🏊) The nearest campground to Les Eyzies, just west of town beside the river. Facilities include a restaurant, bar, laundry and grocery. There are also small apartments (€62-77).

Hôtel des Glycines
HOTEL €€

(☎ 05 53 06 97 07; www.les-glycines-dordogne. com; 4 av de Laugerie; d from €144, lodges from €275; ☺ Jan–mid-Nov; ❀ 🕾 🛋) Les Eyzies' top posh pad: plush rooms range from cream-and-check 'classics' to full-blown lodges with terraces and garden views. Note that classic rooms overlook the main road. The hotel's gastronomic restaurant (lunch *menus* €17, dinner *menus* €62 to €110) is a pampering affair, as is the on-site spa.

Hôtel Le Cro-Magnon
HOTEL €€

(☎ 05 53 06 97 06; www.hostellerie-cro-magnon. com; 54 av de la Préhistoire; d €90-100; ☺ Mar-Oct; 🕾 🛋) This pretty wisteria-clad hotel has been around since the 1850s and was often used as a base by pioneering prehistorians. Flowery rooms are a touch bland, but corridors built straight into the rock face add quirky appeal. Dining is good value in the lovely beam-ceilinged restaurant.

Moulin de la Beaune
FRENCH €€

(Au Vieux Moulin; ☎ 05 53 06 94 33; www.moulinde labeune.com; 2 rue du Moulin Bas; lunch/dinner menus from €30/40; ☺ noon-1.30pm Thu, Fri, Sun, Mon, 7-8.30pm daily mid-Apr–Oct) Reserve ahead for a spot at one of the riverfront terrace tables at this renovated water mill converted into a lovely restaurant and hotel (doubles €75). The most charming family-run establishment in Les Eyzies, it's also the most beautifully situated, and serves up seasonal local fare.

ℹ Information

Tourist Office (☎ 05 53 06 97 05; www. lascaux-dordogne.com; 19 av de la Préhistoire, Les Eyzies; ☺ 9am-6.30pm Jul & Aug, shorter hr rest of year) Small office selling detailed maps of local hikes (€3).

ℹ Getting There & Away

Les Eyzies is 21km west of Sarlat, on the D47. The train station is 700m north of town, with connections to Sarlat (change at Le Buisson; €10.10, one to two hours, three daily), and direct trains to Périgueux (€8.50, 35 minutes, six daily).

Montignac

POP 2807

The charming auburn-stone riverside town of Montignac has become famous for the nearby Grottes de Lascaux, hidden in wooded hills just outside town. Montignac itself, with its crumbling medieval fortress and arching bridges, drapes beautifully along both banks of the Vézère, and is a more peaceful base than Les Eyzies for exploring the valley.

The tiny lanes of the old city sit on the river's west bank; many hotels are on the east bank, near the Lascaux ticket office and place Tourny.

◉ Sights

★ Grotte de Lascaux
HISTORIC SITE

(International Centre for Cave Art; ☎ 05 53 50 99 10; www.lascaux.fr; Montignac; adult/child €16/10.40; ☺ 8.30am-10pm Jul & Aug, shorter hr rest of year) France's most famous prehistoric cave paintings are at the Grotte de Lascaux, 2km southeast of Montignac. Naturally sealed and protected for millennia, it was discovered in 1940 by four teenage boys searching for their dog, Robot. In December 2016, a new interpretation centre and cutting-edge reproduction of the cave was unveiled to the public, allowing visitors to view the entirety of Lascaux' artwork for the first time since 1963.

Popularly known as Lascaux IV, the new International Centre for Cave Art consists of two main sections: an hour-long guided tour through the re-created cave, followed by a self-guided tour. If you're sceptical about visiting a reproduction, don't be: the latest in laser technology and 3D printing was used to reproduce the exact wall contours, engravings (absent in Lascaux II, the previous reproduction) and the nearly 600 paintings down to the very millimetre. It feels remarkably like a real cave – it's damp, dark and chilly, and the whole experience can be legitimately spine-tingling.

After the cave visit, you're turned loose for the self-guided tour, which utilises a personal tablet to help visitors explore the excellent Lascaux Studio. Here you'll find life-size renderings of all the major scenes in the cave, providing context with regard to painting and engraving techniques, superimposed images and more. Don't miss the Shaft (the least accessible part of the cave), where an extremely rare representation of a human, with a bird's head, is depicted. A multimedia show, 3D film and the interactive Galerie de l'Imagination, examining the relationship between cave art and modern art, round out the exhibit.

Advance reservations are highly recommended and can be made online up to two days in advance. A certain number of tickets are only sold on site, so if you can't get a ticket through the website, show up early and you may be in luck. Note that it is still possible to visit Lascaux II (€13; open April through October), though tours are only in French. Lascaux is located 1.2km southeast of Montignac.

Vézère Valley Cave Art

Deep in the Vézère Valley, prehistoric Cro-Magnon artists worked by the light of primitive oil torches, creating some of Europe's first art. Today in the Vézère caves you can see what they created: from simple scratched lines and hand-tracings to complex multicoloured frescoes of leaping horses, mammoths, ibex, aurochs, reindeer and bulls.

Who were the artists?

Most of the Vézère Valley's cave paintings date from the end of the last ice age, between 20,000 BC and 10,000 BC, and were painted by Cro-Magnon people. Until around 20,000 BC much of northern Europe was still covered by vast glaciers and ice sheets, so people lived a hunter-gatherer lifestyle, using the mouths of the natural caves as temporary shelters while they followed the migration routes of prey.

The paintings seem to have come to an abrupt halt around 10,000 BC, around the same time the last ice sheets disappeared and humans hereabouts established a more fixed agricultural lifestyle.

What did they create?

Using flint tools for engraving, natural fibre brushes, pads or sponges for painting, and pigments derived from minerals including magnesium, ochre (red/yellow) and iron (red), Cro-Magnon artists usually depicted animals, though there are occasional mysterious geometric shapes and symbols.

The earliest known cave art in the area is from the Gravettian period, from before 22,000 BC, consisting of abstract engravings, paintings of female genitalia, or 'Venus' figures. It then developed into complex animal figures and friezes such as those at Lascaux, Rouffignac and Font de Gaume, which date from around 17,000 BC to 10,000 BC. These early artists also created jewellery from shells, bones, antlers and scrimshaw, decorated with animal scenes and geometric patterns.

Theories abound as to why Cro-Magnons made this often elaborate art, but in reality, no one knows.

1. Deer detail, Lascaux II (p609)
2. Viewing cave art, Lascaux IV (p609)
3. Animal art detail, Lascaux IV(p609)

WHAT A BOAR!

See wild boars being raised in semi-freedom at **Les Sangliers de Mortemart** (☑ 05 53 03 21 30; www. elevage-sangliers-mortemart.com; St-Felix-de-Reilhac; adult/child €3/1.50; ⊙ 10am-7pm Jul & Aug, 1-5pm Sep-Jun), a farm just outside Mortemart. These porky cousins of the modern pig were once common across France, but their numbers have been reduced by habitat reduction and hunting. The boars are fed a rich diet of *châtaignes* (chestnuts), which gives the meat a distinctive nutty flavour. It's a key ingredient in the hearty stew *civet de sanglier*, as well as pâtés and country terrines. There's a farm shop where you can buy boarthemed goodies.

Le Thot   MUSEUM
(☑ 05 53 50 70 44; www.lascaux.fr; Thonac; adult/child €9.50/6.20, joint ticket with Lascaux €21/13.70; ⊙ 10am-7pm Jul & Aug, to 6pm Apr-Jun & Sep-Oct, shorter hr rest of year) In an effort to bring the prehistoric age to life, Le Thot, 8km southwest of Montignac, places reproduced Lascaux cave scenes alongside displays about Cro-Magnon life and art, as well as real-life descendants of the animals the art depicts (wolves, reindeer, stags, ibex and European bison), which roam the grounds. Note that Le Thot is geared principally towards French-speaking families.

🛏 Sleeping & Eating

Hôtel Le Lascaux   HOTEL €
(☑ 05 53 51 82 81; www.hotel-lascaux-24.fr; 109 av Jean-Jaurès, Montignac; d €74-95; ⊙ Apr-Sep; ⓢ) Despite the old-timey candystripe awnings, rooms at this family-owned hotel are bang up to date, with cool colour schemes, distressed-wood furniture and sparkling bathrooms. Superior rooms have more space, and some overlook the shady back garden.

★ **Bel Estiu**   B&B €€
(☑ 06 50 69 44 04; www.belestiu.com; Le Méjat, St-Genies; d €110-130; ⊙ closed Jan-Mar; ⓢ⊠) A former 18th-century farmhouse and barn, Bel Estiu (Occitan for 'beautiful summer') has been gorgeously reimagined. Relax in the spacious downstairs lounge or prepare

dinner in the fully equipped kitchen before retiring to one of three guest rooms. Outside, the remains of the large stone chicken coop serve as a cool hang-out space. Delectable organic breakfast. It's located 13km southeast of Montignac.

Hostellerie La Roseraie   HOTEL €€
(☑ 05 53 50 53 92; www.laroseraie-hotel.com; 11 place d'Armes, Montignac; d €90-193, tr/q from €159/226; ⊙ Apr-Oct; ⓢ⊠) This mansion in Montignac boasts its own gorgeous rose garden, set around a palm-fringed pool. Rococo rooms are lovely if you like rosy pinks, floral patterns and garden views. Truffles, chestnuts, pork and guinea fowl find their way onto the seasonal menu in the restaurant, and on warm summer nights the terrace is a delight.

ⓘ Information

Tourist Office (☑ 05 53 51 82 60; www. lascaux-dordogne.com; place Bertran de Born, Montignac; ⊙ 9am-6.30pm Jul & Aug, shorter hr rest of year; ⓢ) Around 200m west of place Tourny, next to 14th-century Église St-Georges le Prieuré.

ⓘ Getting There & Away

Montignac is 25km northeast of Les Eyzies on the D706. Buses are inconveniently geared around school times, so you'll need your own car.

LIMOUSIN

With its rolling pastures and little-visited villages, Limousin might be the most overlooked area of southwestern France. It's not nearly as exciting as the Dordogne to the south or the Loire to the north, but it does offer a chance to get off the beaten path, and aficionados will like Limoges for its porcelain and Aubusson for its tapestries.

Technically, Limousin is no longer an official *région,* as it was subsumed by the larger Nouvelle Aquitaine in 2016. However, regional cultural identity still exists, centred around three *départements:* Haute-Vienne, in the west, the capital of which is lively Limoges; the rural Creuse, in the northeast; and, in the southeast, perhaps the most interesting area, the Corrèze, home to Brive-la-Gaillarde and the region's most beautiful villages.

Limoges

POP 133,627

Porcelain connoisseurs will already be familiar with the legendary name of Limoges. For more than 200 years, the city has thrived as the top producer of excellent hard-paste porcelain (china) in France. Several factories continue to make 'limoges' and stunning examples fill city museums and galleries.

Limoges is on the site of the 10 BC Roman city Augustoritum, which took advantage of this strategic position on the River Vienne. The modern-day centre is compact and easy to explore: historic buildings and museums cluster in the medieval Cité quarter, alongside the river, and the partly pedestrianised Château quarter, just to the west.

If you come by train you'll be arriving in style at the city's grand art deco Gare des Bénédictins.

Sights

Château Quarter

This bustling corner of Limoges is the heart of the old city, and is the modern-day shopping centre. It gets its name from the fortified walls that once enclosed the ducal castle and medieval St-Martial abbey, both long gone.

Rue de la Boucherie   HISTORIC SITE

Pedestrianised rue de la Boucherie was named for the butchers' shops that lined the street in the Middle Ages. Today it has many attractive medieval half-timbered houses, and the **Maison de la Boucherie** (36 rue de la Boucherie; ⊙10am-1pm & 2:30-6pm Wed-Sun mid-Jul–mid-Sep) **FREE** operates a small history museum. Tiny 1475 **Chapelle St-Aurélien** (place St-Aurélien; ⊙7am-7pm), dedicated to the patron saint of butchers, is maintained by the butchers' guild.

★ **Église St-Michel des Lions**   CHURCH

(rue Adrien Dubouché; ⊙9am-6pm) Named for the two granite lions flanking its door, Église St-Michel des Lions was built between the 14th and 16th centuries. It contains the relics (including the skull) of St Martial, Limoges' first bishop, who converted the city to Christianity. Look for the huge copper ball perched atop its 65m-high spire.

Cour du Temple   SQUARE

Tucked away between rue du Temple and rue du Consulat, this tiny enclosed courtyard is surrounded by 16th-century *hôtels particuliers* (private mansions). Look out for coats of arms and the 16th-century stone staircase around the edge of the courtyard.

LIMOGES CHINA

For more than 300 years, the name of Limoges has been synonymous with *les arts du feu* (literally 'the fire arts'), especially the production of *émail* (enamel) and *porcelaine* (porcelain).

Limoges had been producing enamel since at least the 12th century, but its fortunes were transformed by the discovery of an extremely pure form of kaolin near St-Yrieix-La-Perche in 1768. This fine white clay, a vital ingredient in porcelain manufacture (along with quartz and feldspar), had previously been imported at huge expense from Asia (the recipe was originally from China, hence porcelain's alternate name). Its discovery on home soil, plus the ease of getting wood on barges on the Vienne to fire kilns, led to an explosion of porcelain production in Limoges in the late 18th and 19th centuries. Three factors distinguish porcelain from other clay-baked ceramics: it's white, extremely hard and translucent.

Buildings around Limoges are often decorated with porcelain and enamel tiles. Check out the Halles Centrales (p616) and the **Pavillon du Verdurier** (place St-Pierre) **FREE**, a beautiful octagonal building dating from 1919 that occasionally hosts art exhibitions.

Many of the city's porcelain makers have factory shops, and outstanding city museums focus on the industry. The tourist office has complete lists.

Porcelaine Royal Limoges (☑05 55 33 28 74; www.royal-limoges.fr; 28 rue Donzelot; guided tour €8; ⊙tours 10am-5pm, shop 10am-6pm Mon-Sat)

Bernardaud (☑05 55 10 55 91; www.bernardaud.fr; 27 av Albert Thomas; tours adult/child €4.50/free; ⊙9.45am-11.15am & 1.30-4.15pm Mon-Sat Jun-Sep)

Haviland (☑05 55 30 21 86; www.haviland.fr; 3 av du Président Kennedy; ⊙10.30am-1pm & 2-6.30pm Mon-Sat, 10.30am-6.30pm daily Jul & Aug) **FREE**

Limoges

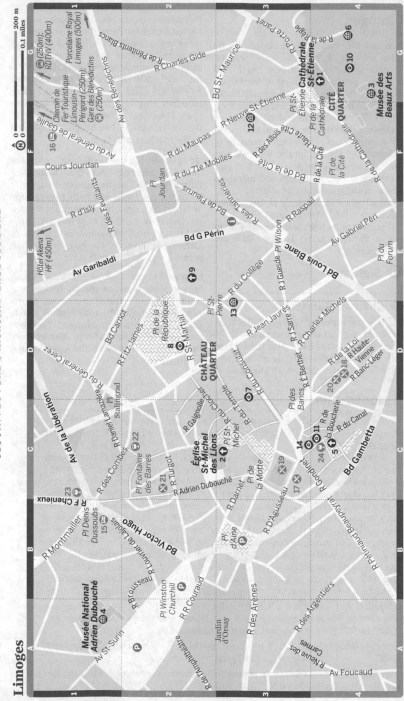

200 m
0.1 miles

Porcelaine Royal
Limoges (500m)
RDTHV (400m)
(250m)

Chemin de
Fer Touristique
Limousin–
Périgord (250m)
Gare des Bénédictins
(250m)

Av du Général de Gaulle

Av des Bénédictins

R de Pénitents Blancs

R Charles Gide

Bd St-Maurice

R de la Règle

R Porte Panet

Cathédrale
St-Étienne

CITÉ
QUARTER

Musée des
Beaux Arts

R Neuve St-Étienne

Pl St-
Étienne

Pl de la
Cathédrale

R de la Cité

R du Maupas

R des Alloi s

R Haute Cité

Bd de la Cité

Pl de
la Cité

R du 71e Mobiles

Cours Jourdan

Pl
Jourdan

R des Tanneries

Bd de Fleurus

Bd G Périn

Av Gabriel Péri

Pl du
Forum

R d'Isly

R des Feuillants

Hôtel Akena
HF (450m)

Av Garibaldi

Bd Louis Blanc

R Raspail

R du Collège

R J Guesde

Pl Wilson

Bd Carnot

R Fitz-James

R du Général Cerez

Av de la Libération

R St-Martial

Pl de la
République

CHÂTEAU
QUARTER

Pl St-
Pierre

R Jean Jaurès

R J Sarre

R Charles Michels

R de la Loi
R Haute-
Vienne
R Banc-Léger

R Daniel Lamazière

Pl
Stalingrad

R Gaignolle

Pl des
Bancs

R É Berthet

Pl Fontaine
des Barres

R des Combes

R Turgot

Église
St-Michel
des Lions

Pl St-
Michel

R du Clocher

R du Temple

R du Consulat

R de
la Boucherie

R du Canal

Bd Gambetta

R Darnet

Pl de
la Motte

R Gondinaud

R d'Aguesseau

Pl
d'Aine

R Adrien Dubouché

R F Chenieux

Pl Denis
Dussoubs

Bd Victor Hugo

R Montmailler

R Louvier de Lajolais

R Brousseau

Pl Winston
Churchill

R R Couraud

R St-Surin

Rue de l'Amphithéâtre

Jardin
d'Orsay

R des Arènes

R Neuve des
Carmes

Av Foucaud

R des Argentiers

R Pétiniaud Beaupeyrat

Musée National
Adrien Dubouché

Limoges

Église St-Pierre du Queyroix   CHURCH
(place St-Pierre; ⊘9am-6pm) The moody late-Gothic Église St-Pierre du Queyroix is notable for its characteristic Limousin belfry and stained glass.

Crypt of St Martial   TOMB
(place de la République) All that remains of the once-great pilgrimage point St-Martial abbey, founded in AD 848, is a faint outline on place de la République, and an underground tomb dedicated to the city's patron saint. The crypt was undergoing renovations at the time of research and will feature a new archaeological centre in the future. Check with tourist office for updates on access to the site.

◉ West of Château Quarter

★**Musée National Adrien Dubouché**   MUSEUM
(☑05 55 33 08 50; www.musee-adriendubouche. fr; 8bis place Winston Churchill; adult/child €7/free; ⊘10am-12.30pm & 2-5.45pm Wed-Mon) This museum, founded in 1845, has one of France's two outstanding ceramics collections (the other is in Sèvres, southwest of Paris), so it's a must for ceramics lovers. Displays illustrate the evolution from earthenware to Limoges hard-paste porcelain, and include 12,000 pieces from Limoges makers as well as Meissen, Royal Doulton, Royal Worcester and others.

◉ Cité Quarter

To the east of the Château quarter, on the bank of the Vienne, la Cité radiates out from the massive cathedral.

★**Musée des Beaux Arts**   GALLERY
(☑05 55 45 98 10; www.museebal.fr; 1 place de l'Évêché; adult/child €5/free; ⊘10am-6pm Wed-Mon Apr-Sep, shorter hr rest of year) The city's wonderful art museum is inside the beautifully restored 18th-century bishops' palace. Get an overview of the town's history through Roman artefacts and medieval treasures, or contemplate the excellent fine arts collection, which ranges from 14th-century Italian masterpieces to entire rooms dedicated to Renoir and Suzanne Valadon. The upper storey displays Limoges enamel and is the pride of the museum.

★**Cathédrale St-Étienne**   CHURCH
(place St-Étienne; ⊘9am-6pm Mon-Sat, 2-6pm Sun Apr-Oct, to 5pm Nov-Mar) Built between 1273 and 1888, Limoges' Gothic cathedral is worth a visit for the Flamboyant-style Portail St-Jean, as well as a glorious rose window, a Renaissance choir screen (beneath the organ loft), and three ornate tombs in the chancel. The bell tower's lower three stories are part of the few remaining Romanesque portions of the cathedral; its top four storeys are Gothic.

Jardin de l'Évêché   GARDENS
FREE Alongside Cathédrale St-Étienne, Limoges' beautiful botanical garden stretches down towards the river, with super views. Medicinal and toxic herbs have been grown here since medieval times.

Musée de la Résistance   MUSEUM
(☑05 55 45 84 44; http://resistance-massif-central.fr; 7 rue Neuve-St-Étienne; adult/child €4/free; ⊘10am-6pm Wed-Mon mid-Jun–mid-Sep,

FROM CATTLE & CLOAKS TO HIGH-CLASS CARS

Limos – stretch or otherwise – may not have originated in Limousin, but the term certainly did. Centuries ago, shepherds who raised Limousin's famed beef cattle wore long cloaks to keep out the cold and rain. Fast-forward to the beginning of the 20th century, when new, luxurious cars were designed with enclosed passenger compartments and open, though roofed, drivers' seats. This open-sided roof resembled the hood of a Limousin cloak, hence the car was named a limousine (the feminine version of *Limousin* in French). The abbreviation 'limo' first appeared in the 1960s. To this day, limo drivers sit in a separate compartment to their passengers (as opposed to other chauffeur-driven cars), just like their horse-drawn carriage predecessors.

9.30am-5pm Wed-Mon rest of year) The Limousin was a stronghold of the Resistance during WWII, and this museum explores the story of their struggle against German occupation through archive film, photography and wartime memorabilia, including photos, letters, diaries and military hardware.

Cité des Métiers et des Arts MUSEUM

(☑ 05 55 32 57 84; www.cma-limoges.com; 5 rue de la Règle; adult/child €4.50/free; ⊙ 2.30-7pm daily Jun–mid-Sep, shorter hr rest of year) Showcases work by top members of France's craft guilds.

🛏 Sleeping

Hôtel Akena HF HOTEL €

(☑ 05 55 77 41 43; www.hotels-akena.com; 16 rue du Général du Bessol; d/tr/q from €69/79/94; 🛜) This 27-room hotel is the pick of the budget places near the station. Forget frills – easy-clean fabrics and pastel colours are the order of the day – but it's good value, especially if you get a room over the back garden. A couple of streets west of the train station. Parking costs €5.

Ibis Limoges Centre HOTEL €

(☑ 05 55 79 03 30; www.accorhotels.com; 6 blvd Victor Hugo; d from €73; ❈🛜) The central, tidy Ibis is an efficient spot to rest your head. Spotless, modern rooms are tucked into a renovated historic building right on the main boulevard around the old town. Parking €11.

Villa 13 APARTMENT €€

(☑ 06 77 56 32 55; www.villa13.fr; 13 av du Général de Gaulle; apt €120-150; 🛜) Swanky contemporary studio apartments fill this townhouse near the train station. Bathrooms are spacious, linens are of high quality, and the kitchenettes are well furnished.

🍴 Eating

Halles Centrales MARKET €

(place de la Motte; ⊙ 7.30am-2pm Mon-Sat, 8am-1pm Sun) Limoges' central market runs the gourmet gamut from local cheese to Limousin beef.

Escrocs SANDWICHES €

(☑ 05 87 07 01 10; www.escrocs.fr; 23 rue Haute Vienne; sandwiches €6-8; ⊙ noon-2.30pm & 7-10pm Tue-Sat) You'll never think about grilled cheese in the same way after a visit to this clever croque monsieur bar. Eight different varieties (think chicken with Cantal cheese, pancetta with Saint-Nectaire and potatoes, or duck confit with Fourme d'Ambert, spinach, pears and chestnuts), plus soup, salad, chips and local Michard beer (p617) on tap.

Chez Alphonse FRENCH €

(☑ 05 55 34 34 14; www.chezalphonse.fr; 5 place de la Motte; menus €16.20-24; ⊙ noon-2pm & 7.30-10.30pm Mon-Sat) Checked tablecloths, laughing locals and blackboards stuffed with regional dishes: what more could you want from a Limoges bistro? Reserve ahead.

★ La Table du Couvent FRENCH €€

(☑ 05 55 32 30 66; www.latableducouvent.com; 15 rue Neuve des Carmes; lunch/dinner/Sunday menus €16.50/25/42; ⊙ noon-2pm Wed-Sun, 7-10pm Tue-Sat) This modish restaurant in a former Carmelite convent is one of the city's most popular eateries, with tables set among rough brick walls. Sit at the open kitchen counter to watch meals being prepared, including locally sourced steaks cooked over an open hearth. Cooking courses (€40-75) are available.

★ Philippe Redon FRENCH €€

(☑ 05 55 79 37 50; 14 rue Adrien Dubouché; dinner menu €48, mains €22-28; ⊙ noon-2pm & 7.30-10pm Tue-Sat) Book ahead for a spot at this romantic modern restaurant that serves some of the best food in the region. Dishes incorporate fresh seasonal produce from truffles to Limousin beef, and service is snappy and welcoming. Leave room for decadent desserts.

Le 27 FRENCH €€

(📞 05 55 32 27 27; www.le27.com; 27 rue Haute-Vienne; lunch/dinner menu from €15.30/27; ⊘ noon-2pm & 7.45-10.30pm Mon-Sat; 🖉) A contemporary bistro with quirky decor to match the inventive cuisine. Teardrop lanterns cast moody lighting, and one wall is taken up by wine. Dishes are French classics with a contemporary spin. A vegan meal is served for €20.

🍷 Drinking & Nightlife

The large student crowd keeps Limoges' nightspots ticking; you'll find most action around the lower end of rue Charles Michels.

Le Duc Étienne BAR

(place St-Aurélien; ⊘ 11am-2am Mon-Sat, 6pm-2am Sun) Hip little bar supplying beers and late-night coffee to a pre-club crowd. In summer, punters spill onto the terrace in front of Église St-Aurélien.

Bacchus WINE BAR

(📞 05 55 79 23 83; 3 rue des Filles Notre Dame; ⊘ 6.30pm-1am Tue-Sat) Small and sophisticated, this wine bar is considerably more grown-up than many of Limoges' drinking options. There are some 200 bottles to choose from, as well as 20 wines by the glass.

Brasserie Michard BREWERY

(📞 05 55 79 37 98; www.bieres-michard.com; 8 pl Denis Dussoubs; ⊘ 4pm-1am Tue-Sat) Absolutely heaving come nightfall, this cavernous brasserie brews four beers, all under €5 a pint. Happy hour blurs into dinner once the *flammekueche* (Alsatian pizza; €6.90-7.40) arrives.

ⓘ Information

Tourist Office (📞 05 55 34 46 87; www.limoges-tourisme.com; 12 bd de Fleurus; ⊘ 10am-7pm Mon-Sat, plus 10am-1pm Sun May-Sep; 🖥)

ⓘ Getting There & Away

AIR

Just off the A20, 10km west of the city, **Limoges Airport** (LIG; 📞 05 55 43 30 30; www.aeroport limoges.com) is a major UK gateway, served by budget carriers including Ryanair and Flybe, as well as Air France. Domestic destinations include Paris Orly, Lyon, Nice and Ajaccio (Corsica).

WORTH A TRIP

ORADOUR-SUR-GLANE – MEMORIAL TO A MASSACRE

On the afternoon of 10 June 1944, the little town of Oradour-sur-Glane, 21km northwest of Limoges, witnessed one of the worst Nazi war crimes committed on French soil. German lorries belonging to the SS 'Das Reich' Division surrounded the town and ordered the population onto the market square. The men were divided into groups and forced into barns, where they were machine-gunned before the structures were set alight. Several hundred women and children were herded into the church, which was set on fire, along with the rest of the town. Only one woman and five men who were in the town that day survived the massacre; 642 people, including 193 children, were killed. The same SS Division committed a similarly brutal act in Tulle two days earlier, in which 99 Resistance sympathisers were strung up from the town's balconies as a warning to others.

Since these events, the entire village has been left untouched, complete with pre-war tram tracks and electricity lines, the blackened shells of buildings and the rusting hulks of 1930s automobiles – an evocative memorial to a village caught up in the brutal tide of war. At the centre of the village is an underground memorial inscribed with the victims' names and displaying their recovered belongings, including watches, wallets, hymnals from the burnt church and children's bikes. Victims were buried in the nearby cemetery.

Entry is via the modern **Centre de la Mémoire** (📞 05 55 43 04 30; www.oradour. org; D3; adult/child €7.80/5.20; ⊘ 9am-6pm May–mid-Sep, to 4pm or 5pm rest of year, closed mid-Dec–Jan), which does an excellent job contextualising the massacre using historical exhibitions, videos and survivors' testimonies. Various theories have been put forward to try to explain the event – perhaps a reaction to the Allied landings four days earlier, or reprisal for sabotage raids committed by the Resistance, or the Resistance's hostage-taking of an SS officer. Those who were ultimately accused of the crime were tried at a 1953 military tribunal in Bordeaux, with outcomes ranging from a death sentence to amnesty (much to the chagrin of Oradour survivors and relatives).

After the war, a new Oradour was rebuilt a few hundred metres west of the ruins. RDTHV (www.rdthv.com) bus 12 serves the Limoges bus station (45 minutes, once or twice Monday to Saturday).

WORTH A TRIP

TRAIN-BUFF TRIP

Clamber aboard carriages pulled by a 1932 steam engine on the **Chemin de Fer Touristique Limousin–Périgord** (www.trainvapeur.com; Gare des Bénédictins; adult/child €28/12) to watch the Limousin's fields and forests roll by. The trains only run on certain days and routes from Limoges and Eymoutiers, June through August. Reservations are essential; make them online or at the tourist office in Limoges, Eymoutiers, Guéret, Pompadour or St-Yrieix.

Taxis (☑ 05 55 38 38 38; www.taxis87.com) from the airport charge a flat-rate fare of €24 during the day, and €34 after 7pm and on Sundays.

BUS

Limoges' bus station is across the tracks from the train station. **RDTHV** (Régie Départementale des Transports de la Haute-Vienne; ☑ 05 55 10 31 00; www.rdthv.com; place des Charentes; ticket €2) buses are geared towards school timetables, so there's only one or two per day during the week. Information and timetables are also available from the tourist office or www.moohv87.fr. SNCF runs additional buses; a map is available at www.regionlimousin.fr.

TRAIN

Limoges' beautiful Gare des Bénédictins is on the Paris–Cahors and Bordeaux–Clermont–Ferrand lines.

Bordeaux €35.40, three hours, five direct daily
Paris €24, three hours, nine daily
Périgueux €17.70, one hour, 15 daily
Toulouse €15 to €27, 3½ hours, three direct daily

Aubusson

POP 3898

Quaint riverside Aubusson has become synonymous with fine tapestries. It was the clacking centre of French production during the 19th century (rivalled only by the Gobelins factories in Paris), producing elegant tapestries renowned for vivid colours, fine detail and exquisite craftsmanship. An exploration of Aubusson's beautiful terraced streets rising above the River Creuse, and its modern-day tapestry museums and studios, is a must for any lover of the art.

⊙ Sights

Cité Internationale de la Tapisserie MUSEUM
(☑ 05 55 83 08 30; www.cite-tapisserie.fr; rue des Arts; adult/child €8/free; ☉10am-6pm Wed-Mon, 2-6pm Tue Jul & Aug, 9.30am-noon & 2-6pm Wed-Mon Feb-Jun & Sep-Dec) This museum moved to a grand new space at the colourfully striped former National School of Decorative Arts in 2016. The building was completely redesigned to explore tapestry worldwide, and Aubusson's particular history and contribution, as well as contemporary tapestry, including artists in residence. It is a good place to get a historical overview as well as see intricate examples of both antique and modern tapestries produced in Aubusson.

Maison du Tapissier MUSEUM
(☑ 05 55 66 32 12; 63 rue Vieille; adult/child €5.50/ free; ☉10am-noon & 2-5pm Mon-Sat) Next to the tourist office, this 16th-century building holds a recreation of a 17th-century weaver's workshop, with tools, original furniture and vintage tapestries.

🛏 Sleeping & Eating

Daytime eateries gear towards the tour bus crowd, but there are several *boulangeries* and the hotel restaurants are reliable.

Hôtel La Beauze BOUTIQUE HOTEL €
(☑ 05 55 66 46 00; www.hotellabeauze.fr; 14 av de la République; d €70-90; ☎) This renovated 19th-century townhouse on the edge of the old town is one of Aubusson's comfiest places to stay. Stylishly furnished rooms have peaceful views across a grassy garden.

L'Hôtel de France HOTEL €€
(☑ 05 55 66 10 22; www.aubussonlefrance.com; 6 rue des Déportés; d €79-110; ☎) This upmarket Logis hotel has 21 plush rooms: some modern, some old-fashioned and frilly, some tucked into the attic with sloping ceilings. Its restaurant (three-course *menus* €22 to €43) is the best in town, with Limousin dishes served to the tunes of a tinkling piano.

ⓘ Information

Tourist Office (☑ 05 55 66 32 12; 63 rue Vieille; ☉10am-noon & 2-6pm; ☎)

ⓘ Getting There & Away

Aubusson is 88km east of Limoges. SNCF buses link Aubusson with Limoges (€20.90, 1¾ hours, four direct Monday to Saturday, two Sunday). The station is about 400m from town, across the river Creuse.

Rochechouart

POP 3789

Meteorites and modern art might be an unlikely combination but they're the twin draws of the pretty walled town of Rochechouart, 45km west of Limoges. It's a fun stop for a quick walk, with its beautiful château and church with a special spiralling spire.

Housed in the town's striking château, overlooking the confluence of two small rivers, the **Musée Départemental d'Art Contemporain** (☑ 05 55 03 77 77; www.musee-rochechouart.com; place du Château; adult/child €4.60/free, 1st Sun of month free; ☺ 10am-12.30pm & 1.30-6pm Wed-Mon, closed mid-Dec–Feb) includes a collection of works by acclaimed Austrian Dadaist Raoul Hausman and a room decorated by 16th-century frescoes.

Two hundred million years ago, a 1.5km-radius intergalactic rock slammed into Earth 4km west of Rochechouart at 72,000km/h with the force of 14 million Hiroshima bombs, creating a crater 20km wide and 6km deep. The **Éspace Météorite Paul Pellas** (☑ 05 55 03 02 70; 16 rue Jean Parvy; adult/child €4/2; ☺ 9am-noon & 1.30-5.30pm Mon-Thu, to 4.30pm Fri, closed mid-Dec–mid-Jan) explores it through minerals, models and videos.

Limoges RDTHV (www.rdthv.com) bus 21 (€2, 80 minutes, two daily Monday to Friday) serves Rochechouart.

Solignac

POP 1551

In the thickly wooded Briance Valley, 10km south of Limoges, the tiny medieval village of Solignac was a major stop on the pilgrimage route to Santiago de Compostela. Its sweet village is made of golden-coloured granite typical of the Limousin, and its 11th-century church, **Abbaye St-Pierre de Solignac** (12 rue de l'Abbaye; ☺ 9am-6pm), is a Romanesque treasure.

Still operational, the church is renowned for its 14m-wide domed roof. The stalls in the nave are decorated with carved wooden sculptures of human heads, fantastical animals and a monk mooning the world, while the columns depict human figures being devoured by dragons.

Five kilometres southeast of Solignac are the moody ruins of **Château de Châlucet** (☑ 05 55 00 96 55; www.chalucet.com; guided tour adult/child €5/free; ☺ guided tours 10:30am-6:30pm Jul & Aug, shorter hr Apr-Jun & Sep-Oct) FREE, a

12th-century keep occupied by the English during the Hundred Years War. The spot, along a pretty little brook with forested hills and tweeting birds, makes a fine picnic stop, with valley views from the tumbledown keep.

The Solignac–Le Vigen train station is on the Limoges (€3.20, 10 minutes, seven daily) to Brive-la-Gaillarde (€15.90, 1¼ hour, five daily) line.

Uzerche

POP 2889

Breathtakingly situated on a spur above the glistening River Vézère, the walled town of Uzerche is one of the Limousin's prettiest hilltop hamlets. Spiky turrets top the walls of 15th- and 16th-century *maisons à tourelles* (turret houses) like witches' hats, and the Porte Bécharie, one of the nine original 14th-century gates, remains remarkably intact.

Uzerche's single street leads uphill past vibrant cafes to the Église St-Pierre, a fortified church with an 11th-century crypt – one of the oldest in the Limousin. From the front, there are fabulous panoramas of the river valley from place de la Lunade (which takes its name from a pagan summer solstice festival now rejigged as a Christian procession). Or view the village afloat: **Vézère Passion** (☑ 05 55 73 02 84; www.vezerepassion.com; Base de la Minoterie, rte de la Minoterie; river trips adult/child from €14/5) rents kayaks and canoes.

🛏 Sleeping & Eating

Those with a riverside picnic in mind can pick up bottles of locally brewed blondes, ambers, organic IPAs and ryes at local craft brewery **Brasserie Vézère** (www.facebook.com/Brasserie.Vezere; 2 allée de la Papeterie; ☺ Thu-Sat 3-7pm).

Hôtel Jean Teyssier   HOTEL €
(☑ 05 55 73 10 05; www.hotel-teyssier.com; rue du Pont-Turgot; d €55-69) The Teyssier's lovely stone exterior conceals a comfortable, modern hotel: the 15 rooms are fresh and well furnished, with magnolia walls and striped fabrics, and the restaurant (*menu* €22) has a nice river-view terrace. It's located near the north entrance to town.

Hôtel Joyet de Maubec   BOUTIQUE HOTEL €€
(☑ 05 55 97 20 60; www.hotel-joyet-maubec.com; place des Vignerons; d/ste from €125/230) Sleek, contemporary design meets French country living at this fine hotel, set in the enchanting

upper village. The elegant restaurant (*menus* €28 to €37) serves elaborate local cuisine, and also has a pastoral terrace.

Le Table de M FRENCH €€
(☑ 05 55 98 17 80; place Alexis Boyer; lunch menu €15, dinner menus €26-40; ☺ noon-2pm Tue-Sun, 7-9pm Wed-Sat) Sup on dishes created from locally sourced ingredients, such as Limousin beef, served by friendly staff on a lively terrace, or in a contemporary dining room dressed in slate grey and rose.

❶ Information

Tourist Office (☑ 05 55 73 15 71; www.paysuzerche.fr; 10 place de la Libération; ☺ 10am-12.30pm & 2-6pm Mon-Sat, 10am-12.30pm & 2.30-5.30pm Sun Jul & Aug, shorter hr rest of year; ☎) Also sells local art, chutneys and honeys.

❶ Getting There & Away

Uzerche's train station, 2km north of the old city along the N20, is on the Limoges (from €9.90, 40 minutes, 12 daily) to Brive-la-Gaillarde (€8, 30 minutes, 12 daily) line.

WORTH A TRIP

TULLE

The industrial town of Tulle, 28km northeast of Brive, is renowned as the world's accordion capital. A single accordion consists of between 3500 and 6800 parts and making one requires up to 200 hours' labour. The very best instruments fetch upwards of €9000.

One of the last remaining traditional accordion makers, **Maugein** (Manufacture d'Accordéons Maugein; ☑ 05 55 20 08 89; www.accordeons-maugein.com; D1089, Zone Industrielle Mulatet; adult/child €5/free; ☺ tours by reservation 2.30pm Tue-Thu), runs guided factory tours by reservation, where you can see the craftspeople at work and browse the accordion museum.

Accordions take centre stage during mid-September's four-day street music festival Nuits de Nacre; Tulle's **tourist office** (☑ 05 55 26 59 61; www.tulle-encorreze.com; 2 place Jean Tavé; ☺ 9.30am-12.30pm & 2-6pm Mon-Sat) has details.

Regular trains run to Tulle from Brive (€5.90, 30 minutes).

Brive-la-Gaillarde
POP 47,349

Navigate the busy outskirts of Brive-la-Gaillarde and you'll eventually be rewarded: a golden sandstone village still forms the town's core, making for an interesting maze of walking streets and cafe life. The main commercial centre for the agricultural Corrèze *département,* its bustling weekly markets draw folk from all around.

◉ Sights

Collégiale St-Martin CHURCH
(place Charles de Gaulle) In the heart of town, the Romanesque Collégiale St-Martin dates from the 11th century. Original parts include the transept and a few decorated columns depicting fabulous beasties and biblical scenes.

Maison Denoix DISTILLERY
(☑ 05 55 74 34 27; www.denoix.com; 9 bd du Maréchal Lyautey; ☺ 9am-noon & 2.30-7pm Tue-Sat) FREE Since 1839, this traditional distillery has produced the favourite Corrèze firewater, *l'eau de noix* (walnut liqueur), alongside concoctions such as chocolate and quince liqueurs. See the copper stills and sample the wares, including grape mustard, or take a free summer-only guided tour (2.30pm Tue-Fri, one hour).

Musée Labenche MUSEUM
(☑ 05 55 18 17 70; http://labenche.brive.fr; 26bis bd Jules-Ferry; adult/child €5/free; ☺ 10am-12.30pm & 1.30-6pm Wed-Mon May-Sep, 2-6pm Oct-Apr) The town's main museum is in the beautiful Renaissance Hôtel de Labenche. Exhibits explore local history and archaeology, and there's a collection of accordions and unique 17th-century English tapestries.

🛏 Sleeping

Auberge de Jeunesse HOSTEL €
(☑ 05 55 24 34 00; www.fuaj.org; 56 av Maréchal Bugeaud; dm €15.60; ☺ reception 4-8pm Apr-Sep; ☎) Brive's hostel makes a striking first impression, with reception inside a former townhouse; however, most dorm rooms are actually in a modern annexe. It's 1.5km from the station.

★ Hôtel le Collonges HOTEL €
(☑ 05 55 74 09 58; www.hotel-collonges.com; 3-5 place Winston Churchill; d €79-89, tr €99; ❋ ☎) Modern rooms are in tip-top condition at this smart hotel at the edge of Brive's town centre.

Rooms upstairs under the eaves can sleep three, and the breakfast buffet (€9) is grand.

★ Cyprès Si Haut
TREEHOUSE €€€

(☑ 06 89 13 58 05; www.cypres-sihaut.com; rue du Fond Bourg, Saint-Mexant; treehouse incl breakfast €230-290; ❋ ☏) Fancy a little treehouse getaway? This luxury cabin on stilts is the perfect spot to power down the mobile phone and go off the grid for a night. Relax in the outdoor hot tub, get rubbed down with essential oils in the spa and order picnic meals to be hauled up via a pulley system. Sleeps four; reserve well ahead.

It's 20 km northeast of Brive, outside the village of Saint-Mexant.

✗ Eating

Georges Brassens Market
MARKET €

(18 Quai Tourny; ⊙ 8.30am-12.30pm Tue, Thu & Sat) A bustling covered market, with the most vendors on Saturday. Stock up on Limousin goodies: goose products, plum brandy, *pâté de pomme de terre* (a rich potato, pork and cream pie) and *galette corrézienne* (walnut and chestnut cake).

La Tavola di Mamma
ITALIAN €

(☑ 05 55 24 33 07; 14 av du 11 Novembre 1918; pizzas & pasta €9-14.90; ⊙ noon-1.45pm Mon-Sat, 7.30-10pm Tue-Sat) For a town of its size, Brive has little to offer in the way of casual, affordable restaurants. If you're saving your centimes, La Tavola is one of the best options.

Borzeix-Besse
DESSERTS €

(☑ 05 55 22 49 98; www.chocolats-borzeix-besse. com; 23 rue Barbecane; mini cakes from €2; ⊙ 10am-noon & 2-7pm Tue-Sat) Divine chocolate and macarons alongside the most beautiful cakes in Limousin.

★ La Table d'Olivier
GASTRONOMY €€€

(☑ 05 55 18 95 95; 3 rue St-Ambroise; lunch/dinner menus from €26/46; ⊙ noon-1.15pm Thu-Sun, 7.30-9.15pm Wed-Sun) Reserve ahead for a seat at Brive's top table, where refined, creative local cuisine is served with charm. Dishes arrive looking like small works of art. Save room for delicate desserts.

ⓘ Information

Tourist Office (☑ 05 55 24 08 80; www. brive-tourisme.com; place du 14 Juillet; ⊙ 9am-12.30pm & 1.30-6.30pm Mon-Sat Jun-Sep, 11am-5pm Sun Jul & Aug, shorter hr rest of year) Housed in a former water tower, locally known as the *phare* (lighthouse), overlooking the market square.

ⓘ Getting There & Away

AIR

Brive-Vallée de la Dordogne Airport (BVE; ☑ 05 55 22 40 00; www.aeroport-brive-vallee-dordogne.com), about 10km south of town, has budget flights to Paris-Orly and London City Airport. The only airport transport is taxi or rental car.

BUS

The **bus station** (place du 14 Juillet) is next to the tourist office. **Trans Périgord** (www.trans perigord.fr) connects Brive with Montignac (€2, 1¼ hours, one daily Monday to Friday).

CFTA (www.cftaco.fr) Regional buses, including a service to Tulle (€2, 45 minutes, six daily Monday to Friday, one Saturday).

Libéo (☑ 05 55 74 20 13; www.libeo-brive.fr; ticket €1.20) Local buses around town; lines 3, N and D serve the train station.

TRAIN

The **train station** (av Jean Jaurès) is located at a major confluence of rail lines 900m southwest of Brive centre. There are lines north to Limoges and Paris, south to Toulouse, west to Périgueux, east to Clermont-Ferrand, and southeast to Figeac.

Cahors from €14, 1¼ hours, nine daily
Limoges from €14.40, one hour, frequent
Paris Austerlitz €40 to €73, 4½ hours, seven daily
Périgueux €14, one hour, seven daily

South of Brive

Rolling countryside unrolls south of Brive to the banks of the Dordogne and the border of the northern Lot. Some of the Limousin's most picturesque villages dot this overtly rural neck of the woods.

Turenne
POP 836

Rising up from a solitary spur of rock, the hilltop village of Turenne is an arresting sight: honey-coloured stone cottages and slanted houses are stacked up like dominoes beneath the towering **Château de Turenne** (☑ 05 55 85 90 66; www.chateau-turenne.com; adult/child €5/3.40; ⊙ 10am-7pm Jul & Aug, shorter hr rest of year), from which viscounts ruled a huge portion of the Limousin, Périgord and Quercy for almost 1000 years. Beautiful views of the surrounding countryside fan out atop the 12th-century **Tour de César**, the arrow-straight tower. Apart from a few ramparts and a 14th-century guard room, the rest of the lordly lodgings have crumbled away, and are now occupied by an ornamental garden.

Behind the 16th-century Flamboyant Gothic façade of Turenne's only hotel, **La Maison des Chanoines** (☑ 05 55 85 93 43; www.maison-des-chanoines.com; rue Joseph Rouveyrol; d €95-120; ☺ mid-Apr–mid-Oct; 🛜), you'll find sparingly decorated countrified rooms and a good restaurant (dinner *menus* €42 to €50).

The **tourist office** (☑ 05 55 24 12 95; www.brive-tourisme.com; D 20; guided visits adult/child €5/2.50; ☺ 10am-12.30pm & 2-6pm Tue-Sun Easter-Sep) at the base of the village runs guided visits and torch-lit night-time promenades in summer.

Turenne is 15km south of Brive. Public transport is limited: there are **CFTA** (www.cftaco.fr) buses from Brive (€2, 30 minutes, three daily Monday to Friday) and trains (€3.70, 15 minutes, two daily) that stop 3km southeast of the village.

Collonges-la-Rouge

POP 491

Built from vibrant rust-red sandstone (hence its name) and topped by fantastical conical turrets and black-slate rooftops, Collonges-la-Rouge is one of the most iconic villages in the Corrèze. In 1942, the entire village received classification as a *monument historique*. Gazing at the gorgeous architecture and browsing Collonges' many artisan shops is a popular pastime, so start early as the village steadily fills with bus-loads of tourists.

◉ Sights & Activities

There are a number of short hikes and bike rides that loop through the countryside around Collonges. Get info from the tourist office; alternatively, maps and descriptions (in French) are signposted in the parking lot at the entrance to town.

St-Pierre Church   CHURCH

(opposite the Covered Market) The fortified St-Pierre church, constructed from the 11th to the 15th centuries on the site of an 8th-century Benedictine priory, is an important stop on the pilgrimage to Santiago de Compostela. In an unusual show of unity during the late 16th century, local Protestants held prayers in the southern nave and their Catholic neighbours prayed in the northern nave. The 12th-century **tympanum** is made from white Turenne limestone, and the bell tower is in the Limousin style.

Covered Market   MARKET

(opposite St-Pierre Church) The slate roof of the ancient covered market shelters an equally ancient baker's oven.

🛏 Sleeping & Eating

La Bastidie   HOTEL €€

(☑ 05 55 88 22 88; www.la-bastidie.fr; 1 rue des Écoles, Noalhac; d €115-155) Escape to pastoral La Bastidie, the stone inn in Noalhac which contains four individually decorated, comfortable rooms, and a tasty **restaurant** (*menus* lunch €21.50, dinner €31 to €60) specialising in local fare with flair. Find it 4.5km northwest of Collonges-la-Rouge.

WORTH A TRIP

CHÂTEAU DE POMPADOUR

Equine aficionados won't want to miss Arnac-Pompadour, home to the **Château de Pompadour** (☑ 05 55 98 55 47; www.pompadour-tourisme.fr; adult/child €9.50/7, with foaling nursery €13/10; ☺ 10am-6.30pm Jul–mid-Sep, reduced hr rest of year), one of France's foremost national *haras* (stud farms). Established in the 18th century by the mistress of Louis XV, Madame de Pompadour (born Jeanne-Antoinette Poisson), the small town is particularly known for its Anglo-Arab pedigrees. Admission to the château includes a peek in 11 rooms on a self-guided tour (the interior was damaged during the Revolution and again during a 19th-century fire) and a visit to the prestigious stables. For an additional charge, you can tour the foaling nursery or take a backstage look at the equine shows (also available as separate admission, adult/child €5/4).

In the Arnac château's right tower, the **tourist office** (☺ 10am-6pm Jul–mid-Sep, reduced hr rest of year) details forthcoming equestrian demonstrations and races, as well as local horse-riding options.

Arnac-Pompadour is on the train line, 60km south of Limoges (€12.80, 1½ hours, four daily). Note the station is in Pompadour, not Arnac.

★ **Auberge de Benges** FRENCH €€
(☑ 05 55 85 76 68; www.aubergedebenges.com; lunch menu €22, mains €15-43; ☺ noon-2pm Wed-Mon & 7-9pm Wed-Sat Mar-Oct) Collonges' top table for locally sourced ingredients, creativity and a relaxed ambience. Step through the wisteria-clad entry to a terrace with sweeping views from the foot of the village.

ℹ Information

Tourist Office (☑ 05 65 33 22 00; www.vallee-dordogne.com; ☺ 9.30am-1pm & 2-7pm Jul & Aug, shorter hr rest of year) Arranges guided tours (adult/child €5/free) of the village.

ℹ Getting There & Away

Collonges is linked by **CFTA** (www.cftaco.fr) bus 4 with Brive (€2, 30 minutes, four to six daily Monday to Friday, one on Saturday), 18km to the northwest along the D38.

Beaulieu-sur-Dordogne

POP 1174

On a tranquil bend of the Dordogne surrounded by agricultural fields, Beaulieu was once an important stop for Compostela pilgrims. Its beautifully preserved medieval quarter is one of the region's finest: a network of curving lanes lined with timber-framed houses and smart mansions, many dating from the 14th and 15th centuries. Its main church is tops.

◉ Sights

★ **Abbatiale St-Pierre** CHURCH
(rue de la République; ☺ 9am-7pm) Beaulieu's most celebrated feature is this 12th-century Romanesque abbey church, with a wonderful tympanum (c 1130) depicting incredible scenes from the Last Judgment, including dancing apostles and resurrected sinners. Also look for its small treasury case filled with 10th- to 13th-century masterworks.

Chapelle des Pénitents CHURCH
(rue de la Chapelle; ☺ mid-Jun–mid-Sep) The pretty riverside Chapelle des Pénitents was built to accommodate pious parishioners – access to the abbey church was strictly reserved for monks and paying pilgrims. Now it hosts temporary exhibitions.

Château de Castelnau-Bretenoux FORTRESS
(☑ 05 65 10 98 00; www.castelnau-bretenoux.fr; Prudhomat; adult/child €8/free, parking €2; ☺ 10am-7pm Jul & Aug, shorter hr rest of year) Not to be confused with the Château de Castelnaud, Castelnau-Bretenoux was constructed in the 12th century and saw heavy action during the Hundred Years War, before being redeveloped in the Middle Ages for newer forms of artillery. It is beautifully (and strategically) set on a promontory above the broad valley. Much of the fortress is in ruins, but you can climb the 15th-century artillery tower, which has great views, and visit 17th- and 18th-century residential rooms (by free guided tour in summer).

Castelnau-Bretenoux fell into disrepair in the 19th century and was refurbished around the turn of the 20th century by Parisian opera singer Jean Mouliérat. It's about 11km south of Beaulieu-sur-Dordogne off the D940.

🛏 Sleeping & Eating

Beaulieu's market is on Wednesday and Saturday mornings. On the second Sunday in May the Fête de la Fraise (Strawberry Festival) is held.

La Ferme du Masvidal CAMPGROUND, B&B €
(☑ 05 55 91 53 14; www.lafermedumasvidal.fr; bd de Turenne, Bilhac; site for 2 adults, tent & car €13, gîte per week €410; ☺ Apr-Sep; 🛜) ✎ This lovely working farm, about 11km southwest of Beaulieu in Bilhac, offers shady camping, B&B rooms and home-cooked meals (per adult/child from €28/14) made with homegrown produce.

Auberge de Jeunesse HOSTEL €
(☑ 05 55 91 13 82; www.hifrance.org; place du Monturuc; dm €15.75; ☺ Apr-Oct, reception 5.30-8pm; 🛜) Parts of this quirky 28-bed hostel, like the latticed windows and square dovecote, date from the 15th century. Inside find a cosy lounge, well-stocked kitchen and dinky four-bed rooms with private bathrooms. Cash only.

ℹ Information

Beaulieu-sur-Dordogne Tourist Office (☑ 05 55 91 09 94; www.vallee-dordogne.com; place Marbot; ☺ 9.30am-12.30pm & 2.30-5pm Mon-Sat Sep-Jun, 9.30am-12.30pm Sun Jul & Aug) On the main square with local and regional maps.

ℹ Getting There & Away

CFTA (www.cftaco.fr) bus 9 links Beaulieu with Brive (€2, one hour, one to two daily) from Monday to Saturday.

THE LOT

Stretching from the River Dordogne in the north to the serpentine River Lot near busy Cahors (and its renowned vineyards) and beyond, the Lot *département* offers an arresting landscape of limestone cliffs and canyons, hilltop towns and undulating hills carpeted in forests, fields or vines. Formerly the northern section of the old province of Quercy, the modern Lot is part of the Occitanie *region*, and makes for great exploring, especially if you have your own wheels.

Cahors

POP 19,340

In a U-shaped curve in the River Lot, Cahors combines the feel of the sunbaked Mediterranean with an alluring old town. Pastel-coloured buildings line the shady squares of the ancient medieval quarter, criss-crossed by a labyrinth of alleyways and cul-de-sacs, and bordered by scenic quays.

Slicing through the centre of Cahors, bd Léon Gambetta – named after the French statesman who was born in Cahors in 1838 – neatly divides Vieux Cahors (old Cahors) to the east and the new city to the west.

⊙ Sights

In the Middle Ages, Cahors was a prosperous commercial centre, and the old city is densely packed with timber-fronted houses and galleried mansions built by the city's medieval merchants. Wandering the old town is a real highlight, with fascinating ancient details around every corner. Don't-miss streets include Dr Bergougnioux, Lastié, St-Priest and St-Urcisse.

Get a copy of *Gardens of Cahors*, a superb free booklet that highlights a walking tour of the town, including many secret gardens. The tourist office offers guided walks in French (€5 to €6).

★ Pont Valentré   BRIDGE
The seven-span Pont Valentré, on the western side of the city, south of the train station, is one of France's most iconic medieval bridges, built as part of the town's defences in the 14th century. The parapets projecting from two of its three tall towers were designed to allow defenders to drop missiles on attackers below. On the bank opposite the bridge, the **Fontaine des Chartreux**, dedicated to the city's Gallo-Roman goddess Divona, was the city's original centre.

★ Cathédrale St-Étienne   CATHEDRAL
(place de la Cathédrale; ⊙7am-6pm) The airy nave of Cahors' Romanesque cathedral, consecrated in 1119, is topped by two cupolas (at 18m wide, the largest in France). Some of the frescoes are from the 14th century, but the side chapels and carvings in the *cloître* (cloister) mainly date from the 16th-century Flamboyant Gothic period. On the north façade, a carved tympanum depicts Christ's ascension surrounded by fluttering angels and pious saints.

Tour du Pape Jean XXII   ARCHITECTURE
(3 bd Léon Gambetta) The Tour du Pape Jean XXII (closed to the public) is the town's tallest building at 34m high. It was originally part of a 14th-century mansion belonging to Jacques Duèse (later Pope John XXII), who constructed the Pont Valentré.

🏃 Activities

Les Crosières Fénelon   BOATING
(☑05 65 30 16 55; www.bateau-cahors.com; quai Valentré; 1¼hr boat tours adult/child €11/5; ⊙May–mid-Oct) Jaunt around on the River Valentré by boat, some going as far as St-Cirq Lapopie (adult/child €62/37) or the vineyards to the west of Cahors (adult/child €59/35).

🛏 Sleeping

★ Auberge de Jeunesse Le Chai   HOSTEL €
(☑05 36 04 00 80; www.hifrance.org; 52 av André Breton; dm incl breakfast €25; @🛜) This new HI hostel, opened in 2017, looks out over the Pont Valentré (p624) from a fabulous rooftop deck. Expect modern hostel amenities including laundry, kitchen, bar, games room and even picnics to go. It's a short walk from the train station.

Hôtel Jean XXII   HOTEL €
(☑05 65 35 07 66; www.hotel-jeanxxii.com; 2 rue Edmond-Albé; s/d/q €62/73.50/98.50; ⊙reception closes 10.30am-4.30pm; 🛜) Next to the Tour du Pape Jean XXII, this excellent nine-room hotel mixes original stone, greenery and well-worn wood with a dash of metropolitan minimalism. Rooms sleep one to four people; there's a reading area on the 1st floor where you can unwind in leather armchairs.

Grand Hôtel Terminus   HOTEL €€
(☑05 65 53 32 00; www.balandre.com; 5 av Charles de Freycinet; d €75-115; ❄🛜) Built c 1920, Cahors' original railway-station hotel evokes an air of faded grandeur. Most of the rooms are large if a little frayed, with hefty radiators, baths and king-size beds. Wi-fi is iffy.

🍴 Eating

Cafes cluster around the modern place François Mitterrand. The park-like banks

Cahors

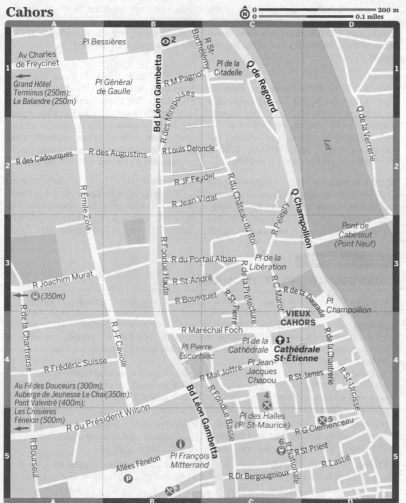

THE DORDOGNE, LIMOUSIN & THE LOT CAHORS

of the Lot are perfect for picnics, especially near the Pont Valentré.

The open-air market is held on place Jean-Jacques Chapou on Wednesdays and Saturdays.

★ **Marché Couvert** MARKET €
(place des Halles; ⏱ 7.30am-12.30pm & 3-7pm Tue-Sat, 9am-noon Sun) The city's main covered market is often simply called Les Halles. There's a not-to-be-missed **open-air**

market on Wednesday and Saturday mornings around the covered market and on place Jean-Jacques Chapou. Excellent food shops cluster around the market and along rue Nationale.

Marie Colline VEGETARIAN €

(☏ 05 65 35 59 96; 173 rue Clémenceau; mains €9; ⊙ noon-1.30pm Mon-Fri; ✔) This super-friendly vegetarian cafe is one of Cahors' most popular lunchtime spots. Join the regulars for homemade creations like spinach rolls, sweet potato soup and apple-prune crumble. Popular dishes sell out quickly – don't arrive late!

★ L'Ô à la Bouche MODERN FRENCH €€

(☏ 05 65 35 65 69; www.loalabouche-restaurant. com; 56 allée Fénelon; lunch menus €27-40, dinner menus €28-42; ⊙ noon-2pm & 7.30-9.30pm Tue-Sat) Book ahead to get a seat in this small,

contemporary restaurant that takes its creative, local cuisine quite seriously. The welcome is warm and the ingredients are the finest the region has to offer.

Au Fil des Douceurs FRENCH €€

(☏ 05 65 22 13 04; 32 av André Breton; lunch menu from €16.50, dinner menus €26-60; ⊙ noon-2pm & 7-9.30pm Tue-Sat) From locally sourced foods to a superb regional wine list, this elegant but fun restaurant serves excellent – and ever-changing – *menus*. Dine inside the modern two-level restaurant or outside on the terrace, with a fabulous view of Pont Valentré.

Le Balandre GASTRONOMY €€€

(☏ 05 65 53 32 00; www.balandre.com; 5 av Charles de Freycinet; lunch menu €23, dinner menus €48-65; ⊙ noon-1.30pm & 7.30-9.15pm Tue-Sat) With chandeliers and stained glass, the deeply

---

LOCAL KNOWLEDGE

WINE COUNTRY: WEST OF CAHORS

Downstream from Cahors, the lower River Lot twists its way through the rich vineyards of the Cahors Appellation d'Origine Contrôlée (AOC) region (www.vindecahors.fr). Pick up the super, free *Vignobles de Cahors et du Lot* map for a comprehensive list of wineries, then visit www.tourisme-lot-vignoble.com and download the map. Malbecs predominate, with some merlot and tannat here and there, and you'll find they're best aged. Local whites don't carry the Cahors AOC.

Snake along the river's northern bank on the D9 for superb views of the vines and the river's many twists and turns. As you go west of Cahors, you'll pass Luzech, the medieval section of which sits at the base of a donjon, and Castelfranc, with a dramatic suspension bridge. Many wineries cluster around Puy l'Évêque.

Château du Cèdre (☏ 05 65 36 53 87; www.chateauducedre.com; Vire-sur-Lot; ⊙ complimentary tastings 9am-noon & 2-6pm Mon-Sat) Casual, organic vineyard in the countryside, 5.5km west of Puy l'Évêque, with award-winning AOC Cahors malbecs.

Château Chambert (☏ 05 65 31 95 75; www.chambert.com; Floressas; ⊙ complimentary tastings 10am-7pm Jul & Aug, shorter hr rest of year) Absolutely iconic château rising above organic vines, 8.5km south of Puy l'Évêque.

Clos Triguedina (☏ 05 65 21 30 81; www.jlbaldes.com; Vire-Sur-Lot; 30min tour & tasting €5; ⊙ 9am-noon & 2-6pm Mon-Sat) In the Baldès family since 1830, this place 5.5km west of Puy l'Évêque produces everything from straight-up malbecs to rosé and a medieval-style black vintage.

Take a Break

Need a break from wine tasting or a bite to eat? Try these spots:

Château de Bonaguil (☏ 05 53 71 90 33; www.chateau-bonaguil.com; Bonaguil; adult/child €9/5; ⊙ 10am-7pm Jul & Aug, 10am-5.30pm Mar-Jun, Sep & Oct)

Le Dodus en Ville (☏ 05 65 22 91 82; http://auxdodus.free.fr; rue Ernest-Marcouly, Puy l'Évêque; 2-/3-course menus €12.50/15; ⊙ noon-2.30pm Tue-Fri, 7-9pm Tue-Sat)

Château de Mercuès (☏ 05 65 20 00 01; www.chateaudemercues.com; rue du Château, Mercuès; d from €225, ste from €260; ⊙ Apr-Oct; ❄ @ 🛜 🏊)

Domaine Le Peyrou (☏ 05 65 30 51 98; www.lepeyrou.com; Luzech; d €68-78, studio/house per week from €525/1080; P 🛜 🏊)

traditional family-run restaurant at Grand Hotel Terminus (p624) commands a devoted following, especially for its foie gras and *confit de canard*. Also offers monthly cooking courses (€100) with chef Gilles Marre.

Drinking & Nightlife

Head to place François Mitterrand where cafe tables spill onto the plaza and fill with people-watching locals.

Le Dousil　　　　　　　　WINE BAR
(☑05 65 53 19 67; http://ledousil.free.fr; 124 rue Nationale; ☺11am-2pm & 7-11pm Tue-Sat) Stop by this convivial *bar à vins* to sample a glass of the local Malbec paired with French tapas (snails!) to nibble on.

ℹ Information

Tourist Office (☑05 65 53 20 65; www. tourisme-cahors.fr; place François Mitterrand; ☺9am-7pm Jun-Aug, shorter hr rest of year; ☎)

ℹ Getting There & Away

Cahors has trains to Paris (from €60, 5½ hours, four direct daily), Limoges (€19, 2¼ hours, five direct daily) and Toulouse (€20.20, 1½ hours, six daily).

North of Cahors

Some of the Lot's most striking sights lie north of Cahors near Limousin and the Dordogne, including the celebrated pilgrimage site of Rocamadour. Public transport is virtually non-existent: you'll need your own wheels to get around.

Rocamadour

POP 628
There are certain places in the world you just may remember for your whole life, and Rocamadour is one of them. From the dramatic silhouette of Rocamadour's steeples and pale stone chapels clamped to 150m of vertical cliffside beneath the ramparts of a 14th-century château, to the magically evocative feeling as you explore this ancient pilgrimage site, this spot makes an impression.

A hugely venerated pilgrimage place through the ages, on holy days as many as 30,000 people would stream into the valley to seek favours from the miraculous statue of the Virgin housed within. Henry Plantagenet (1133–89), King of England and Count of Anjou, was miraculously cured here. Always an important financial and symbolic spot, Rocamadour suffered during the Wars of Religion, when everything was razed. Fortunately, the icon and one bell survived, and they remain today in the rebuilt sanctuaries, which are still an active pilgrimage point.

Pedestrianised Rocamadour climbs the face of a cliff above the River Alzou, ascending from the Cité (old city) to the Sanctuaires to the château on top. You can approach from below or above; each area has car parks, and it's all connected by elevators.

The château on top is connected to the sanctuaries by the switchbacked tree- and cave-lined **Chemin de Croix pathway** (Stations of the Cross) or by **ascenseur incliné** (cable car; ☑05 65 33 67 79; www. ascenseurincline-rocamadour.com; one-way/return €2.60/4.20; ☺9am-10pm Jul & Aug, reduced hr rest of year). The sanctuaries and the Cité below are connected by **Escalier des Pelerins** (223 stairs that the pious once traversed on their knees) or another **ascenseur** (elevator; one-way/return €2.10/3.10; ☺9am-7.30pm Jul & Aug, shorter hr rest of year). A small **tourist train** (www.lepetittraindero-camadour.com; adult/child one-way €2.50/1.75; ☺10.30am-7.30pm Apr-Sep) goes from the lower parking lot about 150m to the Cité.

On the top side of Rocamadour, 1.5km across a spur of the hill, sits the modern conglomeration of shops, hotels and restaurants at touristy hamlet **L'Hospitalet**. Rocamadour is 59km north of Cahors and 51km east of Sarlat.

◉ Sights

You can reserve ahead with the *ascenseur incliné* staff for a one-hour French-only **guided tour** (€8.80) of the site.

In the pedestrianised Cité below the Sanctuaires, the commercial thoroughfare **Grande Rue** is crammed (just as in the pilgrims' heyday) with souvenir shops and touristy restaurants. **Porte du Figuier**, one of the city's original medieval gateways, still exists at the street's far end.

In L'Hospitalet, a cliffside **park** with perfect picnic benches enjoys excellent views to Rocamadour. Nearby the evocative **ruins of an ancient chapel** recall how this was pilgrims' first stop, where they healed and prepared themselves before going to Rocamadour's sanctuary.

★ **Sanctuaires**　　　　　　　HISTORIC SITE
(☺9am-6.30pm) **FREE** The Sanctuaires are seven beautiful 12th- to 14th-century chapels built into the rock-face and surrounding a

DON'T MISS

GOUFFRE DE PADIRAC

Discovered in 1889, the spectacular **Gouffre de Padirac** (☏ 05 65 33 64 56; www.gouffre-de-padirac.com; Padirac; adult/child €12.50/9; ☉ hr vary, approx 9am-7.30pm Apr–Oct) features some of France's spangliest underground caverns. The cave's navigable river, 103m below ground level, is reached through a 75m-deep, 33m-wide chasm. Boat pilots ferry visitors along 1km of subterranean waterways, visiting a series of glorious floodlit caverns, including the soaring **Salle de Grand Dôme** and the **Lac des Grands Gours**, a 27m-wide subterranean lake. You can book online – except for same-day tickets, which must be purchased at the cave.

The caverns are 15km northeast of Rocamadour.

central courtyard. You can see worn stones where pilgrims cycled between the churches. **Chapelle Notre Dame** is the highlight, containing the magical **Vierge Noire** (Black Madonna). Carved from walnut in the 12th century, she drew worshippers from across Europe in the Middle Ages. Overhead, the 9th-century iron bell is said to have rung on its own when somewhere in the world the Virgin performed a miracle.

Outside the chapel are the sites where it is said that the original hermit, St Amadour, was buried, and where **Durandal**, Roland's famous sword, was embedded in the wall. Rocamadour is still an active site; dress appropriately.

Château　　　　　　　　　　FORTRESS
(€2; ☉ 8am-8pm) Perched atop Rocamadour, the château is a series of 14th-century protective ramparts with excellent views of the valley. Exact change is required for the machine operating the entrance.

Grotte des Merveilles　　　　　　CAVE
(☏ 05 65 33 67 92; www.grotte-des-merveilles.com; L'Hospitalet; adult/child €7.50/4.50; ☉ hourly guided visits Apr-Oct) Natural cave with stalactites and 20,000-year-old cave art; in L'Hospitalet.

🛏 Sleeping & Eating

Rocamadour has relatively uninspiring restaurants, with a focus on the tourist trade. Pack a picnic.

★ **Moulin de Latreille**　　　　B&B €€
(☏ 09 65 22 04 03; www.moulindelatreille.com; Calès; d €120; ☉ mid-Mar–Oct; ☏) British expats Giles and Fi Stonor have painstakingly restored this 12th-century watermill on the banks of the River Ouysse, using the mill to power the whole tastefully done property. It's situated 2km down a dirt road from the hilltop village of Calès (17km west of Rocamadour off the D673).

Hôtel Le Troubadour　　　　HOTEL €€
(☏ 05 65 33 70 27; www.hotel-troubadour.com; Belveyre; d €150-200; ☉ mid-Feb–mid-Nov; ☏🏊) Rooms in the renovated stone house at this 17th-century farmstead are kitted out with unique furnishings and modern bathrooms. Grounds are extensive, with a big pool, and half-board (from €72) is available. Find it 2km northeast of Rocamadour, off the D673.

ℹ Information

Cité Tourist Office (Grand Rue, Rocamadour; ☉ 9.30am-1pm & 2-6.30pm; ☏) Small branch in the old city.

Main Tourist Office (☏ 05 65 33 22 00; www.vallee-dordogne.com; L'Hospitalet; ☉ 9.30am-1pm & 2-6.30pm Mon-Sat, 10am-1pm Sun; ☏) In L'Hospitalet. Has smartphone app.

Carennac

POP 407

Tiny Carennac is a sweet cluster of amber houses secluded on the left bank of the emerald Dordogne. Above the square is the Tour de Télémaque, named after the hero of Fénelon's *Les Aventures de Télémaque,* written here in 1699.

Just inside the gateway of the Château du Doyen sit the priory and the Romanesque **Église St-Pierre** (☉ 10am-7pm) with a remarkable Romanesque tympanum of Christ in Majesty. Off the cloître, still beautiful despite being heavily damaged in the Revolution, is a dramatic late-15th-century **Mise au Tombeau** (Statue of the Entombment).

The village's main landmark is 16th-century Château du Doyen, which houses a heritage centre and museum, **L'Espace Patrimoine** (www.pays-vallee-dordogne.com; ☉ 10am-noon & 2-6pm Mon-Fri, 2-6pm Sat & Sun Jul-Sep, Tue-Fri Easter-Jun & Oct) **FREE**, showcasing the art and history of the region.

Martel

POP 1601

Marvellous Martel, 43km east of Sarlat-la-Canéda and 36km south of Brive-la-Gaillarde, is known as *la ville aux sept tours* (the town of seven towers) for its turret-topped skyline. This vibrant pale-stone village was the ancient capital of the Vicomtes de Turenne, and a prosperous judicial centre, and it retains its medieval architecture and charm in its pedestrianised centre.

◉ Sights & Activities

Place des Consuls SQUARE

Martel's central square, place des Consuls, is home to the former fortress of the viscounts, **Hôtel de la Raymondie**, and is filled by a great **market** on Wednesdays and Saturdays. Truffle markets feature in December and January.

Chemin de Fer Touristique du Haut-Quercy RAIL

(☑05 65 37 35 81; www.trainduhautquercy. info; adult/child diesel train €8/5, steam train €10.50/6.50; ⊙Apr-Sep) Runs one-hour trips from Martel east along the precipitous cliff face to St-Denis. It used to transport truffles.

🛏 Sleeping & Eating

Château de Termes HOTEL €

(☑05 65 32 42 03; www.chateau-de-termes.com; St-Denis-lès-Martel; r €75, cabin €110-150; ⊙mid-Mar–Oct; 🖥🏊) This family-friendly cottage complex is set around a manor that originally belonged to winemakers and truffle growers. It has something for everyone: lovely, spacious rooms, two- to six-person cabins, badminton and a heated pool, and the owners organise canoe hire and horse riding. It's 5.3km northwest of Martel.

★ Manoir de Malagorse B&B €€

(☑05 65 27 14 83; www.manoir-de-malagorse.fr; Cuzance; d €160-200, ste €290-320; ⊙Apr–Oct; 🖥🏊) In quiet Cuzance, 8km northwest of Martel, this beauty of a B&B offers luxury normally reserved for top-end hotels. Owners Anna and Abel's period house is a chic combo of sleek lines, soothing colours and fluffy fabrics. It's surrounded by five private hectares, and the four-course home-cooked dinner (€42) is superb.

Relais Sainte-Anne HOTEL €€

(☑05 65 37 40 56; www.relais-sainte-anne.com; rue du Pourtanel; d €95-185, ste €275; ⊙mid-Apr–mid-Nov; 🖥🏊) The pick of places to stay in Martel village, on a quiet lane with 16 individually decorated rooms that blend country comforts with contemporary flair. Its excellent **restaurant** (☑05 65 37 40 56; www.relais-sainte-anne. com; rue du Pourtanel; menus from €30; ⊙noon-1.30pm Sun Nov-Mar, 7.30-9.30pm daily Apr-Oct) uses produce directly from Martel's markets.

★ Au Hasard Balthazar FRENCH €€

(☑05 65 37 42 01; www.auhasardbalthazar.fr; rue Tournemire; lunch/dinner menus from €19/28.50; ⊙noon 1.30pm Tue Sun, 7.30-9.30pm Tue-Sat May-Aug, shorter hours Apr & Sep) Local farm Les Bouriettes operates this wonderful shop and restaurant filled with their super products. Friendly proprietors serve regional specialities in the courtyard below the Tour Tournemire, or in the intimate stone dining room. Imagine ingredients such as walnut oil, pigeon confit, foie gras and wine mustard.

ℹ Information

Buried deep within the pedestrianised centre, the **tourist office** (☑05 65 37 43 44; www. vallee-dordogne.com; place des Consuls; ⊙9.30am-1pm & 2-6.30pm Mon-Sat; 🖥) has a booklet (€.50) and maps of architectural and historical highlights.

East of Cahors

Some of the Lot's most beautiful scenery, with limestone cliffs along the river valley and undulating fields on its hilltops, is crisscrossed by narrow roads east of Cahors.

WORTH A TRIP

GROTTE DU PECH MERLE

Discovered in 1922, the 1200m-long **Grotte du Pech Merle** (☑05 65 31 27 05; www.pechmerle.com; adult/child €13/8; ⊙9.15am-6pm Jul & Aug, shorter hr rest of year) is one of the few decorated caves found around the Lot Valley. It has several wonderful galleries of mammoths, bison and dappled horses, as well as unique hand tracings, fingerprints and human figures. Look out for the beautifully preserved adolescent footprint, clearly imprinted in the clay floor.

Reserve ahead by phone or online in peak season (ask for an English tour); visitors are limited to 700 per day. Entry includes a museum and a 20-minute film (French and English). Find it perched high on the hills above the riverside town of Cabrerets, 30km northeast of Cahors.

THE DORDOGNE, LIMOUSIN & THE LOT EAST OF CAHORS

St-Cirq-Lapopie

POP 208

Teetering at the crest of a sheer cliff high above the River Lot, minuscule St-Cirq-Lapopie's terracotta-roofed houses and vertiginous streets tumble down the steep hillside, affording incredible valley views. It's one of the most magical settings in the Lot, but in high summer it's packed, and in winter it's mostly closed.

◉ Sights & Activities

St-Cirq has one long main street leading up to its highlights: the early-16th-century Gothic **church** (place de l'Église) and a ruined **castle**, where you'll be rewarded with an exquisite panorama across the Lot Valley. Many of the village's houses are now artists' shops producing pottery, leatherwork and jewellery.

Musée Rignault   GALLERY
(☑ 05 65 31 23 22; http://musees.lot.fr; adult/child €2/free; ☉ 10.30am-12.30pm & 2.30-6.30pm Tue-Sun Apr-Sep) Eclectic collection of French furniture, African and Chinese art, and rotating exhibitions. Delightful garden.

Les Croisères de St-Cirq-Lapopie   BOATING
(☑ 05 65 31 72 25; www.croisieres-saint-cirq-lapopie.com; Bouziès; 1hr tour adult/child €12.50/8.50; ☉ Apr-Oct) Runs regular river cruises on its small fleet of boats, including aboard an open-topped *gabarre*, a flat-bottomed barge that was once the traditional mode of river transport in this region of France.

Kalapca   OUTDOORS
(☑ 05 65 24 21 01; www.kalapca.com; Conduché, Bouziès; canoe rental half/full day €20/24; ☉ Apr-Sep) Hires out kayaks and canoes, perfect for experiencing the river scenery at your own pace. Trip lengths range from 4km to 22km; rates include minibus transport to your chosen starting point. Also offers caving, canyoning, climbing and other outdoor activities.

⌂ Sleeping & Eating

La Plage   CAMPGROUND €
(☑ 05 65 30 29 51; www.campingplage.com; sites for tent & 2 people €24; ☉ mid-Apr-mid-Oct; ☎) Riverside campground on the southern bank of the Lot near a small swimming beach, with a slew of amenities including canoe and kayak rental. Also tents and cabanas (€57 to €72).

Auberge de Sombral   HOTEL €
(☑ 05 65 31 26 08; www.lesombral.com; r €60-85; ☎) This central, pretty sienna-stone town-house has seven cosy doubles and a titchy attic room with modern decor. The **restaurant** (*menus* €17 to €31; noon-2pm daily, 7.30-9.30pm Fri & Sat) offers Quercy cuisine, including lamb and trout. Best of all, you'll have the village practically to yourself after dark.

★**Hôtel Le Saint Cirq**   HOTEL €€
(☑ 05 65 30 30 30; www.hotel-lesaintcirq.com; Tour de Faure; d €118-198, f €158; @ ☎ ☜ ☒) This luxurious hotel in the valley below St-Cirq boasts one of the best views of its hilltop profile. Lovely, traditional rooms have terracotta-tiled floors and French windows onto the garden. 'Seigneurale' rooms boast sunken baths, slate bathrooms and the like.

Le Gourmet Quercynois   FRENCH €€
(☑ 05 65 31 21 20; www.restaurant-legourmet quercynois.com; rue de la Peyrolerie; menus €20.80-27.80; ☉ noon-2pm & 7.30-9.30pm mid-Feb-Dec) St-Cirq's top table offers an enormous menu, ranging from *nougat de porc* (pork medallions) to country *cassoulet*. Escape to the little patio to catch evening rays setting over town.

ⓘ Information

Tourist Office (☑ 05 65 31 31 31; www.saint-cirqlapopie.com; place du Sombral; ☉ 10am-1pm & 2-6pm; ☎) In the village hall.

ⓘ Getting There & Away

St-Cirq is 25km east of Cahors and 44km southwest of Figeac.

SNCF buses between Cahors (€6.60, 45 minutes, six daily) and Figeac (€9.10, one hour, five daily) stop at Tour-de-Faure; from there it's 3km uphill to St-Cirq.

Figeac

POP 9826

The buoyant riverside town of Figeac, 70km northeast of Cahors on the River Célé, has a vibrant charm steeped in history. Traffic zips along river boulevards, and the fantastic medieval old town has an appealingly lived-in feel. Winding streets are lined with medieval and ornate Renaissance houses, many with open-air galleries on the top floor (once used for drying goods). Founded by Benedictine monks, the town was later an important medieval trading post and pilgrims' stopover.

◉ Sights

The tourist office offers a changing schedule of **tours** (adult/child €6/free; Apr-Oct) of the old town and nearby countryside.

★ Medieval Figeac   AREA

Enter the historic centre of Figeac at place Vival, where the tourist office occupies the **Hôtel de la Monnaie**, an arcaded 13th-century building where money was exchanged. Purchase the excellent leaflet *Les Clefs de la Ville* (€0.30) for a guide to Figeac's medieval and Renaissance architecture.

Rue de Balène and rue Caviale have the best examples of 14th- and 15th-century houses, many with wooden galleries, timber frames and original stone carvings, while rue de Colomb has fine Renaissance *hôtels particulier*.

Place Champollion is in the heart of the historic quarter, and behind Musée Champollion, **place des Écritures** is surrounded by medieval buildings and features a modern art replica of the Rosetta Stone by Joseph Kosuth.

★ Musée Champollion   MUSEUM

(☑ 05 65 50 31 08; www.musee-champollion.fr; place Champollion; adult/child €5/free; ☺ 10.30am-6.30pm daily Jul & Aug, shorter hr rest of year) This museum is named after Figeac-born Egyptologist and linguist Jean-François Champollion (1790–1832), whose efforts in deciphering the Rosetta Stone provided the key for cracking Egyptian hieroglyphics. The mansion where he was born is now devoted to the history of writing, with exhibits ranging from illustrated medieval manuscripts to the evolution of Chinese characters. Audioguide recommended (€3), unless you read French.

Église St-Sauveur   CHURCH

(place de la Raison; ☺ 9am-6pm) This soaring spot on the Compostela pilgrims' trail, the 11th-century former Benedictine Abbey church, features the exquisite **Notre-Dame-de-Pieté chapel**, a 17th-century woodworking masterpiece.

🛏 Sleeping & Eating

Figeac has a handful of good bistros, plus a lively Saturday morning **market** (place Carnot; ☺ Sat).

Hôtel des Bains   HOTEL €

(☑ 05 65 34 10 89; www.hoteldesbains.fr; 1 rue Griffoul; d €69-87, tr/q €97/108; ✳ 🛜) Basic riverfront hotel with 19 rooms; the best have balconies overlooking the river.

★ Hôtel La Grézalide   HOTEL €€

(☑ 05 65 11 20 40; www.grezalide.com; Grèzes; d €137-162; 🛜 🎱) You'll need a car to reach this beautiful country estate, 21km west of Figeac in the quaint village of Grèzes, but it's

worth the drive. Rooms in the 17th-century manor make maximum use of its architecture, with solid stone and original floorboards. Public rooms display art collections, and the courtyard garden, pool and fantastic regional restaurant round it all out.

Le Seth   BISTRO €

(☑ 05 65 34 50 25; 7 place Champollion; lunch menu €14-18, mains €18, crêpes €9-12; ☺ 11am-1.30pm & 6-9pm Thu-Mon) Climb up to the mezzanine in this ornate and airy townhouse to feast on lamb *tajine*, confit de salmon and sheep's milk fondue. They also run an adjacent crêperie, Sel et Sucre.

Bazilik   BISTRO €

(☑ 06 62 00 21 98; 14 rue Baduel; menus €9-15; ☺ noon-3pm Mon-Fri; ✔) This unusual little find offers a choice between a vegetarian dish (cream of fennel soup, Provençal-style polenta) or a Caribbean dish (coconut chicken, spiced pork stew) on the lunch menu, with a focus on local, seasonal produce.

★ La Dinée du Viguier   GASTRONOMY €€

(☑ 05 65 50 08 08; www.ladineeduviguier.fr; 4 rue Boutaric; lunch menus €23.50, dinner menus €33-48; ☺ noon-2pm Tue-Fri & Sun, 7.45-9pm Tue-Sat) Figeac's top table is a must for foodies into creative cuisine incorporating fresh, regional ingredients. Choose between beautifully prepared dishes including lobster, oysters and locally reared duck.

ℹ Information

Tourist Office (☑ 05 65 34 06 25; www.tourisme-figeac.com; place Vival; ☺ 9am-7pm Jul & Aug, 9am-12.30pm & 2-6pm Mon-Sat Sep-Jun; 🛜)

ℹ Getting There & Away

BUS

SNCF buses run west to Cahors (€13.80, 1¾ hours, five daily) via Tour-de-Faure, and north to Brive-la-Gaillarde (€16, 2¼ hours, three daily).

TRAIN

Figeac's **train station**, on the south side of the river and served by local bus 7, is at a junction. One key line runs north to Brive-la-Gaillarde (€16, 1¼ hours, three daily) and south to Najac (€10.40, 50 minutes, three daily) and Toulouse (€27.10, 2½ hours, two direct daily).

Najac

POP 702

Magical Najac unfurls like a slender ribbon of stone along a rocky saddle high above a bend in the River Aveyron. Its soaring, turreted

AUTOIRE

Walkers and waterfall spotters, tiny Autoire is for you. While the medieval village is pleasant enough, it's the location near the end of a dramatic limestone cirque that makes Autoire stand out. A small 30-metre waterfall cascades through the surrounding forest, while the nearby ruins of a cliff-side fortification overlook the town.

This 30-metre **waterfall** `FREE` is accessed via a pleasant 1km walk through the forest heading upstream. The trail leaves from the parking lot at the north end of the village. On the way back you can cross to the other side of the stream to make it a slightly longer loop.

The return walking loop from Autoire's waterfall (around 1km) passes by a spur trail that climbs another kilometre up to the base of the limestone cliffs, where you'll find **La Roque d'Autoire** (Château des Anglais) `FREE`, the ruins of a 12th-century fortification. Occupied during the Hundred Years War, it's also known as the Château des Anglais. More impressive than the ruins are the fabulous panoramas from this perch – the trail continues along the cliffs in both directions, providing a bird's-eye view of both the waterfall and Autoire.

Autoire is 40km north of Figeac, 50km southeast of Brive and 68km east of Sarlat. You'll need your own car; the car park is €2 per day.

fortress is a must: an evocative journey into the past, with superb views from the central keep.

⊙ Sights

The top of the village revolves around central **place du Faubourg**, a beguiling broad square surrounded by timber-framed houses, some from the 13th century. A pedestrianised lane leads 1.2km down the saddle of the hill to the **Porte de la Pique**, near the fortress. Drivable av de la Gare skirts the edge of town to Église St-Jean and the valley and train station below.

★ **Forteresse Royale de Najac**   FORTRESS
(☑ 05 65 29 71 65; adult/child €5.50/4; ◷ 10.30am-7pm Jul & Aug, 10.30am-1pm & 3-5.30pm Apr-Jun, Sep & Oct) High on a hilltop 150m above a hairpin bend in the River Aveyron, Najac's fortress looks as if it's from a fairy tale: slender towers and fluttering flags rise from crenellated ramparts, surrounded on every side by *falaises* (cliffs) dropping to the valley floor below. Its crumbling architecture is somehow beautifully preserved, and the view from the central keep is superb. Look for the **secret passage** leading out of **St Julian's Chapel**, the **dungeon**, which imprisoned Knights Templar, and **symbols** carved in walls by stonemasons.

A masterpiece of medieval military planning (check out the **extended loopholes** that allowed two archers to fire at once), and practically unassailable thanks to its position, Najac was a key stronghold during the Middle Ages, and was contested by everyone from English warlords to the powerful counts of Toulouse. Richard the Lionheart signed a treaty here in 1185. Reach the fortress via a steep path from the bottom of town.

Église St-Jean   CHURCH
(rue de l'Église; ◷ 10am-noon & 2-6pm May-Sep, Sat & Sun only Apr & Oct) Two hundred metres below the Forteresse Royale de Najac is the austere 13th-century Église St-Jean, constructed and financed by local villagers on the orders of the Inquisition as punishment for their heretical tendencies.

🛏 Sleeping & Eating

Restaurants are largely geared toward tourism, so most close in winter.

Oustal del Barry   HOTEL €
(☑ 05 65 29 74 32; www.oustaldelbarry.com; place du Faubourg; s €53, d €58-79; ❄ 🐾) The best hotel in town is this wonderfully worn and rustic *auberge*, with haphazard rooms filled with trinkets and solid furniture to match its venerable timber-framed façade. Try for a room with a balcony. Visit its renowned country restaurant (*menus* €22 to €28) for traditional southwest cuisine.

ⓘ Information

Najac's tiny **tourist office** (☑ 05 65 29 72 05; www.tourisme-villefranche-najac.com; 25 place du Faubourg; ◷ 9.30am-noon & 2-6pm Mon-Fri, 9.30am-noon Sat & Sun, closed Jan, Sun & Mon Oct-Apr) is on the southern side of the main square. It offers occasional French-language **tours** (adult/child €3/free).

ⓘ Getting There & Away

The train station, served by an automatic machine, is in the valley 1.2km below Najac. Trains go to Figeac (€10.40, 50 minutes, three daily) and Toulouse (€18.90, 1½ hours, six daily)

Atlantic Coast

Best Places to Eat

➡ Magasin Général (p653)

➡ La Co(o)rniche (p665)

➡ Hôtel de la Plage (p666)

➡ Brasserie Le Bordeaux (p654)

➡ Café Lavinal (p661)

➡ La Tupina (p655)

Best Places to Stay

➡ Château Cordeillan-Bages (p661)

➡ Hôtel François 1er (p643)

➡ Hôtel Le Sénéchal (p648)

➡ Hôtel La Cour Carrée (p651)

➡ Le B d'Arcachon (p663)

➡ Quai des Pontis (p649)

Why Go?

With quiet country roads winding through vine-striped hills and wild stretches of coastal sand interspersed with misty islands, the Atlantic coast is where France gets back to nature. Much more laid-back than the Med (but with almost as much sunshine), this is the place to slow the pace right down.

But the Atlantic coast can do cities and culture as well. There's bourgeois Bordeaux with its wonderful old centre, extraordinary wine culture and dynamic dining scene; studenty Nantes with its wealth of fascinating museums; and seafaring La Rochelle with its breathtaking aquarium, beautiful old port and bucolic offshore islands.

A love of the finer things in life unites people in this region, a part of France where *art de vivre* means appreciating exceptional wine, famous worldwide, and feasting on an ocean of oysters and other fresh, salt-of-the-earth seafood.

When to Go
Bordeaux

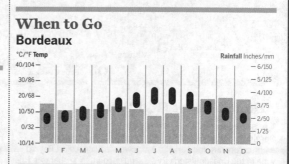

May & Jun Duck-lings are splashing around the Marais Poitevin and it's a prime time to visit La Rochelle.

Jun–Sep The beaches are bathed in sun-shine but there are no high-season crowds.

Sep & Oct Grape-harvesting season around Bordeaux, oyster and *cêpe* mush-room season all over.

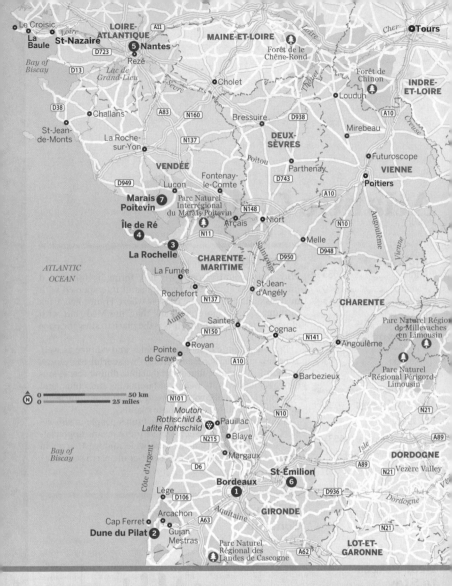

Atlantic Coast Highlights

❶ Bordeaux (p650)
Gorging on exceedingly fine architecture, art, food and wine in the Unesco-listed city that can do no wrong.

❷ Dune du Pilat (p664)
Romping atop Europe's highest sand dune, followed by lunch with sensational sea-and-sand view at La Co(o)rniche.

❸ La Rochelle (p642)
Scaling ancient defensive towers, sailing to Fort Bayard and encountering sharks in this port city's incredible aquarium.

❹ Île de Ré (p647) Cycling smooth, flat bike paths past oyster farms and ancient salt pans on a beautiful island.

❺ Nantes (p635) Riding on the back of a giant heron in

flight or a lumbering 60-tonne mechanical elephant.

❻ St-Émilion (p661)
Learning about and tasting some of the world's most famous wines in the châteaux where they're made.

❼ Marais Poitevin (p642)
Gliding through the emerald-green waterways of western France's 'Green Venice'.

NANTES

POP 303,382

You can take Nantes out of Brittany (as when regional boundaries were redrawn during WWII), but you can't take Brittany out of its long-time capital, Nantes (Naoned in Breton).

Spirited and innovative, this artsy city on the banks of the Loire has a history of reinventing itself. It was founded by Celts around 70 BC and in AD 937 it joined the duchy of Brittany. The Edict of Nantes, a landmark royal charter guaranteeing civil rights to France's Huguenots (Protestants), was signed in Nantes by Henri IV in 1598.

By the 18th century Nantes was France's foremost port, and in the 19th century – following the abolition of slavery – it became an industrial centre; the world's first public transport service, the omnibus, began here in 1826. Shipbuilding anchored the city's economy until the late 20th century and when the shipyards relocated westwards to St-Nazaire, Nantes transformed itself into a thriving student and cultural hub.

◉ Sights

★ Les Machines de l'Île de Nantes
AMUSEMENT PARK

(☑ 08 10 12 12 25, 02 51 17 49 89; www.lesmachines-nantes.fr; blvd Léon Bureau, Parc des Chantiers; adult/child €8.50/6.90, elephant ride €8.50/6.90, carousel visit & ride €8.50/6.90, carousel visit €6.50/5.30; ⊙ 10am-7pm Jul & Aug, to 6pm Apr-Jun, Sep & Oct, 2-5pm or 6pm Nov, Dec, Feb & Mar) Nantes' quirkiest sight is this fantasy world – a serious and seriously wacky workshop with mechanical contraptions galore displayed in plant-filled hothouses – where you can fly giant herons in La Galerie des Machines and prance around like a maharajah on a 12m-tall, 48-tonne mechanical elephant with a secret lounge in its belly. Outside, by the river, Le Carrousel des Mondes Marins (a gigantic funfair carousel) whisks you under the sea on the back of giant crabs, octopuses and other strange sea creatures.

★ Château des Ducs de Bretagne
CASTLE

(☑ 02 40 02 60 11; www.chateaunantes.fr; 4 place Marc Elder; adult/child €8/free; ⊙ château 10am-7pm Jul & Aug, to 6pm Tue-Sun Sep-Jun, ramparts & moat gardens 8.30am-8pm Jul & Aug, to 7pm Sep-Jun) Forget fusty furnishings – light-filled rooms inside the Castle of the Dukes of Brittany house multimedia-rich exhibits detailing the city's history. Look out for sobering documentation of the slave trade, and vintage scale models of Nantes' evolving cityscape.

The château's grassy moat gardens and rampart walk are free to meander and picnic in at leisure. Don't miss the playful summertime slide, built snug against the 15th-century ramparts, by contemporary Breton artist Tangui Robert. Who wouldn't want to whoosh down it?

Musée d'Arts de Nantes
MUSEUM

(☑ 02 51 17 45 00; www.museedartsdenantes.fr; 10 rue Georges Clemenceau; adult/child €8/free, free 1st Sun of month Sep-Jun & 7-9pm Thu; ⊙ 11am-7pm Wed & Fri-Mon, 11am-9pm Thu) A six-year renovation job by London architects Stanton Williams has done wonders for Nantes' art museum, open again since 2017 inside the historic Palais des Beaux Arts, which was built to house the city's collection of fine art between 1891 and 1900. Today's permanent collection spans the 13th to 21st centuries and fills both the palace and the striking new Cube building, linking the palace with 18th-century Chapelle de l'Oratoire (1777). The deconsecrated chapel hosts temporary art exhibitions.

Musée Jules Verne
MUSEUM

(☑ 02 40 69 72 52; www.julesverne.nantes.fr; 3 rue de l'Hermitage; adult/child €6/2.50; ⊙ 10am-7pm Jul & Aug, 2-6pm Mon, Wed-Fri & Sun, 10am-noon & 2-6pm Sat Sep-Jun) Overlooking the river, this is a magical museum with 1st-edition books, hand-edited manuscripts and cardboard theatre cut-outs. Child-friendly interactive displays introduce or reintroduce you to the work of Jules Verne, who was born in Nantes in 1828. Signs are in French but Verne's books, such as *Around the World in 80 Days,* are so well known that it's worthwhile visiting regardless. The museum is a 2km walk down river from the town centre.

Mémorial de l'Abolition de l'Esclavage
MEMORIAL

(☑ 02 40 20 60 11; www.memorial.nantes.fr; quai de la Fosse; ⊙ 9am-8pm mid-Sep–mid-May, to 6pm mid-Sep–mid-May) Down by the water, 2000 brick-sized glass plaques embedded in the quay-side pavement scream out the names of slave-trading ships that regularly

---

ⓘ NANTES CITY PASS

The **Pass Nantes** (24/48/72 hours €25/35/45), available from the tourist office, includes unlimited bus and tram transport, entry to museums and monuments, plus extras such as a free guided tour and shopping discounts.

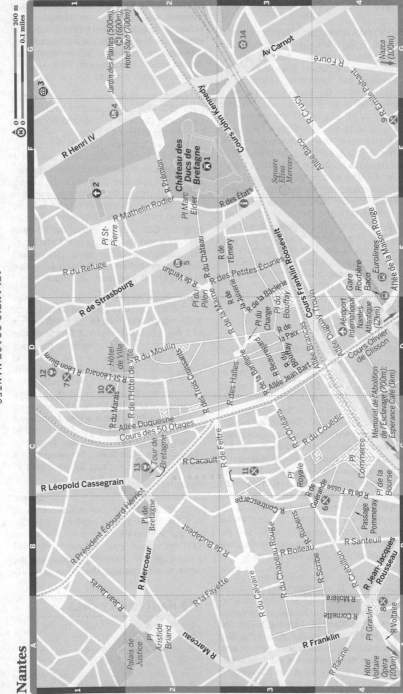

Nantes

Map features and labels:

- Jardin des Plantes (500m); Hôtel Sozo (700m)
- R Henri IV
- Château des Ducs de Bretagne
- Cours John Kennedy
- Av Carnot
- R Fouré
- R de Crucy
- Allée Baco
- Nazca (100m)
- R Émile Péhant
- Square Elisa Mercœur
- Pl St-Pierre
- R Mathelin Rodier
- Pl Marc Elder
- R Prémion
- R du Château
- R des États
- R du Refuge
- R de Strasbourg
- Pl du Pilori
- R de Verdun
- R des Petites-Écuries
- R de la Mame
- R de l'Emery
- R de la Juiverie
- R de la Bâclerie
- Cours Franklin Roosevelt
- Gare Routière Baco
- Eurolines Baco
- Eurolines Rouge
- Allée de la Maison Rouge
- Allée Duguay Trouin
- Aéroport International Nantes Atlantique (12km)
- Cours Olivier de Clisson
- Hôtel de Ville
- R de l'Hôtel de Ville
- R Léonard
- R Léon Blum
- R du Marais
- R des Trois Croissants
- R du Moulin
- Pl du Change
- R Beaurepaire
- R de la Barillerie
- R des Halles
- Allée Jean Bart
- Allée Brancas
- Pl du Bouffay
- R du Bouffay
- R de la Paix
- Allée Duquesne
- Cours des 50 Otages
- Tour de Bretagne
- R Cacault
- R de Feltre
- R d'Orléans
- R du Couédic
- Mémorial de l'Abolition de l'Esclavage (700m); Esperance Café (1km)
- R Léopold Cassegrain
- R Président Édouard Herriot
- Pl de Bretagne
- R de Budapest
- R Contrescarpe
- Pl Royale
- R de la Fosse
- R de Guérande
- Pl du Commerce
- Pl de la Bourse
- R Mercœur
- R la Fayette
- R du Chapeau Rouge
- R Rubens
- R Scribe
- R Crébillon
- Passage Pommeray
- R Santeuil
- R Jean-Jacques Rousseau
- R Jean Jaurès
- Palais de Justice
- Pl Aristide Briand
- R Marceau
- R Calvaire
- R Boileau
- R Molière
- R Corneille
- Pl Graslin
- R Voltaire
- R Franklin
- R Racine
- Hôtel Voltaire Opéra (100m)

Numbered points: 1, 2, 3, 4, 5, 6, 7, 8, 9, 10, 11, 12, 13, 14

Scale: 200 m / 0.1 miles

Nantes

set sail from the port of Nantes from 1750 until the early 19th century. They form part of an emotive Memorial to the Abolition of Slavery, designed in 2014 by Polish artist Krzysztof Wodiczko and American architect Julian Bonder. Steps lead down into a meditative tunnel beneath the quay, etched with abolitionist texts on a 90m-long glass panel.

Jardin des Plantes   PARK
(☑ 02 40 41 65 09; rue Stanislas-Baudry; ⊘ 8.30am-8pm Mar-Oct, shorter hours rest of year) Opened in 1860, this exquisitely landscaped park is among France's most interesting botanical gardens. Century-old magnolia and mulberry trees, Japanese maples, tulip trees, redwoods (sequoias) and magnificent cedars tower above beautiful flower beds, duck ponds, fountains and the enchanting **Serre de l'Île de Palmiers**, a glass 19th-century hothouse filled with palm trees and decked out with tables and chairs for lounging on. There is a **children's playground** and goats to pet at the park's northern end, near the train station.

Cathédrale St-Pierre et St-Paul CATHEDRAL
(☑ 02 40 47 84 64; http://cathedrale-nantes.fr; 1 place St-Pierre; ⊘ 8.30am-7pm Apr-Sep, to 6pm Oct-Mar, garden 8.45am-8pm, crypt 10am-7pm Jul & Aug) Inside Nantes' Flamboyant Gothic cathedral, the tomb of François II (r 1458–88),

Duke of Brittany, and of his second wife, Marguerite de Foix, is a masterpiece of Renaissance art. Enjoy a moment of peace afterwards in Jardin de la Psallette, the secret cathedral garden out back from where you can also access the cathedral crypt.

Sleeping

Hôtel Voltaire Opéra   HOTEL €
(☑ 02 40 73 31 04; www.hotelvoltaireoperanantes.com; 10 rue Gresset; s/d from €50/55; ☎) Rich gold, chocolate and beige palettes adorn compact rooms at this appealing 40-room hotel near the opera. If you don't fancy dragging your suitcase up a flight of stairs, avoid the attic rooms that have no lift. Crisp white and taupe bathrooms are up-to-the-minute, and staff are delightfully welcoming. Breakfast (€12) includes homemade jams and artisan honey.

Okko Hôtels Nantes   DESIGN HOTEL €€
(☑ 02 52 20 00 70; www.okkohotels.com; 15 rue de Strasbourg; d €100-200; ✹@☎) Lifestyle is what four-star, design-driven Okko is all about. Eighty smart, functional rooms stack up on six floors, but it is the ground-floor 'club' with ample sofas to lounge on, iMac desktop and unlimited supply of tea, coffee and soft drinks that is the real lure. Guests mingle here over free drinks and copious nibbles every evening between 6.30pm and 9.30pm. Breakfast €15.

L'Hôtel   HOTEL €€
(☑ 02 40 29 30 31; www.nanteshotel.com; 6 rue Henri IV; d €80-190; ✹@☎) This smart hotel facing Château des Ducs de Bretagne is a breath of fresh air on Nantes' hotel scene. Its 31 rooms are up-to-the-minute, with a clean-cut Scandinavian decor, soft muted colour palettes and the occasional floral or leopard-print papered wall. The lobby, with cactus and tropical plants, doubles as an attractive winter garden and pricier rooms have a balcony or patio. Breakfast €13.

Hotel Sōzō   DESIGN HOTEL €€€
(☑ 02 51 82 40 00; www.sozohotel.fr; 16 rue Frédéric Cailliand; d €125-345; ✹@☎) The architects who designed this place must have been in seventh heaven when asked to transform a graceful old chapel into a luxury boutique hotel. The main features of the chapel have been retained, including the stained-glass windows, but sitting happily alongside are dozens of virgin-white angel wings, garish cartoon art and purple and red lights.

FOLLOW THE GREEN LINE

Meandering around Nantes, you will notice a painted pea-green line snaking along the pavement, zipping up unexpected staircases, sneaking along backstreet alleys and prancing with purpose across cafe pavement terraces. This, ingeniously, is **Le Voyage à Nantes** (www.levoyageanantes.fr), an urban art trail that leads curious visitors to dozens of works of art – sculptures, contemporary art installations, stunning viewpoints, architectural works – all over the city. Many – such as sky-rise bar Le Nid or the slide built into the 15th-century ramparts of Château des Ducs de Bretagne (p635) – are amusingly playful and interactive. The trail is 12km long, but can be traced in sections too. Pick up a city map, marked with the trail, at the tourist office (p640) or simply follow the green line and see where it takes you.

✗ Eating

For cosmopolitan dining, head to the medieval Bouffay quarter, a couple of blocks west of the château around rue de la Juiverie, rue des Petites Écuries and rue de la Bâclerie. Breton crêperies abound. For excellent modern French cuisine, hit rue Fouré.

★**Nazca** SOUTH AMERICAN €

(📞 02 40 35 34 30; http://cebicheria.wixsite.com/nazca; 31 rue Fouré; 2-course lunch menu €16, mains €16; ⏰ noon-1.45pm Mon & Tue, noon-1.45pm & 7.30-9.30pm Wed-Fri) Bruno Triballeau, chef at the French embassy in Bogota for 10 years, and his Colombian wife make a formidable duo at this stylish *cevicheria*. In their bright, two-room restaurant they serve Peruvian-inspired ceviche (raw, cubed, marinated fish) dishes bursting with taste and flavour, accompanied by Pisco cocktails and some lovely Chilean and Argentinian wines. When French cuisine tires, this is the address.

Sugar Blue CAFE €

(📞 09 83 24 19 24; http://sugarbluecafe.fr; 4 rue de l'Arche Sèche; mains €8.50-9, brunch €20; ⏰ 9am-7pm Mon-Sat & 1st Sun of month; 🤚) Everything is *fait maison* (homemade) at this fashionable millennial cafe with bold turquoise-painted brick wall, excellent specialist-roasted coffee and menu chalked on the board. Its gluten-free cakes, chestnut cookies, cinnamon rolls and wholesome lunchtime soups, salads and quiches all brim with local seasonal produce.

Crêperie de Brocéliande CRÊPES €

(📞 02 40 89 04 03; 3 rue de Guerande; crêpes & galettes €3-15; ⏰ noon-2.30pm & 7-10.30pm Tue-Sat) There is no denying the city's Breton roots with crêpes and *galettes de blé noir* (savoury crêpes made with organic buckwheat flour) like this. Both come generously brushed in Breton butter – unsalted for sweet, salted for savoury. The Fondante – a *galette* filled with *andouille* (tripe sausage), melted curé Nantais cheese and creamed leeks – is the local tip.

★**Pickles** MODERN FRENCH €€

(www.pickles-restaurant.com; 2 ru du Marais; 2-/3-course lunch menu €18/22, 4-/6-course dinner menus €40/46; ⏰ noon-2pm Tue, noon-2pm & 7-10pm Wed-Fri, 7-10pm Sat) This buzzing neobistro would be right at home in Paris. Market-sourced, modern and wholly creative cuisine by English chef Dominic Quirke (a Newcastle lad wed to a French lass) is sensational – and extraordinarily good value to boot. Dining is around tightly packed bistro tables or at a *table d'hôte*–style bar, and don't be surprised if Dom comes to chat with you. Advance reservations are essential.

Les Chants d'Avril BISTRO €€

(📞 02 40 89 34 76; www.leschantsdavril.fr; 2 rue Laennec; 2-/3-course lunch menu €19/22.50, dinner menu €27.50; ⏰ noon-1.30pm Mon-Wed, noon-1.30pm & 8-9.15pm Thu & Fri) Follow locals to the iconic bistro of *'chef magicien'* Christophe François, who runs this hugely successful locavore address with his wife Véronique. Everything bar the bread is *fait maison* and there is an exceptional list of natural wines (by the glass €4.50 to €6.50, bottles from €25) to accompany the hearty, top-class fare. Best up, menus are a surprise.

La Cigale BRASSERIE €€€

(📞 02 51 84 94 94; www.lacigale.com; 4 place Graslin; lunch menus €15-26, mains €18-28; ⏰ 7.30am-12.30am) No visit to Nantes is complete without breakfast, brunch, lunch or afternoon tea at the city's legendary brasserie, a sensational feast of ceramic tile mosaics, gilt-framed mirrors and frescoed ceilings in a series of historic salons dating to 1895. Freshly shucked oysters (€40 per dozen), decadent seafood platters (€39-140) and traditional French classics are served nonstop from 11.30am.

🍷 Drinking & Nightlife

Prime drinking areas are the medieval Bouffay quarter; rue Leon Blum; rue Olivettes heading towards the river; and the rejuvenated riverbanks of Île de Nantes. The latter buzzes with atmosphere after dark when the 18 metal rings of **Anneaux de Buren** – a contemporary art installation by French artist Daniel Buren – plot out the water's edge in a rainbow of dazzling colour.

⭐ Le Nid   BAR

(📞 02 40 35 36 49; www.lenidnantes.com; place de Bretagne, 32nd fl, Tour Bretagne; admission €1; ⊙ 2.15pm-midnight Wed, to 4am Thu, to 2am Fri, 10am-2am Sat, 10am-midnight Sun) Far more than just a bar, Le Nid (or The Nest) is an interactive art installation by Nantais artist Jean Jullien. Designer armchairs, with yolk-yellow seat cushions, resemble broken eggs and the bar squats inside a giant white bird, half-stork, half-heron. Panoramic views of the city from floor-to-ceiling windows are predictably magnificent; electro 'Birdy' DJ sets kick off at 10pm every Thursday; and there's jamming sessions every Sunday from 7pm.

Find the bar on the 32nd floor of 144m-high **Tour Bretagne**, built in 1976 to house a 90,000L water reservoir. Cocktails and cheese, charcuterie and seafood platters make Le Nid a tasty spot for a sundown drink.

⭐ Le Jéroboam   WINE BAR

(📞 02 72 02 30 47; 21 rue Léon Blum; ⊙ 6pm-2am Tue-Sat) This enchanting *bar à vin* with vintage green wood facade is the best spot in town to taste regional wines with a laidback, hipster crowd. When the munchies strike, order a perfectly paired tartine (open sandwich). Enticing combos include curried fish with raisins and a citrus onion chutney and grilled *boudin* (black blood sausage) with caramelised shallots.

Hangar à Bananes   BAR, CLUB

(www.hangarabananes.com; 21 quai des Antilles; ⊙ daily till late) This former banana-ripening warehouse on Île de Nantes is home today to a line-up of trendy restaurants, bars and clubs, each hipper than the next. Pavement terraces lounge by the water's edge and are particularly atmospheric after dark when Daniel Buren's riverside rings glow a rainbow of bright colours.

GOURMET SANDWICH STOP

With a summertime pavement terrace basking in the sun and an enchanting interior bursting with antique curiosities, gourmet sandwich shop La Chicorée (📞 02 40 35 56 38; 13 rue Léon Blum; sandwiches €3.80-4.90; ⊙ 10.30am-3.30pm Mon-Fri) is a secret locals would probably rather not share. It is the later-in-life creation of the fabulous Anne and Carole, with long careers in charcuterie and communications already under their belt. They make creatively stuffed baguette sandwiches to order, and the €8 lunch deal includes fantastic homemade soup or dessert as well. If you've never savoured a Real McCoy, traditional French *financier* (succulent, bite-sized almond cake), this is the address.

Esperance Café   COFFEE

(📞 09 82 23 10 98; https://esperancecafe.com; 25 quai François Mitterrand; ⊙ 11am-6pm Mon-Sat, 2-6.30pm Sun) Sacks of raw beans waiting to be roasted fill one corner of this specialist coffee shop, a five-minute walk from Les Machines de l'Île de Nantes. Patrice and Beatrice are the knowledgeable baristas behind the contemporary space where families mingle with hipsters for a salted caramel-laced Latte Maria or coconut-milk Latte Créole spiced with vanilla and lime zest.

The cafe cooks up great homemade cakes, too, and runs coffee roasting workshops (1½ hours, €29).

☆ Entertainment

⭐ Le Lieu Unique   THEATRE

(📞 02 40 12 14 34; www.lelieuunique.com; quai Ferdinand Favre; hammam Wed-Mon €22, Tue free; ⊙ bar 11am-8pm Mon, to 1am Tue & Wed, to 2am Thu, to 3am Fri & Sat, 3-8pm Sun, hammam 11am-9pm) Within the one-time LU biscuit factory (crowned by an iconic angel-sculpted, domed tower, which you can ascend for €2), this industrial-chic *lieu unique* (unique place) is a cutting-edge venue for dance, theatre, art exhibitions and a mixed bag of live music. Its cafe-bar, with great music and laid-back vibe, is laptop central during the day. Deckchairs lounge by the water in summer.

ℹ️ Information

Tourist Office (📞 02 72 64 04 79; www.
nantes-tourisme.com; 9 rue des États; ⊘9am-
7pm Jul & Aug, 10am-6pm Mon-Sat, to 5pm Sun
Sep-Jun)

ℹ️ Getting There & Away

AIR

Aéroport International Nantes-Atlantique
(NTE; www.nantes.aeroport.fr), 12km south-
east of town, is served by budget airline easy-
Jet and others.

BUS

Lila (http://lila.loire-atlantique.fr) buses cover
the surrounding Loire-Atlantique *département*.
Tickets cost €2 per ride.
Eurolines (📞 08 92 89 90 91; www.eurolines.
com; allée de la Maison Rouge) has an office in
town, with buses arriving and departing from
the **Gare Routière Baco** (Bus Station; allée de
la Maison Rouge), 800m from the southern entrance of the train station. Destinations include
elsewhere in France and Europe.

TRAIN

The **train station** (27 bd de Stalingrad), with two
entrances (north and south) in the city centre,
is well connected to most of the country. Destinations include Bordeaux (from €30, 4¼ hours,
three or four daily) and La Rochelle (from €20,
2¼ hours, three or four daily).

Tickets and information are also available at the
SNCF ticket office (12 place de la Bourse; ⊘10am-
6.30pm Mon-Fri, to 6pm Sat) in the city centre.

ℹ️ Getting Around

TO/FROM THE AIRPORT

A *navette* (shuttle bus) links the airport with the
train station's southern entrance (€9, 20 minutes) and place du Commerce every 20 minutes
from about 5.30am until 11pm. Buy tickets in
advance online at www.tan.fr, from the machine
by the bus stop or direct from the driver.

BICYCLE

Nantes' shared bicycle scheme **Bicloo** (www.
bicloo.nantesmetropole.fr) has stations all over
town. The bright orange-and-silver bikes can
be accessed from 4am to 1am, and cost €1/5
per 24 hours/week, plus €0.50 for 30 to 60
minutes, €1.50 for 60 to 90 minutes, €2 over 90
minutes; the first 30 minutes are free.

Poitou

Inland from the coast lies the historic region
of Poitou, governed by the Counts of Poitiers
in the Middle Ages and today embracing the

modern-day *départements* of Deux Sèvres
and Vienne in the Nouvelle-Aquitaine *région*.
Overwhelmingly rural, Poitou is an ancient
slow-paced land specked with centurion goat
farms and dairies, marshes and remarkable
mural-laced Romanesque churches.

Poitiers

POP 90,115

History-steeped Poitiers was founded by the
Pictones, a Gaulish tribe, and rose to prominence as the former capital of Poitou. A
pivotal turning point came in AD 732, when
somewhere near Poitiers (the exact site is
not known) the cavalry of Charles Martel defeated the Muslim forces of Abd ar-Rahman,
governor of Córdoba, thus ending Muslim
attempts to conquer France. Until the Revolution, this sublimely beautiful city was
known as the 'town of 100 bell towers'; the
remarkable Romanesque churches that remain today are in part a legacy of Eleanor of
Aquitaine's financial support.

Poitiers has one of the oldest universities
in the country, established in 1432 and today
a linchpin of this small city: students make
up 25% of the population.

⊙ Sights

Église Notre Dame la Grande　　　CHURCH
(53 place Charles de Gaulle; ⊘9am-7pm, light
show 10.30pm late Jun-Aug, 9.30pm until 3rd
weekend in Sep) FREE The celebrated western facade of this Romanesque church was
exquisitely sculpted in soft gold stone between 1115 and 1130. Spot the temptation
of Adam and Eve, the Nativity, the 12 Apostles and many other biblical scenes – at
their most spectacular in summer when
a colourful 15-minute light show, evoking
the medieval tradition of painting churches, is projected onto the facade. The painted columns inside the church today date
to 1851.

Église St-Hilaire le Grand　　　CHURCH
(📞 05 49 41 21 57; 26 rue St-Hilaire; ⊘9am-7pm
Apr-Nov, to 5.30pm Dec-Mar) FREE Consecrated in 1049, used as a warehouse during the
Revolution and partly rebuilt in the 19th
century, this grandiose Romanesque church
appears on Unesco's list of World Heritage
Sites as a treasured stop on the Chemin de
St-Jacques de Compostelle. The remains of
11th-century decorative paintings – in rich
ochre, ginger and gold tones – in its ornate
sculpted interior are striking.

TIME TRAVEL

Futuristic theme park **Futuroscope** (☑ 05 49 49 11 12; www.futuroscope.com; av René Monory, Chasseneuil-du-Poitou; adult/child €45/37; ☉ 10am-11.15pm Jun–mid-Jul, 9.30am-11pm mid-Jul–early Aug, 8.30am-10.45pm Aug, shorter hours rest of year, closed Jan–mid-Feb) takes you whizzing through space, diving into the deep-blue ocean depths, and racing around city streets and on a close encounter with creatures of the future, among many other space-age cinematic experiences. To keep things cutting edge, one-third of the attractions change annually. Many are motion-seat set-ups requiring a minimum height of 120cm, but there's a play area for younger children with miniature cars and so on.

Allow at least five hours to see the major attractions; two days to see everything. Futuroscope's numerous hotels are bookable through the website, or directly at the lodging desk. Futuroscope is 10km north of Poitiers in Jaunay-Clan (take exit 28 off the A10). TGV trains link the park's TGV station with cities including Paris and Bordeaux. Local Vitalis buses 1 and E link Futuroscope (Parc de Loisirs stop) with Poitiers' train station (€1.50, 30 minutes, twice hourly).

Baptistère St-Jean CHURCH
(rue Jean Jaurès; adult/child €2/1; ☉ 10.30am-12.30pm & 3-6pm Jul & Aug, 10.30am-12.30pm & 3-6pm Wed-Mon Sep & Apr-Jun, 2.30-4.30pm Wed-Mon Oct-Mar) Constructed in the 4th and 5th centuries on Roman foundations, this ginger-stone baptistery formed part of the episcopal ensemble with the cathedral, 100m south. It was redecorated in the 10th century and used as a parish church. The octagonal hole under the frescoes was used for total-immersion baptisms, practised until the 7th century.

Cathédrale St-Pierre CATHEDRAL
(place de la Cathédrale et du Cardinal Pié; ☉ 9am-7.30pm summer, to 5pm winter) FREE The town's grand Gothic cathedral safeguards beautiful 13th-century oak-carved choir stalls, an 18th-century organ with more than 3000 pipes and exceptional stained glass: the 12th-century window (1160–70) illustrating the Crucifixion and the Ascension at the far end of the choir is one of the oldest in France. It was given to the cathedral by Eleanor of Aquitaine and Henry II Plantagenet, King of England, who wed here in 1152.

🛏 Sleeping & Eating

Poitier Centre HISTORIC HOTEL €€
(☑ 05 49 50 50 60; www.poitevins.fr/hotel-mercure-poitiers-centre; 14 rue Édouard Grimaud; d €100-145; ❉@☎) Kip in a Jesuit church built in 1852. Almost half of the 51 designer rooms at this four-star Mercure hotel are situated in the triple nave, vaulted choir or between exquisite stone-sculpted columns of the 55m-long neo-Gothic chapel. Contemporary white-polished concrete walls blend in perfectly with ancient cream stone, and the restaurant **Les Archives** is a memorable dining space beneath stone vaults. Breakfast €16.

Toqué! BISTRO €
(☑ 05 49 62 19 33; www.bistro-toque.com; 44 rue de la Cathédrale; 2-/3-course lunch menu €13/16, 3-course dinner menu €29, mains €16-22; ☉ noon-2pm & 7.30-10.30pm Tue-Fri, 7.30-10.30pm Sat) Be prepared to dine extremely well at this brilliant modern bistro. Chef Grégory Delhaie roots his cuisine firmly in French tradition, infused with a generous dose of contemporary creativity. His signature pâté spiced with Espelette chilli peppers is a must, as is his metre of *crème brûlée* – six different flavours, two of each, served liked shooters – to share for dessert.

La Serrurerie FRENCH €
(☑ 05 49 41 05 14; www.laserrurerie.com; 28 rue des Grandes Écoles; 2-/3-course lunch menu €12/14.50, mains €12-18; ☉ 7.45am-2am Mon-Fri, 8.45-2am Sat, 9.45-2am Sun) Lap up local life at this fabulous industrial-styled lounge restaurant with zinc bar, scrubbed ginger-brick walls and a vintage curiosities collection that would put your grandmother's to shame. Service is swift, and the kitchen caters to every taste and age: creative meal-sized salads, caramelised pork ribs, Brighton-style fish 'n' chips, and French classics like *magret de canard* (duck).

ℹ Information

Tourist office (☑ 05 49 41 21 24; www.ot-poitiers.fr; 45 place Charles de Gaulle; ☉ 10am-7pm Mon-Sat, to 6pm Sun mid-Jun–mid-Sep, 9.30am-6pm Mon-Sat rest of year) Opposite the sculpted western facade of Église Notre Dame la Grande.

POITOU'S ROMANESQUE SISTINE CHAPEL

Nicknamed the 'Romanesque Sistine Chapel', Romanesque **Abbaye de St-Savin sur Gartempe** (☑ 05 49 84 30 00; www.abbaye-saint-savin.fr; place de la Libération, St-Savin; adult/child €8/free; ◷10am-7pm Jul & Aug, 10am-noon & 2-6pm Mon-Sat, 2-6pm Sun May, Jun, Sep & Oct, 10am-noon & 2-5pm Mon-Sat, 2-5pm Sun Feb, Mar, Nov & Dec) – a Unesco World Heritage Site – showcases extraordinarily fine frescoes from the 11th and 12th centuries. The murals, illustrating biblical scenes, are well preserved and cover more than 460 sq metres in the vast barrel-vaulted nave alone. Choir frescoes tell the gory tale of martyr brothers Saints Savin and Cyprien. A multimedia exhibition in the former monk cells explains the murals, and a 25-minute film looks at painting techniques.

The abbey was founded in 800 when 20 monks and an abbot settled in the village of St-Savin under the protection of Charlemagne. Construction work started on the vast abbey-church in 1010, and during the Wars of Religion in the 16th century, it was the only building to miraculously survive. Between 1682 and 1692 Benedictine monks rebuilt the abbey complex – a sacristy, chapter house, refectory, kitchen, monks dormitory and the abbot's residence – in local pink-hued limestone and laid out beautiful gardens.

Find the abbey 45km east of Poitiers via the D951; you'll need your own wheels.

⊙ Getting There & Away

The Poitiers **train station** (☑ 36 35; bd du Grand Cerf) has direct links to Bordeaux (€38, 1¾ hours), La Rochelle (€25.10, 1½ hours) and many other cities including Paris' Gare Montparnasse (from €67, 1¾ hours, 12 daily).

Marais Poitevin

From Poitiers town, an hour's drive southwest along the A10 to Niort and beyond plunges you into the heart of the Marais Poitevin. This *marais* (marshland) – an enchanting web of pea-green waterways overlooked by quaint villages – is a protected nature park. For those seeking somewhere to really melt into rural life, there is no finer spot. Arçais and Coulon – little more than rural, waterfront villages – are the main towns in the park.

Parc Naturel Interrégional du Marais Poitevin (www.parc-marais-poitevin.fr) is a tranquil bird-filled wetland dubbed the Venise Verte (Green Venice) due to the duckweed that turns its maze of waterways emerald green each spring and summer. Covering some 800 sq km of wet and drained marsh, the marshlands are interspersed with villages and woods threaded by canals and bike paths. There are two main bases from which to punt out across the waterways: the small honey-coloured town of Coulon and the romantic village of Arçais.

Boating and cycling are the only ways to satisfactorily explore the area; there's no shortage of operators hiring out bikes and flat-bottomed boats or kayaks for watery tours. Rental outlets in both towns offer identical services for the same price: single kayak per hour/half-day from €12/35, three-place canoe from €15/40, six-person wooden boat €10/45. Guided tours are also possible. Bikes can be hired from several operators in both towns for €5/12/18 per hour/half-day/day.

Getting to either Coulon or Arçais is difficult in anything other than your own car or – for serious cyclists – bike.

La Rochelle

POP 74,998

Known as La Ville Blanche (the White City), La Rochelle's luminous limestone facades glow in the bright coastal sunlight. One of France's foremost seaports from the 14th to 17th centuries, the city has arcaded walkways, half-timbered houses protected from the salt air by slate tiles, ghoulish gargoyles and a fabulous collection of lighthouses – all rich reminders of its magnificent seafaring heritage. The early French settlers of Canada, including the founders of Montreal, set sail from here in the 17th century.

This 'white city' is also commendably green, with efficient public transport and ample open spaces. Its *hôtel de ville* (town hall), built in 1606 and famously the oldest in France, is rising from the ashes after being the victim of a huge fire in 2013. La Rochelle's late-20th-century district of Les Minimes was built on reclaimed land, and now has one of the largest marinas in the country.

◉ Sights

★ Tour de la Lanterne · LIGHTHOUSE
(rue sur les Murs; adult/child €6/free, 3 towers €9/free; ⊙ 10am-6.30pm Apr-Sep, 10am-1pm & 2.15-5.30pm Oct-Mar) Easily mistaken for an ornate church spire, the conical 15th-century Tour de la Lanterne is La Rochelle's beauty queen. It was so named because of its role as the harbour's lighthouse (lit by an enormous candle) and is one of the oldest of its kind in the world. It is sometimes referred to as Tour des Quatre Sergents in memory of four local sergeants, two of whom were held here for plotting to overthrow the newly reinstated monarchy before their execution in Paris in 1822.

Tour St-Nicolas · MONUMENT
(rue de l'Armide; adult/child €6/free, 3 towers €9/free; ⊙ 10am-6.30pm Apr-Sep, 10am-1pm & 2.15-5.30pm Oct-Mar) The only tower to be decked out like a house, this 37m-high pentagonal stone tower has leaned slightly to one side ever since building was complete in 1376. It was originally used for both defensive purposes and as a royal residence, and the different rooms can still be visited. City views from the rooftop terrace are predictably fine – count 120-odd steps in total to the top.

★ Aquarium La Rochelle · AQUARIUM
(☑ 05 46 34 00 00; www.aquarium-larochelle.com; quai Louis Prunier; adult/child €16/12; ⊙ 9am-11pm Jul & Aug, to 8pm Apr-Jun & Sep, 10am-8pm Oct-Mar) La Rochelle's state-of-the-art, family-friendly aquarium is home to 12,000 marine animals and 600 different species. Visits begin by descending in a clunky old 'submarine' to the ocean floor, where you're greeted by the pouting fish of the North Atlantic and serenaded by the sound of crashing waves and classical music. After this you swim through the oceans and seas of the world learning about all its diverse lifeforms. One floor up is the magical Galerie des Lumières (Gallery of Lights).

★ Musée Maritime · MUSEUM
(Maritime Museum; ☑ 05 46 28 03 00; www.museemaritimelarochelle.fr; place Bernard Moitessier; adult/child €9/6.50; ⊙ 10am-6.30pm Apr-Oct) In a series of boldly coloured, red, blue and yellow canopied hangars at the Bassin à Flot, the Maritime Museum evokes the history of La Rochelle port, from the present to the days when Parisians would arrive by train in La Rochelle to then set sail on a steamer to South America and Africa.

⌂ Sleeping

Auberge de Jeunesse · HOSTEL €
(☑ 05 46 44 43 11; www.aj-larochelle.fr/hostel; av des Minimes; dm €18-25, s €39-46, tw €50-54; ⊙ reception 8am-noon, 2-7pm & 9-10pm) This popular 231-bed HI hostel is 2km southwest of the train station in the seaside suburb of Les Minimes. Dorms sport four to six places in bunk beds – or bunk up in a twin. Rates include breakfast, and dinner is available for an additional fee. It's closed for two weeks in December.

Un Hôtel en Ville · BOUTIQUE HOTEL €
(☑ 05 46 41 15 75; www.unhotelenville.fr; 20 place du Maréchal Foch; d €75-85; P ✳ ⊚) Everything about this smart, 11-room boutique hotel at the Vieux Port screams quality. Moderately sized rooms are painted in a startling white, with white bed linens, dark stone furnishings and decorative chocolate, beige and zinc cushion fabrics. Count an extra €11 per person for *le petit dej*, or €13 should you fancy breakfasting on your own private terrace.

★ Hôtel François 1er · DESIGN HOTEL €€
(☑ 05 46 41 28 46; www.hotelfrancois1er.fr; 13-15 rue Bazoges; s €80-100, d €90-125; P ✳ @ ⊚) This 36-room themed hotel, squirrelled away in a centuries-old bourgeois mansion, is a secret museum of street art and rock memorabilia. Monumental portraits by local photographer Marie Monteiro dominate otherwise dazzling white rooms, and original works by France's top street artists pepper public areas. There are numerous acrobatic figures stencilled in white by Jérôme Mesnager and wildly expressive, plaster-cast faces by Gregos.

★ La Fabrique · DESIGN HOTEL €€
(☑ 05 46 41 45 00; www.hotellafabrique.com; 7-11 rue de la Fabrique; d €110-135, tr €160-165; ✳ @ ⊚) At home in an old rope factory, stylish La Fabrique is a nod to its industrial heritage and contemporary design. Fifty-eight rooms are arranged in a quad, above a vast open-plan lounge with made-to-measure furniture, Chesterfield sofas and aerial art

---

ⓘ CITY PASS

The **La Rochelle City Pass** (www.larochelle-citypass.com; 24/48/72 hours €28/38/48) provides admission to all the key city museums, guided tours, unlimited use of public transport and discounts in some boutiques. It can be purchased at the tourist office.

La Rochelle

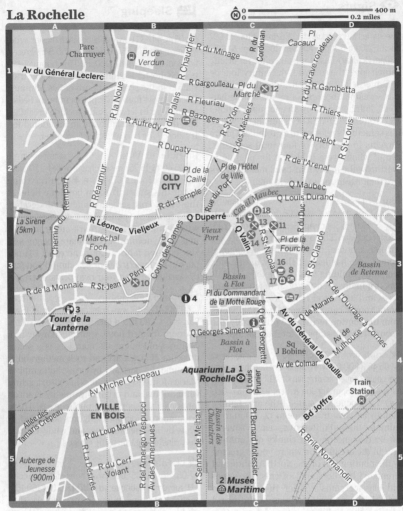

installation. Serene, almost-all-white rooms enjoy walk-in Italian showers and summertime breakfasts (€10) are served on a peaceful patio squirrelled away out back.

Ibis La Rochelle Vieux Port　　HOTEL €€
(☑ 05 46 41 60 22; place du Commandant de la Motte Rouge; d from €75/100; P ✳ @ ☎) Even if you don't usually go for a chain hotel, you might make an exception for this: the 79 bright modern rooms of this contemporary hotel lounge behind the beautiful facade of a 17th-century chapel, built in a Jesuit style in 1628. The church was deconsecrated in

1887 and later became a warehouse. The striking lobby-lounge, with designer bar and sofa-strewn patio in an alfresco interior courtyard, are gorgeous spaces to linger.

✕ Eating

★ **À la Gerbe de Blé**　　SEAFOOD €
(☑ 05 46 41 05 94; 7 rue Thiers; mains €9-16; ☺ 6.30am-4pm Mon-Sat) Lunch local. Between 10am and 1pm buy a dozen oysters from one of the stands in front of the **Marché Central** (rue Thiers, place du Maré; ☺ 7am-1.30pm), pay and ask for them to be shucked, then head around the corner to this buzzing cafe-bar

La Rochelle

built into the red-brick market wall. Tables on the pavement terrace enjoy the morning sun, and a simple menu of steak and fries, omelettes and sandwiches complements the BYO seafood.

Prao   MODERN FRENCH €
(☑ 05 46 37 85 46; http://prao.biz; 10 rue St-Nicolas; 2-/3-course menu lunch €14/16, dinner €23/28, mains €16; ☺ noon-2pm & 7.30-10.30pm Mon-Sat, 11am-3pm Sun; ⊕) Named after the multi-hull proa (*prao* in French) sailboat typical to the Pacific and Indian Oceans, this hipster bistro takes great pride in the products it cooks with, all sourced locally from small, often artisan producers. The result is a light, healthy cuisine packed with lots of vegetables, herbs, seeds and pulses to accompany the daily *effet mer* (fish dish) and *effet terre* (meat dish). Sunday brunch (petit/huge €12/22) buzzes.

Prao Café   CAFE €
(☑ 05 46 29 79 86; http://prao.biz; 21 quai Valin; sandwiches €6, mains €6.50-7.50; ☺ 9.30am-6.30pm Mon-Sat) Across the street from the old-fashioned carousel that spins on the water edge is this hipster cafe. Seating is a mix of sage-green Fermob (pavement terrace) and second-hand vintage (retro interior), and everything on the picnic-perfect menu is also to go. The hot and cold sandwiches, homemade tarts (imagine fennel, cranberry, peanut and chives in one sensational mix) with salad, soups and desserts ooze creativity.

★ **Le Panier de Crabes**   SEAFOOD €€
(☑ 05 46 41 27 31; www.facebook.com/lepanierde crabes; 9 place de la Fourche; 6/12 oysters €11/19, seafood platters €18-30; ☺ noon-2pm & 7-10pm Tue-Sat) The Basket of Crabs is, funnily enough, a self-proclaimed *bistrot de gens de mer* (seafarers' bistro) dishing up sensational Marennes d'Oléron oysters, winkles and whelks, shrimps, crabs and extravagant seafood platters at a price that doesn't break the bank. Local seafarer Olivier Tétaud is the man behind this earthy, no-frills address and works exclusively with local fishermen.

★ **André**   SEAFOOD €€€
(☑ 05 46 41 28 24; www.barandre.com; 5 rue St-Jean du Pérot; menus €23 & €37, mains €18-39; ☺ noon-2.30pm & 7-11pm) Opened in the 1950s as a waterfront seafood cafe, André grew so popular it began buying adjacent shops. It is now an eye-catching maze of eight different interconnecting rooms, each with its own individual ambience (dinner in a port-holed cabin, anyone?) but all serving the same succulent seafood caught the night before.

🍷 Drinking & Nightlife

★ **Chez Garcia – Cave de la Guiguette**   BAR
(https://la-guignette.fr; 8 rue St-Nicolas; ☺ 11am-1.30pm & 5-9pm Mon-Wed, 11am-9pm Thu-Sat, 5-9pm Sun) For a sweet taste of 1930s La Rochelle, follow the hipster crowd to this rough-cut wine bar where little has changed since it opened in 1933 in a blacksmith's yard. Vintage photos and posters evoke the days when fishermen and sailors flocked here from the nearby port. On warm days the drinking action and merriment spill out onto the pedestrian street in front.

La Guiguette – a fruity and fizzy, wine-based drink (€1.70/6.20/9 per glass/pitcher/bottle) unique to this La Rochelle institution – is the drink to order.

ALL AT SEA: FORT BOYARD

The stuff of cinema, Fort Boyard is a 20m-high iceberg of a fortress island lording over the ocean midway between Île d'Aix and Île d'Oléron. It was dreamt up in the 1700s to defend the Bay of Rochefort against the English, but construction of the extraordinary 'stone ship' only began a century later. It then took 19th-century builders 62 years to complete: the first building materials were hauled out to sea in 1802 and the fort was finally completed under Napoléon III (1851–70).

At the end of the Second Empire, Fort Boyard became a prison for Prussian soldiers. Since 1990 the dramatic construction has been the TV studio and film location of the French TV game show *Fort Boyard*. Closed to visitors today, the unique fort is best admired on a boat trip or, in summer, close-up aboard a sea kayak with **Antioche Kayak** (06 63 20 51 44; www.antioche-kayak.com; Port Sud, Fouras; kayak/stand-up paddle board per hour €12/13, lessons per hour from €25), kayak and stand-up paddle guides based 30km south of La Rochelle in Fouras.

Croisières Inter-Îles (08 25 13 55 00; www.inter-iles.com; cours des Dames) has sailings from Easter to early November to Fort Boyard (adult/child €17.50/12) and nearby islands Île d'Aix (€30/18.50) and Île d'Oléron (€25.50/17.50) and Île de Ré (€22.50/15) in July and August. Other companies with kiosks on the same quayside offer identical boat trips.

La Grosse Boîte CAFE
(05 46 52 25 70; www.lagrosseboite.fr; 65 rue Saint-Nicolas; 11am-midnight Tue-Sat;) The Big Box is no ordinary cafe. This is where locals head to play, play and play board and other games to their heart's content – the games cafe is packed every evening. Themed soirées (evenings) include enigmas, cards, adventure in America and so forth – and there are hundreds of different games, brand new and Monopoly-classic to test.

ℹ Information

Tourist Office (05 46 41 14 68; www.larochelle-tourisme.com; 2 quai Georges Simenon; 9am-7pm Jul & Aug, 9am-6pm Mon-Sat, to 5pm Sun Apr-Jun & Sep, shorter hours in winter) Runs some excellent seasonal guided tours and sells the La Rochelle City Pass (24/48/72 hours €28/38/48), which offers various discounts for public transport, sights and activities.

ℹ Getting There & Away

AIR
Aéroport La Rochelle-Île de Ré (La Rochelle Airport; www.larochelle.aeroport.fr), north of the city centre off the N237, has a variety of flights to several British, Irish and European airports.

BUS
From the **bus station** (Gare Routière; place de Verdun), **Les Mouettes** (08 11 36 17 17; www.lesmouettes-transports.com) runs services to regional destinations. Year-round buses to/from Île de Ré (€5) depart from in front of the train station, stopping at place de Verdun en route.

TRAIN
The **train station** (place Pierre Semard) is linked by TGV to Paris' Gare Montparnasse (from €40, 3¼ hours). Other destinations served by regular direct trains include Nantes (from €14, 1¾ hours), Poitiers (from €17.50, 1½ hours) and Bordeaux (from €16, 2¼ hours).

ℹ Getting Around

TO/FROM THE AIRPORT
Yélo (08 10 17 18 17; www.yelo-larochelle.fr; 22 place de Verdun) bus No 7 links the airport with place de Verdun in the town centre (15 minutes, €1.30; on Sunday bus No 47 takes over. In summer there are direct Les Mouettes buses from the airport to/from Île de Ré.

BICYCLE
Greenbike (05 46 29 31 03; www.location-greenbike.com; 41 quai du Gabut; 4/24hr from €12/18; 9am-1pm & 2-7pm Jul & Aug, 10am-noon & 2-6.30pm Sep-Nov & Apr-Jun) Rent pea-green beach cruiser bikes, city bikes, tandems, e-bikes and all the accompanying gear – baskets, helmets, children's seats and trailers – at this shop by Tour St-Nicolas. You'll need to leave your passport and a deposit.

Yélo The city's bike-sharing scheme has dozens of bike stands around town. Pick up a banana-yellow bike at one station and return it to another (€2 plus €3/7/12 for first two/seven/10 hours).

Île de Ré

POP 17,711

Bathed in the southern sun, drenched in a languid atmosphere and scattered with villages of green-shuttered, whitewashed buildings with terracotta roof tiles, Île de Ré is one of the most delightful places on France's west coast. The island spans 30km from its most easterly and westerly points, and just 5km at its widest section. In July and August it is almost impossible to move around and even harder to find a place to stay.

On the northern coast, about 12km from the toll bridge that links the island to La Rochelle, is main town **St-Martin-de-Ré** (population 2600), a quaint fishing port. Surrounded by 17th-century star-shaped fortifications and a citadel (today a prison) built by Vauban, the port town is a mesh of streets filled with Paris-chic fashion boutiques, art galleries and salty sea views.

◉ Sights & Activities

The St-Martin-de-Ré tourist office has plenty of information on water sports, including windsurfing, kite-surfing, paddle-boarding, sailing and canoeing.

★ **Phare des Baleines**   LIGHTHOUSE
(☑ 05 46 29 18 23; www.lepharedesbaleines.fr; 155 rte du Phare; adult/child lighthouse €3.50/2, old tower & museum €8/4, old tower, museum & lighthouse €11/6; ⊙ 9.30am-9pm Jun–mid-Sep, shorter hours rest of year) For an overview of the island, follow the crowds to Phare des Baleines, the island's scarlet-tipped, 59m-tall lighthouse on its northwestern tip. Scale the dizzying, 257-step spiral staircase inside the 19th-century lighthouse (1854) for a sweeping coastal panorama and learn its history in the neighbouring **Musée de la Mer**, snug against a second older lighthouse (1682), now defunct and hence called the **Vieille Tour** (old tower).

Clocher Observatoire   TOWER
(☑ 05 16 19 81 96; 1 rue du Palais; adult/child €2/free; ⊙ 10am-11pm Jul & Aug, to 7pm Sep–mid-Nov & Feb-Jun) A hike up the 117 steps inside the bell stone of fortified Église St-Martin rewards with a mighty fine panorama of St-Martin-de-Ré and the coast. The well-used wooden staircase twists up past the bell tower's trio of bells, the largest of which dates to 1890 and weighs a mighty 1140kg. Be warned: the bells ring for a few minutes every half-hour, in addition to a deafening 10 minutes at 7am, noon and 7pm each day to announce the traditional call to prayer.

Maison du Fier   BIRDWATCHING
(☑ 05 46 29 50 74; https://ile-de-re.lpo.fr/maison-du-fier; rte du Vieux Port, Les Portes-en-Ré; museum adult/child/family €5/3/13; ⊙ 10am-12.30pm & 2.30-7pm Mon-Fri, 2.30-7pm Sat & Sun Jul & Aug, shorter hours rest of year, closed Dec–mid-Mar) A short bike ride from the village of Les Portes-en-Ré brings you to this wooden building, surrounded by marshes and ancient salt pans in the **Réserve Naturelle Lilleau des Niges**. Some 300 different bird species frequent this soggy, sun-flooded nature reserve, and sightings of kestrels, red shanks and blue throats are common. The Maison du Fier runs a small nature museum and organises excellent guided nature walks and activities for both adults and children. Bring binoculars or rent some for €5/3 per day/half-day.

ATLANTIC COAST ÎLE DE RÉ

LOCAL KNOWLEDGE

MADE IN LA ROCHELLE

Souvenir shopping is notably stylish in this seafaring city where boutique shopping is very much grass-roots.

Vinyl collectibles and beautiful objects for the home, many handcrafted in the region, fill the concept store **Prao Boutique** (☑ 05 46 37 24 73; www.prao.biz; 1 rue St-Nicolas; ⊙ 2.30-7pm Mon, 10.30am-7pm Tue-Sat). Design posters inspired by local lighthouses, surfing and shellfish by La Rochelle's very own Prao Studio are a striking addition to any home, while vintage-styled printed notebooks made with recycled paper by Nantes-based Les Éditions du Paon are a stylish gift.

At **Espritvoiles** (☑ 06 33 18 14 47; www.espritvoiles.fr; 67 rue St-Nicolas; ⊙ 10.30am-12.30pm & 2-7pm Tue-Sat), local artist Sylvie Jaquen crafts casual, French-chic bags in all shapes, sizes and colours from the same tough acrylic cloth used to make boat sails at this eye-catching boutique-atelier. Deckchairs in every colour of the rainbow, shopping trolleys, magazine racks, table mats and bins are among the other accessories to tempt.

🛏 Sleeping & Eating

Île de Ré is an easy day trip from La Rochelle. But if you want to spend longer on the island, St-Martin-de-Ré tourist office has a list of boutique hotels, campgrounds and B&Bs; many close in winter and fill up months in advance in high season. Accommodation is limited and expensive – most people camp for a reason!

★ **Hôtel Le Sénéchal**   BOUTIQUE HOTEL €€
(☑ 05 46 29 40 42; www.hotel-le-senechal.com; 6 rue Gambetta, Ars-en-Ré; d €80-355; 🕾🗷) The stunning creation of a Parisian architect, this 22-room boutique hotel on the church square in Ars-en-Ré languishes luxuriantly in several traditional old-stone *maisons de village* and exudes panache and good taste. Scrubbed wooden floorboards, exposed stone walls, designer bathrooms and beautiful fabrics dress each room. Breakfast is served in a flowery courtyard, and there's a pocket-sized heated pool.

La Martinière   ICE CREAM €
(☑ 05 46 09 20 99; www.la-martiniere.fr; 17 quai de la Poithevinière, St-Martin-de-Ré; 1-/2-/3-scoop cones €3/3.80/4.40; ⊙ 10.30am-11pm Jul & Aug, to 9.30pm Sep, Oct, Apr & Jun) No trip to St-Martin-de-Ré is complete without an ice-cream cone from this *glacier* extraordinaire. There are between 250 and 300 incredible flavours to choose from, including madras, caviar and oyster, salted caramel, potato and caramel or rice pudding alongside strawberry, mango, passion fruit, peach and lavender, and other more traditional fruit flavours. Each season a new flavour is launched.

ⓘ Information

Tourist Office (☑ 05 46 09 20 06; www.iledere. com; 2 av Victor Bouthillier, St-Martin-de-Ré; ⊙ 9.30am-1pm & 2-6.30pm Mon-Sat, 9.30am-1.30pm Sun Jul & Aug, shorter hours rest of year) At the entrance to Vieux Port, St-Martin's tourist office has information on the entire island.

ⓘ Getting There & Around

A return ticket to drive across the Pont de Île de Ré (www.pont-ile-de-re.com), the bridge connecting the mainland and island, costs €8 (or €16 mid-June to mid-September); pay on your way to the island from La Rochelle.

Year-round **Les Mouettes** (p646) buses link La Rochelle train station and place de Verdun with the major towns on the island.

A single fare to St-Martin (one hour) or a *forfait journée* covering unlimited travel all day (including the return trip) costs €5. In St-Martin buses stop at the 'Cognacq Jay-Pole d'Échanges' bus stop, a 10-minute walk from the Vieux Port or a five-minute ride on free local shuttle buses.

To reach other towns on the island, you will need to disembark at the Cognacq Jay-Pole d'Échang-

DON'T MISS

PEDALLING AROUND

Criss-crossed by an extensive network of smooth, well-signposted and scenic *pistes cyclables* (bicycle paths) well away from motorised traffic, pancake-flat Île de Ré is a cycling paradise. In St-Martin de Ré pick up a free cycling map (marked with trails, distances and times, online at www.cdciledere.fr) at the tourist office and a pair of chic polka-dotted wheels across the road at **Yoo Too** (☑ 05 46 68 08 09; www.cycles-yootoo.com; 9 av Victor Bouthillier, St-Martin de Ré; per half-day/24hr from €8/11; ⊙ 9am-8pm Jul & Aug, shorter hours rest of year), open year-round; advance reservations are essential for July and August.

In summer, practically every village has somewhere to hire bikes, including trailers and seats for young children. From early July until the end of August, shuttle buses transport cyclists and their bikes between four cycling information points on the island.

From St-Martin, a fabulous 14km (one hour) trail follows the coast west past working oyster beds, before crossing the island past ancient salt pans to the pretty village of Ars-en-Ré where you can buy local rock salt and *fleur de sel* from the island's salt-producers cooperative. From here, it's another 7km to Phare des Baleines (p647), the island's 59m-tall lighthouse on its northwestern tip.

From the lighthouse, a shady 5.5km trail ducks through the protected forest of the Foret Dominiale du Lizay to the north-coast village of Les Portes-en-Ré. Birdwatching enthusiasts (bring binoculars) should not miss the trail from here, via the Maison du Fier (p647), into the marshes and salt pans of the Réserve Naturelle Lilleau des Niges and beyond to Ars-en-Ré. Time the ride with a memorable guided nature walk or activity (for adults and children) organised by the Maison du Fier.

AN OYSTER FARMER'S LUNCH

For an authentic taste of island life, spurn St-Martin's port-side restaurants and pick up the cycling path to Ars-en-Ré – either on foot or by bike. Within seconds of hitting the coast, the path brushes past a twinset of oyster farmer *cabanes* (huts), whose doors are open to the culinary curious. Grab a straw hat to keep off the sun, snag a table overlooking oyster beds and tuck into freshly shucked oysters courtesy of **Auberge de la Mer** (☑ 06 83 08 20 38; chemin de la Galère, St-Martin-de-Ré; oysters per dozen €14; ⊙ 11am-4pm Mar-Oct). Or kick back next door on a brightly coloured bar stool facing the sea at **Ré Ostréa** (☑ 06 63 91 80 19; www.degustationhuitres-iledere.fr; chemin de la Galère, St-Martin-de-Ré; oysters per dozen €12-22; ⊙ 10am-8pm Apr-Sep), a super friendly oyster bar with fresh prawns, whelks, clams and dozens of island oysters to tempt.

es and take a connecting shuttle; timetables are available from the Tourist Office.

Note that taxis are scarce and most people use bikes to get around the island. If you're planning to take a taxi to the airport, reserve well in advance. You can get taxi numbers from the Tourist Office.

Cognac

POP 17,693

On the banks of the River Charente amid vine-covered countryside, Cognac is known worldwide for its double-distilled spirit, on which the local economy thrives. Most visitors head here to visit the famous cognac houses, but it's a picturesque stop even if you are not a fan of the local firewater.

⊙ Sights & Activities

Musée des Arts du Cognac   MUSEUM
(MACO; ☑ 05 45 36 21 10; www.musees-cognac.fr; place de la Salle Verte; adult/child €5/1; ⊙ 11am-6pm Jul & Aug, 2-6pm Tue-Sun Sep-Jun) Inside a contemporary building set into the ramparts alongside the 19th-century Hôtel Perrin de Boussac, this museum explains the production of Cognac from vine to bottle. In the adjoining **Espace Decouverte** (admission free) is a model of Château de Cognac, the castle where François I was born in 1494. Just a fraction of the original riverside edifice remains,

today home to the **Otard** (☑ 05 45 36 88 86; www.otard.com; 127 bd Denfert-Rochereau; ⊙ 10am-noon & 1.30-6pm Jul & Aug, shorter hours rest of year) Cognac house.

Musée d'Art et d'Histoire de Cognac   MUSEUM
(MAH; ☑ 05 45 32 07 25; www.musees-cognac.fr; 48 bd Denfert-Rochereau; adult/child €5/1; ⊙ 11am-6pm Jul & Aug, 2-6pm Wed-Mon Sep-Jun) In the southern corner of the grotto- and pond-clad **Jardin Public**, Cognac's Art and History Museum showcases the town's history. Its interior – magnificent Hôtel Dupuy d'Angec (1837) – is as interesting as the paintings, sculptures and decorative arts on display.

🛏 Sleeping & Eating

Cognac offers excellent accommodation options, laden with charm, in all price ranges. In summer 2018 luxury, five-star **Hôtel Chai Monnet** (http://chaismonnethotel.com) with spa will open in a former *chai* (cellar) on av Paul Firino Martell.

Le Cheval Blanc   HOTEL €
(☑ 05 45 82 09 55; www.hotel-chevalblanc.fr; 6 place Bayard; d/tr/q €70/90/105; ⊙ reception 7am-9.30pm Mon-Fri, 8am-12.30pm & 3-9.30pm Sat, 8am-12.30pm & 5-9.30pm Sun; P❀🐾) A flowery courtyard out back and stylish family rooms are highlights of the unpretentious 27-room White Horse, run by Parisian couple Mylène and Frédéric Personyre, who clearly delight in Cognac's small-town *art de vivre* after fast-paced life in the capital. Rooms are immaculate, with white linens and bright colours; nine open onto the table-bedecked patio garden. Breakfast costs €9.20.

★ **Quai des Pontis**   HOTEL €
(☑ 05 45 32 47 40; www.quaidespontis.com; 16 rue des Pontis; d/tr/q from €78/83/88; P🐾🏊) At home in a former wood factory, this riverside estate is a leafy delight. Pick from one of seven design rooms in the attractive hotel building, an enchanting wooden cabin on stilts right by the water's edge or a romantic *roulotte* (caravan) for two. *Roulottes* and cabins have modern bathrooms, kitchenettes and a serenely peaceful outlook over the River Charente.

★ **L'Arty Show**   INTERNATIONAL €
(☑ 09 87 04 81 77; www.facebook.com/lartyshowcognac; 23 rue du Pont Faumet; mains €15, 2-/3-course menu €18/20; ⊙ noon-2pm Mon-Thu, noon-2pm & 7.30pm-midnight Fri) Cognac brandy invariably stars in the inventive, veg- and pulse-packed dishes of chefs Nathalie and

DON'T MISS

THE HOME OF COGNAC

According to local lore, divine intervention plays a role in the production of Cognac. Made of grape *eaux-de-vie* (brandies) of various vintages, Cognac is aged in oak barrels and blended by an experienced *maître de chai* (cellar master). Each year some 2% of the casks' volume – *la part des anges* (the angels' share) – evaporates through the pores in the wood, nourishing the tiny black mushrooms that thrive on the walls of Cognac warehouses. That 2% might not sound like much, but it amounts to around 20 million bottles a year.

The best-known Cognac houses are open to the public, running tours of their cellars and production facilities, and ending with a tasting session. Opening times vary annually; it's a good idea to reserve in advance. The tourist office has a list of smaller Cognac houses near town; most close October to mid-March.

Delphine at L'Arty Show, an edgy bistro with vintage flea-market furnishings and a name that sounds like *artichaut* ('artichoke' in French). The duo work with local, seasonal and often organic market products, and there is no menu: be prepared for a delicious surprise.

ℹ Information

Cognac Tourist Office (☑ 05 45 82 10 71; www.tourism-cognac.com; 16 rue du 14 Juillet; ☉ 9am-7pm Mon-Sat, 10am-5pm Sun Jul & Aug, shorter hours rest of year)

ℹ Getting There & Away

Cognac **train station** (av du Maréchal Leclerc), 1km south of the town centre, has regular trains to/from Bordeaux (from €17.80, 2¼ hours) and La Rochelle (€12.40, 1¼ hours).

Bordeaux

POP 250,776

An intoxicating cocktail of 18th-century savoir-faire, millennial hi-tech and urban street life on the lower Atlantic Coast, France's sixth largest city is exciting and gutsy. Its city centre on the banks of the River Garonne forms the world's largest urban World Heritage Site (18 sq km), and contemporary architects continue the trend for excellence with breathtakingly wild and beautiful new creations. World-class museums, a vibrant riverside street culture, exceptional dining and a dynamic cafe life buoyed up by Bordeaux's high-spirited university-student population make this a compelling place to linger for a few days. Then there's the glorious wine...

⊙ Sights

★ La Cité du Vin   MUSEUM
(☑ 05 56 16 20 20; www.laciteduvin.com; 134-150 Quai de Bacalan, 1 Esplanade de Pontac; adult/child €20/free; ☉ 10am-7pm Apr-Aug, shorter hours rest of year) The complex world of wine is explored in depth at ground-breaking La Cité du Vin, a stunning piece of contemporary architecture resembling a wine decanter on the banks of the River Garonne. The curvaceous gold building glitters in the sun and its 3000 sq metres of exhibits are equally sensory and sensational. Digital guides lead visitors around 20 themed sections covering everything from vine cultivation, grape varieties and wine production to ancient wine trade, 21st-century wine trends and celebrated personalities.

Tours end with a glass of wine – or grape juice for the kids – in panoramic **Le Belvédère**, with a monumental 30m-long bar and chandelier made out of recycled wine bottles, on the 8th floor. Temporary art exhibitions, cultural events and brilliant, themed one-hour tasting workshops (€15 to €25) are also worth watching out for. To get here, take tram B (direction Bassins à Flots) from Esplanade des Quinconnes, or walk 2.5km north along the river.

★ Cathédrale St-André   CATHEDRAL
(☑ 05 56 44 67 29; www.cathedrale-bordeaux. fr; place Jean Moulin; ☉ 2-7pm Mon, 10am-noon & 2-6pm Tue-Sun) **FREE** The Cathédrale St-André, a Unesco World Heritage Site prior to the city's classification, lords over the city. The cathedral's oldest section dates from 1096; most of what you see today was built in the 13th and 14th centuries. Enjoy exceptional masonry carvings in the north portal.

Even more imposing than the cathedral itself is the gargoyled, 50m-high Gothic belfry, **Tour Pey Berland** (☑ 05 56 81 26 25; www. pey-berland.fr; place Pey-Berland; adult/child €6/ free; ☉ 10am-1.15pm & 2-6pm Tue-Sun Jun-Sep, 10am-12.30pm & 2-5.30pm Tue-Sun Oct-May), erected between 1440 and 1466.

★ Miroir d'Eau   FOUNTAIN
(Water Mirror; place de la Bourse; ☉ 10am-10pm summer) **FREE** A fountain of sorts, the

Miroir d'Eau is the world's largest reflecting pool. Covering an area of 3450 sq metres of black granite on the quayside opposite the imposing Palais de la Bourse, the 'water mirror' provides hours of entertainment on warm sunny days when the reflections in its thin slick of water – drained and re-filled every half-hour – are stunning. Every 23 minutes a dense fog-like vapour is ejected for three minutes to add to the fun (and photo opportunities).

Musée d'Aquitaine
MUSEUM

(☑05 56 01 51 00; www.musee-aquitaine-bordeaux.fr; 20 cours Pasteur; adult/child €5/free; ⏱11am-6pm Tue-Sun) Gallo-Roman statues and relics dating back 25,000 years are among the highlights at this bright and spacious, well-curated history and civilisations museum. Grab a bilingual floor plan at the entrance and borrow an English-language catalogue to better appreciate the exhibits that span prehistory through to 18th-century Atlantic trade and slavery, world cultures and the emergence of Bordeaux as a world port in the 19th century. Temporary exhibitions cost extra.

Musée de la Mer et de la Marine
MUSEUM

(www.museedelamerbordeaux.fr; 95 rue des Étrangers) Slated to open in early 2019, this landmark new museum by the Basins à Flot comprises three floors of exhibition space devoted to almost everything there is to know about Bordeaux's maritime world, including its history, science, culture and traditions. Themes include the history of navigation and discovery, naval battles, the scientific conquest of the Atlantic and the fascinating world of oceanography. The building – a striking work of contemporary architecture designed to look like an ocean liner – was designed by local Bordeaux architect Olivier Brochet.

Musée des Beaux Arts
GALLERY

(☑05 56 10 20 56; www.musba-bordeaux.fr; 20 cours d'Albret; adult/child €5/free; ⏱11am-6pm Wed-Mon) The evolution of Occidental art from the Renaissance to the mid-20th century is on view at Bordeaux's Museum of Fine Arts, which occupies two wings of the 1770s-built Hôtel de Ville, either side of elegant city park Jardin de la Mairie. The museum was established in 1801; highlights include 17th-century Flemish, Dutch and Italian paintings, and the last work painted by one of Bordeaux's earliest (and most celebrated) female artists, Rosa Bonheur (1822–99) who infamously wore men's trousers when she worked.

🛏 Sleeping

Central Hostel
HOSTEL €

(http://centralhostel.fr; 2 place Projet; d €19-30, d €90-150) Urban-chic dorms and swish doubles with USB plugs aplenty and en suite bathrooms are spread across four floors at this dead-central, designer hostel in Saint-Pierre. Glam to the core, the new 97-bed hostel – to open in summer 2018 – promises a bespoke guest experience, bar, sun-drenched terrace designed for summertime chilling and locally sourced restaurant, open 24 hours.

Hôtel de la Presse
DESIGN HOTEL €

(☑05 56 48 53 88, www.hoteldelapresse.com; 8 rue de la Porte-Dijeaux; d €90-160; ❋🛜) Top-to-toe millennial renovations keep this 1920s hotel, wedged between boutiques in Bordeaux's busy shopping heart, right up to date. A monumental bulldog stands sentry in the breakfast room, and its 27 boutique rooms enjoy the same bold murals (albeit featuring vintage printing letter blocks, vintage trainers and the like rather than teeth-bearing canines). The excellent organic breakfast costs €12.50.

★ Hôtel La Cour Carrée
BOUTIQUE HOTEL €€

(☑05 57 35 00 00; www.lacourcarree.com; 5 rue de Lurbe; d €125-250; P❋@🛜) Tucked in an 18th-century house on a quiet side street with little passing traffic, this design-driven boutique hotel oozes natural style and peace. Soft, muted colours and contemporary Scandinavian furnishings complement ancient gold-stone walls in its 16 elegant rooms, and the pièce de résistance is the interior courtyard – a much-appreciated alfresco lounge in summer. Breakfast/parking €12/13.

Mama Shelter
DESIGN HOTEL €€

(☑05 57 30 45 45; www.mamashelter.com/en/bordeaux; 19 rue Poquelin Molière; d/tr from €80/130; ❋@🛜) With personalised iMacs, video booths and free movies in every room, Mama Shelter is up-to-the-minute. White

---

ℹ CITY PASS

Consider investing in the **Bordeaux Métropole City Pass** (www.bordeauxcitypass.com; 24/48/72 hours €29/39/46), covering admission to 20 museums and monuments. It also includes a free guided tour and unlimited use of public buses, trams and boats. Buy it online or at the tourist office (p659).

Bordeaux

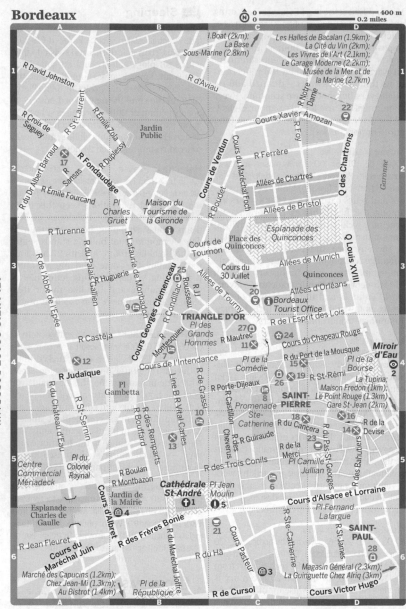

ATLANTIC COAST BORDEAUX

rooms are small, medium or large; XL doubles have a sofa bed. The ground-floor restaurant (mains €13 to €29) sports the same signature rubber rings strung above the bar as other Philippe Starck–designed hotels. Summertime drinks and dinner are served on the sensational rooftop terrace.

Maison Fredon B&B €€
(☎ 05 56 91 56 37; www.latupina.com/maison-dhotes-fredon-bordeaux; 5 rue Porte de La Monnaie; d €90-250; P ☎) In an enchanting 19th-century townhouse of golden stone, this stylish B&B is the accommodation arm of the La Tupina (p655) empire – which translates as five

Bordeaux

bourgeois doubles mixing contemporary furnishings with centuries-old white painted beams, and one of the most delicious breakfasts in town. Some fantastic art pieces decorate the salon where guests can mingle.

★ **Hôtel Continental** HOTEL €€€
(☑05 56 52 66 00; http://en.hotel-le-continental.com; 10 rue Montesquieu; s/d €145/230; ❋ @ ☎) Beautifully located in the chic, shop-laden Triangle d'Or, this enchanting three-star hotel languishes inside an 18th-century *hôtel particulier* (mansion) and first opened its doors as Hôtel du Coq d'Or in 1912. Today part of the sharp and savvy HappyCulture hotel group, its 51 rooms fuse contemporary design with vintage bohemian chic.

✖ Eating

Les Halles de Bacalan FOOD HALL €
(☑05 56 80 63 65; www.facebook.com/hallesdebacalan; 149 quai de Bacalan; ⊙8am-2.30pm & 5.30-8.30pm Tue & Wed, to 10pm Thu & Fri, 8am-2am Sat, 8am-5pm Sun) At home in a waterfront hangar opposite La Cité du Vin, this gleaming state-of-the-art market hall is a fantastic spot to grab a quick gourmet bite. Some 20 upmarket stalls cooking up everything from fish, burgers and meat to oysters, poultry, Italian products and cheese serve a daily menu. Seating is at bar stools or outside overlooking the wet docks.

Woof HOT DOGS €
(www.wearewoof.com; 61 rue St-Rémi; hot dogs €3.50-7; ⊙noon-10.30pm Tue-Sat, 6-10.30pm Sun) For a swift street-food bite between sights, duck into Woof for a gourmet hot dog – to eat in, in the attractive Scandinavian-styled interior, or to take out. Bread is organic, and tasty homemade fillings to accompany your *chien chaud* include caramelised onions, cream cheese, guacamole and sun-dried tomatoes.

★ **Magasin Général** INTERNATIONAL €
(☑05 56 77 88 35; www.magasingeneral.camp; 87 quai des Queyries; mains €10-20; ⊙8am-6pm Mon, to 7pm Tue & Wed, to midnight Thu & Fri, 8.30am-midnight Sat, 8.30am-6pm Sun; ☎) Follow the hip crowd across the river to this huge industrial hangar on the right bank, France's biggest and best organic restaurant with a gargantuan terrace complete with vintage sofa seating, ping-pong table and table football. Everything here, from vegan burgers and superfood salads to smoothies, pizzas, wine and French bistro fare, is *bio* (organic) and sourced locally. Sunday brunch is a bottomless feast.

La Maison du Glacier ICE CREAM €
(☑05 40 54 65 96; www.facebook.com/lamaisonduglacier; 1 place St-Pierre; 1/2/3 scoops €2.70/4.30/5.80; ⊙1.30-6.30pm) Break old-town meanderings in medieval St-Pierre with an ice cream from this local institution. There are 80-odd unusual flavours – all organic – to choose from, including green tea, almond, ginger, apple, quince, chestnut and rhubarb. Summertime seating spills across pretty place St-Pierre.

DON'T MISS

BORDEAUX'S URBAN CHATEAU

Diminutive neighbour to nearby Château Haut-Briond, which is rated among the top 'first growths' in the 1855 classification, **Château Les Carmes Haut Briond** (☑ 07 77 38 10 64; www.les-carmes-haut-brion.com; 20 rue des Carmes; 1½ hour guided visit with tasting €30; ⊘ 9.30am-12.30pm & 2-6pm Mon-Sat) is named after Carmelite monks – Les Carmes – who tended vines here from 1584 until the French Revolution. The 16th-century chateau is very much intact and contrasts beautifully with its millennial cellars and tasting room designed by French designer Philippe Starck. Resembling a majestic ship, the striking building 'floats' in a pool of water and is accessed by footbridges.

Guided visits include a tour of the 19th-century chateau gardens and cellar, and end with wine tasting. Advance reservations online or by telephone are essential. The chateau is 4km southwest of the cathedral, in Pessac. Take tram line A from Hôtel de Ville to the François Mitterrand stop, a 10-minute walk from the chateau.

★**Brasserie Le Bordeaux**　CAFE €€
(☑ 0557304346; https://bordeaux.intercontinental.com; 2-5 place de la Comédie; 2-/3-course lunch menu from €29/39, mains €27; ⊘ 7am-10.30pm) To dine à la Gordon Ramsay without breaking the bank, reserve a table at his elegant belle époque brasserie with an interesting, Anglo-French hybrid cuisine – local Arcachon oysters, fish 'n' chips, Gascon pork pie with piccalilli, braised beef chuck, hand-cut tartare – and a parasol-shaded pavement terrace overlooking busy place de la Comédie. Weekend brunch (€68) is a local hot date.

★**Au Bistrot**　FRENCH €€
(☑ 06 63 54 21 14; www.facebook.com/aubistrotbordeaux; 61 place des Capucins; mains €18-24; ⊘ noon-2.30pm & 7-11pm Wed-Sun) There's nothing flashy or fancy about this hardcore French bistro, an ode to traditional market cuisine with charismatic François front of house and talented French-Thai chef Jacques In'On in the kitchen. Marinated herrings, lentil salad topped with a poached egg, half a roast pigeon or a feisty *andouillette* (tripe sausage) roasted in the oven – 80% of produce is local or from the surrounding Aquitaine region.

★**Mets Mots**　BISTRO €€
(☑ 05 57 83 38 24; www.metsmots.fr; 98 rue Fondaudège; 3-course lunch menu €18.50, 3-/4-course dinner menu €32/40; ⊘ noon-1.30pm Mon & Tue, noon-1.30pm & 7.30-9.30pm Wed-Sat) Talented young chef Léo Forget is turning heads in foodie Bordeaux with his striking new locavore neobistro, with stylish zinc bar, mix of rough chip-wood and retro geometric-tile flooring and a back wall plastered in faded ginger newspapers. The lunchtime *menu*, which might see *confit de canard* with old-

world veg or sweet-and-sour cod chalked on the board, is unbeatable value. Cuisine is strictly seasonal.

★**Le Bouchon Bordelais**　FRENCH €€
(☑ 05 56 44 33 00; www.bouchon-bordelais.com; 2 rue Courbin; 2-/3-course lunch menu from €23/39, 7-course dinner menu €55, mains €21) Seasonal market produce and a generous pinch of creativity form the backbone of this *bistrot coloré* (colourful bistro), tucked down a backstreet lane between place de la Bourse and place de la Comédie. With its exposed stone walls and terracotta floor tiles, interior decor is 100% traditional and quaint – the menu not.

Le Petit Commerce　SEAFOOD €€
(☑ 05 56 79 76 58; 22 rue Parlement St-Pierre; 2-course lunch menu €16, mains €15-26; ⊘ 10am-1am) This iconic bistro, with dining rooms both sides of a narrow pedestrian street and former Michelin-starred chef Stéphane Carrade in the kitchen, is the star turn of the trendy St-Pierre quarter. It's best known for its excellent seafood menu that embraces everything from Arcachon sole and oysters to eels, lobsters and *chipirons* (baby squid) fresh from St-Jean de Luz.

★**Garopapilles**　FRENCH €€
(☑ 09 72 45 55 36; https://garopapilles.com; 62 rue Abbé de l'Épée; 3-/4-course lunch menu €35/45, 5-course dinner menu €90; ⊘ 12.15-2pm Tue & Wed, 12.15-2pm & 7.30-9pm Thu & Fri) Reservations are essential at this Michelin-starred restaurant and wine cellar where *vins d'auteur* (carefully curated wines by small regional wine producers) accompany chef Tanguy Laviale's market-driven *cuisine à la hauteur* (an elevated, tip-top cuisine). Dining is in an elegant, streamlined interior with dark

wood flooring and little decorative distraction. In summer lunch is served in a romantic, herb-fragranced courtyard garden.

Horace   INTERNATIONAL €€
(☑05 56 90 01 93; 40 rue Poquelin Molière; mains €8-14; ⊙8.30am-6.30pm Mon, to 9.30pm Tue-Fri, 9.30am-9.30pm Sat, 9.30am-6.30pm Sun) Whatever the time of day, Horace can do no wrong. Outstanding speciality coffee roasts (including Oven Heaven beans roasted locally), sophisticated fruit- and veg-packed breakfasts, homemade brioches and breads, and lunch/dinner menus bursting with creativity are the quality hallmarks of this coffee shop, owned by the same talented barista as Bordeaux's Black List (☑06 89 91 82 65; www.facebook.com/blacklistcafe; 27 place Pey Berland; ⊙8am-6pm Mon-Fri, 9.30am-6pm Sat). Sunday brunch (€21) is a sell-out every week.

Miles   MODERN FRENCH €€
(☑05 56 81 18 24; http://restaurantmiles.com; 33 rue du Cancera; 3-/4-course lunch menu €27/32, 5-course dinner menu €48; ⊙12.15-1.30pm & 7.30-10pm Tue-Fri, 7.30-10pm Sat) This contemporary oyster-grey space is the creation of four young chefs from France and Vietnam, Israel, Japan and New Caledonia, whose innovative, creative and wholly seasonal kitchen reflects their mixed roots. There's no menu – rather a series of tasting courses (or 'miles' in Miles-speak). Think monkfish with beetroot, *nori* (seaweed) and citrus fruits perhaps, or pork, leek, lemon and smoked dates.

★ La Tupina   FRENCH €€€
(☑05 56 91 56 37; www.latupina.com; 6 rue Porte de la Monnaie; lunch menu €18, dinner menus €44-52, mains €20-32; ⊙noon-2pm & 7-11pm Tue-Sun) Filled with the aroma of soup simmering inside a *tupina* ('kettle' in Basque) over an open fire, this iconic bistro is feted for its seasonal southwestern French fare: calf kidneys with fries cooked in goose fat, milk-fed lamb, tripe and goose wings. Dining is farmhouse-style, in a maze of small elegant rooms decorated with vintage photographs, antique furniture and silver tableware.

🍷 Drinking & Nightlife

Bordeaux places great importance on drinking – be it tasting excellent vintages in a *bar à vin*, guzzling *cacolac* (chocolate milk made in Bordeaux since 1954) in a cafe or glugging local Darwin beer in an industrial hangar. Medieval Saint-Pierre teems with atmospheric cafe pavement terraces, as do Chartrons's riverside quays. Mainstream nightclubs congregate on busy quai du Paladate near the train station.

★ Bar à Vin   WINE BAR
(☑05 56 00 43 47; http://baravin.bordeaux.com; 3 cours du 30 Juillet; ⊙11am-10pm Mon-Sat) The decor – herringbone parquet, grandiose stained glass depicting the godly Bacchus, and sky-high ceiling – matches the reverent air that fills this wine bar inside the hallowed halls of the Maison du Vin de Bordeaux. Dozens of Bordeaux wines are served by the glass (€3.50–8) which, paired with a cheese or charcuterie platter, transport foodies straight to heaven. Gracious sommeliers know their *vin*.

★ Utopia   CAFE, BAR
(☑05 56 79 39 25; www.cinemas-utopia.org; 3 place Camille Jullian; ⊙10am-1am summer, to 10.30pm winter) At home in an old church, this much-venerated art address is a local institution – its sunny terrace alone is fabulous. Art-house cinema, mellow cafe, hot lunch spot and bar rolled into one, it is one of the top addresses in the city to mingle over a drink, tartine (open sandwich, €7), salad (€13), or hot or cold organic veg soup (€6.5) with locals any time of day.

LOCAL KNOWLEDGE

MARKET OYSTERS

If there's one stall at the city's iconic food market that sums up the contagious joie de vivre of Les Capus (as locals call Bordeaux's premier food market), it is *bistrot à huitres* (oyster bar) **Chez Jean-Mi** (place des Capucins, Maré des Capucins; breakfast €1-7.50, seafood €6-25; ⊙7am-2.30pm Tue-Fri, to 3.30pm Sat & Sun) Owner Jean-Mi greets regulars and first-timers with the same huge smile, and his freshly shucked oysters, fish soup and copious seafood platters are of the finest quality money can buy. Arrive early at weekends to snag an alfresco table overlooking the open-air fruit and veg stalls on place des Capucins. Should a dozen oysters and a glass of white tickle your fancy for *petit dej*, Jean-Mi serves breakfast too.

JUSTIN FOULKES/LONELY PLANET ©

Vineyard near St-Émilion (p661) **2.** La Cité du Vin (p650), ⸍rdeaux **3.** Boxed Bordeaux wines

Wine, Glorious Wine

The countryside around the Bordeaux region is full of renowned vineyards and legendary châteaux, many of which can be visited. Venture a little further north and the Cognac region offers a totally different sort of tipple.

Cognac

Bordeaux isn't the only wine party in town. Cognac produces a drink so heavenly that even the angels are said to partake. Learn all about it during a visit to the Musee des Arts du Cognac (p649).

St-Émilion

The quintessential French wine town and the oldest French wine region, St-Émilion (p661) has robust and generous wines that tickle the taste buds; and any number of wine-related tours (available through the tourist office) to get the most from it.

Bordeaux

No wine-tasting tour is complete without an exploration at the groundbreaking La Cité du Vin (p650). Built on the wealth of the grape, Bordeaux lives up to its bourgeois reputation, but today an army of students gives the city a lighter edge.

The Médoc

The Médoc region (p660) encompasses some of the finest wine territory in France, with such grand names as Mouton Rothschild, Latour and Lafite Rothschild hailing from this area. Numerous wine-themed tours are available.

Oysters & Wine

One of the most pleasurable ways of enjoying the region's wines is at Bordeaux' Marché des Capucins (p659), with a glass of chilled white wine in one hand and a fresh, raw oyster in the other.

★**Night Beach** BAR

(https://bordeaux.intercontinental.com; 2-5 place de la Comédie, 7th fl, Grand Hôtel de Bordeaux; ⊙7pm-1am late May-late Sep) There is no finer, more elegant or romantic rooftop bar in Bordeaux than this achingly hip drinking-and-hobnobbing joint on the 7th floor of historic Grand Hôtel de Bordeaux. Views of the city, River Garonne and vineyards beyond are a panoramic 360 degrees, French-chic seating is sofa-style beneath parasols, and DJ sets play at weekends.

★**Symbiose** COCKTAIL BAR

(Old-fashioned Stories; ☑05 56 23 67 15; www.facebook.com/symbiosebordeaux; 4 quai des Chartrons; ⊙noon-2.30pm Mon, noon-2.30pm & 6.30pm-2am Tue-Fri, 6.30pm-2am Sat) There is something inviting about this clandestine address with a soft green facade across from the river on the fringe of the Chartrons district. This is the secret speakeasy that introduced good cocktails with gastronomic food pairings to Bordeaux. The chef uses locally sourced artisan products, and cocktails rekindle old-fashioned recipes packed with homemade syrups and 'forgotten', exotic or unusual ingredients.

Dining here is equally sensational. Reserve in advance to snag a much-sought-after table for lunch (2-/3-course *menu* €17/20) or dinner (5-course *menu* €45).

DON'T MISS

BUNKER ART
....

By far the city's eeriest and most menacing sight, **La Base Sous-Marine** (Submarine Base; ☑05 56 11 11 50; www.facebook.com/Basesousmarinede Bordeaux; bd Alfred Daney; adult/child €5/3, free 1st Sun of month Sep-Jun; ⊙1.30-7pm Tue-Sun) was one of five submarine bases built on the Atlantic Coast by the Germans during the WWII. Designed as a bunker to protect German U-boats from aerial attack, it pens base proved impossible to destroy – by British forces during WWII and subsequently by the city, who now use the reinforced-concrete eyesore as a seriously cool, underground cultural centre, art gallery and music concert venue.

The submarine base is only open during exhibitions and events. Check its Facebook page for details.

★**Le Point Rouge** COCKTAIL BAR

(☑05 56 94 94 40; www.pointrouge-bdx.com; 1 quai de Paludate; ⊙6pm-2am Mon-Sat) A black steel door marked with a small, red doorbell (aka 'le point rouge,' or 'the red dot') heralds the entrance to this trendy speakeasy, a theatrical scarlet affair hidden in the basement of a once-grandiose riverfront *hôtel particulier* (mansion). The encyclopaedia of a cocktail list traces the history of cocktails in some 100 different elaborate creations. Ring the bell to enter.

★**I.Boat** CLUB

(☑05 56 10 48 37; www.iboat.eu; quai Armand Lalande, Bassins à Flot 1; ⊙7.30pm-6am) Hip hop, rock, indie pop, psyche blues rock, punk and hardcore are among the varied sounds that blast out of this fun nightclub and concert venue, on a decommissioned ferry moored in the increasingly trendy, industrial Bassins à Flot district in the north of the city. Live music starts at 7pm, with DJ sets kicking in on the club dance floor from 11.30pm.

☆ **Entertainment**

Get up on the month's cultural events, concerts and happenings with **Sortir** (http://sortirabordeaux.fr), **Bordeaux Les Sorties** (www.bordeaux.sortir.eu) and **Clubs & Concerts** (www.clubsetconcerts.com), freebie listings mags available at the tourist office.

Grand Théâtre THEATRE, OPERA

(☑05 56 00 85 95; www.opera-bordeaux.com; place de la Comédie) Designed by Victor Louis (of Chartres Cathedral fame), this 18th-century theatre stages operas, ballets and concerts of orchestral and chamber music.

Bordeaux Métropole Arena CONCERT VENUE

(www.bordeauxmetropolearena.com; 48-50 ave Jean Alfonséa, Floirac) Up to 11,300 spectators can fit in Bordeaux's sparkling new arena, a curvaceous white 'pebble' designed by French architect Rudy Ricciotti, 5km south of the city centre on the Rive Droite (Right Bank) of the Garonne. Depeche Mode performed at its opening concert in January 2018.

La Guinguette Chez Alriq LIVE MUSIC

(☑05 56 86 58 49; www.laguinguettechezalriq.com; quai des Queyries; admission €5; ⊙7pm-11.30pm Wed, 7pm-midnight Thu & Fri, 5pm-1.30am Sat, noon-7pm Sun May-Sep) For summertime music on the Rive Droite, there is no finer spot than this seasonal *guinguette* (open-air dance hall), with a couple of bars, casual food and live music covering everything from jazz and swing, to pop and beat-rich Balkan bands. Order a homemade punch or artisan beer brewed at Bordeaux's Brasserie de la Lune, and kick back with the hip crowd.

🔓 Shopping

Europe's longest pedestrian shopping street, rue Ste-Catherine, links place de la Victoire and place de la Comédie; 19th-century shopping arcade **Galerie Bordelaise** (rue de la Porte Dijeaux & rue Ste-Catherine; ⊙ hours vary) is nearby. Luxury fashion boutiques lace the Triangle d'Or ('Golden Triangle') formed by cours Georges Clemenceau, cours de l'Intendance and Allées de Tourny. Trendy independent boutiques and design shops are concentrated on rue St-James in the St-Pierre quarter and rue Notre-Dame in Chartrons.

★ L'Intendant   WINE
(www.intendant.com; 2 allées de Tourny; ⊙ 10am-7.30pm Mon-Sat) Welcome to what must be the grandest wine shop in the whole of France. A magnificent central staircase spiralling up five floors is surrounded by cylindrical shelves holding 15,000 bottles of regional wine at this highly respected *caviste* (wine cellar). Bottle prices range from €7 to thousands of euros. Watch for tastings most Saturdays.

★ Chocolaterie Saunion   CHOCOLATE
(☑ 05 56 48 05 75; www.saunion.fr; 56 cours Georges Clemenceau; ⊙ 2-7.15pm Mon, 7.30am-12.30pm & 1.30-7.15pm Tue-Sat) Follow local gourmets to this exquisite, oh-so-bourgeois chocolate shop, run by the same family since 1893. Fourth-generation chocolate-maker Thierry Lalet is at the helm today, crafting gold-foil-wrapped Galliens de Bordeaux (almond nougat, praline and hazelnut chocolate bonbon), Guinettes (kirsch-soaked cherries enrobed in dark chocolate) and chewy Niniches Bordelaises (honey, milk and chocolate caramels).

★ Serendipity   HOMEWARES
(☑ 07 69 60 02 22; www.serendipityshop.fr; 26 rue Buhan; ⊙ 11am-7.30pm Tue-Sat) Romantic and youthful, this delightful *'cabinet de convivialité'* inspires bags of instant feel-good factor. After several years in Paris, Claire Chabellard returned to her native Bordeaux to create this colourful Ali Baba's cave of beautiful, thoughtful objects for the home. Think 'Follow your Dreams' notebooks, Sass & Belle gifts and accessories, personalised jewellery, hanging flower pots and all sorts.

Serendipity also runs craft workshops (origami, candle-making, sewing, flower arranging etc); check its Facebook page.

Marché des Capucins   MARKET
(http://marchedescapucins.com; place des Capucins; ⊙ 6am-1pm Tue-Sun) A classic Bordeaux experience is a Saturday morning spent slurping oysters and white wine from a seafood stand in the city's legendary covered food market. Stalls overflowing with fruit, veg, cheese, meats, fish, bread and all sorts fill the space to bursting.

ℹ️ Information

Tourist Office (☑ 05 56 00 66 00; www.bordeaux-tourisme.com; 12 cours du 30 Juillet; ⊙ 9am-6.30pm Mon-Sat, to 5pm Sun) Runs an excellent range of city and regional tours; reserve in advance online or in situ. It also rents pocket modems to hook you up with wi-fi. There's a small but helpful **branch** (☑ 05 56 00 66 00; rue Charles Domercq, Espace Modalis, Parvis Sud; ⊙ 9.30am-12.30pm & 2-6pm Mon-Fri) at the train station.

Maison du Tourisme de la Gironde (☑ 05 56 52 61 40; www.gironde-tourisme.fr; 9 rue Fondaudège; ⊙ 9am-6pm Mon-Fri, 10am-1pm & 2-6.30pm Sat) Information on the surrounding Gironde *département*.

ℹ️ Getting There & Around

AIR

Aéroport de Bordeaux (Bordeaux Airport; BOD; ☑ Information 05 56 34 50 50; www.bordeaux.aeroport.fr; Mérignac), also known as Bordeaux-Mérignac, is 10km west of the city centre in the suburb of Mérignac.

Urban bus line 1+, operated by public-transport company TBM (www.infotbm.com), links the airport with place Gambetta, place de la Victoire and the Gare St-Jean train station in town. At the airport, buy tickets (€1.60) from the ticket dispenser next to the bus stop, in front of Terminal B, or directly from the driver. Buses run every 10 minutes or so between 6am to 11pm, and the journey time is 40 minutes (longer at rush hour).

BICYCLE

Public bike-sharing scheme V^3 (www.vcub.fr), run by local public transport company TBM, has 1800 banana-yellow bicycles available for use at bike stations all over the city. Pay €1.60 to access a bike for 24 hours, plus €2 per hour after the first 30 minutes (free) is up; you'll need to initially register online or with your credit card at a V^3 station.

BOAT

B^3 (www.infotbm.com) boats, also operated by TBM, shuttle between quai des Maréchal Lyautey (by Palais de la Bourse), quai de Bacalan (by Quai des Marques shopping mall and La Cité du Vin) and quay des Queyries on the right bank (near Magasin Général). Tickets cost €1.60.

DANCING ON THE FRINGE

On sultry summer nights, dance the night away at one of the city's alternative cultural venues in the edgy Bacalan district, a short walk north from La Cité du Vin.

After-work drinks, early-evening parties, cultural events, art exhibitions, concerts and live gigs (hip hop, electro etc) pepper summer evenings at **Le Garage Moderne** (☑05 56 50 91 33; www.legaragemoderne.org; 1 rue des Étrangers; ⊗9am-6pm Mon-Sat) where a trio of dedicated mechanics help locals fix their own cars and bicycles by day. Grab a drink and wander around the vast hangar packed to the rafters with a mesmerising array of vintage curiosities: an old Aquitaine bus, cinema seats, flowery crockery, all sorts.

Nearby, at **Les Vivres de l'Art** (☑05 56 10 80 94; http://lesvivresdelart.org; 4 rue Achard; ⊗10am-6pm), fringe theatre, dance and music events, DJ sets and live gigs enliven weekends. The neoclassical pavilion from 1785 was originally a military base for marines and is a collaborative artist residency today. Fantastical metal sculptures by resident sculptor Jean-François Buisson adorn the shared garden, littered with recycled tables and chairs, a bar and alternative 'dance floor.'

TRAIN

Major services from **Gare St-Jean** (Cours de la Marne) include:

Bayonne (€32, 1¾ hours, at least 10 daily)

La Rochelle (€31.50, 2¼ hours, six daily)

Nantes (from €27, five hours, three daily)

Paris Gare Montparnasse (€69, 3¼ hours, at least 16 daily)

Poitiers (from €27, 1¾ hours, at least hourly)

Toulouse (€39, 2¼ hours, hourly)

Around Bordeaux

Bordeaux's world-famous vineyards surround the city – a perfect day trip. The **Espace Information Routes du Vin** (www.bordeauxwinetrip.fr; 134-150 quai de Bacalan, La Cité du Vin; ⊗10am-7pm Apr-Aug, shorter hours rest of year) inside La Cité du Vin distributes free, colour-coded maps of production areas, driving itineraries along Les Routes des Vins de Bordeaux.

The Médoc

Northwest of Bordeaux, along the western shore of the Gironde Estuary – formed by the confluence of the Garonne and Dordogne rivers – lie some of Bordeaux's most celebrated vineyards. To their west, fine-sand beaches, bordered by dunes and lagoons, stretch from Pointe de Grave south along the Côte d'Argent (Silver Coast) to the Bassin d'Arcachon and beyond, with great surf.

On the banks of the muddy Gironde, the port town of Pauillac (population 1300) is at the heart of the wine country, surrounded by the distinguished Haut-Médoc, Margaux and St-Julien appellations. Extraordinary châteaux pepper these parts, from the world-famous Château Ducru-Braucailllou on its southeast fringe to Château Margaux, with striking cellars designed by Lord Norman Foster of Thames Bank. The Pauillac wine appellation encompasses 18 *crus classés*, including the world-renowned Mouton Rothschild, Latour and Lafite Rothschild.

◉ Sights & Activities

Château Lynch-Bages WINERY

(☑05 56 73 19 31; www.jmcazes.com/en/chateau-lynch-bages; Craste des Jardins, Pauillac; 1hr visit with tasting €9, 2½hr tastings €75; ⊗9.30am-1pm & 2.30-6pm) Gracefully set in the wealthy hamlet of Bages, 2km southwest of Pauillac, this is one of the best-known Médoc wineries – due in no small part to the extraordinary energy, passion and charisma of the Cazes family, who have owned the estate since 1939. It is one of the region's oldest, its wine being among the 18 prestigious *Cinquièmes Crus* classified for the first time in 1855. Each year a contemporary artist is invited to the chateau to create a work of art for it.

In 2017 construction work began on sparkling new, state-of-the-art winemaking facilities for the chateau, promising the very latest in viticultural technology. Designed by renowned architect Chien Chung Pei (son of the celebrated I.M. Pei responsible for the glass pyramid at the Louvre in Paris), the glass-roofed building with several terraces promises to be sensational when complete in 2019. It will house a dedicated reception area for visitors as well as purpose-built fermenting rooms and cellars. Tastings take place in a neighbouring chateau while the renovations take place.

★**La Winery** WINE
(☎05 56 39 04 90; www.winery.fr; rte du Verdon, Rond-point des Vendangeurs, Arsac-en-Médoc; ⏲10.30am-7.30pm Tue-Sun, boutique 10am-8pm Jun-Sep, to 7.30pm Oct-May) Don't miss Philippe Raoux's vast glass-and-steel wine centre, which hosts concerts and contemporary-art exhibits alongside various fee-based tastings, including innovative tastings that determine your *signe œnologique* ('wine sign'), costing €25 (11am and 4pm daily; booking required). Its boutique stocks more than 1000 different wines.

Château Lanessan WINERY
(☎05 56 58 94 80; www.lanessan.com; Cussac-Fort-Medoc; adult/child €15/free; ⏲10am-noon & 2-6pm by advance reservation) With a little advance planning, one of the easiest chateaux to visit is Château Lanessan. Its daily hourlong guided tours take in the neoclassical chateau, its English-style gardens with magnificent 19th-century greenhouse, wine cellars, the stables built in 1880 in the shape of a horseshoe with marble feed troughs, the pine-panelled tack room and a horse museum with several 19th-century horse-drawn carriages. Tours end with wine tasting. Advance reservations, at least one day before, are obligatory.

Sleeping & Eating

★**Château Cordeillan-Bages** DESIGN HOTEL €€€
(☎05 56 59 24 24; www.cordeillanbages.com; rte des Châteaux, Bages; d from €180; ⏲Mar-Nov; ❄@📶🏊) 'A delight for hedonists' is how this luxurious 19th-century mansion describes itself – and understandably so. Right in the heart of Médoc wine country, this Relais & Châteaux hotel-restaurant is the ultimate splurge in viticulture and gastronomic luxury. Twenty-eight modern rooms with designer furniture gaze brazenly at vines, wine tasting is an essential part of every stay, and chef Julien Lefebvre is Michelin-starred.

> **ℹ JOIN A TOUR**
>
> Bordeaux tourist office (p659) organises dozens of different guided tours (in English) in the Médoc including a half-day tour (€42) to two Médoc châteaux with wine tastings; a more specialist half-day 'Classified Growths of Margaux' tour (€89) with tastings at a Cru Bourgeois estate and an 1855 Classified Growth chateau; and a thematic 'Art & Wine' tour (€79). There are dozens to choose from, all detailed on the tourist office website. Advance reservations are essential.

Le Pavillon de Margaux HOTEL €€
(☎05 57 88 77 54; www.le-pavillon-de-margaux.fr; 3 rue Georges Mandel, Margaux; d from €110; 📶) This welcoming, family-run address has 14 country-chic rooms styled according to famous local châteaux; several have their own little *salon* (sitting-room area) and they all come with a much-appreciated courtesy tray with kettle, tea and coffee. Enjoy breakfast with vineyard view and taste local wine over dinner in the hotel restaurant (*menus* from €22).

★**Café Lavinal** FRENCH €€
(☎05 57 75 00 09; www.jmcazes.com/en/cafe-lavinal; place Desquet, Bages; menus €28-38, mains €27-29; ⏲8am-2pm & 7.30-9pm; ❄📶) With Michelin-starred chef Julien Lefebvre from Château Cordeillan-Bages overseeing the menu and 120 wines on the *carte de vin*, a brilliant dining experience is guaranteed at this village bistro near Pauillac. Retro red banquet seating and a zinc bar evoke the 1930s and the menu mixes French classics (veal kidneys, *magret de canard*, fish stew) with burgers, salads and charcuterie platters.

St-Émilion

POP 1956

The medieval village of St-Émilion perches above vineyards renowned for producing full-bodied, deeply coloured red wines and is easily the most alluring of all the region's wine towns. Named after Émilion, a miracle-working Benedictine monk who lived in a cave here between AD 750 and 767, it soon became a stop on pilgrimage routes, and the village and its vineyards are now Unesco-listed. Today, despite masses of tourists descending on to the town, it's worth venturing 47km east from Bordeaux to experience St-Émilion's magic, particularly when the sun sets over the valley and the limestone buildings glow with halo-like golden hues.

Sights & Activities

A variety of hiking and cycling circuits loop through the greater World Heritage jurisdiction; the tourist office (p663) has maps and books detailing itineraries. The tourist office also rents bicycles (half-day/day €15/18) and runs some fantastic guided bike tours; in high season reserve your wheels in advance online.

★ **Maison du Vin de St-Émilion** WINE
(☑ 05 57 55 50 55; www.maisonduvinsaintemilion. com; place Pierre Meyrat; ⊙ 9.30am-6.30pm May-Oct, 9.30am-12.30pm & 2-6pm Nov-Apr) As much information centre and wine school as it is a shop, this excellent wine cellar is owned by the 250 winegrowers whose produce it sells at cellar-door prices. Begin with the small exhibition on the different St-Émilion appellations and test your nose by identifying 12 different aromas: honey, caramel or cocoa? Cherry, plum or blackcurrant? Various 40-minute tastings with sommelier commentary can be reserved in the lounge-like **Salon de Dégustation**, including blind tasting of three wines (€20) or a Grands Crus Classés tasting (€28).

Clocher de l'Église Monolithe TOWER
(Bell Tower; place des Créneaux; €2; ⊙ 9.30am-7.30pm Jul & Aug, shorter hours rest of year) For captivating views of the hilltop hamlet, borrow one of four keys from the tourist office to climb the 196 spiralling steps of this 68m-high bell tower, built to crown subterranean rock church **Église Monolithe** (only open to guided tours) during the 12th to 15th centuries. Village and vineyard views from the top of its Flamboyant Gothic spire are beautiful – on a clear day you can spot Bordeaux.

☞ **Tours**

Some of the town's most interesting historical sites – notably the hermit saint's famous cave **Grotte de l'Ermitage** and early 12th-century church **Église Monolithe**, spectacularly carved in the limestone rock – can only be visited with a guided walking tour run by the tourist office. Tours are themed and vary each season, but there's always a **St-Émilion Souterrain** (Underground St-Émilion; 1½ hours, adult/child €9/free) tour that

delves into the town's fascinating labyrinth of catacombs, a romantic by-night tour (two hours, €15), and several wine-related tours that include tastings and vineyard visits. For those who'd rather not walk, hop aboard an Asia-style **tuk-tuk** (☑ 06 40 83 62 60; www. tuktourevents.com; ⊙ 10am-6pm or 7pm Apr–mid-Nov) for a town or vineyard tour.

✗ **Eating**

St-Émilion is peppered with pricey but average places to eat, albeit with highly atmospheric summer terraces: ample options fill rue de la Porte Bouqueyre and place du Marché. *Lamproie à la Bordelaise* – a type of river eel, sometimes nicknamed 'vampires of the seas' – is the local dish to try, around since the Middle Ages.

★ **L'Envers du Decors** FRENCH €€
(☑ 06 57 74 48 31; www.envers-dudecor.com; 11 rue du Clocher; mains €24-34; ⊙ noon-2.30pm & 7-10.30pm) A few doors down from the tourist office, this wine bar with fire-engine-red facade is one of the finest places to eat – and inevitably drink – in this tasteful wine town. The kitchen cooks up fabulous local classics including *lamproie à la Bordelaise*, duck liver pan-fried in Sauternes and oysters by the dozen.

La Table de Plaisance GASTRONOMY €€€
(Hostellerie de Plaisance; ☑ 05 57 55 07 55; www. hostelleriedeplaisance.com; place du Clocher; lunch/dinner menus from €68/135; ⊙ noon-1.30pm Sat, 7.30-9.30pm Tue-Sat) Wine pairings are naturally in a league of their own at this exquisite Michelin double-starred restaurant, in the heart of the village in a luxurious, five-star hotel, Hostellerie de Plaisance. Tasting *menus* include a mystery eight-course extravaganza served to the whole table or more modest three- and five-course

DON'T MISS

LUNCH BY DESIGN

Knowing foodies adore this spectacular vineyard restaurant **La Terrasse Rouge** (☑ 05 57 24 47 05; www.laterrasserouge.com; 1 Château La Dominique; 3-course menu €39, mains €16-22; ⊙ noon-3pm & 7-10.30pm Jun-Sep, noon-3pm & 7-10.30pm Fri & Sat, noon-3pm Sun-Thu Oct-May) , born out of Jean Nouvel's designer revamp of Château La Dominique's wine cellars, 5km north of St-Émilion. Chefs work with small local producers to source the seasonal produce used in their creative cuisine. Oysters are fresh from Cap Ferret, caviar comes from Neuvic in the Dordogne, and the wine list is naturally extraordinary.

Dining on the uber-chic terrace overlooking a field of dark-red glass pebbles – one of several contemporary art installations on the wine-producing estate – and a sea of vine beyond is nothing short of sublime. Watch for the monthly cooking classes held here, built around lunch and *dégustation* (tasting) of two St-Émilion wines. Advance reservations essential.

feasts. Expect succulent treats like Breton lobster with artichokes, seaweed and aniseed or duck with truffles.

ℹ Information

Tourist Office (📞 05 57 55 28 28; www.saint-emilion-tourisme.com; place des Créneaux; ⏰ 9.30am-7.30pm Jul & Aug, shorter hours rest of year) Upon arriving in town, reserve a spot on one of the tourist office's excellent, themed *visites guidées* (guided tours). Staff are super-friendly and have plenty of maps and brochures on wine-tasting, in both the village and surrounding vineyards, as well as walking and cycling trails. It also rents bicycles (€15/18 per half day/day).

ℹ Getting There & Away

From Bordeaux, direct trains run daily to/from St-Émilion (€9.50, 35 minutes); in the middle of the day, SNCF buses replace the section of the journey between St-Émilion and Libourne.

St-Émilion train station is a scenic 1.7km walk from town. From April to October, call an electric **tuk-tuk** (p662) to shuttle you to/from town.

Arcachon

POP 10,700

A long-time oyster-harvesting area on the southern side of the tranquil, triangular Bassin d'Arcachon (Arcachon Bay), this seaside town lured bourgeois Bordelaise at the end of the 19th century. Its four little quarters are romantically named for each of the seasons, with villas that evoke the town's golden past amid a scattering of 1950s architecture.

Arcachon's generous swathe of golden-sand beach seethes with sun-seekers in summer, but there are plenty of equally sandy but less-crowded beaches, including the lovely Plage des Arbousiers, just a short bike ride away. Arcachon is the perfect launch pad for swashbuckling adventures on nearby Dune du Pilat, Europe's highest sand dune.

◎ Sights & Activities

Beautiful cycling paths wind along the waterfront and through scented pine forests to link Arcachon with the Dune du Pilat (8km south in Pyla-sur-Mer), Biscarosse (30km south) and east to Gujan Mestras (15km) and Le Teich (20km). In Arcachon get a free *carte des pistes cyclables* from the tourist office showing all the trails around the Bassin d'Arcachon. Rent wheels at **Locabeach** (📞 05 56 83 79 11; www.locabeach.com; 34 av du Général de Gaulle; 4hr/1 day €10/13; ⏰ 10am-6pm)

near the train station or **Dingo Vélos** (📞 05 56 83 44 09; www.dingovelos.com; 1 rue Grenier; 4hr/1 day €10/13) by the beachfront.

Plage d'Arcachon   BEACH
In the delightful Ville d'Été (Summer Quarter), Arcachon's deep sandy beach, Plage d'Arcachon, is flanked by two piers. Lively **Jetée Thiers** is at the western end, from where boats yo-yo across the water to Cap Ferret. The eastern pier, **Jetée d'Eyrac** has an old-fashioned carousel, a vintage Big Wheel and the town's turreted casino. The sheltered basin in which Arcachon sits means the water is always absolutely flat calm and ideal for families – a far cry from most Atlantic beaches.

Ville d'Hiver   AREA
On the tree-covered hillside south of the Ville d'Été, the century-old Ville d'Hiver (Winter Quarter) has more than 300 villas, many decorated with delicate wood tracery, ranging in style from neoGothic through to colonial. It's an easy stroll or a short ride up the (free) art-deco public lift in Parc Mauresque.

Union des Bateliers Arcachonnais   BOATING
(UBA; 📞 08 25 27 00 27; www.bateliers-arcachon.com; 75 bd de la Plage; ♿) Buy tickets for a variety of boat tours and themed excursions from the wooden huts next to the jetty from where boats set sail. Year-round it operates regular boats to Cap Ferret (return €14) and excursions to the Île des Oiseaux (1-¾ hours, €16 to €22).

🛏 Sleeping

⭐**Le B d'Arcachon**   DESIGN HOTEL €€
(📞 05 56 83 99 91; www.hotel-b-arcachon.com; 4 rue du Professeur Jolvet; d €110-225; ❄@🛜) A skip from the waterfront by Arcachon's Big Wheel, Le B can do no wrong. Its 56 spacious rooms have serene turquoise, emerald and cream colour palettes, quality fabrics and rain showers. Superior rooms have a balcony with pea-green faux grass and sea views. Late check-out (noon), excellent service, picnics to order (€8), bike rental and a delicious buffet breakfast (adult/child €15/10) too.

⭐**Hôtel Villa d'Hiver**   BOUTIQUE HOTEL €€
(📞 05 56 66 10 36; www.hotelvilledhiver.com; 20 av Victor Hugo; d from €140; ⏰ reception 8am-11pm; ❄@🛜🏊) In the heart of Arcachon's stylish 1860s Ville d'Hiver district, this 12-room boutique hotel seduces with a trio of garden-clad houses a 10-minute walk from the train station. Pricier, balcony-clad rooms on the 1st floor can glimpse the sea, and the

hotel's pop-up Club Plage Pereire is one of the hottest addresses in town.

✗ Eating

The bay's oysters (served raw and accompanied by the local small, flat sausages called *crepinettes*) appear on menus everywhere.

The beachfront promenade between Jetée Thiers and Jetée d'Eyrac is lined with restaurants and places offering pizza and crêpes, plus a couple of places serving seafood.

★ Chez Pierre   SEAFOOD €€
(☑ 05 56 22 52 94; www.cafe-plage-restaurant-pierre.fr; 1 bd Veyrier Montagnères; 2-/3-course menu €27/33, mains €25-35; ⊙ noon-3pm & 7-10.30pm) Stunning shellfish and seafood to suit most budgets, gracious service and an elegant terrace on the seafront with white tablecloths makes this contemporary address the top dining choice in Arcachon. Its fixed *menus* are excellent value, and sunset views – over a dozen deftly shucked oysters from the bay or a decadent shellfish platter fit for a king and queen – are impossibly romantic.

★ Club Plage Pereire   SEAFOOD €€
(☑ 05 57 16 59 13; www.clubplagepereire.com; 12 bd de la Mer; mains €20; ⊙ 10am-midnight Apr-Oct) Each year this pop-up beach hut on sandy Plage Pereire is built afresh, much to the joy of local foodies and bons vivants who flock here for tasty seafood cuisine, the buzzing beach vibe, romantic drinks on the sand and stunning sunset views. To get here from Jetée Thiers, follow the coast west along bd de la Plage and bd de l'Océan for 2km. Reservations essential.

Le Bikini   SEAFOOD €€
(☑ 05 56 83 91 36; 18 allée des Arbousiers, Plage des Arbousiers; mains €20-30; ⊙ 9am-midnight) With comfy, candystriped cushioned seating overlooking kitesurfers on sandy Plage des Arbousiers and an atmospheric bar wrapped around a tree, the Bikini buzzes year-round with energy, fun and locals. Its kitchen cooks up first-class shellfish and seafood, fresh from the ocean – the *barbu* (brill) *à la plancha* is superb. Between meals (reservations essential), it morphs into a hip cafe-bar and waterfront hangout.

To get here, follow the cycling path from Arcachon along the coast towards Dune du Pilat for 4km. Check its Facebook page for summertime soirées on the sand.

ⓘ Information

Tourist Office (☑ 05 57 52 97 97; www.arcachon.com; 21 ave du Général de Gaulle; ⊙ 9am-7pm Jul & Aug, 9am-6pm Mon-Sat, 10am-1pm & 2-5pm Sun May, Jun & Sep, shorter hours in winter) The town's helpful tourist office is positioned between the train station and the seafront.

ⓘ Getting There & Away

The **train station** (bd du Général Leclerc) is a five-minute walk from the seafront along av de la Gaulle. From here there are frequent trains to Bordeaux (€11.50, one hour). To continue to the Dune du Pilat, take local Baia bus line 1 (www.bus-baia.fr) from in front of Arcachon train station (€1, 30 minutes, at least hourly).

Year-round shuttle boats run by **Union des Bateliers Arcachonnais** (p663) sail daily across the water to/from Cap Ferret (adult/child return €14/5, 30 minutes, at least hourly).

Around Arcachon

Pyla-sur-Mer

POP 2127

It is for one reason alone that most people venture as far as pretty Pyla-sur-Mer, the seaside *quartier* of La Teste-de-Buche: to excitedly scamper up, and frolic on, the curvaceous sands of Europe's largest sand dune. Pyla-sur-Mer itself is a coastal patchwork of low-lying, colonial-style summer houses and towering pine trees with, surprisingly and wonderfully so, something of a speakeasy party scene.

◉ Sights

★ Dune du Pilat   NATURAL FEATURE
This colossal sand dune (sometimes referred to as the Dune de Pyla because of its location 4km from the small seaside resort town of Pyla-sur-Mer), 8km south of Arcachon, stretches from the mouth of the Bassin d'Arcachon southwards for 2.7km. Already Europe's largest, the dune is growing eastwards 1.5m a year – it has swallowed trees, a road junction and even a hotel, so local lore claims. The view from the top – approximately 115m above sea level – is magnificent.

To the west you see the sandy shoals at the mouth of the **Bassin d'Arcachon**, including Cap Ferret and the **Banc d'Arguin** bird reserve, where up to 6000 couples of Sandwich terns nest each spring. Dense dark-green forests of maritime pines, oaks, ferns and strawberry trees (whose wood is traditionally used to build oyster-farmer shacks) stretch from the base of the dune eastwards almost as far as the eye can see.

Between Easter and early to mid-November, a wooden staircase – between 150 and 160 steps depending on the year – is erected on one side of the dune to help tourists scramble to its sandy top. Otherwise, clamber exhaustedly up the steep sand mountain – and exercise your inner child by flying down at an exhilarating sprint if you dare. Bare foot is preferable, although the sand can be perishingly cold in winter and as hot as burning coals in the height of summer.

Be warned that it can be desperately windy atop the dune: swirling, whiplashing sand can be particularly unpleasant for younger children. Take care swimming in this area: powerful currents swirl out to sea from deceptively tranquil little bays.

✖ Eating & Drinking

Café Ha(a)ïtza   FRENCH €€
(☑ 05 56 54 02 22; http://haaitza.com; 312 bd de l'Océan; 2-/3-course menu €29/34; ☉ noon-2.30pm & 7-10.30pm winter, to midnight Jul & Aug; ☎) Be it a languid summer lunch on a sun-drenched wooden deck or a snug winter feast beneath steel beams and shelves of books, Café Ha(a)ïtza hits the sweet spot every time. Begin with oysters or tuna tartare, perhaps, followed by meat grilled over a wood fire. Waiters scurry around in fashionable white chinos and Stan Smiths, and straw trilby hats double as dapper lampshades.

In summer the entire place rocks until well after midnight; the cocktail bar serves drinks until 1am.

★ La Co(o)rniche   SEAFOOD €€€
(☑ 05 56 22 72 11; www.lacoorniche-pyla.com; 46 av Louis Gaume; 2-/3-course lunch menu €58/63, seafood platters €40-85) There's no more glamorous address on the Atlantic Coast than this 1930s hunting lodge, reinvented by French designer Philippe Starck. Perfectly placed for a meal or tapas-fuelled drink after a sandy walk on Dune du Pilat, this sensational seaside spot is beach chic at its best. Feasting here on incredible views of the dune and the chef's modern French cuisine is unforgettable.

Snag a table in the infinity pool or, should you prefer a cheaper or lighter dine, flop with a cocktail and seafood tapas in a cushioned canopy in the bar. Should you fall madly in love with the place and find yourself unable to leave, check yourself in to the designer five-star hotel (doubles from €275).

DANCE UNTIL DAWN

Also known as Chez Zézette or Les Goélands by party-loving locals, bar-club hybrid **Le Bal à Papa** (☑ 05 56 22 73 70; www.lebalapapa.fr; 242 bd de l'Océan; ☉ 10pm-2am Thu-Sun) is *the* spot to drink cocktails and dance away summer nights to a wicked mix of 1980s hits until dawn. DJ Christophe Faucampre – aka Papa – and wife Sabrina are the dynamic duo behind this memorable party spot.

ⓘ Information

Espace Accueil (☑ 05 56 22 12 85; www.ladunedupilat.com; Dune du Pilat; ☉ 9.30am-5pm Apr-Oct) Before hiking up the dune, gather information on the flora, fauna and fragility of this protected natural site at the friendly tourist office. It organises free guided dune walks, distributes cycling maps and has information on the entire Bassin d'Arcachon area.

ⓘ Getting There & Away

Cycling is the most invigorating way to get to/from the dune, although there is one hill on the final approach; a beautiful bike path cruises along the waterfront and through scented pine forests to link Arcachon with the Dune du Pilat (8km). Alternatively, local bus line 1 links Arcachon train station with the Dune du Pilat (€1).

Cap Ferret

POP 8087

Hidden within a canopy of pine trees at the tip of the Cap Ferret peninsula, the tiny and deliciously oyster-rich village of Cap Ferret spans a mere 2km between the tranquil bay and the crashing Atlantic waves. Pedalling between oyster shacks and out to the lighthouse on the cape's eastern shore is a deliciously old-fashioned highlight of any visit here.

◉ Sights & Activities

Phare du Cap Ferret   LIGHTHOUSE
(☑ 05 57 70 33 30; adult/child €6/4; ☉ 10am-7.30pm Jul & Aug, 10am-12.30pm & 2-6.30pm Apr-Jun & Sep, 2-5pm Wed-Sun Oct-Mar) Scale 258 steps inside the cape's 53m-tall, red-and-white lighthouse for a stunning view of Cap Ferret, the Bassin d'Arcachon and the stunning Dune du Pilat. Interactive exhibits inside the lighthouse complement the climb. In the surrounding park, a small exhibition inside the **Blockhaus du Parc du Phare** – a concrete bunker with 2m-thick walls built by occupying Germans

in 1940 – explains how the original lighthouse was destroyed by dynamite in 1944. The current lighthouse was built in 1947.

L'École Surf Center
SURFING

(☎05 56 60 61 05; www.surf-center.fr; 22 ave des Goëlands; lessons from €39; ☀Easter-Sep) This surfing school rents out surfboards and runs surfing and bodyboarding lessons on Plage de l'Horizon, a sandy beach on the cape's western coast, near La Pointe du Cap Ferret (the southernmost tip of the cape).

🛏 Sleeping & Eating

Cap Ferret has several campgrounds, many listed on www.bassin-arcachon.com. Otherwise, accommodation is limited – most visitors catch the ferry here from Arcachon.

La Maison du Bassin
BOUTIQUE HOTEL €€

(☎05 56 60 60 63; www.lamaisondubassin.com; 5 rue des Pionniers; s €130-250, d €155-290; ☀closed Jan; @🛜) Cap Ferret's boutique choice mixes muslin-canopied sleigh beds with romantic four-posters, vintage model sail boats, white linens and wooden floors to create a stylish beach-chic ambiance. Breakfast (€15) is served beneath trees in summer on a greenery-draped terrace, and the hotel has a restaurant (*menus* €28 and €42) too. Some rooms are in a second building. Count no more than five minutes to the sand.

★La Canfouine au Canon
SEAFOOD €

(☎06 64 33 23 85; 75 rue Sainte-Catherine, Le Canon; dozen oysters €12-14; ☀noon-3pm & 6-9pm Apr-Sep, noon-3pm Sat & Sun Oct-Dec & Mar) Expect local products the whole way at La Canfouine ('hut' in local dialect), an upmarket 'hut' on the seashore in the fishing village of Le Canon, about 7km north of Cap Ferret along cycling trails. Order oysters, whelks and nail-sized prawns with a Bordeaux rosé or Graves white, and kick back on black sofa seating with world-class views of oyster beds and the Dune du Pilat beyond. Heaven.

★Hôtel de la Plage
FRENCH €€

(☎05 56 60 50 15; www.hoteldelaplage-cap-ferret. fr; 1 av de l'Herbe; dozen oysters €22, mains €14-25; ☀noon-3pm & 7-11pm Tue-Fri, noon-11pm Sat & Sun) Built in the 1860s to feed and accommodate the first oyster farmers who came to settle on Cap Ferret, this attractive wooden mansion oozes historic charm and story. Bordelais restaurateur Nicolas Lascombes is the creative nous behind the hipster restaurant today, known far and wide for its outstanding oyster bar, seafood dishes, nod to tradition and buzzing beach vibe.

🛈 Information

Tourist Office (☎05 56 03 94 49; www. lege-capferret.com; 1 ave du Général de Gaulle, Claouey; ☀9am-12.30pm & 2-6pm Mon-Fri, 9am-12.30pm Sat) Organises a variety of guided tours in English and French, including visits to local oyster farms. Unfortunately it's 12.5km north of the Bélisaire boat jetty, rendering it most useful to visiting motorists.

🛈 Getting There & Away

Cap Ferret is a scenic drive around Bassin d'Arcachon. Alternatively, drive here directly from Bordeaux (72km) along the D106.

Boats run by **Les Bateliers Arcachonnais** (www.bateliers-arcachon.com; Jetée Bélisaire) sail to Cap Ferret's Jetée Bélisaire year-round from Arcachon (adult/child €7/5, 30 minutes, at least hourly). In summer, seasonal boats link Cap Ferret with the Dune du Pilat (adult/child return €26/18, 45 minutes, three daily). Buy e-tickets online up to 15 minutes before departure.

🛈 Getting Around

The easiest and most invigorating way to get around Cap Ferret's seafaring quarters is by bicycle; **Locabeach** (☎05 56 60 49 46; www. locabeach.com; Jetée Bélisaire; 4hr/1 day €10/13; ☀9.45am-6pm Apr–mid-Nov), by the Bélisaire boat jetty, rents wheels.

French Basque Country

POP 288,900

Best Places to Eat

➡ Table de Pottoka (p670)

➡ Ithurria (p688)

➡ Chez Arrambide (p691)

➡ Le Kaiku (p687)

➡ Xaya (p686)

Best Places to Stay

➡ Hôtel du Palais (p678)

➡ Hôtel les Basses Pyrénées (p669)

➡ Baya Hôtel & Spa (p674)

➡ Hôtel de Silhouette (p678)

➡ Hôtel Balea (p683)

➡ Hôtel Txoko (p686)

Why Go?

Edged by the brilliant blue Bay of Biscay and the craggy foothills of the Pyrenees, the Pays Basque (Basque Country) feels one step removed from the rest of France – which is hardly surprising, since it's been an independent nation for much of its history and has more in common with the nearby Basque regions of Spain. Proud, independent and fiery, the people of the Basque Country are fiercely protective of their history and culture, whether it's their passion for *pelota* or their fondness for their spicy chilli pepper, *le piment d'Espelette*. It's a fascinating place.

The region's biggest town is the glitzy beach resort of Biarritz, famous for its sweeping oceanfront and thriving surf scene. Nearby Bayonne is considered the true heart of the Basque Country, and hosts a major Basque festival every July. Along the coast you'll find surf towns and fishing ports, while sleepy hilltop villages nestle among the hills towards the Spanish border.

When to Go
Bayonne

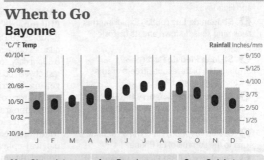

May Chocolate time in Bayonne. Empty beaches and spring flowers in the mountains.

Aug Beaches are packed, and the Fêtes de Bayonne is in full swing.

Sep–Oct Autumnal colours are glorious in the hills, and the surf is as good as it gets.

French Basque Country Highlights

❶ Biarritz (p673) Joining surfers and sunbathers on the famous seafront.

❷ Bayonne (p673) Sampling at one of Bayonne's celebrated chocolate shops.

❸ Sentier du Littoral (p683) Hiking along the wild coast path between Bidart and Hendaye.

❹ St-Jean de Luz (p683) Exploring this charming seaside town and its historic church.

❺ St-Jean Pied de Port (p689) Strolling the picturesque streets of this ancient pilgrimage town.

❻ St-Étienne de Baïgorry (p691) Hiking the hills near this quaint hamlet in a verdant valley.

❼ La Rhune (p688) Catching an antique train to the summit of La Rhune.

❽ Espelette (p688) Picking up some of the Basque Country's famous powdered pimiento pepper.

❾ Les Landes (p674) Seeking out the broad beaches along the coast of Les Landes.

Bayonne

POP 50,000

Stretching along the banks of the Rivers Adour and Nive, the waterside city of Bayonne is one of the prettiest in southwest France, and the capital of the French Basque Country. It's been a strategic stronghold since medieval times, and the old ramparts are still visible around the outskirts of the old town, but it's Bayonne's pretty half-timbered buildings, riverside restaurants and shady cobbled streets that make it worthy of exploration.

The Rivers Adour and Nive split central Bayonne into three: St-Esprit, the area north of the Adour; Grand Bayonne, the oldest and most attractive part of the city, on the western bank of the Nive; and the very Basque quarter of Petit Bayonne to the east.

To the west, Bayonne meets the suburban sprawl of Anglet (famed for its beaches) and the glamorous seaside resort of Biarritz; collectively they're often known as BAB.

◉ Sights

★Cathédrale Ste-Marie CATHEDRAL
(place Louis Pasteur; ⊙ 10-11.45am & 3-6.15pm Mon-Sat, 3.30-6.15pm Sun, cloister 9am-12.30pm & 2-6pm daily) The twin towers of Bayonne's Gothic cathedral soar above the city. Construction began in the 13th century, and was completed in 1451. Above the north aisle are three lovely stained-glass windows; the oldest, in the Chapelle St-Jérôme, dates from 1531. There are also several beautifully restored frescoes. The entrance to the stately 13th-century **cloister** (place Louis Pasteur; ⊙ 9am-12.30pm & 2-6pm) is on place Louis Pasteur.

★Musée Basque et de l'Histoire de Bayonne MUSEUM
(☑ 05 59 59 08 98; www.musee-basque.com; 37 quai des Corsaires; adult/child €7.50/free; ⊙ 10am-6.30pm daily, to 8.30pm Thu Jul & Aug, closed Mon rest of year, open to 6pm Oct-Mar) If you're still getting to grips with the complex culture and history of the Basque region, this excellent ethnographic museum is a great place to start. It's crammed with artefacts, from traditional costumes, artwork and archaeological ephemera to a reconstruction of a typical Basque *etxe* (home). Labelling is in French, Spanish and Basque only – but English information sheets are available.

In July and August free 'nocturnal' visits are possible on Thursday evenings at 8.30pm.

Rue des Faures
STREET

This pretty street was once home to the city's bayonet-making blacksmiths, but it's now reinvented itself as the artisan quarter. It's a lovely place to browse, with galleries, bookshops, a vintage-sewing-machine restorer, a luthier (stringed instrument builder or repairer), a linen shop and one of the last remaining *makhila* makers – the wooden staffs traditionally carried by Basque shepherds.

🛏 Sleeping

Hôtel Côte Basque
HOTEL €

(📞 05 59 55 10 21; www.hotel-cotebasque.fr; 2 rue Maubec; d/tr/f from €76/88/97; ❄ 🛜) A real Bayonne bargain – a historic hotel just steps from the station, set around an enclosed courtyard that would once have divided the nearby houses. There's a clanky old lift that rattles up between the floors, leading to simple but comfy rooms, many of which have a view towards the River Nive and the cathedral's spires.

Hôtel des Arceaux
BOUTIQUE HOTEL €

(📞 05 59 59 15 53; 26 rue Port Neuf; d from €60, without bathroom from €50; 🛜) On the pretty walking street of Port Neuf, this simple hotel offers colourful, no-frills rooms. Some rooms share bathrooms and some are suited to families – they're all different, so ask to see a few. It's a jumble of old furniture, faded prints and chaises longues; there's even a vintage rocking horse in the lounge. Climb to the 1st floor for reception.

★ Hôtel les Basses Pyrénées
BOUTIQUE HOTEL €€

(📞 05 59 25 70 88; www.hotel-bassespyrenees-bayonne.com; 13 rue Tour de Sault; d/f from €90/160; ⊙ closed mid-Feb–early Mar; ❄ @ 🛜) Reception at this chic hotel is tucked into a tower that is part of the town's ramparts. Rooms are blend of high-end antique-styled furnishings and comfy patterned linens. The superb restaurant (open noon to 2.30pm and 7.30pm to 10pm) faces onto place des Victoires, which allows al fresco dining in summer. It's essential to book ahead.

Péniche Djébelle
HOUSEBOAT €€

(📞 05 59 25 77 18; www.djebelle.com; face au 17 Quai de Lesseps; d incl breakfast €150; ⊙ closed Oct-Apr; 🛜) For something completely different, a stay on this *péniche* (houseboat) definitely fits the bill. There are just two rooms, each with roughly half the boat: one

has a Moroccan theme and the other, which has the boat's steering wheel built into the bathroom, is themed after tropical islands. A lavish breakfast is included.

🍴 Eating

Bayonne has some superb places to eat, and costs are generally much lower than in nearby Biarritz.

The **covered market** (Covered Market; quai Commandant Roquebert; ⊙ 7am-1pm Mon-Fri, 6am-1.30pm Sat, 8am-1.30pm Sun) sits on the west bank of the Nive riverfront. There are a number of tempting food shops and delicatessens along rue Port Neuf and rue d'Espagne.

Bistrot Itsaski
BASQUE €

(📞 05 59 46 13 96; www.lebistrotitsaski.com; 43 quai Amiral Jauréguiberry; mains €11-22; ⊙ noon-2pm & 7-9.30pm Thu-Mon) This convivial stone-walled dining room is managed ably by warm proprietors who circulate making sure all guests are happy. And happy they are with the generous portions of light, creative Basque fare with an emphasis on seafood, ham and lamb.

Xurasko
TAPAS €

(📞 05 59 59 21 77; 16 rue Poissonnerie; tapas from €2.50; ⊙ noon-11pm) Rough and ready, and all the better for it, this atmospheric corner bar near the market is guaranteed to be packed with a mix of after-dinner drinkers, market workers and tourists. Pull up a stool by the zinc bar or grab a table on the street and tuck into tapas plates accompanied by a glass of bubbly Txakoli wine or a Bob's beer.

Bakera
BASQUE €

(📞 05 59 25 51 68; 15 rue des Tonneliers; mains €15-18; ⊙ 10am-3pm & 4-10pm Tue-Sat) It might not look like much from the outside, but this is a great place to try classic bistro dishes shot through with some southwestern flavours. The food is big, bold and very Basque.

ⓘ WATCH THIS SPACE!

Bayonne's venerable fine-arts museum **Musée Bonnat-Helleu** (📞 05 59 46 63 60; 5 rue Jacques Laffitte) is undergoing an extensive expansion, which will give it more spacious, modern galleries – veritably doubling its size. It is slated to reopen in mid- to late 2019.

Bayonne

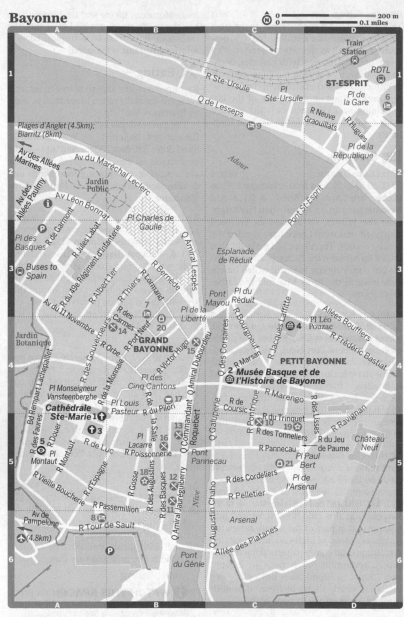

FRENCH BASQUE COUNTRY BAYONNE

Mokofin TEAHOUSE **€**
(☎05 59 59 04 02; www.mokofin.com; 27 rue
Thiers; snacks from €3; ⊗8.30am-7.45pm Tue-Sat,
6.30am-1pm Sun) Beautifully conceived and
created sweets, canapés and finger foods
by Joëlle and Maitena Erguy make this a
special stop for a light snack or pick-me-up,
along with a rich coffee and tea selection.

★ **Table de Pottoka** GASTRONOMY **€€**
(☎05 59 46 14 94; www.pottoka.fr; 21 quai Amiral
Dubourdieu; menu lunch/dinner €21/39, à la carte

Bayonne

mains €22; ⊙ noon-2pm & 7-10pm Tue-Sat) Run by renowned chef Sebastien Gravé (who also runs a place in Paris), this is Bayonne's top spot. It's committed to big Basque flavours, but explores them in all kinds of innovative ways. Inside, things are sleek and minimal, with plain wooden tables and pop-art prints on the walls, and there are dreamy river views through the plate-glass windows.

Ibaia   TAPAS €€
(45 quai Amiral Jauréguiberry; mains from €15; ⊙ noon-2pm & 7-10pm Tue-Sat) This is the place to come to join the Bayonnais for authentic tapas – there's a huge selection, from chorizo sausage to spicy prawns, and loads of local wines by the glass. The riverfront patio is a super spot to linger on hot summer days.

🍸 Drinking & Nightlife

Petit Bayonne is awash with pubs and bars (all generally open from noon to 2am Monday to Saturday), especially along rue Pannecau, rue des Cordeliers and quai Galuperie.

Bar François   CAFE
(🗹 05 59 59 10 38; 14 rue Guilhamin; ⊙ 7am-11pm) As French as a string of onions, this is the classic pavement cafe: tables strewn over the cobbles, waiters rushed off their feet, and more wines by the glass than you could drink in a week's worth of trying. Next to the covered market, this is *the* place to watch town life roll by.

☆ Entertainment

Upcoming cultural events are listed in *À l'Affiche* and the quarterly *Les Saisons de la Culture,* both available free at the tourist office. At 9.30pm every Thursday in July and August, there's free traditional **Basque music** (⊙ 9.30pm) ⸢FREE⸣ in place Charles de Gaulle.

Trinquet St-André   SPECTATOR SPORT
(🗹 05 59 59 18 69; www.ffpb.net; rue des Tonneliers; adult/child €10/2; ⊙ matches 4pm Thu Oct-Jun) Hidden down a backstreet, this atmospheric *trinquet* (indoor court) stages *main nue pelota* (bare-hand *pelota*) matches under an impressive timber-framed roof. It also has a lively bistro and bar for post-match discussion.

La Luna Negra Music   LIVE MUSIC
(🗹 05 59 25 78 05; www.lunanegra.fr; 7 rue des Augustins; ⊙ 7pm-2am Wed-Sat) Down an alley in the old town, this venerable latenight cabaret venue serves up a mixed program of comedy, world music, salsa and live jazz.

🛍 Shopping

Bayonne is famous for two premium products – handmade chocolates, which have been made here for centuries, and the cured ham known as *jambon de Bayonne.* One other local souvenir that you probably won't be able to get through customs is a *baïonnette* (bayonet), developed here in 1640 on rue des Faures (Blacksmiths St).

FÊTES DE BAYONNE

Beginning on either the first Wednesday in August or occasionally the last in July, the **Fêtes de Bayonne** (www.fetes.bayonne.fr; ☉ early Aug or late Jul) attracts thousands of people from across France and Spain for a five-day orgy of drinking, dancing, processions, fireworks and bulls. In many ways it's like a less commercialised version of the famous San Fermín festival in Pamplona (Spain) and, just like in Pamplona, Bayonne also holds bull running. However, here the bulls are actually cows – though they still have horns and they still hurt when they mow you down – and they don't run down the streets, but are instead released on the crowd in front of the Château Neuf.

During the *fête*, bullfights also take place during which bulls are maimed or killed. If you're thinking of attending a bullfight, it's important to understand what you'll witness. The bull's back and neck are repeatedly pierced by the lances, resulting in quite a lot of blood, as well as considerable pain and distress for the animal. The bull gradually becomes weakened through blood loss before the *torero* delivers the final sword thrust. If done properly, the bull dies instantly from this final thrust, albeit after bleeding for some time from its other wounds. If the coup de grâce is not delivered well, the animal dies a slow death. When this happens, the scene can be extremely disturbing.

One of the biggest highlights of the *fête* is the opening ceremony, when huge crowds gather in front of the town hall at 10pm on the Wednesday night for an impressively noisy firework display and the arrival of a 'lion' (the town's mascot).

While the nocturnal activities might be a bit much for children, the daytime processions, marching bands, organised children's picnics and events are tailor-made for the delight of little ones. Thursday daytime has the most child-friendly activities.

If you're planning on attending the *fête*, you'll need to book at least six to eight months in advance for hotel accommodation anywhere in the vicinity of Bayonne. A number of temporary campgrounds (€72 for six days) are erected in and around Bayonne to ease the pressure; otherwise you can just do what most people do and sleep in the back of a car (camping outside one of the campgrounds is forbidden).

Finally, unless you want to stand out like a sore thumb, don't forget to dress all in white with a red sash and neck-scarf.

Pierre Ibaïalde FOOD
(☎ 05 59 25 65 30; www.pierre-ibaialde.com; 41 rue des Cordeliers; ☉ 9am-12.30pm & 2-6pm Mon-Sat, 10am-6.30pm daily Jul & Aug) This is the address to buy Bayonne's celebrated *jambon* – traditionally served wafer thin, and claimed by locals to be every bit as good as *pata negra* or prosciutto. There are afternoon tours (in French) of the shop and drying room in summer if you really want to understand what makes the ham special.

❶ Information

Tourist Office (☎ 05 59 46 09 00, 08 20 42 64 64; www.bayonne-tourisme.com; place des Basques; ☉ 9am-7pm Mon-Sat, 10am-1pm Sun Jul & Aug, 9am-6.30pm Mon-Fri, 10am-1pm & 2-6pm Sat Mar-Jun, Sep & Oct, shorter hr rest of yr) Efficient office providing stacks of informative brochures and bike rental, plus guided city tours.

❶ Getting There & Away

AIR

Aéroport Biarritz Pays Basque (BIQ; ☎ 05 59 43 83 83; www.biarritz.aeroport.fr) is 5km southwest of central Bayonne and 3km southeast of the centre of Biarritz. It's served by low-cost carriers including EasyJet, Flybe and Ryanair, as well as Air France, British Airways, SAS, Voltea and others, with daily domestic flights and flights to the UK and most other areas of Europe.

BUS

Chronoplus (www.chronoplus.eu) buses link Bayonne, Biarritz and Anglet. Services run several times an hour; a single ticket costs €1, while a 24-hour pass is €2. Bus A2 runs between Bayonne and Biarritz, stopping at the Hôtels de Ville and train stations in both towns.

For longer journeys, Transports 64 (www.transports64.fr) buses leave from **place des Basques** for the Spanish border. The 816 travels to St-Jean de Luz (€2, 40 minutes, at least hourly Monday to Saturday, three daily on

Sunday) and Hendaye (€2, one hour). Summer beach traffic can double journey times.

Transportes Pesa (www.pesa.net) buses leave place des Basques twice a day Monday to Saturday for Bilbao (€20.50) in Spain, calling at Biarritz, St-Jean de Luz, Irún and San Sebastián (€8.05).

Conda (www.conda.es) buses travel between Aéroport Biarritz Pays Basque, San Sebastian (€7, one hour, three daily, four on weekends) and Pamplona (€15, three to four hours, three to four daily).

Ouibus (www.ouibus.com) also runs long-distance buses between Bordeaux and San Sebastian, stopping at Bayonne, Biarritz and St-Jean de Luz en route. There are four daily Monday to Saturday and two or three on Sunday. The one-way fare from Bayonne is €14 to €19.

Flixbus (www.flixbus.com) services run to Bilbao from Toulouse (6½ hours, four daily) and Bordeaux (6¾ hours, three daily) via Bayonne, Biarritz, St-Jean de Luz and San Sebastián. Fares start from €5 for Bayonne to San Sebastián.

RDTL (www.rdtl.fr) runs services northwards into Les Landes, including Capbreton/Hossegor (€2, 40 minutes, six daily Monday to Saturday, four on Sunday).

TRAIN

TGVs run between Bayonne and Paris Gare Montparnasse (€66 to €109, four hours, five daily). Other destinations include Bordeaux and Toulouse.

For travel to Biarritz, you're better off catching a bus, as Biarritz' TGV station at La Négresse is way out of town. For destinations further south, trains run at least hourly, including services to St-Jean de Luz (€5.30, 25 minutes) and Hendaye (€7.90, 42 minutes), and twice daily to Irún (€6.50, 1¼ hours).

There are also four trains daily to St-Jean Pied de Port (€10.10, 1½ hours).

ⓘ Getting Around

TO/FROM THE AIRPORT

Chronoplus bus 14 links Bayonne with the airport (€1, buses depart roughly hourly). A taxi from the town centre costs around €25.

Bicycle

Bayonne's tourist office lends out bikes for free (not overnight); you must leave ID as a deposit.

Bus

Three free *navettes* (shuttle buses; www.chrono plus.eu) loop around the heart of town from 7.30am to 7.30pm Monday to Saturday.

Biarritz

POP 25,500

Half ritzy coastal resort, half summer surfers' hang-out, the seaside resort of Biarritz has been a favourite beach getaway since Napoléon III and his Spanish-born wife Eugénie arrived during the mid-19th century. Its elegant villas and heritage-listed residences, which glitter with belle époque and art deco details, have retained their glamour. Unfortunately the 20th century wasn't quite so kind, and the seafront is blessed with its fair share of concrete carbuncles that have done little to enhance

---

DON'T MISS

BAYONNE CHOCOLATE

Bayonne's long association with chocolate stems from a rather unlikely source – the Spanish Inquisition. Fleeing persecution, Jewish chocolate-makers fled their Spanish homeland, settling in Bayonne's St-Esprit neighbourhood, establishing the town's reputation for producing some of the finest chocolate anywhere in France. By 1870, Bayonne boasted 130 chocolatiers, more than in all of Switzerland – although now only around a dozen remain. It even hosts its own chocolate-themed weekend in May, **Les Journées du Chocolat**.

The town's premium makers are **Daranatz** (☑ 05 59 59 03 05; www.chocolat-bayonne-daranatz.fr; 15 rue Port Neuf; ☺ 9.15am-7pm, reduced hours Sep-May) and **Cazenave** (☑ 05 59 59 03 16; www.chocolats-bayonne-cazenave.fr; 19 rue Port Neuf; ☺ 9.15am-noon & 2-7pm Tue-Sat), who are next door to each other on rue Port Neuf, but there are plenty more to try. You can see chocolate being made (Monday to Friday till 4pm; last tour 1½ hours before closing) during a tour of **L'Atelier du Chocolat** (☑ 05 59 55 00 15; www.atelierduchocolat.fr; 1 allée de Gibéléou; adult/child €6/3; ☺ 10am-6.30pm Mon-Sat Jul & Aug, 10am-12.30pm & 2-6pm Sep-Jun), which includes a historical overview of chocolate in Bayonne and, of course, the chance to taste the goods. It also has a shop on rue Port Neuf.

LES LANDES

The *département* of Les Landes, just north of Bayonne and Anglet, is a vast tract of farmed pine forests, lakes and seaside towns. It's great for hiking and biking, but for most people, the reason to visit is its seemingly never-ending beaches. From the mouth of the Ardour at Anglet to the mouth of the Gironde stretches a ribbon of shimmering golden sand, backed by dunes and basking under a deep blue sky.

The combination of sand and waves has made this the heartland of French surfing. The action centres on the small beach towns of **Capbreton** and **Hossegor**, where there are numerous surf schools offering lessons for both novice and experienced riders. Meanwhile the tiny village of **Moliets** may have the best beach of all, with powder-soft sand.

The Landes area is very popular with French holidaymakers in summer, but the accommodation is a bit underwhelming – pricey hotels, busy camp grounds and rough-and-ready surf camps. Contact the tourist offices in **Hossegor** (☑05 58 41 79 00; www.hossegor.fr; 166 av de la Gare; ☉9am-7pm Mon-Sat, 10am-1pm & 4-7pm Sun Jul & Aug, reduced hr rest of yr; ☎) or **Capbreton** (☑05 58 72 12 11; www.capbreton-tourisme.com; av du Président Pompidou; ☉9am-7pm Jul & Aug, reduced hr rest of yr) for details.

Baya Hôtel & Spa (☑05 58 41 80 00; www.bayahotel.com; 85 av Maréchal de Lattre de Tassigny, Capbreton; d from €250) is one of the few hotels smack on the oceanfront in the Landes region. From the ocean-facing rooms, you'll practically feel the waves crash into one of the coast's top surf spots. Rooms are modern, expansive and super-comfortable, and the restaurant serves creative seasonal menus, which means you needn't leave the grounds! Prices plummet in low season.

Seafood bistros and bars can be found in most of the coastal towns, plus a couple of pleasant country restaurants further inland. The top spot to dine is **Jean des Sables** (☑05 58 72 29 82; www.jeandessables.com; 121 bd de la Dune, Hossegor; lunch/dinner menus from €33/50; ☉noon-2pm & 7.30-10pm, closed for lunch Mon, Wed & Fri Jul & Aug, closed Mon & Tue mid-Sep–Jun), right on the beach in Hossegor. Its terrace with views offers sumptuously created fare featuring local seafood – if you want to splash out on a long lunch or a romantic date, you can't go wrong.

From Bayonne's place des Basques, **RDTL** (www.rdtl.fr) bus 7 goes to Capbreton/Hossegor (€2, 40 minutes, five or six Monday to Saturday) and other areas of Les Landes.

its aesthetic appeal. Nevertheless, Biarritz remains one of the southwest's seaside gems and throngs with visitors in summer.

◉ Sights

From art deco mansions to Russian Orthodox churches and 1970s tower-block disasters, Biarritz has a fantastic mish-mash of architectural styles.

To avoid queues, book tickets for most of Biarritz's sights and attractions via the tourist office (p682) website.

Musée de la Mer AQUARIUM
(☑05 59 22 75 40; www.museedelamer.com; esplanade de la Vierge; adult/child €14.90/10.50; joint ticket with Cité de l'Océan €22.50/10.50; ☉9.30am-midnight Jul & Aug, to 8pm Apr, Jun, Sep & Oct, shorter hours rest of year) Housed in a wonderful art deco building near the old port, Biarritz' Musée de la Mer is seething with underwater life from the Bay of Biscay and beyond, including huge aquariums of sharks, playful grey seals and tropical reef fish, as well as exhibits exploring Biarritz' whaling past. In high season it's possible to have the place almost to yourself by visiting late at night.

Cité de l'Océan MUSEUM
(☑05 59 22 75 40; www.citedelocean.com; 1 av de la Plage; adult/child €12.50/8.50, joint ticket with Musée de la Mer €22.50/10.50, discount for large families; ☉10am-10pm Jul & Aug, to 7pm Easter, Apr-Jun, Sep & Oct, shorter hours rest of year) Biarritz' splashiest sea-themed attraction is part museum, part theme park and part educational centre. It takes a fun approach to learning about the sea in all its forms – attractions range from a chance to explore a marine lab to a simulated dive into the depths in a bathysphere. It's good fun, but probably of greater interest to older kids.

In July and August a free *navette* (shuttle bus) runs between Musée de la Mer and the Cité de l'Océan. Tickets can be booked online.

Chapelle Impériale
CHURCH

(☑ 05 59 22 37 10; 15 rue des 100 Gardes; €3; ☉ 2-6pm Thu & Sat Jun-Sep, 2-5pm or 6pm Thu & Sat Oct-Dec & Mar-May) Built in 1864 on the instructions of Empress Eugénie, this glitzy church mixes Byzantine and Moorish styles, and the plaza in front has a superb view of the Grande Plage. Buy tickets on the tourist office website to avoid queues.

Rocher de la Vierge
VIEWPOINT

(Rock of the Virgin) If the swell's big, you might get a drenching as you cross the toy-town-like footbridge (closed in high wind) at the end of Pointe Atalaye to Rocher de la Vierge, named after its white statue of the Virgin and child. Views from this impressive outcrop extend to the mountains of the Spanish Basque Country.

Phare de Biarritz
LIGHTHOUSE

(☑ 05 59 22 37 10; esplanade du Phare Biarritz; adult/child €2.50/2; ☉ 9.30am-12.30pm & 2-6pm Mon-Sat) Climbing the 258 twisting steps inside the 73m-high Phare de Biarritz, the town's 1834 lighthouse, rewards you with sweeping views of the Basque coast. Tickets available at the French-language version of www.anglet-tourisme.com.

Musée d'Art Asiatica
MUSEUM

(☑ 05 59 22 78 79; www.museeasiatica.com; 1 rue Guy Petit; adult/child €10/2; ☉ 10.30am-6.30pm Mon-Fri, 2-7pm Sat & Sun Jul, Aug & during French school holidays, shorter hr rest of yr) Out on the edge of town is this unexpected treasure trove of ancient Indian, Chinese and Tibetan statues, monuments and temple artwork. The layout is a bit haphazard, but the information cards (in several languages) clearly explain the significance of the objects. It's generally considered the finest collection of its type outside Paris.

🏃 Activities

Once the almost exclusive haunt of the rich and pampered, Biarritz is now known more as the capital of European surfing (although in truth, the real centre of European surfing are the small towns of Hossegor and Capbreton, around 25km to the north). The city's main beach, Grande Plage, is good from mid-low tide on a moderate swell, but the 4km-long stretch of beaches that make up Anglet to the south are usually more consistent.

There are loads of surf schools around town that offer lessons from around €35 per hour; the tourist office keeps a list. Make sure your school is registered with the Féderation Française de Surf (FFS; www.surfingfrance.com) to make sure you get the best standard of training.

Grande Plage
BEACH

Grand by name, grand by nature, Biarritz' vast main beach has been the place at which to be seen since the days of Napoléon II and Eugénie. It's wall to wall with bodies on summer days, and dramatically deserted in winter. Hire iconic, striped, 1920s-style beach tents and two beach chairs for €14 per half-day.

Plage Miramar
BEACH

A little bit north of the Grande Plage, on the way to the lighthouse, plage Miramar is packed on summer days.

Plages d'Anglet
BEACH

North of Pointe St-Martin, the adrenaline-pumping surfing beaches of Anglet (the final 't' is pronounced) continue northwards for more than 4km. Take bus 10 from the bottom of av Verdun (just near av Édouard VII).

Plage de Marbella
BEACH

Plage de Marbella is about 2km south of Port Vieux. Bus 10 or 13 heading south will get you here.

SEASIDE WELL-BEING

Thalassotherapy ('sea healing'), using the restorative properties of seawater (along with seaweed and mud), has been popular in Biarritz since the late 18th century and continues to serve as an antidote to 21st-century ailments such as stress and insomnia.

In Biarritz, put thalassotherapy's curative powers to the test – or simply bliss out – at the following:

Thalassa Biarritz (☑ 05 59 41 30 00; www.thalassa.com; 11 rue Louison-Bobet; ☉ 9-11am & 2-4pm) Oceanfront luxury and relaxation at the Sofitel.

Thalmar Biarritz (☑ 08 25 12 64 64, 05 59 52 75 85; www.biarritz-thalasso. com; 80 rue de Madrid; ☉ 8am-8.30pm Mon-Fri, to 7pm Sat, 8.30am-12.30pm & 2-7pm Sun) This spa at Plage de Marbella is part of an established network.

Biarritz

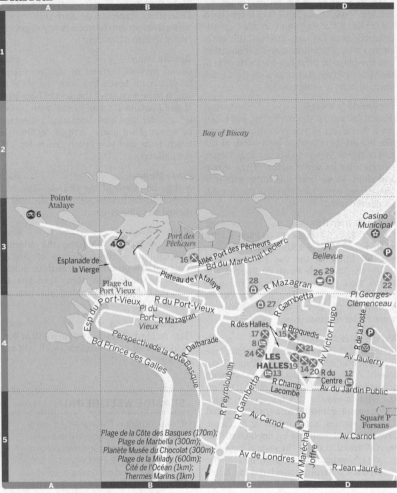

✸ Festivals & Events

Major surfing competitions take place year-round.

Big Festival   MUSIC
(www.facebook.com/bigfestival; ☺mid-Jul) As its name implies, this is Biarritz' largest music festival, attracting big mainstream acts.

🛏 Sleeping

Auberge de Jeunesse de Biarritz   HOSTEL €
(☏05 59 41 76 00; www.hihostels.com; 8 rue Chiquito de Cambo; dm/s incl sheets & breakfast €26/44; ☺reception 9am–noon & 6-10pm, closed mid-Dec–early Jan; @☎) This popular, well-run place has a lot going for it: clean dorms, a lively cafe-bar and a sunny terrace for summer barbecues. From the train station, follow the railway line westwards for 800m.

Maison du Lierre   HERITAGE HOTEL €€
(☏05 59 24 06 00; www.hotel-maisondulierre-biarritz.com; 3 av du Jardin Public; s/d from €102/140; ☎) What a beauty this mansion is: impressively detached, with a balcony and a park view from nearly every room (apart from the very cheapest, which overlook a neighbouring building). It's elegantly simple – wooden floors, cool furnishings,

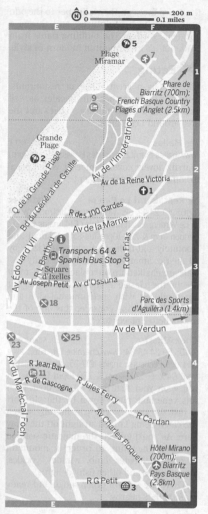

Biarritz

FRENCH BASQUE COUNTRY BIARRITZ

rooms named after flowers – and the central staircase is a listed monument. It's not even expensive for Biarritz. Recommended.

Hôtel Villa Koegui   BOUTIQUE HOTEL €€
(🖉 05 59 50 07 77; www.hotel-villakoegui-biarritz.
fr; 7 rue de Gascogne; s/d from €120/160; 🅿️ 🛜) Big-city style in Biarritz, with cool and minimal rooms spread out over a modern building brimming with quirky furnishings and decor (look out for the pair of fibreglass flamingos in the window). The central courtyard garden is a big plus, but the backstreet location makes parking a pain.

Maison Garnier   BOUTIQUE HOTEL €€
(🖉 05 59 01 60 70; www.hotel-biarritz.com; 29 rue Gambetta; d from €95; 🅿️ 🛜) This corner townhouse has a super location: walk out the door and you'll be right in the thick of the tapas bars around the covered market. It feels soothingly old-world inside, even a touch austere, and still has lots of original features like fireplaces, cornicing and carvings. Reception isn't always staffed, so it's worth ringing ahead.

Hôtel Edouard VII   HISTORIC HOTEL €€
(🖉 05 59 22 39 80; www.hotel-edouardvii.
com; 21 av Carnot; d from €120; 🅿️ 🛜) In a cream-coloured, 19th-century mansion that once belonged to one of Biarritz' mayors, this heritage hotel has a touch of

old-fashioned grandeur about it – from the tick-tocking clocks in the lobby to its antique furniture and floral rugs. There are four room categories – 'Confort' offers the best space-to-price ratio.

Hôtel Mirano
BOUTIQUE HOTEL €€

(☑ 05 59 23 11 63; www.hotelmirano.fr; 11 av Pasteur; d from €84; P ি) Wow, it's like stepping into *Saturday Night Fever* at this '70s retro palace, where everything looks like it's been picked up from the glory days of disco – from the orange perspex light fittings to the leather lounge chairs and squiggly wallpaper (oh, and there's a Betty Boop in the bar). Camp, fun and decently priced too.

To get here, take the D910 southeast out of town, turn left onto av de Grammont and then right onto av Pasteur. It's a good 10-minute walk from the centre.

★ Hôtel du Palais
LUXURY HOTEL €€€

(☑ 05 59 41 64 00; www.hotel-du-palais.com; 1 ave de l'Impératrice; d from €350; P ✲ @ ি ⊛) Biarritz' most glam address is this sumptuous hotel in a grand, historic building fronting directly onto to Grand Plage. Rooms are suitably lavish, and you can expect a gastronomic extravaganza at its several excellent restaurants.

★ Hôtel de Silhouette
BOUTIQUE HOTEL €€€

(☑ 05 59 24 93 82; www.hotel-silhouette-biarritz. com; 30 rue Gambetta; d from €175; ⊛ ি) Come here if you want to splash out. It's just steps from the covered market, but is surprisingly secluded thanks to being set back from the street. It's full of fun, from

---

WORTH A TRIP

MISSION GÂTEAU BASQUE

Rustic bakery **Le Moulin de Bassilour** (☑ 05 59 41 94 49; www.moulindebassilour. com; 1129 rue de Bassilour, Bidart; cakes €1-9; ⊘ 8am-1pm & 2.30-7pm) in a hidden vale 8km south of Biarritz is set in a historic mill that still grinds the flour using the stream that runs beneath the kitchen. From this, the bakery makes delicious, authentic *gâteau Basque* with either a cream or black-cherry filling, creamy cornbread flavoured with anise, and wholesome breads. Sample as the mill wheel spins.

---

the weird faces on the wallpaper to the odd bear and sheep sculptures, and there's a gorgeous garden. The building dates from 1610, but it's metropolitan modern in style.

✖ Eating

Biarritz has a great range of restaurants, from fine dining to beachfront cafes, as well as a cracking tapas culture – check out the area around Les Halles.

Les Halles
MARKET €

(www.halles-biarritz.fr; rue des Halles; ⊘ 7am-2pm) Biarritz' lovely covered market is the place to come for picnic ingredients.

★ Restaurant Le Pim'pi
FRENCH €€

(☑ 05 59 24 12 62; www.lepimpi-bistrot.com; 14 av de Verdun; lunch menu from €14, mains €21-26; ⊘ noon-2pm & 7.30-10pm Tue-Sat) A small and resolutely old-fashioned place unfazed by all the razzamatazz around it. The daily specials are chalked up on a blackboard – most are of the classic French bistro style but are produced with such unusual skill and passion that many consider this one of the town's better places to eat.

Chez Albert
SEAFOOD €€

(☑ 05 59 24 43 84; www.chezalbert.fr; 51bis allée Port des Pêcheurs; mains €17-25, seafood platter from €40; ⊘ 12.15-2pm & 7.30-10pm Thu-Tue) If you want your fish fresh off the boat, then this venerable place down by the old port is just the ticket – you can literally watch the catch being landed straight off the quay here. As you'd expect, the majestic seafood platter is the thing to order: a mountain of oysters, lobster, crab, winkles, cockles, langoustines and other fishy delights.

There are several other rough-and-ready seafood bars nearby.

L'Etable
BASQUE €€

(☑ 05 59 22 10 11; 6 rue Lavernis; mains €16-24; ⊘ 7pm-midnight Wed-Mon) This is one of those places, hidden down an alley and in a cave-like building, that's so discreet that only a local could have pointed it out to you. Despite the less-than-obvious look to the place, it has a solid reputation for basic, traditional local dishes, featuring lots of duck, chilli and seafood. Open daily during French school holidays.

Le Clos Basque
BASQUE €€

(☑ 05 59 24 24 96; 12 rue Louis Barthou; menus €26-31, mains €15; ⊘ noon-2pm & 7.45-9.30pm

BASQUE PINTXOS

Like Bayonne, tapas (or *pintxos* as they're known in Basque Country) is an ever-popular way to eat in Biarritz. Whether it's a quick snack over drinks or a slap-up feast, there are plenty of places to indulge, especially around the covered market.

Les Contrebandiers (☑ 05 59 24 02 27; www.facebook.com/lescontrebandiersbiarritz; 20 av Victor Hugo; tapas €6-11; ☺ 9am-11.45pm Mon-Sat, 10am-2pm Sun) This fashionable spot is attached to a wine shop and offers creative small plates.

Le Comptoir du Foie Gras (☑ 05 59 22 57 42; www.facebook.com/cfgbiarritz; 1 rue du Centre; tapas €2-10; ☺ 8am-2pm & 5-11pm) Foie gras specialist by day, tapas hang-out by night, on a corner next to the covered market. The tapas tends to be heavy on foie gras, but there are other options too.

Bar du Marché (☑ 05 59 23 48 96; 8 rue des Halles; tapas €2 4; ☺ 8am-3pm & 6pm-2am) Established in 1938, this sunny yellow bar is as good for its sit-down meals as for its late-night tapas selection.

Puig & Daro (☑ 05 59 23 30 45; 34 rue Gambetta; mains €6-14; ☺ 6-10pm Tue & Wed, 1-10pm Thu-Sat, 11am-3pm Sun) Take a seat on the wooden patio and dine on a comprehensive tapas selection, from local cheeses to Cantabrian anchovies and sardines in olive oil.

Bar Jean (☑ 05 59 24 80 38; www.barjean-biarritz.fr; 5 rue des Halles; tapas €2-16; ☺ noon-3.30pm & 6.30pm-midnight Wed-Mon) One of the oldest tapas venues in town, Bar Jean is traditional and in summer spills onto the street.

Tue-Sun) One of Biarritz' more traditional tables, with a sweet front patio sheltered by climbing plants and an awning. The menu is proudly Basque, so expect classic dishes such as *axoa* (mashed veal, onions and tomatoes spiced with red Espelette chilli). It gets very busy, so service can be slow.

Milwaukee Café CAFE €€
(☑ 05 59 54 17 04; www.facebook.com/pg/milwaukeecafe; 2 rue du Helder; mains €14-17; ☺ 9am-6.30pm Tue-Sat, to 5pm Sun) A little dose of American deli culture is on offer here: burgers, salads, smoothies and health shakes, followed up by delicious cupcakes and proper barista-made coffees. It's light, fresh and bright inside, and popular with local office workers and ladies-who-lunch. The name is a reference to the owner's family – she's a Milwaukee native, but grew up in Biarritz.

Haragia STEAK €€€
(☑ 05 35 46 68 92; www.facebook.com/haragia 64; 26 rue Gambetta; mains €30-50; ☺ 8pm-1am Thu-Sun, to 5pm Sun) Tucked back in a tiny alley near the central market, this convivial steakhouse has a few small tables and an open kitchen with the grill on show as the friendly brothers cook up your evening meal. The meat menu is simple – steak, veal and pork – but the wine menu is vast!

🍷 Drinking & Nightlife

The area around rue du Port-Vieux and Les Halles (the covered market) tend to be the hotspots for Biarritz' nightlife. Most places will stay open till around 2am, unless otherwise indicated. There are a couple of cheesy nightclubs and lounge bars just behind Grande Plage.

Miremont CAFE
(☑ 05 59 24 01 38; www.miremont-biarritz.com; 1bis place Georges-Clémenceau; hot chocolate from €5; ☺ 9am-8pm) Operating since 1880, this *grande dame* harks back to the time when belle époque Biarritz was the beach resort of choice for the rich and glamorous. Today it still attracts perfectly coiffed hairdos (and that's just on the poodles), but it's the fine tea and cakes that draw in the well-heeled – none of whom seem to mind the sky-high prices.

☆ Entertainment

Free classical-music concerts take place in high summer at various outdoor venues around town; the tourist office has the program.

Parc des Sports d'Aguiléra SPECTATOR SPORT
(☑ 05 59 01 64 60; av Henri Haget) Biarritz' stadium, 2km east of the centre, is home to the local rugby team, Olympique, and hosts professional *pelota* matches in the complex.

Basque Culture

Call a Basque French or Spanish and it's almost certain you'll receive a glare and a stern 'I'm Basque!' in return. It's no surprise, as the Basques *are* different, with their own unique culture and history, and a language – Euskara – unrelated to any other European language. Basque people are genetically different, too: many share the same blood group that can be traced back to Europe's earliest settlers.

Pelote Basque

Pelote Basque (pelota) is the catch-all name for around 16 traditional Basque ball games. The most well-known has players using a scoop-like basket called a *chistera,* while *main nue* is played with an open hand; *jaï alaï* is the most high-octane variant, and has a professional league with games screened on local TV. Every village has its own *pelota* court, called a *fronton.*

Festivals

Basque festivals are the best place to see traditional dress: even if you're not in costume, wearing red and white is mandatory. The big seasonal celebration is the Fêtes de Bayonne, held in July, but there are many smaller celebrations too.

Lauburu

The most visible symbol of Basque culture is the *lauburu,* also known as the Basque cross. Regarded as a symbol of prosperity, it's also used to signify life and death.

Basque Eats

The Basque version of tapas is called *pintxos;* two or three dishes per person is usually enough. Look out for local specialities:

Le Piment d'Espelette This little chilli pepper is an essential spice in cooking.

Fromage des Pyrénées Local cheeses are best bought straight from the farm: look out for varieties such as Ossau-Iraty.

Jambon de Bayonne The Basque version of *pata negra,* sliced wafer-thin.

Axoa Mashed veal with tomato, onions and *le piment d'Espelette.*

Izarra A fiery herb-flavoured liqueur that comes in green and yellow versions.

1. Drying chillies, Espelette (p688) 2. Lauburu symbol , Ainhoa (p688) 3. Crowds celebrating the Fêtes de Bayonne (p672)

LOCAL KNOWLEDGE

SURF'S UP

France's Basque and Atlantic coasts have some of Europe's best surf. Autumn is prime time, with warm(ish) water temperatures, consistently good conditions and few(er) crowds. The big-name spots are Biarritz, Bidart, Hossegor and Capbreton, where you can watch pro surfers battling it out for world-title points in the World Surf League (www.worldsurfleague.com). In fact, decent surf can usually be found almost anywhere between St-Jean de Luz in the south and Soulac-sur-Mer in the north.

The reef breaks around Guéthary, just to the south of Biarritz, are also popular, or you could join Bordeaux' surfers on the beaches around Lacanau.

Less-frequented spots can be found around the pine-forested Cap Ferret peninsula, along with various other remote areas along the coastline of Les Landes.

For beginners, the mellow waves at Hendaye, just to the south of St-Jean de Luz are perfect. There are plenty of surf schools; lessons start at around €35. Contact local tourist offices for details.

🛍 Shopping

Les Sandales d'Eugénie　　　SHOES
(☑ 05 59 24 22 51; 18 rue Mazagran; ⊙ 10am-1pm & 3-6.30pm) Vincent Corbun continues his grandfather's business, established in 1935, making and selling espadrilles in a rainbow of colours and styles (customised with ribbons and laces while you wait).

Jean-Vier　　　HOMEWARES
(☑ 05 59 85 20 55; www.jean-vier.com; 25 rue Mazagran; ⊙ 10am-12.30pm & 2.30-7pm) A sumptuous place to shop for gorgeous Basque linens and lively Basque-inspired designs.

Robert Pariès　　　CHOCOLATE
(☑ 05 59 22 07 52; www.paries.fr; 1 place Bellevue; ⊙ 9am-1pm & 2.30-7.30pm) Scrumptious chocolates and Basque sweets, including *canougas* (chocolate-covered caramels) and *gateaux basques* (cream-filled cakes, often flavoured with cherries).

ℹ Information

In July and August there are tourist-office annexes at the airport and train station, and at the roundabout just off the Biarritz *sortie* (exit) 4 from the A63.

Tourist Office (☑ 05 59 22 37 10; www.tourisme. biarritz.fr; square d'Ixelles; ⊙ 9am-7pm Jul–mid-Sep, shorter hours rest of year) Good source for maps, brochures and transport information, including schedules of buses to Spain.

ℹ Getting There & Away

AIR

Domestic and international flights leave from **Aéroport Biarritz Pays Basque** (p672). Chronoplus (www.chronoplus.eu) Line C buses run from the train station in Biarritz, while Line 14 leaves

from near the Biarritz tourist office. Both run every half-hour or so and take about 10 minutes. A single fare costs €1.

BUS

Buses run frequently between Bayonne and Biarritz. They are much cheaper than taking the train since a bus ticket costs about the same as you'll pay to get from Biarritz' train station to its town centre.

Transports 64 (☑ 08 00 64 24 64, 09 70 80 90 74; www.transports64.fr) line 816 buses travel down the coast to St-Jean de Luz, Urrugne and Hendaye; there's also an express service that runs three times daily. The fare is a flat-rate €2, and buses leave from the **stop** near the tourist office beside square d'Ixelles.

Buses to Spain (p691), including San Sebastián and Bilbao, also depart from that stop.

TRAIN

All trains to Biarritz only stop at the **train station** (☑ 08 92 35 35 35; allée du Moura) about 3.5km southeast of the town centre (the old, central Gare du Midi station is now a cultural centre). Chronoplus bus 10 runs regularly into the city centre, and bus C serves central Bayonne.

Trains serve: Paris Gare Montparnasse (€50 to €109, 4¼ hours, five daily), Bordeaux (€35 to €50, 2¼ hours, 10 daily), St-Jean de Luz (€4, 15 minutes, 15 daily) and Hendaye (€6, 35 minutes, 15 daily).

ℹ Getting Around

Two free Chronoplus (www.chronoplus.eu) shuttle buses trundle around central Biarritz (every 15 minutes, 7.30am to 7.30pm, Monday to Saturday). One travels around the town centre and inland; the other runs north–south along the coast between Plage Miramar, Grande Plage and Plage de la Milady.

Guéthary

POP 1375

Halfway between Biarritz and St-Jean de Luz is the little seaside village of Guéthary, once a whaling station, but now a swish getaway for the Basque Coast's jet set. Set out along a steep hillside that leads down to an attractive harbour and seafront, it's a pretty spot for an afternoon stroll, with a couple of small sandy beaches tucked in under the breakwater and some grand art deco architecture spread along its winding walkways.

◉ Sights

**Musée d'Art Moderne et
Contemporain**   MUSEUM
(✆ 05 59 54 86 37; www.musee-de-guethary.fr; 117 av du Général de Gaulle; €2; ⊗ 10.30am-noon & 3-7pm Mon & Wed-Sat Jul & Aug, 2-6pm Mon & Wed-Sat May, Jun, Sep & Oct) Housed inside the magisterial Villa Saraleguinea, this intriguing little art museum is based around the collection of local poet Paul-Jean Toulet, who lived in Guéthary during the last years of his life, and the sculptor Georges Clément de Swiecinski. It's an eclectic mix that takes in everything from Roman ephemera to abstract sculptures, as well as changing exhibitions of contemporary art, photography and ceramics – but it's the house and grounds that really steal the show.

🛏 Sleeping

Guéthary makes a handy stop-off between Biarritz and St-Jean de Luz and has several small hotels.

★**Hôtel Balea**   BOUTIQUE HOTEL €€
(✆ 05 59 26 08 39; www.hotel-balea-guethary.com; 106 rue Adrien Lahourcade; d from €90; P ❄ 🐾)

Pay attention, class – this cracking hotel receives top marks. It's housed in Guéthary's former public schoolhouse, and the decor echoes its educational heritage in entertaining ways – from an original playground mural and arithmetical room numbers to the vintage maps and pots of pens adorning the breakfast room. It's cool, fun and reasonably priced, even in season. A+.

ℹ Information

Guéthary Tourist Office (✆ 05 59 26 56 60; www.guethary-tourisme.com; 74 rue du Comte de Swiecinski; ⊗ 9am-12.30pm & 2-6.30pm Mon-Sat, 10am-1pm Sun Jul & Aug, reduced hours rest of year) The website has a good map of the Sentier du Littoral.

ℹ Getting There & Away

Transports 64 runs bus 816 between Bayonne, Biarritz and Hendaye. It stops off on the main road in Guéthary; the fare is a flat-rate €2 for anywhere along the coast.

Trains run from Guéthary's tiny station south to St-Jean de Luz (€2, seven minutes, 12 daily) and north to Bayonne (€4, 30 minutes, 11 daily). It's easier to take a bus to Biarritz as the SNCF station is way out of town.

ST-JEAN DE LUZ

POP 13,430

If you're searching for the quintessential Basque seaside town – complete with atmospheric narrow streets, a lively harbour and a sparkling sandy beach – you've found it.

The attractive town of St-Jean de Luz, 24km southwest of Bayonne, grew up around the mouth of the River Nivelle as a fishing port, pulling in large catches of sardines, anchovies and, rather less salubriously, whales

---

A COASTAL HIKE

Running 25km between Bidart and Hendaye is one of the Basque Country's best-kept secrets: the **Sentier du Littoral** (www.guethary-tourisme.com/discover-guethary/path-of-the-coast.php). This coastal hiking trail passes through the region's most beautiful seaside scenery, carpeted with fragrant maquis, pockmarked by rocky coves and backed by the shimmering blue line of the Atlantic horizon. A downloadable route map is available from the Guéthary tourist office website.

There are access points at various locations between Bidart, Guéthary, St-Jean de Luz, Socoa and Hendaye. It's perfectly feasible to just do a couple of sections and then catch a bus or train back to Biarritz or St-Jean de Luz. Interpretative panels are positioned along the trail.

Bring plenty of water and sunscreen, and aim to do your walking in the early morning or late afternoon, as the summer sun can be relentless.

St-Jean de Luz

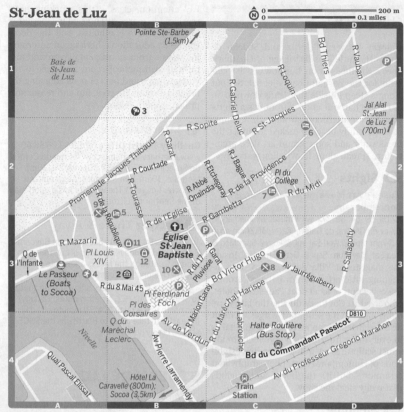

St-Jean de Luz

in bygone days. Later, like the rest of the Basque coastline, it became a fashionable resort for well-to-do French, English and Spanish tourists in the late 19th century, but the town still maintains a sizeable fishing fleet.

St-Jean and its sleepy sister town of Ciboure are linked by busy Pont Charles de Gaulle, which overlooks the fishing port. In summer, the best way to cross the river mouth is to catch one of the regular ferries that chug between the two.

◎ Sights

St-Jean's shady backstreets are great for a wander, especially along the main shopping thoroughfare of rue Gambetta. The town's grandest buildings are around place Louis XIV.

★ **Église St-Jean Baptiste**   CHURCH
(rue Gambetta, St-Jean de Luz; ⊗8.30am-noon & 2-7pm) The plain façade of France's largest

and finest Basque church conceals a splendid interior with a magnificent Baroque altarpiece. It was in front of this very altarpiece that Louis XIV and María Teresa, daughter of King Philip IV of Spain, were married in 1660. After exchanging rings, the couple walked down the aisle and out of the south door, which was then sealed to commemorate peace between the two nations after 24 years of hostilities.

Maison Louis XIV
HISTORIC BUILDING

(☑ 05 59 26 27 58; www.maison-louis-xiv.fr; 6 place Louis XIV, St-Jean de Luz; adult/child €6.50/4; ☺ 10.30am-12.20pm & 2.30-6.30pm Wed-Mon Jul & Aug, 11am-3pm & 4-5pm Wed-Mon Easter, Jun & Sep–mid-Oct) The grandest house in town was built in 1643 by a wealthy shipowner, but its main claim to fame is as the house where Louis XIV lived out his last days of bachelorhood before marrying María Teresa. It's awash with period detail and antiques. Half-hour guided tours (with English text) depart several times daily in July and August.

L'Écomusée Basque Jean-Vier
MUSEUM

(☑ 05 59 51 33 23; www.jean-vier.com; D810; adult/child €7.50/3.20; ☺ 10am-6.30pm Jul & Aug, to 11.15am & 2.30-5.30pm Mon-Sat Apr-Jun, Sep & Oct, closed Nov-Apr) Basque traditions are brought to life at this illuminating multimedia museum, which explores everything from *pelota* and Basque architecture to the art of making Izarra (Basque for 'star'), a liqueur made from 20 different local plants. It's around 2km north of St-Jean de Luz.

Socoa
HISTORIC SITE

(Ciboure) The heart of the historic district of Socoa is about 2.5km west of Ciboure along the continuation of quai Maurice Ravel (named for the *Boléro* composer, who was born in Ciboure in 1875). Its prominent fort was built in 1627 and later improved by Vauban. You can walk out to the Digue de Socoa breakwater or climb to the lighthouse via rue du Phare, then out along rue du Sémaphore for fabulous coastal views.

🏃 Activities

Nivelle V
CRUISE

(☑ 06 09 73 61 81; www.croisiere-saintjeandeluz. com; quai de l'Infante, St-Jean de Luz; adult/child €18/14; ☺ Apr–mid-Oct) Between April and October, the *Nivelle V* runs out along the surrounding coastline all the way towards Spain at 2pm daily, with extra cruises at 10.30am on Tuesdays, Wednesdays and Thursdays from mid-July to mid-September.

BEACH TALK

A superb panorama of St-Jean de Luz unfolds from **Pointe de Ste-Barbe** (St-Jean de Luz), a craggy promontory at the northern end of the Baie de St-Jean de Luz and about 1km beyond the town beach. Go to the end of bd Thiers and keep walking.

The beautiful arcing sands of **St-Jean Plage** (St-Jean de Luz) sprout stripy bathing tents from June to September. It's protected from the wrath of the Atlantic by breakwaters and jetties, and is one of the more child-friendly beaches in the Basque Country.

Or hit the sands at **Plage de Ciboure** (Ciboure), a modest beach 2km west of Socoa on the corniche (the D912), served by Transports 64 buses en route to Hendaye and, in the high season, by Le Passeur (p687) boats.

Shorter cruises on the *Nivelle IV* (adult/child €10/8) depart at 4pm daily, with an extra tour at 5pm daily and at 11am on Sundays in July and August.

Odyssée Bleue
DIVING

(☑ 06 63 54 13 63; www.odyssee-bleue.com; chemin des Blocs, hangar 4, Ciboure) The Basque coast is a great place to learn to dive, and this diving school comes highly recommended. A 20-minute 'baptism' dive costs €55, with longer courses starting from €180. It also offers snorkelling expeditions in summer for €25.

🎉 Festivals & Events

Fêtes de la St-Jean
CULTURAL

(☺ Jun) Bonfires, music and dancing take place on the weekend nearest 24 June in celebration of St John the Baptist.

La Fête du Thon
FOOD & DRINK

(www.saint-jean-de-luz.com/fr/a-voir-a-faire/ evenements-de-saint-jean-de-luz/fete-du-thon; ☺ Jul) The Tuna Festival, on the second weekend in July, fills the streets with brass bands, Basque music and dancing, while stalls sell sizzling tuna steaks.

La Nuit de la Sardine
CULTURAL

(☺ Jul & Aug) The Night of the Sardine – a night of music, folklore and dancing – is held twice each summer, on a Saturday in early July and in August.

THE BASQUE LANGUAGE

According to linguists, Euskara, the Basque language, is unrelated to any other tongue on earth, and is the only language in southwestern Europe to have withstood the onslaught of Latin and its derivatives.

Basque is spoken by about a million people in Spain and France, nearly all of whom are bilingual. In the French Basque Country, the language is widely spoken in Bayonne and the hilly hinterland. However, while it is an official language in Spain, it isn't recognised as such in France (although some younger children are educated in Basque at primary-school level). The language also has a higher survival rate on the Spanish side.

But you'll still encounter the language in France on Basque-language TV and radio stations, and see the occasional sign reading 'Hemen Euskara emaiten dugu' (Basque spoken here) on shop doors. You'll also see the Basque flag (similar stripe arrangement to the UK's but with a red field, a white vertical cross and a green diagonal one) flying throughout the region, as well as another common Basque symbol, the *lauburu* (like a curly four-leaf clover), signifying prosperity, or life and death.

🛏 Sleeping

July to mid-September are packed and reservations are essential; low-season prices drop significantly. There are a couple of cheap and cheerful places opposite the train station.

Between St-Jean de Luz and Guéthary, 7km northeast up the coast, are no fewer than 16 camp grounds. Transports 64's Biarritz and Bayonne buses stop within 1km of them all.

★ Les Almadiès   HOTEL €€
(☑ 05 59 85 34 48; www.hotel-les-almadies.com; 58 rue Gambetta, St-Jean de Luz; d from €105; 🕾) Summer bargains are hard to come by in St-Jean de Luz, but this pretty little hotel definitely ranks as one. It's in a great location on the lively thoroughfare of rue Gambetta, overlooking a little square. Although the rooms are a bit generic – beige carpets, white bathrooms, identikit furniture – there's no doubting the deal here.

★ Hôtel Txoko   BOUTIQUE HOTEL €€
(☑ 05 59 85 10 45; www.hotel-txoko.com; 20 rue de la République, St-Jean de Luz; d from €90; 🟦🕾) This charming hotel is run by an equally charming owner who, when it's not too crowded, will serve you a delicious breakfast in your room. Colours are stripy Basque glorious, there are thoughtful touches like espresso machines and local chocolate in the rooms, and it's on a super-central walking street in the heart of the action and just steps from the beach.

La Devinière   BOUTIQUE HOTEL €€
(☑ 05 59 26 05 51; www.hotel-la-deviniere.com; 5 rue Loquin, St-Jean de Luz; d €120-180; 🕾) You

have to love a place that forsakes TVs for antiquarian books (room 11 even has its own mini-library). Beyond the living room, with its piano and comfy armchairs, there's a delightful small patio equipped with lounges and the rooms are stuffed full of antique and replica antique furnishings. The garden rooms are worth the extra.

Hôtel La Caravelle   BOUTIQUE HOTEL €€
(☑ 05 59 47 18 05; www.hotellacaravelle.com; 1 bd Pierre Benoît, Ciboure; d with/without sea view from €105/70, f €120; 🟦🕾) Stylish and shipshape, this elegant hotel is one step removed from the summertime buzz in St-Jean de Luz, overlooking the water on the opposite side of the port in Ciboure. Originally two fishermen's cottages, it's been spruced up with cream-and-blue colour schemes and nautical knick-knacks. Needless to say, a sea view is a must here. There's free street parking outside.

🍴 Eating

★ Buvette des Halles   SEAFOOD €
(☑ 05 59 26 73 59; bd Victor Hugo, St-Jean de Luz; dishes €7-16; ⊗ 6am-2pm & 7-9pm Sep-Jun, closed Tue) For the full-blown French market experience, this tiny corner restaurant hidden away in Les Halles is a must. Pull up a stool at the counter under its collection of vintage teapots, and tuck into plates of Bayonne ham, grilled sardines, mussels, fish soup and local cheeses. In summer there are tables outside.

★ Xaya   FRENCH €
(☑ 05 59 47 75 48; www.restaurant-saint-jean-de-luz.com; 5 rue St-Jean, St-Jean de Luz; lunch menu €15, mains €16-20; ⊗ noon-1.45pm & 7.30-9.30pm

Tue-Sun, to 10pm Jul & Aug) Duck down a side street into this stone-walled restaurant for excellent French food with a Basque twist. There are two options: order grilled fish or steaks à la carte, or (at dinner-time only) just delve into delectable pintxos (tapas; €7 to €15) for the whole table to share. Inside it's bright and modern, with mirrors, upcycled barrels and blonde wood.

★ **Le Kaiku** BASQUE €€€
(☑ 05 59 26 13 20; www.kaiku.fr; 17 rue de la République, St-Jean de Luz; menu lunch/dinner €36/72, mains €36-48; ⊘ 12.30-2pm & 7.30-10pm Thu-Mon) To spoil yourself, Nicholas Borombo's stellar Michelin-starred address is the place to dine in St-Jean. Known for their modern interpretation of Basque classics, his dishes are full of unusual ingredients, from Asian spices to edible flowers. The setting is lovely too, in an old-town location on a cobbled street near the beach. Reservations and smart attire essential.

☆ Entertainment

Jaï Alaï St-Jean de Luz SPECTATOR SPORT
(☑ 05 59 51 65 36; 18 av André Ithurralde, St-Jean de Luz) In summer, frequent *pelota* matches take place at Jaï Alaï St-Jean de Luz, 1km northeast of the train station. The tourist office can supply times and prices.

🛍 Shopping

★ **Maison Adam** FOOD
(☑ 05 59 26 03 54; 6 rue de la République, St-Jean de Luz; ⊘ 8am-12.30pm & 2-7.30pm) This renowned shop, selling delicious Basque-style macarons (melt-in-the-mouth biscuit-like delicacies), hams and other regional foods, has been trading since 1666 – longer than many a nation has been in existence! It now has other branches, including one in Biarritz.

Sandales Concha SHOES
(☑ 05 59 51 07 56; 2 rue Gambetta, St-Jean de Luz; ⊘ 9am-noon & 2-7pm Tue-Sat) The traditional shoe of the Basque Country is the espadrille and here you can choose from a huge range of handmade shoes starting from €12.

ℹ Information

Tourist Office (☑ 05 59 26 03 16; www.saint-jean-de-luz.com; 20 bd Victor Hugo, St-Jean de Luz; ⊘ 9am-12.30pm & 2-6pm Mon-Sat, 10am-1pm Sun, closed Sun Nov-Mar) Runs

an extensive program of French-language tours around the town and across the Spanish border; ask about English-language tours in summer.

ℹ Getting There & Away

BUS

Transports 64 (p682) buses **stop** near the train station on their way northeast to Biarritz (30 minutes, hourly) and Bayonne (35 minutes). Southwest, there are around 10 services daily to Hendaye (35 minutes). All journeys cost a flat-rate €2.

Hegobus (www.hegobus.fr) bus 23 connects St-Jean de Luz' and Biarritz' train stations (€1) and Ciboure.

Transportes Pesa (p691), **Flixbus** (p691) and **Ouibus** (p691) buses stop in St-Jean de Luz en route to San Sebastián and Bilbao.

TRAIN

There are frequent trains to Bayonne (€5.30, 25 minutes) via Biarritz (€3.50, 20 minutes) and to Hendaye (€3, 10 minutes), with onward connections to Spain.

ℹ Getting Around

The good ship **Le Passeur** (☑ 06 11 69 56 93; www.ciboure-paysbasque.com/cote_detente/ navette_maritime.php; €2.80, complete loop €5; ⊘ 6 daily Apr-Sep) plies the waters between the jetty on the northern edge of St-Jean's beach, quai de l'Infante and Socoa.

> **WORTH A TRIP**
>
> ### GROTTES DE SARE
>
> Who knows what the first inhabitants of the **Grottes de Sare** (www. grottesdesare.fr; off the D306; adult/ child €8.50/5; ⊘ 10am-7pm Aug, to 6pm Apr-Jul & Sep, reduced hours rest of year), some 20,000 years ago, would make of today's whiz-bang technology that now lights up the Stygian gloom in these stunning subterranean caves? Multilingual 45-minute tours take you through a gaping entrance via narrow passages to a huge central cavern, where impressive shows of holograms and laser lights are staged.
>
> Follow the D306 6km south of the village of Sare. Hegobus (www.hegobus. com) bus 21 goes from St-Jean de Luz to the caves (€1, four daily).

OFF THE BEATEN TRACK IN THE BASQUE COUNTRY

There's no doubting the Basque Country's beauty, but unfortunately its good looks mean it's far from a well-kept secret. The coast can be horrendously crowded in summer, but with your own wheels it's possible to escape into the hills to find some of the area's less-frequented corners.

Itxassou This hilltop village is famous for its cherries and its scenic surrounds.

La Bastide-Clairence With whitewashed houses brushed in lipstick red, this is arguably the most beautiful of all Basque mountain villages.

Bidarray A pretty riverside village famed for its white-water-rafting opportunities.

Forêt d'Iraty A vast beech forest that turns the high mountain slopes fire-orange in autumn. A web of walking trails allows for easy exploration.

Larrau This quaint village surrounded by monster hills is another hiker's favourite, with gorges and a monstrous cavern nearby.

LA RHUNE

Traditionally considered the first mountain of the Pyrenees, the 905m-high, antenna-topped and border-straddling La Rhune ('Larrun' in Basque), 10km south of St-Jean de Luz, has always been considered sacred by Basques, though today more people come for the spectacular views than for religious or cultural reasons.

The mountain is best approached from **Col de St-Ignace**, 3km northwest of Sare on the D4 (the St-Jean de Luz road). From here, you can take a fairly strenuous five-hour (return; about 11km) hike, or have all the hikers curse you by hopping on **Le Petit Train de la Rhune** (www.rhune.com; single/return adult €16/19, child €9/12; ☉ mid-Mar–early Nov). This charming little wooden train takes 35 minutes to haul itself up the 4km to the summit. In July and August departures are every 40 minutes; the rest of the time there are about nine per day. Be prepared for a wait of up to an hour in high summer if you haven't bought your ticket online.

Hegobus (www.hegobus.fr) runs bus 21 from St-Jean de Luz train station to the train depot (€1; get off at Col de St-Ignace) for Le Petit Train de la Rhune. Otherwise, reach the mountain with your own wheels.

AINHOA

POP 668

Ainhoa's elongated main street is flanked by imposing 17th-century houses, half-timbered and brightly painted. Look for the rectangular stones set above many of the doors, engraved with the date of construction and the name of the family to whom the house belonged. The fortified church has the Basque trademarks of an internal gallery and an embellished altarpiece.

For a memorable Basque meal, stop at the Michelin-starred **Ithurria** (☎ 05 59 29 92 11; www.ithurria.com; place du Fronton; menus €45-70, mains €30-32; ☉ restaurant noon-2pm Fri-Tue, 7.30-9pm Thu-Tue; P ❖ 🛜), established by the Isabal family in an old pilgrims' hostel and now run by Maurice Isabal's two sons (one the sommelier, the other the chef). To make a night of it, Ithurria's rainbow-hued rooms (doubles from €135) and dreamy swimming pool complement the food perfectly.

Hegobus (www.hegobus.fr) bus line 22 serves St-Jean de Luz train station (€1). The closest train stations are in Cambo-les-Bains (12km away) and St-Jean de Luz (23km away).

ESPELETTE

POP 2000

The whitewashed Basque town of Espelette is famous for its dark-red chillies, an integral ingredient in traditional Basque cuisine. So prized is *le piment d'Espelette* that it's been accorded Appellation d'Origine Contrôlée (AOC) status, like fine wine. In autumn you can scarcely see the walls of the houses under rows of chillies drying in the sun.

The last weekend in October marks Espelette's **Fête du Piment**, with processions, a formal blessing of the chilli peppers and the ennoblement of a *chevalier du piment* (a knight of the pimiento).

🛏 Sleeping & Eating

Maison d'hôte Irazabala B&B €
(📞06 07 14 93 61; www.irazabala.com; 155 Mendiko Bidea; d from €80; 🅿🛜) This beautiful Basque farmhouse is situated in the middle of wildflower meadows. With views over green mountains, it is a bucolic place to rest up. The four rooms are easily the equal of the setting, and you'll struggle to tear yourself away from the garden. There are no TVs in the rooms, but when the setting is as lovely as this, who cares?

It's a couple of kilometres out of town (follow signs for the camp ground and it's signed just on from there).

⭐ **Hôtel Restaurant Euzkadi** FRENCH €€
(📞05 59 93 91 88; www.hotel-restaurant-euzkadi.com; 285 Karrika Nagusia; menus €20-37, mains €14-19; ⊙12.30-2pm & 7.30-9.30pm; 🛜📶) This red-and-white half-timbered hotel is characteristic of the architecture of the Basque Country, and its food is equally classic – *piment d'Espelette* figures heavily in many dishes, and you can try local specialities like *axoa* (tender minced veal simmered with onions and fresh chillies). Rooms are modern (double/triple/quad from €73/100/130), and there's a lovely pool.

🔒 Shopping

L'Atelier du Piment FOOD
(📞05 59 93 90 21; www.atelierdupiment.com; Chemin de l'Eglise; ⊙9am-noon & 2-6pm) FREE This shop on the edge of the village sells a huge variety of chilli-pepper products, from jams to chocolate.

ℹ Information

Tourist Office (📞05 59 93 95 02; www.espelette.fr; 145 Karrika Nagusia; ⊙9.30am-12.30pm & 2-6pm Mon-Sat Jul & Aug, shorter hours rest of year) Helpful office situated within a small stone château.

ℹ Getting There & Away

Transports 64 (p682) runs bus 814 between Bayonne and Espelette (40 minutes, four daily Monday to Friday, three Saturday, two Sunday), via Cambo-les-Bains.

The nearest train station is in Cambo-les-Bains.

St-Jean Pied de Port

POP 1555

At the foot of the Pyrenees, the town of St-Jean Pied de Port (St-Jean at the Foot of the Pass) is a popular waypoint for hikers on the pilgrim trail. The hikers you're bound to see along the main cobbled street of rue de la Citadelle are, in fact, continuing an age-old tradition. For centuries this town, 53km southeast of Bayonne, has been the last stop in France for pilgrims heading south over the Spanish border, a mere 8km away, and on to Santiago de Compostela in western Spain.

The walled town itself is beautifully preserved, ringed by ramparts and topped off by a sturdy citadel. It's an ideal day trip from Bayonne, particularly on Monday when the market is in full swing.

DON'T MISS

MAKHILA TO ORDER

At **L'Atelier Anciart Bergara** (📞05 59 93 03 05; www.makhila.com; Fronton, Larressore; ⊙8am-noon & 2-6pm Mon-Fri, to 5pm Sat) in the village of Larressore, around 6km north of Espelette, craftspeople make the traditional wooden walking sticks known as *makhila*, which have been carried by shepherds, farmers and hillspeople in the Basque Country for as long as anyone cares to remember. Customarily made from medlar wood and topped by a decorative leather pommel capped with steel, bone, horn or bronze, each one is made to order to suit its owner and can take several weeks of work to complete.

Most *makhilas* also have a hidden secret – the hand-grip can be slipped off to reveal a sharp spike, effectively turning a harmless walking stick into a deadly weapon. The workshop offers three core models costing from €280 to €650, or you can order your own custom version for considerably more. Either way, it's a fascinating art that's well worth watching.

You'll need your own wheels to visit Larressore.

◉ Sights & Activities

St-Jean makes a great base for hiking, even if you're not up for the whole Santiago de Compostela route. Two GRs (*grandes randonnées;* long-distance hiking trails) pass through town: the **GR10** (the trans-Pyrenean long-distance trail running from the Atlantic to the Mediterranean over the course of 45 days) and the **GR65** (the Chemin de St-Jacques pilgrim route).

Shorter sections of each route make for a great day-hike from St-Jean; ask at the tourist office for route maps.

★ Walled Town   AREA

Though modern St-Jean has expanded considerably, during medieval times the entire town was enclosed by defensive ramparts guarding France's southwestern corner against incursions from across the Spanish border. The town's four original *portes* (gates) are still in situ, including one at either end of the cobbled rue de la Citadelle.

The traditional entry point for pilgrims is via the **Porte St-Jacques**, at the top end of the street, while at the other, **Porte Notre-Dame** stands next to the town's most famous landmark – the **Pont Romain**, a photogenic arched bridge spanning the River Nive. Despite the name, it's not actually Roman – it was built sometime around 1720.

As you walk along rue de la Citadelle, look out for the dates of construction carved into the lintels above the doorways (the oldest we found was 1510). Also keep your eyes peeled for the motif of the scallop shell – the traditional symbol of the Santiago de Compostela, as pilgrims who completed the route would take a souvenir shell home from the Spanish coast.

La Citadelle   FORTRESS

From the top of rue de la Citadelle, a rough cobblestone path ascends to the massive citadel itself, from where there's a spectacular panorama of the town and the surrounding hills. Constructed in 1628, the fort was rebuilt around 1680 by military engineers of the Vauban school. Nowadays it serves as a secondary school and is closed to the public.

If you've got a head for heights, descend by the steps signed *'escalier poterne'* (rear stairway). Steep and slippery after rain, they plunge down beside the moss-covered ramparts to **Porte de l'Échauguette** (Watchtower Gate).

Prison des Évêques   MONUMENT

(Bishops' Prison; ☑ 05 59 37 00 92; 41 rue de la Citadelle; adult/child €3/free; ☺ 10.30am-7pm Jul-Aug, 11am-12.30pm & 2.30-6.30pm Wed-Mon Apr-Jun, Sep & Oct) Dating back to the 14th century, this vaulted cellar served as the town jail after 1795, as a military lock-up in the 19th century, then as a place of internment during WWII for those caught trying to flee to nominally neutral Spain. The lower section dates from the 13th century, when St-Jean Pied de Port was a bishopric of the Avignon papacy; the building above it dates from the 16th century. There are seasonal exhibitions inside.

🛏 Sleeping

Much of the accommodation is geared towards pilgrims on the long hike to Santiago de Compostela in Galicia, Spain. This type of accommodation is very basic: normally budget dorm beds (around €15 per person). At many places non-pilgrims will be turned away.

If you stay inside the old town, you'll have to haul your luggage on foot from wherever you park.

Itzalpea   PENSION €

(☑ 05 59 37 03 66; www.hotel-itzalpea.com; 5 place du Trinquet; s/d/tr €57/75/105; ❋ 🐾) Outside the walled town, above a popular tearoom, this simple hotel makes a good base, with seven rooms eclectically decorated with puffy bedspreads, vintage furniture and splashes of modern art. It's basic but good for those on a budget. Not all rooms have air-con, and front-facing ones suffer from a bit of road noise.

Hôtel Ramuntcho   HOTEL €€

(☑ 05 59 37 03 91; www.hotel-ramuntcho.com; 1 rue de France; r from €78; ☺ closed Dec; 🐾) In the same hands for generations – and with a suitably old-fashioned feel – this is the only hotel proper inside the walled town. It's in a typical Béarn half-timbered house, with plain, peach-coloured rooms, some of which look over the street, and others of which have views over the Pyrenean foothills. There's also a restaurant on the ground floor. It's part of the Logis de France chain.

🍴 Eating

Monday Market   MARKET €

(place Charles de Gaulle; ☺ 8am-1pm Mon) Farmers from the surrounding hills bring fresh produce – chillies, local cheeses and much

CROSS-BORDER ENCOUNTERS: A DAY IN SAN SEBASTIÁN

Just 33km southwest of St-Jean de Luz, the elegant, sexy and seriously Spanish city of San Sebastián makes a perfect day trip from the French Basque Country. With its twin beaches, lively nightlife and lovely old town, San Sebastián is worth a day of anyone's time, but it's the sensational food that really makes the trip worthwhile. The town has some of the best tapas (or *pintxos*, as they're known here) bars anywhere in Spain, not to mention more Michelin-starred restaurants per capita than anywhere else in the world – including three-starred **Arzak**, the flagship establishment of acclaimed chef Juan Mari Arzak, who frequently features in lists of the world's best chefs.

From St-Jean de Luz, it's just a short 20-minute jump via the A63 (and its many toll-booths); the N10 is toll-free, but turns into one long traffic jam in summer. In high season, it's better to catch a bus or train.

Buses from the French side are easiest: **Transportes Pesa** (☑ Information in Spain +34 900 12 14 00; www.pesa.net), **Ouibus** (www.ouibus.com), **Flixbus** (☑ +49 (0)30 300 137 300; www.flixbus.com) and **Conda** (www.conda.es) services run regularly. Otherwise, trains go from St-Jean de Luz to Hendaye (and occasionally onto Irún in Spain) roughly hourly (€3, 10 minutes). In Hendaye or Irún, board one of the frequent Euskotren metro trains (www.euskotren.es) to San Sebastián Amara station (€2.20, 37 minutes, every 30 minutes). In Hendaye, the metro train stop is just across the car park from the SNCF station.

more – to the town's Monday market. In high summer, a weekly handicraft and food fair is held most Thursdays in the covered market.

Café Ttipia   CAFE €
(☑ 05 59 37 11 96; www.cafettipia.com; 2 place Floquet; mains €12-15; ⊙ 7.30am-2am Thu-Tue, also open Wed Jul & Aug) Fresh, wholesome dishes are served under the plane trees on a beautiful riverfront terrace in summer – expect seasonal local specialities, charcuterie and classics like *steak frites*. It's also one of the best places in town to grab an evening drink.

★ Chez Arrambide   GASTRONOMY €€€
(☑ 05 59 37 01 01; www.hotel-les-pyrenees.com; 19 place Charles de Gaulle; menus €42-110, mains €36-52; ⊙ 12.15-1.45pm & 7.45-9pm daily Jul & Aug, Wed-Mon Sep-Jun) This two-Michelin-starred restaurant at the Hôtel des Pyrénées is renowned for miles around, and is where chef Firmin Arrambide works wonders with market produce. It's a high-class treat, where dishes are as arty as they are edible. Basic rooms (€105 to €255) are available upstairs.

☆ Entertainment

Year-round, variants of *pelota* (admission €7 to €10), including a bare-handed *pelota* tournament, are played at the *trinquet*, *fronton* municipal and *jaï alaï* courts. In summer, these tend to take place at 5pm on a Friday.

In high summer, traditional Basque music and dancing takes place in the *jaï alaï* court or the church. Confirm schedules with the tourist office.

ℹ Information

Tourist Office (☑ 05 59 37 03 57; www.saint-jeanpieddeport-paysbasque-tourisme.com; 14 place Charles de Gaulle; ⊙ 9am-7pm Mon-Sat, 10am-1pm & 2-5pm Sun Jul & Aug, 9am-noon & 2-6pm Mon-Sat Sep-Jun) Maps of local walking trails and schedules for *jaï alaï* matches.

ℹ Getting There & Away

A train is the only public transport to/from Bayonne (€10, 1¼ hours, four daily); this is a spur line and does not go any further than St-Jean Pied de Port. There is also an SNCF bus that runs from Pau's train station to Bayonne, passing through St-Jean Pied de Port en route.

St-Étienne de Baïgorry

POP 1575

The village of St-Étienne de Baïgorry and its outlying hamlets straddle the idyllic Vallée de Baïgorry. This superbly picturesque village stretches along a branch of the River Nive, and like so many Basque settlements, the village has two focal points: its unique church and the *fronton* (*pelota* court). It's also tops for its local hikes…a beautiful spot, indeed.

⊙ Sights & Activities

St-Étienne de Baïgorry makes a good base for hikers, as several spectacular walks start close by (you'll still need a car to reach many of the trailheads). Tourist offices in St-Étienne de Baïgorry and St-Jean Pied de Port (p691) supply route suggestions.

Église St-Étienne de Baïgorry   CHURCH
(☑ 05 59 37 47 28; place de l'Église; ☉ 9am-noon & 2-6pm) The lovely church of St-Étienne was built in the 11th century using the red stone of the nearby Arradoy, and is in the Roman-Byzantine style. It's notable for its three floors of galleries, its painted triumphal arch and the three altars embellished with gilded altarpieces. Keep your eyes open for recycled Roman columns in the nave.

🛏 Sleeping & Eating

You're way off the beaten track here: there are just a couple of hotels to choose from.

Hôtel-Restaurant Arcé   HOTEL €€
(☑ 05 59 37 40 14; www.hotel-arce.com; Route Colonel Ispéguy Baïgorry; d €140-180, ste €200-290; ☉ closed mid-Nov–Apr; 🔊🏊) This impressive hotel has a stunning riverside location and spacious rooms with old-style furnishings. To reach the pool, you stroll past the orange trees and cross the river via a little humpback bridge. The in-house restaurant (*menus* from €28; open for lunch Tuesday and Friday to Sunday, and dinner daily, from April to mid-November) is highly regarded by locals.

The half-board deals offer good value (double/suite from €115/155 per person).

Hôtel-Restaurant Manexenea   HOTEL €
(☑ 05 59 37 41 68; www.manexenea.com; Urdos; s/d from €61/67; ☉ hotel Mar-late Dec; P ✱ 🔊) Five kilometres north of St-Étienne de Baïgorry in the hamlet of Urdos, this rural hotel has cheerful rooms (renovated in 2016) that overlook green fields and a bubbling mountain-fed brook. You can eat some of the denizens of said brook, such as delicious trout, for lunch at the in-house restaurant (open Tuesday to Sunday; two-/three-course *menu* €22/30).

❶ Information

Tourist Office (☑ 05 59 37 47 28; www.saintjeanpieddeport-paysbasque-tourisme.com; 1 place de la Mairie; ☉ 9am-noon & 2-6pm Mon-Sat, 10am-1pm Sun early Jul-Aug, 9am-noon & 2-6pm Mon-Fri rest of year) Local trail maps and info.

❶ Getting There & Away

You'll need your own wheels to reach this village.

The Pyrenees

POP 476,000

Best Places to Eat

➡ Le Viscos (p702)

➡ Le Majestic (p698)

➡ L'Héptaméron des Gourmets (p713)

➡ Lau Tant'hic (p711)

➡ Le Jeu de l'Oie (p715)

Best Places to Stay

➡ Le Castel de la Pique (p712)

➡ Hôtel du Lion d'Or (p710)

➡ Auberge les Myrtilles (p716)

➡ L'Abbaye de Camon (p716)

➡ Eth Béryè Petit (p702)

Why Go?

Spiking the skyline for 430km along the Franco-Spanish border, the snow-dusted Pyrenees offer a glimpse of France's wilder side. This serrated chain of peaks contains some of the country's most pristine landscapes and rarest wildlife, including endangered species such as the griffon vulture, izard (a type of mountain goat) and brown bear. Since 1967, 457 sq km has been protected as the Parc National des Pyrénées, ensuring its valleys, tarns and mountain pastures are preserved for future generations.

Rural and deeply traditional, the Pyrenees' wild landscapes now provide a paradise for skiers, climbers, hikers and bikers. But there's more to the mountains than just outdoor thrills: there are alpine villages to wander, hilltop castles to admire and ancient caves to investigate. They might not be on quite the same scale as the Alps, but the Pyrenees are every bit as stunning. Strap on your boots – it's time to explore.

When to Go
Pau

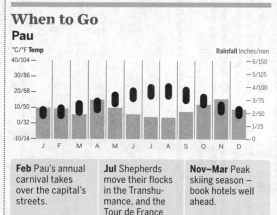

Feb Pau's annual carnival takes over the capital's streets.

Jul Shepherds move their flocks in the Transhumance, and the Tour de France races through.

Nov–Mar Peak skiing season – book hotels well ahead.

The Pyrenees Highlights

1 Pic du Midi (p711)
Admiring the views from the sky-top observatory.

2 Cirque de Gavarnie (p709) Trekking to the mountain amphitheatre.

3 Parc Animalier des Pyrénées (p703) Seeing endangered Pyrenean wildlife.

4 Grotte de Niaux (p714) Marvelling at the prehistoric cave-paintings.

5 Pont d'Espagne (p710) Tackling the trails around Cauterets.

6 Pau's old town (p695) Exploring hidden lanes and chocolate shops.

7 Col du Tourmalet (p697) Driving over the Pyrenees' highest road pass.

8 Labouiche (p714) Floating through the underworld on a subterranean river.

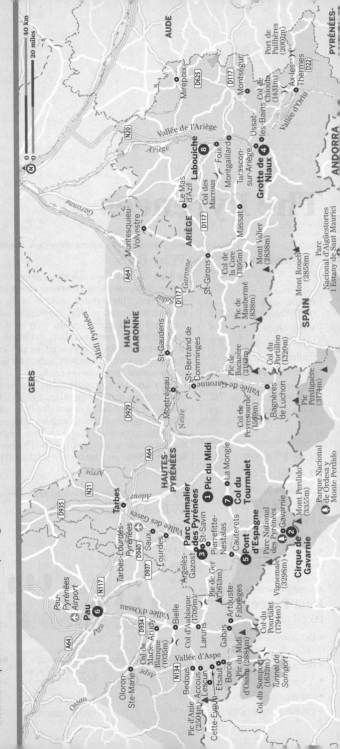

PAU

POP 77,300 / ELEV 220M

In many ways, Pau feels closer to a Riviera resort than a mountain town, with its grand villas, public parks and palm-lined promenades. The largest city in the Pyrenees was once a favourite wintering spot for expat British and Americans, and there's still a touch of fin-de-siècle grandeur around its well-kept streets.

◉ Sights

The town centre sits on a small hill with the Gave de Pau (River Pau) at its base. Along its crest stretches bd des Pyrénées, a wide promenade offering panoramic views of the mountains. A creaky funicular railway dating from 1908 clanks down from bd des Pyrénées to av Napoléon Bonaparte.

Pau's tiny old centre extends for about 500m around the château.

Château de Pau   CHATEAU
(☑ 05 59 82 38 00; www.chateau-pau.fr; 2 rue du Château; adult/child €7/free; ⊙ 9.30am-12.15pm & 1.30-5.45pm, gardens open longer hours) Originally the residence of the monarchs of Navarre, Pau's castle was transformed into a Renaissance château amid lavish gardens by Marguerite d'Angoulême in the 16th century. Marguerite's grandson, Henri de Navarre (the future Henri IV), was born here – cradled, so the story goes, in an upturned tortoise shell (still on display in one of the museum's rooms).

Musée Bernadotte   MUSEUM
(☑ 05 59 27 48 42; 8 rue Tran; adult/child €3/free; ⊙ 10am-noon & 2-6pm Tue-Sun) This townhouse is the birthplace of one of Napoléon's favourite generals, Jean-Baptiste Bernad-otte (nicknamed 'Sergent belle-jambe', on account of his shapely legs). Now a museum, the house explores the strange story of how Bernadotte came to be crowned king of Sweden and Norway in 1810, when the Swedish parliament reckoned that the only way out of the country's dynastic and political crisis was to stick a foreigner on the throne.

Musée des Beaux-Arts   GALLERY
(☑ 05 59 27 33 02; rue Mathieu Lalanne; €5; ⊙ 10am-noon & 2-6pm Wed-Mon) Works by Rubens and El Greco both figure at Pau's fine-arts museum, but the museum's prize piece is a famous Degas canvas, *A New Orleans Cotton Office,* painted in 1873.

✯ Festivals & Events

Carnival Biarnés   CARNIVAL
(www.carnavalbiarnes.com; ⊙ late Feb) Pau holds its annual carnival during the lead-up to Lent. Street parades, costumed processions and general merriment takes over the town, and there's even a mock bear hunt.

Hestiv'Òc   MUSIC
(www.hestivoc.com; ⊙ mid-Aug) Over three days in mid-August (usually the first weekend after the 15th), this massive fest features free concerts and theatre performances all around the city centre. Pau's biggest and best event is always a good time, so don't miss it if you're in the area.

🛏 Sleeping

Brit Hôtel Bosquet   HOTEL €
(☑ 05 59 11 50 11; www.hotel-bosquet.com; 11 rue Valéry Meunier; r €64-85; ❈ 🛜) For the money, this is one of the best-value lodging options in the historic centre. Rooms are a

---

THE REBIRTH OF THE HÉDAS QUARTIER

Although it runs for almost 1km right through Pau's historic centre, the **rue du Hédas** is bafflingly easy to miss. For centuries, the creek that flowed here was used as a sewer, and it retained an air of ill repute right up through the 1950s. Then in 2016, the city launched a rejuvenation projection for this neglected corner of the city, and it was transformed into a sparkling new promenade. Bold, sculpturesque light installations were installed along the 800m lane, gardens and public spaces were added (including *pétanque* courts and a playground), and new businesses arrived. Today, it's a fascinating place to explore, with a handful of eating and drinking spots, and surprising vestiges of the past: the fountain off place Récaborde was once the only source of water in Pau, and was used as a makeshift laundry well into the 20th century. Nearby, at No 20, a doorway beneath a lion sculpture marks the entrance to the home of Pau's last executioner. There are limited access points, though you will find stairs, a lift and slides down to the lane from place d'Espagne.

Pau

Pau

⊚ Sights
1 Château de Pau	A3
2 Musée Bernadotte	B3
3 Musée des Beaux-Arts	D2
4 Rue du Hédas	B3

🛏 Sleeping
5 Brit Hôtel Bosquet	C3
6 Hôtel Bristol	C3

🍴 Eating
7 Café du Passage	A3
8 Chez Canaille	B3
9 Halles de Pau	B2
10 La Fiancée du Desert	B3

11 Le Majestic	B4
12 Les Amants du Marché	B1
Les Papilles Insolites	(see 17)

🍸 Drinking & Nightlife
13 Au Grain de Raisin	A3
14 Le Garage	D2
15 Les Sardines	C3

🛍 Shopping
16 Au Parapluie des Pyrénées	B2
17 BricOTruc	C2
18 Francis Miot	B3
19 Josuat	B2

mix of cheery yellow sponge-painting and exposed stone walls, along with oversized mirrors, touches of artwork and bright bathrooms (with blue and yellow ceramic tiles), though some rooms could use more natural light. Service is friendly.

Hôtel Bristol HOTEL €€
(☎ 05 59 27 72 98; www.hotelbristol-pau.com; 3 rue Gambetta; s €80-100, d €90-110, f €120-130; 🅿 🛜) A classic old French hotel with surprisingly up-to-date rooms, all wrapped up in a fine 19th-century building. Each room is uniquely

ℹ️ ROAD PASSES IN THE PYRENEES

High road passes link the Vallée d'Ossau, the Vallée d'Aspe and the Vallée des Gaves (all of which have regularly featured as punishing mountain stages during the Tour de France). The altitude means that they're often blocked by snow well into summer; signs indicate whether they're *ouvert* (open) or *fermé* (closed).

Col d'Aubisque (1709m; open May to October) The D918 links Laruns in the Vallée d'Ossau with Argelès-Gazost in the Vallée des Gaves. An alternative that's open year-round is the D35 between Louvie-Juzon and Nay.

Col de Marie-Blanque (1035m; open most of year) The shortest link between the Aspe and Ossau valleys is the D294, which corkscrews for 21km between Escot and Bielle.

Col du Pourtalet (1794m; open most of year) The main crossing into Spain generally stays open year-round except during exceptional snowfall.

Col du Tourmalet (2115m; open June to October) Between Barèges and La Mongie, this is the highest road pass in the Pyrenees. If you're travelling east to the Pic du Midi (eg from Cauterets), the only alternative is a long detour north via Lourdes and Bagnères-de-Bigorre.

---

designed, with bold artwork and elegant furniture, while big windows fill the rooms with light. Ask for a mountain view room with balcony. Breakfast is pricey at €12.

Clos Mirabel　　　　　　　B&B €€
(🖉 05 59 06 32 83; www.clos-mirabel.com; 276 av des Frères Barthélémy, Jurançon; d €120-160, ste €260; 🅿️🛜❄️) If you don't mind being 7km west of the city, this 18th-century manor house makes a fine retreat. There are five colour-coded B&B bedrooms with heritage furniture, fireplaces and wood floors: top picks are the Blue Bedroom and the vast Master Bedroom. The gardens and pool are a bonus.

🍴 Eating

La Fiancée du Desert　　MIDDLE EASTERN €
(🖉 05 59 27 27 58; www.la-fiancee-du-desert. com; 21 rue Tran; mains around €9, menus €13-19; ⏰noon-2pm & 7-10pm Tue-Sat) Colourful tapestries, fairy lights and Moroccan lamps set the scene at this rustically chic spot that seems to be everyone's favourite eatery *du jour*. The small plates are best – order a platter with tabouli, hummus, babaganoush, felafel and many other Lebanese delicacies and taste everything. End with mint tea and heavenly baklava.

Les Amants du Marché　　　VEGETARIAN €
(🖉 05 59 02 75 51; www.lesamantsdumarche.fr; 1 rue Bourbaki; menu lunch €15, dinner €18-23, mains around €13; ⏰noon-2pm & 7.30-10pm Tue-Sat; 🖉) Vegetarians have much to celebrate at this delightful little eatery across from the organic market. The chalkboard menu

changes regularly and showcases ingredients often overlooked in traditional French cooking. You'll find deliciously creative dishes along the lines of broccoli and split-pea terrine; bok choy with chickpeas, cumin and peanut sauce; and arancini with squash, feta, sun-dried tomatoes and fennel.

Chez Canaille　　　　　　　FRENCH €€
(🖉 05 59 27 68 65; 3 rue de Hédas; menus lunch €12.50-14.50, dinner €28-35; ⏰noon-1.45pm & 7.45-9.45pm Tue-Fri, 7.45-9.45pm Sat) Hidden down on atmospheric rue de Hédas, Chez Canaille has old-fashioned charm, with burgundy banquettes, red-checked tablecloths and unfussy wooden furniture. The small menu has some fine standouts, including a decadent fois gras, slow-roasted lamb that falls off the bone, and mouth-watering *St-Jacques snackées* (scallops).

Les Papilles Insolites　　　　FRENCH €€
(🖉 05 59 71 43 79; www.lespapillesinsolites.blog spot.co.uk; 5 rue Alexander Taylor; tapas €8-12; ⏰6-10.30pm Wed-Sat) Run by a former Parisian sommelier, this cosy wine bar serves beautifully prepared small plates like Galician-style octopus, scallops with leeks or lamb with cumin. Complete the experience with the owner's choice of one of the 350-odd wines stacked around the shop. Gorgeously Gallic.

Café du Passage　　　　　　FUSION €€
(🖉 05 59 06 29 17; 5 place Reine Marguerite; mains €17-24; ⏰noon-2pm & 7.30-11pm; 🖉) This festive, colourfully decked-out space fits the bill when you seek a bit more *joie de vivre* with your dining experience. Amid low-playing

grooves and whimsical murals, diners tuck into juicy burgers, fish and chips and sizeable vegetable platters. On warm days, join the outdoor diners at tables on the square.

Le Majestic
FRENCH €€€

(☑ 05 59 27 56 83; 9 place Royale; menus lunch €16-25, dinner €28-44; ☺ noon-1.30pm & 7.30-9pm Tue-Sat, noon-1.30pm Sun) This smart restaurant serves top-notch French cuisine. It's formal inside – ice-white tablecloths, razor-sharp napkins, twisted willow – but it suits the sophisticated food, heavy on premium ingredients such as turbot, sea bass, Bigorre pork and Pyrenean lamb. If the sun's out, sit at a table beneath the trees on leafy place Royale.

🍷 Drinking & Nightlife

'Le Triangle', bounded by rue Henri Faisans, rue Émile Garet and rue Castetnau, is the centre of student nightlife, and a string of bars extends along bd des Pyrénées. Pau has some inviting cafes and teahouses – perfect spots to retreat if the weather sours.

Les Sardines
BAR

(9 rue Gachet; ☺ 6pm-2am Tue-Sat) True to name, this festive bar is always packed. Amid vintage signs and a curiously configured ceiling, a mostly 20-something crowd gathers over excellent wine selections (over two dozen by the glass), cocktails lit up by glow sticks and enticing sharing plates. Go early to score a table.

Le Garage
BAR

(☑ 05 59 83 75 17; www.le-garage-bar.fr; 49 rue Émile Garet; ☺ noon-1.30am Mon-Fri, from 3pm Sat & Sun) Le Garage plays heavily on the filling-station theme, with road signs, rockabilly tunes and dangling motorbikes overhead (choose your table carefully). It draws a young and lively crowd, and there's often live music on weekends – and sports shown on multiple screens at other times.

Au Grain de Raisin
WINE BAR

(☑ 05 59 82 98 44; http://barsàvins.com; 11 rue Sully; ☺ 5pm-midnight Wed-Sat, 4-11pm Sun) A welcoming wine bar near the château, which serves a good selection of Continental beers and local wines by the glass (from €3.80 to 6.80), accompanied by plates of tapas.

🛍 Shopping

Pau is famous for its *chocolatiers* (chocolate shops): the top names are Josuat (23 rue Serviez; ☺ 9.30am-12.15pm & 2.30-7.15pm Mon-Sat) and Francis Miot (48 rue Maréchal Joffre; ☺ 10am-7pm Mon-Sat).

ℹ MARKET ALERT!

Pau's once unsightly produce market Halles de Pau (Covered Market; place de la République; ☺ 6am-1pm & 3.30-7.30pm Mon-Fri, 6am-1pm Sat) will soon be housed in a new, beautifully designed, light-filled building adjoining its previous location. Look for the opening in late 2019.

BricOTruc
VINTAGE

(☑ 06 68 32 49 29; 5 rue Taylor; ☺ 2.30-6.30pm Tue, 10am-12.30pm & 2.30-6.30pm Wed-Sat) After browsing the boutiques of nearby rue Serviez, stop by BricOTruc, which has a delightful assortment of recycled jewellery, picture frames, toys, artwork, vases and other assorted bric-a-brac, all handsomely displayed.

Au Parapluie des Pyrénées
FASHION & ACCESSORIES

(12 rue Montpensier; ☺ 8am-noon & 2-7pm Tue-Sat) This lovely old shop makes the beech-handled, rattan-ribbed umbrellas traditionally used by Pyrenean shepherds. Also specialises in the anachronistic art of umbrella repair.

ℹ Information

Tourist Office (☑ 05 59 27 27 08; www.pau-pyrenees.com; place Royale; ☺ 9am-6pm Mon-Sat, 9.30am-1pm Sun) Stocked with useful information on local transport and the Pyrenees generally.

ℹ Getting There & Away

AIR

Aéroport Pau-Pyrénées (☑ 05 59 33 33 00; www.pau.aeroport.fr; rte de l'Aéroport, Uzein) The airport is around 11km northwest of town. There are currently four to six daily flights to Paris Orly (HOP!), three daily to Paris Charles de Gaulle (Air France), one to three daily to Lyon (HOP!), and nine per week to Marseille (Twin Jet).

BUS

Bus services are very limited, although there are at least a couple of daily services to Agen and Mont-de-Marsan, which depart from in front of the train station. Contact Cars Région Aquitaine (☑ 0 800 64 40 47; www.car.aquitaine.fr) for timetables.

TRAIN

Trains arrive at the Gare de Pau, just below the historic centre. There are four TGVs daily from

Paris. In summer, SNCF buses run from Oloron-Ste-Marie into the Vallée d'Aspe.

Bayonne €19 to €27, 1¼ hours

Oloron-Ste-Marie €8, 35 to 52 minutes

Paris Montparnasse €78 to €123, 4½ hours via direct TGV

Toulouse €35, two to 2½ hours

ⓘ Getting Around

TO/FROM THE AIRPORT

Idelis (☑ 05 59 14 15 16; www.reseau-idelis. com) runs an airport shuttle to Pau's train station and town centre. From the airport, buses run roughly hourly from 7.20am to 7.10pm; from the train station, buses run from 6.40am to 7.10pm. Tickets cost €1.30, and the journey time is about half an hour.

Note that buses don't run on Sunday, so you'll need to reserve a taxi at the airport **information desk** (☑ 05 59 33 33 00); expect to pay between €30 and €40.

PUBLIC TRANSPORT

Public transport in Pau is handled by Idelis. Single/day tickets cost €1.30/3.50. Pau's bike-sharing network, **IDEcycle** (www.idecycle. com; per day/week €1/5) is handy for zipping around town.

LOURDES

POP 13,950 / ELEV 400M

The sprawling town of Lourdes, 43km southeast of Pau, has been one of the world's most important pilgrimage sites since 1858, when 14-year-old Bernadette Soubirous (1844–79) is claimed to have been visited 18 times in a rocky grotto by the Virgin Mary.

Now known as the Sanctuaires Notre Dame de Lourdes, the grotto is considered one of the holiest sites in Christendom. Over six million people arrive in Lourdes every year hoping to be healed by the holy waters, but the modern town of Lourdes itself can feel rather dispiriting, with a tatty tangle of neon-signed hotels and souvenir shops selling everything from plastic crucifixes to Madonna-shaped bottles.

Outside the theme-park-like atmosphere of the town, you'll find some intriguing sites, including a hilltop castle and various humble abodes where Soubirous resided – which more than anything illustrate the many hardships the lower classes endured in the late 19th century.

◉ Sights & Activities

★ **Sanctuaires Notre Dame de Lourdes** CAVE

(www.fr.lourdes-france.org; av Monseigneur Théas; ⊗ Porte St-Michel & Porte St-Joseph 5am-midnight, baths 10-11am & 2-3.30pm Mon-Sat, 2.30-4pm Sun & holy days) The spiritual centre of Lourdes is the subterranean grotto where Bernadette Soubirous is believed to have experienced her visions in 1858. From the **Porte St-Michel** (av Monseigneur Théas; ⊗ 10am-6pm), a broad boulevard sweeps towards the gilded spires of the **Basilique du Rosaire** (av Monseigneur Théas; ⊗ 8am-6pm) and the **Basilique Supérieure** (Upper Basilica; av Monseigneur Théas; ⊗ 7am-6pm).

Underneath is the fabled **Grotte de Massabielle** (av Monseigneur Théas; ⊗ 5am-midnight), where people queue for hours to enter and take a blessed dip in the cave's icy-cold baths, while other pilgrims content themselves by lighting candles of remembrance outside.

From Palm Sunday to mid-October, nightly torchlight processions start from the Massabielle Grotto at 9pm, while at 5pm there's the Procession Eucharistique (Blessed Sacrament Procession) along the Esplanade des Processions.

Château Fort MUSEUM

(Fortified Castle; www.chateaufort-lourdes.fr; adult/child €7/3.50; ⊗ 10am-7pm mid-Apr–mid-Oct, to 6pm mid-Oct–mid-Apr) Lourdes' imposing castle stands on a sheer hill just behind the town. There's been a stronghold here since Roman times, but the present building combines a medieval keep with fortifications added during the 17th and 18th centuries. Since the 1920s, the castle has housed the **Musée Pyrénéen**, which displays local artefacts and folk art. Among the exhibitions here, you'll find mid-20th century Pyrenees travel posters, beautiful miniaturised chateaux from France, and intriguing traditional costumes from various valleys near Lourdes.

A free **lift** (rue Baron Duprat; ⊗ 10am-7pm mid-Apr–mid-Oct, to 6pm mid-Oct–mid-Apr) takes you up to the castle.

Pic du Jer VIEWPOINT

(☑ 05 62 94 00 41; www.picdujer.fr; bd d'Espagne; funicular return adult/child €12/9; ⊗ 9.30am-6pm late Mar-early Nov, to 7pm Jul & Aug) Panoramic views of Lourdes and the central Pyrenees are on offer from this rocky outcrop just outside town. There are two routes to the

Lourdes

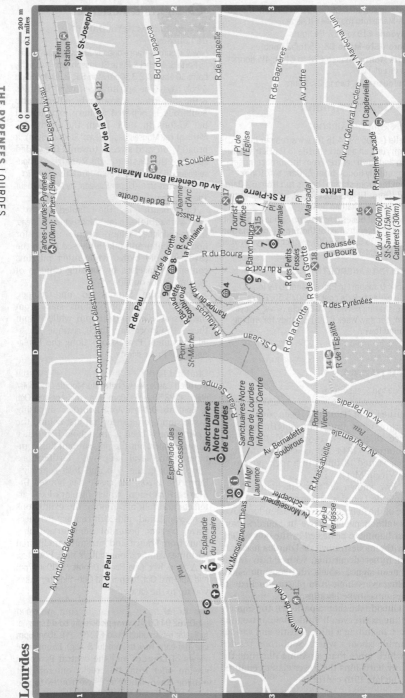

Train Station

Av St-Joseph

Av Eugene Duviau

Av de la Gare

Bd du Lapacca

R de Langelle

R de Bagnères

Av Joffre

Av du Général Leclerc

Av Maréchal Juin

Pl Capdevieille

R Anselme Lacadé

Tarbes-Lourdes-Pyrénées (10km); Tarbes (19km)

R Soubies

Av du Général Baron Maransin

Pl de l'Eglise

Pl St-Pierre

R St-Pierre

R Lafitte

Bd de la Grotte

R de la Fontaine

P Basse

P Jeanne d'Arc

Tourist Office

Pl Peyramale

R Baron Duprat

Marcadal

Pic du Jer (600m); St-Savin (15km); Cauterets (30km)

Bd Commandant Célestin Romain

Bd de la Grotte

R Bertrand Soubirous

Rampe du Fort

R Maupas du Fort

R du Bourg

R du Fort

R des Petits Fossés

R de la Grotte

Chaussée du Bourg

R des Pyrénées

R de Pau

Pont St-Michel

Ô St-Jean

R Jean Sempé

Esplanade des Processions

Sanctuaires Notre Dame de Lourdes

Sanctuaires Notre Dame de Lourdes Information Centre

Av Bernadette Soubirous

Pont Vieux

Av Peyramale

R Massabielle

Av du Paradis

R de l'Egalité

R de l'Egalité

Av Antoine Béguère

R de Pau

Esplanade du Rosaire

Av Monseigneur Theas

Pl Mgr Laurence

Av Monseigneur Schoepfer

Pl de la Merlasse

Chemin de Croix

THE PYRENEES LOURDES

Lourdes

top: a punishing three-hour hike (ideal for penitents) or a speedy six-minute ride on the funicular (ideal for everyone else).

There's a choice of routes back down: a black-run mountain-bike trail, or a more family-friendly option along the **Voie Verte des Gaves**, a decommissioned railway that finishes up at the lower funicular station.

To get to the lower funicular, take bus A1 from Les Halles.

Grottes de Bétharram CAVE
(☑ 05 62 41 80 04; www.betharram.com; chemin Léon Ross, St-Pé-de-Bigorre; adult/child €14.50/9; ⊙ 9am–noon & 1.30-5.30pm late-Mar–Oct) Grottes de Bétharram is a network of subterranean caverns that has been carved out from the limestone, glittering with impressive formations of stalactites and stalagmites. Visits to the cave aboard a combination of minitrain and barge last around 1½ hours, but be warned: the site gets extremely busy in high summer. The site is along the D937, 14km west of Lourdes.

Moulin de Boly MUSEUM
(Boly Mill; 12 rue Bernadette Soubirous; ⊙ 9am–noon & 2-6.30pm Apr-Oct, 3-5pm Nov-Mar) FREE Bernadette was born in this millhouse on 7 January 1844, one year after the marriage of her parents Louise Castérot and François Soubirous. She lived here for the first 10 years of her life; it's still possible to see her childhood bedroom, along with the house's mill machinery.

Le Cachot HISTORIC SITE
(15 rue des Petits Fossés; ⊙ 9am-noon & 2-6.30pm Apr-Oct, 10am-noon & 2-5pm Nov-Mar) FREE In 1857 Bernadette Soubirous' family fell on hard times and were forced to move to this dingy former prison, where they lived communally in a room measuring just 16 sq metres. It was while living here that Bernadette stumbled across the Grotte de Massabielle, having been sent out to collect firewood.

Maison Paternelle de Ste-Bernadette MUSEUM
(2 rue Bernadette Soubirous; €2; ⊙ 9.30am-12.15pm & 2.15-6.30pm late Mar-Oct) After Bernadette Soubirous experienced her visions, Lourdes' abbot bought this house for her family. It's still run by her descendants, and has a collection of memorabilia including family photos and a bed where Bernadette supposedly slept.

Chemin de Croix WALKING
(Way of the Cross; ⊙ 6am-10pm) The Chemin de Croix (sometimes known as the Chemin du Calvaire) leads for 1.5km up the hillside from the Basilique Supérieure past 14 life-size bronze-painted figures representing Stations of the Cross. Seriously devout pilgrims climb to the first station on their knees.

🛏 Sleeping

Lourdes has an enormous number of hotels (second only to Paris in terms of bed space, believe it or not), and you can generally find some good deals by shopping around. Unfortunately, most places are rather plain, with cookie-cutter rooms and services. For something more interesting (but pricier), consider basing yourself outside town.

🛏 Lourdes

Hôtel Saint-Avit HOTEL €
(☑ 05 62 94 06 35; www.hotel-saint-avit.com; 32 rue de l'Egalité; s/d/tr/q from €31/39/45/50; 🖥)

In a peaceful part of town (overlooking the cemetery), this good-value guesthouse has bright but simply furnished rooms, the best of which have views over the rolling hills beyond town. There's also a restaurant with a pleasant terrace.

Hôtel Majestic
HOTEL €

(☎05 62 94 27 23; www.hotel-lourdes-majestic. com; 9 av du Général Baron Maransin; d/tr/q from €40/50/60) Although it's on a busy avenue, the friendly Hôtel Majestic is worth considering for its bright, attractive rooms, with polished wood floors and big windows that let in ample light (but little street noise). It's also quite central, and an easy 300m (downhill) walk from the train station.

Bestwestern Beauséjour
HOTEL €€

(☎05 62 94 38 18; www.hotel-beausejour.com; 16 av de la Gare; s €78, d €88-195; P ⊕ ☒) A step above most Bestwesterns, the Beauséjour is set in an elegant 19th-century building, and has plenty of fine attributes: a bar-brasserie on the main floor, a small heated outdoor pool, good service and a convenient location across from the train station. Rooms range in size and quality; the cheapest are quite compact.

Around Lourdes

Eth Béryè Petit
B&B €

(☎05 62 97 90 02; www.beryepetit.com; 15 rte de Vielle, Beaucens; s/d from €70/75; P ⊕) Twelve kilometres south of Lourdes, this 17th-century farmhouse offers country charm and knockout mountain views. There are three rooms: the most spacious is Era Galeria, which has French windows onto a private balcony, while Poeyaspé and Bédoret are tucked into the beamed attic. Rates are cheaper for subsequent nights. Cash only. It's off the N21 near Beaucens.

Hôtel des Rochers
HOTEL €

(☎05 62 97 09 52; www.lesrochershotel.com; 1 place du Castillou, St-Savin; d €68-73, f €103; P ⊕) In the idyllic village of St-Savin, 16km south of Lourdes, this handsomely landscaped hotel makes a perfect mountain retreat. It's run by an expat English couple, John and Jane, who have renovated the rooms in clean, contemporary fashion – try for one with a mountain view. Half-board is available.

Relais de Saux
B&B €€

(☎05 62 94 29 61; www.lourdes-relais.com; Quartier de Saux; d €80-96; P ⊕) Ruched curtains, antique wardrobes and canopy beds abound

at this ivy-covered mansion, about 4km north of Lourdes. The period house is beautiful, but it's the surroundings that sell the place: grassy lawns and tree-filled gardens set against snowy Pyrenean peaks.

Eating

Lourdes' eating options are generally rather uninspiring, though there is a growing assortment of ethnic restaurants (catering to Lourdes' global visitors).

Les Halles de Lourdes
MARKET €

(place du Champ Commun; ⊙6.30am-1.30pm Mon-Thu, 6.30am-1.30pm & 4-6.30pm Fri, 5.30am-1.30pm Sat) Lourdes' covered market occupies most of the square. It's a fine spot for cheeses, charcuterie, antipasti and other good picnic fare.

Ganapathy
INDIAN €

(☎05 62 45 68 31; 5 rue Baron Duprat; mains €8-13, menu lunch/dinner €12/14; ⊙11am-11pm; ⊘) A favourite of visitors from the subcontinent, this cheerfully decorated restaurant serves up a fine variety of Indian classics. Chicken tikka masala, lamb biryani and prawn curry are among the selections. The *thaalis* (multidish platters) are excellent value for lunch or dinner.

Lung Ta
TIBETAN €

(☎05 62 92 80 45; www.restaurantlungta.fr; 8 rue des Quatre Frères Soulas; mains €10-12; ⊙noon-2pm & 7-10pm Wed-Mon; ⊘) This cosy and warmly lit Tibetan eatery is a surprising find in Lourdes. Amid rice-paper lamps, Tibetan prayer flags and a small Buddha shrine, diners tuck into fragrant dishes from the mountain kingdom. Rich soups like Tsel Thuk (with vegetables and house-made noodles) are quite satisfying. Good vegetarian choices.

O Piment Rouge
BASQUE €€

(☎05 62 41 47 87; www.restaurant-piment-rouge. com; 37 rue de la Grotte; mains €18-22, menu lunch €14-16, dinner €19-29; ⊙noon-1.45pm Thu-Tue, 7-9.30pm Thu-Mon) Dining out can be decidedly hit-and-miss in Lourdes, which makes this delightful eatery a doubly good find. It serves up delicacies from the Basque Country, including squid cooked in ink, tender stewed lamb and a decadent custard sponge cake.

★ Le Viscos
GASTRONOMY €€€

(☎05 62 97 02 28; www.hotel-leviscos.com; 1 rue Lamarque, St-Savin; menus €32-84; ⊙12.30-1.30pm Tue-Sun, 7.30-8.30pm Tue-Sat; P ✴ ⊕) Ex-TV chef Jean-Pierre St-Martin has established his own gastronomic hideaway in St-Savin, 16km south of Lourdes. Known for blending Basque, Breton and Pyrenean cuisine, as well as his unshakeable passion for foie gras, he's now assisted by his son Alexis. Expect very rich, very traditional fine-dining food.

ⓘ Information

Sanctuaires Notre Dame de Lourdes Information Centre (Centre d'Information; ☑ 05 62 42 20 08; www.lourdes-france.com; av Monseigneur Théas; ⊘ 8.30am-12.15pm & 1.45-6.30pm) For information on the Sanctuaires Notre Dame de Lourdes.

Tourist Office (☑ 05 62 42 77 40; www. lourdes-infotourisme.com; place Peyramale; ⊘ 9am-6.30pm) Lourdes' main tourist office has general information on the Pyrenees and advice on accommodation, transport and activities.

ⓘ Getting There & Away

AIR

Tarbes-Lourdes-Pyrénées Airport (www.tlp. aeroport.fr) is 10km north of Lourdes on the N21. There are at least three daily flights to Paris Orly (Air France and HOP!), plus three to four weekly flights to London Stansted, three to Milan and two to Krakow (all Ryanair), as well as several a week to Brussels (TUI Fly) and Rome (AlbaStar).

BUS

The small **bus station** (place Capdevieille) has services northwards to Pau (though trains are much faster and the recommended way to go). Buses running between Tarbes and Argelès-Gazost (at least eight daily), the gateway to the Pyrenean communities of Cauterets, Luz-St-Sauveur and Gavarnie, also stop here.

SNCF buses to Cauterets (€8.20, 54 minutes, at least five daily) leave from the train station.

TRAIN

Gare de Lourdes (33 ave de la Gare) has regular train connections, including direct TGVs to Pau and Paris Montparnasse. Trains to Toulouse often connect through Tarbes.
Bayonne €25 to €37, two hours via Pau
Paris Montparnasse €54 to €132, from 4¾ hours via TGV
Pau €8.30, 28 minutes
Toulouse €30, 2¼ hours

PARC NATIONAL DES PYRÉNÉES

Sprawling for 100km across the Franco-Spanish border, the Parc National des Pyrénées conceals some of the last pockets of true wilderness left in France. In partnership with the 156-sq-km Parque Nacional de Ordesa y Monte Perdido, on the Spanish side of the border, this mountain landscape is a haven for rare flora and fauna, and remains fiercely proud of its culture and heritage: traditional hill-farming and shepherding are still practised here in much the same way as they were a century ago.

Within the park's boundaries are the highest peaks in southwest France, including the loftiest of all, Vignemale (3298m).

WORTH A TRIP

NATURE WATCH

Around 12km south of Lourdes, off the D821 near Argelès-Gazost, fantastic animal park **Parc Animalier des Pyrénées** (☑ 05 62 97 91 07; www.parc-animalier.pyrenees.com; 60bis av des Pyrénées, Argelès-Gazost; adult/child €18/13; ⊘ 9.30am-6pm or 7pm Apr-Oct) is home to many species that were once commonly sighted across the Pyrenees. The animals live on special 'islands' designed to mirror their natural habitat: marmots, chamoix and ibex inhabit rocky hills; beavers and giant otters dart along wooded waterways; and brown bears lord it over their own boulder-strewn mountain kingdom.

There are also flying displays by birds of prey and the park's resident vultures. You can even spend the night in a trapper's cabin (double €390), with windows looking into the wolves' enclosure, or sleep in Le Refuge, a dome-shaped cabin with a floor-to-ceiling window overlooking the bears' habitat (double €390).

The park is doubly important given that many of the species here have either disappeared in the wild or are teetering on the brink of extinction – most notably the brown bear (known in the US as the grizzly; p705), which has all but vanished in the Pyrenees as a result of hunting and habitat loss. Despite fierce opposition from local farmers, a reintroduction program using wild bears from Slovenia has attempted to re-establish a breeding population, and it's thought that there are now around 30 bears roaming wild across the mountains.

🏃 Activities

Mountain Biking

Once the last snows melt around mid-April to May, many of the Pyrenean ski stations open up their trails to VTTs (*vélos tout-terrains;* mountain bikes).

Val d'Azun, Bagnères du Bigorre, Barrousse, Barèges, Ax and several other places all have extensive areas of *sentiers balisés* (marked trails). The useful **Pyrénées Passion** (www.pyrenees-passion.info) website lists the main VTT areas.

There's also a large mountain-bike park near Aude, offering over 900km of trails. Visit **Espace VTT-FFC Aude en Pyrénées** (www.vtt-pyrenees.com/espace-vtt) for directions, trail maps and other details.

Bikes are widely available, and specialist companies such as **La Rébenne** (🖉 05 61 65 20 93; www.larebenne.com; 1 place du 8 Mai 1945, Foix; ⊙ 9am-noon & 2-5.30pm Mon-Fri) offer guided mountain-biking expeditions.

Walking

Three hundred and fifty kilometres of waymarked trails (including the Mediterranean-to-Atlantic GR10) criss-cross the park. Within the park are about 20 *refuges* (mountain huts), primarily run by the Club Alpin Français (CAF). Most are staffed only from July to September but maintain a small crew year-round.

Each of the six park valleys (Vallée d'Aure, Vallée de Luz, Vallée de Cauterets, Val d'Azun, Vallée d'Ossau and Vallée d'Aspe) has a national park folder or booklet in French, *Randonnées dans le Parc National des Pyrénées,* describing 10 to 15 walks.

White-Water Sports

The Gave d'Aspe, Gave d'Oloron and Gave d'Ossau offer excellent white-water rafting. There are several companies based around Oloron-Ste-Marie, including Gaïa Aventure (p706) and **Centre Nautique de Soeix** (🖉 05 59 39 61 00; http://soeix.free.fr; 367 rte du Gave d'Aspe, quartier Soeix, Oloron-Ste-Marie; rafting per person from €25), which both offer canoeing, kayaking and rafting trips. Prices start at between €25 and €35 for a two-hour session.

Skiing

While the Pyrenees' best skiing is across the border at the Spanish resorts (around Baqueira-Beret and Andorra), the French-side resorts still offer good skiing, snow-boarding, *ski nordique* (cross-country skiing) and *raquette à neige* (snowshoeing). Atmospheric Cauterets (p709) is the best known and most stylish.

Grand Tourmalet   SKIING
(www.n-py.com; La Mongie) Home to 69 pistes, the Grand Tourmalet is the largest resort in the Pyrenees. Its 100km of runs trace their way around Col du Tourmalet and the Pic du Midi.

Val d'Azun   SKIING
(www.valdazun.com) The best cross-country skiing in the Pyrenees, 30km southwest of Lourdes.

Ax Trois Domaines   SKIING
(🖉 05 61 64 20 06; www.ax-ski.com; Ax-les-Thermes) Above Ax-les-Thermes, gentle runs snake through pine forest and, higher up, the open spaces of Campels. In summer its trails offer excellent hiking and biking.

ℹ Information

For general information, the PNR Pyrenees (www.pyrenees-parcnational.fr) website, the park's official tourist site, is the place to start. It has comprehensive information on activities, accommodation and sights.

Otherwise visit **Aude Tourist Office** (🖉 04 68 20 07 78; www.pyreneesaudoises.com; Square André Tricoire, Quillan; ⊙ 10am-noon & 2-5pm Mon-Fri). There are also small park visitor centres in Etsaut, Laruns, Arrens-Marsous, Cauterets, Luz-St-Sauveur, Gavarnie and St-Lary-Soulan.

ℹ Getting There & Away

Public transport is quite limited in the area. Getting around without a car is a challenge here, so it's wise to arrange a hire vehicle in Pau or Lourdes.

Vallée d'Aspe

The westernmost of the main Pyrenean valleys, the Vallée d'Aspe draws adventure seekers, hikers and those simply seeking a peaceful retreat from modern life at one of the valley's 13 picturesque cobblestone villages. Majestic peaks and sun-dappled forests make a fine backdrop to trekking, horse riding, mountain biking and paragliding.

Home to just over 3000 people, the valley has been an important thoroughfare since Julius Caesar's Roman legionnaires marched this way. Later, during medieval times, the valley became one of the main routes for pilgrims on the Chemin de St-Jacques, seeking a way across the mountains en route to Santiago de Compostela.

The small town of Oloron-Ste-Marie stands at the valley's northern end. From here, the N134 runs south, roughly following the course of the River Aspe for about 50km to the border, passing through the villages of Sarrance, Bedous, Accous, Cette-Eygun and Etsaut en route.

◉ Sights

Écomusée de la Vallée d'Aspe   MUSEUM
(http://ecomusee.haut-bearn.fr) FREE Four sites around the valley, collectively known as the Écomusée de la Vallée d'Aspe, explore the area's heritage and agricultural traditions. There are small folk museums in the villages of Sarrance, Lourdios-Ichère and Borcé, but the most interesting site is Les Fermiers Basco-Béarnais in Accous.

Opening hours vary by the season; see the website for details.

Les Fermiers Basco-Béarnais   FACTORY
(☑ 05 59 34 76 06; www.ossau-iraty.fr; rue Gambetta, Accous; ☺ 9am-noon & 3-6pm Mon-Thu & Sat, to 5pm Fri) At this farmers' co-op and *fromagerie* (cheese shop), you can sample cheese made from the milk of local ewes, goats and cows.

🏃 Activities

Hiking

For most people, the main reason to visit the Vallée d'Aspe is the chance to tramp the trails. Route suggestions and planning tools are available from the useful Caminaspe (www.caminaspe.fr) website.

The GR10 long-distance trail (part of the iconic Chemin St-Jacques) winds through the valley via the high-altitude village of Lescun, 5.5km from Bedous, which offers westerly views of the stunning Cirque de Lescun, an amphitheatre of jagged limestone mountains, backed by the 2504m Pic d'Anie. The village also marks the start of several fantastic day hikes. One stunning section of the GR10 leads northwest from Lescun via the Refuge de Labérouat and along the base of Les Orgues de Camplong (Camplong Organ Pipes). As long as the weather holds, you'll be guaranteed spectacular views back over the Vallée de Lescun and the distinctive Pic du Midi d'Ossau (2884m), but it's a high-altitude hike, so check the weather forecast, wear proper footwear, and pack wet-weather gear just in case.

Another popular route follows the GR10 south from Borce or Etsaut to Fort du Portalet (Urdos), a 19th-century fortress used as a

THE PYRENEAN BROWN BEAR

In 2004 in the Vallée d'Aspe, the last native brown bear left in France was shot by a boar-hunter, supposedly in self-defence. The demise of the female bear, known as Cannelle to conservationists, marked the extinction of a species that a century ago was still a relatively common sight in the Pyrenees. France was in uproar; the then-President Chirac declared it 'a great loss for French and European biodiversity'.

The species has since been reintroduced using bears imported from Slovenia. They have bred successfully, and it's thought that between 39 and 43 brown bears now roam across the French side of the mountains. Sadly, several have been killed in recent years, including one that fell from a cliff and another that was hit by a car between Argelès-Gazost and Lourdes.

The plight of brown bears in the Pyrenees has become an important touchstone for French conservationists, but it remains a deeply controversial issue, especially for local shepherds and farmers, who see the bears as dangerous predators that pose an unwelcome threat to their flocks and livelihoods. The issue reached a flash point in 2017 when a bear attacked a flock of sheep near Couflens. In a panic, the entire flock of 209 sheep fled over a cliff near the Spanish border and perished. Another 250 died in other bear incidents during the summer.

Despite the outcry by farmers on both sides of the border, the French environment minister Nicolas Hulot announced in 2018 that two more females would be introduced in the Béarn. The move was critical to help boost the faltering bear population – down to just two males – in the western part of the Pyrenees. Meanwhile, even with the new additions, the prospect for the long-term survival of the Pyrenean brown bear remains in a precarious state.

LOCAL KNOWLEDGE

THE TRANSHUMANCE

If you're travelling through the Pyrenees between late May and early June and you happen to find yourself stuck behind an enormous cattle-shaped traffic jam, there's a good chance you may have just got caught up in the age-old tradition of the Transhumance, in which shepherds move their flocks from their winter pastures up to the high grass-rich meadows of the mountain uplands.

This ancient custom has been a fixture on the Pyrenean calendar for hundreds of years, and is still regarded as one of the most important events of the year in the Pyrenees. The Transhumance is carried on in the time-honoured way – usually on foot, assisted by the occasional sheepdog or quad-bike – and several of the valleys host lively festivals to mark the occasion. The whole show is repeated in October, when the flocks are brought back down to the valleys before the snows of winter descend in earnest.

prison in WWII by the Germans and the Vichy government. In summer, 2½-hour tours (€10) in English can be organised through the Bedous tourist office or online (www.tourisme-aspe.com/fort-du-portalet.html).

The Bedous tourist office sells maps and the locally produced guidebook, *Le Topo des 45 Randonnées en Vallée d'Aspe*.

Horse Riding & Donkey Trekking

Randonnées à Cheval

Auberge Cavalière   HORSE RIDING
(05 59 34 72 30; www.auberge-cavaliere.com; quartier Estanguet, Accous; 4-/7-day trip €750/1245) The main centre for horse trips in the valley, run by experienced horse-wranglers Eric and Michel Bonnemazou from their family farm near Accous. They offer a number of guided expeditions through France and Spain throughout the summer, including a four- or seven-day tour of the Pyrenees national park, and a four- or seven-day tour of the spectacular Gavarnie area.

Le Parc Aux Ânes   DONKEY TREKKING
(05 59 34 88 98; www.garbure.net/ane_rando.htm; Etsaut; 4-day trip incl meals adult/child €245/175, plus per donkey €150) Run by the owners of **La Garbure** (05 59 34 88 98; www.garbure.net; Etsaut; per adult €20, half-board €34) *gîte*, this donkey-trekking outfit offers a range of guided trips, staying at remote mountain *gîtes* (self-catering cottages) – or, if you wish, wild camping. It's a fabulous experience, far removed from the hustle of the modern world – and best of all, thanks to your new donkey pal, you don't even have to carry your baggage.

Mountain Biking

Rando Bike   MOUNTAIN BIKING
(05 59 34 79 11; www.rando-bike.fr; Accous; adult/child half-day €24/19, full day €30/24) On

Accous' main street, this experienced firm rents out bikes and also runs its own half- and full-day *randonées VTT* (mountain-bike trips). If you're here in winter, they'll also teach you how to snowshoe.

White-Water Sports

Gaïa Aventure   WATER SPORTS
(06 18 58 08 69; www.gaiaaventure.com; 27 av d'Espagne, Bidos; rafting trips per person from €25) This outfit leads white-water rafting trips on the rivers near Oloron-Ste-Marie. Prices start at between €25 and €35 for a two-hour session.

🎉 Festivals & Events

The valley holds three annual markets in celebration of its local produce: an Easter market in Bedous, a summer market in Aydius on the first Sunday of August, and an autumn food fair in Sarrance.

Other events to look out for are **Le Transhumance de Lourdios** in early June, and the **Fête du Fromage d'Etsaut**, a cheese fair on the last Sunday in July.

🛏 Sleeping

Accommodation is mainly geared towards walkers, with several seasonal campgrounds and *gîtes d'étapes* (walkers' lodges) operating on a *demi-pension* (half-board) basis.

Camping Le Gave d'Aspe   CAMPGROUND €
(05 59 34 88 26; www.campingaspe.com; Urdos; per adult/child/tent €4.25/3/5, bungalow per weekend/week from €125/310; ⊙May-Sep) Beautifully situated alongside the clattering River Aspe, in a forested site near the mountain village of Urdos, this is a superb family-friendly campground. There's a choice of timber bungalows or canvas-roofed chalets, or you can pitch your own tent.

Camping du Lauzart CAMPGROUND €
(☑ 05 59 34 78 80; www.camping-lescun.com; Lescun; per adult/tent/child/car €3.85/5/2.75/1.65; ⊙ Apr-Sep; @ 🗢) Fifty-seven spacious sites pitched under the trees with full-blown mountain views, in a secluded spot just outside Lescun. There's an on-site cafe and fresh bread is delivered daily.

Chambre d'Hôtes Pouquette GUESTHOUSE €
(☑ 05 59 39 48 52; www.chambre-hotes-aspe-bearn-pouquette.com, Cette, Cette-Eygun; s €60-68, d €62-80; 🗢 🖾) Surrounded by undulating peaks, Pouquette makes for a fabulous base while exploring the Vallée d'Aspe. Its five pleasantly furnished rooms are painted in cheerful colours, and the friendly owners have a wealth of information on the region (Madame Ziane speaks excellent English). In the summer, the pool is a fine place to cool off after a day of hiking.

La Toison d'Or B&B €€
(☑ 05 59 34 57 12; place de l'Église de Cette, Cette-Eygun; r €75-105; 🅿 🗢) You'll keep expecting members of Monty Python to pop their heads round the corner at this bizarrely brilliant medieval-era *auberge* (country inn), where the rooms hunker behind arches, block-stones and carved wooden doors. It's been gradually renovated by owner Julie; the breakfast room is the highlight, with its vaulted ceiling and monumental mountain view. It's a 2km drive from Cette-Eygun.

Auberge Cavalière B&B €€
(☑ 05 59 34 72 30; www.auberge-cavaliere.com; quartier Estanguet, Accous; d/tr/f incl breakfast €74/109/139; 🅿 🗢) You'll really feel part of valley life at this rambling old horse farm 3km south of Accous, which offers five floral rooms and a cosy family *gîte*. The stone house is a picture of rustic character. Dinner and picnic baskets can also be arranged.

❶ Information

Pyrenees National Park Visitor Centre
(Maison du Parc National des Pyrénées; ☑ 05 59 34 88 30; Etsaut; ⊙ 10.30am-12.30pm & 2-6.30pm May-Oct) Housed in Etsaut's disused train station. This is a good place to get info on walking paths and other attractions in the area.

Tourist Office (☑ 05 59 34 57 57; www.tourisme-aspe.com; place Sarraillé, Bedous; ⊙ 9am-noon & 2-6pm Mon-Sat) The valley's main tourist office.

❶ Getting There & Away

SNCF buses and trains connect Pau and Oloron-Ste-Marie up to 10 times daily.

Citram Pyrenees (☑ 05 59 27 22 22; www.citrampyrenees.fr) runs a regular bus (three to five daily Monday to Saturday, two daily at weekends) from Oloron into the valley, stopping at all the main villages en route to Somport.

Vallée d'Ossau

Stretching south from Pau to the Spanish border, the Vallée d'Ossau is known for its deep pastoral traditions, sleepy villages and spectacular mountain scenery. The valley tracks its namesake river from its confluence with the Aspe at Oloron-Ste-Marie all the way to the watershed at Col du Pourtalet (1794m), some 60km to the south. The entrance to the valley as far as Laruns is green and pastoral, carpeted with lush fields and farms. Further south, the mountains stack up as the valley draws ever closer to the Spanish border. Aside from magnificent walks amid chiselled peaks and topaz lakes, there's much to explore in this valley: quaint and little-visited mountain settlements, soaring griffon vultures at the Falaise aux Vautours, and the Petit Train d'Artouste, one of Europe's highest train rides.

◉ Sights & Activities

There are 18 tiny villages dotted along the Vallée d'Ossau. The main focus is Laruns, 37km from Pau, a sturdy hamlet that has an excellent tourist office (p709) and national park centre (p709), both stocked with information on hiking, mountain biking, rafting and other outdoor pursuits.

Falaise aux Vautours WILDLIFE RESERVE
(Cliff of the Vultures; ☑ 05 59 82 65 49; www.falaise-aux-vautours.com; Béon; adult/child €6/4; ⊙ 10.30am-12.30pm & 2-6.30pm daily Jul & Aug, 1.30-5.30pm Mon-Fri Apr-Jun & Sep) The griffon vulture *(Gyps fulvus)* was once a familiar sight over the Pyrenees, but habitat loss and hunting have taken their toll on these strange, majestic birds. Now legally protected, over 100 nesting pairs roost around the limestone cliffs of this 82-hectare reserve. It's a thrill watching them swoop and wheel from their nests above the valley, and strategically placed CCTV cameras allow you to see inside their nests from the visitor centre.

Bielle VILLAGE

The former 'capital' of the valley, Bielle is a beautiful village with many fine 15th- and 16th-century houses, linked together via a guided walk.

Rébénacq VILLAGE

Rébénacq is one of the few *bastides* (fortified towns) of the Pyrenees, built in 1347 by a lieutenant of Gaston Fébus, the 11th Count of Foix. Like all *bastides,* it's set around a central square, the place de la Bielle, whose buildings and dimensions have barely changed in seven centuries.

Castet VILLAGE

Perched precariously on a glacial outcrop, this hilltop village boasts a 12th-century keep and a truly magnificent valley view. From the *belvédère* (panoramic viewpoint) known as Port de Castet (868m), hiking and biking trails wind along the hillside.

Eaux-Bonnes VILLAGE

During the 19th century, the small village of Eaux-Bonnes (literally, Good Waters) flourished as a spa resort thanks to its geothermal hot springs, which fed public baths frequented by many illustrious figures including the Empress Eugénie. Even if you're not here for a treatment at the **Thermes des Eaux Bonnes** (☑ 05 59 05 34 02; eaux-bonnes@valvital.fr; rue du Docteur Creignou, Eaux-Bonnes; spa pass adult child €16/8; ☺ 9am–6pm mid-May–Oct), Eaux-Bonnes is worth a stroll through the town's historic centre, which looks all the more striking against the mountainous backdrop of the Pyrenees.

🛏 Sleeping & Eating

L'Arrajou GUESTHOUSE €

(☑ 05 59 82 62 38; www.larrajou.com; quartier de l'Église, Bilhères; s/d/f €60/65/110; ℗ 🛱) Sublime mountain views await at this charming guesthouse set in the tiny village of Bilhères. Expect a warm welcome from the kind-hearted hosts, sunny rooms with bay windows and hearty breakfasts with locally sourced products. During the high season, dinner (€18) is also available.

Le Balcon de l'Ossau GUESTHOUSE €

(☑ 06 09 71 78 06; www.chambres-hotes-ossau.fr; 17 rue du Bourg, Bescat; s/d/tr €60/64/80; 🛱) In Bescat, the owners Kathrin and Michel roll out the welcome mat, with three handsomely set rooms and a peaceful garden where you can take in the views. Outdoors lovers can get loads of tips on hikes and other activities in the area.

Logis Hôtel de France HOTEL €

(☑ 05 59 05 60 16; www.hoteldefrancearudy.com; 1 place de l'Hôtel de Ville, Arudy; s/d/tr/f €61/69/84/90; 🛱) In Arudy, this hotel looks like it's appeared from a vintage postcard. It's on a quiet street leading to the church; outside there are pale green shutters and a pebbledash-and-wood frontage, while inside are pleasant, no-frills rooms and a good country bistro serving regional dishes such as *garbure béarnaise* (a rich meat-and-veg stew).

Casa Paulou GUESTHOUSE €€

(☑ 05 59 05 35 98; 6 rue Bourgneuf Claa, Laruns; s/d €50/80; ℗ 🛱) In the town of Laruns, the friendly Casa Paulou makes a great base for

---

DON'T MISS

SCENIC TRAIN RIDE

A cable car cranks up the Pic de la Sagette (2032m) to reach the start of one of France's most scenic train journeys. The toy-sized Train d'Artouste – affectionately known as **Le Petit Train d'Artouste** (☑ 05 59 05 36 99; www.altiservice.com/excursion/train-artouste; adult/child €25/18; ☺ mid-May–mid-Oct), six kilometres east of Gabas, near the ski resort of Artouste-Fabrèges (1250m), was built for dam workers in the 1920s, but now trundles its way for 10km to Lac d'Artouste, offering heart-stopping views over the valley and the spiky Pic du Midi d'Ossau.

The train gets very busy in summer, carrying over 100,000 passengers in the months it's open – try to visit at the start and end of the season, when it's usually quieter. Tickets can be bought in advance online and by phone. Trains run half-hourly in July and August, and hourly at other times. The return-trip lasts about four hours.

You can also buy a Billet Randonneur (Walker's Ticket), which allows you to get off the train and hike the trails, then get a return train back.

WORTH A TRIP

CIRQUES DE GAVARNIE, TROUMOUSE & D'ESTAUBÉ

Fifty-two kilometres south of Lourdes on the D921 you'll find three of the most breathtaking vistas in the Pyrenees: a trio of natural mountain amphitheatres, carved out by ancient glaciers and framed by sawtoothed, snow-dusted peaks – many of which top out at over 3000m. The town of Gavarnie has a few pleasant lodging options. Most have fireplaces where you can warm up after a day exploring the mountain trails.

The **Cirque de Gavarnie** is the easiest of the area's three mountain amphitheatres to reach – and consequently the most popular – rewarding hikers with a panorama of spiky mountains that provides one of the Pyrenees' most famous vistas. It's especially dramatic after heavy rain, when waterfalls cascade down the mountainsides. The Cirque is about 1½ hours' walk from Gavarnie village. Between Easter and October you can clip-clop along on a horse or donkey (around €25 to €35 for a return-trip). Be sure to wear proper shoes, as the trail can be slippery and rocky.

A second spectacular mountain amphitheatre is the **Cirque de Troumouse**, reached via the minor D922 and a hair-raising 8km toll road near Gèdre, 6.5km northeast of Gavarnie. From the Cirque de Troumouse parking area, there are various signed walks that offer fine views of the cirque, including an easy 30-minute one-way walk to the Lac des Aires. The toll-road itself is steep and quite exposed, with hairpin turns and no barriers, so take it slowly. Snows permitting, it's usually open between April and October; the toll is €5 per vehicle.

Hidden among the mountains between Troumouse and Gavarnie is the **Cirque d'Estaubé**, the most wild and remote of the area's three mountain amphitheatres and only accessible on foot. The trail starts from the turn-off to the barrage des Gloriettes, which you pass on the D922 en route to Troumouse. It's about a 3½-hour return walk; you'll need proper boots, water and snacks.

outdoor adventures in the surrounding countryside. Its five comfy rooms are quite large and painted in cheerful colours; some have magnificent views of the mountains. It's within walking distance of the restaurants of Laruns.

ℹ Information

Tourist Office (La Maison de la Vallée d'Ossau Office de Tourisme; ☏ 05 59 05 31 41; www.valleedossau-tourisme.com; Laruns; ⊙ 9am-noon & 2-6pm Mon-Sat, 9am-noon Sun; 🛜) Located on the square, this spot sells good hiking maps for the area.

National Park Visitor Centre (Maison du Parc National des Pyrénées de Laruns; ☏ 05 59 05 41 59; www.pyrenees-parcnational.fr; Laruns; ⊙ 9am-noon & 2-5.30pm Mon-Fri) Beside the Laruns tourist office.

ℹ Getting There & Away

Citram Pyrénées (p707) runs buses from Pau to Laruns (€2, one hour, two to four daily), stopping at Rébénacq, Arudy, Bielle, Laruns and Eaux Bonnes.

SNCF trains from Pau stop at Buzy-en-Béarn from where there are a few onward bus connections as far as Laruns (40 minutes).

Cauterets

POP 1100 / ELEV 930M

It might not have the altitude of its sister ski stations in the Alps, but in many respects Cauterets is a more pleasant place to hit the slopes. While many of the Alpine resorts have been ruthlessly modernised and are crammed to capacity during the winter and summer seasons, Cauterets has clung on to much of its fin-de-siècle character, with a stately spa and grand 19th-century residences dotted round town.

Snow usually lingers here until early May, returning in late October or early November. In summer the landscape around Cauterets transforms into a hikers' paradise, with trails winding their way into the Parc National des Pyrénées.

◉ Sights & Activities

Cauterets' two ski areas are the Pont d'Espagne and Cirque du Lys; both are great for hiking once the snows melt.

Local guides offer outdoor activities including paragliding, rock-climbing, fishing and via ferrata. Ask at the Cauterets tourist office (p711), or consult the Cauterets website (www.cauterets.com).

Pont d'Espagne
HIKING

(cable cars adult/child €15.50/13) The most popular hike in Cauterets leads to the sparkling **Lac de Gaube**. A one-hour walk from Pont d'Espagne, the brilliantly blue mountain lake lies cradled by serrated peaks. Another trail (90 minutes' walk one way) winds up the **Vallée de Marcadau** to the high-altitude Refuge Wallon-Marcadau (1866m). During the winter, this is a popular spot for Nordic skiing and snowshoeing.

From the giant car park at Pont d'Espagne, 6.4km above Cauterets, a combination *télécabine* (cable car) and *télésiege* (chairlift) provides easy access to the trailheads.

Shuttle buses (adult/child return €8/5) run between Cauterets and the Pont d'Espagne car park every couple of hours in July and August. The car park costs €6.50 for up to 12 hours, or €8 for longer stays.

Cirque du Lys
HIKING, MOUNTAIN BIKING

(cable car adult/child €15/12.50; ⏱ 10am-noon & 1.45-5.15pm Jul & Aug) Cauterets' second most popular hiking area is this mountain amphitheatre, 1850m above sea-level. The best route is to catch the cable car and chairlift from Cambasque up to **Crêtes du Lys**, and walk back down the mountain for 1½ hours via the **Lac d'Ilhéou**, where there's a handy lakeside *refuge* (mountain hut) for lunch. From there it's another 1½ hours back to Cambasque.

The valley is also home to Cauterets' **mountain-bike park** (one-day pass adult/child €17.50/14.50; ⏱ Jul & Aug), with three routes and a drop of 1500m to test your skills.

Bains du Rocher
SPA

(☎ 05 62 92 14 20; www.bains-rocher.fr; av du Docteur Domer; 2hr pass adult/child €18.50/9.50; ⏱ 10am-9pm daily May-Sep, 2-7.15pm Mon-Fri, 10am-12.45pm & 2-7.45pm Sat & Sun Oct & Dec-Apr, closed Nov) It wasn't snow that attracted the first tourists to Cauterets – it was the area's hot springs, which bubble up at temperatures between 36°C and 53°C. The waters are rumoured to have numerous healing properties. At this bath complex, you can treat yourself to a sauna, *hammam* or hot tub, and enjoy the lovely view of the mountains while basking in the pool.

Men need Speedo-style swimwear (sold at the entrance) rather than boardshorts.

🛌 Sleeping

Camping GR10
CAMPGROUND €

(☎ 06 20 30 25 85; www.gr10camping.com; rte de Pierrefitte, Quartier Concé; site for 2 adults €19; ⏱ May-Sep; 🛜) Around 2.5km north of town

on the D920, this is the pick of Cauterets' campgrounds. It's tucked in a flat, grassy site cradled by mountains and forest, and has 69 spacious sites plus great facilities (hook-ups, *pétanque*, tennis courts and heated bathrooms). It even has its own adventure park with a via ferrata.

★Hôtel du Lion d'Or
HOTEL €€

(☎ 05 62 92 52 87; www.liondor.eu; 12 rue Richelieu; d €84-168; 🛜) This Heidi-esque hotel oozes mountain character from every nook and cranny. In business since 1913, it is deliciously eccentric, with charming old rooms in polka-dot pinks, sunny yellows and duck-egg blues, and mountain-themed knick-knacks dotted throughout, from antique sleds to snowshoes. Breakfast includes homemade honey and jams, and the restaurant serves hearty Pyrenean cuisine.

Hôtel Le Bois-Joli
HOTEL €€

(☎ 05 62 92 53 85; www.hotel-leboisjoli.com; 1 place du Maréchal-Foch; d €125-190; 🛜) Above a popular cafe right in the middle of Cauterets, this attractive hotel makes a good central base, with rooms in rich hues of blue, red or green, and mountain views from the upper floors. Breakfast is available in the wood-filled cafe downstairs, but it's a bit steep at €11.

🍴 Eating

Fromagerie du Saloir
DELI €

(av Leclerc; ⏱ 8am-noon & 2-6pm Mon-Sat) Inside the market (Les Halles de Cauterets), cheese lovers can swoon over the seemingly endless varieties of *fromage* as well as liqueurs (including one called Gratte Cul, a traditional wild-rosehip liqueur made in the Pyrenees. It literally translates as 'scratch arse').

La Ferme Basque
FRENCH €

(☎ 05 62 92 54 32; http://fermebasque.free.fr; rte de Cambasque; mains €16-23, menu lunch €21, dinner €26-35; ⏱ 12.30-2.30pm & 7-9pm Mon-Sat, 12.30-2.30pm Sun) This country farmhouse just west of Cauterets has a delightfully rustic restaurant specialising in *garbure* (a rich meat-and-veg stew), omelettes with foie gras and mushrooms, and other hearty mountain cooking. There's also a shop where you can buy homemade pâté, honey, charcuterie and other goodies. It's a pleasant but steep 1km walk from Cauterets – take the trail beside **Pavillon des Abeilles** (www.pavillondesabeilles.com; 23bis av du Mamelon Vert; ⏱ 10.30am-12.30pm & 2.30-7pm Wed-Sat) **FREE**. Call ahead to dine.

Lau Tant'hic
BISTRO €€

(☑05 62 92 02 14; Galerie Aladin, rue de Belfort; mains €16-23, menus €22-27; ◷noon-2.30pm & 7-10pm) Owner Gérant adds his own twist to mountain dishes at his little restaurant, but still favours local ingredients, especially lamb, duck, cured sausages and cheese. His presentation shows a bit of big-city flair too, and the wine list is great.

This is a fine place to try the Pyrenean dish of *garbure*, a belly-filling stew typically made with potatoes, cabbage and pork.

La Cheeserie
FRENCH €€

(☑06 62 62 33 98; www.facebook.com/la cheeserie; Galerie Aladin, rue de Belfort; raclette & fondue per person €18-25; ◷2-10pm; ☑) A *fromage*-lover's paradise, La Cheeserie whips up a dozen varieties of *raclettes* and fondues, served with delicacies like *magret de canard* (seared duck breast), while asparagus and chorizo. There's a suitably impressive wine list, and on warm days you can enjoy those cheeses at one of the outdoor tables on the lane.

La Fruitière
FRENCH €€

(☑05 62 42 13 53; www.hotellerie-fruitiere.csvss. fr; menus lunch €15, dinner from €22; ◷noon-3pm & 7-9pm May-Oct) For dining with a view, nowhere beats the Fruitery. It sits at the head of the Vallée de Lutour, and has a mountain-view terrace that'll blow your thermal socks off. The food is traditional and delicious: tuck into baked trout or grilled duck with a cream of foie gras, and follow with blueberry tart. It's 7km south from town along the D920.

You can make the most of the pretty setting by overnighting here (double room with half-board €120).

La Reine Hortense
FRENCH €€

(☑06 75 67 01 50; Chemin Rural de la Reine Hortense; menus €21-33; ◷10am-7pm Mar-Oct) Although you can drive here, the best way to arrive at this rustic mountaintop eatery is on foot. Take the marked walking path just behind the **Thermes de César** (☑05 62 92 51 60; www. thermesdecauterets.com; av Docteur Domer; ◷8am-12:30pm & 2-5pm Mon-Fri, to noon Sat); it's about two hours return. Once there, you can dine on grilled meats, *raclette* and crêpes while enjoying spectacular views from the outdoor tables.

ℹ Information

Cauterets Tourist Office (☑05 62 92 50 50; www.cauterets.com; place Maréchal Foch; ◷9am-noon & 2-6pm) A helpful office on the main square.

Mountain Information Office (Office de la Montagne; ☑05 62 91 02 83; place Maréchal Foch; ◷8.30am-12.30pm & 5-7.30pm daily Jun-Sep, 4-6.30pm Fri, 9am-12.30pm & 4-6.30pm Sat & Sun Oct-May) On the main square, this handy office is the best place to pick up trail maps and get tips on scenic walks in the area.

Pyrenees National Park Visitor Centre (Maison du Parc National des Pyrénées; ☑05 62 92 52 56; place de la Gare; ◷9.30am-noon & 3-7pm) Sells walking maps and guidebooks, and organises guided walks in summer.

ℹ Getting There & Away

Sadly the last train steamed out of Cauterets' magnificent station in 1947. It now serves as the **bus station** (☑05 62 92 53 70; place de la Gare), with SNCF buses running between Cauterets and Lourdes train station (€8.20, one hour, four to six daily).

VALLÉE DES GAVES

Gentle and pastoral, the Vallée des Gaves (Valley of the Mountain Streams) extends south from Lourdes to Pierrefitte-Nestalas. Here the valley forks: the narrow, rugged eastern tongue twists via Gavarnie while the western tongue corkscrews up to Cauterets.

◉ Sights

★Pic du Midi
VIEWPOINT

(www.picdumidi.com; rue Pierre Lamy de la Chapelle; adult/child €38/23; ◷9am-7pm Jun Sep, 10am-5.30pm Oct-Apr, closed Nov & May) If the Pyrenees has a mustn't-miss view, it's the one from the Pic du Midi de Bigorre (2877m). Once accessible only to mountaineers, since 1878 the Pic du Midi has been home to an important observatory, and on a clear day the sky-top mountain views are out of this world. A cable car climbs to the summit from the nearby ski resort of La Mongie (1800m). Early morning and late evenings generally get the clearest skies and smallest crowds.

At the top, there are several viewing terraces, all offering a different perspective on the serrated mountain landscape. There's also a museum that gives an overview of the observatory and its development over the years. When hunger strikes, you can grab a snack at the sandwich shop or linger over a meal at the restaurant (*menus* €30 to €36).

If you're visiting in the low season, check the website for closures due to bad weather or periodic closures. In summer, if you're travelling from the western valleys via the

Col du Tourmalet, double-check the road is open before you set out – it's usually closed between November and May.

Le Donjon des Aigles
BIRD SANCTUARY

(☏05 62 97 19 59; www.donjon-des-aigles.com; Beaucens; adult/child €14/8.50; ☺10am-noon & 2.30-6.30pm Apr-Sep) Some 15km south of Lourdes, in the spectacular surroundings of the 11th-century Château de Beaucens, you can see one of the world's largest collections of birds of prey. Among the taloned residents are bald eagles, fish eagles, horned owls, vultures and a collection of parrots: flying displays are held at 3.30pm and 5pm (3pm, 4.30pm and 6pm in August).

ⓘ Getting There & Away

Public transport is limited. Most visitors arrive in the area by hired vehicle, which gives the freedom to explore the surrounding countryside.

VALLÉE DE GARONNE

Located in a central swath of the Pyrenees, this picturesque region is home to a few old-fashioned villages, including St-Bertrand de Comminges, which has a famed cathedral. You'll also find one of the most popular ski resorts in the Pyrenees, which doubles as a gateway to fantastic trekking in the summer.

Bagnères de Luchon

POP 2500 / ELEV 630M

Bagnères de Luchon (or simply Luchon) is a trim little town of gracious 19th-century buildings, expanded to accommodate the *curistes* who came to take the waters at its splendid spa. It's now one of the Pyrenees' most popular ski areas, with the challenging runs of Superbagnères right on its doorstep. There are also some fine walks in the area – including some that leave right from town.

🏃 Activities

Thermes de Luchon
BATHHOUSE

(☏05 61 94 52 52; www.thermes-luchon.fr; cours des Quinconces; €15-16.50; ☺7.20am-12.15pm year-round & 3-7.30pm Mon-Sat, 10am-5pm Sun Dec-Feb) You can't leave Luchon without visiting the *vaporarium* of Thermes de Luchon. It's said to be the only natural *hammam* (Turkish bath) in Europe. The experience takes place amid 160m of underground rock-walled corridors where you can sit on (admittedly uncomfortable) benches and breathe in the scented, steamy air. Afterwards, dunk yourself in the warm-water pool, naturally heated to 34°C, then repeat.

Superbagnères
SKIING, CYCLING

(☏05 61 79 21 21; www.luchon-superbagneres. com; rue de Superbagnères; adult/child one way €7.70/6.70, all day access €9.80/7.70; ☺ski-lifts 9.30am-12.30pm & 2-6pm Jul & Aug, 1.30-6pm weekends May-Jun & Sep, 8.45am-6pm or 7pm in winter) Luchon's *télécabine* (ski lift) whisks you up to the mountain plateau known as Superbagnères (1860m), the starting point for the area's winter ski-runs and summer walking trails. The tourist office has lots of information on possible routes, and sells maps and guides.

🛏 Sleeping

Villa d'Alti
HOTEL €

(☏05 61 79 75 54; www.villadalti.com; 3 ave Jacques Barrau; s €58-75, d €63-85, dm/s with shared bathroom €28/32; ⓟ🛜) Set in a former convent in the southern part of town, this large 27-room hotel has bright, generally spacious rooms (but tiny bathrooms) with wide plank floors and fine views over the surrounding greenery. There are also a few dorm rooms and some compact singles that are fine value for budget travellers.

Hospice de France
GUESTHOUSE €

(☏06 88 32 40 64; www.hospicedefrance.com; dm/s/d from €20/55/55, incl half-board from €45/79/109; ☺late Apr-early Nov) Set high in the mountains some 12km southeast of Bagnères de Luchon, the Hospice de France has been welcoming travellers since the 17th century. Today, its comfortable but simply designed rooms make a great base for spectacular hikes and mountain-bike adventures in the region. The on-site restaurant serves traditional Pyrenean cuisine, while access to trails lies right outside the door.

★ Le Castel de la Pique
HOTEL €€

(☏05 61 88 43 66; www.castel-pique.fr; 31 cours des Quinconces; r €72-85; ⓟ🛜) There's a bit of storybook charm to this hotel, with its château corner-turrets and 19th-century façade. Once inside, the lovely rooms don't disappoint, with wood floors, mantelpieces and French windows opening onto decorative balconies; mountain views are practically universal. Owner Alain is a character, and a mine of local knowledge. All in all, it's a bargain – especially with breakfast at €8.

✕ Eating

This mountain town is a fine spot to try Pyrenean dishes like *garbure* (a rich meat-and-veg stew) as well as classic French bistro fare. The best place to browse for a meal is along restaurant-lined allée d'Etigny.

Covered Market   MARKET €
(rue du Docteur Germès; ⊙ 8am-1pm daily Apr-Oct, Wed & Sat Nov-Mar) Luchon's covered market was established in 1897 and is still going strong.

Le Baluchon   BISTRO €€
(📞 05 61 88 91 28; 12 av du Maréchal Foch; menus lunch €18, dinner €28-38, mains €18-22; ⊙ 12.30-2pm & 8-10pm) In contrast to the traditional fare on many Luchon menus, this bistro takes its cue from a more contemporary cookbook. It's run by husband-and-wife team Laura and Thomas, who favour seasonal ingredients and stripped-back presentation: expect dishes such as locally sourced lamb and river trout partnered with delicate vegetable medleys sautéed in white-wine sauce.

L'Héptaméron des Gourmets   GASTRONOMY €€€
(📞 05 61 79 78 55; www.heptamerondesgourmets. com; 2 bd Charles de Gaulle; 7-course menu €65, with wines €100; ⊙ 7-10.30pm Tue-Sat) This swish restaurant is the address for traditional French fine dining. Start with an aperitif in the salon, with its book-lined shelves and leather armchairs, then graduate to the kitschy conservatory for rich cuisine drowned in creamy sauces and truffle butters. Chef Jean-Luc Danjou can also accommodate vegetarian and vegan diners with advance notice. Reserve ahead.

❶ Information

Tourist Office (📞 05 61 79 21 21; www. luchon.com; 18 allée d'Étigny; ⊙ 9am-7pm Mon-Sat, 9am-12.30pm & 2.30-6pm Sun; 🖥) Helpful office with loads of info on activities in the surrounding area. On Luchon's main restaurant- and shop-lined strip.

❶ Getting There & Away

SNCF trains and buses run between Luchon and Montréjeau (€7.70, 50 minutes, five to eight daily), which have frequent connections to Toulouse (€18.40, 70 minutes) and Pau (€20.40, 1½ hours).

St-Bertrand de Comminges

POP 270 / ELEV 520M

On an isolated hillock, St-Bertrand and its **Cathédrale Ste-Marie** (www.cathedrale-saint-bertrand.org; adult/child incl audioguide €5/2; ⊙ 9am-6pm Mon-Sat, 2-6pm Sun May-Sep, 10am-noon & 2-6pm Oct-Apr) loom over the Garonne Valley and the much-pillaged remains of the Gallo-Roman town of Lugdunum Convenarum. Lush hillsides surround the village, and its narrow lanes are lined with photogenic buildings from the 15th and 16th centuries.

The ancient Roman settlement was founded by the Roman general Pompée around 72 BC, and there are a few modest remains from this time located a short stroll from the cathedral. By the 2nd century AD, the town had a population of at least 10,000 inhabitants. The boom days didn't last, however, and the city was sacked by Vandals in 409 and subsequently abandoned. The town saw new life in the 12th century when the cathedral was built, and it became an important stop on the pilgrimage route to Santiago de Compostela.

St-Bertrand de Comminges is located 35km north of Bagnères de Luchon, reachable by taking D125N and N125N.

VALLÉE DE L'ARIÈGE

On the eastern side of the French Pyrenees, the sleepy Vallée de l'Ariège is awash with prehistoric interest: it's home to some of Europe's most impressive underground rivers and subterranean caverns, many of which are daubed with cave paintings left behind by prehistoric people. The most useful bases are Foix, former seat of the Comtes de Toulouse, and Mirepoix, a well-preserved *bastide*.

◉ Sights

Château de Foix   CHATEAU
(📞 05 61 05 10 10; rue du Rocher; adult/child €6.70/4.50; ⊙ 9am-6pm summer, shorter hours rest of year) The Ariège's most unmistakeable landmark is Foix' triple-towered castle, the stronghold of the powerful Comtes de Foix. Built in the 10th century, it survived as their seat of power throughout the medieval era, and served as a prison from the 16th century onwards. The castle is approached via a cobbled causeway from the old town. The interior is rather bare, but the view from the battlements is wonderful.

Rivière Souterraine de Labouiche   RIVER

(✆ 05 61 65 04 11; www.labouiche.com; Baulou; adult/child €11.40/9.40; ⏱10-11am & 2-4.30pm Apr-Jun & Sep, 9.30am-5pm Jul & Aug, 2-4pm Tue-Fri, 10-11am & 2-4.30pm Sat & Sun Oct–mid-Nov) Deep beneath the village of Labouiche, 6km northwest of Foix, flows Europe's longest navigable underground river. Discovered in 1908 by a local doctor, it's been open to the public since 1938. Barge trips lasting 75 minutes run for about 1.5km along its underground course, with guides pulling the boats along by ropes attached to the ceiling, and walkways entering more caverns and eerie chambers.

The highlight of the visit is saved for the end: a clattering waterfall known as the **Cascade Salette**, which tumbles into a sparkling turquoise pool. Depending on rainfall, the waterfall's speed can vary anywhere from 100L to 1500L litres per second. It's all quite touristy, but the kids are bound to love it. On a blazing summer's day, the caves hover at a cool constant temperature of 13˚C.

Grotte du Mas d'Azil   CAVE, MUSEUM

(✆ 05 61 05 10 10; www.sites-touristiques-ariege. fr; ave de la Grotte/D119, Le Mas-d'Azil; adult/child €9/5.50; ⏱cave tours 10.15am-4.45pm mid-Apr–Oct, 9.45am-7pm Jul & Aug, 11.15am-4.30pm mid-Feb–mid-Apr) Twenty-five kilometres northwest of Foix, near Le Mas d'Azil, this rock shelter is famous for its rich finds of prehistoric tools. Visits are by guided tour, which take you through underground galleries and describe the lives of those who lived here as well as some of the artefacts found here by archaeologists over the years. Note that you won't see any original paintings here.

The ticket also includes entry to the **Musée de la Préhistoire** (✆ 05 61 69 99 90; Grand Rue, Le Mas d'Azil; adult/child €4.50/2, combo ticket incl cave tour €9/5.50; ⏱ 9.30am-8pm Jul & Aug, 10am-noon & 1-6pm Mar-Jun, Sep & Oct) in the town of Mas d'Azil (1km north of the cave entrance). English-language tours are available once or twice per day from June to October. Call or go online to reserve a spot. Note that the entrance to the cave is right on the D119 in a vehicular tunnel dug through the mountain. Parking is just south of the tunnel entrance; a pedestrian walkway runs parallel to the road.

Les Forges de Pyrène   MUSEUM

(✆ 05 34 09 30 60; www.forges-de-pyrene.com; rte de Paris, Montgailhard; adult/child €9.50/6.50; ⏱10am-noon & 1-6.30pm Apr-Jun & Sep-Oct, 10am-7pm Jul & Aug, closed Nov-Mar; 🖭) In Montgailhard, 4.5km south of Foix, this 'living museum' explores Ariège folk traditions, with live displays of ancient trades such as blacksmithing, shoe-making, bread baking, tanning and thatching.

Parc de la Préhistoire   MUSEUM

(✆ 05 61 05 10 10; Tarascon-sur-Ariège; adult/child €11.50/8; ⏱10am-7pm Jul & Aug, to 6pm rest of year, closed Nov-Mar) Eighteen kilometres south of Foix, near Tarascon-sur-Ariège, this excellent museum-park provides a useful primer on the area's prehistoric past. The centrepiece is the **Grand Atelier**, which uses film, projections and an audio-visual commentary to explain the story of human settlement. There are also many animal skeletons, including a cave bear and a mammoth, as well as a full-scale reproduction of the Salon Noir in the Grotte de Niaux.

DON'T MISS

PREHISTORIC PAINTERS OF THE PYRENEES

Most people know about the prehistoric artworks of the Dordogne, but far fewer realise that ancient painters left their mark in caves all across the Pyrenees. Halfway up a mountainside about 12km south of Foix, the **Grotte de Niaux** (✆ 05 61 05 10 10; www.sites-touristiques-ariege.fr; adult/child €12/8; ⏱tours hourly 10.15am-4.15pm, extra tours in summer) is the most impressive, with a fabulous gallery of bison, horses and ibex adorning a vast subterranean chamber called the **Salon Noir**. There's also one tiny depiction of a weasel – the only cave painting of the animal yet found.

The Salon Noir is reached via an 800m underground trek through pitch darkness. To preserve the paintings, there's no lighting inside the cave, so you'll be given a torch as you enter. On the way, look out for graffiti left by previous visitors, some of which dates back to the 17th century.

The cave can only be visited with a guide. From April to June and in September and October there's usually one English-language tour a day at 1.30pm. In July and August, English-language tours typically happen at 9.45am and 12.15pm. Visitor numbers are limited, so call or go online to reserve a place.

Outside you can follow a trail around the park's grounds, explore a selection of prehistoric tents and learn to use an ancient spear-thrower.

Château de Montségur CHATEAU

(www.montsegur.fr; Montségur; adult/child Jul & Aug €6.50/3.50, other times €5.50/3; ⏰ 9am-6pm Jul & Aug, 10am-6pm Apr-Jun & Sep, to 5pm Mar & Oct, 11am-4pm Nov & Dec) For the full Monty Python medieval vibe, tackle the steep 20-minute climb to the ruins of this hilltop fortress, 32km east of Foix (and don't forget to bring your own water). It's the westernmost of the string of Cathar castles stretching across into Languedoc; the original castle was razed to rubble after the siege, and the present-day ruins largely date from the 17th century.

It was here, in 1242, that the Cathars suffered their heaviest defeat; the castle fell after a gruelling nine-month siege, and 220 of the defenders were burnt alive when they refused to renounce their faith. A local legend claims that the Holy Grail was smuggled out of the castle in the days before the final battle. Tickets also grant admission to the historical museum in the nearby village of Montségur.

Musée de Montségur MUSEUM

(www.montsegur.fr; Montségur; adult/child €2.50/1.50, combo ticket to Château de Montségur €6.50/3.50; ⏰ 2-5pm Mar, 2-6pm Apr-Jun, Sep & Oct, 10am-noon & 1-6.30pm Jul & Aug, closed Mon) Tucked into the sleepy village of Montségur, this small museum contains a collection of Cathar relics, models of siege weapons and visual displays of what the town's castrum would have looked like during its glory days in 1240. There's also a pair of skeletons found buried together who were likely slain during the town's destruction in 1244.

Sleeping & Eating

There are plenty of appealing lodging options scattered around the Ariège valley. Aside from pretty rural inns, you'll also find good-value guesthouses in Foix, and atmospheric hotels in the heart-tuggingly pretty village of Mirepoix, about 25km to the northeast.

Foix

La Ciboulette B&B €

(☎05 61 01 10 88; www.laciboulette.net; rte St Pierre-de-Rivière, Lieu-Dit La Rochelle; s/d/tr €70/80/100) In a peaceful setting some 3km west of Foix, this small family-run guesthouse has several attractive rooms decorated with artwork and elegant furnishings. Views over the mountains add to the charm. Don't miss a meal of creatively prepared local dishes in the excellent restaurant on-site (open Thursdays to Sundays, mains €17 to €19).

Hôtel Restaurant Lons HOTEL €€

(☎05 34 09 28 00; www.hotel-lons-foix.com; 6 place Dutilh; r €89-110) One of the better hotels in Foix, this is an old-fashioned affair with rambling corridors and functional but comfy rooms, some of which look onto the river, while the others face Foix' shady streets. The riverside restaurant offers good-value regional dishes (*menus* €23 to €36).

Le Jeu de l'Oie FRENCH €€

(☎05 61 02 69 39; 17 rue Lafaurie; menus €18-26; ⏰ noon-2pm & 7-10pm Tue-Sat) Tucked along one of Foix' quiet lanes, Le Jeu de l'Oie serves satisfying plates of *confit de canard* (duck confit) and cassoulet as well as roasted salmon with a chorizo crust and roasted red peppers stuffed with goat's cheese. It has an easy-going atmosphere and excellent-value *menus*.

Mirepoix

Les Minotiers HOTEL €

(☎05 61 69 37 36; www.hotelmirepoix.com; ave Maréchal Foch; r €51-66; P ❄ 📶) This affordable hotel in Mirepoix has clean and simple rooms with big windows, just a short stroll to the village centre. Though the design is fairly generic, it's hard to beat the prices. The on-site restaurant (*menus* €17 to €38) earns

OFF THE BEATEN TRACK

EUROPE'S LARGEST CAVE SYSTEM

Twenty-two kilometres northwest of Ax-les-Thermes on the N20 near Ussat-les-Bains, Europe's largest cave system **Lombrives** (☎06 70 74 32 80; http://grottedelombrives.com; off N20, Ussat-les-Bains; standard tour adult/child €12/8; ⏰ 9am-7pm Jul & Aug, 10am-5pm Jun & Sep, 2-5pm May & Oct) burrows its way through the soft limestone rock beneath the Pyrenees' peaks. Guided tours take in more than 200 stalactite lined tunnels, grottoes and galleries, including a sandy expanse known as the Sahara Desert, and limestone columns variously resembling a mammoth, a wizard and the Virgin Mary.

Standard tours last two hours, but longer 'randonnée spéléologique' expeditions are available for the adventurous (and non-claustrophobic).

SATURDAY SHOPPING SPREE

In the village of St-Girons, the massive **Marché de St-Girons** (rue du Champ de Mars, St-Girons; ☉8am-1pm Sat)spreads along the riverbank every Saturday throughout the year. You'll find beautiful fruits and vegetables, bakery items, cheeses, smoked meats, freshly baked tarts, craft beers and more – nearly all of which is produced in the surrounding region.

Among the food stalls you'll find delicious *galettes* (savoury buckwheat crêpes), meaty sandwiches, pizzas, crêpes and Asian-style dumplings. Edibles aside, the market also has antiques, crafts, clothes, sheepskins, natural beauty products, baskets, books, records and plenty of other finds.

high marks for its Pyrenees-inspired fare (try the pastry-covered lamb with morels).

Maison des Consuls　　　HOTEL €€
(☏05 61 68 81 81; www.maisondesconsuls.com; 6 place du Maréchal Leclerc; d €95-140; P☎) This offbeat hotel has themed all its rooms after notable figures from Mirepoix' past. The best ones are the Louis XVI–style Monseigneur room, with windows overlooking the main square, and the Dame-Louise room, decorated in Louis XIII–style, with a four-poster bed and a superb view over the cathedral. The more modern Voyageur room has its own small balcony (but twin beds).

🛏 Elsewhere

⭐**Auberge les Myrtilles**　　B&B €€
(☏05 61 65 16 46; www.auberge-les-myrtilles.com; Col des Marrous, Le Bosc; d €70-110; P☎☀) You'll feel rather like you're staying in the Canadian wilderness here, with its timber-framed chalet cabins and forested hillside setting. It's a wonderful place to settle yourself: despite the rustic style, there are lots of luxury spoils, including a covered swimming pool with a knockout view, a Swedish-style sauna and, of course, mountain panoramas on every side. It's about 20km west of Foix on the D17.

The restaurant (*menu* €26) is great for local cuisine – don't miss the Azinat (a duck, sausage and vegetable hotpot).

Domaine de Terrac　　GUESTHOUSE €€
(☏05 61 96 39 60; www.domainedeterrac.com; Lieu-Dit Terrac, Rimont; d incl breakfast €95-125; P☎)

Awaken to the sound of birdsong in the valley from this hillside guesthouse 30km west of Foix. Set in a beautifully restored 200-year-old farmhouse, the Domaine de Terrac has five sunny rooms set with quality furnishings and polished wood floors (two rooms also have private balconies). The Welsh-Québecois owners make guests feel right at home.The sauna and hot tub are nice extras.

Château de Beauregard　　HOTEL €€
(☏05 61 66 66 64; www.chateaubeauregard.net; av de la Résistance, St-Girons; r €80-150, ste €200-220, d incl half-board €180-300; P☎☀) In St-Girons, halfway between St-Gaudens and Foix along the D117, this château is ideal for playing lord of the manor: the house is topped by turrets and surrounded by 2.5 hectares of gardens, with grand rooms named after writers (some have their bathrooms hidden in the castle's corner towers). There's also a pool, spa and a great Gascon restaurant (*menus* €30 to €54).

⭐**L'Abbaye de Camon**　　B&B €€€
(☏05 61 60 31 23; www.chateaudecamon.com; 3 place Philippe de Lévis, Camon; d €140-200; ☉Apr-Oct; P☎☀) Wow – what a spot. Founded as a Benedictine abbey in the 12th century, this is now possibly the poshest B&B anywhere in the Pyrenees. The building's decor puts most châteaux to shame, with vaulted archways, winding staircases, a Renaissance-style drawing room, ravishing gardens and a lovely pool – plus five regal rooms oozing antique grandeur. It's around 13km southeast of Mirepoix.

ℹ Information

Information on the main sights is available on the Sites Touristiques Ariège (www.sites-touristiques-ariege.fr) website. If you're visiting several sights, it's worth picking up the free **Pass Multi-Sites** at the first place you visit, which gives discounts at all subsequent places you go to.

Foix Tourist Office (☏05 61 65 12 12; www.tourisme-foix-varilhes.fr; 29 rue Delcassé; ☉9am-noon & 2-6pm Mon-Sat year-round, plus 10am-12.30pm & 2-6pm Sun mid-Jun–Aug)

Mirepoix Tourist Office (☏05 61 68 83 76; www.tourisme-mirepoix.com; place Maréchal Leclerc; ☉9.15am-12.15pm & 2-6pm Mon-Sat; ☎)

ℹ Getting There & Away

Regular trains connect Toulouse and Foix (€15.30, 1¼ hours). You'll need your own wheels, however, if you want to properly explore the villages and scenic back roads of the Ariège.

One or two daily runs of bus 950 go between Mirepoix and Pamiers train station (€6, 30 minutes).

Toulouse Area

Best Places to Eat

➜ Marché Victor Hugo (p725)

➜ La Pente Douce (p725)

➜ Michel Sarran (p725)

➜ L'Ambroisie (p730)

➜ La Table des Cordeliers (p737)

Best Places to Stay

➜ L'Hôtel Particulier Guilhon (p737)

➜ L'Alchimy (p730)

➜ Villa du Taur (p723)

➜ Lacassagne (p737)

➜ Hôtel Albert 1er (p724)

Why Go?

Gastronomy and good living are the passions underpinning this sun-kissed corner of southwestern France.

At the heart of the region's farms and flower-sprinkled meadows is Toulouse, a city of pink stone invigorated by galleries and nightlife aplenty. Beyond here, stocky *bastides* (fortified towns), like hilltop Cordes-sur-Ciel and seductive Lectoure, snooze between vineyards and rolling pastures. Slicing through is the formidable Canal du Midi, a 17th-century feat of engineering now plied by idling houseboaters. Meanwhile tables groan under hefty dishes like *cassoulet* and confit duck, with splashes of complex Gaillac wine.

Once you've enjoyed your fill of Toulouse's festivals, music and cutting-edge art, it's time to slow down. Head west to the Gers *département,* famous for its lush countryside and Armagnac liqueur, or east to magnificent Albi, which remains largely underrated. If at all possible, lose track of time: this delightful region is best experienced at a dawdle.

When to Go
Toulouse

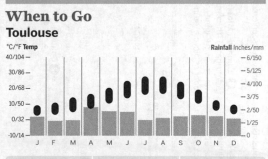

Feb Paint the town purple at Toulouse's violet festival.

May–Aug Prime time for Armagnac distillery and vineyard tours; music festivals ramp up.

Sep Pleasant sunshine and thinner crowds; the Quatre-Cent Coups carnival kicks off in Montauban.

Toulouse Highlights

1 Toulouse's food scene (p724) Ogling fresh produce in covered markets before a duck and *cassoulet* banquet.

2 Condom (p735) Getting acquainted with Armagnac brandy in a scenic, centuries-old distillery.

3 Canal du Midi (p727) Admiring a 17th-century waterway's engineering by boat or bicycle, or in-depth at the canal museum.

4 Cordes-sur-Ciel (p733) Strutting along lofty ramparts at a fortified town in the clouds.

5 Abbaye St-Pierre (p731) Wandering rose-tinted cloisters in Moissac's 12th-century abbey.

6 Vieil Albi (p727) Weaving through medieval laneways to Albi's gargantuan cathedral.

7 Escalier Monumental (p735) Gazing at expansive views from the open-air stairwell in Auch.

8 Lectoure (p736) Soak up the views and atmosphere in this surprisingly seductive village.

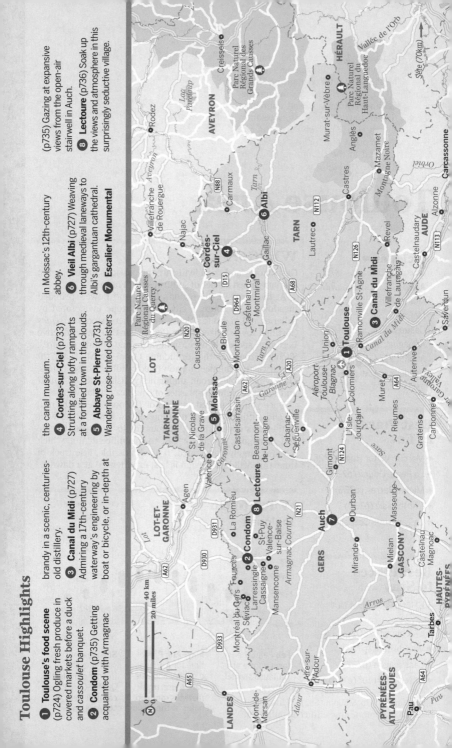

TOULOUSE

POP 458,298

Ochre rooftops and blushing brick churches earned Toulouse the nickname 'La Ville Rose' (The Pink City). Its enchanting Vieux Quartier (Old Quarter) is a dreamy jumble of coral-coloured shopfronts and churches. Beyond the old town, Toulouse sprawls into France's fourth-largest metropolis. It's an animated, hectic place, but Toulouse – nestled between a bend in the Garonne River and the mighty Canal du Midi – is invigorated by its waterways.

Toulouse has one of the largest universities outside Paris: at its core this southwestern French city is home to students and scientists. French aeronautical history continues in the Airbus factory outside town. But Toulouse knows how to have a good time, whether in teeming food markets, *salons de thé* or the thick of its smouldering jazz, techno and rock scenes. From the tips of dusky pink spires to its loudest bars, time spent in Toulouse truly has a rose-tinted sheen.

◉ Sights

Lavish place du Capitole is the classic starting point to explore Toulouse, before wandering south into the pedestrianised Vieux Quartier (Old Quarter). Most of the city's major galleries, museums and religious architecture are easily accessed from metro stops Esquirol, Jean Jaurès and Jeanne d'Arc, all on the red A line.

Place du Capitole   SQUARE
Toulouse's magnificent main square is the city's literal and metaphorical heart, where Toulousiens turn out en masse on sunny evenings to sip a coffee or an early aperitif at a pavement cafe. On the eastern side is the 128m-long façade of the Capitole (⚑05 61 22 34 12; place du Capitole; ⊘8.30am-7pm Mon-Sat, from 10am Sun) FREE, the city hall, built in the 1750s. Inside is the Théâtre du Capitole, one of France's most prestigious opera venues, and the over-the-top, late-19th-century Salle des Illustres (Hall of the Illustrious).

To the south of the square is the city's Vieux Quartier (Old Quarter), a tangle of lanes and leafy squares brimming with cafes, shops and eating options.

Basilique St-Sernin   CHURCH
(place St-Sernin; ambulatory €2.50; ⊘8.30am-6pm Mon-Sat, to 7.30pm Sun) This well-preserved Romanesque edifice is built from golden and rose-hued stonework up to the tip of the octogonal bell tower. Entry is free, but it's worth the additional charge to explore the ambulatory, where marble statues stare from alcoves in the brick walls. The tomb of the basilica's namesake St Sernin (also known as St Saturnin) has pride of place: he was Toulouse's first bishop and met a gruesome end when pagan priests tied him to a bull.

Down in the crypt (accessed from the ambulatory), you can tiptoe among the shadowy rib vaults to view reliquaries containing venerable bones from the likes of St Papoul, another southern French martyr. It also houses various ceremonial objects. Entry hours to the ambulatory and crypt are reduced from October to May (10am to noon and 2pm to 5.30pm).

★ Couvent des Jacobins   CHURCH, MONASTERY
(⚑05 61 22 23 82; www.jacobins.toulouse.fr; rue Lakanal; cloister adult/child €4/free; ⊘10am-6pm Tue-Sun) This elegant ecclesiastical structure is the mother church of the Dominican order, founded in 1215. First admire the Église des Jacobins' ornate stained-glass windows before wandering through the Cloître des Jacobins, in which graceful russet-brick columns surround a green courtyard. Pause in chapels and side rooms along the way, like the echoing Salle Capitulaire, a 14th-century hall ornamented with a haloed lamb and grisaille portraits of Dominican saints. Don't miss Chapelle St-Antonin, with its 14th-century ceiling frescoes showing apocalyptic scenes.

Musée des Augustins   GALLERY
(www.augustins.org; 21 rue de Metz; adult/child €5/free; ⊘10am-6pm Thu-Mon, to 9pm Wed) Located within a former Augustinian monastery, this fine-arts museum spans the

ⓘ CITY PASS

The Pass Tourisme Toulouse (www.toulouse-tourisme.com/pass-tourisme; per 24/48/72 hrs €18/28/35) entitles you to free public transport and entry to various sights, including the Musée des Augustins, the Muséum de Toulouse and Fondation Bemberg. Pass-holders can also enjoy discounts at Cité de l'Espace and Aeroscopia, and in several shops. Buy it at the tourist office or Tisséo agencies at the airport and train station.

Toulouse

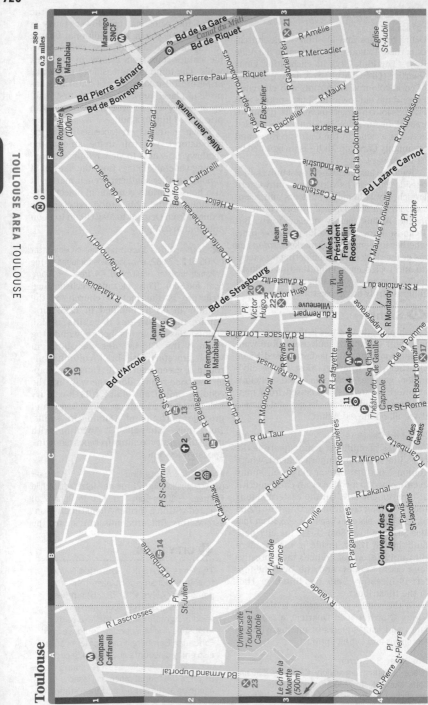

Marengo SNCF

Gare Matabiau

Bd de la Gare

Bd de Riquet

Canal du Midi

R Amélie

R Gabriel Péri

R Mercadier

Église St-Aubin

Bd Pierre Sémard

Bd de Bonrepos

Gare Routière (100m)

R Pierre-Paul Riquet

R des Sept Troubadours

Pl Bachelier

R Bachelier

R Maury

R Palaprat

R de la Colombette

R d'Aubuisson

Bd Lazare Carnot

R Stalingrad

Allée Jean Jaurès

R Caffarelli

R Héliot

Pl de Belfort

R Castellane

R de l'Industrie

Pl Occitane

Pl Matabiau

R Raymond IV

R de Bayard

R Denfert Rochereau

Jean Jaurès

Allées du Président Franklin Roosevelt

R Maurice Fonvieille

Pl Wilson

Bd de Strasbourg

R d'Austerlitz

Pl Victor Hugo

R Victor Hugo

R du Rempart Villeneuve

R St-Antoine du T

R Montardy

R Lapeyrouse

Jeanne d'Arc

Bd d'Arcole

R St-Bernard

R Bellegarde

R du Rempart Matabiau

R du Périgord

R Rémusat

R Montoyal

R Rivals

R d'Alsace-Lorraine

R Lafayette

Capitole

R Charles de Gaulle

Sq Charles de Gaulle

R de la Pomme

R Baour Lormain

Pl St-Sernin

R Cattailhac

R du Taur

R des Lois

Théâtre du Capitole

R St-Rome

R des Gestes

Gambetta

R d'Embarthe

Pl St-Julien

R Deville

Pl Anatole France

R Valade

R Pargaminières

R Romiguières

R Mirepoix

R Lakanal

Parvis St-Jacobins

Couvent des Jacobins

R Lascrosses

Compans Caffarelli

Bd Armand Duportal

Université Toulouse 1 Capitole

Le Cri de la Mouette (500m)

Q St-Pierre

Pl St-Pierre

350 m
0.2 miles

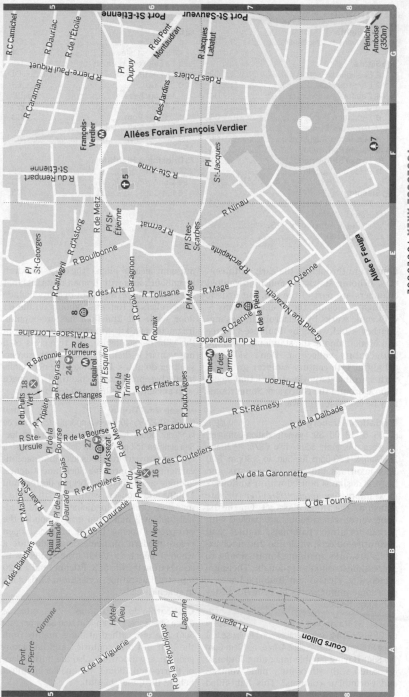

Toulouse

Roman era through to the early 20th century. Echoing stairwells and high-vaulted chambers are part of the fun, but artistic highlights include the French rooms – with some works by Delacroix, Ingres and Courbet – and works by Toulouse-Lautrec and Monet, among the standouts from the 20th-century collection. Don't skip the delightful 14th-century cloister gardens, with gurning gargoyle statues that seem to pose around the courtyard. Some rooms may be closed for renovation.

Fondation Bemberg   MUSEUM
(☏05 61 12 06 89; www.fondation-bemberg. fr; place d'Assézat; adult/child €8/5; ⊙10am-12.30pm & 1.30-6pm Tue-Sun, to 8.30pm Thu) This luxurious museum of fine arts and historic design is housed within Toulouse's most impressive *hôtel particulier* (private mansion), the Hôtel d'Assézat. On the 1st floor, velvet-walled rooms are packed with period furniture, paintings, statues and decorative objects, while the 2nd floor exhibits artworks spanning impressionist to expressionist schools of thought. There are sketches by Picasso and Toulouse-Lautrec, plus some minor works by Pissarro, Sisley and Egon Schiele.

Musée St-Raymond   MUSEUM
(☏05 61 22 31 44; www.saintraymond.toulouse.fr; 1 place St-Sernin; adult/child €4/free; ⊙10am-6pm Tue-Sun) Having trouble imagining Toulouse decorated with 4th-century nude Venuses and Corinthian columns? This light-filled

museum neatly aligns the city's modern neighbourhoods with Roman remnants that once stood there. Standout displays include stone reliefs of Hercules' labours on the 1st floor, while the 2nd floor has eye-popping fragments of a 4th–5th-century mosaic from the villa de St-Rustice, the remnants of a huge, marine-themed design with somersaulting dolphins. Don't skip the necropolis in the basement, an enchantingly lit space with ancient sarcophagi and tomb steles.

Musée Paul Dupuy   MUSEUM
(☏05 31 22 95 40; www.ampdupuy.fr; 13 rue de la Pléau; adult/child €4/free; ⊙10am-6pm Tue-Sun Jun-Sep, to 5pm Tue-Sun Oct-May) Browse a treasure trove of religious art, pharmaceutical items and impressive clocks and watches, lovingly assembled by local collector Paul Dupuy and housed within a 17th-century mansion. Ceramic medicine jars and medical tools will make you grimly ponder the prospect of being lanced or sliced open before modern medicine. Highlights are a wooden bench (c 1500) ornamented with scenes from the life of St Étienne, and a 1320 tapestry illustrating stories from Christ's life in silken thread.

Cathédrale de St-Étienne   CATHEDRAL
(place St-Étienne; ⊙8am-7pm Mon-Sat, from 9am Sun) The city cathedral dates mainly from the 12th and 13th centuries, and has a gorgeous rose window. It's also the burial place of Pierre-Paul Riquet, the master architect behind the Canal du Midi.

DON'T MISS

SPACE TRIP

The fantastic space museum **Cité de l'Espace** (📞 05 67 22 23 24; www.cite-espace.com; av Jean Gonord; adult €21-26, child €15.50-19; ⏰ 10am-7pm daily Jul & Aug, to 5pm or 6pm Sep-Dec & Feb-Jun, closed Mon in Feb, Mar & Sep-Dec, closed Jan; ♿) on the city's eastern outskirts brings Toulouse's illustrious aeronautical history to life through hands-on exhibits, including a moon-running simulator, a rotating pod to test your tolerance for space travel, a planetarium and an observatory, plus a vast cinema to immerse you in a space mission. The showpieces are the full-scale replicas of iconic spacecraft, including the Mir space station and a 52m-high Ariane 5 space rocket.

Since WWII, Toulouse has been the centre of France's aerospace industry, developing many important aircraft (including the Concorde and the 555-seat Airbus A380) as well as components for international space programs.

To reach the museum, catch bus 15 from allée Jean Jaurès to the last stop, from where it's a 500m walk. To avoid queuing, buy your tickets in advance online.

Aeroscopia   MUSEUM
(📞 05 34 39 42 00; www.musee-aeroscopia.fr; allée André Turcat; adult/child under 6yr €12.50/free; ⏰ 9.30am-6pm, closed early Jan; 🚌 Beauzelle) This aviation museum was built on the very spot the A380 Airbus was first completed. Here you can admire commercial and military aircraft and learn behind-the-scenes knowledge about the industry, as well as clamber inside certain vessels.

Jardin des Plantes   PARK
(allée Frédéric Mistral; ⏰ 7.45am-9pm summer, to 6pm winter) These 200-year-old sculpted gardens are a refreshing place to take a breather from hectic central Toulouse. Find the entrance to this 7-hectare park on allée Frédéric Mistral, a 500m-walk south from place St-Jacques.

🏃 Activities

Boat trips along the Garonne run regularly from March to November. In high summer, riverside beach games and sunbathing areas pop up around the city for **Toulouse Plages**, usually from late July to late August.

👉 Tours

Airbus Factory Tours   TOURS
(📞 05 34 39 42 00; www.manatour.fr; allée André Turcat, Blagnac; tours adult/child €15.50/13; ⏰ Mon-Sat by reservation) Plane-spotters can arrange a guided tour of Toulouse's massive JL Lagardère Airbus factory, near the airport in Blagnac, 10km northwest of the city centre. The main factory tour includes a visit to the A380 and A350XWB production lines. You'll also be able to go inside an A400M. Tours must be booked in advance online or by phone.

There's also a 'Panoramic Tour', which takes in other sections of the 700-hectare site via bus. Non-EU visitors must book at least two days ahead. Remember to bring a passport or photo ID. For security reasons, cameras aren't allowed, and you'll have to leave bulky bags behind.

🎉 Festivals & Events

Fête de la Violette   CULTURAL
(⏰ early Feb) Since the 19th century, this street parade and its accompanying revelry have been painting the town purple in a celebration of Toulouse's favourite flower. Everything from sweet and savoury food to liqueurs and wines will have the unmistakable scent of violet. Dress accordingly.

🛏️ Sleeping

La Petite Auberge de St-Sernin   HOSTEL €
(📞 07 60 88 17 17; www.lapetiteaubergedesaintsernin.com; 17 rue d'Embarthe; dm €22-24; ⏰ reception 10am-12.30pm & 2.30-9pm; ❄️📶) No-frills but friendly, secure and great value, this backpacker-filled hostel offers boxy dorm rooms of four, six and eight beds. The decor's plain – tiled floors, bare walls – but there's a garden for barbecues, and you're only a minute's walk from the Basilique St-Sernin. Some rooms have air-con; ask when you book.

⭐ Villa du Taur   BOUTIQUE HOTEL €€
(📞 05 34 25 28 82; www.villadutaur.com; 62 rue du Taur; d €90-180; 🅿️❄️📶) Spitting distance from Basilique St-Sernin, this hip venture with an arty vibe was entirely overhauled in 2017 and the result is spectacular. It's a study in clean lines and all rooms are stylishly furnished. The on-site restaurant and bar is a plus.

★**Hôtel St-Sernin** BOUTIQUE HOTEL €€
(☑05 61 21 73 08; www.hotelstsernin.com; 2 rue St-Bernard; s €63-110, d €90-170; P☎) This tranquil establishment houses 17 soothing and small-but-sleek rooms, some with colourful frescoes on the walls. The two best rooms (10 and 20), great for a romantic getaway, have floor-to-ceiling windows overlooking the Basilique St-Sernin. Ask in advance about parking (€15); there's a limited number of on-site spaces.

★**Hôtel Albert 1er** HOTEL €€
(☑05 61 21 47 49; www.hotel-albert1.com; 8 rue Rivals; d €68-145; ❄☎) ✐ The Albert's central location and eager-to-please staff are a winning combination. A palette of maroon and cream, with marble flourishes here and there, bestows a regal feel on comfortable rooms. The choice rooms are the Classique ones, which are great value. The breakfast buffet (€13) is largely organic. No private parking but ask about preferential rates for the municipal parking nearby

Péniche Amboise B&B €€
(☑06 50 77 64 58; www.peniche-amboise.com; 17 bd Griffoul Dorval; s €80, incl breakfast d €90-130, tr €120-140; P❄☎) Love life on the river? Then how about staying aboard a genuine *péniche* (barge) moored on the banks of the Canal du Midi? There are four cosy, colour-coded rooms, all with tiny private bathrooms and porthole windows. The bathrooms are separated from the bedrooms by a curtain. The best is 'Amboise', with cool cabin-beds and wood floors.

✗ Eating

The city has a flourishing culinary scene, from Michelin-starred establishments to tearooms. For atmospheric dining, head to half-timbered rue Perchepinte for a clutch of classy restaurants. Bd de Strasbourg, place Wilson and the western side of place du Capitole are one long cafe-terrace line-up (though quality varies). Hit rue Pargaminières for kebabs, burgers and other late-night student grub.

★**Flower's Café** CAFE €
(☑05 34 44 93 66; www.theflowerscafe.com; 6 place Roger Salengro; cakes from €4, mains €14-15; ⊙10am-8pm Mon-Sat, from 2pm Sun) Beside a tinkling fountain, this busy cafe is a cake lover's dream – though deciding between glistening raspberry tarts, chocolate cakes or New York–style cheesecake is an exquisite nightmare. Arrive mid-morning for the best chance of grabbing a table. Lunch service is between noon and 2pm from Monday to Saturday only.

L'Oncle Pom BISTRO €
(☑05 61 54 39 86; www.lonclepom.com; 32 rue Gabriel Péri; menus €13-26, mains €11-16; ⊙noon-1.45pm & 7-10pm Tue-Sat, 11am-3pm Sun) Not your average restaurant, L'Oncle Pom is a fine choice. You choose a variety and a recipe of potato, then a side dish of meat, fish or vegetables. All ingredients are

---

WONDROUS WATERWAYS OF TOULOUSE

Whether you're awed by the feats of engineering behind the Canal du Midi or just seeking breezy respite from the city, head to Toulouse's waterways. Here are a few ways to unwind along the water.

Short boat cruises From March to November, boat trips (www.bateaux-toulousains.com; adult/child from €12/6; ⊙Mar-Oct; ♿) run along the Garonne from the quai de la Daurade. Trips start at around €10/5 per adult/child for an hour's cruise. Booking is wise in high summer, or if you're a big group, but you can buy tickets on the boat up to 10 minutes before departure.

Musée et Jardin du Canal du Midi (p727) Sixty kilometres southeast of Toulouse, this museum shines a light on the 17th-century canal that transformed trade in France. The fountain-filled gardens make a refreshing stroll too.

Captain your own canal boat No experience is required to cruise the Canal du Midi under your own steam, if you hire a vessel from **Locaboat** (☑03 86 91 72 72; www.locaboat.com).

Embark on an epic cycle ride Pedal along the 139km Toulouse–Carcassonne stretch of a new cycle route linking the Atlantic and Mediterranean, following the Canal du Midi. Beyond Lauragais, about halfway, the track becomes rough, unmarked and beyond the capabilities of a standard bike. Learn more at www.canaldes2mersavelo.com.

LOCAL KNOWLEDGE

A MARKET LUNCH

A morning spent admiring fresh cheeses, fruits and jars of homemade *cassoulet* at **Marché Victor Hugo** (📞 05 61 22 76 92; www.marche-victor-hugo.fr; place Victor Hugo; ⊘ 7am-1.30pm Tue-Sun) certainly fires the appetite. Fortunately, the upper floor of this covered market houses a handful of lunch places that source their ingredients directly from the produce below. Expect simple, hearty Toulouse fare, from confit duck to beef tartare, served in a hectic setting where you brush elbows with other diners.

Le Louchebem (📞 05 67 00 51 75; www.lelouchebem-toulouse.fr; place Victor Hugo; menus €19-26, mains €16-26; ⊘ noon-2pm Tue-Sun) is the top choice for filling Toulouse favourites like *cassoulet,* while **Le Magret** (📞 05 61 23 21 32; www.restaurant-lemagret.com; place Victor Hugo; menus €20-27, mains €16-21; ⊘ 11.45am-2pm Tue-Fri, to 3pm Sat & Sun) is admired for its expertly seared fish dishes and great-value *menus*. Arrive a few minutes before noon if you want to snag a table, as hungry Toulousiens descend en masse by 1pm.

---

market fresh or locally sourced, and the vintage-chic decor is a treat. Desserts, including carrot cake and panna cotta, are to die for. Locals also rave about the Sunday brunch (€19).

La Faim des Haricots   VEGETARIAN €
(📞 05 61 22 49 25; www.lafaimdesharicots.fr; 3 rue du Puits Vert; menus €12-18; ⊘ noon-2.30pm & 7-10pm; 📷) With confit duck and pâté featuring prominently on restaurant menus across Toulouse, this budget vegetarian canteen provides a much-needed palate cleanser. Faim des Haricots serves everything *à volonté* (all you can eat); simply choose whether you'd prefer to tuck into salads, quiches or the dish of the day.

★La Pente Douce   FRENCH €€
(📞 05 61 46 16 91; www.lapentedouce.fr; 6 rue de la Concorde; menus €23-28, mains €18-24; ⊘ noon-1.30pm Tue & Wed, noon-1.30pm & 8-9.30pm Thu-Sat) La Pente Douce is always packed, generally with gourmet locals who love their food. Smiling chefs in the open kitchen mesmerise with superb dishes like tender veal, Bigorre pork or cod. Presentation is impeccable, the service efficient and the decor playful. Reservations essential.

Balthazar   BISTRO €€
(📞 05 62 72 29 54; www.facebook.com/Balthazar. Toulouse; 50 rue des Couteliers; mains €16-25; ⊘ noon-2pm & 8-9.30pm Wed-Fri, 8-9.30pm Sat) Ask for where's best for lunch and someone will point you in the direction of Balthazar. It's a modern take on an old-style bistro, with classic Gascon cuisine crafted only from seasonal, market-fresh and organic ingredients. Wooden furniture matches the honest food, and the wine list is great.

Le J'Go   BRASSERIE €€
(📞 05 61 23 02 03; www.lejgo.com; 16 place Victor Hugo; menus €18-39, mains €21-27; ⊘ noon-2pm & 7-10.30pm) This much-loved Toulouse favourite won't disappoint. Its delicious menus are designed around what's in season and all ingredients are supplied by small producers. Meats are cooked to perfection and vegetables are flavoursome. Save room for an delectable dessert.

★Michel Sarran   GASTRONOMY €€€
(📞 05 61 12 32 32; www.michel-sarran.com; 21 bd Armand Duportal; menus €60-145; ⊘ noon-1.45pm Mon, Tue, Thu & Fri, 8-9.45pm Mon-Fri Sep-Jul) For a no-expense-spared, food-as-art dining experience, Toulouse's double-Michelin-starred master chef Michel Sarran is your man. He's earned an international reputation for cuisine that takes its cue from the traditional flavours of France's southwest, then spins off in experimental directions. Needless to say, bookings are essential – especially since Michel doesn't open on weekends.

🍷 Drinking & Nightlife

Almost every square in the Vieux Quartier has at least one cafe, that's busy day and night. Other areas lively after dark include rue Castellane, rue Gabriel Péri and near the river around place St-Pierre.

★N°5 Wine Bar   WINE BAR
(📞 05 61 38 44 51; www.n5winebar.com; 5 rue de la Bourse; ⊘ 6pm-1am Mon-Sat) No address buzzes with Toulouse's hip, buoyant crowd more than this fabulous all-rounder wine bar, which was voted the best wine bar in the world in 2017. Take your pick of hundreds of wines by the glass and be sure to order delicious tapas-style platters.

FAMILY FAVE: BEAUMONT-DE-LOMAGNE
....

An easy day trip by car from Toulouse, Auch or Condom, this small town between Toulouse and Condom is blessed with the region's signature *hôtels particuliers* (private mansions), russet church towers and – for something a little different – mathematical heritage.

Beaumont is most famous as the birthplace of 17th-century maths genius and polymath Pierre de Fermat. In honour of Fermat's colossal contribution to world thought – including laying the groundwork for analytic geometry and pioneering probability theory with his contemporary, Blaise Pascal – visitors to his home town will find maths and puzzle trails galore, plus a museum in Fermat's birth house, the **Maison Natale de Pierre Fermat** (Association Fermat-Science; ☑ 05 63 26 52 30; www.fermat-science.com; 3 rue Pierre de Fermat; ☺ 9am-noon & 2-5pm Mon-Fri, 9am-noon Sat Jun-Sep, to 6pm Mon-Fri, 2-5pm Sat Jul & Aug, 2-5pm Mon-Fri Oct-May; 🖼) **FREE**, with ample hands-on displays suited to curious kids.

Reaching Beaumont-de-Lomagne is easiest with your own wheels. A few local buses between Auch and Montauban stop at Beaumont.

★ **Fat Cat**   COCKTAIL BAR
(4 rue de Rémusat; ☺ 7pm-2am) This speakeasy-style cocktail lounge is a wonderful place for a drink thanks to its so-far-above-average cocktails and so-better-looking-than-you clientele. Try the devilish Corpse Reviver (lemon, gin, Cointreau and absinthe).

Au Père Louis   WINE BAR
(45 rue des Tourneurs; ☺ 9am-2.30pm & 6-11.30pm Mon-Sat) This unashamedly retro bar-brasserie in maroon and gold trim has been here since 1889. The left-hand entrance panel reads *'vin blanc'*; the right, *'vin rouge'*. But you needn't pick a side with such a large wine list to choose from. Sip the house speciality, *quinquina*, a powerful fortified wine flavoured with cinchona bark (the source of quinine, the anti-malarial treatment).

Connexion Café   BAR
(www.connexion-cafe.com; 8 rue Gabriel Péri; ☺ 5.30pm-1am Tue-Fri, to 2am Sat) A mash-up of cocktail bar, nightclub and tapas bar in a converted industrial space, this popular spot also hosts live gigs straddling genres from hip-hop to jazz to metal. When the weather's warm, the action spills onto the outdoor terrace. Also serves food.

☆ **Entertainment**

Le Bikini   LIVE MUSIC
(☑ 05 62 24 09 50; www.lebikini.com; rue Théodore Monod, Ramonville St-Agne; ☺ from 8pm) This concert hall has been vibrating with the sounds of rock, pop, world music and DJ sets for more than 30 years. It's at the southern end of metro line B (Ramonville stop).

Le Cri de la Mouette   LIVE MUSIC
(www.lecridelamouette.com; 78 allée de Barcelone; ☺ 11pm-late Thu-Sat) Party hard on a converted canal boat, with regular electro, disco and rock nights. Check its website for events (timings vary depending on the gig).

ℹ Information

Tourist Office (☑ 08 92 18 01 80; www.toulouse-tourisme.com; square Charles de Gaulle; ☺ 9am-7pm Mon-Sat, 10.30am-5.15pm Sun Jun-Sep, 9am-6pm Mon-Fri, 9am-12.30pm & 2-6pm Sat, 10am-12.30pm & 2-5pm Sun Oct-Mar) The modern, multilingual tourist office is housed within a spiky 16th-century belfry.

ℹ Getting There & Away

AIR

Eight kilometres northwest of the city centre, **Toulouse-Blagnac Airport** (TLS; www.toulouse.aeroport.fr/en) has frequent flights to Paris and other large French cities, as well as major hub cities in the UK, Italy and Germany.

BUS

Long-distance bus services are provided by several private operators; destinations include Bordeaux and Paris (overnight coach). Find routes at Eurolines (www.eurolines.fr). All services run to/from Toulouse's **Gare Routière** (Bus Station; bd Pierre Sémard).

TRAIN

Toulouse is served by frequent fast TGVs, which run west to Montauban, Agen and Bordeaux (which has connections to Bayonne and the southwest, plus Paris), and east to Carcassonne, Narbonne, Montpellier and beyond.

Toulouse's main train station, **Gare Matabiau** (bd Pierre Sémard), is 1km northeast of the city centre.

Albi €14.10, one hour, 11 to 16 daily

Auch €16, 1½ hours (direct or with bus), nine daily

Bordeaux from €17, two hours, 13 daily

Carcassonne from €16.50, 45 minutes to one hour, up to 23 daily

Castres €15.70, 70 minutes, up to 11 daily

Montauban €10.30, 30 minutes, up to 26 daily

Pau €34.20, 2¼ to three hours, seven daily

ℹ Getting Around

TO/FROM THE AIRPORT

The airport is linked to the city's metro network (single ticket €1.60); change at Arènes station for the red A line to central Toulouse (Capitole) or Matabiau (the main train station).

Alternatively, the Navette Aéroport shuttlebus links the airport with central Toulouse.The service runs every 20 minutes from 5am to 9.10pm from town, and from 5.45am to 12.10am from the airport. From the airport, buses depart next to the metro stop. From town, catch the bus in front of the bus station, outside the Jean Jaurès metro station or at place Jeanne d'Arc. The trip takes between 20 and 40 minutes, depending on traffic.

Taxis to/from town cost around €30.

PUBLIC TRANSPORT

Local buses and the two-line metro are run by Tisséo (www.tisseo.fr). There are ticket kiosks at the airport, place Jeanne d'Arc and metro stops. A single ticket costs €1.60, a 10-ticket *carnet* (book of tickets) is €13.40 and a one-/three-day pass is €6/12.

ALBI

POP 49,342

The bustling provincial town of Albi has two main claims to fame: a truly mighty cathedral and a truly marvellous painter. Looming up from the centre of Vieil Albi (Old Albi) on the south bank of the River Tarn, the Cathédrale Ste-Cécile is one of France's most monumental Gothic structures and one of the largest brick buildings in the world. Next door is the fantastic Musée Toulouse-Lautrec, dedicated to the ground-breaking artist Henri de Toulouse-Lautrec, who was born here in 1864 and went on to depict the bars and brothels of turn-of-the-century Paris in his own inimitable style.

DON'T MISS

CANAL DU MIDI

Stretching for 241km between Toulouse and the southern port of Sète, the **Canal du Midi** (www.canaldumidi.com) is the queen of French canals. A waterway connecting the Atlantic and Mediterranean had been dreamed of since Roman times, and was finally realised in the 17th century under engineering mastermind Pierre-Paul Riquet. The Canal du Midi was constructed as the first stretch of the mighty 'Canal des Deux Mers' (Canal of the Two Seas).

With an eye on invigorating the Languedoc wine and wheat trades – and dodging the pirate-ridden transport routes around Spain – Louis XIV commissioned the canal in 1666. Riquet, a Languedoc tax farmer and mathematical genius, painstakingly devised a system of dams, bridges, aqueducts, tunnels and locks to overcome the region's difficult terrain.

After years of toil by a workforce of 12,000 women and men, spiralling debts and a loss of faith among Riquet's sponsors, the canal opened in 1681. Riquet died a few months before the official opening of his life's work. Between Toulouse and Castres, in Revel, the **Musée et Jardin du Canal du Midi** (☑ 05 61 80 57 57; www.museecanaldu midi31.blogspot.fr; bd Pierre-Paul Riquet, St-Ferréol; adult/child €5/free; ☉ 10.30am-6.30pm Jul & Aug, 10am-1pm & 2-6pm Tue-Sun Apr-Jun, Sep & Oct, shorter hours rest of year) explores the waterway's remarkable construction and Riquet's life.

Though its commercial importance was eclipsed by the railway in the 19th century, these days the canal, a Unesco World Heritage Site since 1996, is enormously popular with pleasure-boaters. It takes several weeks to sail the whole length, but it's possible to do shorter sections, with especially scenic stretches near Agde, Béziers and Narbonne. Alternatively, hire a bike and appreciate the canal's tranquil, tree-lined scenery from its towpaths.

If you want to cruise, Locaboat (p724) and **Les Canalous** (☑ 03 85 53 76 74; www. canalous-canaldumidi.com; Carnon; weekend/weekly rental from €400/791; ☉ Mar-Oct) rent out small motorboats, while **Minervois Cruisers** (☑ UK +44 1926 811842; www.minervois cruisers.com; ☉ Mar-Oct) offers narrowboats. Prices vary depending on season and boat size, but expect to pay €900 to €1400 a week for a standard four-berth. *Péniches* (motorised, live-aboard narrowboats) are more expensive – around €360 per day.

Albi

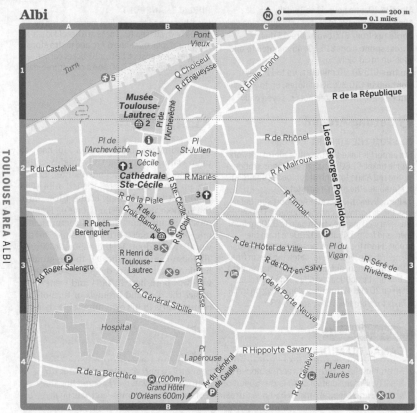

Albi

Top Sights

Sights

Activities, Courses & Tours

Sleeping

Eating

Vieil Albi is also an attractive muddle of winding streets and half-timbered houses. It's wonderful for strolling, especially if you live to leaven your cultural enrichment with excellent food and fine wine.

Sights & Activities

The Albi City Pass (€12), sold at the tourist office, gives free admission to the Musée Toulouse-Lautrec and Cathédrale Ste-Cécile's *grand chœur* and treasury, and offers discounts at local shops and restaurants.

★ Cathédrale Ste-Cécile   CHURCH
(☑ 05 63 38 47 40; www.cathedrale-albi.com; place Ste-Cécile; choir €5, choir & treasury €6; ⊙ 9.30am-5.45pm Mon-Sat, 9.30-10.15am & 1.30-5.15pm Sun) Resembling a castle more than a cathedral, this formidable edifice in orange brick rises above Vieil Albi like an apparition.

Its defensive walls hark back to the many religious wars that scarred medieval Albi. Begun in 1282, the cathedral took well over a century to complete; eight centuries later, it's still one of the world's largest brick buildings, and has been on Unesco's World Heritage list since 2010.

⭐**Musée Toulouse-Lautrec**　MUSEUM
(📞 05 63 49 48 70; www.musee-toulouse-lautrec. com; Palais de la Berbie, place Ste-Cécile; adult/ student €9/free; ☺9am-6pm Jun-Sep, closed noon-2pm rest of year & all day Tue Oct-Mar) Lodged inside the Palais de la Berbie (built in the early Middle Ages for the town's archbishop), this wonderful museum offers an overview of Albi's most celebrated son. The museum owns more than 1000 original works by Toulouse-Lautrec – the largest collection in France outside the Musée d'Orsay – spanning the artist's development, from his early neo-impressionist paintings to his famous Parisian brothel scenes and poster art.

Of particular interest are the early portraits of some of Toulouse-Lautrec's friends and family – including his mother, the Comtesse Adèle de Toulouse-Lautrec, his cousin Gabriel Tapié de Celeyran, and his close friend, Maurice Joyant. They clearly demonstrate the artist's wry eye and playful sense of humour. There are also some delicate animal studies (especially of horses).

Inevitably, however, it's the later works that draw the eye. Toulouse-Lautrec's lifelong fascination with the Parisian underworld, particularly the lives of dancers and prostitutes, is brilliantly represented. Look out for key works including *L'Anglaise du Star au Havre* (Englishwoman of the Star Harbour) and *Les Deux Amies* (The Two Friends), which depicts two prostitutes embracing while they wait for their clients. Pride of place goes to two versions of one of his most famous canvases, *Au Salon de la rue des Moulins,* hung side by side to illustrate changes in the artist's technique.

Toulouse-Lautrec's skills as a cartoonist and caricaturist also made him a pioneer of poster art, and the museum has a fantastic collection of his most famous designs in its permanent collection.

On the top floor is a small collection of works by some of his contemporaries, including Pierre Bonnard, Maurice de Vlaminck and Henri Matisse.

Maison du Vieil Alby　MUSEUM
(1 rue de la Croix Blanche; adult/child €2/free; ☺2-5pm Mon-Sat) Lodged in a timber-framed medieval building, this museum houses a small exhibition on the city's history and its connections with Toulouse-Lautrec.

Collégiale & Cloître Saint-Salvi　CHURCH
(Rue Mariès; ☺church 8.30am-noon & 2-5pm Mon-Wed, 10am-noon & 2-5pm Fri & Sat, 2-5pm Sun, cloister 7am-7pm) This delicate church is worth a look for its lovely 13th-century cloister whose columns are decorated with Gothic and Romanesque flourishes.

Musée de Lapérouse　MUSEUM
(📞 05 63 49 15 55; www.laperouse-france.fr; 41 rue Porta; adult/child €4/free; ☺9am-noon & 2-6pm Tue-Sun, to 7pm Jul & Aug, reduced hours Nov-Feb) This intriguing museum explores the adventures of Albi-born explorer Jean-François de Galaup (aka the Comte de Lapérouse), who made several pioneering naval expeditions around the Pacific between 1785 and 1788. Mysteriously, his ships disappeared without a trace towards the end of their voyage; subsequent expeditions suggested they may have been wrecked on reefs near the island of Vanikoro, halfway between the Solomon Islands and Vanuatu.

Albi Croisières　BOATING
(📞 05 63 43 59 63; www.albi-croisieres.com; ☺May-Oct) Glide down the River Tarn aboard a traditional *gabarre* (flat-bottomed barge). There are regular 30-minute cruises (adult/ child €7.50/5) between 11am and 6pm, a 1½-hour lunchtime cruise (€12/8) leaving at 12.30pm, and full-day return trips (€24/18) to the village of Aiguelèze, near Gaillac.

🛏 Sleeping

Grand Hôtel D'Orléans　HOTEL €
(📞 05 63 54 16 56; www.hotel-orleans-albi.com; 1 place Stalingrad; d €55-77; 🅿 ❄ 🛜) This pleasant three-star opposite Albi's train station, less than 1km south of Vieil Albi, has trim, tidy rooms and friendly service. There's covered parking (€10 per night) but there's usually space to leave your car at the train station. Other perks include a swimming pool (in summer) and Le Goulu, the renowned onsite restaurant (mains from €16).

Hôtel St-Clair　HOTEL €
(📞 05 63 54 25 66; www.hotel-albi-saintclair.com; 8 rue St-Clair; s €40-65, d €48-75; 🅿 🛜) A real rabbit's warren of a hotel, this one – thrillingly creaky rooms with brassy-bordered mirrors

fill an old house slap-bang in the middle of Vieil Albi. The car park has three spaces (€8 per night); if they're full, you'll have to park on the edge of Vieil Albi and walk. There are only 15 rooms, so book ahead.

L'Alchimy　　　　　　　　　BOUTIQUE HOTEL €€
(✉05 63 76 18 18; www.alchimyalbi.fr; 10-12 place du Palais; d/ste from €160/250; P✳🛜) A hushed magnificence greets you in this alluring boutique hotel occupying a lovely art deco building right in the town centre. Rooms are plush and decor is a great blend of modernity and tradition. The ground-floor bar-restaurant (*menus* from €16) serves delicious French specialities with a contemporary twist. There's covered parking (€15). Check online for deals.

✖ Eating

From cafes and bistros to snack bars and chic restaurants, Albi has plenty of well-priced places to eat, including a string of places on rue Henri de Toulouse-Lautrec, just downhill from the cathedral, and around the covered market.

★ L'Ambroisie　　　　　　　　BISTRO €
(✉05 63 76 43 54; 4 rue Henri de Toulouse-Lautrec; mains €17-18, menus €13-26; ⊗noon-2pm & 7.30-10pm) An intimate, colourful dining room sets the tone for this widely acclaimed bistro serving exquisite food. There's an emphasis on veal and chicken. Everything is made in-house with loving care.

L'Epicurien　　　　　　　MODERN FRENCH €€
(✉05 63 53 10 70; www.restaurantlepicurien.com; 42 place Jean Jaurès; mains €19-25, menus €19-65; ⊗noon-2pm & 8-10pm Tue-Sat) This lauded local restaurant serves French comfort food with a refreshing edge. Superbly executed dishes include roasted cod, Pyrénées trout and beef tartare. Desserts are presented with all the flair of a piece of modern art.

Le Lautrec　　　　　　　　　　FRENCH €€
(✉05 63 54 86 55; www.restaurant-le-lautrec. com; 13-15 rue Henri de Toulouse-Lautrec; mains €18, menus €18-42; ⊗noon-2pm Tue-Sun & 7.30-9.30pm Tue-Sat, noon-2pm Sun) Tucked into the back lanes of Vieil Albi, this is the ideal spot to guzzle nourishing flavours of the Tarn region. Try smoky *cassoulet* or *farçous* (dumplings of pork, prunes and Armagnac) alongside platefuls of regional cheese, finishing with mouth-watering desserts like *tartouillat aux fruits de saison* (batter pudding with seasonal fruits).

La Table du Sommelier　　　　　BISTRO €€
(✉05 63 46 20 10; www.latabledusommelier.com; 20 rue Porta; menus €16-60; ⊗noon-1.30pm & 7-9.30pm Tue-Sat) It's in the name – this place is for wine lovers. Owner Daniel Pestre is an experienced sommelier, with an infectious passion for his local vintages: the *menu* 'Autour des Vins' (€39) is themed around wines. The outdoor patio shaded by huge umbrellas is a great spot in summer. On the northern bank of the Tarn, 10 minutes' walk from the cathedral.

ℹ Information

Tourist Office (✉05 63 36 36 00; www. albi-tourisme.fr; place Ste-Cécile; ⊗10am-12.30pm & 1.30-5pm Mon-Sat, to 4.30pm Sun Oct–mid-Jun, 9am-6pm Mon-Sat, 10am-6pm Sun mid-Jun–Sep) Next door to the Musée Toulouse-Lautrec. Ask for one of the themed leaflets covering walks around Vieil Albi.

ℹ Getting There & Away

BUS

TarnBus lines include the 703 to Castres (€2, 50 minutes, at least hourly Monday to Friday) and the 707 to Cordes-sur-Ciel (€2, 35 minutes, five to six Monday to Saturday). Most leave from **place Jean Jaurès** (place Jean Jaurès).

TRAIN

Destinations include Gaillac (€4.80, 20 minutes, frequent), Rodez (€15.30, 1½ hours, six to nine daily) and Toulouse (€14.10, one hour, 11 to 18 daily). For trains to Castres, change at St-Sulpice Tarn station.

MONTAUBAN

POP 56,271

Nestled on the banks of the River Tarn, Montauban is a fine example of a *bastide* (fortified town) in southwest France. There's no shortage of attractive buildings in its distinguished centre, built around a delightful square.

The town was badly battered during both the Hundred Years' War and the Wars of Religion, and famously withstood an 86-day siege imposed by Louis XIII in 1621, during which the defenders resorted to eating horses, rats and dogs to survive.

◉ Sights

Place Nationale　　　　　　　　SQUARE
In the historic upper town, all roads lead to this exquisite square, hemmed in on every

side by magnificent double-vaulted arcades and tall pink buildings.

Musée Ingres GALLERY
(☑ 05 63 22 12 91; www.museeingres.montauban. com; 19 rue de l'Hôtel de Ville; adult/child €7/3.50; ⊙10am-6pm daily Jul & Aug, 10am-noon & 2-6pm Tue-Sun Sep-Jun) Montauban's main focus is this fine-arts museum, which centres on the work of the neoclassical painter (and accomplished violinist) Jean-Auguste-Dominique Ingres, who was born in Montauban in 1780. Inspired by Poussin and David, Ingres became one of the most celebrated portrait painters of his day, and the museum houses many of his key works alongside old masters such as Tintoretto, Van Dyck and Gustave Courbet. The museum was closed for renovation at the time of research, and was due to reopen in early 2020.

ℹ Information

Tourist Office (☑ 05 63 63 60 60; www. montauban-tourisme.com; 4 rue du Collège; ⊙9.30am-6.30pm Mon-Sat, 10am-12.30pm Sun Jul-Aug, 9.30am-noon & 2-6.30pm Mon-Sat Sep-Jun) Book accommodation and grab some local maps at this tourist office in Montauban's old town.

ℹ Getting There & Away

From the **Montauban Ville Bourbon train station** (av Mayenne), about 1km from place Nationale across the River Tarn, direct services reach Toulouse (€10.30, 30 minutes, half-hourly) and Moissac (€6.40, 20 minutes, frequent).

MOISSAC

POP 12,470
Riverside Moissac has been an important stop-off on the Santiago de Compostela trail since the 12th century, thanks to the glorious Abbaye St-Pierre. This standout religious complex is resplendent with some of France's finest Romanesque architecture, especially the apocalyptic scene on its tympanum.

Beyond the abbey, Moissac is a quiet spot best known for local *chasselas de Moissac* grapes. First cultivated by medieval monks, these succulent globes find their way into everything from baked goods to detox remedies.

A COUNTRYSIDE FEAST

Much-lauded hotel-restaurant **Les Boissières** (☑ 05 63 24 50 02; www. lesboissieres.com; 708 route de Caussade, Bioule; mains €15-26, lunch menus €20-60, dinner menus €33-60; ⊙noon-1.30pm & 8-9.30pm Tue-Fri, 8-9.30pm Sat, noon-1.30pm Sun) about 22km northeast of Montauban, in Bioule, is well worth the detour. Chef Cyril Rosenberg blends regional cuisine with contemporary style. Savour duck sautéed in garlic and chardonnay or lamb saddle with chestnut purée in the stone-walled dining room. On warm afternoons, the garden terrace is the place to be. Rooms cost from €90.

◉ Sights

Abbaye St-Pierre ABBEY
(☑ 05 63 04 01 85; www.tourisme.moissac.fr; 6 place Durand de Bredon; cloister adult/child €6.50/4.50; ⊙cloister 10am-7pm Jul-Sep, 2-5pm Oct-Mar, 10am-noon & 2-5pm Apr-Jun) Rosy brick characteristic of the Toulouse area heightens the majesty of this abbey and its exceptional Romanesque cloister. Awarded Unesco World Heritage status in part for its significance along the Santiago de Compostela pilgrimage route, the abbey contains some compelling religious art, in particular a striking frieze of St John's vision of the apocalypse above the elaborate south portal. The **cloister** was completed in 1100, followed a few years later by the **Tour-Porche bell tower**.

The cloister is worth scrutinising on account of the carved capitals topping its slender stone columns: many of them depict biblical scenes in tender detail, such as Samuel pouring holy oil over a kneeling David, as well as animals and plant motifs. Inside the bell tower, look for faint initials carved into the stone – graffiti by the original stone masons.

🛏 Sleeping & Eating

Le Moulin de Moissac HOTEL €€
(☑ 05 63 32 88 88; www.lemoulindemoissac.com; 1 promenade Sancert; d €105-175; P ❄ 🛜) Housed in a 15th-century grain mill overlooking the Tarn, this hotel is a riverside treat. Rooms with distressed wallpaper, lovingly painted furniture and tall French windows open

onto river-view balconies. The restaurant (menus €17 to €59) is one of the best addresses in town to savour beautifully presented regional dishes with a fusion twist. There's a smart sauna-spa and a romantic hot tub, too.

Le Bistrot Gourmand FRENCH €
(☑ 0563041918; www.leflorentin-bistrotgourmand.fr; 8 place Roger Delthil; mains €11-25, menus €15-19; ☺ noon-1.30pm daily, 7-9.30pm Thu-Sat) Moissagais pack into this cosy restaurant opposite Abbaye St-Pierre for the artistically presented, accomplished cooking that doesn't sacrifice substance for style. Top choices are the generous slabs of Aveyron beef and succulent truffle omelette; if you can't decide on dessert, go for the *café gourmand* (coffee with miniature desserts).

ℹ Information

Tourist Office (☑ 05 32 09 69 36; www.tourisme.moissac.fr; 1 bd de Brienne; ☺ 9am-7pm Jul & Aug, 9am-noon & 2-6pm Apr-Jun, Sep & Oct, shorter hours Nov-Mar) Has plenty of info on Moissac and its surrounds.

ℹ Getting There & Away

There are regular direct trains from Moissac to Toulouse (€14.70, 50 minutes, up to seven daily) and Montauban (€6.40, 20 minutes, frequent).

CASTRES

POP 41,600

Local descriptions of Castres, 70km east of Toulouse, as a 'little Venice' slightly oversell its charms. But not only does the town have political pedigree as the birthplace of French Socialism's founding father Jean Jaurès, it also has a superb museum of Spanish art and a landscaped park laid out by the designer of Versailles' gardens. With former tanneries casting fetching reflections in the Agout river flowing through town, Castres is a photogenic spot to explore.

Settled since the Iron Age, Castres rose to prominence with the construction of a Benedictine abbey in the 9th century. Much of its architectural finery dates from the 17th century, and several *hôtels particuliers* (private mansions) from this era remain.

DON'T MISS

A FORAY INTO GAILLAC WINES

Eat out at any restaurant in southwest France and you're guaranteed to stumble across the name Gaillac on the menu. The vineyards rolling around this picturesque town produce the region's best wines – rosés, light whites, fruity reds and the distinctive Gaillac Perlé (semi-sparkling white wine) – which benefit from the area's special microclimate, positioned between the balmy Mediterranean and the cooling rains of the Atlantic. Gaillac itself, on the banks of the River Tarn, is well worth exploring. The old town, with its mix of medieval architecture and *hôtels particuliers* (private mansions), is a delight to amble.

The **Maison des Vins** (☑ 05 63 57 15 40; www.vins-gaillac.com; place Saint-Michel; ☺ 10am-noon & 2-6pm), a well-organised winegrowers' cooperative, is a great place to get acquainted with Gaillac wines. It stocks about 100 local vintages. Friendly, knowledgeable staff, and of course you're welcome to taste the wares and buy the appellations of your dreams. Have lunch afterwards at local favourite **La Table du Sommelier** (☑ 05 63 81 20 10; www.latabledusommelier.com; 34 place du Griffoul; menus €14-33; ☺ noon-2pm & 7-9.30pm Tue-Sat). In a former wine cellar overlooking one of Gaillac's most scenic squares, its 'Autour des Vins' (€32) *menu*, built around around white, rosé or red wines, is a particular delight. Dine outside on warm days.

There are plenty of scenic domaines (wine estates) dotted around Gaillac, offering *dégustation* (tasting) and cellar visits, connected by a signposted **Route des Vins** (Wine Route). Most run year-round. Gaillac's **tourist office** (☑ 08 25 40 08 28; www.tourisme-vignobles-bastides.com; place St-Michel; ☺ 10am-12.30pm & 2-7pm Jul & Aug, 10am-12.30pm & 2-6pm Apr-Jun & Sep, 10am-noon & 2-5pm Wed-Sun Oct-Mar) can supply you with maps and brochures listing wine producers. More information is available at www.tourisme-vignoble-bastides.com.

Local bus 704 runs from Castres to Gaillac (€2, one hour) regularly on weekdays and three times on Saturday, but Gaillac and its surrounds are best explored by car.

CORDES-SUR-CIEL

....

What a gem! Peering above clouds that gather in the valley below, Cordes-sur-Ciel is one of the most spellbinding *bastides* (fortified towns) in the region. Cobbled pathways wiggle their way up to its soaring vantage point over meadows banking the Cérou River. The impossibly cute maze of streets contains galleries, cafes, boutiques and artisans' shops as well as numerous medieval arches and monuments, including stately 13th- and 14th-century Gothic mansions of pink sandstone.

Guided walks run by the **tourist office** (☑ 05 63 56 00 52; www.cordessurciel.fr; 42 Grand Rue Raimond VII; ⊗ 9.30am-1pm & 2-6.30pm Mon-Sat, 10am-1pm & 2-6pm Sun Jul & Aug, shorter hours rest of year) in July and August explore the town's architecture in depth. Special night-time tours conducted by torchlight bring Cordes' medieval character to life. A daily summer night market displays the best local produce, and there are occasional flea markets and crafts fairs. A small but sweet selection of restaurants serving locally sourced farmhouse cuisine peppers place St-Michel and Grand Rue Raimond VII: **L'Escuelle des Chevaliers** (☑ 09 66 86 14 40; www.lescuelledeschevaliers.fr; 87 Grand Rue Raimond VII; menu €20, mains €12-16; ⊗ 7-9pm Mon-Sat & noon-2pm Sun Jul & Aug, noon-2pm & 7-9pm Sat, noon-2pm Sun Apr-Jun, Sep & Oct) plays the medieval theme and specialises in regional dishes with an inventive twist; it has five rooms upstairs (doubles from €70).

Cordes-sur-Ciel is on the D600; take bus 707 from Albi (€2, 35 minutes, five to six Monday to Saturday). Buses arrive at place de la Bouteillerie in Cordes.

For drivers, there are numerous pay-and-display car parks at the bottom of the village – but they can get crowded in high summer.

◉ Sights

Admire the best views in town from quai des Jacobins, which overlooks bridges and historic houses clustered at the river's edge, and the Jardin de l'Évêché, laid out by Le Nôtre, architect of Versailles' gardens.

If you're planning to visit both the Musée Goya and Centre National et Musée Jean Jaurès, it's cheaper with Castres' museum pass (€6.50), available at the tourist office.

**Centre National et Musée
Jean Jaurès** MUSEUM
(☑ 05 63 62 41 83; www.tourisme-castres.fr/musee-jaures; 2 place Pélisson; adult/child €3/1.50; ⊗ 10am-noon & 2-5pm Tue-Sat Sep-Jun, 10am-noon & 2-6pm daily Jul-Aug) If you're wondering why almost every French town seems to have a 'rue Jean Jaurès', this museum has everything you need to know about the father of French Socialism. Castres-born Jean Jaurès lifted the movement for the emancipation of working people into the mainstream. The museum pays tribute to his life and works (most information is in French), while contextualising principles that remain cherished in modern France: press freedom, the right to strike and the importance of leisure for working people.

Musée Goya MUSEUM
(☑ 05 63 71 59 27; rue de l'Hôtel de Ville; adult/child €5/free; ⊗ 10am-6pm Tue-Sun Jul & Aug, 10am-noon & 2-5pm Tue-Sun Sep-Jun) This excellent gallery on the 1st floor of Castres' Hôtel de Ville has a collection of mostly Spanish art, including work by Picasso, Rusiñol, Velázquez and, of course, several works by Goya (including the vast *La Junte des Philippines*). The museum's arms room has interesting collections of old weapons, helmets and fragments of WWII resistance history.

ℹ Information

Tourist Office (☑ 05 63 62 63 62; www.tourisme-castres.fr; 2 place de la République; ⊗ 9.30am-6.30pm Mon-Sat, 10.30am-noon & 2.30-4.30pm Sun Jul & Aug, 9.30am-12.30pm & 2-6pm Mon-Sat, 2.30-4.30pm Sun Sep-Jun) Get your hands on hotel and transport information, plus a money-saving museum pass, at this tourist office overlooking the Jardin de l'Évêché.

ℹ Getting There & Away

Direct trains and a few SNCF buses reach Castres from Toulouse (€15.70, one to 1½ hours, seven to 12 daily). TarnBus line 703 plies the route between Castres and Albi (€2, 50 minutes, at least hourly Monday to Friday). Buses leave from the train station. Line 704 links Castres with Gaillac (€2, one hour).

ARMAGNAC

A carpet of meadows and vineyards unfurls beyond the town of Condom. Welcome to Armagnac. This northern expanse of the Gers *département* is renowned for its centuries-old distilleries. The terrain is ideal for unchallenging road trips: long boulevards lined with birch trees connect regal châteaux with picturesque villages of ancient stone, including La Romieu, Fourcès and Lectoure.

During the Hundred Years' War, the area was pinched between strongholds of the French and English armies, based in Toulouse and Bordeaux respectively. This past tumult has bequeathed it a number of *bastides* (fortified towns), created by wealthier villages as protection against attack.

Auch

POP 22,000

Quaint Auch (rhymes with 'gauche') is a tangle of narrow lanes and half-timbered houses, with architectural treasures that hint at its former glory. Perched on the top of a hill, its snug historic centre is dotted with Gascon restaurants and easy-going bars. Capital of the Gers *département,* named for the river sloshing through the Hautes Pyrénées, Auch was formerly a seat of power for Armagnac's counts.

◉ Sights

Cathédrale Ste-Marie   CATHEDRAL

(place de la République; choir €2; ⊘ 9.30am-7pm Jul & Aug, 9.30am-noon & 2-5.30pm Sep-Jun) Even travellers weary of traipsing around yet another French church will be delighted by Auch's Unesco World Heritage–listed cathedral, a flamboyant late-Gothic to Renaissance building with limestone towers rising imperiously from Auch's main square. Don't miss the astonishing choir, where 67 intricate wood carvings depict apostles, saints, Greek sages and pagan prophetesses. Look for Judith holding the severed head of Holophernes, and St Martha with a tamed *tarasque* (dragon) by her feet. Eighteen impressive stained-glass windows, dating from 1513, beam down from above.

DON'T MISS

TASTING & BUYING ARMAGNAC

Armagnac is best understood as Cognac's sophisticated older sister. While Cognac is world-renowned, Armagnac brandy is produced in smaller quantities for a rapt audience of European digestif connoisseurs. Distilled from white grapes in oaken barrels, Armagnac has the longest history of any French brandy – references to its medicinal qualities date way back to the 14th century.

This sophisticated tipple is distilled in the leafy countryside between France's Garonne and Adour Rivers. There are several atmospheric locations within easy reach of Condom where you can sniff, sample and buy Armagnac. If you're sipping for the first time, keep breathing through your nose to allow its aromas to flood your senses.

Armagnac Ryst-Dupeyron (☑ 05 62 28 08 08; www.maisonrystdupeyron.com; 36 rue Jean Jaurès; ⊘ 10am-noon & 2-5pm Mon-Fri) A turn-of-the-century cellar in Condom offering 45-minute tours and tasting sessions, with commentary in French, English, Spanish or Dutch; you can also buy bottles on-site. Arrive an hour before closing time (better yet, call ahead).

Château de Cassaigne (☑ 05 62 28 04 02; www.chateaudecassaigne.com; Cassaigne; tours adult/child €2.50/free; ⊘ 9am-noon & 2-7pm Jul & Aug, 9am-noon & 2-6pm Tue-Sat Sep-Jun) Fine Armagnac and other regional drops are produced within this beautiful 13th-century château, 6.5km southwest of Condom (off the D931 to Éauze). It's particularly known for its Floc de Gascogne, an aperitif fortified with Armagnac.

Château du Busca Maniban (☑ 05 62 28 40 38; www.buscamaniban.com; Mansencôme; ⊘ 9am-noon & 2-6pm Mon-Thu, to noon Fri) This magnificent château, 10km south of Condom on the D229, has been distilling Armagnac since the mid-17th century. It's not the place for a guided distillery tour, but you can sample and buy fantastic quality Armagnac in the on-site shop.

Escalier Monumental
ARCHITECTURE

These 374 stone steps flow luxuriantly from place Salinis, behind Auch's cathedral, to bd Sadi Carnot by the Gers River, over a drop of 35m. Scenic lookouts from this 1863 staircase overlook Auch's lower town and the surrounding hills. Halfway up there's a chest-puffing statue of Gers-born d'Artagnan, the 17th-century king's guard immortalised in Alexandre Dumas' *The Three Musketeers*. There's also a modern installation by Catalan artist Jaume Plensa, with metallic lettering that tells the biblical story of the flood.

🛏 Sleeping & Eating

Domaine de Baulieu
HOTEL €€

(🖉 05 62 59 97 38; www.ledomainedebaulieu. com; 822 chemin de Lussan; s €79-119, d €94-134; P🅿❄🛜🏊) This haven of peace and tranquillity set in a converted farmhouse is situated in glorious countryside 2.5km east of town. There are 19 immaculate rooms, some with soul-stirring hill views, a superb pool and a relaxing garden. Chef Maxime Deschamps creates mouth-watering menus (€19 to €52) at the on-site restaurant. A safe choice.

La Table d'Oste
FRENCH €€

(🖉 05 62 05 55 62; www.latabledoste.com; 7 rue Lamartine; menus €26-29, mains €20-29; ⊗noon-1.30pm & 7.15-9pm Tue-Fri, noon-1.30pm Sat, 7.15-9pm Mon) Duck, pork and beef feature heavily on the menu at this local favourite in a peaceful street near the cathedral. In the *hamburger Gascon,* different preparations of duck replace both bun and burger. Exquisite execution extends to the small dessert selection: the *pastis gascon* (apple tart with Armagnac) provides an explosion of flavours.

ℹ Information

Tourist Office (🖉 05 62 05 22 89; www. auch-tourisme.com; 3 pl de la République; ⊗9.30am-6.30pm Mon-Sat, 10am-12.30pm & 3-5.30pm Sun Jul & Aug, 10am-12.15pm & 2-6pm Mon-Fri, to 5pm Sat Sep-Jun) Opposite the cathedral in a 15th-century half-timbered building. Pick up a trail map for a self-guided walking tour around Auch's historic buildings.

ℹ Getting There & Away

Direct trains or SNCF buses link Auch with Toulouse (€16, 1½ to two hours, seven to 11 daily). Local buses serve Condom (€1.50, one hour, two to three daily), Montauban (€16.20, 1½ hours, one to three daily), Agen (€13.40, 1½ hours, four

ℹ ONE FOR THE KIDS

Would you have withstood the hardships of medieval warfare, and looked dapper in a chainmail tunic? Find out in Larressingle, the smallest fortified town in France, where replica war machines from the 13th and 14th centuries, including trebuchets and *bombardelle* cannons, are set up around the ramparts and shown off with flash-bang demonstrations at **Camp de Siège Médiéval – Cité des Machines du Moyen Age** (http://larressingle.free.fr; Larress; adult/child €8.20/5.20; ⊗10am-7pm Jul & Aug, 2-6pm mid-Mar–Jun, Sep & Oct, closed Nov-Feb; 🅿).

to eight daily) and Tarbes (€14.70, 1½ to two hours, two to five daily). The train and bus stations are 1km east of the town centre.

Condom
POP 7000

Somewhere between pacing medieval streets and standing beneath a superb Gothic cathedral, amusement over Condom's unfortunate town name quickly turns to awe. It actually derives from the Gallo-Roman word 'Condatomagus', meaning a market town at a river confluence (Condom is situated where the Baïse and Gèle Rivers meet). Locals are well aware of the name's contraceptive meaning, which elicits sniggers among English speakers; town signs are firmly nailed down, to avoid falling prey to souvenir hunters.

While the historic centre needs only a day to explore, Condom is in the midst of Armagnac country, where a potent local brandy has been produced for centuries. This mellow town is a superb base from which to visit distilleries, abbeys and historic ramparts.

◉ Sights & Activities

Cathédrale St-Pierre
CHURCH

(place St-Pierre; ⊗8am-6pm) The foundations of this formidable cathedral date back to 1011, when the site hosted a Benedictine abbey. The cathedral was rebuilt in Flamboyant Gothic style with a lofty nave and elaborate chancel. The 16th-century *cloister*, accessed from rue de l'Evêché, was designed to offer wet-weather protection for

CONDOM DAY TRIPPER

Lectoure It's something of a surprise to come across a place of such historical wealth in such a remote part of the Gers *département,* well away from any major communication route. At the eastern end of Armagnac region, this little charmer perched on a hilltop is Gers' most seductive village, with plenty of medieval buildings as well as handsome *hôtels particuliers* (private mansions). Many of Lectoure's historic buildings are occupied these days by antique dealers, artists, craftsmen, hoteliers and restaurants. Delve in!

Collégiale St-Pierre (☑05 62 28 86 33; www.la-romieu.fr; La Romieu; adult/child €5/2.50; ☺9.30am-6.30pm Mon-Sat, 2-6.30pm Sun May-Oct, 10am-12.30pm & 1.30-6pm Mon-Sat, 2-5.30pm Sun Mar-Apr, 2-5.30pm daily Nov-Feb) A twin-towered medieval church and cloisters is the focal point of tiny La Romieu, 12km northeast of Condom. This lonely village outpost first sprang up as a priory, founded in 1062 by two Benedictine monks returning from a pilgrimage to Rome via Toulouse (the name comes from *roumieu,* meaning 'Roman pilgrim'). Inside the church, the sacristy is lavished with colourful decorations dating from the 19th century; ascend one of the towers (watch your step) for panoramic views of the Gers countryside.

Villa Gallo-Romaine (La Villa de Séviac; ☑05 62 29 48 57; www.elusa.fr; Séviac; adult/child €5/free; ☺10am-1pm & 2-7pm Jul & Aug, 10am-noon & 2-6pm Apr-Jun & Sep, 10am-noon & 2-5pm Oct, 2-5pm Mar & Nov) About 15km west of Condom near the little town of Montréal du Gers lie the excavated remains of a 2nd- to 5th-century Gallo-Roman villa. Discovered in the 19th century, these ancient remnants were once part of a Roman aristocrat's 6500-sq-metre agricultural estate. Archaeologists have revealed the villa's baths, outbuildings and 450 sq metres of geometric mosaic floors, offering a glimpse of the luxurious lifestyle of its owners. After a couple of years of extensive renovations, the site reopened in mid-2018.

Abbaye de Flaran (☑05 62 28 50 19; www.patrimoine-musees-gers.fr; Valence-sur-Baïse; adult/child €5/2; ☺9.30am-7pm Jul-Aug, 9.30am-12.30pm & 2-6pm Sep-Jun) This serene Cistercian abbey is one of the loveliest in the Gers *département.* Founded in 1151 and guarded by a 14th-century fortress door, it was abandoned after the Revolution but the building is remarkably well preserved. Among the rooms on show are the monks' cloister and refectory, and there's a herb garden out the back. On the 2nd floor, the sleeping cells host a superb collection of paintings, including works by Toulouse-Lautrec, Cézanne and Renoir. It's near Valence-sur-Baïse, 10km south of Condom.

Compostela pilgrims; note the weathered scallop shell, the emblem of St James, in stone relief on the wall.

Musée de l'Armagnac   MUSEUM
(☑05 62 28 47 21; 2 rue Jules Ferry; adult/child €2.20/1.10; ☺3-6pm Wed-Sat & Mon Apr-Oct) Located in a turn-of-the-century cellar, this museum is dedicated to the fine art of Armagnac production; it houses a modest collection of vintage bottles, agricultural tools and an 18-tonne press dating from the 19th century.

Gascogne Navigation   BOATING
(☑05 62 28 46 46; www.gascogne-navigation.com; 3 av d'Aquitaine; ☺Apr-Oct) Gascogne Navigation runs one-hour river cruises (adult/child €8.70/6.70) and 2½-hour lunch cruises (€42/28) along the Baïse River, departing from quai Bouquerie. It also rents out small motorboats (€38/85 per hour/half-day).

🛏 Sleeping & Eating

Hôtel-Restaurant Continental   HOTEL €
(☑05 62 68 37 00; www.lecontinental.net; 20 rue Maréchal Foch; d €66-100, ste €140-150; [P][❄][☎]) This lemon-yellow heritage hotel set along the riverfront has small but immaculately clean rooms, all decorated in a palette of cream with occasional vintage flourishes. The quietest rooms overlook the garden. A small wing was added in 2017, with several rooms with modern design. The restaurant (mains from €16) stands out as one of the best in town,

★ **La Ferme de Flaran** HOTEL €€
(☏ 05 62 29 39 83; www.fermedeflaran.com; Bagatelle, Maignaut-Tauzia; d €62-105, ste €117-160; ☺ closed Jan; [P][❀][📶][🏊]) Set in a renovated farm 9km south of Condom, this bucolic gem is one of the most appealing addresses in the area, a bastion of comfort, charm and peace. There are only 12 rooms, which ensures intimacy. The on-site restaurant (*menus* €21 to €41) serves well-executed regional dishes – even if you're not a guest, consider dining here.

★ **La Table des Cordeliers** GASTRONOMY €€€
(☏ 05 62 68 43 82; www.latabledescordeliers. com; 1 rue des Cordeliers; menus €24-90; ☺ noon-1.30pm & 7.15-8.30pm Tue-Sat) Condom's premier restaurant is run by Michelin-starred Eric Sampietro, a culinary magician known for seasonal ingredients assembled in surprising combinations. Tasting *menus* come at a price, but the adjoining bistro offers a three-course *menu* for just €24, with beguiling dishes such as creamy risotto with asparagus. The setting is gorgeous: it's inside a 13th-century chapel, complete with cloister garden.

📧 **Around Condom**

★ **L'Hôtel Particulier**
Guilhon BOUTIQUE HOTEL €€
(☏ 06 27 17 81 65; www.hotel-particulier-guilhon. com; 95 rue Nationale, Lectoure; ste incl breakfast €150-250; [P][❀][📶][🏊]) Stunning! The most luxurious venture for miles around, this

splendid operation occupies a tastefully restored 17th-century aristocratic house. The five gigantic suites are all individually designed and sport every top-end luxury you might desire, and the hotel also has a spa and a pool. Refined meals also available (dinner €45).

Lacassagne B&B €€
(☏ 05 62 28 26 89; www.lacassagnechambres dhotes.fr; Laressingle; d incl breakfast €90-115; ☺ Apr–mid-Nov; [P][📶]) Set in oak-filled countryside just outside Laressingle, this delightful, one-storey hilltop house has shuttered French doors looking out onto the garden, four appealing rooms with romantic trimmings, and a lounge with fireplace. Owner Maïder Papelorey is a fantastic cook; enquire about her €30 *menus,* featuring locally sourced produce. House dogs Bobby and Jacky guarantee a loud welcome.
Find it 6km west of Condom along the D15.

ℹ **Information**

Tourist Office (☏ 05 62 28 00 80; www. tourisme-condom.com; 5 place Saint-Pierre; ☺ 9am-noon & 2-6.30pm Mon-Sat) Opposite the cathedral. Ask about guided cathedral tours and seasonal opening times for Armagnac distilleries.

ℹ **Getting There & Away**

Condom's bus links are limited, but local services run to Auch (€1.50, one hour, two to three daily), from where you can catch trains to Toulouse.

Languedoc-Roussillon

POP 2.7 MILLION

Best Places to Eat

➡ Le Suquet (p758)

➡ Anga (p751)

➡ Chez Bébelle (p757)

➡ La Barbacane (p761)

➡ Halles Vauban (p777)

Best Places to Stay

➡ Hôtel de la Cité (p761)

➡ Château de Creissels (p773)

➡ Domaine Tarbouriech (p754)

➡ Hôtel du Palais (p750)

➡ La Maison d'Uzès (p747)

Why Go?

Stretching from Provence to the Pyrenees, this sultry, sun-baked territory (now part of the greater Occitanie region) feels like a country in its own right. It's been a strategic border since Roman times and is awash with historical reminders, from Roman aqueducts to hilltop Cathar castles. Today it's best known for its vineyards, which produce a third of France's wines, and the busy beaches sprawling along its Mediterranean shore.

Each of Languedoc-Roussillon's three main areas has its own distinct landscape and character. Bas-Languedoc is home to the biggest beaches and the captivating cities of Montpellier and Nîmes. Inland lies the high, wild country of the Grands Causses and Cévennes, with a fascinating mix of hills, caves, gorges, forests and surreal moonscape plateaus. Roussillon, in the southwest, shares close ties with Catalonia just across the Spanish border, including traditional *sardanes* folk dances and a passion for rugby and vibrant summer festivals.

When to Go
Montpellier

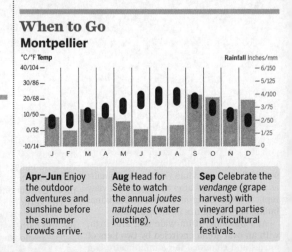

Apr–Jun Enjoy the outdoor adventures and sunshine before the summer crowds arrive.

Aug Head for Sète to watch the annual *joutes nautiques* (water jousting).

Sep Celebrate the *vendange* (grape harvest) with vineyard parties and viticultural festivals.

BAS-LANGUEDOC

The broad, flat plains of Bas-Languedoc take in all of the Languedoc's main towns, as well as its best beaches and richest Roman remains, along with outstanding wines and gourmet produce.

During the Middle Ages, Bas-Languedoc was largely the property of the counts of Toulouse, but it now forms the modern-day *départements* of Gard and Hérault.

Nîmes

POP 154,000

Nîmes is heralded as the 'Rome of France', and it's easy to see why. Two millennia ago it was one of the most important cities of Roman Gaul, as evidenced by its incredible collection of Roman buildings, including a magnificent amphitheatre and a 2000-year-old temple.

There are plenty of museums and markets to explore in Nîmes' palm-lined streets, as well as a host of high-profile festivals throughout the year. Nîmes is also proud of the futuristic Musée de la Romanité, which opened in mid-2018 and is one of the best archaeological museums in Languedoc-Roussillon. In 2018, Nîmes applied – to no avail – to be listed as a Unesco World Heritage Site.

◉ Sights

Save money by purchasing a Pass Nîmes Romaine (Roman Nîmes Pass) combination ticket (adult/child €13/11), which covers admission to Les Arènes, Maison Carrée and Tour Magne at Jardins de la Fontaine. The pass is valid for three days and can be bought at any of these three sites.

★ **Les Arènes**   ROMAN SITE
(☎04 66 21 82 56; www.arenes-nimes.com; place des Arènes; adult/child incl audioguide €10/8; ⊙9am-8pm Jul & Aug, 9am-6.30pm Apr-Jun & Sep, 9am-6pm Mar & Oct, 9.30am-5pm Jan, Feb, Nov & Dec) Nîmes' twin-tiered amphitheatre is the best preserved in France. Built around 100 BC, the arena once seated 24,000 spectators and staged gladiatorial contests and public executions; it's still an impressive venue for gigs and events. An audioguide provides context as you explore the arena, seating areas, stairwells and corridors (known to Romans as *vomitories*), and afterwards you can view replicas of gladiatorial armour and original bullfighters' costumes in the museum.

At 133m long, 101m wide and 21m high, with an oval arena encircled by two tiers of arches and columns, the amphitheatre is a testament to the skill and ingenuity of Roman architects. Despite being adapted, plundered for stone and generally abused over many centuries, the structure of the amphitheatre is still largely intact, and it's not hard to imagine what the atmosphere must have been like when it was filled to capacity.

The seating is divided into four tiers and 34 rows; the posher you were, the closer you sat to the centre. The amphitheatre's oval design meant everyone had an unrestricted view. A system of trapdoors and hoist-lifts beneath the arena enabled animals and combatants to be put into position during the show. Originally, the amphitheatre would have had a canopy to protect spectators from the weather.

Musée de la Romanité   MUSEUM
(☎04 48 21 02 10; 16 bd des Arènes; adult/child €8/3; ⊙10am-8pm Jul & Aug, 10am-7pm Sep-Nov & Apr-Jun, 10am-6pm Wed-Mon Dec-Mar) Opened in mid-2018, this futuristic steel-and-glass structure faces Les Arènes right in the heart of the city. Within, the ambitious archaeological museum's permanent exhibitions are devoted to regional archaeology, with more than 5000 artefacts including well-preserved mosaics and ceramics.

Maison Carrée   ROMAN SITE
(☎04 66 21 82 56; www.maisoncarree.eu; place de la Maison Carrée; adult/child €6/5; ⊙9.30am-8pm Jul & Aug, 10am-6.30pm Apr-Jun & Sep, 10am-6pm Mar & Oct, 10am-1pm & 2-4.30pm Jan, Feb, Nov & Dec) Constructed in gleaming limestone around AD 5, this temple was built to honour Emperor Augustus' two adopted sons. Despite the name, the Maison Carrée (Square House) is actually rectangular – to the Romans, 'square' simply meant a building with right angles. The building is beautifully preserved, complete with stately columns and triumphal steps. There's no need to go inside unless you're interested in the relatively cheesy 22-minute 3D film.

Jardins de la Fontaine   PARK
(quai de la Fontaine; adult/child €3.50/3, garden free; ⊙9am-8pm Jul & Aug, 9am-5pm Sep-Jun) Roman remains in these elegant gardens include the 30m-high **Tour Magne**, raised around 15 BC – the largest of a chain of towers conveying imperial power that once punctuated the city's 7km-long Roman ramparts. At the top of its 140 steps, an orientation table interprets the panoramic views over Nîmes.

The gardens also shelter the **Source de la Fontaine** – once the site of a spring, temple and baths – and the crumbling **Temple de Diane**, located in the northwest corner.

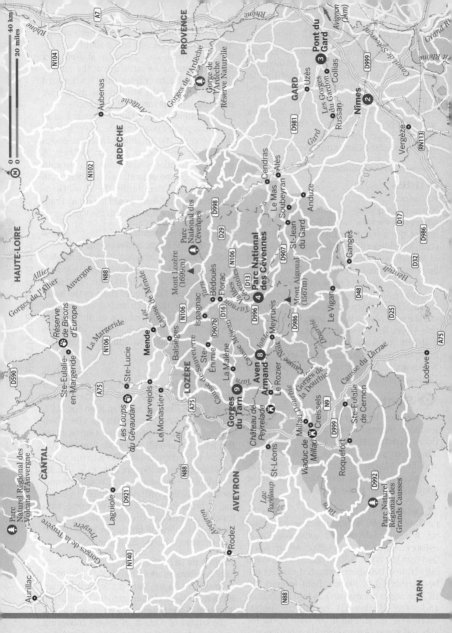

Languedoc-Roussillon Highlights

1 **Musée Fabre** (p748)
Contemplating one of France's richest collections of European art in the exquisite city of Montpellier.

2 **Les Arènes** (p739) Exploring Nîmes' monumental twin-tiered amphitheatre dating from c 100 BC.

3 **Pont du Gard** (p745) Marvelling at the Romans' architectural ambition at this towering aqueduct.

4 **The Cévennes** (p766) Trekking in Robert Louis Stevenson's footsteps with a donkey through wild, rugged countryside.

5 Bouzigues
(p755) Tasting the town's famous oysters and mussels.

6 Château de Peyrepertuse (p774)
Time-travelling back to the Middle Ages at this spectacular Cathar castle.

7 Cité Médiévale (p759)
Strolling through Carcassonne's fairy-tale fortress, ringed by battlements and towers topped by witch's-hat turrets.

8 Aven Armand
(p771) Being awed by the world's greatest concentration of stalagmites.

9 Gorges du Tarn
(p768) Kayaking or canoeing along deeply incised, twisting gorges.

Carré d'Art –
Musée d'Art Contemporain   GALLERY
(☑ 04 66 76 35 70; www.carreartmusee.com; 16 place de la Maison Carrée; ☺10am-6pm Tue-Sun) **FREE** The striking glass-and-steel Carré d'Art was designed by British architect Sir Norman Foster. Inside is the Musée d'Art Contemporain, with permanent and temporary exhibitions covering art from the 1960s onwards. The rooftop restaurant (open Wednesday to Sunday) makes a lovely spot for a drink.

✺ Festivals & Events

Les Grands Jeux Romains   CULTURAL
(www.arenes-nimes.com; ☺late Apr) For three days in April, Romans reconquer the town with an encampment, staged gladiatorial battles in Les Arènes (p739) and a triumphal street parade.

Jeudis de Nîmes   CULTURAL
(☺Jul & Aug) Between 6pm and 10.30pm every Thursday in July and August, food markets and live gigs take over Nîmes' squares.

🛏 Sleeping

Auberge de Jeunesse   HOSTEL €
(☑ 04 66 68 03 20; www.hifrance.org/auberge-de-jeunesse/nimes.html; 257 chemin de l'Auberge de Jeunesse, La Cigale; camping per person €9, dm/d incl breakfast €24/50; ☺reception 7.30am-11pm, hostel closed Nov-Feb; P🛜) It's out in the sticks, 4km northwest of the bus and train stations, but this well-managed hostel has lots in its favour: spacious four- to eight-bed dorms (some with their own bathroom), double rooms, a large garden, a self-catering kitchen, a laundry and a cafe. Take bus 9,

NÎMES FÉRIAS

Nîmes hosts two *férias* (bullfighting festivals): the five-day Féria de Pentecôte (Whitsuntide Festival) in May, and the three-day Féria des Vendanges on the third weekend in September. Thousands of visitors descend on the city for dances, live music and plenty of other cultural events, and each festival is marked by daily *corridas* (bullfights). If you plan to attend a bullfight, be aware the scene can be very disturbing. The bull is first weakened by lances that pierce its back and neck, then put to death by the torero, who delivers the final sword thrust.

direction Alès or Villeverte, and get off at the Stade stop.

Hôtel des Tuileries   HOTEL €
(☑ 04 66 21 31 15; www.hoteldestuileries.com; 22 rue Roussy; d €60-81, tr €70-93, ste €85-118; P🅿❄🛜) Run by an English couple, this well-priced 11-room hotel within strolling distance from Les Arènes (p739) features simple yet satisfyingly equipped rooms, some with covered balconies. Breakfast costs €9. Its private parking garage (€10 to €15) is just down the street, but there are only five car spaces, so reserve ahead.

Hôtel Central   HOTEL €
(☑ 04 66 67 27 75; www.hotel-central.org; 2 place du Château; d €60-95; ❄🛜) Rooms at this aptly named hotel in Nîmes' heart have wooden floors, neutral colours and sleek bathrooms. *Supérieure* rooms offer the most space. Rooms on the top floor have great city views, but the lack of a lift is a drawback considering the number of stairs.

Royal Hôtel   HOTEL €€
(☑ 04 66 58 28 27; www.royalhotel-nimes.com; 3 bd Alphonse Daudet; d €80-125; ❄🛜) Bedrooms here have modern-meets-heritage decor and a choice of street views or an outlook over the grand place d'Assas – fine for the view, though the noise might be intrusive on summer nights. They're split into standard and superior; it's worth bumping up a level for extra space. A few rooms have renovated bathrooms. No lift, alas.

🍴 Eating

A tempting array of restaurants and cafeterias is dotted around the centre. Place aux Herbes, place de l'Horloge and place du Marché are great places to watch the world drift by at bistros, cafes and bars with pavement seating.

La Petite Fadette   TEAHOUSE €
(☑ 04 66 67 53 05; 34 rue du Grand Couvent; menus €15-24, mains €10-20; ☺11am-2.30pm Mon-Wed, 11am-2.30pm & 6-10pm Thu-Sat) *Tartines* (open-face toasted sandwiches) such as ham and tomato or fig jam and goat's cheese, as well as huge salads, are specialities of this cosy *salon de thé* (tearoom), which has a cute rococo interior and outside tables on a small courtyard. A platter of tapas (€20) is also available. Wash it down with a glass of organic wine (€3).

La Marmite   BISTRO €
(☑ 0466299823; www.facebook.com/impeccable. 30; 6 rue de l'Agau; menus €13-25; ☺noon-2pm

Nîmes

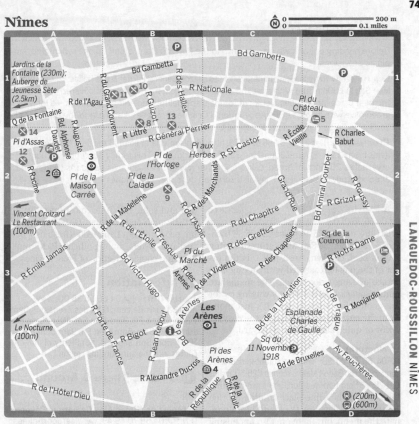

N 0 — 200 m
0 — 0.1 miles

Nîmes

Mon-Sat & 7.30-9.30pm Thu-Sat) The *menu* at La Marmite changes almost daily depending on what the chef considers the best local produce at the nearby Halles (p744), and specials – always flavoursome – are scribbled on the well-worn blackboard. It's always packed with local connoisseurs who won't consider eating anywhere else, so book ahead.

L'Imprévu   FRENCH €

(☑04 66 38 99 59; www.l-imprevu.com; 6 place d'Assas; menus €19-24, mains €13-24; ⊙noon-2pm & 7.30-10.30pm Thu-Tue) Tucked away in the corner of place d'Assas, this fine-dining bistro has a sheltered interior courtyard and a terrace. There's a good choice of seafood, meats and pastas, and some superb desserts such as Breton shortbread with caramelised pears and green-apple sorbet.

Aux Plaisirs des Halles FRENCH €€
(☑ 04 66 36 01 02; www.auxplaisirsdeshalles.com; 4 rue Littré; menus €25-44, mains €23-26; ⊗ noon-2pm & 7.30-10pm Tue-Sat) Market-fresh dining – veal, beef, chicken, fresh fish – is the order of the day here, served with an excellent choice of Languedoc wines. The mains are quite expensive, so consider swinging by for the good-value lunch *menu*. It's just along from the covered market. Eat in the cosy interior or quiet, shaded rear courtyard.

Le Nocturne BISTRO €€
(☑ 04 66 67 20 28; www.restaurant-le-nocturne.com; 29bis rue Benoît Malon; menus €25-50, mains €21-28; ⊗ 8pm-1am Wed-Sun; ☑) Late-opening Le Nocturne is a fine place to dine on rich southwestern flavours. Duck and beef dominate the menu, but there are also appetising fish and veggie options. Rare vintages and limited releases from small-scale producers make up the wine list. There are just 26 seats, so book ahead.

Le Carré d'Art FRENCH €€
(☑ 04 66 67 52 40; www.restaurant-lecarredart.com; 2 rue Gaston Boissier; menus €17-29, mains €23-26; ⊗ noon-1.45pm & 8-10pm Tue-Sat) Open since 1989, this long-standing institution is still going strong. The setting is elegant, in an abstract-art-adorned 19th-century townhouse with a gorgeous shaded courtyard, and the seasonal dishes give traditional French cuisine a modern spin.

Vincent Croizard –
Le Restaurant GASTRONOMY €€€
(☑ 04 66 67 04 99; www.restaurantcroizard.com; 17 rue des Chassaintes; menus €23-58, mains €18-42; ⊗ 12.15-1.30pm & 7.45-9.15pm Wed-Sun) From its discreet façade on a quiet side street, you'd never guess that this restaurant is home to an impossibly romantic lamplit courtyard garden and some of Nîmes' most inventive and artistic high-end cooking. Dishes use premium produce from Languedoc (fresh fish, pork, veal and oysters, among others). Pick from its long and choice selection of French wines.

❶ Information

Tourist Office (☑ 04 66 58 38 00; www.nimes-tourisme.com; 6 bd des Arènes; ⊗ 9am-7.30pm Mon-Fri, 9am-7pm Sat, 10am-6pm Sun Jul & Aug, 9am-6pm Mon-Fri, 9am-5pm Sat, 10am-5pm Sun Sep-Jun; ☎) Plenty of info on Nîmes and the surrounding region.

❶ Getting There & Around

AIR
Aéroport de Nîmes Alès Camargue Cévennes (FNI; ☑ 04 66 70 49 49; www.aeroport-nimes.fr; St-Gilles) Nîmes' airport, 10km southeast of the city on the A54, is served only by Ryanair, which flies to/from London Luton, Liverpool, Brussels-Charleroi and Fez.

An airport bus (€6.80, 30 minutes) to/from the **train station** (p745) connects with all flights.

BICYCLE
Vélo Tango (www.tangobus.fr; bd Sergent Triaire, Train station; bike/electric bike rental per day €3/7.50; ⊗ 7.30am-8pm Mon-Sat) Rents out bikes from the train station; you'll need a credit card to leave a €200 deposit.

BUS
The **bus station** (☑ 08 10 33 42 73; rue Ste-Félicité) is next to the **train station**. Local buses are run by Edgard (www.edgard-transport.fr).

Alès Line 510, €1.50, 1¼ hours, two to six Monday to Saturday

Pont du Gard Line B21, €1.50, 40 minutes, two or three daily Monday to Saturday

Uzès Line E52, €1.50, one hour, eight to 10 daily Monday to Friday, three or four at weekends

TRAIN

TGVs run hourly to/from Paris' Gare de Lyon (from €45, three hours) from the **train station** (bd Sergent Triaire).

Local destinations, with at least hourly departures, include the following:

Alès €9.90, 40 minutes (reduced services Sunday)

Arles €8.80, 25 minutes

Avignon €9.90, 35 minutes

Montpellier €10.10, 30 minutes

Sète €14.40, 55 minutes

AROUND NÎMES

Southern France has no shortage of superb Roman sites, but nothing can top the Unesco World Heritage–listed Pont du Gard, a 30-minute drive northeast of Nîmes.

◉ Sights

★**Pont du Gard**   ROMAN SITE

(☑ 04 66 37 50 99; www.pontdugard.fr; adult/child €8.50/6, Pass Aqueduc incl guided visit of topmost tier €11.50/6; ☺ 9am-11pm Jul & Aug, to 10pm Jun & Sep, to 9pm May, to 8pm Apr & Oct, to 6pm Nov-Mar) The extraordinary three-tiered Pont du Gard was once part of a 50km-long system of channels built around 19 BC to transport water from Uzès to Nîmes. The scale is huge: the bridge is 48.8m high, 275m long and graced with 52 precision-built arches. It was the highest in the Roman Empire. At the visitors centre on the left, northern bank, there's an impressive, high-tech **museum** featuring the bridge, the aqueduct and the role of water in Roman society.

Each block was carved by hand and transported from nearby quarries – no mean feat, considering the largest blocks weighed over 5 tonnes. The height of the bridge descends by 2.5cm across its length, providing just enough gradient to keep the water flowing – an amazing demonstration of the precision of Roman engineering.

You can walk across the tiers for panoramic views over the Gard River, but the best perspective on the bridge is from downstream, along the 1.4km **Mémoires de Garrigue walking trail**. If you buy the Pass Aqueduc, you can walk the bridge's topmost tier, along which the water flowed (guided tour). For children, there's **Ludo**, an activity play area.

Early evening is a good time to visit, as admission is cheaper (adult/child €5/3) and the bridge is stunningly illuminated after dark.

It's 21km northeast of Nîmes.

ℹ Getting There & Away

There are large car parks on both banks of the river that are a 400m level walk from the **Pont du Gard**.

Several buses stop in Collias and Remoulins (near Pont du Gard), including Edgard bus B21 (€1.50, two or three daily Monday to Saturday, one or two on Sunday) between Nîmes and Uzès.

> **WORTH A TRIP**
>
> ### CANOEING ON THE RIVER GARD
>
> For a unique perspective on the Pont du Gard, you need to see it from the water. The Gard River flows from the Cévennes mountains all the way to the aqueduct, passing through the dramatic Gorges du Gardon en route. The best time to do it is between April and June, as winter floods and summer droughts can sometimes make the river impassable.
>
> Most of the local hire companies are based in Collias, 8km from the bridge, a journey of about two hours by kayak. Depending on the season and the height of the river, you can make a longer journey by being dropped upstream at Pont St-Nicholas (19km, about five hours) or Russan (32km, seven to eight hours); the latter option also includes a memorable trip through the Gorges du Gardon.
>
> There's a minimum age of six. Life jackets are always provided, but you must be a competent swimmer. Operators include the following:
>
> **Canoë Collias** (☑ 04 66 22 87 20; www.canoe-collias.com; 194 chemin de St-Privat, Collias; adult/child €23/12; ☺ 8am-8pm mid-Mar–late Oct)
>
> **Canoë Le Tourbillon** (☑ 04 66 22 85 54; www.canoeletourbillon.com; 3 chemin du Gardon, Collias; adult/child from €23/17; ☺ 9am-7pm Apr-Sep)
>
> **Kayak Vert** (☑ 04 66 22 80 76; www.kayakvert.com; 8 chemin de St-Vincent, Collias; adult/child from €23/19; ☺ 9am-6pm mid-May–Oct)

Uzès

POP 8573

Storybook-pretty Uzès is renowned for its Renaissance architecture, a reminder of the days when it was an important trading centre – especially for silk, linen and liquorice. But it also has strong Roman links: water was delivered here via the Pont du Gard aqueduct en route to Nîmes, 25km to the southwest.

Highlights here include the ducal palace, the cathedral, elegant mansions and the arcaded central square, place aux Herbes, which hosts a lively farmers market every Wednesday and Saturday. For foodies, Uzès' biggest appeal is its cache of sublime places to dine.

Sights

★Duché CHATEAU

(☎04 66 22 18 96; www.uzes.fr; place du Duché; €13, incl tour €18; ⏰10am-12.30pm & 2-6.30pm Jul & Aug, 10am-noon & 2-6pm Sep-Jun) This fortified château belonged to the House of Crussol, who were the dukes of Uzès for over 1000 years until the French Revolution. The building is a Renaissance wonder, with a majestic 16th-century façade showing the three orders of classical architecture (Ionic, Doric and Corinthian). Inside, guided tours (in French) take in the lavish ducal apartments and 800-year-old cellars; you can climb the 135-step Bermonde tower for wrap-around town views.

Cathédrale St-Théodont CATHEDRAL

(place de l'Évêché; ⏰9am-6pm May-Sep, to 5pm Oct-Apr) Built in 1090 on the site of a Roman temple, Uzès' cathedral was partially destroyed in both the 13th and 16th centuries and stripped during the French Revolution. All that remains of the 11th-century church is its 42m-high tower, Tour Fenestrelle, the only round bell tower in France, which resembles an upright Leaning Tower of Pisa. The neo-Romanesque façade was built in the 19th century.

Jardin Médiéval GARDENS

(Medieval Garden; http://jardinmedievaluzes.com; rue Port Royal; adult/child garden & Tour du Roi €5.50/3; ⏰10.30am-12.30pm & 2-6pm Jul & Aug, 2-6pm Mon-Fri, 10.30am-12.30pm & 2-6pm Sat & Sun Apr-Jun, Sep & Oct, closed Nov-Mar) This delightful garden contains a wealth of plants and flowers that served a variety of purposes for their medieval planters: medicinal, nutritional and symbolic. Climbing 100 steps inside the Tour du Roi (King's Tower) rewards with panoramic views over Uzès' rooftops.

Musée du Bonbon Haribo MUSEUM

(Sweets Museum; ☎04 66 22 20 25; www.museeharibo.fr; Pont des Charrettes; adult/child €7.50/5.50; ⏰9.30am-7pm Jul & Aug, 10am-1pm & 2-6pm Tue-Sun Sep-Jun) Uzès' history as a confectionery centre lives on at this Wonka-esque museum, which explores the sweets-making process from the early 20th century through to the present day. There's a collection of antique advertising posters and vintage confectionery machinery, but it's the rainbow-coloured sweets shop that takes centre stage. It's 4km southeast of town.

Festivals & Events

Nuits Musicales d'Uzès MUSIC

(www.nuitsmusicalesuzes.org; ⏰Jul) This international festival of Baroque music and jazz takes place during the second half of July.

Sleeping

La Maison Rouge B&B €€

(☎09 50 25 91 06; www.maison-rouge-uzes.com; 6 rue de la Perrine; d €115-160; 📶🏊) The Red House was built from scarlet brick in 1830 for a gentleman-about-town on the edge of old Uzès. Despite its vintage trappings (balconies, stone staircase), the house has been beautifully modernised, with wooden floors, walk-in showers and swish furniture. The owners also run the adjoining **La Maison des Marronniers** (www.maison-des-marronniers-uzes.com), which features four stylish rooms.

Hostellerie Provençale HOTEL €€

(☎04 66 22 11 06; www.hostellerieprovencale.com; 1-3 rue de la Grande Bourgade; d incl breakfast €95-149; P❄📶) This old-style hotel is a trip back in time: the nine rooms of varying size are a mix of wonky floors, sloping ceilings, antique dressers and exposed stone, giving the place a bygone-era vibe. The downstairs restaurant, **La Parenthèse**, serves good regional cuisine (*menus* €23 to €48). Parking costs €15.

Hôtel Entraigues HISTORIC HOTEL €€

(☎04 66 72 05 25; www.hotel-entraigues.com; rue de la Calade; d/ste from €165/235; P❄📶🏊) Trace your way through history at this four-star hotel, an amalgamation of four private houses dating from the 15th to 18th centuries. It's an agreeable mix of odd angles, low beams, arches, crannies and corridors. After a day of exploring, nothing beats sprawling by the big pool or enjoying the panoramic views from the rooftop terrace.

★ La Maison d'Uzès
BOUTIQUE HOTEL €€€

(📞 04 66 20 07 00; www.lamaisonduzes.fr; 18 rue du Dr Blanchard; d from €240; 🅿 ❄ 🛜 🏊) Occupying a 17th-century *hôtel particulier* (private mansion) in Uzès' historical centre, this jewel has beautiful rooms filled with light-toned vintage and contemporary furnishings, and a Michelin-starred restaurant (p747), opening to a gorgeous linden-tree-shaded courtyard with a fountain at its centre. The pièce de résistance is the in-house spa with swimming pool set in an old Roman cellar.

✕ Eating

La Fabrique Givrée
ICE CREAM €

(📞 04 66 57 45 71; www.lafabriquegivree.com; 27 place aux Herbes; 1/2/3 scoops €3.20/5.50/7.30; ⏰ 10am-midnight Jun-Sep, noon-7pm Oct-May) Exquisite seasonal flavours at this late-opening artisanal *glacier* (ice-cream maker) range from chestnut, salted caramel and lemon to exotic Iranian pistachio, Guatemalan coffee, Lebanon orange flower and Tahitian vanilla.

Terroirs
DELI €

(📞 04 66 03 41 90; www.les-terroirs-restaurant-uzes. com; 5 place aux Herbes; tapas €4.70-10, mains €11-15; ⏰ noon-4.30pm & 6.30-10pm) Dine under the arcades or on the cobbled square at this smart deli-cafe. Nearly all that they sell (honey, oil, pâté, wines, herbs) has been locally sourced by the owner. Their *assiettes gourmandes* (gourmet platters) are filled with delights; they also serve up superb tapas and ice creams.

Le Comptoir du 7
BISTRO €€

(📞 04 66 22 11 54; www.maisonsaintgeorges.com; 5 bd Charles Gide; mains €17-28; ⏰ noon-1.30pm & 7.15-9pm Tue-Sat; 🍴) Choose from a barrel-vaulted dining room or a courtyard garden in which to dine on Mediterranean-inspired cuisine. The food is fresh and seasonal, so the menu is dictated by what arrives at the market – always a good sign – and, unusually, there's a choice of veggie options.

La Table d'Uzès
GASTRONOMY €€€

(📞 04 66 20 07 00; www.lamaisonduzes.fr/ restaurant; 18 rue du Dr Blanchard; menus €29-59; ⏰ 12.15-1.30pm & 7.30-8.30pm Wed-Sun) At this Michelin-starred restaurant inside La Maison d'Uzès (p747), Chef Christophe Ducros works his magic with seasonal sun-ripened local produce such as apricots, courgettes, aubergines, tomatoes, green beans, line-caught Mediterranean fish, truffles, Lozère lamb, wild trout, pigeon, and mushrooms foraged from the Parc National des Cévennes. Book

ahead and be sure to request a courtyard seat in fine weather.

ℹ Information

Tourist Office (📞 04 66 22 68 88; www. pays-uzes-tourisme.com; place Albert 1er; ⏰ 10am-6pm Mon-Fri, 10am-1pm & 2-5pm Sat & Sun Jun-Sep, 10am-12.30pm & 2-6pm Mon-Fri, 10am-1pm Sat Oct-May) Just outside the old quarter. Has free leaflets (in English and French) describing walking tours of the historical centre.

ℹ Getting There & Away

Local **buses** (av de la Gare) are run by Edgard (www.edgard-transport.fr).

Alès Line A15, €1.50, one hour, five to six daily Monday to Friday, three on weekends

Avignon Line A15, €1.50, one hour, five daily Monday to Friday, three on weekends

Nîmes Line E52, €1.50, one hour, eight to 10 daily Monday to Friday, three or four on weekends

Montpellier

POP 272,000

Graceful and easy-going, Montpellier is a stylish metropolis with elegant buildings, grand *hôtels particuliers* (private mansions), stately boulevards and shady back-streets, and gorgeous white-sand beaches on its doorstep.

Unlike many southern towns, Montpellier has no Roman heritage. It was founded in the 10th century by the counts of Toulouse and later became a prosperous trading port as well as a scholarly centre – Europe's first medical school was established here in the 12th century.

The population swelled in the 1960s when many French settlers left independent Algeria and relocated here, and it's now France's fastest-growing city and one of its most multicultural. Students make up over a third of the population, giving it a spirited vibe.

ℹ CENT SAVER

The **Montpellier City Card** (1/2/3 days €13.50/19.80/25.20, children half-price) provides unlimited travel on trams and buses, discounts at shops, a guided walking tour and free admission to several museums – with the notable exception of the Musée Fabre. It must be pre-booked on the tourist office (p752) website and collected from the tourist office in person.

Montpellier

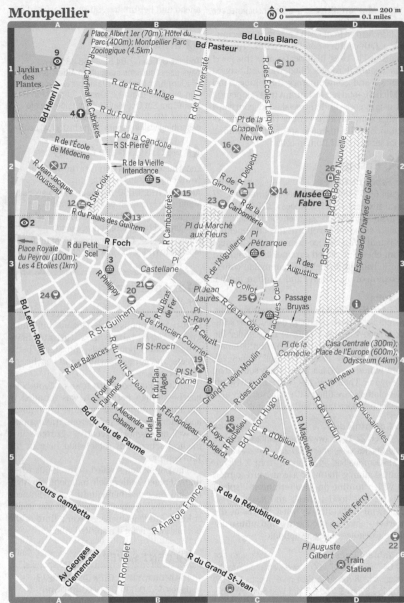

N 0 ——————— 200 m
0 ——————— 0.1 miles

Place Albert 1er (70m); Hôtel du
Parc (400m); Montpellier Parc
Zoologique (4.5km)

Bd Louis Blanc

Bd Pasteur

Jardin
des
Plantes

Bd Henri IV

R du Cardinal de Cabrières

R de l'Ecole Mage

R de l'Université

R des Écoles Laïques

10

R du Four

R de l'École
de Médecine

R de la Candolle
R St-Pierre

Pl de la
Chapelle
Neuve

16

R Jean-Jacques
Rousseau

17

R de la Vieille
Intendance

R Ste-Croix

5

15

R Delpech

R de
Girone

11

14

Musée
Fabre 1

26

R de Bonne Nouvelle

Bd de Bonne Nouvelle

Esplanade Charles de Gaulle

2

12

R du Palais des Guilhem

13

R Cambacérès

23

R de la
Carbonnerie

Pl du Marché
aux Fleurs

R Foch

Place Royale
du Peyrou (100m);
Les 4 Étoiles (1km)

R du Petit
Scel

3

R Philippy

Pl
Castellane

Pl
Pétrarque

6

R de l'Aiguillerie

R des
Augustins

Bd Sarrail

20

21

R du Bras
de Fer

R Collot

Pl Jean
Jaurès

25

R de la Loge

Passage
Bruyas

24

Bd Ledru-Rollin

R St-Guilhem

R du Petit St-Jean

R de l'Ancien Courrier

Pl
St-Ravy

R Cauzit

7

R Jacques Cœur

Casa Centrale (300m);
Place de l'Europe (600m);
Odysseum (4km)

Pl de la
Comédie

R des Balances

R Four des
Flamines

Pl St-Roch

R du Plan
d'Agde

19

Pl St-
Côme

8

Grand R Jean Moulin

R des Étuves

R Vanneau

R de Verdun

R Boussairolles

Bd du Jeu de Paume

R Alexandre
Cabanel

R de la
Fontaine

R En-Gondeau

18

R Loys
R Richelieu

R Diderot

Bd Victor Hugo

R d'Obilion

R Joffre

R Maguelone

R Jules Ferry

22

Cours Gambetta

R de la République

Av Georges
Clemenceau

R Rondelet

R Anatole France

R du Grand St-Jean

Pl Auguste
Gilbert

Train
Station

◉ Sights

Montpellier's beating heart is the huge open
square of place de la Comédie. The city's finest
period architecture and *hôtels particuliers*
are around the old quarter, which lies to the
northeast, bordered by the main roads of bd
Henri IV, rue Foch and bd Louis Pasteur.

★ **Musée Fabre**   GALLERY
(☑ 0467148300; www.museefabre.fr; 39 bd de Bonne
Nouvelle; adult/child €7/5; ◷ 10am-6pm Tue-Sun)

Montpellier

Founded in 1825 by painter François-Xavier Fabre, this exceptional museum houses one of France's richest collections of European art. The galleries collectively showcase the last 600 years of artistic activity in Europe; most of the big names are represented here. Recent renovations have transformed the museum into a light, airy and engaging space.

Highlights of the Old Masters section include three paintings by Rubens, a dreamy *Venus and Adonis* by Nicholas Poussin, and a collection of works by Jacques-Louis David. The Romantic section is strong on French artists – particularly Delacroix, Géricault and Corot – while Courbet, Monet, Degas and Delaunay are among the standouts of the modern section.

Of particular local interest are the works of Marseille-born artist Fréderic Bazille (1841–70), a close contemporary of Monet, Sisley and Manet. The artist has a whole room devoted to him: look out for his portrait of Renoir, seated on a chair with legs tucked up beneath him, and a moody portrait of the artist himself by a very young Monet. Two rooms are also devoted to French painter and sculptor Pierre Soulages, born in 1919 in Rodez.

The lavish **L'Hôtel de Cabrières-Sabatier d'Espeyran** (⊙2-5pm Tue-Sun late-Jun–mid-Sep, 2-5pm Tue, Sat & Sun mid-Sep–late-Jun) mansion is attached to the museum.

Carré Sainte-Anne
GALLERY

(🖉04 67 60 82 11; www.montpellier.fr; 2 rue Philippy; ⊙11am-1pm & 2-7pm Apr-Sep, 10am-1pm & 2-6pm Tue-Sun Oct-Mar) FREE The landmark neogothic St Anne's church, with dazzling stained-glass windows, was deconsecrated in the 1980s and is now a spectacular setting for contemporary-art exhibitions and site-specific installations. It was renovated in 2018. Hours can vary depending on the program.

Cathédrale St-Pierre
CATHEDRAL

(1 rue St-Pierre; ⊙9.30am-noon & 2.30-6.30pm Mon-Sat) Noted for its disproportionately tall porch, Montpellier's monumental Cathédrale St-Pierre began life as a church attached to the 14th-century monastery of St-Benoît; it was raised to cathedral status in 1536. Heavily rebuilt after the Wars of Religion, it's now the seat of the city's archbishops.

Jardin des Plantes
GARDENS

(bd Henri IV; ⊙noon-8pm Tue-Sun Jun-Sep, to 6pm Tue-Sun Oct-May) One of Montpellier's hidden gems, the Jardins des Plantes is the oldest botanical garden in France. Established in 1593, it was used as a model for the much better-known Jardin des Plantes in Paris, laid out nearly 30 years later. Along its shady paths you'll find more than 2500 species, including nine varieties of palm, 250 medicinal plants and an arboretum of rare trees, as well as a glorious greenhouse dating from 1860.

Arc de Triomphe
LANDMARK

(rue Foch; tours adult/child €10/5.50; ⊙tours in English 10am Tue & Sat Jul & Aug) Built in 1695, Montpellier's 52m-high triumphal arch is dedicated to Louis XIV. The tourist office (p752) organises guided tours in summer that take

LOCAL KNOWLEDGE

BEACH LIFE

Strolling around the winding lanes of the old quarter, it's easy to forget that Montpellier is actually a coastal city. Most beaches can be reached in about half an hour by bus or car via the D21, or via a purpose-built cycling track. The sands run for around 10km between the concrete-heavy (and pretty ghastly) beach resorts of **Palavas-les-Flots** and **La Grande-Motte**, and are generally packed in summer.

For much quieter shores, head a few kilometres southeast of La Grande-Motte to **Plage de l'Espiguette** (Le Grau-du-Roi), one of Montpellier's best beaches, although there's no shade. On the western side of an isolated headland, the beach is a designated nature reserve, with dune systems providing a habitat for endangered birds and insects (as well as naturists). It's often windy, which makes it popular with kitesurfers and kite-buggiers, but it's usually much, much emptier than the fleshpot beaches to the west.

Another idea for wildlife spotters is to explore the area of wetlands and coastal lagoons around the small town of **Villeneuve-lès-Maguelone**, on the coastal road to Sète. This is often a good area for flamingo spotting; the birds regularly stop off here en route from the Camargue, some 30km to the east. Tip: it also boasts a wonderfully quiet and scenic beach, **Plage du Pilou** (Villeneuve-lès-Maguelone).

Kayaking is a great way to explore the area at a gentle pace; contact the reputable **Palavas Kayak de Mer** (☑ 04 67 50 79 84; www.palavaskayakdemer.com; Bassin de Plaisance Les 4 Canaux, Palavas-les-Flots; half-/full-day €25/35; ⊘ by reservation).

you up 103 steps inside the arch to the top for panoramic views. The best time to photograph it is just before sunset from **Place Royale du Peyrou** (place Royale du Peyrou; ⊘ 7am-midnight Jun-Aug, to 9.30pm Mar-May, Sep & Oct, to 8pm Nov-Feb), when the entire arch glows in the golden light.

Planet Ocean Montpellier　　　AQUARIUM
(☑ 04 67 13 05 50; www.planetoceanworld.fr; allée Ulysse, Odysseum; adult/child €18/12.50; ⊘ 11am-7pm daily Apr-Aug, Wed-Sun Sep-Mar) Part of the Odysseum shopping centre, this aquarium recreates nine aquatic environments, from polar waters to tropical forests. Kids will love the interactive displays, such as a simulated cargo ship battling through stormy seas. There's also a planetarium. Take tram 1 to the Odysseum station Place de France.

🛌 Sleeping

Auberge de Jeunesse　　　HOSTEL €
(☑ 04 67 60 32 22; www.hifrance.org/auberge-de-jeunesse/montpellier.html; 2 impasse de la Petite Corraterie; dm incl breakfast €22.50; ⊘ reception 7.30am-noon & 2pm-midnight; 🗟) Montpellier's HI-affiliated hostel feels very institutional, but it's a good base for budgeteers, with clean four- to 10-bed dorms and renovated bathrooms. There's a lounge downstairs with table football and pool, and a small garden. It's very close to the centre.

★ **Casa Centrale**　　　GUESTHOUSE €
(☑ 06 28 04 44 29; www.casacentrale.fr; 25 rue Cité Benoît; incl breakfast s €50-60, d €80-100; 🗟) This urban oasis conveniently located near the train station and the historical centre is a great find. The three rooms are meticulously maintained, the bathrooms are impeccable (note that toilets are shared) and you can unwind in the garden. Your host Elodie speaks perfect English and offers plenty of insider tips on the best Montpellier has to offer.

★ **Hôtel du Palais**　　　HOTEL €€
(☑ 04 67 60 47 38; www.hoteldupalais-montpellier. fr; 3 rue du Palais des Guilhem; s €75, d €95-100; ❄🗟) Superbly located near the Arc de Triomphe (p749), this hotel offers a friendly welcome. It has small but beautifully furnished rooms (some with wrought-iron balconies and window boxes) and local art on the walls, plus modernised bathrooms. The setting on a quiet square is delightful; try to get a front-facing room if you can. The nearest car park is on rue Foch.

★ **Baudon de Mauny**　　　BOUTIQUE HOTEL €€€
(☑ 04 67 02 21 77; www.baudondemauny.com; 1 rue de la Carbonnerie; d €145-355; ⊘ reception 4-8pm, closed Feb; ❄🗟) A cross between a palatial B&B and a boutique hotel, this splendid 18th-century house with nine rooms has been given the full designer overhaul: original fireplaces, oak doors and sash windows

sit alongside modern furniture, anglepoise lamps and butterfly wallpaper. The most convenient parking is at Parking du Corum, 500m northeast. Breakfast costs from €10.

✗ Eating

Montpellier is a great destination for foodies. You'll find plenty of cheap and cheerful joints on rue de l'Université, rue des Écoles Laïques and the surrounding streets. The historical centre is also peppered with top restaurants.

Extra Shot CAFE €
(✆07 68 20 18 69; www.extrashot-montpellier. fr; 44 rue de l'Aiguillerie; sandwiches, cakes & salads €4-8; ☺8am-6pm Tue-Thu, to 7pm Fri & Sat, 10.30am-5pm Sun) This upbeat cafe and cake shop is perfect for breakfasts and cake fixes. It also serves wholesome burgers and salads at lunchtime, which you can enjoy with an espresso, a cup of tea or a fruit juice.

Moody Social Club TAPAS €
(✆04 67 60 77 23; www.moody-social-club.fr; 21 rue Vallat; menus €10-15, mains €10-12, tapas from €4; ☺noon-2.30pm & 7-10pm, bar noon-1am Mon-Sat) This *bar à manger* (hybrid bar-restaurant) in a stunning vaulted dining room scores high for atmosphere and is a buzzing spot for fine wine in the company of yummy tapas and other dishes.

★Green Lab VEGETARIAN, LEBANESE €
(✆04 67 57 39 17; www.facebook.com/greenlab montpellier; 2 rue de l'Université; mains €6-10; ☺noon-10pm Tue-Sat; ✈) We defy you not to walk into this easy-to-miss joint in the heart of the old town and not instantly be tempted by the wonderful falafels and delicious vegetarian *assiettes* (salads) on offer. Eat in or take away. Unbeatable value.

★Le Café de la Panacée BISTRO €
(✆04 99 63 45 68; www.lecafedelapanacee.com; 14 rue de l'École de Pharmacie; menus €14-20, Sun brunch €18, tapas €4-8; ☺cafe 10am-midnight Wed-Sat, to 6pm Sun, restaurant 12.15-2pm and 7.30-10.30pm Wed-Sat, brunch 11.30am-3pm Sun) Occupying the top floor of an art gallery, this super-cool venture is an atmospheric spot for digging into superb market-driven dishes. Although the menu is limited, lunch is a real gourmet experience. Locals also rave about the tapas (served in the evening) and Sunday brunch.

★Anga BISTRO €€
(✆04 67 60 61 65; www.facebook.com/restaurant. anga; 19 rue du Palais des Guilhem; menus €21-45; ☺noon-1.45pm & 8-9.30pm Wed-Sat) Drop in to this sweet little gourmet neo-bistro for top-notch market cuisine concocted by a trio of hipsters. The tiny menu changes every day and always involves seasonal, fresh ingredients. The dining area has soft golden-stone walls and only a handful of tables – reservations are essential.

Les Bains de Montpellier MEDITERRANEAN €€
(✆04 67 60 70 87; www.les-bains-de-montpellier. com; 6 rue Richelieu; menus €27-38, mains €17-28; ☺noon-2pm & 8-11pm Mon-Sat) This former public bathhouse is now a hip restaurant that's especially strong on Mediterranean flavours and Italian-influenced dishes. Tables are set around the old perimeter bathrooms, with plush purple chairs and overhead chandeliers,

LANGUEDOC-ROUSSILLON MONTPELLIER

DON'T MISS

HÔTELS PARTICULIERS IN MONTPELLIER

During the 17th and 18th centuries, Montpellier's rich merchants built themselves grand *hôtels particuliers* (private mansions) to show off their power and prodigious wealth. The most important houses are marked by a descriptive plaque in French; you can pick up a map in the tourist office (p752). Many of the houses have fabulous inner courtyards (mostly, alas, closed to the public).

Among the most notable is the **Hôtel de Varennes** (2 place Pétrarque), just off place Pétrarque, a mix of medieval and Renaissance architecture; it's now home to a modest **museum** (✆04 67 66 02 94; 2 place Pétrarque; adult/child €3/free; ☺10.30am-12.30pm & 2-6pm Tue-Sun).

A short walk south on rue Jacques Cœur is the 17th-century **Hôtel des Trésoriers de France** (7 rue Jacques Cœur), one-time residence of King Louis XIII. Just west is the grand **Hôtel St-Côme** (Grand Rue Jean Moulin).

Further west near the Cathédrale St-Pierre (p749) is the early-17th-century **Hôtel de la Vieille Intendance** (rue de la Vieille Intendance), built during the reign of Louis XIII.

but the best are in the interior courtyard, surrounded by ponds and palms.

Le Petit Jardin FRENCH €€
(📞 04 67 60 78 78; www.petit-jardin.com; 20 rue Jean-Jacques Rousseau; menus €32-45, mains €23-32; ⏲ noon-1.30pm & 7.30-9.30pm Tue-Sun) The 'Little Garden' has one of the city's most romantic dining settings – a charmingly green, glass-enclosed secret garden, hidden away behind the amber façade of a typical townhouse in the old quarter. It also has a more relaxed, cheaper bistro (lunch *menu* €21); either way, the food is fresh, seasonal and very French.

🍷 Drinking & Nightlife

You'll find plenty of bars around rue En-Gondeau, off Grand Rue Jean Moulin, around place Jean Jaurès, and around the intersection of rue de l'Université and rue de la Candolle.

Sortir à Montpellier (www.sortiramont-pellier.fr) has nightlife listings in print and online. The big clubs are around Espace Latipolia, 10km out of town on rte de Palavas, and served by night buses.

⭐ **Willie Carter Sharpe** COCKTAIL BAR
(📞 09 84 11 64 53; www.facebook.com/wcs cocktailbar; 3 rue Collot; ⏲ 6pm-1am) Few hob-nobbing spots in Montpellier are as sweet as the vaulted room of this speakeasy-style bar popular with local hipsters. Relax and order a well-prepared cocktail from the moustachioed bartender. There's usually live jazz on Wednesday, Thursday and Sunday.

⭐ **Le Clandestin** WINE BAR
(📞 06 80 40 05 76; www.leclandestin.fr; 18 rue de la Valfère; ⏲ 6pm-1am Tue-Sat) This popular wine and piano bar is a gem. With a wide selection of wines, whiskies and rums, you're sure to find something that will tickle your fancy. It's famed for the quality of its live music sessions featuring pop, rock and jazz sounds.

La Barbote MICROBREWERY
(📞 07 68 31 12 50; www.microbrasserielabarbote. com; 1 rue des Deux Ponts; ⏲ 6pm-1am) In-the-know tourists and locals rub shoulders at Montpellier's best microbrewery, which crafts rich ales and lager, and serves tasty dinner and snacking grub too.

Le Café de la Mer GAY, BAR
(📞 04 67 60 53 92; 5 place du Marché aux Fleurs; ⏲ 8am-1am Mon-Sat, 3pm-1am Sun) One of the city's oldest gay bars now has a mixed clientele and Montpellier's best, sunniest terrace. Ask at the bar for info about where else is hot (or not).

ℹ Information

Tourist Office (📞 04 67 60 60 60; www. montpellier-tourisme.fr; 30 allée Jean de Lattre de Tassigny; ⏲ 9.30am-6pm Mon-Sat, 10am-5pm Sun) Sells the Montpellier City Card (p747) and runs guided tours.

ℹ Getting There & Away

AIR

Montpellier Airport (MPL; 📞 04 67 20 85 00; www.montpellier.aeroport.fr) 8km southeast of town, the airport has regular connections to many French cities, including Ajaccio, Bastia, Bordeaux, Brest, Lille, Nantes, Paris and Strasbourg. There are also flights to London, Amsterdam, Dublin, Berlin, Frankfurt and Munich.

> **LOCAL KNOWLEDGE**
>
> ### THIRD-WAVE COFFEE
>
> Essential for kick-starting the morning after...
>
> **Coffee Club** (📞 07 86 17 81 56; www.coffeeclub.fr; 12 rue St-Guilhem; ⏲ 10am-7pm Tue-Sat, 11am-7pm Sun) Americanos, macchiatos, lattes, chilli mochas, excellent espressos and fluffy flat whites are brewed up at this urban espresso bar. It also has teas, freshly squeezed juices and smoothies and delicious cakes. A handful of tables are scattered on the pavement out the front.
>
> **Café Solo** (📞 04 67 60 36 48; www.facebook.com/cafesolomontpellier; 30 rue St-Guilhem; ⏲ 9am-7pm Mon-Sat) Café Solo roasts its own beans and serves its brews – along with teas, hot chocolates and freshly squeezed juices – in its split-level interior with mezzanine seating, or out on its street terrace with mismatched furniture and warm blankets to wrap up in when it's chilly.

BUS

The **bus station** (☏ 04 67 92 01 43; rue du Grand St-Jean) is an easy walk from the **Montpellier St-Roch train station**. Most regional services provided by **Hérault Transport** (☏ 04 34 88 89 99; www.herault-transport.fr) cost a flat-rate €1.60. Destinations include the following:

La Grande-Motte (20 minutes, half-hourly Monday to Saturday, every 15 minutes on weekends) Catch bus 106 from place de France, in the Antigone quarter. Several buses a day continue to Aigues-Mortes.

Palavas-les-Flots (10 to 20 minutes, at least hourly) Catch the **tram** (☏ 04 67 22 87 87; www.tam-voyages.com) to Station Étang l'Or – the last stop before the coastline, just south of the **airport** (p752), 11km southeast of the city centre – then take bus 131.

Sète (55 minutes, hourly Monday to Saturday, three on Sunday) Take bus 102 from Sabines tram station, 4km southwest of the city centre.

TRAIN

The city's stunning new pleated-concrete and glass **Montpellier Sud-de-France TGV station** (www.oui.sncf; 1521 rue de la Fontaine de la Banquière), designed by French architect Marc Mimram, opened in mid-2018 in the Odysseum quarter, some 4km southeast of the city centre towards the coast, cutting travel time to Paris Gare de Lyon (from €49) to three hours. Trains also run from Montpellier to Barcelona (from €41) and on to Madrid (from €102) up to four times daily.

From **Montpellier St-Roch train station** (www.ter.sncf.com; place Auge Gibert) in the centre, there's at least one hourly connection to the following cities:

Carcassonne €26.70, 1½ hours
Narbonne €17.40, one hour
Nîmes €10.10, 30 minutes
Perpignan €27.20, 1¾ hours

❶ Getting Around

Christian Lacroix contributed designs for Montpellier's four-line tram system. Single tickets (valid on trams and buses) cost €1.60; a one-day pass costs €4.30. There are ticket machines at most tram stops, or you can buy them at the **tourist office** or newsagents.

Sète

POP 45,200

Set alongside the saltwater lagoon of Étang du Thau, Sète is sometimes called the 'Little Venice of Languedoc' – a reference to the many canals that run through town, includ-

GOURMET SHOPPING

Stock up on delicious regional products at **Le Boutik R** (☏ 04 67 66 35 93; www.leboutikr.fr; 41 bd Bonne Nouvelle; ◷ 10am-7pm Tue-Sat): Cévennes chestnut, lavender and garrigue honey, nougat, olives, truffles, olive oils, vinegars, Camargue salt, *Grisettes de Montpellier* (local speciality sweets originating in the Middle Ages and incorporating liquorice powder, honey and sugar) and Languedoc wines and liqueurs.

ing the Canal du Midi, which terminates its 240km journey here from Toulouse, and the Canal du Rhône, whose 98km journey from Beaucaire also ends here. Sète is a bit short on sights, but its honest, workaday atmosphere makes a refreshing change from the built-up tourist towns of the rest of the Languedoc coast. If you like seafood, this is the place to indulge: Sète sports restaurants galore cooking up sea urchins, sardines, cuttlefish and myriad *coquillages* (shellfish). Its centre is a great place to explore on foot. Be sure to walk up Mt St-Clair (the small hill that lords over the centre) for panoramic views and wander around La Pointe Courte, the old fishermen's quarter.

◉ Sights & Activities

Musée Paul Valéry   MUSEUM
(☏ 04 99 04 76 16; www.museepaulvalery-sete.fr; 148 rue François Desnoyer; adult/child €6.10/3.60; ◷ 9.30am-7pm Apr-Oct, 10am-6pm Tue-Sun Nov-Mar) Sète was the birthplace of symbolist poet Paul Valéry (1871–1945), and the town's main museum houses a disappointingly small collection of his works, along with paintings and drawings by other local artists and diverse temporary exhibitions. Valéry is buried in the Cimetière Marin across the street.

Espace Georges Brassens   MUSEUM
(☏ 04 99 04 76 26; www.espace-brassens.fr; 67 bd Camille Blanc; adult/child €5.80/2.30; ◷ 10am-6pm Jun-Sep, 10am-noon & 2-6pm Tue-Sun Oct-May) Sète was the childhood home of singer and poet Georges Brassens (1921–81), whose mellow voice still speaks at this multimedia space.

Kayak Med   KAYAKING, BIKE RENTAL
(☏ 06 95 63 12 75; www.kayakmed.com; 19 promenade Jean-Baptiste Marty; kayak/SUP rental per 3hr €25/30, kayak & SUP tours per 2½hrs from €35, bike rental per 4hr/day €8/12; ◷ 10am-1pm &

OYSTERS & WINE

When romance beckons midway between Sète and Bouzigues, head to **Domaine Tarbouriech** (☑ 04 48 14 00 30; www.domaine-tarbouriech.fr; chemin des Domaines, Marseillan; d/ste from €220/290; P❄🐕🏊), a gem of an address run by the Tarbouriech family on a former *domaine viticole* (wine estate) off the Étang de Thau lagoon. Open since 2018, everything – from its huge rooms and suites to the on-site restaurant and spa – is stylish and impeccable. And there's an oyster bar, of course – Tarbouriech oysters are rated among the world's best by oyster-philes.

Should the surrounding sweep of vineyards inspire further exploration, head to **Vinipolis** (☑ 04 67 77 00 20; www.vinipolis.fr; 5 av des Vendanges, Florensac; ⊙ 9am-noon & 2-6pm Mon & Thu, 9am-5.30pm Tue, Wed, Fri & Sat, 11am-3.30pm Sun), a wonderful wine warehouse in which to get acquainted with Languedoc wines, 11km north of Agde.

2-6pm Apr-Sep) Rent kayaks and SUPs (stand-up paddleboards) or take a guided tour of Sète's waterways with this local outfit. Life jackets and waterproof containers are provided. It also offers bicycle rental.

Sète Croisières BOATING

(☑ 04 67 46 00 46; www.sete-croisieres.com; quai Général Durand; port & coast tour adult/child €12/6, Étang du Thau tour €14/7, town tour €10/5; ⊙ Apr-Oct) Boats run by Sète Croisières cruise around the town, port and coast, plus the Étang du Thau and the local mussel and oyster farms, which you can peer at through the boat's glass-bottomed hulls. All trips leave from quai Général Durand.

🎭 Festivals & Events

Joutes Nautiques SPORTS

(⊙ mid-Jun–Aug) The *joutes nautiques,* when boat crews joust with long poles in an attempt to knock each other into the harbour, run from mid-June and culminate in late August, when the centrepiece La Saint Louis event takes place on quai du Canal Royal.

🛏 Sleeping

Auberge de Jeunesse Sète HOSTEL €

(☑ 04 67 53 46 68; www.hifrance.org/auberge-de-jeunesse/sete.html; 7 rue Général Revest; incl breakfast dm from €23.60, d €57; ⊙ Apr-Sep, reception 9am-noon & 6-9pm; P🐕) This impersonal yet well-run hostel with harbour views houses doubles and four-bed dorms, and a self-catering kitchen. It's a steep 10- to 15-minute walk to get there from the centre.

L'Orque Bleue HOTEL €€

(☑ 04 67 74 72 13; www.hotel-orquebleue-sete.com; 10 quai Aspirant Herber; d €80-140, f €125-145; P❄🐕) To sense Sète as a living port, this

renovated shipping magnate's mansion – a marble-clad 1880s *hôtel particulier* (private mansion) – is the place to sleep, with attractively done-up and spacious rooms. Those with canal outlooks, especially rooms 102, 212 and 323, are prime real estate.

Grand Hôtel HOTEL €€

(☑ 04 67 74 71 77; www.legrandhotelsete.com; 17 quai Maréchal de Lattre de Tassigny; d from €120; P❄🐕) As its name suggests, this 19th-century harbourfront hotel is grand, from the gleaming marble lobby, filled with palms and modern art, all the way through to the stylish rooms arranged around a palm-filled, glass-roofed interior courtyard. The best rooms overlook the harbour. There's an excellent on-site restaurant.

🍴 Eating & Drinking

Cafes and restaurants doubling as bars line Sète's quays.

Oh Gobie SEAFOOD €€

(☑ 04 99 02 61 14; www.facebook.com/ohgobie; 9 quai Maximin Licciardi; mains €10-25; ⊙ noon-1.30pm & 7-9.30pm Thu-Mon) Seafood lovers, you'll find nirvana here: Oh Gobie has a wide assortment of fish delivered daily from the harbour. The quirky terrace complete with seafaring paraphernalia is a good place to soak up the atmosphere of the seafront.

La Méditerranéenne SEAFOOD €€

(☑ 04 67 74 38 37; www.la-mediterraneenne-sete. com; 3 quai Maximin Licciardi; mains €14-20, platters €37-78; ⊙ noon-2.30pm & 7-11pm) Sète is awash with seafood restaurants, but this quayside bistro by local chef Fouzia Sakrani scores highly on friendliness and freshness. Simple but delicious food spans sea bream, sole, red mullet, sardines and sea bass, as well as vast shellfish platters – all served with copious amounts of crusty bread to soak up the rich fish juices.

⭐ **La Coquerie** GASTRONOMY €€€
(☎06 47 06 71 38; www.annemajourel.fr; 1 chemin du Cimetière Marin; 6-course meal €65; ⊙noon-1.15pm & 8-9.30pm Mon-Sat Jun-Sep, noon-1.15pm & 8-9.30pm Thu-Sat, noon-1.15pm Sun Oct-May) Prepare to be wowed: some of Languedoc's most exquisite dining is at chef Anne Majourel's Michelin-starred premises. She shuns *menus* (fixed-price meals) in favour of what's fresh from the fish auction and utilises the region's finest produce. The best views over the harbour aren't from the terrace but inside the dining room opposite the open kitchen. Book *well* ahead.

❶ Information

Tourist office (☎04 99 04 71 71; www.tourisme-sete.com; 60 Grand Rue Mario Roustan; ⊙9.30am-7pm Jul & Aug, 9.30am-6pm Mon-Sat, 10am-5pm Sun Apr-Jun & Sep, 9.30am-5.30pm Mon-Sat, 10am-1pm Sun Oct-Mar) Just back from the waterfront.

❶ Getting There & Away

The regular 102 **bus** (rue de Copenhague; €1.60, hourly Monday to Saturday, three on Sunday) runs between Sète and Montpellier in just under an hour via Montpellier's beaches, or you can catch a **train** (place André Cambon; €6.10, 20 minutes, hourly).

Italian ferry company **Grandi Navi Veloci** (GNV; ☎01 86 26 10 18; www.gnv.it; rte de Pont Martin; seat/cabin/car Sète-Tangier from €76/100/312, Sète-Nador from €91/95/302) operates ferries between Sète and the Moroccan ports of Tangier (32 hours) and Nador (29 hours). There are two to three sailings per week from Sète.

Bouzigues

POP 1398

Oyster and mussel beds occupy the waters of the shimmering Étang de Thau lagoon, which surrounds this little village 15km northwest of Sète, while vineyards crisscross the hillsides above town. Although wine has been produced here since the 6th century, shellfish farming only started in 1925, but it now anchors Bouzigues' economy. It's a wonderful place to soak up the

coastal atmosphere, and there are a few great museums in the area.

⊙ Sights & Activities

⭐ **Musée Parc des Dinosaures et de la Préhistoire** MUSEUM
(☎04 67 43 02 80; www.dinosaure.eu; D613, Mèze; adult/child €12.50/10.50; ⊙10.30am-7pm Jul & Aug, 2-6pm Feb-Jun, Sep & Oct, 2-5pm Nov & Dec, closed Jan) Signs warning of dinosaurs line the drive up, but this dinosaur park is no gimmick – the biggest cache of dinosaur eggs ever discovered in Europe was found here in 1996. Ongoing archaeological digs are unearthing more fossils and footprints. Life-size dinosaur models stand in the parkland and bilingual signs bring exhibits to life. A section of the park focuses on our prehistoric ancestors. The park's 11km west of Bouzigues via the D613.

Musée de Site Gallo-Romain Villa Loupian ROMAN SITE
(☎04 67 18 68 18; www.loupian.fr; Loupian; adult/child €5/3.50; ⊙10am-1pm & 3-9pm Jul & Aug, 10am-noon & 2-6pm Wed-Mon Mar-Jun, Sep & Oct, 10am-noon & 2-5pm Nov & Feb) Dating from the 1st century AD, this extraordinary Roman villa was built on the Via Domitia road linking Italy and Spain. It was occupied for 600 years. Highlights include a wine cellar and the villa's dazzling preserved mosaics with Syrian and Aquitaine influences; they cover 13 ground-floor rooms. Audioguides are included with admission; free tours take place at 3pm Thursday in French, with translation sheets available. The site is 4.5km southwest of Bouzigues off the D613.

Musée de l'Étang de Thau MUSEUM
(☎04 67 78 33 57; www.bouzigues.fr/musee; quai du Port; adult/child €5/3.50; ⊙10am-12.30pm & 2-7.30pm Jul & Aug, 10am-noon & 2-6pm Tue-Sun Sep-Nov & Feb-Jun, closed Dec & Jan) The Musée de l'Étang de Thau has aquarium tanks, sepia photos, vintage fishing equipment and models of the lagoon.

Bateau Promenade BOATING
(☎06 03 31 44 90; www.promenade-bouzigues.fr; quai du Port; adult/child €12/8; ⊙tours 11am, 2.30pm, 4pm & 5.30pm Jul & Aug, 11am, 2.30pm & 4pm May, Jun & Sep, 3pm Apr & Oct) Bateau Promenade takes you out on the water aboard the semi-covered *Bleu Marin* on one-hour cruises to view the shellfish beds; cruises pass the Roquérols lighthouse.

LOCAL KNOWLEDGE

AGDE BEACHES

There are really three Agdes: **Vieux Agde**, the original settlement beside the Hérault River; the fishing port of **Grau d'Agde**; and **Cap d'Agde**, a built-up summer playground.

For most people, the only real reason to stop in Agde is for some swimming and sunbathing, but Vieux Agde is worth a wander, with some imposing *hôtels particuliers* (private mansions) and a pretty riverside setting.

If you're here to sunbathe, Cap d'Agde is the place. Beaches sprawl around the headland; the nicest areas are on the far west (especially around La Tamarissière and St-Vincent) and the far east, home to France's (and the world's) largest nudist colony.

Agde's **train station** (rue de la Digue) is on the northern side of the Hérault River, 300m northwest of Vieux Agde. Services run at least hourly to Montpellier (€10.10, 30 minutes), Perpignan (€19.80, 1¼ hours) and Sète (€5.30, 10 minutes). The Cap d'Agde coast is best accessed with your own wheels.

🛏 Sleeping & Eating

Oyster restaurants line av Louis Tudesq along the waterfront; there are over two dozen in the village and its surrounds.

Lou Labech CAMPGROUND €
(☑04 67 78 30 38; www.lou-labech.fr; rte du Stade; tent, 2 people & car €17-30, chalets, cabins & safari tents per week from €200; ☉Apr-Oct; P🐾) It's worth paying more for a waterfront pitch at this well-spaced beachside campground, which also has chalets and cabins sleeping up to five people, and safari tents sleeping up to four (minimum rental of three nights). There's an on-site shop and bar serving *moules-frites* (mussels and fries) of an evening.

À la Voile Blanche HOTEL €€
(☑04 67 78 35 77; www.alavoileblanche.fr; 1 av Louis Tudesq; d €75-120; ❄🐾) Higher-priced rooms at this family-run waterfront hotel have balconies and panoramic views across the lagoon, marina and oyster beds to Mont St-Clair rising above Sète. All rooms are spacious with contemporary styling, although with a touch of kitsch. Its seafood restaurant (*menus* from €23) downstairs is excellent.

ℹ Information

Sète's **tourist office** can provide information about Bouzigues and its surrounds.

ℹ Getting There & Away

Buses are operated by **Hérault Transport** (p753) and leave from the main square near the town hall. Buses 104 and 103 link Bouzigues with Montpellier (€1.60, 40 minutes, at least three daily). Bus 320 links Bouzigues with Sète (€1.60, 10 minutes, at least three daily).

Narbonne
POP 51,306

These days, Narbonne is a charming mid-size Languedoc market town, but wind the clock back two millennia and you'd be in a major Roman city – the capital of the province of Gallia Narbonensis. Exceptional sights include its cathedral and former archbishops' palace, and the town is now a popular stop-off for boaters. The picturesque Canal de la Robine runs right through the centre of elegant Narbonne and connects the Étang de Bages-Sigean with the Canal du Midi.

By 2020, Narbonne will also benefit from the opening of Narbovia, a cutting-edge museum with a focus on the city's Roman heritage.

◉ Sights

Palais des Archevêques PALACE
(Archbishops' Palace; place de l'Hôtel de Ville; all museums €10, s museum €6; ☉10am-6pm Jun-Sep, 10am-noon & 2-5pm Wed-Mon Oct-May) The former archbishops' palace houses several archaeological museums. Roman mosaics and stucco paintings are on display at the **Musée d'Art et d'Histoire** and **Musée Archéologique**, along with an underground gallery of Gallo-Roman shops in the **Horreum**, and a collection of impressive Roman masonry in the **Musée Lapidaire**. Admission includes access to the keep, with fabulous city views.

Cathédrale St-Just CATHEDRAL
(entry on rue Armand Gauthier; treasury €6; ☉9am-noon & 2-6pm, treasury 10-11.45am & 2-5.45pm) Narbonne's most distinctive landmark is actually only half-finished: construction was

halted in the 14th century, and only the towers and choir reached final completion. Its treasury has a beautiful Flemish tapestry of the Creation, while grotesque gargoyles leer down upon the 16th-century cloister.

🛏 Sleeping & Eating

Will's Hotel   HOTEL €
(✆ 06 45 98 18 80; www.willshotel-narbonne.com; 23 av Pierre Semard; s €61, d €69-79; ✿ 🌐) Once a merchant's house dating from 1860, this basic corner hotel just 150m from the train station is a decent base for overnighting in Narbonne, with uncluttered yet well-kept rooms. There's a bike garage; parking is available at a nearby municipal car park.

La Maison de Gustave   B&B €€
(✆ 06 63 48 29 75; www.lamaisongustave.com; 3-5 rue Gustave Fabre; d €99-139; ✿ 🌐) This character-filled converted townhouse just opposite the cathedral is a great find, with five bright and elegant rooms with all mod cons. The owner is full of information and tips. The only possible downside is that breakfast is served in a compact, dark room.

Les Halles   MARKET
(www.narbonne.halles.fr; 1 cours Mirabeau; ⊙ 7am-2pm) Narbonne's covered market is one of the most beautiful in France. Built at the turn of the 20th century, it's a masterpiece of art nouveau style, with panels of frosted glass, decorative stonework and a wonderful cast-iron roof. Inside, more than 70 stalls sell cheese, charcuterie, poultry, meat and fish as well as fruit, flowers and wine.

★ Chez Bébelle   GRILL €
(✆ 06 85 40 09 01; www.chez-bebelle.fr; 1 bd Docteur Ferroul, Les Halles; mains €14-19; ⊙ noon-2.30pm Tue-Sat) Chez Bébelle is legendary for its convivial atmosphere and top-quality meat dishes, all served with homemade fries and tasty salads. It's the perfect spot for a proper lunch – it's right in Les Halles. A winner.

ℹ Information

Tourist Office (✆ 04 68 65 15 60; www.narbonne-tourisme.com; 31 rue Jean Jaurès; ⊙ 9am-7pm Apr–mid-Sep, 10am-12.30pm & 1.30-6pm Mon-Sat mid-Sep–Mar) Can advise on canal cruises and water sports on the nearby Étang de Bages-Sigean lagoon.

ℹ Getting There & Away

Frequent **trains** (av Carnot) serve Narbonne en route from Béziers (€5.90, 15 minutes), Montpellier (€17.40, one hour) and Perpignan (€15.50, one hour).

Béziers

POP 74,811

Easily Languedoc's most underrated city, Béziers is a great surprise. It's small enough not to be overwhelming, yet has plenty of character. Its historical centre, built on a

---

WORTH A TRIP

NARBONNE DAY TRIPPER

Founded by Cistercian monks in 1093, **Abbaye de Fontfroide** (✆ 04 68 45 11 08; www.fontfroide.com; chemin de Fontfroide, Fontfroide; adult/child abbey, garden & museum €19/15, abbey & gardens only €11.50/7; ⊙ 9.30am-7pm Jul & Aug, 10am-6pm Apr-Jun, Sep & Oct, 10am-12.30pm & 1.30-5pm Nov-Mar) became one of southern France's most powerful ecclesiastical centres during the Middle Ages. Highlights include the tranquil chapter hall, refectory, cloister and monks' dormitory, as well as a rose garden added during the 18th century. Fontfroide also produces its own renowned wine, which you can sample in the on-site wine shop or, better still, in the vaulted **restaurant** (✆ 04 68 41 02 26; www.fontfroide.com; chemin de Fontfroide, Fontfroide; menus €21-40, mains €17-40; ⊙ noon-2pm & 7-9.30pm Tue-Sat, noon-2pm Sun & Mon Jul & Aug, noon-2pm daily mid-Feb-Jun & Sep-late Dec). It's 15km southwest of Narbonne via the D613.

Opened in 1974, 300-hectare wildlife reserve **Réserve Africaine de Sigean** (✆ 04 68 48 20 20; www.reserveafricainesigean.fr; 19 chemin Hameau du Lac, Sigean; adult/child €32/23; ⊙ 9am-6pm May-Aug, 9am-5pm Sep, Oct & Apr, 9am-4.30pm Nov-Mar) aims to recreate the atmosphere of the African savannah – a climate not all that different from the Languedoc's dry and dusty plains. Lions, white rhinos, warthogs, giraffes and zebras are just a few of the 160 species on show, with some 3800 animals here in all. Some areas are drive-through, while others you explore on foot. The reserve is off the A9, 17km south of Narbonne.

hilltop, is a great place for a stroll. Expect a lovely cathedral, great squares, a vast esplanade and picturesque streets lined with magnificent buildings. Béziers has a long history: founded by the Romans and razed during the Albigensian Crusade, it's now best known as the birthplace of Paul Riquet, the man behind the stately Canal du Midi.

⊙ Sights

Pont-Canal
BRIDGE

This 19th-century aqueduct of the Canal du Midi is on the southern edge of town, bridging the Orb River. It affords stupendous views of the city.

Écluses de Fonseranes
ARCHITECTURE

(rue des Écluses; parking incl audioguide €7; ⊙ 3D cinema & shop 10am-7pm mid-Mar–Oct) Situated 1km southwest of town is this famous stepladder of eight locks and nine gates. The whole area was fully renovated in 2017 and is now one of Béziers' highlights. It's connected to the historical centre via a 2km-long walking path. There's a restaurant and a gift shop, and you can watch a 14-minute 3D film that explains the history of the site. You can also rent electric boats or take a boat cruise along the Canal du Midi.

🛏 Sleeping & Eating

You'll find cafes and restaurants on and around place de la Madeleine and near Les Halles covered market.

Le XIX
HOTEL €€

(☑ 04 67 48 04 00; www.hoteldixneuf.com; 19 place Jean Jaurès; d €95-145; ❋ ☎) Disguised by a pale yellow townhouse exterior overlooking classy place Jean Jaurès is this slick, stylish and faultless hotel. The 12 rooms are bright, fresh and airy, and the bathrooms are sparkling. There's a cheerful downstairs cafe. Parking (€11) is at an underground municipal car park just across the street.

L'Hôtel Particulier
BOUTIQUE HOTEL €€€

(☑ 04 67 49 04 47; www.hotelparticulierbeziers.com; 65bis av du 22 Août 1944; d €140-220; ℗❋☎☀) To do Béziers en luxe, nowhere tops this stately 19th-century mansion that has been converted into a boutique hotel with nine fabulously designed and immensely comfortable rooms. It's romantic, chic and intimate, and there's a supremely relaxing garden complete with a lap pool at the back. A winner. Book ahead.

Le Chameau Ivre
TAPAS €€

(☑ 04 67 80 20 20; www.lechameauivre.fr; 15 place Jean Jaurès; menus €20-25, tapas €6.50-9, mains €14-24; ⊙ noon-2pm & 6-11pm Tue-Sat) Easily Béziers' most attractive restaurant and tapas bar, the legendary Drunken Camel serves the best tapas in town – and don't the locals know it. They rush here for the delicate tapas platters and tasty mains. Wine lovers, take note: the wine list has about 3000 vintages. Don't miss it.

OFF THE BEATEN TRACK

GOURMET DINING

If you're looking for a gourmet experience to remember, reserve a table at these hallowed chef tables, tucked away in the countryside.

Le Suquet (☑ 05 65 51 18 20; www.bras.fr; rte de l'Aubrac, Laguiole; menus €145-230, mains €49-90; ⊙ 7-9pm Wed, noon-1.30pm & 7-9pm Thu-Sun Apr-Jun & Sep-Nov, noon-1.30pm & 7-9pm Tue-Sun Jul & Aug, closed Dec-Mar; ☎) Originally opened by superstar chef Michel Bras in the village of Laguiole in 1999, the food here is steeped in the rustic, country flavours of his youth, reinvented in all kinds of outlandish ways. Now run by his son Sébastien, it's worth a trip for the restaurant alone: a modernist, plate-glass marvel, with views over Aubrac's green hills. Double rooms start at €330.

Auberge du Vieux Puits (☑ 04 68 44 07 37; www.aubergeduvieuxpuits.fr; 5 av St-Victor, Fontjoncouse; menus €115-205, mains €70-82; ⊙ noon-1.30pm & 8-9.30pm Wed-Sat, noon-1.30pm Sun Apr-Nov, closed Dec-Mar) Gilles Goujon's wonderfully relaxed Auberge du Vieux Puits is tucked away in the hilltop village of Fontjoncouse, between Narbonne and Perpignan. Goujon's known for his fondness for humble ingredients such as Bigorre pork, Galician beef, sole and John Dory. The menus (fixed-price meals) stretch between four and seven courses and include a 'chariot of cheese' that almost defies belief. Double rooms start at €165.

ⓘ Information

Tourist Office (📞 04 99 41 36 36; www.
beziers-in-mediterranee.com; place du Forum;
⊙10am-6pm Apr-Oct, to 5pm Jan-Mar) Has
multilingual staff. There's an annexe at **Écluses
de Fonseranes**.

ⓘ Getting There & Away

Regular **trains** (Bd de Verdun) run from Montpellier (€13.50, 45 minutes) en route to Narbonne
(€5.90, 15 minutes).

Carcassonne

POP 49,400

Perched on a rocky hilltop and bristling
with zigzag battlements, stout walls and
spiky turrets, the fortified city of Carcassonne looks like something out of a children's storybook when it's seen from afar.
A Unesco World Heritage Site since 1997,
it's most people's idea of the perfect medieval castle.

The Cité Médiévale, as the old walled town
is now known, attracts over four million visitors every year, peaking in high summer.
Time your visit for late in the day (or better
still, for spring or autumn) to truly appreciate the old town's medieval charm.

◉ Sights

Beneath Carcassonne's fortified castle Cité
Médiévale, on the left bank of the Aude River, is the city's second half, **Ville Basse**. It's
a mostly modern town that conceals a medieval heart: the Bastide St-Louis, which was
built during the 13th century using the characteristic grid of streets set around a central
square, place Carnot.

The lower town was later redeveloped
during the 18th and 19th centuries, and is
home to several impressive *hôtels particuliers* (private mansions) and religious buildings, as well as Carcassonne's marvellous
covered market (p761), dating from 1768.

★ Cité Médiévale   AREA

(Map p760; enter via Porte Narbonnaise or Porte
d'Aude; ⊙24hr) **FREE** Built on a steep spur
of rock, Carcassonne's rampart-ringed fortress dates back more than two millennia.
The fortified town is encircled by two sets
of battlements and 52 stone towers, topped
by distinctive 'witch's hat' roofs (added by
architect Viollet-le-Duc during 19th-century
restorations). Note that to actually walk on
the ramparts, you have to pay to enter the

Château et Remparts (Map p760; www.rem
parts-carcassonne.fr; 1 rue Viollet le Duc; adult/child
€9/free; ⊙10am-6.30pm Apr-Sep, 9.30am-5pm
Oct-Mar).

The hill on which the Cité Médiévale
stands has been fortified many times over
the centuries – by Gauls, Romans, Visig-
oths, Moors, Franks and Cathars, to name
a few. Following the annexation of Roussillon by France in 1659, the castle's useful-
ness as a frontier fortress declined and
it slowly crumbled into disrepair. It was
saved from destruction by Viollet-le-Duc,
who left his mark on many of France's medieval landmarks, including Notre Dame
in Paris and Vézelay in Burgundy.

The castle is laid out in a concentric pat-
tern, with the double wall and defensive
towers designed to resist attack from siege
engines. A drawbridge can still be seen in
the main gate of **Porte Narbonnaise** (Map
p760), which leads into the citadel's interi-
or, a maze of cobbled lanes and courtyards,
now mostly lined by shops and restaurants.
The castle's second gate, **Porte d'Aude** (Map
p760), was partly destroyed in 1816 and no
longer has its drawbridge.

In between the walls, an interior space
known as **Les Lices** runs for just over 1km
around the castle. Though designed as a
defensive space to delay would-be attackers, during the medieval era the city's poorest residents would have built a shanty
town of houses and workshops here, which
were cleared out during Viollet-le-Duc's
restorations. It's now the best place to escape the crowds and properly appreciate
the castle's martial architecture.

Pont-Vieux   BRIDGE

(Map p762) Though it's one of several bridges
spanning the Aude River, the Pont-Vieux is
by far the oldest and prettiest. It was built
during the 14th century to provide a quick
link between Carcassonne's lower and upper
towns, and rebuilt in the 19th century. It's
one of the few surviving medieval bridges in France, prized for its graceful arches
and compact dimensions, and is only open
to pedestrians. It's 300m west of the Cité
Médiévale.

🏃 Activities

Several companies offer cruises along the Canal du Midi, providing a beautiful way to appreciate Carcassonne's architecture from afar
while surrounded by gorgeous countryside.

Carcassonne (Cité Médiévale)

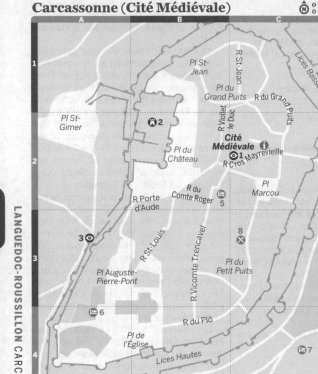

Carcassonne (Cité Médiévale)

The 240km-long canal was awarded Unesco World Heritage Site status for being a marvel of engineering.

The main operators are **Carcassonne Croisière** (Map p762; ☎ 06 80 47 54 33; www.carcassonne-navigationcroisiere.com; Port de Plaisance; 1¼hr cruise adult/child €8.50/6.50; ⊙10.30am & 2pm Jul & Aug, 10.30am & 2.30pm Apr-Jun, Sep & Oct) and **Le Cocagne** (Map p762; ☎06 50 40 78 50; www.bateau-cocagne-canal-carcassonne.fr; Port de Plaisance; 1¼hr cruise adult/child €8/6; ⊙2pm & 6pm daily Jul & Aug, 2pm & 6pm Wed-Mon Apr-Jun, Sep & Oct). Standard cruises last around 1¼ hours, but there are longer trips available. All trips leave from the Port de Plaisance in the Ville Basse.

Evadeo Cycles   CYCLING
(☎04 34 42 88 32; www.evadeocycles.com; 14 rue Jean Monnet; bike hire per 2hr/day from €10/19; ⊙9.30am-noon & 1.30-6pm) Evadeo Cycles hires out bikes and runs excellent guided cycling tours exploring local food, architec-

ture, culture and gastronomy. Kids' bikes, child seats, baby trailers, saddlebags and baggage trailers are all available; one-way Canal du Midi drop-off fees start at €25.

Vins & Vinos
WINE

(Map p762; ☑ 04 68 10 97 04; www.vinsvinos.com; 38 rue Barbès; tastings from €15; ⊙ 10am-6pm Tue-Fri, 9.30am-noon Sat) Most of the wines at cellar/wine-tasting establishment Vins & Vinos come from the south of France, especially the Languedoc-Roussillon and Toulouse areas. Learn more about the *terroirs* and meet the winemakers during tastings and other events.

Vin en Vacances
WINE

(Map p762; ☑ 06 42 33 34 09; www.vinenvacances.com; 10 rue du Pont Vieux; day tours €125-145) Experienced English-speaking company Vin en Vacances runs scheduled minibus tours of local vineyards from Carcassonne.

🛏 Sleeping

The Cité Médiévale has a couple of splendid top-of-the-market choices. Vehicles are banned inside the fortified town: if you're driving you'll have to leave your car outside the city walls overnight. All hotels use porters to lug your bags through the alleyways. It may be more practical to stay outside the walled city.

Auberge de Jeunesse
HOSTEL €

(Map p760; ☑ 04 68 25 23 16; www.hifrance.org/auberge-de-jeunesse/carcassonne.html; rue du Vicomte Trencavel, Cité Médiévale; incl breakfast dm €19-25, d €57; ⊙ closed mid-Dec-Jan & weekends Feb; 🛜) This HI hostel is smack-bang in the centre of the Cité Médiévale (p759) – great for atmosphere, but not great if you're arriving at the train station 4km downhill to the northwest. Facilities include four- to six-bed dorms, a spacious kitchen, an outside terrace and bike rental. It's very popular, so book well ahead.

Hôtel Astoria
HOTEL €

(Map p762; ☑ 04 68 25 31 38; www.astoriacarcassonne.com; 18 rue Tourtel; s €35-69, d €39-95; ⊙ reception 7am-8pm; P🛜) It's not going to win any style awards, but this efficiently run 22-room budget hotel is great value for Carcassonne. Rooms are small but clean and some renovation work started after a change of ownership in 2018. It's just 500m east of the train station, and the private parking (€5 outside, €8 under cover) is a

bonus. Bicycle rental is available for €10 per day.

Pont-Levis Hotel
BOUTIQUE HOTEL €€

(Map p760; ☑ 04 68 72 08 08; www.pontlevishotel.com; 40 chemin des Anglais; d €115-240, ste €210-280; P🛜🅿🅿) This is the area's most welcoming hotel, yet its prices are reasonable for the luxury and amenities it offers. The 12 rooms are smart and snazzy (think sleek surfaces, modern bathrooms, neutral colours) and there's a vast garden at the back with a pool and divine views of the Cité Médiévale (p759).

La Maison Vieille
B&D €€

(☑ 06 23 40 65 34; www.la-maison-vieille.com; 8 rue Trivalle; d/f €95/125; ⊙ mid-Mar–mid-Nov; 🅿🛜) As charming a B&B as you'll find in Carcassonne, this old mansion's beautiful rooms include Barbacane with parquet flooring and walk-in shower; Cité with exposed brick; Prince Noir with an in-room bath; vintage-furnished Dame Carcas; and La Trivalle in whites. Filled with olive trees, its walled courtyard is idyllic for breakfast. It's handy for the walled city and Ville Basse.

⭐Hôtel de la Cité
HISTORIC HOTEL €€€

(Map p760; ☑ 04 68 71 98 71; www.hoteldelacite.fr; place Auguste-Pierre-Pont, Cité Médiévale; d from €250; 🅿🛜🅿) Built in the 19th century in the Gothic Revival style, this is Carcassonne's most magnificent place to stay. Palatial rooms are individually appointed, many with wood panelling and/or timber beams; some have panoramic private terraces. Floor-to-ceiling bookshelves line the private library, which has its own bar, and there's a topiary-flanked swimming pool. Its Michelin-starred restaurant, **La Barbacane** (Map p760; menus €39-85, mains €40-52; ⊙ 12.30-1.45pm & 7.30-9pm), is sublime.

🍴 Eating

Place Marcou in the Cité Médiévale (p759) is hemmed in on three sides by eateries, and throughout the fortified town, every second building seems to be a cafe or restaurant. It's wise to reserve, particularly for lunch. You'll find less-crowded (and better-value) restaurants in the Ville Basse.

Les Halles
MARKET €

(Map p762; place Eggenfelden; ⊙ 7.30am-1.30pm Tue-Sat) Carcassonne's beautiful stone-columned covered market, dating from 1768, sells local wines, cheeses, shellfish and produce.

Carcassonne (Ville Basse)

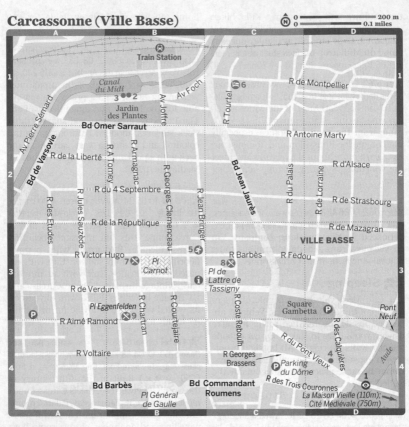

L'Artichaut BISTRO €

(Map p762; ☏09 52 15 65 14; 14 place Carnot; mains €13-20; �) noon-2pm Mon-Wed, noon-2pm & 7-9.30pm Thu-Sat; ☞) This lively local hang-out is full of office workers at lunchtime, so you know you're in good hands. It's great for no-fuss bistro standards, such as roast Camembert, classic *steak-frites* (steak and chips) and tapas platters, along with a few vegetarian options. The location on place Carnot is a winner.

★ **La Table d'Alaïs** FRENCH €€

(Map p760; ☏04 68 71 60 63; www.latabledalais. fr; 32 rue du Plô, Cité Médiévale; menus €20-30, mains €22-25; ☉noon-1.30pm & 7.30-9.30pm Fri-Tue; ☞) Inspired by the market and his region's rich culinary roots, chef Jérémy Thomann has rapidly carved out a grand name for himself at La Table d'Alaïs. The decor is contemporary and the cuisine is a magnificent reworking of local ingredients grown by small producers and farmers. Its desserts and vegetarian menu also get the thumbs up.

★ L'Atelier de Robert Rodriguez
GASTRONOMY €€€

(Map p762; ☑ 04 68 47 37 80; www.restaurant-robertrodriguez.com; 39 rue Coste Reboulh; menus €66-105; ☺ noon-1.30pm & 8-9.30pm Tue-Sat) Robert Rodriguez is an artisan (and character) who works with high-quality, exclusively organic and locally sourced materials. In his *atelier du goût* (taste workshop) with a charmingly old-fashioned decor, he concocts superb traditional Languedoc dishes with a creative twist. His *cassoulet* (rich bean, pork and duck stew) is expensive (€36) but absolutely divine. An original spot. Bookings are essential.

❶ Information

Cité Médiévale Tourist Office (Map p760; ☑ 04 68 10 24 30; www.tourisme-carcassonne.fr; impasse Agnès de Montpellier, Cité Médiévale; ☺ 9.30am-7pm Jul & Aug, 9am-6pm Apr-Jun, Sep & Oct, 9.30am-1pm & 1.30-5.30pm Nov-Mar) In the heart of the **Cité Médiévale** (p759).

Ville Basse Tourist Office (Map p762; ☑ 04 68 10 24 30; www.tourisme-carcassonne.fr; 28 rue de Verdun; ☺ 9am-7pm Jul & Aug, 9am-6pm Mon-Sat, 10am-1pm Sun Apr-Jun, Sep & Oct, 9.30am-12.30pm & 1.30-5.30pm Mon-Sat Nov-Mar) Has plenty of info on Carcassonne and the surrounding region.

❶ Getting There & Around

AIR

Carcassonne Airport (CCF; ☑ 04 68 71 96 46; www.aeroport-carcassonne.com) Situated 5.5km west of town, the airport is used by Ryanair. It serves several UK cities, including London Stansted and Manchester, plus Cork, Dublin, Charleroi and Porto.

The Navette Aéroport (airport shuttle) runs to and from the **airport** (€6, 30 minutes). It only serves arriving and departing flights. It leaves from the **train station** and the **Cité Médiévale** (p759).

TRAIN

Carcassonne's **station** (av Henri Fabre) is on the main line from Toulouse. Buses are geared to school timetables, so it's much easier and quicker to catch a train.

Montpellier €27, 1½ hours, one hourly

Narbonne €11.50, 30 minutes, one hourly

Perpignan €21.20, 1½ hours; change in Narbonne, one hourly

Toulouse €16.50, one hour, up to two hourly

PARC NATIONAL DES CÉVENNES

Dotted with hamlets and cut through by rivers and ravines, this expanse of protected landscape is famous for its biodiversity, with 2300 plant species and 2410 animal species so far recorded. Dry, hot and leafy, the Cévennes has more in common with Mediterranean lands than the Auvergne to its north. It's largely covered by forest, mostly beech, oak and sweet chestnut. Many animals that had disappeared from the area – including vultures, beavers, otters, roe deer and golden eagles – have been reintroduced, either by conservationists or by natural migration. In recognition of its precious natural assets, it's been a Unesco Biosphere Reserve since 1985, and a World Heritage Site since 2011. Needless to say, it's a paradise for nature lovers and outdoorsy types.

In a forested valley, the pretty, peaceful rural village of **Florac** (population 2014) sits at the confluence of three rivers, the Tarnon, Mimente and Tarn. It's the most useful base for exploring the Cévennes and the upper reaches of the Gorges du Tarn. Florac's historical centre, with its narrow streets and elegant stone houses, has charm in spades.

◉ Sights & Activities

In winter there's cross-country skiing on Mont Aigoual and Mont Lozère. Donkey treks are popular in warmer months. There are more than 600km of trails, including 200km of mountain-biking trails and a dozen GR (Grandes Randonnées; hiking) footpaths – most notably, the GR70, also known as the Chemin de Stevenson.

Mont Aigoual Observatory VIEWPOINT
(☑ 04 67 42 59 83; www.aigoual.fr; Valleraugue; ☺ 10am-7pm Jul & Aug, 10am-1pm & 2-6pm May-Jun & Sep) FREE Looming 37km south of Florac off the D18 is the prominent peak of Mont Aigoual (1567m). Its lofty 1894-opened observatory is the last remaining mountain-based meteorological station in France. Inside, you can learn the science behind weather forecasting and cloud formation. There's also an orientation table from where you can take in the wrap-around views of the central Cévennes and beyond. On the very best days, the eye sweeps from the Alps to the Mediterranean and south to the Pyrenees.

Languedoc-Roussillon Architecture

The Languedoc landscape is strewn with spectacular structures that provide a fascinating insight into the region's past.

TRAVELLIGHT/SHUTTERSTOCK ©

During the 2nd century AD, the Languedoc was part of the province of Gallia Narbonensis, a strategically important region of Roman Gaul. As its name suggests, the province's capital was Narbonne, but the most impressive Roman ruins are in Nîmes, including a wonderfully preserved **Roman temple** and a 20,000-seat amphitheatre now known as **Les Arènes** (p739). Just outside the city, the three-tiered Pont du Gard (p745) aqueduct was built to transport water between Uzès and Nîmes, and ranks as one of the great achievements of Roman engineering.

Long after the Romans, the Languedoc remained a strategically important frontier. The legacy of this can be seen in the region's numerous castles and fortified towns – most notably the fortress of **Carcassonne** (p759), with its distinctive 'witch's hat' turrets, and the lonely hilltop castles left behind by the Cathars, an ultra-devout Christian sect persecuted by Rome during the 13th-century Albigensian Crusade.

For much of the medieval era, the neighbouring province of Roussillon was Catalonian rather than French. In 1231, Perpignan became capital of the Kingdom of Mallorca, and it still has a mighty Spanish-style castle, the **Palais des Rois de Majorque** (p775), where the kings and their families lived. A smaller fortress, the **Château Royal** (p781), can be seen in nearby Collioure. Even today, Roussillon still shares strong ties with Catalonia, with *férias* an important part of the festive calendar.

Château Royal (p781), Collioure **2.** Cité Médiévale (p759), Carcassonne **3.** Palais des Rois de Majorque (p775), Perpignan

Mont Lozère MOUNTAIN

The Mont Lozère range is of tough, impenetrable granite, from which the rainfall sluices in small streams. It's the source of the River Tarn, which flows in its early stages through the spectacular Gorges du Tarn. Shrouded in cloud and ice in winter, and bright with bloom in springtime, Mont Lozère is a summertime delight of heather, blueberries and flowing streams. It's crisscrossed by scenic walking trails.

Donkey Trekking

Donkey trekking is a quintessential Cévennes activity – this is Robert Louis Stevenson country, after all. Several local companies situated just outside Florac can provide donkeys and pony rides, either just for the half-day or for longer multiday treks, staying in backcountry *gîtes* (self-catering cottages and villas).

Gentiâne TREKKING

(☑ 04 66 41 04 16; http://ane-et-randonnee.fr; Castagnols; donkey trekking per day €57; ☺ Mar-Nov) Situated 39km east of Florac on the D998, Gentiâne offers donkey trekking on well-marked trails. It also has B&B accommodation (double €70) and camping (free, half-board per person €27).

Tramontane TREKKING

(☑ 04 66 45 92 44, 06 32 56 99 56; chantal.tramontane@wanadoo.fr; St-Martin-de-Lansuscle; donkey trekking per day €50; ☺ Apr-Sep) Tramontane runs donkey treks from its farm 28km southeast of Florac off the D13 in the heart of the Cévennes.

Hiking, Biking & Canyoning

Florac marks the start of numerous walks. The Maison du Tourisme (p767) has plenty of information on trails, most ranging from just a few kilometres up to full-day hikes. Five Grandes Randonnées (GR) trails also cross the Parc National des Cévennes, including GR4, 6, 7, 70 and 700. The IGN Top25 map series covers most of the national park area.

One of the most popular options from Florac is the **Sentier de Gralhon** (7km, 2½ hours), an easy walk that climbs up to the old Gralhon manor and Monteil village before looping back to Florac.

Longer routes take in the nearby peaks, including Mont Lozère (1699m), 14km to the northeast of Florac, the highest peak in the Cévennes.

Cévennes Évasion HIKING

(☑ 04 66 45 18 31; www.cevennes-evasion.com; 6 place Boyer; 3-night hiking or mountain-biking trips from €280; ☺ Apr-Sep) Based in the centre of Florac, Cévennes Évasion runs multiday guided hiking and mountain-biking trips.

Tourisme-Actif OUTDOORS

(☑ 06 83 41 73 08; www.sport-nature-lozere.com; 11 place de l'Esplanade; caving €35-75, canyoning €52-70, via ferrata €35-50; ☺ 10am-6pm Apr-Sep) All equipment is provided on half- and full-day trips organised by this Florac-based adventure company, which can take you on caving, canyoning and via ferrata expeditions of varying levels of difficulty.

WORTH A TRIP

THE CHEMIN DE STEVENSON (GR70)

Famously, the writer Robert Louis Stevenson trekked across the Cévennes in 1878 with his donkey Modestine, a journey recounted in his classic travelogue, *Travels with a Donkey in the Cévennes*.

His route now provides the backbone of the GR70 long-distance trail, which runs for 272km from Le Puy-en-Velay to Alès (slightly longer than Stevenson's original route). It's the Cévennes' most famous walk, and one of the best long-distance routes in France, travelling from the forests of the Cévennes across the Mont Lozère massif into the farmland and valleys of Gévaudan and Velay.

The useful Chemin Stevenson (www.chemin-stevenson.org) and GR70 Stevenson (www.gr70-stevenson.com) websites provide planning information. Free pamphlets and trail maps are widely available once you arrive, or you can rely on the excellent *The Robert Louis Stevenson Trail* guidebook, written by Alan Castle and published by Cicerone.

You don't even need a donkey to carry your baggage these days, as **La Malle Postale** (☑ 04 71 04 21 79, 06 67 79 38 16; www.lamallepostale.com; per luggage item from €8) provides luggage-transfer services.

🛏 Sleeping & Eating

The town of Florac makes the most convenient base. Alternatively, *gîtes* (self-catering cottages and villas) and B&Bs are scattered in and around the Cévennes; the Maison du Tourisme in Florac has a list.

In Florac, restaurants and cafes cluster along rue du Pêcher and av Jean Monestier.

Camping Chantemerle　　CAMPGROUND €
(📞04 66 45 19 66; www.camping-chantemerle. com; Lieu dit la Pontèze, Bédouès; sites for 2 people €20; ☉Apr-Oct; 🅿🛜) Riverside pitches, a private 'beach' and an on-site grocery store, restaurant and bar are highlights of this secluded campground 4.5km northeast of Florac in the village of Bédouès on the banks of the Tarn River. Canoeing, kayak rental and hiking trips can be organised through reception. Also rents chalets (from €400 per week).

La Carline　　HOSTEL €
(📞04 66 45 24 54; www.gite-florac.fr; 18 rue du Pêcher; dm €19, incl breakfast €25; ☉mid-Apr–mid-Sep; 🛜) In an 18th-century house in the centre of Florac, this cute little travellers' *gîte* (self-catering cottage) is run by welcoming hosts Monette and Alain Lagrave. Rooms are colourful and neat, and share bathrooms. There are lots of maps and guidebooks to browse, and Alain makes his own jams for the breakfast table.

La Ferme des Cévennes　　FARMSTAY €
(📞04 66 45 10 90; www.lafermedescevennes. com; La Borie; s €34-43, d €43-55, f €80-95; ☉Apr-Oct; 🅿🛜) 🍴 This large farm boasts an adorable setting on a hillside 5km southeast of Florac. The main building is full of nooks and crannies, and harbours 15 rustic-style rooms of varying sizes and shapes. Organic meals using home-grown produce are available (breakfast/dinner €7/20). Depending on the season, you can milk goats and help make traditional cheese. Great for families.

ℹ Information

Maison du Tourisme (📞04 66 45 01 14; www. cevennes-gorges-du-tarn.com; place de la Gare; ☉9am-12.30pm & 2-6.30pm Mon-Sat, 10am-1pm Sun Jul & Aug, 9am-12.30pm & 2-5pm Mon-Sat Sep-Jun) The Florac-based visitors' centre offers plenty of information on things to see and do inside the park. See www. cevennes-parcnational.fr for more.

ℹ GOURMET CRÊPES & GALETTES

Not your average *crêperie*, Florac's **Au Pêcher Mignon** (📞04 66 45 14 28; 13ter place Louis Dides; crêpes & galettes €10-12; ☉11.30am-2pm & 6.30-9pm Apr-Oct) is renowned for its gourmet crêpes and *galettes* made from what's available on the market. The menu is concise (think two or three items on the chalkboard) but everything's fresh. Tables on the awning-shaded terrace overlook a splashing fountain.

ℹ Getting There & Away

Public transport is very limited in the Cévennes – about the only regular options are the daily (except Sunday) bus that shuttles between Alès and Ispagnac, stopping at Florac en route; and the daily service linking Florac with Mende.

By car, the most spectacular route from the east is the Corniche des Cévennes, a ridge road that winds along the mountain crests of the Cévennes for 56km from St-Jean du Gard to Florac.

If you're approaching Florac from Mende and the north, leave the N106 at Balsièges and drive the much quieter, even prettier D31. This crosses the wild, upland Causse de Sauveterre, then descends to Ispagnac, where you turn left to rejoin the main N106.

Note that petrol stations are few and far between – there are service stations in Florac and Ste-Énimie, but prices here inevitably tend to be high – so it's a good idea to fuel up beforehand.

Mende

POP 12,300

On the northern edge of the Cévennes, Mende is the capital of Lozère, France's least populous *département*. It's a peaceful, rural town with a lovely medieval quarter that would once have been surrounded by defensive walls.

A few half-hidden towers are all that remain of the ramparts, but some interesting medieval buildings still exist. A busy farmers market takes over place Urbain V in front of the **Cathédrale Notre Dame** (place Urbain V; ☉7.30am-6pm) on Saturday morning.

During WWII, Mende (like much of Lozère) was a hotbed of the French Resistance, and local Resistance fighters scored several important victories against the Vichy regime – mainly blowing up railways and disrupting transport links during the run-up

WILDLIFE WATCH

Réserve de Bisons d'Europe (☎04 66 31 40 40; www.bisoneurope.com; Ste-Eulalie-en-Margeride; adult/child horse-drawn carriage €16/9, winter sleigh €19/11, summer walking path €6/4; ⊙10am-5pm Jan-early Nov) Near the small village of Ste-Eulalie-en-Margeride, 45km north of Mende, this vast 200-hectare nature reserve contains more than 30 free-roaming bison. Visits to the reserve are by horse-drawn carriage or, in winter, by sleigh, and last about one hour – an impressive experience. In July and August, you can follow a self-guided 1km walking path around the periphery.

Les Loups du Gévaudan (☎04 66 32 09 22; www.loupsdugevaudan.com; Ste-Lucie; adult/child €9/6, nocturnal visits €12/8; ⊙10am-7pm Jul & Aug, 10am-5.30pm Apr-Jun, Sep & Oct, 10am-5pm Wed, Sat & Sun Nov, Dec & Mar, 10am-5pm Feb, closed Jan) Wolves once prowled freely through the Lozère forests, but today you'll see them only in this sanctuary in Ste-Lucie, 7km north of Marvejols and 36km northeast of Mende off the D809. The 25-hectare park sustains around 80 Mongolian, Canadian, Siberian, Arctic and Polish wolves living in semi-freedom. You can wander around the park or take a free guided tour. Special nocturnal visits are also available in high summer. Feedings take place at 4pm.

to D-Day. Panels around town commemorate several key fighters, including former Mende mayor Henri Bourrillon, the chief of the Lozère Resistance, who was captured in 1944 and died in a Nazi concentration camp.

🛏 Sleeping & Eating

Hôtel de France　　　　　　HOTEL €€
(☎04 66 65 00 04; www.hoteldefrance-mende. com; 9 bd Lucien Arnault; d €98-110; P🅿❄🛜) Clad in shutters and slate, this renovated coaching inn is the best place to stay in Mende, with 38 modern-meets-traditional rooms, all with rustic tiles and some with sweeping views over the garden and valley; three have their own roof terrace. The restaurant (menus €33 to €59) is a fine-dining treat. Covered/uncovered parking costs €7/5.

Le Sanglier　　　　　　　　FRENCH €
(☎04 66 65 12 62; www.restaurant-traiteur-le sanglier.com; 5 av Foch; menus €12-23, mains €11-16; ⊙noon-1.30pm Mon-Sat & 7-9pm Thu-Sat) Freshness and value for money are the hallmarks of this popular eatery near the cathedral (p767). Quintessential dishes include *pavé de bœuf de l'Aubrac* (Aubrac beef) and *saucisse de pays* (local sausage). Small appetite? Opt for a salad. Don't be put off by its modest exterior: it has a beautiful courtyard secreted away out the back.

La Cantine　　　　　　　　BISTRO €€
(☎04 66 32 86 12; http://restaurant-la-cantine. fr; 8 rue St-Privat; menus €16-26; ⊙12.15-1.30pm & 7.30-9.30pm Wed-Sun, noon-1.30pm Tue; 🪑) A daily market-sourced *menu* incorporating local organic ingredients is served on an-

tique crockery at this locals' favourite down a cobbled laneway. Dishes are accompanied by natural wines and *bio* beer. Book ahead.

❶ Information

Tourist Office (☎04 66 94 00 23; www. ot-mende.fr; place du Foirail; ⊙9am-7pm Mon-Sat, 10am-5pm Sun Jul & Aug, 9am-noon & 2-6pm Mon & Wed-Sat Jun & Sep, 9am-noon & 2-6pm Mon-Fri, 9am-noon Sat Oct-May; 🛜) Has free audioguides for city sightseeing walks.

❶ Getting There & Away

BUS

Buses leave from the **train station**. Most pass by place du Foirail, beside the **tourist office**. Timetables change during school holidays.

Clermont-Ferrand €37, 2½ hours, one to three daily

Florac €2, one hour, two to three daily Monday to Saturday, one daily on Sunday in July and August

Le Puy-en-Velay €32, 1¾ hours, one daily

TRAIN

The **train station** (av de la Gare) is 1km north of town across the Lot River.

Alès €20.20, 2½ hours, two daily

Nîmes €28, three hours, one daily

GORGES DU TARN

One of southern France's most inspiring natural sites, the plunging canyons of the Gorges du Tarn wind for some 50km through the high limestone plateaux west from Florac.

Steep cliffs carve through sparkling blue-green waters and limestone escarpments. En route are two villages: medieval Ste-Énimie (a good base for canoeing and walking along the gorges) and La Malène, smaller but equally attractive and with the same opportunities for outdoor fun.

The most spectacular section of the gorges starts at Ste-Énimie, and then winds westwards to Le Rozier, where the River Jonte flows into the Tarn. Motorists and cyclists can take in staggering panoramas from the narrow and twisting cliffside road (expect traffic jams in summer), but piloting your own kayak or canoe is the best way to experience the amazing scenery.

Ste-Énimie

POP 563

Clinging to the cliffside, teeny Ste-Énimie is a charming village with a cobbled quarter full of restored timber houses and stone cottages, along with the 12th-century Église de Ste-Énimie and the old Halle aux Blés (Flour Market).

Situated 27km west of Florac and 56km northeast of Millau, it's the most central base for exploring the Gorges du Tarn. It's a popular starting or finishing point for canoe or kayak explorations of the Tarn. Bear in mind that most activities, accommodation and din-

ing options are only open between April and October.

Should hurling yourself off a 107m-high metal platform attached to a bungee cord float your boat, head 20km southwest to **Le 107** (☑ 06 87 17 12 12; www.le107.com; Le Cirque des Baumes, La Malène; bungee jump €90; ☉ by reservation Thu, Sat & Sun Jul & Aug, Sun Apr-Jun, Sep & Oct). The majestic scenery makes it a spectacular place to take the plunge.

🛌 Sleeping

Many visitors to the Gorges du Tarn decide to camp, and there are plenty of campgrounds to choose from as you travel down the riverside road. Most open from Easter to September. You'll also find a few reliable hotels in Ste-Énimie and Le Rozier. Otherwise, you can base yourself in Florac.

Yelloh Village Camping Nature et Rivière CAMPGROUND €
(☑ 04 66 48 57 36; www.camping-nature-riviere. com; rte des Gorges du Tarn; sites for 2 people for 2 nights €30-38, 4-/6-person chalets for 2 nights from €118; ☉ late Apr-early Sep; P ☏) It's worth paying extra for a riverside site at this small forest campground 3km southwest of Ste-Énimie. Its 57 pitches spread out below beech trees with plenty of space set aside for each site; families also have the option of self-catering timber chalets and cottages. There's a bar, grocery store and laundry service.

DON'T MISS

CANOEING IN THE GORGES DU TARN

Riding the Tarn is best in high summer, when the river is usually low and the descent is a lazy trip over mostly calm water. You can canoe as far as the impassable Pas de Souci, a barrier of boulders about 9km downriver from La Malène. You'll have to arrange for your canoe to be transported beyond the barrier if you want to carry on further.

Tariffs and trip durations depend on how far you want to travel. From Ste-Énimie, destinations include La Malène (from €21, 13km, about four hours) and Cirque des Baumes (from €23, 22km, about six hours). If you want a longer trip, buses can transport you upriver to start in Prades, Montbrun or Ispagnac. Return transport is included in rental prices.

Dozens of companies in Ste-Énimie and La Malène provide canoe and kayak rental from around mid-April to September or October, including **Canoë 2000** (☑ 04 66 48 57 71; www.canoe2000.fr; La Malène; single kayak/2-person canoe rental from €18/34; ☉ Apr-Oct), **Locanoë** (☑ 04 66 48 55 57; www.gorges-du-tarn.fr; Castelbouc; canoe & kayak rental per person from €16; ☉ mid-Apr–late Sep), **Canoë Méjean** (☑ 04 66 48 58 70; www.canoe-mejean.com; rte des Gorges du Tarn; canoe & kayak rental from €15; ☉ 9am-6.30pm May-Sep) and **Le Canophile** (☑ 04 66 48 57 60; www.canoe-tarn.com; rte de Florac; canoe & kayak rental per person from €15; ☉ daily Jul & Aug, Sat & Sun May, Jun & Sep). Most operators also offer stand-up paddleboarding.

If you'd rather someone else did the hard work, let **Les Bateliers de la Malène** (☑ 04 66 48 51 10; www.gorgesdutarn.com; La Malène; per 4 people €92; ☉ 9am-noon & 1.30-5pm Apr-Oct) punt you down an 8km stretch of the gorge in a traditional barge.

OCCITAN

The Languedoc's distinctive language of Occitan is an ancient tongue that is closely related to Catalan. The *langue d'oc* was once widely spoken across most of southern France, while the *langue d'oïl* was the predominant language spoken in the north (the words *oc* and *oïl* meant 'yes' in their respective languages).

Occitan reached its zenith during the 12th century, but it was dealt a blow when Languedoc was annexed by the French kingdom. *Langue d'oïl* became the realm's official language, effectively relegating Occitan to the status of a language spoken only by the poor and uneducated.

Despite the best efforts of the ruling elite to wipe it out, Occitan survived as a distinct language, largely thanks to rural communities keen to hold on to their own regional identity. It enjoyed a literary revival in the 19th century, spearheaded by the poet Frédéric Mistral, who wrote in Occitan's Provençal dialect.

Today Occitan is still widely spoken across southern France, with an estimated 610,000 native speakers and around a million others who have a basic working knowledge. There are six officially recognised dialects: Languedocien *(lengadocian)*, Limousin *(lemosin)*, Auvergnat *(auvernhat)*, Provençal *(provençau)*, Vivaro-Alpine *(vivaroaupenc)* and Gascon *(gascon)*; the latter includes the Aranese sub-dialect spoken in parts of Spanish Catalonia.

L'Auberge du Moulin
HOTEL €

(☑ 04 66 48 53 08; www.aubergedumoulin48.com; rue de la Combe; d €67-95; ⊙ Apr–mid-Nov; P ✱ ☎) This solid, reliable hotel has three-star comforts, a professional and welcoming staff, and an excellent on-site restaurant (*menus* from €15) serving regional fare. Rooms are modern, neat and fresh; rooms 5 to 8 have a private terrace with great valley views.

★ La Maison de Marius
B&B €€

(☑ 04 66 44 25 05; www.maisondemarius.fr; 14 rue Marie et Raymond Martin, Quézac; d €70-120, f €160; ⊙ Apr–Oct; P ☎) In Quézac, 17km east of Ste-Énimie, this cosy place is a proper home away from home. Owner Dany has individually decorated the countrified bedrooms with floral fabrics, watercolours, old luggage and roll-top baths – the Pompeii Suite even has its own jacuzzi, complete with Roman murals. Your hostess also offers *table d'hôte* dinners (€25) with local, seasonal products.

✕ Eating

Le Bel Été
FRENCH €

(☑ 04 66 45 20 75; rue Basse; menus €15-20, mains €12-17; ⊙ noon-1.30pm & 7-8.30pm Tue-Sun Apr-Oct) Sweet and simple, this spot lures diners with its friendly service and tempting menu specialising in regional dishes. Try the *patate lozérienne* (potato gratin with your choice of accompaniment) or grilled sausage. Prices are surprisingly reasonable given the quality of the food. Its shady terrace is a plus.

Aux Petits Galets
FRENCH €

(☑ 09 82 37 70 57; rue du Front du Tarn; menus €16-20, mains €13-18; ⊙ noon-1.45pm & 7-9pm Fri-Wed, 7-9pm Thu Apr-Oct) Forget about presentation and manners; here, it's all about taste. All dishes incorporate locally sourced produce. Highlights include Aubrac beef steak with homemade fries, meal-sized salads and smoked trout.

L'Eden
INTERNATIONAL €

(☑ 04 66 45 66 71; www.eden-bar-restaurant.com; St-Chély-du-Tarn; menus €15-19, mains €8-18; ⊙ noon-10pm Jul & Aug, to 8.30pm Thu-Sun Apr-Jun & Sep) Live music (mainly rock) plays most nights either indoors or on the terrace-facing outdoor stage at this lively bar-restaurant overlooking the Tarn River. It specialises in pizzas (12 kinds), but also dishes up pastas and salads. It's 4.5km southwest of Ste-Énimie.

❶ Information

Tourist office (☑ 04 66 48 53 44; www.cevennes-gorges-du-tarn.com; rte de Mende; ⊙ 9.15am-12.15pm & 2-6pm Mon-Sat, 9am-1pm Sun Jul & Aug, 10am-12.15pm & 2-5pm Tue-Sat Apr-Jun & Sep, closed Oct-Mar) Has info on the Gorges du Tarn.

❶ Getting There & Around

Your own wheels are the best way to explore the gorges. In July and August, there are three daily shuttles between Florac, Ste-Énimie and Le Rozier (€2).

GRANDS CAUSSES

The Grands Causses are part of the same geological formation as the Massif Central to the north. Scorched in summer and windswept in winter, these harsh plateaux hold little moisture, as water filters through the limestone to form an underground world that's ideal for cavers.

The rivers Tarn, Jonte and Dourbie have sliced deep gorges through the 5000-sq-km plateau, creating four *causses* ('plateaux' in the local lingo): Sauveterre, Méjean, Noir and Larzac, each slightly different in geological make-up. All are eerily empty, save for the occasional shepherd and flock, making them perfect for hikers and bikers who like nothing better than to go hours without seeing another soul on the trail.

The wild Gorges de la Jonte are home to a variety of birds of prey that wheel and swoop.

◉ Sights & Activities

The small town of Millau (p772) is the key launch pad for exploring these wild, eerie, adventure-giving plateaux.

Causse de Sauveterre

The northernmost of the *causses* is a gentle, hilly plateau dotted with a few isolated farms and traversed by hiking trails. Every possible patch of fertile earth is cultivated, creating irregular, intricately patterned wheat fields.

Causse Méjean

Causse Méjean, the highest of the *causses*, is also the most barren and isolated. Defined to the north by the Gorges du Tarn and to the south by the Gorges de la Jonte, it looms over Florac, on its eastern flank. It's a land of poor pasture enriched by fertile depressions, where streams gurgle down into the limestone through sinkholes, funnels and fissures.

This combination of water and limestone has created some spectacular underground scenery, particularly at Aven Armand.

★ **Aven Armand**   CAVE
(☑ 04 66 45 61 31; www.aven-armand.com; Hures-la-Parade, Causse Méjean; adult/child €12.50/8.30, combination ticket with Chaos de Montpellier-le-Vieux €17/12.50; ⊙ 9.30am-6pm Jul & Aug, 10am-noon & 1.30-5pm late Mar-Jun & Sep-early Nov) Within the cavern of Aven Armand is the world's greatest concentration of stalagmites, including a gallery of stone columns known as the Forêt Vierge (Virgin Forest). Colourful illuminations create an eerie atmosphere. The cave is accessed via a funicular that drops 60m into the gloom. Guided visits last about one hour. Combination tickets with the Chaos de Montpellier-le-Vieux canyons at Causse Noir are available.

Causse Noir

Rising immediately east of Millau, the Black Causse is best known for the Chaos de Montpellier-le-Vieux.

Chaos de Montpellier-le-Vieux   GORGE
(☑ 05 65 60 66 30; www.montpellierlevieux.com; Le Maubert; adult/child €7/4.90, combination ticket with Aven Armand €17/12.50, tourist train €4.40/3.70; ⊙ 9.30am-6.20pm Jul & Aug, 9.30am-5pm late Mar-Jun & Sep-early Nov) Situated 18km northeast of Millau, overlooking the Gorges de la Dourbie, this maze of canyons was formed by countless millennia of water erosion, which has created more than 120 hectares of tortured limestone formations with fanciful names such as the Sphinx and the Elephant. Five walking trails, lasting one to three hours, cover the site – or you can take a trip aboard the tourist train. There is also ziplining for children (€16) and via ferrata (€32).

Combination tickets with Aven Armand at Causse Méjean are available.

Causse du Larzac

The Causse du Larzac is the largest of the four *causses*. An endless sweep of distant horizons and rocky steppes broken up by medieval villages, it's known as the 'French Desert'.

You'll stumble across venerable fortified villages such as Ste-Eulalie de Cernon, long the capital of the Larzac region, and La Cavalerie. Both were built by the Knights Templar, a religious military order that distinguished itself during the Crusades.

Gorges de la Jonte

The spectacular 20km-long Gorges de la Jonte cleave east–west from Meyrueis to Le Rozier, dividing Causse Noir from Causse Méjean. They're much more lightly trafficked – though busy enough in summer – than the more famous Gorges du Tarn.

Grotte de Dargilan   CAVE
(☑ 04 66 45 60 20; www.grotte-dargilan.com; Dargilan; adult/child €11.50/7.50; ⊙ 10.15am-6pm Jul & Aug, 10.30am-5pm Apr-Jun & Sep, 2-4pm Oct) Just south of the Gorges de la Jonte, Grotte de Dargilan is known as La Grotte Rose (Pink Cave) for its rosy colouring. The most memorable moment of the one-hour, 1km

FAMILY FAVOURITES

Train à Vapeur des Cévennes (☑ 04 66 60 59 00; www.trainavapeur.com; Anduze; adult/child/bike return €16/12/3; ☉ Apr-Oct) Chugging along a 13km stretch of track between St-Jean du Gard and Anduze (15km southwest of Alès), this fabulous steam train follows an old line through the Gardon Valley that was in operation between 1909 and 1971. Restored by enthusiasts, the ride (40 minutes one way) traverses several arched viaducts and subterranean tunnels, including the 833m-long Tunnel d'Anduze.

Micropolis (La Cité des Insectes; ☑ 05 65 58 50 50; www.micropolis-aveyron.com; Le Bourg, St-Léons; adult/child €14.90/10; ☉ 10am-7pm Jul & Aug, to 6pm Apr-Jun, to 5pm Wed-Sun mid-Feb–Mar, Sep & Oct; ⛟) Creepy-crawly-loving kids can indulge their interests at the excellent 'Insect City' of Micropolis, 19km northwest of Millau. This high-tech centre brings the world of insects impressively to life: you can peer inside ant colonies, see the inner workings of beehives and explore the wonderful butterfly pavilion. There are also multimedia exhibits and interactive displays. Afterwards kids can burn off steam at the insect-themed adventure playground while adults unwind in the cafe.

tour through this vast chasm with plenty of stalagmites and stalactites is a sudden, dazzling exit onto a ledge, with a dizzying view of the gorge way below.

Maison des Vautours　　MUSEUM, VIEWPOINT
(☑ 05 65 62 69 69; www.vautours-lozere.com; Le Truel; adult/child €6.80/3; ☉ 9.30am-6.30pm Jul & Aug, 9.30am-5pm Tue-Sun Apr-Jun, Sep & Oct) Birdwatchers won't want to miss the Maison des Vautours, just west of Le Truel on the D996, where a population of more than 200 reintroduced vultures now thrives on the sheer limestone cliffs. You can watch the birds gliding above the Gorges de la Jonte from the viewing point, which also has a live video feed from the nesting sites. Inside the museum, you'll find various exhibitions about the five vulture species that can be found in the area.

Millau

POP 22,000

Famous within France for glove-making, Millau (pronounced *mee-yo*) squeezes between the Grands Causses' Causse Noir and Causse du Larzac at the confluence of the Tarn and Dourbie rivers. The town is an ideal jumping-off point for hiking and adventure sport – particularly hang-gliding and paragliding, which exploit the uplifting thermals.

◉ Sights & Activities

Activities abound around the Grands Causses, with hang-gliding, paragliding, rock climbing, walking and cycling opportunities all accessible from Millau.

The high cliffs of the Gorges de la Jonte (p771) are an internationally renowned venue for climbers. Rock climbing, along with canyoning, via ferrata and caving are among the adventure activities offered by both **Horizon** (☑ 05 65 59 78 60; www.horizon-millau.com; 6 place Lucien Grégoire; rock climbing/canyoning/via ferrata/caving from €150/45/45/33, tandem paragliding from €60; ☉ office hours 9.30am-7pm Jul & Aug, to noon Sep-Jun) and **Roc et Canyon** (☑ 05 65 61 17 77; www.roc-et-canyon.com; 55 av Jean Jaurès; rock climbing/canyoning/via ferrata/rafting/caving from €30/40/34/34/32; ☉ 9am-7pm Jul & Aug, 10am-5pm Sep-Jun).

★ **Aire du Viaduc de Millau**　　BRIDGE
(☑ 05 65 61 61 54; www.leviaducdemillau.com; A75, Millau; guided tour adult/child €4.50/2.50; ☉ visitors centre 9am-7.30pm Jul & Aug, 9.30am-6.30pm Apr-Jun, Sep & Oct, 10am-5pm Nov-Mar) **FREE** The gravity-defying Viaduc de Millau toll bridge hovers 343m above the Tarn valley, making it one of the world's highest road bridges. At its northern end (in Brocuéjouls, about 5km west of the centre of Millau), the **Viaduc Expo** visitor centre explores the story of the bridge's construction and offers 45-minute guided visits (in English on request). There's an upmarket cafeteria and you can walk to a viewpoint to truly appreciate the bridge's astonishing dimensions.

Designed by British architect Sir Norman Foster and opened in 2004, the bridge is a work of imagination as much as engineering: seven slender pylons support 2.5km of the A75 motorway, and despite its heavyweight construction (127,000 cu metres of concrete, 19,000 tonnes of steel, 5000 tonnes of cable), the bridge looks as delicate as a gossamer thread.

Beffroi de Millau   TOWER
(☑ 05 65 59 01 08; 16 rue Droite; adult/child €3.70/ free; ☺ 10am-noon & 2-6pm Jul & Aug, 10am-noon & 2.30-6pm Fri-Wed May, Jun & Sep) The defining landmark of Millau's historical centre is this medieval 12th-century-built square tower topped by an octagonal 17th-century bell tower. It's a 210-step climb to the top for panoramic views of the town, surrounding countryside and, on a clear day, the monumental Viaduc de Millau.

Duverbike   MOUNTAIN BIKING
(☑ 06 23 63 88 66; www.duverbike.com; av de Millau Plage; mountain-bike rental per half-/full day €16/25, guided mountain-bike tours per half-/full day €35/55, mountain-bike-park entry per 1/3hr €4/7; ☺ 10am-8pm Jul & Aug, to 6pm Sep-Jun) Duverbike not only rents out mountain bikes but also offers guided mountain-bike tours and has its own 5000-sq-metre mountain-

bike park with hollows, double bumps, gaps, berms, wall rides and aerial ramps (with a foam pit below).

🛏 Sleeping & Eating

★ Château de Creissels   HOTEL €€
(☑ 05 65 60 16 59; www.chateau-de-creissels.com; place du Prieur, Creissels; d €94-142, ste €143-168; ☺ early Mar-late Dec; P❄🅿📶🐾) In Creissels, 2km southwest of Millau on the D992, this castle's rooms are split between the 12th-century tower (parquet floors, fireplaces, oil paintings) and modern wings (sleek showers, stripped-wood floors, designer lamps; some with balconies overlooking the large garden). Excellent regional cuisine (*menus* from €28) is served in the restaurant's brick-vaulted cellar and on the panoramic terrace.

La Mangeoire   FRENCH €€
(☑ 05 65 60 13 16; www.restaurantmillau.com; 10 bd de la Capelle; menus €17-38, mains €17-26; ☺ noon-1.30pm & 7-9.30pm Tue-Sun; ✍) Fronted

LANGUEDOC-ROUSSILLON MILLAU

WORTH A TRIP

ROQUEFORT

The village of Roquefort (full name Roquefort-sur-Soulzon) is synonymous with its famous blue cheese, produced from ewe's milk in nearby caves. Even if you're not a foodie, it's well worth the trip, if only for its lovely setting at the foot of a majestic limestone plateau.

There are seven Appellation d'Origine Protégée–approved producers in Roquefort, three of which (Gabriel Coulet, Papillon and Roquefort Société) offer cellar visits. The cellars of the four other producers aren't open to the public, but they all have shops where you can sample and buy cheeses.

Marbled with blue-green veins caused by microscopic fungi known as *Penicillium roqueforti* (which are initially grown on leavened bread), pungent Roquefort is one of the region's oldest cheeses. In 1407 Charles VI granted exclusive Roquefort cheesemaking rights to the villagers, and in the 17th century the Sovereign Court of the Parliament of Toulouse imposed severe penalties on cheesemakers fraudulently trading under the Roquefort name. Roquefort was the first cheese in France to be granted its own Appellation d'Origine Contrôlée (AOC) – in 1925 – which became Appellation d'Origine Protégée (AOP) in 1996.

As the cheeses are ripened in natural caves, enlarged and gouged from the mountainside, draughts of air called *fleurines* flow through, encouraging the blue *Penicillium roqueforti* to eat their way through the white cheese curds.

Legend claims the cheese was discovered by accident, when a local lad became distracted by a beautiful girl and left a wheel of cheese behind in one of the village caves. When he returned, it was covered in mould that turned out to be surprisingly tasty. It's now France's second-most-popular cheese after Comté, with an annual production of around 19,000 tonnes.

The **tourist office** (☑ 05 65 58 56 00; www.roquefort-tourisme.fr; av de Lauras; ☺ 9.30am-6.30pm Mon-Sat, 11am-6pm Sun Jul & Aug, 9.30am-12.15pm & 1-5.30pm Mon-Sat Sep, Oct & Apr-Jun, 9.30am-12.15pm & 1-5pm Mon-Fri Nov-Mar) has free cheese tastings and information on the town's cellars. We reccommend **Roquefort Société** (☑ 05 65 58 54 38; www.roquefort-societe.com; 2 av François Galtier; adult/child €6/4; ☺ 10am-noon & 1.30-5pm Apr-Oct, 10am-noon & 1.30-4.30pm Nov-Mar) – the largest producer of Roquefort – who run one-hour tours of the caves, including sampling the company's three main varieties.

CATHAR CASTLES

Dotted across the parched plains of Languedoc are many castles left behind by the Cathars, an ultra-devout Christian sect who were persecuted during the 12th century and eventually crushed by the forces of Pope Innocent III during the Albigensian Crusade.

Perched on rocky outcrops surrounded by orange scrubland, the castles are hugely atmospheric, but many are fast crumbling into dust. They can be explored on a long day's drive from Perpignan or Carcassonne – but pack plenty of water and a hat, as temperatures soar out here in summer.

Château de Peyrepertuse (☑ 04 30 37 00 77; www.chateau-peyrepertuse.com; Duilhac-sous-Peyrepertuse; adult/child €7/4; ☺9am-8pm Jul & Aug, 9am-7pm Apr-Jun & Sep, 10am-6pm Mar & Oct, 10am-4.30pm rest of year) is the largest of the Cathar castles; it's 51km northwest of Perpignan via the D117. Also well worth visiting is **Château de Quéribus** (☑ 04 68 45 03 69; www.cucugnan.fr; Cucugnan; adult/child €7/4; ☺9am-8pm Jul & Aug, 9.30am-7pm May, Jun & Sep, 10am-6pm Apr & Oct, 10am-5pm Nov-Mar), perched 728m up on a rocky hill. It's 42km northwest of Perpignan via the D117. In the same area, 63km northwest of Perpignan via the same D117, turreted **Château de Puilaurens** (☑ 04 68 20 65 26; www.chateau-puilaurens.com; Lapradelle; adult/child €6/3; ☺9am-7pm Jul & Aug, 10am-6pm May, Jun & Sep, 10am-5pm Apr & Oct–mid-Nov) is perhaps the most dramatic of the Cathar fortresses. The smallest of the Cathar castles is **Château d'Aguilar** (☑ 04 68 45 51 00; www.tuchan.fr; Tuchan; adult/child €4/2; ☺10am-7pm Jul & Aug, 10.30am-5.30pm May, Jun & Sep, 11am-5pm Apr & Oct, 11am-4pm Feb & Mar), 35km northwest of Perpignan via the D12.

If you're crossing into the Pyrenees, it's also worth making the trip to the Château de Montségur (p715), another classic (and important) Cathar stronghold.

The *Passeport des Sites du Pays Cathare* (€4) gives a €1 reduction off the admission fee at 21 local sites, including Château d'Aguilar, Château de Peyrepertuse, Château de Quéribus and Château de Puilaurens. Pick it up at any of the 21 sites. No public transport serves the castles, so you'll need your own wheels.

by a shady pavement terrace strung with fairy lights and opening to a romantic vaulted-stone dining room, Millau's best restaurant refines the rich flavours of the region: wood-fire-grilled Trénels sheep-stomach sausage with *aligot* (mashed potato and melted sheep's cheese); Aubrac beef ribs with Roquefort sauce; and spicy spit-roasted local hare (in winter). There's also a vegetarian *menu* (€24).

ⓘ Information

Millau's **tourist office** (☑ 05 65 60 02 42; www.millau-viaduc-tourisme.fr; 1 rue du Beffroi; ☺9am-12.30pm & 2-5.30pm Mon-Sat, 10am-4pm Sun Apr-Sep, 9.30am-12.30pm & 2-5.30pm Mon-Sat Oct-Mar) provides maps and information on hiking, cycling and adventure activities around the Grands Causses.

ⓘ Getting There & Around

Your own wheels (or feet) are the best way to get around. Buses serve the area, but schedules can be erratic, especially outside high summer – contact the **tourist office** in Millau for information.

Most **train** (rue de Belfort) services to/from Millau have been replaced by SNCF coaches. One remaining useful service is the one between Millau and Clermont-Ferrand (€20.50, 4½ hours, once daily).

ROUSSILLON

Dusty scrubland, crimson towns and scorching summer temperatures give Roussillon a distinctly Spanish flavour. Also known as French Catalonia, it incorporates busy beach towns and coastal villages along the Mediterranean as well as the abandoned abbeys and crumbling Cathar strongholds inland among the fragrant maquis. West of Perpignan, Roussillon's only city, the Tech Valley and the Têt Valley offer a heady mix of picturesque villages and stunning mountainscapes.

History

Roussillon's history is inextricably linked with Spain's. After flourishing as the capital of the kingdom of Mallorca, it fell under Aragonese rule for much of the late Middle Ages.

In 1640 the Catalans on both sides of the Pyrenees revolted against the rule of distant Madrid. Peace came in 1659 with the Treaty of the Pyrenees, defining the border between Spain and France once and for all and ceding Roussillon (until then the northern section of Catalonia) to the French, much to the indignation of the locals.

Although it's no longer officially part of Catalonia, Roussillon retains much of its Catalan identity. The *sardane* folk dance is still performed, and the Catalan language, closely related to Provençal, is still commonly spoken.

Perpignan

POP 123,000

Framed by the peaks of the Pyrenees, Perpignan radiates out from the tight knot of the old town's warren of alleys, palm-shaded squares and shabby tenements painted in shades of lemon, peach and tangerine.

Historically, Perpignan (Perpinyà in Catalan) was capital of the kingdom of Mallorca, a Mediterranean power that stretched northwards as far as Montpellier and included all the Balearic Islands. The Mallorcan kings' palace still stands guard at the southern end of the old town.

Perpignan is 13km west of the Mediterranean coastline and 38km north of the border with Spain; this proximity means the town is strong on fiestas.

◉ Sights

Perpignan's old town is roughly contained within the main ring roads of bd des Pyrénées in the west, bd Thomas Wilson in the north, bd Anatole France in the east and bd Henri Poincaré in the south. Its shallow canal skirts its western edge.

★ Palais des Rois de Majorque   PALACE

(☑ 04 68 34 96 26; www.ledepartement66.fr/99-palais-des-rois-de-majorque.htm; 4 rue des Archers; adult/child €4/2; ☉ 10am-6pm Jun-Sep, 9am-5pm Oct-May) Perpignan's most dominant monument, the Palace of the Kings of Mallorca sprawls over a huge area to the south of the old town. Built in 1276, the castle was later refortified with massive red-brick walls by Louis XIV's military engineer, Vauban. These days the star-shaped citadel is sparsely furnished, but its great battlements and strategic defences still give a sense of the Mallorcan kings' might. Views from the ramparts stretch over Perpignan's terracotta rooftops to the coast.

Musée d'Art Hyacinthe Rigaud   MUSEUM

(☑ 04 68 66 19 83; www.musee-rigaud.fr; 21 rue Mailly; adult €8-10, child free; ☉ 10.30am-7pm Jun-Sep, 11am-4.30pm Tue-Sun Oct-May) Occupying two elegant *hôtels particuliers* (private mansions) right in the historical centre, this museum was entirely renovated in 2017 and now ranks as the city's leading cultural institution. The galleries are split into three main sections: Gothic Perpignan, Baroque Perpignan and Modern Perpignan. Highlights include portraits by Perpignan-born painter Hyacinthe Rigaud (1659–1743) as well as paintings and carvings by Banyuls-sur-Mer–born Aristide Maillol (1861–1944).

Cathédrale St-Jean   CATHEDRAL

(place Gambetta; ☉ 7.30am-6pm) Perpignan's old town has several intriguing churches, but the most impressive is the Cathédrale St-Jean, begun in 1324 and not completed until 1509. Topped by a Provençal wrought-iron bell cage, the cathedral has a flat façade of red brick and smooth, zigzagging river stones.

Inside, the fine carving and ornate altarpiece are characteristically Catalan, and the simple statue of the Virgin and child in the north aisle is a venerated relic. Adjacent to the cathedral is a lovely cloister.

🛏 Sleeping

Auberge de Jeunesse   HOSTEL €

(☑ 04 68 34 63 32; www.hifrance.org/auberge-de-jeunesse/perpignan.html; 3 allée Marc Pierre; dm/tw/q incl breakfast €21/43/80; ☉ reception 8-11am & 5-9pm mid-Apr–mid-Oct, hostel closed mid-Oct–mid-Apr; ⓟ 🛜) Perpignan's modern, well-run HI-affiliated hostel has a handy location just north of Parc de la Pépinière, 300m west of the bus station (p778). The single-sex dorms are spartan but well kept; private rooms have showers (but do not have toilets) and there's a self-catering kitchen.

Campanile Perpignan Centre   HOTEL €€

(☑ 04 68 61 42 10; www.campanile.com; 18 bd Jean Bourrat; d €69-75; ⓟ ✳ 🛜) Fresh from a comprehensive refurb, this brilliantly located venture now rates as one of Perpignan's top choices. Its rooms are bright, modern and well equipped, and bathrooms are shiny-clean. There's private parking (€15).

Perpignan

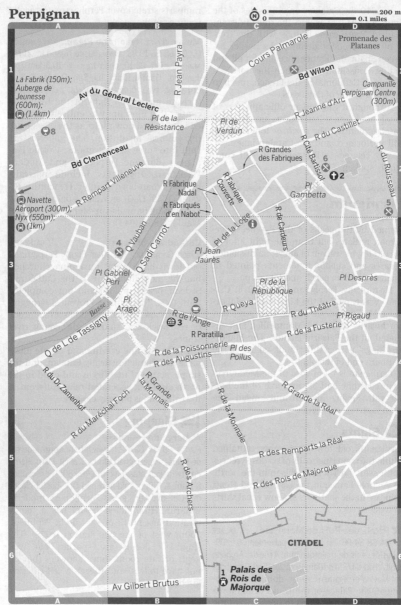

Nyx   HOTEL €€
(☏ 04 68 34 87 48; www.nyxhotel.fr; 62bis av Général de Gaulle; s/d/tr from €83/92/102; P ❄ 🛜) About 500m east of the train station and a 10-minute stroll to the historical centre, this well-managed hotel shelters 17 small but comfortable rooms featuring iridescent fabrics, and themed around the sun, moon, day and night. Two have huge 20-sq-metre terraces; one includes an in-room jacuzzi. Breakfast (€10) includes bacon and eggs and homemade jam.

Perpignan

✗ Eating

★ Halles Vauban   MARKET €
(www.facebook.com/hallesvauban; 37-39 quai
Vauban; mains from €9; ⊗ 9am-8pm Tue & Wed, 8am-
11pm Fri & Sat, 8am-3pm Sun) If only every market was like this. Renovated and now a temple
to fresh local produce, this is the kind of place
where you pop in for a pastry and emerge an
hour later with charcuterie, ripe fruit, desserts
and five different sorts of cheese. Plenty of
stalls sell excellent food, from soups and salads to sushi and grilled fish.

Torcatis en Ville   BURGERS €
(⌨ 06 47 53 59 13; www.facebook.com/torcatisen
ville; allées Maillol, bd Wilson; mains €13; ⊗ noon-
2pm & 7-9pm Tue-Sat) Elevating the humble
burger to high art, this inviting fixed food
truck serves up lusty, made-from-scratch
burgers that come in many variations. The
vegetarian option is tops, especially when
paired with homemade fries and caramelised onions.

Le St-Jean   FRENCH €€
(⌨ 04 68 51 22 25; www.lesaint-jean.com; 1 rue Cité
Bartissol; menus €19-32, mains €22-32; ⊗ noon-
2.30pm Mon & Tue, noon-2.30pm & 7-10.30pm
Wed-Sat) Atmospherically set in the shadow
of its namesake cathedral and opening to a
charming magnolia-shaded cobbled courtyard, Le St-Jean is one of Perpignan's top addresses for inventive French fare. The beef
medallion in Banyuls sauce will linger long
on the palate. The lunch menu (€19) is particularly good value.

Le 17   SEAFOOD €€
(⌨ 04 68 38 56 82; www.restaurant-le17-perpignan.
fr; 17 rue de la Révolution Française; menus €16-23,

mains €16-23; ⊗ noon-2pm & 7.30-9.30pm Tue-Sat
May-Sep, noon-2pm Mon-Wed, noon-2pm & 7.30-
9.30pm Thu-Sat Oct-Apr) The fish practically
flop from the market straight into the pleasantly furnished Le 17 restaurant tucked into
the heart of Perpignan's old town. There is
an agreeable pavement terrace. Service here
is attentive and helpful when it comes to
wine recommendations.

▼ Drinking & Nightlife

Cafes and bars cluster on and around place
de la République and on both banks of
the canal. Av du Général Leclerc has a dynamic drinking and nightlife scene. Halles
Vauban is also hugely popular, with plenty
of congenial bars that attract an eclectic
crowd.

La Cafetière   COFFEE
(⌨ 04 68 51 82 65; www.lacafetiere66.com; 17 rue
de l'Ange; ⊗ 1-7pm Mon, 8am-7pm Tue-Sat) The
aroma of freshly ground coffee wafts from
this wonderful roastery, which sells beans
to take away and brews fantastic espres-
sos to drink at its counter or on the trio
of cherry-red pavement tables. Loose-leaf
teas are also a speciality, along with gourmet chocolates.

Ben Aqui   BAR
(⌨ 04 68 34 79 57; www.facebook.com/acoteduben
aqui; 33 av du Maréchal Leclerc; ⊗ tapas 7-11pm, bar
7pm-2am) It might not look much from the
outside but trust us: Ben Aqui is a wonderful and soulful place to have some great local
tipples (from €3) and excellent traditional
tapas (from €5) in a lively atmosphere.

La Fabrik   BAR
(⌨ 04 68 64 24 04; www.lafabrik66.com; 53 av
du Général Leclerc; ⊗ 11.45am-midnight Mon-
Fri, 5pm-2am Sat) Local Roussillon wines,
French and Spanish beers, rum cocktails
and classic Spanish tapas are served inside this cavernous bar and restaurant
with gorgeous tiled floors, and on its glass-
screened, umbrella-shaded pavement terrace, which overflows with revellers on
warm evenings.

ⓘ Information

Tourist office (⌨ 04 68 66 30 30; www.
perpignantourisme.com; place de la Loge;
⊗ 9.30am-7pm Mon-Sat, 10am-4pm Sun
Jun-Sep, 9am-6pm Mon-Sat, 10am-1pm Sun
Oct-May) Just west of the historical centre
atop a covered section of the canal.

WORTH A TRIP

A DATE WITH PREHISTORY

The cave-riddled cliffs above Tautavel, 34km northwest of Perpignan along the D117, have yielded a host of prehistoric finds, most notably a human skull unearthed in the Arago Cave that's estimated to be 450,000 years old (one of Europe's oldest such discoveries). The fascinating **Musée de Préhistoire de Tautavel** (Tautavel Prehistory Museum; ☑ 04 68 29 07 76; www.450000ans.com; av Léon Jean Grégory, Tautavel; adult/child €8/4; ☉ 10am-7pm Jul & Aug, 10am-12.30pm & 2-6pm Sep-Jun) here delves into the area's prehistoric past, with a full-size cave reproduction, displays of fossilised bones and tools, and multimedia exhibits.

There's no public transport, so you'll need your own wheels.

❶ Getting There & Away

AIR
Perpignan's **airport** (PGF; ☑ 04 68 52 60 70; www.aeroport-perpignan.com; av Maurice Bellonte) is 5km northwest of the town centre. Destinations include London Stansted, Birmingham, Charleroi (Ryanair); Southampton (Flybe); Dublin (Aer Lingus); Paris, Bastia and Lille (Air France); and Nantes (Volotea).

The **Navette Aéroport** (Airport Shuttle; one way €1.30) bus 7 links the airport with place de Catalogne on the northwestern edge of the old town (20 minutes, every 30 minutes Monday to Saturday, three services Sunday).

BUS
Buses anywhere in the Pyrénées-Orientales *département* cost a flat-rate €1. Perpignan's **bus station** (☑ 04 68 80 80 80; bd St-Assiscle) is next to the **train station** (bd St-Assiscle).

Côte Vermeille (hourly Monday to Saturday, one on Sunday) Bus 400 trundles to Collioure (50 minutes), Port-Vendres (65 minutes) and Banyuls-sur-Mer (80 minutes).

Tech Valley (hourly Monday to Saturday, up to three on Sunday) Buses 300/341/342 run regularly to Céret (35 minutes).

Têt Valley (every two hours Monday to Saturday) Regular buses to Villefranche-de-Conflent (1¼ hours) and Vernet-les-Bains (1½ hours); buses are numbered 240/241.

TRAIN
Frequent direct **trains** serve destinations in France and across the border in Spain.

Banyuls-sur-Mer €7.70, 30 minutes
Barcelona from €37, 1½ hours
Collioure €6.10, 20 minutes
Montpellier €27.20, 1¾ hours
Narbonne €15.50, one hour
Paris Gare de Lyon from €86, 5½ hours
Villefranche-de-Conflent €1, 50 minutes

Céret
POP 7885

Tucked in the Pyrenean foothills just off the Tech Valley, the charming little town of Céret conceals an unexpected surprise – one of southern France's best modern art museums, with a collection of stellar canvases donated by some of the 20th century's foremost names in movements from cubism to neorealism.

Lively festivals also take place in the town in spring and summer.

◉ Sights

★ **Musée d'Art Moderne**   GALLERY
(☑ 04 68 87 31 92; www.musee-ceret.com; 8 bd Maréchal Joffre; adult/child €5.50/3.50; ☉10am-7pm Jul-Sep, to 5pm Tue-Sun Oct-Jun) Roussillon had its artistic heyday around the turn of the 20th century, when Fauvist and cubist artists flocked here, attracted by the searing colours and sun-drenched landscapes. This wonderful museum was created in 1950 by Pierre Brune and Frank Burty Haviland, who convinced friends including Picasso, Matisse, Chaïm Soutine and Georges Braque to donate works. The result is one of the finest collections of modern art outside Paris. Take your time – this place is a real treat.

Céret's artistic connections stretch back to 1910, when Catalan sculptor Manolo Hugué, painter Frank Burty Haviland and composer Déodat de Séverac settled here. They were followed in 1911 by Pablo Picasso and Georges Braque, along with other significant figures from the cubist and Fauvist movements, mostly escaping the spiralling rents and stifling atmosphere of the Montmartre art scene.

All the big names passed through Céret, sometimes staying for a short while, sometimes for extended periods. Reading like a who's who of modern art, the list includes André Masson, Max Jacob, Juan Gris, Raoul Dufy, Jean Cocteau, Chaïm Soutine, Amedeo Modigliani, Marc Chagall, Salvador Dalí and Joan Miró.

After the museum's formation in 1950, many of these artists (or their estates) chose to donate their works for free in recognition of Céret's importance to their artistic development (Picasso alone donated 57 pieces, although only one painting, a still life of a dead crane and a jug).

Standout works include a moving *The War* (1943) by Marc Chagall, 29 ceramic cups painted with bullfighting scenes by Picasso, and a famous cubist view of Céret by Chaïm Soutine, painted in 1919 – but there are many more to discover.

🛏 Sleeping & Eating

There are several places to sleep in and around the town, but Céret's proximity to Perpignan, 30km to the northeast, means it's easy to visit as a day trip.

Hôtel des Arcades   HOTEL €
(📞04 68 87 12 30; www.hotelarcadesceret.fr; 1 place Picasso; d €60-78; 🅿❄🛜) This unpretentious hotel is brilliant value, and a great base for exploring Céret and the modern art museum. Rooms are no frills, with simple furniture and plain bathrooms, but renovation works are under way. The best rooms overlook the main square of place Picasso and its century-old plane trees. Breakfast costs €8; parking is €6.

Le Relais des Chartreuses   BOUTIQUE HOTEL €€
(📞04 68 83 15 88; www.relais-des-chartreuses. fr; 106 av d'en Carbouner, Le Boulou; s €70-81, d €80-190, ste €210-275; 🅿❄🛜🏊) A glorious getaway, Le Relais des Chartreuses has 15 glossy rooms inside a Catalan-style house dating from the 17th century. Clutter has been stripped out in favour of a few key antiques, and there's a designer pool, a *table d'hôte* restaurant and an enticing garden. It's 12.5km east of Céret via the D618.

L'Atelier de Fred   BISTRO €€
(📞04 68 95 47 41; 12 rue St-Ferréol; menus €20-41; 🕐12.15-1.45pm & 7.45-9pm Tue-Sat) Céret's best restaurant is a delight from start to finish. Chef Fred has a well-earned reputation for his imaginative versions of traditional dishes, which range from grilled duckling breast to fresh fish and poached pears with hibiscus syrup. It's right in the centre.

ℹ Information

Tourist office (📞04 68 87 00 53; www. vallespir-tourisme.fr; 5 rue St-Ferréol; 🕐9am-

12.30pm & 2-5pm Mon-Sat Nov-Apr, to 6pm May, Jun, Sep & Oct, 9am-7pm Mon-Sat, 9am-1pm Sun Jul & Aug) Can suggest hiking itineraries in the region.

ℹ Getting There & Away

Buses 340, 341 and 342 run to/from Perpignan (€1, 35 minutes, up to 10 daily Monday to Saturday, up to three Sunday). Buses leave from near the **tourist office**.

Têt Valley (Vallée de la Têt)

Fruit orchards carpet the lower reaches of the Vallée de la Têt. Beyond the strategic fortress town of Villefranche-de-Conflent, the scenery becomes wilder, more open and undulating as the valley climbs towards Spanish Catalonia and Andorra. There's no shortage of picturesque villages along the way.

Travelling around the Têt Valley, it's well worth visiting the hilltop village of **Eus**, 12km northeast of Villefranche-de-Conflent. The approach to the village along a quiet road through the vineyards is very scenic. It's one of the most picturesque villages in the region, with narrow, winding streets leading to a medieval church from where it's possible to enjoy spellbinding views of the Pyrenees.

LANGUEDOC-ROUSSILLON TÊT VALLEY (VALLÉE DE LA TÊT)

DON'T MISS

ALL ABOARD THE CANARY

Nicknamed Le Canari (the Canary), bright yellow mountain railway **Le Train Jaune** (📞04 68 96 63 62; www.ter.sncf. com/occitanie/loisirs/patrimoine-culture/train-jaune; place de la Gare; one way €4.20-22.10) trundles along from Villefranche-de-Conflent (427m) through spectacular Pyrenean scenery to Latour de Carol (1231m). One of France's most famous train trips, attracting 400,000 passengers annually, it doesn't take bookings; arrive a good hour before departure. It makes scheduled stops at eight of its 22 stations; alight at the others on request.

At Latour de Carol you can return to Villefranche or change for Toulouse or Barcelona.

DON'T MISS

A DATE WITH THE FAIRIES

The **Orgues d'Ille-sur-Têt** (☑ 04 68 84 13 13; http://lesorgues.ille-sur-tet.com; chemin de Regleilles, Ille-sur-Têt; adult/child €5/3.50) rock formations must be one of the most striking geological wonders in Occitania, though they have remained well under the tourist radar. They consist of clusters of fairy chimneys that were formed when erosion wiped out the softer sandstone covering harder rock, leaving behind isolated pinnacles. Reaching heights of up to 15m, they have conical shapes and are topped by flattish stones of harder rock. Depending on your perspective, they look like giant phalluses, organ pipes or outsized mushrooms.

It's about 2km north of Ille-sur-Têt (follow the signs).

Villefranche-de-Conflent

POP 223

The Unesco-listed town of Villefranche-de-Conflent sits in a breathtaking spot, hemmed in by tall cliffs at the strategic confluence of the valleys of the Têt and Cady rivers. Built by Vauban, its fort dominates the valley and you can walk along the walled town's ramparts. From Villefranche, the famous mountain railway Le Train Jaune (p779) runs through the Pyrenees almost to the Spanish border.

Villefranche's mighty **Fort Liberia** (☑ 04 68 96 34 01; www.fort-liberia.com; adult/child €7/3.80; ☺ 9am-8pm Jul & Aug, 10am-7pm Jun & Sep, 10am-6pm Mar-May & Oct) dominates the skyline above town. Built by Vauban in 1681, it was heavily refortified by Napoléon III between 1850 and 1856. You can wander around its corner turrets and battlements, as well as the defensive keep, the powder magazine and a former prison. A shuttle bus from town (adult/child return €11/5.50) saves you a steep climb up 844 steps in an underground tunnel or a 20-minute walk on a path.

The **tourist office** (☑ 04 68 96 22 96; www. tourisme-canigou.com; 2 rue St-Jean; ☺ 9.30am-6.30pm Jul & Aug, 9.30am-5pm Tue-Sun Jun & Sep, 10am-noon & 2-5pm Tue-Sat Oct-May) plenty of information about the town and the valley.

Buses 240 and 241 link Villefranche-de-Conflent with Perpignan (€1, 1¼ hours, seven daily Monday to Saturday, no services Sunday). They also serve Vernet-les-Bains (€1, 15 minutes, 10 daily Monday to Saturday, no services Sunday). It is also possible to take regional trains between Perpignan and Villefranche-de-Conflent (€1, 50 minutes, up to eight daily).

Vernet-les-Bains

POP 1430

Busy in summer and a ghost town for the rest of the year, the little spa town of Vernet-les-Bains was frequented by the British aristocracy in the late 19th century. You can't help but be dazzled by the fabulous backdrop, with Mont Canigou lording over the valley. No prize for guessing that this rugged terrain offers fantastic hiking opportunities.

Vernet is a great base for mountain biking and hiking, particularly for tackling **Mont Canigou** (2784m). You can get a head start by catching a 4WD up the mountain as far as Les Cortalets (2175m), from where the summit is a three- to four-hour return hike. Local 4WD operators include **Garage Villacèque** (☑ 04 68 05 51 14; louis.villaceque@ orange.fr; rue du Conflent; one way per person €30; ☺ Jun-Sep) and **Canigou En 4x4** (☑ 04 68 05 99 89; www.canigou-en-4x4.com; one way per person €30; ☺ by reservation).

There are few places to stay in or around Vernet; the **tourist office** (☑ 04 68 05 55 35; www.vernet-les-bains.fr; 2 rue de la Chapelle; ☺ 9am-noon & 2-5pm Mon-Fri) can advise on seasonal *gîtes* (self-catering cottages and villas).

Buses 240 and 241 link Vernet-les-Bains with Perpignan (€1, 1½ hours, seven daily Monday to Saturday, no services Sunday). They also serve Villefranche-de-Conflent (€1, 15 minutes, 10 daily Monday to Saturday, no services Sunday). Buses leave from near the tourist office.

Côte Vermeille

Named for its red rock, the Côte Vermeille (Vermilion Coast) runs south from Collioure to Cerbère on the Spanish border, where the Pyrenees foothills dip to the sea. Against a backdrop of vineyards and pinched between the Mediterranean and the mountains, it's riddled with small rocky bays and little ports.

The main town here is Collioure. Three kilometres to its south, Port-Vendres, Roussillon's only natural harbour and deep-water port, has been exploited ever since Greek mariners roamed the rocky coastline. Until the independence of France's North African territories in the 1960s, it was an important port linking them with the mainland. It's still a significant cargo and fishing harbour, however, welcoming everything from small coastal chuggers to giant deep-sea vessels bristling with radar. There's also a large leisure marina, and lots of pleasant walks around the coastline nearby.

❶ Getting There & Away

Buses and trains run regularly along the coast from Perpignan. If you're going by car, you can follow the lovely coastal roads all the way to Banyuls-sur-Mer.

Collioure

POP 3096

Collioure, where boats bob against a backdrop of houses washed in soft pastel colours, is the smallest and most picturesque of the Côte Vermeille resorts. Once Perpignan's port, it found fame in the early 20th century when it inspired the Fauvist artists Henri Matisse and André Derain and, later, Picasso and Braque.

Today the town has more than 30 galleries and workshops, including many on rue de la Fraternité. Collioure is also famed for its wine and its prized Collioure anchovies. Like most beaches along the Côte Vermeille, Collioure's main town beach is shingly, but pleasant enough for a paddle.

◉ Sights & Activities

Château Royal   CHATEAU
(☑04 68 82 06 43; www.ledepartement66.fr/98-chateau-royal-de-collioure.htm; Port Plaisance; adult/child €4/2; ☉10am-7pm Jul & Aug, 9am-5pm Sep-Jun) Collioure's seaside castle was mostly built between 1276 and 1344 by the counts of Roussillon and the kings of Aragon, and was later occupied by the Mallorcan court, although the outer wall was the work of Vauban in the 17th century. Interior furnishings are minimal, but the hybrid Spanish-French architectural styles are striking and the coastal views lovely. Concerts and theatre performances take place in the grounds throughout the year.

Musée d'Art Moderne   GALLERY
(☑04 68 82 10 19; 4 rte de Port-Vendres; adult/child €3/2; ☉10am-noon & 2-6pm Jun-Sep, 10am-noon & 2-6pm Wed-Mon Oct-May) Boat sketches by Matisse and Edouard Pignon along with coastal canvases by Henri Martin and Henri Marre are among the highlights of this small but worthwhile museum. It has a good collection of mainly 20th-century canvases and holds regular exhibitions by local artists.

Moulin de la Cortina   LANDMARK
(www.lemoulindecollioure.com; Parc Pams) The most scenic way to reach this 14th-century windmill is a 950m walk through olive and almond groves from Fort St-Elme along the Cami del Port de Sant Telm (about 20 minutes). Alternatively, it's a steep 150m walk from the Musée d'Art Moderne. Mediterranean views of boats, rocky coast and brilliant blue sea extend from the mill's raised base.

Église Notre-Dame des Anges   CHURCH
(rue de l'Église) At the northern end of the harbour, the medieval belfry of this church once doubled as a lighthouse, although its pink dome – the signature feature of Collioure's skyline – wasn't added until 1810.

Le Chemin du Fauvisme   WALKING
During the early 20th century, Collioure's vibrant coastal hues and piercing light attracted a group of artists known as the Fauves (the Wild Beasts), whose focus was pure colour. The tourist office (p782) has a free map of the Chemin du Fauvisme, a walking trail taking in nine locations featured in works by Henri Matisse and his younger colleague André Derain.

Cellier des Dominicains   WINE
(☑04 68 82 05 63; www.cellierdominicain.com; place Orphila; cellar tours €2; ☉9am-noon & 2-6pm Mon-Sat Apr-Sep) This former monk's cellar now showcases vintages from more than 150 local *vignerons* (winegrowers). Cellar tours lasting 40 minutes, followed by a tasting, take place at 4pm Thursday June to September in French and English.

⌞⌝ Sleeping

Hôtel Le Saint-Pierre   HOTEL €
(☑04 68 82 19 50; www.hotel-stpierre-collioure.fr; 16 av du Général de Gaulle; d €55-70; ☉Feb-Oct; ❈🕸) Bargain! While it doesn't have much of a sea view, this well-run hotel makes up for it by offering some of the most reasonable rates in Collioure, even in high summer. The decor is clean and fresh, if a touch bland, but with only 17 rooms – some with balconies – it doesn't feel crowded even when full.

LANGUEDOC-ROUSSILLON CÔTE VERMEILLE

Casa Païral HOTEL €€

(☎ 04 68 82 05 81; www.hotel-casa-pairal.com; impasse des Palmiers; d from €125; P ❋ ☎ ☎) Set around a secluded jasmine- and rose-perfumed garden sheltering a heated swimming pool and a fountain, this 18th-century house has 27 heritage-style rooms that are all individually decorated. Rooms 4, 22, 26 and 27 have been modernised. Breakfast (€16) is served beneath a century-old magnolia tree. The hotel's conveniently situated in the town centre, a 250m stroll from the beach.

✖ Eating

Collioure gets so many visitors that some of the fancy-looking restaurants along the waterfront can get away with serving poor-quality food. There are several good options tucked away in the backstreets of the centre.

★Chez Paco TAPAS €

(☎ 04 68 82 90 91; 18 rue Rière; tapas €5-14; ⊗ 11am-2pm & 6-10.30pm mid-Jun–mid-Sep) Chez Paco is a snazzy tapas bar tucked in a backstreet away from the madding crowd along the seafront. The tapas (cheese, meat, fish and charcuterie) are varied and tasty, the service excellent and the vibes super-cool. The waiters know their wines and there's a long list to choose from.

Casa Leon SEAFOOD €€

(☎ 04 68 82 10 74; 2 rue Rière; menus €18-38, mains €16-28; ⊗ noon-2pm & 7-10.30pm) Lost in the tangled old quarter, this simple Catalan bistro relies on the quality of its ingredients: bream tartare, cod with mussels and oysters, or king scallops in creamy sauces, along with Collioure's celebrated anchovies.

La 5ème Péché FUSION €€

(☎ 04 68 98 09 76; www.le-cinquieme-peche.com; 16 rue Fraternité; menus €21-62; ⊗ 12.15-1.45pm & 7.30-9pm Tue-Sat) Japan meets France at this creative fusion restaurant hidden away in the old quarter. Chef Masashi Iijima prepares seasonally changing specials using exquisite market-sourced produce. Expect anything from fresh fish to stuffed veal breast in soy sauce. The dining room is small and very popular with locals and visitors – book ahead.

Le Neptune GASTRONOMY €€€

(☎ 04 68 82 02 27; www.leneptune-collioure.com; 9 rte de Port-Vendres; menus €29-99, mains €18-45; ⊗ noon-2pm & 7.30-10pm Apr-Oct, noon-1.30pm & 7.30-9.30pm Thu-Mon Nov-Mar; ☎) It's a toss-up whether the setting or the food steals the show here. Overlooking Collioure's brilliant blue bay and red rooftops, the panoramic seaside terrace (covered and heated in winter) is an absolute stunner, while local ingredients span just-landed turbot to just-cooked lobster. The style is formal, so you'll need to dress up.

❶ Information

Tourist office (☎ 04 68 82 15 47; www.collioure.com; place du 18 Juin; ⊗ 9.15am-6.45pm Jul-Sep, 9.15am-6.45pm Mon-Sat, 10am-5.30pm Sun Apr-Jun & Oct) On the northern side of town near quai de l'Amirauté. It can arrange guided tours (€7).

❶ Getting There & Away

Regular **trains** (rue du Lavoir) link Collioure with Perpignan (€6.10, 20 minutes, hourly) and Banyuls-sur-Mer (€2.40, seven minutes, hourly).

Banyuls-sur-Mer

POP 4749

Banyuls is a small coastal town that began life as a fishing port but is now best known for its wines (Banyuls, Banyuls Grand Cru and Collioure). Grapes grow on the slopes around town on steep, rocky terraces divided by drystone walls, which help retain water and prevent soil erosion.

It's a lovely spot, with three shingly but superb beaches (Centrale, Les Elmes and Centre Hélio Marin) with translucent turquoise waters, and an important marine reserve, the Réserve Naturelle Cerbère-Banyuls, 6km southeast of town, where you can snorkel and scuba dive. Banyuls is also a convenient stop-off if you're heading over the border into Spain, 14km to the south.

◉ Sights

Site de Paulilles ARCHITECTURE, MUSEUM

(www.ledepartement66.fr/60-le-site-de-paulilles.htm; D914; ⊗ Director's House 9am-1pm & 2-9pm) FREE Part industrial relic, part nature walk, this 35-hectare coastal site is remote, as you'd expect of a one-time dynamite factory. It was set up by Nobel Prize founder Alfred Nobel in 1870 and subsequently abandoned in 1984. Haunting photos inside the former director's house depict the hard lives and close community of Catalan workers, whose explosives helped to blast the Panama Canal, Trans-Siberian Railway and Mont Blanc Tunnel. It's 3.2km north of Banyuls-sur-Mer.

Biodiversarium   AQUARIUM
(☑ 04 68 88 73 39; www.biodiversarium.fr; 1 av
Pierre Fabre; adult/child aquarium €9.50/7.50,
joint ticket with Jardin Méditerranéen €12/10;
☉ 10am-12.30pm & 2-6pm) At the southern
end of Banyuls' seafront promenade, this
aquarium, which was modernised in 2017,
houses an intriguing collection of Mediterranean marine life, from sea horses to sea
anemones. Combination tickets are available with the **Jardin Méditerranéen du Mas
de la Serre** (rte des Crêtes; adult/child garden
only €6/4, joint ticket with Biodiversarium €12/10;
☉ 10am-12.30pm & 2-6pm Jul & Aug, 2-6pm Wed-
Sun Apr-Jun & Sep, closed Oct-Mar).

🏃 Activities

Terres des Templiers   WINE
(☑ 04 68 98 36 92; www.terresdestempliers.fr; rte
des Crêtes; ☉ 10.15am-7.30pm late Mar-early Nov)
The best place to try Banyuls' wines is this
vineyard 1.5km west of the seafront via the
D86. Free 30-minute guided tours take in
the century-old oak vats. Tours in English
(€5) depart at 2.30pm, 4pm and 5.30pm.

Aquablue Plongée   DIVING, SNORKELLING
(☑ 04 68 88 17 35; www.aquablue-plongee.com; 5
quai Georges Petit; diving from €39, gear rental per
dive from €6, snorkelling trips from €20; ☉ Apr-
early Nov, by reservation) The Réserve Naturelle
Cerbère-Banyuls is a favourite with underwater photographers for its crabs, lobsters,
starfish, groupers, anemones, ballan wrasse,
damselfish, octopi, sea bream, wolf fish, eels,
orange gorgonians and jellyfish. Immerse
yourself in its crystalline waters with Aquablue Plongée, which offers diving and snor-

kelling as well as PADI courses for beginners
through to experienced divers.

Aleoutes Kayak   KAYAKING
(☑ 04 68 88 34 25; www.kayakmer.net; 11 quai
Georges Petit; trips from €30; ☉ by reservation)
This reputable outfit organises guided kayaking trips along the Côte Vermeille.

🛏 Sleeping & Eating

This seaside resort town has plenty of seasonal
accommodation and several year-round hotels. Banyuls' best restaurants are along the
waterfront.

La Littorine   MEDITERRANEAN €€€
(☑ 04 68 88 03 12; www.restaurant-la-littorine.fr;
Plage des Elmes; menus €26-56, mains €25-40;
☉ noon-1.30pm & 7-9pm) Bang on the beach,
with a sun-drenched glass-enclosed terrace,
the pick of Banyuls' restaurants stocks over
200 Languedoc-Roussillon wines to complement flavour-packed Mediterranean dishes. Above the restaurant, Hôtel des Elmes
(same owner) features 31 luminous rooms
(from €80), some of which have top-notch
sea views.

ℹ️ Information

Tourist office (☑ 04 68 88 31 58; www.
banyuls-sur-mer.com; 4 av de la République;
☉ 9am-7pm Jul & Aug, 9am-noon & 2-6pm Mon-
Sat Sep-Jun) Midway along the beachfront.

ℹ️ Getting There & Away

Trains (av de la Gare) link Banyuls-sur-Mer
with Perpignan (€7.70, 30 minutes, hourly) via
Collioure (€2.40, seven minutes).

Provence

Best Places to Eat

→ Le Sanglier Paresseux (p842)

→ L'Arôme (p841)

→ Le Vivier (p835)

→ Le Champ des Lunes (p836)

Best Places to Stay

→ Mama Shelter (p794)

→ Sous les Figuiers (p820)

→ Les Jardins de Baracane (p825)

→ Les Florets (p833)

→ Le Cloître (p812)

Why Go?

For many people, the pastoral landscapes of Provence are a French fantasy come true. Provence seems to sum up everything enviable about the French lifestyle: fantastic food, hilltop villages, legendary wines, bustling markets and a balmy climate. For decades, it's been a hotspot for holidaymakers and second-homers, inspired by the vision of the rustic good life depicted in Peter Mayle's classic 1989 travelogue, *A Year in Provence*.

For the quintessential Provençal countryside, the best place to begin is inland around the valleys and hills of the Luberon and Var. Further inland rises Provence's highest peak, Mont Ventoux, and beyond it, the snow-capped peaks of the Hautes-Alpes. Meanwhile, along the coast, the rough-and-ready port of Marseille, the dramatic cliffs of the Calanques and the flamingo-rich wetlands of the Camargue are all worthy of a detour.

When to Go
Marseille

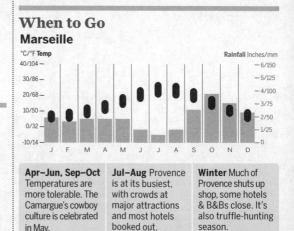

Apr–Jun, Sep–Oct Temperatures are more tolerable. The Camargue's cowboy culture is celebrated in May.

Jul–Aug Provence is at its busiest, with crowds at major attractions and most hotels booked out.

Winter Much of Provence shuts up shop, some hotels & B&Bs close. It's also truffle-hunting season.

MARSEILLE

POP 861,635

Grit and grandeur coexist seamlessly in Marseille, an exuberantly multicultural port city with a pedigree stretching back to classical Greece and a fair claim to the mantle of France's second city. Once seen as somewhat dirty and dangerous, and lacking the glamour of Cannes or St-Tropez, this black sheep of the Provençal coastline has blossomed in cultural confidence since its 2013 stint as European Capital of Culture. The addition of a brace of swanky new museums is just the outward sign of an optimism and self-belief that's almost palpable.

Marseille's heart is the vibrant Vieux Port (old port), mast-to-mast with yachts and pleasure boats. Just uphill is the ancient Le Panier neighbourhood, the oldest section of the city. Also worth an explore is the République quarter, with its stylish boutiques and Haussmannian buildings, and the Joliette area, centred on Marseille's totemic Cathédrale de Marseille Notre Dame de la Major (p790).

⊙ Sights

Greater Marseille is divided into 16 *arrondissements* (districts), which are indicated in addresses (eg 1er for the first *arrondissement* and so on). The city's main thoroughfare, La Canebière (from the Provençal word *canebe*, meaning 'hemp', after the city's traditional rope industry), in the 1st *arrondissement*, stretches eastwards from the Vieux Port towards the train station, a 10-minute walk or two metro stops from the water. North is Le Panier; south is the bohemian concourse of cours Julien; and southwest is the start of the coastal road.

⊙ Central Marseille

★ Vieux Port   PORT

(Old Port; Map p796; Ⓜ Vieux Port) Ships have docked for millennia at Marseille's birthplace, the vibrant Vieux Port. The main commercial docks were transferred to the Joliette area in the 1840s, but the old port remains a thriving harbour for fishing boats, pleasure yachts and tourist boats. Guarded by the forts St-Jean (Map p796; Ⓜ Vieux Port) and St-Nicolas (Map p796; 1 bd Charles Livon; ☐ 83), both sides of the port are dotted with bars, brasseries and cafes, with more to be found around place Thiars and cours Honoré d'Estienne d'Orves, where the action continues until late.

★ Basilique Notre Dame de la Garde   BASILICA

(Montée de la Bonne Mère; Map p792; ☑ 04 91 13 40 80; www.notredamedelagarde.com; rue Fort du Sanctuaire; ⊙ 7am-8pm Apr-Sep, to 7pm Oct-Mar; ☐ 60) Occupying Marseille's highest point, La Garde (154m), this opulent 19th-century Romano-Byzantine basilica is Marseille's most-visited icon. Built on the foundations of a 16th-century fort, which was itself an enlargement of a 13th-century chapel, the basilica is ornamented with coloured marble, superb Byzantine-style mosaics, and murals depicting ships sailing under the protection of La Bonne Mère (The Good Mother). The campanile supports a 9.7m-tall gilded statue of said Mother on a 12m-high pedestal, and the hilltop gives 360-degree panoramas of the city.

The basilica is a steep 1km walk from the Vieux Port; alternatively, take bus 60 or the tourist train.

Musée du Santon   MUSEUM

(Map p796; ☑ 04 91 54 26 58; www.santons marcelcarbonel.com; 49 rue Neuve Ste-Catherine; ⊙ 10am-12.30pm & 2-5pm Mon-Sat; Ⓜ Vieux Port) **FREE** One of Provence's most enduring Christmas traditions is its *santons* (plaster-moulded, kiln-fired nativity figures), first created by Marseillais artisan Jean-Louis Lagnel (1764–1822). This tiny museum displays a collection of 18th- and 19th-century *santons* (from the Provençal word *santoun*, meaning 'little saint'), and runs visits to its workshops. Its boutique sells everything from nail-sized dogs and pigs to a complete *mas* (Provençal farmhouse).

Musée d'Histoire de Marseille   MUSEUM

(History Museum of Marseille; Map p796; ☑ 04 91 55 36 00; http://musee-histoire.marseille.fr; 2 rue Henri-Barbusse; adult/child €6/free; ⊙ 10am-7pm Tue-Sun mid-May–mid-Sep, to 6pm mid-Sep–mid-May; Ⓜ Vieux Port) This intriguing 15,000-sq-metre museum traces the story of 'France's Oldest City' from prehistory (the paintings of the Cosquer Cave) to the present day, across 12 chronological exhibitions. The complex was built beside the remains of a Greek harbour uncovered during construction of the Bourse shopping centre. Highlights include the remains of a 3rd-century merchant vessel discovered in the Vieux Port in 1974: to preserve the soaked and decaying wood, it was freeze-dried where it now sits, behind glass.

PROVENCE MARSEILLE

Provence Highlights

1 **Marseille** (p785) Delving into the multicultural melting pot of this port city.

2 **Arles** (p808) Sitting in the stalls of one of the world's best-preserved Roman amphitheatres.

3 **Camargue** (p808) Spotting candy-pink flamingos and watching cowboys at work.

4 **Gorges du Verdon** (p844) Driving through France's answer to the Grand Canyon.

5 **Avignon** (p822) Exploring the history of papal power at the magnificent Palais des Papes.

HAUTES-
ALPES

Embrun

Gap

Lac de Serre-
Ponçon

Le Lauzet-
Ubaye

D900

Vallée de l'Ubaye

St-Paul-
sur-Ubaye

Larche

Barcelonnette

ITALY

Cuneo

Vinadio

Borgo San
Dalmazzo

PIEDMONT

Pra Loup

Seyne-
les-Alpes

D900

Réserve
Géologique de
Haute-Provence

D2205

Isola

Colmars-
les-Alpes

D902

Lac
d'Allos

D3

Bléone

Isola
2000

Vallée des
Merveilles

steron

Thoard

ALPES
DE HAUTE-PROVENCE

Digne-
les-Bains

Parc National
du Mercantour

D908

Guillaumes

St-Martin-
Vésubie

Vallée de
la Vésubie

N85

Les Mées

yruis

Ganagobie

D953

Barrème

N85

St-André-
les-Alpes

Puget-
Théniers

Entrevaux

Villars-
sur-Var

ALPES-
MARITIMES

D28

D2205

Menton

Lac de
Castillon

Gorges de la Vésubie

Castellane

MONACO

Aurestre

Moustiers
Ste-Marie

D952

Riez

La Palud-
sur-Verdon

Verdon

4 Gorges
du Verdon

Loup

N85

N202

MONACO

Nice

N7

Valensole

Lac de
Ste-Croix

Gorges du Verdon

D21

Comps-sur-Artuby

Grasse

Aéroport
International
Nice–Côte d'Azur

Cagnes-
sur-Mer

Var

gion

Parc Naturel
Régional
du Verdon

Bauduen

Artuby

Cannes

Antibes

Cap
d'Antibes

Quinson

Montmeyan

Aups

D562

Lac de
St-Cassien

Îles de Lérins

Tavernes

D560

Cotignac

Draguignan

Argens

A8

Le Muy

Massif de l'Estérel

Fréjus

Maximin-la-
Ste-Baume

A8

Le Cannet
des Maures

N98

MEDITERRANEAN
SEA

Brignoles

Gontaron

A57

St-Maxime

St- Tropez

Massif des Maures

VAR

Cuers

Domaine
du Rayol

Toulon

Hyères

N98

Côte d'Azur

N
0   20 km
0   10 miles

Vieux Port

AN ITINERARY

Start with an early-morning coffee on the balcony at La Caravelle, with views of the boats bobbing in the harbour and Basilique Notre Dame de la Garde across the way.

Mosey down the quay to the sparkling ❶ **MuCEM** and its cantilevered neighbour ❷ **Villa Méditerranée** for a morning of art and culture. You'll enter through Fort St-Jean, and wind through rooftop gardens to reach the state-of-the-art museums.

Alternatively, take in green-and-white striped ❸ **Cathédrale de la Major** then explore the apricot-coloured alleys of ❹ **Le Panier**, browsing the exhibits at the ❺ **Centre de la Vieille Charité**, and shopping in the neighbourhood's tiny boutiques.

In the afternoon, hop on the cross-port ferry to the harbour's south side and take a ❻ **boat trip** to Château d'If, made famous by the Dumas novel *The Count of Monte Cristo*.

Or stroll under Norman Foster's mirrored pavilion, then wander into the ❼ **Abbaye St-Victor**, to see the bones of martyrs enshrined in gold.

As evening nears, you can catch the sunset from the stone benches in the ❽ **Jardin du Pharo**. Then as the warm southern night sets in, join the throngs on cours Honoré d'Estienne d'Orves, where you can drink pastis and people-watch beneath a giant statue of a lion devouring a man – the ❾ **Milo de Croton**.

Cathédrale de la Major
The striped façade of Marseille's cathedral is made from local Cassis stone and green Florentine marble. Its grand north staircase leads from Le Panier to La Joliette quarter

Villa Méditerranée ❷

MuCEM ❶

Palais & Jardin du Pharo

Musée des Civilisations de l'Europe et de la Méditerranée (MuCEM)
Explore the icon of modern Marseille. This stunning museum was designed by Rudy Ricciotti and Roland Carta, and is linked by a vertigo-inducing footbridge to 13th-century Fort St-Jean. You'll get stupendous views of the Vieux Port and the Mediterranean.

Centre de la Vieille Charité

Before the 18th century, beggar hunters rounded up the poor for imprisonment. The Vieille Charité almshouse, which opened in 1749, improved their lot by acting as a workhouse. It's now an exhibition space and only the barred windows recall its original use.

Le Panier

The site of the Greek town of Massilia, Le Panier woos walkers with its sloping streets. Grand Rue follows the ancient road and opens out into place de Lenche, the location of the Greek market. It is still the place to shop for artisanal products.

Frioul If Express

Catch the Frioul If Express to Château d'If, France's equivalent to Alcatraz. Prisoners were housed according to class: the poorest at the bottom in windowless dungeons, the wealthiest in paid-for private cells, with windows and a fireplace.

Quai des Belges

La Caravelle →

Quai du Port

Cross-Port Ferry

Quai de Rive Neuve

Cours Honoré d'Estienne d'Orves

6

9

4

Fort St-Jean

Bas Fort St-Nicolas

7

Milo de Croton

Subversive local artist Pierre Puget carved the savage *Milo de Croton* for Louis XIV. The statue, whose original is in the Louvre, is a meditation on human pride and shows the Greek Olympian being devoured by a lion, his Olympic cup cast down.

Abbaye St-Victor

St-Victor was built (420–30) to house the remains of tortured Christian martyrs. On Candlemas (2 February) the black Madonna is brought up from the crypt and the archbishop blesses the city and the sea.

Jardin du Pharo

Built by Napoléon III for the Empress Eugénie, the Pharo Palace was designed with its 'feet in the water'. Today it is a congress centre, but the gardens with their magnificent view are open all day.

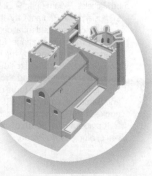

★ **Le Panier**   AREA

(Map p796; M Vieux Port) 'The Basket' is Marseille's oldest quarter – site of the original Greek settlement and nicknamed for its steep streets and buildings. Its close, village-like feel, artsy ambience, cool hidden squares and sun-baked cafes make it a delight to explore. Rebuilt after destruction in WWII, its mishmash of lanes hide artisan shops, *ateliers* (workshops) and terraced houses strung with drying washing. Its centrepiece is La Vieille Charité.

★ **La Vieille Charité**   HISTORIC BUILDING

(Map p796; ☑ 04 91 14 58 80; www.vieille-charite-marseille.com; 2 rue de la Charité; museums adult/child €6/free; ⊙ 10am-6pm Tue-Sun mid-Sep–mid-May, longer hours in summer; M Joliette) In the heart of Marseille's Le Panier quarter is this grand and gorgeous almshouse, built by Pierre Puget (1620–94), an architect and sculptor born just a couple of streets away who rose to become Louis XIV's architect. With its neoclassical central chapel and elegant arcaded courtyard, it's a structure of great harmony and grace. Entry is free, although there's a charge to visit the excellent **Musée d'Archéologie Méditerranéenne** (Museum of Mediterranean Archeology; Map p796; ☑ 04 91 14 58 59; www.culture.marseille.fr; 2 rue de la Charité; adult/child €6/free; ⊙ 10am-7pm Tue-Sun mid-May–mid-Sep, to 6pm mid-Sep–mid-May;

M Joliette) and **Musée d'Arts Africains, Océaniens et Améridiens** (Museum of African, Oceanic & American Indian Art; Map p796; ☑ 04 91 14 58 38; www.marseille.fr/node/630; 2 rue de la Charité; adult/child €6/free; ⊙ 10am-7pm Tue-Sun mid-May–mid-Sep, to 6pm mid-Sep–mid-May; M Joliette), both housed within.

★ **Musée des Civilisations de l'Europe et de la Méditerranée**   MUSEUM

(MuCEM, Museum of European & Mediterranean Civilisations; Map p792; ☑ 04 84 35 13 13; www.mucem.org; 7 promenade Robert Laffont; adult/child incl exhibitions €9.50/free; ⊙ 10am-8pm Wed-Mon Jul & Aug, 11am-7pm Wed-Mon May-Jun & Sep-Oct, 11am-6pm Wed-Mon Nov-Apr; ♿; M Vieux Port, Joliette) The icon of modern Marseille, this stunning museum explores the history, culture and civilisation of the Mediterranean region through anthropological exhibits, rotating art exhibitions and film. The collection sits in a bold, contemporary building designed by Algerian-born, Marseille-educated architect Rudy Ricciotti, and Roland Carta. It is linked by a vertigo-inducing footbridge to the 13th-century Fort St-Jean (p785), from which there are stupendous views of the Vieux Port and the surrounding sea. The fort grounds and gardens are free to explore.

Villa Méditerranée   MUSEUM

(Map p796; ☑ 04 95 09 42 70; www.villa-mediterranee.org; esplanade du J4, off bd du Littoral; ⊙ noon-6pm Tue-Fri, from 10am Sat & Sun; ♿; M Vieux Port, Joliette) FREE This eye-catching white structure next to MuCEM is no ordinary 'villa'. Designed by architect Stefano Boeri in 2013, the sleek white edifice sports a spectacular cantilever overhanging an ornamental pool. Inside, a viewing gallery with glass-panelled floor (look down if you dare!), and two or three temporary multimedia exhibitions evoke aspects of the Mediterranean, be they aquatic, historical or environmental. Not unlike MuCEM, the building itself is the undisputed highlight.

Cathédrale de Marseille Notre Dame de la Major   CATHEDRAL

(Map p796; ☑ 04 91 90 52 87; www.marseille.catholique.fr/La-Major-cathedrale; place de la Major; ⊙ 10am-6.30pm Wed-Sun Apr-Sep, to 5.30pm Oct-Mar; M Joliette) Standing guard between the old and new ports is the striking 19th-century Cathédrale de la Major. After its foundation stone was laid by Napoleon III in 1852, the 'New Major' took over 40 years to complete. It boasts a Byzantine-style

---

WORTH A TRIP

PILGRIMAGE FOR THE ARCHITECTURE-BUFFS

Visionary modernist architect Le Corbusier redefined urban living in 1952 with the completion of a vertical 337-apartment tower, popularly known as **La Cité Radieuse** (Unité d'Habitation; ☑ 04 91 16 78 00; www.marseille-citeradieuse.org; 280 bd Michelet; ⊙ 9am-6pm; 🚌 21, 83, stop Le Corbusier), 'The Radiant City'. Its purpose was to increase residential density to allow for more green space. Today the apartments are joined by the Hôtel Le Corbusier, the high-end restaurant Le Ventre de l'Architecte and a rooftop terrace. English-language tours (10am Friday and Saturday; adult/child €10/5) can be booked through the tourist office (p802).

It's about 5km south of central Marseille, along av du Prado.

striped façade made of local Cassis stone and green Florentine marble.

Beneath the church are **Les Voûtes de la Major**, 19th-century vaulted warehouses repurposed as restaurants and boutiques, while the grand staircase on the northern side makes an impressive gateway to La Joliette.

La Joliette
AREA

(Map p792; Ⓜ Joliette, 🚊 Joliette) The old maritime neighbourhood of La Joliette, moribund since the decline of the 19th-century docks, has been revitalised by bars, shops and restaurants. Ferries still depart for ports around the Med, but the long sweep of 19th-century commercial facades along Quai de la Joliette has been given an impressive scrub. Here you'll find **Marché de la Joliette** (Map p792; place de la Joliette; ⊘ 8am-2pm Mon-Fri; Ⓜ Joliette), one of Marseille's buzziest markets, and **Les Docks** (Map p792; ☎ 04 91 44 25 28; www.lesdocks-marseille.com; 10 place de la Joliette; ⊘ 10am-7pm; Ⓜ Joliette, 🚊 Joliette) – abandoned 19th-century warehouses now filled with boutiques and galleries.

Nearby, **Les Terraces du Port** is a vast new shopping mall filled with upmarket international chains. It has a huge public terrace on level 2 with fab views of the port and coast.

Musée des Beaux Arts
MUSEUM

(☎ 04 91 14 59 30; www.marseille.fr/node/639; 7 rue Édouard Stephan; adult/child €6/free; ⊘ 10am-7pm Tue-Sun mid-May–mid-Sep, to 6pm mid-Sep–mid-May; 🚻; Ⓜ Cinq Avenues-Longchamp, 🚊 Longchamp) Set in the lavish, colonnaded Palais de Longchamp, Marseille's oldest museum owes its existence to an 1801 decree of pre-Napoleonic France's short-lived Consulate, which established 15 museums across the country. A treasure trove of 16th- to 19th- century Italian and Provençal painting and sculpture, it's set in parkland popular with local families seeking shade in Marseille's treeless centre. The spectacular fountains, constructed in the 1860s, in part disguise the water tower at which the Roquefavour Aqueduct terminates.

Musée Cantini
GALLERY

(Map p796; ☎ 04 91 54 77 75; www.culture.marseille.fr; 19 rue Grignan; adult/child €6/free; ⊘ 10am-7pm Tue-Sun mid-May–mid-Sep, to 6pm mid-Sep–mid-May; Ⓜ Estrangin-Préfecture) Donated to the city by the sculptor Jules Cantini on his death in 1916, this 17th-century mansion-turned-museum conceals some superb art behind its wrought-iron gates. The core collection boasts fantastic examples of 17th- and 18th-century Provençal art, including André Derain's *Pinède à Cassis* (1907) and Raoul Dufy's *Paysage de l'Estaque* (1908). Another section is dedicated to work about Marseille, with pieces by Max Ernst, Joan Miró, André Masson and others.

◎ Along the Coast

Mesmerising views of another Marseille unfold along **corniche Président John F Kennedy**, the coastal road that cruises south to the small, beach-volleyball-busy **Plage des Catalans** (Map p792; 3 rue des Catalans; ⊘ 8.30am-6.30pm; 🚌 81, 82) and the boat-filled fishing cove of **Vallon des Auffes** (Map p792; 🚌 83).

Further south, the vast **Prado beaches** are marked by Jules Cantini's 1903 marble replica of Michelangelo's *David*. The beaches, all gold sand, were created from backfill from the excavations for Marseille's metro. They have a world-renowned **skate park**. Nearby lies expansive **Parc Borély** (av du Parc Borély; 🚌 19 or 83, stop Parc Borély).

Promenade Georges Pompidou continues south to **Cap Croisette**, from where the beautiful Parc National des Calanques (p803) can be reached on foot.

To head down the coast, take bus 83 from the Vieux Port. At av du Prado switch to bus 19 to continue further. Espace Infos RTM (p804) sells tickets for ferries between the Vieux Port and La Pointe Rouge, just to the south of the Prado beaches; the City Pass does not cover the ticket.

Château d'If
CASTLE

(☎ 06 03 06 25 26; www.if.monuments-nationaux.fr; Île d'If; adult/child €6/free; ⊘ 10am-6pm Apr-Sep, to 5pm Tue-Sun Oct-Mar) Commanding access to Marseille's Vieux Port, this photogenic island-fortress was immortalised in Alexandre Dumas' 1844 classic *The Count of Monte Cristo*. Many political prisoners were incarcerated here, including the Revolutionary hero Mirabeau and the Communards of 1871. Other than the island itself there's not a great deal to see, but it's worth visiting just for the views of the Vieux Port. **Frioul If Express** (Map p796; ☎ 04 96 11 03 50; www.frioul-if-express.com; 1 quai de la Fraternité) runs boats (return €11, 20 minutes, up to 10 daily) from Quai de la Fraternité.

☞ Tours

Marseille is a natural launch pad for exploring the nearby Parc National des Calanques (p803). Several boat tours depart from the Vieux Port.

Marseille

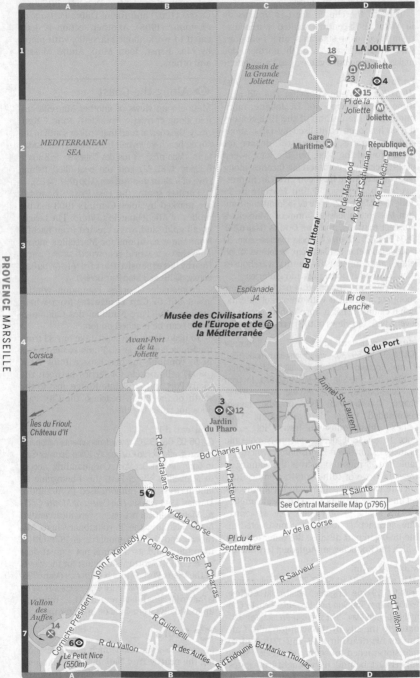

LA JOLIETTE

18

23 Joliette

15

Pl de la
Joliette Joliette

Bassin de
la Grande
Joliette

MEDITERRANEAN
SEA

Gare
Maritime

République
Dames

R de Mazenod
Av Robert Schuman
R de l'Evêche

Bd du Littoral

Esplanade
J4

Pl de
Lenche

Musée des Civilisations 2
de l'Europe et de
la Méditerranée

Q du Port

Avant-Port
de la
Joliette

Corsica

Tunnel St-Laurent

Îles du Frioul;
Château d'If

3
12
Jardin
du Pharo

R des Catalans

Bd Charles Livon

R Sainte

Av Pasteur

See Central Marseille Map (p796)

5

Av de la Corse

Av de la Corse

Bd Charles Livon

John F Kennedy

R Cap Dessemond

Pl du 4
Septembre

R Charras

R Sauveur

Bd Tellène

Vallon
des
Auffes

14

Corniche Président

6

R du Vallon

R Guidicelli

R des Auffes

R d'Endoume Bd Marius Thomas

Le Petit Nice
(550m)

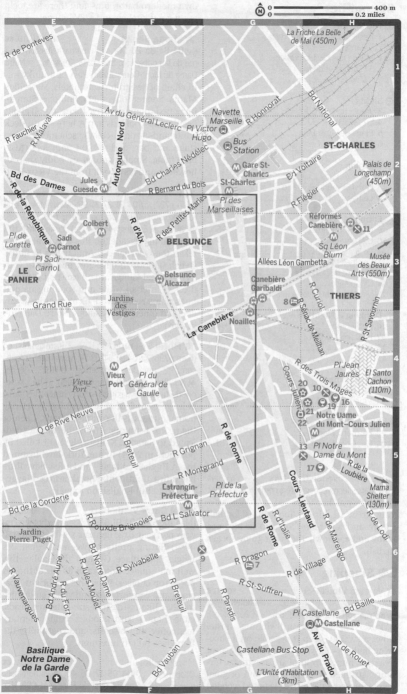

400 m
0.2 miles

La Friche La Belle
de Mai (450m)

R de Ponteves

R Fauchier
R Malaval

Av du Général Leclerc

R Honnorat

Bd National

ST-CHARLES

Pl Victor
Hugo

Navette
Marseille

Bus
Station

Palais de
Longchamp
(450m)

Autoroute Nord

Bd Charles Nédélec

Gare St-
Charles

St-Charles

Pl Voltaire

Bd des Dames

Jules
Guesde

R Bernard du Bois

R Flégier

R de la République

Pl des
Marseillaises

Réformés
Canebière

11

Pl de
Lorette

Sadi
Carnot

Colbert

R d'Aix

R des Petites Maries

BELSUNCE

Sq Léon
Blum

Musée
des Beaux
Arts (550m)

LE
PANIER

Pl Sadi
Carnot

Allées Léon Gambetta

Grand Rue

Belsunce
Alcazar

Canebière
Garibaldi

THIERS

Jardins
des
Vestiges

La Canebière

8

R Curiol

R Sénac de Meilhan

R St-Savournin

Noailles

Vieux
Port

Vieux
Port

Pl du
Général de
Gaulle

R des Trois Mages

Pl Jean
Jaurès

El Santo
Cachon
(110m)

Cours Julien

20

10

19

16

Q de Rive Neuve

R Breteuil

R Grignan

R de Rome

21

22

Notre Dame
du Mont–Cours Julien

13

Pl Notre
Dame du Mont

R Montgrand

17

R de la
Loubière

Estrangin-
Préfecture

Pl de la
Préfecture

Mama
Shelter
(130m)

Bd de la Corderie

R Roux de Brignoles

Bd L Salvator

R de Rome

R d'Italie

Cours Lieutaud

Jardin
Pierre Puget

R Sylvabelle

9

R Dragon

R de Village

R de Marengo

R de Lodi

R Vauvenargues

Bd André Aune

R du Fort

R Jules Moulet

Bd Notre Dame

R Breteuil

R Paradis

7

R St-Suffren

Pl Castellane

Bd Baille

Castellane

Av du Prado

R de Rouet

Basilique
Notre Dame
de la Garde

1

Bd Vauban

Castellane Bus Stop

L'Unité d'Habitation
(3km)

Marseille

Marseille Provence Greeters   WALKING
(www.marseilleprovencegreeters.com)   A great
idea: free walking tours led by locals, covering street art, history, food shops, football
culture and lots more. Sign up in advance
online and check whether your guide speaks
English.

🛏 Sleeping

★ Vertigo Vieux-Port   HOSTEL €
(Map p796; ☑ 04 91 54 42 95; www.hotelvertigo.
fr; 38 rue Fort Notre Dame; dm/tw €26/76; 🛜;
Ⓜ Vieux Port)   This award-winning hostel
shows a swanky sleep is possible on a shoestring budget – for your euro you can expect
breakfast, murals by local artists, vintage furniture, stripped wooden floors and original
architectural details such as exposed wooden
beams and stone arches. All rooms have their
own modern bathrooms, and there are lockers, a good kitchen and a TV lounge.

★ Mama Shelter   DESIGN HOTEL €€
(☑ 04 84 35 20 00; www.mamashelter.com; 64
rue de la Loubière; d from €113; 🅿 ❋ 🛜; Ⓜ Notre
Dame du Mont-Cours Julien)   Part of a funky mi-
ni-chain of design-forward hotels, Marseille's
Mama Shelter offers 125 Philippe Starck–
imagined rooms over five floors. It's all about
keeping the cool kids happy here – with sleek
white-and-chrome colour schemes, a live
stage and bar; and a giant *babi foot* (fuss-
ball) table. Smaller rooms are oddly shaped,
however, and it's a walk from the Vieux Port.

★ Hôtel Edmond Rostand   DESIGN HOTEL €€
(Map p792; ☑ 04 91 37 74 95; www.hoteledmond
rostand.com; 31 rue Dragon; s/d/tr €100/110/135;
❋ @ 🛜; Ⓜ Estrangin-Préfecture)   Push past the
unassuming façade of this great-value hotel in the Quartier des Antiquaires to find a
stylish interior in olive-grey and citrus, with
a communal lounge area, a cafe and 15 rooms
dressed in crisp white and soothing natural
hues. Some rooms overlook a tiny private garden and others the Basilique Notre Dame de
la Garde.

★ Hôtel St-Louis   HISTORIC HOTEL €€
(Map p796; ☑ 04 91 54 02 74; www.hotel-st-louis.
com; 2 rue des Récollettes; d €113; ❋ 🛜;
Ⓜ Noailles, 🚃 Canebière Garibaldi)   The stuc-
coed façade, wrought-iron balconies and
'mini-museum' of this charming hotel pay
homage to its 19th-century origins. Each of
the rooms is unique – from the 'Kenya' (dedicated to Satao, a Kenyan elephant killed by
poachers in 2014) to the 'Yorkshire', inspired
by an English cottage – and a few have little
balconies. Continental breakfasts can be upgraded to full English on request.

Hotel Carré Vieux Port   HOTEL €€
(Map p796; ☑ 04 91 33 02 33; www.hotel-carre-
vieux-port.com; 6 rue Beauvau; s/d/tr €97/111/151;
❋ 🛜)   Sitting pretty between the quai des
Belges and place Général de Gaulle, this
well-maintained hotel rates as one of the old
port's top choices. Its rooms are bright, spacious and comfortable, and you'll enjoy nice
touches like frying-pan-sized shower heads,
cube-shaped bath goodies, complimentary
tea, coffee and biscuits; and (naturally) the
fibreglass bull in reception.

Hotel Bellevue   HOTEL €€
(Map p796; ☑ 04 96 17 05 40; www.hotelbelle
vuemarseille.com; 34 quai du Port; s/d €95/155;
❋ @ 🛜; Ⓜ Vieux Port)   Rooms at this enduring

DON'T MISS

BOUILLABAISSE

Originally cooked by fisherfolk from the scraps of their catch, bouillabaisse is Marseille's signature dish. True bouillabaisse includes at least four kinds of fish, and sometimes shellfish. Don't trust tourist traps that promise cheap bouillabaisse; the real deal costs at least €50 per person. It's served in two parts: the *soupe de poisson* (broth), rich with tomato, saffron and fennel; and the cooked fish, de-boned tableside and presented on a platter. On the side are croutons, *rouille* (a bread-thickened garlic-chilli mayonnaise) and grated cheese, usually Gruyère. Spread *rouille* on the crouton, top with cheese and float it in the soup. Be prepared for a huge meal and tons of garlic.

The *bouillabaisse* at swanky, Michelin-starred **L'Epuisette** (Map p792; ☏04 91 52 17 82; www.l-epuisette.com; 158 rue du Vallon des Auffes; lunch/bouillabaisse menu €75/98; ☺noon-1.30pm & 7.30-9.30pm Tue-Sat; ☐83) – with knock-out sea views to boot – is considered by many to be the finest out there.

1950s hotel are tastefully decorated with midrange simplicity, but the portside views are million-dollar. Breakfast can be delivered to your room for €15, but selecting it from the buffet (€10) on the pocket-sized balcony of the hotel's portside cafe La Caravelle (p800) is a Marseille highlight. Prices can hike during special events.

Le Ryad
BOUTIQUE HOTEL €€
(Map p792; ☏04 91 47 74 54; www.hotelde marseille.fr; 16 rue Sénac de Meilhan; d/ste €111/191; ☏; Ⓜ Noailles, ☐ Canebière Garibaldi) Morocco comes to Marseille at this stylish hotel, which takes its inspiration from the *riads* (traditional houses) of North Africa, all woven cushions, patterned rugs and colourful throws. There's a lovely garden, the top-floor room ('Mogador') has its own mini roof terrace, and the Moroccan breakfast – with North African pancakes and fresh fruit – is worth the extra €7 per person.

Decoh
APARTMENT €€
(Map p792; ☏04 91 37 74 95; www.decoh.fr; 31-33 rue Dragon; apt & studios per night €125-180; ✳@☏; Ⓜ Estrangin-Préfecture) The creative, vintage-loving team at the Hôtel Edmond Rostand (p794) is behind this appealing, self-catering serviced accommodation on rue Paradis, rue Dragon and rue Albert. Studios sleep two people and apartments four; the super-stylish antique furniture recalls eras from the 1950s to '70s. Stay a night, week or month. Cook for yourself, or breakfast at the Hôtel Edmond Rostand.

Intercontinental Marseille – Hôtel Dieu
LUXURY HOTEL €€€
(Map p796; ☏04 13 42 42 42; http://marseille. intercontinental.com; 1 place Daviel; r from €230; Ⓟ✳@☏☲; Ⓜ Colbert, ☐ Sadi Carnot) Occupying a heritage-listed 18th-century hospital,

the Hôtel Dieu, the Intercontinental Marseille has a commanding position in Le Panier overlooking the Vieux Port. The grand U-shaped pile features tall arched windows framed by local golden-hued stone and masonry. Within, the 179 rooms and 15 suites are suitably polished, while the best have either harbour views or private terraces.

✗ Eating

The Vieux Port and surrounding pedestrian streets teem with cafe terraces, but choose carefully (some rely on tourists to pay too much for average food). For world cuisine, try cours Julien and nearby rue des Trois Mages. For pizza, roast chicken, and Middle Eastern food under €10, nose around the streets surrounding **Marché des Capucins** (Marché de Noailles; Map p796; place des Capucins; ☺8am-7pm Mon-Sat; Ⓜ Noailles, ☐ Canebière Garibaldi).

Les Halles de la Major
MARKET €
(Map p796; ☏04 91 45 80 10; www.leshallesde lamajor.com; 12 quai de la Tourette; mains €12-20; ☺9am-7pm; ☐82) This upscale food market inside the newly renovated vaults of La Major Cathedral is great for foodies, self-caterers and simple browsers. Each stall serves a selection of small plated specialities such as local cheeses, freshly shucked oysters and Provençal 'tapas'. There's seating, a terrace and lovely views across the water.

★ El Santo Cachon
CHILEAN €
(☏06 95 99 45 93; 40 rue Ferrari; mains €16-18; ☺7.30pm-midnight Mon-Sat; ☐ Eugene Pierre) Arrive early or reserve a table at Marseille's only Chilean restaurant, because this place fills fast – and after a pisco sour (or three), you'll see why. If you want to make it out of the door walking, combat the frothy

Central Marseille

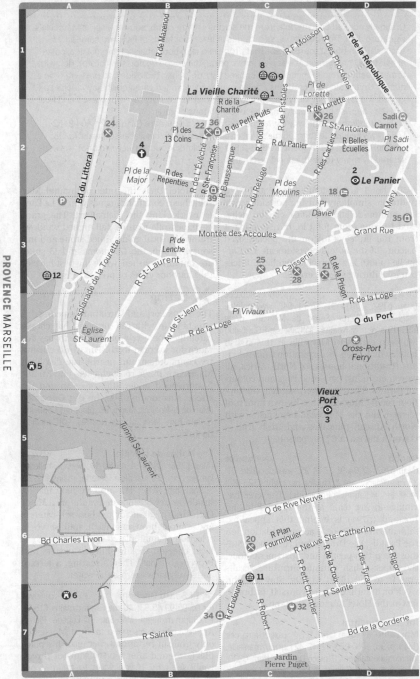

797

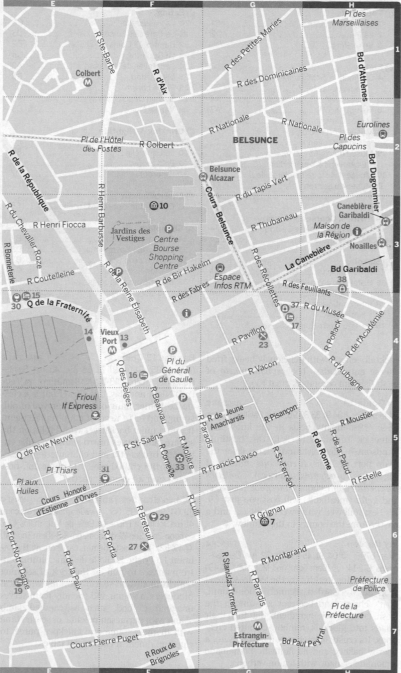

PROVENCE MARSEILLE

Map labels:

Pl des Marseillaises

Bd d'Athènes

Colbert Ⓜ

R Ste-Barbe

R d'Aix

R des Petites Maries

R des Dominicaines

Eurolines

R Nationale

R Nationale

Pl des Capucins

BELSUNCE

Pl de l'Hôtel des Postes

R Colbert

Bd Dugommier

R de la République

R du Chevalier Roze

R Henri Fiocca

R Henri Barbusse

Belsunce Alcazar

R du Tapis Vert

Canebière Garibaldi

R Coutelleine

R Bonneterie

10

Jardins des Vestiges

Centre Bourse Shopping Centre

R Thubaneau

Maison de la Région ℹ

Noailles

Cours Belsunce

R des Récollettes

La Canebière

Bd Garibaldi

R de Bir Hakeim

R des Fabrès

Espace Infos RTM

R des Feuillants

38

R Pollack

R de l'Académie

15
30 Q de la Fraternité

ℹ

R des Fabrès

37 R du Musée

17

R Pavillon

23

R d'Aubagne

R de la Reine Elisabeth

14 Vieux Port **13** Ⓜ

R Vacon

Q des Belges

Pl du Général de Gaulle

16

Frioul If Express

R Beauvau

R de Jeune Anacharsis

R Paradis

R Pisançon

R Moustier

R de la Palud

Q de Rive Neuve

R St-Saëns

R Molière

R Cornelle

R Francis Davso

R St-Férréol

R de Rome

R F stelle

Pl Thiars

31

Cours Honoré d'Estienne d'Orves

Pl aux Huiles

R Breteuil

29

R Lulli

R Grignan

7

R Fort Notre Dame

R de la Paix

R Fortia

27 ✕

R Paradis

R Montgrand

Préfecture de Police

19

R Stanislas Torrents

Pl de la Préfecture

Cours Pierre Puget

R Roux de Brignoles

Ⓜ Estrangin-Préfecture

Bd Paul Peytral

N 0 ――― 200 m
0 ――― 0.1 miles

Central Marseille

PROVENCE MARSEILLE

cocktail's effects with deliciously heavy fried cheese empanadas. The *ceviche mixto* of fresh fish and octopus is great too.

La Goulette   TUNISIAN €
(Map p796; ☏04 91 33 39 90; 1 rue Pavillon; mains €6-9; ◎9am-11pm) Locals in the know and homesick Tunisians flock to this bustling, handsomely tiled restaurant, named for the main port of Tunis. A *couscous maison* of vegetables, *brochettes* (skewers), *côtelettes d'agneau* (lamb chops), *merguez* (sausage) and *kefta* (meatballs) will cost you just €9. It's best followed with sweet mint tea and a pastry from the bounty in the window.

My Garden   FRENCH €
(Map p796; ☏04 91 45 19 74; 32 rue Caisserie; mains €12-14; ◎10am-6pm Wed-Mon; ⊘; ⊟49) For something healthy, try the locally sourced food at My Garden. Fennel, onion confit, goat's cheese and beetroot are among the fresh, farm-to-fork ingredients that turn their salads into glorious, rainbow-coloured creations. Its crusty baguettes come from Sam, a nearby bakery, and its fantastic homemade lemonade is made with lemon verbena.

Bar des 13 Coins   BRASSERIE €
(Map p796; ☏04 91 91 56 49; 45 rue Sainte-Françoise; mains €13-16; ◎9am-11pm; Ⓜ Vieux Port) Night and day, this corner bar is a classic Le Panier hang-out whether you're old, young, hip or in need of a hip replacement. It's on a quiet backstreet with tables on the square, and serves bistro standards like entrecôte, bruschetta and charcuterie plates – but it's the chilled vibe you come for, best tasted over an evening pastis.

★ Les Grandes Tables   INTERNATIONAL €
(☏04 95 04 95 85; www.lesgrandestables.com; 41 rue Jobin, La Friche La Belle de Mai; mains €16; ◎noon-2pm Sun-Wed, noon-2pm & 8-10pm Thu-Sat; ⊟49, 52) The vast former canteen at the vibrant La Friche La Belle de Mai cultural centre manages to pull off the trick of seeming both intimate and stylish. Working with local producers, a young and friendly team serves imaginative food, such as candied lamb shank with parmesan polenta, or seared tuna with thyme, sesame and chickpea puree, to clued-up diners at communal tables.

★ **Place Lorette**   MOROCCAN €
(Map p796; ☑09 81 35 66 75; 3 place de Lorette;
mains €14-16; ◷11am-6pm Thu-Sat, to 4pm Sun;
Ⓜ Colbert) Tucked away on a quiet square in
the middle of polyglot Le Panier, this Moroccan restaurant serves up a fantastic lunch in
an arched and art-strewn stone dining room
– lamb and chicken tagines, semolina bread
and crunchy *pastillas* (sweetly spiced chicken
pastries), all washed down with fresh orange
juice and mint tea. The Sunday brunch (€24)
is a sharing feast.

★ **L'Arôme**   FRENCH €€
(Map p792; ☑04 91 42 88 80; 9 rue de Trois Rois;
menus €23-28; ◷7.30-11pm Mon-Sat; Ⓜ Notre
Dame du Mont) Reserve ahead to snag a table at this fabulous little restaurant just off
cours Julien. From the service – relaxed,
competent and friendly without over familiarity – to the street art on the walls and
the memorable food, it's a complete winner. Well-credentialled chef-owner Romain
achieves sophisticated simplicity in dishes
such as roast duckling served with polenta
and a pecorino *beignet* (doughnut).

★ **Le Café des Épices**   FRENCH €€
(Map p796; ☑04 28 31 70 26; www.lecafedes
epices-by-acdg.com; 4 rue du Lacydon; lunch/dinner
menus €25/35; ◷noon-2pm & 7.30-10pm Tue-Sat;
☐55, Ⓜ Vieux Port) One of Marseille's best
chefs, Arnaud de Grammont, works thoughtfully with great produce and inventive flavours: think gurnard in chickpea broth with
dried tomatoes and radish, or blonde d'Aquitaine beef with polenta and glazed carrots.
Presentation is impeccable, the decor playful
and the outdoor terrace between giant potted
olive trees is superb in good weather.

Café Populaire   BISTRO €€
(Map p792; ☑04 91 02 53 96; 110 rue Paradis;
mains €19-24; ◷noon-2pm & 8-10.30pm Mon-Fri,
8-10.30pm Sat, noon-3pm Sun; Ⓜ Estrangin-Préfecture) Vintage furniture, latticed blinds, old
books and antique soft drink bottles lend a
retro air to this style-conscious, 1950s-styled
jazz *comptoir* (counter) – a restaurant in all
but name. The crowd is chic, and smiling
chefs in the open kitchen churn out international dishes like *tagliata* (steak strips with
rocket and parmesan) and black cod with
miso and *yuzu* (Japanese citrus).

Le Goût des Choses   BISTRO €€
(Map p792; ☑04 91 48 70 62; www.legoutdeschoses.
fr; 4 place Notre Dame du Mont; lunch/dinner menus from €22/29; ◷noon-1.30pm & 7.30-10pm Wed-

Sun) Having previously run restaurants in
Antibes and Fort Lauderdale, husband-and-
wife team Olivier and Sylvie opened this colourful bistro off cours Julien. The generous,
good-value menu mixes Mediterranean and
Middle Eastern flavours with French techniques, in dishes such as steamed salt-cod
with coconut-turmeric sauce.

La Passarelle   PROVENCAL €€
(Map p796; ☑04 91 33 03 27; www.restaurantla
passarelle.fr; 52 rue Plan Fourmiguier; mains €16-
22; ◷noon-2.30pm & 8-10.30pm Mar-Oct, shorter
hours rest of year; ☐82, 83, Ⓜ Vieux Port) This ad-
mirably unpretentious bistro grows most of
its organic veggies in its own *potager* (kitch
en garden), from tomatoes to courgettes, salad leaves and aubergines. It's a cosy, friendly
place for sampling delicious Mediterranean
flavours, with mix-and-match tables and
chairs arranged on a decked terrace beneath
a spreading sail. Charming and simple.

Le Petit Nice   SEAFOOD €€€
(☑04 91 59 25 92; www.passedat.fr; 17 rue des
Braves; menus from €100; ☐83) The flagship restaurant of Marseille-born gastronomic star
Gérald Passedat, Le Petit Nice is a true dining
destination. Set in a 1917 seafront villa on the
Anse de Maldormé, it sets the benchmark for
seafood cookery in Provence. Expect *oursin*
(sea-urchin), *langouste* (crayfish), *rouget* (red
mullet) and other freshly caught Mediterranean delights at their very best.

Le Chalet du Pharo   MEDITERRANEAN €€€
(Map p792; ☑04 91 52 80 11; www.le-chalet-
du-pharo.com; 58 bd Charles Livon, Jardin du
Pharo; menus €39-47; ◷noon-3pm & 7.30-11pm
Mon-Sat, noon-3pm Sun; Ⓜ Vieux Port) Only
Marseillais and the cognoscenti are privy

PROVENCE MARSEILLE

DON'T MISS

BLACK ICE

There are plenty of ice-cream shops
around Marseille, but there's only one
that sells black ice cream (coloured
by vanilla pods, which lend a unique,
bittersweet, custardy flavour). There are
around 30 other flavours of ice cream
and sorbet to try, all made on-site at
Vanille Noire (Map p796; ☑07 77 33 68
19; www.vanillenoire.com; 13 rue Caisserie;
ice cream €2; ◷12.30pm-6.45pm; Ⓜ Vieux
Port) with organic ingredients. Go for the
pastis or lavender to keep it Provençal.

to this little chalet with a very big view, secreted in the Jardin du Pharo. Its hillside terrace, shaded by pines and parasols, stares across the water to Fort St-Jean, MuCEM and the Villa Méditerranée beyond. Grilled fish and meat dominate the menu. Online reservations are essential, and cards aren't accepted.

🍸 Drinking & Nightlife

In the best tradition of Mediterranean cities, Marseille embraces the cafe-lounger lifestyle. Near the Vieux Port, head to place Thiars and cours Honoré d'Estienne d'Orves for cafes that bask in the sun by day and buzz into the night. Cours Julien is a fine place on a sunny day to watch people come and go at the many characterful shops, cafes and restaurants in one of Marseille's most interesting neighbourhoods. Le Panier, place de Lenche and rue des Pistoles are ideal places to while away an afternoon soaking up the area's boho charms.

★ Waaw   BAR

(Map p792; ✆04 91 42 16 33; www.waaw.fr; 17 rue Pastoret; ⊗4pm-midnight Wed & Sat, from 6pm Tue, Thu & Fri; Ⓜ Notre Dame du Mont) Marseille's creative chameleon and the heart of the cours Julien scene, Waaw ('What an Amazing World') has everything you could possibly want for a night out. Whether that's a cold cocktail, a late-night dancehall DJ set or an innovative dinner made from local market produce, the city's unofficial cultural headquarters offers music, film, festivals and much more.

La Caravelle   BAR

(Map p796; ✆04 91 90 36 64; www.lacaravelle-marseille.com; 34 quai du Port; ⊗7am-2am; 🎷; Ⓜ Vieux Port) On the 1st floor of Hôtel Bellevue, this lovely little bar is styled with rich wood and leather, with a zinc bar and yellowing murals that hint of its 1920s pedigree. If it's sunny, snag a coveted spot on the portside terrace, and sip a pastis as you watch the throng below. On Friday there's live jazz from 9pm.

🛈 GAY & LESBIAN MARSEILLE

Visit www.actu-gay.com for information on Marseillais gay life. It's a small scene that is in constant flux and only really converges on weekends, but the city is generally gay friendly.

La Dame du Mont   BAR

(Map p792; ✆04 91 47 35 76; 30-32 place Notre Dame du Mont; ⊗4.30pm-1.30am; Ⓜ Notre Dame du Mont-Cours Julien) Regular DJs bring reggae, soul, funk, rock and much else besides to this friendly, bustling hang-out on place Notre Dame du Mont. Craft beers, cocktails and bonhomie are in ample supply, especially during happy hours (7pm to 9pm).

La Part des Anges   WINE BAR

(Map p796; ✆04 91 33 55 70; www.lapartdes anges.com; 33 rue Sainte; ⊗9am-2am Mon-Sat, 9am-1pm & 6pm-2am Sun; Ⓜ Vieux Port) This fabulously convivial wine bar is named after the alcohol that evaporates through a barrel during wine or whisky fermentation: the 'angels' share'. Take your pick of dozens of wines by the glass, listed by region on a blackboard behind the bar, or buy a bottle to take away. Steak, pasta and other wine-friendly ballast is available.

R2   COCKTAIL BAR

(Map p792; ✆04 91 91 79 39; www.airdemarseille. com; 9 quai du Lazaret; ⊗7pm-2am Tue-Sun Apr-Sep; Ⓜ Joliette) Together, Le Rooftop – a spectacular open-air cocktail bar with rotating DJs playing house, electro, disco and rock – and Reverso – the restaurant space below it, serving from 7pm – make up R2, a slick waterside spot in Joliette.

Polikarpov   BAR

(Map p796; ✆04 91 52 70 30; 24 cours Honoré d'Estienne d'Orves; ⊗8am-1.30am; Ⓜ Vieux Port) Scarcely shut, this al fresco bar with buzzing pavement terrace just a couple of blocks from the Vieux Port markets itself as 'Massilia vodkabar'. From 9pm DJs range across house, electro, R&B and other styles, depending on the night.

U.percut   CLUB

(Map p796; ✆04 91 39 22 15; www.u-percut.fr; 127 rue Sainte; ⊗6pm-2am Tue-Sat; 🚌55) Happy to host anything that will get feet shuffling, U.percut puts on killer jazz bands, crooning soul stars, hip hop maestros and late-night breakbeat DJs under its vaulted stone ceiling. Upstairs it has some excellent local wines, an impressive whisky list and mouth-watering tapas. Cover charges start from €3, and it's also open two Sundays per month.

Le Trash   GAY

(✆04 91 25 52 16; www.letrashbar.com; 28 rue du Berceau; ⊗8.30pm-2am Mon & Wed, from 9.30pm

ℹ **PICNIC PARADISE**

Shop for French-chic foodstuffs, fresh bread and traditional orange-perfumed *navettes de Marseille*, then follow the local crowd to the grassy **Jardin du Pharo** (Map p792; 58 bd Charles Livon; ⊗8am-9pm; ☒81, 82, 83). With unparalleled views over old Marseille, the gardens are a perfect picnic (and sunset-watching) spot.

Farmers Market (Map p792; www.coursjulien.marsnet.org; cours Julien; ⊗7am-1pm Wed; Ⓜ Notre Dame du Mont) Every Wednesday morning the farmers market along cours Julien squawks with life, colour and accordion music as traders flog mounds of organic vegetables, jars of homemade fruit jam, hand-collected quail eggs and bouquets of fragrant herbs. Once your shopping bags are brimming, head to a nearby cafe and watch the mostly boho crowd haggle with the stallholders.

Four des Navettes (Map p796; ☑04 91 33 32 12; www.fourdesnavettes.com; 136 rue Sainte; ⊗7am-8pm Mon-Sat, 9am-1pm & 3-7.30pm Sun; Ⓜ Vieux Port) Opened in 1781, this is the oldest bakery in Marseille; it's been passed down between three families, and it still uses the original 18th-century oven. It is *the* address to pick up Marseille's signature biscuits, the orange-perfumed *navettes de Marseille*, as well as *calissons* (Provençal almond biscuits), nougat and other delights.

Le Bar à Pain (Map p792; ☑06 45 17 37 33; 18 cours Joseph Thierry; lunch €4-5; ⊗8am-8pm Tue-Fri, to 6pm Sat; ☒Canebière) Selling arguably the best baguettes in the city, this charming organic bakery in the Chapitre neighbourhood also rustles together tasty midday snacks like flaky courgette tarts and toasty tomato pizzas, all to be enjoyed on their suntrap of a terrace. The coffee is excellent too, and don't leave without trying a Ti Coco, their rum-laden coconut ball.

Sylvain Depuichaffray (Map p796; ☑04 91 33 09 75; www.sylvaindepuichaffray.fr; 66 rue Grignan; pastries €3-5; ⊗8am-4pm Mon, to 7pm Tue-Sat; Ⓜ Vieux Port) This smart *boulangerie* and patisserie with a *salon du thé* (tearoom) attached produces some of Marseille's best pastries.

Fri & Sat, from 3pm Sun; Ⓜ Baille) Southwest of the cours Julien nightlife area, Le Trash bills itself as Marseille's cruising bar, for good reason. There's a cover charge on special nights (from €10).

Baby Club CLUB
(Map p792; ☑06 48 48 64 17; 2 rue André Poggioli, ⊗midnight-6am Wed-Sun; Ⓜ Notre Dame du Mont) Located in the bohemian neighborhood of La Plaine, Baby Club offers the perfect atmosphere for an abandoned after-hours party. Look for its garish zebra-striped exterior, then head inside to catch the latest French and European house and techno DJs. Some nights are free, but a cover of €10 is more common.

☆ **Entertainment**

Cultural events are covered in *L'Hebdo* (€1.20), available around town, or at www.marseillebynight.com and www.journalventilo.fr. Tickets for some events are sold the tourist office (p802). Cultural centre La Friche La Belle de Mai hosts theatre, cinema and music.

★ **La Friche La Belle de Mai** ARTS CENTRE
(☑04 95 04 95 04; www.lafriche.org; 41 rue Jobin; ⊗ticket kiosk 11am-6pm Mon, to 7pm Tue-Sat, from 12.30pm Sun; ☒49, 52) This 45,000-sq-metre former tobacco factory is now a vibrant arts centre with a theatre, cinema, bar, bookshop, artists' workshops, multimedia displays, skateboard ramps, electro- and world-music parties and much more. Check the program online. The on-site restaurant, Les Grandes Tables (p799), is a great bet for interesting, locally sourced food.

The quickest way to get here by public transport is to catch the metro to Gare St-Charles and walk along rue Guibal, or take line M2 to Cinq Avenues Longchamp, cross Parc Longchamp and then take Rue Bénédit.

★ **Videodrome 2** CINEMA
(Map p792; ☑04 88 44 41 84; www.videodrome2. fr; 49 cours Julien; tickets from €3; ⊗5pm-2am Tue & Thu-Fri, from 3pm Wed & Sat, to 12.30am Sun; Ⓜ Notre Dame du Mont) Fewer video shops would have gone the way of the dodo if they'd followed the lead of Videodrome 2: simultaneously a DVD rental shop, bar-bistro and tiny arthouse movie theatre, it's a treat

> ### ⓘ CENT SAVER
>
> The **Marseille City Pass** (www.resa
> marseille.com; 24/48/72hr €26/33/41)
> covers admission to city museums and
> public transport, and includes a guided
> city tour and a Château d'If boat trip,
> plus other discounts. It's not necessary
> for children under 12, as many attrac-
> tions are greatly reduced or free. Buy it
> online or at the tourist office.

for gregarious cinephiles. As well as stocking some excellent local beers, the cinema
shows rare and cult films and runs retrospectives on notable auteurs.

Opéra Municipal de Marseille   OPERA
(Map p796; ☑ 04 91 55 11 10; http://opera.marseille.
fr; 2 rue Molière; ⊙ box office 10am-5.30pm Tue-Sat;
Ⓜ Vieux Port) Built in the 1920s on the site of
its 18th-century predecessor, this 1800-seat
neoclassical theatre has seen the French premieres of many notable operas, and hosted
some of its most famous performers. The season runs from September to June.

Espace Julien   LIVE MUSIC
(Map p792; ☑ 04 91 24 34 10; www.espace-julien.
com; 39 cours Julien; Ⓜ Notre Dame du Mont-Cours
Julien) Rock, *opérock*, alternative theatre, reggae, hip-hop, Afro groove and other entertainment all appear on the bill at this mainstay of
the cours Julien scene. See the website for the
program and to buy tickets.

🛍 Shopping

Maison Empereur   HOMEWARES
(Map p796; ☑ 04 91 54 02 29; www.empereur.fr;
4 rue des Récolettes; ⊙ 9am-7pm Mon-Sat; ☑ 2,
3) If you only have time to visit one shop in
Marseille, make it this one. Run by the same
family since 1827, France's oldest hardware
store remains a one-stop shop for beautifully made homeware items including Opinel
cutlery, Savon de Marseille soaps, wooden
toy sailing boats and ceramic shaving bowls.

★ Maison de la Boule   GIFTS & SOUVENIRS
(Map p796; ☑ 04 88 44 39 44; www.museede
laboule.com; 4 place des 13 Cantons; ⊙ 10am-7pm
Mon-Sat, to 6pm Sun; ☑ 49, Ⓜ Vieux Port) Pick up
a set of handmade boules (complete with
matching carry bag), plus plenty of other souvenirs of France's iconic game. There's also an
indoor court and a museum exploring the history of the sport, including the curious figure

of Fanny (tradition dictates if you lose a game
13 to nil, you must kiss her bare bum cheeks).

UndARTground   ART
(Map p796; ☑ 06 50 08 28 21; www.undartground.
com; 21 rue des Repenties; ⊙ 11am-7pm Wed-Mon;
☑ 49) As the street-art daubed walls of this
concept store and gallery suggest, it showcases the work of local underground artists.
As well as posters by eBoy and prints by Oaï
of Life, expect anything from urban T-shirts
and thick coffee table books to ghetto blaster
pillow cases designed by AK-LH.

La Grande Savonnerie   COSMETICS
(Map p796; ☑ 09 50 63 80 35; www.lagrande
savonnerie.com; 36 Grande Rue; ⊙ 9am-6pm Tue-
Sun; Ⓜ Vieux Port) Soap-making in Marseille
has been traced by some to the 14th century,
but much of the stuff for sale at the city's
markets is made elsewhere. That's not the
case at this little soap maker, which specialises in the genuine Marseillais article, made
with olive oil and no added perfume, and
shaped into cubes.

ⓘ Information

Tourist Office (Map p796; ☑ 08 26 50 05 00,
box office 04 91 13 89 16; www.marseille-
tourisme.com; 11 La Canebière; ⊙ 9am-6pm;
Ⓜ Vieux Port) Marseille's useful tourist office
has plenty of information on everything, including guided city tours (by foot, bus, electric
tourist train or boat) and trips to Les Calanques. There's free wi-fi too.

Maison de la Région (Map p796; ☑ 04 91
57 50 57; www.regionpaca.fr; 27 place Jules
Guesde; ⊙ 11am-6pm Mon-Sat; Ⓜ Noailles) Info
on Provence and the Côte d'Azur.

Marseille Expos (www.marseilleexpos.com) The
outstanding arts organisation Marseille Expos
distributes an excellent map of hot galleries and
sponsors the festival Printemps de l'Art Contemporain each May. Its website lists what's on.

ⓘ Getting There & Away

AIR

Aéroport Marseille-Provence (Aéroport
Marseille-Marignane; MRS; ☑ 08 20 81 14 14;
www.marseille.aeroport.fr) is 25km northwest
of Marseille in Marignane. There are regular
year-round flights to nearly all major French
cities, plus major hubs in the UK, Germany,
Belgium, Italy and Spain.

BOAT

Gare Maritime de la Major (Marseille Fos;
www.marseille-port.fr; Quai de la Joliette;
Ⓜ Joliette), the passenger ferry terminal, is
located just south of place de la Joliette.

Corsica Linea (☑ 08 25 88 80 88; www.corsica linea.com; quai du Maroc; ⊘ 8.30am-8pm) has regular ferries from Marseille to Corsica and Sardinia, plus long-distance routes to Algeria and Tunisia.

BUS

The **bus station** (Gare Routière; Map p792; ☑ 04 91 08 16 40; www.rtm.fr; 3 rue Honnorat; Ⓜ Gare St-Charles) is on the northern side of the train station. Buy tickets here or from the driver. Services to some destinations, including Cassis, use the **Halte Routière Sud** (p803), south of the centre.

For most destinations along the Côte d'Azur, it's faster and easier to catch the train, but for some smaller towns and villages (especially inland), buses are an alternative. There are several different companies, but you can find comprehensive timetable information on the website Le Pilote (www.lepilote.com). Sample destinations:

Aix-en-Provence (€9, 40 minutes, every 10 minutes Monday to Saturday, less frequent Sunday) Cartreize line 50 express bus leaves from Gare St-Charles. Line 51 also runs frequently to Aix.

Barcelonette (€35, 4¼ hours, one direct daily) LER Line 28

OFF THE BEATEN TRACK

LES CALANQUES

It feels like a miracle to find a refuge such as the **Parc National des Calanques** (☑ 04 20 10 50 00; www.calanques-parcnational.fr; 141 av du Prado, Bâtiment A, Marseille) only a short distance from grimy, pressured Marseille. In parts of this diminutive 85-sq-km patch of scrubby, convoluted promontories, it's easy to believe you're miles from civilisation. This is where the Marseillais come for the sun, to hike over pine-strewn promontories, to mess about on boats and refresh their souls. The region is hugely popular in summer, visited by boats and hikers who schlep for hours to the secluded fishing villages.

Of the many *calanques* along the coastline, the most easily accessible are **Calanque de Sormiou** and **Calanque de Morgiou**, while remote inlets such as **Calanque d'En Vau and Calanque de Port-Miou** take dedication and time to reach – on foot or by kayak.

From October to June the best way to see the *calanques* (including the 500 sq km of the rugged inland **Massif des Calanques**) is to hike the many lined trails through the *maquis* (scrub). Marseille's tourist office (p802) leads guided walks (ages eight and over) and has information about trail and road closures. It also offers an excellent hiking map of the various *calanques*, as does Cassis' **tourist office** (☑ 08 92 39 01 03; www.ot-cassis. com; quai des Moulins; ⊘ 9am-6.30pm Mon-Sat, 9.30am-12.30pm & 3-6pm Sun May-Aug, shorter hours rest of year; ☏). From June to September trails may close due to fire danger.

Operators such as **Destination Calanques Kayak** (☑ 06 07 15 63 86; www.destination-calanques.fr; half/full day €35/55; ⊘ Apr-Oct) and **Raskas Kayak** (☑ 04 91 73 27 16; www.raskas-kayak.com; impasse du Dr Bonfils, Auberge de Jeunesse Marseille; half/full day €40/70) organise sea-kayaking tours; local tourist offices have details of lots of other hire companies. **Calanc'O** (☑ 06 25 78 85 93; www.calanco-kayak-paddle.com; 9 ave Joseph Liautaud; half/full day €35/55; ⊘ 8am-8pm) also offers stand-up paddle-boarding.

During July and August the only real option for accessing individual *calanques* is to take a boat tour with **Croisières Marseille Calanques** (Map p796; ☑ 04 91 58 50 58; www.croisieres-marseille-calanques.com; 1 La Canebière, Vieux Port; Ⓜ Vieux Port) from Marseille or Cassis. Check in advance if you're hoping to be able to stop for a swim, as only a few tours allow this, such as the one offered by **Icard Maritime** (Map p796; ☑ 04 91 33 36 79; www.visite-des-calanques.com; quai des Belges; adult/child from €23/18; Ⓜ Vieux Port).

Getting There & Away

For access to the *calanques* closest to Marseille, drive or take bus 19 from Marseille's **Castellane bus stop** (Halte Routière Sud; Map p792; place Castellane; Ⓜ Castellane) down the coast to its terminus at La Madrague, then switch to bus 20 to Callelongue (note that the road to Callelongue is only open to cars on weekdays from mid-April to May and closed entirely from June to September). From there you can walk to Calanque de la Mounine and Calanque de Marseilleveyre along spectacular trails over the clifftops.

Calanque de Sugiton is also easy to access without a car. Take bus 21 from Castellane towards Luminy and get off at the last stop. From there follow the path (about a 45-minute walk).

Cassis (€2, 45 minutes, hourly Monday to Saturday) La Marcouline Line MO6

Nice (€34, three to five hours, up to five per day) LER Line 20

Eurolines (Map p796; www.eurolines.com; 3 allées Léon Gambetta; Ⓜ Noailles) also has international services.

TRAIN

Eurostar (www.eurostar.com) offers two to 10 weekly services between Marseille and London (from €213, seven hours) via Lille or Paris. As always, the earlier you book, the cheaper the fare.

Regular and TGV trains serve **Gare St-Charles** (🖉 04 91 08 16 40; www.rtm.fr; rue Jacques Bory; Ⓜ Gare St-Charles SNCF), which is a junction for both metro lines. The **left-luggage office** (Consignes Automatiques; ⊘ 8.15am-9pm) is next to platform A. Sample fares:

Avignon €22, 1¼ hours, hourly

Nice €38, 2½ hours, up to six per day

Paris Gare de Lyon From €76, 3½ hours, at least hourly

❶ Getting Around

TO/FROM THE AIRPORT

Navette Marseille (Map p792; www.lepilote. com; one way/return €8.30/14; ⊘ 4.30am-11.30pm) buses link the airport and Gare St-Charles (30 minutes) every 15 to 20 minutes.

The airport's train station has direct services to several cities including Arles and Avignon – a free shuttle bus runs to/from the airport terminal.

BICYCLE

With the **Le Vélo** (🖉 English-language helpline 01 30 79 29 13; www.levelo-mpm.fr) bike-share scheme, you can pick up and drop off bikes from 100-plus stations across the city and along the coastal road to the beaches. Users must first subscribe online (€1/5 per week/year) then the first 30 minutes of every hire is free, after which bikes cost €1 per hour. Stations only take credit cards with chips.

BOAT

Boats run from the old port to the **Îles du Frioul** (p791), as well as to the Parc National des Calanques. There's also a **ferry** (Map p796; one way €0.50; ⊘ 7.30am-8.30pm; Ⓜ Vieux Port) across the Vieux Port.

PUBLIC TRANSPORT

Marseille has two metro lines (Métro 1 and Métro 2), two tram lines (yellow and green) and an extensive network. Bus, metro or tram tickets (one/10 trips €1.70/14) are available from machines in the metro, at tram stops and on buses. Most buses start in front of the **Espace Infos RTM** (Map p796; 🖉 04 91 91 92 10; www.rtm.fr; 6 rue des Fabres; ⊘ 8.30am-6pm Mon-Fri;

Ⓜ Vieux Port), where you can obtain information and tickets.

The metro runs from 5am to 10.30pm Monday to Thursday, and until 12.30am Friday to Sunday. Trams run 5am to 1am daily.

AIX-EN-PROVENCE

POP 142,668

A pocket of left-bank Parisian chic deep in Provence, Aix (pronounced like the letter X) is all class: its leafy boulevards and public squares are lined with 17th- and 18th-century mansions, punctuated by gurgling moss-covered fountains. Haughty stone lions guard its grandest avenue, cafe-laced cours Mirabeau, where fashionable Aixois pose on polished pavement terraces, sipping espresso. While Aix is a student hub, its upmarket appeal makes it pricier than other Provençal towns.

The part-pedestrianised centre of Aix's old town is ringed by busy boulevards, with several large car parks dotted on the edge of town. Whatever you do, don't try and drive into the centre.

◉ Sights

Art, culture and architecture abound in Aix. Of special note are the town's many fountains. Some, like the 1860 **Fontaine de la Rotonde** (pl du Général de Gaulle), are quite grand. Others have simpler charms, such as the 1819 **Fontaine du Roi René** (cours Mirabeau) and the 1734 **Fontaine d'Eau Chaude** (Mossy Fountain; cours Mirabeau) – the former features the king holding a bunch of grapes, while the latter has temperate 18°C (64.4°F) water from a spring and is covered in moss.

Cours Mirabeau   STREET

No streetscape better epitomises Provence's most graceful city than this 440m-long, fountain-studded street, sprinkled with Renaissance *hôtels particuliers* (private mansions) and crowned with a summertime roof of leafy plane trees. It was laid out in the 1650s and later named after the Revolutionary hero the Comte de Mirabeau. Cézanne and Zola hung out at **Les Deux Garçons** (🖉 04 42 26 00 51; http://lesdeuxgarcons.fr; 53 cours Mirabeau; ⊘ 7am-2am), one of a string of busy pavement cafes.

Vieil Aix   HISTORIC SITE

One of Aix's great charms is its historical centre: ramble through it, drinking in divine streetscapes as you choose which historical, cultural or culinary highlight to sample

---

DON'T MISS

TRAILING CÉZANNE
....

Local lad Paul Cézanne (1839–1906) is revered in Aix. To see where he lived, ate, drank, studied and painted, follow the **Circuit de Cézanne** (Cézanne Trail), marked by bronze plaques embedded in the footpath. The essential English-language guide to the circuit, and other artist-related sites, *In the Steps of Cézanne,* is free at the tourist office.

Atelier Cézanne (☑04 42 21 06 53; www.atelier-cezanne.com; 9 av Paul Cézanne; adult/child €6.50/free, audioguide €3; ☉10am-6pm Jun-Sep, 10am-12.30pm & 2-6pm Apr & May, 10.30am-12.30pm & 2-5pm Oct-Mar, closed Sun Dec-Feb; ☐5, 12) Cézanne's last studio, where he worked from 1902 until his death four years later, has been painstakingly preserved. Some elements have been recreated: not all the tools and still-life models strewn around the room were his. Though the studio is inspiring, and home to periodic exhibitions, none of Cezanne's works actually hang there. It's a leisurely walk to the studio at Lauves hill, 1.5km north of central Aix, or you can take the bus.

Terrain des Peintres (www.terrain-des-peintres-aix-en-provence.fr; chemin de la Marguerite; ☐5, 12) A wonderful terraced garden perfect for a picnic, from where Cézanne, among others, painted the Montagne Ste-Victoire. The view of the jagged mountain is inspirational – Cézanne painted over 80 renditions of it, nine of which are immortalised in stone. The gardens are opposite 62 av Paul Cézanne. You'll find them a 10-minute walk uphill from the Atelier Cézanne stop (bus 5 or 12).

Carrières de Bibemus (Bibémus Quarries; ☑04 42 16 11 61; www.cezanne-en-provence. com; 3090 chemin de Bibémus; adult/child €7.70/free; ☉English-language tours 11am Apr, May & Oct; ℙ) In 1895 Cézanne rented a *cabanon* (cabin) at the Carrières de Bibemus, east of Aix, where he painted 27 works. Atmospheric one-hour tours of the ochre quarry take visitors on foot through the dramatic burnt-orange rocks that Cézanne captured so vividly on canvas. Tours are mostly in French, though occasional tours are offered in English; book in advance at the tourist office, wear sturdy shoes and avoid wearing white. The ticket price includes a shuttle from the tourist office.

Bastide du Jas de Bouffan (☑04 42 16 11 61; www.cezanne-en-provence.com; 17 route de Galice; adult/child €6/free; ☉guided tours from 10.30am daily Jun-Sep, Tue, Thu & Sat May & Oct, Wed & Sat Nov-Mar) In 1859 Cézanne's father bought Le Jas de Bouffan, an 18th-century country manor west of Aix where Cézanne painted furiously, producing 36 oils and 17 watercolours depicting the house, farm, chestnut alley, green park and so forth. The manor was closed for renovation when we visited, and is expected to reopen in 2019.

Montagne Ste-Victoire (www.grandsitesaintevictoire.com) East of Aix rises Cézanne's favourite haunt, the magnificent silvery ridge of Montagne Ste-Victoire, its dry slopes carpeted in *garrigue* (scented scrub), bristling with pines, crossed by stone-walled paths and concealing sites such as the 17th-century Sainte-Victoire Priory. The burnt-orange soil supports Coteaux d'Aix-en-Provence vineyards, and hiking, mountain-hiking and other activities can be arranged through the Aix tourist centre. Many hike the 1011m-mountain's north side, but the south side, though steeper, is quite beautiful.

PROVENCE AIX-EN-PROVENCE

---

next. North of the graceful cours Mirabeau, the city's main artery, is the oldest part of town; to the south, the 17th-century **Quartier Mazarin** is home to some of Aix's finest buildings and streets (including the **Place des Quatre Dauphins**, ennobled by a baroque fountain of the same name).

★**Musée Granet**   MUSEUM
(☑04 42 52 88 32; www.museegranet-aixenprovence.fr; place St-Jean de Malte; adult/child €5.50/free; ☉10am-7pm Tue-Sun mid-Jun–Sep, noon-6pm Tue-Sun Oct–mid-Jun) Aix established one of France's first public museums here, on the site of a former Hospitallers' priory, in 1838. Nearly 200 years of acquisitions (including bequests by the eponymous François Marius Granet, himself a painter of note) have resulted in a collection of more than 12,000 works, including pieces by Picasso, Léger, Matisse, Monet, Klee, Van Gogh and, crucially, nine pieces by local boy Cézanne. This fabulous art museum sits right near the top of France's artistic must-sees.

★ **Caumont Centre d'Art**   HISTORIC BUILDING
(📞 04 42 20 70 01; www.caumont-centredart.com; 3 rue Joseph Cabassol; adult/child €6.50/free; ⊙ 10am-7pm May-Sep, to 6pm Oct-Apr) The Caumont is a stellar art space housed inside the Mazarin quarter's grandest 18th-century *hôtel particulier*. While there are three quality exhibitions each year, plus concerts and other events, it's the building itself that's the star of the show. Built from local honey-coloured stone, its palatial rooms are stuffed with antiques and objets d'art attesting to the opulence of the house's aristocratic past.

🎊 Festivals & Events

★ **Festival d'Aix-en-Provence**   MUSIC
(📞 04 34 08 02 17; www.festival-aix.com; ⊙ Jul) Established in the spirit of rebirth following WWII, this world-renowned festival brings opera, orchestral works, chamber music and even buskers to Aix throughout July. The wonderfully atmospheric **Théâtre de l'Archevêché**, created for the first festival in 1948 and still its principal venue, occupies the courtyard of the former Archbishop's Palace.

🛏 Sleeping

★ **L'Épicerie**   B&B €€
(📞 06 74 40 89 73; 12 rue du Cancel; r from €110; 🛜) It's best to connect by phone to this intimate B&B on a backstreet in Vieil Aix. The creation of born-and-bred Aixois lad Luc, the breakfast room re-creates a 1950s grocery store, while the flowery garden out the back is perfect for evening dining and weekend brunch (book ahead for both). Breakfast is a veritable feast. Two rooms accommodate families of four.

★ **Hôtel les Quatre Dauphins**   BOUTIQUE HOTEL €€
(📞 04 42 38 16 39; www.lesquatredauphins.fr; 54 rue Roux Alphéran; s/d €101/123; ✳🛜) This sweet 13-room hotel slumbers in a former 19th-century mansion in one of the loveliest parts of town. Rooms are fresh and clean, decorated with a great eye and equipped with excellent modern bathrooms. Those with sloping, beamed ceilings in the attic are quaint but are not for those who don't pack light – the terracotta-tiled staircase is not suitcase friendly.

★ **Hôtel des Augustins**   HOTEL €€
(📞 04 42 27 28 59; www.hotel-augustins.com; 3 rue de la Masse; s/d €139/159; ✳🛜) Once a 15th-century Augustinian convent – the magnificent stone-vaulted lobby makes visible use of an earlier, 12th-century chapel – this charismatic hotel has volumes of history. Martin Luther even stayed here after his excommunication. Sadly, there's not so much heritage to be found in the modern rooms, though pricier suites have antique furniture and private terraces beneath the bell tower.

★ **Villa Gallici**   HISTORIC HOTEL €€€
(📞 04 42 23 29 23; www.villagallici.com; 18 av de la Violette; r from €560; 🅿✳🛜🍴) Baroque and beautiful, this fabulous villa was built as a private residence in the 18th century and still feels marvellously opulent. Rooms are more like museum pieces, stuffed with gilded mirrors, toile de Jouy wallpaper and filigreed furniture. There's a lovely lavender-filled garden to breakfast in, plus a pool, a superb restaurant and a wine cellar.

🍴 Eating

Aix excels at Provençal cuisine. Restaurant terraces spill out across dozens of charm-heavy old-town squares, many pierced by ancient stone fountains; place des Trois Ormeaux, place des Augustins, place Ramus and vast Forum des Cardeurs are particular favourites.

WORTH A TRIP

A QUINTESSENTIAL PROVENÇAL LUNCH

The delightful hilltop village of Ventabren lies 15km west of Aix-en-Provence, providing a perfect lazy day trip. It's the gorgeous medieval town itself, built as protection from Saracen raids from the 10th century, that's the attraction – but the perfect way to conclude a day exploring its narrow, cobbled lanes is to dine at **La Table de Ventabren** (📞 04 42 28 79 33; www.danb.fr; 1 rue Frédéric Mistral; menus €48-107; ⊙ kitchen noon-1.15pm & 7.45-9.15pm Tue-Sun May-Sep, shorter hours rest of year). Many restaurants with stunning views rest on their laurels in the kitchen: not so La Table de Ventabren. This Michelin-starred restaurant – with a canvas-canopied terrace that's nothing short of magical on summer evenings – serves exquisite food. Chef Dan Bessoudo creates inventive French dishes and out-of-this-world desserts.

★**Farinoman Fou**   BAKERY €
(www.farinomanfou.fr; 3 rue Mignet; bread €1.40-3; ⊙7am-7pm Tue-Sat) To appeal to bread connoisseurs, in Aix as in any part of France, you need to know your dough. Judging by the lines typically spilling out of this shop onto place des Prêcheurs, artisanal *boulanger* Benoît Fradette clearly does. The bakery has no need to invest in a fancy shopfront – customers jostle for space with bread ovens and dough-mixing tubs.

Maison Nosh   CAFE €
(✆06 52 86 22 39; www.maison-nosh.com; 42-44 cours Sextius; lunch menus €10-12; ⊙10am-6pm Mon-Sat) Branching out from its original menu of posh hot dogs and gourmet English muffins, this breezy, youthful cafe now offers healthier breakfast, brunch and lunch options, and it's a pleasant place to linger over excellent coffee. Gourmet hot dogs and muffins still form the core of the lunchtime *formules,* however: for €10 you also get a dessert and a drink.

Le Bistrot   BISTRO €
(✆04 42 23 34 61; 5 Rue Campra; plat du jour €10, lunch menu €16, mains €15-16; ⊙noon-2pm & 7.30-10pm) Locals pack into the tiny vaulted dining room of this hard-to-find place for the superb-value lunch *menus.* All the bistro boxes are ticked: red-and-white tablecloths, friendly old-school service, a chuffing coffee machine and menu classics like *daube provençal* (meat stew), chicken hotpot and grilled entrecôte. Extra points for the witty names: the chocolate mousse is called 'Look out, moustache-wearers'.

★**Le Petit Verdot**   PROVENCAL €€
(✆04 42 27 30 12; www.lepetitverdot.fr; 7 rue d'Entrecasteaux; mains €21-23; ⊙7pm-midnight Mon-Sat) It's all about hearty, honest dining here, with tabletops made out of old wine crates, and a lively chef-patron who runs the place with huge enthusiasm, happily showing how good Provençal food and wine can be. Expect dishes such as *onglet* (skirt steak) in green-pepper sauce or Pata Negra pork with mustard and honey, accompanied by great wines and seasonal veggies.

Jardin Mazarin   FRENCH €€
(✆04 28 31 08 36; www.jardinmazarin.com; 15 rue du 4 Septembre; lunch/dinner menus €23/29; ⊙9am-3pm & 7-10.30pm Mon-Sat) This elegant restaurant is set perfectly on the ground floor of a handsome 18th-century *hôtel particulier* in

---

CALISSONS D'AIX

Aix'a sweetest treat since King René's wedding banquet in 1473 is the marzipan-like local speciality, *calisson d'Aix*, a small, diamond-shaped, chewy delicacy made on a wafer base with ground almonds and fruit syrup, and glazed with icing sugar. Traditional *calissonniers* still make them, including **La Maison du Roy René** (www.calisson.com; 13 rue Gaston de Saporta; calisson boxes from €4.90; ⊙8am-4.30pm Mon-Thu, to 11am Fri).

---

the Quartier Mazarin. Two salons sit beneath splendid beamed ceilings, but the real gem is the verdant fountain-centred garden, which comes into its own in summer. Expect local, seasonal produce (such as truffles and asparagus) from the kitchen.

★**La Table de Pierre Reboul**   GASTRONOMY €€€
(✆04 42 52 27 27; www.chateaudelapioline.com; 260 rue Guillaume du Vair, Château de la Pioline; lunch/dinner menus from €51/72; ⊙noon-2pm & 7-10pm) Pierre Reboul's renowned restaurant has moved from central Aix to aristocratic Château de la Pioline, a suitably smart location for his high-class cuisine. The indulgent French fare meets flavours and ingredients cherry-picked from across the globe (like tempura prawns, or the day's fish with goat's curd and spinach). Rooms are sumptuous too (doubles from €145). The chateau is 5km southwest of town on the D65 towards the TGV station.

🍸 Drinking & Nightlife

The scene is fun but fickle. For nightlife, hit the student-friendly drinking dens on rue de la Verrerie and place Richelme. Open-air cafes crowd the city's squares, especially Forum des Cardeurs, place de Verdun and place de l'Hôtel de Ville (our favourite, for its more intimate scale and shady trees).

🛍 Shopping

★**Book in Bar**   BOOKS
(✆04 42 26 60 07; www.bookinbar.com; 4 rue Joseph Cabassol; ⊙9am-7pm Mon-Sat) Bibliophiles rejoice: this brilliant Anglophile bookshop sells a huge selection of English-language books (among works in other languages) and a thoroughly pleasant tearoom to boot. Look out for occasional book readings, jazz evenings and an English-language book club on the last Thursday of the month (from 5.30pm).

AIX-ELLENT MARKETS

At the daily **food market** (place Richelme; ☉ 7am-noon), trestle tables groan each morning under the weight of marinated olives, goat's cheese, garlic, lavender, honey, peaches, melons, cherries and a bounty of other sun-kissed fruit, veggies and seasonal food. Plane trees provide ample shade on the atmospheric T-shaped square, endowed with a couple of corner cafes where Aixois catch up on the gossip over *un café* once their shopping is done. **Flower markets** fill place des Prêcheurs (Sunday morning) and place de l'Hôtel de Ville (Tuesday, Thursday and Saturday mornings). The **flea market** (place de Verdun; ☉ Tue, Thu & Sat mornings) has quirky vintage items three mornings a week.

❶ Information

Tourist Office (☎ 04 42 16 11 61; www.aixenprovencetourism.com; 300 av Giuseppe Verdi, Les Allées; ☉ 8.30am-7pm Mon-Sat, 10am-1pm & 2-6pm Sun Apr-Sep, 8.30am-6pm Mon-Sat Oct-Mar; ☎) Touch screens add a high-tech air to the usual collection of brochures. Sells tickets for guided tours and cultural events, and has a shop selling regional souvenirs.

❶ Getting There & Around

TO/FROM THE AIRPORT

Aéroport Marseille-Provence (p802) is 25km southwest and served by regular shuttle buses (€8.20, 33 minutes, from 4.40am to 10.30pm).

BICYCLE

Opposite the train station, **AixenVelo** (☎ 04 42 39 90 37; www.aixenvelo.com; 12 rue Gustave Desplaces; per day €45; ☉ 10am-7pm Mon-Sat; ⚡) rents out bikes with electrical motors and has mapped several itineraries around town.

BUS

Aix en Bus (www.aixenbus.fr) runs local buses. Most run until 8pm. La Rotonde is the main hub. The tourist office has schedules.

Half-hourly shuttles link Aix's bus station and the TGV station (€4.30) with the airport (€8.20) from 4.40am to 10.30pm.

TRAIN

The **city centre train station** (☎ 08 00 11 40 23; www.ter.sncf.com/paca; av Maurice Blondel; ☉ 5am-1am Mon-Sat, from 6am Sun), at the southern end of av Victor Hugo, serves Marseille (€8.30, 45 minutes).

Aix's **TGV station** (☎ 0892 35 35 35; www.gares-sncf.com; rte Départementale 9; ☉ 5.30am-1am), 15km from the centre, is a stop on the high-speed Paris–Marseille line. Destinations include Avignon (from €13, 25 minutes, one or two per hour), Lyon (from €33, 1½ hours, around hourly) and Dijon (from €77, 3¼ hours, one or two daily).

Bus 40 runs from the TGV station to Aix's bus station (€4.30, 15 minutes, every 15 minutes).

Note that the direct Eurostar that connects London, Lyon, Avignon and Marseille does not stop at Aix's TGV station; to get to Aix, you have to change onto a connecting TGV at Lille or Paris.

THE CAMARGUE

Where the Petit Rhône and Grand Rhône meet the Mediterranean, the Camargue arises: 930 sq km of *sansouires* (salt flats), *étangs* (small saltwater lakes) and marshlands, interspersed with farmland.

Forget about time in this hauntingly beautiful part of Provence, roamed by black bulls, white horses and pink flamingos. This is slow-go country, a timeless wetland chequered with silver salt pans, waterlogged rice paddies and traditional *gardians* ('cowboys'). But birds are perhaps the delta's greatest feature – flamingos are the obvious star attraction, but there are countless other species to spot.

The main town of the region, diminutive Arles, is a show-stopper. Wander the narrow golden-hued streets, the same ones that famously inspired Van Gogh, to find the town's lovely restored Roman amphitheatre, top-notch art and history museums, and world-class restaurants.

The Camargue's two largest towns are the seaside pilgrim's outpost Stes-Maries-de-la-Mer and, to the northwest, the walled town of Aigues-Mortes.

Arles

POP 52,886

Roman treasures, shady squares and plenty of Camarguais culture make Arles a seductive stepping stone into the Camargue. And if its colourful sun-baked houses evoke a sense of déjà vu, it's because you've seen them already on a Van Gogh canvas – the artist painted 200-odd works around town, though sadly his famous little 'yellow house' at 2 place Lamartine, which he painted in 1888, was destroyed during WWII.

Arles' Saturday market is also a must-see – it's one of Provence's best.

Arles

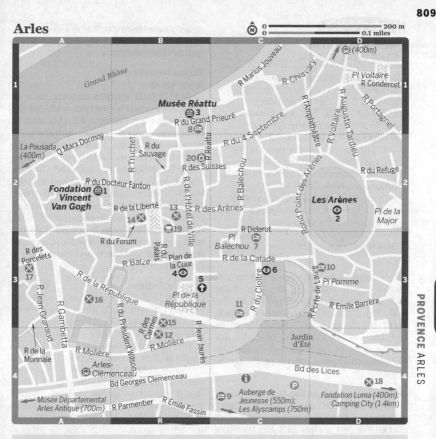

Arles

⊙ Top Sights

1 Fondation Vincent Van Gogh	A2
2 Les Arènes	D2
3 Musée Réattu	B1

⊙ Sights

4 Cryptoportiques	B3
5 Église St-Trophime	B3
6 Théâtre Antique	C3

🛏 Sleeping

7 Hôtel de l'Amphithéâtre	C3
8 Hôtel du Musée	B1
9 Hôtel Jules César	C4
10 Le Calendal	D3
11 Le Cloître	C3

✕ Eating

12 À Côté	B4
13 Fadoli et Fadola	B2
14 Glacier Arlelatis	B2
15 L'Atelier Jean-Luc Rabanel	B3
16 L'Autruche	A3
Le Comptoir du Calendal	(see 10)
17 Le Gibolin	A3
L'Ouvre Boîte	(see 11)
18 Marché d'Arles	D4

🍷 Drinking & Nightlife

19 Le Café Van Gogh	B2

🛍 Shopping

20 La Boutique des Passionnés	B2

⊙ Sights

★ Les Arènes   ROMAN SITE

(Amphithéâtre; ☏ 08 91 70 03 70; www.arenes
-arles.com; Rond-Point des Arènes; adult/child €6/
free, incl Théâtre Antique €9/free; ☺ 9am-8pm Jul

& Aug, to 7pm May, Jun & Sep, shorter hours Oct–
Apr) In Roman Gaul, every important town
had an amphitheatre, where gladiators
and wild animals met their (usually grisly)
ends. Few examples have survived, but Arles

PROVENCE ARLES

DON'T MISS

NEW KID ON THE CULTURAL BLOCK

Arles' already-bulging cultural landscape avidly awaits new cutting-edge gallery and arts centre **Fondation Luma** (04 90 47 76 17; www.luma-arles.org; 45 chemin des Minimes; ⊗Parc des Ateliers 11am-6pm Wed-Sun), rising inexorably at a defunct railway depot in the city's southeastern quarter. Funded by the Swiss-based Luma Foundation, and designed by Frank Gehry, it's set for a high-profile opening in 2019. If you want a scoop, there are French-language guided visits of the site five times a week, and one in English at 11.30am on Saturdays (adult/child €7/free).

(like nearby Nîmes) has preserved its colosseum largely intact. At 136m long, 107m wide and 21m tall, built around AD 90, the oval-shaped amphitheatre would have held 21,000 baying spectators. Though the structure has suffered down the centuries, it's still evocative of the might and capabilities of Roman civilisation. Entry is on the northern side.

★**Fondation Vincent Van Gogh** GALLERY
(04 90 93 08 08; www.fondation-vincentvan-gogh-arles.org; 35ter rue du Docteur Fanton; adult/child €9/free; ⊗10am-7pm Jul & Aug, from 11am Sep-Jun) Housed in a listed 15th-century manor, now twice repurposed (its other incarnation was as a bank), this Van Gogh–themed gallery is a must-see, as much for the architecture as the art. It has no permanent collection – rather, it hosts one or two excellent exhibitions a year, always with a Van Gogh theme and always including at least one Van Gogh masterpiece. Architectural highlights include the rooftop terrace and the coloured-glass bookshop ceiling. Look online for child- and family-centred programs.

★**Musée Réattu** GALLERY
(04 90 49 37 58; www.museereattu.arles.fr; 10 rue du Grand Prieuré; adult/child €8/free; ⊗10am-6pm Tue-Sun, to 5pm Dec-Feb) This superb 150-year-old museum, housed in an exquisitely renovated 15th-century Hospitaller priory by the Rhône, might be assumed old-fashioned, yet its modern collection is truly top-notch. Among its holdings are works by 18th- and 19th-century Provençal artists, two paintings and 57 sketches by Picasso, and of course some works from its namesake, Jacques Réattu. It also stages wonderfully curated cutting-edge exhibitions.

Musée Départemental Arles Antique MUSEUM
(04 13 31 51 03; www.arles-antique.cg13.fr; av de la Première Division Française Libre; adult/child €8/free; ⊗10am-6pm Wed-Mon; P) This striking cobalt-blue museum perches on the edge of what used to be the Roman chariot-racing track (hippodrome), southwest of central Arles. The collection of pagan and Christian finds includes stunning mosaics and an entire wing of treasures highlighting Arles' commercial and maritime prominence. Permanent collections reach back to prehistory, through the arrival of the Greeks in 600 BC to the Roman period and beyond. If you love a proper museum, full of artefacts and history, this is for you.

Théâtre Antique ROMAN SITE
(04 90 49 59 05; rue de la Calade; adult/child, incl entry to Les Arènes, €9/free; ⊗9am-7pm May-Sep, to 6pm Mar, Apr & Oct, 10am-5pm Nov-Feb) It's easy to admire the grace and engineering of this theatre – built at the behest of the unofficial first Roman Emperor, Augustus, in the 1st century BC, despite a semi-ruinous state brought on by centuries of pilfering. It still serves as one of Arles' premier venues, staging summertime concerts and plays where lighting, seating for 10,000 and the few remaining pillars create a magical atmosphere. The entrance and ticket office is on rue de la Calade.

Cryptoportiques ROMAN SITE
(place de la République, Hôtel de Ville; adult/child €4.50/free; ⊗10am-5pm Nov-Feb, 9am-6pm Mar, Apr & Oct, 9am-7pm May-Sep) The origins of these fascinating underground chambers, now sitting below the current city centre, go at least back to the first Roman colony in Arles in 46 BC, and most likely extend to much older Greek caverns. It's a wonderfully literal 2000-year excursion to take the stairs from the gleaming administrative heart of modern Arles, down to three vaulted chambers that may have housed shops or storage cellars under the Roman forum.

Les Alyscamps CEMETERY
(av des Alyscamps; adult/child €4.50/free; ⊗9am-7pm May-Sep, shorter hours rest of year) Testament to the significance of Roman Arles, this grand processional avenue of tombs and sarcophagi holds more than 1500 years

of corpses (which Roman custom insisted were buried outside the city). Van Gogh and Gauguin both painted this necropolis, at the eastern end of which stands the marvellously atmospheric, unfinished 11th-century St-Honorat chapel.

Église St-Trophime   CHURCH
(6 place de la République; ⊘8am-noon & 2-6pm Mon, Fri & Sat, to 5pm Tue-Thu, 2-5pm Sun) Named for Arles' semi-mythical first archbishop, this Romanesque-style church, built over a 5th-century basilica, was a cathedral until the bishopric moved to Aix in 1801. Built between the 12th and 15th centuries, it's considered a masterpiece of Provençal Romanesque. Look for the intricately sculpted western portal, topped by a tympanum depicting the Apocalypse (and St Trophime himself, brandishing his crozier). Inside, the **treasury** contains bone fragments of Arles' bishops. Occasional exhibitions are hosted in neighbouring cloister, **Cloître St-Trophime**.

Tickets to exhibitions in the cloister are sold at the town hall or the tourist office.

✪ Festivals & Events

Fête des Gardians   CULTURAL
(⊘1 May) Mounted *gardians* (Camarguais cowboys) parade and hold games in central Arles during this festival, which affords a fascinating insight into the region's traditions. The show, put on by the Brotherhood of the Gardians, founded in 1512, culminates in the Arena d'Arles.

Fêtes d'Arles   CULTURAL
(www.festivarles.com; ⊘mid-Jun–early Jul) Races, parades, costumes, theatre and music come to Arles over several weeks from mid-June. Highlights include La Course de Satin – a bareback race on purebred Camargue horses dating from 1529 – and the Pegoulado – a torchlight procession of participants dressed in traditional Provençal costume that has wended its way through town to the Roman theatre since at least 1830.

Les Suds   MUSIC
(✆04 90 96 06 27; www.suds-arles.com; ⊘Jul) This wonderfully imaginative and multifaceted world music festival makes use of Arles venues as diverse as the Roman theatre and the abandoned industrial complex Parc des Ateliers. While the main festival occurs over a week in July, the organisers stay busy throughout the year with live events, workshops and more.

Les Rencontres d'Arles Photographie   ART
(www.rencontres-arles.com; adult/child from €28/23; ⊘Jul-Sep) This internationally renowned photography festival, with a pedigree stretching to 1969, makes great use of a number of heritage sites around Arles for its many exhibits, debates, performances and workshops.

🛏 Sleeping

Camping City   CAMPGROUND €
(✆04 90 93 08 86; www.camping-city.com; 67 rte de Crau; 1-/2-person sites €18/20; ⊘Apr-Sep; P☒) On the road to Marseille, 1.5km southeast of town, Camping City is the closest campground to Arles. Bike hire and laundry facilities are available, and there are indoor and outdoor activities for kids. To get here, take bus 2 to the Hermite stop.

Auberge de Jeunesse   HOSTEL €
(✆04 90 96 18 25; www.hifrance.org; 20 av Maréchal Foch; dm incl breakfast & linen €20.30; ⊘Mar-Oct) Modern, shiny and neat, this efficient if uninspiring hostel's drawcard is its location, 10 minutes' walk from the city centre. The usual Fédération Unie des Auberges de Jeunesse (FUAJ) facilities are on offer – kitchen, lounge, cafe and dorms of varying sizes, plus a bar. Bedding is provided, towels aren't, and the doors are locked at 11pm.

La Pousada   B&B €€
(✆06 74 44 39 77; www.lapousada.net; 9 rue Croix Rouge; s/d €90/116; ⊘Mar-Nov; ✴@🐾) Down by the Rhône, this relaxed B&B offers three rustic-chic rooms, all named after spices,

---

FÉRIA D'ARLES

While it unavoidably centres on the ethically questionable 'sport' of bullfighting, the Féria d'Arles is also unavoidably one of the highlights of the city's calendar. Or rather, two of them: one in Easter marking the beginning of the bullfighting season, and one in September, called the Féria du Riz (Festival of Rice), but also involving bullfighting.

Over half a million visitors and bullfighting aficionados descend on Arles for the Easter Féria, with 50,000 cramming into the Roman amphitheatre Les Arènes to see the fights (and the less cruel bull-leaping). But it's in the streets of Arles that the true Féria unfurls: music, feasting, parties, traditional costumes and instruments are all abundant.

with admirable details like brass sinks, open-plan showers and sparkly tiled floors. The complimentary breakfast can be taken in the walled garden in fine weather, and there are bikes and books to borrow.

Le Calendal
HOTEL €€

(☑ 04 90 96 11 89; www.lecalendal.com; 5 rue Porte de Laure; s/d/tr €109/149/159; ⊙ lunch noon-2.30pm, salon de thé 4-6pm; ❉🛜) Hotel, spa and restaurant, this cosy bolthole opposite the Théâtre Antique has bright rooms and an inviting stone-walled garden. Breakfast is a buffet in **Le Comptoir du Calendal** (☑ 04 90 96 11 89; www.lecalendal.com; 5 rue Porte de Laure; mains €12-18; ⊙ 8am-8.30pm; 🛜). A massage in the spa is always a good idea.

Hôtel de l'Amphithéâtre
HISTORIC HOTEL €€

(☑ 04 90 96 10 30; www.hotelamphitheatre.fr; 5-7 rue Diderot; s/d €89/109; ❉@🛜) This elegant address across from the amphitheatre is quite a bargain: the standard of design here far outreaches the reasonable price tag. Antiques, rugs, fireplaces and staircases speak of the building's history, while minimal rooms nod to modern trends, and several have super views over Les Arènes and Arles' rooftops (although you'll pay for the privilege).

Hôtel du Musée
BOUTIQUE HOTEL €€

(☑ 04 90 93 88 88; www.hoteldumusee.com; 11 rue du Grand Prieuré; s/d from €80/110; ❉🛜) In a sensitively preserved 16th- to 17th-century building, this impeccable hotel has 28 peaceful rooms decorated with simple, high-quality furnishings, a chequerboard-tiled breakfast room (breakfast €9.50) and a patio garden brimming with pretty blossoms. Perhaps inspired by the proximity of so many world-class museums, it also has a small exhibition room. Parking is €15 per night.

★ Hôtel Jules César
DESIGN HOTEL €€€

(☑ 04 90 52 52 52; www.hotel-julescesar.fr; 9 bd des Lices; r from €226; ❉🛜🏊) It's not often you can say you've stayed somewhere designed from scratch by a world-famous fashion icon – but that's what you get at this luxe address (part of Sofitel's MGallery collection), renovated by couturier Christian Lacroix. Once a convent for Carmelite nuns, it's now a temple to fashion, glittering with over-the-top mirrors, Roman busts, modern art and trendy textiles.

★ Le Cloître
DESIGN HOTEL €€€

(☑ 04 88 09 10 00; www.hotelducloitre.com; 18 rue du Cloître; r €213; ❉@🛜) The traditional Mediterranean courtyard that greets you on arrival at 'The Cloister' is charming enough, but doesn't betray the inventiveness of the warm, colourful design within. Its 19 rooms are all distinct, with Italian showers and unusual furniture that sacrifices no comfort. Rooms are €14 per person cheaper if you forgo breakfast, and there's a panoramic rooftop terrace.

✗ Eating

Arles and its environs are foodie heaven; reserve ahead. Places often close between 3pm and 6pm, and hours are reduced in winter.

★ Marché d'Arles
MARKET €

(☑ 04 90 49 36 36; bd des Lices; ⊙ 8am-1pm Sat) Plan to be in Arles for the whopping Saturday morning market. You'll find all of Camargue's best produce: salt, rice, goat's cheese, *saucisson d'Arles* (bull-meat sausage) and so much more. Stalls line both sides of the street as visitors and locals alike browse, sample and buy everything from lavender honey to baby chicks.

Glacier Arlelatis
ICE CREAM €

(☑ 06 50 05 74 39; 8 place du Forum; 1/2 scoops €2/4; ⊙ 12.30-11pm) Thirty-eight flavours of artisanal ice cream and sorbet are the mainstays of this *glacier* on busy place du Forum. Buy a cone to take away or treat yourself to a magnificent whipped-cream-topped sundae sitting down. Flavours change but there are always a few distinctly Provençal ones: lavender honey, chestnut and so forth.

Fadoli et Fadola
CAFE €

(☑ 04 90 49 70 73; 44 rue des Arènes; sandwiches €5, salads €7; ⊙ noon-2.30pm; ✍) Well-stuffed sandwiches – made to order, *frotté à l'ail* (rubbed with garlic) and dripping with silken AOC Vallée des Baux olive oil – lure the crowds to this tiny sandwich shop with a hole-in-the-wall takeaway counter. It also sells olive oil by the litre (€12 to €25) and even sushi. Find it footsteps from central 'cafe' square, place du Forum.

★ Le Gibolin
BISTRO €€

(☑ 04 88 65 43 14; 13 rue des Porcelets; 2-/3-course menus €27/34; ⊙ 12.15-2pm & 8-10.30pm Tue-Sat Apr-Jul & Oct, shorter hours rest of year) After spending three decades plying Paris with their passion for organic wines, owners Brigitte and Luc decided to head south and do the same for Arles. Unsurprisingly, it's become a much-loved local fixture, known for its hearty home cooking and peerless wine list (racked up temptingly behind the bar and mostly available by the glass).

★ **L'Autruche** MODERN FRENCH €€
(📞 04 90 49 73 63; 5 rue Dulau; menus €29; ⊘ noon-1.30pm & 7.30-9pm Thu-Sun, noon-1.30pm Wed) 'The Ostrich', run by husband-and-wife team Fabien and Ouria, is a family restaurant in the best tradition. Market-fresh produce is assured, as is the ability of their Michelin-experienced chef to treat it with skill – perhaps plaice with cocoa beans or silky asparagus soup with nuts. Extravagant desserts are a further treat.

L'Ouvre Boîte TAPAS €€
(📞 04 88 09 10 10; 22 rue du Cloître; dishes €8-10; ⊘ 6.30-9.30pm Mon-Fri, 11am-2pm & 6.30-9.30pm Sat & Sun) Alexandre's little joint (the 'Open Box') has become a firm Arlésian favourite for chilled evening eats in the courtyard of the Hôtel du Cloître. It specialises in shared tapas-like 'little plates' – oysters, octopus in herby-tomato sauce, pork in Asian broth – ordered to share. Arrive early for a prime table.

★ **L'Atelier Jean-Luc Rabanel** GASTRONOMY €€€
(📞 04 90 91 07 69; www.rabanel.com; 7 rue des Carmes; menus €55-155; ⊘ noon-1pm & 8-9pm Thu-Sat, noon-1pm Sun, 8-9pm Wed) As much an artistic experience as a double-Michelin-starred adventure, this is the gastronomic flagship of charismatic chef Jean-Luc Rabanel. Many products are sourced from the chef's veggie patch, and wine pairings are an experience in themselves. Saturday-morning cooking classes are also available, working with the kitchen brigade (€200). Next door, Rabanel's À Côté (📞 04 90 47 61 13; www.bistro-acote.com; 21 rue des Carmes; menus €32; ⊘ noon-1.30pm & 7.30-9pm Wed-Sun) offers bistro fare.

🍷 **Drinking & Nightlife**

Le Café Van Gogh CAFE
(Le Café La Nuit; 📞 04 90 96 44 56; www.restaurant-cafe-van-gogh.com; 11 place du Forum; ⊘ 11am-3pm & 6-11pm) Immortalised in Van Gogh's 1888 *Terrasse du Café le Soir,* this cafe trades on its plum spot on the place du Forum and its association with the adopted Arlésian painter. Shaded by plane trees, it turns into a giant terrace at lunch and dinner in summer.

La Guinguette du Patio de Camargue LIVE MUSIC
(📞 04 90 49 51 76; www.chico.fr; 49 chemin de Barriol; ⊘ 11am-midnight) Established in 1995 by Chico, co-founder of the Gypsy Kings, on a patch of industrial wasteland by the banks of the Rhône, this is now a wonderful riverside grill and bar. When the weather's good, it can be very festive, especially if the owner's new band, Chico and the Gypsies, are in a musical mood. Check the site for 'dinner concerts'.

🔒 **Shopping**

La Boutique des Passionnés MUSIC
(📞 04 90 96 59 93; www.passionnes.com; 14 rue Réattu; ⊘ 9am-7pm Tue-Sat) Starting out as a humble record shop, La Boutique des Passionnés has grown into a cultural centre – promoting and selling tickets for shows, hosting intimate performances of Iberian music, selling literature and sculptures, and booking author signings and exhibitions. It's a friendly and important part of Arles' cultural scene.

ℹ️ **Information**

Tourist Office (📞 04 90 18 41 20; www.arles-tourisme.com; 9 blvd des Lices; ⊘ 9am-6.45pm Apr-Sep, 9am-4.45pm Mon-Sat, 10am-1pm Sun Oct-Mar; 🖥️)

ℹ️ **Getting There & Around**

BICYCLE

1Véloc (📞 04 86 32 27 05; www.1veloc.fr; 12 rue de la Cavalerie; bike/ebike per day from €8/25; ⊘ 10am-12.30pm & 3-6pm Tue-Fri, 3-6pm Sat Sep-Jun, plus 10am-noon & 5-6pm Sun Jul & Aug) Rents out bikes and runs tours.

BUS

Buses leave from either the central **bus station** (Gare Routière; www.lepilote.com; av Paulin Talabot) near the train station, or the more central **stop on bd Clémenceau** (bd Clémenceau); many stop at both. There are three different companies, so for up-to-date timetables consult www.lepilote.com, www.edgard-transport.fr or www.envia.fr. Destinations include the following:

Aix-en-Provence Cartreize Line 18, €11, 1¼ hours, up to nine per day from Arles-Clémenceau

Salon-de-Provence Cartreize Line 29, €4.80, 1¼ hours, up to six per day from the central bus station

ℹ️ **CENT SAVER**

Buy a pass for multiple sights at the Arles tourist office or any Roman site: the **Pass Avantage** (€16) covers the museums, both theatres, the baths, crypt, Les Alyscamps and the Cloître St-Trophime; the **Pass Liberté** (€12) gives you the choice of a total of six sights, including two museums.

3 DAYS — Roman Road Trip

Rome really flexed its imperial muscles in Southern France. Roman roads duck and dive across Roman bridges to theatres and arenas where you can grab a seat in the bleachers and watch the curtain rise. Let the show begin!

Though not technically in Provence, **Nîmes'** incredible Roman monuments (p739) are essential viewing. The town's coat of arms – a crocodile chained to a palm tree – recalls the region's first sun-worshipping retirees: Julius Caesar's loyal legionnaires were granted land here to settle after hard years on the Nile campaigns. Two millennia later, Nîmes' intact 1st-century-AD amphitheatre and temple blend seamlessly with the modern town.

The Romans didn't do anything on a small scale and Unesco-listed **Pont du Gard** (p745), 21km northeast along the D9086, is no exception. At 50m this is the world's highest Roman monument. Traverse its awe-inspiring arches, and swim upstream for unencumbered views, or downstream to shaded wooden platforms made for flopping between dips.

Overnight in Uzès, returning south next morning along the D979 to Nîmes and A54 to **Arles** (p808) – count on an hour. Part of the Roman Empire from the 2nd century BC, Roman Arelate has a splendid amphitheatre, theatre and baths. Grab a coffee or ice on place du Forum, the hub of Roman social, political and religious life.

From Arles follow the D17, D78F and D5 north to **Glanum** (p819). Park by the roadside triumphal arch and spend the afternoon exploring the Roman archaeological site. Overnight 2km north in St-Rémy de Provence.

Day three, motor 50km along the A7 to **Orange** (p829). Roman monuments here are stunning and unusually old – from Augustus Caesar's rule (27 BC–AD 14). The stage wall of the Théâtre Antique dominates.

Push on along the D975 to **Vaison-la-Romaine** (p830) for a late lunch. Park on the river banks next to the Roman bridge (Pont Romain). Explore the ruins of the city that flourished here between the 6th and 2nd centuries BC and end with the archaeological museum which revives Vaison's Roman past with incredible swag.

Top: Pont du Gard (p745), near Nîmes
Bottom: Théâtre Antique (p829), Orange

Stes-Marie-de-la-Mer Envia Line 20, €2.50, one hour, up to six per day from the central bus station Monday to Saturday

TRAIN

The **train station** (av Paulin Talabot) has services to Nîmes (from €7.50, 30 minutes to one hour, hourly), Marseille (€13, one hour, at least hourly) and Avignon (€6, 20 minutes, every one to two hours). The closest TGV stations are in Avignon and Nîmes.

Camargue Wetlands

Travelling around the Camargue is tantamount to frolicking with a zillion mosquitoes in a giant nature park. Almost all the Camargue's wetlands are protected by the 863-sq-km Parc Naturel Régional de Camargue, created to preserve its fragile ecosystems by maintaining an equilibrium between ecological considerations and economic mainstays: agriculture, salt and rice production, hunting, grazing and tourism. Pick up information on walking, birdwatching and other activities at the park-run Musée de la Camargue (p816), 10km south of Arles on the D570.

On the periphery, the 600-sq-km lagoon **Étang de Vaccarès** and nearby peninsulas and islands form the 135-sq-km **Réserve Nationale de Camargue** (☑04 90 97 00 97; www.reserve-camargue.org; C134, rte de Fiélouse, La Capelière). Get the full low-down on the reserve and its activities at the **information centre** (☑04 90 97 00 97; www.reserve-camargue.org; C134, rte de Fiélouse, La Capelière; permits adult/child €3/1.50; ⊙9am-1pm & 2-6pm Apr-Sep, to 5pm Wed-Mon Oct-Mar) in La Capelière.

⊙ Sights & Activities

Musée de la Camargue   MUSEUM
(Musée Camarguais; ☑04 90 97 10 82; www.parc-camargue.fr; D570, Mas du Pont de Rousty; adult/child €5/free; ⊙9am-12.30pm & 1-6pm Apr-Sep, 10am-5.30pm Oct-Mar) Inside a 19th-century sheep shed 10km southwest of Arles, this museum evokes traditional life in the Camargue, with exhibitions covering history, culture, ecosystems, farming techniques, flora and fauna. *L'Oeuvre Horizons* by Japanese artist Tadashi Kawamata – aka a wooden observatory shaped like a boat – provides a bird's-eye view of the agricultural estate, which is crossed by a 3.5km walking trail. The headquarters of the **Parc Naturel Régional de Camargue** (PNRC; www.parc-camargue.fr) are also based here.

★**Domaine de la Palissade**   PARK
(☑04 42 86 81 28; www.palissade.fr; 36 chemin Départemental; adult/child €3/free, horse trekking per hour adult/child from €19/16; ⊙9am-6pm mid-Jun–mid-Sep, to 5pm Mar–mid-Jun & mid-Sep–Oct, 9am-5pm Wed-Sun Feb & Nov; ℗) This remote nature centre, 12km south of Salin de Giraud, organises fantastic forays through 702 hectares of protected marshland, scrubby glasswort, flowering sea lavender (in August) and lagoons on foot and horseback (call ahead to book horse treks). Before hitting the scrub, rent binoculars (€2) and grab a free map of the estate's three marked walking trails (1km to 8km) from the office. The tours are as educational as they are enjoyable.

La Maison du Guide   OUTDOORS
(☑04 66 73 52 30, 06 12 44 73 52; www.maisonduguide.camargue.fr; 154 rue du Château de Montcalm, Montcalm; guided tours adult/child €20/free, 4-person cottage per week €270-550; ⊙office 9am-noon Mon; ﹫) Discovery weekends by naturalist Jean-Marie Espuche embrace birdwatching, cycling, horse riding and sunrise nature walks. You'll find 'secret' parts of the Camargue and see much more birdlife than you otherwise might. Jean-Marie also rents out a four-person cottage in Montcalm, a useful base on the edge of the Camargue.

🛏 Sleeping

The most obvious base in the Camargue is Arles, which has a wealth of accommodation. Further out into the countryside hotels are less sophisticated, but there are some attractive B&Bs, cabins and rural campgrounds scattered around.

Ranch-style motel accommodation lines the D570 heading into Stes-Maries-de-la-Mer. The tourist offices can point you towards self-catering *cabanes de gardian* (traditional whitewashed cowboy cottages) and farmstays.

★**Le Mas de Peint**   BOUTIQUE HOTEL €€€
(☑04 90 97 20 62; www.masdepeint.com; rte de Salin de Giraud, Le Sambuc, Manade Jacques Bon; d €250; ⊙mid-Mar–mid-Nov; ❋❂❀) This 17th-century farmhouse has managed to become an upmarket hotel without jettisoning design elements that nod to its rural roots: solid beams, wooden furniture, saddles on the walls, and a bull's head in the lobby. But it's the superb **restaurant** (☑04 90 97 20 62; www.masdepeint.com; rte de Salin de Giraud, Manade Jacques Bon; menus lunch €39, dinner €41-69; ⊙lunch & dinner Sat & Sun, lunch only Fri & Mon-Wed) many come for – watch chefs work from the dining room, or eat on the lovely poolside terrace.

✖ Eating

★ Le Mazet du Vaccarès
SEAFOOD €€

(Chez Hélène et Néné; ☑ 04 90 97 10 79; www.mazet-du-vaccares.fr; rte Albaron Villeneuve; fish/bouillabaisse menu €38/60; ☺ 10am-11pm Fri-Sun mid-Jan–mid-Aug & mid-Sep–mid-Dec; ℗) Shuddering along the low ribbed road past flamingos and Camargue ponies is totally worth it for the seafood at this legendary lakeside cabin. Memorabilia from Hélène and Néné's days as lighthouse keepers in Beauduc fill the restaurant with soul. The jovial couple cook up one fixed *menu,* built from the catch of local fishers. Cash only.

★ La Telline
FRENCH €€

(☑ 04 90 97 01 75; www.restaurantlatelline.fr; Quarter Villeneuve, rte de Gageron, Villeneuve; mains €24-35; ☺ noon-1.15pm & 7.30-9pm Thu-Mon; ℗) A true local favourite, this isolated cottage restaurant with sage-green wooden shutters is one of the best places to sample genuine Camargue food. Summer dining is in a small and peaceful flower-filled garden, where straightforward starters such as *tellines* (molluscs), salad or terrine are followed by grilled fish or meat, or a beef or bull steak. No credit cards.

The owners also run several *chambres d'hôtes* (doubles from €115).

Chez Bob
FRENCH €€

(☑ 04 90 97 00 29; www.restaurantbob.fr; Mas Petite Antonelle, rte du Sambuc, Villeneuve; menu €45; ☺ noon-2pm & 7.30-9pm Wed-Sun; ℗) This house restaurant is an iconic address adored by Arlésians. Feast on grilled bull chops, mullet eggs and *anchoïade* (a powerful Provençal garlic and anchovy emulsion) beneath trees or inside between walls plastered in photos, posters and other memorabilia collected over the years by Jean-Guy, aka 'Bob'. It's 18km south of Arles; reserve ahead.

★ La Chassagnette
GASTRONOMY €€€

(☑ 04 90 97 26 96; www.chassagnette.fr; rte du Sambuc, Domaine de L'Armellière; menus €55-115; ☺ noon-1.30pm & 7-9.30pm Jun-Sep, noon-1.30pm Thu-Sat Oct-May; ♨) Surrounded by a vast *potager* (kitchen garden), which supplies practically all the restaurant's produce, this renowned gourmet table is run by Armand Amal, a former pupil of Alain Ducasse. The multicourse *menus* are full of surprises, and the bucolic setting is among the loveliest anywhere in the Camargue. There's a vegetarian *menu* (unfortunately available only at lunch).

Stes-Maries-de-la-Mer

POP 2680

The saints who give their name to this white-washed seaside town are Marie-Salomé and Marie-Jacobé, persecuted early Christians who escaped here from Palestine. With them, the legend says, was their handmaiden Sara, whose sanctification as Saint Sara the Black makes this a significant place of pilgrimage for Roma and other 'gypsy' peoples, whose patron she is. Stes-Maries has a rough-and-tumble holidaymaker feel, with salt-licked buildings crowding dusty streets. During its Roma pilgrimages, street-cooked pans of paella fuel chaotic crowds of carnivalesque guitarists, dancers and mounted cowboys.

◉ Sights & Activities

Stes-Maries-de-la-Mer is fringed by 30km of fine-sand beaches, easily reached by bicycle. Nudist beaches surround the Gacholle lighthouse off the Digue à la Mer.

Église des Stes-Maries
CHURCH

(☑ 04 90 97 80 25; www.sanctuaire-des-saint-esmaries.fr; 2 place de l'Église; rooftop €2.50; ☺ 10am-noon & 2-5pm Mon-Sat, 2-5pm Sun) Built on the potential first site of Christianity in the Camargue, this fortified church is of uncertain vintage, but probably hails from the 12th century. It draws legions of pilgrims to venerate the statue of Sara, their revered patron saint, during the Pèlerinage des Gitans (p818). The relics of Sara and those of Marie-Salomé and Marie-Jacobé, all found in the crypt by King René in 1448, are enshrined in a wooden chest, stashed in the stone wall above the choir. Don't miss the panorama from the rooftop terrace.

★ Parc Ornithologique du Pont de Gau
WILDLIFE RESERVE

(☑ 04 90 97 82 62; www.parcornithologique.com; D570, Pont du Gau; adult/child €7.50/5; ☺ 9am-7pm Apr-Sep, 10am-6pm Oct-Mar; ℗ ♨) Flamingos are a dime a dozen in the Camargue, but this park is one of the best places to see the many other migratory and seasonal species that thrive in these wetlands. Herons, storks, egrets, teals, avocets and grebes are just some you may spot, depending on the time of year. The reserve has 7km of trails, giving you every chance to see its avian inhabitants, and a care centre for sick and injured birds. Follow the D570 4km north from Stes-Maries-de-la-Mer.

WORTH A TRIP

AIGUES-MORTES

Set in flat marshland and encircled by high stone walls, the picturesque town of Aigues-Mortes was established in the mid-13th century by Louis IX to give the French crown a Mediterranean port under its direct control. Cobbled streets inside the walls are lined with restaurants, cafes and bars, giving the town a festive atmosphere and making it a charming spot from which to explore the Camargue. It's actually located over the border from Provence in the Gard *département,* 28km northwest of Stes-Maries-de-la-Mer at the western extremity of the Camargue.

The **tourist office** (☏04 66 53 73 00; www.ot-aiguesmortes.fr; place St-Louis; ☻9am-6pm) is inside the walled city.

La Digue à la Mer   NATURAL FEATURE

This 2.5m-high dyke was built in the 19th century to cut the delta off from the sea, making the southern Camargue arable. A 20km-long walking and cycling track runs along its length, linking Stes-Maries with the solar-powered **Phare de la Gacholle** (1882), a lighthouse automated in the 1960s. Footpaths cut down to lovely sandy beaches and views of pink flamingos strutting across the marshy planes are second to none. Walking on the fragile sand dunes is forbidden, as is driving.

Manade des Baumelles   FARM

(☏04 90 97 84 14; www.manadedesbaumelles.fr; D38; tour with/without lunch €45/25; ☻tours 10.30am Tue-Sun; ℗) Located on the Petit Rhône, this *manade* (bull farm) lets visitors enter the world of the *gardians* ('cowboys'), watching their strenuous work from the safety of a truck. The braver can ride horses, join in the farm-work, go canoeing and play traditional *gardian* games. Tours end with an optional farm lunch (*menus* €25/37) and a gift shop stocked with Camargue specialities.

Find the *manade* a few kilometres north of Stes-Maries-de-la-Mer, at the end of a gravel track off the D38 towards Aigues-Mortes.

✲✲ Festivals & Events

Pèlerinage des Gitans   RELIGIOUS

(Roma pilgrimages; ☻24-25 May) 'Gypsies' (Romanies, Manouches, Tziganes and Gitans) pour into town for three days from 24 May and again on the Sunday closest to 22 October to celebrate their patron saint, Sara, who according to legend helped bring Christianity to European shores. The festival, rooted in medieval times, still sees the pilgrims camp throughout the town and on the beach.

🛏 Sleeping

Camping Le Clos du Rhône   CAMPGROUND €

(☏04 90 97 85 99; www.camping-leclos.fr; rte d'Aigues Mortes; site €30, mobile home per week €847; ☻late Mar–mid-Nov; @🛜🏊) Right by the beach (yet lavishly embellished with an onshore water park), this large and well-equipped campground sports a range of accommodation options: tent sites, wooden chalets and self-catering cottages. The pool, two-lane water slide, and beachside spa with jacuzzi and *hammam,* plus more mundane services like a grocer, laundry and barbecue, make this a family favourite.

Hôtel Méditerranée   HOTEL €

(☏04 90 97 82 09; www.hotel-mediterranee.camargue.fr; 4 rue Frédéric Mistral; s/d €60/74; ☻mid-Mar–mid-Nov; ❄) This whitewashed cottage hotel, festooned with an abundance of flower pots and just steps from the sea, is truly a steal. Its 14 rooms – three with their own little terrace garden – are spotlessly clean, and breakfast (€8) is served in summer on a pretty vine-covered patio garden, complete with strawberry plants, geraniums and other potted flowers. Bike rental costs €15 per day.

★Cacharel Hotel   HOTEL €€

(☏04 90 97 95 44; www.hotel-cacharel.com; rte de Cacharel, D85A; s/d €151/164, horse riding per hour €30; @🛜🏊) This isolated farmstead, 400m down an unpaved track off the D85A just north of Stes-Maries-de-la-Mer, perfectly balances modern-day comforts with rural authenticity. Photographic portraits of the bull herder who created the hotel in 1955 (son Florian runs the three-star hotel with much love today) give the vintage dining room soul. Rooms sit snug in whitewashed cottages, some overlooking the water.

Swings in the paddock, horse riding with a *gardian* (cowboy), boules to play *pétanque,* and bags of open space make it a perfect family choice. This is Camargue living at its most relaxing.

★Lodge Sainte Hélène   BOUTIQUE HOTEL €€€

(☏04 90 97 83 29; www.lodge-saintehelene.com; chemin Bas des Launes; d for 2 nights €626; ❄@🛜🏊) These pearly-white terraced cottages on a peninsula on the Etang des

Launes are prime real estate for birdwatchers and romance seekers. It's so quiet you can hear flamingos flapping past. Each room comes with a birdwatchers' guide and binoculars, and owner Benoît Noel is a font of local knowledge.

✖ Eating

La Cabane aux Coquillages SEAFOOD €
(☑06 10 30 33 49; 16 av Van Gogh; shellfish €8.50-12.50; ☺noon-3pm & 5-11pm Apr-Nov) Attached to the excellent Ô Pica Pica restaurant, this informal little *cabane* (hut) specialises, unsurprisingly, in *coquillages* (shellfish): oysters, *palourdes* (clams), *coques* (cockles), and *tellines* (a type of local shellfish known elsewhere in France as *pignons*). Or, you could opt for perfectly cooked *fritures* (battered baby prawns, baby squid or anchovies) and a very cooperative glass of wine.

★ Ô Pica Pica SEAFOOD €€
(☑06 10 30 33 49; www.degustationcoquillageslessaintesmariesdelamer.com; 16-18 av Van Gogh; mains €17-25; ☺noon-3pm & 7-11pm Mar-Nov) Fish and shellfish do not come fresher than this. Watch them get gutted, filleted and grilled in the 'open' glass-walled kitchen, then devour your meal on the sea-facing pavement terrace or out the back in the typically Mediterranean white-walled garden. Simplicity is king here: plastic glasses, fish grilled *à la plancha*, and shellfish platters. No coffee and no credit cards.

Local specialities such as *tellines* (shellfish), *langoustines* and fresh *anchois* (anchovies) are worth choosing.

❶ Information

Tourist Office (☑04 90 97 82 55; www.saintesmaries.com; 5 av Van Gogh; ☺9am-8pm Jul & Aug, to 7pm Apr-Jun & Sep, to 6pm Oct, to 5pm Dec-Feb & Mar)

❶ Getting There & Around

Le Vélo Saintois (☑04 90 97 74 56; www.levelosaintois.camargue.fr; 19 rue de la République; per day adult/child/ebike €15/14/30; ☺9am-7pm Mar-Nov) and **Le Vélociste** (☑04 90 97 83 26; www.levelociste.fr; 8 place Mireille; per day adult/child/ebike €15/14/30; ☺9am-7pm Mar-Nov) hire bicycles.

Buses to/from Arles (Line L20, €2.90, one hour, four to eight daily) use the bus shelter at the northern entrance to town on av d'Arles (the continuation of rte d'Arles and the D570).

LES ALPILLES

A silvery chain of low, jagged mountains strung between the Rivers Durance and Rhône, the craggy limestone peaks of Les Alpilles rise impressively to the south of the chic town of St-Rémy de Provence. Designated as the Parc Naturel Régional des Alpilles in 2007, the area's hill villages are best explored by car – or better still on foot, along one of the trails that wind among the peaks. While you walk, look out for eagles and Egyptian vultures soaring overhead.

Covered with scrubby *maquis* and wild almond and olive trees, the area was immortalised by Vincent van Gogh, who created many much-loved paintings here during the later period of his life – especially while he was a resident at the sanatorium of Monastère St-Paul de Mausole (p820).

St-Rémy-de-Provence

POP 10,826

Ravishing St-Rémy is about as cultured and chi-chi as Provence gets, and yet somehow – and in stark contrast to some of the flashier coastal towns (St-Tropez, we're looking at you) – it's managed to cling on to its heart and soul during the gentrification process. Built from honey-coloured stone, and centred on a lovely, plane-shaded square lined by cafes, St-Rémy is a favourite summer haunt of the jet-set – and yet, even in midsummer, it's possible to find pockets of peace and quiet along the streets of the old town.

South of town, the rugged hills of Les Alpilles rise along the horizon, and one of Provence's most impressive Roman ruins can be explored – the incredibly well-preserved ancient town of Glanum.

◉ Sights

Pick up the free Carte St-Rémy at the first sight you visit, get it stamped, then benefit from reduced admission at St-Rémy's other sights.

★ Site Archéologique de Glanum RUINS
(☑04 90 92 23 79; www.site-glanum.fr; rte des Baux-de-Provence; adult/child €7.50/free, parking €2.70; ☺9.30am-6.30pm Apr-Sep, 10am-5pm Oct-Mar, closed Mon Sep-Mar) It might lack the scale and ambition of some of Provence's better-known Roman monuments, but for a glimpse into everyday life in Gaul, this ancient town has no equal. A Roman colony founded around AD 27, the remains of this

once-thriving town have been excavated – complete with baths, forum, columns, marketplace, temples and houses.

Two monuments mark the entrance, 2km south of St-Rémy – a mausoleum (from around 30 BC) and France's oldest triumphal arch, built around AD 20.

★ Monastère St-Paul de Mausole
HISTORIC SITE

(☏04 90 92 77 00; www.saintpauldemausole.fr; adult/child €5/free; ⊙9.30am-6.45pm Apr-Sep, 10.15am-5.15pm Oct-Mar, closed Jan–mid-Feb) This monastery turned asylum is famous for one of its former residents – the ever-volatile Vincent van Gogh, who admitted himself in 1889. Safe within the monastery's cloistered walls, Vincent enjoyed his most productive period, completing 150-plus drawings and around 150 paintings, including his famous *Irises*. A reconstruction of his room is open to visitors, as are a Romanesque **cloister** and **gardens** growing flowers that feature in his work.

Hôtel de Sade
MUSEUM

(☏04 90 92 64 04; www.hotel-de-sade.fr; 1 rue du Parage; adult/child €3.50/free; ⊙9.30am-1pm & 2-6pm Jun-Sep, shorter hours Oct-May) Reopened after an expensive program of renovations, this impressive Renaissance *hôtel particulier* was built in 1513 by Balthazar de Sade (ancestor of the much more notorious Marquis de Sade). Since the early 20th century it has housed the most important archaeological finds from the Roman town of Glanum – including an amazing array of sculptures discovered at the site, such as a striking bust of Livia, wife of Emperor Augustus, thought to have been made between AD 4 and 14.

🛏 Sleeping

★ Le Sommeil des Fées
B&B €

(☏04 90 92 17 66; www.angesetfees-stremy.com; 4 rue du 8 Mai 1945; incl breakfast s €55-70, d €70-90) Upstairs from La Cuisine des Anges (p820), this cosy, colourful B&B has five rooms all named after characters from Arthurian legend, blending Provençal and Andalucian decorative details. It's bright, modern and – considering you're in St-Rémy, and that the rates include breakfast – really quite a steal.

★ Sous les Figuiers
BOUTIQUE HOTEL €€

(☏04 32 60 15 40; www.hotelsouslesfiguiers. com; 3 av Gabriel St-René Taillandier; d €99-191; 🅿❄🛜🏊) 'Under The Fig Trees' nicely captures the languid, leisurely, home-away-from-home feel of this charming, country-

chic house a five-minute walk from the town centre. All the rooms are decorated with great style, blending distressed wood, warm colours and ethnic textiles; some are in the main house, while others are in the gorgeous garden and have cute, private patios. Breakfast costs €15.

La Maison du Village
BOUTIQUE HOTEL €€€

(☏04 32 60 68 20; www.lamaisonduvillage.com; 10 rue du 8 Mai 1945; d €180-220; ❄🛜) The epitome of classy St-Rémy, this 1750s townhouse hotel is like a design magazine come to life. All five suites have their own eclectic decor – four of them have sitting rooms and one has a freestanding tub with a view of the village church tower. The walled garden is a bucolic setting for breakfast, and the hotel even has its own candle shop.

🍴 Eating

St-Rémy has some superb cafes and bakeries, but restaurant prices tend to be on the high side. Market day is on Wednesday and is a magnet for sightseers and locals alike.

Maison Cambillau
BAKERY €

(1 rue Carnot; fougasses & sandwiches €2.60-3; ⊙7.30am-1.30pm & 3-7.30pm Fri-Wed) Well-stuffed *fougasse* (Provençal flatbread) and baguettes with a variety of tasty fillings make this well-established *boulangerie* (bakery) the perfect spot to stock up on a picnic. Complete the takeaway feast with a feisty meringue, bag of nougat, nutty florentine or almond- and pistachio-studded *crousadou*.

Da Peppe
ITALIAN €

(☏04 90 92 11 56; 2 av Fauconnet; pizza €12-16, mains €14-22; ⊙noon-2.30pm & 7-11pm Wed-Mon; 🍴) Excellent pizza and pasta with a Sicilian spin – but the wonderful rooftop terrace is the bit that seals the deal.

La Cuisine des Anges
BISTRO €€

(☏04 90 92 17 66; www.angesetfees-stremy. com; 4 rue du 8 Mai 1945; 2-course menu €27-29, 3-course menu €32; ⊙noon-2.30pm & 7.30-11pm Mon, Wed, Sat & Sun, 7.30-11pm Thu & Fri; ❄🛜) You can't really go too far wrong at the Angels' Kitchen – at least if you're looking for solid, no-nonsense Provençal cooking just like *grande-mère* would have made. Tuck into dishes like slow-cooked lamb, bream fillet, baked St-Marcellin cheese and duck pot-au-feu, and dine either in the courtyard or the stone-walled dining room. Fancy, no; flavoursome, yes.

Gus

BISTRO €€€

(📱 04 90 90 27 61; www.gussaintremy.com; 31 bd Victor Hugo; mains from €19.50; ⊗ noon-2.30pm & 7-10.30pm Tue-Sat) This bright, breezy restaurant is a favourite for the chi-chi summer crowd, and with good reason: the food is classy and the ambience is buzzy, with overtones of a Parisian street cafe. It's particularly good on seafood – big *fruits de mer* platters, lobsters and plates of oysters – but there's a blackboard of French specials too.

🛍 Shopping

★ Joël Durand

CHOCOLATE

(📱 04 90 92 38 25; www.joeldurand-chocolatier. fr; 3 bd Victor Hugo; ⊗ 9.30am-12.30pm & 2.30-7.30pm) Among France's top chocolatiers, using Provençal herbs and plants – lavender, rosemary, violet and thyme – with unexpected flavours such as Earl Grey.

L'Epicerie du Calanquet

FOOD

(📱 04 32 62 09 01; www.moulinducalanquet.fr; 8 rue de la Commune; ⊗ 9.30am-1pm & 2.30-7pm Apr-Sep, 10am-1pm & 2.30-7pm Tue-Sat Oct-Mar) A delectable grocery and fine food emporium, made out to resemble a traditional village shop, and owned by the same people who run the **Moulin à Huile du Calanquet** (📱 04 32 60 09 50; www.moulinducalanquet.fr; vieux chemin d'Arles; ⊗ 9am-noon & 2-7pm Mon-Sat, 10am-noon & 3-6pm Sun Apr-Oct, 9am-noon & 2-6.30pm Mon-Sat Nov-Mar) outside town. Their own olive-oil range takes centre stage, of course, alongside other goodies from the area – and there are tasting sessions and events on the patio during summer.

ℹ Information

St-Rémy Tourist Office (📱 04 90 92 05 22; www.saintremy-de-provence.com; place Jean Jaurès; ⊗ 9.15am-12.30pm & 2-6.30pm Mon-Sat, 10am-12.30pm Sun mid-Apr–mid-Oct, longer hours Jul & Aug, shorter hours mid-Oct–mid-Apr)

ℹ Getting There & Around

BICYCLE

Cycling is a great way to explore the area around St-Rémy – although you'll need strong legs if you want to make it all the way up into Les Alpilles.

There are several bike-rental companies around town, most of which will deliver within a 20km radius of St-Rémy; contact **Telecycles** (📱 04 90 92 83 15; www.telecycles-location.fr; per day €20) or **Vélo-Passion** (📱 04 90 92 49 43; www.velopassion.fr; per day €15, electric bikes from €35).

Alternatively, battery-assisted electric bikes can be hired from **Sun e-Bike** (📱 04 32 62 08 39; www.location-velo-provence.com; 16 bd Marceau; per day €36; ⊗ 9am-6.30pm Apr-Sep, shorter hours Oct-Mar) and Vélo-Passion (from €35).

BUS

Allô Cartreize (📱 08 10 00 13 26; www.lepilote. com) buses depart from place de la République.

Arles (50 minutes, €2.50, two daily) line 54; also stops in Cavaillon for onward travel into the Luberon Valley.

Avignon (€3.60, one hour, at least one every two hours).

Les Baux-de-Provence

POP 436

Clinging precariously to an ancient limestone *baou* (Provençal for 'rocky spur'), this fortified hilltop village is one of the most visited in France (best seen as a day trip, and avoid the summer crowds if you can). It's easy to understand its popularity: narrow cobbled streets wend car-free past ancient houses, up to a splendid ruined castle.

◉ Sights

Château des Baux

CASTLE, RUIN

(📱 04 90 49 20 02; www.chateau-baux-provence. com; adult/child Apr-Sep €10.50/8.50, Oct-Mar €8.50/6.50; ⊗ 9am-8pm Jul & Aug, to 7pm Apr-Jun & Sep, reduced hours Oct-Mar) Crowning the village of Les Baux, these dramatic, maze-like ruins date from the 10th century. The clifftop castle was largely destroyed in 1633, during the reign of Louis XIII, and is a thrilling place to explore – particularly for rambunctious kids. Climb crumbling towers for incredible views, descend into disused dungeons and flex your knightly prowess with giant medieval weapons dotting the open air site. Medieval-themed entertainment and hands-on action – shows, duels, catapult demonstrations and so on – abound in summer.

★ Carrières de Lumières

GALLERY

(📱 04 90 49 20 03; www.carrieres-lumieres.com; rte de Maillane; adult/child €12/10; ⊗ 9.30am-7pm or 7.30pm Apr-Sep, 10am-6pm Oct-Dec & Mar) Inside the chilly galleries of a former limestone quarry, this peculiar but intriguing attraction is like an underground audiovisual art gallery, with giant projections illuminating the walls, floor and ceiling, accompanied by an oration and swelling music. Programs change annually and there are joint tickets (adult/child €18/16 in summer) with the Château des Baux. Dress warmly.

🛏 Sleeping & Eating

⭐ **L'Oustau de Baumanière** GASTRONOMY €€€
(📞 04 90 54 33 07; www.baumaniere.com; menus
€100-215, mains €65-100; ❄🛜) Twice Michelin-starred and luxurious with a capital L, this
legendary hotel-restaurant is the most exclusive – and expensive – place to dine in this
corner of Provence. Head chef Jean-André
Charial revels in the rich flavours of classic
French cooking, and at one of the *table d'hôte*
lunch sessions (€33) you can watch the chef
work and share some food with him.

ℹ Information

Tourist Office (📞 04 90 54 34 39; www.lesbaux-
deprovence.com; Maison du Roy; ⏰ 9.30am-5pm
Mon-Fri, 10am-5.30pm Sat & Sun)

ℹ Getting There & Away

Bus services to Les Baux-de-Provence are
non-existent. Driving is easiest, but parking can be
hellish. Find metered parking spaces (€5 per day)
far down the hill at the village's edge; there's free
parking outside Carrières de Lumières. Good luck.

VAUCLUSE

Named after France's most powerful natural spring, which wells up outside Fontaine-de-Vaucluse, the Vaucluse *département*
sits on Provence's west side, sandwiched between the rumpled mountains of the Hautes-
Alpes and the rocky Var coastline. Crossed by
three great rivers – the Rhône, the Durance
and the Sorgue – Vaucluse is renowned for its
lavender fields and its vineyards, including
the legendary Châteauneuf-du-Pape. The area
has been occupied since ancient times, but it
was the Romans who left the greatest mark in
the form of Orange's ancient theatre and the
remains of two Roman towns, Glanum and
Vasio Vocontiorum. Centuries later, Avignon
became the seat of papal power, and its crenellated ramparts and monumental Palais des
Papes provide a glimpse of medieval majesty.

These days visitors come to explore Vaucluse's hilltop villages, elegant towns and
excellent restaurants – as well as the snowcapped summit of the *géant de Provence,*
Mont Ventoux.

Avignon

POP 91,250

Attention, quiz fans: name the city where the
pope lived during the early 14th century. An-
swered Rome? Bzzz: sorry, wrong answer. For
70-odd years of the early 1300s, the Provençal
town of Avignon was the centre of the Roman
Catholic world, and though its stint as the seat
of papal power only lasted a few decades, it's
been left with an impressive legacy of ecclesiastical architecture, most notably the soaring,
World Heritage–listed fortress-cum-palace
known as the Palais des Papes.

Avignon is now best known for its annual arts festival, the largest in France, which
spans several weeks in July. The rest of the
year, its rampart-ringed old town, medieval bridge, leafy squares and super restaurants are the main attractions. Be warned,
however – the construction of a flashy new
tramway around the old town's edge will
be causing major traffic headaches until at
least 2020.

History

Avignon first gained its ramparts – and
reputation for arts and culture – during the
14th century, when Pope Clement V fled political turmoil in Rome. From 1309 to 1377,
seven French-born popes invested huge
sums in the papal palace and offered asylum
to Jews and political dissidents. Pope Gregory XI left Avignon in 1376, but his death two
years later led to the Great Schism (1378–
1417), during which rival popes (up to three
at one time) resided at Rome and Avignon,
denouncing and excommunicating one another. Even after the matter was settled and
an impartial pope, Martin V, established
himself in Rome, Avignon remained under
papal rule. Avignon and Comtat Venaissin
(now the Vaucluse *département*) were ruled
by papal legates until 1791.

◎ Sights

⭐ **Palais des Papes** PALACE
(Papal Palace; 📞 tickets 04 32 74 32 74; www.
palais-des-papes.com; place du Palais; adult/
child €12/10, with Pont St-Bénézet €14.50/11.50;
⏰ 9am-8pm Jul, to 8.30pm Aug, shorter hours
Sep-Jun) The largest Gothic palace ever
built, the Palais des Papes was erected by
Pope Clement V, who abandoned Rome in
1309 in the wake of violent disorder after
his election. Its immense scale illustrates
the medieval might of the Roman Catholic
church.

Ringed by 3m-thick walls, its cavernous
halls, chapels and antechambers are largely
bare today – but tickets now include tablet
'Histopads' revealing virtual-reality rep-
resentations of how the building would have
looked in all its papal pomp.

Place du Palais SQUARE

This impressive vast square surrounding the Palais des Papes provides knockout photo ops. On top of the Romanesque 17th-century cathedral stands a golden statue of the Virgin Mary (weighing 4.5 tonnes), while next to the cathedral, the hilltop **Rocher des Doms** gardens provide great views of the Rhône, Mont Ventoux and Les Alpilles. Opposite the palace is the 17th-century **Hôtel des Monnaies**, once the papal mint and embellished with elaborate carvings and heraldic beasts.

★**Musée du Petit Palais** MUSEUM

(☑️04 90 86 44 58; www.petit-palais.org; place du Palais; adult/child €6/free; ⏰10am-1pm & 2-6pm Wed-Mon) The archbishops' palace during the 14th and 15th centuries now houses outstanding collections of primitive, pre-Rennaissance, 13th- to 16th-century Italian religious paintings by artists including Botticelli, Carpaccio and Giovanni di Paolo – the most famous is Botticelli's *La Vierge et l'Enfant* (1470).

★**Pont St-Bénézet** BRIDGE

(☑️tickets 04 32 74 32 74; bd de la Ligne; adult/child 24hr ticket €5/4, with Palais des Papes €14.50/11.50; ⏰9am-8pm Jul, to 8.30pm Aug, shorter hours Sep-Jun) Legend says Pastor Bénézet (a former shepherd) had three visions urging him to build a bridge across the Rhône. Completed in 1185, the 900m-long bridge linked Avignon with Villeneuve-lès-Avignon. It was rebuilt several times before all but four of its 22 spans were washed away in the 1600s, leaving the far side marooned in the middle of the Rhône. There are fine (and free) views from Rocher des Doms park, Pont Édouard Daladier, and Île de la Barthelasse's chemin des Berges.

Musée Angladon GALLERY

(☑️04 90 82 29 03; www.angladon.com; 5 rue Laboureur; adult/child €8/6.50; ⏰1-6pm Tue-Sun Apr-Sep, Tue-Sat Oct-Mar) Tiny Musée Angladon harbours an impressive collection of realist, impressionist and expressionist treasures, including works by Cézanne, Sisley, Manet, Modigliani, Degas and Picasso – but the star piece is Van Gogh's *Railway Wagons*, the only painting by the artist on display in Provence. Impress your friends by pointing out that the 'earth' isn't actually paint, but bare canvas.

Musée Calvet GALLERY

(☑️04 90 86 33 84; www.musee-calvet.org; 65 rue Joseph Vernet; adult/child €6/3, joint ticket with Musée Lapidaire €7/3.50; ⏰10am-1pm & 2-6pm Wed-Mon) The elegant Hôtel de Villeneuve-

Martignan (built 1741–54) provides a fitting backdrop for Avignon's fine-arts museum, with 16th- to 20th-century oil paintings, compelling prehistoric pieces, 15th-century wrought iron, and the elongated landscapes of Avignonnais artist Joseph Vernet.

★★ **Festivals & Events**

★**Festival d'Avignon** PERFORMING ARTS

(☑️box office 04 90 14 14 14; www.festival-avignon.com; ⏰Jul) The three-week annual Festival d'Avignon is one of the world's great performing-arts festivals. Over 40 international works of dance and drama play to 100,000-plus spectators at venues around town. Tickets don't go on sale until springtime, but hotels sell out by February.

Festival Off PERFORMING ARTS

(www.avignonleoff.com; ⏰Jul) The Festival d'Avignon is paralleled by a simultaneous fringe event, Festival Off, with eclectic experimental programming.

🛏 **Sleeping**

Péniche Le Hasard HOUSEBOAT €

(☑️06 12 07 47 17, 06 11 62 02 73; www.peniche-le-hasard.fr; chemin des Canotiers, Île de la Barthelasse; r incl breakfast €95; 🅿️❄️📶🏊) Avast, landlubbers: how about spending a night on a riverboat? This lovingly restored *péniche* bobs on the river about 2km from the old town. Two rooms here: the boatman's wheelhouse and the captain's cabin, both quirkily decorated and squeezed into the boat's odd-angled architecture – and up top there's a lovely deck terrace and, believe it or not, a pool.

STREET OF DYERS

Canalside rue des Teinturiers (literally 'street of dyers') is a picturesque pedestrian street known for its alternative vibe in Avignon's old dyers' district. A hive of industrial activity until the 19th century, populated by weavers and tapestry-makers, the street today is renowned for its bohemian bistros, cafes and gallery-workshops. Stone 'benches' in the shade of ancient plane trees make the perfect perch to ponder the irresistible trickle of the River Sorgue, safeguarded since the 16th century by Chapelle des Pénitents Gris. Those in the know dine at **L'Ubu** (p827), with a tiny, daily-changing menu chalked on the blackboard.

Avignon

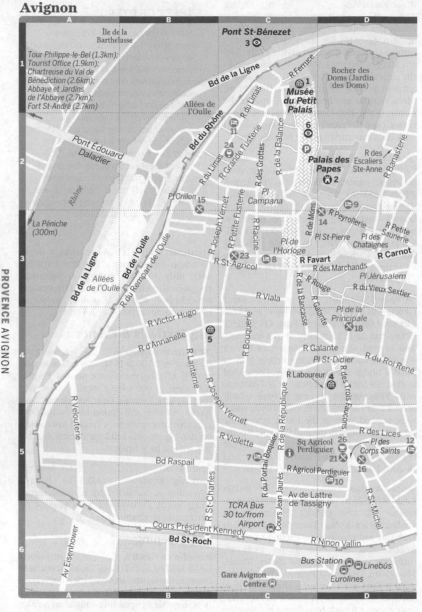

Pont St-Bénezet
3 ⊙

Île de la
Barthelasse

Tour Philippe-le-Bel (1.3km);
Tourist Office (1.9km);
Chartreuse du Val de
Bénédiction (2.6km);
Abbaye et Jardins
de l'Abbaye (2.7km);
Fort St-André (2.7km)

Bd de la Ligne

R Ferruce

Rocher des
Doms (Jardin
des Doms)

Allées de
l'Oulle

Bd du Rhône

R du Limas

**Musée
du Petit
Palais**
1

6 ⊙

Pont Édouard
Daladier

R du Limas

R Grande Fusterie

24

11

R des Grottes

R de la Balance

P

**Palais des
Papes**
2

R des
Escaliers
Ste-Anne

R Banasterie

Rhône

La Péniche
(300m)

Pl Crillon 15

R Joseph Vernet

R Petite Fusterie

R Racine

Pl
Campana

R de Mons

R Peyrollerie

9

14

Pl St-Pierre

Pl des
Chataignes

R Petite
Saunerie

Bd de la Ligne

Bd de l'Oulle

Allées
de l'Oulle

R du Rempart de l'Oulle

R St-Agricol

23

Pl de
l'Horloge

8

R Favart

Pl des Marchands

R Carnot

R Victor Hugo

5

R d'Annanelle

R Lanterne

R Bouquerie

R Viala

R de la Bancasse

R Rouge

R Galante

Pl Jérusalem

R du Vieux Sextier

Pl de la
Principale

18

R Velouterie

R Joseph Vernet

R Violette

R de la République

R Galante

Pl St-Didier

R Laboureur

4

R des Trois Faucons

R du Roi René

Bd Raspail

7

R du Portail Boquier

Sq Agricol
Perdiguier

R Agricol Perdiguier

10

26

21

16

Pl des
Corps Saints

R des Lices

12

R St-Michel

R St-Charles

R Violette

Av de Lattre
de Tassigny

Cours Jean Jaurès

Av Eisenhower

Cours Président Kennedy

TCRA Bus
30 to/from
Airport

Bd St-Roch

R Ninon Vallin

Bus Station

Linebús

Eurolines

**Gare Avignon
Centre**

Le Colbert HOTEL €
(☎ 04 90 86 20 20; www.lecolbert-hotel.com; 7 rue
Agricol Perdiguier; s €78-134, d €93-149; ☉ Apr-Oct;
🛜) One of several hotels on a shaded side
street off rue de la République, this pleasant,
old-fashioned hotel has 15 rooms decked out
in art posters and zingy shades of yellow,
terracotta and tangerine. Rooms are fairly
standard, but it's the sweet interior patio
that sells it – with a palm tree and a tinkling
fountain, it's a dreamy setting for breakfast.

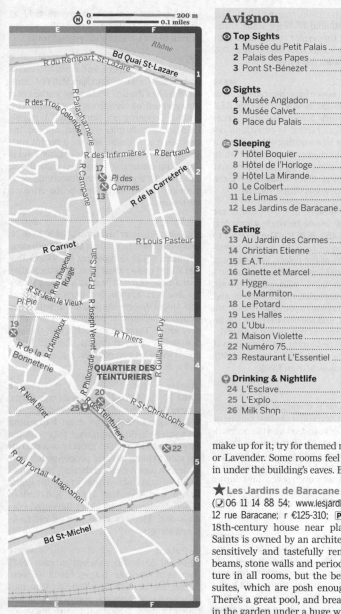

Avignon

◉ Top Sights
1	Musée du Petit Palais	C1
2	Palais des Papes	D2
3	Pont St-Bénezet	C1

◎ Sights
4	Musée Angladon	D4
5	Musée Calvet	B4
6	Place du Palais	C2

🛏 Sleeping
7	Hôtel Boquier	C5
8	Hôtel de l'Horloge	C3
9	Hôtel La Mirande	D2
10	Le Colbert	D5
11	Le Limas	C2
12	Les Jardins de Baracane	D5

✖ Eating
13	Au Jardin des Carmes	E2
14	Christian Etienne	D3
15	E.A.T.	B2
16	Ginette et Marcel	D5
17	Hygge	E2
	Le Marmiton	(see 9)
18	Le Potard	D4
19	Les Halles	E4
20	L'Ubu	E4
21	Maison Violette	D5
22	Numéro 75	F5
23	Restaurant L'Essentiel	C3

◉ Drinking & Nightlife
24	L'Esclave	C2
25	L'Explo	E4
26	Milk Shop	D5

make up for it; try for themed rooms Morocco or Lavender. Some rooms feel a bit squeezed in under the building's eaves. Breakfast is €9.

★ Les Jardins de Baracane
B&B €€

(☎ 06 11 14 88 54; www.lesjardinsdebaracane.fr; 12 rue Baracane; r €125-310; P ❉ 🛜 ⊠) This 18th-century house near place des Corps Saints is owned by an architect, so it's been sensitively and tastefully renovated. Wood beams, stone walls and period detailing feature in all rooms, but the best are the two suites, which are posh enough for a pope. There's a great pool, and breakfast is served in the garden under a huge wisteria tree.

Hôtel Boquier
HOTEL €

(☎ 04 90 82 34 43; www.hotel-boquier.com; 6 rue du Portail Boquier; s €56-78, d €56-80, tr €75-90, q €80-99; ❉ 🛜) It sits on a rather shabby side street, but the owners' infectious enthusiasm and the colourful rooms at this small hotel

Hôtel de l'Horloge
HOTEL €€

(☎ 04 90 16 42 00; www.hotel-avignon-horloge. com; place de l'Horloge; d €140-230; ❉ 🛜) A refined choice: a spacious and well-run hotel in a lovely building near the town hall (and its clock, hence the name), handily placed just off Avignon's main thoroughfare. The decor is fairly standard – beige walls, tasteful prints – but the terrace rooms are worth the extra for their knockout views (room 505 overlooks the Palais des Papes).

Le Limas
B&B €€

(📞 04 90 14 67 19; www.le-limas-avignon.com; 51 rue du Limas; ste €140-250; ❄@🛜) This chic B&B in an 18th-century townhouse, like something out of *Vogue Living,* is everything designers strive for when mixing old and new: a state-of-the-art kitchen and minimalist white decor complementing antique fireplaces and 18th-century spiral stairs. Breakfast on the sun-drenched terrace is divine, darling.

★ Hôtel La Mirande
HOTEL €€€

(📞 04 90 14 20 20; www.la-mirande.fr; 4 place de la Mirande; d from €450; ❄@🛜) The address to sleep in Avignon *en luxe.* It's located literally in the shadow of the palace, and stepping inside feels more like entering an aristocrat's château than a hotel, with oriental rugs, gold-threaded tapestries, marble statues and oil paintings everywhere you look. Rooms are equally opulent, and the best overlook the interior garden where afternoon tea is served.

Its renowned restaurant, Le Marmiton (4 place de la Mirande; menus €75-115, mains €35-40), offers cooking classes (from €90).

🍴 Eating

Place de l'Horloge is crammed with touristy restaurants that don't offer the best cuisine or value in town. Delve instead into the pedestrian old city where ample pretty squares tempt: place des Châtaignes and place de la Principle are two particularly beautiful restaurant-clad squares. Restaurants open seven days during the summer festival season, when reservations become essential. At other times of year many are closed at least two days a week.

★ Maison Violette
BAKERY €

(📞 06 59 44 62 94; place des Corps Saints; ⊙7am-7.30pm Mon-Sat) We simply defy you to walk into this bakery and not instantly be tempted by the stacks of baguettes, *ficelles* and *pains de campagnes* loaded up on the counter, not to mention the orderly ranks of éclairs, *millefeuilles,* fruit tarts and cookies lined up irresistibly behind the glass. Go on, a little bit of what you fancy does you good, *non*?

Les Halles
MARKET €

(www.avignon-leshalles.com; place Pie; ⊙6am-1.30pm Tue-Fri, to 2pm Sat & Sun) Over 40 food stalls showcase seasonal Provençal ingredients. Cooking demonstrations are held at 11am Saturday. Outside on place Pie, admire Patrick Blanc's marvellous vegetal wall.

Hygge
CAFE €

(📞 04 65 81 06 87; 25 place des Carmes; 2-/3-course lunch €13.90/15.90; ⊙8am-3pm Mon-Wed, 8am-3pm & 6-10pm Thu-Sat) 🍴 Having worked at a smorgasbord of high-flying restaurants (including Copenhagen's Noma and Avignon's La Mirande), Jacques Pampiri opened his own place in Avignon, and it's a big hit with the locals. Hearty, wholesome organic food is dished up canteen-style to keep costs down, and the mix-and-match thrift-store decor is great fun. Arrive early for a prime table on the square.

E.A.T.
BISTRO €

(Estaminet, Arômes et Tentations; 📞 04 90 83 46 74; www.restaurant-eat.com; 8 rue Mazan; lunch menu €16, mains €11-17; ⊙noon-2pm & 7-9.45pm Thu-Tue) Weird name; great food. This back-alley bistro near place Crillon is a strong local's tip. It's very French, but borrows flavours and spices freely: smoked hake with pear compôte, perhaps, or one-pot veal in a rich, oozy sauce. There's not much space, though: definitely elbows-in dining. The €16 lunch *menu* includes two courses, a glass of wine and coffee.

Ginette et Marcel
CAFE €

(📞 04 90 85 58 70; 27 place des Corps Saints; tartines €4.30-7.50; ⊙11am-11pm Wed-Mon; 👶) Set on one of Avignon's most happening plane-tree-shaded squares, this vintage cafe styled like a 1950s grocery is a charming spot to hang out and people-watch over a *tartine* (open-face sandwich), tart, salad or other light dish – equally tasty for lunch or an early-evening *apéro.* Kids adore Ginette's cherry- and violet-flavoured cordials and Marcel's glass jars of old-fashioned sweets.

Le Potard
BURGERS €

(📞 04 90 82 34 19; www.lepotard.com; 19-21 place de la Principale; burgers €14-18; ⊙noon-2.30pm Tue-Sat, 6.30-10pm Wed-Sat) Gourmet brioche-based burgers come in a multitude of guises, loaded with tempting goodies from smoked bacon and St-Nectaire cheese to caramelised onions, crunchy rocket and sundried tomato caviar. There's also a range of salad plates served with mini-burgers. In case you're wondering, the name refers to the dial on a guitar (sometimes called a 'pot' in English).

★ Restaurant L'Essentiel FRENCH €€
(☑ 04 90 85 87 12; www.restaurantlessentiel.com; 2 rue Petite Fusterie; menus €32-46; ⊘ noon-2pm & 7-9.45pm Tue-Sat) In the top tier of Avignon's restaurants for many a year, this elegant restaurant remains (as its name suggests) as essential as ever. First there's the setting: a lovely, honey-stoned *hôtel particulier* (mansion) with a sweet courtyard garden. Then there's the food: rich, sophisticated French dining of the first order, replete with the requisite foams, veloutés and reductions.

L'Ubu BISTRO €€
(☑ 04 90 80 01 01; 13 rue des Teinturiers; starters/mains €7.50/16.50; ⊘ noon-2.30pm & 7-10.30pm Mon-Sat) This place is so hip it hurts, from its in-your-face street-art murals to its junk-shop decor and on-trend slogans. The menu changes regularly, so there's no telling what you'll get, but wholefood, organic and fusion often feature on the small menu. Traditional it isn't. Aim for one of the outside tables if you can.

Au Jardin des Carmes FRENCH €€
(☑ 09 54 25 10 67; 21 place des Carmes; 2-/3-course menu €28/33; ⊘ noon-10.30pm Tue-Sat) There's one standout reason to lunch at this homey restaurant, and that's the delightful courtyard garden, shaded by sails, tall bamboo and climbing plants. À la carte starters are €11, mains €21 and desserts €9, plus there's a *plat du jour* at €16. The food is honest rather than *haute cuisine,* but it's prettily presented and packed with flavour.

Numéro 75 MODERN FRENCH €€
(☑ 04 90 27 16 00; www.numero75.com; 75 rue Guillaume Puy; 2-/3-course menus from €31/38; ⊘ noon-2pm & 7.30-9.30pm Mon-Sat) The chic dining room, in the former mansion of absinthe inventor Jules Pernod, is a fitting backdrop to the stylised Mediterranean cooking. *Menus* change nightly and include just a handful of mains, but brevity guarantees freshness. On balmy nights, reserve a table in the elegant courtyard garden.

★ Christian Etienne FRENCH €€€
(☑ 04 90 86 16 50; www.christian-etienne.fr; 10 rue de Mons; lunch/dinner menus from €35/75; ⊘ noon-2pm & 7.30-10pm Tue-Sat) If it's the full-blown, fine-dining French experience you're after, then Monsieur Etienne's much-vaunted (and Michelin-starred) restaurant is the place to go. It's the real deal: truffles and foie gras galore, and the kind of multicourse *menus* that demand a second mortgage. It's

a bit dated inside: go for the lovely, leafy terrace for fine views of the medieval building.

🍷 Drinking & Nightlife

Chic yet laid-back Avignon is awash with gorgeous, tree-shaded pedestrian squares buzzing with cafe life. Favourite options, loaded with pavement terraces and drinking opportunities, include place Crillon, place Pie, place de l'Horloge and place des Corps Saints.

Students tend to favour the many bars dotted along the aptly named rue de la Verrerie (Glassware St).

Milk Shop CAFE
(☑ 09 82 54 16 82; www.milkshop.fr; 26 place des Corps Saints; ⊘ 7.45am-7pm Mon-Fri, 9.30am-7pm Sat; 🖥) Keen to mingle with Avignon students? Make a beeline for this *salon au lait* ('milk bar') where super-thick ice-cream shakes (€4.50) are slurped through extra-wide straws. Bagels (€5 to €7), cupcakes and other American snacks create a deliberate US vibe, while comfy armchairs and wi-fi encourage hanging out.

L'Explo CRAFT BEER
(2 rue des Teinturiers; ⊘ 5pm-midnight Tue-Sat) It's a sunny evening and your inner beer nerd is in the market for a dry rye, hoppy IPA or boozy Belgian wheat beer. Well you're in luck: this groovy little bar on happening rue des Teinturiers serves a big range of artisanal beers, many made locally.

PROVENCE AVIGNON

ℹ CENT SAVER
An excellent-value discount card, **Avignon Passion** yields cheaper admission to big-hitter museums and monuments in Avignon and Villeneuve-lès-Avignon. The first site visited is full price, but each subsequent site is discounted. The reduction depends on each museum, but the discount is at least €1 (it gives you €2 off full price at the Palais des Papes, for example). For maximum savings, pay full price at one of the cheaper museums like the Musée Lapidaire, and benefit from the discount at more expensive ones such as the Palais des Papes and Pont St-Bénézet.

The pass is free and valid for 15 days. It covers a couple of tours too, and is available at the tourist office (p828) and at museums.

L'Esclave GAY
(☑ 04 90 85 14 91; 12 rue du Limas; ☺ 11.30pm-7am Tue-Sun) Avignon's inner-city gay bar rocks well into the wee hours, pulling a clientele that is not always that quiet, based on dozens of neighbour-considerate 'be quiet' signs plastered outside.

ℹ️ Information

Tourist Office (☑ 04 32 74 32 74; www.avignon-tourisme.com; 41 cours Jean Jaurès; ☺ 9am-6pm Mon-Sat, 10am-5pm Sun Apr-Oct, shorter hours Nov-Mar) Offers guided walking tours and information on other tours and activities, including boat trips on the River Rhône and wine-tasting trips to nearby vineyards. Smartphone apps too.

Tourist Office Annexe (Gare Avignon TGV; ☺ Jun-Aug) During summer, Avignon has an information booth at the TGV station.

ℹ️ Getting There & Away

AIR
Aéroport Avignon-Provence (AVN; ☑ 04 90 81 51 51; www.avignon.aeroport.fr; Caumont) is in Caumont, 8km southeast of Avignon, and has direct flights to London, Birmingham and Southampton in the UK.

BUS
Avignon's **bus station** (bd St-Roch; ☺ information window 8am-7pm Mon-Fri, to 1pm Sat) is a major bus hub for the Vaucluse *département*. Long-haul companies **Linebus** (☑ 04 90 85 30 48; www.linebus.com) and **Eurolines** (☑ 04 90 85 27 60; www.eurolines.com) have offices at the far end of bus platforms and serve places like Barcelona. TransVaucluse (www.vaucluse.fr) offers regional bus services in the Avignon area.

Aix-en-Provence €18, LER Line 23, 1¼ hours, six daily Monday to Saturday, two on Sunday
Arles €7.80, LER Line 18, 50 minutes, five daily
Carpentras €2.10, TransVaucluse Line 5, 45 minutes, 11 daily Monday to Saturday, six on Sunday
Orange €2.10, TransVaucluse Line 2, one hour, hourly Monday to Saturday, three on Sunday

TRAIN
Avignon has two train stations: **Gare Avignon Centre** (42 bd St-Roch), on the southern edge of the walled town, and **Gare Avignon TGV** (Courtine), 4km southwest in Courtine.

Local shuttle trains link the two every 15 to 20 minutes (€1.60, six minutes, 6am to 11pm). There is no luggage storage at the train station.

Eurostar (www.eurostar.com) services operate one to five times weekly between Avignon TGV and London St Pancras (from €78, 5¾ hours) en route to/from Marseille.

Aix-en-Provence €12.50 to €21, 25 minutes

Arles €8, 17 minutes
Marseille €12.50 to €19, 40 minutes
Marseille-Provence airport Vitrolles station, €12 to €21, one to 1½ hours
Nice €36 to €62, 3¼ hours
Nîmes €9.90, 30 minutes
Orange €6.60, 22 minutes
Paris Gare du Lyon €45 to €90, 3½ hours

ℹ️ Getting Around

TO/FROM THE AIRPORT
From the airport, **TCRA bus 30** (www.tcra.fr; €1.40; ☺ Mon-Sat) (25 minutes) goes to the post office and LER bus 22 (www.info-ler.fr; €1.50) goes to the Avignon bus station and TGV station.

Taxis cost about €35 to €40.

BICYCLE
Vélopop (☑ 08 10 45 64 56; www.velopop.fr; per half-hour €0.50) Shared-bicycle service, with 17 stations around town. Membership is €1/5 per day/week.

Provence Bike (☑ 04 90 27 92 61; www.provence-bike.com; 7 av St-Ruf; bicycles per day/week from €12/65, scooters €25/150; ☺ 9am-6.30pm Mon-Sat, plus 10am-1pm Sun Jul) Rents out city bikes, mountain bikes, scooters and motorcycles.

Villeneuve-lès-Avignon
POP 12,872

Across the Rhône from Avignon, compact Villeneuve-lès-Avignon has monuments to rival Avignon's but none of the crowds. Meander the cloisters of a medieval monastery, take in hilltop views from Fort St-André and lose yourself in spectacular gardens at Abbaye St-André – reason enough to visit.

◎ Sights

★ Abbaye et Jardins de l'Abbaye
MONASTERY, GARDENS
(☑ 04 90 25 55 95; www.abbayesaintandre.fr; Fort St-André, rue Montée du Fort; adult/child abbey €14/free, garden €7/free; ☺ 10am-6pm Tue-Sun May-Sep, 10am-1pm & 2-5pm Tue-Sun Mar & Oct, to 6pm Apr) The resplendent vaulted halls of this 10th-century abbey, within Fort St-André (p829), can only be visited by guided tour. The stunning terrace gardens, however – built atop the abbey vaults and classed among France's top 100 gardens – can be freely roamed. Pathways meander among fragrant roses, iris-studded olive groves, wisteria-covered pergolas and the ruins of three ancient churches. The views of Avignon and the Rhône are spectacular.

Fort St-André
FORT

(☎ 04 90 25 45 35; rue Montée du Fort; adult/child €6/free, joint ticket with Chartreuse du Val de Bénédiction €9/free; ⊙10am-6pm Jun-Sep, 10am-1pm & 2-5pm Oct-May) King Philip the Fair (aka Philippe le Bel) wasn't messing around when he built defensive 14th-century Fort St-André on the then border between France and the Holy Roman Empire: the walls are 2m thick! Today you can walk a small section of the ramparts and admire 360-degree views from the Tour des Masques (Wizards' Tower) and Tours Jumelles (Twin Towers). You can also tour the Abbaye et Jardins de l'Abbaye.

Chartreuse du Val de Bénédiction
MONASTERY

(☎ 04 90 15 24 24; www.chartreuse.org; 58 rue de la République; adult/child €8/free, joint ticket with Fort St-André €9/free; ⊙9.30am-6.30pm May-Sep, to 5pm Oct-Mar) Shaded from the summer's heat, the three cloisters, 24 cells, church, chapels and nook-and-cranny gardens of the Chartreuse du Val de Bénédiction make up France's biggest Carthusian monastery, founded in 1352 by Pope Innocent VI, who was buried here 10 years later in an elaborate mausoleum.

Tour Philippe-le-Bel
LANDMARK

(☎ 04 32 70 08 57; montée de la Tour; adult/child €2.60/free; ⊙10am-12.30pm & 2-6pm Tue-Sun May-Oct, 2-5pm Feb-Apr) King Philip commissioned the Tour Philippe-le-Bel, 500m outside Villeneuve, to control traffic over Pont St-Bénézet to and from Avignon. The steep steps spiralling to the top reward climbers with stunning river views.

ⓘ Information

Tourist Office (☎ 04 90 25 61 33; www.ot-villeneuvelezavignon.fr; 1 place Charles David; ⊙9.30am-12.30pm & 2-5pm Mon-Fri, 9am-1pm Sat, slightly longer hours in summer) Runs guided tours in English in July and August.

ⓘ Getting There & Away

TCRA (Transports en Commun de la Région d'Avignon; ☎ 04 32 74 18 32; www.tcra.fr) bus 5 links Villeneuve-lès-Avignon with Avignon (it's only 2km, but dull walking).

Orange

POP 29,645

Two thousand years ago, Orange – then known as Arausio – was one of the major settlements in this sunbaked corner of the Gallo-Roman empire. To cement its status, townsfolk constructed an impressive series of structures, including the town's mighty ancient theatre. Once the largest in Gaul, it still steals the show and is rightly (along with Orange's triumphal arch) a World Heritage Site. Unfortunately, despite its massive scale, the limestone structure is surprisingly fragile, and a monumental eight-year restoration project is currently under way to preserve it for the future. Expect scaffolding until at least 2024.

The modern town itself isn't quite as starry – in fact, in places it looks positively unloved – so there's no real reason to spend the night unless you have to.

⊙ Sights

★ Théâtre Antique
HISTORIC SITE

(Ancient Roman Theatre; ☎ 04 90 51 17 60; www.theatre-antique.com; rue Madeleine Roch; adult/child €9.50/7.50; ⊙9am-7pm Jun-Aug, to 6pm Apr, May & Sep, 9.30am-5.30pm Mar & Oct, 9.30am-4.30pm Nov-Feb) Orange's monumental, Unesco-protected Roman theatre is unquestionably one of France's most impressive Roman sights. It's one of only three intact Roman theatres left in the world (the others are in Syria and Turkey), and its sheer size is awe-inspiring: designed to seat 10,000 spectators, its stage wall reaches 37m high, 103m wide and 1.8m thick. Little wonder that Louis XIV called it 'the finest wall in my kingdom'.

★ Colline St-Eutrope
GARDENS

For bird's-eye views of the theatre – and phenomenal vistas of Mont Ventoux and the Dentelles de Montmirail – follow montée Philbert de Chalons or montée Lambert up Colline St-Eutrope (St Eutrope Hill; elevation 97m), once the Romans' lookout point. En route, pass ruins of a 12th-century château, once the residence of the princes of Orange.

Arc de Triomphe
HISTORIC SITE

Orange's 1st-century-AD monumental arch, the Arc de Triomphe – 19m high and wide, and 8m thick – stands on the Via Agrippa. Restored in 2009, its brilliant reliefs commemorate Roman victories in 49 BC with carvings of chained, naked Gauls.

Musée d'Art et d'Histoire
MUSEUM

(www.theatre-antique.com; rue Madeleine Roch; entry incl with Théâtre Antique; ⊙9.15am-7pm Jun-Aug, to 6pm Apr, May & Sep, shorter hours Oct-Mar) This small museum contains various finds relating to the theatre's history, including plaques and friezes that once formed part of the scenery, a range of amphora, busts, columns and vases, and a room displaying three rare engraved *cadastres* (official surveys) dating from 77 BC.

✦ Festivals & Events

Les Chorégies d'Orange PERFORMING ARTS
(www.choregies.asso.fr; ⊙ Jul & Aug) The Théâtre Antique comes alive with all-night concerts, weekend operas and choral performances. Reserve tickets months ahead, and rooms the year before.

🛏 Sleeping & Eating

Hôtel Saint Jean HOTEL €
(✆ 04 90 51 15 16; www.hotelsaint-jean.com; 1 cours Pourtoules; s/d/tr/q €75/85/105/125; ▣✳🖘) An attractive option with bags of Provençal character, half-built into the hillside of the Colline St-Eutrope. Inside, there are checked fabrics and cosy rooms, with windows overlooking a patio; outside, the building is all yellow stone and pistachio-coloured shutters. A few of the rooms have walls cut straight into the hill.

★ **Le Mas Julien** B&B €€
(✆ 04 90 34 99 49; www.mas-julien.com; 704 chemin de St Jean; d €95-125, studio €110-180; ▣✳🖘🏊) Out in the countryside between Orange and Châteauneuf-du-Pape, this delightful farmhouse is the stuff of Provençal dreams: wisteria-clad façade, gorgeous pool, quiet location and rooms that blend contemporary style with rustic charm. There are four rooms and a self-contained studio. Owner Valère caters dinners on request.

Les Saveurs du Marché FRENCH €
(✆ 06 14 44 26 63; 24 place Sylvain; 2-/3-/4-course lunch menu €13/16/24, dinner menu €29; ⊙ noon-2pm Tue-Sun, 7-9pm Tue-Sat) As the name suggests, market flavours underpin the menu here, from delicious homemade tapenades to pan-seared red mullet drizzled with olive oil and fragrant pesto. The menu changes regularly – the four-course lunch is a steal – but quality can suffer a bit when it gets over-busy, so arrive early.

ⓘ CENT SAVER

The Roman Pass (Pass Romain; adult/child €18.50/14) is a joint ticket that allows access to Orange's Roman theatre and museum, plus Nîmes' Les Arènes, the Maison Carrée and Tour Magne. It's valid for seven days, and you can buy it at any of the venues.

ⓘ Information

Tourist Office (✆ 04 90 34 70 88; www.otorange.fr; place des Frères Mounet; ⊙ 9am-6.30pm Mon-Sat, 9am-1pm & 2-6.30pm Sun, closed Sun Oct-Mar) Has lots of brochures and handles hotel bookings, and also sells the Roman Pass.

ⓘ Getting There & Around

BICYCLE

Sport Aventure (✆ 04 90 34 75 08; 1 place de la République; per half-day/day/week €12/18/69) Central bike shop; delivers within 20km radius.

BUS

Most buses depart from Orange's **bus station** (✆ 04 90 34 15 59; 201 cours Pourtoules).

Avignon €2.10, TransVaucluse Line 2, one hour, hourly Monday to Saturday, three on Sunday

Vaison-la-Romaine €2, TransVaucluse Line 4, 45 minutes, eight daily Monday to Saturday, two on Sunday

TRAIN

Orange's **train station** (av Frédéric Mistral) is 1.5km east of the town centre.

Arles €12.60, 40 minutes

Avignon €6.60, 22 minutes

Marseille €26.20, 1¾ hours

Marseille-Provence airport Vitrolles station; €23, 1¼ hours

Vaison-la-Romaine

POP 6275

Tucked between seven hills, Vaison-la-Romaine has long been a traditional exchange centre, and it still has a thriving Tuesday market. The village's rich Roman legacy is obvious – 20th-century buildings rise alongside France's largest archaeological site. A Roman bridge crosses the River Ouvèze, dividing the contemporary town's pedestrianised centre and the spectacular walled, cobbled-street hilltop Cité Médiévale – one of Provence's most magical ancient villages – where the counts of Toulouse built their 12th-century castle. Vaison is a good base for jaunts into the Dentelles de Montmirail or Mont Ventoux, but tourists throng here in summer: reserve ahead.

◉ Sights & Activities

Vaison's position is ideal for village-hopping by bicycle. The tourist office stocks excellent brochures detailing multiple cycling circuits (www.escapado.fr), rated by difficulty, from 26km to 91km.

★ **Gallo-Roman Ruins** RUINS
(☑04 90 36 50 48; www.provenceromaine.com;
adult/child incl all ancient sites, museum & cathedral
€8/4; ☺9.30am-6.30pm Jun-Sep, to 6pm Apr & May,
10am-noon & 2-5.30pm Oct-Mar) The ruined remains of Vasio Vocontiorum, the Roman city
that flourished here between the 6th and 2nd
centuries BC, fill two central Vaison sites. Two
neighbourhoods of this once opulent city,
Puymin and La Villasse, lie on either side of
the tourist office and av du Général de Gaulle.
Admission includes entry to the 12th-cen-
tury Romanesque cloister at **Cathédrale
Notre-Dame de Nazareth** (cloister only
€1.50; ☺10am-12.30pm & 2-6pm Mar-Dec), a five-
minute walk west of La Villasse and a soothing refuge from the summer heat.

In **Puymin**, see houses of the nobility,
mosaics, workers' quarters, a temple and
the still-functioning, 6000-seat **Théâtre
Antique** (c AD 20). To make sense of the
remains (and collect your audioguide; €3),
head for the **Musée Archéologique Gallo-Roman**, which revives Vaison's Roman
past with incredible swag – superb mosaics, carved masks and statues that include a
3rd-century silver bust and marble renderings of Hadrian and wife Sabina.

The Romans shopped at the colonnaded
boutiques and bathed at **La Villasse**, where
you'll find **Maison au Dauphin**, which has
splendid marble-lined fish ponds.

★ **Cité Médiévale** HISTORIC SITE
Wandering around Vaison-la-Romaine's
wonderful medieval quarter, you could be
forgiven for thinking you've stepped into a
forgotten set from *Monty Python and the
Holy Grail*. Ringed by ramparts and accessed
via the pretty **Pont Romain** (Roman Bridge),
it's a fascinating place to explore, criss-crossed
by cobbled alleyways. Look out for the elaborate carvings around many of the doorways
as you climb up towards the 12th-century
château and its wrap-around vistas.

🛏 Sleeping

Camping du Théâtre Romain CAMPGROUND €
(☑04 90 28 78 66; www.camping-theatre.com;
chemin de Brusquet; sites per 2 people with tent &
car €14.90-25.90; ☺mid-Mar–mid-Nov; 🅟≋) A
large, well-run campsite opposite the Théâtre
Antique. It gets lots of sun, and there's a pool.

★ **Hôtel Burrhus** HOTEL €
(☑04 90 36 00 11; www.burrhus.com; 1 place de
Montfort; d €65-96, apt €140; 🅟❋🅟) From the
outside, this looks like a classic town hotel:

shutters, stonework and a prime spot on the
town square. But inside, surprises await: the
arty owners have littered it with modern art,
sculptures, funky furniture and colourful
decorative details, although the white-walled
rooms themselves sometimes feel stark. On
sunny days, take breakfast on the plane-tree-
shaded balcony overlooking the square.

L'École Buissonière B&B €
(☑04 90 28 95 19; www.buissonniere-provence.
com; D75, Buisson; s/d/tr/q from €55/68/83/100;
🅟) Five minutes north of Vaison, in the
countryside between Buisson and Villedieu,
hosts Monique and John have transformed
their stone farmhouse into a tastefully decorated three-bedroom B&B, which is big on
comfort. Breakfast features homemade jam,
and there's an outdoor summer kitchen.

Hostellerie Le Beffroi HISTORIC HOTEL €€
(☑04 90 36 04 71; www.le-beffroi.com; rue de
l'Évêché; d €105-195, tr €205-230; ☺Apr-Jan;
🅟≋≋) This hotel on the narrow streets of
the old town wins hands-down for atmosphere, but you might not feel so enthusiastic
once you've lugged your luggage up from
the car park. Still, it's awash with history:
the two buildings date from 1554 and 1690,
and rooms feel appropriately old-fashioned.
There's a delightful rose garden and (rather
improbably) even a pool.

🍴 Eating

Brasseries on place de Montfort vary in
quality; restaurants on cours Taulignan are
generally better. Dining in Cité Médiévale is
limited and pricey.

Maison Lesage BAKERY €
(2 rue de la République; sandwiches €4-6; ☺7am-
1pm & 3-5pm Mon, Tue & Thu-Sat, 7am-1pm Sun)
For picnics by the river, this excellent bakery
has no shortage of foodie fare: big baguettes,
homemade pastries and nougat, and the
house speciality, bun-sized meringues in a
rainbow of flavours.

★ **Bistro du'O** BISTRO €€
(☑04 90 41 72 90; www.bistroduo.fr; rue du Château;
lunch/dinner menus from €26/38; ☺noon-2pm &
7.30-10pm Tue-Sat) For fine dining in Vaison,
this is everyone's tip. The setting is full of atmosphere, in a vaulted cellar in the medieval
city (once the château stables), and the chef
Philippe Zemour takes his cue from Provençal
flavours and daily market ingredients. Top-
class food, top setting, tops all round.

Le Moulin à Huile
GASTRONOMY €€€

(☑04 90 36 20 67; www.lemoulinahuile84.fr; quai Maréchal Foch, rte de Malaucène; 2-/3-/4-course menus €29/38/45; ☉noon-1.30pm & 7.15-9.30pm Mon, Tue, Fri & Sat, 7.15-9.30pm Thu, noon-1.30pm Sun) This renowned restaurant is still a destination address in Vaison, if only for its lovely riverside setting in a former olive-oil mill. The menus are affordable, and stocked with locally sourced goodies, such as river trout, wood pigeon, and lamb and pork from local farms.

ℹ Information

Tourist Office (☑04 90 36 02 11; www.vaison-ventoux-tourisme.com; place du Chanoine Sautel; ☉9.30am-noon & 2-5.45pm Mon-Sat year-round, plus 9.30am-noon Sun mid-Mar–mid-Oct, longer hours in summer)

ℹ Getting There & Away

The **bus stop** is on av des Choralies, 400m east of the tourist office. Several services are provided by **Cars Comtadin** (☑04 90 67 20 25; www.sudest-mobilites.fr).

Carpentras €2.10, TransVaucluse Line 11, 45 minutes, five daily Monday to Saturday

Vaison-la-Romaine €2, TransVaucluse Line 4, 45 minutes, eight daily Monday to Saturday, two on Sunday

Mont Ventoux

Visible for miles around, Mont Ventoux (1912m) stands like a sentinel over northern Provence. From its summit, accessible by road between May and October, vistas extend to the Alps and, on a clear day, the Camargue.

Because of the mountain's dimensions, every European climate type is represented here, from Mediterranean on its lower southern reaches to Arctic on its exposed northern ridge. As you climb, temperatures can plummet by 20°C, and the fierce mistral wind blows 130 days a year, sometimes at speeds of 250km/h. Bring warm clothes and rain gear, even in summer. You can ascend by road year-round, but you cannot traverse the summit from 15 November to 15 April.

The mountain's diverse fauna and flora have earned the mountain Unesco Biosphere Reserve status. Some species live nowhere else, including the rare snake eagle.

Three gateways – Bédoin, Malaucène and Sault – provide services in summer, but they're far apart.

Biking

Tourist offices distribute *Les Itinéraires Ventoux,* a free map detailing 11 itineraries – graded easy to difficult – and highlighting artisanal farms en route. For more cycling trails, see www.lemontventoux.net. Most cycle-hire outfits also offer electric bikes.

Ventoux Bike Park
CYCLING

(☑04 90 61 84 55; www.facebook.com/Ventoux-BikePark; Chalet Reynard; half/full day €10/14; ☉10am-5pm Sat & Sun, hours vary Mon-Fri) Near the Mont Ventoux summit, at Chalet Reynard, mountain bikers ascend via rope tow (minimum age 10 years), then descend ramps and jumps down three trails (5km in total). In winter it's possible to mountain bike on snow. Bring a bike, helmet and gloves or rent all gear at Chalet Reynard. Call to check opening times, which are highly weather dependent.

Hiking

The GR4 crosses the Dentelles de Montmirail before scaling Mont Ventoux' northern face, where it meets the GR9. Both traverse the ridge. The GR4 branches eastwards to Gorges du Verdon; the GR9 crosses the Vaucluse Mountains to the Luberon. The essential map for the area is *3140ET Mont Ventoux,* by IGN (www.ign.fr). Bédoin's tourist office stocks maps and brochures detailing walks for all levels.

In July and August tourist offices in Bédoin and Malaucène facilitate night-time expeditions up the mountain to see the sunrise (participants must be over 15 years old).

Les Ânes des Abeilles
TOURS

(☑04 90 64 01 52; http://abeilles.ane-et-rando.com; rte de la Gabelle, Col des Abeilles; day/weekend from €50/95) A novel means of exploring the Gorges de la Nesque, a spectacular limestone canyon, or nearby Mont Ventoux, is alongside a donkey from Les Ânes des Abeilles. Beasts carry up to 40kg (ie small children or bags).

ℹ Information

Bédoin Tourist Office (☑04 90 65 63 95; www.bedoin.org; Espace Marie-Louis Gravier, 1 rte de Malaucène; ☉9.30am-12.30pm & 2-6pm Mon-Fri, 9.30am-12.30pm & 3-6pm Sat, 10am-12.30pm Sun mid-Apr–mid-Oct, reduced hours mid-Oct–mid-Apr) Excellent source of information on all regional activities; also helps with lodging.

Malaucène Tourist Office (☑04 90 65 22 59; http://villagemalaucene.free.fr; place de la Mairie; ☉9.15am-12.15pm & 2.30-5.30pm Mon-Fri, 9am-noon Sat) Small village office with info

WORTH A TRIP

GIGONDAS

Wine cellars and cafes surround the sun-dappled central square of Gigondas, famous for its prestigious red wine. Wine tasting here provides an excellent counterpoint to Châteauneuf-du-Pape: both use the same grapes, but the soil is different. In town, **Caveau de Gigondas** (☎04 90 65 82 29; www.caveaudugigondas.com; place Gabrielle Andéol; ⏰10am-noon & 2-6.30pm) represents 100 small producers and offers free tastings – most bottles cost just €12 to €17. The **tourist office** (☎04 90 65 85 46; www.gigondas-dm.fr; rue du Portail; ⏰9am-12.30pm & 2.30-6.30pm Mon-Sat, 10am-1pm Sun Jul & Aug, shorter hours Sep-Jun) has a complete list of wineries.

For exquisite wine pairings to a sensational, traditional Provençal meal, reserve a garden table beneath olive trees at **L'Oustalet** (☎04 90 65 85 30; www.loustalet-gigondas.com; 5 place Gabrielle Andéol; 2-/3-course menu from €36/42; ⏰noon-2pm & 7-9pm Tue-Sat). Should you be unable to move afterwards, **Les Florets** (☎04 90 65 85 01; www.hotel-les-florets.com; 1243 rte des Florêts; r €120-175; P 📶 🏊), 2km from the village with vineyard views, is Gigondas' 'modern-meets-heritage' hotel tip-off.

on Mont Ventoux, but otherwise rather limited on other areas.

Sault Tourist Office (☎04 90 64 01 21; www.ventoux-sud.com; av de la Promenade; ⏰9.30am-12.30pm & 1.30-6.30pm Mon-Fri, 10am-12.30pm & 2-6.30pm Sat & Sun Jun-Aug, 9am-12.30pm & 2.30-5pm or 6pm Mon-Sat Sep-Mar) Good resource for Mont Ventoux information.

ℹ Getting There & Away

Getting up the mountain by public transport isn't feasible – you'll need a car or, if you're feeling fit, a bike.

Carpentras

POP 29,600

Carpentras is a rather run-of-the-mill agricultural town, but it's worth a detour for one very compelling reason – an absolutely wonderful Provençal market, which takes over the entire town every Friday morning, with more than 350 stalls laden with bread, honey, cheese, olives, fruit and a rainbow of *berlingots,* Carpentras' striped, pillow-shaped, hard-boiled sweets. In winter, it's also an important truffle-trading town.

👁 Sights

★Synagogue de Carpentras SYNAGOGUE
(☎04 90 63 39 97; place Juiverie; ⏰10am-noon & 3-4.30pm Mon-Thu, 10-11.30am & 3-3.30pm Fri) Carpentras' remarkable synagogue dates from 1367 and is the oldest still in use in France. Although Jews were initially welcomed into papal territory, by the 17th century they had to live in ghettos in Avignon, Carpentras, Cavaillon and L'Isle-sur-la-Sorgue: the synagogue is deliberately inconspicuous. The wood-panelled prayer hall was rebuilt in 18th-century baroque style; downstairs are bread-baking ovens, used until 1904. For access, ring the doorbell on the half-hour.

★Arc Romain HISTORIC SITE
Hidden behind Cathédrale St-Siffrein, the Arc Romain was built under Augustus in the 1st century AD and is decorated with worn carvings of enslaved Gauls.

Cathédrale St-Siffrein CATHEDRAL
(place St-Siffrein; ⏰8am-noon & 2-6pm Mon-Sat) Carpentras' cathedral was built between 1405 and 1519 in meridional Gothic style, but is crowned by a distinctive contemporary bell tower. Its **Trésor d'Art Sacré** (Treasury of Religious Art) holds precious 14th- to 19th-century religious relics that you can only see during the Foire de St-Siffrein (27 November) or on guided walks with the tourist office.

🛏 Sleeping & Eating

Hôtel du Fiacre HOTEL €€
(☎04 90 63 03 15; www.hotel-du-fiacre.com; 153 rue Vigne; d €70-140, f €105-140; P 📶) Frills, swags and canopies abound at this grand old dame of a hotel, where the old-style decor takes its cue from the 18th-century architecture. Contemporary it ain't, but charming it most surely is. The marble staircase is a thing of beauty too.

★Metafort B&B €€€
(☎04 90 34 46 84; www.metafort-provence.com; 31 Montée du Vieil Hôpital, Méthamis; d €145-195; ❄ 📶 🏊) Wow. This palatial pad pulls out all the stops in terms of architecture, design and out-and-out luxury. It's in a 17th-century

CHÂTEAUNEUF-DU-PAPE

Even in the world of fine wines, Châteauneuf-du-Pape retains a special cachet. It's arguably the best-known of the Rhône appellations, prized by oenophiles the world over. It's mostly based on grenache grapes, with dashes of syrah and mourvèdre sometimes added to the mix. There are numerous vineyards around town offering opportunities to taste.

As its name hints, the hilltop château after which the wine is named was originally built as a summer residence for Avignon's popes, but it's little more than a ruin now – plundered for stone after the Revolution, and bombed by Germany in WWII for good measure. Even so, the wrap-around views of the surrounding Rhône valley are epic, stretching all the way to Mont Ventoux.

The **tourist office** (☑ 04 90 83 71 08; www.ot-chateauneuf-du-pape.mobi; place du Portail; ⊙ 9.30am-6pm Mon-Sat, closed lunch & Wed Oct-May) has a list of wine-producing chateaux and estates such as **Château Mont-Redon** (☑ 04 90 83 72 75; www.chateaumontredon. com; rte d'Orange, D88; ⊙ 9am-7pm Apr-Sep, reduced hours Oct-Mar) or **Domaine de la Solitude** (☑ 04 90 83 71 45; www.domaine-solitude.com; rte de Bédarides, D192; ⊙ 10am-6pm Mon-Fri, by appointment Sat & Sun) who welcome visitors (to taste and buy). In the village, the best place to learn about Châteauneuf-du-Pape wines and refine your palate is the **École de Dégustation** (Tasting School; ☑ 04 90 83 56 15; www.oenologie-mouriesse.com; 2 rue des Papes; 2hr class €40). There are regular classes on Friday evenings and Saturday mornings in French, or if you can get together a group, a bespoke course can be arranged in English.

The local lunch tip-off for Châteauneuf aficionados is **Le Verger des Papes** (☑ 04 90 83 50 40; www.vergerdespapes.com; 4 rue du Château; lunch/dinner menus €22/32; ⊙ noon-2pm Tue-Sat, 7-9pm Thu-Sat), a working vineyard with an excellent restaurant. Dine on typical Provençal country food, with a divine view over the town's rooftops, then educate yourself in the cellars.

By car from Avignon (18km, 30 minutes) take D907 north to D17. From Orange (10km, 15 minutes) take D68 south.

village house in Méthamis, 17km southeast of Carpentras, but the design is unabashedly 21st-century: strikingly minimal rooms, modern art, Scandi-style furniture and an eye-popping rooftop pool overlooking the rocky, maquis-covered hills of the Nesque Valley. Stunning is an understatement.

★ La Maison Jouvaud   PASTRIES €

(40 rue de l'Évêché; boxes of sweets from €10; ⊙ 10am-7pm Mon, 8am-7pm Tue-Fri, 9am-7pm Sat & Sun) If you suffer from a sweet tooth, it's best to not even step inside this patisserie palace, where the glass cases brim with tempting things – from homemade chocolates, petits-fours and cakes to quite possibly the most impressive meringues you will ever see. It's vintage through and through – even the hot chocolate is *à l'ancienne* (old-fashioned).

Chez Serge   FRENCH €€

(☑ 04 90 63 21 24; www.chez-serge.com; 90 rue Cottier; 2-/3-course dinner €29/39; ⊙ noon-2pm & 7.30-10pm Jun-Sep, noon-1.30pm & 7.30-9.30pm Oct-May; ☞ ☐) Run by renowned sommelier Serge Ghokassian, this hip restaurant feels somewhat out of step with the rest

of Carpentras: it's more Parisian chic than Provençal rustic, all sombre tones, swoopy plastic chairs, exposed stone and murals of crocodiles and elephants. The menu zings with southern flavours and, as you'd expect, the wine list is first-rate.

🔒 Shopping

★ Friday Market   MARKET

If you do nothing else in Carpentras, make sure you find time to visit the fabulous Friday market, when several hundred stalls fill rue d'Inguimbert, ave Jean Jaurès and many side streets. It's an institution, and as Provençal as it gets – not to be missed.

ℹ Information

Tourist Office (☑ 04 90 63 00 78; www. carpentras-ventoux.com; 97 place du 25 Août 1944; ⊙ 9.30am-12.30pm & 2-6pm Sat-Mon, 9.30am-12.30pm & 3-7pm Tue)

ℹ Getting There & Away

BUS

The **bus station** (place Terradou) is 150m southwest of the tourist office, which has schedules.

Voyages Arnaud (☑ 04 90 63 01 82; www.voyages-arnaud.com; 8 av Victor-Hugo) provides several services as part of the TransVaucluse network. Nearly all local destinations cost a flat-rate €2.10.

Avignon €2.10, TransVaucluse Line 5, 45 minutes, 11 daily Monday to Saturday, six on Sunday

Marseille-Provence airport €20.40, LER Line 17, two hours 25 minutes, three daily; also travels via L'Isle-sur-la-Sorgue, Cavaillon and Aix-en-Provence.

Orange €2.10, TransVaucluse Line 10, 55 minutes, 10 daily Monday to Saturday

Valson-la-Romaine €2.10, TransVaucluse Line 11, 45 minutes, five daily Monday to Saturday

Trans'CoVe (☑ 04 84 99 50 10; www.transcove.com; 270 ave de la Gare) also runs a number of local buses to destinations including Gigondas, Malaucène and the Venasque – but these are mainly geared around school timetables, although you can reserve bus transport on most routes by calling ahead a day in advance.

TRAIN

Local trains connect Carpentras' **train station** (av de la Gare) to Avignon Centre station (€6.10, 32 minutes, hourly) and Avignon TGV station (38 minutes).

Fontaine-de-Vaucluse

POP 661

Since ancient times, the surging natural spring known as **La Fontaine de Vaucluse** has been a source of wonder and mystery: to prehistoric people it was a site of healing and mysticism, and even to their modern-day counterparts, it's an undeniably impressive sight. The miraculous appearance of this crystal-clear flood draws 1.5 million tourists each year – aim to arrive early in the morning before the trickle of visitors becomes a deluge.

As the origin of the River Sorgue, the village also makes a good base for kayaking and canoeing. Indeed, there is no more enchanting means of meandering from Fontaine-de-Vaucluse 8km downstream to neighbouring **L'Isle-sur-la-Sorgue** than in a canoe or kayak (it can also be done in reverse). Life jackets are provided, but children must be able to swim 25m. Afterwards you're returned by minibus to your car. Trips run from late April to October with **Canoë Évasion** (☑ 04 90 38 26 22; www.canoe-evasion.net; rte de Fontaine-de-Vaucluse/ D24; adult/child €20/10) or **Kayak Vert** (☑ 04 90 20 35 44; www.canoe-france.com; Quartier la Baume; adult/child €20/10).

The village was also once home to the Italian poet Petrarch (1304–74), who wrote his most famous works here: sonnets to his unrequited love, Laura.

❶ Getting There & Away

A **tourist office** (☑ 04 90 20 32 22; www.oti-delasorgue.fr; Résidence Jean Garcin; ☒ 9am-1pm & 2.30-6pm Mon-Sat, 9.30am-1pm Sun) brochure details three easy back-roads biking routes. Bike shops in L'Isle-sur-la-Sorgue deliver to Fontaine.

Voyages Raoux (www.voyages-raoux.fr) runs buses to L'Isle-sur-la-Sorgue (€1.60, 15 minutes, hourly during school term-times, five daily during school holidays).

WORTH A TRIP

L'ISLE-SUR-LA-SORGUE

The Island in the Sorgue is an apt name for this ancient mid-river town, surrounded by a moat of flowing water. L'Isle dates from the 12th century, when fishermen built huts on stilts above what was then a marsh. By the 18th century, canals lined with 70 giant wheels powered silk factories and paper mills. Many of them have been left in place; you'll see them as you walk around the edge of the old town.

These days the 'Venice of Provence' is known for antiques. It's home to several antiques villages, housing 300 dealers between them. Sunday is the big market day, with antique vendors participating, while Thursday offers a smaller market through the village streets.

L'Isle-sur-la-Sorgue has plenty of restaurants, including romantic Michelin-starred **Le Vivier** (☑ 04 90 38 52 80; www.levivier-restaurant.com; 800 cours Fernande Peyre; 2-/3-course weekday menu €26/32, weekend dinner menu €58; ☒ noon-1.30pm Wed-Fri & Sun, 7.30-10pm Tue-Sun, closed Sun evening Oct-Apr), with riverside tables shaded by weeping willows and overhanging oaks.

THE LUBERON

Named after the mountain range running east–west between Cavaillon and Manosque, the Luberon is a Provençal patchwork of hilltop villages, vineyards, ancient abbeys and mile after mile of fragrant lavender fields. It's a rural, traditional region that still makes time for the good things in life – particularly fine food and even finer wine. Nearly every village hosts its own weekly market, packed with stalls selling local specialities, especially olive oil, honey and lavender.

Covering some 600 sq km, the Luberon massif itself is divided into three areas: the craggy Petit Luberon in the west, the higher Grand Luberon mountains, and the smaller hills of the Luberon Oriental in the east. They're all worth exploring, but whatever you do, don't rush – part of the fun of exploring here is getting lost on the back lanes, stopping for lunch at a quiet village cafe, and taking as much time as you possibly can to soak up the scenery.

Apt

POP 11,500 / ELEV 250M

The Luberon's principal town, Apt is edged on three sides by sharply rising plateaus surrounding a river that runs through town. Its Saturday-morning market is full of local colour (and produce), but otherwise Apt is a place you pass through to get somewhere else. Nonetheless, it makes a decent base, if only for a night or two.

Apt is known throughout France for its *fruits confits* (candied fruits, sometimes also known as glacé or crystallised fruit). Strictly speaking, they're not sweets:

they're made with real fruit, from which the water is removed and replaced with a sugar syrup to preserve them. As a result, they still look (and more importantly taste) like pieces of the original fruit. There are several makers around town where you can try and buy.

It's also a hub for the 1650-sq-km **Parc Naturel Régional du Luberon** (www.parcduluberon.fr), a regional nature park criss-crossed by hiking trails.

◎ Sights & Activities

Musée d'Apt   MUSEUM
(Industrial History Museum; ☑04 90 74 95 30; 14 place du Postel; adult/child €5/free; ◎10am-noon & 2-6.30pm Mon-Sat Jun-Sep, to 5.30pm Tue-Sat Oct-May) Apt's various industries – ochre-mining, *fruits confits* and faiences (glazed ceramics) – are explored at this modest but well-curated museum in the middle of town. Exhibits include a reconstructed potter's workshop.

Confiserie Kerry Aptunion   TOURS
(☑04 90 76 31 43; www.lesfleurons-apt.com; D900, Quartier Salignan; ◎shop 9am-12.15pm & 1.30-6pm Mon-Sat, 9am-6pm Jul & Aug) Allegedly the largest *fruits confits* maker in the world, this factory 2.5km outside of Apt produces sweets under the prestigious Les Fleurons d'Apt brand. Free tastings are offered in the shop, and you can watch the process in action on guided factory tours; they run at 2.30pm Monday to Friday in July and August, with an extra tour at 10.30am in August. The rest of the year there's just one weekly tour, usually on Wednesday at 2.30pm; confirm ahead.

LOCAL KNOWLEDGE

PRESTIGE IN PROVENCE

For a once-in-a-lifetime Provençal experience, look no further than the **Domaine de Fontenille** (☑04 13 98 00 00; www.domainedefontenille.com; rte de Roquefraiche; r from €324; ▣🛜), a glorious hotel 2km northwest of Lauris, at home in an 18th-century mansion framed by sweeping, cypress-filled parkland. Contemporary rooms are elegant; there is a luxurious spa; and then there's **Le Champ des Lunes** (☑04 13 98 00 00; www.domainedefontenille.com; lunch menu €35, dinner €42-108; ◎noon-2pm & 7-9.30pm Wed-Sat, noon-2pm Sun).

Overseen by Jérome Faure, who won his first Michelin star at 30, this stellar restaurant is one of the Luberon's most prestigious places to eat. Expect high-class haute cuisine, with impeccably presented dishes dressed with foams, reductions, edible flowers and textural surprises. Lunch is great value – €5 extra buys a glass of wine and coffee.

La Cuisine d'Amelie, the hotel's other restaurant, focuses on simple country flavours and is another lovely spot for lunch (dishes €13 to €18). It's open for lunch and dinner from Friday to Tuesday.

LUBERON BY PEDAL POWER

Don't be put off by the hills – the Luberon is a fantastic destination for cyclists. Several bike routes criss-cross the countryside, including **Les Ocres à Vélo**, a 51km route that takes in the ochre villages of Apt, Gargas, Rustrel, Roussillon and Villars, and the **Véloroute du Calavon**, a purpose-built bike path that follows the route of a disused railway line for 28km between Beaumettes in the west (near Coustellet), via Apt, to La Paraire in the west (near St-Martin-de-Castillon). Plans are under way to extend the trail all the way from Cavaillon to the foothills of the Alps, but it'll be a while before it's completed.

For longer trips, **Le Luberon à Vélo** (☑ 04 90 76 48 05; www.leluberonavelo.com) has mapped a 236km itinerary that takes in pretty much the whole Luberon. Tourist offices stock detailed route leaflets and can provide information on bike rental, luggage transport, accommodation and so on.

Several companies offer e-bikes, which have an electric motor. They're not scooters – you still have to pedal – but the motor helps on the ascents.

🛏 Sleeping & Eating

Hôtel le Palais   HOTEL €
(☑ 04 90 04 89 32; www.hotel-restaurant-apt.fr; 24bis place Gabriel-Péri; s/d/tr/q €55/67/80/90; ☎) Don't go expecting many luxuries at this bargain-basement hotel above a pizza restaurant – but if price is more important than frills, it's a decent option. Rooms are small and very plain, but you're right in the middle of town, and breakfast is a bargain at €6.

★ Le Couvent   B&B €€
(☑ 04 90 04 55 36; www.loucouvent.com; 36 rue Louis Rousset; d €99-140; @ ☎ ☒) Hidden behind a wall in the old town, this enormous *maison d'hôte* occupies a 17th-century former convent. Staying here is as much architectural experience as accommodation: soaring ceilings, stonework, and a grand staircase, plus palatial rooms (one has a sink made from a baptismal font). There's a sweet garden with a little pool, and breakfast is served in the old convent refectory.

Grand Marché d'Apt   MARKET €
(☉ Sat) Apt's huge Saturday-morning market attracts hordes of locals and tourists alike. If you really want to see what a *marché* Provençal is all about, then make it a date in your diary. There is also a **farmer's market** every Tuesday morning.

L'Intramuros   FRENCH €€
(☑ 04 90 06 18 87; 120-124 rue de la République; mains €17-19.50; ☉ noon-2pm & 7-9pm Mon-Sat) What fun this place is: an offbeat French restaurant that's stocked to the gunwales with the owners' bric-a-brac finds, from vintage movie posters, antique shop signs and old radios to a collection of sardine cans. It's run by a father-and-son team, and food is filling –

expect things like rabbit, duck breast and lamb, plus a choice of pastas.

ℹ Information

Tourist Office (☑ 04 90 74 03 18; www. luberon-apt.fr; 788 av Victor Hugo; ☉ 9.30am-12.30pm & 2-6pm Mon-Sat, also 9.30am-12.30pm Sun Jul & Aug) Now located in Apt's former train station, the town's tourist office is an excellent source of information for activities, excursions, bike rides and walks.

Maison du Parc du Luberon (☑ 04 90 04 42 00; www.parcduluberon.fr; 60 place Jean Jaurès; ☉ 8.30am-noon & 1.30-6pm Mon-Fri, 9am-noon Sat Apr-Sep, shorter hours Oct-Mar) A central information source for the Parc Naturel Régional du Luberon, with maps, walking guides and general info. There's also a small fossil museum.

ℹ Getting There & Away

The **bus station** (250 av de la Libération) is just a few blocks east of the town centre. Lignes Express Régionales (www.info-ler.fr) operates local buses.

Avignon (€6.90, Line 22, 1½ hours, four daily Monday to Saturday, two on Sunday) Travels via Bonnieux, Cavaillon and Avignon's TGV station. In the opposite direction, it travels to Forcalquier and Digne-les-Bains.

Bonnieux (€2.10, four daily) TransVaucluse bus 17 stops in Bonnieux, Roussillon and Gordes before continuing to Cavaillon.

Gordes & Around
POP 2130

Arguably the scenic queen of the Luberon's hilltop villages, the tiered village of Gordes seems to teeter improbably on the edge of the sheer rock faces of the Vaucluse plateau from which it rises. A jumble of terracotta rooftops, church towers and winding lanes, it's a living postcard – but unfortunately it's also seethingly popular in summer, so arrive early or late to avoid the worst crowds. Better still, stay for sunset when the village looks at its most beautiful as its honey-coloured stone glows like molten gold.

⊙ Sights

★ Abbaye Notre-Dame de Sénanque
CHURCH

(📷 04 90 72 05 72; www.abbayedesenanque.com; adult/child €7.50/3.50; ⊙ 9-11.30am Mon-Sat Apr-Nov, shorter hours Dec-Mar, guided tours by reservation) If you're searching for that classic postcard shot of the medieval abbey surrounded by a sea of purple lavender, look no further. This sublime Cistercian abbey provides one of the most iconic shots of the Luberon, and it's equally popular these days for selfies. The best displays are usually in July and August. You can wander around the grounds on your own from 9.45am to 11am, but at other times (and to visit the abbey's cloistered interior) you must join a guided tour.

Moulin des Bouillons
DISTILLERY

(📷 04 90 72 22 11; www.moulindesbouillons.com; rte de St-Pantaléon; adult/child €5/3.50; ⊙ 10am-noon & 2-6pm Wed-Mon Apr-Oct) Heading 3.5km south from Gordes along rte de St-Pantaléon (D148), you hit this marvellous rural museum: an olive-oil mill with a 10m-long Gallo-Roman press weighing 7 tonnes – reputedly the world's oldest. The adjoining stained-glass museum showcases beautiful translucent mosaics; a joint ticket costs adult/child €7.50/5.50.

Village des Bories
ARCHITECTURE

(📷 04 90 72 03 48; adult/child €6/4; ⊙ 9am-8pm, shorter hours winter) Beehive-shaped *bories* (stone huts) bespeckle Provence, and at the Village des Bories, 4km southwest of Gordes, an entire village of them can be explored. Constructed of slivered limestone, *bories* were built during the Bronze Age, inhabited by shepherds until 1839, then abandoned until their restoration in the 1970s. Visit early in the morning or just before sunset for the best light. Note that the lower car park is for buses; continue to the hilltop car park to avoid hiking uphill in the blazing heat.

Musée de la Lavande
MUSEUM

(📷 04 90 76 91 23; www.museedelalavande.com; D2; adult/child €6.80/free; ⊙ 9am-7pm May-Sep, 9am-noon & 2-6pm Oct-Apr) To get to grips with Provence's most prestigious crop, this excellent eco-museum makes an ideal first stop. An audioguide and video (in English) explain the lavender harvest, and giant copper stills reveal extraction methods. Afterwards you can take a guided tour of the fields (1pm and 5pm daily May to September). The on-site boutique is an excellent (if pricey) one-stop shop for top-quality lavender products.

There's also a picnic area in the lavender-laden garden. It's located about 7.5km southwest of Gordes on the D2, in the direction of Coustellet.

🛏 Sleeping & Eating

★ Les Balcons du Luberon
B&B €€

(📷 06 38 20 42 13; www.lesbalconsduluberon.fr; rte de Murs; d €110-180; 🛜🌀) The 'Balconies of the Luberon' is an apt name for this lovely B&B: an 18th-century stone farmhouse with five simple, stylish rooms – the best of which have private patios overlooking epic Luberon scenery. Owner Étienne Marty (a trained chef) offers a sumptuous dinner by reservation (€35).

★ Auberge de Carcarille
HOTEL €€

(📷 04 90 72 02 63; www.auberge-carcarille.com; rte d'Apt; d €83-150; 🅿🌼🛜🌀) Old outside, new inside: this country hotel marries the atmosphere of a traditional *bastide familiale* (family house) with spotless, modern rooms. There's a delightful garden to wander, and the restaurant serves superior Provençal food (three-course lunch/dinner *menu* €26/44); half-board deals are great value. It's 3km from Gordes, at the bottom of the valley.

Bastide de Gordes
HERITAGE HOTEL €€€

(📷 04 90 72 12 12; www.bastide-de-gordes.com; Le Village; r from €290; 🌼🛜🌀) Impeccably restored, this deluxe hotel is one of the Luberon's star turns, from the boater-wearing bellboys through to the beamed lobby stuffed with antiques, oil paintings and bookcases. Rooms are enormous and aristocratic (a valley view is essential); spa, gardens, an incredible pool and a trio of restaurants (one Michelin-starred) ice this most indulgent of cakes.

La Boulangerie de Mamie Jane
BAKERY €

(📷 04 90 72 09 34; rue Baptistin Picca; dishes €7-10; ⊙ 6.30am-1pm & 2-6pm Thu-Tue) Those short of time or money in Gordes should follow the locals downhill along rue Baptistin Picca to this pocket-sized *boulangerie* (bakery), which has been in the same family for three generations. Mamie Jane cooks up outstanding bread, pastries, cakes and biscuits, including lavender-perfumed *navettes* and delicious peanut-and-almond brittle known as *écureuil* (from the French for squirrel).

Le Mas Tourteron
GASTRONOMY €€€

(📍04 90 72 00 16; www.mastourteron.com; chemin de St-Blaise les Imberts; menu lunch/dinner €35/76; ⊙12.30-2pm Thu-Sun, 7.30-9.30pm Wed-Sat Apr-Oct) Another one of the Luberon's long-standing tables, overseen by bubbly Elisabeth Bourgeois, it's heavy on Provençal flavours: lots of stuffed aubergines, slow-roasted tomatoes and lashings of olive oil and *herbes de Provence*. The garden setting is lovely, and Elisabeth's husband Philippe handles wine choices. It's 3.5km south of Gordes off the D2.

❶ Information

Tourist Office (📍04 90 72 02 75; contact@luberoncoeurdeprovence.com; place du Château; ⊙9am-12.30pm & 1.30-6pm Mon-Sat, from 10am Sun) is inside Gordes' medieval château, which was enlarged and given its defensive Renaissance towers in 1525.

❶ Getting There & Away

TransVaucluse bus 17 (€2.10, four daily, two on Sunday) stops in Gordes on its way from Apt to Cavaillon. Other stops along the way include Bonnieux and Roussillon.

Roussillon

POP 1291

Red by name, red by nature, that's Roussillon – once the centre of local ochre mining, and still unmistakably marked by its crimson colour (villagers are required to paint their houses according to a prescribed palette of some 40 tints). Today it's home to artists' and ceramicists' workshops, and its charms are no secret: arrive early or late.

During WWII the village was the hideout for playwright Samuel Beckett, who helped the local Resistance by hiding explosives at his house and occasionally going on recce missions.

Parking (€3 March to November) is 300m outside the village.

⊙ Sights & Activities

★ Sentier des Ocres
HIKING

(Ochre Trail; adult/child €2.50/free; ⊙9.30am-5.30pm; 🖼) In Roussillon village, groves of chestnut and pine surround sunset-coloured ochre formations, rising on a clifftop. Two circular trails, taking 30 or 50 minutes to complete, twist through mini-desert landscapes – it's like stepping into a Georgia O'Keeffe painting. Information panels highlight 26 types of flora to spot, the history of local ochre

production, and so on. Wear walking shoes and avoid white!

Ôkhra Conservatoire des Ocres et de la Couleur
ARTS CENTRE

(L'Usine d'Ocre Mathieu; 📍04 90 05 66 69; www.okhra.com; rte d'Apt; tours adult/student €7/5.50; ⊙10am-7pm Jul & Aug, to 6pm Sep-Jun, closed Mon & Tue Jan & Feb; 🖼) This art centre is a great place to see ochre in action. Occupying a disused ochre factory on the D104 east of Roussillon, it explores the mineral's properties through hands-on workshops and guided tours of the factory. The shop upstairs stocks paint pigments and other artists' supplies. Bikes can also be rented here.

Mines de Bruoux
HISTORIC SITE

(📍04 90 06 22 59; www.minesdebruoux.fr; rte de Croagnes, Gargas; adult/child €8.10/6.50; ⊙10am-7pm Jul & Aug, to 6pm Apr-Jun, Sep & Oct) In Gargas, 7km east of Roussillon, this former mine has more than 40km of underground galleries where ochre was once extracted. Around 650m are open to the public, some of which are as much as 15m high. Visits are only by guided tour; reserve ahead as English-language tours are at set times.

🛏 Sleeping & Eating

La Coquillade
FRENCH €€€

(📍04 90 74 71 71; www.coquillade.fr; Le Perrotet; menus lunch €42, dinner €75-95; ⊙12.30-1.30pm & 7.30-9.30pm mid-Apr–mid-Oct) Overnighting at this luxurious hilltop estate won't suit everyone's budget, but everyone should try to fork out for the great-value Bistrot lunch menu. Michelin-starred and run by renowned chef Christophe Renaud, it'll be one of the most memorable meals you'll have in the Luberon. It's a 5km drive south of Roussillon on the D108; look out for signs.

The hotel itself is a stunner, with luxurious rooms (doubles €325 to €390) overlooking a sea of vines.

❶ Information

Tourist Office (📍04 90 05 60 25; http://otroussillon.pagesperso-orange.fr; place de la Poste; ⊙9am-noon & 1.30-5.30pm Mon-Sat) General information on the village's history and suggestions for walking routes through the surrounding area.

❶ Getting There & Away

Roussillon is served by TransVaucluse bus 17 (€2.10, four daily, two on Sunday) which stops in Apt, Bonnieux, Gordes and Cavaillon.

WORTH A TRIP

PROVENCE'S COLORADO

Reds and oranges, scarlets and yellows, purples and crimsons – the fiery colours burned into the earth between Roussillon and Rustrel are astonishing. They're the result of the area's rich mineral deposits, especially hydrated iron oxide, otherwise known as ochre, which has been mined in this part of the Luberon since Roman times. Ochre was traditionally used to colour earthenware and paint buildings. Around the late 18th century, the extraction process was industrialised, and large mines and quarries sprang up. In 1929, at the peak of the ochre industry, some 40,000 tonnes of ochre was mined around Apt.

There are several ochre-themed sites to visit around Roussillon, but for the full technicolour experience, head for the **Colorado Provençal** (☑ 04 32 52 09 75; www.colorado-provencal.com; ◷ 9am–dusk), a quarry site where ochre was mined from the 1880s until 1956. With its weird rock formations and rainbow colours, it's like a little piece of the Southwest USA plonked down amid the hills of Provence. The site is signposted south of Rustrel village, off the D22 to Banon.

For extra thrills, try the treetop assault courses on offer at nearby **Colorado Adventures** (☑ 06 78 26 68 91; www.colorado-adventures.fr; adult/child €19/14; ◷ 9.30am-7.30pm Jul & Aug, 10am-7pm Mar-Jun & Sep-Nov).

Le Petit Luberon

The westernmost extent of the Luberon massif, the Petit Luberon's craggy hills are interspersed with wooded valleys, vineyards and rural farms. It's separated from Le Grand Luberon by the slash of the Combe de Lourmrin, which cuts north–south through the mountains and is tracked by the D943 between Bonnieux and Lourmarin.

Bonnieux

POP 1408

Settled during the Roman era, Bonnieux is another bewitching hilltop town that still preserves its medieval character. It's intertwined with alleys, cul-de-sacs and hidden staircases: from place de la Liberté, 86 steps lead to 12th-century Église Vieille du Haut. Look out for the alarming crack in one of the walls, caused by an earthquake.

The pleasure here is just to wander – especially if you time your visit for the lively Friday market, which takes over most of the old town's streets.

In the scrubby hills about 6km south of Bonnieux, a twisty back road slopes up to a wonderful cedar forest, whose spreading boughs provide welcome relief from Provence's punishing summer heat. Various paths wind through the woods, including a new nature trail that's accessible for wheelchairs. The trip up to the forest is worth the drive by itself: the wrap-around views of the Luberon valley and its *villages perchés* (hilltop towns) are out of this world.

Take the D36 towards Buoux and look out for the signs.

🛏 Sleeping & Eating

⭐ **La Couleur des Vignes**　　　　B&B €€
(☑ 06 77 85 97 92; www.lacouleurdesvignes.com; r €130-150; P 🐾 🖤 🖀) On the northern edge of the village, this is the kind of place that inspires serious life envy. It feels wonderfully secluded, with fragrant lavender-filled gardens overlooking the Luberon hills, and five rooms named after local villages and stuffed with rustic-chic features (thick walls, beams, tiles, fireplaces). But it's the eye-popping 20m infinity pool that has the real wow factor.

⭐ **Maison Valvert**　　　　　　B&B €€€
(☑ 06 72 22 37 89; www.maisonvalvert.com; rte de Marseille; d €205-250, tree house €295; 🖤 🖀) For our money, this could well be the most stylish B&B in the Luberon. On an 18th-century *mas* (farm) and lovingly renovated by Belgian owner Cathy, it's straight out of a designer magazine: neutral-toned rooms, natural fabrics, solar-heated pool and fabulous buffet breakfast. For maximum spoils, go for the ultra-romantic tree house.

Market　　　　　　　　　　MARKET €
(◷ Fri) Bonnieux' huge Friday-morning market is (along with Apt's) one of the biggest and best in the Luberon. It sprawls over several streets in the village centre, with local farmers and producers selling everything from local cheeses, hams and charcuterie to the reddest, ripest tomatoes you could ever hope to see.

⭐ L'Arôme
FRENCH €€€

(📞 04 90 75 88 62; www.laromerestaurant.com; 2 rue Lucien Blanc; menus €35-45, mains €25-34; ⊙ noon-2pm & 7-9.30pm Fri-Tue, 7-9.30pm Thu) Lodged in a charming vaulted cellar in Bonnieux, L'Arôme is a pricey but prestigious address, run by well-respected chef Jean-Michel Pagès. The menu revolves around gourmet ingredients with impeccable local provenance, dashed with spice and surprises, and the romantic stone-walled setting is a winner.

❶ Information

Tourist Office (📞 04 90 75 91 90; www.tourisme-en-luberon.com; 7 place Carnot; ⊙ 9.30am-12.30pm & 2-6pm Mon-Fri, 2-6pm Sat) Covers the entire Petit Luberon.

❶ Getting There & Around

Apt (€1.90, 20 minutes, four daily Monday to Saturday, two on Sunday) LER Line 22 continues on to Cavaillon and Avignon in one direction; Manosque and Digne-les-Bains in the other.

Cavaillon (€2.10, 35 minutes, four daily) From Apt, Transvaucluse bus 17 stops in Roussillon, Bonnieux and Gordes before terminating at Cavaillon.

Ménerbes
POP 1144

Hilltop Ménerbes is another wonder for wandering, with a maze of cobbled alleyways that afford sudden glimpses over the surrounding valleys. It became famous as the home of ex-pat British author Peter Mayle, whose books *A Year in Provence* and *Toujours Provence* recounted his tales of renovating a farmhouse just outside the village in the the late 1980s. He later moved to the nearby villages of Lourmarin and Vaugines, and died in 2018.

◉ Sights & Activities

Musée du Tire-Bouchon
MUSEUM

(📞 04 90 72 41 58; www.domaine-citadelle.com; adult/child €5/free; ⊙ 9am-noon & 2-7pm Apr-Oct, 10am-noon & 2-5pm Mon-Sat Nov-Mar) You have to be a real wine buff to appreciate this museum – dedicated to the art of the humble corkscrew. There are more than 1000 of them on display at Domaine de la Citadelle, a winery on the D3 towards Cavaillon, where you can sample Côtes du Luberon.

Maison de la Truffe et du Vin
WINE

(House of Truffle & Wine; 📞 04 90 72 38 37; www.vin-truffe-luberon.com; place de l'Horloge; ⊙ 10am-noon & 2.30-6pm daily Apr-Oct, Thu-Sat Nov-Mar) In the middle of Ménerbes, opposite the town's 12th-century church, this establishment is home to the Brotherhood of Truffles and Wine of the Luberon, and represents 60 local *domaines*. From April to October, there are free wine-tasting sessions daily, and afterwards you can buy the goods at bargain-basement prices. Winter brings truffle workshops.

🛏 Sleeping & Eating

Bistrot Le 5
BISTRO €€

(📞 04 90 72 31 84; 5 place Albert Roure; mains €15-25; ⊙ noon-2.30pm & 7-9.30pm) Lunch with a view? *Mais oui* – and what a view. On the village's edge, this popular bistro boasts a grandstand, tree-shaded terrace overlooking classic Luberon countryside. The food is decent – mainly French bistro standards – and service can be slapdash, but on a warm summer's night, it'll be hard to take your attention away from the scenery anyway.

La Bastide de Marie
BOUTIQUE HOTEL €€€

(📞 04 90 72 30 20; www.labastidedemarie.com; 64 chemin des Peirelles; d from €350; 🅿 ❄ 🛜 🏊) Run by renowned hotelier Jocelyne Sibuet, this uber-luxurious Provençal bolthole oozes designer style from every corner, from the effortlessly elegant rooms through to the just-so rustic charm of the restaurant. It's all spoils: two-tiered swimming pool, four-poster beds and an utterly lavish breakfast. There's even a swanky villa and cute *roulotte* (wooden caravan) for rent. It's about 5km east of Ménerbes along the D3.

❶ Getting There & Away

TransVaucluse Line 18 (€2.10. three daily Monday to Saturday) runs buses from Apt to Bonnieux, Lacoste, Ménerbes and Oppède-le-Vieux en route to Cavaillon.

Oppède-le-Vieux
POP 1324

Jutting from a craggy hilltop 3km from the modern town of Oppède, Oppède-le-Vieux was abandoned in 1910, when villagers moved down the hill to the valley to cultivate the plains. From the car parks (€3), a wooded path leads up to the village's snaking, atmospheric alleyways. At the very top of town, the village's ruined castle provides a formidable vantage point over the surrounding valley – although the ruins are off limits while the village raises funds for the castle's restoration.

Several artists and ceramicists have set up their studios here, and sell their wares during the summer. Signs from the car parks also direct you to the **Sentier Vigneron**, a 1½-hour viticulture trail through olive groves, cherry orchards and vineyards.

ℹ Getting There & Away

The only bus that stops in Oppède is Transvaucluse Line 18 (€2.10, three daily Monday to Saturday), which travels from Apt via Bonnieux and Ménerbes on its way to Cavaillon.

Le Grand Luberon

Divided from the hills of the Petit Luberon to the west by a deep river canyon, the Combe de Lourmarin, the scenic hills of the Grand Luberon are made for exploring. The main villages of note are Buoux, known for its small medieval fort, and Saignon, a sleepy place with impressive views. Take your time along the winding back roads: the scenery deserves to be savoured.

Buoux

POP 134

Dominated by the ruins of its eponymous Fort de Buoux, the tiny village of Buoux (the 'x' is pronounced) sits across the divide from Bonnieux, 8km south of Apt. The village itself is little more than a collection of a few tumbledown houses, but the valley has spectacular views. The sheer cliffs here are popular with local rock climbers.

OFF THE BEATEN TRACK

LAZY BOAR LUNCH DATE

There's one reason to make a detour to hilltop Caseneuve, 10km east of Saignon, and that's to eat at **Le Sanglier Paresseux** (🕾 04 90 75 17 70; www.sanglierparesseux.com; Caseneuve; 2-/3-/4-course menus €32/39/59; ⊙ 12.30-2.30pm & 7.30-9.30pm Wed-Sun May-Oct, plus Tue Jul & Aug, shorter hours Nov-Apr), one of the Luberon's most talked about tables. Cuisine is inventive, unfussy, seasonal and the perfect showcase for regional ingredients – and the view from the vine-shaded terrace is really unforgettable. Reservations essential.

◉ Sights

Fort de Buoux RUINS
(🕾 04 90 74 25 75; www.lefortdebuoux.e-monsite. com; adult/child €5/4; ⊙ 10am-5pm Wed-Mon) Occupied since prehistoric times, the site of this clifftop fortress commands an incredible view over the surrounding valley. Abandoned in the 17th century, it's an atmospheric place to wander – but is accessed by a winding, crumbling staircase, so take care as you hike up. Note that due to its exposed position, the fort is closed during heavy rain or high winds.

★ Distillerie Les Agnels DISTILLERY
(🕾 04 90 74 34 60; www.lesagnels.com; rte de Buoux, btwn Buoux & Apt; adult/child €6/free; ⊙ 10am-7pm Apr-Sep, to 5.30pm Oct-Mar) This distillery on the edge of Buoux uses locally grown lavender, cypress and rosemary in its products. It also rents out three gorgeous self-contained cottages (€1300 to €2000 per week) that share a glorious heated pool covered by a greenhouse roof.

🛏 Sleeping & Eating

Auberge des Seguins HOTEL €€
(🕾 04 90 74 16 37; www.aubergedesseguins.com; dm incl half-board €44, s €79-89, d €118-138, f €159-239; 🅿🐕🛜❄) Hunkered at the bottom of the valley 2.5km below Buoux, surrounded by sheer cliffs, this lovely old inn feels remarkably secluded. It offers simple, TV-less rooms (some with shared bathrooms) and a dorm in four stone-walled buildings, all with fine valley views. The Provençal restaurant (menu €25) is popular, especially for Sunday lunch; room rates include half-board. The restaurant is open every evening and for lunch on Sunday.

ℹ Getting There & Away

There are no buses to Buoux, so the only way to get here is by car or (if you're up to the hills) by bike.

Saignon

Even in a land of heart-stoppingly pretty villages, little Saignon still manages to raise an admiring eyebrow. Perched on a rocky flank, surrounded by lavender fields and overlooked by a crumbling medieval castle, its cobbled streets and central square (complete with fountain) are the stuff of Provençal dreams.

A short trail leads up to the castle ruins and the aptly titled **Rocher de Bellevue**, a fabulous viewpoint overlooking the entire Luberon range all the way to Mont Ventoux.

PARC NATIONAL DU MERCANTOUR

Created in 1979, this vast national park covers seven alpine valleys and a total area of 685 sq km. Pocked by deep valleys and spiked with jagged peaks, and dominated by the Cime du Gélas (3143m), the third-highest mountain in the Alps-Maritimes, it's a haven for outdoor activities: skiing and snowboarding in winter, hiking and biking in summer, and pretty much everything else besides.

It's also celebrated for its flora and fauna, including rare species such as the ibex, the mouflon, the golden eagle and wild grey wolves, which you can see at the excellent **Alpha wolf park** (☑ 04 93 02 33 69; www.alpha-loup.com; Le Boréon; adult/child €10/8; ☺ 10am-5pm or 6pm Apr-Oct; ⛹) near the mountain village of St-Martin-Vésubie. The park is currently at the forefront over the debate of the return of the wild wolf to France: after more than a century of absence, wolf numbers are increasing – a cause of celebration for conservationists, and of deep anger for local farmers.

For an arresting insight into the forces of nature, a hike up to the massive, fractured stone blocks of **Les Grès d'Annot**, above the town of Annot, is well worth the effort. Caused by volcanic activity around 35 million years ago, they've been sculpted into all kinds of weird and wondrous forms by millennia of erosion. In total, the site covers an area of around 150 hectares criss-crossed by several hiking trails.

The park's deep, high-sided gorges also make for spectacular driving, especially along canyons such as the **Gorges de Daluis**, where the rock glows red from mineral deposits. Note that mountain passes connecting the valleys are usually closed by snow from October to May – roads leading up to the passes indicate whether they are open to road traffic.

🛏 Sleeping & Eating

Le Bastide du Jas　　　　　B&B €€
(☑ 04 32 52 11 54; www.labastidedujas.com; rue du Jas; r €120-180; ☺ Mar-Oct; ⛵) Beams, stone floors, an orchard and a cracking **restaurant** (☑ 04 90 76 64 92; www.labastidedujas.com/dinner; rte du Jas; 3-course menu €45; ☺ 7-9pm Wed-Sat) make this lovely B&B an enormously attractive stay. The 18th-century farmhouse has been converted with care and style, and each of the five rustic-style rooms has a view either over the terrace or the garden. There's also a small apartment, and the pool is a beauty too.

❶ Getting There & Away

Saignon has no public transport.

ALPES-DE-HAUTE-PROVENCE

Provence might conjure up images of rolling fields and gentle hills, but east of the Luberon you'll find yourself travelling through altogether more dramatic landscapes. Rising like a tooth-lined jawbone along the border with Italy, just an hour's drive north of Nice, lie the Alps – France's most famous mountain range, a haven for mountaineers, hikers and wildlife spotters, and home to some of the region's most unforgettable scenery.

Cloaked in snow well into springtime, the mountains of Haute-Provence are divided by six main valleys, connected by some of the highest and most hair-raising road passes anywhere in Europe – an absolute must for road-trippers. At the heart of the area sprawls the huge Parc National du Mercantour, home to a host of rare wildlife, sky-top villages and pristine natural habitats. Keep the camera close by: there's a picture around every corner.

Pays de Forcalquier

An oft-overlooked area between the Luberon valley and the Alpine foothills, the Pays de Forcalquier is well off the main tourist radar, meaning that its hilltop villages and rolling farms are usually relatively tranquil even in high summer. It's the portal to Haute-Provence from the Luberon, and the fastest way in from Marseille too. At its heart lies namesake Forcalquier, famous for its market and absinthe. Saffron grows here, as well as swathes of lavender.

◉ Sights

★**Prieuré de Salagon**　　MONASTERY, GARDENS
(☑ 04 92 75 70 50; www.musee-de-salagon.com; adult/child €8/6; ☺ 10am-8pm Jun-Aug, to 7pm May & Sep, to 6pm Oct–mid-Dec & Feb-Apr; ⛹) Situated 4km south of Forcalquier near Mane, this peaceful priory dates from the 13th

century. It's well worth a visit to wander around its medieval herb gardens, fragrant with native lavender, mint, mugwort and other medicinal plants. There's also a show garden of plants from around the world, and a *jardin de senteurs* that's been planted especially for its fragrances.

Château de Simiane-la-Rotonde CASTLE (www.simiane-la-rotonde.fr; Simiane-la-Rotonde; adult/12-18yr/under 12yr €5.50/3.50/free; ⏱10.30am-1pm & 2-7pm May-Aug, 1.30-6pm Wed-Sun Mar, Apr & Sep–mid-Nov) Forming part of the 12th-century fortified castle built by the Simiane-Agoult family, who were one of the region's most powerful medieval dynasties, this castle is notable for its magnificent central cupola, graced by a soaring dome, 12 supporting ribs and a forest of decorative columns and intricate stonework. It's a masterpiece of medieval engineering, and every August provides the unforgettable setting for classical-music festival **Les Riches Heures Musicales de la Rotonde.**

Ecomusée l'Olivier MUSEUM (☑04 92 72 66 91; www.ecomusee-olivier.com; adult/child €4/free; ⏱10am-1pm & 2-6pm Tue-Sat) 🖋 If all the olive groves around Provence have inspired your curiosity, head 15km southeast of Foraclaquier to Volx, where this intriguing eco-museum explains the extraction process and the olive tree's importance to Mediterranean culture. There's also a posh shop where you can pick up souvenirs, and taste various olive-oil varieties, as well as an excellent Provençal restaurant, **Les Petites Tables** (☑04 86 68 53 14; www.lespetitestables. net; Écomusée l'Olivier, Volx; mains €10-16; ⏱noon-3pm Tue-Sat), that's perfect for lunch.

🛏 Sleeping & Eating

Relais d'Elle B&B € (☑04 92 75 06 87, 06 75 42 33 72; www.relaisdelle. com; rte de la Brillane, Niozelles; s/d/tr/q from €60/70/90/115; 🕿🗷) For peace and tranquillity, you can't really quibble with this cosy, ivy-covered farmhouse, surrounded by gardens and a cracking pool. The rooms err towards the traditional, with old furniture and rather dated decor – but the gorgeous grounds and friendly owners make up for what the house lacks in luxury. *Table d'hôte* dinners are available by reservation, and are served in the garden in summer.

Café de Niozelles PROVENCAL, ITALIAN €€ (☑04 92 73 10 17; www.bistrot-niozelles.fr; place du Village, Niozelles; set menu €26; ⏱12.30-2.30pm &

7-9pm Fri-Wed; 🌐) For just-like-mama-made-it French cuisine, it's worth the 5km drive from Forcalquier to this unapologetically old-school bistro in Niozelles. You'll need an appetite, and a taste for all the traditional trimmings, like offal, tripe and sheep trotters, but you won't find a more authentic French meal in the Pays de Forcalquier.

ℹ Information

Tourist Office (☑04 92 75 10 02; www.haute-provence-tourisme.com; 13 place du Bourguet; ⏱9am-noon & 2-6pm Mon-Sat)

ℹ Getting There & Around

Bachelas Cycles (☑04 92 75 12 47; www. bachelas-cycles.com; 5 bd de la République; per day/week from €19/81; ⏱9am-12.30pm & 2-7pm Mon-Wed, Fri & Sat) rents out mountain, road, tandem and electric bicycles.

LER (www.info-ler.fr) operates buses to/from Forcalquier.

LER Bus 25 (four daily Monday to Saturday, two on Sunday) Runs direct from Marseille (€18.60, two hours) and Aix-en-Provence (€12, 1½ hours) to Forcalquier, stopping at Volx and Manosque.

LER Line 22 (four daily, one or two on Sundays) Travels to Avignon (€16.80, 2 hours 20 minutes), and to Digne-les-Bains (€9.80, one hour) in the opposite direction.

Gorges du Verdon

For sheer, jaw-dropping drama, few sights in France can match the epic Gorges du Verdon. The 'Grand Canyon of Europe' slices a 25km swath through Haute-Provence's limestone plateau all the way to the foothills of the Alps. Etched out over millions of years by the Verdon River, the gorges have formed the centrepiece of the Parc Naturel Régional du Verdon since 1997. With their sheer, plunging cliffs – in some places 700m high, twice the height of the Eiffel Tower – the gorges are a haven for birds, including a colony of reintroduced *vautours fauves* (griffon vultures).

The main gorge begins at Rougon, near the confluence of the Verdon and Jabron Rivers. The most useful jumping-off points are Moustiers Ste-Marie, in the west, and Castellane, in the east.

Cycling & Driving

A complete circuit of the Gorges du Verdon from Moustiers Ste-Marie involves 140km of driving, not to mention a relentless series of hairpin turns. There's a cliffside road on either side of the gorges, but passing spots are rare, roads are narrow and rockfalls are possible – so take it slow and enjoy the scenery.

Spring and autumn are ideal times to visit: the roads can be traffic-clogged in summer and icy in winter. The Route des Crêtes is snowbound from mid-November to mid-March. The only village en route is La Palud-sur-Verdon (930m), so make sure you've got a full tank of petrol before setting out.

★ **Route des Crêtes**   DRIVING TOUR
(D952 & D23; ☉ mid-Mar–mid-Nov) A 23km-long loop with 14 lookouts along the northern rim with drop-dead vistas of the plunging Gorges du Verdon. En route the most thrilling view is from **Belvédère de l'Escalès** – one of the best places to spot vultures overhead.

You'll see signs for the route as you drive through La Palud-sur-Verdon. Note that the road is generally closed outside April to October due to snowfall.

Outdoor Sports

Castellane is the main water-sports base (April to September); its tourist office has lists of local operators. Most charge similar rates for rafting, canyoning, kayaking and hydrospeed expeditions: around €35 for two hours, €55 for a half-day and €75 for a full day. Safety kit is provided, but you'll get (very) wet, so dress appropriately. Reservations are required.

Lac de Castillon's beaches are popular for swimming and paddle boating, while St-André-les-Alpes, on the lakeshore, is France's leading paragliding centre.

Walking & Hiking

Dozens of blazed trails traverse the wild countryside around Castellane and Moustiers. Tourist offices carry the excellent, English-language *Canyon du Verdon* (€4.70), detailing 28 walks, as well as maps of five principal walks (€2.40).

Note that wild camping anywhere in the gorges is illegal. Don't cross the river, except at bridges, and always stay on marked trails, lest you get trapped when the upstream dam opens, which happens twice weekly. Check water levels and the weather forecast with local tourist offices before embarking.

★ **Verdon Nature**   WALKING
(☎ 06 82 23 21 71; www.verdon-nature.com; per person €25) Local man Laurent Pichard runs excellent guided walks into the gorges, including vulture-spotting trips, nature hikes and guided routes following several classic

STARGAZING IN HAUTE-PROVENCE

Driving through the scrubby back roads south of Forcalquier, an unexpected sight appears on the hills: the **Observatoire de Haute-Provence** (☎ 04 92 70 64 00; www.obs-hp.fr; adult/child €5/3; ☉ guided visits 2-5pm Tue-Thu Jul & Aug, 2.15-4pm Wed Sep-Jun), a small dome-shaped observatory built in 1937 near the village of St-Michel-Observatoire to take advantage of Haute-Provence's wonderfully clear night skies. Several times a week in summer (and on Wednesdays the rest of the year), you can take a guided tour of the observatory and learn more about its work. Sometimes, there are night-time star-spotting sessions, too.

Tickets are sold at the **tourist office** (☎ 04 92 76 69 09; astronomie@ haute-provence-tourisme.com; place de la Fontaine; ☉ 9am-noon & 2-6pm Mon & Wed-Sat) in St-Michel-Observatoire.

hiking paths. He also offers a sunset walk and a night sleeping under the stars including the gorges' highest summit, Le Grand Margès. He's based in Castellane, but meeting points vary depending on the walk. He speaks some English.

🛏 Sleeping & Eating

Most accommodation is located in or around the main towns of Moustiers Ste-Marie and Castellane, at the western and eastern ends of the gorges respectively.

Gîte de Chasteuil   B&B €
(☎ 04 92 83 72 45; www.gitedechasteuil.com; Hameau de Chasteuil; s €75, d €82-89, tr €102, q €122; ☉ Mar-Nov) Around 12km west of Castellane, this excellent-value *chambre d'hôte* resides in a former schoolhouse with gorgeous mountain views. It is an ideal stop for hikers along the GR4. You're welcome to bring in your own food for dinner, and they'll pack you a hiker's picnic for €11.

Gîte de la Baume   HOSTEL, B&B €€
(☎ 04 92 83 70 82; www.gite-de-la-baume.com; La Baume; dm €25, d €75-90; P 🛜) What a cracking retreat this is, 9km north of Castellane. It's a friendly *auberge* (country inn) that offers surprisingly smart rooms

THE STAR OF PROVENCE

Huddled at the base of soaring cliffs, the picturesque village of Moustiers Ste-Marie is unquestionably the prettiest spot anywhere near the Gorges du Verdon, for which it serves as a useful gateway. Lining either side of a river valley, the village's main claim to fame is the **Chapelle Notre Dame de Beauvoir**, a 14th-century chapel that teeters precariously on the edge of a steep canyon.

A steep trail climbs beside a waterfall to the chapel, passing 14 stations of the cross en route. High above, a 227m-long chain bearing a shining gold star is stretched between the cliff walls – a tradition, legend has it, begun by the Knight of Blacas, in return for his safe return from the Crusades. It gives rise to the village's local nickname, 'Étoile de Provence' (Star of Provence).

(nearly all with some kind of a view) and a delicious, rustic *table d'hôte* (set menu) dinner (€20) in its restaurant, Aux Delices du Verdon. Half-board rates are available if you're staying overnight, or you can just visit for supper.

⭐ **La Fabrique** B&B €€
(📞 06 95 36 08 31; www.lafabrique04360.com; La Maladrerie, rte de Riez; d €98-135, f €135-150; 🅿️🛜) If you enjoy architectural grand designs, you'll adore this wonderful B&B. Inside the handsome brick shell (a former factory) are gorgeous, clean-lined, elegant rooms, with industrial touches like exposed brick and industrial-style sliding doors. Downstairs is the former factory floor, now a design-mag dream, with a steel staircase, floor-to-ceiling windows, pendant lights and a vast refectory table.

⭐ **La Bastide de Moustiers** GASTRONOMY €€€
(📞 04 92 70 47 47; www.bastide-moustiers.com; chemin de Quinson; menus €60-90; ⏱️ 12.30-1.30pm & 7.30-9pm, closed Oct-Feb) A legendary table of Provence, founded by chef supremo Alain Ducasse. As you'd expect from this Michelin-starred, much-lauded restaurant, it's a temple to French cuisine – and much of the produce comes from the inn's kitchen garden. Dress very smartly, and reserve well ahead.

ℹ️ Information

Castellane Tourist Office (📞 04 92 83 61 14; www.castellane-verdontourisme.com; rue Nationale; ⏱️ 9am-7.30pm daily Jul & Aug, 9am-noon & 2-6pm Mon-Sat, 10am-1pm Sun May-Jun & Sep, closed Sun rest of year) On the east side of the gorges, this is the best source for info on river trips and climbing expeditions, as well as general info on the Gorges du Verdon.

Moustiers Ste-Marie Tourist Office (📞 04 92 74 67 84; www.moustiers.eu; passage du Cloître; ⏱️ 9.30am-7pm Mon-Fri, 9.30am-12.30pm & 2-7pm Sat & Sun Jul & Aug, 10am-noon & 2-6pm Apr-Jun & Sep, closes around 5pm Oct-Mar; 📶) This pretty town acts as the gateway point to the western side of the gorges. Its tourist office is extremely well informed, organises activities and has free wi-fi.

Verdon Tourisme (www.verdontourisme.com) Excellent online resource for exploring the gorges.

ℹ️ Getting There & Away

Public transport in the gorges is limited, but the useful **Navette des Gorges du Verdon** (📞 04 92 34 22 90; autocars.delaye@orange.fr) shuttle bus links Castellane with Point Sublime, La Palud and La Maline (but not Moustiers). Services run twice daily in July and August and on weekends April to June and in September. The fare costs between €2 and €6.

There are also three daily **buses** (📞 08 21 20 22 03; www.info-ler.fr) from Marseille to Riez (€17.50). At least one bus a day continues to Moustiers, La Palud and Castellane, then returns along the same route. The single fare from Moustiers to Castellane is €7.30.

French Riviera & Monaco

Best Places to Eat

➡ Le Mirazur (p897)

➡ Peixes (p858)

➡ La Vague d'Or (p881)

➡ Table 22 (p867)

➡ L'Amandier (p872)

Best Places to Stay

➡ Hostel Meyerbeer Beach (p855)

➡ Les Rosées (p872)

➡ Hôtel La Pérouse (p856)

➡ Château Eza (p888)

➡ Hôtel de Provence (p865)

Why Go?

Once upon a time, everyone called this glamorous stretch of Mediterranean coast the French Riviera; then in 1888 author Stéphen Liégeard dubbed it *La Côte d'Azur,* the name stuck and the rest is history.

Whatever you prefer to call it, the seashore that extends from St-Tropez to the French-Italian border is one of the world's great seaside destinations, packed with gorgeous beaches, luxury hotels, designer bars, belle époque villas, coastal trails, red-rock headlands and offshore islands. From Monte Carlo's casino and Nice's Promenade des Anglais to the Cannes film festival and St-Tropez's yacht harbour, the Côte d'Azur is home to some of the most iconic spots in Europe's collective consciousness.

Beyond the coast, the region is also home to some spectacular hilltop villages and mountain scenery, along with vineyards, flower farms that feed the French perfume industry and more than its fair share of great art museums.

When to Go
Monaco

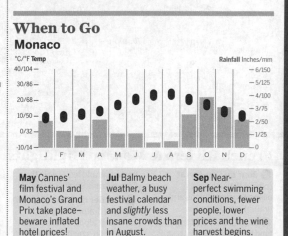

May Cannes' film festival and Monaco's Grand Prix take place—beware inflated hotel prices!

Jul Balmy beach weather, a busy festival calendar and *slightly* less insane crowds than in August.

Sep Near-perfect swimming conditions, fewer people, lower prices and the wine harvest begins.

French Riviera & Monaco Highlights

① **Tour du Cap-Ferrat** (p860) Walking past billionaires' mansions and dramatic rocky coves.

② **Nice** (p850) Splitting your time between beaches, bistros,

museums and festivals in the Côte d'Azur's unofficial capital.

③ **Sentier du Littoral** (p896) Taking a dramatic cape-to-cape walk along Roquebrune-Cap Martin's high drama coastal path.

④ **St-Tropez** (p878) Sipping pastis and watching *pétanque* players under the plane trees in picturesque place des Lices.

⑤ **St-Paul de Vence** (p875) Prowling the backstreets of this stunning hilltop village.

6 Antibes (p869) Visiting the Musée Picasso and viewing the Mediterranean.

7 Monaco (p888) Trying your luck at the Monte Carlo roulette tables.

8 Grasse (p872) Retracing three millennia of perfume-making at museums, factories and fragrant flower farms.

9 Corniche de l'Estérel (p877) Losing yourself in the scarlet sunset glow of this seaside massif.

10 Gorges du Loup (p875) Navigating the hairpin turns of this dramatic river gorge.

NICE

POP 342,522

With its mix of real-city grit, old-world opulence, year-round sunshine, vibrant street life and stunning seaside location, no place in France compares with Nice.

A magnet for sun-seekers and society jet-setters since the 19th century, this bewitching coastal queen has everything going for it – fabulous street markets, an enticing old town, glorious architecture, world-class modern-art museums (thanks to Chagall, Matisse, Picasso and Renoir who fell in love with the place) and a delicious wealth of epicurean restaurants. Nice is far from perfect – it's scruffy in spots, the summertime traffic is horrendous and the beach is made entirely of bum-numbing pebbles – but if you're in town to soak up Riviera vibe, there's no finer spot.

Orientation

Av Jean Médecin runs south from near the main train station to place Masséna, close to the beach and old town.

From the airport, 6km west, promenade des Anglais runs along the curving beachfront (Baie des Anges), becoming quai des États-Unis near the old town. Vieux Nice (Old Nice) is crunched into a 500m-by-500m area enclosed by bd Jean Jaurès, quai des États-Unis and the hill known as Colline du Château. The trendy Port Lympia-Place Garibaldi area lies to the east of Colline du Château.

The wealthy residential neighbourhood of Cimiez, home to some outstanding museums and belle époque architecture, is north of the centre.

⊙ Sights

★ **Promenade des Anglais** ARCHITECTURE
(▣8, 52, 62) The most famous stretch of seafront in Nice – if not France – is this vast paved promenade, which gets its name from the English expat patrons who paid for it in 1822. It runs for the whole 4km sweep of the Baie des Anges with a dedicated lane for cyclists and skaters; if you fancy joining them, you can rent skates, scooters and bikes from **Roller Station** (✆04 93 62 99 05; www.roller-station.fr; 49 quai des États-Unis; skates, boards & scooters per hour/day €5/12, bicycles €5/15; ⊘9am-8pm Jul & Aug, 10am-7pm May, Jun, Sep & Oct, to 6pm Nov-Apr).

A more unusual way to cruise along is an electric Segway from **Mobilboard Nice** (✆04 93 80 21 27; www.mobilboard.com/nice-promenade; 2 rue Halévy, Batiment Ruhl Méridien; 30min/1hr/2hr tour €20/30/50; ⊘9.30am-6pm; ▣8, 52, 62 to Massenet); the same agency also rents out bikes.

Along the way, keep an eye out for a few of the promenade's landmarks, including the **Hôtel Negresco** (✆04 93 16 64 00; www.hotel-negresco-nice.com; 37 Promenade des Anglais; ▣8, 52, 62 to Gambetta/Promenade), the art-deco **Palais de la Méditerranée** (✆04 93 27 12 34; www.lepalaisdelamediterranee.com; 13 promenade des Anglais; d €149-879; ❋@➚❊; ▣8, 52, 62 to Congrès/Promenade) (1929) and Niçoise sculptor Sabine Géraudie's giant iron sculpture *La Chaise de SAB* (2014), which pays homage to the city's famous blue-and-white beach chairs.

In 2015 the city of Nice submitted the Promenade des Anglais as a candidate for Unesco World Heritage status – the process can take up to 10 years to complete.

★ **Vieux Nice** HISTORIC SITE
(▣1 to Opéra-Vieille Ville/Cathédrale-Vieille Ville) Getting lost among the dark, narrow, winding alleyways of Nice's old town is a highlight. The layout has barely changed since the 1700s, and it's now packed with delis, restaurants, boutiques and bars, but the centrepiece remains **cours Saleya**: a massive market square that's permanently thronging in summer. The **food market** (⊘6am-1.30pm Tue-Sun) is perfect for fresh produce and foodie souvenirs, while the

---

ⓘ PORTSIDE MEANDER

Nice's **Port Lympia** (▣2 to Port Lympia), with its beautiful Venetian-coloured buildings, is often overlooked, but a stroll along its quays is lovely, as is the walk to get here: come down through Parc du Château or follow quai Rauba Capeu, where a massive war memorial hewn from the rock commemorates the 4000 Niçois who died in both world wars.

Nice's coolest new gallery space, **Galerie Lympia** (✆04 89 04 53 10; http://galerielympia.departement06.fr; 52 bd Stalingrad; ⊘2-7pm Wed-Sat, 10am-noon & 2-7pm Sun; ▣2 to Port Lympia) **FREE**, is housed in a former galley slaves' prison down by the port. Opened in 2017 by the Alpes-Maritimes' departmental government after a €2.1 million restoration project, it hosts regular free exhibitions of works by contemporary Niçois artists such as Patrick Moya, along with artists from further afield.

DON'T MISS

MODERN ART IN CIMIEZ
....

When you've had your fill of waterfront thrills, escape to the residential neighbourhood of Cimiez, north of Nice-Ville train station, for a low-key dose of local colour and exceptional modern art.

Musée Matisse (☑ 04 93 81 08 08; www.musee-matisse-nice.org; 164 av des Arènes de Cimiez; museum pass 24hr/7 days €10/20; ⊙ 10am-6pm Wed-Mon late Jun–mid-Oct, from 11am rest of year; ☐ 15, 17, 20, 22 to Arènes/Musée Matisse) This museum, 2km north of the city centre in the leafy Cimiez quarter, houses a fascinating assortment of works by Matisse, including oil paintings, drawings, sculptures, tapestries and Matisse's famous paper cutouts. The permanent collection is displayed in a red-ochre 17th-century Genoese villa in an olive grove. Temporary exhibitions are in the futuristic basement building. Matisse is buried in the **Monastère Notre Dame de Cimiez** (place du Monastère; ⊙ 8.30am-12.30pm & 2.30-6.30pm) cemetery, across the park from the museum.

Musée National Marc Chagall (☑ 04 93 53 87 20; www.musee-chagall.fr; 4 av Dr Ménard; adult/child €10/8; ⊙ 10am-6pm Wed-Mon May-Oct, to 5pm Nov-Apr; ☐ 15, 22 to Musée Chagall) The strange, dreamlike and often unsettling work of the Belarusian painter Marc Chagall (1887–1985) is displayed at this museum, which owns the largest public collection of the painter's work. The main hall displays 12 huge interpretations (1954–67) of stories from Genesis and Exodus. From the city centre, allow about 20 minutes to walk to the museum (signposted from av de l'Olivetto), or take the bus.

flower market (6am-5.30pm Tue-Sat, 6.30am-1.30pm Sun) is worth visiting just for the colours and fragrances. A **flea market** (Marché à la Brocante; ⊙ 7am-6pm Mon) is held on Monday.

Baroque aficionados will adore architectural gems **Cathédrale Ste-Réparate** (☑ 04 93 92 01 35; place Rossetti; ⊙ 2-6pm Mon, 9am-noon & 2-6pm Tue-Sun), honouring the city's patron saint; exuberant 16th-century **Chapelle de la Miséricorde** (☑ 04 92 00 41 90; cours Saleya; ⊙ 2.30-5pm Tue Sep-Jun); and 17th-century **Palais Lascaris** (☑ 04 93 62 72 40; 15 rue Droite; museum pass 24hr/7 days €10/20, guided visit adult/child €6/free; ⊙ 10am-6pm Wed-Mon late Jun–mid-Oct, from 11am mid-Oct–late Jun), a frescoed riot of Flemish tapestries, faience (tin-glazed earthenware), gloomy religious paintings and 18th-century pharmacy.

There's also a lively – and very smelly – **fish market** (⊙ 6am-1pm Tue-Sun) on place St-François.

★**Colline du Château**   PARK
(Castle Hill; ⊙ 8.30am-8pm Apr-Sep, to 6pm Oct-Mar) **FREE** For the best views over Nice's red-tiled rooftops, climb the winding staircases up to this wooded outcrop on the eastern edge of the old town. It's been occupied since ancient times; archaeological digs have revealed Celtic and Roman remains, and the site was later occupied by a medieval castle that was razed by Louis XIV in 1706 (only the 16th-century **Tour Bellanda** remains). There are various entrances, including one beside the tower, or

you can cheat and ride the free **lift** (Ascenseur du Château; rue des Ponchettes; ⊙ 9am-8pm Jun-Aug, to 7pm Apr, May & Sep, 10am-6pm Oct-Mar).

★**Musée Masséna**   MUSEUM
(☑ 04 93 91 19 10; 65 rue de France; museum pass 24hr/7 days €10/20; ⊙ 10am-6pm Wed-Mon late Jun–mid-Oct, from 11am rest of year; ☐ 8, 52, 62 to Congrès/Promenade) Originally built as a holiday home for Prince Victor d'Essling (the grandson of one of Napoléon's favourite generals, Maréchal Massena), this lavish belle époque building is another of the city's iconic architectural landmarks. Built between 1898 and 1901 in grand neoclassical style with an Italianate twist, it's now a fascinating museum dedicated to the history of the Riviera – taking in everything from holidaying monarchs to expat Americans, the boom of tourism and the enduring importance of Carnaval.

★**Musée d'Art Moderne et d'Art Contemporain**   GALLERY
(MAMAC; ☑ 04 97 13 42 01; www.mamac-nice.org; place Yves Klein; museum pass 24hr/7 days €10/20; ⊙ 10am-6pm Tue-Sun late Jun–mid-Oct, from 11am rest of year; ☐ 1 to Garibaldi) European and American avant-garde works from the 1950s to the present are the focus of this sprawling multi-level museum. Highlights include works by Christo and Nice's neorealists: Niki de Saint Phalle, César, Arman and Yves Klein. The building's rooftop also works as an exhibition space with knockout panoramas of Nice).

Nice

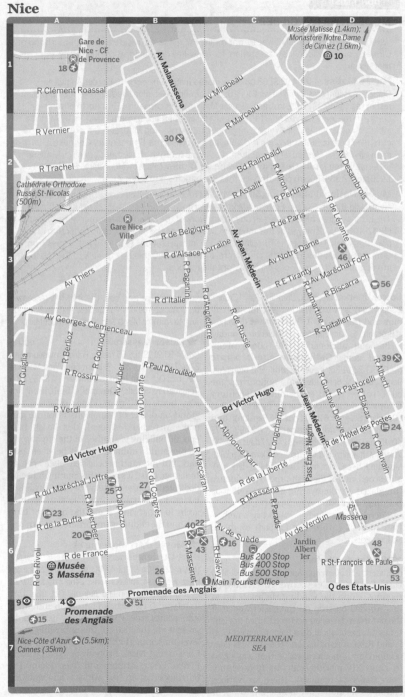

Nice map labels:

- Gare de Nice - CF de Provence
- 18
- R Clément Roassal
- Av Malaussena
- Av Mirabeau
- Musée Matisse (1.4km); Monastère Notre Dame de Cimiez (1.6km);
- 10
- R Vernier
- R Marceau
- 30
- R Trachel
- Bd Raimbaldi
- R Miron
- Av Desambrois
- Cathédrale Orthodoxe Russe St-Nicolas (500m)
- R Assalit
- R Pertinax
- R de Paris
- R de Lépante
- Gare Nice Ville
- R de Belgique
- R d'Alsace-Lorraine
- Av Jean Médecin
- Av Notre Dame
- 46
- Av Maréchal Foch
- Av Thiers
- R Paganini
- R d'Angleterre
- R E Tiranty
- R Lamartine
- R Biscarra
- 56
- R d'Italie
- R de Russie
- R Spitalieri
- Av Georges Clemenceau
- R Berlioz
- R Gounod
- R Paul Déroulède
- R Alberti
- 39
- R Guiglia
- R Rossini
- Av Auber
- Av Durante
- R Gustave Deloye
- R Pastorelli
- R Verdi
- R Blacas
- Bd Victor Hugo
- Av Jean Médecin
- R de l'Hôtel des Postes
- 24
- R Alphonse Karr
- R Longchamp
- Pass Émile Negrin
- 28
- R Chauvain
- Bd Victor Hugo
- R Maccarani
- R de la Liberté
- R du Maréchal Joffre
- R Meyerbeer
- R Dalpozzo
- R du Congrès
- R Masséna
- R Paradis
- Pl Masséna
- 25
- 27
- 40
- 22
- Av de Suède
- Av de Verdun
- 48
- R de la Buffa
- 20
- R de Rivoli
- R de France
- 43
- R Massenet
- R Halévy
- 16
- Jardin Albert 1er
- R St-François de Paule
- 53
- 26
- Bus 200 Stop
- Bus 400 Stop
- Bus 500 Stop
- Main Tourist Office
- Musée Masséna
- 3
- Promenade des Anglais
- Q des États-Unis
- 9
- 4
- 51
- Promenade des Anglais
- 15
- Nice-Côte d'Azur (5.5km); Cannes (35km)
- MEDITERRANEAN SEA

FRENCH RIVIERA & MONACO NICE

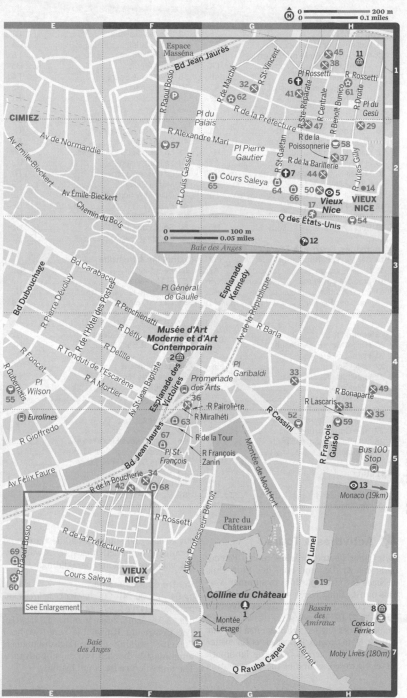

Nice

🏃 Activities & Tours

Swimming at the beaches along Promenade des Anglais and quai des États-Unis is Nice's favourite pastime in summer. Various outfits along Nice's waterfront rent out water-sports equipment. **Glisse Evasion** (☑06 10 27 03 91; www.glisse-evasion.com; 29 Promenade des Anglais; ☺8.30am-7pm May-Sep; ☒8, 52, 62 to Congrès/Promenade or Gambetta/Promenade), just across from the landmark Hôtel Negresco, is one of the best, renting out kayaks and stand-up paddleboards and organising other activities such as waterskiing, wakeboarding and paragliding.

Centre du Patrimoine   WALKING
(☑04 92 00 41 90; www.nice.fr/fr/culture/patrimoine; 14 rue Jules Gilly; tours adult/child €5/free; ☺9am-1pm & 2-5pm Mon-Thu, to 3.45pm Fri) The Centre du Patrimoine runs two-hour thematic walking tours. English-language tours must be booked two days in advance. The tourist office has a full listing.

❶ BEACH TALK

Officially there are 25 named beaches strung out along the Baie des Anges, some of which are free, others of which are reserved solely for paying clientele. All are pebbly, so sensitive behinds might opt for one of the private beaches (€15 to €25 per day), which come with sun-loungers and comfy mattresses.

Free cold-water showers, lifeguards and first-aid posts are available most of the way along the bay, including on the public beaches; there are also a few public toilets for which you have to pay a small charge. Most beaches also offer activities, from beach volleyball to jet-skis and pedalos.

Something else worth noting: nudity is perfectly acceptable on Nice's beaches, and locals certainly aren't shy about letting it all hang out – but of course, there's no obligation to bare all (or anything).

Right opposite Vieux Nice, **Plage Publique des Ponchettes** is generally the busiest beach of all, with oiled bodies either baking in the sun or punching a ball on the beach volleyball court.

Trans Côte d'Azur
BOATING

(www.trans-cote-azur.com; quai Lunel; ⊘ Apr-Oct; 🚊2 to Port Lympia) Trans Côte d'Azur runs one-hour boat cruises along the Baie des Anges and Rade de Villefranche (adult/child €18/13) from April to October. From late May to September it also sails to Île Ste-Marguerite (€40/31, one hour), St-Tropez (€65/51, 2½ hours), Monaco (€38.50/30, 45 minutes) and Cannes (€40/31, one hour).

🎊 Festivals & Events

★ Carnaval de Nice
CARNIVAL

(www.nicecarnaval.com; ⊘ Feb-Mar) Held over a two-week period in late February and early March since 1294. Highlights include the *batailles de fleurs* (battles of flowers) and the ceremonial burning of the carnival king on Promenade des Anglais, followed by a fireworks display.

Nice Jazz Festival
MUSIC

(www.nicejazzfestival.fr; ⊘ Jul) France's original jazz festival has taken on a life of its own, with a jam-packed six-night calendar of performances on two stages in Jardin Albert 1er, and fringe concerts popping up all around town, from Vieux Nice to Massena and the shopping streets around rue de France.

🛏 Sleeping

Accommodation in Nice is excellent and caters to all budgets, unlike many cities on the Côte d'Azur. Hotels charge substantially more during the Monaco Grand Prix. Book well in advance in summer.

★ Hostel Meyerbeer Beach
HOSTEL €

(📋04 93 88 95 65; www.hostelmeyerbeer.com; 15 rue Meyerbeer; dm €25-50, s €80-90, d €90-100; 🚊7, 9, 22, 27, 59, 70 to Rivoli) It's easy to see why this cosy little hostel got voted Best in France in 2018. A welcoming mood prevails throughout, thanks to the congenial, international staff of four, a kitchen small enough to make you feel like you're cooking at home, and a cheerful, immaculate mix of private rooms and four- to eight-bed dorms, each with its own en-suite bathroom.

Villa Saint-Exupéry Beach Hostel
HOSTEL €

(📋04 93 16 13 45; www.villahostels.com; 6 rue Sacha Guitry; dm €30-50, d €100; ❄@🛜; 🚊1 to Masséna) Five blocks from the beach, this long-standing, centrally located city hostel has plenty of pluses: bar, kitchen, gym, sauna, ping-pong, games room and friendly multilingual staff. Dorms sleeping four to 16 all come equipped with private en-suite bathrooms, and there's a host of activities on offer, including yoga, sailing, scuba diving, canyoning and free city walking tours.

Hôtel Solara
HOTEL €

(📋04 93 88 09 96; www.hotelsolara.com; 7 rue de France; s €65-75, d €85-115; ⊘reception 8am-9pm; ❄🛜; 🚊7, 9, 22, 27, 59, 70 to Grimaldi) With a fantastic location on pedestrianised rue de France, small personal fridges for that evening glass of rosé, and sensational terraces on half the rooms, the Solara is pure budget gold. Rooms are small but spotless, and you're right in the heart of the action, a mere block from the beachfront.

THE PINE CONE TRAIN

Chugging between the mountains and the sea, the **Train des Pignes** (Pine Cone Train; www.trainprovence.com; single/ return Nice to Digne €24.10/48.20; 🚇1 to Libération) is one of Provence's most picturesque train rides. The 151km track between Nice and Digne-les-Bains rises to 1000m for breathtaking views as it passes through Haute-Provence's scarcely populated backcountry. The service runs four times daily from **Gare de Nice-CF de Provence** (rue Alfred Binet; 🚇1 to Libération) and is ideal for a day trip inland.

The beautiful medieval village of **Entrevaux** is just 1½ hours from Nice (return fare €24.40), perfect for a picnic and a wander through its historic centre and citadel.

Hôtel Wilson   HOTEL €

(📞 04 93 85 47 79; www.hotel-wilson-nice.com; 39 rue de l'Hôtel des Postes; s €35-57, d €42-82; 🛜; 🚌7, 9 to Wilson or Pastorelli) Generations of travellers have passed through Jean-Marie's rambling 3rd-floor apartment, where all the rooms have been decorated with potted plants and items collected on his travels in a faintly bohemian, hippie-hangover style (one room's styled after Frida Kahlo, another is stuffed with '70s kitsch, while others have African and Asian flavours). It's faded but winningly friendly and family-run. Cheaper rooms share bathrooms.

⭐**Hôtel Windsor**   BOUTIQUE HOTEL €€

(📞 04 93 88 59 35; www.hotelwindsornice.com; 11 rue Dalpozzo; d €92-290; ❋ @ 🛜 ☸; 🚌7, 9, 22, 27, 59, 70 to Grimaldi or Rivoli) Don't be fooled by the staid stone exterior: inside, owner Odile Redolfi has enlisted the collective creativity of several well-known artists to make each of the 57 rooms uniquely appealing. Some are frescoed and others are adorned with experimental chandeliers or photographic murals. The garden and pool out the back are delightful, as are the small bar and attached restaurant.

⭐**Nice Garden Hôtel**   BOUTIQUE HOTEL €€

(📞 04 93 87 35 62; www.nicegardenhotel.com; 11 rue du Congrès; s €75-85, d €110-140; ⏱reception 8.30am-9pm; ❋ 🛜; 🚌7, 9, 22, 27, 59, 70 to Grimaldi) Behind heavy iron gates hides this gem: the nine beautifully appointed rooms – the work of the exquisite Marion – are a subtle blend of old and new and overlook a delightful garden with a glorious orange tree. Amazingly, all this charm and peacefulness is just two blocks from the promenade. Breakfast costs €9.

Hôtel Villa Rivoli   BOUTIQUE HOTEL €€

(📞 04 93 88 80 25; www.villa-rivoli.com; 10 rue de Rivoli; s €69, d €114-208; ❋ 🛜; 🚌7, 9, 22, 27, 59, 70 to Rivoli) This charming but strangely shaped villa dates back to 1890, and it's packed with period detail – gilded mirrors, fireplaces, cast-iron balconies and old-world wallpapers, as well as little conifer trees on the balconies and a sweeping marble staircase. Rooms are on the small side, and some are showing their age. There's a small garden and car park beside the hotel.

⭐**Hôtel La Pérouse**   BOUTIQUE HOTEL €€€

(📞 04 93 62 34 63; www.hotel-la-perouse.com; 11 quai Rauba Capeu; d €247-665; ❋ @ 🛜 ☸) A prime seaside location and boutique hotel style put La Pérouse in a league of its own. Built into the rock cliff-face of Colline du Château, it evokes the spirit of a genteel villa. Lower-floor rooms face a citrus-tree-shaded courtyard and pool; upper-floor rooms have magnificent sea vistas. Smart accent colours and Italian marble bathrooms add flair to the traditional decor.

🍴 Eating

Booking is advisable at most restaurants, particularly during the busy summer season. To lunch with locals, grab a pew in the midday sun on one of the many place Garibaldi cafe terraces. There are lots of restaurants on cours Saleya, but quality can be variable, so choose carefully.

⭐**Mama Baker**   BAKERY €

(📞 06 23 91 33 86; www.facebook.com/Mama bakernice; 13 rue de Lépante; items from €2; ⏱7am-2pm & 3-7pm Mon-Fri, 7am-6pm Sat; 🚌4 to Toselli) Great bakeries abound in France, but even here, truly creative artisanal ones stand out. Witness Mama Baker, where organic grains and speciality ingredients go into a host of unique goodies. Don't miss the delectable *bouchées aux olives,* soft and crispy bite-sized bits of olive-studded cheesy dough, or *pompe à l'huile,* a semi-sweet roll flavoured with olive oil and orange blossoms.

La Fougasserie BAKERY €

(☑ 04 93 80 92 45; www.lafougasserie.com; 5 rue de la Poissonnerie; items from €1; ⊙ 7am-7pm Fri-Tue) Vieux Nice's finest baked goods emanate from this little corner *boulangerie,* which also operates a stall in the Cours Saleya food market. Quality organic ingredients go into a full spectrum of sweet and savoury delights, including croissants, *pan bagnat* (Niçois tuna sandwich), pizza and *pissaladière* (onion tart). At Carnaval time, don't miss its dreamy *bugnes de Carnaval,* doughnut-like fritters delicately scented with orange blossoms.

★ **Chez Palmyre** FRENCH €

(☑ 04 93 85 72 32; 5 rue Droite; 3-course menu €18; ⊙ noon-1.30pm & 7-9.30pm Mon, Tue, Thu & Fri) Look no further for authentic Niçois cooking than this packed, cramped, convivial little space in the heart of the old town. The menu is very meat-heavy, with plenty of tripe, veal, pot-cooked chicken and the like, true to the traditional tastes of Provençal cuisine. It's a bargain, and understandably popular. Book well ahead, even for lunch.

★ **La Rossettisserie** FRENCH €

(☑ 04 93 76 18 80; www.larossettisserie.com; 8 rue Mascoïnat; mains €16.50-19.50; ⊙ noon-2pm & 7-10pm Mon-Sat) Roast meat is the order of the day here: make your choice from beef, chicken, veal or lamb, and pair it with a choice of mashed or sautéed potatoes, ratatouille or salad. Simple and sumptuous, with cosy, rustic decor and a delightful vaulted cellar.

Acchiardo FRENCH €

(☑ 04 93 85 51 16; 38 rue Droite; mains €16-19; ⊙ noon-2pm & 7-10pm Mon-Fri) Warm service and irreproachable quality are the hallmarks of this traditional neighbourhood restaurant, in the same family since 1927. Locals and tourists pack into the three stone-walled rooms for Niçois delights such as *merda di can* (little green gnocchi – nicknamed 'dog poop' for the shape, not the flavour, mind you!), red mullet with parsleyed green beans and olive tapenade, and tiramisu.

Koko Green VEGETARIAN €

(☑ 07 81 63 14 88; www.kokogreen.com; 1 rue de la Loge; weekly specials €15; ⊙ noon-5pm Thu, Fri & Sun, noon-4pm & 7.30-10pm Sat; ✔) At this popular Vieux Nice newcomer, a New Zealander and a naturopath whip up an awesome array of veggie, raw and vegan treats. Weekly specials are globally inspired: Mexican *sopa de tortilla,* Middle Eastern falafel, Vietnamese crêpes – all organic, gluten-free and accompanied by fresh-blended juices. The ultimate showstopper is the vegan cheesecake; dairy-lovers can only marvel at the faux-creaminess!

Badaboom VEGAN €

(☑ 06 71 48 24 01; www.badaboom-nice.net; 11 rue François Guisol; plat du jour €14, with juice €17; ⊙ 8.30am-6pm Mon-Wed, to 10pm Thu & Fri, 10am-5pm Sat; ✔; ⬛ 1 to Garibaldi, 2 to Port Lympia) Vegans and vegetarians are in heaven at this little cafe specialising in fresh cold-pressed juices, whole grains, local organic produce

---

ℹ NICE ICE STOPS

Fenocchio (☑ 04 93 80 72 52; www.fenocchio.fr; 2 place Rossetti; 1/2 scoops €2.50/4; ⊙ 9am-midnight Mar-Nov) There's no shortage of ice-cream sellers in the old town, but this *maître glacier* (master ice-cream maker) has been king of the scoops since 1966. The array of flavours is mind-boggling – olive, tomato, fig, beer, lavender and violet to name a few. Dither too long over the 70-plus flavours and you'll never make it to the front of the queue. The queues at the main branch are long on hot summer days, but they're generally shorter at the **second branch** (☑ 04 93 62 88 80; 6 rue de la Poissonnerie; ⊙ 9am-midnight Wed-Mon Mar-Nov) around the corner.

Gelateria Azzurro (☑ 04 93 13 92 24; www.facebook.com/Gelateriazzurro; 1 rue Ste-Réparate; ice cream from €2.70; ⊙ 11am-midnight) Next door to the cathedral, this venerable Vieux Nice *gelateria* is beloved for its ice cream, yes – but even more so for its homemade waffle cones, made here on the hot griddle right before your eyes!

Arlequin Gelati (☑ 04 93 04 69 88; www.arlequin-gelati.com; 9 av Malausséna; 1/2/3/4 scoops €3/5/7/9; ⊙ 10am-midnight Apr-mid-Oct; ✱; ⬛ 1 to Libération or Gare Thiers) A five-minute walk from Nice Ville train station brings you to this fab ice-cream shop founded by Milanese gelato master Roberto. Grab a scoop of chocolate-orange, hazelnut, pistachio, panna cotta or cinnamon-infused *spéculoos,* take it to the pavement tables out the front, and watch the world go by.

and raw desserts. The menu features salads, wraps and daily *plats du jour,* each served with juice for an extra €3.

⭐ Bar des Oiseaux   FRENCH €€

(☎04 93 80 27 33; 5 rue St-Vincent; 3-course lunch menu €20, dinner menus from €30; ⏱noon-1.45pm & 7.15-9.45pm Tue-Sat) Hidden down a narrow backstreet, this old-town classic has been in business since 1961, serving as a popular nightclub before reincarnating itself as a restaurant (some of its original saucy murals have survived the transition). Nowadays it's a lively bistro serving superb traditional French cuisine spiced up with modern twists. The weekday lunch special offers phenomenal value. Book ahead.

⭐ La Femme du Boulanger   BISTRO €€

(☎04 89 03 43 03; www.facebook.com/femmeduboulanger; 3 rue Raffali; mains €20-25, tartines €16-22; ⏱9am-3pm & 7-11pm; 🚌8, 52, 62 to Massenet) This back-alley gem with pavement seating is a vision of French bistro bliss. Mains like duck *à l'orange*, honey-balsamic glazed lamb shank, or perfect *steak au poivre* with *gratin dauphinois* (cheesy potatoes) and perfectly tender veggies are followed up with raspberry clafoutis, tiramisu and other scrumptious desserts. Tartines on wood-fired homemade bread are the other house speciality.

⭐ Peixes   SEAFOOD €€

(☎04 93 85 96 15; 4 rue de l'Opéra; small plates €12-19, mains €17-35; ⏱noon-10pm Tue-Sat) This chic modern seafood eatery is the latest jewel in the crown of Niçois master restaurateur Armand Crespo. All done up in white-and-turquoise nautical decor, with dangling fish eyeball light fixtures and murals of a tentacle-haired mermaid ensnaring a fishing boat, it specialises in fresh local fish turned into delicious ceviches, tartares and Japanese-style tatakis by chefs in the open kitchen.

⭐ Franchin   FRENCH €€

(☎04 93 87 15 74; www.franchin.fr; 10 rue Massenet; mains €24-31; ⏱noon-2pm & 7-10pm Wed-Sun; 🚌8, 52, 62 to Massenet) White linen tablecloths give this upmarket brasserie an air of formality, but the friendly service dispels any notions of stuffiness, and the food is simply divine. Don't miss the octopus salad with potatoes and chorizo (one of the best appetisers you'll find anywhere on the Côte d'Azur), and ask about the €16 weekday specials (excellent value for money when available).

Olive et Artichaut   PROVENCAL €€

(☎04 89 14 97 51; www.oliveartichaut.com; 6 rue Ste-Réparate; 3-course menu €32, mains €16-28; ⏱noon-2pm & 7.30-10pm Wed-Sun) There's barely enough room to swing a pan in this tiny street bistro, especially when it's full of diners (as it often is), but it doesn't seem to faze young Niçois chef Thomas Hubert and his friendly team. He sources as much produce as possible from close-to-home suppliers (Sisteron lamb, Niçoise olives, locally caught fish) and likes to give the old classics his own spin. Wise diners reserve.

Café Paulette   TAPAS €€

(☎04 92 04 74 48; 15 rue Bonaparte; tapas €6-10, mains €11-29; ⏱8am-12.30am Wed-Sat; 🚌1 to Garibaldi) Chilled and classy Café Paulette has become one of the Petit Marais's favourite hang-outs since opening in 2017. Part cafe, part convivial lunch spot and part evening wine bar, it's especially beloved for its tasty international tapas such as roast squid and barley 'risotto' or Japanese-style sesame-crusted tuna tataki. An ample array of cocktails supplements the solid wine list.

LOCAL KNOWLEDGE

NIÇOIS SPECIALITIES

Niçois specialities include *socca* (a savoury, griddle-fried pancake made from chickpea flour and olive oil, sprinkled with a liberal dose of black pepper), *petits farcis* (stuffed vegetables), *pissaladière* (onion tart topped with black olives and anchovies) and the many vegetable *beignets* (fritters). Try them at **Chez René Socca** (☎04 93 92 05 73; 2 rue Miralhéti; small plates €3-6; ⏱9am-9pm Tue-Sun, to 10.30pm Jul & Aug, closed Nov; 🖉), **Socca d'Or** (☎04 93 56 52 93; www.restaurant-soccador-nice.fr; 45 rue Bonaparte; socca €3; ⏱11am-2pm & 6-10pm Mon, Tue & Thu-Sat; 🚌1 to Garibaldi, 2 to Port Lympia) or **Chez Pipo** (☎04 93 55 88 82; www.chezpipo.fr; 13 rue Bavastro; socca €2.90; ⏱11.30am-2.30pm & 5.30-10pm Wed-Sun; 🚌1 to Garibaldi, 2 to Port Lympia).

At the Cours Saleya market, **Socca du Cours** (place Charles Félix; socca €3, other snacks from €2; ⏱9.30am-1pm) is the go-to, snack-attack address.

Flaveur GASTRONOMY €€€

(📞 04 93 62 53 95; www.restaurant-flaveur.com; 25 rue Gubernatis; 2-course lunch menus €62, 3-/4-course dinner menus €85/99; ☺noon-2pm Tue-Fri, 7.30-10pm Tue-Sat; 🚊3, 7, 9, 27 to Pastorelli) Run by brothers Gaël and Mickaël Tourteau, this small restaurant has big culinary ambitions (and a second Michelin star as of 2018). In a Zen dining room with bold fabrics and wooden platters artfully arranged on the walls, it's a haute-cuisine temple, with dishes dressed in foams, creams, reductions and snows, and presented with the precision of museum exhibits.

🍸 Drinking & Nightlife

Cafe terraces on cours Saleya are lovely for an early-evening aperitif. Vieux Nice's bounty of pubs attracts a noisy, boisterous crowd; most bars have a happy hour from 6pm to 8pm. The trendy area to drink these days is Le Petit Marais in the Port Lympia area, where a clutch of new bars and bistros have opened up.

⭐La Part des Anges WINE BAR

(📞 04 93 62 69 80; www.lapartdesanges-nice. com; 17 rue Gubernatis; ☺10am-8.30pm Mon-Thu, to midnight Fri & Sat; 🚊7, 9 to Pastorelli or Wilson) The focus at this classy wine shop-bar is organic wines – a few are sold by the glass, but the best selection is available by the bottle, served with homemade tapenades and charcuterie platters. The name means 'the Angel's Share', referring to the alcohol that evaporates as wines age. There are only a few tables, so arrive early or reserve ahead.

⭐Beer District CRAFT BEER

(📞 06 75 10 26 36; www.beerdistrict.fr; 13 rue Cassini; ☺6pm-1am Tue-Sat; 🚊1 to Garibaldi, 2 to Port Lympia) One of Nice's coolest new nightspots, Beer District pours a regularly rotating lineup of 16 draught microbrews and 50 bottled beers from all over the world. The vibe is chilled and friendly, with free tastes cheerfully offered and little bowls of peanuts for snacking.

⭐La Ronronnerie CAFE

(📞 09 51 51 26 50; www.laronronnerie.fr; 4 rue de Lépante; ☺11.30am-6pm Tue-Sat; 🚊4 to Sasserno) Kitties rule the roost at this one-of-a-kind cafe, an absolute must for cat-lovers. Five free-range felines roam about the tables, seeking the right lap to sit in, yawning and stretching on plush pedestals or climbing the tree branch overhead. Meanwhile, humans sip hot beverages and nibble on bagels and cake. It's all squeaky clean, without a flea in sight.

Les Distilleries Idéales CAFE

(📞 04 93 62 10 66; www.facebook.com/ldinice; 24 rue de la Préfecture; ☺9am-12.30am) The most atmospheric spot for a tipple in the old town, whether you're after one of the many beers on tap or a local wine by the glass. Brick-lined and set out over two floors (with a little balcony that's great for people-watching), it's packed until late. Happy hour is from 6pm to 8pm.

El Merkado BAR

(📞 04 93 62 30 88; www.el-merkado.com; 12 rue St-François de Paule; ☺11am-1.30am Oct-Apr, 10am-2.30am May-Sep) Footsteps from cours Saleya, this hip tapas bar (strapline: 'In Sangria We Trust') struts its vintage stuff on the ground floor of a quintessential Niçois town house. Lounging on its pavement terrace or a sofa with an after-beach cocktail is the thing to do here.

La Movida COCKTAIL BAR

(📞 04 93 80 48 04; www.movidanice.com; 41 quai des États-Unis; ☺10am-2am) No place in Vieux Nice offers better people-watching than the beach-facing tables on La Movida's streetside deck and upstairs terrace. Snag one in time for sunset if you can, and stick around for cocktails, tapas, DJs and live music.

Rosalina Bar BAR

(📞 04 93 89 34 96; www.facebook.com/bar.rosalina; 16 rue Lascaris; ☺6.30pm-12.30am Mon-Sat; 🚊1 to Garibaldi, 2 to Port Lympia) Way back before Le Port-Garibaldi became so trendy, Rosalina was the neighbourhood's nightlife pioneer. A decade later, it's still an inviting, friendly spot for drinks or dinner, whether you're sipping wine and nibbling complimentary crostini with killer olive tapenade on the outdoor terrace, or downing a cocktail beside the piano and the swing in the whimsically decorated interior.

Le 6 GAY

(📞 04 93 62 66 64; www.le6.fr; 6 rue Raoul Bosio; ☺10pm-5am Wed-Sat) Primped and pretty A-gays crowd shoulder to shoulder at Nice's compact, perennially popular gay bar. Le 6 keeps a busy event and party schedule: guest DJs, karaoke and shower shows.

ST-JEAN-CAP FERRAT

A world unto itself, the prosperous seaside village of St-Jean-Cap-Ferrat sits aloof from the hustle and bustle of the main coast road, astride a dreamy peninsula that juts into the Mediterranean midway between Nice and Monaco. Away from the town centre, the Cap Ferrat peninsula is dotted with the villas of millionaires and billionaires, including the extraordinarily lavish, belle époque confection **Villa Ephrussi de Rothschild** (✉04 93 01 33 09; www.villa-ephrussi.com/en; adult/child €14/11; ⊙10am-6pm Feb-Jun, Sep & Oct, to 7pm Jul & Aug, 2-6pm Mon-Fri, 10am-6pm Sat & Sun Nov-Jan) with stunning gardens.

Some 14km of eucalyptus-scented walking paths lace the peninsula, affording magnificent views of the wonderfully rugged coastline. Encompassing the heart and soul of the cape's coastline, the **Tour du Cap Ferrat** is a 7km loop circumnavigating the most rugged and scenic part of the peninsula; one trailhead starts on Plage de Passable behind St-Jean's **tourist office** (✉04 93 76 08 90; www.saintjeancapferrat-tourisme.fr; 5 av Denis Séméria; ⊙9.30am-6.30pm Mon-Sat, 9am-1pm & 2-5pm Sun May-Sep, shorter hours rest of year). Highlights include the series of rocky, secluded coves on the peninsula's western shoreline and the lighthouse at the far southern tip. Allow about two hours to walk the trail in either direction.

Bus 81, operated by Lignes d'Azur, provides direct services from Nice's Promenade des Arts stop to the centre of St-Jean-Cap-Ferrat (€1.50, 30 minutes).

☆ Entertainment

Opéra de Nice   OPERA
(✉04 92 17 40 79; www.opera-nice.org; 4-6 rue St-François de Paule) The vintage 1885 grande dame hosts opera, ballet and orchestral concerts.

Shapko   LIVE MUSIC
(✉06 15 10 02 52; www.shapkobar.fr; 5 rue Rossetti; ⊙6pm-2.30am) Near the cathedral square, Shapko stages live music nightly in a variety of genres: blues, funk, jazz, R&B, soul, rock and more. Happy hour runs from 6pm to 9pm.

Wayne's   LIVE MUSIC
(✉04 93 13 46 99; www.waynes.fr; 15 rue de la Préfecture; ⊙10am-2am) One of a strip of raucous drinking holes on the edge of the old town, Wayne's is a proper pub, through and through: plenty of beers on tap, a nightly roster of bands and big-screen sports action. Scruffy as it comes, but great fun if that's what you're in the mood for.

🛍 Shopping

Shops abound in Nice, ranging from the boutiques of Vieux Nice and the New Town's designer fashion temples to the enormous Nice Étoile shopping mall. For vintage fashion and contemporary art, meander the hip Petit Marais near place Garibaldi. For gourmet gifts to take home, head for Vieux Nice, where you'll find olive oil, wine, candied fruits and much more.

★ Maison Auer   FOOD
(✉04 93 85 77 98; www.maison-auer.com; 7 rue St-François de Paule; ⊙9am-6pm Tue-Sat) With its gilded counters and mirrors, this opulent shop – run by the same family for five generations – looks more like a 19th-century boutique than a sweets shop, but this is where discerning Niçois have been buying their *fruits confits* (crystallised fruit) and *amandes chocolatées* (chocolate-covered almonds) since 1820.

Cave de la Tour   WINE
(✉04 93 80 03 31; www.cavedelatour.com; 3 rue de la Tour; ⊙7am-8pm Tue-Sat, to 12.30pm Sun) Since 1947, locals have been trusting the owners of this atmospheric *cave* (wine cellar) to find the best wines from across the Alpes-Maritimes and Var. It's a ramshackle kind of place, with upturned wine barrels and blackboard signs, and a loyal clientele, including market traders and fishmongers getting their early-morning wine fix. Lots of wines are available by the glass.

Friperie Caprice   VINTAGE
(✉09 83 48 05 43; www.facebook.com/Caprice VintageShop; 12 rue Droite; ⊙2-7pm Mon, 11am-1.30pm & 2.30-7pm Tue-Sat) Nice's favourite vintage shop is a treasure trove of clothing, jewellery and accessories spanning much of the 20th century; what really sets it apart is the generous advice and assistance of amiable owner Madame Caprice, who knows every piece in the shop.

ℹ Information

Tourist Office (☑ 04 92 14 46 14; www.
nicetourisme.com; 5 Promenade des Anglais;
⊙9am-7pm daily Jun-Sep, to 6pm Mon-Sat
Oct-May; ☎; ▣ 8, 52, 62 to Massenet) Nice's
main tourist office on Promenade des Anglais
provides a wealth of resources, including maps,
brochures, information about attractions and
help booking accommodation.

ℹ Getting There & Away

AIR

Nice-Côte d'Azur Airport (NCE; ☑ 08 20 42
33 33; www.nice.aeroport.fr; ☎, ▣ 98, 99,
▣ 2) is France's second-largest airport and has
international flights to Europe, North Africa
and the USA, with regular and low-cost airlines.
The airport has two terminals, linked by a free
shuttle bus.

BOAT

Corsica Ferries (☑ 04 92 00 42 76; www.corsi-
caferries.com; quai du Commerce; ▣ 2 to Port
Lympia) and **Moby Lines** (☑ 08 00 90 11 44;
www.mobylines.fr; Quai du Commerce; ▣ 2 to
Port Lympia) offer regular ferry services from
Nice to Corsica. Corsica Ferries also serves
Golfo Aranci in Sardinia.

BUS

Lignes d'Azur (☑ 08 10 06 10 06; www.lignes-
dazur.com) operates an excellent intercity bus
service from Nice; tickets cost just €1.50.
Bus 100 (place de l'Île de Beauté; ▣ 2 to Port
Lympia) To Menton (1¼ to 1½ hours) via the
Corniche Inférieure and Monaco (45 minutes).
Bus 200 (av de Verdun) To Cannes (1½ to 1¾
hours).
Bus 400 (av de Verdun) To Vence (70 minutes)
via St-Paul de Vence (one hour).
Bus 500 (av de Verdun) To Grasse (1½ hours).
Eurolines (☑ 08 92 89 90 91; www.eurolines.fr;
27 rue de l'Hotel des Postes; ▣ 7, 9 to Wilson)
serves long-haul European destinations.

ℹ Getting Around

TO/FROM THE AIRPORT

Nice-Côte d'Azur airport is about 7km west of
Nice, by the sea. The following buses depart
from there:
Buses 98 and 99 link the airport's terminal
with Promenade des Anglais and Nice train
station respectively (€6, 35 minutes, every 20
minutes).
Bus 110 (one way/return €22/33) links the
airport with Monaco (45 minutes, half-hourly)
and Menton (1¼ hours, hourly).
Bus 210 goes to Cannes (one way/return
€22/33, 50 minutes, half-hourly).

Bus 250 goes to Antibes (one way/return
€11/16.50, 40 minutes, half-hourly).
From 2019, Nice's new east–west tram line
2 will provide direct services from the airport
to Nice's port (26 minutes), with intermediate
stops granting access to other city centre
destinations.
Taxis from the airport to Nice's centre charge a
flat rate of €32.

BICYCLE

Vélo Bleu (☑ 04 93 72 06 06; www.velobleu.
org) is Nice's shared-bicycle service. It's great
value and very convenient for getting round
town, with 100-plus stations around the city –
pick up your bike at one, return it at another.
One-day/weeklong subscriptions cost
€1.50/5, plus usage: free for the first 30 minutes, €1 for the next 30, then €2 per hour thereafter. Some stations are equipped with terminals
to register directly with a credit card; otherwise
you'll need a mobile phone.
The handy Vélo Bleu app allows you to find
your nearest station, gives real-time information
about the number of bikes available at each and
calculates itineraries.

BUS & TRAM

Buses and trams in Nice are run by **Lignes
d'Azur**. Tickets cost just €1.50 and include one
connection, including intercity buses within
the Alpes-Maritimes *département*. If you're
using Nice's buses and trams a lot, consider
purchasing a money-saving all-day ticket or
multi-day pass. Buses are particularly handy
for getting to the Musée Matisse and Musée
Chagall in Cimiez.
Buses typically run every 10 to 15 minutes
between 6am and 9pm. Between 9pm and 1am
or 2am, night buses – numbered N1 to N5 and
running every 30 to 60 minutes – fan out to
various destinations around the city from their
central terminus at **Promenade des Arts**.
Bus stops throughout the city have clear signs
indicating which buses stop there. Tickets can
be purchased at machines on the platform or
on board the bus. All tickets (including day and
week passes) must be validated at the beginning
of each ride by inserting them into the machines
provided on board.

CAR & MOTORCYCLE

Traffic, a confusing one-way system, and pricey
parking mean driving in Nice is a bad idea – it's
better to explore the city first, then head back
out to the airport and rent your car for onward
travel there.
Holiday Bikes (☑ 04 93 16 01 62; www.loca-
bike.fr; 34 av Auber; 24hr rental 50cc/125cc
scooter from €32/57; ⊙ 9.30am-12.30pm &
2.30-6.30pm Mon-Sat year-round, plus 10am-
noon & 5-6.30pm Sun Jun-Aug; ▣ 1 to Gare

Thiers) rents out scooters and motorcycles. It has another **office** (☑ 04 93 04 15 36; 6 rue Massenet; ⊙ 9.30am-12.30pm & 2.30-6.30pm Mon-Sat year-round, plus 10am-noon & 5-6.30pm Sun Jun-Aug; ☐ 8, 52, 62 to Massenet) just off the Promenade des Anglais.

CANNES

POP 74,285

Glamorous Cannes sets camera flashes popping at its film festival in May, when stars pose in tuxes and full-length gowns on the red carpet. But the glitz doesn't end there. Throughout the year, as you walk among the designer bars, couture shops and palaces of La Croisette, the wealth and glamour of this city cannot fail to impress. Admiring Ferraris and Porsches and celebrity-spotting on the chic sunlounger-striped beaches and liner-sized yachts moored at the port are perennial Cannes pastimes.

Whether Cannes' soul has managed to survive its celebrity-playground status is another question, but there's still enough natural beauty to make a trip worthwhile: the harbour, the bay, the clutch of offshore islands and the old quarter, Le Suquet, all spring into life on a sunny day. And with the city's famous beaches benefiting from a serious facelift in 2019, there's suddenly lots more space to lay your towel!

NEW BEACH BUILD

At the time of writing, Cannes was undertaking its largest urban renewal project since 1960 – and the city's beaches are the lucky beneficiaries! In phase one of the project, barges have been hauling in boatloads of new sand (95,000 cu metres to be exact) to significantly enlarge Plage de la Croisette and protect it from erosion. When work is completed (scheduled for April 2019), the average beach width will have effectively doubled, to 40m.

Phases two and three, scheduled for completion by 2022, call for further beautification of Cannes' public spaces, with a new emphasis on aesthetic harmony and accessibility, including the widening of pedestrian walkways and bike lanes. Stay tuned!

⊙ Sights

★ La Croisette   ARCHITECTURE

The multi-starred hotels and couture shops lining the iconic bd de la Croisette (aka La Croisette) may be the preserve of the rich and famous, but anyone can enjoy strolling the palm-shaded promenade – a favourite pastime among Cannois at night, when it twinkles with bright lights. Views of the Baie de Cannes and nearby Estérel mountains are beautiful, and seafront hotel palaces dazzle in all their stunning art deco glory.

Palais des Festivals et des Congrès   LANDMARK

(Festival & Congress Palace; 1 bd de la Croisette; guided tour adult/child €6/free) Posing for a selfie on the 22 steps leading up to the main entrance of this concrete bunker – unlikely host to the world's most glamorous film festival – at the western end of La Croisette is an essential Cannes experience. Afterwards, wander along the **Allée des Étoiles du Cinéma**, a footpath of 46 celebrity hand imprints in the pavement; it begins with the hands of Meryl Streep in front of the tourist office.

The only way to enter the festival building and walk into the auditorium, tread the stage and learn about cinema's most glamorous event is with a **Palais des Festivals guided tour** (☑ 04 92 99 84 22; www.cannes-destination.com/guided-tour/visit-palais-festival-cannes; adult/child €6/free) organised by the Cannes tourist office. Check dates and get booking instructions on the tourist office website.

La Malmaison   NOTABLE BUILDING

(☑ 04 97 06 44 90, 04 97 06 45 21; www.cannes.com/fr/culture/centre-d-art-la-malmaison.html; 47 bd de la Croisette; ⊙ 10am-7pm daily Jul-Sep, 10am-1pm & 2-6pm Tue-Sun Oct-Apr, closed May & Jun) On La Croisette, La Malmaison is a seaside pavilion in the former games and tea room of Cannes' grandest hotel of the 1860s, the Grand Hôtel (opened in 1864, shut in 1950, then demolished and rebuilt in the 1960s). Modern art exhibitions fill part of La Malmaison today; admission price varies depending on the exhibit.

Le Suquet   HISTORIC SITE

Follow rue St-Antoine and snake your way up through the narrow streets of Le Suquet, Cannes' oldest district. Up top you'll find the site of Cannes' medieval castle, place de la Castre, flanked by the 17th-century Église Notre-Dame de l'Esperance. Climb the adjacent ramparts for great views of the bay.

CANNES DAY TRIPPER

For a culturally enriching day trip, head to the towns of Cagnes-sur-Mer, Ville-neuve-Loubet and Le Cannet – all within 15 to 30 minutes of Cannes – where you'll find a trio of highlights.

Just outside Cagnes-sur-Mer, the evocative **Musée Renoir** (☑ 04 93 20 61 07; www.cagnes-tourisme.com; chemin des Colettes, Cagnes-sur-Mer; adult/child €6/free; ⊙ 10am-1pm & 2-6pm Jun-Sep, 10am-noon & 2-6pm Apr & May, to 5pm Oct-Mar, closed Tue year-round) is housed in the Domaine des Collettes, former home and studio to an arthritis-crippled Pierre-Auguste Renoir (1841–1919), who lived here with his wife and three sons from 1907 until his death. Works of his on display include *Les Grandes Baigneuses* (The Women Bathers; 1892), a reworking of the 1887 original, and rooms are dotted with photographs and personal possessions. The magnificent olive and citrus groves are as much an attraction as the museum itself. Many visitors set up their own easel to paint.

Equally wonderful is **Musée Escoffier de l'Art Culinaire** (Escoffier Museum of Culinary Arts; ☑ 04 93 20 80 51; http://fondation-escoffier.org; 3 rue Auguste Escoffier, Ville-neuve-Loubet; adult/child €6/free; ⊙ 10am-1pm & 2-7pm daily Jun-Sep, to 6pm Oct-May), which retraces the history of modern gastronomy. Auguste Escoffier (1846–1935), inventor of the *pêche Melba* among other things, was France's first great chef and a celebrity among Europe's well heeled.

Finally, there's Le Cannet's **Musée Bonnard** (☑ 04 93 94 06 06; www.museebonnard.fr; 16 bd Sadi Carnot, Le Cannet; adult/child €5/3.50; ⊙ 10am-6pm Tue-Sun Sep-Jun, to 8pm Jul & Aug), in a restored belle époque villa with a striking contemporary extension. Instantly recognisable by their intense colour, the works of neo-impressionist painter Pierre Bonnard (1867–1947) form the backbone of the museum's permanent collection. Bonnard arrived in Le Cannet fresh from Paris in 1910 and lived in a seafront villa with his wife, Martha, until his death. It was in Le Cannet that Bonnard painted his best works, including several landscapes of St-Tropez, Antibes and other Riviera resorts.

🏖 Beaches

Cannes is blessed with sandy beaches, although much of the bd de la Croisette stretch is taken up by private enterprises, leaving just a small strip of free sand near the Palais des Festivals for the bathing hoi polloi.

Z Plage BEACH
(☑ 04 93 90 12 34; 73 bd de la Croisette; ⊙ 9.30am-6pm Apr-Sep, to 7pm Jul & Aug) Expect to pay €60/45/70 in July and August (€40/30/50 in other months) for the blue sunloungers on the front row/other rows/pier of the super-stylish Z Plage, the beach of Hôtel Martinez. Booking ahead is advised.

Plage du Midi BEACH
(bd Jean Hibert) This urban beach just west of Vieux Port enjoys gorgeous sunset views across to the red rock formations of the Corniche de l'Esterel.

Plage Vegaluna BEACH
(☑ 04 93 43 67 05; www.vegaluna.com; La Croisette; sunloungers €15-25; ⊙ 9.30am-7pm; ⊕) Family-friendly private beach.

👉 Tours

Trans Côte d'Azur Cruises BOATING
(☑ 04 92 98 71 30; www.trans-cote-azur.com; quai Max Laubeuf) From June to September this boat company offers all-day cruises to St-Tropez (adult/child return €50/40) and Monaco (€54/40). Shorter two-hour cruises set sail for the Corniche d'Or (€27/18), where you can take in the dramatic contrasts of the Estérel's red cliffs, green forests and intense azure waters.

🎉 Festivals & Events

Cannes lives for music in the summer, so come prepared to party hard.

Festival de Cannes FILM
(www.festival-cannes.com; ⊙ May) Cannes' world-famous celebration of cinema. You won't get in to any of the premieres, but it's still fun because you see all the celebs walking around.

Festival d'Art Pyrotechnique FIREWORKS
(www.festival-pyrotechnique-cannes.com; ⊙ Jul & Aug) Around 200,000 people cram onto La Croisette every summer to admire the

Cannes

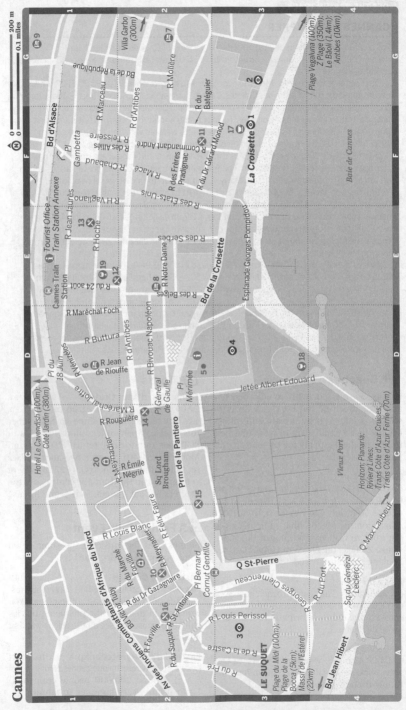

Cannes

outstanding fireworks display over the Baie de Cannes. Magical. Held on six nights in July and August (see the website for exact dates).

Les Plages Électroniques MUSIC
(www.plages-electroniques.com; 1-day pass €30-37, 2-/3-day pass €57/77; ⊙ Aug) DJs spin on the sand at the Plage du Palais des Festivals during this relaxed festival, held over a three-day weekend in mid-August.

🛏 Sleeping

Cannes is an important conference centre, and when an event swings into town (there are a dozen or so during the year, including the film festival), hotels book up and prices soar. Many hotels sell out in summer as well, so plan ahead. During film-festival season you won't be able to find a bed for love nor money, but you can always stay in nearby Nice and catch the train to Cannes.

★ **Hôtel de Provence** HOTEL €€
(☑ 04 93 38 44 35; www.hotel-de-provence.com; 9 rue Molière; s €93-140, d €110-247, ste €246-340; ⊙ closed mid-Jan–early Mar; ❄ 🕸) This traditional Provençal townhouse with buttermilk walls, lavender-blue shutters and a palm-lined entryway disguises a minimalist-chic interior. Almost every room sports a balcony, climaxing with a 7th-floor suite with stunning rooftop terrace. The Provence also has self-catering studios in the neighbourhood for three to six people. Breakfast costs €10.80.

Hôtel Alnea HOTEL €€
(☑ 04 93 68 77 77; www.hotel-alnea.com; 20 rue Jean de Riouffe; s €79-120, d €85-145; ❄ 🕸) A breath of fresh air in a town of stars, Noémi and Cédric's hotel offers bright, colourful two-star rooms, original paintings and numerous little details, such as the afternoon coffee break, the honesty bar, and the bike or boules (to play *pétanque*) loans. Book directly with the hotel to save 15% over other internet booking sites.

Hôtel Le Mistral BOUTIQUE HOTEL €€
(☑ 04 93 39 91 46; www.mistral-hotel.com; 13 rue des Belges; r €89-159; ❄ 🕸) For super-pricey Cannes, this little three-star offers amazing value. The 10 rooms are small but decked out in flattering red and plum tones – Privilege rooms have quite a bit more space, plus a fold-out sofa bed. There are sea views from two rooms on the 4th floor, and the hotel is just 50m from La Croisette. There's no lift, though.

Hôtel Villa Claudia HOTEL €€
(☑ 04 93 38 34 33; www.villa-claudia-cannes.com; 37 bd d'Alsace; d €100-190; ❄ 🕸) Completely renovated in 2018, this dusky rose villa just east of the train station offers comfortable, refined digs within easy walking distance of everything. The high-ceilinged rooms are hung with photos of film stars, and there's a pleasant outdoor patio for soaking up the sun. Reserve ahead for hassle-free parking in the enclosed courtyard (€10 per night).

Hotel Le Cavendish HERITAGE HOTEL €€€
(☑ 04 97 06 26 00; www.cavendish-cannes.com; 11 bd Carnot; d €170-310) With its rotunda rooms and Napoleon III–era architecture, this grand dame of a hotel can't fail to impress. It's classic in style – plenty of taffeta, tassels and swags, and a monumental marble staircase – but there's a civilised air of old-world grandeur about the place, with special touches such as complimentary evening aperitifs and a private beach on La Croisette.

ISLAND ESCAPES

Although just 20 minutes away by boat, Cannes' tranquil Îles de Lérins islands feel far from the madding crowd. Île Ste-Marguerite, where the mysterious Man in the Iron Mask was incarcerated during the late 17th century, is known for its bone-white beaches, eucalyptus groves and small marine museum. Tiny Île St-Honorat has been a monastery since the 5th century; you can visit the church and small chapels and stroll through the monks' vineyards.

Boats leave Cannes from quai des Îles on the western side of the harbour. **Trans Côte d'Azur** (☑04 92 98 71 30; www.trans-cote-azur.com; quai Max Laubeuf), **Riviera Lines** (☑04 92 98 71 31; www.riviera-lines.com; quai Max Laubeuf) and **Horizon** (☑04 92 98 71 36; www.horizon-lerins.com; quai Laubeuf) all run ferries to Île Ste-Marguerite, while **Planaria** (☑04 92 98 71 38; www.cannes-ilesdelerins.com; quai Max Laubeuf) covers Île St-Honorat.

✘ Eating

Most private beaches have restaurants, which are particularly delightful on warm sunny days, although you pay for the privilege of eating *les pieds dans l'eau* (on the waterfront). Expect to pay around €25 to €30 for a main of grilled fish or meat, or a gourmet salad.

Several streets just inland, such as rue Hoche, are filled with restaurants and bistros. Cheaper eats can be found in and around Cannes' atmospheric food market, Marché Forville.

★ PhilCat   SANDWICHES €
(☑04 93 38 43 42; promenade de la Pantiéro; sandwiches & salads €3.50-5.50; ⏰7am-7pm mid-Mar–Oct; ✈) Phillipe and Catherine's prefab cabin on the waterfront is a perfect lunch spot. This is fast-food, Cannes-style – giant salads, toasted panini and the best *pan bagna* (€5.30; a gargantuan bun filled with tuna, onion, red pepper, lettuce and tomato, and dripping in olive oil) on the Riviera. The 'super' version (€5.50) throws anchovies into the mix.

La Boulangerie par Jean-Luc Pelé   BAKERY €
(☑04 93 99 45 82; www.jeanlucpele.com; 3 rue du 24 Août; sandwiches €5, lunch menus €5.50-10.50; ⏰7.30am-7.30pm Mon-Sat) This swanky bakery by Cannois *chocolatier* and *pâtissier* Jean-Luc Pelé casts a whole new spin on eating cheaply in Cannes. Creative salads, sandwiches, wraps and bagels – to eat in or out – burst with local flavours and provide the perfect prelude to the utterly sensational cakes and desserts Pelé is best known for.

Côté Jardin   BISTRO €
(☑04 93 38 60 28; www.facebook.com/pg/cote jardinbychristopheferre; 12 ave St-Louis; plats du jour €12-14, other mains €12-22; ⏰noon-2pm & 7-9.30pm Tue-Sat) Craving a break from Cannes' glitz and grandiosity? This down-to-earth bistro on a residential backstreet is the perfect antidote. Enjoy superb-value *plats du jour* in an enclosed garden overhung with flowering trees, the menu changing based on what chef Christian Ferré finds at the market: Provençal beef stew, chicken curry, codfish aïoli...all updated daily on the Facebook page.

★ Bobo Bistro   MEDITERRANEAN €€
(☑04 93 99 97 33; www.facebook.com/Bobo BistroCannes; 21 rue du Commandant André; pizzas €14-20, mains €18-31; ⏰noon-3pm & 7-11pm) Predictably, it's a 'bobo' (bourgeois bohemian) crowd that gathers at this achingly cool bistro in Cannes' fashionable Carré d'Or. Decor is stylishly retro, with attention-grabbing objets d'art including a tableau of dozens of spindles of coloured yarn. Cuisine is local, seasonal and invariably organic: artichoke salad, tuna carpaccio with passion fruit, roasted cod with mash *fait masion* (homemade).

Le Grain de Sel   BISTRO €€
(☑04 93 38 83 65; www.legraindesel-cannes.com; 25 rue Hoche; lunch menus €19, mains €24-32; ⏰noon-2pm Mon-Sat, 7-10pm Tue-Sat) Vietnamese-born, French-trained chef Nhut Nguyen is at the helm of this delightful new bistro on Cannes' pedestrianised restaurant row. The high-ceilinged interior dining room, done up with modern lighting and faux bookshelves, creates a relaxed backdrop for inventive offerings such as shrimp tempura with Provençal zucchini fritters or roast lamb with herbes de Provence, parsnip mousse, dates and candied lemon.

Aux Bons Enfants   FRENCH €€
(☑06 18 81 37 47; www.aux-bons-enfants-cannes.com; 80 rue Meynadier; 2-/3-course menus €24/31, mains €18; ⏰noon-2pm & 7-10pm Tue-Sat) A people's-choice place since 1935, this informal restaurant cooks up regional dishes, such as *aïoli*

garni (garlic and saffron mayonnaise served with fish and vegetables), *daube* (a Provençal beef stew) and *rascasse meunière* (pan-fried rockfish), all in a convivial atmosphere. No credit cards or reservations.

New York, New York BRASSERIE €€
(☎04 93 06 78 27; www.nynycannes.com; 1 allée de la Liberté; pizzas €13-19, mains €18-39; ⏲8.30am-11pm; 📶✍) Very trendy and very popular, this Manhattan-style diner with its vast front terrace is a favourite hang-out for Cannes' young and beautiful crowd, who tuck into huge pizzas, steaks, club sandwiches and gourmet burgers. The bare brick and industrial decor are straight outta Brooklyn, but the setting is classic Côte d'Azur.

★**Table 22** MODERN EUROPEAN €€€
(Mantel; ☎04 93 39 13 10; www.restaurantmantel.com; 22 rue St-Antoine; menus €39-65, mains €35-46; ⏲noon-2pm Wed-Sun, 7.30-10pm daily) Discover why Noël Mantel is the hotshot of the Cannois gastronomic scene at his refined old-town restaurant. Service is stellar and the seasonally inspired cuisine divine – Mantel's food maximises local ingredients but isn't afraid to experiment with unusual flavours and cooking techniques. Spot the classic film stars on the walls, from Cary Grant to Alfred Hitchcock.

Drinking & Nightlife

Going out in Cannes is taken seriously: dress to impress.

Bars around the Carré d'Or (Golden Sq) – bordered by rue Commandant André, rue des Frères Pradignac, rue du Batéguier and rue du Dr Gérard Monod – tend to be young, trendy and busy. Beach and hotel bars are more upmarket. Download the free **Cannes Agenda** app (www.cannes.com/fr/mairie/espace-communication/le-mois-a-cannes.html) for listings.

★**L'Epicurieux** WINE BAR
(☎04 93 99 93 94; 6 rue des Frères Casanova; ⏲10am-10pm Mon-Thu, to 11pm Fri & Sat) A cosy little spot for a glass or two of a local vintage – the wine list here is great, with hand-picked choices from local *domaines*

STARRING AT CANNES

For 12 days in May, all eyes turn to Cannes, centre of the cinematic universe, where 33,000 producers, distributors, directors, publicists, stars and hangers-on descend to buy, sell or promote more than 2000 films. As the premier film event of the year, the Festival de Cannes (p863) attracts around 4000 journalists from all over the world.

At the centre of the whirlwind is the colossal, 60,000-sq-metre Palais des Festivals (p862), where the official selections are screened. The palace opened in 1982, replacing the original Palais des Festivals – since demolished. The inaugural festival was scheduled for 1 September 1939, as a response to Mussolini's fascist-propaganda film festival in Venice, but Hitler's invasion of Poland brought the festival to an abrupt end. It restarted in 1946 – and the rest is history.

Over the years the festival split into 'in competition' and 'out of competition' sections. The goal of 'in competition' films is the prestigious Palme d'Or, awarded to the festival's best film as chosen by the jury and its president. Notable winners include Francis Ford Coppola's *Apocalypse Now* (1979), Quentin Tarantino's cult *Pulp Fiction* (1994) and American activist Michael Moore's anti-Bush-administration polemic *Fahrenheit 9/11* (2004). More recent winners include *La Classe* (2008), a film by Laurent Cantet about teaching in tough Parisian suburbs; *Dheepan* (2015) by French director Jacques Audiard, which tells the tale of how a former Tamil Tiger from Sri Lanka gains asylum in France and *Shoplifters* (2018), by Japanese director Hirokazu Kore-eda, about an impoverished family that takes in an abused girl.

The vast majority of films are 'out of competition'. Behind the scenes the **Marché du Film** (www.marchedufilm.com) sees nearly $1 billion worth of business negotiated in distribution deals. And it's this hard-core commerce, combined with all the televised Tinseltown glitz, that gives the film festival its special magic.

Tickets to the film festival are off limits to average Joes. What you can get are same-day free tickets to selected individual films, usually after their first screening. Availability is limited, and all arrangements must be made through **Cannes Cinéma** (☎04 97 06 45 15; www.cannes-cinema.com; 10 av de Vallauris; ⏲10am-noon & 2-4pm).

DON'T MISS

PICNIC PERFECT

Marché Forville (11 rue du Marché Forville; ⊙ 7.30am-1pm Tue-Fri, to 2pm Sat & Sun) For local culture, head to Cannes' busy food market, a couple of blocks back from the port. In the biz since 1934, it is one of the most important markets in the region and the supplier of choice for restaurants – and for your beach picnic! On Monday the food stalls are replaced by an all-day *brocante* (flea market).

Fromagerie Ceneri (☑ 04 93 39 63 68; www.fromagerie-ceneri.com; 22 rue Meynadier; ⊙ 10am-6pm Mon, 8am-7pm Tue-Sat, 8.30am-12.30pm Sun) With cowbells strung from the wooden ceiling, and a stunning array of cheeses, this is the only place to shop for dairy products in Cannes. A master *fromager-affineur* (cheesemonger and ripener) in business since 1968, Ceneri is a rare and precious breed on the Riviera. Its selection of *chèvre* (goat's cheese) from Provence is second to none.

including Côtes de Provence and Côtes du Rhône. Bistro snacks and live bands at weekends make it doubly attractive.

Armani Caffè   CAFE
(☑ 04 93 99 44 05; www.armanirestaurants. com/cannes-armani-caffe; 42 bd de la Croisette; ⊙ 8.30am-7pm Mon-Sat) The al fresco cafe of Italian fashion design house Armani is predictably chic, stylish and full of panache. Sit beneath taupe parasols in a prettily manicured garden and enjoy the comings and goings of La Croisette over a chilled glass of prosecco (€10). Salads, pasta and panini too.

Gotha Club   CLUB
(☑ 04 93 45 11 11; www.gotha-club.com; place Franklin Roosvelt, Casino Palm Beach; cover €25-50; ⊙ midnight-dawn May, Jul & Aug) Only open in May during the film festival and again in July and August, this club is a hot ticket in DJ land. Bringing together some of the most happening names in music with a spectacular setting at the seafaring end of La Croisette, Gotha is a glitzy VIP favourite. Door policy is tight: no guys without girls and only fabulous-looking people.

KA Club   BAR
(☑ 07 60 17 20 10; www.ka-cannes.com; 1 jetée Albert Edouard; ⊙ 7.30pm-5am daily May-Sep, Thu-Sat Oct-Apr) Perched atop the Palais des Festivals, this trendy bar and club with dropdead Mediterranean views is one of Cannes' choicest and chicest nightspots. Sunset on the rooftop terrace is not to be missed, and DJs keep things hopping till dawn.

Bâoli   CLUB
(☑ 04 93 43 03 43; www.baolicannes.com; Port Pierre Canto, bd de la Croisette; ⊙ 8pm-6am Fri & Sat) This is Cannes' coolest, trendiest and most selective nightspot – so selective, in fact,

that your entire posse might not get in unless you're dressed to the nines. It's part club, part restaurant, so one way to ensure you'll get in is to book a table and make a night of it. Located at the eastern end of La Croisette.

ℹ Information

Tourist Office (☑ 04 92 99 84 22; www. cannes-destination.fr; 1 bd de la Croisette; ⊙ 9am-7pm Mar-Oct, to 8pm Jul & Aug, 10am-6pm Nov-Feb; 🛜) Runs the informative 'Once Upon a Time: Cannes' guided walking tour (€6) in English at 9.15am (June to September) or 2.30pm (October to May) every Monday, as well as a host of fun themed tours (in English).

Tourist Office – Train Station Annexe (8 bis place de la Gare; ⊙ 9am-1pm & 2-6pm Mon-Sat)

ℹ Getting There & Around

BUS

From bus stops in front of Cannes' train station, **Lignes d'Azur** (p861) runs express services to Nice (bus 200; €1.50, 1¾ hours, every 15 minutes), Nice-Côte d'Azur airport (bus 210; one way/return €22/23, 50 minutes, half-hourly), Mougins (bus 600; €1.50, 25 minutes, every 20 minutes) and Grasse (bus 600; €1.50, one hour).

Palmbus (☑ 08 25 82 55 99; www.palmbus. fr) operates local buses serving Cannes and the surrounding region from a separate **bus station** (place Bernard Cornut Gentille) near the waterfront.

BICYCLE

Mistral Location (☑ 06 20 33 87 64, 04 93 39 33 60; www.mistral-location.com; 4 rue Georges Clémenceau) rents out bicycles/scooters for €20/30 per day.

TRAIN

Cannes' gleaming white train station is well connected with other towns along the coast.

Antibes €3.10, 12 minutes, at least twice hourly

Marseille €33, 2¼ hours, half-hourly
Monaco €10, one hour, at least twice hourly
Nice €7.20, 40 minutes, every 15 minutes
St-Raphaël €7.60, 30 minutes, hourly

ANTIBES

POP 76,119

With its boat-bedecked port, 16th-century ramparts and narrow cobblestone streets festooned with flowers, it's little wonder that lovely Antibes has stolen the hearts of so many artists and writers: they include Graham Greene, Max Ernst and Picasso, who featured the town in many paintings and now has a museum dedicated to him here.

Only Antibes' attractive old town would be recognisable to any of its famous former residents. The modern town, like many along the Riviera, has sprawled rather unbecomingly along the coast and inland, so the best vantage point is from the sea – ideally in one of the many posh yachts that pull into port throughout summer, or from the long series of beaches south of town.

Beyond the city limits, save some time to explore beautiful **Cap d'Antibes**, a wooded cape studded with seaside mansions and pretty walking trails.

Sights

Vieil Antibes   HISTORIC SITE
Ringed by sturdy medieval walls and crisscrossed with lanes and shady squares, old Antibes is a delightful place for a wander. The wonderful **Marché Provençal** (cours Masséna; ⊙7am-1pm Tue-Sun Sep-Jun, daily Jul & Aug) is old Antibes' beating heart, sheltered by a 19th-century cast-iron roof and packed with stalls selling olives, cheese, vegetables, tapenades and other Provençal goodies until around 1pm.

Musée Picasso   MUSEUM
(☑04 92 90 54 26; www.antibes-juanlespins.com/culture/musee-picasso; Château Grimaldi, 4 rue des Cordiers; adult/concession €6/3; ⊙10am-6pm Tue-Sun mid-Jun–mid-Sep, 10am-1pm & 2-6pm Tue-Sun rest of year) Picasso himself said, 'If you want to see the Picassos from Antibes, you have to see them in Antibes'. The 14th-century Château Grimaldi was Picasso's studio from July to December 1946 and now houses an excellent collection of his works and fascinating photos of him. The sheer variety – lithographs, paintings, drawings and ceramics – shows how versatile and curious

an artist Picasso was. The museum also has a room dedicated to Nicolas de Staël, another painter who adopted Antibes as home.

Fort Carré   MONUMENT
(☑04 92 90 52 13; av 11 Novembre; guided tour adult/child €3/free; ⊙10am-1pm & 2-6pm Tue-Sun Jun-Oct, 10am-12.30pm & 1.30-4.30pm Tue-Sun Nov-May) The impregnable 16th-century Fort Carré, enlarged by Vauban in the 17th century, dominates the approach to Antibes from Nice. It served as a border defence post until 1860, when Nice, until then in Italian hands, became French. Tours depart half-hourly; some guides speak English.

Jardin Botanique de la Villa Thuret   GARDENS
(☑04 97 21 25 00; www6.sophia.inra.fr/jardin_thuret; 90 chemin Raymond; ⊙8am-6pm Mon-Fri Jun-Sep, 8.30am-5.30pm Mon-Fri Oct-May) **FREE** In the centre of Cap d'Antibes, this serene, 3.5-hectare botanical garden was created in 1856 and showcases 2500 species – the perfect opportunity to study the sun-rich cape's lush and invariably exotic flora up close.

☂ Beaches

Plage de la Gravette   BEACH
(quai Henri Rambaud) Right in the centre of Antibes, you'll find Plage de la Gravette, a small patch of sand by the *remparts* (ramparts).

Plage de la Garoupe   BEACH
This stretch of Cap d'Antibes was first raked clear of seaweed in 1922 by Cole Porter and American artist Gerald Murphy to create a sandy beach. Its golden sand is shared today by a small public beach overlooked by the excellent-value terrace of **Le Rocher** (☑04 93 67 51 36; 925 chemin de la Garoupe, Plage de la Garoupe; crepes €11-16, salads & mains €15-20; ⊙9am-6pm) and the private **Plage Keller** (with white-tablecloth dining, and sun loungers on a jetty).

Plage de la Salis   BEACH
This beach, with unbeatable views of old Antibes and the Alps, is 20 minutes from Antibes.

🛏 Sleeping

Old Antibes has some pleasant hotels, but things get seriously pricey once you head out towards Cap d'Antibes.

Hôtel La Jabotte   B&B €€
(☑04 93 61 45 89; www.jabotte.com; 13 av Max Maurey; d €154-214, q €254; 🅿 @ 🖣) Just 150m inland from Plage de la Salis and 2km south of the old town towards Cap d'Antibes, this

AN AFTER-DARK STROLL

Stroll along the rampart walkway to the harbour, where luxury yachts jostle for the limelight with *Nomade* (2010), an 8m-tall sculpture of a man looking out to sea. The work of Catalan artist Jaume Plensa, the mirage-like **Bastion St-Jaume** (quai Henri Rambaud; ⏰10am-11pm Jun-Aug, to 6pm Sep-May) is built from thousands of white letters and is lit at night – a magnificent sight. It squats on the terrace of the Bastion St-Jaume, the former site of a Roman temple, a 17th-century fortified tower and, until 1985, a shipyard.

pretty little hideaway makes a cosy base. Hot pinks, sunny yellows and soothing mauves dominate the homey, feminine decor, and there's a sweet patio where breakfast is served on sunny days. There's a minimum stay of three nights in summer.

Le Relais du Postillon HOTEL €€
(☎04 93 34 20 77; www.relaisdupostillon.com; 8 rue Championnet; s from €65, d €85-149; ⏰reception 7.30am-11pm; ❀🐾) This stone-walled former coaching hotel has a great location opposite a small park and square on the edge of the old town. Rooms are rather charming, especially if you bag one at the front, which have their own dinky balconies overlooking the square. The ground-floor cafe is a lovely spot for breakfast, too.

Hôtel La Place HOTEL €€
(☎04 97 21 03 11; www.la-place-hotel.com; 1 av du 24 Août; d €89-195; ❀@🐾) It's rare to find contemporary chic decor and a warm, professional welcome next to a city bus station, but La Place does it awfully well. Its 14 rooms are spacious, stylish and dressed in soothing taupe and aubergine or aniseed green. Three have bijou balconies. Breakfast (€13) and an evening buffet of antipasti (€15) are served in the airy lounge.

✗ Eating

Vieil Antibes is the place to eat, both for atmosphere and for its diversity of restaurants. To build your own picnic, hit Antibes' **Fromagerie l'Etable** (☎04 93 34 51 42; 1 rue Sade; ⏰8am-1pm & 4-7pm Tue-Sat, 8am-1pm Sun) for cheese and deli products, and dazzling morning market Marché

Provençal (p869) for everything else. If you have access to your own kitchen, head down to the waterfront quai des Pêcheurs, where fishers sell their morning's catch from 9am to 12.30pm.

★**L'Atelier Jean-Luc Pelé** SANDWICHES €
(☎04 92 95 78 21; www.jeanlucpele.com; 27 rue de la République; sandwiches from €5; ⏰7am-7pm) This branch of Jean-Luc Pelé's stellar Cannes bakery is a welcome addition to Antibes' lunch line-up. Gourmet bagels, wraps, soups, quiches and sandwiches come in all kinds of creative combos (€7.50 to €11) including a drink and a sinful cake from the patisserie counter. There's also a divine array of chocolates.

La Badiane FUSION €
(☎04 93 34 45 41; 3 traverse du 24 Août; lunch menus €18-20, mains €13-15; ⏰11am-3pm Mon-Fri) The little side street behind Antibes' bus station has a clutch of great lunchtime restaurants, including this exotic Moroccan-tinged diner, which serves up yummy treats such as chicken tagine, crispy *pastillas* (filled pastries) and spicy quiches. Shame it's only open for lunch on weekdays.

★**Nacional** INTERNATIONAL €€
(☎04 93 61 77 30; www.restaurant-nacional-antibes.com; 61 place Nationale; tapas €8-21, mains €21-38; ⏰noon-2pm & 7-10pm Tue-Thu, to 10.30pm Fri & Sat) 'Beef & Wine' is the strapline of this contemporary wine-bar-styled space, so that should give you some idea of the focus here. It's popular for its burgers, steaks in pepper or port sauce, and other grilled meats. The in-crowd adores it for aperitifs and tapas, best sampled on the walled patio garden hidden away at the back.

l'Arazur FRENCH €€€
(☎04 93 34 75 60; www.larazur.fr; 8 rue des Palmiers; lunch menus €29-34, dinner menus €60; ⏰12.15-2pm Thu-Sun, 7.15-10pm Wed-Sun) After years polishing his skills in double- and triple-starred Michelin restaurants, young chef Lucas Marini recently launched his own gastronomic venture in Vieil Antibes' pedestrian zone. Fresh seafood, local veggies and classic Provençal ingredients are incorporated into dishes such as grilled squid with artichokes, candied lemon and olive powder. The stone-walled cellar is especially cosy; come at lunchtime for best value.

🍷 Drinking & Nightlife

Pedestrian bd d'Aguillon heaves with merry Anglophones falling out of the busy 'English' and 'Irish' pubs.

La Siesta Beach Club　　　　CLUB
(📞 04 93 33 31 31; www.joa-casino.com; 2000 rte du Bord de Mer; ⊙ 6pm-1am Sun-Thu, to 2am Fri & Sat mid-Jun–early Sep) This legendary establishment is famous up and down the coast for its summer beachside nightclub and late-night dancing under the stars. There are DJs nightly, plus live music on Fridays and Saturdays. Find it 4km north of Vieil Antibes on the D6098.

ℹ️ Information

Tourist Office (📞 04 22 10 60 10; www. antibesjuanlespins.com; 42 av Robert Soleau; ⊙ 9am-7pm daily Jul & Aug, 9.30am-12.30pm & 2-5pm Mon-Sat, 9am-1pm Sun Sep-Jun) By Antibes train station; an excellent source of tourist information and offers guided walking tours of old Antibes and 'Painters on the French Riviera' (adult/child €7/3.50).

ℹ️ Getting There & Away

BUS

The Nice–Cannes bus service (route 200, €1.50) operated by **Lignes d'Azur** (p861) has a **stop** (bd Général Vautrin) just west of Antibes' train station (cross the tracks via the pedestrian overpass).

Envibus (📞 04 89 87 72 00; www.envibus.fr) operates local bus services for Cap d'Antibes, Biot, Vence and St-Paul de Vence from a separate **bus station** (Gare Routière d'Antibes; place Guynemer; ⊙ ticket office 9am-12.30pm & 2-5pm Mon-Sat) on the western edge of Vieil Antibes, 700m south of Antibes' train station. Tickets cost €1 from machines or €1.50 from the bus driver.

TRAIN

Antibes' train station is on the main line between Nice (€4.80, 15 to 30 minutes, four hourly) and Cannes (€3.10, 10 to 15 minutes, four hourly).

MOUGINS & MOUANS-SARTOUX

Spiralling up its hilltop in the shape of a snail shell, pinprick Vieux Mougins looks almost too perfect to be real. Picasso discovered the medieval village in 1935 with lover Dora Marr and lived here with his final love, Jacqueline Roque, from 1961 until his death. Mougins has since become something of an elite location, with prestigious hotel-restaurants, the country's most-sought-after international school and Sophia Antipolis (France's Silicon Valley) nearby.

Nearby Mouans-Sartoux (population 10,490) is equally charming and more down to earth, with a cluster of popular eateries and its own excellent museum to explore.

◉ Sights

★ Musée d'Art Classique de Mougins　　　　GALLERY

(MACM; 📞 04 93 75 18 22; www.mouginsmusee.com; 32 rue Commandeur; adult/child €12/5; ⊙ 10am-6pm Oct-Jun, to 8pm Jul-Sep) The brainchild of compulsive art collector and British entrepreneur Christian Levett, this outstanding museum contains 600 works spanning 5000 years. The collection aims to show how ancient civilisations inspired neoclassical, modern and contemporary art, thus the collection is organised by civilisations – Roman, Greek and Egyptian – with antiquities juxtaposed with seminal modern works. The top floor is dedicated to armoury, with excellent interactive displays bringing to life the helmets, spears and shields. There's also a fascinating Roman and Greek coin collection.

Musée de la Photographie André Villers　　　　MUSEUM

(📞 04 93 75 85 67; Porte Sarrazine; ⊙ 10am-12.30pm & 2-6pm) **FREE** The small but perfectly formed Musée de la Photographie has some fascinating black-and-white photos of Picasso, snapped by celebrated photographers such as André Villers and Jacques Henri Lartigue. It also hosts regular exhibitions on anything from fashion to war photography.

DON'T MISS

JAZZ À JUAN

The beach resort of **Juan-les-Pins**, 2km southwest of Antibes, was famously the home of F Scott Fitzgerald, who lived here with his wife Zelda and daughter Scottie in 1926–27 (their house is now a posh hotel). The waterfront draws steady crowds of beachgoers in summer, along with music fans who descend en masse for the **Jazz à Juan** (www.jazzajuan.com; Les Jardins du Jazz, bd Baudoin; ⊙ mid-Jul) festival in July.

Espace de l'Art Concret   GALLERY
(www.espacedelartconcret.fr; Château de Mouans,
Mouans-Sartoux; adult/child €7/free; ⊙11am-7pm
daily Jul & Aug, 1-6pm Wed-Sun Sep-Jun) Modern-
art and architecture lovers shouldn't miss
Mouans-Sartoux' contemporary-art centre, housed in the 16th-century Château de
Mouans and the purpose-built Donation
Albers-Honegger extension, a brilliant and
brilliantly controversial lime-green concrete
block ferociously clashing with its historic
surroundings. All the old familiars (Eduar-
do Chillida, Yves Klein, Andy Warhol, César,
Philippe Starck) are here, along with lesser-known practitioners and temporary exhibitions. It's 4km northwest of Mougins.

★**Les Jardins du MIP**   GARDENS
(☑04 92 98 62 69; www.museesdegrasse.com; 979
chemin des Gourettes, Mouans-Sartoux; adult/child
€4/free, combo ticket incl MIP €6/free; ⊙10am-
7pm May-Aug, to 5.30pm Apr & Sep-Nov, closed
Dec-Mar) 🌿 These gorgeous gardens belonging to Grasse's Musée International de la
Parfumerie (p873) showcase plants used in
scent-making. Half the garden is displayed
as fields to show how roses, jasmine and lavender are grown; the other half is organised
by olfactory families (woody, floral, amber
etc), which you can rub and smell on your
way around. The gardens are 5km northwest
of Mougins and 10km southwest of Grasse
on the edge of the Mouans-Sartoux village.

It's half-price if you show your ticket for the
Musée International de la Parfumerie. From
Grasse bus station, take bus 20 (€1.50), oper-
ated by Sillages (sillages.paysdegrasse.fr).

🛏 Sleeping & Eating

★**Les Rosées**   B&B €€€
(☑04 92 92 29 64; www.lesrosees.com; 238 chemin
de Font Neuve; d €280-360; 🅿✳🛜🏊) You
know that dreamy Provençal getaway you've
been looking for? The one in the little village,
set among gardens filled with lavender and
honeysuckle, and peaceful wood-beamed
rooms looking out over Provençal hills? Well,
this place is it. Throw in luxuries including
Bose sound systems, designer bathrooms,
home-cooked food and a gorgeous pool, and
you really won't ever want to leave.

There's even a gypsy caravan in the garden if you're looking for something really
different.

★**Le Sot l'y Laisse**   PROVENCAL €€
(☑04 93 75 54 50; www.sotlylaisse.fr; 1 place Suzanne de Villeneuve, Mouans-Sartoux; lunch menus

€20-25, dinner menus €25-35, mains €17-28;
⊙noon-2pm & 7-10pm Thu-Mon) You won't
find a more authentic Provençal restaurant
than this place, on the shady town square of
Mouans-Sartoux, 4km northwest of Mougins.
The signature dish, a hearty chicken stew,
gives the place its name (it means 'the fool
leaves it there', referring to the juicy oyster
of meat most people miss in poultry). Fish,
meats and desserts are all superb.

★**L'Amandier**   MODERN FRENCH €€€
(☑04 93 90 00 91; www.amandier.fr; 48 av Jean-
Charles Mallet; lunch menus €22, dinner menus
€35-55; ⊙noon-2pm & 7-9.30pm; ✳) Young chef
Denis Fétisson has brought Roger Vergé's
baby back to its former glory. Set in an old
mill, it's considered casual in these parts,
but comes with chandeliers and breathtaking views. Various fixed-price meals let
you shape your culinary experience, but the
underlying theme is classic French. Lunch
menus (€22 including wine, coffee and mini-
desserts) offer outstanding value.

❶ Information

Tourist Office (☑04 92 92 14 00; www.
mougins-tourisme.com; 39 place des Patriotes;
⊙10am-7pm daily Jul & Aug, to 6pm daily Jun
& Sep, to 6pm Mon-Sat Apr & May, to 5pm
Mon-Sat Oct-Mar) Located at the entrance
of the old village. Pick up the free map to the
town's historic centre, and borrow a free set of
boules to play *pétanque* with the locals (or your
friends); just leave an ID.

❶ Getting There & Away

Bus 600 (€1.50), operated by **Lignes d'Azur**
(p861), runs every 20 minutes, connecting
Mougins and Mouans-Sartoux with Cannes (20
minutes) and Grasse (35 minutes). Drivers can
park free at the **Moulin de la Croix** car park at
the foot of town.

GRASSE

POP 50,937

Up in the hills to the north of Nice, the town
of Grasse has been synonymous with perfumery since the 16th century, and the town
is still home to around 30 makers – a few of
which offer guided tours of their factories,
and the chance to hone your olfactory skills.
The perfumes of Provence are something
that linger long after you leave for home –
especially if you happen to have bought a
few soaps, body sprays and *eaux de toilette*
to take home with you.

⊙ Sights

Fragonard's Usine Historique & Musée du Parfum
MUSEUM

(☑ 04 93 36 44 65; www.fragonard.com/fr/usines/musee-du-parfum; 20 bd Fragonard; ⊙9am-6pm) **FREE** At the entrance to the old town, next to the Jardin des Plantes, this ochre-coloured mansion is where the Fragonard perfumery began in 1926 – though perfumers were at work here as early as 1782. Guided visits take in the original equipment used for extraction and distilling, and end at the shop where you can buy Fragonard scents. Upstairs there's a small, self-guided Musée du Parfum (Perfume Museum) tracing perfume's history. Fragonard also offers 90-minute English-language perfume-making workshops (€65; book ahead).

★Musée International de la Parfumerie
MUSEUM

(MIP, ☑ 04 97 05 58 11; www.museesdegrasse.com; 2 bd du Jeu de Ballon; adult/child €4/free, combo ticket incl Les Jardins du MIP €6/free; ⊙10am-7pm May-Sep, to 5.30pm Oct-Apr; ⊕) This whiz-bang museum is a work of art: housed in an 18th-century mansion enlarged with a modern glass structure, it retraces three millennia of perfume history through beautifully presented artefacts (including Marie Antoinette's travelling case), bottles, videos, vintage posters, olfactive stations and explanatory panels. The museum offers interesting insights into how the industry developed in Grasse. Kids are well catered for with dedicated multimedia stations, a fragrant garden, a film testing sense of smell and a reconstructed 19th-century perfume shop.

Musée Fragonard
MUSEUM

(Collection Hélène et Jean-François Costa; ☑04 93 36 02 07; www.fragonard.com/fr/usines/musee-fragonard; 14 rue Jean Ossola; ⊙10am-6pm) **FREE** On Grasse's main pedestrian street, this small museum explores the work of Grassois painter Fragonard (1732–1806), whose risqué paintings of love scenes shocked and titillated 18th-century France with their licentiousness. Paintings by Marguerite Gérard (1761–1837), Fragonard's sister-in-law and protégée, and Jean-Baptiste Mallet (1759–1835), another Grasse native, fill other rooms on the 1st floor.

Musée Molinard
MUSEUM

(☑ 04 93 36 01 62; www.molinard.com; 60 bd Victor Hugo; ⊙9.30am-6.30pm Mon-Sat, 10am-6pm Sun) **FREE** Visitors can admire a fine collection of vintage perfume bottles and learn about perfume ingredients on a self-guided tour of this small museum tracing the 200-year history of Molinard, one of Grasse's longest-standing perfumeries. A more extensive guided tour takes you into Molinard's original 19th-century factory, where you'll see the historical distillery and the still-functioning soap factory. Afterwards you're invited to shop to your heart's content in the attached showroom. Molinard also runs an in-town boutique on place aux Aires.

Musée d'Art et d'Histoire de Provence
MUSEUM

(☑ 04 93 36 80 20; www.museesdegrasse.com; 2 rue Mirabeau; adult/child €2/free; ⊙10am-7pm May-Sep, to 5.30pm Oct-Apr) This local-history museum, at home since 1921 in an aristocratic *hôtel particulier* (mansion), is a wonderful evocation of life in the 18th century. Rooms are laid out pretty much as they were when the marquise of Clapiers-Cabris lived here – he loathed his mother, who lived opposite, so much that he had a Gorgon's head carved over his door to leer through her windows. Don't miss the ground-floor kitchen, decorative art collection and gardens with beautiful springtime wisteria. Admission also includes entry to the **Villa Musée Jean-Honoré Fragonard** (☑ 04 93 36 52 98; www.museesdegrasse.com/vmjhf/presentation; 23 blvd Fragonard; adult/child €2/free; ⊙1-7pm Jul, Aug & school holidays).

🛏 Sleeping & Eating

There is a dire lack of decent accommodation in Grasse town, but there are some lovely options in the surrounding countryside, especially around the nearby villages of Mougins, Mouans-Sartoux, Le Rouret and Cabris.

Le Mas du Naoc
B&B €€

(☑ 04 93 60 63 13; www.lemasdunaoc.com; 580 chemin du Migrané, Cabris; d €160-220, tr €230; ⊕≋) This vine-covered, 18th-century *chambre d'hôte* 6km west of Grasse slumbers in the shade of century-old olive, jasmine, fig and orange trees. Soft natural hues dress Sandra and Jérôme Maingret's three lovely rooms – all with access to fully equipped kitchens – and the coastal panorama from the pool is inspirational. No children under seven; minimum two-night stay April to October.

★Hotel du Clos
HOTEL €€€

(☑ 0493407885; www.hotel-du-clos.com; 3 Chemin des Écoles, Le Rouret; r €169-260; 🅿❄⊕≋) Hidden in the hills 10km east of Grasse, this

FLOWER FARM VISIT

For a different spin on Grasse's perfume production, plan a trip to **Domaine de Manon** (📞 06 12 18 02 69; www.le-domaine-de-manon.com; 36 chemin du Servan, Plascassier; adult/child €6/free), a lovely flower farm 7km southeast of the centre of Grasse. Centifolia roses and jasmine have been cultivated here for three generations, and the farm now supplies Dior exclusively. Tours only take place during flowering: Tuesday at 9am from early May to mid-June for roses, and late August to mid-October for jasmine; contact Carole Biancalana at domainedemanon@yahoo.fr or ring to reserve and verify times, which vary from year to year.

The farm is in the small village of Plascassier (officially part of Grasse). Head in the direction of Valbonne along the D4 as you leave Grasse, and then follow signs for 'Vieux Village' when you get to Plascassier. The *domaine* will be on your left.

village retreat began as a restaurant (now Michelin-starred) and has since expanded with a second bistro and this lovely hotel, housed in a 17th-century farmhouse and barn. It's effortlessly tasteful, with chic rooms, cosy country decor and swanky bathrooms. The best rooms have views over gardens and olive trees.

Café des Musées   MODERN FRENCH €
(1 rue Jean Ossola; lunch specials from €11; ⏰ 9am-6.30pm Mon-Sat, to 6pm Sun) This stylish, well-situated cafe is the perfect stop between sights for lunch (creative salads, carefully crafted daily specials, soup or pasta of the day) or a gourmet coffee break (€6 for crêpes with coffee, tea or *chocolat chaud*).

ℹ Information

Tourist Office (📞 04 93 36 66 66; www.grasse.fr; place de la Buanderie; ⏰ 9am-1pm & 2-5pm Mon-Fri, from 10am Sat; 📶) Takes reservations for guided tours and workshops of the perfume factories, and provides maps and information on the town. Adjacent to the Grasse bus station.

ℹ Getting There & Around

Local bus company **Lignes d'Azur** (p861) departs regularly from Grasse's **bus station** (place de la Buanderie). Fares for all destinations are a flat-rate €1.50. Bus 600 goes to Cannes (one hour, every 20 minutes) via Mouans-Sartoux (30 minutes) and Mougins (35 minutes). Bus 500 goes to Nice (1½ hours, hourly).

The train station is a short distance downhill from the centre; shuttle buses (€1.50) to 'Centre Ville' depart from in front of the train station. There are regular rail services to Nice (€9.60, one hour, hourly) via Cannes (€4.60, 25 minutes).

VENCE

POP 18,393

Some visitors only come to Vence to see Matisse's otherworldly Chapelle du Rosaire at the edge of town. Yet Vence deserves more than a flying visit. It's well worth lingering a while to explore the city's charming and well-preserved medieval centre, much of which dates back to the 13th century. Sample some of Vence's gastronomic talent on restaurant-fringed place du Peyra, stroll through lovely place du Frêne with its 500-year-old ash tree, or take time to appreciate the Marc Chagall mosaic in Vieux Vence's cathedral. A fruit-and-veg market fills place du Jardin several mornings a week, with antiques on Wednesday.

◉ Sights

★**Chapelle du Rosaire**   ARCHITECTURE
(Rosary Chapel; 📞 04 93 58 03 26; www.vence.fr/the-rosaire-chapel; 466 av Henri Matisse; adult/child €7/4; ⏰ 10am-noon & 2-6pm Tue, Thu & Fri, 2-6pm Wed & Sat Apr-Oct, to 5pm Nov-Mar) An ailing Henri Matisse moved to Vence in 1943 to be cared for by his former nurse and model, Monique Bourgeois, who'd since become a Dominican nun. She persuaded him to design this extraordinary chapel for her community. The artist designed everything from the decor to the altar and the priests' vestments. From the road, you can see the blue-and-white ceramic roof tiles, wrought-iron cross and bell tower. Inside, light floods through the glorious blue, green and yellow stained-glass windows.

Musée de Vence   MUSEUM
(Fondation Émile Hugues; 📞 04 93 24 24 23; www.museedevence.com; 2 place du Frêne; adult/child €6/3; ⏰ 11am-6pm Tue-Sun) With its wonderful 20th-century art exhibitions, this daring art museum inside the imposing Château de Villeneuve offers a nice contrast to Vence's

historic quarter. Matisse-lovers will appreciate the recently opened permanent exhibit on the 2nd floor, which showcases the city of Vence's private collection of six dozen works by the great artist, displayed on a rotating basis.

🛏 Sleeping & Eating

⭐ La Maison du Frêne
B&B €€

(📱 06 88 90 49 69; www.lamaisondufrene.com; 1 place du Frêne; d €135-170; ⊘ Feb-Dec; ❄ 🛜) Named for the gorgeous 500-year-old ash tree out the front, this arty guesthouse is a labour of love for avid art collectors Thierry and Guy. Yes, that Niki de Saint Phalle is an original. And yes, the César too. It's an essential sleepover for true art-lovers, who will thoroughly appreciate the superb, sprawling rooms that boldly mix classic and contemporary styles.

⭐ Restaurant La Litote
MODERN FRENCH €€

(📱 04 93 24 27 82; www.lalitote-vence.com; 5 rue de l'Évêché; 2-/3-course lunch menus €18/22, dinner menus €29/34; ⊘ noon-2.30pm & 7-10pm, closed Tue Jun-Sep, closed Sun evening & Mon Oct-May) In the heart of Vence's old town, La Litote is the very picture of a village bistro, with tables set out on the square and blackboard menus filled with seasonal classics. Expect stews, supremes and steaks in winter, grilled fish and salads in summer, and delicious desserts year-round. Homey and lovely.

ℹ Information

Tourist Office (📱 04 93 58 06 38; www.vence-tourisme.fr; 8 place du Grand Jardin; ⊘ 9am-6pm Mon-Sat) Has several good leaflets on self-guided tours in and around Vence.

ℹ Getting There & Away

Lignes d'Azur (p861) bus 400 to/from Nice (€1.50, 1¼ hours, once or twice hourly) stops on place du Grand Jardin. Medieval Vence is pedestrianised; park in the paid **lot** underneath place du Grand Jardin or in the streets leading to the historical centre.

ST-PAUL DE VENCE
POP 3451

Once upon a time, St-Paul de Vence was a small medieval village atop a hill looking out to sea. Then came the likes of Picasso in the postwar years, followed by showbiz stars such as Yves Montand and Roger Moore, and St-Paul shot to fame. The village is now home to dozens of art galleries as well as the renowned Fondation Maeght.

Among the many artists who have lived in or passed through St-Paul over the years are Soutine, Léger, Cocteau, Matisse and Chagall. The latter is buried with his wife, Vava, in the cemetery at the village's southern end (immediately to the right as you enter).

WORTH A TRIP

GORGES DU LOUP

A combination of perilously perched villages, sheer cliffs, waterfalls, densely wooded slopes and gushing rivers, the Gorges du Loup is a scenic, unspoiled part of the world, known for spectacular drives and walking trails.

The highlight of the gorge's western side (reached via the D3) is the fortified village of **Gourdon**, teetering on a rocky summit 14km north of Grasse. Lunch on the splendid home cooking of chef Stephan Lucas at **Au Vieux Four** (📱 04 93 09 68 60; www.facebook.com/auvieuxfourgourdon; 4 rue Basse, Gourdon; lunch menus €22-28, dinner menus €38-42; ⊘ noon-2pm Fri-Tue, 7.15-9pm Fri & Sat).

Way down below, along the D2210, bitter-orange trees are cultivated on terraces around the beautifully intact medieval village of **Le Bar-sur-Loup**. Further north along the rushing river's edge, via the D3, tucked beneath the remnants of an old railway bridge (bombed during WWII), you'll find the hamlet of **Le Pont du Loup**.

End in **Tourrettes-sur-Loup**, a postcard-perfect medieval village, a further 10 minutes' drive east along the D2210. **Bistrot Gourmand Clovis** (📱 04 93 58 87 04; www.clovisgourmand.fr; 21 Grand Rue; 2-/3-/4-course menus €40/49/58, tasting menus with/without wine €105/67; ⊘ 12.30-1.30pm & 7.30-9.30pm Wed-Fri & Sun, 7.30-9.30pm Sat; 📱), in its cobbled heart, cooks up a stylish contemporary decor and creative seasonal cuisine that's been honoured with a Michelin star. Bookings essential.

BIOT

This 15th-century hilltop village (population 9876) was once an important pottery-manufacturing centre specialising in earthenware oil and wine containers. Metal containers brought an end to this, but Biot is still active in handicraft production, especially glass-making. See the blowers in action and pick up some premium glassware at the renowned **Verrerie de Biot** (🕿 04 93 65 03 00; www.verreriebiot.com; chemin des Combes; guided tour adult/child €6/3, museum adult/child €3/1.50; ⊙9.30am-8pm Mon-Sat, 10.30am-1.30pm & 2.30-7.30pm Sun May-Sep, to 6pm Oct-Apr) FREE, at the foot of the village. One and a half kilometres south of town, there's also a **museum** (🕿 04 92 91 50 20; www.musee-fernandleger.fr; chemin du Val de Pôme; adult/child incl audioguide €5.50/free, special exhibitions additional €2; ⊙10am-6pm Wed-Mon May-Oct, to 5pm Nov-Apr) devoted to the experimental artist Fernand Léger, a major inspiration for pop art.

St-Paul's tiny cobbled lanes get overwhelmingly crowded in high season – come early or late to beat the rush.

◉ Sights & Activities

Across from the entrance to the fortified village, the *pétanque* pitch, where many a star has had a spin, is the hub of village life. The tourist office rents out balls (€2) and organises one-hour *pétanque* lessons (€5 per person; reserve in advance).

Fondation Maeght   MUSEUM
(🕿 04 93 32 81 63; www.fondation-maeght.com; 623 chemin des Gardettes; adult/child €15/10; ⊙10am-7pm Jul-Sep, to 6pm Oct-Jun) St-Paul's renowned art museum features works by a who's who of 20th-century artists – including many who found inspiration along the Côte d'Azur. From pieces by Georges Braque, Vassily Kandinsky and Marc Chagall to spooky sculptures by Alberto Giacometti and glassworks by Joan Miró, it's a treasure trove – although works from the permanent collection are often disappointingly confined to a single room to make room for temporary exhibits. The innovative building designed by Josep Lluís Sert is fittingly experimental, and the gardens are delightful.

🛏 Sleeping & Eating

Villa St Paul   B&B €€
(🕿 04 93 72 58 71; www.villasaintpauldevence.com; 293 Chemin Fontmurado; r €78-150, apt €98-240; 🛜🌊) At this attractive oasis 1km below St-Paul, friendly young hosts David and Jeannette welcome guests with three spacious, comfortable rooms and a grassy pool area for lounging. Days begin with abundant breakfasts featuring fresh-squeezed orange juice, croissants, a variety of cheeses and

eggs cooked to order. The pricier adjoining Étoile de St-Paul features six more rooms and its own *hammam*.

★**Les Cabanes d'Orion**   B&B €€€
(🕿 06 75 45 18 64; www.orionbb.com; Impasse des Peupliers, 2436 chemin du Malvan; d €230-285; 🛜🌊) Dragonflies flit above water lilies in the natural swimming pool, while guests slumber amid a chorus of frogs and cicadas in luxurious cedar-wood tree houses at this enchanting, ecofriendly B&B. Children are well catered for with mini-*cabanes* in two of the tree houses. There's a minimum two- to four-night stay from May to September.

La Colombe d'Or   HOTEL €€€
(🕿 04 93 32 80 02; www.la-colombe-dor.com; place de Gaulle; d €250-430; ❄🛜🌊) This world-famous inn could double as the Fondation Maeght's annexe: the 'Golden Dove' was party HQ for dozens of 20th-century artists (Chagall, Braque, Matisse, Picasso etc) who paid for their meals in kind, resulting in an extraordinary private art collection. Rooms are strung with unique pieces, as are the **restaurant** (🕿 04 93 32 80 02; www.la-colombe-dor.com; mains €29-49; ⊙noon-2.30pm & 7.30-10.30pm late Dec-Oct) and garden.

★**Le Tilleul**   MODERN FRENCH €€
(🕿 04 93 32 80 36; www.restaurant-letilleul.com; place du Tilleul; menus €25-29, mains €15-32; ⊙8.30am-10.30pm; 🖉) Considering its location on the *remparts,* this place could have easily plumbed the depths of a typical tourist trap. But it hasn't. Instead, divine and beautifully presented dishes grace your table, complemented by an all-French wine list and blissful terrace seating under the shade of a big lime-blossom tree. Open for breakfast and afternoon tea too.

ℹ️ Information

Tourist Office (✏️ 04 93 32 86 95; www.
saint-pauldevence.com; 2 rue Grande; ⏱️10am-
7pm Jun-Sep, to 6pm Oct-May, closed 1-2pm
Sat & Sun) Runs a series of informative,
themed guided tours that delve into the village's illustrious past. Some tours are also
available in English. Book ahead. Also organises
pétanque lessons.

ℹ️ Getting There & Away

Bus 400, operated by **Lignes d'Azur** (p861),
serves St-Paul once or twice hourly, running between Nice (€1.50, one hour) and Vence (€1.50,
seven minutes). The town is closed to traffic,
but there are several car parks (€2.70 per hour)
surrounding the village.

CORNICHE DE L'ESTÉREL

A walk or drive along the winding Corniche
de l'Estérel, opened by the Touring Club de
France in 1903, is an attraction in its own
right. Also known as the Corniche d'Or,
'Golden Coast', and signposted as the N98 or
the D559, it offers spectacular views of rugged red rock formations juxtaposed against
the blue-green Mediterranean. Small summer resorts and dreamy inlets (perfect for
swimming), all accessible by bus or train,
dot its 30km length stretching from Fréjus and St-Raphaël to Cannes. The most
dramatic stretch is between Anthéor and
Théoule-sur-Mer, where the tortuous, narrow road skirts through sparsely built areas.

🏃 Activities

With its lush green Mediterranean forests,
intensely red peaks and sterling sea views,
the Massif de l'Estérel is a walker's paradise.
Local tourist offices have leaflets detailing
the most popular walks, including Pic de
l'Ours (496m) and Pic du Cap Roux (452m).
Buy IGN's Carte de Randonnée (1:25,000)
No 3544ET *Fréjus, Saint-Raphaël & Corniche de l'Estérel* for more serious walks.

Those preferring a more informed hike
can sign up for a three-hour guided walk
with a forest ranger from the Office National des Forêts (National Forestry Office) or
nature guide at **St-Raphaël tourist office**
(✏️ 04 94 19 52 52; www.saint-raphael.com; 99
quai Albert 1er; ⏱️ 9am-12.30pm & 2-6.30pm Mon-
Sat Sep-Jun, 9am-7pm Jul & Aug). Access to the
range is prohibited on windy or particularly
hot days because of fire risks; check with the
tourist office before setting off.

With its 30km of coastline, the corniche
has more than 30 beaches running the gamut of possibilities: sandy, pebbly, nudist, cove-
like... you name it. But wherever you go, the
sea remains that crystal-clear turquoise and
deep blue, an irresistible invitation to swim.

The Estérel is also a leading dive centre,
with numerous WWII shipwrecks and pristine waters. Much of the coast is protected,
meaning its fauna and flora are among the
best around.

Sentier du Littoral   HIKING
Running 11km between Port Santa Lucia
(the track starts behind the naval works)
and Agay, this coastal path (yellow markers)
takes in some of the area's most scenic spots.
It takes roughly 4½ hours to complete, but
from May to October you could make a day
of it by stopping at some of the idyllic beaches scattered along the way.

Fréjus

POP 52,897

Once an important province of Roman Gaul
(when it was known as Forum Julii), the little
town of Fréjus is a quiet spot that has some
surprisingly big attractions – including some
Roman ruins, a chapel decorated by the film-
maker-artist Jean Cocteau (of *Les Enfants
du Paradis* fame), and an impressive Gothic
cathedral whose cloister houses a unique collection of medieval ceiling frescoes.

It's particularly worth a visit on Wednesday and Saturday morning, when the old-
town market is in full swing.

👁️ Sights

If you're visiting several sights in Fréjus, it's
worth buying a **Fréjus Pass** (€6), which
grants entry to all municipal museums, or
the **Fréjus Pass Integral** (€9), which also includes the town's top attraction, the cathedral
cloister. You can buy the pass at the first sight
you visit.

⭐ Cloître de la
Cathédrale de Fréjus   CATHEDRAL
(✏️ 04 94 51 26 30; www.cloitre-frejus.fr; 48 rue de
Fleury; adult/child €6/free; ⏱️10am-12.30pm &
1.45-6.30pm Jun-Sep, 10am-1pm & 2-5pm Tue-Sun
Oct-May) Fréjus' star sight is its 11th- and
12th-century cathedral, one of the region's
first Gothic buildings. Its **cloister** features
rare 14th- and 15th-century painted wood-
en ceiling panels depicting angels, devils,
hunters, acrobats and monsters in vivid

comic-book fashion. The meaning and origin of these are unknown. Only 500 of the original 1200 frames survive. Afterwards, peek at the octagonal 5th-century **baptistery**, which incorporates eight Roman columns; it's one of the oldest Christian buildings in France and is exceptionally well preserved.

Les Arènes   RUINS
(Amphitheatre; ☑ 04 94 51 34 31; rue Henri Vadon; adult/child €3/free; ⊙ 9.30am-12.30pm & 2-6pm Tue-Sun Apr-Sep, 9.30am-noon & 2-4.30pm Tue-Sat Oct-Mar) In comparison to some of Provence's other Roman ruins, Fréjus' amphitheatre is a little underwhelming – it was badly damaged during archaeological digs, and some half-hearted reconstruction hasn't quite recaptured the atmosphere of what was once one of Gaul's largest amphitheatres (seating 10,000 spectators). Plans have been mooted to rebuild it properly, but so far no joy.

Musée Archéologique   MUSEUM
(☑ 04 94 52 15 78; 3 place Calvini; adult/child €3/free; ⊙ 9.30am-12.30pm & 2-6pm Tue-Sun Apr-Sep, 9.30am-noon & 2-4.30pm Tue-Sat Oct-Mar) Fréjus' Roman remains have seen better days, so the town's archaeological museum makes a useful accompaniment. There are some fascinating treasures on display dating all the way back to the town's Grecian and Roman beginnings, from everyday objects to rare finds, such as a double-faced marble statue of Hermes, a head of Jupiter and a stunning 3rd-century mosaic depicting a leopard.

🛏 Sleeping & Eating

Fréjus has a few hotels in the town centre, with other options spread out along the coast and in the surrounding countryside. It's the least-expensive home base for exploring the Estérel region.

**Auberge de Jeunesse
Fréjus-St-Raphaël**   HOSTEL €
(☑ 04 94 53 18 75; www.fuaj.org; chemin du Counillier; dm €19-24; ⊙ Mar-Oct; ☎) This is a rambling, basic HI-affiliated hostel set in 10 hectares of pine trees and parkland, where you can also pitch your tent. Take bus 2 or 3 from St-Raphaël or Fréjus train stations to stop Les Chênes, then cross the roundabout and take chemin du Counillier on your left (600m). Daily lockout applies between noon and 5.30pm; rates include breakfast and sheets.

Hôtel Les Calanques   HOTEL €€
(☑ 04 98 11 36 36; www.hotel-les-calanques.com; rue du Nid au Soleil, Les Issambres; s €72-104, d €83-148, tr €118-145, f €149-168) Thirteen kilometres south of Fréjus towards St-Tropez along the winding coast road, this family-run three-star sits on the rocks above its own quiet cove, accessed via the hotel's palm-filled garden. Many of the 12 rooms sport brand-new bathrooms and other upgrades from a recent makeover, and 10 boast stunning sea views – don't even consider the two facing the busy road.

★ Mon Fromager   DELI €
(☑ 04 94 40 67 99; www.mon-fromager.fr; 38 rue Siéyès; plat du jour €15.60, 5-cheese platter €12.70; ⊙ shop 9.30am-12.30pm & 2-7pm Tue-Sat, lunch noon-2pm Tue-Sat; ☑) Enterprising cheesemonger Philippe Daujam not only sells cheese – he also cooks it into tasty lunches in his deli-style restaurant by the cheese counter and on the street outside. Locals flock for the excellent-value *plat du jour* and can't-go-wrong cheese platters with salad. The faux cow-skin table mats are a fun touch, and Philippe is a font of *fromage* knowledge.

ℹ Information

Tourist Office (☑ 04 94 51 83 83; www.frejus.fr; 249 rue Jean Jaurès; ⊙ 9.30am-7pm Jul & Aug, 9.30am-12.30pm & 2.30-6.30pm Mon-Sat Jun & Sep, 9.30am-noon & 2-6pm Mon-Sat Oct-May)

ℹ Getting There & Away

Bus 4, operated by **AggloBus** (☑ 04 94 44 52 70, 04 94 53 78 46; www.agglobus-cavem.com), links Fréjus' little **bus station** (rue Gustave Bret) with St-Raphaël (€1.50).

From Fréjus' small **train station**, in summer there are hourly services to/from St-Raphaël (€1.40, three minutes), Cannes (€8.10, 30 to 45 minutes) and Nice (from €12.40, one hour).

ST-TROPEZ

POP 4305

Pouting sexpot Brigitte Bardot came to St-Tropez in the 1950s to star in *Et Dieu Créa la Femme* (And God Created Woman; 1956) and overnight transformed the peaceful fishing village into a sizzling jet-set favourite. Tropeziens have thrived on their sexy image ever since: at the Vieux Port, yachts like spaceships jostle for millionaire moorings, and infinitely more tourists jostle to admire them.

Yet there is a serene side to this village trampled by 60,000 summertime inhabitants and visitors on any given day. In the low season, the St-Tropez of mesmerising quaint beauty and 'sardine scales glistening like pearls on the cobblestones' that charmed Guy de Maupassant (1850–93) comes to life. Meander cobbled lanes in the old fishing quarter of La Ponche, sip pastis at a place des Lices cafe, watch old men play *pétanque* beneath plane trees, or walk in solitary splendour from beach to beach along the coastal path.

Sights

Vieux Port   PORT

Yachts line the harbour (as their uniformed crews diligently scrub them) and visitors stroll the quays at the picturesque old port. In front of the sable-coloured townhouses, the Bailli de Suffren statue (quai Suffren) of a 17th-century naval hero, cast from a 19th-century cannon, peers out to sea. Duck beneath the archway, next to the tourist office, to uncover St-Tropez' daily morning fish market, on place aux Herbes.

★ Musée de l'Annonciade   GALLERY

(🎫 04 94 17 84 10; www.saint-tropez.fr/fr/culture/ musee-de-lannonciade; place Grammont; adult/ child €6/free; ☺ 10am-6pm daily mid-Jun–Sep, Tue-Sun Oct–mid-Jun) In a gracefully converted 16th-century chapel, this small but famous museum showcases an impressive collection of modern art infused with that legendary Côte d'Azur light. Pointillist Paul Signac bought a house in St-Tropez in 1892 and introduced other artists to the area. The museum's collection includes his *St-Tropez, Le Quai* (1899) and *St-Tropez, Coucher de Soleil au Bois de Pins* (1896). Vuillard, Bonnard and Maurice Denis (the self-named 'Nabis' group) have a room to themselves.

★ La Ponche   HISTORIC SITE

Shrug off the hustle of the port in St-Tropez's historic fishing quarter, La Ponche, northeast of the Vieux Port. From the southern end of quai Frédéric Mistral, place Garrezio sprawls east from 10th-century Tour Suffren to place de l'Hôtel de Ville. From here, rue Guichard leads southeast to iconic Église de St-Tropez (Eglise Notre Dame de l'Assomption; rue Commandant Guichard). Follow rue du Portail Neuf south to Chapelle de la Miséricorde (1-5 rue de la Miséricorde; ☺ 10am-6pm).

Place des Lices   SQUARE

St-Tropez' legendary and very charming central square is studded with plane trees, cafes and *pétanque* players. Simply sitting on

a cafe terrace watching the world go by or jostling with the crowds at its twice-weekly market (p881) extravaganza, jam-packed with everything from fruit and veg to antique mirrors and sandals, is an integral part of the St-Tropez experience.

Place des Lices has seen artists and intellectuals fraternising for decades here, most frequently in the famous Café des Arts, now simply called Le Café (🎫 04 94 97 44 69; www. lecafe.fr; Traverse des Lices; 2-course lunch menu €18, mains €22-29; ☺ 8am-11pm) – and not to be confused with the newer, green-canopied Café des Arts on the corner of the square. Aspiring *pétanque* players can borrow a set from the bar.

★ Citadelle de St-Tropez   MUSEUM

(🎫 04 94 97 59 43; www.saint-tropez.fr/fr/ culture/citadelle; 1 montée de la Citadelle; adult/ child €3/free; ☺ 10am-6.30pm Apr-Sep, to 5.30pm Oct-Mar; ▣) Built in 1602 to defend the coast against Spain, the citadel dominates the hillside overlooking St-Tropez to the east. The views are fantastic, as are the exotic peacocks wandering the grounds. Its dungeons are home to the excellent Musée de l'Histoire Maritime, an interactive museum that traces the history of humans at sea through fishing, trading, exploration, travel and the navy. The particular focus, of course, is Tropezienne and Provençal seafarers.

Beaches

★ Plage de Pampelonne   BEACH

The 5km-long, celebrity-studded Plage de Pampelonne sports a line-up of exclusive beach restaurants and clubs in summer. Find public entries (and parking for €5.50) at one of six access points: rte de Tahiti, chemin des Moulins, chemin de Tamaris, bd Patch, chemin des Barraques and rte de Bonne Terrasse. The northern edge of the beach begins 4km southeast of St-Tropez with Plage de Tahiti.

Plage des Salins   BEACH

(chemin des Salins) Just east of St-Tropez, Plage des Salins is a 600m-wide pine-fringed beach at the southern foot of Cap des Salins. At the northern end of the beach, on a rock jutting out to sea, is the tomb of Émile Olivier (1825–1913), who served as first minister to Napoleon III until his exile in 1870. It looks out towards La Tête de Chien, named after the legendary dog who declined to eat St Torpes' remains.

✈ Activities & Tours

Sentier du Littoral   WALKING
A spectacular coastal path wends past rocky outcrops and hidden bays 35km south from St-Tropez, around the peninsula to the beach at Cavalaire-sur-Mer. In St-Tropez, the yellow-flagged path starts at **La Ponche**, immediately east of Tour du Portalet, and curves around Port des Pêcheurs, past the citadel. It then leads past the walled **Cimitière Marin** (Marine Cemetery; Pointe du Cimetière), **Plage des Graniers** and beyond.

The tourist office has maps with distances and walking times (eg, Plage des Salins is 8.5km or around 2½ hours' walk).

Les Bateaux Verts   BOATING
(☑ 04 94 49 29 39; www.bateauxverts.com; 7 quai Jean Jaurès) Les Bateaux Verts offers trips around Baie des Cannebiers (dubbed 'Bay of Stars' after the celebrity villas dotting its coast) from April to September (adult/child from €11/6), as well as seasonal boats to Cannes (€39/25, 1½ hours) and Porquerolles (€43/28, two hours), and regular shuttle boats to Marines de Cogolin, Port Grimaud, Ste-Maxime and Les Issambres.

🛌 Sleeping

St-Tropez is home to celebrity-studded hangs, with prices to match – this is no shoestring destination, though campgrounds do sit southeast along Plage de Pampelonne. Most hotels close in winter; the tourist office lists what's open, and also has a list of B&Bs. If you're driving, double-check the parking arrangements.

La Vigneraie 1860   CAMPGROUND €
(☑ 04 94 97 17 03; www.la-vigneraie-1860.fr; chemin des Moulins; site for 2 people €53.50, apt per week from €800; ☺ Apr-Oct, reception 8am-noon & 5-8pm; ℗) This simple caravan and campground just off Plage de Pampelonne offers one of the few ways to live cheaply and still get a chance to hang out in one of the most exclusive locales in the region. Surrounded by vineyards, it has basic showers and apartments.

Hôtel Lou Cagnard   HOTEL €€
(☑ 04 94 97 04 24; www.hotel-lou-cagnard.com; 30 av Paul Roussel; r from €95; ☺ Apr-Oct; ℗ ✳ 📶) This old-school hotel stands in stark contrast to most of the swanky hotels around St-Tropez. Located in an old house shaded by lemon and fig trees, its 18 rooms are unashamedly frilly and floral, but some have garden patios, and the lovely jasmine-scented garden and welcoming family feel make it a home away from home. The cheapest rooms share toilets.

Hôtel Ermitage   BOUTIQUE HOTEL €€€
(☑ 04 94 81 08 10; www.ermitagehotel.fr; 14 av Paul Signac; r from €320; ✳ 📶) Well, if you really want to hang with the jet set, the hip Hermitage is your kind of place. Self-consciously retro, the decor draws inspiration from St-Tropez's midcentury heyday: bold primary colours, vintage design pieces and big prints of '60s icons on the walls. The bar's as cool as they come, with sweeping views over St-Trop.

Pastis   HOTEL €€€
(☑ 04 98 12 56 50; www.pastis-st-tropez.com; 75 av du Général Leclerc; d from €575; ✳ ✖) This stunning townhouse-turned-hotel is the brainchild of an English couple besotted with Provence and passionate about modern art. You'll love the pop-art-inspired interior (if that's your thing) and long for a swim in the emerald-green pool. Every room is beautiful, although those overlooking av du Général Leclerc are noisy. Low-season deals make it much more affordable.

🍴 Eating

Prices are high: the glamour dust sprinkled on fish and chips doesn't come cheap! Quai Jean Jaurès is lined with mediocre restaurants with great portside views. Cheaper eats cluster near quai de l'Épi and the new port. Reservations are essential in high season; many restaurants close in winter.

Don't leave town without sampling *tarte Tropézienne*, an orange-blossom-flavoured double sponge cake filled with thick cream, created by Polish baker A Mickla in 1955.

La Tarte Tropézienne   CAFE €
(☑ 04 94 97 94 25; www.latartetropezienne.fr; place des Lices; tarts/snacks from €5.50/3; ☺ 6.30am-10pm; 📶) This smart, bustling cafe-bakery is the creator of St Tropez' eponymous sugar-crusted, orange-perfumed cake, but also does decent breads and light meals. There are smaller branches on **rue Clémenceau** (☑ 04 94 97 71 42; www.latartetropezienne.fr; 36 rue Clémenceau; tarts/snacks €5.50/3; ☺ 7am-10pm) and near the **new port** (☑ 04 94 97 19 77; www.latartetropezienne.fr; 9 bd Louis Blanc; tarts/snacks €5.50/3; ☺ 6.30am-7.30pm), plus various other towns around Provence and the Île de France.

Le Gorille
CAFE €

(📞 04 94 97 03 93; www.legorille.com; 1 quai Suffren; sandwiches/mains €7/17; ⏱ 7am-7pm) This portside hang-out gets its name from its previous owner – the short, muscular and apparently very hairy Henri Guérin! Stop here for breakfast or a post-clubbing *croque-monsieur* and fries. It's anything but pretentious.

La Pesquière
SEAFOOD €

(📞 04 94 97 05 92; http://pesquiere.mazagran. free.fr; 1 rue des Remparts; menus adult/child €29/14; ⏱ 9am-midnight late Mar-Oct) It's no surprise this old-fashioned place survives in restless, modish St Tropez: since 1962 the one family has made an art of buying the day's freshest catch – whether that be dourade, red mullet, bass or prawns – and cooking it to simple perfection. Locals love it, as do visitors, and you feel you've had your money's worth.

★ Bistro Canaille
FUSION €€

(📞 04 94 97 40 96; 28 rue des Remparts; plates €12-24; ⏱ 7-11pm Tue-Sun Jun-Sep, Fri & Sat Mar-May & Oct-Dec) Probably the pick of the modern places to eat in town – creative, cosy and great value while still hitting the gourmet heights. It's got the soul of a bistro, but specialises in fusion-style tapas dishes inspired by the owners' travels – like local dourade with olives and *yuzu* (Japanese citrus). More tempting combinations are chalked on the board.

Bistro Pastis
BISTRO €€

(📞 04 94 49 36 96; www.bistropastis.fr; 18 rue Henri Seillon; mains €22-25; ⏱ 8pm-midnight) With a plum position near the Viex Port and such an obvious name, you'd be forgiven for thinking this bistro was nothing but a tourist trap, but the food and service are top-notch. Monkfish with lobster sauce, penne with prawns, salt-roasted bone marrow with toast: we guarantee you'll come away happy, and not much lighter in the pocket.

★ La Vague d'Or
GASTRONOMY €€€

(📞 04 94 55 91 00; www.residencepinede.com; Résidence de la Pinède, Plage de la Bouillabaisse; menus from €130; ⏱ 7.30-10pm mid-Apr–mid-Oct; 📶) Triple-starred chef Arnaud Donckele has established a gastronomic temple at the Résidence de la Pinède: expect exquisite ingredients treated with the utmost cheffy cleverness. But with offerings such as the Balade Epicurienne setting you back half a grand for seven courses with matched wines, expectations can rise to dangerous heights. Then again, this *is* St Topez.

ℹ Information

Tourist Office (📞 08 92 68 48 28; www. sainttropeztourisme.com; quai Jean Jaurès; ⏱ 9.30am-1.30pm & 3-7.30pm Jul & Aug, 9.30am-12.30pm & 2-7pm Apr-Jun, Sep & Oct, to 6pm Mon-Sat Nov-Mar) Runs occasional walking tours April to October, and also has a **kiosk** (⏱ 9am-6pm Jul & Aug) in Parking du Port in July and August.

ℹ Getting There & Around

BICYCLE
Rolling Bikes (📞 04 94 97 09 39; www. rolling-bikes.com; 50 av du Général Leclerc; per day bikes/scooters/motorcycles from €17/46/120; ⏱ 9am-12.30pm & 3-7pm Tue-Sat Sep-Jun, daily Jul & Aug) Do as the locals do and opt for two wheels.

DON'T MISS

ST-TROPEZ SHOPPING ICONS

Market (place des Lices; ⏱ 8am-1pm Tue & Sat) Forget the fancy side of St-Tropez for a while, and re-enter a more traditional Provence at this twice-weekly market, offering everything from cheese trucks and veg stalls to bric-a-brac sellers, sandal-makers and vintage clothes.

Atelier Rondini (📞 04 94 97 19 55; www.rondini.fr; 18 rue Georges Clémenceau; ⏱ 10.30am-1pm & 3-6.30pm Tue-Sun) Colette brought a pair of sandals from Greece to Atelier Rondini (open since 1927) to be replicated. It's still making the iconic sandals today (from about €145).

K Jacques (📞 04 94 97 41 50; www.kjacques.com; 39bis rue Allard; ⏱ 10am-1pm & 2.30-8.30pm Mon-Sat, 10.30am-1pm & 3-8.30pm Sun) Hand-crafting sandals (from €240) since 1933 for such clients as Picasso and Brigitte Bardot. There's another branch (📞 04 94 97 41 50; www.kjacques.fr; 16 rue Seillon; ⏱ 10am-1pm & 2.30-8.30pm Mon-Sat, 10.30am-1pm & 3-8.30pm Sun) nearby.

LAZY DAYS

BEACHES

Whoever you are, the Côte d'Azur has a beach with your name on it. Play with your kids beneath the pines and soaring cliffs at **Plage Petite Afrique** in Beaulieu-sur-Mer, lounge among the chic and stylish at **Z Plage** (p863) in Cannes, bring your wheelchair to the water's edge (and beyond) at **Plage du Centenaire** in Nice, or trade Nice's pebbles for the sandy shores of **Plage de Pampelonne** (p879) in St-Tropez.

SEASIDE DRINKING & DINING

Sip a drink without leaving your sun lounger at private beaches such as **Sporting Plage** (☑ 04 93 87 18 10; www.sportingplage.fr; 25 Promenade des Anglais; mains €18-25; ☺ noon-5pm late Dec–mid-Oct; ☐ 8, 52, 62 to Congrès/Promenade) in Nice, or snack on seafood by the water's edge at idyllic **Paloma Beach** (☑ 04 93 01 64 71; www.paloma-beach.com; 1 rte de Sainte-Hospice; mains €21-47.50; ☺ Easter-Sep) in St-Jean-Cap-Ferrat. More-ambitious souls can leave Vieux Nice's urban beach and cross the street for cocktails on the beach-facing balcony at **La Movida** (p859) or go gastronomic on the sea-view terrace at Michelin-starred **La Rastègue** (p886).

CÔTE D'AZUR CLASSICS

Don't forget the timeless Côte d'Azur classics: whiling away a lazy afternoon people-watching from a blue chair on the **Promenade des Anglais** (p850), or trying your luck at roulette and *trente et quarante* at the gaming tables at **Casino de Monte Carlo** (p889).

1. Promenade des Anglais (p850)
2. Pampelonne beach (p879), St-Tropez
3. Paloma Beach, St-Jean-Cap-Ferrat (p860)

If there was ever a perfect place to take life easy, the Côte d'Azur is it. Here you can follow proudly in the footsteps of 19th-century aristocrats and immerse yourself in a life of unapologetic leisure any day of the week.

BOAT

Les Bateaux de St-Raphaël (☑ 04 94 95 17 46; www.bateauxsaintraphael.com; ☺ Apr-late Nov) Seasonal boats between St-Tropez (Nouveau Port) and St-Raphaël (one way adult/child €15/10, one hour).

Les Bateaux Verts (p880)

Sea Taxi (☑ 06 12 40 28 05; www.taxi-boat-saint-tropez.com) Taxi boat for hire around St-Tropez. A crossing from St Tropez to Ste-Maxime is €80 during the day, and €100 after 10pm.

Trans Côte d'Azur (☑ 04 92 98 71 30; www.trans-cote-azur.co.uk; ☺ May-Oct) Ferries from Nice and Cannes.

BUS

VarLib (☑ 09 70 83 03 80; www.varlib.fr) tickets cost €3 from the **bus station** (Gare Routière; ☑ 04 94 56 25 74; av du Général de Gaulle) for anywhere within the Var département (except Toulon-Hyères airport). Destinations include Ramatuelle (35 minutes, up to six daily) and St-Raphaël (1¼ to three hours, depending on traffic, hourly) via Grimaud and Port Grimaud, and Fréjus.

Buses to Toulon (two hours, seven daily, fewer in summer) stop at Le Lavandou (one hour) and Hyères (1½ hours).

Buses serve Toulon-Hyères airport (€15, 1½ hours), but some require a transfer.

MASSIF DES MAURES

A wild range of wooded hills rumpling the landscape inland between Hyères and Fréjus, the Massif des Maures is a pocket of surprising wilderness just a few miles from the summer hustle of the Côte d'Azur. Shrouded by pine, chestnut and cork oak trees, its near-black vegetation gives rise to its name, derived from the Provençal word *mauro* (dark pine wood).

Traditional industries (chestnut harvests, cork, pipe-making) are still practised here, and the area is criss-crossed by hiking trails that offer spectacular views of the surrounding coastline.

Hidden in the forest, the leafy village of **Collobrières** is *the* place to taste chestnuts. Across its 11th-century bridge, the **tourist office** (☑ 04 94 48 08 00; www.collobrieres-tourisme.com; bd Charles Caminat; ☺ 9am-12.30pm & 2-5.30pm Mon-Wed & Fri-Sat, 2-5.30pm Thu, 9am-12.30pm Sun Jul & Aug, shorter hours rest of year) can help you participate in the October chestnut harvest, celebrated with the **Fête de la Châtaigne**, or join a guided forest walk.

⊙ Sights & Activities

Local tourist offices can supply hiking guides and route suggestions, but note that from June to September, access to many areas is limited due to the risk of forest fire. Depending on the risk, trails are graded yellow, orange, red and black, with yellow meaning some minor restrictions at certain times of day, and black meaning total closure. Ask at a tourist office before you set out.

★**Monastère de la Verne**   MONASTERY
(Chartreuse de la Verne; ☑ 04 94 43 45 51; off D14; adult/child €6/3; ☺ 11am-6pm Wed-Mon Jun-Aug, to 5pm Feb-May & Sep-Dec; [P]) The majestic 12th-century Monastère de la Verne sits on a forested ridge in the Massif des Maures, rising like an island of honeyed stone in a sea of green. The Carthusian institution was founded in 1170, possibly on the site of a temple to the goddess Laverna, protector of the bandits who hid in the Maures. It has been ravaged by fire and rebuilt several times over the years (much of the reconstruction dates from the 17th and 18th centuries).

Village des Tortues   WILDLIFE RESERVE
(☑ 04 89 29 14 10; www.villagedestortues.fr; 1065 rte du Luc (D97), Carnoules; adult/child €15/10; ☺ 9am-7pm mid-Mar–mid-Oct, 9.30am-5pm mid-Oct–mid-Mar; [P]) This sanctuary protects one of France's most endangered species, the Hermann tortoise *(Testudo hermanni)* today found only in the Massif des Maures and on Corsica. In summer, the best time to see the tortoises is in the morning and late afternoon. Watch them hatch from mid-May to the end of June; they hibernate from November to early March. Guided tours at 10.30am and 2pm are enlightening.

🛏 Sleeping & Eating

The tourist office lists local *gîtes* (cottages), hotels and B&Bs online.

★**La Petite Fontaine**   FRENCH €€
(☑ 04 94 48 00 12; 6 place de la République; menus €27-33; ☺ noon-1.30pm & 7.30-9pm Tue-Sat, noon-1.30pm Sun) Locals travel from miles around to sit at a tree-shaded table on place de la République and feast on *daube de boeuf* (beef stew), forest mushrooms and housemade terrine at one of southern France's most charming, relaxed village inns. The walls inside are exposed stone, and the fruit tarts are out of this world. Reservations are essential, as is cash.

Ferme de Peïgros
FRENCH €€

(☑04 94 48 03 83; http://fermedepeigros.
pagesperso-orange.fr; Col de Babaou; menus €29;
⊙noon-2pm Jan-Dec, 7-9.30pm Jul & Aug; [P])
Treat yourself to real mountain food: wild
boar, pheasant, capon, kid, *cèpes* (porcini
mushrooms) and other delicacies. Finish
with chestnut ice cream and superb views
at this goat farm, 1.8km along a gravel track
from the top of the Col de Babaou (8km
from Collobrières). You can also stay at one
of two *gîtes* (€305 per week). Bring cash.

❶ Getting There & Away

Public transport is pretty much non-existent up
in the hills. You'll need your own wheels.

CORNICHE DES MAURES

The Corniche des Maures (D559) unwinds
beautifully southwest from La Croix-Valmer
to Le Lavandou along a shoreline trimmed
with sandy beaches ideal for swimming,
sunbathing and windsurfing.

Tiny **Plage du Rayol** and **Plage de l'Escale** are particularly enchanting beaches:
they're backed by pine trees and have a restaurant on the sand. As the D559 hugs the
coast going west, you'll reach Plage du Layet, the beautiful beach at **Cavalière** (not to
be confused with Cavalaire-sur-Mer).

Once a fishing village, **Le Lavandou** is
now now an overbuilt family-oriented beach
resort with a small intact old town and 12km
of golden sand; opposite the **tourist office**
(☑04 94 00 40 50; www.ot-lelavandou.fr; quai
Gabriel Péri; ⊙9am-12.30pm & 2-7pm Mon-Sat,
9.30am-12.30pm & 3.30-6.30pm Jul & Aug, short-

er hours rest of year) boats sail to the **Îles des
Hyères**. Inland, the flower-strewn hilltop
village of **Bormes-les-Mimosas** is the jewel
in the Corniche des Maures' crown.

◉ Sights & Activities

Bormes-les-Mimosas' **tourist office** (☑04
94 01 38 38; www.bormeslesmimosas.com; 1 place
Gambetta; ⊙9am-12.30pm & 2.30-6.30pm Jul &
Aug, 9am-12.30pm & 2-5pm Mon-Sat Oct-Mar; ☎)
takes bookings for botanical walks (€9) and
hikes (€7) with a forest warden in the village's nearby **Forêt du Dom**.

★ Domaine du Rayol
GARDENS

(Le Jardin des Méditerranées; ☑04 98 04 44 00;
www.domainedurayol.org; av des Belges, Rayol-
Canadel-sur-Mer; adult/child €11/8; ⊙9.30am-
7.30pm Jul & Aug, to 6.30pm Apr-Jun, Sep & Oct,
to 5.30pm Nov-Mar; [P]🚻) ✎ Growing continuously since its conception in 1910, this
stunning garden, with plants from all Mediterranean climates, is wonderful for a stroll
or a themed nature walk. The dense flora
cascades down the hillside to the sea, and
while the flowers are at their best in April
and May, it's always worth a visit. In summer, at the estate's petite gem of a beach,
you can snorkel around underwater flora
and fauna with an experienced guide (adult/
child €28/20; bookings essential).

Fort de Brégançon
FORT

(☑04 94 01 38 38; www.bormeslesmimosas.com;
av Guy Iezenas, Cap de Brégançon; adult/child €10/
free, parking €6-9; ⊙9.15am-4.15pm late Jun-late
Sep, shorter hours rest of year) A private residence of the president from 1968 to 2013,
the Fort de Brégançon is now an accessible
national monument. Located on a scenic

OFF THE BEATEN TRACK

ROUTE DES CRÊTES

For breathtaking views of the Med and the Îles d'Hyères, follow rte des Crêtes as it winds its
way through maquis-covered hills some 400m above the sea. From Bormes-les-Mimosas,
follow the D41 uphill (direction Collobrières) past the Chapelle St-François and, 1.5km north
of the village centre, turn immediately right after the sign for Col de Caguo-Ven (237m).

The **Relais du Vieux Sauvaire** (☑04 94 22 02 32; www.relaisduvieuxsauvaire.com; rte
des Crêtes, corniche de la pierre d'Avenoun; menu €45, mains €32-38; ⊙noon-2.30 & 7-9.30pm
Mon-Sat, noon-12.30pm Sun May-Nov; [P]) is the hidden gem of these hills. With dreamy
180-degree views, this restaurant and pool (most people come for lunch and then stay
all afternoon) is one of a kind. The food is as sunny as the views: pizzas, melon and Par-
ma ham, or whole sea bass in salt crust.

Past the restaurant, rte des Crêtes joins the final leg of the panoramic Col du Canadel
road. On the *col* (mountain pass), turn left to descend into the heart of the forested Massif des Maures, or right to the sea and the coastal Corniche des Maures (D559).

peninsula 20 minutes' drive from Bormes-les-Mimosas, the imposing fort dates back to the 11th century and has featured in numerous conflicts since, from the tensions between Provence and France to the French Revolution and WWI. Tickets must be booked in advance via the Bormes tourist office (p885), either in person or online.

ⓘ Getting There & Away

The coastal D559 is served by **VarLib** (www. varlib.fr) buses 7801 and 7802, running between St-Tropez and Toulon (€3, two hours, up to 20 per day).

THE THREE CORNICHES

This trio of corniches (coastal roads) hugs the cliffs between Nice and Monaco, each higher than the last, with dazzling views of the Med. For the grandest views, it's the Grande Corniche you want, but the Moyenne Corniche runs a close scenic second. The lowest of all, the Corniche Inférieure, allows access to a string of snazzy coastal resorts.

With Nice, Monaco and Menton nearby, there's no really compelling reason to

---

LOCAL KNOWLEDGE

LAZY LUNCH CALL

This Corniche des Maures squirrels away a couple of memorable addresses that beg long, lazy lunches.

On the southwestern end of nudist Plage du Layet, bare-bones **Chez Jo** (Restaurant Plage du Layet; ☑ 04 94 05 85 06; Plage du Layet, Cavalière; mains €20-30; ☉ noon-3pm May-Sep) is the ultimate summer seafood, suntan and socialisation shack on the sand – buzzes come noon with tanned, barefoot beach-lovers sipping Bandol whites and devouring the fresh seafood.

At the other end of the spectrum, in Bormes-les-Mimosas, is Michelin-starred **La Rastègue** (☑ 04 94 15 19 41; www. larastegue.com; 48 bd du Levant; menus €49; ☉ 7.30-9pm Tue-Sat, noon-1.45pm Sun Apr-Nov) with its ever-changing menu of superb Provençal fare and sensational sea-view terrace. Jérôme Masson rules the kitchen; his wife, Patricia, the dining room – and they sure do excel. The open kitchen lets you see the chef at work.

---

stay overnight on the Corniches. A few cafes and bistros pepper the clifftop roads, or picnic-shop at Nice's tasty Cours Saleya market (p850) before hitting the high road.

Skimming the villa-lined waterfront between Nice and Monaco, the **Corniche Inférieure**, built in the 1860s, passes through the towns of Villefranche-sur-Mer, St-Jean-Cap Ferrat, Beaulieu-sur-Mer, Èze-sur-Mer and Cap d'Ail.

Cut through rock in the 1920s, the **Moyenne Corniche** takes drivers from Nice past the Col de Villefranche (149m), the hilltop village of Èze and Beausoleil (the French town bordering Monaco's Monte Carlo). Èze is linked to its lower coastal counterpart, Èze-sur-Mer, by the steep Sentier Nietzsche (p887) footpath.

Views from Napoléon's spectacular cliff-hanging **Grande Corniche** are mesmerising. Hitchcock was sufficiently impressed to use it as a backdrop for his film *To Catch a Thief* (1956), starring Cary Grant and Grace Kelly. Ironically, Kelly died in 1982 after crashing her car on this very same road. There are no villages of note along the Grande Corniche until you reach hilltop La Turbie, best known for its imposing Roman triumphal monument.

ⓘ Getting There & Away

Bus 100 (€1.50, every 15 minutes from 6am to 8pm) runs the length of the Corniche Inférieure between Nice and Menton, stopping at all the villages along the way, including Villefranche-sur-Mer (15 minutes), Beaulieu-sur-Mer (20 minutes) and Cap d'Ail (35 minutes). Bus 81 serves Villefranche (20 minutes) and St-Jean-Cap Ferrat (30 minutes).

From Nice, trains to Ventimiglia in Italy (half-hourly 5am to 11pm) stop at Villefranche-sur-Mer (€1.90, seven minutes), Beaulieu-sur-Mer (€2.30, 10 minutes) and Cap d'Ail (€3.50, 20 minutes).

Bus 82 serves the Moyenne Corniche from Nice all the way to Èze (20 minutes); bus 112 carries on to Beausoleil (40 minutes, Monday to Saturday).

Bus 116 links the town of La Turbie with Nice (€1.50, 35 minutes, five daily), and bus 114 goes to Monaco (€1.50, 30 minutes, six daily).

Èze

POP 2343

This rocky little village perched on an impossibly steep peak is the jewel in the Riviera's crown. The main attraction is the medieval village itself, with small higgledy-piggledy

ÎLES D'HYÈRES

Lying intriguingly offshore from the coast between Toulon to Hyères, the Îles d'Hyères are also known as the Îles d'Or (Islands of Gold) – not just due to their mica-rich rock but also for the golden beaches that fringe their forested hinterland. They're overrun in July and August, but for much of the rest of the year you might have them largely to yourself, with plenty of good weather too.

Île de Porquerolles is the largest; Île de Port-Cros is a national park with fantastic snorkelling; and Île du Levant is both an army camp and a nudist colony. Wild camping and cars are forbidden throughout the archipelago.

There are a plenty of bistros and cafes on Porquerolles and Port-Cros, but if you're cycling round and exploring the beaches, packing a picnic is both cheaper and more convenient.

The main ports for travelling to the islands are La Tour Fondue (at the southern end of the Presqu'île de Giens), Port d'Hyères (further north) and Le Lavandou (east of Hyères). From June to September seasonal ferries also run from other locations, including Toulon and St-Tropez.

Vedettes Îles d'Or et Le Corsaire (✆ 04 94 71 01 02; www.vedettesilesdor.fr; quai des Îles d'Or, Le Lavandou, Gare Maritime; ⊘ 8.30am-12.15pm & 2-6.30pm Mon, Tue, Thu, Sat & Sun, from 1.15pm Wed & Fri) runs boats to the Îles d'Hyères from Le Lavandou, Cavalaire and La Croix-Valmer.

From Le Lavandou, boats go to Île du Levant (return adult/child €28/23, 35 to 55 minutes), Île de Port-Cros (€28/23, 35 to 55 minutes) and Île de Porquerolles (€36/28, 45 to 75 minutes). Trips from Cavalaire and La Croix-Valmer cost about €5 extra.

There are also multi-island cruises (adult/child €48/39) on high-speed La Croisière Bleue vessels, which stop at both Île de Porquerolles and Île de Port-Cros. The company also runs a summer-only ferry to St-Tropez from Le Lavandou (adult/child €47/37), Cavalaire (€32/26) and La Croix-Valmer. Note that in winter, boats only connect Le Lavandou, Île du Levant and Île de Port-Cros.

stone houses and winding lanes (and plenty of galleries and shops), and mesmerising views of the coast.

The village gets very crowded during the day; for a quieter wander, come early in the morning or late afternoon. You'll get the best panorama from Jardin Exotique d'Èze, a cactus garden at the top of the village where you'll also find the old castle ruins.

⊙ Sights

Jardin Exotique d'Èze   GARDENS
(✆ 04 93 41 10 30; www.jardinexotique-eze.fr; rue du Château; adult/child €6/3.50; ⊘ 9am-7.30pm Jul-Sep, to 6.30pm Apr-Jun & Oct, to 4.30pm Nov-Mar) The best panorama in Èze village is from this cactus garden right at the top of the craggy hilltop village. Take time to relax in the ruins of Èze's castle and contemplate the stunning view from the garden's Zen area – few places offer such a wild panorama.

Fort de la Revère   VIEWPOINT
Sitting just below Èze, this fort is the perfect place to revel in 360-degree views. An orientation table helps you get your bearings. The fort was built in 1870 to protect Nice (it served as an allied prisoner camp during WWII). There are picnic tables under the trees for an al fresco lunch and dozens of trails in the surrounding Parc Naturel Départemental de la Grande Corniche, a protected area that stretches along the D2564 from Col d'Èze to La Turbie.

Sentier Nietzsche   WALKING
This incredibly steep downhill hike takes you all the way from the hilltop village of Èze (elevation 427m) to the seaside village of Èze-sur-Mer in just 45 minutes, with some spectacular views en route. Bring sturdy hiking shoes and plenty of water, and take care with loose rocks underfoot. The trail is clearly signposted near the bottom of Èze village.

🛏 Sleeping & Eating

Domaine Pins Paul   B&B €€
(✆ 04 93 41 22 66; www.domainepinspaul.fr; 4530 av des Diables Bleus; d/ste €190/290; ❄ ⬤ ⬛) Swimming in the panoramic pool of the Domaine Pins Paul comes complete with views of the sea and Èze village. Rooms in the grand Provençal *bastide* (country house) are beautiful (each with their own little wine fridge), and the surrounding fragrant woods are perfect for a stroll.

★ **Château Eza**   LUXURY HOTEL €€€

(✆ 04 93 41 12 24; www.chateaueza.com; rue de la Pise; d from €370; ❄ 🛜) If you're looking for a place to propose, well, there can be few more memorable settings than this wonderful clifftop hotel, perched dramatically above the glittering blue Mediterranean. There are only 12 rooms, so it feels intimate, but the service is impeccable, and the regal decor (gilded mirrors, sumptuous fabrics, antiques) explains the sky-high price tag.

Even if you're not staying, it's worth experiencing a sundown at the stylish bar or – even better – a meal at the hotel's luxurious **restaurant** (lunch menus €52-62, tasting menus €120).

La Turbie

POP 3160

Perched high above the Mediterranean, the village of La Turbie is a key stop along the Grande Corniche scenic drive. Its main attraction is the spectacular **Trophée des Alpes** (✆ 04 93 41 20 84; www.trophee-auguste.fr; 18 av Albert 1er; adult/child €6/free; ⊙ 9.30am-1pm & 2.30-6.30pm Tue-Sun mid-May–mid-Sep, 10am-1.30pm & 2.30-5pm rest of year), a monument built by Emperor Augustus at the high point of the ancient Via Julia Augusta to celebrate the Romans' pivotal victory over the surrounding mountain tribes.

There are some attractive pedestrianised streets and good restaurants in the immediate vicinity of the monument, but the heart of town is less attractive due to the steady flow of traffic along the busy D2564.

✗ Eating

★ **Café de la Fontaine**   MODERN FRENCH €€

(✆ 04 93 28 52 79; www.hostelleriejerome.com; 4 av Général de Gaulle; mains €18-24; ⊙ noon-3pm & 7-11pm) Passers-by might not give this inconspicuous village bistro a second glance. But what they don't know is that it is Michelin-starred chef Bruno Cirino's baby – somewhere for him to go back to his culinary roots with simple yet delicious dishes reflecting *le terroir* (land) and season. Blackboard *plats* (dishes) are crafted from market produce.

MONACO

POP 37,550

Squeezed into just 200 hectares, Monaco might be the world's second-smallest country (only the Vatican is smaller), but what it lacks in size it makes up for in attitude. A magnet for high-rollers and hedonists since the early 20th century, it's also renowned as one of the world's most notorious tax havens and home to the annual Formula One Grand Prix.

Despite its prodigious wealth, Monaco is far from being the French Riviera's prettiest town. World-famous Monte Carlo is basically an ode to concrete and glass, dominated by high-rise hotels, super yachts and apartment blocks that rise into the hills like ranks of dominoes, plonked into an utterly bewildering street layout seemingly designed to confound lowly pedestrians.

In dramatic contrast, the rocky outcrop known as Le Rocher, jutting out on the south side of the port, is crowned by a rather charming old town, home to the principality's royal palace.

⊙ Sights & Activities

A major construction project is under way on the the north side of the port, where the foundations for Monaco's brand new Museum of the Automobile (and a large car park) are currently being laid; the work is expected to continue until at least 2020.

★ **Le Rocher**   HISTORIC SITE

Monaco Ville, also called Le Rocher, is the only part of Monaco to have retained its original old town, complete with small, windy medieval lanes. The old town thrusts skywards on a pistol-shaped rock, its strategic location overlooking the sea that became the stronghold of the Grimaldi dynasty. There are various staircases up to Le Rocher; the best route up is via Rampe Major, which starts from place d'Armes near the port.

Palais Princier de Monaco   PALACE

(✆ 93 25 18 31; www.palais.mc; place du Palais; adult/child €8/4, incl Collection de Voitures Anciennes car museum €11.50/5, incl Musée Océanographique €19/11; ⊙ 10am-6pm Apr-Jun & Sep–mid-Oct, to 7pm Jul & Aug) Built as a fortress atop Le Rocher in the 13th century, this palace is the private residence of the Grimaldi family. It is protected by the blue-helmeted, white-socked Carabiniers du Prince; changing of the guard takes place daily at 11.55am, when crowds gather outside the gates to watch.

Most of the palace is off limits, but you can get a glimpse of royal life on a tour of the glittering **state apartments**, where you can see some of the lavish furniture and priceless artworks collected by the family over the centuries. It's a good idea to buy tickets online in advance to avoid queuing.

Combined tickets including Monaco's oceanographic museum (p889) or the Prince's **classic car collection** (Monaco Top Cars Collection; ☑ 92 05 28 56; www.mtcc.mc; Terrasses de Fontvieille; adult/child €6.50/3, incl Palais Princier de Monaco €11.50/5; ☉ 10am-6pm) are also available.

Cathédrale de Monaco   CATHEDRAL
(4 rue Colonel Bellando de Castro; ☉ 8.30am-6.45pm) FREE An adoring crowd continually shuffles past Prince Rainier's and Princess Grace's flower-adorned graves, located inside the cathedral choir of Monaco's 1875 Romanesque-Byzantine cathedral.

★ **Musée Océanographique**
de Monaco   AQUARIUM
(☑ 93 15 36 00; www.oceano.mc; av St-Martin; adult/child high season €16/12, low season €11/7; ☉ 9.30am-8pm Jul & Aug, 10am-7pm Apr-Jun & Sep, to 6pm Oct-Mar) Stuck dramatically to the edge of a cliff since 1910, the world-renowned Musée Océanographique de Monaco, founded by Prince Albert I (1848–1922), is a stunner. Its centrepiece is its aquarium with a 6m-deep lagoon where sharks and marine predators are separated from colourful tropical fish by a coral reef. Upstairs, two huge colonnaded rooms retrace the history of oceanography and marine biology (and Prince Albert's contribution to the field) through photographs, old equipment, numerous specimens and interactive displays.

★ **Jardin Exotique**   GARDENS
(☑ 93 15 29 80; www.jardin-exotique.mc; 62 bd du Jardin Exotique; adult/child €7.20/3.80; ☉ 9am-7pm mid-May–mid-Sep, to 6pm rest of year) Home to the world's largest succulent and cactus collection, from small echinocereus to 10m-tall African candelabras, the gardens tumble down the slopes of Moneghetti through a maze of paths, stairs and bridges. Views of the principality are spectacular. Admission includes the **Musée d'Anthropologie**, which displays prehistoric remains unearthed in Monaco, and a 35-minute guided tour of the **Grotte de l'Observatoire**. The prehistoric, stalactite- and stalagmite-laced cave is the only one in Europe where the temperature rises as you descend.

★ **Casino de Monte Carlo**   CASINO
(☑ 98 06 21 21; www.casinomontecarlo.com; place du Casino; morning visit incl audioguide adult/child Oct-Apr €14/10, May-Sep €17/12, salons ordinaires gaming Oct-Apr €14, May-Sep €17; ☉ visits 9am-1pm, gaming 2pm-late) Peeping inside Monte Carlo's legendary marble-and-gold casino is a Monaco essential. The building, open to visitors every morning, including the exclusive *salons privés*, is Europe's most lavish example of belle époque architecture. Prince Charles III spearheaded the casino's development and in 1866, three years after its inauguration, the name 'Monte Carlo' – Ligurian for 'Mount Charles' in honour of the prince – was coined. To gamble here, visit after 2pm (when a strict over-18s-only admission rule kicks in).

✦ Festivals & Events

Formula One Grand Prix   SPORTS
(www.formula1monaco.com; ☉ late May) Formula One's most iconic event spans four days in late May, when Monaco goes completely car crazy and every street in town is closed for the race. At other times of the year, fans can walk the 3.2km circuit through town; the tourist office has maps. Friday's cheapest tickets go for €30, but figure €1400 for a prime casino-side Sunday spot.

Grand Prix Historique de Monaco   SPORTS
(www.monacograndprixticket.com/grand-prix-historique; ☉ May) Held every other year (in even-numbered years), this fun event features vintage racing cars navigating Monte Carlo's twists and turns two weeks before the Formula One Grand Prix begins.

🛏 Sleeping & Eating

Relais International de la
Jeunesse Thalassa   HOSTEL €
(☑ 04 93 78 18 58; www.clajsud.com/relaisclajcap dail.html; 2 av Gramaglia, Cap d'Ail; dm €20; ☉ Apr-Oct) Perched at the Mediterranean's edge, this hostel in Cap d'Ail, France (2km from Monaco, or five minutes by bus or train) has a fab beachside location, clean four- to 10-bed dorms, home-cooked meals (€12), takeaway picnics (€9) and a handy location 300m from the station. The one possible downside? Large school groups occasionally overrun the place.

★ **Pierre Geronimi**   ICE CREAM
(☑ 97 98 69 11; www.glacespierregeronimi.com; 36 bd d'Italie; 1/2/3 scoops €3.80/6/8; ☉ 8am-7pm Mon-Sat Oct-Apr, 7.30am-7.30pm Mon-Sat & 10am-6pm Sun May-Sep) A bit of a local secret: Monaco's best ice creams and sorbets, made by its eponymous Corsican *maître glacier*. Try chestnut flour, beetroot, matcha tea or honey and pine nut flavour– and for the ultimate indulgence, ask for it to be served cocktail-style in a glass *verrine*. He also creates delicious ice-cream cakes and patisseries.

Monte Carlo Casino

TIMELINE

1863 Charles III inaugurates the first Casino on Plateau des Spélugues. The ❶ **atrium** is a small room with a wooden podium from which an orchestra entertains while punters purchase entrance tickets.

1864 Hôtel de Paris opens and the area becomes known as the 'Golden Square'.

1865 Construction of ❷ **Salle Europe**. Cathedral-like, it is lined with onyx columns and lit by eight Bohemian crystal chandeliers weighing 150kg each.

1868 The steam train arrives in Monaco and ❸ **Café de Paris** is completed.

1878–79 Gambling moves to Hôtel de Paris while Charles Garnier is charged with building a new casino with a miniature replica of the Paris Opera House, ❹ **Salle Garnier**.

1890 The advent of electricity casts a glow on architect Jules Touzet's newly added ❺ **gaming rooms** for high rollers.

1903 Inspired by female gamblers, Henri Schmit decorates ❻ **Salle Blanche** with caryatids and the painting *Les Grâces Florentines*.

1904 Smoking is banned in the gaming rooms and ❼ **Salon Rose**, a new smoking room, is added.

1910 ❽ **Salle Médecin**, immense and grand, hosts the high-spending Private Circle.

1966 Celebrations mark 100 years of uninterrupted gambling despite two world wars.

TOP TIPS

➡ After 2pm when gaming begins, admission is strictly for 18 years and over. Rooms beyond the Salle Europe are closed to the general public. Photo ID is obligatory.

➡ Don't wear trainers. A jacket for men is not obligatory (but is recommended) in the gaming rooms.

➡ In the main room, the minimum bet is €5/25 for roulette/blackjack.

➡ In the *salons privés*, there is no maximum bet.

S-F/SHUTTERSTOCK ©

Atrium
The casino's 'lobby', so to speak, is paved in marble and lined with 28 Ionic columns, which support a balustraded gallery canopied with an engraved glass ceiling.

Hôtel de Paris

HÔTEL DE PARIS

Notice the horse's shiny leg (and testicles) on the lobby's statue of Louis XIV on horseback? Legend has it that rubbing them brings good luck in the casino.

Salon Rose
Smoking was banned in the gaming rooms following a fraud involving a croupier letting his ash fall on the floor. The Salon Rose (Pink Room; today a restaurant) was therefore opened in 1903 for smokers – the gaze of Gallelli's famous cigarillo-smoking ladies follows you around the room.

Salle Garnier
Taking eight months to build and two years to restore (2004–06), the opera's original statuary is rehabilitated using original moulds saved by the creator's grandson. Individual air-con and heating vents are installed beneath each of the 525 seats.

DEA/G. DAGLI ORTI/GETTY IMAGES ©

Salle Europe

The oldest part of the casino, where they continue to play *trente-et-quarante* and European roulette, which have been played here since 1865. Tip: the bull's-eye windows around the room originally served as security observation points.

Café de Paris

With the arrival of Diaghilev as director of the Monte Carlo Opera in 1911, Café de Paris becomes the go-to address for artists and gamblers. It retains the same high-glamour ambience today. Tip: snag a seat on the terrace and people-watch.

LABORANT/SHUTTERSTOCK ©

Jardins des Boulingrins

Place du Casino

③

Salles Touzet

This vast partitioned hall, 21m by 24m, is decorated in the most lavish style: oak, Tonkin mahogany and oriental jasper panelling are offset by vast canvases, Marseille bronzes, Italian mosaics, sculptural reliefs and stained-glass windows.

Jardins du Casino

①

② ⑤

⑦

④

⑧

⑥

Salle Médecin

Also known as Salle Empire because of its extravagant Empire-style decor, Monégasque architect François Médecin's gaming room was originally intended for the casino's biggest gamblers. Part of it still remains hidden from prying eyes as a Super Privé room.

Terraces, Gardens & Walkways

Fairmont Monte Carlo

Salle Blanche

Today a superb bar-lounge, the Salle Blanche (White Room) opens onto an outdoor gaming terrace. The caryatids on the ceiling were modelled on fashionable courtesans such as La Belle Otéro, who placed her first bet here aged 18.

BEST VIEWS

Wander behind the casino through manicured gardens and gaze across Victor Vasarely's vibrant op-art mosaic, *Hexagrace*, to views of the harbour and the sea.

Hexagrace Mosaic

Monaco

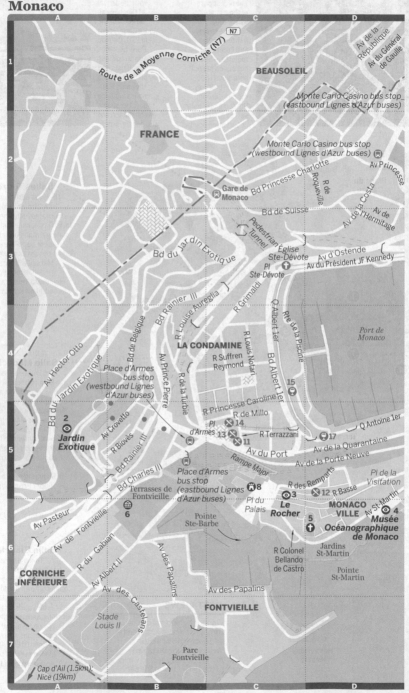

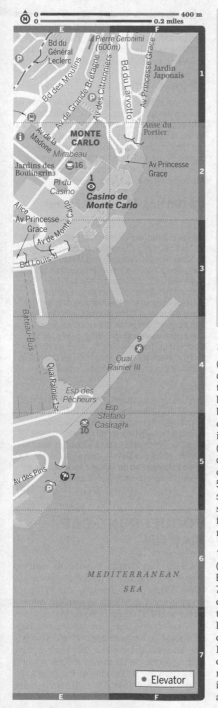

N
0 ____ 400 m
0 ____ 0.2 miles

★ **Marché de la Condamine**　　MARKET €

(www.facebook.com/marche.condamine; 15 place d'Armes; ⊙7am-3pm Mon-Sat, to 2pm Sun) For tasty, excellent-value fare around shared tables, hit Monaco's fabulous food court, tucked beneath the arches behind the open-air place d'Armes market. Rock-bottom budget faves include fresh pasta from **Maison des Pâtes** (☏93 50 95 77; Marché de la Condamine, 15 place d'Armes; pasta €6.40-12; ⊙7am-3.30pm) and traditional Niçois *socca* from **Chez Roger** (☏93 50 80 20; Marché de la Condamine, 15 place d'Armes; socca €3; ⊙10am-3pm); there's also pizza and seafood from **Le Comptoir**, truffle cuisine from **Truffle Bistrot**, a deli, a cafe, a cheesemonger and more.

★ **La Montgolfière**　　FUSION €€€

(☏97 98 61 59; www.lamontgolfiere.mc; 16 rue Basse; 3-/4-course menu €47/54; ⊙noon-2pm & 7.30-9.30pm Mon, Tue & Thu-Sat) Monégasque chef Henri Geraci has worked in some of the Riviera's top restaurants, but he's now happily settled at his own establishment down a shady alleyway near the palace. Escoffier-trained, he's faithful to the French classics, but his travels have inspired a fondness for Asian flavours, so expect some exotic twists. The restaurant's small and sought after, so reserve ahead.

OFF THE BEATEN TRACK

FLEE THE CROWDS

A serene alternative to the sweaty hike with the crowds up Rampe Majeur to Le Rocher is a panoramic stroll along the port's **dyke** (Monaco Dyke), the world's largest floating dyke, 28m wide and 352m long. Scale the steps at the end of quai Antoine 1er and bear left to the viewpoint at the dyke's far end, next to the cruiseship terminal, for an outstanding Monte Carlo panorama.

Backtrack to **Esplanade Stefano Casiraghi** for a quick flop in the sun on the contemporary sun deck here; ladders allow you to dip into the water. Then weave your way along the coastal path and up through the shady Jardins St-Martin to Le Rocher. Look out for stone steps leading down to a **secret shingle beach** (Plage des Pêcheurs) only locals know about.

🍷 Drinking & Nightlife

Much of Monaco's superchic drinking goes on in its designer restaurants and the bars of luxury hotels. For a lower-key ambience, head to the relaxed bars located behind the port. Monégasque people are fond of wine and will drink it almost any time of day. The signature after-dinner drink is limoncello, sometimes homemade with lemons grown in the region.

Brasserie de Monaco MICROBREWERY
(📞97 98 51 20; www.facebook.com/brasseriede monacomc; 36 rte de la Piscine; ⏰noon-2am) This bar down by La Condamine is Monaco's only microbrewery, and its organic lagers and ales pack the punters in. Inside it's all chrome, steel and big-screen TVs, and live sport and DJs keep the weekends extra busy. For a more chilled experience, head for the portside patio out the front. Happy hour's from 6pm to 8pm.

Rascasse BAR
(📞06 16 16; www.larascassemontecarlo.com; 1 quai Antoine; ⏰4pm-5am) This two-storey lounge bar down by the port draws the crowds at aperitif time, then morphs into Monaco's liveliest nightspot, with live music Monday through Friday and all-night DJs on weekends.

Café de Paris CAFE
(📞98 06 76 23; www.facebook.com/cafedeparis montecarlo; place du Casino; ⏰8am-2am) The *grande dame* of Monaco's cafes (founded in 1882), it's perfect for *un petit café* and a spot of people-watching. Everything is chronically overpriced, and the waiters can be horrendously snooty, but it's the price you pay for a front-row view of Monte Carlo's razzamatazz.

ℹ️ Information

Get maps and info – along with your semi-official Monaco passport stamp – at the helpful **tourist office** (📞92 16 61 16; www.visitmonaco.com; 2a bd des Moulins; ⏰9am-7pm Mon-Sat, 11am-1pm Sun) just above the casino. For tourist information by the port, head to the seasonal kiosk near the cruise-ship terminal on Esplanade des Pêcheurs, open mid-June to mid-September.

ℹ️ Getting There & Around

BUS

Lignes d'Azur (www.lignesdazur.com) runs bus 100 (€1.50, every 15 minutes from 6am to 9pm) to/from Nice (45 minutes) and Menton (40 minutes) along the Corniche Inférieure; bus 110 (one way/return €22/33, hourly) goes to/from Nice-Côte d'Azur airport (45 minutes). Eastbound, both services stop at the tunnel entrance near **place d'Armes** and the **Monte Carlo Casino bus stop** in front of the tourist office. Westbound, the **casino stop** is diagonally opposite the tourist office near Jardins des Boulingrins, and the **place d'Armes stop** is on bd Charles III. Night services run Thursday to Saturday.

TRAIN

Services run about every 20 minutes east to Menton (€2.30, 12 minutes) and west to Nice (€4.10, 25 minutes). Access to the **station** (av Prince Pierre) is through pedestrian tunnels, lifts and escalators from **allée Lazare Sauvaigo**, **pont Ste-Dévote**, **place Ste-Dévote** (place Ste-Dévote) and **bd de Belgique/bd du Jardin Exotique**. There are no trains between midnight and 5.30am.

ROQUEBRUNE-CAP MARTIN

POP 12,679

Beautiful Cap Martin nestles its languid shores into the sea of crystalline water between Monaco and Menton. The village of Roquebrune-Cap-Martin is actually centred on the medieval village of Roquebrune, which towers over the cape (the village and cape are linked by innumerable *very* steep steps). The amazing thing about this place is that, despite Monaco's proximity, it feels a world away from the urban glitz of the principality: the coastline around Cap Martin remains relatively unspoiled and it's as if Roquebrune had left its clock on medieval time.

◉ Sights & Activities

It takes 30 to 45 minutes to climb from Cap Martin to Roquebrune, depending on your fitness level (and a lot less the other way around since it's downhill). You'll find several staircases linking the two parts of town.

★ **Cabanon Le Corbusier**   ARCHITECTURE
(☑ 06 48 72 90 53; www.capmoderne.com; Promenade Le Corbusier; guided tours adult/child €18/ free; ☉ guided tours 10am & 2pm May-Sep) The only building French architect Le Corbusier (1887–1965) ever built for himself is this rather simple – but very clever – beach hut on Cap Martin. The *cabanon* (small beach hut), which he completed in 1952, became his main holiday home until his death. The hut can be visited on excellent two-hour guided tours run by the Association Cap Moderne; tours depart on foot from Roquebrune-Cap-Martin train station and must be reserved in advance by email.

★ **Villa E-1027**   ARCHITECTURE
(☑ 06 48 72 90 53; www.capmoderne.com; guided tours adult/child €18/free; ☉ tours 10am & 2pm May-Sep) Irish modernist architect Eileen Gray designed this tour de force of a Mediterranean villa, complete with highly inventive furniture and fixtures, in the late 1920s. Nearly a century later, after an extensive renovation, it is once again open to the public for guided tours. Other noteworthy features of the villa include its beautiful landscaping and seaside location, along with the murals added by Le Corbusier against Gray's wishes in the 1930s. Reserve ahead online; tour size is limited to 12 people.

🛏 Sleeping & Eating

Hôtel Victoria   DESIGN HOTEL €€€
(☑ 04 93 35 65 90; www.hotel-victoria.fr; 7 promenade du Cap Martin; d €133-291; ⊛ @ 🛜) Well placed on the waterfront, between Roquebrune's urban attractions and the wilder shores of Cap Martin, this recently remodelled four-star hotel features immaculate blue and white rooms, with balconies on the sea-facing units. It's next to the bus 100 stop (going to Menton, Nice and Monaco) and 500m from Roquebrune-Cap-Martin train station (on the Nice–Ventimille route). Rates are cheaper online.

Les Deux Frères   MODERN FRENCH €€
(☑ 04 93 28 99 00, 06 80 86 22 41; www.lesdeux freres.com; 1 place des Deux Frères; lunch/dinner menus €28/53; ☉ noon-1.30pm & 7.30-9.30pm Wed-Sun; 🛜) This gourmet hotel-restaurant with panoramic terrace is super stylish. Eight chic boutique rooms (doubles €75 to €110) – two with sea view – slumber up top, while waiters in black serve magnificent dishes (dishes for two such as huge pieces of meat or whole fish, delicate fish fillets in hollandaise sauce or spinach and basil olive oil) hidden beneath silver domed platters.

ℹ Information

Tourist Office (☑ 04 93 35 62 87; www.roque brune-cap-martin.com; 218 av Aristide Briand; ☉ 9am-12.30pm & 2-5.30pm Mon-Sat) Local information on the Roquebrune area.

ℹ Getting There & Away

Bus 100 (€1.50) goes to Monaco (15 minutes), Nice (1¼ hours) and Menton (15 minutes); it stops on av de la Côte d'Azur, which lies below Roquebrune and above Cap Martin (you'll see steps near the bus stop).

The Roquebrune-Cap-Martin **train station** is at the western end of Cap Martin, adjacent to the coastal path and steeply downhill from Château de Roquebrune. Destinations include Monaco (€1.60, four minutes), Nice (€4.80, 30 minutes), Menton (€1.40, six minutes) and Ventimiglia (€3.90, 25 minutes). Trains run half-hourly.

MENTON

POP 28,231

Last stop on the Côte d'Azur before Italy, the seaside town of Menton offers a glimpse of what the high life on the Riviera must have been like before the developers moved in. With its sunny climate, shady streets and pastel mansions – not to mention a lovely old port – it's one of the most attractive towns on the entire coast. Menton's old town is a cascade of pastel-coloured buildings. Add a fantastic museum dedicated to the great artist and film director Jean Cocteau, as well as several excellent restaurants, and Menton really is a must.

To French people, the town is also known for its lemons, which are renowned for their flavour and celebrated every February with a big lemon-themed party.

A COASTAL HIKE

With the exception of a 4km stretch through Monaco, you can walk the entire 13km coastal strip between Roquebrune-Cap Martin and Cap d'Ail without passing a car. Starting west of Menton, the **Sentier du Littoral** follows Cap Martin's rugged coastline past beaches and wooded shores, including beautiful **Plage Buse**, all the way to Monaco's **Plage Larvotto**. Resuming at **Plage Marquet** near Monaco's western edge, the path skirts dramatic coastal bluffs all the way to hedonistic **Plage Mala** in Cap d'Ail.

The walk is easy going, but visitors should note that the stretch of coast between Monaco and Cap d'Ail is inaccessible in bad weather. The path is well signposted and you can easily walk small sections or make a day trip out of it, including beach stops and lunch in Monaco. The Roquebrune-Cap Martin and Cap d'Ail train stations both make ideal starting points, depending on which section you wish to tackle first. If you don't fancy walking through Monaco, you can catch bus 6 from Larvotto to Fontvieille.

⊙ Sights & Activities

The town's epicentre is the bustling, pedestrianised rue St-Michel, with its ice-cream parlours and souvenir shops.

★ Musée Jean Cocteau
Collection Séverin Wunderman　　　GALLERY

(☑ 04 89 81 52 50; www.museecocteaumenton.fr; 2 quai de Monléon; adult/child Jun-Oct €10/free, Nov-May €8/free; ⊙ 10am-6pm Wed-Mon) Art collector Séverin Wunderman donated some 1500 Cocteau works to Menton in 2005 on the condition that the town build a dedicated Cocteau museum. And what a museum Menton built: this futuristic, low-rise building is a wonderful space to make sense of Cocteau's eclectic work. Its collection includes drawings, ceramics, paintings and cinematographic work, with exhibits rotating annually. Admission includes the Cocteau-designed Musée du Bastion.

Musée du Bastion　　　GALLERY
(quai Napoléon III; adult/child Jun-Oct €10/free, Nov-May €8/free; ⊙ 10am-6pm Wed-Mon) Cocteau loved Menton. It was following a stroll along the seaside that he got the idea of turning a disused 17th-century bastion (1636) on the seafront into a monument to his work. He restored the building himself, decorating the alcoves, outer walls, reception hall and floors with pebble mosaics. The works on display change regularly. Admission includes entry to the Musée Jean Cocteau.

Jardin de la Serre de la Madone　　　GARDENS
(☑ 04 93 57 73 90; www.serredelamadone.com; 74 rte de Gorbio; adult/child €8/4; ⊙ 10am-6pm Tue-Sun Apr-Oct, to 5pm Jan-Mar, closed Nov & Dec) Beautiful if slightly unkempt, this garden was designed by American botanist Lawrence Johnston. He planted dozens of rare plants picked up from his travels around the world. Abandoned for decades, it has been mostly restored to its former glory. Guided tours (1½ hours) take place daily at 3pm. Take Zest bus 7 (€1.50, 15 minutes) from Menton's train or bus station to the Serre de la Madone stop.

✖ Festivals & Events

Fête du Citron　　　CARNIVAL
(Lemon Festival; www.fete-du-citron.com; ⊙ Feb) Menton's quirky two-week Fête du Citron sees sculptures and decorative floats made from tonnes of lemons weave along the seafront. Afterwards, the monumental lemon creations are dismantled and the fruit sold off at bargain prices in front of Palais de l'Europe. Each year the festival follows a different theme.

⌂ Sleeping & Eating

In the old town, pedestrianised rue du Vieux Collège is worth a meander for its tasty lineup of eateries. Rue St-Michel is littered with touristy shops selling lemon-based products, including limoncello, lemonade, lemon-infused olive oil and lemon preserves.

Hôtel Lemon　　　HOTEL €
(☑ 04 93 28 63 63; www.hotel-lemon.com; 10 rue Albert 1er; s €65, d €73-85; ☎) Hôtel Lemon sits in an attractive 19th-century villa with a pretty garden, opposite a school. Its spacious minimalist rooms are decked out in shades of white with bright red or lemon-yellow bathrooms. Breakfast costs €9.

★ Hôtel Napoléon　　　BOUTIQUE HOTEL €€
(☑ 04 93 35 89 50; www.napoleon-menton.com; 29 porte de France; d €95-330, junior ste €149-450; ✳ @ ☎ ☎) Standing tall on the seafront, the Napoléon is Menton's most stylish sleeping option. Everything from the pool to the

restaurant-bar and the back garden (a haven of freshness in summer) has been beautifully designed. Rooms are decked out in white and blue, with Cocteau drawings on headboards. Sea-facing rooms have balconies but are a little noisier because of the traffic.

Au Baiser du Mitron BAKERY €
(The Baker's Kiss; ☑ 04 93 57 67 82; www.au-baiserdumitron.com; 8 rue Piéta; items from €1; ☺ 8am-7pm Tue-Sun) This one-of-a-kind *boulangerie* showcases breads from the Côte d'Azur, inland Provence and other favourite spots from baker-owner Kevin Le Meur's world travels. Everything is baked in a traditional *four à bois* (wood bread oven) from 1906, using 100% natural ingredients and no preservatives. The *tarte au citron de Menton* (Menton lemon tart) is the best there is.

Le Bistrot des Jardins PROVENCAL €€
(☑ 04 93 28 28 09; www.le-bistrot-des-jardins.fr; 14 av Boyer; 2-/3-course menus lunch €27/33, dinner €33/40; ☺ noon-2pm & 7.30-9.30pm Tue-Sat, noon-2pm Sun) Reservations are required at this delightful patio garden restaurant with tables clothed in lilac languishing al fresco between flowering magnolias and aromatic pots of thyme, sage and other Provençal herbs. The traditional, market-inspired cuisine is equally attractive.

★ **Le Mirazur** GASTRONOMY €€€
(☑ 04 92 41 86 86; www.mirazur.fr; 30 av Aristide Briand; lunch menus €80-110, dinner menus €110-210; ☺ 12.15-2pm & 7.15-10pm Wed-Sun Mar-Dec) Design, cuisine and sea views (the full sweep of the Med) are all spectacular at this 1930s villa with a twinset of Michelin stars. This is the culinary kingdom of daring Argentinian chef Mauro Colagreco, who flavours dishes not with heavy sauces but with herbs and flowers from Le Mirazur's dazzling herb and flower garden, citrus orchard and vegetable patch.

Find it 3km northeast of Menton off the coastal D6007 to Italy. Cooking classes too.

HOT LUNCH DATE

Drop-dead-gorgeous **Gorbio** (population 1387), just a few kilometres inland from Menton and the Mediterranean coast, is a classic Provençal *village perché* (hilltop village). Strolling through the town's narrow medieval streets is the main entertainment here, along with the scenic climb to the neighbouring village of **Ste-Agnès** or a meal to remember at **Le Beauséjour** (☑ 04 93 41 46 15; 14 place de la République; lunch/dinner menus €29/47, mains €20-28; ☺ noon-2.30pm Thu-Tue Apr-Oct, 7.15-9.30pm Jul-Sep). The stuff of Provençal lunch dreams, 'Beautiful Stay' serves delicious local fare in a buttermilk house with front terrace overlooking Gorbio's village square. The interior dining room, straight out of a design magazine, proffers panoramic views of the tumbling vale. Every item, from salade niçoise to duck breast glazed with local honey, is a work of art. No credit cards.

ℹ Information

Tourist Office (☑ 04 92 41 76 76; www.tourisme-menton.fr; 8 av Boyer; ☺ 9am-7pm Jul & Aug, 9am-12.30pm & 2-6pm Mon-Sat Sep-Jun)

ℹ Getting There & Away

Bus 100, operated by **Lignes d'Azur** (p861), runs frequently to Nice (€1.50, 1½ hours) via Monaco (40 minutes) and the Corniche Inférieure. Bus 110 links Menton with Nice-Côte d'Azur airport (one way/return €22/33, 1¼ hours, hourly). **Zest** (☑ 04 93 35 93 60; www.zestbus.fr) offers additional bus service to inland villages such as Gorbio, Roquebrune and Ste-Agnès.

There are regular train services (half-hourly) to Ventimiglia in Italy (€2.70, 10 minutes), Monaco (€2.30, 11 minutes) and Nice (€5.50, 40 minutes).

Corsica

POP 338,000

Includes ➡

Best Places to Eat

- La Sassa (p906)
- A Pignata (p926)
- U Casanu (p911)
- La Rivière Des Vins (p927)
- Kissing Pigs (p922)

Best Places to Stay

- Hôtel Demeure Les Mouettes (p916)
- Auberge U n'Antru Versu (p925)
- Maison Battisti (p905)
- Hôtel Demeure Castel Brando (p904)
- Les Roches Rouges (p913)

Why Go?

Jutting from the foaming Mediterranean like an impregnable fortress, Corsica resembles a miniature continent, with astounding geographical diversity. Within half an hour's drive, the landscape ranges from glittering bays, vibrant coastal cities and fabulous beaches to sawtooth mountain ridges, verdant valleys, dense forests and time-forgotten hilltop villages. Holidays in Corsica offer tremendously varying opportunities: from hiking and canyoning to snorkelling and sunbathing, enjoying a leisurely boat trip, delving into the island's multifaceted history and sampling local delicacies.

Though Corsica has been part of France for more than 200 years, it feels different from the mainland in everything from customs and cuisine to language and character. Locals love to explain their Corsican identity so plenty of engaging evenings await, especially if the holy trilogy of food, wine and harmonious Corsican music are involved.

When to Go
Ajaccio

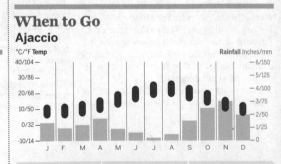

Easter Marked by solemn processions and colourful passion plays.

May & Jun The maquis is in blossom and while it's warm enough to swim, it's not too hot to hike.

Jul–Sep Enjoy the summer party vibe at beach restaurants and nightclubs.

Corsica Highlights

1 Réserve Naturelle de Scandola (p912) Cruising the sapphire waters off Corsica's northwestern coast.

2 Cap Corse (p900) Exploring this wild and remote peninsula by way of winding coastal roads.

3 Les Calanques de Piana (p913) Seeing red, blazing red, flaming between fantastic rock formations.

4 Vallée du Tavignano (p928) Hiking through this gorgeous, road-free mountain valley near Corte.

5 Plage de Palombaggia (p923) Slipping into serene turquoise waters at Corsica's prettiest beach.

6 Filitosa (p918) Meeting the amazing megalithic builders, face to face.

7 Ajaccio (p913) Boning up on Bonaparte around Napoléon's home town.

8 Îles Lavezzi (p922) Discovering island paradises, halfway to Italy.

9 Bonifacio (p919) Marvelling at Corsica's most dramatic fortified town, perched on the edge of a cliff.

10 Aiguilles de Bavella (p925) Walking and canyoning among the rocky 'needles' of this soaring massif.

ℹ Getting There & Away

AIR

Corsica's four airports – Ajaccio, Bastia, Calvi and Figari (north of Bonifacio) – are served by regular year-round flights from the French mainland airports, and in summer from other European countries as well.

BOAT
To/from Mainland France

Corsica's five ferry ports (Ajaccio, Bastia, Île Rousse, Porto-Vecchio and Propriano) can be reached from Nice, Marseille and Toulon. Journeys last between 5½ and 15½ hours, depending on the route, size of vessel and time of day. There are numerous crossings in summer, but far fewer in winter. Always book in advance.

Fares vary dramatically – anything from €30 to €100 for a foot passenger – depending on route, degree of comfort, need for overnight accommodation, and size of vehicle (if any). Expect to pay around €500 return for a car and two passengers from Nice to Ajaccio in July and August.

Ferry companies include **Corsica Ferries** (☑ 08 25 09 50 95; www.corsica-ferries.fr), **La Méridionale** (☑ 04 91 99 45 09, 09 70 83 13 20; www.lameridionale.com) and **Corsica Linea** (☑ 08 25 88 80 88; www.corsicalinea.com).

To/from Italy

Ferries operated by **Corsica Ferries** (p900), **La Méridionale** (p900) and **Moby** (☑ 09 74 56 20 75, 04 95 34 84 94; www.mobycorse.fr) link Corsica with the mainland Italian ports of Genoa, Livorno and Savona, and Porto Torres in Sardinia year-round. From April to October, Moby and **Blu Navy** (☑ 05 65 26 97 10; www.blunavytraghetti.com) also sail between Bonifacio and Santa Teresa di Gallura in Sardinia.

GETTING AROUND

By far the best way to get around Corsica is by car, but rental and fuel costs can quickly add up. Even with the help of sat-nav, you'll need a detailed road map, such as Michelin's yellow-jacketed *Corse-du-Sud, Haute-Corse* (map 345), covering the entire island at a scale of 1:150,000.

Public transport only connects the larger towns and cities, from which local explorations can continue on foot or by bike or scooter

---

ℹ **SEASONAL WARNING**

Corsica's tourism is heavily seasonal. Most hotels, restaurants and even sights open only from Easter to October, so winter visitors will need patience, a good book and an appetite for walking...

(both readily available for hire). Corsica's only train line, the **Chemin de Fer de la Corse** (www.cf-corse.corsica), is an attractive if limited option, running across the stunning mountainous interior between Bastia and Ajaccio, with a branch route to Calvi and Île Rousse. The bus network is more comprehensive but often there's only one bus per day, and none on Sunday.

Corsica Bus & Train (www.corsicabus.org) is a tip-top, one-stop website displaying up-to-date bus and train timetables, island-wide.

THE NORTHEAST

Northeastern Corsica encapsulates the island at its very best. Historic Bastia, Corsica's second city and largest ferry port, is not just a great point of arrival; with its maze of alleyways, bustling medieval harbour, and imposing citadel, it's also a place where you could happily linger for several days. Immediately north, the enchanting Cap Corse peninsula boasts spectacular coastal scenery, as well as delightful villages like Nonza, Centuri and Erbalunga, while to the west St-Florent is an exquisite little port-cum-resort.

Bastia

POP 43,675

As France's second busiest passenger port, after Calais, the dynamic city of Bastia remains lively year-round, and offers a wonderful welcome to Corsica. While it may not have the relaxed charm of its long-term rival Ajaccio, and is home to fewer people, it's much larger to stroll around, and has the feel of a genuine lived-in city that refuses to sell its soul just to please the tourists.

Bastia's historic core consists of two distinct neighbourhoods: Terra Vecchia, surrounding the small original harbour; and Terra Nova, the high-walled citadel above. Although those names mean 'Old Land' and 'New Land', the hilltop fortress is actually much older, built from the 15th century onwards as the stronghold of Bastia's Genoese overlords. What's now the Terra Vecchia replaced the tiny fishing village below with a tangle of alleyways, an ensemble of splendidly top-heavy tenement blocks, and some fine churches.

⊙ Sights

★ Terra Vecchia OLD TOWN

Criss-crossed by narrow lanes, Terra Vecchia is Bastia's heart and soul. Shady **place de l'Hôtel de Ville** hosts a lively morning market on Saturday and Sunday. One block west, baroque **Chapelle de l'Immaculée Conception** (rue des Terrasses; ⊙8am-7pm), with its elaborately painted barrel-vaulted ceiling, served as the seat of the short-lived Anglo-Corsican parliament in 1795. Further north, **Chapelle St-Roch** (rue Napoléon; ⊙8am-7pm) holds an 18th-century organ and *trompe l'œil* roof.

★ Vieux Port HARBOUR

Bastia's Vieux Port is ringed by precariously tall, pastel-coloured tenements and buzzy brasseries, and overlooked by the twin-towered **Église St-Jean Baptiste** (4 rue du Cardinal Viale Préla; ⊙8am-noon & 3-7pm Mon-Sat). The best views of the harbour are from the citadel or the hillside park of **Jardin Romieu**, reached via a stately old staircase that twists up from the waterfront.

★ Terra Nova OLD TOWN

Looming above the harbour, Bastia's stern-walled citadel was built between the 15th and 17th centuries for the city's Genoese masters. Known as the Terra Nova, despite looking much older than the lower town, it's largely residential and uncommercialised. The amber-hued **Palais des Gouverneurs** now houses the **Musée de Bastia** (☑04 95 31 09 12; www.musee-bastia.com; place du Donjon; adult/child €5/2.50, Oct-Apr free; ⊙10am-6.30pm daily Jul & Aug, Tue-Sun May-Jun & Sep, 9am-noon & 2-5pm Tue-Sun Oct-Apr), while the majestic **Cathédrale Ste-Marie** (rue de l'Évêché; ⊙8am-noon & 2-6.30pm Mon-Sat, to 5.30pm Oct-Mar, 8am-noon Sun) and the rococo **Église Ste-Croix** (rue de l'Évêché; ⊙9am-noon & 2-6pm Mon-Sat, to 5pm Oct-Mar), home to a mysterious black-oak crucifix found in the sea in 1428, stand side by side a few streets south.

🛏 Sleeping

Hôtel Central HOTEL €€

(☑04 95 31 71 12; www.centralhotel.fr; 3 rue Miot; d €120-150, apt €160; ❄🕙) From the black-and-white tiled floor in the entrance to the sweeping central staircase – there's no lift – this family-run hotel oozes vintage charm. Guest rooms come in all shapes and sizes, but like the appealing breakfast room, they're kitted out with idiosyncratic

DON'T MISS

SUMMER COOLER

A Bastia institution, still going strong after more than 80 years, glorious ice-cream parlour **Raugi** (☑04 95 31 22 31; 2 rue du Chanoine Colombani; ice cream from €2; ⊙9.30am-11pm Tue-Sat, 9.30am-noon & 2-11pm Sun Oct-May, 9.30am-12.30pm & 4.30pm-1am Tue-Sun Jun-Sep, closed mid-Feb–mid-Mar) tempts with Corsican flavours including chestnut, mandarin, fig, aromatic *senteur de maquis* (the herbal scent of the wilderness) and sweet *myrte* (myrtle). In summer, they open an annex by the old port.

1940s fixtures and furnishings. The three apartments, with fully equipped kitchen, are great for longer stays.

★ Hôtel-Restaurant La Corniche HOTEL €€

(☑04 95 31 40 98; www.hotel-lacorniche.com; D31, San Martino di Lota; d €88-130; ⊙mid-Feb–Dec; ❄🕙🏊) Perched high in the hills, 8km along a tortuous road northwest of Bastia, this veteran family-run hotel makes a brilliant halfway house between city and wilderness. Summertime ushers in dreamy lounging in the bijou back garden, by the pool or on the panoramic terrace – the sea views will leave you smitten.

★ Hôtel des Gouverneurs HOTEL €€€

(☑04 95 47 10 10; www.hotel-desgouverneurs.com; 3 rue des Turquines; d €260-320, ste €430-510; ⊙Feb-Dec; ❄🕙🏊) The only hotel within Bastia's hilltop citadel is a stylish contemporary gem. Tiers of peaceful, spacious rooms and suites drop down the seaward slope, with tremendous views over the port and along the coast. There's a spa and indoor pool, but no restaurant. Set in a pedestrian enclave, guests will need to walk the final 200m from the nearest car park.

🍴 Eating

Chez Vincent PIZZA, FRENCH €

(☑04 95 31 62 50; www.facebook.com/chez.vincent.1; 12 rue St-Michel; pizzas €9.50-12.50, mains €18-26; ⊙noon-2pm Mon-Fri, 6.30-11pm Mon-Sat; ☑) The great selling point of this long-standing local favourite is its location, with a terrace perched at the edge of the citadel and glorious views of the port. Its reputation rests on its excellent pizzas, but changing daily specials include well-executed French classics like mussels and steaks.

Bastia

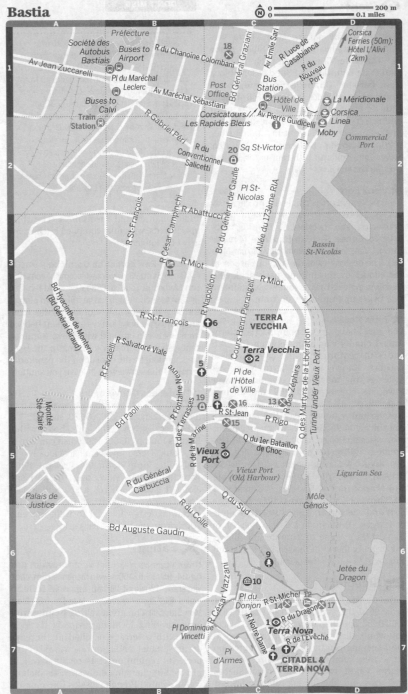

N 0 — 200 m
0 — 0.1 miles

Préfecture

Av Jean Zuccarelli

Société des Autobus Bastiais

Buses to Airport

Pl du Maréchal Leclerc

Buses to Calvi

Train Station

R du Chanoine Colombani

R Gabriel Péri

Av Maréchal Sébastiani

18

Post Office

Corsicatours
Les Rapides Bleus

Bus Station

Hôtel de Ville

Av Pierre Guidicelli

La Méridionale

Corsica
Linea

Moby

Corsica Ferries (50m);
Hôtel L'Alivi (2km)

R Luce de Casabianca

Av Émile Sari

Bd Général Graziani

R du Nouveau Port

Commercial Port

20 Sq St-Victor

R du Conventionnel Salicetti

Pl St-Nicolas

Bd du Général de Gaulle

Allée du 173ème RIA

Bassin St-Nicolas

R Abattucci

R César Campinchi

R St-François

R Miot

11

R Miot

R Napoléon

Cours Henri Pierangeli

TERRA VECCHIA

R St-François

6

R Salvatoré Viale

R Favalelli

R Favalelli

R Fontaine Neuve

5

Terra Vecchia 2

Pl de l'Hôtel de Ville

R des Zéphirs

Q des Martyrs de la Libération

Tunnel under Vieux Port

Bd Paoli

Montée Ste-Claire

Bd Hyacinthe de Montera
(Bd Général Giraud)

19 8

16

R St-Jean

15

13

R Rigo

R des Terrasses

R de la Marine

Vieux Port 3

Q du 1er Bataillon de Choc

Vieux Port
(Old Harbour)

Ligurian Sea

R du Général Carbuccia

Palais de Justice

R du Collé

Q du Sud

Môle Génois

Bd Auguste Gaudin

9

Jetée du Dragon

10

Pl du Donjon

R St-Michel

R du Dragon

12

14

17

R César-Vazzani

Pl Dominique Vincetti

Pl d'Armes

R Notre Dame

1

4

Terra Nova

7

R de l'Évêché

CITADEL & TERRA NOVA

Bastia

◎ **Top Sights**

◎ **Sights**

🛌 **Sleeping**

🍴 **Eating**

🛍 **Shopping**

Petit Vincent   SEAFOOD €€
(☑ 04 20 00 14 67; 1 rue du Dragon; mains €21-27; ⊘ 6.30-11pm Mon, noon-2.30pm & 6.30-11pm Tue-Sat; 🐾) The fishier, fine-dining little brother of Chez Vincent (p901) stands lower down the citadel slope, with tables on a lovely garden terrace overlooking the port as well as a very cosy indoor dining room. The changing menu concentrates on seafood, using Asian flavours to subtle and delicious effect, but usually includes a straightforward grilled fish, and at least one meat option.

Col Tempo   SEAFOOD €€
(☑ 04 95 58 14 22; www.facebook.com/coltempo bastia; 4 rue St-Jean, Vieux Port; mains €24-30; ⊘ noon-2pm & 8-10pm Tue-Sat, noon-2pm Sun) The scrumptious market-fresh cuisine served here, beside Bastia's Vieux Port, has rightly earned kudos from locals. Watch the boats bobbing in the harbour as you tuck into specialities like *rillettes de crabe au citron vert* (lime-marinated crabmeat pâté), *risotto 'retour de la pêche'* (risotto studded with fresh-caught seafood) and codfish fillet with truffled polenta and asparagus-leek fondue.

A Scudella   CORSICAN €€
(☑ 09 51 70 79 46, 06 25 27 26 25; 10 rue Pino; mains €13-18, menu €25; ⊘ 6-11.30pm Tue-Sat) Tucked down a back alley near the Vieux Port, this is a superb spot to sample traditional mountain cuisine, from appetisers of fine Corsican charcuterie and *beignets de brocciu* (sweet, lemon-scented fritters filled with ricotta-like Brocciu cheese) to *veau aux olives* (stewed veal with olives) and *flan à la châtaigne* (chestnut flan).

La Table du Marché   FRENCH €€€
(☑ 04 95 31 64 25; place de l'Hôtel de Ville; mains €22-45, menus €32 & €74; ⊘ noon-3pm & 7-10.30pm Mon-Sat) Classic, deeply traditional French restaurant, with indoor and outdoor tables surveying the old-town market square. Beautifully presented meat and seafood dishes are at their best value on the €32 set menu, while €74 buys three separate lobster courses – soup, salad and grilled – plus a dessert.

🛍 Shopping

★**LN Mattei**   FOOD & DRINKS
(☑ 04 95 32 44 38; www.capcorsemattei.com; 15 bd Général de Gaulle; ⊘ 9.30am-12.30pm & 2-7pm Mon-Sat) Run by Bastia's famous distillery, this iconic boutique has the look and feel of a grocer from the 1900s. The enticing array of bottles naturally includes Mattei's signature aperitif, Cap Corse, while gourmets can also stock up on locally milled chestnut flour, *sel à la figue* (fig-scented salt) and Corsican *marrons* (chestnuts) preserved in *eau-de-vie* (brandy).

Isula Crea   ARTS & CRAFTS
(☑ 04 95 44 02 07; 3 rue St Jean; ⊘ 10am-7pm Tue-Sat, to 1pm Sun) A fine spot to pick up authentic Corsican handicrafts, this gorgeous little old-town boutique displays and sells the work of 30 craftspeople from all over the island. There's everything from jewellery and graphic art to woodcarving and glassware.

ℹ️ Information

Tourist Office (📞 04 95 54 20 40; www.
bastia-tourisme.com; place St-Nicolas; ⏰ 8am-
8pm Mon-Sat, 8am-1pm & 3-7pm Sun Jul &
Aug, 8am-6pm Mon-Sat, to noon Sun May, Jun,
Sep & Oct, 8.30am-noon & 2-6pm Mon-Fri Nov-
Apr; 📶) Information on Bastia and Cap Corse,
plus guided tours of the city, ticket sales and
help with hotel reservations.

ℹ️ Getting There & Around

TO/FROM THE AIRPORT

Aéroport Bastia-Poretta (www.bastia.aeroport.
fr) is 20km south of the city. **Société des Autobus Bastiais** (📞 04 95 31 06 65; www.bastiabus.
com) operates frequent shuttles (€9, 35 minutes) between the airport and Bastia's **Place du
Maréchal Leclerc**, where it stops across from
the train station outside the city's Préfecture.
Taxi Aéroport Poretta (📞 04 95 36 04 65; www.
corsica-taxis.com) charges €48/66 by day/night.

BOAT

Ferry companies including **Corsica Ferries**
(p900), **Corsica Linea** (📞 08 25 88 80 88; www.
corsicalinea.com), **La Méridionale** (📞 04 91 99
45 09, 09 70 83 13 20; www.lameridionale.com)
and **Moby** (p900) have information offices at
Bastia Port (www.bastia.port.fr); they usually
open for same-day ticket sales a couple of hours
before sailings. Ferries sail to/from Marseille,
Toulon and Nice (mainland France), and Livorno,
Savona and Genoa (Italy).

BUS

Bastia's **bus station** (1 rue du Nouveau Port)
– really just a couple of open-air bus stops – is
immediately north of place St-Nicolas, behind
the Hôtel de Ville (town hall), and is used by
buses to Cap Corse as well as **Corsicatours/
Les Rapides Bleus** (📞 04 95 31 03 79; www.
rapides-bleus.com) services to Porto-Vecchio.
Buses to the airport and to **Calvi** run from the
roundabout outside the train station.

TRAIN

Services from the **train station** (www.cf-corse.
corsica; av Maréchal Sébastiani) run to Ajaccio
(€21.60, 3¾ hours, five daily) via Corte (€10.10,
1¾ hours), and Calvi (€16.40, 3¼ hours, two
daily) via Île Rousse (€13.50, 2¾ hours).

Cap Corse

Poking like a giant finger from Corsica's
northeastern corner, the Cap Corse peninsula is a world apart. Measuring 40km long by
just 10km wide, it's easily seen in a day trip
from Bastia, but you could spend your entire holiday exploring its two very different
sides. The east coast, with its rolling green
hills, pretty little ports and beautiful beaches, has a languorous feel, while the west,
across the craggy central spine, is much
more dramatic, all rocky cliffs, perched villages and strong winds.

As it loops around Cap Corse, the narrow
D80 coastal road crams in 120km of switchback curves and hair-raising drop-offs; expect slow but exhilarating driving.

Erbalunga

POP 400

North of Bastia, the coast road winds past
small beaches to reach this harbour village
after 9km. As tiny as it is picturesque, Erbalunga squeezes onto a pocket-sized promontory and centres on a cute seafront square,
strewn with well-worn fishing boats and
tempting restaurants. Narrow alleys lead
to a romantic and totally derelict **Genoese
tower** by the water.

🛏️ Sleeping & Eating

⭐ **Hôtel Demeure Castel Brando**   HOTEL €€€
(📞 04 95 30 10 30; www.en.castelbrando.com;
rte Principale; d from €200; ⏰ mid-Mar–Oct;
❄️📶🏊) Set in a stately, cream-coloured,
mid-19th-century mansion overlooking the
main road, this historic hotel offers soothing
rustic-chic rooms set around a bewitching
courtyard, plus palm-shaded gardens, two
pools (one heated) and bike rental. Some,
less charming, rooms are in a modern annexe at the back.

A Piazzetta   BISTRO €
(📞 04 95 33 28 69; place d'Erbalunga; mains €13-
23; ⏰ noon-2pm & 7-10pm daily Jul & Aug, Wed-Mon
Mar-Jun, Sep & Oct, Thu-Sun Feb & Nov, closed Jan &
Dec) With its cosy stone-walled interior and
a summertime terrace beneath an ancient
plane tree on the plaza, this good-value Corsican bistro has a quintessential village-square
vibe. It serves everything from stuffed mussels and steaks to pizzas, pasta and salads.

Le Pirate   CORSICAN €€€
(📞 04 95 33 24 20; www.restaurantlepirate.com;
lunch menu €42, dinner menus €75-90; ⏰ noon-
2pm & 7.30-10pm Jun-Sep, closed 2 days weekly –
usually Mon & Tue – Apr, May & Oct) For a meal
to remember, dine on the waterfront terrace
at this Michelin-starred restaurant, right by
the harbour. It's quite magical on a starry
summer evening, with seafood-rich *haute
cuisine* to match.

Macinaggio

POP 570

The coastal road swings inland, westwards, at little Macinaggio, well short of the peninsula's northern tip. You can only explore the seashore further north on foot, along the magnificent 24km-long **Sentier des Douaniers** (Customs Officers' Trail). A port since Roman times, Macinaggio now centres on a pleasure marina used by summer excursion boats.

🛏 Sleeping & Eating

Casa di Babbo   B&B €€

(📞 04 95 35 43 36; www.casa-di-babbo.com; Tomino; d/tr €100/120; ❄ 🐶 🌳) This lovely B&B, surrounded by fruit trees on the hillside 1km south of Macinaggio – follow the yellow signs – operates a two-night minimum stay in July and August. That's no hardship, though: its six rooms are themed and beautifully decorated, and besides the pool it has several terraces where you can while away an afternoon. The breakfasts are something to remember.

La Vela d'Oro   SEAFOOD €€

(📞 04 95 35 42 46; mains €16-32, menus €18-20; ⊘ noon-2.30pm & 7.30-10pm, closed Wed in low season & Jan–mid-Mar) Macinaggio's finest restaurant lurks in a narrow alleyway, one block back from the waterfront. Seafood is the main attraction; the best stuff, like lobster or crab, is sold by weight, so prices can soar. They do offer two set menus though: an €18 'meat' one with charcuterie and veal; and a €20 'fish' one with soup followed by fresh catch.

ℹ Information

Tourist Office (📞 04 95 35 40 34; www.macinagglorogliano-capcorse.fr; port de Plaisance de Macinaggio; ⊘ 9am-noon & 2-6pm Mon-Fri, 10am-noon Sat, shorter hours in winter) The helpful local tourist office, on the jetty poking out from the harbour, has information on Cap Corse activities of all kinds.

ℹ Getting There & Away

It takes up to an hour to drive the 37km from Bastia to Macinaggio along the D80, a route that's followed by one or two buses per day (€8, one hour, no Sunday service).

Centuri

POP 215

Rough-hewn but ravishing, the tiny harbour of Centuri, near the northwestern tip of Cap Corse, is home to one of Europe's most

---

OFF THE BEATEN TRACK

CONCHIGLIO ESCAPE

For dreamy views and a taste of rural life, check out the two B&B rooms in gloriously romantic, vintage-furnished, golden-stone **Maison Battisti** (📞 04 95 35 10 40; www.maisonbattisti.com; Conchiglio, Barrettali; r incl breakfast €95) in tiny Conchiglio, between Nonza and Centuri. The owners also rent out two enchanting self-catering cottages by the week, and sell local products in the lovely shop alongside. A 1.5km trail leads down to the beach.

CORSICA CAP CORSE

---

important lobster fleets: eight boats worked by three rival families. During lobster season, early April to early October, a cluster of waterfront restaurants compete to serve the best *pâtes à la langouste* (pasta with lobster).

🛏 Sleeping & Eating

Hôtel du Pêcheur   HOTEL €

(📞 04 95 35 60 14; port de Centuri; d €65-85; ⊘ May-Oct) Set in a four-square cream-and-red house that stands proudly at water's edge in the heart of the old port, the Auberge du Pêcheur has an unassuming retro charm. Its rooms may be simple, with old-fashioned bathrooms, double glazing not air-con, and no wi-fi, but they're great value for this pricey neck of the woods, and three have full-on harbour views.

Au Vieux Moulin   HOTEL €€

(📞 04 95 35 60 15; www.le-vieux-moulin.net; port de Centuri; d annex €135, main house €235; @ 🛜) Poised just up from the harbour, this upmarket hotel-restaurant is based in a glorious old mansion. The two nicest rooms are upstairs in the house itself, overlooking the port; the rest are in a modern annex, where some but not all have fabulous sea-view balconies. The restaurant front terrace also enjoys wonderful views.

La Bella Vista   SEAFOOD €€

(📞 04 95 35 62 60; port de Centuri; menus €21-69; ⊘ noon-2pm & 7-10pm Apr–mid-Nov) Run by a long-established fishing family, La Bella Vista is a great spot for fresh seafood and sports a sweet sunny terrace directly above the boats in the harbour. Specialities include bouillabaisse and mixed platters like the €39.50 Misto Bella Vista, a smorgasbord of squid, scallops, shrimp, grilled fish and – of course – locally caught lobster.

Nonza

POP 70

Arrayed around a rocky pinnacle that's crowned with the remains of a Genoese watchtower, Nonza is much the most attractive village on the western coast of Cap Corse. Its diminutive central square, at a sharp curve in the D80 – high above the coast at this point – is a hubbub of activity in summer, while its schist-roofed stone houses look ready to tumble down the hillside onto the black-pebble beach far below.

That beach, accessible via a rocky footpath, is a legacy of an asbestos mine that closed 50 years ago. Locals don't seem to worry about potential pollution, though – it's packed with holidaying families in high season.

Sleeping & Eating

Casa Lisa   B&B €

(04 95 37 83 52, 06 11 70 45 73; www.casalisa.fr; r €75; Apr-Oct;) Walk three minutes downhill from Nonza's central square, via a series of signposted staircases, to reach this venerable old house. Delightful views down to the shoreline unfold from the garden patio and the five simple, immaculate guest rooms. Breakfast costs €7 extra.

Le Relais du Cap   B&B €

(04 95 37 86 52; www.relaisducap.com; Marine de Negru; d with shared bathroom €85; Apr-Oct;) For the ultimate seaside escape, this friendly little B&B is hard to beat. Squeezed beside a pocket-size pebble beach, beneath a towering cliff 4km south of Nonza, it holds four neat, unpretentious doubles (sharing bathrooms), all with staggering sunset-facing views. No air-con, but who needs it with the sea breezes puffing in?

Casa Maria   B&B €€

(04 95 37 80 95; www.casamaria-corse.com; chemin de la Tour; d/q €105/175; Apr-Oct;) This bewitching hideaway is in the heart of the village, just below the tower in a coolly refurbished 18th-century mansion. Four of its five rooms revel in sea views, while three – including the family suite – sit harmoniously beneath the sloping roof. Enjoy summer breakfasts beneath a vine-clad pergola in the bijou back garden.

★ La Sassa   GRILL €€

(04 95 38 55 26; www.lasassa.com; Tour de Nonza; mains €20-40; noon-3pm & 7.30-midnight May-Sep) In a magnificent setting, on a rocky spur immediately below Nonza's Genoese watchtower, this entirely outdoor restaurant serves up succulent meat and seafood cooked on an open Argentinian-style grill. Colourfully spotlit after dark, it puts on live music weekly, with DJs other nights. The sea views and sunsets are unforgettable.

St-Florent

POP 1650

The pretty little resort of St-Florent is the principal town of the hugely fertile region known as the Nebbio, an amphitheatre-shaped valley that's ringed by high mountains and renowned for its olives, wheat and chestnuts.

Though little more than a village, St-Florent boasts its own Romanesque **cathedral** (chemin de la Cathédrale; adult/child €1.50/free; 9.30am-noon & 3-6.30pm Mon-Fri, 9.30am-noon Sat, 3-6.30pm Sun Jun–mid-Oct) dating from 1140 when Corsica was under Pisan rule. The town's picturesque 15th-century citadel was bombarded by Nelson and is closed to visitors. In summer, St-Florent springs to life as a bustling, rather upmarket holiday destination, attracting visitors with a string of restaurants, a marina crammed with pleasure boats, and a reasonable beach, **Plage de la Roya**, 2km southwest. Better beaches, best accessed by boat, lie between the isolated headlands further west.

Sleeping & Eating

Villa Serena   B&B €

(04 95 39 04 94; les Hauts de Fromentica; d incl breakfast €85; Apr-Oct;) Villa Serena comprises three simple, modern B&B rooms in a spectacular hilltop setting 1km up from the beach and 3km southwest of the town centre. Each room has outside space and its own independent entrance, and rates include breakfast, served on the wonderful sea-view terrace.

Hôtel de l'Europe   HOTEL €€

(04 95 35 32 91; www.hotel-europe2.com; port de Plaisance; d/q €118/160;) Several of the no-frills rooms in this bright, nicely refurbished quayside hotel have balconies facing the water, though noise-wise that can be a mixed blessing in the hubbub of high summer. Doubles tend to be smallish, and there are some larger quadruples; off-season rates are great value. The downstairs restaurant is pretty good.

★ **Auberge de Pecheur**   SEAFOOD **€€**
(☑06 24 36 30 42; www.aubergedupecheur.net; rte de Bastia; mains €25-38; ☺7-11.30pm Mon-Sat May–mid-Oct, open Sun July & Aug) Entering this irresistible seafood restaurant via the owners' fish shop, St-Cristophe – also the name of their boat – you get a chance to inspect the day's fresh catch before you settle into the lovely courtyard dining area. Expect exquisitely presented fishy delights of all kinds, including, for those partial to Japanese flavours, sashimi-style tuna tartare and teppanyaki grilled swordfish.

ℹ Information

Tourist Office (☑04 95 37 06 04; www.corsica-saintflorent.com; rte de Bastia; ☺9am-noon & 1.30-5.30pm Mon-Fri) Offers information on the Nebbio region as well as St-Florent itself.

ℹ Getting There & Away

St-Florent is not on a train line, but **Autocars Santini** (☑04 95 37 02 98; www.autocars santini.fr) run at least two buses daily all year to Bastia (€10, 45 minutes, no service weekends October to May), and also two daily, in July and August only, to Île Rousse (€15, 1¼ hours).

LA BALAGNE

This striking region blends history, culture and beach, with a healthy dash of Mediterranean glam to seal the deal. Whether you're looking for *la dolce vita* or *la vida loca,* you should be able to find it in Calvi or Île Rousse. But try, if you can spare the time, to venture inland, for a day trip at least. Hidden among the valleys and spurs of La Balagne's spectacular hinterland, even on the hillsides lining the coast, you'll come across cute-as-can-be villages, Romanesque chapels, olive groves and lush vineyards. A signposted route, the **Strada di l'Artigiani** (www.routedesartisans.fr), spotlights craftspeople and producers who welcome visitors, ranging from potters and woodcarvers to beekeepers and biscuit-makers.

Île Rousse

POP 3610

Straddling a long, sandy curve of coastline, and backed by maquis-cloaked mountains, the attractive little beach town of Île Rousse fills up in summer with sun-worshippers and holidaying yachties. Founded by Pascal Paoli in 1758, hoping to eclipse the Genoese-ruled port of Calvi, it has finally achieved that goal; unlike Île Rousse, Calvi no longer has ferry service from the mainland. The ferry port is just north of the centre, over a causeway on the tiny Île de la Pietra.

◉ Sights & Activities

Old Town   HISTORIC SITE
Île Rousse's delightful old town centres on tree-shaded **place Paoli**, with its daily food market (p908), designed to resemble a Greek temple, alongside.

Promenade de la Marinella   BEACH
This coastal promenade follows the seafront east from Île Rousse. The beach right by the town centre is actually very pleasant, with fine broad sand, but inevitably it can get very crowded in summer. More peaceful beaches nearby include Plage de Bodri, immediately southwest; Algajola, 8km southwest; and the magnificent Plage de Lozari, 8km east.

Île de la Pietra   ISLAND
Low, rocky Île de la Pietra, the 'russet island' that gave Île Rousse its name, is a pleasant 15-minute stroll from the centre, across a short causeway. Apart from the ferry terminal and a solitary hotel, it's uninhabited. Walk up to the **Genoese watchtower** above the port, then follow the footpath that winds to the **lighthouse** at its far end.

Club Nautique d'Île Rousse   WATER SPORTS
(☑04 95 60 22 55; www.cnir.org; rte du Port; ☺9am-6pm Jul & Aug, by arrangement Sep-Jun) Offers water-sports equipment rentals (kayaks, sailboards, stand-up paddleboards, catamarans), plus two-hour sea-kayak trips (€35) around the promontory and its islets.

🛏 Sleeping

L'Escale Côté Sud   HOTEL **€€**
(☑04 95 63 01 70; www.hotel-ilerousse.com/escale-cote-sud; 22 rue Notre-Dame; r €95-195) Open year-round, and right in the heart of town, this well-equipped modern hotel is an excellent midrange option. Four of its rooms enjoy dreamy views of limpid turquoise waters lapping the beach, just across the promenade. Besides the large lounge bar downstairs, the place also has a good restaurant just down the street.

Hôtel Perla Rossa   BOUTIQUE HOTEL **€€€**
(☑04 95 48 45 30; www.hotelperlarossa.com; 30 rue Notre-Dame; ste €290-590; ☺late Apr–mid-

Oct; ✳🛜) With its soft-apricot façade and oyster-grey shutters, this boutique old-town option adds a touch of chic to the hotel scene. All its 10 rooms are opulent suites, decorated in a soothing cream-and-orange palette, and the best have swoon-inducing sea-view balconies.

✖️ Eating

Food Market
MARKET €

(place Paoli; ⊙8am-1pm mid-Apr–Sep, shorter hours rest of year) Modelled on a Greek temple, with its open sides, tiled roof and 21 classical columns, Île Rousse's covered food market opens every morning. Outside summer, it's busiest on Fridays.

★ A Casa Corsa
CORSICAN €

(📱04 95 60 23 63; 6 place Paoli; sandwiches & salads €5-10; ⊙9am-midnight Tue-Sun mid-Mar–mid-Nov; 🖋️) With a prime location – and outdoor tables – on gorgeous place Paoli, this wine bar does a brisk trade in salads, cheese and charcuterie platters and other stalwart Corsican dishes. All the excellent, all-Corsican wines are available by the glass.

L'Escale
SEAFOOD €€

(📱04 95 60 10 53; www.hotel-ilerousse.com; 28 rue Notre-Dame; mains €22-28, menu €26; ⊙noon-3pm & 6-10pm) You'd never guess from its crisp modern appearance, with huge sea-facing windows and outdoor terrace, but this family-run restaurant has been open since 1903. Though big, it's usually full enough to keep its energetic young staff scurrying to

deliver massive helpings of fresh meat and seafood. Shellfish is a speciality, available in tapas-style sharing plates; try the delicious baked oysters.

★ Pasquale Paoli
GASTRONOMY €€€

(📱04 95 47 67 70; www.pasquale-paoli.fr; 2 place Paoli; mains €25-39, 3-course lunch/dinner menu €28/58; ⊙noon-2pm & 8-10pm daily Jun-Sep, Tue-Sat May & Oct-Dec) Whether you choose to dine in the whitewashed, vaulted dining room, or al fresco on the wood-decked terrace on the main square, this Michelin-starred gastronomic restaurant guarantees a sophisticated experience. The maître d' expertly introduces each dish, with the provenance of its ingredients, and for this quality the prices are extremely reasonable.

🍷 Drinking & Nightlife

Café des Platanes
CAFE

(place Paoli; ⊙6am-2am Jun-Sep, 7am-8.30pm Oct-May) With its wood panelling and art nouveau touches, this venerable main-square cafe has a real old-time charm. Sipping an aperitif beneath its namesake sycamores, and watching the local gents play boules – Île Rousse doesn't get any better than that.

ℹ️ Information

Tourist Office (📱04 95 60 04 35; www.ot-ile-rousse.fr; ⊙9am-7pm Mon-Sat, 10am-1pm & 3-6pm Sun Jun-Sep; 9am-noon & 2-6pm Mon-Sat Apr, May & Oct, closed Sat Nov-Mar) Information on Île Rousse and the whole Balagne region.

ℹ️ Getting There & Away

BOAT
Corsica Linea (📱08 25 88 80 88; www.corsicalinea.com) and **Corsica Ferries** (📱08 25 09 50 95; www.corsica-ferries.fr) operate ferries between Île Rousse and the mainland French ports of Marseille, Nice and Toulon, as well as Savona in Italy.

BUS
One or two buses each day head to Calvi (€4, 30 minutes) and Bastia (€14, 1¾ hours).

TRAIN
From the **train station**, at the inland end of the causeway to the ferry port, four or five daily trains run west to Calvi (€6, 40 minutes), while at least two daily services to Ponte Leccia offer onward connections to Bastia (€13.50, 2½ hours) or Ajaccio (€22.20, four hours).

DON'T MISS

THE TREMBLER

You may well tremble as the *trinighellu* (trembler) – the affectionate nickname for the dinky little coastal train **U Trinighellu** (📱04 95 32 80 57; www.cf-corse.corsica; one way €6) between Île Rousse and Calvi – trundles along its sand-covered tracks. Running six to seven times daily, and calling at 15 stations by request only, it's the easiest way to access numerous hidden coves and beaches: no traffic jams and a low-key, scenic journey.

Hop off at whichever rocky cove takes your fancy, or, for fine golden sand, at Algajola or Plage de Bodri, the closest stop to Île Rousse.

PLAGE DE L'ARINELLA

If there's one crescent of Corsican sand not to miss, it's this serene cove, tucked into the rocks with dramatic views across the bay to the citadel of Calvi, and boasting one of the island's finest beach-dining experiences.

White-clothed tables, strung along the sand and topped with straw parasols, evoke a tropical paradise at **Le Matahari** (☑ 04 95 60 78 47; www.lematahari.com; mains €18-37, dinner menu €45; ☺ noon-3pm Apr-Sep, 7-10.30pm Tue-Sun Jun-Sep). The stylish interior is shabby-chic, the waiters wear white and boaters, and the food is Mediterranean fusion: penne à la langouste (spiny lobster with pasta), sesame-coated tuna steak, fish teriyaki. Opening hours are weather-dependent, so call ahead; reservations are essential.

To drive to Plage de l'Arinella, turn off the T30 in Lumio, 6km south of Algajola and 9km east of Calvi. Follow the signs and twist 3km downhill, past leafy walled-garden second homes, to the turquoise water.

Algajola

POP 340

Historic little Algajola centres on a delightful walled enclave, on a sea-girt headland tipped by a tiny Genoese castle that's now a private home. Just 7km west of Île Rousse, and 16km from Calvi, Algajola makes a great alternative to its larger neighbours, not least because of the long, golden beach that stretches away eastwards.

🛏 Sleeping & Eating

⭐**U Castellu** B&B €€
(☑ 04 95 36 26 13; www.ucastelluchambresdhotes. com; 8 place du Château; d incl breakfast €98-166; ☺ Apr-Oct; ❄ 🤶) The five light-filled rooms in this lovely B&B, set in an old village home on the main square and right beside the ancient castle, are a wonderful blend of old and new. Maud's welcome is another drawcard, as is the panoramic rooftop terrace where they lay out the copious buffet breakfast.

The excellent **restaurant** (☑ 04 95 60 78 75; 10 place du Château; mains €16-22, menus €22-27; ☺ noon-2.30pm & 7-10.30pm Wed-Mon, 7-10.30pm Tue mid-Apr–mid-Oct) alongside serves sunny, reliable Mediterranean cuisine.

Hôtel de la Plage Santa Vittoria HOTEL €€
(☑ 04 95 35 17 03; www.hotelplage-vittoria-corse. com; A Marina; d €123-135; ☺ mid-Apr–mid-Oct; ❄ 🤶) You can't get any closer to the beach than this family-run hotel; cross the pathway beneath its ochre arcades and you're standing on yellow sand. Guest rooms are crisp and clean, and slightly larger on the town side, but those sea views are irresistible. Downsides? The beach gets *very* crowded in summer, and the wi-fi is patchy.

Le Padula SEAFOOD, PIZZA €€
(☑ 04 95 60 75 22; Plage d'Aregno; pizza from €12, mains €16-25; ☺ 8am-11pm Easter-Oct) Spectacular views and tasty, unpretentious food bring the crowds flocking to this informal beach terrace restaurant, 1km east of the centre. The menu ranges from pizza – served day and night – and the daily *plat du jour* (€16) to classic seafood snacks like fried squid or mussels cooked in wine.

ℹ Getting There & Away

Poised beside the T30, Algajola is less than half an hour from either Île Rousse or Calvi by car or train.

Calvi

POP 5300

Basking between the fiery orange bastions of its medieval citadel and a glittering moon-shaped bay that's lined by a magnificent beach, Calvi has a long and venerable history. Locals insist that Christopher Columbus was born here, in the one Genoese city on Corsica that the French could never capture, while Admiral Nelson lost his right eye besieging the citadel on behalf of Pascal Paoli.

Since the 1920s, Calvi has been a tourist hotspot, to the point where it now has the feel – and, in high season, the crowds and prices – of a chi-chi French Riviera resort. Palatial yachts jostle in its marina, overlooked by upmarket brasseries, while higher up, the citadel watchtowers stand aloof.

Come in spring or autumn, though, and there's a lot to like about Calvi. The beach is emptier, it's easier to get into a restaurant, and cooler temperatures mean you can hike along the superb coastline.

PRETTY PIGNA

The charming village of Pigna, a mirage of burnt-orange rooftops and blue-shuttered houses, nestles on the hillside 8km southwest of Île Rousse. Thanks to its auditorium, Centre Culturel Voce, it's become a high-profile destination for Corsican music fans. Artisan workshops are scattered among the sweet cobbled streets both here and in the cute hamlet of **Sant'Antonino** a little higher up, precariously perched on a rocky outcrop that commands incredible views.

In Pigna, both **Casa Musicale** (☑ 04 95 61 77 31; www.casa-musicale.org; Pigna; d €90-125; ⊙ mid-Feb–Dec; ☜) and **U Palazzu** (☑ 04 95 47 32 78; www.hotel-corse-palazzu. com; d €158-250, ste €290; ⊙ Apr-Oct) have romantic restaurant terraces worthy of a million marriage proposals, but the prize for best lunch spot has go to **A Casarella** (☑ 04 95 61 78 08; snacks from €4, mains €8-10; ⊙ 10.30am-sunset, Apr–mid-Oct).

Up the hill in pretty Sant'Antonino, stop in for a freshly squeezed lemon juice at **Cave Antonini** (☑ 06 09 58 94 01; Sant'Antonino; ⊙ 9am-6pm Apr-Oct, to 8pm Jul & Aug).

⊙ Sights & Activities

★ Citadel   HISTORIC SITE

Crowning a rocky headland, Calvi's massive citadel was fortified by Corsica's Genoese rulers from the 12th century onwards, and has fended off everyone from Franco-Turkish raiders to Anglo-Corsican besiegers. While it holds little commercial activity to match the modern town below, a scenic hour-long stroll is rewarded with superb views from its five bastions. Don't miss the **Caserne Sampiero**, once home to the Genoese governor and now used by the legendary Foreign Legion, and the 13th-century **Cathédrale St-Jean Baptiste**, home to the ebony *Christ des Miracles,* credited with saving Calvi from Saracen invasion in 1553.

Plage de Calvi   BEACH

Sun worshippers don't have far to stroll. Backed by a grove of pine trees, Calvi's stellar white-sand beach curves eastwards for 4.5km around the Golfe de Calvi from the marina.

Colombo Line   BOATING

(☑ 04 95 65 32 10; www.colombo-line.com; quai Landry, Port de Plaisance; ⊙ Apr-Oct) Colombo Line runs a bevy of seasonal boat excursions, heading along the coast from the marina – a fine way to beat the summer traffic. Highlights include day trips to the Réserve Naturelle de Scandola, with beach stopovers at Girolata (adult/child €64/32) or Ajaccio (€90/45).

🛏 Sleeping

Relais International de la
Jeunesse U Carebellu   HOSTEL €

(☑ 04 95 65 14 16; www.clajsud.fr; rte de Pietra Maggiore; dorm €20, cash only; ⊙ Apr-Oct; Ⓟ ☜) This good-value hostel spreads through two buildings on the hillside 4km south of the centre, near the start (or end) of the GR20 footpath. As well as two large dorms, it offers smaller three- to five-person rooms. Rates include breakfast, other meals also available. You'll need a vehicle to get here, but station pick-ups are sometimes available.

Hôtel Le Magnolia   HOTEL €€

(☑ 04 95 65 19 16; www.hotel-le-magnolia.com; rue Alsace Lorraine; d from €125; ⊙ Apr-Oct; ❄☜) Right by the church in the heart of town, this attractive mansion sits in a beautiful high-walled courtyard garden adorned by a handsome magnolia tree. Pretty much every room has a lovely outlook – rooftops, garden or sea – while connecting doubles make it a hit with families.

Hôtel La Villa   LUXURY HOTEL €€€

(☑ 04 95 65 10 10; www.hotel-lavilla.com; chemin Notre-Dame de la Serra; d from €550, ste from €1090; ⊙ late Apr-early Oct; ❄@☜❄) The last word in Calvi chic, this lavish hilltop hideaway is brimming with boutique trappings. Clean lines, cappuccino-and-chocolate colour schemes, designer fabrics and minimalist motifs distinguish the rooms, while facilities include a pool, spa, tennis courts and Michelin-starred restaurant.

✕ Eating

Annie Traiteur _DELI €_

(✆ 04 95 65 49 67; 5 rue Clemenceau; snacks from €3; ⊙ 6am-midnight Jul & Aug, 8.30am-7pm Apr-Jun & Sep-Nov) With its dazzling array of Corsican charcuterie, cheeses, prepared deli foods, jams, wines, liqueurs, olive oils and chestnut-flour cakes, this beautifully stocked deli is the perfect place to pick up a picnic.

★ U Casanu _CORSICAN €€_

(✆ 04 95 65 00 10; 18 bd Wilson; mains €16-25; ⊙ noon-1.30pm & 8-10pm Mon-Sat Jan-Oct) For an unforgettable lunch, grab a booth at this cosy hole-in-the-wall, cheerily decorated in yellow and green, and hung with watercolours by septuagenarian artist-owner Monique Luciani. Tuck into home-cooked fish couscous, roast lamb, codfish aioli or octopus salad, and don't miss the exquisite _fiadone_, a classic Corsican cheesecake made with lemon-scented Brocciu cheese soaked in _eau de vie_ (brandy).

A Candella _CORSICAN €€_

(✆ 04 95 65 42 13; 9 rue St-Antoine; mains €17-29; ⊙ noon-2.30pm & 7-10.30pm mid-May–Sep) Of the few eating options within the citadel, A Candella stands out for the stupendous views from its romantic, golden-hued stone terrace, strewn with pretty flowers in pots and olive trees. The food tends to be Corsican hearty, with rich sauces on chunks of meat and fish, but they do decent salads if you fancy lingering over a light lunch.

🍷 Drinking & Nightlife

★ Chez Tao _BAR_

(✆ 04 95 65 00 73; www.cheztao.com; rue St-Antoine; ⊙ 9pm-6am Jun-Sep) Eight decades on, hedonistic hipsters still flock to this super-smooth piano bar, a Calvi institution founded high in the citadel by White Russian émigré Tao Kanbey de Kerekoff in 1935. Enjoy a cocktail in the lavish, vaulted 16th-century interior, where there's usually live music or a DJ, or better still, soak up the amazing sea views from the terrace.

ℹ Information

Tourist Office (✆ 04 95 65 16 67; www.balagne-corsica.com; Port de Plaisance; ⊙ 9am-7pm Mon-Sat, to 1pm Sun Jul & Aug; 9am-noon & 2-6pm Mon-Sat, 9.30am-12.30pm Sun May, Jun & Sep; shorter hours rest of year; 🛜) Very dynamic, with excellent resources on La Balagne, including detailed walk itineraries, with maps (€2 each or €6 for four). There's a summer-only annex in the citadel.

ℹ Getting There & Away

AIR

Calvi's **Aéroport Calvi Ste-Catherine** (www.calvi.aeroport.fr), 7km southeast of the centre, has flights to mainland France and continental Europe. Count on paying €25 for a taxi in to town.

BUS

There's a year-round bus service to Bastia (€16, 2½ hours, two daily in summer; one daily Monday to Friday otherwise) via Île Rousse (€4, 30 minutes). Between May and mid-October there's also a daily bus to Porto, with Sunday service in July and August only (€16, 2½ hours).

WORTH A TRIP

POINTE DE LA REVELLATA

Thrill your senses with a short scenic drive west along the coastal D81B (signposted 'Route de Porto – bord de mer' from just below Calvi's citadel) to Pointe de la Revellata, the nearest point on Corsica to the French mainland. Within seconds of leaving town, you're deep in the hot, sun-baked maquis, with only a low stone wall separating white-knuckled passenger from the scrubby green drop down to the sparkling emerald water far below. Suddenly, after 4km, the majestic cape pops into view, with a toy-like white lighthouse at its tip, and dusty walking trails etched in ginger. Park in the lay-by, then walk downhill for 20 minutes for a lunch of grilled seafood and salad at **Mar A Beach** (✆ 06 33 62 17 64; www.marabeach.fr; Plage de l'Alga; mains €12-25; ⊙ restaurant noon-5pm May-Oct, noon-5pm Thu-Sun Mar & Apr; bar noon-7pm May-Oct), a Robinson Crusoe–style beach hut beside **Plage de l'Alga**; call ahead to check it's open, and make a booking.

To enjoy even better views of the bay of Calvi, drive another 1.5km uphill (signposted) towards **Chapelle Notre Dame de la Serra**.

CORSICA CALVI

TRAIN

From Calvi train station, south of the harbour, there are at least two departures daily to Bastia (€16.40, 3¼ hours) and Ajaccio (€25.10, 4¾ hours), in each case involving a change at Ponte Leccia, and four or five direct trains to Île Rousse (€6, 40 minutes).

NORTHWEST CORSICA

The coastline that stretches away northwards from the classy and historic city of Ajaccio holds some of the most breathtaking scenery in all Corsica. Successive bays unfold in dazzling splendour, each peppered with villages that spring to life in summer. Many of the beaches are superb, and the sea is consistently enticing, but it's the breathtaking coastal cliffscape, culminating in the iconic red-rock extravaganza of the Calanques de Piana, that you'll never forget.

Porto

POP 550

The setting could hardly be more magnificent. The village of Porto stands amid the west coast's most spectacular scenery, facing the stunning Golfe de Porto – a Unesco World Heritage Site, cradled between flame-red cliffs – and with a thickly forested valley to its rear, where the Gorges de Spelunca offers superb hiking.

Very much a summer resort, and all but deserted in winter, Porto sprawls a long way back from the sea, up the slopes of the valley. All action centres on its picturesque waterfront, punctuated by a pocket-sized red-rock headland that's topped by an oh-so-cute 16th-century watchtower, built to guard against Barbary pirates. Frequent boat trips set off to explore the shimmering seas of the gulf.

◉ Sights & Activities

Waterfront PORT

Porto's main sights are clustered around the harbour. Once you've climbed the higgledy-piggledy headland up to the **Genoese tower** (€2.50; ⊙9am-7pm Apr-Oct, to 8pm Jul & Aug), stroll round to the bustling marina, from where an arched footbridge crosses the estuary to an impressive eucalyptus grove and Porto's pebbly patch of beach.

★**Réserve Naturelle de Scandola** NATURE RESERVE

The jewel of the Golfe de Porto World Heritage Site, the Réserve Naturelle de Scandola extends both above and below the water, from the russet-hued cliffs down to their submarine counterparts. With no road or trail access, you can only explore this majestic wilderness by boat.

Several Porto-based boat operators, including **Via Mare** (☑06 07 28 72 72, 06 09 51 15 25; www.viamare-promenades.com; tours €26-47), **L'Eivissa** (☑06 75 30 96 27; www.portoeivissa. com; tours €25-60) and **Corse Émotion** (☑06 68 58 94 94; www.corse-emotion.com; tours €26-60), run half-day excursions into the reserve, in some cases combining it with Les Calanques de Piana.

★**Gorges de la Spelunca** HIKING

Just inland from Porto, the awesome Gorges de la Spelunca offers splendid hiking, plus freshwater swimming on hot days. A 45-minute trail, marked with orange blazes, leads eastwards through the heart of the canyon from the bridge over the Porto River, 2km east of Ota on the D124, to the Pont de Zaglia, an 18th-century Genoan stone bridge.

🛏 Sleeping

Camping Les Oliviers CAMPGROUND €

(☑04 95 26 14 49; www.camping-oliviers-porto. com; Pont de Porto; per adult/child/tent or car €11.80/6/4; ⊙late Mar-early Nov; @🛜🏊) Idyllically set amid overhanging olive trees, this steeply terraced site climaxes with a landscaped swimming pool, surrounded by artificial rocks. It's by the main road, 2km up from the harbour, but you can swim in the river. There's a large fitness centre, and wooden chalets and *roulottes* (caravans) can be rented by the week. Expect lively group-participation events in summer.

Le Bon Accueil HOTEL €

(☑04 95 26 19 50; www.bonaccueilporto.com; rte de la Marine; d €70-75; ❉🛜) With a warm welcome from owners Didier and Claire, who run the *tabac* (tobacconists) downstairs, this family hotel, near the top of the road down to the port, offers simple, well-priced rooms, a guest fridge and a sweet upstairs terrace that's ideal for picnics and al fresco drinks.

LES CALANQUES DE PIANA

No amount of praise can do justice to the astonishing beauty of Les Calanques de Piana (E Calanche in Corsican). These sculpted cliffs rear above the Golfe de Porto in staggering scarlet pillars, teetering columns, and irregularly shaped outcrops of pink, ochre and ginger. Flaming red in the sunlight, they're one of the great sights of Corsica. And as you sway around switchback after switchback along the rock-riddled 10km stretch of the D81 between Porto and the village of Piana, one mesmerising vista piggybacks on another.

There are two ways to discover the Calanques: by boat or on foot. Numerous operators offer boat trips from Porto; allow €25 for a 1½-hour excursion. For a land-based perspective, don your walking boots. Several trails start near the municipal stadium, 3km north of Piana on the D81. Piana's **tourist office** (☑ 09 66 92 84 42; www.otpiana.com; place de la Mairie; ⊗ 9am-noon & 1-5pm Mon-Fri, to noon Sat & Sun Jul & Aug, shorter hours rest of year; 🛜) sells a €1 leaflet detailing six walks.

Afterwards, flop on the sand on the idyllic beaches of **Ficajola** or **Arone**, 5km north and 12km southwest of Piana respectively. The **Camping de la Plage d'Arone** (☑ 04 95 20 64 54; Plage d'Arone, Piana; 2 people with tent & car €29; ⊗ Jun-Sep) is as tranquil a campground as you'll find in Corsica. Or splurge on lunch (mains €35, lunch *menu* €25) or sundowners with epic views at Corsica's original luxury hotel, **Les Roches Rouges** (☑ 04 95 27 81 81; www.lesrochesrouges.com; D81; d €140-160; ⊗ Apr-Oct; ❄ 🛜), an eccentric vintage property that opened in 1912.

Hôtel-Restaurant Le Belvédère HOTEL €€
(☑ 04 95 26 12 01; www.hotelrestaurant-lebelve-dere-porto.com; rte de la Marine; d/q €93/150; 🛜) In a great location beside the harbour, near the steps up to the little watchtower, this small hotel holds bright, clean, tiled-floor rooms; several have full-on sea views, some have private terraces. Family rooms sleep up to five, with a double bed, two bunks and a trundle bed

✖ Eating

Le Moulin CORSICAN €
(☑ 04 95 26 12 09; Pont de Porto; mains €15-24, menus €19-28; ⊗ noon-10.30pm Apr-Oct) Pleasantly situated above a rushing river, immediately south of the bridge at the start of the D84 towards Evisa, 'The Mill' serves solid Corsican food in an unpretentious, family-friendly setting. Specialities include zucchini *beignets,* Corsican bean-and-vegetable soup, polenta, local cheese and charcuterie, cannelloni and grilled meats.

Le Maquis CORSICAN €€
(☑ 04 95 26 12 19; rte de Galéria; mains €22-29; ⊗ noon-2pm & 7-10pm, closed Dec) Propped on the hillside beside the main road, this welcoming restaurant is much loved by locals and tourists alike. The food is a delight, with a changing daily menu that's rooted in traditional Corsican recipes but extends to Mediterranean classics like seafood risotto.

Sit in the cosy interior or, for brilliant views, reserve a table on the balcony.

ℹ Information

Tourist Office (☑ 04 95 26 10 55; www.por-to-tourisme.com; place de la Marine; ⊗ 9am-7pm Mon-Sat, to 1pm Sun mid-Jun–mid-Sep, 9am-6pm Mon-Fri, to 4pm Sat, to 1pm Sun May–mid-Jun & 2nd half of Sep, 9am-5pm Mon-Fri Oct-Apr) Helpful office set in the former gunpowder store that belonged to Porto's Genoese watchtower.

ℹ Getting There & Away

Face it: there's no fast or easy way to reach Porto. Whether you're driving the coastal D81 from Calvi (75km north) or Ajaccio (80km south), you can expect two hours of switchbacks and jaw-dropping vistas.

Bus services:

Ajaccio €12, two hours, two daily
Calvi €16, 2½ hours, one or two daily
Piana €3, 20 minutes, two daily

Ajaccio

POP 68,490

Commanding a lovely sweep of bay, the handsome city of Ajaccio has the self-confidence that comes with a starring role in world history. In summer, there's more than a whiff of the Côte d'Azur to its pastel-toned, cafe-filled historic core and the trendy waterfront promenade that stretches west,

Ajaccio

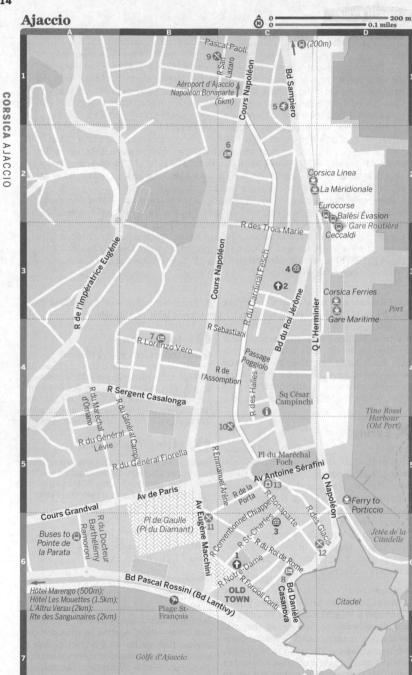

0   200 m
0   0.1 miles

Pascal Paoli
9
R San Lazaro

Aéroport d'Ajaccio
Napoléon Bonaparte
(6km)

(200m)

Bd Sampiero

Cours Napoléon

5

6

Corsica Linea
La Méridionale
Eurocorse
Balési Évasion
Gare Routière
Ceccaldi

R des Trois Marie

4

2

R du Cardinal Fesch

Corsica Ferries
Gare Maritime

Port

Cours Napoléon

R Sebastiani

7
R Lorenzo Vero

R de
l'Assomption

Passage
Poggiolo

R des Halles

Bd du Roi Jérôme

Q L'Herminier

R de l'Impératrice Eugénie

R Sergent Casalonga

R du Maréchal d'Ornano

R du Général
Lévie

R du Général Campi

R du Général Fiorella

10

Sq César
Campinchi

Tino Rossi
Harbour
(Old Port)

Av de Paris

Cours Grandval

R du Docteur
Barthélémy
Ramoroni

Buses to
Pointe de
la Parata

Pl de Gaulle
(Pl du Diamant)

Av Eugène Macchini

R Emmanuel Arène

Pl du Maréchal
Foch

Av Antoine Sérafini

R de la
Porta

13

R Conventionnel Chiappe

R Bonaparte

R St-Charles
3

Q Napoléon

R des Glacis

Ferry to
Porticcio

Jetée de la
Citadelle

11

1
R Notre-Dame

R du Roi de Rome

12

Hôtel Marengo (500m);
Hôtel Les Mouettes (1.5km);
L'Altru Versu (2km);
Rte des Sanguinaires (2km)

Bd Pascal Rossini (Bd Lantivy)

OLD
TOWN

R Forcioli Conti

8

Bd Danièle
Casanova

Citadel

Plage St-
François

Golfe d'Ajaccio

Ajaccio

buzzing with beachgoers by day and party people later on. But it's in the tangled old-town lanes that the spectre of Napoléon Bonaparte looms largest, with the house where he was born in 1769 now serving as a museum to his memory. The headland alongside is dominated by a redoubtable citadel that's sadly off limits to visitors, while a palace amid the newer boulevards to the north displays magnificent art collected by Napoléon's uncle. With ferries from mainland France mooring right alongside, Ajaccio's always bustling with activity.

Sights

Palais Fesch –
Musée des Beaux-Arts   GALLERY
(04 95 26 26 26; www.musee-fesch.com; 50-52 rue du Cardinal Fesch; adult/child €8/5; ⏱9.15am-6pm May-Sep, 9am-5pm Oct-Apr) Established by Napoléon's uncle, cardinal Joseph Fesch (1763–1839), Ajaccio's superb art museum holds the largest French collection of Italian paintings outside the Louvre. Masterpieces by Titian, Fra Bartolomeo, Veronese, Bellini and Botticelli – look out for his *Vierge à l'Enfant Soutenu par un Ange* (Mother and Child Supported by an Angel) – are complemented by temporary exhibitions. Several rooms are devoted to Napoléon and his family, with one unlikely painting showing Napoléon atop a dromedary.

Chapelle Impériale   CHAPEL
(Imperial Chapel; 04 95 21 43 89; www.musees-nationaux-napoleoniens.org; 50-52 rue du Cardinal Fesch; €3; ⏱10am-12.30pm & 1.15-5.30pm Tue-Sun Apr-Sep) The crypt of the imperial chapel, across the courtyard from the Palais Fesch, holds the tombs of Napoléon's parents and several other relatives. Don't expect to find the man himself, though – he's buried in Les Invalides in Paris. The chapel is open in summer only; to visit, buy a ticket in the Palais Fesch.

Maison Bonaparte   MUSEUM
(04 95 21 43 89; www.musees-nationaux-napoleoniens.org; rue St-Charles; adult/child €7/free; ⏱10am-12.30pm & 1.15-5.30pm Tue-Sun Apr-Sep, 10.30am-12.30pm & 1.15-4.30pm Tue-Sun Oct-Mar) Unremarkable from the outside, the old-town house where Napoléon was born and spent his first nine years was ransacked by Corsican nationalists in 1793, requisitioned by English troops from 1794 to 1796, and eventually rebuilt by his mother. It's now preserved as a museum, filled with interesting displays and memorabilia despite the loss of its original furnishings and decor. Highlights include a glass medallion containing a lock of Napoléon's hair.

Cathédrale Ste-Marie   CATHEDRAL
(rue Forcioli Conti; ⏱8-11.30am & 2.30-5.45pm Mon-Sat, to 9.30am Sun) Surprisingly small but in a commanding position facing out to sea, Ajaccio's ochre-coloured cathedral dates from the 16th century. As well as a depiction of the Virgin of the Sacred Heart by Eugène Delacroix (1798–1863), it claims to contain Napoléon's baptismal font, though some historians dispute that he was baptised here at all.

Activities

Kiosks on the quayside at the foot of place du Maréchal Foch sell tickets for seasonal **boat trips** around the Golfe d'Ajaccio and Îles Sanguinaires (adult/child €27/15), and excursions to the Réserve Naturelle de Scandola (adult/child €58/38).

Pointe de la Parata   WALKING
This slender promontory, 12km west of Ajaccio, is a magnet for walkers. A much-trodden trail around the cape rewards with great sea views and tantalising close-ups of the four islets of the Îles Sanguinaires (Bloody Islands). **Bus 5** (€1, 30 minutes) runs to the trailhead from just west of Ajaccio's Pl de Gaulle.

LSP 2 Roues   CYCLING
(✆06 07 28 84 81; www.lsp2roues.com; 13 bd Sampiero; bike/electric bike/scooter per day €20/30/43; ⏱9am-noon & 2-7pm Mon-Fri, to noon Sat Jul-Aug, rest of year shorter hours, with some weekend availability) To pedal to the Pointe de la Parata (p915) from downtown Ajaccio, pick up two wheels from LSP 2 Roues.

✯ Festivals & Events

Fêtes Napoléoniennes   STREET CARNIVAL
(⏱15 Aug) Ajaccio's biggest bash celebrates Napoléon's birthday on 15 August – which coincides with the Assumption of Mary, a national bank holiday – with military-themed parades, street spectacles and a huge fireworks display.

🛏 Sleeping

Hôtel Kallisté   HOTEL €
(✆04 95 51 34 45; www.hotel-kalliste-ajaccio.com; 51 cours Napoléon; s/d €72/92; ✳🖥) Low rates and a central location on Ajaccio's main shopping street, just up from both train station and port, are the main appeals of this 19th-century townhouse, which holds 60 plain rooms of all sizes. They can arrange car and scooter rental.

Hôtel Napoléon   HOTEL €€
(✆04 95 51 54 00; www.hotel-napoleon-ajaccio.fr; 4 rue Lorenzo Vero; d €130-150; ✳🖥) The warmth of a family-run hotel, coupled with a prime location on a side street in the heart of town, make the Napoléon an excellent midrange choice. Rooms are clean, bright and comfortable, despite their rather uninspiring decor; some of the nicest are on the 7th floor, with high ceilings and tall shuttered windows looking out on a leafy backyard.

ICE CREAM PITSTOP
....
Sample the extraordinary creations of Pierre Geronimi, Corsica's most celebrated *glacier* (ice-cream maker) at **Glaces Geronimi** (✆04 95 28 04 13; www.glacespierregeronimi.com; résidence de la Plage, Sagone; scoop €3, sundae €15; ⏱7.30am-2.30am Apr-Sep, to 6.30pm Oct-Mar) – violet tutti-frutti, Camembert or mustard ice cream, anyone? – in this beachfront cafe, 13km southeast of Cargèse towards Ajaccio.

Hôtel San Carlu Citadelle   HOTEL €€
(✆04 95 21 13 84; www.hotel-sancarlu.com; 8 bd Danièle Casanova; d €126-149, f €156-188; ✳🖥) This cream-coloured townhouse, smack opposite the citadel and featuring matching oyster-grey shutters, is a solid bet. Rooms are clean and modern, while the views over citadel and sea get better with every floor. The family room sleeps up to five comfortably. Traffic noise could be an issue for light sleepers.

★**Hôtel Demeure Les Mouettes**   BOUTIQUE HOTEL €€€
(✆04 95 50 40 40; www.hotellesmouettes.fr; 9 cours Lucien Bonaparte; d €170-520; ⏱Apr-Oct; ✳🖥🏊) Nestled right at the water's edge, 1.5km west of the old town, this colonnaded, peach-coloured 19th-century mansion is a dream. Views of the bay from its terraces – some rooms have their own private ones – and (heated) pool are exquisite; you may spot dolphins at dawn or dusk. Inside, the decor is elegantly understated and the service superb.

🍴 Eating

Boulangerie Galeani   BAKERY €
(✆04 95 21 39 68; 3 rue du Cardinal Fesch; pastries €2-3, sandwiches €5.50; ⏱6.30am-7.30pm Tue-Sat, to 1pm Sun) Ajaccio's office workers queue outside the town's finest bakery at midday for fresh-made sandwiches and delicious pastries; tourists with more time on their hands linger over breakfast or a bargain lunch at the pavement tables outside. Be sure to try one of the chestnut-flour specialities.

★**L'Altru Versu**   BISTRO €€
(✆04 95 50 05 22; www.facebook.com/mezzacquiresto; rte des Sanguinaires; mains €18-38, menus €29-54; ⏱12.30-2pm & 7.30-10.30pm Thu-Mon, plus 7.30-10.30pm Tue & Wed mid-May–mid-Oct, closed Jan & Feb) At this perennial favourite on Ajaccio's waterfront, 2.5km west of the old town, magnificent sea views complement the exquisite gastronomic creations of the Mezzacqui brothers (Jean-Pierre front of house, David powering the kitchen), from crispy minted prawns with pistachio cream to pork with honey and clementine zest.

★**Le 20123**   CORSICAN €€
(✆04 95 21 50 05; www.20123.fr; 2 rue du Roi de Rome; menu €36.50; ⏱7-11pm Apr-Oct, closed Mon Nov-Mar) This fabulous, one-of-a-kind restaurant originated in the village of Pila Canale (postcode 20123). When the owner moved to Ajaccio, the village came too – water

fountain, life-sized dolls, central square and all. That might sound tacky, but it works; lively year-round, it's a charming, characterful night out, where everyone feasts on a seasonal four-course menu that's rich in meaty traditional cuisine.

The price might seem a little steep, but given the sheer quantity of food that's served, you won't feel short-changed.

A Nepita BISTRO €€

(☑04 95 26 75 68; 4 rue San Lazaro; 2-/3-course menus lunch €28/33, dinner €35/42; ⏱noon-1.30pm Mon-Wed, noon-1.30pm & 7.30-9.30pm Thu & Fri, 7.30-9.30pm Sat, closed Aug) With its modern French cuisine and elegant setting, it's no wonder A Nepita keeps winning plaudits and loyal followers. While it makes a nice change from hearty traditional Corsican food, the island's not forgotten. The changing daily menu includes just two appetisers, two mains and two desserts, and draws on the freshest local ingredients, including seasonal seafood and vegetables.

Le Cabanon FRENCH €€

(☑04 95 22 55 90; 4 bd Danièle Casanova; mains €18-29, menu €38; ⏱noon-2pm & 7.30-10pm Tue-Sat) Loïc fishes, Nadine cooks – a winning combination if there ever was one. Nestled across from the citadel in the old town, 'The Shed' offers a sunny cuisine inspired by Loïc's catch of the day in a charming bistro-like dining room. On summer evenings, the seats on the pavement terrace facing the citadel are irresistible.

🛍 Shopping

U Stazzu FOOD & DRINKS

(☑04 95 51 10 80; www.ustazzu.com; 1 rue Bonaparte; ⏱9am-7.30pm Mon-Sat, to 3pm Sun) For Corsican goodies, there's only one address that matters: U Stazzu, famous for its handmade charcuterie and Corsican delicacies (olive oil, jams, liqueurs, honey) crafted by small producers. Owner Paul Marcaggi has been honoured as the best charcutier in France, and in summer customers line up just to get in the door.

ℹ Information

Tourist Office (☑04 95 51 53 03; www.ajaccio-tourisme.com; 3 bd du Roi Jérôme; ⏱8am-8pm Mon-Sat, 9am-1pm Sun Jul-Aug, shorter hours Sep-June, closed Sun Nov-Mar; 🖥) Ajaccio's helpful tourist office, in the former fish market, is a great source of information on town and island alike.

ℹ AJACCIO BEACH LIFE

Ajaccio's most popular beach, **Plage de Ricanto** (aka Tahiti Plage), is 5km east of town, just short of the airport. Dedicated beach bums tend to prefer the sands of **Porticcio** (Porticcio) further east, which is 15km by road from Ajaccio, but only 6km if you sail straight across the bay, on the 20-minute **ferry** (Navette Maritime; ☑04 95 21 06 16, 06 03 13 46 80; www.promenades-en-mer.org; one way/return €5/9) that runs six to nine times daily.

Heading west along the waterfront from the old town, on the other hand, the coast road leads past several smaller beaches – Ariane, Neptune, Palm Beach and Marinella – before culminating after 12km at the slender, rocky **Pointe de la Parata**. This popular hiking destination gives grandstand views of the **Îles Sanguinaires** (Bloody Islands), named for their vivid crimson colours at sunset.

ℹ Getting There & Away

AIR

The **Aéroport d'Ajaccio Napoléon Bonaparte** (☑04 95 23 56 56; www.2a.cci.fr/Aeroport-Napoleon-Bonaparte-Ajaccio), 6km east of the town centre around the bay, is connected with the French mainland, and in summer with London Stansted, by Air Corsica. It's linked by the hourly bus 8 (€5, 30 minutes) with Ajaccio's train station (bus stop Marconajo). A taxi into town will cost around €25.

BOAT

Corsica Linea (☑04 95 57 69 10, 08 25 88 80 88; www.corsicalinea.com), **Corsica Ferries** (☑08 25 09 50 95; www.corsica-ferries.fr) and **La Méridionale** (p900) sail to the French mainland ports of Toulon (seven to 11 hours), Nice (6¼ to 10 hours) and Marseille (12 hours) from Ajaccio's **Gare Maritime** (☑04 95 51 55 45; quai L'Herminier). Buy tickets before sailings inside the combined bus and ferry terminal.

BUS

Long-distance buses from Ajaccio only serve destinations to the south and west of the city that can't be reached by train, including Bonifacio, Porto and Sartène. Buses arrive and depart immediately outside the ferry terminal, while local bus companies including **Ceccaldi** (☑04 95 21 38 06; www.autocars-ceccaldi-ajaccio.fr), **Eurocorse** (☑04 95 71 24 64; www.eurocorse.com)

PREHISTORIC CORSICA: FILITOSA & CAURIA

Southern Corsica boasts the island's most astonishing prehistoric sites, set amid stunning landscapes and essential viewing for anyone with an interest in Europe's earliest civilisations.

The granite menhirs (standing stones) at **Filitosa** (☑ 04 95 74 00 91; www.filitosa.fr; D57; €7; ☉ 9am-sunset Apr-Oct), 20km north of Propriano, were first erected as much as 6000 years ago, perhaps to mark communal tombs. Many were re-carved during the Bronze Age to hold detailed faces and weaponry, and thus, uniquely, appear to depict specific individuals, perhaps warriors or chieftains. Current theories suggest that the so-called 'Sea Peoples', long-standing enemies of the ancient Egyptians, may have sailed west across the Mediterranean to Corsica at this time, and taken over pre-existing settlements such as Filitosa.

The desolate and beautiful **Cauria plateau** (off D48), 15km south of Sartène and reached by turning right onto the D48 just south of town, holds further megalithic curiosities. To find them, follow signs to Stantari, then walk 10 minutes down a dirt track, where they're set along a 40-minute loop trail, close to a fantastic jumble of naturally eroded boulders that surely served as an ancient landmark. Both **Stantari** and **Renaghju** are short *alignements* (lines) of standing stones that show similar anatomical details and weaponry to those at Filitosa; **Funtanaccia** is a dolmen, one of Corsica's few burial chambers, with its pillars and capstones fully exposed.

Both sites can easily be visited from Sartène; alternatively, **U Mulinu di Calzola** (☑ 06 84 79 21 86, 04 95 24 32 14; www.umulinu.net; Pont de Calzola, Casalabriva; d/tr €110/€125; ☉ May-Oct) is a gorgeous inn located right on the banks of the Taravo river, less than 10 minutes' drive from Filitosa. Dinner on the shaded terrace is certain to win you over after a day sightseeing.

and **Balési Évasion** (☑ 04 95 70 15 55; www.balesievasion.com) sell tickets inside the adjoining bus terminal. Sunday services operate in July and August only.

Bonifacio €20, 3 hours, twice daily Mon-Sat

Porto €12, 2 hours, twice daily Mon-Sat

Porto-Vecchio €20, 3¼ hours, twice daily Mon-Sat

Zonza €12, 2 hours, twice daily Mon-Sat

TRAIN

Services from the **train station** (☑ 04 95 23 11 03; www.cf-corse.corsica; place de la Gare), 1km north of the old town and 500m north of the ferry terminal, include the following:

Bastia €21.60, 3¾ hours, five daily

Calvi €25.10, 4¾ hours, two daily (change at Ponte Leccia)

Corte €11.50, two hours, five daily

THE SOUTH

A microcosm of Corsica itself, the south boasts two of the island's most alluring port towns – the cliff-hugging citadel of Bonifacio and the glamorous resort of Porto-Vecchio – along with its most remarkable megalithic sites (Filitosa and Cucuruzzu), some of its most

breathtaking mountains (Aiguilles de Bavella) and its most beautiful beach (Palombaggia).

Sartène

POP 3405

With its grey granite houses, secretive dead-end alleys and sombre, introspective air, the hill village of Sartène has long been renowned for encapsulating Corsica's rugged spirit. To French novelist Prosper Mérimée, this was the 'most Corsican of Corsican towns'. It certainly feels a long way from the glitter of the Corsican coast; the hillside houses are endearingly ramshackle, the streets scruffy and shady, and life still crawls along at a traditional tilt. Even if the banditry and bloody vendettas for which it was formerly notorious now lie firmly in the past, Sartène continues to offer an authentic glimpse of how life used to be lived in rural Corsica.

◉ Sights

Musée de Préhistoire Corse et d'Archéologie   MUSEUM
(☑ 04 95 77 01 09; bd Jacques Nicolaï; adult/child €4.50/2.50; ☉ 10am-6pm Jun-Sep, to 5pm Mon-Fri Oct-May) This modern museum traces

Corsica's prehistory from its original fauna through the megalithic, Bronze Age and Roman eras. Much of it is rather dry, with cases of tiny, symmetrically arrayed arrowheads, though an interesting section on marine archaeology displays huge jars salvaged from shipwrecks. There are also full-sized granite-carved replica menhirs, with good explanations of the cultures that created them.

✦✦ Festivals & Events

Procession du Catenacciu　　　　RELIGIOUS
(◉ Good Friday) Every Good Friday since the Middle Ages, a chained, barefoot penitent has re-enacted Christ's journey to Calvary by lugging a massive oak cross on a 1.8km circuit through the streets of Sartène. Wearing red robes and cowled to preserve his anonymity, the Catenacciu (literally 'chained one'), is chosen by the parish priest, often to atone for a grave sin.

Both the 34kg cross and 16kg chain are displayed year-round inside Sartène's granite **Église Ste-Marie** (place Porta), on the main square.

🛏 Sleeping & Eating

Hôtel des Roches　　　　HOTEL €€
(☎ 04 95 77 07 61; www.sartenehotel.fr; av Jean-Jaurès; d €113-160; ◉ Feb–mid-Dec; P ✳ 🤶) This large hotel, just a few steps from the main square, may look a little drab as you approach, but the views from the balconies and terraces on its other side, down over the valley towards the sea, are stupendous. All the rooms are crisp, simple and light; those that face out cost extra.

Le Jardin de l'Echauguette　　CORSICAN €€
(☎ 06 20 40 71 49; place de la Vardiola; mains €16-22, menus €22.50-30; ◉ noon-2pm & 7-10pm mid-Apr–Sep) This cheerful restaurant, downstairs from Sartène's main square, centres on a dreamy walled garden terrace, overhung by trees. Linger over rich Corsican specialities like *beignets de courgette* (zucchini fritters), cannelloni with Brocciu cheese, or veal stew.

❶ Information

Tourist Office (☎ 04 95 77 15 40; www.lacorsedesorigines.com; cours Sœur Amélie; ◉ 9am-6pm Mon-Fri, 10am-5pm Sat Jun-Sep, 10am-5pm Mon-Fri Oct-May) Helpful regional tourist office on Sartène's main street, 200m south of the town square.

❶ Getting There & Away

Sartène is 80km (1½ hours' drive) south of Ajaccio and 50km (one hour) north of Bonifacio. At least twice daily, buses run by **Eurocorse** and/or **Balési Évasion** (p918) head for Ajaccio, Bonifacio, L'Alta Rocca and Porto-Vecchio.

Bonifacio

POP 3015

Thanks to its stunning natural setting, the ancient fortress town of Bonifacio is an essential stop for all visitors to Corsica. Protected by vast smooth walls, the town itself stretches along a narrow, top-heavy promontory, undercut by creamy-white limestone cliffs hollowed out by centuries of ceaseless waves. Down below, connected by steep footpaths and a single winding road, and lapped by cornflower-blue waters, its harbour and modern marina shelters at the landward end of a snaking fjord-like inlet.

It's down by the port where much of Bonifacio's tourist trade is concentrated, including ferries across to nearby Sardinia, boat tours to Corsica's southerly beaches and the Îles Lavezzi, and a busy clutch of bars, clubs and brasseries along the quayside. The old city, though, is what truly lingers in the mind, a ravishingly romantic web of alleyways lined with ramshackle medieval houses and chapels with faded pastel plasterwork.

◉ Sights & Activities

★ Citadel　　　　HISTORIC SITE
(Haute Ville) The great joy of visiting Bonifacio lies in strolling the tangled medieval lanes of the citadel. The paved steps of montée du Rastello and montée St-Roch lead up from the marina to its old gateway, the **Porte de Gênes**, complete with an original 16th-century drawbridge. Immediately inside, the **Bastion de l'Étendard** (adult/child €2.50/free, incl Escalier du Roi d'Aragon €3.50/free; ◉ 9am-8pm mid-Apr–Sep, 10am-5pm rest of year) was the main stronghold of the fortified town. Built to hold heavy artillery, it now houses a small museum, and provides access to the ramparts, which offer jaw-dropping views.

Several of the town's streets are spanned by arched aqueducts, designed to collect rainwater to fill the communal cistern opposite **Église Ste-Marie Majeure**. On the southern side of the citadel, the **Escalier du Roi d'Aragon** (adult/child €2.50/free, incl Bastion de l'Étendard €3.50/free; ◉ 9am-sunset Apr-Oct) cuts down the cliff-face.

Aiguilles de
Bavella

Zonza

Cucuruzzu &
Capula

Ste-Lucie
de Tallano

Levie

Sartène

Porto-
Vecchio

Plage de
San Ciprianu

Plage de
Palombaggia

Cauria

Tyrrhenian
Sea

MEDITERRANEAN
SEA

Bonifacio

Îles Lavezzi

 Exploring Southern Corsica

Southern Corsica encapsulates the very best the island has to offer: mountains and beaches, culture, history and plenty of fabulous restaurants for epicurean travellers.

Start your trip in **Bonifacio** (p919): perched atop dramatic chalky cliffs that plunge into the sea, it is undoubtedly Corsica's most spectacular town. Allow a day to wander the streets of the citadel, descend (and then re-climb!) the precipitous Escalier du Roi d'Aragon, and hike to the Phare de Pertusato for views of the town's amazing setting.

The next day, pack a picnic and snorkelling gear and join a boat trip to the **Îles Lavezzi** (p922), an idyllic archipelago southeast of Bonifacio towards Sardinia, where you can walk the island paths and swim in turquoise waters, amid schools of colourful fish.

On the third day, head north from Bonifacio towards **Sartène** (p918) – taking a small detour to the remote and rural prehistoric sites of **Cauria** (p918) on your way to a late lunch on the panoramic terrace at Le Jardin de l'Echauguette. Continue to **Levie** (p926), up in the mountainous region of L'Alta Rocca. Your overnight destination is the exquisite boutique inn A Pignata – half-board is compulsory, and what a good idea!

The next morning, visit the Bronze-Age forts of **Cucuruzzu and Capula** (p926), deep in the woods five minutes' drive from the hotel. Spend the rest of the day exploring the picturesque villages of **Levie** and **Ste-Lucie de Tallano**, or simply enjoying the creature comforts and views of A Pignata.

On day five: action! Go canyoning, hiking or mountain biking in the **Aiguilles de Bavella** (p925), a stunning mountain fastness characterised by steep, serrated peaks, forested slopes and deep canyons. Spend the night in **Zonza** (p925) to recover, before driving down to **Porto-Vecchio** (p923) the next day and flopping on one of its paradisiacal beaches: Plage de Palombaggia or Plage de San CVecchiu get our vote.

For your last day, enjoy a spot of shopping in Porto-Vecchio's pretty boutiques, feast on fresh pasta or seafood at the harbourside U Molu and check out whichever beaches you missed out on the day before.

Top: Mountain biking in the Aiguilles de Bavella (p925)
Bottom: Limestone cliffs, Bonifacio (919)

> ### ℹ BEACH TALK
>
> Bonifacio's town beaches – such as **Plage de Sotta Rocca**, a small pebbly cove reached by steps that drop from av Charles de Gaulle – are a little underwhelming. For something nicer, explore **Plage Fazzio** and the other sandy inlets on the northern side of Bouches de Bonifacio, accessed via a 3km footpath that leaves av Sylvère Bohn just north of the Esso petrol station at the harbour's eastern edge. Even better stretches of sand can be found in **Sperone**, 8km southeast of Bonifacio.

Bonifacio doesn't fill the entire headland. Just beyond the old core as you head west, beyond the Gothic **Église Ste-Dominique** and massive defunct barracks, you come to an eerily quiet **marine cemetery**. At the western tip of the peninsula, an underground passage dug during WWII leads down to a 'window' cut into the rock just 12m above the sea, at a rudder-shaped rock formation known as the **Gouvernail de la Corse**.

Îles Lavezzi ISLAND
(day trips from Bonifacio adult/child €35/17.50) Paradise! If you love to splash in tranquil lapis-lazuli waters, this protected clutch of uninhabited islets was made for you. The largest, the 65-hectare Île Lavezzi itself, is the most accessible. In summer, operators based at Bonifacio's marina (and also in Porto-Vecchio) offer boat trips; bring a picnic.

Phare de Pertusato WALKING
For an enjoyable hike with magnificent views, head south along the cliffs to the Phare (Lighthouse) de Pertusato. Clearly signposted off the road up to the citadel, the trail leads past the deceptively lighthouse-like Semaphore de Pertusato before following a rudimentary road to Pertusato. Count on 2½ hours, without shelter or other facilities, for the 5.6km return trip.

🛌 Sleeping

Hôtel Le Colomba HOTEL €€
(☑04 95 73 73 44; www.hotel-bonifacio-corse.fr; 4-6 rue Simon Varsi; d €167; 🅿❄🛜) Occupying a tastefully renovated 14th-century building, this hotel enjoys a prime location on a picturesque (steep) street, bang in the heart of the old town. Rooms are simple and smallish, but fresh and decorated with amenities including wrought-iron bedsteads, country fabrics, carved bedheads and/or chequerboard tiles. Other pluses include friendly staff and breakfast served in a medieval vaulted cellar.

Hôtel Genovese HOTEL €€€
(☑04 95 73 12 34; www.hotel-genovese.com; place de l'Europe, Haute-Ville; d €270-310; ste €350-610; 🅿❄🛜🏊) Built into Bonifacio's northern ramparts, just west of the historic core, this ultra-cool hotel is hard to resist. Its rooftop swimming pool and bijou garden are stunning, and the interior stylish and bright. Standard rooms are comfortable but a bit underwhelming, while the poolside terrace and some fancier rooms and suites offer spectacular views over town and harbour.

🍴 Eating

⭐ Kissing Pigs CORSICAN €
(☑04 95 73 56 09; 15 quai Banda del Ferro; mains €9-23, menus €21-23; ⏱11.30am-2.30pm & 6.30-11pm Tue-Sun) At water's edge beneath the citadel, and festooned with swinging sausages, this seductively cosy and friendly restaurant-cum-wine bar serves wonderfully rich and predominantly meaty Corsican dishes. Hearty casseroles include pork stewed with muscat and chestnuts, while the cheese and charcuterie platters are great for sharing. The Corsican wine list is another hit.

La Bodega CORSICAN €
(☑06 73 75 94 70; www.facebook.com/LaBodega Bonifacio; place Bonaparte; mains €13-19; ⏱noon-10pm Mar-Oct) At this cute wood-beamed hole-in-the-wall, just up from the tourist office, gregarious owner Jean-Marie whips up no-nonsense Corsican classics, from veal with olives to *civet de sanglier* (wild boar stew). Don't miss his *aubergine à la bonifacienne* (roasted aubergine, stuffed with garlic, breadcrumbs, egg and Corsican cheese), or sample a bit of everything with an *assiette dégustation* (tasting plate; €19).

Sorba BAKERY €
(☑06 22 51 70 12; 3 rue St-Erasme; ⏱8am-12.30pm & 3-6pm Tue-Sun Apr-Oct) Before a boat trip, drop in at this artisanal patisserie-gelateria down by the water, run by the same family since 1921, and splash out on a bag of lemon- or aniseed-flavoured *canistrelli* (Corsican biscuits), a loaf of *pain des morts* (literally 'death bread' but actually sweet nut-and-raisin bread) or some giant-sized chestnut and orange *fugazzi* (cookies) to nibble aboard.

Les Quatres Vents
SEAFOOD €€

(☑ 04 95 73 07 50; 29 quai Banda del Ferro; mains €16-39; ☺ noon-2.30pm & 7-11pm Wed-Sun, closed mid-Nov–early Feb; ❄) Surveying the harbour through giant windows, the 'Four Winds' has an appropriately nautical theme, with lots of yachting photos, plus a spiral ship's staircase and even a funnel above the open kitchen. Breton owned, it's the finest seafood restaurant in town, offering classic preparations of shellfish and fresh catch, or a 'petit' bouillabaisse for €29.

ⓘ Information

Tourist Office (☑ 04 95 73 11 88; www. bonifacio.fr; 2 rue Fred Scamaroni; ☺ 9am-8pm Jul & Aug, shorter hours rest of year, closed Sat & Sun Nov-Mar; 🛜) Bonifacio's tourist office, in the old-town walls, is complemented by summer-only annexes in the Bastion de l'Étendard and down by the port.

ⓘ Getting There & Around

AIR

Aéroport de Figari-Sud-Corse (☑ 04 95 71 10 10; www.2a.cci.fr/Aeroport-Figari-Sud-Corse), 20km north of Bonfacio, welcomes domestic flights from France, plus seasonal services from London Stansted on Air Corsica, and London Gatwick on Easyjet. There's no shuttle-bus service to Bonifacio, though **Transports Rossi** (☑ 04 95 73 11 88; www.corsicabus.org) runs shuttles to Porto-Vecchio. Car rental is available, while a taxi into Bonifacio costs about €45.

BOAT

Italian ferry operators **Moby** (☑ 04 95 34 84 94, 09 74 56 20 75; www.mobycorse.fr) and **Blu Navy** (p900) run seasonal boats between Bonifacio and Santa Teresa Gallura (Sardinia); sailing time is 50 minutes.

BUS

Eurocorse Voyages (☑ 04 95 21 06 30; www. eurocorse.com) runs daily buses to Porto-Vecchio (€8, 30 minutes) and Ajaccio (€20, three hours).

Porto-Vecchio

POP 12,645

Shamelessly seductive, fashionably alluring, Porto-Vecchio has been dubbed the Corsican St-Tropez. The kind of summer resort that entices French A-listers and wealthy tourists, it's split between the ancient core, aloof on a hilltop; the modern marina in the marvellous bay below; and enough urban sprawl across the inland plain to mean it's now Corsica's third most populous town. The old town's picturesque backstreets, lined with restaurants and designer shops, have charm in spades, and are presided over by the ruined vestiges of an old Genoese citadel. Although there's no beach in Porto-Vecchio itself, some of Corsica's finest beaches are close by.

CORSICA PORTO-VECCHIO

CORSICA'S MOST BEAUTIFUL BEACH

Lapped by turquoise waters, fringed with pine trees and graced with gorgeous views of the Îles Corbicale, the long sandy crescent of **Plage de Palombaggia**, 10km southeast of Porto-Vecchio, is widely acknowledged to be Corsica's most beautiful beach. To officially make it to paradise, reserve a table at oh-so-chic beach restaurant **Tamaricciu** (☑ 04 95 70 49 89; www.tamaricciu.com; Plage de Palombaggia; mains €17-37; ☺ 12.30-6pm mid-Apr–mid-Jun & Sep–mid-Oct, 12.30-10.30pm mid-Jun–Aug), with unsurpassable views of the turquoise surf. Coming from Porto-Vecchio, follow the T10 south then turn left onto rte de Palombaggia, which winds around the coast.

Across the first headland south of Plage de Palombaggia, **Plage de la Folacca** (also known as Plage de Tamaricciu) is no less impressive. Continue a few kilometres further south, over the Bocca di L'Oru pass, to reach another gem of a beach, the gently curving **Plage de Santa Giulia**.

The coast north of Porto-Vecchio is also peppered with scenic expanses of sand. The gorgeous, translucent seas off the beaches at **Cala Rossa** and **Baie de San Ciprianu** are sure to set your heart aflutter. Further north lies the stunning **Golfe de Pinarello**, with its Genoese tower and yet more beautiful expanses of sand lapped by shallow waters.

Various operators offer boat excursions from Porto-Vecchio's marina to Bonifacio and the Îles Lavezzi.

🛏 Sleeping & Eating

A Littariccia B&B €€
(📞 04 95 70 41 33; www.littariccia.com; rte de Palombaggia; d €145-225; 🅿🅟🌐🏊) The twin trump cards here are the fabulous hillside location, overlooking Plage de Palombaggia 9km southeast of Porto-Vecchio, and the dreamy pool. Spread through adjacent villas that can also be rented in their entirety, the rooms are pretty and bright, but not all come with a sea view. Wi-fi is available in the pool area only.

Le Goéland HOTEL €€€
(📞 04 95 70 14 15; www.hotelgoeland.com; av Georges-Pompidou, port de Plaisance; d from €330; 🕓 early Apr-early Nov; 🅿🌐) If you've the urge – and the budget – to stay in Porto-Vecchio itself, there's no better option than this cream-coloured waterfront hotel, arrayed around verdant lawns and its own little artificial beach 1km below the old town, and 500m from the harbour. Most of the light-filled rooms have great views, and there's a good restaurant.

La Table de Nathalie BISTRO €€
(📞 04 95 71 65 25; www.facebook.com/restaurant latabledenahalie; 4 rue Jean Jaures; mains €24-42; 🕓 7-11pm Mon, noon-2pm & 7-11pm Tue-Sat Mar-Nov, plus 7-11pm Sun Jul & Aug) Locals and tourists alike flock to the front terrace of this chic little bistro, just south of the tourist office. The menu abounds in seasonally inspired, locally sourced treats such as slow-cooked fish in citrus-herb crust, terrine of rabbit with Cervione hazelnuts or home-made foie gras with muscat from Cap Corse.

A Cantina di l'Orriu CORSICAN €€
(📞 04 95 70 26 21; www.lorriu.fr; 5 cours Napoléon; mains €18-29; 🕓 6-11pm Tue, noon-2pm & 6-11pm Wed-Sun mid-Mar–Oct) The atmospheric old-stone interior of this wine-bar-turned-restaurant is packed to the rafters with sausages and cold meats hung up to dry, cheeses, jars of jam and honey, and other tasty Corsican produce, and there's a spacious outdoor terrace too. Lunch platters range from light to feisty – ravioli is a speciality – and desserts are sumptuous.

🍷 Drinking & Nightlife

Le Glacier de la Place BAR
(📞 04 95 70 21 42; www.leglacierdelaplace.com; 4 place de la République; 🕓 8am-11pm Jun-Aug, shorter hours rest of year) It may call itself an ice-cream parlour, and it does serve a month's worth of sundaes, but this place on Porto-Vecchio's main square is more famous for its staggering selection of beers from all over the world, as well as its numerous rums and whiskies.

Via Notte CLUB
(📞 04 95 72 02 12; www.vianotte.com; rte de Porra; 🕓 8pm-5am Jun-Sep) Corsica's hottest club, on Porto-Vecchio's southern outskirts, Via Notte claims to be the largest open-air nightclub in Europe. With up to 5000 revellers and superstar DJs most nights in summer, it has to be seen to be believed.

ℹ Information

Tourist Office (📞 04 95 70 09 58; www.ot-porto vecchio.com; rue Général Leclerc; 🕓 9am-11pm Jun-Sep, 9am-noon & 2-6pm Oct-May; 📶) Helpful tourist office on the inland edge of the old town.

ℹ Getting There & Away

AIR

From **Aéroport de Figari-Sud-Corse** (p923), 20km southwest of Porto-Vecchio, **Transports Rossi** (p923) operates a shuttle bus to Porto-Vecchio's bus station (€4, 30 minutes, two to four daily). A taxi will cost around €50.

BOAT

Corsica Linea (p900) and **Corsica Ferries** (📞 08 25 09 50 95; www.corsica-ferries.fr) operate seasonal ferries to Porto-Vecchio from the mainland French ports of Marseille (12 to 13½ hours), Nice (nine to 10 hours) and Toulon (11 to 13½ hours).

BUS

All buses leave from the bus station – Gare Routière – at the northern end of the harbour.
Balési Évasion (📞 04 95 70 15 55; www.balesievasion.com) Buses to Ajaccio (€20, 3¼ hours) via L'Alta Rocca (€8, one hour).
Eurocorse (📞 04 95 71 24 64; www.eurocorse.com) Twice-daily services to Bonifacio (€8, 30 minutes) and to Ajaccio (€20, 3½ hours) via Sartène, and summer-only shuttles to Plage de Palombaggia (€9 return).
Corsicatours/Les Rapides Bleus (📞 04 95 72 35 57; www.rapides-bleus.com) Two daily buses to Bastia (€25, three hours), plus summer-only shuttles to Plage de Santa Giulia (€9 return, 20 minutes, four daily July and August).

L'Alta Rocca

When you've seen enough superb seascapes for the moment, take the time to explore the wilderness of L'Alta Rocca, the mountainous country that looms inland north of Porto-Vecchio. At the southern end of Corsica's long spine, a world away from the bling and bustle of the coast, it's a beguiling combination of dense evergreen and deciduous forests and granite villages strung along rocky ledges.

⊙ Sights

★ Aiguilles de Bavella   MOUNTAIN

The high pass by which the D268 crosses the mountains, the **Col de Bavella** (Bavella Pass; 1218m), is overlooked by the magnificent silhouettes of the serrated Aiguilles de Bavella (Bavella Needles). Soaring to over 1600m, and also known as the Cornes d'Asinao (Asinao Horns), these jagged points vary in colour from grey to ochre to golden as the sun moves across the sky.

The Bavella massif offers wonderful climbing, canyoning and walking. From the parking area at the pass, alongside the white marble statue of **Notre Dame des Neiges** (Our Lady of the Snows), a high-mountain spur of the GR20 hiking trail splits off northwards to approach Monte Incudine (2134m). Alternatively, a red-marked trail leads one hour south, mostly along a wide dirt road, to culminate with a last-minute scramble to reach the **Trou de la Bombe**, a giant hole in the rock. If you're lucky you may spot a few of the mouflons (wild mountain sheep) that frequent the area.

🛏 Sleeping & Eating

Auberge du Col de Bavella   CORSICAN €

(☑ 04 95 72 09 87; www.auberge-bavella.com; Col de Bavella, D268; mains €10-23, menu €24; ⊙ noon-3pm & 7-9.30pm Apr-Oct) Rustic roadside inn, near the summit, where you can feast on roasted baby goat, wild boar stew and other hearty Corsican favourites. The central fireplace is welcome on cooler spring and autumn days. For overnight guests, it holds impeccable four- to eight-bed dorms (€20 per person; breakfast/half-board/full board €27/44/53) and private doubles (€128 with half-board).

ⓘ Getting There & Away

Much the best way to see this magnificent landscape is by driving your own vehicle. In July and August, though, **Balési Évasion** (p924) run daily buses that call at Zonza and Quenza en route between Ajaccio and Porto-Vecchio, and loop up from Zonza to the Col and back both morning and evening. For the rest of the year, the route operates on Monday and Friday only, and there's no service up to the Col.

Zonza

POP 2635

A bustling little mountain crossroads, the attractive village of Zonza (pronounced 'tzonz') makes a perfect base for exploring L'Alta Rocca. Summer tourists stroll back and forth along the narrow main street, home to a good crop of restaurants and accommodation. Tiny **Quenza**, nearby, is another charmer, cradled by thickly wooded mountains with the Aiguilles de Bavella looming on the horizon.

🛏 Sleeping & Eating

Le Pré aux Biches   CAMPGROUND €

(☑ 06 27 52 48 03; www.lodges-yourtes-corse.com; d/tr/q yurt €50/60/80, d/q lodge €70/120; ⊙ May–mid-Sep) The quilted, sumptuously furnished Mongolian yurts are the star attraction on this peaceful, meadow-like organic farm, 2km west of Zonza. Larger safari-style tent lodges are also available, and everyone has their own dedicated toilet and showers in a shared block. They serve breakfast (€6) and dinner (€22) using products from the farm. Note that access to electricity is limited.

★ Auberge U n'Antru Versu   B&B €€

(☑ 04 95 78 31 47; www.aubergeunantruversu.com; San Gavinu di Carbini; incl breakfast d €80-125, q €160; ⊙ Mar-Dec; ❄ 🐾 📶) This delightful family-run B&B hides in a pretty village house in tiny San Gavinu di Carbini, between Levie and Zonza. The rooms are exquisite, blending modern fittings, antique furniture and colourful fabrics, while the downstairs restaurant serves delicious pizzas plus French classics (mains €15 to €20; *menu* €25).

Eternisula   CAFE €

(☑ 04 95 27 44 71; www.facebook.com/leternisula; rte de Quenza; sandwiches, soups & snacks €5-19.50; ⊙ 11am-10pm Tue-Sat, to 5pm Sun May-Oct) The brainchild of an Anglo-Corsican couple, this gorgeous, central cafe-cum-gourmet deli offers charcuterie and cheese platters, espresso, sandwiches, soups and a suggestion of the day, served in the pretty dining room or on the terrace.

ⓘ Getting There & Away

Zonza sits at the junction of the D268 and D368, 9km below Col de Bavella. **Balési Évasion** (p924) runs daily buses in July and August to Ajaccio (€12), and Porto-Vecchio (€8), which also loop to the Col and back. For the rest of the year services are on Monday and Friday only, with no Col detour.

WORTH A TRIP

LEVIE

The small mountain village of Levie, home to a fine Corsican archaeology **museum** (☑ 04 85 78 00 78; off D59, quartier Prato; adult/child €4/free; ⊙ 10am-6pm Jun-Sep, to 5pm Tue-Sat Oct-May), makes a worthwhile stop. Post-museum, archaeological buffs can track down the real thing at **Cucuruzzu** (☑ 04 95 78 48 21; Levie; adult/child €4/free; ⊙ 9.30am-7pm Jun-Sep, to 6pm Apr, May & Oct): a side turning north from the D268, 3km west of Levie, arrives after 4km at a beautiful forest, where an easy 2.5km loop trail leads past two remarkable *castelli* (Bronze Age hillforts). Cucuruzzuis a rocky hillock that was fortified around 1200 BC by cramming boulders into every crevice, and topping the walled ensemble with a round tower. **Capula**, a similar fortress further along, was strengthened by the Romans and altered and then levelled during the Middle Ages.

Near Cucuruzzu, boutique farmhouse **A Pignata** (☑ 04 95 78 41 90; www.apignata. com; rte du Cucuruzzu; incl half-board, d/cabin from €260/€480; ⊙ Apr-Dec; ❄ 🛜 ≋) has 16 rooms, two stilt-perched, family-friendly tree house cabins and a wonderful rustic restaurant (*menu* €53). As well as a vegetable garden and herd of pigs (spoiler alert – they end up as charcuterie), there's a heated indoor pool, with vast mountain-view windows.

CORTE

POP 6800

Blessed with a stunning natural setting, circled by jagged peaks at the confluence of several rivers, the mountain stronghold of Corte is as forbidding as it is spectacular. Centring on a towering pinnacle that's been fortified for over 2000 years, it still stands at the heart of Corsican identity. When Pascal Paoli made it the capital of his short-lived Corsican republic in 1755, most of Corte's population lived within its hilltop citadel. French invaders devastated the upper town 14 years later; fleeing refugees included Napoléon's mother, pregnant with the future emperor.

These days, life focuses on the newer town below, linked to the citadel by steep stairways and cobbled alleys. While Corte remains a nationalist stronghold, famous for being secretive and inward-looking, it's also home to Corsica's only university, founded by Paoli and reopened in 1981. Its strong youthful energy is boosted in summer when hikers, bikers and climbers flock in to explore the nearby valleys.

◉ Sights & Activities

Citadel HISTORIC SITE
(adult/child incl Musée de la Corse €5.30/1.50; ⊙ 10am-7pm daily late Jun-late Sep, to 5pm Tue-Sun Apr-late Jun & late Sep-Oct, to 4pm Tue-Sat Nov-Mar) Corte's citadel occupies a stark rocky crag that juts above the Tavignano and Restonica rivers. Its oldest portion – the château known as the Nid d'Aigle, meaning 'Eagle's Nest' – was built at the highest point in 1419. It can only be accessed by paying for admission to the Musée de la Corse, an anthropological museum housed in the modernised 19th-century barracks below.

Place Gaffory SQUARE
Below the citadel, place Gaffory is a lively little square that's dominated by the 15th-century **Église de l'Annonciation**. The bullet holes that pockmark nearby houses date from Corsica's war of independence. Napoléon's parents were living just down from the square when his elder brother Joseph, later King of Spain, was born in 1768.

Musée de la Corse MUSEUM
(☑ 04 95 45 25 45; www.musee-corse.com; Citadel; adult/child incl citadel €5.30/1.50; ⊙ 10am-8pm daily late Jun-late Sep, to 6pm Tue-Sun Apr-late Jun & late Sep-Oct, to 5pm Tue-Sat Nov-Mar) Housed in the converted and expanded former barracks of the citadel, this intriguing museum is devoted to Corsican anthropology rather than history. The two main galleries cover everything from pottery and agriculture to religious fraternities and tourism – and don't miss the listening booths that play different genres of Corsican music – while a third stages temporary exhibitions.

🛏 Sleeping & Eating

Busy with students year round, Corte is bursting with restaurants. Menus tend to be meat-heavy, and prices generally lower than elsewhere on the island.

Camping Saint-Pancrace CAMPGROUND €
(☑ 04 95 46 09 22, 06 22 73 74 86; www.camping-saintpancrace.fr; place St-Pancrace; adult/tent/car €6/4/3; ☉ mid-Apr–Sep) The pick of Corte's campgrounds, this pretty site has only 25 pitches, all sheltering under olive trees and green oaks, plus a snack bar. Set in a peaceful neighbourhood, a 20-minute walk north of town, it's not suitable for camper vans or caravans.

L'Albadu B&B €
(☑ 04 95 46 24 55; www.hebergement-albadu.fr; ancienne rte d'Ajaccio; d incl half-board per person €60, camping adult/tent/car €6.50/3.50/3.50) The friendly owners of this horse farm, 2km south of Corte, offer assorted accommodation – camping, a 10-bed dorm and five double rooms – at bargain prices. Abundant *table d'hôte* dinners (included with half-board; €25 otherwise) come with appetiser, main course, cheese, dessert, aperitif, wine and coffee. Horse-riding excursions into the surrounding countryside are the icing on the cake.

★ Osteria di l'Orta B&B €€
(☑ 04 95 61 06 41; www.osteria-di-l-orta.com; av du Pont de l'Orta; d €107, ste €137-200; ❊ @ 🛜 ♒) Set in a powder-blue house on Corte's northern edge, this peach of a B&B is run by a charming couple, Marina and Antoine. The three rooms and two suites are lovely, with polished wooden floors and great showers, while the guest kitchen, dining room and DVD lounge are a welcome bonus.

Marina cooks delicious and copious Corsican dinners (€35) using produce from their adjoining farm, and they also make their own aperitifs and wine.

★ La Rivière des Vins BISTRO €
(☑ 04 95 46 37 04; 5 rampe Ste-Croix; mains €8-19, menus €13.50-19; ☉ noon-2pm & 7-11pm Mon-Fri, 7-11pm Sat & Sun; ♒) Diners flock to this fab bistro, on a staircase climbing from Corte's main street, for its relaxed atmosphere, unbeatable value and sumptuous food. The meat skewers and Corsican sausages, grilled in the open fireplace, are wonderful, while the *patatines* (chunks of roast potato), omelettes and salads will make vegetarians weep for joy. Excellent wines by the glass or jug.

🍷 Drinking & Nightlife

Thanks in large part to Corte's many students, there's a lively year-round bar scene along cours Paoli.

Bar de la Haute Ville BAR
(☑ 04 95 61 06 20; www.bardelahauteville.fr; pl Gaffory; sandwiches €5.50; ☉ 8am-2am; 🛜) Known to all as 'BHV', this legendary bar spills out across the town's small upper square, with local beers on tap and plenty of fine wines too, along with a snack menu. Live local musicians play several nights per week in summer.

La Vieille Cave WINE BAR
(☑ 04 95 46 33 79; 2 ruelle de la Fontaine; ☉ 11am-7pm) Sit round a barrel on a low stool in this jewel of a wine cellar, and let the formidable Emmanuel Simonini guide you through the innumerable vintages on offer, either to sip right there and then with a charcuterie platter, or to take home as a souvenir. Closing times are subject to the convivial atmosphere, and often extend later.

ℹ Information

Tourist Office (☑ 04 95 46 26 70; www.corte-tourisme.com; Citadel; ☉ 9am-6pm Mon-Sat, to 1.30pm Sun Jul & Aug, to 6pm Mon-Fri Sep-Jun) The helpful local tourist office is just above the southern approach to the citadel, diagonally across the courtyard from the museum.

ℹ Getting There & Away

Corte's **train station** (☑ 04 95 46 00 97; www.cf-corse.corsica; pl de la Gare), across the Tavignano River 800m below the town centre, has five daily services (three on Sunday) to both Bastia to the northeast (€10.10, 1¾ hours) and Ajaccio to the southwest (€11.50, two hours), via Vizzavona.

The T20 road also connects Corte with Bastia and Ajaccio, again running via Vizzavona (32km), while the T50 heads southeast to the coast, where it meets the T10 south towards Porto-Vecchio and Bonifacio.

The only public transport into the Restonica valley is a summer shuttle bus from Corte along the D623; otherwise, you'll need your own vehicle. All travel into the Tavignano valley is on foot.

LOCAL KNOWLEDGE

LONG-DISTANCE TRAIL TASTER

Corsica's long-distance trails, especially the north–south, two-week GR20, are legendary. For those who can't – or don't want to! – fit two weeks of walking into their holiday, you can get a wonderful taste of the hiker's life by spending a single night at the **Refuge A Sega** (📞 09 88 99 35 57, 06 10 71 77 26; www.pnr.corsica; dm €14; ⓧ Jun-Sep), and combining two of the island's most scenic valleys in an easy, two-day itinerary.

Day one consists of a five-hour walk from Corte up the stunning Vallée du Tavignano, following the orange waymarks of the famous cross-island Mare a Mare itinerary, and breaking for a picnic at the Passerelle de Rossolino. Once at the refuge – be sure to book in advance online – take a dip in the nearby natural pools, then enjoy a home-cooked Corsican dinner.

After breakfast on day two, head east to the Bergeries d'Alzu (sheepfold, two hours), before heading down to the Vallée de la Restonica (one hour), and then back to Corte along the scenic D623 (two hours).

AROUND CORTE

Rearing to astonishing heights, the craggy mountains of central Corsica are in every sense the core of the island. Even when foreign powers like the Genoese controlled the citadel ports along the coast, a uniquely Corsican way of life persisted deep in the interior.

Vallée de la Restonica

Crashing down from the grey-green mountains southwest of Corte, the Restonica River has carved a gorgeous pine-forested valley that extends right to the edge of town. To see the full majesty of the Vallée de la Restonica, follow the tortuous D623 for 15km to the Bergeries de Grotelle (1375m), where it dead-ends at a car park (€6), and a huddle of shepherds' huts that sell drinks, cheeses and snacks. So narrow that it's effectively single file for much of the way, and fringed by steep drop-offs, it's no road for the faint-hearted, and gets so crowded in summer that marshals struggle to keep traffic flowing at all. At quieter times, though, the valley is idyllic, with river-scoured basins in the rock making perfect settings for bathing and sunbathing.

Vallée du Tavignano

If you have a day to spare, don't miss the opportunity to hike into the deliciously peaceful, car-free wonderland of the Vallée du Tavignano, the deepest gorge in Corsica. Even though it's right on Corte's doorstep, it's only accessible on foot and remains well off the beaten track. The signposted trail from Corte leads in around 2½ hours to the Passerelle de Rossolino footbridge, a fabulous spot for a picnic that's surrounded by translucent green natural bathing pools.

Vizzavona

South of Corte, the T20 climbs steeply in the shadow of Monte d'Oro (2389m) before arriving at the cool mountain hamlet of Vizzavona. No more than a cluster of houses around a train station, Vizzavona is an ideal base from which to explore the 16-sq-km Forêt de Vizzavona. A short, gentle and well-signed path meanders to **Cascade des Anglais** (off T20), gleaming waterfalls with shallow family-friendly dipping pools.

Understand
France

France Today

Having confronted terrorism and the rise of the far right in Europe, 'France is back' as the country's young and dynamic, highly eloquent president has asserted more than once with dazzling confidence. And indeed, as French cities reinvent themselves to meet future challenges and urban strategists prepare for a greener future, this ancient country of Gallic pride and tradition has every reason to hold its head high.

Best In Print

Paris (Edward Rutherford; 2013) Eight centuries of Parisian history.

A Moveable Feast (Ernest Hemingway; 1964) Beautiful evocation of 1920s Paris.

Life: A User's Manual (Georges Perec; 1978) Intricately structured novel about an apartment block's inhabitants between 1833 and 1975.

The Horseman on the Roof (Jean Giono; 1951) An Italian exile in 1830s Provence, which is ravaged by a cholera epidemic.

Best in Film

Hugo (2011) Martin Scorsese's Oscar-winning children's film pays tribute to Parisian film pioneer Georges Méliès through the adventure of an orphan boy in the 1930s who tends clocks at a Paris train station.

La Haine (Hate; 1995) Mathieu Kassovitz' prescient take on social tensions in modern Paris.

Aurore (I Got Life!; 2017) Heart-warming French comedy about a mother's lot.

La Môme (La Vie en Rose; 2007) Story of singer Edith Piaf starring French actress Marion Cotillard.

Back on the World Stage

Presidential elections in 2017 placed the country squarely on an upward path to renewal and regeneration. All the traditional parties were eliminated in the first round of voting, paving the way for savvy Emmanuel Macron – a former investment banker – to win the second round of voting and form a centrist government with his freshly formed, pro-EU movement En Marche (since repackaged as political party La République en Marche). Not only did Macron's overwhelming victory mark a dramatic political break from political tradition in France, but it also delivered a resoundingly blow to the country's far-right hopes of gaining power: Macron defeated the Front National's Marine Le Pen by a decisive 66.1% to 33.9% in the presidential second round.

With an absolute majority in the National Assembly, Macron is pursuing a rigorous reform program. His agenda: to reboot the economy, reduce taxes for businesses and make the country's notoriously rigid labour laws more flexible. Moves to privatise the heavily indebted, state-run railway company SNCF in 2018 were met with months of hugely disruptive strikes by transport workers countrywide, but Macron remains bent on reform. On the world stage, he is an eloquent global statesman and champion of a unified Europe.

Start-Up Nation

As the country's youngest-ever president (aged 39 when he moved into the Élysée Palace), Macron is a digital native and innovator. He tweets and shares videos on Facebook in English and French, and speaks English at ease in public (describing the then Australian prime minister's wife as 'delicious' – a wonderful faux pas derived from the high-society French *'délicieux'* meaning 'delightful' – during a diplomatic visit to Australia in May 2018). In 2017 he unveiled the world's largest start-up campus in Paris, Station F, conceived by French billionaire businessman Xavier Niel, where 3000 international entrepreneurs beaver away on new tech ideas and businesses. Inside a gargantuan steel, glass and concrete hangar built in the 1920s as a railway depot, it proves Macron's determination to lure world talent – be it in science, tech or banking – to France. A similar digital eco-system, French Tech Totem, will open in Lyon in 2019.

Urban Renaissance

Cities are enjoying a renaissance as brave new worlds mushroom on industrial wastelands and derelict riverbanks. In Lyon, the multimillion-euro Confluence project continues apace on the slip of land where the Rhône meets the Saône. Phase One is complete and Phase Two, overseen by Swiss architects Herzog and de Mcuron (of Tate Modern and Beijing Olympic Stadium fame), is now introducing hi-tech residential buildings and landscaped leisure spaces into the environmentally sustainable mix. Ultimately, 50km of riverbanks along the Saône will sport pedestrian walkways, cycling lanes, picnic areas and parks peppered with art works for public recreational use.

Further south in Bordeaux, an equally ambitious urban-renewal project is under way at Euratlantique, a sizzling new business and residential district boasting glass-and-steel office towers, eco-smart skyscrapers, a groundbreaking arts incubator and old abattoirs upcycled as luxe shopping malls when complete in 2020. Riverbanks will likewise be greened up, with bags of space for urban walkers and cyclists to experience their city at a grassroots level.

A Greener France

Tackling climate change is of tantamount importance to President Emmanuel Macron who has made France's commitment to limiting global warming very clear. Following the withdrawal of the USA from the Paris climate-change agreement in June 2017, Macron openly invited American scientists and researchers to France to continue their vital climate research. During a subsequent official visit to the USA in April 2018, the French president urged the USA to reconsider its withdrawal, warning Congress, 'There is no Planet B'. (It was in Paris, at the United Nations Climate Change Conference (COP21) in 2015, that world leaders agreed to limit global warming to less than 2°C by the end of the century.)

National measures recently introduced in France include banning single-use plastic bags, reducing supermarket food waste, banning the sale of all petrol and diesel cars by 2040 (currently just 1.2% and 3.5% of French cars are electric or hybrid) and introducing financial incentives to low-level income households to change polluting oil-fired boilers to renewable energies. In the capital €150 million is being invested in its environmentally friendly cycling infrastructure. However, this fell short of satisfying French Environment Minister Nicolas Hulot, who resigned on live radio in August 2018, citing his frustration at the government's 'small steps' to combat climate change as his reason for stepping down.

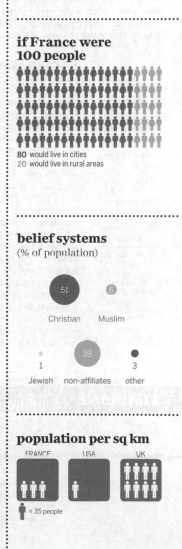

AREA: **551,000 SQ KM**

POPULATION: **67.2 MILLION**

GDP: **€2163 BILLION**

INFLATION: **1.03%**

UNEMPLOYMENT: **8.9%**

if France were 100 people

80 would live in cities
20 would live in rural areas

belief systems
(% of population)

51 Christian

6 Muslim

1 Jewish

39 non-affiliates

3 other

population per sq km

FRANCE   USA   UK

= 35 people

History

The history of France mirrors that of much of Europe. Its beginnings saw the mass migration of the nomadic Celts, the subjugation by the Romans, and their civilising influence, and the rise of a local nobility. Christianity brought a degree of unity, but nowhere else would such a strongly independent church continue to coexist under a powerful central authority (think Charles 'The Hammer' Martel or Louis XIV's claim to be the state itself). This is the essence of France's story.

Roman Gaul

Best Roman Sights

Pont du Gard (near Nîmes)

Les Arènes & Maison Carrée (Nîmes)

Musée Gallo-Romain & Théâtre Romain (Vienne)

Théâtre Antique (Orange)

Théâtre Antique (Arles)

Musée Gallo-Romain Vesunna (Périgueux)

Fourvière (Lyon)

What is now France was settled by several different groups of people in the Iron Age, but the largest and most organised were the Celtic Gauls. The subjugation of these people and their territory by Rome was gradual, and within a few centuries Rome had imposed its government, roads, trade, culture and even language. A Gallo-Roman culture emerged and Gaul was increasingly integrated into the Roman Empire.

It began in the 1st millennium BC as the Greeks and Romans established colonies on the Mediterranean coast, including Massilia (Marseille). Centuries of conflict between the Gauls and the Romans ended in 52 BC when Julius Caesar's legions crushed a revolt by many Gallic tribes led by Celtic Arverni tribe chief Vercingétorix at Gergovia, near present-day Clermont-Ferrand – no site better evokes the drama and bloodshed of this momentous point in history than the MuséoParc Alésia in Burgundy. For the next couple of years, during the Gallic Wars, the Gauls hounded the Romans with guerrilla warfare and fought them in several match-drawn pitched battles. But gradually Gallic resistance collapsed and the Romans reigned supreme.

The stone architecture left by the occupiers was impressive and Roman France is magnificent, climaxing with the mighty Pont du Gard aqueduct, built to bring water to the city of Nîmes in southern France. Splendid theatres and amphitheatres dating from this period are still extant in that city as well as at Autun, Arles and Orange. Some Roman remains were reused: in an early form of recycling, the 1st-century

TIMELINE	**c 30,000 BC**	**c 7000 BC**	**1500–500 BC**
	During the middle Palaeolithic period, Cro-Magnon people start decorating their homes in the Vézère Valley of the Dordogne with colourful scenes of animals, human figures and geometric shapes.	Neolithic people turn their hands to monumental menhirs and dolmen during the New Stone Age, creating a fine collection in Brittany that continues to baffle historians.	Celtic Gauls move into the region and establish trading links with the Greeks, whose colonies included Massilia (Marseille) on the Mediterranean coast; the latter bring grapes and olives.

Roman amphitheatre at Périgueux in the Dordogne was dismantled in the 3rd century and its stones used to build the city walls.

Sophisticated urban centres with markets and baths of hot and cold running water began to emerge. The Romans planted vineyards, notably in Burgundy and Bordeaux; introduced techniques to process wine; and introduced the newfangled faith of Christianity.

Later the Franks would adopt these important elements of Gallo-Roman civilisation (including Christianity), and their eventual assimilation resulted in a fusion of Germanic culture with that of the Celts and the Romans.

The Agony & the Ecstasy: Medieval France

When the Roman Empire collapsed, the gates to a wave of Franks and other Germanic tribes under Merovius opened to the north and northeast. Merovius' grandson, Clovis I, converted to Christianity, giving him greater legitimacy and power over his Christian subjects, and made Paris his seat; his successors founded the abbey of St-Germain des Prés in Paris and later the one at St-Denis to the north, which would become the richest, most important monastery in France and the final resting place of its kings.

The Frankish tradition, by which the king was succeeded by all of his sons, led to power struggles and the eventual disintegration of the kingdom into a collection of small feudal states. The dominant house to emerge was that of the Carolingians.

Carolingian power reached apogee under Charlemagne, who extended the boundaries of the kingdom and was crowned Holy Roman Emperor (Emperor of the West) in AD 800. But during the 9th century Scandinavian Vikings (also called Norsemen, thus Normans) raided France's western coast, settling in the lower Seine Valley and later forming the duchy of Normandy. This would be a century of disunity in France, marked politically by the rise of Norman power and religiously by the foundation of influential abbeys such as the Benedictine one at Cluny. By the time Hugh Capet ascended the throne in 987, the king's domain was a humble parcel of land around Paris and Orléans.

The tale of how William the Conqueror and his forces mounted a successful invasion of England from their base in Normandy in 1066 is told on the Bayeux Tapestry, showcased inside Bayeux' Musée de la Tapisserie de Bayeux. In 1152 Eleanor of Aquitaine wed Henry of Anjou, bringing a further third of France under the control of the English crown. The subsequent rivalry between France and England for control of Aquitaine and the vast English territories in France lasted three centuries.

Prehistory Sights

Vézère Valley (Dordogne)

Carnac (Brittany)

Filitosa (Corsica)

Vallée de l'Ariège (Pyrenees)

Musée de Préhistoire de Solutré (near Mâcon)

Musée de Tautavel (near Perpignan)

Le Carroi Musée (Chinon)

3rd century BC	121 BC	55–52 BC	c 455–70
The Celtic Parisii tribe builds a handful of wattle-and-daub huts on what is now the Île de la Cité in Paris; the capital city is christened Lutetia by the Romans.	The Romans begin taking Gallic territory, annexing southern Gaul as the province of Gallia Narbonensis (in modern Provence and Languedoc), with its capital at the present-day town of Narbonne.	Julius Caesar launches his invasion of Britain from the Côte d'Opale in far northern France; the Gauls defeat the Romans at Gergovia near present-day Clermont-Ferrand, but ultimately the Romans prevail.	France remains under Roman rule until the 5th century, when the Franks (hence the name 'France') and the Alemanii invade and overrun the country from the east.

Hundred Years War

In 1337 hostility between Capetians and Anglo-Normans degenerated into the Hundred Years War, fought on and off until the middle of the 15th century. The Black Death, which broke out a decade after the hostilities began and lasted more than two years, killed more than a third (an estimated 80,000 souls) of Paris' population alone.

The French suffered particularly nasty defeats at Crécy and Agincourt. Abbey-studded Mont St-Michel in present-day Normandy was the only place in northern and western France not to fall into English hands. The dukes of Burgundy (allied with the English) occupied Paris and in 1422 John Plantagenet, duke of Bedford, was made regent of France for England's King Henry VI, then an infant. Less than a decade later Henry was crowned king of France.

THE VIRGIN WARRIOR

Many stories surround the origins of Jeanne d'Arc (Joan of Arc), the virgin warrior burned at the stake by the English, and France's patron saint. Some say she was the bastard child of Louis d'Orléans, King Charles VI's brother. The more accurate account pinpoints Domrémy in northeastern France (Domrémy-la-Pucelle today) as the place where she was born to a peasant family in 1412.

Revelations delivered by the Archangel Michael prompted Jeanne d'Arc to flee the fold in 1428. Her mission: to raise a siege against the city of Orléans and see the future Charles VII crowned king of France. An enquiry conducted by clergy and university clerks in Poitiers tried to establish if Jeanne d'Arc was a fraud or a gift, as she claimed, from the king of Heaven to the king of France. Her virginity was likewise certified. Following the six-week interrogation Jeanne was sent by Charles VII to Tours, where she was equipped with intendants, a horse, a sword and her own standard featuring God sitting in judgement on a cloud. In Blois the divine warrior collected her army, drummed up by Charles VII from his Royal Army Headquarters there. In April 1429, just 17 years old, Jeanne d'Arc started her attack on Orléans, besieged by the English from October of the previous year. On 5 and 6 May the French gained control of Bastille St-Loup and Bastille des Augustins, followed the next day by Fort des Tourelles – a fort guarding the only access to the city from the left bank. This last shattering defeat prompted the English to lay down the siege on 8 May and was a decisive turning point in the Hundred Years War.

From Orléans Jeanne d'Arc went on to defeat the English at Jargeau, Beaugency and Patay. Despite Charles' promised coronation in July 1429, battles between the English and the French waged until 1453, by which time the virginal warrior responsible for turning the war around was dead: Jeanne d'Arc was captured by the Burgundians, sold to the English, convicted of witchcraft and heresy in Rouen in 1431 and burned at the stake. She was canonised in 1920.

732	800–900	987	1066
Somewhere near Poitiers, Charles Martel and his cavalry repel the Muslim Moors. His grandson, Charlemagne, extends the boundaries of the kingdom and is crowned Holy Roman Emperor.	Scandinavian Vikings (also called Norsemen, thus Normans) raid France's western coast and settle in the lower Seine Valley where they later form the Duchy of Normandy.	Five centuries of Merovingian and Carolingian rule ends with the crowning of Hugh Capet; a dynasty that will rule one of Europe's most powerful countries for the next eight centuries is born.	Duke of Normandy William the Conqueror and his Norman forces occupy England, making Normandy and, later, Plantagenet-ruled England formidable rivals of the kingdom of France.

Luckily for the French, 17-year-old Jeanne d'Arc (Joan of Arc) came along with the outlandish tale that she had a divine mission from God to expel the English from France and bring about the coronation of French Charles VII in Reims.

The Rise of the French Court

With the arrival of Italian Renaissance culture during the reign of François I (r 1515–47), the focus of French attention became the Loire Valley. Italian artists decorated royal castles at Amboise, Azay-le-Rideau, Blois, Chambord and Chaumont.

Renaissance ideas of scientific and geographic scholarship and discovery assumed a new importance, as did the value of secular matters over religious life. Writers such as Rabelais, Marot and Ronsard of La Pléiade were influential, as were artist and architect disciples of Michelangelo and Raphael. Evidence of this architectural influence can be seen in François I's château at Fontainebleau – where superb artisans, many of them brought over from Italy, blended Italian and French styles to create the First School of Fontainebleau – and the Petit Château at Chantilly, both near Paris. This new architecture reflected the splendour of the monarchy, which was fast moving towards absolutism. But all this grandeur and show of strength was not enough to stem the tide of Protestantism that was flowing into France.

The Reformation swept through Europe in the 1530s, spearheaded by the ideas of Jean (John) Calvin, a Frenchman born in Picardy but exiled to Geneva. Following the Edict of January 1562, which afforded the Protestants certain rights, the Wars of Religion broke out between the Huguenots (French Protestants who received help from the English), the Catholic League (led by the House of Guise) and the Catholic monarchy, and lasted three dozen years.

Henri IV, founder of the Bourbon dynasty, issued the controversial Edict of Nantes in 1598, guaranteeing the Huguenots civil and political rights, notably freedom of conscience. Ultra-Catholic Paris refused to allow the new Protestant king to enter the city, and a siege of the capital continued for almost five years. Only when Henri IV embraced Catholicism at the cathedral in St-Denis did the capital submit to him.

France's most famous king of this or any other century, Louis XIV (r 1643–1715), called Le Roi Soleil (the Sun King), ascended the throne at the tender age of five. Bolstered by claims of divine right, he involved the kingdom in a series of costly wars with Holland, Austria and England, which gained France territory but nearly bankrupted the treasury. State taxation to refill the coffers caused widespread poverty and vagrancy. In Versailles, Louis XIV built an extravagant palace and made his courtiers compete with each other for royal favour, thereby quashing the ambitious,

Best History Museums

MuCEM (Marseille)

Musée Carnavalet (Paris)

Musée d'Art et d'Histoire (Bayeux)

Mémorial – Un Musée pour la Paix (Caen)

Centre d'Histoire de la Résistance et de la Déportation (Lyon)

Musée d'Aquitaine (Bordeaux)

HISTORY THE RISE OF THE FRENCH COURT

1095	1152	1309	1337
Pope Urban II preaches the First Crusade in Clermont-Ferrand, prompting France to take a leading role and giving rise to some splendid cathedrals, including those at Reims, Strasbourg, Metz and Chartres.	Eleanor of Aquitaine weds Henry of Anjou, bringing a further third of France under the control of the English crown and sparking a French–English rivalry that will last three centuries.	French-born pope Clément V moves papal headquarters from Rome to Avignon, where the Holy Seat remains until 1377; 'home' is the resplendent Palais des Papes built under Benoît XII.	Incessant struggles between the Capetians and England's King Edward III, a Plantagenet, over the powerful French throne degenerate into the Hundred Years War, which will last until 1453.

feuding aristocracy and creating the first centralised French state. In 1685 he revoked the Edict of Nantes.

The Seven Years War (1756–63) was one of a series of ruinous military engagements pursued by Louis XV, the Sun King's grandson. It led to the loss of France's flourishing colonies in Canada, the West Indies and India. It was in part to avenge these losses that his successor Louis XVI sided with the colonists in the American War of Independence a dozen years later. But the Seven Years War cost France a fortune and, more disastrously for the monarchy, it helped to disseminate at home the radical democratic ideas that were thrust upon the world stage by the American Revolution.

**Paris:
Revolution
Encounters**

Jeu de Paume
....
Place de Bastille
....
Hôtel des Invalides
....
*Place de la
Concorde*
....
Conciergerie

Revolution to Republic

At the beginning of the 18th century, new economic and social circumstances began to render the *ancien régime* (old order) dangerously out of step with the needs of the country. The regime was further weakened by the anti-establishment and anticlerical ideas of the Enlightenment, whose leading lights included Voltaire, Rousseau and Diderot. But entrenched vested interests, a cumbersome power structure and royal lassitude prevented change from starting until the 1770s, by which time the monarchy's moment had passed.

By the late 1780s, the indecisive Louis XVI and his dominating consort, Marie Antoinette, had managed to alienate virtually every segment of society, and the king became increasingly isolated as unrest and dissatisfaction reached boiling point. When he tried to neutralise the power of the more reform-minded delegates at a meeting of the États-Généraux (States-General) in Versailles in May and June 1789, the masses took to the streets of Paris. On 14 July, a mob raided the armoury at the Hôtel des Invalides for rifles, seizing 32,000 muskets, then stormed the prison at Bastille – the ultimate symbol of the despotic *ancien régime*. The French Revolution had begun.

At first, the Revolution was in the hands of moderate republicans called the Girondins. France was declared a constitutional monarchy and various reforms were introduced, including the adoption of the Déclaration des Droits de l'Homme et du Citoyen (Declaration of the Rights of Man and of the Citizen) modelled on the American Declaration of Independence. But as the masses armed themselves against the external threat to the new government – posed by Austria, Prussia and the exiled French nobles – patriotism and nationalism mixed with extreme fervour, popularising and radicalising the Revolution. It was not long before the Girondins lost out to the extremist Jacobins, who abolished the monarchy and declared the First Republic after Louis XVI proved unreliable as

The Sun King was yet another Louis named after France's patron saint. Paintings in Versailles' Royal Chapel evoke the idea that the king was chosen by God, thus was His lieutenant on earth.

1358	1422	1431	1515
The war between France and England and the devastation and poverty caused by the plague lead to the ill-fated peasants' revolt led by Étienne Marcel.	John Plantagenet, duke of Bedford, is made regent of France for England's King Henry VI, then an infant; in less than a decade Henry is crowned king of France at Paris' Notre Dame.	Jeanne d'Arc (Joan of Arc) is burned at the stake in Rouen for heresy; the English are not driven out of France until 1453.	With the reign of François I the royal court moves to the Loire Valley, where a rash of stunning Renaissance châteaux and hunting lodges is built.

A DATE WITH THE REVOLUTION

Along with standardising France's system of weights and measures with the now almost universal metric system, the revolutionary government adopted a new, 'more rational' calendar from which all 'superstitious' associations (ie saints' days and mythology) were removed. Year 1 began on 22 September 1792, the day the First Republic was proclaimed.

The names of the 12 months – Vendémaire, Brumaire, Frimaire, Nivôse, Pluviôse, Ventôse, Germinal, Floréal, Prairial, Messidor, Thermidor and Fructidor – were chosen according to the seasons. The autumn months, for instance, were Vendémaire (derived from *vendange,* grape harvest), Brumaire (from *brume,* mist or fog) and Frimaire (from *frimas,* wintry weather). In turn, each month was divided into three 10-day 'weeks' called *décades,* the last day of which was a rest day. The five remaining days of the year were used to celebrate Virtue, Genius, Labour, Opinion and Rewards. These festivals were initially called *sans-culottides* in honour of the *sans-culottes,* the extreme revolutionaries who wore pantaloons rather than the short breeches favoured by the upper classes.

While the republican calendar worked well in theory, it caused no end of confusion for France in its communications and trade abroad because the months and days kept changing in relation to those of the Gregorian calendar. The revolutionary calendar was abandoned and the old system restored in 1806 by Napoléon Bonaparte.

a constitutional monarch. The Assemblée Nationale (National Assembly) was replaced by an elected Revolutionary Convention.

In January 1793, Louis XVI was convicted of 'conspiring against the liberty of the nation' and guillotined on place de la Révolution, today's place de la Concorde, in Paris. Two months later the Jacobins set up the Committee of Public Safety to deal with national defence and to apprehend and try 'traitors'. This body had dictatorial control over the country during the so-called Reign of Terror (September 1793 to July 1794), which saw religious freedoms revoked and churches desecrated, cathedrals turned into 'Temples of Reason', and thousands incarcerated in dungeons in Paris' Conciergerie on Île de la Cité before being beheaded.

After the Reign of Terror faded, a five-man delegation of moderate republicans set itself up to rule the republic as the Directoire (Directory).

Napoléon & Empire

It was true happenstance that brought dashing young Corsica-born general Napoléon Bonaparte to the attention of France. In October 1795 a group of royalist youths bent on overthrowing the Directoire were intercepted on rue St-Honoré in Paris by forces under Bonaparte, who fired into the crowd. For this 'whiff of grapeshot' he was put in command of

Best Walled Towns

Carcassonne
(Languedoc)

Avignon
(Provence)

St-Malo
(Brittany)

Domme
(Dordogne)

Uzerche
(Limousin)

1530s	1572	1588	1589
The Reformation, spurred by the writings of French Jean (John) Calvin, sweeps through France, pitting Catholics against Protestants and eventually leading to the Wars of Religion (1562–98).	Some 3000 Huguenots visiting Paris to celebrate the wedding of the Protestant Henri of Navarre (the future Henri IV) are slaughtered on 23–24 August, in the so-called St Bartholomew's Day Massacre.	The Catholic League forces Henri III (r 1574–89), the last of the Valois kings, to flee the royal court at the Louvre; the next year he is assassinated by a fanatical Dominican friar.	Henri IV, the first Bourbon king, ascends the throne after renouncing Protestantism; *'Paris vaut bien une messe'* (Paris is well worth a Mass), he is reputed to have said upon taking communion.

the French forces in Italy, where he was particularly successful in the campaign against Austria.

In 1799 Napoléon overthrew the Directoire and assumed power as First Consul, chosen by popular vote. A referendum three years later declared him 'Consul for Life' and his birthday became a national holiday. In 1804, when he crowned himself 'Emperor of the French' in the presence of Pope Pius VII at Notre Dame in Paris, the scope of Napoléon's ambitions were obvious to all.

To legitimise his authority, Napoléon needed more battlefield victories. So began a series of wars and victories by which France would come to control most of Europe. In 1812 his troops captured Moscow, only to be killed off by the Russian winter. Two years later Allied armies entered Paris, exiled Napoléon to Elba in the Mediterranean and restored the House of Bourbon to the French throne at the Congress of Vienna.

In early 1815 Napoléon escaped Elba, landed in southern France and gathered a large army as he marched towards Paris. On 1 June he reclaimed the throne. But his reign ended just three weeks later when his forces were defeated at Waterloo in Belgium. Napoléon was exiled again, this time to St Helena in the South Atlantic, where he died in 1821. In 1840 his remains were moved to the Hôtel des Invalides in Paris.

Although reactionary in some ways – he re-established slavery in France's colonies in 1802, for example – Napoléon instituted a number of important reforms, including a reorganisation of the judicial system; the promulgation of a new legal code, the Code Napoléon (or civil code), which forms the basis of the French legal system to this day; and the establishment of a new education system. More importantly, he preserved the essence of the changes brought about by the Revolution.

A struggle between extreme monarchists seeking a return to the *ancien régime,* people who saw the changes wrought by the Revolution as irreversible, and the radicals of the poor working-class neighbourhoods of Paris dominated the reign of Louis XVIII (r 1814–24). His successor Charles X responded to the conflict with ineptitude and was overthrown in the so-called July Revolution of 1830. Those who were killed in the accompanying Paris street battles are buried in vaults under the Colonne de Juillet in the centre of place de la Bastille. Louis-Philippe, a constitutional monarch of bourgeois sympathies who followed him, was subsequently chosen as ruler by parliament, only to be ousted by the 1848 Revolution.

The Second Republic was established and elections brought in Napoléon's inept nephew, the German-reared (and accented) Louis Napoléon Bonaparte, as president. In 1851 he staged a coup d'état and proclaimed himself Emperor Napoléon III of the Second Empire, which lasted until 1870.

Napoleonic Sights

Maison Bonaparte (Ajaccio)

Salon Napoléonien (Ajaccio)

Arc de Triomphe (Paris)

Hôtel des Invalides (Paris)

Napoléon III apartments (Musée du Louvre, Paris)

1598	1643	1756–63	1789
Henri IV gives French Protestants freedom of conscience with the Edict of Nantes – much to the horror of staunchly Catholic Paris, where many refuse to acknowledge the forward-thinking document.	The Roi Soleil (Sun King), Louis XIV, all of five years old, assumes the French throne. In 1682 he moves his court – lock, stock and satin slipper – from Paris' Palais des Tuileries to Versailles.	The Seven Years War against Britain and Prussia sees Louis XV engage in several ruinous wars resulting in the loss of France's colonies in Canada, the West Indies and India.	The French Revolution begins when a mob arms itself with weapons taken from the Hôtel des Invalides and storms the prison at Bastille, freeing a total of just seven prisoners.

THE KINDEST CUT

Hanging, then drawing and quartering – roping the victim's limbs to four oxen, which then ran in four different directions – was once the favoured method of publicly executing commoners. In a bid to make public executions more humane, French physician Joseph Ignace Guillotin (1738–1814) came up with the guillotine.

Several tests on dead bodies down the line, highwayman Nicolas Jacques Pelletier was the first in France to have his head sliced off by the 2m-odd falling blade on 25 April 1792 on place de Grève (today's place de l'Hôtel de Ville) in Paris. During the Reign of Terror, at least 17,000 met their death by guillotine.

By the time the last person in France to be guillotined (murderer Hamida Djandoubi in Marseille) was given the chop in 1977 (behind closed doors – the last public execution was in 1939), the lethal contraption had been sufficiently refined to slice off a head in 2/100 of a second. A real McCoy guillotine is displayed in the Galerie de la Méditerraneé of Marseille's MuCEM. France abolished capital punishment in 1981.

Like his uncle before him, Napoléon III embroiled France in a number of costly conflicts, including the disastrous Crimean War (1854–56). In 1870, Otto von Bismarck goaded Napoléon III into declaring war on Prussia. Within months the thoroughly unprepared French army was defeated and the emperor had been taken prisoner.

The Belle Époque

Though it ushered in the glittering belle époque (beautiful age), there was little else attractive about the start of the Third Republic. Born as a provisional government of national defence in September 1870, it was quickly besieged by the Prussians, who blockaded Paris and demanded National Assembly elections be held. The first move made by the resultant monarchist-controlled assembly was to ratify the Treaty of Frankfurt. The terms of the treaty – a huge war indemnity and surrender of the provinces of Alsace and Lorraine – prompted immediate revolt (known as the Paris Commune), during which several thousand Communards were killed and another 20,000 executed.

The belle époque launched art-nouveau architecture, a whole field of artistic 'isms' from impressionism onwards, and advances in science and engineering, including the construction of the first metro line in Paris. World Exhibitions were held in the capital in 1889 (showcased by the Eiffel Tower) and again in 1901 in the purpose-built Petit Palais.

But all was not well in the republic. France was consumed with a desire for revenge after its defeat by Germany, and looking for scapegoats. The so-called Dreyfus Affair began in 1894 when Jewish army captain

Paris in the 1920s and '30s was a centre of the avant-garde, with painters pushing into new fields of art such as cubism and surrealism, Le Corbusier rewriting the architecture textbook, foreign writers such as Ernest Hemingway drawn by the city's liberal atmosphere (and cheap booze), and nightlife establishing a cutting-edge reputation.

1793	1795	1799	1815
Louis XVI is tried and convicted as citizen 'Louis Capet' (as all kings since Hugh Capet were declared to have ruled illegally) and executed; Marie Antoinette's turn comes nine months later.	A five-man delegation of moderate republicans led by Paul Barras sets itself up as the Directoire (Directory) and rules the First Republic for five years.	Napoléon Bonaparte dismisses the Directoire and seizes control of the government in a coup d'état, opening the doors to 16 years of despotic rule, and victory and then defeat on the battlefield.	British and Prussian forces under the Duke of Wellington defeat Napoléon at Waterloo; he is exiled to a remote island in the South Atlantic where he dies six years later.

Alfred Dreyfus was accused of betraying military secrets to Germany; he was then court-martialled and sentenced to life imprisonment on Devil's Island in French Guiana. Liberal politicians succeeded in having the case reopened despite opposition from the army command, right-wing politicians and many Catholic groups, and Dreyfus was vindicated in 1900. This resulted in more rigorous civilian control of the military and, in 1905, the legal separation of church and state.

The Two World Wars

A full 20% of all Frenchmen – one out of every five males – between 20 and 45 years of age were killed in WWI.

Central to France's entry into World War I against Austria-Hungary and Germany had been its desire to regain Alsace and Lorraine, lost to Germany in the Franco-Prussian War – but it would prove to be a costly piece of real estate in terms of human life. By the time the armistice was signed in November 1918, some 1.3 million French soldiers had been killed and almost one million crippled. At the Battle of Verdun alone, the French (under the command of General Philippe Pétain) and the Germans each lost about 400,000 men.

The naming of Adolf Hitler as Germany's chancellor in 1933 signalled the end of a decade of compromise between France and Germany over border guarantees. Initially the French tried to appease Hitler, but two days after Germany invaded Poland in 1939 France joined Britain in declaring war on Germany. By June 1940 France had capitulated. The Maginot Line had proved useless, with German armoured divisions outflanking it by going through Belgium.

Key War Museums

Mémorial de la Shoah (Paris)

Centre d'Histoire de la Résistance et de la Déportation (Lyon)

Mémorial – Un Musée pour la Paix (Caen)

Musée Mémorial de la Bataille de Normandie (Bayeux)

The Germans divided France into a zone under direct German rule (along the western coast and the north, including Paris), and a puppet-state based in the spa town of Vichy and led by General Pétain, the ageing WWI hero of the Battle of Verdun. The Vichy regime was viciously anti-Semitic, and local police helped the Nazis in rounding up French Jews and others for deportation to Auschwitz and other death camps. While many people either collaborated with the Germans or passively waited out the occupation, the underground movement known as the Résistance, or Maquis, whose active members never amounted to more than about 5% of the French population, engaged in such activities as sabotaging railways, collecting intelligence for the Allies, helping Allied airmen who had been shot down, and publishing anti-German leaflets.

An 80km-long stretch of beach was the site of the D-Day landings on 6 June 1944, when more than 100,000 Allied troops stormed the coastline to liberate most of Normandy and Brittany. Paris was liberated on 25 August by a force spearheaded by Free French units, sent in ahead of the Americans so the French would have the honour of liberating their own capital.

1851	1871	1903	1904
Louis Napoléon leads a coup d'état and proclaims himself Emperor Napoléon III of the Second Empire (1852–70), a period of significant economic growth and building under Baron Haussmann.	The Treaty of Frankfurt is signed, the harsh terms of which (a 5-billion-franc war indemnity, surrender of the provinces of Alsace and Lorraine) prompt immediate revolt.	The world's biggest sporting event after the Olympics and the World Cup sprints around France for the first time; Tour de France riders pedal throughout the night to cover 2500km in 19 days.	Colonial rivalry between France and Britain in Africa ends with the Entente Cordiale (Cordial Understanding), marking the start of a cooperation that continues, more or less, to this day.

THE MAGINOT LINE

The Ligne Maginot, named after France's minister of war from 1929 to 1932, was one of the most spectacular blunders of WWII. This elaborate, mostly subterranean defence network, built between 1930 and 1940 (and, in the history of military architecture, second only to the Great Wall of China in sheer size), was the pride of prewar France. It included everything France's finest military architects thought would be needed to defend the nation in a 'modern war' of poison gas, tanks and aeroplanes: reinforced concrete bunkers, subterranean lines of supply and communication, minefields, antitank canals, floodable basins and even artillery emplacements that popped out of the ground to fire and then disappeared. The only things visible above ground were firing posts and lookout towers. The line stretched along the Franco-German frontier from the Swiss border all the way to Belgium where, for political and budgetary reasons, it stopped. The Maginot Line even had a slogan: *Ils ne passeront pas* (They won't get through).

'They' – the Germans – never did. Rather than attack the Maginot Line straight on, Hitler's armoured divisions simply circled around through Belgium and invaded France across its unprotected northern frontier. They then attacked the Maginot Line from the rear.

The war ruined France. More than one-third of industrial production fed the German war machine during WWII, the occupiers requisitioning practically everything that wasn't (and was) nailed down: ferrous and nonferrous metals, statues, iron grills, zinc bar tops, coal, leather, textiles and chemicals. Agriculture, strangled by the lack of raw materials, fell by 25%.

In their retreat, the Germans burned bridges (2600 destroyed) and the Allied bombardments tore up railroad tracks (40,000km). The roadways had not been maintained since 1939, ports were damaged, and nearly half a million buildings and 60,000 factories were destroyed. The French had to pay for the needs of the occupying soldiers to the tune of 400 million francs a day, prompting an inflation rip tide.

Rebuilding & the Loss of the Colonies

The magnitude of France's postwar economic devastation required a strong central government with broad powers to rebuild the country's industrial and commercial base. Soon after liberation most banks, insurance companies, car manufacturers and energy-producing companies fell under government control. Other businesses remained in private hands, the objective being to combine the efficiency of state planning with the dynamism of private initiative. But progress was slow. By 1947

France has always drawn immigrants: 4.3 million from Europe between 1850 and WWI, and another three million between the world wars. Post-WWII, several million unskilled workers followed from North Africa and French-speaking sub-Saharan Africa.

1905	1918	1920s	1939
The emotions aroused by the Dreyfus Affair and the interference of the Catholic Church lead to the promulgation of *lacité* (secularism), the legal separation of church and state.	The armistice ending WWI signed at Fôret de Compiègne near Paris sees the return of lost territories (Alsace and Lorraine), but the war brings about the loss of more than a million French soldiers.	Paris sparkles as the centre of the avant-garde. The luxurious Train Bleu (Blue Train) makes its first run, and Sylvia Beach of the Shakespeare & Company bookshop publishes James Joyce's *Ulysses*.	Nazi Germany occupies France and divides it into a zone under direct German occupation (along the north and western coasts), and a puppet state led by General Pétain, based in the spa town of Vichy.

rationing remained in effect and France had to turn to the USA for loans as part of the Marshall Plan to rebuild Europe.

One aim of the plan was to stabilise postwar Europe financially and politically, thus thwarting the expansion of Soviet power. As the Iron Curtain fell over Eastern Europe, the pro-Stalinist bent of France's Communist Party put it in a politically untenable position. Seeking at once to exercise power within the government and at the same time oppose its measures as insufficiently Marxist, the communists found themselves on the losing end of disputes involving the colonies, workers' demands and American aid. In 1947 they were booted out of government.

The economy gathered steam in the 1950s. The French government invested in hydroelectric and nuclear-power plants, oil and gas exploration, petrochemical refineries, naval construction, auto factories and building construction to accommodate a boom in babies and consumer goods. The future at home was looking brighter; the situation of *la France d'outre-mer* (overseas France) was another story altogether.

France's humiliation at the hands of the Germans had not been lost on its restive colonies. As the war economy tightened its grip, native-born people, poorer to begin with, noticed that they were bearing the brunt of the pain. In North Africa the Algerians coalesced around a movement for greater autonomy, which blossomed into a full-scale independence movement by the end of the war. The Japanese moved into strategically important Indochina in 1940. The Vietnamese resistance movement that developed quickly took on an anti-French, nationalistic tone, setting the stage for Vietnam's eventual independence.

The 1950s spelled the end of French colonialism. When Japan surrendered to the Allies in 1945, nationalist Ho Chi Minh launched a push for an autonomous Vietnam that became a drive for independence. Under the brilliant General Giap, the Vietnamese perfected a form of guerrilla warfare that proved highly effective against the French army. After their defeat at Dien Bien Phu in 1954, the French withdrew from Indochina.

The struggle for Algerian independence was nastier. Technically a French *département,* Algeria was in effect ruled by a million or so French settlers who wished at all costs to protect their privileges. Heads stuck firmly in the Saharan sands, the colonial community and its supporters in the army and the right wing refused all Algerian demands for political and economic equality.

The Algerian War of Independence (1954–62) was brutal. Nationalist rebel attacks were met with summary executions, inquisitions, torture and massacres, which made Algerians more determined to gain their independence. The government responded with half-hearted reform. International pressure on France to pull out of Algeria came from the UN, the USSR and the USA, while *pieds noirs* (literally 'black feet', as

Paris was transformed under urban planner Baron Haussmann (1809–91), who created the 12 huge boulevards radiating from the Arc de Triomphe. Napoléon III, who had commissioned Haussmann's work, threw glittering parties at the royal palace in Compiègne, and breathed in fashionable sea air at Biarritz and Deauville.

1944	1949	1951	1946–62
Normandy and Brittany are the first to be liberated by Allied troops following the D-Day landings in June, followed by Paris on 25 August by a force spearheaded by Free French units.	France signs the Atlantic Pact uniting North America and Western Europe in a mutual defence alliance (NATO); the Council of Europe, of which France is part, is born.	Fear of communism and a resurgent Germany prompts the first steps towards European integration with the European Coal and Steel Community and military accords three years later.	French colonialism ends with war in Indochina (1946–54) followed by the Algerian War of Independence (1954–62), brought to a close with the signing of the Accord d'Évian (Evian Accord) in Évian-les-Bains.

THE BIRTH OF THE BIKINI

Almost called *atome* (atom) rather than bikini, after its pinprick size, the scanty little two-piece bathing suit was the 1946 creation of Cannes fashion designer Jacques Heim and automotive engineer Louis Réard. It made its first appearance poolside in Paris at the Piscine Molitor, a mythical art deco pool complex that reopened – with original pool – as the stunning Hôtel Molitor in 2014.

Top-and-bottom swimsuits had existed for centuries, but it was the French duo who made them briefer than brief and plumped for the name 'bikini' – after Bikini, an atoll in the Marshall Islands chosen by the USA in the same year as the testing ground for atomic bombs.

Once wrapped top and bottom around the curvaceous 1950s sex-bomb Brigitte Bardot on St-Tropez' Plage de Pampelonne, there was no looking back. The bikini was here to stay.

Algerian-born French people are known in France), elements of the military and extreme right-wingers became increasingly enraged at what they saw as defeatism in dealing with the problem. A plot to overthrow the French government and replace it with a military-style regime was narrowly avoided when General Charles de Gaulle, France's undersecretary of war who had fled Paris for London in 1940 after France capitulated and had spent more than a dozen years in opposition to the postwar Fourth Republic, agreed to assume the presidency in 1958.

De Gaulle's initial attempts at reform – according the Algerians political equality and recognising their right in principle to self-determination – infuriated right-wingers without quenching the Algerian thirst for independence. Following a failed coup attempt by military officers in 1961, the Organisation de l'Armée Secrète (OAS; a group of French settlers and sympathisers opposed to Algerian independence) resorted to terrorism. It tried to assassinate de Gaulle several times and in 1961 violence broke out on the streets of Paris. Police attacked Algerian demonstrators, killing more than 100 people. Algeria was granted independence the following year.

Since the end of WWII France has been one of the five permanent members of the UN Security Council. Follow its movements at www.un.org/en/sc.

The Road to Prosperity & Europe

In the late 1960s Charles de Gaulle was appearing more and more like yesterday's man. The loss of the colonies, a surge in immigration and a rise in unemployment had weakened his government. De Gaulle's government by decree was starting to gall the anti-authoritarian baby-boomer generation, now at university and agitating for change. Students reading Herbert Marcuse and Wilhelm Reich found much to admire in Fidel

1966	1968	1981	1989
France withdraws from NATO's joint military command in 1966; it has maintained an independent arsenal of nuclear weapons since 1960. A year later NATO moves out of its headquarters near Paris.	Large-scale anti-authoritarian student protests (known as 'May 1968'), aimed at Charles de Gaulle's style of government by decree, escalate into a countrywide protest that eventually brings down the president.	The superspeedy TGV makes its first commercial journey from Paris to Lyon, breaking all speed records to complete the train journey in two hours instead of six.	President Mitterrand's *grand projet*, Opéra Bastille, opens to mark the bicentennial of the French Revolution; IM Pei's love-it-or-leave-it Grande Pyramide is unveiled at the Louvre.

Castro, Che Guevara and the black struggle for civil rights in America, and vociferously denounced the war in Vietnam.

Student protests of 1968 climaxed with a brutal overreaction by police to a protest meeting at the Sorbonne, Paris' most renowned university. Overnight, public opinion turned in favour of the students, while the students themselves occupied the Sorbonne and erected barricades in the Latin Quarter. Within days a general strike by 10 million workers countrywide paralysed France.

But such comradeship between workers and students did not last long. While the former wanted a greater share of the consumer market, the latter wanted to destroy it. After much hesitancy de Gaulle took advantage of this division by appealing to people's fear of anarchy. Just as the country seemed on the brink of revolution and an overthrow of the Fifth Republic, stability returned. The government decentralised the higher-education system and followed through in the 1970s with a wave of other reforms (lowering the voting age to 18, instituting legalised abortion and so on). De Gaulle meanwhile resigned from office in 1969 and suffered a fatal heart attack the following year.

Georges Pompidou stepped onto the presidential podium in 1969. Despite embarking on an ambitious modernisation program, investing in aerospace, telecommunications and nuclear power, he failed to stave off inflation and social unrest following the global oil crisis of 1973. He died the following year.

In 1974 Valéry Giscard d'Estaing inherited a deteriorating economic climate and sharp divisions between the left and the right. His friendship with emperor and alleged cannibal Jean-Bédel Bokassa of the Central African Republic did little to win him friends, and in 1981 he was ousted by long-time head of the Parti Socialiste (PS; Socialist Party), François Mitterrand.

Despite France's first socialist president instantly alienating the business community by setting out to nationalise several privately owned banks, industrial groups and other parts of the economy, Mitterrand gave France a sparkle. Potent symbols of France's advanced technological savvy – the Minitel, a proto-personal computer in everyone's home, and high-speed TGV train service between Paris and Lyon – were launched in 1980 and 1981 respectively; a clutch of *grands projets* were embarked upon in the French capital. The death penalty was abolished, homosexuality was legalised, a 39-hour work week was instituted, annual holiday time was upped from four to five weeks and the right to retire at 60 was guaranteed.

But by 1986 the economy was weakening and in parliamentary elections that year the right-wing opposition, led by Jacques Chirac (mayor of Paris since 1977), won a majority in the National Assembly. For the

The French invented the first digital calculator, the hot-air balloon, Braille and margarine, not to mention Grand Prix racing and the first public interactive computer network.

1994	1995	1998	2001
The 50km-long Channel Tunnel linking France with Britain opens after seven years of hard graft by 10,000 workers.	After twice serving as prime minister, Jacques Chirac becomes president of France, winning popular acclaim for his direct words and actions in matters relating to the EU and the war in Bosnia.	After resuming nuclear testing in the South Pacific in the early 1990s, France signs the worldwide test-ban treaty, bringing an end to French nuclear testing once and for all.	Socialist Bertrand Delanoë becomes the first openly gay mayor of Paris (and any European capital); he is wounded in a knife attack by a homophobic assailant the following year.

next two years Mitterrand worked with a prime minister and cabinet from the opposition, an unprecedented arrangement known as *cohabitation*. The extreme-right Front National (FN; National Front) meanwhile quietly gained ground by loudly blaming France's economic woes on immigration.

Presidential elections in 1995 ushered Chirac (an ailing Mitterrand did not run and died the following year) into the Élysée Palace. However, Chirac's attempts to reform France's colossal public sector in order to meet the criteria of the European Monetary Union (EMU) were met with the largest protests since 1968, and his decision to resume nuclear testing on the Polynesian island of Mururoa and a nearby atoll was the focus of worldwide outrage. Always the maverick, Chirac called early parliamentary elections in 1997 – only for his party, the Rassemblement pour la République (RPR; Rally for the Republic), to lose out to a coalition of socialists, communists and greens. Another period of *cohabitation* ensued.

The 2002 presidential elections surprised everybody. The first round of voting saw left-wing PS leader Lionel Jospin eliminated and the FN's Jean-Marie Le Pen win 17% of the national vote. But in the subsequent run-off ballot, Chirac enjoyed a landslide victory, echoed in parliamentary elections a month later when the president-backed coalition UMP (Union pour un Mouvement Populaire) won a healthy majority, leaving Le Pen's FN without a seat in parliament and ending years of *cohabitation*.

Sarkozy's France

Presidential elections in 2007 ushered out old-school Jacques Chirac (in his 70s with two terms under his belt) and brought in Nicolas Sarkozy. Dynamic, ambitious and media savvy, the former interior minister and chairman of centre-right party UMP wooed voters with policies about job creation, lower taxes, crime crackdown and help for France's substantial immigrant population – issues that had particular pulling power coming from the son of a Hungarian immigrant father and Greek Jewish–French mother. However, his first few months in office were dominated by personal affairs as he divorced his wife Cecilia and wed Italian multimillionaire singer Carla Bruni a few months later.

The 2008 global banking crisis saw the government inject €10.5 billion into France's six major banks. Unemployment hit the 10% mark in 2010 and in regional elections the same year, Sarkozy's party lost badly. The left won 54% of votes and control of 21 out of 22 regions on mainland France and Corsica. Government popularity hit an all-time low.

Riots ripped through the Alpine town of Grenoble in 2010 after a 27-year-old man was shot dead by police while allegedly trying to rob a casino. The incident echoed bloodshed five years earlier in a Parisian suburb following the death of two teenage boys of North African origin,

Nicolas Sarkozy became the first French president to be held in police custody after being detained over allegations of corruption in July 2014. He was subsequently released, but placed under formal investigation over allegations of accepting campaign donations in 2007 from former Libyan leader Colonel Gaddafi. In March 2018 Sarkozy was ordered to stand trial on corruption charges.

2002	2004	2005	2007
The French franc, first minted in 1360, is thrown onto the scrap heap of history as the country adopts the euro as its official currency along with 14 other EU member-states.	France bans the wearing of crucifixes, the Islamic headscarf and other overtly religious symbols in state schools.	The French electorate overwhelmingly rejects the EU Constitution. Parisian suburbs are wracked by rioting Arab and African youths.	Pro-American pragmatist Nicolas Sarkozy beats Socialist candidate Ségolène Royal to become French president.

electrocuted after hiding in an electrical substation while on the run from the police. In Grenoble the burning cars and street clashes with riot police were seen as a measurement of just how volatile France had become.

Hollande's France

The President of the Republic has a website (www.elysee.fr), posts regularly on his Facebook page and is active on Twitter @elysee. He is also highly prolific on his personal accounts @EmmanuelMacron.

Presidential elections in 2012 ushered in France's first socialist president since François Mitterand left office in 1995. Nicolas Sarkozy ran for a second term in office, but lost against left-wing candidate François Hollande (b 1954) of the Socialist party whose ambitious talk of reducing unemployment, clearing the country's debts, upping tax on corporations and salaries over €1 million per annum and increasing the minimum salary clearly won over the electorate. Parliamentary elections a month later sealed Hollande's grip on power: the Socialists won a comfortable majority in France's 577-seat National Assembly, paving the way for Hollande to govern France during Europe's biggest economic crisis in decades.

His term got off to a rocky start. Scandal broke in 2013 after finance minister Jérôme Cahuzac admitted to having a safe-haven bank account in Switzerland and was forced to resign. Two months later France officially entered recession again. France's AA+ credit rating was downgraded still further to AA and unemployment dipped to 11.1% – the highest in 15 years. Rising anger at Hollande's failure to get the country's economy back on track saw his popularity plunge fast and furiously, and his Socialist party was practically wiped out in the 2014 municipal elections as the vast majority of the country swung decisively to the right. Paris, with the election of Spanish-born socialist Anne Hidalgo as Paris' first female mayor, was one of the few cities to remain on the political left.

French presidents have spent summer holidays at 17th-century Fort de Brégançon, on a rocky islet off the Mediterranean coast, since 1968. It was abandoned as a state residence in 2013 and a year later opened its historic doors to visitors.

Hollande's handling of his personal affairs proved equally inelegant. The same year French tabloid magazine *Closer* published photographs of the French president arriving at the Paris apartment of his alleged mistress, actress Julie Gayet, on a scooter – prompting public concern about both presidential security (or rather, lack of) and the well-being of the president's relationship with long-term partner and official First Lady, journalist Valérie Trierweiler. The presidential couple soon after announced the end of their relationship. Hollande's popularity plummeted to rock-bottom.

Terrorism & State of Emergency

On 7 January 2015, the Paris offices of newspaper *Charlie Hebdo* were attacked in response to satirical images it had published of the prophet Muhammad. Eleven staff and one police officer were killed and a further 22 people injured. #JeSuisCharlie ('I am Charlie') became a worldwide slogan of support.

2010	2011	2012	2013
Country-wide strikes and protests briefly paralyse the country after Sarkozy unveils plans to push the retirement age back from 60 to 62 by 2018.	French parliament bans burkas in public. Muslim women publicly wearing the face-covering veil can be fined and required to attend 'citizenship classes'.	France loses its top AAA credit rating. Economic policy is the big issue in presidential elections which usher in François Hollande, France's first Socialist president in 17 years.	Same-sex marriage is legalised in France. By the end of the year, 7000 gay couples have tied the knot.

On 13 November 2015 terrorist attacks occurred in Paris and St-Denis. During a football match watched by 80,000 spectators, three explosions were heard outside the stadium. Soon after, gunmen fired on customers drinking on pavement terraces outside several cafes and restaurants in Paris' 10e and 11e arrondissements. At 9.40pm three gunmen stormed concert hall Le Bataclan and fired into the audience. In all that evening 130 people lost their lives and 368 were injured. *Fluctuat nec mergitur* (tossed but not sunk) – etched on Paris' city coat of arms – assumed a vital new meaning after the attacks and became the rallying cry of French people countrywide who stood in complete solidarity with Parisians.

More was to follow. In Nice on 14 July 2016, while thousands of people were gathered on Promenade des Anglais to celebrate Bastille Day, a lorry ploughed through the crowd. Hundreds were injured and 86 killed. France entered three days of official mourning.

Following the fatal terrorist attacks in Paris, France declared a state of emergency, essentially allowing authorities to carry out police raids and place suspects under house arrest without prior court authorisation. This heightened security measure remained in place until November 2017 when it was effectively replaced by a new anti-terrorism law giving authorities similar rights: to search private homes, restrict free movement of individuals (41 people were placed under house arrest during the initial two-year state of emergency), and close mosques if necessary.

The Rise of the Far Right

In 2017 French president François Hollande's popularity hovered at a record all-time low. As the country geared up for presidential elections in May that year, all eyes were on the increasingly powerful Front National (now known as Rassemblement national; RN), known for its fervent anti-immigrant stance. In 2014 municipal elections, the far-right party led by Marine Le Pen won 7% of votes, trumping the ruling left-centre Socialists in several towns. In European elections a month later, the party won a quarter of votes, ahead of the main opposition party UMP (21%) and governing left-wing Socialists (14%). Prime Minister Manuel Valls was reported in the press as describing the victory as a political 'earthquake'. During parliamentary elections a few months later the then FN won its first ever two seats in the French Senate and the Socialists lost majority control of the Upper Chamber. The far right was clearly a force to be reckoned with, though the 2017 presidential elections saw Marine Le Pen convincingly defeated by 39-year-old centrist Emmanuel Macron.

France today maintains a rigid distinction between church and state. The country is a secular republic, meaning there can be no mention of religion on national school syllabuses.

Keep tabs on the moves and motions of France's National Assembly at www2.assemblee-nationale.fr.

2014	2015	2016	2017
Municipal elections result in Paris' first female mayor Anne Hidalgo, who is Spanish-born to boot. In European elections a month later, the far-right National Front wins almost a quarter of votes.	Deadly terrorist attacks in Paris: at satirical newspaper *Charlie Hebdo* on 7 January and at multiple locations including concert hall Le Bataclan on 13 November. The next year terrorists target Nice on Bastille Day.	France's 22 administrative *régions* are reduced to 13. French people are not impressed.	Centrist Emmanuel Macron wins presidential elections to become, at the age of 39, France's youngest-ever president. Paris wins its bid to host the Summer Olympics and Paralympics in 2024.

The French

Stylish, sexy, chic, charming, arrogant, rude, bureaucratic, chauvinistic... France is a country whose people attract more stubborn myths and stereotypes than any other. Over the centuries dozens of tags, true or otherwise, have been pinned on the garlic-eating, beret-wearing, *sacrebleu*-swearing French. (The French, by the way, don't wear berets or use old chestnuts like *sacrebleu* anymore.) So what precisely does it mean to be French?

Superiority Complex

Most French people are proud to be French and are staunchly nationalistic, a result of the country's republican stance that places nationality – rather than religion, for example – atop the self-identity list. This has created an overwhelmingly self-confident nation, culturally and intellectually, that can appear as a French superiority complex.

Such natural confidence is the backbone to being French. Never was this demonstrated more passionately or fervently than during the terrorist attacks that rocked the French capital in November 2015 and Nice during Bastille Day celebrations in 2016. Far from cowering in a corner, the shock attacks prompted the French to get out there and defiantly brandish their culture and national pride as their greatest weapon against terrorism: the hashtag slogan #JeSuisEnTerrasse spread like wildfire on the internet while in Paris, Parisians took to cafe pavement terraces and public spaces in typical quiet and elegant defiance.

Many French speak a foreign language fairly well, travel, and are happy to use their language skills should the need arise. Of course, if monolingual English-speakers don't try to speak French, there is no way proud French linguists will reveal they speak English! Many French men, incidentally, deem an English-speaking gal's heavily accented French as irresistibly sexy as many people deem a Frenchman speaking English.

Sixty Million Frenchmen Can't Be Wrong: What Makes the French so French ask Jean-Benoît Nadeau and Julie Barlow in their witty, well-written and at times downright comical musings on the French.

Tradition v Innovation

Suckers for tradition, the French are slow to embrace new ideas and technologies: it took the country an age to embrace the internet, clinging on to its own at-the-time-advanced Minitel system. Yet the French innovate. They came up with microchipped credit cards long before anyone else. The lead pencil, refrigerator, tinned foods, calculator, spirit level and little black dress (*merci,* Chanel) are all French inventions.

Naturally Sexy

When it comes to sex, not all French men ooze romance or light Gitane cigarettes all day. Nor are they as civilised about adultery as French cinema would have you believe. Adultery, illegal in France until 1975, was actually grounds for automatic divorce until as late as 2004. Today, some 45% of marriages in France end in divorce (making France the ninth most divorced country in the world) – with women, interestingly, being the ones to file for divorce in three out of four cases. As with elsewhere in Europe, couples are marrying later – at the average age of 32 and 31 for men and women respectively today, compared to 30 and 28 a decade ago. Almost 60% of babies in France are born out of wedlock, and one-fifth are raised by a single parent.

Kissing is an integral part of French life. (The expression 'French kissing' doesn't exist in French, incidentally.) Countrywide, people who know each other really well, reasonably well, a tad or barely at all greet each other with a glancing peck on each cheek. Southern France aside (where everyone kisses everyone), two men rarely kiss (unless they are related or artists) but always shake hands. Boys and girls start kissing as soon as they're out of nappies, or so it seems.

Lifestyle

Be a fly on the wall in the 5th-floor bourgeois apartment of Monsieur et Madame Tout le Monde and you'll see them dunking croissants in bowls of *café au lait* for breakfast, buying a baguette every day from the boulangerie (Monsieur nibbles the end off on his way home) and recycling nothing bar a few glass bottles and the odd cardboard box.

They go to the movies once a month, work 35 hours a week (many French still toil 39 hours or more a week – employers can enforce a 39-hour work week for a negotiable extra cost), and enjoy five weeks' holiday and almost a dozen bank (public) holidays a year. The couple view the start-up launched by their 24-year-old son in Paris with a bemusing mix of pride, scepticism and non-comprehension. Their 20-year-old daughter is a student: France's overcrowded state-run universities are free and open to anyone who passes the baccalaureate. Then there's their youngest, aged 10 and one of France's many children who have no school on Wednesday – the four-day week is a ball for kids, but not so easy for working parents who have to sort out childcare for that one day each week.

Madame buys a load of hot-gossip weekly magazines, Monsieur meets his mates to play boules, and the first two weeks of August is the *only* time to go on a summer holiday (with the rest of France). Dodging dog poo on pavements is a sport practised from birth and everything goes on the *carte bleue* (credit or debit card) when shopping. The couple have a landlord, although they are in the minority: 65% of households own their own home; the rest rent.

Les Femmes

Women were granted suffrage in 1945, but until 1964 a woman needed her husband's permission to open a bank account or get a passport. Younger French women in particular are quite outspoken and emancipated. But this self-confidence has yet to translate into equality in the workplace, where women hold few senior and management positions. Sexual harassment is addressed with a law imposing financial penalties on the offender. A great achievement in the last decade has been *Parité,*

FRANCE'S FIRST LADY

Not only are many French naturally sexy, but this enviable look is ageless. Or it has been unofficially declared so among older women following the arrival of President Emmanuel Macron who brought into office a glamorous first lady 24 years his senior (and over 60 to boot). Confidently stylish and sexy to the core, Brigitte Trogneux was a married mum-of-three and teacher at a school in small-town Amiens when she first met Macron, then a 15-year-old school pupil. The pair fell in love, prompting enormous scandal at the time, and subsequently married. They are the embodiment of open mindedness.

the law requiring political parties to fill 50% of their slates in all elections with female candidates.

Abortion is legal during the first 12 weeks of pregnancy, and girls under 16 do not need parental consent provided they are accompanied by an adult of their choice: 30 abortions take place in France for every 100 live births.

Above all else French women are known for their natural chic, style and class. And there's no doubt that contemporary French women are sassier than ever. Take the Rykiel women: in the 1970s, legendary Parisian knitwear designer Sonia Rykiel (1930–2016) designed the skin-tight, boob-hugging sweater worn with no bra beneath. In the new millennium, daughter Nathalie created Rykiel Woman, a sensual label embracing everything from lingerie to sex toys and aimed squarely at women who know what they want.

Then, of course, there is Spanish-born Anne Hidalgo, Paris' first ever female mayor, elected in 2014. *Allez les femmes!*

Linguistic Patriotism

Speaking a language other than their own is an emotional affair for the French, memorably illustrated a few years back when the-then French president Jacques Chirac walked out of an EU summit session after a fellow countryman had the audacity to address the meeting in English. French newspapers and the French blogosphere seethed with debate on linguistic patriotism the following day, with French bloggers – many of whom write in English – rightly pointing out that French has not been the primary international language for a long, long time.

Since the arrival of Emmanuel Macron – a fluent English speaker – on the political scene in 2017, English has assumed a new *de rigueur* in France. Since assuming the French presidency, Macron's silver-tongued ability to speak at ease in both English and French has won over the world.

French was the main language of the EU until 1995 when Sweden and Finland came into the EU fold. French broadcasting laws restrict the amount of airtime radio and TV stations can devote to non-French music, but nothing can be done to restrict who airs what on the internet. With English words like 'weekend', 'jogging', 'stop' and 'OK' firmly entrenched in daily French usage, language purists might just have lost the battle.

Multiculturalism

France is multicultural (immigrants make up around 9% of the population), yet its republican code, while inclusive and nondiscriminatory, has been criticised for doing little to accommodate a multicultural

---

FRENCH KISSING

Kissing French-style is not straightforward, with 'how many' and 'which side first' being potentially problematic. In Paris it is two: unless parties are related, *very* close friends or haven't seen each other in an age, anything more is deemed affected. That said, in hipster 20-something circles, friends swap three or four cheek-skimming kisses.

Travel south and *les bises* (kisses), or *les bisous* as the French colloquially say, multiply; three or four is the norm in Provence. The bits of France neighbouring Switzerland around Lake Geneva tend to be three-kiss country (in keeping with Swiss habits); and in the Loire Valley it is four. Corsicans, bizarrely, stick to two but kiss left cheek first – which can lead to locked lips given that everyone else in France starts with the right cheek.

society (and, interestingly, none of the members of France's National Assembly represents the immigrant population, first or second generation). Nothing reflects this dichotomy better than the law, in place since 2004, banning the Islamic headscarf, Jewish skullcap, crucifix and other religious symbols in French schools, or the more recent 2017 burkini ban on beaches in southern France.

Some 90% of the French Muslim community – Europe's largest – are noncitizens. Most are illegal immigrants living in poverty-stricken *bidonvilles* (shanty towns) around Paris, Lyon, Marseille and other metropolitan centres. Many are unemployed (youth unemployment in many suburbs is as high as 40%) and face little prospect of getting a job.

Good Sports

Most French wouldn't be seen dead walking down the street in trainers and tracksuits. But contrary to appearances, they love sport. Shaved-leg cyclists toil up Mont Ventoux, football fans fill stadiums and anyone who can flits off for the weekend to ski or snowboard.

Les 24 Heures du Mans and the F1 Grand Prix in Monaco are the world's raciest dates in motor sports; the French Open, aka Roland Garros, in Paris in late May to early June is the second of the year's four grand-slam tennis tournaments; and the Tour de France is – indisputably – the world's most prestigious bicycle race. Bringing together 189 of the world's top male cyclists (21 teams of nine) and 15 million spectators in July each year for a spectacular 3000-plus-kilometre cycle around the country, the three-week race always labours through the Alps and Pyrenees and finishes on Paris' Champs-Élysées. The route in between changes each year but wherever it goes, the French systematically turn out in droves – armed with tables, chairs and picnic hampers – to make a day of it. The serpentine publicity caravan preceding the cyclists showers roadside spectators with coffee samples, logo-emblazoned balloons, pens and other free junk-advertising gifts and is easily as much fun as watching the cyclists themselves speed through – in 10 seconds flat.

France's greatest moment in football history came at the 1998 World Cup, which the country hosted and won. The son of Algerian immigrants, Marseille-born midfielder Zinedine Zidane (b 1972) wooed the nation with a sparkling career of goal-scoring headers and extraordinary footwork that unfortunately ended with him head-butting an Italian player during the 2006 World Cup final. But such was the power of his humble Marseillais grin (since used to advertise Adidas sports gear, Volvic mineral water and Christian Dior fashion) that the French nation instantly forgave this 'golden boy' of French football.

Recent years have seen a crop of new French stars emerge: in 2016 French midfielder Paul Pogba (b 1993) was signed by Manchester United for a then-record €105 million, a price tag equalled by Les Bleus' striker Ousmane Dembélé (b 1997) a year later when he moved to Barcelona. Paris-born Kylian Mbappé (b 1998) then put pen to paper the same year and signed for Paris Saint-Germain, eclipsing both transfer fees with a deal worth around €180 million. French football is clearly back in the spotlight.

France's second-greatest moment in football history came at the 2018 World Cup, which Les Bleues won – almost 20 years to the day since their first World Cup win. At the tender age of 19, Mbappé became the youngest player to score in a World Cup final since the 17-year-old Brazilian player Pelé in 1958. The team's coach Didier Deschamps made history by becoming just the third person in the world to first captain a World Cup winning team and then win it again as manager of the national side.

Following France's ban on face covering, burka included, in 2010, municipalities in 30 coastal resorts on the Côte d'Azur and in Corsica banned burkinis in 2016. The French Council of State declared the ruling illegal, but the body-covering beach wear still remains banned on some beaches in Cannes, Nice and elsewhere.

France's traditional ball games include *pétanque* and the more formal boules, which has a 70-page rule book. Both are played by men on a gravel pitch.

The French Table

Few Western cuisines are so envied, aspired to or seminal. The freshness of ingredients, natural flavours, regional variety and range of cooking methods in French cuisine is phenomenal. The very word 'cuisine' was borrowed from the French – no other language could handle all the nuances. The French table waltzes taste buds through a dizzying array of dishes sourced from aromatic street markets, seaside oyster farms, sun-baked olive groves and ancient vineyards mirroring the beauty of each season. Discovering these varied regional cuisines is an enriching, essential experience.

Terroir

No country so blatantly bundles up cuisine with its *terroir* (land). *'Le jardin de France'* (the garden of France), a poetic phrase coined by the French writer Rabelais in the 16th century to describe his native Touraine in the Loire Valley, has been exploited ever since. Yet it is the serene valley, tracing the course of the River Loire west of the French capital, which remains most true to the Rabelais image of a green and succulent landscape laden with lush fruits, flowers, nuts and vegetables.

It was in the Renaissance kitchens of the Loire's celebrated châteaux that French cooking was refined: *coq au vin* (chicken in wine) and *cuisses de grenouilles* (frogs' legs) were common dishes, and poultry and game dishes were the pride and joy. Once or twice a year a fattened pig was slaughtered and prepared dozens of different ways – roasts, sausages, *boudin noir* (black pudding), charcuterie (cold meats), pâtés and so on. No single part, offal et al, was wasted.

Sauces

With plenty of game and poultry going into châteaux kitchens, it was natural that medieval cooks should whip up a sauce to go with it. In the 14th to 16th centuries, *sauce verte* (green sauce) – a rather crude, heavily spiced mix of vinegar and green grape juice – accompanied meat dishes. In 1652 François-Pierre de la Varenne published his cook book *Le Cuisinier François* in which he dismissed bread and breadcrumbs as thickening agents in favour of *roux* (a more versatile mixture of flour and fat). This paved the way for the creation, a century later, of classic French sauces such as béchamel (a milk-based sauce thickened with *roux*) and *velouté* (a velvety mix of chicken or other stock and melted butter, seasoned and thickened with *roux*) a century later. *Velouté* is the base for dozens of other sauces made to accompany meat, fish and game dishes today.

Bread

In northern France wheat fields shade vast swaths of agricultural land a gorgeous golden copper, and nothing is more French than *pain* (bread). Starved peasants demanded bread on the eve of the French Revolution when the ill-fated Queen Marie Antoinette is purported to have said 'let them eat cake'. And bread today – no longer a matter of life or death but a cultural icon – accompanies every meal. It's rarely served with butter, but when it is, the butter is always *doux* (unsalted).

Cooking Classes

La Terrasse Rouge
(St-Émilion)

Le St-James
(near Bordeaux)

L'Atelier Jean-Luc Rabanel
(Arles)

Le Mirazur
(Menton)

Le Grand Bleu
(Sarlat-la-Canéda)

La Table du Couvent
(Limoges)

Every town and almost every village has its own *boulangerie* (bakery) that sells bread in all manner of shapes, sizes and variety. Artisan *boulangeries* bake their bread in a wood-fired, brick bread oven pioneered by Loire Valley châteaux in the 16th century.

Plain old *pain* is a 400g, traditional-shaped loaf, soft inside and crusty out. The iconic classic is *une baguette,* a long thin crusty loaf weighing 250g. Anything fatter and it becomes *une flûte,* thinner *une ficelle.* While French baguettes are impossibly good, they systematically turn unpleasantly dry within four hours, and unbelievably rock-hard within 12.

Charcuterie & Foie Gras

Charcuterie, the backbone of every French picnic and a bistro standard, is traditionally made from pork, though other meats are used in making *saucisse* (small fresh sausage, boiled or grilled before eating), *saucisson* (salami), *saucisson sec* (air-dried salami), *boudin noir* (blood sausage or pudding made with pig's blood, onions and spices) and other cured and salted meats. Pâtés, terrines and rillettes are also considered charcuterie. The difference between a pâté and a terrine is academic: a pâté is removed from its container and sliced before it is served, while a terrine is sliced from the container itself. Rillettes, spread cold over bread or toast, is potted meat or even fish that has been shredded with two forks, seasoned and mixed with fat.

The key component of *pâté de foie gras* is foie gras, which is the liver of fattened ducks and geese who are force-fed in almost every case. It was first prepared *en croûte* (in a pastry crust) around 1780 by one Jean-Pierre Clause, chef to the military governor of Alsace, who was impressed enough to send a batch to the king of Versailles. Today, it is a traditional component of celebratory or festive meals – particularly Christmas and New Year's Eve – in family homes countrywide, and is consumed with relish year-round in regions in southwest France where it is primarily made, namely Aquitaine (the Dordogne), Limousin, Auvergne and the Midi-Pyrénées.

Patisserie

Patisserie is a general French term for pastries and includes *tartes* (tarts), *flans* (custard pies), *gâteaux* (cakes) and *biscuits* (cookies) as well as traditional croissants, *pains au chocolats* (chocolate-filled croissants) and other typical pastries. *Sablés* are shortbread biscuits, *tuiles* are delicate wing-like almond cookies, madeleines are small scallop-shaped cakes often flavoured with a hint of vanilla or lemon, and *tarte tatin* is an upside-down caramelised apple pie that's been around since the late 19th century. Louis XIV (r 1643–1715), known for his sweet tooth, is credited with introducing the custom of eating dessert – once reserved for feast days and other celebrations – at the end of a meal.

No sweet treat evokes the essence of French patisserie quite like the elegant, sophisticated and zany macaron, a legacy of Catherine de Médicis who came to France in 1533 with an entourage of Florentine chefs and pastry cooks adept in the subtleties of Italian Renaissance cooking and armed with delicacies such as aspic, truffles, quenelles (dumplings), artichokes – and macarons. Round and polished smooth like a giant Smartie, the macaron (nothing to do with coconut) is a pair of crisp-shelled, chewy-inside discs – egg whites whisked stiff with sugar and ground almonds – sandwiched together with a smooth filling. Belying their egg-shell fragility, macarons are created in a rainbow of lurid colours and flavours, wild and inexhaustible: rose petal, cherry blossom, caramel with coconut and mango, mandarin orange and olive oil...

The Food of France by Waverley Root, first published in 1958, remains the seminal work in English on *la cuisine française,* with a focus on historical development, by a long-time Paris-based American foreign correspondent.

Foodie Towns

Le Puy-en-Velay (lentils)

Dijon (mustard)

Privas (chestnuts)

Cancale (oysters)

Espelette (red chillies)

Colmar (chocolate stork eggs)

Lyon (piggy-part cuisine)

Cheese

No French food product is a purer reflection of *terroir* than cheese, an iconic staple that – with the exception of most coastal areas – is made all over the country, tiny villages laying claim to ancient variations made just the way *grand-père* (grandfather) did it. France boasts more than 500 varieties, made with *lait cru* (raw milk), pasteurised milk or *petit-lait* ('little-milk', the whey left over after the fats and solids have been curdled with rennet).

Chèvre, made from goat's milk, is creamy, sweet and faintly salty when fresh, but hardens and gets saltier as it matures. Among the best is Ste-Maure de Touraine, a mild creamy cheese from the Loire Valley; Cabécou de Rocamadour from Midi-Pyrénées, often served warm with salad or marinated in oil and rosemary; and Lyon's St-Marcellin, a soft white cheese that should be served impossibly runny.

Roquefort, a ewe's-milk veined cheese from Languedoc, is the king of blue cheeses and vies with Burgundy's pongy Époisses for the strongest taste award. Soft, white, orange-skinned Époisses, created in the 16th century by monks at Abbaye de Cîteaux, takes a month to make, using washes of saltwater, rainwater and Marc de Bourgogne – a local pomace brandy and the source of the cheese's final fierce bite.

Equal parts of Comté, Beaufort and Gruyère – a trio of hard fruity, cow's milk cheeses from the French Alps – are grated and melted in a garlic-smeared pot with a dash of nutmeg, white wine and *kiersch* (cherry liqueur) to create fondue Savoyarde. Hearty and filling, this pot of melting glory originated from the simple peasant need of using up cheese scraps. It is now the chic dish to eat on the ski slopes.

Wine Schools

École des Vins de Bourgogne (Beaune)

La Cité du Vin & École du Vin de Bordeaux (Bordeaux)

La Winery (the Médoc)

Maison du Vin de St-Émilion (St-Émilion)

École de Dégustation (Châteauneuf-du-Pape)

Langlois-Chateau (Saumur)

Wine

Viticulture in France is an ancient art and tradition that bears its own unique trademark. The French thirst for wine goes back to Roman times when techniques to grow grapes and craft wine were introduced, and *dégustation* (tasting) has been an essential part of French wine culture ever since.

APERITIFS & DIGESTIFS

Meals in France are preceded by an aperitif such as a *kir* (white wine sweetened with a sweet fruit syrup like blackcurrant or chestnut), *kir royale* (Champagne with blackcurrant syrup), *pineau* (cognac and grape juice) or a glass of sweet white Coteaux du Layon from the Loire Valley. In southern France aniseed-flavoured pastis (clear in the bottle, cloudy when mixed with water) is the aperitif to drink al fresco; in the southwest, go local with a Floc de Gascogne, a liqueur wine made from Armagnac and red or white grape juice. In Corsica, Cap Corse Mattei – a fortified wine whose recipe has stood the test of time (nearly 150 years!) – is the choice *apéro*.

After-dinner drinks accompany coffee. France's most famous brandies are Cognac and Armagnac, both made from grapes in the regions of those names. *Eaux de vie* (literally 'waters of life') can be made with grape skins and the pulp left over after being pressed for wine (Marc de Champagne, Marc de Bourgogne), apples (Calvados) and pears (Poire William), as well as such fruits as plums *(eau de vie de prune)* and even raspberries *(eau de vie de framboise)*. In the Loire Valley a shot of orange (aka a glass of local Cointreau liqueur) ends the meal.

When in Normandy, do as the festive Normans do: refresh the palate between courses with a *trou normand* (literally 'Norman hole') – traditionally a shot of *calva* (Calvados) or a contemporary scoop of apple sorbet doused in the local apple brandy.

Quality wines in France are designated as Appellation d'Origine Contrôlée (AOC; literally, 'label of inspected origin'), equivalent since 2012 to the European-wide Appellation d'Origine Protégée (AOP). Both labels mean the same: that the wine has met stringent regulations governing where, how and under what conditions it was grown and bottled. French AOC can cover a wide region (such as Bordeaux), a sub-region (such as Haut-Médoc), or a commune or village (such as Pomerol). Some regions only have a single AOC (such as Alsace), while Burgundy has dozens.

Some viticulturists have honed their skills and techniques to such a degree that their wine is known as a *grand cru* (literally 'great growth'). If this wine has been produced in a year of optimum climatic conditions, it becomes a *millésime* (vintage) wine. *Grands crus* are aged in small oak barrels then bottles, sometimes for 20 years or more, to create those memorable bottles (with price tags to match) that wine experts enthuse about with such passion.

There are dozens of wine-producing regions throughout France, but the principal ones are Burgundy, Bordeaux, the Rhône and Loire Valleys, Champagne, Languedoc, Provence and Alsace. Wines are generally named after the location of the vineyard rather than the grape varietal. Organic and biodynamic wines are increasingly popular.

Red

France's most respected reds are from Burgundy (Bourgogne in French), Bordeaux and the Rhône Valley.

Monks in Burgundy began making wine in the 8th century during the reign of Charlemagne. Today vineyards remain small, rarely more than 10 hectares, with vignerons (winegrowers) in Côte d'Or, Chablis, Châtillon and Mâcon producing small quantities of excellent reds from pinot noir grapes. The best Bourgogne vintages demand 10 to 20 years to age.

In the sun-blessed south, Bordeaux has the perfect climate for producing wine: its 1100 sq km of vineyards produce more fine wine than any other region in the world. Well-balanced Bordeaux reds blend several grape varieties, predominantly merlot, cabernet sauvignon and cabernet franc. The Médoc, Pomerol, St-Émilion and Graves are key winegrowing areas.

The most renowned red in the Côtes du Rhône appellation from the Rhône Valley – a vast 771-sq-km winegrowing area with dramatically different soils, climates, topography and grapes – is Châteauneuf du Pape, a strong full-bodied wine bequeathed by the Avignon popes who planted the distinctive stone-covered vineyards.

Further south on the coast near Toulon, deep-flavoured Bandol reds have been produced from dark-berried mourvèdre grapes since Roman times. These wines were famous across Gaul, their ability to mature at sea ensuring they travelled far beyond their home shores in the 16th and 17th centuries.

White

Some of France's finest whites come from the Loire Valley. This large winegrowing region produces the country's greatest variety of wines, and light delicate whites from Pouilly-Fumé, Vouvray, Sancerre, Bourgueil and Chinon are excellent. Muscadet, cabernet franc and chenin

THE FRENCH TABLE WINE

Top Self-Drive Wine Trips

Marne & Côte des Bar Champagne Routes (Champagne)

Route des Grands Crus (Burgundy)

Route des Vins d'Alsace (Alsace)

Route Touristique des Vignobles (Loire Valley)

Route des Vins de Jura (the Jura)

blanc are key grape varieties, contrasting with the chardonnay grapes that go into some great Burgundy whites.

Vines were planted by the Greeks in Massilia (Marseille) around 600 BC and crisp Cassis whites remain the perfect companion to the coast's bounty of shellfish and seafood.

Alsace produces almost exclusively white wines – mostly varieties produced nowhere else in France – that are known for their clean, fresh taste. Unusually, some of the fruity Alsatian whites also go well with red meat. Alsace's four most important varietal wines are riesling (known for its subtlety), gewürztraminer (pungent and highly regarded), pinot gris (robust and high in alcohol) and muscat d'Alsace (less sweet than muscats from southern France).

Rosé

Chilled, fresh pink rosé wines – best drunk al fresco beneath a vine-laced pergola – are synonymous with the hot south. Côtes de Provence, with 20 hectares of vineyards between Nice and Aix-en-Provence, is the key appellation (and France's sixth-largest).

Other enticing rosé labels from Provence include Coteaux d'Aix-en-Provence, Palette and Coteaux Varois.

Champagne

Champagne has been produced northeast of Paris since the 17th century when innovative monk Dom Pierre Pérignon perfected a technique for making sparkling wine. It's made from the white chardonnay, red pinot noir or black pinot meunier grape. Each vine is vigorously pruned and trained to produce a small quantity of high-quality grapes.

If the final product is labelled *brut,* it is extra dry, with only 1.5% sugar content. *Extra-sec* means very dry (but not as dry as *brut*), *sec* is dry and *demi-sec* slightly sweet. The sweetest Champagne is labelled *doux*. Whatever the label, it is sacrilege to drink it out of anything other than a traditional Champagne flute, narrow at the bottom to help the bubbles develop, wider in the middle to promote the diffusion of aromas, and narrower at the top again to concentrate those precious aromas.

Britons have had a taste for Bordeaux' full-bodied red wines, known as clarets in the UK, since the 12th century when King Henry II, who controlled the region through marriage, gained the favour of locals by granting them tax-free trade status with England.

The Arts

Literature, music, painting, cinema: France's vast artistic heritage is the essence of French *art de vivre*. Contemporary French writers might struggle to be published abroad, but Voltaire, Victor Hugo, Marcel Proust and Simone de Beauvoir walk the hall of fame. Music is embedded in the French soul, with world-class rap, dance and electronica coming out of Paris. French painting, with its roots in prehistoric cave art, continues to break new ground with provocative street art, while French film is enjoying a marvellous renaissance.

Literature

Courtly Love to Symbolism

Troubadours' lyric poems of courtly love dominated medieval French literature, while the *roman* (literally 'romance', now meaning 'novel') drew on old Celtic tales. With the *Roman de la Rose,* a 22,000-line poem by Guillaume de Lorris and Jean de Meun, allegorical figures like Pleasure, Shame and Fear appeared.

French Renaissance literature was extensive and varied. La Pléiade was a group of lyrical poets active in the 1550s and 1560s. The exuberant narrative of Loire Valley–born François Rabelais (1494–1553) blends coarse humour with encyclopedic erudition in a vast panorama of every kind of person, occupation and jargon in 16th-century France. Michel de Montaigne (1533–92) covered cannibals, war horses, drunkenness and the resemblance of children to their fathers, along with other themes.

The *grand siècle* (golden age) ushered in classical lofty odes to tragedy. François de Malherbe (1555–1628) brought a new rigour to rhythm in poetry, and Marie de La Fayette (1634–93) penned the first French novel, *La Princesse de Clèves* (1678).

The philosophical Voltaire (1694–1778) dominated the 18th century. A century on, Besançon gave birth to French Romantic Victor Hugo (1802–85). The breadth of interest and technical innovations exhibited in his poems and novels – *Les Misérables* and *The Hunchback of Notre Dame* among them – was phenomenal.

In 1857 literary landmarks *Madame Bovary* by Gustave Flaubert (1821–80), and Charles Baudelaire's (1821–67) poems *Les Fleurs du Mal* (The Flowers of Evil), were published. Émile Zola (1840–1902) saw novel-writing as a science in his powerful series, *Les Rougon-Macquart.*

FRENCH CINEMA

1920s

French film flourishes. Sound ushers in René Clair's (1898–1981) world of fantasy and satirical surrealism. **Watch** Abel Gance's antiwar blockbuster *J'Accuse!* (I Accuse!; 1919), filmed on WWI battlefields.

1930s

WWI inspires a new realism: portraits of ordinary lives dominate film. **Watch** *La Grande Illusion* (The Great Illusion; 1937), a devastating evocation of war's folly based on the trench warfare experience of director Jean Renoir.

1940s

Surrealists eschew realism. WWII saps the film industry of both talent and money. **Watch** Jean Cocteau's *La Belle et la Bête* (Beauty and the Beast; 1945) and *Orphée* (Orpheus; 1950).

1950s

Nouvelle Vague (New Wave) sees small budgets, no stars and real-life subject matter. **Watch** A petty young criminal on the run in Jean-Luc Godard's *À Bout de Souffle* (Breathless; 1958) and adolescent rebellion in François Truffaut's *Les Quatre Cents Coups* (The 400 Blows; 1959).

1960s

France as the land of romance. **Watch** Claude Lelouch's *Un Homme et une Femme* (A Man and a Woman; 1966) and Jacques Demy's bittersweet *Les Parapluies de Cherbourg* (The Umbrellas of Cherbourg; 1964).

Evoking mental states was the dream of symbolists Paul Verlaine (1844–96) and Stéphane Mallarmé (1842–98). Verlaine shared a tempestuous homosexual relationship with poet Arthur Rimbaud (1854–91): enter French literature's first modern poems.

Modern Literature

The world's longest novel – a seven-volume 9,609,000-character giant by Marcel Proust (1871–1922) – dominated the early 20th century. *À la Recherche du Temps Perdu* (Remembrance of Things Past) explores in evocative detail the true meaning of past experience recovered from the unconscious by involuntary memory.

Surrealism proved a vital force until WWII. André Breton (1896–1966) captured the spirit of surrealism – a fascination with dreams, divination and all manifestations of the imaginary – in his autobiographical narratives. In Paris the bohemian Colette (1873–1954) captivated and shocked with her titillating novels detailing the amorous exploits of heroines such as schoolgirl Claudine. In New York meanwhile, what would become one of the bestselling French works of all time was published in 1943: *Le Petit Prince* (The Little Prince), by Lyon-born writer and pilot, Antoine de Saint-Exupéry (1900–44). He captured the hearts of millions with his magical yet philosophical tale for children about an aviator's adventures with a little blonde-haired Prince from Asteroid B-612.

After WWII, existentialism developed around the lively debates of Jean-Paul Sartre (1905–80), Simone de Beauvoir (1908–86) and Albert Camus (1913–60) in Paris' Left Bank cafes.

The *nouveau roman* of the 1950s saw experimental young writers seek new ways of organising narratives, with Nathalie Sarraute slashing identifiable characters and plot in *Les Fruits d'Or* (The Golden Fruits). *Histoire d'O* (Story of O), an erotic sadomasochistic novel written by Dominique Aury under a pseudonym in 1954, sold more copies outside France than any other contemporary French novel.

Another writer to turn heads was radical young writer Françoise Sagan (1935–2004) who shot to fame overnight at the age of 18 with her first novel, *Bonjour Tristesse* (Hello Sadness), published in 1954. The subsequent fast-paced, hedonistic lifestyle pursued by the party-loving, bourgeois-born writer ensured she remained in the spotlight until her death in 2004.

Best Literary Sights

Maison de Victor Hugo (Paris)

Sartre's and de Beauvoir's graves, Cimetière du Montparnasse (Paris)

Oscar Wilde's grave, Cimetière du Père Lachaise (Paris)

Musée Colette (Burgundy)

Musée Jules Verne (Nantes & Amiens)

Les Charmettes (Chambéry)

READING LIST

One way of ensuring your beach reading is right up to the minute is to plump for the latest winner of the Prix Goncourt, France's most prestigious literary prize awarded annually since 1903 and reflective, in recent years, of the occupation in contemporary French literature with issues of race, multiculturalism and immigration.

Winners include Marcel Proust in 1919 for *À l'Ombre des Jeunes Filles en Fleurs* (Within a Budding Grove; 1924) and Simone de Beauvoir in 1954 for *Les Mandarins* (The Mandarins; 1957). The first black woman to win the award, NDiaye stunned the literary world at the age of 21 with *Comédie Classique* (Classic Comedy;1988), a 200-page novel comprising one single sentence. Eric Vuillard's realist *L'Ordre du Jour* (The Order of the Day), a historical work about the rise of Hitler and Nazi annexation of Austria in 1938, landed the 2017 prize.

Add to your reading list the laureate of France's other big literary award, the Grand Prix du Roman de l'Académie Française, around since 1914. In 2017 Daniel Rondeau won the esteemed prize with *Mécaniques du chaos* (Mechanics of Chaos), a polyphonic novel layering together dozens of different contemporary worlds.

Contemporary Literature

Marc Levy (www.marclevy.info) is France's bestselling writer. The film rights of his first novel were snapped up for the Stephen Spielberg box-office hit, *Just Like Heaven* (2005), and his novels have since been translated into 49 languages. His 16th novel, *Elle & Lui* (2015) was quickly published in English as *PS from Paris* (2017), as will no doubt be the case with *La Dernière des Stanfield* (The Last of the Stanfields; 2018) and *Une Fille Comme Elle* (A Girl Like Her; 2018).

No French writer better delves into the mind, mood and politics of France's notable ethnic population than Faïza Guène (b 1985; http://faizaguene.fr), sensation of the French literary scene who writes in a notable 'urban slang' style. Born and bred on a ghetto housing estate outside Paris, she stunned critics with her debut novel, *Kiffe Kiffe Demain* (2004), sold in 27 countries and published in English as *Just Like Tomorrow* (2006). Faïza Guène's father moved from a village in western Algeria to northern France in 1952, aged 17, to work in the mines. Her latest novel *Millenium Blues* (2018) opens with an accident in Paris during a heatwave in the capital in 2003.

Delphine de Vigan (b 1966) is another female Parisian writer to be widely translated in English. Her eight novels today include the psychological thriller *D'après une histoire vraie* (2015), published in English as *Based On a True Story* (2017), about a writer named Delphine living in Paris with her teenage kids and famous journalist husband.

Jean-Marie Gustave Le Clézio, born during WWII in Nice to a Niçois mother and Mauritian father, addresses ethnic issues engagingly. The bulk of his childhood was spent in Nigeria and he studied in Bristol, England, and Aix-en-Provence. In 2008 he won the Nobel Prize in Literature.

The work of Paris-born Patrick Modiano (b 1945) was only really discovered by an Anglophone audience after the novelist was awarded the Nobel Prize in Literature in 2014. His most famous novel remains Prix Goncourt winner *Rue des Boutiques Obscures* (1978), translated in English as *Missing Person* (1980). His latest novel is *Souvenirs dormants* (Sleeping Memories; 2017).

Music

Jazz & French Chansons

Jazz hit 1920s Paris in the banana-clad form of Josephine Baker, an African American cabaret dancer. Post-WWII ushered in a much-appreciated bunch of musicians, mostly black Americans who opted to remain in Paris' bohemian Montmartre rather than return to the brutal racism and segregation of the USA: Sidney Bechet called Paris home from 1949, jazz drummer Kenny 'Klook' Clarke followed in 1956, pianist Bud Powell in 1959, and saxophonist Dexter Gordon in the early 1960s.

1970s

The limelight baton goes to lesser-known directors like Éric Rohmer (b 1920), who make beautiful but uneventful films in which the characters endlessly analyse their feelings.

1980s

Big-name stars, slick production values and nostalgia: generous state subsidies see film-makers switch to costume dramas and comedies in the face of growing competition from the USA. **Watch** Luc Besson strikes gold with *Subway* (1985) and *Le Grand Bleu* (The Big Blue; 1988).

1990s

French actor Gérard Depardieu wins huge audiences in France and abroad. **Watch** *Cyrano de Bergerac* (1990) and *Astérix et Obélix: Mission Cléopâtre* (2002). Besson continues to stun with *Nikita* (1990) and *Jeanne d'Arc* (Joan of Arc; 1999).

New Millennium

'New French Extremity' is the tag given to the socially conscious, transgressive films of talented Paris-born, Africa-raised film-maker Claire Denis. **Watch** *Chocolat* (1988) and *Matériel Blanc* (White Material; 2009), scripted by Parisian novelist Marie NDiaye, to explore the legacy of French colonialism.

2011

Renaissance of French film. **Watch** *The Artist* (2011), a silent B&W, French-made romantic comedy set in 1920s Hollywood that scooped five Oscars and seven BAFTAs to become the most awarded film in French film history.

2014

Female film-maker Pascale Ferran (b 1960) makes her mark with *Bird People* (2014), set in and around a hotel at Paris' Charles de Gaulle airport.

In 1934 a chance meeting between Parisian jazz guitarist Stéphane Grappelli and three-fingered Roma guitarist Django Reinhardt in a Montparnasse nightclub led to the formation of the Hot Club of France quintet. Claude Luter and his Dixieland band were hot in the 1950s.

The *chanson française*, a French folk-song tradition dating from the troubadours of the Middle Ages, was eclipsed by the music halls and burlesque of the early 20th century, but was revived in the 1930s by Édith Piaf and Charles Trenet. In the 1950s, Paris' Left Bank cabarets nurtured *chansonniers* (cabaret singers) such as Léo Ferré, Georges Brassens, Claude Nougaro, Jacques Brel and the very charming, very sexy, very French Serge Gainsbourg. A biopic celebrating his life, *Serge Gainsbourg: Une Vie Héroïque* (Serge Gainsbourg: A Heroic Life), was released in 2009 to wide acclaim.

In the 1980s irresistible crooners Jean-Pierre Lang and Pierre Bachelet revived the *chanson* tradition with classics such as 'Les Corons' (1982), a passionate ode to northern France's miners. Contemporary performers include Vincent Delerm, Bénabar, Jeanne Cherhal, Camille, Soha, Les Têtes Raides and Arnaud Fleurent-Didier.

Jazz fans will adore the gypsy jazz style of young French pop singer Zaz – an experimental voice from Tours in the Loire Valley, often compared to Édith Piaf – who stormed to the top of the charts with her debut album *Zaz* (2010). Her subsequent third album, *Paris* (2014) is a musical ode to the French capital with 13 songs evoking Paris' irresistible charm and romance. Her first live album, *Sur la Route* (2015), only confirms that Zaz is one of France's hottest contemporary female voices.

Rap

France is known for its rap, an original 1990s sound spearheaded by Senegal-born, Paris-reared rapper MC Solaar and Suprême NTM (NTM being an acronym for a French expression far too offensive to print). Most big-name rappers are French twenty-somethings of Arabic or African origin whose prime preoccupations are the frustrations and fury of fed-up immigrants in the French *banlieues* (suburbs).

Disiz La Peste, born in Amiens to a Senegalese father and French mother, portrayed precisely this in his third album, aptly entitled *Histoires Extra-Ordinaires d'un Jeune de Banlieue* (The Extraordinary Stories of a Youth in the Suburbs; 2005), as did his 'last' album *Disiz the End* (2009), after which he morphed into Peter Punk (www.disizpeterpunk. com) and created a very different rock-punk-electro sound. In 2011 he returned as rap artist Disiz La Peste, releasing a rash of albums culminating in 2017 with *Pacifique*, his 11th album.

France's other big rap band is Marseille's home-grown IAM (www.iam. tm.fr), around since 1989 and still going strong. In 2017 the group released its eighth album, *Révolution*, and went on tour for the first time in several years; tickets for concerts in Paris and Marseille sold out within seconds of going online. A ninth album is expected in 2018, followed by a world tour in 2019 to celebrate the band's 30th birthday. Djadja & Dinaz from Meaux, 40km northeast of Paris, is a hip-hop duo to watch; their 2018 album *Le revers de la médaille* raced to the top of the French charts.

French rap continues to inspire fresh talent. Congolese rapper Maître Gims (b 1986) arrived in France at the age of two, grew up in squats in the Parisian suburbs and is one of France's best-known rappers today. The millennial rap scene is notably prolific in Bordeaux in southwest France where talented young rappers like 20-something Joey Larsé – originally from the Parisian suburb of Montreuil – have chosen to live and work.

Musical Pilgrimage

Serge Gainsbourg's grave, Cimetière du Montparnasse (Paris)

Jim Morrison's grave, Cimetière du Père Lachaise (Paris)

Former home of Josephine Baker, Château des Milandes (Dordogne)

Espace Georges Brassens (Sète)

Jazz à Juan, Juan-les-Pins (French Riviera)

Rock & Pop

One could be forgiven for thinking that French pop is becoming dynastic. The distinctive M (for Mathieu) is the son of singer Louis Chédid; Arthur H is the progeny of pop-rock musician Jacques Higelin; and Thomas Dutronc is the offspring of 1960s idols Jacques and Françoise Hardy. Serge Gainsbourg's daughter with Jane Birkin, Charlotte Gainsbourg (b 1971), made her musical debut in 1984 with the single 'Lemon Incest' and – several albums later – released a cover version of the song 'Hey Joe' as soundtrack to the film *Nymphomaniac* (2013) in which she also starred as the leading lady. For her latest album, *Rest,* released in 2017, she collaborated with Guy Man from Daft Punk and Paul McCartney among others.

Indie rock band Phoenix, from Versailles, headlines festivals in the USA and UK. The band was born in the late 1990s in a garage in the Paris suburbs; lead singer Thomas Mars, school mate Chris Mazzalai (guitar), his brother Laurent Brancowitz (guitar and keyboards) and Deck d'Arcy (keyboards/brass) have six hugely successful albums under their belt, including *Ti Amo* (2017) and a much coveted Grammy award.

Always worth a listen is Louise Attaque who, after a 10-year break, released its new album, *L'Anomalie,* with huge success in 2016. Nosfell (www.nosfell.com), one of France's most creative and intense musicians, sings in his own invented language called *le klokobetz.* In 2015 Nosfell wrote the music for *Contact,* a musical comedy by French dancer and choreographer Philippe Decouflé. His fifth album, *Echo Zulu* (2017), woos listeners with powerful lyrics in English and French, some written by French sound poet Anne-James Chaton.

Christophe Maé (www.christophe-mae.fr) mixes acoustic pop with soul, with stunning success. His jazzy third album, *Je Veux du Bonheur* (2013), was heavily influenced by the time the Provence-born singer spent travelling in New Orleans; his last album *L'attrape-rêves* (2016) included the song 'Ballerine' that he sung to propose to his now-wife. Travels abroad likewise provided the inspiration for the 2016 album *Palermo Hollywood,* by talented singer-songwriter Benjamin Biolay (b 1973).

Marseille born Marina Kaye (b 1998) won *France's Got Talent* TV show at the age of 13, as well as huge acclaim with her debut single 'Homeless'; she released her first album *Fearless* in 2015. Celebrity singer Nolwenn Leroy (b 1982) performs in Breton, English and Irish as well as French, while Paris' very own Indila (b 1984) woos France with her edgy pop and *rai* (a style derived from Algerian folk music). Then there's Louane (b. 1996), the idol of many a young French teen.

> Despite the English name, solo band Christine & the Queens is firmly French. Hailing from Nantes on the Atlantic Coast, Héloïse Letissier (b 1988) woos music lovers with her edgy rock and pop, outspoken attitudes and brazen pansexuality.

World

With styles from Algerian *rai* to other North African music (artists include Cheb Khaled, Natacha Atlas, Jamel, Cheb Mami) and Senegalese *mbalax* (Youssou N'Dour), West Indian zouk (Kassav', Zouk Machine) and Cuban salsa, France's world beat is strong. Manu Chao (www.manuchao.net), the Paris-born son of Spanish parents, uses world elements to stunning effect.

Magic System from Côte d'Ivoire popularised *zouglou* (a kind of West African rap and dance music) with its album *Premier Gaou,* and Congolese Koffi Olomide still packs the halls. Also try to catch blind singing couple, Amadou and Mariam; Rokia Traoré from Mali; and Franco-Algerian DJ turned singer Rachid Taha (www.rachidtaha.fr) whose music mixes Arab and Western musical styles with lyrics in English, Berber and French.

No artist has sealed France's reputation in world music more than Paris-born, Franco-Congolese rapper, slam poet and three-time Victoire de la Musique–award winner, Abd al Malik (b 1975). His albums *Gibraltar* (2006), *Dante* (2008), *Château Rouge* (2010) and *Scarifications* (2015) are classics.

Painting

Prehistoric to Landscape

France's oldest known prehistoric cave paintings (created 31,000 years ago) adorn the Grotte Chauvet-Pont-d'Arc in the Rhône Valley (and its stunning replica, Caverne du Pont d'Arc) and the underwater Grotte Cosquer near Marseille. In the Dordogne, it is the prehistoric art in caves at Lascaux that stuns.

According to Voltaire, French painting proper began with Baroque painter Nicolas Poussin (1594–1665), known for his classical mythological and biblical scenes bathed in golden light. Wind forward a couple of centuries and modern still life popped up with Jean-Baptiste Chardin (1699–1779). A century later, neoclassical artist Jacques Louis David (1748–1825) wooed the public with vast history paintings.

While Romantics like Eugène Delacroix (1798–1863; buried in Paris' Cimetière du Père Lachaise) revamped the subject picture, the Barbizon School effected a parallel transformation of landscape painting. Jean-François Millet (1814–75), the son of a peasant farmer from Normandy, took many of his subjects from peasant life, and reproductions of his *L'Angélus* (The Angelus; 1857) – the best-known painting in France after the *Mona Lisa* – are strung above mantelpieces all over rural France. The original hangs in Paris' Musée d'Orsay.

Realism & Impressionism

The realists were all about social comment: Édouard Manet (1832–83) evoked Parisian middle-class life and Gustave Courbet (1819–77) depicted working-class drudgery.

It was in a flower-filled garden in a Normandy village that Claude Monet (1840–1926) expounded impressionism, a term of derision taken from the title of his experimental painting *Impression: Soleil Levant* (*Impression: Sunrise;* 1874). A trip to the Musée d'Orsay unveils a rash of other members of the school – Boudin, Sisley, Pissarro, Renoir, Degas and more.

An arthritis-crippled Renoir painted out his last impressionist days in a villa on the French Riviera, a part of France that inspired dozens of artists: Paul Cézanne (1839–1906) is particularly celebrated for his post-impressionist still lifes and landscapes done in Aix-en-Provence, where he was born and worked; Paul Gauguin (1848–1903) worked in Arles; while Dutch artist Vincent van Gogh (1853–90) painted Arles and St-Rémy de Provence. In St-Tropez, pointillism took off: Georges Seurat (1859–91) was the first to apply paint in small dots or uniform brush strokes of unmixed colour, but it was his pupil Paul Signac (1863–1935) who is best known for pointillist works.

20th Century to Present Day

Twentieth-century French painting is characterised by a bewildering diversity of styles, including cubism, and Fauvism, named after the slur of a critic who compared the exhibitors at the 1906 autumn Salon in Paris with *fauves* (wild animals) because of their radical use of intensely bright colours. Spanish cubist Pablo Picasso (1881–1973) and fauvist Henri Matisse (1869–1954) both chose southern France to set up studio, Matisse living in Nice and Picasso in Antibes.

The early 20th century also saw the rise of the Dada movement, and no piece of French art better captures its rebellious spirit than Marcel Duchamp's *Mona Lisa,* complete with moustache and goatee. In 1922 German Dadaist Max Ernst moved to Paris and worked on surrealism, a Dada offshoot that drew on the theories of Freud to reunite the conscious and unconscious realms and permeate daily life with fantasies and dreams.

Best Modern Art

Monet's garden (Giverny)

Musée Renoir (Cagnes-sur-Mer)

Musée Picasso (Paris & Antibes)

Musée Matisse & Musée Chagall (Nice)

Musée Jean Cocteau Collection Séverin Wunderman (Menton)

Atélier Cézanne (Aix-en-Provence)

Chemin du Fauvisme (Collioure)

Setting the Trends

Palais de Tokyo (Paris)

Centre Pompidou (Paris)

Fondation Louis Vuitton (Paris)

Fondation Maeght (St-Paul de Vence)

Centre Pompidou-Metz (Metz)

Musée d'Art Moderne et d'Art Contemporain (Nice)

With the close of WWII, Paris' role as artistic world capital ended. The focus shifted back to southern France in the 1960s with new realists such as Arman (1928–2005) and Yves Klein (1928–62), both from Nice. In 1960 Klein famously produced *Anthropométrie de l'Époque Bleue,* a series of imprints made by naked women (covered from head to toe in blue paint) rolling around on a white canvas, in front of an orchestra of violins and an audience in evening dress.

Artists turned to the minutiae of everyday urban life to express social and political angst. Conceptual artist Daniel Buren (b 1938) reduced his painting to a signature series of vertical 8.7cm-wide stripes that is applied to any surface imaginable – white marble columns in the courtyard of Paris' Palais Royal included. The painter (who in 1967, as part of the radical *groupe BMPT,* signed a manifesto declaring he was not a painter) was the *enfant terrible* of French art in the 1980s. Partner-in-crime Michel Parmentier (1938–2000) insisted on monochrome painting – blue in 1966, grey in 1967 and red in 1968.

Paris-born conceptual artist Sophie Calle (b 1953) brazenly exposes her private life in public with eye-catching installations such as *Prenez Soin de Vous* (Take Care of Yourself; 2007), a compelling and addictive work of art in book form exposing the reactions of 107 women to an email Calle received from her French lover, dumping her. Her *Rachel, Monique* (2010) evoked the death and lingering memory of her mother in the form of a photographic exhibition first shown at Paris' Palais de Tokyo, later as a live reading performance at the Festival d'Avignon, and most recently in a chapel in New York. In 2015 *Suite Vénitienne* was published, a beautiful hardback edition, on gilt-edged Japanese paper, of her first art book in 1988 in which she followed Henri B around Venice for two weeks, anonymously photographing the enigmatic stranger. The publication of *Sophie Calle: My All* (2017), a photo-book documenting all 54 of her artworks to date, confirmed her reputation as France's most famous conceptual artist.

Street art is big, thanks in part to the pioneering work of Blek Le Rat (http://bleklerat.free.fr) in the 1980s. The Parisian artist, born as Xavier Prou, began by spraying tiny rats in hidden corners of the streets of Paris, went on to develop stencil graffiti as a recognised form, and notably inspired British street artist Banksy. Other blockbuster names to look out for include Gregos (b 1972) whose 3D clay faces protrude out of walls and other unexpected places all over France; Jérôme Mesnager (b 1961) known for his stencilled white figures; and Monsieur Chat (aka Thoma Vuille) who leaves cartoon cats with huge Cheshire-cat grins all over the place.

Then there is digital art. In 2013 the world's largest collective street-art exhibition, La Tour Paris 13 (www.tourparis13.fr), opened in a derelict apartment block in Paris' 13e *arrondissement.* Its 36 apartments on 13 floors showcased works by 100 international artists. The blockbuster exhibition ran for one month, after which the tower was shut and demolished. Itself an art work, the three-day demolition was filmed and streamed live on the internet – where the street artworks remain. This initial foray into digital art was followed in 2018 by the Paris opening of EP7 – a cultural cafe showcasing a vast interactive pixel screen as its main façade – and Atelier des Lumières, the capital's first digital-art centre inside a 19th-century smelting factory.

Cinematic Experiences

....

Cinémathèque Française (Paris)

Set in Paris, film-location tours (Paris)

....

Fondation Jérôme Seydoux-Pathé (Paris)

....

Musée Lumière (Lyon)

....

Cannes Film Festival (Cannes)

....

American Film Festival (Deauville)

....

Futuroscope (Poitiers)

In 2020 Lille will be the World Design Capital, the first French city to do so. Watch for a year laden with exhibitions and festivities.

Architecture

From prehistoric megaliths around Carnac in Brittany to Vauban's 33 star-shaped citadels dotted around France to defend its 17th-century frontiers, French architecture has always been of *grand-projet* proportions. In the capital, the skyline shimmers with Roman arenas, Gothic cathedrals, postmodernist cubes and futuristic skyscrapers, while provincial France cooks up the whole gamut of mainstream architectural styles along with regional idiosyncrasies.

Prehistoric to Roman

No part of France better demonstrates the work of the country's earliest architects than Brittany, which has more megalithic menhirs (monumental upright stones), tombs, cairns and burial chambers than anywhere else on earth. Many date from around 3500 BC and the most frequent structure is the dolmen, a covered burial chamber consisting of vertical menhirs topped by a flat capstone. Bizarrely, Brittany's ancient architects had different architectural tastes from their European neighbours – rather than the cromlechs (stone circles) commonly found in Britain, Ireland, Germany and Spain, they were much keener on building arrow-straight rows of menhirs known as *alignements*. And, indeed, Carnac's monumental Alignements de Carnac is the world's largest known prehistoric structure.

The Romans left behind a colossal architectural legacy in Provence and the French Riviera. Thousands of men took three to five years to haul the 21,000 cu metres of local stone needed to build the Pont du Gard near Nîmes. Other fine pieces of Roman architecture, still operational, include amphitheatres in Nîmes and Arles, open-air theatres in Orange and Fréjus, and Nîmes' Maison Carrée.

Romanesque

Catch up with southern France's prehistoric architects at Marseille's Centre de la Vieille Charité, Quinson's Musée de Préhistoire des Gorges du Verdon, and the beehive-shaped huts called *bories* at the Village des Bories near Gordes in the Luberon.

A religious revival in the 11th century led to the construction of Romanesque churches, so-called because their architects adopted many architectural elements (eg vaulting) from Gallo-Roman buildings still standing at the time. Romanesque buildings typically have round arches, heavy walls, few windows and a lack of ornamentation that borders on the austere.

Romanesque masterpieces include Toulouse's Basilique St-Sernin, Poitiers' Église Notre Dame la Grande, the exquisitely haunting Basilique St-Rémi in Reims, Caen's twinset of famous Romanesque abbeys, and Provence's trio in the Luberon (Sénanque, Le Thoronet and Silvacane). In Normandy the nave and south transept of the abbey-church on Mont St-Michel are beautiful examples of Norman Romanesque.

Then there is Burgundy's astonishing portfolio of Romanesque abbeys, among the world's finest: Abbaye de Pontigny, Abbaye de Cîteaux and Vézelay's Basilique Ste-Madeleine are highlights.

Gothic

Avignon's pontifical palace is Gothic architecture on a gargantuan scale. The Gothic style originated in the mid-12th century in northern France, where the region's great wealth attracted the finest architects, engineers and artisans. Gothic structures are characterised by ribbed vaults carved with great precision, pointed arches, slender verticals, chapels (often built or endowed by the wealthy or by guilds), galleries and arcades along the nave and chancel, refined decoration and large stained-glass windows. If you look closely at certain Gothic buildings, however, you'll notice minor asymmetrical elements introduced to avoid monotony.

The world's first Gothic building was the Basilique de St-Denis near Paris, which combined various late-Romanesque elements to create a new kind of structural support in which each arch counteracted and complemented the next. The basilica served as a model for many other 12th-century French cathedrals, including Notre Dame de Paris and Chartres' cathedral – both known for their soaring flying buttresses. No Gothic belfry is finer to scale than that of Bordeaux' Cathédrale St-André.

In the 14th century, the Radiant Gothic style developed, named after the radiating tracery of the rose windows, with interiors becoming even lighter thanks to broader windows and more translucent stained glass. One of the most influential Rayonnant buildings was Paris' Ste-Chapelle, whose stained glass forms a curtain of glazing on the 1st floor.

Renaissance

The Renaissance, which began in Italy in the early 15th century, set out to realise a 'rebirth' of classical Greek and Roman culture. It had its first impact on France at the end of that century, when Charles VIII began a series of invasions of Italy, returning with some new ideas.

To trace the shift from late Gothic to Renaissance, travel along the Loire Valley. During the very early Renaissance period, châteaux were used for the first time as pleasure palaces rather than defensive fortresses. Many edifices built during the 15th century to early 16th century in the Loire Valley – including Château d'Azay-le-Rideau and Château de Villandry – were built as summer or hunting residences for royal financiers, chamberlains and courtiers. Red-patterned brickwork – such as that on the Louis XII wing of Château Royal de Blois – adorned the façade of most châteaux dating from Louis XII's reign (1498–1515).

The quintessential French Renaissance château is a mix of classical components and decorative motifs (columns, tunnel vaults, round arches, domes etc) with the rich decoration of Flamboyant Gothic. It ultimately showcased wealth, ancestry and refinement. Defensive towers (a historical seigniorial symbol) were incorporated into a new decorative architecture, typified by its three-dimensional use of pilasters and arcaded loggias, terraces, balconies, exterior staircases, turrets and gabled chimneys. Heraldic symbols were sculpted on soft stone façades, above

Renaissance architecture stamped châteaux with a new artistic form: the monumental staircase. The most famous of these splendid ceremonial (and highly functional) creations are at Azay-le-Rideau, Blois, and Chambord in the Loire Valley.

FRANCE'S MOST BEAUTIFUL VILLAGES

One of French architecture's signature structures popped up in rural France from the 13th century, 'up' being the operative word for these *bastides* or *villages perchés* (fortified hilltop villages), built high on a hill to afford maximum protection for previously scattered populations. Provence and the Dordogne are key regions to hike up, down and around one medieval hilltop village after another, but you can find them in almost every French region. Many of the most dramatic and stunning are among Les Plus Beaux Villages de France (The Most Beautiful Villages in France; www.les-plus-beaux-villages-de-france.org).

doorways and fireplaces, and across coffered ceilings. Symmetrical floor plans broke new ground and heralded a different style of living: Château de Chambord contained 40 self-contained apartments, arranged on five floors around a central axis. This ensured easy circulation in a vast edifice that many rank as the first modern building in France.

Mannerism

Mannerism, which followed the Renaissance, was introduced by Italian architects and artists brought to France around 1530 by François I, whose royal château at Fontainebleau was designed by Italian architects. Over the following decades, French architects who had studied in Italy took over from their Italian colleagues.

The Mannerist style lasted until the early 17th century, when it was subsumed by the Baroque style.

Baroque

No single museum presents a finer overview of French architecture than Paris' Cité de l'Architecture et du Patrimoine inside the 1937-built Palais de Chaillot.

During the Baroque period (the tail end of the 16th to late 18th centuries), painting, sculpture and classical architecture were integrated to create structures and interiors of great subtlety, refinement and elegance. Architecture became more pictorial, with the painted ceilings in churches illustrating the Passion of Christ to the faithful, and palaces invoking the power and order of the state.

Salomon de Brosse, who designed Paris' Palais du Luxembourg in 1615, set the stage for two of France's most prominent early-Baroque architects: François Mansart (1598–1666), who designed the classical wing of Château Royal de Blois, and his younger rival Louis Le Vau (1612–70), who worked on France's grandest palace at Versailles.

Neoclassicism

Nancy's place Stanislas in northern France is the country's loveliest neoclassical square. Neoclassical architecture, which emerged in about 1740 and remained popular until well into the 19th century, had its roots in the renewed interest in the classical forms and conventions of Greco-Roman antiquity: columns, simple geometric forms and traditional ornamentation.

Hotels for Architecture Buffs

Les Bains & Hôtel Molitor (Paris)

Hôtel Le Corbusier (Marseille)

Hôtel Oscar (Le Havre)

Hotel Sôzô (Nantes)

La Co(o)rniche (Pyla-sur-Mer)

La Fabrique (Provence)

Among the earliest examples of this style is the Italianate façade of Paris' Église St-Sulpice, designed in 1733 by Giovanni Servandoni, which took inspiration from Christopher Wren's St Paul's Cathedral in London; and the Petit Trianon at Versailles, designed by Jacques-Ange Gabriel for Louis XV in 1761. France's greatest neoclassical architect of the 18th century was Jacques-Germain Soufflot, the man behind the Panthéon in Left Bank Paris.

Neoclassicism peaked under Napoléon III, who used it extensively for monumental architecture intended to embody the grandeur of imperial France and its capital: the Arc de Triomphe, La Madeleine, the Arc du Carrousel at the Louvre, the Assemblée Nationale building and the Palais Garnier. It was during this period moreover that urban planner Baron Haussmann, between 1850 and 1870 as Prefect of the Seine, completely redrew Paris' street plan, radically demolishing the city's maze of narrow, cramped medieval streets and replacing it with wide boulevards, sweeping parks and attractive *passages couverts* (covered passages).

The true showcase of this era though is Casino de Monte Carlo in Monaco, created by French architect Charles Garnier (1825–98) in 1878.

Art Nouveau

Art nouveau (1850–1910) combined iron, brick, glass and ceramics in ways never before seen. The style emerged in Europe and the USA under various names (Jugendstil, Sezessionstil, Stile Liberty) and caught on quickly in Paris. The style was characterised by sinuous curves and flowing asymmetrical forms reminiscent of creeping vines, water lilies, the patterns on insect wings and the flowering boughs of trees. Influenced by the arrival of exotic objets d'art from Japan, its French name came from a Paris gallery that featured works in the 'new art' style. The Piscine Saint-Georges (1923–26) in Rennes is a perfect example. True buffs should make a beeline for the art-nouveau tourist trail in Nancy.

The Belle Époque

The glittering belle époque, hot on the heels of art nouveau, heralded an eclecticism of decorative stucco friezes, *trompe l'œil* paintings, glittering wall mosaics, brightly coloured Moorish minarets and Turkish towers. Immerse yourself in its fabulous and whimsical designs with a stroll along Promenade des Anglais in Nice, where the pink-domed Hôtel Negresco (1912) is the icing on the cake; or, up north, around the colourful Imperial Quarter of Metz. Or flop in a beautiful belle époque spa like Vichy.

Modern

The Fondation Victor Vasarely, by the father of op art Victor Vasarely (1908–97), was an architectural coup when unveiled in Aix-en-Provence in 1976. Its 14 giant monumental hexagons reflected what Vasarely had already achieved in art: the creation of optical illusion and changing perspective through the juxtaposition of geometrical shapes and colours.

France's best-known 20th-century architect, Charles-Édouard Jeanneret (better known as Le Corbusier; 1887–1965), was born in Switzerland but settled in Paris in 1917 at the age of 30. A radical modernist, he tried to adapt buildings to their functions in industrialised society without ignoring the human element, thus rewriting the architectural style book with his sweeping lines and functionalised forms adapted to fit the human form. No single building has redefined urban living more than Le Corbusier's vertical 337-apartment 'garden city' known as La Cité Radieuse (the Radiant City) – today Hôtel Le Corbusier – that he designed on the coast in Marseille in 1952.

Most of Le Corbusier's work was done outside Paris, though he did design several private residences and the Pavillon Suisse, a dormitory for Swiss students at the Cité Internationale Universitaire in the 14e *arrondissement* of the capital. Elsewhere, Chapelle de Notre-Dame du Haut in the Jura and Couvent Ste-Marie de la Tourette near Lyon are 20th-century architectural icons.

Until 1968, French architects were still being trained almost exclusively at the conformist École des Beaux-Arts, reflected in most of the acutely unimaginative and impersonal 'lipstick tube' structures erected in the Parisian skyscraper district of La Défense, the Unesco building (1958) in the 7e, and Montparnasse's ungainly 210m-tall Tour Montparnasse (1973).

Interesting and alarming were Le Corbusier's plans for Paris that thankfully never left the drawing board. Called Plan Voisin (Neighbour Project; 1925), it envisaged wide boulevards linking the Gare Montparnasse with the Seine and lined with skyscrapers. The project would have required bulldozing much of the Latin Quarter.

GRANDS PROJETS

For centuries French political leaders sought to immortalise themselves through the erection of huge public edifices (aka *grands projets*) in Paris. Georges Pompidou commissioned the once reviled, now much-loved Centre Pompidou (1977) in which the architects – in order to keep the exhibition halls as uncluttered as possible – put the building's insides out. His successor, Valéry Giscard d'Estaing, was instrumental in transforming the derelict Gare d'Orsay train station into the glorious Musée d'Orsay (1986).

François Mitterrand commissioned the capital's best-known contemporary architectural landmarks (taxpayers' bill: a whopping €4.6 billion), including the Opéra Bastille, the Grande Arche in La Défense, the four glass towers of the national library, and IM Pei's glass pyramid at the hitherto sacrosanct and untouchable Louvre (an architectural cause célébre that paved the way, incidentally, for Mario Bellini and Rudy Ricciotti's magnificent flying carpet roof atop the Louvre's Cour Visconti in 2012).

JEAN NOUVEL

France's leading and arguably most talented architect, Jean Nouvel (b 1945), is the creative talent behind both Paris' ambitious Gare d'Austerlitz project and a succession of landmark buildings in Paris: the Institut du Monde Arabe (1987), successfully mixing modern and traditional Arab and Western elements; riverside Musée du Quai Branly, an iconic glass, wood-and-sod structure; and experimental concert hall Philharmonie de Paris (2015).

Nouvel also designed Périgueux' glass-and-steel Musée Gallo-Romain Vesunna (2003) in the Dordogne. His most recent work is Ycone (2018), a dazzling, 14-storey residential block of coloured glass with modular apartments and digital concierge in Lyon's Confluence district.

Contemporary

Glass has been a big feature of millennial architecture in the capital. Canadian architect Frank Gehry used 12 enormous glass sails to design the Fondation Louis Vuitton (2014) in the Bois de Bologne. The transformation of Forum des Halles (2016) by architects Patrick Berger and Jacques Anziutti saw the 1970s-eyesore shopping centre crowned with a spectacular gold-coloured canopy made of 18,000 glass shingles. One-third of the €600 million budget to restore Gare d'Austerlitz, to be complete in 2021, will be used to restore the historic train station's amazing glass roof.

At Porte de Versailles, the Tour Triangle (2019) is a glittering triangular glass tower designed by Jacques Herzog and Pierre de Meuron. It will be the first skyscraper in Paris since 1973's eyesore Tour Montparnasse, itself set to get a new reflective façade and green rooftop.

Glass will be likewise combined with green architecture in the Mille Arbres (Thousand Trees) project. Japanese architect Sou Fujimoto and French architect Manal Rachdi will transform Porte Maillot into a spectacular tree-topped glass structure by 2022.

Notable pieces of architecture in the provinces include Lyon's sparkling glass-and-steel cloud on the confluence of the Rhône and Saône Rivers, aka the cutting-edge Musée des Confluences (2014); Strasbourg's European Parliament; Dutch architect Rem Koolhaas' Euralille and a 1920s art-deco swimming pool turned art museum in Lille; and the fantastic Louvre II in Lens, 37km south of Lille.

In Strasbourg, Italian architect Paolo Portoghesi designed France's biggest mosque, large enough to seat 1500 worshippers. Topped by a copper dome and flanked by wings resembling a flower in bud, the riverside building took 20 years of political to-ing and fro-ing for the groundbreaking project – a landmark for Muslims in France – to come to fruition.

Looking south, Frank Gehry is the big-name architect behind Arles' innovative new cultural centre: all a shimmer in the bright southern sun, rocklike Luma Fondation (2018) evokes the nearby Alpilles mountain range with its two linked towers topped with aluminium. Nearby in Roman Nîmes, architect Elizabeth de Portzamparc is the creative talent behind the Roman city's striking €59.4 million archaeological museum, the Musée de la Romanité (2018).

In Lyon, Swiss architects Herzog and de Meuron (of Tate Modern and Beijing National Stadium fame) are hard at work on phase two of the exciting Confluence project, begun in 2016, which will add a notable residential district, market and new bridges to the former wasteland.

Art Nouveau in Paris

Hector Guimard's noodle-like metro entrances

The interior of the Musée d'Orsay

Department stores Le Bon Marché and Galeries Lafayette

The glass roof over the Grand Palais

Landscapes and Wildlife

France is a land of art. Fantastic portraits adorn the walls of galleries, villages resemble oil paintings plucked from a bygone rural age, and the people are naturally stylish. But as gorgeous as the art of France is, it fades when compared to the sheer beauty of the countryside itself.

The Land

Hexagon-shaped France, Europe's third-largest country (after Russia and Ukraine), is fringed by water or mountains along every side except in the northeast.

The country's 3427km-long coastline is incredibly diverse, ranging from white-chalk cliffs (Normandy) and treacherous promontories (Brittany) to broad expanses of fine sand (Atlantic Coast) and pebbly beaches (the Mediterranean Coast).

Western Europe's highest peak, Mont Blanc (4810m), spectacularly crowns the French Alps, which stagger along France's eastern border. North of Lake Geneva, the gentle limestone Jura Mountains run along the Swiss frontier to reach heights of around 1700m, while the rugged Pyrenees guard France's 450km-long border with Spain and Andorra, peaking at 3404m.

Five major river systems criss-cross the country: the Garonne (which includes the Tarn, the Lot and the Dordogne) empties into the Atlantic; the Rhône links Lake Geneva and the Alps with the Mediterranean; Paris is licked in poetic verse by the Seine, which slithers through the city en route from Burgundy to the English Channel; and tributaries of the North Sea–bound Rhine drain much of the area north and east of the capital. Then there's France's longest river, the château-studded Loire, which meanders through history from the Massif Central to the Atlantic.

From butterfly-spotting in the Cévennes to exploring bird-rich wetlands in the Camargue, UK-based tour company Nature Trek (www.naturetrek. co.uk) organises inspirational wildlife-watching holidays.

Wildlife

France is blessed with a rich variety of flora and fauna, although few habitats have escaped human impacts: intensive agriculture, wetland draining, urbanisation, hunting and the encroachment of industry and tourism infrastructure menace dozens of species.

Animals

France has more mammal species (around 135) than any other European country. Couple this with around 500 bird species (depending on which rare migrants are included), 40 types of amphibian, 36 varieties of reptile and 72 kinds of fish, and wildlife-watchers are in seventh heaven. Of France's 40,000 identified insects, 10,000 creep and crawl in the Parc National du Mercantour in the southern Alps.

High-altitude plains in the Alps and the Pyrenees shelter the marmot, which hibernates from October to April and has a shrill and distinctive whistle; the nimble chamois (mountain antelope), with its dark-striped head; and the *bouquetin* (Alpine ibex), seen in large numbers in the Parc National de la Vanoise. Mouflons (wild mountain sheep), introduced in the 1950s, clamber over stony sunlit scree slopes in the mountains, while red and roe deer and wild boar are common in lower-altitude forested areas. The Alpine hare welcomes winter with its white coat, while 19 of Europe's 29 bat species hang out in the dark in the Alpine national parks.

The *loup* (wolf), which disappeared from France in the 1930s, returned to the Parc National du Mercantour in 1992 – much to the horror of the mouflon (on which it preys) and local sheep farmers. Dogs, corrals and sound machines have been used as an effective, nonlethal way of keeping the growing free-roaming wolf population of the Mercantour and other Alpine areas from feasting on domesticated sheep herds. The wolf is a government-protected species, hence farmers are powerless to shoot an attacking wolf.

A rare but wonderful treat is the sighting of an *aigle royal* (golden eagle): 40 pairs nest in the Mercantour, 20 pairs nest in the Vanoise, 30-odd in the Écrins and some 50 in the Pyrenees. Other birds of prey include the peregrine falcon, the kestrel, the buzzard and the bearded vulture – Europe's largest bird of prey, with an awe-inspiring wingspan of 2.8m. More recently, the small, pale-coloured Egyptian vulture has been spreading throughout the Alps and Pyrenees.

Even the eagle-eyed will have difficulty spotting the ptarmigan, a chickenlike species that moults three times a year to ensure a foolproof seasonal camouflage (brown in summer, white in winter). It lives on rocky slopes and in Alpine meadows above 2000m. The nutcracker, with its loud, buoyant singsong and larch-forest habitat, the black grouse, rock partridge, the very rare eagle owl and the three-toed woodpecker are among the other 120-odd species keeping birdwatchers glued to the skies in highland realms.

Elsewhere, there are now around 2700 pairs of white storks; 10% of the world's flamingo population hangs out in the Camargue; giant black cormorants – some with a wingspan of 1.7m – reside on an island off Pointe du Grouin on the north coast of Brittany; and there are unique seagull and fishing-eagle populations in the Réserve Naturelle de Scandola on Corsica. The *balbuzard pêcheur* (osprey), a migratory hunter that flocks to France in February or March, today only inhabits two regions of France: Corsica and the Loire Valley.

Follow the progress of France's precious wolf, bear and lynx populations with Ferus (www.ferus.org), France's conservation group for these protected predators.

Plants

About 140,000 sq km of forest – beech, oak and pine in the main – covers 20% of France, and there are 4900 different species of native flowering plants countrywide (2250 alone grow in the Parc National des Cévennes).

The Alpine and Pyrenean regions nurture fir, spruce and beech forests on north-facing slopes between 800m and 1500m. Larch trees, mountain and arolla pines, rhododendrons and junipers stud shrubby subalpine zones between 1500m and 2000m; and a brilliant riot of spring and summertime wildflowers carpets grassy meadows above the treeline in the alpine zone (up to 3000m).

BEARS, OH MY!

The brown bear disappeared from the Alps in the mid-1930s. The 150-odd native bears living in the Pyrenees a century ago had dwindled to one orphaned cub following the controversial shooting of its mother – the last female bear of Pyrenean stock – by a hunter in 2004. Today an estimated 39 to 43 bears of Slovenian origin live in the Pyrenees, and this is set to increase if government plans, announced in 2018, to release two more female bears into the wild to help boost the dwindling bear population come off.

WILDLIFE WATCH

The national parks and their regional siblings are great for observing animals in their natural habitat. The following are also worth a gander:

Flamingos The Camargue, France's best-known wetland site, attracts 10,000 pink flamingos and over 400 other bird species including rollers and glossy ibises.

Vultures Found in the Pyrenees at Falaise aux Vautours, the Vallée d'Ossau and in Languedoc at the Belvédère des Vautours in the Parc Naturel Régional des Grands Causses.

Storks In Alsace at the Centre de Réintroduction Cigognes & Loutres, in Hunawihr, and the Enclos aux Cigognes in Munster; on the Atlantic Coast at Réserve Ornithologique du Teich, near Arcachon; and at the Parc des Oiseaux outside Villars-les-Dombes near Lyon.

Dolphins and whales Playful bottlenose dolphins splash around in the Mediterranean, and whales are sometimes sighted too. Prime viewing from boat trips on the French Riviera and Corsica.

Alpine blooms include the single golden-yellow flower of the arnica, long used in herbal and homeopathic bruise-relieving remedies; the flame-coloured fire lily; and the hardy Alpine columbine, with its delicate blue petals. The protected 'queen of the Alps' (aka the Alpine eryngo) bears an uncanny resemblance to a purple thistle but is, in fact, a member of the parsley family (to which the carrot also belongs).

Corsica and the Massif des Maures, west of St-Tropez on the Côte d'Azur, are closely related botanically: both have chestnut and cork-oak trees and are thickly carpeted with garrigues and maquis – heavily scented scrubland, where dozens of fragrant shrubs and herbs find shelter.

Of France's 150 orchids, the black vanilla orchid is one to look out for – its small red-brown flowers exude a sweet vanilla fragrance.

National Parks

The proportion of protected land in France is surprisingly low: seven *parcs nationaux* (www.parcsnationaux.fr) fully protect just 0.8% of the country. Another 13% (70,000 sq km) in metropolitan France and its overseas territories is protected to a substantially lesser degree by 48 *parcs naturels régionaux* (www.parcs-naturels-regionaux.tm.fr), and a further few per cent by 320 smaller *réserves naturelles* (www.reserves-naturelles.org), some of them under the eagle eye of the Conservatoire du Littoral.

Select pockets of nature – the Pyrenees, Mont St-Michel and its bay, part of the Loire Valley, the astonishingly biodiverse Cévennes, a clutch of capes on Corsica and vineyards in Burgundy and Champagne – have been declared Unesco World Heritage Sites.

Environmental Issues

As elsewhere in the world, wetlands in France – incredibly productive ecosystems that are essential for the survival of birds, reptiles, fish and amphibians – are shrinking. More than 20,000 sq km (3% of French territory) are considered important wetlands but only 4% of this land is currently protected.

Great tracts of forest burn each summer, often because of careless day trippers but more often than not by arson that accounts for 39% of forest fires. Since the mid-1970s, between 31 sq km and 615 sq km of land has been reduced to black stubble each year by an average of 540 fires. Soaring summer temperatures combined with no rain saw 2017 go down as one of the worst years on record: thousands of residents in Provence and Corsica were evacuated from their homes, with 12,000 locals and tourists in Bormes-les-Mimosas spending one night in July in emergency shelters

LIFE & DEATH OF THE IBEX

Often spotted hanging out on sickeningly high crags and ledges, the nippy *bouquetin des Alpes* (Alpine ibex), with its imposingly large, curly-wurly horns, is the animal most synonymous with the French Alps. Higher altitudes were loaded with the handsome beast in the 16th century but, three centuries on, its extravagant horns had become a must-have item in any gentleman's trophy cabinet, and within a few years it had been hunted to the brink of extinction.

In 1963 the Parc National de la Vanoise was created in the Alps to stop hunters in the massif from shooting the few Alpine ibex that remained. The creation of similar nature reserves and rigorous conservation campaigns have seen populations surely and steadily recover – to the point where today the Alpine ibex is thriving. Not that you're likely to encounter one: the canny old ibex has realised that some mammals are best avoided.

Green initiatives in Paris include the creation of 100 hectares of green roofs, façades and vertical walls in the capital city, a third of which will be devoted to urban agriculture.

as forest fires spread dangerously close to the seaside resort. Some 70 sq km of forest in all were destroyed.

Dogs and guns also pose a threat to French animal life, brown bears included. While the number of hunters has fallen by more than 20% in the last decade, there are still a lot more hunters in France (1.3 million) than in any other Western European country. Despite the 1979 Brussels Directive for the protection of wild birds, their eggs, nests and habitats in the EU, the French government has been very slow to make its provisions part of French law, meaning birds that can fly safely over other countries can still be hunted as they cross France.

The state-owned electricity company, Electricité de France (EDF), has an enviable record on minimising greenhouse-gas emissions – fossil-fuel-fired power plants account for just 4.6% of its production. Clean, renewable hydropower, generated by 220 dams, comprises 8.8% of the company's generating capacity but this does affect animal habitats. And no less than 75% (the highest in the world) of France's electricity comes from another controversial carbon-zero source: nuclear power, generated by 58 nuclear reactors at 20 sites. In 2012 François Hollande's socialist government had promised to reduce France's reliance on nuclear energy to 50% by 2025, but under President Emmanuel Macron's centrist government this target date has been pushed back to 2035.

This said, the government has agreed to closing down France's oldest nuclear reactor from the 1970s at Fessenheim in Alsace by 2020 once the new state-of-the-art Flamanville 3 reactor, under construction at a cost of €10.5 billion on Normandy's west coast, opens in late 2018.

Europe's largest solar-powered electricity-generating farm sits 1000m-high on a south-facing slope near the tiny village of Curbans in Provence. The farm's 150-hectare array of photovoltaic cells – 145,000 panels in all – removes 120,000 metric tonnes of carbon dioxide annually from the French energy bill.

Global warming might translate as an increasingly shorter, uncertain and riskier season for ski enthusiasts in the French Alps as snowfall becomes more erratic and avalanches occur more often. But for Alpine flora and fauna, it is even more serious. Alpine plants are fleeing up their warming mountainsides at between 0.5m and 4m per decade, reports the WWF, making way for invasive species and the pathogens and animal life that come with them. France's largest glacier meanwhile, the Mer de Glace near Chamonix, is retreating by 4m to 5m each year.

Survival Guide

Directory A–Z

Accessible Travel

While France presents evident challenges for *visiteurs handicapés* (disabled visitors), particularly those with mobility issues – cobblestones, cafe-lined streets that are a nightmare to navigate in a wheelchair *(fauteuil roulant)*, a lack of kerb ramps, older public facilities and many budget hotels without lifts – don't let that stop you from visiting. Efforts are being made to improve the situation and with a little careful planning, a hassle-free accessible stay is possible.

➜ Paris' tourist office runs the excellent 'Tourisme & Handicap' initiative whereby museums, cultural attractions, hotels and restaurants that provide access or special assistance or facilities for those with physical, mental, visual and/or hearing disabilities display a special logo at their entrances. For a list of qualifying places, go to www.parisinfo.com and click on 'Practical Paris'.

➜ Paris metro, most of it built decades ago, is hopeless. Line 14 of the metro was built to be wheelchair-accessible, although in reality it remains extremely challenging to navigate in a wheelchair – unlike Paris buses which are 100% accessible.

➜ Parisian taxi company Horizon, part of Taxis G7 (www.taxisg7.fr), has cars especially adapted to carry wheelchairs and drivers trained in helping passengers with disabilities.

➜ Countrywide, many SNCF train carriages are accessible to people with disabilities. A traveller in a wheelchair can travel in both the TGV and in the 1st-class carriage with a 2nd-class ticket on mainline trains provided they make a reservation by phone or at a train station at least a few hours before departure. Details are available in the SNCF booklet *Le Mémento du Voyageur Handicapé* (Handicapped Traveller Summary) available at all train stations.

Accès Plus (☑03 69 32 26 26, 08 90 64 06 50; www. accessibilite.sncf.com) The SNCF assistance service for rail travellers with disabilities. Can advise on station accessibility and arrange a *fauteuil roulant* or help getting on or off a train.

Access Travel (☑UK 07973 114 365; www.access-travel.co.uk) Specialised UK-based agency for accessible travel.

Infomobi.com (☑09 70 81 93 95; www.vianavigo.com/accessibilite) Has comprehensive information on accessible travel in Paris and the surrounding Île de France area.

Mobile en Ville (☑09 52 29 60 51; www.mobileenville.org; 8 rue des Mariniers, 14e) Association that works hard to make independent travel within Paris easier for people in wheelchairs. Among other things it organises some great family *randonnées* (walks) in and around Paris.

Tourisme et Handicaps (☑01 44 11 10 41; www.tourisme-handicaps.org; 43 rue Marx Dormoy, 18e) Issues the 'Tourisme et Handicap' label to tourist sites, restaurants and hotels that comply with strict accessibility and usability standards. Different symbols indicate the sort of access afforded to people with physical, mental, hearing and/or visual disabilities.

Accommodation

Be it a fairy-tale château, a boutique hideaway or floating pod on a lake, France has accommodation to suit every taste and pocket. If you're visiting in high season (especially

BOOKING SERVICES

Drop by lonelyplanet.com/france/hotels for recommendations and accommodation bookings all over France.

B&Bs

Bienvenue à la Ferme (www.bienvenue-a-la-ferme.com) Farmstay accommodation options for a taste of French rural life.

Chambres d'Hôtes France (www.chambresdhotesfrance.com) Comprehensive, France-wide B&B listings.

Fleurs de Soleil (www.fleursdesoleil.fr) Selective collection of 550 stylish *maisons d'hôte*, mainly in rural France.

Gîtes de France (www.gites-de-france.com) France's primary umbrella organisation for B&Bs and self-catering properties *(gîtes);* search by region, theme (charm, with kids, by the sea, gourmet, great garden etc.), activity (fishing, wine tasting etc) or facilities (pool, dishwasher, fireplace, baby equipment etc).

iGuide Rivages (www.iguide-hotels.com) Gorgeous presentation of France's most charming and often-times most upmarket B&Bs, organised by region and/or theme (romantic, gastronomic, green, oenological and so forth)

Samedi Midi Éditions (www.samedimidi.com) Country, mountain, seaside…choose your *chambre d'hôte* by location or theme (romance, golf, design, cooking courses).

Camping

Websites with campsite listings searchable by location, theme and facilities:

Bienvenue à la Ferme (www.bienvenue-a-la-ferme.com)

Camping en France (www.camping.fr)

Camping France (www.campingfrance.com)

Gîtes de France (www.gites-de-france.com)

HPA Guide (http://camping.hpaguide.com)

August), reserve ahead – the best addresses on the coast fill up months in advance.

Categories

As a rule of thumb, budget covers everything from basic hostels to small family-run places; midrange means a few extra creature comforts such as a lift; while top-end places stretch from luxury five-star palaces with air-conditioning, swimming pools and restaurants to boutique-chic Alpine chalets.

Costs

Accommodation costs vary wildly between seasons and regions: what will buy you a night in a romantic *chambre d'hôte* (B&B) in the country-side may get a dorm bed in a major city or high-profile ski resort.

Reservations

Midrange, top-end and many budget hotels require a credit card number to secure an advance reservation made by phone; some hostels do not take bookings. Many tourist offices can advise on availability and reserve for you, often for a fee of €5 and usually only if you stop by in person. In the Alps, ski-resort tourist offices run a central reservation service for booking accommodation.

Seasons

➡ In ski resorts, high season is Christmas, New Year and the February–March school holidays.

➡ On the coast, high season is summer, particularly August.

➡ Hotels in inland cities often charge low-season rates in summer.

➡ Rates often drop outside the high season – in some cases by as much as 50%.

➡ In business-oriented hotels in cities, rooms are most expensive from Monday to Thursday and cheaper over the weekend.

➡ In the Alps, hotels usually close between seasons, from around May to mid-June and from mid-September to early December; many addresses in Corsica only open Easter to October.

B&Bs

For charm, a heartfelt *bien-venue* (welcome) and solid home cooking, it's hard to beat France's privately run *chambres d'hôte* (B&Bs) – urban rarities but as common as muck in rural areas. By law a *chambre d'hôte* must have no more than five rooms and breakfast must be included in the price; some hosts prepare a meal *(table d'hôte)* for an extra charge of around €30 including wine. Pick up lists of *chambres d'hôte* at tourist offices, or find one to suit online.

Camping

Be it a Mongolian yurt, boutique tree house or simple canvas beneath stars, camping in France is in vogue. Thousands of well-equipped campgrounds dot the country, many considerately placed by rivers, lakes and the sea.

➡ Most campgrounds open March or April to late September or October; popular spots fill up fast in summer so it is wise to call ahead.

➡ 'Sites' refer to fixed-price deals for two people including a tent and a car. Otherwise the price is broken down per adult/tent/car. Factor in a few extra euro per night for *taxe de séjour* (holiday tax) and electricity.

➡ Euro-economisers should look out for local, good-value but no-frills *campings municipaux* (municipal campgrounds).

➡ Many campgrounds rent out mobile homes with mod cons such as heating, fitted kitchen and TV.

➡ Pitching up 'wild' in nondesignated spots *(camping sauvage)* is illegal in France.

➡ Campground offices often close during the day.

➡ Accessing many campgrounds without your own transport can be slow and costly, or simply impossible.

Homestays

One of the best ways to brush up your *français* and immerse yourself in local life is by staying with a French family under an arrangement known as *hôtes payants* or *hébergement chez l'habitant*. Popular among students and young people, this set-up means you rent a room and usually have access (sometimes limited) to the bathroom and the kitchen; meals may also be available. If you are sensitive to smoke or pets, make sure you mention this.

Hostels

Hostels in France range from funky to threadbare, although with a wave of design-driven, up-to-the-minute hostels opening in Paris, Marseille and other big cities, hip hangouts with perks aplenty seem to easily outweigh the threadbare these days.

➡ In university towns, *foyers d'étudiant* (student dormitories) are sometimes converted for use by travellers during summer.

➡ A dorm bed in an *auberge de jeunesse* (hostel) costs €20 to €50 in Paris, and anything from €15 to €40 in the provinces, depending on location, amenities and

facilities; sheets are always included, as is breakfast more often than not.

➡ To prevent outbreaks of bedbugs, sleeping bags are not permitted.

➡ Hostels by the sea or in the mountains sometimes offer seasonal outdoor activities.

➡ French hostels are 100% nonsmoking.

➡ Official *auberges de jeunesse* affiliated to the Fédération Unie des Auberges de Jeunesse (www.fuaj.org) or Ligue Française pour les Auberges de la Jeunesse (www.auberges-de-jeunesse.com) require guests to have an annual Hostelling International (HI) card (€7/11 for under/over 26s) or a nightly Welcome Stamp (up to €3; maximum of six per year).

Hotels

Hotels in France are rated with one to five stars, although the ratings are based on highly objective criteria (eg the size of the entry hall), not the quality of the service, the decor or cleanliness.

➡ French hotels almost never include breakfast in their rates. Unless specified otherwise, prices quoted don't include breakfast, which costs around €8/12/25 in a budget/ midrange/top-end hotel.

➡ When you book, hotels usually ask for a credit card number; some require a deposit.

➡ A double room generally has one double bed (sometimes two singles pushed together!); a room with twin beds *(deux lits)* is usually more expensive, as is a room with a bathtub instead of a shower.

➡ Feather pillows are practically nonexistent in France, even in top-end hotels.

➡ All hotel restaurant terraces allow smoking; if you are sensitive to smoke, you may need to sit inside.

GLAMPING

Farewell clammy canvas, adieu inflatable mattress… Glamping in France is cool and creative, with *écolo chic* (ecochic) and adventurous alternatives springing up all the time. If you fancy doing a Robinson Crusoe by staying in a tree house with an incredible view over the treetops, visit Cabanes de France (www.cabanes-de-france.com), which covers leafy options between branches all over France. Prefer to keep your feet firmly on the ground? Keep an eye out for ecoconscious campsites where you can snooze in a *tipi* (tepee) or in a giant hammock.

Refuges & Gîtes d'Étape

➜ *Refuges* (mountain huts or shelters) are basic cabins established along walking trails in uninhabited mountainous areas and operated by national-park authorities, the Club Alpin Français (www.ffcam.fr) or other private organisations.

➜ *Refuges* are marked on hiking and climbing maps.

➜ A bunk in a dorm generally costs €10 to €25. Hot meals are sometimes available (and, in a few cases, mandatory), pushing the price up to €30 or beyond.

➜ Advance reservations and a weather check are essential before setting out.

➜ *Gîtes d'étape*, better equipped and more comfortable than *refuges* (some even have showers), are situated along walking trails in less remote areas, often in villages.

➜ Check out Gîtes d'Étape et Refuges (www.gites-refuges. com), an online listing of 4000 *gîtes d'étape* and *refuges* in France.

Rental Accommodation

If you are planning on staying put for more than a few days or are travelling in a group, then renting a furnished studio, apartment or villa can be an economical alternative. You will have the chance to live like a local, with trips to the farmers market and the *boulangerie* (bakery).

Finding an apartment for long-term rental can be gruelling. Landlords usually require substantial proof of financial responsibility and sufficient funds in France; many ask for a *caution* (guarantee) and a hefty deposit.

➜ Cleaning, linen rental and electricity fees usually cost extra.

➜ Classified ads appear in *De Particulier à Particulier* (www. pap.fr, in French), published

on Thursday and sold at news stands.

➜ For apartments outside Paris it's best to search at your destination.

➜ Check places like bars and *tabacs* (tobacconists) for free local newspapers (often named after the number of the *département*) with classifieds listings.

Discount Cards

Discount cards yield fantastic benefits and easily pay for themselves. As well as the card fee, you'll often need a passport-sized photo and some form of ID with proof of age (eg passport or birth certificate).

People over 60 or 65 are entitled to discounts on things like public transport, museum admission fees and theatres.

Discount card options:

Camping Card International (www.campingcardinternational. com; €10) Used as ID for checking into campsites; the annual card includes third-party liability insurance and covers up to 11 people in a party; it usually yields up to 20% discount. Available at automobile associations, camping federations and campgrounds.

European Youth Card (www. eyca.org; €10) Wide range of discounts for under 26 year olds. Available online.

International Student Identity Card (www.isic.org; €13)

Discounts on travel, shopping, attractions and entertainment for full-time students. Available at ISIC points listed online.

International Teacher Identity Card (www.isic.org; €18) Travel, shopping, entertainment and sightseeing discounts for full-time teachers.

International Youth Travel Card (www.isic.org; €13) Discounts on travel, tickets and so forth for under 31 year olds.

Electricity

Plugs have two round pins; electrical current is 230V/50Hz AC.

Type E
230V/50Hz

FRENCH-CHIC SLEEPING

A château, a country manor, Parisian opulence in the shade of the Eiffel Tower – whether you want to live like a lord, sleep like a log or blow the budget, there's a room with your name on it.

Alistair Sawday's (www.sawdays.co.uk) Boutique retreats and *chambres d'hôte*, placing the accent on originality and authentic hospitality.

Châteaux & Hôtels Collection (www.chateauxhotels.com) Châteaux and other historic properties, now boutique hotels, with a thousand tales to tell.

Grandes Étapes Françaises (www.grandesetapes.fr) Beautiful châteaux-hotels and multistar residences.

iGuide (www.iguide-hotels.com) Abbeys, manors, châteaux – a real mixed bag of charming hotels.

Logis de France (www.logis-de-france.fr) Small, often family-run hotels with charm and a warm welcome.

Relais & Châteaux (www.relaischateaux.com) Seductive selection of top-end villas, châteaux and historic hotels.

Relais du Silence (www.relaisdusilence.com) Fall asleep to complete silence in a gorgeous château, spa-clad *auberge* (country inn), or vineyard hotel...

Small Luxury Hotels of the World (www.slh.com) Super-luxurious boutique hotels, chalets and resorts.

Type C
220V/50Hz

Embassies & Consulates

All foreign embassies are in Paris.

➡ Many countries – including Canada, Japan, the UK, USA and most European countries – also have consulates in other major cities such as Bordeaux, Lyon, Nice, Marseille and Strasbourg.

➡ To find a consulate or an embassy, visit www.embassiesabroad.com or look up *'ambassade'* in the super user-friendly Pages Jaunes (www.pagesjaunes.fr).

Emergency & Important Numbers

France country code	♪33
International access code	♪00
Europe-wide emergency	♪112
Ambulance (SAMU)	♪15
Police	♪17

Customs Regulations

Goods brought in and out of countries within the EU incur no additional taxes provided duty has been paid somewhere within the EU and the goods are for personal consumption. Duty-free shopping is available only if you are leaving the EU.

Duty-free allowances (for adults) coming from non-EU countries (including the Channel Islands):

➡ 200 cigarettes or 50 cigars or 250g tobacco

➡ 1L spirits or 2L of sparkling wine/other alcoholic drinks less than 22% alcohol

➡ 4L still wine

➡ 16L beer

➡ other goods up to the value of €300/430 when entering by land/air or sea (€150 for under 15 year olds)

Higher limits apply if you are coming from Andorra; anything over these limits must be declared. For further details, see www.douane.gouv.fr (partly in English).

Food

This guide includes options for all tastes and budgets, reviewed in order of preference and categorised according to type of cuisine, or price range, or both.

For the complete tastebud tour of France's varied regional cuisines and accompanying tipples, see the essay The French Table (p952). To understand how to eat and drink like a local, see the tip-loaded section at the front of this book (p35).

Health

France is a healthy place, so your main risks are likely to be sunburn, foot blisters, insect bites and mild stomach problems from eating and drinking with too much gusto.

No vaccinations are required to travel to France, but the World Health Organization (WHO) recommends that all travellers be covered for diphtheria, tetanus, measles, mumps, rubella and polio, regardless of their destination.

Before You Go

➡ Bring your medications in their original, clearly labelled, containers.

➡ A signed and dated letter from your physician describing your medical conditions and medications, including generic names (French medicine names are often completely different from those in other countries), is also a good idea.

➡ Dental care in France is usually good; however, it is sensible to have a dental check-up before a long trip.

Availability & Cost of Health Care

For basic requirements, chemists (*pharmacies*) in France are extremely helpful and sell a wide range of

medicines not requiring a prescription (*ordonnance*).

As a visitor, you can either make an appointment or sit in line (depending on the doctor's practice) to see a *médecin généraliste* (doctor or general practitioner). Expect to pay between €35 and €50 up front, part or all of which your health insurance will then reimburse.

Providing you can prove you have valid insurance (ie to reimburse the cost of health treatment), you don't have to pay up front to receive emergency treatment at a hospital.

Tap Water

Tap water country-wide is drinkable.

Some fountains in villages and towns also spout drinking water – '*eau potable*' means 'drinking water', '*non potable*' means undrinkable. In the chic capital, there is even the odd drinking fountain gushing sparkling water.

Insurance

➡ Comprehensive travel insurance to cover theft, loss and medical problems is highly recommended.

➡ Some policies specifically exclude dangerous activities such as scuba diving, motorcycling, skiing and even trekking: read the fine print.

➡ Check that the policy covers ambulances or an emergency flight home.

➡ Find out in advance if your insurance plan will

make payments directly to providers or reimburse you later for overseas health expenditures.

➡ If you have to claim later, make sure you keep all documentation.

➡ Paying for your airline ticket with a credit card often provides limited travel accident insurance – ask your credit card company what it is prepared to cover.

➡ Worldwide travel insurance is available at www.lonelyplanet.com/travel-insurance. You can buy, extend and claim online anytime – even if you're already on the road.

Internet Access

➡ Wi-fi (pronounced 'wee-fee' in French) is available at major airports, in most hotels, and at many cafes, restaurants, museums and tourist offices.

➡ In cities free wi-fi is available in hundreds of public places, including parks, libraries and municipal buildings. In Paris look for a purple 'Zone Wi-Fi' sign. To connect, select the 'PARIS_WI-FI_' network. Sessions are limited to two hours (renewable). For complete details and a map of hotspots, see www.paris.fr/wifi.

➡ To search for free wi-fi hotspots in France, visit www.hotspot-locations.com.

➡ Tourist offices is some larger cities, including

Lyon and Bordeaux, rent out pocket-sized mobile wi-fi devices that you carry around with you, ensuring a fast wi-fi connection while roaming the city.

➡ Alternatively, rent a mobile wi-fi device online before leaving home and arrange for it to be delivered by post to your hotel in France through HipPocketWifi (http://hippocketwifi.com), Travel WiFi (http://travel-wifi.com) or My Webspot (http://my-webspot.com).

➡ Co-working cafes providing unlimited, fast internet access are increasingly rife; at least one can usually be tracked down in cities. Expect to pay about €5 per hour for a desk, plug and unlimited hot drinks and snacks.

WHAT THE 🛜 ICON MEANS

Only accommodation providers that have an actual computer that guests can use to access the internet are flagged with a comput-er icon. The wi-fi icon (🛜) indicates anywhere with wi-fi access. Where this icon appears, assume the wi-fi is free unless otherwise specified.

Language Courses

➡ The website www.studyabroad.com can help you find specific courses and summer programs.

➡ All manner of French-language courses are available in Paris and provincial towns and cities; most also arrange accommodation.

➡ Prices and courses vary greatly; the content can often be tailored to your specific needs (for a fee).

➡ The website www.europa-pages.com/france lists language schools in France.

Aix-Marseille Université (Uni-versité de Provence; 🗹04 13 55 32 23; https://sufle.univ-amu.fr; 29 av Robert Schumann) A hot choice, also known as Univer-sité de Provence, in lovely Aix: semester-long language courses as well as shorter summer classes.

Alliance Française (🗹01 42 84 90 00; www.alliancefr.org; 101 bd Raspail, 6e; intensive/ex-tensive courses per week from €253/113; Ⓜ St-Placide) French courses (minimum one week) for all levels. Intensif courses meet for four hours a day five days a week; extensif courses involve nine hours' tuition a week.

Centre Méditerranéen d'Études Françaises (www.cmef-monaco.fr; chemin des Oliviers, Cap d'Ail) Legendary French Riviera school around since 1952, with a stunning open-air amphitheatre, designed by Jean Cocteau and overlooking the sparkling blue Med.

Eurocentres (www.eurocentres.com) This affiliation of small, well-organised schools has three addresses in France: in Amboise in the charming Loire Valley, in La Rochelle, and in Paris.

Legal Matters
Police

➡ French police have wide powers of search and seizure and can ask you to prove your identity at any time – whether or not there is 'probable cause'.

➡ Foreigners must be able to prove their legal status in France (eg with a passport, visa or residency permit) without delay.

➡ If the police stop you for any reason, be polite and remain calm. Verbally (and of course physically) abusing a police officer can lead to a hefty fine, and even imprisonment.

➡ You may refuse to sign a police statement, and have the right to ask for a copy.

➡ People who are arrested are considered innocent until proven guilty, but can be held in custody until trial.

Drugs & Alcohol

➡ French law does not distinguish between 'hard' and 'soft' drugs.

➜ The penalty for any personal use of *stupéfiants* (including cannabis, amphetamines, ecstasy and heroin) can be a one-year jail sentence and a €3750 fine but, depending on the circumstances, it might be anything from a stern word to a compulsory rehab program.

➜ Importing, possessing, selling or buying drugs can get you up to 10 years in prison and a fine of up to €500,000.

➜ Police have been known to search chartered coaches, cars and train passengers for drugs just because they're coming from Amsterdam.

➜ *Ivresse* (drunkenness) in public is punishable by a fine.

LGBTIQ+ Travellers

The rainbow flag flies high in France, a country that left its closet long before many of its European neighbours. *Laissez-faire* perfectly sums up France's liberal attitude towards homosexuality and people's private lives in general; in part because of a long tradition of public tolerance towards unconventional lifestyles.

➜ Paris has been a thriving gay and lesbian centre since the late 1970s, and most major organisations are based there today.

➜ Bordeaux, Lille, Lyon, Montpellier, Toulouse and many other towns also have an active queer scene.

➜ Attitudes towards homosexuality tend to be more conservative in the countryside and villages.

➜ France's lesbian scene is less public than its gay male counterpart and is centred mainly on women's cafes and bars.

➜ Same-sex marriage has been legal in France since May 2013.

➜ Gay Pride marches are held in major French cities mid-May to early July.

Publications

Damron (www.damron.com) Has published English-language travel guides since the 1960s, including *Damron Women's Traveller* for lesbians and *Damron Men's Travel Guide* for gays.

Spartacus International Gay Guide (www.spartacusworld. com) A male-only guide to just about every country in the world, with more than 70 pages devoted to France, almost half of which cover Paris. There's a smartphone app too.

Websites

Gaipied (www.gayvox.com/ guide3) Online travel guide to France, with listings by region, by Gayvox.

Gay Travel & Life in France (www. gay-france.net) Insider tips on gay life in France.

Tasse de Thé (www.tassedethe. com) A *webzine lesbien* with lots of useful links.

Money

ATMs

Automated Teller Machines (ATMs) – known as *distributeurs automatiques de billets* (DAB) or *points d'argent* in French – are the cheapest and most convenient way to get money. ATMs connected to international networks are situated in all cities and towns and usually offer an excellent exchange rate.

Cash

You always get a better exchange rate in-country, but it is a good idea to arrive in France with enough euros to take a taxi to a hotel if you have to.

Credit & Debit Cards

➜ Credit and debit cards, accepted almost everywhere in France, are convenient, relatively secure and usually offer a better exchange rate than travellers cheques or cash exchanges.

➜ Credit cards issued in France have embedded chips – you have to type in a PIN to make a purchase.

➜ Visa, MasterCard and Amex can be used in shops and supermarkets and for train travel, car hire and motorway tolls.

➜ Don't assume that you can pay for a meal or a budget hotel with a credit card – enquire first.

➜ Cash advances are a supremely convenient way to stay stocked up with euros, but getting cash with a credit card involves both fees (sometimes US$10 or more) and interest – ask your credit-card issuer for details. Debit-card fees are usually much lower.

➜ For lost cards, these numbers operate 24 hours:

Amex ☏01 47 77 72 00

MasterCard ☏08 00 90 13 87

Visa ☏08 00 90 11 79

AMERICANS, TAKE NOTE

US-issued 'smart' credit/debit cards with embedded chips (a technology pioneered in France in the 1980s) and PINs work virtually everywhere in France, including autoroute toll plazas, but cards with a chip but no PIN may occasionally leave you unable to pay – for instance, at unstaffed, 24/7 petrol (gas) stations with self-pay pumps. If your credit card is of the old type, ie with a magnetic strip but no chip, ask your issuer to send you a new, chip-equipped card – they're usually happy to oblige as the new technology is much more secure.

Exchange Rates

Australia	A$1	€0.64
Canada	C$1	€0.66
Japan	¥100	€0.76
NZ	NZ$1	€0.59
UK	UK£1	€1.14
USA	US$1	€0.85

For current exchange rates see www.xe.com.

Money Changers

➡ Commercial banks charge up to €5 per foreign-currency transaction – if they even bother to offer exchange services any more.

➡ In Paris and major cities, *bureaux de change* (exchange bureaus) are faster and easier, open longer hours and often give better rates than banks.

Opening Hours

Opening hours vary throughout the year. We list high-season opening hours, but remember these longer summer hours often decrease in shoulder and low seasons.

Banks 9am–noon and 2pm–5pm Monday to Friday or Tuesday to Saturday

Bars 7pm–1am

Cafes 7am–11pm

Clubs 10pm–3am, 4am or 5am Thursday to Saturday

Restaurants Noon–2.30pm and 7pm–11pm six days a week

Shops 10am–noon and 2pm–7pm Monday to Saturday; longer, and including Sunday, for shops in defined ZTIs (international tourist zones)

Post

French post offices are flagged with a yellow or brown sign reading 'La Poste'. Since La Poste (www.laposte. fr) also has banking, finance and bill-paying functions, queues can be long, but automatic machines dispense postage stamps.

Public Holidays

The following *jours fériés* (public holidays) are observed in France:

New Year's Day (Jour de l'An) 1 January

Easter Sunday & Monday (Pâques & Lundi de Pâques) Late March/April

May Day (Fête du Travail) 1 May

Victoire 1945 8 May

Ascension Thursday (Ascension) May; on the 40th day after Easter

Pentecost/Whit Sunday & Whit Monday (Pentecôte & Lundi de Pentecôte) Mid-May to mid-June; on the seventh Sunday after Easter

Bastille Day/National Day (Fête Nationale) 14 July

Assumption Day (Assomption) 15 August

All Saints' Day (Toussaint) 1 November

Remembrance Day (L'onze Novembre) 11 November

Christmas (Noël) 25 December
The following are *not* public holidays in France: Shrove Tuesday (Mardi Gras; the first day of Lent); Maundy (or Holy) Thursday and Good Friday, just before Easter; and Boxing Day (26 December).
Note: Good Friday and Boxing Day *are* public holidays in Alsace.

Safe Travel

France is generally a safe place, despite a rise in crime and terrorism in recent years.

➡ Never leave baggage unattended, especially at airports or train stations.

➡ At museums and monuments, bags are routinely checked on entry.

➡ Sporadic train strikes and striking taxi drivers can disrupt travel.

➡ France's hunting season is September to February: if you see signs reading *'chasseurs'* or *'chasse gardée'* tacked to trees, don't enter the area.

➡ In the Alps and Pyrenees, check the day's avalanche report and stick to groomed pistes. Summer thunderstorms can be sudden and violent.

➡ On the Atlantic Coast watch for powerful tides and undertows; only swim on beaches with lifeguards.

Taxes & Refunds

The standard value-added tax (VAT) rate of 20% is levied on most goods and services in France. Restaurants and hotels must always include 10% VAT in their prices.
Non-EU residents can claim a VAT refund on same-day purchases over €175, providing the goods are for personal consumption and are being personally transported home; retailers have details.

Telephone
Mobile Phones

➡ French mobile phone numbers begin with 06 or 07.

➡ France uses GSM 900/1800, which is compatible with the rest of Europe and Australia but not with the North American GSM 1900 or the totally different system in Japan (though some North Americans have tri-band phones that work here).

➡ Check with your service provider about roaming charges – dialling a mobile phone from a fixed-line phone or another mobile can be incredibly expensive.

➡ It is usually cheaper to buy a local SIM card from a French provider such as Orange, SFR, Bouygues or Free Mobile, which gives you

CHARGING DEVICES

Carrying your own charger and cable is the only sure way of ensuring you don't run out of juice. Don't be shy to ask in cafes and restaurants if you can plug in and charge – if you ask nicely, most will oblige. In Paris the odd cafe lends cables to customers, savvy taxi drivers stock a selection of smartphone-compatible cables and chargers for passengers to use, and newer RATP bus stops are equipped with USB ports (bring your own cable).

On TGV trains, all 1st-class carriages (and occasionally 2nd-class depending on how new the train is) have plugs. On every TGV irrespective of age, there is at least one 'office' space between carriages with mini-desk and double plug. Otherwise, upon arrival, an increasing number of SNCF train stations have charging stations: in Paris, Gare de Nord, Gare de Montparnasse and Gare de St-Lazare all have pedal-powered charging stations, as do several other stations countrywide including Lille, Lyon, Strasbourg and Avignon TGV.

a local phone number. To do this, ensure your phone is unlocked.

➡ If you already have a compatible phone, you can slip in a SIM card and rev it up with prepaid credit, though this is likely to run out fast as domestic prepaid calls cost about €0.50 per minute.

➡ Recharge cards are sold at most *tabacs* (tobacconist-newsagents), supermarkets and online through websites such as Topengo (www.topengo.fr) or Sim-OK (https://recharge.sim-ok.com).

Phone Codes
Calling France from abroad Dial your country's international access code, then 33 (France's country code), then the 10-digit local number *without* the initial zero.

Calling internationally from France Dial 00 (the international access code), the *indicatif* (country code), the area code (without the initial zero if there is one) and the local number. Some country codes are posted in public telephones.

Directory enquiries For national *service des renseignements* (directory inquiries) dial 11 87 12 or use the service for free online at www.118712.fr.

International directory inquiries For numbers outside France, dial 11 87 00.

Phone Cards
➡ Public phones still exist, but are hard to find. Phones accept calling cards or credit cards.

➡ **Emergency numbers** (p978) can be dialled from public phones without a card.

➡ Prepaid calling cards with codes *(tickets téléphones)*, sold at *tabacs* (tobacconists), are the cheapest way to call. When purchasing, *tabacs* can tell you which type is best for the country you want to call. Or buy online at www.topengo.fr (click on *cartes appels internationaux* and select the *ticket téléphone* for the geographic zone you'll call).

➡ Using calling cards from a home phone is much cheaper than using them from public phones or mobile phones.

➡ Hotels, *gîtes*, hostels and *chambres d'hôte* are free to meter their calls as they like. The surcharge is usually around €0.30 per minute but can be higher.

Time
France uses the 24-hour clock and is on Central European Time, which is one hour ahead of GMT/UTC. During daylight-saving time, which runs from the last Sunday in March to the last Sunday in October, France is two hours ahead of GMT/UTC.

The following times do not take daylight saving into account:

Paris	noon
Auckland	11pm
Berlin	noon
Cape Town	noon
London	11am
New York	6am
San Francisco	3am
Sydney	9pm
Tokyo	8pm

Toilets
Public toilets, signposted WC or *toilettes*, are not always plentiful in France, especially outside the big cities.

Love them (as a sci-fi geek) or loathe them (as a claustrophobe), France's 24-hour self-cleaning toilets are here to stay. Outside Paris these mechanical WCs are free, but in Paris they cost around €0.50 a go. Don't even think about nipping in after someone else to avoid paying unless you fancy a *douche* (shower) with disinfectant. There is no time for dawdling either; you have precisely 15 minutes before being (ooh-la-la!) exposed to passers-by. Green means *libre* (vacant) and red means *occupé* (occupied).

Some older establishments and motorway stops still have the hole-in-the-floor *toilettes à la turque* (squat toilets). Provided you hover, these are actually very hygienic, but take care not to get soaked by the flush.

Keep some loose change handy for tipping toilet attendants, who keep a hawk-like eye on many of France's public toilets.

The French are completely blasé about unisex toilets, so save your blushes when tiptoeing past the urinals to reach the ladies' loo.

Tourist Information

Almost every city, town and village has an *office de tourisme* (a tourist office run by some unit of local government) or *syndicat d'initiative* (a tourist office run by an organisation of local merchants). Both are excellent resources and can supply you with local maps as well as details on accommodation, restaurants and activities. If you have a special interest such as walking, cycling, architecture or wine sampling, ask about it.

➡ Many tourist offices make local hotel and B&B reservations, sometimes for a nominal fee.

➡ *Comités régionaux de tourisme* (CRTs; regional tourist boards), their *départemental* analogues (CDTs) and their websites are a superb source of information and hyperlinks.

➡ French government tourist offices (usually called Maisons de la France) provide every imaginable sort of tourist information on France.
Useful websites include the following:

French Government Tourist Office (www.france.fr/en) The low-down on sights, activities, transport and special-interest holidays in all of France's regions.

French Tourist Offices (www.tourisme.fr) Website of tourist offices in France, with mountains of inspirational information organised by theme and region.

Visas

Generally not required for stays of up to 90 days (or at all for EU nationals); some nationalities need a Schengen visa.

Visa Requirements

➡ For up-to-date details on visa requirements, see the website of the **Ministère des Affaires Étrangères** (Ministry of Foreign Affairs; www.diplomatie.gouv.fr; 37 quai d'Orsay, 7e; Ⓜ Assemblée Nationale) and click 'Coming to France'.

➡ EU nationals and citizens of Iceland, Norway and Switzerland need only a passport or a national identity card to enter France and stay in the country, even for stays of more than 90 days. However, citizens of new EU member states may be subject to various limitations on living and working in France.

➡ Citizens of Australia, the USA, Canada, Hong Kong, Israel, Japan, Malaysia, New Zealand, Singapore, South Korea and many Latin American countries do not need visas to visit France as tourists for up to 90 days. For long stays of more than 90 days, contact your nearest French embassy or consulate and begin your application well in advance, as it can take months.

➡ Other people wishing to come to France as tourists have to apply for a Schengen Visa, named after the agreements that have abolished passport controls between 26 European countries. It allows unlimited travel throughout the entire zone for a 90-day period. Apply to the consulate of the country you are entering first, or your main destination. Among other things, you need travel and repatriation insurance and to be able to show that you have sufficient funds to support yourself.

➡ Tourist visas cannot be changed into student visas after arrival. However, short-term visas are available for students sitting university-entrance exams in France.

➡ Tourist visas cannot be extended except in emergencies (such as medical problems). When your visa expires you'll need to leave and reapply from outside France.

Carte de Séjour

➡ EU passport holders and citizens of Switzerland, Iceland and Norway do not need a *carte de séjour* (residence permit) to reside or work in France.

➡ Nationals of other countries with long-stay visas must contact the local *mairie* (city hall) or *préfecture* (prefecture) to apply for a *carte de séjour*. Usually, you are required to do so within eight days of arrival in France. Make sure you have all the necessary documents before you arrive.

➡ Students of all nationalities studying in France need a *carte de séjour*.

Working Holiday Visa

Citizens of Australia, Canada, Japan, New Zealand, Russia (and a handful of others) aged between 18 and 30 (35 for Canadians) are eligible for a 12-month, multiple-entry Working Holiday Visa (*Permis Vacances-Travail*), allowing combined tourism and employment in France.

➡ Apply to the embassy or consulate in your home country. Do this early as there are annual quotas.

➡ You must be applying for a Working Holiday Visa for France for the first time.

➡ You will need comprehensive travel insurance for the duration of your stay.

Régions & Départements

NOUVELLE-AQUITAINE
16 Charente
17 Charente-Maritime
19 Corrèze
23 Creuse
24 Dordogne
33 Gironde
40 Landes
47 Lot-et-Garonne
64 Pyrénées-Atlantiques
79 Deux-Sèvres
86 Vienne
87 Haute-Vienne

AUVERGNE-RHÔNE ALPES
01 Allier
03 Ain
07 Ardèche
15 Cantal
26 Drôme
38 Isère
42 Loire
43 Haute-Loire
63 Puy-de-Dôme
69 Rhône
73 Savoie
74 Haute-Savoie

BOURGOGNE-FRANCHE-COMTÉ
14 Calvados
25 Doubs
39 Jura
50 Manche
61 Orne
70 Haute Saône
90 Territoire de Belfort

BRETAGNE
22 Côte-d'Armor
29 Finistère
35 Ille-et-Vilaine
56 Morbihan

CENTRE-VAL DE LOIRE
18 Cher
28 Eure-et-Loir
36 Indre
37 Indre-et-Loire
41 Loir-et-Cher
45 Loiret

CORSE
2A Corse-du-Sud
2B Haute-Corse

GRAND-EST
08 Ardennes
10 Aube
51 Marne
52 Haute-Marne
54 Meurthe-et-Moselle
55 Meuse
57 Moselle
67 Bas-Rhin
68 Haut-Rhin
88 Vosges

HAUTS-DE-FRANCE
02 Aisne
59 Nord
60 Oise
62 Pas-de-Calais
80 Somme

ÎLE-DE-FRANCE
91 Essonne
92 Hauts-de-Seine
75 Paris
78 Seine-et-Marne
93 Seine-St-Denis
94 Val-de-Marne
95 Val-d'Oise
77 Yvelines

OCCITANIE
09 Ariège
11 Aude
12 Aveyron
30 Gard
31 Haute-Garonne
32 Gers
34 Hérault
46 Lot
48 Lozère
65 Hautes-Pyrénées
66 Pyrénées-Orientales
81 Tarn
82 Tarn-et-Garonne

NORMANDIE
21 Côte-d'Or
27 Eure
58 Nièvre
71 Saône-et-Loire
76 Seine-Maritime
89 Yonne

PAYS DE LA LOIRE
44 Loire-Atlantique
49 Maine-et-Loire
53 Mayenne
72 Sarthe
85 Vendée

PROVENCE-ALPES-CÔTE D'AZUR
04 Alpes-de-Haute-Provence
06 Alpes-Maritimes
13 Bouches-du-Rhône
05 Hautes-Alpes
83 Var
84 Vaucluse

International Boundary
Région Boundary
Département Boundary

PRACTICALITIES

Classifieds Visit FUSAC (www.fusac.fr) for classified ads about housing, babysitting, jobs and language exchanges in and around Paris.

Laundry Virtually all French cities and towns have at least one *laverie libre-service* (self-service laundrette). Machines run on coins.

Newspapers and magazines Locals read their news in centre-left *Le Monde* (www.lemonde.fr), right-leaning *Le Figaro* (www.lefigaro.fr) or left-leaning *Libération* (www.liberation.fr).

Radio For news, tune in to the French-language France Info (105.5MHz; www.franceinfo.fr) and multilanguage RFI (738kHz or 89MHz in Paris; www.rfi.fr). Popular national FM music stations include NRJ (www.nrj.fr), Virgin (www.virginradio.fr), La Radio Plus (www.laradioplus.com) and Nostalgie (www.nostalgie.fr).

Weights and measures France uses the metric system.

➡ You must meet all health and character requirements.

➡ You will need a return plane ticket and proof of sufficient funds (usually around €3800) to get you through the start of your stay.

➡ Once you have arrived in France and have found a job, you must apply for an *autorisation provisoire de travail* (temporary work permit), which will only be valid for the duration of the employment offered. The permit can be renewed under the same conditions up to the limit of the authorised length of stay.

➡ You can also study or do training programs but the visa cannot be extended, nor can it be turned into a student visa.

➡ After one year you *must* go home.

Volunteering

Online resources like Go Abroad (www.goabroad.com) and Transitions Abroad (www.transitionsabroad.com) throw up a colourful selection of volunteering opportunities in France: helping out on a family farm in the Alps, restoring an historic monument in Provence or participating in a summertime archaeological excavation are but some of the golden opportunities awaiting those keen to volunteer their skills and services.

Some interesting volunteer organisations:

Club du Vieux Manoir (www.clubduvieuxmanoir.fr) Restore a medieval fortress, an abbey or a historic château at a summer work camp.

GeoVisions (www.geovisions.org) Volunteer 15 hours a week to teach a French family English in exchange for room and board.

Rempart (www.rempart.com) Brings together 170 organisations countrywide committed to preserving France's religious, military, civil, industrial and natural heritage.

Volunteers For Peace (www.vfp.org) US-based nonprofit organisation. Can link you up with a voluntary service project dealing with social work, the environment, education or the arts.

World Wide Opportunities on Organic Farms (WWOOF; www.wwoof.org) Work on a small farm or other organic venture (harvesting chestnuts, renovating an abandoned olive farm near Nice etc).

Work

➡ EU nationals have an automatic right to work in France.

➡ Most others will need a hard-to-get work permit, issued at the request of your employer, who will have to show that no one in France – or the entire European Economic Area – can do your job.

➡ Exceptions may be made for artists, computer engineers and translation specialists.

➡ Some travellers aged between 18 and 30 may be eligible for a 12-month, multiple-entry Working Holiday Visa (p984), which allows combined tourism and employment in France.

➡ Working 'in the black' (ie, without documents) is difficult and risky for non-EU nationals.

➡ The only instance in which the government might turn a blind eye to workers without documents is during fruit harvests (mid-May to November) and the *vendange* (grape harvest; mid-September to mid- or late October). Though, of course, undocumented workers harvest at their own risk.

➡ Au pair work is also very popular and can be done legally even by non-EU citizens. To apply, contact a placement agency at least three months in advance.

Transport

GETTING THERE & AWAY

Flights, cars and tours can be booked online at www.lonelyplanet.com/bookings.

Entering the Country

Entering France from other parts of the EU is usually a breeze – no border check-points and no customs – thanks to the Schengen Agreement, signed by all of France's neighbours except the UK, the Channel Islands and Andorra.

For these three entities, old-fashioned document and customs checks are still the norm, at least when exiting France (when entering France in the case of Andorra).

Air

Airports & Airlines

Air France (www.airfrance.com) is the national carrier, with plenty of both domestic and international flights in and out of major French airports.

Smaller provincial air-ports with international flights, mainly to/from the UK, continental Europe and North Africa, include Paris-Beauvais, Bergerac, Biarritz, Brest, Brive-la-Gaillarde (Vallée de la Dordogne), Caen, Carcassonne, Clermont-Ferrand, Deauville, Dinard, Grenoble, La Rochelle, Le Touquet (Côte d'Opale), Limoges, Montpellier, Nîmes, Pau, Perpignan, Poitiers, Rennes, Rodez, St-Étienne, Toulon and Tours.

Aéroport de Charles de Gaulle, Paris (CDG; ☑01 70 36 39 50; www.parisaeroport.fr)

Aéroport d'Orly, Paris (ORY; ☑01 70 36 39 50; www.parisaeroport.fr)

Aéroport de Bordeaux (Bordeaux Airport; BOD; ☑Information 05 56 34 50 50; www.bordeaux.aeroport.fr; Mérignac)

Aéroport de Lille (LIL; www.lille.aeroport.fr; rte de L'Aéroport, Lesquin)

Aéroport International Strasbourg (SXB; www.strasbourg.aeroport.fr)

Aéroport Lyon-St Exupéry (LYS; www.lyonaeroports.com)

Aéroport Marseille-Provence (Aéroport Marseille-Marignane; MRS; ☑08 20 81 14 14; www.marseille.aeroport.fr)

Aéroport Montpellier (MPL; ☑04 67 20 85 00; www.montpellier.aeroport.fr)

Aéroport Nantes Atlantique (NTE; www.nantes.aeroport.fr)

Aéroport Nice-Côte d'Azur (NCE; ☑08 20 42 33 33; www.nice.aeroport.fr; ☎; ☐98, 99, ☐2)

Aéroport Toulouse-Blagnac (TLS; www.toulouse.aeroport.fr/en)

EuroAirport, Basel (MLH or BSL, ☑+33 3 89 90 31 11; www.euroairport.com)

CLIMATE CHANGE & TRAVEL

Every form of transport that relies on carbon-based fuel generates CO_2, the main cause of human-induced climate change. Modern travel is dependent on aeroplanes, which might use less fuel per kilometre per person than most cars but travel much greater distances. The altitude at which aircraft emit gases (including CO_2) and particles also contributes to their climate change impact. Many websites offer 'carbon calculators' that allow people to estimate the carbon emissions generated by their journey and, for those who wish to do so, to offset the impact of the greenhouse gases emitted with contributions to portfolios of climate-friendly initiatives throughout the world. Lonely Planet offsets the carbon footprint of all staff and author travel.

Land

Bicycle

Transporting a bicycle to France is a breeze.

On **Eurotunnel Le Shuttle** (☎France 08 10 63 03 04, UK 08443 35 35 35; www.eurotunnel.com) trains through the Channel Tunnel, the fee for a bicycle, including its rider, is from £20 one way; reservations must be made at least 48 hours in advance of departure.

A bike that's been dismantled to the size of a suitcase can be carried on board a **Eurostar** (☎France 08 92 35 35 39, UK 08432 186 186; www.eurostar.com) train from London or Brussels just like any other luggage. Otherwise, there's a £40 charge and you'll need advance reservations.

On ferries, foot passengers – where allowed – can usually (but not always) bring along a bicycle for no charge.

European Bike Express (☎iUK 01430 422 111; www.bike-express.co.uk) transports cyclists and their bikes from the UK to places around France.

Bus

Eurolines (☎08 92 89 90 91; www.eurolines.eu), a grouping of 32 long-haul coach operators (including the UK's National Express), links France with cities all across Europe, Morocco and Russia. Discounts are available to people under 26 and over 60. Make advance reservations, especially in July and August.

A single Paris–London fare starts at €17, including a Channel crossing by ferry or the Channel Tunnel. Book as far ahead as possible to bag the cheapest ticket.

Flixbus (www.flixbus.com) offers low-cost, intercity bus travel between 27 countries in Europe aboard comfy buses equipped with a toilet, snacks, plug sockets to keep devices charged and free wi-fi, and runs night services too. Sample fares include €48 for a one-way Bordeaux–Annecy or Paris–Strasbourg ticket.

Car & Motorcycle

A right-hand-drive vehicle brought to France from the UK or Ireland must have deflectors affixed to the headlights to avoid dazzling oncoming traffic. In the UK, information on driving in France is available from the RAC (www.rac.co.uk/driving-abroad/france) and the AA (www.theaa.com).

A foreign motor vehicle entering France must display a sticker or licence plate identifying its country of registration.

EUROTUNNEL

The Channel Tunnel (Chunnel), inaugurated in 1994, is the first dry-land link between England and France since the last ice age.

High-speed **Eurotunnel Le Shuttle** (☎France 08 10 63 03 04, UK 08443 35 35 35; www.eurotunnel.com) trains whisk bicycles, motorcycles, cars and coaches in 35 minutes from Folkestone through the Channel Tunnel to Coquelles, 5km southwest of Calais. Shuttles run 24 hours a day, with up to three departures an hour during peak periods. LPG and CNG tanks are not permitted, meaning gas-powered cars and many campers and caravans have to travel by ferry.

Eurotunnel sets its fares the way budget airlines do: the further in advance you book and the lower the demand for a particular crossing, the less you pay; same-day fares can cost a small fortune. Fares for a car, including up to nine passengers, start at £30 (€37).

Train

Rail services link France with virtually every country in Europe.

➡ Book tickets and get train information from Rail Europe (www.raileurope.com). In the UK contact Railteam (www.railteam.co.uk).

➡ A very useful train-travel resource is the information-packed website The Man in Seat 61 (www.seat61.com). Certain rail services between France and its continental neighbours are marketed under unique brand names:

Elipsos Luxurious, overnight 'train-hotel' from Paris to Madrid and Barcelona in Spain; book through France's **SNCF** (Société Nationale des Chemins de fer Français, French National Railway Company; ☎from abroad +33 8 92 35 35 35, in France 36 35; http://en.voyages-sncf.com).

TGV Lyria (high-speed train; www.tgv-lyria.fr) To Switzerland.

Thalys (www.thalys.com) Thalys trains pull into Paris' Gare du Nord from Brussels, Amsterdam and Cologne.

Thello (www.thello.com) Overnight train service from Paris to Milan, Brescia, Verona and Venice in Italy.

EURAIL PASS

Rail passes are worthwhile if you plan to clock up the kilometres.

SAMPLE TRAIN FARES

ROUTE	FULL FARE (€)	DURATION (HR)
Paris-Amsterdam	135	3¼
Paris-Berlin	147	8
Bordeaux-London	87	5½
Paris-Brussels	115	1½
Dijon-Milan	131	7
Marseille-Barcelona	100	4½
Paris-Venice	213	11¾
Strasbourg-Vienna	171	9¾

Available only to people who don't live in Europe, the Eurail Pass (www.eurail.com) is valid in up to 21 countries, including France. People 25 and under get the best deals. Passes must be validated at a train-station ticket window before you begin your first journey.

EUROSTAR

The **Eurostar** (☑France 08 92 35 35 39, UK 08432 186 186; www.eurostar.com) whisks you from London to Paris in 2¼ hours.

Except late at night, trains link London (St Pancras International) with Paris (Gare du Nord; hourly), Calais (Calais-Fréthun; one hour, three daily), Lille (Gare Lille-Europe; 1½ hours, eight daily), Disneyland Resort Paris (2½ hours, one direct daily), Lyon (4¾ hours, one to five per week), Avignon (5¾ hours, one to five per week), Marseille (6½ hours, one to five per week) and Bordeaux (six hours with change of train in Paris, four daily), with less frequent services departing from Ebbsfleet and Ashford in Kent. Weekend ski trains connect England with the French Alps from late December to mid-April.

Eurostar offers a bewildering array of fares. A standard, 2nd-class single ticket from Paris to London starts at €44.

For the best deals, buy a return ticket, stay over a Saturday night, book up to 120 days in advance and don't mind non-exchangeability and non-refundability. Discount fares are available for under 26s or over 60s.

Sea

Some ferry companies have started setting fares the way budget airlines do: the longer in advance you book and the lower the demand for a particular sailing, the less you pay. Seasonal demand is a crucial factor (Christmas, Easter, UK and French school holidays, and July and August are especially busy), as is the time of day (an early-evening ferry can cost much more than one at 4am). People under 25 and over 60 may qualify for discounts.

To get the best fares, check Ferry Savers (www.ferrysavers.com).

Foot passengers are not allowed on Dover–Boulogne, Dover–Dunkirk or Dover–Calais car ferries except for daytime (and, from Calais to Dover, evening) crossings run by P&O Ferries. On ferries that do allow foot passengers, taking a bicycle is usually free. Several ferry companies ply the waters between Corsica and Italy.

GETTING AROUND

Driving is the simplest way to get around France, but a car is a liability in traffic-plagued, parking-starved city centres, and petrol bills and *autoroute* (dual carriageway/divided highway) tolls add up.

France is famous for its excellent public-transport network, which serves everywhere bar some very rural areas. The state-owned Société Nationale des Chemins de Fer Français (SNCF) takes care of almost all land transport between *départements* (counties). Transport within *départements* is handled by a combination of short-haul trains, SNCF buses and local bus companies.

INTERNATIONAL FERRY COMPANIES

COMPANY	CONNECTION	WEBSITE
Brittany Ferries	England-Normandy, England-Brittany, Ireland-Brittany	www.brittany-ferries.co.uk; www.brittanyferries.ie
Condor Ferries	England-Normandy, England-Brittany, Channel Islands-Brittany	www.condorferries.co.uk
Corsica Linea	Algeria-France, Sardinia-France, Tunisia-France	www.corsicalinea.com
CTN	Tunisia-France	www.ctn.com.tn
DFDS Seaways	England-Normandy, England-Channel Ports	www.dfdsseaways.co.uk
Grandi Navi Veloci (GNV)	Morocco-Sète (Languedoc-Roussillon)	www.gnv.it
Irish Ferries	Ireland-Normandy, Ireland-Brittany	www.irishferries.com
Manche Îles Express	Channel Islands-Normandy	www.manche-iles.com
Norfolk Line (DFDS Seaways)	England-Channel Ports	www.norfolkline.ferries.org
P&O Ferries	England-Channel Ports	www.poferries.com
Stena Line Ferries	Ireland-Normandy	www.stenaline.ie

Air

France's high-speed train network renders rail travel between some cities (eg from Paris to Lyon, Marseille and Bordeaux) faster and easier than flying.

Air France (www.airfrance. com) and its subsidiaries Hop! (www.hop.com) and Transavia (www.transavia.com) control the lion's share of France's domestic airline industry.

Budget carriers offering flights within France include EasyJet (www.easyjet.com), Twin Jet (www.twinjet.net) and Air Corsica (www.aircorsica.com).

Bicycle

France is great for cycling. Much of the countryside is drop-dead gorgeous and the country has a growing number of urban and rural *pistes cyclables* (bike paths and lanes; see Voies Vertes online at www.voievertes.com) and an extensive network of secondary and tertiary roads with relatively light traffic.

French law requires that bicycles must have two functioning brakes, a bell, a red reflector on the back and yellow reflectors on the pedals. After sunset and when visibility is poor, cyclists must turn on a white headlamp and a red tail lamp. When being overtaken by a vehicle, cyclists must ride in single file. Towing children in a bike trailer is permitted.

Never leave your bicycle locked up outside overnight if you want to see it – or at least most of its parts – again. Some hotels offer enclosed bicycle parking.

Bicycle Transport

The SNCF does its best to make travelling with a bicycle easy; see www.velo.sncf.com for full details.

Bicycles (not disassembled) can be taken along on virtually all intraregional TER trains and most long-distance intercity trains, subject to space availability. The charge for TER and Corail Intercité trains is either free, €5 or €10 depending on the route; TGV, Téoz and Lunéa trains require a €10 reservation fee that must be made when you purchase your passenger ticket. Bike reservations can be made by phone (36 35) or at an SNCF ticket office but not via the internet.

Bicycles that have been partly disassembled and put in a box *(housse)*, with maximum dimensions of 120cm by 90cm, can be taken along for no charge in the baggage compartments of TGV, Téoz, Lunéa and Corail Intercité trains.

In the Paris area, bicycles are allowed aboard Transilien and RER trains except Monday to Friday during the following times:

➡ 6.30am to 9am for trains heading into Paris

➡ 4.30pm to 7pm for trains travelling out of Paris

➡ 6am to 9am and 4.30pm to 7pm on RER lines A and B With precious few exceptions, bicycles are not allowed on metros, trams and local, intra-*département* and SNCF buses (the latter replace trains on some runs).

Hire

Most French cities and towns have at least one bike shop that rents out *vélos tout terrains* (mountain bikes; around €15 a day), known as VTTs, as well as more road-oriented *vélos tout chemin* (VTCs), or cheaper city bikes. You usually have to leave ID and/or a deposit (often a credit-card slip of €250) that you forfeit if the bike is damaged or stolen.

A growing number of cities – including Paris, Aix-en-Provence, Amiens, Besançon, Bayonne, Bordeaux, Caen, Clermont-Ferrand, Dijon, La Rochelle, Lille, Lyon, Marseille, Montpellier, Mulhouse, Nancy, Nantes, Nice, Orléans, Rennes, Rouen, Toulouse, Strasbourg and Vannes – have automatic bike-rental systems, intended to encourage cycling as a form of urban transport, with computerised pick-up and drop-off sites all over town. In general, you have to sign up either short term or long term, providing credit-card details, and can then use the bikes for no charge for the first half-hour; after that, hourly charges rise quickly.

Boat

There are boat services along France's coasts and to its offshore islands, and ferries aplenty to/from Corsica.

Canal Boating

Transportation and tranquillity are usually mutually exclusive – but not if you rent a houseboat and cruise along France's canals and navigable rivers, stopping at whim to pick up supplies, dine at a village restaurant or check out a local château by bicycle. Changes in altitude are taken care of by a system of *écluses* (locks).

Boats generally accommodate from two to 12 passengers and are fully outfitted with bedding and cooking facilities. Anyone over 18 can pilot a riverboat, but first-time skippers are given a short instruction session so they qualify for a *carte de plaisance* (a temporary cruising permit). The speed limit is 6km/h on canals and 8km/h on rivers.

Prices start at around €650 a week for a small boat and easily top €3500 a week for a large, luxurious craft. Except in July and August, you can often rent over a weekend.

Advance reservations are essential for holiday periods, over long weekends and in July and August, especially for larger boats.

Rental agencies include the following:

France Afloat (https://franceafloat.com) Anglophone, canal-boat specialist in France.

Free Wheel Afloat (www.
freewheelafloat.com) UK-based,
self-drive barge specialist.

H2olidays (www.barginginfrance.
com) Hotel barges, river cruises
and self-drive barges.

Worldwide River Cruise (www.
worldwide-river-cruise.com)
River-cruiser rental, price-com-
parison website.

Bus

Buses are widely used for
short-distance travel within
départements, especially in
rural areas with relatively few
train lines (eg Brittany and
Normandy). Unfortunately,
services in some regions
are infrequent and slow,
in part because they were
designed to get children to
their schools in the towns
rather than transport visitors
around the countryside.

Some less-busy train lines
have been replaced by SNCF
buses, which, unlike regional
buses, are free if you've got a
rail pass.

Car & Motorcycle

Having your own wheels gives
you exceptional freedom
and makes it easy to visit
more remote parts of France.
Depending on the number of
passengers, it can also work
out cheaper than the train.
For example, by *autoroute*,
the 930km drive from Paris to
Nice (9½ hours of driving) in
a small car costs about €75
for petrol and another €77 in
tolls – by comparison, a one-
way, 2nd-class TGV ticket for
the 5½-hour Paris to Nice run
costs anything from €69 to
€120 per person.

In the cities, traffic and
finding a place to park can be
a major headache. During holiday periods and bank-holiday
weekends, roads throughout
France also get backed up
with traffic jams (*bouchons*).

Motorcyclists will find
France great for touring,
with winding roads of good
quality and lots of stunning
scenery. Just make sure your

wet-weather gear is up to
scratch.

France (along with Bel-
gium) has the densest highway network in Europe. There
are four types of intercity
roads:

Autoroutes (highway names
beginning with A) Multilane
divided highways, usually (except
near Calais and Lille) with tolls
(*péages*). Generously outfitted
with rest stops.

Routes Nationales (N, RN) National highways. Some sections
have divider strips.

Routes Départementales (D)
Local highways and roads.

Routes Communales (C, V)
Minor rural roads.

For information on *autoroute*
tolls, rest areas, traffic and
weather, go to the Sociétés
d'Autoroutes website (www.
autoroutes.fr).

Bison Futé (www.bison-
fute.gouv.fr) is also a good
source of information about
traffic conditions. Plot itineraries between your departure
and arrival points, and calcu-
late toll costs with an online
mapper such as Via Michelin
(www.viamichelin.com) or
Mappy (https://fr.mappy.
com).

Theft from cars can be
a major problem in France,
especially in the south.

Driving Licences & Documents

An International Driving
Permit (IDP), valid only if
accompanied by your original licence, is good for a year
and can be issued by your
local automobile association
before you leave home.

Drivers must carry the
following at all times:

➜ passport or an EU national
ID card

➜ valid driving licence
(*permis de conduire;* most
foreign licences can be used
in France for up to a year)

➜ car-ownership papers,
known as a *carte grise* (grey
card)

➜ proof of third-party liability
assurance (insurance)

Fuel

Essence (petrol), also known
as *carburant* (fuel), costs
between €1.48 and €1.65 per
litre for 95 unleaded (Sans
Plomb 95 or SP95, usually
available from a green pump)
and €1.35 to €1.60 for diesel
(*diesel, gazole* or *gasoil,* usually available from a yellow
pump). Check and compare
current prices countrywide at
www.prix-carburants.gouv.fr.

Filling up (*faire le plein*) is
most expensive at *autoroute*
rest stops, and usually
cheapest at hypermarkets.

Many small petrol stations
close on Sunday afternoons
and, even in cities, it can be
hard to find a staffed station
open late at night. In general,
after-hours purchases (eg
at hypermarkets' fully automatic, 24-hour stations) can
only be made with a credit
card that has an embedded
PIN chip, so if all you've got
is cash or a magnetic-strip
credit card, you could be
stuck.

Hire

To hire a car in France, you'll
generally need to be over 21
years old, have had a driving
licence for at least a year, and
have an international credit
card. Drivers under 25 usually have to pay a surcharge
(*frais jeune conducteur*) of
€25 to €35 per day.

Car-hire companies provide
mandatory third-party liability
insurance, but things such
as collision-damage waivers
(CDW, or *assurance tous
risques*) vary greatly from
company to company. When
comparing rates and conditions (ie the fine print), the
most important thing to check

ROAD CHECK

In many areas, Auto-
route Info (107.7MHz;
www.autorouteinfo.fr)
has round-the-clock
traffic information.

ROAD DISTANCES (KM)

	Bayonne	Bordeaux	Brest	Caen	Cahors	Calais	Chambéry	Cherbourg	Clermont-Ferrand	Dijon	Grenoble	Lille	Lyon	Marseille	Nantes	Nice	Paris	Perpignan	Strasbourg	Toulouse
Bordeaux	184																			
Brest	811	623																		
Caen	764	568	376																	
Cahors	307	218	788	661																
Calais	164	876	710	339	875															
Chambéry	860	651	120	800	523	834														
Cherbourg	835	647	399	124	743	461	923													
Clermont-Ferrand	564	358	805	566	269	717	295	689												
Dijon	807	619	867	548	378	572	273	671	279											
Grenoble	827	657	1126	806	501	863	56	929	300	302										
Lille	997	809	725	353	808	112	767	476	650	505	798									
Lyon	831	528	1018	698	439	755	103	820	171	194	110	687								
Marseille	700	651	1271	1010	521	1067	344	1132	477	506	273	999	314							
Nantes	513	326	298	292	491	593	780	317	462	656	787	609	618	975						
Nice	858	810	1429	1168	679	1225	410	1291	636	664	337	1157	473	190	1131					
Paris	771	583	596	232	582	289	565	355	424	313	571	222	462	775	384	932				
Perpignan	499	451	1070	998	320	1149	478	1094	441	640	445	1081	448	319	773	476	857			
Strasbourg	1254	1066	1079	730	847	621	496	853	584	335	551	522	488	803	867	804	490	935		
Toulouse	300	247	866	865	116	991	565	890	890	727	533	923	536	407	568	564	699	205	1022	
Tours	536	348	490	246	413	531	611	369	369	418	618	463	449	795	197	952	238	795	721	593

is the *franchise* (deductible/ excess), which for a small car is usually around €600 for damage and €800 for theft. With many companies, you can reduce the excess by half, and perhaps to zero, by paying a daily insurance supplement of up to €20. Your credit card may cover CDW if you use it to pay for the rental, but the car-hire company won't know anything about this – verify conditions and details with your credit-card issuer to be sure.

Arranging your car hire or fly/drive package before you leave home is usually considerably cheaper than a walk-in rental, but beware of website offers that don't include a CDW or you may be liable for up to 100% of the car's value.

International car-hire companies:

➜ Avis (www.avis.com)

➜ Budget (www.budget.fr)

➜ EasyCar (www.easycar.com)

➜ Europcar (www.europcar.com)

➜ Hertz (www.hertz.com)

➜ Sixt (www.sixt.fr)
French car-hire companies:

➜ ADA (www.ada.fr)

➜ DLM (www.dlm.fr)

➜ France Cars (www.francecars.fr)

➜ Locauto (www.locauto.fr)

➜ Renault Rent (www.renault-rent.com)

➜ Rent a Car (www.rentacar.fr)
Deals can be found on the internet and through companies such as the following:

➜ Auto Europe (www.autoeurope.com)

➜ DriveAway Holidays (www.driveaway.com.au)

➜ Holiday Autos (www.holidayautos.co.uk)
Rental cars with automatic transmission are very much the exception in France; they usually need to be ordered well in advance and are more expensive than manual cars.

For insurance reasons, it is usually forbidden to take rental cars on ferries, eg to Corsica.

All rental cars registered in France have a distinctive number on the licence plate, making them easily identifiable – including to thieves. *Never* leave anything of value in a parked car, even in the boot (trunk).

Insurance

Third-party liability insurance (*assurance au tiers*) is compulsory for all vehicles in France, including cars brought in from abroad. Normally, cars registered and insured in other European countries can circulate freely in France, but it's a good idea to contact your insurance company before you leave home to make sure you have coverage – and to check whom to contact in case of a breakdown or accident.

If you get into a minor accident with no injuries, the easiest way for drivers to sort things out with their insurance companies is to fill out a Constat Aimable d'Accident Automobile (European Accident Statement), a standardised way of recording important details about what happened. In rental cars it's usually in the packet of documents in the glove compartment. Make sure the report includes any information that will help you prove that the accident was not your fault. Remember, if it *was* your fault you may be liable for a hefty insurance deductible/excess. Don't sign anything you don't fully understand. If problems crop up, call the police (17).

French-registered cars have details of their insurance company printed on a little green square affixed to the windscreen.

Purchase-Repurchase Plans

If you don't live in the EU and need a car in France (or Europe) for 17 days to six months (up to one year if you'll be studying), by far the cheapest option is to 'purchase' a new one and then 'sell' it back at the end of your trip. In reality, you pay only for the number of days you have the vehicle but the 'temporary transit' (TT) paperwork means that the car is registered under your name – and that the whole deal is exempt from all sorts of taxes.

Companies offering purchase-repurchase (*achat-rachat*) plans:

Eurocar TT (www.eurocartt.com)

Peugeot OpenEurope (www.peugeot-openeurope.com)

Renault Eurodrive (www.eurodrive.renault.com) Eligibility is restricted to people who are not residents of the EU (citizens of EU countries are eligible if they live outside the EU); the minimum age is 18 (in some cases 21). Pricing and special offers depend on your home country. All the plans include unlimited kilometres, 24-hour towing and breakdown service, and comprehensive insurance with absolutely no deductible/excess, so returning the car is hassle-free, even if it's damaged.

Extending your contract (up to a maximum of 165 days) after you start using the car is possible, but you'll end up paying about double the prepaid per-day rate.

Purchase-repurchase cars, which have special red licence plates, can be picked up at about three-dozen cities and airports all over France and dropped off at the agency of your choosing. For a fee, you can also pick up or return your car in certain cities outside France.

Parking

In city centres, most on-street parking places are *payant* (metered) from about 9am to 7pm (sometimes with a break from noon to 2pm) Monday to Saturday, except bank holidays.

Road Rules

Enforcement of French traffic laws (see www.securiteroutiere.gouv.fr) has been stepped up considerably in recent years. Speed cameras are common, as are radar traps and unmarked police vehicles. Fines for many infractions are given on the spot, and serious violations can lead to the confiscation of your driving licence and car.

Speed limits outside built-up areas (except where signposted otherwise):

Undivided N and D highways 80km/h (70km/h when raining)

Non-autoroute divided highways 110km/h (100km/h when raining)

Autoroutes 130km/h (110km/h when raining, 60km/h in icy conditions)

ENVIRONMENTAL ZONES

Two types of environmental zones aim to reduce the road-traffic pollution in heavily built-up or busy areas by permanently or temporarily restricting road traffic.

ZPAs (air protection zones) can cover an entire *département* or region and usually only apply for a few days, often during hot or bad weather, when air pollution peaks.

In ZCR zones, all cars, motorcycles and trucks registered after 1997 have to display a Crit'Air sticker to enter. This applies to the city of Paris within the *périphérique* (ring road) between 8am and 8pm Monday to Friday. Stickers can be ordered online (www.crit-air.fr); you'll need to upload a copy of your vehicle's registration certificate and allow time for it to be mailed to your home. Prices for a Crit'Air Vignette start at €3.11. Fines for not displaying a valid sticker start at €68. Check www.green-zones.eu or download the Green Zone App to check current zones.

PRIORITY TO THE RIGHT

Under the *priorité à droite* ('priority to the right') rule, any car entering an intersection (including a T-junction) from a road (including a tiny village backstreet) on your right has the right of way. Locals assume every driver knows this, so don't be surprised if they courteously cede the right of way when you're about to turn from an alley onto a highway – and boldly assert their rights when you're the one zipping down a main road.

Priorité à droite is suspended (eg on arterial roads) when you pass a sign showing an upended yellow square with a black square in the middle. The same sign with a horizontal bar through the square lozenge reinstates the *priorité à droite* rule.

When you arrive at a roundabout at which you do not have the right of way (ie the cars already in the roundabout do), you'll often see signs reading *vous n'avez pas la priorité* (you do not have right of way) or *cédez le passage* (give way).

To reduce carbon emissions, *autoroute* speed limits have recently been reduced to 110km/h in some areas.

Unless otherwise signposted, a limit of 50km/h applies in *all* areas designated as built up, no matter how rural they may appear. You must slow to 50km/h the moment you come to a white sign with a red border and a place name written on it; the speed limit applies until you pass an identical sign with a horizontal bar through it.

Other important driving rules:

➡ Blood-alcohol limit is 0.05% (0.5g per litre of blood) – the equivalent of two glasses of wine for a 75kg adult. Police often conduct random breathalyser tests and penalties can be severe, including imprisonment.

➡ All passengers, including those in the back seat, must wear seat belts.

➡ Mobile phones may be used only if they are equipped with a hands-free kit or speakerphone.

➡ Turning right on a red light is illegal.

➡ Cars from the UK and Ireland must have deflectors affixed to their headlights to avoid dazzling oncoming motorists.

➡ Radar detectors, even if they're switched off, are illegal; fines are hefty.

➡ Children under 10 are not permitted to ride in the front seat (unless the back is already occupied by other children under 10).

➡ A child under 13kg must travel in a backward-facing child seat (permitted in the front seat only for babies under 9kg and if the airbag is deactivated).

➡ Up to age 10 and/or a minimum height of 140cm, children must use a size-appropriate type of front-facing child seat or booster.

➡ All vehicles driven in France must carry a high-visibility reflective safety vest (stored inside the vehicle, not in the trunk/boot), a reflective triangle, and a portable, single-use breathalyser kit.

➡ If you'll be driving on snowy roads, make sure you have snow chains (*chaînes neige*), required by law whenever and wherever the police post signs.

➡ Riders of any type of two-wheeled vehicle with a motor (except motor-assisted bicycles) must wear a helmet. No special licence is required to ride a motorbike whose engine is smaller than 50cc, which is why rental scooters are often rated at 49.9cc.

Hitching & Ride-Sharing

Hitching is never entirely safe in any country in the world, and we don't recommend it. Travellers who decide to hitch should understand that they are taking a small but potentially serious risk. Remember that it's safer to travel in pairs and be sure to inform someone of your intended destination. Hitching is not really part of French culture.

Hitching from city centres is pretty much hopeless, so your best bet is to take public transport to the outskirts. It is illegal to hitch on *autoroutes,* but you can stand near an entrance ramp as long as you don't block traffic. Hitching in remote rural areas is better, but once you get off the *routes nationales,* traffic can be light and local. If your itinerary includes a ferry crossing, it's worth trying to score a ride before the ferry since vehicle tickets usually include a number of passengers free of charge. At dusk, give up and think about finding somewhere to stay.

A number of organisations around France arrange *covoiturage* (car sharing), ie, putting people looking for rides in touch with drivers going to the same destination:

➡ Covoiturage (www.covoiturage.fr)

➡ Bla Bla Car (www.blablacar.fr)

➡ Karzoo (www.karzoo.eu) International journeys.

Local Transport

France's cities and larger towns have world-class public-transport systems. There are *métros* (underground subway systems) in Paris, Lille, Lyon, Marseille, Toulouse and Rennes, and tramways in cities such as Bordeaux, Grenoble, Lille, Lyon, Nancy, Nantes, Nice, Reims, Rouen and Strasbourg.

In addition to a *billet à l'unité* (single ticket), you can purchase a *carnet* (booklet or bunch) of 10 tickets or a *pass journée* (all-day pass).

Taxi

All medium and large train stations – and many small ones – have a taxi stand out the front. In small cities and towns, where taxi drivers are unlikely to find another fare anywhere near where they let you off, one-way and return trips often cost the same. Tariffs are about 30% higher at night and on Sundays and holidays. A surcharge is usually charged to get picked up at a train station or airport, and there's a small additional fee for a fourth passenger and/or for suitcases.

Providing you're able to connect to the app and order a car on your smartphone, Uber can be a cheaper alternative to regular city taxis. While Uber fares in Paris are not dramatically cheaper than an official taxi, Uber fares in other French cities can be up to one-third cheaper.

Train

Travelling by train in France is a comfortable and environmentally sustainable way to see the country. Since many train stations have car-hire agencies, it's easy to combine rail travel with rural exploration by car.

The jewel in the crown of France's public-transport system – alongside the Paris *métro* – is its extensive rail network, almost all of it run by the heavily indebted, state-rail operator **SNCF** (Société Nationale des Chemins de fer Français, French National Railway Company; ☎from abroad +33 8 92 35 35 35, in France 36 35; http://en.voyages-sncf.com) (French President Macron announced plans

to reform and privatise the company in 2018, prompting huge strikes). The SNCF employs the most advanced rail technology, but its network reflects the country's centuries-old Paris-centric nature: most of the principal rail lines radiate out from Paris like the spokes of a wheel, the result being that services between provincial towns situated on different spokes can be infrequent and slow.

Since its inauguration in the 1980s, the pride and joy of SNCF is the TGV (Train à Grande Vitesse; www.tgv.com), which zips passengers along at speeds of up to 320km/h.

The main TGV lines (or LGVs, short for *lignes à grande vitesse*, ie high-speed rail lines) head north, east, southeast and southwest from Paris (trains use slower local tracks to get to destinations off the main line):

TGV Nord, Thalys and Eurostar Link Paris Gare du Nord with Arras, Lille, Calais, Brussels (Bruxelles-Midi), Amsterdam, Cologne and, via the Channel Tunnel, Ashford, Ebbsfleet and London St Pancras.

LGV Est Européene (www.lgv-est.com) Connects Paris Gare de l'Est with Reims, Nancy, Metz, Strasbourg, Zurich and Germany, including Frankfurt and Stuttgart. The super-high-speed track stretches as far east as Strasbourg.

TGV Sud-Est and TGV Midi-Méditerranée Link Paris Gare de Lyon with the southeast, including Dijon, Lyon, Geneva, the Alps, Avignon, Marseille, Nice and Montpellier.

TGV Atlantique Sud-Ouest and TGV Atlantique Ouest Link Paris Gare Montparnasse with western and southwestern France, including Brittany (Rennes, Brest, Quimper), Tours, Nantes, Poitiers, La Rochelle, Bordeaux, Biarritz and Toulouse.

LGV Rhin-Rhône High-speed rail route that bypasses Paris altogether in its bid to better link the provinces. Six services a day speed between Strasbourg and Lyon, with most continuing south

to Marseille or Montpellier on the Mediterranean.

TGV tracks are interconnected, making it possible to go directly from, for example, Lyon to Nantes or Bordeaux to Lille without having to switch in Paris or transfer from one of Paris' six main train stations to another. Stops on the link-up, which runs east and south of Paris, include Charles de Gaulle airport and Disneyland Resort Paris.

Long-distance trains sometimes split at a station ie, each half of the train heads off for a different destination. Check the destination panel on your car as you board or you could wind up very far from where you intended to go. Other types of train:

TER (Train Express Régional; www.ter-sncf.com) A train that is not a TGV is often referred to as a *corail*, a *classique* or, for intraregional services, a TER.

Transilien (www.transilien.com) SNCF services in the Île de France area in and around Paris.

Tickets & Reservations

Large stations often have separate ticket windows for *international, grandes lignes* (long-haul) and *banlieue* (suburban) lines, and for people whose train is about to leave (*départ immédiat* or *départ dans l'heure*). Nearly every SNCF station has one *borne libre-service* (self-service terminal) or *billeterie automatique* (automatic ticket machine) that accepts both cash and PIN-chip credit cards.

You can buy a ticket by phone or via the SNCF booking website Voyages SNCF (www.voyages-sncf.com), and either have it sent to you by post (in France) or collect it from any SNCF ticket office or from ticket machines. Alternatively, download the SNCF app and buy/store your ticket on your smartphone.

Before boarding the train, paper tickets must be validated (*composter*) by time-stamping them in a

Trains & Ferries

NON-TGV PARIS DEPARTURE STATIONS

- Gare du Nord
- Gare de l'Est
- Gare de Lyon
- Gare d'Austerlitz
- Gare Montparnasse
- Gare St-Lazare

TGV LINES & DEPARTURE STATIONS

TGV Fast Track	TGV Non-Fast Track	
		TGV Nord, Thalys & Eurostar – departure from Paris Gare du Nord
		TGV Atlantique Sud-Ouest & TGV Atlantique Ouest – departure from Paris Gare Montparnasse
		TGV Sud-Est & TGV Midi-Mediterranée – departure from Paris Gare de Lyon
		TGV Est Européen – departure from Paris Gare de l'Est
		TGV Rhin-Rhône - no departures from Paris; fast-speed link between Strasbourg and Lyon

Normal SNCF track

composteur, a yellow post located on the way to the platform. If you forget (or don't have a ticket for some other reason), find a conductor on the train before they find you – otherwise you can be fined.

CHANGES & REIMBURSEMENTS

For trains that do not assign reserved seats (such as regional TER trains), full-fare tickets are usable whenever you like for 61 days from the

date they were purchased. Like all SNCF tickets, they cannot be replaced if lost or stolen.

Prem's, Intercités 100% Éco and other promotional tickets cannot be changed or reimbursed.

If you have a full-fare Loisir ticket, you can change your reservation by phone, internet or at train stations for a charge of €5 as of 30 days from departure; changes made the day before or day of your reserved trip incur a charge of €15/12 for TGV/Intercity tickets.

Pro tickets allow full reimbursement up to 30 minutes *after* the time of departure (by calling ⏴36 35) and can be cancelled up to two hours before.

SNCF Fares & Discounts

Full-fare tickets can be quite expensive. Fortunately, a dizzying array of discounts are available and station staff are very good about helping travellers find the very best fare.

➡ First-class travel, where available, costs 20% to 30% extra.

➡ Ticket prices for some trains, including most TGVs, are pricier during peak periods.

➡ The further in advance you reserve, the lower the fares.

➡ Children under four travel for free, or pay €9 with a *forfait bambin* to any destination if they need a seat.

➡ Children aged four to 11 travel for half-price.

OUIGO

Run by the SNCF, Ouigo (www.ouigo.com) is a low-cost TGV service whereby you can travel on high-speed TGVs for a snip of the usual price to 17 destinations in France, including Aix-en-Provence TGV, Angers-St Laud, Avignon TGV, Le Mans, Lyon, Marseille, Montpellier, Nantes, Nîmes, Paris, Paris Disneyland's Marne-La Vallée-Chessy TGV station and Paris' Aéroport Charles de Gaulle.

➡ Tickets can only be purchased online from three weeks until four hours before departure; tickets are emailed four days before departure and must be printed out or readable on a smartphone

with the Ouigo app (iPhone and Android).

➡ The minimum single fare is €10. Children under 12 pay a flat €5 single fare.

➡ Each passenger is allowed to bring on board one piece of cabin luggage (35cm x 55cm x 25cm), one piece of hand luggage (27cm x 36cm x 15cm) and a child's pushchair for free; an extra bag and/or a larger bag costs €5 (€20 if you rock up at the train without registering the bag online in advance).

➡ If you want to plug in while aboard, be sure to reserve a seat with electric plug socket for an additional €2.

DISCOUNT TICKETS

The SNCF's most heavily discounted tickets are called Prem's, available online, at ticket windows and from ticket machines: 100% Prem's are available from Thursday evening to Monday night, for last-minute travel that weekend; Saturday-return Prem's are valid for return travel on a Saturday; and three-month Prem's can be booked a maximum of 90 days in advance. Prem's are nonrefundable and nonchangeable.

Intercités 100% Éco can be booked from three months to the day of departure, and offer cheap tickets between any stops, in any direction, on four main lines: Paris–Toulouse, Paris–Bordeaux, Paris–Nantes and Paris–Strasbourg. A single fare costs €15 to €35.

On regional trains, discount fares requiring neither a discount card nor advance purchase include the following:

Loisir rates Good for return travel that includes a Saturday night at your destination or involves travel on a Saturday or Sunday.

Découverte fares Available for low-demand 'blue-period' trains to people aged 12 to 25, seniors and the adult travel companions of children under 12.

Mini-Groupe tickets In some regions, these bring big savings for three to six people travelling together, provided you spend a Saturday night at your destination.

DISCOUNT CARDS

Reductions of at least 25% (for last-minute bookings), and of 40%, 50% or even 60% (if you reserve well ahead or travel during low-volume 'blue' periods), are available with several discount cards (valid for one year):

Carte Jeune (€50) Available to travellers aged 12 to 27.

Carte Enfant+ (€75) For one to four adults travelling with a child aged four to 11.

Carte Weekend (€75) For people aged 26 to 59. Offers discounts on return journeys of at least 200km that either include a Saturday night away or only involve travel on a Saturday or Sunday.

Carte Sénior+ (€60) For travellers over 60.

Left-Luggage Facilities

Because of security concerns, few French train stations have *consignes automatiques* (left-luggage lockers). In larger stations you can leave your bags in a *consigne manuelle* (staffed left-luggage facility) where items are handed over in person and X-rayed before being stowed. Charges are around €7 for up to 10 hours and €12 for 24 hours; payment must be made in cash.

Rail Passes

Residents of Europe (who do not live in France) can purchase an **InterRail One Country Pass** (www.interrail.eu; three/four/six/eight days €170/197/242/281, 12 to 25 years €148/171/210/243), which entitles its bearer to unlimited travel on SNCF trains for three to eight days over the course of a month.

For non-European residents, Rail Europe (www.raileurope-world.com) offers the France Rail Pass (two/four/five days over one month €123.50/184.50/209.50, 12 to 25 years €101.50/151/171.50). You need to really rack up the kilometres to make these passes worthwhile.

Language

Standard French is taught and spoken throughout France. This said, regional accents and dialects are an important part of identity in certain regions, but you'll have no trouble being understood anywhere if you stick to standard French, which we've also used in this chapter.

The sounds used in spoken French can almost all be found in English. There are a couple of exceptions: nasal vowels (represented in our pronunciation guides by o or u followed by an almost inaudible nasal consonant sound m, n or ng), the 'funny' *u* (ew in our guides) and the deep-in-the-throat *r*. Bearing these few points in mind and reading our pronunciation guides below as if they were English, you'll be understood just fine.

BASICS

French has two words for 'you' – use the polite form *vous* unless you're talking to close friends, children or animals in which case you'd use the informal *tu*. You can also use *tu* when a person invites you to use *tu*.

All nouns in French are either masculine or feminine, and so are the adjectives, articles *le/la* (the) and *un/une* (a), and possessives *mon/ma* (my), *ton/ta* (your) and *son/sa* (his, her) that go with the nouns. In this chapter we have included masculine and femine forms where necessary, separated by a slash and indicated with 'm/f'.

WANT MORE?

For in-depth language information and handy phrases, check out Lonely Planet's *French Phrasebook*. You'll find it at **shop.lonelyplanet.com**, or you can buy Lonely Planet's iPhone phrasebooks at the Apple App Store.

Hello.	Bonjour.	bon·zhoor
Goodbye.	Au revoir.	o·rer·vwa
Excuse me.	Excusez-moi.	ek·skew·zay·mwa
Sorry.	Pardon.	par·don
Yes.	Oui.	wee
No.	Non.	non
Please.	S'il vous plaît.	seel voo play
Thank you.	Merci.	mair·see
You're welcome.	De rien.	der ree·en

How are you?
Comment allez-vous?   ko·mon ta·lay·voo

Fine, and you?
Bien, merci. Et vous?   byun mair·see ay voo

You're welcome.
De rien.   der ree·en

My name is ...
Je m'appelle ...   zher ma·pel ...

What's your name?
Comment vous   ko·mon voo·
appelez-vous?   za·play voo

Do you speak English?
Parlez-vous anglais?   par·lay·voo ong·glay

I don't understand.
Je ne comprends pas.   zher ner kom·pron pa

ACCOMMODATION

Do you have any rooms available?
Est-ce que vous avez   es·ker voo za·vay
des chambres libres?   day shom·brer lee·brer

How much is it per night/person?
Quel est le prix   kel ay ler pree
par nuit/personne?   par nwee/per·son

Is breakfast included?
Est-ce que le petit   es·ker ler per·tee
déjeuner est inclus?   day·zher·nay ayt en·klew

KEY PATTERNS

To get by in France, mix and match these simple patterns with words of your choice:

Where's (the entry)?
Où est (l'entrée)?   oo ay (lon·tray)

Where can I (buy a ticket)?
Où est-ce que je peux   oo es·ker zher per
(acheter un billet)?   (ash·tay un bee·yay)

When's (the next train)?
Quand est   kon ay
(le prochain train)?   (ler pro·shun trun)

How much is (a room)?
C'est combien pour   say kom·buyn poor
(une chambre)?   (ewn shom·brer)

Do you have (a map)?
Avez-vous (une carte)?   a·vay voo (ewn kart)

Is there (a toilet)?
Y a-t-il (des toilettes)?   ee a teel (day twa·let)

I'd like (to book a room).
Je voudrais   zher voo·dray
(réserver   (ray·ser·vay
une chambre).   ewn shom·brer)

Can I (enter)?
Puis-je (entrer)?   pweezh (on·tray)

Could you please (help)?
Pouvez-vous   poo·vay voo
(m'aider),   (may·day)
s'il vous plaît?   seel voo play

Do I have to (book a seat)?
Faut-il (réserver   fo·teel (ray·ser·vay
une place)?   ewn plas)

campsite	camping	kom·peeng
dorm	dortoir	dor·twar
guest house	pension	pon·syon
hotel	hôtel	o·tel
youth hostel	auberge de jeunesse	o·berzh der zher·nes
a ... room	une chambre ...	ewn shom·brer ...
single	à un lit	a un lee
double	avec un grand lit	a·vek un gron lee
twin	avec des lits jumeaux	a·vek day lee zhew·mo
with (a)...	avec ...	a·vek ...
air-con	climatiseur	klee·ma·tee·zer
bathroom	une salle de bains	ewn sal der bun
window	fenêtre	fer·nay·trer

DIRECTIONS

Where's ...?
Où est ...?   oo ay ...

What's the address?
Quelle est l'adresse?   kel ay la·dres

Could you write the address, please?
Est-ce que vous pourriez   es·ker voo poo·ryay
écrire l'adresse,   ay·kreer la·dres
s'il vous plaît?   seel voo play

Can you show me (on the map)?
Pouvez-vous m'indiquer   poo·vay·voo mun·dee·kay
(sur la carte)?   (sewr la kart)

at the corner	au coin	o kwun
at the traffic lights	aux feux	o fer
behind	derrière	dair·ryair
in front of	devant	der·von
far (from)	loin (de)	lwun (der)
left	gauche	gosh
near (to)	près (de)	pray (der)
next to ...	à côté de ...	a ko·tay der...
opposite ...	en face de ...	on fas der ...
right	droite	drwat
straight ahead	tout droit	too drwa

EATING & DRINKING

What would you recommend?
Qu'est-ce que vous   kes·ker voo
conseillez?   kon·say·yay

What's in that dish?
Quels sont les   kel son lay
ingrédients?   zun·gray·dyon

I'm a vegetarian.
Je suis végétarien/   zher swee vay·zhay·ta·ryun/
végétarienne.   vay·zhay·ta·ryen (m/f)

I don't eat ...
Je ne mange pas ...   zher ner monzh pa ...

Cheers!
Santé!   son·tay

That was delicious.
C'était délicieux!   say·tay day·lee·syer

Please bring the bill.
Apportez-moi   a·por·tay·mwa
l'addition,   la·dee·syon
s'il vous plaît.   seel voo play

I'd like to reserve a table for ...	Je voudrais réserver une table pour ...	zher voo·dray ray·zair·vay ewn ta·bler poor ...
(eight) o'clock	(vingt) heures	(vungt) er
(two) people	(deux) personnes	(der) pair·son

LANGUAGE EATING & DRINKING

Key Words

appetiser	entrée	on·tray
bottle	bouteille	boo·tay
breakfast	petit déjeuner	per·tee day·zher·nay
children's menu	menu pour enfants	mer·new poor on·fon
cold	froid	frwa
delicatessen	traiteur	tray·ter
dinner	dîner	dee·nay
dish	plat	pla
food	nourriture	noo·ree·tewr
fork	fourchette	foor·shet
glass	verre	vair
grocery store	épicerie	ay·pees·ree
highchair	chaise haute	shay zot
hot	chaud	sho
knife	couteau	koo·to
local speciality	spécialité locale	spay·sya·lee·tay lo·kal
lunch	déjeuner	day·zher·nay
main course	plat principal	pla prun·see·pal
market	marché	mar·shay
menu (in English)	carte (en anglais)	kart (on ong·glay)
plate	assiette	a·syet
spoon	cuillère	kwee·yair
wine list	carte des vins	kart day vun
with/without	avec/sans	a·vek/son

Meat & Fish

beef	bœuf	berf
chicken	poulet	poo·lay
crab	crabe	krab
lamb	agneau	a·nyo
oyster	huître	wee·trer
pork	porc	por
snail	escargot	es·kar·go
squid	calmar	kal·mar
turkey	dinde	dund
veal	veau	vo

Fruit & Vegetables

apple	pomme	pom
apricot	abricot	ab·ree·ko
asparagus	asperge	a·spairzh
beans	haricots	a·ree·ko
beetroot	betterave	be·trav
cabbage	chou	shoo
cherry	cerise	ser·reez
corn	maïs	ma·ees
cucumber	concombre	kong·kom·brer
grape	raisin	ray·zun
lemon	citron	see·tron
lettuce	laitue	lay·tew
mushroom	champignon	shom·pee·nyon
peach	pêche	pesh
peas	petit pois	per·tee pwa
(red/green) pepper	poivron (rouge/vert)	pwa·vron (roozh/vair)
pineapple	ananas	a·na·nas
plum	prune	prewn
potato	pomme de terre	pom der tair
prune	pruneau	prew·no
pumpkin	citrouille	see·troo·yer
shallot	échalote	eh·sha·lot
spinach	épinards	eh·pee·nar
strawberry	fraise	frez
tomato	tomate	to·mat
vegetable	légume	lay·gewm

Other

bread	pain	pun
butter	beurre	ber
cheese	fromage	fro·mazh
egg	œuf	erf
honey	miel	myel
jam	confiture	kon·fee·tewr
lentils	lentilles	lon·tee·yer
pasta/noodles	pâtes	pat
pepper	poivre	pwa·vrer
rice	riz	ree
salt	sel	sel
sugar	sucre	sew·krer
vinegar	vinaigre	vee·nay·grer

SIGNS

Entrée	Entrance
Femmes	Women
Fermé	Closed
Hommes	Men
Interdit	Prohibited
Ouvert	Open
Renseignements	Information
Sortie	Exit
Toilettes/WC	Toilets

Drinks

beer	*bière*	bee·yair
coffee	*café*	ka·fay
(orange) juice	*jus (d'orange)*	zhew (do·ronzh)
milk	*lait*	lay
tea	*thé*	tay
(mineral) water	*eau (minérale)*	o (mee·nay·ral)
(red) wine	*vin (rouge)*	vun (roozh)
(white) wine	*vin (blanc)*	vun (blong)

EMERGENCIES

Help!
Au secours!   o skoor

I'm lost.
Je suis perdu/perdue.   zhe swee·pair·dew (m/f)

Leave me alone!
Fichez-moi la paix!   fee·shay·mwa la pay

There's been an accident.
Il y a eu un accident.   eel ya ew un ak·see·don

Call a doctor.
Appelez un médecin.   a·play un mayd·sun

Call the police.
Appelez la police.   a·play la po·lees

I'm ill.
Je suis malade.   zher swee ma·lad

It hurts here.
J'ai une douleur ici.   zhay ewn doo·ler ee·see

I'm allergic to ...
Je suis allergique ...   zher swee za·lair·zheek ...

SHOPPING & SERVICES

I'd like to buy ...
Je voudrais acheter ...   zher voo·dray ash·tay ...

May I look at it?
Est-ce que je   es·ker zher
peux le voir?   per ler vwar

I'm just looking.
Je regarde.   zher rer·gard

I don't like it.
Cela ne me plaît pas.   ser·la ner mer play pa

How much is it?
C'est combien?   say kom·byun

QUESTION WORDS

How?	*Comment?*	ko·mon
What?	*Quoi?*	kwa
When?	*Quand?*	kon
Where?	*Où?*	oo
Who?	*Qui?*	kee
Why?	*Pourquoi?*	poor·kwa

It's too expensive.
C'est trop cher.   say tro shair

Can you lower the price?
Vous pouvez baisser   voo poo·vay bay·say
le prix?   ler pree

There's a mistake in the bill.
Il y a une erreur dans   eel ya ewn ay·rer don
la note.   la not

ATM	*guichet automatique de banque*	gee·shay o·to·ma·teek der bonk
credit card	*carte de crédit*	kart der kray·dee
internet cafe	*cybercafé*	see·bair·ka·fay
post office	*bureau de poste*	bew·ro der post
tourist office	*office de tourisme*	o·fees der too·rees·mer

TIME & DATES

What time is it?
Quelle heure est-il?   kel er ay til

It's (eight) o'clock.
Il est (huit) heures.   il ay (weet) er

It's half past (10).
Il est (dix) heures   il ay (deez) er
et demie.   ay day·mee

morning	*matin*	ma·tun
afternoon	*après-midi*	a·pray·mee·dee
evening	*soir*	swar
yesterday	*hier*	yair
today	*aujourd'hui*	o·zhoor·dwee
tomorrow	*demain*	der·mun

Monday	*lundi*	lun·dee
Tuesday	*mardi*	mar·dee
Wednesday	*mercredi*	mair·krer·dee
Thursday	*jeudi*	zher·dee
Friday	*vendredi*	von·drer·dee
Saturday	*samedi*	sam·dee
Sunday	*dimanche*	dee·monsh

January	*janvier*	zhon·vyay
February	*février*	fayv·ryay
March	*mars*	mars
April	*avril*	a·vreel
May	*mai*	may
June	*juin*	zhwun
July	*juillet*	zhwee·yay
August	*août*	oot
September	*septembre*	sep·tom·brer
October	*octobre*	ok·to·brer
November	*novembre*	no·vom·brer
December	*décembre*	day·som·brer

TRANSPORT

Public Transport

boat	bateau	ba·to
bus	bus	bews
plane	avion	a·vyon
train	train	trun

I want to go to ...
Je voudrais aller à ...   zher voo·dray a·lay a ...

Does it stop at (Amboise)?
Est-ce qu'il s'arrête à   es·kil sa·ret a
(Amboise)?   (om·bwaz)

At what time does it leave/arrive?
À quelle heure est-ce   a kel er es
qu'il part/arrive?   kil par/a·reev

Can you tell me when we get to ...?
Pouvez-vous me   poo·vay·voo mer
dire quand   deer kon
nous arrivons à ...?   noo za·ree·von a ...

I want to get off here.
Je veux descendre   zher ver day·son·drer
ici.   ee·see

first	premier	prer·myay
last	dernier	dair·nyay
next	prochain	pro·shun
a ... ticket	un billet ...	un bee·yay ...
1st-class	de première classe	der prem·yair klas
2nd-class	de deuxième classe	der der·zyem las
one-way	simple	sum·pler
return	aller et retour	a·lay ay rer·toor

aisle seat	côté couloir	ko·tay kool·war
delayed	en retard	on rer·tar
cancelled	annulé	a·new·lay
platform	quai	kay
ticket office	guichet	gee·shay
timetable	horaire	o·rair
train station	gare	gar
window seat	côté fenêtre	ko·tay fe·ne·trer

Driving & Cycling

I'd like to hire a ...	Je voudrais louer ...	zher voo·dray loo·way ...
4WD	un quatre-quatre	un kat·kat
car	une voiture	ewn vwa·tewr
bicycle	un vélo	un vay·lo

NUMBERS

1	un	un
2	deux	der
3	trois	trwa
4	quatre	ka·trer
5	cinq	sungk
6	six	sees
7	sept	set
8	huit	weet
9	neuf	nerf
10	dix	dees
20	vingt	vung
30	trente	tront
40	quarante	ka·ront
50	cinquante	sung·kont
60	soixante	swa·sont
70	soixante-dix	swa·son·dees
80	quatre-vingts	ka·trer·vung
90	quatre-vingt-dix	ka·trer·vung·dees
100	cent	son
1000	mille	meel

motorcycle	une moto	ewn mo·to
child seat	siège-enfant	syezh·on·fon
diesel	diesel	dyay·zel
helmet	casque	kask
mechanic	mécanicien	may·ka·nee·syun
petrol/gas	essence	ay·sons
service station	station-service	sta·syon·ser·vees

Is this the road to ...?
C'est la route pour ...?   say la root poor ...

(How long) Can I park here?
(Combien de temps)   (kom·byun der tom)
Est-ce que je peux   es·ker zher per
stationner ici?   sta·syo·nay ee·see

The car/motorbike has broken down (at ...).
La voiture/moto est   la vwa·tewr/mo·to ay
tombée en panne (à ...).   tom·bay on pan (a ...)

I have a flat tyre.
Mon pneu est à plat.   mom pner ay ta pla

I've run out of petrol.
Je suis en panne   zher swee zon pan
d'essence.   day·sons

I've lost my car keys.
J'ai perdu les clés de   zhay per·dew lay klay der
ma voiture.   ma vwa·tewr

GLOSSARY

(m) indicates masculine gender, (f) feminine gender and (pl) plural

accueil (m) – reception

alignements (m pl) – a series of standing stones, or menhirs, in straight lines

AOC – Appellation d'Origine Contrôlée; system of French wine and olive oil classification showing that items have met government regulations as to where and how they are produced

AOP – Appellation d'Origine Protégée; Europe-wide equivalent to *AOC*

arrondissement (m) – administrative division of large city; abbreviated on signs as 1er (1st arrondissement), 2e (2nd) etc

atelier (m) – workshop or studio

auberge – inn

auberge de jeunesse (f) – youth hostel

baie (f) – bay

bassin (m) – bay or basin

bastide (f) – medieval settlement in southwestern France, usually built on a grid plan and surrounding an arcaded square; fortified town; also a country house in Provence

belle époque (f) – literally 'beautiful age'; era of elegance and gaiety characterising fashionable Parisian life in the period preceding WWI

billet (m) – ticket

billetterie (f) – ticket office or counter

bouchon – Lyonnais bistro

boulangerie (f) – bakery or bread shop

boules (f pl) – a game similar to lawn bowls played with heavy metal balls on a sandy pitch; also called *pétanque*

brasserie (f) – restaurant similar to a *café* but usually serving full meals all day (original meaning: brewery)

bureau de change (m) – exchange bureau

bureau de poste (m) – post office

carnet (m) – a book of five or 10 bus, tram or metro tickets sold at a reduced rate

carrefour (m) – crossroad

carte (f) – card; menu; map

cave (f) – wine cellar

chambre (f) – room

chambre d'hôte (f) – B&B

charcuterie (f) – butcher's shop and delicatessen; the prepared meats it sells

cimetière (m) – cemetery

col (m) – mountain pass

consigne or **consigne manuelle** (f) – left-luggage office

consigne automatique (f) – left-luggage locker

correspondance (f) – linking tunnel or walkway, eg in the metro; rail or bus connection

cour (f) – courtyard

crémerie (f) – dairy or cheese shop

dégustation (f) – tasting

demi (m) – 330mL glass of beer

demi-pension (f) – half board (B&B with either lunch or dinner)

département (m) – administrative division of France

donjon (m) – castle keep

église (f) – church

épicerie (f) – small grocery store

ESF – École de Ski Français; France's leading ski school

fest-noz or **festoù-noz** (pl) – night festival

fête (f) – festival

Fnac – retail chain selling entertainment goods, electronics and tickets

forêt (f) – forest

formule or **formule rapide** (f) – lunchtime set similar to a *menu* but with two of three courses on offer (eg starter and main or main and dessert)

fromagerie (f) – cheese shop

FUAJ – Fédération Unie des Auberges de Jeunesse; France's major hostel association

funiculaire (m) – funicular railway

galerie (f) – covered shopping centre or arcade

gare or **gare SNCF** (f) – railway station

gare maritime (f) – ferry terminal

gare routière (f) – bus station

gendarmerie (f) – police station; police force

gîte d'étape (m) – hikers accommodation, usually in a village

golfe (m) – gulf

GR – *grande randonnée;* long-distance hiking trail

grand cru (m) – wine of exceptional quality

halles (f pl) – covered market; central food market

halte routière (f) – bus stop

horaire (m) – timetable or schedule

hostellerie – hostelry

hôtel de ville (m) – city or town hall

hôtel particulier (m) – private mansion

intra-muros – old city (literally 'within the walls')

jardin (m) – garden

jardin botanique (m) – botanic garden

laverie (f) or **lavomatique** (m) – laundrette

libre – vacant, available

mairie (f) – city or town hall

maison du parc (f) – a national park's headquarters and/or visitors centre

marché (m) – market

marché aux puces (m) – flea market

marché couvert (m) – covered market

mas (m) – farmhouse in southern France

menu (m) – fixed-price meal with two or more courses

mistral (m) – strong north or northwest wind in southern France

musée (m) – museum

GLOSSARY

navette (f) – shuttle bus, train or boat

occupé – occupied

palais de justice (m) – law courts

parapente – paragliding

parlement (m) – parliament

parvis (m) – square

patisserie (f) – cake and pastry shop

pétanque (f) – a game similar to lawn bowls played with heavy metal balls on a sandy pitch; also called *boules*

petit déjeuner – breakfast

place (f) – square or plaza

plage (f) – beach

plan (m) – city map

plan du quartier (m) – map of nearby streets (hung on the wall near metro exits)

plat du jour (m) – daily special in a restaurant

pont (m) – bridge

porte (f) – gate in a city wall

poste (f) – post office

préfecture (f) – prefecture (capital of a *département*)

presqu'île (f) – peninsula

puy (m) – volcanic cone or peak

quai (m) – quay or railway platform

quartier (m) – quarter or district

refuge (m) – mountain hut, basic shelter for hikers

région (f) – administrative division of France

rond point (m) – roundabout

salon de thé – tearoom

sentier (m) – trail

service des urgences (f) – casualty ward

ski de fond – cross-country skiing

SNCF – Société Nationale des Chemins de Fer; state-owned railway company

SNCM – Société Nationale Maritime Corse-Méditerranée; state-owned ferry company linking Corsica and mainland France

sortie (f) – exit

square (m) – public garden

tabac (m) – tobacconist (also selling bus tickets, phonecards etc)

table d'hôte – set menu at a fixed price

taxe de séjour (f) – municipal tourist tax

télécarte (f) – phonecard

télécabine – gondola

téléphérique (m) – cableway or cable car

téléski (m) – chairlift

téléski (m) – ski lift or tow

terroir – land

TGV – *Train à Grande Vitesse*; high-speed train or bullet train

tour (f) – tower

vallée (f) – valley

VF (f) – *version française*; a film dubbed in French

vieille ville (f) – old town or old city

ville neuve (f) – new town or new city

VO (f) – *version originale*; a nondubbed film with French subtitles

VTT – *vélo tout terrain*; mountain bike

winstub – traditional Alsatian eatery

Behind the Scenes

SEND US YOUR FEEDBACK

We love to hear from travellers – your comments keep us on our toes and help make our books better. Our well-travelled team reads every word on what you loved or loathed about this book. Although we cannot reply individually to your submissions, we always guarantee that your feedback goes straight to the appropriate authors, in time for the next edition. Each person who sends us information is thanked in the next edition – the most useful submissions are rewarded with a selection of digital PDF chapters.

Visit **lonelyplanet.com/contact** to submit your updates and suggestions or to ask for help. Our award-winning website also features inspirational travel stories, news and discussions.

Note: We may edit, reproduce and incorporate your comments in Lonely Planet products such as guidebooks, websites and digital products, so let us know if you don't want your comments reproduced or your name acknowledged. For a copy of our privacy policy visit lonelyplanet.com/privacy.

OUR READERS

Many thanks to the travellers who used the last edition and wrote to us with helpful hints, useful advice and interesting anecdotes: Adam Powell, Alessandra Furlan, Bill Leddy, Bruce Stillard, Dan Bostrom, George Moss, Jeremie Pinard Saint-Pierre, Jorden Summers, Joseph Clarke, Laura Heemeryck, Linda Moss, Maya Zane Kaisth, Nelly Stanko, Shannon Mekuly, Vicki Lloyd

WRITER THANKS

Nicola Williams

Heartfelt *bisous* to the many friends and professionals who aided and abetted in tracking down the best in Paris, Bordeaux and elsewhere on the Atlantic Coast, including: in Paris, Elodie Berta, Mary Winston-Nicklin, Kasia Dietz, Rachel Vanier and Stéphanie Ruch; in and around Bordeaux, Pauline Versace (La Cité du Vin), Emmeline Azra (St-Émilion) and Alexia Guelte. Kudos to my ever-fabulous co-writers and my ever-faithful, trilingual 'France *en famille*' research team, Matthias, Niko, Mischa and Kaya Luefkens.

Alexis Averbuck

I am deeply indebted to Didier Ageorges of excellent restaurant Pascaline in Sebastopol, California and Christophe Algieri who generously led me to many a fabulous new Basque locale. Big hugs to Alexandra Miliotis and Margarita Kontzia who made my exit through Paris a party on the Seine. And – as always – the ideal travel companion, Ryan Ver Berkmoes, the trip was a peachy delight!

Oliver Berry

Un grand merci to everyone who helped me with my research in Provence this time around, including Jérome Coustellet, Marie Lafarge, Sophie Casticci, James Clarke, Agnès Caron and Aurelie Martin. Back home, thanks to Rosie Hillier for putting up with long days and nights of write up, and to everyone in the LP team putting the project together, especially Destination Editor Dan Fahey for fielding myriad questions about taxonomy, topography, Typefi and plenty more besides.

Jean-Bernard Carillet

A huge thanks to everyone who made trips to Occitanie a pure joy, including Sarah D, Elodie and Sarah K, as well as Céline, Sabrina, Jean-François, Caroline and Loriane. And big thanks to Daniel at LP for his trust.

Kerry Christiani

A big *merci* to all the travel professionals and acquaintances who made my road to research in Alsace, Lorraine and Champagne all the smoother. In particular I would like to thank Apollonia Gontero in Troyes, Géraldine Amar in Strasbourg, and the Champagne-making pros at maisons Taittinger, Veuve Clicquot, Moët & Chandon and Boizel.

Gregor Clark

Merci beaucoup to the many French and Monégasque locals who shared their insights about France and Monaco with me, especially Marion Pansiot, Clara Diaz Campuzano, Lucie Richard, Did Kwo, Claire Bouvrot, Bruno Rouganne and Eric Demeester. Back home, hugs to Gaen, Meigan and Chloe, who always make coming home the best part of the trip.

Damian Harper

Thanks to Myriam, Frederica Forte, Michael Egan, Sophie and Isobel, Veronique, Thomas, Antonin, Louis Chow, Diane and Clive and of course endless gratitude to Daisy, Tim and Emma for all your help and support. Thanks also to the people of France, who made this trip so engaging, refreshing and fun.

Anita Isalska

My time in France was enriched by many productive detours and chance encounters. A big thank you to Vanessa Michy and her colleagues at Auvergne-Rhône-Alpes Tourisme for the helpful suggestions. I'm grateful to Nicola Williams, Tom Hewitson and Jane Atkin for tips (or morale-boosting), and my parents, Barbara and Harry, for enthusiastically joining the research on cuisine dauphinoise. For scrutiny of piste maps and stunt driving in national parks, my partner Normal Matt excelled himself – *merci infiniment*.

Catherine Le Nevez

Merci mille fois first and foremost to Julian and to the innumerable Parisians and those in northern France who provided insights, inspiration and great times. Huge thanks too to my Paris co-authors Chris and Nicola, Destination Editor Daniel Fahey and everyone at LP. As ever, a heartfelt *merci encore* to my parents, brother, belle-sœur, neveu and nièce for sustaining my lifelong love of Paris and of France.

Hugh McNaughtan

As always, I must thank Tasmin, Maise and Willa, my endlessly patient family, plus my editor Dan, and the support team at Lonely Planet. I'd also like to thank Audrey, Isabelle and the many people in Provence who made this project a success and a pleasure.

Christopher Pitts

Special thanks to all the crew at LP who have put so much hard work into making this book what it is. *Un très grand merci* to Marcel in Najac for helping me get my car unstuck; I thought it was a goner. *Bises* also to Alain and Anne-Marie in Calviac, the rest of the Pavillard clan, and my dearest partners in crime: Perrine, Elliot and Céleste.

Daniel Robinson

Special thanks to (from east to west) Yoann Ivanoff (Sully-sur-Loire), Marie-Laure de Brem (Bourges), Laetitia Marion (Saint-Viâtre), Louise Floch (Chambord), Lyne Coutellier (Blois), Mélodie Pesneau (Amboise), Marion Moulun and Serrat Mehretab (Tours), Sébastien Guessard (Tourquant), Olivier Thibault and Jean-Claude Freléchoux (Saumur), Patrick and Annick Rivière (Le Mans) and Anny Monet (Le Mans, Saumur and Angers). This project would not have been possible without the support, enthusiasm and forbearance of my wife Rachel and our sons Yair and Sasson (New London, Connecticut).

Regis St Louis

Countless chefs, winemakers, baristas, innkeepers and others helped along the way – and I am deeply grateful to the people in the south of France. Special thanks go to Michele and Roland Skripnikoff, Richard Lengsfeld and family, Bruno Eldin, Madame Ziane, and the Lyon Running Crew. Thanks to the support of Cassandra and daughters Magdalena and Genevieve, who made this endeavour worthwhile.

Greg Ward

Thanks to the many wonderful people who helped me as I criss-crossed Corsica, and took the time to tell me about the history, legends and hiking trails of the island. Thanks too to my editor Daniel Fahey for giving me this opportunity, and to my dear wife Sam for everything else.

ACKNOWLEDGEMENTS

Climate map data adapted from Peel MC, Finlayson BL & McMahon TA (2007) 'Updated World Map of the Köppen-Geiger Climate Classification', Hydrology and Earth System Sciences, 11, 1633-44.

Cover photograph: Lavender fields, Alpes-de-Haute-Provence, Michel Cavalier/AWL ©

Illustrations p82-3, p98-9, p104-5, p190-1, p272-3, p788-9 , p890-1 by Javier Zarracina

THIS BOOK

This 13th edition of Lonely Planet's *France* guidebook was curated by Nicola Williams and researched and written by Nicola Williams, Alexis Averbuck, Oliver Berry, Jean-Bernard Carillet, Kerry Christiani, Gregor Clark, Damian Harper, Anita Isalska, Catherine Le Nevez, Christopher Pitts, Daniel Robinson, Regis St Louis and Greg Ward. This guidebook was produced by the following:

Destination Editor
Daniel Fahey

Senior Product Editor
Genna Patterson

Product Editor Jessica Ryan

Senior Cartographer
Mark Griffiths

Book Designer Gwen Cotter

Assisting Editors Sarah Bailey, Judith Bamber, Michelle Bennett, Lucy Cowie, Peter Cruttenden, Andrea Dobbin, Samantha Forge, Carly Hall, Gabrielle Innes, Jodie Martire, Anne Mulvaney, Rosie Nicholson, Kristin Odijk, Monique Perrin, Sarah Reid, Tamara Sheward, Fionnuala Twomey, Sam Wheeler and Simon Williamson

Cartographer Rachel Imeson

Cover Researcher
Naomi Parker

Thanks to Ronan Abayawickrema, Ben Buckner, Heather Champion, Grace Dobell, Evan Godt, Alicia Johnson, Sandie Kestell, Jenna Myers, Catherine Naghten, Claire Naylor, Karyn Noble, Matt Phillips, Angela Tinson

Index

1020

Map Legend

Sights

- Beach
- Bird Sanctuary
- Buddhist
- Castle/Palace
- Christian
- Confucian
- Hindu
- Islamic
- Jain
- Jewish
- Monument
- Museum/Gallery/Historic Building
- Ruin
- Shinto
- Sikh
- Taoist
- Winery/Vineyard
- Zoo/Wildlife Sanctuary
- Other Sight

Activities, Courses & Tours

- Bodysurfing
- Diving
- Canoeing/Kayaking
- Course/Tour
- Sento Hot Baths/Onsen
- Skiing
- Snorkelling
- Surfing
- Swimming/Pool
- Walking
- Windsurfing
- Other Activity

Sleeping

- Sleeping
- Camping
- Hut/Shelter

Eating

- Eating

Drinking & Nightlife

- Drinking & Nightlife
- Cafe

Entertainment

- Entertainment

Shopping

- Shopping

Information

- Bank
- Embassy/Consulate
- Hospital/Medical
- @ Internet
- Police
- Post Office
- Telephone
- Toilet
- Tourist Information
- • Other Information

Geographic

- Beach
- Gate
- Hut/Shelter
- Lighthouse
- Lookout
- Mountain/Volcano
- Oasis
- Park
-)(Pass
- Picnic Area
- Waterfall

Population

- Capital (National)
- Capital (State/Province)
- City/Large Town
- Town/Village

Transport

- Airport
- Border crossing
- Bus
- Cable car/Funicular
- Cycling
- Ferry
- Metro station
- Monorail
- Parking
- Petrol station
- S-Bahn/Subway station
- Taxi
- T bane/Tunnelbana station
- Train station/Railway
- Tram
- Tube station
- U-Bahn/Underground station
- • Other Transport

Routes

- Tollway
- Freeway
- Primary
- Secondary
- Tertiary
- Lane
- Unsealed road
- Road under construction
- Plaza/Mall
- Steps
- Tunnel
- Pedestrian overpass
- Walking Tour
- Walking Tour detour
- Path/Walking Trail

Boundaries

- International
- State/Province
- Disputed
- Regional/Suburb
- Marine Park
- Cliff
- Wall

Hydrography

- River, Creek
- Intermittent River
- Canal
- Water
- Dry/Salt/Intermittent Lake
- Reef

Areas

- Airport/Runway
- Beach/Desert
- Cemetery (Christian)
- Cemetery (Other)
- Glacier
- Mudflat
- Park/Forest
- Sight (Building)
- Sportsground
- Swamp/Mangrove

Note: Not all symbols displayed above appear on the maps in this book

Christopher Pitts

Paris; The Dordogne, Limousin & the Lot Born in the year of the Tiger, Chris's first expedition in life ended in failure when he tried to dig from Pennsylvania to China at the age of six. Hardened by reality but still infinitely curious about the other side of the world, he went on to study Chinese in university, living for several years in Kunming, Taiwan and Shanghai. A chance encounter in an elevator led to a Paris relocation, where he lived with his wife and two children for over a decade before the lure of Colorado's sunny skies and outdoor adventure proved too great to resist.

Daniel Robinson

The Loire Valley Over the past 25 years, Daniel has worked on dozens of Lonely Planet projects, including the first editions of *Cambodia* and *Paris* (co-authored with Tony Wheeler) and 12 of the 13 editions of *France*, researched in rain, sleet, snow and, when he's lucky the kind of glorious sunlight that inspired the post-impressionists. His latest projects include *Israel & the Palestinian Territories* and *Borneo*, both as coordinating author, as well as *Germany* and *Southeast Asia on a Shoestring*. Daniel's travel writing has appeared in *National Geographic Traveler*, the *New York Times* and the *Los Angeles Times*, and has been translated into 10 foreign languages.

Regis St Louis

Lyon & the Rhône Valley, The Pyrenees Regis grew up in a small town in the American Midwest – the kind of place that fuels big dreams of travel – and he developed an early fascination with foreign dialects and world cultures. He spent his formative years learning Russian and a handful of Romance languages, which served him well on journeys across much of the globe. Regis has contributed to more than 50 Lonely Planet titles, covering destinations across six continents. His travels have taken him from the mountains of Kamchatka to remote island villages in Melanesia, and to many grand urban landscapes. When not on the road, he lives in New Orleans. Follow him on www.instagram.com/regisstlouis.

Greg Ward

Corsica Since whetting his appetite for travel by following the hippy trail to India, and later living in northern Spain, Greg Ward has written guides to destinations all over the world. As well as covering the USA from the Southwest to Hawaii, he has ranged on recent assignments from Corsica to the Cotswolds, and Japan to Corfu. See his website, www.gregward.info, for his favourite photos and memories.

Kerry Christiani
Champagne, Alsace & Lorraine Kerry is an award-winning travel writer, photographer and Lonely Planet author, specialising in Central and Southern Europe. Based in Wales, she has authored/co-authored more than a dozen Lonely Planet titles. An adventure addict, she loves mountains, cold places and true wilderness. She features her latest work at https://its-a-small-world.com and tweets @kerrychristiani.

Gregor Clark
Burgundy, Provence, French Riviera & Monaco Gregor Clark is a US-based writer whose love of foreign languages and curiosity about what's around the next bend have taken him to dozens of countries on five continents. Chronic wanderlust has also led him to visit all 50 states and most Canadian provinces on countless road trips through his native North America. Since 2000, Gregor has regularly contributed to Lonely Planet guides, with a focus on Europe and the Americas. Titles include *Italy*, *France*, *Brazil*, *Costa Rica*, *Argentina*, *Portugal*, *Switzerland*, *Mexico*, *South America on a Shoestring*, *Montreal & Quebec City*, *France's Best Trips*, *New England's Best Trips*, cycling guides to Italy and California and coffee-table pictorials such as *Food Trails*, the *USA Book* and the *Lonely Planet Guide to the Middle of Nowhere*.

Damian Harper
Normandy, Brittany Damian has been writing for Lonely Planet for over two decades, contributing to titles as diverse as *China*, *Beijing*, *Shanghai*, *Vietnam*, *Thailand*, *Ireland*, *London*, *Mallorca*, *Malaysia*, *Singapore & Brunei*, *Hong Kong*, *China's Southwest* and *Great Britain*. A seasoned guidebook writer, Damian has penned articles for numerous newspapers and magazines, including the *Guardian* and the *Daily Telegraph*, and currently makes Surrey, England, his home. A self-taught trumpet novice, his other hobbies include collecting modern first editions, photography and Taekwondo. Follow Damian on Instagram (damian.harper).

Anita Isalska
French Alps & the Jura Mountains, Auvergne Anita Isalska is a travel journalist, editor and copywriter. After several merry years as a staff writer and editor – a few of them in Lonely Planet's London office – Anita now works freelance between Australia, the UK and any Alpine chalet with good wi-fi. Anita writes about France, Eastern Europe, Southeast Asia and off-beat travel. Read her stuff on www.anitaisalska.com.

Catherine Le Nevez
Paris Catherine's wanderlust kicked in when she roadtripped across Europe from her Parisian base, aged four, and she's been hitting the road at every opportunity since, travelling to around 60 countries and completing her Doctorate of Creative Arts in Writing, Masters in Professional Writing, and postgrad qualifications in Editing and Publishing along the way. Over the past dozen-plus years she's written scores of Lonely Planet guides and articles covering Paris, France, Europe and far beyond. Her work has also appeared in numerous online and print publications. Topping Catherine's list of travel tips is to travel without any expectations.

Hugh McNaughtan
Provence, French Riviera A former English lecturer, Hugh swapped grant applications for visa applications, and turned his love of travel into a full-time thing. Having done a bit of restaurant-reviewing in his home town (Melbourne) he's now eaten his way across four continents. He's never happier than when on the road with his two daughters. Except perhaps on the cricket field.

...and a sense of
...Wheeler needed
...Asia overland to
...nd – broke but
...ng and stapling
...*on the Cheap*.
...lanet was born.
Today, Lonely Planet has offices in Franklin, London,
Melbourne, Oakland, Dublin, Beijing and Delhi, with more than 600 staff and writers. We share
Tony's belief that 'a great guidebook should do three things: inform, educate and amuse'.

OUR WRITERS

Nicola Williams
Paris, Atlantic Coast Border-hopping is way of life for British writer, runner, foodie,
art aficionado and mum-of-three Nicola Williams who has lived in a French village
on the southern side of Lake Geneva for more than a decade. Nicola has authored
more than 50 guidebooks for Lonely Planet, and covers France as a destination
expert for the *Telegraph*. She also writes for the *Independent*, *Guardian*, *Lonely
Planet* magazine, *French Magazine*, *Cool Camping France* and others. Catch her on the road on Twitter and Instagram at @tripalong. Nicola also wrote the Plan Your Trip, Understand and Survival Guide
chapters of this book.

Alexis Averbuck
French Basque Country Alexis Averbuck has travelled and lived all over the world,
from Sri Lanka to Ecuador, Zanzibar and Antarctica. In recent years she's been
living on the Greek island of Hydra and exploring her adopted homeland; sampling
oysters in Brittany and careening through hill-top villages in Provence; and adven-
turing along Iceland's surreal lava fields, sparkling fjords and glacier tongues. A
travel writer for over two decades, Alexis has lived in Antarctica for a year, crossed
the Pacific by sailboat and written books on her journeys through Asia, Europe and the Americas.

Oliver Berry
Provence, French Riviera Oliver Berry is a writer and photographer from Cornwall.
He has worked for Lonely Planet for more than a decade, covering destinations from
Cornwall to the Cook Islands, and has worked on more than thirty guidebooks. He
is also a regular contributor to many newspapers and magazines, including Lonely
Planet *Traveller*. His writing has won several awards, including the Guardian Young
Travel Writer of the Year and the TNT Magazine People's Choice Award.

Jean-Bernard Carillet
Toulouse Area, Languedoc-Roussillon Jean-Bernard is a Paris-based freelance
writer and photographer who specialises in Africa, France, Turkey, the Indian
Ocean, the Caribbean and the Pacific. He loves adventure, remote places, islands,
outdoors, archaeological sites and food. His insatiable wanderlust has taken
him to 114 countries across six continents, and it shows no sign of waning. It has
inspired lots of articles and photos for travel magazines and some 70 Lonely
Planet guidebooks, both in English and in French.

OVER PAGE | MORE WRITERS

Published by Lonely Planet Global Limited
CRN 554153
13th edition – March 2019
ISBN 978 1 78657 379 7
© Lonely Planet 2019   Photographs © as indicated 2019
10 9 8 7 6 5 4 3 2 1
Printed in China